Praise for *Upgrading and Repairing PCs* and Scott Mueller from Readers Around the World...

"**I can't stop reading it.** It is SO well written, documented, outlined, etc. I just wanted you to know how satisfied I am with your book."

JOHN P. COWAN, CHIEF OPERATING OFFICER
WEB Alive Enterprises

"Once again thank you for an outstanding book without which I feel I would not have been able to pass the CompTIA tests."

WES DIDYK, CERTIFIED PC TECHNICIAN

"I just purchased the Tenth Edition of *Upgrading and Repairing PCs*, and it is better than ever!! **I have a dog-eared copy** of the Sixth Edition that has been of great help in understanding hardware components, and I use it frequently in my work."

LARRY ROBERTS

"I am grateful for all the quality information you have included here, and **I am convinced that your book is the best and most detailed on the subject** that I have ever come across."

WIESLAW (WES) WALAWENDER, PRESIDENT
Global Interception Systems & Services,
Europe

"I just purchased your 10th Anniversary Edition of *Upgrading and Repairing PC's*. Masterpiece of work. **If I had to have one book on a desert island, this would be it.** (I'd have to hire a valet to carry it around - ha ha!)"

CURTISS CLARKE, APPLICATIONS DEVELOPER
Ontario, Canada

"What a great book. Thanks for everything in it. [I'm] Now in semi-retirement from newspaper journalism, I love to mess with computers, mostly old ones, an interest helped by being a radio ham too, I guess. **Your book is a *vade mecum* I couldn't imagine being without.**"

GENE DONNELLY, JOURNALIST
South Africa

"As a confirmed Mac head, I was not happy when a job change (from academic to industrial) forced me to start using PCs. But, **Scott's book is a lifesaver** and allows you to successfully deal with all those PC head-banging situations."

KAREN LEBENS

"**Your book will become my bible...**"

KATE MULLIS, SUPPORT SERVICES
Lease Link

"I must say you that I have never seen such a comprehensive book on PC hardware. Thank you very much for this book. Besides a lot of very useful and interesting information, reading it was very enjoyable for me. **It is a real masterpiece.** I am sure that every computer expert must have this book, and not only those who maintain and repair computer systems. I recommend your book to my students as a very good book not only on hardware, and not only on PCs, but on Computer Science as a whole also. I am looking forward to having the next edition of your book."

SERGE SILKIN, PROFESSOR-ASSISTANT
Department of Information and
Computer Science,
Yaroslavl State University, Russia

"I just wanted to say thank you. I first read the Upgrading and Repairing PC's, the first edition. Because of this edition being taught at the Technical School I attended back in 1991, I changed careers. I spent the next six years repairing computers for a living and learning all about computers that I could. I just want-

W9-BPN-089

ed you to know how much I have enjoyed your books on Upgrading and Repairing PC's."

RAMONA ALLEN

"This is the most concise and yet exhaustive upgrade book I have ever laid my eyes on. I could not put it down. I was overwhelmed by how up-to-date the information is for every-day practical use. The terms are easy to use for anyone just getting starting in the PC world. PC books for dummies, look out...this new edition is a knockout."

MARK BARBOUR, FINANCIAL SYSTEMS CONSULTANT

"There are approximately 12 lineal feet of book-shelf in the den devoted to computer technology. They are generally nice and clean and properly arranged. There is one tattered book handy on the workbench, and that is the **Gospel according to St. Scott**. This one is the motherload. You realize of course that it is roughly analogous to giving the keys to a new Lamborgini to one of my grandkids! I wonder if you have any idea how many thousands of us out here really depend on you?"

JACK WILLIAMS

"Once again, Scott has produced **THE defini-tive book on computers**. It is not only the most comprehensive and informative comput-er book that I have come across, but it also is written in a style that it is easy to understand. This is a must-read for anyone interested in this subject."

RICHARD DRAKE, PRESIDENT, Compucycle

"I haven't found a computing book more thor-ough and precise than *Upgrading and Repairing PCs*. Many hours of frustration have been saved through this book!"

PHILLIP DAVIS

"The writing style of Scott Mueller has no equal that I have found in the computer book world so far. I would recommend *Upgrading and Repairing PCs* to *anyone* interested in knowing what goes on in his or her computer and how

to fix it without having to depend on—or more importantly—*pay* someone else to do it."

GREGORY A. MACK

"Scott Mueller has an uncanny ability to take very complex and wide-ranging material and make it VERY understandable. His newest book is yet another example of his thorough-ness, being up-to-date, and hitting the mark for those of us involved with PCs. Scott's books always answer my questions. **I would-n't touch, buy, open, or use a PC with-out having Scott's newest edition at my side.**"

JOHN P. COWAN, INTERNET FACILITATOR, Business Insurance Group

"If I'd had the book as a reference in the field, there is no doubt in my mind that I would have saved many hours of time. For me, this would more than justify three times the books price in saved time for my small, one-man operation."

BRETT HAVENER, COMPUTER TECH/ BUSINESS OWNER

"Never have I felt compelled to send anyone a thank you until I touched Upgrading and Repairing PCs. If you're like me and your company depends on this information, you'll appreciate the value of having all this knowl-edge in just one place."

NELSON G. COE, PRESIDENT, Nelco Distribution Inc.

"With the new information, this is one book that will not be gathering dust on a book-shelf."

JAY BRATCHER, SYSTEM TECHNICIAN, Strategic Supply, Inc.

"The book is all I thought it would be—plus a lot more. It is easy to understand and is thor-ough and very good for someone who wants to maintain and upgrade his own PC. It is worth the money if you are serious about PC care and maintenance."

JOE T. DEFELICE JR.

UPGRADING AND REPAIRING PCS,

Eleventh Edition

Scott Mueller

201 West 103rd Street,
Indianapolis, Indiana 46290

Contents at a Glance

Upgrading and Repairing PCs, 11th Edition

Copyright © 1999 by Que® Corporation

International Standard Book Number: 0-7897-1903-7

Library of Congress Catalog Card Number: 98-87630

Printed in the United States of America

First Printing: August 1999

01   00   99   4   3   2   1

Trademarks

Warning and Disclaimer

Associate Publisher
Jim Minatel

Acquisitions Editor
Jill Byus

Senior Development Editor
Rick Kughen

Technical Editors
Mark Soper
Jeff Sloan
Joe Curley
Anthony Armstrong
Doug Klippert
Pete Lenges
Karen Weinstein
Kent Easley
Ariel Silverstone

Managing Editor
Lisa Wilson

Project Editor
Natalie Harris

Copy Editors
Pamela Woolf
Michael Dietsch
JoAnna Kremer
Kelly Talbot
Kelli Brooks
Lisa Lord

Indexer
Kevin Kent

Proofreader
Benjamin Berg

Software Development Specialist
Brandon Penticuff

Interior Design
Glenn Larsen

Cover Design
Karen Ruggles

Layout Technician
Mark Walchle

Formatter
Katie Robinson

Contents

4 Motherboards and Buses   203

5 BIOS   345

24 Building or Upgrading Systems   1251

25 PC Diagnostics, Testing, and Maintenance   1287

To Lynn:

Another year, another edition... Now ist der time ven ve dahnce!

About the Author

Scott Mueller is president of Mueller Technical Research, an international research and corporate training firm. Since 1982, MTR has specialized in the industry's longest running, most in-depth, accurate and effective corporate PC hardware and technical training seminars, maintaining a client list that includes Fortune 500 companies, the U.S. and foreign governments, major software and hardware corporations, as well as PC enthusiasts and entrepreneurs. His seminars have been presented to thousands of PC support professionals throughout the world.

Scott Mueller has developed and presented training courses in all areas of PC hardware and software. He is an expert in PC hardware, operating systems, and data-recovery techniques. For more information about a custom PC hardware or data recovery training seminar for your organization, contact Lynn at

Mueller Technical Research
21 Spring Lane
Barrington Hills, IL 60010-9009
(847) 854-6794
(847) 854-6795 Fax
Internet: scottmueller@compuserve.com
Web: http://www.m-tr.com

Scott has many popular books, articles, and course materials to his credit, including *Upgrading and Repairing PCs*, which has sold more than 2 million copies, making it by far the most popular PC hardware book on the market today. His two hour video titled *Your PC—The Inside Story* is available through LearnKey, Inc. For ordering information, contact

LearnKey, Inc.
1845 West Sunset Boulevard
St. George, UT 84770
(800) 865-0165
(801) 674-9733
(801) 674-9734 Fax

If you have questions about PC hardware, suggestions for the next edition of the book, or any comments in general, send them to Scott via email at scottmueller@compuserve.com.

When he is not working on PC-related books or teaching seminars, Scott can usually be found in the garage working on vehicle performance projects. This year a Harley Road King is taking most of his time, and he promises to finish the Impala next.

Special Thanks to...

Mark Edward Soper is a writer, editor, and trainer who has worked with IBM-compatible PCs since 1984. Mark spent plenty of time in the trenches as a technical support specialist and technical salesman before his first computer-related articles were published in 1988. He has written over 100 articles on a wide variety of topics from scanner upgrades to Web-enabled presentations for major industry publications including *WordPerfect Magazine*, *PCNovice Guides*, *PCToday*, and *SmartComputing*. Since 1992 he has taught thousands of students across the country how to troubleshoot and upgrade their computers, create Web sites, and build basic networks. Mark is a rail fan from way back, and has also had his photos published in *Passenger Train Journal* magazine. You can learn more about Mark at his company's Web site, www.selectsystems.com, and you can write to him at mesoper@selectsystems.com.

Jeff Sloan is the Dimension OEM BIOS development manager for Dell Computers. Prior to Dell, he worked at IBM PC Company for 15 years, the last eight of which were spent in PS/2 BIOS development and the Problem Determination SWAT team. He has a BS in computer science from University of Pittsburgh, 1979, and is currently working on an MS in Software Engineering at Southwest Texas State. Jeff has tech edited numerous Que books.

Joe Curley is an engineering manager at Dell Computer Corporation, working in audio, motion video, and graphics development. Prior to Dell, Joe worked for Tseng Labs, Inc. and was a pioneer in Super VGA graphics development in numerous roles, including general manager for Advanced Systems development. Joe has spoken at several leading industry conferences, including the Windows Hardware Engineering Conference, about topics ranging from I/O bus and PC architecture to graphics memory architecture.

Anthony Armstrong is a development engineer working for Dell Computer Corporation on PC motherboards for the Dimension and Optiplex lines of business. Anthony has previously worked for IBM in the PowerPC reference platform test group and currently has one personal computer-related patent pending. Anthony is a computer engineering graduate of the University of Texas at Austin.

Doug Klippert is an independent contract trainer living in Tacoma, Washington. He is a Microsoft Certified Software Engineer (MCSE) and a Microsoft Certified Trainer (MCT). He is also a Microsoft Office User Specialist, Master in Office 97. Doug has a BA in accounting and an MBA in public administration. He can be reached at doug@klippert.com. Doug has tech edited numerous Que books.

Pete Lenges is a technical software instructor for New Horizons Computer Learning Centers, one of the world's largest training integrators. He is an A+ certified technician with a specialty in Microsoft operating systems as well as an MCT (Microsoft Certified Trainer) and MCP (Microsoft Certified Professional). He currently conducts both hardware and software classes at the Indianapolis facility and also assists in the everyday management of his company's LAN/WAN.

Karen Weinstein is an independent computer consultant living in North Potomac, Maryland. She has had over a decade of experience in PC sales and support. Karen has a BS in business administration from the University of Maryland.

Kent Easley is an assistant professor of computer information systems at Howard College in Big Spring, Texas. He teaches introductory computer science, networking, and programming. He is a Microsoft Certified Professional and supervises the Microsoft Authorized Academic Training Program (AATP) at Howard College. He has experience as a network administrator and as a systems librarian. Kent has tech edited numerous Que books. He can be reached by email at keasley@hc.cc.tx.us.

Ariel Silverstone has been involved in the computer industry for over 15 years. He has consulted nationally for Fortune 1000 firms on the implementation of management information systems and networking systems. He has designed and set up hundreds of networks over the years, including using all versions of NetWare and Windows NT Server. For five years, he has been the chief technical officer for a computer systems integrator in Indiana. While no longer a professional programmer, he is competent in a variety of computer languages, including both low- and high-level languages. He has been a technical reviewer over 20 books, including titles on Windows NT, NetWare, networking, Windows 2000, Cisco routers, and firewalls.

Acknowledgments

This Eleventh Edition is the product of a great deal of additional research and development over the previous editions. Several people have helped me with both the research and production of this book. I would like to thank the following people:

First, a very special thanks to my wife and partner, Lynn. This book continues to be an incredible burden on both our business and family life, and she has to put up with a lot! Apparently I can be slightly incorrigible after staying up all night writing, drinking Jolt, and eating chocolate covered raisins. <g> Lynn is also excellent at dealing with the many companies we have to contact for product information and research. She is the backbone of MTR.

Thanks to Lisa Carlson of Mueller Technical Research for helping with product research and office management. She has fantastic organizational skills that have been a tremendous help in managing all of the information that comes into and goes out of this office.

I must give a special thanks to Jill Byus, Rick Kughen, and Jim Minatel at Que. They are my editorial and publishing team, and have all worked so incredibly hard to make this the best book possible. They have consistently pressed me to improve the content of this book. You guys are the best!

I would also like to say thanks to Mark Soper, who added expertise in areas that I might tend to neglect. Also thanks to all the technical editors who checked my work and questioned me at every turn, as well as the numerous other editors, illustrators, and staff at Que who work so hard to get this book out!

Thanks to all the companies who have provided hardware, software, and research information that has been helpful in developing this book. Thanks to David Means for feedback from the trenches about various products and especially data recovery information.

Thanks to all the readers who have emailed me with suggestions concerning this book; I welcome all your comments. A special thanks to Paul Reid who always has many suggestions to offer for improving the book and making it more technically accurate.

Finally, I would like to thank the more than 10,000 people who have attended my seminars; you may not realize how much I learn from each of you and all your questions! Thanks also to those of you on the Internet and CompuServe forums with both questions and answers, from which I have also learned a great deal.

Tell Us What You Think!

As the reader of this book, *you* are our most important critic and commentator. We value your opinion and want to know what we're doing right, what we could do better, what areas you'd like to see us publish in, and any other words of wisdom you're willing to pass our way.

As the associate publisher for this book, I welcome your comments. You can fax, email, or write me directly to let me know what you did or didn't like about this book—as well as what we can do to make our books stronger.

While I cannot help you with technical problems related to the topics covered in this book, Scott Mueller welcomes your technical questions. The best way to reach him is by email at scottmueller@compuserve.com.

When you write, please be sure to include this book's title and author as well as your name and phone or fax number. I will carefully review your comments and share them with the author and editors who worked on the book.

Fax:	317.817.7070
Email:	hardware@mcp.com
Mail:	Macmillan Computer Publishing
	201 West 103rd Street
	Indianapolis, IN 46290 USA

Introduction

Welcome to *Upgrading and Repairing PCs, Eleventh Edition*. More than just a minor revision, this new edition contains hundreds of pages of new material and extensive updates. The PC industry is moving faster than ever, and this book is the most accurate, complete, and up-to-date book of its type on the market today.

This book is for people who want to upgrade, repair, maintain, and troubleshoot computers or for those enthusiasts who want to know more about PC hardware. This book covers the full range of PC-compatible systems from the oldest 8-bit machines to the latest in high-end 64-bit PC-based workstations. If you need to know about everything from the original PC to the latest in PC technology on the market today, this book is definitely for you.

This book covers state-of-the-art hardware and accessories that make the most modern personal computers easier, faster, and more productive to use. Hardware coverage includes all the Intel and Intel-compatible processors through the latest Pentium III, Celeron, and AMD CPU chips; new cache and main memory technology; PCI and AGP local bus technology; CD-ROM drives; tape backups; sound boards; PC-card and Cardbus devices for laptops; IDE and SCSI interface devices; larger and faster hard drives; and new video adapter and display capabilities.

The comprehensive coverage of the PC-compatible personal computer in this book has consistently won acclaim since debuting as the first book of its kind on the market in 1988. Now with the release of this 11th Edition, *Upgrading and Repairing PCs* continues its role as not only the best-selling book of its type, but also the most comprehensive and complete reference on even the most modern systems—those based on cutting-edge hardware and software. This book examines PCs in depth, outlines the differences among them, and presents options for configuring each system.

Sections of this book provide detailed information about each internal component of a personal computer system, from the processor to the keyboard and video display. This book examines the options available in modern, high-performance PC configurations and how to use them to your advantage; it focuses on much of the hardware and software available today and specifies the optimum configurations for achieving maximum benefit for the time and money you spend. At a glance, here are the major system components, peripherals, technologies, and processes covered in this edition of *Upgrading and Repairing PCs*:

- Pentium III, Pentium II, Celeron, Xeon, and earlier central processing unit (CPU) chips as well as Intel-compatible processors from AMD, Cyrix, and other vendors. The processor is one of the most important parts of a PC, and this book features more extensive and updated processor coverage than ever before.
- The latest processor-upgrade socket and slot specifications, including expanded coverage of Super7 motherboards and Intel's new Socket 370.

- New motherboard designs, including the ATX, WTX, micro-ATX, and NLX form factors. This new edition features the most accurate, detailed and complete reference to PC motherboards that you will find.

- The latest chipsets for current processor families, including all new coverage of the Intel 810 chipset, as well as new members of the 440 chipset family, including the 440ZX, 440GX, and 440NX.

- Special bus architectures and devices, including high-speed PCI (Peripheral Component Interconnect), AGP (Accelerated Graphics Port), and the 100MHz processor bus.

- Bus and system resources that often conflict such as interrupt request (IRQ) lines, Direct Memory Access (DMA) channels, and input/output (I/O) port addresses.

- Plug-and-Play (PnP) architecture for setting system resources automatically, including features such as IRQ steering, which allows you to share the IRQ lines—the resource most in-contention in a modern PC.

- All new coverage of the BIOS, including detailed coverage of BIOS setup utilities, Flash upgradable BIOSes, and Plug-and-Play BIOS. The CD accompanying this book also contains BIOS error codes, beep codes, and error messages for Phoenix, AMI, Award, Microid Research, and IBM BIOSes.

- Greatly expanded coverage of IDE and SCSI includes in-depth looks at hard drive interfaces and technologies, including new IDE specifications such as Ultra ATA/33, Ultra-ATA/66, and the latest on SCSI-3.

- Floppy drives and other removable storage devices such as Zip and LS-120 (SuperDisk) drives, tape drives, and recordable CDs.

- New coverage of drive installation and configuration, including steps for partitioning hard drives, mapping drive letters, and transferring data from an old drive to a new drive.

- Expanded coverage of burgeoning CD technologies, including the newest MultiBeam CD-ROMs. CD-R/CD-RW coverage now includes detailed steps and advice for avoiding buffer under-runs, creating bootable CDs, and selecting the most reliable media.

- Increasing system memory capacity with SIMM, DIMM, and RIMM modules and increasing system reliability with ECC RAM.

- New types of memory, including Synchronous Pipeline Burst cache, EDO RAM, Burst EDO, Synchronous DRAM, and Rambus DRAM.

- Large-screen Super VGA monitors, flat-panel LED displays, high-speed graphics adapters, and 3D graphics accelerators. Includes advice for choosing a 3D accelerator to optimize your system for game play, as well as coverage of 3D technologies, chipsets and APIs.

- Peripheral devices such as sound cards, modems, DVD drives, and network interface cards.

- PC-card and Cardbus devices for laptops.

- Laser and dot-matrix printer features, maintenance, and repair. Also includes all new coverage of scanners and scanning technology.

The Eleventh Edition includes more detailed troubleshooting advice that will help you track down problems with your memory, system resources, new drive installations, BIOS, I/O addresses, video and audio performance, modems, and much more.

This book also focuses on software problems, starting with the basics of how an operating system such as DOS or Windows works with your system hardware to start your system. You also learn how to troubleshoot and avoid problems involving system hardware, the operating system, and applications software.

This book is the result of years of research and development in the production of my PC hardware, operating system, and data recovery seminars. Since 1982, I have personally taught (and still teach) thousands of people about PC troubleshooting, upgrading, maintenance, repair, and data recovery. This book represents the culmination of many years of field experience and knowledge culled from the experiences of thousands of others. What originally started out as a simple course workbook has over the years grown into a complete reference on the subject. Now you can benefit from this experience and research.

What Are the Main Objectives of This Book?

Upgrading and Repairing PCs focuses on several objectives. The primary objective is to help you learn how to maintain, upgrade, and repair your PC system. To that end, *Upgrading and Repairing PCs* helps you fully understand the family of computers that has grown from the original IBM PC, including all PC-compatible systems. This book discusses all areas of system improvement such as floppy disks, hard disks, central processing units, and power-supply improvements. The book discusses proper system and component care; it specifies the most failure-prone items in different PC systems and tells you how to locate and identify a failing component. You'll learn about powerful diagnostics hardware and software that enable a system to help you determine the cause of a problem and how to repair it.

PCs are moving forward rapidly in power and capabilities. Processor performance increases with every new chip design. *Upgrading and Repairing PCs* helps you gain an understanding of all the processors used in PC-compatible computer systems.

This book covers the important differences between major system architectures from the original Industry Standard Architecture (ISA) to the latest in PCI and AGP systems. *Upgrading and Repairing PCs* covers each of these system architectures and their adapter boards to help you make decisions about which kind of system you want to buy in the future, and to help you upgrade and troubleshoot such systems.

The amount of storage space available to modern PCs is increasing geometrically. *Upgrading and Repairing PCs* covers storage options ranging from larger, faster hard drives to state-of-the-art storage devices. In addition, it provides detailed information on upgrading and troubleshooting system RAM.

When you finish reading this book, you should have the knowledge to upgrade, troubleshoot, and repair almost all systems and components.

Who Should Use This Book?

Upgrading and Repairing PCs is designed for people who want a thorough understanding of how their PC systems work. Each section fully explains common and not-so-common problems, what causes problems, and how to handle problems when they arise. You will gain an understanding of disk configuration and interfacing, for example, that can improve your diagnostics and troubleshooting skills. You'll develop a feel for what goes on in a system so that you can rely on your own judgment and observations and not some table of canned troubleshooting steps.

Upgrading and Repairing PCs is written for people who will select, install, configure, maintain, and repair systems they or their companies use. To accomplish these tasks, you need a level of knowledge much higher than that of an average system user. You must know exactly which tool to use for a task and how to use the tool correctly. This book can help you achieve this level of knowledge.

What Is in This Book?

This book is organized into chapters that cover the components of a PC system. There are a few chapters that serve to introduce or expand in an area not specifically component-related, but most parts in the PC will have a dedicated chapter or section, which will aid you in finding the information you want. Also note that the index has been improved greatly over previous editions, which will further aid in finding information in a book of this size.

Chapters 1 and 2 of this book serve primarily as an introduction. Chapter 1, "Personal Computer Background," begins with an introduction to the development of the original IBM PC and PC-compatibles. This chapter incorporates some of the historical events that led to the development of the microprocessor and the PC. Chapter 2, "PC Components, Features, and System Design," provides information about the different types of systems you encounter and what separates one type of system from another, including the types of system buses that differentiate systems. Chapter 2 also provides an overview of the types of PC systems that help build a foundation of knowledge essential for the remainder of the book, and it offers some insight as to how the PC market is driven and where components and technologies are sourced.

Chapters 3–6 cover the primary system components of a PC. Chapter 3, "Microprocessors," goes into detail about the central processing unit, or main processor, including those from Intel, AMD, and other companies. Chapter 4, "Motherboards and Buses," covers the motherboard, chipsets, motherboard components, and system buses in detail. Because the processor and motherboard are perhaps the most significant parts of the PC, Chapters 3 and 4 were a primary focus of mine when rewriting this book. They have received extensive updates and a great deal of new material has been added.

Chapter 5, "BIOS," has a detailed discussion of the system BIOS including types, features, and upgrades. This has grown from a section of the book to a complete chapter, with more information on this subject than ever before. Be sure to see the exhaustive list of BIOS codes and error messages I've included on the CD-ROM. They're all printable, so be sure to print the codes for your BIOS in case you need them later.

Chapter 6, "Memory," gives a detailed discussion of PC memory, including the latest in cache and main memory specifications. Next to the processor and motherboard, the system memory is one of the most important parts of a PC. Memory is also one of the most difficult things to understand, as it is somewhat intangible and not always obvious how it works. This chapter has received extensive updates in order to make memory technology more understandable, as well as to cover the newest technologies on the market today. Coverage of cache memory has been updated in order to help you understand this difficult subject and know exactly how the different levels of cache in a modern PC function, interact, and affect system performance.

Chapter 7, "The IDE Interface," gives a detailed discussion of ATA/IDE, including types and specifications. This includes coverage of the new Ultra-ATA modes that allow 33MB/sec and 66MB/sec operation. Chapter 8, "The SCSI Interface," includes a discussion of SCSI including the new higher speed modes possible with SCSI-3. The SCSI chapter covers the new Low Voltage Differential signaling used by some of the higher speed devices on the market, as well as the latest information on cables, terminators, and SCSI configurations.

Chapter 9, "Magnetic Storage Principles," details the inner workings of magnetic storage devices such as disk and tape drives. Chapter 10, "Hard Disk Storage," details the function and operation of hard disk drives, while Chapter 11, "Floppy Disk Storage," does the same thing for floppy drives. Chapter 12, "High-Capacity Removable Disk Storage," covers removable storage drives such as SuperDisk (LS-120), Zip, and tape drives. Chapter 13, "Optical Storage," covers optical drives and storage using CD and DVD technology, including CD recorders, rewritable CDs, and other optical technologies. This chapter features extensive updates on DVD as well as all the CD recording technology. Chapter 14, "Physical Drive Installation and Configuration," covers how to install drives of all kinds in a PC system.

Chapter 15, "Video Hardware," covers everything there is to know about video cards and displays. Chapter 16, "Serial, Parallel, and Other I/O Interfaces," covers the standard serial and parallel ports still found in most systems, as well as newer technology such as USB and iLink (FireWire). Chapter 17, "Input Devices," covers keyboards, pointing devices, and game ports used to communicate with a PC. Chapter 18, "Internet Connectivity," covers all the different methods for connecting to the Net. Chapter 19, "Local Area Networking," covers PC-based local area networks in detail. Chapter 20, "Audio Hardware," covers sound and sound-related devices, including sound boards and speaker systems. Chapter 21, "Power Supply and Chassis/Case," is a detailed investigation of the power supply, which still remains the primary cause for PC system problems and failures. Chapter 22, "Printers and Scanners," covers the various types of printers and scanners in detail.

Chapter 23, "Portable PCs," covers portable systems including laptop and notebook systems. It also focuses on all the technology unique and peculiar to portable systems, such as mobile processors, display, battery, and other technologies.

Chapter 24, "Building or Upgrading Systems," focuses on buying or building a PC-compatible system as well as system upgrades and improvements. This information is useful, especially if you make purchasing decisions, and also serves as a general guideline for features that make a certain compatible computer a good or bad choice. The more adventurous can use this information to assemble their own custom system from scratch. Physical disassembly and assembly procedures are also discussed.

Chapter 25, "PC Diagnostics, Testing, and Maintenance," covers diagnostic and testing tools and procedures. This chapter also adds more information on general PC troubleshooting and problem determination. Chapter 26, "Operating Systems Software and Troubleshooting," covers operating system software and troubleshooting. Chapter 27, "File Systems and Data Recovery," covers file systems and data recovery procedures.

Chapter 28, "A Final Word," offers closure by tying all the technologies together and providing suggestions on additional places to find information.

What's New and Special About the Eleventh Edition

Many of you who are reading this have purchased one or more of the previous editions. Based on your letters, emails, and other correspondence, I know that as much as you value each new edition, you want to know what new information I'm bringing you. So here is a short list of the major improvements to this edition:

- As the PC industry continues to move further away from "IBM compatible" thinking and nomenclature, this edition is doing the same. In Chapter 2 I discuss who controls the PC hardware industry and what effect this control has on you.

- The updating of Chapter 3 involved a major reorganization of the chapter and many pages of new coverage. The new organization looks at all the relevant processors (and coprocessors and processor upgrades) in terms of the family of processor they belong to. The coverage of Pentium II, III, and Celeron processors has been strengthened with up-to-date listings of steppings, processors from AMD, Cyrix, and other vendors have been given more coverage. Cutting-edge features such as on-die L2 cache are explained in more detail as well. The latest processor slots and sockets are covered, including Slot 1, Slot 2, Socket 370, and the Super7 socket architecture. I hope you will like the substantial additions of illustrations and photographs that better show items such as socket types, processor features, and markings.

- Chapter 4 takes the new approach of covering the motherboards and the buses found on the motherboards together as one topic. In addition, you will find extensive new coverage of the latest chipsets, which form the basis of all modern motherboards. This chapter includes detailed coverage of the features, capabilities, and limitations of the chipsets in common use today.

- Chapter 5 is a new addition to the lineup that delves into how the drivers in a system work together to act as an interface between the hardware and the operating system software. This chapter also explains ROM chips installed on adapter cards, as well as all the additional drivers loaded when your system starts up. You'll also find an in-depth look at working with the BIOS Setup utility.

■ Chapter 6 has been reorganized to begin by looking at types of memory and how they are installed. All of the more recent types of memory, including SDRAM and RDRAM, are explained in more detail in this edition. You'll also find answers to often-asked questions relating memory speed to processor speed and a more thorough explanation of why error checking is still an important memory feature. This chapter also contains new coverage of RIMMs, continuity modules, and Rambus memory in general.

■ Chapter 7 and 8 also contain a great deal of new information. Here, you'll find in-depth coverage of both interfaces, including ATA/66 and SCSI-3.

■ Chapters 9 and 10 contain expanded coverage of hard drive mechanics and principles of electromagnetism. Chapter 12 contains the latest information on the SuperDisk drives and investigates problems with other removable formats such as the Iomega Zip "Click of Death" syndrome.

■ Chapter 13 contains expanded coverage of CD-R and CD-RW drives, including advice for writing CDs more reliably and creating bootable CDs. This chapter also includes improved coverage of DVD and new MultiBeam technology.

■ Chapter 14 walks you through installing drives—hard drives, floppy drives, CD-ROM, magnetic tape—and helps you set map a letter to the drive.

■ Chapter 15 includes enhanced coverage of video displays—including flat-panel LEDs—and video cards for gaming and multimedia enthusiasts.

■ Chapter 18 contains a greatly expanded coverage of Internet connectivity options, including more coverage of 56K connections, ISDN, DSL, DirecPC, and leased lines.

■ Chapter 19 is the perfect primer for those new to networking—at home or in the office. This chapter provides the background you'll need to be productive on a network—whether you're part of a corporate-wide LAN or simply networking a pair of computers at home.

■ Chapter 20 helps you optimize your computer's sound output, whether you are a hardcore gamer, a MIDI musician, or if you want to learn about the MP3 format that is revolutionizing the way musical artists distribute music via the Internet.

■ Chapters 25 and 26 both have new and different coverage. Much of this is a reflection of newer operating systems such as Windows 98, NT, and Windows 2000. The fact that troubleshooting and configuration tools are less dependent on hardware system vendors (such as IBM or Compaq) and more generally are third-party software tools necessitates a new way to look at setup and testing.

■ Chapter 27 takes an in-depth look at the file system, including new examples that explain how FAT16, FAT32, and NTFS work. If you're upgrading to Windows 2000, you'll find that choosing the right file system is an important decision to make up-front. This chapter provides the in-depth background you need to make a sound decision.

Although these are the major changes to the core of the book, every chapter has seen substantial updates. If you thought the additions to the Tenth Anniversary Edition were incredible, wait until you see what I've done with the Eleventh Edition. It is the most comprehensive overhaul this book has seen since I wrote the first edition 11 years ago!

The Eleventh Edition CD-ROM

As if everything included in the printed book isn't enough, this edition contains an all-new CD-ROM. You'll find the new content on this CD to be an indispensable addition to this book. The CD contains

- *Que's edition of PartitionMagic.* Create and manage multiple hard disk partitions with this powerful application. PartitionMagic allows you to create partitions without first backing up your data and deleting existing partitions. PartitionMagic also allows you to create and manage partitions using a native Windows 95/98 and NT executable that operates from within the Windows interface. The best part is that because you can work within the Windows interface from the same drive you are partitioning, you don't have to spend hours reloading your operating system, applications, and data files.

  PartitionMagic allows you to switch between FAT and FAT32 file systems with ease. It also enables you to manage multiple operating systems in separate partitions. PartitionMagic includes support for FAT, FAT32, NTFS, HPFS, and Linux ext2 file systems.

  You can use PartitionMagic as a replacement to FDISK or use it to tweak your drive partitioning after completing your drive setup with FDISK. If you decide to change partitioning later, run PartitionMagic and reallocate your partitions.

▶▶ See Appendix C, "Making the Most of PartitionMagic and Drive Image" p. 1529.

- *Que's Edition of Drive Image.* Rest easy knowing your data is secure because you've created compressed backups of your hard drives and stored them safely to your Zip, LS-120 SuperDrive, or CD-R. Drive Image creates a carbon copy of your drive, including all optimizations and configurations, allowing you to make a complete backup you can use to restore your system or make exact duplicates of a system. Drive Image saves all passwords, Registry settings, user profiles, and customizations with the image, saving you hours of down time.

  Create compressed hard-disk image files that are about 40 percent smaller than the used space on the drive. You can even create and image of your primary partition, store it to a separate partition, and restore your primary partition in an emergency.

  Drive Image supports FAT, FAT32, NTFS, and HPFS file systems, and allows for sector-by-sector copying of data from Windows, Linux, UNIX, and NetWare drives.

▶▶ See Appendix C, "Making the Most of PartitionMagic and Drive Image" p. 1529.

Note

PartitionMagic and Drive Image would cost more than $100 if purchased separately. The Que Editions of both applications are yours for the price of this book. These are fully licensed products, not demos or timeout versions.

- *A+ Testing Questions from Heathkit.* Study for the A+ exams using 150 training questions from Heathkit Educational Systems, a leader in technical-based education.

  The questions appear in an interactive, Windows-based format that allows you to answer questions as if your were taking the actual tests. Use this book to learn the concepts and technologies then use the test questions to sharpen your skills and point out areas in which you need more study.

Note

If you need additional help studying for A+ Certification, see my *Upgrading and Repairing PCs: A+ Certification Study Guide*, also published by Que, ISBN 0-7897-2095-7.

■ *Hard Drive Specifications from Blue-Planet.com.* This database contains hard drive specifications for more than 4,000 hard drives from Seagate, Quantum, Western Digital, Maxtor, IBM, and many others. This incredibly useful database puts thousands of drive specifications at your fingertips, and the elegant database design allows you to quickly find and print just the specs you need.

Note

The CD also includes a wealth of legacy PC technical information. See the Technical Reference section on the CD.

Note

If you are a field technician or someone who frequently works on PCs away from your desk, I recommend picking up a copy of *Upgrading and Repairing PCs: Technician's Portable Reference*, also published by Que (ISBN: 0-7897-2096-5). This handy book is filled with many of the tables and technical detail from this book, as well as boiled down versions of these chapters that put crucial details and technical specifications at your fingertips—all in a portable book that fits easily in your toolkit or briefcase.

■ *Vendor List Database.* Use Scott Mueller's fully searchable database of vendors to locate addresses, phone numbers, and URLs for all the manufacturers discussed in this book. This keyword searchable database allows you to search for any vendor or product using any keyword. Instead of searching through 70+ pages of vendors, search and extract the data you need.

■ *BIOS Codes, Beep Codes, and Error Message.* Find complete listings of BIOS codes, beep codes and error messages from Phoenix, AMI, Award, Microid Research (MR BIOS), and IBM—as well as some of those used by OEM vendors. If you are service technician, you'll find these lists to be an integral part of your troubleshooting arsenal. If you a are a private user, I recommend that you print the codes for your BIOS and keep them in a safe place in case you need to troubleshoot BIOS errors.

■ *Third-Party Software.* Use Que's extensive library of software, including overclocking, Y2K, and performance benchmarking utilities to tune and optimize your PC.

■ *Previous Editions of This Book.* If you're looking for legacy coverage of older technologies, be sure to check the previous editions of this book that are in PDF format on the CD (the Fourth, Sixth, and Tenth Anniversary editions are included in their entirety and are fully printable). Simply use the included Adobe Acrobat Reader software to open and print the pages you need from the selected editions of this book.

■ *IBM Personal Computer Family Hardware Reference.* Many of the technologies used in today's PCs originated from the original IBM PC, XT, and AT systems. This chapter serves as a technical reference will prove valuable if you are service technician who is required to work on all types of computers. If you want to learn how the original PC evolved into what you use today, this is an excellent place to start.

A Personal Note

I am so excited about all the new changes in this edition, I can hardly wait for everybody to see it. The last few months before the release of this new edition were more difficult than usual, not only in meeting the deadlines that are required to bring it out on schedule, but also while corresponding with readers and teaching my classes using the previous edition and knowing I had all the great new information written for this edition. This has been more noticeable to me this time around because this is perhaps the most extensive update I have done; there is so much new material added. Well now the wait is over, and this new edition is now available.

When asked what year was his favorite Corvette, Dave McLellan, former manager of the Corvette platform at GM, always said "Next year's model." Now with the new Eleventh Edition, next year's model has just become this year's model, until next year that is...

During the months leading up to the release of the Eleventh Edition, I and everybody else at Que have worked hard to make this the best edition ever. I am so grateful to everybody who has helped me with this book over the last 11 years as well as all the loyal readers who have been reading this book, many of you since the first edition came out. I have had personal contact with many thousands of you in the seminars I have been teaching since 1982, and all I can say is I enjoy your comments and even criticisms tremendously. Using this book in a teaching environment has been a major factor in its development. Some of you might be interested to know that I originally began writing this book in 1985; back then it was used exclusively in my PC hardware seminars before being published by Que in 1988. In one way or another I have been writing and rewriting this book almost continuously for more than 15 years! In the more than 11 years since it was first published, *Upgrading and Repairing PCs* has proven to be not only the first but absolutely the best book of its kind. With the new Eleventh Edition, it is even better than ever. Your comments, suggestions, and support have helped this book to become the best PC hardware book on the market. I look forward to hearing your comments after you see this exciting new edition.

Scott

Personal Computer Background

1

Many discoveries and inventions have directly and indirectly contributed to the development of the personal computer. Examining a few important developmental landmarks can help bring the entire picture into focus.

Computer History—Before Personal Computers

The first computers of any kind were simple calculators. Even these evolved from mechanical devices to electronic digital devices.

Timeline

The following is a timeline of some significant events in computer history. It is not meant to be complete, just a representation of some of the major landmarks in computer development.

- *1617.* John Napier creates "Napiers Bones," wooden or ivory rods used for calculating.

- *1642.* Blaise Pascal introduces the Pascaline digital adding machine.

- *1822.* Charles Babbage conceives the Difference Engine, and later the Analytical Engine, a true general purpose computing machine.

- *1906.* Lee DeForest patents the vacuum tube triode, used as an electronic switch in the first electronic computers.

- *1945.* John von Neumann wrote "First Draft of a Report on the EDVAC," in which he outlined the architecture of the modern stored-program computer.

- *1946.* ENIAC was introduced, an electronic computing machine built by John Mauchly and J. Presper Eckert.

- *1947.* On December 23, William Shockley, Walter Brattain, and John Bardeen successfully tested the point-contact transistor, setting off the semiconductor revolution.

- *1949.* Maurice Wilkes assembled the EDSAC, the first practical stored-program computer, at Cambridge University.

- *1950.* Engineering Research Associates of Minneapolis built the ERA 1101, one of the first commercially produced computers.

- *1952.* The UNIVAC I delivered to the U.S. Census Bureau was the first commercial computer to attract widespread public attention.

- *1953.* IBM shipped its first electronic computer, the 701.

- *1954.* A Silicon-based junction transistor, perfected by Gordon Teal of Texas Instruments Inc., brought the price of this component down to $2.50.

- *1954.* The IBM 650 magnetic drum calculator established itself as the first mass-produced computer, with the company selling 450 in one year.

- *1955.* Bell Laboratories announced the first fully transistorized computer, TRADIC.

- *1956.* MIT researchers built the TX-0, the first general-purpose, programmable computer built with transistors.

- *1956.* The era of magnetic disk storage dawned with IBM's shipment of a 305 RAMAC to Zellerbach Paper in San Francisco.

- *1958.* Jack Kilby created the first integrated circuit at Texas Instruments to prove that resistors and capacitors could exist on the same piece of semiconductor material.

- *1959*. IBM's 7000 series mainframes were the company's first transistorized computers.

- *1959*. Robert Noyce's practical integrated circuit, invented at Fairchild Camera and Instrument Corp., allowed printing of conducting channels directly on the silicon surface.

- *1960*. Bell Labs designed its Dataphone, the first commercial modem, specifically for converting digital computer data to analog signals for transmission across its long-distance network.

- *1960*. The precursor to the minicomputer, DEC's PDP-1 sold for $120,000.

- *1961*. According to *Datamation* magazine, IBM had an 81.2-percent share of the computer market in 1961, the year in which it introduced the 1400 Series.

- *1964*. CDC's 6600 supercomputer, designed by Seymour Cray, performed up to three million instructions per second—a processing speed three times faster than that of its closest competitor, the IBM Stretch.

- *1964*. IBM announced System/360, a family of six mutually compatible computers and 40 peripherals that could work together.

- *1964*. Online transaction processing made its debut in IBM's SABRE reservation system, set up for American Airlines.

- *1965*. Digital Equipment Corp. introduced the PDP-8, the first commercially successful minicomputer.

- *1966*. Hewlett-Packard entered the general purpose computer business with its HP-2115 for computation, offering a computational power formerly found only in much larger computers.

- *1970*. Computer-to-computer communication expanded when the Department of Defense established four nodes on the ARPAnet: the University of California-Santa Barbara and UCLA, SRI International, and the University of Utah.

- *1971*. A team at IBM's San Jose Laboratories invented the 8-inch floppy disk.

- *1971*. The first advertisement for a microprocessor, the Intel 4004, appeared in *Electronic News*.

- *1971*. The Kenbak-1, one of the first personal computers, advertised for $750 in *Scientific American*.

- *1972*. Hewlett-Packard announced the HP-35 as "a fast, extremely accurate electronic slide rule" with a solid-state memory similar to that of a computer.

- *1972*. Intel's 8008 microprocessor made its debut.

- *1972*. Steve Wozniak built his "blue box," a tone generator to make free phone calls.

- *1973*. Robert Metcalfe devised the Ethernet method of network connection at the Xerox Palo Alto Research Center.

- *1973*. The Micral was the earliest commercial, non-kit personal computer based on a microprocessor, the Intel 8008.

- *1973*. The TV Typewriter, designed by Don Lancaster, provided the first display of alphanumeric information on an ordinary television set.

- *1974*. Researchers at the Xerox Palo Alto Research Center designed the Alto—the first workstation with a built-in mouse for input.

- *1974*. Scelbi advertised its 8H computer, the first commercially advertised U.S. computer based on a microprocessor, Intel's 8008.

- *1975.* Telenet, the first commercial packet-switching network and civilian equivalent of ARPAnet, was born.

- *1975.* The January edition of *Popular Electronics* featured the Altair 8800, based on Intel's 8080 microprocessor, on its cover.

- *1975.* The visual display module (VDM) prototype, designed by Lee Felsenstein, marked the first implementation of a memory-mapped alphanumeric video display for personal computers.

- *1976.* Steve Wozniak designed the Apple I, a single-board computer.

- *1976.* The 5 1/4-inch flexible disk drive and diskette were introduced by Shugart Associates.

- *1976.* The Cray I made its name as the first commercially successful vector processor.

- *1977.* Tandy Radio Shack introduces the TRS-80.

- *1977.* Apple computer introduces the Apple II.

- *1977.* Commodore introduces the PET (Personal Electronic Transactor).

- *1978.* The VAX 11/780 from Digital Equipment Corp. featured the capability to address up to 4.3 gigabytes of virtual memory, providing hundreds of times the capacity of most minicomputers.

- *1979.* Motorola introduces the 68000 microprocessor.

- *1980.* John Shoch, at the Xerox Palo Alto Research Center, invented the computer "worm," a short program that searched a network for idle processors.

- *1980.* Seagate Technology created the first hard disk drive for microcomputers.

- *1980.* The first optical data storage disk had 60 times the capacity of a 5 1/4-inch floppy disk.

- *1981.* Adam Osborne completed the first portable computer, the Osborne I, which weighed 24 pounds and cost $1,795.

- *1981.* IBM introduced its PC, igniting a fast growth of the personal computer market.

- *1981.* Sony introduced and shipped the first 3 1/2-inch floppy drives and diskettes.

- *1983.* Apple introduced its Lisa. The first personal computer with a graphical user interface (GUI).

- *1983.* Compaq Computer Corp. introduced their first PC clone that used the same software as the IBM PC.

- *1984.* Apple Computer launched the Macintosh, the first successful mouse-driven computer with a GUI, with a single $1.5 million commercial during the 1984 Super Bowl.

- *1984.* IBM released the PC-AT. Several times faster than original PC and based on the Intel 286 chip. This is the computer all modern PCs are based on.

- *1985.* CD-ROM was introduced from CDs on which music is recorded.

- *1986.* Compaq announced the Deskpro 386, the first computer on the market to use Intel's new 386 chip.

- *1987.* IBM introduced its PS/2 machines, which made the 3 1/2-inch floppy disk drive and VGA video standard for IBM computers.

- *1988.* Apple cofounder Steve Jobs, who left Apple to form his own company, unveiled the NeXT.

- *1988*. Compaq and other PC-clone makers developed enhanced industry standard architecture, which was better than microchannel and retained compatibility with existing machines.

- *1988*. Robert Morris' worm flooded the ARPAnet. Then 23-year-old Morris, the son of a computer security expert for the National Security Agency, sent a nondestructive worm through the Internet, causing problems for about 6,000 of the 60,000 hosts linked to the network.

- *1989*. Intel released the 486 microprocessor, which contained more than 1 million transistors.

- *1990*. The World Wide Web (WWW) was born when Tim Berners-Lee, a researcher at CERN, the high-energy physics laboratory in Geneva, developed Hypertext Markup Language (HTML).

Mechanical Calculators

One of the earliest calculating devices on record is the Abacus, which has been known and widely used for more than 2,000 years. The Abacus is a simple wooden rack holding parallel rods on which beads are strung. When these beads are manipulated back and forth according to certain rules, several different types of arithmetic operations can be performed.

Math with standard Arabic numbers found its way to Europe in the eighth and ninth centuries. In the early 1600s a man named Charles Napier (the inventor of logarithms) developed a series of rods (later called Napier's Bones) that could be used to assist with numeric multiplication.

Blaise Pascal is normally credited with building the first digital calculating machine in 1642. It could perform the addition of numbers entered on dials and was intended to help his father, who was a tax collector. Then in 1671, Gottfried Wilhelm von Leibniz invented a calculator that was finally built in 1694. His calculating machine could not only add, but by successive adding and shifting, it could also multiply.

In 1820, Charles Xavier Thomas developed the first commercially successful mechanical calculator that could not only add but also subtract, multiply, and divide. After that, a succession of ever improving mechanical calculators created by various other inventors followed.

The First Mechanical Computer

Charles Babbage, a mathematics professor in Cambridge England, is considered by many as being the father of computers because of his two great inventions—each a different type of mechanical computing engine.

The Difference Engine as he called it was conceived in 1812, and solved polynomial equations by the method of differences. By 1822, he had built a small working model of his Difference Engine for demonstration purposes. With financial help from the British government, Babbage started construction of a full-scale model in 1823. It was intended to be steam-powered, and fully automatic, and would even print the resulting tables.

Babbage continued work on it for 10 years, however, by 1833 he had lost interest because he now had an idea for an even better machine, something he described as a general-purpose, fully program-controlled, automatic mechanical digital computer. Babbage called his new machine an Analytical Engine. The plans for the Analytical Engine specified a parallel decimal computer operating on numbers (words) of 50 decimal digits and with a storage capacity (memory) of 1,000 such numbers. Built-in operations were to include everything that a modern general-purpose computer would need, even the all-important conditional function, which would allow instructions to be executed in an order depending on certain conditions, not just in numerical sequence. In modern computers this conditional capability is manifested in the IF statement found in modern computer languages. The Analytical Engine was also intended to use punched cards, which would control or program the machine. The machine was to operate automatically, by steam power, and would require only one attendant.

This Analytical Engine would have been the first true general-purpose computing device. It is regarded as the first real predecessor to a modern computer because it had all the elements of what is considered a computer today. These included

- *An input device.* Using an idea similar to the looms used in textile mills at the time, a form of punched cards supplied the input.

- *A control unit.* A barrel shaped section with many slats and studs was used to control or program the processor.

- *A processor (or calculator).* A computing engine containing hundreds of axles and thousands of gears about 10 feet tall.

- *Storage.* A unit containing more axles and gears that could hold 1,000 50-digit numbers.

- *An output device.* Plates designed to fit in a printing press, used to print the final results.

Alas, this potential first computer was never actually completed because of the problems in machining all the precision gears and mechanisms required. The tooling of the day was simply not good enough.

An interesting side note is that the punched card idea first proposed by Babbage finally came to fruition in 1890. That year a competition was held for a better method to tabulate the U.S. Census information, and Herman Hollerith, a Census Department employee, came up with the idea for punched cards. Without these cards, they had estimated the census data would take years to tabulate, with it they were able to finish in about six weeks. Hollerith went on to found the Tabulating Machine Company, which later became known as IBM.

IBM and other companies at the time developed a series of improved punch-card systems. These systems were constructed of electromechanical devices such as relays and motors. Such systems included features to automatically feed in a specified number of cards from a "read-in" station; perform operations such as addition, multiplication, and sorting; and feed out cards punched with results. These punched-card computing machines could process from 50–250 cards per minute, with each card holding up to 80-digit numbers. The punched cards provided a means of not only input and output, but they also served as a form of memory storage. Punched card machines did the bulk of the world's computing for more than 50 years and gave many of the early computer companies their start.

Electronic Computers

A physicist named John V. Atanasoff is credited with creating the first true digital electronic computer in 1942, while he worked at Iowa State College. His computer was the first to use modern digital switching techniques and vacuum tubes as the switches.

Military needs during World War II caused a great thrust forward in the evolution of computers. Systems were needed to calculate weapons trajectory and other military functions. In 1946, John P. Eckert, John W. Mauchly, and their associates at the Moore School of Electrical Engineering at the University of Pennsylvania built the first large scale electronic computer for the military. This machine became known as *ENIAC*, the *Electrical Numerical Integrator and Calculator*. It operated on 10-digit numbers, and could multiply two such numbers at the rate of 300 products per second by finding the value of each product from a multiplication table stored in its memory. ENIAC was about 1,000 times faster than the previous generation of electromechanical relay computers.

ENIAC used about 18,000 vacuum tubes, occupied 1,800 square feet (167 square meters) of floor space, and consumed about 180,000 watts of electrical power. Punched cards served as the input and output; registers served as adders and also as quick-access read-write storage.

The executable instructions composing a given program were created via specified wiring and switches that controlled the flow of computations through the machine. As such, ENIAC had to be rewired and switched for each different program to be run.

Earlier in 1945, the mathematician John Von Neumann demonstrated that a computer could have a very simple, fixed physical structure and yet be capable of executing any kind of computation effectively by means of proper programmed control without the need for any changes in hardware. In other words, you could change the program without rewiring the system. Von Neumann's ideas, often referred to as the *stored-program technique*, became fundamental for future generations of high-speed digital computers and were universally adopted.

The first generation of modern programmed electronic computers to take advantage of these improvements appeared in 1947. This group of machines included EDVAC and UNIVAC, the first commercially available computers. These computers included, for the first time, the use of true random access memory (RAM) for storing parts of the program and data that is needed quickly. Typically, they were programmed directly in machine language, although by the mid-1950s progress had been made in several aspects of advanced programming. The standout of the era is the UNIVAC (UNIVersal Automatic Computer), which was the first true general-purpose computer designed for both alphabetical and numerical uses. This made the UNIVAC a standard for business, not just science and the military.

Modern Computers

From UNIVAC to the present, computer evolution has moved very rapidly. The first generation computers were known for using vacuum tubes in their construction. The generation to follow would use the much smaller and more efficient transistor.

From Tubes to Transistors

Any modern digital computer is largely a collection of electronic switches. These switches are used to represent and control the routing of data elements called binary digits (or bits). Because of the on or off nature of the binary information and signal routing used by the computer, an efficient electronic switch was required. The first electronic computers used vacuum tubes as switches, and although the tubes worked, they had many problems.

The type of tube used in early computers was called a *triode* and was invented by Lee DeForest in 1906. It consists of a cathode and a plate, separated by a control grid, suspended in a glass vacuum tube. The cathode is heated by a red-hot electric filament, which causes it to emit electrons that are attracted to the plate. The control grid in the middle can control this flow of electrons. By making it negative, the electrons are repelled back to the cathode; by making it positive, they are attracted toward the plate. Thus by controlling the grid current, you could control the on/off output of the plate

Unfortunately, the tube was inefficient as a switch. It consumed a great deal of electrical power and gave off enormous heat—a significant problem in the earlier systems. Primarily because of the heat they generated, tubes were notoriously unreliable—one failed every couple of hours or so in the larger systems.

The invention of the transistor, or semiconductor, was one of the most important developments leading to the personal computer revolution. The transistor was invented in 1947, and announced in 1948, by Bell Laboratories engineers John Bardeen, Walter Brattain, and William Shockley. The transistor, which essentially functions as a solid-state electronic switch, replaced the much less suitable vacuum tube. Because the transistor was so much smaller and consumed significantly less power, a computer system built with transistors was also much smaller, faster, and more efficient than a computer system built with vacuum tubes.

Transistors are made primarily from the elements silicon and germanium, with certain impurities added. Depending on the impurities added and its electron content, the material becomes known as either N-Type (negative) or P-Type (positive). Both types are conductors, allowing electricity to flow in either direction. However, when the two types are joined, a barrier is formed where they meet that allows current to flow only in one direction when a voltage is present in the right polarity. This is why they are normally called semiconductors.

A transistor is made from placing two P-N junctions back to back. They are made by sandwiching a thin wafer of one type of semiconductor material between two wafers of the other type. If the wafer in-between is made from P-type material, the transistor is designated a NPN. If the wafer in-between is N-type, the transistor is designated PNP.

In an NPN transistor, the N-type semiconductor material on one side of the wafer is called the *emitter* and is normally connected to a negative current. The P-type material in the center is called the *base*. And the N-type material on the other side of the base is called the *collector*.

An NPN transistor compares to a triode tube such that the emitter is equivalent to the cathode, the base is equivalent to the grid, and the collector is equivalent to the plate. By controlling the current at the base, you can control the flow of current between the emitter and collector.

Compared to the tube, the transistor is much more efficient as a switch, and in addition can be miniaturized to microscopic scale. The latest Pentium II and III microprocessors consist of more than 27 million transistors on a single chip die!

The conversion from tubes to transistors began the trend toward miniaturization that continues to this day. Today's small laptop (or palmtop) PC systems, which run on batteries, have more computing power than many earlier systems that filled rooms and consumed huge amounts of electrical power.

Integrated Circuits

The third generation of modern computers is known for using integrated circuits instead of individual transistors. In 1959, engineers at Texas Instruments invented the integrated circuit (IC), a semiconductor circuit that contains more than one transistor on the same base (or substrate material) and connects the transistors without wires. The first IC contained only six transistors. By comparison, the Intel Pentium Pro microprocessor used in many of today's high-end systems has more than 5.5 million transistors, and the integral cache built into some of these chips contains as many as an additional 32 million transistors! Today, many ICs have transistor counts in the multimillion range.

The First Microprocessor

In 1998, Intel celebrated its 30th anniversary. Intel was founded on July 18, 1968, by Robert Noyce, Gordon Moore, and Andrew Grove. They had a specific goal: to make semiconductor memory practical and affordable. This was not a given at the time considering that Silicon chip-based memory was at least 100 times more expensive than the magnetic core memory commonly used in those days. At the time, semiconductor memory was going for about a dollar a bit, whereas core memory was about a penny a bit. Noyce said, "All we had to do was reduce the cost by a factor of a hundred, then we'd have the market; and that's basically what we did."

By 1970, Intel was known as a successful memory chip company, having introduced a 1Kbit memory chip much larger than anything else available at the time. (1Kbit equals 1,024 bits, and a byte equals 8 bits. This chip, therefore, stored only 128 bytes—not much by today's standards.) Known as the 1103 dynamic random access memory (DRAM), it became the world's largest-selling semiconductor device by the end of the following year. By this time Intel had also grown from the core founders and a handful of others to more than 100 employees.

Because of Intel's success in memory chip manufacturing and design, Japanese manufacturer Busicom asked Intel to design a set of chips for a family of high-performance programmable calculators. At the time, all logic chips were custom-designed for each application or product. Because most chips had to be custom designed specific to a particular application, no one chip could have any widespread usage.

Busicom's original design for their calculator called for at least 12 custom chips. Intel engineer Ted Hoff rejected the unwieldy proposal and instead designed a single-chip, general-purpose logic device that retrieved its application instructions from semiconductor memory. As the core of a four-chip set, this central processing unit could be controlled by a program that could essentially tailor the function of the chip to the task at hand. The chip was generic in nature, meaning it could function in designs other than calculators. Previous designs were hard-wired for one purpose, with built-in instructions; this chip would read a variable set of instructions from memory, which would control the function of the chip. The idea was to design almost an entire computing device on a single chip that could perform different functions, depending on what instructions it was given.

There was one problem with the new chip: Busicom owned the rights to it. Hoff and others knew that the product had almost limitless application, bringing intelligence to a host of "dumb" machines. They urged Intel to repurchase the rights to the product. While Intel founders Gordon Moore and Robert Noyce championed the new chip, others within the company were concerned that the product would distract Intel from its main focus, making memory. They were finally convinced by the fact that every four-chip microcomputer set included two memory chips. As the director of marketing at the time recalled, "Originally, I think we saw it as a way to sell more memories, and we were willing to make the investment on that basis."

Intel offered to return Busicom's $60,000 investment in exchange for the rights to the product. Struggling with financial troubles, the Japanese company agreed. Nobody else in the industry at the time, even at Intel, realized the significance of this deal. Of course it paved the way for Intel's future in processors. The result was the 1971 introduction of the 4-bit Intel 4004 microcomputer set (the term *microprocessor* was not coined until later). Smaller than a thumbnail and packing 2300 transistors, the $200 chip delivered as much computing power as the first electronic computer, ENIAC. By comparison, ENIAC relied on 18,000 vacuum tubes packed into 3,000 cubic feet (85 cubic meters) when it was built in 1946. The 4004 executed 60,000 operations in one second, primitive by today's standards, but a major breakthrough at the time.

Intel introduced the 8008 microcomputer in 1972, which processed eight bits of information at a time, twice as much as the original chip. By 1981, Intel's microprocessor family had grown to include the 16-bit 8086 and the 8-bit 8088 processors. These two chips garnered an unprecedented 2,500 design wins in a single year. Among those designs was a product from IBM that was to become the first PC.

In 1982, Intel introduced the 286 chip. With 134,000 transistors, it provided about three times the performance of other 16-bit processors of the time. Featuring on-chip memory management, the 286 was the first microprocessor that offered software compatibility with its predecessors. This revolutionary chip was first used in IBM's benchmark PC-AT.

In 1985 came the Intel386 processor. With a new 32-bit architecture and 275,000 transistors, the chip could perform more than 5 million instructions every second (MIPS). Compaq's DESKPRO 386 was the first PC based on the new microprocessor.

Next out of the block was the Intel486 processor in 1989. The new chip had 1.2 million transistors and the first built-in math coprocessor. The 486 was some 50 times faster than the original 4004, equaling the performance of powerful mainframe computers.

In 1993, Intel introduced the first Pentium processor, setting new performance standards with up to five times the performance of the Intel486 processor. The Pentium processor uses 3.1 million transistors to perform up to 90 MIPS—now up to about 1,500 times the speed of the original 4004.

The first processor in the P6 family, called the Pentium Pro processor, was introduced in 1995. With 5.5 million transistors, it was the first to be packaged with a second die containing high-speed memory cache to accelerate performance. Capable of performing up to 300 MIPS, the Pentium Pro continues to be a popular choice for multiprocessor servers and high-performance workstations.

Intel introduced the Pentium II processor in May 1997. Pentium II processors have 7.5 million transistors packed into a cartridge rather than a conventional chip. The Pentium II family was augmented in April 1998, with both the low-cost Celeron processor for basic PCs and the high-end Pentium II Xeon processor for servers and workstations.

Sometime during the year 2000 we expect to see the new P7 processor, code-named Merced.

This will be Intel's first processor with 64-bit instructions, and will spawn a whole new category of operating systems and applications, while still remaining backward-compatible with 32-bit software.

Personal Computer History

The fourth and current generation of modern computer includes those that incorporate micro-processors in their designs. Of course, part of this fourth generation of computers is the personal computer, which itself was made possible by the advent of low cost microprocessors and memory.

Birth of the Personal Computer

In 1973, some of the first microcomputer kits based on the 8008 chip were developed. These kits were little more than demonstration tools and didn't do much except blink lights. In late 1973, Intel introduced the 8080 microprocessor, which was 10 times faster than the earlier 8008 chip and addressed 64K of memory. This was the breakthrough the personal computer industry had been waiting for.

A company called MITS introduced the Altair kit in a cover story in the January 1975 issue of *Popular Electronics*. The Altair kit, considered to be the first personal computer, included an 8080 processor, a power supply, a front panel with a large number of lights, and 256 bytes (not kilo-bytes) of memory. The kit sold for $395 and had to be assembled. Assembly back then meant you got out your soldering iron to actually finish the circuit boards, not like today where you can assemble a system of pre-made components with nothing more than a screwdriver.

The Altair included an open architecture system bus called the S-100 bus because it had 100 pins per slot. The open architecture meant that anybody could develop boards to fit in these slots and interface to the system. This prompted various add-ons and peripherals from numerous aftermar-ket companies. The new processor inspired software companies to write programs, including the CP/M (Control Program for Microprocessors) operating system and the first version of the Microsoft BASIC (Beginners All-purpose Symbolic Instruction Code) programming language.

IBM introduced what can be called its first personal computer in 1975. The Model 5100 had 16K of memory, a built-in 16-line by 64-character display, a built-in BASIC language interpreter, and a built-in DC-300 cartridge tape drive for storage. The system's $9,000 price placed it out of the mainstream personal computer marketplace, which was dominated by experimenters (affectionately referred to as hackers) who built low-cost kits ($500 or so) as a hobby. Obviously, the IBM system was not in competition for this low-cost market and did not sell as well by comparison.

The Model 5100 was succeeded by the 5110 and 5120 before IBM introduced what we know as the IBM Personal Computer (Model 5150). Although the 5100 series preceded the IBM PC, the older systems and the 5150 IBM PC had nothing in common. The PC IBM turned out was more closely related to the IBM System/23 DataMaster, an office computer system introduced in 1980. In fact, many of the engineers who developed the IBM PC had originally worked on the DataMaster.

In 1976, a new company called Apple Computer introduced the Apple I, which originally sold for $666. The selling price was an arbitrary number selected by one of the co-founders, Steve Jobs. This system consisted of a main circuit board screwed to a piece of plywood. A case and power supply were not included. Only a few of these computers were made, and they reportedly have sold to collectors for more than $20,000. The Apple II, introduced in 1977, helped set the standard for nearly all the important microcomputers to follow, including the IBM PC.

The microcomputer world was dominated in 1980 by two types of computer systems. One type, the Apple II, claimed a large following of loyal users and a gigantic software base that was growing at a fantastic rate. The other type, CP/M systems, consisted not of a single system but of all the many systems that evolved from the original MITS Altair. These systems were compatible with one another and were distinguished by their use of the CP/M operating system and expansion slots, which followed the S-100 standard. All these systems were built by a variety of companies and sold under various names. For the most part, however, these systems used the same software and plug-in hardware. It is interesting to note that none of these systems were PC-compatible or Macintosh-compatible, the two primary standards in place today.

A new competitor looming on the horizon was able to see that in order to be successful, a personal computer needed to have an open architecture, slots for expansion, a modular design, and healthy support from both hardware and software companies other than the original manufacturer of the system. This competitor turned out to be IBM, which was quite surprising at the time because IBM was not known for systems with these open architecture attributes! IBM in essence became more like the early Apple, and Apple themselves became like everybody expected IBM to be. The open architecture of the forthcoming IBM PC and the closed architecture of the forthcoming Macintosh caused a complete turnaround in the industry.

The IBM Personal Computer

At the end of 1980, IBM decided to truly compete in the rapidly growing low-cost personal computer market. The company established what was called the Entry Systems Division, located in

Boca Raton, Florida, to develop the new system. The division was located intentionally far away from IBM's main headquarters in New York, or any other IBM facilities, in order that this new division be able to operate independently as a separate unit. This small group consisted of 12 engineers and designers under the direction of Don Estridge. The team's chief designer was Lewis Eggebrecht. The Entry Systems Division was charged with developing IBM's first real PC. (IBM considered the previous 5100 system, developed in 1975, to be an intelligent programmable terminal rather than a genuine computer, even though it truly was a computer.) Nearly all these engineers had been moved into the new division from the System/23 DataMaster project, which was a small office computer system introduced in 1980, and was the direct predecessor at IBM to the IBM PC.

Much of the PC's design was influenced by the DataMaster design. In the DataMaster's single-piece design, the display and keyboard were integrated into the unit. Because these features were limiting, they became external units on the PC, although the PC keyboard layout and electrical designs were copied from the DataMaster.

Several other parts of the IBM PC system also were copied from the DataMaster, including the expansion bus (or input/output slots), which included not only the same physical 62-pin connector, but also almost identical pin specifications. This copying of the bus design was possible because the PC used the same interrupt controller as the DataMaster and a similar direct memory access (DMA) controller. Also, expansion cards already designed for the DataMaster could easily be redesigned to function in the PC.

The DataMaster used an Intel 8085 CPU, which had a 64KB address limit, and an 8-bit internal and external data bus. This arrangement prompted the PC design team to use the Intel 8088 CPU, which offered a much larger (1MB) memory address limit and an internal 16-bit data bus, but only an 8-bit external data bus. The 8-bit external data bus and similar instruction set allowed the 8088 to be easily interfaced into the earlier DataMaster designs.

Estridge and the design team rapidly developed the design and specifications for the new system. In addition to borrowing from the System/23 DataMaster, the team studied the marketplace, which also had enormous influence on the IBM PC's design. The designers looked at the prevailing standards and successful systems available at the time, learned from the success of those systems, and incorporated into the new PC all the features of the popular systems, and more. With the parameters for design made obvious by the market, IBM produced a system that quite capably filled its niche in the market.

IBM brought its system from idea to delivery of functioning systems in one year by using existing designs and purchasing as many components as possible from outside vendors. The Entry Systems Division was granted autonomy from IBM's other divisions and could tap resources outside the company, rather than go through the bureaucratic procedures that required exclusive use of IBM resources. IBM contracted out the PC's languages and operating system to a small company named Microsoft. That decision was the major factor in establishing Microsoft as the dominant force in PC software today.

Note

It is interesting to note that IBM had originally contacted Digital Research (the company that created CP/M, then the most popular personal computer operating system) to have them develop an operating system for the new IBM PC, but they were leery of working with IBM, and especially balked at the nondisclosure agreement IBM wanted them to sign. Microsoft jumped on the opportunity left open by Digital Research, and as a result has become one of the largest software companies in the world. IBM's use of outside vendors in developing the PC was an open invitation for the aftermarket to jump in and support the system—and it did.

On Wednesday, August 12, 1981, a new standard was established in the microcomputer industry with the debut of the IBM PC. Since then, hundreds of millions of PC-compatible systems have been sold, as the original PC has grown into an enormous family of computers and peripherals. More software has been written for this computer family than for any other system on the market.

The PC Industry 18 Years Later

In the more than 18 years since the original IBM PC was introduced, many changes have occurred. The IBM-compatible computer, for example, advanced from a 4.77MHz 8088-based system to 500MHz or faster Pentium II-based systems—nearly 4,000 times faster than the original IBM PC (in actual processing speed, not just clock speed). The original PC had only one or two single-sided floppy drives that stored 160KB each using DOS 1.0, whereas modern systems easily can have 20GB (20 billion bytes) or more of hard disk storage.

A rule of thumb in the computer industry (called Moore's Law, originally set forth by Intel co-founder Gordon Moore) is that available processor performance and disk-storage capacity doubles every two years, give or take.

Since the beginning of the PC industry, this pattern has shown no sign of changing.

In addition to performance and storage capacity, another major change since the original IBM PC was introduced is that IBM is not the only manufacturer of "PC-compatible" systems. IBM originated the PC-compatible standard, of course, but today they no longer set the standards for the system they originated. More often than not, new standards in the PC industry are developed by companies and organizations other than IBM. Today, it is Intel and Microsoft who are primarily responsible for developing and extending the PC hardware and software standards, respectively. Some have even taken to calling PCs "Wintel" systems, owing to the dominance of those two companies.

In more recent years Intel and Microsoft have carried the evolution of the PC forward. The introduction of hardware standards such as the PCI (Peripheral Component Interconnect) bus, AGP (Accelerated Graphics Port) bus, ATX and NLX motherboard form factors, Socket 1 through 8 as well as Slot 1 and 2 processor interfaces, and numerous others show that Intel is really pushing PC hardware design these days. In a similar fashion, Microsoft is pushing the software side of things with the continual evolution of the Windows operating system as well as applications such as the Office suite.

Today there are literally hundreds of system manufacturers following the collective PC standard and producing computers that are fully PC-compatible. There are also thousands of peripheral manufacturers whose components expand and enhance PC-compatible systems.

PC-compatible systems have thrived, not only because compatible hardware can be assembled easily, but also because the primary operating system was available not from IBM but from a third party (Microsoft). The core of the system software is the BIOS (basic input/output system), and this was also available from third-party companies such as AMI, Award, Phoenix, and others. This situation allowed other manufacturers to license the operating system and BIOS software and to sell their own compatible systems. The fact that DOS borrowed the functionality and user inter-face from both CP/M and UNIX probably had a lot to do with the amount of software that became available. Later, with the success of Windows, there would be even more reasons for soft-ware developers to write programs for PC-compatible systems.

One of the reasons why Apple Macintosh systems will likely never enjoy the success of PC sys-tems is that Apple controls all the primary systems software (BIOS and OS), and has never licensed it to other companies for use in compatible systems.

At some point in their development, Apple seemed to recognize this flawed stance, and in the mid-1990s, licensed its software to third-party manufacturers such as Power Computing. After a short time, Apple cancelled its licensing agreements with other manufacturers. Since Apple remains essentially a closed system, other companies cannot develop compatible machines, meaning Macintosh systems are only available from one source—Apple. As such, it seems too late for them to effectively compete with the PC-compatible juggernaut. It is fortunate for the com-puting public as a whole that IBM created a more open and extendible standard, which today finds systems being offered by hundreds of companies in thousands of configurations. This kind of competition among manufacturers and vendors of PC-compatible systems is the reason why such systems offer so much performance and so many capabilities for the money.

The IBM-compatible market continues to thrive and prosper. New technology continues to be integrated into these systems, enabling them to grow with the times. These systems offer a high value for the money and have plenty of software available to run on them. It's a safe bet that PC-compatible systems will dominate the personal computer marketplace for the next 15–20 years.

Moore's Law

In 1965, Gordon Moore was preparing a speech about the growth trends in computer memory, and he made an interesting observation. When he began to graph the data, he realized there was a striking trend. Each new chip contained roughly twice as much capacity as its predecessor, and each chip was released within 18–24 months of the previous chip. If this trend continued, he reasoned, computing power would rise exponentially over relatively brief periods of time (see Figure 1.1).

Moore's observation, now known as Moore's Law, described a trend that has continued to this day and is still remarkably accurate. It was found to not only describe memory chips, but also accurately describe the growth of processor power and disk-drive storage capacity. It has become the basis for many industry performance forecasts. In 26 years, the number of transistors on a chip has increased more than 3,200 times, from 2,300 on the 4004 in 1971 to more than 7.5 million on the Pentium II processor.

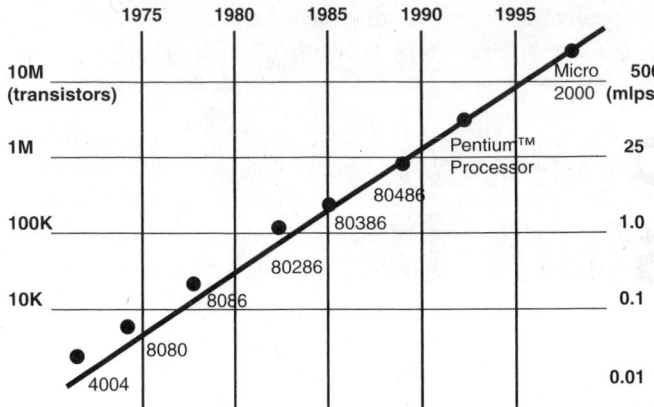

Figure 1.1 Moore's Law as applied to processors, showing that transistor count doubles about every two years.

What does the future hold? For PCs, one thing is sure: They will continue to become faster, smaller, and cheaper. According to Gordon Moore, computing power continues to increase at a rate of about double the power every two years. This has held true not only for speed but storage capacity as well. This means that computers you will be purchasing two years from now will be about twice as fast and store twice as much as what you can purchase today. The really amazing part is that this rapid pace of evolution shows no signs of letting up.

PC Components, Features, and System Design

SOME OF THE MAIN TOPICS IN THIS CHAPTER ARE

What Is a PC?

System Types

System Components

This chapter defines what a *PC* really is, and then continues by defining the types of PCs on the market. In addition, the chapter gives an overview of the components found in a modern PC.

What Is a PC?

I normally ask the question, "What exactly is a PC?" when I begin one of my PC hardware seminars. Of course, most people immediately answer that PC stands for *personal computer*, which in fact it does. They might then continue by defining a personal computer as any small computer system purchased and used by an individual. Unfortunately, that definition is not nearly precise or accurate enough for our purposes. I agree that a PC is a personal computer, but not all personal computers are PCs. For example, an Apple Macintosh system is clearly a personal computer, but nobody I know would call a Mac a PC, least of all Mac users! For the true definition of what a PC is, you must look deeper.

Calling something a PC implies that it is something much more specific than just any personal computer. One thing it implies is a family relation to the first IBM PC from 1981. In fact, I'll go so far as to say that IBM literally *invented* the PC; that is, they designed and created the very first one, and it was IBM who originally defined and set all the standards that made the PC distinctive from other personal computers. Note that it is very clear in my mind—as well as in the historical record—that IBM did *not* invent the personal computer. (Most recognize the historical origins of the personal computer in the MITS Altair, introduced in 1975.) IBM did not invent the personal computer, but they did invent the PC. Some people might take this definition a step further and define a PC as any personal computer that is "IBM compatible." In fact, many years back PCs were called either IBM compatibles or IBM clones, in essence paying homage to the origins of the PC at IBM.

The reality today is that although IBM clearly designed and created the first PC in 1981 and controlled the development and evolution of the PC standard for several years thereafter, IBM is no longer in control of the PC standard; that is, they do not dictate what makes up a PC today. IBM lost control of the PC standard in 1987 when they introduced their PS/2 line of systems. Up until then, other companies that were producing PCs literally copied IBM's systems right down to the chips, connectors, and even the shapes (form factors) of the boards, cases, and power supplies; after 1987, IBM abandoned many of the standards they created in the first place. That's why for many years now I have refrained from using the designation "IBM compatible" when referring to PCs.

If a PC is no longer an IBM compatible, what is it? The real question seems to be, "Who is in control of the PC standard today?" That question is best broken down into two parts. First, who is in control of PC software? Second, who is in control of PC hardware?

Who Controls PC Software?

Most of the people in my seminars don't even hesitate for a split second when I ask this question; they immediately respond "Microsoft!" I don't think there is any argument with that answer. Microsoft clearly controls the operating systems that are used on PCs, which have migrated from the original MS-DOS to Windows 95/98, Windows NT, and Windows 2000.

Microsoft has effectively used their control of the PC operating system as leverage to also control other types of PC software, such as utilities and applications. For example, many utility programs that were originally offered by independent companies such as disk caching, disk compression, defragmentation, file structure repair, and even calculators and notepads are now bundled (included with) in Windows. They have even bundled applications such as Web browsers, insuring an automatic installed base for these applications—much to the dismay of companies that produce competing versions. Microsoft has also leveraged their control of the operating system to integrate their own networking software and applications suites more seamlessly into the operating system than others. That's why they now dominate most of the PC software universe, from operating systems to utilities, from word processors to spreadsheets.

In the early days of the PC, when IBM was clearly in control of the PC hardware standard, they hired Microsoft to provide most of the core software for the PC. IBM developed the hardware, wrote the BIOS (basic input/output system), and then hired Microsoft to develop the Disk Operating System (DOS) as well as several other programs and utilities for IBM. In what was later viewed as perhaps the most costly business mistake in history, IBM failed to secure exclusive rights to the DOS they had contracted from Microsoft, either by purchasing it outright or by an exclusive license agreement. Instead, IBM licensed it non-exclusively, which subsequently allowed Microsoft to sell the same MS-DOS code they developed for IBM to any other company that was interested. Early PC cloners such as Compaq eagerly licensed this same operating system code, and suddenly you could purchase the same basic MS-DOS operating system with several different company names on the box. In retrospect, that single contractual error made Microsoft into the dominant software company it is today, and subsequently caused IBM to lose control of the very PC standard they had created.

As a writer myself (words, not software) I can appreciate what an incredible oversight this was. Imagine that a book publisher comes up with a great idea for a very popular book, and then contracts with and subsequently pays an author to write it. Then, by virtue of a poorly written contract, the author discovers that he can legally sell the very same book (perhaps with a different title) to all the competitors of the original publisher. Of course no publisher I know would allow this to happen, yet that is exactly what IBM allowed Microsoft to do back in 1981. By virtue of their deal with Microsoft, IBM had essentially lost control of the software they commissioned for their new PC from day one.

▶▶ See "BIOS," p. 345.

It is interesting to note that in the PC business software enjoys copyright protection, whereas hardware can only be protected by patents, which are difficult and time consuming to get and which expire after 17 years. To patent something requires that it be a unique and substantially new design. This made it impossible to patent most aspects of the IBM PC because it was designed using previously existing parts that anybody could purchase off the shelf! In fact, most of the important parts for the original PC came from Intel, such as the 8088 processor, 8284 clock generator, 8253/54 timer, 8259 interrupt controller, 8237 DMA (Direct Memory Access) controller, 8255 peripheral interface, and the 8288 bus controller. These are the chips that made up the heart and soul of the original PC.

Because the design of the original PC was not wholly patentable, anybody could duplicate the hardware of the IBM PC. All they had to do was purchase the same chips from the same manufacturers and suppliers that IBM used and design a new motherboard with a similar circuit. Seemingly as if to aid in this, IBM even published complete schematic diagrams of their motherboards and all their adapter cards in very detailed and easily available Technical Reference manuals. I have several of these early IBM manuals and still refer to them from time to time for specific component-level PC design information. In fact, I still recommend these original manuals to anybody who wants to delve deeply into PC design.

The difficult part of copying the IBM PC was the software, which is protected by copyright law. Phoenix Software was among the first to develop a legal way around this problem, which enabled them to functionally duplicate (but not exactly copy) software such as the BIOS (basic input/output system). The *BIOS* is defined as the core set of control software, which drives the hardware devices in the system directly. These types of programs are normally called *device drivers*, so in essence the BIOS is a collection of all the core device drivers used to operate and control the system hardware. What is called the operating system (such as DOS or Windows) uses the drivers in the BIOS to control and communicate with the various hardware and peripherals in the system.

Phoenix's method for duplicating the BIOS legally was an ingenious form of reverse-engineering. They hired two teams of software engineers, the second of which had to be specially screened to consist only of people who had never seen or studied the IBM BIOS code. The first team did study the IBM BIOS, and wrote as complete a description of what it did as possible. The second team read the description written by the first team, and set out to write from scratch a new BIOS that did everything the first team described. The end result was a new BIOS written from scratch with code that, although not identical to IBM's, had exactly the same functionality.

Phoenix called this a "clean room" approach to reverse engineering software, and it can escape any legal attack. Because IBM's original PC BIOS consisted of only 8KB of code and had limited functionality, duplicating it through the clean room approach was not very difficult or time consuming. As the IBM BIOS evolved, Phoenix—as well as the other BIOS companies—found it relatively easy to keep in step with any changes IBM might make. Discounting the POST (power on self test) or BIOS Setup program (used for configuring the system) portion of the BIOS, most BIOSes, even today, have only about 32K of active code. Today not only Phoenix, but also others such as AMI and Microid Research, are producing BIOS software for PC system manufacturers.

After the hardware and the BIOS of the IBM PC were duplicated, all that was needed to produce a fully IBM-compatible system was DOS. Reverse engineering DOS—even with the clean room approach—would have been a daunting task because DOS is much larger than the BIOS and consists of many more programs and functions. Also, the operating system has evolved and changed more often than the BIOS, which by comparison has remained relatively constant. This means that the only way to get DOS on an IBM compatible is to license it. This is where Microsoft comes in. Because IBM (who hired Microsoft to write DOS in the first place) did not ensure that Microsoft signed an exclusive license agreement, Microsoft was free to sell the same DOS to anybody. With a licensed copy of MS-DOS, the last piece was in place and the floodgates were open for IBM-compatible systems to be produced whether IBM liked it or not.

In retrospect, this is exactly why there are no clones or compatibles of the Apple Macintosh system. It is not that Mac systems cannot be duplicated; in fact, the Mac hardware is fairly simple and easy to produce using off-the-shelf parts. The real problem is that Apple owns the MAC OS as well as the BIOS, and because they have seen fit not to license them, no other company can sell an Apple-compatible system. Also, note that the Mac BIOS and OS are very tightly integrated; the Mac BIOS is very large and complex, and it is essentially a part of the OS, unlike the much more simple and easily duplicated BIOS found on PCs. The greater complexity and integration has allowed both the Mac BIOS and OS to escape any clean room duplication efforts. This means that without Apple's blessing (in the form of licensing), no Mac clones are likely to ever exist.

It might be interesting to note that during '96–'97 there was an effort by the more liberated thinkers at Apple to license their BIOS/OS combination, and several Mac compatible machines were not only developed, but also were produced and sold. Companies such as Sony, Power Computing, Radius, and even Motorola had invested millions of dollars in developing these systems, but shortly after these first Mac clones were sold, Apple rudely canceled all licensing! This was apparently the result of an edict from Steve Jobs, who had been hired back to run the company and who was one of the original architects of the closed-box proprietary design Macintosh system in the first place. By canceling these licenses, Apple has virtually guaranteed that their systems will never be a mainstream success. Along with their smaller market share come much higher system costs, fewer available software applications, and fewer hardware upgrades as compared to PCs. The proprietary design also means that major repair or upgrade components such as motherboards, power supplies, and cases are available only from Apple at very high prices, and upgrades of these components are normally not cost effective.

I often think that if Apple had a different view and had licensed their OS and BIOS early-on, this book might be called "Upgrading and Repairing Macs" instead!

In summary, because IBM did not own DOS (or Windows) but licensed it non-exclusively from Microsoft, anybody else who wanted to put MS-DOS or Windows on their system could license the code from Microsoft. This enabled any company who wanted to develop an IBM-compatible system to circumvent IBM completely, and yet produce a functionally identical machine. Because people desire backward compatibility, when one company controls the operating system, they naturally control all the software that goes around it, including everything from drivers to application programs. As long as PCs are used with Microsoft operating systems, they will have the upper hand in controlling PC software.

Who Controls PC Hardware?

Although it is clear that Microsoft has always controlled PC software by virtue of their control over the PC operating system, what about the hardware? It is easy to see that IBM controlled the PC hardware standard up through 1987. After all, IBM invented the core PC motherboard design, expansion bus slot architecture (8/16-bit ISA bus), serial and parallel port design, video card design through VGA and XGA standards, floppy and hard disk interface and controller designs, power supply design, keyboard interface and design, mouse interface, and even the physical shapes (form factors) of everything from the motherboard to the expansion cards, power supplies, and system chassis. All these pre-1987 IBM PC, XT and AT system design features are still influencing modern systems today.

But to me the real question is what company has been responsible for creating and inventing new and more recent PC hardware designs, interfaces, and standards? When I ask people that question, I normally see some hesitation in their response—some people say Microsoft (but they control the software, not the hardware), some say Compaq or name a few other big name system manufacturers. Only a few surmise the correct answer—Intel.

I can see why many people don't immediately realize this; I mean, how many people actually own an Intel brand PC? No, not just one that says "intel inside" on it (which refers only to the system having an Intel processor), but a system that was designed and built by Intel or even purchased through them. Believe it or not, I think that many, if not most, people today do have Intel PCs!

Certainly this does not mean that they have purchased their systems from Intel because it is well known that Intel does not sell complete PCs direct to end users. You cannot currently order a system from Intel, nor can you purchase an Intel brand system from somebody else. What I am talking about is the motherboard. In my opinion, the single most important part in a PC system is the motherboard, and I'd say that whoever made your motherboard should be considered the legitimate manufacturer of your system. Even back when IBM was the major supplier of PCs, they only made the motherboard, and contracted the other components of the system (power supply, disk drives, and so on) out to others.

▶▶ See "Motherboards and Buses," p. 203.

The top tier system manufacturers do make their own motherboards. According to *Computer Reseller News* magazine, the top three desktop systems manufacturers for the last several years have consistently been Compaq, Packard Bell, and IBM. These companies, for the most part, do design and manufacture their own motherboards, as well as many other system components. In some cases they even design their own chips and chipset components for their own boards. Although sales are high for these individual companies, there is a larger overall segment of the market that can be called the second tier.

In the second tier are companies who do not really manufacture systems, but assemble them instead. That is, they purchase motherboards, cases, power supplies, disk drives, peripherals, and so on, and assemble and market the components together as complete systems. Dell, Gateway, and Micron are some of the larger system assemblers today, but there are hundreds more who can be listed. In overall total volume, this ends up being the largest segment of the PC marketplace today. What is interesting about the second tier systems is that, with very few exceptions, you and I can purchase the same motherboards and other components any of the second tier manufacturers can (although we pay more than they do). We can also assemble a virtually identical system from scratch ourselves, but that is a story for another chapter, and is covered in Chapter 24, "Building or Upgrading Systems."

If Gateway, Dell, Micron, and others do not manufacture their own motherboards, who does? You guessed it—Intel. Not only do those specific companies use pretty much exclusively Intel motherboards, if you check around you'll find today that many, if not most, of the systems on the market in the second tier come with Intel motherboards. The only place Intel doesn't dominate is the low-end market Socket 7 type systems, which is mainly because Intel had originally abandoned the Socket 7 design and the low end market in general. Now they are coming back strong in the low end PC market with the newer Socket 370 design, with which they intend to dominate the low end market as well.

I checked a review of 10 different Pentium II systems in the current *Computer Shopper* magazine, and I'm not kidding, eight out of the 10 systems they evaluated had Intel motherboards. In fact, those eight used the exact same Intel motherboard. That means that these systems differ only in the cosmetics of the exterior case assembly and by what video card, disk drives, keyboards, and so on the assembler used that week.

The other two systems in the sample review had boards from manufacturers other than Intel, but even those boards used Intel Pentium II processors and Intel motherboard chipsets, which together comprise more than 90 percent of the motherboard cost. This review was not an anomaly; it is consistent with what I have been seeing under the hood of mail-order and mainstream "white box" PC systems for years.

▶▶ See "Pentium II Processors," p. 162.

▶▶ See "Chipsets," p. 235.

How and when did this happen? Intel has been the dominant PC processor supplier since IBM chose the Intel 8088 CPU in the original IBM PC in 1981. By controlling the processor, Intel naturally had control of the chips needed to integrate their processors into system designs. This naturally led Intel into the chipset business. They started their chipset business in 1989 with the 82350 EISA (Extended Industry Standard Architecture) chipset, and by 1993 they had become— along with the debut of the Pentium processor—the largest volume major motherboard chipset supplier. Now I imagine them sitting there, thinking that they make the processor and all the other chips needed to produce a motherboard, so why not just eliminate the middle man and make the entire motherboard too? The answer to this, and a real turning point in the industry, came about in 1994 when Intel became the largest-volume motherboard manufacturer in the world. And they have remained solidly on top ever since. They don't just lead in this category by any small margin; in fact, during 1997 Intel made more motherboards than the next eight largest motherboard manufacturers combined, with sales of more than 30 million boards, worth more than $3.6 billion! Note that this figure does not include processors or chipsets—only the boards themselves. These boards end up in the various system assembler brand PCs you and I buy, meaning that most of us are now essentially purchasing Intel-manufactured systems, no matter who actually wielded the screwdriver.

Table 2.1 shows the top 10 motherboard manufacturers, ranked by 1997 sales (1998 sales reports were not available at the time this book was printed).

Note

These figures reflect sales in millions.

Table 2.1   Top Motherboard Manufacturers (*Computer Reseller News*)

Motherboard Manufacturer	1997 Sales	1996 Sales
Intel	$3,600	$3,200
Acer	$825	$700
AsusTek	$640	$426
Elitegroup	$600	$600
First International Computer (FIC)	$550	$450
QDI Group	$320	$246
Soyo	$254	$123
Giga-Byte	$237	$165
Micro-Star	$205	$180
Diamond Flower (DFI)	$160	$100

Without a doubt, Intel controls the PC hardware standard because they control the PC motherboard. They not only make the vast majority of motherboards being used in systems today, but they also supply the vast majority of processors and motherboard chipsets to other motherboard manufacturers. This means that even if you don't have an actual Intel motherboard, the motherboard you do have probably has an Intel processor or chipset.

Intel also has a hand in setting several of the more recent PC hardware standards. It was Intel who originally created the PCI (Peripheral Component Interconnect) local bus interface and the new AGP (Accelerated Graphics Port) interface for high performance video cards. Intel designed the ATX motherboard form factor that replaces the (somewhat long in the tooth) IBM-designed Baby-AT form factor that has been used since the early `80s. Intel also created the NLX motherboard form factor to replace the proprietary and limited LPX design used by many lower-cost systems, which finally brought motherboard upgradability to those systems. Intel also created the DMI (Desktop Management Interface) for monitoring system hardware functions and the DPMA (Dynamic Power Management Architecture) and APM (Advanced Power Management) standards for managing power usage in the PC.

Intel has pushed for advancements in motherboard chipsets; supporting new types of memory such as EDO (Extended Data Out), SDRAM (Synchronous Dynamic RAM), and RDRAM (Rambus Dynamic RAM); new and faster bus interfaces; and faster memory access. They are also having a major effect in the portable market, bringing out special low-power processors, chipsets, and mobile modules (combining processor and chipset together on a daughterboard) to ease portable system design and improve functionality and performance. It doesn't take much to see that Intel is clearly in as much control of the PC hardware standard as Microsoft is in control of the PC software standard.

These days, the Intel processor and chipsets are so ubiquitous that these components are being reverse-engineered, and so called "Intel-compatible" versions are being produced. Companies such as AMD, Cyrix, and others have a variety of processors, which are direct pin-compatible replacements for Intel processors; furthermore, some chipset manufacturers have even produced pin for pin copies of Intel chipsets.

Whoever controls the operating system controls the software for the PC, and whoever controls the processor—and therefore the motherboard—controls the hardware. Because it seems to be a Microsoft and Intel combination for the software and hardware control in the PC today, it is no wonder the modern PC is often called a "Wintel" system.

PC 9x Specifications

Even though Intel has full control of PC hardware, Microsoft recognizes their power over the PC from the operating system perspective and has been releasing a series of documents called the "PC 9x Design Guides" (where 9x designates the year) as a set of standard specifications to guide both hardware and software developers who are creating products that work with Windows. The requirements in these guides are part of Microsoft's "Designed for Windows" logo requirement. In other words, if you produce either a hardware or software product and you want the official "Designed for Windows" logo to be on your box, your product has to meet the PC 9x minimum requirements.

Following are the documents that have been produced so far:

- Hardware Design Guide for Microsoft Windows 95
- Hardware Design Guide Supplement for PC 95
- PC 97 Hardware Design Guide
- PC 98 System Design Guide
- PC 99 System Design Guide
- PC 2000 System Design Guide

All these documents are available for download from Microsoft's Web site, and they have also been available as published books from Microsoft Press.

These system design guides present information for engineers who build personal computers, expansion cards, and peripheral devices that are to be used with Windows 95, 98, and NT operating systems. The requirements and recommendations for PC design in these guides form the basis for the requirements of the "Designed for Microsoft Windows" logo program for hardware that Microsoft sponsors.

These guides include requirements for basic (desktop and mobile) systems, workstations, and even entertainment PCs. They also address Plug-and-Play device configuration and power management in PC systems, requirements for universal serial bus (USB) and IEEE 1394, and new devices supported under Windows, including new graphics and video device capabilities, DVD, scanners and digital cameras, and other devices.

Note

Note that these guides do not mean anything directly for the end user; instead, they are meant to be guides for PC manufacturers to build their systems. As such, they are only recommendations, and they do not have to be followed to the letter. In some ways they are a market control tool for Intel and Microsoft to further wield their influence on PC hardware and software. In reality, the market often dictates that some of these recommendations are disregarded, which is one reason why they continue to evolve with new versions year after year.

System Types

PCs can be broken down into many different categories. I like to break them down in two different ways—one by the type of software they can run, the other by the motherboard host bus, or processor bus design and width. Because this book concentrates mainly on hardware, let's look at that first.

When a processor reads data, the data moves into the processor via the processor's external data bus connection. The processor's data bus is directly connected to the processor host bus on the motherboard. The processor data bus or host bus is also sometimes referred to as the *local bus* because it is local to the processor that is connected directly to it. Any other devices that are connected to the host bus essentially appear as if they are directly connected to the processor as well. If the processor has a 32-bit data bus, the motherboard must be wired to have a 32-bit processor host bus. This means that the system can move 32-bits worth of data into or out of the processor in a single cycle.

▶▶ See "Data Bus," p. 50.

Different processors have different data bus widths, and the motherboards that are designed to accept them require a processor host bus with a matching width. Table 2.2 lists all the Intel processors and their data bus widths.

Table 2.2   Intel Processors and Their Data Bus Widths

Processor	Data Bus Width
8088	8-bit
8086	16-bit
286	16-bit
386SX	16-bit
386DX	32-bit
486 (all)	32-bit
Pentium	64-bit
Pentium MMX	64-bit
Pentium Pro	64-bit
Pentium Celeron/II/III	64-bit
Pentium II/III Xeon	64-bit

A common misconception arises in discussions of processor widths. Although the Pentium processors all have 64-bit data bus widths, their internal registers are only 32 bits wide, and they process 32-bit commands and instructions. Thus, from a software point of view, all chips from the 386 to the Pentium III have 32-bit registers and execute 32-bit instructions. From the electronic or physical perspective, these 32-bit software capable processors have been available in physical forms with 16-bit (386SX), 32-bit (386DX, 486), and 64-bit (Pentium) data bus widths. The data bus width is the major factor in motherboard and memory system design because it dictates how many bits move in and out of the chip in one cycle.

▶▶ See "Internal Registers," p. 51.

The future P7 processor, code-named Merced, will have a new Intel Architecture 64-bit (IA-64) instruction set, but it will also process the same 32-bit instructions as 386 through Pentium processors do. It is not known whether Merced will have a 64-bit data bus like the Pentium or whether it will include a 128-bit data bus.

▶▶ See "Processor Specifications," p. 39.

From Table 2.2 you can see that 486 systems have a 32-bit processor bus, which means that any 486 motherboard would have a 32-bit processor host bus. Pentium processors, whether they are the original Pentium, Pentium MMX, Pentium Pro, or even the Pentium II and III, all have 64-bit data busses. This means that Pentium motherboards have a 64-bit processor host bus. You cannot put a 64-bit processor on a 32-bit motherboard, which is one reason that 486 motherboards cannot accept true Pentium processors.

As you can see from this table, we can break systems down into the following hardware categories:

- 8-bit
- 16-bit
- 32-bit
- 64-bit

What is interesting is that besides the bus width, the 16- through 64-bit systems are remarkably similar in basic design and architecture. The older 8-bit systems are very different, however. This gives us two basic system types, or classes, of hardware:

- 8-bit (PC/XT-class) systems
- 16/32/64-bit (AT-class) systems

PC stands for personal computer, XT stands for an eXTended PC, and AT stands for an advanced technology PC. The terms PC, XT, and AT, as they are used here, are taken from the original IBM systems of those names. The XT was basically a PC system that included a hard disk for storage in addition to the floppy drives found in the basic PC system. These systems had an 8-bit 8088 processor and an 8-bit Industry Standard Architecture (ISA) Bus for system expansion. The bus is the name given to expansion slots in which additional plug-in circuit boards can be installed.

The 8-bit designation comes from the fact that the ISA Bus found in the PC/XT class systems can send or receive only eight bits of data in a single cycle. The data in an 8-bit bus is sent along eight wires simultaneously, in parallel.

▶▶ See "The ISA Bus," p. 283.

16-bit and greater systems are said to be AT-class, which indicates that they follow certain standards, and that they follow the basic design first set forth in the original IBM AT system. AT is the designation IBM applied to systems that first included more advanced 16-bit (and later, 32- and 64-bit) processors and expansion slots. AT-class systems must have a processor that is compatible with Intel 286 or higher processors (including the 386, 486, Pentium, Pentium Pro, and Pentium II processors), and they must have a 16-bit or greater system bus. The system bus architecture is central to the AT system design, along with the basic memory architecture, Interrupt ReQuest (IRQ), DMA (Direct Memory Access), and I/O port address design. All AT-class systems are similar in the way these resources are allocated and how they function.

The first AT-class systems had a 16-bit version of the ISA Bus, which is an extension of the original 8-bit ISA Bus found in the PC/XT-class systems. Eventually, several expansion slot or bus designs were developed for AT-class systems, including those in the following list:

- 16-bit ISA bus
- 16/32-bit Extended ISA (EISA) bus
- 16/32-bit PS/2 Micro Channel Architecture (MCA) bus
- 16-bit PC-Card (PCMCIA) bus
- 32-bit Cardbus (PCMCIA) bus
- 32-bit VESA Local (VL) bus
- 32/64-bit Peripheral Component Interconnect (PCI) bus
- 32-bit Accelerated Graphics Port (AGP)

A system with any of these types of expansion slots is by definition an AT-class system, regardless of the actual Intel or Intel-compatible processor that is used. AT-type systems with 386 or higher processors have special capabilities that are not found in the first generation of 286-based ATs. The 386 and higher systems have distinct capabilities regarding memory addressing, memory management, and possible 32- or 64-bit wide access to data. Most systems with 386DX or higher chips also have 32-bit bus architectures to take full advantage of the 32-bit data transfer capabilities of the processor.

Most PC systems today incorporate 16-bit ISA slots for backward compatibility and lower function adapters, and PCI slots for truly high performance adapters. Most portable systems use PC-Card and Cardbus slots in the portable unit, and ISA and PCI slots in optional docking stations.

Chapter 4, "Motherboards and Buses," contains a great deal of in-depth information on these and other PC system buses, including technical information such as pinouts, performance specifications, and bus operation and theory.

Table 2.3 summarizes the primary differences·between the older 8-bit (PC/XT) systems and a modern AT system. This information distinguishes between these systems and includes all IBM and compatible models.

Table 2.3   Differences Between PC/XT and AT Systems

System Attributes	(8-bit) PC/XT Type	(16/32/64-bit) AT Type
Supported processors	All x86 or x88	286 or higher
Processor modes	Real	Real/ Protected/Virtual Real
Software supported	16-bit only	16- or 32-bit
Bus slot width	8-bit	16/32/64-bit
Slot type	ISA only	ISA, EISA, MCA, PC-Card, Cardbus, VL-Bus, PCI
Hardware interrupts	8 (6 usable) ·	16 (11 usable)
DMA channels	4 (3 usable)	8 (7 usable)
Maximum RAM	1MB	16MB/4GB or more
Floppy controller speed	250 Kbit/sec	250/300/500/1,000 Kbit/sec
Standard boot drive	360KB or 720KB	1.2MB/1.44MB/2.88MB
Keyboard interface	Unidirectional	Bidirectional
CMOS memory/clock	None standard	MC146818-compatible
Serial-port UART	8250B	16450/16550A

The easiest way to identify a PC/XT (8-bit) system is by the 8-bit ISA expansion slots. No matter what processor or other features the system has, if all the slots are 8-bit ISA, the system is a PC/XT. AT (16-bit plus) systems can be similarly identified—they have 16-bit or greater slots of any type. These can be ISA, EISA, MCA, PC-card (formerly PCMCIA), Cardbus, VL-Bus, or PCI. Using this information, you can properly categorize virtually any system as a PC/XT type or an AT type. There really have been no PC/XT type (8-bit) systems manufactured for many years. Unless you are in a computer museum, virtually every system you encounter today is based on the AT type design.

System Components

A modern PC is both simple and complicated. It is simple in the sense that over the years many of the components used to construct a system have become integrated with other components into fewer and fewer actual parts. It is complicated in the sense that each part in a modern system performs many more functions than did the same types of parts in older systems.

This section briefly examines all the components in a modern PC system. Each of these components is discussed further in later chapters.

Here are the components needed to assemble a basic modern PC system:

- Motherboard
- Processor
- Memory (RAM)

- Case (chassis)
- Power supply
- Floppy drive
- Hard disk
- CD-ROM, CD-R, or DVD-ROM drive
- Keyboard
- Mouse
- Video card
- Monitor (display)
- Sound card
- Speakers

Motherboard

The motherboard is the core of the system. It really is the PC—everything else is connected to it, and it controls everything in the system. Motherboards are available in several different shapes or form factors. The motherboard usually contains the following individual components:

- Processor socket (or slot)
- Processor voltage regulators
- Motherboard chipset
- Level 2 cache (normally found in the CPU today)
- Memory SIMM or DIMM sockets
- Bus slots
- ROM BIOS
- Clock/CMOS battery
- Super I/O chip

The chipset contains all the primary circuitry that makes up the motherboard; in essence, the chipset *is* the motherboard. The chipset controls the CPU or processor bus, the L2 cache and main memory, the PCI (Peripheral Component Interconnect) bus, the ISA (Industry Standard Architecture) bus, system resources, and more. If the processor represents the engine of your system, the chipset represents the chassis in which the engine is installed. As such, the chipset dictates the primary features and specifications of your motherboard, including what types of processors, memory, expansion cards, disk drives, and so on the system supports.

Note that most newer (Pentium Celeron/II/III class) systems include the L2 cache inside the processor rather than on the motherboard. In the newest and best designs, the L2 cache is actually a part of the processor die just like the L1 cache, whereas in others it is simply a separate chip (or chips) in the processor module.

The chipset plays a big role in determining what sorts of features a system can support. For example, which processors you can use, which types and how much memory you can install, what speeds you can run the machine, and what types of system buses your system can support are all tied in to the motherboard chipset. The ROM BIOS contains the initial POST (Power-On Self Test) program, bootstrap loader (which loads the operating system), drivers for items that are built into the board (the actual BIOS code), and usually a system setup program (often called CMOS setup) for configuring the system. Motherboards are covered in detail in Chapter 4.

Processor

The processor is often thought of as the "engine" of the computer. Also called the CPU (Central Processing Unit), it is the single most important chip in the system because it is the primary circuit that carries out the program instructions of whatever software is being run. Modern processors contain literally millions of transistors, etched onto a tiny square of silicon called a die, which is about the size of your thumbnail. The processor has the distinction of being one of the most expensive parts of most computers, even though it is also one of the smallest parts. In most modern systems, the processor costs from two to ten times more than the motherboard it is plugged into.

Microprocessors are covered in detail in Chapter 3, "Microprocessor Types and Specifications."

Memory (RAM)

The system memory is often called RAM (for Random Access Memory). This is the primary memory, which holds all the programs and data the processor is using at a given time. RAM requires power to maintain storage, so when you turn off the computer everything in RAM is cleared; when you turn it back on the memory must be reloaded with programs for the processor to run. The initial programs for the processor come from a special type of memory called ROM (Read Only Memory), which is not erased when the power to the system is turned off.

The ROM contains instructions to get the system to load or *boot* an operating system and other programs from one of the disk drives into the main RAM memory so that the system can run normally and perform useful work. Newer operating systems allow several programs to run at one time, with each program or data file that is loaded using some of the main memory. Generally, the more memory your system has, the more programs you can run simultaneously.

Memory is normally purchased and installed in a modern system in SIMM (Single Inline Memory Module) or DIMM (Dual Inline Memory Module) form. Formerly very expensive, memory prices have dropped recently, significantly reducing the cost of memory as compared to other parts of the system. Even so, the cost of the recommended amount of memory for a given system is usually equal or greater than that of the motherboard.

Memory is covered in detail in Chapter 6, "Memory."

Case (Chassis)

The case is the frame or chassis that houses the motherboard, power supply, disk drives, adapter cards, and any other physical components in the system. There are several different styles of cases available, from small or slim versions that sit horizontally on a desktop to huge tower types that stand vertically on the floor, and even some that are designed to be rackmounted for industrial use. In addition to the physical styles, different cases are designed to accept different form factor motherboards and power supplies. Some cases have features that make installing or removing components easy, such as a screwless design that requires no tools to disassemble, side open panels or trays that allow easy motherboard access, removable cages or brackets that give easy access to disk drives, and so on. Some cases include additional cooling fans for heavy duty systems, and some are even available with air filters that ensure that the interior will remain clean and dust free. Most cases include a power supply, but you can also purchase bare cases and power supplies separately.

The case is covered in detail in Chapter 21, "Power Supply and Chassis/Case."

Power Supply

The power supply is what feeds electrical power to every single part in the PC. As such, it has a very important job, but it is one of the least glamorous parts of the system so it receives little attention. Unfortunately, this often means that it is one of the components that is most skimped on when a system is constructed. The main function of the supply is to convert the 110v AC wall current into the 3.3v, 5v, or 12fv power that the system requires for operation.

The power supply is covered in detail in Chapter 21.

Floppy Disk Drive

The floppy drive is a simple, inexpensive, low capacity removable media magnetic storage device. For many years floppy disks were the primary medium for software distribution and system backup. However, with the advent of CD-ROM and DVD-ROM discs as the primary method of installing or loading new software in a system, and with inexpensive high capacity tape drives for backup, the floppy drive is not used very often in most modern systems, except perhaps by a system builder, installer, or technician. Because the floppy drive is the first device from which a PC attempts to boot, it is still the primary method that is used for loading initial operating systems' startup software and core hardware diagnostics. Recent advancements in technology have created new types of floppy drives with up to 120MB or more of storage, making the drive much more usable for temporary backups or for moving files from system to system.

Floppy disk drives are covered in detail in Chapter 11, "Floppy Disk Storage."

Hard Disk Drive

The hard disk is the primary archival storage memory for the system. It contains copies of all programs and data that are not currently active in main memory. A hard drive is so named because it consists of spinning platters of aluminum or ceramic that are coated with a magnetic medium. Hard drives can be created with many different storage capacities, depending on the density, size, and number of platters. Most desktop systems today use drives with 3 1/2-inch platters, whereas most laptop or notebook computers use 2 1/2-inch platter drives.

Hard disk drives are also covered in detail in Chapter 10, "Hard Disk Storage."

CD-ROM Drive

CD- (Compact Disc) and DVD- (Digital Versatile Disc) ROM (Read Only Memory) drives are relatively high capacity removable media optical drives. They are primarily a read-only medium, which means the drives can only read information, and the data on the discs cannot altered or rewritten. There are writable or rewritable versions of the discs and drives available, but they are much more expensive than their read-only counterparts, and therefore are not included standard in most PCs. CD-ROM and DVD-ROM are the most popular media for distributing software or large amounts of data because they are very inexpensive when produced in quantity and they can hold a great deal of information.

CD-ROM drives are covered in detail in Chapter 13, "Optical Storage."

Keyboard

The keyboard is the primary device on a PC that is used by a human being to communicate with and control a system. Keyboards are available in a large number of different languages, layouts, sizes, shapes, and with numerous special features or characteristics. One of the best features of the PC as designed by IBM is that it was one of the first personal computers to use a detached keyboard. Most systems prior to the PC had the keyboard as an integral part of the system chassis, which severely limited flexibility. Because the PC uses a detached keyboard with a standardized connector and signal design, in most cases it is possible to connect any PC compatible keyboard you want to your system, which gives you the freedom to choose the one that suits you best.

Keyboards are covered in detail in Chapter 17, "Input Devices."

Mouse

With the advent of computer operating systems that used a Graphical User Interface (GUI), it became necessary to have a device that enabled a user to point at or select items that were shown on the screen. Although there are many different types of pointing devices on the market today, the first and most popular device for this purpose is the mouse. By moving the mouse across a desk or tabletop, a corresponding pointer can be moved across the computer screen, allowing items to be more easily selected or manipulated than they can with a keyboard alone. Standard mice, as used on PCs, have two buttons: one for selecting items under the pointer, and the other for activating menus. Mice are also available with a third button, a wheel, or a stick, which can be used to scroll the display or for other special functions.

The mouse is covered in detail in Chapter 17.

Video Card

The video card controls the information you see on the monitor. All video cards have four basic parts: a video chip or chipset, Video RAM, a DAC (Digital to Analog Converter), and a BIOS. The video chip actually controls the information on the screen by writing data to the video RAM. The DAC reads the video RAM and converts the digital data there into analog signals to drive the monitor. The BIOS holds the primary video driver that allows the display to function during boot time and at a DOS prompt in basic text mode. More enhanced drivers are then usually loaded from disk to enable advanced video modes for Windows or applications software.

Video cards are covered in detail in Chapter 15, "Video Hardware."

Monitor (Display)

In most systems, the monitor is housed in its own protective case, separate from the system case and chassis. In portable systems and some low-cost PCs, however, the monitor is built into the system case. Monitors are generally classified by three major criteria: diagonal size in inches, resolution in pixels, and refresh rate in hertz (Hz). Desktop monitors usually range from 14" to 21" diagonal measure (although as you will see in Chapter 8, "The SCSI Interface," the actual viewable area is smaller than the advertised measure). LCD monitors in portable systems range from 11" to 14". Resolution ranges from 640×480 pixels (horizontal measurement first, and then vertical) to 1600×1200 pixels. Each pixel in the monitor is made up of a trio of dots, one each for the colors red, blue, and green. An average monitor is capable of refreshing 60 times per second (60Hz), whereas higher quality monitors might refresh at 100Hz. The refresh rate measures how often the display of the screen is redrawn from the contents of the video adapter memory. Both the resolution and refresh rate of the monitor are tied to the capability of the system video adapter. Most monitors are capable of supporting several different resolutions and refresh rates (with the common exception of LCD screens in portables).

Monitors are covered in detail in Chapter 15.

Microprocessor Types and Specifications

SOME OF THE MAIN TOPICS IN THIS CHAPTER ARE

Processor Specifications
SSE (Streaming SIMD Extensions)
Dual Independent Bus (DIB) Architecture
Processor Manufacturing
PGA Chip Packaging
Single Edge Contact (SEC) and Single Edge Processor (SEP) Packaging
Processor Sockets
Processor Slots
CPU Operating Voltages
Heat and Cooling Problems
Intel-Compatible Processors (AMD and Cyrix)
P1 (086) First-Generation Processors
P2 (286) Second-Generation Processors
P3 (386) Third-Generation Processors
P4 (486) Fourth-Generation Processors
P5 (586) Fifth-Generation Processors
Intel P6 (686) Sixth-Generation Processors
P7 (786) Seventh-Generation Processors
Processor Troubleshooting Techniques

Microprocessors

The brain or engine of the PC is the processor (sometimes called microprocessor), or Central Processing Unit (CPU). The CPU performs the system's calculating and processing. The processor is easily the most expensive single component in the system, costing up to four or more times greater than the motherboard it plugs into. Intel is generally credited with creating the first microprocessor in 1971 with the introduction of a chip called the 4004. Today they have almost total control over the processor market, at least for PC systems. This means that all PC-compatible systems use either Intel processors or Intel-compatible processors from a handful of competitors (such as AMD or Cyrix).

Intel's dominance in the processor market had not always been assured. Although they are generally credited with inventing the processor and introducing the first one on the market, by the late 70s the two most popular processors for PCs were *not* from Intel (although one was a clone of an Intel processor). Personal computers of that time primarily used the Z-80 by Zilog and the 6502 by MOS Technologies. The Z-80 was noted for being an improved and less expensive clone of the Intel 8080 processor, similar to the way companies today such as AMD, Cyrix, IDT, and Rise Technologies have cloned Intel's Pentium processors.

Back then I had a system containing both of those processors, consisting of a 1MHz (yes, that's one as in 1MHz!) 6502-based Apple main system with a Microsoft Softcard (Z-80 card) plugged into one of the slots. The Softcard contained a 2MHz Z-80 processor. This allowed me to run software for both types of processors on the one system. The Z-80 was used in systems of the late 70s and early 80s that ran the CP/M operating system, while the 6502 was best known for its use in the early Apple computers (before the Mac).

The fate of both Intel and Microsoft were dramatically changed in 1981 when IBM introduced the IBM PC, which was based on a 4.77MHz Intel 8088 processor running the Microsoft Disk Operating System (DOS) 1.0. Since that fateful decision was made, PC-compatible systems have used a string of Intel or Intel compatible processors, each new one capable of running the software of the processor before it, from the 8088 to the current Pentium III. The following sections cover the different types of processor chips that have been used in personal computers since the first PC was introduced almost two decades ago. These sections provide a great deal of technical detail about these chips and explain why one type of CPU chip can do more work than another in a given period of time.

Pre-PC Microprocessor History

It is interesting to note that the microprocessor had only existed for 10 years prior to the creation of the PC! The microprocessor was invented by Intel in 1971. The PC was created by IBM in 1981. Now nearly 20 years later, we are still using systems based on the design of that first PC (and mostly backward compatible with it). The processors powering our PCs today are still backward compatible with the one selected by IBM in 1981.

The story of the development of the first microprocessor, the Intel 4004, can be read in Chapter 1, "Personal Computer Background." The 4004 processor was introduced on November 15, 1971, and originally ran at a clock speed of 108KHz (108,000 cycles per second, or 0.108MHz). The 4004 contained 2,300 transistors and was built on a 10 micron process. This means that each line, trace, or transistor could be spaced about 10 microns (millionths of a meter) apart. Data was transferred four bits at a time, and the maximum addressable memory was only 640 bytes. The 4004 was designed for use in a calculator, but proved to be useful for many other functions because of its inherent programmability.

In April 1972, Intel released the 8008 processor, which originally ran at a clock speed of 200KHz (0.2MHz). The 8008 processor contained 3,500 transistors and was built on the same 10 micron process as the previous processor. The big change in the 8008 was that it had an 8-bit data bus, which meant it could move data 8 bits at a time—twice as much as the previous chip. It could also address more memory, up to 16KB. This chip was primarily used in dumb terminals and general-purpose calculators.

The next chip in the lineup was the 8080, introduced in April 1974, running at a clock rate of 2MHz. Due mostly to the faster clock rate, the 8080 processor had 10 times the performance of the 8008. The 8080 chip contained 6,000 transistors and was built on a 6 micron process. Like the previous chip, the 8080 had an 8-bit data bus, so it could transfer 8 bits of data at a time. The 8080 could address up to 64KB of memory, significantly more than the previous chip.

It was the 8080 that helped start the PC revolution, as this was the processor chip used in what is generally regarded as the first personal computer, the Altair 8800. The CP/M operating system was written for the 8080 chip, and Microsoft was founded and delivered their first product: Microsoft BASIC for the Altair. These initial tools provided the foundation for a revolution in software because thousands of programs were written to run on this platform.

In fact, the 8080 became so popular that it was cloned. A company called Zilog formed in late 1975, joined by several ex-Intel 8080 engineers. In July of 1976, they released the Z-80 processor, which was a vastly improved version of the 8080. It was not pin compatible, but instead combined functions such as the memory interface and RAM refresh circuitry, which allowed cheaper and simpler systems to be designed. The Z-80 also incorporated a superset of 8080 instructions, meaning it could run all 8080 programs. It also included new instructions and new internal registers, so software that was designed for the Z-80 would not necessarily run on the older 8080. The Z-80 ran initially at 2.5MHz (later versions ran up to 10MHz), and contained 8,500 transistors. The Z-80 could access 64KB of memory.

Radio Shack selected the Z-80 for the TRS-80 Model 1, their first PC. The chip was also the first to be used by many pioneering systems including the Osborne and Kaypro machines. Other companies followed suit, and soon the Z-80 was the standard processor for systems running the CP/M operating system and the popular software of the day.

Intel released the 8085, their follow up to the 8080, in March of 1976. Even though it pre-dated the Z-80 by several months, it never achieved the popularity of the Z-80 in personal computer systems. It was popular as an embedded controller, finding use in scales and other computerized equipment. The 8085 ran at 5MHz and contained 6,500 transistors. It was built on a 3 micron process and incorporated an 8-bit data bus.

Along different architectural lines, MOS Technologies introduced the 6502 in 1976. This chip was designed by several ex-Motorola engineers who had worked on Motorola's first processor, the 6800. The 6502 was an 8-bit processor like the 8080, but it sold for around $25, whereas the 8080 cost about $300 when it was introduced. The price appealed to Steve Wozniak who placed the chip in his Apple I and Apple II designs. The chip was also used in systems by Commodore and other system manufacturers. The 6502 and its successors were also used in computer games, including the original Nintendo Entertainment System (NES) among others. Motorola went on to create the 68000 series, which became the basis for the Apple Macintosh line of computers. Today those systems use the PowerPC chip, also by Motorola, and a successor to the original 68000 series.

All these previous chips set the stage for the first PC chips. Intel introduced the 8086 in June 1978. The 8086 chip brought with it the original x86 instruction set that is still present on x86-compatible chips such as the Pentium III. A dramatic improvement over the previous chips, the 8086 was a full 16-bit design with 16-bit internal registers and a 16-bit data bus. This meant that it could work on 16-bit numbers and data internally and also transfer 16-bits at a time in and out of the chip. The 8086 contained 29,000 transistors and initially ran at up to 5MHz. The chip also used 20-bit addressing, meaning it could directly address up to 1MB of memory. Although not directly backward compatible with the 8080, the 8086 instructions and language was very similar and allowed older programs to be ported over quickly to run. This later proved important to help jumpstart the PC software revolution with recycled CP/M (8080) software.

Although the 8086 was a great chip, it was expensive at the time and more importantly required an expensive 16-bit support chips and board design. To help bring costs down, in 1979, Intel released a crippled version of the 8086 called the 8088. The 8088 processor used the same internal core as the 8086, had the same 16-bit registers, and could address the same 1MB of memory, but the external data bus was reduced to 8 bits. This allowed support chips from the older 8-bit 8085 to be used, and far less expensive boards and systems could be made. It is for these reasons that IBM chose the crippled chip, the 8088, for the first PC.

This decision would affect history in several ways. The 8088 was fully software compatible with the 8086, so it could run 16-bit software. Also, because the instruction set was very similar to the previous 8085 and 8080, programs written for those older chips could be quickly and easily modified to run. This allowed a large library of programs to be quickly released for the IBM PC, thus helping it become a success. The overwhelming blockbuster success of the IBM PC left in its wake the legacy of requiring backward compatibility with it. In order to maintain the momentum, Intel has pretty much been forced to maintain backward compatibility with the 8088/8086 in most of the processors they have released since then.

In some ways the success of the PC, and the Intel architecture it contains, has limited the growth of the personal computer. In other ways, however, its success has caused a huge number of programs, peripherals, and accessories to be developed, and the PC to become a de facto standard in the industry. The original 8088 processor used in the first PC contained close to 30,000 transistors and ran at less than 5MHz. The most recent processors from Intel contain close to 30 million transistors and run at over 500MHz. Intel has already demonstrated processors running at 1GHz. According to Moore's Law, these will be commonplace in only a few years, along with transistor counts in the hundreds of millions.

Processor Specifications

Many confusing specifications often are quoted in discussions of processors. The following sections discuss some of these specifications, including the data bus, address bus, and speed. The next section includes a table that lists the specifications of virtually all PC processors.

Processors can be identified by two main parameters: how wide they are and how fast they are. The speed of a processor is a fairly simple concept. Speed is counted in megahertz (MHz), which means millions of cycles per second—and faster is better! The width of a processor is a little more complicated to discuss because there are three main specifications in a processor that are expressed in width. They are

- Data input and output bus
- Internal registers
- Memory address bus

Table 3.1 lists the primary specifications for the Intel family of processors used in IBM and compatible PCs. Table 3.2 lists the Intel compatible processors from AMD, Cyrix, Nexgen, IDT, and Rise. The following sections explain these specifications in detail.

Note that most Pentium II and III processors include 512KB of 1/2-core speed L2 cache on the processor card, while the Xeon includes 512KB, 1MB, or 2MB of full-core speed L2 cache. The Celeron and Pentium II PE processors, as well as the K6-3 from AMD, all include on-die L2 cache, which runs at the full core speed of the processor. Most all future processors will contain the L2 cache directly in the CPU die and run it at full core speed.

The transistor count figures do not include the standard 256KB or 512KB L2 cache built in to the Pentium Pro and Pentium II CPU packages. The L2 cache contains an additional 15.5 (256KB), 31 (512KB), or optionally 62 million (1MB) transistors!

Table 3.1   Intel Processor Specifications

Processor	CPU Clock	Voltage	Internal Register Size	Data Bus Width	Max. Memory	L1 Cache
8088	1x	5v	16-bit	8-bit	1MB	-
8086	1x	5v	16-bit	16-bit	1MB	-
286	1x	5v	16-bit	16-bit	16MB	-
386SX	1x	5v	32-bit	16-bit	16MB	-
386SL	1x	3.3v	32-bit	16-bit	16MB	0KB[1]
386DX	1x	5v	32-bit	32-bit	4GB	-
486SX	1x	5v	32-bit	32-bit	4GB	8KB
486SX2	2x	5v	32-bit	32-bit	4GB	8KB
487SX	1x	5v	32-bit	32-bit	4GB	8KB
486DX	1x	5v	32-bit	32-bit	4GB	8KB
486SL[2]	1x	3.3v	32-bit	32-bit	4GB	8KB
486DX2	2x	5v	32-bit	32-bit	4GB	8KB
486DX4	2-3x	3.3v	32-bit	32-bit	4GB	16KB
486Pentium OD	2.5x	5v	32-bit	32-bit	4GB	2×16KB
Pentium 60/66	1x	5v	32-bit	64-bit	4GB	2×8KB
Pentium 75-200	1.5-3x	3.3-3.5v	32-bit	64-bit	4GB	2×8KB
Pentium MMX	1.5-4.5x	1.8-2.8v	32-bit	64-bit	4GB	2×16KB
Pentium Pro 512KB 1MB	2-3x	3.3v	32-bit	64-bit	64GB	2×8KB
Pentium II MMX	3.5-4.5x	1.8-2.8v	32-bit	64-bit	64GB	2×16KB
Pentium II Celeron	3.5-4.5x	1.8-2.8v	32-bit	64-bit	64GB	2×16KB
Pentium II Celeron	3.5-7x	1.8-2v	32-bit	64-bit	64GB	2×16KB
Pentium II PE[3]	3.5-6x	1.6v	32-bit	64-bit	64GB	2×16KB
Pentium II Xeon 1MB 2MB	4-4.5x	1.8-2.8v	32-bit	64-bit	64GB	2×16KB
Pentium III	4.5-6x	1.8-2v	32-bit	64-bit	64GB	2×16KB
Pentium III Xeon 1MB 2MB	5-6x	1.8-2v	32-bit	64-bit	64GB	2×16KB

Table 3.2   Intel Compatible Processors

Processor	CPU Clock	Voltage	Internal Register Size	Data Bus Width	Max. Memory	L1 Cache
AMD K5	1.5-1.75x	3.5v	32-bit	64-bit	4GB	16+8KB
AMD-K6	2.5-4.5x	2.2-3.2v	32-bit	64-bit	4GB	2×32KB
AMD-K6-2	3.5-5x	2.2-2.4v	32-bit	64-bit	4GB	2×32KB
AMD-K6-3	4-5x	2.2-2.4v	32-bit	64-bit	4GB	2×32KB
Cyrix 6x86	2x	2.5-3.5v	32-bit	64-bit	4GB	16KB
Cyrix 6x86MX/MII	2-3.5x	2.9v	32-bit	64-bit	4GB	64KB
Nexgen Nx586	2x	4v	32-bit	64-bit	4GB	2×16KB
IDT Winchip	3-4x	3.3-3.5v	32-bit	64-bit	4GB	2×32KB
IDT Winchip2/2A	2.33-4x	3.3-3.5v	32-bit	64-bit	4GB	2×32KB
Rise mP6	2-3.5x	2.8v	32-bit	64-bit	4GB	2×8KB

FPU = Floating-Point Unit (internal math coprocessor)

WT = Write-Through cache (caches reads only)

WB = Write-Back cache (caches both reads and writes)

Bus = Processor external bus speed (motherboard speed)

Core = Processor internal core speed (CPU speed)

MMX = Multimedia extensions, 57 additional instructions for graphics and sound processing

L1 Cache Type	L2 Cache	L2 Cache Speed	Integral FPU	Multimedia Instructions	No. of Transistors	Date Introduced
-	-	-	-	-	29,000	June '79
-	-	-	-	-	29,000	June '78
-	-	-	-	-	134,000	Feb. '82
-	-	Bus	-	-	275,000	June '88
WT	-	Bus	-	-	855,000	Oct. '90
-	-	Bus	-	-	275,000	Oct. '85
WT	-	Bus	-	-	1.185M	April '91
WT	-	Bus	-	-	1.185M	April '94
WT	-	Bus	Yes	-	1.2M	April '91
WT	-	Bus	Yes	-	1.2M	April '89
WT	-	Bus	Opt.	-	1.4M	Nov. '92
WT	-	Bus	Yes	-	1.2M	March '92
WT	-	Bus	Yes	-	1.6M	Feb. '94
WB	-	Bus	Yes	-	3.1M	Jan. '95
WB	-	Bus	Yes	-	3.1M	March '93
WB	-	Bus	Yes	-	3.3M	Oct. '94
WB	-	Bus	Yes	MMX	4.5M	Jan. '97
WB	256KB	Core	Yes	-	5.5M	Nov. '95
WB	512KB	1/2 Core	Yes	MMX	7.5M	May '97
WB	0KB	-	Yes	MMX	7.5M	April '98
WB	128KB	Core	Yes	MMX	19M	Aug. '98
WB	256KB	Core	Yes	MMX	27.4M	Jan. '99
WB	512KB	Core	Yes	MMX	7.5M	April '98
WB	512KB	1/2 Core	Yes	SSE	9.5M	Feb. '99
WB	512KB	Core	Yes	SSE	9.5M	March '99

L1 Cache Type	L2 Cache	L2 Cache Speed	Integral FPU	Multimedia Instructions	No. of Transistors	Date Introduced
WB	-	Bus	Yes	-	4.3M	March '96
WB	-	Bus	Yes	MMX	8.8M	April '97
WB	-	Bus	Yes	3DNow	9.3M	May '98
WB	256KB	Core	Yes	3DNow	21.3M	Feb. '99
WB	-	Bus	Yes	-	3M	Feb. '96
WB	-	Bus	Yes	MMX	6.5M	May '97
WB	-	Bus	Yes	-	3.5M	March '94
WB	-	Bus	Yes	MMX	5.4M	Oct. '97
WB	-	Bus	Yes	3DNow	5.9M	Sept. '98
WB	-	Bus	Yes	MMX	3.6M	Oct. '98

3DNow = MMX plus 21 additional instructions for graphics and sound processing

SSE = Streaming SIMD (Single Instruction Multiple Data) Extensions, MMX plus 70 additional instructions for graphics and sound processing

[1] The 386SL contains an integral-cache controller, but the cache memory must be provided outside the chip.

[2] Intel later marketed SL Enhanced versions of the SX, DX, and DX2 processors. These processors were available in both 5v and 3.3v versions and included power-management capabilities.

[3] The Enhanced mobile PII has on-die L2 cache similar to the Celeron.

Note

Note in Table 3.1, that the Pentium Pro processor includes 256KB, 512KB, or 1MB of full core speed L2 cache in a separate die within the chip. The Pentium II/III processors include 512KB of 1/2 core speed L2 cache on the processor card. The Celeron and Pentium II PE processors include full core speed L2 cache integrated directly within the processor die.

The transistor count figures do not include the external (off-die) 256KB, 512KB, 1MB, or 2MB L2 cache built in to the Pentium Pro and Pentium II/III or Xeon CPU packages. The external L2 cache contains an additional 15.5 (256KB), 31 (512KB), 62 million (1MB), or 124 million (2MB) transistors!

Processor Speed Ratings

A common misunderstanding about processors is their different speed ratings. This section covers processor speed in general, and then provides more specific information about Intel processors.

A computer system's clock speed is measured as a frequency, usually expressed as a number of cycles per second. A crystal oscillator controls clock speeds using a sliver of quartz sometimes contained in what looks like a small tin container. Newer systems include the oscillator circuitry in the motherboard chipset, so it might not be a visible separate component on newer boards. As voltage is applied to the quartz, it begins to vibrate (oscillate) at a harmonic rate dictated by the shape and size of the crystal (sliver). The oscillations emanate from the crystal in the form of a current that alternates at the harmonic rate of the crystal. This alternating current is the clock signal that forms the time base on which the computer operates. A typical computer system runs millions of these cycles per second, so speed is measured in megahertz. (One hertz is equal to one cycle per second.) An alternating current signal is like a sine wave, with the time between the peaks of each wave defining the frequency (see Figure 3.1).

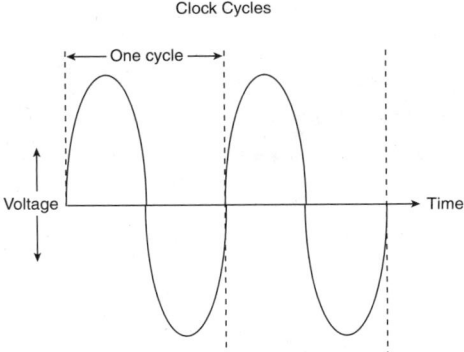

Figure 3.1   Alternating current signal showing clock cycle timing.

Note

The hertz was named for the German physicist Heinrich Rudolf Hertz. In 1885, Hertz confirmed the electromagnetic theory, which states that light is a form of electromagnetic radiation and is propagated as waves.

A single cycle is the smallest element of time for the processor. Every action requires at least one cycle and usually multiple cycles. To transfer data to and from memory, for example, a modern processor such as the Pentium II needs a minimum of three cycles to set up the first memory transfer, and then only a single cycle per transfer for the next three to six consecutive transfers. The extra cycles on the first transfer are normally called *wait states*. A wait state is a clock tick in which nothing happens. This ensures that the processor isn't getting ahead of the rest of the computer.

▶▶ See "SIMMs and DIMMs," p. 437.

The time required to execute instructions also varies:

- *8086 and 8088.* The original 8086 and 8088 processors take an average of 12 cycles to execute a single instruction.
- *286 and 386.* The 286 and 386 processors improve this rate to about 4.5 cycles per instruction.
- *486.* The 486 and most other fourth generation Intel compatible processors such as the AMD 5x86 drop the rate further, to about two cycles per instruction.
- *Pentium.* The Pentium architecture and other fifth generation Intel compatible processors such as those from AMD and Cyrix include twin instruction pipelines and other improvements that provide for operation at one or two instructions per cycle.
- *Pentium Pro, Pentium II/III, Celeron and Xeon.* These Intel P6 class processors, as well as other sixth generation processors such as those from AMD and Cyrix, can execute as many as three or more instructions per cycle.

Different instruction execution times (in cycles) make it difficult to compare systems based purely on clock speed, or number of cycles per second. How can two processors that run at the same clock rate perform differently with one running "faster" than the other? The answer is simple: efficiency.

The main reason why the 486 was considered fast relative to a 386 is that it executes twice as many instructions in the same number of cycles. The same thing is true for a Pentium; it executes about twice as many instructions in a given number of cycles as a 486. This means that given the same clock speed, a Pentium will be twice as fast as a 486, and consequently a 133MHz 486 class processor (such as the AMD 5x86-133) is not even as fast as a 75MHz Pentium! That is because Pentium megahertz are "worth" about double what 486 megahertz are worth in terms of instructions completed per cycle. The Pentium II and III are about 50 percent faster than an equivalent Pentium at a given clock speed because they can execute about that many more instructions in the same number of cycles.

Comparing relative processor performance, you can see that a 600MHz Pentium III is about equal to a (theoretical) 900MHz Pentium, which is about equal to an 1,800MHz 486, which is about equal to a 3,600MHz 386 or 286, which is about equal to a 7,200MHz 8088. The original PCs' 8088 ran at only 4.77MHz; today, we have systems that are comparatively about 1,500 times faster. As you can see, you have to be careful in comparing systems based on pure MHz alone, because many other factors affect system performance.

Evaluating CPU performance can be tricky. CPUs with different internal architectures do things differently and may be relatively faster at certain things and slower at others. To fairly compare different CPUs at different clock speeds, Intel has devised a specific series of benchmarks called the iCOMP (Intel Comparative Microprocessor Performance) index that can be run against processors to produce a relative gauge of performance. The iCOMP index benchmark has been updated twice and released in original iCOMP, iCOMP 2.0, and now iCOMP 3.0 versions.

Table 3.3 shows the relative power, or iCOMP 2.0 index, for several processors.

Table 3.3   Intel iCOMP 2.0 Index Ratings

Processor	iCOMP 2.0 Index	Processor	iCOMP 2.0 Index
Pentium 75	67	Pentium Pro 200	220
Pentium 100	90	Celeron 300	226
Pentium 120	100	Pentium II 233	267
Pentium 133	111	Celeron 300A	296
Pentium 150	114	Pentium II 266	303
Pentium 166	127	Celeron 333	318
Pentium 200	142	Pentium II 300	332
Pentium-MMX 166	160	Pentium II Overdrive 300	351
Pentium Pro 150	168	Pentium II 333	366
Pentium-MMX 200	182	Pentium II 350	386
Pentium Pro 180	197	Pentium II Overdrive 333	387
Pentium-MMX 233	203	Pentium II 400	440
Celeron 266	213	Pentium II 450	483

The iCOMP 2.0 index is derived from several independent benchmarks and is a stable indication of relative processor performance. The benchmarks balance integer with floating point and multimedia performance.

Recently Intel discontinued the iCOMP 2.0 index and released the iCOMP 3.0 index. iCOMP 3.0 is an updated benchmark that incorporates an increasing use of 3D, multimedia, and Internet technology and software, as well as the increasing use of rich data streams and compute-intensive applications, including 3D, multimedia, and Internet technology. iCOMP 3.0 combines six benchmarks: WinTune 98 Advanced CPU Integer test, CPUmark 99, 3D WinBench 99-3D Lighting and Transformation Test, MultimediaMark 99, Jmark 2.0 Processor Test, and WinBench 99-FPU WinMark. These newer benchmarks take advantage of the SSE (Streaming SIMD Extensions), additional graphics and sound instructions built in to the PIII. Without taking advantage of these new instructions, the PIII would benchmark at about the same speed as a PII at the same clock rate.

The following table shows the iCOMP Index 3.0 ratings for newer Intel processors.

Processor	iCOMP 3.0 Index
Pentium II 450MHz	1240
Pentium III 450MHz	1500
Pentium III 500MHz	1650
Pentium III 550MHz	1780

Considerations When Interpreting iCOMP Scores

Each processor's rating is calculated at the time the processor is introduced, using a particular, well-configured, commercially available system. Relative iCOMP Index 3.0 scores and actual system performance might be affected by future changes in software design and configuration. Relative scores and actual system performance also may be affected by differences in components or characteristics of microprocessors such as L2 cache, bus speed, extended multimedia or graphics instructions, or improvements in the microprocessor manufacturing process.

Differences in hardware components other than microprocessors used in the test systems also can affect how iCOMP scores relate to actual system performance. iCOMP 3.0 ratings cannot be compared with earlier versions of the iCOMP index because different benchmarks and weightings are used in calculating the result.

Processor Speeds and Markings Versus Motherboard Speed

Another confusing factor when comparing processor performance is that virtually all modern processors since the 486DX2 run at some multiple of the motherboard speed. For example, a Celeron 466 runs at a multiple of seven times the motherboard speed of 66MHz, while a Pentium III 550 runs at five and a half times the motherboard speed of 100MHz. Up until early 1998, most motherboards ran at 66MHz or less because that is all Intel supported with their processors until then. Starting in April 1998, Intel released both processors and motherboard chipsets designed to run at 100MHz. Cyrix has a few processors designed to run on 75MHz motherboards, and many Pentium motherboards are capable of running that speed as well, although technically Intel never supported it. AMD also has versions of the K6-2 designed to run at motherboard speeds of 100MHz.

By late 1999, motherboards running at 133MHz should be available, which is the next step in board speed.

Normally, you can set the motherboard speed and multiplier setting via jumpers or other configuration mechanism (such as CMOS setup) on the motherboard.

Modern systems use a variable-frequency synthesizer circuit usually found in the main motherboard chipset to control the motherboard and CPU speed. Most Pentium motherboards will have three or four speed settings. The processors used today are available in a variety of versions that run at different frequencies based on a given motherboard speed. For example, most of the Pentium chips run at a speed that is some multiple of the true motherboard speed. For example, Pentium processors and motherboards run at the speeds shown in Table 3.4.

For information on specific AMD or Cyrix processors, see their respective sections later in this chapter.

Table 3.4   Intel Processor and Motherboard Speeds

CPU Type	CPU Speed (MHz)	Clock Multiplier	Motherboard Speed (MHz)
Pentium	60	1x	60
Pentium	66	1x	66
Pentium	75	1.5x	50
Pentium	90	1.5x	60
Pentium	100	1.5x	66
Pentium	120	2x	60
Pentium	133	2x	66
Pentium	150	2.5x	60
Pentium/Pentium Pro	166	2.5x	66
Pentium/Pentium Pro	180	3x	60
Pentium/Pentium Pro	200	3x	66
Pentium/Pentium II	233	3.5x	66
Pentium(Mobile)/Pentium-II/Celeron	266	4x	66
Pentium II/Celeron	300	4.5x	66
Pentium II/Celeron	333	5x	66
Pentium II/Celeron	366	5.5x	66
Pentium Celeron	400	6x	66
Pentium Celeron	433	6.5x	66
Pentium Celeron	466	7x	66
Pentium Celeron	500	7.5x	66
Pentium II	350	3.5x	100
Pentium II/Xeon	400	4x	100
Pentium II/III/Xeon	450	4.5x	100
Pentium III/Xeon	500	5x	100
Pentium III/Xeon	533	4x	133
Pentium III/Xeon	550	5.5x	100
Pentium III/Xeon	600	4.5x	133

If all other variables are equal—including the type of processor, the number of wait states (empty cycles) added to different types of memory accesses, and the width of the data bus—you can compare two systems by their respective clock rates. However, the construction and design of the memory controller (contained in the motherboard chipset) as well as the type and amount of memory installed can have an enormous effect on a system's final execution speed.

In building a processor, a manufacturer tests it at different speeds, temperatures, and pressures. After the processor is tested, it receives a stamp indicating the maximum safe speed at which the unit will operate under the wide variation of temperatures and pressures encountered in normal operation. The rating system usually is simple. For example, the top of the processor in one of my systems is marked like this:

A80486DX2–66

The A is Intel's indicator that this chip has a Ceramic Pin Grid Array form factor, or an indication of the physical packaging of the chip.

The 80486DX2 is the part number, which identifies this processor as a clock-doubled 486DX processor.

The -66 at the end indicates that this chip is rated to run at a maximum speed of 66MHz. Because of the clock doubling, the maximum motherboard speed is 33MHz. This chip would be acceptable for any application in which the chip runs at 66MHz or slower. For example, you could use this processor in a system with a 25MHz motherboard, in which case the processor would happily run at 50MHz.

Most 486 motherboards also had a 40MHz setting, in which case the DX2 would run at 80MHz internally. Because this is 14MHz beyond its rated speed, many would not work; or if it worked at all, it would be only for a short time. On the other hand, I have found that most of the newer chips marked with –66 ratings seem to run fine (albeit somewhat hotter) at the 40/80MHz settings. This is called overclocking and can end up being a simple, cost-effective way to speed up your system. However, I would not recommend this for mission-critical applications where the system reliability is of the utmost importance; a system pushed beyond specification like this can often exhibit erratic behavior under stress.

Note

One good source of online overclocking information is located at `http://www.sysopt.com`. It includes, among other things, fairly thorough overclocking FAQs and an ongoing survey of users who have successfully (and sometimes unsuccessfully) overclocked their CPUs. Note that many of the newer Intel processors incorporate fixed bus multipliers, which effectively prevent or certainly reduce the ability to overclock. Unfortunately this can be overridden with a simple hardware fix, and many counterfeit processor vendors are selling remarked (overclocked) chips.

Sometimes, however, the markings don't seem to indicate the speed directly. In the older 8086, for example, -3 translates to 6MHz operation. This marking scheme is more common in some of the older chips, which were manufactured before some of the marking standards used today were standardized.

The Processor Heat Sink Might Hide the Rating

Most processors have heat sinks on top of them, which can prevent you from reading the rating printed on the chip.

A *heat sink* is a metal device that draws heat away from an electronic device. Most processors running at 50MHz and faster should have a heat sink installed to prevent the processor from overheating.

Fortunately, most CPU manufacturers are placing marks on the top and bottom of the processor. If the heat sink is difficult to remove from the chip, you can take the heat sink and chip out of the socket together and read the markings on the bottom of the processor to determine what you have.

Cyrix P-Ratings

Cyrix/IBM 6x86 processors use a PR (Performance Rating) scale that is not equal to the true clock speed in megahertz. For example, the Cyrix 6x86MX/MII-PR366 actually runs at only 250MHz (2.5 × 100MHz). This is a little misleading—you must set up the motherboard as if a 250MHz processor were being installed, not the 366MHz you might suspect. Unfortunately this leads people to believe these systems are faster than they really are. Table 3.5 shows the relationship between the Cyrix 6x86, 6x86MX, and M-II P-Ratings versus the actual chip speeds in MHz.

Table 3.5   Cyrix P-Ratings Versus Actual Chip Speeds in MHz

Cyrix CPU Type	P-Rating	Actual CPU Speed (MHz)	Clock Multiplier	Motherboard Speed (MHz)
6x86	PR90	80	2x	40
6x86	PR120	100	2x	50
6x86	PR133	110	2x	55
6x86	PR150	120	2x	60
6x86	PR166	133	2x	66
6x86	PR200	150	2x	75
6x86MX	PR133	100	2x	50
6x86MX	PR133	110	2x	55
6x86MX	PR150	120	2x	60
6x86MX	PR150	125	2.5x	50
6x86MX	PR166	133	2x	66
6x86MX	PR166	137.5	2.5x	55
6x86MX	PR166	150	3x	50
6x86MX	PR166	150	2.5x	60
6x86MX	PR200	150	2x	75
6x86MX	PR200	165	3x	55
6x86MX	PR200	166	2.5x	66
6x86MX	PR200	180	3x	60
6x86MX	PR233	166	2x	83
6x86MX	PR233	187.5	2.5x	75
6x86MX	PR233	200	3x	66
6x86MX	PR266	207.5	2.5x	83
6x86MX	PR266	225	3x	75
6x86MX	PR266	233	3.5x	66
M-II	PR300	225	3x	75
M-II	PR300	233	3.5x	66
M-II	PR333	250	3x	83
M-II	PR366	250	2.5x	100

Note that a given P-Rating can mean several different actual CPU speeds, for example a Cyrix 6x86MX-PR200 might actually be running at 150MHz, 165MHz, 166MHz, or 180MHz, but *not* at 200MHz.

This P-Rating was supposed to indicate speed in relation to an Intel Pentium processor, but the processor they are comparing to is the original non-MMX, small L1 cache version running on an older motherboard platform with an older chipset and slower technology memory. The P-Rating does not compare well against the Celeron, Pentium II, or Pentium III processors. In that case these chips are more comparative at their true speed. In other words, the MII-PR366 really runs at only 250MHz, and compares well against Intel processors running at closer to that speed. I consider calling a chip an MII-366 when it really runs at only 250MHz very misleading, to say the least.

AMD P-Ratings

Although both AMD and Cyrix concocted this misleading P-Rating system, AMD thankfully only used it for a short time and only on the older K5 processor. They still have the PR designation stamped on their newer chips, but all K6 processors have PR numbers that match their actual CPU speed in MHz. Table 3.6 shows the P-Rating and actual speeds of the AMD K5 and K6 processors.

Table 3.6   AMD P-Ratings Versus Actual Chip Speeds in MHz

Cyrix CPU Type	P-Rating	Actual CPU Speed (MHz)	Clock Multiplier	Motherboard Speed (MHz)
K5	PR75	75	1.5x	50
K5	PR90	90	1.5x	60
K5	PR100	100	1.5x	66
K5	PR120	90	1.5x	60
K5	PR133	100	1.5x	66
K5	PR166	116.7	1.75x	66
K6	PR166	166	2.5x	66
K6	PR200	200	3x	66
K6	PR233	233	3.5x	66
K6	PR266	266	4x	66
K6	PR300	300	4.5x	66
K6-2	PR233	233	3.5x	66
K6-2	PR266	266	4x	66
K6-2	PR300	300	4.5x	66
K6-2	PR300	300	3x	100
K6-2	PR333	333	5x	66
K6-2	PR333	333	3.5x	95
K6-2	PR350	350	3.5x	100
K6-2	PR366	366	5.5x	66
K6-2	PR380	380	4x	95
K6-2	PR400	400	4x	100
K6-2	PR450	450	4.5x	100
K6-2	PR475	475	5x	95
K6-3	PR400	400	4x	100
K6-3	PR450	450	4.5x	100

Data Bus

Perhaps the most common ways to describe a processor is by the speed at which it runs and the width of the processor's external data bus. This defines the number of data bits that can be moved into or out of the processor in one cycle. A *bus* is a series of connections that carry common signals. Imagine running a pair of wires from one end of a building to another. If you connect a 110v AC power generator to the two wires at any point and place outlets at convenient locations along the wires, you have constructed a power bus. No matter which outlet you plug the wires into, you have access to the same signal, which in this example is 110v AC power. Any transmission medium that has more than one outlet at each end can be called a bus. A typical computer system has several internal and external buses.

The processor bus discussed most often is the external data bus—the bundle of wires (or pins) used to send and receive data. The more signals that can be sent at the same time, the more data can be transmitted in a specified interval and, therefore, the faster (and wider) the bus. A wider data bus is like having a highway with more lanes, which allows for greater throughput.

Data in a computer is sent as digital information consisting of a time interval in which a single wire carries 5v to signal a 1 data bit, or 0v to signal a 0 data bit. The more wires you have, the more individual bits you can send in the same time interval. A chip such as the 286 or 386SX, which has 16 wires for transmitting and receiving such data, has a 16-bit data bus. A 32-bit chip, such as the 386DX and 486, has twice as many wires dedicated to simultaneous data transmission as a 16-bit chip; a 32-bit chip can send twice as much information in the same time interval as a 16-bit chip. Modern processors such as the Pentium series have 64-bit external data buses. This means that Pentium processors including the original Pentium, Pentium Pro, and Pentium II can all transfer 64 bits of data at a time to and from the system memory.

A good way to understand this flow of information is to consider a highway and the traffic it carries. If a highway has only one lane for each direction of travel, only one car at a time can move in a certain direction. If you want to increase traffic flow, you can add another lane so that twice as many cars pass in a specified time. You can think of an 8-bit chip as being a single-lane highway because one byte flows through at a time. (One byte equals eight individual bits.) The 16-bit chip, with two bytes flowing at a time, resembles a two-lane highway. You may have four lanes in each direction to move a large number of automobiles; this structure corresponds to a 32-bit data bus, which has the capability to move four bytes of information at a time. Taking this further, a 64-bit data bus is like having an 8-lane highway moving data in and out of the chip!

Just as you can describe a highway by its lane width, you can describe a chip by the width of its data bus. When you read an advertisement that describes a 32-bit or 64-bit computer system, the ad usually refers to the CPU's data bus. This number provides a rough idea of the chip's performance potential (and, therefore, the system).

Perhaps the most important ramification of the data bus in a chip is that the width of the data bus also defines the size of a bank of memory. This means that a 32-bit processor, such as the 486 class chips, reads and writes memory 32 bits at a time. Pentium class processors, including the Pentium II, read and write memory 64 bits at a time. Because standard 72-pin SIMMs (Single

Inline Memory Modules) are only 32 bits wide, they must be installed one at a time in most 486 class systems; they're installed two at a time in most Pentium class systems. Newer DIMMs (Dual Inline Memory Modules) arc 64 bits wide, so they are installed one at a time in Pentium class systems. Each DIMM is equal to a complete bank of memory in Pentium systems, which makes system configuration easy, because they can then be installed or removed one at a time.

▶▶ See "Memory Banks," p. 451.

Internal Registers (Internal Data Bus)

The size of the internal registers indicate how much information the processor can operate on at one time and how it moves data around internally within the chip. This is sometimes also referred to as the internal data bus. The register size is essentially the same as the internal data bus size. A register is a holding cell within the processor; for example, the processor can add numbers in two different registers, storing the result in a third register. The register size determines the size of data the processor can operate on. The register size also describes the type of software or commands and instructions a chip can run. That is, processors with 32-bit internal registers can run 32-bit instructions that are processing 32-bit chunks of data, but processors with 16-bit registers cannot. Most advanced processors today—chips from the 386 to the Pentium II— use 32-bit internal registers and can therefore run the same 32-bit operating systems and software.

Some processors have an internal data bus (made up of data paths and storage units called registers) that is larger than the external data bus. The 8088 and 386SX are examples of this structure. Each chip has an internal data bus twice the width of the external bus. These designs, which sometimes are called hybrid designs, usually are low-cost versions of a "pure" chip. The 386SX, for example, can pass data around internally with a full 32-bit register size; for communications with the outside world, however, the chip is restricted to a 16-bit–wide data path. This design enables a systems designer to build a lower-cost motherboard with a 16-bit bus design and still maintain software and instruction set compatibility with the full 32-bit 386.

Internal registers often are larger than the data bus, which means that the chip requires two cycles to fill a register before the register can be operated on. For example, both the 386SX and 386DX have internal 32-bit registers, but the 386SX has to "inhale" twice (figuratively) to fill them, whereas the 386DX can do the job in one "breath." The same thing would happen when the data is passed from the registers back out to the system bus.

The Pentium is an example of this type of design. All Pentiums have a 64-bit data bus and 32-bit registers—a structure that might seem to be a problem until you understand that the Pentium has two internal 32-bit pipelines for processing information. In many ways, the Pentium is like two 32-bit chips in one. The 64-bit data bus provides for very efficient filling of these multiple registers. Multiple pipelines are called *superscalar* architecture, which was introduced with the Pentium processor.

▶▶ See "Pentium Processors," p.129.

More advanced sixth-generation processors such as the Pentium Pro and Pentium II/III have as many as six internal pipelines for executing instructions. Although some of these internal pipes are dedicated to special functions, these processors can still execute as many as three instructions in one clock cycle.

Address Bus

The address bus is the set of wires that carry the addressing information used to describe the memory location to which the data is being sent or from which the data is being retrieved. As with the data bus, each wire in an address bus carries a single bit of information. This single bit is a single digit in the address. The more wires (digits) used in calculating these addresses, the greater the total number of address locations. The size (or width) of the address bus indicates the maximum amount of RAM that a chip can address.

The highway analogy can be used to show how the address bus fits in. If the data bus is the highway and the size of the data bus is equivalent to the number of lanes, the address bus relates to the house number or street address. The size of the address bus is equivalent to the number of digits in the house address number. For example, if you live on a street in which the address is limited to a two-digit (base 10) number, no more than 100 distinct addresses (00–99) can exist for that street (10 to the power of 2). Add another digit, and the number of available addresses increases to 1,000 (000–999), or 10 to the power of 3.

Computers use the binary (base 2) numbering system, so a two-digit number provides only four unique addresses (00, 01, 10, and 11) calculated as 2 to the power of 2. A three-digit number provides only eight addresses (000–111), which is 2 to the third power. For example, the 8086 and 8088 processors use a 20-bit address bus that calculates as a maximum of 2 to the 20th power or 1,048,576 bytes (1MB) of address locations. Table 3.7 describes the memory-addressing capabilities of Intel processors.

Table 3.7   Intel and Intel Compatible Processor Memory-Addressing Capabilities

Processor Family	Address Bus	Bytes	KB	MBs	GB
8088/8086	20-bit	1,048,576	1,024	1	—
286/386SX	24-bit	16,777,216	16,384	16	—
386DX/486/P5 Class	32-bit	4,294,967,296	4,194,304	4,096	4
P6 Class	36-bit	68,719,476,736	67,108,864	65,536	64

The data bus and address bus are independent, and chip designers can use whatever size they want for each. Usually, however, chips with larger data buses have larger address buses. The sizes of the buses can provide important information about a chip's relative power, measured in two important ways. The size of the data bus is an indication of the chip's information-moving capability, and the size of the address bus tells you how much memory the chip can handle.

Internal Level 1 (L1) Cache

All modern processors starting with the 486 family include an integrated (L1) cache and controller. The integrated L1 cache size varies from processor to processor, starting at 8KB for the original 486DX and now up to 32KB, 64KB, or more in the latest processors.

Since L1 cache is always built in to the processor die, it runs at the *full core speed* of the processor internally. By full core speed, I mean this cache runs at the higher clock multiplied internal processor speed rather than the external motherboard speed. This cache basically is an area of very fast memory built in to the processor and is used to hold some of the current working set of code and data. Cache memory can be accessed with no wait states because it is running at the same speed as the processor core.

Using cache memory reduces a traditional system bottleneck because system RAM often is much slower than the CPU. This prevents the processor from having to wait for code and data from much slower main memory therefore improving performance. Without the L1 cache, a processor frequently would be forced to wait until system memory caught up.

L1 cache is even more important in modern processors because it is often the only memory in the entire system that can truly keep up with the chip. Most modern processors are clock multiplied, which means they are running at a speed that is really a multiple of the motherboard they are plugged into. The Pentium II 333MHz, for example, runs at a very high multiple of five times the true motherboard speed of 66MHz. Because the main memory is plugged in to the motherboard, it can also run at only 66MHz maximum. The only 333MHz memory in such a system is the L1 cache built into the processor core. In this example, the Pentium II 333MHz processor has 32KB of integrated L1 cache in two separate 16KB blocks.

▶▶ See "Memory Speeds," p. 424.

If the data that the processor wants is already in the internal cache, the CPU does not have to wait. If the data is not in the cache, the CPU must fetch it from the Level 2 cache or (in less sophisticated system designs) from the system bus, meaning main memory directly.

In order to understand the importance of cache, you need to know the relative speeds of processors and memory. The problem with this is that processor speed is normally expressed in MHz (millions of cycles per second), while memory speeds are often expressed in nanoseconds (billionths of a second per cycle).

Both are really time or frequency based measurements, and a chart comparing them can be found in Chapter 6, "Memory," Table 6.3. In this table you will note that a 200MHz processor equates to five nanosecond cycling, which means you would need 5ns memory to keep pace with a 200MHz CPU. Also note that the motherboard of a 200MHz system will normally run at 66MHz, which corresponds to a speed of 15ns per cycle, and require 15ns memory to keep pace. Finally note that 60ns main memory (common on many Pentium class systems) equates to a clock speed of approximately 16MHz. So in a typical Pentium 200 system, you have a processor running at 200MHz (5ns per cycle), a motherboard running at 66MHz (15ns per cycle), and main memory running at 16MHz (60ns per cycle).

To learn how the L1 and L2 cache work, consider the following analogy.

This story involves a person (in this case you) eating food to act as the processor requesting and operating on data from memory. The kitchen where the food is prepared is the main memory (SIMM/DIMM) RAM. The cache controller is the waiter, and the L1 cache is the table you are seated at. L2 cache will be introduced as a food cart, which is positioned between your table and the kitchen.

Okay, here's the story. Say you start to eat at a particular restaurant every day at the same time. You come in, sit down, and order a hot dog. To keep this story proportionately accurate, let's say you normally eat at the rate of one bite (byte? <g>) every five seconds (200MHz = 5ns cycling). It also takes 60 seconds for the kitchen to produce any given item that you order (60ns main memory).

So, when you first arrive, you sit down, order a hot dog, and you have to wait for 60 seconds for the food to be produced before you can begin eating. Once the waiter brings the food, you start eating at your normal rate. Pretty quickly you finish the hot dog, so you call the waiter and order a hamburger. Again you wait 60 seconds while the hamburger is being produced. When it arrives again you begin eating at full speed. After you finish the hamburger, you order a plate of fries. Again you wait, and after it is delivered 60 seconds later you eat it at full speed. Finally, you decide to finish the meal and order cheesecake for dessert. After another 60-second wait, you can again eat dessert at full speed. Your overall eating experience consists of mostly a lot of waiting, followed by short bursts of actual eating at full speed.

After coming into the restaurant for two consecutive nights at exactly 6 p.m. and ordering the same items in the same order each time, on the third night the waiter begins to think; "I know this guy is going to be here at 6 p.m., order a hot dog, a hamburger, fries, and then cheesecake. Why don't I have these items prepared in advance and surprise him, maybe I'll get a big tip." So you enter the restaurant, order a hot dog, and the waiter immediately puts it on your plate, with no waiting! You then proceed to finish the hot dog and right as you were about to request the hamburger, the waiter deposits one on your plate. The rest of the meal continues in the same fashion, and you eat the entire meal, taking a bite every five seconds, and never have to wait for the kitchen to prepare the food. Your overall eating experience this time consists of all eating, with no waiting for the food to be prepared, due primarily to the intelligence and thoughtfulness of your waiter.

This analogy exactly describes the function of the L1 cache in the processor. The L1 cache itself is the table that can contain one or more plates of food. Without a waiter, the space on the table is a simple food buffer. When stocked, you can eat until the buffer is empty, but nobody seems to be intelligently refilling it. The waiter is the cache controller who takes action and adds the intelligence to decide what dishes are to be placed on the table in advance of your needing them. Like the real cache controller, he uses his skills to literally guess what food you will require next, and if and when he guesses right, you never have to wait.

Let's now say on the fourth night you arrive exactly on time and start off with the usual hot dog. The waiter, by now really feeling confident, has the hot dog already prepared when you arrive, so there is no waiting.

Just as you finish the hot dog, and right as he is placing a hamburger on your plate, you say "Gee, I'd really like a bratwurst now; I didn't actually order this hamburger." The waiter guessed wrong, and the consequence is that this time you have to wait the full 60 seconds as the kitchen prepares your brat. This is known as a cache miss, where the cache controller did not correctly fill the cache with the data the processor actually needed next. The result is waiting, or in the case of a sample 200MHz Pentium system, the system essentially throttles back to 16MHz (RAM speed) whenever there is a cache miss. According to Intel, the L1 cache in most of their processors has approximately a 90 percent hit ratio. This means that the cache has the correct data 90 percent of the time and consequently the processor runs at full speed, 200MHz in this example, 90 percent of the time. However, 10 percent of the time the cache controller guesses wrong and the data has to be retrieved out of the significantly slower main memory, meaning the processor has to wait. This essentially throttles the system back to RAM speed, which in this example was 60ns or 16MHz.

Level 2 (L2) Cache

To mitigate the dramatic slowdown every time there is a cache miss, a secondary or L2 cache can be employed.

Using the restaurant analogy I used to explain L1 cache in the previous section, I'll equate the L2 cache to a cart of additional food items placed strategically such that the waiter can retrieve food from it in 15 seconds. In an actual Pentium class system, the L2 cache is mounted on the motherboard, which means it runs at motherboard speed—66MHz or 15ns in this example. Now if you ask for an item the waiter did not bring in advance to your table, instead of making the long trek back to the kitchen to retrieve the food and bring it back to you 60 seconds later, he can first check the cart where he has placed additional items. If the requested item is there, he will return with it in only 15 seconds. The net effect in the real system is that instead of slowing down from 200MHz to 16MHz waiting for the data to come from the 60ns main memory, the data can instead be retrieved from the 15ns (66MHz) L2 cache instead. The effect is that the system slows down from 200MHz to 66MHz.

Most L2 caches have a hit ratio also in the 90 percent range, which means that if you look at the system as a whole, 90 percent of the time it will be running at full speed (200MHz in this example) by retrieving data out of the L1 cache. Ten percent of the time it will slow down to retrieve the data from the L2 cache. Ninety percent of that time the data will be in the L2, and 10 percent of that time you will have to go to the slow main memory to get the data due to an L2 cache miss. This means that our sample system runs at full processor speed 90 percent of the time 77(200MHz in this case), motherboard speed 9 percent of the time (66MHz in this case), and RAM speed about 1 percent of the time (16MHz in this case). You can clearly see the importance of both the L1 and L2 caches; without them the system will be using main memory more often, which is significantly slower than the processor.

In Pentium (P5) class systems, the L2 cache is normally found on the motherboard and must therefore run at motherboard speed. Intel made a dramatic improvement to this in the P6 class systems by migrating the L2 cache from the motherboard directly into the processor. In the Xeon and Celeron processors, the L2 cache runs at full processor core speed, which means there is no waiting or slowing down after an L1 cache miss. In the mainstream Pentium II processors, for economy reasons, the L2 cache runs at half the core processor speed, which is still significantly faster than the motherboard.

Cache Organization

The organization of the cache memory in the 486 and Pentium family is called a four-way set associative cache, which means that the cache memory is split into four blocks. Each block also is organized as 128 or 256 lines of 16 bytes each.

To understand how a four-way set associative cache works, consider a simple example. In the simplest cache design, the cache is set up as a single block into which you can load the contents of a corresponding block of main memory. This procedure is similar to using a bookmark to locate the current page of a book that you are reading. If main memory equates to all the pages in the book, the bookmark indicates which pages are held in cache memory. This procedure works if the required data is located within the pages marked with the bookmark, but it does not work if you need to refer to a previously read page. In that case, the bookmark is of no use.

An alternative approach is to maintain multiple bookmarks to mark several parts of the book simultaneously. Additional hardware overhead is associated with having multiple bookmarks, and you also have to take time to check all the bookmarks to see which one marks the pages of data you need. Each additional bookmark adds to the overhead, but also increases your chance of finding the desired pages.

If you settle on marking four areas in the book, you have essentially constructed a four-way set associative cache. This technique splits the available cache memory into four blocks, each of which stores different lines of main memory. Multitasking environments, such as Windows, are good examples of environments in which the processor needs to operate on different areas of memory simultaneously and in which a four-way cache would improve performance greatly.

The contents of the cache must always be in sync with the contents of main memory to ensure that the processor is working with current data. For this reason, the internal cache in the 486 family is a *write-through* cache. Write-through means that when the processor writes information out to the cache, that information is automatically written through to main memory as well.

By comparison, the Pentium and later chips have an internal write-back cache, which means that both reads and writes are cached, further improving performance. Even though the internal 486 cache is write-through, the system can employ an external write-back cache for increased performance. In addition, the 486 can buffer up to four bytes before actually storing the data in RAM, improving efficiency in case the memory bus is busy.

Another feature of improved cache designs is that they are non-blocking. This is a technique for reducing or hiding memory delays by exploiting the overlap of processor operations with data accesses. A non-blocking cache allows program execution to proceed concurrently with cache misses as long as certain dependency constraints are observed. In other words, the cache can handle a cache miss much better and allow the processor to continue doing something non-dependent on the missing data.

The cache controller built into the processor also is responsible for watching the memory bus when alternative processors, known as busmasters, are in control of the system. This process of watching the bus is referred to as *bus snooping*. If a busmaster device writes to an area of memory that also is stored in the processor cache currently, the cache contents and memory no longer agree. The cache controller then marks this data as invalid and reloads the cache during the next memory access, preserving the integrity of the system.

A secondary external L2 cache of extremely fast static RAM (SRAM) chips also is used in most 486 and Pentium-based systems. It further reduces the amount of time that the CPU must spend waiting for data from system memory. The function of the secondary processor cache is similar to that of the onboard cache. The secondary processor cache holds information that is moving to the CPU, thereby reducing the time that the CPU spends waiting and increasing the time that the CPU spends performing calculations. Fetching information from the secondary processor cache rather than from system memory is much faster because of the SRAM chips' extremely fast speed—15 nanoseconds (ns) or less.

Pentium systems incorporate the secondary cache on the motherboard, while Pentium Pro and Pentium II systems have the secondary cache inside the processor package. By moving the L2 cache into the processor, systems are capable of running at speeds higher than the motherboard—up to as fast as the processor core.

As clock speeds increase, cycle time decreases. Most SIMM memory used in Pentium and earlier systems was 60ns, which works out to be only about 16MHz! Standard motherboard speeds are now 66MHz, 100MHz, or 133MHz, and processors are available at 600MHz or more. Newer systems don't use cache on the motherboard any longer, as the faster SDRAM or RDRAM used in modern Pentium Celeron/II/III systems can keep up with the motherboard speed. The trend today is toward integrating the L2 cache into the processor die just like the L1 cache. This allows the L2 to run at full core speed because it is now a part of the core. Cache speed is always more important than size. The rule is that a smaller but faster cache is always better than a slower but bigger cache. Table 3.8 illustrates the need for and function of L1 (internal) and L2 (external) caches in modern systems.

Table 3.8   CPU Speeds Relative to Cache, SIMM/DIMM, and Motherboard

CPU Type:	Pentium	Pentium Pro	Pentium II 333
CPU speed:	233MHz	200MHz	333MHz
L1 cache speed:	4ns (233MHz)	5ns (200MHz)	3ns (333MHz)
L2 cache speed:	15ns (66MHz)	5ns (200MHz)	6ns (167MHz)
Motherboard speed:	66MHz	66MHz	66MHz
SIMM/DIMM speed:	60ns (16MHz)	60ns (16MHz)	15ns (66MHz)
SIMM/DIMM type:	FPM/EDO	FPM/EDO	SDRAM

(continues)

Table 3.8   Continued

CPU Type:	Celeron 500	Pentium III 500	Pentium III 600
CPU speed:	500 Hz	500MHz	600MHz
L1 cache speed:	2ns (500MHz)	2ns (500 Hz)	1.7ns (600MHz)
L2 cache speed:	2ns (500MHz)	4ns (250MHz)	1.7ns (600MHz)
Motherboard speed:	66MHz	100MHz	133MHz
SIMM/DIMM speed:	15ns (66MHz)	10ns (100MHz)	7.5ns (133MHz)
SIMM/DIMM type:	SDRAM	SDRAM	SDRAM/RDRAM

As you can see, having two levels of cache between the very fast CPU and the much slower main memory helps minimize any wait states the processor might have to endure. This allows the processor to keep working closer to its true speed.

Processor Modes

All Intel 32-bit and later processors, from the 386 on up, can run in several modes. Processor modes refer to the various operating environments and affect the instructions and capabilities of the chip. The processor mode controls how the processor sees and manages the system memory and the tasks that use it.

Three different modes of operation possible are

- Real mode (16-bit software)
- Protected mode (32-bit software)
- Virtual Real mode (16-bit programs within a 32-bit environment)

Real Mode

The original IBM PC included an 8088 processor that could execute 16-bit instructions using 16-bit internal registers, and could address only 1MB of memory using 20 address lines. All original PC software was created to work with this chip and was designed around the 16-bit instruction set and 1MB memory model. For example, DOS and all DOS software, Windows 1.x through 3.x, and all Windows 1.x through 3.x applications are written using 16-bit instructions. These 16-bit operating systems and applications are designed to run on an original 8088 processor.

◀◀ See "Internal Registers," p. 51.

◀◀ See "Address Bus," p. 52.

Later processors such as the 286 could also run the same 16-bit instructions as the original 8088, but much faster. In other words, the 286 was fully compatible with the original 8088 and could run all 16-bit software just the same as an 8088, but, of course, that software would run faster. The 16-bit instruction mode of the 8088 and 286 processors has become known as real mode. All software running in real mode must use only 16-bit instructions and live within the 20-bit (1MB) memory architecture it supports. Software of this type is normally single-tasking, which means that only one program can run at a time. There is no built-in protection to keep one program from overwriting another program or even the operating system in memory, which means that if more than one program is running, it is possible for one of them to bring the entire system to a crashing halt.

Protected (32-bit) Mode

Then came the 386, which was the PC industry's first 32-bit processor. This chip could run an entirely new 32-bit instruction set. To take full advantage of the 32-bit instruction set you needed a 32-bit operating system and a 32-bit application. This new 32-bit mode was referred to as protected mode, which alludes to the fact that software programs running in that mode are protected from overwriting one another in memory. Such protection helps make the system much more crash-proof, as an errant program cannot very easily damage other programs or the operating system. In addition, a crashed program can be terminated, while the rest of the system continues to run unaffected.

Knowing that new operating systems and applications—which take advantage of the 32-bit protected mode—would take some time to develop, Intel wisely built in a backward compatible real mode into the 386. That allowed it to run unmodified 16-bit operating systems and applications. It ran them quite well—much faster than any previous chip. For most people, that was enough; they did not necessarily want any new 32-bit software—they just wanted their existing 16-bit software to run faster. Unfortunately, that meant the chip was never running in the 32-bit protected mode, and all the features of that capability were being ignored.

When a high-powered processor such as a Pentium III is running DOS (real mode), it acts like a "Turbo 8088." Turbo 8088 means that the processor has the advantage of speed in running any 16-bit programs; it otherwise can use only the 16-bit instructions and access memory within the same 1MB memory map of the original 8088. This means if you have a 128MB Pentium III system running Windows 3.x or DOS, you are effectively using only the first megabyte of memory, leaving the other 127MB largely unused!

New operating systems and applications that ran in the 32-bit protected mode of the modern processors were needed. Being stubborn, we resisted all the initial attempts at getting switched over to a 32-bit environment. It seems that as a user community, we are very resistant to change and would be content with our older software running faster rather than adopting new software with new features. I'll be the first one to admit that I was one of those stubborn users myself!

Because of this resistance, 32-bit operating systems such as UNIX or variants such as Linux, OS/2, and even Windows NT and Windows 2000 have had a very hard time getting any mainstream share in the PC marketplace. Out of those, Windows 2000 is the only one that will likely become a true mainstream product, and that is mainly because Microsoft has coerced us in that direction with Windows 95 and 98. Windows 3.x was the last full 16-bit operating system. In fact, it was not a complete operating system because it ran on top of DOS.

Microsoft realized how stubborn the installed base of PC users was so it developed Windows 95 as a bridge to a full 32-bit world. Windows 95 is a mostly 32-bit operating system, but it retains enough 16-bit capability to fully run our old 16-bit applications. Windows 95 came out in August

1995, a full 10 years later than the introduction of the first 32-bit PC processor! It has taken us only 10 years to migrate to software that can fully use the processors we have in front of us.

Virtual Real Mode

The key to the backward compatibility of the Windows 95 32-bit environment is the third mode in the processor: virtual real mode. Virtual real is essentially a virtual real mode 16-bit environment that runs inside 32-bit protected mode. When you run a DOS prompt window inside Windows 95/98, you have created a virtual real mode session. Because protected mode allows true multitasking, you can actually have several real mode sessions running, each with its own software running on a virtual PC. This can all run simultaneously, even while other 32-bit applications are running.

Note that any program running in a virtual real mode window can access up to only 1MB of memory, which that program will believe is the first and only megabyte of memory in the system. In other words, if you run a DOS application in a virtual real window, it will have a 640KB limitation on memory usage. That is because there is only 1MB of total RAM in a 16-bit environment, and the upper 384KB is reserved for system use. The virtual real window fully emulates an 8088 environment, so that aside from speed, the software runs as if it were on an original real mode-only PC. Each virtual machine gets its own 1MB address space, an image of the real hardware BIOS routines, and emulation of all other registers and features found in real mode.

Virtual real mode is used when you use a DOS window or run a DOS or Windows 3.x 16-bit program in Windows 95/98. When you start a DOS application, Windows 95 creates a virtual DOS machine under which it can run.

One interesting thing to note is that all Intel (and Intel compatible—such as AMD and Cyrix) processors power up in real mode. If you load a 32-bit operating system, it will automatically switch the processor into 32-bit mode and take control from there.

Some DOS and Windows 3.x applications misbehave, which means they do things that even virtual real mode will not support. Diagnostics software is a perfect example of this. Such software will not run properly in a real mode (virtual real) window under Windows 95/98 or NT, and Windows 2000. In that case, you can still run your Pentium II in the original no-frills real mode by interrupting the boot process and commanding the system to boot plain DOS. This is accomplished on most Windows 95/98/NT systems by pressing the F8 key when you see the prompt Starting Windows... on the screen. You will then see the Startup menu; you can select one of the command prompt choices, which tell the system to boot plain 16-bit real mode DOS. The choice of Safe Mode Command Prompt is best if you are going to run true hardware diagnostics, which do not normally run in protected mode and should be run with a minimum of drivers and other software loaded.

Although real mode is used by DOS and "standard" DOS applications, there are special programs available that "extend" DOS and allow access to extended memory (over 1MB). These are sometimes called DOS extenders and are usually included as a part of any DOS or Windows 3.x software that uses them. The protocol that describes how to make DOS work in protected mode is called DPMI (DOS protected mode interface). DPMI was used by Windows 3.x to access extended memory for use with Windows 3.x applications. It allowed them to use more memory even though they were still 16-bit programs. DOS extenders are especially popular in DOS games, because they allow them to access much more of the system memory than the standard 1MB most real mode programs can address. These DOS extenders work by switching the processor in and out of real mode, or in the case of those that run under Windows, they use the DPMI interface built in to Windows, allowing them to share a portion of the system's extended memory.

Another exception in real mode is that the first 64KB of extended memory is actually accessible to the PC in real mode, despite the fact that it's not supposed to be possible. This is the result of a bug in the original IBM AT with respect to the 21st memory address line, known as A20 (A0 is the first address line). By manipulating the A20 line, real mode software can gain access to the first 64KB of extended memory—the first 64KB of memory past the first megabyte. This area of memory is called the high memory area (HMA).

SMM (Power Management)

Spurred on primarily by the goal of putting faster and more powerful processors in laptop computers, Intel has created power management circuitry. This circuitry enables processors to conserve energy use and lengthen battery life. This was introduced initially in the Intel 486SL processor, which is an enhanced version of the 486DX processor. Subsequently, the power-management features were universalized and incorporated into all Pentium and later processors. This feature set is called SMM, which stands for System Management Mode.

SMM circuitry is integrated into the physical chip but operates independently to control the processor's power use based on its activity level. It allows the user to specify time intervals after which the CPU will be partially or fully powered down. It also supports the suspend/resume feature that allows for instant power on and power off, used mostly with laptop PCs. These settings are normally controlled via system BIOS settings.

Superscalar Execution

The fifth-generation Pentium and newer processors feature multiple internal instruction execution pipelines, which enable them to execute multiple instructions at the same time. The 486 and all preceding chips can perform only a single instruction at a time. Intel calls the capability to execute more than one instruction at a time superscalar technology. This technology provides additional performance compared with the 486.

▶▶ See "Pentium Processor," p. 129.

Superscalar architecture usually is associated with high-output RISC (Reduced Instruction Set Computer) chips. An RISC chip has a less complicated instruction set with fewer and simpler instructions. Although each instruction accomplishes less, overall the clock speed can be higher, which can usually increase performance. The Pentium is one of the first CISC (Complex

Instruction Set Computer) chips to be considered superscalar. A CISC chip uses a more rich, full-featured instruction set, which has more complicated instructions. As an example, say you wanted to instruct a robot to screw in a light bulb. Using CISC instructions you would say

1. Pick up the bulb.
2. Insert it into the socket.
3. Rotate clockwise until tight.

Using RISC instructions you would say something more along the lines of

1. Lower hand.
2. Grasp bulb.
3. Raise hand.
4. Insert bulb into socket.
5. Rotate clockwise one turn.
6. Is bulb tight? If not repeat step 5.
7. End.

Overall many more RISC instructions are required to do the job because each instruction is simpler and does less. The advantage is that there are fewer overall commands the robot (or processor) has to deal with, and it can execute the individual commands more quickly, and thus in many cases execute the complete task (or program) more quickly as well. The debate goes on whether RISC or CISC is really better, but in reality there is no such thing as a pure RISC or CISC chip.

Intel and compatible processors have generally been regarded as CISC chips, although the fifth and sixth generation versions have many RISC attributes, and internally break CISC instructions down into RISC versions.

MMX Technology

MMX technology is named for multi-media extensions, or matrix math extensions, depending on whom you ask. Intel states that it is actually not an acronym and stands for nothing special; however, the internal origins are probably one of the preceding. MMX technology was introduced in the later fifth-generation Pentium processors (see Figure 3.2) as a kind of add-on that improves video compression/decompression, image manipulation, encryption, and I/O processing—all of which are used in a variety of today's software.

MMX consists of two main processor architectural improvements. The first is very basic; all MMX chips have a larger internal L1 cache than their non-MMX counterparts. This improves the performance of any and all software running on the chip, regardless of whether it actually uses the MMX-specific instructions.

The other part of MMX is that it extends the processor instructions set with 57 new commands or instructions, as well as a new instruction capability called Single Instruction, Multiple Data (SIMD).

Figure 3.2   An Intel Pentium MMX chip shown from the top and bottom (exposing the die). Photograph used by permission of Intel Corporation.

Modern multimedia and communication applications often use repetitive loops that, while occupying 10 percent or less of the overall application code, can account for up to 90 percent of the execution time. SIMD enables one instruction to perform the same function on multiple pieces of data, similar to a teacher telling an entire class to "sit down," rather than addressing each student one at a time. SIMD allows the chip to reduce processor-intensive loops common with video, audio, graphics, and animation.

Intel also added 57 new instructions specifically designed to manipulate and process video, audio, and graphical data more efficiently. These instructions are oriented to the *highly parallel* and often repetitive sequences often found in multimedia operations. Highly parallel refers to the fact that the same processing is done on many different data points, such as when modifying a graphic image.

Intel licensed the MMX capabilities to competitors such as AMD and Cyrix, who were then able to upgrade their own Intel-compatible processors with MMX technology.

SSE (Streaming SIMD Extensions)

The Pentium III processor introduced in February 1999 included an update to MMX called Streaming SIMD Extensions (SSE). SSE includes 70 new instructions for graphics and sound processing over what MMX provided. SSE is similar to MMX, in fact, it was originally called MMX-2 before it was released. Besides adding more MMX style instructions, the SSE instructions allow for floating-point calculations, and now use a separate unit within the processor instead of sharing the standard floating-point unit as MMX did.

The Streaming SIMD Extensions consist of 70 new instructions, including Single Instruction Multiple Data (SIMD) floating-point, additional SIMD integer, and cacheability control instructions. Some of the technologies that benefit from the Streaming SIMD Extensions include advanced imaging, 3D, streaming audio and video (DVD playback), and speech recognition applications. The benefits of SSE include the following:

- Higher resolution and higher quality image viewing and manipulation
- High quality audio, MPEG2 video, and simultaneous MPEG2 encoding and decoding
- Reduced CPU utilization for speech recognition, as well as higher accuracy and faster response times

The SSE instructions are particularly useful with MPEG2 decoding, which is the standard scheme used on DVD video discs. This means that SSE equipped processors should be capable of doing MPEG2 decoding in software at full speed without requiring an additional hardware MPEG2 decoder card. SSE-equipped processors are much better and faster than previous processors when it comes to speech recognition.

Note that for any of the SSE instructions to be beneficial, they must be encoded in the software, which means that SSE-aware applications must be used to see the benefits. Most software companies writing graphics and sound-related software have updated those applications to be SSE-aware and utilize the features of SSE. The processors, which include SSE, will also include MMX, so standard MMX-enabled applications will still run as they did on processors without SSE.

Dynamic Execution

First used in the P6 or sixth-generation processors, dynamic execution is an innovative combination of three processing techniques designed to help the processor manipulate data more efficiently. Those techniques are multiple branch prediction, data flow analysis, and speculative execution. Dynamic execution enables the processor to be more efficient by manipulating data in a more logically ordered fashion rather than simply processing a list of instructions, and it is one of the hallmarks of all sixth-generation processors.

The way software is written can dramatically influence a processor's performance. For example, performance will be adversely affected if the processor is frequently required to stop what it is doing and jump or branch to a point elsewhere in the program. Delays also occur when the processor cannot process a new instruction until the current instruction is completed. Dynamic execution allows the processor to not only dynamically predict the order of instructions, but execute them out of order internally, if necessary, for an improvement in speed.

Multiple Branch Prediction

Multiple branch prediction predicts the flow of the program through several branches. Using a special algorithm, the processor can anticipate jumps or branches in the instruction flow. It uses this to predict where the next instructions can be found in memory with an accuracy of 90 percent or greater. This is possible because while the processor is fetching instructions, it is also looking at instructions further ahead in the program.

Data Flow Analysis

Data flow analysis analyzes and schedules instructions to be executed in an optimal sequence, independent of the original program order. The processor looks at decoded software instructions and determines whether they are available for processing or are instead dependent on other instructions to be executed first. The processor then determines the optimal sequence for processing and executes the instructions in the most efficient manner.

Speculative Execution

Speculative execution increases performance by looking ahead of the program counter and executing instructions that are likely to be needed later. Because the software instructions being processed are based on predicted branches, the results are stored in a pool for later referral. If they are to be executed by the resultant program flow, the already completed instructions are retired and the results are committed to the processor's main registers in the original program execution order. This technique essentially allows the processor to complete instructions in advance, and then grab the already completed results when necessary.

Dual Independent Bus (DIB) Architecture

The Dual Independent Bus (DIB) architecture was first implemented in the first sixth-generation processor. DIB was created to improve processor bus bandwidth and performance. Having two (dual) independent data I/O buses enables the processor to access data from either of its buses simultaneously and in parallel, rather than in a singular sequential manner (as in a single-bus system). The second or backside bus in a processor with DIB is used for the L2 cache, allowing it to run at much greater speeds than if it were to share the main processor bus.

Note

The DIB architecture is explained more fully in Chapter 4, "Motherboards and Buses." To see the typical Pentium II system architecture, see Figure 4.34.

Two buses make up the DIB architecture: the L2 cache bus and the processor-to-main-memory, or system, bus. The P6 class processors from the Pentium Pro to the Celeron and Pentium II/III processors can use both buses simultaneously, eliminating a bottleneck there. The Dual Independent Bus architecture enables the L2 cache of the 500MHz Celeron processor, for example, to run seven and a half times faster than the L2 cache of older Pentium processors. Because the backside or L2 cache bus is coupled to the speed of the processor core, as the frequency of future P6 class processors (Celeron, Pentium II/III) increases, so will the speed of the L2 cache.

The key to implementing DIB was to move the L2 cache memory off of the motherboard and into the processor package. L1 cache has always been directly a part of the processor die, but L2 was larger and had to be external. By moving the L2 cache into the processor, the L2 cache could run at speeds more like the L1 cache, much faster than the motherboard or processor bus. To move the L2 cache into the processor initially, modifications had to be made to the CPU socket or slot. There are two socket-based processors that fully support DIB. The Pentium Pro, which plugs into Socket 8, and the Celeron, which is available in Socket 370 or Slot 1 versions. In the Pentium Pro, the L2 cache is contained within the chip package but on separate die(s). This, unfortunately, made the chip expensive and difficult to produce, although it did mean that the L2 cache ran at full processor speed. The Celeron updates this design and includes both the L1 and L2 caches directly on the processor die. This allows the L1 and L2 to both run at full processor speed, and makes the chip much less expensive to produce.

The Pentium II/III adopted an initially less expensive and easier-to-manufacture approach called the Single Edge Contact (SEC) or Single Edge Processor (SEP) package, which are covered in more detail later in this chapter.

Most Pentium II/III processors run the L2 cache at exactly 1/2-core speed, but that can easily be scaled up or down in the future. For example the 300MHz and faster Pentium IIPE (Performance Enhanced) processors used in laptop or mobile applications and the 600MHz Pentium III have on-die L2 cache like the Celeron, which runs at full core speed. Also, most have 512KB of L2 cache internally, but the PII/III processors with on-die L2 cache only use 256KB. Even so, they are faster than the 512KB versions, because it is better to have a cache that is twice as fast than one that is twice as large.

Cache design can be easily changed in the future because Intel makes Xeon versions of the PII and PIII that include 512KB, 1MB, or even 2MB of full core speed L2 cache. These aren't on-die, but consist of special high-speed Intel manufactured cache chips located within the cartridge. The flexibility of the P6 processor design will allow Intel to make Pentium IIIs with any amount of cache they like.

The Pentium II/III SEC processor connects to a motherboard via a single-edge connector instead of the multiple pins used in existing Pin Grid Array (PGA) socket packages.

DIB also allows the system bus to perform multiple simultaneous transactions (instead of singular sequential transactions), accelerating the flow of information within the system and boosting performance. Overall DIB architecture offers up to three times the bandwidth performance over a single-bus architecture processor.

Processor Manufacturing

Processors are manufactured primarily from silicon, the second most common element on Earth—only oxygen is more abundant. Silicon is the primary ingredient in beach sand; however, in that form it isn't pure enough to be used in chips.

To be made into chips, raw silicon is purified, melted down, and then processed in special ovens where a seed crystal is used to grow large cylindrical crystals called boules (see Figure 3.3). Each boule is larger than eight inches in diameter and over 50 inches long, weighing hundreds of pounds.

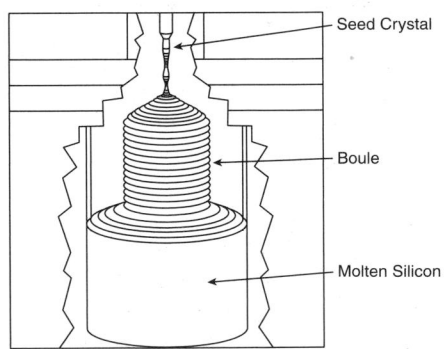

— Seed Crystal

— Boule

— Molten Silicon

Figure 3.3   Growing a pure silicon boule in a high pressure, high temperature oven.

The boule is then ground into a perfect 200mm-diameter cylindrical ingot (the current standard), with a flat cut on one side for positioning accuracy and handling. Each ingot is then cut with a high-precision diamond saw into over a thousand circular wafers, each less than a millimeter thick (see Figure 3.4). Each wafer is polished to a mirror-smooth surface.

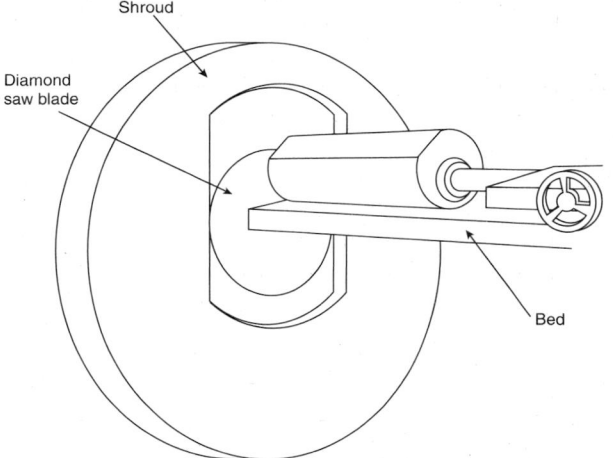

Figure 3.4 Slicing a silicon ingot into wafers with a diamond saw.

Chips are manufactured from the wafers using a process called *photolithography*. Through this photographic process, transistors and circuit and signal pathways are created in semiconductors by depositing different layers of various materials on the chip, one after the other. Where two specific circuits intersect, a transistor or switch can be formed.

The photolithographic process starts when an insulating layer of silicon dioxide is grown on the wafer through a vapor deposition process. Then a coating of photoresist material is applied and an image of that layer of the chip is projected through a mask onto the now light-sensitive surface.

Doping is the term used to describe chemical impurities added to silicon (which is naturally a non-conductor), creating a material with semiconductor properties. The projector uses a specially created mask, which is essentially a negative of that layer of the chip etched in chrome on a quartz plate. The Pentium III currently uses five masks and has as many layers, although other processors may have six or more layers. Each processor design requires as many masks as layers to produce the chips.

As the light passes through the first mask, the light is focused on the wafer surface, imprinting it with the image of that layer of the chip. Each individual chip image is called a die. A device called a stepper then moves the wafer over a little bit and the same mask is used to imprint another chip die immediately next to the previous one. After the entire wafer is imprinted with chips, a caustic solution washes away the areas where the light struck the photoresist, leaving the mask imprints of the individual chip vias (interconnections between layers) and circuit pathways.

Then, another layer of semiconductor material is deposited on the wafer with more photoresist on top, and the next mask is used to produce the next layer of circuitry. Using this method, the layers of each chip are built one on top of the other, until the chips are completed.

The final masks add the *metallization* layers, which are the metal interconnects used to tie all the individual transistors and other components together. Most chips use aluminum interconnects today, although many will be moving to copper in the future. Copper is a better conductor than aluminum and will allow smaller interconnects with less resistance, meaning smaller and faster chips can be made. The reason copper hasn't been used up until recently is that there were difficult corrosion problems to overcome during the manufacturing process that were not as much a problem with aluminum.

A completed circular wafer will have as many chips imprinted on it as can possibly fit. Because each chip is normally square or rectangular, there are some unused portions at the edges of the wafer, but every attempt is made to use every square millimeter of surface.

The standard wafer size used in the industry today is 200mm in diameter, or just under 8 inches. This results in a wafer of about 31,416 square millimeters. The current Pentium II 300MHz processor is made up of 7.5 million transistors using a 0.35 micron (millionth of a meter) process. This process results in a die of exactly 14.2mm on each side, which is 202 square millimeters of area. This means that about 150 total Pentium II 300MHz chips on the .35 micron process can be made from a single 200mm-diameter wafer.

The trend in the industry is to go to both larger wafers and a smaller chip die process. Process refers to the size of the individual circuits and transistors on the chip. For example, the Pentium II 333MHz and faster processors are made on a newer and smaller .25 micron process, which reduces the total chip die size to only 10.2mm on each side, or a total chip area of 104 square millimeters. On the same 200mm (8-inch) wafer as before, Intel can make about 300 Pentium II chips using this process, or double the amount over the larger .35 micron process 300MHz version.

The Pentium III is currently built on a .25 micron process and has a die size of 128 square millimeters, which is about 11.3mm on each side. This is slightly larger than the Pentium II because the III has about two million more transistors.

In the future, processes will move from .25 micron to .18, and then .13 micron. This will allow for more than double the number of chips to be made on existing wafers, or more importantly, will allow more transistors to be incorporated into the die, yet it will not be larger overall than die today. This means the trend for incorporating L2 cache within the die will continue, and transistor counts will rise up to 100 million per chip or more in the future.

The trend in wafers is to move from the current 200mm (8-inch) diameter to a bigger, 300mm (12-inch) diameter wafer. This will increase surface area dramatically over the smaller 200mm design and boost chip production to about 675 chips per wafer. Intel and other manufacturers expect to have 300mm wafer production in place just after the year 2000. After that happens, chip prices should continue to drop dramatically as supply increases.

Note that not all the chips on each wafer will be good, especially as a new production line starts. As the manufacturing process for a given chip or production line is perfected, more and more of the chips will be good. The ratio of good to bad chips on a wafer is called the yield. Yields well under 50 percent are common when a new chip starts production; however, by the end of a given chip's life, the yields are normally in the 90 percent range. Most chip manufacturers guard their yield figures and are very secretive about them because knowledge of yield problems can give their competitors an edge. A low yield causes problems both in the cost per chip and in delivery delays to their customers. If a company has specific knowledge of competitors' improving yields, they can set prices or schedule production to get higher market share at a critical point. For example, AMD was plagued by low-yield problems during 1997 and 1998, which cost them significant market share. They have been solving the problems, but it shows that yields are an important concern.

After a wafer is complete, a special fixture tests each of the chips on the wafer and marks the bad ones to be separated out later. The chips are then cut from the wafer using either a high-powered laser or diamond saw.

After being cut from the wafers, the individual die are then retested, packaged, and retested again. The packaging process is also referred to as bonding, because the die is placed into a chip housing where a special machine bonds fine gold wires between the die and the pins on the chip. The package is the container for the chip die, and it essentially seals it from the environment.

After the chips are bonded and packaged, final testing is done to determine both proper function and rated speed. Different chips in the same batch will often run at different speeds. Special test fixtures run each chip at different pressures, temperatures, and speeds, looking for the point at which the chip stops working. At this point, the maximum successful speed is noted and the final chips are sorted into bins with those that tested at a similar speed. For example, the Pentium III 450, 500, and 550 are all exactly the same chip made using the same die. They were sorted at the end of the manufacturing cycle by speed.

One interesting thing about this is that as a manufacturer gains more experience and perfects a particular chip assembly line, the yield of the higher speed versions goes way up. This means that out of a wafer of 150 total chips, perhaps more than 100 of them check out at 550MHz, while only a few won't run at that speed. The paradox is that Intel often sells a lot more of the lower priced 450 and 500MHz chips, so they will just dip into the bin of 550MHz processors and label them as 450 or 500 chips and sell them that way. People began discovering that many of the lower-rated chips would actually run at speeds much higher than they were rated, and the business of overclocking was born. Overclocking describes the operation of a chip at a speed higher than it was rated for. In many cases, people have successfully accomplished this because, in essence, they had a higher-speed processor already—it was marked with a lower rating only because it was sold as the slower version.

Intel has seen fit to put a stop to this by building overclock protection into most of their newer chips. This is usually done in the bonding or cartridge manufacturing process, where the chips are intentionally altered so they won't run at any speeds higher than they are rated. Normally this involves changing the bus frequency (BF) pins on the chip, which control the internal multipliers the chip uses. Even so, enterprising individuals have found ways to run their motherboards at bus speeds higher than normal, so even though the chip won't allow a higher multiplier, you can still run it at a speed higher than it was designed.

Be Wary of PII and PIII Overclocking Fraud

Also note that unscrupulous individuals have devised a small logic circuit that bypasses the overclock protection, allowing the chip to run at higher multipliers. This small circuit can be hidden in the PII or PIII cartridge, and then the chip can be remarked or relabeled to falsely indicate it is a higher speed version. This type of chip remarketing fraud is far more common in the industry than people want to believe. In fact, if you purchase your system or processor from a local computer flea market type show, you have an excellent chance of getting a remarked chip. I recommend purchasing processors only from more reputable direct distributors or dealers. Contact Intel, AMD, or Cyrix, for a list of their reputable distributors and dealers.

I recently installed a 200MHz Pentium processor in a system that is supposed to run at a 3x multiplier based off a 66MHz motherboard speed. I tried changing the multiplier to 3.5x but the chip refused to go any faster; in fact, it ran at the same or lower speed than before. This is a sure sign of overclock protection inside, which is to say that the chip won't support any higher level of multiplier. My motherboard included a jumper setting for an unauthorized speed of 75MHz, which when multiplied by 3x resulted in an actual processor speed of 225MHz. This worked like a charm, and the system is now running fast and clean. Note that I am not necessarily recommending overclocking for everybody; in fact, I normally don't recommend it at all for any important systems. If you have a system you want to fool around with, it is interesting to try. Like my cars, I always seem to want to hotrod my computers.

PGA Chip Packaging

PGA packaging has been the most common chip package used until recently. It was used starting with the 286 processor in the 1980s and is still used today for Pentium and Pentium Pro processors. PGA takes its name from the fact that the chip has a grid-like array of pins on the bottom of the package. PGA chips are inserted into sockets, which are often of a ZIF (Zero Insertion Force) design. A ZIF socket has a lever to allow for easy installation and removal of the chip.

Most Pentium processors use a variation on the regular PGA called SPGA (Staggered Pin Grid Array), where the pins are staggered on the underside of the chip rather than in standard rows and columns. This was done to move the pins closer together and decrease the overall size of the chip when a large number of pins is required. Figure 3.5 shows a Pentium Pro that uses the dual-pattern SPGA (on the right) next to an older Pentium 66 that uses the regular PGA. Note that the right half of the Pentium Pro shown here has additional pins staggered among the other rows and columns.

Figure 3.5   PGA on Pentium 66 (left) and dual-pattern SPGA on Pentium Pro (right).

Single Edge Contact (SEC) and Single Edge Processor (SEP) Packaging

Abandoning the chip-in-a-socket approach used by virtually all processors until this point, the Pentium II/III chips are characterized by their Single Edge Contact (SEC) cartridge design. The processor, along with several L2 cache chips, is mounted on a small circuit board (much like an oversized memory SIMM), which is then sealed in a metal and plastic cartridge. The cartridge is then plugged into the motherboard through an edge connector called Slot 1, which looks very much like an adapter card slot.

By placing the processor and L2 cache as separate chips inside a cartridge, they now have a CPU module that is easier and less expensive to make than the Pentium Pro that preceded it. The Single Edge Contact (SEC) cartridge is an innovative—if a bit unwieldy—package design that incorporates the backside bus and L2 cache internally. Using the SEC design, the core and L2 cache are fully enclosed in a plastic and metal cartridge. These subcomponents are surface mounted directly to a substrate (or base) inside the cartridge to enable high-frequency operation. The SEC cartridge technology allows the use of widely available, high-performance industry standard Burst Static RAMs (BSRAMs) for the dedicated L2 cache. This greatly reduces the cost compared to the proprietary cache chips used inside the CPU package in the Pentium Pro.

A less expensive version of the SEC is called the Single Edge Processor (SEP) package. The SEP package is basically the same circuit board containing processor and (optional) cache as the Pentium II, but without the fancy plastic cover. The SEP package plugs directly into the same Slot 1 connector used by the standard Pentium II. Four holes on the board allow for the heat sink to be installed.

Slot 1 is the connection to the motherboard and has 242 pins. The Slot 1 dimensions are shown in Figure 3.6. The SEC cartridge or SEP processor is plugged into Slot 1 and secured with a processor-retention mechanism, which is a bracket that holds it in place. There may also be a retention mechanism or support for the processor heat sink. Figure 3.7 shows the parts of the cover that make up the SEC package. Note the large thermal plate used to aid in dissipating the heat from this processor. The SEP package is shown in Figure 3.8.

Processor Sockets

Intel has created a set of socket designs—Socket 1 through Socket 8, and the new Socket 370—used for their chips from the 486 through the Pentium Pro and Celeron. Each socket is designed to support a different range of original and upgrade processors. Table 3.9 shows the specifications of these sockets.

Table 3.9   Intel 486/Pentium CPU Socket Types and Specifications

Socket Number	Pins	Pin Layout	Voltage	Supported Processors
Socket 1	169	17×17 PGA	5v	486 SX/SX2, DX/DX2*, DX4 Overdrive
Socket 2	238	19×19 PGA	5v	486 SX/SX2, DX/DX2*, DX4 Overdrive, 486 Pentium Overdrive
Socket 3	237	19×19 PGA	5v/3.3v	486 SX/SX2, DX/DX2, DX4, 486 Pentium Overdrive, AMD 5x86
Socket 4	273	21×21 PGA	5v	Pentium 60/66, Overdrive
Socket 5	320	37×37 SPGA	3.3/3.5v	Pentium 75-133, Overdrive
Socket 6**	235	19×19 PGA	3.3v	486 DX4, 486 Pentium Overdrive
Socket 7	321	37×37 SPGA	VRM	Pentium 75-233+, MMX, Overdrive, AMD K5/K6, Cyrix M1/II
Socket 8	387	dual pattern SPGA	Auto VRM	Pentium Pro
PGA370	370	37×37 SPGA	Auto VRM	Celeron
Slot 1	242	Slot	Auto VRM	Pentium II/III, Celeron
Slot 2	330	Slot	Auto VRM	Pentium II/III Xeon

Non-overdrive DX4 or AMD 5x86 also can be supported with the addition of an aftermarket 3.3v voltage-regulator adapter.

**Socket 6 was a paper standard only and was never actually implemented in any systems.*

PGA = Pin Grid Array.

SPGA = Staggered Pin Grid Array.

VRM = Voltage Regulator Module.

Sockets 1, 2, 3, and 6 are 486 processor sockets and are shown together in Figure 3.10 so you can see the overall size comparisons and pin arrangements between these sockets. Sockets 4, 5, 7, and 8 are Pentium and Pentium Pro processor sockets and are shown together in Figure 3.11 so you can see the overall size comparisons and pin arrangements between these sockets. More detailed drawings of each socket are included throughout the remainder of this section with the thorough descriptions of the sockets.

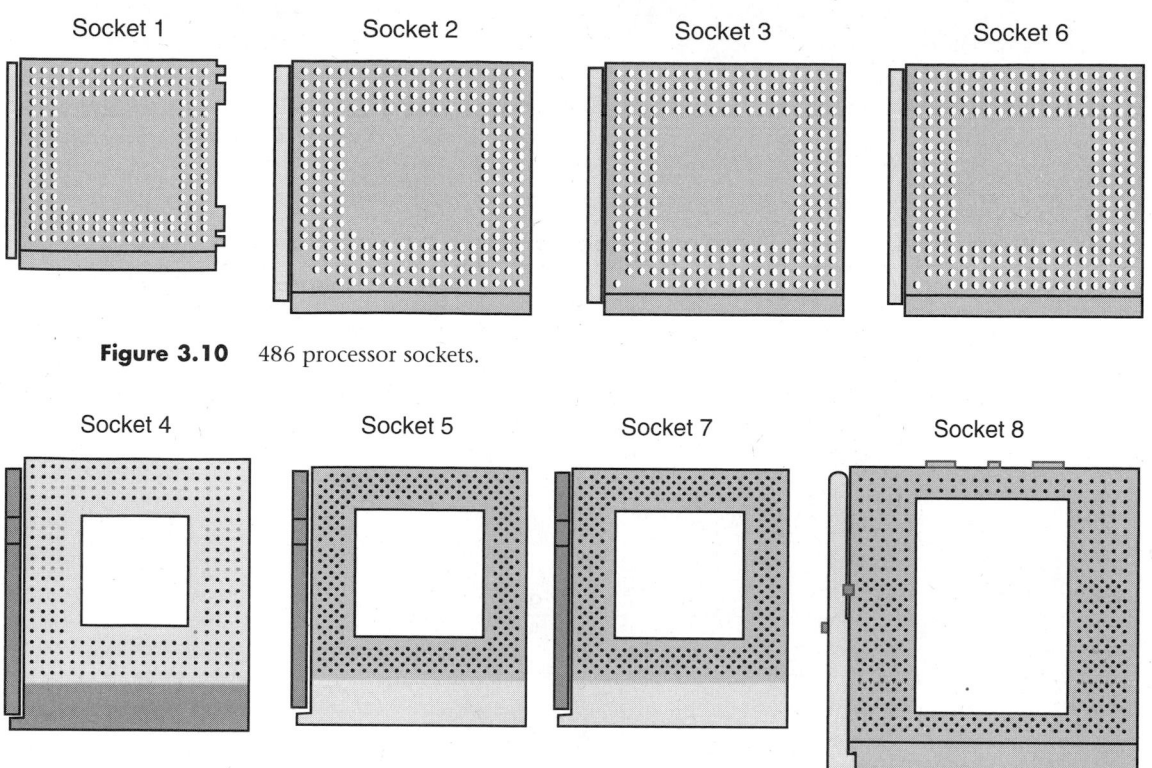

Figure 3.10   486 processor sockets.

Figure 3.11   Pentium and Pentium Pro processor sockets.

Socket 1

The original OverDrive socket, now officially called Socket 1, is a 169-pin PGA socket. Motherboards that have this socket can support any of the 486SX, DX, and DX2 processors, and the DX2/OverDrive versions. This type of socket is found on most 486 systems that originally were designed for OverDrive upgrades. Figure 3.12 shows the pinout of Socket 1.

The original DX processor draws a maximum 0.9 amps of 5v power in 33MHz form (4.5 watts) and a maximum 1 amp in 50MHz form (5 watts). The DX2 processor, or OverDrive processor, draws a maximum 1.2 amps at 66MHz (6 watts). This minor increase in power requires only a passive heat sink consisting of aluminum fins that are glued to the processor with thermal transfer epoxy. Passive heat sinks don't have any mechanical components like fans. Heat sinks with fans or other devices that use power are called active heat sinks. OverDrive processors rated at 40MHz or less do not have heat sinks.

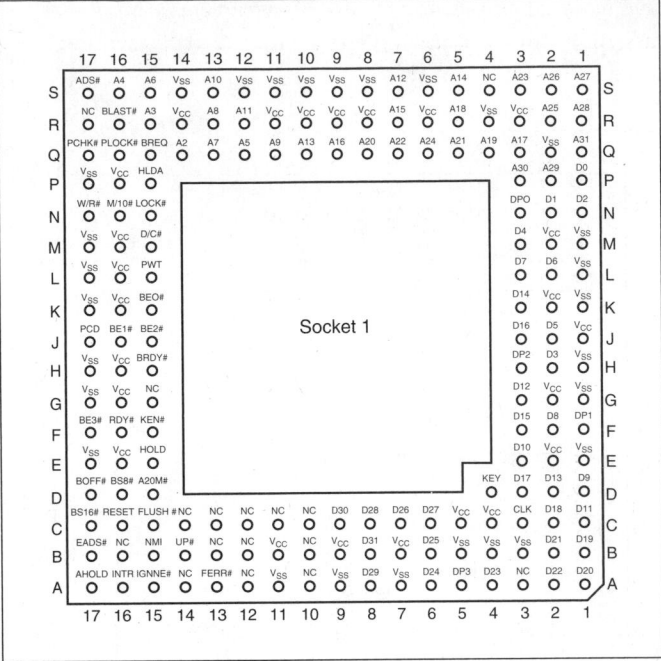

Figure 3.12 Intel Socket 1 pinout.

Socket 2

When the DX2 processor was released, Intel was already working on the new Pentium processor. The company wanted to offer a 32-bit, scaled-down version of the Pentium as an upgrade for systems that originally came with a DX2 processor. Rather than just increasing the clock rate, Intel created an all new chip with enhanced capabilities derived from the Pentium.

The chip, called the Pentium OverDrive processor, plugs into a processor socket with the Socket 2 or Socket 3 design. These sockets will hold any 486 SX, DX, or DX2 processor, as well as the Pentium OverDrive. Because this chip is essentially a 32-bit version of the (normally 64-bit) Pentium chip, many have taken to calling it a Pentium-SX. It is available in 25/63MHz and 33/83MHz versions. The first number indicates the base motherboard speed; the second number indicates the actual operating speed of the Pentium OverDrive chip. As you can see, it is a clock-multiplied chip that runs at 2.5 times the motherboard speed. Figure 3.13 shows the pinout configuration of the official Socket 2 design.

Notice that although the new chip for Socket 2 is called Pentium OverDrive, it is not a full-scale (64-bit) Pentium. Intel released the design of Socket 2 a little prematurely and found that the chip ran too hot for many systems. The company solved this problem by adding a special active heat sink to the Pentium OverDrive processor. This active heat sink is a combination of a standard heat sink and a built-in electric fan. Unlike the aftermarket glue-on or clip-on fans for processors that you might have seen, this one actually draws 5v power directly from the socket to drive the fan. No external connection to disk drive cables or the power supply is required. The fan/heat sink assembly clips and plugs directly into the processor and provides for easy replacement if the fan fails.

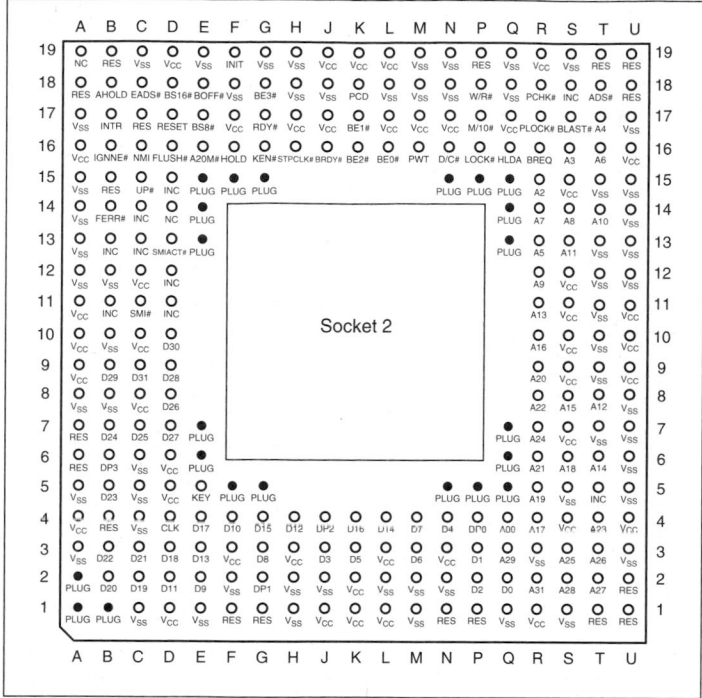

Figure 3.13   238-pin Intel Socket 2 configuration.

Another requirement of the active heat sink is additional clearance—no obstructions for an area about 1.4 inches off the base of the existing socket to allow for heat-sink clearance. The Pentium OverDrive upgrade will be difficult or impossible in systems that were not designed with this feature.

Another problem with this particular upgrade is power consumption. The 5v Pentium OverDrive processor will draw up to 2.5 amps at 5v (including the fan) or 12.5 watts, which is more than double the 1.2 amps (6 watts) drawn by the DX2 66 processor. Intel did not provide this information when it established the socket design, so the company set up a testing facility to certify systems for thermal and mechanical compatibility with the Pentium OverDrive upgrade. For the greatest peace of mind, ensure that your system is certified compatible before you attempt this upgrade.

Note

See Intel's Web site (http://www.intel.com) for a comprehensive list of certified OverDrive-compatible systems.

Figure 3.14 shows the dimensions of the Pentium OverDrive processor and the active heat sink/fan assembly.

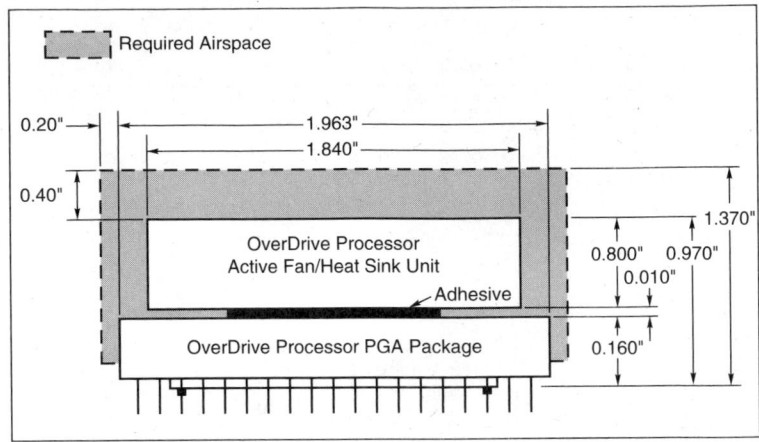

Figure 3.14   The physical dimensions of the Intel Pentium OverDrive processor and active heat sink.

Socket 3

Because of problems with the original Socket 2 specification and the enormous heat the 5v version of the Pentium OverDrive processor generates, Intel came up with an improved design. The new processor is the same as the previous Pentium OverDrive processor, except that it runs on 3.3v and draws a maximum 3.0 amps of 3.3v (9.9 watts) and 0.2 amp of 5v (1 watt) to run the fan—a total 10.9 watts. This configuration provides a slight margin over the 5v version of this processor. The fan will be easy to remove from the OverDrive processor for replacement, should it ever fail.

Intel had to create a new socket to support both the DX4 processor, which runs on 3.3v, and the 3.3v Pentium OverDrive processor. In addition to the new 3.3v chips, this new socket supports the older 5v SX, DX, DX2, and even the 5v Pentium OverDrive chip. The design, called Socket 3, is the most flexible upgradable 486 design. Figure 3.15 shows the pinout specification of Socket 3.

Notice that Socket 3 has one additional pin and several others plugged compared with Socket 2. Socket 3 provides for better keying, which prevents an end user from accidentally installing the processor in an improper orientation. However, one serious problem exists: This socket cannot automatically determine the type of voltage that will be provided to it. A jumper is likely to be added on the motherboard near the socket to enable the user to select 5v or 3.3v operation.

Caution

Because this jumper must be manually set, however, a user could install a 3.3v processor in this socket when it is configured for 5v operation. This installation will instantly destroy a very expensive chip when the system is powered on. So, it is up to the end user to make sure that this socket is properly configured for voltage, depending on which type of processor is installed. If the jumper is set in 3.3v configuration and a 5v processor is installed, no harm will occur, but the system will not operate properly unless the jumper is reset for 5v.

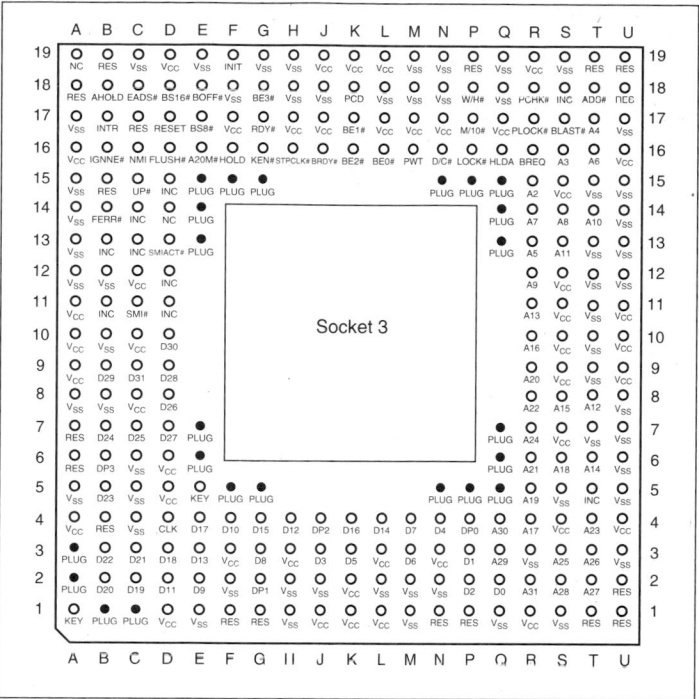

Figure 3.15   237-pin Intel Socket 3 configuration.

Socket 4

Socket 4 is a 273-pin socket that was designed for the original Pentium processors. The original Pentium 60MHz and 66MHz version processors had 273 pins and would plug into Socket 4—a 5v-only socket, because all the original Pentium processors run on 5v. This socket will accept the original Pentium 60MHz or 66MHz processor, and the OverDrive processor. Figure 3.16 shows the pinout specification of Socket 4.

Somewhat amazingly, the original Pentium 66MHz processor consumes up to 3.2 amps of 5v power (16 watts), not including power for a standard active heat sink (fan). The 66MHz OverDrive processor that replaced it consumes a maximum 2.7 amps (13.5 watts), including about 1 watt to drive the fan. Even the original 60MHz Pentium processor consumes up to 2.91 amps at 5v (14.55 watts). It might seem strange that the replacement processor, which is twice as fast, consumes less power than the original, but this has to do with the manufacturing processes used for the original and OverDrive processors.

Although both processors will run on 5v, the original Pentium processor was created with a circuit size of 0.8 micron, making that processor much more power-hungry than the newer 0.6 micron circuits used in the OverDrive and the other Pentium processors. Shrinking the circuit size is one of the best ways to decrease power consumption. Although the OverDrive processor for Pentium-based systems will draw less power than the original processor, additional clearance

Socket 6

The last 486 socket was created especially for the DX4 and the 486 Pentium OverDrive processor. Socket 6 is a slightly redesigned version of Socket 3, which has an additional two pins plugged for proper chip keying. Socket 6 has 235 pins and will accept only 3.3v 486 or OverDrive processors. This means that Socket 6 will accept only the DX4 and the 486 Pentium OverDrive processor. Because this socket provides only 3.3v, and because the only processors that plug into it are designed to operate on 3.3v, there's no chance that damaging problems will occur, such as those with the Socket 3 design. In practice, Socket 6 has seen very limited use. Figure 3.18 shows the Socket 6 pinout.

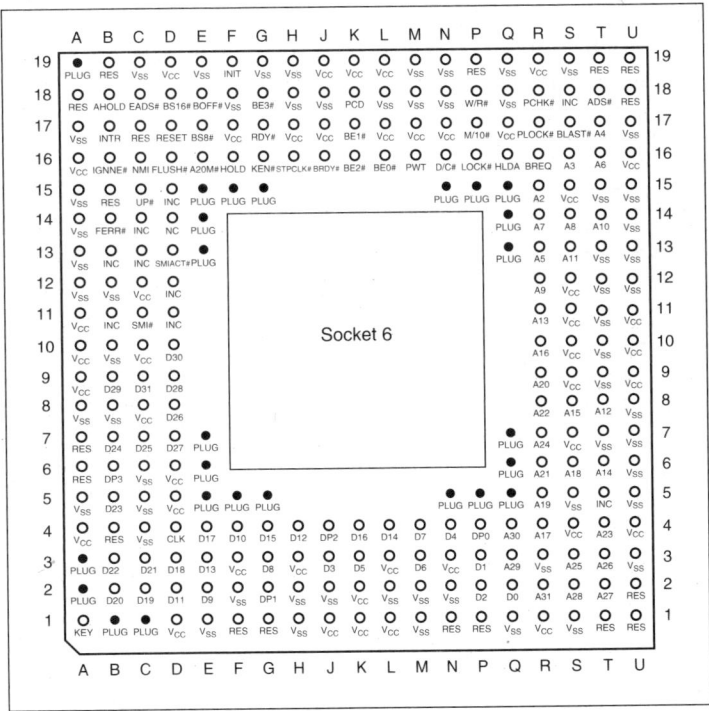

Figure 3.18   235-pin Intel Socket 6 configuration.

Socket 7 (and Super7)

Socket 7 is essentially the same as Socket 5 with one additional key pin in the opposite inside corner of the existing key pin. Socket 7, therefore, has 321 pins total in a 21×21 SPGA arrangement. The real difference with Socket 7 is not the socket but with the companion VRM (Voltage Regulator Module) that must accompany it.

The VRM is a small circuit board that contains all the voltage regulation circuitry used to drop the 5v power supply signal to the correct voltage for the processor. The VRM was implemented for several good reasons. One is that voltage regulators tend to run hot and are very failure-prone.

Soldering these circuits on the motherboard, as has been done with the Pentium Socket 5 design, makes it very likely that a failure of the regulator will require a complete motherboard replacement. Although technically the regulator could be replaced, many are surface-mount soldered, which would make the whole procedure very time-consuming and expensive. Besides, in this day and age, when the top-of-the-line motherboards are worth only $150, it is just not cost-effective to service them. Having a replaceable VRM plugged into a socket will make it easy to replace the regulators should they ever fail.

Although replacability is nice, the main reason behind the VRM design is that Intel and other manufacturers have built Pentium processors to run on a variety of voltages. Intel has several different versions of the Pentium and Pentium-MMX processors that run on 3.3v (called VR), 3.465v (called VRE), or 2.8v, while AMD, Cyrix and others use different variations. Because of this, most newer motherboard manufacturers are either including VRM sockets or building adaptable VRMs into the motherboard.

Figure 3.19 shows the Socket 7 pinout.

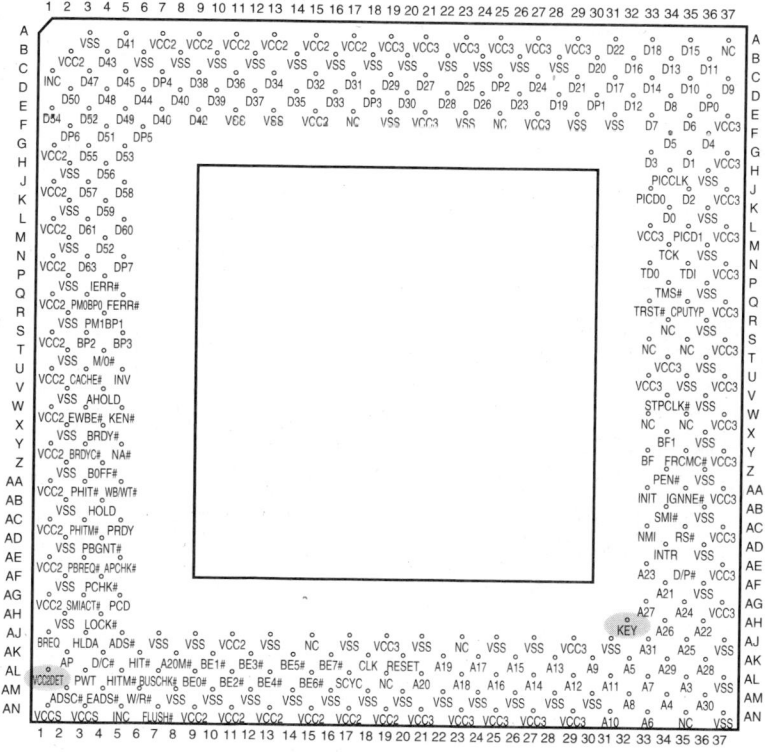

Figure 3.19 Socket 7 (Pentium) Pinout (top view).

AMD, along with Cyrix and several chipset manufacturers, pioneered an improvement or extension to the Intel Socket 7 design called Super Socket 7 (or Super7), taking it from 66MHz to

95MHz and 100MHz. This allows for faster Socket 7 type systems to be made, which are nearly as fast as the newer Slot 1 and Socket 370 type systems using Intel processors. Super7 systems also have support for the AGP video bus, as well as Ultra-DMA hard disk controllers, and advanced power management.

New chipsets are required for Super7 boards. Major third-party chipset suppliers, including Acer Laboratories Inc. (Ali), VIA Technologies, and SiS, are supporting the Super7 platform. ALi has the Aladdin V, VIA the Apollo MVP3, and SiS the SiS530 chipset for Super7 boards. Most of the major motherboard manufacturers are making Super7 boards in both Baby-AT and ATX form factors.

If you want to purchase a Pentium class board that can be upgraded to the next generation of even higher speed Socket 7 processors, look for a system with a Super7 socket and an integrated VRM that supports different voltage selections.

Socket 8

Socket 8 is a special SPGA socket featuring a whopping 387 pins! This was specifically designed for the Pentium Pro processor with the integrated L2 cache. The additional pins are to allow the chipset to control the L2 cache that is integrated in the same package as the processor. Figure 3.20 shows the Socket 8 pinout.

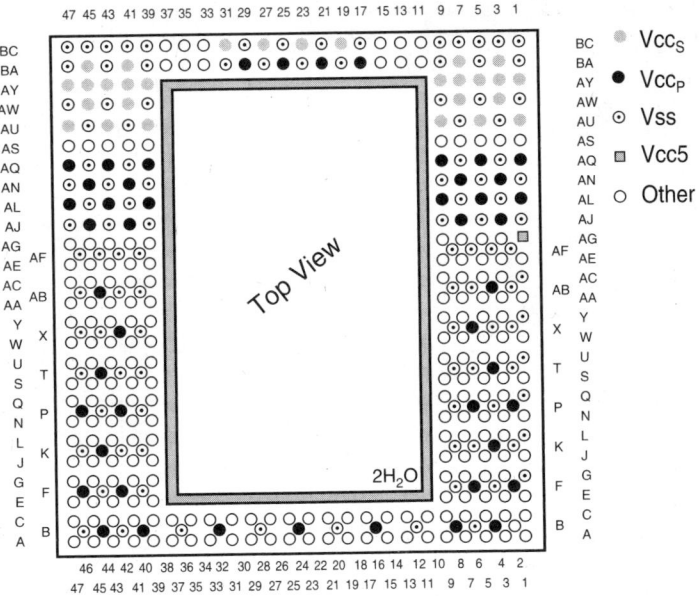

Figure 3.20 Socket 8 (Pentium Pro) Pinout showing power pin locations.

Socket PGA-370

In January 1999, Intel introduced a new socket for P6 class processors. The new socket is called PGA-370, because it has 370 pins and was designed for lower cost PGA (Pin Grid Array) versions of the Celeron and Pentium III processors. PGA-370 is designed to directly compete in the lower end system market along with the Super7 platform supported by AMD and Cyrix. PGA-370 brings the low cost of a socketed design, with less expensive processors, mounting systems, heat sinks, etc. to the high performance P6 line of processors.

Initially all the Celeron and Pentium III processors were made in SECC (Single Edge Contact Cartridge) or SEPP (Single Edge Processor Package) formats. These are essentially circuit boards containing the processor and separate L2 cache chips on a small board that plugs into the motherboard via Slot 1. This type of design was necessary when the L2 cache chips were made a part of the processor, but were not directly integrated into the processor die. Intel did make a multi-die chip package for the Pentium Pro, but this proved to be a very expensive way to package the chip, And, a board with separate chips was cheaper, which is why the Pentium II looks different from the Pentium Pro.

Starting with the Celeron 300A processor introduced in August 1998, Intel began combining the L2 cache directly on the processor die; it was no longer in separate chips. With the cache fully integrated into the die, there was no longer a need for a board-mounted processor. Because it costs more to make a Slot 1 board or cartridge-type processor instead of a socketed type, Intel moved back to the socket design to reduce the manufacturing cost—especially with the Celeron, which competes on the low end with Socket 7 chips from AMD and Cyrix.

The Socket PGA-370 pinout is shown in Figure 3.21.

The Celeron is gradually being shifted over to PGA-370, although for a time both were available. All Celeron processors at 333MHz and lower were only available in the Slot 1 version. Celeron processors from 366MHz–433MHz were available in both Slot 1 and Socket PGA-370 versions; all Celeron processors from 466MHz and up are only available in the PGA-370 version.

A motherboard with a Slot 1 can be designed to accept almost any Celeron, Pentium II, or Pentium III processor. To use the newer 466MHz and faster Celerons, which are only available in PGA-370 form, a low-cost adapter called a "slot-ket" has been made available by several manufacturers. This is essentially a Slot 1 board containing only a PGA-370 socket, which allows you to use a PGA-370 processor in any Slot 1 board. A typical slot-ket adapter is shown in the "Celeron" section, later in this chapter.

▶▶ See "Celeron," p. 174.

Figure 3.21 Socket PGA-370 (PGA Celeron) pinout (top view).

Zero Insertion Force (ZIF) Sockets

When Intel created the Socket 1 specification, they realized that if users were going to upgrade processors, they had to make the process easier. They found that it typically takes 100 pounds of insertion force to install a chip in a standard 169-pin screw Socket 1 motherboard. With this much force involved, you easily could damage either the chip or socket during removal or rein- stallation. Because of this, some motherboard manufacturers began using Low Insertion Force (LIF) sockets, which typically required only 60 pounds of insertion force for a 169-pin chip. With the LIF or standard socket, I usually advise removing the motherboard—that way you can sup- port the board from behind when you insert the chip. Pressing down on the motherboard with 60–100 pounds of force can crack the board if it is not supported properly. A special tool is also required to remove a chip from one of these sockets. As you can imagine, even the low insertion force was relative, and a better solution was needed if the average person was going to ever replace their CPU.

Manufacturers began inserting special Zero Insertion Force (ZIF) sockets in their later Socket 1 motherboard designs. Since then, virtually all processor sockets have been of the ZIF design. Note, however, that a given Socket X specification has nothing to do with whether it is ZIF, LIF, or standard; the socket specification covers only the pin arrangement. These days, nearly all motherboard manufacturers are using ZIF sockets. These sockets almost eliminate the risk involved in upgrading because no insertion force is necessary to install the chip. Most ZIF sockets are handle-actuated; you lift the handle, drop the chip into the socket, and then close the handle. This design makes replacing the original processor with the upgrade processor an easy task.

Because of the number of pins involved, virtually all CPU sockets from Socket 2 through the present are implemented in ZIF form. This means that since the 486 era, removing the CPU from most motherboards does not require any tools.

Processor Slots

After introducing the Pentium Pro with its integrated L2 cache, Intel discovered that the physical package they chose was very costly to produce. They were looking for a way to easily integrate cache and possibly other components into a processor package, and they came up with a cartridge or board design as the best way to do this. In order to accept their new cartridges, Intel designed two different types of slots that could be used on motherboards.

Slot 1 is a 242-pin slot that is designed to accept Pentium II, Pentium III, and most Celeron processors. Slot 2 is a more sophisticated 330-pin slot that is designed for the Pentium II and III Xeon processors, which are primarily for workstations and servers. Besides the extra pins, the biggest difference between Slot 1 and Slot 2 is the fact that Slot 2 was designed to host up to four-way or more processing in a single board. Slot 1 only allows single or dual processing functionality.

Note that Slot 2 is also called SC330, which stands for Slot Connector with 330 pins.

Slot 1

Slot 1 is used by the SEC (Single Edge Cartridge) design used with the Pentium II processors. Inside the cartridge is a substrate card that includes the processor and L2 cache. Unlike the Pentium Pro, the L2 cache is mounted on the circuit board and not within the same chip package as the processor. This allows Intel to use aftermarket SRAM chips instead of making them internally, and also allows them to make Pentium II processors with different amounts of cache easily. For example, the Celeron versions of the Pentium II have no L2 cache, whereas other future versions will have more than the standard 512KB included in most Pentium II processors. Figure 3.22 shows the Slot 1 connector dimensions and pin layout.

◄◄ See "Single Edge Cartridge (SEC) and Single Edge Processor (SEP)," p. 71.

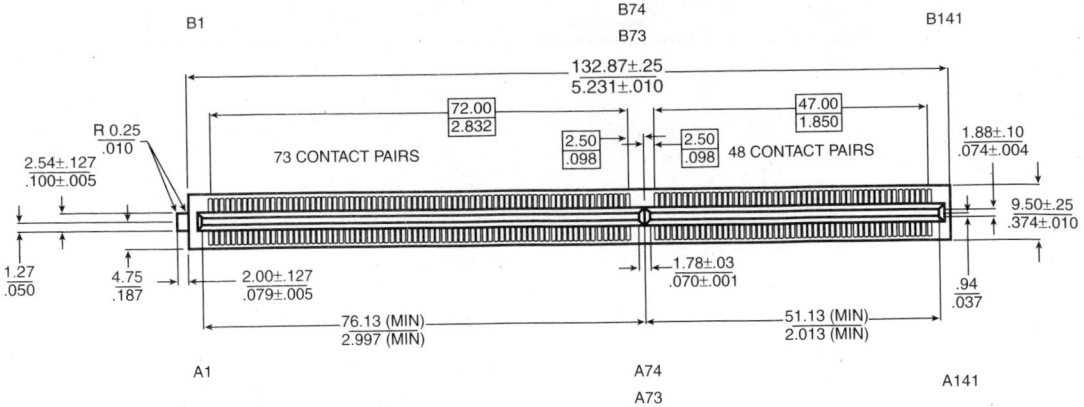

Figure 3.22   Slot 1 connector dimensions and pin layout.

Table 3.10 lists the names of each of the pins in the Slot 1 connector.

Table 3.10   Signal Listing in Order by Pin Number

Pin No.	Pin Name	Pin No.	Pin Name	Pin No.	Pin Name
A1	VCC_VTT	A25	DEP#[0]	A49	D#[37]
A2	GND	A26	GND	A50	GND
A3	VCC_VTT	A27	DEP#[1]	A51	D#[33]
A4	IERR#	A28	DEP#[3]	A52	D#[35]
A5	A20M#	A29	DEP#[5]	A53	D#[31]
A6	GND	A30	GND	A54	GND
A7	FERR#	A31	DEP#[6]	A55	D#[30]
A8	IGNNE#	A32	D#[61]	A56	D#[27]
A9	TDI	A33	D#[55]	A57	D#[24]
A10	GND	A34	GND	A58	GND
A11	TDO	A35	D#[60]	A59	D#[23]
A12	PWRGOOD	A36	D#[53]	A60	D#[21]
A13	TESTHI	A37	D#[57]	A61	D#[16]
A14	GND	A38	GND	A62	GND
A15	THERMTRIP#	A39	D#[46]	A63	D#[13]
A16	Reserved	A40	D#[49]	A64	D#[11]
A17	LINT[0]/INTR	A41	D#[51]	A65	D#[10]
A18	GND	A42	GND	A66	GND
A19	PICD[0]	A43	D#[42]	A67	D#[14]
A20	PREQ#	A44	D#[45]	A68	D#[9]
A21	BP#[3]	A45	D#[39]	A69	D#[8]
A22	GND	A46	GND	A70	GND
A23	BPM#[0]	A47	Reserved	A71	D#[5]
A24	BINIT#	A48	D#[43]	A72	D#[3]

Pin No.	Pin Name	Pin No.	Pin Name	Pin No.	Pin Name
A73	D#[1]	A113	Reserved	B32	D#[63]
A74	GND	A114	GND	B33	VCC_CORE
A75	BCLK	A115	ADS#	B34	D#[56]
A76	BR0#	A116	Reserved	B35	D#[50]
A77	BERR#	A117	AP#[0]	B36	D#[54]
A78	GND	A118	GND	B37	VCC_CORE
A79	A#[33]	A119	VID[2]	B38	D#[59]
A80	A#[34]	A120	VID[1]	B39	D#[48]
A81	A#[30]	A121	VID[4]	B40	D#[52]
A82	GND	B1	EMI	B41	EMI
A83	A#[31]	B2	FLUSH#	B42	D#[41]
A84	A#[27]	B3	SMI#	B43	D#[47]
A85	A#[22]	B4	INIT#	B44	D#[44]
A86	GND	B5	VCC_VTT	B45	VCC_CORE
A87	A#[23]	B6	STPCLK#	B46	D#[36]
A88	Reserved	B7	TCK	B47	D#[40]
A89	A#[19]	B8	SLP#	B48	D#[34]
A90	GND	B9	VCC_VTT	B49	VCC_CORE
A91	A#[18]	B10	TMS	B50	D#[38]
A92	A#[16]	B11	TRST#	B51	D#[32]
A93	A#[13]	B12	Reserved	B52	D#[28]
A94	GND	B13	VCC_CORE	B53	VCC_CORE
A95	A#[14]	B14	Reserved	B54	D#[29]
A96	A#[10]	B15	Reserved	B55	D#[26]
A97	A#[5]	B16	LINT[1]/NMI	B56	D#[25]
A98	GND	B17	VCC_CORE	B57	VCC_CORE
A99	A#[9]	B18	PICCLK	B58	D#[22]
A100	A#[4]	B19	BP#[2]	B59	D#[19]
A101	BNR#	B20	Reserved	B60	D#[18]
A102	GND	B21	BSEL#	B61	EMI
A103	BPRI#	B22	PICD[1]	B62	D#[20]
A104	TRDY#	B23	PRDY#	B63	D#[17]
A105	DEFER#	B24	BPM#[1]	B64	D#[15]
A106	GND	B25	VCC_CORE	B65	VCC_CORE
A107	REQ#[2]	B26	DEP#[2]	B66	D#[12]
A108	REQ#[3]	B27	DEP#[4]	B67	D#[7]
A109	HITM#	B28	DEP#[7]	B68	D#[6]
A110	GND	B29	VCC_CORE	B69	VCC_CORE
A111	DBSY#	B30	D#[62]	B70	D#[4]
A112	RS#[1]	B31	D#[58]	B71	D#[2]

(continues)

Table 3.10   **Continued**

Pin No.	Pin Name	Pin No.	Pin Name	Pin No.	Pin Name
B72	D#[0]	B89	VCC_CORE	B106	LOCK#
B73	VCC_CORE	B90	A#[15]	B107	DRDY#
B74	RESET#	B91	A#[17]	B108	RS#[0]
B75	BR1#	B92	A#[11]	B109	VCC5
B76	FRCERR	B93	VCC_CORE	B110	HIT#
B77	VCC_CORE	B94	A#[12]	B111	RS#[2]
B78	A#[35]	B95	A#[8]	B112	Reserved
B79	A#[32]	B96	A#[7]	B113	VCC_L2
B80	A#[29]	B97	VCC_CORE	B114	RP#
B81	EMI	B98	A#[3]	B115	RSP#
B82	A#[26]	B99	A#[6]	B116	AP#[1]
B83	A#[24]	B100	EMI	B117	VCC_L2
B84	A#[28]	B101	SLOTOCC#	B118	AERR#
B85	VCC_CORE	B102	REQ#[0]	B119	VID[3]
B86	A#[20]	B103	REQ#[1]	B120	VID[0]
B87	A#[21]	B104	REQ#[4]	B121	VCC_L2
B88	A#[25]	B105	VCC_CORE		

Slot 2 (SC330)

Slot 2 (otherwise called SC330) is used on high-end motherboards that support the Pentium II and III Xeon processors. Figure 3.23 shows the Slot 2 connector.

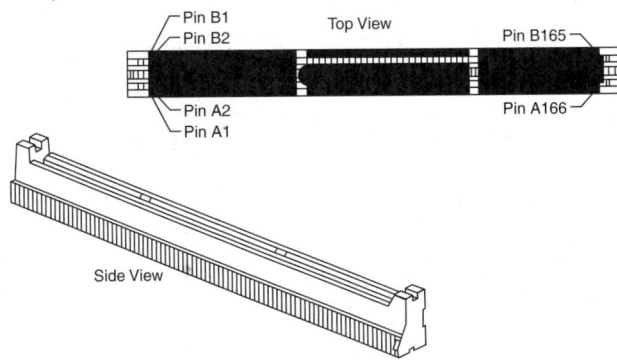

Figure 3.23   Slot 2 (SC330) connector dimensions and pin layout.

The Pentium II or III is designed in a cartridge similar to, but larger than, that used for the Pentium II. Figure 3.24 shows the Xeon cartridge.

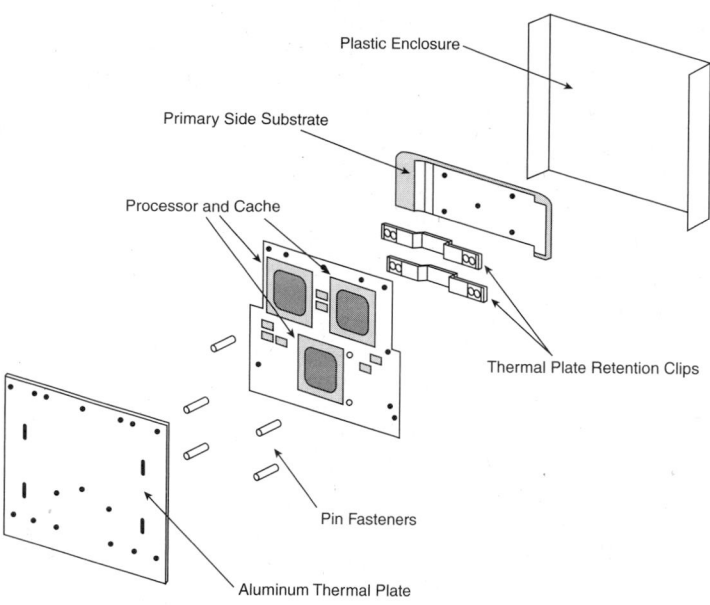

Figure 3.24   Pentium II/III Xeon cartridge.

Motherboards featuring Slot 2 are primarily found in higher end systems such as workstations or servers, which use the Pentium II or III Xeon processors. These are Intel's high-end chips, which differ from the standard Pentium II/III mainly by virtue of having full core-speed L2 cache, and more of it.

CPU Operating Voltages

One trend that is clear to anybody that has been following processor design is that the operating voltages have gotten lower and lower. The benefits of lower voltage are threefold. The most obvious is that with lower voltage comes lower overall power consumption. By consuming less power, the system will be less expensive to run, but more importantly for portable or mobile systems, it will run much longer on existing battery technology. The emphasis on battery operation has driven many of the advances in lowering processor voltage, because this has a great effect on battery life.

The second major benefit is that with less voltage and therefore less power consumption, there will be less heat produced. Processors that run cooler can be packed into systems more tightly and will last longer. The third major benefit is that a processor running cooler on less power can be made to run faster. Lowering the voltage has been one of the key factors in allowing the clock rates of processors to go higher and higher.

Until the release of the mobile Pentium and both desktop and mobile Pentium MMX, most processors used a single voltage level to power both the core as well as run the input/output circuits. Originally, most processors ran both the core and I/O circuits at 5 volts, which was later was reduced to 3.5 or 3.3 volts to lower power consumption. When a single voltage is used for both the internal processor core power as well as the external processor bus and I/O signals, the processor is said to have a single or unified power plane design.

When originally designing a version of the Pentium processor for mobile or portable computers, Intel came up with a scheme to dramatically reduce the power consumption while still remaining compatible with the existing 3.3v chipsets, bus logic, memory, and other components. The result was a dual-plane or split-plane power design where the processor core ran off of a lower voltage while the I/O circuits remained at 3.3v. This was originally called Voltage Reduction Technology (VRT) and first debuted in the Mobile Pentium processors released in 1996. Later, this dual-plane power design also appeared in desktop processors such as the Pentium MMX, which used 2.8v to power the core and 3.3v for the I/O circuits. Now most recent processors, whether for mobile or desktop use, feature a dual-plane power design. Some of the more recent Mobile Pentium II processors run on as little as 1.6v for the core while still maintaining compatibility with 3.3v components for I/O.

Knowing the processor voltage requirements is not a big issue with Pentium Pro (Socket 8) or Pentium II (Slot 1 or Slot 2) processors, because these sockets and slots have special voltage ID (VID) pins that the processor uses to signal to the motherboard the exact voltage requirements. This allows the voltage regulators built in to the motherboard to be automatically set to the correct voltage levels by merely installing the processor.

Unfortunately, this automatic voltage setting feature is not available on Socket 7 and earlier motherboard and processor designs. This means you must normally set jumpers or otherwise configure the motherboard according to the voltage requirements of the processor you are installing. Pentium (Socket 4, 5, or 7) processors have run on a number of voltages, but the latest MMX versions are all 2.8v, except for mobile Pentium processors, which are as low as 1.8v. Table 3.11 lists the voltage settings used by Intel Pentium (non-MMX) processors that use a single power plane. This means that both the CPU core and the I/O pins run at the same voltage.

Table 3.11 shows voltages used by Socket 7 processors.

Table 3.11   Socket 7 Single- and Dual-Plane Processor Voltages

Voltage Setting	Processor	Core Voltage	I/O Voltage	Voltage Planes
VRE (3.5v)	Intel Pentium	3.5v	3.5v	Single
STD (3.3v)	Intel Pentium	3.3v	3.3v	Single
MMX (2.8v)	Intel MMX Pentium	2.8v	3.3v	Dual
VRE (3.5v)	AMD K5	3.5v	3.5v	Single
3.2v	AMD-K6	3.2v	3.3v	Dual
2.9v	AMD-K6	2.9v	3.3v	Dual
2.4v	AMD-K6-2/K6-3	2.4v	3.3v	Dual
2.2v	AMD-K6/K6-2	2.2v	3.3v	Dual
VRE (3.5v)	Cyrix 6x86	3.5v	3.5v	Single
2.9v	Cyrix 6x86MX/M-II	2.9v	3.3v	Dual
MMX (2.8v)	Cyrix 6x86L	2.8v	3.3v	Dual
2.45v	Cyrix 6x86LV	2.45v	3.3v	Dual

Normally, the acceptable range is plus or minus five percent from the nominal intended setting.

Most Socket 7 and later Pentium motherboards supply several voltages (such as 2.5v, 2.7v, 2.8v, and 2.9v) for compatibility with future devices. A voltage regulator built into the motherboard converts the power supply voltage into the different levels required by the processor core. Check the documentation for your motherboard and processor to find the appropriate settings.

The Pentium Pro and Pentium II processors automatically determine their voltage settings by controlling the motherboard-based voltage regulator through built-in voltage ID (VID) pins. Those are explained in more detail later in this chapter.

▶▶ See "Pentium Pro Processors," p. 156.

▶▶ See "Pentium II Processors," p. 162.

Note that on the STD or VRE settings, the core and I/O voltages are the same; these are single plane voltage settings. Anytime a different voltage other than STD or VRE is set, the motherboard defaults to a dual-plane voltage setting where the core voltage can be specifically set, while the I/O voltage remains constant at 3.3v no matter what.

Socket 5 was only designed to supply STD or VRE settings, so any processor that can work at those settings can work in Socket 5 as well as Socket 7. Older Socket 4 designs can only supply 5v, plus they have a completely different pinout (fewer pins overall), so it is not possible to use a processor designed for Socket 7 or Socket 5 in Socket 4.

Most Socket 7 and later Pentium motherboards supply several voltages (such as 2.2v, 2.4v, 2.5v, 2.7v, 2.8v, and 2.9v as well as the older STD or VRE settings) for compatibility with many processors. A voltage regulator built into the motherboard converts the power supply voltage into the different levels required by the processor core. Check the documentation for your motherboard and processor to find the appropriate settings.

The Pentium Pro, Celeron, and Pentium II/III processors automatically determine their voltage settings by controlling the motherboard-based voltage regulator. That's done through built-in voltage ID (VID) pins.

For hot rodding purposes, many newer motherboards for these processors have override settings that allow for manual voltage adjustment if desired. Many people have found that when attempting to overclock a processor, it often helps to increase the voltage by a tenth of a volt or so. Of course this increases the heat output of the processor and must be accounted for with adequate heat sinking.

Heat and Cooling Problems

Heat can be a problem in any high-performance system. The higher speed processors normally consume more power and therefore generate more heat. The processor is usually the single most power-hungry chip in a system, and in most situations, the fan inside your computer case might not be capable of handling the load without some help.

Heat Sinks

To cool a system in which processor heat is a problem, you can buy (for less than $5, in most cases) a special attachment for the CPU chip called a heat sink, which draws heat away from the CPU chip. Many applications may need only a larger standard heat sink with additional or longer fins for a larger cooling area. Several heat-sink manufacturers are listed in the Vendor List, on the CD.

A heat sink works like the radiator in your car, pulling heat away from the engine. In a similar fashion, the heat sink conducts heat away from the processor so that it can be vented out of the system. It does this by using a thermal conductor (usually metal) to carry heat away from the processor into fins that expose a high amount of surface area to moving air. This allows the air to be heated, thus cooling the heat sink and the processor as well. Just like the radiator in your car, the heat sink depends on airflow. With no moving air, a heat sink is incapable of radiating the heat away. To keep the engine in your car from overheating when the car is not moving, auto engineers incorporate a fan. Likewise, there is always a fan somewhere inside your PC helping to move air across the heat sink and vent it out of the system. Sometimes the fan included in the power supply is enough, other times an additional fan must be added to the case, or even directly over the processor to provide the necessary levels of cooling.

The heat sink is clipped or glued to the processor. A variety of heat sinks and attachment methods exist. Figure 3.25 shows various passive heat sinks and attachment methods.

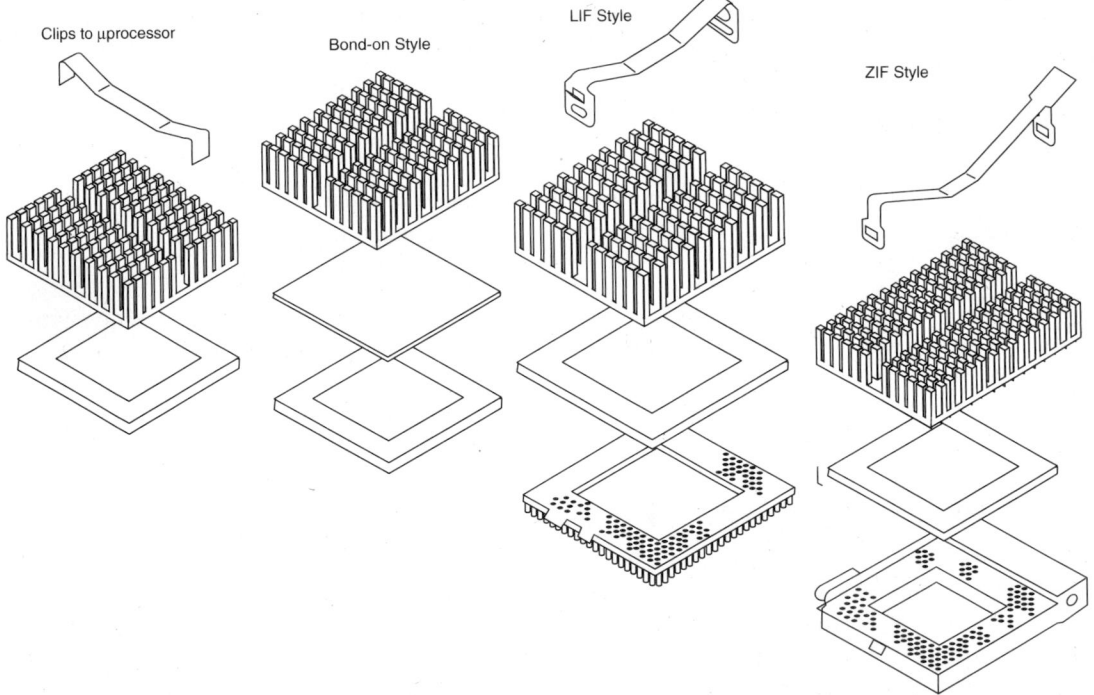

Figure 3.25   Passive heat sinks for socketed processors showing various attachment methods.

Tip

According to data from Intel, heat sink clips are the number two destroyer of motherboards (screwdrivers are number one). When installing or removing a heat sink that is clipped on, make sure you don't scrape the surface of the motherboard. In most cases, the clips hook over protrusions in the socket, and when installing or removing the clips, it is very easy to scratch or scrape the surface of the board right below where the clip ends attach. I like to place a thin sheet of plastic underneath the edge of the clip while I work, especially if there are board traces that can be scratched in the vicinity.

Heat sinks are rated for their cooling performance. Typically the ratings are expressed as a resistance to heat transfer, in degrees centigrade per watt (°C/W), where lower is better. Note that the resistance will vary according to the airflow across the heat sink. To ensure a constant flow of air and more consistent performance, many heat sinks incorporate fans so they don't have to rely on the airflow within the system. Heat sinks with fans are referred to as active heat sinks (see Figure 3.26). Active heat sinks have a power connection, often using a spare disk drive power connector, although most newer motherboards now have dedicated heat sink power connections right on the board.

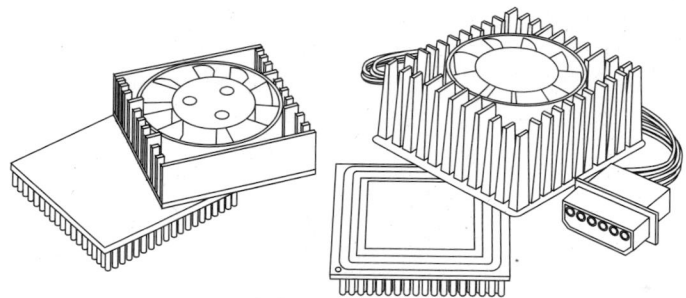

Figure 3.26 Active heat sinks for socketed processors.

Active heat sinks use a fan or other electric cooling device, which require power to run. The fan type is most common but some use a peltier cooling device, which is basically a solid-state refrigerator. Active heat sinks require power and normally plug into a disk drive power connector or special 12v fan power connectors on the motherboard. If you do get a fan type heat sink, be aware that some on the market are very poor quality. The bad ones have motors that use sleeve bearings, which freeze up after a very short life. I only recommend fans with ball-bearing motors, which will last about 10 times longer than the sleeve-bearing types. Of course, they cost more, but only about twice as much, which means you'll save money in the long run.

Figure 3.27 shows an active heat sink arrangement on a Pentium II/III type processor. This is common on what Intel calls their "boxed processors," which are sold individually and through dealers.

The passive heat sinks are 100 percent reliable, as they have no mechanical components to fail. Passive heat sinks (see Figure 3.28) are basically an aluminum-finned radiator that dissipates heat through convection. Passive types don't work well unless there is some airflow across the fins, normally provided by the power supply fan or an extra fan in the case. If your case or power supply is properly designed, you can use a less expensive passive heat sink instead of an active one.

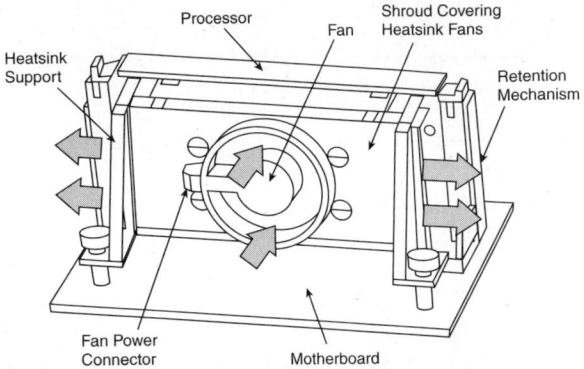

Figure 3.27 An active (fan powered) heat sink and supports used with Pentium II/III type processors.

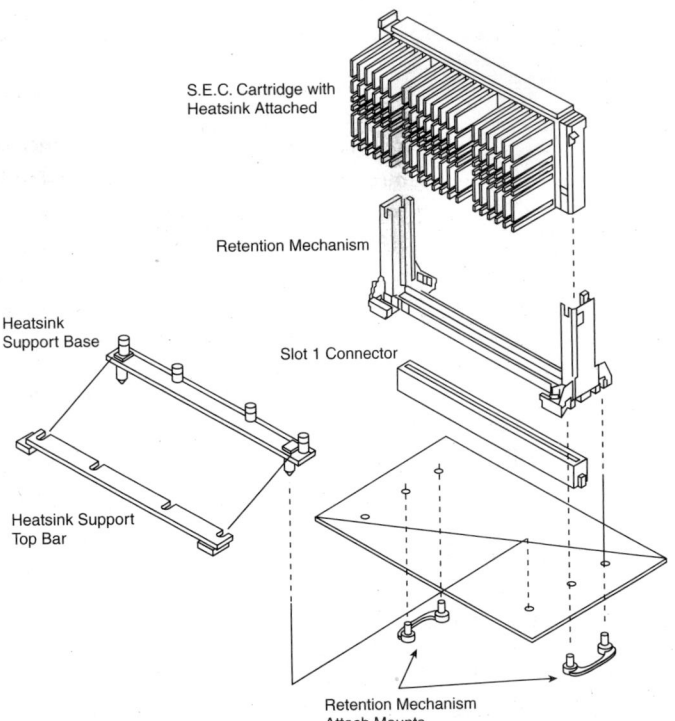

Figure 3.28 A passive heat sink and supports used with Pentium II/III type processors.

Tip

To function effectively, a heat sink must be as directly attached to the processor as possible. To eliminate air gaps and ensure a good transfer of heat, in most cases, you should put a thin coating of thermal transfer grease on the surface of the processor where the heat sink attaches. This will dramatically decrease the thermal resistance properties and is required for maximum performance.

In order to have the best possible transfer of heat from the processor to the heat sink, most heat sink manufacturers specify some type of thermal interface material to be placed between the processor and the heat sink. This normally consists of a zinc-based white grease (similar to what skiers put on their noses to block the sun), but can also be a special pad or even a type of double-stick tape. Using a thermal interface aid such as thermal grease can improve heat sink performance dramatically. Figure 3.29 shows the thermal interface pad or grease positioned between the processor and heat sink.

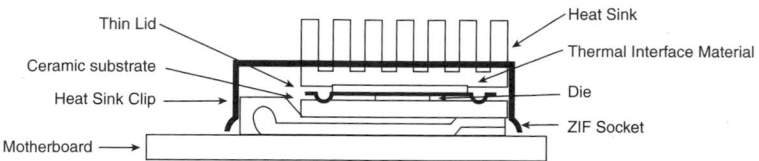

Figure 3.29   Thermal interface material helps transfer heat from the processor die to the heat sink.

Most of the newer systems on the market use an improved motherboard form factor (shape) design called ATX. Systems made from this type of motherboard and case allow for improved cooling of the processor due to the processor being repositioned in the case near the power supply. Also, most of these cases now feature a secondary fan to further assist in cooling. Normally the larger case mounted fans are more reliable than the smaller fans included in active heat sinks. A properly designed case can move sufficient air across the processor, allowing for a more reliable and less expensive passive (no fan) heat sink to be used.

▶▶ See "ATX," p. 214.

Math Coprocessors (Floating-Point Units)

This section covers the floating-point unit (FPU) contained in the processor, which was formerly a separate external math coprocessor in the 386 and older chips. Older central processing units designed by Intel (and cloned by other companies) used an external math coprocessor chip. However, when Intel introduced the 486DX, they included a built-in math coprocessor, and every processor built by Intel (and AMD and Cyrix, for that matter) since then includes a math coprocessor. Coprocessors provide hardware for floating-point math, which otherwise would create an excessive drain on the main CPU. Math chips speed your computer's operation only when you are running software designed to take advantage of the coprocessor. All the subsequent fifth and sixth generation Intel and compatible processors (such as those from AMD and Cyrix) have featured an integrated floating-point unit, although the Intel ones are known for having the best performance.

Math chips (as coprocessors sometimes are called) can perform high-level mathematical operations—long division, trigonometric functions, roots, and logarithms, for example, at 10 to 100 times the speed of the corresponding main processor. The operations performed by the math chip are all operations that make use of noninteger numbers (numbers that contain digits after the decimal point). The need to process numbers in which the decimal is not always the last character leads to the term *floating point* because the decimal (point) can move (float), depending on the operation. The integer units in the primary CPU work with integer numbers, so they perform addition, subtraction, and multiplication operations. The primary CPU is designed to handle such computations; these operations are not offloaded to the math chip.

The instruction set of the math chip is different from that of the primary CPU. A program must detect the existence of the coprocessor, and then execute instructions written explicitly for that coprocessor; otherwise, the math coprocessor draws power and does nothing else. Fortunately, most modern programs that can benefit from the use of the coprocessor correctly detect and use the coprocessor. These programs usually are math-intensive: spreadsheet programs, database applications, statistical programs, and graphics programs, such as computer-aided design (CAD) software. Word processing programs do not benefit from a math chip and therefore are not designed to use one. Table 3.12 summarizes the coprocessors available for the Intel family of processors.

Table 3.12 matches processors and the coprocessor it uses.

Table 3.12   Math Coprocessor Summary

Processor	Coprocessor
8086	8087
8088	8087
286	287
386SX	387SX
386DX	387DX
486SX	487SX, DX2/OverDrive*
487SX*	Built-in FPU
486SX2	DX2/OverDrive**
486DX	Built-in FPU
486DX2	Built-in FPU
486DX4/5x86	Built-in FPU
Intel Pentium/Pentium MMX	Built-in FPU
Cyrix 6x86/MI/MII	Built-in FPU
AMD K5/K6	Built-in FPU
Pentium II/III/Celeron/Xeon	Built-in FPU

FPU = Floating-point unit

*The 487SX chip is a modified pinout 486DX chip with the math coprocessor enabled. When you plug in a 487SX chip, it disables the 486SX main processor and takes over all processing.

**The DX2/OverDrive is equivalent to the SX2 with the addition of a functional FPU.

Although virtually all processors since the 486 series have built-in floating-point units, they vary in performance. Historically the Intel processor FPUs have dramatically outperformed those from AMD and Cyrix, although AMD and Cyrix are achieving performance parity in their newer offerings.

Within each of the original 8087 group, the maximum speed of the math chips varies. A suffix digit after the main number, as shown in Table 3.13, indicates the maximum speed at which a system can run a math chip.

Table 3.13   Maximum Math Chip Speeds

Part	Speed	Part	Speed
8087	5MHz	287	6MHz
8087-3	5MHz	287-6	6MHz
8087-2	8MHz	287-8	8MHz
8087-1	10MHz	287-10	10MHz

The 387 math coprocessors, and the 486 or 487 and Pentium processors, always indicate their maximum speed rating in MHz in the part number suffix. A 486DX2-66, for example, is rated to run at 66MHz. Some processors incorporate clock multiplication, which means that they can run at different speeds compared with the rest of the system.

Tip

The performance increase in programs that use the math chip can be dramatic—usually, a geometric increase in speed occurs. If the primary applications that you use can take advantage of a math coprocessor, you should upgrade your system to include one.

Most systems that use the 386 or earlier processors are socketed for a math coprocessor as an option, but they do not include a coprocessor as standard equipment. A few systems on the market don't even have a socket for the coprocessor because of cost and size considerations. These systems are usually low cost or portable systems, such as older laptops, the IBM PS/1, and the PCjr. For more specific information about math coprocessors, see the discussions of the specific chips—8087, 287, 387, and 487SX—in the later sections. Table 3.14 shows the specifications of the various math coprocessors.

Table 3.14   Older Intel Math Coprocessor Specifications

Name	Power Consumption	Case Minimum Temperature	Case Maximum Temperature	No. of Trans-istors	Date Intro-duced
8087	3 watts	0°C, 32°F	85°C, 185°F	45,000	1980
287	3 watts	0°C, 32°F	85°C, 185°F	45,000	1982
287XL	1.5 watts	0°C, 32°F	85°C, 185°F	40,000	1990
387SX	1.5 watts	0°C, 32°F	85°C, 185°F	120,000	1988
387DX	1.5 watts	0°C, 32°F	85°C, 185°F	120,000	1987

Most often, you can learn what CPU and math coprocessor are installed in a particular system by checking the markings on the chip.

Processor Bugs

Processor manufacturers use specialized equipment to test their own processors, but you have to settle for a little less. The best processor-testing device to which you have access is a system that you know is functional; you then can use the diagnostics available from various utility software companies or your system manufacturer to test the motherboard and processor functions.

Companies such as Diagsoft, Symantec, Micro 2000, Trinitech, Data Depot, and others offer specialized diagnostics software that can test the system, including the processor. If you don't want to purchase this kind of software, you can perform a quick-and-dirty processor evaluation by using the diagnostics program supplied with your system.

Perhaps the most infamous of these is the floating-point division math bug in the early Pentium processors. This and a few other bugs are discussed in detail later in this chapter.

Because the processor is the brain of a system, most systems don't function with a defective processor. If a system seems to have a dead motherboard, try replacing the processor with one from a functioning motherboard that uses the same CPU chip. You might find that the processor in the original board is the culprit. If the system continues to play dead, however, the problem is elsewhere, most likely in the motherboard, memory, or power supply. See the chapters that cover those parts of the system for more information on troubleshooting those components. I must say that in all my years of troubleshooting and repairing PCs, I have rarely encountered defective processors.

A few system problems are built in at the factory, although these bugs or design defects are rare. By learning to recognize these problems, you can avoid unnecessary repairs or replacements. Each processor section describes several known defects in that generation of processors, such as the infamous floating-point error in the Pentium. For more information on these bugs and defects, see the following sections, and check with the processor manufacturer for updates.

Processor Update Feature

All processors can contain design defects or errors. Many times, the effects of any given bug can be avoided by implementing hardware or software workarounds. Intel documents these bugs and workarounds well for their processors in their processor Specification Update manuals; this manual is available from their Web site. Most of the other processor manufacturers also have bulletins or tips on their Web sites listing any problems or special fixes or patches for their chips.

Previously, the only way to fix a processor bug was to work around it or replace the chip with one that had the bug fixed. Now, a new feature built into the Intel P6 processors, including the Pentium Pro and Pentium II, can allow many bugs to be fixed by altering the *microcode* in the processor. Microcode is essentially a set of instructions and tables in the processor that control how the processor operates. These processors incorporate a new feature called reprogrammable microcode, which allows certain types of bugs to be worked around via microcode updates. The microcode updates reside in the system ROM BIOS and are loaded into the processor by the system BIOS during the power on self test (POST). Each time the system is rebooted, the fix code is reloaded, ensuring that it will have the bug fix installed anytime the processor is operating.

The easiest method for checking the microcode update is to use the Pentium Pro and Pentium II processor update utility, which is developed and supplied by Intel. This utility can verify whether the correct update is present for all Pentium Pro processor-based motherboards. The utility displays the processor *stepping* and version of the microcode update. A stepping is the processor hardware equivalent of a new version. In software, we refer to minor version changes as 1.0, 1.1, 1.2, etc., while in processors we call these minor revisions steppings.

To install a new microcode update, however, the motherboard BIOS must contain the routines to support the microcode update, which virtually all Pentium Pro and Pentium II BIOSes do have. The Intel processor update utility determines whether the code is present in the BIOS, compares the processor stepping with the microcode update currently loaded, and installs the new update, if needed. Use of this utility with motherboards containing the BIOS microcode update routine allows just the microcode update data to be changed; the rest of the BIOS is unchanged. A version of the update utility is provided with all Intel boxed processors. The term *boxed processors* refers to processors packaged for use by system integrators, that is, people who build systems. If you want the most current version of this utility, you have to contact an Intel processor dealer to download it, because Intel only supplies it to their dealers.

Note that if the BIOS in your motherboard does not include the processor microcode update routine, you should get a complete system BIOS upgrade from the motherboard vendor.

When you are building a system with a Pentium Pro, Celeron, or Pentium II/III processor, you must use the processor update utility to check that the system BIOS contains microcode updates that are specific to particular silicon stepping of the processor you are installing. In other words, you must ensure that the update matches the processor stepping being used.

Table 3.15 contains the current microcode update revision for each processor stepping. These update revisions are contained in the microcode update database file that comes with the Pentium Pro processor and Pentium II processor update utility. Processor steppings are listed in the sections on the Pentium, Pentium Pro, and Pentium II processors later in this chapter.

Table 3.15   Processor Steppings (Revisions) and Microcode Update Revisions Supported by the Update Database File PEP6.PDB

Processor	Stepping	Stepping Signature	Microcode Update Revision Required
Pentium Pro	C0	0x612	0xC6
Pentium Pro	sA0	0x616	0xC6
Pentium Pro	sA1	0x617	0xC6
Pentium Pro	sB1	0x619	0xD1
Pentium II	C0	0x633	0x32
Pentium II	C1	0x634	0x33
Pentium II	dA0	0x650	0x15

Using the processor update utility (CHECKUP3.EXE) available from Intel, a system builder can easily verify that the correct microcode update is present in all systems based on the P6 (Pentium Pro, Celeron, Pentium II/III and Xeon) processors. For example, if a system contains a processor with stepping C1 and stepping signature 0x634, the BIOS should contain the microcode update revision 0x33. The processor update utility identifies the processor stepping, signature, and microcode update revision that is currently in use.

If a new microcode update needs to be installed in the system BIOS, the system BIOS must contain the Intel-defined processor update routines so the processor update utility can permanently install the latest update. Otherwise, a complete system BIOS upgrade is required from the motherboard manufacturer. It is recommended that the processor update utility be run after upgrading a motherboard BIOS and before installing the operating system when building a system based on any P6 processor. The utility is easy to use and executes in just a few seconds. Because the update utility may need to load new code into your BIOS, ensure that any jumper settings on the motherboard are placed in the "enable flash upgrade" position. This enables writing to the flash memory.

After running the utility, turn off power to the system and reboot—do not warm boot—to ensure that the new update is correctly initialized in the processor. Also ensure that all jumpers, such as any flash upgrade jumpers and so on, are returned to their normal position.

Intel Processor Codenames

Intel has always used codenames when talking about future processors. The codenames are normally not supposed to become public, but often they do. They can often be found in magazine articles talking about future generation processors. Sometimes, they even appear in motherboard manuals because the manuals are written before the processors are officially introduced. Table 3.16 lists Intel processor codenames for reference.

Table 3.16   Intel Processors and Codenames

Codename	Processor
P4	486DX
P4S	486SX
P23	486SX
P23S	487SX
P23N	487SX
P23T	486 OverDrive for the 80486 (169-pin PGA)
P4T	486 OverDrive for the 486 (168-pin PGA)
P24	486DX2
P24S	486DX2
P24D	486DX2WB (Write Back)
P24C	486DX4
P24CT	486DX4WB (Write Back)
P5	Pentium 60 or 66MHz, Socket 4, 5v

Codename	Processor
P24T	486 Pentium OverDrive, 63 or 83MHz, Socket 3
P54C	Classic Pentium 75–200MHz, Socket 5/7, 3.3v
P55C	Pentium MMX 166–266MHz, Socket 7, 2.8v
P54CTB	Pentium MMX OverDrive 125+, Socket 5/7, 3.3v
Tillamook	Mobile Pentium MMX 0.25 micron, 166–266MHz, 1.8v
P6	Pentium Pro, Socket 8
Klamath	Original Pentium II, 0.35 micron, Slot 1
Deschutes	Pentium II, 0.25 micron, Slot 1 or 2
Covington	Celeron, PII w/ no L2 cache
Mendocino	Celeron, PII w/ 128KB L2 cache on die
Dixon	Pentium IIPE (mobile), 256KB on-die L2 cache
Katmai	Pentium III, PII w/ SSE instructions
Willamette	Pentium III w/ on-die L2
Tanner	Pentium III Xeon
Cascades	PIII, 0.18 micron, on-die L2
Merced	P7, First IA-64 processor, on-die L2, 0.18 micron
McKinley	1GHz, Improved Merced, IA-64, 0.18 micron w/ copper interconnects
Foster	Improved PIII, IA-32
Madison	Improved McKinley, IA-64, 0.13 micron

Intel-Compatible Processors (AMD and Cyrix)

Severalcompanies—mainly AMD and Cyrix—have developed processors that are compatible with Intel processors. These chips are fully Intel-compatible, so they emulate every processor instruction in the Intel chips. Most of the chips are pin-compatible, which means that they can be used in any system designed to accept an Intel processor; others require a custom motherboard design. Any hardware or software that works on Intel-based PCs will work on PCs made with these third-party CPU chips. A number of companies currently offer Intel-compatible chips, and I will discuss some of the most popular ones here.

AMD Processors

Advanced Micro Devices (AMD) has become a major player in the Pentium-compatible chip market with their own line of Intel-compatible processors. AMD ran into trouble with Intel several years ago because their 486-clone chips used actual Intel microcode. These differences have been settled and AMD now has a five-year cross-license agreement with Intel. In 1996, AMD finalized a deal to absorb NexGen, another maker of Intel-compatible CPUs. NexGen had been working on a chip they called the Nx686, which was renamed the K6 and introduced by AMD. Since then, AMD has refined the design as the K6-2 and K6-3. Their new chip, called the K7, is designed similarly to the Pentium II and III, and uses the same cartridge design. AMD currently offers a wide variety of CPUs, from 486 upgrades to the K6 series and the new K7. Table 3.17 lists the basic processors offered by AMD and their Intel socket.

Table 3.17 AMD CPU Summary

AMD CPU Type	P-Rating	Actual CPU Speed (MHz)	Clock Multiplier	Motherboard Speed (MHz)	Socket
Am486DX4-100	n/a	100	3x	33	Socket 1,2,3
Am486DX4-120	n/a	120	3x	40	Socket 1,2,3
Am5x86-133	75	133	4x	33	Socket 1,2,3
K5	PR75	75	1.5x	50	Socket 5,7
K5	PR90	90	1.5x	60	Socket 5,7
K5	PR100	100	1.5x	66	Socket 5,7
K5	PR120	90	1.5x	60	Socket 5,7
K5	PR133	100	1.5x	66	Socket 5,7
K5	PR166	116.7	1.75x	66	Socket 5,7
K6	PR166	166	2.5x	66	Socket 7
K6	PR200	200	3x	66	Socket 7
K6	PR233	233	3.5x	66	Socket 7
K6	PR266	266	4x	66	Socket 7
K6	PR300	300	4.5x	66	Socket 7
K6-2	PR233	233	3.5x	66	Socket 7
K6-2	PR266	266	4x	66	Socket 7
K6-2	PR300	300	4.5x	66	Socket 7
K6-2	PR300	300	3x	100	Super7
K6-2	PR333	333	5x	66	Socket 7
K6-2	PR333	333	3.5x	95	Super7
K6-2	PR350	350	3.5x	100	Super7
K6-2	PR366	366	5.5x	66	Socket 7
K6-2	PR380	380	4x	95	Super7
K6-2	PR400	400	4x	100	Super7
K6-2	PR450	450	4.5x	100	Super7
K6-2	PR475	475	5x	95	Super7
K6-3	PR400	400	4x	100	Super7
K6-3	PR450	450	4.5x	100	Super7

Notice in the table that for the K5 PR120 through PR166 the model designation does not match the CPU clock speed. This is called a PR rating instead and is further described earlier in this chapter.

Starting with the K6, the P-Rating equals the true MHz clock speed.

The model designations are meant to represent performance comparable with an equivalent Pentium-based system. AMD chips, particularly the new K6, have typically fared well in performance comparisons and usually have a much lower cost. There is more information on the respective AMD chips in the sections for each different type of processor.

As you can see from the table, most of AMD's newer processors are designed to use the Super7 interface they pioneered with Cyrix. Super7 is an extension to the standard Socket 7 design, allowing for increased board speeds of up to 100MHz.

Cyrix

Cyrix has become an even larger player in the market since being purchased by National Semiconductor in November 1997. Prior to that they had been a fabless company, meaning they had no chip-manufacturing capability. All the Cyrix chips were manufactured for Cyrix first by Texas Instruments, and then mainly IBM up through the end of 1998. Starting in 1999, National Semiconductor has taken over manufacturing of the Cyrix processors. More recently, National has been looking to sell the Cyrix division, as the PC business has not been what they thought it would be. For now the future of Cyrix is a little unclear.

Like Intel, Cyrix has begun to limit its selection of available CPUs to only the latest technology. Cyrix is currently focusing on the Pentium market with the M1 (6x86) and M2 (6x86MX) processors. The 6x86 has dual internal pipelines and a single, unified 16KB internal cache. It offers speculative and out-of-order instruction execution, much like the Intel Pentium Pro processor. The 6x86MX adds MMX technology to the CPU. The chip is Socket 7 compatible, but some require modified chipsets and new motherboard designs. Table 3.18 lists Cyrix M1 processors and bus speeds.

Table 3.18   Cyrix Processor Ratings Versus Actual Speeds

Cyrix CPU Type	P-Rating	Actual CPU Speed (MHz)	Clock Multiplier	Motherboard Speed (MHz)	Socket
6x86	PR90	80	2x	40	Socket 5,7
6x86	PR120	100	2x	50	Socket 5,7
6x86	PR133	110	2x	55	Socket 5,7
6x86	PR150	120	2x	60	Socket 5,7
6x86	PR166	133	2x	66	Socket 5,7
6x86	PR200	150	2x	75	Super7
6x86MX	PR133	100	2x	50	Socket 7
6x86MX	PR133	110	2x	55	Socket 7
6x86MX	PR150	120	2x	60	Socket 7
6x86MX	PR150	125	2.5x	50	Socket 7
6x86MX	PR166	133	2x	66	Socket 7
6x86MX	PR166	137.5	2.5x	55	Socket 7
6x86MX	PR166	150	3x	50	Socket 7
6x86MX	PR166	150	2.5x	60	Socket 7
6x86MX	PR200	150	2x	75	Super7
6x86MX	PR200	165	3x	55	Socket 7
6x86MX	PR200	166	2.5x	66	Socket 7
6x86MX	PR200	180	3x	60	Socket 7
6x86MX	PR233	166	2x	83	Super7
6x86MX	PR233	187.5	2.5x	75	Super7
6x86MX	PR233	200	3x	66	Socket 7

(continues)

Table 3.18   Continued

Cyrix CPU Type	P-Rating	Actual CPU Speed (MHz)	Clock Multiplier	Motherboard Speed (MHz)	Socket
6x86MX	PR266	207.5	2.5x	83	Super7
6x86MX	PR266	225	3x	75	Super7
6x86MX	PR266	233	3.5x	66	Socket 7
M-II	PR300	225	3x	75	Super7
M-II	PR300	233	3.5x	66	Socket 7
M-II	PR333	250	3x	83	Super7
M-II	PR366	250	2.5x	100	Super7

Not all motherboards support bus speeds such as 40MHz or 55MHz.

A Super7 motherboard is required to support the 100MHz bus speed

Most Super7 motherboards support bus speeds lower than 100MHz

The 6x86MX features 64KB of unified L1 cache and more than double the performance of the previous 6x86 CPUs. The 6x86MX is offered in clock speeds ranging from 180–266MHz, and like the 6x86, it is Socket 7 compatible. When running at speeds of 300MHz and higher, the 686MX was renamed as the MII. Besides the higher speeds, all other functions are virtually identical. All Cyrix chips were manufactured by other companies such as IBM, who also markets the 6x86 chips under its own name. National began manufacturing Cyrix processors during 1998, but now that Cyrix is selling them off, the future is unclear.

Note that later versions of the 6x86MX chip have been renamed the MII to deliberately invoke comparisons with the Pentium II, instead of the regular Pentium processor. The MII chips are not redesigned; they are, in fact, the same 6x86MX chips as before, only running at higher clock rates. The first renamed 6x86MX chip is the MII 300, which actually runs at only 233MHz on a 66MHz Socket 7 motherboard. There is also an MII 333, which will run at a 250MHz clock speed on newer 100MHz Super7 motherboards.

Cyrix also has made an attempt at capturing even more of the low-end market than they already have by introducing a processor called the MediaGX. This is a low-performance cross between a 486 and a Pentium combined with a custom motherboard chipset in a two-chip package. These two chips contain everything necessary for a motherboard, except the Super I/O chip, and make very low-cost PCs possible. Expect to see the MediaGX processors on the lowest end, virtually disposable-type PCs. Later versions of these chips will include more multimedia and even network support.

IDT Winchip

Another offering in the chip market is from Integrated Device Technology (IDT). A longtime chip manufacturer who was more well-known for making SRAM (cache memory) chips, IDT acquired Centaur Technology, who had designed a chip called the C6 Winchip. Now with IDT's manufacturing capability, the C6 processor became a reality.

Featuring a very simple design, the C6 Winchip is more like a 486 than a Pentium. It does not have the superscalar (multiple instruction pipelines) of a Pentium; it has a single high-speed pipeline instead. Internally, it seems the C6 has little in common with other fifth- and sixth-generation x86 processors. Even so, according to Centaur, it closely matches the performance of a Pentium MMX when running the Winstone 97 business benchmark, although that benchmark does not focus on multimedia performance. It also has a much smaller die (88 mm^2) than a typical Pentium, which means it should cost significantly less to manufacture.

The C6 has two large internal caches (32KB each for instructions and data), and will run at 180, 200, 225, and 240MHz. The power consumption is very low—14W maximum at 200MHz for the desktop chip, and 7.1 to 10.6W for the mobile chips. This processor will likely have some success in the low-end market.

P-Ratings

To make it easier to understand processor performance, the P-Rating system was jointly developed by Cyrix, IBM Microelectronics, SGS-Thomson Microelectronics, and Advanced Micro Devices. This new rating, titled the (Performance) P-Rating, equates delivered performance of microprocessor to that of an Intel Pentium. To determine a specific P-Rating, Cyrix and AMD use benchmarks such as Winstone 9x. Winstone 9x is a widely used, industry-standard benchmark that runs a number of Windows-based software applications.

The idea is fine, but in some cases it can be misleading. A single benchmark or even a group of benchmarks cannot tell the whole story on system or processor performance. In most cases, the companies selling PR-rated processors have people believing that they are really running at the speed indicated on the chip. For example, a Cyrix/IBM 6x86MX-PR200 does not really run at 200MHz; instead, it runs at 166MHz. I guess the idea is that it "feels" like 200MHz, or compares to some Intel processor running at 200MHz (which one?). I am not in favor of the P-Rating system and prefer to just report the processor's true speed in MHz. If it happens to be 166 but runs faster than most other 166 processors, so be it—but I don't like to number it based on some comparison like that.

Note

See "Cyrix P-Ratings" and "AMD P-Ratings" earlier in this chapter to see how P-Ratings stack up against the actual processor speed in MHz.

The Ziff-Davis Winstone benchmark is used because it is a real-world, application-based benchmark that contains the most popular software applications (based on market share) that run on a Pentium processor. Winstone also is a widely used benchmark and is freely distributed and available.

P1 (086) First-Generation Processors
8088 and 8086 Processors

Intel introduced a revolutionary new processor called the 8086 back in June of 1978. The 8086 was one of the first 16-bit processor chips on the market; at the time virtually all other processors were 8-bit designs. The 8086 had 16-bit internal registers and could run a new class of software using 16-bit instructions. It also had a 16-bit external data path, which meant it could transfer data to memory 16 bits at a time.

The address bus was 20 bits wide, meaning that the 8086 could address a full 1MB (2 to the 20th power) of memory. This was in stark contrast to most other chips of that time that had 8-bit internal registers, an 8-bit external data bus, and a 16-bit address bus allowing a maximum of only 64KB of RAM (2 to the 16th power).

Unfortunately, most of the personal computer world at the time was using 8-bit processors, which ran 8-bit CP/M (Control Program for Microprocessors) operating systems and software. The board and circuit designs at the time were largely 8-bit as well. Building a full 16-bit motherboard and memory system would be costly, pricing such a computer out of the market.

The cost was high because the 8086 needed a 16-bit data bus rather than a less expensive 8-bit bus. Systems available at that time were 8-bit, and slow sales of the 8086 indicated to Intel that people weren't willing to pay for the extra performance of the full 16-bit design. In response, Intel introduced a kind of crippled version of the 8086, called the 8088. The 8088 essentially deleted 8 of the 16 bits on the data bus, making the 8088 an 8-bit chip as far as data input and output were concerned. However, because it retained the full 16-bit internal registers and the 20-bit address bus, the 8088 ran 16-bit software and was capable of addressing a full 1MB of RAM.

For these reasons, IBM selected the 8-bit 8088 chip for the original IBM PC. Years later, they were criticized for using the 8-bit 8088 instead of the 16-bit 8086. In retrospect, it was a very wise decision. IBM even covered up the physical design in their ads, which at the time indicated their new PC had a "high-speed 16-bit microprocessor." They could say that because the 8088 still ran the same powerful 16-bit software the 8086 ran, just a little more slowly. In fact, programmers universally thought of the 8088 as a 16-bit chip because there was virtually no way a program could distinguish an 8088 from an 8086. This allowed IBM to deliver a PC capable of running a new generation of 16-bit software, while retaining a much less expensive 8-bit design for the hardware. Because of this, the IBM PC was actually priced less at its introduction than the most popular PC of the time, the Apple II. For the trivia buffs out there, the IBM PC listed for $1,265 and included only 16KB of RAM, while a similarly configured Apple II cost $1,355.

The original IBM PC used the Intel 8088. The 8088 was introduced in June 1979, but the IBM PC did not appear until August 1981. Back then, there was often a significant lag time between the introduction of a new processor and systems that incorporated it. That is unlike today, when new processors and systems using them are often released on the same day.

The 8088 in the IBM PC ran at 4.77MHz, or 4,770,000 cycles (essentially computer heartbeats) per second. Each cycle represents a unit of time to the system, with different instructions or operations requiring one or more cycles to complete. The average instruction on the 8088 took 12 cycles to complete.

Computer users sometimes wonder why a 640KB conventional-memory barrier exists if the 8088 chip can address 1MB of memory. The conventional-memory barrier exists because IBM reserved 384KB of the upper portion of the 1,024KB (1MB) address space of the 8088 for use by adapter cards and system BIOS. The lower 640KB is the conventional memory in which DOS and software applications execute.

80186 and 80188 Processors

After Intel produced the 8086 and 8088 chips, it turned its sights toward producing a more powerful chip with an increased instruction set. The company's first efforts along this line—the 80186 and 80188—were unsuccessful. But incorporating system components into the CPU chip was an important idea for Intel because it led to faster, better chips, such as the 286.

The relationship between the 80186 and 80188 is the same as that of the 8086 and 8088; one is a slightly more advanced version of the other. Compared CPU to CPU, the 80186 is almost the same as the 8088 and has a full 16-bit design. The 80188 (like the 8088) is a hybrid chip that compromises the 16-bit design with an 8-bit external communications interface. The advantage of the 80186 and 80188 is that they combine on a single chip 15 to 20 of the 8086–8088 series system components—a fact that can greatly reduce the number of components in a computer design. The 80186 and 80188 chips were used for highly intelligent peripheral adapter cards of that age, such as network adapters.

8087 Coprocessor

Intel introduced the 8086 processor in 1976. The math coprocessor that was paired with the chip—the 8087—often was called the numeric data processor (NDP), the math coprocessor, or simply the math chip. The 8087 is designed to perform high-level math operations at many times the speed of the main processor. The primary advantage of using this chip is the increased execution speed in number-crunching programs, such as spreadsheet applications.

P2 (286) Second-Generation Processors
286 Processors

The Intel 80286 (normally abbreviated as 286) processor did not suffer from the compatibility problems that damned the 80186 and 80188. The 286 chip, first introduced in 1981, is the CPU behind the original IBM AT. Other computer makers manufactured what came to be known as IBM clones, many of these manufacturers calling their systems AT-compatible or AT-class computers.

When IBM developed the AT, it selected the 286 as the basis for the new system because the chip provided compatibility with the 8088 used in the PC and the XT. That means that software written for those chips should run on the 286. The 286 chip is many times faster than the 8088 used in the XT, and it offered a major performance boost to PCs used in businesses. The processing speed, or throughput, of the original AT (which ran at 6MHz) was five times greater than that of the PC running at 4.77MHz. The die for the 286 is shown in Figure 3.30.

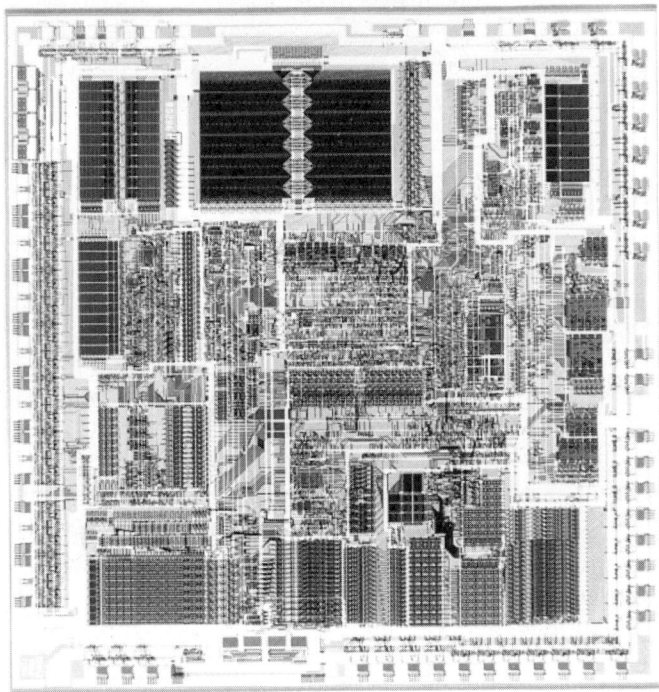

Figure 3.30   286 Processor die. Photograph used by permission of Intel Corporation.

286 systems are faster than their predecessors for several reasons. The main reason is that 286 processors are much more efficient in executing instructions. An average instruction takes 12 clock cycles on the 8086 or 8088, but an average 4.5 cycles on the 286 processor. Additionally, the 286 chip can handle up to 16 bits of data at a time through an external data bus twice the size of the 8088.

The 286 chip has two modes of operation: real mode and protected mode. The two modes are distinct enough to make the 286 resemble two chips in one. In real mode, a 286 acts essentially the same as an 8086 chip and is fully *object-code compatible* with the 8086 and 8088. (A processor with object-code compatibility can run programs written for another processor without modification and execute every system instruction in the same manner.)

In the protected mode of operation, the 286 was truly something new. In this mode, a program designed to take advantage of the chip's capabilities believes that it has access to 1GB of memory (including virtual memory). The 286 chip, however, can address only 16MB of hardware memory. A significant failing of the 286 chip is that it cannot switch from protected mode to real mode without a hardware reset (a warm reboot) of the system. (It can, however, switch from real mode to protected mode without a reset.) A major improvement of the 386 over the 286 is that software can switch the 386 from real mode to protected mode, and vice versa. See the section "Processor Modes," earlier in this chapter for more information.

Only a small amount of software that took advantage of the 286 chip was sold until Windows 3.0 offered standard mode for 286 compatibility; by that time, the hottest-selling chip was the 386. Still, the 286 was Intel's first attempt to produce a CPU chip that supported multitasking, in which multiple programs run at the same time. The 286 was designed so that if one program locked up or failed, the entire system didn't need a warm boot (reset) or cold boot (power off or on). Theoretically, what happened in one area of memory didn't affect other programs. Before multitasked programs could be "safe" from one another, however, the 286 chip (and subsequent chips) needed an operating system that worked cooperatively with the chip to provide such protection.

80287 Coprocessor

The 80287, internally, is the same math chip as the 8087, although the pins used to plug them into the motherboard are different. Both the 80287 and the 8087 operate as though they were identical.

In most systems, the 80286 internally divides the system clock by two to derive the processor clock. The 80287 internally divides the system-clock frequency by three. For this reason, most AT-type computers run the 80287 at one-third the system clock rate, which also is two-thirds the clock speed of the 80286. Because the 286 and 287 chips are asynchronous, the interface between the 286 and 287 chips is not as efficient as with the 8088 and 8087.

In summary, the 80287 and the 8087 chips perform about the same at equal clock rates. The original 80287 is not better than the 8087 in any real way—unlike the 80286, which is superior to the 8086 and 8088. In most AT systems, the performance gain that you realize by adding the coprocessor is much less substantial than the same type of upgrade for PC- or XT-type systems or for the 80386.

286 Processor Problems

After you remove a math coprocessor from an AT-type system, you must rerun your computer's Setup program. Some AT-compatible SETUP programs do not properly unset the math coprocessor bit. If you receive a POST error message because the computer cannot find the math chip, you might have to unplug the battery from the system board temporarily. All Setup information will be lost, so be sure to write down the hard drive type, floppy drive type, and memory and video configurations before unplugging the battery. This information is critical in reconfiguring your computer correctly.

P3 (386) Third-Generation Processors

386 Processors

The Intel 80386 (normally abbreviated as 386) caused quite a stir in the PC industry because of the vastly improved performance it brought to the personal computer. Compared with 8088 and 286 systems, the 386 chip offered greater performance in almost all areas of operation.

The 386 is a full 32-bit processor optimized for high-speed operation and multitasking operating systems. Intel introduced the chip in 1985, but the 386 appeared in the first systems in late 1986 and early 1987. The Compaq Deskpro 386 and systems made by several other manufacturers introduced the chip; somewhat later, IBM used the chip in its PS/2 Model 80. The 386 chip rose in popularity for several years, which peaked around 1991. Obsolete 386 processor systems are mostly retired or scrapped, having been passed down the user chain. If they are in operating condition, they can be useful for running old DOS or Windows 3.x-based applications, which they can do quite nicely.

The 386 can execute the real-mode instructions of an 8086 or 8088, but in fewer clock cycles. The 386 was as efficient as the 286 in executing instructions, which means that the average instruction took about 4.5 clock cycles. In raw performance, therefore, the 286 and 386 actually seemed to be at almost equal clock rates. Many 286 system manufacturers were touting their 16MHz and 20MHz 286 systems as being just as fast as 16MHz and 20MHz 386 systems, and they were right! The 386 offered greater performance in other ways, mainly because of additional software capability (modes) and a greatly enhanced memory management unit (MMU). The die for the 386 is shown in Figure 3.31.

The 386 can switch to and from protected mode under software control without a system reset— a capability that makes using protected mode more practical. In addition, the 386 has a new mode, called virtual real mode, which enables several real mode sessions to run simultaneously under protected mode.

The protected mode of the 386 is fully compatible with the protected mode of the 286. The protected mode for both chips often is called their native mode of operation, because these chips are designed for advanced operating systems such as OS/2 and Windows NT, which run only in protected mode. Intel extended the memory-addressing capabilities of 386 protected mode with a new MMU that provided advanced memory paging and program switching. These features were extensions of the 286 type of MMU, so the 386 remained fully compatible with the 286 at the system-code level.

The 386 chip's virtual real mode was new. In virtual real mode, the processor could run with hardware memory protection while simulating an 8086's real-mode operation. Multiple copies of DOS and other operating systems, therefore, could run simultaneously on this processor, each in a protected area of memory. If the programs in one segment crashed, the rest of the system was protected. Software commands could reboot the blown partition.

Numerous variations of the 386 chip exist, some of which are less powerful and some of which are less power-hungry. The following sections cover the members of the 386-chip family and their differences.

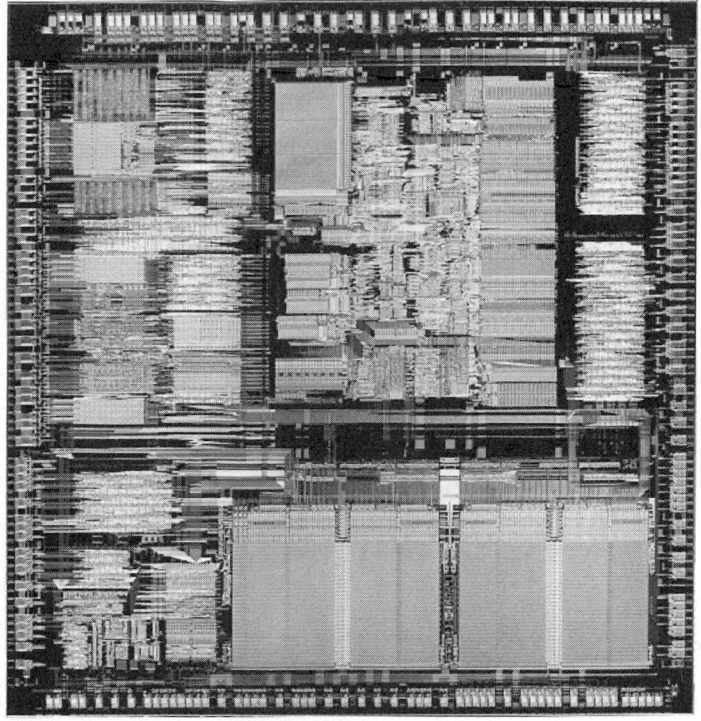

Figure 3.31   386 processor die. Photograph used by permission of Intel Corporation.

386DX Processors

The 386DX chip was the first of the 386 family members that Intel introduced. The 386 is a full 32-bit processor with 32-bit internal registers, a 32-bit internal data bus, and a 32-bit external data bus. The 386 contains 275,000 transistors in a VLSI (very large scale integration) circuit. The chip comes in a 132-pin package and draws approximately 400 milliamperes (ma), which is less power than even the 8086 requires. The 386 has a smaller power requirement because it is made of CMOS (complementary metal oxide semiconductor) materials. The CMOS design enables devices to consume extremely low levels of power.

The Intel 386 chip was available in clock speeds ranging from 16–33MHz; other manufacturers, primarily AMD and Cyrix, offered comparable versions with speeds up to 40MHz.

The 386DX can address 4GB of physical memory. Its built in virtual memory manager enables software designed to take advantage of enormous amounts of memory to act as though a system has 64TB of memory. (A terabyte (TB) is 1,099,511,627,776 bytes of memory, or about 1,000GB.)

386SX Processors

The 386SX was designed for systems designers who were looking for 386 capabilities at 286 system prices. Like the 286, the 386SX is restricted to only 16 bits when communicating with other system components, such as memory. Internally, however, the 386SX is identical to the DX chip;

the 386SX has 32-bit internal registers and can therefore run 32-bit software. The 386SX uses a 24-bit memory-addressing scheme like that of the 286, rather than the full 32-bit memory address bus of the standard 386. The 386SX, therefore, can address a maximum 16MB of physical memory rather than the 4GB of physical memory that the 386DX can address. Before it was discontinued, the 386SX was available in clock speeds ranging from 16–33MHz.

The 386SX signaled the end of the 286 because of the 386SX chip's superior MMU and the addition of the virtual real mode. Under a software manager such as Windows or OS/2, the 386SX can run numerous DOS programs at the same time. The capability to run 386-specific software is another important advantage of the 386SX over any 286 or older design. For example, Windows 3.1 runs nearly as well on a 386SX as it does on a 386DX.

Note

One common fallacy about the 386SX is that you can plug one into a 286 system and give the system 386 capabilities. This is not true; the 386SX chip is not pin-compatible with the 286 and does not plug into the same socket. Several upgrade products, however, have been designed to adapt the chip to a 286 system. In terms of raw speed, converting a 286 system to a 386 CPU chip results in little performance gain—286 motherboards are built with a restricted 16-bit interface to memory and peripherals. A 16MHz 386SX is not markedly faster than a 16MHz 286, but it does offer improved memory management capabilities on a motherboard designed for it, and the capability to run 386-specific software.

386SL Processors

The 386SL is another variation on the 386 chip. This low-power CPU had the same capabilities as the 386SX, but it was designed for laptop systems in which low power consumption was needed. The SL chips offered special power-management features that were important to systems that ran on batteries. The SL chip also offered several sleep modes to conserve power.

The chip included an extended architecture that contained a System Management Interrupt (SMI), which provided access to the power-management features. Also included in the SL chip was special support for LIM (Lotus Intel Microsoft) expanded memory functions and a cache controller. The cache controller was designed to control a 16–64KB external processor cache.

These extra functions account for the higher transistor count in the SL chips (855,000) compared with even the 386DX processor (275,000). The 386SL was available in 25MHz clock speed.

Intel offered a companion to the 386SL chip for laptops called the 82360SL I/O subsystem. The 82360SL provided many common peripheral functions such as serial and parallel ports, a direct memory access (DMA) controller, an interrupt controller, and power-management logic for the 386SL processor. This chip subsystem worked with the processor to provide an ideal solution for the small size and low power-consumption requirements of portable and laptop systems.

80387 Coprocessor

Although the 80387 chips ran asynchronously, 386 systems were designed so that the math chip runs at the same clock speed as the main CPU. Unlike the 80287 coprocessor, which was merely an 8087 with different pins to plug into the AT motherboard, the 80387 coprocessor was a high-performance math chip designed specifically to work with the 386.

All 387 chips used a low power-consumption CMOS design. The 387 coprocessor had two basic designs: the 387DX coprocessor, which was designed to work with the 386DX processor, and the 387SX coprocessor, which was designed to work with the 386SX, SL, or SLC processors.

Intel originally offered several speeds for the 387DX coprocessor. But when the company designed the 33MHz version, a smaller mask was required to reduce the lengths of the signal pathways in the chip. This increased the performance of the chip by roughly 20 percent.

Note

Because Intel lagged in developing the 387 coprocessor, some early 386 systems were designed with a socket for a 287 coprocessor. Performance levels associated with that union, however, leave much to be desired.

Installing a 387DX is easy, but you must be careful to orient the chip in its socket properly; otherwise, the chip will be destroyed. The most common cause of burned pins on the 387DX is incorrect installation. In many systems, the 387DX was oriented differently from other large chips. Follow the manufacturer's installation instructions carefully to avoid damaging the 387DX; Intel's warranty does not cover chips that are installed incorrectly.

Several manufacturers developed their own versions of the Intel 387 coprocessors, some of which were touted as being faster than the original Intel chips. The general compatibility record of these chips was very good.

Weitek Coprocessors

In 1981, several Intel engineers formed the Weitek Corporation. Weitek developed math coprocessors for several systems, including those based on Motorola processor designs. Intel originally contracted Weitek to develop a math coprocessor for the Intel 386 CPU, because Intel was behind in its own development of the 387 math coprocessor. The result was the Weitek 1167, a custom math coprocessor that uses a proprietary Weitek instruction set, which is incompatible with the Intel 387.

To use the Weitek coprocessor, your system must have the required additional socket, which was different from the standard Intel coprocessor sockets.

80386 Bugs

Some early 16MHz Intel 386DX processors had a small bug that appeared as a software problem. The bug, which apparently was in the chip's 32-bit multiply routine, manifested itself only when you ran true 32-bit code in a program such as OS/2 2.x, UNIX/386, or Windows in enhanced mode. Some specialized 386 memory-management software systems also may invoke this subtle bug, but 16-bit operating systems (such as DOS and OS/2 1.x) probably will not.

The bug usually causes the system to lock up. Diagnosing this problem can be difficult because the problem generally is intermittent and software-related. Running tests to find the bug is difficult; only Intel, with proper test equipment, can determine whether your chip has a bug. Some programs can diagnose the problem and identify a defective chip, but they cannot identify all defective chips. If a program indicates a bad chip, you certainly have a defective one; if the program passes the chip, you still might have a defective one.

Intel requested that its 386 customers return possibly defective chips for screening, but many vendors did not return them. Intel tested returned chips and replaced defective ones. The defective chips later were sold to bargain liquidators or systems houses that wanted chips that would not run 32-bit code. The defective chips were stamped with a 16-bit SW Only logo, indicating that they were authorized to run only 16-bit software.

Chips that passed the test, and all subsequent chips produced as bug-free, were marked with a double-sigma code (SS). 386DX chips that are not marked with either of these designations have not been tested by Intel and might be defective.

The following marking indicates that a chip has not yet been screened for the defect; it might be either good or bad.

> 80386-16

The following marking indicates that the chip has been tested and has the 32-bit multiply bug. The chip works with 16-bit software (such as DOS) but not with 32-bit, 386-specific software (such as Windows or OS/2).

> 80386-16
>
> 16-bit SW Only

The following mark on a chip indicates that it has been tested as defect-free. This chip fulfills all the capabilities promised for the 80386.

> 80386-16
>
> SS

This problem was discovered and corrected before Intel officially added DX to the part number. So, if you have a chip labeled as 80386DX or 386DX, it does not have this problem.

Another problem with the 386DX can be stated more specifically. When 386-based versions of XENIX or other UNIX implementations are run on a computer that contains a 387DX math coprocessor, the computer locks up under certain conditions. The problem does not occur in the DOS environment, however. For the lockup to occur, all the following conditions must be in effect:

- Demand page virtual memory must be active.
- A 387DX must be installed and in use.
- DMA (direct memory access) must occur.
- The 386 must be in a wait state.

When all these conditions are true at the same instant, the 386DX ends up waiting for the 387DX and vice versa. Both processors will continue to wait for each other indefinitely. The problem is in certain versions of the 386DX, not in the 387DX math coprocessor.

Intel published this problem (Errata 21) immediately after it was discovered to inform its OEM customers. At that point, it became the responsibility of each manufacturer to implement a fix in its hardware or software product. Some manufacturers, such as Compaq and IBM, responded by modifying their motherboards to prevent these lockups from occurring.

The Errata 21 problem occurs only in the B stepping version of the 386DX and not in the later D stepping version. You can identify the D stepping version of the 386DX by the letters DX in the part number (for example, 386DX-20). If DX is part of the chip's part number, the chip does not have this problem.

P4 (486) Fourth-Generation Processors

486 Processors

In the race for more speed, the Intel 80486 (normally abbreviated as 486) was another major leap forward. The additional power available in the 486 fueled tremendous growth in the software industry. Tens of millions of copies of Windows, and millions of copies of OS/2, have been sold largely because the 486 finally made the GUI of Windows and OS/2 a realistic option for people who work on their computers every day.

Four main features make a given 486 processor roughly twice as fast as an equivalent MHz 386 chip. These features are

- *Reduced instruction-execution time.* A single instruction in the 486 takes an average of only two clock cycles to complete, compared with an average of more than four cycles on the 386. Clock-multiplied versions such as the DX2 and DX4 further reduced this to about two cycles per instruction.

- *Internal (Level 1) cache.* The built-in cache has a hit ratio of 90–95 percent, which describes how often zero-wait-state read operations will occur. External caches can improve this ratio further.

- *Burst-mode memory cycles.* A standard 32-bit (4-byte) memory transfer takes two clock cycles. After a standard 32-bit transfer, more data up to the next 12 bytes (or three transfers) can be transferred with only one cycle used for each 32-bit (4-byte) transfer. Thus, up to 16 bytes of contiguous, sequential memory data can be transferred in as little as five cycles instead of eight cycles or more. This effect can be even greater when the transfers are only 8 bits or 16 bits each.

▶▶ See "Burst EDO," p. 428.

- *Built-in (synchronous) enhanced math coprocessor (some versions).* The math coprocessor runs synchronously with the main processor and executes math instructions in fewer cycles than previous designs did. On average, the math coprocessor built into the DX-series chips provides two to three times greater math performance than an external 387 chip.

The 486 chip is about twice as fast as the 386, which means that a 386DX-40 is about as fast as a 486SX-20. This made the 486 a much more desirable option, primarily because it could more easily be upgraded to a DX2 or DX4 processor at a later time. You can see why the arrival of the 486 rapidly killed off the 386 in the marketplace.

Before the 486, many people avoided GUIs because they didn't have time to sit around waiting for the hourglass, which indicates that the system is performing behind-the-scenes operations that the user cannot interrupt. The 486 changed that situation. Many people believe that the 486 CPU chip spawned the widespread acceptance of GUIs.

With the release of its faster Pentium CPU chip, Intel began to cut the price of the 486 line to entice the industry to shift over to the 486 as the mainstream system. Intel later did the same thing with its Pentium chips, spelling the end of the 486 line. The 486 is now offered by Intel only for use in embedded microprocessor applications, used primarily in expansion cards.

Most of the 486 chips were offered in a variety of maximum speed ratings, varying from 16MHz up to 120MHz. Additionally, 486 processors have slight differences in overall pin configurations. The DX, DX2, and SX processors have a virtually identical 168-pin configuration, whereas the OverDrive chips have either the standard 168-pin configuration or a specially modified 169-pin OverDrive (sometimes also called 487SX) configuration. If your motherboard has two sockets, the primary one likely supports the standard 168-pin configuration, and the secondary (OverDrive) socket supports the 169-pin OverDrive configuration. Most newer motherboards with a single ZIF socket support any of the 486 processors except the DX4. The DX4 is different because it requires 3.3v to operate instead of 5v, like most other chips up to that time.

A processor rated for a given speed always functions at any of the lower speeds. A 100MHz-rated 486DX4 chip, for example, runs at 75MHz if it is plugged into a 25MHz motherboard. Note that the DX2/OverDrive processors operate internally at two times the motherboard clock rate, whereas the DX4 processors operate at two, two and a half, or three times the motherboard clock rate. Table 3.19 shows the different speed combinations that can result from using the DX2 or DX4 processors with different motherboard clock speeds.

Table 3.19   Intel DX2 and DX4 Operating Speeds Versus Motherboard Clock Speeds

Processor speed	DX2 (2× mode) Speed	DX4(2.5× mode) Speed	DX4 (3× mode) Speed	DX4
16MHz Motherboard	32MHz	32MHz	40MHz	48MHz
40MHz Motherboard	80MHz	80MHz	100MHz	120MHz
20MHz Motherboard	40MHz	40MHz	50MHz	60MHz
50MHz Motherboard	n/a	100MHz	n/a	n/a
25MHz Motherboard	50MHz	50MHz	63MHz	75MHz
33MHz Motherboard	66MHz	66MHz	83MHz	100MHz

The internal core speed of the DX4 processor is controlled by the CLKMUL (Clock Multiplier) signal at pin R-17 (Socket 1) or S-18 (Socket 2, 3, or 6). The CLKMUL input is sampled only during a reset of the CPU, and defines the ratio of the internal clock to the external bus frequency CLK signal at pin C-3 (Socket 1) or D-4 (Socket 2, 3, or 6). If CLKMUL is sampled low, the internal core speed will be two times the external bus frequency. If driven high or left floating (most motherboards would leave it floating), triple speed mode is selected. If the CLKMUL signal is connected to the BREQ (Bus Request) output signal at pin Q-15 (Socket 1) or R-16 (Socket 2, 3, or 6), the CPU internal core speed will be two and a half times the CLK speed. To summarize, here is how the socket has to be wired for each DX4 speed selection:

CPU Speed	CLKMUL (Sampled Only at CPU Reset)
2x	Low
2.5x	Connected to BREQ
3x	High or Floating

You will have to determine how your particular motherboard is wired and whether it can be changed to alter the CPU core speed in relation to the CLK signal. In most cases, there would be one or two jumpers on the board near the processor socket. The motherboard documentation should cover these settings if they can be changed.

One interesting capability here is to run the DX4-100 chip in a doubled mode with a 50MHz motherboard speed. This would give you a very fast memory bus, along with the same 100MHz processor speed, as if you were running the chip in a 33/100MHz tripled mode.

Note

One caveat is that if your motherboard has VL-Bus slots, they will have to be slowed down to 33 or 40MHz to operate properly.

Many VL-Bus motherboards can run the VL-Bus slots in a buffered mode, add wait states, or even selectively change the clock only for the VL-Bus slots to keep them compatible. In most cases, they will not run properly at 50MHz. Consult your motherboard—or even better, your chipset documentation—to see how your board is set up.

Caution

If you are upgrading an existing system, be sure that your socket will support the chip that you are installing. In particular, if you are putting a DX4 processor in an older system, you need some type of adapter to regulate the voltage down to 3.3v. If you put the DX4 in a 5v socket, you will destroy the chip! See the earlier section on processor sockets for more information.

The 486-processor family is designed for greater performance than previous processors because it integrates formerly external devices, such as cache controllers, cache memory, and math coprocessors. Also, 486 systems were the first designed for true processor upgradability. Most 486 systems can be upgraded by simple processor additions or swaps that can effectively double the speed of the system.

486DX Processors

The original Intel 486DX processor was introduced on April 10, 1989, and systems using this chip first appeared during 1990. The first chips had a maximum speed rating of 25MHz; later versions of the 486DX were available in 33MHz- and 50MHz-rated versions. The 486DX originally was available only in a 5v, 168-pin PGA version, but now is also available in 5v, 196-pin PQFP (Plastic Quad Flat Pack) and 3.3v, 208-pin SQFP (Small Quad Flat Pack). These latter form factors are available in SL Enhanced versions, which are intended primarily for portable or laptop applications in which saving power is important.

Two main features separate the 486 processor from older processors:

- The 486DX integrates functions such as the math coprocessor, cache controller, and cache memory into the chip.
- The 486 also was designed with upgradability in mind; double-speed OverDrive are upgrades available for most systems.

The 486DX processor is fabricated with low-power CMOS (complementary metal oxide semiconductor) technology. The chip has a 32-bit internal register size, a 32-bit external data bus, and a 32-bit address bus. These dimensions are equal to those of the 386DX processor. The internal register size is where the "32-bit" designation used in advertisements comes from. The 486DX chip contains 1.2 million transistors on a piece of silicon no larger than your thumbnail. This figure is more than four times the number of components on 386 processors and should give you a good indication of the 486 chip's relative power. The die for the 486 is shown in Figure 3.32.

The standard 486DX contains a processing unit, a floating-point unit (math coprocessor), a memory-management unit, and a cache controller with 8KB of internal-cache RAM. Due to the internal cache and a more efficient internal processing unit, the 486 family of processors can execute individual instructions in an average of only two processor cycles. Compare this figure with the 286 and 386 families, both of which execute an average 4.5 cycles per instruction. Compare it also with the original 8086 and 8088 processors, which execute an average 12 cycles per instruction. At a given clock rate (MHz), therefore, a 486 processor is roughly twice as efficient as a 386 processor; a 16MHz 486SX is roughly equal to a 33MHz 386DX system; and a 20MHz 486SX is equal to a 40MHz 386DX system. Any of the faster 486s are way beyond the 386 in performance.

The 486 is fully instruction-set–compatible with previous Intel processors, such as the 386, but offers several additional instructions (most of which have to do with controlling the internal cache).

Like the 386DX, the 486 can address 4GB of physical memory and manage as much as 64TB of virtual memory. The 486 fully supports the three operating modes introduced in the 386: real mode, protected mode, and virtual real mode.

- *In real mode*, the 486 (like the 386) runs unmodified 8086-type software.
- *In protected mode*, the 486 (like the 386) offers sophisticated memory paging and program switching.

■ *In virtual real mode*, the 486 (like the 386) can run multiple copies of DOS or other operating systems while simulating an 8086's real mode operation. Under an operating system such as Windows or OS/2, therefore, both 16-bit and 32-bit programs can run simultaneously on this processor with hardware memory protection. If one program crashes, the rest of the system is protected, and you can reboot the blown portion through various means, depending on the operating software.

Figure 3.32   486 processor die. Photograph used by permission of Intel Corporation.

The 486DX series has a built-in math coprocessor that sometimes is called an MCP (math coprocessor) or FPU (floating-point unit). This series is unlike previous Intel CPU chips, which required you to add a math coprocessor if you needed faster calculations for complex mathematics. The FPU in the 486DX series is 100 percent software-compatible with the external 387 math coprocessor used with the 386, but it delivers more than twice the performance. It runs in synchronization with the main processor and executes most instructions in half as many cycles as the 386.

486SL

The 486SL was a short-lived, standalone chip. The SL enhancements and features became available in virtually all the 486 processors (SX, DX, and DX2) in what are called SL enhanced versions. SL enhancement refers to a special design that incorporates special power-saving features.

The SL enhanced chips originally were designed to be installed in laptop or notebook systems that run on batteries, but they found their way into desktop systems, as well. The SL enhanced chips featured special power-management techniques, such as sleep mode and clock throttling, to reduce power consumption when necessary. These chips were available in 3.3v versions, as well.

Intel designed a power-management architecture called system management mode (SMM). This mode of operation is totally isolated and independent from other CPU hardware and software. SMM provides hardware resources such as timers, registers, and other I/O logic that can control and power down mobile-computer components without interfering with any of the other system resources. SMM executes in a dedicated memory space called system management memory, which is not visible and does not interfere with operating system and application software. SMM has an interrupt called system management interrupt (SMI), which services power-management events and is independent from, and higher priority than, any of the other interrupts.

SMM provides power management with flexibility and security that were not available previously. For example, an SMI occurs when an application program tries to access a peripheral device that is powered down for battery savings, which powers up the peripheral device and reexecutes the I/O instruction automatically.

Intel also designed a feature called suspend/resume in the SL processor. The system manufacturer can use this feature to provide the portable computer user with instant-on-and-off capability. An SL system typically can resume (instant on) in one second from the suspend state (instant off) to exactly where it left off. You do not need to reboot, load the operating system, load the application program, and then load the application data. Simply push the Suspend/Resume button and the system is ready to go.

The SL CPU was designed to consume almost no power in the suspend state. This feature means that the system can stay in the suspend state possibly for weeks and yet start up instantly right where it left off. An SL system can keep working data in normal RAM memory safe for a long time while it is in the suspend state, but saving to a disk still is prudent.

486SX

The 486SX, introduced in April 1991, was designed to be sold as a lower cost version of the 486. The 486SX is virtually identical to the full DX processor, but the chip does not incorporate the FPU or math coprocessor portion.

As you read earlier in this chapter, the 386SX was a scaled-down (some people would say crippled) 16-bit version of the full-blown 32-bit 386DX. The 386SX even had a completely different pinout and was not interchangeable with the more powerful DX version. The 486SX, however, is a different story. The 486SX is, in fact, a full-blown 32-bit 486 processor that is basically pin-compatible with the DX. A few pin functions are different or rearranged, but each pin fits into the same socket.

The 486SX chip is more a marketing quirk than new technology. Early versions of the 486SX chip actually were DX chips that showed defects in the math-coprocessor section. Instead of being scrapped, the chips were packaged with the FPU section disabled and sold as SX chips. This arrangement lasted for only a short time; thereafter, SX chips got their own mask, which is different from the DX mask. (A *mask* is the photographic blueprint of the processor and is used to etch the intricate signal pathways into a silicon chip.) The transistor count dropped to 1.185 million (from 1.2 million) to reflect this new mask.

The 486SX chip is twice as fast as a 386DX with the same clock speed. Intel marketed the 486SX as being the ideal chip for new computer buyers, because fewer entry-level programs of that day used math-coprocessor functions.

The 486SX was normally available in 16, 20, 25, and 33MHz-rated speeds, and there was also a 486 SX/2 that ran at up to 50 or 66MHz. The 486SX normally comes in a 168-pin version, although other surface-mount versions are available in SL enhanced models.

Despite what Intel's marketing and sales information implies, no technical provision exists for adding a separate math coprocessor to a 486SX system; neither is a separate math coprocessor chip available to plug in. Instead, Intel wanted you to add a new 486 processor with a built-in math unit and disable the SX CPU that already was on the motherboard. If this situation sounds confusing, read on, because this topic brings you to the most important aspect of 486 design: upgradability.

487SX

The 487SX math coprocessor, as Intel calls it, really is a complete 25MHz 486DX CPU with an extra pin added and some other pins rearranged. When the 487SX is installed in the extra socket provided in a 486SX CPU-based system, the 487SX turns off the existing 486SX via a new signal on one of the pins. The extra key pin actually carries no signal itself and exists only to prevent improper orientation when the chip is installed in a socket.

The 487SX takes over all CPU functions from the 486SX and also provides math coprocessor functionality in the system. At first glance, this setup seems rather strange and wasteful, so perhaps further explanation is in order. Fortunately, the 487SX turned out to be a stopgap measure while Intel prepared its real surprise: the OverDrive processor. The DX2/OverDrive speed-doubling chips, which are designed for the 487SX 169-pin socket, have the same pinout as the 487SX. These upgrade chips are installed in exactly the same way as the 487SX; therefore, any system that supports the 487SX also supports the DX2/OverDrive chips.

Although in most cases you can upgrade a system by removing the 486SX CPU and replacing it with a 487SX (or even a DX or DX2/OverDrive), Intel originally discouraged this procedure. Instead, Intel recommended that PC manufacturers include a dedicated upgrade (OverDrive) socket in their systems, because several risks were involved in removing the original CPU from a standard socket. (The following section elaborates on those risks.) Now Intel recommends—or even insists on—the use of a single processor socket of a ZIF design, which makes upgrading an easy task physically.

◄◄ See "Zero Insertion Force (ZIF) Sockets," p. 86.

Very few early 486 systems had a socket for the Weitek 4167 coprocessor chip for 486 systems that existed in November 1989.

DX2/OverDrive and DX4 Processors

On March 3, 1992, Intel introduced the DX2 speed-doubling processors. On May 26, 1992, Intel announced that the DX2 processors also would be available in a retail version called OverDrive. Originally, the OverDrive versions of the DX2 were available only in 169-pin versions, which meant that they could be used only with 486SX systems that had sockets configured to support the rearranged pin configuration.

On September 14, 1992, Intel introduced 168-pin OverDrive versions for upgrading 486DX systems. These processors could be added to existing 486 (SX or DX) systems as an upgrade, even if those systems did not support the 169-pin configuration. When you use this processor as an upgrade, you install the new chip in your system, which subsequently runs twice as fast.

The DX2/OverDrive processors run internally at twice the clock rate of the host system. If the motherboard clock is 25MHz, for example, the DX2/OverDrive chip runs internally at 50MHz; likewise, if the motherboard is a 33MHz design, the DX2/OverDrive runs at 66MHz. The DX2/OverDrive speed doubling has no effect on the rest of the system; all components on the motherboard run the same as they do with a standard 486 processor. Therefore, you do not have to change other components (such as memory) to accommodate the double-speed chip. The DX2/OverDrive chips have been available in several speeds. Three different speed-rated versions have been offered:

- 40MHz DX2/OverDrive for 16MHz or 20MHz systems
- 50MHz DX2/OverDrive for 25MHz systems
- 66MHz DX2/OverDrive for 33MHz systems

Notice that these ratings indicate the maximum speed at which the chip is capable of running. You could use a 66MHz-rated chip in place of the 50MHz- or 40MHz-rated parts with no problem, although the chip will run only at the slower speeds. The actual speed of the chip is double the motherboard clock frequency. When the 40MHz DX2/OverDrive chip is installed in a 16MHz 486SX system, for example, the chip will function only at 32MHz—exactly double the motherboard speed. Intel originally stated that no 100MHz DX2/OverDrive chip would be available for 50MHz systems—which technically has not been true, because the DX4 could be set to run in a clock-doubled mode and used in a 50MHz motherboard (see the discussion of the DX4 processor in this section).

The only part of the DX2 chip that doesn't run at double speed is the bus interface unit, a region of the chip that handles I/O between the CPU and the outside world. By translating between the differing internal and external clock speeds, the bus interface unit makes speed doubling transparent to the rest of the system. The DX2 appears to the rest of the system to be a regular 486DX chip, but one that seems to execute instructions twice as fast.

DX2/OverDrive chips are based on the 0.8 micron circuit technology that was first used in the 50MHz 486DX. The DX2 contains 1.1 million transistors in a three-layer form. The internal 8KB cache, integer, and floating-point units all run at double speed. External communication with the PC runs at normal speed to maintain compatibility.

Besides upgrading existing systems, one of the best parts of the DX2 concept was the fact that system designers could introduce very fast systems by using cheaper motherboard designs, rather than the more costly designs that would support a straight high-speed clock. This means that a 50MHz 486DX2 system was much less expensive than a straight 50MHz 486DX system. The system board in a 486DX-50 system operates at a true 50MHz. The 486DX2 CPU in a 486DX2-50 system operates internally at 50MHz, but the motherboard operates at only 25MHz.

You may be thinking that a true 50MHz DX processor–based system still would be faster than a speed-doubled 25MHz system, and this generally is true. But, the differences in speed actually are very slight—a real testament to the integration of the 486 processor and especially to the cache design.

When the processor has to go to system memory for data or instructions, for example, it has to do so at the slower motherboard operating frequency (such as 25MHz). Because the 8KB internal cache of the 486DX2 has a hit rate of 90–95 percent, however, the CPU has to access system memory only 5–10 percent of the time for memory reads. Therefore, the performance of the DX2 system can come very close to that of a true 50MHz DX system and cost much less. Even though the motherboard runs only at 33.33MHz, a system with a DX2 66MHz processor ends up being faster than a true 50MHz DX system, especially if the DX2 system has a good L2 cache.

Many 486 motherboard designs also include a secondary cache that is external to the cache integrated into the 486 chip. This external cache allows for much faster access when the 486 chip calls for external-memory access. The size of this external cache can vary anywhere from 16KB to 512K or more. When you add a DX2 processor, an external cache is even more important for achieving the greatest performance gain. This cache greatly reduces the wait states that the processor will have to add when writing to system memory or when a read causes an internal cache miss. For this reason, some systems perform better with the DX2/OverDrive processors than others, usually depending on the size and efficiency of the external-memory cache system on the motherboard. Systems that have no external cache will still enjoy a near-doubling of CPU performance, but operations that involve a great deal of memory access will be slower.

This brings us to the DX4 processor. Although the standard DX4 technically was not sold as a retail part, it could be purchased from several vendors, along with the 3.3v voltage adapter needed to install the chip in a 5v socket. These adapters have jumpers that enable you to select the DX4 clock multiplier and set it to 2x, 2.5x, or 3x mode. In a 50MHz DX system, you could install a DX4/voltage-regulator combination set in 2x mode for a motherboard speed of 50MHz and a processor speed of 100MHz! Although you may not be able to take advantage of certain VL-Bus adapter cards, you will have one of the fastest 486-class PCs available.

Intel also sold a special DX4 OverDrive processor that included a built-in voltage regulator and heat sink that are specifically designed for the retail market. The DX4 OverDrive chip is essentially the same as the standard 3.3v DX4 with the main exception that it runs on 5v because it includes an on-chip regulator. Also, the DX4 OverDrive chip will run only in the tripled speed mode, and not the 2x or 2.5x modes of the standard DX4 processor.

Note

As of this writing, Intel has discontinued all 486 and DX2/DX4/OverDrive processors, including the so-called Pentium OverDrive processor.

Pentium OverDrive for 486SX2 and DX2 Systems

The Pentium OverDrive Processor became available in 1995. An OverDrive chip for 486DX4 systems had been planned, but poor marketplace performance of the SX2/DX2 chip meant that it never saw the light of day. One thing to keep in mind about the 486 Pentium OverDrive chip is that although it is intended primarily for SX2 and DX2 systems, it should work in any upgradable 486SX or DX system that has a Socket 2 or Socket 3. If in doubt, check Intel's online upgrade guide for compatibility.

The Pentium OverDrive processor is designed for systems that have a processor socket that follows the Intel Socket 2 specification. This processor also will work in systems that have a Socket 3 design, although you should ensure that the voltage is set for 5v rather than 3.3v. The Pentium OverDrive chip includes a 32KB internal L1 cache, and the same superscalar (multiple instruction path) architecture of the real Pentium chip. Besides a 32-bit Pentium core, these processors feature increased clock-speed operation due to internal clock multiplication and incorporate an internal write-back cache (standard with the Pentium). If the motherboard supports the write-back cache function, increased performance will be realized. Unfortunately, most motherboards, especially older ones with the Socket 2 design, only support write-through cache.

Most tests of these OverDrive chips show them to be only slightly ahead of the DX4-100 and behind the DX4-120 and true Pentium 60, 66, or 75. Unfortunately, these are the only solutions still offered by Intel for upgrading the 486. Based on the relative affordability of low-end "real" Pentiums (in their day), it was hard not to justify making the step up to a Pentium system. At the time, I did not recommend the 486 Pentium OverDrive chips as a viable solution for the future.

"Vacancy"—Secondary OverDrive Sockets

Perhaps you saw the Intel advertisements—both print and television—that featured a 486SX system with a neon Vacancy sign pointing to an empty socket next to the CPU chip. Unfortunately, these ads were not very informative, and they made it seem that only systems with the extra socket could be upgraded. I was worried when I first saw these ads because I had just purchased a 486DX system, and the advertisements implied that only 486SX systems with the empty OverDrive socket were upgradable. This, of course, was not true, but the Intel advertisements did not communicate that fact very well.

I later found that upgradability does not depend on having an extra OverDrive socket in the system and that virtually any 486SX or DX system can be upgraded. The secondary OverDrive socket was designed to make upgrading easier and more convenient. Even in systems that have the second socket, you can actually remove the primary SX or DX CPU and plug the OverDrive processor directly into the main CPU socket, rather than into the secondary OverDrive socket.

In that case, you would have an upgraded system with a single functioning CPU installed; you could remove the old CPU from the system and sell it or trade it in for a refund. Unfortunately, Intel does not offer a trade-in or core-charge policy; it does not want your old chip. For this reason, some people saw the OverDrive socket as being a way for Intel to sell more CPUs. Some valid reasons exist, however, to use the OverDrive socket and leave the original CPU installed.

One reason is that many PC manufacturers void the system warranty if the CPU has been removed from the system. Also, most manufacturers require that the system be returned with only the original parts when systems are serviced; you must remove all add-in cards, memory modules, upgrade chips, and similar items before sending the system in for servicing. If you replace the original CPU when you install the upgrade, returning the system to its original condition will be much more difficult.

Another reason for using the upgrade socket is that the system will not function if the main CPU socket is damaged when you remove the original CPU or install the upgrade processor. By contrast, if a secondary upgrade socket is damaged, the system still should work with the original CPU.

80487 Upgrade

The Intel 80486 processor was introduced in late 1989, and systems using this chip appeared during 1990. The 486DX integrated the math coprocessor into the chip.

The 486SX began life as a full-fledged 486DX chip, but Intel actually disabled the built-in math coprocessor before shipping the chip. As part of this marketing scheme, Intel marketed what it called a 487SX math coprocessor. Motherboard manufacturers installed an Intel-designed socket for this so-called 487 chip. In reality, however, the 487SX math chip was a special 486DX chip with the math coprocessor enabled. When you plugged this chip into your motherboard, it disabled the 486SX chip and gave you the functional equivalent of a full-fledged 486DX system.

AMD 486 (5x86)

AMD makes a line of 486-compatible chips that install into standard 486 motherboards. In fact, AMD makes the fastest 486 processor available, which they call the Am5x86(TM)-P75. The name is a little misleading, as the 5x86 part makes some people think that this is a fifth-generation Pentium-type processor. In reality, it is a fast clock-multiplied (4x clock) 486 that runs at four times the speed of the 33MHz 486 motherboard you plug it into.

The 5x85 offers high-performance features such as a unified 16KB write-back cache and 133MHz core clock speed; it is approximately comparable to a Pentium 75, which is why it is denoted with a P-75 in the part number. It is the ideal choice for cost-effective 486 upgrades, where changing the motherboard is difficult or impossible.

Not all motherboards support the 5x86. The best way to verify that your motherboard supports the chip is by checking with the documentation that came with the board. Look for keywords such as "Am5X86," "AMD-X5," "clock-quadrupled," "133MHz," or other similar wording. Another good way to determine whether your motherboard supports the AMD 5x86 is to look for it in the listed models on AMD's Web site.

There are a few things to note when installing a 5x86 processor into a 486 motherboard:

- The operating voltage for the 5x86 is 3.45v +/- 0.15v. Not all motherboards may have this setting, but most that incorporate a Socket 3 design should. If your 486 motherboard is a Socket 1 or 2 design, you cannot use the 5x86 processor directly. The 3.45 volt processor will not operate in a 5-volt socket and may be damaged. To convert a 5-volt motherboard to 3.45 volts, adapters can be purchased from several vendors including Kingston, Evergreen, and AMP. In fact, Kingston and Evergreen sell the 5x86 complete with a voltage regulator adapter attached in an easy-to-install package. These versions are ideal for older 486 motherboards that don't have a Socket 3 design.

- It is generally better to purchase a new motherboard with Socket 3 than to buy one of these adapters; however, 486 motherboards are hard to find these days, and your old board may be in a proprietary form factor for which it is impossible to find a replacement. Buying a new motherboard is also better than using an adapter because the older BIOS may not understand the requirements of the processor as far as speed is concerned. BIOS updates are often required with older boards.

- Most Socket 3 motherboards have jumpers, allowing you to set the voltage manually. Some boards don't have jumpers, but have voltage autodetect instead. These systems check the VOLDET pin (pin S4) on the microprocessor when the system is powered on.

- The VOLDET pin is tied to ground (Vss) internally to the microprocessor. If you cannot find any jumpers for setting voltage, you can check the motherboard as follows: Switch the PC off, remove the microprocessor, connect pin S4 to a Vss pin on the ZIF socket, power on, and check any Vcc pin with a voltmeter. This should read 3.45 (± 0.15) volts. See the previous section on CPU sockets for the pinout.

- The 5x86 requires a 33MHz motherboard speed, so be sure the board is set to that frequency. The 5x86 operates at an internal speed of 133MHz. Therefore, the jumpers must be set for "clock-quadrupled" or "4x clock" mode. By setting the jumpers correctly on the motherboard, the CLKMUL pin (pin R17) on the processor will be connected to ground (Vss). If there is no 4x clock setting, the standard DX2 2x clock setting should work.

- Some motherboards have jumpers that configure the internal cache in either write-back (WB) or write-through (WT) mode. They do this by pulling the WB/WT pin (pin B13) on the microprocessor to logic High (Vcc) for WB or to ground (Vss) for WT. For best performance, configure your system in WB mode; however, reset the cache to WT mode if there are problems running applications or the floppy drive doesn't work right (DMA conflicts).

- The 5x86 runs hot, so a heat sink is required; it normally must have a fan.

In addition to the 5x86, the AMD enhanced 486 product line includes 80MHz, 100MHz, and 1,20MHz CPUs. These are the A80486DX2-80SV8B (40MHz×2), A80486DX4-100SV8B (33MHz×3), and the A80486DX4–120SV8B (40MHz×3).

Cyrix/TI 486

The Cyrix 486DX2/DX4 processors were available in 100MHz, 80MHz, 75MHz, 66MHz, and 50MHz versions. Like the AMD 486 chips, the Cyrix versions are fully compatible with Intel's 486 processors and work in most 486 motherboards.

The Cx486DX2/DX4 incorporates an 8KB write-back cache, an integrated floating-point unit, advanced power management, and SMM, and was available in 3.3v versions.

Note

TI originally made all the Cyrix-designed 486 processors, and under their agreement they also sold them under the TI name. Eventually, TI and Cyrix had a falling out, and now IBM makes most of the Cyrix chips, although that might change since National Semiconductor has purchased Cyrix, and is now attempting to sell it.

P5 (586) Fifth-Generation Processors

Pentium Processors

On October 19, 1992, Intel announced that the fifth generation of its compatible microprocessor line (code-named P5) would be named the Pentium processor rather than the 586, as everybody had been assuming. Calling the new chip the 586 would have been natural, but Intel discovered that it could not trademark a number designation, and the company wanted to prevent other manufacturers from using the same name for any clone chips that they might develop. The actual Pentium chip shipped on March 22, 1993. Systems that use these chips were only a few months behind.

The Pentium is fully compatible with previous Intel processors, but it also differs from them in many ways. At least one of these differences is revolutionary: The Pentium features twin data pipelines, which enable it to execute two instructions at the same time. The 486 and all preceding chips can perform only a single instruction at a time. Intel calls the capability to execute two instructions at the same time superscalar technology. This technology provides additional performance compared with the 486.

The standard 486 chip can execute a single instruction in an average of two clock cycles—cut to an average of one clock cycle with the advent of internal clock multiplication used in the DX2 and DX4 processors. With superscalar technology, the Pentium can execute many instructions at a rate of two instructions per cycle. Superscalar architecture usually is associated with high-output RISC (Reduced Instruction Set Computer) chips. The Pentium is one of the first CISC (Complex Instruction Set Computer) chips to be considered superscalar. The Pentium is almost like having two 486 chips under the hood. Table 3.20 shows the Pentium processor specifications.

Table 3.20 Pentium Processor Specifications

Introduced	March 22, 1993 (first generation); March 7, 1994 (second generation)
Maximum rated speeds	60, 66, 75, 90, 100, 120, 133, 150, 166, 200MHz (second generation)
CPU clock multiplier	1x (first generation), 1.5x–3x (second generation)
Register size	32-bit
External data bus	64-bit
Memory address bus	32-bit
Maximum memory	4GB
Integral-cache size	8KB code, 8KB data
Integral-cache type	Two-way set associative, write-back Data
Burst-mode transfers	Yes

(continues)

Table 3.20   Continued

Number of transistors	3.1 million
Circuit size	0.8 micron (60/66MHz), 0.6 micron (75–100MHz), 0.35 micron (120MHz and up)
External package	273-pin PGA, 296-pin SPGA, tape carrier
Math coprocessor	Built-in FPU (floating-point unit)
Power management	SMM (system management mode), enhanced in second generation
Operating voltage	5v (first generation), 3.465v, 3.3v, 3.1v, 2.9v (second generation)

PGA = Pin Grid Array

SPGA = Staggered Pin Grid Array

The two instruction pipelines within the chip are called the u- and v-pipes. The *u-pipe*, which is the primary pipe, can execute all integer and floating-point instructions. The *v-pipe* is a secondary pipe that can execute only simple integer instructions and certain floating-point instructions. The process of operating on two instructions simultaneously in the different pipes is called *pairing*. Not all sequentially executing instructions can be paired, and when pairing is not possible, only the u-pipe is used. To optimize the Pentium's efficiency, you can recompile software to allow more instructions to be paired.

The Pentium is 100 percent software-compatible with the 386 and 486, and although all current software will run much faster on the Pentium, many software manufacturers want to recompile their applications to exploit even more of the Pentium's true power. Intel has developed new compilers that will take full advantage of the chip; the company will license the technology to compiler firms so that software developers can take advantage of the Pentium's superscalar (parallel processing) capability. This optimization rapidly started to appear in the software on the market. Optimized software improved performance by allowing more instructions to execute simultaneously in both pipes.

The Pentium processor has a Branch Target Buffer (BTB), which employs a technique called branch prediction. It minimizes stalls in one or more of the pipes caused by delays in fetching instructions that branch to nonlinear memory locations. The BTB attempts to predict whether a program branch will be taken, and then fetches the appropriate instructions. The use of branch prediction enables the Pentium to keep both pipelines operating at full speed. Figure 3.33 shows the internal architecture of the Pentium processor.

The Pentium has a 32-bit address bus width, giving it the same 4GB memory-addressing capabilities as the 386DX and 486 processors. But the Pentium expands the data bus to 64 bits, which means that it can move twice as much data into or out of the CPU, compared with a 486 of the same clock speed. The 64-bit data bus requires that system memory be accessed 64 bits wide, which means that each bank of memory is 64 bits.

On most motherboards, memory is installed via SIMMs (Single Inline Memory Modules) or DIMMs (Dual Inline Memory Modules). SIMMs are available in 8-bit-wide and 32-bit-wide versions, while DIMMs are 64 bits wide. There are also versions with additional bits for parity or ECC (error correcting code) data. Most Pentium systems use the 32-bit-wide SIMMs—two of these

SIMMs per bank of memory. Most Pentium motherboards have at least four of these 32-bit SIMM sockets, providing for a total of two banks of memory. The newest Pentium systems and most Pentium II systems today use DIMMs, which are 64 bits wide—just like the processor's external data bus so only one DIMM is used per bank. This makes installing or upgrading memory much easier because DIMMs can go in one at a time and don't have to be matched up in pairs.

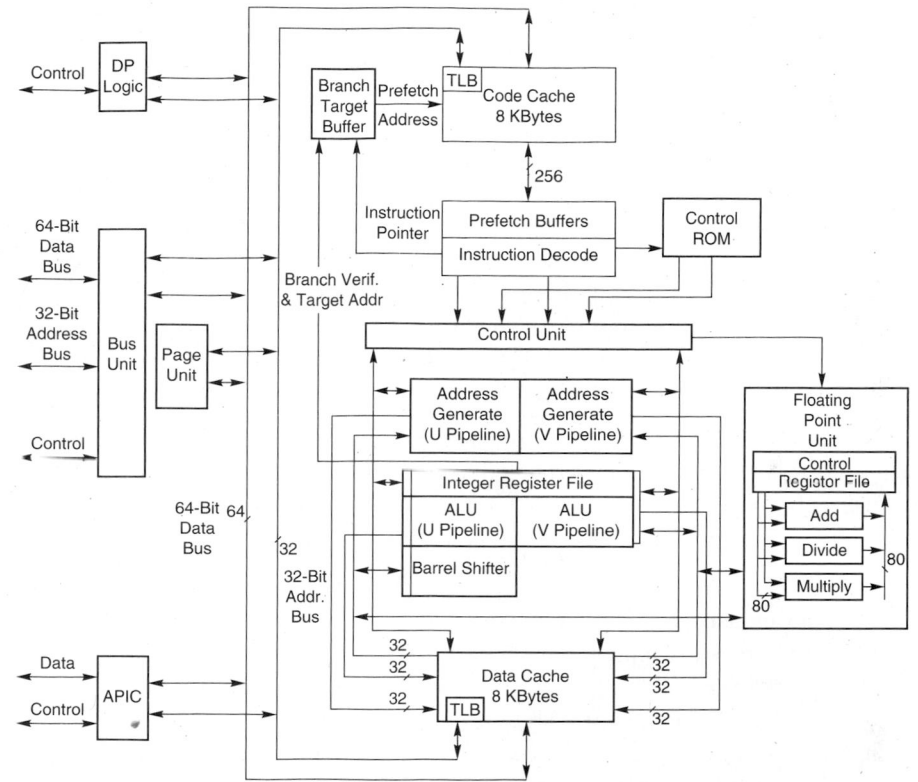

Figure 3.33   Pentium processor internal architecture.

▶▶ See "SIMMs and DIMMs," p. 437, and "Memory Banks," p. 451.

Even though the Pentium has a 64-bit data bus that transfers information 64 bits at a time into and out of the processor, the Pentium has only 32-bit internal registers. As instructions are being processed internally, they are broken down into 32-bit instructions and data elements, and processed in much the same way as in the 486. Some people thought that Intel was misleading them by calling the Pentium a 64-bit processor, but 64-bit transfers do indeed take place. Internally, however, the Pentium has 32-bit registers that are fully compatible with the 486.

The Pentium has two separate internal 8KB caches, compared with a single 8KB or 16KB cache in the 486. The cache-controller circuitry and the cache memory are embedded in the CPU chip. The cache mirrors the information in normal RAM by keeping a copy of the data and code from different memory locations. The Pentium cache also can hold information to be written to memory when the load on the CPU and other system components is less. (The 486 makes all memory writes immediately.)

The separate code and data caches are organized in a two-way set associative fashion, with each set split into lines of 32 bytes each. Each cache has a dedicated Translation Lookaside Buffer (TLB) that translates linear addresses to physical addresses. You can configure the data cache as write-back or write-through on a line-by-line basis. When you use the write-back capability, the cache can store write operations and reads, further improving performance over read-only write-through mode. Using write-back mode results in less activity between the CPU and system memory—an important improvement, because CPU access to system memory is a bottleneck on fast systems. The code cache is an inherently write-protected cache because it contains only execution instructions and not data, which is updated. Because burst cycles are used, the cache data can be read or written very quickly.

Systems based on the Pentium can benefit greatly from secondary processor caches (L2), which usually consist of up to 512KB or more of extremely fast (15ns or less) Static RAM (SRAM) chips. When the CPU fetches data that is not already available in its internal processor (L1) cache, wait states slow the CPU. If the data already is in the secondary processor cache, however, the CPU can go ahead with its work without pausing for wait states.

The Pentium uses a BiCMOS (bipolar complementary metal oxide semiconductor) process and superscalar architecture to achieve the high level of performance expected from the chip. BiCMOS adds about 10 percent to the complexity of the chip design, but adds about 30–35 percent better performance without a size or power penalty.

All Pentium processors are SL enhanced, meaning that they incorporate the SMM to provide full control of power-management features, which helps reduce power consumption. The second-generation Pentium processors (75MHz and faster) incorporate a more advanced form of SMM that includes processor clock control. This allows you to throttle the processor up or down to control power use. You can even stop the clock with these more advanced Pentium processors, putting the processor in a state of suspension that requires very little power. The second-generation Pentium processors run on 3.3v power (instead of 5v), reducing power requirements and heat generation even further.

Many current motherboards supply either 3.465v or 3.3v. The 3.465v setting is called VRE (Voltage Reduced Extended) by Intel and is required by some versions of the Pentium, particularly some of the 100MHz versions. The standard 3.3v setting is called STD (Standard), which most of the second-generation Pentiums use. STD voltage means anything in a range from 3.135v to 3.465v with 3.3v nominal. There is also a special 3.3v setting called VR (Voltage Reduced), which reduces the range from 3.300v to 3.465v with 3.38v nominal. Some of the processors require this narrower specification, which most motherboards provide. Here is a summary:

Voltage Specification	Nominal	Tolerance	Minimum	Maximum
STD (Standard)	3.30v	±0.165	3.135v	3.465v
VR (Voltage Reduced)	3.38v	±0.083	3.300v	3.465v
VRE (VR Extended)	3.50v	±0.100	3.400v	3.600v

For even lower power consumption, Intel introduced special Pentium processors with Voltage Reduction Technology in the 75 to 266MHz family; the processors are intended for mobile computer applications. They do not use a conventional chip package and are instead mounted using a new format called tape carrier packaging (TCP). The tape carrier packaging does not encase the chip in ceramic or plastic as with a conventional chip package, but instead covers the actual processor die directly with a thin, protective plastic coating. The entire processor is less than 1mm thick, or about half the thickness of a dime, and weighs less than 1 gram. They are sold to system manufacturers in a roll that looks very much like a filmstrip. The TCP processor is directly affixed (soldered) to the motherboard by a special machine, resulting in a smaller package, lower height, better thermal transfer, and lower power consumption. Special solder plugs on the circuit board located directly under the processor draw heat away and provide better cooling in the tight confines of a typical notebook or laptop system—no cooling fans are required. For more information on mobile processors and systems, see Chapter 23, "Portable PCs."

The Pentium, like the 486, contains an internal math coprocessor or FPU. The FPU in the Pentium has been rewritten and performs significantly better than the FPU in the 486, yet it is fully compatible with the 486 and 387 math coprocessor. The Pentium FPU is estimated at two to as much as 10 times faster than the FPU in the 486. In addition, the two standard instruction pipelines in the Pentium provide two units to handle standard integer math. (The math coprocessor handles only more complex calculations.) Other processors, such as the 486, have only a single-standard execution pipe and one integer math unit. Interestingly, the Pentium FPU contains a flaw that received widespread publicity. See the discussion in the section "Pentium Defects," later in this chapter.

First-Generation Pentium Processor

The Pentium has been offered in three basic designs, each with several versions. The first-generation design, which is no longer available, came in 60 and 66MHz processor speeds. This design used a 273-pin PGA form factor and ran on 5v power. In this design, the processor ran at the same speed as the motherboard—in other words, a 1x clock is used.

The first-generation Pentium was created through an 0.8 micron BiCMOS process. Unfortunately, this process, combined with the 3.1 million transistor count, resulted in a die that was overly large and complicated to manufacture. As a result, reduced yields kept the chip in short supply; Intel could not make them fast enough. The 0.8 micron process was criticized by other manufacturers, including Motorola and IBM, which had been using 0.6 micron technology for their most advanced chips. The huge die and 5v operating voltage caused the 66MHz versions to consume up to an incredible 3.2 amps or 16 watts of power, resulting in a tremendous amount of heat and problems in some systems that did not employ conservative design techniques. Fortunately, adding a fan to the processor would solve most cooling problems, as long as the fan kept running.

Much of the criticism leveled at Intel for the first-generation Pentium was justified. Some people realized that the first-generation design was just that; they knew that new Pentium versions, made in a more advanced manufacturing process, were coming. Many of those people advised against purchasing any Pentium system until the second-generation version became available.

Tip

A cardinal rule of computing is never buy the first generation of any processor. Although you can wait forever because something better always will be on the horizon, a little waiting is worthwhile in some cases.

If you do have one of these first-generation Pentiums, do not despair. As with previous 486 systems, Intel offers OverDrive upgrade chips that effectively double the processor speed of your Pentium 60 or 66. These are a single-chip upgrade, meaning they replace your existing CPU. Because subsequent Pentiums are incompatible with the Pentium 60/66 Socket 4 arrangement, these OverDrive chips were the only way to upgrade an existing first-generation Pentium without replacing the motherboard.

Rather than upgrading the processor with one only twice as fast, you should really consider a complete motherboard replacement, which would accept a newer design processor that would potentially be many times faster.

Second-Generation Pentium Processor

Intel announced the second-generation Pentium on March 7, 1994. This new processor was introduced in 90 and 100MHz versions, with a 75MHz version not far behind. Eventually, 120, 133, 150, 166, and 200MHz versions were also introduced. The second-generation Pentium uses 0.6 micron (75/90/100MHz) BiCMOS technology to shrink the die and reduce power consumption. The newer, faster 120MHz (and higher) second-generation versions incorporate an even smaller die built on a 0.35 micron BiCMOS process. These smaller dies are not changed from the 0.6 micron versions; they are basically a photographic reduction of the P54C die. The die for the Pentium is shown in Figure 3.34. Additionally, these new processors run on 3.3v power. The 100MHz version consumes a maximum 3.25 amps of 3.3v power, which equals only 10.725 watts. Further up the scale, the 150MHz chip uses 3.5 amps of 3.3v power (11.6 watts); the 166MHz unit draws 4.4 amps (14.5 watts); and the 200MHz processor uses 4.7 amps (15.5 watts).

The second-generation Pentium processors come in a 296-pin SPGA form factor that is physically incompatible with the first-generation versions. The only way to upgrade from the first generation to the second is to replace the motherboard. The second-generation Pentium processors also have 3.3 million transistors—more than the earlier chips. The extra transistors exist because additional clock-control SL enhancements were added, along with an on-chip Advanced Programmable Interrupt Controller (APIC) and dual-processor interface.

The APIC and dual-processor interface are responsible for orchestrating dual-processor configurations in which two second-generation Pentium chips can process on the same motherboard simultaneously. Many of the Pentium motherboards designed for file servers come with dual Socket 7 specification sockets, which fully support the multiprocessing capability of the new chips. Software support for what usually is called Symmetric Multi-Processing (SMP) is being integrated into operating systems such as Windows NT and OS/2.

Figure 3.34   Pentium processor die. *Photograph used by permission of Intel Corporation.*

The second-generation Pentium processors use clock-multiplier circuitry to run the processor at speeds faster than the bus. The 150MHz Pentium processor, for example, can run at 2.5 times the bus frequency, which normally is 60MHz. The 200MHz Pentium processor can run at a 3x clock in a system using a 66MHz bus speed.

Note

Some Pentium systems support 75MHz or even up to 100MHz with newer motherboard and chipset designs.

Virtually all Pentium motherboards have three speed settings: 50, 60, and 66MHz. Pentium chips are available with a variety of internal clock multipliers that cause the processor to operate at various multiples of these motherboard speeds. Table 3.21 lists the speeds of currently available Pentium processors and motherboards.

Table 3.21   Pentium CPU and Motherboard Speeds

CPU Type/Speed	CPU Clock	Motherboard Speed (MHz)
Pentium 75	1.5x	50
Pentium 90	1.5x	60
Pentium 100	1.5x	66
Pentium 120	2x	60
Pentium 133	2x	66

(continues)

Table 3.21 Continued

CPU Type/Speed	CPU Clock	Motherboard Speed (MHz)
Pentium 150	2.5x	60
Pentium 166	2.5x	66
Pentium 200	3x	66
Pentium 233	3.5x	66
Pentium 266	4x	66

The core-to-bus frequency ratio or clock multiplier is controlled in a Pentium processor by two pins on the chip labeled BF1 and BF2. Table 3.22 shows how the state of the BFx pins will affect the clock multiplication in the Pentium processor.

Table 3.22 Pentium BFx Pins and Clock Multipliers

BF1	BF2	Clock Multiplier	Bus Speed (MHz)	Core Speed (MHz)
0	1	3x	66	200
0	1	3x	60	180
0	1	3x	50	150
0	0	2.5x	66	166
0	0	2.5x	60	150
0	0	2.5x	50	125
1	0	2x/4x	66	133/266*
1	0	2x	60	120
1	0	2x	50	100
1	1	1.5x/3.5x	66	100/233*
1	1	1.5x	60	90
1	1	1.5x	50	75

The 233 and 266MHz processors have modified the 1.5x and 2x multipliers to 3.5x and 4x, respectively.

Not all chips support all the bus frequency (BF) pins or combinations of settings. In other words, some of the Pentium processors will operate only at specific combinations of these settings, or may even be fixed at one particular setting. Many of the newer motherboards have jumpers or switches that allow you to control the BF pins and, therefore, alter the clock multiplier ratio within the chip. In theory, you could run a 75MHz-rated Pentium chip at 133MHz by changing jumpers on the motherboard. This is called overclocking, and is discussed in the "Processor Speed Ratings" section of this chapter. What Intel has done to discourage overclockers in its most recent Pentiums is discussed near the end of the "Processor Manufacturing" section of this chapter.

A single-chip OverDrive upgrade is currently offered for second-generation Pentiums. These OverDrive chips are fixed at a 3x multiplier; they replace the existing Socket 5 or 7 CPU, increase processor speed up to 200MHz (with a 66MHz motherboard speed), and add MMX capability, as well. Simply stated, this means that a Pentium 100, 133, or 166 system equipped with the OverDrive chip will have a processor speed of 200MHz. Perhaps the best feature of these Pentium OverDrive chips is that they incorporate MMX technology. MMX provides greatly enhanced performance while running the multimedia applications that are so popular today.

If you have a Socket 7 motherboard, you might not need the special OverDrive versions of the Pentium processor that have built-in voltage regulators. Instead, you can purchase a standard Pentium or Pentium-compatible chip and replace the existing processor with it. You will have to be sure to set the multiplier and voltage settings so that they are correct for the new processor.

Pentium-MMX Processors

A third generation of Pentium processors (code-named P55C) was released in January 1997, which incorporates what Intel calls MMX technology into the second-generation Pentium design (see Figure 3.35). These Pentium-MMX processors are available in clock rates of 66/166MHz, 66/200MHz, and 66/233MHz, and a mobile-only version, which is 66/266MHz. The MMX processors have a lot in common with other second-generation Pentiums, including superscalar architecture, multiprocessor support, on-chip local APIC controller, and power-management features. New features include a pipelined MMX unit, 16KB code, write-back cache (versus 8KB in earlier Pentiums), and 4.5 million transistors. Pentium-MMX chips are produced on an enhanced 0.35 micron CMOS silicon process that allows for a lower 2.8v voltage level. The newer mobile 233MHz and 266MHz processors are built on a 0.25 micron process and run on only 1.8 volts. With this newer technology, the 266 processor actually uses less power than the non-MMX 133.

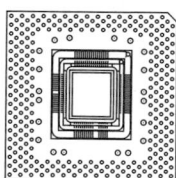 

Figure 3.35   Pentium MMX. The left side shows the underside of the chip with the cover plate removed exposing the processor die. *Photograph used by permission of Intel Corporation.*

To use the Pentium-MMX, the motherboard must be capable of supplying the lower (2.8v or less) voltage these processors use. To allow a more universal motherboard solution with respect to these changing voltages, Intel has come up with the Socket 7 with VRM. The VRM is a socketed module that plugs in next to the processor and supplies the correct voltage. Because the module is easily replaced, it is easy to reconfigure a motherboard to support any of the voltages required by the newer Pentium processors.

Of course, lower voltage is nice, but MMX is what this chip is really all about. MMX technology was developed by Intel as a direct response to the growing importance and increasing demands of multimedia and communication applications. Many such applications run repetitive loops of instructions that take vast amounts of time to execute. As a result, MMX incorporates a process Intel calls Single Instruction Multiple Data (SIMD), which allows one instruction to perform the same function on many pieces of data. Furthermore, 57 new instructions that are designed specifically to handle video, audio, and graphics data have been added to the chip.

If you want maximum future upgradability to the MMX Pentiums, make sure that your Pentium motherboard includes 321-pin processor sockets that fully meet the Intel Socket 7 specification. These would also include the VRM (Voltage Regulator Module) socket. If you have dual sockets, you can add a second Pentium processor to take advantage of SMP (Symmetric Multiprocessing) support in some newer operating systems.

Also make sure that any Pentium motherboard you buy can be jumpered or reconfigured for both 60 and 66MHz operation. This will enable you to take advantage of future Pentium OverDrive processors that will support the higher motherboard clock speeds. These simple recommendations will enable you to perform several dramatic upgrades without changing the entire motherboard.

Pentium Defects

Probably the most famous processor bug in history is the now legendary flaw in the Pentium FPU. It has often been called the FDIV bug, because it affects primarily the FDIV (floating-point divide) instruction, although several other instructions that use division are also affected. Intel officially refers to this problem as Errata No. 23, titled "Slight precision loss for floating-point divides on specific operand pairs." The bug has been fixed in the D1 or later steppings of the 60/66MHz Pentium processors, as well as the B5 and later steppings of the 75/90/100MHz processors. The 120MHz and higher processors are manufactured from later steppings, which do not include this problem. There are tables listing all the different variations of Pentium processors and steppings and how to identify them later in this chapter.

This bug caused a tremendous fervor when it first was reported on the Internet by a mathematician in October, 1994. Within a few days, news of the defect had spread nationwide, and even people who did not have computers had heard about it. The Pentium would incorrectly perform floating-point division calculations with certain number combinations, with errors anywhere from the third digit on up.

By the time the bug was publicly discovered outside of Intel, they had already incorporated the fix into the next stepping of both the 60/66MHz and the 75/90/100MHz Pentium processor, along with the other corrections they had made.

After the bug was made public and Intel admitted to already knowing about it, a fury erupted. As people began checking their spreadsheets and other math calculations, many discovered that they had also encountered this problem and did not know it. Others who had not encountered the problem had their faith in the core of their PCs very shaken. People had come to put so much trust in the PC that they had a hard time coming to terms with the fact that it might not even be capable of doing math correctly!

One interesting result of the fervor surrounding this defect is that people are less likely to implicitly trust their PCs, and are therefore doing more testing and evaluating of important results. The bottom line is that if your information and calculations are important enough, you should implement some results tests. Several math programs were found to have problems. For example, a bug was discovered in the yield function of Excel 5.0 that some were attributing to the Pentium processor. In this case, the problem turned out to be the software, which has been corrected in later versions (5.0c and later).

Intel finally decided that in the best interest of the consumer and their public image, they would begin a lifetime replacement warranty on the affected processors. This means that if you ever encounter one of the Pentium processors with the Errata 23 floating-point bug, they will replace the processor with an equivalent one without this problem. Normally, all you have to do is call Intel and ask for the replacement. They will ship you a new part matching the ratings of the one you are replacing in an overnight shipping box. The replacement is free, including all shipping charges. You merely remove your old processor, replace it with the new one, and put the old one back in the box. Then you call the overnight service who will pick it up and send it back. Intel will take a credit card number when you first call for the replacement only to ensure that the original defective chip is returned. As long as they get the original CPU back within a specified amount of time, there will be no charges to you. Intel has indicated that these defective processors will be destroyed and will not be remarketed or resold in another form.

Testing for the FPU Bug

Testing a Pentium for this bug is relatively easy. All you have to do is execute one of the test division cases cited here and see if your answer compares to the correct result.

The division calculation can be done in a spreadsheet (such as Lotus 1-2-3, Microsoft Excel, or any other), in the Microsoft Windows built-in calculator, or in any other calculating program that uses the FPU. Make sure that for the purposes of this test the FPU has not been disabled. That would normally require some special command or setting specific to the application, and would, of course, ensure that the test came out correct, no matter whether the chip is flawed or not.

The most severe Pentium floating-point errors occur as early as the third significant digit of the result. Here is an example of one of the more severe instances of the problem:

962,306,957,033 / 11,010,046 = 87,402.6282027341 (correct answer)

962,306,957,033 / 11,010,046 = 87,399.5805831329 (flawed Pentium)

Note

Note that your particular calculator program may not show the answer to the number of digits shown here. Most spreadsheet programs limit displayed results to 13 or 15 significant digits.

As you can see in the previous case, the error turns up in the third most significant digit of the result. In an examination of over 5,000 integer pairs in the 5- to 15-digit range found to produce Pentium floating-point division errors, errors beginning in the sixth significant digit were the most likely to occur.

Here is another division problem that will come out incorrectly on a Pentium with this flaw:

4,195,835 / 3,145,727 = 1.33382044913624100 (correct answer)

4,195,835 / 3,145,727 = 1.33373906890203759 (flawed Pentium)

This one shows an error in the fifth significant digit. A variation on the previous calculation can be performed as follows:

$$x = 4,195,835$$

$$y = 3,145,727$$

$$z = x - (x/y) \times y$$

$$4,195,835 - (4,195,835 / 3,145,727) \times 3,145,727 = 0 \text{ (correct answer)}$$

$$4,195,835 - (4,195,835 / 3,145,727) \times 3,145,727 = 256 \text{ (flawed Pentium)}$$

With an exact computation, the answer here should be zero. In fact, you will get zero on most machines, including those using Intel 286, 386, and 486 chips. But, on the Pentium, the answer is 256!

Here is one more calculation you can try:

$$5,505,001 / 294,911 = 18.66665197 \text{ (correct answer)}$$

$$5,505,001 / 294,911 = 18.66600093 \text{ (flawed Pentium)}$$

This one represents an error in the sixth significant digit.

There are several workarounds for this bug, but they extract a performance penalty. Because Intel has agreed to replace any Pentium processor with this flaw under a lifetime warranty replacement program, the best workaround is a free replacement!

Power Management Bugs

Starting with the second-generation Pentium processors, Intel added functions that allow these CPUs to be installed in energy-efficient systems. These are usually called *Energy Star systems* because they meet the specifications imposed by the EPA Energy Star program, but they are also unofficially called *green PCs* by many users.

Unfortunately, there have been several bugs with respect to these functions, causing them to either fail or be disabled. These bugs are in some of the functions in the power-management capabilities accessed through SMM. These problems are applicable only to the second-generation 75/90/100MHz processors, because the first-generation 60/66MHz processors do not have SMM or power-management capabilities, and all higher speed (120MHz and up) processors have the bugs fixed.

Most of the problems are related to the STPCLK# pin and the HALT instruction. If this condition is invoked by the chipset, the system will hang. For most systems, the only workaround for this problem is to disable the power-saving modes, such as suspend or sleep. Unfortunately, this means that your green PC won't be so green anymore! The best way to repair the problem is to replace the processor with a later stepping version that does not have the bug. These bugs affect the B1 stepping version of the 75/90/100MHz Pentiums, and were fixed in the B3 and later stepping versions.

Pentium Processor Models and Steppings

We know that like software, no processor is truly ever perfect. From time to time, the manufacturers will gather up what problems they have found and put into production a new stepping, which consists of a new set of masks that incorporate the corrections. Each subsequent stepping is better and more refined than the previous ones. Although no microprocessor is ever perfect, they come closer to perfection with each stepping. In the life of a typical microprocessor, a manufacturer may go through half a dozen or more such steppings.

Table 3.23 shows all the versions of the Pentium processor Model 1 (60/66MHz version), indicating the various steppings that have been available.

Table 3.23   Pentium Processor Model 1 (60/66MHz Version) Steppings

Type	Family	Model	Stepping	Mfg. Stepping	Speed	Comments Specification	Number
0	5	1	3	B1	50	Q0399	ES
0	5	1	3	B1	60	Q0352	
0	5	1	3	B1	60	Q0400	ES
0	5	1	3	B1	60	Q0394	ES, HS
0	5	1	3	B1	66	Q0353	5v1
0	5	1	3	B1	66	Q0395	ES, HS, 5v1
0	5	1	3	B1	60	Q0412	
0	5	1	3	B1	60	SX753	
0	5	1	3	B1	66	Q0413	5v2
0	5	1	3	B1	66	SX754	5v2
0	5	1	5	C1	60	Q0466	HS
0	5	1	5	C1	60	SX835	HS
0	5	1	5	C1	60	SZ949	HS, BOX
0	5	1	5	C1	66	Q0467	HS, 5v2
0	5	1	5	C1	66	SX837	HS, 5v2
0	5	1	5	C1	66	SZ950	HS, BOX, 5v2
0	5	1	7	D1	60	Q0625	HS
0	5	1	7	D1	60	SX948	HS
0	5	1	7	D1	60	SX974	HS, 5v3
0	5	1	7	D1	60	—*	HS, BOX
0	5	1	7	D1	66	Q0626	HS, 5v2
0	5	1	7	D1	66	SX950	HS, 5v2
0	5	1	7	D1	66	Q0627	HS, 5v3
0	5	1	7	D1	66	SX949	HS, 5v3
0	5	1	7	D1	66	—*	HS, BOX, 5v2

Tables 3.24, 3.25, 3.26, and 3.28 show all the different variations of Pentium

75/90/100/120/133/150/166/200/233/266MHz, classic and MMX processors. Table 3.24 lists classic (non-MMX) desktop models. Table 3.25 lists MMX desktop models. Explanations of all the specifications and the comments in the comments column follow Table 3.26, the listing of Pentium OverDrive models.

Table 3.24   Pentium Processor Versions and Steppings

Type	Family	Model	Stepping	Core Stepping	Speed (MHz) Core-Bus	S-Spec	Comments
0	5	2	1	B1	75-50	Q0540	ES
2	5	2	1	B1	75-50	Q0541	ES
0	5	2	1	B1	90-60	Q0542	STD
0	5	2	1	B1	90-60	Q0613	VR
2	5	2	1	B1	90-60	Q0543	DP
0	5	2	1	B1	100-66	Q0563	STD
0	5	2	1	B1	100-66	Q0587	VR
0	5	2	1	B1	100-66	Q0614	VR
0	5	2	1	B1	90-60	SX879	STD
0	5	2	1	B1	90-60	SX885	STD, MD
0	5	2	1	B1	90-60	SX909	VR
2	5	2	1	B1	90-60	SX874	DP, STD
0	5	2	1	B1	100-66	SX886	STD, MD
0	5	2	1	B1	100-66	SX910	VR, MD
0	5	2	2	B3	90-60	Q0628	STD
0/2	5	2	2	B3	90-60	Q0611	STD
0/2	5	2	2	B3	90-60	Q0612	VR
0	5	2	2	B3	100-66	Q0677	VRE
0	5	2	2	B3	90-60	SX923	STD
0	5	2	2	B3	90-60	SX922	VR
0	5	2	2	B3	90-60	SX921	STD
2	5	2	2	B3	90-60	SX942	DP, STD
2	5	2	2	B3	90-60	SX943	DP, VR
2	5	2	2	B3	90-60	SX944	DP, MD
0	5	2	2	B3	90-60	SZ951	BOX, STD
0	5	2	2	B3	100-66	SX960	VRE, MD
0/2	5	2	4	B5	75-50	Q0666	STD
0/2	5	2	4	B5	90-60	Q0653	STD
0/2	5	2	4	B5	90-60	Q0654	VR
0/2	5	2	4	B5	90-60	Q0655	STD, MD
0/2	5	2	4	B5	100-66	Q0656	STD, MD
0/2	5	2	4	B5	100-66	Q0657	VR, MD
0/2	5	2	4	B5	100-66	Q0658	VRE, MD
0	5	2	4	B5	120-60	Q0707	VRE

Type	Family	Model	Stepping	Core Stepping	Speed (MHz) Core-Bus	S-Spec	Comments
0	5	2	4	B5	120-60	Q0708	STD
0/2	5	2	4	B5	75-50	SX961	SID
0/2	5	2	4	B5	75-50	SZ977	BOX, STD
0/2	5	2	4	B5	90-60	SX957	STD
0/2	5	2	4	B5	90-60	SX958	VR
0/2	5	2	4	B5	90-60	SX959	STD, MD
0/2	5	2	4	B5	90-60	SZ978	BOX, STD
0/2	5	2	4	B5	100-66	SX962	VRE, MD
0/2	5	2	5	C2	75-50	Q0700	STD
0/2	5	2	5	C2	75-50	Q0749	STD, MD
0/2	5	2	5	C2	90-60	Q0699	STD
0/2	5	2	5	C2	100-50/66	Q0698	VRE, MD
0/2	5	2	5	C2	100-50/66	Q0697	STD
0	5	2	5	C2	120-60	Q0711	VRE, MD
0	5	2	5	C2	120-60	Q0732	VRE, MD
0	5	2	5	C2	133-66	Q0733	STD, MD
0	5	2	5	C2	133-66	Q0751	STD, MD
0	5	2	5	C2	133-66	Q0775	VRE, MD
0/2	5	2	5	C2	75-50	SX969	STD
0/2	5	2	5	C2	75-50	SX998	STD, MD
0/2	5	2	5	C2	75-50	SZ994	BOX, STD
0/2	5	2	5	C2	75-50	SU070	BOXF, STD
0/2	5	2	5	C2	90-60	SX968	STD
0/2	5	2	5	C2	90-60	SZ995	BOX, STD
0/2	5	2	5	C2	90-60	SU031	BOXF, STD
0/2	5	2	5	C2	100-50/66	SX970	VRE, MD
0/2	5	2	5	C2	100-50/66	SX963	STD
0/2	5	2	5	C2	100-50/66	SZ996	BOX, STD
0/2	5	2	5	C2	100-50/66	SU032	BOXF, STD
0	5	2	5	C2	120-60	SK086	VRE, MD
0	5	2	5	C2	120-60	SX994	VRE, MD
0	5	2	5	C2	120-60	SU033	BOXF, VRE, MD
0	5	2	5	C2	133-66	SK098	STD, MD
0/2	5	2	B	cB1	120-60	Q0776	STD, No, STP
0/2	5	2	B	cB1	133-66	Q0772	STD, No, STP
0/2	5	2	B	cB1	133-66	Q0773	STD,STP
0/2 MD	5	2	B	cB1	133-66	Q0774	VRE, No, STP,
0/2	5	2	B	cB1	120-60	SK110	STD, No, STP

(continues)

Table 3.24   Continued

Type	Family	Model	Stepping	Core Stepping	Speed (MHz) Core-Bus	S-Spec	Comments
0/2	5	2	B	cB1	133-66	SK106	STD, No, STP
0/2	5	2	B	cB1	133-66	S106J	STD, No, STP
0/2	5	2	B	cB1	133-66	SK107	STD, STP
0/2	5	2	B	cB1	133-66	SU038	BOXF, STD, No, STP
0/2	5	2	C	cC0	133-66	Q0843	STD, No
0/2	5	2	C	cC0	133-66	Q0844	STD
0/2	5	2	C	cC0	150-60	Q0835	STD
0/2	5	2	C	cC0	150-60	Q0878	STD, PPGA
0/2	5	2	C	cC0	150-60	SU122	BOXF, STD
0/2	5	2	C	cC0	166-66	Q0836	VRE, No
0/2	5	2	C	cC0	166-66	Q0841	VRE
0/2	5	2	C	cC0	166-66	Q0886	VRE, PPGA
0/2	5	2	C	cC0	166-66	Q0890	VRE, PPGA
0	5	2	C	cC0	166-66	Q0949	VRE, PPGA
0/2	5	2	C	cC0	200-66	Q0951F	VRE, PPGA
0	5	2	C	cC0	200-66	Q0951	VRE, PPGA
0	5	2	C	cC0	200-66	SL25H	BOXF, VRE, PPGA
0/2	5	2	C	cC0	120-60	SL22M	BOXF, STD
0/2	5	2	C	cC0	120-60	SL25J	BOX, STD
0/2	5	2	C	cC0	120-60	SY062	STD
0/2	5	2	C	cC0	133-66	SL22Q	BOXF, STD
0/2	5	2	C	cC0	133-66	SL25L	BOX, STD
0/2	5	2	C	cC0	133-66	SY022	STD
0/2	5	2	C	cC0	133-66	SY023	STD, No
0/2	5	2	C	cC0	133-66	SU073	BOXF, STD, No
0/2	5	2	C	cC0	150-60	SY015	STD
0/2	5	2	C	cC0	150-60	SU071	BOXF, STD
0/2	5	2	C	cC0	166-66	SL24R	VRE, No, MAXF
0/2	5	2	C	cC0	166-66	SY016	VRE, No
0/2	5	2	C	cC0	166-66	SY017	VRE
0/2	5	2	C	cC0	166-66	SU072	BOXF, VRE, No
0	5	2	C	cC0	166-66	SY037	VRE, PPGA
0/2	5	2	C	cC0	200-66	SY044	VRE, PPGA
0	5	2	C	cC0	200-66	SY045	BOXUF, VRE, PPGA
0	5	2	C	cC0	200-66	SU114	BOX, VRE, PPGA

Type	Family	Model	Stepping	Core Stepping	Speed (MHz) Core-Bus	S-Spec	Comments
0	5	2	C.	cC0	200-66	SL24Q	VRE, PPGA, No, MAXF
0/2	5	2	6	E0	75-50	Q0837	STD
0/2	5	2	6	E0	90-60	Q0783	STD
0/2	5	2	6	E0	100-50/66	Q0784	STD
0/2	5	2	6	E0	120-60	Q0785	VRE
0/2	5	2	6	E0	75-50	SY005	STD
0/2	5	2	6	E0	75-50	SU097	BOX, STD
0/2	5	2	6	E0	75-50	SU098	BOXF, STD
0/2	5	2	6	E0	90-60	SY006	STD
0/2	5	2	6	E0	100-50/66	SY007	STD
0/2	5	2	6	E0	100-50/66	SU110	BOX, STD
0/2	5	2	6	E0	100-50/66	SU099	BOXF, STD
0/2	5	2	6	E0	120-60	SY033	STD
0/2	5	2	6	E0	120-60	SU100	BOXF, STD

Table 3.25   Pentium MMX Processor Versions and Steppings

Type	Family	Model	Stepping	Core Stepping	Core Speed (MHz)	S-Spec	Comments
0/2	5	4	4	xA3	150	Q020	ES, PPGA
0/2	5	4	4	xA3	166	Q019	ES, PPGA
0/2	5	4	4	xA3	200	Q018	ES, PPGA
0/2	5	4	4	xA3	166	SL23T	BOXF, SPGA
0/2	5	4	4	xA3	166	SL23R	BOX, PPGA
0/2	5	4	4	xA3	166	SL25M	BOXF, PPGA
0/2	5	4	4	xA3	166	SY059	PPGA
0/2	5	4	4	xA3	166	SL2HU	BOX, SPGA
0/2	5	4	4	xA3	166	SL239	SPGA
0/2	5	4	4	xA3	166	SL26V	SPGA, MAXF
0/2	5	4	4	xA3	166	SL26H	PPGA, MAXF
0/2	5	4	4	xA3	200	SL26J	BOXUF, PPGA, MAXF
0/2	5	4	4	xA3	200	SY060	PPGA
0/2	5	4	4	xA3	200	SL26Q	BOX, PPGA, MAXF
0/2	5	4	4	xA3	200	SL274	BOXF, PPGA, MAXF
0/2	5	4	4	xA3	200	SL23S	BOX, PPGA
0/2	5	4	4	xA3	200	SL25N	BOXF, PPGA

(continues)

Table 3.25 **Continued**

Type	Family	Model	Stepping	Core Stepping	Core Speed (MHz)	S-Spec	Comments
0/2	5	4	3	xB1	166	Q125	ES, PPGA
0/2	5	4	3	xB1	166	Q126	ES, SPGA
0/2	5	4	3	xB1	200	Q124	ES, PPGA
0/2	5	4	3	xB1	233	Q140	ES, PPGA
0/2	5	4	3	xB1	166	SL27H	PPGA
0/2	5	4	3	xB1	166	SL27K	SPGA
0/2	5	4	3	xB1	166	SL2HX	BOX, SPGA
0/2	5	4	3	xB1	166	SL23X	BOXF, SPGA
0/2	5	4	3	xB1	166	SL2FP	BOX, PPGA
0/2	5	4	3	xB1	166	SL23V	BOXF, PPGA
0/2	5	4	3	xB1	200	SL27J	PPGA
0/2	5	4	3	xB1	200	SL2FQ	BOX, PPGA
0/2	5	4	3	xB1	200	SL23W	BOXF, PPGA
0/2	5	4	3	xB1	233	SL27S	PPGA
0/2	5	4	3	xB1	233	SL2BM	BOX, PPGA
0/2	5	4	3	xB1	233	SL293	BOXF, PPGA
0	5	4	3	mxB1	120	Q230	ES, TCP
0	5	4	3	mxB1	133	Q130	ES, TCP
0	5	4	3	mxB1	133	Q129	ES, PPGA
0	5	4	3	mxB1	150	Q116	ES, TCP
0	5	4	3	mxB1	150	Q128	ES, PPGA
0	5	4	3	mxB1	166	Q115	ES, TCP
0	5	4	3	mxB1	166	Q127	ES, PPGA
0	5	4	3	mxB1	200	Q586	PPGA
0	5	4	3	mxB1	133	SL27D	TCP
0	5	4	3	mxB1	133	SL27C	PPGA
0	5	4	3	mxB1	150	SL26U	TCP
0	5	4	3	mxB1	150	SL27B	PPGA
0	5	4	3	mxB1	166	SL26T	TCP
0	5	4	3	mxB1	166	SL27A	PPGA
0	5	4	3	mxB1	200	SL2WK	PPGA
0	5	8	1	myA0	166	Q255	TCP
0	5	8	1	myA0	166	Q252	TCP
0	5	8	1	myA0	166	SL2N6	TCP
0	5	8	1	myA0	200	Q146	TCP
0	5	8	1	myA0	233	Q147	TCP
0	5	8	1	myA0	200	SL28P	TCP
0	5	8	1	myA0	233	SL28Q	TCP

Type	Family	Model	Stepping	Core Stepping	Core Speed (MHz)	S-Spec	Comments
0	5	8	1	myA0	266	Q250	TCP
0	5	8	1	myA0	266	Q251	TCP
0	5	8	1	myA0	266	SL2N5	TCP
0	5	8	1	myA0	266	Q695	TCP
0	5	8	1	myA0	266	SL2ZH	TCP
0	5	8	2	myB2	266	Q766	TCP
0	5	8	2	myB2	266	Q767	TCP
0	5	8	2	myB2	266	SL23M	TCP
0	5	8	2	myB2	266	SL23P	TCP
0	5	8	2	myB2	300	Q768	TCP
0	5	8	2	myB2	300	SL34N	TCP

All the Pentium MMX processors listed in this table run on a 66MHz bus except for 150MHz models, which run on a 60MHz bus.

Table 3.26 shows all the versions of the Pentium OverDrive processors, indicating the various steppings that have been available. Note that the Type 1 chips in this table are 486 Pentium OverDrive processors, which are designed to replace 486 chips in systems with Socket 2 or 3. The other OverDrive processors are designed to replace existing Pentium processors in Socket 4 or 5/7.

Table 3.26   Pentium OverDrive Steppings

Type	Family	Model	Stepping	Mfg. Stepping	Speed	Spec. Number	Product	Version
1	5	3	1	B1	63	SZ953	PODP5v63	1.0
1	5	3	1	B2	63	SZ990	PODP5v63	1.1
1	5	3	2	C0	83	SU014	PODP5v83	2.1
0	5	1	A	tA0	133	SU082	PODP5v133	1.0
0	5	2	C	aC0	125	SU081	PODP3v125	1.0
0	5	2	C	aC0	150	SU083	PODP3v150	1.0
0	5	2	C	aC0	166	SU084	PODP3v166	1.0
1	5	4	4	oxA3	125/50, 150/60	SL24V	PODPMT60X150	1.0
1	5	4	4	oxA3	166/66	SL24VV	PODPMT66X166	1.0
1	5	4	3	oxB1	180/60	SL2FE	PODPMT60X180	2.0
1	5	4	3	oxB1	200/66	SL2FF	PODPMT66X200	2.0

The following list explains all the entries in the Comments columns of these Tables 3.22–3.24.

*These chips have no specification number.

ES = Engineering Sample. These chips were not sold through normal channels but were designed for development and testing purposes.

HS = Heat Spreader Package. This indicates a chip with a metal plate on the top, which is used to spread heat away from the center part of the chip. The heat spreader helps the chip run cooler; however, most later chips use a smaller, more powerful and efficient die, and Intel has been able to eliminate the heat spreader from these.

DP = Dual Processor version where Type 0 is primary only, Type 2 is secondary only, and Type 0 or 2 is either.

MD = Minimum Delay timing restrictions on several processor signals.

STD = Standard voltage range. The range for the C2 and subsequent steppings of the Pentium processor is 3.135v to 3.6v. The voltage range for B-step parts remains at 3.135v–3.465v. Note that all E0-step production parts are standard voltage.

VR = Voltage Reduced (3.300v–3.465v).

VRE = VR and Extended (3.45v–3.60v).

VRT = Voltage Reduction Technology.

TCP = Tape Carrier Package.

BOX = A retail boxed processor with a standard passive heat sink.

BOXF = A retail boxed processor with an active (fan-cooled) heat sink.

The absence of a package type in the comments column means the processor is SPGA by default.

2.285v = This is a mobile Pentium processor with MMX technology with a core operating voltage of 2.285v–2.665v.

MAXF = The part may run only at the maximum specified frequency. Specifically, a 200MHz may be run at 200MHz +0/-5 MHz (195–200MHz), and a 166MHz may be run at 166MHz +0/-5MHz (161–166MHz).

BOXUF = This part also ships as a boxed processor with an unattached fan heat sink.

1.8v = This is a mobile Pentium processor with MMX technology with a core operating voltage of 1.665v–1.935v and an I/O operating voltage of 2.375v–2.625v.

2.2v = This Pentium processor with MMX technology with a core operating voltage of 2.10v–2.34v.

2.0v = This is a mobile Pentium processor with MMX technology with a core operating voltage of 1.850v–2.150v and an I/O operating voltage of 2.375v–2.625v.

STP = The cB1 stepping is logically equivalent to the C2-step, but on a different manufacturing process. The mcB1 step is logically equivalent to the cB1 step (except it does not support DP, APIC, or FRC). The mcB1, mA1, mA4, and mcC0-steps also use Intel's VRT (Voltage Reduction Technology), and are available in the TCP and SPGA package, primarily to support mobile applications. The mxA3 is logically equivalent to the xA3 stepping, except it does not support DP or APIC.

NO = Part meets the specifications but is not tested to support 82498/82493 and 82497/82492 cache timings.

In these tables, the processor Type heading refers to the dual processor capabilities of the Pentium. Versions indicated with a Type 0 can be used only as a primary processor, while those marked as Type 2 can be used only as the secondary processor in a pair. If the processor is marked as Type 0/2, it can serve as the primary or secondary processor, or both.

The Family designation for all Pentiums is 5 (for 586), while the model indicates the particular revision. Model 1 indicates the first-generation 60/66MHz version, whereas Model 2 or later indicates the second-generation 75+MHz version. The stepping number is the actual revision of the particular model. The family, model, and stepping number can be read by software such as the Intel CPUID program. These also correspond to a particular manufacturer stepping code, which is how Intel designates the chips in-house. These are usually an alphanumeric code. For example, stepping 5 of the Model 2 Pentium is also known as the C2 stepping inside Intel.

Manufacturing stepping codes that begin with an m indicate a mobile processor. Most Pentium processors come in a standard Ceramic Pin Grid Array (CPGA) package; however, the mobile processors also use the tape carrier package (TCP). Now there is also a Plastic Pin Grid Array (PPGA) package being used to reduce cost.

To determine the specifications of a given processor, you need to look up the S-spec number in the table of processor specifications. To find your S-spec number, you have to read it off of the chip directly. It can be found printed on both the top and bottom of the chip. If your heat sink is glued on, remove the chip and heat sink from the socket as a unit and read the numbers from the bottom of the chip. Then you can look up the S-spec number in the table; it will tell you the specifications of that particular processor. Intel is introducing new chips all the time, so visit their Web site and search for the Pentium processor "Quick Reference Guide" in the developer portion of their site. There you will find a complete listing of all current processor specifications by S-spec number.

One interesting item to note is that there are several subtly different voltages required by different Pentium processors. Table 3.27 summarizes the different processors and their required voltages:

Table 3.27   Pentium Processor Voltages

Model	Stepping	Voltage Spec.	Voltage Range
1	—	Std.	4.75–5.25v
1	—	5v1	4.90–5.25v
1	—	5v2	4.90–5.40v
1	—	5v3	5.15–5.40v
2+	B1-B5	Std.	3.135–3.465v
2+	C2+	Std.	3.135–3.600v
2+	—	VR	3.300–3.465v
2+	B1-B5	VRE	3.45–3.60v
2+	C2+	VRE	3.40–3.60v
4+	—	MMX	2.70–2.90v
4	3	Mobile	2.285–2.665v
4	3	Mobile	2.10–2.34v
8	1	Mobile	1.850–2.150v
8	1	Mobile	1.665–1.935v

Many of the newer Pentium motherboards have jumpers that allow for adjustments to the different voltage ranges. If you are having problems with a particular processor, it may not be matched correctly to your motherboard voltage output.

If you are purchasing an older, used Pentium system today, I recommend using only Model 2 (second generation) or later version processors that are available in 75MHz or faster speeds. I would definitely want stepping C2 or later. Virtually all the important bugs and problems were fixed in the C2 and later releases. The newer Pentium processors have no serious bugs to worry about.

AMD-K5

The AMD-K5 is a Pentium-compatible processor developed by AMD and available as the PR75, PR90, PR100, PR120, PR133, and PR-166. Because it is designed to be physically and functionally compatible, any motherboard that properly supports the Intel Pentium should support the AMD-K5. However, a BIOS upgrade might be required to properly recognize the AMD-K5. AMD keeps a list of motherboards that have been tested for compatibility.

The K5 has the following features:

- 16KB instruction cache, 8KB write-back data cache
- Dynamic execution—branch prediction with speculative execution
- Five-stage RISC-like pipeline with six parallel functional units
- High-performance floating-point unit (FPU)
- Pin-selectable clock multiples of 1.5x and 2x

The K5 is sold under the P-Rating system, which means that the number on the chip does not indicate true clock speed, only apparent speed when running certain applications.

◀◀ See "AMD P-Ratings," p. 49.

Note that several of these processors do not run at their apparent rated speed. For example, the PR-166 version actually runs at only 117 true MHz. Sometimes this can confuse the system BIOS, which may report the true speed rather than the P-Rating, which compares the chip against an Intel Pentium of that speed. AMD claims that because of architecture enhancements over the Pentium, they do not need to run the same clock frequency to achieve that same performance. Even with such improvements, AMD markets the K5 as a fifth-generation processor, just like the Pentium.

The AMD-K5 operates at 3.52 volts (VRE Setting). Some older motherboards default to 3.3 volts, which is below specification for the K5 and could cause erratic operation.

Pseudo Fifth-Generation Processors

There is at least one processor that, while generally regarded as a fifth-generation processor, lacks many of the functions of that class of chip—the IDT Centaur C6 Winchip. True fifth-generation chips would have multiple internal pipelines, which is called superscalar architecture, allowing more than one instruction to be processed at one time. They would also feature branch prediction, another fifth-generation chip feature. As it lacks these features, the C6 is more closely related to a 486; however, the performance levels and the pinout put it firmly in the class with Pentium processors. It has turned out to be an ideal Pentium Socket 7-compatible processor for low-end systems.

IDT Centaur C6 Winchip

The C6 processor is a recent offering from Centaur, a wholly owned subsidiary of IDT (Integrated Device Technologies). It is Socket 7-compatible with Intel's Pentium, includes MMX extensions, and is available at clock speeds of 180, 200, 225, and 240MHz. Pricing is below Intel on the Pentium MMX.

Centaur is led by Glenn Henry, who spent more than two decades as a computer architect at IBM and six years as chief technology officer at Dell Computer Corp. The company is a well-established semiconductor manufacturer well-known for SRAM and other components.

As a manufacturer, IDT owns its own fabs (semiconductor manufacturing plants), which will help keep costs low on the C6 Winchip. Their expertise in SRAM manufacturing may be applied in new versions of the C6, which integrate onboard L2 cache in the same package as the core processor, similar to the Pentium Pro.

The C6 has 32KB each of instruction and data cache, just like AMD's K6 and Cyrix's 6x86MX, yet it has only 5.4 million transistors, compared with the AMD chip's 8.8 million and the Cyrix chip's 6.5 million. This allows for a very small processor die, which also reduces power consumption. Centaur achieved this small size with a streamlined design. Unlike competitor chips, the C6 is not superscalar—it issues only one instruction per clock cycle like the 486. However, with large caches, an efficient memory-management unit, and careful performance optimization of commonly used instructions, the C6 achieves performance that's comparable to a Pentium. Another benefit of the C6's simple design is low power consumption—low enough for notebook PCs. Neither AMD nor Cyrix has a processor with power consumption low enough for most laptop designs.

To keep the design simple, Centaur compromised on floating-point and MMX speed and focused instead on typical application performance. As a result, the chip's performance trails the other competitors' on some multimedia applications and games.

Intel P6 (686) Sixth-Generation Processors

The P6 (686) processors represent a new generation with features not found in the previous generation units. The P6 processor family began when the Pentium Pro was released in November 1995. Since then, many other P6 chips have been released by Intel, all using the same basic P6 core processor as the Pentium Pro. Table 3.28 shows the variations in the P6 family of processors.

Table 3.28   Intel P6 Processor Variations

Pentium Pro	Original P6 processor, includes 256KB, 512KB, or 1MB of full core-speed L2 cache
Pentium II	P6 with 512KB of half core speed L2 cache
Pentium II Xeon	P6 with 512KB, 1MB, or 2MB of full-core speed L2 cache
Celeron	P6 with no L2 cache
Celeron-A	P6 with 128KB of on-die full-core speed L2 cache
Pentium III	P6 with SSE (MMX2), 512KB of half-core speed L2 cache
Pentium IIPE	P6 with 256KB of full-core speed L2 cache
Pentium III Xeon	P6 with SSE (MMX2), 512KB, 1MB, or 2MB of full-core speed L2 cache

Even more are expected in this family, including versions of the Pentium III with on-die full-core speed L2 cache, and faster versions of the Celeron.

The main new feature in the fifth-generation Pentium processors was the superscalar architecture, where two instruction execution units could execute instructions simultaneously in parallel. Later fifth-generation chips also added MMX technology to the mix, as well. So then what did Intel add in the sixth-generation to justify calling it a whole new generation of chip? Besides many minor improvements, the real key features of all sixth-generation processors are Dynamic Execution and the Dual Independent Bus (DIB) architecture, plus a greatly improved superscalar design.

Dynamic Execution enables the processor to execute more instructions on parallel, so that tasks are completed more quickly. This technology innovation is comprised of three main elements:

■ *Multiple branch prediction*, to predict the flow of the program through several branches

■ *Dataflow analysis*, which schedules instructions to be executed when ready, independent of their order in the original program

■ *Speculative execution*, which increases the rate of execution by looking ahead of the program counter and executing instructions that are likely to be needed

Branch prediction is a feature formerly found only in high-end mainframe processors. It allows the processor to keep the instruction pipeline full while running at a high rate of speed. A special fetch/decode unit in the processor uses a highly optimized branch prediction algorithm to predict the direction and outcome of the instructions being executed through multiple levels of branches, calls, and returns. It is like a chess player working out multiple strategies in advance of game play by predicting the opponent's strategy several moves into the future. By predicting the instruction outcome in advance, the instructions can be executed with no waiting.

Dataflow analysis studies the flow of data through the processor to detect any opportunities for out-of-order instruction execution. A special dispatch/execute unit in the processor monitors many instructions and can execute these instructions in an order that optimizes the use of the multiple superscalar execution units. The resulting out-of-order execution of instructions can keep the execution units busy even when cache misses and other data-dependent instructions might otherwise hold things up.

Speculative execution is the processor's capability to execute instructions in advance of the actual program counter. The processor's dispatch/execute unit uses dataflow analysis to execute all available instructions in the instruction pool and store the results in temporary registers. A retirement unit then searches the instruction pool for completed instructions that are no longer data dependent on other instructions to run, or which have unresolved branch predictions. If any such completed instructions are found, the results are committed to memory by the retirement unit or the appropriate standard Intel architecture in the order they were originally issued. They are then retired from the pool.

Dynamic Execution essentially removes the constraint and dependency on linear instruction sequencing. By promoting out-of-order instruction execution, it can keep the instruction units working rather than waiting for data from memory. Even though instructions can be predicted and executed out of order, the results are committed in the original order so as not to disrupt or change program flow. This allows the P6 to run existing Intel architecture software exactly as the P5 (Pentium) and previous processors did, just a whole lot more quickly!

The other main P6 architecture feature is known as the Dual Independent Bus. This refers to the fact that the processor has two data buses, one for the system (motherboard) and the other just for cache. This allows the cache memory to run at speeds previously not possible.

Previous P5 generation processors have only a single motherboard host processor bus, and all data, including cache transfers, must flow through it. The main problem with that is the cache memory was restricted to running at motherboard bus speed, which was 66MHz until recently and has now moved to 100MHz. We have cache memory today that can run 500MHz or more, and main memory (SDRAM) that runs at 66 and 100MHz, so a method was needed to get faster memory closer to the processor. The solution was to essentially build in what is called a backside bus to the processor, otherwise known as a dedicated cache bus. The L2 cache would then be connected to this bus and could run at any speed. The first implementation of this was in the Pentium Pro, where the L2 cache was built right into the processor package and ran at the full core processor speed. Later, that proved to be too costly, so the L2 cache was moved outside of the processor package and onto a cartridge module, which we now know as the Pentium II/III. With that design, the cache bus could run at any speed, with the first units running the cache at half-processor speed.

By having the cache on a backside bus directly connected to the processor, the speed of the cache is scalable to the processor. In current PC architecture—66MHz Pentiums all the way through the 333MHz Pentium IIs—the motherboard runs at a speed of 66MHz. Newer Pentium II systems run a 100MHz motherboard bus and have clock speeds of 350MHz and higher. If the cache were restricted to the motherboard as is the case with Socket 7 (P5 processor) designs, the cache memory would have to remain at 66MHz, even though the processor was running as fast as 333MHz. With newer boards, the cache would be stuck at 100MHz, while the processor ran as fast as 500MHz or more. With the Dual Independent Bus (DIB) design in the P6 processors, as the processor runs faster, at higher multiples of the motherboard speed, the cache would increase by the same amount that the processor speed increases. The cache on the DIB is coupled to processor speed, so that doubling the speed of the processor also doubles the speed of the cache.

The DIB architecture is necessary to have decent processor performance in the 300MHz and beyond range. Older Socket 7 (P5 processor) designs will not be capable of moving up to these higher speeds without suffering a tremendous performance penalty due to the slow motherboard-bound L2 cache. That is why Intel is not developing any Pentium (P5 class) processors beyond 266MHz; however, the P6 processors will be available in speeds of up to 500MHz or more.

Finally, the P6 architecture upgrades the superscalar architecture of the P5 processors by adding more instruction execution units, and by breaking down the instructions into special micro-ops. This is where the CISC (Complex Instruction Set Computer) instructions are broken down into more RISC (Reduced Instruction Set Computer) commands. The RISC-level commands are smaller and easier for the parallel instruction units to execute more efficiently. With this design, Intel has brought the benefits of a RISC processor—high-speed dedicated instruction execution—to the CISC world. Note that the P5 had only two instruction units, while the P6 has at least six separate dedicated instruction units. It is said to be three-way superscalar, because the multiple instruction units can execute up to three instructions in one cycle.

Other improvements in efficiency also are included in the P6 architecture: built-in multiprocessor support, enhanced error detection and correction circuitry, and optimization for 32-bit software.

Rather than just being a faster Pentium, the Pentium Pro, Pentium II/III, and other sixth-generation processors have many feature and architectural improvements. The core of the chip is very RISC-like, while the external instruction interface is classic Intel CISC. By breaking down the CISC instructions into several different RISC instructions and running them down parallel execution pipelines, the overall performance is increased.

Compared to a Pentium at the same clock speed, the P6 processors are faster—as long as you're running 32-bit software. The P6 Dynamic Execution is optimized for performance primarily when running 32-bit software such as Windows NT. If you are using 16-bit software, such as Windows 95 or 98 (which operate part time in a 16-bit environment) and most older applications, the P6 will not provide as marked a performance improvement over similarly speed-rated Pentium and Pentium-MMX processors. That's because the Dynamic Execution capability will not be fully exploited. Because of this, Windows NT is often regarded as the most desirable operating system for use with Pentium Pro/II/III/Celeron processors. While this is not exactly true (a Pentium Pro/II/III/Celeron will run fine under Windows 95/98), Windows NT does take better advantage of the P6's capabilities. Note that it is really not so much the operating system but which applications you use. Software developers can take steps to gain the full advantages of the sixth-generation processors. This includes using modern compilers that can improve performance for all current Intel processors, writing 32-bit code where possible, and making code as predictable as possible to take advantage of the processor's Dynamic Execution multiple branch prediction capabilities.

Pentium Pro Processors

Intel's successor to the Pentium is called the Pentium Pro. The Pentium Pro was the first chip in the P6 or sixth-generation processor family. It was introduced in November 1995, and became widely available in 1996. The chip is a 387-pin unit that resides in Socket 8, so it is not pin-compatible with earlier Pentiums. The new chip is unique among processors as it is constructed in a Multi-Chip Module (MCM) physical format, which Intel is calling a Dual Cavity PGA (Pin Grid Array) package. Inside the 387-pin chip carrier are two dies. One contains the actual Pentium Pro processor (shown in Figure 3.36), and the other a 256KB (the Pentium Pro with 256KB cache is shown in Figure 3.37), 512KB, or 1MB (the Pentium Pro with 1MB cache is shown in Figure 3.37) L2 cache. The processor die contains 5.5 million transistors, the 256KB cache die contains 15.5 million transistors, and the 512KB cache die(s) have 31 million transistors each, for a potential total of nearly 68 million transistors in a Pentium Pro with 1MB of internal cache! A Pentium Pro with 1MB cache has two 512KB cache die and a standard P6 processor die (see Figure 3.38).

The main processor die includes a 16KB split L1 cache with an 8KB two-way set associative cache for primary instructions, and an 8KB four-way set associative cache for data.

Another sixth-generation processor feature found in the Pentium Pro is the Dual Independent Bus (DIB) architecture, which addresses the memory bandwidth limitations of previous-generation processor architectures. Two buses make up the DIB architecture: the L2 cache bus (contained entirely within the processor package) and the processor-to-main memory system bus. The speed of the dedicated L2 cache bus on the Pentium Pro is equal to the full core speed of the processor. This was accomplished by embedding the cache chips directly into the Pentium Pro package. The DIB processor bus architecture addresses processor-to-memory bus bandwidth limitations. It offers up to three times the performance bandwidth of the single-bus, "Socket 7" generation processors, such as the Pentium.

Figure 3.36   Pentium Pro processor die. *Photograph used by permission of Intel Corporation.*

Figure 3.37   Pentium Pro processor with 256KB L2 cache (the cache is on the left side of the processor die). *Photograph used by permission of Intel Corporation.*

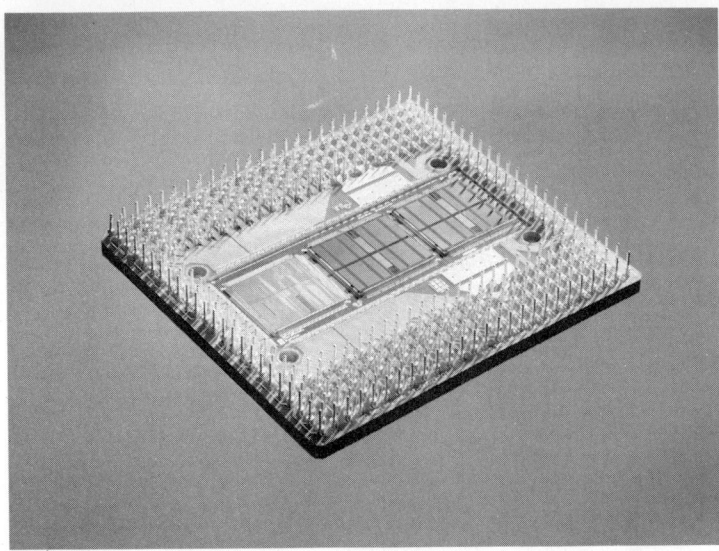

Figure 3.38   Pentium Pro processor with 1MB L2 cache (the cache is in the center and right portions of the die). *Photograph used by permission of Intel Corporation.*

Table 3.29 shows Pentium Pro processor specifications. Table 3.30 shows the specifications for each model within the Pentium Pro family, as there are many variations from model to model.

Table 3.29   Pentium Pro Family Processor Specifications

Introduced	November 1995
Maximum rated speeds	150, 166, 180, 200MHz
CPU	2.5x, 3x
Internal registers	32-bit
External data bus	64-bit
Memory address bus	36-bit
Addressable memory	64GB
Virtual memory	64TB
Integral L1-cache size	8KB code, 8KB data (16KB total)
Integrated L2-cache bus	64-bit, full core-speed
Socket/Slot	Socket 8
Physical package	387-pin Dual Cavity PGA
Package dimensions	2.46 (6.25cm) × 2.66 (6.76cm)
Math coprocessor	Built-in FPU
Power management	SMM (system management mode)
Operating voltage	3.1v or 3.3v

Table 3.30   Pentium Pro Processor Specifications by Processor Model

Pentium Pro Processor (200MHz) with 1MB Integrated Level 2 Cache

Introduction date	August 18, 1997
Clock speeds	200MHz (66MHz × 3)
Number of transistors	5.5 million (0.35 micron process), plus 62 million in 1MB L2 cache (0.35 micron)
Cache Memory	8Kx2 (16KB) L1, 1MB core-speed L2
Die Size	0.552 (14.0mm)

Pentium Pro Processor (200MHz)

Introduction date	November 1, 1995
Clock speeds	200MHz (66MHz × 3)
iCOMP Index 2.0 rating	220
Number of transistors	5.5 million (0.35 micron process), plus 15.5 million in 256KB L2 cache (0.6 micron), or 31 million in 512KB L2 cache (0.35 micron)
Cache Memory	8Kx2 (16KB) L1, 256KB or 512KB core-speed L2
Die Size	0.552 inches per side (14.0mm)

Pentium Pro Processor (180MHz)

Introduction date	November 1, 1995
Clock speeds	180MHz (60MHz × 3)
iCOMP Index 2.0 rating	197
Number of transistors	5.5 million (0.35 micron process), plus 15.5 million in 256KB L2 cache (0.6 micron)
Cache Memory	8Kx2 (16KB) L1, 256KB core-speed L2
Die Size	0.552 inches per side (14.0mm)

Pentium Pro Processor (166MHz)

Introduction date	November 1, 1995
Clock speeds	166MHz (66MHz × 2.5)
Number of transistors	5.5 million (0.35 micron process), plus 31 million in 512KB L2 cache (0.35 micron)
Cache Memory	8Kx2 L1, 512KB core-speed L2
Die Size	0.552 inches per side (14.0mm)

Pentium Pro Processor (150MHz)

Introduction date	November 1, 1995
Clock speeds	150MHz (60MHz × 2.5)
Number of transistors	5.5 million (0.6 micron process), plus 15.5 million in 256KB L2 cache (0.6 micron)
Cache Memory	8Kx2 speed L2
Die Size	0.691 inches per side (17.6mm)

As you saw in Table 3.3, performance comparisons on the iCOMP 2.0 Index rate a classic Pentium 200MHz at 142, whereas a Pentium Pro 200MHz scores an impressive 220. Just for comparison, note that a Pentium MMX 200MHz falls right about in the middle in regards to performance at 182. Keep in mind that using a Pentium Pro with any 16-bit software applications will nullify much of the performance gain shown by the iCOMP 2.0 rating.

Like the Pentium before it, the Pentium Pro runs clock multiplied on a 66MHz motherboard. The following table lists speeds for Pentium Pro processors and motherboards.

CPU Type/Speed	CPU Clock	Motherboard Speed
Pentium Pro 150	2.5x	60
Pentium Pro 166	2.5x	66
Pentium Pro 180	3x	60
Pentium Pro 200	3x	66

The integrated L2 cache is one of the really outstanding features of the Pentium Pro. By building the L2 cache into the CPU and getting it off the motherboard, they can now run the cache at full processor speed rather than the slower 60 or 66MHz motherboard bus speeds. In fact, the L2 cache features its own internal 64-bit backside bus, which does not share time with the external 64-bit frontside bus used by the CPU. The internal registers and data paths are still 32-bit, as with the Pentium. By building the L2 cache into the system, motherboards can be cheaper because they no longer require separate cache memory. Some boards may still try to include cache memory in their design, but the general consensus is that L3 cache (as it would be called) would offer less improvement with the Pentium Pro than with the Pentium.

One of the features of the built-in L2 cache is that multiprocessing is greatly improved. Rather than just SMP, as with the Pentium, the Pentium Pro supports a new type of multiprocessor configuration called the Multiprocessor Specification (MPS 1.1). The Pentium Pro with MPS allows configurations of up to four processors running together. Unlike other multiprocessor configurations, the Pentium Pro avoids cache coherency problems because each chip maintains a separate L1 and L2 cache internally.

Pentium Pro-based motherboards are pretty much exclusively PCI and ISA bus-based, and Intel is producing their own chipsets for these motherboards. The first chipset was the 450KX/GX (code-named Orion), while the most recent chipset for use with the Pentium Pro is the 440LX (Natoma). Due to the greater cooling and space requirements, Intel designed the new ATX motherboard form factor to better support the Pentium Pro and other future processors, such as the Pentium II. Even so, the Pentium Pro can be found in all types of motherboard designs; ATX is not mandatory.

▶▶ See "Motherboard Form Factors," p. 204, and "Sixth-Generation (P6 Pentium Pro/Pentium II Class) Chipsets," p. 252.

Some Pentium Pro system manufacturers have been tempted to stick with the Baby-AT form factor. The big problem with the standard Baby-AT form factor is keeping the CPU properly cooled. The massive Pentium Pro processor consumes more than 25 watts and generates an appreciable amount of heat.

Four special Voltage Identification (VID) pins are on the Pentium Pro processor. These pins can be used to support automatic selection of power supply voltage. This means that a Pentium Pro motherboard does not have voltage regulator jumper settings like most Pentium boards, which greatly eases the setup and integration of a Pentium Pro system. These pins are not actually signals, but are either an open circuit in the package or a short circuit to voltage. The sequence of opens and shorts define the voltage required by the processor. In addition to allowing for automatic voltage settings, this feature has been designed to support voltage specification variations on future Pentium Pro processors. The VID pins are named VID0 through VID3 and the definition of these pins is shown in Table 3.31. A 1 in this table refers to an open pin and 0 refers to a short to ground. The voltage regulators on the motherboard should supply the voltage that is requested or disable itself.

Table 3.31   Pentium Pro Voltage Identification Definition

VID[3:0]	Voltage Setting		VID[3:0]	Voltage Setting
0000	3.5		1000	2.7
0001	3.4		1001	2.6
0010	3.3		1010	2.5
0011	3.2		1011	2.4
0100	3.1		1100	2.3
0101	3.0		1101	2.2
0110	2.9		1110	2.1
0111	2.8		1111	No CPU present

Most Pentium Pro processors run at 3.3v, but a few run at 3.1v. Although those are the only versions available now, support for a wider range of VID settings will benefit the system in meeting the power requirements of future Pentium Pro processors. Note that the 1111 (or all opens) ID can be used to detect the absence of a processor in a given socket.

The Pentium Pro never did become very popular on the desktop, but has found a niche in file server applications due primarily to the full core-speed high-capacity internal L2 cache. It is expected that Intel will introduce only one or two more variations of the Pentium Pro, primarily as upgrade processors for those who want to install a faster CPU in their existing Pentium Pro motherboard. In most cases, it would be wiser to install a new Pentium II motherboard instead.

The following tables list the unique specifications of the different models of the Pentium Pro.

As with other processors, the Pentium Pro has been available in a number of different revisions and steppings. The following table shows all the versions of the Pentium Pro. They can be identified by the Specification number printed on the top and bottom of the chip.

Type	Family	Model	Stepping	Mfg. Stepping	L2 Size/ Stepping	Speed Core/Bus	Spec. (+/-5%)	Voltage	Notes
0	6	1	1	B0	256/a	133/66	Q0812	3.1v	3,4
0	6	1	1	B0	256/a	150/60	Q0813	3.1v	3,4
0	6	1	1	B0	256/a	133/66	Q0815	3.1v	3,4
0	6	1	1	B0	256/a	150/60	Q0816	3.1v	3,4

(continues)

(continued)

Type	Family	Model	Stepping	Mfg. Stepping	L2 Size/ Stepping	Speed Core/Bus	Spec. (+/-5%)	Voltage	Notes
0	6	1	1	B0	256/a	150/60	SY002	3.1v	3
0	6	1	1	B0	256/a	150/60	SY011	3.1v	
0	6	1	1	B0	256/a	150/60	SY014	3.1v	
0	6	1	2	C0	256/a	150/60	Q0822	3.1v	3,4
0	6	1	2	C0	256/a	150/60	Q0825	3.1v	4
0	6	1	2	C0	256/a	150/60	Q0826	3.1v	4
0	6	1	2	C0	256/a	150/60	SY010	3.1v	
0	6	1	6	sAO 2	256/a	180/60	Q0858	3.3v	4
0	6	1	6	sAO 2	256/a	200/66	Q0859	3.3v	4
0	6	1	6	sAO 2	256/a	180/60	Q0860	3.3v	4,5
0	6	1	6	sAO 2	256/a	200/66	Q0861	3.3v	4,5
0	6	1	6	sAO 2	512/ Pre 6	166/66	Q0864	3.3v	4
0	6	1	6	sAO 2	512/ Pre 6	200/66	Q0865	3.3v	4
0	6	1	6	sAO 2	256/a	180/60	Q0873	3.3v	4
0	6	1	6	sAO 2	256/a	200/66	Q0874	3.3v	4
0	6	1	6	sAO 2	256/a	180/60	Q0910	3.3v	
0	6	1	6	sAO 2	256/a	180/60	SY012	3.3v	
0	6	1	6	sAO 2	256/a	200/66	SY013	3.3v	
0	6	1	7	sA1	256/a	200/66	Q076	3.3v	7
0	6	1	7	sA1	256/a	180/60	Q0871	3.3v	4
0	6	1	7	sA1	256/a	200/66	Q0872	3.3v	4
0	6	1	7	sA1	256/a	180/60	Q0907	3.3v	4
0	6	1	7	sA1	256/a	200/66	Q0908	3.3v	4
0	6	1	7	sA1	256/b	200/66	Q0909	3.3v	4
0	6	1	7	sA1	512/ Pre 6	166/66	Q0918	3.3v	4
0	6	1	7	sA1	512/ Pre 6	200/66	Q0920	3.3v	4
0	6	1	7	sA1	512/ Pre 6	200/66	Q0924	3.3v	4
0	6	1	7	sA1	512/a	166/66	Q0929	3.3v	4
0	6	1	7	sA1	512/a	200/66	Q932	3.3v	4
0	6	1	7	sA1	512/b	166/66	Q935	3.3v	4
0	6	1	7	sA1	512/b	200/66	Q936	3.3v	4
0	6	1	7	sA1	256/a	200/66	SL245	3.5v	7
0	6	1	7	sA1	256/a	200/66	SL247	3.5v	7
0	6	1	7	sA1	256/b	180/60	SU103	3.3v	8
0	6	1	7	sA1	256/b	200/66	SU104	3.3v	8
0	6	1	7	sA1	256/b	180/60	SY031	3.3v	
0	6	1	7	sA1	256/b	200/66	SY032	3.3v	

Type	Family	Model	Stepping	Mfg. Stepping	L2 Size/ Stepping	Speed Core/Bus	Spec. (+/-5%)	Voltage	Notes
0	6	1	7	sA1	512/a	166/66	SY034	3.3v	
0	6	1	7	sA1	256/a	180/60	SY039	3.3v	
0	6	1	7	sA1	256/b	200/66	SY040	3.3v	
0	6	1	7	sA1	512/b	166/66	SY047	3.3v	
0	6	1	7	sA1	512/b	200/66	SY048	3.3v	
0	6	1	9	sB1	512/b	166/66	Q008	3.3v	4
0	6	1	9	sB1	512/b	166/66	Q009	3.3v	4
0	6	1	9	sB1	512/b	200/66	Q010	3.3v	4
0	6	1	9	sB1	512/b	200/66	Q011	3.3v	4
0	6	1	9	sB1	256/b	180/60	Q033	3.3v	4
0	6	1	9	sB1	256/b	200/66	Q034	3.3v	4
0	6	1	9	sB1	256/b	180/60	Q035	3.3v	4
0	6	1	9	sB1	256/b	200/66	Q036	3.3v	4
0	6	1	9	sB1	256/b	200/66	Q083	3.5v	7
0	6	1	9	sB1	256/b	200/66	Q084	3.5v	7
0	6	1	9	sB1	256/b	180/60	SL22S	3.3v	
0	6	1	9	sB1	256/b	200/66	SL22T	3.3v	
0	6	1	9	sB1	256/b	180/60	SL22U	3.3v	
0	6	1	9	sB1	256/b	200/66	SL22V	3.3v	9
0	6	1	9	sB1	512/b	166/66	SL22X	3.3v	
0	6	1	9	sB1	512/b	200/66	SL22Z	3.3v	
0	6	1	9	sB1	256/b	180/60	SL23L	3.3v	8
0	6	1	9	sB1	256/b	200/66	SL23M	3.3v	8
0	6	1	9	sB1	256/b	200/66	SL254	3.5v	7
0	6	1	9	sB1	256/b	200/66	SL255	3.5v	7
0	6	1	9	sB1	512/b	166/66	SL2FJ	3.3v	8
0	6	1	9	sB1	1024/g	200/66	SL259	3.3v	
0	6	1	9	sB1	1024/g	200/66	SL25A	3.3v	

1. *L2 cache stepping refers to the silicon revision of the 256KB, 512KB, or 1MB on-chip L2 cache. The "a" designation refers to the first production steppings; the "b" to the second production steppings, and so on.*

2. *The sA0 stepping is logically equivalent to the C0 stepping, but on a different manufacturing process.*

3. *The VID pins are not supported on these parts.*

4. *These are engineering samples only, provided under a Pentium Pro processor nondisclosure loan agreement.*

5. *The VID pins are functional but not tested on these parts.*

6. *These sample parts are equipped with a preproduction 512KB L2 cache.*

7. *These components have additional specification changes associated with them:*

a. *Primary Voltage = 3.5v*

b. *Max Thermal Design Power = 39.4W @ 200MHz, 256KB L2*

c. *Max Current = 11.9A*

d. *The VID pins are not supported on these parts.*

8. *This is a boxed Pentium Pro processor with an unattached fan heat sink.*

9. *This part also ships as a boxed processor with an unattached fan heat sink.*

Pentium II Processors

Intel revealed the Pentium II in May 1997. Prior to its official unveiling, the Pentium II processor was popularly referred to by its code name Klamath, and was surrounded by much speculation throughout the industry. The Pentium II is essentially the same sixth-generation processor as the Pentium Pro, with MMX technology added (which included double the L1 cache and 57 new MMX instructions); however, there are a few twists to the design. The Pentium II processor die is shown in Figure 3.39.

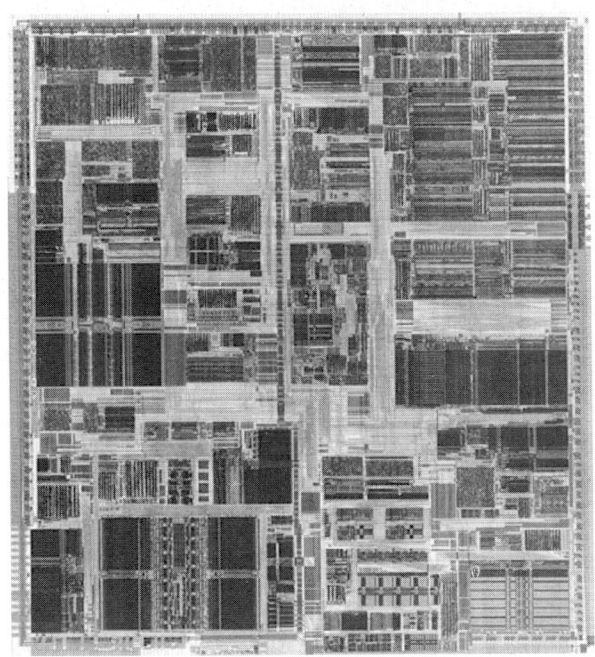

Figure 3.39   Pentium II Processor die. *Photograph used by permission of Intel Corporation.*

From a physical standpoint, it is truly something new. Abandoning the chip in a socket approach used by virtually all processors up until this point, the Pentium II chip is characterized by its Single Edge Contact (SEC) cartridge design. The processor, along with several L2 cache chips, is mounted on a small circuit board (much like an oversized-memory SIMM) as shown in Figure 3.40, which is then sealed in a metal and plastic cartridge. The cartridge is then plugged into the motherboard through an edge connector called Slot 1, which looks very much like an adapter card slot.

There are two variations on these cartridges, called SECC (Single Edge Contact Cartridge) and SECC2. Figure 3.41 shows a diagram of the SECC package. Figure 3.42 shows the SECC2 package.

Figure 3.40   Pentium II Processor Board (inside SEC cartridge). *Photograph used by permission of Intel Corporation.*

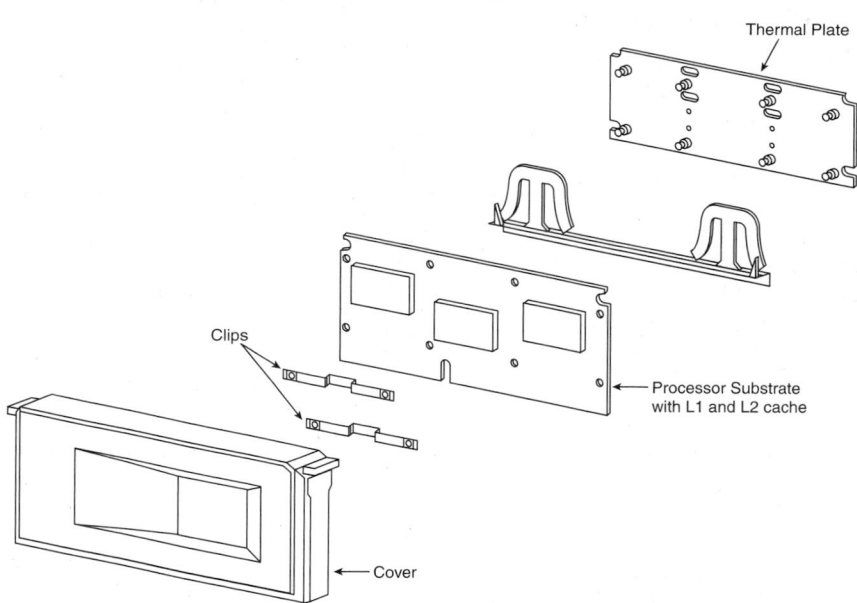

Figure 3.41   SECC components showing enclosed processor board.

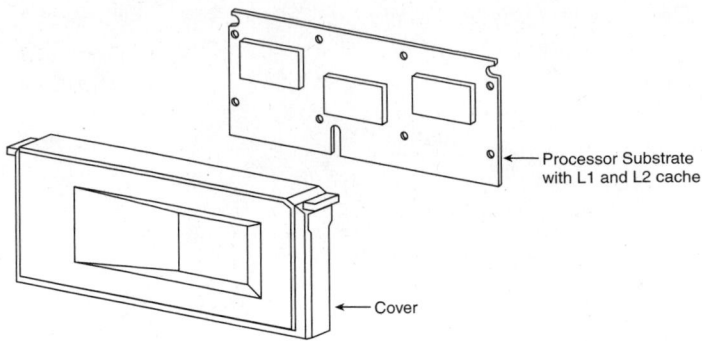

Processor Substrate
with L1 and L2 cache

Cover

Figure 3.42 2 Single Edge Contact Cartridge, rev. 2 components showing half-enclosed processor board.

As you can see from these figures, the SECC2 version is cheaper to make because it uses fewer overall parts. It also allows for a more direct heat sink attachment to the processor for better cooling. Intel transitioned from SECC to SECC2 in the beginning of 1999; all newer PII/PIII cartridge processors use the improved SECC2 design.

By using separate chips mounted on a circuit board, Intel can build the Pentium II much less expensively than the multiple die within a package used in the Pentium Pro. They can also use cache chips from other manufacturers, and more easily vary the amount of cache in future processors compared to the Pentium Pro design.

At present, Intel is offering Pentium II processors with the following speeds:

CPU Type/Speed	CPU Clock	Motherboard Speed
Pentium II 233MHz	3.5x	66MHz
Pentium II 266MHz	4x	66MHz
Pentium II 300MHz	4.5x	66MHz
Pentium II 333MHz	5x	66MHz
Pentium II 350MHz	3.5x	100MHz
Pentium II 400MHz	4x	100MHz
Pentium II 450MHz	4.5x	100MHz

The Pentium II processor core has 7.5 million transistors and is based on Intel's advanced P6 architecture. The Pentium II started out using .35 micron process technology, although the 333MHz and faster Pentium IIs are based on 0.25 micron technology. This enables a smaller die, allowing increased core frequencies and reduced power consumption. At 333MHz, the Pentium II processor delivers a 75–150 percent performance boost, compared to the 233MHz Pentium processor with MMX technology, and approximately 50 percent more performance on multimedia benchmarks. These are very fast processors, at least for now. As shown in Table 3.3, the iCOMP 2.0 Index rating for the Pentium II 266MHz chip is more than twice as fast as a classic Pentium 200MHz.

Aside from speed, the best way to think of the Pentium II is as a Pentium Pro with MMX technology instructions and a slightly modified cache design. It has the same multiprocessor scalability as the Pentium Pro, as well as the integrated L2 cache. The 57 new multimedia-related instructions carried over from the MMX processors and the capability to process repetitive loop commands more efficiently are also included. Also included as a part of the MMX upgrade is double the internal L1 cache from the Pentium Pro (from 16KB total to 32KB total in the Pentium II).

The original Pentium II processors were manufactured using a 0.35 micron process. More recent models, starting with the 333MHz version, have been manufactured using a newer 0.25 micron process. Intel is considering going to a 0.18 micron process in the future. By going to the smaller process, power draw is greatly reduced.

Maximum power usage for the Pentium II is shown in the following table.

Core Speed	Power Draw	Process	Voltage
450MHz	27.1w	0.25 micron	2.0v
400MHz	24.3w	0.25 micron	2.0v
350MHz	21.5w	0.25 micron	2.0v
333MHz	23.7w	0.25 micron	2.0v
300MHz	43.0w	0.35 micron	2.8v
266MHz	38.2w	0.35 micron	2.8v
233MHz	34.8w	0.35 micron	2.8v

You can see that the highest speed 450MHz version of the Pentium II actually uses less power than the slowest original 233MHz version! This was accomplished by using the smaller 0.25 micron process and running the processor on a lower voltage of only 2.0v. Future Pentium III processors will use the 0.25- and 0.18 micron processes and even lower voltages to continue this trend.

The Pentium II includes Dynamic Execution, which describes unique performance-enhancing developments by Intel and was first introduced in the Pentium Pro processor. Major features of Dynamic Execution include Multiple Branch Prediction, which speeds execution by predicting the flow of the program through several branches; Dataflow Analysis, which analyzes and modifies the program order to execute instructions when ready; and Speculative Execution, which looks ahead of the program counter and executes instruction that are likely to be needed. The Pentium II processor expands on these capabilities in sophisticated and powerful new ways to deliver even greater performance gains.

Like the Pentium Pro, the Pentium II also includes DIB architecture. The term *Dual Independent Bus* comes from the existence of two independent buses on the Pentium II processor—the L2 cache bus and the processor-to-main-memory system bus. The Pentium II processor can use both buses simultaneously, thus getting as much as 2× more data in and out of the Pentium II processor than a single-bus architecture processor. The DIB architecture enables the L2 cache of the 333MHz Pentium II processor to run 2 1/2 times as fast as the L2 cache of Pentium processors. As the frequency of future Pentium II processors increases, so will the speed of the L2 cache. Also, the pipelined system bus enables simultaneous parallel transactions instead of singular sequential transactions. Together, these DIB architecture improvements offer up to three times the bandwidth performance over a single-bus architecture as with the regular Pentium.

Table 3.32 shows the general Pentium II processor specifications. Table 3.33 shows the specifications that vary by model for the models that have been introduced to date.

Table 3.32   Pentium II General Processor Specifications

Bus Speeds	66MHz, 100MHz
CPU clock multiplier	3.5x, 4x, 4.5x, 5x
CPU Speeds	233MHz, 266MHz, 300MHz, 333MHz, 350MHz, 400MHz, 450MHz
Cache Memory	16Kx2 (32KB) L1, 512KB 1/2-speed L2
Internal Registers	32-bit
External Data Bus	64-bit system bus w/ ECC; 64-bit cache bus w/ optional ECC
Memory Address Bus	36-bit
Addressable Memory	64GB
Virtual Memory	64TB
Physical package	Single Edge Contact Cartridge (S.E), 242 pins
Package Dimensions	5.505 in. (12.82cm)x2.473 inches (6.28cm)x0.647 in. (1.64cm)
Math coprocessor	Built-in FPU (floating-point unit)
Power management	SMM (System Management Mode)

Table 3.33   Pentium II Specifications by Model

Pentium II MMX Processor (350, 400 and 450MHz)	
Introduction date	April 15, 1998
Clock speeds	350MHz (100MHzx3.5), 400MHz (100MHz x4), and 450MHz (100MHzx4.5)
iCOMP Index 2.0 rating	386 (350MHz), 440 (400MHz), and 483 (450MHz)
Number of transistors	7.5 million (0.25 micron process), plus 31 million in 512KB L2 cache
Cacheable RAM	4GB
Operating voltage	2.0v
Slot	Slot 2
Die Size	0.400 inches per side (10.2mm)

Mobile Pentium II Processor (266, 300, 333, and 366MHz)	
Introduction date	January 25, 1999
Clock speeds	266, 300, 333, and 366MHz
Number of transistors	27.4 million (0.25 micron process), 256KB on-die L2 cache
Ball Grid Array (BGA)	Number of balls = 615
Dimensions	Width = 31mm; Length = 35mm
Core voltage	1.6 volts
Thermal design power ranges by frequency	366MHz = 9.5 watts; 333MHz = 8.6 watts; 300MHz = 7.7 watts; 266MHz = 7.0 watts

Pentium II MMX Processor (333MHz)

Introduction date	January 26, 1998
Clock speeds	333MHz (66MHzx5)
iCOMP Index 2.0 rating	366
Number of transistors	7.5 million (0.25 micron process), plus 31 million in 512KB L2 cache
Cacheable RAM	512MB
Operating voltage	2.0v
Slot	Slot 1
Die Size	0.400 inches per side (10.2mm)

Pentium II MMX Processor (300MHz)

Introduction date	May 7, 1997
Clock speeds	300MHz (66MHzx4.5)
iCOMP Index 2.0 rating	332
Number of transistors	7.5 million (0.35 micron process), plus 31 million in 512KB L2 cache
Cacheable RAM	512MB
Die Size	0.560 inches per side (14.2mm)

Pentium II MMX Processor (266MHz)

Introduction date	May 7, 1997
Clock speeds	266MHz (66MHzx4)
iCOMP Index 2.0 rating	303
Number of transistors	7.5 million (0.35 micron process), plus 31 million in 512KB L2 cache
Cacheable RAM	512MB
Slot	Slot 1
Die Size	0.560 inches per side (14.2mm)

Pentium II MMX Processor (233MHz)

Introduction date	May 7, 1997
Clock speeds	233MHz (66MHzx3.5)
iCOMP Index 2.0 rating	267
Number of transistors	7.5 million (0.35 micron process), plus 31 million in 512KB L2 cache
Cacheable RAM	512MB
Slot	Slot 1
Die Size	0.560 inches per side (14.2mm)

As you can see from the table, the Pentium II can handle up to 64GB of physical memory. Like the Pentium Pro, the CPU incorporates Dual Independent Bus architecture. This means the chip has two independent buses: one for accessing the L2 cache, the other for accessing main memory. These dual buses can operate simultaneously, greatly accelerating the flow of data within the system. The L1 cache always runs at full core speeds because it is mounted directly on the processor die. The L2 cache in the Pentium II normally runs at 1/2-core speed, which saves money and allows for less expensive cache chips to be utilized. For example, in a 333MHz Pentium II, the L1 cache runs at a full 333MHz, while the L2 cache runs at 167MHz. Even though the L2 cache is not at full core speed as it was with the Pentium Pro, this is still far superior to having cache memory on the motherboard running at the 66MHz motherboard speed of most Socket 7 Pentium designs. Intel claims that the DIB architecture in the Pentium II allows up to three times the bandwidth of normal single-bus processors like the original Pentium.

By removing the cache from the processor's internal package and using external chips mounted on a substrate and encased in the cartridge design, Intel can now use more cost-effective cache chips and more easily scale the processor up to higher speeds. The Pentium Pro was limited in speed to 200MHz, largely due to the inability to find affordable cache memory that runs any faster. By running the cache memory at 1/2-core speed, the Pentium II can run up to 400MHz while still using 200MHz rated cache chips. To offset the 1/2-core speed cache used in the Pentium II, Intel doubled the basic amount of integrated L2 cache from 256KB standard in the Pro to 512KB standard in the Pentium II.

Note that the tag-RAM included in the L2 cache will allow up to 512MB of main memory to be cacheable in PII processors from 233MHz to 333MHz. The 350MHz, 400MHz, and faster versions include an enhanced tag-RAM that allows up to 4GB of main memory to be cacheable. This is very important if you ever plan on adding more than 512MB of memory. In that case, you would definitely want the 350MHz or faster version; otherwise, memory performance would suffer.

The system bus of the Pentium II provides "glueless" support for up to two processors. This enables low-cost, two-way on the L2 cache bus. These system buses are designed especially for servers or other mission-critical system use where reliability and data integrity are important. All Pentium IIs also include parity-protected address/request and response system bus signals with a retry mechanism for high data integrity and reliability.

To install the Pentium II in a system, a special processor-retention mechanism is required. This consists of a mechanical support that attaches to the motherboard and secures the Pentium II processor in Slot 1 to prevent shock and vibration damage. Retention mechanisms should be provided by the motherboard manufacturer. (For example, the Intel Boxed AL440FX and DK440LX motherboards include a retention mechanism, plus other important system integration components.)

The Pentium II can generate a significant amount of heat that must be dissipated. This is accomplished by installing a heat sink on the processor. Many of the Pentium II processors will use an active heat sink that incorporates a fan. Unlike heat sink fans for previous Intel boxed processors, the Pentium II fans draw power from a three-pin power header on the motherboard. Most motherboards provide several fan connectors to supply this power.

Special heat sink supports are needed to furnish mechanical support between the fan heat sink and support holes on the motherboard. Normally, a plastic support is inserted into the heat sink holes in the motherboard next to the CPU, before installing the CPU/heat sink package. Most fan heat sinks have two components: a fan in a plastic shroud and a metal heat sink. The heat sink is attached to the processor's thermal plate and should not be removed. The fan can be removed and replaced if necessary, for example, if it has failed. Figure 3.43 shows the SEC assembly with fan, power connectors, mechanical supports, and the slot and support holes on the motherboard.

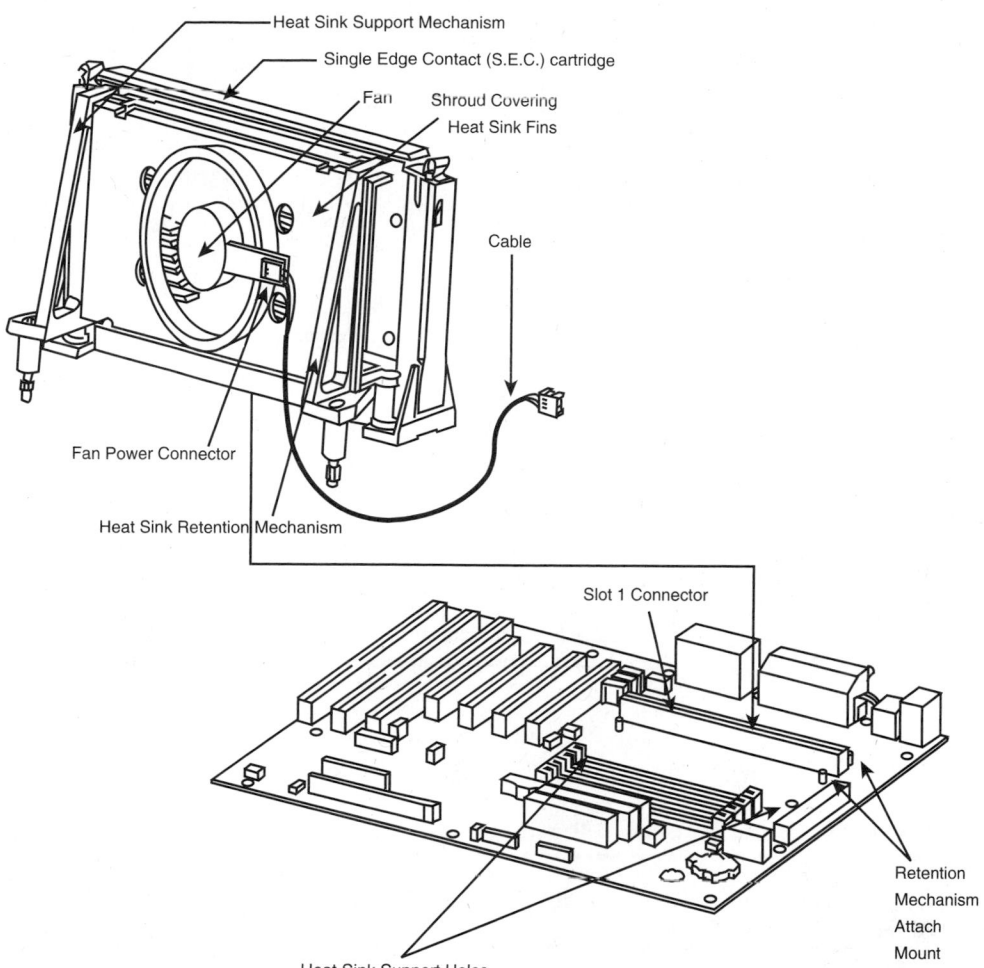

Heat Sink Support Mechanism

Single Edge Contact (S.E.C.) cartridge

Fan   Shroud Covering

Heat Sink Fins

Cable

Fan Power Connector

Heat Sink Retention Mechanism

Slot 1 Connector

Retention
Mechanism
Attach
Mount

Heat Sink Support Holes

Figure 3.43   Pentium II processor and heat sink assembly.

The following tables show the specifications unique to certain versions of the Pentium II processor.

To identify exactly which Pentium II processor you have and what its capabilities are, look at the specification number printed on the SEC cartridge. You will find the specification number in the dynamic mark area on the top of the processor module. See Figure 3.44 to locate these markings.

After you have located the specification number (actually, it is an alphanumeric code), you can look it up in Table 3.34 to see exactly which processor you have.

For example, a specification number of SL2KA identifies the processor as a Pentium II 333MHz running on a 66MHz system bus, with an ECC L2 cache—and that this processor runs on only 2.0 volts. The stepping is also identified, and by looking in the Pentium II Specification Update Manual published by Intel, you could figure out exactly which bugs were fixed in that revision.

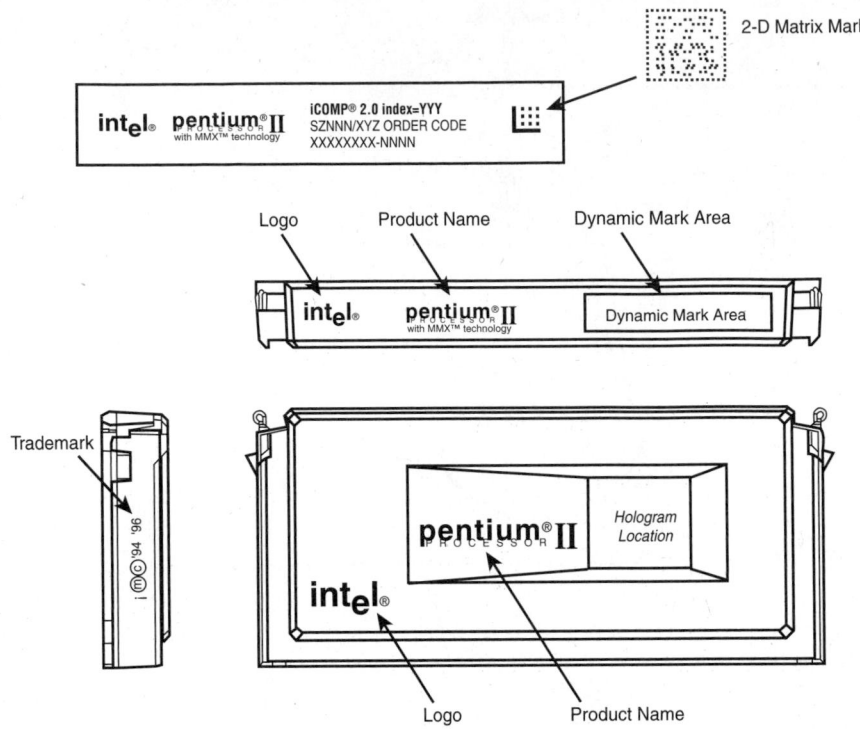

Figure 3.44 Pentium II single edge contact cartridge.

Table 3.34 Basic Pentium II Processor Identification Information

S-spec	Core Stepping	CPUID	Core/Bus Speed (MHz)	L2 Cache Size (MB)	L2 Cache Type	CPU Package	Notes (see foonotes)
SL264	C0	0633h	233/66	512	non-ECC	SECC 3.00	5
SL265	C0	0633h	266/66	512	non-ECC	SECC 3.00	5
SL268	C0	0633h	233/66	512	ECC	SECC 3.00	5
SL269	C0	0633h	266/66	512	ECC	SECC 3.00	5
SL28K	C0	0633h	233/66	512	non-ECC	SECC 3.00	1, 3, 5
SL28L	C0	0633h	266/66	512	non-ECC	SECC 3.00	1, 3, 5
SL28R	C0	0633h	300/66	512	ECC	SECC 3.00	5
SL2MZ	C0	0633h	300/66	512	ECC	SECC 3.00	1, 5
SL2HA	C1	0634h	300/66	512	ECC	SECC 3.00	5
SL2HC	C1	0634h	266/66	512	non-ECC	SECC 3.00	5
SL2HD	C1	0634h	233/66	512	non-ECC	SECC 3.00	5
SL2HE	C1	0634h	266/66	512	ECC	SECC 3.00	5
SL2HF	C1	0634h	233/66	512	ECC	SECC 3.00	5
SL2QA	C1	0634h	233/66	512	non-ECC	SECC 3.00	1, 3, 5
SL2QB	C1	0634h	266/66	512	non-ECC	SECC 3.00	1, 3, 5

S-spec	Core Stepping	CPUID	Core/Bus Speed (MHz)	L2 Cache Size (MB)	L2 Cache Type	CPU Package	Notes (see foonotes)
SL2QC	C1	0634h	300/66	512	ECC	SECC 3.00	1, 5
SL2KA	dA0	0650h	333/66	512	ECC	SECC 3.00	5
SL2QF	dA0	0650h	333/66	512	ECC	SECC 3.00	1
SL2K9	dA0	0650h	266/66	512	ECC	SECC 3.00	
SL35V	dA1	0651h	300/66	512	ECC	SECC 3.00	1, 2
SL2QH	dA1	0651h	333/66	512	ECC	SECC 3.00	1, 2
SL2S5	dA1	0651h	333/66	512	ECC	SECC 3.00	2, 5
SL2ZP	dA1	0651h	333/66	512	ECC	SECC 3.00	2, 5
SL2ZQ	dA1	0651h	350/100	512	ECC	SECC 3.00	2, 5
SL2S6	dA1	0651h	350/100	512	ECC	SECC 3.00	2, 5
SL2S7	dA1	0651h	400/100	512	ECC	SECC 3.00	2, 5
SL2SF	dA1	0651h	350/100	512	ECC	SECC 3.00	1, 2
SL2SH	dA1	0651h	400/100	512	ECC	SECC 3.00	1, 2
SL2VY	dA1	0651h	300/66	512	ECC	SECC 3.00	1, 2
SL33D	dB0	0652h	266/66	512	ECC	SECC 3.00	1, 2, 5
SL2YK	dB0	0652h	300/66	512	ECC	SECC 3.00	1, 2, 5
SL2WZ	dB0	0652h	350/100	512	ECC	SECC 3.00	1, 2, 5
SL2YM	dB0	0652h	400/100	512	ECC	SECC 3.00	1, 2, 5
SL37G	dB0	0652h	400/100	512	ECC	SECC2 OLGA	1, 2, 4
SL2WB	dB0	0652h	450/100	512	ECC	SECC 3.00	1, 2, 5
SL37H	dB0	0652h	450/100	512	ECC	SECC2 OLGA	1, 2
SL2KE	TdB0	1632h	333/66	512	ECC	PGA	2, 4
SL2W7	dB0	0652h	266/66	512	ECC	SECC 2.00	2, 5
SL2W8	dB0	0652h	300/66	512	ECC	SECC 3.00	2, 5
SL2TV	dB0	0652h	333/66	512	ECC	SECC 3.00	2, 5
SL2U3	dB0	0652h	350/100	512	ECC	SECC 3.00	2, 5
SL2U4	dB0	0652h	350/100	512	ECC	SECC 3.00	2, 5
SL2U5	dB0	0652h	400/100	512	ECC	SECC 3.00	2, 5
SL2U6	dB0	0652h	400/100	512	ECC	SECC 3.00	2, 5
SL2U7	dB0	0652h	450/100	512	ECC	SECC 3.00	2, 5
SL356	dB0	0652h	350/100	512	ECC	SECC2 PLGA	2, 5
SL357	dB0	0652h	400/100	512	ECC	SECC2 OLGA	2, 5
SL358	dB0	0652h	450/100	512	ECC	SECC2 OLGA	2, 5
SL37F	dB0	0652h	350/100	512	ECC	SECC2 PLGA	1, 2, 5
SL3FN	dB0	0652h	350/100	512	ECC	SECC2 OLGA	2, 5
SL3EE	dB0	0652h	400/100	512	ECC	SECC2 PLGA	2, 5
SL3F9	dB0	0652h	400/100	512	ECC	SECC2 PLGA	1, 2
SL38M	dB1	0653h	350/100	512	ECC	SECC 3.00	1, 2, 5
SL38N	dB1	0653h	400/100	512	ECC	SECC 3.00	1, 2, 5

(continues)

Table 3.34   Continued

S-spec	Core Stepping	CPUID	Core/Bus Speed (MHz)	L2 Cache Size (MB)	L2 Cache Type	CPU Package	Notes (see foonotes)
SL36U	dB1	0653h	350/100	512	ECC	SECC 3.00	2, 5
SL38Z	dB1	0653h	400/100	512	ECC	SECC 3.00	2, 5
SL3D5	dB1	0653h	400/100	512	ECC	SECC2 OLGA	1, 2

SECC = Single Edge Contact Cartridge

SECC2 = Single Edge Contact Cartridge revision 2

PLGA = Plastic Land Grid Array

OLGA = Organic Land Grid Array

CPUID = The internal ID returned by the CPUID instruction

ECC = Error Correcting Code

1. This is a boxed Pentium II processor with an attached fan heat sink.

2. These processors have an enhanced L2 cache, which can cache up to 4GB of main memory. Other standard PII processors can only cache up to 512MB of main memory.

3. These boxed processors may have packaging which incorrectly indicates ECC support in the L2 cache.

4. This is a boxed Pentium II OverDrive processor with an attached fan heat sink, designed for upgrading Pentium Pro (Socket 8) systems.

5. These parts will only operate at the specified clock multiplier frequency ratio at which they were manufactured. They can only be overclocked by increasing bus speed.

The two variations of the SECC2 cartridge vary by the type of processor core package on the board. The PLGA (Plastic Land Grid Array) is the older type of packaging used in previous SECC cartridges as well, and is being phased out. Taking its place is the newer OLGA (Organic Land Grid Array), which is a processor core package that is smaller and easier to manufacture. It also allows better thermal transfer between the processor die and the heat sink, which is attached directly to the top of the OLGA chip package. Figure 3.45 shows the open back side (where the heat sink would be attached) of SECC2 processors with PLGA and OLGA cores.

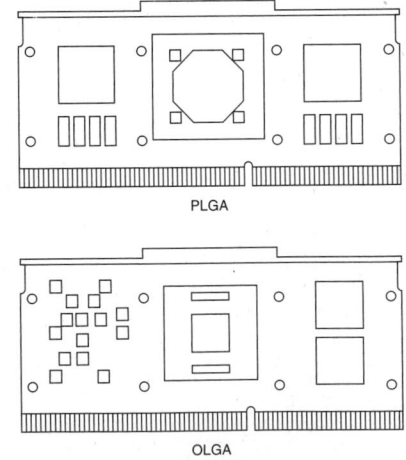

PLGA

OLGA

Figure 3.45   SECC2 processors with PLGA and OLGA cores.

Pentium II motherboards have an onboard voltage regulator circuit that is designed to power the CPU. Currently, there are Pentium II processors that run at several different voltages, so the regulator must be set to supply the correct voltage for the specific processor you are installing. As with the Pentium Pro and unlike the older Pentium, there are no jumpers or switches to set; the voltage setting is handled completely automatically through the Voltage ID (VID) pins on the processor cartridge. Table 3.35 shows the relationship between the pins and the selected voltage.

Table 3.35   Pentium II Voltage ID Definition

Processor Pins

VID4	VID3	VID2	VID1	VID0	Voltage
0	1	1	1	1	Reserved
0	1	1	1	0	Reserved
0	1	1	0	1	Reserved
0	1	1	0	0	Reserved
0	1	0	1	1	Reserved
0	1	0	1	0	Reserved
0	1	0	0	1	Reserved
0	1	0	0	0	Reserved
0	0	1	1	1	Reserved
0	0	1	1	0	Reserved
0	0	1	0	1	**1.80**
0	0	1	0	0	**1.85**
0	0	0	1	1	**1.90**
0	0	0	1	0	**1.95**
0	0	0	0	1	**2.00**
0	0	0	0	0	**2.05**
1	1	1	1	1	**No CPU**
1	1	1	1	0	**2.1**
1	1	1	0	1	**2.2**
1	1	1	0	0	**2.3**
1	1	0	1	1	**2.4**
1	1	0	1	0	**2.5**
1	1	0	0	1	**2.6**
1	1	0	0	0	**2.7**
1	0	1	1	1	**2.8**
1	0	1	1	0	2.9
1	0	1	0	1	3.0
1	0	1	0	0	3.1
1	0	0	1	1	3.2
1	0	0	1	0	3.3
1	0	0	0	1	3.4
1	0	0	0	0	3.5

0 = Processor pin connected to Vss
1 = Open on processor

To ensure the system is ready for all Pentium II processor variations, the values in **bold** must be supported. Most Pentium II processors run at 2.8v, with some newer ones at 2.0v.

The Pentium II Mobile Module is a Pentium II for notebooks that includes the North Bridge of the high-performance 440BX chipset. This is the first chipset on the market that allows 100MHz processor bus operation, although that is currently not supported in the mobile versions. The 440BX chipset was released at the same time as the 350 and 400MHz versions of the Pentium II; it is the recommended minimum chipset for any new Pentium II motherboard purchases.

▶▶ See "Mobile Pentium II," p. 1218.

Newer variations on the Pentium II include the Pentium IIPE, which is a mobile version that includes 256KB of L2 cache directly integrated into the die. This means that it runs at full core speed, making it faster than the desktop Pentium II, because the desktop chips use half-speed L2 cache.

Celeron

The Celeron processor is a P6 with the same processor core as the Pentium II. It is mainly designed for lower cost PCs in the $1,000 or less price category. The best "feature" is that although the cost is low, the performance is not. In fact, due to the superior cache design, the Celeron outperforms the Pentium II at the same speed and at a lower cost.

Most of the features for the Celeron are the same as the Pentium II because it uses the same internal processor core. The main differences are in packaging and L2 cache design.

Up until recently, all Celeron processors were available in a package called the Single Edge Processor Package (SEPP or SEP package). The SEP package is basically the same Slot 1 design as the SECC (Single Edge Contact Cartridge) used in the Pentium II/III, with the exception of the fancy plastic cartridge cover. This cover is deleted in the Celeron, making it cheaper to produce and sell. Essentially the Celeron uses the same circuit board as is inside the Pentium II package.

◀◀ See "Single Edge Contact (SEC) and Single Edge Processor (SEP) Packaging," p. 71.

Even without the plastic covers, the Slot 1 packaging was more expensive than it should be. This was largely due to the processor retention mechanisms (stands) required to secure the processor into Slot 1 on the motherboard, as well as the larger and more complicated heat sinks required. This, plus competition from the lower end Socket 7 systems using primarily AMD processors, led Intel to introduce the Celeron in a socketed form. The socket is called PGA-370 or Socket 370, because it has 370 pins. The processor package designed for this socket is called the Plastic Pin Grid Array (PPGA) package (see Figure 3.46). The PPGA package plugs into the 370 pin socket and allows for lower cost, lower profile, and smaller systems because of the less expensive processor retention and cooling requirements of the socketed processor.

◀◀ See "Socket PGA-370," p. 85.

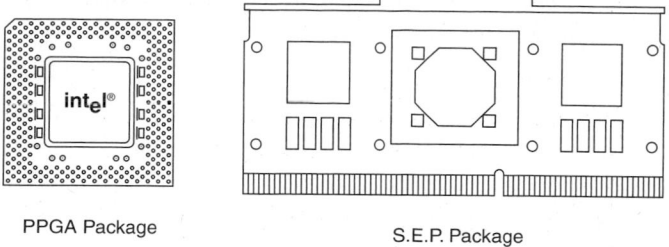

PPGA Package   S.E.P. Package

Figure 3.46   Celeron processors in the PPGA and SEP packages.

All Celeron processors at 433MHz and lower have been available in the SEPP that plugs into the 242-contact slot connector. The 300MHz and higher versions are also available in the PPGA package. This means that the 300MHz–433MHz have been available in both packages, while the 466MHz and higher speed versions are only available in the PPGA.

Motherboards that include Socket 370 cannot accept Slot 1 versions of the Celeron, and would also be unable to accept Pentium II or III processors. I normally recommend people use Slot 1 motherboards even for Celerons, because they can later upgrade to Pentium III processors without changing the board. That is because most motherboards that include a Slot 1 can accept Pentium II, Pentium III, or SEPP (Slot 1 board type) Celeron processors. Since the newest and fastest Celerons are only available in the socketed form, you would think this would make them unusable in a Slot 1 motherboard. Fortunately, there are slot-to-socket adapters (usually called slot-kets) available for about $10 that plug into Slot 1 and incorporate a Socket 370 on the card. Figure 3.47 shows a typical slot-ket adapter.

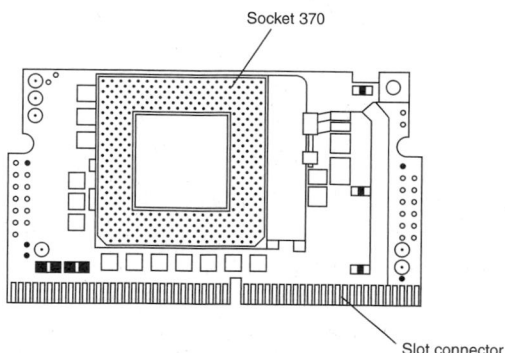

Socket 370

Slot connector

Figure 3.47   Slot-ket adapter for installing PPGA processors in Slot 1 motherboards.

Highlights of the Celeron include

- Available at 300MHz (300A) and higher core frequencies with 128KB L2 cache; 300MHz and 266MHz core frequencies without L2 cache
- Uses same P6 core processor as the Pentium Pro and Pentium II
- Dynamic execution microarchitecture

- Operates on a 66MHz CPU bus (future versions will likely also use the 100MHz bus)
- Specifically designed for lower cost value PC systems
- Includes MMX technology
- More cost-effective packaging technology including Single Edge Processor (SEP) or Plastic Pin Grid Array (PPGA) packages
- Integrated 32KB L1 cache, implemented as separate 16KB instruction and 16KB data caches
- Integrated thermal diode for temperature monitoring

Table 3.36 shows the specifications for all the Celeron processors.

Table 3.36 Intel Celeron Processor Specifications

Intel Celeron Processor (466MHz)

Introduction date	April 26, 1999
Clock speeds	466MHz
Number of transistors	19 million (0.25 micron process)
Cache: 128KB on-die packaging	Plastic Pin Grid Array (PPGA), 370 pins
Bus Speed	66MHz
Bus Width	64-bit system bus
Addressable Memory	4GB
Typical Use	Value PCs

Mobile Intel Celeron Processor (366MHz)

Introduction date	May 17, 1999
Clock speeds	366MHz
Number of transistors	18.9 million (0.25 micron process), 128KB on-die L2 cache
Ball Grid Array (BGA) number of balls	615
Dimensions	Width = 32mm; Length = 37mm
Core voltage	1.6 volts
Thermal design power	300MHz = 8.6 watts
Typical use	Value/low-cost mobile PCs

Mobile Intel Celeron Processor (333MHz)

Introduction date	April 5, 1999
Clock speeds	333MHz
Number of transistors	18.9 million (0.25 micron process), 128KB on-die L2 cache
Ball Grid Array (BGA) number of balls	615
Dimensions	Width = 31mm; Length = 35mm
Core voltage	1.6 volts
Thermal design power	300MHz = 8.6 watts
Typical use	Value/low-cost mobile PCs

Intel Celeron Processor (433MHz)

Introduction date	March 22, 1999
Clock speeds	433MHz
Number of transistors	19 million (0.25 micron process)
Cache	128KB on-die Single Edge Processor Package (SEPP), 242 pins
Plastic Pin Grid Array (PPGA)	370 pins
Bus Speed	66MHz
Bus Width	64 bit system bus
Addressable Memory	4GB
Typical Use	Value PCs

Mobile Intel Celeron Processor (266 and 300MHz)

Introduction date	January 25, 1999
Clock speeds	266 and 300MHz
Number of transistors	18.9 million (0.25 micron process), 128KB on-die L2 cache
Ball Grid Array (BGA) number of balls	615
Dimensions	Width = 31mm; Length = 35mm
Core voltage	1.6 volts
Thermal design power	300MHz = 7.7 watts; 266MHz = 7.0 watts
Typical use	Value/low-cost mobile PCs

Intel Celeron Processor (400, 366MHz)

Introduction date	January 4, 1999
Clock speeds	400, 366MHz
Number of transistors	19 million (0.25 micron process)
Single Edge Processor Package (SEPP)	242 pins
Plastic Pin Grid Array (PPGA)	370 pins
Bus Speed	66MHz
Bus Width	64-bit system bus
Addressable Memory	4GB
Typical Use	Low-cost PCs

Intel Celeron Processor (333MHz)

Introduction date	August 24, 1998
Clock speeds	333MHz
Number of transistors	19 million (0.25 micron process)
Single Edge Processor Package (SEPP)	242 pins
Bus Speed	66MHz
Bus Width	64-bit system bus
Addressable Memory	4GB
Package Dimensions	5" × 2.275" × .208"
Typical Use	Low-cost PCs

(continues)

Table 3.36   Continued

Intel Celeron Processor (300A-MHz)

Introduction date	August 24, 1998
Clock speeds	300MHz
Number of transistors	19 million (0.25 micron process)
Single Edge Processor Package (SEPP)	242 pins
Bus Speed	66MHz
Bus Width	64-bit system bus
Addressable Memory	4GBs
Package Dimensions	5" × 2.275" × .208"
Typical Use	Low-cost PCs

Intel Celeron Processor (300 MHz)

Introduction date	June 8, 1998
Clock speeds	300 MHz
Number of transistors	7.5 million (0.25 micron process)
Single Edge Processor Package (SEPP)	242 pins
Bus Speed	66MHz
Bus Width	64-bit system bus
Addressable Memory	4GB
Virtual Memory	64TB
Package Dimensions	5" × 2.275" × .208"
Typical Use	Low-cost PCs

Intel Celeron Processor (266MHz)

Introduction date	April 15, 1998
Clock speeds	266MHz
Number of transistors	7.5 million (0.25 micron process)
Single Edge Processor Package (SEPP)	242 pins
Bus Speed	66MHz
Bus Width	64-bit system bus
Addressable Memory	4GB
Virtual Memory	64TB
Package Dimensions	5" × 2.275" × .208"
Typical Use	Low-cost PCs

The Intel Celeron processors at 466, 433, 400, 366, 333, and 300A-MHz include integrated L2 cache 128KB. The core for the 466, 433, 400, 366, 333, and 300A-MHz processors have a whopping 19 million transistors due to the addition of the integrated 128KB L2 cache.

All the Celerons are manufactured using the .25 micron process, which reduces processor heat and enables the Intel Celeron processor to use a smaller heat sink compared to some of the Pentium II processors. Table 3.37 shows the power consumed by the various Celeron processors.

Table 3.37   Intel Celeron Processor Power Consumption

Processor Speed	Current (amps)	Voltage	Watts
266MHz	8.2	2.0	16.4
300MHz	9.3	2.0	18.6
300A-MHz	9.3	2.0	18.6
333MHz	10.1	2.0	20.2
366MHz	11.2	2.0	22.4
400MHz	12.2	2.0	24.4
433MHz	12.6	2.0	25.2
466MHz	13.4	2.0	26.8

Figure 3.48 shows the Intel Celeron processor identification information. Figure 3.49 shows the Celeron's PPGA processor markings.

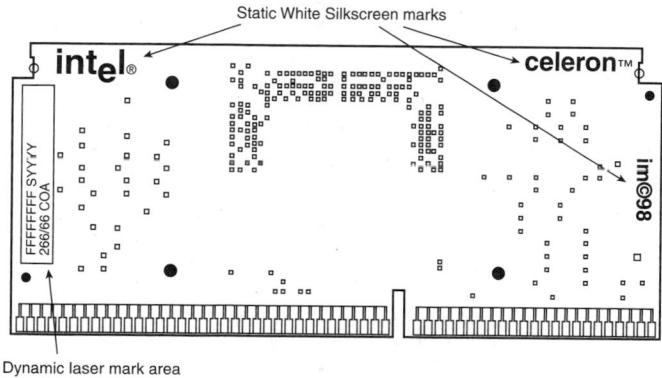

Figure 3.48   Celeron SEPP (Single Edge Processor Package) processor markings.

Note

The markings on the processor identify the following information:

SYYYY = S-spec. number

FFFFFFFF = FPO # (test lot tracability #)

COA = Country of assembly

Figure 3.49   Celeron PPGA processor markings.

Note

The PPGA processor markings identify the following information:

AAAAAAA = Product pode

ZZZ = Processor speed (MHz)

LLL = Integrated L2 cache size (in Kilobytes)

SYYYY = S-spec. number

FFFFFFFF-XXXX = Assembly lot tracking number

Table 3.38 shows all the available variations of the Celeron, indicated by the S-specification number.

Table 3.38   Intel Celeron Variations

S-spec	Core Stepping	L2 Size	CPUID	Speed Core/Bus	Package	Notes (see foonotes)
SL2SY	dA0	0	0650h	266/66MHz	SEPP	
SL2YN	dA0	0	0650h	266/66MHz	SEPP	1
SL2YP	dA0	0	0650h	300/66MHz	SEPP	
SL2Z7	dA0	0	0650h	300/66MHz	SEPP	1
SL2TR	dA1	0	0651h	266/66MHz	SEPP	
SL2QG	dA1	0	0651h	266/66MHz	SEPP	1
SL2X8	dA1	0	0651h	300/66MHz	SEPP	
SL2Y2	dA1	0	0651h	300/66MHz	SEPP	1
SL2Y3	dB0	0	0652h	266/66MHz	SEPP	1
SL2Y4	dB0	0	0652h	300/66MHz	SEPP	1
SL2WM	mA0	128KB	0660h	300A/66MHz	SEPP	3
SL32A	mA0	128KB	0660h	300A/66MHz	SEPP	1
SL2WN	mA0	128KB	0660h	333/66MHz	SEPP	3
SL32B	mA0	128KB	0660h	333/66MHz	SEPP	1
SL376	mA0	128KB	0660h	366/66MHz	SEPP	
SL37Q	mA0	128KB	0660h	366/66MHz	SEPP	1
SL39Z	mA0	128KB	0660h	400/66MHz	SEPP	
SL37V	mA0	128KB	0660h	400/66MHz	SEPP	1
SL3BC	mA0	128KB	0660h	433/66MHz	SEPP	
SL35Q	mB0	128KB	0665h	300A/66MHz	PPGA	2
SL36A	mB0	128KB	0665h	300A/66MHz	PPGA	
SL35R	mB0	128KB	0665h	333/66MHz	PPGA	2
SL36B	mB0	128KB	0665h	333/66MHz	PPGA	
SL36C	mB0	128KB	0665h	366/66MHz	PPGA	
SL35S	mB0	128KB	0665h	366/66MHz	PPGA	2
SL3A2	mB0	128KB	0665h	400/66MHz	PPGA	

S-spec	Core Stepping	L2 Size	CPUID	Speed Core/Bus	Package	Notes (see foonotes)
SL37X	mB0	128KB	0665h	400/66MHz	PPGA	2
SL3BA	mB0	128KB	0665h	433/66MHz	PPGA	
SL3BS	mB0	128KB	0665h	433/66MHz	PPGA	2
SL3EH	mB0	128KB	0665h	466/66MHz	PPGA	
SL3FL	mB0	128KB	0665h	466/66MHz	PPGA	2

SEPP = Single Edge Processor Package

PPGA = Plastic Pin Grid Array

1. Boxed processor with an attached fan heat sink

2. Boxed processor with an unattached fan heat sink

3. Also available as a boxed processor with an attached fan heat sink

Pentium III

The Pentium III processor, shown in Figure 3.50, was released in February 1999 and introduced several new features to the P6 family. The most important advancements are the streaming SIMD extensions (SSE), consisting of 70 new instructions that dramatically enhance the performance and possibilities of advanced imaging, 3D, streaming audio, video, and speech-recognition applications.

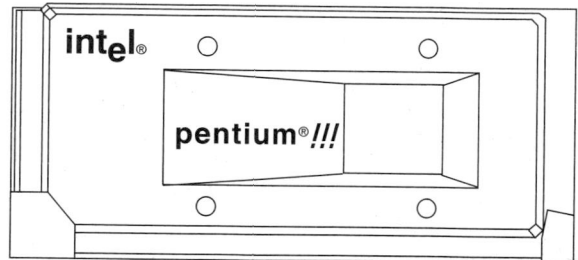

Figure 3.50 Pentium III processor. *Photograph used by permission of Intel Corporation.*

Based on Intel's advanced 0.25 micron CMOS process technology, the PIII core has over 9.5 million transistors. The Pentium III is available in 450MHz, 500MHz, and 550MHz versions, as well as in 500MHz and 550MHz Xeon versions. The Pentium III also incorporates advanced features such as a 32KB L1 cache and half core speed 512KB L2 cache with cacheability for up to 4GB of addressable memory space. The PIII also can be used in dual-processing systems with up to 64GB of physical memory. A self-reportable processor serial number gives security, authentication, and system management applications a powerful new tool for identifying individual systems.

Pentium III processors are available in Intel's Single Edge Contact Cartridge 2 (SECC2) form factor, which is replacing the more expensive older SEC packaging. The SECC2 package covers only one side of the chip, and allows for better heat sink attachment and less overall weight. It is also less expensive.

Architectural features of the Pentium III processor include

- *Streaming SIMD Extensions.* Seventy new instructions for dramatically faster processing and improved imaging, 3D streaming audio and video, Web access, speech recognition, new user interfaces, and other graphics and sound rich applications.

- *Intel Processor Serial Number.* The processor serial number, the first of Intel's planned building blocks for PC security, serves as an electronic serial number for the processor and, by extension, its system or user. This enables the system/user to be identified by networks and applications. The processor serial number will be used in applications that benefit from stronger forms of system and user identification, such as the following:

  - *Applications using security capabilities.* Managed access to new Internet content and services; electronic document exchange

  - *Manageability applications.* Asset management; remote system load and configuration

  - *Intel MMX Technology*

  - *Dynamic Execution Technology*

  - *Incorporates an on-die diode.* This can be used to monitor the die temperature for thermal management purposes.

Most of the Pentium III processors will be made in the improved SECC2 packaging, which is less expensive to produce and allows for a more direct attachment of the heat sink to the processor core for better cooling.

All Pentium III processors have 512KB of L2 cache, which runs at half of the core processor speed. Xeon versions have 512KB, 1MB, or 2MB of L2 cache that runs at full core speed. These are more expensive versions designed for servers and workstations.

All PIII processor L2 caches can cache up to 4GB of addressable memory space, and include Error Correction Code (ECC) capability.

Table 3.39 shows the Pentium III specifications by model.

Table 3.39   Pentium III Processor Specifications

Pentium III Processor (550MHz)	
Introduction date	May 17, 1999
Clock Speeds	450, 500MHz
Number of transistors	9.5 million (0.25 micron process)
L2 cache	512KB
Processor Package Style	Single Edge Contact (SEC) Cartridge 2
System Bus Speed	100MHz
System Bus Width	64-bit system bus
Addressable Memory	64GB
Typical Use	Business and consumer PCs, one- and two-way servers and workstations

Pentium III Processor (450 and 500MHz)

Introduction date	February 26, 1999
Clock Speeds	450, 500MHz
Number of transistors	9.5 million (0.25 micron process)
L2 cache	512KB
Processor Package Style	Single Edge Contact (SEC) Cartridge 2
System Bus Speed	100MHz
System Bus Width	64-bit system bus
Addressable Memory	64GB
Typical Use	Business and consumer PCs, one- and two-way servers and workstations

Pentium III processors can be identified by their markings, which are found on the top edge of the processor cartridge. Figure 3.51 shows the format and meaning of the markings.

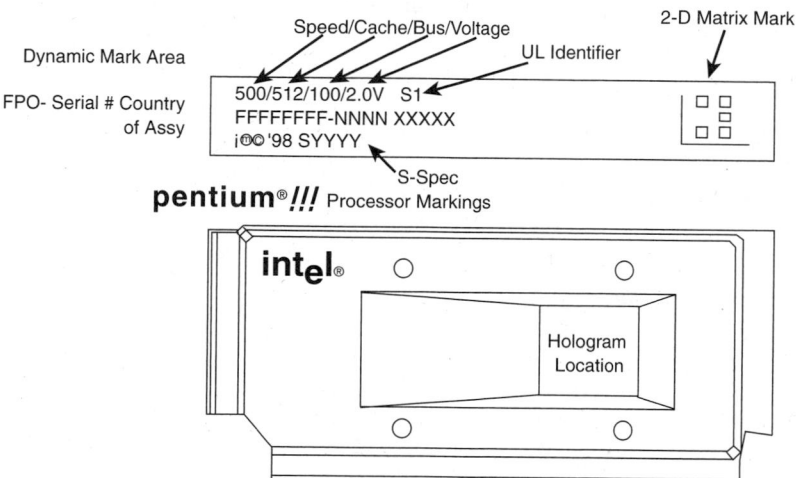

Figure 3.51   Pentium III processor markings.

Table 3.40 shows the available variations of the Pentium III, indicated by the S-specification number.

Table 3.40   Intel Pentium III Processor Variations

S-Spec	Core Stepping	CPUID	Core/Bus Speed (MHz)	L2 Cache Size	L2 Cache Type	Package	Notes (see footnotes)
SL364	kB0	672	450/100	512	ECC	SECC2	
SL365	kB0	672	500/100	512	ECC	SECC2	
SL3CC	kB0	672	450/100	512	ECC	SECC2	1

(continues)

Table 3.40   Continued

S-Spec	Core Stepping	CPUID	Core/Bus Speed (MHz)	L2 Cache Size	L2 Cache Type	Package	Notes (see footnotes)
SL3CD	kB0	672	500/100	512	ECC	SECC2	1
SL38E	kB0	672	450/100	512	ECC	SECC	
SL38F	kB0	672	500/100	512	ECC	SECC	
SL35D	kC0	673	450/100	512	ECC	SECC2	
SL35E	kC0	673	500/100	512	ECC	SECC2	
SL3F7	kC0	673	550/100	512	ECC	SECC2	

SECC = Single Edge Contact Cartridge
SECC2 = Single Edge Contact Cartridge revision 2
CPUID = The internal ID returned by the CPUID instruction
ECC = Error Correcting Code
1. This is a boxed processor with an attached heat sink

Pentium III processors are all clock multiplier locked. This is a means to prevent processor fraud and overclocking by making the processor work only at a given clock multiplier. Unfortunately, this feature can be bypassed by making modifications to the processor under the cartridge cover, and unscrupulous individuals have been selling lower speed processors remarked as higher speeds. It pays to purchase your systems or processors from direct Intel distributors or high-end dealers that do not engage in these practices.

Pentium II/III Xeon

The Pentium II and III processors are available in special high-end versions called Xeon processors. These differ from the standard Pentium II and III in three ways: packaging, cache size, and cache speed.

Xeon processors use a larger SEC (Single Edge Contact) cartridge than the standard PII/III processors, mainly to house a larger internal board with more cache memory. The Xeon processor is shown in Figure 3.52; the Xeon's SEC is shown in Figure 3.53.

Figure 3.52   Pentium III Xeon processor. *Photograph used by permission of Intel.*

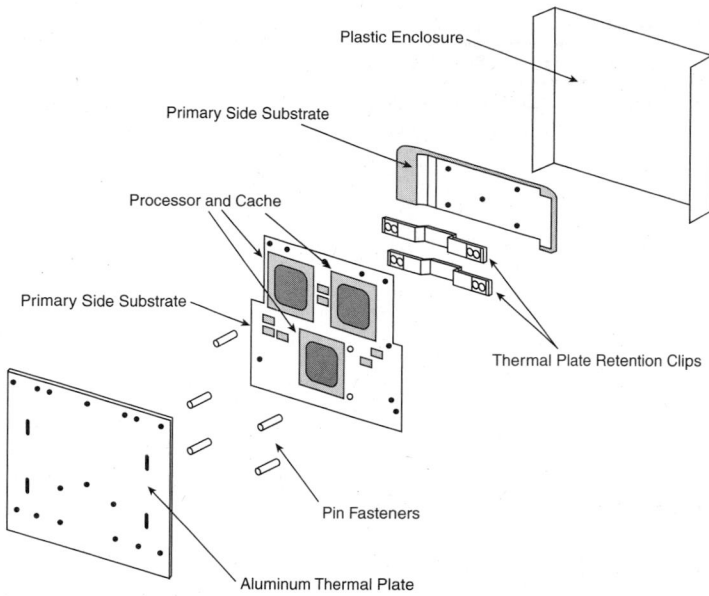

Figure 3.53   Xeon processor internal components.

Besides the larger package, the Xeon processors also include more L2 cache. They are available in three variations, with 512KB, 1MB, or 2MB of L2 cache. This cache is costly; the list price of the 2MB version is over $3,000!

Even more significant than the size of the cache is its speed. All the cache in the Xeon processors run at the full core speed. This is difficult to do considering that the cache chips are separate chips on the board; they are not integrated into the processor die like the Celeron. With the amount of cache, that would be impossible today but might be possible in the future.

Table 3.41 shows the Xeon processor specifications for each model.

Table 3.41   Intel Pentium II and III Xeon Specifications

Pentium III Xeon Processor (500 and 550MHz)	
Introduction date	March 17, 1999
Clock Speeds	500, 550MHz
Number of transistors	9.5 million (0.25 micron process)
L2 cache	512KB, 1 and 2MB for 500MHz
Processor Package Style	Single Edge Contact (SEC) Cartridge 2
System Bus Speed	100MHz
System Bus Width	64-bit system bus
Addressable Memory	64GB
Typical Use	Business PCs, two-, four- and eight-way (and higher) servers and workstations

(continues)

Table 3.41   Continued

Pentium II Xeon Processor (450MHz)

Introduction date	January 5, 1999
Clock speed	450MHz
L2 cache	512KB, 1MB, and 2MB
Number of transistors	7.5 million
Processor Package Style	Single Edge Contact (SEC) Cartridge
System Bus Speed	100MHz
System Bus Width	8 bytes
Addressable Memory	64GB
Virtual Memory	64TB
Package Dimensions	Height 4.8" × Width 6.0" × Depth .73"
Typical Use	Four-way servers and workstations

Pentium II Xeon Processor (450MHz)

Introduction date	October 6, 1998
Clock speed	450MHz
L2 cache	512KB
Number of transistors	7.5 million
Processor Package Style	Single Edge Contact (SEC) Cartridge
System Bus Speed	100MHz
System Bus Width	8 bytes
Addressable Memory	64GB
Virtual Memory	64TB
Package Dimensions	Height 4.8" × Width 6.0" × Depth .73"
Typical Use	Dual-processor workstations and servers

Pentium II Xeon Processor (400MHz)

Introduction date	June 29, 1998
Clock speed	400MHz
L2 cache versions	512KB and 1MB
Number of transistors	7.5 million
Processor Package Style	Single Edge Contact (SEC) Cartridge
System Bus Speed	100MHz
System Bus Width	8 bytes
Addressable Memory	64GB
Virtual Memory	64TB
Package Dimensions	Height 4.8" × Width 6.0" × Depth .73"
Typical Use	Midrange and higher servers and workstations

Note that the Slot 2 Xeon processors do not replace the Slot 1 processors. Xeon processors for Slot 2 are targeted at the mid-range to high-end server and workstation market segments, offering larger, full-speed L2 caches and four-way multiprocessor support. Pentium III processors for Slot 1 will continue to be the processor used in the business and home desktop market segments, and for entry-level servers and workstations (single and dual processor systems).

Pentium III Future

There are several new developments on target for the Pentium III processors. The primary trend seems to be the integration of L2 cache into the processor die, which also means it runs at full core speed.

There will also be further reductions in the process size used to manufacture the processors. Pentium II processors at 333MHz and up were the first members of the Pentium II processor family to be based on the "Deschutes" core (0.25 micron technology). Currently, through the Pentium III 550, they are still using a 0.25 micron process, but will be shifting to a 0.18, and then 0.13 micron process in the future. The shift to the 0.13 micron process will also include a shift from aluminum interconnects on the chip die to copper instead.

Other Sixth-Generation Processors

Besides Intel, many other manufacturers are now making P6 type processors, but often with a difference. Most of them are designed to interface with P5 class motherboards and for the lower end markets. AMD has recently offered up the K7, which is a true sixth-generation design using its own proprietary connection to the system.

This section examines the various sixth-generation processors from manufacturers other than Intel.

Nexgen Nx586

Nexgen was founded by Thampy Thomas who hired some of the people formerly involved with the 486 and Pentium processors at Intel. At Nexgen, they created the Nx586, a processor that was functionally the same as the Pentium but not pin compatible. As such, it was always supplied with a motherboard; in fact, it was normally soldered in. Nexgen did not manufacture the chips or the motherboards they came in; for that they hired IBM Microelectronics. Later Nexgen was bought by AMD, right before they were ready to introduce the Nx686, a greatly improved design done by Greg Favor, and a true competitor for the Pentium. AMD took the Nx686 design and combined it with a Pentium electrical interface to create a drop-in Pentium compatible chip called the K6, which actually outperformed the original from Intel.

The Nx586 had all the standard fifth-generation processor features, such as superscalar execution with two internal pipelines and a high performance integral L1 cache with separate code and data caches. One advantage is that the Nx586 includes separate 16KB instruction and 16KB data caches compared to 8KB each for the Pentium. These caches keep key instruction and data close to the processing engines to increase overall system performance.

The Nx586 also included branch prediction capabilities, which are one of the hallmarks of a sixth-generation processor. Branch prediction means the processor has internal functions to predict program flow to optimize the instruction execution.

The Nx586 processor also featured an RISC (Reduced Instruction Set Computer) core. A translation unit dynamically translates x86 instructions into RISC86 instructions. These RISC86 instructions were specifically designed with direct support for the x86 architecture while obeying RISC performance principles. They are thus simpler and easier to execute than the complex x86 instructions. This type of capability is another feature normally found only in P6 class processors.

The Nx586 was discontinued after the merger with AMD, who then took the design for the successor Nx686 and released it as the AMD-K6.

AMD-K6 Series

The AMD-K6 processor is a high-performance sixth-generation processor that is physically installable in a P5 (Pentium) motherboard. It was essentially designed for them by Nexgen, and was first known as the Nx686. The Nexgen version never appeared because they were purchased by AMD before the chip was due to be released. The AMD-K6 delivers performance levels somewhere between the Pentium and Pentium II processor due to its unique hybrid design. Because it is designed to install in Socket 7, which is a fifth-generation processor socket and motherboard design, it cannot perform quite as a true sixth-generation chip because the Socket 7 architecture severely limits cache and memory performance. However, with this processor, AMD is giving Intel a lot of competition in the low- to mid-range market, where the Pentium is still popular.

The K6 processor contains an industry-standard, high-performance implementation of the new multimedia instruction set (MMX), enabling a high level of multimedia performance. The K6-2 introduced an upgrade to MMX AMD calls 3DNow, which adds even more graphics and sound instructions. AMD designed the K6 processor to fit the low-cost, high-volume Socket 7 infrastructure. This enables PC manufacturers and resellers to speed time to market and deliver systems with an easy upgrade path for the future. AMD's state-of-the-art manufacturing facility in Austin, Texas (Fab 25) makes the AMD-K6 series processors. Initially they used AMD's 0.35 micron, five-metal layer process technology; newer variations use the 0.25 micron processor to increase production quantities because of reduced die size, as well as to decrease power consumption.

AMD-K6 processor technical features include

- Sixth-generation internal design, fifth-generation external interface
- Internal RISC core, translates x86 to RISC instructions
- Superscalar parallel execution units (seven)
- Dynamic execution
- Branch prediction
- Speculative execution
- Large 64KB L1 cache (32KB instruction cache plus 32KB write-back dual-ported data cache)
- Built-in floating-point unit (FPU)
- Industry-standard MMX instruction support
- System Management Mode (SMM)
- Ceramic Pin Grid Array (CPGA) Socket 7 design
- Manufactured using a 0.35 micron and 0.25 micron, five-layer design

The K6-2 adds

- Higher clock speeds
- Higher bus speeds of up to 100MHz (Super7 motherboards)
- 3DNow; 21 new graphics and sound processing instructions

The K6-3 adds

- 256KB of on-die full core speed L2 cache

The addition of the full speed L2 cache in the K6-3 is significant. It brings the K6 series to a level where it can fully compete with the Intel Celeron and Pentium II processors. The 3DNow capability added in the K6-2/3 is also being exploited by newer graphics programs, making these processors ideal for lower cost gaming systems.

The AMD-K6 processor architecture is fully x86 binary code compatible, which means it runs all Intel software, including MMX instructions. To make up for the lower L2 cache performance of the Socket 7 design, AMD has beefed up the internal L1 cache to 64KB total, twice the size of the Pentium II or III. This, plus the dynamic execution capability, allows the K6 to outperform the Pentium and come close to the Pentium II in performance for a given clock rate. The K6-3 is even better with the addition of full core speed L2 cache.

Both the AMD-K5 and AMD-K6 processors are Socket 7 bus-compatible. However, certain modifications might be necessary for proper voltage setting and BIOS revisions. To ensure reliable operation of the AMD-K6 processor, the motherboard must meet specific voltage requirements.

The AMD processors have specific voltage requirements. Most older split-voltage motherboards default to 2.8v Core/3.3v I/O, which is below specification for the AMD-K6 and could cause erratic operation. To work properly, the motherboard must have Socket 7 with a dual-plane voltage regulator supplying 2.9v or 3.2v (233MHz) to the CPU core voltage (Vcc2) and 3.3v for the I/O (Vcc3). The voltage regulator must be capable of supplying up to 7.5A (9.5A for the 233MHz) to the processor. When used with a 200MHz or slower processor, the voltage regulator must maintain the core voltage within 145 mv of nominal (2.9v+/-145 mv). When used with a 233MHz processor, the voltage regulator must maintain the core voltage within 100 mv of nominal (3.2v+/-100 mv).

If the motherboard has a poorly designed voltage regulator that cannot maintain this performance, unreliable operation can result. If the CPU voltage exceeds the absolute maximum voltage range, the processor can be permanently damaged. Also note that the K6 can run hot. Ensure your heat sink is securely fitted to the processor and the thermally conductive grease or pad is properly applied.

The motherboard must have an AMD-K6 processor-ready BIOS with support for the K6 built in. Award has that support in their March 1, 1997 or later BIOS, AMI had K6 support in any of their BIOS with CPU Module 3.31 or later, and Phoenix supports the K6 in version 4.0, release 6.0, or release 5.1 with build dates of 4/7/97 or later.

Because these specifications can be fairly complicated, AMD keeps a list of motherboards that have been verified to work with the AMD-K6 processor on their Web site. All the motherboards on that list have been tested to work properly with the AMD-K6. So, unless these requirements can be verified elsewhere, it is recommended that you only use a motherboard from that list with the AMD-K6 processor.

The multiplier, bus speed, and voltage settings for the K6 are shown in Table 3.42. You can identify which AMD-K6 you have by looking at the markings on this chip, as shown in Figure 3.57.

Table 3.42   AMD-K6 Processor Speeds and Voltages

Processor	Core Speed	Clock Multiplier	Bus Speed	Core Voltage	I/O Voltage
K6-III	450MHz	4.5x	100MHz	2.4v	3.3v
K6-III	400MHz	4x	100MHz	2.4v	3.3v
K6-2	475MHz	5x	95MHz	2.4v	3.3v
K6-2	450MHz	4.5x	100MHz	2.4v	3.3v
K6-2	400MHz	4x	100MHz	2.2v	3.3v
K6-2	380MHz	4x	95MHz	2.2v	3.3v
K6-2	366MHz	5.5x	66MHz	2.2v	3.3v
K6-2	350MHz	3.5x	100MHz	2.2v	3.3v
K6-2	333MHz	3.5x	95MHz	2.2v	3.3v
K6-2	333MHz	5.0x	66MHz	2.2v	3.3v
K6-2	300MHz	3x	100MHz	2.2v	3.3v
K6-2	300MHz	4.5x	66MHz	2.2v	3.3v
K6-2	266MHz	4x	66MHz	2.2v	3.3v
K6	300MHz	4.5x	66MHz	2.2v	3.45v
K6	266MHz	4x	66MHz	2.2v	3.3v
K6	233 MHz	3.5x	66MHz	3.2v	3.3v
K6	200MHz	3x	66MHz	2.9v	3.3v
K6	166MHz	2.5x	66MHz	2.9v	3.3v

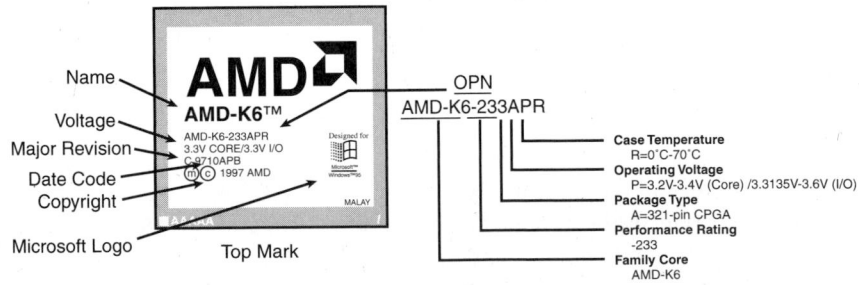

Figure 3.54   AMD-K6 processor markings.

Older motherboards achieve the 3.5x setting by setting jumpers for 1.5x. The 1.5x setting for older motherboards equates to a 3.5x setting for the AMD-K6 and newer Intel parts. To get the 4x and higher setting requires a motherboard that controls three BF (bus frequency) pins, including BF2. Older motherboards can only control two BF pins. The settings for the multipliers are shown in Table 3.43.

Table 3.43   AMD-K6 Multiplier Settings

Multiplier Setting	BF0	BF1	BF2
2.5x	Low	Low	High
3x	High	Low	High
3.5x	High	High	High
4x	Low	High	Low
4.5x	Low	Low	Low
5x	High	Low	Low
5.5x	High	High	Low

These settings are normally controlled by jumpers on the motherboard. Consult your motherboard documentation to see where they are and how to set them for the proper multiplier and bus speed settings.

Unlike Cyrix and some of the other Intel competitors, AMD is a manufacturer and a designer. This means they design and build their chips in their own fabs. Like Intel, AMD is migrating to 0.25 micron process technology and beyond. The original K6 has 8.8 million transistors and is built on a 0.35 micron, five-layer process. The die is 12.7mm on each side, or about 162 square mm. The K6-3 uses a 0.25 micron process and now incorporates 21.3 million transistors on a die only 10.9mm on each side, or about 118 square mm. Further process improvements will enable even more transistors, smaller die, higher yields, and greater numbers of processors. AMD has recently won contracts with several high-end system suppliers, which gives them an edge on the other Intel competitors. AMD has delivered more than 50 million Windows-compatible CPUs in the last five years.

Because of its performance and compatibility with the Socket 7 interface, the K6 series is often looked at as an excellent processor upgrade for motherboards currently using older Pentium or Pentium MMX processors. Although they do work in Socket 7, the AMD-K6 processors have different voltage and bus speed requirements than the Intel processors. Before attempting any upgrades, you should check the board documentation or contact the manufacturer to see if your board will meet the necessary requirements. In some cases, a BIOS upgrade will also be necessary.

3DNow

3DNow technology was introduced in May 1998 in the K6-2 as a set of instructions that extend the multimedia capabilities of the AMD chips. This allows greater performance for 3D graphics, multimedia, and other floating-point-intensive PC applications.

3DNow technology is a set of 21 instructions that use SIMD (Single Instruction Multiple Data) techniques to operate on arrays of data rather than single elements. Positioned as an extension to MMX technology, 3DNow is similar to the SSE (streaming SIMD extensions) found in the Pentium III processors from Intel. SSE consists of 70 new SIMD type instructions.

3DNow is well supported by software including Microsoft Windows 95/98, Windows NT 4.0, and all newer Microsoft operating systems. Application programming interfaces such as Microsoft's DirectX 6.x API and SGI's Open GL API have been optimized for 3DNow technology, as have the drivers for many leading 3D graphic accelerator suppliers, including 3Dfx, ATI, Matrox, and nVidia.

AMD-K7

The K7 is AMD's successor to the K6 series. The K7 is a whole new chip from the ground up and does not interface via the Socket 7 or Super7 sockets like their previous chips. Instead AMD seems to be taking a lesson from Intel, as the K7 looks almost exactly like a Pentium II/III cartridge. Unfortunately it doesn't plug into the same motherboards as the Pentium II/III; instead the K7 slot is a proprietary design requiring specific K7 motherboards with specific K7 chipsets.

The K7 is available in speeds from 550MHz and up, and uses a sideways 200MHz bus called the EV6 to connect to the motherboard North Bridge chip as well as other processors. Licensed from Digital Equipment, the EV6 bus is the same as that used for the Alpha 21264 processor, now owned by Compaq.

The K7 has a very large 128KB of L1 cache on the processor die, and 200MHz L2 cache from 512KB to 8MB in the cartridge. As expected, the K7 has support for MMX and 3DNow instructions, but not for the newer SSE (streaming SIMD extensions) instructions from Intel.

The initial production will utilize 0.25 micron technology, and clock speeds will exceed 500MHz. Subsequent versions will use a 0.18 micron process, and speeds will continue to increase. AMD chairman and CEO William J. (Jerry) Sanders III has previously stated the goal of delivering 1GHz K7 chips by 2000, utilizing copper interconnect manufacturing.

Cyrix MediaGX

The Cyrix MediaGX is designed for low-end sub-$1,000 retail store systems that must be highly integrated and low priced. The MediaGX integrates the sound, graphics, and memory control by putting these functions directly within the processor. With all these functions pulled "on chip," MediaGX-based PCs are priced lower than other systems with similar features.

The MediaGX processor integrates the PCI interface, coupled with audio, graphics, and memory control functions, right into the processor unit. As such, a system with the MediaGX doesn't require a costly graphics or sound card. Not only that, but on the motherboard level, the MediaGX and its companion chip replace the processor, North and South Bridge chips, the memory control hardware, and L2 cache found on competitive Pentium boards. Finally, the simplified PC design of the MediaGX, along with its low-power and low-heat characteristics, allow the OEM PC manufacturer to design a system in a smaller form factor with a reduced power-supply requirement.

processor. If you have an SX system, you also will have t
se you must inform the CMOS memory that a math copr
so require you to run the setup program.) Intel provides a
n to verify that the new chip is installed and functioning

functions correctly, you have nothing more to do. You do
ware on your system for the new chip. The only difference
ything works nearly twice as fast as it did before the upgra

Problems

lder 486SX or 486DX systems with the OverDrive process
can make an OverDrive upgrade difficult or impossible:

dependent timing loops

erDrive heat sink (25MHz and faster)

n rather than socketed

occur in systems that should be upgradable but are not. Or
OM BIOS. A few 486 systems have a BIOS that regulates har
oops based on how long it takes the CPU to execute a series
enly is running twice as fast, the prescribed timing interval
ystem operation or even hardware lockups. Fortunately, you
upgrading the system's BIOS. Intel offers BIOS updates with

ysical clearance. All OverDrive chips have heat sinks glued o
he heat sink can add 0.25 to 1.2 inches to the top of the chi
th other components in the system, especially in small desk
o this problem must be determined on a case-by-case basis.
sion card or disk drive, or even modify the chassis slightly to
the interference cannot be resolved, leaving you only the
ut the heat sink. Needless to say, removing the glued-on hea
y provided by Intel and will at worst damage the chip or the
recommend removing the heat sink.

up to twice the heat of the chips that they replace. Even wi
the faster OverDrive chips, some systems do not have enou
eep the OverDrive chip within the prescribed safe

all desktop systems or portables are most likely to have cooli
oper testing can indicate whether a system will have a heat
as been running an extensive test program to certify systems
an OverDrive upgrade.

Intel has indicated that the new 64-bit Merced processor will be available in sample volumes in 1999, with planned production volumes moving from 1999 to mid-2000. The Merced processor will be the first processor in Intel's IA-64 (Intel Architecture 64-bit) product family, and will incorporate innovative performance-enhancing architecture techniques, such as predication and speculation.

Merced

The most current generation of processor is the P6, which was first seen in the Pentium Pro introduced in November of 1995, and most recently found in the latest Pentium III processors. Obviously, then, the next generation processor from Intel will be called the P7.

Although the Merced processor program is still far from being released, the program has made considerable progress to date according to Intel, including

- Definition of the 64-bit instruction set architecture with Hewlett-Packard
- Completion of the fundamental microarchitecture design
- Completion of functional model and initial physical layout
- Completion of mechanical and thermal design and validation with system vendors
- Specifications complete and designs underway for chipset and other system components
- Progress on 64-bit compiler development and IA-64 software development kits
- Real-time software emulation capability to speed the development of IA-64 optimized software
- Multiple operating systems running in Merced simulation environment
- All required platform components planned for alignment with 1999 Merced processor samples for initial system assembly and testing

Intel's IA-64 product family is expected to expand the capabilities of the Intel architecture to address the high-performance server and workstation market segments. A variety of industry players—among them leading workstation and server-system manufacturers, leading operating system vendors, and dozens of independent software vendors—have already publicly committed their support for the Merced processor and the IA-64 product family.

As with previous new processor introductions, the P7 will not replace the P6 or P5, at least not at first. It will feature an all new design that will be initially expensive and found only in the highest end systems such as file servers or workstations. Intel expects the P7 will become the mainstream processor by the year 2004 and that the P6 will likely be found in low-end systems only. Intel is already developing an even more advanced P7 processor, due to ship in 2001, which will be significantly faster than Merced.

Intel and Hewlett-Packard began jointly working on the P7 processor in 1994. It was then that they began a collaboration on what will eventually become Intel's next-generation CPU. Although we don't know exactly what the new CPU will be like, Intel has begun slowly releasing information about the new processor to prepare the industry for its eventual release. In October of 1997, more than three years after they first disclosed their plan to work together on a new microprocessor architecture, Intel and HP officially announced some of the new processor's technical details.

The MediaGX processor is not a Socket 7 processor; in fact, it does not go in a socket at all—it is permanently soldered into its motherboard. Because of the processor's high level of integration, motherboards supporting MediaGX processors and its companion chip (Cx5510) are of a different design than conventional Pentium boards. As such, a system with the MediaGX processor is more of a disposable system than an upgradable system. You will not be able to easily upgrade most components in the system, but that is often not important in the very low-end market. If upgradability is important, look elsewhere. On the other hand, if you need the lowest-priced system possible, one with the MediaGX might fill the bill.

The MediaGX is fully Windows-compatible and will run the same software as an equivalent Pentium. You can expect a MediaGX system to provide equivalent performance as a given Pentium system at the same megahertz. The difference with the MediaGX is that this performance level is achieved at a much lower cost. Because the MediaGX processor is soldered into the motherboard and requires a custom chipset, it is only sold in a complete motherboard form.

There is also an improved MMX-enhanced MediaGX processor that features MPEG1 support, Microsoft PC97 compliance for Plug-and-Play access, integrated game port control, and AC97 audio compliance. It supports Windows 95 and DOS-based games, and MMX software as well. Such systems will also include two universal serial bus (USB) ports, which will accommodate the new generation of USB peripherals such as printers, scanners, joysticks, cameras, and more.

The MediaGX processor is offered at 166 and 180MHz, while the MMX-enhanced MediaGX processor is available at 200MHz and 233 MHz. Compaq is using the MMX-enhanced MediaGX processor in its Presario 1220 notebook PCs, which is a major contract win for Cyrix. Other retailers and resellers are offering low-end, low-cost systems in retail stores nationwide.

Cyrix/IBM 6x86 (M1) and 6x86MX (MII)

The Cyrix 6x86 processor family consists of the now-discontinued 6x86 and the newer 6x86MX processors. They are similar to the AMD-K5 and K6 in that they offer sixth-generation internal designs in a fifth-generation P5 Pentium compatible Socket 7 exterior.

The Cyrix 6x86 and 6x86MX (renamed MII) processors incorporate two optimized superpipelined integer units and an on-chip floating-point unit. These processors include the dynamic execution capability that is the hallmark of a sixth-generation CPU design. This includes branch prediction and speculative execution.

The 6x86MX/MII processor is compatible with MMX technology to run the latest MMX games and multimedia software. With its enhanced memory-management unit, a 64KB internal cache, and other advanced architectural features, the 6x86MX processor achieves higher performance and offers better value than competitive processors.

Features and benefits of the 6x86 processors include

- *Superscalar architecture.* Two pipelines to execute multiple instructions in parallel.
- *Branch prediction.* Predicts with high accuracy the next instructions needed.

■ *Speculative execution.* Allows the pipelines to continuously execute instructions following a branch without stalling the pipelines.

■ *Out-of-order completion.* Lets the faster instruction exit the pipeline out of order, saving processing time without disrupting program flow.

The 6x86 incorporates two caches: a 16KB dual-ported unified cache and a 256-byte instruction line cache. The unified cache is supplemented with a small quarter-K sized high-speed, fully associative instruction line cache. The improved 6x86MX design quadruples the internal cache size to 64KB, which significantly improves performance.

The 6x86MX also includes the 57 MMX instructions that speed up the processing of certain computing-intensive loops found in multimedia and communication applications.

All 6x86 processors feature support for System Management Mode (SMM). This provides an interrupt that can be used for system power management or software transparent emulation of I/O peripherals. Additionally, the 6x86 supports a hardware interface that allows the CPU to be placed into a low-power suspend mode.

The 6x86 is compatible with x86 software and all popular x86 operating systems, including Windows 95/98, Windows NT, OS/2, DOS, Solaris, and UNIX. Additionally, the 6x86 processor has been certified Windows 95 compatible by Microsoft.

As with the AMD-K6, there are some unique motherboard requirements for the 6x86 processors. Cyrix maintains a list of recommended motherboards on their Web site that should be consulted if you are considering installing one of these chips in a board.

When installing or configuring a system with the 6x86 processors, you have to set the correct motherboard bus speed and multiplier settings. The Cyrix processors are numbered based on a P-rating scale, which is not the same as the true megahertz clock speed of the processor.

See "Cyrix P-Ratings" earlier in this chapter to see the correct and true speed settings for the Cyrix 6x86 processors.

Note that because of the use of the P-rating system, the actual speed of the chip is not the same number at which it is advertised. For example, the 6x86MX-PR300 is not a 300MHz chip; it actually runs at only 263MHz or 266MHz, depending on exactly how the motherboard bus speed and CPU clock multipliers are set. Cyrix says it runs as fast as a 300MHz Pentium, hence the P-rating. Personally, I wish they would label the chips at the correct speed, and then say that it runs faster than a Pentium at the same speed.

To install the 6x86 processors in a motherboard, you also have to set the correct voltage. Normally, the markings on top of the chip indicate which voltage setting is appropriate. Various versions of the 6x86 run at 3.52v (use VRE setting), 3.3v (VR setting), or 2.8v (MMX) settings. The MMX versions use the standard split-plane 2.8v core 3.3v I/O settings.

P7 (786) Seventh-Generation Processors

What is coming after the Pentium III? The next processor is code-named either P7 or Merced.

For example, if your motherboard has a Pentium Socket 5, you can install a Pentium M 233MHz processor with a 2.8v voltage regulator adapter, or optionally an AMD-K6, also voltage regulator adapter. If you have Socket 7, your motherboard should be capable of ing the lower voltage Pentium MMX or AMD-K6 series directly without any adapters. T and K6-3 are the fastest and best processors for Socket 7 motherboards.

Rather than purchasing processors and adapters separately, I normally recommend you them together in a module from companies such as Kingston or Evergreen (see the Ven on the CD).

Upgrading the processor can, in some cases, double the performance of a system, such a were going from a Pentium 100 to an MMX 233. However, if you already have a Pentiu you already have the fastest processor that goes in that socket. In that case, you really s look into a complete motherboard change, which would let you upgrade to a Pentium I sor at the same time. If your chassis design is not proprietary and your system uses an i standard Baby-AT or ATX motherboard design, I normally recommend changing the mc and processor rather than trying to find an upgrade processor that will work with your board.

OverDrive Processors

Intel has stated that all its future processors will have OverDrive versions available for u at a later date. Often these are repackaged versions of the standard processors, sometim ing necessary voltage regulators and fans. Usually they are more expensive than other s but they are worth a look.

OverDrive Processor Installation

You can upgrade many systems with an OverDrive processor. The most difficult aspect c installation is having the correct OverDrive processor for your system. Currently, 486 Pc OverDrive processors are available for replacing 486SX and 486DX processors. Pentium Pentium-MMX OverDrive processors are also available for some Pentium processors. Unfortunately, Intel no longer offers upgrade chips for 168-pin socket boards. Table 3.4 current OverDrive processors offered by Intel.

Table 3.45   Intel OverDrive Processors

Processor Designation	Replaces	Socket	Heat Sink
486 Pentium OverDrive	486SX/DX/SX2/DX2	Socket 2 or 3	Active
120/133 Pentium	Pentium 60/66	Socket 4	Active OverDrive
200MHz Pentium OverDrive	Pentium 75/90/100	Socket 5/7	Active with MMX

Upgrades that use the newer OverDrive chips for Sockets 2–7 are likely to be much easic these chips almost always go into a ZIF socket and, therefore, require no tools. In most cial configuration pins in the socket and on the new OverDrive chips take care of any j tings for you. In some cases, however, you might have to set some jumpers on the mot

Finally, some systems have a proprietary design that p This would, for example, include virtually all portable their processor soldered into the motherboard. Some c Module, which is potentially upgradable.

To clarify which systems are tested to be upgradable w extensive list of compatible systems. To determine who processor, contact Intel via its FAXback system (see the OverDrive Processor Compatibility Data documents. T Web site. These documents list the systems that have b and indicate which other changes you might have to r a newer ROM BIOS or Setup program).

Note

If your system is not on the list, the warranty on the OverDrive p upgrades only for systems that are in the compatibility list. The li require a ROM upgrade, a jumper change, or perhaps a new s

After upgrading your system, I suggest running a diagn to verify that the new processor is running correctly.

▶▶ See "Norton Utilities Diagnostics," p. 1296.

Processor Benchmarks

People love to know how fast (or slow) their computers speed; it is human nature. To help us with this quest, v used to measure different aspects of processor and syste numerical measurement can completely describe the pe processor or a complete PC, benchmarks can be useful t and systems.

However, the only truly accurate way to measure your s using the actual software applications you use. Though ponent of a system, often other parts of the system can systems with different processors, for example, if they a memory, different hard disks, video cards, and so on. Al results.

Benchmarks can normally be divided into two kinds: co benchmarks measure the performance of specific parts o hard disk, video card, or CD-ROM drive, while system be mance of the entire computer system running a given ap

Benchmarks are, at most, only one kind of information purchasing process. You are best served by testing the sy operating systems and applications, and in the configura

There are several companies that specialize in benchmark tests and software. The following table lists the company and the benchmarks they are known for. You can contact these companies via the information in the Vendor List on the CD.

Company	Benchmarks Published	Benchmark Type
Intel	iCOMP index 2.0	Processor
Intel	iCOMP index 2.0	System Intel Media Benchmark
Business Applications Performance Corporation	SYSmark/NT (BAPCo)	System
Business Applications Performance Corporation for Windows	SYSmark/NT, SYSmark95 (BAPCo)	System
Standard Performance Evaluation Corporation	SPECint95 (SPEC)	Processor
Standard Performance Evaluation Corporation	SPECint95, SPECfp95	Processor (SPEC)
Ziff-Davis Benchmark	CPUmark32	Processor Operation
Ziff-Davis Benchmark	Winstone 98	System Operation
Ziff-Davis Benchmark	WinBench 98	System Operation
Ziff-Davis Benchmark	CPUmark32, Winstone 98, WinBench 98, 3D WinBench 98	System Operation
Symantec Corporation	Norton SI32	Processor
Symantec Corporation Norton Multimedia	Norton SI32, Benchmark	System

Processor Troubleshooting Techniques

Processors are normally very reliable. Most PC problems will be with other devices, but if you suspect the processor, there are some steps you can take to troubleshoot it. The easiest thing to do is to replace the microprocessor with a known good spare. If the problem goes away, the original processor is defective. If the problem persists, the problem is likely elsewhere.

Table 3.46 provides a general troubleshooting checklist for processor-related PC problems.

Table 3.46   Troubleshooting Processor-Related Problems

Problem Identification	Possible Cause	Resolution
System is dead, no cursor, no beeps, no fan	Power cord failure	Plug in or replace power cord. Power cords can fail even though they look fine.
	Power supply Failure	Replace the power supply. Use a known-good spare for testing.

(continues)

Table 3.46   Troubleshooting Processor-Related Problems

Problem Identification	Possible Cause	Resolution
	Motherboard failure	Replace motherboard. Use a known good spare for testing.
	Memory failure	Remove all memory except 1 bank and retest. If the system still won't boot replace bank 1.
System is dead, no beeps, or locks up before POST begins	All components either not installed or incorrectly installed	Check all peripherals, especially memory and graphics adapter. Reseat all boards and socketed components.
System beeps on startup, fan is running, no cursor on screen.	Improperly Seated or Failing Graphics Adapter	Reseat or replace graphics adapter. Use known good spare for testing.
Locks up during or shortly after POST	Poor Heat Dissipation	Check CPU heat sink/fan; replace if necessary, use one with higher capacity
	Improper voltage settings	Set motherboard for proper core processor voltage
	Wrong motherboard bus speed	Set motherboard for proper speed
	Wrong CPU clock multiplier	Jumper motherboard for proper clock multiplier
Improper CPU identification during POST	Old BIOS	Update BIOS from manufacturer
	Board is not configured properly	Check manual and jumper board accordingly to proper bus and multiplier settings
Operating system will not boot	Poor heat dissipation	Check CPU fan; replace if necessary, may need higher capacity heat sink
	Improper voltage settings	Jumper motherboard for proper core voltage
	Wrong motherboard bus speed	Jumper motherboard for proper speed
	Wrong CPU clock multiplier	Jumper motherboard for proper clock multiplier
	Applications will not install or run	Improper drivers or incompatible hardware; update drivers and check for compatibility issues
System appears to work, but no video is displayed	Monitor turned off or failed	Check monitor and power to monitor. Replace with known, good spare for testing

If during the POST the processor is not identified correctly, your motherboard settings might be incorrect or your BIOS might need to be updated. Check that the motherboard is jumpered or configured correctly for the processor that you have, and make sure that you have the latest BIOS for your motherboard.

If the system seems to run erratically after it warms up, try setting the processor to a lower speed setting. If the problem goes away, the processor might be defective or overclocked.

Many hardware problems are really software problems in disguise. Make sure you have the latest BIOS for your motherboard, as well as the latest drivers for all your peripherals. Also it helps to use the latest version of your given operating system since there will normally be fewer problems.

Motherboards and Buses

SOME OF THE MAIN TOPICS IN THIS CHAPTER ARE

Motherboard Form Factors

Without a doubt, the most important component in a PC system is the main board or motherboard. Some companies refer to the motherboard as a system board or planar. The terms, *motherboard*, *main board*, *system board*, and *planar* are interchangeable. In this chapter, we will examine the different types of motherboards available and those components usually contained on the motherboard and motherboard interface connectors.

There are several common form factors used for PC motherboards. The form factor refers to the physical dimensions and size of the board, and dictates what type of case the board will fit into. Some are true standards (meaning that all boards with that form factor are interchangeable), while others are not standardized enough to allow for true interchangeability. Unfortunately these nonstandard form factors preclude any easy upgrade, which generally means they should be avoided. The more commonly known PC motherboard form factors include the following:

Obsolete Form Factors

- Baby-AT
- Full-size AT
- LPX (semi-proprietary)

All Others

- Proprietary Designs (Compaq, Packard Bell, Hewlett-Packard, notebook/portable systems, etc.)

Modern Form Factors

- ATX
- Micro-ATX
- Flex-ATX
- NLX
- WTX

Motherboards have evolved over the years from the original Baby-AT size and shape boards used in the original IBM PC and XT, to the current ATX, NLX, and WTX boards used in most full-size desktop and tower systems. ATX has a number of variants, including Micro-ATX (which is a smaller version of the ATX form factor used in the smaller systems) to Flex-ATX (an even smaller version for the lowest-cost home PCs). NLX is designed for corporate desktop type systems; WTX is for workstations and medium duty servers. The following table shows the modern industry-standard form factors and their recommended uses.

Form Factor	Use
ATX	Standard desktop, mini-tower and full-tower systems, most common form factor today, most flexible design
Micro-ATX	Lower cost desktop or mini-tower systems
Flex-ATX	Least expensive small desktop or mini-tower systems
NLX	Corporate desktop or mini-tower systems, integrated 10/100 Ethernet, easiest and quickest to service
WTX	High performance workstations, midrange servers

Although the Baby-AT, Full-size AT, and LPX boards were once popular, they have all but been replaced by more modern and interchangeable form factors. The modern form factors are true standards, which guarantees improved interchangeability within each type. This means that ATX boards will interchange with other ATX boards, NLX with other NLX and so on. The additional features found on these boards as compared to the obsolete form factors, combined with true interchangeability, has made the migration to these newer form factors quick and easy. Today I only recommend purchasing systems with one of the modern industry-standard form factors.

Anything that does not fit into one of the industry standard form factors is considered proprietary. Unless there are special circumstances, I do not recommend purchasing systems with proprietary board designs. They will be virtually impossible to upgrade and very expensive to repair later, because the motherboard, case, and often power supply will not be interchangeable with other models. I call proprietary form factor systems "disposable" PCs, since that's what you must normally do with them when they are too slow or need repair out of warranty.

The following sections detail each of the standard form factors.

Baby-AT

The first popular PC motherboard was, of course, the original IBM PC released in 1981. Figure 4.1 shows how this board looked. IBM followed the PC with the XT motherboard in 1983, which had the same basic shape as the PC board, but had eight slots instead of five. Also, the slots were spaced 0.8 inch apart instead of 1 inch apart as in the PC (see Figure 4.2). The XT also eliminated the weird cassette port in the back, which was supposed to be used to save BASIC programs on cassette tape instead of the much more expensive (at the time) floppy drive.

▶▶ See "An Introduction to the PC (5150)," in "IBM Personal Computer Family Hardware" on the CD

▶▶ See "An Introduction to the XT (5160)," in "IBM Personal Computer Family Hardware" on the CD

The minor differences in the slot positions and the now lonesome keyboard connector on the back required a minor redesign of the case. This motherboard became very popular and many other PC motherboard manufacturers of the day copied IBM's XT design and produced similar boards. By the time most of these clones or compatible systems came out, IBM had released their AT system, which initially used a larger form factor motherboard. Due to the advances in circuit miniaturization, these companies found they could fit all the additional circuits found on the 16-bit AT motherboard into the XT motherboard form factor. Rather than call these boards XT-sized, which may have made people think they were 8-bit designs, they referred to them as Baby-AT, which ended up meaning an XT-sized board with AT motherboard design features (16-bit or greater).

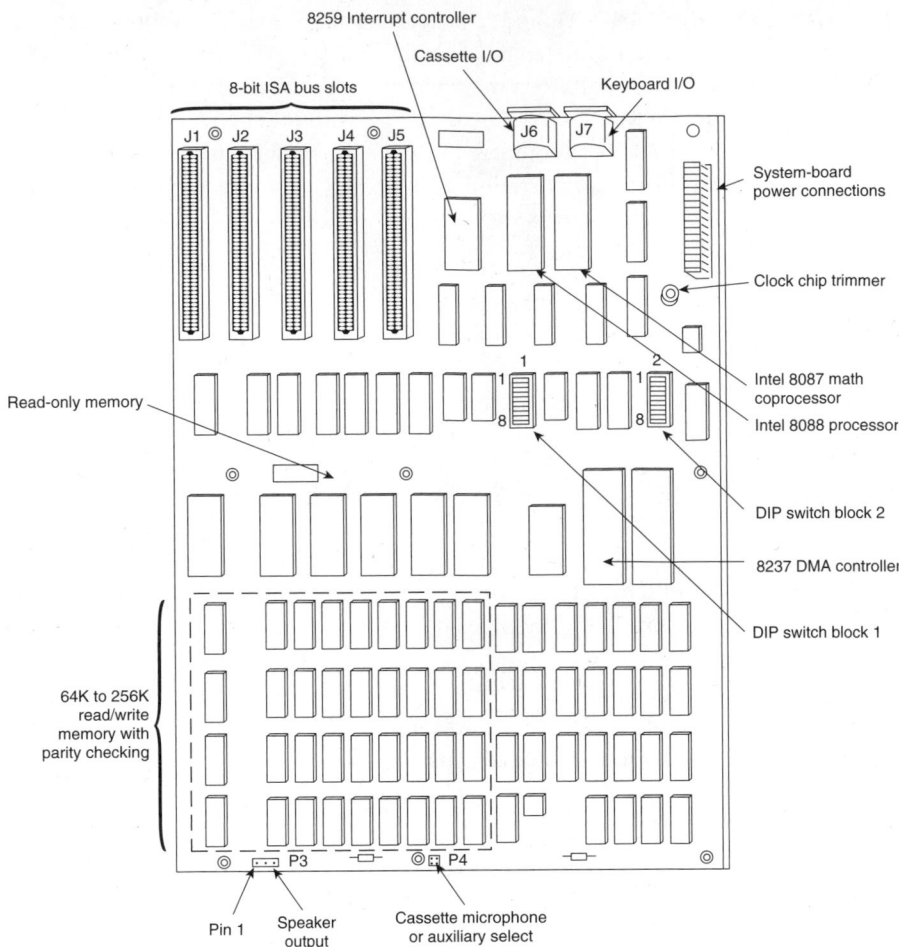

Figure 4.1 IBM PC motherboard (circa 1981).

Thus, the Baby-AT form factor is essentially the same as the original IBM XT motherboard. The only difference is a slight modification in one of the screw hole positions to fit into an AT-style case (see Figure 4.3). These motherboards also have specific placement of the keyboard and slot connectors to match the holes in the case. Note that virtually all full-size AT and Baby-AT motherboards use the standard 5-pin DIN type connector for the keyboard. Baby-AT motherboards can be used to replace full-sized AT motherboards and will fit into a number of different case designs. Because of their flexibility, from 1983 into early 1996 the Baby-AT form factor was the most popular motherboard type. Starting in mid-1996, Baby-AT was replaced by the superior ATX motherboard design, which is not directly interchangeable. Most systems sold since 1996 have used the improved ATX, micro-ATX, or NLX designs, and Baby-AT is getting harder and harder to come by. Figure 4.3 shows the dimensions and layout of a Baby-AT motherboard.

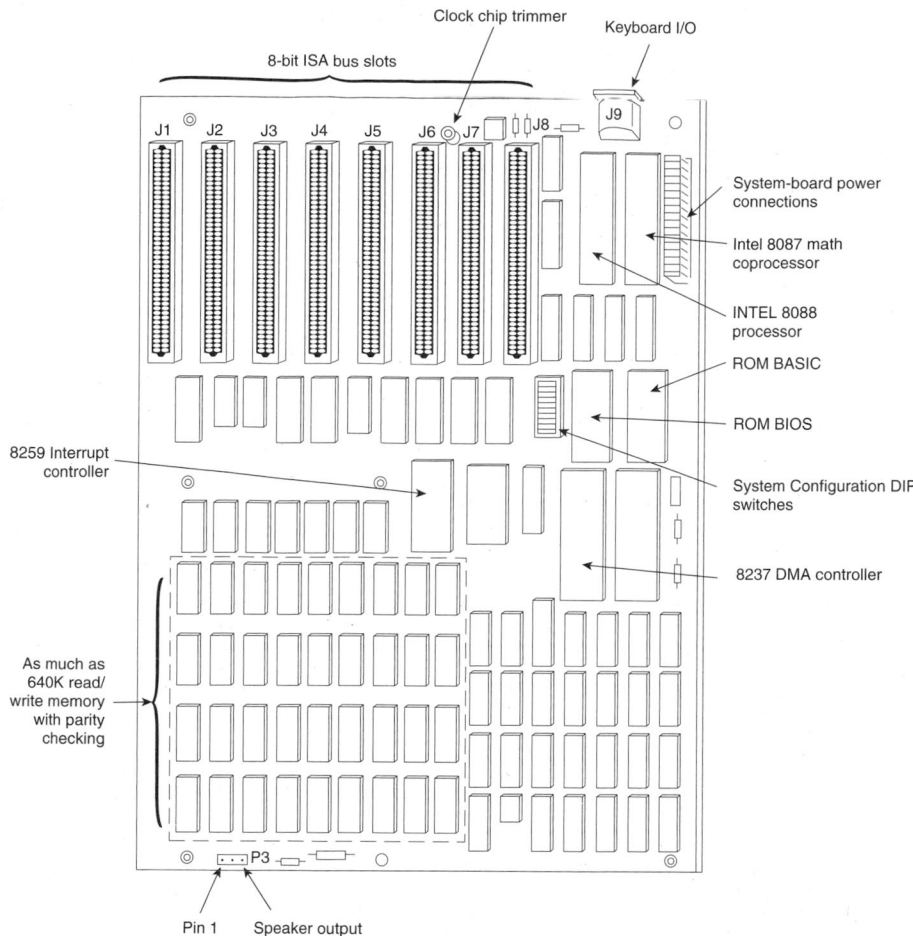

Figure 4.2 IBM PC-XT motherboard (circa 1983).

Any case that accepts a full-sized AT motherboard will also accept a Baby-AT design. Since its debut in the IBM XT motherboard in 1983 and lasting well into 1996, the Baby-AT motherboard form factor was, for that time, the most popular design. You can get a PC motherboard with virtually any processor from the original 8088 to the fastest Pentium III in this design, although the pickings are slim in the Pentium II/III category. As such, systems with Baby-AT motherboards are virtually by definition upgradable systems. Because any Baby-AT motherboard can be replaced with any other Baby-AT motherboard, this is an interchangeable design.

Until mid-1996 I had recommended to most people that they make sure any PC system they purchased had a Baby-AT motherboard. They would sometimes say, "I've never heard of that brand before." "Of course," I'd tell them, "that's not a brand, but a shape!" The point being that if they had a Baby-AT board in their system, when a year or so goes by and they longed for something faster, it would be easy and inexpensive to purchase a newer board with a faster processor and simply swap it in. If they purchased a system with a proprietary or semi-proprietary board, they would be out of luck when it came time to upgrade, because they had a disposable PC. Disposable PCs may be cheaper initially, but they are usually much more expensive in the long run because they can't easily or inexpensively be upgraded or repaired.

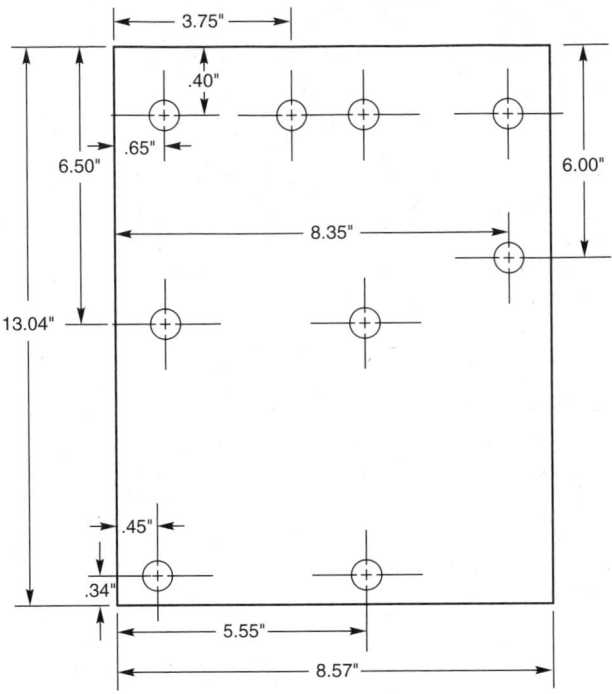

Figure 4.3   Baby-AT motherboard form factor dimensions.

The easiest way to identify a Baby-AT form factor system without opening it is to look at the rear of the case. In a Baby-AT motherboard, the cards plug directly into the board at a 90-degree angle; in other words, the slots in the case for the cards are perpendicular to the motherboard. Also, the Baby-AT motherboard has only one visible connector directly attached to the board, which is the keyboard connector. Normally this connector is the full-sized 5-pin DIN type connector; although, some Baby-AT systems will use the smaller 6-pin min-DIN connector (sometimes called a PS/2 type connector) and may even have a mouse connector. All other connectors will be mounted on the case or on card edge brackets and attached to the motherboard via cables.

Figure 4.4 shows the connector profile at the rear of Baby-AT boards. The keyboard connector is visible through an appropriately placed hole in the case.

▶▶ See "Keyboard/Mouse Interface Connectors," p. 920.

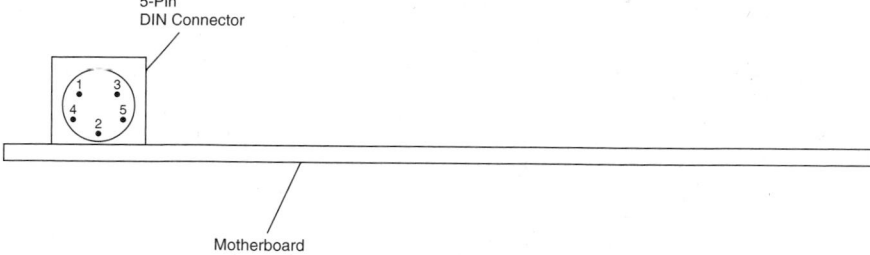

Figure 4.4   The Baby-AT motherboard rear connector profile showing keyboard connector position.

Baby-AT boards all conform to specific width, screw hole, slot, and keyboard connector locations, but one thing that can vary is the length of the board. Versions have been built that are shorter than the full 13-inch length; these are often called Mini-AT, Micro-AT, or even things such as 2/3-Baby or 1/2-Baby. Even though they may not have the full length, they still bolt directly into the same case as a standard Baby-AT board, and can be used as a direct replacement for one.

Full-Size AT

The full-size AT motherboard matches the original IBM AT motherboard design. This allows for a very large board of up to 12 inches wide by 13.8 inches deep. When the full-size AT board debuted in 1984, IBM needed more room for additional circuits when they migrated from the 8-bit architecture of the PC/XT to the 16-bit architecture of the AT. So, IBM started with an XT board and extended it in two directions (see Figure 4.5).

The board was redesigned to make it slightly smaller a little over a year after being introduced. Then it was redesigned again as IBM shrank it down to XT-size in a system they called the XT-286 (see Figure 28.14 in Chapter 28). The XT-286 board size was virtually identical to the original XT, and was adopted by most PC-compatible manufacturers when it became known as Baby-AT.

▶▶ See "An Introduction to the AT," in "IBM Personal Computer Family Hardware" on the CD

▶▶ See "An Introduction to the XT Model 286," in "IBM Personal Computer Family Hardware" on the CD

The keyboard connector and slot connectors in the full-sized AT boards still conformed to the same specific placement requirements to fit the holes in the XT cases already in use, but a larger case was still required to fit the larger board. Due to the larger size of the board, a full-size AT motherboard will fit into full-size AT desktop or Tower cases only. Because these motherboards will not fit into the smaller Baby-AT or Mini-Tower cases, and because of advances in component miniaturization, they are no longer being produced by most motherboard manufacturers, except in some cases for dual processor server applications.

Note that you can always replace a full-size AT motherboard with a Baby-AT board, but the opposite is not true unless the case is large enough to accommodate the full-size AT design.

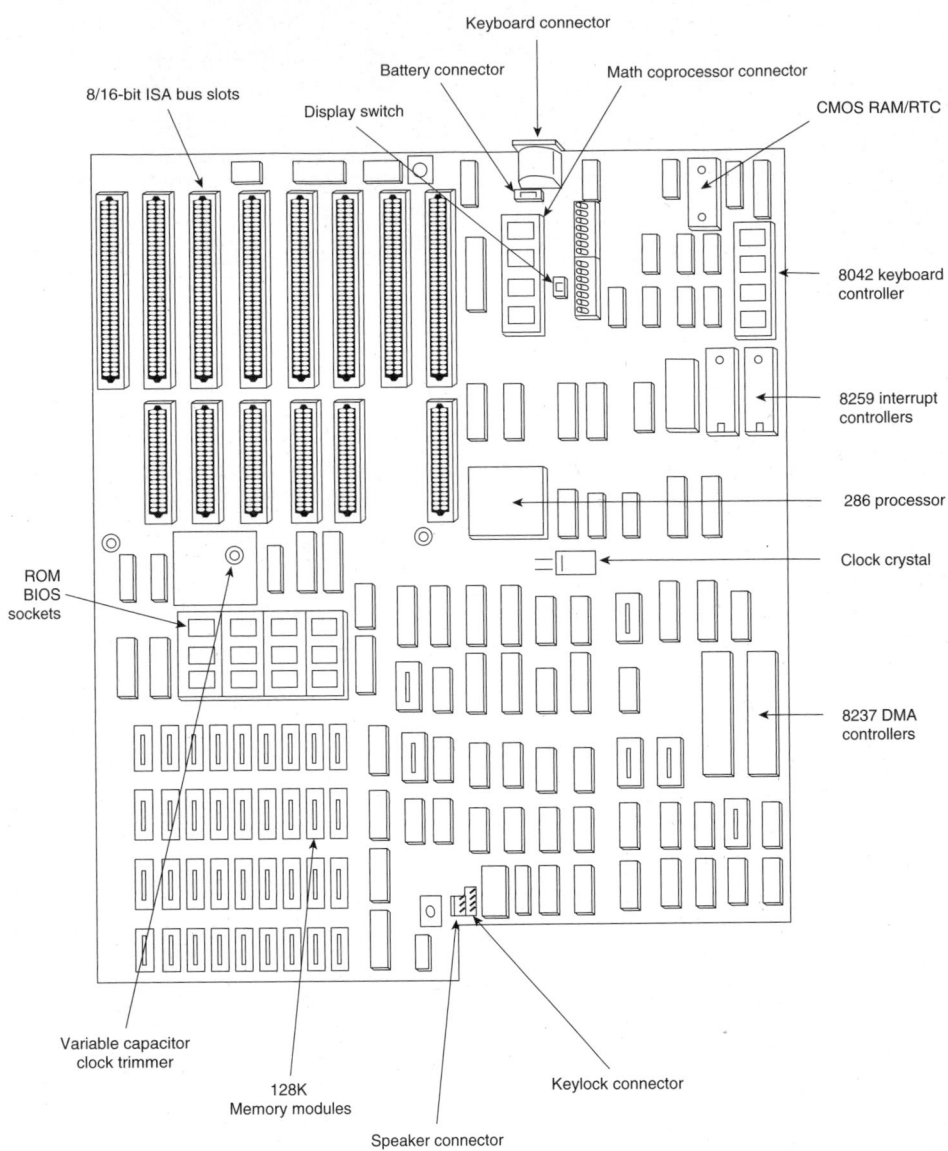

Figure 4.5 IBM AT motherboard (circa 1984).

LPX

The LPX and Mini-LPX form factor boards are a semi-proprietary design originally developed by Western Digital in 1987 for some of their motherboards. The LP in LPX stands for Low Profile, which is so named because these boards incorporated slots that were parallel to the main board, allowing the expansion cards to install sideways. This allowed for a slim or low profile case design and overall a smaller system than the Baby-AT.

Although Western Digital no longer produces PC motherboards, the form factor lives on and has been duplicated by many other motherboard manufacturers. Unfortunately, because the specifications were never laid out in exact detail—especially with regard to the bus riser card portion of the design—these boards are termed semi-proprietary and are not interchangeable between manufacturers. This means that if you have a system with an LPX board, in most cases you will not be able to replace the motherboard with a different LPX board later. You essentially have a system that you cannot upgrade or repair by replacing the motherboard with something better. In other words, you have what I call a disposable PC, something I would not normally recommend that anybody purchase.

Most people are not aware of the semi-proprietary nature of the design of these boards, and they have been extremely popular in what I call "retail store" PCs from the late '80s through the late '90s. This would include primarily Compaq and Packard Bell systems, as well as any others who used this form factor. These boards wer most often used in Low Profile or Slimline case systems, but can also be found in Tower cases, too. These are often lower cost systems such as those sold at retail electronics superstores. Due to their proprietary nature, I recommend staying away from any system that uses an LPX motherboard.

LPX boards are characterized by several distinctive features (see Figure 4.6). The most noticeable is that the expansion slots are mounted on a bus riser card that plugs into the motherboard. Expansion cards must plug sideways into the riser card. This sideways placement allows for the low profile case design. Slots will be located on one or both sides of the riser card depending on the system and case design.

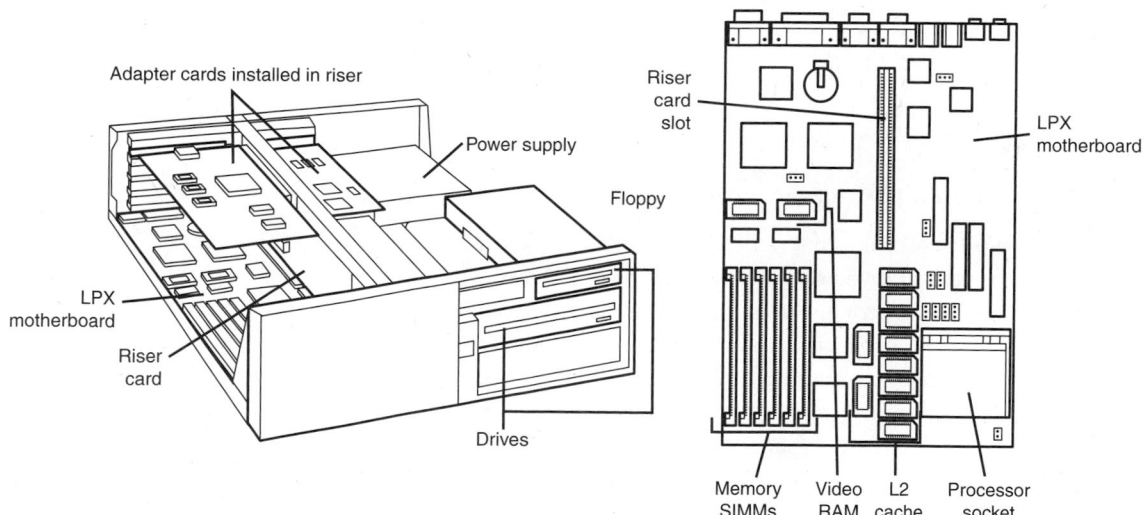

Figure 4.6 Typical LPX system chassis and motherboard.

Another distinguishing feature of the LPX design is the standard placement of connectors on the back of the board. An LPX board will have a row of connectors for video (VGA 15-pin), parallel

(25-pin), two serial ports (9-pin each), and mini-DIN PS/2 style mouse and keyboard connectors. All these connectors are mounted across the rear of the motherboard and protrude through a slot in the case. Some LPX motherboards may have additional connectors for other internal ports such as Network or SCSI adapters. Figure 4.7 shows the standard form factors for the LPX and Mini-LPX motherboards used in many systems today.

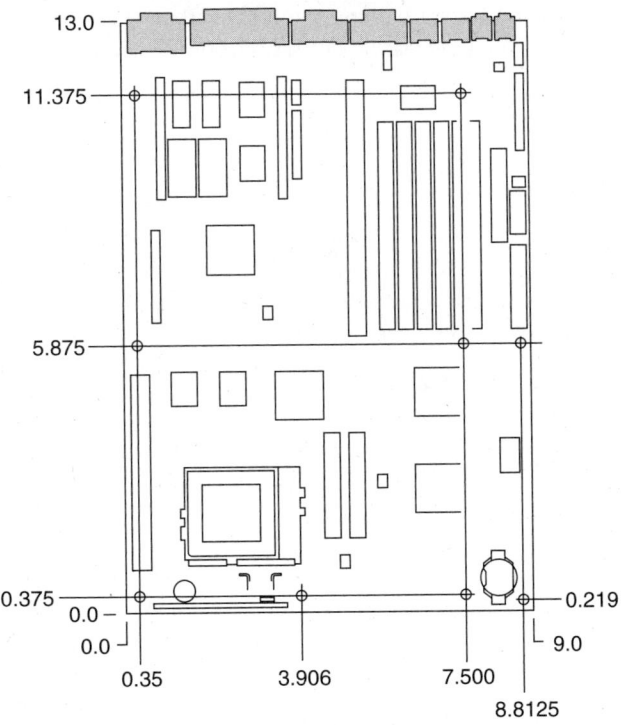

Figure 4.7 LPX motherboard dimensions.

I am often asked, "How can I tell if a system has an LPX board before I purchase it?" Fortunately, this is easy, and you don't even have to open the system up or remove the cover. LPX motherboards have a very distinctive design with the bus slots on a riser card that plugs into the motherboard. This means that any card slots will be parallel to the motherboard, because the cards stick out sideways from the riser. Looking at the back of a system, you should be able to tell whether the card slots are parallel to the motherboard. This implies a bus riser card is used, which also normally implies that the system is an LPX design.

The use of a riser card no longer directly implies that the motherboard is an LPX design. More recently, a newer form factor called NLX has been released which also uses a riser card.

On an LPX board, the riser is placed in the middle of the motherboard while NLX boards have the riser to the side (the motherboard actually plugs into the riser in NLX).

Because the riser card is no longer used only on LPX boards, perhaps the easiest feature to distinguish is the single height row of connectors along the bottom of the board. The NLX boards have a different connector area with both single-row and double-row connector areas.

See the section on NLX motherboards later in this chapter for more information on NLX.

See Figure 4.8 for an example of the connectors on the back of an LPX board. There are two connector arrangements shown, for systems without or with USB ports. Note that not all LPX boards will have the built-in audio, so those connectors might be missing. Other ports can be missing from what is shown in these diagrams, depending on exactly what options are included on a specific board.

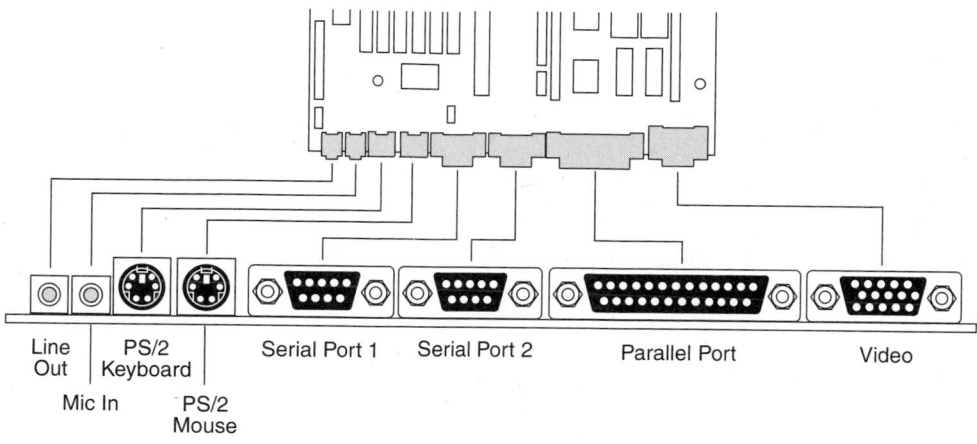

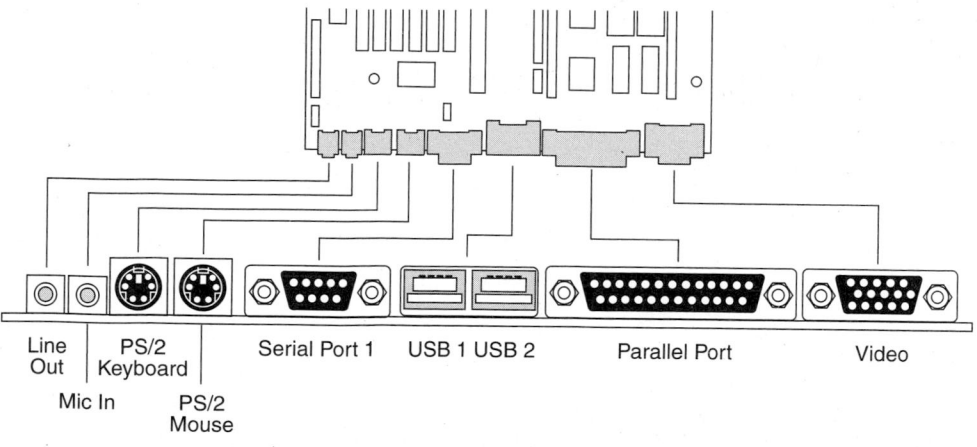

Figure 4.8 LPX motherboard back panel connectors.

The connectors along the rear of the board prevent expansion cards from being plugged directly into the motherboard, which accounts for why riser cards are used for adding expansion boards.

While the built-in connectors on the LPX boards were a good idea, unfortunately, the LPX design was proprietary (not a fully interchangeable standard) and thus, not a good choice. Newer motherboard form factors such as ATX, Micro-ATX, and NLX have both built-in connectors and use a standard board design. In fact, the NLX form factor was developed as a modern replacement for LPX.

ATX

The ATX form factor was the first of a dramatic evolution in motherboard form factors. ATX is a combination of the best features of the Baby-AT and LPX motherboard designs, with many new enhancements and features thrown in. The ATX form factor is essentially a Baby-AT motherboard turned sideways in the chassis, along with a modified power supply location and connector. The most important thing to know initially about the ATX form factor is that it is physically incompatible with either the previous Baby-AT or LPX designs. In other words, a different case and power supply are required to match the ATX motherboard. These new case and power supply designs have become common, and can be found in many new systems.

The official ATX specification was initially released by Intel in July 1995 and was written as an open specification for the industry. ATX boards didn't hit the market in force until mid-1996 when they rapidly began replacing Baby-AT boards in new systems. The ATX specification was updated to version 2.01 in February 1997. The latest revision is ATX version 2.03, released in December 1998. Intel has published detailed specifications so other manufacturers can use the ATX design in their systems. Currently, ATX is the most popular motherboard form factor for new systems, and it is the one I recommend most people get in their systems today. An ATX system will be upgradable for many years to come, exactly like Baby-AT was in the past.

ATX improves on the Baby-AT and LPX motherboard designs in several major areas:

- *Built-in double high external I/O connector panel.* The rear portion of the motherboard includes a stacked I/O connector area that is 6 1/4-inches wide by 1 3/4-inches tall. This allows external connectors to be located directly on the board and negates the need for cables running from internal connectors to the back of the case as with Baby-AT designs.

- *Single keyed internal power supply connector.* This is a boon for the average end user who always had to worry about interchanging the Baby-AT power supply connectors and subsequently blowing the motherboard! The ATX specification includes a single keyed and shrouded power connector that is easy to plug in, and which cannot be installed incorrectly. This connector also features pins for supplying 3.3v to the motherboard, which means that ATX motherboards will not require built-in voltage regulators that are susceptible to failure.

▶▶ See "Power Supply Connectors," p. 1102.

- *Relocated CPU and memory.* The CPU and memory modules are relocated so they cannot interfere with any bus expansion cards, and they can easily be accessed for upgrade without removing any of the installed bus adapters. The CPU and memory are relocated next to the power supply, which is where the primary system fan is located. The improved airflow concentrated over the processor often eliminates the need for extra-cost and sometimes failure-prone CPU cooling fans. There is room for a large passive heat sink on the CPU with more than adequate clearance provided in that area.

Note

Note that systems from smaller vendors might still include CPU fans even in ATX systems, as Intel supplies processors with attached high-quality (ball bearing) fans for CPUs sold to smaller vendors. These are so-called "boxed" processors because they are sold in single-unit box quantities instead of pallets of 100 or more like the raw CPUs sold to the larger vendors. Intel includes the fan as insurance because most smaller vendors and system assemblers lack the engineering knowledge necessary to perform thermal analysis, temperature measurements, and the testing required to select the properly sized passive heat sink. By putting a fan on these "boxed" processors, Intel is covering their bases, as the fan will ensure adequate CPU cooling. This allows them to put a warranty on the boxed processors that is independent of the system warranty. Larger vendors have the engineering talent to select the proper passive heat sink, thus reducing the cost of the system as well as increasing reliability. With an OEM non-boxed processor, the warranty is with the system vendor and not Intel directly. Intel normally includes heat sink mounting instructions with their motherboards if non-boxed processors are used.

- *Relocated internal I/O connectors.* The internal I/O connectors for the floppy and hard disk drives are relocated to be near the drive bays and out from under the expansion board slot and drive bay areas. This means that internal cables to the drives can be much shorter, and accessing the connectors will not require card or drive removal.

- *Improved cooling.* The CPU and main memory are positioned so they can be cooled directly by the power supply fan, eliminating the need for separate case or CPU cooling fans. Note that the ATX specification originally specified that the ATX power supply fan blows into the system chassis instead of outward. This reverse flow, or positive pressure design, pressurizes the case, which greatly minimizes dust and dirt intrusion. With the positive pressurized reverse flow design, an air filter can be easily added to the air intake vents on the power supply, creating a system that is even more immune to dirt and dust. More recently, the ATX specification was revised to allow the more normal standard flow, which negatively pressurizes the case by having the fan blow outward. Because the specification technically allows either type of airflow, and because some overall cooling efficiency is lost with the reverse flow design, most power supply manufacturers provide ATX power supplies with standard airflow fans that exhaust air from the system, otherwise called a negative pressure design.

- *Lower cost to manufacture.* The ATX specification eliminates the need for the rat's nest of cables to external port connectors found on Baby-AT motherboards, additional CPU or chassis cooling fans, or onboard 3.3v voltage regulators. Instead, ATX uses a single power supply connector and allows for shorter internal drive cables. These all conspire to greatly reduce the cost of the motherboard the cost of a complete system—including the case and power supply.

Figure 4.9 shows the new ATX system layout and chassis features, as you would see them looking in with the lid off on a desktop, or sideways in a tower with the side panel removed. Notice how virtually the entire motherboard is clear of the drive bays, and how the devices such as CPU, memory, and internal drive connectors are easy to access and do not interfere with the bus slots. Also notice the power supply orientation and the single power supply fan that blows into the case directly over the high heat, cooling items such as the CPU and memory.

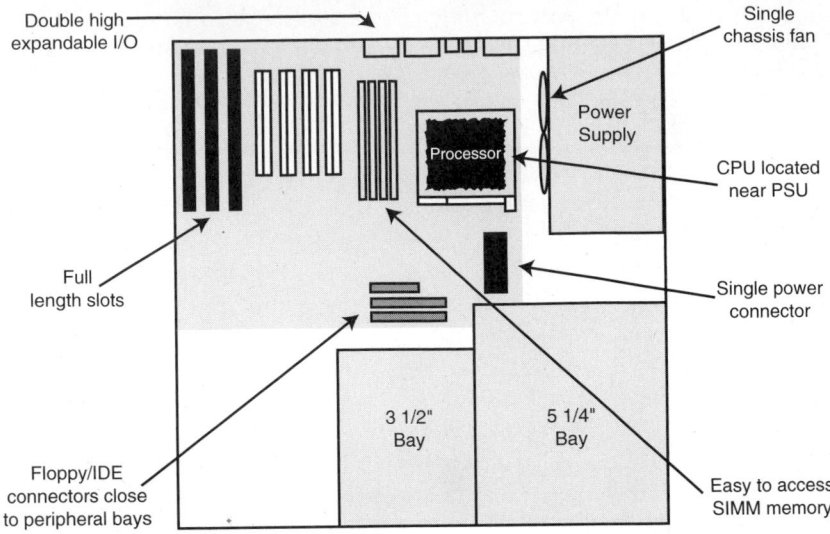

Figure 4.9 ATX system chassis layout and features.

The ATX motherboard is basically a Baby-AT design rotated sideways. The expansion slots are now parallel to the shorter side dimension and do not interfere with the CPU, memory, or I/O connector sockets. There are actually two basic sizes of ATX boards. In addition to a full-sized ATX layout, Intel also has specified a mini-ATX design, which is a fully compatible subset in size and will fit into the same case. A full size ATX board is 12" wide × 9.6" deep (305mm × 244mm). The mini-ATX board is 11.2" × 8.2" (284mm × 208mm).

Although the case holes are similar to the Baby-AT case, cases for the two formats are generally not compatible. The power supplies would require a connector adapter to be interchangeable, but the basic ATX power supply design is similar to the standard Slimline power supply. The ATX and mini-ATX motherboard dimensions are shown in Figure 4.10.Clearly, the advantages of the ATX form factor make it the best choice for new systems. For backward compatibility, you can still find Baby-AT boards for use in upgrading older systems, but the choices are becoming slimmer every day. I would never recommend building or purchasing a new system with a Baby-AT motherboard, as you will severely limit your future upgrade possibilities. In fact, I have been recommending only ATX systems for new system purchases since late 1996 and will probably continue to do so for the next several years.

The best way to tell whether your system has an ATX-board design without removing the lid is to look at the back of the system. There are two distinguishing features that identify ATX. One is that the expansion boards plug directly into the motherboard. There is no riser card like with LPX or NLX and so the slots will be perpendicular to the plane of the motherboard. Also, ATX boards have a unique double-high connector area for all the built-in connectors on the motherboard (see Figure 4.11). This will be found just to the side of the bus slot area, and can be used to easily identify an ATX board.

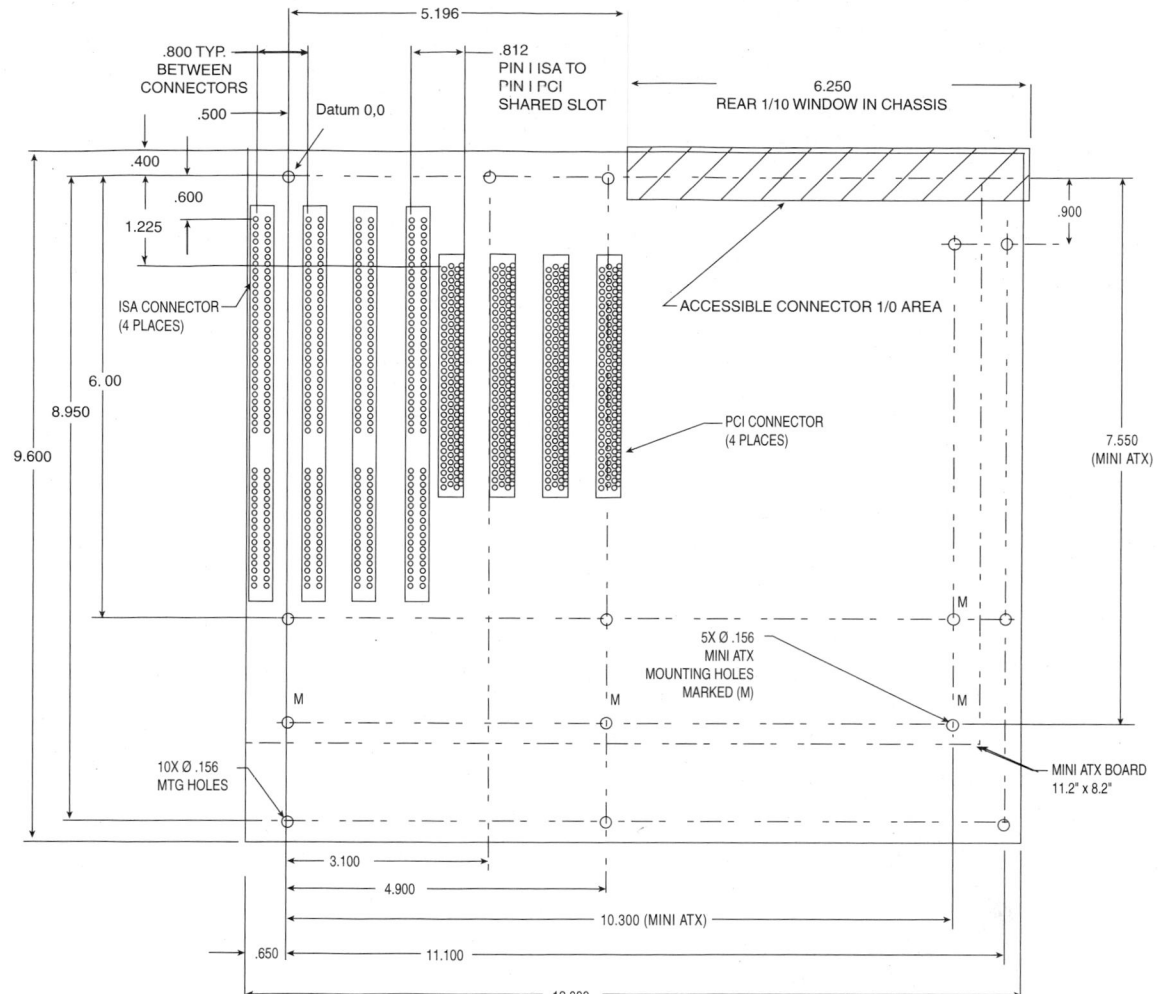

Figure 4.10 ATX specification version 2.03, showing ATX and mini-ATX dimensions.

The specification and related information about the ATX, mini-ATX, micro-ATX, flex-ATX, or NLX form factor specifications are available from the Platform Development Support Web site at `http://www.teleport.com/~ffsupprt/`. This single public site replaces the previous independent sites dedicated to those form factors. The Platform Developer site provides form factor specifications and design guides, as well as design considerations for new technologies, information on initiative supporters, vendor products through a "One-Stop-Shopping" mall link, and a form factor bulletin board.

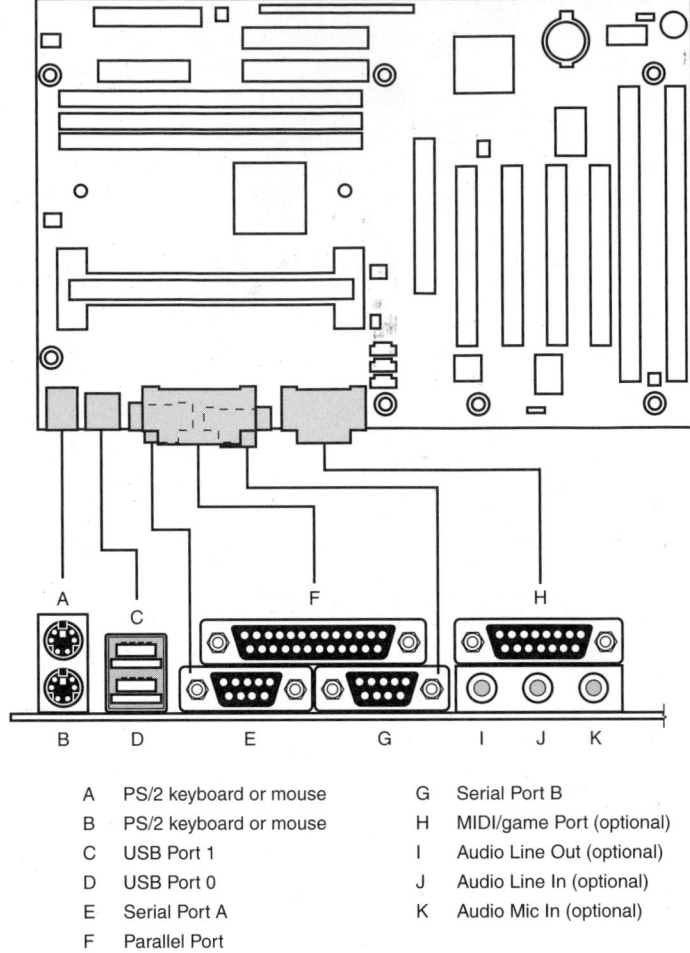

A	PS/2 keyboard or mouse	G	Serial Port B
B	PS/2 keyboard or mouse	H	MIDI/game Port (optional)
C	USB Port 1	I	Audio Line Out (optional)
D	USB Port 0	J	Audio Line In (optional)
E	Serial Port A	K	Audio Mic In (optional)
F	Parallel Port		

Figure 4.11 Typical ATX motherboard rear panel connectors.

Micro-ATX

Micro-ATX is a motherboard form factor originally introduced by Intel in December of 1997 as an evolution of the ATX form factor for smaller and lower cost systems. The reduced size as compared to standard ATX allows for a smaller chassis, motherboard, and power supply, reducing the cost of entire system. The micro-ATX form factor is also backward compatible with the ATX form factor and can be used in full-size ATX cases. During early 1999 this form factor began to really catch on in the low-cost, sub-$1,000 PC market.

The main differences between micro-ATX and standard or mini-ATX are as follows:

- Reduced width motherboard (9.6" [244mm] instead of 12" [305mm] or 11.2" [284mm])
- Fewer I/O bus expansion slots
- Smaller power supply (SFX form factor)

The micro-ATX motherboard maximum size is only 9.6" × 9.6" (244 × 244 mm) as compared to the full-size ATX size of 12" × 9.6" (305 × 244 mm) or the mini-ATX size of 11.2" × 8.2" (284mm × 208mm). Even smaller boards can be designed as long as they conform to the location of the mounting holes, connector positions, etc. as defined by the standard. Fewer slots aren't a problem because more components such as sound and video are likely to be integrated on the motherboard and therefore won't require separate slots. This higher integration reduces motherboard and system costs. External buses such as USB, 10/100 Ethernet, and optionally 1394 (FireWire) will provide additional expansion out of the box.

The specifications for micro-ATX motherboard dimensions are shown in Figure 4.12.

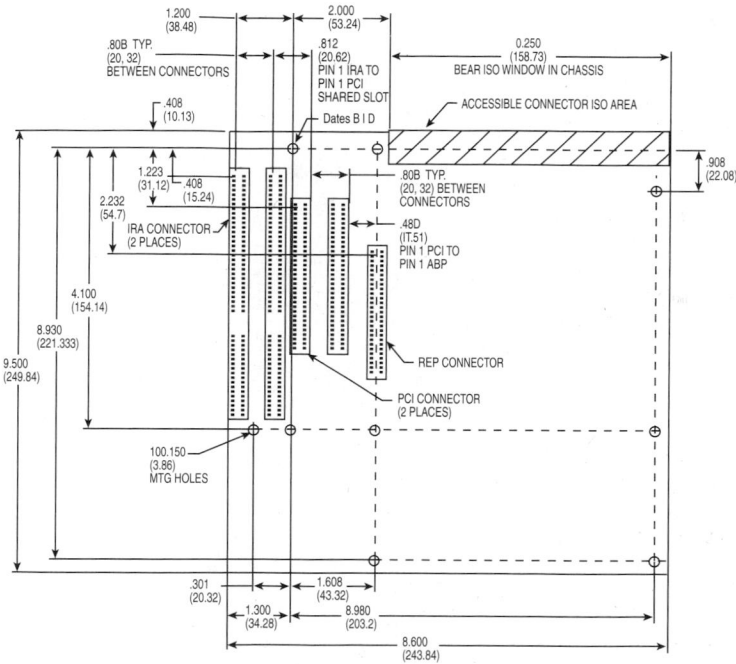

Figure 4.12   Micro-ATX specification 1.0 motherboard dimensions.

A new, small form factor (called SFX) power supply has been defined for use with micro-ATX systems. The smaller size of this power supply encourages flexibility in choosing mounting locations within the chassis, and will allow for smaller systems which consume less power overall.

▶▶ See "SFX Style (micro-ATX Motherboards)," p. 1099.

The micro-ATX form factor is similar to ATX for compatibility. The similarities include the following:

- Standard ATX 20-pin power connector
- Standard ATX I/O panel
- Mounting holes are a subset of ATX

These similarities will ensure that a micro-ATX motherboard will easily work in a standard ATX chassis with a standard ATX power supply, as well as the smaller micro-ATX chassis and SFX power supply.

The overall system size for a micro-ATX is very small. A typical case will be only 12" to 14" tall, about 7" wide, and 12" deep. This results in a kind of micro-tower or desktop size. A typical micro-ATX tower is shown in Figure 4.13.

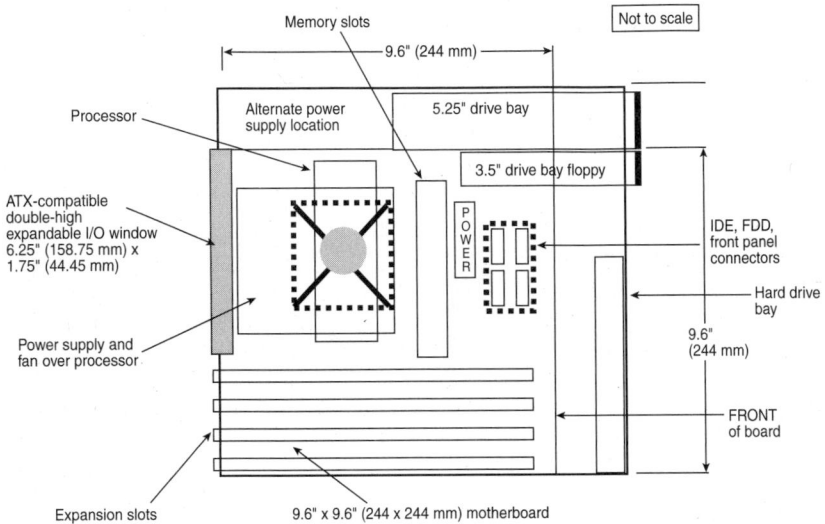

Figure 4.13   Micro-ATX system side view showing typical internal layout.

As with ATX, micro-ATX was released to the public domain by Intel so as to facilitate adoption as a de facto standard. The specification and related information on micro-ATX are available through the Platform Developer Web site (`http://www.teleport.com/~ffsupprt/`).

Flex-ATX

In March of 1999, Intel released the flex-ATX addendum to the micro-ATX specification. This added a new and even smaller variation of the ATX form factor to the motherboard scene. Flex-ATX is smaller design intended to allow a variety of new PC designs, especially extremely inexpensive, smaller, consumer-oriented, appliance type systems.

Flex-ATX defines a board that is only 9.0" × 7.5" (229mm × 191mm) in size, which is the smallest of the ATX family boards. Besides the smaller size, the other biggest difference between the flex-ATX form factor and the micro-ATX is that flex-ATX will only support socketed processors. This means that a flex-ATX board will not have a Slot 1 or Slot 2 type connector for the cartridge versions of the Pentium II/III processors. However, it can have Socket 7 or the newer Socket 370, which supports up through the AMD K6-3 and Intel Celeron (Pentium II/III class) processors. Future versions of the Pentium III will most likely become available in the Socket 370 design and will be usable in flex-ATX boards.

Besides the smaller size and socketed-processor only requirement, the rest of flex-ATX is backward compatible with standard ATX, using a subset of the mounting holes and the same I/O and power supply connector specifications (see Figure 4.14).

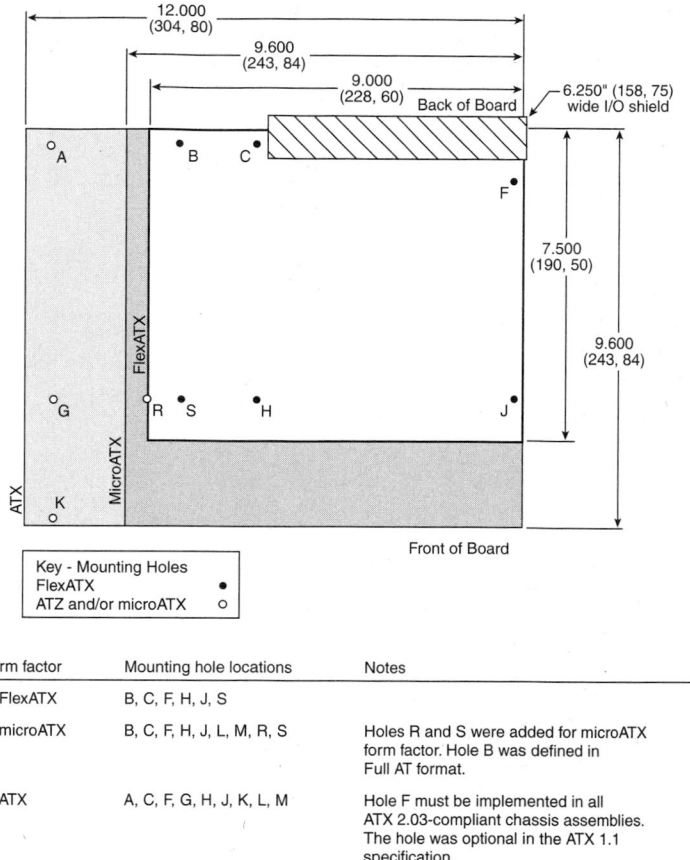

Figure 4.14   Size and mounting hole comparison between ATX, micro-ATX, and flex-ATX motherboards.

Most flex-ATX systems will likely use the SFX (small form factor) type power supplies (introduced in the micro-ATX specification), although if the case allows, a standard ATX power supply can also be used.

With the addition of flex-ATX, the family of ATX boards has now grown to include four definitions of size, as shown in Table 4.1:

Table 4.1 ATX Motherboard Form Factors

Form Factor	Max. Width	Max. Depth
ATX	12.0" (305mm)	9.6" (244mm)
Mini-ATX	11.2" (284mm)	8.2" (208mm)
Micro-ATX	9.6" (244mm)	9.6" (244mm)
Flex-ATX	9.0" (229mm)	7.5" (191mm)

Note that these dimensions are the maximum the board can be. It is always possible to make a board smaller as long as it conforms to the mounting hole and connector placement requirements detailed in the respective specifications. Each of these have the same basic screw hole and connector placement requirements, so if you have a case that will fit a full-sized ATX board, you could also mount a mini-, micro-, or flex-ATX board in that same case. Obviously if you have a smaller case designed for micro-ATX or flex-ATX, it will not be possible to put the larger mini-ATX or full sized ATX boards in that case.

NLX

NLX is a new low-profile form factor designed to replace the non-standard LPX design used in previous low-profile systems. First introduced in November of 1996 by Intel, NLX is proving to be the form factor of choice for Slimline corporate desktop systems now and in the future. NLX is similar in initial appearance to LPX, but with numerous improvements designed to allow full integration of the latest technologies. NLX is basically an improved version of the proprietary LPX design, and it is fully standardized, which means you should be able to replace one NLX board with another from a different manufacturer—something that was not possible with LPX.

Another limitation of LPX boards is the difficulty in handling the physical size of the newer Pentium II/III processors and their higher output thermal characteristics as well as newer bus structures such as AGP for video. The NLX form factor has been designed specifically to address these problems (see Figure 4.15).

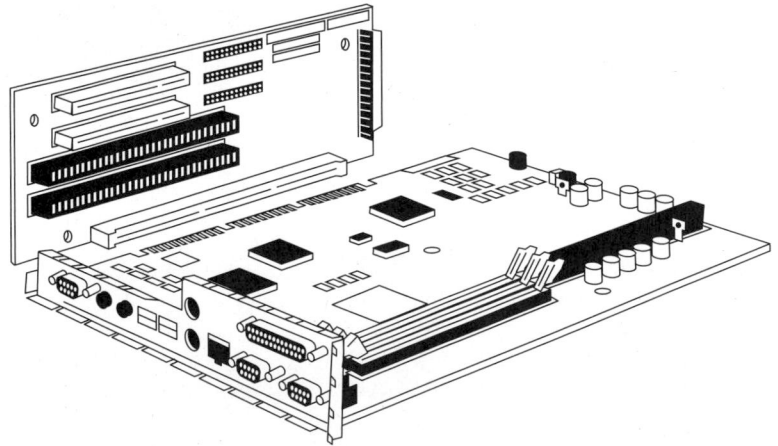

Figure 4.15 NLX motherboard and riser combination.

The main characteristic of an NLX system is that the motherboard plugs into the riser, unlike LPX where the riser plugs into the motherboard. This means the motherboard can be removed from the system without disturbing the riser or any of the expansion cards plugged into it. In addition, the motherboard in an NLX system literally has no internal cables or connectors attached to it! All devices that normally plug into the motherboard, such as drive cables, the power supply, front panel light and switch connectors, etc., all plug into the riser instead (see Figure 4.16). By using the riser card as a connector concentration point, it is possible to remove the lid on an NLX system and literally slide the motherboard out the left side of the system without unplugging a single cable or connector on the inside. This allows for unbelievably quick motherboard changes; in fact, I have swapped motherboards in less than 30 seconds on NLX systems!

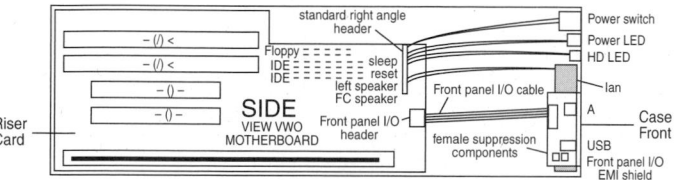

Figure 4.16   Orientation of the riser card in an NLX system.

In addition to being able to remove the motherboard so easily, you can also remove a power supply or any disk drive without removing any other boards from the system. Such a design is a boon for the corporate market, where ease and swiftness of servicing is a major feature. Not only can components be replaced with lightening speed, but because of the industry standard design, motherboards, power supplies, and other components will be interchangeable even among different systems.

Specific advantages of the NLX form factor include

- *Support for all desktop system processor technologies.* This is especially important in Pentium II/III systems, because the size of the Single Edge Contact cartridge this processor uses can run into physical fit problems on existing Baby-AT and LPX motherboards.

- *Flexibility in the face of rapidly changing processor technologies.* Backplane-like flexibility has been built into the form by allowing a new motherboard to be easily and quickly installed without tearing your entire system to pieces. But unlike traditional backplane systems, many industry leaders are putting their support behind NLX.

- *Support for newer technologies.* This includes Accelerated Graphics Port (AGP) high-performance graphic solutions, Universal Serial Bus (USB), and memory modules in DIMM or RIMM form.

- *Ease and speed of servicing and repair.* Compared to other industry standard interchangeable form factors, NLX systems are by far the easiest to work on, and allow component swaps or other servicing in the shortest amount of time.

Furthermore, with the importance of multimedia applications, connectivity support for such things as video playback, enhanced graphics, and extended audio have been built into the motherboard. This should represent a good cost savings over expensive daughterboard arrangements that have been necessary for many advanced multimedia uses in the past. Although ATX also has this support, LPX and Baby-AT don't have the room for these additional connectors.

Figure 4.17 shows the basic NLX system layout, while the NLX motherboard dimensions are shown in Figure 4.18. Notice that, like ATX, the system is clear of the drive bays and other chassis-mounted components. Also, the motherboard and I/O cards (which, like the LPX form factor, are mounted parallel to the motherboard) can easily be slid in and out of the side of the chassis, leaving the riser card and other cards in place. The processor can be easily accessed and enjoys greater cooling than in a more closed-in layout.

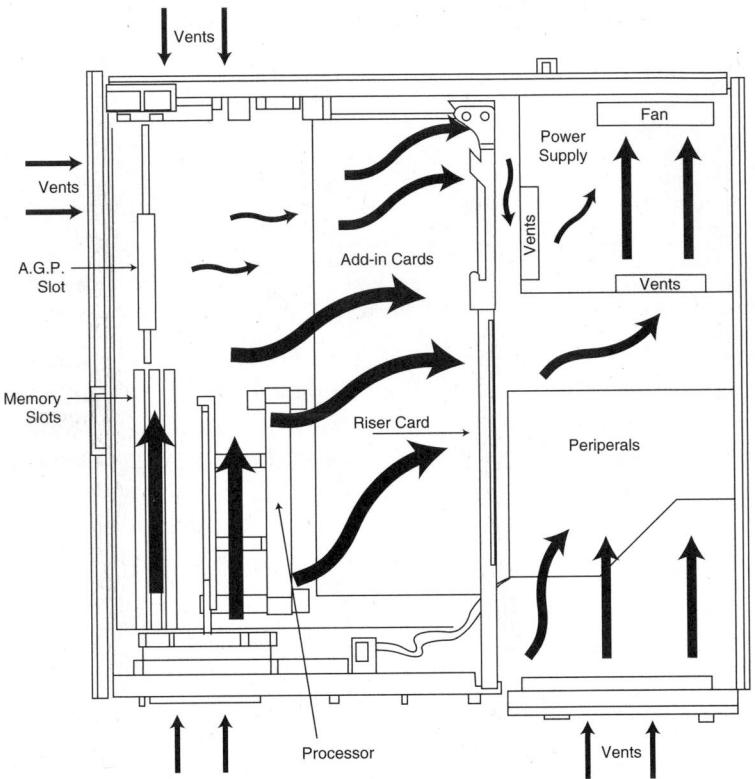

Figure 4.17   NLX system chassis layout and cooling airflow.

The NLX motherboard is specified in three different lengths front to back of 13.6", 11.2" or 10" total (see Figure 4.18). With proper bracketry, the shorter boards can go into a case designed for a longer board.

As with most of the different form factors, you can identify NLX via the unique I/O shield or connector area at the back of the board (see Figure 4.19). I only need a quick look at the rear of any given system to determine what type of board is contained within. The following figure shows the unique stepped design of the NLX I/O connector area. This allows for a row of connectors all along the bottom, and has room for double-stacked connectors on one side.

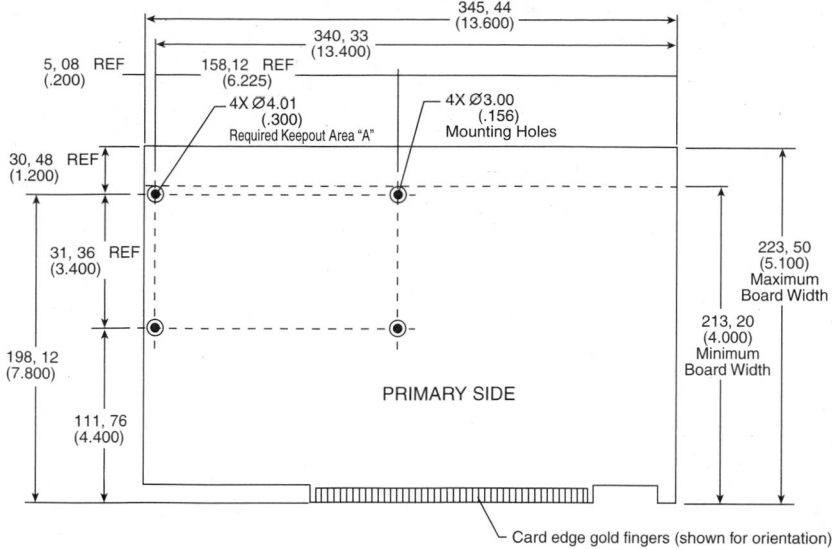

Figure 4.18 NLX form factor. This shows a 13.6-inch long NLX board. The NLX specification also allows shorter 11.2-inch and 10-inch versions.

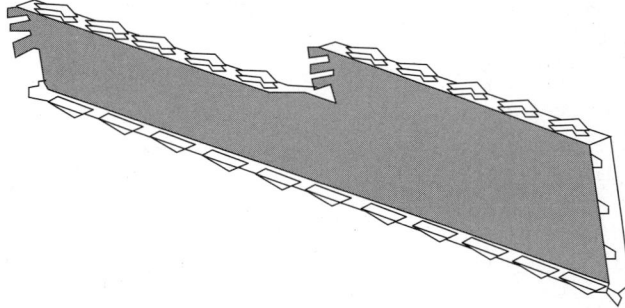

Figure 4.19 NLX motherboard I/O shield and connector area as seen from behind.

As you can see, the NLX form factor has been designed for maximum flexibility and space efficiency. Even extremely long I/O cards will fit easily, without getting in the way of other system components—a problem with Baby-AT form factor systems.

The specification and related information about the NLX form factor are available through the Platform Developer Web site located at http://www.teleport.com/~ffsupport/.

ATX, mini-ATX, micro-ATX, flex-ATX, and NLX form factors will be the predominant form factors used in virtually all future systems. Since these are well-defined standards that have achieved acceptance in the marketplace, I would avoid the older, obsolete standards such as Baby-AT. I recommend avoiding LPX or other proprietary systems if upgradability is a factor because it is not only difficult to locate a new motherboard that will fit, but LPX systems are also limited in expansion slots and drive bays. Overall ATX is still the best choice for most new systems where expandability, upgradability, low cost, and ease of service are of prime importance.

WTX

WTX is a new board and system form factor developed for the mid-range workstation market. WTX goes beyond ATX and defines the size and shape of the board and the interface between the board and chassis, as well as required chassis features.

WTX was first released in September 1998 (1.0) and updated in February of 1999 (1.1). The specification and other information on WTX are available at the following Web site: http://www.wtx.org.

The WTX form factor is designed to support

- Future Intel-based 32- and 64-bit processor technologies
- Dual processor motherboards
- Future memory technologies
- Future graphics technologies
- Flex Slot I/O (double-wide PCI) cards
- Deskside (tower) form factor
- Rack mount capability
- Easy accessibility to memory and expansion slots
- High-capacity power supplies

Figure 4.20 shows a typical WTX system with the cover removed. Note that easy access is provided to internal components via pull out drawers and swinging side panels.

WTX introduces a new slot called the Flex Slot, which is really a double-wide PCI slot designed to allow larger, more power hungry, multifunction cards to be utilized. The Flex Slot is primarily designed for a removable, customizable I/O card for WTX systems. By using the Flex Slot, the I/O signals are moved farther away from the processor, chipset, and memory in the system. This allows for improved Electromagnetic Interference (EMI) performance because I/O connectors and their associated cables are moved away from the strongest signal generators in the system. A Flex Slot I/O card can include features such as PCI, audio, LAN, SCSI, serial and parallel ports, keyboard and mouse connections, USB, 1394, and system management features such as fan speed control, all on a single card. Figure 4.21 shows an example Flex Slot I/O card for a WTX system.

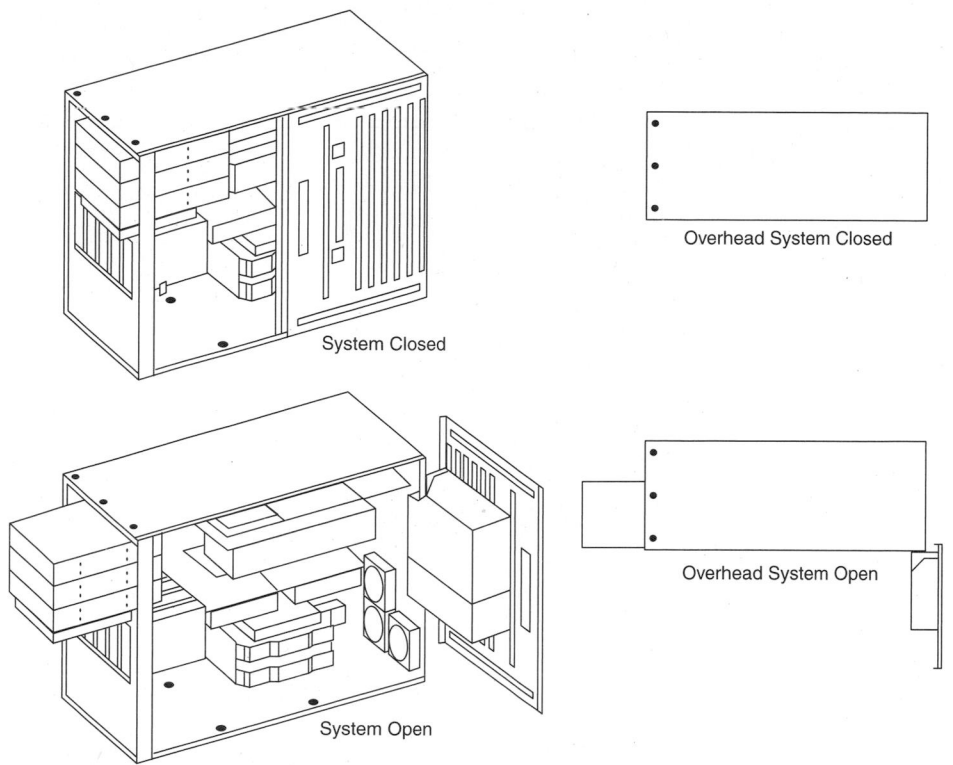

Overhead System Closed

System Closed

Overhead System Open

System Open

Figure 4.20 Typical WTX system chassis showing internal layout and ease of access.

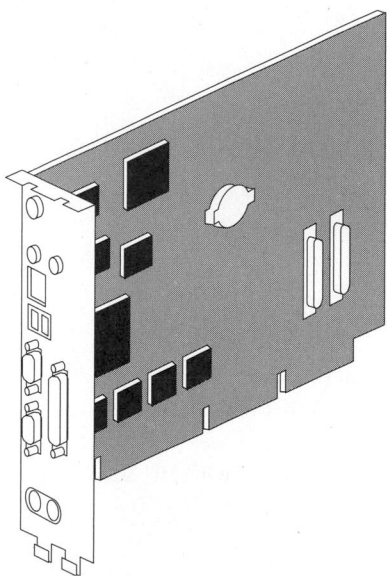

Figure 4.21 Flex Slot I/O card for a WTX system.

WTX motherboards can be a maximum width of 14 inches (356mm) and a maximum length of 16.75 inches (425 mm), which is significantly larger than ATX. There are no minimum motherboard dimensions, so board designers are free to design smaller boards as long as they meet the mounting criteria. Figure 4.22 shows WTX maximum board dimensions, sample connector locations, and mounting hole restrictions.

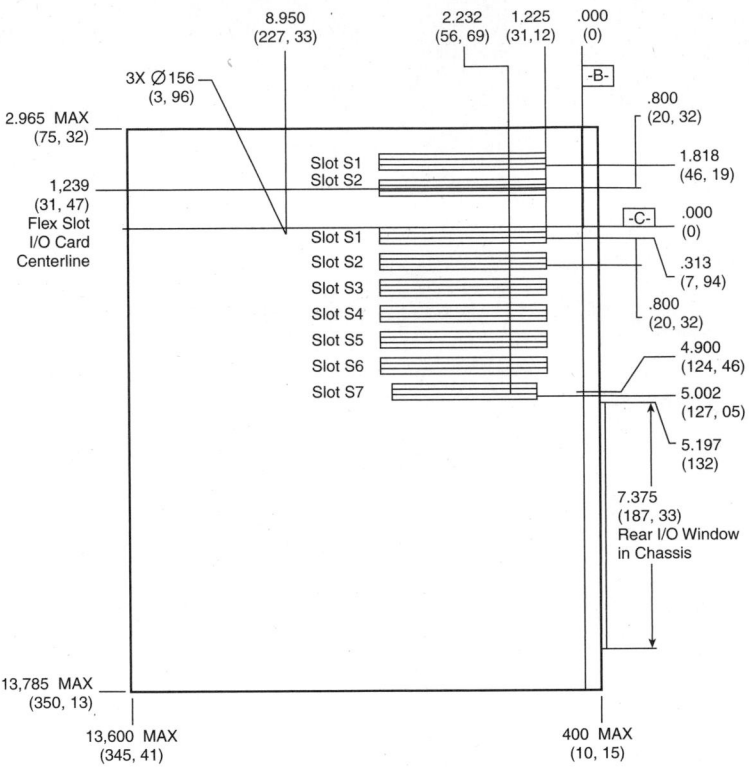

Figure 4.22   WTX motherboard dimensions and sample connector layout.

The WTX specification offers flexibility by leaving motherboard mounting features and locations undefined. Instead of defining exact screw hole positions, WTX motherboards must mount to a standard mounting adapter plate, which must be supplied with the board. The WTX chassis is designed to accept the mounting plate with attached motherboard and not just a bare board alone. Figure 4.23 shows the WTX motherboard mounting plate dimensions.

The WTX specification also defines keep-out zones or areas over the motherboard that must be free of any physical restrictions. This is to allow adequate clearance for tall or large items on the motherboard, and for proper cooling as well. Figure 4.24 shows the motherboard and plate as it would be installed in the system, along with the keep-out zones over the board.

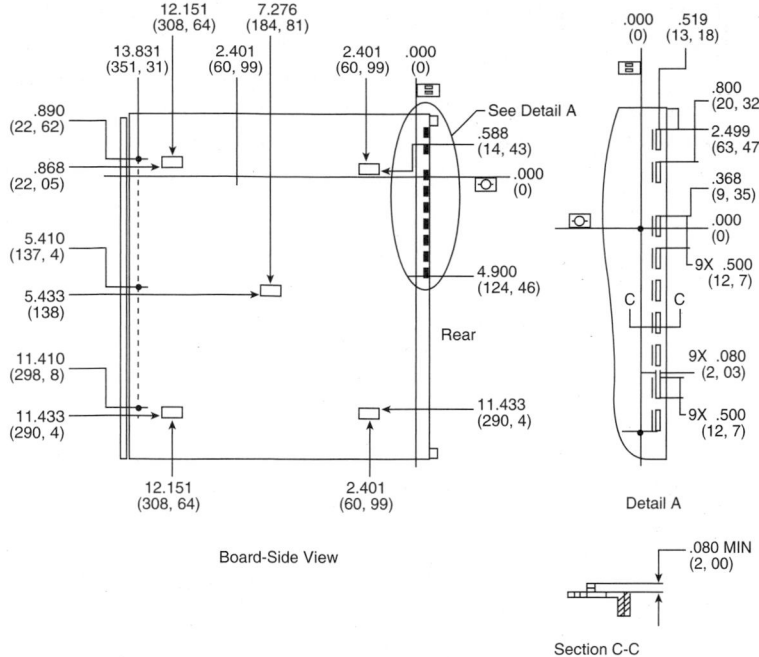

Figure 4.23 WTX motherboard mounting plate.

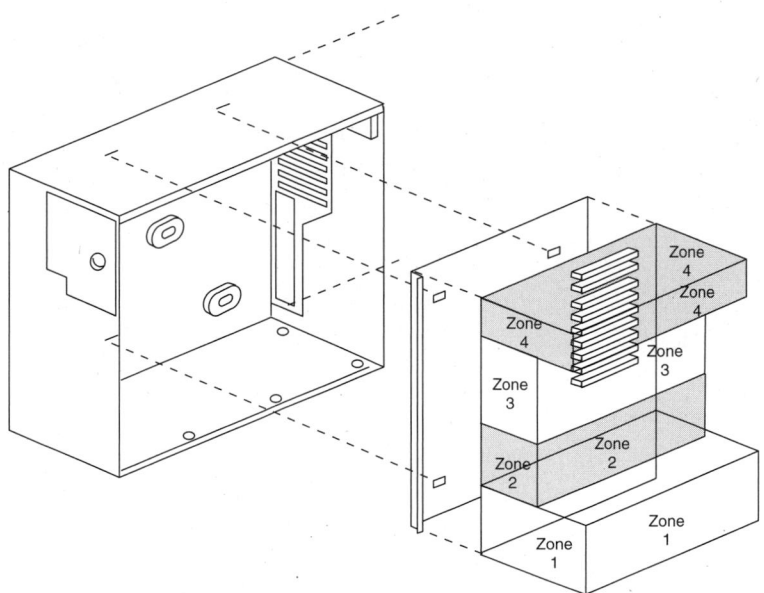

Figure 4.24 Typical WTX chassis showing board installation and keep-out zones.

To run a heavy-duty WTX system, new power supply designs are required. WTX specifically defines two power supply form factors and power levels in order to meet the power requirements of WTX systems. They are single fan 350w nominal and dual fan 850w nominal units respectively. The single fan power supply is intended for the lower power (around 350w) configurations of WTX systems. The dual fan power supply is for higher power configured workstations (up to around 850w). These will normally be supplied with the chassis, and are mounted on a swing out panel on one of the chassis sides.

With WTX we now have five industry standard form factors. Listed in order of cost/power from most to least they are as follows:

- WTX—For mid- to high-end workstations/servers
- ATX (and mini-ATX)—For power users, enthusiasts, low-end servers/workstations, higher-end home systems
- NLX—For corporate desktop, business workstations
- Micro-ATX—For midrange home systems, entertainment systems
- Flex-ATX—For low-end home systems, starter PCs, PC-based appliances

As you can see, WTX isn't a replacement for ATX, it is for much more expensive and much higher end type systems than ATX.

Proprietary Designs

Motherboards that are not one of the standard form factors such as Full-sized or Baby-AT, ATX, mini-ATX, micro-ATX, or NLX are deemed proprietary. Most people purchasing PCs should avoid proprietary designs because they do not allow for a future motherboard, power supply, or case upgrade, which limits future use and serviceability of the system. To me, proprietary systems are disposable PCs, because you can neither upgrade them, nor can you easily repair them. The problem is that the proprietary parts can only come from the original system manufacturer, and they usually cost many times more than non-proprietary parts. This means that after your proprietary system goes out of warranty, it is not only un-upgradable, but it is also essentially no longer worth repairing. If the motherboard or any component on it goes bad, you will be better off purchasing a completely new standard system than paying five times the normal price for a new proprietary motherboard. In addition, a new motherboard in a standard form factor system would be one or more generations newer and faster than the one you would be replacing. In a proprietary system, the replacement board would not only cost way too much, but it would be the same as the one that failed.

Note that it might be possible to perform limited upgrades to older systems with proprietary motherboards, in the form of custom (non-OEM) processor replacements with attached voltage regulators, usually called "overdrive" chips. Unfortunately these often overtax the board, power supply, and other components in the system, and because the board was not originally designed to work with them, they usually don't perform up to the standards of a less expensive new processor and motherboard combination. As such, I normally recommend upgrading the motherboard and processor together—something that can't be done with a proprietary system.

Most proprietary systems will still allow for disk drive, memory, or other simple upgrades, but even those can be limited because of board design and BIOS issues. The popular LPX motherboard design is at the heart of most proprietary systems. These systems are or were sold primarily in the retail store channel. This class of system has traditionally been dominated by Compaq and Packard Bell, and, as such, virtually all their systems have the problems inherent with their proprietary designs.

Some of these manufacturers seem to go out of their way to make their systems as physically incompatible as possible with any other system. Then, replacement parts, repairs, and upgrades are virtually impossible to find—except, of course, from the original system manufacturer and at a significantly higher price than the equivalent part would cost to fit a standard PC-compatible system.

For example, if the motherboard in my current ATX form factor system (and any system using a Baby-AT motherboard and case) dies, I can find any number of replacement boards that will bolt directly in—with my choice of processors and clock speeds—at great prices. If the motherboard dies in a newer Compaq, Packard Bell, Hewlett-Packard, or other proprietary form factor system, you'll pay for a replacement available only from the original manufacturer, and you have little or no opportunity to select a board with a faster or better processor than the one that failed. In other words, upgrading or repairing one of these systems via a motherboard replacement is difficult and usually not cost-effective.

Systems sold by the leading mail-order suppliers such as Dell, Gateway, Micron, and others are available in industry standard form factors such as ATX, micro-ATX, and NLX. This allows for easy upgrading and system expansion in the future. These standard factors allow you to replace your own motherboards, power supplies, and other components easily and select components from any number of suppliers other than where you originally bought the system.

Backplane Systems

One type of proprietary design is the backplane system. These systems do not have a motherboard in the true sense of the word. In a backplane system, the components normally found on a motherboard are located instead on an expansion adapter card plugged into a slot.

In these systems, the board with the slots is called a backplane, rather than a motherboard. Systems using this type of construction are called backplane systems.

Backplane systems come in two main types—passive and active. A passive backplane means the main backplane board does not contain any circuitry at all except for the bus connectors and maybe some buffer and driver circuits. All the circuitry found on a conventional motherboard is contained on one or more expansion cards installed in slots on the backplane. Some backplane systems use a passive design that incorporates the entire system circuitry into a single mothercard. The mothercard is essentially a complete motherboard that is designed to plug into a slot in the passive backplane. The passive backplane/mothercard concept allows the entire system to be easily upgraded by changing one or more cards. Because of the expense of the high-function mothercard, this type of system design is rarely found in PC systems. The passive backplane design does enjoy popularity in industrial systems, which are often rack-mounted. Some high-end file servers also feature this design. Figure 4.25 shows Pentium II/III card-based systems for passive backplane systems. Figure 4.26 shows a rack-mount chassis with a passive backplane.

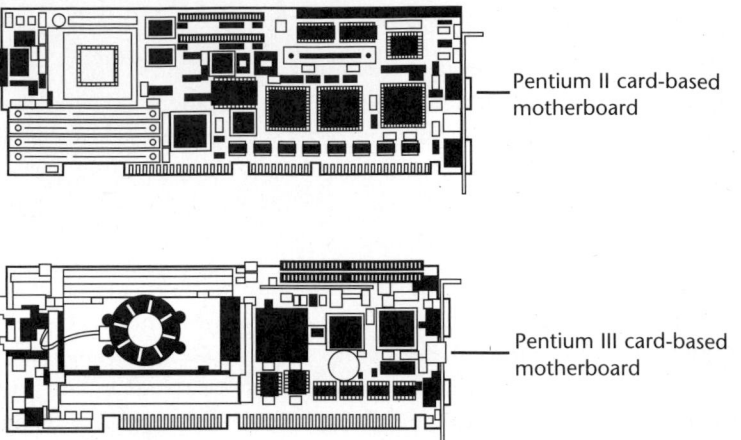

Pentium II card-based motherboard

Pentium III card-based motherboard

Figure 4.25 Pentium and Pentium II/III card-based motherboards (mothercards) for passive backplane systems.

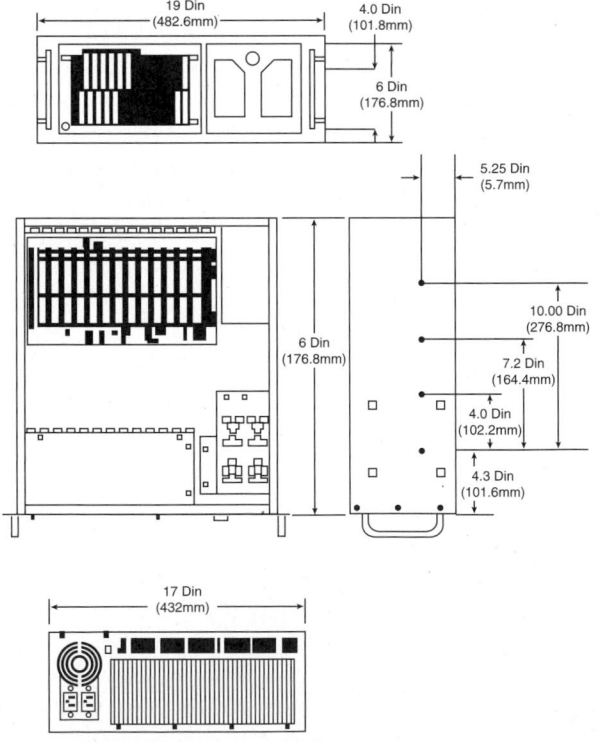

Figure 4.26 A rack-mount chassis with passive backplane.

Passive backplane systems with mothercards (often called single-board computers) are by far the most popular backplane design. They are used in industrial or laboratory type systems, and are normally rack mountable. They usually have a large number of slots, extremely heavy-duty power supplies, and feature high-capacity, reverse flow cooling designed to pressurize the chassis with cool, filtered air.

An active backplane means the main backplane board contains bus control and usually other circuitry as well. Most active backplane systems contain all the circuitry found on a typical motherboard except for what is then called the *processor complex*. The processor complex is the name of the circuit board that contains the main system processor and any other circuitry directly related to it, such as clock control, cache, and so forth. The processor complex design allows the user to easily upgrade the system later to a new processor type by changing one card. In effect, it amounts to a modular motherboard with a replaceable processor section.

Many large PC manufacturers have built systems with an active backplane/processor complex. Both IBM and Compaq, for example, have used this type of design in some of their high-end (server class) systems. This allows an easier and generally more affordable upgrade than the passive backplane/mothercard design because the processor complex board is usually much cheaper than a mothercard. Unfortunately, because there are no standards for the processor complex interface to the system, these boards are proprietary and can only be purchased from the system manufacturer. This limited market and availability causes the prices of these boards to be higher than most complete motherboards from other manufacturers.

The motherboard system design and the backplane system design have advantages and disadvantages. Most original personal computers were designed as backplanes in the late 1970s. Apple and IBM shifted the market to the now traditional motherboard with a slot-type design because this type of system generally is cheaper to mass-produce than one with the backplane design. The theoretical advantage of a backplane system, however, is that you can upgrade it easily to a new processor and level of performance by changing a single card. For example, you can upgrade a system's processor just by changing the card. In a motherboard-design system, you often must change the motherboard, a seemingly more formidable task. Unfortunately, the reality of the situation is that a backplane design is often much more expensive to upgrade. For example, because the bus remains fixed on the backplane, the backplane design precludes more comprehensive upgrades that involve adding local bus slots.

Another nail in the coffin of backplane designs is the upgradable processor. Starting with the 486, Intel began standardizing the sockets or slots in which processors were to be installed, allowing a single motherboard to support a wider variety of processors and system speeds. Because board designs could be made more flexible, changing only the processor chip for a faster standard OEM type (not one of the kludgy "overdrive" chips) is the easiest and generally most cost-effective way to upgrade without changing the entire motherboard. To allow processor upgrades, Intel has standardized on a number of different types of CPU sockets and slots that allow for upgrading to any faster processors designed to fit the same common socket or slot.

Because of the limited availability of the processor-complex boards or mothercards, they usually end up being more expensive than a complete new motherboard that uses an industry-standard form factor. The bottom line is that unless you have a requirement for a large capacity industrial or laboratory type system, especially one that would be rack mounted, you are better off sticking with standard ATX form factor PCs. They will certainly be far less expensive.

Motherboard Components

A modern motherboard has several components built in, including various sockets, slots, connectors, chips, and so on. This section examines the components found on a typical motherboard.

Most modern motherboards have at least the following major components on them:

- Processor socket/slot
- Chipset (North and South Bridges)
- Super I/O chip
- ROM BIOS (Flash ROM)
- SIMM/DIMM/RIMM sockets
- ISA/PCI/AGP bus slots
- CPU voltage regulator
- Battery

These components are discussed in the following sections.

Processor Sockets/Slots

The CPU is installed in a socket for all systems up to and including the Pentium Pro processor. The Pentium II processors and beyond use a slot where the processor card or cartridge plugs in.

Starting with the 486 processors, Intel designed the processor to be a user installable and replaceable part, and developed standards for CPU sockets that would allow different models of the same basic processor to plug in. These socket specifications were numbered and based on the socket or slot number you have on your motherboard. This means that you will know exactly what types of processors can be installed.

◀◀ See "Processor Sockets," 74.

Sockets for processors prior to the 486 were not numbered, and interchangeability was limited. Table 4.2 shows the relationship between the various processor sockets/slots and the chips designed to go into them.

Table 4.2   CPU Socket Specifications

Socket Number	Pins	Pin Layout	Voltage	Supported Processors
Socket 1	169	17×17 PGA	5v	486 SX/SX2, DX/DX2*, DX4 OverDrive
Socket 2	238	19×19 PGA	5v	486 SX/SX2, DX/DX2*, DX4 OverDrive, 486 Pentium OverDrive
Socket 3	237	19×19 PGA	5v/3.3v	486 SX/SX2, DX/DX2, DX4, 486 Pentium OverDrive, 5x86

Socket Number	Pins	Pin Layout	Voltage	Supported Processors
Socket 4	273	21×21 PGA	5v	Pentium 60/66, OverDrive
Socket 5	320	37×37 SPGA	3.3v/3.5v	Pentium 75-133, OverDrive
Socket 6**	235	19×19 PGA	3.3v	486 DX4, 486 Pentium OverDrive
Socket 7	321	37×37 SPGA	VRM	Pentium 75-266+, MMX, OverDrive, 6x86, K6
Socket 8	387	dual pattern SPGA	Auto VRM	Pentium Pro
Socket PGA370	370	37×37 SPGA	Auto VRM	PGA Celeron, future PIII
Slot 1	242	SEC/SEP Slot	Auto VRM	Pentium II, SEP Celeron, Pentium III
Slot 2/SC330	330	SEC Slot	Auto VRM	Pentium II Xeon, Pentium III Xeon

*Non-OverDrive DX4 also can be supported with the addition of an aftermarket 3.3v voltage regulator adapter.

**Socket 6 was a proposed standard only and was never actually implemented in any systems.

PGA = Pin Grid Array.

SPGA = Staggered Pin Grid Array.

VRM = Voltage Regulator Module.

SEC = Single Edge Contact cartridge.

SEP = Single-Edge Processor package (Pentium II without the plastic cartridge, for example, Celeron)

Chipsets

When the first PC motherboards were created by IBM, they used several discrete chips to complete the design. Besides the processor and optional math coprocessor, there were many other components required to complete the system. These other components included things such as the clock generator, bus controller, system timer, interrupt and DMA controllers, CMOS RAM and clock, and the keyboard controller. There were also a number of other simple logic chips used to complete the entire motherboard circuit, plus, of course, things such as the actual processor, math coprocessor (floating-point unit), memory, and other parts. Table 4.3 lists all the primary chip components used on the original PC/XT and AT motherboards.

Table 4.3   Primary Chip Components on Motherboards

Chip Function	PC/XT Version	AT Version
Processor	8088	80286
Math Coprocessor (Floating-Point Unit	8087	80287
Clock Generator	8284	82284
Bus Controller	8288	82288
System Timer	8253	8254
Low-order Interrupt Controller	8259	8259
High-order Interrupt Controller	—	8259
Low-order DMA Controller	8237	8237
High-order DMA Controller	—	8237
CMOS RAM/Real-time Clock	—	MC146818
Keyboard Controller	8255	8042

In addition to the processor/coprocessor, a six-chip set was used to implement the primary motherboard circuit in the original PC and XT systems. IBM later upgraded this to a nine-chip design in the AT and later systems, mainly by adding additional Interrupt and DMA controller chips, and the non-volatile CMOS RAM/Real-time Clock chip. All these motherboard chip components came from Intel or an Intel-licensed manufacturer, except the CMOS/Clock chip, which came from Motorola. To build a clone or copy of one of these IBM systems back would require all these chips plus many smaller discrete logic chips to glue the design together, totaling to 100 or more individual chips. This kept the price of a motherboard high, and left little room on the board to integrate other functions.

In 1986, a company called Chips and Technologies introduced a revolutionary component called the 82C206—the main part of the first PC motherboard chipset. This was a single chip that integrated into it all the functions of the main motherboard chips in an AT-compatible system. This chip included the functions of the 82284 Clock Generator, 82288 Bus Controller, 8254 System Timer, dual 8259 Interrupt Controllers, dual 8237 DMA Controllers, and even the MC146818 CMOS/Clock chip. Besides the processor, virtually all the major chip components on a PC motherboard could now be replaced by a single chip. Four other chips augmented the 82C206 acting as buffers and memory controllers, thus completing virtually the entire motherboard circuit with five total chips. This first chipset was called the CS8220 chipset by Chips and Technologies. Needless to say, this was a revolutionary concept in PC motherboard manufacturing. Not only did it greatly reduce the cost of building a PC motherboard, but it also made it much easier to design a motherboard. The reduced component count meant the boards had more room for integrating other items formerly found on expansion cards. Later the four chips augmenting the 82C206 were replaced by a new set of only three chips, and the entire set was called the New Enhanced AT (NEAT) CS8221 chipset. This was later followed by the 82C836 Single Chip AT (SCAT) chipset, which finally condensed all the chips in the set down to a single chip.

The chipset idea was rapidly copied by other chip manufacturers. Companies such as Acer, Erso, Opti, Suntac, Symphony, UMC, and VLSI each gained an important share of this market. Unfortunately for many of them, the chipset market has been a volatile one, and many of them have long since gone out of business. In 1993, VLSI had become the dominant force in the chipset market and had the vast majority of the market share; by the next year, they, along with virtually everybody else in the chipset market, would be fighting to stay alive. This is because a new chipset manufacturer had come on the scene, and within a year or so of getting serious, they were totally dominating the chipset market. That company is Intel, and since 1994 they have had a virtual lock on the chipset market. If you have a motherboard built since 1994, chances are good that it has an Intel chipset on it along with an Intel processor. There are very few chipset competitors left, and the ones that are left are scratching for the lower end of the market. Today, that would include primarily ALi (Acer Laboratories, Inc.), VIA Technologies, and SiS (Silicon integrated Systems). It is interesting to note that Chips and Technologies survived by changing course to design and manufacture video chips, and found a niche in that market specifically for laptop and notebook video chipsets. They were bought out by Intel in 1998 as a way for Intel to get into the video chipset business.

Intel Chipsets

You cannot talk about chipsets today without discussing Intel. They currently own well over 90 percent of the chipset market, and virtually 100 percent of the higher end Pentium II/III chipset market. It is interesting to note that we probably have Compaq to thank for forcing Intel into the chipset business in the first place!

The thing that really started it all was the introduction of the EISA bus designed by Compaq in 1989. At that time, they had shared the bus with other manufacturers in an attempt to make it a market standard. However, they refused to share their EISA bus chipset—a set of custom chips needed to implement this bus on a motherboard.

Enter Intel, who decided to fill the chipset void for the rest of the PC manufacturers wanting to build EISA bus motherboards. As is well known today, the EISA bus failed to become a market success except for the niche server business, but Intel now had a taste of the chipset business and this they apparently wouldn't forget. With the introduction of the 286 and 386 processors, Intel became impatient with how long it took the other chipset companies to create chipsets around their new processor designs; this delayed the introduction of motherboards that supported the new processors. For example, it took more than two years after the 286 processor was introduced for the first 286 motherboards to appear, and just over a year for the first 386 motherboards to appear after the 386 had been introduced. Intel couldn't sell their processors in volume until other manufacturers made motherboards that would support them, so they thought that by developing motherboard chipsets for a new processor in parallel with the new processor, they could jumpstart the motherboard business by providing ready-made chipsets for the motherboard manufacturers to use.

Intel tested this by introducing the 420 series chipsets along with their 486 processor in April of 1989. This allowed the motherboard companies to get busy right away, and it was only a few months before the first 486 motherboards appeared. Of course, the other chipset manufacturers weren't happy; now they had Intel as a competitor, and Intel would always have their new processor chipsets on the market first!

Intel then realized that they now made both processors *and* chipsets, which were 90 percent of the components on a motherboard. What better way to ensure that motherboards were available for their Pentium processor when it was introduced than by making their own motherboards as well, and having these boards ready on the new processor's introduction date. When the first Pentium processor debuted in 1993, Intel also debuted the 430LX chipset and a fully finished motherboard as well. Now not only were the chipset companies upset, but the motherboard companies weren't too happy either. Intel was not only the major supplier of parts needed to build finished boards (processors and chipsets), but Intel was now building and selling finished boards as well. By 1994, Intel had not only dominated the processor market, but they had cornered the chipset and motherboard markets as well.

Since then, Intel has remained on top in these markets, always introducing new chipsets and motherboards to go with their new processors. Their success in processors prompted them to take additional steps—making chipsets and then complete PC motherboards.

Now as Intel develops new processors, they develop chipsets and even complete motherboards simultaneously, which means they can be announced and shipped in unison. This eliminates the delay between introducing new processors and having motherboards and systems be capable of using them, which was common in the industry's early days. This delay is virtually eliminated today. It was amazing to me that on the day they introduced the first Pentium, Pentium II, and Pentium III processors, not only were there new chipsets available to support them, but complete motherboards were available as well. That very day, you could call Dell, Gateway, or Micron and order a complete "Intel" system using the new Intel processor, chipset, and motherboard. This has not made companies such as Compaq (who still like to make their own motherboards rather than purchase somebody else's off-the-shelf product) very happy, to say the least.

First, with the advent of the Pentium, Pentium Pro, Pentium II, and now the Pentium III processor, not only do more than 90 percent of the systems sold use Intel processors, but their motherboards also most likely have an Intel chipset on them. In fact, their entire motherboard was most likely made by Intel. In my seminars, I ask how many people in the class have Intel brand PCs. Of course, Intel does not sell or market a PC under their own name, so nobody thinks they have an "Intel brand" PC. But, if your motherboard was made by Intel, for all intents and purposes you sure seem to have an Intel brand PC, as far as I am concerned. Does it really matter whether Dell, Gateway, or Micron put that same Intel motherboard into a slightly different looking case with their name on it?

Intel Chipset Model Numbers

Intel started a pattern of numbering their chipsets as follows:

Chipset Number	Processor Family
420xx	P4 (486)
430xx	P5 (Pentium)
440xx	P6 (Pentium Pro/Pentium II/III)
450xx	P6 Server (Pentium Pro/Pentium II/III Xeon)

The chipset numbers listed here are an abbreviation of the actual chipset numbers stamped on the individual chips. For example, one of the current popular Pentium II/III chipsets is the Intel 440BX chipset, which really consists of two components, the 82443BX North Bridge and the 82371EX South Bridge. The North Bridge is so named because it is the connection between the high-speed processor bus (66 or 100MHz) and the slower AGP (66MHz) and PCI (33MHz) buses. The South Bridge is so named because it is the bridge between the PCI bus (33MHz) and the even slower ISA bus (8MHz). By reading the number and letter combinations on the larger chips on your motherboard, you can usually quickly identify the chipset your motherboard uses.

Most of Intel's chipsets (and those of Intel's competitors) are broken into a two-tiered architecture incorporating a North Bridge and South Bridge section. The North Bridge is the main portion of the chipset and incorporates the interface between the processor and the rest of the motherboard. The North Bridge components are what the chipset is named after, meaning that, for example, what we call the 440BX chipset is actually derived from the fact that the actual North

Bridge chip part number for that set is 82443BX. Figure 4.27 shows a sample motherboard (in this case an Intel SE440BX-2) with the locations of all chips and components.

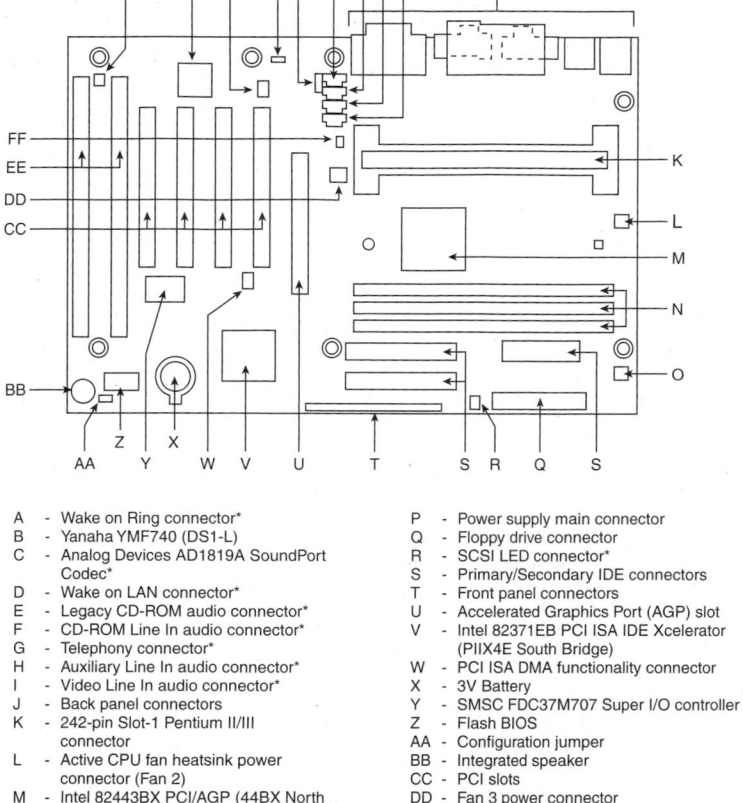

A   - Wake on Ring connector*
B   - Yanaha YMF740 (DS1-L)
C   - Analog Devices AD1819A SoundPort
       Codec*
D   - Wake on LAN connector*
E   - Legacy CD-ROM audio connector*
F   - CD-ROM Line In audio connector*
G   - Telephony connector*
H   - Auxiliary Line In audio connector*
I   - Video Line In audio connector*
J   - Back panel connectors
K   - 242-pin Slot-1 Pentium II/III
       connector
L   - Active CPU fan heatsink power
       connector (Fan 2)
M   - Intel 82443BX PCI/AGP (44BX North
       Bridge) controller
N   - DIMM sockets
O   - Fan 1 power connector

P   - Power supply main connector
Q   - Floppy drive connector
R   - SCSI LED connector*
S   - Primary/Secondary IDE connectors
T   - Front panel connectors
U   - Accelerated Graphics Port (AGP) slot
V   - Intel 82371EB PCI ISA IDE Xcelerator
       (PIIX4E South Bridge)
W   - PCI ISA DMA functionality connector
X   - 3V Battery
Y   - SMSC FDC37M707 Super I/O controller
Z   - Flash BIOS
AA - Configuration jumper
BB - Integrated speaker
CC - PCI slots
DD - Fan 3 power connector
EE - ISA slots
FF - Chassis intrusion switch connector*

* = Optional features

Figure 4.27   Intel SE440BX-2 motherboard showing component locations. *Used by permission of Intel.*

The North Bridge contains the cache and main memory controllers and the interface between the high-speed (33MHz, 50MHz, 66MHz, or 100MHz) processor bus and the 33MHz PCI (Peripheral Component Interconnect) or 66MHz AGP (Accelerated Graphics Port) buses. Intel often refers to the North Bridge of their more recent chipsets as the PAC (PCI/AGP Controller). The North Bridge is essentially the main component of the motherboard and is the only motherboard circuit besides the processor that normally runs at full motherboard (processor bus) speed. Most modern chipsets use a single-chip North Bridge; however, some of the older ones actually consisted of up to three individual chips to make up the complete North Bridge circuit.

The South Bridge is the lower speed component in the chipset and has always been a single individual chip. The South Bridge is a somewhat interchangeable component in that different North Bridge chipsets often are designed to use the same South Bridge component. This modular design of the chipset allows for lower cost and greater flexibility for motherboard manufacturers. The South Bridge connects to the 33MHz PCI bus and contains the interface to the 8MHz ISA bus. It also normally contains the dual IDE hard disk controller interfaces, the USB (Universal Serial Bus) interface, and even the CMOS RAM and clock functions. The South Bridge contains all the components that make up the ISA bus, including the interrupt and DMA controllers.

Let's start by examining the Intel 486 motherboard chipsets and then work our way through the latest Pentium II sets.

Intel's Early 386/486 Chipsets

Intel's first real PC motherboard chipset was the 82350 chipset for the 386DX and 486 processors. This chipset was not very successful, mainly because the EISA bus was not very popular, and because there were many other manufacturers making standard 386 and 486 motherboard chipsets at the time. The market changed very quickly, and Intel dropped the EISA bus support and introduced follow-up 486 chipsets that were much more successful.

Table 4.4 shows the Intel 486 chipsets.

Table 4.4   Intel 486 Motherboard Chipsets

Chipset	420TX	420EX	420ZX
Codename	Saturn	Aries	Saturn II
Date Introduced	Nov. '92	March '94	March '94
Processor	5v 486	5v/3.3v 486	5v/3.3v 486
Bus Speed	up to 33 MHz	up to 50 MHz	up to 333 MHz
SMP (dual CPUs)	No	No	No
Memory Types	FPM	FPM	FPM
Parity/ECC	Parity	Parity	Parity
Max. Memory	128MMB	128MMB	160MMB
L2 Cache Type	Async	Async	Async
PCI Support	2.0	2.0	2.1
AGP Support	No	No	No

SMP = Symmetric Multiprocessing (Dual Processors)
FPM = Fast Page Mode
PCI = Peripheral Component Interconnect
AGP = Accelerated Graphics Port
Note: PCI 2.1 supports concurrent PCI operations.

Intel had pretty good success with their 486 chipsets. They had developed their current two-tiered approach to system design even back then. This design is such that all Intel 486, Pentium,

Pentium Pro, and Pentium II have been designed using two main components, which are commonly called the North Bridge and South Bridge.

Fifth-Generation (P5 Pentium Class) Chipsets

With the advent of the Pentium processor in March of 1993, Intel also introduced their first Pentium chipset, the 430LX chipset (code-named Mercury). This was the first Pentium chipset on the market and set the stage as Intel took this lead and ran with it. Other manufacturers took months to a year or more to get their Pentium chipsets out the door. Since the debut of their Pentium chipsets, Intel has dominated the chipset market with nobody even coming close. Table 4.5 shows the Intel Pentium motherboard chipsets.

Table 4.5   Intel Pentium Motherboard Chipsets (North Bridge)

Chipset	430LX	430NX	430FX	430MX	430HX	430VX	430TX
Codename	Mercury	Neptune	Triton	Mobile Triton	Triton II	Triton III	n/a
Date Introduced	Mar. '93	Mar. '94	Jan. '95	Oct. '95	Feb. '96	Feb. '96	Feb. '97
Bus Speed	66 MHz	66MHz	66MHz	66MHz	66MHz	66MHz	66MHz
CPUs Supported	P60/66	P75+	P75+	P75+	P75+	P75+	P75+
SMP (dual CPUs)	No	Yes	No	No	Yes	No	No
Memory Types	FPM	FPM	FPM/ EDO	FPM/ EDO	FPM/ EDO	FPM/ EDO/ SDRAM	FPM/ EDO/ SDRAM
Parity/ECC	Parity	Parity	Neither	Neither	Both	Neither	Neither
Max. Memory	192MB	512MB	128MB	128MB	512MB	128MB	256MB
Max. Cacheable	192MB	512MB	64MB	64MB	512MB	64MB	64MB
L2 Cache Type	Async	Async	Async/ Pburst	Async/ Pburst	Async/ Pburst	Async/ Pburst	Async/ Pburst
PCI Support	2.0	2.0	2.0	2.0	2.1	2.1	2.1
AGP Support	No	No	No	No	No	No	No
South Bridge	SIO	SIO	PIIX	MPIIX	PIIX3	PIIX3	PIIX4

SMP = Symmetric Multiprocessing (Dual Processors)
FPM = Fast Page Mode
EDO = Extended Data Out
BEDO = Burst EDO
SDRAM = Synchronous Dynamic RAM

Note

PCI 2.1 supports concurrent PCI operations.

Table 4.6 shows all the applicable Intel South Bridge chips, which are the second part of the modern Intel motherboard chipsets.

Table 4.6   Intel South Bridge Chips

Chip Name	SIO	PIIX	PIIX3	PIIX4	PIIX4E	ICH0	ICH
Part Number	82378IB /ZB	82371FB	82371SB	82371AB	82371EB	82801AB	82801AA
IDE Support	None	BMIDE	BMIDE	UDMA-33	UDMA-33	UDMA-33	UDMA-66
USB Support	None	None	Yes	Yes	Yes	Yes	Yes
CMOS/Clock	No	No	No	Yes	Yes	Yes	Yes
Power Management	SMM	SMM	SMM	SMM	SMM/ ACPI	SMM/ ACPI	SMM/ ACPI

SIO = System I/O   BMIDE = Bus Master IDE
PIIX = PCI ISA IDE Xcelerator   UDMA = Ultra-DMA IDE
ICH = I/O Controller Hub   SMM = System Management Mode
USB = Universal Serial Bus   ACPI = Advanced Configuration and Power Interface
IDE = Integrated Drive Electronics (AT Attachment)

The following sections detail all the Pentium motherboard chipsets and their specifications.

Intel 430LX (Mercury)

The 430LX was introduced in March of 1993, concurrent with the introduction of the first Pentium processors. This chipset was only used with the original Pentiums, which came in 60MHz and 66MHz versions. These were 5v chips and were used on motherboards with Socket 4 processor sockets.

◄◄ See "Processor Sockets," p. 79.

◄◄ See "First-Generation Pentium Processor," p. 133.

The 430LX chipset consisted of three total chips for the North Bridge portion. The main chip was the 82434LX system controller. This chip contained the processor-to-memory interface, cache controller, and PCI bus controller. There was also a pair of PCI bus interface accelerator chips, which were identical 82433LX chips.

The 430LX chipset was noted for the following:

■ Single processor
■ Support for up to 512KB of L2 cache
■ Support for up to 192MB of standard DRAM

This chipset died off along with the 5v 60/66MHz Pentium processors.

Intel 430NX (Neptune)

Introduced in March of 1994, the 430NX was the first chipset designed to run the new 3.3v second generation Pentium processor. These were noted by having Socket 5 processor sockets, and an on-board 3.3v/3.5v voltage regulator for both the processor and chipset. This chipset was primarily designed for Pentiums with speeds from 75MHz to 133MHz, although mostly it was used with 75MHz to 100MHz systems. Along with the lower voltage processor, this chipset ran faster, cooler, and more reliably than the first-generation Pentium processor and the corresponding 5v chipsets.

◄◄ See "CPU Operating Voltages," p. 91.

◄◄ See "Second-Generation Pentium Processor," p. 134.

The 430NX chipset consisted of three chips for the North Bridge component. The primary chip was the 82434NX, which included the cache and main memory (DRAM) controller and the control interface to the PCI bus. The actual PCI data was managed by a pair of 82433NX chips called local bus accelerators. Together, these two chips, plus the main 82434NX chip, constituted the North Bridge.

The South Bridge used with the 430NX chipset was the 82378ZB System I/O (SIO) chip. This component connected to the PCI bus and generated the lower speed ISA bus.

The 430NX chipset introduced the following improvements over the Mercury (430LX) chipset:

- Dual processor support
- Support for 512MB of system memory (up from 192MB for the LX Mercury chipset)

This chipset rapidly became the most popular chipset for the early 75MHz to 100MHz systems, overshadowing the older 60MHz and 66MHz systems that used the 430LX chipset.

Intel 430FX (Triton)

The 430FX (Triton) chipset rapidly became the most popular chipset ever, after it was introduced in January of 1995. This chipset is noted for being the first to support EDO (Extended Data Out) memory, which also became popular at the time. EDO was slightly faster than the standard FPM (Fast Page Mode) memory that had been used up until that time, but cost no more than the slower FPM. Unfortunately, while being known for faster memory support, the Triton chipset was also known as the first Pentium chipset without support for parity checking for memory. This was a major blow to PC reliability, although many did not know it at the time.

►► See "EDO RAM," p. 427.

►► See "Parity Checking," p. 459.

The Triton chipset lacked not only parity support from the previous 430NX chipset, but it also would only support a single CPU. The 430FX was designed as a low-end chipset, for home or non–mission-critical systems. As such, it did not replace the 430NX, which carried on in higher end network file servers and other more mission-critical systems.

The 430FX consisted of a three-chip North Bridge. The main chip was the 82437FX system controller that included the memory and cache controllers, CPU interface, and PCI bus controller, along with dual 82438FX data path chips for the PCI bus. The South Bridge was the first PIIX (PCI ISA IDE Xcelerator) chip that was the 82371FB. This chip acted not only as the bridge between the 33MHz PCI bus and the slower 8MHz ISA bus, but also incorporated for the first time a dual-channel IDE interface. By moving the IDE interface off of the ISA bus and into the PIIX chip, it was now effectively connected to the PCI bus, allowing for much faster Bus Master IDE transfers. This was key in supporting the ATA-2 or Enhanced IDE interface for better hard disk performance.

The major points on the 430FX are

■ Support for EDO memory

■ Support for higher speed—pipelined burst cache

■ PIIX South Bridge with high-speed Bus Master IDE

■ Lack of support for parity-checked memory

■ Only single CPU support

■ Supported only 128MB of RAM, of which only 64MB could be cached

That last issue is one that many people are not aware of. The 430FX chipset can only cache up to 64MB of main memory. This means that if you install more than 64MB of RAM in your system, performance will suffer greatly. Now, many think this won't be that much of a problem—after all, they don't normally run enough software to load past the first 64MB anyway. That is another misunderstanding, because Windows 9x and NT/2000 (as well as all other protected mode operating systems including Linux, etc.) load from the top down. This means, for example, that if you install 96MB of RAM (one 64MB and one 32MB bank), virtually all your software, including the main operating system, will be loading into the non-cached region above 64MB. Only if you use more than 32MB would you begin to see an improvement in performance. Try disabling the L2 cache via your CMOS setup to see how slow your system will run without it. That is the performance you can expect if you install more than 64MB of RAM in a 430FX-based system.

This lack of cacheable memory, plus the lack of support for parity or ECC (error correcting code) memory, make this a non-recommended chipset in my book. Fortunately, this chipset became obsolete when the more powerful 430HX was introduced.

Intel 430HX (Triton II)

The Triton II 430HX chipset was created by Intel as a true replacement for the powerful 430NX chip. It added some of the high-speed memory features from the low-end 430FX, such as support for EDO memory and pipeline burst L2 cache. It also retained dual-processor support. In addition to supporting parity checking to detect memory errors, it also added support for ECC (error correcting code) memory to detect and correct single bit errors on-the-fly. And the great thing was that this was implemented using plain parity memory.

This was a chipset suitable for high-end or mission-critical system use such as file servers; it also worked well for lower end systems. Parity or ECC memory was not required—the chipset could easily be configured to use less expensive, nonparity, noncorrecting memory as well.

The HX chipset's primary advantages over the FX are

- Symmetric Multiprocessor (dual processor) support.
- Support for ECC (error correcting code) and parity memory.
- 512MB maximum RAM support (versus 128MB).
- L2 cache functions over 512MB RAM versus 64MB (providing optional cache Tag RAM is installed).
- Memory transfers in fewer cycles overall.
- PCI level 2.1 compliance that allows concurrent PCI operations.
- PIIX3 supports different IDE/ATA transfer speed settings on a single channel.
- PIIX3 South Bridge component supports USB.

The memory problems with caching in the 430FX were corrected in the 430HX. This chipset allowed for the possibility of caching the full 512MB of possible RAM as long as the correct amount of cache *tag* was installed. Tag is a small cache memory chip used to store the index to the data in the cache. Most 430HX systems shipped with a tag chip that could only manage 64MB of cached main memory, while you could optionally upgrade it to a larger capacity tag chip that would allow for caching the full 512MB of RAM.

The 430HX chipset was a true one-chip North Bridge. It was also one of the first chips out in a ball-grid array package, where the chip leads were configured as balls on the bottom of the chip. This allowed for a smaller chip package than the previous PQFP (Plastic Quad Flat Pack) packaging used on the older chips, and, because there was only one chip for the North Bridge, a very compact motherboard was possible. The South Bridge was the PIIX3 (82371SB) chip, which allowed for independent timing of the dual IDE channels. This meant that you could install two different speed devices on the same channel and configure their transfer speeds independently. Previous PIIX chips allowed both devices to work at the lowest common denominator speed supported by both. The PIIX3 also incorporated the USB for the first time on a PC motherboard. Unfortunately at the time, there were no devices available to attach to USB, nor was there any operating systems or driver support for the bus. USB ports were a curiosity at the time, and nobody had a use for them.

▶▶ See "USB (Universal Serial Bus)," p. 892.

The 430HX supports the newer PCI 2.1 standard, which allowed for concurrent PCI operations and greater performance. Combined with the support for EDO and pipelined burst cache, this was perhaps the best Pentium chipset for the power user's system. It offered not only excellent performance, but with ECC memory it offered a truly reliable and stable system design.

The 430HX was the only modern Intel Pentium-class chipset to offer parity and error-corrected memory support. This made it the recommended Intel chipset for mission-critical applications such as file servers, database servers, business systems, and so on. Of course, today few would recommend using any type of Pentium system as a file server in lieu of a more powerful, and yet not much more expensive, Pentium II/III system.

As this chipset and most of the Pentium processors are being phased out, you should look toward Pentium II systems for this kind of support.

Intel 430VX (Triton III)

The 430VX chipset never had an official code-name, although many in the industry began calling it the Triton III. The 430VX was designed to be a replacement for the low-end 430FX chipset. It was not a replacement for the higher powered 430HX chipset. As such, the VX has only one significant technical advantage over the HX, but in almost all other respects is more like the 430FX than the HX.

The VX has the following features:

- Support for 66MHz SDRAM (synchronous DRAM)
- No parity or ECC memory support
- Single processor only
- Supports only 128MB RAM
- Supports only 64MB of cached RAM

Although the support for SDRAM is a nice bonus, the actual speed derived from such memory is limited. This is because with a good L2 cache, there will only be a cache miss about 5 percent of the time the system is reading or writing memory, which means that the cache performance is actually more important than main memory performance. This is why most 430HX systems are faster than 430VX systems even though the VX can use faster SDRAM memory. Also, note that because the VX was designed as a low-end chipset for low-cost retail systems, most of them would never see any SDRAM memory anyway.

Like with the 430FX, the VX has the limitation of being capable to cache only 64MB of main memory. With the memory price crash of 1996 bringing memory prices down to where more than 64MB is actually affordable for most people, and with Windows software using more and more memory, this is really becoming a limitation.

The 430VX chipset was rapidly made obsolete in the market by the 430TX chipset that followed.

Intel 430TX

The 430TX chipset never had a code-name that I am aware of; however, some persisted in calling it the Triton IV. The 430TX was Intel's last Pentium chipset. It was designed not only to be used in desktop systems, but to replace the 430MX mobile Pentium chipset for laptop and notebook systems.

The 430TX has some refinements over the 430VX, but, unfortunately, it still lacks support for parity or ECC memory, and retains the 64MB cacheable RAM limitation of the older FX and VX chipsets. The 430TX was not designed to replace the high-end 430HX chipset, which still remained the chipset of choice for mission-critical systems. This is probably because of Intel's de-emphasizing of the Pentium; they are trying to wean us from Pentium processors and force the market—especially for higher end mission-critical systems—to the more powerful Pentium II/III.

The TX chipset features include the following:

- 66MHz SDRAM support
- Cacheable memory still limited to 64MB
- Support for Ultra-ATA, or Ultra-DMA 33 (UDMA) IDE transfers
- Lower power consumption for mobile use
- No parity or ECC memory support
- Single processor only

▶▶ See "ATA/ATAPI-4," p. 526

Because the Pentium processor has been relegated to low-end system use only, the fact that it lacks parity or ECC memory support, as well as the lack of support for cacheable memory over 64MB, has not been much of a problem for the market for which this chipset is intended. You should not use it for business-class systems, especially those that are mission-critical.

Those seeking a true high-performance chipset and a system that is robust—and which has support for mission-critical features such as ECC memory or for caching more than 64MB of memory—should be looking at Pentium II systems and not the lowly Pentium. Intel has recently stopped all further Pentium processor manufacturing and is only continuing to sell what they have in inventory.

Third-Party (Non-Intel) P5 Pentium Class Chipsets

VIA Technologies

VIA Technologies, Inc. was founded in 1987, and has become a major designer of PC motherboard chipsets. VIA employs state-of-the-art manufacturing capability through foundry relationships with leading silicon manufacturers, such as Toshiba and Taiwan Semiconductor Manufacturing Corporation.

Apollo VP-1

The VT82C580VP Apollo VP-1 is a four-chip set released in October of 1995 and used in older Socket 5 and Socket 7 systems. The Apollo VP-1 is an equivalent alternative to the Intel 430VX chipset, and features support for SDRAM, EDO, or Fast Page Mode memory as well as pipeline-burst SRAM cache. The VP-1 consists of the VT82C585VP 208-pin PQFP (Plastic Quad Flat Pack), two VT82C587VP 100-pin PQFP chips acting as the North Bridge, and the VT82C586 208-pin PQFP South Bridge chip.

Apollo VP2

The two-chip Apollo VP2 chipset was released in May of 1996. The VP2 is a high-performance Socket 7 chipset including several features over the previous VP-1 chipset. The VP2 adds support for ECC (error correcting code) memory over the VPX. The VP2 has also been licensed by AMD as their AMD 640 chipset. Motherboards using the Apollo VP2 can support P5 class processors, including the Intel Pentium and Pentium MMX, AMD K5 and K6, and Cyrix/IBM 6x86 and 6x86MX (MII) processors.

The VP2 chipset consists of the VT82C595 328 pin BGA (Ball Grid Array) package North Bridge chip, which supports up to 2MB of L2 cache and up to 512MB DRAM. Additional performance-related features include a fast DRAM controller with support for SDRAM, EDO, BEDO, and FPM DRAM types in mixed combinations with 32/64-bit data bus widths and row and column addressing, a deeper buffer with enhanced performance, and an intelligent PCI bus controller with Concurrent PCI master/CPU/IDE (PCI 2.1) operations. For data integrity and server use, the VP2/97 incorporates support for ECC or parity memory.

The Apollo VP2 features the VIA VT82C586B PCI-IDE South Bridge controller chip, which complies with the Microsoft PC97 industry specification by supporting ACPI/OnNow, Ultra DMA/33, and USB technologies.

Apollo VPX

The VT82C580VPX Apollo VPX is a four-chip set for Socket 7 motherboards released in December of 1996. The Apollo VPX is functionally equivalent to the Intel 430TX chipset, but also has specific performance enhancements relative to the 430TX. The VPX was designed as a replacement for the VP-1 chipset, and is an upgrade of that set designed to add support for the newer AMD and Cyrix P5 processors.

The Apollo VPX consists of the VT82C585VPX North Bridge and VT82C586B South Bridge chips. There are also two 208-pin PQFP frame buffers that go with the North Bridge memory interface. The Apollo VPX/97 features the VIA VT82C586B PCI-IDE South Bridge controller chip that complies with the Microsoft PC97 industry standard by supporting ACPI/OnNow, Ultra-DMA/33, and USB technologies. VIA also offers a non-PC97 version of the Apollo VPX that includes the older VT82C586A South Bridge and which was used in more entry-level PC designs.

Motherboards using the Apollo VPX can support P5 class processors, including the Intel Pentium and Pentium MMX, AMD K5 and K6, and Cyrix/IBM 6x86 and 6x86MX (MII) processors. To enable proper implementation of the Cyrix/IBM 6x86 200+ processor, the chipset features an asynchronous CPU bus that operates at either 66 or 75MHz speeds. The Apollo VPX is an upgrade over the Apollo VP-1 with the additional feature of Concurrent PCI master/CPU/IDE operations (PCI 2.1). The VPX also supports up to 2MB of L2 cache and up to 512MB DRAM.

Apollo VP3

The Apollo VP3 is one of the first P5 class chipsets to implement the Intel AGP (Advanced Graphics Port) specification. Intel offers that interface with their Pentium II (P6) class chipsets. This allows a higher performance Socket 7 motherboard to be built that can accept the faster AGP video cards. The Socket 7 interface allows P5 class processors such as the Intel Pentium and Pentium MMX, AMD K5 and K6, and Cyrix/IBM 6x86 and 6x86MX (MII) to be utilized.

The Apollo VP3 chipset consists of the VT82C597 North Bridge system controller (472-pin BGA) and the VT82C586B South Bridge (208-pin PQFP). The VT82C597 North Bridge provides superior performance between the CPU, optional synchronous cache, DRAM, AGP bus, and the PCI bus with pipelined, burst, and concurrent operation. The VT82C597 complies with the Accelerated Graphics Port Specification 1.0 and features a 66MHz master system bus.

Apollo MVP3

The Apollo MVP3 adds to the VP3 chip by supporting the new Super-7 100MHz Socket-7 specification. This allows the newer high-speed P5 processors such as the AMD K6 and Cyrix/IBM MII processors to be supported. The Apollo MVP3 chipset is a two-chip chipset that consists of the VT82C598AT North Bridge system controller and the VT82C586B South Bridge. The VT82C598AT chip is a 476-pin BGA (Ball Grid Array) package and the VT82C586B chip is a 208-pin PQFP (Plastic Quad Flat Pack) package.

The VT82C598AT North Bridge chip includes the CPU-to-PCI bridge, the L2 cache and buffer controller, the DRAM controller, the AGP interface, and the PCI IDE controller. The VT82C598AT North Bridge provides superior performance between the CPU, optional synchronous cache, DRAM, AGP bus, and the PCI bus with pipelined, burst, and concurrent operation. The DRAM controller supports standard Fast Page Mode (FPM), EDO, SDRAM, and DDR (Double Data Rate) SDRAM. The VT82C598AT complies with the Accelerated Graphics Port Specification 1.0 and features support for 66/75/83/100MHz CPU bus frequencies and the 66MHz AGP bus frequency.

The VT82C586B South Bridge includes the PCI-to-ISA bridge, ACPI support, SMBus, the USB host/hub interface, the Ultra-33 IDE Master controller, PS/2 Keyboard/Mouse controller, and the I/O controller. The chip also contains the keyboard and PS/2 mouse controller.

This chipset is closest to the Intel 430TX in that it supports Socket 7 chips (Pentium and P5-compatible processors), SDRAM DIMM memory, and is physically a two-chip set. It differs mainly in that it allows operation at speeds up to 100MHz and supports AGP—features only available with the Pentium II boards and chipsets from Intel. This is an attempt to make the Socket 7 motherboards and processors more competitive with the lower-end Pentium II chips such as the Celeron. The South Bridge is compatible with the newer Intel PIIX4e in that it includes UDMA IDE, USB, CMOS RAM, plus ACPI 1.0 power management.

One big benefit over the Intel 430TX is support for ECC (error correcting code) memory or parity checking can be selected on a bank-by-bank basis, which allows mixing of parity and ECC modules. The 430TX from Intel doesn't support any ECC or parity functions at all. Memory timing for FPM is X-3-3-3, whereas EDO is X-2-2-2, and SDRAM is X-1-1-1, which is similar to the Intel 430TX.

Another benefit over the 430TX is in memory cacheability. The 430TX allows caching up to only 64MB of main memory, a significant limitation in higher end systems. The maximum cacheable range is determined by a combination of cache memory size and the number of cache tag bits used. The most common L2 cache sizes will be 512KB or 1MB of L2 cache on the motherboard, allowing either 128MB or 256MB of main memory to be cached. The maximum configuration of 2MB of L2 cache will allow up to 512MB of main memory to be cacheable. Intel solves this in the Pentium II by including sufficient cache tag RAM in the L2 cache built in to the Pentium II processors to allow either 512MB of main memory or 4GB of main memory to be cached.

The MVP3 seems to be the chipset of choice in the higher end Socket 7 motherboards from DFI, FIC, Tyan, Acer, and others.

Acer Laboratories, Inc (ALi)

Acer Laboratories, Inc. was originally founded in 1987 as an independent research and development center for the Acer Group. In 1993, ALi separated financially and legally from Acer Inc. and became a member company of the Acer Group. ALi has rapidly claimed a prominent position among PC chipset manufacturers.

Aladdin IV

The Aladdin IV from Acer Labs is a two-chip set for P5 class processors consisting of the M1531 North Bridge and either an M1533 or M1543 South Bridge chip. The Aladdin IV supports all Intel, AMD, Cyrix/IBM and other P5-class CPUs including the Intel Pentium and Pentium MMX, AMD K5 and K6, and the Cyrix/IBM 6x86 and 6x86MX (MII) processors. The Aladdin IV is equivalent to the Intel 430TX chipset, with the addition of error-correcting memory support and higher-speed 75MHz and 83.3MHz operation. Also, when using the M1543 South Bridge, an additional Super I/O chip is not necessary as those functions are included in the M1543 South Bridge.

The M1531 North Bridge is a 328-pin BGA (Ball Grid Array) chip that supports CPU bus speeds of 83.3 MHz, 75 MHz, 66 MHz, 60 MHz, and 50MHz. The M1531 also supports Pipelined-Burst SRAM cache in sizes of up to 1MB, allowing either 64MB (with 8-bit Tag SRAM) or up to 512MB (with 11-bit Tag SRAM) of cacheable main memory. FPM, EDO, or SDRAM main memory modules are supported for a total capacity of 1GB in up to four total banks. Memory timing is 6-3-3-3 for back-to-back FPM reads, 5-2-2-2 for back-to-back EDO reads, and 6-1-1-1 for back-to-back SDRAM reads. For reliability and integrity in mission-critical or server applications, ECC (Error Correcting Code) or parity is supported. PCI spec. 2.1 is also supported, allowing concurrent PCI operations.

The M1533 South Bridge integrates ACPI support, two-channel Ultra-DMA 33 IDE master controller, two-port USB controller, and a standard Keyboard/Mouse controller. A more full-function M1543 South Bridge is also available that has everything in the M1533 South Bridge plus all the functions of a normally separate Super I/O controller. The M1543 integrates ACPI support, two-channel Ultra-DMA 33 IDE controller, two-port USB controller, and a standard keyboard/mouse controller. Also included is an integrated Super I/O including a 2.88MB floppy disk controller, two high-performance serial ports, and a multi-mode parallel port. The serial ports incorporate 16550-compatible UARTs (Universal Asynchronous Receiver Transmitters) with 16-byte FIFO (First In First Out) buffers and Serial Infra Red (SIR) capability. The multimode Parallel Port includes support for Standard Parallel Port (SPP) mode, PS/2 bidirectional mode, Enhanced Parallel Port (EPP) mode, and the Microsoft and Hewlett Packard Extended Capabilities Port (ECP) mode.

Aladdin V

The Acer Labs (ALi) Aladdin V Chipset is a two-chip set that consists of the M1541 North Bridge chip and the M1543 South Bridge/Super I/O controller combo chip. The M1541 North Bridge is a 456-pin BGA package chip while the M1543 South Bridge is a 328-pin BGA package chip. The M1541 chipset is similar to the previous M1532 chipset with the addition of higher speed (up to 100MHz) operation and AGP (Accelerated Graphics Port) support.

The M1541 North Bridge includes the CPU-to-PCI bridge, the L2 cache and buffer controller, the DRAM controller, the AGP interface, and the PCI controller. The M1541 supports the Super-7 high-speed 100MHz Socket 7 processor interface used by some of the newer AMD and Cyrix/IBM P5 processors. It will also run the processor bus at 83.3MHz, 75MHz, 66MHz, 60MHz, and 50MHz for backward compatibility. When running the CPU bus at 75MHz, the PCI bus only runs at 30MHz; however, when the CPU bus is running at 83.3MHz or 100MHz, the PCI bus will run at full 33MHz PCI standard speed.

The M1541 also integrates enough cache Tag RAM (16K×10) internally to support 512KB of L2 cache, simplifying the L2 cache design and further reducing the number of chips on the mother-board. Cacheable memory is up to 512MB of RAM when using 512KB L2 cache and 1GB of RAM when using 1MB of L2 cache. FPM, EDO, or SDRAM memory is supported, in up to four banks and up to 1GB total RAM. ECC/Parity is also supported for mission-critical or fileserver applications to improve reliability. Memory timing is 6-3-3-3-3-3-3-3 for back-to-back FPM reads, 5-2-2-2-2-2-2-2 for back-to-back EDO reads, and 6-1-1-1-2-1-1-1 for back-to-back SDRAM reads. For more information on memory timing, see chapter 6.

Finally, Accelerated Graphics Port (AGP) Interface specification V1.0 is supported, along with 1x and 2x modes, allowing the latest graphics cards to be utilized.

The M1543 South Bridge and Super I/O combo chip includes ACPI support, the USB host/hub interface, dual channel Ultra-DMA/33 IDE host interface, keyboard and mouse controller, and the Super I/O controller. The built-in Super I/O consists of an integrated floppy disk controller, two serial ports with infrared support, and a multimode parallel port.

Silicon integrated Systems (SiS)

Silicon integrated Systems (SiS) was formerly known as Symphony Labs and is one of the three largest non-Intel PC motherboard chipset manufacturers.

5581 and 5582

The SiS5581 and 5582 chips are both 553-pin BGA package single-chip sets incorporating both North and South Bridge functions. The SiS5582 is targeted for AT/ATX form factor motherboards while the SiS5581 is intended to be used on LPX/NLX form factor boards. In all other ways, the two North Bridge chips are identical. The SiS 5581/5582 is a single-chip set designed to be a high-performance, low-cost alternative that is functionally equivalent to Intel's 430TX chipset. By having everything in a single chip, a low-cost motherboard can be produced.

The 5581/5582 consists of both North and South Bridge functions, including PCI to ISA bridge function, PCI IDE function, Universal Serial Bus host/hub function, Integrated RTC, and Integrated Keyboard Controller. These chips support a CPU bus speed of 50, 55, 60, 66, and 75MHz.

A maximum of 512KB of L2 cache is supported, with a maximum cacheable range of 128MB of main memory. The maximum cacheable range is determined by a combination of cache memory size, and the number of Tag bits used. The most common cache size that will allow caching of up to 128MB of RAM will be 512KB, although up to 384MB of RAM can technically be installed in up to three total banks. Because this is designed for low-cost systems, ECC (Error Correcting Code) or parity functions are not supported. Main memory timing is x-3-3-3 for FPM, while EDO timing is x-2-2-2, and SDRAM timing is x-1-1-1.

The 5581/5582 chipset also includes Advanced Configuration and Power Interface (ACPI) power management, a dual channel Ultra-DMA/33 IDE interface, USB controller, and even the CMOS RAM and Real Time Clock (RTC). PCI v2.1 is supported that allows concurrent PCI operation; however, AGP is not supported in this chipset.

5591 and 5592

The SiS 5591/5592 is a three-chip set consisting of either a 5591 or 5592 North Bridge chip along with a SiS5595 South Bridge. The 5591/5592 North Bridge chips are both 3.3v 553-pin BGA package chips, while the 5595 South Bridge chip is a 5v 208-pin PQFP (Plastic Quad Flat Pack) package chip. The SiS5591 North Bridge is targeted for ATX form factor motherboards while the SiS5592 version is intended to be used on the NLX form factor. In all other ways, the two North Bridge chips are identical.

The 5591/5592 North Bridge chips include the Host-to-PCI bridge, the L2 cache controller, the DRAM controller, the Accelerated Graphics Port interface, and the PCI IDE controller. The SiS5595 South Bridge includes the PCI-to-ISA bridge, the ACPI/APM power management unit, the Universal Serial Bus host/hub interface, and the ISA bus interface that contains the ISA bus controller, the DMA controllers, the interrupt controllers, and the Timers. It also integrates the Keyboard controller and the Real Time Clock (RTC).

The 5591/5592 North Bridge chips support CPU bus speeds of up to 75MHz. They also support up to 1MB of L2 cache allowing up to 256MB of main memory to be cacheable. The maximum cacheable main memory amount is determined by a combination of cache memory size and the number of Tag bits used. Most common cache sizes will be 512KB and 1MB. The 512KB cache with 7 Tag bits will allow only 64M of memory to be cached, while 8 Tag bits will allow caching of up to 128MB. With 1MB of cache onboard, the cacheable range is doubled to a maximum of 256MB.

A maximum of 256MB of total RAM is allowed in up to three banks. Both ECC and parity are supported for mission-critical or file server applications. Main memory timing for FPM memory is x-3-3-3, EDO timing is x-2-2-2, and SDRAM is x-1-1-1.

PCI specification 2.1 is supported at up to 33MHz, and AGP specification 1.0 is supported in both 1x and 2x modes. The separate 5595 South Bridge includes a dual-channel Ultra-DMA/33 interface and support for USB.

Sixth-Generation (P6 Pentium Pro/Pentium II/III Class) Chipsets

Although Intel clearly dominated the Pentium chipset world, they are virtually the only game in town for the Pentium Pro and Pentium II/III chipsets. The biggest reason for this is that since the

Pentium first came out in 1993, Intel has been introducing new chipsets (and even complete ready-to-go motherboards) simultaneously with their new processors. This makes it hard for anybody else to catch up. Another problem for other chipset manufacturers is that Intel has been reluctant to license the Slot 1 and Socket 370 interface used by the Celeron and Pentium II/III processors, while the Socket 7 interface used by the Pentium has been freely available for license. Still, some licenses have been granted, and you should see other chipmakers developing Socket 370 or Slot 1 processors in the future. For now, Intel has most of the Celeron/Pentium II/III market to themselves.

Several of the third-party chipset manufacturers such as VIA Technologies, Acer Laboratories, Inc (ALi), and Silicon integrated Systems (SiS) have recently introduced chipsets for Slot 1 or Socket 370 motherboards.

Note that because the Pentium Pro, Celeron, and Pentium II/III are essentially the same processor with different cache designs, the same chipset can be used for Socket 8 (Pentium Pro), Socket 370 (Celeron), and Slot 1 (Celeron/Pentium II/III) designs. Of course, the newer P6 class chipsets are optimized for the Slot 1/Socket 370 architecture and nobody is doing any new Socket 8 designs. This is also true for the Pentium Pro, which is essentially obsolete compared to the Celeron/Pentium II/III and is currently being used only in limited file server applications.

Although there are a few newcomers to the P6 chipset market, virtually all Pentium Pro, Celeron, and Pentium II/III motherboards use Intel chipsets; their market share here is for all practical purposes near 100 percent.

The sixth-generation P6 (Pentium Pro/Celeron/Pentium II/III) motherboard chipsets continue with the North Bridge/South Bridge design first debuted in the Pentium processor chipsets. In fact, the South Bridge portion of the chipset is the same as that used in many of the Pentium chipsets.

Table 4.7 shows the chipsets used on Pentium Pro motherboards.

Table 4.7   Pentium Pro Motherboard Chipsets (North Bridge)

Chipset	450KX	450GX	440FX
Codename	Orion	Orion Server	Natoma
Workstation Date Introduced	Nov. 1995	Nov. 1995	May 1996
Bus Speed	66 MHz	66 MHz	66 MHz
SMP (dual CPUs)	Yes	Yes (4 CPUs)	Yes
Memory Types	FPM	FPM	FPM/EDO/BEDO
Parity/ECC	Both	Both	Both
Maximum Memory	8GB	1GB	1GB
L2 Cache Type	In CPU	In CPU	In CPU
Maximum Cacheable	1GB	1GB	1GB
PCI Support	2.0	2.0	2.1

(continues)

Table 4.7 Continued

Chipset	450KX	450GX	440FX
AGP Support	No	No	No
AGP Speed	n/a	n/a	n/a
South Bridge	various	various	PIIX3

SMP = Symmetric Multiprocessing (Dual Processors)   Pburst = Pipeline Burst (Synchronous)
FPM = Fast Page Mode   PCI = Peripheral Component Interconnect
EDO = Extended Data Out   AGP = Accelerated Graphics Port
BEDO = Burst EDO   SIO = System I/O
SDRAM = Synchronous Dynamic RAM   PIIX = PCI ISA IDE Xcelerator

Note

PCI 2.1 supports concurrent PCI operations.

For the Celeron and Pentium II/III motherboards, Intel offers the chipsets in Table 4.8.

Table 4.8 Celeron and Pentium II/III Motherboard Chipsets (North Bridge)

Chipset	440FX	440LX	440EX	440BX
Codename	Natoma	none	none	none
Date Introduced	May 1996	Aug. 1997	April 1998	April 199
Part Numbers	82441FX 82442FX	82443LX	82443EX	82443BX
Bus Speed	66 MHz	66 MHz	66 MHz	66/100 MHz
Optimum Processor	Pentium II	Pentium II	Celeron	Pentium II/III, Celeron
SMP (dual CPUs)	Yes	Yes	No	Yes
Memory Types	FPM/EDO/BEDO	FPM/EDO/SDRAM	EDO/SDRAM	SDRAM
Parity/ECC	Both	Both	Neither	Both
Maximum Memory	1GB	1GB EDO/ 512 MB SDRAM	256MB	1GB
Memory Banks	4	4	2	4
PCI Support	2.1	2.1	2.1	2.1
AGP Support	No	AGP-2x	AGP-2x	AGP-2x
South Bridge	82371SB (PIIX3)	82371AB (PIIX4)	82371EB (PIIX4E)	82371EB (PIIX4E)

Chipset	440GX	450NX	440ZX	810
Codename	none	none	none	Whitney
Date Introduced	June 1998	June '98	November '98	April '99
Part Numbers	82443GX	82451NX 82452NX 82453NX 82454NX	82443ZX	82810/ 82810-DC100 82802AB/AC
Bus Speed	100 MHz	100 MHz	66/100 MHz*	66/100 MHz

Chipset	440GX	450NX	440ZX	810
Optimum Processor	Pentium II/III, Xeon	Pentium II/III, Xeon	Celeron, Pentium II/III	Celeron, Pentium II/III
SMP (dual CPUs)	Yes	Yes, up to 4	No	No
Memory Types	SDRAM	FPM/EDO	SDRAM	SDRAM
Parity/ECC	Both	Both	Neither	Neither
Maximum Memory	2GB	8 GB	256 MB	256 MB
Memory Banks	4	4	2	2
PCI Support	2.1	2.1	2.1	2.2
AGP Support	AGP-2x	No	AGP-2x	Direct AGP
South Bridge	82371EB (PIIX4E)	82371EB (PIIX4E)	82371EB (PIIX4E)	82801AA/AB (ICH/ICH0)

* Note the 440ZX is available in a cheaper 440ZX-66 version, which will only run 66MHz

SMP = Symmetric Multiprocessing (Dual Processors)

FPM = Fast Page Mode   *PCI = Peripheral Component Interconnect*

EDO = Extended Data Out   *AGP = Accelerated Graphics Port*

BEDO = Burst EDO   *SIO = System I/O*

SDRAM = Synchronous Dynamic RAM   *PIIX = PCI ISA IDE Xcelerator*

Pburst = Pipeline Burst (Synchronous)   *ICH = I/O Controller Hub*

Note

Pentium Pro, Celeron, and Pentium II/III CPUs have their secondary cache integrated into the CPU package. Therefore, cache characteristics for these machines are not dependent on the chipset but are quite dependent on the processor instead.

Most Intel chipsets are designed as a two-part system, using a North Bridge and a South Bridge component. Often the same South Bridge component can be used with several different North Bridge chipsets. Table 4.9 shows a list of all the current Intel South Bridge components and their capabilities.

Table 4.9   Intel South Bridge Chips

Chip Name	SIO	PIIX	PIIX3	PIIX4	PIIX4E	ICH0	ICH
Part Number	82378IB/ZB	82371FB	82371SB	82371AB	82371EB	82801AB	82801AA
IDE Support	None	BMIDE	BMIDE	UDMA-33	UDMA-33	UDMA-33	UDMA-66
USB Support	None	None	Yes	Yes	Yes	Yes	Yes
CMOS/Clock	No	No	No	Yes	Yes	Yes	Yes
Power Management	SMM	SMM	SMM	SMM	SMM/ACPI	SMM/ACPI	SMM/ACPI

SIO = System I/O   *BMIDE = Bus Master IDE*

PIIX = PCI ISA IDE Xcelerator   *UDMA = Ultra-DMA IDE*

ICH = I/O Controller Hub   *SMM = System Management Mode*

USB = Universal Serial Bus   *ACPI = Advanced Configuration and Power Interface*

IDE = Integrated Drive Electronics (AT Attachment)

The following sections examine the P6 chipsets for both the Pentium Pro and Pentium II processors.

Intel 450KX/GX (Orion Workstation/Server)

The first chipsets to support the Pentium Pro were the 450KX and GX, both code-named Orion. The 450KX was designed for networked or standalone workstations; the more powerful 450GX was designed for file servers. The GX server chipset was particularly suited to the server role, as it supports up to four Pentium Pro processors for Symmetric Multiprocessing (SMP) servers, up to 8GB of four-way interleaved memory with ECC or parity, and two bridged PCI buses. The 450KX is the workstation or standalone user version of Orion and as such it supports fewer processors (one or two) and less memory (1GB) than the GX. The 450GX and 450KX both have full support for ECC memory—a requirement for server and workstation use.

The 450GX and 450KX North Bridge is comprised of four individual chip components—an 82454KX/GX PCI Bridge, an 82452KX/GX Data Path (DP), an 82453KX/GX Data Controller (DC), and an 82451KX/GX Memory Interface Controller (MIC). Options for QFP (Quad Flat Pack) or BGA (Ball Grid Array) packaging were available on the PCI Bridge and the DP. BGA uses less space on a board.

The 450's high reliability is obtained through ECC from the Pentium Pro processor data bus to memory. Reliability is also enhanced by parity protection on the processor bus, control bus, and on all PCI signals. In addition, single-bit error correction is provided, thereby avoiding server downtime because of spurious memory errors caused by cosmic rays.

▶▶ See "Parity and ECC," p. 457.

Until the introduction of the following 440FX chipset, these were used almost exclusively in file servers. After the debut of the 440FX, the expensive Orion chips all but disappeared due to their complexity and high cost.

Intel 440FX (Natoma)

The first popular mainstream P6 (Pentium Pro or Pentium II) motherboard chipset was the 440FX, which was code-named Natoma. The 440FX was designed by Intel to be a lower cost and somewhat higher performance replacement for the 450KX workstation chipset. It offered better memory performance through support of EDO memory, which the prior 450KX lacked.

The 440FX uses half the number of components than the previous Intel chipset. It offers additional features such as support for the PCI 2.1 (Concurrent PCI) standard, Universal Serial Bus (USB) support, and reliability through error checking and correction (ECC).

The Concurrent PCI processing architecture maximizes system performance with simultaneous activity on the CPU, PCI, and ISA buses. Concurrent PCI provides increased bandwidth to better support 2D/3D graphics, video and audio, and processing for host-based applications. ECC memory support delivers improved reliability to business system users.

The main features of this chipset include

- Support for up to 1GB of EDO memory
- Full 1GB cacheability (based on the processor because the L2 cache and tag are in the CPU)
- Support for USB
- Support for BusMaster IDE
- Full parity/ECC support

The 440FX consists of a two-chip North Bridge. The main component is the 82441FX PCI Bridge and Memory controller, along with the 82442FX Data Bus accelerator for the PCI bus. This chipset uses the PIIX3 82371SB South Bridge chip that supports high-speed busmaster DMA IDE interfaces and USB, and it acts as the bridge between the PCI and ISA buses.

Note that this was the first P6 chipset to support EDO memory, but it lacked support for the faster SDRAM. Also, the PIIX3 used with this chipset does not support the faster Ultra DMA IDE hard drives.

The 440FX was the chipset used on the first Pentium II motherboards, which have the same basic architecture as the Pentium Pro. The Pentium II was released several months before the chipset that was supposedly designed for it was ready, and so early PII motherboards used the older 440FX chipset. This chipset was never designed with the Pentium II in mind, whereas the newer 440LX was optimized specifically to take advantage of the Pentium II architecture. For that reason, I normally recommended that people stay away from the original 440FX-based PII motherboards and wait for Pentium II systems that used the forthcoming 440LX chipset. When the new chipset was introduced, the 440FX was quickly superseded by the improved 440LX design.

Intel 440LX

The 440LX quickly took over in the marketplace after it debuted in August of 1997. This was the first chipset to really take full advantage of the Pentium II processor. Compared to the 440FX, the 440LX chipset offers several improvements:

- Support for the new Advanced Graphics Port (AGP) video card bus
- Support for 66MHz SDRAM memory
- Support for the Ultra DMA IDE interface
- Support for Universal Serial Bus (USB)

The 440LX rapidly became the most popular chip for all new Pentium II systems from the end of 1997 through the beginning of 1998.

Intel 440EX

The 440EX is designed to be a low-cost lower performance alternative to the 440LX chipset. It was introduced in April 1998 along with the Intel Celeron low-end Pentium II processor. The 440EX lacks several features in the more powerful 440LX, including dual processor and ECC or parity memory support. This chipset is basically designed for low-end 66MHz bus-based systems that use the new Intel Celeron low-end Pentium II processor. Note that boards with the 440EX will fully support a full-blown Pentium II but lack some of the features of the more powerful 440LX or 440BX chipsets.

The main things to note about the 440EX are listed here:

- Designed with a feature set tuned for the low-end PC market
- Primarily for the Intel Celeron processor
- Supports AGP
- Does not support ECC or parity memory
- Single processor support only

Although it is based on the core technology of the Intel 440LX, the 440EX is basically considered a lower-feature, lower-reliability version of that chipset designed for non-mission-critical systems.

The 440EX consists of a 82443EX PCI AGP Controller (PAC) North Bridge component and the new 82371EB (PIIX4E) South Bridge chip. Although this chipset is fine for most low-end use, I would normally recommend the faster, more powerful, and more reliable (with ECC memory) 440BX instead.

Intel 440BX

The Intel 440BX chipset was introduced in April of 1998 and was the first chipset to run the processor host bus (and basically the motherboard) at 100MHz. The 440BX was designed specifically to support the faster Pentium II/III processors at 350MHz, 400MHz, 450MHz, or 500MHz. A mobile version of this chipset also is the first Pentium II/III chipset for notebook or laptop systems.

The main change from the previous 440LX to the BX is that the 440BX chipset improves performance by increasing the bandwidth of the system bus from 66MHz to 100MHz. The chipset can run at either 66- or 100MHz, allowing one basic motherboard design to support all Pentium II/III processor speeds from 233MHz to 500MHz and beyond.

Intel 440BX highlights

- Support for 100MHz SDRAM (PC100)
- Support for both 100MHz or 66MHz system and memory bus designs
- Support for up to 1GB of memory in up to four banks (four DIMMs)
- Support for ECC (Error Correcting Code) memory
- Support for ACPI (Advanced Configuration and Power Interface specification)
- The first chipset to support the Mobile Intel Pentium II processor

▶▶ See "Mobile Pentium II," p. 1218.

The Intel 440BX consists of a single North Bridge chip called the 82443BX Host Bridge/Controller, which is paired with a new 82371EB PCI-ISA/IDE Xcelerator (PIIX4E) South Bridge chip. The new South Bridge adds support for the ACPI specification version 1.0. Figure 4.28 shows a typical system block diagram using the 440BX.

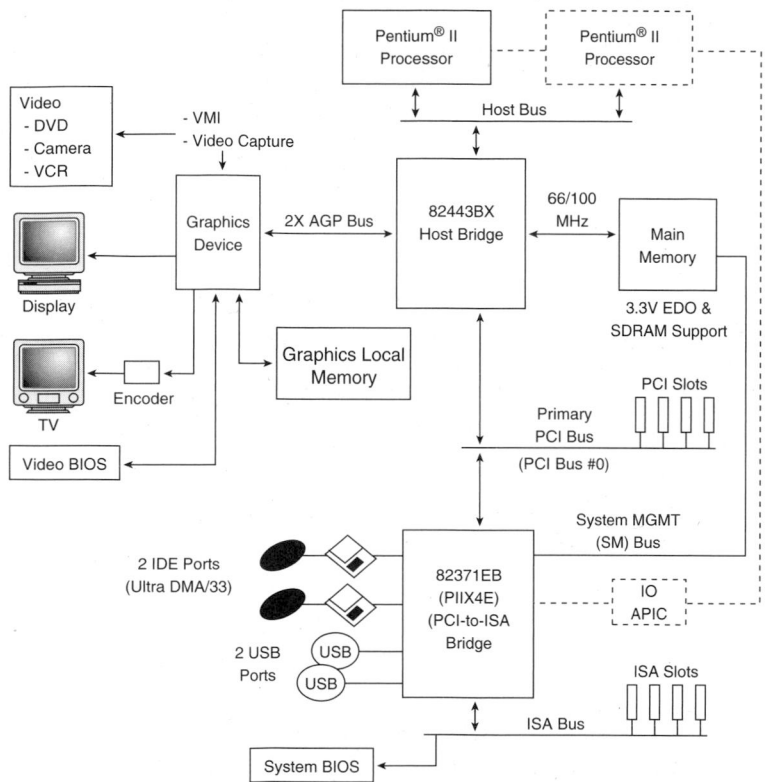

Figure 4.28 System block diagram using the Intel 440BX chipset.

The 440BX is currently the most popular high-end chipset in the Intel arsenal for standard desktop users. It offers superior performance and high reliability through the use of ECC (Error Correcting Code), SDRAM (Synchronous DRAM), and DIMMs (Dual Inline Memory Modules).

Intel 440ZX and 440ZX-66

The 440ZX is designed to be a low-cost version of the 440BX. The 440ZX brings 66 or 100MHz performance to entry-level Celeron and low-end Pentium II/III systems. The 440ZX is pin-compatible with the more expensive 440BX, meaning existing 440BX motherboards can be easily redesigned to use this lower cost chipset.

Note that there are two versions of the 440ZX, the standard one, will run at 100MHz or 66MHz, and the 440ZX-66, which will only run at the slower 66MHz.

The features of the 440ZX include the following:

- Optimized for the micro-ATX form factor
- Support for Celeron and Pentium II/III processors at up to 100MHz bus speeds
- The main differences from the 440BX include
  - No parity or ECC memory support
  - Only two banks of memory (two DIMMs) supported
  - Maximum memory only 256MB
  - Only runs up to 66MHz (440ZX-66)

The 440ZX is not a replacement for the 440BX; instead, it is designed to be used in less expensive systems where the greater memory capabilities, performance, and data integrity functions (ECC memory) of the 440BX are not needed.

Intel 440GX

The Intel 440GX AGPset is the first chipset optimized for high-volume midrange workstations and lower cost servers. The 440GX is essentially a version of the 440BX that has been upgraded to support the Slot 2 (also called SC330) processor slot for the Pentium II/III Xeon processor. The 440GX can still be used in Slot 1 designs as well. It also supports up to 2GB of memory, twice that of the 440BX. Other than these items, the 440GX is essentially the same as the 440BX. Because the 440GX is core-compatible with the 440BX, motherboard manufacturers will be able to quickly and easily modify their existing Slot 1 440BX board designs into Slot 1 or 2 440GX designs.

The main features of the 440GX include

- Support for Slot 1 and Slot 2
- Support for 100MHz system bus
- Support for up to 2GB of SDRAM memory

This chipset allows for lower cost, high-performance workstations and servers using the Slot 2 based Xeon processors.

Intel 450NX

The 450NX chipset is designed for multiprocessor systems and standard high-volume servers based on the Pentium II/III Xeon processor. The Intel 450NX chipset consists of four components: the 82454NX PCI Expander Bridge (PXB), 82451NX Memory and I/O Bridge Controller (MIOC), 82452NX RAS/CAS Generator (RCG), and 82453NX Data Path Multiplexor (MUX).

The 450NX supports up to four Pentium II/III Xeon processors at 100MHz. Two dedicated PCI Expander Bridges (PXBs) can be connected via the Expander Bus. Each PXB provides two independent 32-bit, 33MHz PCI buses, with an option to link the two buses into a single 64-bit, 33MHz bus.

Figure 4.29 shows a typical high-end server block diagram using the 450NX chipset.

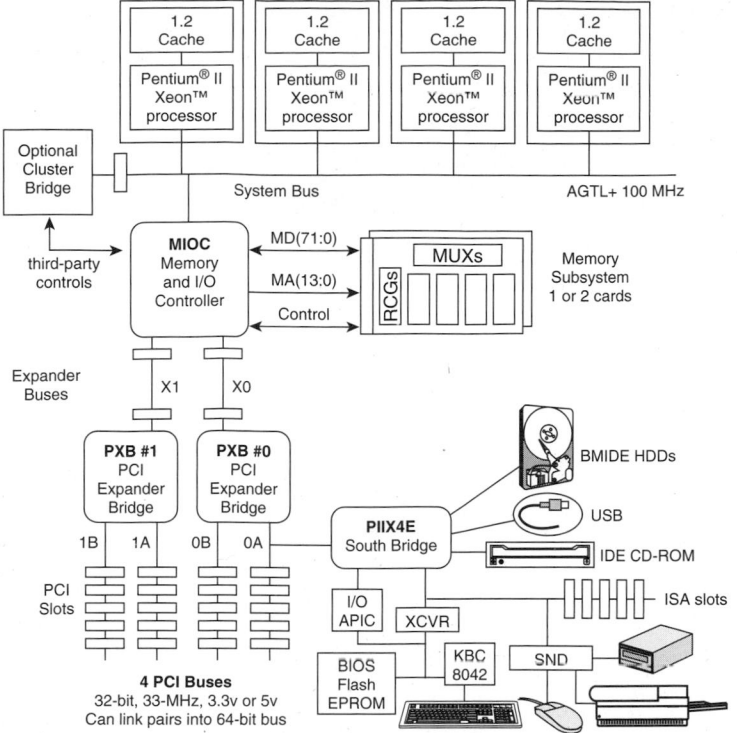

Figure 4.29   High-end server block diagram using the Intel 440NX chipset.

The 450NX supports one or two memory cards. Each card incorporates an RCG chip and two MUX chips, in addition to the memory DIMMs. Up to 8GB of memory is supported in total.

The primary features of the 450NX include the following:

- Slot 2 (SC330) processor bus interface at 100MHz
- Supports up to four-way processing
- Support for two dedicated PCI expander bridges (PXBs)
- Up to four 32-bit PCI buses or two 64-bit PCI buses

The 450NX chipset does not support AGP, because high-end video is not an issue in network file servers.

Intel 810

Introduced in April of 1999, the Intel 810 chipset (code-named Whitney) represents a major change in chipset design from the standard North and South Bridges that have been used since the 486 days. The 810 chipset allows for improvements in system performance, all for less cost and system complexity.

The major features of the 810 chipset include

- 440BX chipset technology foundation
- 66/100MHz System Bus capability
- Integrated Intel 3D graphics with Direct AGP for 2D and 3D graphics
- Efficient use of system memory for graphics performance
- Optional 4MB of dedicated display cache video memory
- Digital Video Out port compatible with DVI specification for flat panel displays
- Software MPEG-2 DVD playback with Hardware Motion Compensation
- Accelerated Hub Architecture for increased 66MHz I/O performance
- Supports UDMA-66 for high performance IDE drives
- Integrated Audio-Codec 97 (AC97) controller
- Supports low-power sleep modes
- Random Number Generator (RNG) for stronger security products
- Integrated USB controller
- Elimination of ISA Bus

The 810 chipset (see Figure 4.30) consists of three major components:

- *82810 Graphics Memory Controller Hub (GMCH)*. 421 Ball Grid Array (BGA) package
- *82801 Integrated Controller Hub (ICH)*. 241 Ball Grid Array (BGA) package
- *82802 Firmware Hub (FWH)*. In either 32-pin Plastic Leaded Chip Carrier (PLCC) or 40-pin Thin Small Outline Package (TSOP) packages

Figure 4.30   Intel 810 chipset showing the 82810 (GMCH), 82801 (ICH), and 82802 (FWH) chips. *Photograph used by permission of Intel Corporation.*

Compared to the previous North/South Bridge designs, there are some fairly significant changes in the 810 chipset. The previous system designs had the North Bridge acting as the memory controller, talking to the South Bridge chip via the PCI bus. This new design has the Graphics Memory Controller Hub (GMCH) taking the place of the North Bridge, which talks to the I/O

Controller Hub (ICH) via a 66MHz dedicated interface called the Accelerated Hub Architecture (AHA) bus. In particular, implementing a direct connection between the North and South Bridges in this manner was key in implementing the new UDMA-66 high-speed IDE interface for hard disks, DVD drives, and other IDE devices.

Figure 4.31 shows a system block diagram for the 810 chipset.

Overall there is still a three-tier system approach as with the previous North/South Bridge and super I/O chip circuits used in previous motherboard designs. The big difference is that the lowest speed in this new design is the 33MHz PCI bus. The old 8MHz ISA bus is finally put out to pasture, as there is no direct provision for ISA in this chipset. It is possible to integrate an ISA bridge chip in an 810 motherboard, so you might yet see some of these boards with ISA slots, but it is doubtful due to the extra cost and little benefit this would provide.

With the 810 chipset, ISA is finally dead.

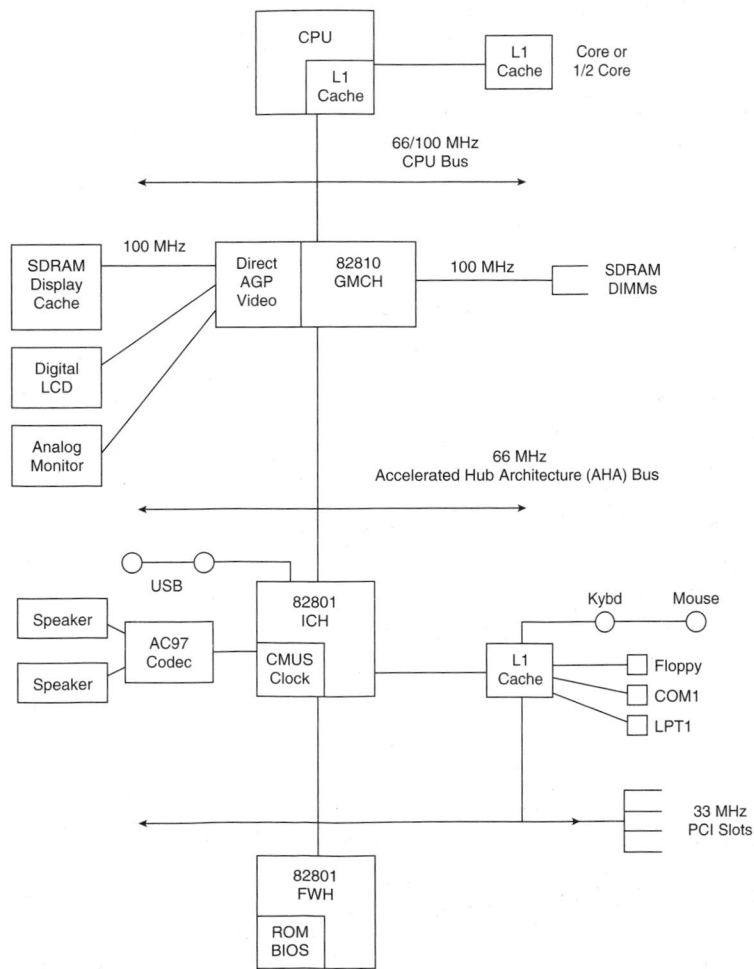

Figure 4.31   Intel 810 Chipset system block diagram.

The 82810 Graphics Memory Controller Hub (GMCH) uses an internal Direct AGP (integrated AGP) interface to create 2D and 3D effects and images. The video capability integrated into the 82810 chip features Hardware Motion Compensation to improve software DVD video quality and both analog and direct digital video out ports, which enable connections to either traditional TVs (via an external converter module) or the new direct digital flat panel displays. The GMCH chip also incorporates the System Manageability Bus, which allows networking equipment to monitor the 810 chipset platform. Using ACPI specifications, the system manageability function enables low-power sleep mode and conserves energy when the system is idle.

Note that there are two versions of the GMCH, known as the 82810 and 82810-DC100. The latter DC100 (Display Cache 100MHz) version has the option for up to 4MB of 100MHz SDRAM to be directly connected as a dedicated display cache. The regular 82810 GMCH chip lacks this provision.

The 82801 I/O Controller Hub (ICH) employs Accelerated Hub Architecture for a direct connection from the GMCH chip. This is twice as fast (266MB/sec) as the previous North/South Bridge connections that used the PCI bus. Plus, the AHA bus is dedicated, meaning that no other devices will be on it. The AHA bus also incorporates optimized arbitration rules allowing more functions to run concurrently, enabling better video and audio performance.

The ICH also integrates dual IDE controllers, which run up to either 33MB/s (UDMA-33 or Ultra-ATA/33) or 66MB/s (UDMA-66 or Ultra-ATA/66). Note that there are two versions of the ICH chip. The 82801AA (ICH) incorporates the 66MB/s capable IDE and supports up to six PCI slots, while the 82801AB (ICH0) only supports 33MB/sec maximum and supports up to four PCI slots.

The ICH also integrates an interface to an Audio-Codec 97 (AC97) controller, dual USB ports, and the PCI bus with up to four or six slots. The Integrated Audio-Codec 97 controller enables software audio and modem by using the processor to run sound and modem software. By reusing existing system resources, this lowers the system cost by eliminating components.

The 82802 Firmware Hub (FWH) incorporates the system BIOS and video BIOS, eliminating a redundant nonvolatile memory component. The BIOS within the FWH is flash type memory, so it can be field updated at any time. In addition, the 82802 contains a hardware Random Number Generator (RNG). The RNG provides truly random numbers to enable fundamental security building blocks supporting stronger encryption, digital signing, and security protocols. There are two versions of the FWH, called the 82802AB and 82802AC respectively. The AB version incorporates 512KB (4Mbit) of flash BIOS memory, and the AC version incorporates a full 1MB (8Mbit) of BIOS ROM.

With the Intel 810 chipset, Intel has done something that many in the industry were afraid of—they have integrated the video and graphics controller directly into the motherboard chipset. This means that systems using the 810 chipset won't have an AGP slot, and won't be able to use conventional AGP video cards. From a performance standpoint, this is not really a problem. The video they have integrated is an outstanding performer, and it has direct access to the rest of the chipset at a data rate even faster than standard AGP. The direct AGP interface built-in to the 810 chipset runs at 100MHz, rather than the 66MHz of standard AGP. Intel calls the integrated interface Direct AGP, and it describes the direct connection between the memory and processor controllers with the video controller all within the same chip.

This probably dictates the future of mainstream PCs, which means the video card, as we know it, will be reserved only for higher end systems. With the 810 chipset, Intel has let it be known in a big way that they have entered the PC video business. If I were a video chip or board manufacturer, I would be carefully studying my options in other areas for the future!

In fact, the theme with the 810 chipset is one of integration. The integrated video means no video cards are required; the integrated AC97 interface means that conventional modems and sound cards are not required. Plus, there is an integrated CMOS/Clock chip (in the ICH), and even the BIOS is integrated in the FWH chip. All in all the 810 should be taken as a sign for things to come in the PC industry, which means more integration, better overall performance, and less cost.

Third-Party (non-Intel) P6 Class Chipsets

Acer Laboratories, Inc. (ALi)

Aladdin Pro II

The Acer Labs (ALi) Aladdin Pro II M1621 is a two-chip set for P6 (Pentium Pro and Pentium II) processors consisting of two BGA package chips, the 456-pin BGA package M1621 North Bridge, and either the M1533 or M1543 South Bridge. This is one of the first Slot 1 P6 processor chipsets from a company other than Intel.

The M1621 North Bridge includes an AGP, memory and I/O controller, and a data path with multiport buffers for data acceleration. It can support multiple Pentium II processors with bus speeds of 60, 66, and 100MHz. This chipset is equivalent to the 440BX chipset from Intel.

The integrated memory controller supports FPM, EDO, and SDRAM with a total capacity of up to 1GB (SDRAM) or 2GB (EDO). ECC (Error Correcting Code) memory is supported, allowing use in mission-critical or fileserver applications. Memory timing is x-1-1-1-1-1-1-1 in back-to-back SDRAM reads, or x-2-2-2-2-2-2-2 in back-to-back EDO reads.

The M1621 supports AGP v1.0, in both 1x and 2x modes, and is fully compliant with PCI Rev. 2.1, allowing for concurrent PCI operations. The M1621 can be used with either the M1533 South Bridge or M1543 South Bridge/Super I/O combo chips.

The M1533 South Bridge includes the following features:

- PCI-to-ISA Bridge
- Built-in keyboard/mouse controller
- Enhanced Power Management, featuring ACPI (Advanced Configuration and Power Interface)
- Two-port USB interface
- Dual channel Ultra-DMA/33 IDE host adapter
- 328-pin BGA package

M1543 includes all features in the 1533 plus fully integrated Super I/O, including a Floppy Disk Controller, two high-speed serial ports, and one multimode parallel port.

VIA Technologies

Apollo P6/97

The VT82C680 Apollo P6 is a high-performance, cost-effective, and energy-efficient chipset for the implementation of PCI/ISA desktop and notebook personal computer systems based on 64-bit Intel P6 processors. This was one of the first non-Intel P6 chipsets of any kind available and is functionally equivalent to the Intel 440FX chipset. The Apollo P6 chipset supports dual processor configurations with up to 66MHz external CPU bus speed. The DRAM and PCI bus are also independently powered so that each of the buses can be run at 3.3v or 5v. The ISA bus always runs at 5v. The Apollo P6 supports up to 1GB of DRAM. This chipset never really achieved much popularity in the market.

Apollo Pro

The Apollo Pro is a high-performance chipset for Slot 1 mobile and desktop PC systems. The Apollo Pro includes support for advanced system power management capability for both desktop and mobile PC applications, PC100 SDRAM, AGP 2x mode, and multiple CPU/DRAM timing configurations. The Apollo Pro chipset is comparable in features to the 440BX and PIIX4e chipset from Intel, and represents one of the first non-Intel chipsets to support the Socket 1 architecture.

The VIA Apollo Pro consists of two devices—the VT82C691 North Bridge chip and the VT82C596, a BGA-packaged South Bridge with a full set of mobile, power-management features. For cost-effective desktop designs, the VT82C691 can also be configured with the VT82C586B South Bridge.

The VT82C691 Apollo Pro North Bridge supports all Slot-1 (Intel Pentium II) and Socket 8 (Intel Pentium Pro) processors. The Apollo Pro also supports the 66MHz and the newer 100 MHz CPU external bus speed required by the 350MHz and faster Pentium II processors. AGP v1.0 and PCI 2.1 are also supported, as are FPM, EDO, and SDRAM. Different DRAM types may be used in mixed combinations in up to eight banks and up to 1GB of DRAM. EDO memory timing is 5-2-2-2-2-2-2-2 for back-to-back accesses, and SDRAM timing is 6-1-1-1-2-1-1-1 for back-to-back accesses.

The VT82C596 South Bridge supports both ACPI (Advanced Configuration and Power Interface) and APM (Advanced Power Management), and includes an integrated USB Controller and dual UltraDMA-66 EIDE ports.

Silicon integrated Systems (SiS)

SiS5600/5595

The 5600/5595 chipset was introduced in June 1998, and is designed for low-cost Celeron CPUs with a 66MHz or 100MHz host bus. SiS intends to use this low-cost chipset to help push the Pentium II PC technology toward the sub-$1,000 PC market.

Super I/O Chips

The third major chip seen on most PC motherboards is called the Super I/O chip. This is a chip that normally integrates devices formerly found on separate expansion cards in older systems.

Most Super I/O chips contain, at a minimum, the following components:

- Floppy controller
- Dual serial port controllers
- Parallel port controller

The floppy controllers on most Super I/O chips will handle two drives, but some of them can only handle one. Older systems often required a separate floppy controller card.

The dual serial port is another item that was formerly on one or more cards. Most of the better Super I/O chips implement a buffered serial port design known as a UART (Universal Asynchronous Receiver Transmitter), one for each port. Most mimic the standalone NS16550A high-speed UART, which was created by National Semiconductor. By putting the function of two of these chips into the Super I/O chip, we essentially have these ports built-in to the motherboard.

Virtually all Super I/O chips also include a high-speed multimode parallel port. The better ones allow three modes, called standard (bidirectional), Enhanced Parallel Port (EPP), and the Enhanced Capabilities Port (ECP) modes. The ECP mode is the fastest and most powerful, but selecting it also means your port will use an ISA bus 8-bit DMA channel, usually DMA channel 3. As long as you account for this and don't set anything else to that channel (such as a sound card, and so on), the EPC mode parallel port should work fine. Some of the newer printers and scanners that connect to the system via the parallel port will use ECP mode, which was initially invented by Hewlett-Packard.

The Super I/O chip may contain other components, as well. For example, currently the most popular Pentium II motherboard on the market—the Intel SE440BX ATX motherboard—uses an SMC (Standard Microsystems Corp.) FDC37C777 Super I/O chip. This chip incorporates the following functions:

- Single floppy drive interface
- Two high-speed serial ports
- One ECP/EPP multimode parallel port
- 8042-style keyboard and mouse controller

Only the keyboard and mouse controller are surprising here; all the other components are in most Super I/O chips. The integrated keyboard and mouse controller saves the need to have this chip as a separate part on the board.

One thing I've noticed over the years is that the role of the Super I/O chip has decreased more and more in the newer motherboards. This is primarily due to Intel moving Super I/O functions such as IDE directly into the chipset South Bridge component, where these devices can attach to the PCI bus rather than the ISA bus. One of the shortcomings of the Super I/O chip is that it is interfaced to the system via the ISA bus, and shares all the speed and performance limitations of that 8MHz bus. Moving the IDE over to the PCI bus allowed higher speed IDE drives to be developed that could transfer at the faster 33MHz PCI bus speed.

As Intel combines more and more functions into their main chipset, and as USB-based peripherals replace standard serial, parallel, and floppy controller-based devices, you will probably see the Super I/O chip fade away on some future motherboard designs. At least one of the third-party chipsets has already combined the South Bridge and Super I/O chip into a single component, saving space and reducing parts count on the motherboard.

Motherboard CMOS RAM Addresses

In the original AT system, a Motorola 146818 chip was used as the RTC (Real-time Clock) and CMOS (Complementary Metal-Oxide Semiconductor)RAM chip. This is a special chip that had a simple digital clock, which used 10 bytes of RAM, and an additional 54 more bytes of leftover RAM in which you could store anything you wanted. The designers of the IBM AT used these extra 54 bytes to store the system configuration.

Modern PC systems don't use the Motorola chip; instead, they incorporate the functions of this chip into the motherboard chipset (South Bridge), Super I/O chip, or they use a special battery and NVRAM (Non-Volatile RAM) module from companies such as Dallas or Benchmarq.

Table 4.10 shows the standard format of the information stored in the 64-byte standard CMOS RAM module. This information controls the configuration of the system and is read and written by the system Setup program.

Table 4.10   AT CMOS RAM Addresses

Offset Hex	Offset Dec	Field Size	Function
00h	0	1 byte	Current second in binary coded decimal (BCD)
01h	1	1 byte	Alarm second in BCD
02h	2	1 byte	Current minute in BCD
03h	3	1 byte	Alarm minute in BCD
04h	4	1 byte	Current hour in BCD
05h	5	1 byte	Alarm hour in BCD
06h	6	1 byte	Current day of week in BCD
07h	7	1 byte	Current day in BCD
08h	8	1 byte	Current month in BCD
09h	9	1 byte	Current year in BCD
0Ah	10	1 byte	Status register A Bit 7 = Update in progress 0 = Date and time can be read 1 = Time update in progress Bits 6–4 = Time frequency divider 010 = 32.768khz Bits 3–0 = Rate selection frequency 0110 = 1.024KHz square wave frequency

Offset Hex	Offset Dec	Field Size	Function
0Bh	11	1 byte	Status register B Bit 7 = Clock update cycle 0 = Update normally 1 = Abort update in progress Bit 6 = Periodic interrupt 0 = Disable interrupt (default) 1 = Enable interrupt Bit 5 = Alarm interrupt 0 = Disable interrupt (default) 0 = Disable interrupt (default) 1 = Enable interrupt Bit 4 = Update-ended interrupt 0 = Disable interrupt (default) 1 = Enable interrupt Bit 3 = Status register A square wave frequency 0 = Disable square wave (default) 1 = Enable square wave Bit 2 = Date format 0 = Calendar in BCD format (default) 1 = Calendar in binary format Bit 1 = 24-hour clock 0 = 24-hour mode (default) 1 = 12-hour mode Bit 0 = Daylight Savings Time 0 = Disable Daylight Savings (default) 1 = Enable Daylight Savings
0Ch	12	1 byte	Status register C Bit 7 = IRQF flag Bit 6 = PF Bit 5 = AF flag Bit 4 = UF flag Bits 3–0 = Reserved
0Dh	13	1 byte	Status register D Bit 7 = Valid CMOS RAM bit 0 = CMOS battery dead 1 = CMOS battery power good Bits 6–0 = Reserved
0Eh	14	1 byte	Diagnostic status Bit 7 = Real-time clock power status 0 = CMOS has not lost power 1 = CMOS has lost power Bit 6 = CMOS checksum status 0 = Checksum is good 1 = Checksum is bad Bit 5 = POST configuration information status 0 = Configuration information is valid 1 = Configuration information is invalid Bit 4 = Memory size compare during POST 0 = POST memory equals configuration 1 = POST memory not equal to configuration Bit 3 = Fixed disk/adapter initialization 0 = Initialization good 1 = Initialization failed Bit 2 = CMOS time status indicator 0 = Time is valid 1 = Time is Invalid Bits 1–0 = Reserved

(continues)

Table 4.10   Continued

Offset Hex	Offset Dec	Field Size	Function
0Fh	15	1 byte	Shutdown code 00h = Power on or soft reset 01h = Memory size pass 02h = Memory test past 03h = Memory test fail 04h = POST end; boot system 05h = JMP double word pointer with EOI 06h = Protected mode tests pass 07h = Protected mode tests fail 07h = Protected mode tests fail 08h = Memory size fail 09h = Int 15h block move 0Ah = JMP double word pointer without EOI 0Bh = used by 80386
10h	16	1 byte	Floppy disk drive types Bits 7–4 = Drive 0 type Bits 3–0 = Drive 1 type 0000 = None 0001 = 360KB 0010 = 1.2MB 0011 = 720KB 0100 = 1.44MB
11h	17	1 byte	Reserved
12h	18	1 byte	Hard disk types Bits 7–4 = Hard disk 0 type (0–15) Bits 3–0 = Hard disk 1 type (0–15)
13h	19	1 byte	Reserved
14h	20	1 byte	Installed equipment Bits 7–6 = Number of floppy disk drives 00 = 1 floppy disk drive 01 = 2 floppy disk drives Bits 5–4 = Primary display 00 = Use display adapter BIOS 01 = CGA 40-column 10 = CGA 80-column 11 = Monochrome Display Adapter Bits 3–2 = Reserved Bit 1 = Math coprocessor present Bit 0 = Floppy disk drive present
15h	21	1 byte	Base memory low-order byte
16h	22	1 byte	Base memory high-order byte
17h	23	1 byte	Extended memory low-order byte
18h	24	1 byte	Extended memory high-order byte
19h	25	1 byte	Hard Disk 0 Extended Type (0–255)
1Ah	26	1 byte	Hard Disk 1 Extended Type (0–255)
1Bh	27	9 bytes	Reserved
2Eh	46	1 byte	CMOS checksum high-order byte
2Fh	47	1 byte	CMOS checksum low-order byte
30h	48	1 byte	Actual extended memory low-order byte
31h	49	1 byte	Actual extended memory high-order byte

Offset Hex	Offset Dec	Field Size	Function
32h	50	1 byte	Date century in BCD
33h	51	1 byte	POST information flag Bit 7 = Top 128KB base memory status 0 = Top 128KB base memory not installed 1 = Top 128KB base memory installed Bit 6 = Setup program flag 0 = Normal (default) 1 = Put out first user message Bits 5–0 = Reserved
34h	52	2 bytes	Reserved

Note that many newer systems have more than 64 bytes of CMOS RAM; in fact, in some systems they might have 2KB or 4KB. The extra room is used to store the Plug-and-Play information detailing the configuration of adapter cards and other options in the system. As such, there is no 100 percent standard for how CMOS information is stored in all systems. Table 4.10 only shows how the original systems did it; newer BIOS versions and motherboard designs can do things differently. You should consult the BIOS manufacturer for more information if you want the full details of how CMOS is stored, because the CMOS configuration and Setup program is normally a part of the BIOS. This is another example of how close the relationship is between the BIOS and the motherboard hardware.

There are backup programs and utilities in the public domain for CMOS RAM information, which can be useful for saving and later restoring a configuration. Unfortunately, these programs would be BIOS specific and would only function on a BIOS they are designed for. As such, I don't normally rely on these programs because they are too motherboard and BIOS specific and will not work on all my systems seamlessly.

Table 4.11 shows the values that can be stored by your system BIOS in a special CMOS byte called the diagnostics status byte. By examining this location with a diagnostics program, you can determine whether your system has set trouble codes, which indicate that a problem previously has occurred.

Table 4.11   CMOS RAM Diagnostic Status Byte Codes

Bit Number 7 6 5 4 3 2 1 0	Hex	Function
1 • • • • • • •	80	Real-time clock (RTC) chip lost power
• 1 • • • • • •	40	CMOS RAM checksum is bad
• • 1 • • • • •	20	Invalid configuration information found at POST
• • • 1 • • • •	10	Memory size compare error at POST
• • • • 1 • • •	08	Fixed disk or adapter failed initialization
• • • • • 1 • •	04	Real-time clock (RTC) time found invalid
• • • • • • 1 •	02	Adapters do not match configuration
• • • • • • • 1	01	Time-out reading an adapter ID
• • • • • • • •	00	No errors found (Normal)

If the Diagnostic status byte is any value other than zero, you will normally get a CMOS configuration error on startup. These types of errors can be cleared by rerunning the Setup program.

Motherboard Interface Connectors

There are a variety of different connectors on a modern motherboard. Figure 4.32 shows the location of these connectors on a typical motherboard (using the Intel SE440BX model as the example). Several of these connectors such as power supply connectors, serial and parallel ports, and keyboard/mouse connectors are covered in other chapters. Tables 4.12–4.16 contain the pinouts of most of the other different interface and I/O connectors you will find.

▶▶ See "Power Supply Connectors," p. 1102.

▶▶ See "Serial Ports," p. 872, and "Parallel Ports," p. 883.

▶▶ See "Keyboard/Mouse Interface Connectors," p. 920.

▶▶ See "USB (Universal Serial Bus)," p. 892.

▶▶ See "ATA I/O Connector," p. 514.

Table 4.12   Infrared Data (IrDA) Pin-Header Connector

Pin	Signal	Pin	Signal
1	+5 V	4	Ground
2	Key	5	IrTX
3	IrRX	6	CONIR (Consumer IR)

Table 4.13   Battery Connector

Pin	Signal	Pin	Signal
1	Gnd	3	KEY
2	Unused	4	+6v

Table 4.14   LED and Keylock Connector

Pin	Signal	Pin	Signal
1	LED Power (+5v)	4	Keyboard Inhibit
2	KEY	5	Gnd
3	Gnd		

Table 4.15   Speaker Connector

Pin	Signal	Pin	Signal
1	Ground	3	Board-Mounted Speaker
2	KEY	4	Speaker Output

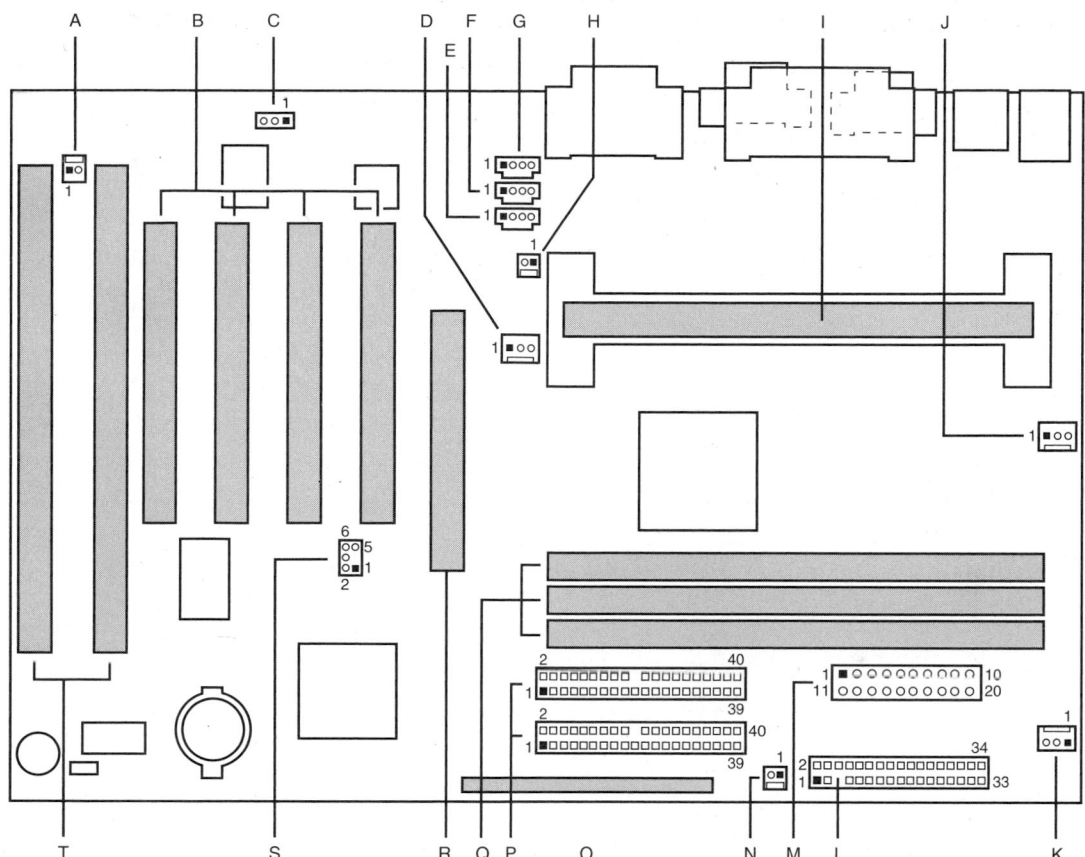

A	Wake on Ring (J1A1)	K	Fan 1 (J8M1)
B	PCI slots (J4D2, J4D1, J4C1, J4B1)	L	Diskette drive (J8K1)
C	Optional Wake on LAN technology (J1C1)	M	Power supply (J7L1)
D	Fan 3 (J3F2)	N	Optional SCSI LED (J8J1)
E	Optional Auxiliary Line In (J2F2)	O	Front panel (J8G2)
F	Optional telephony (J2F1)	P	Primary and secondary IDE (J7G1, J8G1)
G	Optional CD-ROM audio (J1F1)	Q	DIMMs (J6J1, J6J2, J7J1)
H	Optional chassis intrusion (J3F1)	R	A.G.P. (J4E1)
I	Slot 1 (J4J1)	S	PC/PCI (J6D1)
J	Fan 2 (J4M1)	T	ISA slots (J4B2, J4A1)

Figure 4.32 Typical motherboard connectors (Intel SE440BX shown).

Table 4.16   Microprocessor Fan Power Connector

Pin	Signal Name
1	Ground
2	+12V
3	Sense tachometer

Caution

Do not place a jumper on this connector; serious board damage will result if the 12v is shorted to ground.

Note that some boards have a board mounted piezo speaker. It is enabled by placing a jumper over pins 3 and 4, which routes the speaker output to the board-mounted speaker. Removing the jumper allows a conventional speaker to be plugged in.

Some other connectors that you might find on some newer motherboards are listed in Tables 4.17–4.22.

Table 4.17   Chassis Intrusion (Security) Pin-Header

Pin	Signal Name
1	Ground
2	CHS_SEC

Table 4.18   Wake on LAN Pin-Header

Pin	Signal Name
1	+5 VSB
2	Ground
3	WOL

Table 4.19   CD Audio Connector

Pin	Signal Name	Pin	Signal Name
1	CD_IN-Left	3	Ground
2	Ground	4	CD_IN-Right

Table 4.20   Telephony Connector

Pin	Signal Name	Pin	Signal Name
1	Audio Out (monaural)	3	Ground
2	Ground	4	Audio In (monaural)

Table 4.21   ATAPI-Style Line In Connector

Pin	Signal Name	Pin	Signal Name
1	Left Line In	3	Ground
2	Ground	4	Right Line In (monaural)

Table 4.22   Wake on Ring Pin-Header

Pin	Signal Name
1	Ground
2	RINGA

Intel and several other motherboard manufacturers like to place all the front-panel motherboard connectors in a single row as shown in Figure 4.33.

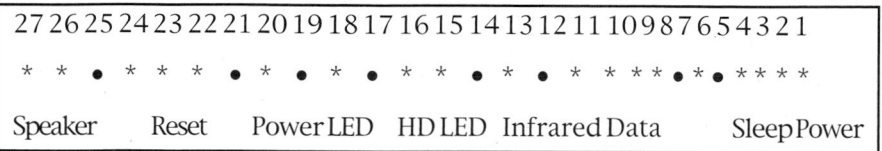

Figure 4.33   Typical ATX motherboard front panel connectors (Intel motherboard shown).

Table 4.23 shows the designations for the front-panel motherboard connectors commonly used on Intel ATX motherboards.

Table 4.23   ATX Motherboard Front Panel Connectors

Connector	Pin	Signal Name
Speaker	27	SPKR_HDR
	26	PIEZO_IN
	25	Key
	24	Ground
Reset	23	SW_RST
	22	Ground
none	21	No connect/Key
Sleep/Power LED	20	PWR_LED
	19	Key
	18	Ground
none	17	No connect/Key
Hard Drive LED	16	HD_PWR
	15	HD Active#
	14	Key
	13	HD_PWR +5 V
none	12	No connect
IrDA	11	CONIR (Consumer IR)
	10	IrTX
	9	Ground
	8	IrRX
	7	Key
	6	+5V

(continues)

Table 4.23   Continued

Connector	Pin	Signal Name
none	5	No connect
Sleep/Resume	4	SLEEP_PU (pullup)
	3	SLEEP
Power On	2	Ground
	1	SW_ON#

System Bus Functions and Features

At the heart of every motherboard are the buses that make it up. A *bus* is a common pathway across which data can travel within a computer. This pathway is used for communication and can be established between two or more computer elements.

The PC has a hierarchy of different buses. Most modern PCs have at least three different buses; some have four or more. They are hierarchical because each slower bus is connected to the faster one above it. Each device in the system is connected to one of the buses, and some devices (primarily the chipset) act as bridges between the various buses.

The main buses in a modern system are as follows:

- *The Processor Bus*. This is the highest-speed bus in the system and is at the core of the chipset and motherboard. This bus is used primarily by the processor to pass information to and from cache or main memory and the North Bridge of the chipset. The processor bus in Pentium II systems runs at either 66 or 100MHz and has the full 64-bit data path width of the processor.

- *The AGP (Accelerated Graphics Port) Bus*. This is a high-speed 66MHz, 32-bit bus specifically for a video card. It is connected to the North Bridge of the chipset and is manifested as a single AGP slot in systems that support it.

- *The PCI (Peripheral Component Interconnect) Bus*. This is a 33Mhz, 32-bit bus found in virtually all newer 486 systems and Pentium and higher processor systems. This bus is generated by the chipset North Bridge, which acts as the PCI controller. This bus is manifested in the system as a collection of 32-bit slots, normally about four on most motherboards. High-speed peripherals such as SCSI adapters, network cards, video cards, and more can be plugged in to PCI bus slots. The chipset South Bridge is plugged in to the PCI bus, and from there generates the IDE and USB ports.

- *The ISA (Industry Standard Architecture) Bus*. This is an 8MHz, 16-bit bus that remains in systems today after first appearing in the original PC in 8-bit, 5MHz form, and in the 1984 IBM AT in full 16-bit form. It is a very slow-speed bus, but is still ideal for certain slow-speed or older peripherals. The PC industry has been loath to give up this bus, despite pressure from Microsoft and Intel to do away with it in future PC designs. Most people have used it in recent times for plug-in modems, sound cards, and various other low-speed peripherals. The ISA bus is generated by the South Bridge part of the motherboard chipset, which acts as the ISA bus controller and the interface between the ISA bus and the faster PCI bus above it. The motherboard's Super I/O chip is normally connected to this bus.

The system chipset is the conductor that controls the orchestra of system components, allowing each to have their turn on their respective buses.

Bus Type	Width (bits)	Speed (MHz)	Bandwidth (M MB/sec)
8-bit ISA	8	4.77	2.39
16-bit ISA	16	8.33	8.33
EISA*	32	8.33	33.3
VLB*	32	33.33	133.33
PCI	32	33.33	133.33
PCI-2x**	32	66.66	266.66
PCI 64-bit**	64	33.33	266.66
PCI-2x 64-bit**	64	66.66	533.33
AGP	32	66.66	266.66
AGP-2x	32	66.66	533.33
AGP-4x*	32	66.66	1,066.66

* EISA and VLB are no longer used in current motherboard designs.

** Note that these bus types are proposed and have not yet been implemented in PC systems.

The PCI bus has two proposed extensions. One is to go from 32 bits to 64 bits. The other is to double the clock speed of the bus to 66MHz. So far, neither of these has been implemented in PC systems, and it doesn't seem likely they will in the near future. More likely we will see improvements in other areas such as AGP, which has already moved to 2x mode and will move to a 4x mode in the future.

Interestingly enough, these faster modes will be achieved at the same clock rate; the only difference is that 2 or 4 bits will be transferred for every hertz (cycle) rather than the 1 bit per cycle standard today. This will allow the AGP bus to keep pace with future video needs, all the way to over 1,066MB/sec!

The following sections discuss the processor and other subset buses in the system, and the main I/O buses mentioned in the previous table.

The Processor Bus

The processor bus is the communication pathway between the CPU and motherboard chipset, more specifically the North Bridge. This bus runs at the full motherboard speed—normally 66MHz, 75MHz, or 100MHz—and is used to transfer data between the CPU and the chipset North Bridge. It also transfers data between the CPU and an external memory cache on Pentium (P5 class) systems. Figure 4.19 shows how this bus fits into a typical Pentium (P5 class) PC system.

Later in this chapter, Figure 4.34 shows where and how the other main buses, such as the PCI and IDE buses, fit into the system. As you can see, there is clearly a three-tier architecture with the fastest CPU bus on top, the PCI bus next, and the ISA bus at the bottom. Different components in the system are connected to one of these three main buses.

Pentium (P5) class systems have an external cache for the CPU; these caches are connected to the processor bus that runs at the motherboard speed (normally 66MHz). Thus, as the Pentium processors have been getting faster and faster, the L2 cache has unfortunately remained at the relatively slow motherboard speed. This was solved in the Pentium Pro and Pentium II systems. They have moved the L2 cache off of the motherboard and directly onto the CPU. By incorporating the L2 cache in the CPU, they can run it at a speed closer to the true CPU speed. In the Pentium Pro, the L2 cache actually does run at full CPU speed, but in the Pentium II it runs at one half of the processor speed. This is still much faster than the motherboard-bound cache on the Socket 7 P5 class systems. The built-in L2 CPU cache is one of the main reasons the Socket 8 and Slot 1 architecture is superior to the Socket 7 designs.

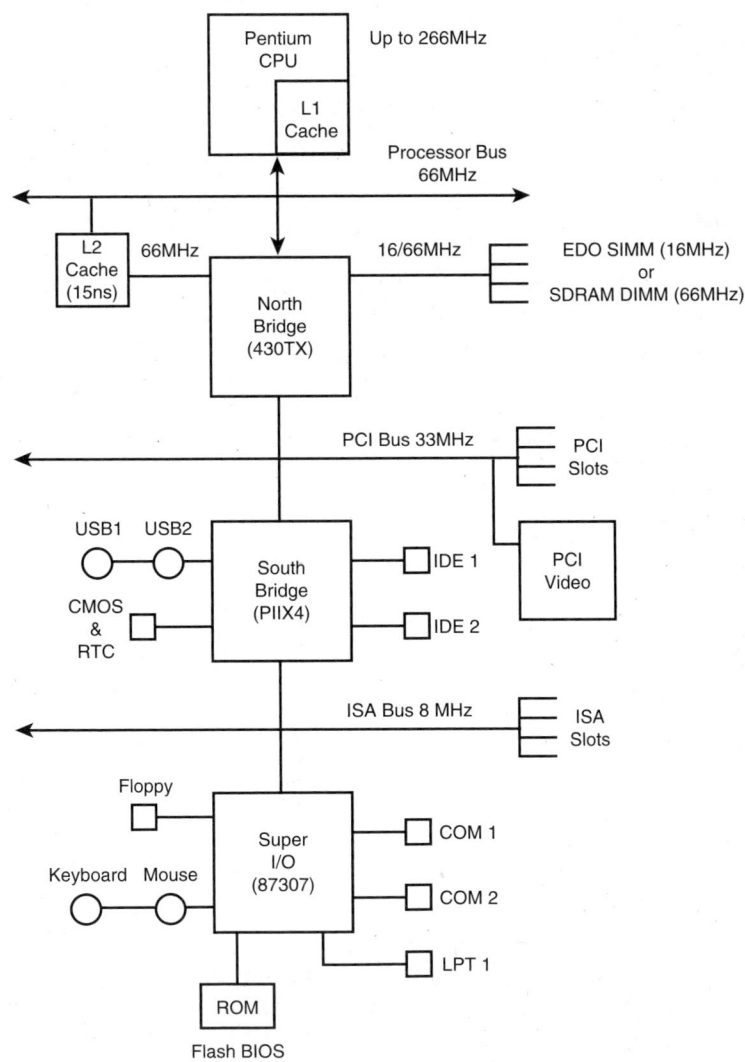

Figure 4.34 Typical Pentium (P5 Class) system architecture showing the different bus levels in the system.

Note that recently there is a new version of the Socket 7 architecture called *Super-7*. It is designed primarily by AMD and Cyrix for their new Socket 7 P5 class processors that run at motherboard speeds up to 100MHz. This is definitely better than 66MHz, but still not quite up to the Slot-1 architecture where the L2 cache automatically scales up in speed along with the processor. By moving the L2 cache off the motherboard, the Slot 1 designs offer greater performance.

Figure 4.35 shows the typical Pentium III system design. You can see the two main changes: One is that the L2 cache now runs at half processor core speed rather than motherboard speed. Also note that the motherboard speed has been increased to 100MHz, which dramatically improves main memory performance combined with 100MHz SDRAM memory. The other main change is the addition of a new single slot bus called AGP (Accelerated Graphics Port). This allows the video card to be on its own dedicated high-speed bus, which runs at twice the speed of PCI. Actually, the speed is misleading, as AGP has 2x and 4x modes that allow a further doubling or quadrupling of the speed over the base of 66MHz. This results in incredible video bandwidth, which is necessary for full-motion video capture and display.

Because the purpose of the processor bus is to get information to and from the CPU at the fastest possible speed, this bus operates at a much faster rate than any other bus in your system; no bottleneck exists here. The bus consists of electrical circuits for data, addresses (the address bus, which is discussed in the following section), and control purposes. In a Pentium-based system, the processor bus has 64 data lines, 32 address lines, and associated control lines. The Pentium Pro and Pentium II have 36 address lines, but otherwise are the same as the Pentium and Pentium MMX.

The processor bus operates at the same base clock rate as the CPU does externally. This can be misleading because most CPUs these days run internally at a higher clock rate than they do externally. For example, a Pentium 266 system has a Pentium CPU running at 266MHz internally, but only 66.6MHz externally, while a Pentium II 450 runs at 450MHz internally but only 100MHz externally. A Pentium 133, 166, 200, and even a Pentium 233 also run the processor external bus at 66.6MHz. In most newer systems, the actual processor speed is some multiple (1.5x, 2x, 2.5x, 3x, and so on) of the processor bus.

◀◀ See "Processor Speed Ratings," p. 42.

The processor bus is tied to the external processor pin connections and can transfer one bit of data per data line every one or two clock cycles. Thus, a Pentium, Pentium Pro, or Pentium II can transfer 64 bits of data at a time.

To determine the transfer rate for the processor bus, you multiply the data width (64 bits for a Pentium, Pentium Pro, or Pentium II) by the clock speed of the bus (the same as the base or unmultiplied clock speed of the CPU). If you are using a Pentium, Pentium MMX, Pentium Pro, or Pentium II chip that runs at a 66MHz motherboard speed, and it can transfer a bit of data each clock cycle on each data line, you have a maximum instantaneous transfer rate of roughly 528MB/sec. You get this result by using the following formula:

$$66\text{MHz} \times 64 \text{ bits} = 4{,}224\text{Mbit/sec}$$

$$4{,}224\text{Mbit/sec} \div 8 = 528\text{MB/sec}$$

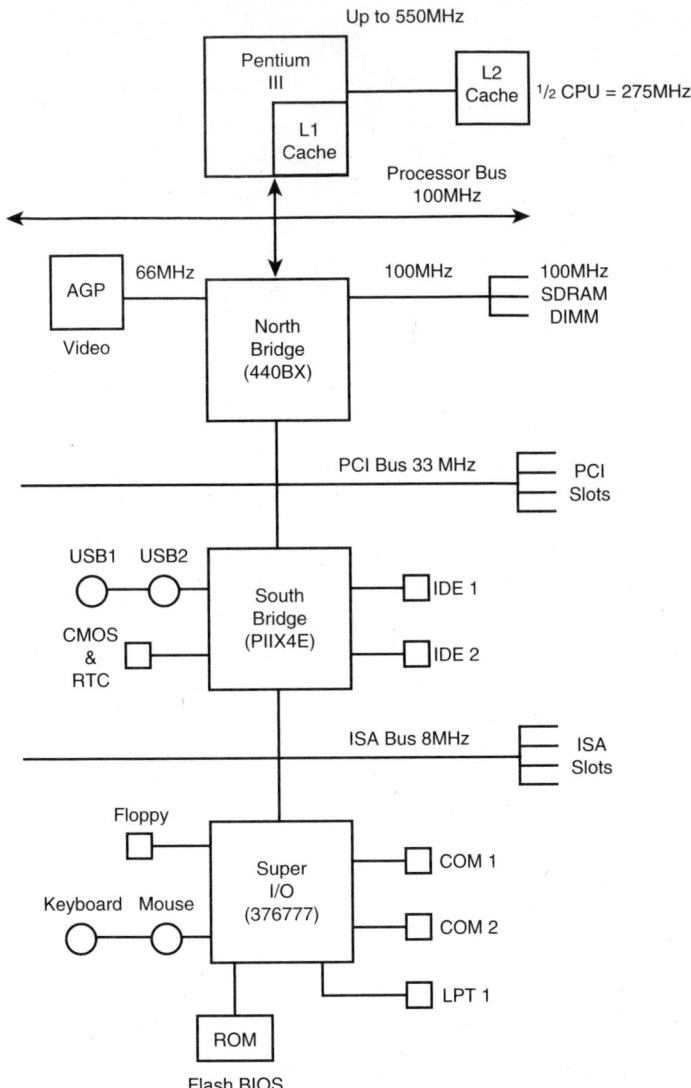

Figure 4.35   Typical Pentium III system architecture showing the different bus levels in the system.

This transfer rate, often called the *bandwidth of the bus*, represents a maximum. Like all maximums, this rate does not represent the normal operating bandwidth; you should expect much lower average throughput. Other limiting factors such as chipset design, memory design and speed, and so on conspire to lower the effective average throughput.

The Memory Bus

The memory bus is used to transfer information between the CPU and main memory—the RAM in your system. This bus is connected to the motherboard chipset North Bridge chip. Depending on the type of memory your chipset (and therefore motherboard) is designed to handle, the North Bridge will run the memory bus at different speeds. Systems that use FPM (Fast Page Mode) or EDO (Extended Data Out) memory with a 60ns access time run the memory bus at only 16MHz. That is because 16MHz results in about 60ns cycling speed. Newer chipsets and motherboards that support SDRAM can run the memory bus at 66MHz (15ns) or up to 100MHz (10ns). This obviously results in faster memory performance and virtually negates the need for having cache memory on the motherboard. That is why the Pentium II processor was designed to include a higher speed L2 cache built in, as the SDRAM memory on the motherboard already runs at the same speed as the motherboard cache found in older Pentium systems. Figure 4.32 and Figure 4.33 show how the memory bus fits into your PC.

Note

Notice that the main memory bus is always the same width as the processor bus. This will define the size of what is called a "bank" of memory. Memory banks and their width relative to processor buses are discussed in the "Memory Banks" section in Chapter 6.

The Need for Expansion Slots

The I/O bus or expansion slots are what enables your CPU to communicate with peripheral devices. The bus and its associated expansion slots are needed because basic systems cannot possibly satisfy all the needs of all the people who buy them. The I/O bus enables you to add devices to your computer to expand its capabilities. The most basic computer components, such as sound cards and video cards, can be plugged into expansion slots; you also can plug in more specialized devices, such as network interface cards, SCSI host adapters, and others.

Note

In most modern PC systems, a variety of basic peripheral devices are built into the motherboard. Most systems today have at least dual (primary and secondary) IDE interfaces, dual USB (Universal Serial Bus) ports, a floppy controller, two serial ports, a parallel port, keyboard, and mouse controller built directly into the motherboard. These devices are normally distributed between the motherboard chipset South Bridge and the Super I/O chip. (Super I/O chips are discussed earlier in this chapter.)

Many will even add more items such as a built-in sound card, video adapter, SCSI host adapter, or network interface also built into the motherboard. Those items are not built into the motherboard chipset or Super I/O chip, but would be configured as additional chips installed on the board. Nevertheless, these built-in controllers and ports still use the I/O bus to communicate with the CPU. In essence, even though they are built in, they act as if there are cards plugged into the system's bus slots, including using system resources in the same manner.

Types of I/O Buses

Since the introduction of the first PC, many I/O buses have been introduced. The reason is simple: Faster I/O speeds are necessary for better system performance. This need for higher performance involves three main areas:

- Faster CPUs
- Increasing software demands
- Greater multimedia requirements

Each of these areas requires the I/O bus to be as fast as possible. Surprisingly, virtually all PC systems shipped today still incorporate the same basic bus architecture as the 1984 vintage IBM PC/AT. However, most of these systems now also include a second high-speed local I/O bus such as VL-Bus or PCI, which offer much greater performance for adapters that need it. Many of the newest systems also include a third high-speed bus called AGP for improved video performance beyond what PCI offers.

One of the primary reasons why new I/O-bus structures have been slow in coming is compatibility—that old catch-22 that anchors much of the PC industry to the past. One of the hallmarks of the PC's success is its standardization. This standardization spawned thousands of third-party I/O cards, each originally built for the early bus specifications of the PC. If a new high-performance bus system was introduced, it often had to be compatible with the older bus systems so that the older I/O cards would not be obsolete. Therefore, bus technologies seem to evolve rather than make quantum leaps forward.

You can identify different types of I/O buses by their architecture. The main types of I/O architecture are

- ISA
- Micro Channel Architecture (MCA)
- EISA
- VESA Local Bus (VL-Bus)
- PCI Local Bus
- AGP
- PC-Card (formerly PCMCIA)
- FireWire (IEEE-1394)
- Universal Serial Bus (USB)

▶▶ See "PC Cards" pg. 1236.

▶▶ See "IEEE 1394 (Also called i.link or FireWire)" pg. 896.

▶▶ See "USB (Universal Serial Bus)" pg. 892.

The differences among these buses consist primarily of the amount of data that they can transfer at one time and the speed at which they can do it. Each bus architecture is implemented by a chipset that is connected to the processor bus. Typically, this chipset also controls the memory bus (refer to Figure 4.18 earlier in this chapter). The following sections describe the different types of PC buses.

The ISA Bus

ISA, which is an acronym for *Industry Standard Architecture*, is the bus architecture that was introduced as an 8-bit bus with the original IBM PC in 1981; it was later expanded to 16 bits with the IBM PC/AT in 1984. ISA is the basis of the modern personal computer and the primary architecture used in the vast majority of PC systems on the market today. It may seem amazing that such a presumably antiquated architecture is used in today's high-performance systems, but this is true for reasons of reliability, affordability, and compatibility, plus this old bus is still faster than many of the peripherals that we connect to it!

Two versions of the ISA bus exist, based on the number of data bits that can be transferred on the bus at a time. The older version is an 8-bit bus; the newer version is a 16-bit bus. The original 8-bit version ran at 4.77MHz in the PC and XT. The 16-bit version used in the AT ran at 6MHz, and then 8MHz. Later, the industry as a whole agreed on an 8.33MHz maximum standard speed for 8/16-bit versions of the ISA bus for backward compatibility. Some systems have the capability to run the ISA bus faster than this, but some adapter cards will not function properly at higher speeds. ISA data transfers require anywhere from two to eight cycles. Therefore, the theoretical maximum data rate of the ISA bus is about 8MB/sec, as the following formula shows:

$$8MHz \times 16 \text{ bits} = 128Mbit/sec$$

$$128Mbit/sec \div 2 \text{ cycles} = 64Mbit/sec$$

$$64Mbit/sec \div 8 = 8MB/sec$$

The bandwidth of the 8-bit bus would be half this figure (4MB/sec). Remember, however, that these figures are theoretical maximums; because of I/O bus protocols, the effective bandwidth is much lower—typically by almost half. Even so, at 8MB/sec, the ISA bus is still faster than many of the peripherals we connect to it.

The 8-Bit ISA Bus

This bus architecture is used in the original IBM PC computers. Although virtually nonexistent in new systems today, this architecture still exists in hundreds of thousands of PC systems in the field.

Physically, the 8-bit ISA expansion slot resembles the tongue-and-groove system that furniture makers once used to hold two pieces of wood together. It is specifically called a *card/edge connector*. An adapter card with 62 contacts on its bottom edge plugs into a slot on the motherboard that has 62 matching contacts. Electronically, this slot provides eight data lines and 20 addressing lines, enabling the slot to handle 1MB of memory.

Figure 4.36 describes the pinouts for the 8-bit ISA bus.

Figure 4.37 shows how these pins are oriented in the expansion slot.

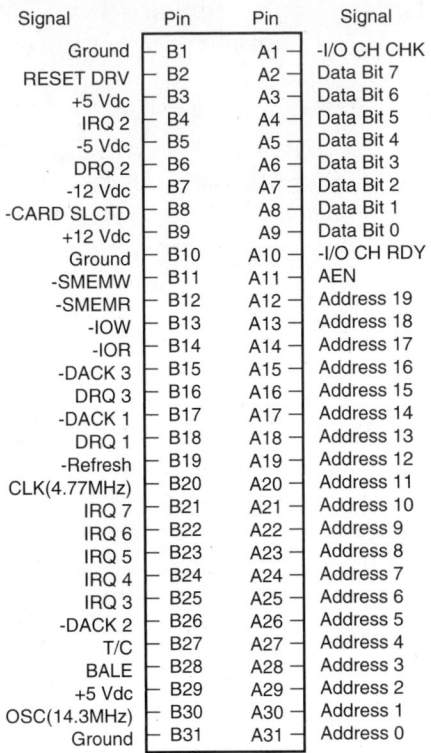

Signal	Pin	Pin	Signal
Ground	B1	A1	-I/O CH CHK
RESET DRV	B2	A2	Data Bit 7
+5 Vdc	B3	A3	Data Bit 6
IRQ 2	B4	A4	Data Bit 5
-5 Vdc	B5	A5	Data Bit 4
DRQ 2	B6	A6	Data Bit 3
-12 Vdc	B7	A7	Data Bit 2
-CARD SLCTD	B8	A8	Data Bit 1
+12 Vdc	B9	A9	Data Bit 0
Ground	B10	A10	-I/O CH RDY
-SMEMW	B11	A11	AEN
-SMEMR	B12	A12	Address 19
-IOW	B13	A13	Address 18
-IOR	B14	A14	Address 17
-DACK 3	B15	A15	Address 16
DRQ 3	B16	A16	Address 15
-DACK 1	B17	A17	Address 14
DRQ 1	B18	A18	Address 13
-Refresh	B19	A19	Address 12
CLK(4.77MHz)	B20	A20	Address 11
IRQ 7	B21	A21	Address 10
IRQ 6	B22	A22	Address 9
IRQ 5	B23	A23	Address 8
IRQ 4	B24	A24	Address 7
IRQ 3	B25	A25	Address 6
-DACK 2	B26	A26	Address 5
T/C	B27	A27	Address 4
BALE	B28	A28	Address 3
+5 Vdc	B29	A29	Address 2
OSC(14.3MHz)	B30	A30	Address 1
Ground	B31	A31	Address 0

Figure 4.36   Pinouts for the 8-bit ISA bus.

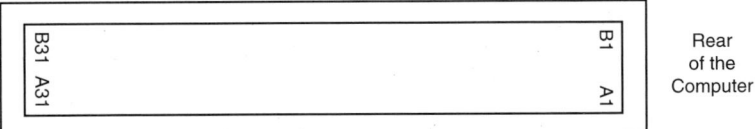

Figure 4.37   The 8-bit ISA bus connector.

Although the design of the bus is simple, IBM waited until 1987 to publish full specifications for the timings of the data and address lines, so in the early days of PC compatibles, manufacturers had to do their best to figure out how to make adapter boards. This problem was solved, however, as PC-compatible personal computers became more widely accepted as the industry standard and manufacturers had more time and incentive to build adapter boards that worked correctly with the bus.

The dimensions of 8-bit ISA adapter cards are as follows:

4.2 inches (106.68mm) high

13.13 inches (333.5mm) long

0.5 inch (12.7mm) wide

The 16-Bit ISA Bus

IBM threw a bombshell on the PC world when it introduced the AT with the 286 processor in 1984. This processor had a 16-bit data bus, which meant that communications between the processor and the motherboard as well as memory would now be 16 bits wide instead of only 8. Although this processor could have been installed on a motherboard with only an 8-bit I/O bus, that would have meant a huge sacrifice in the performance of any adapter cards or other devices installed on the bus.

The introduction of the 286 chip posed a problem for IBM in relation to its next generation of PCs: Should the company create a new I/O bus and associated expansion slots to try to come up with a system that could support both 8- and 16-bit cards? IBM opted for the latter solution, and the PC/AT was introduced with a set of expansion slots with 16-bit extension connectors. You can plug an 8-bit card into the forward part of the slot or a 16-bit card into both parts of the slot.

Note

The expansion slots for the 16-bit ISA bus also introduced access keys to the PC environment. An *access key* is a cutout or notch in an adapter card that fits over a corresponding tab in the connector into which the adapter card is inserted. Access keys typically are used to keep adapter cards from being inserted into a connector improperly.

The extension connector in each 16-bit expansion slot adds 36 connector pins to carry the extra signals necessary to implement the wider data path. In addition, two of the pins in the 8-bit portion of the connector were changed. These two minor changes do not alter the function of 8-bit cards.

Figure 4.38 describes the pinouts for the full 16-bit ISA expansion slot.

Figure 4.39 shows the orientation and relation of 8-bit and 16-bit ISA bus slots.

The extended 16-bit slots physically interfere with some 8-bit adapter cards that have a *skirt*—an extended area of the card that drops down toward the motherboard just after the connector. To handle these cards, IBM left two expansion ports in the PC/AT without the 16-bit extensions. These slots, which are identical to the expansion slots in earlier systems, can handle any skirted PC or XT expansion card. This is not a problem today, as no skirted 8-bit cards have been manufactured for years.

Note

Sixteen-bit ISA expansion slots were introduced in 1984. Since then, virtually every manufacturer of 8-bit expansion cards has designed them without drop-down skirts so that they fit properly in 16-bit slots. Most new systems do not have any 8-bit only slots, because a properly designed 8-bit card will work in any 16-bit slot.

Note that some poorly designed motherboards or adapter cards may have fitment problems. It is not uncommon to find that a full-length card will not work in a particular slot due to interference with the processor heat sink, SIMM or DIMM memory, voltage regulators, or other components on the board. Systems using the LPX motherboard and even the Baby-AT motherboard form factors are especially prone to these types of problems. This is another reason I recommend ATX form factor systems—things fit so much better.

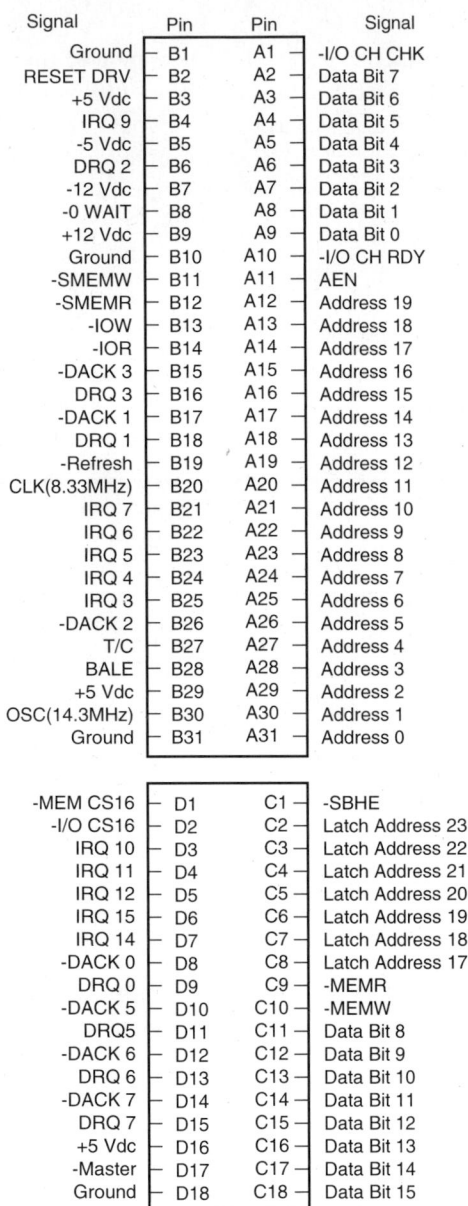

Signal	Pin	Pin	Signal
Ground	B1	A1	-I/O CH CHK
RESET DRV	B2	A2	Data Bit 7
+5 Vdc	B3	A3	Data Bit 6
IRQ 9	B4	A4	Data Bit 5
-5 Vdc	B5	A5	Data Bit 4
DRQ 2	B6	A6	Data Bit 3
-12 Vdc	B7	A7	Data Bit 2
-0 WAIT	B8	A8	Data Bit 1
+12 Vdc	B9	A9	Data Bit 0
Ground	B10	A10	-I/O CH RDY
-SMEMW	B11	A11	AEN
-SMEMR	B12	A12	Address 19
-IOW	B13	A13	Address 18
-IOR	B14	A14	Address 17
-DACK 3	B15	A15	Address 16
DRQ 3	B16	A16	Address 15
-DACK 1	B17	A17	Address 14
DRQ 1	B18	A18	Address 13
-Refresh	B19	A19	Address 12
CLK(8.33MHz)	B20	A20	Address 11
IRQ 7	B21	A21	Address 10
IRQ 6	B22	A22	Address 9
IRQ 5	B23	A23	Address 8
IRQ 4	B24	A24	Address 7
IRQ 3	B25	A25	Address 6
-DACK 2	B26	A26	Address 5
T/C	B27	A27	Address 4
BALE	B28	A28	Address 3
+5 Vdc	B29	A29	Address 2
OSC(14.3MHz)	B30	A30	Address 1
Ground	B31	A31	Address 0

Signal	Pin	Pin	Signal
-MEM CS16	D1	C1	-SBHE
-I/O CS16	D2	C2	Latch Address 23
IRQ 10	D3	C3	Latch Address 22
IRQ 11	D4	C4	Latch Address 21
IRQ 12	D5	C5	Latch Address 20
IRQ 15	D6	C6	Latch Address 19
IRQ 14	D7	C7	Latch Address 18
-DACK 0	D8	C8	Latch Address 17
DRQ 0	D9	C9	-MEMR
-DACK 5	D10	C10	-MEMW
DRQ5	D11	C11	Data Bit 8
-DACK 6	D12	C12	Data Bit 9
DRQ 6	D13	C13	Data Bit 10
-DACK 7	D14	C14	Data Bit 11
DRQ 7	D15	C15	Data Bit 12
+5 Vdc	D16	C16	Data Bit 13
-Master	D17	C17	Data Bit 14
Ground	D18	C18	Data Bit 15

Figure 4.38 Pinouts for the 16-bit ISA bus.

The dimensions of a typical AT expansion board are as follows:

4.8 inches (121.92mm) high

13.13 inches (333.5mm) long

0.5 inch (12.7mm) wide

8/16-bit ISA Bus Pinouts.

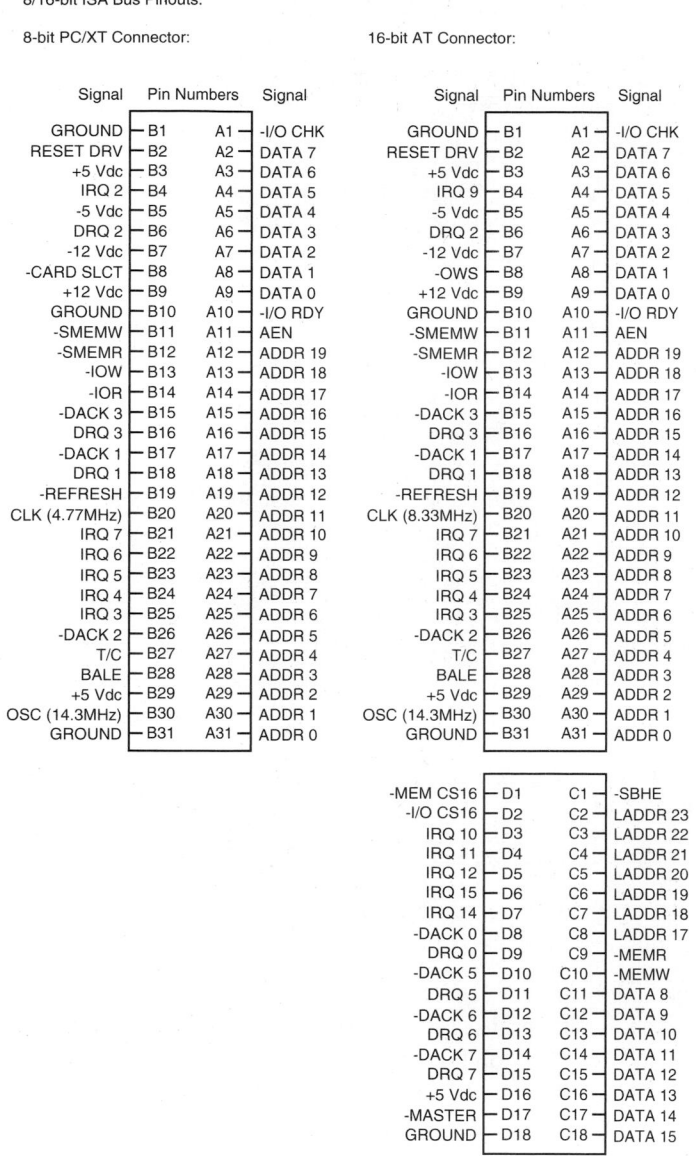

8-bit PC/XT Connector:

Signal	Pin Numbers		Signal
GROUND	B1	A1	-I/O CHK
RESET DRV	B2	A2	DATA 7
+5 Vdc	B3	A3	DATA 6
IRQ 2	B4	A4	DATA 5
-5 Vdc	B5	A5	DATA 4
DRQ 2	B6	A6	DATA 3
-12 Vdc	B7	A7	DATA 2
-CARD SLCT	B8	A8	DATA 1
+12 Vdc	B9	A9	DATA 0
GROUND	B10	A10	-I/O RDY
-SMEMW	B11	A11	AEN
-SMEMR	B12	A12	ADDR 19
-IOW	B13	A13	ADDR 18
-IOR	B14	A14	ADDR 17
-DACK 3	B15	A15	ADDR 16
DRQ 3	B16	A16	ADDR 15
-DACK 1	B17	A17	ADDR 14
DRQ 1	B18	A18	ADDR 13
-REFRESH	B19	A19	ADDR 12
CLK (4.77MHz)	B20	A20	ADDR 11
IRQ 7	B21	A21	ADDR 10
IRQ 6	B22	A22	ADDR 9
IRQ 5	B23	A23	ADDR 8
IRQ 4	B24	A24	ADDR 7
IRQ 3	B25	A25	ADDR 6
-DACK 2	B26	A26	ADDR 5
T/C	B27	A27	ADDR 4
BALE	B28	A28	ADDR 3
+5 Vdc	B29	A29	ADDR 2
OSC (14.3MHz)	B30	A30	ADDR 1
GROUND	B31	A31	ADDR 0

16-bit AT Connector:

Signal	Pin Numbers		Signal
GROUND	B1	A1	-I/O CHK
RESET DRV	B2	A2	DATA 7
+5 Vdc	B3	A3	DATA 6
IRQ 9	B4	A4	DATA 5
-5 Vdc	B5	A5	DATA 4
DRQ 2	B6	A6	DATA 3
-12 Vdc	B7	A7	DATA 2
-OWS	B8	A8	DATA 1
+12 Vdc	B9	A9	DATA 0
GROUND	B10	A10	-I/O RDY
-SMEMW	B11	A11	AEN
-SMEMR	B12	A12	ADDR 19
-IOW	B13	A13	ADDR 18
-IOR	B14	A14	ADDR 17
-DACK 3	B15	A15	ADDR 16
DRQ 3	B16	A16	ADDR 15
-DACK 1	B17	A17	ADDR 14
DRQ 1	B18	A18	ADDR 13
-REFRESH	B19	A19	ADDR 12
CLK (8.33MHz)	B20	A20	ADDR 11
IRQ 7	B21	A21	ADDR 10
IRQ 6	B22	A22	ADDR 9
IRQ 5	B23	A23	ADDR 8
IRQ 4	B24	A24	ADDR 7
IRQ 3	B25	A25	ADDR 6
-DACK 2	B26	A26	ADDR 5
T/C	B27	A27	ADDR 4
BALE	B28	A28	ADDR 3
+5 Vdc	B29	A29	ADDR 2
OSC (14.3MHz)	B30	A30	ADDR 1
GROUND	B31	A31	ADDR 0
-MEM CS16	D1	C1	-SBHE
-I/O CS16	D2	C2	LADDR 23
IRQ 10	D3	C3	LADDR 22
IRQ 11	D4	C4	LADDR 21
IRQ 12	D5	C5	LADDR 20
IRQ 15	D6	C6	LADDR 19
IRQ 14	D7	C7	LADDR 18
-DACK 0	D8	C8	LADDR 17
DRQ 0	D9	C9	-MEMR
-DACK 5	D10	C10	-MEMW
DRQ 5	D11	C11	DATA 8
-DACK 6	D12	C12	DATA 9
DRQ 6	D13	C13	DATA 10
-DACK 7	D14	C14	DATA 11
DRQ 7	D15	C15	DATA 12
+5 Vdc	D16	C16	DATA 13
-MASTER	D17	C17	DATA 14
GROUND	D18	C18	DATA 15

Figure 4.39   The 8-bit and 16-bit ISA bus connectors.

Two heights actually are available for cards that are commonly used in AT systems: 4.8 inches and 4.2 inches (the height of older PC-XT cards). The shorter cards became an issue when IBM introduced the XT Model 286. Because this model has an AT motherboard in an XT case, it needs AT-type boards with the 4.2-inch maximum height. Most board makers trimmed the height of their boards; many manufacturers now make only 4.2-inch tall (or less) boards so that they will work in systems with either profile.

32-Bit Buses

After 32-bit CPUs became available, it was some time before 32-bit bus standards became available. Before MCA and EISA specs were released, some vendors began creating their own proprietary 32-bit buses, which were extensions of the ISA bus. Although the proprietary buses were few and far between, they do still exist.

The expanded portions of the bus typically are used for proprietary memory expansion or video cards. Because the systems are proprietary (meaning that they are nonstandard), pinouts and specifications are not available.

The Micro Channel Bus

The introduction of 32-bit chips meant that the ISA bus could not handle the power of another new generation of CPUs. The 386DX chips can transfer 32 bits of data at a time, but the ISA bus can handle a maximum 16 bits. Rather than extend the ISA bus again, IBM decided to build a new bus; the result was the MCA bus. *MCA* (an acronym for *Micro Channel Architecture*) is completely different from the ISA bus and is technically superior in every way.

IBM not only wanted to replace the old ISA standard, but also to receive royalties on it; the company required vendors that licensed the new MCA bus to pay IBM royalties for using the ISA bus in all previous systems. This requirement led to the development of the competing EISA bus (see the next section on the EISA bus) and hindered acceptance of the MCA bus. Another reason why MCA has not been adopted universally for systems with 32-bit slots is that adapter cards designed for ISA systems do not work in MCA systems.

Note

The MCA bus is not compatible with the older ISA bus, so cards designed for the ISA bus do not work in an MCA system.

MCA runs asynchronously with the main processor, meaning that fewer possibilities exist for timing problems among adapter cards plugged into the bus.

MCA systems produced a new level of ease of use, as anyone who has set up one of these systems can tell you. An MCA system has no jumpers and switches—neither on the motherboard nor on any expansion adapter. You don't need an electrical engineering degree to plug a card into a PC. What you do need is the Reference disk, which goes with the particular system, and the Options disks, which go with each of the cards installed in the system. Once a card is installed, you can load the Options disks files onto the Reference disk; after that, you don't need the Options disks anymore. The Reference disk contains the special BIOS and system setup program needed for an MCA system, and the system cannot be configured without it. IBM maintains a library of all of their Reference and Options disks at `ftp://ftp.pc.ibm.com/pub/pccbbs`. Check this site if you need any of these files.

The MCA bus also supports bus mastering. Through implementing bus mastering, the MCA bus provides significant performance improvements over the older ISA buses. (Bus mastering is also implemented in the EISA bus. General information related to bus mastering is discussed in the

"Bus Mastering" section later in this chapter.) In the MCA bus mastering implementation, any bus mastering devices can request unobstructed use of the bus in order to communicate with another device on the bus. The request is made through a device known as the *Central Arbitration Control Point (CACP)*. This device arbitrates the competition for the bus, making sure all devices have access and that no single device monopolizes the bus.

Each device is given a priority code to ensure that order is preserved within the system. The main CPU is given the lowest priority code. Memory refresh has the highest priority, followed by the DMA channels, and then the bus masters installed in the I/O slots. One exception to this is when an NMI (non-maskable interrupt) occurs. In this instance, control returns to the CPU immediately.

The MCA specification provides for four adapter sizes, which are described in Table 4.24.

Table 4.24   Physical Sizes of MCA Adapter Cards

Adapter Type	Height (in Inches)	Length (in Inches)
Type 3	3.475	12.3
Type 3 half	3.475	6.35
Type 5	4.825	13.1
Type 9	9.0	13.1

Four types of slots are involved in the MCA design:

- 16-bit
- 16-bit with video extensions
- 16-bit with memory-matched extensions
- 32-bit

IBM still has all the technical reference manuals for MCA available; however, development has stopped for MCA devices because other faster and more feature-rich buses are available today.

The EISA Bus

EISA is an acronym for *Extended Industry Standard Architecture*. This standard was announced in September 1988 as a response to IBM's introduction of the MCA bus—more specifically, to the way that IBM wanted to handle licensing of the MCA bus. Vendors did not feel obligated to pay retroactive royalties on the ISA bus, so they turned their backs on IBM and created their own buses.

The EISA standard was developed primarily by Compaq, and was intended as being their way of taking over future development of the PC bus away from IBM. Compaq knew that nobody would clone their bus if they were the only company that had it, so they essentially gave the design away to other leading manufacturers. They formed the EISA committee, a non-profit organization designed specifically to control development of the EISA bus. Very few EISA adapters were ever developed. Those that were developed centered mainly around disk array controllers and server type network cards.

The EISA bus provides 32-bit slots for use with 386DX or higher systems. The EISA slot enables manufacturers to design adapter cards that have many of the capabilities of MCA adapters, but the bus also supports adapter cards created for the older ISA standard. EISA provides markedly faster hard drive throughput when used with devices such as SCSI bus-mastering hard drive controllers. Compared with 16-bit ISA system architecture, EISA permits greater system expansion with fewer adapter conflicts.

The EISA bus adds 90 new connections (55 new signals) without increasing the physical connector size of the 16-bit ISA bus. At first glance, the 32-bit EISA slot looks a lot like the 16-bit ISA slot. The EISA adapter, however, has two rows of connectors. The first row is the same kind used in 16-bit ISA cards; the other, thinner row extends from the 16-bit connectors. This means that ISA cards can still be used in EISA bus slots. Although this compatibility was not enough to ensure the popularity of EISA buses, it is a feature that was carried over into the newer VL-Bus standard. The physical specifications of an EISA card are as follows:

- 5 inches (127mm) high
- 13.13 inches (333.5mm) long
- 0.5 inches (12.7mm) wide

The EISA bus can handle up to 32 bits of data at an 8.33MHz cycle rate. Most data transfers require a minimum of two cycles, although faster cycle rates are possible if an adapter card provides tight timing specifications. The maximum bandwidth on the bus is 33MB/sec, as the following formula shows:

- 8.33MHz×32 bits = 266.56Mbit/sec
- 266.56Mbit/sec÷8 = 33.32MB/sec

Data transfers through an 8- or 16-bit expansion card across the bus would be reduced appropriately. Remember, however, that these figures represent theoretical maximums. Wait states, interrupts, and other protocol factors can reduce the effective bandwidth—typically, by half.

Figure 4.40 describes the pinouts for the EISA bus.

Figure 4.41 shows the locations of the pins.

Lower Signal	Upper Signal	Pin	Pin	Upper Signal	Lower Signal
Ground	Ground	B1	A1	-I/O CH CHK	-CMD
+5 Vdc	RESET DRV	B2	A2	Data Bit 7	-START
+5 Vdc	+5 Vdc	B3	A3	Data Bit 6	EXRDY
Reserved	IRQ 9	B4	A4	Data Bit 5	-EX32
Reserved	-5 Vdc	B5	A5	Data Bit 4	Ground
KEY	DRQ 2	B6	A6	Data Bit 3	KEY
Reserved	-12 Vdc	B7	A7	Data Bit 2	-EX16
Reserved	-0 WAIT	B8	A8	Data Bit 1	-SLBURST
+12 Vdc	+12 Vdc	B9	A9	Data Bit 0	-MSBURST
M-IO	Ground	B10	A10	-I/O CH RDY	W-R
-LOCK	-SMEMW	B11	A11	AEN	Ground
Reserved	-SMEMR	B12	A12	Address 19	Reserved
Ground	-IOW	B13	A13	Address 18	Reserved
Reserved	-IOR	B14	A14	Address 17	Reserved
-BE 3	-DACK 3	B15	A15	Address 16	Ground
KEY	DRQ 3	B16	A16	Address 15	KEY
-BE 2	-DACK 1	B17	A17	Address 14	-BE 1
-BE 0	DRQ 1	B18	A18	Address 13	Latch Address 31
Ground	-Refresh	B19	A19	Address 12	Ground
+5 Vdc	CLK(8.33MHz)	B20	A20	Address 11	-Latch Address 30
Latch Address 29	IRQ 7	B21	A21	Address 10	-Latch Address 28
Ground	IRQ 6	B22	A22	Address 9	-Latch Address 27
Latch Address 26	IRQ 5	B23	A23	Address 8	-Latch Address 25
Latch Address 24	IRQ 4	B24	A24	Address 7	Ground
KEY	IRQ 3	B25	A25	Address 6	KEY
Latch Address 16	-DACK 2	B26	A26	Address 5	Latch Address 15
Latch Address 14	T/C	B27	A27	Address 4	Latch Address 13
+5 Vdc	BALE	B28	A28	Address 3	Latch Address 12
+5 Vdc	+5 Vdc	B29	A29	Address 2	Latch Address 11
Ground	OSC(14.3MHz)	B30	A30	Address 1	Ground
Latch Address 10	Ground	B31	A31	Address 0	Latch Address 9

Lower Signal	Upper Signal	Pin	Pin	Upper Signal	Lower Signal
Latch Address 8	-MEM CS16	D1	C1	-SBHE	Latch Address 7
Latch Address 6	-I/O CS16	D2	C2	Latch Address 23	Ground
Latch Address 5	IRQ 10	D3	C3	Latch Address 22	Latch Address 4
+5 Vdc	IRQ 11	D4	C4	Latch Address 21	Latch Address 3
Latch Address 4	IRQ 12	D5	C5	Latch Address 20	Ground
KEY	IRQ 15	D6	C6	Latch Address 19	KEY
Data Bit 16	IRQ 14	D7	C7	Latch Address 18	Data Bit 17
Data Bit 18	-DACK 0	D8	C8	Latch Address 17	Data Bit 19
Ground	DRQ 0	D9	C9	-MEMR	Data Bit 20
Data Bit 21	-DACK 5	D10	C10	-MEMW	Data Bit 22
Data Bit 23	DRQ5	D11	C11	Data Bit 8	Ground
Data Bit 24	-DACK 6	D12	C12	Data Bit 9	Data Bit 25
Ground	DRQ 6	D13	C13	Data Bit 10	Data Bit 26
Data Bit 27	-DACK 7	D14	C14	Data Bit 11	Data Bit 28
KEY	DRQ 7	D15	C15	Data Bit 12	KEY
Data Bit 29	+5 Vdc	D16	C16	Data Bit 13	Ground
+5 Vdc	-Master	D17	C17	Data Bit 14	Data Bit 30
+5 Vdc	Ground	D18	C18	Data Bit 15	Data Bit 31
-MAKx		D19	C19		-MREQx

Figure 4.40 Pinouts for the EISA bus.

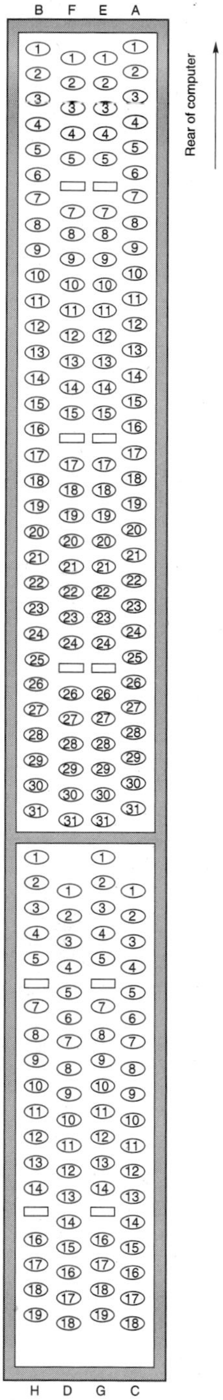

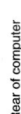

Figure 4.41 The card connector for the EISA bus.

Automated Setup

EISA systems also use an automated setup to deal with adapter-board interrupts and addressing issues. These issues often cause problems when several different adapter boards are installed in an ISA system. EISA setup software recognizes potential conflicts and automatically configures the system to avoid them. EISA does, however, enable you to do your own troubleshooting, as well as to configure the boards through jumpers and switches. This concept was not new to EISA; IBM's MCA bus also supported configuration via software. Another new feature of EISA systems is *IRQ sharing*, meaning that multiple bus cards can share a single interrupt. This feature has also been implemented in PCI bus cards.

Similar to the MCA bus and the Reference disk required there, systems with an EISA bus require an EISA Configuration disk, along with options disks containing files specific to each EISA adapter installed. You can get the EISA Configuration disk from the manufacturer of your system or motherboard and the Options disks from the manufacturer of the specific boards you are using. Just as with MCA based systems, without these disks and files, you cannot properly configure an EISA system.

Note

Although automated setup traditionally has not been available in ISA systems, it is now available with Plug-and-Play (PnP) systems and components. PnP systems are discussed toward the end of this chapter in the section titled "Plug-and-Play Systems."

Local Buses

The I/O buses discussed so far (ISA, MCA, and EISA) have one thing in common: relatively slow speed. The three newer bus types that we will look at in the following few sections all use the *local bus* concept explained in this section to address the speed issue. The three main local buses found in PC systems are

- VL-Bus (VESA Local Bus)
- PCI (Peripheral Component Interconnect)
- AGP (Accelerated Graphics Port)

The speed limitation of ISA, MCA, and EISA is a carryover from the days of the original PC, when the I/O bus operated at the same speed as the processor bus. As the speed of the processor bus increased, the I/O bus realized only nominal speed improvements, primarily from an increase in the bandwidth of the bus. The I/O bus had to remain at a slower speed, because the huge installed base of adapter cards could operate only at slower speeds.

Figure 4.42 shows a conceptual block diagram of the buses in a computer system.

The thought of a computer system running slower than it could is very bothersome to some computer users. Even so, the slow speed of the I/O bus is nothing more than a nuisance in most cases. You don't need blazing speed to communicate with a keyboard or mouse—you gain nothing in performance. The real problem occurs in subsystems in which you need the speed, such as video and disk controllers.

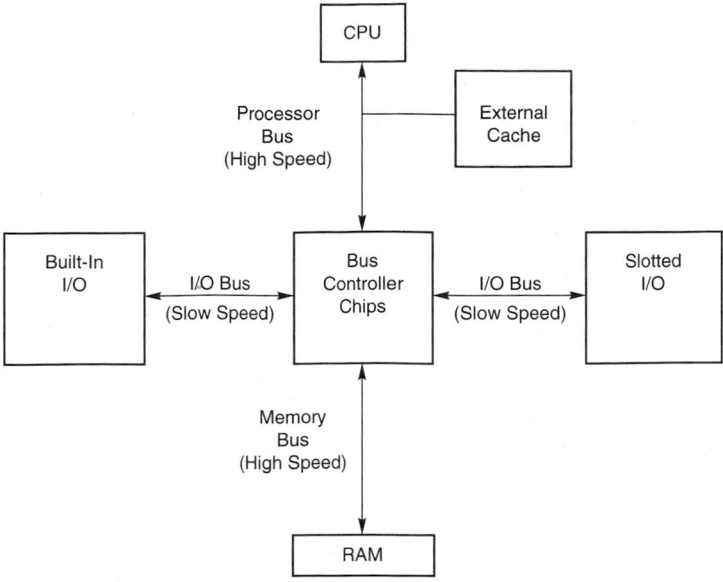

Figure 4.42   Bus layout in a traditional PC.

The speed problem became acute when graphical user interfaces (such as Windows) became prevalent. These systems required the processing of so much video data that the I/O bus became a literal bottleneck for the entire computer system. In other words, it did little good to have a processor that was capable of 66MHz to 450MHz or faster if you could put data through the I/O bus at a rate of only 8MHz.

An obvious solution to this problem is to move some of the slotted I/O to an area where it could access the faster speeds of the processor bus—much the same way as the external cache. Figure 4.43 shows this arrangement.

This arrangement became known as *local bus*, because external devices (adapter cards) now could access the part of the bus that was local to the CPU—the processor bus. Physically, the slots provided to tap this new configuration would need to be different from existing bus slots to prevent adapter cards designed for slower buses from being plugged into the higher bus speeds, which this design made accessible.

It is interesting to note that the very first 8-bit and 16-bit ISA buses were a form of local bus architecture. These systems had the processor bus as the main bus, and everything ran at full processor speeds. When ISA systems ran faster than 8MHz, the main ISA bus had to be decoupled from the processor bus because expansion cards, memory, and so on could not keep up. In 1992, an extension to the ISA bus called the *VESA local bus* (VL-Bus) started showing up on PC systems, indicating a return to local bus architecture. Since then, the *Peripheral Component Interconnect* (PCI) local bus has supplanted VL-Bus and the Accelerated Graphics Port (AGP) bus has been introduced to complement PCI.

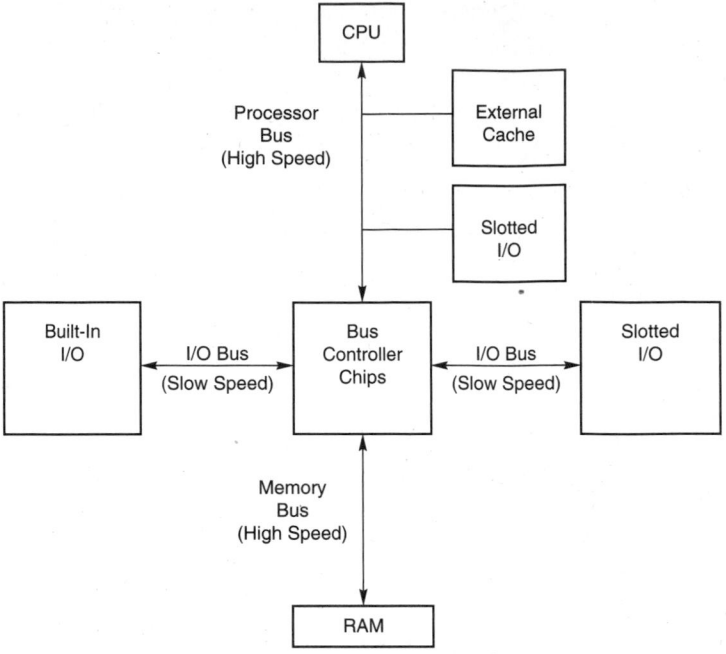

Figure 4.43   How a local bus works.

Note

A system does not have to have a local bus expansion slot to incorporate local bus technology; instead, the local bus device can be built directly into the motherboard. (In such a case, the local bus-slotted I/O shown in Figure 4.41 would in fact be built-in I/O.) This built-in approach to local bus is the way the first local bus systems were designed.

Local bus solutions do not replace earlier standards, such as ISA; they are designed into the system as a bus that is closer to the processor in the system architecture. Older buses such as ISA have been kept around for backward compatibility with slower types of adapters that don't need any faster connection to the system (such as modems). Therefore, a typical system will have AGP, PCI and ISA slots. Older cards still are compatible with the system, but high-speed adapter cards can take advantage of the AGP and PCI local bus slots as well.

The performance of graphical user interfaces such as Windows and OS/2 have been tremendously improved by moving the video cards off of the slow ISA bus and onto faster PCI and now AGP local buses.

VESA Local Bus

The VESA local bus was the most popular local bus design from its debut in August 1992 through 1994. It was created by the VESA committee, a non-profit organization founded by NEC to further develop video display and bus standards. In a similar fashion to how EISA evolved, NEC had

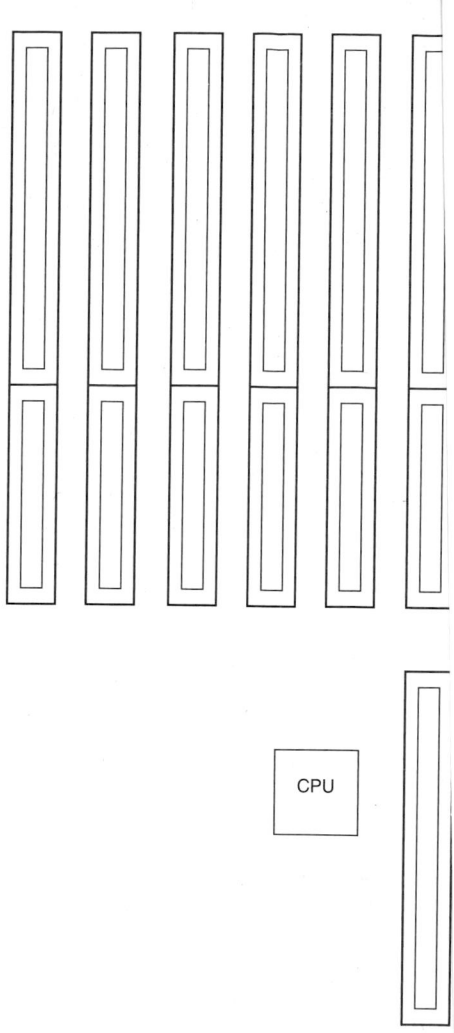

Figure 4.44   An example of VL-Bus slots in an ISA sys

done most of the work on the VL-Bus (as it would be called), and after founding the non-profit VESA committee, they turned over future development to VESA. At first, the local bus slot seemed primarily designed to be used for video cards. Improving video performance was a top priority at NEC to help sell their high-end displays as well as their own PC systems. By 1991, video performance had become a real bottleneck in most PC systems.

The Video Electronics Standards Association (VESA) developed a standardized local bus specification known as *VESA local bus (VL-Bus)*. As in earlier local bus implementations, the VL-Bus slot offers direct access to system memory at the speed of the processor itself. The VL-Bus can move data 32 bits at a time, enabling data to flow between the CPU and a compatible video subsystem or hard drive at the full 32-bit data width of the 486 chip. The maximum rated throughput of the VL-Bus is 128MB to 132MB/sec. In other words, local bus went a long way toward removing the major bottlenecks that existed in earlier bus configurations.

Additionally, VL-Bus offers manufacturers of hard-drive interface cards an opportunity to overcome another traditional bottleneck: the rate at which data can flow between the hard drive and the CPU. The average 16-bit IDE drive and interface can achieve throughput of up to 5MB/sec, whereas VL-Bus hard drive adapters for IDE drives are touted as providing throughput of as much as 8MB/sec. In real-world situations, the true throughput of VL-Bus hard drive adapters is somewhat less than 8MB/sec, but VL-Bus still provides a substantial boost in hard-drive performance.

Despite all the benefits of the VL-Bus (and, by extension, of all local buses), this technology has a few drawbacks, which are described in the following list:

- *Dependence on a 486 CPU.* The VL-Bus inherently is tied to the 486 processor bus. This bus is quite different from that used by Pentium and later processors. A VL-Bus that operates at the full rated speed of a Pentium has not been developed, although stopgap measures (such as stepping down speed or developing bus bridges) are available. Unfortunately, these result in poor performance. Some systems have been developed with both VL-Bus and PCI slots, but because of design compromises, performance often suffers.

- *Speed limitations.* The VL-Bus specification provides for speeds of up to 66MHz on the bus, but the electrical characteristics of the VL-Bus connector limit an adapter card to no more than 40–50MHz. In practice, running the VL-Bus at speeds over 33MHz cause many problems, so 33MHz has become the acceptable speed limit. Systems that use faster processor bus speeds must buffer and step down the clock on the VL-Bus or add wait states. Note that if the main CPU uses a clock modifier (such as the kind that doubles clock speeds), the VL-Bus uses the unmodified CPU clock speed as its bus speed.

- *Electrical limitations.* The processor bus has very tight timing rules that may vary from CPU to CPU. These timing rules were designed for limited loading on the bus, meaning that the only elements originally intended to be connected to the local bus are elements such as the external cache and the bus controller chips. As you add more circuitry, you increase the electrical load. If the local bus is not implemented correctly, the additional load can lead to problems such as loss of data integrity and timing problems between the CPU and the VL-Bus cards.

- *Card limitations.* Depending on the electrical loading of a system, the number of VL-Bus cards is limited. Although the VL-Bus specification provides for as many as three cards, this can be achieved only at clock rates of up to 40MHz with an otherwise low system-board load. As the system-board load and clock rate increases, the number of cards supported decreases. Only one VL-Bus card can be supported at 50MHz with a high system-board load. In practice, these limits could not usually be reached without problems.

The VL-Bus did not seem to be a well-enginee[...]
take the pins from the 486 processor and run[...]
words, the VL-Bus is essentially the raw 486 p[...]
design, because no additional chipsets or inte[...]
could add VL-Bus slots to their 486 motherbo[...]
these slots appeared on virtually all 486 syste[...]

Unfortunately, the 486 processor bus was not[...]
plugged into it at one time. Problems arose w[...]
duced into the circuit by different cards. Since[...]
bus, different processor speeds meant differen[...]
achieve. Although the VL-Bus could be adapte[...]
the Pentium, it was designed for the 486, and[...]
cost, after a new bus called *PCI (Peripheral Con[...]*
vor very quickly. It never did catch on with P[...]
development of the VL-Bus in the PC industry[...]
or systems today.

For a used system, or as an inexpensive upgra[...]
and can provide an acceptable solution for hig[...]

Physically, the VL-Bus slot is an extension of t[...]
have. If you have an ISA system, the VL-Bus is[...]
ISA slots. Likewise, if you have an EISA system[...]
those existing slots. Figure 4.44 shows how th[...]
The VESA extension has 112 contacts and use[...]

The VL-Bus adds a total 116 pin locations to t[...]
Table 4.25 lists the pinouts for only the VL-Bu[...]
pins for which two purposes are listed, the sec[...]
transfer mode.)

Table 4.25   Pinouts for the VL-Bus

Pin	Signal	Pin	Signal
B1	Data 0	A1	Data 1
B2	Data 2	A2	Data 3
B3	Data 4	A3	Ground
B4	Data 6	A4	Data 5
B5	Data 8	A5	Data 7
B6	Ground	A6	Data 9
B7	Data 10	A7	Data 11
B8	Data 12	A8	Data 13
B9	VCC	A9	Data 15
B10	Data 14	A10	Ground
B11	Data 16	A11	Data 17
B12	Data 18	A12	VCC
B13	Data 20	A13	Data 19
B14	Ground	A14	Data 21
B15	Data 22	A15	Data 23
B16	Data 24	A16	Data 25
B17	Data 26	A17	Ground
B18	Data 28	A18	Data 27
B19	Data 30	A19	Data 29
B20	VCC	A20	Data 31
B21	Address 31 or Data 63	A21	Address 30 or Data 62
B22	Ground	A22	Address 28 or Data 60
B23	Address 29 or Data 61	A23	Address 26 or Data 58
B24	Address 27 or Data 59	A24	Ground
B25	Address 25 or Data 57	A25	Address 24 or Data 56
B26	Address 23 or Data 55	A26	Address 22 or Data 54
B27	Address 21 or Data 53	A27	VCC
B28	Address 19 or Data 51	A28	Address 20 or Data 52
B29	Ground	A29	Address 18 or Data 50
B30	Address 17 or Data 49	A30	Address 16 or Data 48
B31	Address 15 or Data 47	A31	Address 14 or Data 46
B32	VCC	A32	Address 12 or Data 44
B33	Address 13 or Data 45	A33	Address 10 or Data 42
B34	Address 11 or Data 43	A34	Address 8 or Data 40
B35	Address 9 or Data 41	A35	Ground
B36	Address 7 or Data 39	A36	Address 6 or Data 38
B37	Address 5 or Data 37	A37	Address 4 or Data 36
B38	Ground	A38	Write Back
B39	Address 3 or Data 35	A39	Byte Enable 0 or 4

Pin	Signal	Pin	Signal
B40	Address 2 or Data 34	A40	VCC
B41	Unused or LBS64#	A41	Byte Enable 1 or 5
B42	Reset	A42	Byte Enable 2 or 6
B43	Data/Code Status	A43	Ground
B44	Memory-I/O Status or Data 33	A44	Byte Enable 3 or 7
B45	Write/Read Status or Data 32	A45	Address Data Strobe
B46	Access key	A46	Access key
B47	Access key	A47	Access key
B48	Ready Return	A48	Local Ready
B49	Ground	A49	Local Device
B50	IRQ 9	A50	Local Request
B51	Burst Ready	A51	Ground
B52	Burst Last	A52	Local Bus Grant
B53	ID0	A53	VCC
B54	ID1	A54	ID2
B55	Ground	A55	ID3
B56	Local Clock	A56	ID4 or ACK64#
B57	VCC	A57	Unused
B58	Local Bus Size 16	A58	Loc/Ext Address Data Strobe

Figure 4.45 shows the locations of the pins.

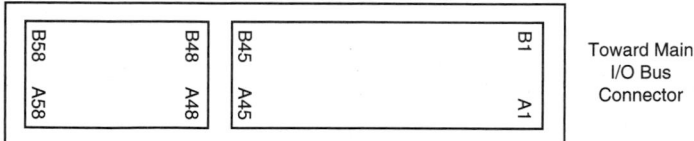

Figure 4.45   The card connector for the VL-Bus.

The PCI Bus

In early 1992, Intel spearheaded the creation of another industry group. It was formed with the same goals as the VESA group in relation to the PC bus. Recognizing the need to overcome weaknesses in the ISA and EISA buses, the PCI Special Interest Group was formed.

The Peripheral Component Interconnect (PCI) bus specification was released in June 1992 as version 1.0; it was later updated in April 1993 as version 2.0, and in early 1995 the latest revision 2.1 appeared. PCI redesigned the traditional PC bus by inserting another bus between the CPU and the native I/O bus by means of bridges. Rather than tap directly into the processor bus, with its delicate electrical timing (as was done in the VL-Bus), a new set of controller chips was developed to extend the bus, as shown in Figure 4.46.

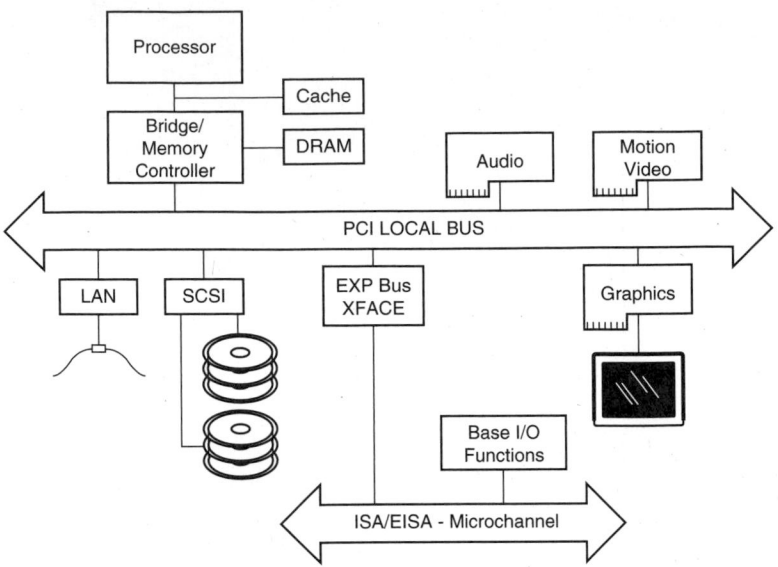

Figure 4.46   Conceptual diagram of the PCI bus.

The PCI bus often is called a *mezzanine bus* because it adds another layer to the traditional bus configuration. PCI bypasses the standard I/O bus; it uses the system bus to increase the bus clock speed and take full advantage of the CPU's data path. Systems that integrate the PCI bus became available in mid 1993 and have since become the mainstay high-end systems.

Information is transferred across the PCI bus at 33MHz, at the full data width of the CPU. When the bus is used in conjunction with a 32-bit CPU, the bandwidth is 132MB per second, as the following formula shows:

$$33\text{MHz}\times32 \text{ bits} = 1{,}056\text{Mbit/sec}$$

$$1{,}056\text{Mbit/sec}\div8 = 132\text{MB/sec}$$

When the bus is used in future 64-bit implementations, the bandwidth doubles, meaning that you can transfer data at speeds up to 264MB/sec. Real-life data transfer speeds necessarily will be lower, but still much faster than anything else that is currently available. Part of the reason for this faster real-life throughput is the fact that the PCI bus can operate concurrently with the processor bus; it does not supplant it. The CPU can be processing data in an external cache while the PCI bus is busy transferring information between other parts of the system—a major design benefit of the PCI bus.

A PCI adapter card uses its own unique connector. This connector can be identified within a computer system because it typically is offset from the normal ISA, MCA, or EISA connectors. See Figure 4.47 for an example. The size of a PCI card can be the same as that of the cards used in the system's normal I/O bus.

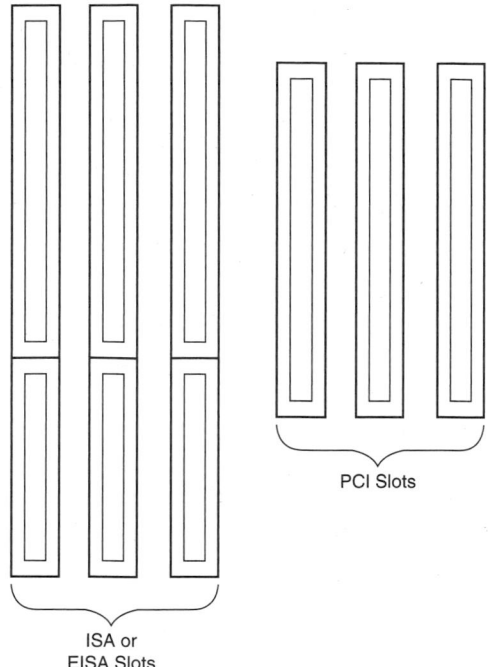

Figure 4.47 Possible configuration of PCI slots in relation to ISA or EISA slots.

The PCI specification identifies three board configurations, each designed for a specific type of system with specific power requirements. The 5v specification is for stationary computer systems, the 3.3v specification is for portable machines, and the universal specification is for motherboards and cards that work in either type of system.

Table 4.26 shows the 5v PCI pinouts, and Figure 4.48 shows the pin locations. Table 4.27 shows the 3.3v PCI pinouts; the pin locations are indicated in Figure 4.49. Finally, Table 4.28 shows the pinouts, and Figure 4.50 shows the pin locations for a universal PCI slot and card. Notice that each figure shows both the 32-bit and 64-bit variations on the respective specifications.

Note

If the PCI card supports only 32 data bits, it needs only pins B1/A1 through B62/A62. Pins B63/A63 through B94/A94 are used only if the card supports 64 data bits.

Table 4.26   Pinouts for a 5v PCI Bus

Pin	Signal Name	Pin	Signal Name
B1	−12v	A1	Test Reset
B2	Test Clock	A2	+12v
B3	Ground	A3	Test Mode Select

(continues)

Table 4.26 Continued

Pin	Signal Name	Pin	Signal Name
B4	Test Data Output	A4	Test Data Input
B5	+5v	A5	+5v
B6	+5v	A6	Interrupt A
B7	Interrupt B	A7	Interrupt C
B8	Interrupt D	A8	+5v
B9	PRSNT1#	A9	Reserved
B10	Reserved	A10	+5v I/O
B11	PRSNT2#	A11	Reserved
B12	Ground	A12	Ground
B13	Ground	A13	Ground
B14	Reserved	A14	Reserved
B15	Ground	A15	Reset
B16	Clock	A16	+5v I/O
B17	Ground	A17	Grant
B18	Request	A18	Ground
B19	+5v I/O	A19	Reserved
B20	Address 31	A20	Address 30
B21	Address 29	A21	+3.3v
B22	Ground	A22	Address 28
B23	Address 27	A23	Address 26
B24	Address 25	A24	Ground
B25	+3.3v	A25	Address 24
B26	C/BE 3	A26	Init Device Select
B27	Address 23	A27	+3.3v
B28	Ground	A28	Address 22
B29	Address 21	A29	Address 20
B30	Address 19	A30	Ground
B31	+3.3v	A31	Address 18
B32	Address 17	A32	Address 16
B33	C/BE 2	A33	+3.3v
B34	Ground	A34	Cycle Frame
B35	Initiator Ready	A35	Ground
B36	+3.3v	A36	Target Ready
B37	Device Select	A37	Ground
B38	Ground	A38	Stop
B39	Lock	A39	+3.3v
B40	Parity Error	A40	Snoop Done
B41	+3.3v	A41	Snoop Backoff
B42	System Error	A42	Ground

Pin	Signal Name	Pin	Signal Name
B43	+3.3v	A43	PAR
B44	C/BE 1	A44	Address 15
B45	Address 14	A45	+3.3v
B46	Ground	A46	Address 13
B47	Address 12	A47	Address 11
B48	Address 10	A48	Ground
B49	Ground	A49	Address 9
B50	Access key	A50	Access key
B51	Access key	A51	Access key
B52	Address 8	A52	C/BE 0
B53	Address 7	A53	+3.3v
B54	+3.3v	A54	Address 6
B55	Address 5	A55	Address 4
B56	Address 3	A56	Ground
B57	Ground	A57	Address 2
B58	Address 1	A58	Address 0
B59	+5v I/O	A59	+5v I/O
B60	Acknowledge 64-bit	A60	Request 64-bit
B61	+5v	A61	+5v
B62	+5v Access key	A62	+5v Access key
B63	Reserved	A63	Ground
B64	Ground	A64	C/BE 7
B65	C/BE 6	A65	C/BE 5
B66	C/BE 4	A66	+5v I/O
B67	Ground	A67	Parity 64-bit
B68	Address 63	A68	Address 62
B69	Address 61	A69	Ground
B70	+5v I/O	A70	Address 60
B71	Address 59	A71	Address 58
B72	Address 57	A72	Ground
B73	Ground	A73	Address 56
B74	Address 55	A74	Address 54
B75	Address 53	A75	+5v I/O
B76	Ground	A76	Address 52
B77	Address 51	A77	Address 50
B78	Address 49	A78	Ground
B79	+5v I/O	A79	Address 48
B80	Address 47	A80	Address 46
B81	Address 45	A81	Ground

(continues)

Table 4.26 Continued

Pin	Signal Name	Pin	Signal Name
B82	Ground	A82	Address 44
B83	Address 43	A83	Address 42
B84	Address 41	A84	+5v I/O
B85	Ground	A85	Address 40
B86	Address 39	A86	Address 38
B87	Address 37	A87	Ground
B88	+5v I/O	A88	Address 36
B89	Address 35	A89	Address 34
B90	Address 33	A90	Ground
B91	Ground	A91	Address 32
B92	Reserved	A92	Reserved
B93	Reserved	A93	Ground
B94	Ground	A94	Reserved

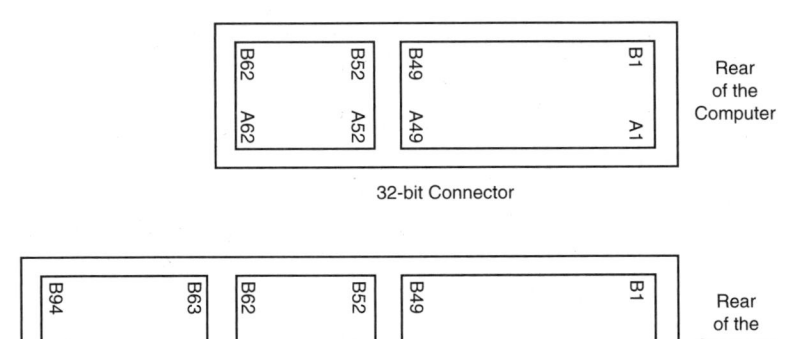

Figure 4.48 The 5v PCI slot and card configuration.

Table 4.27 Pinouts for a 3.3v PCI Bus

Pin	Signal Name	Pin	Signal Name
B1	−12v	A1	Test Reset
B2	Test Clock	A2	+12v
B3	Ground	A3	Test Mode Select
B4	Test Data Output	A4	Test Data Input
B5	+5v	A5	+5v
B6	+5v	A6	Interrupt A
B7	Interrupt B	A7	Interrupt C
B8	Interrupt D	A8	+5v

Pin	Signal Name	Pin	Signal Name
B9	PRSNT1#	A9	Reserved
B10	Reserved	A10	+3.3v
B11	PRSNT2#	A11	Reserved
B12	Access key	A12	Access key
B13	Access key	A13	Access key
B14	Reserved	A14	Reserved
B15	Ground	A15	Reset
B16	Clock	A16	+3.3v
B17	Ground	A17	Grant
B18	Request	A18	Ground
B19	+3.3v	A19	Reserved
B20	Address 31	A20	Address 30
B21	Address 29	A21	+3.3v
B22	Ground	A22	Address 28
B23	Address 27	A23	Address 26
B24	Address 25	A24	Ground
B25	+3.3v	A25	Address 24
B26	C/BE 3	A26	Init Device Select
B27	Address 23	A27	+3.3v
B28	Ground	A28	Address 22
B29	Address 21	A29	Address 20
B30	Address 19	A30	Ground
B31	+3.3v	A31	Address 18
B32	Address 17	A32	Address 16
B33	C/BE 2	A33	+3.3v
B34	Ground	A34	Cycle Frame
B35	Initiator Ready	A35	Ground
B36	+3.3v	A36	Target Ready
B37	Device Select	A37	Ground
B38	Ground	A38	Stop
B39	Lock	A39	+3.3v
B40	Parity Error	A40	Snoop Done
B41	+3.3v	A41	Snoop Backoff
B42	System Error	A42	Ground
B43	+3.3v	A43	PAR
B44	C/BE 1	A44	Address 15
B45	Address 14	A45	+3.3v
B46	Ground	A46	Address 13
B47	Address 12	A47	Address 11

(continues)

Table 4.27   Continued

Pin	Signal Name	Pin	Signal Name
B48	Address 10	A48	Ground
B49	Ground	A49	Address 9
B50	Ground	A50	Ground
B51	Ground	A51	Ground
B52	Address 8	A52	C/BE 0
B53	Address 7	A53	+3.3v
B54	+3.3v	A54	Address 6
B55	Address 5	A55	Address 4
B56	Address 3	A56	Ground
B57	Ground	A57	Address 2
B58	Address 1	A58	Address 0
B59	+3.3v	A59	+3.3v
B60	Acknowledge 64-bit	A60	Request 64-bit
B61	+5v	A61	+5v
B62	+5v Access key	A62	+5v Access key
B63	Reserved	A63	Ground
B64	Ground	A64	C/BE 7
B65	C/BE 6	A65	C/BE 5
B66	C/BE 4	A66	+3.3v
B67	Ground	A67	Parity 64-bit
B68	Address 63	A68	Address 62
B69	Address 61	A69	Ground
B70	+3.3v	A70	Address 60
B71	Address 59	A71	Address 58
B72	Address 57	A72	Ground
B73	Ground	A73	Address 56
B74	Address 55	A74	Address 54
B75	Address 53	A75	+3.3v
B76	Ground	A76	Address 52
B77	Address 51	A77	Address 50
B78	Address 49	A78	Ground
B79	+3.3v	A79	Address 48
B80	Address 47	A80	Address 46
B81	Address 45	A81	Ground
B82	Ground	A82	Address 44
B83	Address 43	A83	Address 42
B84	Address 41	A84	+3.3v
B85	Ground	A85	Address 40
B86	Address 39	A86	Address 38

Pin	Signal Name	Pin	Signal Name
B87	Address 37	A87	Ground
B88	+3.3v	A88	Address 36
B89	Address 35	A89	Address 34
B90	Address 33	A90	Ground
B91	Ground	A91	Address 32
B92	Reserved	A92	Reserved
B93	Reserved	A93	Ground
B94	Ground	A94	Reserved

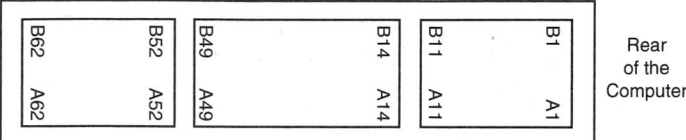

32-bit Connector

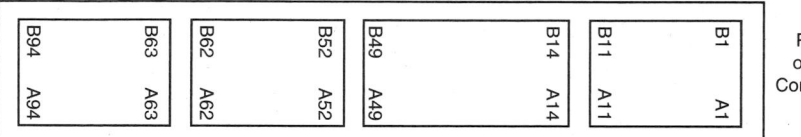

64-bit Connector

Figure 4.49   The 3.3v PCI slot and card configuration.

Table 4.28   Pinouts for a Universal PCI Bus

Pin	Signal Name	Pin	Signal Name
B1	−12v	A1	Test Reset
B2	Test Clock	A2	+12v
B3	Ground	A3	Test Mode Select
B4	Test Data Output	A4	Test Data Input
B5	+5v	A5	+5v
B6	+5v	A6	Interrupt A
B7	Interrupt B	A7	Interrupt C
B8	Interrupt D	A8	+5v
B9	PRSNT1#	A9	Reserved
B10	Reserved	A10	+v I/O
B11	PRSNT2#	A11	Reserved
B12	Access key	A12	Access key
B13	Access key	A13	Access key

(continues)

Table 4.28   Continued

Pin	Signal Name	Pin	Signal Name
B14	Reserved	A14	Reserved
B15	Ground	A15	Reset
B16	Clock	A16	+v I/O
B17	Ground	A17	Grant
B18	Request	A18	Ground
B19	+v I/O	A19	Reserved
B20	Address 31	A20	Address 30
B21	Address 29	A21	+3.3v
B22	Ground	A22	Address 28
B23	Address 27	A23	Address 26
B24	Address 25	A24	Ground
B25	+3.3v	A25	Address 24
B26	C/BE 3	A26	Init Device Select
B27	Address 23	A27	+3.3v
B28	Ground	A28	Address 22
B29	Address 21	A29	Address 20
B30	Address 19	A30	Ground
B31	+3.3v	A31	Address 18
B32	Address 17	A32	Address 16
B33	C/BE 2	A33	+3.3v
B34	Ground	A34	Cycle Frame
B35	Initiator Ready	A35	Ground
B36	+3.3v	A36	Target Ready
B37	Device Select	A37	Ground
B38	Ground	A38	Stop
B39	Lock	A39	+3.3v
B40	Parity Error	A40	Snoop Done
B41	+3.3v	A41	Snoop Backoff
B42	System Error	A42	Ground
B43	+3.3v	A43	PAR
B44	C/BE 1	A44	Address 15
B45	Address 14	A45	+3.3v
B46	Ground	A46	Address 13
B47	Address 12	A47	Address 11
B48	Address 10	A48	Ground
B49	Ground	A49	Address 9
B50	Access key	A50	Access key
B51	Access key	A51	Access key
B52	Address 8	A52	C/BE 0
B53	Address 7	A53	+3.3v

Pin	Signal Name	Pin	Signal Name
B54	+3.3v	A54	Address 6
B55	Address 5	A55	Address 4
B56	Address 3	A56	Ground
B57	Ground	A57	Address 2
B58	Address 1	A58	Address 0
B59	+5 I/O	A59	+v I/O
B60	Acknowledge 64-bit	A60	Request 64-bit
B61	+5v	A61	+5v
B62	+5v Access key	A62	+5v Access key
B63	Reserved	A63	Ground
B64	Ground	A64	C/BE 7
B65	C/BE 6	A65	C/BE 5
B66	C/BE 4	A66	+v I/O
B67	Ground	A67	Parity 64-bit
B68	Address 63	A68	Address 62
B69	Address 61	A69	Ground
B70	+v I/O	A70	Address 60
B71	Address 59	A71	Address 58
B72	Address 57	A72	Ground
B73	Ground	A73	Address 56
B74	Address 55	A74	Address 54
B75	Address 53	A75	+v I/O
B76	Ground	A76	Address 52
B77	Address 51	A77	Address 50
B78	Address 49	A78	Ground
B79	+v I/O	A79	Address 48
B80	Address 47	A80	Address 46
B81	Address 45	A81	Ground
B82	Ground	A82	Address 44
B83	Address 43	A83	Address 42
B84	Address 41	A84	+v I/O
B85	Ground	A85	Address 40
B86	Address 39	A86	Address 38
B87	Address 37	A87	Ground
B88	+v I/O	A88	Address 36
B89	Address 35	A89	Address 34
B90	Address 33	A90	Ground
B91	Ground	A91	Address 32
B92	Reserved	A92	Reserved
B93	Reserved	A93	Ground
B94	Ground	A94	Reserved

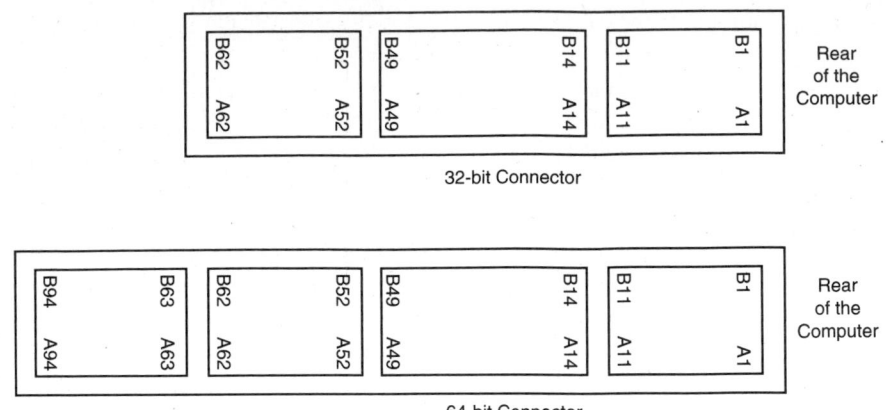

Figure 4.50   The universal PCI slot and card configuration.

Notice that the universal PCI board specifications effectively combine the 5v and 3.3v specifications. For pins for which the voltage is different, the universal specification labels the pin simply V I/O. This type of pin represents a special power pin for defining and driving the PCI signaling rail.

Another important feature of PCI is the fact that it was the model for the Intel PnP specification. This means that PCI cards do not have jumpers and switches, and are instead configured through software. True PnP systems are capable of automatically configuring the adapters, while non-PnP systems with ISA slots have to configure the adapters through a program that is usually a part of the system CMOS configuration. Starting in late 1995, most PC-compatible systems have included a PnP BIOS that allows the automatic PnP configuration.

Accelerated Graphics Port (AGP)

The Accelerated Graphics Port (AGP) was created by Intel as a new bus specifically designed for high performance graphics and video support. AGP is based on PCI, but contains a number of additions and enhancements, and is physically, electrically, and logically independent of PCI. For example the AGP connector is similar to PCI, although it has additional signals and is positioned differently in the system. Unlike PCI, which is a true bus with multiple connectors (slots), AGP is more of a point-to-point high performance connection designed specifically for a video card in a system, as only one AGP slot is allowed for a single video card.

The AGP specification 1.0 was originally released by Intel in July of 1996, and defined a 66MHz clock rate with 1x or 2x signaling using 3.3 volts. AGP version 2.0 was released in May 1998, and added 4x signaling as well as a lower 1.5v operating capability. There is also a new AGP Pro specification that defines a slightly longer slot with additional power pins at each end to drive bigger and faster AGP cards which consume more than 25 watts of power, up to a maximum of 110 watts. AGP Pro cards would likely be used for high-end graphics workstations. AGP Pro slots are backward compatible, meaning standard AGP card will plug in.

AGP is a high-speed connection, and runs at a base frequency of 66MHz (actually 66.66MHz), which is double that of standard PCI. In the basic AGP mode called 1x, a single transfer is done every cycle. Since the AGP bus is 32 bits (4 bytes) wide, at 66 million times per second it would be capable of transferring data at a rate of about 266MB/sec (million bytes per second)! The original AGP specification also defines a 2x mode, where two transfers are done every cycle, resulting in 533 MB/sec. Using an analogy where every cycle is equivalent to the back and forth swing of a pendulum, the 1x mode is thought of as transferring information at the start of each swing. In 2x mode, an additional transfer would occur every time the pendulum completed half a swing, thereby doubling performance while technically maintaining the same clock rate, or in this case, the same number of swings per second. Most modern AGP cards work in the 2x mode.

The newer AGP 2.0 specification adds the capability for 4x transfers, which transfers data four times per cycle and equals a data transfer rate of 1,066 MB/sec. The Table 4.29 shows the differences in clock rates and data transfer speeds for the various AGP modes.

Table 4.29   Clock Rates Versus Data Transfer Speeds

AGP Mode	Base Clock Rate	Effective Clock Rate	Data Transfer Rate
1x	66MHz	66MHz	266MB/sec
2x	66MHz	133MHz	533MB/sec
4x	66MHz	266MHz	1,066MB/sec

Because AGP is independent of PCI, using an AGP video card will free up the PCI bus for more traditional input and output, such as for IDE/ATA or SCSI controllers, USB controllers, sound cards, etc.

Besides faster video performance, one of the main reasons Intel designed AGP was to allow the video card to have a high-speed connection directly to the system RAM. This will allow an AGP video card to have direct access to the system RAM, reducing the need for more and more video memory. This is especially important because memory hungry 3D video becomes more and more prevalent on PCs.

AGP will allow the speed of the video card to pace the requirements for high-speed 3D graphics rendering as well as full motion video on the PC in the future.

System Resources

System resources are the communications channels, addresses, and other signals used by hardware devices to communicate on the bus. At their lowest level, these resources typically include the following:

- Memory addresses
- IRQ (interrupt request) channels
- DMA (direct memory access) channels
- I/O port addresses

The best solution is to purchase a multiport serial I/O card that will allow non-conflicting interrupt settings, or an intelligent card with its own processor that can handle the multiple ports on-board and only use one interrupt in the system.

▶▶ See "Serial Ports" p. 872.

If a device listed in the table is not present, such as the motherboard mouse port (IRQ 12) or parallel port 2 (IRQ 5), you can consider those interrupts as available. For example, a second parallel port is a rarity, and most systems will have a sound card installed and set for IRQ 5. Also, on most systems IRQ 15 is assigned to a secondary IDE controller. If you do not have a second IDE hard drive, you could disable the secondary IDE controller to free up that IRQ for another device.

Note that an easy way to check your interrupt settings is to use the Device Manager in Windows 95/98, NT, or Windows 2000. By double-clicking on the Computer Properties icon in the Device Manager, you can get concise lists of all used system resources. Microsoft has also included a program called HWDIAG on Windows 95B and newer versions, which does an excellent job of reporting system resource usage.

DMA Channels

DMA (Direct Memory Access) channels are used by high-speed communications devices that must send and receive information at high speed. A serial or parallel port does not use a DMA channel, but a sound card or SCSI adapter often does. DMA channels sometimes can be shared if the devices are not the type that would need them simultaneously. For example, you can have a network adapter and a tape backup adapter sharing DMA channel 1, but you cannot back up while the network is running. To back up during network operation, you must ensure that each adapter uses a unique DMA channel.

8-Bit ISA Bus DMA Channels

In the 8-bit ISA bus, four DMA channels support high-speed data transfers between I/O devices and memory. Three of the channels are available to the expansion slots. Table 4.32 shows the typical uses of these DMA channels.

Table 4.32   8-Bit ISA Default DMA-Channel Assignments

DMA	Standard Function	Bus Slot
0	Dynamic RAM Refresh	No
1	Available	Yes (8-bit)
2	Floppy disk controller	Yes (8-bit)
3	Hard disk controller	Yes (8-bit)

Because most systems typically have both a floppy and hard disk drive, only one DMA channel is available in 8-bit ISA systems.

16-Bit ISA DMA Channels

Since the introduction of the 286 CPU, the ISA bus has supported eight DMA channels, with seven channels available to the expansion slots. Like the expanded IRQ lines described earlier in this chapter, the added DMA channels were created by cascading a second DMA controller to the first one. DMA channel 4 is used to cascade channels 0–3 to the microprocessor. Channels 0–3 are available for 8-bit transfers, and channels 5–7 are for 16-bit transfers only. Table 4.33 shows the typical uses for the DMA channels.

Table 4.33   16/32-Bit ISA/PCI Default DMA-Channel Assignments

DMA	Standard Function	Bus Slot	Card Type	Transfer	Recommended Use
0	Available	Yes	16-bit	8-bit	Integrated Sound
1	Available	Yes	8/16-bit	8-bit	8-bit Sound
2	Floppy Disk Controller	Yes	8/16-bit	8-bit	Floppy Controller
3	Available	Yes	8/16-bit	8-bit	LPT1: in ECP Mode
4	1st DMA Controller Cascade	No	-	16-bit	
5	Available	Yes	16-bit	16-bit	16-bit Sound
6	Available	Yes	16-bit	16-bit	ISA SCSI Adapter
7	Available	Yes	16-bit	16-bit	Available

Note that PCI adapters don't use these ISA DMA channels these are only for ISA cards.

The only standard DMA channel used in all systems is DMA 2, which is universally used by the floppy controller. DMA 4 is not usable and does not appear in the bus slots. DMA channels 1 and 5 are most commonly used by ISA sound cards such as the Sound Blaster 16. These cards use both an 8- and a 16-bit DMA channel for high-speed transfers.

Note

Although DMA channel 0 appears in a 16-bit slot connector extension and therefore can only be used by a 16-bit card, it only does 8-bit transfers! Because of this, you will generally not see DMA 0 as a choice on 16-bit cards. Most 16-bit cards (such as SCSI host adapters) that use DMA channels have their choices limited to DMA 5–7.

EISA

Realizing the shortcomings inherent in the way DMA channels are implemented in the ISA bus, the creators of the EISA specification created a specific DMA controller for their new bus. They increased the number of address lines to include the entire address bus, thus allowing transfers anywhere within the address space of the system. Each DMA channel can be set to run 8-, 16-, or 32-bit transfers. In addition, each DMA channel can be separately programmed to run any of four types of bus cycles when transferring data:

- *Compatible*. This transfer method is included to match the same DMA timing as used in the ISA bus. This is done for compatibility reasons; all ISA cards can operate in an EISA system in this transfer mode.

- *Type A.* This transfer type compresses the DMA timing by 25 percent over the Compatible method. It was designed to run with most (but not all) ISA cards and still yield a speed increase.

- *Type B.* This transfer type compresses timing by 50 percent over the Compatible method. Using this method, most EISA cards function properly, but only a few ISA cards will be problem-free.

- *Type C.* This transfer method compresses timing by 87.5 percent over the Compatible method; it is the fastest DMA transfer method available under the EISA specification. No ISA cards will work using this transfer method.

EISA DMA also allows for special reading and writing operations referred to as *scatter write* and *gather read.* Scattered writes are done by reading a contiguous block of data and writing it to more than one area of memory at the same time. Gathered reads involve reading from more than one place in memory and writing to a device. These functions are often referred to as *buffered chaining,* and they increase the throughput of DMA operations.

MCA

It might be assumed that because MCA is a complete rebuilding of the PC bus structure that DMA in an MCA environment would be better constructed. This is not so. Quite the contrary, DMA in MCA systems were for the most part all designed around one DMA controller with the following issues:

- It can only connect to two 8-bit data paths. This can only transfer one or two bytes per bus cycle.

- It is only connected to AO:A23 on the address bus. This means it can only make use of the lower 16MB of memory.

- Runs at 10MHz.

The incapability of the DMA controller to address more than two bytes per transfer severely cripples this otherwise powerful bus.

I/O Port Addresses

Your computer's I/O ports enable communications between devices and software in your system. They are equivalent to two-way radio channels. If you want to talk to your serial port, you need to know what I/O port (radio channel) it is listening on. Similarly, if you want to receive data from the serial port, you need to listen on the same channel it is transmitting on.

Unlike IRQs and DMA channels, we have an abundance of I/O ports in our systems. There are 65,535 ports to be exact—numbered from 0000h to FFFFh—and this is an artifact of the Intel processor design more than anything else. Even though most devices use up to eight ports for themselves, with that many to spare, we aren't going to run out anytime soon. The biggest problem you have to worry about is setting two devices to use the same port.

Most modern plug-and-play systems will resolve any port conflicts and select alternative ports for one of the conflicting devices.

One confusing issue is that I/O ports are designated by hexadecimal addresses similar to memory addresses. They are not memory; they are ports. The difference is that when you send data to memory address 1000h, it gets stored in your SIMM or DIMM memory. If you send data to I/O port address 1000h, it gets sent out on the bus on that "channel" and anybody listening in would then "hear" it. If nobody was listening to that port address, the data would reach the end of the bus and be absorbed by the bus terminating resistors.

Driver programs are primarily what interact with devices at the different port addresses. The driver must know which ports the device is using to work with it, and vice versa. That is not usually a problem because the driver and device both come from the same company.

Motherboard and chipset devices are normally set to use I/O port addresses from 0h to FFh, and all other devices use from 100h to FFFFh. Table 4.34 shows the commonly used motherboard and chipset based I/O port usage:

Table 4.34   Motherboard and Chipset-based Device Port Addresses

Address (hex)	Size	Description
0000 - 000F	16 bytes	Chipset - 8237 DMA 1
0020 - 0021	2 bytes	Chipset - 8259 interrupt controller 1
002E - 002F	2 bytes	Super I/O controller Configuration registers
0040 - 0043	4 bytes	Chipset - Counter/Timer 1
0048 - 004B	4 bytes	Chipset - Counter/Timer 2
0060	1 byte	Keyboard/Mouse controller byte - reset IRQ
0061	1 byte	Chipset - NMI, speaker control
0064	1 byte	Keyboard/Mouse Controller, CMD/STAT Byte
0070, bit 7	1 bit	Chipset - Enable NMI
0070, bits 6:0	7 bits	MC146818 - Real-time clock, Address
0071	1 byte	MC146818 - Real-time clock, Data
0078	1 byte	Reserved - Board configuration
0079	1 byte	Reserved - Board configuration
0080 - 008F	16 bytes	Chipset - DMA page registers
00A0 - 00A1	2 bytes	Chipset - 8259 interrupt controller 2
00B2	1 byte	APM control port
00B3	1 byte	APM status port
00C0 - 00DE	31 bytes	Chipset - 8237 DMA 2
00F0	1 byte	Math Coprocessor Reset Numeric Error

To find out exactly what port addresses are being used on your motherboard, consult the board documentation or look these settings up in the Windows Device Manager.

Bus-based devices normally use the addresses from 100h on up. Table 4.35 lists the commonly used bus-based device addresses and some common adapter cards and their settings:

Table 4.35   Bus-based Device Port Addresses

Address (hex)	Size	Description
0130 - 0133	4 bytes	Adaptec SCSI adapter (alternate)
0134 - 0137	4 bytes	Adaptec SCSI adapter (alternate)
0168 - 016F	8 bytes	Fourth IDE interface
0170 - 0177	8 bytes	Secondary IDE interface
01E8 - 01EF	8 bytes	Third IDE interface
01F0 - 01F7	8 bytes	Primary IDE / AT (16-bit) Hard Disk Controller
0200 - 0207	8 bytes	Gameport or Joystick adapter
0210 - 0217	8 bytes	IBM XT expansion chassis
0220 - 0233	20 bytes	Creative Labs Sound Blaster 16 audio (default)
0230 - 0233	4 bytes	Adaptec SCSI adapter (alternate)
0234 - 0237	4 bytes	Adaptec SCSI adapter (alternate)
0238 - 023B	4 bytes	MS bus mouse (alternate)
023C - 023F	4 bytes	MS bus mouse (default)
0240 - 024F	16 bytes	SMC Ethernet adapter (default)
0240 - 0253	20 bytes	Creative Labs Sound Blaster 16 audio (alternate)
0258 - 025F	8 bytes	Intel above board
0260 - 026F	16 bytes	SMC Ethernet adapter (alternate)
0260 - 0273	20 bytes	Creative Labs Sound Blaster 16 audio (alternate)
0270 - 0273	4 bytes	Plug-and-Play I/O read ports
0278 - 027F	8 bytes	Parallel Port 2 (LPT2)
0280 - 028F	16 bytes	SMC Ethernet adapter (alternate)
0280 - 0293	20 bytes	Creative Labs Sound Blaster 16 audio (alternate)
02A0 - 02AF	16 bytes	SMC Ethernet adapter (alternate)
02C0 - 02CF	16 bytes	SMC Ethernet adapter (alternate)
02E0 - 02EF	16 bytes	SMC Ethernet adapter (alternate)
02E8 - 02EF	8 bytes	Serial Port 4 (COM4)
02EC - 02EF	4 bytes	Video, 8514 or ATI standard ports
02F8 - 02FF	8 bytes	Serial Port 2 (COM2)
0300 - 0301	2 bytes	MPU-401 MIDI Port (secondary)
0300 - 030F	16 bytes	SMC Ethernet adapter (alternate)
0320 - 0323	4 bytes	XT (8-bit) hard disk controller
0320 - 032F	16 bytes	SMC Ethernet adapter (alternate)
0330 - 0331	2 bytes	MPU-401 MIDI port (default)
0330 - 0333	4 bytes	Adaptec SCSI adapter (default)
0334 - 0337	4 bytes	Adaptec SCSI adapter (alternate)
0340 - 034F	16 bytes	SMC Ethernet adapter (alternate)
0360 - 036F	16 bytes	SMC Ethernet adapter (alternate)
0366	1 byte	Fourth IDE command port
0367, bits 6:0	7 bits	Fourth IDE status port

Address (hex)	Size	Description
0370 - 0375	6 bytes	Secondary floppy controller
0376	1 byte	Secondary IDE command port
0377, bit 7	1 bit	Secondary floppy controller Disk Change
0377, bits 6:0	7 bits	Secondary IDE status port
0378 - 037F	8 bytes	Parallel Port 1 (LPT1)
0380 - 038F	16 bytes	SMC Ethernet adapter (alternate)
0388 - 038B	4 bytes	Audio - FM synthesizer
03B0 - 03BB	12 bytes	Video, Mono/EGA/VGA standard ports
03BC - 03BF	4 bytes	Parallel Port 1 (LPT1) in some systems
03BC - 03BF	4 bytes	Parallel Port 3 (LPT3)
03C0 - 03CF	16 bytes	Video, EGA/VGA standard ports
03D0 - 03DF	16 bytes	Video, CGA/EGA/VGA standard ports
03E6	1 byte	Third IDE command port
03E7, bits 6:0	7 bits	Third IDE status port
03E8 - 03EF	8 bytes	Serial Port 3 (COM3)
03F0 - 03F5	6 bytes	Primary floppy controller
03F6	1 byte	Primary IDE command port
03F7, bit 7	1 bit	Primary Floppy controller disk Change
03F7, bits 6:0	7 bits	Primary IDE status port
03F8 - 03FF	8 bytes	Serial Port 1 (COM1)
04D0 - 04D1	2 bytes	Edge/level triggered PCI interrupt controller
0530 - 0537	8 bytes	Windows sound system (default)
0604 - 060B	8 bytes	Windows sound system (alternate)
0678 - 067F	8 bytes	LPT2 in ECP mode
0778 - 077F	8 bytes	LPT1 in ECP mode
0A20 - 0A23	4 bytes	IBM Token-Ring adapter (default)
0A24 - 0A27	4 bytes	IBM Token-Ring adapter (alternate)
0CF8 - 0CFB	4 bytes	PCI Configuration address Registers
0CF9	1 byte	Turbo and Reset control register
0CFC - 0CFF	4 bytes	PCI configuration data registers
FF00 - FF07	8 bytes	IDE bus master registers
FF80 - FF9F	32 bytes	Universal Serial Bus (USB)
FFA0 - FFA7	8 bytes	Primary bus master IDE registers
FFA8 - FFAF	8 bytes	Secondary bus master IDE registers

To find out exactly what your devices are using, again I recommend consulting the documentation for the device or looking the device up in the Windows Device Manager.

Virtually all devices on your system buses use I/O port addresses. Most of these are fairly standardized, meaning you won't often have conflicts or problems with these settings. In the next section, you learn more about working with I/O addresses.

Resolving Resource Conflicts

The resources in a system are limited. Unfortunately, the demands on those resources seem to be unlimited. As you add more and more adapter cards to your system, you will find that the potential for resource conflicts increases. If your system is fully PnP-compatible, potential conflicts should be resolved automatically.

How do you know whether you have a resource conflict? Typically, one of the devices in your system stops working. Resource conflicts can exhibit themselves in other ways, though. Any of the following events could be diagnosed as a resource conflict:

- A device transfers data inaccurately.
- Your system frequently locks up.
- Your sound card doesn't sound quite right.
- Your mouse doesn't work.
- Garbage appears on your video screen for no apparent reason.
- Your printer prints gibberish.
- You cannot format a floppy disk.
- The PC starts in Safe mode (Windows 95).

Windows 9x and Windows 2000 will also show conflicts by highlighting a device in yellow or red in the Device Manager representation. By using the Windows Device Manager, you can usually spot the conflicts quickly.

In the following sections, you learn some of the steps that you can take to head off resource conflicts or track them down when they occur.

Caution

Be careful in diagnosing resource conflicts; a problem might not be a resource conflict at all, but a computer virus. Many computer viruses are designed to exhibit themselves as glitches or periodic problems. If you suspect a resource conflict, it may be worthwhile to run a virus check first to ensure that the system is clean. This procedure could save you hours of work and frustration.

Resolving Conflicts Manually

Unfortunately, the only way to resolve conflicts manually is to take the cover off your system and start changing switches or jumper settings on your adapter cards. Each of these changes then must be accompanied by a system reboot, which implies that they take a great deal of time. This situation brings us to the first rule of resolving conflicts: When you set about ridding your system of resource conflicts, make sure that you allow a good deal of uninterrupted time.

Also make sure that you write down your current system settings before you start making changes. That way, you will know where you began and can go back to the original configuration (if necessary).

Finally, dig out the manuals for all your adapter boards; you will need them. If you cannot find the manuals, contact the manufacturers to determine what the various jumper positions and switch settings mean. Additionally, you could look for more current information online at the manufacturers' Web sites.

Now you are ready to begin your detective work. As you try various switch settings and jumper positions, keep the following questions in mind; the answers will help you narrow down the conflict areas:

- *When did the conflict first become apparent?* If the conflict occurred after you installed a new adapter card, that new card probably is causing the conflict. If the conflict occurred after you started using new software, chances are good that the software uses a device that is taxing your system's resources in a new way.

- *Are there two similar devices in your system that do not work?* For example, if your modem, integrated serial ports, or mouse—devices that use a COM port—do not work, chances are good that these devices are conflicting with each other.

- *Have other people had the same problem, and if so, how did they resolve it?* Public forums—such as those on CompuServe, Internet newsgroups, and America Online—are great places to find other users who might be able to help you solve the conflict.

Whenever you make changes in your system, reboot and see whether the problem persists. When you believe that you have solved the problem, make sure that you test all your software. Fixing one problem often seems to cause another to crop up. The only way to make sure that all problems are resolved is to test everything in your system.

One of the best pieces of advice I can give you is to try changing one thing at a time, and then retest. That is the most methodical and simplest way to isolate a problem quickly and efficiently.

As you attempt to resolve your resource conflicts, you should work with and update a system-configuration template, as discussed in the following section.

The motherboard BIOS is most often associated with hardware rather than software. This is because the BIOS on the motherboard is contained in a ROM (read-only memory) chip on the board, which contains the initial software drivers needed to get the system running. Years ago, when running only DOS on basic PCs, this was enough so that no other drivers were needed; the motherboard BIOS had everything that was necessary. The motherboard BIOS normally includes drivers for all the basic system components, including the keyboard, the floppy drive, the hard drive, the serial and parallel ports, and more. As systems became more complex, new hardware was added for which no motherboard BIOS drivers existed. These included devices such as newer video adapters, CD-ROM drives, SCSI hard disks, and so on.

Rather than requiring a new motherboard BIOS that would specifically support the new devices, it was far simpler and more practical to copy any new drivers that were needed onto the system hard disk and configure the operating system to load them at boot time. This is how most CD-ROM drives, sound cards, scanners, printers, PC-card (PCMCIA) devices, and so on are supported. Because these devices don't need to be active during boot time, the system can boot up from the hard disk and wait to load the drivers during the initial operating system load.

Some drivers, however, must be active during boot time. For example, how will you be able to see anything on the screen if your video card doesn't have a set of drivers in a ROM somewhere, rather than waiting to load them from the hard disk? The solution to this could be to provide a motherboard ROM with the appropriate video drivers built in; however, this is impractical because of the variety of cards, each needing its own drivers. You would end up with hundreds of different motherboard ROMs, depending on which video card you had. Instead, when IBM was designing the original PC, it created a better solution. It designed the PC's motherboard ROM to scan the slots looking for adapter cards with ROMs on them. If a card was found with a ROM on it, the ROM was executed during the initial system startup phase, well before the system began loading the operating system from the hard disk.

By putting the ROM-based drivers right on the card, you didn't have to change your mother-board ROM to have built-in support for new devices, especially those that needed to be active during boot time. A few different cards (adapter boards) will almost always have a ROM onboard, including the following:

- *Video cards*. All will have an onboard BIOS.
- *SCSI adapters*. Those that support booting from SCSI hard drives have an onboard BIOS. Note that, in most cases, the SCSI BIOS does not support any SCSI devices other than a hard disk; if you use a SCSI CD-ROM, scanner, zip drive, and so on, you still need to load the appropriate drivers for those devices from your hard disk.
- *Network cards*. Those that support booting directly from a file server will have what is usually called a boot ROM or IPL (Initial Program Load) ROM onboard. This allows for PCs to be configured on a LAN as diskless workstations—also called Net PCs, NCs (Network Computers), or even smart terminals.
- *IDE or floppy upgrade boards*. Boards that allow you to attach more or different types of drives that what is normally supported by the motherboard alone. These cards require an onboard BIOS to enable these drives to be bootable.

■ *Y2K boards.* Boards that incorporate BIOS fixes to update the century byte in the CMOS RAM. These boards have a small driver contained in a BIOS, which monitors the year byte for a change from 99 to 00. When this is detected, the driver updates the century byte from 19 to 20, correcting a flaw in some older motherboard BIOSes.

BIOS and CMOS RAM

Some people confuse BIOS with the CMOS RAM in a system. This confusion is aided by the fact that the Setup program in the BIOS is used to set and store the configuration settings in the CMOS RAM. They are, in fact, two totally separate components.

The BIOS on the motherboard is stored in a fixed ROM chip. Also on the motherboard is a chip called the RTC/NVRAM chip, which stands for Real-Time Clock/Non-Volatile Memory. This is actually a digital clock chip with a few extra bytes of memory thrown in.

The first one ever used in a PC was the Motorola MC146818 chip, which had 64 bytes of storage, of which 10 bytes were dedicated to the clock function. Although it is called nonvolatile, it is actually volatile, meaning that without power, the time/date settings and the data in the RAM portion will, in fact, be erased. It is called non-volatile because it is designed using CMOS (complementary metal-oxide semiconductor) technology, which results in a chip that runs on very little power, and that power is provided by a battery in the system, not by the AC wall current. This is also why most people incorrectly call this chip the CMOS RAM chip; although not technically accurate, that is easier to say than the RTC/NVRAM chip. Most RTC/NVRAM chips run on as little as 1 micro-amp (millionth of an amp), which means they use very little battery power to run. Most will last five years before the lithium battery runs out and the information stored gets erased.

When you enter your BIOS Setup, configure your hard disk parameters or other BIOS Setup settings, and save them, these settings are written to the storage area in the RTC/NVRAM (otherwise called CMOS RAM) chip. Every time your system boots up, it reads the parameters stored in the CMOS RAM chip to determine how the system should be configured. A relationship exists between the BIOS and CMOS RAM, but they are two distinctly different parts of the system.

Motherboard BIOS

All motherboards must have a special chip containing software we call the BIOS or ROM BIOS. This ROM chip contains the startup programs and drivers that are used to get the system running and act as the interface to the basic hardware in the system. A POST (power on self test) in the BIOS also tests the major components in the system when you turn it on, and normally a setup program used to store system configuration data in the CMOS (complementary metal-oxide semiconductor) memory powered by a battery on the motherboard. This CMOS RAM is often called NVRAM (Non-Volatile RAM) because it runs on about 1 millionth of an amp of electrical current and can store data for years when powered by a tiny lithium battery.

▶▶ See "ROM Hardware," p. 350.

The BIOS is a collection of programs embedded in one or more chips, depending on the design of your computer. That collection of programs is the first thing loaded when you start your computer, even before the operating system. Simply put, the BIOS in most PCs has four main functions:

- *POST (power on self test).* The POST tests your computer's processor, memory, chipset, video adapter, disk controllers, disk drives, keyboard, and other crucial components.

- *BIOS Setup.* System configuration and setup program. This is usually a menu-driven program activated by pressing a special key during the POST, which allows you to configure the motherboard and chipset settings along with the date and time, passwords, disk drives, and other basic system settings. You also can control the power-management settings and boot-drive sequence from the BIOS Setup. Some older 286 and 386 systems did not have the Setup program in ROM and required that you boot from a special setup disk.

- *Bootstrap loader.* A routine that reads the disk drives looking for a valid master boot sector. If one meeting certain minimum criteria (ending in the signature bytes 55AAh) is found, then the code within is executed. This master boot sector program then continues the boot process by loading an operating system boot sector, which then loads the operating system core files.

- *BIOS (basic input/output system).* This refers to the collection of actual drivers used to act as a basic interface between the operating system and your hardware when the system is booted and running. When running DOS or Windows in safe mode, you are running almost solely on ROM-based BIOS drivers because none are loaded from disk.

ROM Hardware

Read-only memory, or ROM, is a type of memory that can permanently or semi-permanently hold data. It is called read-only because it is either impossible or difficult to write to. ROM is also often called nonvolatile memory because any data stored in ROM will remain even if the power is turned off. As such, ROM is an ideal place to put the PC's startup instructions—that is, the software that boots the system—the BIOS.

Note that ROM and RAM are not opposites, as some people seem to believe. In fact, ROM is technically a subset of the system's RAM. In other words, a portion of the system's random access memory address space is mapped into one or more ROM chips. This is necessary to contain the software that enables the PC to boot up; otherwise, the processor would have no program in memory to execute when it is powered on.

For example, when a PC is turned on, the processor automatically jumps to address FFFF0h, expecting to find instructions to tell the processor what to do. This location is exactly 16 bytes from the end of the first megabyte of RAM space, as well as the end of the ROM itself. If this location were mapped into regular RAM chips, any data stored there would have disappeared when the power was previously turned off, and the processor would subsequently find no instructions to run the next time power was turned on. By placing a ROM chip at this address, a system startup program can be permanently loaded into the ROM and will be available every time the system is turned on.

▶▶ See "The Boot Process," p. 1353.

▶▶ For more information about Dynamic RAM, see "DRAM," p. 418.

Normally the system ROM will start at address F0000h, which is 64KB prior to the end of the first megabyte. Because the ROM chip is normally 64KB in size, the ROM programs occupy the entire last 64KB of the first megabyte, including the critical FFFF0h startup instruction address.

Some think it is strange that the PC would start executing instructions 16 bytes from the end of the ROM, but this design was intentional. All the ROM programmer has to do is to place a JMP (jump) instruction at that address that instructs the processor to jump to the actual beginning of the ROM—in most cases close to F0000h—which is about 64KB earlier in the memory map. It's like deciding to read every book starting 16 pages from the end, and then having all book publishers agree to place an instruction there to jump back the necessary number of pages to get to page 1. By setting the startup location in this way, Intel allowed the ROM to grow to be any size, all the while keeping it at the upper end of addresses in the first megabyte of the memory address space.

The main ROM BIOS is contained in a ROM chip on the motherboard, but adapter cards with ROMs are also on them as well. ROMs on adapter cards contain auxiliary BIOS routines and drivers needed by the particular card, especially for those cards that must be active early in the boot process, such as video cards, for example. Cards that don't need drivers active during boot (such as sound cards) will not normally have a ROM because those drivers can be loaded from the hard disk later in the boot process.

Because the BIOS is the main portion of the code stored in ROM, we often call the ROM the ROM BIOS. In older PCs, the motherboard ROM BIOS could consist of up to five or six total chips, but most PCs have only required a single chip for many years now.

Adapter cards that require drivers during the boot process need to have ROM onboard. This includes cards such as video cards, most SCSI (small computer systems interface) cards (if you want to boot from a SCSI hard drive), enhanced IDE controller cards, and some network cards (for booting from the server). The ROM chip on these cards contains drivers and startup programs that will be executed by the motherboard ROM at boot time. This, for example, is how a video card can be recognized and initialized, even though your motherboard ROM does not contain specific drivers for it. You wouldn't want to load the initial VGA mode drivers from disk because the screen would remain dark until those drivers were loaded.

Adapter card ROMs are automatically scanned and read by the motherboard ROM during the early part of the boot process, during the POST (power on self test). The motherboard ROM scans a special area of RAM reserved for adapter ROMs (addresses C0000-DFFFFh) looking for a 55AAh signature byte pair that indicates the start of a ROM.

All adapter ROMs must start with 55AAh or they won't be recognized by the motherboard. The third byte indicates the size of the ROM in 512-byte units called paragraphs, and the fourth byte is the actual start of the driver programs. The size byte is used by the motherboard ROM for testing purposes. The motherboard ROM adds all the bytes in the ROM and divides the sum by the number of bytes. The result should produce a remainder of 100h. Thus, when creating a ROM for an adapter, the programmer uses a "fill" byte at the end to get the checksum to come out right. Using this checksum the motherboard tests each adapter ROM during the POST and flags any that appear to have been corrupted.

The motherboard BIOS automatically runs the programs in any adapter ROMs it finds during the scan. You see this in most systems when you turn your system on, and during the POST, you see the video card BIOS initialize and announce its presence.

ROM Shadowing

ROM chips by their nature are very slow, with access times of 150ns (nanoseconds, or billionths of a second), compared to DRAM access times of 60ns or less. Because of this, in many systems the ROMs are *shadowed*, which means they are copied into DRAM chips at startup to allow faster access during normal operation. The shadowing procedure copies the ROM into RAM and then assigns that RAM the same address as the ROM originally used, disabling the actual ROM in the process. This makes the system seem as though it has 60ns (or whatever the RAM speed is) ROM.

The performance gain from shadowing is often very slight, and it can cause problems if not set up properly, so in most cases, it is wise to shadow only the motherboard and maybe the video card BIOS, and leave the others alone.

Mostly, shadowing is useful only if you are running 16-bit operating systems such as DOS or Windows 3.x. If you are running a 32-bit operating system such as Windows 95, Windows 98, Windows 2000, or Windows NT, shadowing is virtually useless because those operating systems do not use the 16-bit ROM code while running. Instead, those operating systems load 32-bit drivers into RAM, which replace the 16-bit BIOS code used only during system startup.

Shadowing controls are found in the CMOS Setup program in the motherboard ROM, which is covered in more detail later in this chapter.

There are four types of ROM chips:

- *ROM.* Read-only memory
- *PROM.* Programmable ROM
- *EPROM.* Erasable PROM
- *EEPROM.* Electrically-erasable PROM, also called a flash ROM

No matter which type of ROM your system uses, the data stored in a ROM chip is nonvolatile and will remain indefinitely unless intentionally erased or overwritten (in those where that is possible).

Table 5.1 lists the identifying part numbers typically used for each type of ROM chip, along with any other identifying information.

Table 5.1   ROM Chip Part Numbers

ROM Type	Part Number	Other
ROM	No longer in use	
PROM	27nnnn	
EPROM	27nnnn	Quartz Window
EEPROM	28xxxx or 29xxxx	

Mask ROM

Originally, most ROMs were manufactured with the binary data (0s and 1s) already "cast in" or integrated into the die. The die represents the actual silicon chip itself. These are called Mask ROMs because the data is formed into the mask from which the ROM die is photolithographically produced. This type of manufacturing method is economical if you are making hundreds of thousands of ROMs with the same information. If you have to change a single bit, however, you must remake the mask, which is an expensive proposition. Because of costs and inflexibility, nobody uses Mask ROMs anymore.

Mask ROMs are exactly analogous to prerecorded CD-ROMs. Some people think a CD-ROM is first manufactured as a blank and then the data is written to it by laser, but that is not true. A CD-ROM is literally a piece of plastic that is stamped in a press, and the data is directly molded in, not written. The only actual recording was done with the master disc from which the molds or stamps are made.

PROM

PROMs are a type of ROM that is blank when new and that must be programmed with whatever data you want. The PROM was invented in the late 1970s by Texas Instruments and has been available in sizes from 1KB (8Kb) to 2MB (16Mb) or more. They can be identified by their part numbers, which are usually 27nnnn—where the 27 indicates the TI type PROM, and the nnnn indicates the size of the chip in kilobits (not bytes). For example, most PCs that used PROMs came with 27512 or 271000 chips, which indicate 512Kb (64KB) or 1Mb (128KB).

Note

Since 1981, all cars sold in the US have used onboard computers with some form of ROM containing the control software. My '89 Pontiac Turbo Trans Am came with an onboard computer containing a 2732 PROM, which was a 32Kb (4KB) chip in the ECM (Electronic Control Module or vehicle computer) under the dash. This chip contained a portion of the vehicle operating software as well as all the data tables describing spark advance, fuel delivery, and other engine and vehicle operating parameters. Many devices with integrated computers use PROMs to store their operating programs.

Although we say these chips are blank when new, they are technically preloaded with binary 1s. In other words, a 1Mb ROM chip used in a modern PC would come with 1 million (actually 1,048,576) bit locations, each containing a binary 1. A blank PROM can then be programmed, which is the act of writing to it. This normally requires a special machine called a device programmer, a ROM programmer, or a ROM burner (see Figure 5.2).

We sometimes refer to programming the ROM as "burning" it, because that is technically an apt description of the process. Each binary 1 bit can be thought of as a fuse, which is intact. Most chips run on 5 volts, but when we program a PROM, we place a higher voltage (normally 12 volts) at the various addresses within the chip. This higher voltage actually blows or burns the fuses at the locations we desire, thus turning any given 1 into a 0. Although we can turn a 1 into a 0, you should note that the process is irreversible; that is, we cannot turn a 0 back into a 1.

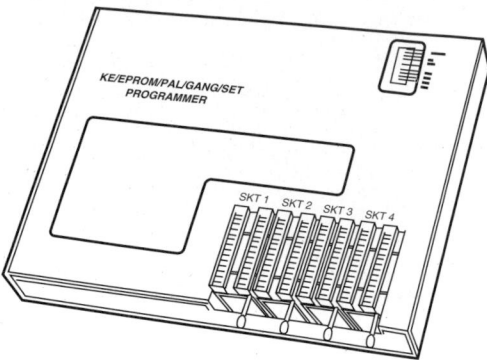

Figure 5.2   Typical gang (multisocket) device programmer (PROM burner).

The device programmer examines the program you want to write into the chip and then selectively changes only the 1s to 0s where necessary in the chip.

PROM chips are often referred to as OTP (one time programmable) chips for this reason. They can be programmed once and never erased. Most PROMs are very inexpensive, about $3 for a typical PC motherboard PROM, so if you want to change the program in a PROM, you discard it and program a fresh one with the new data.

The act of programming a PROM takes anywhere from a few seconds to a few minutes, depending on the size of the chip and the algorithm used by the programming device. Figure 5.2 shows an illustration of a typical PROM programmer that has multiple sockets. This is called a gang programmer and can program several chips at once, saving time if you have several chips to write with the same data. Less expensive programmers are available with only one socket, which is fine for most individual use.

I use and recommend a very inexpensive programmer from a company called Andromeda Research (see Vendor List on the CD). Besides being economical, their unit has the advantage of connecting to a PC via the parallel port for fast and easy data transfer of files between the PC and the programming unit. Their unit is also portable and comes built into a convenient carrying case. It is operated by an included menu-driven program you install on the connected PC. The program contains several features, including a function that allows you to read the data from a chip and save it in a file on your system, as well as to write a chip from a data file, verify that a chip matches a file, and verify that a chip is blank before programming begins.

Chapter 4, "Motherboards and Buses," shows how I used my PROM programmer to modify the BIOS in some of my older PCs. With today's systems primarily using flash ROMs, this capability is somewhat limited, but I include the information because I think it is very interesting.

Note

I even used my PROM programmer to reprogram the PROM in my 1989 Turbo Trans Am, changing the factory preset speed and rpm limiters, turbocharger boost, torque converter lockup points, spark advance, fuel delivery, idle speed, and much more! I also incorporated a switch box under the dash that allows me to switch among four different chips, even while the vehicle is running. One chip I created I call the "valet chip," which, when engaged, cuts off the fuel injectors at a preset speed of 36 miles per hour and restarts them when the vehicle coasts down to 35mph. I imagine this type of modification would be useful for those with teenagers driving, because you could set the mph or engine rpm limit to whatever you want! Another chip I created cuts off fuel to the engine altogether, which I engage for security purposes when the vehicle is parked. No matter how clever, a thief will not be able to steal this car unless he tows it away. If you are interested in such a chip-switching device or custom chips for your Turbo Trans Am or Buick Grand National, contact Casper's Electronics (see the Vendor List on the CD-ROM accompanying this book). For other vehicles with replaceable PROMs, companies such as Superchips, Hypertech, or Evergreen offer custom PROMs for improved performance (see the Vendor List on the CD). I installed a Superchips chip in a Ford Explorer I had, and it made a dramatic improvement in engine operation and vehicle performance.

EPROM

One variation of the PROM that has been very popular is the EPROM. An EPROM is a PROM that is erasable. An EPROM chip can be easily recognized by the clear quartz crystal window set in the chip package directly over the die (see Figure 5.3). You can actually see the die through the window! EPROMs have the same 27xxxx part-numbering scheme as the standard PROM, and they are functionally and physically identical except for the clear quartz window above the die.

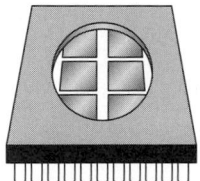

Figure 5.3   An EPROM showing the quartz window for ultraviolet erasing.

The purpose of the window is to allow ultraviolet light to reach the chip die because the EPROM is erased by exposure to intense UV light. The window is quartz crystal because regular glass blocks UV light. You can't get a suntan through a glass window!

Note

The quartz window makes the EPROMS more expensive than the OTP (One Time Programmability) PROMs. This extra expense is needless if erasability is not important.

The UV light erases the chip by causing a chemical reaction, which essentially melts the fuses back together! Thus, any binary 0s in the chip become 1s, and the chip is restored to new condition with binary 1s in all locations. To work, the UV exposure must be at a specific wavelength (2,537 angstroms), at a fairly high intensity (12,000 uw/cm^2), in close proximity (2–3cm, or about 1 inch), and last for between 5 and 15 minutes duration. An EPROM eraser (see Figure 5.4) is a device that contains a UV light source (usually a sunlamp-type bulb) above a sealed compartment drawer where you place the chip or chips.

Figure 5.4 shows a professional type EPROM eraser that can handle up to 50 chips at a time. I use a much smaller and less expensive one called the DataRase by Walling Co. (see the Vendor List on the CD). This device erases up to four chips at a time and is both economical and portable.

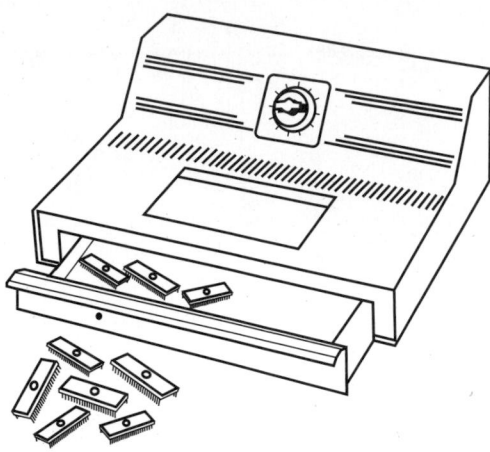

Figure 5.4   A professional EPROM eraser.

The quartz crystal window on an EPROM is normally covered by tape, which prevents accidental exposure to UV light. UV light is present in sunlight, of course, and even in standard room lighting, so that over time a chip exposed to the light may begin to degrade. For this reason after a chip is programmed, it is a good idea to put a sticker over the window to protect it.

EEPROM/Flash ROM

A newer type of ROM is the EEPROM, which stands for Electrically Erasable PROM. These chips are also called flash ROMs and are characterized by their capability to be erased and reprogrammed directly in the circuit board they are installed in, with no special equipment required. By using an EEPROM, or flash ROM, it is possible to erase and reprogram the motherboard ROM in a PC without removing the chip from the system or even opening up the system chassis!

With a flash ROM or EEPROM, you don't need a UV eraser or device programmer to program or erase chips. Not only do virtually all PC motherboards built since 1994 use flash ROMs or EEPROMs, most automobiles built since then also use them as well. For example my `94 Chevy Impala SS has a PCM (Powertrain Control Module) with an integral flash ROM.

The EEPROM or flash ROM can be identified by a 28xxxx or 29xxxx part number, as well as by the absence of a window on the chip. Having an EEPROM or flash ROM in your PC motherboard means you can now easily upgrade the motherboard ROM without having to swap chips. In most cases, you will download the updated ROM from the motherboard manufacturer's Web site and then run a special program they provide to update the ROM. This procedure is described in more detail later in this chapter.

I recommend that you periodically check with your motherboard manufacturer to see whether an updated BIOS is available for your system. An updated BIOS may contain bug fixes or enable new features not originally found in your system. You might find fixes for a potential year 2000 date problem, for example, or new drivers to support booting from LS-120 (120MB floppy) drives.

Note

For the auto enthusiasts out there, you might want to do the same for your car; that is, check to see whether ROM upgrades are available for your vehicle's computer. Now that updates are so easy and inexpensive, vehicle manufacturers are releasing bug-fix ROM upgrades that correct operational problems or improve vehicle performance. In most cases, you will have to check with your dealer to see whether any new vehicle ROMs are available. If you have a GM car, GM has a site on the Web where you can get information about the BIOS revisions available for your car, which it calls Vehicle Calibrations. The GM Vehicle Calibration Information site address is

```
http://207.74.147.14/vci/
```

When you enter your VIN (vehicle identification number), this page displays the calibration history for the vehicle, which is a list of all the different flash ROM upgrades (calibrations) developed since the vehicle was new. For example, when I entered the VIN on my 1994 Impala, I found that five flash ROM calibrations had been released over the years, and my car had only the second revision installed originally, meaning there had been three newer ROMs than the one I had! The fixes in the various calibration updates are also listed. A trip to the dealer with this information enabled them to use their diagnostic computer to connect to my car and reflash the PCM with the latest software, which, in my case, fixed several problems including engine surging under specific conditions, shift clunks, erroneous "check engine" light warnings, and several other minor problems.

With the flash ROM capability, I began experimenting with running calibrations originally intended for other vehicles, and I now run a modified Camaro calibration loaded into the flash ROM in my Impala. The spark-advance curve and fuel delivery parameters are much more aggressive in the Camaro calibration, as are the transmission shift points and other features. If you are interested in having a custom program installed in your flash ROM equipped vehicle, I recommend you contact Wright Automotive or Evergreen Performance (see the Vendor List on the CD).

These days, many objects with embedded computers controlling them are using flash ROMs. Pretty soon you'll be taking your toaster in for flash ROM upgrades as well! The method for locating and updating your PC motherboard flash ROMs is shown in Chapter 4.

Other devices may have flash ROMs as well; for example, I have updated the flash ROMs in my Motorola ISDN modem as well as in my Kodak digital camera. Both of these items had minor quirks that were fixed by updating their internal ROM code, which was as easy as downloading a file from their respective Web sites and running the update program included in the file.

Flash ROMs are also frequently used to add new capabilities to peripherals or to update peripherals, such as modems, to the latest standards; for example, updating a modem from X2 or Kflex to v.90.

ROM BIOS Manufacturers

A number of popular BIOS manufacturers in the market today supply the majority of motherboard and system manufacturers with the code for their ROMs. This section discusses the various versions available.

Several companies have specialized in the development of a compatible ROM BIOS product. The three major companies that come to mind in discussing ROM BIOS software are American Megatrends, Inc. (AMI), Award Software, and Phoenix Software. Each company licenses its ROM

BIOS to motherboard manufacturers so those manufacturers can worry about the hardware rather than the software. To obtain one of these ROMs for a motherboard, the OEM (Original Equipment Manufacturer) must answer many questions about the design of the system so that the proper BIOS can be either developed or selected from those already designed. Combining a ROM BIOS and a motherboard is not a haphazard task. No single, generic, compatible ROM exists, either. AMI, Award, Microid Research, and Phoenix ship many variations of their BIOS code to different board manufacturers, each one custom- tailored to that specific motherboard.

Recently, some big changes have occurred in the BIOS industry. Phoenix landed a contract with Intel and now provides all of Intel's motherboard BIOSes, replacing AMI, who previously had the contract. This is a big deal because Intel sells about 80 percent or more of all PC motherboards. What that basically means is that if you purchase a PC today, you will probably be getting an Intel-made motherboard with the new Phoenix BIOS.

Another development is that in late 1998, Phoenix bought Award, and all its new products will be under the Phoenix name. Thus, the big-three BIOS developers are now reduced to the big two—Phoenix and AMI. Many of the offshore motherboard manufacturers still continue to use the AMI or Award BIOS. However, Phoenix is currently the leading BIOS company. It is not only developing the BIOS for most newer systems on the market, but it also is the primary BIOS developer responsible for new BIOS development and new BIOS standards.

OEMs

Many OEMs (original equipment manufacturers) have developed their own compatible ROMs independently. Companies such as Compaq and AT&T have developed their own BIOS products that are comparable to those offered by AMI, Phoenix, Award, and others. These companies also offer upgrades to newer versions that often can offer more features and improvements or fix problems with the older versions. If you use a system with a proprietary ROM, make sure that it is from a larger company with a track record and one that will provide updates and fixes as necessary. Ideally, upgrades should be available for download from the Internet.

Most OEMs have their BIOS written for them by a third-party company. For example, Hewlett Packard contracts with Phoenix, a well-known BIOS supplier, to develop the motherboard BIOSes used in all the HP Vectra PCs. Note that even though Phoenix may have done the development, you still have to get any upgrades or fixes from Hewlett Packard. This is really true for all systems because all motherboard manufacturers customize the BIOS for their boards.

Intel, today the largest manufacturer of motherboards in the world, used to use AMI for its BIOS, but during 1997, it switched over to Phoenix for all its newer systems. Today Intel supplies versions of the Phoenix BIOS with all its boards. Phoenix is again the largest BIOS supplier in the world; it is found in the majority of motherboards today.

AMI

Although AMI customizes the ROM code for a particular system, it does not sell the ROM source code to the OEM. An OEM must obtain each new release as it becomes available. Because many

OEMs don't need or want every new version developed, they might skip several version changes before licensing a new one. The AMI BIOS is currently the most popular BIOS in PC systems. Newer versions of the AMI BIOS are called Hi-Flex because of the high flexibility found in the BIOS configuration program. The AMI Hi-Flex BIOS is used in Intel, AMI, and many other manufacturers' motherboards. One special AMI feature is that it is the only third-party BIOS manufacturer to make its own motherboard.

During powerup, the BIOS ID string is displayed on the lower-left part of the screen. This string tells you valuable information about which BIOS version you have and about certain settings that are determined by the built-in setup program.

Tip

A good trick to help you view the BIOS ID string is to shut down and either unplug your keyboard or hold down a key as you power back on. This causes a keyboard error, and the string will remained displayed.

The primary BIOS Identification string (ID String 1) is displayed by any AMI BIOS during the POST (power on self test) at the bottom-left corner of the screen, below the copyright message. Two additional BIOS ID strings (ID Strings 2 and 3) can be displayed by the AMI Hi-Flex BIOS by pressing the Insert key during POST. These additional ID strings display the options that are installed in the BIOS.

The general BIOS ID String 1 format for older AMI BIOS versions is shown in Table 5.2.

Table 5.2   ABBB-NNNN-mmddyy-KK

Position	Description
A	BIOS Options: D = Diagnostics built in S = Setup built in E = Extended Setup built in
BBB	Chipset or Motherboard Identifier: C&T = Chips & Technologies chipset NET = C&T NEAT 286 chipset 286 = Standard 286 motherboard SUN = Suntac chipset PAQ = Compaq motherboard INT = Intel motherboard AMI = AMI motherboard G23 = G2 chipset 386 motherboard
NNNN	The manufacturer license code reference number
mmddyy	The BIOS release date, mm/dd/yy
KK	The AMI keyboard BIOS version number.

The BIOS ID String 1format for AMI Hi-Flex BIOS versions is shown in Table 5.3.

Table 5.3   AB-CCcc-DDDDDD-EFGHIJKL-mmddyy-MMMMMMMM-N

Position	Description

A	Processor Type:
	    0 = 8086 or 8088
	    2 = 286
	    3 = 386
	    4 = 486
	    5 = Pentium
	    6 = Pentium Pro/II

B	Size of BIOS:
	    0 = 64KB BIOS
	    1 = 128KB BIOS

CCcc	Major and minor BIOS version number

DDDDDD	Manufacturer license code reference number
	    0036xx = AMI 386 motherboard, xx = Series #
	    0046xx = AMI 486 motherboard, xx = Series #
	    0056xx = AMI Pentium motherboard, xx = Series #
	    0066xx = AMI Pentium Pro motherboard, xx = Series #

E	1 = Halt on POST Error
F	1 = Initialize CMOS every boot
G	1 = Block pins 22 and 23 of the keyboard controller
H	1 = Mouse support in BIOS/keyboard controller
I	1 = Wait for <F1> key on POST errors
J	1 = Display floppy error during POST
K	1 = Display video error during POST
L	1 = Display keyboard error during POST
mmddyy	BIOS Date, mm/dd/yy
MMMMMMMM	Chipset identifier or BIOS name
N	Keyboard controller version number

AMI Hi-Flex BIOS ID String 2 is shown in Table 5.4.

Table 5.4   AAB-C-DDDD-EE-FF-GGGG-HH-II-JJJ

Position	Description
AA	Keyboard controller pin number for clock switching.

B	Keyboard controller clock switching pin function:
	    H = High signal switches clock to high speed.
	    L = High signal switches clock to low speed.
	    C = Clock switching through chipset registers:
	    0 = Disable.
	    1 = Enable.

DDDD	Port address to switch clock high.
EE	Data value to switch clock high.
FF	Mask value to switch clock high.
GGGG	Port address to switch clock low.
HH	Data value to switch clock low.
II	Mask value to switch clock low.
JJJ	Pin number for Turbo Switch Input.

AMI Hi-Flex BIOS ID String 3 is shown in Table 5.5.

Table 5.5   AAB-C-DDD-EE-FF-GGGG-HH-II-JJ-K-L

Position	Description
AA	Keyboard controller pin number for cache control.
B	Keyboard controller cache control pin function:
	H = High signal enables the cache.
	L = High signal disables the cache.
C	1 = High signal is used on the keyboard controller pin.
DDD	Cache control through chipset registers:
	0 = Cache control off.
	1 = Cache control on.
EE	Port address to enable cache.
FF	Data value to enable cache.
GGGG	Mask value to enable cache.
HH	Port address to disable cache.
II	Data value to disable cache.
JJ	Mask value to disable cache.
K	Pin number for resetting the 82335 memory controller.
L	BIOS Modification Flag:
	0 = The BIOS has not been modified.
	1–9, A–Z = Number of times the BIOS has been modified.

The AMI BIOS has many features, including a built-in setup program activated by pressing the Delete or Esc key in the first few seconds of booting up your computer. The BIOS prompts you briefly as to which key to press and when to press it. The AMI BIOS offers user-definable hard disk types, essential for optimal use of many IDE or ESDI drives. The 1995 and newer BIOS versions also support enhanced IDE drives and will autoconfigure the drive parameters.

A unique feature of some of the AMI BIOS versions was that in addition to the setup, they had a built-in, menu-driven diagnostics package, essentially a very limited version of the standalone AMIDIAG product. The internal diagnostics are not a replacement for more comprehensive disk-based programs, but they can help in a pinch. The menu-driven diagnostics do not do extensive memory testing, for example, and the hard disk low-level formatter works only at the BIOS level rather than at the controller register level. These limitations often have prevented it from being capable of formatting severely damaged disks. Most newer AMI BIOS versions no longer include the full diagnostics.

AMI doesn't produce BIOS documentation; it leaves that up to the motherboard manufacturers who include their BIOS on the motherboard. However, AMI has published a detailed version of its documentation called the *Programmer's Guide to the AMIBIOS*, published by Windcrest/McGraw-Hill and available under the ISBN 0-07-001561-9. This is a book written by AMI engineers that describes all the BIOS functions, features, error codes, and more. I recommend this book for users with an AMI BIOS in their system because this provides a complete version of the documentation for which they may have been looking.

The AMI BIOS is sold through distributors, a list of which is available at its Web site. However, keep in mind that you cannot buy upgrades and replacements directly from AMI, and AMI produces upgrades only for its own motherboards. If you have a non-AMI motherboard with a customized AMI BIOS, you will have to contact the motherboard manufacturer for an upgrade.

Award

Award is unique among BIOS manufacturers because it sells its BIOS code to the OEM and allows the OEM to customize the BIOS. Of course, then the BIOS no longer is Award BIOS, but rather a highly customized version. AST uses this approach on its systems, as do other manufacturers, for total control over the BIOS code without having to write it from scratch. Although AMI and Phoenix customize the ROM code for a particular system, they do not sell the ROM's source code to the OEM. Some OEMs that seem to have developed their own ROM code started with a base of source code licensed to them by Award or some other company.

The Award BIOS has all the normal features you expect, including a built-in setup program activated by pressing Ctrl+Alt+Esc or a particular key on startup (normally prompted on the screen). This setup offers user-definable drive types, required to fully use IDE or ESDI hard disks. The POST is good, and Award runs technical support on its Web site at http://www.award.com.

Award was purchased by Phoenix in late 1998, and in the future, its BIOS will be available under the Phoenix name. However, it will continue to support its past BIOS versions and develop updates if necessary.

Phoenix

The Phoenix BIOS for many years has been a standard of compatibility by which others are judged. It was one of the first third-party companies to legally reverse-engineer the IBM BIOS using a "clean room" approach. In this approach, a group of engineers studied the IBM BIOS and wrote a specification for how that BIOS should work and what features should be incorporated. This information then was passed to a second group of engineers who had never seen the IBM BIOS. They could then legally write a new BIOS to the specifications set forth by the first group. This work would then be unique and not a copy of IBM's BIOS; however, it would function the same way.

The Phoenix BIOS excels in two areas that put it high on my list of recommendations. One is that the POST is excellent. The BIOS outputs an extensive set of beep codes that can be used to diagnose severe motherboard problems that would prevent normal operation of the system. In fact, with beep codes alone, this POST can isolate memory failures in Bank 0 right down to the individual SIMM or DIMM module. The Phoenix BIOS also has an excellent setup program free from unnecessary frills, but one that offers all the features the user would expect, such as user-definable drive types, and so on. The built-in setup is activated by pressing Ctrl+Alt+S, Ctrl+Alt+Esc, or a particular key on startup, such as F2 on most newer systems, depending on the version of BIOS you have.

The second area in which Phoenix excels is the documentation. Not only are the manuals that you get with the system detailed, but Phoenix has also written a set of BIOS technical-reference manuals that are a standard in the industry. The set consists of three books, titled *System BIOS for IBM PC/XT/AT Computers and Compatibles*, *CBIOS for IBM PS/2 Computers and Compatibles*, and *ABIOS for IBM PS/2 Computers and Compatibles*. In addition to being an excellent reference for the Phoenix BIOS, these books serve as an outstanding overall reference to the BIOS in general.

Phoenix has extensive technical support and documentation on its Web site at http://www.phoenix.com, as does its largest nationwide distributor, Micro Firmware, Inc. at http://www.firmware.com, or check the phone numbers listed in the Vendor list on the CD. Micro Firmware offers upgrades to some older systems with a Phoenix BIOS, including many Packard Bell, Gateway 2000 (with Micronics motherboards), Micron Technologies, and other systems. For most systems, especially newer ones, you will need to get any BIOS updates from the system or motherboard manufacturer.

These companies' products are established as ROM BIOS standards in the industry, and frequent updates and improvements ensure that a system containing these ROMs will have a long life of upgrades and service.

Microid Research (MR) BIOS

Microid Research is an interesting BIOS supplier. It primarily markets upgrade BIOSes for older Pentium and 486 motherboards that were abandoned by their original manufacturers. As such, it is an excellent upgrade for adding new features and performance to an older system. Microid Research BIOS upgrades are sold through Unicore Software.

Upgrading the BIOS

In this section, you learn that ROM BIOS upgrades can improve a system in many ways. You also learn that the upgrades can be difficult and may require much more than plugging in a generic set of ROM chips.

The ROM BIOS, or read-only memory basic input/output system, provides the crude brains that get your computer's components working together. A simple BIOS upgrade can often give your computer better performance and more features.

The BIOS is the reason that different operating systems can operate on virtually any PC-compatible system despite hardware differences. Because the BIOS communicates with the hardware, the BIOS must be specific to the hardware and match it completely. Instead of creating their own BIOSes, many computer makers buy a BIOS from specialists such as American Megatrends, Inc. (AMI), Award Software (now part of Phoenix), Microid Research, or Phoenix Technologies Ltd. A motherboard manufacturer that wants to license a BIOS must undergo a lengthy process of working with the BIOS company to tailor the BIOS code to the hardware. This process is what makes upgrading a BIOS somewhat problematic; the BIOS usually resides on ROM chips on the motherboard and is specific to that motherboard model or revision. In other words, you must get your BIOS upgrades from your motherboard manufacturer.

Often, in older systems, you must upgrade the BIOS to take advantage of some other upgrade. To install some of the larger and faster IDE (Integrated Drive Electronics) hard drives and LS-120 (120MB) floppy drives in older machines, for example, you may need a BIOS upgrade. Some machines are still being sold with older BIOSes that do not support hard drives larger than 8GB, for example.

The following list shows the primary functions of a ROM BIOS upgrade:

- Adding LS-120 (120MB) floppy drive support (also known as a SuperDrive)
- Adding support for hard drives greater than 8GB
- Adding support for Ultra-DMA/33 IDE hard drives
- Adding support for bootable ATAPI CD-ROM drives
- Adding or improving Plug-and-Play support and compatibility
- Correcting year-2000 and leap-year bugs
- Correcting known bugs or compatibility problems with certain hardware and software
- Adding support for newer types of processors

If you are installing newer hardware or software, and even though you follow all the instructions properly, you can't get it to work, specific problems may exist with the BIOS that an upgrade might fix. This is especially true for newer operating systems. Many systems need to have a BIOS update to properly work with the plug-and-play features of Windows 95 and 98, and the same is true for Windows 2000. Because these things are random and vary from board to board, it pays to periodically check the board manufacturer's Web site to see if any updates are posted and what problems they will fix.

Where to Get Your BIOS Update

For most BIOS upgrades, you must contact the motherboard manufacturer by phone or download the upgrade from its Web site. The BIOS manufacturers do not offer BIOS upgrades because the BIOS in your motherboard did not actually come from them. In other words, although you think you have a Phoenix, AMI, or Award BIOS, you really don't! Instead, you have a custom version of one of these BIOSes, which was licensed by your motherboard manufacturer and uniquely customized for its board. As such, you must get any BIOS upgrades from the motherboard manufacturer because they must be customized for your board as well.

In the case of Phoenix or Award, another option may exist. A company called Unicore specializes in providing Award BIOS upgrades. Unicore may be able to help you out if you can't find your motherboard manufacturer or if it is out of business. Phoenix has a similar deal with MicroFirmware, a company it has licensed to provide various BIOS upgrades. If you have a Phoenix or an Award BIOS and your motherboard manufacture can't help you, contact one of these companies for a possible solution. Microid Research (sold through Unicore) is another source of BIOS upgrades for a variety of older and otherwise obsolete boards. They are available for boards that originally came with AMI, Award, or Phoenix BIOSes, and they add new features to older boards that have been abandoned by their original manufacturers. Contact them or Unicore for more information.

When seeking a BIOS upgrade for a particular motherboard (or system), you will need to know the following information:

- The make and model of the motherboard (or system)
- The version of the existing BIOS
- The type of CPU (for example, Pentium MMX, AMD K6, Cyrix/IBM 6x86MX, MII, Pentium II, and so on)

You can usually identify the BIOS you have by watching the screen when the system is first powered up. It helps to turn the monitor on first because some take a few seconds to warm up, and often the BIOS information is displayed for only a few seconds.

Tip

Look for any copyright notices or part number information. Sometimes you can press the Pause key on the keyboard to freeze the POST, allowing you to take your time to write down the information. Pressing any other key will then cause the POST to resume.

You can also often find the BIOS ID information in the BIOS Setup screens.

After you have this information, you should be able to contact the motherboard manufacturer to see whether a new BIOS is available for your system. If you go to the Web site, check to see whether a version exists that is newer than the one you have. If so, you can download it and install it in your system.

Determining Your BIOS Version

Most BIOSes display version information on the screen when the system is first powered up. In some cases the monitor takes too long to warm up, and you may miss this information because it is only displayed for a few seconds. Try turning your monitor on first, and then your system, which will make it easier to see. You can usually press the Pause key on the keyboard when the BIOS ID information is being displayed; this freezes it so you can record the information. Pressing any other key will allow the system startup to resume.

Backing Up Your BIOS's CMOS Settings

A motherboard BIOS upgrade will usually wipe out the BIOS Setup settings in the CMOS RAM. Therefore, you should record these settings, especially the important ones such as hard disk parameters. Some software programs, such as the Norton Utilities, can save and restore CMOS settings, but unfortunately, these types of programs are often useless in a BIOS upgrade situation. This is because sometimes the new BIOS will offer new settings or change the positions of the stored data in the CMOS RAM, which means you don't want to do an exact restore. Also with the variety of different BIOSes out there, I have yet to find a CMOS RAM backup and restore program that worked on more than just a few specific systems.

You are better off manually recording your BIOS Setup parameters, or possibly connecting a printer to your system and using the Shift+Prtsc (Print Screen) function to print out each of the setup screens. Some shareware programs could print or even save and restore the BIOS Setup settings stored in the CMOS RAM, but these were BIOS version specific and would not work on any system. Most of these programs were useful during the 286-386 era, but the increasing variety of newer systems, especially those with Plug-and-Play capabilities, have rendered most of these older programs useless.

Keyboard-Controller Chips

In addition to the main system ROM, older AT-class (286 and later) computers also have a keyboard controller or keyboard ROM, which is a keyboard-controller microprocessor with its own built-in ROM. This is often found in the Super I/O or South Bridge chips on most newer boards. The keyboard controller was originally an Intel 8042 microcontroller, which incorporates a microprocessor, RAM, ROM, and I/O ports. This was a 40-pin chip that often had a copyright notice identifying the BIOS code programmed into the chip. Modern motherboards have this function integrated into the chipset, specifically the Super I/O or South Bridge chips, so you won't see the old 8042 chip anymore.

The keyboard controller controls the reset and A20 lines and also deciphers the keyboard scan codes. The A20 line is used in extended memory and other protected-mode operations. In many systems, one of the unused ports is used to select the CPU clock speed. Because of the tie-in with the keyboard controller and protected-mode operation, many problems with keyboard controllers became evident on these older systems when upgrading from DOS to Windows 95/98, NT, or Windows 2000.

Problems with the keyboard controller were solved in most systems in the early 1990s, so you shouldn't have to deal with this issue in systems newer than that. With older systems, when you upgraded the BIOS in the system, the BIOS vendor often included a new keyboard controller.

Using a Flash BIOS

Virtually all PCs built since 1996 include a flash ROM to store the BIOS. A flash ROM is a type of EEPROM (Electrically Erasable Programmable Read-Only Memory) chip that you can erase and reprogram directly in the system without special equipment. Older EPROMs required a special ultraviolet light source and an EPROM programmer device to erase and reprogram them, whereas flash ROMs can be erased and rewritten without even removing them from the system.

Using flash ROM enables a user to download ROM upgrades from a Web site or to receive them on disk; you then can load the upgrade into the flash ROM chip on the motherboard without removing and replacing the chip. Normally, these upgrades are downloaded from the manufacturer's Web site, and then an included utility is used to create a bootable floppy with the new BIOS image and the update program. It is important to run this procedure from a boot floppy so that no other software or drivers are in the way that might interfere with the update. This method saves time and money for both the system manufacturer and the end user.

Sometimes the flash ROM in a system is write-protected, and you must disable the protection before performing an update, usually by means of a jumper or switch that controls the lock on the ROM update. Without the lock, any program that knows the right instructions can rewrite the ROM in your system—not a comforting thought. Without the write-protection, it is conceivable that virus programs could be written that copy themselves directly into the ROM BIOS code in your system. Even without a physical write-protect lock, modern flash ROM BIOSes have a security algorithm that helps to prevent unauthorized updates. This is the technique that Intel uses on its motherboards.

Note that motherboard manufacturers will not notify you when they upgrade the BIOS for a particular board. You must periodically log in to their Web sites to check for updates. Normally, any flash updates are free.

Before proceeding with a BIOS upgrade, you must first locate and download the updated BIOS from your motherboard manufacturer. Consult the Vendor List on the CD to find the Web site address or other contact information for your motherboard manufacturer. Log in to their Web site and follow the menus to the BIOS updates page, and then select and download the new BIOS for your motherboard.

The BIOS upgrade utility is contained in a self-extracting archive file that can initially be downloaded to your hard drive, but it must be extracted and copied to a floppy before the upgrade can proceed. Different motherboard manufacturers have slightly different procedures and programs to accomplish a flash ROM upgrade, so it is best if you read the directions usually included with the update. I include instructions here for Intel motherboards because they are by far the most common.

The Intel BIOS upgrade utility will fit on a floppy disk and provides the capability to save, verify, and update the system BIOS. The upgrade utility also provides the capability to install alternative languages for BIOS messages and the SETUP utility.

The first step in the upgrade after downloading the new BIOS file is to enter the CMOS setup and write down your existing CMOS settings because they will be erased during the upgrade. Then you create a DOS boot floppy and uncompress or extract the BIOS upgrade files to the floppy from the file you downloaded. Then you reboot on the newly created upgrade disk and follow the menus for the actual reflash procedure.

Here is a step-by-step procedure for the process:

1. Save your CMOS RAM setup configuration. You can do so by pressing the appropriate key during boot (F1 with an AMI BIOS, F2 with a Phoenix BIOS) and write down all your current CMOS settings. You may also be able to print the screens if you have a printer connected, using the PrtSc key on the keyboard. You will need to reset these settings after you have upgraded to the latest BIOS. Write down all settings that are unique to the system. These settings will be needed later to reconfigure the system. Pay special attention to any hard drive settings; these are very important. If you fail to restore these properly, you may not be able to boot from the drive or access the data on it.

2. Exit the BIOS Setup and restart the system. Allow the system to fully start Windows and bring up a DOS prompt window or boot directly to a DOS prompt via the Windows Start menu (for example, press F8 when you see "Starting Windows," and select Command Prompt).

3. Place a floppy disk in the A: floppy drive and format the floppy using the /S option on the FORMAT command as follows:

   ```
   C:\>FORMAT A: /S
   ```

4. Alternatively, if you have an otherwise blank preformatted floppy in the floppy drive, use the SYS command to make it bootable as follows:

   ```
   C:\>SYS A:
   ```

5. The file you originally downloaded from the Intel Web site is a self-extracting compressed archive that includes other files that need to be extracted. Put the file in a temporary directory, then from within this directory, double-click the BIOS file you downloaded or type the file name of the file and press Enter. This causes the file to self-extract. For example, if the file you downloaded was called SEBIOS04.EXE (for the Intel SE440BX motherboard), you would enter the following command:

   ```
   C:\TEMP>SEBIOS04 <enter>
   ```

6. The extracted files resulting from this should contain a file named BIOS.EXE and a software license text file. You then do another extract on the BIOS.EXE file to the bootable floppy you created using the following command:

   ```
   C:\TEMP>BIOS A:
   ```

7. Now you can restart the system with the bootable floppy in drive A: containing the new BIOS files you just extracted. Upon booting from this disk, the IFLASH program will automatically start; press Enter when prompted.

8. Highlight Save Flash Memory Area to a File and press Enter. Follow the prompts to enter a filename. This creates a backup of your existing BIOS, which will be valuable should the new BIOS cause unexpected problems.

9. Highlight Update Flash Memory From a File and press Enter. Follow the prompts to select the name of the BIOS image file you will use to update the flash ROM. Press the Tab key to highlight the filename, and press Enter.

10. The system now gives a warning stating that continuing will destroy the current contents of the flash memory area. Press Enter to continue—the update should take about three minutes. Do not interrupt this procedure or the flash BIOS will be corrupted.

11. When you're told that the BIOS has been successfully loaded, remove the bootable floppy from the drive and press Enter to reboot the system.

12. Press F1 or F2 to enter Setup. On the first screen within SETUP, check the BIOS version to ensure that it is the new version.

13. In Setup, load the default values. If you have an AMI BIOS, press the F5 key; with a Phoenix BIOS, go to the Exit submenu and highlight Load Setup Defaults, and then press Enter.

Caution

If you do not set the values back to default, the system may function erratically.

14. If the system had unique settings, re-enter those settings now. Press F10 to save the values, exit Setup, and restart the system. Your system should now be fully functional with the new BIOS.

Note

If you encounter a CMOS checksum error or other problems after rebooting, try rebooting the system again. CMOS checksum errors require that you enter Setup, check and save your settings, and exit Setup a second time.

Flash BIOS Recovery

When you performed the flash reprogramming, you should have seen a warning message on the screen similar to the following:

> The BIOS is currently being updated. DO NOT REBOOT OR POWER DOWN until the update is completed (typically within three minutes)...

If you fail to heed this warning or something interrupts the update procedure, you will be left with a system that has a corrupted BIOS. This means you will not be able to restart the system and redo the procedure, at least not easily. Depending on the motherboard, you may have to replace the flash ROM chip with one that was preprogrammed by the motherboard manufacturer because your board will be nonfunctional until a noncorrupted ROM is present. This is why I still keep my trusty ROM burner around; it is very useful for those motherboards with socketed flash ROM chips. In minutes, I can use the ROM burner to reprogram the chip and reinstall it in the board. If you need a ROM programmer, I recommend either Andromeda Research or Bytek (see the Vendor List on the CD).

In most systems today, the flash ROM is soldered into the motherboard so it cannot be replaced, rendering the reprogramming idea moot. However, this doesn't mean that the only way out is a complete motherboard replacement. Most motherboards with soldered-in flash ROMs have a special BIOS Recovery procedure that can be performed. This hinges on a special unerasable part of the flash ROM that is reserved for this purpose.

In the unlikely event that a flash upgrade is interrupted catastrophically, the BIOS may be left in an unusable state. Recovering from this condition requires the following steps. A minimum of a power supply, a speaker, and a floppy drive configured as drive A: should be attached to the motherboard for this procedure to work.

1. Change the Flash Recovery jumper to the recovery mode position. Virtually all Intel motherboards and many third-party motherboards have a jumper or switch for BIOS recovery, which is normally labeled "Recover/Normal." Figure 5.5 shows this jumper on the Intel SE440BX, a typical motherboard.

2. Install the bootable BIOS upgrade disk you previously created to do the flash upgrade into drive A: and reboot the system.

Because of the small amount of code available in the nonerasable flash boot block area, no video prompts are available to direct the procedure. In other words, you will see nothing on the screen. In fact, it is not even necessary for a video card to be connected for this procedure to work. The procedure can be monitored by listening to the speaker and look-ing at the floppy drive LED. When the system beeps and the floppy drive LED is lit, the sys-tem is copying the BIOS recovery code into the flash device.

3. As soon as the drive LED goes off, the recovery should be complete. Power the system off.

4. Change the flash recovery jumper back to the default position for normal operation.

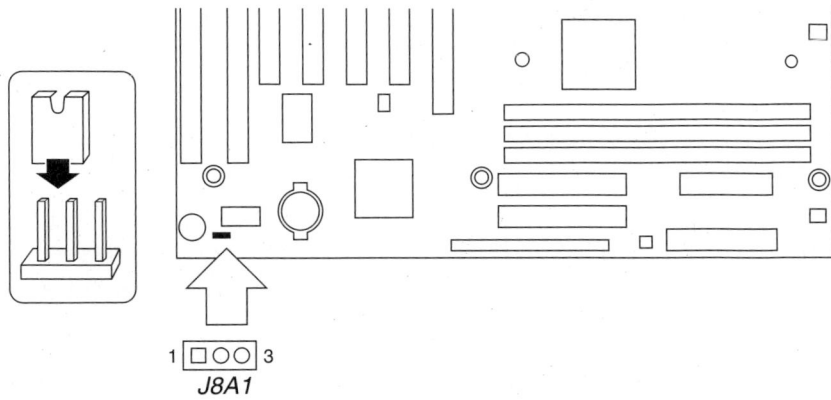

1 □○○ 3
J8A1

Figure 5.5   Typical Intel motherboard BIOS recovery jumper.

When you power the system back on, the new BIOS should be installed and functional. However, you might want to leave the BIOS upgrade floppy in drive A: and check to see that the proper BIOS version was installed.

Note

Note that this BIOS recovery procedure is often the fastest way to update a large number of machines, especially if you are performing other upgrades at the same time. This is how it is normally done in a system assembly or production environment.

Using IML System Partition BIOS

IBM and Compaq used a scheme similar to a flash ROM, called Initial Microcode Load (IML), in some of their older Pentium and 486 systems. IML is a technique in which the BIOS code is installed on the hard disk in a special hidden-system partition and is loaded every time the system is powered up. Of course, the system still has a core BIOS on the motherboard, but all that BIOS does is locate and load updated BIOS code from the system partition. This technique enabled Compaq and IBM to distribute ROM updates on disk for installation in the system parti-tion. The IML BIOS is loaded every time the system is reset or powered on.

Along with the system BIOS code, the system partition contains a complete copy of the Setup and Diagnostics or Reference Disk, which provides the option of running the setup and system-configuration software at any time during a reboot operation. This option eliminates the need to boot from this disk to reconfigure the system and gives the impression that the entire Setup and Diagnostics or Reference Disk is contained in ROM.

One drawback to this technique is that the BIOS code is installed on the hard disk; the system cannot function properly without the correctly set-up hard disk connected. You always can boot from the Reference Disk floppy should the hard disk fail or become disconnected, but you cannot boot from a standard floppy disk.

Caution

This scheme makes hard drive updates problematic and causes all kinds of support nightmares. I recommend avoiding any system with an IML BIOS, especially if you are buying it used, because support for these types of configurations is hard to come by and not many people know how to deal with them.

Motherboard CMOS RAM Addresses

In the original AT system, a Motorola 146818 chip was used as the RTC (real-time clock) and CMOS (complementary metal-oxide semiconductor) RAM chip. This is a special chip that had a simple digital clock that used 10 bytes of RAM and an additional 54 more bytes of leftover RAM in which you could store anything you wanted. The designers of the IBM AT used these extra 54 bytes to store the system configuration.

Modern PC systems don't use the Motorola chip; instead, they incorporate the functions of this chip into the motherboard chipset (South Bridge) or Super I/O chip, or they use a special battery and NVRAM (nonvolatile RAM) module from companies such as Dallas or Benchmarq.

Table 5.6 shows the standard format of the information stored in the 64-byte standard CMOS RAM module. This information controls the configuration of the system and is read and written by the system setup program.

Table 5.6 AT CMOS RAM Addresses

Offset Hex	Offset Dec	Field Size	Function
00h	0	1 byte	Current second in binary coded decimal (BCD)
01h	1	1 byte	Alarm second in BCD
02h	2	1 byte	Current minute in BCD
03h	3	1 byte	Alarm minute in BCD
04h	4	1 byte	Current hour in BCD
05h	5	1 byte	Alarm hour in BCD
06h	6	1 byte	Current day of week in BCD
07h	7	1 byte	Current day in BCD
08h	8	1 byte	Current month in BCD
09h	9	1 byte	Current year in BCD
0Ah	10	1 byte	Status register A Bit 7 = Update in progress 0 = Date and time can be read 1 = Time update in progress Bits 6-4 = Time frequency divider 010 = 32.768KHz Bits 3–0 = Rate selection frequency 0110 = 1.024KHz square wave frequency

(continues)

Table 5.6   Continued

Offset Hex	Offset Dec	Field Size	Function

0Bh	11	1 byte	Status register B
			Bit 7 = Clock update cycle
			    0 = Update normally
			    1 = Abort update in progress
			Bit 6 = Periodic interrupt
			    0 = Disable interrupt (default)
			    1 = Enable interrupt
			Bit 5 = Alarm interrupt
			    0 = Disable interrupt (default)
			    0 = Disable interrupt (default)
			    1 = Enable interrupt
			Bit 4 = Update-ended interrupt
			    0 = Disable interrupt (default)
			    1 = Enable interrupt
			Bit 3 = Status register A square wave frequency
			    0 = Disable square wave (default)
			    1 = Enable square wave
			Bit 2 = Date format
			    0 = Calendar in BCD format (default)
			    1 = Calendar in binary format
			Bit 1 = 24-hour clock
			    0 = 24-hour mode (default)
			    1 = 12-hour mode
			Bit 0 = Daylight Savings Time
			    0 = Disable Daylight Savings (default)
			    1 = Enable Daylight Savings

0Ch	12	1 byte	Status register C Bit 7 = IRQF flag Bit 6 = PF Bit 5 = AF flag Bit 4 = UF flag Bits 3–0 = Reserved

0Dh	13	1 byte	Status register D
			Bit 7 = Valid CMOS RAM bit
			    0 = CMOS battery dead
			    1 = CMOS battery power good
			Bits 6–0 = Reserved

0Eh	14	1 byte	Diagnostic status
			Bit 7 = Real-time clock power status
			    0 = CMOS has not lost power
			    1 = CMOS has lost power
			Bit 6 = CMOS checksum status
			    0 = Checksum is good
			    1 = Checksum is bad
			Bit 5 = POST configuration information status
			    0 = Configuration information is valid
			    1 = Configuration information is invalid
			Bit 4 = Memory size compare during POST
			    0 = POST memory equals configuration
			    1 = POST memory not equal to configuration
			Bit 3 = Fixed disk/adapter initialization
			    0 = Initialization good
			    1 = Initialization failed
			Bit 2 = CMOS time status indicator
			    0 = Time is valid
			    1 = Time is invalid
			Bits 1-0 = Reserved

Offset Hex	Offset Dec	Field Size	Function
0Fh	15	1 byte	Shutdown code 00h = Power on or soft reset 01h = Memory size pass 02h = Memory test past 03h = Memory test fail 04h = POST end; boot system 05h = JMP double word pointer with EOI 06h = Protected mode tests pass 07h = Protected mode tests fail 07h = Protected mode tests fail 08h = Memory size fail 09h = Int 15h block move 0Ah = JMP double word pointer without EOI 0Bh = used by 80386

10h	16	1 byte	Floppy disk drive types
			Bits 7–4 = Drive 0 type
			Bits 3–0 = Drive 1 type
			    0000 = None
			    0001 = 360KB
			    0010 = 1.2MB
			    0011 = 720KB
			    0100 = 1.44MB

11h	17	1 byte	Reserved
12h	18	1 byte	Hard disk types Bits 7–4 = Hard disk 0 type (0–15) Bits 3–0 = Hard disk 1 type (0–15)
13h	19	1 byte	Reserved

14h	20	1 byte	Installed equipment
			Bits 7–6 = Number of floppy disk drives
			    00 = 1 floppy disk drive
			    01 = 2 floppy disk drives
			Bits 5–4 = Primary display
			    00 = Use display adapter BIOS
			    01 = CGA 40-column
			    10 = CGA 80-column
			    11 = Monochrome Display Adapter
			Bits 3–2 = Reserved
			Bit 1 = Math coprocessor present
			Bit 0 = Floppy disk drive present

15h	21	1 byte	Base memory low-order byte
16h	22	1 byte	Base memory high-order byte
17h	23	1 byte	Extended memory low-order byte
18h	24	1 byte	Extended memory high-order byte
19h	25	1 byte	Hard Disk 0 Extended Type (0–255)
1Ah	26	1 byte	Hard Disk 1 Extended Type (0–255)
1Bh	27	9 bytes	Reserved
2Eh	46	1 byte	CMOS checksum high-order byte
2Fh	47	1 byte	CMOS checksum low-order byte
30h	48	1 byte	Actual extended memory low-order byte
31h	49	1 byte	Actual extended memory high-order byte
32h	50	1 byte	Date century in BCD

(continues)

Table 5.6   Continued

Offset Hex	Offset Dec	Field Size	Function

33h	51	1 byte	POST information flag
			    Bit 7 = Top 128KB base memory status
			        0 = Top 128KB base memory not installed
			        1 = Top 128KB base memory installed
			    Bit 6 = Setup program flag
			        0 = Normal (default)
			        1 = Put out first user message
			    Bits 5–0 = Reserved

34h	52	2 bytes	Reserved

Note that many newer systems have more than 64 bytes of CMOS RAM; in fact, in some systems they may have 2KB or 4KB. The extra room is used to store the Plug-and-Play information detailing the configuration of adapter cards and other options in the system. As such, no 100% standard exists for how CMOS information is stored in all systems. Table 5.6 shows only how the original systems did it; newer BIOS versions and motherboard designs can do things differently. You should consult the BIOS manufacturer for more information if you want the full details of how CMOS is stored as the CMOS configuration and the setup program is normally a part of the BIOS. This is another example of how close the relationship is between the BIOS and the motherboard hardware.

Backup programs and utilities are in the public domain for CMOS RAM information, which can be useful for saving and later restoring a configuration. Unfortunately, these programs are BIOS specific and would only function on a BIOS for which they are designed. As such, I don't normally rely on these programs because they are too motherboard- and BIOS-specific and will not work seamlessly on all my systems.

Table 5.7 shows the values that may be stored by your system BIOS in a special CMOS byte called the diagnostics status byte. By examining this location with a diagnostics program, you can determine whether your system has set trouble codes, which indicate that a problem previously has occurred.

Table 5.7   CMOS RAM Diagnostic Status Byte Codes

| Bit Number | | | | | | | | Hex | Function |
7	6	5	4	3	2	1	0		
1	•	•	•	•	•	•	•	80	Real-time clock (RTC) chip lost power
•	1	•	•	•	•	•	•	40	CMOS RAM checksum is bad
•	•	1	•	•	•	•	•	20	Invalid configuration information found at POST
•	•	•	1	•	•	•	•	10	Memory size compare error at POST
•	•	•	•	1	•	•	•	08	Fixed disk or adapter failed initialization
•	•	•	•	•	1	•	•	04	Real-time clock (RTC) time found invalid
•	•	•	•	•	•	1	•	02	Adapters do not match configuration
•	•	•	•	•	•	•	1	01	Time-out reading an adapter ID
•	•	•	•	•	•	•	•	00	No errors found (Normal)

If the Diagnostic status byte is any value other than zero, you will normally get a CMOS configuration error on bootup. These types of errors can be cleared by rerunning the setup program.

Replacing a BIOS ROM

Systems dating from 1995 or earlier usually won't have a flash ROM and instead will use an EPROM. To upgrade the BIOS in one of these systems is to replace the EPROM chip with a new one preloaded with the new BIOS. As with a flash ROM upgrade, you must get this from your motherboard manufacturer. There is usually a fee for this because they will have to custom burn a chip just for you and mail it out. Most boards older than 1995 are probably not worth upgrading the BIOS on, so weigh this option carefully! It doesn't make sense to spend $50 on a new BIOS for an ancient board when a new Pentium or Pentium II board can be had for $75, and that new board will include a flash BIOS and many other new features.

To replace the BIOS chip, follow these steps:

1. Back up the CMOS RAM settings.

2. Power the system down and unplug the power cord.

3. Remove the cover and any other components in the way of the BIOS EPROM chip. Remember to use caution with respect to static discharges; it is a good idea to wear an antistatic wrist strap for this procedure, or ground yourself to the chassis before touching any internal components.

4. Using a chip puller or a thin flat-blade screwdriver, gently pry the chip out of its socket.

5. Remove the new EPROM from the anti-static packing material it came in.

6. Install the new EPROM chip into the socket.

7. Reinstall anything you removed to gain access to the chip.

8. Put the cover back on, plug the system in, and power on.

9. Enter the BIOS setup information you saved earlier.

10. Reboot and enjoy the new BIOS!

As you can see, things are much easier with a modern motherboard with a flash ROM because normally you don't even have to remove the lid.

CMOS Setting Specifications

Running or Accessing the CMOS Setup Program

If you want to run the BIOS Setup program, you usually have to reboot and press a particular key or key combination during the POST. The major vendors have standardized the following keystrokes to enter the BIOS Setup:

- *AMI BIOS.* Press Delete during POST.
- *Phoenix BIOS.* Press F2 during POST.
- *Award BIOS.* Press Delete or Ctrl+Alt+Esc during POST.
- *Microid Research BIOS.* Press Esc during POST.

If your system will not respond to one of these common keystroke settings, you may have to contact the manufacturer or read the system documentation to find the correct keystrokes.

Some unique ones are as follows:

- *IBM Aptiva/Valuepoint.* Press F1 during POST.
- *Older Phoenix BIOS.* Boot to a safe mode DOS command prompt, and then press Ctrl+Alt+Esc or Ctrl+Alt+S.
- *Compaq.* Press F10 during POST.

After you are in the BIOS Setup main screen, you'll usually find a main menu allowing access to other menus and submenus of different sections or screens. Using the Intel SE440BX-2 motherboard as an example (one of the most popular motherboards in the world) we will go through all the menus and submenus of this typical motherboard. Although other motherboards may feature slightly different settings, most will be very similar.

BIOS Setup Menus

Most modern BIOSes offer a menu bar at the top of the screen when you're in the BIOS Setup that controls navigation through the various primary menus. A typical menu bar offers the choices shown in Table 5.8.

Note

Because most common BIOSes use similar settings, I've chosen the Phoenix BIOS—used by all modern Intel motherboards—to use as an example in the following tables. If your machine uses another BIOS—AMI, Award, or a proprietary BIOS—these settings will be different. These settings will, however, help you get a general idea of the type of settings to expect and how the BIOS Setup settings affect your computer.

Table 5.8   Typical BIOS Setup Menus*

Setup Menu Screen	Description
Maintenance	Specifies the processor speed and clears the setup passwords. This menu is only available in Configure mode, set by a jumper on the board.
Main	Allocates resources for hardware components.
Advanced	Specifies advanced features available through the chipset.
Security	Specifies passwords and security features.
Power	Specifies power management features.
Boot	Specifies boot options and power supply controls.
Exit	Saves or discards changes to the setup program options.

*Based on the Phoenix BIOS used by the Intel SE440BX-2 motherboard. Used by permission of Intel Corporation.

Choosing each of these selections takes you to another menu with more choices. We'll examine all the choices available in a typical motherboard, such as the Intel SE440BX-2.

Maintenance Menu

The Maintenance menu is a special menu for setting the processor speed and clearing the setup passwords. Older motherboards used jumpers to configure the processor bus speed (motherboard speed) and processor multiplier. Most newer boards from Intel and others now offer this control via the BIOS Setup rather than moving jumpers. In the case of Intel, one jumper still remains on the board called the configuration jumper, which must be set to Configure mode for the Maintenance menu to be available.

Setup displays this menu only if the system is set in Configure mode. To set Configure mode, power the system off and move the configuration jumper on the motherboard from *Normal* to *Configure* (see Figure 5.5 earlier in this chapter). Because this is the only jumper on a modern Intel board, it is pretty easy to find. When the system is powered back on, the BIOS Setup automatically runs, and you will be able to select the Maintenance menu shown in Table 5.9. After making changes and saving, power the system off and reset the jumper to Normal mode for normal operation.

Table 5.9   Typical Maintenance Menu Settings*

Feature	Options	Description
Processor Speed	233 266 300 333 350 400 450 500 550	Specifies the processor speed in megahertz. This setup screen shows only speeds up to and including the maximum speed of the processor installed on the motherboard.
Clear All Passwords	No options	Clears the user and supervisor passwords.

Based on the Phoenix BIOS used by the Intel SE440BX-2 motherboard. Used by permission of Intel Corporation.

Note that most newer Intel processors are designed to allow operation only at or below their rated speed, whereas others allow higher-than-rated speeds to be selected.

If users forget their password, all they have to do is set the configuration jumper, enter the Maintenance menu in BIOS Setup, and use the option provided to clear the password. This function will not tell the user what the password was; it will simply clear it, allowing a new one to be set if desired. This means the security is only as good as the lock on the system case because anybody who can get to the configuration jumper can clear the password and access the system. This is why most better cases come equipped with locks.

Main Menu

The standard CMOS Setup menu dates back to the 286 days, when the complete BIOS Setup consisted of only one menu. In the standard menu you can set the system clock, record hard disk and floppy drive parameters and the basic video type. Newer BIOSes have more complicated setups with more menus and submenus, so the main menu often is fairly sparse compared to older systems.

Security Menu

Most BIOSes include two passwords for security, called the Supervisor and User passwords. These passwords help control who is allowed to access the BIOS Setup program and who is allowed to boot the computer. The supervisor password is also called a setup password because it controls access to the setup program. The user password is also called a system password because it controls access to the entire system.

If a supervisor password is set, a password prompt is displayed when an attempt is made to enter the BIOS Setup menus. When entered correctly, the supervisor password gives unrestricted access to view and change all the Setup options in the Setup program. If the supervisor password is not entered or is entered incorrectly, access to view and change Setup options in the Setup program will be restricted.

If the user password is set, the password prompt is displayed before the computer boots up. The password must be entered correctly before the system is allowed to boot. Note that if only the supervisor password is set, the computer boots without asking for a password because the supervisor password controls access only to the BIOS Setup menus. If both passwords are set, the password prompt is displayed at boot time, and either the user or the supervisor password can be entered to boot the computer. In most systems, the password can be up to seven or eight characters in length.

If you forget the password, most systems have a jumper on the board which allows all passwords to be cleared. This means that for most systems, the password security also requires that the system case be locked to prevent users from opening the cover and accessing the password-clear jumper. This jumper is often not labeled on the board for security reasons, but it can be found in the motherboard or system documentation.

Note that provided you know the password and can get into the BIOS Setup, a password can also be cleared by entering the BIOS Setup and selecting the Clear Password function. If there is no Clear function, you can still clear the password by selecting the Set Password function and pressing Enter (for no password) at the prompts.

Table 5.21 shows the security functions in a typical BIOS Setup.

Table 5.21   Typical Security Settings*

Feature	Options	Description
User Password Is	No options	Reports if there is a user password set.
Supervisor Password Is	No options	Reports if there is a supervisor password set.
Set User Password	Password can be up to seven alphanumeric characters.	Specifies the user password.
Set Supervisor Password	Password can be up to seven alphanumeric characters.	Specifies the supervisor password.
Clear User Password	No Options	Clears the user password.

Feature	Options	Description
User Setup Access	None View Only Limited Access Full Access (default)	Controls the user's capability to run the BIOS Setup program.
Unattended Start	Disabled (default) Enabled	Enables the unattended start feature. When enabled, the computer boots, but the keyboard is locked. The user must enter a password to unlock the computer or boot from a diskette.

*Based on the Phoenix BIOS used by the Intel SE440BX-2 motherboard. Used by permission of Intel Corporation.

To clear passwords if the password is forgotten, most motherboards will have a password-clear jumper or switch. Intel motherboards require that you set the configuration jumper, enter the Maintenance menu in BIOS Setup, and select the Clear Password feature there. If you can't find the documentation for your board and aren't sure how to clear the passwords, you can try removing the battery for 15 minutes or so, which will clear the CMOS RAM. It can take that long for the CMOS RAM to clear on some systems because they have capacitors in the circuit that retain a charge. Note that this will also erase all other BIOS settings, including the hard disk settings, so they should be recorded beforehand.

Power Management Menu

Power management is defined as the capability of the system to automatically enter power-conserving modes during periods of inactivity. There are two main classes of power management; the original standard was called APM (Advanced Power Management) and had been supported by most systems since the 386 and 486 processors. More recently, a new type of power management called ACPI (Advanced Configuration and Power Interface) has been developed and began appearing in systems during 1998. Most systems sold in '98 or later support the more advanced ACPI type of power management. In APM, the hardware does the actual power management, and the operating system or other software had little control. With ACPI, the power management is now done by the operating system and BIOS, and not the hardware. This makes the control more centralized and easier to access and allows applications to work with the power management.

Table 5.22 shows the typical power settings found in most motherboard BIOSes.

Table 5.22   Typical Power Settings*

Feature	Options	Description
Power Management	Disabled Enabled (default)	Enables or disables the BIOS power-management feature.
Inactivity Timer	Off (default) 1 Minute 5 Minutes 10 Minutes 20 Minutes 30 Minutes 60 Minutes 120 Minutes	Specifies the amount of time before the computer enters Standby mode.
Hard Drive	Disabled Enabled (default)	Enables power management for hard disks during Standby and Suspend modes.
VESA Video Power Down	Disabled Standby (default) Suspend Sleep	Specifies power management for video during Standby and Suspend modes.
Fan Always On	No (default) Yes	Select Yes to force the fan to remain on when the system is in a power-managed state.

*Based on the Phoenix BIOS used by the Intel SE440BX-2 motherboard. Used by permission of Intel Corporation.

When in Standby mode, the BIOS reduces power consumption by spinning down hard drives and reducing power to or turning off VESA (Video Electronics Standards Organization) DPMS (Display Power Management Signaling)-compliant monitors. While in Standby mode, the system can still respond to external interrupts, such as those from keyboards, mice, fax/modems or network adapters. For example, any keyboard or mouse activity brings the system out of Standby mode and immediately restores power to the monitor.

In most systems, the operating system takes over most of the power-management settings, and in some cases, it can even override the BIOS settings. This is definitely true if the operating system and the motherboard both support ACPI.

Some systems feature additional power management settings in their BIOS. Some of the more common ones are shown in Table 5.23.

Table 5.23   Typical Power Management Settings*

ACPI Function	Select Enabled only if your computer's operating system supports the Advanced Configuration and Power Interface (ACPI) specification. Currently, Windows 98 and Windows 2000 support ACPI.
Power Management	This option enables you to select the type (or degree) of power saving for Doze, Standby, and Suspend modes. Following are the individual mode settings: Max Saving—Maximum power savings. Inactivity period is 1 minute in each mode. User Define—Set each mode individually. Select timeout periods in the section for each mode. Min Saving—Minimum power savings. Inactivity period is 1 hour in each mode (except the hard drive).

PM Control by APM	If Advanced Power Management (APM) is installed on your system, selecting Yes gives better power savings.
Video Off Method	Determines the manner in which the monitor is blanked.
V/H SYNC+Blank	System turns off vertical and horizontal synchronization ports and writes blanks to the video buffer.
DPMS Support	Select this option if your monitor supports the Display Power Management Signaling (DPMS) standard of the Video Electronics Standards Association (VESA). Use the software supplied for your video subsystem to select video power-management values.
Blank Screen	System writes only blanks to the video buffer.
Video Off After	As the system moves from lesser to greater power-saving modes, select the mode in which you want the monitor to blank.
MODEM Use IRQ	Name the interrupt request (IRQ) line assigned to the modem (if any) on your system. Activity of the selected IRQ always awakens the system.
Doze Mode	After the selected period of system inactivity, the CPU clock throttles to a small percentage of its duty cycle: between 10 percent and 25 percent for most chipsets. All other devices still operate at full speed.
Standby Mode	After the selected period of system inactivity, the CPU clock stops, the hard drive enters an idle state, and the L2 cache enters a power-save mode. All other devices still operate at full speed.
Suspend Mode	After the selected period of system inactivity, the chipset enters a hardware suspend mode, stopping the CPU clock and possibly causing other system devices to enter power-management modes.
HDD Power Down	After the selected period of drive inactivity, any system IDE devices compatible with the ATA-2 specification or later power manage themselves, putting themselves into an idle state after the specified timeout and then waking themselves up when accessed.
Throttle Duty Cycle	When the system enters Doze mode, the CPU clock runs only part of the time. You may select the percent of time that the clock runs.
VGA Active Monitor	When Enabled, any video activity restarts the global timer for Standby mode.
Soft-Off by PWR-BTTN	When you select Instant Off or Delay 4 Sec., turning the system off with the On/Off button places the system in a very low power-usage state, either immediately or after 4 seconds, with only enough circuitry receiving power to detect power button activity or Resume by Ring activity.
CPUFAN Off in Suspend	When Enabled, the CPU fan turns off during Suspend mode.
Resume by Ring	When Enabled, an input signal on the serial Ring Indicator (RI) line (in other words, an incoming call on the modem) awakens the system from a soft off state.
Resume by Alarm	When Enabled, you can set the date and time at which the RTC (real-time clock) alarm awakens the system from Suspend mode.
Date (of Month) Alarm	Select a date in the month when you want the alarm to go off.
Time (hh:mm:ss) Alarm	Set the time you want the alarm to go off.
Wake Up On LAN	When Enabled, an input signal from a local area network (LAN) awakens the system from a soft off state.
IRQ8 Break [Event From] Suspend	You can select Enabled or Disabled for monitoring of IRQ8 (the real-time clock) so it does not awaken the system from Suspend mode.

(continues)

Table 5.23 Continued

Reload Global Timer Events	When Enabled, an event occurring on each device listed below restarts the global timer for Standby mode.
	IRQ3-7, 9-15, NMI
	Primary IDE 0
	Primary IDE 1
	Secondary IDE 0
	Secondary IDE 1
	Floppy Disk
	Serial Port
	Parallel Port

Based on the Phoenix BIOS used by the Intel SE440BX-2 motherboard. Used by permission of Intel Corporation.

Boot Menu (Boot Sequence, Order)

The Boot menu is used for setting the boot features and the boot sequence. If your operating system includes a bootable CD—Windows 2000, for example—use this menu to change the boot drive order to check your CD before your hard drive. Table 5.24 shows the functions and settings available on a typical motherboard.

Table 5.24 Typical Boot Menu Settings*

Feature	Options	Description
Boot-time Diagnostic Screen	Disabled (default) Enabled	Displays the diagnostics screen during boot.
Quick Boot Mode	Disabled Enabled (default)	Enables the computer to boot without running certain POST tests.
Scan User Flash Area	Disabled (default) Enabled	Enables the BIOS to scan the flash memory for user binary files that are executed at boot time.
After Power Failure	Power On Stay Off Last State (default)	Specifies the mode of operation if an AC/Power loss occurs. Power On restores power to the computer. Stay Off keeps the power off until the power button is pressed. Last State restores the previous power state before power loss occurred.
On Modem Ring	Stay Off Power On (default)	Specifies how the computer responds to an incoming call on an installed modem when the power is off.
On LAN	Stay Off Power On (default)	Specifies how the computer responds to a LAN wakeup event when the power is off.
First Boot Device Second Boot Device Third Boot Device Fourth Boot Device	Removable devices Hard Drive ATAPI CD-ROM Drive Network Boot	Specifies the boot sequence from the available devices.

Feature	Options	Description
		To specify boot sequence:
		1. Select the boot device with _ or ⁻.
		2. Press + to move the device up the list or - to move the device down the list.
		The operating system assigns a drive letter to each boot device in the order listed. Changing the order of the devices changes the drive lettering.
Hard Drive	No options	Lists available hard drives. When selected, displays the Hard Drive submenu.
Removable Devices	No options	Lists available removable devices. When selected, displays the Removable Devices submenu.

Based on the Phoenix BIOS used by the Intel SE440BX-2 motherboard. Used by permission of Intel Corporation.

Using this menu, you can configure which devices your system boots from and in which order the devices are sequenced. From this menu, you can also access Hard Drive and Removable Devices submenus, which allow you to configure the ordering of these devices in the boot sequence. For example, you can set hard drives to be the first boot choice, and then in the hard drive submenu, decide to boot from the secondary drive first and the primary drive second. Normally, the default with two drives would be the other way around.

Exit Menu

The Exit menu is for exiting the Setup program, saving changes, and for loading and saving defaults. Table 5.25 shows the typical selections found in most motherboard BIOSes.

Table 5.25   Typical Exit Menu Settings*

Feature	Description
Exit Saving Changes	Exits and saves the changes in CMOS RAM.
Exit Discarding Changes	Exits without saving any changes made in Setup.
Load Setup Defaults	Loads the factory default values for all the Setup options.
Load Custom Defaults	Loads the custom defaults for Setup options.
Save Custom Defaults	Saves the current values as custom defaults. Normally, the BIOS reads the Setup values from flash memory. If this memory is corrupted, the BIOS reads the custom defaults. If no custom defaults are set, the BIOS reads the factory defaults.
Discard Changes	Discards changes without exiting Setup. The option values present when the computer was turned on are used.

Based on the Phoenix BIOS used by the Intel SE440BX-2 motherboard. Used by permission of Intel Corporation.

After you have selected an optimum set of BIOS Setup settings, you can save these settings using the Save Custom Defaults option. This will enable you to quickly restore your settings if they are corrupted or lost. All BIOS settings are stored in the CMOS RAM memory, which is powered by a battery attached to the motherboard.

Additional BIOS Setup Features

Some systems have additional features in their BIOS Setup screens, which may not be found in all BIOSes. Some of the more common features you might see are shown in Table 5.26.

Table 5.26   Additional BIOS Setup Features*

Virus Warning	When enabled, you receive a warning message if a program attempts to write to the boot sector or the partition table of the hard disk drive. If you get this warning during normal operation, you should run an antivirus program to see whether an infection has occurred. This feature protects only the master boot sector, not the entire hard drive. Note that programs which usually write to the master boot sector, such as FDISK, can trigger the virus warning message.
CPU Internal Cache/ External Cache	This allows you to disable the L1 (internal) and L2 (external) CPU cache. This is often used when testing memory, in which case you don't want the cache functioning. For normal operation, both caches should be enabled.
Quick Power On Self Test	When enabled, this reduces the amount of time required to run the power on self test (POST). A quick POST skips certain steps such as the memory test. If you trust your system, you can enable the quick POST, but in most cases I recommend leaving it disabled so you get the full-length POST version.
Swap Floppy Drive	This field is functional only in systems with two floppy drives. Selecting Enabled assigns physical drive B: to logical drive A, and physical drive A: to logical drive B:.
Boot Up Floppy Seek	When Enabled, the BIOS tests (seeks) floppy drives to determine whether they have 40 or 80 tracks. Only 360KB floppy drives have 40 tracks; drives with 720KB, 1.2MB, and 1.44MB capacity all have 80 tracks. Because very few modern PCs have 40-track floppy drives, you can disable this function to save time.
Boot Up System Speed	Select High to boot at the default CPU speed; select Low to boot at a simulated 8MHz speed. The 8MHz option was often used in the past with certain copy-protected programs, which would fail the protection scheme if booted at full speed. This option is not used today.
Gate A20 Option	Gate A20 refers to the way the system addresses memory above 1MB (extended memory). When set to Fast, the system chipset controls Gate A20. When set to Normal, a pin in the keyboard controller controls Gate A20. Setting Gate A20 to Fast improves system speed, particularly with protected-mode operating systems such as Win9x and Win2000.
Typematic Rate Setting	When Disabled, the following two items (Typematic Rate and Typematic Delay) are irrelevant. Keystrokes repeat at a rate determined by the keyboard controller in your system. When Enabled, you can select a typematic rate and typematic delay.
Typematic Rate (Chars/Sec)	When the typematic rate setting is enabled, you can select a typematic rate (the rate at which characters repeat when you hold down a key) of 6, 8, 10, 12, 15, 20, 24, or 30 characters per second.
Typematic Delay (Msec)	When the typematic rate setting is Enabled, you can select a typematic delay (the delay before key strokes begin to repeat) of 250, 500, 750 or 1,000 milliseconds.
Security Option	If you have set a password, select whether the password is required every time the system boots, or only when you enter Setup.
PS/2 Mouse Function Control	If your system has a PS/2 (motherboard) mouse port and you install a serial pointing device, select Disabled.

PCI/VGA Palette Snoop	Allows multimedia boards to read data from video RAM. Normally set to Disabled unless specifically instructed when installing a multimedia board.
HDD S.M.A.R.T. capability	S.M.A.R.T. is an acronym for Self-Monitoring Analysis and Reporting Technology system. S.M.A.R.T. is a hard drive self-diagnostic feature available on some IDE hard drives.
Report No FDD For WIN 95	Select Yes to release IRQ6 when the system contains no floppy drive, for compatibility with Windows 95 logo certification. In the Integrated Peripherals screen, select Disabled for the Onboard FDC Controller field.
ROM Shadowing	ROM chips are typically very slow, around 150ns (nanoseconds), and operate only 8 bits at a time, whereas RAM runs 60ns or even 10ns or less and is either 32 bits or 64 bits wide in most systems. Shadowing is the copying of BIOS code from ROM into RAM, where the CPU can read the BIOS drivers at the higher speed of RAM.

Year 2000 BIOS Issues

Everybody is concerned about the year 2000 problem. In a nutshell, the problem stems from the fact that the clock in the PC was originally designed to automatically update the year digits only, and the century had to be manually updated. This meant that if the PC was off during the transition from 1999 to 2000, the clock would be reset to 1900 instead. Newer PCs have a redesigned clock that automatically updates the century digits as well as the year digits.

When the PC is running, the system BIOS receives the date and time from the RTC. The first time a non-year 2000 compliant PC is turned on after January 1, 2000, 12:00 a.m., the BIOS will be told by the RTC that the year is 1900. Some BIOSes will convert this to 1980 or some other more recent date. With most of these systems, the user can then manually set the year to 2000, and the BIOS will update the century digits in the RTC. At that point the problem won't reoccur until 2099.

When the operating system (OS) is loaded, it receives the time and date from the system BIOS. An application can request the date and time from the OS, the BIOS, or the RTC. Most applications get the date and time from the OS, some get it from the BIOS, and a few get it from the RTC. An application can be Y2K compliant but report a bad date if it is sent from either a non-year 2000 compliant BIOS or RTC.

To test your operating system for Y2K compatibility:

1. If you are using DOS, boot your system to a safe mode command prompt (no other drivers loaded).

2. Set the date to December 31, 1999 by typing the following command at the DOS prompt:
   ```
   DATE 12-31-1999 <enter>
   ```

3. Then set the time to 11:59 p.m. by typing
   ```
   TIME 23:59 <enter>
   ```

4. Verify that the date and time are set correctly by typing
   ```
   DATE <enter>
   ```
   and then
   ```
   TIME <enter>
   ```

5. Observe the output. Now wait more than one minute, and then check the date by typing

DATE <enter>

If the date has changed to January 1, 2000, then your version of DOS does not have a Y2K problem.

1. If you are running Windows 9x, NT, or Windows 2000, boot to the operating system desktop.

2. Open the control panel by selecting Start, Settings, Control Panel.

3. Select the Date/Time icon and set the date to December 31, 1999 and set the time to 11:59 p.m. Watch for a minute to see what happens. If after a minute the date and time correctly change, you have a Y2K-compliant operating system.

Note

This test does not guarantee that your applications are Y2K compliant. This test only checks the operating system for Y2K compliance.

Now you can check your BIOS with the following procedure:

1. First enter your BIOS setup.

◄◄ See "Running or Accessing the CMOS Setup Program," p. 375

2. Then set the date to December 31, 1999.

3. Set the time to 11:59 p.m. Watch for a minute to see what happens. If after a minute the date and time correctly change, you have a Y2K-compliant BIOS.

Note

Again, this does not mean that you won't have any problems with applications; this checks only the BIOS. If the date and time do not correctly change, your BIOS is not Y2K compliant.

Finally, you can check your real-time clock (RTC) using the following procedure:

1. Enter your BIOS setup the same as in the previous example.

2. Set the date to December 31, 1999 and the time to 11:59 p.m.

3. Save and exit BIOS setup.

4. Power off the system.

5. Wait more than one minute, turn the system back on, and again enter the BIOS setup. If the date has correctly changed, you have a Y2K-compliant RTC. This verifies only the clock and does not affect applications. If the date and time did not correctly change, your clock is not Y2K compliant.

Note that many systems will not have compliant clocks, and some may not have compliant BIOSes; in that case, the simple workaround is either to ensure the system is running at midnight on December 31, 1999, or if the system is off or the BIOS is the problem, the first time booting on or after January 1, 2000, run the BIOS Setup and enter the correct date.

Another solution is to purchase one of the Y2K adapter cards being sold today, which have an onboard BIOS that will correctly handle the date change. They can also help correct the problem of the clock by watching for 1900 from the BIOS, in which case they automatically correct the CMOS clock and pass the correct date on to the operating system.

Admittedly, these tests are fairly simple. For more serious testing, I recommend that you check out programs such as Y2000.EXE by the National Software Testing Laboratories (NSTL). This program can be downloaded for free from its Web site, and it will give an accurate picture of the compliance level of your PC. Most of the BIOS manufacturers also offer more comprehensive test programs free for the downloading.

The following sections examine some of the larger BIOS manufacturers and whether their BIOSes are Y2K compliant.

Award

Award states that its BIOS correctly handles the changeover from 1999 to 2000 and correctly reads and reports dates beyond Year 2000 from the system real-time clock, including leap year dates. This compliance depends on the release date:

If your Award BIOS was released before April 26, 1994, you need to reset your system clock only once after the change:

1. Turn the system off before midnight on December 31, 1999.
2. Turn it back on some time after midnight on January 1, 2000.
3. Then set the system date correctly in the BIOS setup.

If your Award BIOS was released between April 26, 1994 and May 31, 1995, you will need to obtain a BIOS upgrade or reset your system clock every day! BIOSes between these dates have a bug where they assume the century is fixed at 19.

If your Award BIOS was released after May 31, 1995, its calendar automatically rolls from 1999 to 2000 at midnight, even though it may fail the NSTL 2000.EXE test. Award Software has modified its BIOS source code to accommodate the requirements of 2000.EXE and other applications that invoke INT1Ah function 04h. Award BIOS source code issued later than November 18, 1996 passes the NSTL 2000.EXE test program.

In addition to BIOS upgrades through Unicore Software, Award is also offering a hardware/software solution called the Millennium/Pro BIOS upgrade card. This card is also available through Unicore Software (see the vendor list).

AMI

AMI states that BIOS products shipped by AMI before 1998 and with versions earlier than 6.31.01 may require updates.

Note

Note that some OEMs may have changed the version and must be consulted to determine the true AMI version number.

Detection of an AMI BIOS is performed with a power-on boot process, which will display the AMI logo and date of that BIOS version. For any AMIBIOS with a date older than 1998 and with a version less than 6.31.01, it recommends an upgrade to ensure Y2K readiness.

Phoenix

Phoenix states that, in general, many (but not all) machines equipped with PhoenixBIOS 4.0 Release 5 and later versions have support for automatic date update when the system is first switched on after December 31, 1999. (The change to support automatic updates was made available to manufacturers in mid 1995). I recommend that you test with a program such as Y2000.exe to be sure that the system is compliant. If not, upgrades should be available from your motherboard manufacturer or MicroFirmware (see the vendor list).

Plug-and-Play BIOS

Traditionally, installing and configuring devices in PCs has been a difficult process. During installation, the user is faced with the task of configuring the new card by selecting the IRQ, I/O ports, and DMA channel. In the past, users were required to move jumpers or set switches on the add-in cards to control these settings. They needed to know exactly what resources were already in use so they could find a set of resources that did not conflict with the devices already in the system. If a conflict exists, the system may not boot, the device may fail or cause the conflicting hardware to fail.

PnP is technology designed to prevent configuration problems and provide users with the capability to easily expand a PC. With PnP, the user simply plugs in the new card and the system configures it automatically for proper operation.

PnP is composed of three principal components:

■ Plug-and-Play BIOS
■ Extended System Configuration Data (ESCD)
■ Plug-and-Play operating system

The PnP BIOS initiates the configuration of the PnP cards during the boot-up process. If the cards were previously installed, the BIOS reads the information from ESCD and initializes the cards, then boots the system. During the installation of new PnP cards, the BIOS consults the ESCD to determine what system resources are available and needed for the add-in card. If the BIOS is capable of finding sufficient available resources, it configures the card. However, if the BIOS is incapable of locating sufficient available resources, the Plug-and-Play routines in the operating system complete the configuration process. During the configuration process, the configuration registers (in flash BIOS) on the card as well as the ESCD are updated with the new configuration data.

PnP Device IDs

All Plug-and-Play devices must contain a Plug-and-Play device ID to allow the operating system to uniquely recognize the device so that it can load the appropriate driver software. Each device manufacturer is responsible for assigning the Plug-and-Play ID for each product and storing it in the hardware.

Plug-and-Play three-character Vendor ID followed by a four-digit product ID (for example, XYZ1234).

Each manufacturer of Plug-and-Play devices must be assigned an industry-unique, three-character Vendor ID. Then the device manufacturer is responsible for assigning a unique product ID to each individual product model. After an ID is assigned to a product model, it must not be assigned to any other product model manufactured by the same company (that is, one that uses the same Vendor ID).

Many devices have no standard ID, such as the interrupt controller or keyboard controller. In that case, Microsoft has reserved a prefix of PNP to identify various devices that do not have an existing ID, as well as defining compatibility devices. These IDs are shown in Table 5.27.

Table 5.27   PnP Device IDs

Device ID	Description
PNPOxxx	System Devices
	Interrupt Controllers
PNP0000	AT Interrupt Controller
PNP0001	EISA Interrupt Controller
PNP0002	MCA Interrupt Controller
PNP0003	APIC
PNP0004	Cyrix SliC MP interrupt controller
	Timers
PNP0100	AT Timer
PNP0101	EISA Timer
PNP0102	MCA Timer
	DMA
PNP0200	AT DMA Controller
PNP0201	EISA DMA Controller
PNP0202	MCA DMA Controller
	Keyboards
PNP0300	IBM PC/XT keyboard controller (83-key)
PNP0301	IBM PC/AT keyboard controller (86-key)
PNP0302	IBM PC/XT keyboard controller (84-key)
PNP0303	IBM Enhanced (101/102-key, PS/2 mouse support)
PNP0304	Olivetti Keyboard (83-key)
PNP0305	Olivetti Keyboard (102-key)
PNP0306	Olivetti Keyboard (86-key)
PNP0307	Microsoft Windows(R) Keyboard
PNP0308	General Input Device Emulation Interface (GIDEI) legacy

(continues)

Table 5.27   Continued

Device ID	Description
PNP0309	Olivetti Keyboard (A101/102 key)
PNP030A	AT&T 302 keyboard
PNP030B	Reserved by Microsoft
PNP0320	Japanese 106-key keyboard A01
PNP0321	Japanese 101-key keyboard
PNP0322	Japanese AX keyboard
PNP0323	Japanese 106-key keyboard 002/003
PNP0324	Japanese 106-key keyboard 001
PNP0325	Japanese Toshiba Desktop keyboard
PNP0326	Japanese Toshiba Laptop keyboard
PNP0327	Japanese Toshiba Notebook keyboard
PNP0340	Korean 84-key keyboard
PNP0341	Korean 86-key keyboard
PNP0342	Korean Enhanced keyboard
PNP0343	Korean Enhanced keyboard 101b
PNP0343	Korean Enhanced keyboard 101c
PNP0344	Korean Enhanced keyboard 103
	Parallel Devices
PNP0400	Standard LPT printer port
PNP0401	ECP printer port
	Serial Devices
PNP0500	Standard PC COM port
PNP0501	16550A-compatible COM port
PNP0502	Multiport serial device (nonintelligent 16550)
PNP0510	Generic IRDA-compatible device
PNP0511	Generic IRDA-compatible device
	Disk Controllers
PNP0600	Generic ESDI/IDE/ATA compatible hard disk controller
PNP0601	Plus Hardcard II
PNP0602	Plus Hardcard IIXL/EZ
PNP0603	Generic IDE supporting Microsoft Device Bay Specification
PNP0700	PC standard floppy disk controller
PNP0701	Standard floppy controller supporting MS Device Bay Spec
	Display Adapters
PNP0900	VGA Compatible
PNP0901	Video Seven VRAM/VRAM II/1024i
PNP0902	8514/A Compatible
PNP0903	Trident VGA
PNP0904	Cirrus Logic Laptop VGA
PNP0905	Cirrus Logic VGA
PNP0906	Tseng ET4000
PNP0907	Western Digital VGA
PNP0908	Western Digital Laptop VGA
PNP0909	S3 Inc. 911/924
PNP090A	ATI Ultra Pro/Plus (Mach 32)
PNP090B	ATI Ultra (Mach 8)
PNP090C	XGA Compatible
PNP090D	ATI VGA Wonder

Device ID	Description
PNP090E	Weitek P9000 Graphics Adapter
PNP090F	Oak Technology VGA
PNP0910	Compaq QVision
PNP0911	XGA/2
PNP0912	Tseng Labs W32/W32i/W32p
PNP0913	S3 Inc. 801/928/964
PNP0914	Cirrus Logic 5429/5434 (memory mapped)
PNP0915	Compaq Advanced VGA (AVGA)
PNP0916	ATI Ultra Pro Turbo (Mach64)
PNP0917	Reserved by Microsoft
PNP0918	Matrox MGA
PNP0919	Compaq QVision 2000
PNP091A	Tseng W128
PNP0930	Chips & Technologies Super VGA
PNP0931	Chips & Technologies Accelerator
PNP0940	NCR 77c22e Super VGA
PNP0941	NCR 77c32blt
PNP09FF	Plug-and-Play Monitors (VESA DDC)
	Peripheral buses
PNP0A00	ISA bus
PNP0A01	EISA bus
PNP0A02	MCA bus
PNP0A03	PCI bus
PNP0A04	VESA/VL bus
PNP0A05	Generic ACPI bus
PNP0A06	Generic ACPI Extended-I/O bus (EIO bus)
	Real-time clock, BIOS, system board devices
PNP0800	AT-style speaker sound
PNP0B00	AT real-time clock
PNP0C00	Plug-and-Play BIOS (only created by the root enumerator)
PNP0C01	System board
PNP0C02	General ID for reserving resources required by Plug-and-Play motherboard registers. (Not specific to a particular device.)
PNP0C03	Plug-and-Play BIOS Event Notification Interrupt
PNP0C04	Math Coprocessor
PNP0C05	APM BIOS (Version independent)
PNP0C06	Reserved for identification of early Plug-and-Play BIOS implementation.
PNP0C07	Reserved for identification of early Plug-and-Play BIOS implementation.
PNP0C08	ACPI system board hardware
PNP0C09	ACPI embedded controller
PNP0C0A	ACPI control method battery
PNP0C0B	ACPI fan
PNP0C0C	ACPI power button device
PNP0C0D	ACPI lid device
PNP0C0E	ACPI sleep button device
PNP0C0F	PCI interrupt link device
PNP0C10	ACPI system indicator device

(continues)

Table 5.27 Continued

Device ID	Description
PNP0C11	ACPI thermal zone
PNP0C12	Device bay controller
PNP0C13	Plug-and-Play BIOS (used when ACPI mode cannot be used)
	PCMCIA controller chipsets
PNP0E00	Intel 82365-compatible PCMCIA controller
PNP0E01	Cirrus Logic CL-PD6720 PCMCIA controller
PNP0E02	VLSI VL82C146 PCMCIA controller
PNP0E03	Intel 82365-compatible CardBus controller
	Mice
PNP0F00	Microsoft Bus mouse
PNP0F01	Microsoft Serial mouse
PNP0F02	Microsoft InPort mouse
PNP0F03	Microsoft PS/2-style mouse
PNP0F04	Mouse Systems mouse
PNP0F05	Mouse Systems 3-Button mouse (COM 2)
PNP0F06	Genius mouse (COM 1)
PNP0F07	Genius mouse (COM 2)
PNP0F08	Logitech Serial mouse
PNP0F09	Microsoft BallPoint Serial mouse
PNP0F0A	Microsoft Plug-and-Play mouse
PNP0F0B	Microsoft Plug-and-Play BallPoint mouse
PNP0F0C	Microsoft-compatible Serial mouse
PNP0F0D	Microsoft-compatible InPort-compatible mouse
PNP0F0E	Microsoft-compatible PS/2-style mouse
PNP0F0F	Microsoft-compatible Serial Ballpoint-compatible mouse
PNP0F10	Texas Instruments QuickPort mouse
PNP0F11	Microsoft-compatible bus mouse
PNP0F12	Logitech PS/2-style mouse
PNP0F13	PS/2 Port for PS/2-style mice
PNP0F14	Microsoft kids mouse
PNP0F15	Logitech bus mouse
PNP0F16	Logitech SWIFT device
PNP0F17	Logitech-compatible serial mouse
PNP0F18	Logitech-compatible bus mouse
PNP0F19	Logitech-compatible PS/2-style mouse
PNP0F1A	Logitech-compatible SWIFT device
PNP0F1B	HP Omnibook mouse
PNP0F1C	Compaq LTE Trackball PS/2-style mouse
PNP0F1D	Compaq LTE Trackball Serial mouse
PNP0F1E	Microsoft Kids Trackball mouse
PNP0F1F	Reserved by Microsoft Input Device Group
PNP0F20	Reserved by Microsoft Input Device Group
PNP0F21	Reserved by Microsoft Input Device Group
PNP0F22	Reserved by Microsoft Input Device Group
PNP0F23	Reserved by Microsoft Input Device Group
PNP0FFF	Reserved by Microsoft Systems

Device ID	Description
PNP8xxx	**Network Adapters**
PNP8001	Novell/Anthem NE3200
PNP8004	Compaq NE3200
PNP8006	Intel EtherExpress/32
PNP8008	HP EtherTwist EISA LAN Adapter/32 (HP27248A)
PNP8065	Ungermann-Bass NIUps or NIUps/EOTP
PNP8072	DEC (DE211) EtherWorks MC/TP
PNP8073	DEC (DE212) EtherWorks MC/TP_BNC
PNP8078	DCA 10 Mb MCA
PNP8074	HP MC LAN Adapter/16 TP (PC27246)
PNP80c9	IBM Token Ring
PNP80ca	IBM Token Ring II
PNP80cb	IBM Token Ring II/Short
PNP80cc	IBM Token Ring 4/16Mbs
PNP80d3	Novell/Anthem NE1000
PNP80d4	Novell/Anthem NE2000
PNP80d5	NE1000 Compatible
PNP80d6	NE2000 Compatible
PNP80d7	Novell/Anthem NE1500T
PNP80d8	Novell/Anthem NE2100
PNP80dd	SMC ARCNETPC
PNP80de	SMC ARCNET PC100, PC200
PNP80df	SMC ARCNET PC110, PC210, PC250
PNP80e0	SMC ARCNET PC130/E
PNP80e1	SMC ARCNET PC120, PC220, PC260
PNP80e2	SMC ARCNET PC270/E
PNP80e5	SMC ARCNET PC600W, PC650W
PNP80e7	DEC DEPCA
PNP80e8	DEC (DE100) EtherWorks LC
PNP80e9	DEC (DE200) EtherWorks Turbo
PNP80ea	DEC (DE101) EtherWorks LC/TP
PNP80eb	DEC (DE201) EtherWorks Turbo/TP
PNP80ec	DEC (DE202) EtherWorks Turbo/TP_BNC
PNP80ed	DEC (DE102) EtherWorks LC/TP_BNC
PNP80ee	DEC EE101 (Built-in)
PNP80ef	DECpc 433 WS (Built-in)
PNP80f1	3Com EtherLink Plus
PNP80f3	3Com EtherLink II or IITP (8- or 16-bit)
PNP80f4	3Com TokenLink
PNP80f6	3Com EtherLink 16
PNP80f7	3Com EtherLink III
PNP80f8	3Com Generic Etherlink Plug-and-Play device
PNP80fb	Thomas Conrad TC6045
PNP80fc	Thomas Conrad TC6042
PNP80fd	Thomas Conrad TC6142
PNP80fe	Thomas Conrad TC6145

(continues)

Table 5.27   Continued

Device ID	Description
PNP80ff	Thomas Conrad TC6242
PNP8100	Thomas Conrad TC6245
PNP8105	DCA 10 MB
PNP8106	DCA 10 MB fiber optic
PNP8107	DCA 10 MB twisted pair
PNP8113	Racal NI6510
PNP811C	Ungermann-Bass NIUpc
PNP8120	Ungermann-Bass NIUpc/EOTP
PNP8123	SMC StarCard PLUS (WD/8003S)
PNP8124	SMC StarCard PLUS with onboard hub (WD/8003SH)
PNP8125	SMC EtherCard PLUS (WD/8003E)
PNP8126	SMC EtherCard PLUS with boot ROM socket (WD/8003EBT)
PNP8127	SMC EtherCard PLUS with Boot ROM Socket (WD/8003EB)
PNP8128	SMC EtherCard PLUS TP (WD/8003WT)
PNP812a	SMC EtherCard PLUS 16 with Boot ROM Socket (WD/8013EBT)
PNP812d	Intel EtherExpress 16 or 16TP
PNP812f	Intel TokenExpress 16/4
PNP8130	Intel TokenExpress MCA 16/4
PNP8132	Intel EtherExpress 16 (MCA)
PNP8137	Artisoft AE-1
PNP8138	Artisoft AE-2 or AE-3
PNP8141	Amplicard AC 210/XT
PNP8142	Amplicard AC 210/AT
PNP814b	Everex SpeedLink /PC16 (EV2027)
PNP8155	HP PC LAN Adapter/8 TP (HP27245)
PNP8156	HP PC LAN Adapter/16 TP (HP27247A)
PNP8157	HP PC LAN Adapter/8 TL (HP27250)
PNP8158	HP PC LAN Adapter/16 TP Plus (HP27247B)
PNP8159	HP PC LAN Adapter/16 TL Plus (HP27252)
PNP815f	National Semiconductor Ethernode *16AT
PNP8160	National Semiconductor AT/LANTIC Ethernode 16-AT3
PNP816a	NCR Token-Ring 4Mbs ISA
PNP816d	NCR Token-Ring 16/4Mbs ISA
PNP8191	Olicom 16/4 Token-Ring Adapter
PNP81c3	SMC EtherCard PLUS Elite (WD/8003EP)
PNP81c4	SMC EtherCard PLUS 10T (WD/8003W)
PNP81c5	SMC EtherCard PLUS Elite 16 (WD/8013EP)
PNP81c6	SMC EtherCard PLUS Elite 16T (WD/8013W)
PNP81c7	SMC EtherCard PLUS Elite 16 Combo (WD/8013EW or 8013EWC)
PNP81c8	SMC EtherElite Ultra 16
PNP81e4	Pure Data PDI9025-32 (Token Ring)
PNP81e6	Pure Data PDI508+ (ArcNet)
PNP81e7	Pure Data PDI516+ (ArcNet)
PNP81eb	Proteon Token Ring (P1390)
PNP81ec	Proteon Token Ring (P1392)
PNP81ed	Proteon ISA Token Ring (1340)
PNP81ee	Proteon ISA Token Ring (1342)

PNP81ef	Proteon ISA Token Ring (1346)
PNP81f0	Proteon ISA Token Ring (1347)
PNP81ff	Cabletron E2000 Series DNI
PNP8200	Cabletron E2100 Series DNI
PNP8209	Zenith Data Systems Z-Note
PNP820a	Zenith Data Systems NE2000-compatible
PNP8213	Xircom Pocket Ethernet II
PNP8214	Xircom Pocket Ethernet I
PNP821d	RadiSys EXM-10
PNP8227	SMC 3000 series
PNP8228	SMC 91C2 controller
PNP8231	Advanced Micro Devices AM2100/AM1500T
PNP8263	Tulip NCC-16
PNP8277	Exos 105
PNP828A	Intel '595 based Ethernet
PNP828B	TI2000-style Token Ring
PNP828C	AMD PCNet Family cards
PNP828D	AMD PCNet32 (VL version)
PNP8294	IrDA Infrared NDIS driver (Microsoft-supplied)
PNP82bd	IBM PCMCIA-NIC
PNP82C2	Xircom CE10
PNP82C3	Xircom CEM2
PNP8321	DEC Ethernet (All types)
PNP8323	SMC EtherCard (All types except 8013/A)
PNP8324	ARCNET Compatible
PNP8326	Thomas Conrad (All Arcnet types)
PNP8327	IBM Token Ring (All types)
PNP8385	Remote Network Access driver
PNP8387	RNA Point-to-point Protocol driver
PNP8388	Reserved for Microsoft Networking components
PNP8389	Peer IrLAN infrared driver (Microsoft-supplied)
PNP8390	Generic network adapter

PNPAxxx	**SCSI, Proprietary CD Adapters**
PNPA002	Future Domain 16-700 compatible controller
PNPA003	Panasonic proprietary CD-ROM adapter (SBPro/SB16)
PNPA01B	Trantor 128 SCSI controller
PNPA01D	Trantor T160 SCSI controller
PNPA01E	Trantor T338 Parallel SCSI controller
PNPA01F	Trantor T348 Parallel SCSI controller
PNPA020	Trantor Media Vision SCSI controller
PNPA022	Always IN-2000 SCSI controller
PNPA02B	Sony proprietary CD-ROM controller
PNPA02D	Trantor T13b 8-bit SCSI controller
PNPA02F	Trantor T358 Parallel SCSI controller
PNPA030	Mitsumi LU-005 single-speed CD-ROM controller + drive
PNPA031	Mitsumi FX-001 single-speed CD-ROM controller + drive
PNPA032	Mitsumi FX-001 double-speed CD-ROM controller + drive

(continues)

Table 5.27   Continued

Device ID	Description
PNPBxxx	**Sound/Video-Capture, Multimedia**
PNPB000	Sound Blaster 1.5 sound device
PNPB001	Sound Blaster 2.0 sound device
PNPB002	Sound Blaster Pro sound device
PNPB003	Sound Blaster 16 sound device
PNPB004	Thunderboard-compatible sound device
PNPB005	AdLib-compatible FM synthesizer device
PNPB006	MPU401 compatible
PNPB007	Microsoft Windows sound system-compatible sound device
PNPB008	Compaq Business Audio
PNPB009	Plug-and-Play Microsoft Windows sound system device
PNPB00A	MediaVision Pro Audio Spectrum
PNPB00B	MediaVision Pro Audio 3D
PNPB00C	MusicQuest MQX-32M
PNPB00D	MediaVision Pro Audio Spectrum Basic
PNPB00E	MediaVision Pro Audio Spectrum
PNPB00F	MediaVision Jazz-16 chipset (OEM Versions)
PNPB010	Auravision VxP500 chipset—Orchid Videola
PNPB018	MediaVision Pro Audio Spectrum 8-bit
PNPB019	MediaVision Pro Audio Spectrum Basic
PNPB020	Yamaha OPL3-compatible FM synthesizer device
PNPB02F	Joystick/Game port
PNPCxxx-Dxxx	**Modems**
PNPC000	Compaq 14400 Modem (TBD)
PNPC001	Compaq 2400/9600 Modem (TBD)

Initializing a PnP Device

One responsibility of a Plug-and-Play BIOS during POST is to isolate and initialize all Plug and Play cards and assign them with a valid Card Select Number (*CSN*). After a CSN is assigned, the system BIOS can then designate resources to the cards. The BIOS is responsible only for the configuration of boot devices; all the remaining Plug and Play devices may be configured dynamically by the operating system software.

The following steps outline a typical flow of a Plug-and-Play BIOS during the POST:

1. Disable all configurable devices.

2. Identify all Plug-and-Play devices.

3. Construct a resource map of resources that are statically allocated to devices in the system.

4. Enable input and output devices.

5. Perform ISA ROM scan.

6. Configure the boot device.

7. Enable Plug-and-Play ISA and other configurable devices.

8. Start the bootstrap loader.

If the loaded operating system is Plug-and-Play compliant, it will take over management of the system resources. Any unconfigured Plug-and-Play devices will be configured by the appropriate system software or the Plug-and-Play-operating system.

At this point, the operating system is loaded and takes control over Plug-and-Play system resources. Using the Device Manager in the operating system such as Windows, the user can now control any Plug-and-Play devices.

BIOS Error Messages

When a PC system is first powered on, the system runs a power on self test (POST). If errors are encountered during the POST, in most cases you will see a text error message displayed on the screen. Errors that occur very early in the POST may happen before the video card is initialized. These types of errors cannot be displayed, so the system uses two other alternatives for communicating the error message. One is beeping; that is, the system will beep the speaker in a specific pattern that indicates which error has occurred.

The other alternative is to send a hexadecimal error code to I/O port address 80h, which can be read by a special card in one of the bus slots. When the ROM BIOS is performing the POST, in most systems the results of these tests are continuously sent to I/O Port 80h so they can be monitored by special diagnostics cards called POST cards. These tests sometimes are called manufacturing tests because they were designed into the system for testing systems on the assembly line without a video display attached.

The POST-code cards have a two-digit hexadecimal display used to report the number of the currently executing test routine. Before executing each test, a hexadecimal numeric code is sent to the port, and then the test is run. If the test fails and locks up the machine, the hexadecimal code of the last test being executed remains on the card's display.

Many tests are executed in a system before the video display card is enabled, especially if the display is EGA or VGA. Therefore, many errors can occur that would lock up the system before the system could possibly display an error code through the video system. Because not all these errors generate beep codes, to most normal troubleshooting procedures, a system with this type of problem (such as a memory failure in Bank 0) would appear completely "dead." By using one of the commercially available POST-code cards, however, you can often diagnose the problem.

These codes are completely BIOS dependent because the card does nothing but display the codes sent to it. Some BIOSes have more detailed POST procedures and therefore send more informative codes. POST cards can be purchased from JDR Microdevices or other sources.

For simple but otherwise fatal errors that cannot be displayed on the screen, most of the BIOS versions also send audio codes that can be used to help diagnose such problems. The audio codes are similar to POST codes, but they are read by listening to the speaker beep rather than by using a special card.

The following sections detail the text, beep, and I/O port 80h error codes for all the popular BIOS versions.

Note

The CD accompanying this book contains an exhaustive listing of BIOS error codes, error messages, and beep codes for BIOSes from Phoenix, AMI, Award, Microid Research, and IBM.

General BIOS Boot Text Error Messages

The ROM maps of most PCs are similar to the original IBM systems with which they are compatible—with the exception of the Cassette BASIC portion (also called ROM BASIC). It may come as a surprise to some PC users, but the original IBM PC actually had a jack on the rear of the system for connecting a cassette tape recorder. This was to be used for loading programs and data to or from a cassette tape. Tapes were used at the time because floppy drives were very costly, and hard disks were not even an option yet. Floppy drives came down in price quickly at the time, and the cassette port never appeared on any subsequent IBM systems. The cassette port also never appeared on any compatible system.

The original PC came standard with only 16KB of memory in the base configuration. No floppy drives were included, so you could not load or save files from disks. Most computer users at the time would either write their own programs in the BASIC (Beginner's All-Purpose Symbolic Instruction Code) language or run programs written by others. A BASIC language interpreter was built into the ROM BIOS of these early IBMs and was designed to access the cassette port on the back of the system.

What is really strange is that IBM kept this ROM BASIC relationship all the way into the early 1990s! I liken this to humans having an appendix. The ROM BASIC in those IBM systems is a sort of vestigial organ—a leftover that had some use in prehistoric ancestors but that has no function today.

You can catch a glimpse of this ROM BASIC on older IBM systems that have it by disabling all the disk drives in the system. In that case, with nothing to boot from, most IBM systems unceremoniously dump you into the strange (vintage 1981) ROM BASIC screen. When this occurs, the message looks like this:

```
The IBM Personal Computer Basic
Version C1.10 Copyright IBM Corp 1981
62940 Bytes free
Ok
```

Many people used to dread seeing this because it usually meant that your hard disk had failed to be recognized! Because no compatible systems ever had the Cassette BASIC interpreter in ROM, they had to come up with different messages to display for the same situations in which an IBM system would invoke this BASIC. Compatibles that have an AMI BIOS in fact display a confusing message, as follows:

```
NO ROM BASIC - SYSTEM HALTED
```

This message is a BIOS error message that is displayed by the AMI BIOS when the same situations occur that would cause an IBM system to dump into Cassette BASIC, which, of course, is not present in an AMI BIOS (or any other compatible BIOS, for that matter). Other BIOS versions display different messages. For example, under the same circumstances, a Compaq BIOS displays the following:

```
Non-System disk or disk error
replace and strike any key when ready
```

This is somewhat confusing on Compaq's part because this very same (or similar) error message is contained in the DOS Boot Sector and would normally be displayed if the system files were missing or corrupted.

In the same situations in which you would see Cassette BASIC on an IBM system, a system with an Award BIOS would display the following:

```
DISK BOOT FAILURE, INSERT SYSTEM DISK AND PRESS ENTER
```

Phoenix BIOS systems will display either

```
No boot device available -
strike F1 to retry boot, F2 for setup utility
```

or

```
No boot sector on fixed disk -
strike F1 to retry boot, F2 for setup utility
```

The first or second Phoenix message displays depending on which error actually occurred.

Although the message displayed varies from BIOS to BIOS, the cause is the same for all of them. Two things can generally cause any of these messages to be displayed, and they both relate to specific bytes in the Master Boot Record, which is the first sector of a hard disk at the physical location Cylinder 0, Head 0, Sector 1.

The first problem relates to a disk that has either never been partitioned or that has had the Master Boot Sector corrupted. During the boot process, the BIOS checks the last two bytes in the Master Boot Record (the first sector of the drive) for a "signature" value of 55AAh. If the last two bytes are not 55AAh, an Interrupt 18h is invoked. This calls the subroutine that displays the message you received, and the others indicated, or on an IBM system invokes Cassette (ROM) BASIC.

The Master Boot Sector (including the signature bytes) is written to the hard disk by the DOS FDISK program. Immediately after you low-level format a hard disk, all the sectors are initialized with a pattern of bytes, and the first sector does not contain the 55AAh signature. In other words, these ROM error messages are exactly what you see if you attempt to boot from a hard disk that has been low-level formatted but has not yet been partitioned.

Now consider the second situation that can cause these messages. If the signature bytes are correct, the BIOS executes the Master Partition Boot Record code, which performs a test of the Boot Indicator Bytes in each of the four partition table entries. These bytes are at offset 446 (1BEh), 462 (1CEh), 478 (1DEh), and 494 (1EEh), respectively. They are used to indicate which of the four possible partition table entries contains an active (bootable) partition. A value of 80h in any of these byte offsets indicates that table contains the active partition, whereas all other values must be 00h. If more than one of these bytes is 80h (indicating multiple active partitions), or any of the byte values is anything other than 80h or 00h, you see the following error message:

```
Invalid partition table
```

If all these four Boot Indicator Bytes are 00h, indicating no active (bootable) partitions, then you also see Cassette BASIC on an IBM system or the other messages indicated earlier, depending on which BIOS you have. This is exactly what occurs if you were to remove the existing partitions from a drive using FDISK but had not created new partitions on the drive, or had failed to make one of the partitions Active (bootable) with FDISK before rebooting your system.

Unfortunately, no easy way exists to clear out the partition table on a system where it is damaged. You can try to use FDISK to remove damaged partitions, but FDISK will not always allow it. In that case, you have to resort to something more powerful, such as the DISKEDIT command found in the Norton Utilities package by Symantec.

Memory

6

SOME OF THE MAIN TOPICS IN THIS CHAPTER ARE

Memory Basics

ROM

DRAM

Cache Memory: SRAM

RAM Memory Speeds

Future DRAM Memory Technologies

Physical RAM Memory

Installing RAM Upgrades

Troubleshooting Memory

The System Logical Memory Layout

Memory Basics

This chapter looks at memory from both a physical and logical point of view. First, you will look at what memory is, where it fits into the PC architecture, and how it works. Then I'll discuss the different types of memory, speeds, and packaging of the chips and memory modules you can buy and install.

This chapter also covers the logical layout of memory, defining the different areas and their uses from the system's point of view. Because the logical layout and uses are within the "mind" of the processor, memory mapping and logical layout remain perhaps the most difficult subjects to grasp in the PC universe. This chapter contains useful information that removes the mysteries associated with memory and enables you to get the most out of your system.

Memory is the workspace for the computer's processor. It is a temporary storage area where the programs and data being operated on by the processor must reside. Memory storage is considered temporary because the data and programs remain there only as long as the computer has electrical power or is not reset. Before being shut down or reset, any data that has been changed should be saved to a more permanent storage device of some type (usually a hard disk) so it can be reloaded into memory again in the future.

We often call memory *RAM*, for *random access memory*. Main memory is called RAM because you can randomly (and quickly) access any location in memory. This designation is somewhat misleading and often misinterpreted. Read-only memory (ROM), for example, is also randomly accessible, yet is normally differentiated from the system RAM because it cannot normally be written to. Also, disk memory is randomly accessible too, but we don't consider that RAM either.

Over the years, the definition of RAM has changed from a simple acronym to become something that means the primary memory workspace used by the processor to run programs, which usually is constructed of a type of chip called DRAM (Dynamic RAM). One of the characteristics of DRAM chips (and therefore RAM in general) is that they store data dynamically, which means information can be written to RAM over and over again at any time. An important characteristic of RAM is that data is stored only as long as the memory has electrical power.

Therefore, when we talk about a computer's memory, we usually mean the RAM or physical memory in the system, which is primarily the memory chips or modules used by the processor to store primary active programs and data. This is often confused with the term *"storage,"* which should be used when referring to things such as disk and tape drives (although they can be used as a form of RAM called virtual memory).

RAM can refer to both the physical chips that make up the memory in the system and the logical mapping and layout of that memory. Logical mapping and layout refer to how the memory addresses are mapped to actual chips and what address locations contain which types of system information.

People new to computers often confuse main memory with disk storage because both have capacities that are expressed in similar megabyte or gigabyte terms. The best analogy to explain the relationship between memory and disk storage I've found is to think of a small office with a desk and a file cabinet.

In this popular analogy, the file cabinet represents the system's hard disk, where both programs and data are stored for long-term safekeeping. The desktop represents the system's main memory, which allows the person working at the desk (acting as the processor) direct access to any files placed on it. Files represent the programs and documents you can "load" into the memory. To work on a particular file, it must first be retrieved from the cabinet and placed on the desktop. If the desktop is large enough, you might be able to have several files open on it at one time; likewise, if your system has more memory, you can run more or larger programs and work on more or larger documents.

Adding hard disk space to a system is like putting a bigger file cabinet in the office; more files can be permanently stored. Adding more memory to a system is like getting a bigger desk; you can work on more programs and data at the same time.

One difference between this analogy and the way things really work in a computer is that when a file is loaded into memory, it is a copy of the file that is actually loaded; the original still resides on the hard disk. Note that because of the temporary nature of memory, any files that have been changed after being loaded into memory must then be saved back to the hard disk before the system is powered off and the memory subsequently cleared. If the changed file is not saved, then the original copy of the file on the hard disk remains unaltered. This is like saying that any changes made to files left on the desktop are discarded when the office is closed, although the original files themselves are still in the cabinet.

Memory temporarily stores programs when they are running, along with the data being used by those programs. RAM chips are sometimes termed *volatile storage* because when you turn off your computer or an electrical outage occurs, whatever is stored in RAM is lost unless you saved it to your hard drive. Because of the volatile nature of RAM, many computer users make it a habit to save their work frequently. (Some software applications can do timed backups automatically.)

Launching a computer program brings files into RAM, and as long as they are running, computer programs reside in RAM. The CPU executes programmed instructions in RAM, and also stores results in RAM. RAM stores your keystrokes when you use a word processor and also stores numbers used in calculations. Telling a program to save your data instructs the program to store RAM contents on your hard drive as a file.

Physically, the *main memory* in a system is a collection of chips or modules containing chips that are normally plugged into the motherboard. These chips or modules vary in their electrical and physical design and must be compatible with the system into which they are being installed to function properly. In this chapter, I'll discuss the different types of chips and modules that can be installed in different systems.

Next to the processor, memory can be one of the more expensive components in a modern PC, although the total amount spent on memory for a typical system has declined over the past few years. Even after the price drops, you should still be spending more on the memory for your system than for your motherboard—in fact, up to twice as much. Before the memory price crash in mid-'96, memory had maintained a fairly consistent price for many years of about $40 per megabyte. A typical configuration back then of 16MB cost more than $600. In fact, memory was so expensive at that time, it was worth more than its weight in gold. These high prices caught the attention of criminals as memory module manufacturers were robbed at gunpoint in several large heists. These robberies were partially induced by the fact that memory was so valuable, the demand was high, and stolen chips or modules were virtually impossible to trace. After the rash of armed robberies and other thefts, memory module manufacturers began posting armed guards and implementing beefed-up security procedures.

By the end of 1996, memory prices had cooled considerably to about $4 a megabyte, a tenfold price drop in less than a year. Prices continued to fall after the major crash and recently have reached about a dollar per megabyte, or about $125 for 128MB, a typical configuration today. This means that of all the money spent on a PC system today, we are now installing about four times more memory in a system compared to a few years ago and, at the same time, are spending about 1/6 of its previous cost.

Memory costs less now than a few years ago, but its useful life has become much shorter. New types of memory are being adopted more quickly than before, and any new systems you purchase now most likely will not accept the same memory as your existing ones. In an upgrade or repair situation, that means you often have to change the memory if you change the motherboard. The chance that you can reuse the memory in an existing motherboard when upgrading to a new one is slim. This is likely to continue in the future, meaning that the system or upgrade motherboard you buy next year most likely can't use the memory in your current systems.

Because of this, you should understand all the different types of memory on the market today, so you can best determine which types are required by which systems, and thus more easily plan for future upgrades and repairs.

To better understand physical memory in a system, you should see where and how it fits into the system. There are three main types of physical memory used in modern PCs:

- *ROM*. Read-only memory
- *DRAM*. Dynamic random access memory
- *SRAM*. Static RAM

ROM

Read-only memory, or ROM, is a type of memory that can permanently or semipermanently hold data. It is called read-only because it is either impossible or difficult to write to. ROM is also often referred to as *nonvolatile memory* because any data stored in ROM remains there, even if the power is turned off. As such, ROM is an ideal place to put the PC's startup instructions—that is, the software that boots the system.

Note that ROM and RAM are not opposites, as some people seem to believe. In fact, ROM is technically a subset of the system's RAM. In other words, a portion of the system's Random Access Memory address space is mapped into one or more ROM chips. This is necessary to contain the software that enables the PC to boot up; otherwise, the processor would have no program in memory to execute when it was powered on.

▶▶ See "The Boot Process," p. 1351.

For example, when a PC is turned on, the processor automatically jumps to address FFFF0h, expecting to find instructions to tell the processor what to do. This location is exactly 16 bytes from the end of the first megabyte of RAM space and the end of the ROM. If this location were mapped into regular memory chips, any data stored there would have disappeared when the power was turned off previously, and the processor would subsequently find no instructions to run the next time power was turned on. By placing a ROM chip at this address, a system startup program can be permanently loaded into the ROM and is available every time the system is turned on.

◀◀ For more information about Dynamic RAM, see "DRAM," p. 418.

Normally, the system ROM starts at address F0000h, which is 64KB prior to the end of the first megabyte. Because the ROM chip is normally 64KB, the ROM programs occupy the entire last 64KB of the first megabyte, including the critical FFFF0h startup instruction address.

Some think it strange that the PC would start executing instructions 16 bytes from the end of the ROM, but this design was intentional. All the ROM programmer has to do is place a JMP (jump) instruction at that address, which instructs the processor to jump to the actual beginning of the ROM—in most cases close to F0000h, which is about 64KB earlier in the memory map. It's kind of like deciding to read every book starting 16 pages from the end, and then having all book publishers agree to place an instruction there to jump back the necessary number of pages to get to page 1. By setting the startup location in this way, Intel allowed the ROM to grow to be any size, all the while keeping it at the upper end of addresses in the first megabyte of the memory address space.

The main ROM BIOS is contained in a ROM chip on the motherboard, but there are also adapter cards with ROMs on them as well. ROMs on adapter cards contain auxiliary BIOS routines and drivers needed by the particular card, especially for those cards that must be active early in the boot process, such as video cards. Cards that don't need drivers active at boot time normally do not have a ROM because those drivers can be loaded from the hard disk later in the boot process.

The motherboard ROM normally contains four main programs, including the following in most systems:

- *POST (power on self test)*. A series of test routines that ensure the system components are operating properly.
- *CMOS Setup*. A menu-driven application that allows the user to set system configuration parameters, options, security settings, and preferences.
- *Bootstrap Loader*. The routine that first scans the floppy drive and then the hard disk, looking for an operating system to load.
- *BIOS (basic input/output system)*. A series of device driver programs designed to present a standard interface to the basic system hardware, especially hardware that must be active during the boot process.

Because the BIOS is the main portion of the code stored in ROM, we often call the ROM the *ROM BIOS*. In older PCs, the motherboard ROM BIOS could consist of up to five or six total chips, but most PCs have required only a single chip for many years now. For more information on the motherboard ROM, see Chapter 4, "Motherboards and Buses," and Chapter 5 "BIOS."

Adapter cards that require startup drivers also have ROMs on them. This includes cards such as video cards, most SCSI (Small Computer Systems Interface) cards, Enhanced IDE controller cards, and some network cards. The ROM chip on these cards contains drivers and startup programs that are executed by the motherboard ROM at boot time.

This, for example, is how a video card can be recognized and initialized, even though your motherboard ROM does not contain specific drivers for it. You wouldn't want to load the initial VGA mode drivers from disk because the screen would remain dark until those drivers were loaded. What happens is the motherboard ROM scans a special adapter ROM area of RAM (addresses C0000–DFFFFh), looking for a 55AAh signature byte pair that indicates the start of a ROM. The motherboard BIOS automatically runs the programs in any adapter ROMs it finds during the scan. You see this in most systems when you turn your system on, and during the POST you see the video card BIOS initialize and announce its presence.

There are four different types of ROM chips:

■ *ROM.* Read-only memory

■ *PROM.* Programmable ROM

■ *EPROM.* Erasable PROM

■ *EEPROM.* Electrically Erasable PROM, also called flash ROM

No matter which type of ROM you use, the data stored in a ROM chip is non-volatile and remains indefinitely unless intentionally erased or overwritten.

For more information on these types of chips, see Chapter 5.

DRAM

Dynamic RAM (DRAM) is the type of memory chip used for most of the main memory in a modern PC. The main advantages of DRAM are that it is very dense, meaning you can pack a lot of bits into a very small chip, and it is inexpensive, which makes it affordable for large amounts of memory.

The memory cells in a DRAM chip are tiny capacitors that retain a charge to indicate a bit. The problem with DRAM is that it is dynamic, and because of the design it must be constantly refreshed or the electrical charges in the individual memory capacitors will drain and the data will be lost. Refresh occurs when the system memory controller takes a tiny break and accesses all the rows of data in the memory chips. Most systems have a memory controller (normally built into the North Bridge portion of the motherboard chipset), which is set for an industry-standard refresh rate of 15µs (microseconds). The memory is accessed in such a way that all rows of data will be accessed after exactly 128 of these special refresh cycles. This means that every 1.92ms (milliseconds or 128×15µsec), all the rows in the memory are read to refresh the data.

◀◀ See "Chipsets," p. 235.

Refreshing the memory unfortunately takes processor time away from other tasks because each refresh cycle takes several CPU cycles to complete. In older systems, the refresh cycling could take up to 10 percent or more of the total CPU time, but with modern systems running in the hundreds of megahertz, refresh overhead is now on the order of 1 percent or less of the total CPU time. Some systems allow you to alter the refresh timing parameters via the CMOS Setup, but be aware that increasing the time between refresh cycles to speed up your system can allow some of the memory cells to begin draining, which can cause random soft memory errors to appear. A *soft error* is a data error that is not caused by a defective chip. It is usually safer to stick with the recommended or default refresh timing. Because refresh consumes less than 1 percent of modern system overall bandwidth, altering the refresh rate has little effect on performance.

DRAMs use only one transistor and capacitor pair per bit, which makes them very dense, offering more memory capacity per chip than other types of memory. There are currently DRAM chips available with densities of up to 256Mbits or more. This means that there are DRAM chips with 256 million or more transistors! Compare this to a Pentium II, which has 7.5 million transistors, and it makes the processor look wimpy by comparison. The difference is that in a memory chip, the transistors and capacitors are all consistently arranged in a (normally square) grid of simple repetitive structures, unlike the processor, which is a much more complex circuit of different structures and elements interconnected in a highly irregular fashion. At least one manufacturer is working on chips, intended for the 2001–2002 timeframe, with 256-gigabit densities using circuit line widths of 0.05 micron, indicating that memory densities will continue to rise as they have for years.

The transistor for each DRAM bit cell reads the charge state of the adjacent capacitor. If the capacitor is charged, the cell is read to contain a 1; no charge indicates a 0. The charge in the tiny capacitors is constantly draining, which is why the memory must be refreshed constantly. Even a momentary power interruption, or anything that interferes with the refresh cycles, can cause a DRAM memory cell to lose the charge and therefore the data.

DRAM is used in PC systems because it is inexpensive and the chips can be densely packed, meaning that a lot of memory capacity can fit in a small space. Unfortunately, DRAM is also slow, normally much slower than the processor. For this reason, there have been many different types of DRAM architectures developed to improve performance.

Cache Memory: SRAM

There is another distinctly different type of memory that is significantly faster than most types of DRAM. *SRAM* stands for *Static RAM*, which is so named because it does not need the periodic refresh rates like DRAM (Dynamic RAM). Because of SRAM's design, not only are refresh rates unnecessary, but SRAM is much faster than DRAM and fully able to keep pace with modern processors.

SRAM memory is available in access times of 2ns or less, which means it can keep pace with processors running 500MHz or faster! This is because of the SRAM design, which calls for a cluster of six transistors for each bit of storage. The use of transistors but no capacitors means that refresh rates are not necessary because there are no capacitors to lose their charges over time. As long as there is power, SRAM remembers what is stored. With these attributes, why don't we use SRAM for all system memory? The answers are simple:

Type	Speed	Density	Cost
DRAM	Slow	High	Low
SRAM	Fast	Low	High

Compared to DRAM, SRAM is much faster, but also much lower in density and much more expensive. The lower density means that SRAM chips are physically larger and store many fewer bits overall. The high number of transistors and the clustered design means that SRAM chips are both physically larger and much more expensive to produce than DRAM chips. For example, a DRAM module might contain 64MB of RAM or more, while SRAM modules of the same approximate physical size would have room for only 2MB or so of data and would cost the same as the 64MB DRAM module. Basically, SRAM is up to 30 times larger physically and up to 30 times more expensive than DRAM. The high cost and physical constraints have prevented SRAM from being used as the main memory for PC systems.

Even though SRAM is too expensive for PC use as main memory, PC designers have found a way to use SRAM to dramatically improve PC performance. Rather than spend the money for all RAM to be SRAM memory, which can run fast enough to match the CPU, it is much more cost-effective to design in a small amount of high-speed SRAM memory, called *cache memory*. The cache runs at speeds close to or even equal to the processor and is the memory from which the processor normally directly reads from and writes to. During read operations, the data in the high-speed cache memory is resupplied from the lower-speed main memory or DRAM in advance. Up until recently, DRAM was limited to about 60ns (16MHz) in speed. To convert access time in nanoseconds to MHz, use the following formula:

1 / nanoseconds × 1000 = MHz

Likewise to convert from MHz to nanoseconds, use the following inverse formula:

1 / MHz × 1000 = nanoseconds

When PC systems were running 16MHz and less, it was possible for the DRAM to fully keep pace with the motherboard and system processor, and there was no need for cache. However, as soon as processors crossed the 16MHz barrier, it was no longer possible for DRAM to keep pace, and that is exactly when SRAM began to enter PC system designs. This occurred back in 1986–1987 with the debut of systems with the 386 processor running at 16MHz and 20MHz. These were among the first PC systems to employ what's called *cache memory*, a high-speed buffer made up of SRAM that directly feeds the processor. Because the cache can run at the speed of the processor, the system is designed so that the cache controller will anticipate the processor's memory needs and preload the high-speed cache memory with that data. Then, as the processor calls for a memory address, the data can be retrieved from the high-speed cache rather than the much lower speed main memory.

Cache effectiveness is expressed as a hit ratio. This is the ratio of cache hits to total memory accesses. A *hit* happens when the data the processor needs has been preloaded into the cache from the main memory, meaning that the processor can read it from the cache. A *cache miss* is when the cache controller did not anticipate the need for a specific address; the desired data was not preloaded into the cache; therefore, the processor must retrieve the data from the slower main memory, instead of the faster cache. Anytime the processor reads data from main memory, the processor must wait because the main memory cycles at a much slower rate than the processor. If the processor is running at 233MHz, then it is cycling at nearly 4ns, while the main memory might be 60ns, which means it is running at only 16MHz. Therefore, every time the processor reads from main memory, it would effectively slow down to 16MHz! The slowdown is accomplished by having the processor execute what are called *wait states*, which are cycles in which nothing is done; the processor essentially cools its heels while waiting for the slower main memory to return the desired data. Obviously, we don't want our processors slowing down, so cache function and design become important as system speeds increase.

To minimize the processor being forced to read data from the slow main memory, there are normally two stages of cache in a modern system, called Level 1 (L1) and Level 2 (L2). The L1 cache is also called *integral* or *internal cache* because it is directly built into the processor and is actually a part of the processor die (raw chip). Because of this, L1 cache always runs at the full speed of the processor core and is the fastest cache in any system. All 486 and higher processors incorporate integral L1 cache, making them significantly faster than their predecessors. L2 cache is also called *external cache* because it is external to the processor chip. Originally, this meant it was installed on the motherboard, as was the case with all 386, 486, and Pentium systems. In those systems, the L2 cache runs at motherboard speed because it is installed on the motherboard. You can normally find the L2 cache directly next to the processor socket in Pentium and earlier systems.

In the interest of improved performance, later processor designs from Intel, including the Pentium Pro and Pentium II/III, have included the L2 cache as a part of the processor. It is still external to the actual CPU die and is instead a separate die or chip mounted inside the processor package or module. As such, Pentium Pro or Pentium II systems will not have any cache on the motherboard; it is all contained in the processor module, instead.

The key to understanding both cache and main memory is to see where they fit in the overall system architecture.

Figure 6.1 shows a typical Pentium MMX system with the Intel 430TX chipset.

See Figure 4.35 in Chapter 4 for a diagram showing a typical Pentium III system with integrated L2 cache.

Table 6.1 illustrates the need for and function of L1 (internal) and L2 (external) cache in modern systems.

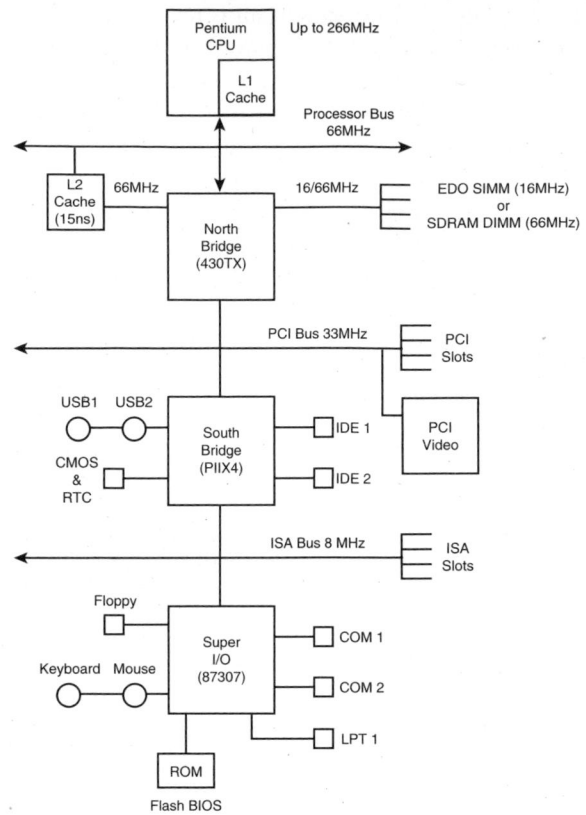

Figure 6.1 System architecture, Pentium MMX system with an Intel 430TX chipset.

Table 6.1   The Relationship Between L1 (Internal) and L2 (External) Cache in Modern Systems

CPU Type	486 DX4	Pentium	Pentium Pro	Pentium II (1997)	Pentium II (1998)
Typical CPU speed	100MHz	233MHz	200MHz	300MHz	400MHz
L1 cache speed	10ns	4.3ns	5.0ns	3.3ns	2.5ns
	(100MHz)	(233MHz)	(200MHz)	(300MHz)	(400MHz)
L2 cache speed	30ns	15ns	5ns	6ns	5ns
	(33MHz)	(66MHz)	(200MHz)	(150MHz)	(200MHz)
Motherboard speed	33MHz	66MHz	66MHz	66MHz	100MHz
SIMM/DIMM speed	60ns (16MHz)	60ns (16MHz)	60ns (16MHz)	15ns (66MHz)	10ns (100MHz)

Cache designs were originally *asynchronous*, meaning they ran at a clock speed that was not identical or in sync with the processor bus. Starting with the 430FX chipset released in early 1995, a new type of synchronous cache design was supported. It required that the chips now run in sync or at the same identical clock timing as the processor bus, further improving speed and performance. Also added at that time was a feature called *pipeline burst mode*, which reduced overall cache latency (wait states) by allowing single-cycle accesses for multiple transfers after the first one. Because both synchronous and pipeline burst capability came at the same time in new modules, usually specifying one implies the other. Overall synchronous pipeline burst cache allowed for about a 20 percent improvement in overall system performance, which was a significant jump.

The cache controller for a modern system is contained in either the North Bridge of the chipset, as with Pentium and lesser systems, or within the processor, as with the Pentium Pro/II and newer systems. The capabilities of the cache controller dictate the cache's performance and capabilities. One important thing to note is that most cache controllers have a limitation on the amount of memory that can be cached. Often, this limit can be quite low, as with the 430TX chipset-based Pentium systems. The 430TX chipset can cache data only within the first 64MB of system RAM. If you have more memory than that, you will see a noticeable slowdown in system performance because all data outside the first 64MB is never cached, and is always accessed with all the wait states required by the slower DRAM. Depending on what software you use and where data is stored in memory, this can be significant. For example, 32-bit operating systems, such as Windows 9x and NT, load from the top down, so if you had 96MB of RAM, the operating system and applications would load directly into the upper 32MB (past 64MB), which is not cached. This results in a dramatic slowdown in overall system use. Removing the additional memory to bring the system total down to the cacheable limit of 64MB is the solution. In short, it is unwise to install more main RAM memory than your system (chipset) can cache. Consult your system documentation or the chipset section in Chapter 4 for more information.

AMD K6-2	AMD K6-3	Celeron	Pentium III	Pentium III Xeon
475MHz	450MHz	466MHz	550MHz	550MHz
2.1ns	2.2ns	2.1ns	1.8ns	1.8ns
(475MHz)	(450MHz)	(466MHz)	(550MHz)	(550MHz)
10ns	2.2ns	2.1ns	3.6ns	1.8ns
(100MHz)	(450MHz)	(466MHz)	(275MHz)	(550MHz)
95MHz	100MHz	66MHz	100MHz	100MHz
10.5ns	10ns	15ns	10ns	10ns
(95MHz)	(100MHz)	(66MHz)	(100MHz)	(100MHz)

RAM Memory Speeds

The speed and performance issue with memory is confusing to some because memory speed is usually expressed in ns (nanoseconds), and processor speed has always been expressed in MHz (megahertz). Recently, however, some newer and faster types of memory have speeds expressed in MHz, adding to the confusion. Let's see if we can come up with a way to translate one to the other.

A *nanosecond* is defined as one billionth of a second—a very short time indeed. To put some perspective on that, the speed of light is 186,282 miles (299,792 kilometers) per second in a vacuum. In one billionth of a second, a beam of light travels a mere 11.80 inches or 29.98 centimeters, less than the length of a typical ruler!

Chip and system speed has been expressed in megahertz (MHz), which is millions of cycles per second. There are systems today with processors running 600MHz or faster, and we should see gigahertz (GHz, or billions of cycles per second) speeds within a few years.

Because it is confusing to speak in these different terms for speeds, I thought it would be interesting to see how they compare. Table 6.2 shows the relationship between nanoseconds (ns) and megahertz (MHz) for the speeds associated with PCs from yesterday to today and tomorrow.

Table 6.2   The Relationship Between Megahertz (MHz) and Cycle Times in Nanoseconds (ns)

Clock Speed	Cycle Time	Clock Speed	Cycle Time	Clock Speed	Cycle Time
4.77MHz	210ns	120MHz	8.3ns	433MHz	2.3ns
6MHz	167ns	133MHz	7.5ns	450MHz	2.2ns
8MHz	125ns	150MHz	6.7ns	466MHz	2.1ns
10MHz	100ns	166MHz	6.0ns	500MHz	2.0ns
12MHz	83ns	180MHz	5.6ns	533MHz	1.9ns
16MHz	63ns	200MHz	5.0ns	550MHz	1.8ns
20MHz	50ns	225MHz	4.4ns	600MHz	1.7ns
25MHz	40ns	233MHz	4.3ns	650MHz	1.5ns
33MHz	30ns	250MHz	4.0ns	700MHz	1.4ns
40MHz	25ns	266MHz	3.8ns	750MHz	1.3ns
50MHz	20ns	300MHz	3.3ns	800MHz	1.3ns
60MHz	17ns	333MHz	3.0ns	850MHz	1.2ns
66MHz	15ns	350MHz	2.9ns	900MHz	1.1ns
75MHz	13ns	366MHz	2.7ns	950MHz	1.1ns
80MHz	13ns	400MHz	2.5ns	1000MHz	1.0ns
100MHz	10ns				

As you can see from this table, as clock speeds increase, cycle time decreases proportionately.

If you examine this table, you can clearly see that the 60ns DRAM memory used in the typical PC for many years is totally inadequate when compared to processor speeds of 400MHz and higher. Up until 1998, most DRAM memory used in PCs has been rated at an access time of 60ns or higher, which works out to be 16.7MHz or slower! This super-slow 16MHz memory has been installed in systems running up to 300MHz or faster, and you can see what a mismatch there has been between processor and main memory performance. More recently we have 100MHz and even 133MHz memory, called PC100 and PC133 respectively.

System memory timing is a little more involved than simply converting nanoseconds to megahertz. The transistors for each bit in a memory chip are most efficiently arranged in a grid, using a row and column scheme to access each transistor. All memory accesses involve selecting a row address and then a column address, and then transferring the data. The initial setup for a memory transfer where the row and column addresses are selected is a necessary overhead normally referred to as *latency*. The access time for memory is the cycle time plus latency for selecting the row and column addresses. For example, memory rated at 60ns normally has a latency of about 25ns (to select the row and column address) and a cycle time of about 35ns to actually transfer the data. Therefore, the true memory clock rate in a system with 60ns memory would be on the order of 28.5MHz (35ns = 28.5MHz). Even so, a single memory transfer still requires a full 60ns, so consecutive transfers happen at a rate of only 16.7MHz (60ns) because of the added latency.

What happens when a 300MHz processor is trying to read multiple bytes of data from 16MHz memory? A lot of wait states! A wait state is an additional "do nothing" cycle that the processor must execute while waiting for the data to become ready. With memory cycling every 60ns (16MHz) and a processor cycling every 3ns (300MHz), the processor has to execute approximately 19 wait states before the data is ready on the twentieth cycle. Adding wait states in this fashion effectively slows the processing speed to that of the memory, or 16MHz in this example. To reduce the number of wait states required, several types of faster memory and cache are available, all of which are discussed in this chapter.

Over the development life of the PC, memory has had a difficult time keeping up with the processor, requiring several levels of high-speed cache memory to intercept processor requests for the slower main memory. Table 6.3 shows the progress and relationship between system board (motherboard) speeds in PCs and the different types and speeds of main memory or RAM used.

Table 6.3   Relationship of Motherboard Speeds to RAM Speeds

Motherboard Speeds	Processor Speeds	RAM Type	RAM Speeds	Timeframe
5MHz–66MHz	5MHz–200MHz	FPM/EDO	5MHz–16MHz	1981–1996
66MHz–100MHz	200MHz–450MHz	SDRAM	66MHz or 100MHz	1997–1998
100MHz+	500MHz+	RDRAM	600MHz or 800MHz	1999+

FPM = Fast Page Mode
EDO = Extended Data Out
SDRAM = Synchronous Dynamic RAM
RDRAM = Rambus DRAM

As you can see from this table, memory development was very slow for the first 15 years of PC history, with speeds accelerating from 200ns (5MHz) to 60ns (16MHz). By 1996, PC processor speeds had increased from 5MHz to 200MHz, but main memory had increased from 5MHz to only 16MHz in that same timeframe! More recently, main memory has caught up to the processor speed with the introduction of the RDRAM (Rambus DRAM) in new systems for 1999 and beyond.

Fast Page Mode (FPM) DRAM

Standard DRAM is accessed through a technique called *paging*. Normal memory access requires that a row and column address be selected, which takes time. Paging allows faster access to all the data within a given row of memory by keeping the row address the same and changing only the column. Memory that uses this technique is called *Page Mode* or *Fast Page Mode* memory. Other variations on Page Mode were called *Static Column* or *Nibble Mode* memory.

Paged memory is a simple scheme for improving memory performance that divides memory into pages ranging from 512 bytes to a few kilobytes long. The paging circuitry then enables memory locations in a page to be accessed with fewer wait states. If the desired memory location is outside the current page, one or more wait states are added while the system selects the new page.

To improve further on memory access speeds, systems have evolved to allow faster access to DRAM. One important change was the implementation of burst mode access in the 486 and later processors. Burst mode cycling takes advantage of the consecutive nature of most memory accesses. After setting up the row and column addresses for a given access, using burst mode, you can then access the next three adjacent addresses with no additional latency or wait states. A burst access is normally limited to four total accesses. To describe this, we often refer to the timing in the number of cycles for each access. A typical burst mode access of standard DRAM is expressed as x-y-y-y; x is the time for the first access (latency plus cycle time), and y represents the number of cycles required for each consecutive access.

Standard 60ns DRAM normally runs 5-3-3-3 burst mode timing. This means the first access takes a total of five cycles (on a 66MHz system bus, this is about 75ns total or 5×15ns cycles), and the consecutive cycles take three cycles each (3×15ns = 45ns). As you can see, the actual system timing is somewhat less than the memory is technically rated for. Without the bursting technique, memory access would be 5-5-5-5 because the full latency is needed for each memory transfer.

DRAM memory that supports paging and this bursting technique is called *Fast Page Mode* (FPM) memory. The term comes from the ability of memory accesses to data on the same page to be done with less latency. Most 486 and Pentium systems from 1995 and earlier use FPM memory.

Another technique for speeding up FPM memory was a technique called *interleaving*. In this design, two separate banks of memory are used together, alternating access from one to the other as even and odd bytes. While one is being accessed, the other is being precharged, when the row and column addresses are being selected. Then, by the time the first bank in the pair is finished returning data, the second bank in the pair is finished with the latency part of the cycle and is now ready to return data. While the second bank is returning data, the first bank is being precharged, selecting the row and column address of the next access. This overlapping of accesses in two banks reduces the effect of the latency or precharge cycles and allows for faster overall data retrieval. The only problem is that to use interleaving, you must install identical pairs of banks together, doubling the amount of SIMMs or DIMMs required. This method was popular on 32-bit wide memory systems on 486 processors, but fell out of favor on Pentiums because of their 64-bit wide memory width. To do interleaving on a Pentium machine, you would need to install memory 128 bits at a time, meaning four 72-pin SIMMs or two DIMMs at a time.

EDO (Extended Data Out) RAM

A new type of memory called *EDO (Extended Data Out)* RAM became available for Pentium systems in 1995. EDO, a modified form of FPM memory, is also referred to as *Hyper Page Mode*. EDO was invented and patented by Micron Technology, although it has licensed production to many other memory manufacturers. EDO memory consists of specially manufactured chips that allow a timing overlap between successive accesses. The name *Extended Data Out* refers specifically to the fact that unlike FPM, the data output drivers on the chip are not turned off when the memory controller removes the column address to begin the next cycle. This allows the next cycle to overlap the previous one, saving approximately 10ns per cycle.

The effect of EDO is that cycle times are improved by allowing the memory controller to begin a new column address instruction while it is reading data at the current address. This is almost identical to what was achieved in older systems by interleaving banks of memory, but unlike interleaving, you don't need to install two identical banks of memory in the system at a time.

EDO RAM allows for burst mode cycling of 5-2-2-2, compared to the 5-3-3-3 of standard Fast Page Mode memory. To do four memory transfers, then, EDO would require 11 total system cycles, compared to 14 total cycles for FPM. This is a 22 percent improvement in overall cycling time, but in actual testing EDO normally increases overall system benchmark speed by about 5 percent. Even though the overall system improvement might seem small, the important thing about EDO is that it uses the same basic DRAM chip design as FPM, meaning that there is practically no additional cost over FPM. As such, EDO costs about the same as FPM and offers higher performance.

To actually use EDO memory, your motherboard chipset must support it. Most motherboard chipsets since the Intel 430FX (Triton), which debuted in 1995, have offered support for EDO. Because EDO memory chips cost the same to manufacture as standard chips, combined with Intel's support of EDO in all their chipsets, the PC market jumped on the EDO bandwagon full force.

◄◄ See "Fifth-Generation (P5 Pentium Class) Chipsets," p. 129, and "Sixth-Generation (P6 Pentium Pro/Pentium II/III Class) Chipsets," p. 151.

EDO RAM is ideal for systems with bus speeds of up to 66MHz, which fit perfectly with the PC market up through 1997. However, since 1998, the market for EDO has rapidly declined as the newer and faster SDRAM (Synchronous DRAM) architecture has become the standard for new PC system memory.

Burst EDO

A variation of EDO is *Burst Extended-Data-Out Dynamic Random Access Memory (BEDO DRAM)*. BEDO is basically EDO memory with special burst features for even speedier data transfers than standard EDO. Unfortunately, only one chipset (Intel 440FX Natoma) supported it, and it was quickly overshadowed by SDRAM, which seemed to be favored among PC system chipset and system designers. As such, you won't see BEDO being used in systems today, and it is no longer in production.

SDRAM

SDRAM stands for *Synchronous DRAM*, a type of DRAM that runs in synchronization with the memory bus. SDRAM delivers information in very high-speed bursts using a high-speed, clocked interface. SDRAM removes most of the latency involved in asynchronous DRAM because the signals are already in synchronization with the motherboard clock.

Like EDO RAM, your chipset must support this type of memory for it to be usable in your system. Starting in 1997 with the 430VX and 430TX, most of Intel's subsequent chipsets support SDRAM, making it the most popular type of memory for new systems. SDRAM is especially suited to the Pentium II/III architecture and the high-performance motherboards that run them.

SDRAM's performance is dramatically improved over FPM or EDO RAM. Because SDRAM is still a type of DRAM, the initial latency is the same, but overall cycle times are much faster than with FPM or EDO. SDRAM timing for a burst access would be 5-1-1-1, meaning that four memory reads would complete in only eight system bus cycles, compared to 11 cycles for EDO and 14 cycles for FPM.

Besides being able to work in fewer cycles, SDRAM is also capable of supporting 100MHz (10ns) or faster system bus cycling, which since 1998 has become the new standard for system speed. As such, almost all new PC systems sold in 1998 and for probably three years thereafter will include SDRAM memory. Recently SDRAM was updated to a revised PC133 specification, where the memory runs at up to 133MHz. This will be used in lower cost systems in lieu of faster RDRAM.

In the near future, this figure will probably be pushed to 200MHz to keep up with faster systems of the future.

SDRAM is sold in DIMM form and is often rated by megahertz speed rather than nanosecond cycling time, so you see SDRAM sold as 66MHz or 15ns, 83MHz or 12ns, or 100MHz or 10ns. Because of the extreme timing at the 100MHz level, Intel has created a PC/100 standard that defines the performance criteria a 100MHz memory module must meet to be reliable in a 100MHz system. To meet the criteria with enough overhead to spare, most PC/100-certified memory will be 8ns, or 125MHz. Even though they are technically capable of 125MHz, they will be PC/100 or 100MHz "certified." Although 10ns memory might work, Intel feels that it will not be reliable enough because the margins are too close.

Although SDRAM is much faster than previous types of memory, prices are not appreciably higher, which has made SDRAM's acceptance even more rapid.

►► See "SIMMs and DIMMs," p. 437.

Future DRAM Memory Technologies

RDRAM

The *RDRAM*, or *Rambus DRAM*, is a radical new memory design found in high-end PC systems starting in 1999. It is endorsed by Intel and is supported in most of their new PC motherboard chipsets for 1999 and beyond.

Rambus developed what is essentially a chip-to-chip memory bus, with specialized devices that communicate at very high rates of speed. What may be interesting to some is that this technology was first developed for game systems and first made popular by the Nintendo 64 game system!

Conventional memory systems that use FPM/EDO or SDRAM are known as *wide channel systems*. They have memory channels as wide as the processor's data bus, which for the Pentium and up is 64 bits. The DIMM (Dual Inline Memory Module) is a 64-bit wide device, meaning data can be transferred to it 64 bits (or 8 bytes) at a time. The fastest DIMMs are the SDRAM type, which run at 100MHz, meaning the overall throughput is 100 × 8, or 800Mbytes/sec. Most SDRAM controllers (built into the motherboard chipset North Bridge component) can handle only a single channel of memory with up to three or four banks total.

RDRAMs, on the other hand, are a narrow channel device. They transfer data only 16 bits (2 bytes) at a time (plus 2 optional parity bits), but at much faster speeds. They normally run 800MHz, meaning the overall throughput is 800 × 2, or 1.6GB per second, twice that of SDRAM. Also, there is far less latency between transfers because they all run synchronously in a looped system and in only one direction, meaning that the actual overall throughput of an RDRAM bus is nearly triple that of standard 100MHz SDRAM. For further increases in speed, it is possible to use two or four RDRAM channels simultaneously, increasing memory throughput to 3.2GB/sec or 6.4GB/sec if necessary.

A single Rambus memory channel can support up to 32 individual RDRAM devices (the RDRAM chips), more if buffers are used. Each individual chip is serially connected to the next on a package called a *RIMM* (*Rambus Inline Memory Module*), but all memory transfers are done between the memory controller and a single device, not between devices. The individual RDRAM chips are contained on RIMMs, and a single channel normally has three RIMM sockets. The RDRAM memory bus is a continuous path through each device and module on the bus, with each module having input and output pins on opposite ends. Therefore, any RIMM sockets not containing a RIMM must then be filled with a continuity module to ensure that the path is completed. The signals that reach the end of the bus are terminated on the motherboard.

Each RDRAM on a RIMM essentially operates as a standalone module sitting on the 16-bit data bus. Internally, each RDRAM chip has a core that operates on a 128-bit wide bus split into eight 16-bit banks running at 100MHz. In other words, every 10ns (100MHz), each RDRAM chip can transfer 16 bytes to and from the core. This internally wide, yet externally narrow, high-speed interface is the key to RDRAM. Because of this design, the same type of silicon chip technology can be used to increase speeds dramatically, while maintaining the same overall cost as the SDRAM type memory that preceded it. In other words, RDRAM, which is three times faster than SDRAM overall, costs about the same and is easy to manufacture.

Other improvements to the design include separating control and data signals on the bus. There are independent control and address buses split into two groups of pins for row and column commands, while data is transferred across the 2-byte wide data bus. The actual memory bus clock runs at 400MHz; however, data is transferred on both the falling and rising edge of the clock signal, or twice per clock pulse. The falling edge is called an *even cycle* and the rising edge is called an *odd cycle*. Complete memory bus synchronization is achieved by sending packets of data beginning on an even cycle interval. The overall wait before a memory transfer can begin (latency) is only one cycle, or 2.5ns maximum.

Figure 6.2 shows the relationship between clock and data cycles; you can see 5 total clock cycles (each with a falling and rising edge) and 10 data cycles in the same time. An RDRAM data packet always begins on an even (falling) transition for synchronization purposes.

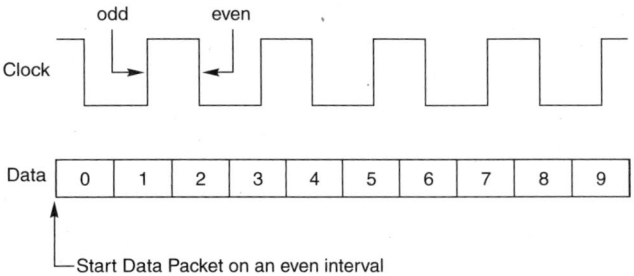

Figure 6.2 RDRAM clock and data cycle relationship.

The architecture also supports multiple, simultaneous interleaved transactions in multiple separate time domains. This means that before a transfer has even completed, another can begin.

Another important feature of RDRAM is that it is a low-power memory system. The RIMMs themselves as well as the RDRAM devices run on only 2.5 volts and use low voltage signal swings from 1.0v to 1.8v, a swing of only 0.8v total. Combine this with RDRAMs also having four power-down modes and automatically transitioning into standby at the end of a transaction, and you can see why total module power is slightly lower than an SDRAM's at the desktop and similar to EDO for mobile systems.

RDRAM chips will be installed in modules called RIMMs. A RIMM (shown in Figure 6.3) is similar in size and physical form to current DIMMs, but they are not interchangeable. RIMMs are available in 32MB, 64MB, 128MB, and soon 256MB and larger capacities. They can be added to a system one at a time because each individual RIMM represents multiple banks to a system.

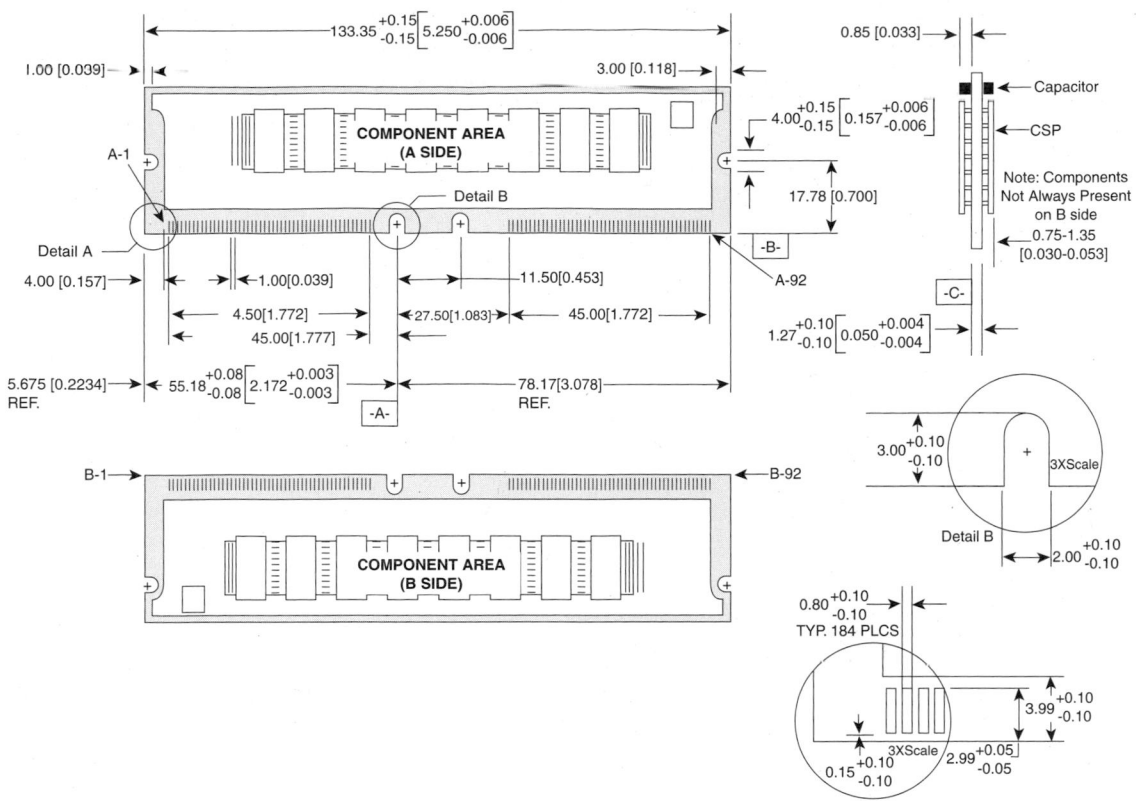

Figure 6.3 A 168-pin RIMM module.

An RDRAM memory controller with a single Rambus channel supports up to three RIMM modules, which at the 64Mbit-chip density level supports 256MB per RIMM. Future RIMM versions will be available in higher capacities, up to 1GB or more, and it will be possible to develop chipsets (with integral Rambus memory controllers) that can support more Rambus channels, allowing more RIMM sockets per board. There will also be a Small Outline (SO) version of the RIMM called an *SO-RIMM*, specifically designed to be used in notebook and portable computers.

RIMM modules and sockets are gold-plated and designed for 25 insertion/removal cycles. Each RIMM has 184 pins, split into two groups of 92 pins on opposite ends and sides of the module. The pinout of the RIMM is shown in Table 6.4.

Table 6.4   RIMM Pinout

Pin	Pin Name	Pin	Pin Name	Pin	Pin Name	Pin	Pin Name
A1	Gnd	B1	Gnd	A47	NC	B47	NC
A2	LDQA8	B2	LDQA7	A48	NC	B48	NC
A3	Gnd	B3	Gnd	A49	NC	B49	NC
A4	LDQA6	B4	LDQA5	A50	NC	B50	NC
A5	Gnd	B5	Gnd	A51	Vref	B51	Vref
A6	LDQA4	B6	LDQA3	A52	Gnd	B52	Gnd
A7	Gnd	B7	Gnd	A53	SCL	B53	SA0
A8	LDQA2	B8	LDQA1	A54	Vdd	B54	Vdd
A9	Gnd	B9	Gnd	A55	SDA	B55	SA1
A10	LDQA0	B10	LCFM	A56	SVdd	B56	SVdd
A11	Gnd	B11	Gnd	A57	SWP	B57	SA2
A12	LCTMN	B12	LCFMN	A58	Vdd	B58	Vdd
A13	Gnd	B13	Gnd	A59	RSCK	B59	RCMD
A14	LCTM	B14	NC	A60	Gnd	B60	Gnd
A15	Gnd	B15	Gnd	A61	RDQB7	B61	RDQB8
A16	NC	B16	LROW2	A62	Gnd	B62	Gnd
A17	Gnd	B17	Gnd	A63	RDQB5	B63	RDQB6
A18	LROW1	B18	LROW0	A64	Gnd	B64	Gnd
A19	Gnd	B19	Gnd	A65	RDQB3	B65	RDQB4
A20	LCOL4	B20	LCOL3	A66	Gnd	B66	Gnd
A21	Gnd	B21	Gnd	A67	RDQB1	B67	RDQB2
A22	LCOL2	B22	LCOL1	A68	Gnd	B68	Gnd
A23	Gnd	B23	Gnd	A69	RCOL0	B69	RDQB0
A24	LCOL0	B24	LDQB0	A70	Gnd	B70	Gnd
A25	Gnd	B25	Gnd	A71	RCOL2	B71	RCOL1
A26	LDQB1	B26	LDQB2	A72	Gnd	B72	Gnd
A27	Gnd	B27	Gnd	A73	RCOL4	B73	RCOL3
A28	LDQB3	B28	LDQB4	A74	Gnd	B74	Gnd
A29	Gnd	B29	Gnd	A75	RROW1	B75	RROW0
A30	LDQB5	B30	LDQB6	A76	Gnd	B76	Gnd
A31	Gnd	B31	Gnd	A77	NC	B77	RROW2
A32	LDQB7	B32	LDQB8	A78	Gnd	B78	Gnd
A33	Gnd	B33	Gnd	A79	RCTM	B79	NC
A34	LSCK	B34	LCMD	A80	Gnd	B80	Gnd
A35	Vcmos	B35	Vcmos	A81	RCTMN	B81	RCFMN
A36	SOUT	B36	SIN	A82	Gnd	B82	Gnd
A37	Vcmos	B37	Vcmos	A83	RDQA0	B83	RCFM
A38	NC	B38	NC	A84	Gnd	B84	Gnd
A39	Gnd	B39	Gnd	A85	RDQA2	B85	RDQA1

Pin	Pin Name	Pin	Pin Name	Pin	Pin Name	Pin	Pin Name
A40	NC	B40	NC	A86	Gnd	B86	Gnd
A41	Vdd	B41	Vdd	A87	RDQA4	B87	RDQA3
A42	Vdd	B42	Vdd	A88	Gnd	B88	Gnd
A43	NC	B43	NC	A89	RDQA6	B89	RDQA5
A44	NC	B44	NC	A90	Gnd	B90	Gnd
A45	NC	B45	NC	A91	RDQA8	B91	RDQA7
A46	NC	B46	NC	A92	Gnd	B92	Gnd

RIMMs are keyed with two notches in the center. This prevents a backward insertion and prevents the wrong type (voltage) RIMM from being used in a system. Currently, all RIMMs run on 2.5v, but there might be new versions in the future that run on less. To allow for these new types of RIMMs, there are three possible keying options in the design (see Figure 6.4). The left key (indicated as "DATUM A" in the following figure) is fixed in position, but the center key can be in three different positions spaced 1 or 2mm to the right, indicating different types of RIMMs. The current default is option A, as shown in Figure 6.6 and Table 6.5, which corresponds to 2.5v operation.

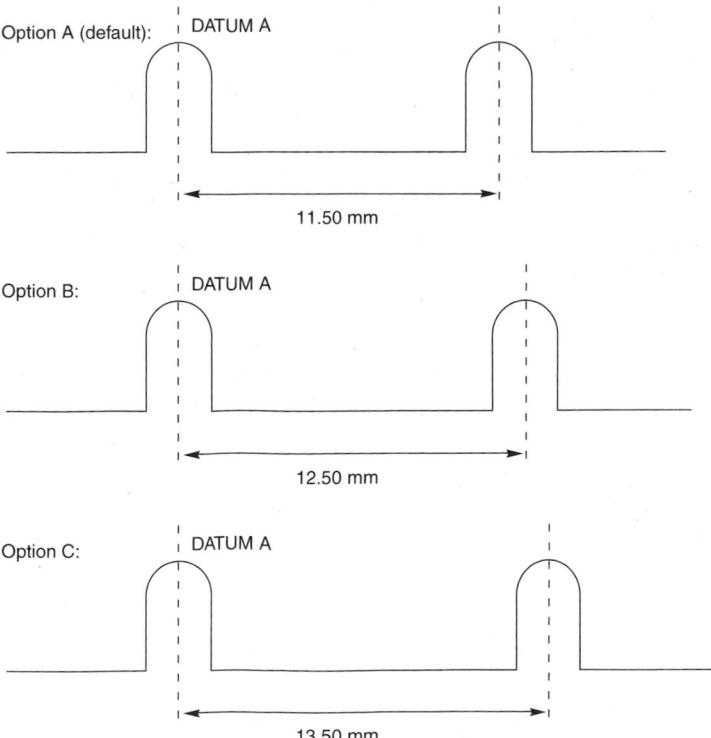

Figure 6.4 RIMM keying options.

Table 6.5—Possible Keying Options for RIMMs

Option	Notch Separation	Description
A	11.5mm	2.5v RIMM
B	12.5mm	Reserved
C	13.5mm	Reserved

RIMMs incorporate a Serial Presence Detect (SPD) device, which is essentially a flash ROM on board. This ROM contains information about the RIMM's size and type, including detailed timing information for the memory controller. The memory controller automatically reads the data from the SPD ROM to configure the system to match the RIMMs installed.

Figure 6.5 shows a typical PC RIMM installation. The RDRAM controller and clock generator are typically in the motherboard chipset North Bridge component. As you can see, the Rambus memory channel flows from the memory controller through each of up to three RIMM modules in series. Each module contains 4, 8, 16, or more RDRAM devices (chips), also wired in series, with an onboard SPD ROM for system configuration. Any RIMM sockets without a RIMM installed must have a continuity module, shown in the last socket in this figure. This allows the memory bus to remain continuous from the controller through each module (and, therefore, each RDRAM device on the module) until the bus finally terminates on the motherboard. Note how the bus loops from one module to another. For timing purposes, the first RIMM socket must be 6 inches or less from the memory controller, and the entire length of the bus must not be more than it would take for a signal to go from one end to another in four data clocks, or about 5ns.

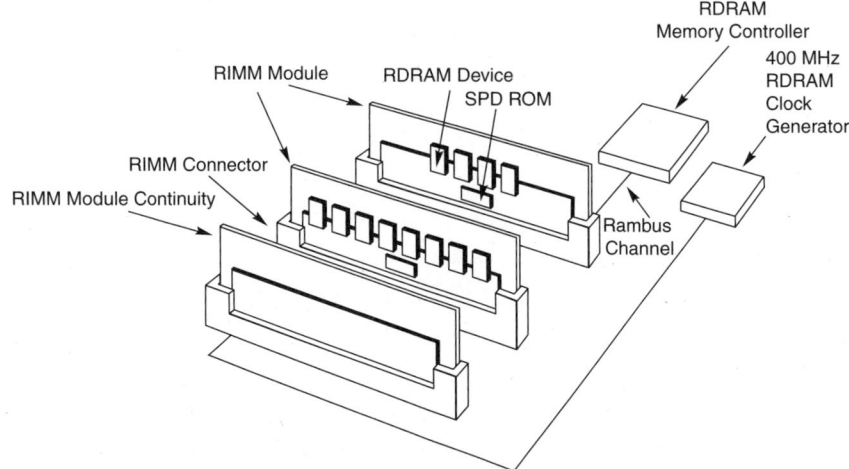

Figure 6.5 Typical RDRAM bus layout, showing two RIMMs and one continuity module installed.

Interestingly, Rambus does not manufacture the RDRAM devices (the chips) or the RIMMs; that is left to other companies. Rambus is merely a design company, and it has no chip fabs or manufacturing facilities of its own. It licenses its technology to other companies who then manufacture the devices and modules. There are currently at least 13 RDRAM licensees, including Fujitsu Ltd., Hitachi Ltd., Hyundai Electronics Industry Co. Ltd., IBM Microelectronics, LG Semiconductor Co. Ltd., Micron Technology Inc., Mitsubishi Electric Corp., NEC Corp., Oki Electric Industry Co. Ltd., Samsung Electronics Corp., Siemens AG, and Toshiba Corp. All these companies are manufacturing both the RDRAM devices and the RIMMs that contain them.

With Intel throwing its full weight behind the Rambus memory, and the outstanding performance of RDRAM combined with low cost, low power consumption, and small size, RDRAM is positioned to be the standard for PC memory into the next millennium and beyond.

DDR SDRAM

Double Data Rate (*DDR*) SDRAM memory is an evolutionary design of standard SDRAM in which data is transferred twice as fast. Instead of doubling the actual clock rate, DDR memory achieves the doubling in performance by transferring twice per transfer cycle, once at the leading (falling) and once at the trailing (rising) edge of the cycle (see Figure 6.2). This is similar to the way RDRAM operates and effectively doubles the transfer rate, even though the same overall clock and timing signals are used.

DDR is being proposed by processor companies, including AMD and Cyrix, and chipset manufacturers, including VIA Technologies, ALi (Acer Labs, Inc.), and SiS (Silicon Integrated Systems), as a low-cost license-free alternative to RDRAMs. Intel is officially supporting only RDRAMs for new high-end systems in 1999 and beyond, but DDR seems destined for the lower-end commodity PCs as an alternative. The DDR Consortium, an industry panel consisting of Fujitsu, Ltd., Hitachi, Ltd., Hyundai Electronics Industries Co., Mitsubishi Electric Corp., NEC Corp., Samsung Electronics Co., Texas Instruments, Inc., and Toshiba Corp. undertook official standardization of DDR.

Expect DDR SDRAM to make an appearance during late 1999, primarily in non-Intel processor–based systems.

Physical RAM Memory

The CPU and motherboard architecture (chipset) dictates a particular computer's physical memory capacity and the types and forms of memory that can be installed. Over the years, two main changes have occurred in computer memory—it has gradually become faster and wider! The CPU and the memory controller circuitry indicate the speed and width requirements. The memory controller in a modern PC resides in the motherboard chipset. Even though a system may physically support a given amount of memory, the type of software you run could dictate whether all the memory can be used.

The 8088 and 8086, with 20 address lines, can use as much as 1MB (1,024KB) of RAM. The 286 and 386SX CPUs have 24 address lines; they can keep track of as much as 16MB of memory. The 386DX, 486, Pentium, Pentium-MMX, and Pentium Pro CPUs have a full set of 32 address lines; they can keep track of 4GB of memory, and the Pentium II/III with 36 address lines can manage an impressive 64GB!

◄◄ See "Processor Specifications," p. 39.

When the 286 and higher chips emulate the 8088 chip (as they do when running 16-bit software, such as DOS or Windows 3.x), they implement a hardware operating mode called *real mode*. Real mode is the only mode available on the 8086 and 8088 chips used in PC and XT systems. In real mode, all Intel processors—even the mighty Pentium—are restricted to using only 1MB of memory, just as their 8086 and 8088 ancestors were, and the system design reserves 384KB of that amount. Only in protected mode can the 286 or better chips use their maximum potential for memory addressing.

◄◄ See "Processor Modes," p. 58.

Pentium-based systems can address as much as 4GB of memory, and P6 class (Pentium Pro/II/Celeron/III) systems can address 64GB. To put these memory-addressing capabilities into perspective, 64GB (65,536MB) of memory would cost about $70,000! Even if you could afford all this memory, some of the largest memory modules available today are 168-pin DIMMs with 256MB capacity. To install 64GB of RAM would require 256 of the largest 256MB DIMMs available, and most systems today can support up to only four or maybe eight DIMM sockets.

Most Pentium II/Celeron/III motherboards have a maximum of only three to six DIMM sockets, which allows a maximum of .75–1.5GB if all the sockets are filled. These limitations are from the chipset, not the processor. Technically, a Pentium can address 4GB of memory and a Pentium II/Celeron/III can address 64GB, but there isn't a chipset on the market that will allow that! Most of the Pentium II/III chipsets today are limited to 1GB of memory, some will handle up to 4GB.

Pentium systems have even more limitations. Pentium systems have been available since 1993, but only those built in 1997 or later use a motherboard chipset that supports SDRAM DIMMs. Even those using the newest 430TX chipset from Intel will not support more than 256MB of total memory and should not have more than 64MB actually installed because of memory-caching limitations. Don't install more than 64MB of RAM in your Pentium system unless you are sure the motherboard and chipset will allow the L2 cache to function with the additional memory.

Note

See the "Chipsets" section in Chapter 4 for the maximum cacheable limits on all the Intel and other motherboard chipsets.

Older 386 and 486 motherboards could have problems addressing memory past 16MB because of DMA (Direct Memory Access) controller problems. If you install an ISA adapter that uses a DMA channel (such as a busmaster SCSI adapter) and you have more than 16MB of memory, you have the potential for problems because the ISA bus allows only DMA access to 16MB. Attempted transfers beyond 16MB cause the system to crash. This should not be an issue with newer 32-bit operating systems and 32-bit slots such as PCI. The 32-bit operating systems automatically remap ISA bus DMA transfers beyond 16MB properly, and PCI simply doesn't have any such limitations.

SIMMs and DIMMs

Originally, systems had memory installed via individual chips. They are often referred to as *DIP* (*Dual Inline Package*) chips because of their design. The original IBM XT and AT had 36 sockets on the motherboard for these individual chips, and then more of them were installed on the memory cards plugged into the bus slots. I remember spending hours populating boards with these chips, which was a tedious job.

Besides being a time-consuming and labor-intensive way to deal with memory, DIP chips had one notorious problem—they crept out of their sockets over time as the system went through thermal cycles. Every day, when you powered the system on and off, the system heated and cooled, and the chips gradually walked their way out of the sockets. Eventually, good contact was lost and memory errors resulted. Fortunately, reseating all the chips back in their sockets usually rectified the problem, but that method was labor intensive if you had a lot of systems to support.

The alternative to this at the time was to have the memory soldered into either the motherboard or an expansion card. This prevented the chips from creeping and made the connections more permanent, but that caused another problem. If a chip did go bad, you had to attempt desoldering and resoldering a new one or resort to scrapping the motherboard or memory card where the chip was installed. This was expensive and made memory troubleshooting difficult.

What was needed was a chip that was both soldered yet removable, and that is exactly what was found in the chip called a *SIMM*. For memory storage, most modern systems have adopted the Single Inline Memory Module (SIMM) or Dual Inline Memory Module (DIMM) as an alternative to individual memory chips. These small boards pluginto special connectors on a motherboard or memory card. The individual memory chips are soldered to the SIMM/DIMM, so removing and replacing them is impossible. Instead, you must replace the entire module if any part of it fails. The SIMM/DIMM is treated as though it were one large memory chip.

PC systems use two main physical types of SIMMs—30-pin (8 bits plus 1 optional parity bit) and 72-pin (32 bits plus 4 optional parity bits)—with various capacities and other specifications. The 30-pin SIMMs are smaller than the 72-pin versions and may have chips on one or both sides. The 30-pin SIMMs are basically obsolete and are being followed rapidly by the 72-pin versions. This is true primarily because the 64-bit systems, which are now the industry standard, would require eight 30-pin SIMMs or two 72-pin SIMMs per bank.

DIMMs, which are popular on Pentium-MMX, Pentium Pro, and Pentium II–based systems, are 168-pin units with 64-bit (non-parity) or 72-bit (parity or ECC) data paths. A 168-pin DIMM is physically one inch longer than a 72-pin SIMM, and can be recognized by having a secondary keying notch, but the main physical difference is that DIMMs have different signal pins on each side of the module. That is why they are called Dual Inline Memory Modules, and why with only an inch of additional length, they have many more pins than a SIMM.

Figures 6.6, 6.7, and 6.8 show typical 30-pin (8-bit) and 72-pin (32-bit) SIMMs and a 168-pin (64-bit) DIMM, respectively. The pins are numbered from left to right and are connected through to both sides of the module on the SIMMs. The pins on the DIMM are different on each side, but on a SIMM, each side is the same as the other, and the connections carry through. Note that all dimensions are in both inches and millimeters (in parentheses).

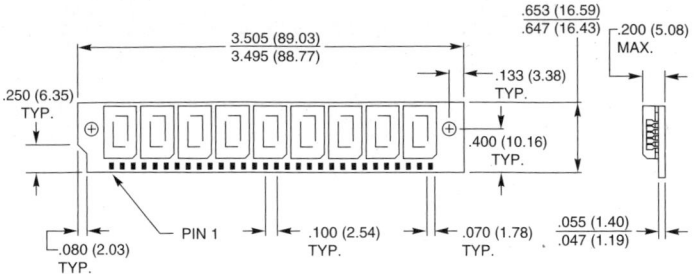

Figure 6.6 A typical 30-pin SIMM. The one shown here is 9-bit, although the dimensions would be the same for 8-bit.

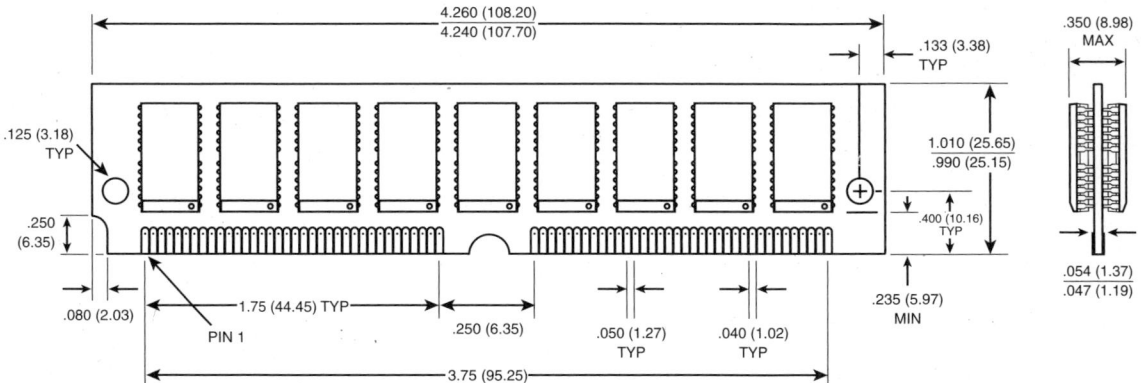

Figure 6.7 A typical 72-pin SIMM, although the dimensions would be the same for 32 bit.

Single inline pinned packages, sometimes called *SIPPs*, really are SIMMs with pins, not contacts. The pins are designed to be installed in a long connector socket that is much cheaper than the standard SIMM socket. SIPPs are inferior to SIMMs because they lack the positive latching mechanism that retains the module, and the connector lacks the high-force wiping contacts that resist corrosion. SIPPs are rarely used today.

Note

You could convert a SIPP to a SIMM by cutting off the pins or convert a SIMM to a SIPP by soldering pins on. Also, some companies have made SIPP-to-SIMM converters that allow the SIPPs to be plugged into 30-pin SIMM sockets.

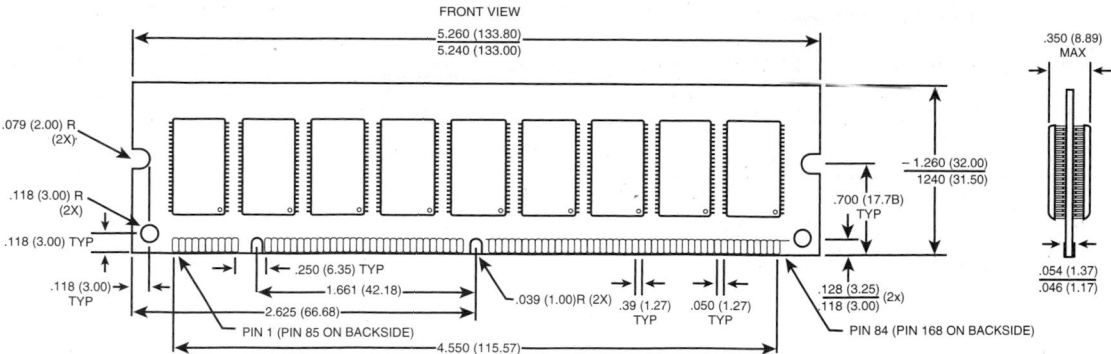

Figure 6.8   A typical 168-pin DIMM. The one shown here is 72-bit, although the dimensions would be the same for 64-bit.

These memory modules are extremely compact, considering the amount of memory they hold. SIMMs and DIMMs are available in several capacities and speeds. Table 6.6 lists the different capacities available for the 30-pin and 72-pin SIMMs and 168-pin DIMMs.

Table 6.6   SIMM and DIMM Capacities

30-Pin SIMM Capacities

Capacity	Parity SIMM	Non-Parity SIMM
256KB	256KBx9	256KBx8
1MB	1MBx9	1MBx8
4MB	4MBx9	4MBx8
16MB	16MBx9	16MBx8

72-Pin SIMM Capacities

Capacity	Parity SIMM	Non-Parity SIMM
1MB	256KBx36	256KBx32
2MB	512KBx36	512KBx32
4MB	1MBx36	1MBx32
8MB	2MBx36	2MBx32
16MB	4MBx36	4MBx32
32MB	8MBx36	8MBx32
64MB	16MBx36	16MBx32
128MB	32MBx36	32MBx32

168-Pin DIMM Capacities

Capacity	Parity DIMM	Non-Parity DIMM
8MB	1MB×72	1MB×64
16MB	2MB×72	2MB×64
32MB	4MB×72	4MB×64
64MB	8MB×72	8MB×64
128MB	16MB×72	16MB×64
256MB	32MB×72	32MB×64

Dynamic RAM (DRAM) SIMMs and DIMMs of each type and capacity are available in different speed ratings. SIMMs have been available in many different speed ratings, ranging from 120ns for some of the slowest, to 50ns for some of the fastest available. DIMMs are available in speeds from 60ns to 10ns or faster. Many of the first systems to use SIMMs used versions rated at 120ns. They were quickly replaced in the market by 100ns and even faster versions. Today, you generally purchase EDO SIMMs rated at 60ns and SDRAM DIMMs rated at 10ns. Both faster and slower ones are available, but they are not often required and are difficult to get.

If a system requires a specific speed, you can almost always substitute faster speeds if the one specified is not available. There are no problems in mixing SIMM speeds, as long as you use SIMMs equal to or faster than what the system requires. Because there's little price difference between the different speed versions, I usually buy faster SIMMs than are needed for a particular application. This may make them more usable in a future system that could require the faster speed.

Since DIMMs have an onboard ROM which reports their speed to the system, most systems will run the memory controller and memory bus at the speed matching the slowest DIMM installed.

Note

Most DIMMs are Synchronous DRAM (SDRAM) memory, which means they deliver data in very high-speed bursts using a clocked interface. SDRAM supports bus speeds of up to 133MHz, with data transfer rates of up to 200MHz or higher possible in the future.

Several variations on the 30-pin SIMMs can affect how they work (if at all) in a particular system. First, there are actually two variations on the pinout configurations. Most systems use a generic type of SIMM, which has an industry-standard pin configuration. Many older IBM systems used a slightly modified 30-pin SIMM, starting with the XT-286 introduced in 1986 through the PS/2 Model 25, 30, 50, and 60. These systems require a SIMM with different signals on five of the pins. They are known as IBM-style 30-pin SIMMs. You can modify a generic 30-pin SIMM to work in the IBM systems and vice versa, but purchasing a SIMM with the correct pinouts is much easier. Be sure you tell the SIMM vendor if you need the specific IBM-style versions.

Another issue for the 30-pin SIMMs is the chip count. The SIMM acts as though it were a single chip of 8 bits wide (with optional parity), and it really does not matter how this total is derived.

Older SIMMs were constructed with eight or nine individual 1-bit-wide chips to make up the module, but many newer SIMMs use two 4-bit-wide chips and optionally one 1-bit-wide chip for parity, making a total of two or three chips on the SIMM. Accessing the two- or three-chip SIMMs can require adjustments to the refresh timing circuits on the motherboard, and many older 386 and 486 motherboards could not cope. Most newer motherboards automatically handle the slightly different refresh timing of both the two- and three-chip or eight- and nine-chip SIMMs. The two- and three-chip versions are more reliable, use less power, and generally cost less. If you have an older system, most likely it will work with the two- and three-chip SIMMs, but some do not. Unfortunately, the only way to know is to try them. To avoid the added time of changing to the eight/nine-chip versions if the two- and three-chip versions don't work in an older system, it seems wise to stick with the eight- and nine-chip variety in any older system.

The 72-pin SIMMs do not have different pinouts and are differentiated only by capacity and speed. The number of chips on them does not affect these SIMMs. The 72-pin SIMMs are ideal for 32-bit systems, such as 486 machines, because they compose an entire bank of memory (32 data bits plus 4 parity bits). When you configure a 32-bit (486) system that uses 72-pin SIMMs, you can usually add or remove memory as single SIMM modules (except on systems that use inter-leaved memory schemes to reduce wait states). This is because a 32-bit chip such as a 486 reads and writes banks of memory 32 bits wide, and a 72-pin SIMM is exactly 32 bits wide (36 bits with optional parity).

In 64-bit systems—which includes any Pentium or newer processor—72-pin SIMMs must be used in pairs to fill a single bank. A few motherboard manufacturers offer "SIMM-saver" motherboards that are designed for newer Pentium processors, but have both 72- and 30-pin SIMM sockets. Although this is not the most desirable arrangement, it allows users on a budget to reuse their old 30-pin SIMMs. In this situation, eight 30-pin SIMMs can be used at a time to fill one bank. Alternatively, you could pair four 30-pin SIMMs with one 72-pin SIMM to create one bank. This setup, however, really is not very because it consumes large amounts of space on the mother-board.

Other options available are SIMM stackers and converters. These items allow you to use 30-pin SIMMs in 72-pin sockets, thereby saving you the expense of having to scrap all those old 30-pin SIMMs you have lying around. Again, such adapters can cause problems—especially if overhead clearance is tight—so investigate carefully before you buy. With the falling prices of SIMMs today, you are probably better off staying with 72-pin SIMMs and 168-pin DIMMs.

Remember that some older high-performance 486 systems use interleaved memory to reduce wait states. This requires a multiple of two 72-pin 36-bit (32-bit) SIMMs because interleaved memory access is alternated between the SIMMs to improve performance. Thus, a 32-bit processor ends up using two 32-bit banks together in an alternating fashion.

If a Pentium system using 72-pin SIMMs were to use interleaving, you would have to install four 72-pin (32-bit) SIMMs at a time because it takes two of them to make up a single bank. Similarly, with DIMMs, you would have to install two at a time because normally a single DIMM represents a bank on a Pentium, but interleaving requires that two banks be installed at a time and that they be identical. Most Pentium and higher systems don't use interleaving, as first EDO and then SDRAM eliminated the advantages it would offer.

Note

A bank is the smallest amount of memory that can be addressed by the processor at one time and usually corresponds to the data bus width of the processor. If the memory is interleaved, a virtual bank may be twice the absolute data bus width of the processor.

You cannot always replace a SIMM with a higher capacity unit and expect it to work. Systems might have specific design limitations for the maximum capacity of SIMM they can take. A larger capacity SIMM works only if the motherboard is designed to accept it in the first place. Consult your system documentation to determine the correct capacity and speed to use.

All systems on the market today use SIMMs, and many use DIMMs. The SIMM/DIMM is not a proprietary memory system, but an industry-standard device. As mentioned, some SIMMs have slightly different pinouts and specifications other than speed and capacity, so be sure you get the correct SIMMs for your system.

SIMM Pinouts

Tables 6.7 and 6.8 show the interface connector pinouts for 30-pin SIMM varieties and the standard 72-pin version. They also include a special presence detect table that shows the configuration of the presence detect pins on various 72-pin SIMMs. The presence detect pins are used by the motherboard to detect exactly what size and speed SIMM is installed. Industry-standard 30-pin SIMMs do not have a presence detect feature, but IBM did add this capability to their modified 30-pin configuration. Note that all SIMMs have the same pins on both sides of the module.

Table 6.7   Industry-Standard and IBM 30-Pin SIMM Pinouts

Pin	Standard SIMM Signal Names	IBM SIMM Signal Names
1	+5 Vdc	+5 Vdc
2	Column Address Strobe	Column Address Strobe
3	Data Bit 0	Data Bit 0
4	Address Bit 0	Address Bit 0
5	Address Bit 1	Address Bit 1
6	Data Bit 1	Data Bit 1
7	Address Bit 2	Address Bit 2
8	Address Bit 3	Address Bit 3
9	Ground	Ground
10	Data Bit 2	Data Bit 2
11	Address Bit 4	Address Bit 4
12	Address Bit 5	Address Bit 5
13	Data Bit 3	Data Bit 3
14	Address Bit 6	Address Bit 6

Pin	Standard SIMM Signal Names	IBM SIMM Signal Names
15	Address Bit 7	Address Bit 7
16	Data Bit 4	Data Bit 4
17	Address Bit 8	Address Bit 8
18	Address Bit 9	Address Bit 9
19	Address Bit 10	Row Address Strobe 1
20	Data Bit 5	Data Bit 5
21	Write Enable	Write Enable
22	Ground	Ground
23	Data Bit 6	Data Bit 6
24	No Connection	Presence Detect (Ground)
25	Data Bit 7	Data Bit 7
26	Data Bit 8 (Parity) Out	Presence Detect (1MB = Ground)
27	Row Address Strobe	Row Address Strobe
28	Column Address Strobe Parity	No Connection
29	Data Bit 8 (Parity) In	Data Bit 8 (Parity) I/O
30	+5 Vdc	+5 Vdc

Table 6.8 Standard 72-Pin SIMM Pinout

Pin	SIMM Signal Name	Pin	SIMM Signal Name
1	Ground	21	Data Bit 20
2	Data Bit 0	22	Data Bit 5
3	Data Bit 16	23	Data Bit 21
4	Data Bit 1	24	Data Bit 6
5	Data Bit 17	25	Data Bit 22
6	Data Bit 2	26	Data Bit 7
7	Data Bit 18	27	Data Bit 23
8	Data Bit 3	28	Address Bit 7
9	Data Bit 19	29	Address Bit 11
10	+5 Vdc	30	+5 Vdc
11	Presence Detect 5	31	Address Bit 8
12	Address Bit 0	32	Address Bit 9
13	Address Bit 1	33	Address Bit 12
14	Address Bit 2	34	Address Bit 13
15	Address Bit 3	35	Parity Data Bit 2
16	Address Bit 4	36	Parity Data Bit 0
17	Address Bit 5	37	Parity Data Bit 1
18	Address Bit 6	38	Parity Data Bit 3
19	Address Bit 10	39	Ground
20	Data Bit 4	40	Column Address Strobe 0

(continues)

Table 6.8   Standard 72-Pin SIMM Pinout

Pin	SIMM Signal Name	Pin	SIMM Signal Name
41	Column Address Strobe 2	57	Data Bit 12
42	Column Address Strobe 3	58	Data Bit 28
43	Column Address Strobe 1	59	+5 Vdc
44	Row Address Strobe 0	60	Data Bit 29
45	Row Address Strobe 1	61	Data Bit 13
46	Reserved	62	Data Bit 30
47	Write Enable	63	Data Bit 14
48	ECC Optimized	64	Data Bit 31
49	Data Bit 8	65	Data Bit 15
50	Data Bit 24	66	EDO
51	Data Bit 9	67	Presence Detect 1
52	Data Bit 25	68	Presence Detect 2
53	Data Bit 10	69	Presence Detect 3
54	Data Bit 26	70	Presence Detect 4
55	Data Bit 11	71	Reserved
56	Data Bit 27	72	Ground

Notice that the 72-pin SIMMs use a set of four or five pins to indicate the type of SIMM to the motherboard. These presence detect pins are either grounded or not connected to indicate the type of SIMM to the motherboard. Presence detect outputs must be tied to the ground through a zero-ohm resistor or jumper on the SIMM—to generate a high logic level when the pin is open or low logic level when the pin is grounded by the motherboard. This produces signals that can be decoded by the memory interface logic. If the motherboard uses presence detect signals, then a POST procedure can determine the size and speed of the installed SIMMs and adjust control and addressing signals automatically. This allows the memory size and speed to be autodetected.

Note

In many ways, the presence detect pin function is similar to the industry-standard DX coding used on modern 35mm film rolls to indicate the ASA (speed) rating of the film to the camera. When you drop the film into the camera, electrical contacts can read the film's speed rating via an industry standard configuration.

Table 6.9 shows the JEDEC industry standard presence detect configuration listing for the 72-pin SIMM family. *JEDEC* is the Joint Electronic Devices Engineering Council, an organization of the U.S. semiconductor manufacturers and users that sets package outline dimension and other standards for chip and module packages.

Table 6.9   Presence Detect Pin Configurations for 72-Pin SIMMs

Size	Speed	Pin 67	Pin 68	Pin 69	Pin 70	Pin 11
1MB	100ns	Gnd	—	Gnd	Gnd	—
1MB	80ns	Gnd	—	—	Gnd	—
1MB	70ns	Gnd	—	Gnd	—	—
1MB	60ns	Gnd	—	—	—	—
2MB	100ns	—	Gnd	Gnd	Gnd	—
2MB	80ns	—	Gnd	—	Gnd	—
2MB	70ns	—	Gnd	Gnd	—	—
2MB	60ns	—	Gnd	—	—	—
4MB	100ns	Gnd	Gnd	Gnd	Gnd	—
4MB	80ns	Gnd	Gnd	—	Gnd	—
4MB	70ns	Gnd	Gnd	Gnd	—	—
4MB	60ns	Gnd	Gnd	—	—	—
8MB	100ns	—	—	Gnd	Gnd	—
8MB	80ns	—	—	—	Gnd	—
8MB	70ns	—	—	Gnd	—	—
8MB	60ns	—	—	—	—	—
16MB	80ns	Gnd	—	—	Gnd	Gnd
16MB	70ns	Gnd	—	Gnd	—	Gnd
16MB	60ns	Gnd	—	—	—	Gnd
16MB	50ns	Gnd	—	Gnd	Gnd	Gnd
32MB	80ns	—	Gnd	—	Gnd	Gnd
32MB	70ns	—	Gnd	Gnd	—	Gnd
32MB	60ns	—	Gnd	—	—	Gnd
32MB	50ns	—	Gnd	Gnd	Gnd	Gnd

— = No Connection (open)

Gnd = Ground

Pin 67 = Presence detect 1

Pin 68 = Presence detect 2

Pin 69 = Presence detect 3

Pin 70 = Presence detect 4

Pin 11 = Presence detect 5

Unfortunately, unlike the film industry, not everybody in the computer industry follows established standards. As such, presence detect signaling is not a standard throughout the PC industry. Different system manufacturers sometimes use different configurations for what is expected on these four pins. Compaq, IBM (mainly PS/2 systems), and Hewlett-Packard are notorious for this type of behavior. Many of the systems from these vendors require special SIMMs that are basically the same as standard 72-pin SIMMs, except for special presence detect requirements. Table 6.10 shows how IBM defines these pins.

Table 6.10   72-Pin SIMM Presence Detect Pins

67	68	69	70	SIMM Type	IBM Part Number
—	—	—	—	Not a valid SIMM	n/a
Gnd	—	—	—	1MB 120ns	n/a
—	Gnd	—	—	2MB 120ns	n/a
Gnd	Gnd	—	—	2MB 70ns	92F0102
—	—	Gnd	—	8MB 70ns	64F3606
Gnd	—	Gnd	—	Reserved	n/a
—	Gnd	Gnd	—	2MB 80ns	92F0103
Gnd	Gnd	Gnd	—	8MB 80ns	64F3607
—	—	—	Gnd	Reserved	n/a
Gnd	—	—	Gnd	1MB 85ns	90X8624
—	Gnd	—	Gnd	2MB 85ns	92F0104
Gnd	Gnd	—	Gnd	4MB 70ns	92F0105
—	—	Gnd	Gnd	4MB 85ns	79F1003 (square notch) L40-SX
Gnd	—	Gnd	Gnd	1MB 100ns	n/a
Gnd	—	Gnd	Gnd	8MB 80ns	79F1004 (square notch) L40-SX
—	Gnd	Gnd	Gnd	2MB 100ns	n/a
Gnd	Gnd	Gnd	Gnd	4MB 80ns	87F9980
Gnd	Gnd	Gnd	Gnd	2MB 85ns	79F1003 (square notch) L40SX

— = No Connection (open)

Gnd = Ground

Pin 67 = Presence detect 1

Pin 68 = Presence detect 2

Pin 69 = Presence detect 3

Pin 70 = Presence detect 4

Because these pins can have custom variations, you must often specify IBM, Compaq, HP, or generic SIMMs when you order memory.

DIMM Pinouts

Table 6.11 shows the pinout configuration of a 168-pin standard unbuffered SDRAM DIMM. Note again that the pins on each side of the DIMM are different.

Table 6.11   168-Pin SDRAM DIMM Pinouts

Pin	x64 Non-Parity	x72 Parity/ECC	Pin	x64 Non-Parity	x72 Parity/ECC
1	Gnd	Gnd	85	Gnd	Gnd
2	Data Bit 0	Data Bit 0	86	Data Bit 32	Data Bit 32
3	Data Bit 1	Data Bit 1	87	Data Bit 33	Data Bit 33
4	Data Bit 2	Data Bit 2	88	Data Bit 34	Data Bit 34

Pin	x64 Non-Parity	x72 Parity/ECC	Pin	x64 Non-Parity	x72 Parity/ECC
5	Data Bit 3	Data Bit 3	89	Data Bit 35	Data Bit 35
6	+5v	+5v	90	+5v	+5v
7	Data Bit 4	Data Bit 4	91	Data Bit 36	Data Bit 36
8	Data Bit 5	Data Bit 5	92	Data Bit 37	Data Bit 37
9	Data Bit 6	Data Bit 6	93	Data Bit 38	Data Bit 38
10	Data Bit 7	Data Bit 7	94	Data Bit 39	Data Bit 39
11	Data Bit 8	Data Bit 8	95	Data Bit 40	Data Bit 40
12	Gnd	Gnd	96	Gnd	Gnd
13	Data Bit 9	Data Bit 9	97	Data Bit 41	Data Bit 41
14	Data Bit 10	Data Bit 10	98	Data Bit 42	Data Bit 42
15	Data Bit 11	Data Bit 11	99	Data Bit 43	Data Bit 43
16	Data Bit 12	Data Bit 12	100	Data Bit 44	Data Bit 44
17	Data Bit 13	Data Bit 13	101	Data Bit 45	Data Bit 45
18	+5v	+5v	102	+5v	+5v
19	Data Bit 14	Data Bit 14	103	Data Bit 46	Data Bit 46
20	Data Bit 15	Data Bit 15	104	Data Bit 47	Data Bit 47
21	—	Check Bit 0	105	—	Check Bit 4
22	—	Check Bit 1	106	—	Check Bit 5
23	Gnd	Gnd	107	Gnd	Gnd
24	—	—	108	—	—
25	—	—	109	—	—
26	+5V	+5V	110	+5v	+5v
27	Write Enable Address Strobe	Write Enable Address Strobe	111	Column	Column
28	Byte Mask 0	Byte Mask 0	112	Byte Mask 4	Byte Mask 4
29	Byte Mask 1	Byte Mask 1	113	Byte Mask 5	Byte Mask 5
30	S0	S0	114	S1	S1
31	Reserved Strobe	Reserved Strobe	115	Row Address	Row Address
32	Gnd	Gnd	116	Gnd	Gnd
33	Address Bit 0	Address Bit 0	117	Address Bit 1	Address Bit 1
34	Address Bit 2	Address Bit 2	118	Address Bit 3	Address Bit 3
35	Address Bit 4	Address Bit 4	119	Address Bit 5	Address Bit 5
36	Address Bit 6	Address Bit 6	120	Address Bit 7	Address Bit 7
37	Address Bit 8	Address Bit 8	121	Address Bit 9	Address Bit 9
38	Address Bit 10	Address Bit 10	122	Bank Address 0	Bank Address 0
39	Bank Address 1	Bank Address 1	123	Address Bit 11	Address Bit 11
40	+5v	+5v	124	+5v	+5v
41	+5v	+5v	125	Clock 1	Clock 1
42	Clock 0	Clock 0	126	Address Bit 12	Address Bit 12

(continues)

Table 6.11   Continued

Pin	x64 Non-Parity	x72 Parity/ECC	Pin	x64 Non-Parity	x72 Parity/ECC
43	Gnd	Gnd	127	Gnd	Gnd
44	Reserved	Reserved	128	Clock Enable 0	Clock Enable 0
45	S2	S2	129	S3	S3
46	Byte Mask 2	Byte Mask 2	130	Byte Mask 6	Byte Mask 6
47	Byte Mask 3	Byte Mask 3	131	Byte Mask 7	Byte Mask 7
48	Reserved	Reserved	132	Address Bit 13	Address Bit 13
49	+5v	+5v	133	+5v	+5v
50	—	—	134	—	—
51	—	—	135	—	—
52	—	Check Bit 2	136	—	Check Bit 6
53	—	Check Bit 3	137	—	Check Bit 7
54	Gnd	Gnd	138	Gnd	Gnd
55	Data Bit 16	Data Bit 16	139	Data Bit 48	Data Bit 48
56	Data Bit 17	Data Bit 17	140	Data Bit 49	Data Bit 49
57	Data Bit 18	Data Bit 18	141	Data Bit 50	Data Bit 50
58	Data Bit 19	Data Bit 19	142	Data Bit 51	Data Bit 51
59	+5v	+5v	143	+5v	+5v
60	Data Bit 20	Data Bit 20	144	Data Bit 52	Data Bit 52
61	—	—	145	—	—
62	Voltage Reference	Voltage Reference	146	Voltage Reference	Voltage Reference
63	Clock Enable 1	Clock Enable 1	147	—	—
64	Gnd	Gnd	148	Gnd	Gnd
65	Data Bit 21	Data Bit 21	149	Data Bit 53	Data Bit 53
66	Data Bit 22	Data Bit 22	150	Data Bit 54	Data Bit 54
67	Data Bit 23	Data Bit 23	151	Data Bit 55	Data Bit 55
68	Gnd	Gnd	152	Gnd	Gnd
69	Data Bit 24	Data Bit 24	153	Data Bit 56	Data Bit 56
70	Data Bit 25	Data Bit 25	154	Data Bit 57	Data Bit 57
71	Data Bit 26	Data Bit 26	155	Data Bit 58	Data Bit 58
72	Data Bit 27	Data Bit 27	156	Data Bit 59	Data Bit 59
73	+5v	+5v	157	+5v	+5v
74	Data Bit 28	Data Bit 28	158	Data Bit 60	Data Bit 60
75	Data Bit 29	Data Bit 29	159	Data Bit 61	Data Bit 61
76	Data Bit 30	Data Bit 30	160	Data Bit 62	Data Bit 62
77	Data Bit 31	Data Bit 31	161	Data Bit 63	Data Bit 63
78	Gnd	Gnd	162	Gnd	Gnd
79	Clock 2	Clock 2	163	Clock 3	Clock 3
80	—	—	164	—	—

Pin	x64 Non-Parity	x72 Parity/ECC	Pin	x64 Non-Parity	x72 Parity/ECC
81	—	—	165	Serial PD	Serial PD
	Address 0	Address 0			
82	Serial Data I/O	Serial Data I/O	166	Serial PD	Serial PD
Address 1		Address 1			
83	Serial Clock Input	Serial Clock Input	167	Serial PD	Serial PD
Address 2		Address 2			
84	+5v	+5v	168	+5v	+5v

— = No Connection (open)

Gnd = Ground

The DIMM uses a completely different type of presence detect called *serial presence detect*. It consists of a small EEPROM (Electrically Erasable Programmable Read Only Memory) or flash memory chip on the DIMM that contains specially formatted data indicating the DIMM's features. This serial data can be read via the serial data pins on the DIMM, and it allows the motherboard to autoconfigure to the exact type of DIMM installed.

Physical RAM Capacity and Organization

Several types of memory chips have been used in PC system motherboards. Most of these chips are single-bit–wide chips, available in several capacities. The following table lists available RAM chips and their capacities:

RAM Chip	Capacity
16KB by 1 bit	These devices were used in the original IBM PC with a Type 1 motherboard.
64KB by 1 bit	These chips were used in the standard IBM PC Type 2 motherboard and in the XT Type 1 and 2 motherboards. Many memory adapters of the era, such as the popular vintage AST six-pack boards, also used these chips.
128KB by 1 bit	These chips, used in the IBM AT Type 1 motherboard, often were a strange physical combination of two 64KB chips stacked one on top of the other and soldered together. Single-chip versions were also used for storing the parity bits in the IBM XT 286.
256KB by 1 bit (or 64KB by 4 bits)	These chips were once very popular in motherboards and memory cards. The IBM XT Type 2 and IBM AT Type 2 motherboards, and most compatible systems of that era, used these chips.
1MB by 1 bit (or 256KB by 4 bits)	1MB chips were very popular for a number of years and were most often used in 256KB to 8MB SIMMs.
4MB by 1 bit (or 1MB by 4 bits)	4MB chips are used primarily in SIMMs from 1MB to 16MB in capacity. They are used primarily in 4MB and 8MB SIMMs and generally are not sold as individual chips.
16MB by 1 bit (or 4MB by 4 bits)	16MB chips are often used in 72-pin SIMMs of 16MB to 32MB capacity.
64MB by 1 bit (or 16MB by 4 bits)	64MB chips are popular in high-capacity 16MB or larger memory modules, especially for notebook systems.

RAM Chip	Capacity
256MB by 1 bit (or 64MB by 4 bits)	256MB chips are the most recent on the market. These chips allow enormous SIMM capacities of 128MB or larger! Because of the high expense and limited availability of these chips, you see them only in the most expensive and highest capacity modules on the market.

Note that chip capacity normally goes up by factors of 4 because the die that make up the chips are square. When they increase capacity, this normally results in four times more transistors and four times more capacity. Most modern SIMMs and DIMMs use 16Mbit to 256Mbit chips onboard.

Figure 6.9 shows the markings on a typical older memory chip. Many memory manufacturers use similar schemes for numbering their chips; however, if you are really trying to identify a particular chip, it is best to consult the manufacturer catalog for more information.

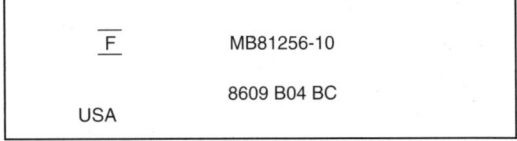

Figure 6.9   The markings on a typical older memory chip.

The -10 on the chip corresponds to its speed in nanoseconds (a 100-nanosecond rating). MB81256 is the chip's part number, which usually contains a clue about the chip's capacity. The key digits are 1256, which indicate that this chip is 1 bit wide and has a depth of 256KB. The 1 means that to make a full byte with parity, you need nine of these single-bit–wide chips. A chip with a part number of KM4164B-10 indicates a 64KB by 1-bit chip at a speed of 100 nanoseconds. The following list matches common chips with their industry-standard part numbers:

Part Number	Chip
4164	64KB by 1 bit
4464	64KB by 4 bits
41128	128KB by 1 bit
44128	128KB by 4 bits
41256	256KB by 1 bit
44256	256KB by 4 bits
41000	1MB by 1 bit
44000	1MB by 4 bits

Chips wider than 1 bit are used to construct banks of less than 9, 18, or 36 chips (depending on the system architecture). For example, a 32-bit SIMM can be constructed of only eight 4-bit–wide chips.

In Figure 6.9, the "F" symbol centered between two lines is the manufacturer's logo for Fujitsu Microelectronics. The 8609 indicates the date of manufacture (ninth week of 1986). Some manufacturers, however, use a Julian date code. To further decode the chip, contact the manufacturer or chip vendor.

SIMMs and DIMMs also have part numbers that can be difficult to decode. Unfortunately, there is no industry standard for numbering these modules, so you have to contact the manufacturer if you want to decode the numbers. Figure 6.10 shows how Micron Technology (also Crucial Technology) SIMMs are encoded.

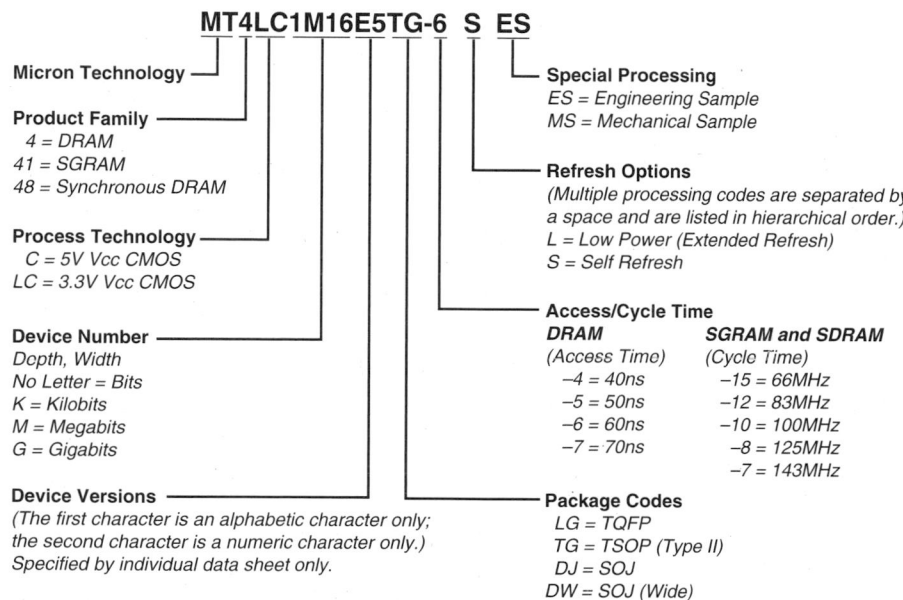

Figure 6.10   Typical SIMM part numbers for Micron (Crucial Technology) SIMMs.

Memory Banks

Memory chips (DIPs, SIMMs, SIPPs, and DIMMs) are organized in banks on motherboards and memory cards. You should know the memory bank layout and position on the motherboard and memory cards.

You need to know the bank layout when adding memory to the system. In addition, memory diagnostics report error locations by byte and bit addresses, and you must use these numbers to locate which bank in your system contains the problem.

The banks usually correspond to the data bus capacity of the system's microprocessor. Table 6.12 shows the widths of individual banks based on the type of PC.

Table 6.12   Memory Bank Widths on Different Systems

Processor	Data Bus	Memory Bank Size (No Parity)	Memory Bank Size (Parity)	30-pin SIMMs per Bank	72-pin SIMMs per Bank	168-pin DIMMs per Bank
8088	8-bit	8 bits	9 bits	1	n/a	n/a
8086	16-bit	16 bits	18 bits	2	n/a	n/a
286	16-bit	16 bits	18 bits	2	n/a	n/a
386SX, SL, SLC	16-bit	16 bits	18 bits	2	n/a	n/a
486SLC, SLC2	16-bit	16 bits	18 bits	2	n/a	n/a
386DX	32-bit	32 bits	36 bits	4	1	n/a
486SX, DX, DX2, DX4, 5x86	32-bit	32 bits	36 bits	4	1	n/a
Pentium, K6	64-bit	64 bits	72 bits	8	2	1
Pentium Pro, II, Celeron, III	64-bit	64 bits	72 bits	8	2	1

The number of bits for each bank can be made up of single chips, SIMMs, or DIMMs. Modern systems don't use individual chips; instead, they use only SIMMs or DIMMs. If the system has a 16-bit processor such as a 386SX, it would probably use 30-pin SIMMs and have two SIMMs per bank. All the SIMMs in a single bank must be the same size and type.

A 486 system requires four 30-pin SIMMs or one 72-pin SIMM to make up a bank. A single 72-pin SIMM is 32 bits wide or 36 bits wide if it supports parity. You can often tell whether a SIMM supports parity by counting its chips. To make a 32-bit SIMM, you could use 32 individual 1-bit–wide chips, or you could use eight individual 4-bit–wide chips to make up the data bits. If the system used parity, then four extra bits are required (36 bits total), so you would see one more 4-bit–wide or four individual 1-bit–wide chips added to the bank for the parity bits.

As you might imagine, 30-pin SIMMs are less than ideal for 32-bit or 64-bit systems (that is, 486 or Pentium) because you must use them in increments of four or eight per bank! Because these SIMMs are available in 1MB, 4MB, and 16MB capacities today, this means that a single bank of 30-pin SIMMs in a 486 system would be 4MB, 16MB, or 64MB; for a Pentium system, this would be 8MB, 32MB, or 128MB of memory, with no in-between amounts. Using 30-pin SIMMs in 32- and 64-bit systems artificially constrains memory configurations and such systems are not recommended. If a 32-bit system (such as any PC with a 486 processor) uses 72-pin SIMMs, each SIMM represents a separate bank, and the SIMMs can be added or removed on an individual basis rather than in groups of four, as would be required with 30-pin SIMMs. This makes memory configuration much easier and more flexible. In modern 64-bit systems that use SIMMs, two 72-pin SIMMs are required per bank.

DIMMs are ideal for Pentium and higher systems, as the 64-bit width of the DIMM exactly matches the 64-bit width of the Pentium processor data bus. This means that each DIMM represents an individual bank, and they can be added or removed one at a time.

The physical orientation and numbering of the SIMMs or DIMMs used on a motherboard is arbitrary and determined by the board's designers, so documentation covering your system or card comes in handy. You can determine the layout of a motherboard or adapter card through testing, but that takes time and might be difficult, particularly after you have a problem with a system.

RAM Chip Speed

PC memory speeds vary from about 10ns to 200ns. When you replace a failed memory module, you must install a module of the same type and speed as the failed module. You can substitute a chip with a different speed only if the replacement chip's speed is equal to or faster than that of the failed chip.

Some people have had problems when "mixing" chips because they used a chip that did not meet the minimum required specifications (for example, refresh timing specifications) or was incompatible in pinout, depth, width, or design. Chip access time can always be less (that is, faster) as long as your chip is the correct type and meets all other specifications.

Substituting faster memory usually doesn't cause improved performance because the system still operates the memory at the same speed. In systems not engineered with a great deal of "forgiveness" in the timing between memory and system, however, substituting faster memory chips might improve reliability.

To place more emphasis on timing and reliability, Intel has created standards for the new high-speed 100MHz and 133MHz memory supported by their newer chipsets. Called the PC/100 and PC/133 standards, these are standards for certifying that memory modules perform within Intel's timing and performance guidelines. At 100MHz or higher, there is not much "forgiveness" or slop allowed in memory timing.

The same common symptoms result when the system memory has failed or is simply not fast enough for the system's timing. The usual symptoms are frequent parity check errors or a system that does not operate at all. The POST might report errors, too. If you're unsure of what chips to buy for your system, contact the system manufacturer or a reputable chip supplier.

▶▶ See "Parity Checking," p. 459.

Gold Versus Tin

Many people don't understand the importance of the SIMM and DIMM electrical contacts in a computer system. Both SIMMs and DIMMs are available in gold- or tin-plated contact form. I initially thought that gold contact SIMMs or DIMMs were the best way to go for reliability in all situations, but that is not true. To have the most reliable system, you must install SIMMs or DIMMs with gold-plated contacts into gold-plated sockets and SIMMs or DIMMs with tin-plated contacts into only tin-plated sockets.

If you don't heed this warning and install memory with gold-plated contacts into tin sockets or vice versa, you will get memory errors. In my experiences, they occur six months to one year after installation. I have encountered this problem several times in my own systems and in several systems I have serviced. I have even been asked to assist one customer in a lawsuit. The customer had bought several hundred machines from a vendor, and severe memory failures began appearing in most of the machines approximately a year after delivery. The cause was traced to dissimilar metals between the memory modules and sockets (gold SIMMs in tin sockets, in this case). The vendor refused to replace the SIMMs with tin-plated versions, hence the lawsuit.

Most Intel Pentium and 486 motherboards that were designed to accept 72-pin SIMMs have tin-plated sockets, so they must have tin-plated memory. Intel now specifically recommends not mixing dissimilar metals in a system's memory. Studies done by the connector manufacturers show that a type of corrosion called *fretting* occurs when tin comes in pressure contact with gold or any other metal. With fretting corrosion, tin oxide transfers to the gold surface and hardens, eventually causing a high-resistance connection. This happens when gold comes into contact with tin, no matter how thick or thin the gold coating. Over time, depending on the environment fretting, corrosion can and will cause high resistance at the contact point and thus cause memory errors.

You would think tin makes a poor connector material because it readily oxidizes. Even so, electrical contact is easily made between two tin surfaces under pressure because the oxides on both soft surfaces bend and break, ensuring contact. This is especially true in SIMMs or DIMMs where a lot of pressure is placed on the contacts.

When tin and gold come into contact, because one surface is hard, the oxidation builds up and does not break easily under pressure. Increased contact resistance ultimately results in memory failures. The bottom line is that you should place only gold SIMMs into gold sockets and only tin SIMMs into tin sockets.

The connector manufacturer AMP has published several documents from the AMP Contact Physics Research Department that discuss this issue, but two are the most applicable. One is titled *Golden Rules: Guidelines for the Use of Gold on Connector Contacts*, and the other is called *The Tin Commandments: Guidelines for the Use of Tin on Connector Contacts*. Both can be downloaded in .PDF form from the AMP Web site. Here is an excerpt from the Tin Commandments, specifically commandment Number Seven, which states "7. Mating of tin-coated contacts to gold-coated contacts is not recommended." For further technical details, you can contact Intel or AMP at the sites I have recommended.

Certainly, the best type of setup is gold to gold, as in having gold-plated SIMMs or DIMMs and gold-plated sockets on the motherboard. Most high-end file servers or other high-reliability systems are designed this way. In fact, most systems that require SDRAM DIMMs use gold-plated sockets and therefore require SDRAM DIMMs with gold-plated contacts.

If you have mixed metals in your memory now, the correct solution is to replace the memory modules with the appropriate contact type to match the socket. Another much less desirable solution is to wait until problems appear (about six months to a year, in my experience), and then remove the modules, clean the contacts, reinstall, and repeat the cycle. This is probably fine if you are an individual with one or two systems, but it is not fine if you are maintaining hundreds of systems. If your system does not feature parity or ECC memory (most systems sold today do not), when the problems do occur, you might not be able to immediately identify them as memory related (General Protection Faults, crashes, file and data corruption, and so on).

One problem with cleaning is that the hard tin oxide deposits that form on the gold surface are difficult to remove and often require abrasive cleaning (by using an eraser or crocus cloth, for example). This should never be done dry because it generates static discharges that can damage the chips. Instead, use a contact cleaner to lubricate the contacts; wet contacts minimize the potential for static discharge damage when rubbing the eraser or other abrasive on the surface.

To further prevent this problem from occurring, I highly recommend using a liquid contact enhancer and lubricant called Stabilant 22 from DW Electrochemicals when installing SIMMs or DIMMs. Its Web site has a detailed application note on this subject if you are interested in more technical details, see the Vendor List on the CD-ROM.

Some people have accused me of being too picky by insisting that the memory match the socket. On several occasions, I have returned either memory or motherboards because the vendor putting them together did not have a clue that this is a problem. When I tell some people about it, they tell me they have a lot of PCs with mixed metal contacts that run fine and have been doing so for many years.

Of course, that is certainly a poor argument against doing the right thing. Many people are running SCSI buses that are way too long, with improper termination, and they say it runs "fine." Parallel port cables are by the spec limited to 10 feet, yet I see many have longer cables, which they claim work "fine." The IDE cable limit is 18 inches; that spec is violated and people get away with it, saying their drive runs just "fine." I see cheap, crummy power supplies that put out noise, hash, and loosely regulated voltages, and I have even measured up to 69 volts AC of ground leakage, and yet the systems were running "fine." I have encountered numerous systems without proper CPU heat sinks, or where the active heat sink (fan) was stalled, and the system ran "fine." This reminds me of when Johnny Carson would interview 100-year-old people and often got them to admit that they drank heavily and smoked cigarettes every day, as if those are good practices that ensure longevity!

The truth is I am often amazed at how poorly designed or implemented some systems are, and yet they do seem to work… for the most part. The occasional lockup or crash is just written off by the user as "that's they way they all are." All except my systems, of course. In my systems, I adhere to proper design and engineering practices. In fact, I am often guilty of engineering or specifying overkill into things. Although it adds to the cost, they do seem to run better because of it.

In other words, what one individual can "get away" with does not change the laws of physics. It does not change the fact that for those supporting many systems or selling systems where the maximum in reliability and service life is desired, the gold/tin issue does matter.

Another issue that was brought to my attention was the thickness of the gold on the contacts; people are afraid that it is so thin, it will wear off after one or two insertions. Certainly, the choice of gold coating thickness depends on the durability required by the application; because of gold's high cost, it is prudent to keep the gold coating thickness as low as is appropriate for the durability requirements.

To improve durability, a small amount of cobalt or nickel added to the gold usually hardens the gold coatings. Such coatings are defined as "hard gold" and produce coatings with a low coefficient of friction and excellent durability characteristics. Hard gold-coated contacts can generally withstand hundreds to thousands of durability cycles without failing. Using an underlayer with a hardness value greater than that of gold alone that provides additional mechanical support can enhance the durability of hard gold coatings. Nickel is generally recommended as an underlayer for this purpose. Lubricants are also effective at increasing the durability of gold coatings. Generally, lubrication can increase the durability of a gold contact by an order of magnitude.

Increasing the thickness of a hard gold coating increases durability. The following laboratory results were obtained by AMP for the wear-through of a hard gold coating to the 1.3 micron (50 microinch) thick nickel underplate. The following data is for a 0.635cm. (0.250 in.) diameter ball wiped a distance of 1.27cm. (0.500 in.) under a normal force of 100 grams for each cycle.

Thickness Microns	Thickness Microinch	Cycles to Failure
0.4	15	200
0.8	30	1000
1.3	50	2000

As you can see from this table, an 0.8 micron (30 microinches) coating of hard gold results in durability that is more than adequate for most connector applications, as it allows 1,000 insertion and removal cycles before wearing through. I studied the specification sheets for DIMM and SIMM sockets produced by AMP and found that their gold-plated sockets come mostly as .000030 (30 microinches) thick gold over .000050 (50 microinches) thick nickel in the contact area. As far as I can determine, the coating on virtually all SIMM and DIMM contacts would be similar in thickness, allowing for the same durability.

AMP also has a few gold-plated sockets with specifications of .001020 (1,020 microinches)-thick gold over .001270 (1,270 microinches)-thick nickel. I'd guess that the latter sockets were for devices such as SIMM testers, where many insertions were expected over the life of the equipment. They could also be used in high-vibration or high-humidity environments.

For reference, all their tin-contact SIMM and DIMM sockets have the following connector plating specifications: .000030 (30 microinches) minimum thick tin on mating edge over .000050 (50 microinches) minimum thick nickel on entire contact.

The bottom line is that the thickness of the coating in current SIMM and DIMM sockets and modules is not an issue for the expected use of these devices. The thickness of the plating used in current SIMM and DIMM systems is also not relevant to the tin versus gold matability issue. The only drawback to a thinner gold plating is that it will wear after fewer insertion/removal cycles, exposing the nickel underneath and allowing the onset of fretting corrosion.

In my opinion, this tin/gold issue will be even more important for those using DIMMs, for two reasons. With SIMMs, you really have two connections for each pin (one on each side of the module), so if one of them goes high resistance, it will not matter; there is a built-in redundancy.

With DIMMs, you have many, many more connections (168 versus 72) and no redundant connections. The chance for failure is much greater. Also, most DIMM applications will be SDRAM, where the timing is down in the 15–10ns range for 66MHz and 100MHz boards, respectively. At these speeds, the slightest additional resistance in the connection causes problems.

Because of these issues, for the future I would specify only motherboards that have gold-plated SDRAM DIMM connectors, and then, of course, use only SDRAMs with gold-plated contacts. I noted that, for example, Micron produces only SDRAM DIMMs with gold-plated contacts, and all the DIMM sockets I've seen so far are gold plated, too. I would not currently recommend any motherboards using tin-lead SDRAM DIMM connectors, nor would I recommend purchasing tin-lead SDRAM DIMMs.

Parity and ECC

Part of the nature of memory is that it inevitably fails. These failures are usually classified as two basic types: hard fails and soft errors.

The most well understood are *hard fails*, in which the chip is working and then, because of some flaw, physical damage, or other event, becomes damaged and experiences a permanent failure. Fixing this type of failure normally requires replacing some part of the memory hardware, such as the chip, SIMM, or DIMM. Hard error rates are known as *HERs*.

The other more insidious type of failure is the *soft error*, which is a nonpermanent failure that might never reoccur or could occur only at infrequent intervals. (Soft fails are effectively "fixed" by powering the system off and back on.) Soft error rates are known as *SERs*.

About 20 years ago, Intel made a discovery about soft errors that shook the memory industry. It found that alpha-particles were causing an unacceptably high rate of soft errors or Single Event Upsets (*SEUs*, as they are sometimes called) in the 16KB DRAMs that were available at the time. Because alpha-particles are low-energy particles that can be stopped by something as thin and light as a sheet of paper, it became clear that for alpha-particles to cause a DRAM soft error, they would have to be coming from within the semiconductor material. Testing showed trace elements of thorium and uranium in the plastic and ceramic chip packaging materials used at the time. This discovery forced all the memory manufacturers to evaluate their manufacturing process to produce materials free from contamination.

Today, memory manufacturers have all but totally eliminated the alpha-particle source of soft errors. Many people believed that was justification for the industry trend to drop parity checking. The argument is that, for example, a 16MB memory subsystem built with 4MB technology would experience a soft error caused by alpha-particles only about once every 16 years! The real problem with this thinking is that it is seriously flawed, and many system manufacturers and vendors were coddled into removing parity and other memory fault-tolerant techniques from their systems even though soft errors continue to be an ongoing problem. More recent discoveries prove that alpha-particles are now only a small fraction of the cause of DRAM soft errors!

As it turns out, the biggest cause of soft errors today are cosmic rays. IBM researchers began investigating the potential of terrestrial cosmic rays in causing soft errors similar to alpha-particles.

The difference is that cosmic rays are very high-energy particles and cannot be stopped by sheets of paper or other more powerful types of shielding. The leader in this line of investigation was Dr. J.F. Ziegler of the IBM Watson Research Center in Yorktown Heights, New York. He has produced landmark research into understanding cosmic rays and their influence on soft errors in memory.

One example of the magnitude of the cosmic ray soft-error phenomenon demonstrated that with a certain sample of non-IBM DRAMs, the Soft Error Rate (SER) at sea level was measured at 5950 FIT (Failures in Time, which is measured at 1 billion hours) per chip. This was measured under real-life conditions with the benefit of millions of device hours of testing. In an average system with 36 memory chips among the SIMMs, this would result in a soft error occurring every six months! In power user or server systems with a larger amount of memory, it could mean an error per month or more. When the exact same test setup and DRAMs were moved to an underground vault shielded by over 50 feet of rock, thus eliminating all cosmic rays, absolutely no soft errors were recorded! This not only demonstrates how troublesome cosmic rays can be, but it also proves that the packaging contamination and alpha-particle problem has indeed been solved.

Cosmic ray–induced errors are even more of a problem in SRAMs than DRAMS because the amount of charge required to flip a bit in an SRAM cell is less than is required to flip a DRAM cell capacitor. Cosmic rays are also more of a problem for higher-density memory. As chip density increases, it becomes easier for a stray particle to flip a bit. It has been predicted by some that the Soft Error Rate of a 64MB DRAM will be double that of a 16MB chip, and a 256MB DRAM will have a rate four times higher.

Unfortunately, the PC industry has largely failed to recognize this new cause of memory errors. Electrostatic discharge, power surges, or unstable software can much more easily explain away the random and intermittent nature of a soft error, especially right after a new release of an operating system or major application.

Studies have shown that the soft-error rate for ECC systems is on the order of 30 times greater than the hard-error rate. This is not surprising to those familiar with the full effects of cosmic ray–generated soft errors. There is now data suggesting that some 16MB DRAM chip designs will actually experience soft errors numbering in the 24,000 FIT range. This would result in a soft error about once a month for most systems today!

Although cosmic rays and other radiation events are the biggest cause of soft errors, others can be caused by the following:

- *Power glitches or noise on the line.* This can be caused by a defective power supply in the system or by defective power at the outlet.
- *Incorrect type or speed rating.* The memory must be the correct type for the chipset, and match the system access speed.
- *RF (Radio Frequency) interference.* Caused by radio transmitters in close proximity to the system, which can generate electrical signals in system wiring and circuits.
- *Static discharges.* Causes momentary power spikes, which alters data.

■ *Timing glitches*. Data doesn't arrive at the proper place at the proper time, causing errors. Often caused by improper settings in the BIOS setup, by memory that is rated slower than the system requires, or by overclocked processors and other system components.

Most of these problems don't cause chips to permanently fail (although bad power or static can damage chips permanently), but they can cause momentary problems with data.

How can you deal with these errors? Just ignoring them is certainly not the best way to deal with them, but unfortunately that is what many system manufacturers and vendors are doing today. The best way to deal with this problem is to increase the system's fault tolerance. This means implementing ways of detecting and possibly correcting errors in PC systems. There are basically three levels and techniques for fault tolerance used in modern PCs:

■ Non-parity

■ Parity

■ ECC (Error Correcting Code)

Non-parity systems have no fault tolerance at all. The only reason they are used is because they have the lowest inherent cost. No additional memory is necessary, as is the case with parity or ECC techniques. Because a parity-type data byte has 9 bits versus 8 for non-parity, memory cost is 12.5 percent higher. Also, the non-parity memory controller is simplified because it does not need the logic gates to calculate parity or ECC check bits. Portable systems that place a premium on minimizing power might benefit from the reduction in memory power resulting from fewer DRAM chips. Finally, the memory system data bus is narrower, which reduces the amount of data buffers. The statistical probability of memory failures in a modern office desktop computer is now estimated at about one error every few months. Errors will be more or less frequent depending on how much memory you have.

This error rate might be tolerable for low-end systems that are not used for mission-critical applications. In this case, their extreme market cost sensitivity probably can't justify the extra cost of parity or ECC memory, and such errors then have to be tolerated.

At any rate, having no fault tolerance in a system is simply gambling that memory errors are unlikely. You further gamble that if they do occur, memory errors will result in an inherent cost less than the additional hardware necessary for error detection. However, the risk is that these memory errors can lead to serious problems. A memory error in a calculation could cause the wrong value to go into a bank check. In a server, a memory error could force a system hang and bring down all LAN-resident client systems with subsequent loss of productivity. Finally, with a non-parity or non-ECC memory system, tracing the problem is difficult, which is not the case with parity or ECC. These techniques at least isolate a memory source as the culprit, thus reducing both the time and cost of resolving the problem.

Parity Checking

One standard IBM set for the industry is that the memory chips in a bank of nine each handle 1 bit of data: 8 bits per character plus 1 extra bit called the *parity bit*. The parity bit enables memory-control circuitry to keep tabs on the other 8 bits—a built-in cross-check for the integrity of each byte in the system. If the circuitry detects an error, the computer stops and displays a message informing you of the malfunction. If you are running a GUI operating system such as Windows or OS/2, a parity error generally manifests itself as a locked system. When you reboot, the BIOS should detect the error and display the appropriate error message.

SIMMs and DIMMs are available both with and without parity bits. Originally, all PC systems used parity-checked memory to ensure accuracy. Starting in 1994, a disturbing trend developed in the PC-compatible marketplace. Most vendors began shipping systems without parity checking or any other means of detecting or correcting errors! These systems can use cheaper non-parity SIMMs, which saves about 10–15 percent on memory costs for a system. Parity memory results in increased initial system cost, primarily because of the additional memory bits involved. Parity cannot correct system errors, but because parity can detect errors, it can make the user aware of memory errors when they happen. This has two basic benefits:

- Parity guards against the consequences of faulty calculations based on incorrect data.
- Parity pinpoints the source of errors, which helps with problem resolution, thus improving system serviceability.

PC systems can easily be designed to function using either parity or non-parity memory. The cost of implementing parity as an option on a motherboard is virtually nothing; the only cost is in actually purchasing the parity SIMMs or DIMMs, which are about 10–15 percent more expensive than non-parity versions. This enables a system manufacturer to offer its system purchasers the choice of parity if they feel the additional cost is justified for their particular application.

Unfortunately, several of the big names began selling systems without parity to reduce their prices, and they did not make it well known that the lower cost meant parity memory was no longer included as standard. This began happening mostly in 1994–1995, and has continued until recently, with few people understanding the full implications. After one or two major vendors did this, most of the others were forced to follow to remain price-competitive.

Because nobody wanted to announce this information, it remained sort of a dirty little secret within the industry. Originally, when this happened, you could still specify parity memory when you ordered a system, even though the default configurations no longer included it. There was a 10–15 percent surcharge on the memory, but those who wanted reliable, trustworthy systems could at least get them, provided they knew to ask, of course. Then a major bomb hit the industry, in the form of the Intel Triton 430FX Pentium chipset, which was the first major chipset on the market that did not support parity checking at all! It also became the most popular chipset of its time and was found in practically all Pentium motherboards sold in the 1995 timeframe. This set a disturbing trend for the next few years. All but one of Intel's Pentium processor chipsets after the 430FX did not support parity-checked memory; the only one that did was the 430HX Triton II. The good news is that this trend now seems to be over, and the system manufacturers and users are finally coming around to the importance of fault-tolerant memory. As such, all the Pentium Pro and Pentium II chipsets currently available do support parity and ECC, and more and more people are realizing that this type of memory is worthwhile. I do expect new low-end chipsets even for the Pentium II to emerge that do not support parity, but they are designed for the sub-$1,000 market, where price, not system integrity, is the most important concern.

Let's look at how parity checking works, and then examine in more detail the successor to parity checking, called ECC (Error Correcting Code), which can not only detect but correct memory errors on-the-fly.

IBM originally established the odd parity standard for error checking. The following explanation may help you understand what is meant by odd parity. As the 8 individual bits in a byte are stored in memory, a parity generator/checker, which is either part of the CPU or located in a special chip on the motherboard, evaluates the data bits by adding up the number of 1s in the byte. If an even number of 1s is found, the parity generator/checker then creates a 1 and stores it as the ninth bit (parity bit) in the parity memory chip. That makes the sum for all 9 bits (including the parity bit) an odd number. If the original sum of the 8 data bits were an odd number, then the parity bit created would be a 0, keeping the sum for all 9 bits an odd number. The basic rule is that the value of the parity bit is always chosen so that the sum of all 9 bits (8 data bits plus 1 parity bit) is stored as an odd number. If the system used even parity, then the example would be the same except the parity bit would be created to ensure an even sum. It doesn't matter whether even or odd parity is used; the system will use one or the other, and it is completely transparent to the memory chips involved. Remember that the 8 data bits in a byte are numbered 0 1 2 3 4 5 6 7. The following examples might make it easier to understand:

```
Data bit number:    0 1 2 3 4 5 6 7    Parity bit
Data bit value:     1 0 1 1 0 0 1 1    0
```

In this example, because the total number of data bits with a value of 1 is an odd number (5), the parity bit must have a value of 0 to ensure an odd sum for all nine bits.

Here is another example:

```
Data bit number:    0 1 2 3 4 5 6 7    Parity bit
Data bit value:     1 1 1 1 0 0 1 1    1
```

In this example, because the total number of data bits with a value of 1 is an even number (6), the parity bit must have a value of 1 to create an odd sum for all 9 bits.

When the system reads memory back from storage, it checks the parity information. If a (9-bit) byte has an even number of bits with a parity bit value of 1, that byte must have an error. The system cannot tell which bit has changed or if only a single bit has changed. If 3 bits changed, for example, the byte still flags a parity-check error; if 2 bits changed, however, the bad byte could pass unnoticed. Because multiple bit errors (in a single byte) are rare, this scheme gives you a reasonable and inexpensive ongoing indication that memory is good or bad.

The following examples show parity-check messages for three types of older systems:

```
For the IBM PC:                       PARITY CHECK x
For the IBM XT:                       PARITY CHECK x    yyyyy (z)
For the IBM AT and late model XT:     PARITY CHECK x    yyyyy
```

Where x is 1 or 2:

> 1 = Error occurred on the motherboard
>
> 2 = Error occurred in an expansion slot

In this example, *yyyyy* represents a number from 00000 through FFFFF that indicates, in hexadecimal notation, the byte in which the error has occurred.

Where (z) is (S) or (E):

(S) = Parity error occurred in the system unit

(E) = Parity error occurred in an optional expansion chassis

Note

An expansion chassis was an option IBM sold for the original PC and XT systems to add more expansion slots. This unit consisted of a backplane motherboard with eight slots; one slot contained a special extender/receiver card cabled to a similar extender/receiver card placed in the main system. Because of the extender/receiver cards in the main system and the expansion chassis, the net gain was six slots. Although the IBM version has long since been discontinued, other companies have since produced 8-bit and 16-bit ISA expansion chassis, allowing more ISA slots to be added to a system.

When a parity-check error is detected, the motherboard parity-checking circuits generate a *nonmaskable interrupt* (*NMI*), which halts processing and diverts the system's attention to the error. The NMI causes a routine in the ROM to be executed. The routine clears the screen and then displays a message in the screen's upper-left corner. The message differs depending on the type of computer system. On some older IBM systems, the ROM parity-check routine halts the CPU. In such a case, the system locks up, and you must perform a hardware reset or a power-off/power-on cycle to restart the system. Unfortunately, all unsaved work is lost in the process.

Most systems do not halt the CPU when a parity error is detected; instead, they offer you the choice of rebooting the system or continuing as though nothing happened. Additionally, these systems may display the parity error message in a different format from IBM, although the information presented is basically the same. For example, most systems with a Phoenix BIOS display one of these messages:

```
Memory parity interrupt at xxxx:xxxx
Type (S)hut off NMI, Type (R)eboot, other keys to continue
```

or

```
I/O card parity interrupt at xxxx:xxxx
Type (S)hut off NMI, Type (R)eboot, other keys to continue
```

The first of these two messages indicates a motherboard parity error (Parity Check 1), and the second indicates an expansion-slot parity error (Parity Check 2). Notice that the address given in the form *xxxx:xxxx* for the memory error is in a segment:offset form rather than a straight linear address, such as with IBM's error messages. The segment:offset address form still gives you the location of the error to a resolution of a single byte.

You have three ways to proceed after viewing this error message:

- You can press S, which shuts off parity checking and resumes system operation at the point where the parity check first occurred.

- Pressing R forces the system to reboot, losing any unsaved work.
- Pressing any other key causes the system to resume operation with parity checking still enabled.

If the problem occurs, it is likely to cause another parity-check interruption. It's usually prudent to press S, which disables the parity checking so that you can then save your work. In this case, it's best to save your work to a floppy disk to prevent the possible corruption of the hard disk. You should also avoid overwriting any previous (still good) versions of whatever file you are saving, because you could be saving a bad file caused by the memory corruption. Because parity checking is now disabled, your save operations will not be interrupted. Then you should power the system off, restart it, and run whatever memory diagnostics software you have to try to track down the error. In some cases, the POST finds the error on the next restart, but you usually need to run a more sophisticated diagnostics program, perhaps in a continuous mode, to locate the error.

Systems with an AMI BIOS displays the parity error messages in the following forms:

```
ON BOARD PARITY ERROR ADDR (HEX) = (xxxxx)
```

or

```
OFF BOARD PARITY ERROR ADDR (HEX) = (xxxxx)
```

These messages indicate that an error in memory has occurred during the POST, and the failure is located at the address indicated. The first one indicates that the error occurred on the motherboard, and the second message indicates an error in an expansion slot adapter card. The AMI BIOS can also display memory errors in the following manner:

```
Memory Parity Error at xxxxx
```

or

```
I/O Card Parity Error at xxxxx
```

These messages indicate that an error in memory has occurred at the indicated address during normal operation. The first one indicates a motherboard memory error, and the second indicates an expansion slot adapter memory error.

Although many systems enable you to continue processing after a parity error and even allow disabling further parity checking, continuing to use your system after a parity error is detected can be dangerous. The idea behind letting you continue using either method is to give you time to save any unsaved work before you diagnose and service the computer, but be careful how you do this.

Caution

When you are notified of a memory parity error, remember the parity check is telling you that memory has been corrupted. Do you want to save potentially corrupted data over the good file from the last time you saved? Definitely not! Make sure you save your work with a different filename. In addition, after a parity error, save only to a floppy disk if possible and avoid writing to the hard disk; there is a slight chance that the hard drive could become corrupted if you save the contents of corrupted memory.

After saving your work, determine the cause of the parity error and repair the system. You might be tempted to use an option to shut off further parity checking and simply continue using the system as though nothing were wrong. Doing so is like unscrewing the oil pressure warning indicator bulb on a car with an oil leak so that the oil pressure light won't bother you anymore!

A few years ago, when memory was more expensive, there were a few companies marketing SIMMs with bogus parity chips. Instead of actually having the extra memory chips needed to store the parity bits, these "logic parity" or parity "emulation" SIMMs used an onboard parity generator chip. This chip ignored any parity the system was trying to store on the SIMM, but when data was retrieved, it always ensured that the correct parity was returned, thus making the system believe all was well even though there might be a problem.

These bogus parity modules were used because memory was much more expensive, and a company could offer a "parity" SIMM for only a few dollars more with the fake chip. Unfortunately, identifying them can be difficult. The bogus parity generator doesn't look like a memory chip, and has different markings from the other memory chips on the SIMM. Most of them had a "GSM" logo, which indicated the original manufacturer of the parity logic device, not necessarily the SIMM itself.

One way to positively identify these bogus fake parity SIMMs is by using a hardware SIMM test machine, such as those by Darkhorse Systems or Aristo. Of course, I don't recommend using bogus parity SIMMs. Fortunately, the problem has mostly subsided because honest-to-gosh memory is much cheaper these days.

ECC (Error Correcting Code)

ECC goes a big step beyond simple parity error detection. Instead of just detecting an error, ECC allows a single bit error to be corrected, which means the system can continue without interruption and without corrupting data. ECC, as implemented in most PCs, can only detect, not correct, double-bit errors. Because studies have indicated that approximately 98% of memory errors are the single-bit variety, the most commonly used type of ECC is one in which the attendant memory controller detects and corrects single-bit errors in an accessed data word (double-bit errors can be detected, but not corrected). This type of ECC is known as *SEC-DED* (*Single-Bit Error Correction-Double-bit Error Detection*) and requires an additional 7 check bits over 32 bits in a 4-byte system and an additional 8 check bits over 64 bits in an 8-byte system. ECC in a 4-byte (32-bit, such as a 486) system obviously costs more than non-parity or parity, but in an 8-byte (64-bit, such as Pentium) system, ECC and parity costs are equal because the same number of extra bits (8) are required for either parity or ECC. Because of this, you can purchase parity SIMMs (36-bit) or DIMMs (72-bit) for Pentium systems and use them in an ECC mode if the chipset supports ECC functionality. If the Pentium system uses SIMMs, then two 36-bit (parity) SIMMs are added for each bank (for a total of 72-bits), and ECC is done at the bank level. If the Pentium system uses DIMMs, then a single parity/ECC 72-bit DIMM is used as a bank and provides the additional bits.

ECC entails the memory controller calculating the check bits on a memory-write operation, performing a compare between the read and calculated check-bits on a read operation, and, if necessary, correcting bad bits. The additional ECC logic in the memory controller is not very significant in this age of inexpensive, high-performance VLSI logic, but ECC actually affects memory performance on writes. This is because the operation must be timed to wait for the calculation of check bits and, when the system waits for corrected data, reads. On a partial-word write, the entire word must first be read, the affected byte(s) rewritten, and then new check bits calculated. This turns partial-word write operations into slower read-modify writes. Fortunately this performance hit is very small, on the order of a few percent at maximum, so the tradeoff for increased reliability is a good one.

Most memory errors are of a single-bit nature, which can be corrected by ECC. Incorporating this fault-tolerant technique provides high system reliability and attendant availability. An ECC-based system is a good choice for servers, workstations, or mission-critical applications in which the cost of a potential memory error outweighs the additional memory and system cost to correct it, along with ensuring that it does not detract from system reliability. If you value your data and use your system for important (to you) tasks, then you'll want ECC memory. No self-respecting manager would build or run a network server, even a lower end one, without ECC memory.

By designing a system that allows the user to make the choice of ECC, parity, or non-parity, users can choose the level of fault tolerance desired, as well as how much they want to gamble with their data.

Installing RAM Upgrades

Adding memory to a system is one of the most useful upgrades you can perform, and also one of the least expensive, especially when you consider the increased capabilities of Windows 9x, Windows NT, Windows 2000, and OS/2 when you give them access to more memory. In some cases, doubling the memory can practically double the speed of a computer.

The following sections discuss adding memory, including selecting memory chips, installing memory chips, and testing the installation.

Upgrade Options and Strategies

Adding memory can be an inexpensive solution; at this writing, the cost of memory has fallen to about $1.50 per megabyte. A small dose can give your computer's performance a big boost.

How do you add memory to your PC? You have three options, listed in order of convenience and cost:

- Adding memory in vacant slots on your motherboard.
- Replacing your current motherboard's memory with higher-capacity memory.
- Purchasing a memory expansion card (not a cost-effective or performance-effective solution for any system currently on the market).

Adding expanded memory to PC- or XT-type systems is not a good idea, mainly because an expanded memory board with a couple of megabytes of expanded memory installed can cost more than the entire system is worth. Also, this memory does not function for Windows, and a PC- or XT-class system cannot run OS/2. Instead, purchase a more powerful system—for example, an inexpensive Pentium II 266—with greater expansion capabilities.

If you decide to upgrade to a more powerful computer system, you normally cannot salvage the memory from a PC or XT system. The 8-bit memory boards are useless in 16-bit systems, and the speed of the memory chips is usually inadequate for newer systems. All new systems use high-speed SIMM or DIMM modules rather than chips. A pile of 150ns (nanoseconds), 64KB, or 256KB chips is useless if your next system is a high-speed system that uses SIMMs, DIMMs or any memory devices faster than 70ns.

Be sure to carefully weigh your future needs for computing speed and for a multitasking operating system (OS/2, Windows 9x, Windows NT, Windows 2000, or Linux, for example) against the amount of money you spend to upgrade current equipment.

Before you add RAM to a system (or replace defective RAM chips), you must determine the memory chips required for your system. Your system documentation has this information.

If you need to replace a defective SIMM or DIMM and do not have the system documentation, you can determine the correct module for your system by inspecting the ones that are already installed. Each module has markings that indicate the module's capacity and speed. RAM capacity and speed are discussed in detail earlier in this chapter.

If you do not have the documentation for your system and the manufacturer does not offer technical support, open your system case and carefully write down the markings that appear on your memory chips. Then contact a local computer store or module vendor, such as Kingston, Micron (Crucial), PNY, or others, for help in determining the proper RAM chips for your system. Adding the wrong modules to a system can make it as unreliable as leaving a defective module installed and trying to use the system in that condition.

Note

Before upgrading a system beyond 64MB of RAM, be sure that your chipset supports caching more than 64MB. Adding RAM beyond the amount your system can cache slows performance rather than increases it. See the section "Cache Memory: SRAM" earlier in this chapter and the discussion of chipsets in Chapter 4 for a more complete explanation of this common system limitation. This limitation was mostly with Pentium (P5) class chipsets. Pentium II/III processors have the L2 cache controller integrated in the processor (not the chipset) which will support caching up to 1GB, or 4GB on most newer models.

Selecting and Installing Motherboard Memory with Chips, SIMMs, or DIMMs

If you are upgrading a motherboard by adding memory, follow the manufacturer's guidelines on which memory chips or modules to buy. As you learned earlier, memory comes in various form factors, including individual chips known as DIP memory chips, SIMMs, and DIMMs. Your computer may use one or possibly a mixture of these form factors.

No matter what type of memory chips you have, the chips are installed in memory banks. A *memory bank* is a collection of memory chips that make up a block of memory. Your processor reads each bank of memory in one pass. A memory bank does not work unless it is filled with memory chips. (Banks are discussed in more detail earlier in this chapter in the section "Memory Banks.")

Pentium and newer systems through the Pentium III normally have between two and four banks of memory, but each bank usually requires two 72-pin (32- or 36-bit) SIMMs or most likely one 168-pin DIMM.

Installing extra memory on your motherboard is an easy way to add memory to your computer. Most systems have at least one vacant memory bank where you can install extra memory at a later time and speed up your computer.

Replacing SIMMS and DIMMs with Higher Capacity

If all the SIMM or DIMM slots on your motherboard are occupied, your best option is to remove an existing bank of memory and replace it with higher-capacity memory. For example, if you have 16MB of RAM in a Pentium system with four SIMM slots filled with 4MB 72-pin SIMMs, you may be able to replace all four SIMMs with 8MB SIMMs and increase the system memory to 32MB. Alternatively, you could keep two of the existing 4MB SIMMs and replace two with 8MB SIMMs, increasing the total RAM to 24MB. Remember that just as when you install SIMMs, they need to be replaced in a full bank and all the SIMMs in the bank need to be the same capacity. The requirement for multiple modules is not an issue with DIMMs because in all current systems, a DIMM constitutes at least one full bank of memory.

However, just because there are higher-capacity SIMMs or DIMMs available that are the correct pin count to plug into your motherboard, don't automatically assume the higher-capacity memory will work. Your system's chipset and BIOS will set limits on the capacity of the memory you can use. Check your system or motherboard documentation to see what size SIMMs or DIMMs work with it before purchasing the new RAM. It is a good idea to make sure you have the latest BIOS when installing new memory.

Adding Adapter Boards

Memory expansion boards typically are a last-resort way to add memory. For many systems (such as older models from Compaq) with proprietary local bus memory-expansion connectors, you must purchase all memory-expansion boards from that company. Similarly, IBM used proprietary memory connectors in many of the PS/2 systems. For other industry-standard systems that use nonproprietary memory expansion, you can purchase from hundreds of vendors' memory-expansion boards that plug into the standard bus slots.

Unfortunately, any memory expansion that plugs into a standard bus slot runs at bus speed rather than at full-system speed. For this reason, most systems today provide standard SIMM or

DIMM connector sockets directly on the motherboard so that the memory can be plugged directly into the system's local bus. Using memory adapter cards in these systems only slows them down. Other systems use proprietary local bus connectors for memory-expansion adapters, which can cause additional problems and expense when you have to add or service memory. Upgrading a system by using a memory adapter card is no longer cost-effective, either. Because most systems and motherboards built on 486 or later processors can be upgraded with SIMMs or DIMMs, the only systems that would be upgraded with an adapter card are so old, it would be less expensive to replace the entire motherboard than to upgrade these old systems.

Installing Memory

This section discusses installing memory—specifically, new SIMM or DIMM modules. It also covers the problems you are most likely to encounter and how to avoid them. You will also get information on configuring your system to use new memory.

When you install or remove memory, you are most likely to encounter the following problems:

- Electrostatic discharge
- Broken or bent pins
- Incorrectly seated SIMMs and DIMMs
- Incorrect switch and jumper settings

To prevent electrostatic discharge (ESD) when you install sensitive memory chips or boards, do not wear synthetic-fiber clothing or leather-soled shoes. Remove any static charge you are carrying by touching the system chassis before you begin, or better yet, wear a good commercial grounding strap on your wrist. You can order one from an electronics parts store or mail-order house. A grounding strap consists of a conductive wristband grounded at the other end by a wire clipped to the system chassis. Leave the system unit plugged in—but turned off—to keep it grounded.

Caution

Be sure to use a properly designed commercial grounding strap; do not make one yourself. Commercial units have a one-meg ohm resistor that serves as protection if you accidentally touch live power. The resistor ensures that you do not become the path of least resistance to the ground and therefore become electrocuted. An improperly designed strap can cause the power to conduct through you to the ground, possibly killing you.

Broken or bent leads are another potential problems associated with installing individual memory chips (DIPs) or SIPP modules. Fortunately, this is not a problem you have when installing a SIMM or DIMM. Sometimes, the pins on new chips are bent into a V, making them difficult to align with the socket holes. If you notice this problem on a DIP chip, place the chip on its side on a table, and press gently to bend the pins so that they are at a 90-degree angle to the chip. For a SIPP module, you might want to use needle-nose pliers to carefully straighten the pins so that they protrude directly down from the edge of the module, with equal amounts of space between pins. Then you should install the chips in the sockets one at a time.

Caution

Straightening the pins on a DIP chip or SIPP module is not difficult work, but if you are not careful, you could easily break off one of the pins, rendering the chip or memory module useless. Use great care when you straighten the bent pins on any memory chip or module. You can use chip-insertion and pin-straightening devices to ensure that the pins are straight and aligned with the socket holes; these inexpensive tools can save you a great deal of time.

Each memory chip or module must be installed to point in a certain direction. Each device has a polarity marking on one end. This is normally a notch on SIMMs or DIMMs and could be a notch, circular indentation, or mark on any individual chip. The chip socket might have a corresponding notch. Otherwise, the motherboard may have a printed legend that indicates the chip's orientation. If the socket is not marked, you should use other chips as a guide. The orientation of the notch indicates the location of Pin 1 on the device. Aligning this notch correctly with the others on the board ensures that you do not install the chip backward. Gently set each chip into a socket, ensuring that every pin is properly aligned with the connector into which it fits. Then push the chip in firmly with both thumbs until it is fully seated.

SIMM memory is oriented by a notch on one side of the module that is not present on the other side, as shown in Figure 6.11. The socket has a protrusion that must fit into this notched area on one side of the module. This protrusion makes it impossible to install a SIMM backward unless you break the connector. Figure 6.11 shows a detailed blowup of the backside of the SIMM, showing the notch and the locking clip. Figure 6.12 shows a close-up of a SIMM (note that it, too, is keyed to ensure proper expansion socket installation).

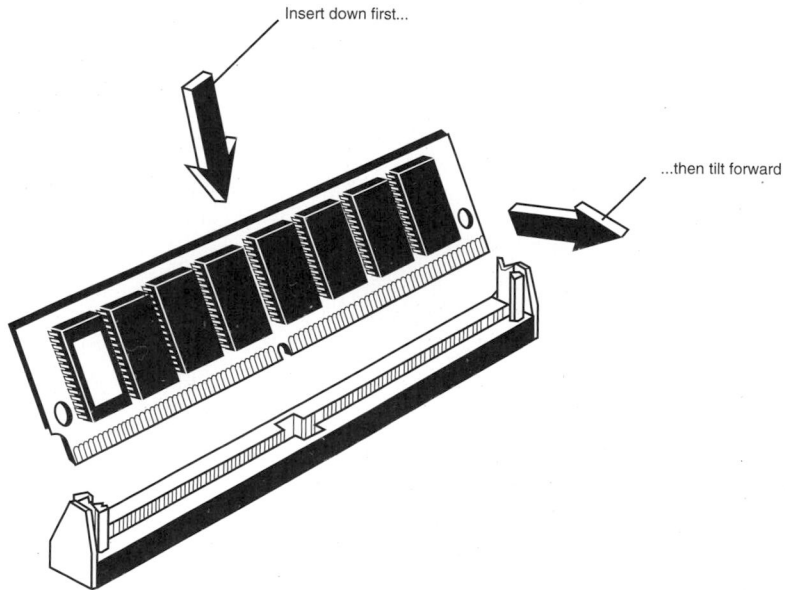

Figure 6.11   The notch on this SIMM is shown on the left end. Insert the SIMM at an angle and then tilt it forward until the locking clips snap into place.

Similarly, DIMMs are keyed by notches along the bottom connector edge that are offset from center so that they can be inserted in only one direction, as shown in Figure 6.13. SIPP modules, however, do not plug into a keyed socket; you have to orient them properly. The system documentation can be helpful if the motherboard has no marks to guide you. You can also use existing SIPP modules as a guide.

The DIMM ejector tab locks into place in the notch on the side of the DIMM when it is fully inserted. Some DIMM sockets have ejector tabs on both ends. When installing SIMMs and DIMMs, take care not to force the module into the socket. If the module does not slip easily into the slot and then snap into place, there is a good chance the module is not oriented or aligned correctly. Forcing the module could break the module or the socket. If the retaining clips on the socket break, the memory isn't held firmly in place, and there is a good chance you will get random memory errors because the module can't make consistent electrical contact if it is loose.

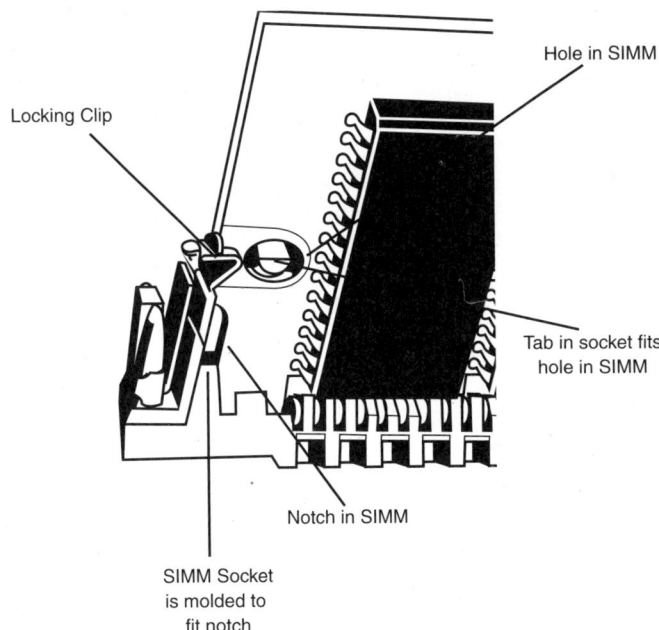

Figure 6.12 This close-up shows the backside of a SIMM inserted in the SIMM socket with the notch aligned, the locking clip locked, and the hole in the SIMM aligned with the tab that sticks out from the socket.

As explained earlier in this chapter, DIMMs can come in several different varieties, including unbuffered or buffered and 3.3v or 5v. Buffered DIMMs have additional buffer chips on them to interface to the motherboard. Unfortunately, these buffer chips slow the DIMM down and are not effective at higher speeds. For this reason, all PC systems use unbuffered DIMMs. The voltage is simple—DIMM designs for PCs are almost universally 3.3v. If you install a 5v DIMM in a 3.3v socket, it would be damaged, but fortunately, keying in the socket and on the DIMM prevents that.

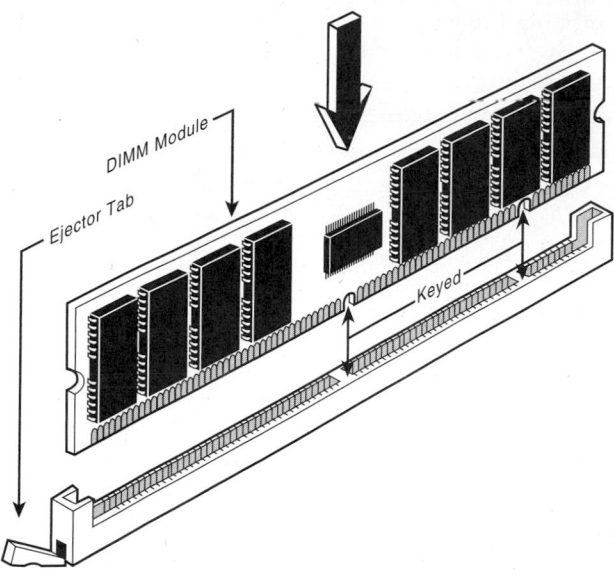

Figure 6.13   DIMM keys match the protrusions in the DIMM sockets.

Modern PC systems use only unbuffered 3.3v DIMMs. Apple and other non-PC systems may use the buffered 5v versions. Fortunately, the key notches along the connector edge of a DIMM are spaced differently for RFU and buffered DIMMs and 5.0v DIMMs, as shown in Figure 6.14. This prevents inserting a DIMM of the wrong type into a socket.

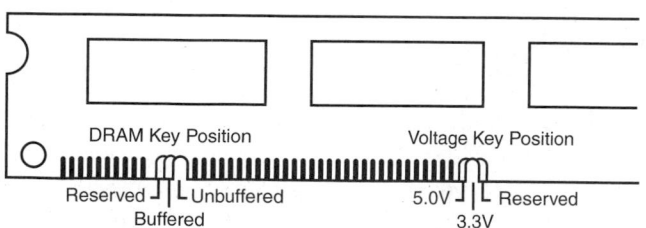

Figure 6.14   168-pin DRAM DIMM notch key definitions.

Before installing memory, make sure the system power is off. Then remove the PC cover and any installed cards. SIMMs and DIMMs snap easily into place, but chips can be more difficult to install. A chip-installation tool is not required, but it can make inserting the chips into sockets much easier. To remove chips, use a chip extractor or small screwdriver. Never try removing a RAM chip with your fingers because you can bend the chip's pins or poke a hole in your finger with one of the pins. You remove SIMMs and DIMMs by releasing the locking tabs and either pulling or rolling them out of their sockets.

After adding the memory and putting the system back together, you might have to run the CMOS Setup and resave with the new amount of memory. Most newer systems automatically detect the new amount of memory and reconfigure it for you. Most newer systems also don't require setting any jumpers or switches on the motherboard to configure them for your new memory. Older motherboards that use individual RAM chips rather than SIMMs or DIMMs for memory are more likely to need changes to jumper and switch settings. If you install individual RAM chips on a motherboard and the CMOS does not recognize the new RAM, check the system documentation to see if changes to motherboard jumpers or switches are required.

Note

Information on installing memory on older memory-expansion cards can be found in Chapter 7 of the Sixth Edition of *Upgrading and Repairing PCs* on the CD-ROM accompanying this book.

After configuring your system to work properly with the additional memory, you should run a memory-diagnostics program to make sure the new memory works properly. At least two and sometimes three memory-diagnostic programs are available for all systems. In order of accuracy, these programs are as follows:

- POST (power on self test)
- Disk-based advanced diagnostics software

The POST is used every time you power up the system.

Many additional diagnostics programs are available from aftermarket utility software companies. More information on aftermarket testing facilities can be found in Chapter 25, "PC Diagnostics, Testing, and Maintenance."

Troubleshooting Memory

Memory problems can be difficult to troubleshoot. For one thing, computer memory is still mysterious to people, as it is a kind of "virtual" thing that can be hard to grasp. The other difficulty is that memory problems can be intermittent and often look like problems with other areas of the system, even software. This section will show simple troubleshooting steps you can perform if you suspect you are having a memory problem.

To troubleshoot memory, you first need some memory diagnostics testing programs. You already have several, and might not know it! Every motherboard BIOS has a memory diagnostic in the POST that runs when you first turn on the system. In most cases, you also received a memory diagnostic on a utility disk that came with your system. Finally, a commercial program called Check-It is included on one of the CD-ROMs with this book. Many other commercial diagnostics programs are on the market, and almost all of them include memory tests.

When the POST runs, it not only tests memory, but also counts it. The count is compared to the amount counted the last time BIOS SETUP was run; if it is different, an error message is issued. As the POST runs, it writes a pattern of data to all the memory locations in the system and reads that pattern back to verify that the memory works. If any failure is detected, you see or hear a message. Audio messages (beeping) are used for critical or "fatal" errors that occur in areas important for the system's operation. If the system can access enough memory to at least allow video to function, then you see error messages instead of hearing beep codes.

See Chapter 5 for detailed listings of the BIOS beep and other error codes, which are specific to the type of BIOS you have. For example, most Intel motherboards use the Phoenix BIOS. Several different beep codes are used in that BIOS to indicate fatal memory errors.

If your system makes it through the POST with no memory error indications, then there might not be a hardware memory problem, or the POST might not be able to detect the problem. Intermittent memory errors are often not detected during the POST, and other subtle hardware defects can be hard for the POST to catch. The POST is designed to run quickly, so the testing is not nearly as thorough as it could be. That is why you often have to boot from a DOS or diagnostic disk and run a true hardware diagnostic to do more extensive memory testing. These types of tests can be run continuously, and left running for days if necessary to hunt down an elusive intermittent defect.

Still, even these programs do only pass/fail type testing; that is, all they can do is write patterns to memory and read them back. They cannot determine how close the memory is to failing—only that it worked or not. For the highest level of testing, the best thing to have is a dedicated memory test machine, normally called a *SIMM/DIMM tester*. These devices allow you to insert a module and test it thoroughly at a variety of speeds, voltages, and timings to let you know for certain whether the memory is good or bad. I have defective SIMMs, for example, that work in some systems (slower ones) but not others. What I mean is that the *same* memory test program fails the SIMM in one machine but passes it in another. In the SIMM tester, it is always identified as bad right down to the individual bit, and it even tells me the actual speed of the device, not just its rating. Several companies that offer SIMM/DIMM testers are included in the vendor list, including Darkhorse Systems and Aristo. They can be expensive, but for a professional in the PC repair business, using one of these SIMM/DIMM testers is the only way to go.

After your operating system is running, memory errors can still occur, normally identified by error messages you might receive. These are the most common:

- *Parity errors.* Indicates that the parity checking circuitry on the motherboard has detected a change in memory since the data was originally stored.(See the "Parity Checking" section earlier in this chapter.)

- *General or global protection faults.* A general-purpose error indicating that a program has been corrupted in memory, usually resulting in immediate termination of the application. This can also be caused by buggy or faulty programs.

- *Fatal exception errors.* Error codes returned by a program when an illegal instruction has been encountered, invalid data or code has been accessed, or the privilege level of an operation is invalid.

- *Divide error.* A general-purpose error indicating that a division by zero was attempted or the result of an operation does not fit in the destination register.

If you are encountering these errors, they could be caused by defective or improperly configured memory, but they can also be caused by software bugs (especially drivers), bad power supplies, static discharges, close proximity radio transmitters, timing problems, and more.

If you suspect the problems are caused by memory, there are ways to test the memory to determine whether that is the problem. Most of this testing involves running one or more memory test programs.

I am amazed that most people make a critical mistake when they run memory test software. The biggest problem I see is that people run memory tests with the system caches enabled. This effectively invalidates memory testing because most systems have what is called a *write-back cache*. This means that data written to main memory is first written to the cache. Because a memory test program first writes data and then immediately reads it back, the data is read back from the cache, not the main memory. It makes the memory test program run very quickly, but all you tested was the cache. The bottom line is that if you test memory with the cache enabled, then you aren't really writing to the SIMM/DIMMs, but only to the cache. Before you run any memory test programs, be sure your cache is disabled. The system will run very slowly when you do this, and the memory test will take much longer to complete, but you will be testing your actual RAM, not the cache.

The following steps will allow you to effectively test and troubleshoot your system RAM. Figure 6.15 provides a boiled-down procedure to help you step through the process quickly.

First, let's cover the memory testing and troubleshooting procedures.

1. Power up the system and observe the POST. If the POST completes with no errors, then basic memory functionality has been tested. If errors are encountered, go to the defect isolation procedures.

2. Restart the system, and enter your BIOS (or CMOS) Setup. In most systems, this is done by pressing the F2 key during the POST but before the boot process begins. Once in BIOS setup, verify that the memory count is equal to the amount that has been installed. If the count does not match what has been installed, go to the defect isolation procedures.

3. Find the BIOS setup options for cache, and set all cache options to disabled. Save the settings and reboot to a DOS formatted system disk (floppy) containing the diagnostics program of your choice. If your system came with a diagnostics disk, you can use that, or you can use one of the many commercial PC diagnostics programs on the market, such as PC-Technician by Windsor Technologies (which comes in self-booting form), the Norton Utilities by Symantec, or others.

4. Follow the instructions that came with your diagnostic program to have it test the system base and extended memory. Most programs have a mode that allows them to loop the test—that is, to run it continuously, which is great for finding intermittent problems. If the program encounters a memory error, proceed to the defect isolation procedures.

5. If no errors are encountered in the POST or in the more comprehensive memory diagnostic, then your memory has tested okay in hardware. Be sure at this point to reboot the system, enter the BIOS setup, and re-enable the cache. The system will be running very slowly until the cache is turned back on.

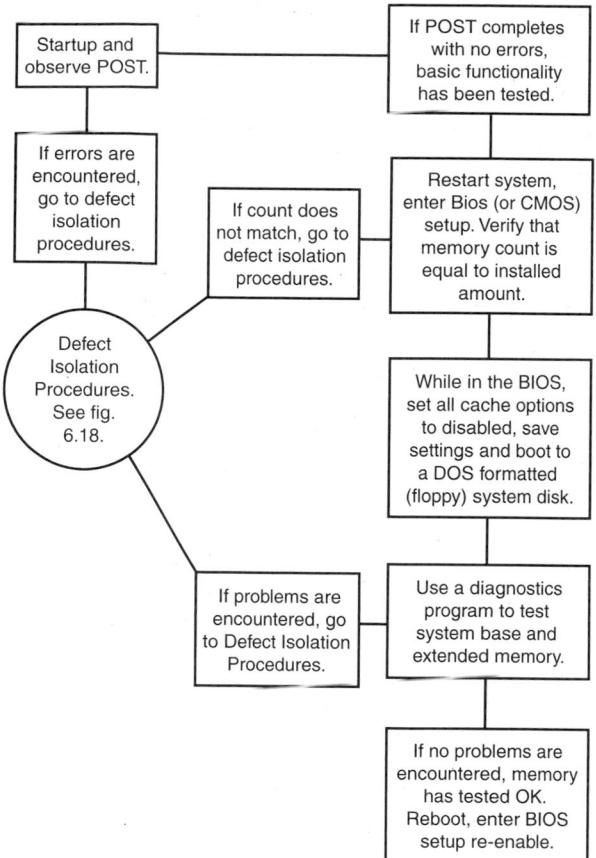

Figure 6.15   Testing and troubleshooting memory.

6. If you are having memory problems yet the memory still tests okay, then you might have a problem undetectable by simple pass/fail testing, or your problems are caused by software or one of many other defects or problems in your system. You might want to bring the memory to a SIMM/DIMM tester for a more accurate analysis. Most PC repair shops have such a tester. I would also check the software (especially drivers, which might need updating), power supply, and system environment for problems such as static, radio transmitters, and so forth.

Memory Defect Isolation Procedures

To use these steps, I am assuming you have identified an actual memory problem that is being reported by the POST or disk-based memory diagnostics. If this is the case, see the following steps and Figure 6.16 to see the steps to identify or isolate which SIMM or DIMM in the system is causing the problem.

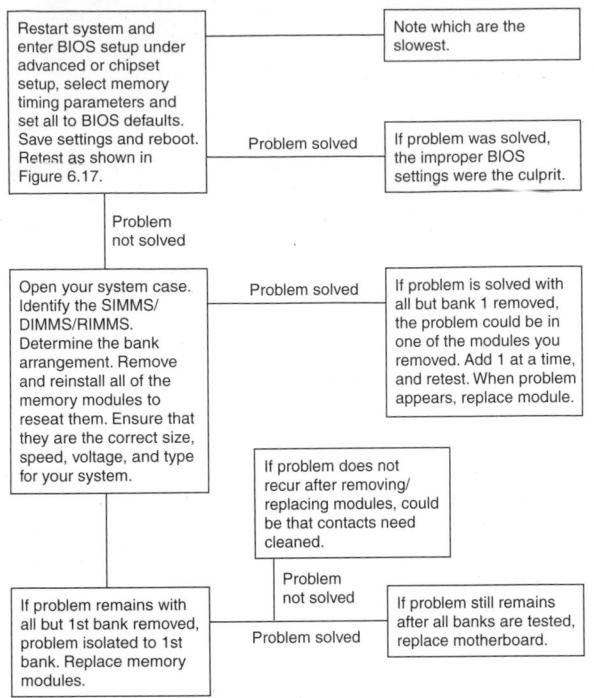

Figure 6.16 Follow these steps if you are still encountering memory errors after completing the steps in Figure 6.17.

1. Restart the system and enter the BIOS setup. Under a menu usually called Advanced or Chipset Setup, there may be memory timing parameters. Select BIOS or Setup defaults, which are usually the slowest settings. Save the settings, reboot, and retest using the testing and troubleshooting procedures listed earlier. If the problem has been solved, improper BIOS settings were the problem. If the problem remains, you likely do have defective memory, so continue to the next step.

2. Open the system up for physical access to the SIMM/DIMMs on the motherboard. Identify the bank arrangement in the system. For example, Pentium systems use 64-bit banks, which means two 72-pin SIMMs or one 168-pin DIMM per bank. Using the manual or the legend silk-screened on the motherboard, identify which SIMMs or DIMM correspond to which bank. Most Pentium boards that use SIMMs have four, six, or eight total SIMMs installed in two, three, or four banks. Most boards using DIMMs have two, three, or four total DIMMs, each of which represents a single bank.

3. Remove all the memory except the first bank, and retest using the troubleshooting and testing procedures listed earlier. If the problem remains with all but the first bank removed, then the problem has been isolated to the first bank, which must be replaced.

4. Replace the memory in the first bank, preferably with known good spare modules, but you can also swap in others that you have removed and retest. If the problem *still* remains after testing all the memory banks (and finding them all to be working properly), it is likely the

motherboard itself is bad (probably one of the memory sockets). Replace the motherboard and retest.

5. At this point, the first (or previous) bank has tested good, so the problem must be in the remaining modules that have been temporarily removed. Install the next bank of memory and retest. If the problem resurfaces now, then the memory in that bank is defective. Continue testing each bank until you find the defective module.

6. Repeat the preceding step until all remaining banks of memory are installed and have been tested. If the problem has not resurfaced after removing and reinstalling all the memory, then the problem was likely intermittent or caused by poor conduction on the memory contacts. Often simply removing and replacing memory can resolve problems because of the self-cleaning action between the SIMM/DIMM and the socket during removal and reinstallation.

The System Logical Memory Layout

The original PC had a total of 1MB of addressable memory, and the top 384KB of that was reserved for use by the system. Placing this reserved space at the top (between 640KB and 1024KB instead of at the bottom, between 0KB and 640KB) led to what is often called the *conventional memory barrier*. The constant pressures on system and peripheral manufacturers to maintain compatibility by never breaking from the original memory scheme of the first PC has resulted in a system memory structure that is (to put it kindly) a mess. Almost two decades after the first PC was introduced, even the newest Pentium II–based systems are limited in many important ways by the memory map of the first PCs.

What we end up with is a PC with a split personality. There are two primary modes of operation that are very different from each other. The original PC used an Intel 8088 processor that could run only 16-bit instructions or code, which ran in what was called the *real mode* of the processor. These early processors had only enough address lines to access up to 1MB of memory, and the last 384KB of that was reserved for use by the video card as video RAM, other adapters (for on-card ROM BIOS), and finally the motherboard ROM BIOS.

The 286 processor brought more address lines, enough to allow up to 16MB of RAM to be used, and a new mode called *protected mode* that you had to be in to use it. Unfortunately, all the operating systems software at the time was designed to run only within the first 1MB, so extender programs were added and other tricks performed to eventually allow DOS and Windows 3.x access up to the first 16MB. One area of confusion was that RAM was now noncontiguous; that is, the operating system could use the first 640KB and the last 15MB, but not the 384KB of system reserved area that sat in between.

When the first 32-bit processor was released by Intel in 1985 (the 386DX), the memory architecture of the system changed dramatically. There were now enough address lines for the processor to use 4GB of memory, but this was accessible only in a new 32-bit *protected mode* in which only 32-bit instructions or code could run. This mode was designed for newer, more advanced operating systems, such as Windows 9x, NT, OS/2, Linux, UNIX, and so forth. With the 386 came a whole new memory architecture in which this new 32-bit software could run. Unfortunately, it took 10 years for the mainstream user to upgrade to 32-bit operating systems and applications, which shows how stubborn we are! From a software instruction perspective, all of the processors since the 386 are really just faster versions of the same. Other than the recent addition of MMX and MMX2 (Katmai) instructions to the processor, for all intents and purposes, a Pentium II is just a turbo-386.

The real problem now is that from that point on, the machine has two distinctly different modes, with different memory architectures in each. For backward compatibility, you could still run the 386 and higher processors in real mode, but only 16-bit software could run in that mode, and such software could access only the first 1MB or 16MB, depending on how it was written. For example, 16-bit drivers could load into and access only the first 1MB. Also, it is worth noting that the system ROM BIOS, including the POST, BIOS configuration, boot code, and all the internal drivers, is virtually all 16-bit software. This is because all Intel processors, even including the latest Pentium IIs, all begin operation in 16-bit real mode when they are powered on. When a 32-bit operating system loads, it is that operating system code that instructs the processor to switch into 32-bit protected mode.

When an operating system like Windows 9x is loaded, the processor is switched into 32-bit protected mode early in the loading sequence. Then 32-bit drivers for all the hardware can be loaded, and then the rest of the operating system can load. In 32-bit protected mode, the operating systems and applications can access all the memory in the system, up to the maximum limit of the processor (64TB for a Pentium II).

Unfortunately, one problem with protected mode is just that: It is protected. The name comes from the fact that only driver programs are allowed to talk directly to the hardware in this mode; programs loaded by the operating system, such as by clicking on an icon in Windows, are not allowed to access memory or other hardware directly. This protection is provided so that a single program cannot crash the machine by doing something illegal. You may have seen the error message in Windows 9x indicating this, and that the program will be shut down.

Diagnostics software by nature must talk to the hardware directly. This means that little intensive diagnostics testing can be done while a protected mode operating system like Windows 9x, NT, Linux, and so forth is running. For system testing, you normally have to boot from a DOS floppy or interrupt the loading of Windows (press the F8 key when "Starting Windows" appears during the boot process) and select Command Prompt Only, which boots you into DOS, or by executing a shutdown and select "Restart the computer in MS-DOS mode." Many of the higher end hardware diagnostics programs include their own special limited 16-bit operating system so they can more easily access memory areas even DOS would use.

When you boot from a Windows 9x startup disk you are running 16-bit DOS, for example, and if you want to access your CD-ROM drive to install Windows, for example, you need to load a 16-bit CD-ROM driver program from that disk as well. In this mode, you can do things like partition and format your hard disk, install Windows, or test the system completely.

The point of all this is that although you might not be running DOS or Windows 3.x very much these days, at least for system configuration and installation, as well as for high-level hardware diagnostics testing, data recovery, and so forth, you will still need to boot a 16-bit OS occasionally. When you are in that mode, the systems architecture changes, there is less memory accessible, and some of the software you are running (16-bit drivers and most application code) will have to fight over the first 1MB or even 640KB for space.

The system memory areas discussed in this chapter, including the 384KB at the top of the first megabyte, which is used for video, adapter BIOS, and motherboard BIOS, as well as the remaining extended memory, are all part of the PC hardware design. They exist whether you are running 16-bit or 32-bit software; however, the limitations on their use in 16-bit (real) mode are much more severe. Because most people run 32-bit operating systems like Windows 9x, NT, Linux, and so on, these operating systems automatically manage the use of RAM, meaning you don't have to interact with and manage this memory yourself as you often did with the 16-bit operating systems.

The following sections are intended to give you an understanding of the PC hardware memory layout, which is consistent no matter which operating system you use. The only thing that changes is how your operating system uses these areas and how they are managed by the OS.

Someone who wants to become knowledgeable about personal computers must at one time or another come to terms with the types of memory installed on his system—the small and large pieces of different kinds of memory, some accessible by software application programs and some not. The following sections detail the different kinds of memory installed on a modern PC. The kinds of memory covered in the following sections include the following:

- Conventional (base) memory
- Upper memory area (UMA)
- High memory area (HMA)
- Extended memory (XMS)
- Expanded memory (obsolete)
- Video RAM memory (part of UMA)
- Adapter ROM and special purpose RAM (part of UMA)
- Motherboard ROM BIOS (part of UMA)

Subsequent sections also cover preventing memory conflicts and overlap, using memory managers to optimize your system's memory, and making better use of memory. In a 16-bit or higher system, the memory map extends beyond the 1MB boundary and can continue to 16MB on a system based on the 286 or higher processor, 4GB (4,096MB) on a 386DX or higher, or as much as 64GB (65,536MB) on a Pentium II. Any memory past 1MB is called extended memory.

Figure 6.17 shows the logical address locations for a 16-bit or higher system. If the processor is running in real mode, only the first megabyte is accessible. If the processor is in protected mode, the full 16MB, 4,096MB, or 65,536MB are accessible. Each symbol is equal to 1KB of memory, and each line or segment is 64KB. This map shows the first two megabytes of system memory.

```
    . = Program-accessible memory (standard RAM)
    G = Graphics Mode Video RAM
    M = Monochrome Text Mode Video RAM
    C = Color Text Mode Video RAM
    V = Video ROM BIOS (would be a   in PS/2)
    a = Adapter board ROM and special-purpose RAM (free UMA space)
    r = Additional PS/2 Motherboard ROM BIOS (free UMA in non-PS/2 systems)
    R = Motherboard ROM BIOS
    b = IBM Cassette BASIC ROM (would be R  in IBM compatibles)
    h = High Memory Area (HMA), if HIMEM.SYS is loaded.

    Conventional (Base) Memory:

         : 0---1---2---3---4---5---6---7---8---9---A---B---C---D---E---F---
    000000: ................................................................
    010000: ................................................................
    020000: ................................................................
    030000: ................................................................
    040000: ................................................................
    050000: ................................................................
    060000: ................................................................
    070000: ................................................................
    080000: ................................................................
    090000: ................................................................

    Upper Memory Area (UMA):

         : 0---1---2---3---4---5---6---7---8---9---A---B---C---D---E---F---
    0A0000: GGGGGGGGGGGGGGGGGGGGGGGGGGGGGGGGGGGGGGGGGGGGGGGGGGGGGGGGGGGGGGGG
    0B0000: MMMMMMMMMMMMMMMMMMMMMMMMMMMMMMMMCCCCCCCCCCCCCCCCCCCCCCCCCCCCCCCC
         : 0---1---2---3---4---5---6---7---8---9---A---B---C---D---E---F---
    0C0000: VVVVVVVVVVVVVVVVVVVVVVVVVVVVVVVVaaaaaaaaaaaaaaaaaaaaaaaaaaaaaaaa
    0D0000: aaaaaaaaaaaaaaaaaaaaaaaaaaaaaaaaaaaaaaaaaaaaaaaaaaaaaaaaaaaaaaaa
         : 0---1---2---3---4---5---6---7---8---9---A---B---C---D---E---F---
    0E0000: rrrrrrrrrrrrrrrrrrrrrrrrrrrrrrrrrrrrrrrrrrrrrrrrrrrrrrrrrrrrrrrr
    0F0000: RRRRRRRRRRRRRRRRRRRRRRRRRRRRRRRRbbbbbbbbbbbbbbbbbbbbbbbbbRRRRRRRR

    Extended Memory:

         : 0---1---2---3---4---5---6---7---8---9---A---B---C---D---E---F---
    100000: hhhhhhhhhhhhhhhhhhhhhhhhhhhhhhhhhhhhhhhhhhhhhhhhhhhhhhhhhhhhhhhh

    Extended Memory Specification (XMS) Memory:

    110000: ................................................................
    120000: ................................................................
    130000: ................................................................
    140000: ................................................................
    150000: ................................................................
    160000: ................................................................
    170000: ................................................................
    180000: ................................................................
    190000: ................................................................
    1A0000: ................................................................
    1B0000: ................................................................
    1C0000: ................................................................
    1D0000: ................................................................
    1E0000: ................................................................
    1F0000: ................................................................
```

Figure 6.17 The logical memory map of the first 2MB.

◄◄ See "Processor Modes," p. 58.

> **Note**
>
> To save space, this map stops after the end of the second megabyte. In reality, this map continues to the maximum of addressable memory.

Conventional (Base) Memory

The original PC/XT-type system was designed to use 1MB of RAM. This 1MB of RAM is divided into several sections, some of which have special uses. DOS can read and write to the entire megabyte, but can manage the loading of programs only in the portion of RAM space called conventional memory, which was 512KB at the time the first PC was introduced. The other 512KB was reserved for use by the system, including the motherboard and adapter boards plugged into the system slots.

After introducing the system, IBM decided that only 384KB was needed for these reserved uses, and the company began marketing PCs with 640KB of user memory. Therefore, 640KB became the standard for memory that can be used by DOS for running programs, and is often termed the 640KB memory barrier. The remaining memory after 640KB was reserved for use by the graphics boards, other adapters, and the motherboard ROM BIOS.

This barrier largely affects 16-bit software, such as DOS and Windows 3.1, and is much less of a factor with 32-bit software and operating systems, such as Windows 9x, NT/2000, and so on.

Upper Memory Area (UMA)

The term *Upper Memory Area (UMA)* describes the reserved 384KB at the top of the first megabyte of system memory on a PC/XT and the first megabyte on an AT-type system. This memory has the addresses from A0000 through FFFFF. The way the 384KB of upper memory is used breaks down as follows:

■ The first 128KB after conventional memory is called video RAM. It is reserved for use by video adapters. When text and graphics are displayed onscreen, the data bits that make up those images reside in this space. Video RAM is allotted the address range from A0000–BFFFF.

■ The next 128KB is reserved for the adapter BIOS that resides in read-only memory chips on some adapter boards plugged into the bus slots. Most VGA-compatible video adapters use the first 32KB of this area for their onboard BIOS. Any other adapters installed can use the rest. Many network adapters also use this area for special-purpose RAM called *Shared Memory*. Adapter ROM and special-purpose RAM is allotted the address range from C0000–DFFFF.

■ The last 128KB of memory is reserved for motherboard BIOS (the basic input/output system, which is stored in read-only RAM chips or ROM). The POST (power on self test) and bootstrap loader, which handles your system at boot-up until the operating system takes over, also reside in this space. Most systems use only the last 64KB (or less) of this space, leaving the first 64KB or more free for remapping with memory managers. Some systems also include the CMOS Setup program in this area. The motherboard BIOS is allotted the address range from E0000–FFFFF.

Not all the 384KB of reserved memory is fully used on most 16-bit and higher systems. For example, according to the PC standard, reserved video RAM begins at address A0000, which is right at the 640KB boundary. Normally, it is used for VGA graphics modes, while the monochrome and color text modes use B0000–B7FFF and B8000–BFFFF, respectively. Older non-VGA adapters used memory only in the B0000 segment. Different video adapters use varying amounts of RAM for their operations, depending mainly on the mode they are in. To the processor, however, it always appears as the same 128KB area, no matter how much RAM is really on the video card. This is managed by bank switching areas of memory on the card in and out of the A0000–BFFFF segments.

Although the top 384KB of the first megabyte was originally termed *reserved memory*, it is possible to use previously unused regions of this memory to load 16-bit device drivers (such as the ANSI.SYS screen driver that comes with DOS) and memory-resident programs (such as MOUSE.COM, the DOS mouse driver), which frees up the conventional memory they would otherwise require. Note that this does not affect 32-bit device drivers such as those used with Windows 9x, NT/2000, and so forth because they load into extended memory with no restrictions. The amount of free UMA space varies from system to system, depending mostly on the adapter cards installed on the system. For example, most video adapters, SCSI adapters, and some network adapters require some of this area for built-in ROMs or special-purpose RAM use.

Segment Addresses and Linear Addresses

One thing that can be confusing is the difference between a segment address and a full linear address. The use of segmented address numbers comes from the internal structure of the Intel processors and is used primarily by older, 16-bit operating systems. They use a separate register for the segment information and another for the offset. The concept is very simple. For example, assume that I am staying in a hotel room, and somebody asks for my room number. The hotel has 10 floors, numbered from zero through nine; each floor has 100 rooms, numbered from 00 to 99. A segment is defined as any group of 100 rooms starting at a multiple of 10, and indicated by a two-digit number. So a segment address of 54 would indicate the actual room 540, and you could have an offset of 00 to 99 rooms from there.

In this hotel example, then, each segment is specified as a two-digit number from 00–99, and an offset can be specified from any segment starting with a number from 00–99.

Say that I'm staying in room 541. If the person needs this information in segment:offset form, and each number is two digits, I could say that I am staying at a room segment starting address of 54 (room 540), and an offset of 01 from the start of that segment. I could also say that I am in room segment 50 (room 500), and an offset of 41. You could even come up with other answers, such as I am at segment 45 (room 450) offset 91 (450+91=541). Here is an example of how this adds up:

Segment	Offset	Total
54	01	541
50	41	541
45	91	541

As you can see, although the particular segment and offset are different, they all add up to the same room address. In the Intel x86 processors, a similar scheme is used when a segment and offset are added internally to produce the actual address. It can be somewhat confusing, especially if you are writing assembly language or machine language software!

This is exactly how segmented memory in an Intel processor works. Notice that the segment and offset numbers essentially overlap on all digits except the first and last. By adding them together with the proper alignment, you can see the linear address total.

With 32-bit operating systems, segment addresses are not an issue. A linear address is one without segment:offset boundaries, such as saying room 541. It is a single number, not two numbers added together. For example, a SCSI host adapter might have 16KB ROM on the card addressed from D4000 to D7FFF. These numbers expressed in segment:offset form are D400:0000 to D700:0FFF. The segment portion is composed of the most significant four digits, and the offset portion is composed of the least significant four digits. Because each portion overlaps by one digit, the ending address of its ROM can be expressed in four different ways, as follows:

```
D000:7FFF =    D000    segment
+   7FFF   offset
- - - -
= D7FFF   total
D700:0FFF =    D700    segment
+   0FFF   offset
- - - -
= D7FFF   total
D7F0:00FF =    D7F0    segment
+   00FF   offset
- - - -
= D7FFF   total
D7FF:000F =    D7FF    segment
+   000F   offset
- - - -
= D7FFF   total
```

As you can see, although the segment and offset differ slightly in each case, the total ends up being the same. Adding the segment and offset numbers makes even more combinations possible, as in the following examples:

```
D500:2FFF =    D500    segment
+   2FFF   offset
- - - -
= D7FFF   total
D6EE:111F =    D6EE    segment
+   111F   offset
- - - -
= D7FFF   total
```

As you can see, several combinations are possible. The correct and generally accepted way to write this address as a linear address is D7FFF, although most would write the segment:offset address as D000:7FFF. Keeping the segment mostly zeros makes the segment:offset relationship easier to understand and the number easier to comprehend. If you understand the segment:offset relationship to the linear address, you now know why when a linear address number is discussed it is five digits, but a segment number is only four.

Video RAM Memory

A video adapter installed in your system uses a portion of your system's first megabyte of memory to hold graphics or character information for display, but this is normally used or active only when in basic VGA mode. A video card can have 4MB, 8MB, or more on board, but most of that is used by the video chipset on the card, not directly accessed by your system processor. When in basic VGA mode, such as when at a DOS prompt or when running in Windows safe mode, your processor can directly access up to 128KB of the video RAM from address A0000–BFFFFh. All modern video cards also have onboard BIOS normally addressed at C0000–C7FFFh, which is part of the memory space reserved for adapter card BIOS. Generally, the higher the resolution and color capabilities of the video adapter, the more system memory the video adapter uses, but again, that additional memory (past 128KB) is not normally accessible by the processor. Instead, the system tells the video chip what should be displayed, and the video chip generates the picture by putting data directly into the video RAM on the card.

In the standard system-memory map, a total of 128KB is reserved for use by the video card to store currently displayed information when in basic VGA mode. The reserved video memory is located in segments A000 and B000. The video adapter ROM uses additional upper memory space in segment C000. Even with the new multiple monitor feature in Windows 98, only one video card (the primary video card) is in the memory map; all others use no low system memory.

Note

The location of video adapter RAM is responsible for the 640KB DOS conventional memory barrier. DOS can use all available contiguous memory in the first megabyte of memory up to the point where the video adapter RAM is encountered. The use of ancient video adapters, such as the MDA and CGA, can allow DOS access to more than 640KB of system memory. For more information, see Chapter 5 of *Upgrading and Repairing PCs, Tenth Anniversary Edition*, included on the CD.

To learn how standard video adapters use the system's memory, see "Obsolete Video Adapter Types," also in Chapter 5 of the *Tenth Edition*.

Video Graphics Array (VGA) Memory

All VGA-compatible cards, including Super VGA cards, are almost identical to the EGA in terms of memory use. Just as with the EGA, they use all 128KB of the video RAM from A0000–BFFFF, but not all at once. Again, the video RAM area is split into three distinct regions, and each of these regions is used only when the adapter is in the corresponding mode. One minor difference with the EGA cards is that virtually all VGA cards use the full 32KB allotted to them for onboard ROM (C0000 to C7FFF). Figure 6.18 shows the VGA adapter memory map.

You can see that the typical VGA card uses a full 32KB of space for the onboard ROM containing driver code. Some VGA cards might use slightly less, but this is rare. Just as with the EGA card, the video RAM areas are active only when the adapter is in the particular mode designated. In other words, when a VGA adapter is in graphics mode, only segment A000 is used; when it is in color text mode, only the last half of segment B000 is used. Because the VGA adapter is almost never run in monochrome text mode, the first half of segment B000 remains unused (B0000–B7FFF). Figure 6.18 shows the standard motherboard ROM BIOS so that you can get an idea of how the entire UMA is laid out with this adapter.

```
       . = Empty Addresses
       G = Video Graphics Array (VGA) Adapter Graphics Mode Video RAM
       M = VGA Monochrome Text Mode Video RAM
       C = VGA Color Text Mode Video RAM
       V = Standard VGA Video ROM BIOS
       R = Standard Motherboard ROM BIOS


       : 0---1---2---3---4---5---6---7---8---9---A---B---C---D---E---F---
0A0000: GGGGGGGGGGGGGGGGGGGGGGGGGGGGGGGGGGGGGGGGGGGGGGGGGGGGGGGGGGGGGGGGG
0B0000: MMMMMMMMMMMMMMMMMMMMMMMMMMMMMMMMCCCCCCCCCCCCCCCCCCCCCCCCCCCCCCCCCC
       : 0---1---2---3---4---5---6---7---8---9---A---B---C---D---E---F---
0C0000: VVVVVVVVVVVVVVVVVVVVVVVVVVVVVVVVV...............................
0D0000: ................................................................
       : 0---1---2---3---4---5---6---7---8---9---A---B---C---D---E---F---
0E0000: ................................................................
0F0000: RRRRRRRRRRRRRRRRRRRRRRRRRRRRRRRRRRRRRRRRRRRRRRRRRRRRRRRRRRRRRRRRRR
```

Figure 6.18 The VGA (and Super VGA) adapter memory map.

Systems that use the LPX (Low Profile) motherboard design in an LPX- or Slimline-type case incorporate the video adapter into the motherboard. In these systems, even though the video BIOS and motherboard BIOS may be from the same manufacturer, they are always set up to emulate a standard VGA-type adapter card. In other words, the video BIOS appears in the first 32KB of segment C000 just as though a standalone VGA-type card were plugged into a slot. The built-in video circuit in these systems can be easily disabled with a switch or jumper, which then allows a conventional VGA-type card to be plugged in. By having the built-in VGA act exactly as though it were a separate card, disabling it allows a new adapter to be installed with no compatibility problems that might arise if the video drivers had been incorporated into the motherboard BIOS.

If you were involved with the PC industry in 1987, you might remember how long it took for clone video card manufacturers to accurately copy the IBM VGA circuits. It took nearly two years (almost to 1989) before you could buy an aftermarket VGA card and expect it to run everything an IBM VGA system would with no problems. Some of my associates who bought some of the early cards inadvertently became members of the video card manufacturer's "ROM of the week" club! They were constantly finding problems with the operation of these cards, and many updated and patched ROMs were sent to try and fix the problems. Not wanting to pay for the privilege of beta testing the latest attempts at VGA compatibility, I bit the bullet and took the easy way out. I bought the IBM VGA card (PS/2 Display Adapter) for $595. Note that a top-of-the-line AGP video card today normally runs for less than half that!

Although the card worked very well in most situations, I did find compatibility problems with the memory use of this card and a few other cards, mainly SCSI adapters. This was my first introduction to what I call "scratch pad memory use" by an adapter. I found that many different types of adapters might use some areas in the UMA for mapping scratch pad memory. This refers to memory on the card that stores status information, configuration data, or any other temporary type information of a variable nature. Most cards keep this scratch pad memory to themselves and do not attempt to map it into the processor's address space. However, some cards do place this type of memory in the address space so that the driver programs for the card can use it. Figure 6.19 shows the memory map of the IBM PS/2 Display Adapter (IBM's original VGA card).

```
     . = Empty Addresses
     G = Video Graphics Array (VGA) Adapter Graphics Mode Video RAM
     M = VGA Monochrome Text Mode Video RAM
     C = VGA Color Text Mode Video RAM
     V = IBM VGA Video ROM BIOS
     v = IBM VGA Scratch Pad memory (used by the card)
     R = Standard Motherboard ROM BIOS


        : 0---1---2---3---4---5---6---7---8---9---A---B---C---D---E---F---
0A0000: GGGGGGGGGGGGGGGGGGGGGGGGGGGGGGGGGGGGGGGGGGGGGGGGGGGGGGGGGGGGGGGGGG
0B0000: MMMMMMMMMMMMMMMMMMMMMMMMMMMMMMMMMMCCCCCCCCCCCCCCCCCCCCCCCCCCCCCCCC
        : 0---1---2---3---4---5---6---7---8---9---A---B---C---D---E---F---
0C0000: VVVVVVVVVVVVVVVVVVVVVVVVV..vvvvvv........vv......................
0D0000: ................................................................
        : 0---1---2---3---4---5---6---7---8---9---A---B---C---D---E---F---
0E0000: ................................................................
0F0000: RRRRRRRRRRRRRRRRRRRRRRRRRRRRRRRRRRRRRRRRRRRRRRRRRRRRRRRRRRRRRRRRRR
```

Figure 6.19   IBM's ISA-bus VGA card (PS/2 Display Adapter) memory map.

There is nothing different about this VGA card or any other with respect to the video RAM area. What *is* different is that the ROM code that operates this adapter consumes only 24KB of memory from C0000–C5FFF. Also strange is the 2KB "hole" at C6000, the 6KB of scratch pad memory starting at C6800, and the additional 2KB of scratch pad memory at CA000. In particular, the 2KB "straggler" area really caught me off guard when I installed a SCSI host adapter in this system that had a 16KB onboard BIOS with a default starting address of C8000. I immediately ran into a conflict that completely disabled the system. In fact, it would not boot, had no display at all, and could only beep out error codes that indicated the video card had failed. At first I thought I had somehow "fried" the card, but removing the new SCSI adapter had everything functioning normally. I could get the system to work with the SCSI adapter and an old CGA card substituting for the VGA, so I immediately knew a conflict was afoot. This scratch pad memory use was not documented clearly in the technical-reference information for the adapter, so it was something I had to find out by trial and error. If you have ever had two cards that don't work together in the same system, this is one example of a potential conflict that can disable the system completely!

▶▶ See "Adapter Memory Configuration and Optimization," p. 499.

Needless to say, nothing could be done about this 2KB of scratch pad memory hanging out there, and I had to work around it as long as I had this card in the system. I solved my SCSI adapter problem by merely moving the SCSI adapter BIOS to a different address.

Note

I have seen other VGA-type video adapters use scratch pad memory, but they have all kept it within the C0000–C7FFF 32KB region allotted normally for the video ROM BIOS. By using a 24KB BIOS, I have seen other cards with up to 8KB of scratch pad area, but none—except for IBM's—in which the scratch pad memory goes beyond C8000.

Adapter ROM and Special Purpose RAM Memory

The second 128KB of upper memory beginning at segment C000 is reserved for the software programs, or BIOS (basic input/output system), on the adapter boards plugged into the system slots. These BIOS programs are stored on special chips known as read-only memory (ROM). Most adapters today use EEPROM (Electrically Erasable Programmable ROM) or flash ROM, which can be erased and reprogrammed right in the system without removing the chip or card. Updating the flash ROM is as simple as running the update program you get from the manufacturer and following the directions onscreen. It pays to check periodically with your card manufacturers to see if they have flash ROM updates for their cards.

ROM is useful for semipermanent programs that must always be present while the system is running, and especially for booting. Graphics boards, hard disk controllers, communications boards, and expanded memory boards, for example, are adapter boards that might have adapter ROM. These adapter ROMs are in an area of memory separate from the VGA video RAM and motherboard ROM areas.

On systems based on the 386 CPU chip or higher, memory managers that are included with DOS 6 or third-party programs can load device drivers and memory-resident programs into unused regions in the UMA.

To actually move the RAM usage on any given adapter requires that you consult the documentation for the card. Most older cards require that specific switches or jumpers be changed, and the settings will probably not be obvious without the manual. Most newer cards, especially those that are Plug and Play, allow these settings to be changed by software that comes with the card or the Device Manager program that goes with some of the newer operating systems, such as Windows 9x or Windows 2000 and newer.

Video Adapter BIOS

The video adapter BIOS handles the translation between the video card and basic VGA mode graphics instructions. Remember that your system is in a basic VGA mode during boot and whenever you are running Windows in safe mode. Although 128KB of upper memory beginning at segment C000 is reserved for use by adapter BIOSes, not all this space is used by video adapters commonly found on PCs. Table 6.13 details the amount of space used by the BIOS on each type of common video adapter card.

Table 6.13   Memory Used by Different Video Cards

Type of Adapter	Adapter BIOS Memory Used
Monochrome display adapter (MDA)	None; drivers in motherboard BIOS
Color graphics adapter (CGA)	None; drivers in motherboard BIOS
Enhanced graphics adapter (EGA)	16KB onboard (C0000–C3FFF)
Video graphics array (VGA)	32KB onboard (C0000–C7FFF)
Super VGA (SVGA)	32KB onboard (C0000–C7FFF)

Depending on the basic VGA mode selected (color text, monochrome text, or VGA graphics), the video card uses all the 128KB of upper memory beginning at segment C000. In addition, these graphics cards can contain up to 8MB or more of onboard memory for use in their native high-resolution modes in which to store currently displayed data and more quickly fetch new screen data for display.

Hard Disk Controller and SCSI Host Adapter BIOS

The upper memory addresses C0000 to DFFFF are also used for the built-in BIOS contained on many hard drive and SCSI controllers. Table 6.14 lists the amount of memory and the addresses commonly used by the BIOS contained on hard drive adapter cards.

Table 6.14   Memory Addresses Used by Different Hard Drive Adapter Cards

Disk Adapter Type	Onboard BIOS Size	BIOS Address Range
Most XT compatible controllers	8KB	C8000–C9FFF
Most AT controllers	None	Drivers in motherboard BIOS
Most standard IDE adapters	None	Drivers in motherboard BIOS
Most enhanced IDE adapters	16KB	C8000–CBFFF
Some SCSI host adapters	16KB	C8000–CBFFF
Some SCSI host adapters	16KB	DC000–DFFFF

The hard drive or SCSI adapter card used on a particular system might use a different amount of memory, but it is most likely to use the memory segment beginning at C800 because this address is considered part of the IBM standard for personal computers. Virtually all the disk controller or SCSI adapters today that have an onboard BIOS allow the BIOS starting address to be easily moved in the C000 and D000 segments. The locations listed in Table 6.14 are only the default addresses that most of these cards use. If the default address is already in use by another card, you have to consult the documentation for the new card to see how to change the BIOS starting address to avoid any conflicts.

Figure 6.20 shows a sample memory map for an Adaptec AHA-2940 SCSI adapter.

```
      . = Empty Addresses
      G = Video Graphics Array (VGA) Adapter Graphics Mode Video RAM
      M = VGA Monochrome Text Mode Video RAM
      C = VGA Color Text Mode Video RAM
      V = Standard VGA Video ROM BIOS
      S = SCSI Host Adapter ROM BIOS
      R = Standard Motherboard ROM BIOS


        : 0---1---2---3---4---5---6---7---8---9---A---B---C---D---E---F---
 0A0000: GGGGGGGGGGGGGGGGGGGGGGGGGGGGGGGGGGGGGGGGGGGGGGGGGGGGGGGGGGGGGGGGG
 0B0000: MMMMMMMMMMMMMMMMMMMMMMMMMMMMMMMMCCCCCCCCCCCCCCCCCCCCCCCCCCCCCCCCCC
        : 0---1---2---3---4---5---6---7---8---9---A---B---C---D---E---F---
 0C0000: VVVVVVVVVVVVVVVVVVVVVVVVVVVVVVVV.................................
 0D0000: ..............................................SSSSSSSSSSSSSSSSSS
        : 0---1---2---3---4---5---6---7---8---9---A---B---C---D---E---F---
 0E0000: ................................................................
 0F0000: RRRRRRRRRRRRRRRRRRRRRRRRRRRRRRRRRRRRRRRRRRRRRRRRRRRRRRRRRRRRRRRRR
```

Figure 6.20   Adaptec AHA-2940U SCSI adapter default memory use.

Note how this SCSI adapter fits in here. Although no conflicts are in the UMA memory, the free regions have been fragmented by the placement of the SCSI BIOS. Because most systems do not have any BIOS in segment E000, that remains as a free 64KB region. With no other adapters using memory, this example shows another free UMB (Upper Memory Block) starting at C8000 and continuing through DBFFF, which represents an 80KB free region. Using the EMM386 driver that comes with DOS or Windows, memory can be mapped into these two regions for loading 16-bit memory-resident drivers and programs. Note that this has no effect on 32-bit Windows 9x or NT drivers, as those are loaded into extended memory automatically. Unfortunately, because programs cannot be split across regions, the largest 16-bit driver program you could load is 80KB, which is the size of the largest free region. It would be much better if you could move the SCSI adapter BIOS so that it was next to the VGA BIOS, as that would bring the free UMB space to a single region of 144KB. It is much easier and more efficient to use a single 144KB region than two regions of 80KB and 64KB. Again, manipulating memory in this manner is not necessary with 32-bit drivers because they are automatically loaded into extended memory anyway.

Fortunately, it is possible to move this particular SCSI adapter because it is a Plug-and-Play card. This means you can control the resource settings with the Win9x Device Manager.

If you have an older non–Plug-and-Play card, you probably need the documentation to discover the switch and jumper settings for the card; most manufacturers don't clearly label them. If you can't find your original documentation, consult the Micro House PC Hardware Library on the CD-ROM with this book, which has an extensive database of adapter cards, motherboards, and hard drives showing jumper settings, configuration information, manufacturer information, and so on.

Most cards sold since 1996 have been Plug and Play, meaning that they are fully software configurable.

After changing the appropriate switches to move the SCSI adapter BIOS to start at C8000, the optimized map would look like Figure 6.21.

```
. = Empty Addresses
G = Video Graphics Array (VGA) Adapter Graphics Mode Video RAM
M = VGA Monochrome Text Mode Video RAM
C = VGA Color Text Mode Video RAM
V = Standard VGA Video ROM BIOS
S = SCSI Host Adapter ROM BIOS
R = Standard Motherboard ROM BIOS


        : 0---1---2---3---4---5---6---7---8---9---A---B---C---D---E---F---
0A0000: GGGGGGGGGGGGGGGGGGGGGGGGGGGGGGGGGGGGGGGGGGGGGGGGGGGGGGGGGGGGGGGGG
0B0000: MMMMMMMMMMMMMMMMMMMMMMMMMMMMMMMMMMCCCCCCCCCCCCCCCCCCCCCCCCCCCCCCCC
        : 0---1---2---3---4---5---6---7---8---9---A---B---C---D---E---F---
0C0000: VVVVVVVVVVVVVVVVVVVVVVVVVVVVVVVVVVSSSSSSSSSSSSSSSSSS..............
0D0000: ................................................................
        : 0---1---2---3---4---5---6---7---8---9---A---B---C---D---E---F---
0E0000: ................................................................
0F0000: RRRRRRRRRRRRRRRRRRRRRRRRRRRRRRRRRRRRRRRRRRRRRRRRRRRRRRRRRRRRRRRRR
```

Figure 6.21 Adaptec AHA-2940U SCSI adapter with optimized memory use.

Notice how the free space is now a single contiguous block of 144KB. This represents a far more optimum setup than the default settings.

Network Adapters

Network adapter cards can also use upper memory in segments C000 and D000. The exact amount of memory used and the starting address for each network card vary with the card's type and manufacturer. Some network cards do not use any memory at all. A network card might have two primary uses for memory. They are as follows:

- IPL (Initial Program Load or Boot) ROM
- Shared Memory (RAM)

An IPL ROM is usually an 8KB ROM that contains a bootstrap loader program that allows the system to boot directly from a file server on the network. This allows the removal of all disk drives from the PC, creating a diskless workstation. Because no floppy or hard disk is in the system to boot from, the IPL ROM gives the system the instructions necessary to locate an image of the operating system on the file server and load it as though it were on an internal drive. If you are not using your system as a diskless workstation, it is beneficial to disable any IPL ROM or IPL ROM socket on the adapter card. Note that many network adapters do not allow this socket to be disabled, which means that you lose the 8KB of address space for other hardware, even if the ROM chip is removed from the socket!

Shared memory refers to a small portion of RAM contained on the network card that is mapped into the PC's upper memory area. This region is used as a memory window onto the network and offers rapid data transfer from the network card to the system. IBM pioneered the use of shared memory for its first Token-Ring network adapters, and now shared memory is commonly used in other companies' network adapters. Shared memory was first devised by IBM because it found that transfers using the DMA channels were not fast enough in most systems. This had mainly to do with some quirks in the DMA controller and bus design, which especially affected 16-bit ISA bus systems. Network adapters that do not use shared memory use DMA or Programmed I/O (PIO) transfers to move data to and from the network adapter.

Although shared memory is faster than either DMA or PIO for ISA systems, it does require 16KB of UMA space to work. Most standard performance network adapters use PIO because it makes them easier to configure, and they require no free UMA space, but most high-performance adapters use shared memory. The shared memory region on most network adapters that use one is usually 16KB in size and can be located at any user-selected 4KB increment of memory in segments C000 or D000.

Figure 6.22 shows the default memory addresses for the IPL ROM and shared memory of an IBM Token-Ring network adapter, although many other network adapters, such as Ethernet adapters, are similar. One thing to note is that most Ethernet adapters use either a DMA channel or standard PIO commands to send data to and from the network, and don't use shared memory, as many Token-Ring cards do.

```
     . = Empty Addresses
     G = Video Graphics Array (VGA) Adapter Graphics Mode Video RAM
     M = VGA Monochrome Text Mode Video RAM
     C = VGA Color Text Mode Video RAM
     V = Standard VGA Video ROM BIOS
     I = Token Ring Network Adapter IPL ROM
     N = Token Ring Network Adapter Shared RAM
     R = Standard Motherboard ROM BIOS


        : 0---1---2---3---4---5---6---7---8---9---A---B---C---D---E---F---
 0A0000: GGGGGGGGGGGGGGGGGGGGGGGGGGGGGGGGGGGGGGGGGGGGGGGGGGGGGGGGGGGGGGGGG
 0B0000: MMMMMMMMMMMMMMMMMMMMMMMMMMMMMMMMMMCCCCCCCCCCCCCCCCCCCCCCCCCCCCCCCC
        : 0---1---2---3---4---5---6---7---8---9---A---B---C---D---E---F---
 0C0000: VVVVVVVVVVVVVVVVVVVVVVVVVVVVVVVVV................IIIIIIII........
 0D0000: ................................NNNNNNNNNNNNNNNN................
        : 0---1---2---3---4---5---6---7---8---9---A---B---C---D---E---F---
 0E0000: ................................................................
 0F0000: RRRRRRRRRRRRRRRRRRRRRRRRRRRRRRRRRRRRRRRRRRRRRRRRRRRRRRRRRRRRRRRRRR
```

Figure 6.22 Network adapter default memory map.

I have also included the standard VGA video BIOS in Figure 6.22 because nearly every system would have a VGA-type video adapter as well. Note that these default addresses for the IPL ROM and the shared memory can easily be changed by reconfiguring the adapter. Most other network adapters are similar in that they also have an IPL ROM and a shared memory address, although the sizes of these areas and the default addresses might be different. Most network adapters that incorporate an IPL ROM option can disable the ROM and socket so that those addresses are not needed at all. This helps conserve UMA space and prevent possible future conflicts if you are never going to use the function.

Notice in this case that the SCSI adapter used in Figure 6.23 fits both at its default BIOS address of DC000 and the optimum address of C8000. The Token-Ring shared memory location is not optimal and causes fragmentation of the UMB space. By adjusting the location of the shared memory, this setup can be greatly improved. Figure 6.23 shows an optimal setup with the Token-Ring adapter and the SCSI adapter in the same machine.

```
    . = Empty Addresses
    G = Video Graphics Array (VGA) Adapter Graphics Mode Video RAM
    M = VGA Monochrome Text Mode Video RAM
    C = VGA Color Text Mode Video RAM
    V = Standard VGA Video ROM BIOS
    S = SCSI Host Adapter ROM BIOS
    I = Token Ring Network Adapter IPL ROM
    N = Token Ring Network Adapter Shared RAM
    R = Standard Motherboard ROM BIOS


        : 0---1---2---3---4---5---6---7---8---9---A---B---C---D---E---F---
0A0000: GGGGGGGGGGGGGGGGGGGGGGGGGGGGGGGGGGGGGGGGGGGGGGGGGGGGGGGGGGGGGGGGG
0B0000: MMMMMMMMMMMMMMMMMMMMMMMMMMMMMMMMCCCCCCCCCCCCCCCCCCCCCCCCCCCCCCCCCC
        : 0---1---2---3---4---5---6---7---8---9---A---B---C---D---E---F---
0C0000: VVVVVVVVVVVVVVVVVVVVVVVVVVVVVVVVSSSSSSSSSSSSSSSSSSNNNNNNNNNNNNNNNN
0D0000: IIIIIIII........................................................
        : 0---1---2---3---4---5---6---7---8---9---A---B---C---D---E---F---
0E0000: ................................................................
0F0000: RRRRRRRRRRRRRRRRRRRRRRRRRRRRRRRRRRRRRRRRRRRRRRRRRRRRRRRRRRRRRRRRRR
```

Figure 6.23 Adaptec AHA-2940U SCSI adapter and network adapter with optimized memory use.

This configuration allows a single 120KB UMB that can be efficiently used to load software drivers. Notice that the IPL ROM was moved to D0000, which places it as the last item installed before the free memory space. This is done because if the IPL function is not needed, it can be disabled and the UMB space would increase to 128KB and still be contiguous. If the default settings are used for both the SCSI and network adapters, the UMB memory is fragmented into three regions of 16KB, 40KB, and 64KB. The memory still functions, but it is hardly an optimal situation.

Note that the Plug-and-Play feature in Win9x, Windows NT, and Windows 2000 does not attempt to optimize memory use, only to resolve conflicts. Of course, with 32-bit drivers, the location and size of free Upper Memory Blocks don't really matter because 32-bit drivers will be loaded into extended memory. If you are still occasionally running DOS-based programs, such as games, you should manually optimize the upper memory area configuration for maximum memory and performance.

Other ROMs in the Upper Memory Area

In addition to the BIOS for hard drive controllers, SCSI adapters, and network cards, upper memory segments C000 and D000 are used by some terminal emulators, security adapters, memory boards, and other devices and adapter boards. Some adapters might require memory only for BIOS information, and others could require RAM in these upper memory segments. For information on a specific adapter, consult the manufacturer's documentation.

Motherboard BIOS Memory

The last 128KB of reserved memory is used by the motherboard BIOS. The BIOS programs in ROM control the system during the boot-up procedure and remain as drivers for various hardware in the system during normal operation. Because these programs must be available immediately, they cannot be loaded from a device such as a disk drive. Four main programs stored in most motherboard ROMs are as follows:

- The POST is a set of routines that test the motherboard, memory, disk controllers, video adapters, keyboard, and other primary system components. This routine is useful when you troubleshoot system failures or problems.

▶▶ See "The Power On Self Test (POST)," p. 1289.

- The bootstrap loader routine initiates a search for an operating system on a floppy disk or hard disk. If an operating system is found, it is loaded into memory and given control of the system.

▶▶ See "The Boot Process," p. 1351.

- The BIOS is the software interface to all the hardware in the system. The BIOS is a collection of individual drivers for the hardware in the system. With the BIOS, a program can easily access features in the system by calling on a standard BIOS driver function instead of talking directly to the device.

◀◀ See "BIOS," p. 345.

- The CMOS Setup program is a menu-driven application used for system configuration and setup. It is normally activated at boot time by pressing the proper key. This program is used to set basic system configuration parameters and BIOS features, motherboard and chipset features, user preferences, and security features (passwords), and in some cases to run limited diagnostics. Not all systems have the CMOS Setup program in ROM; some must load it from a floppy disk or hard disk.

Both segments E000 and F000 in the memory map are considered reserved for the motherboard BIOS, but only some systems actually use this entire area. Older 8-bit systems require only segment F000 and enable adapter card ROM or RAM to use segment E000. Most 16-bit or greater systems use all F000 for the BIOS and may decode but not use any of segment E000. By decoding an area, the motherboard essentially grabs control of the addresses, which precludes installing any other hardware in this region. In other words, it is not possible to configure adapter cards to use this area. That is why you will find that most adapters that use memory simply do not allow any choices for memory use in segment E000. Although this might seem like a waste of 64KB of memory space, any 386 or higher system can use the powerful MMU in the processor to map RAM from extended memory into segment E000 as an Upper Memory Block. The system can subsequently load 16-bit driver software in this UMB if necessary. This is a nice solution to what otherwise would be wasted memory, although it is not important if you use 32-bit drivers.

Many different ROM-interface programs are in the IBM motherboards, but the location of these programs is mostly consistent.

Figure 6.24 shows the motherboard ROM BIOS memory use of most 16-bit or greater systems.

```
. = Empty Addresses
R = Standard Motherboard ROM BIOS

        : 0---1---2---3---4---5---6---7---8---9---A---B---C---D---E---F---
0E0000: ................................................................
0F0000: RRRRRRRRRRRRRRRRRRRRRRRRRRRRRRRRRRRRRRRRRRRRRRRRRRRRRRRRRRRRRRRRRR
```

Figure 6.24 Motherboard ROM BIOS memory use of most systems.

Note that the standard system BIOS uses only segment F000 (64KB). In almost every case, the remainder of the BIOS area (segment E000) is completely free and can be used as UMA block space.

Extended Memory

As mentioned previously in this chapter, the memory map on a system based on the 286 or higher processor can extend beyond the 1MB boundary that exists when the processor is in real mode. On a 286 or 386SX system, the extended memory limit is 16MB; on a 386DX, 486, Pentium, Pentium MMX, or Pentium Pro system, the extended memory limit is 4GB (4,096MB). Systems based on the Pentium II processor have a limit of 64GB (65,536MB).

For a system to address memory beyond the first megabyte, the processor must be in protected mode—the native mode of 286 and higher processors. On a 286, only programs designed to run in protected mode can take advantage of extended memory; 386 and higher processors offer another mode, called virtual real mode, which enables extended memory to be, in effect, chopped into 1MB pieces (each its own real-mode session). Virtual real mode also allows for several of these sessions to be running simultaneously in protected areas of memory. They can be seen as DOS prompt sessions or windows within Windows 9x, NT, or OS/2. Although several DOS programs can be running at once, each is still limited to a maximum of 640KB of memory because each session simulates a real-mode environment, right down to the BIOS and Upper Memory Area. Running several programs at once in virtual real mode, called *multitasking*, requires software that can manage each program and keep them from crashing into one another. OS/2, Windows 9x, and Windows NT all do this.

The 286 and higher CPU chips also run in what is termed *real mode*, which enables full compatibility with the 8088 CPU chip installed on the PC/XT-type computer. Real mode enables you to run DOS programs one at a time on an AT-type system just as you would on a PC/XT. However, an AT-type system running in real mode, particularly a 386-, 486-, Pentium-, Pentium Pro–, or Pentium II–based system, is really functioning as little more than a turbo PC. In real mode, these processors can emulate the 8086 or 8088, but they cannot operate in protected mode at the same time. For that reason, the 386 and above also provide a virtual real mode that operates under protected mode. This allows real-mode programs to execute under the control of a protected-mode operating system, such as Win9x, NT/2000, or OS/2.

Note

Extended memory is basically all memory past the first megabyte, which can be accessed only while the processor is in protected mode.

XMS Memory

Microsoft, Intel, AST Corp., and Lotus Development developed the extended memory specification (XMS) in 1987 to specify how programs would use extended memory. The XMS specification functions on systems based on the 286 or higher and allows real-mode programs (those designed to run in DOS) to use extended memory and another block of memory usually out of the reach of DOS.

Before XMS, there was no way to ensure cooperation between programs that switched the processor into protected mode and used extended memory. There was also no way for one program to know what another had been doing with the extended memory because none of them could see that memory while in real mode. HIMEM.SYS becomes an arbitrator of sorts that first grabs all the extended memory for itself and then doles it out to programs that know the XMS protocols. In this manner, several programs that use XMS memory can operate together under DOS on the same system, switching the processor into and out of protected mode to access the memory. XMS rules prevent one program from accessing memory that another has in use. Because Windows 3.x is a program manager that switches the system to and from protected mode in running several programs at once, it has been set up to require XMS memory to function. Windows 95 operates mostly in protected mode, but still calls on real mode for access to many system components. Windows NT and Windows 2000 are true protected-mode operating systems, as is OS/2.

Extended memory can be made to conform to the XMS specification by installing a device driver in the CONFIG.SYS file. The most common XMS driver is HIMEM.SYS, which is included with Windows 3.x and later versions of DOS, starting with 4.0 and up. Windows 9x and NT automatically allow XMS functions in DOS prompt sessions, and you can configure full-blown DOS-mode sessions to allow XMS functions as well.

Note

To learn more about the High Memory Area (HMA) and Expanded Memory, see Chapter 5 of *Upgrading and Repairing PCs, Tenth Anniversary Edition*, on the CD.

Preventing ROM BIOS Memory Conflicts and Overlap

As explained previously, C000 and D000 are reserved for use by adapter-board ROM and RAM. If two adapters have overlapping ROM or RAM addresses, usually neither board operates properly. Each board functions if you remove or disable the other one, but they do not work together.

With many adapter boards, you can change the actual memory locations to be used with jumpers, switches, or driver software, which might be necessary to allow two boards to coexist in one system. This type of conflict can cause problems for troubleshooters. You must read the documentation for each adapter to find out what memory addresses the adapter uses and how to change the addresses to allow coexistence with another adapter. Most of the time, you can work around these problems by reconfiguring the board or changing jumpers, switch settings, or software-driver parameters. This change enables the two boards to coexist and stay out of each other's way.

Additionally, you must ensure that adapter boards do not use the same IRQ (Interrupt Request Line), DMA (direct memory access) channel, or I/O port address. You can easily avoid adapter board memory, IRQ, DMA channel, and I/O port conflicts by creating a chart or template to mock up the system configuration by penciling on the template the resources already used by each installed adapter. You end up with a picture of the system resources and the relationship of each adapter to the others. This procedure helps you anticipate conflicts and ensures that you configure each adapter board correctly the first time. The template also becomes important documentation when you consider new adapter purchases. New adapters must be configurable to use the available resources in your system.

◀◀ See "System Resources," p. 311.

If your system has Plug-and-Play capabilities, and you use PnP adapters, it can resolve conflicts between the adapters by moving the memory usage on any conflict. Unfortunately, this routine is not intelligent and still requires human intervention—that is, manual specification of addresses to achieve the most optimum location for the adapter memory.

ROM Shadowing

Virtually all 386 and higher systems enable you to use what is termed *shadow memory* for the motherboard and possibly some adapter ROMs as well. Shadowing essentially moves the programming code from slow ROM chips into fast 32-bit system memory. Shadowing slower ROMs by copying their contents into RAM can greatly speed up these BIOS routines—sometimes making them four to five times faster.

Note that shadowing ROMs is not very important when running a 32-bit operating system, such as Win9x or NT. This is because those operating systems use only the 16-bit BIOS driver code during booting; then they load 32-bit replacement drivers into faster extended memory and use them. Therefore, shadowing normally affects only DOS or other 16-bit software and operating systems. Because of this, some people are tempted to turn off the Video BIOS shadowing feature in the BIOS setup. Unfortunately, it won't gain you any memory back (you've lost it anyway) and will make the system slightly slower to boot up and somewhat slower when in Windows safe mode. The 16-bit BIOS video driver code is used at those times.

Note

To learn more about ROM shadowing, see Chapter 5 of *Upgrading and Repairing PCs, Tenth Anniversary Edition*, on the CD accompanying this book.

Total Installed Memory Versus Total Usable Memory

Most people don't realize that not all the SIMM or other RAM memory you purchase and install in a system is available. Because of some quirks in system design, the system usually has to "throw away" up to 384KB of RAM to make way for the Upper Memory Area.

For example, most systems with 16MB of RAM (which is 16,384KB) installed show a total of only 16,000KB installed during the POST or when running Setup. This indicates that 16,384KB–16,000KB = 384KB of missing memory! Some systems might show 16,256KB with the same 16MB installed, which works out to 16,384KB–16,256KB = 128KB missing.

If you run your Setup program and check out your base and extended memory values, you will find more information than just the single figure for the total shown during the POST. In most systems with 4,096KB (4MB), you have 640KB base and 3,072KB extended. In some systems, Setup reports 640KB base and 3,328KB extended memory, which is a bonus. In other words, most systems come up 384KB short, but some come up only 128KB short.

This shortfall is not easy to explain, but it is consistent from system to system. Say that you have a 486 system with two installed 72-pin (32-bit) 16MB SIMMs. This results in a total installed memory of 32MB in two separate banks because the processor has a 32-bit data bus. Each SIMM is a single bank in this system. Most cheaper 486 systems use the 30-pin (8-bit) SIMMs; four are required to make a single bank. The first bank (or SIMM, in this case) starts at address 0000000h (the start of the first megabyte), and the second starts at 1000000 (the start of the seventeenth megabyte).

One of the cardinal rules of memory is that you absolutely cannot have two hardware devices wired to the same address. This means that 384KB of the first memory bank in this system would be in direct conflict with the video RAM (segments A000 and B000), any adapter card ROMs (segments C000 and D000), and of course the motherboard ROM (segments E000 and F000). That means all SIMM RAM that occupies these addresses must be shut off or the system will not function! Actually, a motherboard designer can do three things with the SIMM memory that would overlap from A0000–FFFFF:

- Use the faster RAM to hold a copy of any slow ROMs (shadowing), disabling the ROM in the process.
- Turn off any RAM not used for shadowing, eliminating any UMA conflicts.
- Remap any RAM not used for shadowing, adding to the stack of currently installed extended memory.

Most systems shadow the motherboard ROM (usually 64KB) and the video ROM (32KB), and simply turn off the rest. Some motherboard ROMs allow additional shadowing to be selected between C8000–DFFFF, usually in 16KB increments.

Note

You can shadow only ROM, never RAM, so if any card (such as a network card) has a RAM buffer in the C8000–DFFFF area, you must not shadow the RAM buffer addresses or the card will not function. For the same reason, you cannot shadow the A0000–BFFFF area because it is the video adapter RAM buffer.

Most motherboards do not do any remapping, which means that any of the 384KB not shadowed is simply turned off. That is why enabling shadowing does not seem to use any memory. The memory used for shadowing would otherwise be discarded in most systems. These systems would appear to be short by 384KB compared to what is physically installed in the system. For example, in a system with 32MB, no remapping would result in 640KB of base memory and 31,744KB of extended memory, for a total of 32,384KB of usable RAM—384KB short of the total (32,768KB–384KB).

Some systems shadow what they can and then remap any segments that do not have shadowing into extended memory so as not to waste the nonshadowed RAM. PS/2 systems, for example, shadow the motherboard BIOS area (E0000–FFFFF or 128KB in these systems) and remap the rest of the first bank of SIMM memory (256KB from A0000–DFFFF) to whatever address follows the last installed bank.

Note

Many newer systems don't allow selecting ROM shadowing functions, nor do they do any remapping. These days, the small amount of memory or performance gain just isn't worth the trouble in system engineering and design to accomplish it.

In my sample system with two 16MB (32-bit) SIMMs, the 256KB not used for shadowing would be remapped to 2000000–203FFFF, which is the start of the 33rd megabyte. This affects diagnostics because if you had any memory error reported in those addresses (2000000–203FFFF), it would indicate a failure in the first SIMM, even though the addresses point to the end of installed extended memory. The addresses from 1000000–1FFFFFF would be in the second SIMM, and the 640KB base memory 0000000–009FFFF would be back in the first SIMM. As you can see, figuring out how the SIMMs are mapped into the system is not easy!

Most systems that do remapping can remap an entire segment only if no shadowing is going on within it. The video RAM area in segments A000 and B000 can never contain shadowing, so at least 128KB can be remapped to the top of installed extended memory in any system that supports remapping. Because most systems shadow in segments F000 (motherboard ROM) and C000 (video ROM), these two segments cannot be remapped. This leaves 256KB maximum for remapping. Any system remapping the full 384KB must not be shadowing at all, which would slow down the system and is not recommended. Shadowing is always preferred over remapping, and remapping what is not shadowed is definitely preferred over simply turning off the RAM.

Systems that have 384KB of "missing" memory do not do remapping. If you want to determine whether your system has any missing memory, all you need to know are three things. One is the total physical memory actually installed. Running your Setup program can discover the other two items. You want to know the total base and extended memory numbers recognized by the system. Then simply subtract the base and extended memory from the total installed to determine the missing memory. You will usually find that your system is "missing" 384KB, but you could be lucky and have a system that remaps 256KB of what is missing and thus shows only 128KB of memory missing.

Virtually all systems use some of the missing memory for shadowing ROMs, especially the motherboard and video BIOS, so what is missing is not completely wasted. Systems "missing" 128KB will find that it is being used to shadow your motherboard BIOS (64KB from F0000–FFFFF) and video BIOS (32KB from C0000–C8000). The remainder of segment C0000 (32KB from C8000–CFFFF) is simply being turned off. All other segments (128KB from A0000–BFFFF and 128KB from D0000–EFFFF) are being remapped to the start of the fifth megabyte (400000–43FFFF). Most systems simply disable these remaining segments rather than take the trouble to remap them.

Note

If your system is doing remapping, any errors reported near the end of installed extended memory are likely in the first bank of memory because that is where they are remapped from. The first bank in a 32-bit system would be constructed of either four 30-pin (8-bit) SIMMs or one 72-pin (32-bit) SIMM. The first bank in a 64-bit system would be constructed of either two 72-pin (32-bit) SIMMs or one 168-pin (64-bit) DIMM.

Adapter Memory Configuration and Optimization

Ideally, all adapter boards would be Plug-and-Play devices that require you to merely plug the adapter into a motherboard slot and then use it. With the Plug-and-Play specification, we are moving toward that goal. However, sometimes it almost seems that adapter boards are designed as though they were the only adapter likely to be on a system. They usually require you to know the upper memory addresses and IRQ and DMA channels already on your system and how to configure the new adapter so that it does not conflict with your already installed adapters.

Adapter boards use upper memory for their BIOS and as working RAM. If two boards attempt to use the same BIOS area or RAM area of upper memory, a conflict occurs that can keep your system from booting. The following sections cover ways to avoid these potential conflicts and how to troubleshoot if they do occur. In addition, these sections discuss moving adapter memory to resolve conflicts and provide some ideas on optimizing adapter memory use.

How to Determine What Adapters Occupy the UMA

You can determine what adapters are using space in upper memory in the following two ways:

- Study the documentation for each adapter on your system to determine the memory addresses they use.
- Use a software utility that can quickly determine for you what upper memory areas your adapters are using.

The simplest way (although by no means always the most foolproof) is to use a software utility to determine the upper memory areas used by the adapters installed on your system. One such utility, Microsoft Diagnostics (MSD), comes with Windows 3.x and DOS 6 or higher versions. The Device Manager under System in the Windows 95 Control Panel also supplies this information, as does the new System Information utility that comes with Windows 98. These utilities examine your system configuration and determine not only the upper memory used by your adapters, but also the IRQs used by each of these adapters.

True Plug-and-Play systems also shut down one of the cards involved in a conflict to prevent a total system lockup. This could cause Windows to boot in safe mode.

After you run MSD, Device Manager, or another utility to determine your system's upper memory configuration, make a printout of the memory addresses used. Thereafter, you can quickly refer to the printout when you are adding a new adapter to ensure that the new board does not conflict with any devices already installed on your system.

Moving Adapter Memory to Resolve Conflicts

After you identify a conflict or potential conflict using one of the two methods discussed in the previous section, you might have to reconfigure one or more of your adapters to move the upper memory space used by a problem adapter.

Most adapter boards make moving adapter memory a somewhat simple process, enabling you to change a few jumpers or switches to reconfigure the board. With Plug-and-Play cards, use the configuration program that comes with the board or the Windows Device Manager to make the changes. The following steps help you resolve most problems that arise because adapter boards conflict with one another:

1. Determine the upper memory addresses currently used by your adapter boards and write them down.

2. Determine if any of these addresses are overlapping, which results in a conflict.

3. Consult the documentation for your adapter boards to determine which boards can be reconfigured so that all adapters have access to unique memory addresses.

4. Configure the affected adapter boards so that no conflict in memory addresses occurs.

For example, if one adapter uses the upper memory range C8000–CBFFF and another adapter uses the range CA000–CCFFF, you have a potential address conflict. One of them must be changed. Note that Plug-and-Play cards allow these changes to be made directly from the Windows Device Manager.

Optimizing Adapter Memory Use

On an ideal PC, adapter boards would always come configured so that the upper memory addresses they use immediately follow the upper memory addresses used by the previous adapter, with no overlap that could cause conflicts. Such an upper memory arrangement would not only be "clean," but would make it much easier to use available upper memory for loading device drivers and memory-resident programs. However, this is not the case. Adapter boards often leave gaps of unused memory between one another—this is, of course, preferable to an overlap, but still is not the best use of upper memory.

Those who wanted to make the most of their upper memory might consider studying the documentation for each adapter board installed on their systems to determine a way to compact the upper memory used by each of these devices. For example, the use of upper memory could be simpler if you configured your adapter boards so that the blocks of memory they use fit together like bricks in a wall, rather than like a slice of Swiss cheese, as is the case on most systems. The more you can reduce your free upper memory to as few contiguous chunks as possible, the more completely and efficiently you can take advantage of the UMA.

Memory optimization in this manner is not really necessary if you are running 32-bit drivers as you would in a normal Win9x or NT system. This is mostly useful for running older DOS applications, games, and so on.

Note

On systems using an older 16-bit operating system, such as Windows 3.1 or DOS, memory-resident programs and device drivers can be moved into the UMA by using a memory manager such as the MEMMAKER utility or some other aftermarket utility. See Chapter 5 of *Upgrading and Repairing PCs, Tenth Anniversary Edition*, on the CD.

The IDE Interface

7

SOME OF THE MAIN TOPICS IN THIS CHAPTER ARE

An Overview of the IDE Interface

The primary interface used to connect a hard disk drive to a modern PC is called IDE. This stands for Integrated Drive Electronics and refers to the fact that the interface electronics or controller is built into the drives themselves. IDE did not spring up overnight; it is actually an evolutionary version of earlier interfaces that used separate drives and controllers.

Today IDE is used to connect not only hard disks, but also CD-ROM drives, DVD drives, high-capacity floppy drives, and tape drives. Even so, IDE is still thought of primarily as a hard disk interface, and it evolved directly from the separate controller and hard drive interfaces that were used prior to IDE. This chapter covers the IDE interface in detail, as well as the original interfaces from which IDE evolved.

Precursors to IDE

This section covers the different hard disk drive interfaces used prior to IDE, giving you all the technical information you need to deal with them in any way—troubleshooting, servicing, upgrading, and even mixing the different types.

A variety of hard disk interfaces have been available for PC hard disks over the years. As time has passed, the number of choices has increased, and many of the older designs are no longer viable in newer systems. You need to know about all these interfaces, from the oldest to the newest designs, because you will encounter all of them whenever upgrading or repairing systems is necessary.

These interfaces have different cabling and configuration options, and the setup and format of drives will vary as well. Special problems might arise when you are trying to install more than one drive of a particular interface type or (especially) when you are mixing drives of different interface types in one system.

The primary job of the hard disk controller or interface is to transmit and receive data to and from the drive. The different interface types limit how fast data can be moved from the drive to the system and offer different levels of performance. If you are putting together a system in which performance is a primary concern, you need to know how these different interfaces affect performance and what you can expect from them. Many of the statistics that appear in technical literature are not indicative of the real performance figures you will see in practice. I will separate the myths presented by some of these overly optimistic figures from the reality of what you will actually see.

With regard to disk drives, and especially hard disk drives, the specification on which people seem to focus the most is the drive's reported average *seek time*—the (average) time it takes for the heads to be positioned from one track to another. Unfortunately, the importance of this specification often is overstated, especially in relation to other specifications, such as the data transfer rate.

The transfer rate of data between the drive and the system is more important than access time, because most drives spend more time reading and writing information than they do moving the heads around. The speed at which a program or data file is loaded or read is affected most by the data transfer rate. Specialized operations such as sorting large files, which involves a lot of random access to individual records of the file (and, therefore, many seek operations), are helped greatly by a faster-seeking disk drive. Seeking performance is important in these cases. Most normal file load and save operations, however, are affected mainly by the rate at which data can be read and written to and from the drive. The data transfer rate depends on both the drive and the interface.

Several types of hard disk interfaces have been used in PC systems over the years, as shown in the following table.

Interface	When Used
ST-506/412	1978–1989
ESDI	1986–1991
SCSI	1986–Present
IDE	1988–Present

As you can see, only IDE and SCSI remain popular today. Of these interfaces, only ST-506/412 and ESDI are what you could call true disk-controller-to-drive interfaces. SCSI and IDE are system-level interfaces that usually incorporate a chipset-based variation of one of the other two types of disk controller interfaces internally. For example, most SCSI and IDE drives incorporate the same basic controller circuitry used in separate ESDI controllers. The SCSI interface adds another layer of interface that attaches the controller to the system bus, whereas IDE is a direct bus-attachment interface. Even so, virtually all modern disk drives use either IDE or SCSI interfaces to connect to a system.

In data recovery, it helps to know the disk interface you are working with, because many data-recovery problems involve drive setup and installation problems. Each interface requires a slightly different method of installation and drive configuration. If the installation or configuration is incorrect or accidentally altered by the system user, it may prevent access to data on a drive. Accordingly, anyone who wants to become proficient in data recovery must be an expert on installing and configuring various types of hard disks and controllers.

The PC's reliance on industry-standard interfaces such as IDE allows a great deal of cross-system and cross-manufacturer compatibility. The use of industry-standard interfaces such as IDE allows you to pick up a mail-order catalog, purchase a hard disk, CD-ROM drive, high-capacity floppy, etc. for the lowest possible price, and be assured that it will work with your system. This Plug-and-Play capability results in affordable hard disk storage and a variety of options in capacities and speed.

The ST-506/412 Interface

The ST-506/412 interface was developed by Seagate Technologies around 1980. The interface originally appeared in the Seagate ST-506 drive, which was a 5MB formatted (or 6MB unformatted) drive in a full-height, 5 1/4-inch form factor. By today's standards, this drive is a tank! In 1981, Seagate introduced the ST-412 drive, which added a feature called buffered seek to the interface. This drive was a 10MB formatted (12MB unformatted) drive that also qualifies as a tank by today's standards. Besides the Seagate ST-412, IBM also used the Miniscribe 1012 as well as the International Memories, Inc. (IMI) model 5012 drive in the XT. IMI and Miniscribe are long gone, but Seagate remains as one of the largest drive manufacturers. Since the original XT, Seagate has supplied drives for numerous systems made by many different manufacturers.

Most drive manufacturers that made hard disks for PC systems adopted the Seagate ST-506/412 standard, a situation that helped make this interface popular. One important feature is the interface's Plug-and-Play design. No custom cables or special modifications are needed for the drives, which means that virtually any ST-506/412 drive will work with any ST-506/412 controller. The only real compatibility issue with this interface is the level of BIOS support provided by the system.

When introduced to the PC industry by IBM in 1983, ROM BIOS support for this hard disk interface was provided by a BIOS chip on the controller. Contrary to what most believed, the PC and XT motherboard BIOS had no inherent hard disk support. When the AT system was introduced, IBM placed the ST-506/412 interface support in the motherboard BIOS and eliminated it from the controller. All 16-bit and higher systems since then have an enhanced version of the same support in the motherboard BIOS as well. Because this support has been limited, especially in the older BIOS versions, many disk controller manufacturers also placed BIOS support for their controllers directly on the controllers themselves. In some cases, you would use the controller BIOS and motherboard BIOS together; in other cases, you would disable the controller or motherboard BIOS and then use one or the other. These issues will be discussed more completely in Chapter 14, "Physical Drive Installation and Configuration."

◄◄ See "Motherboard BIOS," p. 349.

The ST-506/412 interface does not quite make the grade in today's high-performance PC systems. This interface was designed for a 5MB drive, and I have not seen any drives larger than 152MB (Modified Frequency Modulation encoding) or 233MB (Run-Length Limited encoding) available for this type of interface. Because the capacity, performance, and expandability of ST-506/412s are so limited, this interface is obsolete and generally unavailable in new systems. However, many older systems still use drives that have this interface.

Disk Drive Encoding Schemes and Problems

As indicated in Chapter 9, "Magnetic Storage Principles," in the section "Data Encoding Schemes," encoding schemes are used in communications for converting digital data bits to various tones for transmission over a telephone line. For disk drives, the digital bits are converted, or encoded, in a pattern of magnetic impulses, or flux transitions (also called flux reversals), which are written on the disk. These flux transitions are decoded later, when the data is read from the disk.

A device called an *endec* accomplishes the conversion to flux transitions for writing on the media and the subsequent reconversion back to digital data during read operations. The function of the endec is very similar to that of a modem (modulator/demodulator) in that digital data is converted to an analog waveform, which then is converted back to digital data. Sometimes, the endec is called a data separator, because it is designed to separate data and clocking information from the flux-transition pulse stream read from the disk.

One of the biggest problems with the original ST-506/412 interface used in the first PC hard disks was the fact that this endec resided on the disk controller (rather than the drive), which resulted in the possibility of corruption of the analog data signal before it reached the media. This problem became especially pronounced when the ST-506/412 controllers later switched to using RLL endecs to store 50 percent more data on the drive. With the RLL encoding scheme, the actual density of magnetic flux transitions on the disk media remains the same as with MFM encoding, but the timing between the transitions must be measured much more precisely.

In RLL encoding, the intervals between flux changes are approximately the same as with MFM, but the actual timing between them is much more critical. As a result, the transition cells in which signals must be recognized are much smaller and more precisely placed than with MFM. RLL encoding places more stringent demands on the timing of the controller and drive electronics. With RLL encoding, accurately reading the timing of the flux changes is paramount. Additionally, because RLL encodes variable-length groups of bits rather than single bits, a single error in one flux transition can corrupt two to four bits of data. For these reasons, an RLL controller usually has a more sophisticated error-detection and error-correction routine than an MFM controller.

The bottom line is that other than improved precision, there is no real difference between an ST-506/412 drive that is sold as an MFM model and one that is sold as an RLL model.

One method for avoiding reliability problems in the conversion process is to place an endec directly on the drive rather than on the controller. This method reduces the susceptibility to noise and interference that can plague some drive systems running RLL encoding. IDE and SCSI drives both have the endec (and often the entire controller) built into the drive by default. Because the endec is attached to the drive without cables and with an extremely short electrical distance, the propensity for timing- and noise-induced errors is greatly reduced or eliminated. This situation is analogous to a local telephone call between the endec and the disk platters. This local communication makes the ESDI, IDE, and SCSI interfaces much more reliable than the older ST-506/412 interface; they share none of the reliability problems that were once associated with RLL encoding over the ST-506/412 interface. Virtually all ESDI, IDE, and SCSI drives use RLL encoding today with tremendously increased reliability over even MFM ST-506/412 drives.

Note

For a complete historical reference covering the original ST-506/412 controllers used in the PC environment, see *Upgrading and Repairing PCs, Sixth Edition*, found in its entirety on the CD included with this book.

The ESDI Interface

ESDI, or Enhanced Small Device Interface, is a specialized hard disk interface established as a standard in 1983, primarily by Maxtor Corporation. Maxtor led a consortium of drive manufacturers to adopt its proposed interface as a high-performance standard to succeed ST-506/412. ESDI later was adopted by the ANSI (American National Standards Institute) organization and published under the ANSI X3T9.2 Committee. The latest version of the ANSI ESDI document is known as X3.170a-1991. You can obtain this document, and other ANSI-standard documents, from ANSI or from Global Engineering Documents. These companies are listed in the Vendor List database on the CD included with this book.

Compared with ST-506/412, ESDI has provisions for increased reliability, such as building the endec into the drive. ESDI was much faster than the older ST-506/412 that preceded it, and was capable of a maximum 24Mbit/sec transfer rate. Most drives running ESDI, however, are limited to a maximum 10- or 15Mbit/sec. Unfortunately, compatibility problems between different ESDI implementations, combined with pressure from low-cost, high-performance IDE interface drives, served to make the ESDI interface obsolete by the early '90s. ESDI became somewhat popular in high-end (especially file server) systems during the late '80s.

Enhanced commands enabled some ESDI controllers to read a drive's capacity parameters directly from the drive and control defect mapping, but several manufacturers had different methods for writing this information on the drive. When you install an ESDI drive, in some cases the controller automatically reads the parameter and defect information directly from the drive. In other cases, however, you still have to enter this information manually, as with ST-506/412.

The ESDI's enhanced defect-mapping commands provide a standard way for the PC system to read a defect map from a drive, which means that the manufacturer's defect list can be written to the drive as a file. The defect list file then can be read by the controller and low-level format software, eliminating the need for the installer to type these entries from the keyboard. This also enables the format program to update the defect list with new entries if it finds new defects during the low-level format or the surface analysis.

Most ESDI implementations have drives formatted to 32 sectors or more per track (80 or more sectors per track are possible)—many more sectors per track than the standard ST-506/412 implementation of 17 to 26. The greater density results in two or more times the data-transfer rate, with a 1:1 interleave. Almost without exception, ESDI controllers support a 1:1 interleave, which allows for a transfer rate of 1MB/sec or greater.

Because ESDI is much like the ST-506/412 interface, it can replace that interface without affecting software in the system. Most ESDI controllers are register-compatible with the older ST-506/412 controllers, which enables OS/2 and other non-DOS operating systems to run with few or no problems. The ROM BIOS interface to ESDI is similar to the ST-506/412 standard; many low-level disk utilities that run on one interface will run on the other. To take advantage of ESDI defect mapping and other special features, however, use a low-level format and surface-analysis utility designed for ESDI (such as the ones usually built into the controller ROM BIOS and called by DEBUG).

During the late 1980s, most high-end systems from major manufacturers were equipped with ESDI controllers and drives. Starting with the early 1990s, manufacturers began equipping high-end systems such as network file servers and workstations with SCSI. The SCSI interface allows for much greater expandability, supports more types of devices thanESDI does, and offers equal or greater performance.

Note

For a complete historical reference covering the ESDI controllers used in the PC environment, see *Upgrading and Repairing PCs, Sixth Edition,* found in its entirety on the CD included with this book.

The IDE Interface

Integrated Drive Electronics (IDE) is a generic term applied to any drive with an integrated (built-in) disk controller. The IDE interface, as we know it, is officially called *ATA* (*AT Attachment*) and is an ANSI standard. However, IDE can roughly apply to any disk drive with a built-in controller. Note that the "AT" in the name AT Attachment comes from the original IBM AT that debuted the 16-bit ISA (Industry Standard Architecture) bus. ATA therefore refers basically to a hard disk drive that plugs directly into a version of the AT-bus, otherwise known as the ISA bus.

The first drives with integrated ISA (AT-bus) controllers were called hardcards; they consisted of a hard disk bolted directly to an ISA bus controller card and plugged into a slot as a single unit. Today, a variety of drives with integrated controllers are available. In a drive with IDE, the disk controller is integrated into the drive, and this combination drive/controller assembly usually plugs into a bus connector on the motherboard or bus adapter card. Combining the drive and controller greatly simplifies installation, because there are no separate power or signal cables from the controller to the drive. Also, when the controller and drive are assembled as a unit, the number of total components is reduced, signal paths are shorter, and the electrical connections are more noise-resistant. This results in a more reliable design than is possible when a separate controller, connected to the drive by cables, is used.

Placing the controller, including the digital to analog encoder/decoder (endec) on the drive gives IDE drives an inherent reliability advantage over interfaces with separate controllers. Reliability is increased because the data encoding, from digital to analog, is performed directly on the drive in a tight noise-free environment. The timing-sensitive analog information does not have to travel along crude ribbon cables that are likely to pick up noise and insert propagation delays into the signals. The integrated configuration allows for increases in the clock rate of the encoder and the storage density of the drive.

Integrating the controller and drive also freed the controller and drive engineers from having to adhere to the strict standards imposed by the earlier interface standards. Engineers can design what essentially are custom drive and controller implementations because no other controller would ever have to be connected to the drive. The resulting drive and controller combinations can offer higher performance than earlier standalone controller and drive setups. IDE drives sometimes are called drives with embedded controllers.

The IDE connector on motherboards in many systems is nothing more than a stripped-down bus slot. In ATA IDE installations, these connectors normally contain a 40-pin subset of the 98 pins that would be available in a standard 16-bit ISA bus slot. Note that smaller 2 1/2-inch ATA drives use a superset 44-pin connection, which includes pins for power and configuration. The pins used are only the signal pins required by a standard-type XT or AT hard disk controller. For example, because an AT-style disk controller uses only interrupt line 14, the motherboard ATA IDE connector supplies only that interrupt line; no other interrupt lines are needed. The XT IDE motherboard connector supplies interrupt line 5 because that is what an XT controller would use. Note that even if your ATA interface is connected to the South Bridge chip and runs at PCI bus speeds, the pinout and functions of the pins are still the same.

◄◄ See "Motherboard Interface Connectors," p. 272.

◄◄ See "The ISA Bus," p. 283.

Note

Many people who use systems with IDE connectors on the motherboard believe that a hard disk controller is built into their motherboard, but the controller really is in the drive. I do not know of any PC systems that have hard disk controllers built into the motherboard.

When IDE drives are discussed, the ATA IDE variety usually is the only kind mentioned because it is so popular. But other forms of IDE drives exist, based on other buses. For example, several PS/2 systems came with Micro-Channel (MCA) IDE drives that plug directly into a Micro-Channel Bus slot (through an angle adapter or interposer card). An 8-bit ISA form of IDE also existed >but was never very popular. Most IBM-compatible systems with the ISA or EISA bus use AT-Bus (16-bit) IDE drives. The ATA IDE interface is by far the most popular type of drive interface available.

Note

IDE is a generic name that could be given to any interface where the controller portion of the circuit is on the drive; ATA refers to a specific type of IDE interface. Because the only popular form of IDE interface is ATA, the terms are often used interchangeably, even though on a technical level that is not correct.

The primary advantage of IDE drives over the older separate controller based interfaces and newer host bus interface alternatives such as SCSI or IEEE-1394 (iLink or FireWire) is cost. Because the separate controller or host adapter is eliminated and the cable connections are simplified, IDE drives cost much less than a standard controller and drive combination. These drives also are more reliable because the controller is built into the drive. Therefore, the endec or data separator (the converter between the digital and analog signals on the drive) stays close to the media. Because the drive has a short analog signal path, it is less susceptible to external noise and interference.

Another advantage is performance. IDE drives are some of the highest performance drives available—but they also are among the lowest performance drives. This apparent contradiction is a result of the fact that all IDE drives are different. You cannot make a blanket statement about the performance of IDE drives because each drive is unique. The high-end models, however, offer performance that is equal or superior to that of any other type of drive on the market for a single-user, single-tasking operating system.

IDE Origins

The earliest IDE drives were called hardcards—nothing more than hard disks and controllers bolted directly together and plugged into a slot as a single unit. Companies such as the

Plus Development Division of Quantum took small 3 1/2-inch drives (either ST-506/412 or ESDI) and attached them directly to a standard controller. The assembly then was plugged into an ISA bus slot as though it were a normal disk controller. Unfortunately, the mounting of a heavy, vibrating hard disk in an expansion slot with nothing but a single screw to hold it in place left a lot to be desired. Not to mention the possible interference with adjacent cards due to the fact that many of these units were much thicker than a controller card alone.

Several companies got the idea that you could redesign the controller to replace the logic-board assembly on a standard hard disk, and then mount it in a standard drive bay just like any other drive. Because the built-in controller in these drives still needed to plug directly into the expansion bus just like any other controller, a cable was run between the drive and one of the slots.

These connection problems were solved in different ways. Compaq was the first to incorporate a special bus adapter in its system to adapt the 98-pin AT (ISA) bus edge connector on the motherboard to a smaller 40-pin header style connector that the drive would plug into. The 40-pin connectors were all that was needed, because it was known that a disk controller never would need more than 40 of the ISA-bus lines.

In 1987, IBM developed its own MCA IDE drives and connected them to the bus through a bus adapter device called an interposer card. These bus adapters (sometimes called paddle boards or angle boards) needed only a few buffer chips and did not require any real circuitry because the drive-based controller was designed to plug directly into the bus. The paddle board nickname came from the fact that they resembled game paddle or joystick adapters, which do not have much circuitry on them. Another 8-bit variation of IDE appeared in 8-bit ISA systems such as the PS/2 Model 30. The XT IDE interface uses a 40-pin connector and cable that is similar to, but not compatible with, the 16-bit version.

IDE Bus Versions

Three main types of IDE interfaces were available at one time, with the differences based on three different bus standards:

- AT Attachment (ATA) IDE (16-bit ISA)
- XT IDE (8-bit ISA)
- MCA IDE (16-bit Micro Channel)

Of these, only the ATA version is used today, and it has evolved with newer, faster, and more powerful versions becoming available. These improved versions of ATA are referred to as ATA-2 and higher. They are also called EIDE, which stands for Enhanced IDE, Fast-ATA, or ultra-ATA.

Note

Many people are confused about 16- versus 32-bit bus connections and 16- versus 32-bit hard drive connections. A PCI connection allows for a 32-bit (and possibly 64-bit in the future) bandwidth from the bus to the IDE host interface, which is normally in the motherboard chipset South Bridge. However, the actual ATA-IDE interface between the host connector on the motherboard and the drive (or drives) themselves is only a 16-bit interface. Thus, in an IDE (or EIDE) drive configuration, you are still getting only 16-bit bandwidth between the drive and the motherboard-based host interface. This usually does not create a bottleneck, because one or two hard drives cannot supply the controller enough data to saturate even a 16-bit channel.

The XT and ATA versions have standardized on 40-pin connectors and cables, but the connectors have slightly different pinouts, rendering them incompatible with one another. MCA IDE uses a completely different 72-pin connector and is designed for MCA bus systems only.

In most cases, you must use the type of IDE drive that matches your system bus. This situation means that XT IDE drives work only in XT-class, 8-bit ISA slot systems (obsolete today). AT IDE (ATA) drives work only in AT-class, 16-bit or greater ISA/PCI slot systems. MCA IDE drives work only in obsolete Micro-Channel systems (such as the IBM PS/2 Model 50 or higher). A company called Silicon Valley offers adapter cards for XT systems that will run ATA IDE drives. Other companies, such as Arco Electronics and Sigma Data, have IDE adapters for Micro-Channel systems that allow ATA IDE drives to be used on MCA systems. (You can find these vendors in Appendix A.) These adapters are useful for older XT or PS/2 systems, because there is a very limited selection of XT or MCA IDE drives, whereas the selection of ATA IDE drives is virtually unlimited.

In most modern ISA/PCI systems, you will find an ATA connector on the motherboard. If your motherboard does not have one of these connectors and you want to attach an AT IDE drive to your system, you can purchase an adapter card that adds an ATA interface (or two) to a system via the ISA or PCI bus slots. Some of the cards offer additional features, such as an on-board ROM BIOS or cache memory.

Because the ATA variety of IDE is the primary one in use today, that is what most of this chapter discusses.

ATA IDE

CDC, Western Digital, and Compaq actually created what could be called the first ATA-type IDE interface drive and were the first to establish the 40-pin IDE connector pinout. The first ATA IDE drives were 5 1/4-inch half-height CDC 40MB units with integrated WD controllers sold in the first Compaq 386 systems in 1986.

Eventually, the 40-pin IDE connector and drive interface method was placed before one of the ANSI standards committees which, in conjunction with drive manufacturers, ironed out some deficiencies, tied up some loose ends, and published what is known as the CAM ATA (Common Access Method AT Attachment) interface. The CAM Committee was formed in October 1988, and the first working document of the AT Attachment interface was introduced in March 1989. Before the CAM ATA standard, many companies that followed CDC, such as Conner Peripherals, made proprietary changes to what had been done by CDC. As a result, many older ATA drives from the late '80s are very difficult to integrate into a dual-drive setup that has newer drives. By the early '90s, most drive manufacturers brought their drives into full compliance with the official standard, which eliminated many of these compatibility problems.

Some areas of the ATA standard have been left open for vendor-specific commands and functions. These vendor-specific commands and functions are the main reason why it is so difficult to low-level format IDE drives. To work to full capability, the formatter you are using usually must know the specific vendor-unique commands for rewriting sector headers and remapping defects. Unfortunately, these and other specific drive commands differ from OEM to OEM, clouding the "standard" somewhat. Most ATA drive manufacturers have formatting software available on their Web sites.

Note

It is important to note that only the ATA IDE interface has been standardized by the industry. The XT IDE and MCA IDE never were adopted as industry-wide standards and never became very popular. These interfaces no longer are in production, and no new systems of which I am aware come with these non-standard IDE interfaces.

ATA Standards

Today what we call the ATA interface is controlled by an independent group of representatives from major PC, drive, and component manufacturers. This group is called Technical Committee T13, and is responsible for all interface standards relating to the AT Attachment (ATA) storage interface. T13 is a part of the National Committee on Information Technology Standards (NCITS), which operates under rules approved by the American National Standards Institute (ANSI), a governing body that sets rules which control non-proprietary standards in the computer industry as well as many other industries.

The rules are designed to ensure that voluntary industry standards are developed by the consensus of people and organizations in the affected industry. NCITS specifically develops Information Processing System standards, whereas ANSI approves the process under which they are developed and publishes them. Since T13 is essentially a public organization, all the working drafts, discussions, and meetings of T13 are open for all to see.

The ATA interface has evolved into several successive standard versions introduced as follows:

- ATA-1 (1988–1994)
- ATA-2 (1996, also called Fast-ATA, Fast-ATA-2, or EIDE)
- ATA-3 (1997)
- ATA-4 (1998, also called ultra-ATA/33)
- ATA-5 (1999–present, also called ultra-ATA/66)

Each version of ATA is backward compatible with the previous versions. In other words older ATA-1 or ATA-2 devices will work fine on ATA-4 or ATA-5 interfaces. In cases where the device version and interface version don't match, they will work together at the capabilities of the lesser of the two. Newer versions of ATA are built on older versions, and with few exceptions can be thought of as extensions of the previous versions. This means that ATA-5, for example, is equal to ATA-4 with the addition of additional features. The following sections describe all the ATA versions in more detail.

ATA-1 (AT Attachment Interface for Disk Drives)

Although first published and used since 1988 in various draft forms, ATA-1 wasn't officially approved until 1994 (committees often work slowly). ATA-1 defined the original AT Attachment interface, which was an integrated bus interface between disk drives and host systems based on the ISA (AT) bus. The major features that were introduced and documented in the ATA-1 specification are

- 40/44-pin connectors and cabling
- Master/slave/cable Select drive configuration options
- Signal timing for basic PIO (Programmed I/O) and DMA (Direct Memory Access) modes
- CHS (Cylinder Head Sector) and LBA (Logical Block Address) drive parameter translations

ATA-1 has been officially published as ANSI X3.221-1994, AT Attachment Interface for Disk Drives.

You can obtain the current version of these or virtually any other computer standards from Global Engineering Documents, which is listed in the Vendor's List on the CD-ROM accompanying this book. The ATA standards have gone a long way toward eliminating incompatibilities and problems with interfacing IDE drives to ISA/PCI bus systems. The ATA specifications define the signals on the 40-pin connector, the functions and timings of these signals, cable specifications, and so on. The following section lists some of the elements and functions defined by the ATA specification.

ATA I/O Connector

The ATA interface connector is a 40- or 44-pin header-type connector that generally is keyed to prevent the possibility of installing it upside down (see Figures 7.1 and 7.2). To create a keyed connector, the manufacturer removes pin 20 to prevent the user from installing the cable backward. The use of keyed connectors and cables is highly recommended; plugging an IDE cable in backward can damage both the drive and the bus adapter circuits (although I have done it myself many times with no smoked parts yet!).

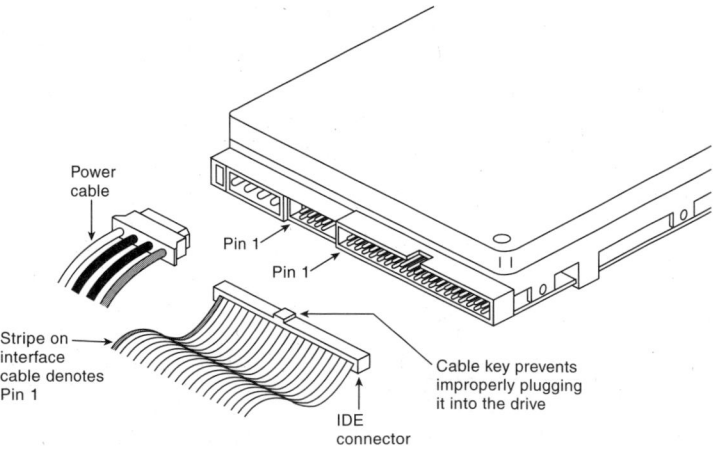

Figure 7.1 Typical ATA (IDE) hard drive connectors.

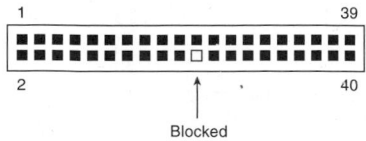

Figure 7.2   ATA (IDE) 40-pin interface connector detail.

Table 7.1 shows the ATA-IDE interface connector pinout.

Table 7.1   ATA Connector

Signal Name	Pin	Pin	Signal Name
-RESET	1	2	GROUND
Data Bit 7	3	4	Data Bit 8
Data Bit 6	5	6	Data Bit 9
Data Bit 5	7	8	Data Bit 10
Data Bit 4	9	10	Data Bit 11
Data Bit 3	11	12	Data Bit 12
Data Bit 2	13	14	Data Bit 13
Data Bit 1	15	16	Data Bit 14
Data Bit 0	17	18	Data Bit 15
GROUND	19	20	KEY (pin missing)
DRQ 3	21	22	GROUND
-IOW	23	24	GROUND
-IOR	25	26	GROUND
I/O CH RDY	27	28	SPSYNC:CSEL
-DACK 3	29	30	GROUND
IRQ 14	31	32	-IOCS16
Address Bit 1	33	34	-PDIAG
Address Bit 0	35	36	Address Bit 2
-CS1FX	37	38	-CS3FX
-DA/SP	39	40	GROUND
+5 Vdc (Logic)	41	42	+5 Vdc (Motor)
GROUND	43	44	-TYPE (0=ATA)

Note that the connector pinout shows 44 total pins, although only the first 40 are used on most 3 1/2-inch or larger ATA drives. The additional four pins shown (pins 41–44) are a superset found primarily on the smaller 2 1/2-inch drives used in notebook and laptop systems. Those drives don't have room for a separate power connector, so the additional pins are primarily designed to supply power to the drive.

ATA I/O Cable

A 40-conductor ribbon cable is specified to carry signals between the bus adapter circuits and the drive (controller). To maximize signal integrity and eliminate potential timing and noise problems, the cable should not be longer than 0.46 meters (18 inches).

Note that the newer high-speed IDE interfaces are especially susceptible to cable problems and cables that are too long. If the cable is too long, you will experience data corruption and other errors that can be maddening. This will be manifested in any type of problems reading from or writing to the drive. I always keep a special high-quality short IDE cable in my toolbox for testing drives where I suspect this problem. Figure 7.3 shows the typical ATA cable layout and dimensions.

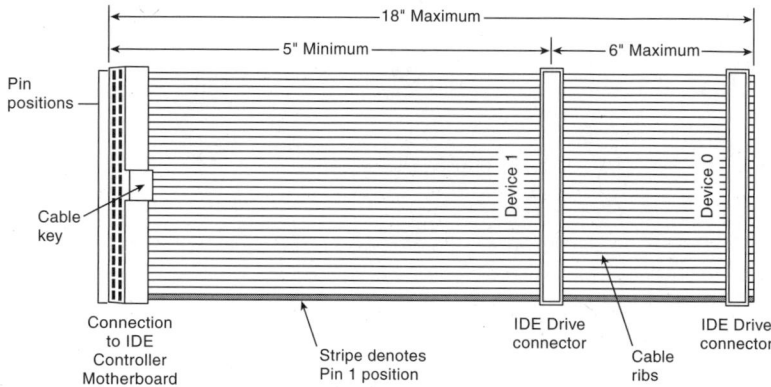

Figure 7.3   ATA (IDE) cable.

ATA Signals

This section describes some of the most important signals in more detail.

Pin 20 is used as a key pin for cable orientation and is not connected through in the interface. This pin should be missing from any ATA connectors, and the cable should have the pin-20 hole in the connector plugged off to prevent the cable from being plugged in backward.

Pin 39 carries the Drive Active/Slave Present (DASP) signal, which is a dual-purpose, time-multiplexed signal. During power-on initialization, this signal indicates whether a slave drive is present on the interface. After that, each drive asserts the signal to indicate that it is active. Early drives could not multiplex these functions and required special jumper settings to work with other drives. Standardizing this function to allow for compatible dual-drive installations is one of the features of the ATA standard. This is why some drives require a slave present (SP) jumper, while others do not.

Pin 28 carries the Cable Select or Spindle Synchronization signal (CSEL or SPSYNC), which is a dual-purpose conductor; a given installation, however, may use only one of the two functions. The CSEL function is the most widely used and is designed to control the designation of a drive as master (drive 0) or slave (drive 1) without requiring jumper settings on the drives. If a drive sees the CSEL as being grounded, the drive is a master; if CSEL is open, the drive is a slave.

You can install special cabling to ground CSEL selectively. This installation normally is accomplished through a Y-cable arrangement, with the IDE bus connector in the middle and each drive at opposite ends of the cable. One leg of the Y has the CSEL line connected through, indicating a master drive; the other leg has the CSEL line open (conductor interrupted or removed), making the drive at that end the slave.

Dual-Drive Configurations

Dual-drive ATA installations can be problematic because each drive has its own controller, and both controllers must function while being connected to the same bus. There has to be a way to ensure that only one of the two controllers will respond to a command at a time.

The ATA standard provides the option of operating on the AT bus with two drives in a daisy-chained configuration. The primary drive (drive 0) is called the master, and the secondary drive (drive 1) is the slave. You designate a drive as being master or slave by setting a jumper or switch on the drive or by using a special line in the interface called the Cable Select (CSEL) pin, and by setting the CS jumper on the drive.

When only one drive is installed, the controller responds to all commands from the system. When two drives (and, therefore, two controllers) are installed, all commands from the system are received by both controllers. Each controller then must be set up to respond only to commands for itself. In this situation, one controller then must be designated as the master and the other as the slave. When the system sends a command for a specific drive, the controller on the other drive must remain silent while the selected controller and drive are functioning. Setting the jumper to master or slave allows discrimination between the two controllers by setting a special bit (the DRV bit) in the Drive/Head Register of a command block.

Configuring IDE drives can be simple, as is the case with most single-drive installations, or troublesome, especially when it comes to mixing two drives from different manufacturers on a single cable.

Most IDE drives can be configured with four possible settings:

- Master (single-drive)
- Master (dual-drive)
- Slave (dual-drive)
- Cable Select

Because each IDE drive has its own controller, you must specifically tell one drive to be the master and the other to be the slave. There is no functional difference between the two, except that the drive that's specified as the slave will assert a signal called DASP (Drive Active/Slave Present) after a system reset informs the master that a slave drive is present in the system. The master drive then pays attention to the Drive Select line, which it otherwise ignores. Telling a drive that it's the slave also usually causes it to delay its spinup for several seconds to allow the master to get going, and thus to lessen the load on the system's power supply.

Until the ATA IDE specification, no common implementation for drive configuration was in use. Some drive companies even used different master/slave methods for different models of drives. Because of these incompatibilities, some drives work together only in a specific master/slave or slave/master order. This situation affects mostly older IDE drives that were introduced before the ATA specification.

Most drives that fully follow the ATA specification now need only one jumper (master/slave) for configuration. A few also need a slave present jumper as well. Table 7.2 shows the jumper settings required by most ATA IDE drives.

Table 7.2   Jumper Settings for Most ATA IDE-Compatible Drives

Jumper Name	Single-Drive	Dual-Drive Master	Dual-Drive Slave
Master (M/S)	On	On	Off
Slave Present (SP)	Off	On	Off

Figure 7.4 shows the jumpers on a typical ATA drive.

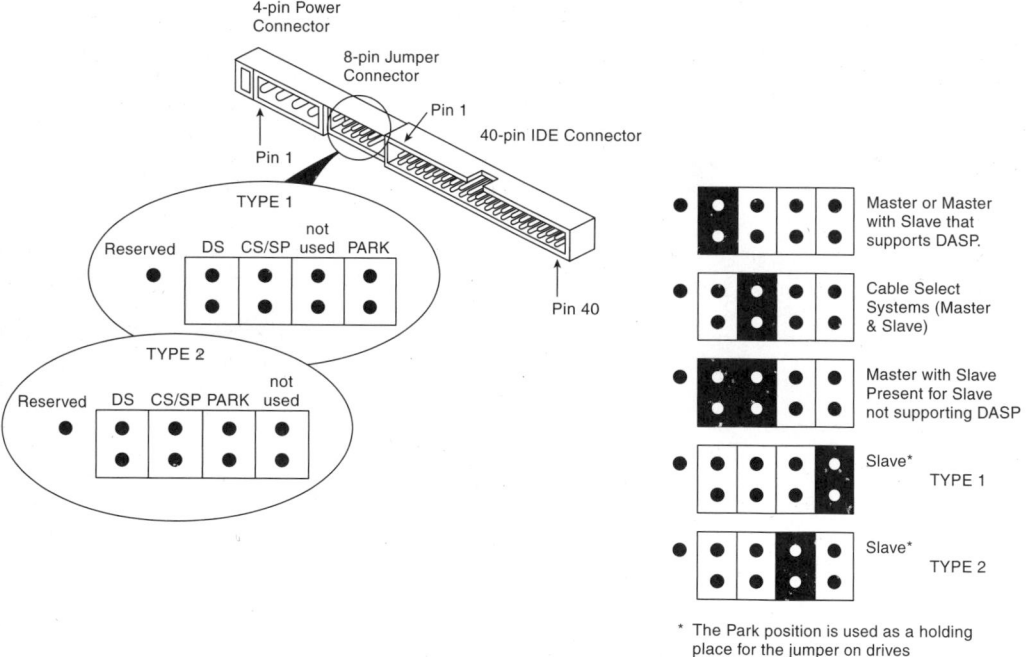

Figure 7.4   ATA (IDE) drive jumpers.

The Master jumper indicates that the drive is a master or a slave. Some drives also require a Slave Present jumper, which is used only in a dual-drive setup and then installed only on the master drive, which is somewhat confusing. This jumper tells the master that a slave drive is attached.

With many ATA IDE drives, the Master jumper is optional and may be left off. Installing this jumper doesn't hurt in these cases and may eliminate confusion; I recommend that you install the jumpers listed here.

ATA Commands

One of the best features of the ATA IDE interface is the enhanced command set. The ATA IDE interface was modeled after the WD1003 controller that IBM used in the original AT system. All ATA IDE drives must support the original WD command set (eight commands) with no exceptions, which is why IDE drives are so easy to install in systems today. All IBM-compatible systems have built-in ROM BIOS support for the WD1003, which means that essentially they support ATA IDE as well.

In addition to supporting all the WD1003 commands, the ATA specification added numerous other commands to enhance performance and capabilities. These commands are an optional part of the ATA interface, but several of them are used in most drives available today and are very important to the performance and use of ATA drives in general.

Perhaps the most important is the Identify Drive command. This command causes the drive to transmit a 512-byte block of data that provides all details about the drive. Through this command, any program (including the system BIOS) can find out exactly what type of drive is connected, including the drive manufacturer, model number, operating parameters, and even the serial number of the drive. Many modern BIOSes use this information to automatically receive and enter the drive's parameters into CMOS memory, eliminating the need for the user to enter these parameters manually during system configuration. This arrangement helps prevent mistakes that can later lead to data loss when the user no longer remembers what parameters he or she used during setup.

The Identify Drive data can tell you many things about your drive, including the following:

- Number of cylinders in the recommended (default) translation mode
- Number of heads in the recommended (default) translation mode
- Number of sectors per track in the recommended (default) translation mode
- Number of cylinders in the current translation mode
- Number of heads in the current translation mode
- Number of sectors per track in the current translation mode
- Manufacturer and model number
- Firmware revision
- Serial number
- Buffer type, indicating sector buffering or caching capabilities

Several public-domain programs can execute this command to the drive and report the information onscreen. I use the IDEINFO (available at http://www.dc.ee/Files/Utils/IDEINFO.ARJ) or IDEDIAG (available from many of the popular shareware sites) program. I find these programs especially useful when I am trying to install IDE drives and need to know the correct parameters for a user-definable BIOS type. These programs get the information directly from the drive.

Two other very important commands are the Read Multiple and Write Multiple commands. These commands permit multiple-sector data transfers and, when combined with block-mode Programmed I/O (PIO) capabilities in the system, can result in incredible data-transfer rates many times faster than single-sector PIO transfers.

There are many other enhanced commands, including room for a given drive manufacturer to implement what are called vendor-unique commands. These commands often are used by a particular vendor for features unique to that vendor. Often, features such as low-level formatting and defect management are controlled by vendor-unique commands. This is why low-level format programs can be so specific to a particular manufacturer's IDE drives and why many manufacturers make their own LLF programs available.

ATA-2 (AT Attachment Interface with Extensions)

Approved in 1996, ATA-2 was a major upgrade to the original ATA standard. Perhaps the biggest change was almost a philosophical one. ATA-2 was updated to define an interface between host systems and storage devices in general and not only disk drives. The major features added to ATA-2 as compared to the original ATA standard include

- Faster PIO and DMA transfer modes
- Support for power management
- Support for removable devices
- PCMCIA (PC card) device support
- Defined drive support for up to 137.4GB
- Defined standard CHS/LBA (Cylinder Head Sector/Logical Block Address) translation methods for drives up to 8.4GB in capacity

ATA-2 is also known by unofficial marketing terms such as fast-ATA or fast-ATA-2 (Seagate/Quantum) and EIDE (Enhanced IDE, Western Digital). ATA-2 was officially published as ANSI X3.279-1996 AT Attachment Interface with Extensions.

ATA-3 (AT Attachment 3 Interface)

First published in 1997, ATA-3 was a comparatively minor revision to the ATA-2 standard that preceded. It consisted of a general cleanup of the specification and had mostly minor clarifications and revisions. The most major changes included the following:

- Eliminated single word (8-bit) DMA transfer protocols
- Added S.M.A.R.T. (Self-Monitoring, Analysis, and Reporting Technology) support for prediction of device performance degradation
- Added security mode, allowing password protection for device access
- Recommendations for source and receiver bus termination to solve noise issues at higher transfer speeds

ATA-3 has been officially published as ANSI X3.298-1997, AT Attachment 3 Interface.

ATA-2 and ATA-3 are extensions of the original ATA (IDE) specification. The most important additions are performance-enhancing features such as fast PIO and DMA modes. ATA-2 also features improvements in the Identify Drive command allowing a drive to tell the software exactly what its characteristics are; this is essential for both Plug and Play (PnP) and compatibility with future revisions of the standard. ATA-3 adds improved reliability, especially of the faster mode 4 transfers; note that ATA-3 does not define any faster modes. ATA-3 also adds a simple password-based security scheme, more sophisticated power management, and Self Monitoring Analysis and Report Technology (S.M.A.R.T.). This allows a drive to keep track of problems that might result in a failure.

ATA-2 and 3 are often called Enhanced IDE (or EIDE). EIDE is technically a marketing program from Western Digital. Fast-ATA and Fast-ATA-2 are similar Seagate-inspired marketing programs, which are also endorsed by Quantum. As far as the hard disk and BIOS are concerned, these are all different terms for basically the same thing.

There are four main areas where ATA-2 (EIDE), ATA-3, and ATA-4 have improved the original ATA/IDE interface in several ways:

- Increased maximum drive capacity
- Faster data transfer
- Secondary two-device channel
- ATAPI (ATA Program Interface)

The following sections describe these improvements.

Increased Drive Capacity

ATA-2/EIDE allows for increased drive capacity over the original ATA/IDE specification. This is done through an Enhanced BIOS, which makes it possible to use hard disks exceeding the 504MB barrier. The origin of this limit is the disk geometry (cylinders, heads, sectors) supported by the combination of an IDE drive and the BIOS' software interface. Both IDE and the BIOS are capable of supporting huge disks, but their combined limitations conspire to restrict the useful capacity to 504MB.

An Enhanced BIOS circumvents this by using a different geometry when talking to the drive than when talking to the software. What happens in between is called *translation*. For example, if your drive has 2,000 cylinders and 16 heads, a translating BIOS will make programs think that the drive has 1,000 cylinders and 32 heads.

You can usually tell if your BIOS is enhanced by the capability to specify more than 1,024 cylinders in the BIOS setup, although this is inconclusive. If you see drive-related settings such as LBA, ECHS, or even Large, these are telltale signs of a BIOS with translation support. Most BIOSes with a date of 1994 or later are enhanced. If your system currently does not have an Enhanced BIOS, you may be able to get an upgrade.

Table 7.3 shows the three ways today's BIOSes can handle translation: Standard CHS addressing, Extended CHS addressing, and LBA addressing. They are summarized in the following table.

Table 7.3   ATA-2 Translation Methods

BIOS Mode	Operating System to BIOS	BIOS to Drive Ports
Standard CHS	Logical CHS Parameters	Logical CHS Parameters
Extended CHS	Translated CHS Parameters	Logical CHS Parameters
LBA	Translated CHS Parameters	LBA Parameters

In Standard CHS, there is only one possible translation step internal to the drive. The drive's actual physical geometry is completely invisible from the outside with all zoned recorded ATA drives today. The Cylinders, Heads, and Sectors printed on the label for use in the BIOS setup are purely logical geometry, and do not represent the actual physical parameters. Standard CHS addressing is limited to 16 heads and 1,024 cylinders, which gives us a limit of 504MB.

This is often called "Normal" in the BIOS setup, and causes the BIOS to behave like an old-fashioned one without translation. Use this setting if your drive has fewer than 1,024 cylinders or if you want to use the drive with a non-DOS operating system that doesn't understand translation.

In Extended CHS, a translated logical geometry is used to communicate between the drive and the BIOS, while a different translated geometry is used to communicate between the BIOS and everything else. In other words, there are normally two translation steps. The drive still translates internally, but has logical parameters that exceed the 1,024 cylinder limitation of the standard BIOS. In this case, the drive's cylinder count is usually divided by 2, and the head count is multiplied by 2 to get the translated values from those actually stored in the CMOS Setup. This type of setting breaks the 504/528MB barrier.

This is often called "Large" or "ECHS" in the BIOS setup, and tells the BIOS to use Extended CHS translation. It uses a different geometry (cylinders/heads/sectors) when talking to the drive than when talking to the BIOS. This type of translation should be used with drives that have more than 1,024 cylinders but that do not support LBA (Logical Block Addressing). Note that the geometry entered in your BIOS setup is the logical geometry, not the translated one.

LBA is a means of linearly addressing sector addresses, beginning at Cylinder 0, Head 0, Sector 1 as LBA 0, and proceeding on to the last physical sector on the drive. This is new in ATA-2, but has always been the one and only addressing mode in SCSI.

With LBA, each sector on the drive is numbered starting from 0. The number is a 28-bit binary number internally, which translates to a sector number from 0 to 268,435,456. Because each sector represents 512 bytes, this results in a maximum drive capacity of exactly 128GB, or 137 billion bytes. Unfortunately, the operating system still needs to see a translated CHS, so the BIOS determines how many sectors there are and comes up with Translated CHS to match. The BIOS CHS limits are 1,024 cylinders, 256 heads, and 63 sectors per track, which limits total drive capacity to just under 8GB.

In other words, this breaks the 528MB barrier in essentially the same way as Extended CHS does. Because it is somewhat simpler to use a single linear number to address a sector on the hard disk compared to a CHS type address, this is the preferred method if the drive supports LBA.

Caution

A word of warning with these BIOS translation settings: If you switch between Standard CHS, Extended CHS, or LBA, the BIOS may change the (translated) geometry. The same thing can happen if you transfer a disk that has been formatted on an old, non-LBA computer to a new one that uses LBA. This causes the logical CHS geometry seen by the operating system to change and the data to appear in the wrong locations from where it actually is! This can cause you to lose access to your data if you are not careful. I always recommend recording the CMOS Setup screens associated with the hard disk configuration so that you can properly match the setup of a drive to the settings to which it was originally set.

Systems using ATA drives have been plagued by size limitations because of ATA interface and BIOS issues. The first two limits were mostly BIOS related, the first was at 528MB, and the second at 8.4GB. Along with ATA-4 and ATA-5, the T13 committee has also defined an extension or enhancement to the BIOS originally designed by Phoenix called Enhanced BIOS Services for Disk Drives. This document describes new services provided by the BIOS to support storage devices of over 9.4 trillion GB (9.4×10 to the 21st power, or to be more precise 9,444,732,965,739,292,000,000 bytes!) Older BIOS services have a compatibility limit of 528MB and a theoretical limit of 8.4GB. Starting in mid-1998, most systems incorporated the enhanced BIOS services. Note that even though the BIOS can handle drives with up to 2^{64}th sectors, an ATA drive is still currently limited in size to 2^{28}th sectors, or 137.4GB maximum.

Faster Data Transfer

ATA-2/EIDE and ATA-3 define several high-performance modes for transferring data to and from the drive. These faster modes are the main part of the new specifications and were the main reason they were initially developed. The following section discusses these modes.

The PIO mode determines how fast data is transferred to and from the drive. In the slowest possible mode, PIO mode 0, the data cycle time cannot exceed 600 nanoseconds (ns). In a single cycle, 16 bits are transferred in to or out of the drive making the theoretical transfer rate of PIO Mode 0 (600ns cycle time) 3.3MB/sec. Most of the high-performance ATA-2 (EIDE) drives today support PIO Mode 4, which offers a 16.6MB/sec transfer rate.

Table 7.4 shows the PIO modes, with their respective transfer rates.

Table 7.4—PIO Modes and Transfer Rates

PIO Mode	Cycle Time (ns)	Transfer Rate (MB/sec)	Specification
0	600	3.33	ATA
1	383	5.22	ATA
2	240	8.33	ATA
3	180	11.11	ATA-2, EIDE, fast-ATA
4	120	16.67	ATA-2, EIDE, fast-ATA

To run in Mode 3 or 4 requires that the IDE port on the system be a local bus port. This means that it must operate through either a VL-Bus or PCI bus connection. Most motherboards with

ATA-2/EIDE support have dual IDE connectors on the motherboard, and most of them now allow full throughput. Most of the motherboard chipsets include the ATA interface in their South Bridge component, which in modern systems is tied into the PCI bus.

Older 486 and some early Pentium boards have only the primary connector running through the system's PCI local bus. The secondary connector on those boards usually runs through the ISA bus, and therefore supports up to Mode 2 operation only.

When interrogated with an Identify Drive command, a hard disk returns, among other things, information about the PIO and DMA modes it is capable of using. Most enhanced BIOSes will automatically set the correct mode to match the capabilities of the drive. If you set a mode faster than the drive can handle, data corruption will result.

ATA-2 and newer drives also perform Block Mode PIO, which means that they use the Read/Write Multiple commands that greatly reduce the number of interrupts sent to the host processor. This lowers the overhead, and the resulting transfers are even faster.

DMA Transfer Modes

ATA-2 and newer drives also support *Direct Memory Access* (DMA) transfers. DMA means that the data is transferred directly between drive and memory without using the CPU as an intermediary, as opposed to PIO. This has the effect of offloading much of the work of transferring data from the processor, in effect allowing the processor to do other things while the transfer is taking place.

There are two distinct types of direct memory access: DMA and busmastering DMA. Ordinary DMA relies on the legacy DMA controller on the system's mainboard to perform the complex task of arbitration, grabbing the system bus and transferring the data. In the case of busmastering DMA, all this is done by logic in the interface.

Systems using the Intel PIIX (PCI IDE ISA eXcelerator) and later South Bridge chips have the capability of supporting busmaster IDE. This uses the busmaster mode on the PCI bus to execute data transfers. The busmaster IDE modes and transfer rates are shown in Table 7.5.

Table 7.5   Busmaster IDE Modes and Transfer Rates

BMIDE Mode	Cycle Time (ns)	Transfer Rate (MB/sec)	Specifications
0	480	4.16	ATA-1
1	150	3.33	ATA-2, EIDE, fast-ATA
2	120	16.67	ATA-2, EIDE, fast-ATA

Note that busmaster DMA modes are also called multiword DMA modes because they do 16-bit transfers. Unfortunately, even the fastest multiword DMA mode 2 results in the same 16.67MB/sec transfer speed as PIO Mode 4, so DMA never really caught on as being desirable. However, even though the transfer speed is the same as PIO, since DMA offloads much of the work from the processor, overall system performance would be higher. Even so, multiword DMA modes were never very popular and have now been superseded by the newer ultra-DMA modes supported in ATA-4 compatible devices.

The following table shows the ultra-DMA modes now supported in the ATA-4 and ATA-5 specifications.

UDMA Mode	Cycle Time (ns)	Transfer Rate (MB/sec)	Specification
0	240	16.67	ATA-4, ultra-ATA/33
1	160	25.00	ATA-4, ultra-ATA/33
2	120	33.33	ATA-4, ultra-ATA/33
3	90	44.44	ATA-5, ultra-ATA/66
4	60	66.67	ATA-5, ultra-ATA/66

ATAPI (ATA Packet Interface)

ATAPI is a standard designed for devices such as CD-ROMs and tape drives that plug into an ordinary ATA (IDE) connector. The principal advantage of ATAPI hardware is that it's cheap and works on your current adapter. For CD-ROMs, it has a somewhat lower CPU usage compared to proprietary adapters, but there's no performance gain otherwise. For tape drives, ATAPI has potential for superior performance and reliability compared to the popular floppy controller attached tape devices. ATAPI is also used to run other removable storage devices such as the LS-120 superdisk drives and internal Iomega Zip and Jaz drives.

Although ATAPI CD-ROMs use the hard disk interface, this does not mean they look like ordinary hard disks; to the contrary, from a software point of view, they are a completely different kind of animal. They actually most closely resemble a SCSI device. All modern IDE CD-ROMs support the ATAPI protocols and generally the terms are synonymous. In other words, an ATAPI CD-ROM is an IDE CD-ROM and vice versa.

Caution

ATAPI support is not found directly in the BIOS of many systems. Systems without ATAPI support in the BIOS cannot boot from an ATAPI CD-ROM and you still must load a driver to use ATAPI under DOS or Windows. Windows 95 and Windows NT have native ATAPI support, and newer systems with ATAPI-aware BIOS are now available, which will allow booting from an ATAPI CD-ROM. Some versions of the Windows 98 and Windows 2000 CD-ROMs are directly bootable on those systems, greatly easing installation.

I normally recommend keeping different types of IDE devices on separate channels. Some older chipsets cannot support setting different transfer rates for different devices, which means the channel must be set to the speed of the slowest device. Because most CD-ROM and tape drives run at lower IDE mode speeds, this would force your hard disk to run slower if they shared a single cable. Even if the chipset you have supports separate speed settings for devices on the same channel (cable), I still recommend keeping them separate because IDE does not normally support overlapping access such as SCSI. In other words, when one drive is running, the other cannot be accessed. By keeping the CD-ROM and hard disk on separate channels, you can more effectively overlap accessing between them.

ATA/ATAPI-4 (AT Attachment 4 with Packet Interface Extension)

First published in 1998, ATA-4 includes several important additions to the standard. It includes the Packet Command feature known as the AT Attachment Packet Interface (ATAPI), which allows devices such as CD-ROM drives, LS-120 SuperDisk floppy drives, tape drives, and other types of storage devices to be attached through a common interface. Until ATA-4 came out, ATAPI was a separately published standard. ATA-4 also adds the 33MB/sec transfer mode known as ultra-DMA or ultra-ATA. ATA-4 is backward compatible with ATA-3 and earlier definitions of the ATAPI. The major revisions added in ATA-4 are as follows:

- Ultra-DMA (UDMA) transfer modes up to 33MB/sec (called UDMA/33 or ultra-ATA/33)
- Integral ATAPI support
- Advanced power management support
- Defined an optional 80-conductor, 40-pin cable for improved noise resistance
- Compact Flash Adapter (CFA) support
- Introduced enhanced BIOS support for drives over 9.4 trillion GB in size (even though ATA is still limited to 137.4GB)

ATA-4 has been published as ANSI NCITS 317-1998, ATA-4 with Packet Interface Extension.

The newer PIIX4 and later South Bridge chips from the Intel motherboard chipsets support ATA-4, and many of the new drives support the high-speed UDMA (ultra-DMA) transfer mode.

◀◀ See "Chipsets," p. 235.

ATA-4 makes ATAPI support a full part of the ATA standard, and thus ATAPI is no longer an auxiliary interface to ATA but is merged completely within. This should promote ATA for use as an interface for many other types of devices. ATA-4 also adds support for new ultra-DMA modes (also called ultra-ATA) for even faster data transfer. The highest-performance mode, called UDMA/33, has 33MB/second bandwidth, twice that of the fastest programmed I/O mode or DMA mode previously supported. In addition to the higher transfer rate, because UDMA modes relieve the load on the processor, further performance gains are realized.

Also included is support for queuing commands, which is similar to that provided in SCSI-2. This allows for better multitasking as multiple programs make requests for IDE transfers.

▶▶ See "SCSI Versus IDE," p. 557.

ATA/ATAPI-5 (AT Attachment 5 with Packet Interface)

This version of the ATA standard is still in the draft stages, and builds on ATA-4. The major additions in the draft standard so far include the following:

- Ultra-DMA (UDMA) transfer modes up to 66MB/sec (called UDMA/66 or ultra-ATA/66)
- 80-conductor cable required for UDMA/66 operation

- Added automatic detection of 40 or 80-conductor cables
- UDMA modes faster than UDMA/33 are enabled only if an 80-conductor cable is detected

Each of the standards from the original ATA to ATA-5 are compatible; in other words, you can plug a so-called ATA-5 drive into an ATA-1 system or an ATA-1 drive into an ATA-5 system. In such cases, the drive or system will operate at the lowest common denominator with regard to performance and features.

Another standard recently approved by the T13 committee is an IEEE-1394 (iLink or FireWire) extension to the ATA interface protocol. This specifies a bridge protocol between the iLink/FireWire bus and ATA, allowing ATA drives to be adapted to this newer interface.

▶▶ See "IEEE-1394 (Also called i.Link or FireWire)," p. 896.

Copies of any of the published standards can be purchased from ANSI or Global Engineering Documents (see the Vendor's List on the CD).

ATA-5 includes ultra-ATA/66, which doubles the ultra-ATA burst transfer rate by reducing setup times and increasing the clock rate. The faster clock rate increases interference, which causes problems with the standard 40-pin cable used by ATA and ultra-ATA. To eliminate noise and interference, a new 40-pin, 80-conductor cable was developed. This cable was first announced in ATA-4, but is now mandatory in ATA-5 to support the ultra-ATA/66 mode. This cable adds 40 additional ground lines between each of the original 40 ground and signal lines, which help shield the signals from interference. Note that this cable works with older non–ultra-ATA devices as well, because it still has the same 40-pin connectors.

The 40-pin, 80-conductor cables will support the Cable Select feature and have color coded connectors. The blue (end) connector should be connected to the ATA host interface (usually the motherboard). The black (opposite end) connector is known as the master position, which is where the primary drive will plug in. The gray (middle) connector is for slave devices.

To use any of the ultra-DMA modes, both your ATA interface and drive must support the mode you want to use. The operating system must also be capable of handling Direct Memory Access (DMA); Windows 95 OSR2 or later, Windows 98, and Windows 2000 are ready out of the box, but older versions of Windows 95 and NT will require additional or updated drivers. To use the fastest ultra-ATA/66 mode, you will also need an ultra-ATA/66-capable, 80-conductor cable.

For reliability, ultra-DMA modes incorporate an error-detection mechanism known as cyclical redundancy checking (CRC). CRC is an algorithm that calculates a checksum used to detect errors in a stream of data. Both the host (controller) and the drive calculate a CRC value for each ultra-DMA transfer. After the data is sent, the drive calculates a CRC value and this is compared to the original host CRC value. If a difference is reported, the host might be required to select a slower transfer mode and retry the original request for data.

Obsolete IDE Versions

As mentioned earlier, other versions of the IDE interface were used in some early systems. While you may find some systems based on these interfaces if you are supporting legacy hardware, none of these has been used in any new system since the approval of the ATA-1 standard in 1994.

XT-Bus (8-bit) IDE

Many systems with XT ISA bus architecture used XT IDE hard drives. The IDE interface in these systems usually is built into the motherboard. The IBM PS/2 Models 25, 25-286, 30, and 30-286 systems used an 8-bit XT IDE interface. These 8-bit XT IDE drives are difficult to find. Few manufacturers other than IBM, Western Digital, and Seagate made them; none of these drives were available in capacities beyond 40MB.

Because the ATA IDE interface is a 16-bit design, it could not be used in 8-bit (XT type) systems, so some of the drive manufacturers standardized an XT-Bus (8-bit) IDE interface for XT class systems. These drives were never very popular, and were usually only available in capacities from 20MB–40MB.

MCA IDE

The IBM PS/2 Models 50 and higher come with Micro-Channel Architecture (MCA) bus slots. IBM used a type of MCA IDE drive in many of these systems. MCA IDE is a form of IDE interface, but it is designed for the MCA bus and is not compatible with the more industry-standard ATA IDE interface. Few companies other than IBM and Western Digital make replacement MCA IDE drives for these systems. I recommend replacing these drives with ATA IDE drives, using adapters from Arco Electronics or Sigma Data or switching to SCSI drives instead. The IBM MCA IDE drives are expensive for the limited capacity they offer.

The SCSI Interface

SOME OF THE MAIN TOPICS IN THIS CHAPTER ARE

Small Computer System Interface (SCSI)

ANSI SCSI Standards

Single-Ended or Differential SCSI

SCSI-1 and SCSI-2

SCSI-3

SCSI Cables and Connectors

SCSI Cable and Connector Pinouts

SCSI Drive Configuration

Plug-and-Play (PnP) SCSI

SCSI Configuration Troubleshooting

SCSI Versus IDE

Small Computer System Interface (SCSI)

SCSI (pronounced "scuzzy") stands for Small Computer System Interface, and is a general-purpose interface used for connecting many types of devices to a PC. This interface has its roots in SASI, the Shugart Associates System Interface. SCSI is the most popular interface for attaching high-speed disk drives to higher performance PCs such as workstations or network servers. SCSI is also very flexible; it is not only a disk interface, but also a systems-level interface allowing many different types of devices to be connected. SCSI is a bus that supports as many as 7 or 15 total devices. Multichannel adapters exist that can support up to 7 or 15 devices per channel.

The SCSI controller, called the *host adapter*, functions as the gateway between the SCSI bus and the PC system bus. Each device on the bus has a controller built in. The SCSI bus does not talk directly with devices such as hard disks; instead, it talks to the controller that is built into the drive.

A single SCSI bus can support as many as 8 or 16 physical units, usually called SCSI IDs. One of these units is the SCSI host adapter card in your PC; the other 7 or 15 can be other peripherals. You could have hard disks, tape drives, CD-ROM drives, a graphics scanner, or other devices (up to 7 or 15 additional devices) attached to a single SCSI host adapter. Most systems can support up to four host adapters, each with up to 15 devices, for a total of 60 devices! There are even dual channel adapters which could double that figure.

When you purchase an SCSI device such as an SCSI hard disk, you usually are purchasing the device, controller, and SCSI adapter in one circuit; as such the device is ready to connect directly to the SCSI bus. This type of drive usually is called an embedded SCSI device—the SCSI interface is built in. For example, most SCSI hard drives are technically the same as their IDE counterparts except for the addition of the SCSI bus adapter circuits (normally a single chip) added to the controller board. You do not need to know what type of controller is inside the SCSI drive, because your system cannot talk directly to the controller as though it were plugged into the system bus, like on a standard IDE drive. Instead, communications go through the SCSI host adapter installed in the system bus. You can access the drive only with the SCSI protocols.

Apple originally rallied around SCSI as being an inexpensive way out of the bind in which it put itself with the Macintosh. When the engineers at Apple realized the problem in making the Macintosh a closed system (with no expansion slots), they decided that the easiest way to gain expandability was to build an SCSI port into the system, which is how external peripherals can be added to the slotless Macs. Now that they are designing their newest systems with slots, SCSI has dropped from most of them as a built-in option. Because PC systems always have been expandable, the push toward SCSI has not been as urgent. With up to eight or more bus slots supporting different devices and controllers in PC compatible systems, it seemed as though SCSI was not needed as much.

SCSI has since become popular in the PC-based workstation market because of the performance and expandability that it offers. One block that stalled acceptance of SCSI in the PC marketplace was the lack of a real standard; the SCSI standard was originally designed by one company, and then taken over by a committee. Since then no single manufacturer has controlled it. Originally, companies had their own interpretation of how SCSI should be implemented, particularly at the host-adapter level.

SCSI today is a standard, in much the same way that RS-232 (the serial communications port for modems, and so on) is a standard. The SCSI standard (like the RS-232 standard), however, defines only the hardware connections, not the driver specifications required to communicate with the devices. Software ties the SCSI subsystem into your PC, but unfortunately, most of the driver programs work only for a specific device and host adapter. With an SCSI driver for most common adapters and devices built into Windows 95 and 98, it is now much easier to get multiple SCSI devices to work using a single adapter.

Note

Some SCSI host adapters bundled with hardware, such as graphics scanners or a "bargain" SCSI CD-ROM drive, will not include all the features needed to support multiple SCSI devices or bootable SCSI hard drives. This has nothing to do with any limitations in the SCSI specification. The situation is simply that the manufacturer has included the most stripped-down version of an SCSI adapter available to save money. It has all the functionality needed to support the device it came with, but nothing else. Fortunately, with the right adapter and drivers, one card could do it all, most likely the one used for the hard disk, as it would be the most full-featured of the bunch.

SCSI can be troublesome at times because of the lack of a single host-adapter standard, a software interface standard, and standard ROM BIOS support for hard disk drives attached to the SCSI bus. Fortunately, some simple recommendations can keep you from living this compatibility nightmare!

In the beginning, SCSI lacked the capability to run hard disks off the SCSI bus. To boot from these drives and use a variety of operating systems was a problem that resulted from the lack of an interface standard. The standard BIOS software is designed to talk to ST-506/412, ESDI, or ATA (IDE) hard disks and devices. SCSI is so different from IDE that a new set of ROM BIOS routines are necessary to support the system so it can self-boot. Also, this BIOS support is unique to the SCSI host adapter you are using; so, unless the host adapter is built into your motherboard, this support won't be in your motherboard BIOS. Instead, SCSI host adapters are available with BIOS support right on the SCSI host adapter itself.

▶▶ See "The ST-506/412 Interface," p. 505.

▶▶ See "The ESDI Interface," p. 507.

Because of the lead taken by Apple in developing systems software (operating systems and ROM) support for SCSI, peripherals connect to Apple systems in fairly standard ways. Until recently, this kind of standard-setting leadership was lacking for SCSI in the PC world. This situation changed dramatically with Windows 95 and later versions, which include drivers for most standard SCSI adapters and peripherals on the market. These days Windows 98 and Windows 2000 include drivers and support for most SCSI adapters and devices built in.

Many PC manufacturers have standardized SCSI for high-end systems. In these systems, an SCSI host adapter card is placed in one of the slots, or the system has an SCSI host adapter built into the motherboard. This arrangement is similar in appearance to the IDE interface, because a single cable runs from the motherboard to the SCSI drive. SCSI supports as many as 7 or 15 additional devices (some of which may not be hard disks), whereas IDE supports only four devices (two per controller). Additionally, SCSI supports more types of devices other than hard disks than IDE supports. IDE devices must be either a hard disk, IDE-type CD-ROM drive, or a tape drive, LS-120 SuperDisk drive, Zip drive, and so on. Systems with SCSI drives are easy to upgrade, because virtually any third-party SCSI drive will plug in and function.

ANSI SCSI Standards

The SCSI standard defines the physical and electrical parameters of a parallel I/O bus used to connect computers and peripheral devices in daisy-chain fashion. The standard supports devices such as disk drives, tape drives, and CD-ROM drives. The original SCSI standard (ANSI X3.131-1986) was approved in 1986, SCSI-2 was approved in January 1994, and the first portions of SCSI-3 were approved in 1995. Note that SCSI-3 has evolved into an enormous standard with numerous different sections, and is an evolving, growing standard still very much under development. Since it has been broken down into multiple standards, there really is no single SCSI-3 standard.

The SCSI interface is defined as a standard by ANSI (American National Standards Institute), specifically a committee currently known as T10. T10 is a technical committee of the National Committee on Information Technology Standards (NCITS, pronounced "insights"). NCITS is accredited by, and operates under rules that are approved by ANSI. These rules are designed to ensure that voluntary standards are developed by the consensus of industry groups. NCITS develops information processing system standards, while ANSI approves the process under which they are developed and publishes them.

NCITS was formerly known as the X3 Committee, and SCSI was originally published under the T9 Committee. NCITS was formerly known as the X3 Task Group. The original SCSI-1 standard was published by the X3T9 ANSI group in 1986, and is officially published by ANSI as X3.131-1986.

One problem with the original SCSI-1 document was that many of the commands and features were optional, and there was little or no guarantee that a particular peripheral would support the expected commands. This problem caused the industry as a whole to define a set of 18 basic SCSI commands called the Common Command Set (CCS) to become the minimum set of commands supported by all peripherals. CCS became the basis for what is now the SCSI-2 specification.

Along with formal support for CCS, SCSI-2 provided additional definitions for commands to access CD-ROM drives (and their sound capabilities), tape drives, removable drives, optical drives, and several other peripherals. In addition, an optional higher speed called Fast SCSI-2 and a 16-bit version called Wide SCSI-2 were defined. Another feature of SCSI-2 is *command queuing*, which enables a device to accept multiple commands and execute them in the order that the device deems to be most efficient. This feature is most beneficial when you are using a multitasking operating system that could be sending several requests on the SCSI bus at the same time.

The X3T9 group approved the SCSI-2 standard as X3.131-1990 in August 1990, but the document was recalled in December 1990 for changes before final ANSI publication. Final approval for the SCSI-2 document was finally made in January 1994, although it has changed little from the original 1990 release. The SCSI-2 document is now called ANSI X3.131-1994. The official document is available from Global Engineering Documents or the ANSI committee—both are listed in the Vendor List on the CD. You can also download working drafts of these documents from the NCR SCSI BBS, listed in the Vendor List on the CD under "NCR Microelectronics."

Most companies indicate that their host adapters follow both the ANSI X3.131-1986 (SCSI-1) as well as the x3.131-1994 (SCSI-2) standards. Note that because virtually all parts of SCSI-1 are supported in SCSI-2, virtually any SCSI-1 device is also considered SCSI-2 by default. Many manufacturers advertise that their devices are SCSI-2, but this does not mean that they support any of the additional optional features that were incorporated in the SCSI-2 revision.

For example, an optional part of the SCSI-2 specification includes a fast synchronous mode that doubles the standard synchronous transfer rate from 5MB/sec to 10MB/sec. This Fast SCSI transfer mode can be combined with 16-bit Wide SCSI for transfer rates of up to 20MB/sec. There was an optional 32-bit version defined in SCSI-2, but component manufacturers have shunned this as too expensive. In essence, 32-bit SCSI was a stillborn specification, as it has been withdrawn from the SCSI-3 standards. Most SCSI implementations are 8-bit standard SCSI or 16-bit Fast/Wide SCSI. Even devices which support none of the Fast or Wide modes can still be considered SCSI-2.

The first SCSI-3 standards were approved in 1998. Even before it was fully completed, portions of this specification, although not final, have been sold in products. These include the Fast-20 and Fast-40 modes, which are also called Ultra-SCSI and Ultra2-SCSI respectively.

Table 8.1 shows the maximum transfer rates for the SCSI bus at various speeds and widths, and the cable type required for the specific transfer widths.

Note

The A cable is the standard 50-pin SCSI cable, whereas the P cable is a 68-pin cable designed for 16-bit transfers. High Voltage Differential (HVD) signaling was never popular and is now considered obsolete. LVD (Low Voltage Differential) signaling is used in the Ultra2 and Ultra3 modes to increase performance and cabling lengths. Pinouts for the cable connections are listed in this chapter in Tables 8.2 through 8.5.

SCSI is both forward and backward compatible, meaning one can run faster devices on buses with slower host adapters or vice versa. In each case, the entire bus will run at the lowest common denominator speed. In fact, as was stated earlier, virtually any SCSI-1 device can also legitimately be called SCSI-2 (or even SCSI-3). Of course you can't take advantage of the faster modes on an older, slower host adapter. By the same token, you can purchase an Ultra3 capable SCSI host adapter and still run older standard SCSI devices. You can even mix standard 8-bit and wide 16-bit devices on the same bus using cable adapters.

Table 8.1   SCSI Types, Data-Transfer Rates, and Cables

SCSI Technology	Marketing Term	Clock Speed	Transfer Width	Transfer Speed (MHz)
Fast-5	Standard	5	8-bit	5
Fast-5/Wide	Wide	5	16-bit	10
Fast-10	Fast	10	8-bit	10
Fast-10/Wide	Fast/Wide	10	16-bit	20
Fast-20	Ultra	20	8-bit	20
Fast-20/Wide	Ultra/Wide	20	16-bit	40
Fast-40	Ultra2	40	8-bit	40
Fast-40/Wide	Ultra2/Wide	40	16-bit	80
Fast-80	Ultra3	40^3	8-bit	80
Fast-80/Wide	Ultra3/Wide	40^3	16-bit	160

Cable Lengths are in meters, 25M = 80ft., 12M = 40ft., 6M = 20ft., 3M = 10ft., 1.5M = 5ft.
SE = Single-ended signaling
HVD = High Voltage Differential signaling, obsolete
LVD = Low Voltage Differential signaling

SCSI Signaling

"Normal" or standard SCSI uses a signaling technique called Single-ended (SE) signaling. SE signaling is a low cost technique, but it also has performance and noise problems.

Single-ended signaling is also called unbalanced signaling. Each signal is carried on a pair of wires, normally twisted to help reduce noise. With SE one of the pair is grounded, often to a common ground for all signals, and the other carries the actual voltage transitions. It is up to a receiver at the other end of the cable to detect the voltage transitions, which are really just changes in voltage.

Unfortunately, this type of unbalanced signaling is very prone to problems with noise, electromagnetic interference, and ground leakage; these problems get worse the longer the cable. This is the reason that Ultra SCSI was limited to such short maximum bus lengths, as little as 1 1/2 meters or 5 feet.

When SCSI was first developed, a signaling technique called High Voltage Differential (HVD) signaling was also introduced into the standard. Differential signaling, also known as balanced signaling, is still done with a pair of wires. In fact, the first in the pair carries the same type of signal that single-ended SCSI carries. The second in the pair, however, carries the logical inversion of that signal. The receiving device detects the difference between the pair (hence the name differential). By using the wires in a balanced pair, it no longer becomes necessary for the receiver to detect voltage magnitude, only the differential between voltage in two wires. This is

Max. No. of Devices	Cable Type	Max. Length (SE)	Max. Length (HVD)	Max. Length (LVD)
7	A (50-pin)	6MB	25M	-
15	P (68-pin)	6MB	25M	-
7	A (50-pin)	3MB	25M	-
15	P (68-pin)	3MB	25M	-
7	A (50-pin)	3/1.5M[1]	25M	-
7[1]	P (68-pin)	3/1.5M[1]	25M	-
7	A (50-pin)	-	-	12M[2]
15	P (68-pin)	-	-	12M[2]
7	A (50-pin)	-	-	12M[2]
15	P (68-pin)	-	-	12M[2]

1 = *Ultra SCSI cable total length is restricted to 1.5M if there are more than three devices on the bus (not including the host adapter). A maximum of seven devices are allowed.*
2 = *A 25MB cable may be used with Ultra2 and Ultra3 SCSI if there is only one device.*
3 = *Ultra3 SCSI transfers twice per clock cycle.*

much easier for circuits to do reliably, which makes them less susceptible to noise and allows for greater cable length. Because of this, differential SCSI can be used with cable lengths of up to 25 meters, whereas single-ended SCSI is good only for 6 meters maximum, or as little as 1 1/2 meters in the faster modes.

Figure 8.1 shows the circuit differences between balanced (differential) and unbalanced (single-ended) transmission lines.

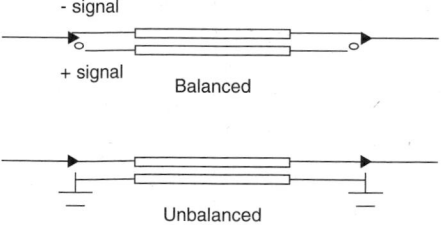

Figure 8.1 *Balanced (differential) versus unbalanced (single-ended) signaling.*

Unfortunately the original standard for HVD signaling called for high voltage differentials between the two wires. This means that small, low-power, single chip interfaces using HVD signaling could not be developed. Instead circuits using several chips were required. This works at both ends, meaning both the host adapter and device circuitry had to be larger and more expensive.

Another problem with HVD SCSI is that although the cables and connectors look (and are) exactly the same as for SE SCSI, both types of devices cannot be mixed on the same bus. If they are, the high voltage from the HVD device will burn out the receiver circuits on all SE devices attached to the bus. In other words, the result will be smoked hardware— not a pretty sight.

Because SE SCSI worked well enough for the speeds that were needed up until recently, HVD SCSI signaling never really caught on. It was only used in minicomputers and very rarely, if at all, in PCs. Because of this, the extra cost of this interface, and the fact that it is electrically incompatible with standard SE SCSI devices, HVD signaling was removed from the SCSI specification in the latest SCSI-3 documents. In other words, as far as you are concerned, it is obsolete.

Still, there was a need for a more reliable signaling technique that would allow for longer cable lengths. The answer came in the form of LVD, or Low Voltage Differential signaling. By designing a new version of the differential interface, it can be made to work with inexpensive and low power SCSI chips. Another advantage of LVD is that because it uses low-voltage, if you plug an LVD device into an SE SCSI bus, nothing will be damaged. In fact, as an optional part of the LVD standard, the LVD device can be designed as a multimode device, which means it will work on both SE or LVD buses. In the case of installing a multimode LVD device into an SE bus, the device will detect that it is installed in an SE bus and will default to SE mode.

This means that all multimode LVD/SE SCSI devices can be used on either LVD or SE SCSI buses. However, when on a bus with even one other SE device, all the LVD devices on the bus will run only in SE mode. Because SE mode only supports SCSI speeds of up to 20MHz (Fast-20 or UltraSCSI), and cable lengths of up to 1 1/2 or 3 meters, the devices will also work only at that speed or lower; you might also have problems with longer cables. Although you can purchase an Ultra3 SCSI multimode LVD/SE drive and install it on an SCSI bus along with single-ended devices, you will certainly be wasting the capabilities of the faster device.

Note that all Ultra2 and Ultra3 devices support LVD signaling, as that is the only way they can be run at the Ultra2 (40MHz) or Ultra3 (80MHz) speeds. It is possible for Ultra SCSI (20MHz) or slower devices to support LVD signaling, but in most cases LVD is synonymous with Ultra2 or Ultra3 only.

Table 8.1, shown earlier, lists all the SCSI speeds and maximum lengths for each speed using the supported signaling techniques for that speed.

Because the connectors are the same for SE, HVD, LVD, or multimode SE/LVD devices, and because putting an HVD device on any bus with SE or LVD devices will cause damage, it would be nice to be able to tell them apart. One way is to look for a special symbol on the unit; the industry has adopted different universal symbols for single-ended and differential SCSI. Figure 8.2 shows these symbols.

If you do not see such symbols, you can tell whether you have a high voltage differential device by using an ohmmeter to check the resistance between pins 21 and 22 on the device connector.

- On a single-ended or low voltage differential device, the pins should be tied together and also tied to the ground.

■ On a high voltage differential device, the pins should be open or have significant resistance between them.

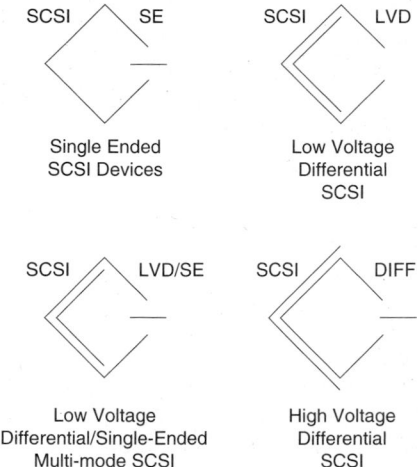

Figure 8.2 Universal symbol icons identifying SE, LVD, multimode LVD/SE, and HVD devices.

Although you will blow stuff up if you plug HVD devices into LVD or SE buses, this generally should not be a problem, because virtually all devices used in the PC environment are SE, LVD, or LVD/SE.

SCSI-1 and SCSI-2

The SCSI-2 specification essentially is an improved version of SCSI-1 with some parts of the specification tightened and several new features and options added. Normally, SCSI-1 and SCSI-2 devices are compatible, but SCSI-1 devices ignore the additional features in SCSI-2.

Some of the changes in SCSI-2 are very minor. For example, SCSI-1 allowed SCSI Bus parity to be optional, whereas parity must be implemented in SCSI-2. Parity is an extra bit that is sent as a verification bit to ensure that the data is not corrupted. Another requirement is that initiator devices, such as host adapters, provide terminator power to the interface; most devices already did so.

SCSI-2 also added several optional features:

■ Fast SCSI (10MHz)

■ Wide SCSI (16-bit transfers)

■ Command queuing

■ High-density cable connectors

■ Improved Active (Alternative 2) termination

Command queuing is where commands can stack up at a device, which can then decide on the quickest way to execute them. This allows the initiator to disconnect and move on to something else while the device accomplishes the task(s). The high-density connectors allow for smaller more efficient connector and cable designs, and active termination uses a powered terminator that is much better at controlling noise than passive designs. These features are not required; they are optional under the SCSI-2 specification. If you connect a standard SCSI host adapter to a Fast SCSI drive, for example, the interface will work, but only at standard SCSI speeds.

SCSI-3

SCSI-3 is a term used to describe a set of standards currently being developed. Simply put, it is the next generation of documents a product conforms to. See the section "New Commands" later in this chapter. Unlike SCSI-1 and SCSI-2, SCSI-3 is not one document that covers everything in SCSI, but is instead a collection of documents that covers the physical connections, electrical interface, primary command set, and specific protocols. The specific protocols include hard disk interface commands, commands for tape drives, controller commands for RAID (Redundant Arrays of Inexpensive Drives), and other commands as well. There is also an overall SCSI Architectural Model (SAM). Each document within the standard is now a separate publication with its own revision level. Normally we don't refer to SCSI-3 anymore as a specific interface, and instead refer to the specific variations in SCSI-3 such as Ultra-2 SCSI.

The main additions to SCSI-3 include

- Ultra2 (Fast-40) SCSI
- Ultra3 (Fast-80) SCSI
- Low Voltage Differential (LVD) signaling

By breaking up SCSI-3 into many smaller individual standards, it has allowed the standard as a whole to develop more quickly. The individual sub-standards can now be published rather than waiting for the entire standard to be approved.

Figure 8.3 shows the main parts of SCSI-3.

The primary changes being seen in the marketplace from SCSI-3 are the new Fast-40 (Ultra2) and Fast-80 (Ultra3) high-speed drives and adapters. These have taken the performance of SCSI up to 160MB/sec. Also new is the Low Voltage Differential (LVD) electrical standard, which allows for greater cable lengths.

A number of people are confused over the speed variations in SCSI. Part of the problem is that speeds are quoted as either clock speeds (MHz) or transfer speeds. With 8-bit transfers you get one byte per transfer, so if the clock is 40MHz (Fast-40 or Ultra2 SCSI), the transfer speed is 40 megabytes per second (MB/sec). On the other hand, if you are using a Wide (16-bit) interface, the transfer speed doubles to 80MB/sec even though the clock speed remains at 40MHz. Finally, there is confusion because SCSI speeds or modes are often discussed using either the official terms such as Fast-10, Fast-20, Fast-40, Fast-80 or the equivalent marketing terms such as Fast, Ultra, Ultra2, and Ultra3. Refer to Table 8.1 for a complete breakdown of SCSI official terms, marketing terms, and speeds.

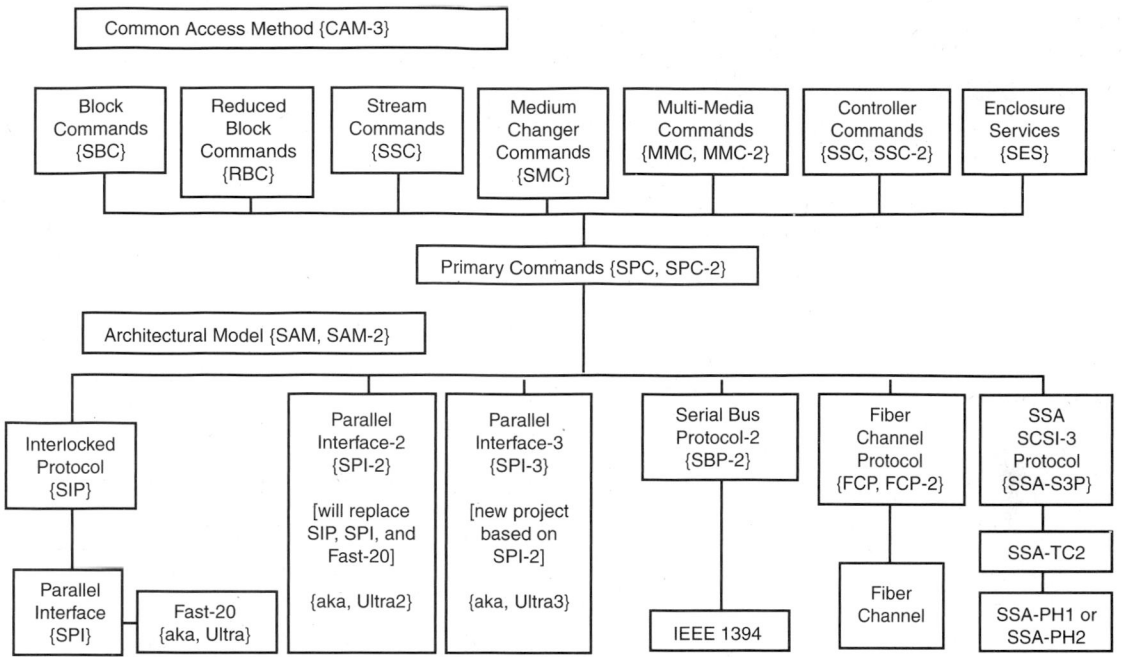

SCSI-3 Architecture Roadmap

Figure 8.3   The SCSI-3 architecture.

Fast and Fast-Wide SCSI

Fast SCSI refers to high-speed synchronous transfer capability. Fast SCSI achieves a 10MB/sec transfer rate on the standard 8-bit SCSI cabling. When combined with a 16-bit Wide SCSI interface, this configuration results in data-transfer rates of 20MB/sec (called Fast/Wide).

Fast-20 (Ultra) SCSI

Fast-20 or Ultra SCSI refers to high-speed synchronous transfer capability that is twice as fast as Fast-SCSI. This has been introduced in the Draft (unfinished) SCSI-3 specification and has already been adopted by the marketplace, especially for high-speed hard disks. Ultra SCSI achieves a 20MB/sec transfer rate on the standard 8-bit SCSI cabling. When combined with a 16-bit Wide SCSI interface, this configuration results in data-transfer rates of 40MB/sec (called Ultra/Wide).

Fast-40 (Ultra2) SCSI

Fast-40 or Ultra2 SCSI is a part of SCSI-3 and is capable of achieving a 40MB/sec transfer rate over an 8-bit (narrow) SCSI bus, and 80MB/sec over a 16-bit (wide) SCSI bus.

Fast-80 SCSI

Fast-80 or Ultra3 SCSI is a part of SCSI-3 and is capable of achieving an 80MB/sec transfer rate over an 8-bit (narrow) SCSI bus, and 160MB/sec over a 16-bit (wide) SCSI bus.

Wide SCSI

Wide SCSI allows for parallel data transfer at a bus width of 16 bits. The wider connection requires a new cable design. The standard 50-conductor 8-bit cable is called the A cable. SCSI-2 originally defined a special 68-conductor B cable that was supposed to be used in conjunction with the A cable for 32-bit wide transfers. However, because of a lack of industry support and the added expenses involved, 32-bit SCSI was never actually implemented and was finally removed as a part of the SCSI-3 specifications. As such there are two different types of SCSI cables, called the A cable and the P cable. A cables are any SCSI cables with 50-pin connectors, whereas P cables are any SCSI cables with 68-pin connectors. You need a P cable if you are connecting a Wide SCSI device and want it to work in 16-bit mode.

Fiber Channel SCSI

Fiber Channel SCSI is a specification for a serial interface using a fiber channel physical and protocol characteristic, with SCSI command set. It can achieve 100MB/sec over either fiber or coaxial cable.

Termination

The single-ended SCSI bus depends on very tight termination tolerances to function reliably. Unfortunately, the original 132-ohm passive termination defined in the SCSI-1 document was not designed for use at the higher synchronous speeds now possible. These passive terminators can cause signal reflections to generate errors when transfer rates increase or when more devices are added to the bus. SCSI-2 defines an active (voltage-regulated) terminator that lowers termination impedance to 110 ohms and improves system integrity. Note that LVD SCSI requires special LVD terminators. If you use SE terminators on a bus with LVD devices, they either won't work or, if they are multimode devices, will default to SE operation.

Command Queuing

In SCSI-1, an initiator device, such as a host adapter, was limited to sending one command per device. In SCSI-2, the host adapter can send as many as 256 commands to a single device, which will store and process those commands internally before responding on the SCSI bus. The target device even can resequence the commands to allow for the most efficient execution or performance possible. This is especially useful in multitasking environments, such as OS/2 and Windows NT, which can take advantage of this feature.

New Commands

SCSI-2 took the Common Command Set that was being used throughout the industry and made it an official part of the standard. The CCS was designed mainly for disk drives and did not include specific commands designed for other types of devices. In SCSI-2, many of the old commands are reworked, and several new commands have been added. New command sets have been added for CD-ROMs, optical drives, scanners, communications devices, and media changers (jukeboxes).

SCSI Cables and Connectors

The SCSI standards are very specific when it comes to cables and connectors. The most common connectors specified in this standard are the 50-position unshielded pin header connector for internal SCSI connections and the 50-position shielded Centronics latch-style connectors for external connections. The shielded Centronics style connector also is called Alternative 2 in the official specification. Passive or Active termination (Active is preferred) is specified for both single-ended and differential buses. The 50-conductor bus configuration is defined in the SCSI-2 standard as the A cable.

Older narrow (8-bit) SCSI adapters and external devices use a full size Centronics type connector that normally has wire latches on each side to secure the cable connector. Figure 8.4 shows what the low-density 50-pin SCSI connector looks like.

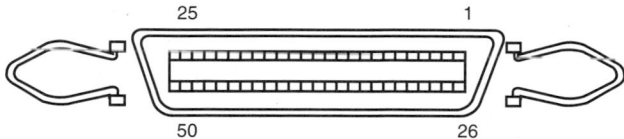

Figure 8.4   Low-density, 50-pin SCSI connector.

The SCSI-2 revision added a high-density, 50-position, D-shell connector option for the A-cable connectors. This connector now is called Alternative 1. Figure 8.5 shows the 50-pin high-density SCSI connector.

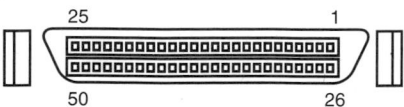

Figure 8.5   High-density, 50-pin SCSI connector.

The Alternative 2 Centronics latch-style connector remains unchanged from SCSI-1. A 68-conductor B cable specification was added to the SCSI-2 standard to provide for 16- and 32-bit data transfers; the connector, however, had to be used in parallel with an A cable. The industry did not widely accept the B-cable option, which has been dropped from the SCSI-3 standard.

To replace the ill-fated B cable, a new 68-conductor P cable was developed as part of the SCSI-3 specification. Shielded and unshielded high-density D-shell connectors are specified for both the A and P cable. The shielded high-density connectors use a squeeze-to-release latch rather than the wire latch used on the Centronics-style connectors. Active termination for single-ended buses is specified, providing a high level of signal integrity. Figure 8.6 shows the 68-pin high-density SCSI connector.

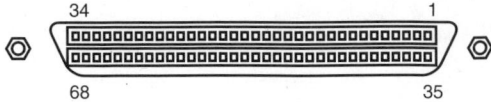

Figure 8.6 High-density, 68-pin SCSI connector.

Drive arrays normally use special SCSI drives with what is called an 80-pin Alternative-4 connector, which is capable of Wide SCSI and also includes power signals. Drives with the 80-pin connector are normally *hot swappable*—they can be removed and installed with the power on—in drive arrays. The 80-pin Alt-4 connector is shown in Figure 8.7.

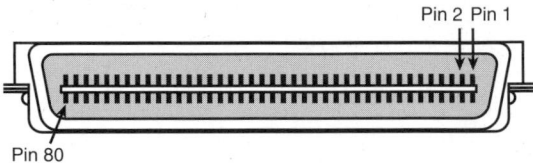

Figure 8.7 80-pin Alt-4 SCSI connector.

Apple and some other non-standard implementations from other vendors used a 25-pin cable and connector for SCSI devices.

They did this by eliminating most of the grounds from the cable, which unfortunately results in a noisy, error prone connection. I don't recommend using 25-pin cables and connectors; you should avoid them if possible. The connector used in these cases was a standard female DB-25 connector, which looks exactly like a PC parallel port (printer) connector. Unfortunately, it is possible to damage equipment by plugging printers into DB-25 SCSI connectors or by plugging SCSI devices into DB-25 printer connectors. So, if you use this type of SCSI connection, be sure it is marked well, as there is no way to tell DB-25 SCSI from DB-25 parallel printer connectors by looking at them. The DB-25 connector is shown Figure 8.8.

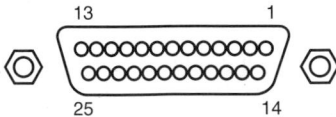

Figure 8.8 DB-25 SCSI connector.

Again I recommend you avoid making SCSI connections using this type of cable or connector.

SCSI Cable and Connector Pinouts

The following section details the pinouts of the various SCSI cables and connectors. There are two electrically different versions of SCSI: Single-ended and Differential. These two versions are electrically incompatible and must not be interconnected or damage will result. Fortunately, there are very few Differential SCSI applications available in the PC industry, so you will rarely (if ever) encounter one. Within each electrical type (Single-ended or Differential), there are basically two SCSI cable types:

- A Cable (Standard 8-bit SCSI)
- P Cable (16-bit Wide SCSI)

The 50-pin A-cable is used in most SCSI-1 and SCSI-2 installations, and is the most common cable you will encounter. SCSI-2 Wide (16-bit) applications use a P cable instead, which has 68-pins. You can intermix standard and Wide SCSI devices on a single SCSI bus by interconnecting A and P cables with special adapters. SCSI-3 applications that are 32-bit wide would have used an additional Q cable, but this was finally dropped from the SCSI-3 standard after it was never implemented in actual products.

SCSI cables are specially shielded with the most important high-speed signals carried in the center of the cable, and less important, slower ones in two additional layers around the perimeter. A typical SCSI cable is constructed as shown in Figure 8.9.

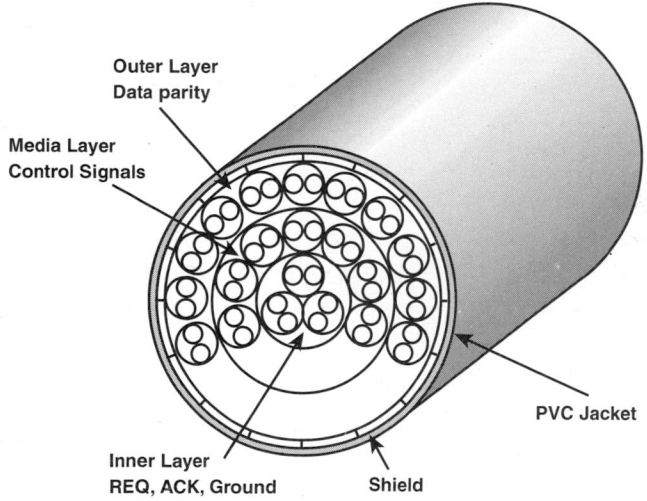

Figure 8.9 Cross section of a typical SCSI cable.

This specialized construction is what makes SCSI cables so expensive as well as thicker than other types of cables. Note this specialized construction is only necessary for external SCSI cables. Cables used to connect devices inside a shielded enclosure (such as inside a PC) can use much less expensive ribbon cables.

The A cables can have Pin Header (Internal) type connectors or External Shielded connectors, each with a different pinout. The P cables feature the same connector pinout on either Internal or External cable connections.

Single-Ended SCSI Cables and Connectors

The single-ended electrical interface is the most popular type for PC systems. Tables 8.2 and 8.3 show all the possible single-ended cable and connector pinouts. The A cable is available in both internal unshielded and external shielded configurations. A hyphen preceding a signal name indicates the signal is Active Low. The RESERVED lines have continuity from one end of the SCSI bus to the other. In an A cable bus, the RESERVED lines should be left open in SCSI devices (but may be connected to ground), and are connected to ground in the bus terminator assemblies. In the P and Q cables, the RESERVED lines are left open in SCSI devices and in the bus terminator assemblies.

Table 8.2   A-Cable (Single-Ended) Internal Unshielded Header Connector

Signal	Pin	Pin	Signal
GROUND	1	2	-DB(0)
GROUND	3	4	-DB(1)
GROUND	5	6	-DB(2)
GROUND	7	8	-DB(3)
GROUND	9	10	-DB(4)
GROUND	11	12	-DB(5)
GROUND	13	14	-DB(6)
GROUND	15	16	-DB(7)
GROUND	17	18	-DB(Parity)
GROUND	19	20	GROUND
GROUND	21	22	GROUND
RESERVED	23	24	RESERVED
Open	25	26	TERMPWR
RESERVED	27	28	RESERVED
GROUND	29	30	GROUND
GROUND	31	32	–ATN
GROUND	33	34	GROUND
GROUND	35	36	-BSY
GROUND	37	38	-ACK
GROUND	39	40	-RST
GROUND	41	42	-MSG
GROUND	43	44	-SEL
GROUND	45	46	-C/D
GROUND	47	48	-REQ
GROUND	49	50	-I/O

Table 8.3   A Cable (Single-Ended) External Shielded Connector

Signal	Pin	Pin	Signal
GROUND	1	26	-DB(0)
GROUND	2	27	-DB(1)
GROUND	3	28	-DB(2)
GROUND	4	29	-DB(3)
GROUND	5	30	-DB(4)
GROUND	6	31	-DB(5)
GROUND	7	32	-DB(6)
GROUND	8	33	-DB(7)
GROUND	9	34	-DB(Parity)
GROUND	10	35	GROUND
GROUND	11	36	GROUND
RESERVED	12	37	RESERVED
Open	13	38	TERMPWR
RESERVED	14	39	RESERVED
GROUND	15	40	GROUND
GROUND	16	41	-ATN
GROUND	17	42	GROUND
GROUND	18	43	-BSY
GROUND	19	44	-ACK
GROUND	20	45	-RST
GROUND	21	46	-MSG
GROUND	22	47	-SEL
GROUND	23	48	-C/D
GROUND	24	49	-REQ
GROUND	25	50	-I/O

IBM used the SCSI interface in virtually all PS/2 systems introduced after 1990. These systems use a Micro-Channel SCSI adapter or have the SCSI Host Adapter built into the motherboard. In either case, IBM's SCSI interface uses a special 60-pin mini-Centronics type external shielded connector that is unique in the industry. A special IBM cable is required to adapt this connector to the standard 50-pin Centronics style connector used on most external SCSI devices. The pinout of the IBM 60-pin mini-Centronics style External Shielded connector is shown in Table 8.4. Notice that although the pin arrangement is unique, the pin-number-to-signal designations correspond with the standard unshielded internal pin header type of SCSI connector. IBM has discontinued this design and all their systems because after the PS/2 series, all have used conventional SCSI connectors.

Table 8.4 **IBM PS/2 SCSI External**

Signal Name	Pin	Pin	Signal Name
GROUND	1	60	Not Connected
–DB(0)	2	59	Not Connected
GROUND	3	58	Not Connected
–DB(1)	4	57	Not Connected
GROUND	5	56	Not Connected
–DB(2)	6	55	Not Connected
GROUND	7	54	Not Connected
–DB(3)	8	53	Not Connected
GROUND	9	52	Not Connected
-DB(4)	10	51	GROUND
GROUND	11	50	-I/O
-DB(5)	12	49	GROUND
GROUND	13	48	-REQ
-DB(6)	14	47	GROUND
GROUND	15	46	–C/D
-DB(7)	16	45	GROUND
GROUND	17	44	-SEL
-DB(Parity)	18	43	GROUND
GROUND	19	42	-MSG
GROUND	20	41	GROUND
GROUND	21	40	-RST
GROUND	22	39	GROUND
RESERVED	23	38	-ACK
RESERVED	24	37	GROUND
Open	25	36	-BSY
TERMPWR	26	35	GROUND
RESERVED	27	34	GROUND
RESERVED	28	33	GROUND
GROUND	29	32	-ATN
GROUND	30	31	GROUND

The P cable (Single-ended) and connectors are used in 16-bit wide SCSI-2 applications (see Table 8.5 for the pinout).

Table 8.5 **P Cable (Single-Ended) Internal or External Shielded Connector**

Signal Name	Pin	Pin	Signal Name
GROUND	1	35	-DB(12)
GROUND	2	36	-DB(13)

Signal Name	Pin	Pin	Signal Name
GROUND	3	37	-DB(14)
GROUND	4	38	-DB(15)
GROUND	5	39	-DB(Parity 1)
GROUND	6	40	-DB(0)
GROUND	7	41	-DB(1)
GROUND	8	42	-DB(2)
GROUND	9	43	-DB(3)
GROUND	10	44	-DB(4)
GROUND	11	45	-DB(5)
GROUND	12	46	-DB(6)
GROUND	13	47	-DB(7)
GROUND	14	48	-DB(Parity 0)
GROUND	15	49	GROUND
GROUND	16	50	GROUND
TERMPWR	17	51	TERMPWR
TERMPWR	18	52	TERMPWR
RESERVED	19	53	RESERVED
GROUND	20	54	GROUND
GROUND	21	55	-ATN
GROUND	22	56	GROUND
GROUND	23	57	-BSY
GROUND	24	58	-ACK
GROUND	25	59	-RST
GROUND	26	60	-MSG
GROUND	27	61	-SEL
GROUND	28	62	-C/D
GROUND	29	63	-REQ
GROUND	30	64	-I/O
GROUND	31	65	-DB(8)
GROUND	32	66	-DB(9)
GROUND	33	67	-DB(10)
GROUND	34	68	-DB(11)

Differential SCSI Signals

High Voltage Differential (HVD) SCSI is not normally used in a PC environment, but is very popular with minicomputer installations due to the very long bus lengths that are allowed. Recently, this is changing with the introduction of Low Voltage Differential signaling for SCSI.

Differential signaling uses drivers on both the initiator and target ends of the bus and makes each signal work in a push/pull arrangement, rather than a signal/ground arrangement as with standard single-ended SCSI. This allows for much greater cable lengths and eliminates some of the problems with termination.

Most all PC peripherals produced since the beginning of SCSI have been SE (single-ended) types. These are incompatible with HVD devices, although HVD devices can be used on a SE bus with appropriate (and expensive) adapters. The new LVD (Low-Voltage Differential) devices, on the other hand, can be used on a SE bus if they are multimode devices, in which case they will switch into SE mode. If all devices including the host adapter support LVD mode, all the devices will switch into that mode and much longer cable lengths and higher speeds can be used. The normal limit for an SE SCSI bus is 1.5 to 3 meters maximum (about 5–10 feet) and up to 20MHz. If run in LVD mode, the maximum bus length goes up to 12 meters (about 40 feet) and speeds can go up to 80MHz. HVD SCSI supports bus lengths of up to 25 meters (about 80 feet).

Note that almost all recently introduced SCSI hard disks are Ultra2 or Ultra3 devices, which means by default they are also LVD or multimode LVD/SE devices.

Expanders

SCSI expanders separate an SCSI bus into more than one physical segment, each of which can have the full SCSI cable length for that type of signaling. They provide a complete regeneration of the SCSI bus signals, allowing greater cable lengths and incompatible devices to essentially share the same bus. An expander can also be used to separate incompatible parts of an SCSI bus, for example to keep SE and HVD SCSI devices in separate domains.

Expanders are transparent to the software and firmware on the bus and they don't take up a device ID. They are normally capable of providing termination if located at the end of a bus segment, or they can have termination disabled if they are in the middle of a bus segment.

Due to their expense, expanders are not normally used except in extreme situations where no other alternative remains. In most cases it is better to stick within the recommended cable and bus length requirements, and keep incompatible devices such as High Voltage Differential (HVD) devices off of a standard SE (single-ended) or LVD (Low Voltage Differential) bus.

Termination

All buses need to be electrically terminated at each end; the SCSI bus is no exception. Improper termination still is one of the most common problems in SCSI installations. Three types of terminators typically are available for the SCSI bus:

- Passive
- Active (also called Alternative 2)
- Forced Perfect Termination (FPT): FPT-3, FPT-18, and FPT-27
- LVD (Low Voltage Differential) termination

Typical passive terminators (a network of resistors) allow signal fluctuations in relation to the terminator power signal on the bus. Usually, passive terminating resistors suffice over short distances, such as two or three feet, but for longer distances, active termination is a real advantage. Active termination is required with Fast SCSI.

An active terminator actually has one or more voltage regulators to produce the termination voltage, rather than resistor voltage dividers. This arrangement helps ensure that the SCSI signals always are terminated to the correct voltage level. Active terminators will usually have some sort of LED indicating the termination activity. The SCSI-2 specification recommends active termination on both ends of the bus and requires active termination whenever Fast or Wide SCSI devices are used. Most high-performance host adapters have an "auto-termination" feature, so if it is the end of a chain, it will terminate itself.

A variation on active termination is available for single-ended buses: *Forced Perfect Termination.* Forced Perfect Termination is an even better form of active termination, in which diode clamps are added to eliminate signal overshoot and undershoot. The trick is that instead of clamping to +5 and Ground, these terminators clamp to the output of two regulated voltages. This arrangement enables the clamping diodes to eliminate signal overshoot and undershoot, especially at higher signaling speeds and over longer distances.

FPT terminators are available in several versions. FPT-3 and FPT-18 versions are available for 8-bit standard SCSI, while the FPT-27 is available for 16-bit (Wide) SCSI. The FPT-3 version forces perfect the three most highly active SCSI signals on the 8-bit SCSI bus, while the FPT-18 forces perfect all the SCSI signals on the 8-bit bus except grounds. FPT-27 also forces perfect all the 16-bit Wide SCSI signals except grounds.

Note that LVD buses that you want to run in LVD mode require LVD terminators. If you use SE terminators, the bus will default into SE mode.

▶▶ See "SCSI Drive Configuration," p. 549.

Note

Several companies make high-quality terminators for the SCSI bus, including Aeronics and the Data Mate division of Methode. Both of these companies make a variety of terminators. Aeronics is well-noted for some unique FPT versions that are especially suited to problem configurations that require longer cable runs or higher signal integrity. One of the best investments you can make in any SCSI installation is in high-quality cables and terminators. Contact information for both of these companies is listed in the Vendor List on the CD.

Special terminators are also required for LVD and HVD SCSI, so if you are using those interfaces, make sure your terminators are compatible.

SCSI Drive Configuration

SCSI drives are not too difficult to configure, but they are more complicated than IDE drives. The SCSI standard controls the way the drives must be set up. You need to set two or three items when you configure an SCSI drive:

- SCSI ID setting (0–7 or 0–15)
- Terminating resistors

The SCSI ID setting is very simple. Up to 7 SCSI devices can be used on a single narrow SCSI bus or up to 15 devices on a wide SCSI bus, and each device must have a unique SCSI ID address. There are 8 or 16 addresses respectively, and the host adapter takes one address, so the rest are free for up to 7 or 15 SCSI peripherals. Most SCSI host adapters are factory-set to ID 7 or 15, which is the highest priority ID. All other devices must have unique IDs that do not conflict with one another. Some host adapters boot only from a hard disk set to a specific ID. Older Adaptec host adapters required the boot hard disk to be ID 0; newer ones can boot from any ID.

Setting the ID usually involves changing jumpers on the drive. If the drive is installed in an external chassis, the chassis might have an ID selector switch that is accessible at the rear. This selector makes ID selection a simple matter of pressing a button or rotating a wheel until the desired ID number appears. If no external selector is present, you must open the external device chassis and set the ID via the jumpers on the drive.

Three jumpers are required to set the SCSI ID; the particular ID selected actually is derived from the binary representation of the jumpers themselves. For example, setting all three ID jumpers off results in a binary number of 000b, which translates to an ID of 0. A binary setting of 001b equals ID 1, 010b equals 2, 011b equals 3, and so on. (Notice that as I list these values, I append a lowercase b to indicate binary numbers.)

Unfortunately, the jumpers can appear either forward or backward on the drive, depending on how the manufacturer set them up. To keep things simple, I have recorded all the different ID jumper settings in the following tables. Table 8.6 shows the settings for drives that order the jumpers with the Most Significant Bit (MSB) to the left; Table 8.7 shows the settings for drives that have the jumpers ordered so that the MSB is to the right.

Table 8.6   SCSI ID Jumper Settings with the Most Significant Bit to the Left

SCSI	ID	Jumper	Settings
0	0	0	0
1	0	0	1
2	0	1	0
3	0	1	1
4	1	0	0
5	1	0	1
6	1	1	0
7	1	1	1

1 = Jumper On, 0 = Jumper Off

SCSI termination is very simple. Termination is required at both ends of the bus; there are no exceptions. If the host adapter is at one end of the bus, it must have termination enabled. If the host adapter is in the middle of the bus, and if both internal and external bus links are present, the host adapter must have its termination disabled, and the devices at each end of the bus must have terminators installed. Unfortunately, the majority of problems that I see with SCSI installations are the result of improper termination.

Figure 8.10 shows a representation of an SCSI bus with several devices attached. In this case the host adapter is at one end of the bus and a CD-ROM drive is at the other. For the bus to work properly, those devices must be terminated while the others do not.

When installing an external SCSI device, you will usually find the device in a storage enclosure with both input and output SCSI connectors, so that you can use the device in a daisy chain. If the enclosure is at the end of the SCSI bus, an external terminator module most likely will have to be plugged into the second (outgoing) SCSI port to provide proper termination at that end of the bus (see Figure 8.11).

External terminator modules are available in a variety of connector configurations, including pass-through designs, which are needed if only one port is available. Pass-through terminators also are commonly used in internal installations in which the device does not have built-in terminating resistors. Many hard drives use pass-through terminators for internal installations to save space on the logic-board assembly (see Figure 8.12).

The pass-through models are required when a device is at the end of the bus and only one SCSI connector is available.

Table 8.7   SCSI ID Jumper Settings with the Most Significant Bit to the Right

SCSI	ID	Jumper	Settings
0	0	0	0
1	1	0	0
2	0	1	0
3	1	1	0
4	0	0	1
5	1	0	1
6	0	1	1
7	1	1	1

1 = Jumper On, 0 = Jumper Off

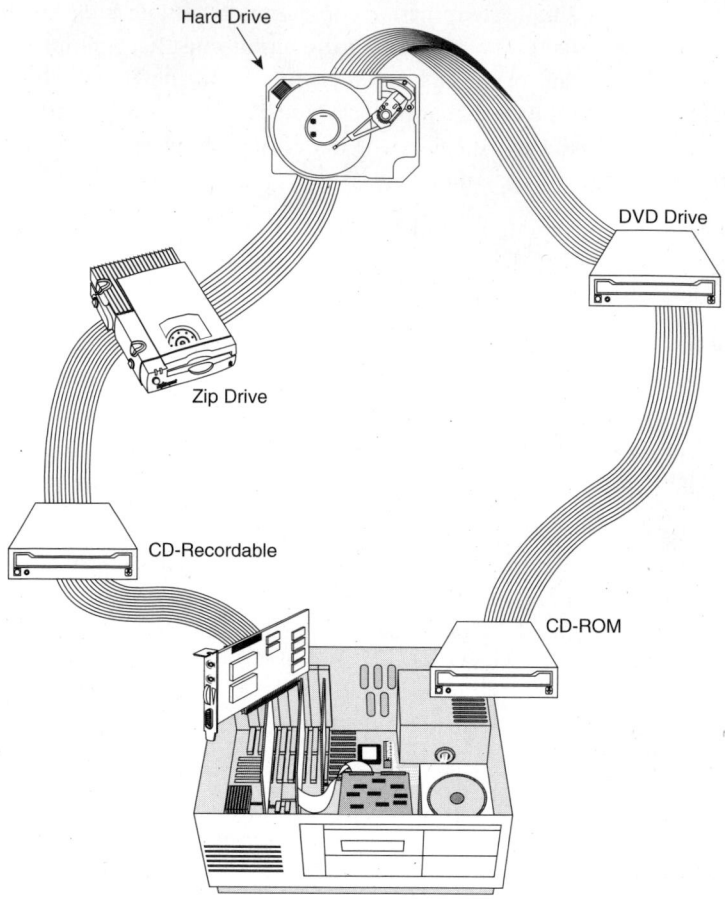

Figure 8.10 SCSI bus daisy-chain connections; the first and last devices must be terminated.

Other configuration items on an SCSI drive can be set via jumpers. Following are several of the most common additional settings that you will find:

- Start on Command (delayed start)
- SCSI Parity
- Terminator Power
- Synchronous Negotiation

These configuration items are described in the following sections.

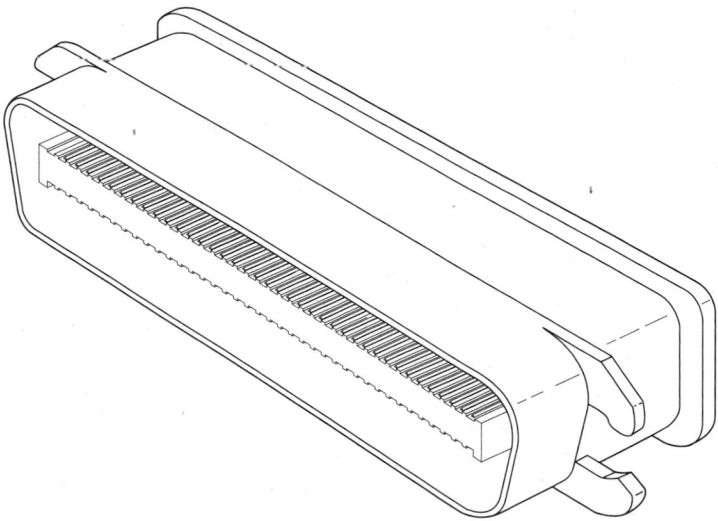

Figure 8.11   External SCSI device terminator.

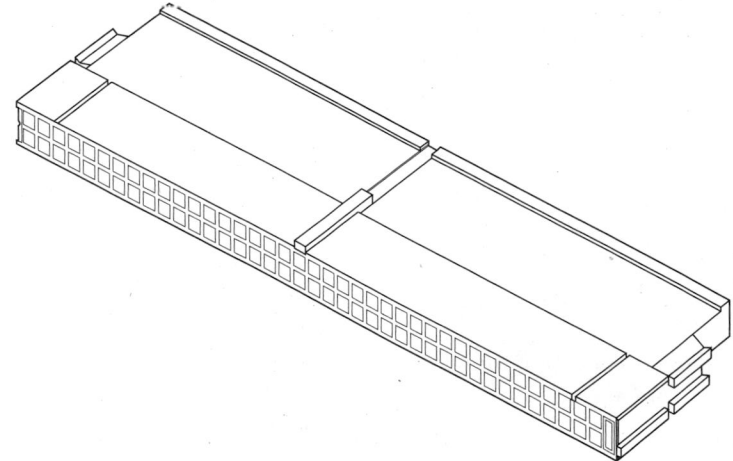

Figure 8.12   Internal pin-header connector pass-through SCSI terminator.

Start On Command (Delayed Start)

If you have multiple drives installed in a system, it is wise to set them up so that all the drives do not start to spin immediately when the system is powered on. A hard disk drive can consume three or four times more power during the first few seconds after power-on than during normal operation. The motor requires this additional power to get the platters spinning quickly. If several drives are drawing all this power at the same time, the power supply may be overloaded, which can cause the system to hang or have intermittent startup problems.

Nearly all SCSI drives provide a way to delay drive spinning so that this problem does not occur. When most SCSI host adapters initialize the SCSI bus, they send out a command called Start Unit to each of the ID addresses in succession. By setting a jumper on the hard disk, you can prevent the disk from spinning until it receives the Start Unit command from the host adapter. Because the host adapter sends this command to all the ID addresses in succession, from the highest priority address (ID 7) to the lowest (ID 0), the higher priority drives can be made to start first, with each lower priority drive spinning up sequentially. Because some host adapters do not send the Start Unit command, some drives might simply delay spinup for a fixed number of seconds rather than wait for a command that never will arrive.

If drives are installed in external chassis with separate power supplies, you need not implement the delayed-start function. This function is best applied to internal drives that must be run from the same power supply that runs the system. For internal installations, I recommend setting Start on Command (delayed start) even if you have only one SCSI drive; this setting will ease the load on the power supply by spinning the drive up after the rest of the system has full power. This method is especially good for portable systems and other systems in which the power supply is limited.

SCSI Parity

SCSI Parity is a limited form of error checking that helps ensure that all data transfers are reliable. Virtually all host adapters support SCSI parity checking, so this option should be enabled on every device. The only reason why it exists as an option is that some older host adapters do not work with SCSI parity, so the parity must be turned off.

Terminator Power

The terminators at each end of the SCSI bus require power from at least one device on the bus. In most cases, the host adapter supplies this terminator power; in some cases, however, it does not. For example, parallel port SCSI host adapters typically do not supply terminator power. It is not a problem if more than one device supplies terminator power because each source is diode-protected. For simplicity's sake, many will configure all devices to supply terminator power. If no device supplies terminator power, the bus will not be terminated correctly and will not function properly.

SCSI Synchronous Negotiation

The SCSI bus can run in two modes: asynchronous (the default) and synchronous. The bus actually switches modes during transfers through a protocol called *synchronous negotiation*. Before data is transferred across the SCSI bus, the sending device (called the *initiator*) and the receiving device (called the *target*) negotiate how the transfer will take place. If both devices support synchronous transfers, they will discover this fact through the negotiation, and the transfer will take place at the faster synchronous rate.

Unfortunately, some older devices do not respond to a request for synchronous transfer and can actually be disabled when such a request is made. For this reason, both host adapters and devices that support synchronous negotiation often have a jumper that can be used to disable this negotiation so it can work with older devices. By default, all devices today should support synchronous negotiation, and this function should be enabled.

Plug-and-Play (PnP) SCSI

Plug-and-Play SCSI was originally released in April 1994. This specification allows SCSI device manufacturers to build PnP peripherals that will automatically configure when used with a PnP operating system. This will allow you to easily connect or reconfigure external peripherals, such as hard disk drives, backup tapes, and CD-ROMs.

To connect SCSI peripherals to the host PC, the specification requires a PnP SCSI host adapter such as PnP ISA or PCI. PnP add-in cards enable a PnP operating system to automatically configure software device drivers and system resources for the host bus interface.

The PnP SCSI specification version 1.0 includes these technical highlights:

- A single cable connector configuration
- Automatic termination of the SCSI bus
- SCAM (SCSI configured automagically) automatic ID assignment
- Full backward compatibility of PnP SCSI devices with the installed base of SCSI systems.

This should go a long way in making SCSI easier to use for the normal user.

Each SCSI peripheral that you add to your SCSI bus (other than hard disk drives) requires an external driver to make the device work. Hard disks are the exception; driver support for them normally is provided as part of the SCSI host adapter BIOS. These external drivers are specific not only to a particular device, but also to the host adapter.

Recently, two types of standard host adapter interface drivers have become popular, greatly reducing this problem. By having a standard host adapter driver to write to, peripheral makers can more quickly create new drivers that support their devices, and then talk to the universal host adapter driver. This arrangement eliminates dependence on one particular type of host adapter. These primary or universal drivers link the host adapter and the operating system.

The Advanced SCSI Programming Interface (ASPI) currently is the most popular universal driver, with most peripheral makers writing their drivers to talk to ASPI. The *A* in ASPI used to stand for Adaptec, the company that introduced it, but other SCSI device vendors have licensed the right to use ASPI with their products. DOS does not support ASPI directly, but it does when the ASPI driver is loaded. Windows 95, Windows 98, Windows NT, and OS/2 2.1 and later versions provide automatic ASPI support for several SCSI host adapters.

Future Domain and NCR have created another interface driver called the Common Access Method (CAM). CAM is an ANSI-approved protocol that enables a single driver to control several host adapters. In addition to ASPI, OS/2 2.1 and later versions currently offer support for CAM. Future Domain also provides a CAM-to-ASPI converter in the utilities that go with its host adapters.

SCSI Configuration Troubleshooting

When you are installing a chain of devices on a single SCSI bus, the installation can get complicated very quickly. If you have a problem during installation, check these items first:

- Make sure you are using the latest BIOS from your motherboard manufacturer. Some have had problems with their PCI bus slots not working properly.

- Check to be sure that all SCSI devices attached to the bus powered on.

- Make sure all SCSI cables and power cables properly connected. Try removing and reseating all the connectors to be sure.

- Check that the host adapter and each device on each SCSI bus channel have a unique SCSI ID setting.

- Make sure the SCSI bus is terminated properly. Remember there should only be two terminators on the bus, one at each end. All other termination should be removed or disabled.

- If your system BIOS setup has settings for controlling PCI bus configuration, make sure the PCI slot containing the SCSI adapter is configured for an available interrupt. If your system is Plug and Play, use the Windows Device Manager to check and possibly change the resource configuration.

- Make sure the host adapter installed in a PCI slot that supports bus mastering. Some older motherboards did not allow bus mastering to work in all PCI slots. Check your motherboard documentation and try moving the SCSI host adapter to a different PCI slot.

- If you have an SCSI hard disk installed and your system will not boot from the SCSI drive, there can be several causes for this problem. Note that if both SCSI and non-SCSI disk drives are installed in your computer; in almost all cases the non-SCSI drive will be the boot device. If you want to boot from an SCSI drive, check the boot sequence configuration in your BIOS. If your system allows, change the boot sequence to allow SCSI devices to boot first. If not, try removing the non-SCSI drives from your system.

If the system has only SCSI disk drives and it still won't boot, check the following items:

- Make sure your computer's BIOS Setup drive configuration is set to "No Drives Installed". The PC BIOS supports only ATA (IDE) drives; by setting this to no drives, the system will then try to boot from another device such as SCSI.

- Make sure the drive is partitioned and that a primary partition exists. Use FDISK from DOS or Windows to check.

- Make sure the boot partition of the boot hard disk is set to active. This can be checked or changed with the FDISK program.

- Finally as a last resort, you can try backing up all data on the SCSI hard disk, and then perform a low-level format with the Format utility built into or included with the host adapter.

Here are some tips for getting your setup to function quickly and efficiently:

- *Start by adding one device at a time.* Rather than plug numerous peripherals into a single SCSI card and then try to configure them at the same time, start by installing the host adapter and a single hard disk. Then you can continue installing devices one at a time, checking to make sure that everything works before moving on.

- *Keep good documentation.* When you add an SCSI peripheral, write down the SCSI ID address and any other switch and jumper settings, such as SCSI Parity, Terminator Power, and Delayed or Remote Start. For the host adapter, record the BIOS addresses, Interrupt, DMA channel, and I/O Port addresses used by the adapter, and any other jumper or configuration settings (such as termination) that might be important to know later.

- *Use proper termination.* Each end of the bus must be terminated, preferably with active or Forced Perfect (FPT) terminators. If you are using any Fast SCSI-2 device, you must use active terminators rather than the cheaper passive types. Even with standard (slow) SCSI devices, active termination is highly recommended. If you have only internal or external devices on the bus, the host adapter and last device on the chain should be terminated. If you have external and internal devices on the chain, you generally will terminate the first and last of these devices but not the SCSI host adapter (which is in the middle of the bus).

- *Use high-quality shielded SCSI cables.* Make sure that your cable connectors match your devices. Use high-quality shielded cables, and observe the SCSI bus-length limitations. Use cables designed for SCSI use, and if possible, stick to the same brand of cable throughout a single SCSI bus. Different brands of cables have different impedance values; this situation sometimes causes problems, especially in long or high-speed SCSI implementations.

Following these simple tips will help minimize problems and leave you with a trouble-free SCSI installation.

SCSI Versus IDE

When you compare the performance and capabilities of IDE and SCSI interfaced drives, you need to consider several factors. These two types of drives are the most popular drives used in PC systems today, and a single manufacturer may make identical drives in both interfaces. Deciding which drive type is best for your system is a difficult decision that depends on many factors.

In most cases, you will find that an IDE drive using the same head-disk assembly as an SCSI drive from the same manufacturer will perform about the same or outperform the equivalent SCSI drive at a given task or benchmark. This is mainly true when using a single drive with a single user operating system such as Windows 95/98. More powerful operating systems such as NT or Windows 2000 can more effectively use the command queuing and other features of SCSI, thus improving performance over IDE, especially when supporting multiple drives.

It is interesting to see that SCSI really evolved from IDE, or you could say that both evolved from the ST-506/412 and ESDI interfaces that were once used.

◄◄ See "The ESDI Interface," p. 507.

◄◄ See "The ST-506/412 Interface," p. 505.

SCSI Hard Disk Evolution and Construction

SCSI is not a disk interface, but a bus that supports SCSI bus interface adapters connected to disk and other device controllers. The first SCSI drives for PCs were standard ST-506/412 or ESDI drives with a separate SCSI bus interface adapter (sometimes called a bridge controller) that converted the ST-506/412 or ESDI interfaces to SCSI. This interface originally was in the form of a secondary logic board, and the entire assembly often was mounted in an external case.

The next step was to build the SCSI bus interface "converter" board directly into the drive's own logic board. Today, we call these drives embedded SCSI drives, because the SCSI interface is built in.

At that point, there was no need to conform to the absolute specifications of ST-506/412 or ESDI on the internal disk interface, because the only other device that the interface ever would have to talk to was built in as well. Thus, the disk-interface and controller-chipset manufacturers began to develop more customized chipsets that were based on the ST-506/412 or ESDI chipsets already available, but offered more features and higher performance.

Today, if you look at a typical SCSI drive, you often can identify the chip or chipset that serves as the disk controller on the drive as being exactly the same kind that would be used on an ST-506/412 or ESDI controller, or as some evolutionary customized variation thereof.

Consider some examples. An ATA IDE drive must fully emulate the system-level disk-controller interface introduced with the Western Digital WD1003 controller series that IBM used in the AT. These drives must act as though they have a built-in ST-506/412 or ESDI controller; in fact, they actually do. Most of these built-in controllers have more capabilities than the original WD1003 series (usually in the form of additional commands), but they must at least respond to all the original commands that were used with the WD1003.

If you follow the hard drive market, you usually will see that drive manufacturers offer most of their newer drives in both ATA-IDE and SCSI versions. In other words, if a manufacturer makes a particular 20GB IDE drive, you invariably will see that the company also makes an SCSI model with the same capacity and specifications, which uses the same HDA (Head Disk Assembly) and even looks the same as the IDE version. If you study these virtually identical drives, the only major difference you will find is the additional chip on the logic board of the SCSI version, called an SCSI Bus Adapter Chip (SBIC).

Figures 8.13 and 8.14 show the logic-block diagrams of the WD-AP4200 (a 200MB ATA-IDE drive) and WD-SP4200 (a 200MB SCSI drive), respectively. These drives use the same HDA; they differ only in their logic boards, and even the logic boards are the same except for the addition of an SBIC on the SCSI drive's logic board.

Notice that even the circuit designs of these two drives are almost identical. Both drives use an LSI (Large Scale Integrated circuit) chip called the WD42C22 Disk Controller and Buffer manager chip. In the ATA drive, this chip is connected through a DMA control chip directly to the AT bus. In the SCSI version, a WD33C93 SCSI bus interface controller chip is added to interface the disk-controller logic to the SCSI bus. In fact, the logic diagrams of these two drives differ only in the fact that the SCSI version has a complete subset of the ATA drive, with the SCSI bus interface controller logic added. This essentially is a very condensed version of the separate drive and bridge controller setups that were used in the early days of PC SCSI.

◀◀ See "DMA Transfer Modes," p. 524.

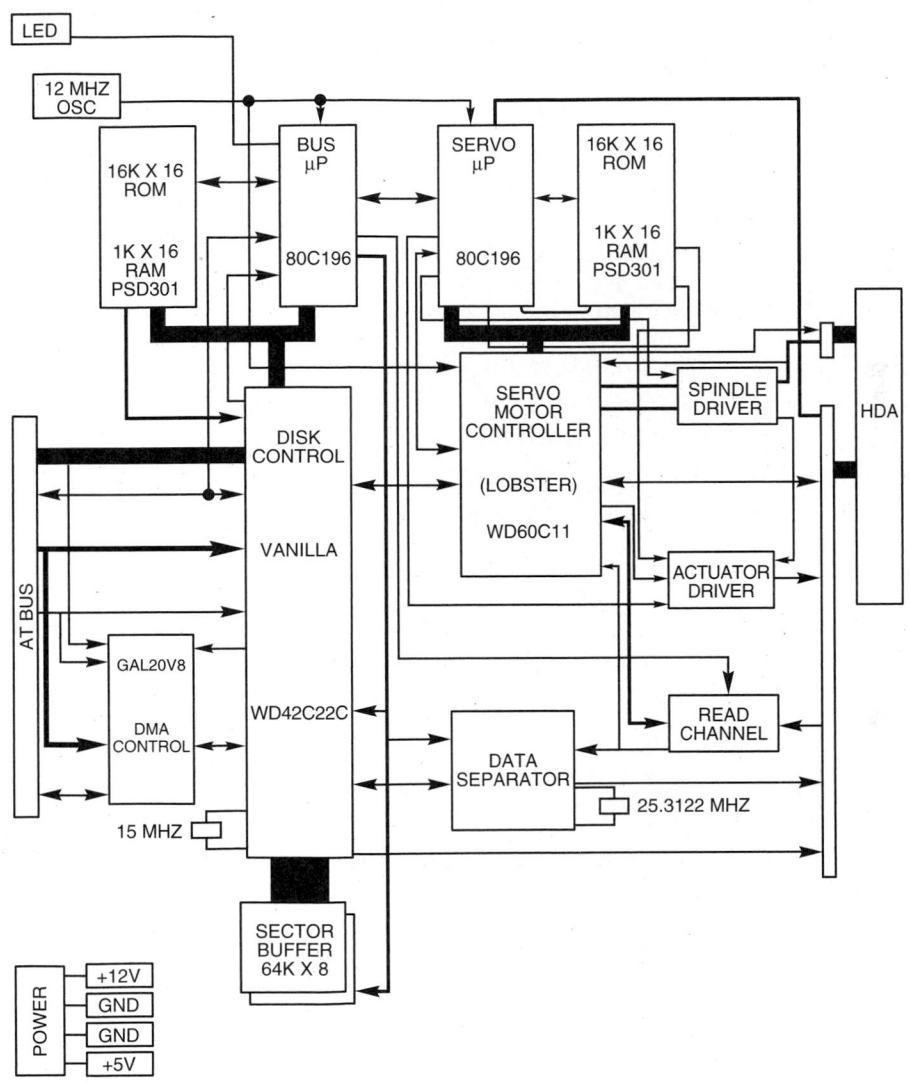

Figure 8.13 *Western Digital WD-AP4200 200MB ATA-IDE drive logic-board block diagram.*

To top off this example, study the logic diagram in Figure 8.15 for the WD 1006V-MM1, which is an ST-506/412 controller.

You can clearly see that the main LSI chip onboard is the same WD42C22 disk controller chip used in the IDE and SCSI drives. Here is what the technical reference literature says about that chip:

The WD42C22 integrates a high performance, low cost Winchester controller's architecture. The WD42C22 integrates the central elements of a Winchester controller subsystem such as the host interface, buffer manager, disk formatter/controller, encoder/decoder, CRC/ECC (Cyclic Redundancy Check/Error Correction Code) generator/checker, and drive interface into a single 84-pin PQFP (Plastic Quad Flat Pack) device.

The virtually identical design of ATA-IDE and SCSI drives is not unique to Western Digital. Most drive manufacturers design their ATA-IDE and SCSI drives the same way, often using these very same WD chips, and disk controller and SCSI bus interface chips from other manufacturers. You now should be able to understand that most SCSI drives are "regular" ATA-IDE drives with SCSI bus logic added. This fact will come up again later in this chapter in the section "SCSI Versus IDE: Advantages and Limitations," which discusses performance and other issues differentiating these interfaces.

For another example, I have several old IBM 320MB and 400MB embedded SCSI-2 hard disks; each of these drives has onboard a WD-10C00 Programmable Disk Controller in the form of a 68-pin PLCC (Plastic Leaded Chip Carrier) chip. The technical literature states:

This chip supports ST412, ESDI, SMD and Optical interfaces. It has 27Mbit/sec maximum transfer rate and an internal, fully programmable 48- or 32-bit ECC, 16-bit CRC-CCITT or external user defined ECC polynomial, fully programmable sector sizes, and 1.25 micron low power CMOS design.

In addition, these particular embedded SCSI drives include the 33C93 SCSI Bus Interface Controller chip, which also is used in the other SCSI drive that I mentioned. Again, there is a distinctly separate disk controller, and the SCSI interface is added on.

So again, most embedded SCSI drives have a built-in disk controller (usually based on previous ST-506/412 or ESDI designs) and additional logic to interface that controller to the SCSI bus (a built-in bridge controller, if you like). Now think about this from a performance standpoint. If virtually all SCSI drives really are ATA-IDE drives with an SCSI Bus Interface Controller chip added, what conclusions can you draw?

First, no drive can perform sustained data transfers faster than the data can actually be read from the disk platters. In other words, the HDA limits performance to whatever it is capable of achieving. Drives can transmit data in short bursts at very high speeds, because they often have built-in cache or read-ahead buffers that store data. Many of the newer high-performance SCSI and ATA-IDE drives have 1M or more of cache memory onboard. No matter how big or intelligent the cache is, however, sustained data transfer still will be limited by the HDA.

▶▶ See "ATA IDE," p. 512.

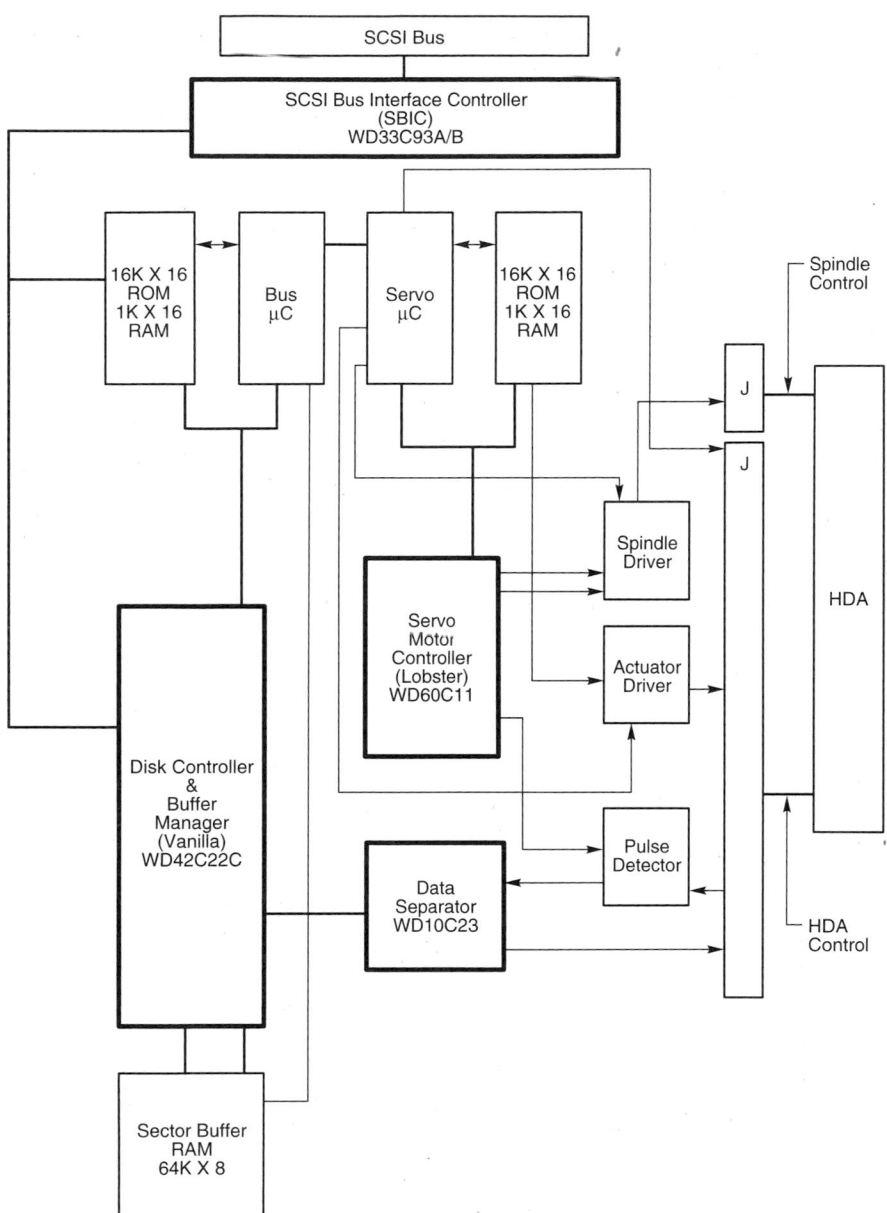

Figure 8.14   Western Digital WD-SP4200 200MB SCSI drive logic-board block diagram.

Data from the HDA must pass through the disk controller circuits, which, as you have seen, are virtually identical between similar SCSI and ATA-IDE drives. In the ATA-IDE drive, this data then is presented directly to the system bus. In the SCSI drive, however, the data must pass through an

Magnetic Storage

Permanent or semi-permanent computer data storage works by way of either optical or magnetic principles, or in some cases a combination of the two. In the case of magnetic storage, a stream of binary computer data bits (zeros and ones) are stored by magnetizing tiny pieces of metal embedded on the surface of a disk or tape in a pattern that represents the data. Later this magnetic pattern can be read and converted back into the exact same stream of bits you started with. This is the principle of magnetic storage, and the subject of this chapter.

Magnetic storage is often difficult for people to understand because magnetic fields cannot be seen by the human eye. This chapter explains the principles, concepts, and techniques behind modern computer magnetic storage, allowing you to understand what is happening behind the scenes. This information is designed for those who have an insatiable curiosity about how these things work; it is not absolutely necessary to use a PC or perform routine troubleshooting, maintenance, or upgrades. Since the data I store on my hard drives, tape drives, floppy drives, and other magnetic storage devices happens to be far more important to me than the devices themselves, knowing how my data is handled makes me feel much more comfortable with the system in general. Having an understanding of the underlying technology does help when it comes to dealing with problems that might arise.

This chapter covers magnetic storage principles and technology, and can be considered an introduction to several other chapters in the book, including the following:

- *Chapter 10.* "Hard Disk Storage"
- *Chapter 11.* "Floppy Disk Storage"
- *Chapter 12.* "High-Capacity Removable Disk Storage"
- *Chapter 14.* "Physical Drive Installation and Configuration"

Note

Optical Storage—CD-ROM technology—is covered in Chapter 14.

Consult these chapters for more specific information on different types of magnetic and optical storage, as well as drive installation and configuration.

History of Magnetic Storage

Before there was magnetic storage for computers, the primary storage medium was punched cards. What is amazing to me is that I missed contact with punched cards by about a year; the college I went to discontinued using them during my freshman year, before I was able to take any computer-related courses. I have to believe that this was more a reflection on their budget and lack of focus on current technology at the time (in 1979, there really weren't many punch-card readers being used in the field) than it is on my age!

The history of magnetic storage dates back to June 1949, when a group of IBM engineers and scientists began working on a new storage device. What they were working on was the first magnetic storage device for computers, and it revolutionized the industry. On May 21, 1952, IBM announced the IBM 726 Tape Unit with the IBM 701 Defense Calculator, marking the transition from punched-card calculators to electronic computers.

Four years later, on September 13, 1956, a small team of IBM engineers in San Jose, California introduced the first computer disk storage system—the 305 RAMAC (Random Access Method of Accounting and Control).

The 305 RAMAC could store 5 million characters (that's right, only 5MB!) of data on 50 disks, each a whopping 24 inches in diameter. Unlike tape drives, RAMAC's recording heads could go directly to any location on a disk surface without reading all the information in between. This random accessibility had a profound effect on computer performance at the time, allowing data to be stored and retrieved significantly faster than if on tape.

From these beginnings, the magnetic storage industry has progressed such that today you can store 50GB or more on tiny 3.5-inch drives that fit into a single computer drive bay.

IBM's contributions to the history and development of magnetic storage are incredible; in fact, most have either come directly from IBM or as a result of IBM research. Not only did IBM invent computer magnetic tape storage as well as the hard disk drive, but they also invented the floppy drive. The same San Jose facility where the hard drive was created introduced the first floppy drive, then using 8-inch diameter floppy disks, in 1971. The team that developed the drive was led by Alan Shugart, a now legendary figure in computer storage.

Since then, IBM has pioneered advanced magnetic data encoding schemes such as MFM (Modified Frequency Modulation) and RLL (Run Length Limited); drive head designs such as Thin Film, Magneto-Resistive (MR), and Giant Magneto-Resistive (GMR) heads; and drive technologies such as PRML (Partial Response Maximum Likelihood), No-ID recording, and Self-Monitoring Analysis and Reporting Technology (S.M.A.R.T.). Today, IBM is arguably the leader in developing and implementing new drive technology, and is second in sales only to Seagate Technology in PC hard drives.

How Magnetic Fields Are Used to Store Data

All magnetic storage devices, such as floppy disk drives and hard disk drives, read and write data by using electromagnetism. This basic principle of physics states that as an electric current flows through a conductor (wire), a magnetic field is generated around the conductor (see Figure 9.1).

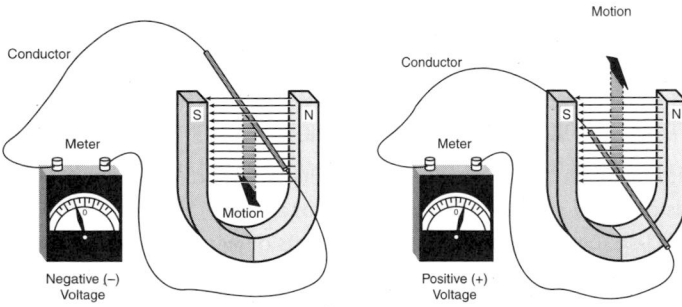

Figure 9.1   Current is induced in a wire when passed through a magnetic field.

Magneto-Resistive (MR) Heads

A more recent development in magnetic recording, or more specifically, the read phase of magnetic recording, is the magneto-resistive head. All heads are detectors, that is they are designed to detect the flux transitions in the media and convert them back to an electrical signal that can be interpreted as data. One problem with magnetic recording is the ever increasing desire for more and more density, which is putting more information (flux transitions) in a smaller and smaller space. As the magnetic domains on the disk get smaller, the signal from the heads during reading operations becomes weaker; it becomes difficult to distinguish the true signal from the random noise or stray fields present. What is needed is a more efficient read head, which is a more efficient way to detect these transitions on the disk.

Long ago another effect of magnetism on a wire was discovered. When a wire was passed through a magnetic field, not only did the wire generate a small current, but the resistance of the wire also changed. Standard read heads use the head as a tiny generator, relying on the fact that the heads will generate a pulsed current when passed over magnetic flux transitions. A newer type of head design pioneered by IBM instead relies on the fact that the resistance in the head wires will also change.

Rather than use the head to generate tiny currents, which must then be filtered, amplified, and decoded, a magnetoresistive (MR) head uses the head as a resistor. A circuit passes a voltage through the head and watches for the voltage to change, which will occur when the resistance of the head changes as it passes through the flux reversals on the media. This mechanism for using the head results in a much stronger and clearer signal of what was on the media, and makes it possible for density to be increased.

Note that the MR scheme only works for reading—any time an MR read head is employed there is a separate standard inductive head used for writing the data. By incorporating separate read and write heads, they can both be optimized for their purpose and made to work much more efficiently than a single head that does both. In the last few years, virtually all modern hard disks have converted to using MR heads for reading. MR heads are capable of increasing density four times over the previous inductive-only heads. IBM introduced the first drive with MR heads in 1991, with their 1GB 3.5-inch models.

In the quest for even more density, a new type of MR head was introduced by IBM in 1997. Called giant magnetoresistive (GMR) heads, they are physically smaller than standard MR heads, but are so named for the GMR effect on which they are based.

The GMR effect was first discovered in 1988 in crystal samples exposed to very high-powered magnetic fields (1,000 times the fields used in HDDs). It was discovered that there were very large resistance changes occurring in materials comprised of alternating very thin layers of various metallic elements. The key structure in GMR materials is a spacer layer of a non-magnetic metal between two magnetic metals. Magnetic materials tend to align themselves in the same direction. So if the spacer layer is thin enough, changing the orientation of one of the magnetic layers can cause the next one to align itself in the same direction. What was determined was that the magnetic alignment of the magnetic layers periodically swung back and forth from being aligned in the same magnetic direction to being aligned in opposite magnetic directions. The overall resistance is relatively low when the layers were in the same alignment and relatively high when in opposite alignment.

When a weak magnetic field, such as that from a bit on a hard disk, passes beneath a GMR head, the magnetic orientation of one of the magnetic layers rotates relative to that of the other, generating a significant change in electrical resistance due to the GMR effect. Since the physical nature of the resistance change was determined to be caused by the relative spin of the electrons in the different layers, GMR heads are often referred to as *spin-valve heads*.

In December 1997, IBM announced a 16.8GB 3.5-inch HDD product using GMR heads for the high-performance desktop market—the industry's first GMR storage product. Currently GMR heads are found in many drives, and GMR will become the dominant head technology for the year 2000 and beyond.

Data Encoding Schemes

Magnetic storage is essentially an analog medium. The data that a PC stores on it, however, is digital information—that is, ones and zeros. When the drive sends digital information to a magnetic recording head, the head creates magnetic domains on the storage medium with specific polarities corresponding to the positive and negative voltages that the drive applies to the head. It is the flux reversals that form the boundaries between the areas of positive and negative polarity that the drive controller uses to encode the digital data onto the analog medium. During a read operation, each flux reversal that the drive detects generates a positive or negative pulse that the device uses to reconstruct the original binary data.

To optimize the placement of flux transitions during magnetic storage, the drive passes the raw digital input data through a device called an encoder/decoder (endec), which converts the raw binary information to a waveform that is designed to optimally place the flux transitions (pulses) on the media. During a read operation, the endec reverses the process and decodes the pulse train back into the original binary data. Over the years, several different schemes for encoding data in this manner have been developed; some are better or more efficient than others, which you see later in this section.

Other descriptions of the data encoding process may be much simpler, but they omit the facts that make some of the issues related to hard drive reliability so critical—namely, timing. Engineers and designers are constantly "pushing the envelope" to stuff more and more bits of information into the limited quantity of magnetic flux reversals per inch. What they came up with, essentially, is a design in which the bits of information are not only decoded from the presence or absence of flux reversals, but from the timing between them. The more accurately they can time the reversals, the more information that can be encoded (and subsequently decoded) from that timing information.

In any form of binary signaling, the use of timing is significant. When interpreting a read or write waveform, the timing of each voltage transition event is critical. Timing is what defines a particular bit or transition cell, that is the time window within which the drive is either writing or reading a transition. If the timing is off, a given voltage transition may be recognized at the wrong time as being in a different cell, which would throw the conversion or encoding off, resulting in bits being missed, added, or misinterpreted. To ensure that the timing is precise, the transmitting and receiving devices must be in perfect synchronization. For example, if recording a zero is done by placing no transition on the disk for a given time period or cell, imagine recording 10 zero bits in a row—you would have a long period of 10 time periods or cells with no transitions.

Imagine now that the clock on the encoder was slightly off when reading from when the data was actually written. If it were fast, it might think that during this long stretch of 10 cells with no transitions only nine cells had elapsed. Or if it were slow, it might think that 11 cells had elapsed instead. In either case this would result in a read error, meaning the same bits would not be read as they were written. To prevent timing errors in drive encoding/decoding, perfect synchronization is necessary between the reading and writing processes. This synchronization is often accomplished by adding a separate timing signal, called a *clock signal*, to the transmission between the two devices. It is also possible for the clock and data signals to be combined and transmitted as a single signal. Most magnetic data encoding schemes use this type of combination of clock and data signals.

Adding a clock signal to the data ensures that the communicating devices can accurately interpret the individual bit cells. Each bit cell is bounded by two other cells containing the clock transitions. By sending clock information along with the data, the clocks remain in synch, even if the medium contains a long string of identical zero bits. Unfortunately, the transition cells that are used solely for timing take up space on the medium that could otherwise be used for data.

Because the number of flux transitions that a drive can record in a given space on a particular medium is limited by the physical nature or density of the medium and the head technology, drive engineers have developed various ways of encoding the data by using a minimum number of flux reversals (taking into consideration the fact that some flux reversals used solely for clocking are required). Signal encoding enables the system to make the maximum use of a given drive hardware technology.

Although various encoding schemes have been tried, only a few are popular today. Over the years, these three basic types have been the most popular:

- Frequency Modulation (FM)
- Modified Frequency Modulation (MFM)
- Run Length Limited (RLL)

The following sections examine these codes, discuss how they work, where they are used, and any advantages or disadvantages that apply to them. It will help to refer to Figure 9.5 (later in the chapter) as you read the descriptions of each of these encoding schemes, as this figure depicts how each of these schemes would store an "X" on the same media.

FM Encoding

One of the earliest techniques for encoding data for magnetic storage is called Frequency Modulation (FM) encoding. This encoding scheme, sometimes called Single Density encoding, was used in the earliest floppy disk drives installed in PC systems. The original Osborne portable computer, for example, used these Single-Density floppy disk drives, which stored about 80KB of data on a single disk. Although it was popular until the late 1970s, FM encoding is no longer used.

MFM Encoding

Modified Frequency Modulation (MFM) encoding was devised to reduce the number of flux reversals used in the original FM encoding scheme and, therefore, to pack more data onto the disk. MFM encoding minimizes the use of clock transitions, leaving more room for the data. MFM records clock transitions only when a stored zero bit is preceded by another zero bit; in all other cases, a clock transition is not required. Because MFM minimizes the use of clock transitions, it can double the clock frequency used by FM encoding, enabling it to store twice as many data bits in the same number of flux transitions.

Because it is twice as efficient as FM encoding, MFM encoding also has been called Double-Density recording. MFM is used in virtually all PC floppy disk drives today and was used in nearly all PC hard disks for a number of years. Today, virtually all hard disks use RLL (Run Length Limited) encoding, which provides even greater efficiency than MFM.

Because MFM encoding writes twice as many data bits by using the same number of flux reversals as FM, the clock speed of the data is doubled, so the drive actually sees the same number of total flux reversals as with FM. This means that a drive using MFM encoding reads and writes data at twice the speed of FM, even though the drive sees the flux reversals arriving at the same frequency as in FM.

The only caveat is that MFM encoding requires improved disk controller and drive circuitry, because the timing of the flux reversals must be more precise than in FM. These improvements were not difficult to achieve, and MFM encoding became the most popular encoding scheme for many years.

Table 9.1 shows the data bit to flux reversal translation in MFM encoding.

Table 9.1   MFM Data to Flux Transition Encoding

Data Bit Value	Flux Encoding
1	NT
0 preceded by 0	TN
0 preceded by 1	NN

T = Flux transition
N = No flux transition

RLL Encoding

Today's most popular encoding scheme for hard disks, called RLL (Run Length Limited), packs up to two times more information on a given disk than MFM does and three times as much information as FM. In RLL encoding, the drive combines groups of bits into a unit to generate specific patterns of flux reversals. By combining the clock and data signals in these patterns, the clock rate can be further increased while maintaining the same basic distance between the flux transitions on the storage medium.

IBM invented RLL encoding and first used the method in many of its mainframe disk drives. During the late 1980s, the PC hard disk industry began using RLL encoding schemes to increase the storage capabilities of PC hard disks. Today, virtually every drive on the market uses some form of RLL encoding.

Instead of encoding a single bit, RLL normally encodes a group of data bits at a time. The term *Run Length Limited* is derived from the two primary specifications of these codes, which are the minimum number (the run length) and maximum number (the run limit) of transition cells allowed between two actual flux transitions. Several variations of the scheme are achieved by changing the length and limit parameters, but only two have achieved any real popularity: RLL 2,7 and RLL 1,7.

You can even express FM and MFM encoding as a form of RLL. FM can be called RLL 0,1, because there are as few as zero and as many as one transition cells separating two flux transitions. MFM can be called RLL 1,3, because there are as few as one and as many as three transition cells separating two flux transitions. (Although these codes can be expressed as variations of RLL form, it is not common to do so.)

RLL 2,7 was initially the most popular RLL variation because it offers a high-density ratio with a transition detection window that is the same relative size as that in MFM. This method provides high storage density and fairly good reliability. In very high-capacity drives, however, RLL 2,7 did not prove to be reliable enough. Most of today's highest capacity drives use RLL 1,7 encoding, which offers a density ratio 1.27 times that of MFM and a larger transition detection window relative to MFM. Because of the larger relative timing window or cell size within which a transition can be detected, RLL 1,7 is a more forgiving and more reliable code, which is important when media and head technology are being pushed to their limits.

Another little-used RLL variation called RLL 3,9—sometimes called ARLL (Advanced RLL)—allows an even higher density ratio than RLL 2,7. Unfortunately, reliability suffered too greatly under the RLL 3,9 scheme; the method was used by only a few now-obsolete controllers and has all but disappeared.

It is difficult to understand how RLL codes work without looking at an example. Within a given RLL variation such as RLL 2,7 or 1,7, you can construct many different flux transition encoding tables to demonstrate how particular groups of bits are encoded into flux transitions.

In the conversion table shown in Table 9.2, specific groups of data bits 2, 3, and 4 bits long are translated into strings of flux transitions 4, 6, and 8 transition cells long, respectively. The selected transitions for a particular bit sequence are designed to ensure that flux transitions do not occur too close together or too far apart.

It is necessary to limit how close two flux transitions can be because of the fixed resolution capabilities of the head and the storage medium. Limiting how far apart two flux transitions can be ensures that the clocks in the devices remain in sync.

Table 9.2   RLL 2,7 Data to Flux Transition Encoding

Data Bit Values	Flux Encoding
10	NTNN
11	TNNN
000	NNNTNN
010	TNNTNN
011	NNTNNN
0010	NNTNNTNN
0011	NNNNTNNN

T = Flux transition
N = No flux transition

In studying this table, you might think that encoding a byte value such as 00000001b would be impossible because no combinations of data bit groups fit this byte. Encoding this type of byte is not a problem, however, because the controller does not transmit individual bytes; instead, the controller sends whole sectors, making it possible to encode such a byte by including some of the bits in the following byte. The only real problem occurs in the last byte of a sector, if additional bits are needed to complete the final group sequence. In these cases, the endec in the controller adds excess bits to the end of the last byte. These excess bits are truncated during any reads so the controller always decodes the last byte correctly.

Encoding Scheme Comparisons

Figure 9.5 shows an example of the waveform written to store the ASCII character X on a hard disk drive by using three different encoding schemes.

In each of these encoding scheme examples, the top line shows the individual data bits (01011000b, for example) in their bit cells separated in time by the clock signal, which is shown as a period (.). Below that line is the actual write waveform, showing the positive and negative voltages as well as head voltage transitions that result in the recording of flux transitions. The bottom line shows the transition cells, with T representing a transition cell that contains a flux transition and N representing a transition cell that is empty.

The FM encoding example shown in Figure 9.5 is easy to explain. Each bit cell has two transition cells: one for the clock information and one for the data itself. All the clock transition cells contain flux transitions, and the data transition cells contain a flux transition only if the data is a 1 bit. No transition is present when the data is a 0 bit. Starting from the left, the first data bit is 0, which decodes as a flux transition pattern of TN. The next bit is a 1, which decodes as TT. The next bit is 0, which decodes as TN, and so on.

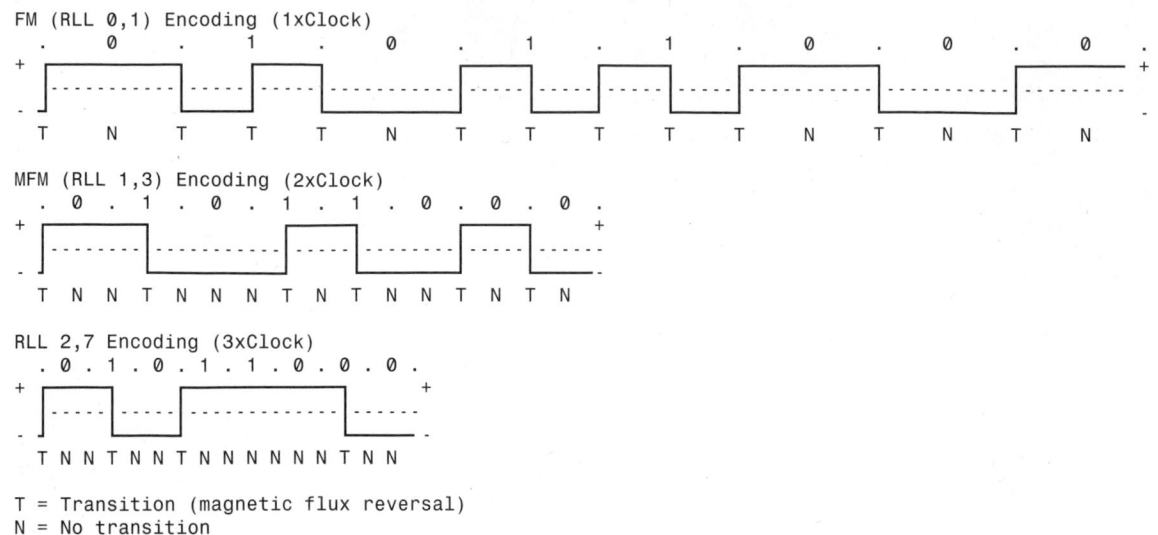

FM (RLL 0,1) Encoding (1xClock)

MFM (RLL 1,3) Encoding (2xClock)

RLL 2,7 Encoding (3xClock)

T = Transition (magnetic flux reversal)
N = No transition
. = Data bit window boundaries (Clock timing)

Figure 9.5 ASCII character "X" write waveforms using FM, MFM, and RLL 2,7 encoding.

The MFM encoding scheme also has clock and data transition cells for each data bit to be recorded. As you can see, however, the clock transition cells carry a flux transition only when a zero bit is stored after another zero bit. Starting from the left, the first bit is a 0, and the preceding bit is unknown (assume 0), so the flux transition pattern is TN for that bit. The next bit is a 1, which always decodes to a transition-cell pattern of NT. The next bit is 0, which was preceded by 1, so the pattern stored is NN. By using Table 9.1 (shown earlier), you can easily trace the MFM encoding pattern to the end of the byte. You can see that the minimum and maximum number of transition cells between any two flux transitions are one and three, respectively, which explains why MFM encoding can also be called RLL 1,3.

The RLL 2,7 pattern is more difficult to see because it encodes groups of bits rather than individual bits. Starting from the left, the first group that matches the groups listed in Table 9.2 are the first three bits, 010. These bits are translated into a flux transition pattern of TNNTNN. The next two bits, 11, are translated as a group to TNNN; and the final group, 000 bits, is translated to NNNTNN to complete the byte. As you can see in this example, no additional bits were needed to finish the last group.

Notice that the minimum and maximum number of empty transition cells between any two flux transitions in this example are 2 and 6, although a different example could show a maximum of seven empty transition cells. This is where the RLL 2,7 designation comes from. Because even fewer transitions are recorded than in MFM, the clock rate can be increased to three times that of FM or 1.5 times that of MFM, thus storing more data in the same space. Notice, however, that the resulting write waveform itself looks exactly like a typical FM or MFM waveform in terms of the number and separation of the flux transitions for a given physical portion of the disk. In other words, the physical minimum and maximum distances between any two flux transitions remain the same in all three of these encoding scheme examples.

PRML (Partial-Response, Maximum-Likelihood) Decoders

Another feature in high-end hard disk drives involves the disk read circuitry. Read channel circuits using Partial-Response, Maximum-Likelihood (PRML) technology enable disk drive manufacturers to increase the amount of data stored on a disk platter by up to 40 percent. PRML replaces the standard "detect one peak at a time" approach of traditional analog peak-detect, read/write channels with digital signal processing.

As the data density of hard drives increase, the drive must necessarily record the flux reversals closer together on the medium. This makes it more difficult to read the data on the disk, because the adjacent magnetic peaks can begin to interfere with each other. PRML modifies the way that the drive reads the data from the disk. The controller analyzes the analog data stream it receives from the heads by using digital signal sampling, processing, and detection algorithms (this is the partial response element) and predicts the sequence of bits that the data stream is most likely to represent (the maximum likelihood element). PRML technology can take an analog waveform, which might be filled with noise and stray signals, and produce an accurate reading from it.

This may not sound like a very precise method of reading data that must be bit-perfect to be usable, but the aggregate effect of the digital signal processing filters out the noise efficiently enough to enable the drive to place the flux change pulses much closer together on the platter, thus achieving greater densities. Most modern drives now use PRML technology in their endec circuits.

Capacity Measurements

The industry standard abbreviations for the units used to measure the capacity of magnetic (and other) drives are shown in Table 9.3.

Table 9.3   Standard Abbreviations and Meanings

Abbreviation	Description	Decimal Power	Decimal Value	Binary Power	Binary Value
Kbit or Kb	Kilobit	10^3	1,000	2^{10}	1,024
K or KB	Kilobyte	10^3	1,000	2^{10}	1,024
Mbit or Mb	Megabit	10^6	1,000,000	2^{20}	1,048,576
M or MB	Megabyte	10^6	1,000,000	2^{20}	1,048,576
Gbit or Gb	Gigabit	10^9	1,000,000,000	2^{30}	1,073,741,824
G or GB	Gigabyte	10^9	1,000,000,000	2^{30}	1,073,741,824
Tbit or Tb	Terabit	10^{12}	1,000,000,000,000	2^{40}	1,099,511,627,776
T or TB	Terabyte	10^{12}	1,000,000,000,000	2^{40}	1,099,511,627,776

As you can see, each of these units of measurement has two possible values: a decimal (or metric) and a binary. Unfortunately, there are no differences in the abbreviations used to indicate these two types of values. In other words, M can indicate both "millions of bytes" and megabytes. In general, memory values are expressed by using the binary values, although disk capacities can go either way. This often leads to confusion in reporting disk capacities, because many manufacturers tend to use whichever value makes their products look better. Note also that when bits and bytes are used as part of some other measurement, the difference between bits and bytes is often distinguished by the use of a lower- or uppercase B. For example, megabits are typically abbreviated with a lowercase b, resulting in the abbreviation Mbps for megabits per second, while MBps indicates megabytes per second.

I hope that this examination of the basic principles of magnetic storage and the different encoding schemes that magnetic devices use has taken some of the mystery out of the way data is recorded on a drive.

Hard Disk Storage

SOME OF THE MAIN TOPICS IN THIS CHAPTER ARE

Definition of a Hard Disk

Hard Drive Advancements

Areal Density

Hard Disk Drive Operation

Basic Hard Disk Drive Components

Hard Disk Features

Definition of a Hard Disk

To many users, the hard disk drive is the most important and yet the most mysterious part of a computer system. A *hard disk drive* is a sealed unit that a PC uses for nonvolatile data storage. *Nonvolatile*, or permanent storage, in this case, means that the storage device retains the data even when there is no power supplied to the computer. Because the hard disk drive is expected to retain its data until a user deliberately erases it, the PC uses it to store its most crucial programming and data. As a result, when the hard disk fails, the consequences are usually very serious. To maintain, service, and expand a PC system properly, you must understand how the hard disk unit functions.

Most computer users want to know how hard disk drives work and what to do when a problem occurs. However, few books about hard disks cover this subject in the detail necessary for the PC technician or sophisticated user. This section corrects that situation by thoroughly describing the hard disk drive from a physical, mechanical, and electrical point of view.

A hard disk drive contains rigid, disk-shaped platters, usually constructed of aluminum or glass. Unlike floppy disks, the platters cannot bend or flex—hence the term hard disk. In most hard disk drives, you cannot remove the platters, which is why they are sometimes called fixed disk drives. Removable hard disk drives are also available. Sometimes this term refers to a device in which the entire drive unit (that is, the disk and the drive) is removable, but it is more commonly used to refer to cartridge drives, such as the Iomega Zip and Jaz drives, that have removable storage media.

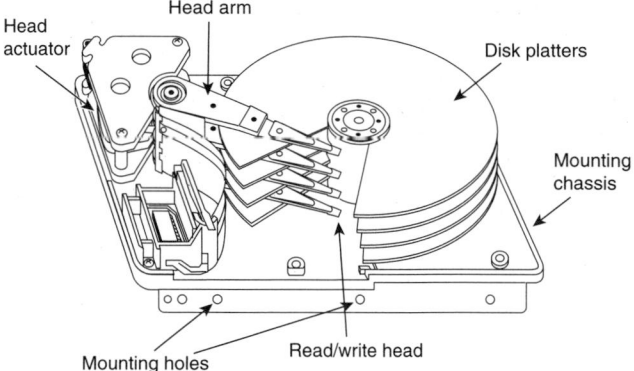

Figure 10.1   Hard disk heads and platters.

Note

Hard disk drives were at one time called *Winchester drives*. This term dates back to the 1960s, when IBM developed a high-speed hard disk drive that had 30MB of fixed-platter storage and 30MB of removable-platter storage. That drive soon received the nickname Winchester after the famous Winchester 30-30 rifle. For a time after that, all drives that used a high-speed spinning platter with a floating head were known colloquially as Winchester drives.

Hard Drive Advancements

In the 15 or more years that hard disks have commonly been used in PC systems, they have undergone tremendous changes. To give you an idea of how far hard drives have come in that time, I've outlined some of the more profound changes in PC hard disk storage:

- Maximum storage capacities have increased from the 10MB 5 1/4-inch full-height drives available in 1982 to 40GB or more for small 3 1/2-inch half-height drives, and 20GB or more for notebook system 2 1/2-inch drives. Hard drives smaller than 4GB are rare in today's personal computers.

- Data transfer rates from the media (sustained transfer rates) have increased from 85 to 102KBytes/sec for the original IBM XT in 1983 to 30MBytes/sec or more for some of the fastest drives today.

- Average seek times have decreased from more than 85ms (milliseconds) for the 10MB XT hard disk in 1983 to 5ms or less for some of the fastest drives today.

- In 1982, a 10MB drive cost more than $1,500 ($150 per megabyte). Today, the cost of hard drives has dropped to between 1 and 2 cents per megabyte or less!

Areal Density

Areal density is often used as a technology growth-rate indicator for the hard disk drive industry. *Areal density* is defined as the product of the linear bits per inch (BPI), measured along the length of the tracks around the disk, multiplied by the number of tracks per inch (TPI), measured radially on the disk. The results are expressed in units of megabits or gigabits per square inch (Mbit/sq.-inch or Gbit/sq.-inch) and are used as a measure of efficiency in drive recording technology. Current high-end 3 1/2-inch drives record at areal densities of nearly 6Gbit/sq.-inch. Prototype drives with densities as high as 20Gbit/sq.-inch now exist, providing capacities of more than 10GB on a single 2 1/2-inch platter.

During 1998, IBM introduced a drive they call the MicroDrive, which can store 340MB on a single platter the size of a quarter! This type of drive can be used in information appliances, digital cameras, and anywhere else that flash memory cards have been used.

Areal density (and, therefore, drive capacity) has been doubling approximately every two to three years, which will soon enable manufacturers to build 20 or 30GB drives that fit in the palm of your hand. Companies are also developing new media and head technologies to support these higher areal densities, such as ceramic or glass platters, MR (Magneto-Resistive) heads, pseudo-contact recording, and PRML (Partial-Response, Maximum-Likelihood) electronics. The primary challenge in achieving higher densities is manufacturing drive heads and disks to operate at closer tolerances. To fit more data on a platter of a given size, the tracks must be placed closer together, and the heads must be capable of achieving greater precision in their placement over the tracks. This means that as hard disk capacities increase, heads must ride ever closer to the disk surface.

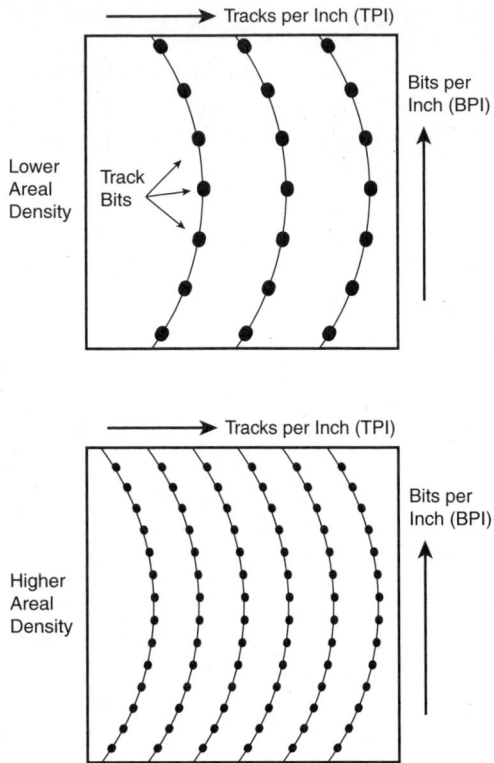

Figure 10.2 Areal density, combining tracks per inch and bits per inch.

Hard Disk Drive Operation

The basic physical construction of a hard disk drive consists of spinning disks with heads that move over the disks and store data in tracks and sectors. The heads read and write data in concentric rings called tracks, which are divided up into segments called sectors, which normally store 512 bytes each (see Figure 10.3).

Hard disk drives usually have multiple disks, called platters, that are stacked on top of each other and spin in unison, each with two sides on which the drive stores data. Most drives have at least two or three platters, resulting in four or six sides, and some drives have up to 11 or more platters. The identically positioned tracks on each side of every platter together make up a cylinder (see Figure 10.4). A hard disk drive normally has one head per platter side, with all the heads mounted on a common carrier device or rack. The heads move radially in and out across the disk in unison; they cannot move independently, because they are mounted on the same rack.

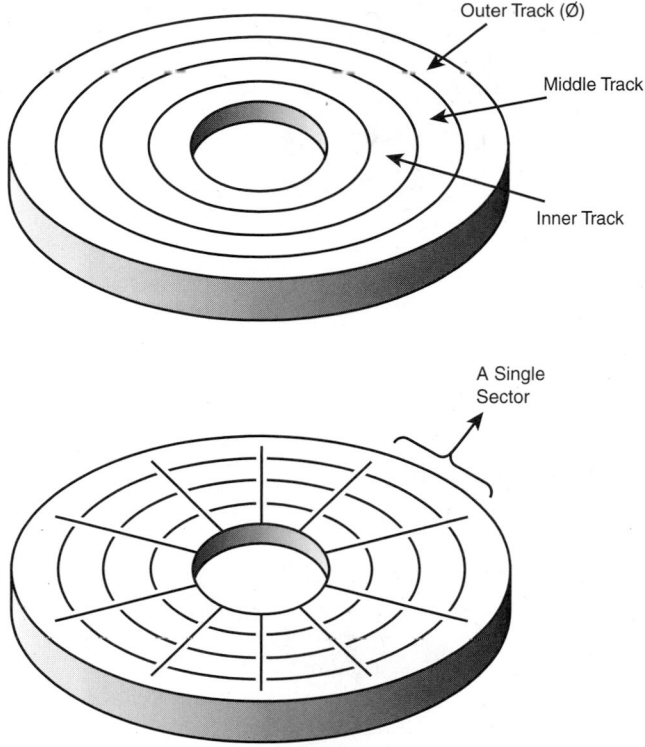

Figure 10.3 The tracks and sectors on a disk.

Originally, most hard disks spun at 3,600 rpm—approximately 10 times faster than a floppy disk drive. Until recently, 3,600rpm was pretty much a constant among hard drives. Now, however, quite a few hard drives spin the disks even faster. The Toshiba 3.3G drive in one of my notebook computers spins at 4,852rpm; other drives spin as fast as 5,400, 5,600, 6,400, 7,200, and even 10,000rpm. High rotational speeds combined with a fast head-positioning mechanism and more sectors per track are what make one hard disk faster than another.

The heads in most hard disk drives do not (and should not!) touch the platters during normal operation. When the heads are powered off, however, in most drives they land on the platters as they stop spinning. While the drive is running, a very thin cushion of air keeps each head suspended a short distance above or below the platter. If the air cushion is disturbed by a particle of dust or a shock, the head may come into contact with the platter while it is spinning at full speed. When contact with the spinning platters is forceful enough to do damage, the event is called a *head crash*. The result of a head crash can be anything from a few lost bytes of data to a completely ruined drive. Most drives have special lubricants on the platters and hardened surfaces that can withstand the daily "takeoffs and landings" as well as more severe abuse.

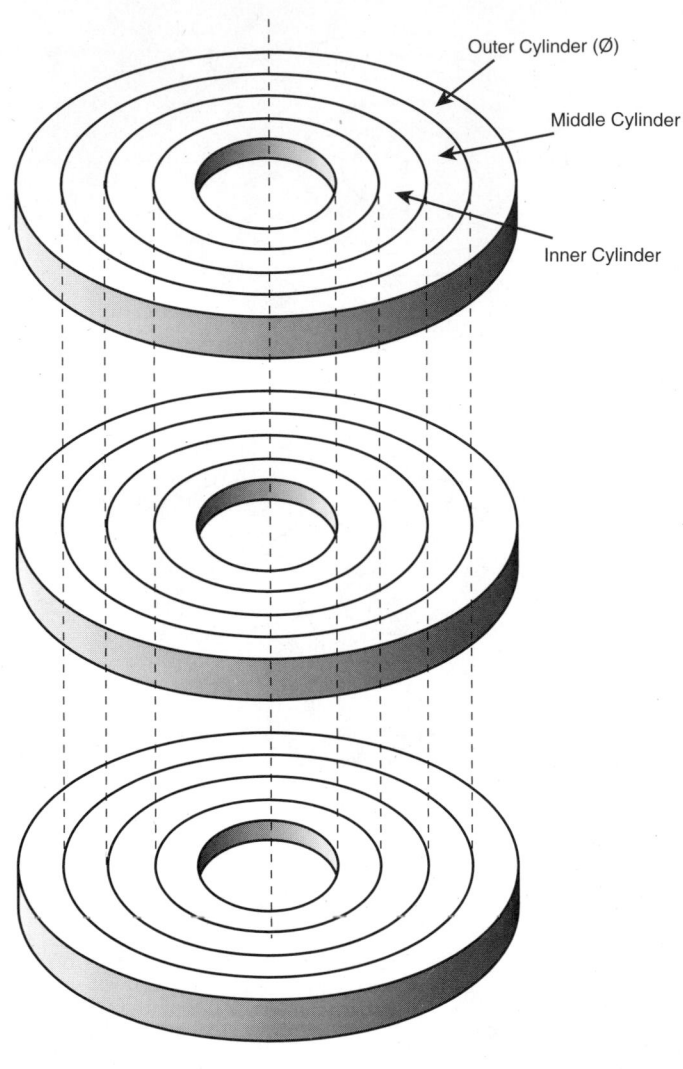

Cylinders

Figure 10.4 Cylinders.

Because the platter assemblies are sealed and non-removable, the track densities on the disk can be very high. Hard drives today have up to 20,000 or more TPI (tracks per inch) recorded on the media. Head Disk Assemblies (HDAs), which contain the platters, are assembled and sealed in clean rooms under absolutely sanitary conditions. Because few companies repair HDAs, repair or replacement of the parts inside a sealed HDA can be expensive. Every hard disk ever made eventually fails. The only questions are when the failure will occur and whether your data is backed up.

Caution

It is strongly recommended that you do not even attempt to open a hard disk drive's HDA unless you have the equipment and the expertise to make repairs inside. Most manufacturers deliberately make the HDA difficult to open, to discourage the intrepid do-it-yourselfer. Opening the HDA almost certainly voids the drive's warranty.

Many PC users think that hard disks are fragile, and comparatively speaking, they are one of the more fragile components in your PC. In my weekly PC Hardware and Troubleshooting or Data Recovery seminars, however, I have run various hard disks for days with the lids off, and have even removed and installed the covers while the drives were operating. Those drives continue to store data perfectly to this day with the lids either on or off. Of course, I do not recommend that you try this test with your own drives, nor would I do this with my larger, more expensive drives.

The Ultimate Hard Disk Drive Analogy

There is an old analogy that compares the interaction of the heads and the medium in a typical hard disk drive as being similar in scale to a 747 flying a few feet off the ground at cruising speed (500+ mph). I have heard this analogy used over and over again for years, and I've even used it in my seminars many times without checking to see whether the analogy is technically accurate with respect to modern hard drives. It isn't.

One highly inaccurate aspect of the 747 analogy has always bothered me—the use of an airplane of any type to describe the head-and-platter interaction. This analogy implies that the heads fly very low over the surface of the disk, but technically, this is not true. The heads do not fly at all in the traditional aerodynamic sense; instead, they float on a cushion of air that's being dragged around by the platters.

A much better analogy would use a hovercraft instead of an airplane; the action of a hovercraft much more closely emulates the action of the heads in a hard disk drive. Like a hovercraft, the drive heads rely somewhat on the shape of the bottom of the head to capture and control the cushion of air that keeps them floating over the disk. By nature, the cushion of air on which the heads float forms only in very close proximity to the platter, and is often called an *air bearing* by the disk drive industry.

I thought it was time to come up with a new analogy that more correctly describes the dimensions and speeds at which a hard disk drive operates today. I looked up the specifications on a specific hard disk drive, and then magnified and rescaled all the dimensions involved to make the head floating height equal to 1 inch. For my example, I used a Seagate model ST-12550N Barracuda 2 drive, which is a 2GB (formatted capacity), 3 1/2-inch SCSI-2 drive, hardly state of the art by today's rapidly changing standards. Table 10.1 shows the specifications of the Barracuda drive, as listed in the technical documentation.

Table 10.1 Seagate ST-12550N Barracuda 2, 3 1/2-inch, SCSI-2 Drive Specifications

Specification	Value	Unit of Measure
Linear density	52,187	Bits per inch (BPI)
Bit spacing	19.16	Micro-inches (μ-in)
Track density	3,047	Tracks per inch (TPI)
Track spacing	328.19	Micro-inches (μ-in)
Total tracks	2,707	Tracks
Rotational speed	7,200	Revolutions per minute (rpm)
Average head linear speed	53.55	Miles per hour (mph)
Head slider length	0.08	Inches
Head slider height	0.02	Inches
Head floating height	5	Micro-inches (μ-in)
Average seek time	8	Milliseconds (ms)

By interpreting these specifications, you can see that in this drive, the head sliders are about 0.08-inch long and 0.02-inch high. The heads float on a cushion of air about 5μ-in (millionths of an inch) from the surface of the disk while traveling at an average speed of 53.55mph (figuring an average track diameter of 2 1/2-inches). These heads read and write individual bits spaced only 19.16μ-in apart on tracks separated by only 328.19μ-in. The heads can move from one track to any other in only 8ms during an average seek operation.

To create my analogy, I magnified the scale to make the head floating height equal to 1 inch. Because 1 inch is 200,000 times greater than 5μ-in, I scaled up everything else by the same amount.

Magnified to such a scale, the heads of this typical hard disk in my analogy would be more than 1,300 feet long and 300 feet high (about the size of the Sears Tower lying sideways!) The heads would float on a cushion of air that travels at a speed of more than 10.7 million mph (2,975 miles per second), only 1 inch above the ground and reads data bits spaced a mere 3.83 inches apart on tracks separated by only 5.47 feet.

Because the average seek time of 8ms (.008 seconds) is defined as the time it takes to move the heads over one-third of the total tracks (about 902, in this case), each skyscraper-size head could move sideways to any track within a distance of 0.93 miles (902 tracks×5.47 feet). This results in an average sideways velocity of more than 420,000 mph (116 miles per second)!

The forward speed of this imaginary head is difficult to comprehend, so I'll elaborate. The diameter of the Earth at the equator is 7,926 miles, which means a circumference of about 24,900 miles. At 2,975 miles per second, this imaginary head would circle the Earth about once every 8 seconds!

This analogy should give you a new appreciation of the technological marvel that the modern hard disk drive actually represents. It makes the 747 analogy look rather archaic (not to mention totally inaccurate), doesn't it?

Tracks and Sectors

A *track* is a single ring of data on one side of a disk. A disk track is too large to manage data effectively as a single storage unit. Many disk tracks can store 100,000 or more bytes of data, which would be very inefficient for storing small files. For that reason, tracks are divided into several numbered divisions known as sectors. These sectors represent slices of the track.

Various types of disk drives split their disk tracks into different numbers of sectors, depending on the density of the tracks. For example, floppy disk formats use 8–36 sectors per track, although hard disks usually store data at a higher density and can use 17–100 or more sectors per track. The sectors created by the standard formatting procedure on a PC system have a capacity of 512 bytes, which has been one constant throughout the history of the PC.

The sectors on a track are numbered starting with 1, unlike the heads or cylinders that are numbered starting with 0. For example, a 1.44MB floppy disk contains 80 cylinders numbered from 0–79 and two heads numbered 0 and 1, while each track on each cylinder has 18 sectors numbered from 1–18.

When a disk is formatted, the formatting program creates ID areas before and after each sector's data that the disk controller uses for sector numbering and for identifying the start and end of each sector. These areas precede and follow each sector's data area, and consume some of the disk's total storage capacity. This accounts for the difference between a disk's unformatted and formatted capacities. Note that most modern hard drives are sold preformatted and only advertise the formatted capacity. The unformatted capacity is usually not mentioned anymore. Another interesting development is that IBM and others now make drives with ID-less recording, which means that the sectors are recorded without ID marks before and after each sector. This means that more of the disk can be used for actual data.

Each sector on a disk has a prefix portion, or header, that identifies the start of the sector and contains the sector number, as well as a suffix portion, or trailer, that contains a checksum (which helps ensure the integrity of the data contents). Each sector also contains 512 bytes of data. The low-level formatting process normally fills the data bytes with some specific value, such as F6h (hex), or some other test pattern used by the drive manufacturer. Some patterns are more difficult for the drive to encode/decode, so these patterns are normally used when the manufacturer is testing the drive during initial formatting. A special test pattern might cause errors to surface that a normal data pattern would not show. This way, the manufacturer can more accurately identify marginal sectors during testing.

Note

The type of disk formatting discussed here is a physical or low-level format, not the high-level format that you perform when you use the Windows 9x Explorer or the DOS FORMAT program on a disk. See the "Disk Formatting" section later in this chapter to learn about the difference between these two types of formatting.

The sector headers and trailers are independent of the operating system, the file system, and the files stored on the drive. In addition to the headers and trailers, there are gaps within the sectors, between the sectors on each track, and also between tracks, but none of these gaps contain usable

The Sector ID data consists of the Cylinder, Head, and Sector Number fields, as well as a CRC field used to verify the ID data. Most controllers use bit 7 of the Head Number field to mark a sector as bad during a low-level format or surface analysis. This convention is not absolute, however. Some controllers use other methods to mark a bad sector, but usually the mark involves one of the ID fields.

The WRITE TURN-ON GAP follows the ID field's CRC bytes and provides a pad to ensure a proper recording of the user data area that follows, as well as to allow full recovery of the ID CRC.

The user DATA field consists of all 512 bytes of data stored in the sector. This field is followed by a CRC field to verify the data. Although many controllers use two bytes of CRC here, the controller may implement a longer Error Correction Code (ECC) that requires more than two CRC bytes to store. The ECC data stored here provides the possibility of correcting errors in the DATA field as well as detecting them. The correction/detection capabilities depend on the ECC code the drive uses and its implementation by the controller. The WRITE TURN-OFF GAP is a pad that enables the ECC (CRC) bytes to be fully recovered.

The INTER-RECORD GAP provides a means to accommodate variances in drive spindle speeds. A track may have been formatted while the disk was running slightly slower than normal, and then written to while the disk was running slightly faster than normal. In such cases, this gap prevents the accidental overwriting of any information in the next sector. The actual size of this padding varies, depending on the speed of the DATA disk's rotation when the track was formatted and each time the DATA field is updated.

The PRE-INDEX GAP allows for speed tolerance over the entire track. This gap varies in size, depending on the variances in disk rotation speed and write-frequency tolerance at the time of formatting.

This sector prefix information is extremely important, because it contains the numbering information that defines the cylinder, head, and sector. So this information—except the DATA field, DATA CRC bytes, and WRITE TURN-OFF GAP—is written only during a low-level format.

Disk Formatting

There are two formatting procedures required before you can write user data to a disk:

- Physical, or low-level formatting
- Logical, or high-level formatting

When you format a blank floppy disk, the Windows 9x Explorer or the DOS FORMAT command performs both kinds of formats simultaneously. If the floppy was already formatted, DOS and Windows will default to doing only a high-level format.

A hard disk, however, requires two separate formatting operations. Moreover, a hard disk requires a third step, between the two formatting procedures, to write the partitioning information to the disk. Partitioning is required because a hard disk is designed to be used with more than one operating system. It is possible to use multiple operating systems on one hard drive by separating the physical formatting into a procedure that is always the same, regardless of the operating system used and the high-level format (which is different for each operating system). Partitioning enables a single hard disk drive to run more than one type of operating system or it can enable a single operating system to use the disk as several volumes or logical drives. A volume or logical drive is any section of the disk to which the operating system assigns a drive letter or name.

Consequently, preparing a hard disk drive for data storage involves three steps:

1. Low-level formatting (LLF)
2. Partitioning
3. High-level formatting (HLF)

Low-Level Formatting

During a low-level format, the formatting program divides the disk's tracks into a specific number of sectors, creating the intersector and intertrack gaps and recording the sector header and trailer information. The program also fills each sector's data area with a dummy byte value or a pattern of test values. For floppy disks, the number of sectors recorded on each track depends on the type of disk and drive. For hard disks, the number of sectors per track depends on the drive and the controller interface.

Originally, PC hard disk drives used a separate controller that took the form of an expansion card or was integrated into the motherboard. Because the controller could be used with various disk drives and might even have been made by a different manufacturer, there had to be some uniformity in the communications between the controller and the drive. For this reason, the number of sectors written to a track tended to be relatively consistent.

The original ST-506/412 MFM controllers always placed 17 sectors per track on a disk, although ST-506/412 controllers with RLL encoding increased the number of sectors to 25 or 26 per track; ESDI drives had 32 or more sectors per track. The IDE and SCSI drives found in PCs today can have anywhere from 17 to 100 or more sectors per track because these drives have the controller integrated into the drive unit. This is what Integrated Drive Electronics (IDE) means. A SCSI drive is basically the same as an IDE, except for the addition of a SCSI bus adapter circuit. Because the drive and the controller are a matched set, there is no need for manufacturers to maintain any uniformity in the communications between them, and they can use any number of sectors per track they want.

Virtually all IDE and SCSI drives use a technique called *zoned recording*, which writes a variable number of sectors per track. Without zoned recording, the number of sectors, and therefore bits, on each track is a constant. This means the actual number of bits per inch will vary. There will be more bits per inch on the inner tracks and less on the outer. The data rate and rotational speed will remain constant, as is the number of bits per track. The following figure shows a drive recorded with the same number of sectors per track.

A standard recording wastes capacity on the outer tracks, because it is longer and yet holds the same amount of data (more loosely spaced) as the inner tracks. One way to increase the capacity of a hard drive during the low-level format is to create more sectors on the disks' outer cylinders than on the inner ones. Because they have a larger circumference, the outer cylinders can hold more data. Drives without zoned bit recording store the same amount of data on every cylinder, even though the tracks of the outer cylinders might be twice as long as those of the inner cylinders. The result is wasted storage capacity, because the disk medium must be capable of storing data reliably at the same density as on the inner cylinders. When the number of sectors per track is fixed, as in older controllers, the drive capacity is limited by the density of the innermost (shortest) track.

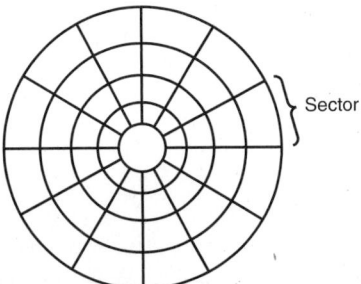

Figure 10.5   Standard recording, where the same number of sectors comprise every track.

Drives that use zoned bit recording split the cylinders into groups called zones, with each successive zone having more sectors per track as you move outward from the center of the disk. All the cylinders in a particular zone have the same number of sectors per track. The number of zones varies with specific drives, but most drives have 10 or more zones.

Figure 10.6 shows a drive with a zoned recording.

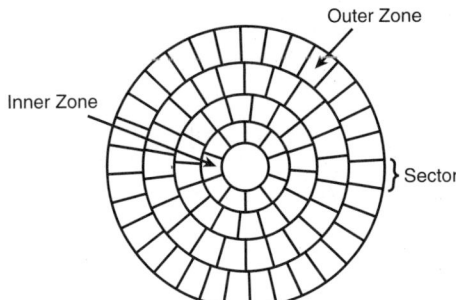

Figure 10.6   Zoned recording, where the number of sectors per track increases within each zone moving out from the center.

Another effect of zoned bit recording is that transfer speeds vary depending on what zone the heads are in. A drive with a zoned recording still spins at a constant speed, however, because there are more sectors per track in the outer zones, data transfer will be fastest there. Consequently, data transfer will be slowest when reading or writing to the inner zones. That is why virtually all drives today report minimum and maximum sustained transfer rates, which depend on where on the drive you are reading from or writing to.

As an example, see Table 10.3, which shows the zones defined for one particular 3.8GB Quantum drive, the sectors per track for each zone, and its data transfer rate.

Table 10.3   Zoned Bit Recording Information for the Quantum Fireball 3.8GB Hard Disk Drive

Zone	Tracks in Zone	Sectors Per Track	Data Transfer Rate (Mbit/s)
0	454	232	92.9
1	454	229	91.7
2	454	225	90.4
3	454	225	89.2
4	454	214	85.8
5	454	205	82.1
6	454	195	77.9
7	454	185	74.4
8	454	180	71.4
9	454	170	68.2
10	454	162	65.2
11	454	153	61.7
12	454	142	57.4
13	454	135	53.7
14	454	122	49.5

This drive has a total of 6,810 tracks on each platter surface and, as you can see, the tracks are divided into 15 zones of 454 tracks each. It is not essential for all the zones to be the same size; this is simply how this drive is arranged. Zone 0 consists of the outermost 454 tracks, which are the longest and contain the most sectors: 232. Each track in this zone can therefore provide 118,784 bytes or 116KB of user data storage, although the 122 sector tracks in zone 14 can hold only 62,464 bytes, or 61KB.

Thus, with zoned bit recording, each platter surface in this disk drive contains 1,259,396 sectors, for a storage capacity of 644,810,752 bytes or 614.94MB. Without zoned bit recording, the number of sectors per track would be limited to 122 over the entire surface of each platter, for a total of 830,820 sectors, storing 425,379,840 bytes or 405.67MB. Zoned bit recording, therefore, provides a 51.59 percent increase in the storage capacity of this particular drive.

Notice also the difference in the data transfer rates for each of the zones. The tracks in the outermost zone (0) yield a transfer rate of 92.9Mbit/sec, which is 87.67 percent higher than the 49.5Mbit/sec of the innermost zone (14). This is one reason why you might notice huge discrepancies in the results produced by disk drive benchmark programs. A test that reads or writes files on the outer tracks of the disk naturally yields far better results than one conducted on the inner tracks. It may appear as though your drive is running slower, when the problem is actually that the test results you are comparing result from disk activity on different zones.

Drives with separate controllers used in the past could not handle zoned bit recording because there was no standard way to communicate information about the zones from the drive to the controller.

With SCSI and IDE disks, however, it became possible to format individual tracks with different numbers of sectors, because these drives have the disk controller built in. The built-in controllers on these drives are fully aware of the zoning algorithm, and can translate the physical Cylinder, Head, and Sector numbers to logical Cylinder, Head, and Sector numbers so the drive appears to have the same number of sectors on each track. Because the PC BIOS is designed to handle only a single number of sectors per track throughout the entire drive, a zoned drive must run by using a sector translation scheme.

The use of zoned bit recording enables drive manufacturers to increase the capacity of their hard drives by 20–50 percent compared with a fixed–sector-per-track arrangement. Virtually all IDE and SCSI drives today use zoned bit recording.

Partitioning

Creating a partition on a hard disk drive enables it to support separate file systems, each in its own partition.

Each file system can then use its own method to allocate file space in logical units called clusters or allocation units. Every hard disk drive must have at least one partition on it and can have up to four partitions, each of which can support the same or different type file systems. There are three common file systems used by PC operating systems today:

- *FAT (File Allocation Table).* The standard file system supported by DOS, Windows 9x, and Windows NT. FAT partitions support filenames of 11 characters maximum (8+3 character extension) under DOS, and 255 characters under Windows 9x or Windows NT 4.0 (or later). The standard FAT file system uses 12- or 16-bit numbers to identify clusters, resulting in a maximum volume size of 2GB.

  Using FDISK, you can create only two physical FAT partitions on a hard disk drive—primary and extended—but you can subdivide the extended partition into as many as 25 logical volumes. Alternative partitioning programs such as Partition Magic can create up to four primary partitions or three primary and one extended.

- *FAT32 (File Allocation Table, 32-bit).* An optional file system supported by Windows 95 OSR2 (OEM Service Release 2), Windows 98, and Windows 2000.

  FAT32 uses 32-bit numbers to identify clusters, resulting in a maximum single volume size of 2TB or 2,048GB in size.

- *NTFS (Windows NT File System).* The native file system for Windows NT that supports filenames up to 256 characters long and partitions up to (a theoretical) 16 exabytes. NTFS also provides extended attributes and file system security features that do not exist in the FAT file system. Of these three file systems, the FAT file system still is by far the most popular and is accessible by nearly every operating system, which makes it the most compatible as well. FAT32 and NTFS provide additional features but are not universally accessible by other operating systems.

▶▶ See "FAT Disk Structures," p. 1380 and "FAT32," p. 1399.

Partitioning is accomplished by running the FDISK program that comes with your operating system. FDISK allows you to select the amount of space on the drive to use for a partition, from a single megabyte or one percent of the drive up to the entire capacity of the drive, or as much as the particular file system will allow. Normally it is recommended to have as few partitions as possible, and many people (myself included) try to stick with only one or two at the most. This was more difficult before FAT32, as the maximum partition size for a FAT16 partition was only 2GB. With FAT32, the maximum partition size can be up to 2,048GB.

Once a drive is partitioned, each partition must then be high-level formatted by the operating system that will use it.

High-Level Formatting

During the high-level format, the operating system (such as Windows 9x, Windows NT, or DOS) writes the structures necessary for managing files and data on the disk. FAT partitions have a Volume Boot Sector (VBS), two copies of a file allocation table (FAT), and a root directory on each formatted logical drive. These data structures enable the operating system to manage the space on the disk, keep track of files, and even manage defective areas so they do not cause problems.

High-level formatting is not really a physical formatting of the drive, but rather the creation of a table of contents for the disk. In low-level formatting, which is the real physical formatting process, tracks and sectors are written on the disk. As mentioned, the DOS FORMAT command can perform both low-level and high-level format operations on a floppy disk, but it performs only the high-level format for a hard disk. Low-level formats of IDE and SCSI hard disk drives are performed by the manufacturer, and should almost never be performed by the end user. The only time I low-level IDE or SCSI drives is when I am attempting to repair a format that has become damaged (parts of the disk become unreadable), or in some cases when I want to wipe away all data on the drive.

Basic Hard Disk Drive Components

Many types of hard disk drives are on the market, but nearly all share the same basic physical components. There might be some differences in the implementation of these components (and in the quality of the materials used to make them), but the operational characteristics of most drives are similar. The basic components of a typical hard disk drive (see Figure 10.5) are as follows:

- Disk platters
- Logic board
- Read/write heads
- Cables and connectors
- Head actuator mechanism
- Configuration items (such as jumpers or switches)
- Spindle motor

The platters, spindle motor, heads, and head actuator mechanisms are usually contained in a sealed chamber called the Head Disk Assembly (HDA). The HDA is usually treated as a single component; it is rarely opened. Other parts external to the drive's HDA, such as the logic boards, bezel, and other configuration or mounting hardware, can be disassembled from the drive.

Hard Disk Platters (Disks)

A typical hard disk drive has one or more platters, or disks. Hard disks for PC systems have been available in a number of form factors over the years. Normally, the physical size of a drive is expressed as the size of the platters. Following are the platter sizes that have been associated with PC hard disk drives:

- 5 1/4-inch (actually 130mm, or 5.12 inches) ·
- 3 1/2-inch (actually 95mm, or 3.74 inches)
- 2 1/2-inch
- 1.8-inch
- 1-inch (MicroDrive)

Larger hard disk drives that have 8-inch, 14-inch, or even larger platters are available, but these drives are not used with PC systems. Currently, the 3 1/2-inch drives are the most popular for desktop and some portable systems, while the 2 1/2-inch and smaller drives are very popular in portable or notebook systems. These little drives are quite amazing, with current capacities typically in the 4GB–14GB range, and capacities of 20GB or more expected by the year 2000. Figure 10.7 shows an expanded view of a typical, 3 1/2-inch hard drive.

Most hard disk drives have two or more platters, although some of the smaller drives have only one. The number of platters that a drive can have is limited by the drive's vertical physical size. The maximum number of platters I have seen in any 3 1/2-inch drive is 11.

Platters have traditionally been made from an aluminum alloy, which provides both strength and light weight. However, manufacturers' desire for higher and higher densities and smaller drives has led to the use of platters made of glass (or, more technically, a glass-ceramic composite). One such material, produced by the Dow Corning Corporation, is called MemCor. MemCor is composed of glass with ceramic implants, enabling it to resist cracking better than pure glass. Glass platters offer greater rigidity than metal (because metal can be bent and glass cannot) and can therefore be machined to one-half the thickness of conventional aluminum disks—sometimes less. Glass platters are also much more thermally stable than aluminum platters, which means that they do not expand or contract very much with changes in temperature. Several hard disk drives made by companies such as IBM, Seagate, Toshiba, Areal Technology, and Maxtor currently use glass or glass-ceramic platters. For most manufacturers, glass disks will probably replace the standard aluminum substrate over the next few years, especially in high-performance 2 1/2- and 3 1/2-inch drives.

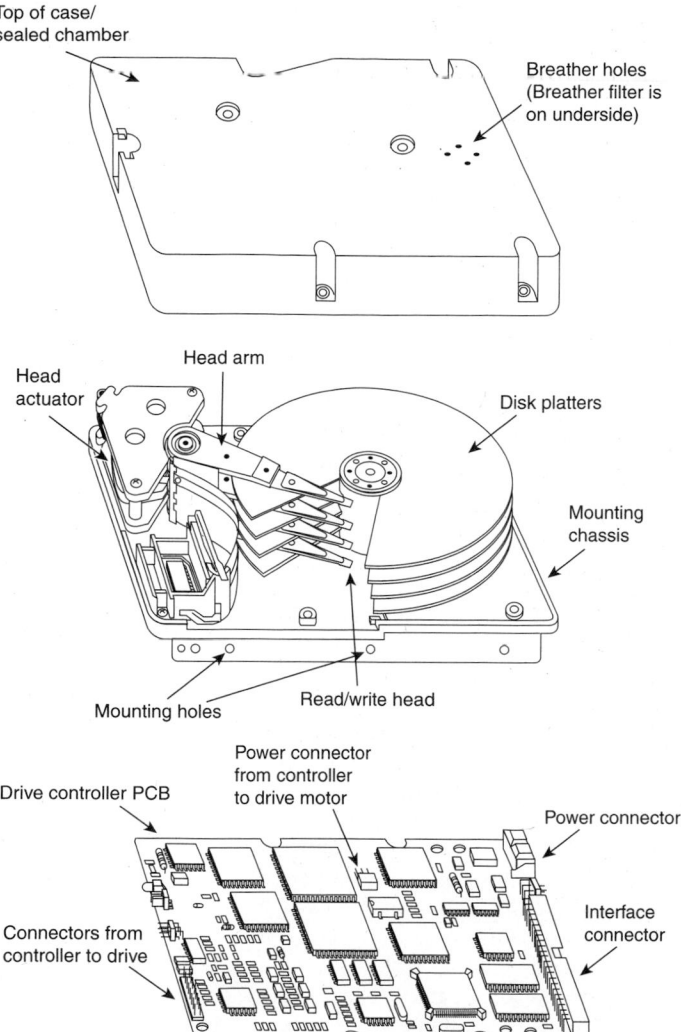

Figure 10.7   Hard disk drive components.

Recording Media

No matter what substrate is used, the platters are covered with a thin layer of a magnetically retentive substance, called the medium, on which magnetic information is stored. Two popular types of magnetic media are used on hard disk platters:

- Oxide media
- Thin-film media

The oxide medium is made of various compounds, containing iron oxide as the active ingredient. The magnetic layer is created on the disk by coating the aluminum platter with a syrup containing iron-oxide particles. This syrup is spread across the disk by spinning the platters at high speed; centrifugal force causes the material to flow from the center of the platter to the outside, creating an even coating of the material on the platter. The surface is then cured and polished. Finally, a layer of material that protects and lubricates the surface is added and burnished smooth. The oxide coating is normally about 30 millionths of an inch thick. If you could peer into a drive with oxide-coated platters, you would see that the platters are brownish or amber.

As drive density increases, the magnetic media needs to be thinner and more perfectly formed. The capabilities of oxide coatings have been exceeded by most higher capacity drives. Because the oxide medium is very soft, disks that use it are subject to head-crash damage if the drive is jolted during operation. Most older drives, especially those sold as low-end models, use oxide media on the drive platters. Oxide media, which have been used since 1955, remained popular because of their relatively low cost and ease of application. Today, however, very few drives use oxide media.

The thin-film media is thinner, harder, and more perfectly formed than oxide media. Thin film was developed as a high-performance medium that enabled a new generation of drives to have lower head floating heights, which in turn made increases in drive density possible. Originally, thin-film media were used only in higher capacity or higher quality drive systems, but today, virtually all drives use thin-film media.

The thin-film media is aptly named. The coating is much thinner than can be achieved by the oxide-coating method. Thin-film media are also known as plated, or sputtered, media because of the various processes used to deposit the thin film on the platters.

Thin-film plated media are manufactured by depositing the magnetic medium on the disk with an electroplating mechanism, in much the same way that chrome plating is deposited on the bumper of a car. The aluminum platter is immersed in a series of chemical baths that coat the platter with several layers of metallic film. The magnetic medium layer itself is a cobalt alloy about 3μ-in. thick.

Thin-film sputtered media are created by first coating the aluminum platters with a layer of nickel phosphorus, and then applying the cobalt-alloy magnetic material in a continuous vacuum-deposition process called *sputtering*. This process deposits magnetic layers as thin as 1 or 2μ-in. on the disk, in a fashion similar to the way that silicon wafers are coated with metallic films in the semiconductor industry. The same sputtering technique is then used again to lay down an extremely hard, 1μ-in. protective carbon coating. The need for a near-perfect vacuum makes sputtering the most expensive of the processes described here.

The surface of a sputtered platter contains magnetic layers as thin as 1μ-in. Because this surface also is very smooth, the head can float closer to the disk surface than was possible previously. Floating heights as small as 3μ-in. above the surface are possible. When the head is closer to the platter, the density of the magnetic flux transitions can be increased to provide greater storage capacity. Additionally, the increased intensity of the magnetic field during a closer-proximity read provides the higher signal amplitudes needed for good signal-to-noise performance.

Both the sputtering and plating processes result in a very thin, hard film of magnetic media on the platters. Because the thin-film media is so hard, it has a better chance of surviving contact with the heads at high speed. In fact, modern thin-film media are virtually uncrashable. If you could open a drive to peek at the platters, you would see that platters coated with the thin-film media look like the silver surfaces of mirrors.

The sputtering process results in the most perfect, thinnest, and hardest disk surface that can be produced commercially, which is why it has largely replaced plating as the preferred method of creating thin-film media. Having a thin-film media surface on a drive results in increased storage capacity in a smaller area with fewer head crashes and a drive that typically will provide many years of trouble-free use.

Read/Write Heads

A hard disk drive usually has one read/write head for each platter surface (meaning that each platter has two sets of read/write heads—one for the top side and one for the bottom side). These heads are connected, or ganged, on a single movement mechanism. The heads, therefore, move across the platters in unison.

Mechanically, read/write heads are simple. Each head is on an actuator arm that is spring-loaded to force the head into contact with a platter. Few people realize that each platter actually is "squeezed" by the heads above and below it. If you could open a drive safely and lift the top head with your finger, the head would snap back down into the platter when you released it. If you could pull down on one of the heads below a platter, the spring tension would cause it to snap back up into the platter when you released it.

Figure 10.8 shows a typical hard disk head-actuator assembly from a voice coil drive.

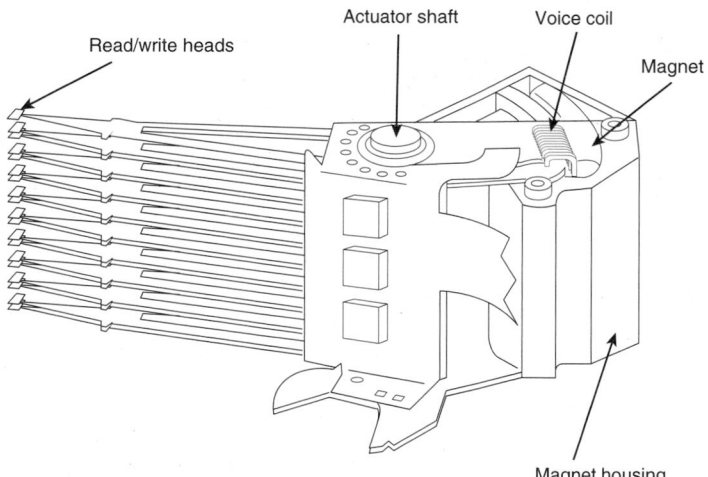

Figure 10.8   Read/write heads and rotary voice coil actuator assembly.

When the drive is at rest, the heads are forced into direct contact with the platters by spring tension, but when the drive is spinning at full speed, air pressure develops below the heads and lifts them off the surface of the platter. On a drive spinning at full speed, the distance between the heads and the platter can be anywhere from 3 to 20μ-in. or more.

In the early 1960s, hard disk drive recording heads operated at floating heights as large as 200–300μ-in.; today's drive heads are designed to float as low as 3-5μ-in. above the surface of the disk. To support higher densities in future drives, the physical separation between the head and disk is expected to be as little as 0.5μ-in. by the end of the century.

Caution

The small size of the gap between the platters and the heads is why you should never open the disk drive's HDA except in a clean-room environment. Any particle of dust or dirt that gets into this mechanism could cause the heads to read improperly, or possibly even to strike the platters while the drive is running at full speed. The latter event could scratch the platter or the head.

To ensure the cleanliness of the interior of the drive, the HDA is assembled in a class-100 or better clean room. This specification means that a cubic foot of air cannot contain more than 100 particles that measure up to 0.5 microns (19.7μ-in.). A single person breathing while standing motionless spews out 500 such particles in a single minute! These rooms contain special air-filtration systems that continuously evacuate and refresh the air. A drive's HDA should not be opened unless it is inside such a room.

Although maintaining a clean-room environment may seem to be expensive, many companies manufacture tabletop or bench-size clean rooms that sell for only a few thousand dollars. Some of these devices operate like a glove box; the operator first inserts the drive and any tools required, and then closes the box and turns on the filtration system. Inside the box, a clean-room environment is maintained, and a technician can use the built-in gloves to work on the drive.

In other clean-room variations, the operator stands at a bench where a forced-air curtain maintains a clean environment on the bench top. The technician can walk in and out of the clean-room field by walking through the air curtain. This air curtain is much like the curtain of air used in some stores and warehouses to prevent heat from escaping in the winter while leaving a passage wide open.

Because the clean environment is expensive to produce, few companies, except those that manufacture the drives, are properly equipped to service hard disk drives.

Read/Write Head Designs

As disk drive technology has evolved, so has the design of the read/write head. The earliest heads were simple iron cores with coil windings (electromagnets). By today's standards, the original head designs were enormous in physical size and operated at very low recording densities. Over the years, head designs have evolved from the first simple Ferrite Core designs into the several types and technologies available today. This section discusses the different types of heads found in PC hard disk drives, including the applications and relative strengths and weaknesses of each.

Four types of heads have been used in hard disk drives over the years:

- Ferrite
- Metal-In-Gap (MIG)
- Thin Film (TF)
- Magneto-Resistive (MR)

Ferrite

Ferrite heads, the traditional type of magnetic-head design, evolved from the original IBM 30-30 Winchester drive. These heads have an iron-oxide core wrapped with electromagnetic coils. The drive produces a magnetic field by energizing the coils or by passing a magnetic field near them. This gives the heads full read/write capability. Ferrite heads are larger and heavier than thin-film heads and therefore require a larger floating height to prevent contact with the disk while it is spinning.

Manufacturers have made many refinements to the original (monolithic) ferrite head design. One type of ferrite head called a composite ferrite head has a smaller ferrite core bonded with glass in a ceramic housing. This design permits a smaller head gap, which allows higher track densities. These heads are less susceptible to stray magnetic fields than the older monolithic design heads.

During the 1980s, composite ferrite heads were popular in many low-end drives, such as the Seagate ST-225. As density demands grew, the competing MIG and thin-film head designs came to be used in place of ferrite heads, which are virtually obsolete today. Ferrite heads cannot write to the higher coercivity media needed for high-density disk designs and have poor frequency response with higher noise levels. The main advantage of ferrite heads is that they are the cheapest type available.

Metal-In-Gap

Metal-In-Gap (MIG) heads are a specially enhanced version of the composite ferrite design. In MIG heads, a metal substance is applied to the head's recording gap. Two versions of MIG heads are available: single-sided and double-sided. Single-sided MIG heads are designed with a layer of magnetic alloy placed along the trailing edge of the gap. Double-sided MIG designs apply the layer to both sides of the gap. The metal alloy is applied through a vacuum-deposition process called sputtering, which was discussed in the previous section on recording media.

This magnetic alloy has twice the magnetization capability of raw ferrite and enables the head to write to the higher coercivity thin-film media needed at the higher densities. MIG heads also produce a sharper gradient in the magnetic field for a better-defined magnetic pulse. Double-sided MIG heads offer even higher coercivity capability than the single-sided designs.

Because of these increases in capabilities through improved designs, MIG heads were for a time the most popular head design, and were used in all but very high-capacity drives. Due to market pressures demanding higher and higher densities, however, MIG heads have been largely displaced in favor of thin-film heads.

Thin Film

Thin-film (TF) heads are manufactured much the same way as a semiconductor chip—through a photolithographic process. This process creates many thousands of heads on a single circular wafer and produces a very small, high-quality product.

TF heads have an extremely narrow and controlled head gap that is created by sputtering a hard aluminum material. Because this material completely encloses the gap, the area is very well protected, minimizing the chance of damage from contact with the spinning disk. The core is a combination of iron and nickel alloy that has two to four times more magnetic power than a ferrite head core.

TF heads produce a sharply defined magnetic pulse that enables them to write at extremely high densities. Because they do not have a conventional coil, TF heads are more immune to variations in coil impedance. These small, lightweight heads can float at a much lower height than the ferrite and MIG heads; in some designs, the floating height is 2μ-in. or less. Because the reduced height enables the heads to pick up and transmit a much stronger signal from the platters, the signal-to-noise ratio increases, improving accuracy. At the high track and linear densities of some drives, a standard ferrite head would not be capable of picking out the data signal from the background noise. Another advantage of TF heads is that their small size enables the platters to be stacked closer together, making it possible to fit more platters into the same space.

Until the past few years, TF heads were relatively expensive compared with older technologies, such as ferrite and MIG. Better manufacturing techniques and the need for higher densities, however, have driven the market to TF heads. The widespread use of these heads has also made them cost-competitive with, if not cheaper than, MIG heads.

Many of the drives in the 100MB to 1,000MB range manufactured today use TF heads, especially in the smaller form factors. TF heads displaced MIG heads as the most popular head design, but they are now themselves being displaced by newer technologies, such as magneto-resistive heads.

Magneto-Resistive

Magneto-Resistive (MR) heads are the latest technology. Invented and pioneered by IBM, MR heads currently offer the highest performance available. Most 3 1/2-inch drives with capacities in excess of 1GB currently use MR heads. As areal densities continue to increase, the MR head eventually will become the head of choice for nearly all hard drives, displacing the popular MIG and TF head designs.

MR heads rely on the fact that the resistance of a conductor changes slightly when an external magnetic field is present. Rather than put out a voltage by passing through a magnetic-field flux reversal, as a normal head would, the MR head senses the flux reversal and changes resistance. A small current flows through the heads, and this sense current measures the change in resistance. This design provides an output that is three or more times more powerful than a TF head during a read. In effect, MR heads are power-read heads, acting more like sensors than generators.

MR heads are more costly and complex to manufacture than other types of heads, because several special features or steps must be added. Among them are

- Additional wires must be run to and from the head to carry the sense current.
- Four to six more masking steps are required.
- Because MR heads are so sensitive, they are very susceptible to stray magnetic fields and must be shielded.

Because the MR principle can only read data and is not used for writing, MR heads really are two heads in one. The assembly includes a standard inductive TF head for writing data and an MR head for reading. Because two separate heads are built into one assembly, each head can be optimized for its task. Ferrite, MIG, and TF heads are known as single-gap heads because the same gap is used for both reading and writing, while the MR head uses a separate gap for each operation.

The problem with single-gap heads is that the gap length is always a compromise between what is best for reading and what is best for writing. The read function needs a thin gap for higher resolution; the write function needs a thicker gap for deeper flux penetration to switch the medium. In a dual-gap MR head, the read and write gaps can be optimized for both functions independently. The write (TF) gap writes a wider track than the read (MR) gap reads. Thus, the read head is less likely to pick up stray magnetic information from adjacent tracks.

Drives with MR heads require better shielding from stray magnetic fields, which can affect these heads more easily than they do the other head designs. All in all, however, the drawback is minor compared with the advantages that the MR heads offer.

More recently, improved MR designs called giant Magneto-Resistive or spin valve heads have been introduced. These use the effect of a magnetic field capable of changing the direction of electron spin in certain materials to alter the resistance of the material. This results in a Magneto-Resistive effect that is even more sensitive, and which can be used to read even higher density recordings.

Head Sliders

The term *slider* is used to describe the body of material that supports the actual drive head itself. The slider is what actually floats or slides over the surface of the disk, carrying the head at the correct distance from the medium for reading and writing. Most sliders resemble a trimaran, with two outboard pods that float along the surface of the disk media and a central "hull" portion that actually carries the head and the read/write gap. The following figure shows a typical slider. Note the actual head, with the read/write gap, is on the trailing end of the slider.

The trend toward smaller and smaller form factor drives has forced sliders to become smaller and smaller as well. The typical mini-Winchester slider design is about .160×.126×.034 inches in size. Most head manufacturers have now shifted to 50 percent smaller nanosliders, which have dimensions of about .08×.063×.017 inches. The nanoslider is being used in both high-capacity and small form-factor drives. The next evolution in slider design, called the picoslider, is smaller still—70 percent smaller than the original design. Picosliders are assembled by using flex interconnect cable (FIC) and chip on ceramic (COC) technology that enables the process to be completely automated.

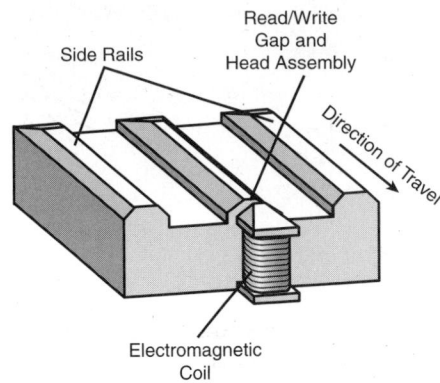

Figure 10.9   The underside of a typical head slider.

Smaller sliders reduce the mass carried at the end of the head actuator arms, providing increased acceleration and deceleration, leading to faster seek times. The smaller sliders also require less area for a landing zone, thus increasing the usable area of the disk platters. Further, the smaller slider contact area reduces the slight wear on the platter surface that occurs during normal startup and spindown of the drive platters.

The newer nanoslider designs also have specially modified surface patterns that are designed to maintain the same floating height above the disk surface, whether the slider is positioned above the inner or outer cylinders. Conventional sliders increase or decrease their floating height considerably, according to the velocity of the disk surface traveling beneath them. Above the outer cylinders, the velocity and floating height are higher. This arrangement is undesirable in newer drives that use zoned bit recording, in which the bit density is the same on all the cylinders. When the bit density is uniform throughout the drive, the head floating height should be relatively constant as well for maximum performance. Special textured surface patterns and manufacturing techniques enable the nanosliders to float at a much more consistent height, making them ideal for zoned bit recording drives.

Head Actuator Mechanisms

Possibly more important than the heads themselves is the mechanical system that moves them: the head actuator. This mechanism moves the heads across the disk and positions them accurately above the desired cylinder. There are many variations on head actuator mechanisms in use, but all fall into one of two basic categories:

- Stepper motor actuators
- Voice coil actuators

The use of one or the other type of actuator has profound effects on a drive's performance and reliability. The effects are not limited to speed; they also include accuracy, sensitivity to temperature, position, vibration, and overall reliability. The head actuator is the single most important specification in the drive, and the type of head actuator mechanism in a drive tells you a great deal about the drive's performance and reliability characteristics. Table 10.4 shows the two types of hard disk drive head actuators and the affected performance characteristics.

Table 10.4   Characteristics of Stepper Motor Versus Voice Coil Drives

Characteristic	Stepper Motor	Voice Coil
Relative access speed	Slow	Fast
Temperature sensitive	Yes (very)	No
Positionally sensitive	Yes	No
Automatic head parking	Not usually	Yes
Preventive maintenance	Periodic format	None required
Relative reliability	Poor	Excellent

Generally, a stepper motor drive has a slower average access rating, is temperature-sensitive during read and write operations, is sensitive to physical orientation during read and write operations, does not automatically park its heads above a save zone during power-down, and usually requires annual or biannual reformats to realign the sector data with the sector header information due to mistracking. To put it bluntly, a drive equipped with a stepper motor actuator is much less reliable (by a large margin) than a drive equipped with a voice coil actuator.

Floppy disk drives position their heads by using a stepper motor actuator. The accuracy of the stepper mechanism is suited to a floppy disk drive, because the track densities are usually nowhere near those of a hard disk. The track density of a 1.44MB floppy disk is 135 tracks per inch, while hard disk drives have densities of over 5,000 tracks per inch. Virtually all the hard disk drives being manufactured today use voice coil actuators, because stepper motors cannot achieve the degree of accuracy needed.

Stepper Motor Actuators

A stepper motor is an electrical motor that can "step," or move from position to position, with mechanical detents or click-stop positions. If you were to grip the spindle of one of these motors and spin it manually, you would hear a clicking or buzzing sound as the motor passed each detent position with a soft click.

Stepper motors cannot position themselves between step positions; they can stop only at the predetermined detent positions. The motors are small (between 1 and 3 inches) and can be square, cylindrical, or flat. Stepper motors are outside the sealed HDA, although the spindle of the motor penetrates the HDA through a sealed hole.

Stepper motor mechanisms are affected by a variety of problems; the greatest problem is temperature. As the drive platters heat and cool, they expand and contract, and the tracks on the platters move in relation to a predetermined track position. The stepper mechanism cannot move in increments of less than a single track to correct for these temperature-induced errors. The drive positions the heads to a particular cylinder according to a predetermined number of steps from the stepper motor, with no room for nuance.

Figure 10.10 shows a common stepper motor design, where a split metal band is used to transfer the movement from the rotating motor shaft to the head actuator itself.

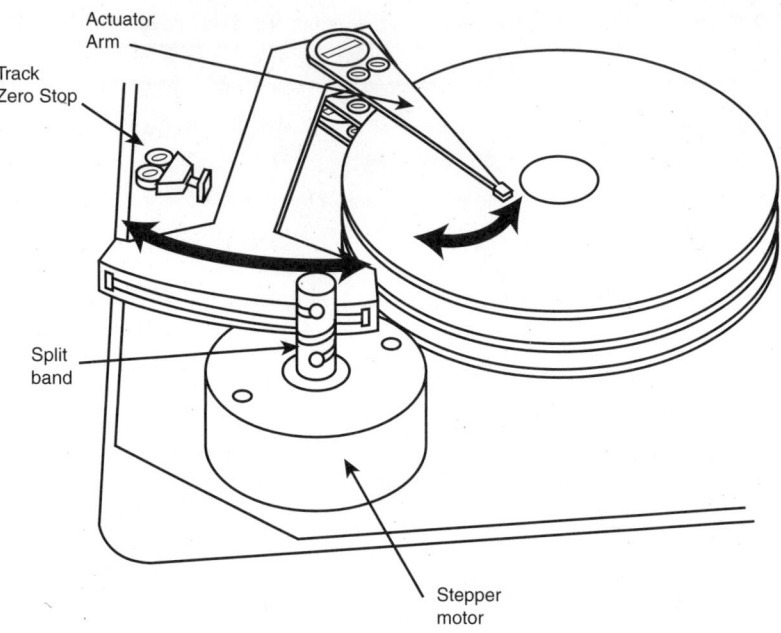

Track Zero Stop

Actuator Arm

Split band

Stepper motor

Figure 10.10 A stepper motor actuator.

Voice Coil Actuators

The voice coil actuators used in virtually all hard disk drives made today, unlike stepper motor actuators, use a feedback signal from the drive to accurately determine the head positions and adjust them, if necessary. This arrangement provides significantly greater performance, accuracy, and reliability than traditional stepper motor actuator designs.

A voice coil actuator works by pure electromagnetic force. The construction of the mechanism is similar to that of a typical audio speaker, from which the term voice coil is derived. An audio speaker uses a stationary magnet surrounded by a voice coil, which is connected to the speaker's paper cone. Energizing the coil causes it to move relative to the stationary magnet, which produces sound from the cone. In a typical hard disk drive's voice coil system, the electromagnetic coil is attached to the end of the head rack and placed near a stationary magnet. There is no physical contact between the coil and the magnet; instead, the coil moves by pure magnetic force. As the electromagnetic coils are energized, they attract or repulse the stationary magnet and move the head rack. Systems like these are extremely quick and efficient, and usually much quieter than systems driven by stepper motors.

Unlike a stepper motor, a voice coil actuator has no click-stops, or detent positions; rather, a special guidance system stops the head rack above a particular cylinder. Because it has no detents, the voice coil actuator can slide the heads in and out smoothly to any position desired. Voice coil actuators use a guidance mechanism called a *servo* to tell the actuator where the heads are in relation to the cylinders and to place the heads accurately at the desired positions. This positioning system often is called a *closed loop feedback mechanism*. It works by sending the index (or servo) signal to the positioning electronics, which return a feedback signal that is used to position the heads accurately. The system is also called servo-controlled, which refers to the index or servo information that is used to dictate or control head-positioning accuracy.

A voice coil actuator with servo control is not affected by temperature changes, as a stepper motor is. When temperature changes cause the disk platters to expand or contract, the voice coil system compensates automatically because it never positions the heads in predetermined track positions. Rather, the voice coil system searches for the specific track, guided by the prewritten servo information, and then positions the head rack precisely above the desired track, wherever it happens to be. Because of the continuous feedback of servo information, the heads adjust to the current position of the track at all times. For example, as a drive warms up and the platters expand, the servo information enables the heads to "follow" the track. As a result, a voice coil actuator is sometimes called a *track following system*.

The two main types of voice-coil positioner mechanisms are

- Linear voice-coil actuators
- Rotary voice-coil actuators

The two types differ only in the physical arrangement of the magnets and coils.

A linear actuator (see Figure 10.11) moves the heads in and out over the platters in a straight line. The coil moves in and out on a track surrounded by the stationary magnets. The primary advantage of the linear design is that it eliminates the head *azimuth* variations that occur with rotary positioning systems. (Azimuth refers to the angular measurement of the head position relative to the tangent of a given cylinder.) A linear actuator does not rotate the head as it moves from one cylinder to another, thus eliminating this problem.

Although the linear actuator seems to be a good design, it has one fatal flaw: The devices are much too heavy. As drive performance has increased, the desire for lightweight actuator mechanisms has become very important. The lighter the mechanism, the faster it can accelerate and decelerate from one cylinder to another. Because they are much heavier than rotary actuators, linear actuators were popular only for a short time; they are virtually nonexistent in drives manufactured today.

Rotary actuators (refer to Figure 10.8) also use stationary magnets and a movable coil, but the coil is attached to the end of an actuator arm. As the coil moves relative to the stationary magnet, it swings the head arms in and out over the surface of the disk. The primary advantage of this mechanism is its light weight, which means that the heads can accelerate and decelerate very quickly, resulting in very fast average seek times. Because of the lever effect on the head arm, the heads move faster than the actuator, which also helps to improve access times. (Refer to Figure 10.8, which shows a rotary voice coil actuator.)

The disadvantage of a rotary system is that as the heads move from the outer to the inner cylinders, they rotate slightly with respect to the tangent of the cylinders. This rotation results in an azimuth error and is one reason why the area of the platter in which the cylinders are located is somewhat limited. By limiting the total motion of the actuator, the azimuth error is contained to within reasonable specifications. Virtually all voice coil drives today use rotary actuator systems.

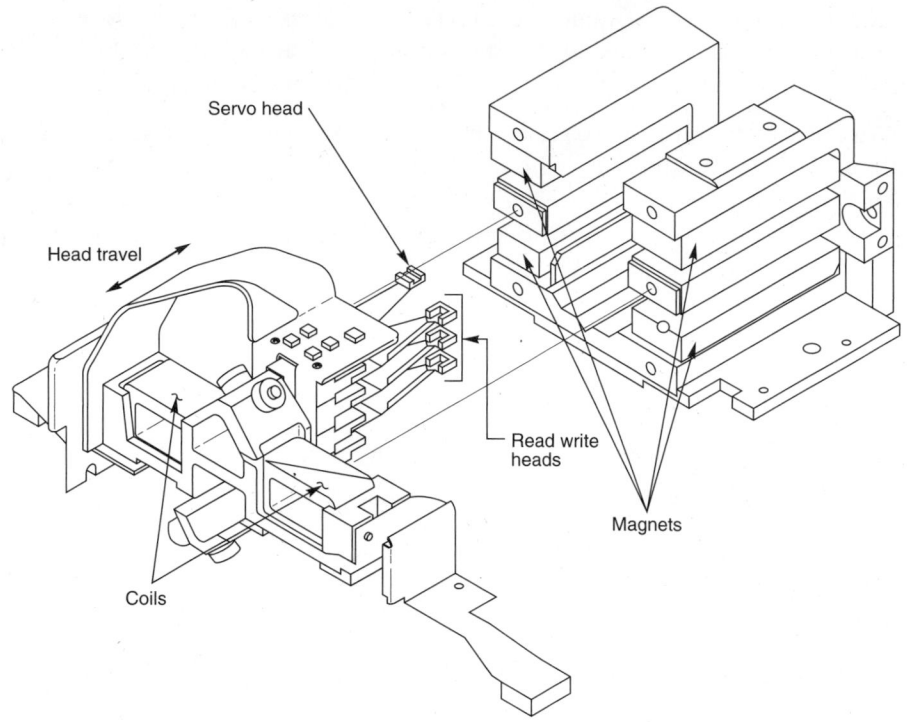

Servo head

Head travel

Read write
heads

Magnets

Coils

Figure 10.11   A linear voice coil actuator.

Servo Mechanisms

Three servo mechanism designs have been used to control voice coil positioners over the years:

- Wedge servo
- Embedded servo
- Dedicated servo

The three designs are slightly different, but they accomplish the same basic task: They enable the head positioner to adjust continuously so it is precisely positioned above a given cylinder on the disk. The main difference between these servo designs is where the gray code information is actually written on the drive.

All servo mechanisms rely on special information that is written to the disk when it is manufactured. This information is usually in the form of a special code called a *gray code*. A gray code is a special binary notational system in which any two adjacent numbers are represented by a code that differs in only one bit place or column position. This system makes it easy for the head to read the information and quickly determine its precise position.

At the time of manufacture, a special machine called a servowriter writes the servo gray code on the disk. The servowriter is basically a jig that mechanically moves the heads to a given reference position, and then writes the servo information at that position. Many servowriters are themselves guided by a laser-beam reference that calculates its own position by calculating distances in wavelengths of light. Because the servowriter must be capable of moving the heads mechanically, the process requires either that the lid of the drive be removed or that access be available through special access ports in the HDA. After the servowriting is complete, these ports are usually covered with sealing tape. You often see these tape-covered holes on the HDA, usually accompanied by warnings that you will void the warranty if you remove the tape. Because servowriting exposes the interior of the HDA, it requires a clean-room environment.

A servowriter is an expensive piece of machinery, costing up to $50,000 or more, and often must be custom-made for a particular make or model of drive. Some drive-repair companies have servowriting capability, which means that they can rewrite the servo information on a drive if it becomes damaged. If a servowriter is not available, a drive with servo-code damage must be sent back to the drive manufacturer for the servo information to be rewritten.

Fortunately, it is impossible to damage the servo information through disk read and write processes. Drives are designed so the heads cannot overwrite the servo information, even during a low-level format. One myth that has been circulating (especially with respect to IDE drives) is that you can damage the servo information by improper low-level formatting. This is not true. An improper low-level format can compromise the performance of the drive, but the servo information is totally protected and cannot be overwritten. Even so, it is possible for the servo information on some drives to be damaged by a strong adjacent magnetic field or by jarring the drive while it is writing, causing the heads to move off track.

The track-following capabilities of a servo-controlled voice coil actuator eliminate the positioning errors that occur over time with stepper motor drives. Voice coil drives are not affected by conditions such as thermal expansion and contraction of the platters. In fact, many voice coil drives today perform a special thermal-recalibration procedure at predetermined intervals while they run. This procedure usually involves seeking the heads from cylinder 0 to some other cylinder one time for every head on the drive. As this sequence occurs, the control circuitry in the drive monitors how much the track positions have moved since the last time the sequence was performed, and a thermal-recalibration adjustment is calculated and stored in the drive's memory. This information is then used every time the drive positions the heads to ensure the most accurate positioning possible.

Most drives perform the thermal-recalibration sequence every five minutes for the first half-hour that the drive is powered on, and then once every 25 minutes after that. With some drives, this thermal-recalibration sequence is very noticeable; the drive essentially stops what it is doing, and you hear rapid ticking for a second or so. Some people think that this is an indication that their drive is having a problem reading something and perhaps is conducting a read retry, but this is not true. Most of the newer intelligent drives (IDE and SCSI) employ this thermal-recalibration procedure to maintain positioning accuracy.

As multimedia applications grew in popularity, thermal recalibration became a problem with some manufacturers' drives. The thermal-recalibration sequence sometimes interrupted the transfer of a large data file, such as an audio or video file, which resulted in audio or video playback jitter. Some companies released special A/V (audio visual) drives that hide the thermal-recalibration sequences so they never interrupt a file transfer. Most of the newer IDE and SCSI drives are A/V capable, which means that the thermal-recalibration sequences will not interrupt a transfer such as a video playback.

While we are on the subject of automatic drive functions, most of the drives that perform thermal-recalibration sequences also automatically perform a function called a *disk sweep*. Also called *wear leveling* by some manufacturers, this procedure is an automatic head seek that occurs after the drive has been idle for a period of time. The disk-sweep function moves the heads to a cylinder in the outer portion of the platters, which is where the head float-height is highest (because the head-to-platter velocity is highest). Then, if the drive continues to remain idle for another period, the heads move to another cylinder in this area, and the process continues indefinitely as long as the drive is powered on.

The disk-sweep function is designed to prevent the head from remaining stationary above one cylinder in the drive for too long, where friction between the head and platter eventually would dig a trench in the medium. Although the heads are not in direct contact with the medium, they are so close that the constant air pressure from the head floating above a single cylinder could cause friction and excessive wear.

Wedge Servo

Some early servo-controlled drives used a technique called a *wedge servo*. In these drives, the gray-code guidance information is contained in a "wedge" slice of the drive in each cylinder immediately preceding the index mark. The index mark indicates the beginning of each track, so the wedge-servo information was written in the PRE-INDEX GAP, which is at the end of each track. This area is provided for speed tolerance and normally is not used by the controller. Figure 10.12 shows the servo-wedge information on a drive.

Some controllers had to be notified that the drive was using a wedge servo so they could shorten the sector timing to allow for the wedge-servo area. If they were not correctly configured, these controllers would not work properly with the drive.

Another problem was that the servo information appears only one time every revolution, which means that the drive often needed several revolutions before it could accurately determine and adjust the head position. Because of these problems, the wedge servo never was a popular design; it no longer is used in drives.

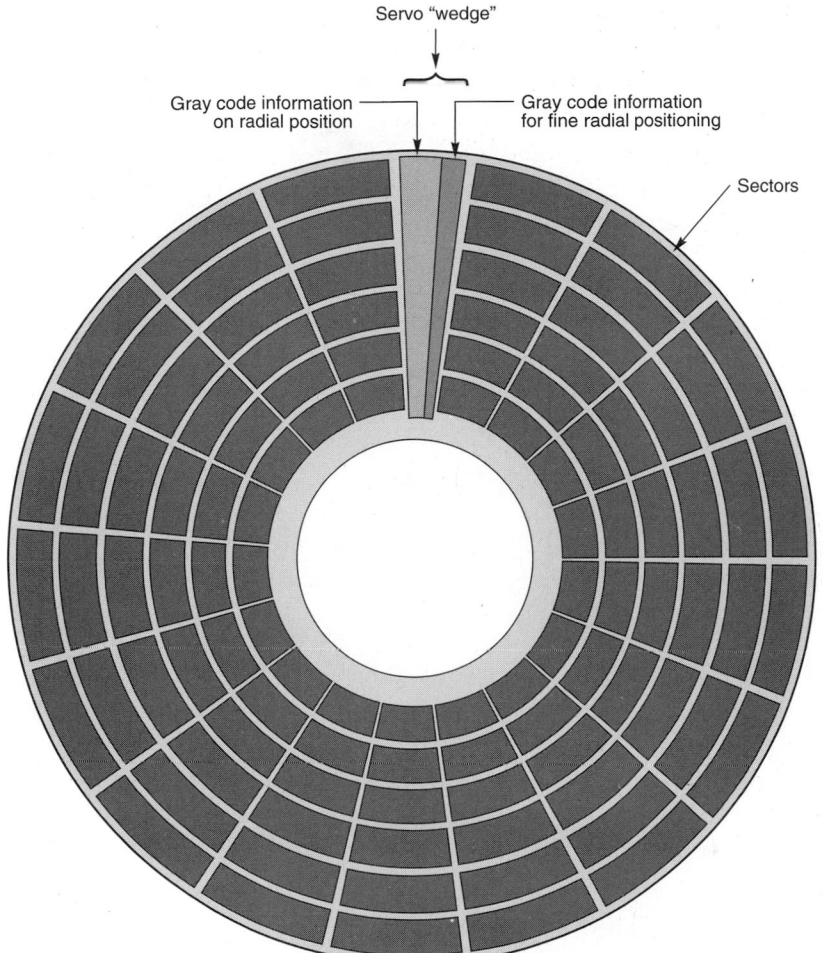

Servo "wedge"

Gray code information
on radial position

Gray code information
for fine radial positioning

Sectors

Figure 10.12   A wedge servo.

Embedded Servo

An embedded servo (see Figure 10.13) is an enhancement of the wedge servo. Instead of placing the servo code before the beginning of each cylinder, an embedded servo design writes the servo information before the start of each sector. This arrangement enables the positioner circuits to receive feedback many times in a single revolution, making the head positioning much faster and more precise. Another advantage is that every track on the drive has its own positioning information, so each head can quickly and efficiently adjust position to compensate for any changes in the platter or head dimensions, especially for changes due to thermal expansion or physical stress.

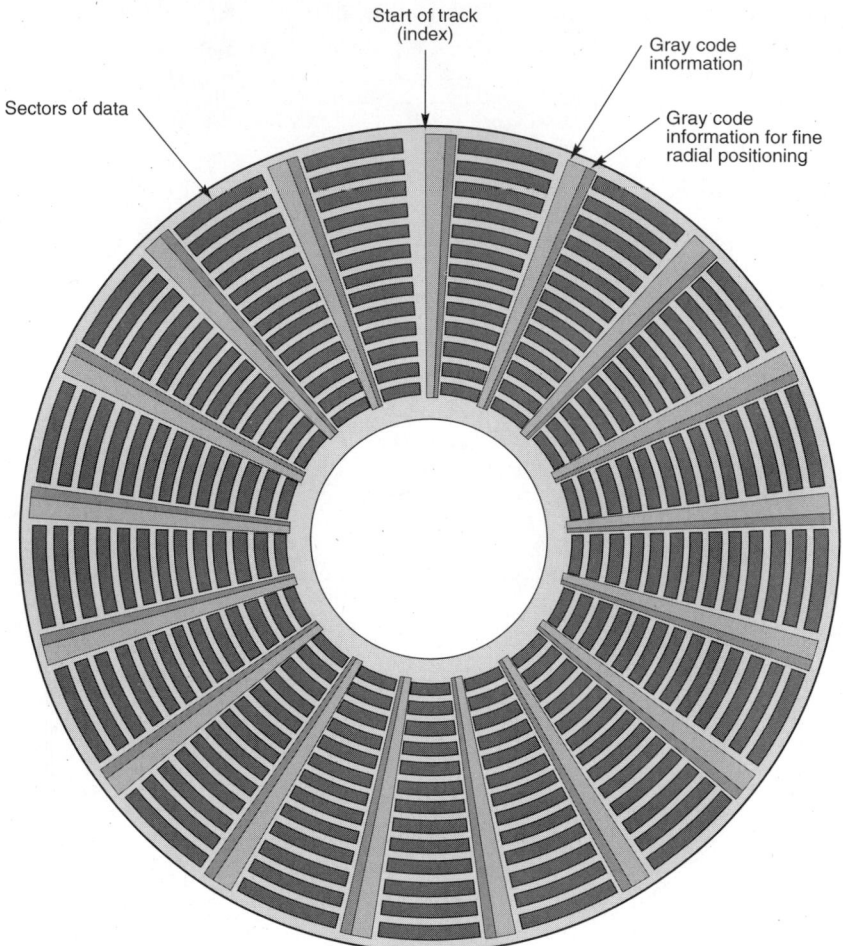

Figure 10.13 An embedded servo.

Most drives today use an embedded servo to control the positioning system. As in the wedge servo design, the embedded servo information is protected by the drive circuits, and any write operations are blocked whenever the heads are above the servo information. Thus, it is impossible to overwrite the servo information with a low-level format, as some people incorrectly believe.

Although the embedded servo works much better than the wedge servo because the servo feedback information is made available several times in a single disk revolution, a system that offered continuous servo feedback information would be better.

Dedicated Servo

A dedicated servo is a design in which the servo information is written continuously throughout the entire track, rather than just once per track or at the beginning of each sector. Unfortunately, if this procedure were used on the entire drive, no room would be left for data. For this reason, a *dedicated servo* uses one side of one of the platters exclusively for the servo-positioning information. The term "dedicated" comes from the fact that this platter side is completely dedicated to the servo information and cannot contain any data.

When building a dedicated servo drive, the manufacturer deducts one side of one platter from normal read/write usage, and records a special set of gray-code data there that indicates the proper track positions. Because the head that rests above this surface cannot be used for normal reading and writing, the gray code can never be erased, and the servo information is protected, as in the other servo designs. No low-level format or other procedure can possibly overwrite the servo information. Figure 10.14 shows a dedicated servo mechanism. Normally the head on top or one in the center is dedicated for servo use.

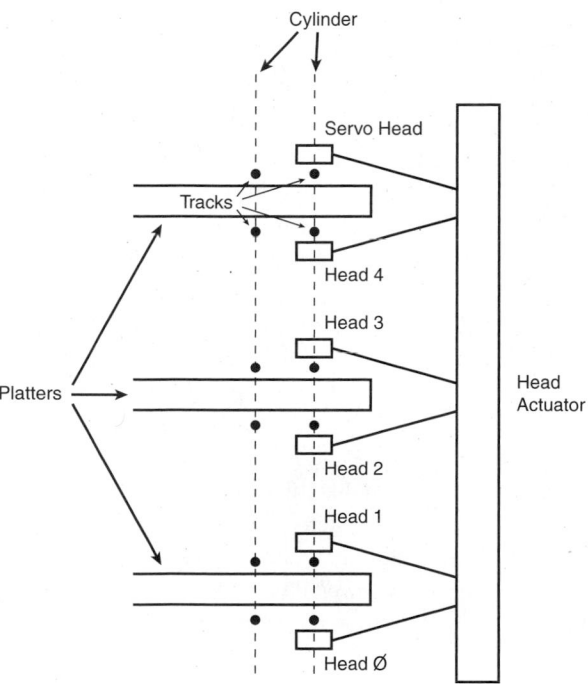

Figure 10.14   A dedicated servo, showing one entire head/side used for servo reading.

When the drive moves the heads to a specific cylinder, the internal drive electronics use the signals received by the servo head to determine the position of the read/write heads. As the heads move, the track counters are read from the dedicated servo surface. When the servo head detects the requested track, the actuator stops. The servo electronics then fine-tune the position so the heads are positioned precisely above the desired cylinder before any writing is permitted. Although only one head is used for servo tracking, the other heads are attached to the same rack so if one head is above the desired cylinder, all the others will be as well.

One way of telling if a drive uses a dedicated servo platter is if it has an odd number of heads. For example, the Toshiba MK-538FB 1.2GB drive that I have on my computer has eight platters, but only 15 read/write heads. The drive uses a dedicated-servo positioning system, and the sixteenth head is the servo head. The advantage of the dedicated servo concept is that the servo information is continuously available to the drive, making the head positioning process faster and more precise. The drawback is that dedicating an entire platter surface to servo information can be wasteful. More drives today use embedded servo information than dedicated servo. Some drives combine a dedicated servo with an embedded servo, but this type of hybrid design is rare.

Of course, as mentioned earlier, today's IDE and SCSI drives have head, track, and sector-per-track parameters that are translated from the actual physical numbers. Therefore, it is not usually possible to tell from the published numbers exactly how many heads or platters are contained within a drive.

Automatic Head Parking

When you power off a hard disk drive, the spring tension in each head arm pulls the heads into contact with the platters. The drive is designed to sustain thousands of takeoffs and landings, but it is wise to ensure that the landing occurs at a spot on the platter that contains no data. Older drives required manual head parking; you had to run a program that positioned the drive heads to a landing zone, usually the innermost cylinder, before turning the system off. Modern drives automatically park the heads, so park programs are no longer needed.

Some amount of abrasion occurs during the landing and takeoff process, removing just a "micro puff" from the magnetic medium; but if the drive is jarred during the landing or takeoff process, real damage can occur.

One benefit of using a voice coil actuator is automatic head parking. In a drive that has a voice coil actuator, the heads are positioned and held by magnetic force. When the power to the drive is removed, the magnetic field that holds the heads stationary over a particular cylinder dissipates, enabling the head rack to skitter across the drive surface and potentially cause damage. In the voice coil design, the head rack is attached to a weak spring at one end and a head stop at the other end. When the system is powered on, the spring is overcome by the magnetic force of the positioner. When the drive is powered off, however, the spring gently drags the head rack to a park-and-lock position before the drive slows down and the heads land. On some drives, you can actually hear the "ting...ting...ting...ting" sound as the heads literally bounce-park themselves, driven by this spring.

On a drive with a voice coil actuator, you activate the parking mechanism by turning off the computer; you do not need to run a program to park or retract the heads. In the event of a power outage, the heads park themselves automatically. (The drives unpark automatically when the system is powered on.)

Air Filters

Nearly all hard disk drives have two air filters. One filter is called the recirculating filter, and the other is called either a barometric or breather filter. These filters are permanently sealed inside the drive and are designed never to be changed for the life of the drive, unlike many older mainframe hard disks that had changeable filters.

A hard disk on a PC system does not circulate air from inside to outside the HDA or vice versa. The recirculating filter that is permanently installed inside the HDA is designed to filter only the small particles scraped off the platters during head takeoffs and landings (and possibly any other small particles dislodged inside the drive). Because PC hard disk drives are permanently sealed and do not circulate outside air, they can run in extremely dirty environments (see Figure 10.15).

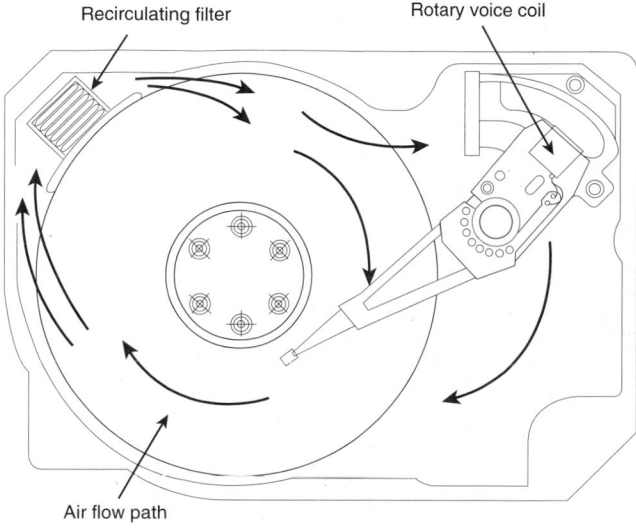

Figure 10.15 Air circulation in a hard disk.

The HDA in a hard disk drive is sealed but not airtight. The HDA is vented through a barometric or breather filter element that allows for pressure equalization (breathing) between the inside and outside of the drive. For this reason, most hard drives are rated by the drive's manufacturer to run in a specific range of altitudes, usually from 1,000 feet below to 10,000 feet above sea level. In fact, some hard drives are not rated to exceed 7,000 feet while operating, because the air pressure would be too low inside the drive to float the heads properly. As the environmental air pressure changes, air bleeds into or out of the drive so internal and external pressures are identical. Although air does bleed through a vent, contamination usually is not a concern, because the barometric filter on this vent is designed to filter out all particles larger than 0.3 microns (about 12μ-in.) to meet the specifications for cleanliness inside the drive. You can see the vent holes on most drives, which are covered internally by this breather filter. Some drives use even finer grade filter elements to keep out even smaller particles.

I conducted a seminar in Hawaii several years ago, and several of the students were from the Mauna Kea astronomical observatory. They indicated that virtually all the hard disk drives they had tried to use at the observatory site had failed very quickly, if they worked at all. This was no surprise, because the observatory is at the 13,800-foot peak of the mountain, and at that altitude, even people don't function very well! At the time, it was suggested that the students look into solid-state (RAM) disks, tape drives, or even floppy disk drives as their primary storage medium. Since this time, IBM's Adstar division (which produces all IBM hard drives) introduced a line of rugged 3 1/2-inch drives that are hermetically sealed (airtight), although they do have air inside the HDA. Because they carry their own internal air under pressure, these drives can operate at any altitude, and can also withstand extremes of shock and temperature. The drives are designed for military and industrial applications, such as systems used aboard aircraft and in extremely harsh environments.

Hard Disk Temperature Acclimation

Because hard drives have a filtered port to bleed air into or out of the HDA, moisture can enter the drive, and after some period of time, it must be assumed that the humidity inside any hard disk is similar to that outside the drive. Humidity can become a serious problem if it is allowed to condense—and especially if you power up the drive while this condensation is present. Most hard disk manufacturers have specified procedures for acclimating a hard drive to a new environment with different temperature and humidity ranges, and especially for bringing a drive into a warmer environment in which condensation can form. This situation should be of special concern to users of laptop or portable systems. If you leave a portable system in an automobile trunk during the winter, for example, it could be catastrophic to bring the machine inside and power it up without allowing it to acclimate to the temperature indoors.

The following text and Table 10.5 are taken from the factory packaging that Control Data Corporation (later Imprimis and eventually Seagate) used to ship with its hard drives:

> If you have just received or removed this unit from a climate with temperatures at or below 50°F (10°C) do not open this container until the following conditions are met, otherwise condensation could occur and damage to the device and/or media may result. Place this package in the operating environment for the time duration according to the temperature chart.

Table 10.5   Hard Disk Drive Environmental Acclimation Table

Previous Climate Temperature	Acclimation Time
+40°F (+4°C)	13 hours
+30°F (-1°C)	15 hours
+20°F (-7°C)	16 hours
+10°F (-12°C)	17 hours
0°F (-18°C)	18 hours
-10°F (-23°C)	20 hours
-20°F (-29°C)	22 hours
-30°F (-34°C) or less	27 hours

As you can see from this table, you must place a hard disk drive that has been stored in a colder-than-normal environment into its normal operating environment for a specified amount of time to allow it to acclimate before you power it on.

Spindle Motors

The motor that spins the platters is called the spindle motor because it is connected to the spindle around which the platters revolve. Spindle motors in hard disk drives are always connected directly; there are no belts or gears involved. The motor must be free of noise and vibration; otherwise, it can transmit a rumble to the platters that can disrupt reading and writing operations.

The spindle motor must also be precisely controlled for speed. The platters in hard disk drives revolve at speeds ranging from 3,600 to 7,200rpm or more, and the motor has a control circuit with a feedback loop to monitor and control this speed precisely. Because the speed control must be automatic, hard drives do not have a motor-speed adjustment. Some diagnostics programs claim to measure hard drive rotation speed, but all these programs do is estimate the rotational speed by the timing at which sectors pass under the heads.

There is actually no way for a program to measure the hard disk drive's rotational speed; this measurement can be made only with sophisticated test equipment. Don't be alarmed if some diagnostics program tells you that your drive is spinning at an incorrect speed; most likely the program is wrong, not the drive. Platter rotation and timing information is not provided through the hard disk controller interface. In the past, software could give approximate rotational speed estimates by performing multiple sector read requests and timing them, but this was valid only when all drives had the same number of sectors per track and spun at the same speed. Zoned bit recording—combined with the many different rotational speeds used by modern drives, not to mention built-in buffers and caches—means that these calculation estimates cannot be performed accurately by software.

On most drives, the spindle motor is on the bottom of the drive, just below the sealed HDA. Many drives today, however, have the spindle motor built directly into the platter hub inside the HDA. By using an internal hub spindle motor, the manufacturer can stack more platters in the drive, because the spindle motor takes up no vertical space.

Note

Spindle motors, particularly on the larger form-factor drives, can consume a great deal of 12-volt power. Most drives require two to three times the normal operating power when the motor first spins the platters. This heavy draw lasts only a few seconds or until the drive platters reach operating speed. If you have more than one drive, you should try to sequence the start of the spindle motors so the power supply does not have to provide such a large load to all the drives at the same time. Most SCSI and IDE drives have a delayed spindle-motor start feature.

Logic Boards

All hard disk drives have one or more logic boards mounted on them. The logic boards contain the electronics that control the drive's spindle and head actuator systems and present data to the controller in some agreed-upon form. On IDE drives, the boards include the controller itself, while SCSI drives include the controller and the SCSI bus adapter circuit.

Many disk drive failures occur in the logic board not in the mechanical assembly. (This statement does not seem logical, but it is true.) Therefore, you can sometimes repair a failed drive by replacing the logic board rather than the entire drive. Replacing the logic board, moreover, enables you to regain access to the data on the drive—something that replacing the entire drive does not.

In many cases, logic boards plug into the drive and are easily replaceable. These boards are usually mounted with standard screw hardware. If a drive is failing and you have a spare, you might be able to verify a logic-board failure by taking the board off the known good drive and mounting it on the bad one. If your suspicions are confirmed, you can order a new logic board from the drive manufacturer, but unless you have data on the drive you need to recover, it may make more sense to buy a new drive, considering today's low disk drive costs.

To reduce costs further, many third-party vendors can also supply replacement logic-board assemblies. These companies often charge much less than the drive manufacturers for the same components. (See the Vendor List on the CD, for vendors of drive components, including logic boards.)

Cables and Connectors

Hard disk drives typically have several connectors for interfacing to the computer, receiving power, and sometimes grounding to the system chassis. Most drives have at least these three types of connectors:

- Interface connector(s)
- Power connector
- Optional ground connector (tab)

Of these, the interface connectors are the most important, because they carry the data and command signals between the system and the drive. In most cases, the drive interface cables can be connected in a daisy chain or bus-type configuration. Most interfaces support at least two devices, and SCSI (Small Computer System Interface) can support up to seven (Wide SCSI-2 can support up to 15) devices in the chain, in addition to the host adapter. Older interfaces, such as ST-506/412 or ESDI (Enhanced Small Device Interface), used separate cables for data and control signals, but today's SCSI and IDE (Integrated Drive Electronics) drives have a single connector.

◀◀ See "ATA I/O Connector," p. 514, and "SCSI Cables and Connectors," p. 541.

The power connector is usually the same four-pin type that is used in floppy disk drives, and the same power-supply connector plugs into it. Most hard disk drives use both 5- and 12-volt power, although some of the smaller drives designed for portable applications use only 5-volt power. In most cases, the 12-volt power runs the spindle motor and head actuator, and the 5-volt power runs the circuitry. Make sure that your power supply can supply adequate power for the hard disk drives installed in your system.

The 12-volt power consumption of a drive usually varies with the physical size of the unit. The larger the drive is, the faster it spins, and the more platters there are to spin, the more power that it requires. For example, most of the 3 1/2-inch drives on the market today use roughly one-half to one-fourth the power (in watts) of the older 5 1/4-inch drives. Some of the very small (2 1/2- or 1.8-inch) hard disks barely sip electrical power and actually use one watt or less!

A grounding tab provides a positive ground connection between the drive and the system's chassis. In most computers, the hard disk drive is mounted directly to the chassis using screws, so the ground wire is unnecessary. On some systems, the drives are installed on plastic or fiberglass rails, which do not provide proper grounding. These systems must provide a grounding wire plugged into the drive at this grounding tab. Failure to ground the drive may result in improper operation, intermittent failure, or general read and write errors.

Configuration Items

To configure a hard disk drive for installation in a system, you usually must set several jumpers (and, possibly, terminating resistors) properly. These items vary from interface to interface and often from drive to drive as well. A complete discussion of the configuration settings for each interface appears in the section "Hard Disk Installation Procedures" later in this chapter.

The Faceplate or Bezel

Many hard disk drives offer as an option a front faceplate, or bezel (see Figure 10.16). A bezel usually is supplied as an option for the drive rather than as a standard item. In most cases today, the bezel is a part of the case and not the drive itself.

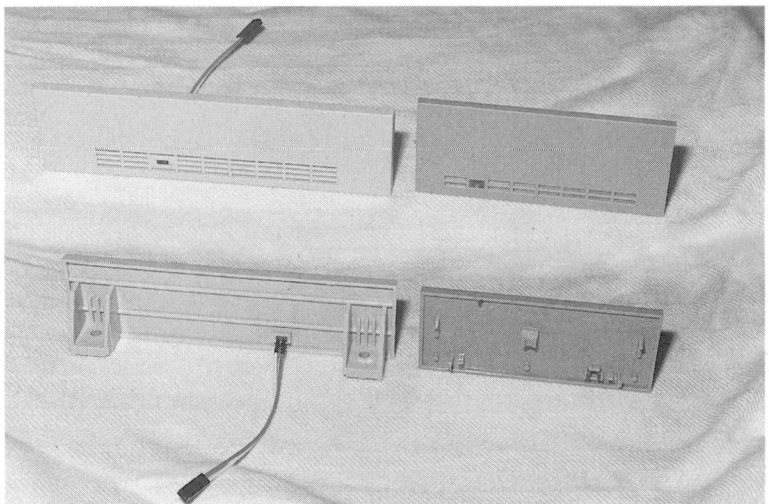

Figure 10.16   Typical 5 1/4- and 3 1/2-inch hard drives bezel shown from the front (as seen on the outside of the PC case) (top) and from the back (bottom) (the inside mounting and LED wiring).

Older systems had the drive installed so it was visible outside the system case. To cover the hole in the case, you would use an optional bezel or faceplate. Bezels often come in several sizes and colors to match various PC systems. Many faceplate configurations for 3 1/2-inch drives are available, including bezels that fit 3 1/2-inch drive bays as well as 5 1/4-inch drive bays. You even have a choice of colors (usually black, cream, or white).

Some bezels feature a light-emitting diode (LED) that flickers when your hard disk is in use. The LED is mounted in the bezel; the wire hanging off the back of the LED plugs into the drive. In some drives, the LED is permanently mounted on the drive, and the bezel has a clear or colored window so you can see the LED flicker while the drive is being accessed.

In systems in which the hard disk is hidden by the unit's cover, a bezel is not needed. In fact, using a bezel may prevent the cover from resting on the chassis properly, in which case the bezel will have to be removed. If you are installing a drive that does not have a proper bezel, frame, or rails to attach to the system, check Appendix C on the CD; several listed vendors offer these accessories for a variety of drives.

Hard Disk Features

To make the best decision in purchasing a hard disk for your system or to understand what differentiates one brand of hard disk from another, you must consider many features. This section examines some of the issues that you should consider when you evaluate drives:

- Reliability
- Shock mounting
- Speed
- Cost

Reliability

When you shop for a drive, you might notice a statistic called the Mean Time Between Failures (MTBF) described in the drive specifications. MTBF figures usually range from 20,000–500,000 hours or more. I usually ignore these figures because they are derived theoretically.

In understanding the MTBF claims, it is important to understand how the manufacturers arrive at them and what they mean. Most manufacturers have a long history of building drives and their drives have seen millions of hours of cumulative use. They can look at the failure rate for previous drive models with the same components and calculate a failure rate for a new drive based on the components used to build the drive assembly. For the electronic circuit board, they can also use industry standard techniques for predicting the failure of the integrated electronics. This enables them to calculate the predicted failure rate for the entire drive unit.

To understand what these numbers mean, it is important to know that the MTBF claims apply to a population of drives, not an individual drive. This means that if a drive claims to have a MTBF of 500,000 hours, you can expect a failure in that population of drives in 500,000 hours of total running time. If there are 1,000,000 drives of this model in service and all 1,000,000 are running at once, you can expect one failure out of this entire population every 1/2 hour. MTBF statistics are not useful for predicting the failure of any individual drive or a small sample of drives.

It is also important to understand the meaning of the word failure. In this sense, a failure is a fault that requires the drive to be returned to the manufacturer for repair, not an occasional failure to read or write a file correctly.

Finally, as some drive manufacturers point out, this measure of MTBF should really be called mean time to first failure. "Between failures" implies that the drive fails, is returned for repair, and then at some point fails again. The interval between repair and the second failure here would be the MTBF. Because in most cases, a failed hard drive that would need manufacturer repair is replaced rather than repaired, the whole MTBF concept is misnamed.

The bottom line is that I do not really place much emphasis on MTBF figures. For an individual drive, they are not accurate predictors of reliability. However, if you are an information systems manager considering the purchase of thousands of PCs or drives per year, or a system vendor building and supporting thousands of systems, it is worth your while to examine these numbers and study the methods used to calculate them by each vendor. If you can understand the vendor's calculations and compare the actual reliability of a large sample of drives, you can purchase more reliable drives and save time and money in service and support.

S.M.A.R.T.

S.M.A.R.T. (Self-Monitoring, Analysis and Reporting Technology) is an industry standard providing failure prediction for disk drives. When S.M.A.R.T. is enabled for a given drive, the drive monitors predetermined attributes that are susceptible to or indicative of drive degradation. Based on changes in the monitored attributes, a failure prediction can be made. If a failure is deemed likely to occur, S.M.A.R.T. makes a status report available so that the system BIOS or driver software can notify the user of the impending problems, perhaps allowing the user to back up the data on the drive before any real problems occur.

Predictable failures are the types of failures that S.M.A.R.T. will attempt to detect. These failures result from the gradual degradation of the drive's performance. According to Seagate, 60 percent of drive failures are mechanical, which are exactly the type of failures S.M.A.R.T. is designed to predict.

Of course, not all failures are predictable, and S.M.A.R.T. cannot help with unpredictable failures that happen without any advance warning. These can be caused by static electricity, improper handling or sudden shock, or circuit failure such as thermal-related solder problems or component failure.

S.M.A.R.T. was originally created by IBM in 1992. That year IBM began shipping 3 1/2-inch hard disk drives equipped with Predictive Failure Analysis (PFA), an IBM-developed technology that periodically measures selected drive attributes and sends a warning message when a predefined threshold is exceeded. IBM turned this technology over to the ANSI organization and it subsequently became the ANSI-standard S.M.A.R.T. protocol for SCSI drives as defined in the ANSI-SCSI Informational Exception Control (IEC) document X3T10/94-190.

Interest in extending this technology to IDE/ATA drives led to the creation of the S.M.A.R.T. Working Group in 1995. Besides IBM, other companies represented in the original group were Seagate Technology, Conner Peripherals (now a part of Seagate), Fujitsu, Hewlett-Packard, Maxtor, Quantum, and Western Digital. The S.M.A.R.T. specification produced by this group and placed in the public domain covers both IDE/ATA and SCSI hard disk drives, and can be found in most of the more recently produced drives on the market.

The S.M.A.R.T. design of attributes and thresholds is similar in IDE/ATA and SCSI environments, but the reporting of information differs.

In an IDE/ATA environment, driver software on the system interprets the alarm signal from the drive generated by the S.M.A.R.T. "report status" command. The driver polls the drive on a regular basis to check the status of this command and, if it signals imminent failure, sends an alarm to the operating system where it will be passed on via an error message to the end user. This structure also allows for future enhancements, which might allow reporting of information other than drive failure conditions. The system can read and evaluate the attributes and alarms reported in addition to the basic "report status" command.

SCSI drives with S.M.A.R.T. only communicate a reliability condition as either good or failing. In a SCSI environment, the failure decision occurs at the disk drive, and the host notifies the user for action. The SCSI specification provides for a sense bit to be flagged if the drive determines that a reliability issue exists. The system then alerts the end user via a message.

The basic requirements for S.M.A.R.T. to function in a system are simple. All you need are a S.M.A.R.T. capable hard disk drive and a S.M.A.R.T. aware BIOS or hard disk driver for your particular operating system. If your BIOS does not support S.M.A.R.T., there are utility programs that can support S.M.A.R.T. on a given system. These include Norton Smart Doctor from Symantec, EZ Drive from Microhouse International, or Data Advisor from Ontrack Data International.

Note that traditional disk diagnostics such as Scandisk and Norton Disk Doctor work only on the data sectors of the disk surface and do not monitor all the drive functions that are monitored by S.M.A.R.T. Most modern disk drives keep spare sectors available to use as substitutes for sectors which have errors. When one of these spares is reallocated, the drive reports the activity to the S.M.A.R.T. counter but still looks completely defect-free to a surface analysis utility such as Scandisk.

Drives with S.M.A.R.T. monitor a variety of attributes that vary from one manufacturer to another. Attributes are selected by the device manufacturer based on their capability to contribute to the prediction of degrading or fault conditions for that particular drive. Most drive manufacturers consider the specific set of attributes being used and the identity of those attributes as vendor specific and proprietary.

Some drives monitor the floating height of the head above the magnetic media. If this height changes from a nominal figure, the drive could fail. Other drives can monitor different attributes such as ECC (error correcting code) circuitry that indicates whether soft errors are occurring when reading or writing data. Some of the attributes monitored on different drives include the following:

- Head floating height
- Data throughput performance
- Spin-up time
- Reallocated (spared) sector count
- Seek error rate
- Seek time performance
- Drive spin-up retry count
- Drive calibration retry count

Each attribute has a threshold limit that is used to determine the existence of a degrading or fault condition. These thresholds are set by the drive manufacturer and cannot be changed.

When there are sufficient changes in the monitored attributes to trigger a S.M.A.R.T. alert, the drive will send an alert message via an IDE/ATA or SCSI command (depending on the type of hard disk drive you have) to the hard disk driver in the system BIOS, which then forwards the message to the operating system. The operating system will then display a warning message as follows:

Caution

Immediately back up your data and replace your hard disk drive. A failure may be imminent.

The message might contain additional information, such as which physical device initiated the alert, a list of the logical drives (partitions) that correspond to the physical device, and even the type, manufacturer, and serial number of the device.

The first thing to do when you receive such an alert would be to heed the warning and back up all the data on the drive. It would be wise to back up to new media and not overwrite any previous good backups you might have, just in case the drive fails before the backup is complete.

After backing up your data, what should you do? S.M.A.R.T warnings can be caused by an external source and may not actually indicate the drive itself is going to fail. For example, environmental changes such as high or low ambient temperatures can trigger a S.M.A.R.T. alert, as can excessive vibration in the drive caused by an external source. Additionally, electrical interference from motors or other devices on the same circuit as your PC can also induce these alerts.

If the alert was not caused by an external source, a drive replacement may be indicated. If the drive is under warranty, contact the vendor and ask them whether they will replace it. If no further alerts occur, the problem may have been an anomaly and you might not need to replace the drive. If you receive further alerts, replacing the drive is recommended. If you can connect both the new and existing (failing) drive to the same system, you might be able to copy the entire contents of the existing drive to the new one, saving you from having to install or reload all the applications and data from your backup.

Performance

When you select a hard disk drive, one of the important features you should consider is the performance (speed) of the drive. Hard drives can have a wide range of performance capabilities. As is true of many things, one of the best indicators of a drive's relative performance is its price. An old saying from the automobile-racing industry is appropriate here: "Speed costs money. How fast do you want to go?"

You can measure the speed of a disk drive in two ways:

- Average seek time
- Transfer rate

Average seek time, normally measured in milliseconds (ms), is the average amount of time it takes to move the heads from one cylinder to another a random distance away. One way to measure this specification is to run many random track-seek operations, and then divide the timed results by the number of seeks performed. This method provides an average time for a single seek.

The standard method used by many drive manufacturers to measure the average seek time involves measuring the time it takes the heads to move across one-third of the total cylinders. Average seek time depends only on the drive itself; the type of interface or controller has little effect on this specification. The rating is a gauge of the capabilities of the head actuator.

Note

Be wary of benchmarks that claim to measure drive seek performance. Most IDE and SCSI drives use a scheme called sector translation, so any commands that the drive receives to move the heads to a specific cylinder may not actually result in the intended physical movement. This situation renders some benchmarks meaningless for those types of drives. SCSI drives also require an additional step, because the commands first must be sent to the drive over the SCSI bus. These drives may seem to have the fastest access times because the command overhead is not factored in by most benchmarks. However, when this overhead is factored in by benchmark programs, these drives receive poor performance figures.

A slightly different measurement, called average access time, involves another element called *latency*. Latency is the average time (in milliseconds) that it takes for a sector to be available after the heads have reached a track. On average, this figure is half the time that it takes for the disk to rotate once, which is 8.33ms at 3,600rpm. A drive that spins twice as fast would have half the latency. A measurement of a drive's average access time is the sum of its average seek time and its latency. This number provides the average amount of time required before the drive can access a randomly requested sector.

Latency is a factor in disk read and write performance. Decreasing the latency increases the speed of access to data or files and is accomplished only by spinning the drive platters faster. I have a drive that spins at 4,318rpm, for a latency of 6.95ms. Some drives spin at 7,200rpm, resulting in an even shorter latency time of only 4.17ms, while others spin at 10,000rpm, resulting in an incredible 3.00ms latency. In addition to increasing performance where real-world access to data is concerned, spinning the platters faster also increases the data-transfer rate after the heads arrive at the desired sectors.

The transfer rate is probably more important to overall system performance than any other statistic. Transfer rate is the rate at which the drive and controller can send data to the system. The transfer rate depends primarily on the drive's HDA and secondarily on the controller. Transfer rates used to be bound more to the limits of the controller, meaning that drives that were connected to newer controllers often outperformed those connected to older controllers. This situation is where the concept of interleaving sectors came from. Interleaving refers to the ordering of the sectors so they are not sequential, enabling a slow controller to keep up without missing the next sector.

Modern drives with integrated controllers are fully capable of keeping up with the raw drive transfer rate. In other words, they no longer have to interleave the sectors to slow the data for the controller. Interleaving was done when slower controllers were used that were not ready for the next sector immediately after the previous one had been read, causing it to go by before the controller was ready, and the drive to spin another complete revolution just to read it. By numbering the sectors out of order, skipping one or more at a time, the controller would only have to read every second or third sector, which actually made things faster because additional revolutions would not be required. Modern controllers are very fast, and interleaving is no longer necessary since the controller can read the sectors one after the other in consecutive order. Interleaving is covered in more detail later in this chapter.

Another performance issue is the raw interface performance which, in IDE or SCSI drives, is usually far higher than any of the drives themselves are capable of sustaining. Be wary of transfer specifications that are quoted for the interface and not the drive, because they may have little effect on what the drive can actually produce. The drive interface limits the maximum theoretical transfer rate; the actual drive and controller generate the real limits on performance.

To calculate the true transfer rate of a drive, you have to know several important specifications. The two most important specifications are the true rotational speed of the drive (in rpm) and the average number of physical sectors on each track (SPT). I say "average" because most drives today use a zoned bit recording technique that creates different numbers of sectors on the cylinders. The transfer rate on zoned bit recording drives always is fastest in the outermost zone, where the sector per track count is highest. Also, be aware that many drives (especially zoned bit recording drives) are configured with sector translation, so the number of sectors per track reported by the BIOS has little to do with the actual physical characteristics of the drive. You must know the drive's true physical parameters, rather than the values that the BIOS uses.

When you know these figures, you can use the following formula to determine the maximum data transfer rate in millions of bits per second (Mbps):

$$\text{Maximum Transfer Rate (Mbps)} = \text{SPT} \times 512 \text{ bytes} \times \text{rpm}/60 \text{ seconds}/1{,}000{,}000 \text{ bits}$$

For example, the Seagate ST-12551N 2G 3 1/2-inch drive spins at 7,200rpm and has an average of 81 sectors per track. The maximum transfer rate for this drive is figured as follows:

$$81 \times 512 \times 7{,}200/60/1{,}000{,}000 = 4.98\text{Mbps}$$

Using this formula, you can calculate the true maximum sustained transfer rate of any drive.

Cache Programs and Caching Controllers

At the software level, disk cache programs such as SMARTDRV (in DOS) or VCACHE (in Windows 9x, Windows NT, and Windows 2000) can have a major effect on disk drive performance. These cache programs hook into the BIOS hard drive interrupt and intercept the read and write calls to the disk BIOS from application programs and device drivers.

When an application program wants to read data from a hard drive, the cache program intercepts the read request, passes the read request to the hard drive controller in the usual way, saves the data read from the disk in its cache memory buffer, and then passes the data back to the application program. Depending on the size of the cache buffer, data from numerous sectors can be read into and saved in the buffer.

When the application wants to read more data, the cache program again intercepts the request and examines its buffers to see whether the requested data is still in the cache. If so, the program passes the data back from the cache to the application immediately, without another hard drive operation. Because the cached data is stored in memory, this method speeds access tremendously and can greatly affect disk drive performance measurements.

Most controllers now have some form of built-in hardware buffer or cache that doesn't intercept or use any BIOS interrupts. Instead, the drive caches data at the hardware level, which is invisible to normal performance-measurement software. Manufacturers originally included track read-ahead buffers in controllers to permit 1:1 interleave performance. Some manufacturers now increase the size of these read-ahead buffers in the controller, while others add intelligence by using a cache instead of a simple buffer.

Many IDE and SCSI drives have cache memory built directly into the drive's on-board controller. For example, the Seagate Hawk 4GB drive on which I am saving this chapter has 512KB of built-in cache memory. Other drives have even larger built-in caches, such as the Seagate Barracuda 4GB with 1MB of integrated cache memory. I remember when 640KB was a lot of memory for an entire system. Now, tiny 3 1/2-inch hard disk drives have more than that built right in! These integrated caches are part of the reason many IDE and SCSI drives perform so well.

Although software and hardware caches can make a drive faster for routine transfer operations, a cache will not affect the true maximum transfer rate that the drive can sustain.

Interleave Selection

In a discussion of disk performance, the issue of interleave often comes up. Although traditionally this was more a controller performance issue than a drive issue, modern IDE and SCSI hard disk drives with built-in controllers are fully capable of processing the data as fast as the drive can send it. In other words, all modern IDE and SCSI drives are formatted with no interleave (sometimes expressed as a 1:1 interleave ratio). On older hard drive types, such as MFM and ESDI, you could modify the interleave during a low-level format to optimize the drive's performance. Today, drives are low-level formatted at the factory and interleave adjustments are a moot topic. Since altering the interleave or sector ordering in any way requires a low-level format to be performed, all data is normally lost in this process.

When a disk is low-level formatted, numbers are assigned to the sectors. These numbers are written in the Sector ID fields in the Sector header and can be written or updated only by a low-level format. With older drive interfaces that used discrete controllers such as ST-506/412 or ESDI, you often had to calculate the best interleave value for the particular controller and system that you were using. This allowed you to low-level format the drive and number the sectors to offer optimum performance.

Notice that nearly all IDE and SCSI drives have interleave ratios fixed at 1:1 and built-in controllers that can handle these ratios with no problem. In these drives, there no longer is a need to calculate or specify an interleave ratio, but knowing about interleaving can give you some further insight into the way these drives function.

Many older ST-506/412 controllers could not handle the sectors as quickly as the drive could send them. Suppose that you have a standard ST-5096/412 drive with 17 sectors on each track and you low-level formatted the drive and specified a 1:1 interleave—numbered the sectors on each track consecutively.

Now suppose that you want to read some data from the drive. The controller commands the drive to position the heads at a specific track and to read all 17 sectors from that track. The heads move and arrive at the desired track. The time it takes for the heads to move is called the seek time. When the heads arrive at the desired track, you have to wait for an average half-revolution of the disk for the first sector to arrive. This wait is called *latency*. After an average latency of half of a disk revolution, the sector numbered 1 arrives below the heads. While the disk continues to spin at 3,600rpm (60 revolutions per second), the data is read from Sector 1, and as the data is being transferred from the controller to the system board, the disk continues to spin. Finally, the data is completely moved to the motherboard, and the controller is ready for Sector 2. Figure 10.17 shows what is happening.

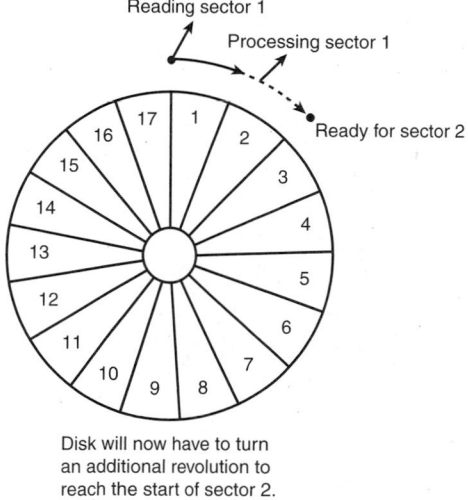

Figure 10.17   A hard disk interleave ratio (1:1) too low for the controller.

But wait, there's a problem here. Because the disk continues to spin at such a high rate of speed, the Sector 2 passed below the head while the controller was working, and by the time the controller is ready again, the heads will be coming to the start of Sector 3. Because the controller needs to read sector 2 next, however, the controller must wait for the disk to spin a full revolution, or until the start of Sector 2 comes below the heads. After this additional disk revolution, Sector 2 arrives below the heads and is read. While the controller is transferring the data from

Sector 2 to the motherboard, Sector 3 passes below the heads. When the controller finally is ready to read Sector 3, the heads are coming to the start of Sector 4, so another complete revolution is required, and the controller will have to get Sector 4 on the next go-around. This scenario continues, with each new revolution allowing only one sector to be read and missing the next sector because that sector passes below the heads before the controller is ready.

As you can see, the timing of this procedure is not working out very well. At this pace, 17 full revolutions of the disk will be required to read all 17 sectors. Because each revolution takes 1/60 of one second, it will take 17/60 of one second to read this track, or almost one-third of a second—a very long time, by computer standards.

Can this performance be improved? You notice that after reading a specific sector from the disk, the controller takes some time to transfer the sector data to the motherboard. The next sector that the controller can catch in this example is the second sector away from the first one. In other words, the controller seems to be capable of catching every second sector.

I hope that you now can imagine the perfect solution to this problem: Number the sectors out of order. The new numbering scheme takes into account how fast the controller works; the sectors are numbered so that each time the controller is ready for the next sector, the sector coming below the heads is numbered as the next sector that the controller will want to read. Figure 10.18 shows this new interleaved sector-numbering scheme.

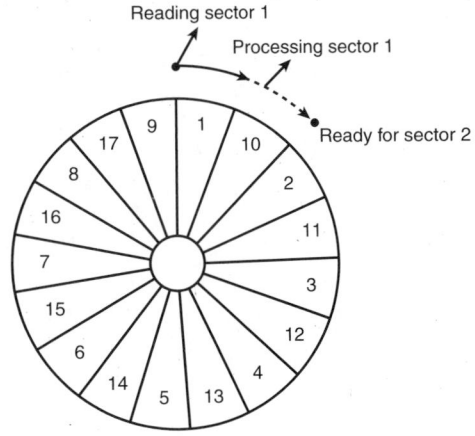

Figure 10.18 A hard disk interleave ratio (2:1) matching the controller's capabilities.

The new numbering system eliminates the extra disk revolution that previously was required to pick up each sector. Under the new scheme, the controller will read all 17 sectors on the disk in only two complete revolutions. Renumbering the sectors on the disk in this manner is called *interleaving*, which normally is expressed as a ratio. The interleave ratio in this example is 2:1, which means that the next numbered sector is 2 sectors away from the preceding one. If the controller is capable of handling this, only two complete revolutions are needed to read an entire track. Thus, reading the track takes only 2/60 of one second at the 2:1 interleave, rather than the

17/60 of one second required to read the disk at the 1:1 interleave—an improvement of 800 percent in the data transfer rate.

This example depicts a system in which the ideal interleave is 2:1. I used this example because most controllers that came in older 286 and 386 class systems worked in exactly this manner. If you set such a controller for a 1:1 interleave, you likely would make the drive eight times slower than it should be. This situation, however, has changed with newer controller technology.

The correct interleave for an older system depends primarily on the controller and secondarily on the speed of the system into which the controller is plugged. A controller and system that can handle a *consecutive sector interleave* (a 1:1 interleave) must transfer data as fast as the disk drive can present it; this used to be quite a feat but now is standard. Any 286 or faster system easily can handle the 1:1 interleave data transfer rate. The only types of systems that truly were too slow to handle a 1:1 interleave effectively are the original 4.77MHz PC- and XT-type systems. Those systems have a maximum throughput to the slots of just under 400KB per second—not fast enough to support a 1:1 interleave controller.

Head and Cylinder Skewing

Another performance adjustment that you could make at one time during a low-level format of a drive was to adjust the skew of the drive's heads and cylinders. Head skew is the offset in logical sector numbering between the same physical sectors on two tracks below adjacent heads of the same cylinder. The number of sectors skewed when switching from head to head within a single cylinder compensates for head switching and controller overhead time. *Cylinder skew* is the offset in logical sector numbering between the same physical sectors on two adjacent tracks on two adjacent cylinders.

Note that just as with interleaving, neither of these parameters is adjustable on modern IDE or SCSI drives. This information is relevant only for older drive technology. The discussion is included here to help understand what happens inside the drive. IDE and SCSI drives do use skewing, but it is factory preset and impossible to change.

With a 1:1 interleave controller, the maximum data transfer rate can be maintained when reading and writing sectors to the disk. Although it would seem that there is no other way to further improve efficiency and the transfer rate, there are two other factors that are similar to interleave: head and cylinder skewing.

When a drive is reading (or writing) data sequentially, all the sectors on a given track are read, and then the drive must electronically switch to the next head in the cylinder to continue the operation. If the sectors are not skewed from head to head within the cylinder, no delay occurs after the last sector on one track and before the arrival of the first sector on the next track. Because all drives require some time (although a small amount) to switch from one head to another, and because the controller also adds some overhead to the operation, it is likely that by the time the drive is ready to read the sectors on the newly selected track, the first sector will already have passed by. By skewing the sectors from one head to another—that is, rotating their arrangement on the track so that the arrival of the first sector is delayed relative to the preceding

Floppy Disk Drives

This chapter examines floppy disk drives and disks. It explores the different types of drives and disks that have been and are now available, how they function, and how to properly install and service these drives and disks.

Alan Shugart is generally credited with inventing the floppy disk drive in 1967 while working for IBM. One of Shugart's senior engineers, David Noble, actually proposed the flexible medium (then 8 inches in diameter) and the protective jacket with the fabric lining. Shugart left IBM in 1969, and in 1976 his company, Shugart Associates, introduced the minifloppy (5 1/4-inch) disk drive. It, of course, became the standard eventually used by personal computers, rapidly replacing the 8-inch drives. He also helped create the Shugart Associates System Interface (SASI), which was later renamed SCSI (Small Computer System Interface) when approved as an ANSI standard.

Sony introduced the first 3 1/2-inch microfloppy drives and diskettes in 1983. The first significant company to adopt the 3 1/2-inch floppy for general use was Hewlett-Packard in 1984 with their partially PC-compatible HP-150 system. The industry adoption of the 3 1/2-inch drive was furthered by Apple using it in the first Macintosh systems in 1984, and IBM putting it into their entire PC product line starting in 1986.

Note that all PC floppy disk drives are still based on (and mostly compatible with) the original Shugart designs, including the electrical and command interfaces. Compared to other parts of the PC, the floppy disk drive has undergone relatively few changes over the years.

Drive Components

All floppy disk drives, regardless of type, consist of several basic common components. To properly install and service a disk drive, you must be able to identify these components and understand their functions (see Figure 11.1).

Read/Write Heads

A floppy disk drive normally has two read/write heads, one for each side of the disk, with both heads being used for reading and writing on their respective disk sides (see Figure 11.2). At one time, single-sided drives were available for PC systems (the original PC had such drives), but today single-sided drives are a fading memory.

Note

Many people do not realize that the first head on a floppy disk drive is the bottom one. Single-sided drives, in fact, used only the bottom head; the top head was replaced by a felt pressure pad. Another bit of disk trivia is that the top head (Head 1) is not directly over the bottom head (Head 0). The top head is offset either four or eight tracks inward from the bottom head, depending on the drive type.

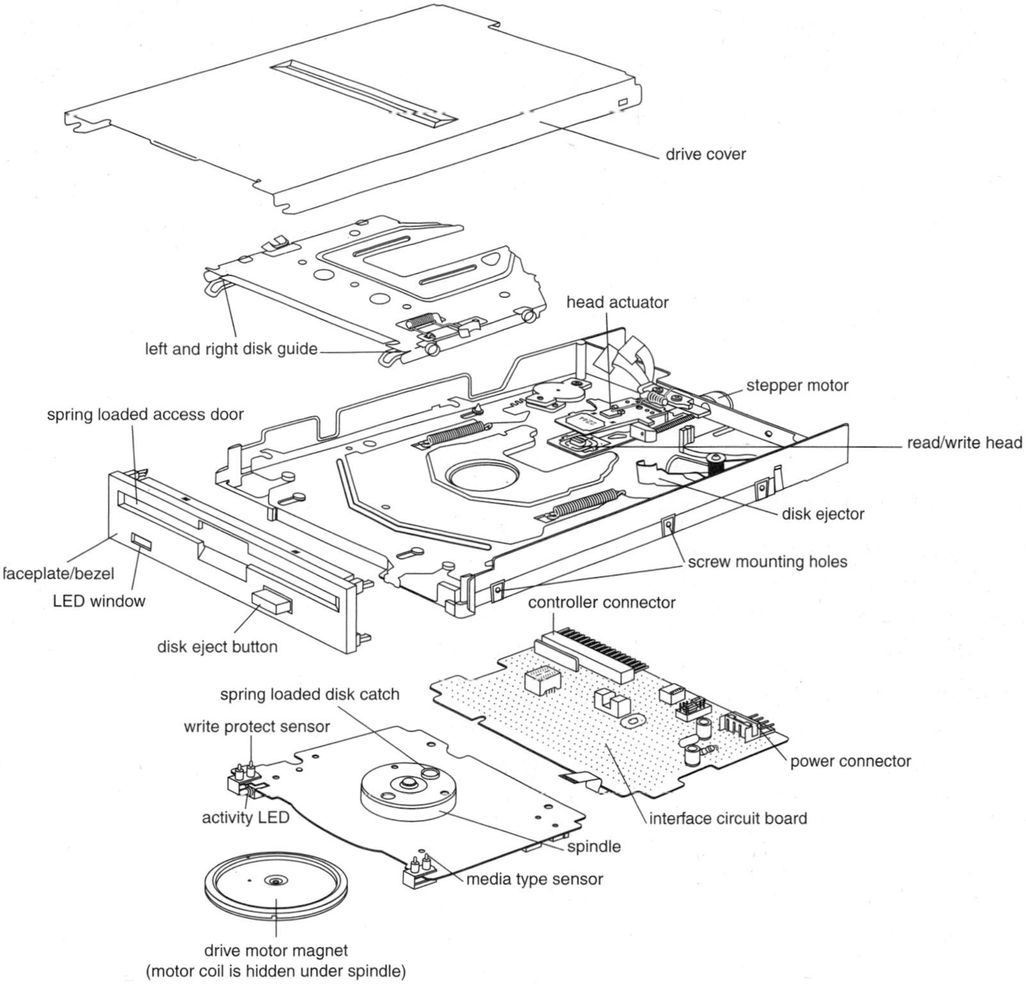

drive cover

head actuator

stepper motor

left and right disk guide

read/write head

spring loaded access door

disk ejector

screw mounting holes

faceplate/bezel

LED window

controller connector

disk eject button

spring loaded disk catch

write protect sensor

power connector

activity LED

interface circuit board

spindle

media type sensor

drive motor magnet
(motor coil is hidden under spindle)

Figure 11.1   A typical floppy disk drive.

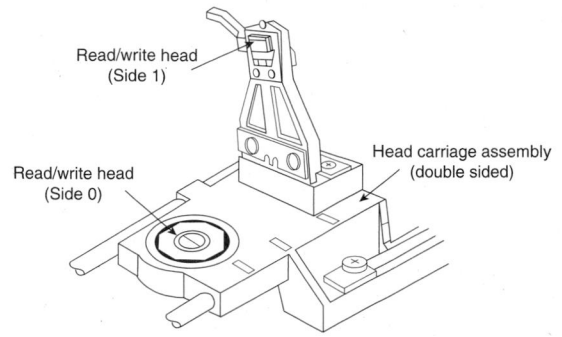

Read/write head
(Side 1)

Head carriage assembly
(double sided)

Read/write head
(Side 0)

Figure 11.2   A double-sided drive head assembly.

The head mechanism is moved by a motor called a *head actuator*. The heads can move in and out over the surface of the disk in a straight line to position themselves over various tracks. On a floppy drive, the heads move in and out tangentially to the tracks that they record on the disk. This is different from hard disks where the heads move on a rotating arm similar to the tone-arm of a record player. Because the top and bottom heads are mounted on the same rack, or mechanism, they move in unison and cannot move independently of each other. Both the upper and lower heads each define tracks on their respective side of the disk medium, while at any given head position, the tracks under the top and bottom head simultaneously are called a *cylinder*. Most floppy disks are recorded with 80 tracks on each side (160 tracks total), which would be 80 cylinders.

The heads themselves are made of soft ferrous (iron) compounds with electromagnetic coils. Each head is a composite design, with a read/write head centered within two tunnel-erase heads in the same physical assembly (see Figure 11.3).

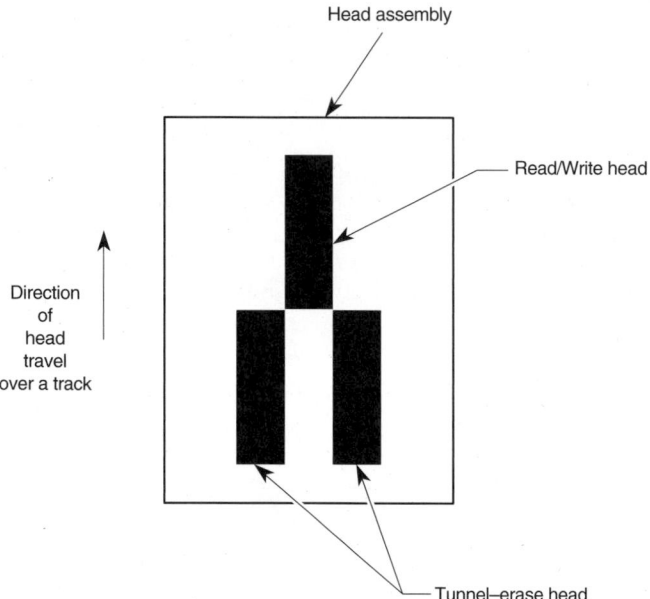

Figure 11.3   Composite construction of a typical floppy disk drive head.

Floppy disk drives use a recording method called *tunnel erasure*. As the drive writes to a track, the trailing tunnel-erase heads erase the outer bands of the track, trimming it cleanly on the disk. The heads force the data into a specified narrow "tunnel" on each track. This process prevents the signal from one track from being confused with the signals from adjacent tracks, which would happen if the signal were allowed to naturally "taper off" to each side. *Alignment* is the placement of the heads with respect to the tracks they must read and write. Head alignment can be checked only against some sort of reference-standard disk recorded by a perfectly aligned machine. These types of disks are available, and you can use one to check your drive's alignment. However, this is usually not practical for the end user, because one calibrated analog alignment disk can cost more than a new drive.

The floppy disk drive's two heads are spring-loaded and physically grip the disk with a small amount of pressure, which means that they are in direct contact with the disk surface while reading and writing to the disk. Because floppy disk drives spin at only 300 or 360rpm, this pressure does not present an excessive friction problem. Some newer disks are specially coated with Teflon or other compounds to further reduce friction and enable the disk to slide more easily under the heads. Because of the contact between the heads and disk, a buildup of the magnetic material from the disk eventually forms on the heads. The buildup should periodically be cleaned off the heads as part of a preventive-maintenance or normal service program. Most manufacturers recommend cleaning the heads after every 40 hours of drive operation, which, considering how many people use these drives today, could be a lifetime.

To read and write to the disk properly, the heads must be in direct contact with the magnetic medium. Very small particles of loose oxide, dust, dirt, smoke, fingerprints, or hair can cause problems with reading and writing the disk. Disk and drive manufacturers' tests have found that a spacing as little as .000032 inch (32 millionths of an inch) between the heads and medium can cause read/write errors. You now can understand why it is important to handle disks carefully and avoid touching or contaminating the surface of the disk medium in any way. The rigid jacket and protective shutter for the head access aperture on 3 1/2-inch disks is excellent for preventing problems caused by contamination. Disks that are 5 1/4-inch do not have the same protective elements, which is perhaps one reason why they have fallen into disuse. If you still use 5 1/4-inch floppy disks, you should exercise extra care in their handling.

The Head Actuator

The head actuator for a floppy disk drive uses a special kind of motor, called a *stepper motor*, that rotates in discrete increments or steps (see Figure 11.4). This type of motor does not spin around continuously; rather, the motor turns a precise specified distance and stops. Stepper motors are not infinitely variable in their positioning; they move in fixed increments, or *detents*, and must stop at a particular detent position. This is ideal for disk drives, as the location of each track on the disk can then be defined by moving one or more increments of the motor's motion. The disk controller can instruct the motor to position itself any number of steps within the range of its travel. To position the heads at cylinder 25, for example, the controller instructs the motor to go to the 25th detent position or step from Cylinder 0.

The stepper motor can be linked to the head rack in one of two ways. In the first, the link is a coiled, split-steel band. The band winds and unwinds around the spindle of the stepper motor, translating the rotary motion into linear motion. Some drives, however, use a worm-gear arrangement rather than a band. In this type of drive, the head assembly rests on a worm gear driven directly off the stepper motor shaft. Because this arrangement is more compact, you normally find worm-gear actuators on the smaller 3 1/2-inch drives.

Most stepper motors used in floppy disk drives can step in specific increments that relate to the track spacing on the disk. Older 48 Track Per Inch (TPI) drives have a motor that steps in increments of 3.6 degrees. This means that each 3.6 degrees of stepper motor rotation moves the heads from one track to the next. Most 96 or 135 TPI drives have a stepper motor that moves in 1.8 degree increments, which is exactly half of what the 48 TPI drives use. Sometimes you see this information actually printed or stamped right on the stepper motor itself, which is useful if you are trying to figure out what type of drive you have. 5 1/4-inch 360K drives were the only 48 TPI drives that used the 3.6 degree increment stepper motor. All other drive types normally use the 1.8 degree stepper motor. On most drives, the stepper motor is a small cylindrical object near one corner of the drive.

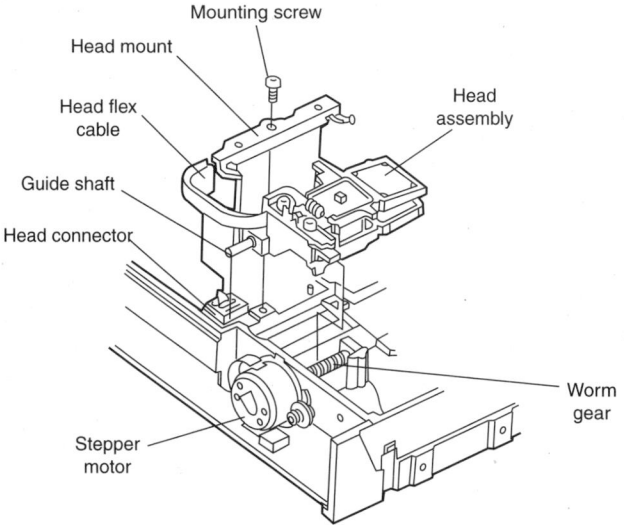

Figure 11.4 An expanded view of a stepper motor and head actuator.

A stepper motor usually has a full travel time of about 1/5 of a second—about 200ms. On average, a half-stroke is 100ms, and a one-third stroke is 66ms. The timing of a one-half or one-third stroke of the head-actuator mechanism is often used to determine the reported average-access time for a disk drive. Average-access time is the normal amount of time the heads spend moving at random from one track to another.

The Spindle Motor

The spindle motor is what spins the disk. The normal speed of rotation is either 300 or 360rpm, depending on the type of drive. The 5 1/4-inch high-density (HD) drive is the only drive that spins at 360rpm; all others, including the 5 1/4-inch double-density (DD), 3 1/2-inch DD, 3 1/2-inch HD, and 3 1/2-inch extra-high density (ED) drives, spin at 300rpm. This is a slow speed when compared to a hard disk drive, which helps to explain why floppy disk drives have much lower data transfer rates. However, this slow speed also makes it possible for the drive heads to be in physical contact with the disk while it is spinning, without causing friction damage.

Most earlier drives used a mechanism by which the spindle motor physically turned the disk spindle with a belt, but all modern drives use a direct-drive system with no belts. The direct-drive systems are more reliable and less expensive to manufacture, as well as smaller in size. The earlier belt-driven systems did have more rotational torque available to turn a sticky disk because of the torque multiplication factor of the belt system. Most newer direct-drive systems use an automatic torque compensation capability that sets the disk-rotation speed to a fixed 300 or 360rpm, and compensates with additional torque for high-friction disks or less torque for more slippery ones. Besides compensating for different amounts of friction, this arrangement eliminates the need to adjust the rotational speed of the drive, something that was frequently required on older drives.

Circuit Boards

A disk drive always incorporates one or more *logic boards*, which are circuit boards that contain the circuitry used to control the head actuator, read/write heads, spindle motor, disk sensors, and other components on the drive. The logic board implements the drive's interface to the controller board in the system unit.

The standard interface used by all PC floppy disk drives is termed the Shugart Associates SA-400 interface, which was invented in the 1970s and is based on the NEC 765 controller chip. All modern floppy controllers contain circuits that are compatible with the original NEC 765 chip. This industry-standard interface is why you can purchase "off-the-shelf" drives (raw, or bare, drives) that can plug directly into your controller.

Tip

Logic boards for a drive can fail and usually are difficult to obtain as a spare part. One board often costs more than replacing the entire drive. I recommend keeping failed or misaligned drives that might otherwise be discarded so they can be used for their remaining good parts, such as logic boards. You can use the parts to restore a failing drive very cost-effectively.

The Controller

At one time, the controller for a computer's floppy disk drives took the form of a dedicated expansion card installed in an ISA bus slot. Later implementations used a multifunction card that provided the IDE/ATA, parallel, and serial port interfaces in addition to the floppy disk drive controller. Today's PCs have the floppy controller integrated into the motherboard, usually in the form of a Super I/O chip that also includes the parallel and serial interfaces, among other things. Even though the floppy controller can be found in the Super I/O chip on the motherboard, it is still interfaced to the system via the ISA (Industry Standard Architecture) bus, and functions exactly as if it were a card installed in an ISA slot. These built-in controllers are normally configured via the system BIOS Setup routines, and can be disabled if an actual floppy controller card is going to be installed.

Whether it is built-in or not, all primary floppy controllers use a standard set of system resources as follows:

- IRQ 6 (Interrupt Request)
- DMA 2 (Direct Memory Address)
- I/O ports 3F0-3F5, 3F7 (Input/Output)

On the other (right) side of the disk from the write-protect hole, there is usually another hole called the media-density-selector hole. If this hole is present, the disk is constructed of a special medium and is therefore an HD or ED disk. If the media-sensor hole is exactly opposite the write-protect hole, it indicates a 1.44MB HD disk. If the media-sensor hole is located more toward the top of the disk (the metal shutter is at the top of the disk), it indicates an ED disk. No hole on the right side means that the disk is a low-density disk. Most 3 1/2-inch drives have a media sensor that controls recording capability based on the absence or presence of these holes.

The actual magnetic medium in both the 3 1/2-inch and 5 1/4-inch disks is constructed of the same basic materials. They use a plastic base (usually Mylar) coated with a magnetic compound. High-density disks use a cobalt-ferric compound; extended-density disks use a barium-ferric media compound. The rigid jacket material on the 3 1/2-inch disks often causes people to believe incorrectly that these disks are some sort of "hard disk" and not really a floppy disk. The disk "cookie" inside the 3 1/2-inch case is just as floppy as the 5 1/4-inch variety.

Floppy Disk Media Types and Specifications

This section examines the types of disks that have been available to PC owners over the years. Especially interesting are the technical specifications that can separate one type of disk from another, as Table 11.6 shows. The following sections define all the specifications used to describe a typical disk.

Table 11.6   Floppy Disk Media Specifications

	5 1/4-inch			3 1/2-inch		
Media Parameters	**Double-Density (DD)**	**Quad Density (QD)**	**High Density (HD)**	**Double Density (DD)**	**High Density (HD)**	**Extra High Density (ED)**
Tracks Per Inch (TPI)	48	96	96	135	135	135
Bits Per Inch (BPI)	5,876	5,876	9,646	8,717	17,434	34,868
Media Formulation	Ferrite	Ferrite	Cobalt	Cobalt	Cobalt	Barium
Coercivity (Oersteds)	300	300	600	600	720	750
Thickness (Micro-in.)	100	100	50	70	40	100
Recording Polarity	Horiz.	Horiz.	Horiz.	Horiz.	Horiz.	Vert.

Density

Density, in simplest terms, is a measure of the amount of information that can be reliably packed into a specific area of a recording surface. The keyword here is reliably.

Disks have two types of densities: longitudinal density and linear density. *Longitudinal density* is indicated by how many tracks can be recorded on the disk, and is often expressed as a number of tracks per inch (TPI). *Linear density* is the capability of an individual track to store data, and is often indicated as a number of bits per inch (BPI). Unfortunately, these types of densities are often confused when discussing different disks and drives.

Media Coercivity and Thickness

The *coercivity* specification of a disk refers to the magnetic-field strength required to make a proper recording. Coercivity, measured in oersteds, is a value indicating magnetic strength. A disk with a higher coercivity rating requires a stronger magnetic field to make a recording on that disk. With lower ratings, the disk can be recorded with a weaker magnetic field. In other words, the lower the coercivity rating, the more sensitive the disk.

HD media demands higher coercivity ratings so the adjacent magnetic domains don't interfere with each other. For this reason, HD media is actually less sensitive and requires a stronger recording signal strength.

Another factor is the thickness of the disk. The thinner the disk, the less influence a region of the disk has on another adjacent region. The thinner disks, therefore, can accept many more bits per inch without eventually degrading the recording.

Caring for and Handling Floppy Disks and Drives

Most computer users know the basics of disk care. Disks can be damaged or destroyed easily by the following:

- Touching the recording surface with your fingers or anything else
- Writing on a disk label (which has been affixed to a disk) with a ball-point pen or pencil
- Bending the disk
- Spilling coffee or other substances on the disk
- Overheating a disk (leaving it in the hot sun or near a radiator, for example)
- Exposing a disk to stray magnetic fields

Despite all these cautions, disks are rather hardy storage devices; I can't say that I have ever destroyed one by just writing on it with a pen, because I do so all the time. I am careful, however, not to press too hard, so I don't put a crease in the disk. Also, touching a disk does not necessarily ruin a disk, but rather makes the disk and your drive head dirty with oil and dust. The real danger to your disks comes from magnetic fields that, because they are unseen, can sometimes be found in places you never imagined.

For example, all color monitors (and color TV sets) have a degaussing coil around the face of the tube that demagnetizes the shadow mask when you turn the monitor on. If you keep your disks anywhere near (within one foot) of the front of the color monitor, you expose them to a strong magnetic field every time you turn on the monitor. Keeping disks in this area is not a good idea because the field is designed to demagnetize objects, and indeed works well for demagnetizing disks. The effect is cumulative and irreversible.

Another source of powerful magnetic fields is an electric motor found in vacuum cleaners, heaters, air conditioners, fans, electric pencil sharpeners, and so on. Do not place these devices near areas where you store disks. Audio speakers also contain magnets, but most of the speakers sold for use with PCs are shielded to minimize disk corruption.

Three and a half-inch disks should be stored between 40–127° Fahrenheit. Five and a 1/4-inch disks should be stored between 40–140° Fahrenheit. In both cases, humidity should not exceed 90 percent.

Airport X-ray Machines and Metal Detectors

People associate myths with things they cannot see, and we certainly cannot see data as it is stored on a disk or the magnetic fields that can alter the data.

One of my favorite myths to dispel is that the airport X-ray machine somehow damages disks. I have a great deal of experience in this area from having traveled around the country for the past 10 years or so with disks and portable computers in hand. I fly about 150,000 miles per year, and my portable computer equipment and disks have been through X-ray machines more than 100 times each year.

The biggest problem people have when they approach the airport X-ray machines with disks or computers is that they don't pass the stuff through! Seriously, X-rays are essentially just a form of light, and disks and computers are not affected by X-rays at anywhere near the levels found in these machines.

What can damage your magnetic media is the metal detector. Time and time again, someone with magnetic media or a portable computer approaches the security check. They freeze and say, "Oh no, I have disks and a computer—they have to be hand-inspected." The person then refuses to place the disk and computer on the X-ray belt, and either walks through the metal detector with disks and computer in hand or passes the items over to the security guard, in very close proximity to the metal detector.

Metal detectors work by monitoring disruptions in a weak magnetic field. A metal object inserted in the field area causes the field's shape to change, which the detector observes. This principle, which is the reason that the detectors are sensitive to metal objects, can be dangerous to your disks; the X-ray machine, however, is the safest area through which to pass either your disk or your computer.

The X-ray machine is not dangerous to magnetic media because it merely exposes the media to electromagnetic radiation at a particular (very high) frequency. Blue light is an example of electromagnetic radiation of a different frequency. The only difference between X-rays and blue light is in the frequency, or wavelength, of the emission.

Some people worry about the effect of X-ray radiation on their system's EPROM (Erasable Programmable Read-Only Memory) chips. This concern might actually be more valid than worrying about disk damage because EPROMs are erased by certain forms of electromagnetic radiation. In reality, however, you do not need to worry about this effect either. EPROMs are erased by direct exposure to very intense ultraviolet light. Specifically, to be erased an EPROM must be exposed to a 12,000 uw/cm^2 UV light source with a wavelength of 2,537 angstroms for 15 to 20 minutes, and at a distance of 1 inch. Increasing the power of the light source or decreasing the distance from the source can shorten the erasure time to a few minutes.

The airport X-ray machine is different by a factor of 10,000 in wavelength. The field strength, duration, and distance from the emitter source are nowhere near what is necessary for EPROM erasure. Many circuit-board manufacturers even use X-ray inspection on circuit boards (with components including EPROMs installed) to test and check quality control during manufacture.

In my own experiences, I have passed one disk through different airport X-ray machines for two years, averaging two or three passes a week. The same disk still remains intact with all the original files and data and has never been reformatted. I also have a portable computer that has gone through X-ray machines safely every week for more than four years. I prefer to pass computers and disks through the X-ray machine because it offers the best shielding from the magnetic fields produced by the metal detector standing next to it. Doing so may also lessen the "hassle factor" with the security personnel because if I have the computer X-rayed, they often do not require that I unpack it and turn it on. Unfortunately, with the greater emphasis on airport security these days, even when the computer is X-rayed, some airlines require that the system be demonstrated (turned on) anyway.

Now you may not want to take my word for it, but there has been scientific research published that corroborates what I have stated. A few years ago, a study was published by two scientists, one of whom actually designs X-ray tubes for a major manufacturer. Their study was titled "Airport X-rays and Floppy Disks: No Cause for Concern," and was published in 1993 in the journal *Computer Methods and Programs in Biomedicine*. According to the abstract,

> A controlled study was done to test the possible effects of X-rays on the integrity of data stored on common sizes of floppy disks. Disks were exposed to doses of X-rays up to seven times that to be expected during airport examination of baggage. The readability of nearly 14 megabytes of data was unaltered by X-irradiation, indicating that floppy disks need not be given special handling during X-ray inspection of baggage.

In fact, the disks were retested after two years of storage, and there has still been no measurable degradation since the exposure.

Drive-Installation Procedures

In most cases, installing a floppy disk drive is a matter of physically attaching the drive to the computer chassis or case, and then plugging the power and signal cables into the drive. Some type of bracket and screws are normally required to attach the drive to the chassis. These are normally included with the chassis or case itself. Several companies listed in Appendix A specialize in cases, cables, brackets, screw hardware, and other items useful in assembling systems or installing drives.

Note

Because floppy disk drives are generally installed into the same half-height bays as hard disk drives, the physical mounting of the drive in the computer case is the same for both units. See "Hard Disk Installation Procedures," in Chapter 14, "Physical Drive Installation and Configuration," for more information on the process.

When you connect a drive, make sure the power cable is installed properly. The cable is normally keyed so you cannot plug it in backward. Also, install the data and control cable. If there is no key is in this cable, use the colored wire in the cable as a guide to the position of pin 1. This cable is oriented correctly when you plug it in so the colored wire is plugged into the disk drive connector toward the cut-out notch in the drive edge connector.

Older drives used to require various jumpers to be set to allow the drive to work properly. The two most common jumpers were the Drive Select (DS) jumper and the Disk Change (DC) jumper. If you encounter an older drive with these jumpers, there are a few simple rules to follow. The DS (Drive Select) jumper will normally have two positions, labeled 0 and 1 or in some cases 1 and 2. In all PC installations, the DS jumper should be set on the second position, no matter what it is numbered. This will allow the drive on the cable before the twist to function as drive B: and the drive at the end of the cable after the twist to function as drive A:. The DC jumper setting is normally an on or off setting. For PC usage, if the drive has a DC jumper, it must be set on or enabled.

Troubleshooting Floppy Drives

Because of their very low cost, floppy drives have become a fairly disposable item these days. Also their connection to the system has become simpler over the years as drives today come preconfigured with no jumpers or switches to set. The cables are fairly standardized as well. What all this means is that if the drive or cable are suspected as being defective, they should be replaced rather than repaired. This section discusses some of the most common problems floppy drives can have and how to troubleshoot them.

Problem

Dead drive—the drive does not spin and the LED never comes on.

Cause/Solution

Drive or controller not properly configured in BIOS setup. Check BIOS setup for proper drive type and make sure the controller is enabled if built-in to the motherboard.

Other causes for a dead drive include:

- Bad power supply or power cable—Measure the power at the cable with a voltmeter, ensure that 12v and 5v are available to the drive.
- Bad data cable—Replace the cable and retest.
- Defective drive—Replace the drive and retest.
- Defective controller—Replace the controller and retest. If the controller is built-in to the motherboard, disable it via the BIOS setup, install a card-based controller and retest, or replace the entire motherboard and retest.

Problem

Drive LED remains on continuously.

Cause/Solution

Data cable is on backward at either the drive or controller connection. Reinstall the cable properly and retest.

Also, the data cable could be offset on the connector by one or more pins. Reinstall the cable properly and retest. If this does not solve the problem, it could be a defective cable. Replace the cable and retest.

Problem

Phantom directories—you have exchanged disks in the drive, but the system still believes the previous disk is inserted, and even shows directories of the previous disk.

Cause/Solution

There are several possible causes and solutions:

- *Defective cable (pin 34).* Replace the cable and retest.
- *Improper drive configuration.* If the drive is an older model and has a DC jumper, it must be set enabled.
- *Defective drive.* Replace the drive and retest.

Common Floppy Drive Error Messages—Causes and Solutions

Error Message

Invalid Media or Track Zero Bad, Disk Unusable

Cause/Solution

You are formatting the disk and the disk media type does not match the format parameters. Make sure you are using the right type of disk for your drive and formatting the disk to its correct capacity. Other causes and solutions are:

- *Defective or damaged disk.* Replace the disk and retest.
- *Dirty heads.* Clean the drive heads and retest.

Error Message

CRC Error or Disk Error 23

Cause/Solution

The data read from the diskette does not match the data that was originally written. (CRC stands for Cyclic Redundancy Check.) Replace the disk and retest. Possibly clean the drive heads. Use the Norton Utilities for possible data recovery from the disk.

Error Message

General Failure Reading Drive A, Abort, Retry, Fail; or Disk Error 31

Cause/Solution

The disk is not formatted or has been formatted for a different operating system (Macintosh, for example). Reformat the disk and retest. Another cause could be that there are damaged areas on the disk medium. Replace the disk and retest. Use the Norton Utilities for possible data recovery from the disk.

Error Message

Access Denied

Cause/Solution

You are trying to write to a write-protected disk or file. Move the write-protect switch to allow writing on the disk, or remove the read-only file attribute from the file(s). File attributes can be changed by the ATTRIB command.

Error Message

Insufficient Disk Space or Disk Full

Cause/Solution

The disk is filled, or the root directory is filled. Check to see if sufficient free space is available on the disk for your intended operation.

Error Message

Bytes in Bad Sectors

Cause/Solution

This is displayed after formatting or running the CHKDSK command, and shows that the disk has several allocation units that are marked bad. This is not a problem in itself because when they are marked in this fashion, the operating system will not use them for file storage. Even so, I normally don't recommend using disks with bad sectors.

Error Message

Disk Type or Drive Type Incompatible or Bad

Cause/Solution

You are attempting to DISKCOPY between two incompatible drive or disk types. Disks can only be copied between drives using the same disk density and size.

Repairing Floppy Disk Drives

Attitudes about repairing floppy disk drives have changed over the years, primarily because of the decreasing cost of drives. When drives were more expensive, people often considered repairing the drive rather than replacing it. With the cost of drives decreasing every year, however, certain labor- or parts-intensive repair procedures have become almost as expensive as replacing the drive with a new one. Because of cost considerations, repairing floppy disk drives usually is limited to cleaning the drive and heads and lubricating the mechanical mechanisms.

Cleaning Floppy Disk Drives

Sometimes read and write problems are caused by dirty drive heads. Cleaning a drive is easy; you can proceed in two ways:

- *Use one of the simple head-cleaning kits available from computer- or office-supply stores.* These devices are easy to operate and don't require you to open the computer case to access the drive.

- *The manual method: Use a cleaning swab with a liquid such as pure alcohol or trichloroethane.* With this method, you must open the system unit to expose the drive and, in many cases (especially in earlier full-height drives), also remove and partially disassemble the drive.

The manual method can result in a better overall job, but usually the work required is not worth the difference.

The cleaning kits come in two styles: The wet type uses a liquid squirted on a cleaning disk to wash off the heads; the dry kit relies on abrasive material on the cleaning disk to remove head deposits. I recommend that you never use the dry drive-cleaning kits. Always use a wet system in which a liquid solution is applied to the cleaning disk. The dry disks can prematurely wear the heads if used improperly or too often; wet systems are very safe to use.

The manual drive-cleaning method requires that you have physical access to the heads to swab them manually with a lint-free foam swab soaked in a cleaning solution. This method requires some level of expertise: Simply jabbing at the heads incorrectly with a cleaning swab might knock the drive heads out of alignment. You must use a careful in-and-out motion, and lightly swab the heads. No side-to-side motion (relative to the way the heads travel) should be used; this motion can snag a head and knock it out of alignment. Because of the difficulty and danger of this manual cleaning, for most applications I recommend a simple wet-disk cleaning kit because it is the easiest and safest method.

One question that comes up repeatedly in my seminars is "How often should you clean a disk drive?" Most drive and disk manufacturers recommend cleaning after every 40 hours of drive operation. Since the floppy drives are rarely used except for file backups or system configuration and setup or diagnostics, it is hard to gauge when this much time will have elapsed. Depending on the number and size of fans in the system, there might be a large amount of air flowing through the floppy drive, which means it can be subject to contamination even though it is not being used. In some cases this means cleaning is often required more frequently than the recommendations suggest.

What type of environment is the system in? Do you smoke cigarettes near the system? If so, more frequent cleaning would be required. Usually, a safe rule of thumb is to clean drives about once a year if the system is in a clean office environment in which no smoke or other particulate matter is in the air. In a heavy-smoking environment, you might have to clean every six months or perhaps even more often. In dirty industrial environments, you might have to clean every month or so. Your own experience is your guide in this matter. If the operating system reports drive errors such as the familiar DOS Abort, Retry, Ignore prompt, you should clean your drive to try to solve the problem. If cleaning does solve the problem, you probably should step up the interval between preventive-maintenance cleanings.

In some cases, you might want to place a very small amount of lubricant on the door mechanism or other mechanical contact point inside the drive. Do not use oil; use a pure silicone lubricant. Oil collects dust rapidly after you apply it and usually causes the oiled mechanism to gum up later. Silicone does not attract dust in the same manner and can be used safely. Use very small amounts of silicone; do not drip or spray silicone inside the drive. You must make sure that the lubricant is applied only to the part that needs it. If the lubricant gets all over the inside of the drive, it can cause unnecessary problems.

Aligning Floppy Disk Drives

If your disk drives are misaligned, you will notice that other drives cannot read disks created in your drive, and you might not be able to read disks created in other drives. This situation can be dangerous if you allow it to progress unchecked. If the misalignment is bad enough, you will probably notice it first in the drive's inability to read original application-program disks, while still being able to read the disks you have created yourself.

To solve this problem, you can have the drive realigned. I usually don't recommend realigning drives because of the low cost of replacing the drive compared to aligning one. Also, an unforeseen circumstance catches many people off-guard: You may find that your newly aligned drive might not be capable of reading all the disks you created while the drive was out of alignment. If you replace the misaligned drive with a new one, and keep the misaligned drive, you can use it for DISKCOPY purposes to transfer the data to newly formatted disks in the new drive.

Aligning disk drives is usually no longer performed because of the high relative cost. In the past, aligning a drive properly required access to an oscilloscope (for about $500), a special analog-alignment disk ($75), the OEM service manual for the drive, and a half hour to an hour of time.

Some programs on the market evaluate the condition of floppy disk drives by using a disk created or formatted on the same drive. A program that uses this technique cannot make a proper evaluation of a disk drive's alignment. To do this, you must use a specially created disk produced by a tested and calibrated machine. You can use this type of disk as a reference standard by which to judge a drive's performance. Accurite, the primary manufacturer of reference standard floppy disks, helps specify floppy disk industry standards. Accurite produces the following three main types of reference standard disks used for testing drive function and alignment:

- Digital Diagnostic Diskette (DDD)
- Analog Alignment Diskette (AAD)
- High-Resolution Diagnostic Diskette (HRD)

The HRD disk, introduced in 1989, represented a breakthrough in floppy disk drive testing and alignment. The disk is accurate to within 50μ-inches (millionths of an inch)—accurate enough to use not only for precise testing of floppy disk drives, but also for aligning drives. With software that uses this HRD disk, you can align a floppy disk drive without having to use special tools or an oscilloscope. Other than the program and the HRD disk, you need only a PC to which to connect the drive. This product has significantly lowered the cost of aligning a floppy disk drive and has eliminated the need for special test equipment.

The Accurite program Drive Probe is designed to work with the HRD disks. Drive Probe is the most accurate and capable floppy disk testing program on the market, thanks to the use of HRD disks. Until other programs utilize the HRD disks for testing, Drive Probe is my software of choice for floppy disk drive testing and alignment. Because the Drive Probe software also acts as a disk exerciser for use with AAD disks and an oscilloscope, you can move the heads to specific tracks for controlled testing.

With the price of most types of floppy disk drives hovering at or below the $25 mark, aligning drives usually is not a cost-justified alternative to replacement. The Drive Probe and HRD system can make alignment more cost-effective than before, but it is still a labor- and cost-intensive operation. Weigh this cost against the replacement cost and age of the drive. I have purchased brand-new 1.44MB floppy disk drives for as low as $15. At these prices, alignment is no longer a viable option.

High-Capacity Removable Storage

SOME OF THE MAIN TOPICS IN THIS CHAPTER ARE

Why Use Removable Drives?

Types of Removable Media Drives

Removable Drive Letter Assignments

Comparing Removable Drives

Tape Drives

Why Use Removable Drives?

The reason for the shortage of storage space on today's PCs is easy enough to understand. With fancier user interfaces and more and more features being added, both operating systems and applications continue to grow in size. Take a look at the sheer number and size of the files stored in the two main directories used by Windows 9x (usually C:\WINDOWS and C:\WINDOWS\ SYSTEM). The amount of disk space used by the files in those two directories alone can quickly balloon to 200MB or more after you also install a few Windows applications. The reason is simple: Nearly all Windows applications place files in one of the Windows directories that the application will use later. These files include those with extensions such as DLL, 386, VBX, DRV, TTF, and many others. Similarly other operating systems—such as Windows NT, OS/2, Linux, and UNIX—as well as the software applications that run in these operating systems can require enormous amounts of storage space.

Applications also use more graphics and sound. Digital cameras and video recorders allow you to capture and store images that can easily consume hundreds of megabytes of space.

This section focuses on some of the more advanced data storage options on the market: high capacity removable media storage, including both disk and tape drives. This chapter focuses on magnetic or magneto-optical storage. Pure optical storage—such as CD-R, CD-RW, DVD-R, DVD-RAM, and others—is covered in Chapter 13, "Optical Storage."

Some removable media drives use media as small as a 3 1/2-inch floppy disk, whereas others use larger media up to 5 1/4-inches. Most popular removable storage drives today have capacities that range from 100MB to 70GB or more. These drives offer fairly speedy performance and the capability to store anything from a few data files or less frequently used programs to complete hard disk images on a removable disk or tape. Besides backup this allows the capability to easily transport huge data files—Computer Aided Drawing (CAD) files and graphics files, for example—from one computer to another. Or, you can use a removable cartridge to take sensitive data away from your office so you can lock it safely away from prying eyes.

There are two basic categories of removable media: disk and tape. Disk media is much more expensive, usually has a lower capacity, and is more easily used on a file-by-file basis as compared to tape. Disk media is faster for copying a few files, but normally slower for copying large numbers of files or entire drives. Tape media is much less expensive overall, has a higher total capacity, and is more easily used on an image or multiple file basis. Such tape drives are more suited for complete backups of entire hard disks including all applications and data. Because it is suited for mass backup, tape can be painstaking to use for copying single files. This chapter covers both removable disk and tape storage.

Note

Removable media disk drives can be used as system backup devices similar to tape. However, the higher price of the medium itself (disks or cartridges) and the generally slower speed at which they perform can make this use somewhat prohibitive on a large scale. For file-by-file backups, disk media is ideal; if, however, you're completely backing up entire drives or systems, tape is faster and more economical.

Types of Removable Media Drives

There are two commonly used types of removable media disk drives: magnetic media and optical media, also called magneto-optical media. Magnetic media drives use technology very much like that of a floppy or hard disk drive to encode data for storage. Magneto-optical media drives encode information on disk by using newer technology—a combination of traditional magnetic and laser technologies.

There are also several connection options for the leading removable drives. Although SCSI has been, and continues to be, a popular solution, most of the removable drives today connect to an IDE port, a parallel port, or a USB (Universal Serial Bus) port. The parallel and USB connections are external, which allows you to share one drive between several different computers. Unfortunately, the parallel port drives generally provide relatively poor performance levels, and although USB is better, it still cannot match the performance of IDE or SCSI. For a high-performance connection, SCSI is still the ultimate for external high-capacity drives. Although SCSI can work internally as well, most internal drives use IDE because it is less expensive.

Note

Connecting or installing removable media drives is similar to connecting and installing other internal and external peripherals.

The external USB or parallel port drives are the simplest of the available interfaces, requiring only a special cable that comes with the drive and installation of special software drivers. See the instructions that come with each drive for the specifics of its installation.

A small group of companies dominates the market for magnetic and magneto-optical removable media drives. 3M's spin-off company Imation and Iomega are the leading names in removable magnetic media drives.

Removable magnetic media drives are usually floppy or hard disk based. For example, the popular Zip drive is a 3 1/2-inch version of the original Bernoulli floppy disk drive made by Iomega. The new 3M LS-120 drive is a floppy-based drive that stores 120MB on a disk that looks exactly like a 1.44MB floppy! The former SyQuest drive and current Iomega Jaz drive are both hard disk–based designs.

Both the Iomega and SyQuest designs are proprietary standards, while the LS-120 is a true industry standard supported by many companies. However, the Iomega Zip drive has become a de facto standard in the industry. Many new PCs sold today include a Zip drive as standard equipment. Even so, because the LS-120 SuperDisk is supported as a bootable direct floppy replacement by virtually all new systems today, and many vendors supply them as standard equipment, I expect the market to shift to the LS-120 and derivatives as the de facto standard for the future.

The following sections provide information about both magnetic media and magneto-optical drive types.

High-Capacity Floptical Drives

There is a special type of high-capacity floppy disk drive being marketed by several companies that is sometimes called a floptical drive. These drives are unique in that they can both read and write standard floppy disks as well as higher-capacity floptical disks. A 21MB version was originally available but more recently a 120MB version has become popular; with 250MB and 500MB versions coming, the 21MB version has become obsolete. The older 21MB version was created by Insite Peripherals, and packed 21MB of data on the same size disk as a 3 1/2-inch floppy. The 21MB floptical drive is an ancestor of the newer SuperDisk (LS-120) drives, which can store 120MB on a 3 1/2-inch floppy disk.

In addition, all floptical drives can read and write 1.44MB and 720KB floppy disks (although they cannot handle 2.88MB disks). Because of their greatly increased storage capacity and capability to use common floppy disks, the newer 120MB flopticals are considered by many as the perfect replacement floppy disk drive.

The name floptical might suggest the use of laser beams to burn or etch data onto the disk or to excite the media in preparation for magnetic recording—as is the case with the CD-R and Write Once, Read Many (WORM) drives—but this suggestion is erroneous. The read/write heads of a floptical drive use magnetic recording technology, much like that of floppy disk drives.

The floptical disk itself is composed of the same ferrite materials common to floppy and hard disks. Floptical drives are capable of such increased capacity because many more tracks are packed on each disk, compared with a standard 1.44MB floppy. Obviously, to fit so many tracks on the floptical disk, the tracks must be much more narrow than those on a floppy disk.

That's where optical technology comes into play. Flopticals use a special optical mechanism to properly position the drive read/write heads over the data tracks on the disk. Servo information, which specifically defines the location of each track, is embedded in the disk during the manufacturing process. Each track of servo information is actually etched or stamped on the disk and is never disturbed during the recording process. Each time the floptical drive writes to the disk, the recording mechanism (including the read/write heads) is guided by a laser beam precisely into place by this servo information. When the floptical drive reads the encoded data, the laser uses this servo information again to guide the read/write heads precisely into place.

21MB Floptical Drives

The original Insite 21MB floptical disks used tracks formatted to 27 sectors of 512 bytes. The disks revolved at 720rpm. Flopticals are capable of nearly 10MB per minute data throughput, using a SCSI interface.

Unfortunately, the 21MB drives by Insite never really caught on due to several reasons. One is that no leading manufacturer has included these drives in a standard configuration with built-in BIOS drivers and support. Also, Microsoft, IBM, and Apple have not built support for these drives directly into their operating systems.

LS-120 (120MB) SuperDisk Drives

The LS-120 drive (also called a SuperDisk drive) was designed to become the new standard floppy disk drive in the PC industry. LS-120 technology was developed by Imation (3M) Corporation; Matsushita-Kotobuki Industries, Ltd. (MKE); and O.R. Technology and stores 120MB of data, or about 83 times more data than current 1.44MB floppy disks. In addition to storing more, these drives read and write at up to five times the speed of standard floppy disk drives.

The LS-120 floppy disk drive can act as the PC's bootable A: drive (in newer systems with BIOS support) and is fully compatible with Windows NT, Windows 2000, Windows 95/98. Macintoshes can also use SuperDisk drives, so data can be exchanged between PCs and Macs.

In addition to the new 120MB floppy disks, the LS-120 drive accepts standard 720KB and 1.44MB floppy disks, and actually reads and writes those disks up to three times faster than standard floppy disk drives. Iomega Zip drives are not backward compatible and cannot use existing floppy disks; the proprietary Zip media stores less and is more expensive than the 3M LS-120 media. Many people in the computer industry believe that LS-120 technology will replace the 1.44MB floppy disk in new computers.

The LS-120 normally uses the standard IDE interface, which is already built into most existing systems, and it is perfect for portable systems. There are also USB and parallel versions for an easy external connection. The LS-120 provides a solution that not only replaces the existing floppy, but can even replace the floppy disk drive internally. Having one of these high-capacity drives in a portable allows the use of relatively inexpensive 120MB removable disks while on the road. They are perfect for storing entire applications or datasets and can be removed and secured when the portable system is not in use.

LS-120 specifications are compared to standard 1.44MB floppy disks in Table 12.1.

Table 12.1   LS-120 Specifications

Drive Type	LS-120 Floppy	Standard 1.44MB Floppy Disk
Formatted Capacity	120MB	1.44MB
Transfer Rate: parallel port	290KB/sec	45KB/sec
Transfer Rate: internal IDE	484KB/sec	n/a
Average seek time	70ms	84ms
Disk rotational speed	720rpm	300rpm
Track density	2,490tpi	135tpi
Number of tracks	1,736 × 2 sides	80 × 2 sides

The 3MB LS-120 disk has the same shape and size as a standard 1.44MB 3 1/2-inch floppy disk; however, it uses a combination of magnetic and optical technology to enable greater capacity and performance. Named after the Laser Servo (LS) mechanism it employs, LS-120 technology places optical reference tracks on the disk that are both written and read by a laser system. The optical sensor in the drive enables the read/write head to be precisely positioned over the magnetic data tracks, enabling track densities of 2,490tpi versus 135tpi for a 1.44MB floppy disk.

Virtually all new PCs now come with LS-120 support directly in the BIOS, which means that these drives are easy to install, they can directly replace the A: floppy disk drive, and they're bootable, as well. Many newer laptop systems come with LS-120 drives that replace and yet are fully compatible with the standard floppy disk drive. Unlike Zip, you can install the LS-120 in your laptop and leave the standard floppy disk drive at home.

Many PC manufacturers are incorporating LS-120 drives in their products as standard equipment. Besides coming in new systems, these drives are also available separately at a cost of about $75 or less in internal or external versions for upgrading older systems. The 120MB floppy disks are available for about $10 per disk or less, almost half the cost of the proprietary Zip media.

Bernoulli Drives

In the early 1980s, Iomega introduced the Bernoulli drive. The disk used in the original Bernoulli drive was a thick cartridge roughly the same size as a 5 1/4-inch floppy disk, although a large shutter, similar to the shutter on a 3 1/2-inch floppy disk, easily distinguished Bernoulli disks from standard floppy disks. Bernoulli cartridges were originally available in 10MB capacities, but those were replaced by 35MB, 65MB, 105MB, and 150MB capacities.

Bernoulli disks were originally known as the most durable of the removable media drive types. For example it is probably safer to mail a Bernoulli cartridge than another type of removable disk because the media is well protected inside the cartridge. Bernoulli encases a magnetic-media-covered flexible disk (in effect, a floppy disk) in a rigid cartridge in the same way the thin disk of a 1.44MB floppy is encased in a rigid plastic shell.

When it rotates in the drive, the disk is pulled by air pressure toward the drive heads. Many people think that there is no head-to-disk contact in a Bernoulli drive, but indeed there is. As the disk spins, the airflow generated by the disk movement encounters what is called a Bernoulli plate, which is a stationary plate designed to control the air flow so the disk is pulled toward the read/write head. At full speed, the head touches the disk, which causes wear. Bernoulli drives have built-in random seek functions that prevent any single track on the disk from wearing excessively during periods of inactivity. Bernoulli disk cartridges should be replaced periodically because they can wear out. The disk itself spins at speeds approaching the 3,600rpm of relatively slow hard drives. The drive has an average seek time of 18ms, not a great deal slower than today's medium-priced hard drives.

Zip Drives

Another form of Bernoulli drive from Iomega is the popular Zip drive. This device is available as a internal SCSI or IDE unit, or as an external SCSI or parallel port device. There is also a low-power version designed for use in notebook computers and a "plus" version that features both SCSI and parallel interfaces. The drive is capable of storing up to 100MB of data on a small removable magnetic cartridge that resembles a 3 1/2-inch floppy disk. The drive has approximately a 29ms access time and a 1MB/sec transfer rate when used with a SCSI connection. When using the parallel connection, the drive's speed is often limited by the speed of the parallel port.

Zip drives use a proprietary 3 1/2-inch disk made by Iomega. It is about twice as thick as a standard 3 1/2-inch floppy disk.

The Zip drives do not accept standard 1.44MB or 720KB floppy disks, making this an unlikely candidate for a floppy disk drive replacement. Internal Zip drives have become popular options in new PCs, and the external models are an effective solution for exchanging data between systems, but the major PC manufacturers have not recognized the proprietary format directly in the system BIOS, meaning you cannot boot from a Zip drive, nor can it replace the A: floppy disk drive.

Zip drives have also suffered from reliability problems, such as the so called "click death," which occurs when the drive begins a rhythmic ticking sound. At this point, the data on the disk can be corrupted and both the drive and the media must be replaced.

▶▶ See "Zip Drive 'Click of Death,'" p. 678.

Finally, the media costs of Zip are almost double that of the higher-capacity LS-120 drives, which are an industry standard fully supported by the system BIOS in modern PCs. Table 12.2 lists the Zip specifications.

Table 12.2   Zip Specifications (100 and 250MB Capacity)

Model (Interface)	SCSI and/or Parallel	EIDE
Formatted capacity	100MB or 250MB	100MB or 250MB
Sustained transfer rate	1.40MB/sec	1.40 maximum MB/sec
Sustained transfer rate	0.79MB/sec	0.79 minimum MB/sec
Maximum throughput	60MB/min (SCSI); 20MB/min (parallel)	84MB/min
Average seek time	29ms	29ms
Disk rotational speed	2,941rpm	2,941rpm
Buffer size	32KB	16KB

Figure 12.1 shows the interior of a Zip drive, listing the various components within.

The interior assembly forms a tray that is mounted on a sliding track. This allows the entire tray to move with the disk.

Iomega also introduced a smaller and lower capacity version of Zip called the Clik! drive, primarily for notebook computers. Unfortunately, these drives never became popular because of their low capacity and proprietary nature, compared to the industry standard SuperDisk (LS-120) drives. Most newer desktop and laptop systems support the SuperDisk drives internally as a direct and compatible replacement for the standard floppy drive. SuperDisk drives can be connected externally to all systems via USB or parallel interfaces.

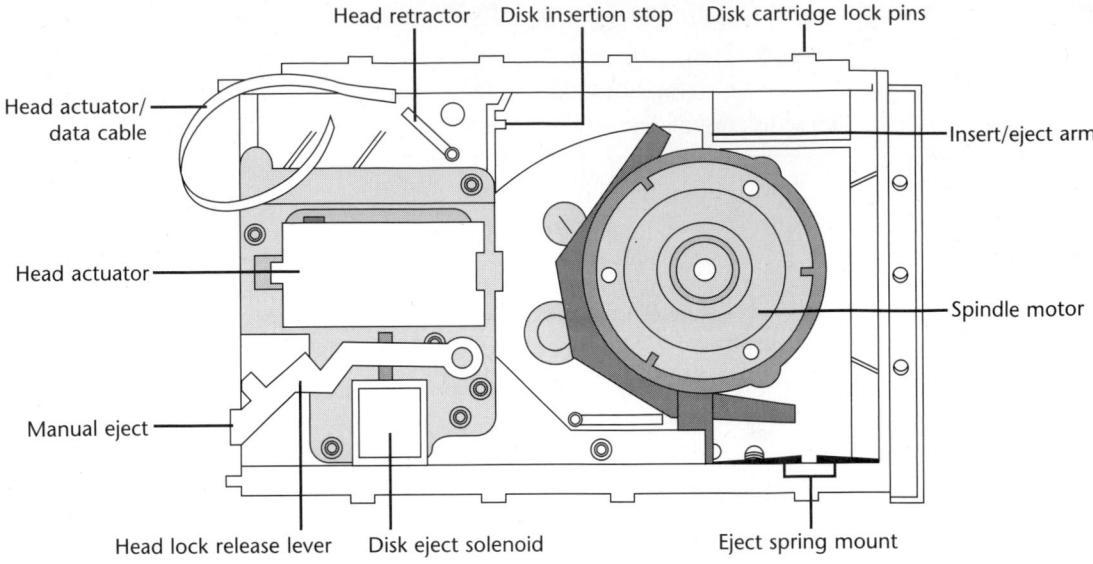

Figure 12.1 Iomega Zip drive internal view.

Zip Drive "Click of Death"

Iomega has acknowledged that as many as 100,000 users of Zip drives have suffered what is called the "Click of Death." The name refers to a sharp clicking sound which is heard from the drive as the heads are continually loaded and unloaded as they try to read a disk. This unfortunately means at a minimum that the disk, and possibly the drive, is likely trashed.

In fact many have found that the disk cartridge can be damaged in such a way that if you attempt to read it on another Zip drive, that drive will be damaged as well. The only solution is to get a new disk and drive, and do not try to read damaged disks in new drives.

If you believe your drive or disk has been damaged, call Iomega technical support (see the Vendor List on the CD) and they should replace the defective disk and possibly the drive as well.

Iomega lists these precautions to help prevent damaged disks and drives.

- Eject disks prior to transporting any Iomega drive. This allows the drive heads (which read and write to the disks) to park in a natural position.
- Avoid dropping your drive; it can damage internal structures.
- Be especially careful to transport and store Jaz disks only in the Jaz disk cases.

Note

Iomega offers utility diagnostics software that tests the integrity of the Zip heads and Zip media. You can download this from their Web site.

Another company, Gibson Research, has developed a unique program for diagnosing problems with Zip and Jaz drives. It is called Trouble In Paradise (TIP), and can also be downloaded free from the Gibson Research site. They are well known as the manufacturers of the Spinrite program for hard disks. See the Vendor List in the CD for their URL and address.

Because of the high frequency of this problem, many data recovery companies have had a large business in recovering data from damaged Zip cartridges. In fact the problem has even prompted a class action suit. The law firm of Dodge, Fazio, Anderson, and Jones, P.C. has announced that a nationwide class action was commenced on September 10, 1998 in the Superior Court of New Castle County in Delaware on behalf of all owners of the Iomega Zip drive. The complaint contains claims for breach of warranty, negligence in manufacturing and design, consumer fraud, and failure to warn.

Investigation has shown that the Click of Death has three main causes.

1. Magnetic particles corrupt the read/write mechanism of the drive, as well as any disk it is attempting to read.

2. Lubricant on the disk decomposes, forming a solid material, which accumulates on the heads of the drive. This prevents the heads from reading the disk, and subsequently corrupts it.

3. The drive heads come in contact with the edge of the spinning disk, which can dislodge the drive heads and/or tear the storage media and render the disk useless.

This latter point is especially troublesome, because if damaged media is inserted into a new drive, it can damage the new drive as well, in some cases tearing the heads off their mount.

Data recovery from a damaged Zip disk can run $400 or more, so I suggest you keep backups of any important data you store on these disks.

Zip 250 (SCSI and Parallel)

The Zip 250 drive is an extension of Iomega's popular Zip product line, offering enhanced features such as increased capacity and performance, as well as compatibility with existing Zip 100 disks.

The SCSI version of the Zip 250 runs about 1.6 times faster than the Zip 100; however, the parallel port version has about the same performance due to limitations of the parallel interface.

Jaz Drives

Another type of removable hard disk drive is the Jaz drive from Iomega. This is physically and functionally identical to the SyQuest drives in that it is a true removable cartridge hard disk, except that the capacity of the cartridge has been increased; 1GB and 2GB models are available. Unfortunately, the cartridges themselves cost $100 to $125, which is about seven times the cost of a digital audio tape (DAT) cartridge that stores up to four times more data! The high cost of the media makes the Jaz drive unsuitable for backup when compared to traditional tape media, but possibly useful as an add-on external SCSI hard disk drive. Jaz drives are available in SCSI interface versions only. Table 12.3 lists the specifications for Jaz drives.

Table 12.3   Jaz Specifications

Model	1GB	2GB
Formatted Capacity	1070 million bytes	2000 million bytes
Transfer rate:		
Maximum	6.62MB/sec	8.7MB/sec
Average	5.4MB/sec	7.35MB/sec
Minimum	3.41MB/sec	3.41MB/sec
Burst	10MB/sec	20MB/sec
Average seek time read	10 ms	10 ms
Average seek time write	12 ms	12 ms
Access Time	15.5–17.5ms	15.5–17.5ms
Disk Rotational speed	5400rpm	5394rpm
Buffer size	256KB	512KB
Interface	Fast SCSI II	Ultra SCSI

SyQuest Drives

SyQuest has filed for bankruptcy, but they do continue to support their existing products. All their technology was purchased by Iomega. SyQuest manufactured some drives that use 5 1/4-inch cartridges and others that use 3 1/2-inch cartridges. But the SyQuest disks, like the Bernoulli cartridges, are easily distinguished from floppy disks. The 5 1/4-inch 44MB and 88MB cartridges used in some SyDOS drives are encased in clear plastic, as are the SyDOS 3 1/2-inch 105MB and SyQuest 270MB cartridges. The disk spins inside the cartridge at several thousand rpm. SyQuest claims a 14ms average access time for the drives it manufactures.

The disks for the SyQuest and SyDOS drives are composed of a rigid platter inside a plastic cartridge but are not as well-protected as the disk in a Bernoulli cartridge. Some people consider these disks fragile. If the SyQuest and SyDOS cartridges are not severely jostled or dropped, however, they can be transported safely. These cartridges must be carefully protected when you mail or ship them.

The SyQuest/SyDOS drives are available in internal and external models. The internal models require a connection to the existing IDE hard drive interface card. The external models require a SCSI interface card with an external connector and are powered by a transformer that connects to a grounded AC wall plug.

SyQuest filed a Chapter 11 petition with the United States Bankruptcy Court in Oakland, California on November 17, 1998. On January 13, 1999 SyQuest announced that it had entered into an agreement with Iomega Corporation to sell certain assets including all its intellectual property, its U.S. inventory, and its U.S. fixed assets.

SyQuest has commenced limited sales and support operations. This includes online technical support via the World Wide Web, warranty returns, and product service operations. This means that you should still be able to purchase blank cartridges and get repairs, but it is doubtful they will be making any new products in the future. Note that Iomega did not take on support of their older products, they only purchased their technology.

SparQ Drives

The SparQ drive is a removable hard disk drive by SyQuest that was designed to be a low-cost alternative to other technologies with similar capacities, such as the Jaz and the SyJet. The medium is a proprietary cartridge containing a single disk platter with a 1GB capacity. At $99 for a three pack of cartridges, the cost per megabyte of the SparQ is substantially less than that of comparable removable hard disk media, although it still does not approach that of tape or CD-R.

The drive was available in internal IDE and external parallel port versions. The parallel port version, like all drives using this interface, is limited by the throughput of the port itself, but the IDE version of the SparQ provides data transfer rates that are faster than most competing drives. EIDE burst transfer rates can be as high as 16.6MB/sec by using PIO mode 4, with sustained rates ranging from 3.7 to 6.8MB/sec. Table 12.4 lists the specifications for the SparQ drive.

Table 12.4   SparQ Specifications

Formatted Capacity	1008 million bytes
Transfer rate: EIDE version	
Maximum	6.9MB/sec
Minimum	3.7MB/sec
Burst (PIO mode 4)	16.6MB/sec
Sustained transfer rate: parallel version	1.25MB/sec
Average seek time	12ms
Disk rotational speed	5,400rpm

Because SyQuest has declared bankruptcy, there will likely not be any further developments in the SparQ line, although they do intend to continue to support the existing products sold.

Removable Drive Letter Assignments

One problem people have when installing new drives is confusion with drive letter assignments. This becomes especially true when adding a new drive moves the assignments of previous drives, something that most people don't expect. Some simple rules govern drive letter assignments in Windows and DOS, which I will discuss here. These basic rules apply to all versions of Windows through Win98 and NT (Windows 2000) and DOS as well, although in some operating systems and with some drivers you can have specific control over certain drives.

The basic rule is that devices supported by ROM BIOS-based drivers come first, and those assigned by disk-loaded drivers come second. Because floppy drives and hard drives are normally ROM BIOS supported, these would come first, before any other removable drives.

The system therefore assigns the drive letter A to the first physical floppy drive. If a second physical floppy drive is present, it is assigned drive letter B. If there is no second floppy drive, the system automatically reserves B: as a logical drive representation of the same physical drive A:. This allows files to be copied from one disk to another by specifying COPY file.ext A: B:.

The system then checks for installed hard drives and begins by assigning C: to the master partition on the first drive. If you have only one hard disk, any extended partitions on that drive are read, and any volumes in them are assigned consecutive letters after C:. For example, if you have a hard disk with a primary partition as C: and an extended partition divided into two logical volumes, they will be assigned D: and E:.

After the hard drive partitions and logical volumes are assigned, the system begins assigning letters to devices that are driver controlled such as CD-ROM drives, PCMCIA attached devices, parallel port devices, SCSI devices, and so on.

Here is how it works with only one hard drive split into three volumes, and a CD-ROM drive:

One Drive Primary Partition	C:
One Drive Extended Partition 1st Volume	D:
One Drive Extended Partition 2nd Volume	E:
CD-ROM Drive	F:

When a removable drive is added to this mix, it is assigned either F: or G: depending on the driver and when it is loaded. If the CD-ROM driver is loaded first, the removable drive is G:. If the removable drive driver is loaded first, it becomes F: and the CD-ROM drive is bumped to G:.

In DOS, you control the driver load order by rearranging the DEVICE= statements in the CONFIG.SYS file. This doesn't work in Windows because Win 9x and NT use 32-bit drivers, which aren't loaded via CONFIG.SYS. You can exert control over the drive letters in Windows by manually assigning drive letters to the CD-ROM or removable drives. You do this as follows:

1. Right-click My Computer, and choose Properties.

2. Choose the Device Manager tab.

3. Click the + next to the CD-ROM drive icon. Right-click the CD-ROM drive, choose Properties, and select the Settings tab.

4. Select and change the Start Drive Letter.

5. Select the same letter for End Drive Letter.

6. Click OK and allow your system to reboot for changes to take effect.

7. Repeat the previous steps by clicking the + next to Disk Drives and assign a different drive letter to your removable drive.

Using these steps you can interchange the removable drive with the CD-ROM drive, but you cannot set either type to a drive letter below any of your existing floppy or hard drives.

So far this seems just as everybody would expect, but from here forward is where it can get strange. The rule is that the system always assigns a drive letter to all primary partitions first, and all logical volumes in extended partitions second. This means that if you have a second hard disk, it also has primary and extended partitions, and the extended partition has two logical volumes, the primary partition on the second drive becomes D:, with the extended partition logical volumes becoming G: and H:.

Here is how it works with two hard drives, each split into three volumes, and a CD-ROM drive:

First Drive Primary Partition	C:
Second Drive Primary Partition	D:
First Drive Extended Partition 1st Volume	E:
First Drive Extended Partition 2nd Volume	F:
Second Drive Extended Partition 1st Volume	G:
Second Drive Extended Partition 2nd Volume	H:
CD-ROM Drive	I:

In this example if a removable drive were added it would become either I: or J:. Using the same procedure outlined previously, you could swap I: or J: or assign them higher (but not lower) letters as well.

Drive Remapping Utilities

While some utilities are available for remapping drive letters under Windows, I normally don't recommend them. This is because if you boot under DOS or via a floppy, these remappings will no longer be in place and the standard BIOS mapping will prevail. Since one often boots to DOS to do setup, diagnostics, configuration or formatting/partitioning, confusion about which drive letters are what can lead to mistakes and lost data!

Comparing Removable Drives

Deciding on a removable drive is getting tougher, because many removable drives are currently on the market. Iomega and SyQuest lead the pack, but new entries from Exabyte and Avatar Peripherals provide their own proprietary drives, as well. Unfortunately, all these drives use their own proprietary media that are universally incompatible. If you want to exchange files with another user, that user must have a drive made by the same manufacturer. The ease of portability is one reason why the parallel port models of many of these drives are popular.

Table 12.5 shows a direct comparison between the most popular removable drives on the market.

Table 12.5   Removable Drive Specifications

Drive Type	Disk/Cartridge Capacity	Average Seek Time	Data Transfer Rate
Iomega Zip Parallel	100MB	29ms	1.4MB/sec
Iomega Zip IDE	100MB	29ms	1.4Mb/sec
Iomega Zip SCSI	100MB	29ms	1.4MB/sec
Imation LS-120 Internal	120MB	70ms	4.0MB/sec
SyQuest 235 Parallel	235MB	13.5ms	1.25MB/sec
Avatar Shark 250 Parallel	250MB	12ms	1.2MB/sec
Avatar Shark PCMCIA	250MB	12ms	2.0MB/sec
SyQuest 235 SCSI/IDE	235MB	13.5ms	2.4MB/sec
Iomega Jaz (SCSI)	2GB	12ms	5.4MB/sec
Avatar Shark IDE	250MB	12ms	2.5MB/sec
SyQuest SyJet SCSI	1.5GB	12ms	5.3MB/sec
SyQuest Syjet IDE	1.5GB	12ms	5.3MB/sec
SyQuest SparQ IDE	1GB	12ms	6.9MB/sec
SyQuest SparQ Parallel	1GB	12ms	1.25MB/sec
CD-R Drives	650MB	<150ms	150KB/sec–2.4MB/sec

When shopping for a removable drive, keep the following in mind:

- *Price per megabyte of storage.* Take the cost of the drive's cartridge or disk and divide it by the storage capacity to see how much you are paying per megabyte of storage. This difference in price will become quite apparent as you buy more cartridges or disks for the drive. (Don't forget to factor in the cost of the drive itself!)

- *Access time versus need of access.* The access and data transfer speeds are important only if you need to access the data frequently or quickly. If your primary use is archiving data, a slower drive might be fine. However, if you plan to run programs off the drive, choose a faster drive instead.

- *Compatibility and portability.* Opt for an external SCSI or parallel port solution if you need to move the drive between various computers. Also verify that there are drivers available for each type of machine and operating system you want to use with the drive. Also consider whether you have to exchange disks with other users. The Iomega Zip disk is rapidly becoming the standard for removable cartridge media, but the graphic design industry has long used SyQuest drives. For some users, this might be the most important factor in choosing a drive.

- *Internal versus external.* Most users find external parallel port or USB drives the easiest to install; additionally they give you the option of using the drive on several systems. Internal drives are usually faster because their IDE or SCSI interfaces and are more cleanly integrated into the system from a physical perspective.

- *Bootable or not.* The LS-120 SuperDisk drives are BIOS supported in almost all new systems, and they are fully compatible with existing floppy drives. This means they can completely replace the floppy, a decided advantage over Zip and the others.

Tape Drives

The data backup and archive needs of a personal computer can be overwhelming. People with large hard drives and numerous applications installed and those who generate a large amount of data might find it necessary to back up their computers on a weekly or even a daily basis.

In addition, a critical need on today's PCs is data storage space. Sometimes it seems as though the storage requirements of a PC can never be satisfied. On nearly any PC used for business, study, or even fun, the amount of software installed can quickly overwhelm even a large hard drive. To save space on the primary storage devices, you can archive infrequently used data to another storage medium.

This section focuses on tape backup drives, which can solve the problems of the growing need for data storage space and the need for a fast and efficient way to back up many megabytes of data.

Any computer book worth reading warns repeatedly that you should back up your system regularly. Backups are necessary because at any time a major problem, or even some minor ones, can corrupt the important information and the programs stored on your computer's hard disk drive, rendering this information useless. A wide range of problems can damage the data on your hard drive. Here is a list of some of these data-damaging problems:

- Sudden fluctuations in the electricity that powers your computer (power spikes) resulting in data damage or corruption.
- Overwriting a file by mistake.
- Mistakenly formatting your hard disk when you meant to format a floppy.
- Hard drive failure resulting in loss of data that has not been backed up. Not only do you have to install a new drive but, because you have no backup, you also must reinstall all your software.
- Catastrophic damage to your computer (storm, flood, lightning strike, fire, theft). A single lightning strike near your office or home can destroy the circuitry of your computer, including your hard drive. Theft of your computer, of course, is equally devastating. A recent, complete backup greatly simplifies the process of setting up a replacement computer.
- Loss of valuable data due to a computer-related virus. One single download or floppy disk can contain a virus that can damage valuable files and even your entire hard disk. With several hundred new viruses appearing each month, no antivirus software program can keep you entirely safe. A recent backup of uninfected, critical files can help repair even the worst damage.

Backups are also the cure for such common headaches as a full hard drive and the need to transfer data between computers. By backing up data you rarely use and deleting the original data from your hard drive, you free up space once occupied by that data. If you later need a particular data file, you can retrieve that file from your backup. You can also more easily share large amounts of data between computers—as when you send data from one city to another, for example—by backing up the data to a tape and sending the tape.

Regardless of how important regular backups are, many people avoid making them. A major reason for this lapse is that for many people, backing up their system is tedious work when they have to use floppy disks or other low-capacity media. When you use these media, you might have to insert and remove many disks to back up all the important programs and data.

Tape backup drives are the most simple and efficient device for backing up your system. With a tape backup drive installed in your computer, you insert a tape into the drive, start your backup software, and select the drive and files you want to back up. The backup software copies your selected files onto the tape while you attend to other business. Later, when you need to retrieve some or all the files on the backup tape, you insert the tape in the drive, start your backup program, and select the files you want to restore. The tape backup drive takes care of the rest of the job.

This section examines the various types of tape backup drives on the market, describing the capacities of different drives as well as the system requirements for installation and use of a tape drive. The following topics are covered in this section:

- Common standards for tape backup drives
- Common backup tape capacities
- Newer higher capacity tape drives
- Common tape drive interfaces
- The QIC standards for tape backup drives
- Portable tape drives
- Tape backup software

The Origins of Tape Backup Standards

The evolution of tape backup standards is similar to that of standards for many computer components. Using tape to back up computer data became a common practice long before accepted tape backup standards existed. At first, computers used reel-to-reel tape systems (somewhat similar to old reel-to-reel audio tape recorders) to store data. The most commonly used tape—quarter-inch—eventually developed into a de facto standard. But each tape system manufacturer used its own data-encoding specifications for backup tapes. Variations included not only the number of tracks and data density on the tape, but also the interface used to connect the drive to the computer.

In 1972, more than a decade before the introduction of the first IBM PC, 3M introduced the first quarter-inch tape cartridge designed for data storage. The cartridge measured 6×4×5/8 inches. Inside this cartridge, the tape was threaded onto two reels. The tape was moved from one reel to another during the recording or read-back process by a drive belt. Because of the reliability of this tape cartridge, the demand for tape backup systems began to grow, despite the lack of established standards for storing data on these cartridges.

The result of this lack of standardization was that quarter-inch tapes written on one manufacturer's tape backup drive generally could not be read by another manufacturer's quarter-inch tape drive. One problem created by this situation was that the way particular manufacturers encoded data on a tape continued to change. If a particular model of tape drive became disabled and the manufacturer had discontinued that particular drive and no longer used its encoding format, the data stored on tapes written on the disabled drive would be unavailable until the drive was repaired. In the event the manufacturer could not repair the drive, the data was lost forever.

As with other computer components, such as hard drive interface cards, consumers were the force behind standardization. Consumers clamored for standardized tape drives that could read tapes created on different tape drives manufactured by different companies.

The QIC Standards

In response to this demand for standardization, the tape drive industry formed the Quarter-Inch Cartridge Drive Standards Inc., sometimes referred to as the Quarter-Inch Committee (QIC). In 1983–84, the first tape drive based on a QIC standard was shipped: the QIC-02, which stored 60MB of data encoded in nine data tracks on roughly 300 feet of tape.

As the technology improved, and because the 4×6×5/8-inch size of the first tape cartridges was difficult to adapt to the 5 1/2-inch drive bays in most PCs, QIC adopted a second standard for tape cartridges roughly the size of an audio cassette. These minicartridges measure 3 1/4×2 1/2×3/5 inches.

These two cartridge sizes are currently used in various QIC-standard tape drives. A two-letter code at the end of the QIC standard number designates whether the tape standard is based on the full-sized cartridge or the minicartridge. These two-letter codes are as follows:

- DC in a QIC standard number stands for data cartridge, the 4×6×5/8-inch cassette.
- MC in a QIC standard number stands for minicartridge, the 3 1/4×2 1/2×3/5-inch cassette.

The new QIC-5B-DC, for example, is a 5GB-capacity tape based on the QIC standard for the full-sized cartridge. The new QIC-5010-MC, which has 13GB capacity, is based on the minicartridge standard.

Table 12.6 shows the common QIC-standard tape formats and their technical specifications.

Table 12.6 Specifications of QIC-Standard Quarter-Inch Tape Cassettes and Minicartridges QIC Minicartridge Tape Standards DC-2000 QIC Tape Standards (Approximate Dimensions 3 1/4 by 2 1/2 by 3/5)

QIC Standard Number	Capacity (w/o Compression) (1)	Tracks	Data Transfer Rate (Approximate)
QIC-40	40MB/60MB	20	2MB-to-8MB/minute
QIC-80	80MB/120MB	28	3MB-to-9MB/minute
QIC-100 (obsolete)	20MB/40MB	12 or 24	—
QIC-128	86MB/128MB	32	—
QIC-3010	255MB	40	9MB/minute
QIC-3020	500MB	40	9MB/minute
QIC-3030	555MB	40	—
QIC-3040	840MB (3)	42 or 52	—
QIC-3050	750MB	40	—
QIC-3060 (inactive)	875MB	38	—
QIC-3070	4GB	144	—
QIC-3080	1.6GB	50	—
QIC-3095	2–5GB	72	30–60MB*
QIC-3110	2GB	48	—
QIC-3210	2.3/5.7GB	72	30MB*
QIC-5010	13GB	144	—

(1) Tape capacity can vary according to tape length.   *(2) Tape lengths can vary by manufacturer.*
*Compressed

Table 12.7 shows the full-size data cartridge standards.

Table 12.7 QIC Full-Sized Data Cartridge Standards DC-300a/DC-600/DC-6000 QIC Tape Standards (Approximate Dimensions 4×6× 5/8)

QIC Standard Number	Capacity (w/o Encoding Compression)	Tracks	Max. Data Transfer Rate (Approximate)
QIC-11 (DC-300)	45MB	9	—
QIC-24	45MB/60MB	9	—
QIC-120	125MB	15	—
QIC-150	150MB/250MB	18	—
QIC-525	320MB/525MB	26	12MB/minute
QIC-1000	1GB	30	18MB/minute
QIC-1350	1.35GB	30	18MB/minute
QIC-2100	2.1GB	30	18MB/minute
QIC-2GB	2.0GB	42	18MB/minute
QIC-5GB	5GB	44	18MB/minute
QIC-5010	13GB	144	18MB/minute
QIC-5210	25GB	144	120MB/minute

(1) Tape capacity can vary according to tape length.   *(2) Tape lengths can vary by manufacturer.*

Data Density	Tape Length (2)	Encoding Method	Interface Type
—	205 ft.v or 307.5 ft.	MFM	Floppy or optional adapter card
—	205 ft. or 307.5 ft.	MFM	Floppy or optional adapter card
10,000bpi	—	MFM	SCSI (4) or QIC
16,000bpi	—	MFM	SCSI or QIC
22,000bpi	300 ft.	MFM	Floppy or IDE
42,000bpi	400 ft.	MFM	Floppy or IDE
51,000bpi	275 ft.	MFM	SCSI-2 or QIC
41,000bpi	400 ft.	RLL	SCSI-2 or QIC
—	295 ft.	RLL	SCSI-2 or QIC
—	295 ft.	RLL	—
68,000bpi	295 ft.	RLL	SCSI-2 or QIC
60,000bpi	—	RLL	SCSI-2 or QIC
67,733bpi	Various	RLL	IDE or SCSI
—	—	RLL	SCSI 2 or QIC
60,960bpi	740 ft.	GCR	SCSI or SCSI-2
—	—	RLL	SCSI-2 or QIC

(3) 1GB with drives based on 0.315-inch tape cartridge   *(4) SCSI: Small Computer Systems Interface*

Data Density	Tape Length (1)	Encoding Method	Interface Type
—	450 ft.	MFM	QIC-02
8,000	450 ft. or 600 ft.	MFM	SCSI or QIC-02
10,000	600 ft.	MFM	SCSI or QIC-02
10,000bpi	600 ft. or 1,000 ft.	MFM	SCSI or QIC-02
16,000bpi	1,000 ft.	MFM	SCSI or SCSI-2
36,000bpi	760 ft.	MFM	SCSI or SCSI-2
51,000bpi	760 ft.	RLL	SCSI-2
68,000bpi	875 ft.	RLL	SCSI-2
40,640bpi	900 ft.	MFM	SCSI-2
96,000bpi	1,200 ft.	RLL	SCSI-2
68,000bpi	—	RLL	SCSI-2
101,600bpi	1,200–1,500 ft	RLL	SCSI or SCSI-2

Unlike software with version numbers (1.0, 1.1, 2.0, 2.1) that tell you which version of the software is the most recent, the QIC number designation does not serve as an accurate guide to understanding which QIC-standard tape drives are the latest technology. The designations QIC-100 and QIC-128, for example, were used for tape drives marketed long before today's QIC-40 and QIC-80 drives. Furthermore, the QIC-standard version numbers frequently have no correlation with the capacity of the tape cassettes or minicartridges used by the drive. For example, the QIC-40 tapes have a capacity of 60MB; the QIC-80 tapes, a capacity of 120MB.

QIC-standard backup tapes are magnetic media, primarily ferric oxide, and are recorded in a manner similar to the way data is encoded on your hard drive, using either Modified Frequency Modulation (MFM) or Run-Length Limited (RLL) technology.

Early QIC Tape Backup Types

The original QIC-standard drives, QIC-40 and QIC-80, are based on minicartridges. There are several reasons for the success of QIC-40 and QIC-80, not the least of which is that these two standards resulted in the first generation of economically attractive tape drives that store data in a manner that is compatible with products made by different manufacturers. In other words, QIC-40 and QIC-80 tape drives and tapes are quite affordable, and backups made on one QIC-40 or QIC-80 tape drive can be read in a tape drive built by another manufacturer.

In addition, the compact size of the minicartridge used for QIC-40 and QIC-80 tapes has resulted in drives made by numerous manufacturers that fit easily into both 5 1/2-inch half-height drive bays and 3 1/2×1-inch drive bays.

Backup tapes, such as floppy disks and hard drives, must be formatted before use, and one aspect of using a QIC-80 tape drive that was never improved was the time it takes to format a tape. Formatting a 125MB-capacity QIC-80 tape can take more than three hours. It's almost impossible to find a preformatted tape because of these long format times. The industry has been preformatting tapes since 1994. Other tape formats have the capability to format on-the-fly, which means they don't require preformatted tapes.

Data is stored on QIC-40 and QIC-80 tapes in MFM format, the format used on floppy disks (and older hard drives). Another similarity between formatting a backup tape, floppy disks, and a hard drive is that the formatting process creates a record-keeping system. The record-keeping system used on QIC-40 and QIC-80 tapes is similar to that on a hard drive or floppy disk.

The QIC standard calls for a file allocation table (FAT) that keeps track of where data is stored on the tape and keeps bad sectors from being used for data storage. A QIC-40 tape is divided into 20 tracks, with each track divided into 68 segments of 29 sectors each. Each sector stores 1KB (1,024 bytes). This record-keeping system and the error-correcting system that ensures reliably stored backup data use a total of 30% or more of each QIC-40 tape.

Despite the slow backup speeds of tape backup drives on some computers and the time it takes to format tapes, the ease of using a backup tape drive makes it easy to understand why the QIC-40 and QIC-80 tape drives were very popular.

High-Capacity QIC-Standard Drives

Using a QIC-80 tape drive to back up a network server's 4GB drive or other large hard drive packed with data can be nearly as frustrating as swapping floppy disks during a backup, because you have to switch media many times to protect the whole drive.

The solution to this tape-swapping problem is to use a larger capacity tape drive system. QIC has established a number of standards for higher-capacity tape drive systems ranging from 86MB to 13GB. Generally, these larger capacity systems pack data more densely on the tape, using as many as 144 tracks to pack 60,000 bits per inch (bpi) or more onto the tape (compared to the QIC-40's 20 tracks and 10,000bpi). To achieve these higher capacities, QIC-standards call for tape media with a higher coercivity level of 1,300 oersteds or more (compared to QIC-40 and QIC-80 tape media, which has a coercivity level of 550 oersteds). High-capacity tapes are also longer. QIC-5010 tapes, for example, are 1,200 feet long (compared to QIC-40 and QIC-80 tapes, both of which are roughly 300 feet long).

Note

Just as the higher coercivity level of 1.44MB floppy disks enables an HD drive to write more densely packed tracks than is possible with 720KB floppy disks, higher coercivity tape media enables higher densities, as well.

Although tape systems based on the minicartridge dominate the market for lower capacity tape drives, high-capacity tape backup systems are based on both minicartridge-sized tapes and full-sized data cartridge tapes. For example, the QIC-525 standard, which has a capacity of 525MB (without data compression), is based on the full-sized (4×6×5/8) cartridge. The QIC-5010 standard is based on a minicartridge (3 1/4×2 1/2×3/5).

QIC-Tape Compatibility

Although QIC-standard drives are based on the standard minicartridge and the full-sized data cartridge, it would be a mistake to assume that tapes based on the same cartridge standard are always compatible. For example, QIC-5010-standard tapes are incompatible with QIC-40 and QIC-80 tape backup systems, although both standards are based on the minicartridge. Similarly, QIC-525-standard tapes are incompatible with earlier standards based on the full-sized data cartridge. The lack of compatibility between tapes based on the same sized cartridge is due to differences in tape drive mechanisms, as well as the coercivity differences between tape standards. Table 12.8 shows the compatibility of common QIC-standard backup tapes.

Table 12.8   QIC-Tape-Standard Compatibility

QIC Minicartridge Standard	Compatibility
QIC-40	n/a
QIC-80	QIC-40 (read-only)
QIC-3010	QIC-40 and QIC-80 (read-only)
QIC-3020	QIC-40, QIC-80, and QIC-3010 (read only)
QIC-3030	QIC-3010 (read-only)

(continues)

Table 12.8   Continued

QIC Minicartridge Standard	Compatibility
QIC-3040	n/a
QIC-3050	n/a
QIC-3070	QIC-3030 (read-only)
QIC-3080	n/a
QIC-3095	QIC-3010 and QIC-3020 (read-only)
QIC-3210	QIC-3040 (read-only)
QIC-3230	QIC-3040, QIC-3095, and QIC-3210 (read-only)
QIC Full-Sized Cartridge	
QIC-24	n/a
QIC-120	QIC-24 (read-only)
QIC-150	QIC-24 and QIC-120 (read-only)
QIC-525	QIC-24, QIC-120, and QIC-150 (read-only)
QIC-1000	QIC-120, QIC-150, and QIC-525 (read-only)
QIC-1350	QIC-525 and QIC-1000 (read-only)
QIC-2G	QIC-120, QIC-150, QIC-525, and QIC-1000 (read-only)
QIC-2100	QIC-525 and QIC-1000 (read-only)
QIC-5G	QIC-24, QIC-120, QIC-150, QIC-525, and QIC-1000 (read-only)
QIC-5010	QIC-150, QIC-525, and QIC-1000 (read-only)

Tape compatibility is an important issue to consider when you choose a tape backup system. For example, as you can see from Table 12.8, the 4GB QIC-3070-standard drive can read only its own tapes and those that conform to the QIC-3030 standard. If you have many QIC-80 tapes containing data that you must continue to access, a better choice might be a drive based on the 2GB QIC-3010 standard. The QIC-3010 can read QIC-40 and QIC-80 tapes.

Other High-Capacity Tape Drive Standards

Ferric oxide QIC-standard tapes have declined in popularity in recent years, whereas two other types of tape backup systems are becoming increasingly popular for backing up networks and other systems with large amounts of data: 4mm digital audio tape (DAT) and 8mm videotape.

Sony introduced DAT, and licenses DAT technologies to other manufacturers, in effect setting the standard for drives and tapes manufactured by those companies. There is only one company, Exabyte, that manufactures 8mm tape drive assemblies. As a result, you're assured compatibility. Table 12.9 shows the basic specifications of the DAT and 8mm technology tapes.

Table 12.9   DAT and 8mm Tape Specifications

Tape Standard	Capacity (w/o Compression)	Data Density	Tracks (Approx-imate)	Tape Length	Recording Technology	Encoding Format	Interface
DAT (4mm metal particle)	2GB/4GB	114MB/in	1,869	195 ft./ 300 ft.	Helical Scan DataDAT	DDS*	SCSI
8mm video tape	14GB	n/a	n/a	120m	Helical Scan		

DDS: Digital data storage

Helical scan recording is similar in many ways to the way video images are recorded to videotape. As with QIC-standard tape drives, DAT and 8mm tapes move past the recording heads, which are mounted on a drum. These read/write heads rotate at a slight angle to the tape, writing a section of a helix, or spiral. The tape drive mechanism wraps the tape about halfway around the read/write heads, causing the heads to touch the tape at an angle. With helical scan technology, the entire surface of the tape is used to record data, unlike other technologies in which data tracks are separated by areas of unrecorded tape. This use of the entire tape surface enables helical scan backup drives to pack a much greater amount of data on a particular length of tape.

The DAT Tape Drive Standard

Digital audio tape (DAT) is a tape standard that has primarily been developed and marketed by Hewlett-Packard. HP chairs the DDS (digital data storage) Manufacturers Group, and has led the development of the DDS standards.

The technology behind digital audio tape is similar in many ways to the techniques used to record music and encode it on audio compact discs (CDs). DAT drives do not record data on the tape in the MFM or RLL formats used by QIC-standard drives; rather, bits of data received by the tape drive are assigned numerical values, or digits. Then the drive translates these digits into a stream of electronic pulses that are written to the tape. Later, when you restore information to a computer from the tape, the DAT tape drive translates these digits back into the original binary bits.

DAT tapes can store up to 12GB of uncompressed data, or about 24GB compressed. Two types of data formats—digital data storage (DDS) and DataDAT—are used for DAT tapes; however, DDS-type drives are by far the most common. DDS drives are available in three types:

- DDS-1 drives store 2GB of uncompressed data (4GB compressed).
- DDS-2 drives can store 4GB of uncompressed data (up to 8GB with compression).
- DDS-3 drives have a native 12GB capacity, or 24GB compressed.

DDS-3 drives offer full read and write compatibility with all DDS-2 and DDS-1 drives, as well as three times the capacity and double the data-transfer rate of current DDS-2 drives. DDS-3 drives are designed to provide reliable high-performance backup for medium to large networks at a substantially lower price than 8mm or DLT (digital linear tape) products with similar capacities.

The new HP DDS-3 drive (Model C1537A) has a native capacity of 12GB with a transfer rate of 1MB/sec. The DDS-3 drive typically can store 24GB on a single 125m tape at a rate of 2MB/sec by using built-in hardware data compression. The new HP DDS-3 drive incorporates several innovations, including the use of a partial response maximum likelihood (PRML) data-channel detection scheme that enables the tape's read head to differentiate between bits of data picked up simultaneously.

A typical DDS-2 drive costs about $800, whereas DDS-3 drives are approximately $1,300. DDS technology has an excellent track record and a reputation for reliability that has made it the technology of choice for workstation, end user, and network backups.

The 8mm Tape Drive

A single manufacturer, Exabyte, offers tape backup drives that use 8mm tape cartridges like those used for videotape. However, although the cartridge design is the same as a videotape, the actual magnetic medium is not. It is strongly recommended that you do not use videotapes for backing up your data. You should use only tapes that are intended for use as a data storage medium. Exabyte offers drives in several capacities—1.5GB (3GB with hardware data compression), 5GB (10GB with hardware compression), 7GB (14GB with hardware compression), and 20GB (40GB with hardware compression).

Although these drives use 8mm videotapes, they do not use video technology for the process of writing computer data to the tape. Rather, Exabyte developed its own technology for encoding information on the tapes, using the helical scan method to record the data.

The 6MB/sec data throughput rate of the Exabyte 8mm tape backup drive, compared with the 10MB per minute throughput of the DAT drive, makes the 8mm tape drive a more attractive choice. The extraordinary speed and huge capacity of these 8mm tape drives makes them extremely attractive for backing up network servers and for backing up workstations from the server.

DLT (Digital Linear Tape)

Digital linear tape (DLT) is now considered one of the hottest products in the high-end tape-backup market, because of its capability to provide high-capacity, high-speed, and highly reliable backups. DLT started as a proprietary technology belonging to Digital Equipment Corporation. The technology has been on the market since 1991, but in December 1994, Quantum purchased Digital's DLT and magneto-resistive drive technology.

DLT has a capacity of up to 35–70GB compressed, and a data-transfer rate of 5–10MB/sec or more. This is approximately the same speed as a high-speed 8mm drive; however, 8mm has a slight performance advantage in real-world tests.

DLT segments the tape into parallel horizontal tracks and records data by streaming the tape across a single stationary head at 100–150 inches/sec during read/write operations. This is a dramatic contrast to traditional helical-scan technology, in which the data is recorded in diagonal stripes with a rotating drumhead while a much slower tape motor draws the media past the recording head.

The result is a very durable drive and a robust medium. DLT drive heads have a minimum life expectancy of 15,000 hours under worst-case temperature and humidity conditions, and the tapes have a life expectancy of 500,000 passes. DLT drives are designed primarily for network server backup, and cost $6,000 to $8,000 or more depending on capacity. With automatic tape changers, DLT drives can be left unattended for many network backup tasks.

Travan Cartridge Tape

3M has created an entirely new tape cartridge standard based on the QIC format called Travan. Tape drives based on Travan technology have had a significant impact on the tape market for PCs and workstations, and drives based on this technology should have a prominent place in this market over the next several years.

The Travan platform features a unique drive/minicartridge interface that is patented by 3M. The Travan platform fits in a 3 1/2-inch form factor, making it easy to install in a variety of systems and enclosures. Travan drives can accept current QIC and Travan minicartridges—a critical need for users, given the installed base of more than 200 million QIC-compatible minicartridges worldwide.

Travan cartridges contain 750 feet of .315-inch wide tape. There are currently several different levels of Travan cartridges and drives available called TR-1 through TR-4, each based on a particular QIC standard:

- The TR-1 minicartridge provides users with 400MB of uncompressed storage, more than doubling the capacity of the QIC-80 minicartridge (125MB).
- The TR-2 minicartridge, a new modified QIC-3010 drive/cartridge, stores 800MB of uncompressed data, which is significantly more than the 340MB capacity of QIC-3010 tapes.
- The capacity of the TR-3 minicartridge, a new modified 3020 drive/cartridge, is 1.6GB of uncompressed data (up from 670MB in the QIC-3020).
- The newest Travan cartridge, TR-4, stores 4GB of uncompressed data and is compatible with the QIC-3095 standard.

Notice that virtually all Travan drives offer 2:1 data compression, which doubles the uncompressed native capacity. This means that a Travan TR-4 drive can store up to 8GB on a single cartridge! A typical TR-4 based drive, such as those from Hewlett-Packard's Colorado Memory Systems Division, sell for about $300. Because Travan tapes sell in the $35 price range and are available through many distributors and resellers, the low cost and high availability of these drives and cartridges make Travan one of the best backup solutions possible for most individuals.

The TR-1 through TR-3 drives usually interface to the system via the floppy controller or parallel port. I recommend using an EPP or ECP parallel port for ease of use and performance. The higher-end TR-4 drives often use a SCSI-2 interface, which offers greater performance than either the floppy or parallel port interface. A typical TR-4 system such as the HP T4000 drive operates at 514KB/sec, which is approximately four times faster than floppy-interface systems, providing backup speeds up to 31MB per minute native and up to 62MB per minute with 2:1 data compression. Using a typical Pentium system, users can back up a 1GB hard drive in about 30 minutes. If you use the floppy controller or parallel port, you can expect backup times about four times longer or about two hours for a 1GB drive.

Storage industry leaders such as 3M, HP/Colorado, Iomega, Exabyte, Tandberg Data, and Sony offer Travan drives and support future development of Travan drive and recording formats.

Choosing a Tape Backup Drive

Choosing a tape backup drive can be a simple job if you need to back up a single standalone system with a relatively small hard drive. The decision becomes more complex if the system has a larger hard drive, or if you must back up not only a desktop system but also a laptop. Choosing a tape backup drive type can be an even more complex program if you must back up a network server's hard drives and perhaps even back up the workstations from the server. As you ponder which backup tape drive type you should choose, consider the following factors:

- The amount of data you must back up
- The data throughput you need
- The tape standard that is best for your needs
- The cost of the drive and tapes
- The capabilities and compatibility of the included driver and backup software

By balancing the considerations of price, capacity, throughput, compatibility, and tape standard, you can find a tape drive that best meets your needs.

Note

When purchasing a tape backup drive, take the time to look through magazines where dealers or distributors advertise. Several publications specialize in PCs and carry advertising from many hardware and software distributors. I recommend publications such as the *Computer Reseller News* and *Computer Shopper*.

These publications cater to people or companies willing to go around the middlemen and buy direct. By reading such publications, you can get an excellent idea of the drives available and the price you can expect to pay.

While reading about drive capabilities and prices, don't neglect to read reviews of the software included with each drive. Verify that the software capabilities match your expectations and needs. This is especially important if you intend to use the drive on a non-Windows 9x system, because most backup software today is tailored for Windows 9x.

Capacity

The first rule for choosing a tape backup drive is to buy a drive whose capacity is large enough for your needs, now and for the foreseeable future. The ideal is to buy a drive with enough capacity so you can start your backup software, insert a blank tape in the drive, walk away from the system, and find the backup completed when you return.

No matter the capacity needs for a workstation, I generally recommend either DAT drives or the newer Travan drives. These are the most cost-effective and highest-performing drives on the market today. The tapes are preformatted, which saves a lot of time, and can store up to 8GB on a single Travan TR-4 tape or 24GB on a single DDS-3 DAT tape.

You should always make sure that your tape backup medium supports a capacity larger than your largest single drive or partition. This makes automated backups possible because you won't have to change a tape in the middle of a backup. Because the DAT drives normally interface via SCSI, you can use a parallel port SCSI adapter to connect the drive to a system's parallel port or a standard internal SCSI adapter. Of course, the internal adapter performs better, but a portable DAT drive connected via the parallel port can be used to back up many different systems. The DAT medium is also cheaper than any other tape medium on the market when you consider its cost per megabyte.

Tape Standards

The next most important consideration, after adequate capacity, is choosing a drive whose tapes meet a standard that is useful to you. For example, if you must be able to restore backup data by using any of a number of different tape backup drives, you should make sure that all these drives can at least read the tapes. For this reason, if you have several systems to work with, you should choose a tape standard that will work in them all.

There is no quick, simple answer as to which standard is the best. Many people stick with QIC-standard drives because QIC created the first standards and continues to develop new standards for large-capacity tape backups. But if you need a large-capacity backup tape system, DAT or 8mm might be the correct choice.

If you need backward compatibility with tapes or tape drives you already have, you will need to buy drives that are the same standard or a higher compatible standard. For example, if you need a large-capacity tape drive that is backward compatible with your QIC-80 tapes, you should consider the 2GB-capacity QIC-3010, which reads QIC-40 and QIC-80 tapes. If, on the other hand, you don't have to worry about data already stored on old tapes, the important considerations might be capacity and performance. Therefore, DAT or 8mm drives might be the best choice.

Tip

It is important that you make a choice you can live with. If you manage a large installation of computers, mixing QIC, Travan, DAT, and 8mm drives among systems is seldom a good idea.

Software Compatibility

Equally important to your consideration is the software required to operate each drive. Currently, most drives come with software that runs under the Windows 9x operating system. However, finding software that runs equally well under Windows NT or UNIX might be difficult.

Most operating systems have their own software for backing up data to a tape drive. If you intend to use this software, you should verify that the drive you purchase is supported by each piece of software on each system that you intend to use with the drive.

Data Throughput

You should consider the 8mm or DLT drives if performance is more important to you than price or compatibility. These drives offer huge capacity and tremendous data throughput—as high as 6MB/sec. Large-capacity drives based on newer QIC-standards are capable of 18MB per minute throughput. DAT tape drives offer throughput of 10MB per minute.

The low end of the tape backup drive performance spectrum is the older QIC-80 standard drives. When linked to a floppy controller, these drives achieve 3MB to 4MB per minute throughput. Even with a dedicated interface card purchased at added cost, QIC-80 drives are lucky to achieve their advertised throughput of 9MB per minute. Portable QIC-80 drives are advertised at 3MB to 8MB per minute, but 2MB or 3MB a minute is a more realistic figure.

The Cost of the Drive and Tapes

The price of tape drives varies considerably based on where you buy, so it pays to shop enthusiastically for a good price after you have settled on the type of drive you want to buy.

The cost of backup tapes also varies widely, depending on where you buy. Because many computer retailers and direct channel vendors offer lower prices when you buy three or more tapes at a time, it pays to shop for price and buy the largest quantity of tapes you expect to need.

Tip

One point worth remembering when you evaluate whether to buy a tape drive is that the cost of the tapes and drive, taken as a whole, is nowhere near as high as the costs (in terms of frustration and lost productivity) of a single data-damaging hard drive problem. Considering that most people are more likely to back up their system if they have a tape drive installed than if they must use another medium for the backup, the cost of a drive and tapes is quite small, even on a standalone PC used mostly for fun.

Portable Tape Drives

The portable tape drive is one of the most popular tape drive configurations because portables can be moved easily from system to system—desktops, laptops, a single system, or multisystem installations. Portable tape drives are particularly useful to people who use laptops (in which an internal tape backup drive will not fit) and those who want to back up a number of systems on a single tape backup drive. Portable tape drives are good also for people who want to use a tape backup drive for their desktop system but whose system has no available drive bay, as is often the case with small profile, or Slimline, desktop systems.

Portable tape drives can meet so many needs because these drives are self-contained. The unit connects to the computer's parallel port and is powered by a transformer that plugs into a standard AC socket.

To set up a portable tape drive, you plug the transformer cord into the system unit and an AC socket, connect the data cable to the computer's parallel port, and run the backup software. One limitation of portable units is availability of compatible backup software. Although portable tape drive manufacturers include software that operates the drive, some popular third-party backup software cannot be used with portable drives.

Tape Drive Installation Issues

Each of the tape drive standards covered in this chapter provides a range of options for installation, usually including both internal and external models. Whether to choose an internal or external drive, and which external drive to choose if that appears to be the best choice for you, is not always a cut-and-dried issue. If you must back up a single computer with a relatively small hard drive, an internal drive might be your best choice. If you have to back up several computers, or if you must be able to share data between several computers, a portable would be preferable. If your backup needs are not that simple, however, here are some additional considerations:

- If your computer has a large hard drive and you back up often, or if you administer a large number of systems, you should consider installing large-capacity QIC, DAT, or 8mm tape drives. Using these tape formats minimizes the amount of work you must do and the number of tapes you have to store for each computer.

- If your best choice is a large capacity QIC, DAT, or 8mm tape drive and almost all the computers you administer have an available drive bay, you might choose a portable DAT or 8mm tape system, which you can move from system to system.

The following sections cover some important installation issues for internal and external mounted drives.

Internal Installation

Virtually all internal tape backup drives available today are designed to be installed in a half-height drive bay. Many are designed to be installed in either half-height drive bays or the smaller drive bays generally used for 3 1/2-inch floppy disk drives. Drives that can be installed in 3 1/2-inch floppy disk drive bays generally are shipped in a cage, or frame, that also enables them to be installed in a 5 1/4-inch bay. To install the drive in a 3 1/2-inch bay, you remove the cage and the 5 1/4-inch bay faceplate. Most tape drives are between 5 and 9 inches deep and require that much clearance inside the system case. To mount tape drives inside the system, use the same rails or cage apparatus used for floppy disk drives, hard drives, and other devices such as CD-ROM drives.

Internal tape drives require a spare power connector, usually the larger connector used for hard drives, although some might require the smaller power connector used by 3 1/2-inch floppy disk drives. If a power connector is not available inside your system, you can buy a power splitter from a computer store or cable supply vendor.

Internal tape drives also require an interface to the system. QIC-40 and QIC-80 drives most often connect to the system through the floppy controller. On a system with only one floppy disk drive, you connect the tape drive to an unused connector on the floppy disk data cable. On systems with two floppy disk drives, you use a special cable linked to the floppy disk data cable, in effect a splitter cable.

Internal drives other than QIC-40s and QIC-80s usually connect to either a SCSI adapter or the IDE interface integrated into the system's motherboard.

External Installation

If you want to move an external tape drive from computer to computer, you must have the appropriate interface installed in each system on which you want to use the drive. Portable tape backup drives such as the DAT portables use either a standard SCSI connection or have a SCSI-to-parallel port converter that uses the computer's parallel port connector. There are no external IDE devices.

Power is supplied to external units by a transformer that plugs into an ordinary 120v AC wall socket. Generally, the transformer connects to the external tape drive with a small connector. When you choose an external tape drive, be sure you have enough AC power sockets available for your computer, its peripherals, and the tape drive.

Tape Drive Backup Software

The most important decision you can make after you choose the tape standard and capacity of your backup tape drive is the backup software you will use with it. Most tape drives are shipped with backup software that generally is adequate for your basic backup needs.

Often, however, third-party software compatible with the drive you have chosen gives you greater flexibility and functionality. For example, some tape drives might not ship with software for the operating system that you want to use. If you want to use one of these drives with another operating system, you might need to purchase third-party backup software. And if you will be backing up network workstations from a server, you must make sure that the drive is shipped with software capable of performing this function; otherwise, you will need to acquire third-party software. The most important issue when selecting a third-party backup software package is compatibility with your drive. Be sure to check the software company's list of certified tape drives for the exact manufacturer and model number for your unit before you make a purchase. Some software manufacturers even certify specific firmware revisions in a tape drive.

One important issue with backup software is data compression, special programming that stores data on the backup tape in less space than is needed on the original source disk. Some companies produce backup software that is well-known for especially efficient data compression. In other words, backup software produced by these companies does a better job of compressing large data files into a small amount of space. However, if your tape drive provides compression at the hardware level, this point is moot, as far as the software is concerned. You can compress data only once, and hardware compression is always preferable to software compression.

You might want to take the time to read reviews on backup software in one of the many monthly computer magazines, such as *PC Magazine*, *Windows Magazine*, or *BYTE*. The reviews can help you determine which backup software does the best job of compressing data; they also provide information on how quickly backup software programs perform a typical backup. The speed of the backup software and its data-compression capabilities are important considerations. Also of great importance is whether the software is easy to use. If your backup software makes backing up more difficult than it has to be, chances are you won't back up as often as you should.

Tip

Some of the more recent software for tape drives include a "Disaster Recovery" feature. This feature creates a boot disk (floppy) that can quickly reformat a drive and perform a basic operating system installation. Look for this feature when considering your purchase decision.

Bundled Software

Before you buy a backup tape drive, you should always check whether the drive includes software that will meet your needs and, if it doesn't, be sure to buy third-party software that does the job. Generally, the software bundled with most tape backup drives will do the job for you—provided that you don't plan to place great demands on the tape drive.

Third-Party Software

A large number of companies manufacture backup software designed for different types of tape drives and different uses. For example, many manufacturers design their backup software to be compatible with most networks. Others specialize in DOS and Windows backup software. Some specialize in OS/2 software. Others are well-known among those whose computers run in UNIX. You might need to call the software company to determine whether a particular type of software is compatible not only with the tape drive you have chosen, but also with your network and operating environment.

Often, third-party software is easier to use than the software designed by a tape manufacturer. The tape manufacturer's software might have an unfamiliar interface or its commands might seem cryptic to you, even if you have used backup software for years. It is not uncommon for tape manufacturers to include inadequate or even incomplete documentation for the backup software included with the drive, although this is generally the case only with lower-cost models. In such a case, you might be able to solve the problem by purchasing third-party software.

Third-party software often does a better job of data compression than the software designed by a tape manufacturer. In addition, third-party software often includes capabilities not included with the software bundled with many drives. Some of the capabilities you might want to look for include the following:

- *Unattended backup scheduling.* Enables you to schedule a backup for a time when you won't need to use your computer.
- *Macro capability.* Use when selecting options and the files to back up.
- *A quick tape-erase capability.* Use when erasing the entire contents of a tape.
- *Partial tape-erase capability.* Use when erasing only part of a tape.
- *Tape unerase capability.* Use when recovering erased data.
- *Password-protect capability.* Enables you to protect backup data from access by unauthorized persons.

You can find backup software manufacturers by reading some of the many monthly computer magazines, paying particular attention to their usability reviews. Generally, if a backup software product gets good reviews, works on a system configuration such as yours, and has the features you need, it is worth the price you pay.

Tape Drive Troubleshooting

Tape drives can be troublesome to install and operate. Any type of removable media is more susceptible to problems or damage, and tape is no exception. This section lists some common problems and resolutions. After each problem or symptom there is a list of troubleshooting steps.

Backup or Restore Operation Failure

If your tape drive suffers a backup or restore operation failure, follow these steps:

1. Make sure you are using the correct type of tape cartridge.

2. Remove and replace the cartridge.

3. Restart the system.

4. Retension the tape.

5. Try a new tape.

6. Clean the tape heads.

7. Make sure all cables are securely connected.

Bad Block or Other Tape Media Errors

To troubleshoot bad block or other types of media errors, follow these steps:

1. Retension the tape.

2. Clean the heads.

3. Try a new tape.

4. Restart the system.

5. Try initializing the tape.

6. Perform a Secure Erase on the tape (previous data will no longer be retrievable from the tape).

Note that most minicartridge tapes are preformatted, and cannot be reformatted by your drive. Do not attempt to bulk erase preformatted tapes, as this will render the tapes unusable.

System Lockup or System Freezing when Running a Tape Backup

If your system locks up or freezes while running a tape backup, follow these steps:

1. Ensure that your system meets at least the minimum requirements for both the tape drive and the backup software.

2. Check for driver or resource (IRQ, DMA, or I/O port address) conflicts with your tape drive controller card or interface.

3. Set the CD-ROM to master and the tape drive to slave if both are using the same IDE port.

4. Check the BIOS boot sequence; make sure it is not set to ATAPI (tape/CD-ROM) devices if the tape drive is configured as a master device or as a slave with no master.

5. Make sure the hard drive has sufficient free space; most backup programs temporarily use hard drive space as a buffer for data transfer.

6. Hard drive problems can cause the backup software to lock up. Check your hard disk for errors with SCANDISK or a comparable utility.

7. Check for viruses.

8. Check for previous tape drive installations; make sure any drivers from previous installations are removed.

9. Temporarily disable the current VGA driver and test with the standard 640×480×16 VGA driver supplied by Microsoft. If the problem does not reoccur, contact your graphics board manufacturer for an updated video driver.

10. Files in some third-party Recycle Bins can cause backup software to lock up. Empty the Recycle Bin before attempting a backup.

11. Disable antivirus programs and Advanced Power Management.

12. Try the tape drive on another computer system and different operating system, or try swapping the drive, card, and cable with known good, working equipment.

Other Tape Drive Problems

Other issues that might cause problems in general with tape backups include

- Corrupted data or ID information on the tape.
- Incorrect BIOS (CMOS) settings.
- Networking problems (outdated network drivers, etc.).
- The tape was made by another tape drive. If the other drive can still read the tape, this might indicate a head alignment problem or incompatible environment.

Tape Retensioning

Retensioning a tape is the process of fast forwarding and then rewinding the tape, to ensure there is even tension on the tape and rollers throughout the entire tape travel. Retensioning is recommended as a preventive maintenance operation when using a new tape or after an existing tape has been exposed to temperature changes or shock (for example, dropping the tape). Retensioning restores the proper tension to the media and removes unwanted tight spots that can develop.

Some general rules for retensioning include the following:

- Retension any tapes that have not been used for over a month or two.
- Retension tapes if you have errors reading them.
- Retension any tapes that have been dropped.
- In some cases, it may be necessary to perform the retension operation several times to achieve the proper effect. Most tape drive or backup software include a Retension feature as a menu selection.

Optical Storage

13

SOME OF THE MAIN TOPICS IN THIS CHAPTER ARE

What Is a CD-ROM?

Within minutes of inserting a plastic and aluminum, sandwich-coated data disc into your computer, you have access to information that might have taken you days or even weeks to find a few short years ago. Science, medicine, law, business profiles, and educational materials—every conceivable form of human endeavor or pursuit of knowledge—are making their way to CD-ROM, or *compact disc read-only memory*. Other formats such as CD-R and CD-RW are expanding the compact disc's capabilities by making them writable, and new technologies such as DVD are making it possible to store more data than ever on the same size disc.

CD-ROM drives are now considered standard equipment on most PCs. The primary exception to this rule is PCs that are intended for use on business networks. Server hard drives and shared network CD-ROMs can be much more economical than individual CD-ROM drives on every computer. However, nearly all standalone systems can benefit from some sort of optical storage device.

The CD-ROM is a read-only optical storage medium capable of holding up to 682MB of data (approximately 333,000 pages of text), 74 minutes of high-fidelity audio, or some combination of the two, on a single side of a five-inch disc. The CD-ROM is similar to the familiar audio compact disc and can, in fact, play in a normal audio player. The result, however, would be noise— unless audio tracks accompany the data on the CD-ROM (see the section "Enhanced Music CDs," later in this chapter). Accessing data from a CD-ROM is quite a bit faster than from a floppy disk but considerably slower than a modern hard drive. The term CD-ROM refers to both the discs themselves and the drive that reads them.

Although only a few dozen CD-ROMs, or titles, were published for personal computer users in all of 1988, there are currently hundreds of thousands of individual titles containing data and programs, ranging from worldwide agricultural statistics to preschool learning games. Individual businesses, local and federal government offices, and small businesses also publish thousands of their own limited-use titles. As one example, consider that the storage space and expense that so many business offices once dedicated to the maintenance of a telephone book library can now be replaced by two discs containing the telephone listings for the entire United States.

CDs: A Brief History

In 1978, the Philips and Sony corporations joined forces to produce the current audio CD. Philips had already developed commercial laser-disc players, and Sony had a decade of digital recording research under its belt. The two companies were poised for a battle—the introduction of potentially incompatible audio laser disc formats—when they came to terms on an agreement to formulate a single audio technology.

Sony pushed for a 12-inch platter. Philips wanted to investigate smaller sizes, especially when it became clear that they could pack an astonishing 12 hours of music on the 12-inch discs.

By 1982, the companies announced the standard, which included the specifications for recording, sampling, and—above all—the 4.72-inch format you live with today. This size was chosen, legend has it, because it could contain all of Beethoven's approximately 70-minute Ninth Symphony without interruption.

With the continued cooperation of Sony and Philips through the 1980s, additional specifications were announced concerning the use of CD technology for computer data. These recommendations evolved into the computer CD-ROM drives in use today, which use the same technology and disc format as audio CDs. Where engineers used to struggle to find the perfect fit between disc form and a great symphony, software developers and publishers began cramming these little discs with the world's information.

CD-ROM Technology

Although identical in appearance to audio CDs, CD-ROMs store data instead of (or in addition to) audio. The CD-ROM drives in PCs that read the data discs bear a strong resemblance to an audio CD player. The procedures for handling the CDs (inserting them into the CD drive and ejecting them when finished) are all familiar to anyone who has used an audio CD. Both forms of CDs operate on the same general mechanical principles.

The disc is made of a polycarbonate wafer, 120mm in diameter and 1.2mm thick, with a 15mm hole in the center. This wafer base is coated with a metallic film, usually an aluminum alloy. The aluminum film is the portion of the disc that the CD-ROM drive reads for information. The aluminum film or strata is then covered by a plastic polycarbonate coating that protects the underlying data. A label is usually placed on the top of the disc, and all reading occurs from the bottom. CD-ROMs are single-sided.

Note

CD-ROM media should be handled with the same care as a photographic negative. The CD-ROM is an optical device and degrades as its optical surface becomes dirty or scratched. If your drive uses a caddy—a container for the disc that does not require handling the disc itself—you might want to purchase a sufficient supply of these to reduce the handling of the actual discs. Most of the drives produced today no longer use caddies, however, and improper handling of the discs can shorten their life.

Mass-Producing CD-ROMs

Although a laser etches data onto a master disc, this technique would be impractical for the reproduction of hundreds or thousands of copies. Each production of a master disc can take over 30 minutes to encode. In addition, these master discs are made of materials that aren't as durable as a mass-produced disc for continued or prolonged use.

For limited-run CD production, an original master is coated with metal in a process similar to electroplating. After the metal is formed and separated from the master, the metal reverse image imprint of the original can be used to stamp copies, not unlike the reproduction of vinyl records. This process works effectively for small quantities; eventually the stamp wears out.

(continues)

To produce a large volume of discs, manufacturers use the following three-step process:

1. The master is once again plated and a stamp is produced.

2. This stamp creates a duplicate master, made of a more resilient metal.

3. The duplicate master can then be used to produce numerous stamps.

This technique makes it possible to create a great many production stamps from the duplicate master, preserving the original integrity of the first encoding. It also allows for mass production using inexpensive materials. The CDs you buy are coated with aluminum after they are stamped into polycarbonate, and then are protected with a thin layer of plastic. The thin aluminum layer that coats the etched pits as well as the smooth surfaces enables the reading laser to determine the presence or absence of strongly reflected light.

This mass-manufacturing process is identical for both data CD-ROMs and audio CDs.

Reading the information back is a matter of reflecting a low-powered laser off the aluminum strata. A receiver or light receptor notes where light is strongly reflected or where it is absent or diffused. Diffused or absent light is caused by the pits etched in the CD. Strong reflection of the light indicates no pit—this is called a *land*. The light receptors within the player collect the reflected and diffused light as it is refracted from the surface. As the light sources are collected from the refraction, microprocessors translate the light patterns back into data or sound.

The individual pits on a CD are 0.12 microns deep and about 0.6 microns wide (one micron equals one-millionth of a meter). The pits are etched into a spiral track with a spacing of 1.6 microns between turns, corresponding to a track density of nearly 16,000 tracks per inch. The pits and lands run from 0.9 to 3.3 microns long. The track starts at the inside of the disc and ends as close as 5mm from the edge of the disc. This single spiral track is nearly three miles long.

When a CD—audio or data—seeks out a specific datum on the disc, it looks up the address of the datum from a table of contents and positions itself near the beginning of this datum across the spiral, waiting for the right string of bits to flow past the laser beam.

CD-ROM data is recorded using a technique called *Constant Linear Velocity* (*CLV*). This means that the track data is always moving past the read laser at the same linear speed. In other words, the disk must spin faster when reading the inner track area and slower when reading the outer track area. Because CDs were originally designed to record audio, the speed at which the drive reads the data had to be constant. Thus, each disc is broken up into blocks, or sectors, that are stored at the rate of 75 blocks per second on a disc that can hold a total of 74 minutes of information, resulting in a maximum of 333,000 blocks (sectors).

New multispeed CD-ROM readers still read the same CLV-recorded CDs, but play them back at a *Constant Angular Velocity* (*CAV*). This means that the track data is moving past the read laser at a different speed, depending on where the track is physically located on the CD (inner or outer track). This type of drive reads the tracks at the edge of the disk faster than ones near the center because the CD is rotating at a constant speed, similar to old record players. CAV drives are also quieter than CLV drives, as a rule. A drive that combines CLV and CAV technologies is referred to as Partial-CAV or P-CAV. Table 13.1 compares CLV and CAV.

Table 13.1   CLV Versus CAV Technology Quick Reference

	CLV	CAV
Speed of CD rotation	Varies with data position on CD—faster on inner tracks than on outer tracks	Constant
Data Transfer rate	Constant	Varies with data position on CD—faster on inner tracks than on outer tracks
Noise level	High	Low
Price	High	Low
Availability	Limited	Common

At one time, people wanting the fastest CD-ROM drives preferred to purchase CLV drives, but a better option is available today: drives using Zen Research's TrueX drive technology, which uses multiple laser beams to achieve constant high transfer rates without the limitations or very high expense of CLV technology.

▶▶ See "TrueX/MultiBeam Technology," p. 709.

In an audio disc, each block stores 2,352 bytes. In a CD-ROM, 304 of these bytes are used for Sync (Synchronizing bits), ID (Identification bits), ECC (Error Correcting Code), and EDC (Error Detection Code) information, leaving 2,048 bytes for user data. Because these blocks are read at a constant speed of 75 per second, this results in a standard CD-ROM transfer rate of 153,600 bytes per second, which is exactly 150KB/sec.

Because a typical disc can hold a maximum of 74 minutes of data, and each second contains 75 blocks of 2,048 bytes each, you can calculate the absolute maximum storage capacity of a CD-ROM at 681,984,000 bytes (rounded as 682 million bytes or 650MB—megabytes—a.k.a. *binary megabytes*).

TrueX/MultiBeam Technology

As you've seen in previous sections, choosing a CD-ROM drive on the basis of its X-rating (speed multiple of the original 1x CD-ROM drive) can be highly misleading. Because CAV or P-CAV drives are common, most high-speed drives (16x or faster) don't achieve their rated maximum speed until the outer areas of the CD-ROM are read. Vibration can cause conventional CD-ROMs to reduce their spin rates to get reliable data reading, but at a sacrifice in speed.

A new approach to high-speed CD-ROM and DVD mechanisms changes the way that high speeds are achieved: instead of reading one track at a time, why not read more? This method, known as TrueX/MultiBeam, was developed by a company called Zen Research, which licenses the technology to CD-ROM and DVD drive makers, similar to the way that motherboard and video card chipset vendors license their technology to other companies. Thus, drives using this technology won't be sold under the Zen Research name.

CD-ROM and forthcoming DVD drives based Zen's TrueX/MultiBeam technology work in a completely different manner than typical CAV drives, which increase their transfer rates by increasing their spin rates. Instead, TrueX drives use a relatively modest constant spin rate and split the data-reading laser beam into seven paths, allowing the beam to read seven tracks at the same time, rather than only one as with conventional drives (hence the term MultiBeam). Figure 13.1 illustrates how the data is split into seven paths.

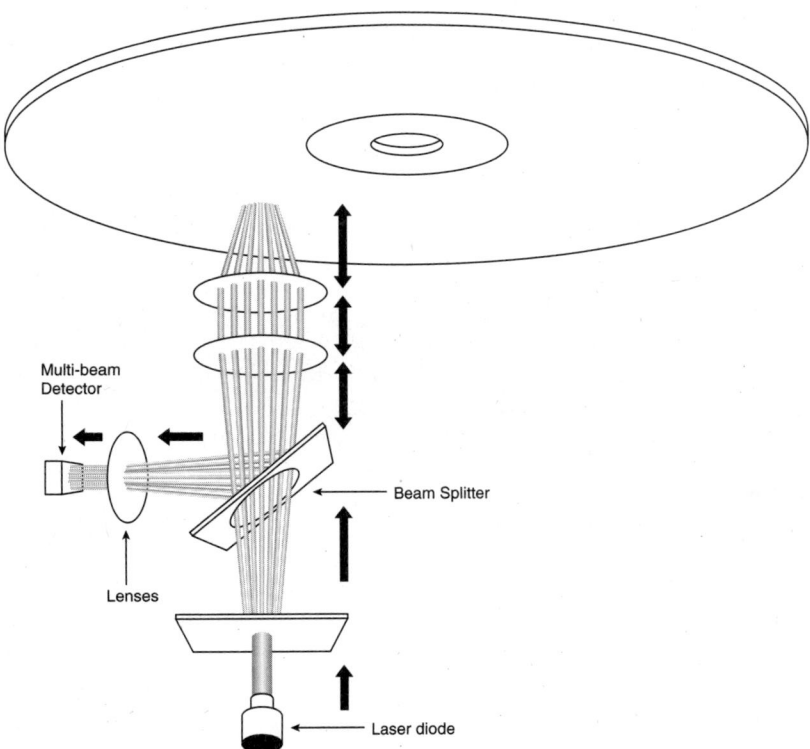

Figure 13.1   MultiBeam technology allows seven tracks to be read at once.

By using a lower spin rate, the problems of vibration are avoided. By using CLV, the problems of variable data-transfer rates across the CD surface are avoided. And, by reading seven tracks at once, TrueX/MultiBeam drives can achieve true, constant X-ratings of 40x, 52x, or higher. Also, transfer rates are at a high, constant speed. In Table 13.1, the transfer rates listed for 40x and 52x drives (40x@6,000KB per second, 52x@7,500 KB per second) represent seldom-achieved rates for conventional CAV 40x Max and 52x Max drives from most vendors. However, drives using TrueX/MultiBeam technology achieve these transfer rates across the entire surface of the CD-ROM. Table 13.2 compares two CD ROM drives—one P-CAV and one TrueX.

Table 13.2   P-CAV and TrueX Compared

Drive	Factory X-Rating	Avg. X-Rating	Technology	CPU Utilization	Average Access Time
Acer CD-640A	40x	24-27x	P-CAV	8% (near center of CD) -> 82% (outer tracks of CD at 40x)	75ms
Kenwood 40x	40x	42-47x	TrueX	18% constant across CD	80ms

Source: Emedia Professional, January 1999

TrueX/MultiBeam products are available from various vendors. Kenwood Technologies (whose products are sold under both the Kenwood and HiVal names) was the first company to sell retail CD-ROM drives using the TrueX/MultiBeam technology. Some Compaq models also offer TrueX/MultiBeam drives. Because Zen Research doesn't manufacture drives but provides the technology to other drive makers it's likely that other drive vendors will offer both CD-ROM and DVD-type drives using this or improved versions of this technology in the future.

Note

DVD drives using a variation of this technology are expected to be released in 1999, and future versions might include as many as 20-beam reading, compared to the seven-beam reading now in use.

Inside Data CDs

The microprocessor that decodes the electrical impulses is the key difference between audio CD players and CD-ROM drives. Audio CDs convert the digital information stored on the disc into analog signals for a stereo amplifier to process. In this scheme, some imprecision is acceptable because it would be virtually impossible to hear in the music. CD-ROMs, however, cannot tolerate any imprecision. Each bit of data must be read accurately. For this reason, CD-ROM discs have a great deal of additional Error Correcting Code (ECC) information written to the disc along with the actual stored information. The ECC can detect and correct most minor errors, improving the reliability and precision to levels that are acceptable for data storage.

CD-ROM drives operate in the following manner (see Figure 13.2):

1. The laser diode emits a low-energy infrared beam toward a reflecting mirror.

2. The servo motor, on command from the microprocessor, positions the beam onto the correct track on the CD-ROM by moving the reflecting mirror.

3. When the beam hits the disc, its refracted light is gathered and focused through the first lens beneath the platter, bounced off the mirror, and sent toward the beam splitter.

4. The beam splitter directs the returning laser light toward another focusing lens.

5. The last lens directs the light beam to a photo detector that converts the light into electric impulses.

6. These incoming impulses are decoded by the microprocessor and sent along to the host computer as data.

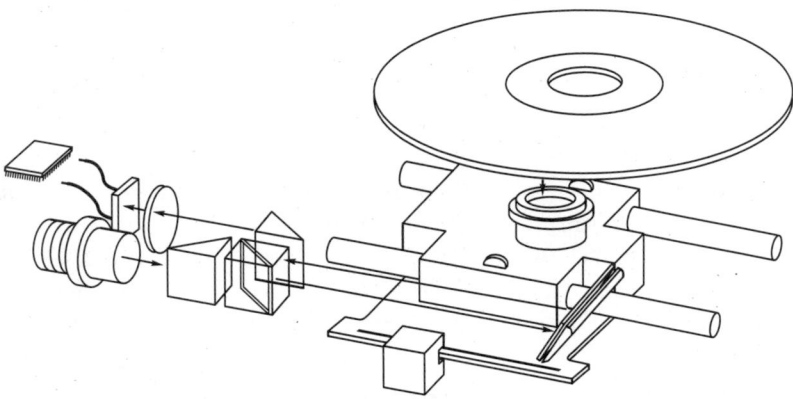

Figure 13.2 *Typical components inside a CD-ROM drive.*

The pits that are etched into the CD-ROM vary in length. The reflected light beam changes in intensity as it crosses over from a land to a pit area. The corresponding electrical signal from the photodetector varies with the reflected light intensity. The transitions between high and low signals, physically recorded as the start and end of each pit area, form a signaling code that the drive interprets as data bits.

Because a single bit error can be disastrous in a program or data file, the error detection and correction algorithms used by a CD-ROM drive are extensive. These routines allow for the probability of an undetected error to be fewer than 1 in 1,025. In more physical terms, this means that there would be only one undetected error in 2 quadrillion discs (this would form a stack 1 billion miles high!).

The error-correction data alone requires 288 bytes for every 2,048 bytes of informational content on the disc. This allows for the correction of numerous bad bits, including bursts of bad data over 1,000 bits long. This powerful error-correction capability is required because physical defects can cause errors and because the CD medium was originally designed for audio reproduction, in which minor errors or even missing data are tolerable.

In the case of an audio CD, missing data can be interpolated—that is, the information follows a predictable pattern that enables the drive to guess the missing values. For example, if three values are stored on an audio disc, say 10, 13, and 20 appearing in a series, and the middle value is missing—due to damage or dirt on the CD's surface—you can interpolate a middle value of 15, which is midway between 10 and 20. Although this might not be exactly correct, in the case of audio recording it will not be noticeable to the listener. If those same three values appear on a CD-ROM in an executable program, there is no way to guess at the correct value for the middle sample. Interpolation cannot work because executable program instructions or data must be exact or the program will crash or improperly read data needed for a calculation. To guess 15 is not merely slightly off; it is completely wrong.

Because of the need for such precision, CD-ROM drives for use on PCs were later to market than their audio counterparts. When first introduced, CD-ROM drives were too expensive for widespread adoption. In addition, drive manufacturers were slow in adopting standards, causing a lag time for the production of CD-ROM titles. Without a wide base of software to drive the industry, acceptance was slow.

After the production costs of both drives and discs began to drop, however, CD-ROMs were rapidly assimilated into the PC world. This was particularly due to the ever-expanding size of PC applications. Virtually all software is now supplied on CD-ROM, even if the disc doesn't contain data representing a tenth of its potential capacity. As the industry stands now, if a software product requires more than two or three floppy disks, it is more economical to put it on a CD-ROM.

For large programs, the advantage is obvious. The Windows 98 operating system would require more than 70 floppy disks, and even that is only when Microsoft uses its proprietary 1.71MB disk format. The cost of producing, packaging, and shipping that many floppy disks instead of a single CD-ROM would drive up the price of the product substantially.

What Types of Drives Are Available?

When purchasing a CD-ROM drive for your PC, you should consider three distinct sets of criteria, as follows:

- The drive's performance specifications
- The interface the drive requires for connection to your PC
- The physical disc-handling system the drive uses

The variance in all these categories is enormous; in fact, single vendors offer entire lines of drives that vary in performance specifications, disc-handling mechanisms, and type of interface to the PC. For these reasons, drive prices can also vary widely. Before you buy, know the drive's characteristics.

CD-ROM Drive Specifications

Drive specifications tell you the drive's performance capabilities. If you're shopping for a sports car, for example, and the dealer tells you the car can accelerate from a standing stop to 60 miles per hour in five seconds, you know you've got a hot car. You can use the car's horsepower, weight, suspension design, and other specifications to understand more about the vehicle's performance.

CD-ROM drive specifications tell the shopper much the same thing. Typical performance figures published by manufacturers are the data transfer rate, access time, internal cache or buffers (if any), and the interface the drive uses.

Data Transfer Rate

The data transfer rate tells you how much data the drive can read from a CD-ROM and transfer to the host computer in a given amount of time. Normally, transfer rates indicate the drive's capability for reading large, sequential streams of data.

The standard measurement in the industry is kilobytes per second, usually abbreviated as KB/sec or, for today's faster drives, megabytes per second (MB/sec). If a manufacturer claims a drive can transfer data at 150KB/sec, it means that a drive reading a sequential stream of data from the CD will achieve 150KB/sec after it has come up to speed. Note that this is a sustained and sequential read, as of a single large file, not access across the data disc from different portions of the platter. Obviously, the data transfer specification is meant to convey the drive's peak data-reading capabilities. A higher rate of transfer might be better, but a number of other factors come into play as well.

The standard compact disc format dictates that there should be 75 blocks (or sectors) of data per second, with each block containing 2,048 bytes of data. This gives a transfer rate of exactly 150KB/sec. This is the standard for CD-DA (Digital Audio) drives and is also called single-speed in CD-ROM drives. The term *single-speed* refers to the original 150KB/sec drives because CDs are recorded in a Constant Linear Velocity (CLV) format, which means that the rotational speed of the disc varies to keep the track speed constant. This is also the rate at which music CDs are played by any speed of CD-ROM drive. A double-speed (or 2x) drive simply attains a transfer rate of 300KB/sec, two times that of the single-speed drive.

Because CD-ROM drives do not read and play data in real-time as audio drives do, it is possible to speed up the data transfer rate by spinning the disc at a higher linear velocity. CD-ROM drive speeds have accelerated rapidly over the years, and many different drive speeds are currently available, all of which are multiples of the original single-speed drives. Table 13.3 shows the speeds at which CD-ROM drives can operate.

Table 13.3   CD-ROM Drive Speeds and Data Transfer Rates

Drive Speed	Transfer Rate (bps)	Transfer Rate (KB/sec)
Single-speed (1x)	153,600	150
Double-speed (2x)	307,200	300
Triple-speed (3x)	460,800	450
Quad-speed (4x)	614,400	600
Six-speed (6x)	921,600	900
Eight-speed (8x)	1,228,800	1,200
Ten-speed (10x)	1,536,000	1,500
Twelve-speed (12x)	1,843,200	1,800
Sixteen-speed (16x)	2,457,600	2,400
Eighteen-speed (18x)	2,764,800	2,700
Twenty-four-speed (24x)	3,686,400	3,600
Thirty-two-speed (32x)	4,915,200	4,800
Thirty-six-speed (36x)	5,529,600	5,400
Forty-speed (40x)	6,144,000	6,000
Forty-eight-speed (48x)	7,372,800	7,200
Fifty-two-speed (52x)	7,987,200	7,500
One-hundred-speed (100x)	15,360,000	15,000
CAV drives (12x–24x)	1,843,200–3,686,400	1,800–3,600

bps = bytes per second

KB/sec = kilobytes per second

Note

Starting with 16x drives and above, the rated speeds for conventional (CAV) drives are maximum speeds. For example, a so-called 32x CD-ROM drive will achieve this 32x speed only on the outer edges of a CD-ROM platter. Depending on the drive model, most of the CD will be read at 12x–16x speeds. Because CD-ROMs can hold over 650MB of information, but most CD-ROMs are used to distribute information that occupies only a fraction of the total CD space, this maximum speed is seldom reached because CDs are created from the center of the disc outwards.

Note

So-called 100x CD-ROM drives actually achieve these high transfer rates by copying the contents of the CD-ROM to your hard disk and then running the copy from the (much faster) hard drive. This treats the hard drive as a very large CD-ROM cache. The "100x" drive-caching technology and Smart100 CD-ROM were developed by Taiwan's Elitegroup.

The 32x and faster drives are currently the most popular, and are standard equipment in most new PCs on the market today. A 4x drive is the minimum required to meet the MPC-3 (Multimedia Personal Computer) standard, and the fact that 48x and faster drives are now available goes to show that the hardware industry moves much more quickly than the standards-making process. In fact, it would probably be relatively difficult to find a new 4x drive today. New systems typically include a 32x or faster CD-ROM drive.

The way that CD-ROM drive speeds have constantly increased makes the thought of performing upgrades problematic. The drive speed of a CD-ROM has a different effect on different types of users. If you use CDs primarily to install applications or look up textual information in reference products such as dictionaries and telephone directories, the speed of the drive is not critical. A few more seconds spent performing a one-time program installation is not worth making sure you always have the fastest drive on the market.

Multimedia and game titles that contain a lot of music, animation, and video are another story, however. The multimedia experience can be greatly enhanced by a faster CD-ROM drive, and some software products specify a recommended minimum drive speed. It certainly is not necessary, however, to buy a new drive each time a faster speed is introduced. For gamers and other heavy CD-ROM users, a good rule of thumb is that an upgrade is not worthwhile unless you would be at least doubling your present speed. For light CD-ROM users, upgrading might never be necessary, because quad-speed drives are adequate for almost any application. Of course it is virtually impossible to purchase anything less than a 12x drive today because the manufacturers have discontinued all the slower drives due to competition in the marketplace making them uneconomical to produce. When installing a large office suite such as Microsoft Office 2000, Corel WordPerfect Office 2000, or an operating system such as Windows 98 or Windows 2000, using at least a 12x drive will greatly speed up the installation process.

Despite these speed increases, however, even the fastest CD-ROM drives pale in comparison to hard disk drive transfer rates, which can be as high as 21MB/sec. The SCSI or ATA/IDE interfaces that CD-ROM drives use today support data transfer rates reaching 80MB/sec, meaning that they are more than up to the task of maintaining CD-ROM transfer rates. If you expect to run a variety of CD-based software on your system, you need a drive with a high data-transfer rate. Applications that employ full-motion video, animation, and sound require high transfer rates, and you'll be disappointed in the results with a slower drive.

Vibration problems can cause high-speed drives to drop to lower speeds to allow reliable reading of CD-ROMs. Your CD-ROM can become unbalanced if you apply a small paper label to its surface to identify the CD or affix its serial number or code for easy reinstallation. For this reason, some 40x and faster CD-ROM drives such as the Plextor UltraPleX 40max and Acer CD-640A come with auto-balancing or vibration-control mechanisms to overcome these problems.

As drive makers seek to increase maximum speed ratings above 50x by increasing spin rates, vibration can become an even greater problem.

Access Time

The access time for a CD-ROM drive is measured the same way as for PC hard disk drives. In other words, the access time is the delay between the drive receiving the command to read and its actual first reading of a bit of data. The time is recorded in milliseconds; a typical manufacturer's rating for a 24x drive would be listed as 95ms. This is an average access rate; the true access rate depends entirely on where the data is located on the disc. When the read mechanism is positioned to a portion of the disc nearer to the narrower center, the access rate is faster than when it is positioned at the wider outer perimeter. Access rates quoted by many manufacturers are an average taken by calculating a series of random reads from a disc.

Obviously, a faster (that is, a lower) average access rate is desirable, especially when you rely on the drive to locate and pull up data quickly. Access times for CD-ROM drives are steadily improving, and the advancements are discussed later in this chapter. Note that these average times are significantly slower than PC hard drives, ranging from 200ms to below 100ms, compared to the 8ms access time of a typical hard disk drive. Most of the speed difference lies in the construction of the drive itself. Hard drives have multiple-read heads that range over a smaller surface area of the medium; CD-ROM drives have only one laser-read beam, and it must be able to access the entire range of the disc. In addition, the data on a CD is organized in a single long spiral. When the drive positions its head to read a track, it must estimate the distance into the disc and skip forward or backward to the appropriate point in the spiral. Reading off the outer edge requires a longer access time than the inner segments, unless you have a Constant Angular Velocity (CAV) drive, which spins at a constant rate so the access time to the outer tracks is equal to that of the inner tracks.

Access times have been falling since the original single-speed drives came out. With each increase in data transfer speed, you have usually seen an increase in access time as well. But as you can see in Table 13.4, these improvements are much less significant because of the physical limitation of the drive's single-read mechanism design.

Table 13.4 Typical CD-ROM Drive Access Times

Drive Speed	Access Time (ms)
Single-speed (1x)	400
Double-speed (2x)	300
Triple-speed (3x)	200
Quad-speed (4x)	150
Six-speed (6x)	150
Eight-speed (8x)	100
Ten-speed (10x)	100
Twelve-speed (12x)	100

(continues)

Table 13.4   Continued

Drive Speed	Access Time (ms)
Sixteen-speed (16x)	90
Eighteen-speed (18x)	90
Twenty-four-speed (24x)	90
Thirty-two-speed (32x)	85
Forty-speed (40x)	75
Forty-eight-speed (48x)	75
CAV (12/24x)	150–90

The times listed here are typical examples for good drives; within each speed category some drives are faster and some are slower.

Buffer/Cache

Most CD-ROM drives include internal buffers or caches of memory installed on-board. These buffers are actual memory chips installed on the drive's circuit board that enable it to stage or store data in larger segments before sending it to the PC. A typical buffer for a CD-ROM drive is 256KB, although drives are available that have either more or less (more is usually better). Generally, the faster drives come with more buffer memory to handle the higher transfer rates. However, many low-cost (under $100) CD-ROM drives are shipping with buffers as small as 128KB, which saves money but can limit performance. The Kenwood drives using the Zen Research TrueX/MultiBeam technology, discussed earlier in the chapter, use a 2MB cache buffer, but this is required in part because the seven different data streams from the seven-beam laser must be recombined before transfer to the CPU.

Having buffer or cache memory for the CD-ROM drive offers a number of advantages. Buffers can ensure that the PC receives data at a constant rate; when an application requests data from the CD-ROM, the data can be found in files scattered across different segments of the disc. Because the drive has a relatively slow access time, the pauses between data reads can cause a drive to send data to the PC sporadically. You might not notice this in typical text applications, but on a drive with a slower access rate coupled with no data buffering, it is very noticeable—and even irritating—during the display of video or some audio segments. In addition, a drive's buffer, when under the control of sophisticated software, can read and have ready the disc's table of contents, speeding up the first request for data. A minimum size of 512KB for a built-in buffer or cache is recommended, and is standard on many 24x and faster drives. However, keep in mind that large buffers don't always result in faster data transfer rates overall.

CPU Utilization

A once-neglected but very real issue in calculating computer performance is the impact that any piece of hardware or software has on the CPU (central processing unit). This CPU utilization factor refers to how much attention the CPU (such as Pentium III, K6-3, and so on) must provide to the hardware or software to help it work. A low CPU utilization percentage score is desirable because the less time a CPU spends on any given hardware or software process provides more time for other tasks, and thus greater performance for your system. On CD-ROM drives, three factors influence CPU utilization: CAV drive speed, drive buffer size, and interface type.

A good example of the impact of CAV drive speed can be seen in comparing the CPU utilization rates of the Acer and Kenwood 40x drives I looked at earlier.

Drive	Type	Minimum CPU-Utl	Maximum CPU-Utl
Acer 40x	P-CAV	8% (inner tracks)	82% (40x reads)
Kenwood 40x	TrueX	18% at all times	

The Acer 40x drive required most of the CPU's attention when reading at 40x, but the Kenwood used less than 20 percent of the CPU's attention no matter where the data was on the CD.

Drive buffer size also influences CPU utilization. For CD-ROM drives with similar performance ratings, the drive with a larger buffer is likely to require less CPU time (lower CPU Utilization percentage) than the one with a smaller buffer.

A third factor influencing CPU utilization is the interface type. Traditionally, SCSI-interface CD-ROM drives have had far lower CPU utilization rates than IDE/ATAPI drives of similar ratings. One review of 12x drives done several years ago rated CPU utilization for IDE/ATAPI CD-ROM drives at 65–80 percent, whereas SCSI CD-ROM drives checked in at less than 11 percent.

DMA (Direct Memory Access)

Today, the introduction of bus-mastering IDE controller circuits on current-model Pentium-class motherboards has substantially changed the picture. Bus-mastering IDE controllers use Direct Memory Access (DMA) transfers to improve performance and reduce CPU utilization. Now, CPU utilization for IDE/ATAPI and SCSI CD-ROM drives is about equal at around 11 percent. Thus, it's to your benefit to enable DMA access for your CD-ROM drives (and your IDE hard drives, too) if your system permits it.

Most recent IDE/ATAPI CD-ROM drives (12x and above) support DMA transfers, as does Windows 95 and above and most recent Pentium-class motherboards. To determine whether your Win9x system has this feature enabled, check the System Properties' Device Manager tab and click the + mark next to Hard Disk Controllers. A drive interface capable of handling DMA transfers will list Bus Master in the name. Next, check the hard drive and CD-ROM information for your system. You can use the properties sheet for your system's CD-ROM drives under Windows 9x to find this information; you might need to open the system to determine your hard drive brand and model. Hard disk drives and CD-ROM drives that support MultiWord DMA Mode 2 (16.6MB/second), UltraDMA Mode 2 (33MB/second), or faster can use DMA transfers. Check your product literature or the manufacturer's Web sites for information.

To enable DMA transfers if your motherboard and drives support it, open the System Properties sheet in Windows 9x, click the Device Manager tab, and open the Properties sheet for your hard drive. Click the Settings tab, and place a check mark in the box labeled DMA.

Repeat the same steps to enable DMA transfers for any additional hard drives and ATAPI/IDE CD-ROM drives in your computer. Restart your computer after making these changes.

Note

I strongly recommend that you back up your drives and your Windows 9x Registry before you enable DMA support or before you install and enable the driver to allow DMA support. If your system hangs up after you enable this feature, you'll need to replace the Registry after enabling DMA with the pre-DMA copy. Otherwise, you'll be faced with editing Registry keys by hand to start your system again. Because DMA transfers bypass the CPU to achieve greater speed, DMA problems could result in data loss. Make backups first, instead of wishing you had later.

Drive interfaces that don't mention bus mastering can't perform this speedup or need to have the correct driver installed. Windows 95 OSR 2.x and Windows 98 will automatically install the correct driver for Intel chipsets that support bus mastering. However, if you have a non-Intel chipset, or have Windows 95 (original version) or Windows 95a (OSR1), you will need to determine whether your system can support bus mastering and download the correct drivers. A good Web site for both Intel and non-Intel chipset support of this important feature is www.bmdrivers.com. Follow the links at this site to the motherboard chipset vendors, their technical notes (to determine whether your chipset supports bus mastering), and the drivers you need to download. Table 13.5 provides a list of chipsets that support DMA.

Table 13.5   Bus-Mastering Chipsets by Vendor and Operating System

Vendor	Chipsets	Driver Source by Operating System
Intel	430FX 430HX 430VX 440FX 430TX 440LX 440BX 440EX 440GX 440ZX 440ZX-66 450NX	(Same driver for all Intel chipsets) Windows 95 original & OSR1 (95a): Download from the Intel Web site Windows 95B, 95C (OSR 2.x), Windows 98: included on Windows CD-ROM
VIA	MVP3 VP3 VP2 VPX VP1	For Windows 95 (any version) and NT 3.51 & higher: Download the drivers from the VIA Web site. For Windows 98: included on CD-ROM

Vendor	Chipsets	Driver Source by Operating System
SiS	611 85c496 5513, 5571, 5581/5582, 5591, 5597/5598, 5600 IDE Driver* SiS530/5595 & SiS620/5595 IDE Driver	Download the drivers from the SiS Web site. *(For SiS chipsets 5511/5512/ 5513, 5596/5513, 5571, 5581/5582, 5598/5597, 5591/5595, 600/5595)
ETEQ	Various motherboard models	See **www.soyo.com.tw** to look up models and drivers; download there or from related FTP site.
PCChips	TXPRO	Download DOS, Windows 3.1, Windows 95, and Windows NT 4 drivers from the PCChips FTP site
	HXPRO	Download DOS, Windows 3.1, Windows 95, Windows NT 3.51 and 4.0 drivers from the PCChips FTP site.
	VXPRO	Download DOS, Windows 3.1, Windows 95, UNIX, OS/2, Windows NT 3.5, or NetWare drivers from the PCChips FTP site
Ali	See note at right	Drivers are available from the motherboard makers using ALi chipsets.

All Intel chipsets which contain a PIIXn device (PIIX, PIIX3, PIIX4, PIIX4E, and so on) are bus-mastering chipsets.

Although PCChips chipset names are similar to certain Intel Pentium chipsets (Triton series TX, HX, and VX), the drivers listed are strictly for PCChips chipsets, not Intel's.

A replacement for manufacturer-specific bus-mastering drivers is available from HighPoint Technologies. This product, XStore Pro, supports bus-mastering chipsets made by Intel, Via, SiS, and ALi, and has proven to more than double disk performance as measured by the Ziff-Davis Business WinMark 98. For more information, visit the HighPoint Web site.

Interface

A CD-ROM's interface is the physical connection of the drive to the PC's expansion bus. The interface is the data pipeline from the drive to the computer, and its importance shouldn't be minimized. There are four different types of interfaces available for attaching a CD-ROM, CD-R, or CD-RW drive to your system:

- SCSI/ASPI (Small Computer System Interface/Advanced SCSI Programming Interface)
- IDE/ATAPI (Integrated Drive Electronics/AT Attachment Packet Interface)
- Parallel port
- USB port

The following sections examine these different interface choices.

SCSI/ASPI

SCSI (pronounced *scuzzy*), or the Small Computer System Interface, is a name given to a special interface bus that allows many different types of peripherals to communicate. The current implemented version of the standard is called SCSI-3, which actually consists of several standards, each defining a part of the interface.

A standard software interface called ASPI (Advanced SCSI Programming Interface) enables CD-ROM drives (and other SCSI peripherals) to communicate with the SCSI host adapter installed in the computer. SCSI offers the greatest flexibility and performance of the interfaces available for CD-ROM drives, and can be used to connect many other types of peripherals to your system as well.

The SCSI bus enables computer users to string a group of devices along a chain from one SCSI host adapter, avoiding the complication of installing a separate adapter card into the PC bus slots for each new hardware device, such as a tape unit or additional CD-ROM drive added to the system. These traits make the SCSI interface preferable for connecting a peripheral such as a CD-ROM to your PC.

Not all SCSI adapters are created equal, however. Although they might share a common command set, they can implement these commands differently, depending on how the adapter's manufacturer designed the hardware. ASPI was created to eliminate these incompatibilities. ASPI was originally developed by Adaptec, Inc., a leader in the development of SCSI controller cards and adapters who originally named it the Adaptec SCSI Programming Interface before it became a de facto standard. ASPI consists of two main parts. The primary part is an ASPI-Manager program, which is a driver that functions between the operating system and the specific SCSI host adapter. The ASPI-Manager sets up the ASPI interface to the SCSI bus.

The second part of an ASPI system is the individual ASPI device drivers. For example, you would get an ASPI driver for your SCSI CD-ROM drive. You can also get ASPI drivers for your other SCSI peripherals, such as tape drives and scanners. The ASPI driver for the peripheral talks to the ASPI-Manager for the host adapter. This is what enables the devices to communicate together on the SCSI bus.

The bottom line is that if you are getting an SCSI interface CD-ROM, be sure that it includes an ASPI driver that runs under your particular operating system. Also, be sure that your SCSI host adapter has the corresponding ASPI-Manager driver as well. There are substantial differences between different SCSI adapters because SCSI can be used for a wide variety of peripherals. Low-cost, SCSI-3 compliant ISA or PCI adapters can be used for CD-ROM interfacing, but higher-performance PCI adapters that support more advanced SCSI standards such as Wide, Ultra, UltraWide, Ultra2Wide, and so on can be used with both CD-ROM drives and other devices such as CD-R/CD-RW drives, hard drives, scanners, tape backups, and so forth. To help you choose the appropriate SCSI adapter for both your CD-ROM drive and any other SCSI-based peripheral you're considering, visit Adaptec's Web site.

The SCSI interface offers the most powerful and flexible connection for CD-ROMs and other devices.

It provides better performance, and seven or more drives can be connected to a single host adapter. The drawback is cost. If you do not need SCSI for other peripherals and intend on connecting only one CD-ROM drive to the system, you will be spending a lot of money on unused potential. In that case, an IDE/ATAPI interface CD-ROM drive would be a more cost-effective choice.

IDE/ATAPI

The IDE/ATAPI (Integrated Drive Electronics/AT Attachment Packet Interface) is an extension of the same ATA (AT Attachment) interface most computers use to connect to their hard disk drives. Specifically, ATAPI is an industry-standard enhanced IDE interface for CD-ROM drives. ATAPI is a software interface that adapts the SCSI/ASPI commands to the IDE/ATA interface. This enables drive manufacturers to take their high-end CD-ROM drive products and quickly adapt them to the IDE interface. This also enables the IDE CD-ROM drives to remain compatible with the MSCDEX (Microsoft CD-ROM Extensions) that provide a software interface with DOS. With Windows 9x, the CD-ROM extensions are contained in the CDFS (CD File System) VxD (virtual device) driver.

ATAPI drives are sometimes also called enhanced IDE (EIDE) drives because this is an extension of the original IDE (technically the ATA) interface. In most cases, an IDE/ATA CD-ROM drive will connect to the system via a second IDE interface connector and channel, leaving the primary one for hard disk drives only. This is preferable because IDE does not share the single channel well and would cause a hard disk drive to wait for CD-ROM commands to complete and vice versa. SCSI does not have this problem because an SCSI host adapter can send commands to different devices without having to wait for each previous command to complete.

Caution

If you decide to purchase a writable CD-ROM drive, such as a CD-R or CD-RW, the SCSI interface is most definitely recommended over IDE/ATA because of IDE's problems in sharing a channel between two devices. Writing to a compact disc requires a steady stream of data that the IDE interface often is not capable of delivering.

The IDE/ATAPI interface represents the most cost-effective and high-performance interface for CD-ROM drives. Most new systems that include a CD-ROM drive will have it connected through IDE/ATAPI. To prevent performance problems, be sure that your CD-ROM drive is connected on the secondary IDE channel, which is separate from the primary channel used by your hard disk drives. Some sound cards include an ATAPI interface driver and the requisite secondary IDE interface connector specifically for a CD-ROM drive. You can connect up to two drives to the secondary IDE connector; for more than that, SCSI is your only choice, and provides better performance as well.

Many systems on the market today can use the IDE/ATAPI CD-ROM drive as a bootable device, which allows the vendor to supply a recovery CD that can restore the computer's software to its factory-shipped condition. Later, you'll see how bootable CDs differ from ordinary CDs and how you can use low-cost CD-R/CD-RW drives, CD-R mastering software, and imaging software to make your own bootable CDs with your own preferred configuration.

Parallel Port

One of the easiest types of CD-ROM drive to install is one that uses a parallel port interface, and parallel port drives can be used on virtually any computer running Windows 9x.

Rather than opening the case to insert an SCSI adapter or connect an internal drive, you can install some CD-ROM drives simply by connecting a cable to the PC's parallel port and loading the appropriate software.

Obviously, the advantages of CD-ROMs that use the parallel port interface are their ease of installation and their portability. In an office environment where the primary function of CD-ROMs is to install software, you can easily move one parallel port drive from machine to machine, rather than purchase a drive for each system. If you use an operating system that supports Plug and Play (PnP), such as Windows 9x, simply plugging a PnP drive into the parallel port causes the OS to detect the new hardware and load the appropriate driver for you automatically.

For best performance, it's recommended that you set your printer port to use IEEE-1284 standards such as ECP/EPP or ECP before connecting your parallel-port CD-ROM. These are bidirectional, high-speed extensions to the standard Centronics parallel-port standard and will provide better performance for virtually any recent parallel device, including printers, tape backups, and Zip and LS-120 drives (also known as SuperDrives), as well as CD-ROM, CD-R, and CD-RW drives.

Using the IEEE-1284 enhanced settings can make a tremendous difference in parallel-port CD-ROM performance. For example, bidirectional (PS/2 style) can achieve data transfer rates of 100 to 530KB/second, whereas EPP can achieve rates of about 1,200Kb/second—12 times that of standard (unidirectional).

▶▶ See "IEEE 1284 Parallel Port Standard," p. 884.

Note

Parallel port CD-ROM drives nearly always include a cable with a pass-through connector. This connector plugs into the parallel port and, if necessary, a printer cable can plug into the connector. This enables you to continue using the port to connect to your printer while sharing the interface with the CD-ROM drive.

Not surprisingly, you pay a price for all this convenience. Parallel port drives typically have somewhat lower data-transfer rates and higher access times than their SCSI or IDE/ATA counterparts, they are slightly more expensive, and, of course, they require their own power supply. Parallel port devices can also be subject to compatibility problems, particularly on older systems. These performance levels can make the drives unsuitable for high-end gaming and multimedia applications, but for general use they are more than adequate.

I generally do not recommend that you purchase a parallel port device simply to save the trouble of opening up the computer. Installing an internal drive is not terribly difficult, and the performance increase is more than worth the extra effort. However, if you can take advantage of the portability that these devices provide, they are an excellent CD-ROM solution.

USB Interface

The newest type of interface, USB, the Universal Serial Bus, has proven to be extremely flexible and has been used for everything from keyboards and joysticks to CD-RW drives from several vendors. These drives can function as CD-ROM drives for data reading, but their real benefit comes in their transportability to different computers for use as a backup or archiving device with CD-R or CD-RW media.

USB CD-RW drives provide read and write transfer rates that match the fastest rates possible with IEEE-1284 parallel ports, with read rates on typical 6x models ranging from 1,145 to 1,200KB/second. They offer the same PnP ease of other modern peripherals used on a Windows 9x system. USB also provides a benefit that no parallel-port drive can match: hot-swappability, the capability to be moved from one computer to another without powering down either system.

For Windows 98 systems with USB ports, USB-based CD-RW drives are an excellent solution for backup and archiving of data onto low-cost, durable optical media. Although Windows 95 OSR 2.1 and above also support USB, at least in theory, USB device support with Windows 95 is chancy at best. This operating-system limitation should be a minimal issue as time passes and Windows 95 is replaced by Windows 98 and Windows 2000.

▶▶ See "USB and 1394 (i.Link) FireWire—Serial and Parallel Port Replacements," p. 891.

Loading Mechanism

There are two distinctly different mechanisms for loading a CD into a CD-ROM drive: the tray and the caddy . Each one offers some benefits and features. Which type you select has a major impact on your use of the drive because you interact with this mechanism every time you load a disc.

Multiple CD-ROM drives on the market allow you to insert more than one disc at a time. Some of these use a special cartridge that you fill with discs, much like a multidisc CD player used in automobiles. Newer models are slot-loading, allowing you to push a button to select which internal cartridge slot you want to load with a CD. The drive's door opens and you slide in the CD, which the drive mechanism grabs and pulls into place. Typical capacities range from 3–5 CDs or more, and these are available in both SCSI and IDE/ATAPI interfaces.

Tray

Most current SCSI and IDE/ATAPI CD-ROM drives use a tray loading mechanism. This is similar to the mechanism used with a stereo system. Because you don't need to put each disc into a separate caddy, this mechanism is much less expensive overall. However, it also means that you have to handle each disc every time you insert or remove it.

Tray loading is more convenient than a caddy system (see the section, "Caddy," later in this chapter) because you don't need a caddy. However, this can make it much more difficult for young children to use the discs without smudging or damaging them due to excess handling.

The tray loader itself is also subject to damage. The trays can easily break if bumped or if something is dropped on them while they are extended. Also, any contamination you place on the tray or disc is brought right into the drive when the tray is retracted. Tray-loaded drives should not be used in a harsh environment such as a commercial or industrial application. Make sure both the tray and the data surface of the CD are clean whenever you use a tray-loading CD.

Note

One of the classic legends among PC technical support engineers is that of the user who called to complain that the cup holder on his computer retracted every time he restarted the machine. After careful questioning, the puzzled engineer determined that the caller had been using the CD-ROM tray to hold his coffee cup. Needless to say, this practice is not recommended.

The tray mechanism also does not hold the disc as securely as the caddy. If you don't have the disc placed in the tray properly when it retracts, the disc or tray can be damaged. Even a slight misalignment can prevent the drive from reading the disc properly, forcing you to open the tray and reset the disc.

Some tray drives cannot operate in a vertical (sideways) position because gravity prevents proper loading and operation. Check to see whether the drive tray has retaining clips on the outer edge of the CD seat, such as the Hitachi drive I have in my HP Vectra. If so, you can run the drive in either horizontal or vertical position.

Some CD-ROM drives equipped with retaining clips still aren't able to run CD-ROMs reliably in the vertical position. If this is a critical feature for you, be sure to test a unit before you install it in a system, or make sure you can return it if it doesn't work properly.

Apart from the convenience, the other advantage of the tray mechanism over the caddy system is in cost, and that is a big factor. If you do not have young children and you plan to use the drive in a clean environment where careful handling and cleanliness can be assured, the tray mechanism is recommended due to its significantly lower cost.

Caddy

At one time, the caddy system was used on most high-end CD-ROM drives as well as the early CD-R (recordable CD) drives. It has since declined in popularity due to the convenience of the tray. The caddy system requires that you place the CD itself into a special caddy, which is a sealed container with a metal shutter. The caddy has a hinged lid that you open to insert the CD, but after that the lid remains shut. When you insert the caddy containing the CD into the drive, the drive opens a metal shutter on the bottom of the caddy, allowing access to the CD by the laser.

The caddy is not the most convenient loading mechanism, although if all your CDs are in their own caddies, all you have to do is grab the caddy containing the disc you want and insert it into the drive. This makes the CD operate much like a 3.5-inch disk. You can handle the caddy without worrying about touching or contaminating the disc or the drive, making this the most accurate and durable mechanism as well. Young children can easily handle the caddies and don't have to touch the compact discs themselves.

Because the caddy is sealed, the discs are protected from damage caused by handling. The only time you actually handle the disc is when you first put it into the caddy. The caddy loading system also ensures that the disc is properly located when inside the drive. This allows for more accurate laser-head positioning mechanisms, and caddy drives generally have faster access times, as well.

The drawbacks to the caddy system are the expense and the inconvenience. You only get one caddy with the drive, so if you want to store your CD-ROMs in their own caddies, you must buy many more. Additional caddies can cost from $4–$10 each, which can lead to a significant expense if you have a large number of CD-ROMs. Most people do not buy caddies for all their discs. The alternative is that each time you insert a new disc into the drive, you first have to eject the caddy/disc, remove the disc from the caddy, put the disc back into the original jewel case, open the jewel case for the new disc, put the new disc into the caddy, and finally insert the caddy/disc back into the drive.

A final advantage of caddy-loaded drives is that they can function when mounted either horizontally or vertically, meaning that the drive can be installed sideways. You cannot do this with the cheaper tray-loaded drives, although some newer tray-loaded drives have small retaining tabs that allow both horizontal or vertical mounting.

Caddy-based CD-ROM and CD-R systems have declined drastically in popularity in recent years.

Other Drive Features

Although drive specifications are of the utmost importance, you should also consider other factors and features when evaluating CD-ROM drives. Besides quality of construction, the following criteria bear scrutiny when making a purchasing decision:

- Drive sealing
- Self-cleaning lenses
- Internal versus external drive

Drive Sealing

Dirt is your CD-ROM's biggest enemy. Dust or dirt, when it collects on the lens portion of the mechanism, can cause read errors or severe performance loss. Many manufacturers seal off the lens and internal components from the drive bay in airtight enclosures. Other drives, although not sealed, have double dust doors—one external and one internal—to keep dust from the inside of the drive. All these features help prolong the life of your drive.

Caddy-loaded drives are inherently sealed better and are much more resistant to the external environment than tray-loaded drives. Always use a caddy-loaded drive in harsh industrial or commercial environments.

Self-Cleaning Lenses

If the laser lens gets dirty, so does your data. The drive will spend a great deal of time seeking and reseeking or will finally give up. Lens-cleaning discs are available, but built-in cleaning mechanisms are now included on virtually all good-quality drives. This might be a feature you'll want to consider, particularly if you work in a less-than-pristine work environment, or you have trouble keeping your desk clean, let alone your CD-ROM drive lens.

Internal Versus External Drives

When deciding whether you want an internal or external drive, think about where and how you're going to use your CD-ROM drive. What about the future expansion of your system? Both types of drives have advantages and disadvantages, such as the following:

■ *External enclosure.* These tend to be rugged, portable, and large—in comparison to their internal versions. Buy an external drive only if you lack the space inside the system or if your computer's power supply cannot support the additional load. You might also consider an external if you want to be able to move the drive from one PC to another easily. Parallel port drives are very portable and supported on a broad range of machines, but USB drives are a better choice for Windows 98 systems that have USB ports.
SCSI drives can also be portable. If each PC has its own SCSI adapter with an external connection, all you need to do is unplug the drive from one adapter and plug it in to the other. Parallel port and USB-based drives must be external, and SCSI CD-ROM drives can be external, so if you are looking for an IDE type interface, you must use the internal IDE connector.

■ *Internal enclosure.* Internal drives will clear off a portion of your desk. Buy an internal drive if you have a free drive bay and a sufficient power supply and you plan to keep the CD-ROM drive exclusively on one machine. The internal drives are also nice because you can connect the audio connector to your sound card and leave the external audio connectors free for other inputs. Internal drives can be IDE or SCSI.

CD-ROM Disc and Drive Formats

Compact discs are pitted to encode the binary bit values 0 and 1. Without a logical organization to this disc full of digits, the CD-ROM drive and PC would be at a loss to find any discernible data amid all those numbers. To this end, the data is encoded to conform to particular standards. When a drive encounters particular patterns, it—and the PC—can recognize the organization of the disc and find its way around the platter. Without standard data formats, the CD-ROM industry would be dead in the water; vendors of discs and disc drives would produce hardware and software that was incompatible with that of other vendors, thereby limiting the number of units that could be sold.

Formats are also needed to advance the technology. For example, hard rubber wheels and no suspension were fine for the first automobiles as they cruised along at the breakneck speed of 30mph. But hitting a pothole at 60mph could cause serious damage to the vehicle—and the riders. Inflatable tires and shock absorbers became necessary components of the modern car.

Similarly, the standards for disc formats have evolved as well. The first compact data discs stored only text information, which is relatively easy to encode. Graphics produced a greater challenge, and the standards evolved to accommodate them. The use of animation with synchronized sound and live-motion video called for other expansions to the standards by which data is stored on CDs.

It is extremely important to note that advanced CD-ROM standards are in the process of evolution right now. Multiple vendors are deploying a number of different techniques for expanding the capabilities of CD-ROM technology. They might be incompatible with each other or immature in their development, but acceptance of these newer standards by software vendors is essential to the widespread use of these standards. It is important that you be familiar with these issues before you purchase a drive. Consider the formats it is capable of reading now—and in the future.

The majority of drives available today, however, do comply with earlier CD-ROM formats, ensuring that the vast library of CD-ROM titles available today can be used on these drives.

Table 13.6 describes the differing CD-ROM formats.

Table 13.6 CD-ROM Formats

Format	Used For	Notes
Red Book	Digital audio CDs	This standard, a.k.a. CDDA (Compact Disc Digital Audio), was codeveloped by Philips and Sony
Yellow Book	Computer CDs	Specifics physical arrangement of sectors. ISO Mode 1:9660
		Level 1: PC, Apple, UNIX, DVI
		Level 2: CDTV
		ISO 9660, HFS, and HFS-ISO are used with Yellow Book to define file and directory structures. See also Mode 1, Mode 2, and CD-ROM/XA, which define sector fomats.
White Book	VideoCD	Stores MPEG-1, MPEG-2, and similar video sources. Has replaced VHS video in southeast Asia for film distribution.
Orange Book	Writable CDs including CD-R, magneto-optical, single and multisession recording and packet writing	Part I—Magneto-Optical Drives Part II—CD-R
Green Book	Combination of Red Book and Yellow Book—for CD-I (Interactive CD)	CD-ROM/XA can be played on either CD-I or CD-ROM drives; CD-I has been used for interactive sales presentations and kiosks
CD+ (Enhanced CD)	Combines music and computer data on single CD	Used by musical artists to incorporate videos and interviews on music CDs

Data Standard: ISO 9660

Manufacturers of the first CD-ROM data discs produced their discs for one particular drive. In other words, a data disc produced for company A's drive could not be read by anyone who had purchased company B's CD-ROM drive—the disc needed to be formatted for each manufacturer's drive. Obviously, this stalled the development of the industry. Philips and Sony developed the "Yellow Book" specifications for data CD-ROMs.

When Philips and Sony first published the audio CD specifications, the material was released in a red binder and became known as the "Red Book." Subsequent CD-ROM specifications have been dubbed by color as well, such as the "Orange Book" and the "Green Book."

The Yellow Book specifications are an extension of the way in which audio data can be stored on disc, and detail how data—rather than audio—can be organized on a disc for its later retrieval. The International Organization for Standardization (ISO) refined this specification (called ISO 9660) so that every vendor's products could expect to find a table of contents in the same place on a data disc. This is known as a Volume Table of Contents, and is quite similar in theory to a printed book's table of contents. ISO 9660 did not completely solve compatibility problems, however. The method for incorporating additional data to aid and refine the disc search process and even the format of the data blocks was still left to each separate vendor's design.

High Sierra Format

It was in all manufacturers' interests to resolve this standardization issue. In a meeting in 1985 at the High Sierra Hotel and Casino in Lake Tahoe, California, leading manufacturers of CD-ROM drives and CD-ROM discs came together to resolve the differences in their implementation of the ISO 9660 format. The agreement has become known as the High Sierra format and is now a part of the ISO 9660 specification document. This agreement enabled all drives to read all ISO 9660–compliant discs, opening the way for the mass production of CD-ROM software publishing. Adoption of this standard also enabled disc publishers to provide cross-platform support for their software, easily manufacturing discs for DOS, UNIX, and other operating system formats. Without this agreement, the maturation of the CD-ROM marketplace would have taken years longer and stifled the production of CD-ROM–based information.

The exact and entire specifications for how to format the compact disc medium are complex, strewn with jargon you might never need, and superfluous to your understanding of a drive's capabilities. You should know the basics, however, because you get a glimpse into the inner workings of how data can be retrieved so quickly from such an enormous well.

To put the basic High Sierra format in perspective, the disc layout is roughly analogous to that of a floppy disk. A floppy disk has a system track that not only identifies itself as a floppy disk and reveals its density and operating system, but also tells the computer how it's organized—into directories, which are made up of files.

Basic CD-ROM formats are much the same. The initial track of a data CD identifies it as a CD and begins the synchronization between the drive and the disc. Beyond the synchronization lies a system area that details how the entire disc is structured. This system area identifies the location of the volume area—where the actual data is stored. The system area also lists the directories in this volume, with pointers or addresses to various named areas, as illustrated in Figure 13.3. A significant difference between the CD directory structure and that of DOS is that the CD's system area also contains direct addresses of the files within the subdirectories, allowing the CD to seek specific locations on the spiral data track.

Because the CD data is all on one long spiral track, when speaking of tracks in the context of a CD, I'm actually talking about sectors or segments of data along that spiral.

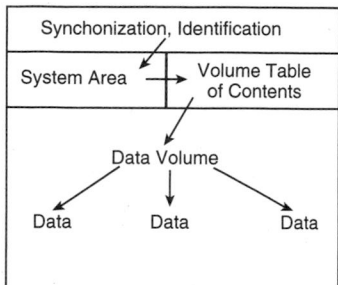

Figure 13.3 A diagram of CD-ROM basic file organizational format.

CD-DA (Digital Audio)

Data drives that can read both data and audio are called CD-DA. Virtually all the data drives now being sold read both types of discs. When you insert a disc, the drive reads the first track to determine what type of disc you've loaded. Most drives ship with audio CD software that enables you to play music CDs from your PC; Windows 9x and Windows NT have this capability built in. You can use headphones or, with an installed sound card, connect speakers to the system. Some external drives ship with standard Left/Right audio plugs; simply plug them into any external amplifier.

CD-ROM XA or Extended Architecture

CD-ROM XA, or Extended Architecture, is backward-compatible with the earlier High Sierra or ISO 9660 CD-ROMs. It adds another dimension to the world of CD-ROM technology: multiple-session recording.

Multiple Sessions

You will remember from the High Sierra format discussion that each CD-ROM disc has a VTOC (or Volume Table of Contents) in its system area, which tells the CD reader where and how the data is laid out on disc. Until this point, CD data was single-session in its encoding. In other words, when a CD was mastered, all the data that will ever reside on the disc had to be recorded in one session. The format, or the medium, had no provision for returning later to append more information.

Single-session CDs are no longer the only option, however. The CD-ROM XA format includes the capability to create multiple sessions on a single disc, each with its own VTOC. A drive that is CD-ROM XA–compliant is capable of finding the multiple VTOCs located on different areas of the disc and reading the data from those multiple sessions. This means that you can record a small amount of data on a CD, remove the CD from the drive, and then return to it later to record more data until the disc is filled. This is a vast improvement over the single-session concept, which forced you to wait until you had a sufficient amount of data to make burning a disc worthwhile. This technique is used by photofinishers who provide you with a CD with your pictures and ask you to return the CD to them with your next roll until the CD is full of electronic versions of your photos.

Multisession CD-ROMs Versus CD-RW

Although CD-ROM XA recording (see the section "CD-R" later in this chapter) allows you to reuse a CD-R until it's full by multisession recording, there is no way to remove data from the CD-R but to simply replace it with updated versions until the CD-R is full. CD-RW (Rewritable CD) drives allow you to add, edit, and delete data from CD/RW media, as well as use CD-R media as with CD-R–only drives.

Interleaving

CD-ROM XA drives employ a technique known as interleaving. The specification calls for the capability to encode on disc whether the data directly following an identification mark is graphics, sound, or text. Graphics can include standard graphics pictures, animation, or full-motion video. In addition, these blocks can be interleaved, or interspersed, with each other. For example, a frame of video can start a track followed by a segment of audio, which would accompany the video, followed by yet another frame of video. The drive picks up the audio and video sequentially, buffering the information in memory, and then sending it along to the PC for synchronization.

In short, the data is read off the disc in alternating pieces and then synchronized at playback so that the result is a simultaneous presentation of the data. Without interleaving, it would be necessary for the drive to read and buffer the entire video track before it could read the audio track and synchronize the two for playback.

Mode 1 and Mode 2, Form 1 and Form 2

To achieve this level of sophistication, the CD format is broken up so that the data types are layered. Mode 1 is the standard Yellow Book CD sector format with error correction. Each 2,352-byte sector consists of four fields (see Figure 13.4), as follows:

- Synchronization (12 bytes)
- Header (8 bytes)
- User Data (2,048 bytes)
- Error Correction Code (ECC) and Error Detection Code (EDC) (284 bytes)

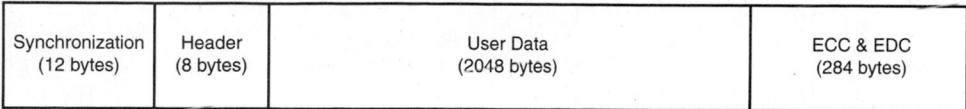

Synchronization (12 bytes)	Header (8 bytes)	User Data (2048 bytes)	ECC & EDC (284 bytes)

Figure 13.4 CD-ROM Yellow Book (Mode 1) sector format.

Mode 2, which was newly defined for the XA format, is CD data without error correction. The Mode 2 track, however, allows what are called Form 1 and Form 2 tracks to exist one after the other on the Mode 2 track, thereby permitting the interleaving. These interleaved tracks can include their own error correction and can contain any type of data. Figure 13.5 shows a visual representation of the breakdowns of Mode and Form structure.

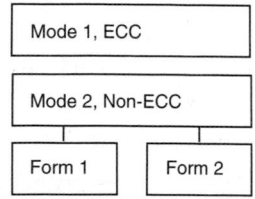

Figure 13.5 A diagrammatic view of Mode and Form format for CD-ROM XA.

A Mode 2, Form 1 sector contains six fields (see Figure 13.6), as follows:

- Synchronization (12 bytes)
- Header (8 bytes)
- Subheader (8 bytes)
- User Data (2,048 bytes)
- Error Correction Code (280 bytes)
- Error Detection Code (4 bytes)

Synchronization (12 bytes)	Header (8 bytes)	Subheader (8 bytes)	User Data (2048 bytes)	ECC (280 bytes)	EDC (4 bytes)

Figure 13.6 CD-ROM Yellow Book (Mode 2, Form 1) sector format.

A Mode 2, Form 2 sector contains only five fields (see Figure 13.7), as follows:

- Synchronization (12 bytes)
- Header (8 bytes)
- Subheader (8 bytes)
- User Data (2,324 bytes)
- Error Detection Code (4 bytes)

Synchronization (12 bytes)	Header (8 bytes)	Subheader (8 bytes)	User Data (2324 bytes)	EDC (4 bytes)

Figure 13.7 CD-ROM Yellow Book (Mode 2, Form 2) sector format.

Both sector formats add a subheader field that identifies the type of information (such as audio or video) carried in the user data field. The Form 2 sector lacks the Error Correction Code of the Form 1 sector and increases the size of the user data field instead.

Because they use less control data, CD-ROMs that use the Mode 2, Form 2 sector format (such as MPEG video CDs) can hold more user information than other CD-ROM types in the same number of sectors, resulting in a data transfer rate of 172KB/sec instead of the standard 150KB/sec.

For a drive to be truly XA-compatible, the Form 2 data encoded on the disc as audio must be Adaptive Differential Pulse Code Modulation (ADPCM) audio—specially compressed and encoded audio. This requires that the drive or the SCSI controller have a signal processor chip that can decompress the audio during the synchronization process.

What all this translates into is that many of the CD-ROM drives currently available are only partially XA-compliant. They might be capable of reading the interleaved data and multisession discs but might not have the ADPCM audio component on the disc or its controller.

Presently, the only drives with full XA compliance are produced by Sony and IBM. The Sony drive incorporates the ADPCM chip on its drive. The IBM XA drive is for IBM's proprietary Micro Channel bus and is designed for its high-end PS/2 Model computers.

Manufacturers might claim that their drives are XA-ready, which means that they are capable of multisession and Mode 1 and Mode 2, Form 1 and Form 2 reading, but they do not incorporate the ADPCM chip. This is not a devastating shortcoming, however, because the CD-ROM XA format has not been very successful in itself. Software developers have not produced many XA software titles. IBM has a few under its Multimedia program, but when compared to the thousands of CD-ROM titles produced each year, very few of them take full advantage of XA capabilities.

However, although you might not find many XA discs on the market, the multisession capabilities and the Mode 2 sector formats defined by the standard are the basis for other CD-ROM formats that have been somewhat more successful, such as CD Extra (or CD PLUS) and PhotoCD.

If you purchase a drive that is fully mode- and form-compatible and is capable of reading multiple sessions, you have the technology needed to take advantage of the most popular formats available at this time. Audio and video interleaving is possible without full XA compliance, as MPC (Multimedia PC) applications under Microsoft Windows demonstrate.

Mixed-Mode CDs

There are several CD-ROM formats that combine different mode sectors on a single disc. Usually, these discs include both standard CD audio and CD-ROM data sectors and originate from the music side (rather than the data side) of the compact disc industry. The intention is for a user to be able to play only the audio tracks in a standard audio CD player while remaining unaware of the data track. However, a user with a PC or a dedicated combination audio/data player can access both the audio and data tracks on the same disc. The audio portion of the disc can consist of up to 98 standard Red Book audio tracks, whereas the data track is typically composed of XA Mode 2 sectors, and can contain video, song lyrics, still images, or other multimedia content.

The fundamental problem with these mixed-mode CDs is that when an audio player tries to play the data track, the result is static that could conceivably damage speakers. Different manufacturers have addressed this problem in different ways, resulting in a number of format names, including CD-ROM Ready, Enhanced Music CDs, CD Extra, and CD Plus.

CD-ROM Ready

One solution, the CD-ROM Ready disk, hides the data track in a pause before the first audio track on the disc. Inserting the CD into an audio player and pressing the Play button simply skips past the pause and plays the first audio track. However, if you start the audio playing and then rewind past the beginning of the first audio track, the player will access the data track, possibly with disastrous results (depending on the volume level). CD-ROM Ready is therefore not a completely effective solution.

Enhanced Music CDs

Philips and Sony, in conjunction with other companies such as Microsoft and Apple, have developed another solution, the Enhanced Music CD specification, as defined in the Blue Book standard. Enhanced music CDs are often marketed under the names CD Plus (CD PLUS) or CD Extra and use the multisession technology defined in the CD-ROM XA standard to separate the audio and data tracks. Sometimes the markings are quite obscure, and you might not know that an audio CD contains data tracks until you play it in a CD-ROM drive.

The first session on an Enhanced Music CD contains up to 98 standard Red Book audio tracks, whereas the second session contains a single track of CD-ROM XA Mode 2 sectors. Because audio CD players are only single-session capable, they play only the audio tracks and ignore the additional session containing the XA data. An XA-ready CD-ROM drive in a PC, however, can see both of the sessions on the disc and access both the audio and data tracks.

PhotoCD

First announced back in 1990 but not available until 1992, CD drives or players that display your own CD-ROM–recorded photographs over your television are now being sold by Kodak. You simply drop off a roll of film at a participating Kodak developer; later you take home a PhotoCD and drop it into your PC or a Kodak PhotoCD-compatible disc player.

A PhotoCD-compatible player is a home A/V (audio/visual) entertainment system component that is designed to play both PhotoCDs and audio CDs.

Because virtually all data-ready CD drives can also interpret audio, it was not difficult for Kodak to design the CD players to play audio discs as well. The player merely reads the first track and determines what type of disc you've fed it.

Using the PhotoCD player, you can view your photographs at any one of several resolutions; with a PC, you can both view your images and manipulate them using standard graphics software packages.

When you drop off your roll of film, the Kodak developers produce prints, as they normally do. After prints are made, however, the process goes high-tech. Using high-speed SUN SPARCstations, they scan the prints with ultra-high-resolution scanners. To give you an idea of the amount of information each scan carries, one color photograph can take 15–20MB of storage. The compressed, stored images are then encoded onto special writable CDs. The finished product is packaged in a familiar CD case and shipped back to your local developer for pickup.

PhotoCD Disc Types

The images on the disc are compressed and stored using Kodak's own PhotoYCC encoding format, which includes up to six different resolutions for each image, as shown in Table 13.7. Kodak has defined several different types of PhotoCD discs to accommodate the needs of different types of users. The PhotoCD Master disc is the standard consumer format, and contains up to 100 of your photos in all the resolutions shown in the table except for base x64.

Table 13.7   PhotoCD Resolutions

Base	Resolution (pixels)	Description
/16	128×192	Thumbnail
/4	256×384	Thumbnail
x1	512×768	TV resolution
x4	1024×1536	HDTV resolution
x16	2048×3072	Print size
x64	4096×6144	Pro PhotoCD master only

The different resolutions supply you with images appropriate for different applications. If, for example, you want to include a PhotoCD image on a Web page, you would choose a low-resolution image. A professional photographer shooting photos for a print ad would want to use the highest resolution possible.

The Pro PhotoCD Master disc is intended for professional photographers using larger film formats, such as 70mm, 120mm, or 4×5 inch. This type of disc adds an even higher-resolution image (4,096×6,144 pixels) to those already furnished on the PhotoCD Master disc. Because of this added high-resolution image, this type of disk can hold anywhere from 25–100 images, depending on the film format.

The PhotoCD Portfolio disc is designed for interactive presentations that include sound and other multimedia content. The high-resolution images that take up the most space are not needed here, so this type of disc can contain up to 700 images, depending on how much other content is included.

The PhotoCD Catalogue disc uses even lower-resolution images, designed for use in thumbnail displays. Up to 600 images of this type can be stored on a single disc.

The Print PhotoCD disc is intended for users in the printing industry and includes the same five resolutions as the PhotoCD Master disc, plus a platform-independent CMYK image that can be used by virtually any imaging software or publishing system.

Multiple Session Photo CDs

One of the breakthroughs of the PhotoCD concept is that each of the disc types is capable of containing multiple sessions. Because the average consumer would not usually have enough film processed to fill an entire disc, you can bring back your partially filled CDs each time you have more film to develop. A new session is then added to your existing CD until the entire disc is filled. You pay less for the processing because a new CD is not needed, and all your images are stored on a smaller number of disks.

Any XA-compliant or XA-ready CD-ROM drive can read the multiple sessions on a PhotoCD disc, and even if your drive is not multisession capable, it can still read the first session on the disc. If this is the case, you'll have to purchase a new disc for each batch of film you process, but you can still take advantage of PhotoCD technology.

Kodak provides software that enables you to view the PhotoCD images on your PC, and licenses a PhotoCD import filter to the manufacturers of many different desktop publishing, image editing, and paint programs. This means that you can modify your PhotoCD images using a program such as Adobe Photoshop and integrate them into documents for printing or electronic publication with a page layout program such as Adobe PageMaker.

Picture CD

Although Kodak still offers PhotoCD services, its high cost has led to limited popularity. Kodak now offers the simpler Picture CD and Picture Disk services. Unlike PhotoCD, these services use the industry-standard JPEG file format. Picture CD uses a CD-R, with images stored at a single medium-resolution scan of 1,024 by 1,536 pixels. This resolution is adequate for 4×6 and 5×7 prints. The less-expensive Picture Disk service stores images on a 1.44MB floppy disk at a resolution of 400×600, suitable for screensavers and slide shows.

The software provided with Picture CD allows the user to manipulate images with various automatic or semiautomatic operations, but unlike PhotoCD, the standard JPEG (JPG) file format used for storage allows any popular image-editing program to work with the images without conversion. Although the image quality of Picture CD isn't as high as with Photo CD, the much lower price of the service should make it far more popular with amateur photographers.

Writable CD-ROM Drives

It is now possible to create your own CD-ROMs—and audio CDs as well—using one of the new breeds of recordable CD-ROM devices. By purchasing writable CD-ROM disks and recording (or burning) your own CDs, you can store large amounts of data at a cost that is lower than any other removable, random-access medium.

You might find that cartridge drives such as Iomega's Zip and Jaz are priced comparably to writable CD-ROM drives, but recordable CD-ROM disks typically cost from $1–$10 each, whereas a 1GB Jaz cartridge costs about $100. Also, if you want to transport the data, the other system must have the same type of drive, as there is no industry standard for cartridge data formats.

Magnetic tape media can provide a lower cost per megabyte, but tapes are linear-access devices. Accessing files from tape is a time-consuming process and does not provide anywhere near the convenience of a CD-ROM.

Compared with either tape or other removable media, using a CD-ROM burner is a very cost-effective and easy method for transporting large files or making archival copies. Another benefit of the CD for archiving data is that CDs have a much longer shelf life than tapes or other removable media.

Most writable CD-ROM drives are WORM (write-once, read many) devices, meaning that after you fill a CD with data, it is permanently stored. The de facto standard for this technology is the CD-R (CD-Recordable) drive. The write-once limitation makes this type of device less than ideal for system backups or other purposes in which it would be preferable to reuse the same media over and over. However, because of its low media costs, you might find that making permanent backups to CD-ROMs is as economically feasible as tape or other media.

In any case, there are now also CD-ROM burners on the market that are rewritable. CD-RW (CD-Rewritable) drives can reuse the same discs, making them suitable for almost any type of data storage task. All CD-RW drives can also be used to create CD-Rs. The following sections examine these two standards and how you can use them for your own data storage needs.

CD-R

CD-R drives are indeed WORM devices; however, they use a special recordable CD-ROM disc that, once recorded, can be played back or read in any standard CD-ROM drive. CD-R drives are useful for archival storage or for creating master CDs, which can be duplicated for distribution within a company.

Note

Because of the technical changes in the way the CD is made, there can sometimes be problems reading CDs made by CD-R devices in a standard CD-ROM player. Most of these problems result in poor play performance as the CD-ROM drive tries to align itself to the CD. However, some very old CD-ROM drives can't handle CD-R media.

CD-Rs function using the same principle as standard CD-ROMs, by reading the light reflected by a laser striking the surface of the disc. Light is either returned from the disc or not, forming a binary code. However, the CD-R disc itself is different from a standard CD-ROM.

Instead of the recording beam burning pits into a metallic or glass strata, the CD-R media is coated with a photosensitive organic dye that has the same reflective properties as a *virgin* CD. In other words, a CD reader would see an unrecorded CD-R disc as one long land. When the recording laser begins to burn data into the CD-R media, it heats the gold layer and the dye layer beneath. The result of heating these areas causes the dye and gold areas to diffuse light in exactly the same way that a pit would on a glass master disc or a mass-produced CD. The reader is fooled into thinking a pit exists, but there is no actual pit, simply a spot of less-reflective disc caused by the chemical reaction of heating the dye and gold. This use of heat to create the pits in the disc is why the recording process is often referred to as *burning* a CD.

Most recordable CD-ROM drives can write discs using any of the formats discussed thus far—from ISO 9660 all the way through CD-ROM XA. In addition, these drives can read the formats as well, and therefore serve as general-purpose CD-ROM readers. Prices have been falling steadily and now can be $250 or less for a drive, and under $2 for the blank media.

CD-R Capacity

All CD-R drives can work with the standard 650MB CD-R media (equal to 74 minutes of recorded music), but recently some companies have developed 700MB capacity (equal to 80 minutes of recorded music) CD-R blanks. Although the extra 50MB of storage can be useful, current media cost (over $4 each) makes them much more expensive per MB than the 650MB standard. Two other considerations are that a capacity beyond 650MB/74 minutes is beyond the Orange Book specification, according to Adaptec, so compatibility of these extra-large CD-Rs in many drives is questionable. Also, many CD-R/CD-RW drives can't handle the extra capacity, and an update to popular CD-R mastering programs such as Adaptec's Easy CD Creator Pro might be necessary for some users. If you're concerned about industry-standard compatibility, I'd recommend sticking with the standard 650MB/74 minute media.

CD-R Media Color

There's controversy among CD-R users about which colors of CD-R media provide the best performance. Table 13.8 shows the most common color combinations, along with which brands use them and some technical information.

Some brands are listed with more than one color combination, due to production changes or different product lines. You should check color combinations whenever you purchase a new batch of CD-R media if you've found that particular color combinations work better for you in your applications.

Table 13.8   CD-R Media Color and Its Effect on Recording

Media Color (first color is reflective layer; second is die layer)	Brands	Technical Notes
Gold-gold	Mitsui Kodak Maxell	Phthalocyanine dye Less tolerance for power variations Might be less likely to work in a wide variety of drives
	Ricoh	Invented by Mitsui Toatsu Chemicals
		Works best in drives that use a Long Write Strategy (longer laser pulse) to mark media
Gold-green	Imation (nee 3M) Memorex	Cyanine dye; more forgiving of disk-write and disk-read variations
	Kodak	Has a rated lifespan of 10 years
	BASF	Color combination developed by Taiyo Yuden
	TDK	Used in the development of the original CD-R standards
		De facto standard for CD-R industry and was the original color combination used during the development of CD-R technology
		Works best in drives that use a Short Write Strategy (shorter laser pulse) to mark media
Silver-blue	Verbatim DataLifePlus HiVal Maxell TDK	Process developed by Verbatim Azo dye Similar performance to green media plus rated to last up to 100 years
		A good choice for long-term archiving

Ultimately, although the different color combinations each have their advantages, the best way to choose a media type is to try a major brand of media in your CD-R/CD-RW drive with both full-disk and small-disk recording jobs and then try the completed CD-R in as wide a range of CD-ROM drive brands and speeds as you can.

The perfect media for you will be the ones that offer you

- High reliability in writing
- No dye or reflective surface dropouts
- Durability through normal handling (scratch-resistant coating on media surface)
- Compatibility across the widest range of CD-ROM drives
- Lowest unit cost

Choosing the Best Media

After you determine which media works the best for you and your target drives, you might still be faced with a wide variety of choices, including conventional surface, printable surface, unbranded, jewel-case, bulk on spindle. The following list discusses these options:

- *Conventional surface.* Choose this type of media if you want to use a marker to label the CD rather than adding a paper label. This type of CD often has elaborate labeling, including areas to indicate CD title, date created, and other information as well as prominent brand identification. Because of the surface marking, it's not suitable for relabeling unless you use very opaque labels. It's a good choice for internal backups and data storage, though, where labeling is less important.

- *Printable surface.* Choose this type of media if you have a CD printer (a special type of inkjet printer that can print directly onto the face of the CD). Because the brand markings are usually low-contrast or even nonexistent (to allow overprinting), this type also works well with labeling kits such as NEATO and others.

- *Unbranded.* Usually sold in bulk on spindle, these are good choices for economy or use with labeling kits. They are not usually suitable for CD printers.

- *Jewel case.* Any of the preceding versions can be sold with jewel cases (the same type of case used for CD-ROM software and music CDs). This is a good choice if you plan to distribute the media in a jewel case, but it raises your costs if you plan to distribute or store the media in paper, Tyvek, or plastic sleeves. Hint: use extra jewel cases to replace your broken jewel cases on your CD software or music collection!

- *Bulk on spindle.* This media generally comes with no sleeves and no cases. It is usually the lowest-priced packaging within any brand of media. This is an excellent choice for mass duplication, or for those who don't use jewel cases for distribution.

CD-R Media Recording Speed Rating (X-Rating)

With CD-R mastering speeds ranging from 1x (now-discontinued first generation units) up through fast 4x and state-of-the-art 8x rates, it's important to check the speed rating of your CD-R media before you try the latest 4x and 8x units.

Most branded media on the market today is rated to work successfully at up to 4x recording speeds. Some brands indicate this specifically on their packaging, whereas you must check the Web sites for others to get this information.

If speed ratings are unavailable, assume the media is capable of reliable writing at no more than a 4x speed. Media that is 8x-rated is becoming more popular, but is often not available at retail stores. Check on the Web or with the drive vendor. At this point, 8x-rated media is somewhat more expensive than 4x or less-rated media. If you have problems recording at 4x on media of an unknown X-rating, try recording at 2x.

Writing a CD with a CD-R/CD-RW Drive

CD-R/CD-RW drives come in slower speeds than their CD-ROM reader counterparts. The fastest CD-R drives write at 8x normal speed—given the system performance to do so. However, some can read at up to 24x normal speed. This is obviously no competition for the 24x and 32x CD-ROM reader drives on the market today, but many CD-R users already have a read-only CD-ROM drive.

Whenever a CD-R drive writes data, it creates one long spiral track on the CD, alternating on and off to etch the pattern into the raw media. Because the CD-R can't realign itself like a hard drive, when it starts writing it must continue until it's finished with the track, or the CD is ruined. This means that the CD-R recording software, in combination with your system hardware, must be able to deliver a consistent stream of data to the CD-R drive while it's writing. To aid in this effort, the software uses a buffer that it creates on your hard disk to temporarily store the data as it is being sent to the CD-R drive.

You'll recall that the normal data transfer rate for a single-speed CD-ROM is 150KB/sec. When writing at a 4x speed, the computer must feed data to the CD-R drive at 600KB/sec. If any part of the computer isn't able to maintain that data rate, you'll receive a buffer under-run message, and the recording attempt will fail.

The buffer under-run message indicates that the CD-R drive had to abort recording because it ran out of data in its buffer to write to the CD. This is the biggest problem that people have with CD-R devices. Providing a fast source to write from—usually a fast SCSI drive—on a system with plenty of RAM will generally help avoid buffer under-runs.

How to Reliably Make CD-Rs

With typical burn times for full CD-Rs ranging from 10 minutes (8x) to as much as 80 minutes (1x), it is frustrating to have a buffer under-run turn your CD-R media to a coffee coaster—an unreadable blank.

Five major factors influence your ability to create a working CD-R: interface type, drive buffer size, the location and condition of the data you want to record to CD-R, the recording speed, and whether the computer is performing other tasks while trying to create the CD-R.

In general, SCSI-interface CD-R/CD-RW drives can burn CD-Rs at faster rates and more reliably than IDE/ATAPI drives. This is because the SCSI interface can work at higher sustained transfer rates, requires less CPU attention (lower CPU utilization rate), and can multitask multiple devices on the same SCSI interface card (daisy-chained devices). However, there are far more IDE/ATAPI CD-R/CD-RW drives than SCSI-interface drives on the market today, especially in the under-$300 market. This is because IDE/ATAPI drives can use the standard IDE interfaces found on virtually all Pentium-class and higher motherboards. The drives are also lower in cost, due to their simpler design. Thus, with a "free" interface and low-cost drive design, a user willing to use a 2x writer can start CD-R mastering for less than $200 in some cases.

To improve the odds of getting reliable CD-R creation with IDE/ATAPI drives, look for drives with

- *A large data buffer (1MB or larger).* The data buffer in the drive will hold information read from the original data source, so that even if there's a pause in data reading, there's no possibility of a buffer under-run until the on-drive buffer runs empty. A larger buffer minimizes the chance of "running out of data."

- *Drives that support DMA or UDMA operating modes.* As you've already seen, DMA/UDMA modes transfer data faster and with less CPU intervention than earlier versions of IDE. To use this feature, you'll also need a motherboard with a bus-mastering IDE interface with the appropriate drivers installed.

Tip

Also, if you have problems with reliable CD-R creation at the drive's maximum speed, try using a lower speed (2x instead of 4x, for example). Your mastering job will take twice as long, but better to create a working CD-R slowly than ruin a blank quickly.

An alternative approach is to use packet-writing software to create your CD-R. Many late-model CD-R/CD-RW drives support packet writing, which allows drag-and-drop copying of individual files to the CD-R rather than transferring all the files at once as with normal mastering software. This "a little at a time" approach means that less data must be handled in each write, and can make the difference between success and failure. If your drive supports this feature, it might come with Adaptec's DirectCD software (which performs packet writing), or you might need to buy it separately (about $70.00 direct from Adaptec). Check Adaptec's Web site to see whether your drive can work with DirectCD. Note that although packet-written CDs can be read with Windows 95/98/NT/2000, they cannot be read with Windows 3.1/MS-DOS because these operating systems don't support packet-written CDs.

If your CD-R/CD-RW drive is SCSI-based, make sure you have the correct type of SCSI interface card! Although many drive vendors take the uncertainty out of this issue by supplying an appropriate card, others don't. When faced with SCSI interface card prices ranging from as little as $50 to over $500, it's easy to choose the lowest-priced adapter to save money. If your SCSI card isn't made for the task of creating CD-Rs, you'll also wind up with buffer under-runs and a nice collection of $2.00 coffee coaster blanks instead of working CD-Rs.

If you must buy your own SCSI card for your recorder, follow these tips:

- *Forget about ISA cards.* Although ISA (Industry Standard Architecture) cards still work in today's Pentium III and AMD K6-3 computers, their long-term outlook is terminal. By the early 2000s, new computers built to the latest PC99 standards will no longer have any ISA slots. If you like to move expensive hardware to the new machines to get the longest lifespan from it, ISA will soon see a No Vacancy sign on new computers. Even for current machines, ISA cards with acceptable performance for CD-R mastering are far too expensive.

- *PCI is better, but not all PCI will work!* As discussed in Chapter 16, "Serial, Parallel, and Other I/O Interfaces," PCI's 32-bit data bus and 33MHz typical performance is far faster than ISA's 16-bit data bus and 8.33 MHz typical performance. Because PCI slots are now more common than ISA slots and are about to completely replace ISA slots your SCSI-based drive should be attached to a PCI card.

■ *Any SCSI interface card used for CD-R/CD-RW drives should offer a feature called bus-mastering.* As discussed earlier in this chapter, bus-mastering allows data transfers to bypass the CPU for faster system performance. Very low-cost PCI-based SCSI cards don't offer this feature. Note that you can find some bus-mastering PCI cards that are less expensive than ISA bus-mastering cards, although they're faster.

You need to use a bus-mastering PCI-based card to get highly reliable CD-R creation at a low cost with your SCSI-based CD-R/CD-RW drive.

Tip

A number of CD-R manufacturers offer bus mastering SCSI cards for PCI slots, including Adaptec, Amedia, Promise Tech, SIIG, Tekram, DTC, and Advansys.

CD-R/CD-RW Drive Buffer Size

When you purchase a CD-R/CD-RW drive, you should consider the size of the drive's internal RAM buffer. With otherwise identically configured systems, the drive with the larger RAM buffer should provide more reliable mastering.

Most CD-R/CD-RW drives offer buffer sizes of at least 1MB. I recommend purchasing drives that contain buffers of at least 2MB. Regardless of your interface type (IDE/ATAPI or SCSI), a buffer under-run (the drive's buffer runs out of data) is a fatal end to your CD-R mastering attempt.

Organizing Data for a CD-R

If you have the following conditions in place whenever you want to make a CD-R at highest speed, you'll seldom have any problems:

■ High-speed DMA bus-mastering SCSI interface card

■ SCSI-interface CD-R

■ Data residing on a defragmented SCSI-interface local hard disk

If you're groaning because your CD-R mastering environment isn't anything like this, you're not alone. Many users don't have any SCSI-based devices, and yet a few simple precautions can help your IDE-based CD-R mastering attempts to succeed.

To ready your system for mastering a CD, follow these recommendations:

■ Whenever possible, move all data you want to put onto a CD-R to a fast local hard drive. If you can't do this, avoid using the following sources for data: floppy drives, parallel-port Zip or other removable-storage drives, CD-ROM drives (especially 8x or slower), or Network drives (especially if you use ISA network cards on standard Ethernet or Token-Ring networks). These locations for data usually can't feed data quickly enough to maintain data flow to the CD-R drive.

■ Before you master the CD-R, use disk-repair tools on your C: drive, CD-R mastering drive, CD-R data drive, and swap drives, followed by full defragmentation of each drive. This assures that disk errors or file fragmentation, both of which slow down disk access, won't be a factor in program or data search and retrieval.

- Avoid trying to master from active files or zero-byte files (often used for temporary storage). If you must master these files to make an archival copy of your current system configuration, use a program such as Norton Ghost or PowerQuest Drive Image, which create a single compressed file from your drive's contents. Then, master the CD-R using the resulting compressed file.

- Turn off power management for your hard disk and other peripherals. You can normally do this through the Power icon in Windows 9x. A few Seagate IDE drives require that you install a TSR program into AUTOEXEC.BAT to accomplish this because their built-in firmware does the power management.

- Make sure your temporary drive has at least twice the empty space of your finished CD-R. Your CD-R's estimated space requirements are shown during the mastering process with programs such as Adaptec Easy CD-Creator. Thus, if you're creating a CD-R with 500MB of data, your temporary drive must have at least 1GB of empty space.

- With Windows 9x, you'll improve disk caching by adjusting the typical role of the computer from workstation to server in the Performance tab of the System Properties dialog box. Note that this change works correctly with Windows 95B & 95C (OSR 2.x) and Windows 98, but the registry keys are incorrect in Windows 95 original retail and OSR1 (95a) versions. Check Microsoft's Web site for the correct registry key settings for Windows 95/95a, back up and edit the Registry, and restart the computer before making this change with those versions.

- If your original data is coming from a variety of sources, consider using the Create Disk Image option in Adaptec Easy CD-Creator or your software's most similar feature. This feature creates an image file on your hard drive that contains all the files you want to put onto a CD-R. Then, use Create CD from Disk Image to actually master the CD-R from that information.

- If you're uncertain of success, why waste a CD-R blank? Most mastering programs offer a test-then-create option that does a simulated burn of the CD-R before the actual creation. After the simulation, you're warned of any problems before the actual process begins. This option takes twice as long as the normal mastering process, so you might want to use it only when you're especially concerned about problems.

- Small files are harder to use in mastering a CD-R than large ones because of the excessive drive tracking necessary to find them and load them. You might want to use a packet-writing program such as Adaptec's DirectCD instead if your drive supports it.

- Keep your CD-R and other drives clean and free from dust. Use a cleaning CD if necessary. Dirty drives cause data-read errors or data-write errors if your CD-R drive is the dirty one.

Even with all these considerations, you might still have problems recording at your drive's top speed. In that case, it might be necessary to slow down the recording speed.

Setting the CD-R Recording Speed

The steady climb in CD-R mastering speeds from the old 1x to current 4x and 8x speeds has helped fuel the rush to CD-R mastering. But many users whose first CD-R drive was a slow-but-reliable 1x or 2x unit might have problems when switching to the newer 4x or faster recording rates. As the speed of the CD-R recording process increases, the likelihood of problems also increases. You've already seen that using the fastest interface and largest buffer size available can help you create CD-Rs more reliably. Unfortunately, in some cases you might also want to reduce the recording rate of your drive.

If you're having buffer under-run problems despite taking all the precautions listed in the previous section, try dropping down a speed. CD-R mastering speeds run 1x, 2x, 4x, 8x. Go to the next lower speed and see how you do.

Using a lower speed than the drive is rated for can be frustrating, but it's preferable to take twice the time and actually get a CD-R than to ruin one in half the time.

Avoid Multitasking While Mastering a CD-R

Even with a fast hard drive, a fast host adapter, and a fast CD-R drive, you can still have buffer under-runs if you try to run more than one program while making your CD-R. If you run another program during the mastering process, the computer is forced to perform time-slicing, which causes it to start a process, switch away from it to start the next process, switch back to the first process, and so forth. This switching process could cause the CD-R drive to run out of data because it isn't receiving data in a steady stream. Forget about surfing the net, playing Solitaire, or creating a label for your new CD-R during the mastering process if you want reliable mastering.

CD-R Software

Another difficulty with CD-R devices is that they require special software to write them. Although most cartridge drives and other removable media mount as standard devices in the system and can be accessed exactly like a hard drive, the CD-R drive uses special CD-ROM burning software to write to the disk. This software handles the differences between how data is stored on a CD and how it is stored on a hard drive. As you learned earlier, there are several CD-ROM standards for storing information. The CD-ROM–burning software arranges the data into one of these formats so the CD can be read later by a CD-ROM reader.

At one time, CD recording technology required that you have what amounted to a replica of the CD on a local hard drive. In fact, some software packages even required a separate, dedicated disk partition for this purpose. You would copy all the files to the appropriate place on the hard drive, creating the directory structure for the CD, and then the software would create an exact replica of every sector for the proposed CD-ROM—including every file, all the directory information, and the volume information—and copy it to the CD-R drive. The result was that you had to have about 1.5GB of storage to burn a single CD (650MB/CD $\times$ 2 = 1.3GB + overhead = 1.5GB). This is no longer a requirement because most software supports virtual images. You select the files and directories that you want to write to the CD from your hard drive and create a virtual directory structure for the CD-ROM in the software. This means that you can select files from different directories on different hard drives, or even files from network or other CD-ROM drives, and combine them any way you want on the CD-R. This works well provided the drives have adequate speed and your CD-R drive has a large buffer. If you have problems, follow the advice given earlier to overcome slow data sources.

The software assembles the directory information, burns it onto the CD, opens each file on the CD, and copies the data directly from the original source. This generally works well, but you must be aware of the access times for the media you select as data sources. If, for example, you select directories from a slow hard drive or from a busy network, the software might not be able to read the data fast enough to maintain a consistent stream to the recorder. This causes the write to fail, resulting in a wasted disc.

CD-R drives that support several writing speeds typically come equipped with software that can simulate the recording process for testing purposes. The software reads the source data from the various media you've selected and determines the maximum possible speed for the recording process. Even this is not foolproof, however. Conditions might change between the time of the test and the actual disc write process, resulting in a failed recording attempt. For this reason, it is best to burn CDs from source data on a local hard drive rather than network drives. SCSI is preferable to IDE for both the CD-R burner and the source drive because SCSI is better suited to devices sharing the same interface.

Don't Forget the Software!

If you have persistent problems with making CD-Rs, your mastering software might be to blame. Check the vendor's Web site for tips and software updates. Make sure that your mastering software is compatible with your drive and your drive's firmware revision. Some drives offer software-upgradable firmware similar to the motherboard's flash BIOS.

Each of the major CD-R/CD-RW drive vendors provides extensive technical notes to help you achieve reliable recordings. You can also find helpful information on SCSI adapter vendors' Web sites and the Web sites of the CD-R media vendors.

Creating Music CDs

Newer CD-R, CD-RW, and CD-ROM drives are making it possible for you to create a customized archive of your favorite prerecorded music. Adaptec's Easy CD-Creator Deluxe Edition, for example, features the SpinDoctor utility to build music CDs, and even removes pops, hiss, and other problems from old analog cassette tapes and vinyl LPs.

Digital audio extraction allows the digital tracks on commercial CDs to be transformed into WAV files by compatible mastering programs. Those WAV files, exactly like the ones created from older music sources via your sound card, can then create a CD-R, which can be played back in any popular CD stereo system.

A contributor to this chapter used this technique to combine several audio sources into a single rehearsal CD for a Christmas cantata at his church. Note that the church had purchased the music books and the original rehearsal cassette and CD recordings.

This exciting technology is not intended to give you a way to create a free music library. Instead, use it to give the music recordings you've paid for an extra dimension of usefulness.

Don't confuse this with the new breed of standalone digital CD copying machines, which don't require a computer and use a different, and more expensive, type of media.

Creating Digital Photo Albums

Photo-realistic printers from Epson, Canon, HP, and other vendors need a source for images. Scanners provide a start, but where will you store your photos? CD-Rs are the answer. Software such as the PhotoRelay utility bundled with Adaptec's Easy CD-Creator, Kai's Power Show, or customized solutions designed with Adobe Acrobat or other products provide a great place to store and show off your photos.

Creating a Rescue CD

A number of programs on the market today allow you to make a compressed image file of the contents of any drive. These programs, such as the Ghost program sold by Symantec's Peter Norton group or PowerQuest's Drive Image, allow you to lock in the condition of any drive as of a particular time.

Note

See the CD accompanying this book for Que's edition of DriveImage.

This allows you to create an image file of your system when it's working and use the image-restore feature to reset your system when it fails.

Note

Don't confuse this with a popular Norton Utilities option called Norton Image. This program makes a backup copy of your drives' partition table, master boot record, FATs, and root directory to the end of each drive's data area. This very small file can recover from virus attacks or other problems with the first few sectors of a drive.

The perfect place to store a compressed image file is on a CD-R. At a minimum, your rescue disk should contain the compressed image file (a 650MB CD-R could contain the equivalent of a 1.5GB drive's normal contents if Drive Image's maximum compression option is used). It's also desirable to place a copy of the image-restore program on the CD-R. Mastering this type of rescue CD-R is done exactly the same as a conventional CD-R mastering process. To use the rescue CD-R, you must boot your system with drivers that allow the CD-ROM drive to work, run the restore program to read the data from the CD-R, and overwrite the drive's existing contents.

If you're looking for a single-CD solution to rescuing your system, one that won't require you to lug around a bootable floppy disk, I'll cover that later in this chapter after discussing the kinds of software a CD-ROM drive needs to operate.

▶▶ See "Making a Bootable CD-ROM for Emergencies," p. 763.

Multiple Session CD-R Drives

Although it is true that a CD-R disc can only be filled with data once, most of the CD-R drives and software packages support multiple sessions on a single disk. This means you can partially fill a disk and then add other sessions later. As with any multisession disk, you must have an XA-compliant or XA-ready CD-ROM drive to read all the sessions on a CD-R disc. Otherwise, your access is limited to the data in the first session.

About the only CD-ROM drives that can't read a multisession CD-R are first-generation single-speed and a few of the 2x drives. These drives are so old that they're extremely scarce and overdue for replacement (as are the computers they're found in). In practice, then, you can treat multisession CD-Rs as being as compatible as any other CD-R you create.

CD-RW

CD-RW (CD-Rewritable) drives, as defined in Part III of the Orange Book standard, are rapidly becoming a popular alternative to CD-Rs. CD-RWs use a different type of disc that the drive can rewrite at least one thousand times. Although they're slightly more expensive than CD-R media, CD-RWs are still far cheaper than optical cartridges and other removable formats. This makes CD-RW a viable technology for system backups, file archiving, and virtually any other data storage task.

Note

CD-RW drives are sometimes referred to as erasable CDs, or CD-E.

The drawback of the CD-RW is that the lower reflectivity of the disc itself limits its readability. Many standard CD-ROM and CD-R drives cannot read CD-RWs. However, a multiread capability is now found in virtually all CD-ROM drives of 24x speed or above, enabling them to read CD-RWs. Look for the "Multi-read" label on the drive to determine which of your drives have this capability. What's more, CD-RW drives are also capable of writing to CD-R discs and of reading standard CD-ROM discs. This means that by spending a little bit more for a CD-RW drive, you can get the best of both worlds: fully compatible WORM capability as well as rewritable storage.

The CD-RW Medium

The photosensitive dye within a CD-R disk changes from a reflective state to a nonreflective state when it is exposed to the laser recording beam of a CD-R drive. The change of state is permanent, which is why CD-R is a WORM medium. CD-RW disks also contain a substance that changes its reflective state when exposed to a laser, but unlike a CD-R, its change is not permanent.

The active layer of a CD-RW disk is an Ag-In-Sb-Te (silver-indium-antimony-tellurium) alloy that, in its original state, has a polycrystalline structure that makes it reflective. The active material is deposited on top of a polycarbonate substrate that is grooved in a spiral pattern to ensure precise servo guidance, resulting in accurate alignment of the lands and pits and absolute time information.

When the CD-RW drive writes to the disk, the laser uses its highest power setting, known as Pwrite, to heat the active material to a temperature between 500 and 700 degrees Celsius, causing it to liquefy. In its liquid state, the molecules of the active material flow freely, losing their polycrystalline structure and taking on an amorphous state. When the material solidifies in this amorphous state, it loses its reflectivity. By selectively firing the laser, the drive leaves parts of the disc in the polycrystalline state, forming the lands, and parts in the amorphous state, forming the pits.

To reverse the phase of a specific area on a disc, the laser operates at a lower power setting (Perase) and heats the active material to approximately 200° Celsius, well below its liquefaction temperature, but above the temperature at which it reverts back from its amorphous to its poly-crystalline state and becomes reflective again.

Note that despite the name of the Perase power setting, there is no explicit erasure performed to a CD-RW disk when it is rewritten. The drive pulses the laser at the appropriate power levels to produce polycrystalline and amorphous areas (lands and pits) at the appropriate locations, regardless of the previous state of those locations. Thus, the drive is writing both lands and pits. It is impossible to "erase" a CD-RW disk without writing new data over the old.

The formatting process for a CD-RW disk, which deletes the old contents and make the disk ready for new data, was very tedious with early CD-RW drives. New developments allow a rapid format in about 30 seconds, which is comparable to the quick format time on an ordinary floppy disk.

Reading CD-RW Discs

The original CD standards specify that on a compact disc the lands should have a minimum reflectance value of 70 percent, meaning that the area of a disc that represents a land should reflect back no less than 70 percent of the light directed at it. The pits should have a maximum reflectance value of 28 percent. In the early 1980s when these standards were developed, the pho-todiodes used in CD players were relatively insensitive, and these reflectance requirements were deliberately made stringent to accommodate them.

On a CD-RW disk, the reflectance of a land is approximately 15–25 percent, obviously well below the original minimum requirement. All the reflectance levels of CD-RW disks are approximately one-third of those defined in the original standard. However, the difference in the reflectance of a CD-RW disc's lands and the pits meets the 60 percent required by the original CD-ROM stan-dard, and the photodiodes available today are more than capable of discerning between the CD-RW reflectance values. Thus, although some CD-ROM drives are not capable of reading CD-RW discs, it is not a difficult matter to modify the existing designs to make it possible for them to do so.

Philips, the company that is largely responsible for the development of CD-RW technology, in conjunction with Hewlett-Packard, has developed a multiread specification that has been approved by the Optical Storage Technology Association. This specification defines the levels of amplification needed for standard CD-ROM drives to read CD-RW discs.

Because only recent CD-ROM drives (many 24x drives and virtually all 32x and above) are multi-read (capable of reading CD-RW media), many early DVD drives can't read CD-RW, and because CD-RW media is about 3x the cost of CR-R blanks, I recommend using CD-R media in CD-RW drives when you want to send data to other users. Use the CD-RW media for drag-and-drop file copying or for temporary backup storage. Remember, every CD-RW drive is also a CD-R drive. Many vendors of CD-RW/CD-R media sell CD-R/CD-RW bundle packages which feature both types of media, recognizing the dual nature of the drives and the different purposes of the two types of media—often at a savings that makes the CD-R media essentially free.

If you are wondering whether a CD-ROM drive can read a CD-RW disc, look for the "Multi-read" label on the drive—and, of course, test an actual CD-RW of your own creation if possible.

DVD (Digital Versatile Disc)

The future of CD-ROM is called DVD (Digital Versatile Disc). This is a new standard that dramatically increases the storage capacity of, and therefore the useful applications for, CD-ROM–size disks. A CD-ROM can hold a maximum of about 650MB of data, which might sound like a lot but is simply not enough for many up-and-coming applications, especially where the use of video is concerned.

One of the primary applications for DVDs is as a replacement for videotapes. DVDs can be rented or purchased like prerecorded VCR tapes, but offer much higher resolution and quality and greater content. DVD has applications not only in computers, but in the consumer entertainment market as well.

DVD History

DVD had a somewhat confusing beginning. During 1995, two competing standards for high-capacity CD-ROM drives emerged to compete with each other for future market share. A standard called Multimedia CD was introduced and backed by Sony and Philips Electronics, whereas a competing standard called the Super Density (SD) disk was introduced and backed by Toshiba, Time Warner, and several other companies. If both of these standards had hit the market as is, consumers as well as entertainment and software producers would have been in a quandary over which one to choose.

Fearing a repeat of the Beta/VHS situation, several organizations, including the Hollywood Video Disc Advisory Group and the Computer Industry Technical Working Group, banded together. They insisted on a single format and refused to endorse either competing proposal. With this incentive, both groups worked out an agreement on a single, new, high-capacity CD-ROM in September of 1995. The new standard combined elements of both previously proposed standards and was called DVD, which originally stood for Digital Video Disk, but which has since been changed to Digital Versatile Disc. The single DVD standard has avoided a confusing replay of the VHS/Beta fiasco and has given the software, hardware, and movie industries a single, unified standard to support.

DVD Specifications

DVD offers an initial storage capacity of 4.7GB of digital information on a single-sided, single-layer disc the same diameter and thickness of a current CD-ROM. With MPEG-2 (Motion Picture Experts Group–standard 2) compression, that's enough to contain 135 minutes of video, enough for a full-length, full-screen, full-motion feature film—including three channels of CD-quality audio and four channels of subtitles. With only one audio track, a single disk could easily hold 160 minutes of video or more. This initial capacity is no coincidence; the creation of DVD was driven by the film industry, which has long sought a storage medium cheaper and more durable than videotape.

Note

It is important to know the difference between the DVD-Video and DVD-ROM standards. DVD-Video discs contain only video programs and are intended to be played in a DVD player, connected to a television and possibly an audio system. DVD-ROM is a data storage medium intended for use by PCs and other types of computers. The distinction is much like that between an audio CD and a CD-ROM. Computers might be able to play audio CDs as well as CD-ROMs, but dedicated audio CD players cannot use a CD-ROM's data tracks.

Current models of DVD are compatible with 8.5GB dual-layer discs as well as double-sided discs that will store 9.4GB in a single layer and 17GB in a dual-layer format.

DVD's initial storage capacity is made possible by several factors, including

- A smaller pit length (~2.08x, from 0.972 to 0.4 microns)
- A reduced track pitch (~2.16x, from 1.6 to 0.74 microns)
- A larger data area on the disc (~1.02x, from 86 to 87.6 square centimeters)
- More efficient channel bit modulation (~1.06x)
- More efficient error correction code (~1.32x)
- Less sector overhead (~1.06x, from 2048/2352 to 2048/2060 bytes)

The DVD drive's data markings are much smaller and closer together than those on CD, allowing the same physical-sized platter to hold much more information (see Figure 13.8).

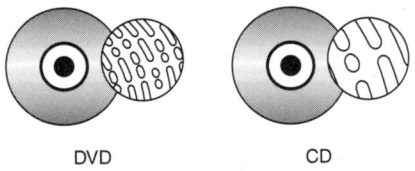

DVD   CD

Figure 13.8 DVD data markings versus those of a standard CD-R or CD-RW.

The drive uses a shorter wavelength laser to read these smaller pits and lands. DVD can double its initial capacity by using both sides of the disc, and double it again by writing two separate layers of data on each side. The second data layer is written to a separate substrate below the first layer, which is semireflective to allow the laser to penetrate to the substrate beneath it. By focusing the laser on one of the two substrates, the drive can read roughly twice the amount of data from the same surface area.

With advancements coming in blue-light lasers, this capacity might be increased several-fold in the future. DVD drives are also very fast compared to current CD-ROM technology. The standard transfer rate is 1.3MB/sec, which is approximately equivalent to that of a 9x CD-ROM drive. Access times are typically in the 150–200ms range, with burst transfer rates of 12MB/sec or higher. DVD drives spin at a base speed that is about three times as fast as a single speed CD-ROM. 5x drives are now available. DVD drives use either the IDE/ATA or SCSI interface, exactly like CD-ROMs, and include audio connectors for playing audio CDs through headphones or speakers.

DVD drives are fully backward-compatible, and as such will be able to play today's CD-ROMs as well as audio CDs. When playing existing CDs, the performance of current models is equivalent to a 20x or faster CD-ROM drive. As such, users who currently own 4x CD-ROM drives might want to consider a DVD drive instead of upgrading to a faster CD-ROM drive. Several manufacturers have announced plans to phase out their CD-ROM drive products in favor of DVD. In a few years, DVDs might make CD-ROMs obsolete, in the same way that audio CDs displaced vinyl records in the 1980s.

The current DVD drives feature several improvements over the first-generation models of 1997. Those units were expensive, slow, and incompatible with either CD-R or CD-RW media. Many early units asked your overworked video card to try to double as a MPEG decoder to display DVD movies, with mediocre results in speed and image quality. As is often the case with "leading edge" devices, their deficiencies make them eminently avoidable.

Many PC vendors have integrated DVD-ROM drives into their new high-end computers, usually as an option. The typical package also includes an MPEG-2 decoder board for processing the compressed video on DVD disks. This offloads the intensive MPEG calculations from the system processor and makes it possible to display full-screen, full-motion video on a PC.

Some manufacturers of video display adapters have begun to include MPEG decoder hardware on their products. These adapters are called "DVD MPEG-2 accelerated," and call for some of the MPEG decoding tasks to be performed by software. Any software decoding involved in an MPEG solution places a greater burden on the main system processor, and can therefore yield less satisfactory results.

Adding a DVD Drive to Your System

A DVD drive installs in a manner similar to that of a CD-ROM or any other type of drive. See Chapter 14, "Physical Drive Installation and Configuration," to learn how to install a 5 1/4–inch DVD drive.

Following, are some basic principles to keep in mind when installing a DVD drive:

- Most DVD drives are IDE/ATAPI devices, meaning that you have the issue of master/slave setups on the dual-connector 40-pin IDE cable. If you're replacing an old CD-ROM drive, simply note its master-slave configuration when you remove it from your system, set the new DVD drive the same way, attach it to the data cable, connect the power, and you're finished.

- Many current DVD drives require that you connect them to a bus-mastering IDE interface. If your drive requires a bus-mastering interface, check out the tips earlier in this chapter.

- The other half of DVD, the MPEG decoder card, can be tougher. You must have an open PCI expansion slot, the card usually requires an IRQ (which might force you to disable an existing port to free up an IRQ), and you must connect the decoder card to your existing VGA card. Because of the high hardware demands that MPEG decoder cards place on many users' systems, new VGA video cards with high-quality MPEG movie playback are looking more and more interesting to users. Table 13.9 compares MPEG decoder cards to video cards with built-in MPEG players.

Table 13.9   MPEG Decoder Cards Versus Video Cards with MPEG Players

Consideration	MPEG Decoder	MPEG Player
PCI Slot usage	1 for decoder; 1 for VGA	1 slot only
Movie Image Quality	High	Varies
Playback Speed	High	Varies
MPEG Game Compatibility	Yes	No

DVD Standards

DVD is still a young technology, and the standards situation is more confused than usual. Just about the only certain element in the DVD picture is the DVD-ROM format itself. Nearly all other aspects of the technology are caught up in conflicts between rival standards.

DVD video currently exists as a standard supported by most of the movie industry. Movie titles and DVD players are widely available in North America and Japan. DVD's one-time rival, DIVX, which was supported by only a few major studios, was discontinued in the summer of 1999.

Why DIVX Died

DIVX required a different player—the DVD players available now cannot play DIVX discs—and, even more shocking, required that the player be connected to Digital Video Express's computerized billing system via a built-in modem to play a DIVX disc or go through an on-line payment system. Fortunately, every DIVX player can also play standard DVD and audio CDs.

DIVX had several shortcomings that contributed to its failure, including the rental system, which rendered the DIVX movie useless after 48 hours unless you paid to view it again or purchased it. Other shortcomings included modem and online ordering hassles, and the lack of outlets for DIVX movies (mostly Circuit City stores).

Low-cost rentals for DVD movies and the increasing popularity of DVD movies at public libraries give you plenty of places to find DVD movies to try, and they are sold by virtually every major consumer electronics store.

What to do with your DIVX player? Use it for DVD movies, and check with the Circuit City or DIVX Web sites for details about a $100 rebate, which will compensate you for the extra cost of the now-useless DIVX enhancements in your player.

DVD Standards

In a war that brings back unhappy memories of the VHS/Beta struggle of the 1980s, the computer and movie industries are locked in a struggle to see which enhancements to the basic DVD standard will actually exist. Table 13.10 compares the competing DVD standards.

Table 13.10   DVD Standards

Standard	Capacity	Compatible With	Notes
DVD-RAM	2.6GB per side	Not compatible with DVD-ROM drives unless they are very recent models; check with your vendor	Most popular and lowest-priced recordable DVD- type technology; several models now shipping; media about $25 per disk; requires Windows 95 OSR 2.x or Windows 98 with FAT-32 to exceed 2GB per side
DVD-R	3.95GB (original) 4.7GB (1999 version)	Almost all DVD players can read these	Original 3.95GB drives were $17,000; new 4.7GB drives sell for under $5500; media about $40 per disk; future versions of the 1999-model drive are expected to work with DVD-RW media
DVD-RW (originally called DVD-R/W)	4.7GB	Almost all DVD players will be able to read these	Media about $40 per disk; phase-change technology; first drives expected in late 1999
DVD+RW	2.8GB per side	A few current DVD-ROM drives from Sony and Philips can read these	Media is about $30 per disk; no cartridge is needed; HP, Philips and Sony introduced shipping models in mid-1999; list about $700

There are also conflicts between standards for writable versions of DVD drives. Right now, the most likely candidates for acceptance are DVD-R and DVD-RAM, both based on specifications published in August 1997. DVD-R is comparable to CD-R in that it is a WORM technology that uses an organic dye as its active medium. The first DVD-R drives were released by Pioneer in October 1997 with a price of $17,000; blank discs are now about $40.

DVD-RAM is a rewritable drive type that uses a phase-change technology such as that of CD-RW. However, DVD-RAM discs cannot be read by standard DVD-ROM drives because of differences in both reflectivity of the medium and the data format. (DVD-R, by comparison, is backward-compatible with DVD-ROM.) DVD-ROM drives that can read DVD-RAM discs began to come on the market in early 1999. Neither DVD-R nor DVD-RAM can write disks using dual layers, but there will be double-sided DVD-RAM discs available. Some manufacturers have matched the standard 4.7GB capacity for a single-sided, single-layer disc with their DVD-R and DVD-RAM products, but most implementations hold slightly less.

Apart from DVD-R and DVD-RAM, several other writable DVD standards are in various stages of development. DVD+RW, also called DVD Phase Change Rewritable, is a competing rewritable format championed by Philips, Sony, and Hewlett-Packard. It is more closely based on CD-RW and is incompatible with DVD-RAM, although DVD+RW drives can read DVD-ROMs and CDs. These drives began to ship in the summer of 1999.

Pioneer has its own rewritable format, originally called DVD-R/W and now referred to as DVD-RW, that also uses a phase-change technology and is somewhat more compatible than DVD-RAM. Drives based on this technology are expected in late 1999. Although newer DVD-type drives have become more compatible with the CD-R/CD-RW standards, there still exists a major problem in harmonizing the many different types of writable DVD formats. As with the old Beta versus VHS battle, even the introduction of a superior specification complicates the process of accepting a single specification as an industry standard.

CD-ROM Software on Your PC

After you've physically installed the drive, you're ready for the last step—installing the drivers and other CD-ROM/DVD-ROM software. As usual, this process can be simple with a PnP operating system such as Windows 9x or rather painful with DOS and Windows 3.1. The optical drive needs the following three software components for it to operate on a PC:

- A SCSI adapter driver (not needed for ATAPI IDE CD-ROM drives). Most popular SCSI adapter drivers are built into Windows 9x.
- A SCSI driver for the specific CD-ROM drive you've installed. An ASPI driver is built into Windows 9x, as is an ATAPI IDE CD-ROM driver.
- MSCDEX—Microsoft CD Extensions for DOS, which is built into Windows 9x as the CDFS VxD.

If you still use DOS, you can have the first two drivers—the SCSI adapter driver and CD-ROM driver—load into your system at startup by placing command lines in your CONFIG.SYS file. The MSCDEX, or DOS extension, is an executable file added into your system through your AUTOEXEC.BAT file. This is not required in Windows 9x; the operating system will autodetect the drive on startup and prompt you to install the correct drivers if it can't find them in its standard arsenal of device drivers.

Using Windows 9x along with a CD-ROM or DVD-ROM drive that conforms to the ATAPI (AT Attachment Packet Interface) IDE specification does not require you to do anything. All the driver support for these drives is built into Windows 9x, including the ATAPI driver and the CDFS VxD driver.

If you are running an SCSI CD-ROM drive under Windows 9x, you will still need the ASPI (Advanced SCSI Programming Interface) driver that goes with your drive. The ASPI driver for your drive will normally come from the drive manufacturer and is included with the drive in most cases. However, by arrangement with hardware manufacturers, Windows 9x usually includes the ASPI driver for most SCSI host adapters, and also automatically runs the CDFS VxD virtual device driver. In some rare cases, you might have to install an updated driver that you have obtained from the manufacturer.

When you install a PnP SCSI host adapter in a Windows 9x system, simply booting the computer should cause the operating system to detect, identify, and install drivers for the new device. When the driver for the host adapter is active, the system should detect the SCSI devices connected to the adapter and again load the appropriate drivers automatically.

The only problem you might encounter is if you are installing a new device, such as a DVD-ROM drive, on an older version of Windows. Windows 98 includes drivers for most of the DVD-ROM drives on the market, but Windows 95 was released before these devices existed. In this case, you will probably have to supply a device driver on floppy disk, in response to a request from the OS, during the installation process.

DOS SCSI Adapter Driver

For DOS users, of course, the installation process is not so easy. Each SCSI adapter model has a specific driver that enables communication between the PC and the SCSI interface. Normally, these drivers conform to the ASPI. The ASPI driver for the drive connects with the ASPI driver for the SCSI host adapter; this is how the adapter and the drive communicate. An ASPI driver should be provided both with your SCSI drive and with the host adapter. Documentation should also have been included that walks you through the installation of the software.

Most SCSI adapters come with an installation program that automates the process of installing the appropriate ASPI drivers, both for the adapter and for the devices connected to the SCSI bus. However, you can manually add the SCSI device driver to your CONFIG.SYS file. In the CONFIG.SYS file, add the name and path of the appropriate driver with the DEVICE= command (replace C:\DRIVERS with the actual location of your files, and MYSCSI.SYS with the actual name of your SCSI driver):

```
DEVICE=C:\DRIVERS\MYSCSI.SYS
```

C:\DRIVERS is the subdirectory into which you copied the SCSI ASPI device drivers. Some drivers have option switches or added commands that, for example, enable you to view the progress of the driver being loaded.

DOS CD-ROM Device Driver

This driver should be a part of your basic installation kit as well. If not, contact the drive's manufacturer for the proper device driver for your SCSI card.

The device driver should come with an installation program that prompts you for the memory I/O address for the SCSI adapter to which you've connected the CD-ROM drive. This device driver enables the adapter to communicate with the drive through the SCSI bus. Installation programs add a line similar to the following to your CONFIG.SYS file (replace MYCDROM.SYS with the actual name of your CD-ROM driver file, and C:\DRIVERS with the actual location of your files):

```
DEVICE=C:\DRIVERS\MYCDROM.SYS /D:mscd001
```

C:\DRIVERS is the subdirectory that contains the driver MYCDROM.SYS, the driver for your specific CD-ROM drive.

Note the /D:mscd001 option after the preceding statement. This designation, called the device signature, identifies this CD-ROM driver as controlling the first (001), and only, CD-ROM drive on the system. This portion of the device driver statement is for the Microsoft DOS Extensions driver, which designates CD-ROM drives in this fashion. In fact, you could use any designation here, as long as the MSCDEX command line uses the same one.

MSCDEX: Adding CDs to DOS

The Microsoft CD Extensions for DOS allow the DOS operating system (and by extension, Windows 3.1) to identify and use data from CD-ROMs attached to the system. The original DOS operating system had no provisions for this technology, so "hooks" or handling of this unique media are not part of the basic operating environment. Using these extensions is convenient for all involved, however. As CD-ROM technology changes, the MSCDEX can be changed, independently of DOS. For example, most PhotoCD, multiple-session CD-ROM drives require MSCDEX.EXE version 2.21 or higher, which has been modified from earlier versions to accommodate the newer CD-ROM format.

MSCDEX.EXE should be in your software kit with your drive. If not, you can obtain the latest copy directly from Microsoft. If you are a registered user of DOS or Windows 3.1, MSCDEX.EXE is free. Read the licensing agreement that appears on the disc or in your manual concerning the proper licensing of the MSCDEX files.

Your installation software should add a line similar to the following to your AUTOEXEC.BAT file:

```
C:\WINDOWS\COMMAND\MSCDEX.EXE /d:mscd001
```

C:\WINDOWS\COMMAND is the directory in which the MSCDEX.EXE file is located by default with Windows 95 and 98; with MS-DOS and Windows 3.1, it could be located in the \DOS directory, or in the directory containing the CD-ROM drivers. The /d:mscd001 portion of the command line supplies the MSCDEX extension with the device signature defined in the CD-ROM device driver of your CONFIG.SYS file.

Note*

The MSCDEX and CD-ROM device signatures must match. The defaults that most installations provide are used in this example. As long as the two names are the same, the drivers can find one another.

As long as you have these three drivers—the SCSI adapter driver, the CD-ROM driver, and the DOS CD extensions—loaded properly in your system, the CD-ROM drive will operate as transparently as any other drive in your system.

Table 13.11 lists the options that you can add to the MSCDEX.EXE command line.

Table 13.11   MSCDEX Command-Line Options

Switch	Function
/V	Called Verbose; when this option is added to the command line, it displays information about memory allocation, buffers, drive letter assignments, and device driver names on your screen at boot time.
/L:\<letter\>	Designates which DOS drive letter you want to assign to the drive. For example, /L:G assigns the drive letter G: to your CD-ROM drive. Two conditions apply: First, you must not have another drive assigned to that letter; and second, your **lastdrive=** statement in your CONFIG.SYS file must be equal to or greater than the drive letter you're assigning. **LASTDRIVE=G** would be fine. **LASTDRIVE=F** would cause an error if you attempt to assign the CD-ROM drive to the G: drive with the /L: switch.
/M:\<buffers\>	Enables you to buffer the data from the CD-ROM drive. This is useful if you want faster initial access to the drive's directory. Buffers of 10 to 15 are more than enough for most uses. Any more is overkill. Each buffer, however, is equal to 2KB of memory. So a /M:10 buffer argument, for example, would take 20KB of memory. Note that this does not significantly increase the overall performance of the drive, just DOS's initial access to the drive and the access of large data blocks when the drive is reading live-motion video files, for example. You can't turn a 400ms drive into a speed demon by adding a 200KB buffer. With no /M: argument added, MSCDEX will add six buffers as a default. That might be fine for most PCs and CD-ROM drives.
/E	Loads the aforementioned buffers into DOS high memory, freeing up space in the conventional 640KB. Early versions of MSCDEX—anything below version 2.1—do not load into extended memory. You must have DOS 5.0 for this option to load.
/K	Provides Kanji (Japanese) language support.
/S	Enables you to share your CD-ROM drive on a peer-to-peer network, such as Windows for Workgroups.

Note that Windows 9x uses a built-in CDFS (CD File System) driver that takes the place of MSCDEX. It is configured through the Windows 9x Registry and requires no AUTOEXEC.BAT command. USB-based CD-ROM/CD-R/CD-RW drives are also configured through the Windows 9x Registry and use no CONFIG.SYS or AUTOEXEC.BAT commands.

Loading CD-ROM Drivers

As mentioned earlier, your drive should come with installation software that copies the device driver files to your hard drive. It should also add the necessary command lines to your CONFIG.SYS and AUTOEXEC.BAT files.

When the process is complete, you can reboot your machine and look for signs that all went smoothly in the software installation.

Following is a series of sample portions of your startup screens to give you an idea of what messages you'll receive when a given driver is properly loaded into the system.

When you're sure that the software is loaded correctly, try the drive by inserting a disc into the drive. Then get a directory of the disc from the DOS prompt by issuing the following command:

```
DIR/w G:
```

This command gives you a directory of the CD you've inserted, if your CD has been assigned the drive letter G.

You can log in to the CD-ROM drive, as you would any DOS drive. The only DOS commands not possible on a CD-ROM drive are those that write to the drive. Remember that CDs are media that cannot be overwritten, erased, or formatted.

If you logged in to the CD-ROM and received a directory of a sample CD, you're all set.

Now you can power down the PC and replace the cover.

CD-ROM in Microsoft Windows 3.x

When your drive is added to your system, Windows already knows about it through the device drivers and DOS. The CD-ROM drive is accessible through File Manager by double-clicking its file cabinet icon. You see your CD-ROM drive among the drive icons across the top. Windows knows that the drive is a CD-ROM drive through the DOS extensions discussed earlier.

You can set your CD-ROM player to play audio CDs while you are working in Windows. You need to hook up your drive to a sound card and speakers or connect the CD's audio ports to a stereo first. Go to Windows' control panel and select Drivers. If you do not see [MCI] CD Audio among the files in the driver's list, choose Add. Insert the Windows installation disk that contains the CDAUDIO driver and add the driver. When the driver appears on the list, close the Drivers and control panel windows.

Double-click the Media Player icon. Under Devices, select CD. A listing of the track numbers on your audio CD appears along the bottom edge of the Media Player. The controls on Media Player are similar to those of an audio CD player, including track select, continuous play, and pause.

Many drive manufacturers supply DOS-based CD audio players with their systems. Check your installation manual and software discs for these utilities.

Optical Drives in Windows 9x and Windows NT 4.0

As stated earlier, Windows 9x and Windows NT include virtually all the drivers you will need to run your optical drive, making the software installation automatic. Windows automatically recognizes most IDE drives, and with the addition of the appropriate drive-specific ASPI driver, most SCSI drives as well.

There are several new capabilities with CDs and DVDs in Windows 9x/NT. The most dramatic is the Autoplay feature, which is available on Windows 95/98 and some versions of Windows NT 4.0.

Autoplay is a feature integrated into Windows 9x that enables you to simply insert a disc into the drive, and Windows will automatically run it without any user intervention. It will also detect whether that particular disc has already been installed on your system, and if not, it will automatically start the install program. If the disc has already been installed, it will start the application program on the disc.

The Autoplay feature is simple. When you insert a disc, Windows 9x automatically spins it and looks for a file called AUTORUN.INF. If this file exists, Windows 9x opens it and follows the instructions contained within. As you can see, this Autoplay feature will only work on discs that have this file. Most software companies are now shipping CD-ROM and DVD-ROM titles that incorporate the Autoplay feature.

Tip

You can disable the Autoplay feature for all CD-ROMs by opening the Windows 9x System control panel to the Device Manager page, highlighting your CD-ROM drive, and clicking the Properties button. The Properties dialog box for the drive has a Settings page that contains an Auto Insert Notification checkbox. Clearing this box prevents the operating system from processing the AUTORUN.INF file.

If you want to use Autoplay for some CDs, but not others, hold down the Shift key when inserting a CD you don't want to Autoplay.

Windows 9x/NT includes a new version of the Media Player found in Windows 3.x called the CD Player. This application allows you to play audio CDs in your drive while you work at the computer. The CD Player features graphical controls that look like a standard audio CD-ROM drive and even has advanced features found in audio drives, such as random play, programmable playback order, and the capability to save play list programs.

MS-DOS Drivers and Windows 9x

Many users have discovered that their CD-ROM drives didn't come with MS-DOS drivers at a very unfortunate time: when their Windows 9x system wouldn't start up. All too often, the "cure" for a "dead" Windows 9x system is a complete reinstallation from the Windows 9x CD, to replace defective files and settings with new copies. Of course, if Windows isn't working, its 32-bit CD-ROM device drivers aren't working either. And, if you don't have your CONFIG.SYS and AUTOEXEC.BAT files and the files listed earlier either, you can't reload Windows! You should have a bootable disk ready that has the appropriate drivers included to allow you to rebuild your Windows 9x installation in case of emergencies.

If you have Windows 98, the Emergency Startup disk that you create during installation or later already has the appropriate drivers, AUTOEXEC.BAT, and CONFIG.SYS included to run most popular SCSI and ATAPI/IDE-based CD-ROMs. However, a Windows 95 bootable disk doesn't include the AUTOEXEC.BAT, CONFIG.SYS, or drivers; you'll have to add these yourself (see the next section).

Note

If you can't find any references to the MS-DOS drivers needed for your CD-ROM drive on your Windows 9x computer, check for an installation disk that might have been shipped with the drive. To install the CD-ROM device driver files you need, use that disk to perform an MS-DOS/Windows 3.1 installation, which will add the appropriate lines to your CONFIG.SYS and AUTOEXEC.BAT files and copy the drivers to your system.

Creating a Bootable Disk with CD-ROM Support

If you use Windows 95 (any version), take a moment and create a bootable disk. I'll assume that your CD-ROM drive uses the following CD-ROM device driver: MYCDROM.SYS, located in C:\CDROM.

Note

Your actual CD-ROM device driver will have a different name, but it almost always has *CD* or *CD-ROM* in the name somewhere!

You need to copy the following files to your bootable disk in A: drive:

- MYCDROM.SYS

  Use the actual driver name for your CD-ROM drive and copy it from the file's actual location.

- MSCDEX.EXE

  Copy from C:\WINDOWS\COMMAND; same file for any CD-ROM drive.

Then, you need to create a CONFIG.SYS file that loads the CD-ROM device driver and an AUTOEXEC.BAT that loads the MSCDEX.EXE CD-ROM extensions for MS-DOS program. Use a text editor such as the Windows Notepad.

- Contents of CONFIG.SYS:

  DEVICE=MYCDROM.SYS /D:mscd001

- Contents of AUTOEXEC.BAT:

  MSCDEX.EXE /d:mscd001 (other optional switches if you like as noted earlier)

note

Note that the **/d:** switch refers to the same device name, which could be "Charlie" or "Kumquat" or anything that matches! A mismatch would cause the loading process to fail.

Add these four files added to your bootable floppy (listed again here for clarity):

- MYCDROM.SYS (or whatever your CD-ROM driver is called)
- MSCDEX.EXE
- AUTOEXEC.BAT (references MSCDEX.EXE)
- CONFIG.SYS (references MYCDROM.SYS)

Also, add the COMMAND.COM file and the hidden boot files to the disk to complete your bootable disk that can both start your computer and give you access to the CD-ROM drive.

With the disk still in the A: drive, check your BIOS setup, change the drive boot order to allow A: to be first if needed, and then save any changes if necessary. The computer reboots, and if you've done your work properly, you should boot up to an A: prompt and be able to access your CD-ROM drive at whatever drive letter was displayed when MSCDEX.EXE ran. This will be the next drive letter after your last hard drive letter. If your latest hard drive letter is C:, the CD-ROM is D:.

Put your Windows 95 CD-ROM in the CD-ROM drive and see whether you can display a directory listing. If you can, your bootable disk is a success! Put the disk away for a rainy day. Sooner or later, you'll need it.

Note

The same basic procedure works for MS-DOS and Windows 3.1 users.

Windows 98 users can normally use their Emergency Startup disk created during upgrade installation or through the Windows Programs tab in the Add/Remove Software dialog box. Unlike the Windows 95 version, the Windows 98 version has an elaborate multipart CONFIG.SYS file that tries the most common IDE and SCSI CD-ROM drivers to find one that works with your drive.

If you did not create an emergency disk when installing Windows 98 or have misplaced the disk, you can create one at any time by opening the Add/Remove Programs control panel, selecting the Startup Disk tab and choosing Create Disk.

If you use Windows 2000, your CD is bootable. Be sure to set the boot order in your BIOS so that your system scans your CD-ROM before your hard drive. See Chapter 5, "BIOS," for more information on accessing the BIOS Setup utility.

Making a Bootable CD-ROM for Emergencies

With the rise of low-cost CD-R/CD-RW drives and low-cost drive imaging products such as Norton's Ghost and PowerQuest's Drive Image, it's now possible for individual PC owners to create their own version of what is standard with more and more new computers: a bootable CD-ROM that can be used to start up a system and restore it to a previously saved state. This is a step beyond the rescue CD that I discussed earlier, in which the image file was placed on a standard data CD-R. To recover from a system crash with that type of CD, you'd need to boot your system with a boot disk similar to the one I described making in the previous section.

But wouldn't it be great if you didn't need a bootable disk? They're easy to erase, damage, or lose. What if the CD-R itself could be bootable? You might have even seen a computer manufacturer's recovery CD boot itself before restoring a drive. With most CD-R mastering software, you can make one too.

Bootable CDs contain a special version of the boot files found on any disk or hard drive used to start a system. Because these files take less than 100KB (in the case of Windows 95B), the remainder of the 650MB can be used to store a compressed image of the system hard drive (made with Ghost, Drive Image, or similar products), a copy of the original operating system installation files, or anything else that you'd find useful.

By creating a bootable CD, you can

■ Have a bootable "super-sized floppy" that can't be erased or altered (if you write-protect it during creation).

■ Create your own recovery CD by creating a compressed image file of your system when it's in top working condition and placing the image file on the CD along with the restore program. In the event of disaster, boot with the CD and restore the image file.

■ Switch between operating systems by creating compressed image files of each operating system after you install it and copying each to a separate CD along with the recovery utility. It isn't necessary to make the CD bootable with the same operating system because you'll need to restart the computer after restoring the image file.

Files Needed for a Bootable CD

The minimum requirements for a bootable CD include

■ A system in which the CD-ROM can be designated as a boot drive

Note

Check your BIOS under Advanced Setup or similar options. Recent and current BIOS code supplied by AMI, Award Software, and Phoenix Technologies typically support the CD-ROM as a bootable device.

■ A CD-ROM drive which can be treated as a bootable device (see the sidebar after this list)
■ A CD-R or CD-RW drive (you'll use CD-R media in either case)
■ Mastering software that allows creation of a bootable CD

Note

If your current CD-mastering software lacks this option, consider changing to Adaptec's Easy CD-Creator Pro. This low-cost software program supports most CD-R/CD-RW drives, offers high performance, many features for creating music as well as data CDs, and can make bootable CD-Rs.

■ A floppy disk containing your operating system boot files

Note

You can use the ERU disk created by Windows 95, the startup disk created by Windows 95/98, or any bootable disk made by your operating system. Note that you'll need to add the CD-ROM drivers to the disk, or verify that the Windows 98 startup disk will work with your CD-ROM drive (discussed later in this chapter).

ATAPI/IDE Drives are Bootable

Most ATAPI/IDE drives connected to a motherboard IDE interface can be used as a bootable device if the BIOS permits it. If your CD-ROM is connected to a sound card, this procedure won't work. If your CD-ROM is connected to an SCSI interface, you'll need an SCSI interface with a BIOS chip that permits booting as well as a bootable CD.

Here's a quick test to see whether your system can handle treating an IDE/ATAPI CD as a bootable device:

1. Place a data CD into your CD-ROM drive.

2. Start your computer.

3. Enter the BIOS Setup program.

4. Go to the appropriate screen (as mentioned earlier) and select CD-ROM as first boot device.

5. Select first hard disk (a.k.a. C:) as second boot device.

6. Exit BIOS setup screens and save changes.

7. On computer restart, see whether CD-ROM drive is being read for boot files. If so, eject data CD and allow computer to boot from hard disk. You should be able to boot from a bootable CD if your system tries to read the boot files from the CD-ROM drive.

The basic procedure for creating a bootable CD is as follows:

1. Create a bootable floppy for the operating system you want to install on the CD.

2. Get a blank CD-R and place it into your CD-R/CD-RW drive.

3. Start your mastering software.

4. Under disk layout, make sure that ISO 9660 is selected. This CD format doesn't permit long filenames, so make sure that any additional files you add to the CD have no more than eight characters plus up to three characters for the filename extension.

5. Make sure that the bootable option is enabled in the disk layout.

6. When prompted, insert the disk containing boot files into A: drive.

7. These files are copied to your CD layout. Note that the names of these files are not the same as the normal operating system boot files. The files are called BOOTCAT.BIN and BOOTIMG.BIN.

8. Add any additional files (image files, operating system install files, and so on) you want to the layout.

9. Start the CD Creation process.

10. When the process is completed, view the contents of the finished CD-R.

11. Close your mastering program, saving the layout if you desire.

12. Insert the bootable CD you just created into your CD-ROM drive.

13. Restart the computer and see whether your system boots from the CD.

If you follow these directions, you will discover two interesting things when you reboot:

- Your CD-ROM drive is called drive A:.

- You won't be able to see any of your files on drive A: (the CD-ROM) except for COMMAND.COM if you made the CD-R with Windows 9x boot files.

Even though the bootable CD was able to start the computer, a CD-ROM, regardless of BIOS version, is still primarily a software-controlled peripheral. Without the appropriate driver software (the CD-ROM device driver in CONFIG.SYS and the MSCDEX.EXE program in AUTOEXEC.BAT), the CD-ROM drive cannot function at all (normal mode) or cannot do any more than boot the computer as if it's a 650MB shiny round floppy disk (bootable CD mode).

The CONFIG.SYS and AUTOEXEC.BAT statements needed on a bootable CD are similar to the standard examples you saw earlier, but with special modifications that allow them to work on a CD and change the drive letter assignments back to normal.

1. Start with a bootable disk containing the AUTOEXEC.BAT, CONFIG.SYS, MYCDROM.SYS (substitute your driver for this one), and MSCDEX.EXE as I discussed earlier.

2. Edit the CONFIG.SYS to read:

   ```
   Lastdrive=Z
   Device=mycdrom.sys /d:mscd001
   ```

3. Edit the AUTOEXEC.BAT to read:

   ```
   MSCDEX /d:mscd001 /l:z
   ```

   The /l:z statement "locks" your CD-ROM drive letter at Z:.

4. Boot the computer with the modified boot disk, and make sure the CD-ROM drive is accessible as Z:.

5. Start the CD-R mastering software program.

6. Create your CD-layout. If you're trying to make a rescue CD from an image file made with Norton Ghost, Drive Image, and so on, place the image file into the CD layout, along with the image-file-restore program.

7. Open the File menu and select CD Properties. Check mark the box that says Bootable CD.

8. Under Data type, select ISO 9660 and select Any 8+3 Character MS-DOS Filename under Properties

   Note that with ISO 9660 that any Windows 9x-style long file names are shortened to their MS-DOS alias names ("Program Files" = "Progra~1", and so on).

9. Create the CD. Insert the bootable disk you created in steps 1–4 when prompted.

10. Note that even though the bootable floppy contains four additional files, the two files in the CD layout are still called BOOTCAT.BIN and BOOTIMG.BIN. These files contain all bootable information from the floppy.

11. Remove the bootable floppy, and restart the computer (change the boot sequence to CD-ROM first and hard disk second).

12. Success means the system boots from CD-ROM and CD-ROM drivers load to allow access to entire CD.

Caring for Optical Media

Some people believe that optical discs and drives are indestructible when compared to their magnetic counterparts. Actually, modern optical drives are far less reliable than modern hard disk drives. Reliability is the bane of any removable media, and CD-ROMs and DVD-ROMs are no exception.

By far the most common causes of problems with optical discs and drives are scratches, dirt, and other contamination. Small scratches or fingerprints on the bottom of the disc should not affect performance because the laser focuses on a point inside the actual disk, but dirt or deep scratches can interfere with reading a disc.

To remedy this type of problem, you can clean the bottom surface of the CD with a soft cloth, but be careful not to scratch the surface in the process. The best technique is to wipe the disc in a radial fashion, using strokes that start from the center of the disc and emanate toward the outer edge. This way, any scratches will be perpendicular to the tracks rather than parallel to them, minimizing the interference they might cause. You can use any type of solution on the cloth to clean the disc, so long as it will not damage plastic. Most window cleaners are excellent at removing fingerprints and other dirt from the disc and will not damage the plastic surface.

If there are deep scratches, they can often be buffed or polished out. A commercial plastic cleaner such as that sold in auto parts stores for cleaning plastic instrument cluster and tail-lamp lenses is very good for removing these types of scratches. This type of plastic polish or cleaner has a very mild abrasive that polishes scratches out of a plastic surface. Products labeled as cleaners are usually designed for more serious scratches, whereas those labeled as polishes are usually milder and work well as a final buff after using the cleaner. Polishes can be used alone if the surface is not scratched very deeply.

Read errors can also occur when dust accumulates on the read lens of your CD-ROM drive. You can try to clean out the drive and lens with a blast of "canned air," or by using a drive cleaner (which can be purchased at most music stores that sell audio CDs).

If your discs and your drive are clean, but you still can't read a particular disc, your trouble might be due to disc capacity. Early CD-ROM discs had a capacity of about 550MB (equivalent to about 60 minutes of CD audio). More recently, the capacity of a standard CD has been pushed to 650MB (74 minutes of CD audio). Many older CD-ROM drives are unreliable when they try to read the outermost tracks of newer discs where the last bits of data are stored. You're more likely to run into this problem with a CD that has lots of data—including some multimedia titles. If you have this problem, you might be able to solve it with a firmware or driver upgrade for your CD-ROM drive, but it's possible that the only solution will be to replace the drive.

Sometimes too little data on the disc can be problematic as well. Some older CD-ROM drives use an arbitrary point on the disc's surface to calibrate their read mechanism, and if there happens to be no data at that point on the disc, the drive will have problems calibrating successfully. Fortunately, this problem can usually be corrected by a firmware or driver upgrade for your drive.

Many older drives have had problems working under Windows 9x. If you are having problems, contact your drive manufacturer to see whether there is a firmware or software-driver upgrade that might take care of your problem. With new high-speed drives available for well under $100, it might not make sense to spend any time messing with an older drive that is having problems. It would be more cost-effective to upgrade to a new drive instead.

If you are having problems with only one particular disc and not the drive in general, you might find that your difficulties are in fact caused by a defective disc. See whether you can exchange the disc for another to determine whether that is indeed the cause.

Troubleshooting Optical Drives

Failure Reading a CD

If your CD fails to read a CD, try the following solutions:

- Check for scratches on CD data surface.
- Check drive for dust, dirt; use cleaning CD.
- Make sure drive shows up as working device in System Properties.
- Try a CD that you know to work.
- Restart computer (the magic cure-all).
- Remove drive from Device Manager in Windows 9x, allow system to redetect drive and reinstall drivers (if PnP-based system).

Failure to Read CD-R, CD-RW Disks in CD-ROM or DVD Drive

If your CD-ROM or DVD drive fails to read CD-R and CD-RW disks, try the following solutions:

- Check compatibility; some very old 1x CD-ROM drives can't read CD-R media. Replace drive with newer, faster, cheaper model.
- Many early-model DVD drives can't read CD-R, CD-RW media; check compatibility.
- CD-ROM drive must be Multi-Read compatible to read CD-RW due to lower reflectivity of media; replace drive.
- If some CD-Rs but not others can be read, check media color combination to see whether some color combinations work better than others; change brand of media.
- Packet-written CD-Rs (from Adaptec DirectCD and backup programs) can't be read on MS-DOS/Windows 3.1 CD-ROM drives due to limitations of operating system.

IDE/ATAPI CD-ROM Drive Runs Slowly

If your IDE/ATAPI CD-ROM drive performs poorly, check the following items:

- Check cache size in the Performance tab of the System Properties control panel. Select the quad-speed setting (largest cache size)
- Check to see whether the CD-ROM drive is set as the slave to your hard disk; move CD-ROM to the secondary controller if possible.

- Your PIO or UDMA mode might not be set correctly for your drive in the BIOS; check drive specs and use autodetect in BIOS for best results (see Chapter 5).

- Check to see that you are using bus-mastering drivers on compatible systems; install appropriate drivers for motherboard's chipset and operating system in use. See "DMA (Direct Memory Access)" earlier in this chapter.

- Check to see whether you are using the CD-ROM interface on your sound card instead of IDE connection on motherboard. Move drive connection to the IDE interface on motherboard and disable sound card IDE if possible to free up IRQ and I/O port address ranges.

- Open the System Properties control panel and select the Performance tab to see whether system is using MS-DOS Compatibility Mode for CD-ROM drive. If all IDE drives are running in this mode, see www.microsoft.com and query on "MS-DOS Compatibility Mode" for a troubleshooter. If only the CD-ROM drive is in this mode, see whether you're using CD-ROM drivers in CONFIG.SYS and AUTOEXEC.BAT. Remove the lines containing references to the CD-ROM drivers (don't actually delete the lines—REM them), reboot the system and verify that your CD-ROM drive still works and that it's running in 32-bit mode. Some older drives require at least the CONFIG.SYS driver to operate.

Poor Results When Writing to CD-R Media

If you are having problems successfully writing data to a CD-R disk, see "How to Reliably Make CD-Rs" earlier in this chapter.

Trouble Reading CD-RW Disks on CD-ROM

If you cannot read CD-RW disks in your CD-ROM, check the vendor specifications to see whether your drive is multi-read compliant. Some drives are not compliant.

If your drive is multi-read compliant, try the CD-RW disk on known-compliant CD-ROM drive (drive with multi-read feature).

Trouble Reading CD-R Disks on DVD Drive

If your DVD drive cannot read a CD-R disk, check drive compliance—original DVDs cannot read CD-R media. Newer, faster DVD drives support CD-R media.

Trouble Making Bootable CDs

If you are having problems creating a bootable CD, try these possible solutions:

- Check the contents of bootable floppy disk from which you copied the boot image. To access entire contents of a CD-R, a bootable disk must contain CD-ROM drivers, AUTOEXEC.BAT, and CONFIG.SYS.

- Use ISO 9660 format. Don't use Joliet format because it is for long-filename CDs and can't boot.

- Check your system's BIOS for boot compliance and boot order; CD-ROM should be listed first.

- Check drive for boot compliance.

- SCSI CD-ROMs need SCSI card with BIOS and bootable capability as well as special motherboard BIOS settings.

Physical Drive Installation and Configuration

SOME OF THE MAIN TOPICS IN THIS CHAPTER ARE

Hard Disk Installation Procedures

Hard Drive Physical Installation—Step by Step

Replacing an Existing Drive

Hard Disk Drive Troubleshooting and Repair

Installing an Optical Drive (CD-ROM, CD-R)

Floppy Drive Installation Procedures

Tape Drive Installation Issues

This chapter covers the actual installation of hard drives, optical drives (CD/DVD), floppy drives, and tape drives. This includes everything from the preparation of the components to setting jumpers to the actual cabling and physical installation. Also the initial system software configuration issues will be covered as well, right up until the start of the operating system installation. From that point on the steps you take would depend on which operating system you are installing.

For more information on drive interfaces, magnetic storage, drive operation, and operating system issues, see the following chapters:

- *Chapter 7*. "The IDE Interface"
- *Chapter 8*. "The SCSI Interface"
- *Chapter 9*. "Magnetic Storage Principles"
- *Chapter 10*. "Hard Disk Storage"
- *Chapter 11*. "Floppy Disk Storage"
- *Chapter 12*. "High-Capacity Removable Disk Storage"
- *Chapter 13*. "Optical Storage"
- *Chapter 26*. "Operating System Software and Troubleshooting"

Although most of the drives you would install in a PC are covered here, the primary emphasis is on hard disks.

Hard Disk Installation Procedures

This section describes the hard disk drive installation process, particularly the configuration, physical installation, and formatting of a hard disk drive.

To install a hard drive in a PC, you must perform some or all of the following procedures:

- Configure the drive
- Configure the host adapter
- Physically install the drive
- Configure the system
- Partition the drive
- High-level format the drive

As you perform the setup procedure, you may need to know various details about the hard disk drive, the host adapter, and the system ROM BIOS, as well as many of the other devices in the system. This information usually appears in the various OEM manuals that come with these devices. Make sure when you purchase these items that the vendor includes these manuals. (Many do not include the manuals unless you ask for them.) For most equipment sold today, you will get enough documentation from the vendor or reseller of the equipment to enable you to proceed.

If you are like me, however, and want all the technical documentation on the device, you will want to contact the original manufacturer of the device and order the technical specification manual. For example, if you purchase a system that comes with a Western Digital IDE hard disk, the seller probably will give you some limited information on the drive, but not nearly the amount that the actual Western Digital technical specification manual provides. To get this documentation, you have to call Western Digital and order it. The same rule applies for any of the other components in most of the systems sold today. I find the OEM technical manuals to be essential in providing the highest level of technical support possible.

For reference, you can look up the hard disk manufacturer names in Vendor List, on the CD, and you will find numbers to call for technical support, as well as URLs for their Web sites.

Drive Configuration

Before you physically install a hard disk drive into the computer, you must be sure that it is properly configured. For an IDE drive, this generally means designating the drive as a master/slave or using the Cable Select feature and a special cable to determine the relationship. For SCSI drives, you must set the device's SCSI ID and possibly its SCSI bus termination state.

◄◄ These procedures are covered in "The IDE Interface," p. 509, and "The SCSI Interface," p. 529.

Host Adapter Configuration

Older hard disk drive types used separate disk controller cards that you had to install in a bus slot. The IDE and SCSI hard disk drives used in today's PCs have the disk controller integrated into the drive assembly. For IDE drives, the I/O interface is nearly always integrated into the system's motherboard, and you configure the interface through the system BIOS. There is no separate host adapter, therefore, if you have an IDE drive you can proceed to "Physical Installation," later in this chapter. Some systems might use ATA/IDE adapters in lieu of the built-in interface, because some of the motherboard-integrated ATA interfaces will not support the faster modes some newer drives (such as ATA/33 and ATA/66) are capable of achieving. In most cases, I would recommend upgrading the motherboard rather than getting an IDE host adapter, because there are other benefits to a new motherboard and the cost isn't much higher.

SCSI drives, however, usually require a host adapter card that you must install in a bus slot like any other card. A few motherboards have integrated SCSI adapters, but these are rare. Configuring a SCSI host adapter card involves setting the different system resources that the adapter requires. As with most expansion cards, a SCSI host adapter will require some combination of the following system resources:

- ROM addresses
- Interrupt requests (IRQ)
- DMA (Direct Memory Access) channel (DRQ)
- I/O port addresses

Not all adapters use every one of these resources, but some may use them all. In most cases, these resources will be automatically configured by the BIOS and your operating system.

When you install a host adapter that supports Plug and Play in a system with a Plug-and-Play BIOS and operating system, such as Windows 9x, the configuration process is completely automatic. The computer sets the required hardware resource settings to values that do not conflict with other devices in the computer.

◀◀ See "Plug-and-Play BIOS," p. 400.

If your hardware or operating system does not support Plug and Play, you have to manually configure the adapter to use the appropriate resources. Some adapters provide software that enables you to reconfigure or change the hardware resources, while others use jumpers or DIP switches.

◀◀ See "System Resources," p. 311.

The IDE interface is part of the standard PC BIOS, which makes it possible to boot from an IDE drive. The BIOS provides the device driver functionality that the system needs to access the drive before any files can be loaded from disk. The SCSI interface is not part of the standard PC BIOS, so most SCSI host adapters have their own ROM BIOS that enables SCSI drives to function as boot devices.

Use of the SCSI BIOS is usually optional. If you are not booting from a SCSI drive, you can load a standard device driver for your operating system to access the SCSI devices. Most host adapters have DIP switches that you use to enable or disable SCSI BIOS support.

In addition to providing boot functionality, the SCSI BIOS can provide many other functions, including any or all of the following:

- Low-level formatting
- Drive-type (parameter) control
- Host adapter configuration
- SCSI diagnostics
- Support for nonstandard I/O port addresses and interrupts

If the adapter's onboard BIOS is enabled, it will use specific memory address space in the upper memory area (UMA). The UMA is the top 384KB in the first megabyte of system memory. The UMA is divided into three areas of two 64KB segments each, with the first and last areas being used by the video adapter circuits and the motherboard BIOS, respectively. Segments C000h and D000h are reserved for use by adapter ROMs such as those found on disk controllers or SCSI host adapters.

Note

You must ensure that any adapters using space in these segments of the HMA (high memory area) do not overlap with another adapter that uses this space. No two adapters can share this memory space. Most adapters have software, jumpers, or switches that can adjust the configuration of the board and change the addresses it uses to prevent conflict.

Physical Installation

The procedure for the physical installation of a hard disk drive is much the same as that for installing any other type of drive. You must have the correct screws, brackets, and faceplates for the specific drive and system before you can install the drive.

Some computer cases require plastic or metal rails that are secured to the sides of a hard disk drive so it can slide into the proper place in the system (see Figure 14.1). When you purchase a drive, vendors often give you the option to purchase a kit as opposed to the bare drive. For slightly more money, the kit includes mounting rails, screws, and often a ribbon cable that you should be able to use in most systems. Be careful when purchasing a SCSI drive, however, as the kit might include a host adapter that can add substantially to the price.

Because cables can vary for both IDE and SCSI interfaces, be sure you have the proper cable for both your drive and controller. For example, to run the newer Fast-ATA/66 modes, you need a special 80-conductor cable. This cable is also recommended if you are running Fast-ATA/33; it will work for all slower modes as well.

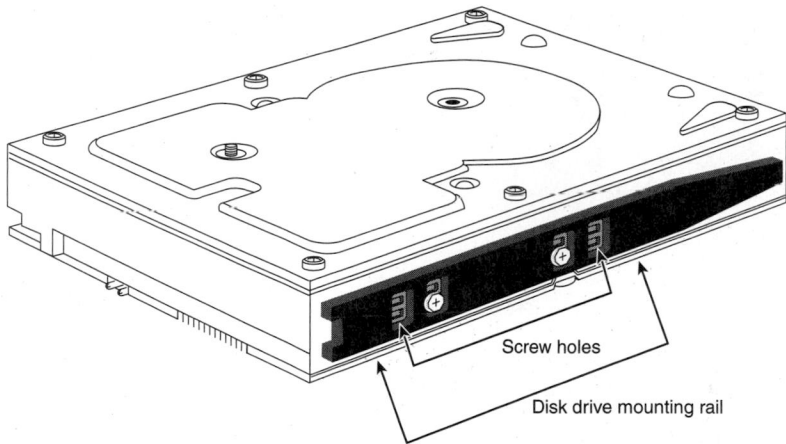

Screw holes

Disk drive mounting rail

Figure 14.1   A typical hard disk with mounting rails.

If you cannot purchase a drive kit, there are several companies listed in the Vendor List (on the CD) that specialize in drive-mounting brackets, cables, and other hardware accessories. Also, many newer aftermarket computer cases have eliminated the need for drive rails altogether by building the expansion slot itself to the 3 1/2- or 5 1/4-inch drive specification, enabling you to bolt the new drive directly to the case. Most 3 1/2-inch hard drives sold in boxed packaging in retail outlets do include the mounting bracket required to mount a 3 1/2-inch drive in a 5 1/4-inch bay (as shown in Figure 14.2).

Note

You should also note the length of the drive cable itself when you plan on adding a hard disk drive. It can be very annoying to assemble everything that you think you'll need to install a drive, and then find that the drive cable is not long enough to reach the new drive location. You can try to reposition the drive to a location closer to the interface connector on the host adapter or motherboard, or just get a longer cable. IDE cables are limited to 18 inches in overall length; if they are shorter, that is all the better. This is most important if your drive is going to use the faster ATA/33 and ATA/66 modes. Using a cable that is too long will cause timing errors and signal degradation, possibly corrupting the data on your drive.

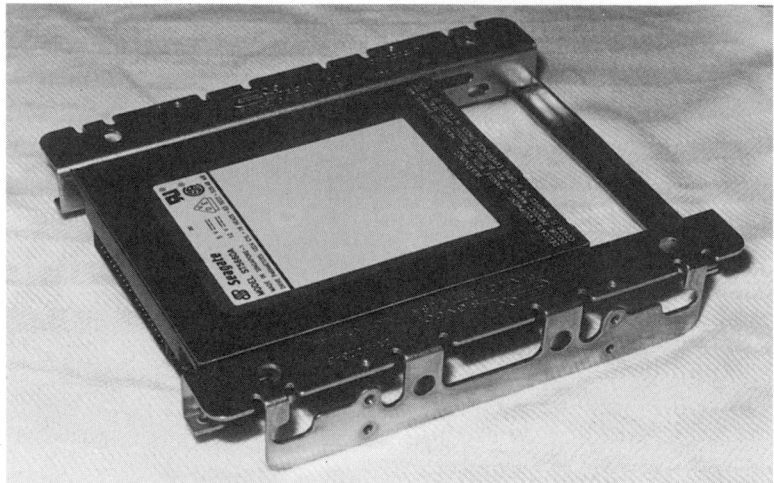

Figure 14.2   A typical bracket used to mount a 3 1/2-inch drive in a 5 1/4-inch drive bay. The bracket is screwed to the drive, and then mounted in the bay by using screws or rails as determined by the case.

Different faceplate, or bezel, options are also available. Make sure that you have the correct bezel for your application. Some systems, for example, do not need a bezel; if there is a bezel on the drive, you must remove it.

Caution

Make sure you use only the screws that come with your new drive. Many drives come with a special short-length screw that can have the same size thread as other screws you might use in your system. If you use screws that are too long, they might protrude too far into the drive casing and cause problems.

Hard Drive Physical Installation—Step by Step

The step-by-step procedures for installing a hard drive are as follows:

1. Check your computer for an unused IDE connector. Typical Pentium-class and above PCs have provision for four IDE devices; if you have less, add your drive to an unused 40-pin

connector on an IDE cable. (You will need to attach a cable if you have only one IDE cable in the computer and both connectors on the cable already have drives or devices attached.)

2. Double-check the pin configuration. The colored (normally red or red-flecked) stripe on one edge of the cable goes to pin 1 of the hard drive's data connector. Reverse this, and the drive won't be capable of accepting any commands, such as identify, FDISK, or FORMAT. Most cables will be keyed to prevent improper installation, but many are not.

3. Slide the drive carefully into a drive bay of the correct size. Most hard drives, except for a few very high-capacity SCSI drives meant for servers and the Quantum Bigfoot series, are 3 1/2-inch wide and 1-inch high. If you have no 3 1/2-inch drive bays left for your hard disk, attach a drive-adapter kit to the sides of the drive to make it wide enough to fit into a 5 1/4-inch wide drive bay (refer to Figure 14.2). Some case designs require that you attach rails to the side of the hard drive. If so, attach them to the drive using the screws supplied with either the case or the drive. Be sure the screws aren't too long, if you bottom the screws in the drive, you can damage it. Then slide the drive into the bay in the case until the rails latch into place. Note that most cases include the screws and rails to install drives, but if not you may have to purchase them separately.

4. Attach the existing data cable connector to the back of the drive, unless you are adding the drive and cable at the same time. In that case, attach the cable to the drive before you slide it into the drive bay and fasten it into place (step 2 above).

5. Attach the appropriate power connector to the drive. Most hard drives use the larger, or "Molex" four-wire power connector. If necessary, purchase a Y-splitter cable to create two power connectors from one (many computers have fewer power connectors than drive bays).

6. Turn on the computer and listen for the new hard disk to spin up. While today's drives are very quiet compared to early hard disks, you should still hear a faint rattling or clicking as the new hard disk starts to run. If you don't hear anything from the drive, double-check the data and power cables.

7. Restart the computer and access the BIOS setup screens to configure the new hard disk. At a minimum, you'll need to detect (or set) the following parameters: cylinders, heads, sectors per track, and write precompensation. If your BIOS has an autodetect or auto type setting, I recommend you use it as it will configure most parameters automatically. For IDE hard drives above 528 million bytes, you'll also need to set LBA translation to access the drive's full capacity. If autodetect was selected LBA translation should already be set correctly. Many systems have a Peripherals Configuration screen, which also allows you to set UDMA, PIO, and block mode configurations for maximum drive performance. See your drive's documentation for the correct settings. Save the BIOS configuration, and exit the BIOS setup screen to continue. The following section has more information on this step, as it can be complicated.

8. Restart the computer, and prepare to run FDISK to prepare the hard drive for formatting and use. Or, you can use drive partitioning software, such as PowerQuest's Partition Magic to automatically create and manage disk partitions.

Note

See the CD accompanying this book for Macmillan editions of Partition Magic and Drive Image, which allows you to image a drive for emergency restoration or for multiple installations.

System Configuration

After your drive is physically installed, you have to provide the computer with basic information about the drive so the system can access it and boot from it. How you set and store this information depends on the type of drive and system you have. Standard (IDE) setup procedures apply for most hard disks except SCSI drives. SCSI drives normally follow a custom setup procedure that varies depending on the host adapter that you are using. If you have a SCSI drive, follow the instructions included with the host adapter to configure the drives.

Automatic Drive Typing

For IDE drives, virtually all new BIOS versions in today's PCs have automatic typing. The BIOS sends a special Identify Drive command to all the devices connected to the IDE interface during the system startup sequence; the drives are intelligent enough to respond with the correct parameters. The BIOS then automatically enters the parameter information returned by the drive. This procedure eliminates errors or confusion in parameter selection. However, even with automatic drive typing, some BIOSes will alert you that you need to enter the system Setup program and configure the drive. In these situations, just enter the system BIOS configuration utility and save the settings that the BIOS has detected for the drive. You don't need to enter any settings yourself.

If your system supports automatic drive typing but no drive information appears onscreen, you might have forgotten to attach the power cable to the drive, or you may have reversed the IDE interface cable at either the motherboard or the hard drive connections. The red stripe on the 40-pin IDE cable is supposed to be aligned with pin 1 at both ends. Without power or proper data connection the drive will never spin up and, therefore, cannot be detected.

Even though most new BIOSes support automatic drive typing at startup, there are a couple of benefits to performing this task within the BIOS configuration screen:

- In the event that you need to move the drive to another system, you'll know the drive geometry and translation scheme (such as LBA) that was used to access the drive. If the drive is moved to another computer, the identical drive geometry (cylinder, head, sectors per track) and translation scheme must be used in the other computer, or the data on the drive will not be accessible and can be lost. Because many systems with auto-configuration don't display these settings during the startup process, performing the drive-typing operation yourself might be the only way to get this information.
- Even if you never expect to move the drive, you'll gain several seconds on every startup by detecting the drive in the BIOS configuration screens and saving the setting there. You can also save time by setting unused drive interfaces to Not Installed. Otherwise, the computer will try to detect devices on all four IDE ports (primary master, primary slave, secondary master, and secondary slave) each time you start the computer.

Manual Drive Typing

If you are dealing with a motherboard that does not support automatic typing, you must enter the appropriate drive information in the system BIOS manually. The BIOS has a selection of pre-configured drive types, but these are woefully outdated in most cases, providing support only for drives holding a few hundred megabytes or less. In nearly every case, you will have to select the user-defined drive type and provide values for the following settings:

- Cylinders
- Heads
- Sectors per track
- Write precompensation

The values that you use for these settings should be provided in the documentation for the hard disk drive, or they might be printed on the drive itself. It's a good idea to check for these settings and write them down, because they may not be visible once you've installed the drive. You should also maintain a copy of these settings in case your system BIOS should lose its data due to a battery failure. One of the best places to store this information is inside the computer itself. Taping a note with vital settings like these to the inside of the case can be a lifesaver.

In the event that you are not able to determine the correct settings for your hard drive from either the drive case or from the Technical Reference, there are utility programs available from the Internet that can query the drive for this information. Western Digital's TBLCHK.EXE has been updated to handle LBA-mode hard drives, unlike many older utilities, and can be obtained from Western Digital's Web site.

Note

The setup parameters for over 1,000 popular drive models are included in the Technical Reference on the CD. Additionally, there is a generic table of parameters included in the appendix that will work (although they may not work optimally) with any IDE drive up to 528MB.

Depending on the maker and the version of your system BIOS, there may be other settings to configure as well, such as what transfer mode to use, and whether or not the BIOS should use logical block addressing.

◀◀ See "Increased Drive Capacity," p. 521.

Formatting

Proper setup and formatting are critical to a drive's performance and reliability. This section describes the procedures used to format a hard disk drive correctly. Use these procedures when you install a new drive in a system or immediately after you recover data from a hard disk that has been exhibiting problems.

There are three major steps in the formatting process for a hard disk drive subsystem:

1. Low-level formatting
2. Partitioning
3. High-level formatting

Low-Level Formatting

All new hard disk drives are low-level formatted by the manufacturer, and you do not have to perform another LLF before you install the drive. In fact, under normal circumstances, you should not ever have to perform a low-level format on an IDE or SCSI drive. Most manufacturers no longer recommend that you low-level format any IDE type drive.

This recommendation has been the source of some myths about IDE. Many people say, for example, that you cannot perform a low-level format on an IDE drive, and that if you do, you will destroy the drive. This statement is untrue! What can happen is that you may lose the optimal head and cylinder skew factors for the drive that were set by the manufacturer, as well as the map of drive defects. This situation is not good and will definitely have a negative effect on the drive's performance, but you still can use the drive with no problems.

However, there may be times when you must perform a low-level format on an IDE or SCSI drive. The following sections discuss the software that you can use to do this.

SCSI Low-Level Format Software

If you are using an SCSI drive, you must use the LLF program provided by the manufacturer of the SCSI host adapter. The design of these devices varies enough that a register-level program can work only if it is tailored to the individual controller. Fortunately, all SCSI host adapters include low-level format software, either in the host adapter's BIOS or in a separate disk-based program.

The interface to the SCSI drive is through the host adapter. SCSI is a standard, but there are no true standards for what a host adapter is supposed to look like. This means that any formatting or configuration software will be specific to a particular host adapter.

Note

Notice that SCSI format and configuration software is keyed to the host adapter and is not specific in any way to the particular SCSI hard disk drive that you are using.

IDE Low-Level Format Software

IDE drive manufacturers have defined extensions to the standard WD1002/1003 AT interface, which was further standardized for IDE drives as the ATA (AT Attachment) interface. The ATA specification provides for vendor-unique commands, which are manufacturer proprietary extensions to the standard. To prevent improper low-level formatting, many of these IDE drives have special codes that must be sent to the drive to unlock the format routines. These codes vary among manufacturers. If possible, you should obtain LLF and defect-management software from the drive manufacturer; this software usually is specific to that manufacturer's products, and often is model-specific. Check the brand and model number of your hard disk to determine the utility program you need.

Most ATA IDE drives are protected from any alteration to the skew factors or defect map erasure because they are in a translated mode. Zoned bit recording drives are always in translation mode and are fully protected. Most ATA drives have a custom command set that must be used in the format process; the standard format commands defined by the ATA specification usually do not work, especially with intelligent or zoned bit recording IDE drives. Without the proper manufacturer-specific format commands, you can't perform the defect management by the manufacturer-specified method, in which bad sectors often can be spared.

Most manufacturers supply low-level format programs for their drives. Here are a few examples:

- *Seagate.* `ftp://ftp.seagate.com/techsuppt/seagate_utils/sgatfmt4.zip`
- *IBM.* `http://www.storage.ibm.com/techsup/hddtech/welcome.htm`
- *Quantum.* `<http://support.quantum.com/menus/soft_menu.htm`
- *Western Digital.* `http://www.wdc.com/service/ftp/wddiag/wd_diag.exe`
- *Maxtor.* `http://www.maxtor.com/library/ide.html`

I would try the manufacturer specific format programs first. They are free and can often work at a lower level and handle defects in ways that the more generic ones can't. If formatting software is not available from your drive's manufacturer, I recommend Disk Manager by Ontrack and the MicroScope program by Micro 2000. Another excellent, inexpensive, general-purpose PC hardware diagnostic that includes low-level format capability is #1 TuffTEST Pro from #1-PC Diagnostics. These programs can format many IDE drives because they know the manufacturer-specific IDE format commands and routines. They also can perform defect-mapping and surface-analysis procedures.

Note

While Ontrack Disk Manager can be purchased in a "generic" version that works with any manufacturer's hard drives, brand-specific OEM versions are often available free of charge on the utility disks or CD-ROMs shipped with new retail-packaged hard disk drives. You should also check your drive maker's Web site for updated versions of Disk Manager. These OEM versions are designed to check for a particular brand's drive firmware, and will not work on any other brand than the one for which they were modified.

Nondestructive Formatters

General-purpose, BIOS-level, nondestructive formatters, such as Calibrate and SpinRite, are not recommended in most situations where a real LLF is required. These programs have several limitations and problems that limit their effectiveness; in some cases, they can even cause problems with the way that defects are handled on a drive. These programs attempt to perform a track-by-track LLF by using BIOS functions, while backing up and restoring the track data as they go. These programs do not actually perform a complete LLF, because they do not even try to low-level format the first track (Cylinder 0, Head 0) due to problems with some controller types that store hidden information on the first track.

These programs also do not perform defect mapping in the way that standard LLF programs do, and they can even remove the carefully applied sector header defect marks during a proper LLF. This situation potentially allows data to be stored in sectors that originally were marked defective and may actually void the manufacturer's warranty on some drives. Another problem is that these programs only work on drives that have already been formatted and can format only drives that are formattable through BIOS functions.

Note

Spinrite is, however, useful for recovering data found on drives with read errors, because of its thorough method of repeatedly rereading the errors and analyzing the results to reconstruct the missing data. This process is called *Dynastat Data Recovery*.

A true LLF program bypasses the system BIOS and sends commands directly to the disk controller hardware. For this reason, many LLF programs are specific to the disk controller hardware for which they are designed. It is virtually impossible to have a single format program that will run on all different types of controllers. Many hard drives have been incorrectly diagnosed as being defective because the wrong format program was used and the program did not operate properly.

Drive Partitioning with FDISK

Partitioning a hard disk is the act of defining areas of the disk for an operating system to use as a volume.

When you partition a disk, the partitioning software writes a master partition boot sector at Cylinder 0, Head 0, Sector 1—the first sector on the hard disk. This sector contains data that describes the partitions by their starting and ending cylinder, head, and sector locations. The partition table also indicates to the ROM BIOS which of the partitions is bootable and, therefore, where to look for an operating system to load.

▶▶ See "File Systems and Data Recovery," p. 1379.

The FDISK program is the accepted standard for partitioning hard disk drives for use with all versions of Windows 9x and DOS. Partitioning prepares the boot sector of the disk in such a way that the FORMAT.COM program or the Windows GUI format utility can operate correctly. FDISK also makes it possible for different operating systems to coexist on a single hard disk. No matter which operating system you use, it should come with an FDISK program that can be used to partition the drive.

Note

Because FDISK depends on BIOS information about the hard disk to determine the size and drive geometry of the hard disk, correct BIOS settings are vital to a correct operation of FDISK. If a 10GB hard drive is defined in the BIOS as a 10MB hard drive, for example, all that FDISK will prepare for use, and all that FORMAT will ultimately prepare, is 10MB.

With any version of Windows, as with MS-DOS, FDISK allows you to create two different types of disk partitions: primary and extended. A primary partition can be bootable but an extended partition cannot. If you have only a single hard disk in your system, at least part of the drive must be prepared as a primary partition if you want to start your computer from the hard disk (and who doesn't?). A primary partition equals a single drive letter (C: on one-drive systems), whereas an extended partition acts as a sort of logical container for additional drive letters (D: and beyond). A single extended partition can contain a single drive letter (also referred to as a *logical DOS drive*), or more than one logical DOS drive of different sizes.

Don't get hung up on the fact that FDISK calls partitions "DOS" partitions or "DOS" drives. This is true even though the operating system you are installing is Windows 95, 98, NT, 2000, Linux, etc.

Depending on the version of Windows in use (and with any version of MS-DOS), it might be necessary to subdivide a hard drive through the use of FDISK. The original release of Windows 95 and MS-DOS supports FAT16, which allows no more than 65,536 files per drive and a single drive letter of no more than 2.1GB in size. Thus, a 10.1GB hard disk prepared with MS-DOS or the original Windows 95 must have at a minimum of five drive letters, and could have more. See Figure 14.3.

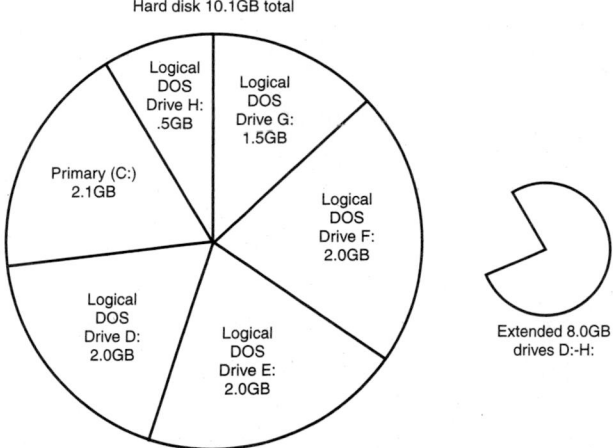

Figure 14.3   Adding a hard drive above 2.1GB in size to an MS-DOS or original Windows 95 computer forces the user to create multiple drive letters to use the entire drive capacity. The logical DOS drives are referenced like any other drive, although they are portions of a single physical hard disk.

▶▶ See "FAT Disk Structures" p. 1380.

Another reason for subdividing a single drive into letters is for increased data security. For example, PowerQuest (the creators of PartitionMagic) suggests a three-drive partitioning scheme that looks like this:

> C: for the operating system and utilities
>
> D: for applications
>
> E: and above for data

In this example, primary and extended partitions would be assigned as shown here:

> C: the primary partition
>
> D: and E: in the extended partition as logical DOS drives

If a catastrophic failure to the disk structure wipes out C: or D:, Drive E:, which contains the data, will normally still be intact. This method also makes backing up the data easier; just set the backup program to back up all of E:, or all the changed files on E:.

Large Hard Disk Support

If you use the Windows 95B or above (Win95 OSR 2.x) or Windows 98 versions of FDISK with a hard drive greater than 512MB, FDISK will offer to enable large disk support.

Choosing to enable large disk support provides several benefits:

- You can use a large hard disk (greater than 2.1GB) as a single drive letter; in fact, your drive can be as large as 2TB and still be identified by a single drive letter. This is due to the FAT32 file system, which allows for many more files per drive than FAT16.

▶▶ See "FAT32," p. 1399.

- Because of the more efficient storage methods of FAT-32, your files will use less hard disk space overall.

However, keep in mind that all disk operations must be done through Windows 95B or Windows 98 for any drive FDISKed with large hard drive support (FAT32). If you have old MS-DOS games or applications that require you to boot with MS-DOS rather than with Windows' command-prompt mode, they can't access a FAT32 drive.

A drive prepared with the large hard disk support (FAT32) option enabled can still be partitioned into primary and secondary partitions with FDISK, as with FAT16 for the data-security reasons listed earlier.

Another type of file system is NTFS, which is supported only by Windows NT and Windows 2000. This is a high performance file system with additional security and networking features. It is discussed in more detail in Chapter 27, "File Systems and Data Recovery". Note that Windows 9x cannot read NTFS partitions, and Windows NT cannot read FAT32 partitions. Windows 2000 can handle both FAT32 and NTFS.

Assigning Drive Letters with FDISK

There are many ways to use FDISK, depending on the number of hard drives you have in your system and the number of drive letters you want to create.

With a single drive, creating a primary partition (C:) and an extended partition with two logical DOS drives within it will result in the following drive letters:

Partition Type	Drive letter(s)
Primary	C:
Extended volumes	D: and E:

Most people would think that a second physical drive added to this system should have drive letters that follow the E: drive.

However, you need to understand how drive letters are allocated by the system to know how to use FDISK correctly in this situation. Table 14.1 shows how FDISK assigns drive letters by drive and partition type.

Table 14.1   Drive Letter Allocations by Drive and Partition Type

Drive	Partition	Order	First drive letter
1st	Primary	1st	C:
1st	Extended	3rd	E:
2nd	Primary	2nd	D:
2nd	Extended	4th	F:

How does this affect you when you add another hard drive? If you prepare the second hard drive with a primary partition and your first hard drive has an extended partition on it, the second hard drive will take the primary partition's D: drive letter. This moves all the drive letters in the first hard drive's extended partition up one drive letter.

In the first example, we listed a drive with C: (primary partition), D:, and E: (extended partition volumes) as the drive letters (D: and E: were in the extended partition). Table 14.2 indicates what happens if a second drive is added with a primary partition and an extended partition with two volumes (same setup as the first drive):

Table 14.2   Drive Letter Changes Caused by Addition of Second Drive with Primary Partition

Drive	Partition Type	Order	Original drive letter(s) (first drive only)	New drive letter(s) after adding second drive
1st	Primary	1st	C:	C:
1st	Extended	3rd	D:, E:	E:, F:
2nd	Primary	2nd		D:
2nd	Extended	4th		G:, H:

After adding the second drive, the original drive letters D: and E: have now become E: and F:. The primary partition on the new drive has become D:, and the extended partition volumes on the second drive are G: and H:. Confused? Well you better not be or you'll find yourself deleting or copying data to or from the wrong drive.

This principle extends to third and fourth physical drives as well: the primary partitions on each drive get their drive letters first, followed by logical DOS drives in the extended partitions.

One way to affect this is to only partition additional drives with extended partitions, in other words, do not create primary partitions on them. That way the new drive's partitions will be seen only as additional letters, and the letters used by the first drive's partitions will remain unchanged.

If you're *adding* a drive to your system, you should now understand why preparing that second, third, or fourth drive with a primary partition is a bad idea. If you're installing an additional hard drive (not a replacement), remember that it can't be a bootable drive. If it can't be bootable, there's no reason to make it a primary partition. FDISK will allow you to create an extended partition using 100 percent of the space on any drive. Table 14.3 shows the same example used in the Table 14.2 with the second drive installed as an extended partition:

Table 14.3 Drive Letter Allocations after Addition of Second Drive with Extended Partition Only

Drive	Partition Type	Order	Original drive letter(s) (first drive only)	New drive letter(s) after adding second drive
1st	Primary	1st	C:	C:
1st	Extended	3rd	D:, E:	D:, E:
2nd	Primary	2nd	—	—
2nd	Extended	4th		F:

When a new drive is added with only extended partition volumes, then you can see that the original drive letters remain undisturbed. This is a much easier to understand arrangement, and prevents accidents with data due to drive letters changing. This operating-system behavior also explains why some of the first computers with IDE-based (ATAPI) Iomega Zip drives had the Zip drive as D:, with a single hard disk identified as C: and E:; the Zip drive was treated as the second hard drive with a primary partition.

Drive Partitioning with Partition Magic

PowerQuest's Partition Magic allows you to take an existing hard drive and perform the following changes to it without loss of data:

- Change primary partition size (larger or smaller)
- Turn empty space on hard drive into additional drive letters
- Convert the inefficient FAT16 partition type into efficient FAT32 on systems with Windows 95B or Windows 98
- Move programs to new drive letters created with PM and change registry keys and other information automatically

Note

As mentioned earlier in the chapter, the CD accompanying this book contains the Que edition of Partition Magic. I still recommend FDISK be used for initial partitioning and setup of any drive, but Partition Magic can be very useful for reconfiguring a system that is already partitioned.

While the program recommends a full backup before starting, I've used Partition Magic many times to turn a single "big drive" into two or more drive letters in less than 10 minutes. Performing the same task with backup software and FDISK/FORMAT can taken several hours.

High-Level (Operating System) Formatting

The final step in the installation of a hard disk drive is the high-level format. Like the partitioning process, the high-level format is specific to the file system you've chosen to use on the drive. On Windows 9x and DOS systems, the primary function of the high-level format is to create a FAT and a directory system on the disk so the operating system can manage files. You must run FDISK before formatting a drive. Each drive letter created by FDISK must be formatted before it can be used for data storage.

Usually, you perform the high-level format with the FORMAT.COM program or the formatting utility in Windows 9x Explorer. FORMAT.COM uses the following syntax:

```
FORMAT C: /S /V
```

This command high-level formats drive C:, writes the hidden operating system files in the first part of the partition, and prompts for the entry of a volume label to be stored on the disk at the completion of the process.

The FAT high-level format program performs the following functions and procedures:

1. Scans the disk (read only) for tracks and sectors marked as bad during the LLF, and notes these tracks as being unreadable.

2. Returns the drive heads to the first cylinder of the partition, and at that cylinder (Head 1, Sector 1) writes a DOS volume boot sector.

3. Writes a FAT at Head 1, Sector 2. Immediately after this FAT, it writes a second copy of the FAT. These FATs essentially are blank except for bad-cluster marks noting areas of the disk that were found to be unreadable during the marked-defect scan.

4. Writes a blank root directory.

5. If the /S parameter is specified, copies the system files, IO.SYS and MSDOS.SYS (or IBM-BIO.COM and IBMDOS.COM, depending on which DOS you run) and COMMAND.COM to the disk (in that order).

6. If the /V parameter is specified, prompts the user for a volume label, which is written as the fourth file entry in the root directory.

Now, the operating system can use the disk for storing and retrieving files, and the disk is a bootable disk.

During the first phase of the high-level format, the program performs a marked defect scan. Defects marked by the LLF operation show up during this scan as being unreadable tracks or sectors. When the high-level format encounters one of these areas, it automatically performs up to five retries to read these tracks or sectors. If the unreadable area was marked by the LLF, the read fails on all attempts.

After five retries, the DOS FORMAT program gives up on this track or sector and moves to the next one. Areas that remain unreadable after the initial read and the five retries are noted in the FAT as being bad clusters.

Note

Because the high-level format doesn't overwrite data areas beyond the root directory of the hard disk, it's possible to use programs such as Norton Utilities to unformat the hard disk that contains data from previous operations, provided no programs or data has been copied to the drive after high-level formatting. Unformatting can be performed because the data from the drive's previous use is still present.

If you create an extended partition, the logical DOS drive letters found there need a simpler FORMAT command, because system files aren't necessary. For example, FORMAT D:/V for drive D:, FORMAT E:/V for drive E:, etc.

FDISK and FORMAT Limitations

The biggest problem with FDISK is that it is destructive. If you change your mind about disk structure, you must back up your system and start over again. That alone is cause for using FDISK with care, but there are other limitations you should keep in mind:

- FDISK doesn't provide any help with issues of drive letter changes.
- FDISK requires FORMAT before the drive is ready for use.
- FORMAT must check the entire drive before making it ready for use. Its error management is rudimentary and can waste a lot of disk space with older drives that have disk errors.
- FDISK and FORMAT are designed for a single operating system environment, with no provision for multiboot options (Windows 9x and NT or Windows 9x and Linux, for example).
- FDISK and FORMAT offer no procedure for migrating data to a new drive, and XCOPY is tricky to use
- FDISK and FORMAT might cause conflicts with existing CD-ROM drives, which often use the next available drive letter after the existing hard drive

For these reasons, many drive vendors offer some sort of automatic disk installation software with their hard drives. These routines can make the task of disk migration a fast, easy, reliable operation.

Typical features of automatic disk installation programs include the following:

- *Replacement for FDISK and FORMAT.* A single program performs both functions more quickly than FDISK and FORMAT separately
- *Database of drive jumpers for major brands and models*

- *Drive copy function.* Copies contents of old MS-DOS or Windows 9x drive to new drive, retaining long filenames, file attributes, etc.

- *CD-ROM drive letter relocation utility.* Moves CD-ROM to new drive letter (to make room for new hard drive letters) and resets Windows Registry and INI file references to new drive letter so CD-ROM software works without reinstallation

- *Menu-driven or wizard-driven process for installing new hard drive*

- *Optional override of BIOS limitations for installation of large hard drives (>504MB, 2.1GB, 8.4GB, etc.)*

The two major vendors in the automated disk-utility business are Ontrack Data International, Inc. and StorageSoft. These companies sell their disk-installation products to OEM hard drive vendors for use with particular brands of drives. They also sell to the public "generic" versions that can be purchased for use with any brand or model of hard disk. Table 14.4 provides a basic overview of the most popular disk installation programs.

Table 14.4   Overview of Automatic Disk-Installation Programs

Vendor	Software	Current Version	OEM	Retail
Ontrack	Disk Manager	9.xx	Yes	Yes
	Disk Manager DiskGo!	2.5x	Yes	Yes
StorageSoft	EZ Drive	9x	Yes	Yes
	DrivePro	3.x	No	Yes
Seagate[1]	DiscWizard	2.4x	Yes	No
Maxtor[2]	MaxBlast!	9.x	Yes	No

1 Seagate's DiscWizard was codeveloped with Ontrack, and contains Ontrack Disk Manager v9.x.

2 Maxtor's MaxBlast! Software v9.x is a customized version of EZ-Drive. Version 7.x and 8.x of MaxBlast! were customized versions of Ontrack's Disk Manager

Disk Manager and EZ-Drive are DOS-based utility programs, whereas DiscWizard and Disk Manager DiskGo! offer a Windows-like interface. Seagate's DiscWizard actually analyzes the system, asks the user questions about the intended installation, and prepares a customized procedure based on the user's responses.

OEM versions of disk-installation programs are available from the drive makers' Web sites; retail versions usable with any combination of drives can be purchased from retail stores or at the vendors' online stores.

Replacing an Existing Drive

Previous sections discuss installing a single hard drive or adding a new hard drive to a system. While formatting and partitioning a new hard disk can be challenging, replacing an existing drive and moving your programs and files to it can be a lot more challenging.

Drive Migration for MS-DOS Users

When MS-DOS 6.x was dominant, many users used this straightforward method to transfer the contents of their old hard drive to their new hard drive:

1. The user created a bootable disk containing FDISK, FORMAT, and XCOPY.

2. The new hard drive was prepared with a primary partition (and possibly an extended partition, depending on the user's desires).

3. The new hard drive was formatted with system files, although the operating system identified it as D:.

4. The XCOPY command was used to transfer all non-hidden files from C:\ (the old hard drive) to D:\ thus:

   ```
   XCOPY C:\ D:\/S/E
   ```

   The XCOPY command also was used as necessary to transfer files from any remaining drive letters on the old hard drive to the corresponding drive letters on the new drive.

Because the only hidden files such a system would have were probably the operating system boot files (already installed) and the Windows 3.1 permanent swap file (which could be recreated after restarting Windows), this "free" data transfer routine worked well for many people.

After the original drive was removed from the system, the new drive would be jumpered as master and assigned C:. You will need to run FDISK from a floppy and set the primary partition on the new C: drive as Active. Then exit FDISK and the drive will boot.

Drive Migration for Windows 9x Users

Windows 95 and 98 have complicated the once simple act of data transfer to a new system by their frequent use of hidden files and folders (such as \Windows\Inf, where Windows 9x hardware drivers are stored). The extensive use of hidden files was a major reason for a greatly enhanced version of XCOPY to be included in Windows 9x.

Note

XCOPY32 is automatically used in place of XCOPY when XCOPY is started within a DOS session under Windows.

XCOPY32 for Windows 9x Data Transfer

Compared to "classic" XCOPY, XCOPY32 can copy hidden files; can preserve file attributes such as system, hidden, read-only, and archive; can automatically create folders, and is compatible with long filenames. Thus, it is possible to use it to duplicate an existing drive, but with these cautions:

1. The XCOPY32 command is much more complex.

2. There may be errors during the copy process because of Windows' use of temporary files during normal operation, but XCOPY32 can be forced to continue.

This command line will call XCOPY32 and transfer all files and folders with their original attributes intact from the original drive (C:) to the new drive (D:). This command must be run from an MS-DOS session under Windows 95 or 98.

```
xcopy32 c:\. d:\ /e/c/h/r/k
```

The command switches are explained here:

- /E. Copies folders, even if empty, also copies all folders beneath the starting folder
- /C. Continues to copy after errors (The Windows swap file can't be copied due to being in use.)
- /H. Copies hidden and system files
- /R. Overwrites read-only files
- /K. Preserves file attributes

Repeat the command with appropriate drive-letter changes for any additional drive letters on your old drive.

After the original drive is removed from the system, the new drive needs to be jumpered as master (or single) and the operating system will assign it C:. You will need to run FDISK from a floppy and set the primary partition on the new C: drive as Active. Then exit FDISK, and the drive will boot.

Note that although the XCOPY method has worked for me, some people have problems with it. A much more automated and easy approach to cloning drives is to use commercial software designed for that purpose, such as Drive Copy by PowerQuest or Norton Ghost by Symantec.

While many users have prepared new hard drives for use with nothing but FDISK and FORMAT, today's more complex systems are presenting increasingly good reasons for looking at alternatives.

Hard Disk Drive Troubleshooting and Repair

If a hard drive has a mechanical problem inside the sealed HAD (head disk assembly), repairing the drive is usually not feasible. It may be doable, but financially it will be far less expensive to purchase a new drive. If the failure is in the logic board, that board can be replaced with one from a donor drive. Normally this is done only for the purposes of reading the information on the failed drive, because you will have to purchase a complete second drive to cannibalize for the logic board. None of the drive manufacturers normally sell spare parts for their drives anymore.

Most hard disk drive problems are not mechanical hardware problems; instead, they are "soft" problems that can be solved by a new LLF and defect-mapping session. Soft problems are characterized by a drive that sounds normal but produces various read and write errors.

Hard problems are mechanical, such as when the drive sounds as though it contains loose marbles. Constant scraping and grinding noises from the drive, with no reading or writing capability, also qualify as hard errors. In these cases, it is unlikely that an LLF will put the drive back into service. If a hardware problem is indicated, first replace the logic-board assembly. You can make this repair yourself and, if successful, you can recover the data from the drive.

If replacing the logic assembly does not solve the problem, contact the manufacturer or a specialized repair shop that has clean-room facilities for hard disk repair. (See the Vendor's List on the CD for a list of drive manufacturers and companies that specialize in hard disk drive repair.) Because of the costs, it will probably be more economical to simply purchase a new drive.

Testing a Drive

When accessing a drive, it is easy to tell if the drive has been partitioned and formatted properly. A simple test will tell you if a st ꞅd drive is in its "raw" condition or has been partitioned and formatted properly. These tests work best if you have a boot disk available and if the spare hard drive is the only hard drive attached.

First, attach the drive to your system. If you can attach power and data cables to it, you need not install it into a drive bay unless you are planning to use it immediately. If the drive will be run loose, I recommend placing it on a non-conductive foam pad or other soft surface. This will insulate the drive from potential shocks and other hazards. After detecting the drive in the BIOS and saving the changes, start your operating system from the boot disk.

Then, from the A: prompt, enter the following command:

```
DIR C:
```

This will produce one of the following responses:

- *Invalid Drive Specification.* This indicates the drive does not have a valid partition (created by FDISK), or that the existing Master Boot Sector or partition tables have been damaged. No matter what, the drive must be partitioned and FORMATted before use. You will also get this warning on a FAT32 or NTFS partitioned drive if you use a Windows 95 (original version) or MS-DOS boot disk when checking. Use a Windows 95B, Windows 98, or Windows 2000 boot disk to avoid this false message from FAT32 partitions. Or use a Windows NT or Windows 2000 boot disk to detect NTFS partitions.

- *Invalid media type.* This drive has been partitioned but not FORMATted, or the format has been corrupted. You will want to use FDISK's #4 option to examine the drive's existing partitions, and either delete them and create new ones or keep the existing partitions and run FORMAT on each drive letter.

- *Directory of C:....* The contents of C: drive are listed, indicating the drive was stored with a valid FDISK and FORMAT structure and data.

Installing an Optical Drive (CD-ROM, CD-R)

Installation of a CD-ROM or DVD-ROM drive can be as difficult or as easy as you make it. If you plan ahead, the installation should go smoothly.

This section walks you through the installation of a typical internal (SCSI or IDE) and external (SCSI only) optical drive, with tips that often aren't included in the manufacturer's installation manuals. After you install the hardware, your job may be finished if you are running Windows 9x and using a Plug-and-Play drive, or you may have to manually load the software needed to access the drive.

Note

CD-ROM and DVD-ROM drives use the same IDE and SCSI system interfaces and can be installed using the same basic procedures. Some DVD-ROM drives come with an MPEG-2 decoder board that enables you to view DVD movies and video on your PC. This board installs in a PCI bus slot like any other expansion card and performs the video decoding process that would otherwise fall to the system processor.

Avoiding Conflict: Get Your Cards in Order

Regardless of the type of installation—internal or external drive—you must have a functioning IDE or SCSI host adapter before the drive can function. In most cases, you will be connecting the optical drive to an existing IDE or SCSI adapter. If so, the adapter should already be configured not to conflict with other devices in your system. All you have to do is connect the drive with the appropriate cable and proceed from there.

Most computers today have an IDE adapter integrated into the motherboard. However, if you are adding SCSI to your system for the first time, you must install a SCSI host adapter into an expansion slot and make sure it is configured to use the appropriate hardware resources, such as the following:

- IRQ
- DMA channel
- I/O port address

As always, Windows 9x and PnP hardware can completely automate this process, but if you're using another operating system, you may have to configure the adapter manually.

Drive Configuration

Configuration of your new optical drive is paramount to its proper functioning. Examine your new drive (see Figure 14.4) and locate any jumpers. For an IDE drive, here are the typical ways to jumper the drive:

- As the primary (master) drive on the secondary IDE connection
- As the secondary (slave) drive to a current hard disk drive

If the drive is to be the only device on your secondary EIDE interface, the factory settings are usually correct. Consult the manual to make sure this is so.

When you use the CD-ROM or DVD-ROM as a secondary drive—that is, the second drive on the same ribbon cable with another device—make sure it is jumpered as the slave drive, and configure the other device so it is the master drive (see Figure 14.5). In most cases, the drive will show up as the next logical drive, or the D: drive.

Caution

Whenever possible, you should not connect a CD-ROM or DVD-ROM drive to the same channel as a hard disk drive, as sharing the channel can slow down both devices. If your computer has the two IDE channels standard in systems today, you should connect the optical drive to the secondary channel, even if you only have one hard disk drive on the primary.

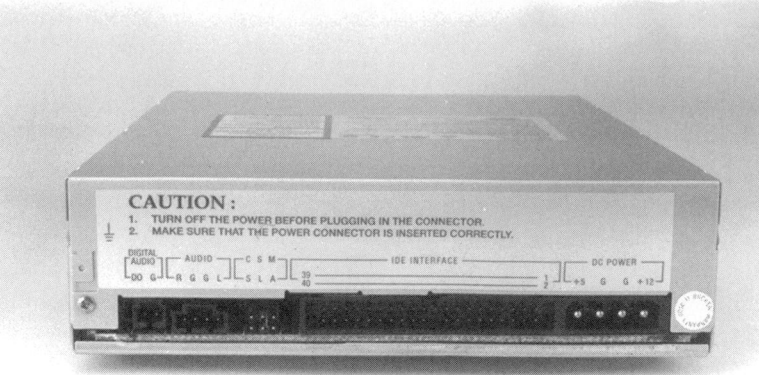

Figure 14.4 The rear connection interfaces of a typical IDE internal CD-ROM drive.

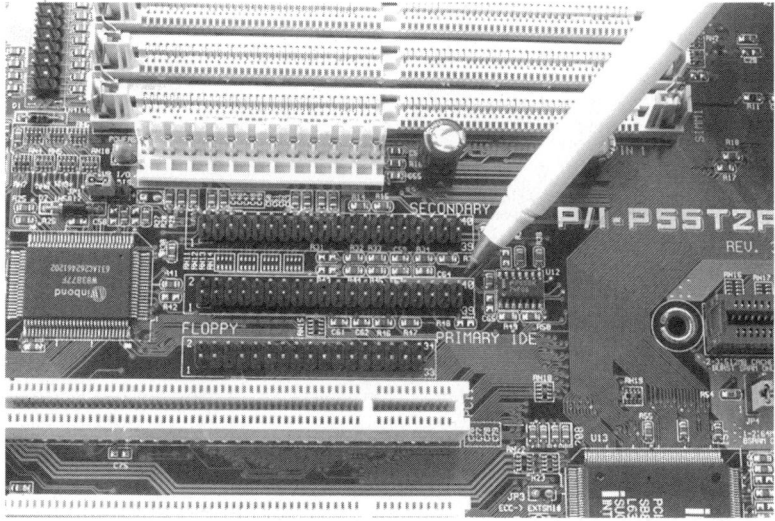

Figure 14.5 An embedded EIDE interface with a primary and secondary IDE connection.

SCSI drives are a bit easier to configure, because you need only to select the proper SCSI ID for the drive. By convention, the boot disk (the C: drive) in a SCSI system is set as ID0, and the host adapter has the ID of 7. You are free to choose any ID in between that is not being used by another device. Most SCSI devices use some sort of rotating or pushbutton selector to cycle between the SCSI IDs, but some may use jumpers.

SCSI devices are cabled together in a bus configuration. If your new SCSI drive falls at the end of the SCSI bus, you will also need to terminate the drive. Note that the SCSI bus refers to the physical arrangement of the devices, and not the SCSI IDs selected for each one.

Note

IDE/EIDE discs and SCSI optical drives can easily coexist in the same system. The optical drive will need to be connected to a SCSI host adapter separate from the IDE subsystem. Some audio adapters have a SCSI interface built in.

External (SCSI) Drive Hook-Up

Unpack the drive carefully. With the purchase of an external drive, you should receive the following items:

- CD-ROM or DVD-ROM drive
- SCSI adapter cable

With the exception of the SCSI host adapter, this is the bare minimum you need to get the drive up and running. You'll probably also find a CD caddy, documentation for the drive, driver software, a SCSI terminator plug, and possibly a sampling of CDs to get you started. SCSI drives almost never come with the SCSI host adapter that you need to connect them to the system. Because SCSI is designed to support up to 7 devices on the same system (or up to 15 devices for Ultra2 SCSI), it would be impractical to include a host adapter with every peripheral. Although a few computers have SCSI interfaces integrated into the motherboard, in most cases you have to purchase a SCSI adapter as a separate expansion card.

To begin the installation, take a look at your work area and the SCSI cable that came with the drive. Where will the drive find a new home? You're limited by the length of the cable. Find a spot for the drive, and insert the power cable into the back of the unit. Make sure that you have an outlet, or preferably a free socket in a surge-suppressing power strip to plug in the new drive.

SCSI devices generally use one of two cable types. Some older drives use a 50-pin Centronics cable, referred to as an A-cable, while most drives today use a 68-connector D-shell cable called a P-cable. Plug one end of the supplied cable into the connector socket of the drive, and one into the SCSI connector on the adapter card. Most external drives have two connectors on the back—either connector can be hooked to the PC (see Figure 14.6). You use the other connector to attach another SCSI device or, if the drive is at the end of the bus, to connect a terminator plug. Secure the cable with the guide hooks on both the drive and adapter connector, if provided.

Note

A SCSI device should include some means of terminating the bus, when necessary. The terminator may take the form of a cableless plug that you connect to the second SCSI connector on the drive, or the drive may be self-terminating, in which case there should be a jumper or a switch that you can set to activate termination.

Finally, your external drive should have a SCSI ID select switch on the back. This switch sets the identification number that the host adapter uses to distinguish the drive from the other devices on the bus. The host adapter, by most manufacturers' defaults, should be set for SCSI ID 7, and some (but not all) manufacturers reserve the IDs 0 and 1 for use by hard disk drives. Make sure you set the SCSI ID for the CD-ROM or DVD-ROM drive to any other number—6, 5, or 4, for example. The only rule to follow is to make sure that you do not set the drive for an ID that is already occupied—by either the adapter or any other SCSI peripheral on the bus.

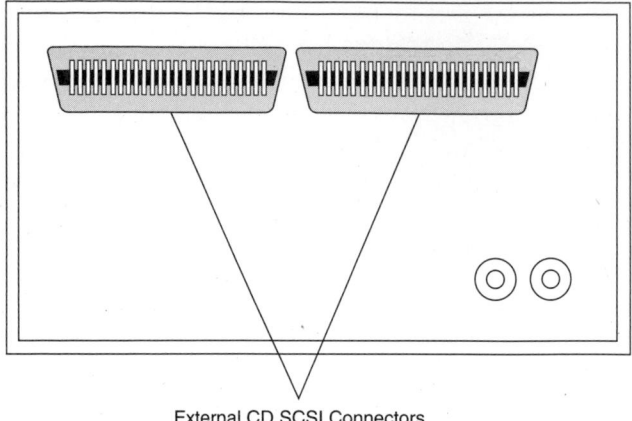

External CD SCSI Connectors

Figure 14.6   Older Centronics-style external CD-ROM drive SCSI connectors.

Internal Drive Installation

Unpack your internal drive kit. You should have the following pieces:

- The drive
- Internal CD-audio cable
- Floppy disks/CD-ROM with device driver software and manual
- Drive rails and mounting screws

Your manufacturer also may have provided a power cable splitter—a bundle of wires with plastic connectors on each of three ends. A disc caddy and owner's manual may also be included. If you do not already have one in the computer, you will also need a SCSI host adapter to connect SCSI peripherals.

Make sure the PC is turned off, and remove the cover from the case. Before installing a SCSI adapter into the PC's expansion bus, connect the SCSI ribbon cable onto the adapter card (see Figure 14.7).

Ribbon Cable and Card Edge Connector

The ribbon cable should be identical on both ends. You'll find a red stripe or dotted line down one side of the outermost edge of the cable. This stripe indicates a pin-1 designation and ensures that the SCSI cable is connected properly into the card and into the drive. If you're lucky, the manufacturer supplied a cable with notches or keys along one edge of the connector. With such a key, you can insert the cable into the card and drive in only one way. Unkeyed cables must be hooked up according to the pin-1 designation.

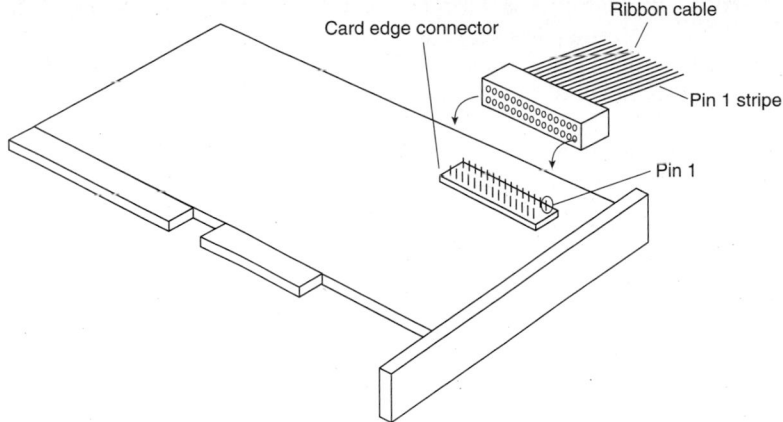

Figure 14.7 Connecting a ribbon cable to a SCSI adapter.

Along one edge of your SCSI adapter, you'll find a double row of 50 brass-colored pins. This is the card edge connector. In small print along the base of this row of pins you should find at least two numbers next to the pins—1 and 50. Aligning the ribbon cable's marked edge over pin 1, carefully and evenly insert the ribbon cable connector.

Now insert the adapter card into a free bus slot in the computer, leaving the drive end of the cable loose for the time being.

Choose a bay in the front of your computer's case for your internal drive. Make sure it's easily accessible from outside and not blocked by other items on your desk. You'll be inserting the CDs or DVDs here, and you'll need the elbow room.

Remove the drive bay cover from the computer case. You may have to loosen some screws to do this, or the cover may just pop out. Inside the drive bay, you should find a metal enclosure with screw holes for mounting the drive. If the drive has mounting holes along its side and fits snugly into the enclosure, you won't need mounting rails. If it's a loose fit, however, mount the rails along the sides of the drive with the rail screws, and then slide the drive into the bay. Secure the drive into the bay with four screws—two on each side. If the rails or drive don't line up evenly with four mounting holes, make sure that you use at least two—one mounting screw on each side. Because you'll be inserting and ejecting many discs over the years, mounting the drive securely is a must.

Once again, find the striped side of the ribbon cable and align it with pin 1 on the drive's edge connector. Either a diagram in your owner's manual or a designation on the connector itself tells you which is pin 1.

The back of the drive has a 4-pin power connector outlet. Inside the case of your PC, at the back of your floppy or hard disk, are power cords—bundled red and yellow wires with plastic connectors on them. You may already have an open power connector lying open in the case. Take the open connector and plug it into the back of the power socket on the CD-ROM or DVD-ROM drive. These connectors can only go in one way. If you do not have an open connector, use the splitter (see Figure 14.8). Disconnect a floppy drive power cord. Attach the splitter to the detached power cord. Plug one of the free ends into the floppy drive, the other into the CD-ROM or DVD-ROM drive.

Note

It's preferable to "borrow" power from the floppy drive connector in this way, rather than from another device. Your hard drive may require more power or be more sensitive to sharing this line than the floppy. If you have no choice—if the splitter and ribbon cable won't reach, for example—you can split off any power cord that hasn't already been split. Check the power cable to ensure that you have a line not already overloaded with another splitter.

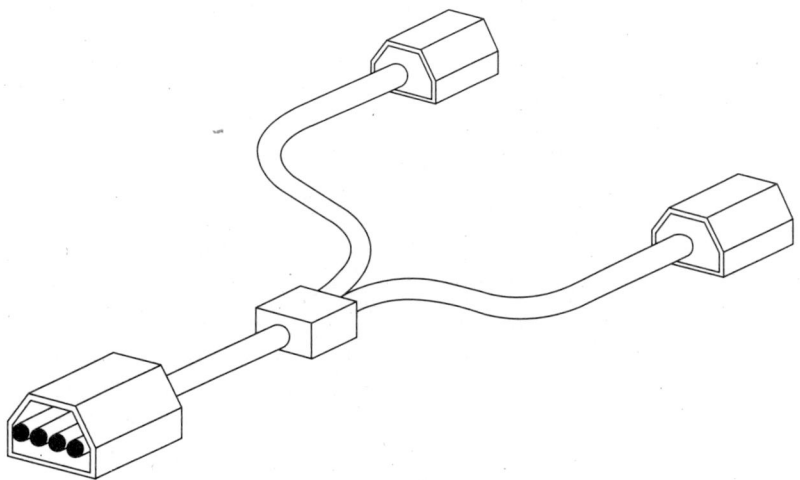

Figure 14.8 Power cord splitter and connector.

Do not replace the PC cover yet—you need to make sure that everything is running perfectly before you seal the case. You're now ready to turn on the computer.

SCSI Chains: Internal, External, or Both

Remember, one of the primary reasons for using the SCSI interface for your CD-ROM or DVD-ROM drive is the ability to connect a string of peripherals from one adapter, thus saving card slots inside the PC and limiting the nightmare of tracking IRQs, DMAs, and I/O memory addresses.

You can add hard drives, scanners, tape backup units, and other SCSI peripherals to this chain (see Figure 14.9). You must keep a few things in mind, however, and chief among them is SCSI termination.

◀◀ See "Termination," p. 540 and 548.

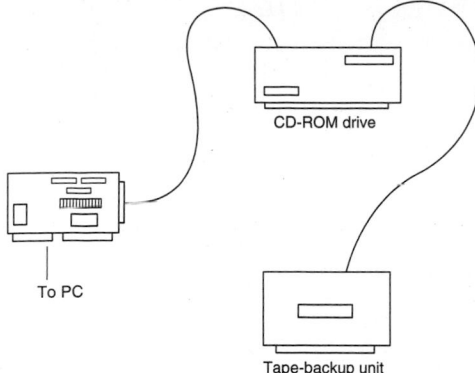

To PC

Figure 14.9 An SCSI chain of devices on one adapter card.

Example One: All External SCSI Devices. Say that you installed your CD-ROM or DVD-ROM drive and added a tape device to the SCSI bus with the extra connector on the back of the optical drive. The first device in this SCSI bus is the adapter card itself. Most modern host adapters are *auto terminating,* meaning they will terminate themselves without your intervention if they are at the end of the bus.

From the card, you ran an external cable to the optical drive, and from the optical drive, you added another cable to the back of the tape unit. You must now terminate the tape unit as well. Most external units are terminated with a SCSI cap—a small connector that plugs into the unused external SCSI connector. These external drive connectors come in two varieties: a SCSI cap and a pass-through terminator. The cap is just that; it plugs over the open connector and covers it. The pass-through terminator, however, plugs into the connector and has an open end into which you can plug the SCSI cable. This type of connector is essential if your external drive has only one SCSI connector; you can plug the drive in and make sure that it's terminated—all with one connector.

Example Two: Internal Chain and Termination. On an internal SCSI bus, the same rules apply: All the internal devices must have unique SCSI ID numbers, and the first and last devices must be terminated. In the case of internal devices, however, you must check for termination. Internal devices typically have DIP switches or terminator packs similar to those on your adapter card. If you install a tape unit as the last device on the chain, it must have some means of terminating the bus. If you place your optical drive in the middle of the bus, you must deactivate its termination. The host adapter at the end of the chain must still be terminated.

Note

Most internal SCSI devices ship with terminating resistors or DIP switches on board, usually the latter. Check your user's manuals for their locations. Any given device may have one, two, or even three such resistors.

Example Three: Internal and External SCSI Devices. If you mix and match external as well as internal devices, follow the same rules. The bottom example shown in Figure 14.10 has an internal CD-ROM drive, terminated and set for SCSI ID 6; the external tape unit also is terminated, and it is using SCSI ID 5. The SCSI adapter itself is set for ID 7 and, most importantly, its termination has been disabled, because it is no longer at the end of the bus.

Note

As with any adapter card, be careful when handling the card itself. Make sure that you ground yourself first.

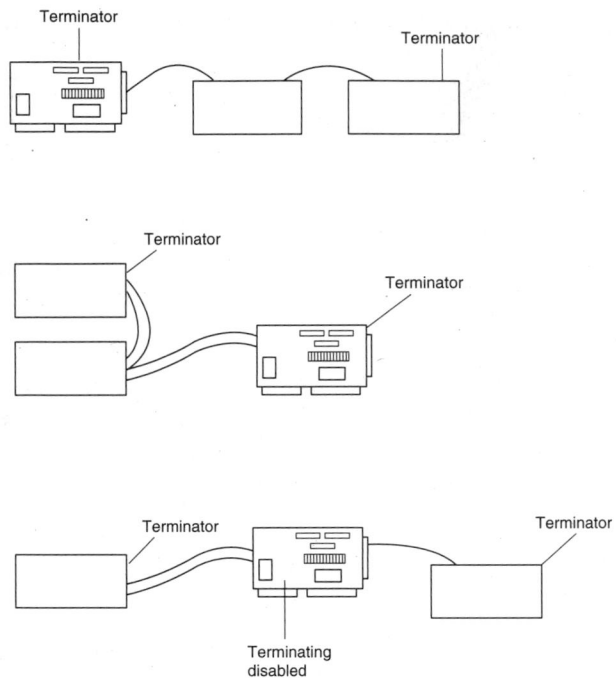

Figure 14.10   Examples of various SCSI termination scenarios.

To help you determine if your SCSI interface card and devices are functioning properly, Adaptec supplies a utility program called the "SCSI Interrogator". Use it to determine which LUN (Logical Unit Numbers) are available for new devices.

If you don't see any devices listed, you might have a termination problem. Shut down your system and your devices. Then, check terminator plugs, switches, or resistor packs. If they appear correct, turn on the external devices about five seconds before you start the system. A multi-switch power director with high-quality surge protection works well for this, since it allows you to turn on individual devices. If the devices fail to show up after you restart the system, you may have a problem with the SCSI device driver software.

One peculiarity of the Adaptec SCSI Interrogator is that it lists a "host adapter #1" that's actually your IDE interface! If your SCSI card isn't working, both "host adapter #0" and "host adapter #1" will actually be IDE. You can tell if this is happening with Windows 9x because it will list "ESDI_506" as the driver version.

Floppy Drive Installation Procedures

A floppy drive is one of the simplest types of drives to install. In most cases, installing a floppy disk drive is a matter of attaching the drive to the computer chassis or case, and then plugging the power and signal cables into the drive. Some type of bracket and screws are normally required to attach the drive to the chassis; however, some chassis are designed to accept the drive with no brackets at all. Any brackets, if needed, are normally included with the chassis or case itself. Several companies listed in the Vendor List, on the CD, specialize in cases, cables, brackets, screw hardware, and other items useful in assembling systems or installing drives.

Note

Because floppy disk drives are generally installed into the same half-height bays as hard disk drives, the physical mounting of the drive in the computer case is the same for both units. See "Hard Disk Installation Procedures," earlier in this chapter, for more information on the process.

When you connect a drive, make sure the power cable is installed properly. The cable is normally keyed so you cannot plug it in backward. Also, install the data and control cable. If there is no key is in this cable, use the colored wire in the cable as a guide to the position of pin 1. This cable is oriented correctly when you plug it in so the colored wire is plugged into the disk drive connector toward the cut-out notch in the drive edge connector. See Chapter 11 for more information about floppy drives and cabling. If the drive LED stays on continuously when the system is running, that is a sure sign you have the floppy cable on backward.

Tape Drive Installation Issues

Tape drives are normally used for backing up data from hard disks, not normally for online storage. There are a wide variety of tape drives on the market, which are discussed in detail in Chapter 12. Each of the tape drive types provide a range of options for installation, usually including both internal and external models. Whether to choose an internal or external drive, and which external drive to choose if that appears to be the best choice for you, is not always a cut-and-dried issue. If you must back up a single computer with a relatively small hard drive, an internal drive might be your best choice. If you have to back up several computers or if you must be able to share data between several computers, a portable would be preferable. If your backup needs are not that simple, however, here are some additional considerations:

■ If your computer has a large hard drive and you backup often or if you administer a large number of systems, you should consider installing large-capacity QIC, DAT or 8mm tape drives. Using these tape formats minimizes the amount of work you must do and the number of tapes you have to store for each computer.

■ If your best choice is a large capacity QIC, DAT, or 8mm tape drive and almost all the computers you administer have an available drive bay, you might choose a portable DAT or 8mm tape system, which you can move from system to system.

The following sections cover some important installation issues for internal and external mounted drives.

Internal Installation

Virtually all internal tape backup drives available today are designed to be installed in a half-height drive bay. Many are designed to be installed in either half-height drive bays or the smaller drive bays generally used for 3 1/2-inch floppy disk drives. Drives that can be installed in 3 1/2-inch floppy disk drive bays generally are shipped in a cage, or frame, which also enables them to be installed in a 5 1/4-inch bay. To install the drive in a 3 1/2-inch bay, remove the cage and the 5 1/4-inch bay faceplate. Most tape drives are between 5 and 9 inches deep and require that much clearance inside the system case. To mount tape drives inside the system, use the same rails or cage apparatus used for floppy disk drives, hard drives, and other devices such as CD-ROM drives.

Internal tape drives require a spare power connector, usually the larger connector used for hard drives, although some may require the smaller power connector used by 3 1/2-inch floppy disk drives. If a power connector is not available inside your system, you can buy a power splitter from a computer store or cable supply vendor.

Internal tape drives also require an interface to the system. Most of the modern drives interface via IDE or SCSI if internally mounted, while externally mounted drives use either parallel, USB, or SCSI. Older drives used the floppy controller to interface to the system, but these are not recommended.

External Installation

If you want to move an external tape drive from computer to computer, you must have the appropriate interface installed in each system on which you want to use the drive. Portable tape backup drives, such as the DAT portables, use either a standard SCSI connection or have an SCSI-to-parallel port converter that uses the computer's parallel port connector. There are no external IDE devices, because that is not allowed in the IDE/ATA standard.

Power is supplied to external units by a transformer that plugs into an ordinary 120v AC wall socket. Generally, the transformer connects to the external tape drive with a small connector. When you choose an external tape drive, be sure you have enough AC power sockets available for your computer, its peripherals, and the tape drive.

Video Hardware

SOME OF THE MAIN TOPICS IN THIS CHAPTER ARE

Video Display Technologies

CRT Monitors

LCD Displays

Flat-Panel LCD Displays

Monitor Selection Criteria

Video Display Adapters

Video Cards for Multimedia

3D Graphics Accelerators

Upgrading or Replacing Your Video Card

Adapter and Display Troubleshooting

Video Display Technologies

As the visual connection between you and your computer, the video display is one of the most important components of your PC. Before CRT monitors came into general use, the teletypewriter was the standard computer interface—a large, loud device that printed the input and output characters on a roll of paper. The first CRT displays were primitive by today's standards; they displayed only text in a single color, but to users at the time they were a great improvement.

Today, PC video displays are much more sophisticated, but you must be careful when selecting video hardware for your computer. Working with even the fastest and most powerful PC can be a chore when the display slows the system down, causes eyestrain, or is not suitable for the tasks you want to accomplish.

The video subsystem of a PC consists of two main components:

■ Monitor (or video display)

■ Video adapter (also called the video card or graphics adapter)

This chapter explores the range of PC video adapters on the market today and the displays that work with them.

Note

The term video, as it is used in this context, does not necessarily imply the existence of a moving image, such as on a television screen. All adapters that feed signals to a monitor or other display are video adapters, whether or not they are used with applications that display moving images, such as multimedia or video-conferencing software.

A monitor may use one of several display technologies. By far the most popular is cathode ray tube (CRT) technology, the same technology used in television sets. CRTs consist of a vacuum tube enclosed in glass. One end of the tube contains an electron gun; the other end contains a screen with a phosphorous coating.

When heated, the electron gun emits a stream of high-speed electrons that are attracted to the other end of the tube. Along the way, a focus control and deflection coil steer the beam to a specific point on the phosphorous screen. When struck by the beam, the phosphor glows. This light is what you see when you watch TV or your computer screen.

The phosphor chemical has a quality called persistence, which indicates how long this glow remains onscreen. Persistence is what causes a faint image to remain on your TV screen for a few seconds after you turn the set off. The scanning frequency of the display specifies how often the image is refreshed. You should have a good match between persistence and scanning frequency so that the image has less flicker (which occurs when the persistence is too low) and no ghost images (which occurs when the persistence is too high).

The electron beam moves very quickly, sweeping the screen from left to right in lines from top to bottom, in a pattern called a raster. The horizontal scan rate refers to the speed at which the electron beam moves laterally across the screen.

During its sweep, the beam strikes the phosphor wherever an image should appear onscreen. The beam also varies in intensity to produce different levels of brightness. Because the glow begins to fade almost immediately, the electron beam must continue to sweep the screen to maintain an image—a practice called redrawing or refreshing the screen.

Most current CRT displays have an ideal refresh rate (also called the vertical scan frequency) of about 85 hertz (Hz), which means that the screen is refreshed 85 times per second. Refresh rates that are too low cause the screen to flicker, contributing to eyestrain. The higher the refresh rate, the better for your eyes.

It is important that the refresh rates expected by your monitor match those produced by your video card. If you have mismatched rates, you will not see an image and may actually damage your monitor.

Although a few monitors have a fixed refresh rate, most monitors support a range of frequencies; this support provides built-in compatibility with future video standards (described in the "Video Display Adapters" section later in this chapter). A monitor that supports many video standards is called a multiple-frequency monitor. Most monitors today are multiple-frequency monitors, which means they support operation with a variety of popular video signal standards. Different vendors call their multiple-frequency monitors by different trade names, including multisync, multifrequency, multiscan, autosynchronous, and autotracking.

Phosphor-based screens come in two styles: curved and flat. The typical display screen is curved; it bulges outward from the middle of the screen. This design is consistent with the vast majority of CRT designs (the same as the tube in most television sets).

The traditional screen is curved both vertically and horizontally. Some models use the Trinitron design, which is curved only horizontally and is flat vertically. Many people prefer this flatter screen because it shows less glare and a higher-quality, more accurate image. The disadvantage is that the technology required to produce flat-screen displays is more expensive, resulting in higher prices for the monitors.

Alternative display designs are available as well, including flat-panel LCD displays.

▶▶ See "LCD Displays," p. 806.

▶▶ See "Flat-Panel LCD Displays," p. 808.

CRT Monitors

A monitor requires a source of input. The signals that run to your monitor come from a video adapter inside or plugged into your computer. Some computers—such as those that use the low profile (LPX) or new low profile (NLX) motherboard form factor—contain this adapter circuitry on the motherboard. Most systems, however, use Baby-AT or ATX-style motherboards and usually incorporate the video adapter on a separate circuit board that is plugged into an expansion or bus slot. The expansion cards that produce video signals are called video cards, or graphics cards. The term video adapter is applicable to either integrated or separate video circuitry. Whether the video adapter is built into the motherboard or found on a separate card, the circuitry operates the same way and generally uses the same components.

All on One

One product, the Cyrix MediaGX, offers a unique two-chip solution that encompasses most of the multiple chips found on a system board, including CPU, memory controller, sound, and video. The video portion of the MediaGX is an external ICS clock/RAMDAC chip.

The CPU portion of the MediaGX chipset contains the graphics interface and acceleration features. The MediaGX uses a shared memory technique for its frame buffer RAM, using some of the system's memory for video operations. The amount of memory used by video operations varies with the amount of video memory required for the current image.

This memory-sharing technique is called Unified Memory Architecture (UMA); it reduces system cost, but also reduces system performance.

▶▶ See "The Digital-to-Analog Converter (RAMDAC)," p. 839.

LCD Displays

Borrowing technology from laptop manufacturers, more and more monitor makers market monitors with LCD (liquid crystal display) displays. LCDs have low-glare screens that are completely flat and low power requirements (5 watts versus nearly 100 watts for an ordinary monitor). The color quality of an active-matrix LCD panel actually exceeds that of most CRT displays.

At this point, however, LCD screens usually are more limited in resolution than typical CRTs and are more expensive; for example, a 15-inch LCD screen can cost more than $1,000—more than twice the cost of a high-quality 17-inch CRT monitor. However, it is important to consider that an LCD screen provides a larger viewable image than a CRT monitor of the same size. Four basic LCD choices are available: passive-matrix monochrome, passive-matrix color, active-matrix analog color, and the latest—active-matrix digital. The passive-matrix designs are also available in single- and dual-scan versions. The passive-matrix monochrome and color panels are primarily found in low-cost notebook computer displays or in industrial-use desktop display panels because of their relatively low cost and enhanced durability compared to active-matrix models. Desktop LCD panels are analog or digital units.

Note

The most common type of passive-matrix display uses a supertwist numatic design, so these panels are often referred to as STNs. Active-matrix panels usually use a thin-film transistor design and are thus referred to as TFTs.

In an LCD, a polarizing filter creates two separate light waves. The polarizing filter allows light waves that are aligned only with the filter to pass through. After passing through the polarizing filter, the remaining light waves are all aligned in the same direction. By aligning a second polarizing filter at a right angle to the first, all those waves are blocked. By changing the angle of the second polarizing filter, the amount of light allowed to pass can be changed. It is the role of the liquid crystal cell to change the angle of polarization and control the amount of light that passes. In a color LCD, an additional filter has three cells for each pixel—one each for displaying red, green, and blue.

The light wave passes through a liquid-crystal cell, with each color segment having its own cell. The liquid crystals are rod-shaped molecules that flow like a liquid. They enable light to pass straight through, but an electrical charge alters their orientation and the orientation of light passing through them. Although monochrome LCDs do not have color filters, they can have multiple cells per pixel for controlling shades of gray.

In a passive-matrix LCD, each cell is controlled by the electrical charges of two transistors, determined by the cell's row and column positions on the display. The number of transistors along the screen's horizontal and vertical edges determines the resolution of the screen. For example, a screen with an 800×600 resolution has 800 transistors on its horizontal edge and 600 on the vertical, for a total of 1,400. As the cell reacts to the pulsing charge from its two transistors, it twists the light wave, with stronger charges twisting the light wave more. Supertwist refers to the orientation of the liquid crystals, comparing on mode to off mode—the greater the twist, the higher the contrast.

Charges in passive-matrix LCDs are pulsed, therefore the displays lack the brilliance of active-matrix, which provides a constant charge to each cell. To increase the brilliance, most vendors have turned to a new technique called double-scan LCD, which splits passive-matrix screens into a top half and bottom half, reducing the time between each pulse. In addition to increasing the brightness, dual-scan designs also increase the response time and therefore the perceptible speed of the display, making this type more usable for full-motion video or other applications where the displayed information changes rapidly.

In an active-matrix LCD, each cell has its own dedicated transistor behind the panel to charge it and twist the light wave. Thus, an 800×600 active-matrix display has 480,000 transistors. This provides a brighter image than passive-matrix displays because the cell can maintain a constant, rather than a momentary, charge. However, active-matrix technology uses more energy than passive-matrix. With a dedicated transistor for every cell, active-matrix displays are more difficult and expensive to produce.

Note

Because an LCD display requires a specified number of transistors to support each cell, there are no multiple frequency displays of this type. All the pixels on an LCD screen are of a fixed size, although CRT pixels are variable. Thus, LCD displays are designed to be operated at a specific resolution. Before purchasing this type of display, be sure your video adapter supports the same resolution as the screen and that the resolution will be sufficient for your needs throughout the life of the monitor.

High-quality LCD displays for desktop computers and their matching video controllers usually feature onboard image scalers to allow different resolutions on the LCD display. This is an important feature to check for before purchasing a flat panel (FP) LCD display.

▶▶ See "Flat-Panel LCD Displays," p. 808.

In both active- and passive-matrix LCDs, the second polarizing filter controls how much light passes through each cell. Cells twist the wavelength of light to closely match the filter's allowable wavelength. The more light that passes through the filter at each cell, the brighter the pixel.

Monochrome LCDs achieve grayscales (up to 64) by varying the brightness of a cell or dithering cells in an on-and-off pattern. Color LCDs, on the other hand, dither the three-color cells and control their brilliance to achieve different colors on the screen. Double-scan passive-matrix LCDs (also known as DSTN) have recently gained in popularity because they approach the quality of active-matrix displays but do not cost much more to produce than other passive-matrix displays. Although DSTN panels offer better on-axis (straight-ahead) viewing quality than straight passive-matrix panels, their off-axis (viewing at an angle) performance is still poor when compared to active-matrix (TFT) panels.

The big problem with active-matrix LCDs is that the manufacturing yields are low, forcing higher prices. This means many of the panels produced have more than a certain maximum number of failed transistors. The resulting low yields limit the production capacity and incurs higher prices.

In the past, several hot, miniature CRTs were needed to light an LCD screen, but portable computer manufacturers now use a single tube the size of a cigarette. Fiber-optic technology evenly spreads light emitted from the tube across an entire display.

Thanks to supertwist and triple-supertwist LCDs, today's screens enable you to see the screen clearly from more angles with better contrast and lighting. To improve readability, especially in dim light, some laptops include backlighting or edgelighting (also called sidelighting). Backlit screens provide light from a panel behind the LCD. Edgelit screens get their light from the small fluorescent tubes mounted along the sides of the screen. Some older laptops excluded such lighting systems to lengthen battery life. Most modern laptops enable you to run the backlight at a reduced power setting that dims the display but that allows for longer battery life.

The best color displays are active-matrix or thin-film transistor (TFT) panels, in which each pixel is controlled by three transistors (for red, green, and blue). Active-matrix screen refreshes and redraws are immediate and accurate, with much less ghosting and blurring than in passive-matrix LCDs (which control pixels via rows and columns of transistors along the edges of the screen). Active-matrix displays are also much brighter and can easily be read at an angle.

Note

An alternative to LCD screens is gas-plasma technology, typically known for its black and orange screens in some of the older Toshiba notebook computers. Some companies are incorporating full-color gas-plasma technology for desktop screens and possibly color high-definition television (HDTV) flat-panel screens, such as the Philips Flat TV.

Flat-Panel LCD Displays

LCD desktop monitors, once seen mainly on the office sets of futuristic TV shows, are now becoming an increasingly reasonable choice for use in today's office computing environment.

LCD desktop monitors offer the following benefits over conventional CRT (Cathode Ray Tube) "glass tube" monitors:

- Virtually 100 percent of LCD size is viewable area, compared to a loss of 1 to 1 1/2-inches of viewable area versus the diagonal tube measurement on CRT monitors. Thus, a 15-inch LCD provides a viewable area roughly equal to a typical 17-inch CRT monitor.

- Small front-to-back dimensions free up desk space.

- Direct addressing of display (each pixel in the picture corresponds with a transistor) and always perfect alignment provide a high-precision image that lacks CRT's problems with pincushion or barrel distortion or convergence errors (halos around the edges of onscreen objects).

- Low power consumption and less heat buildup make LCD units less expensive to operate.

- Because LCD units lack a CRT, no concerns exist about electromagnetic VLF or ELF emissions.

- A number of LCD panels offer a pivoting feature, enabling the unit to swivel 90 degrees, allowing a choice of the traditional "landscape" horizontal mode for Web-surfing and the "portrait" vertical mode for word processing and page-layout programs.

Before you rush to the store to purchase an LCD desktop monitor, you should consider several potential drawbacks:

- If you routinely switch display resolutions (as Web developers do to preview their work), LCD monitors must take one of two approaches to change resolutions: reduce the onscreen image to occupy only the pixels of the new resolution, thus using only a portion of a typical 1024×768 LCD panel to display a 640×480 image, or scale the image to occupy the entire screen. Scaling will be very common in the future because the Digital Display Work Group (DDWG) standard for LCD desktop displays specifies that the scaling must take place in the display panel, the graphics controller, or both places. Look at the quality of a scaled image if using different resolutions is important to you.

- You have a choice between digital and analog LCD panels. Digital LCD panels generally offer higher image quality because no conversion of analog to digital signals occurs, but they require a special digital display card. These display cards may be included in the price of the panel, or they may be an extra-cost item.

Note

Video card and chipset makers such as 3Dfx, nVidia, S3, ATI, and others are rapidly adding support for digital and analog display panels to their newest 3D chipsets and video cards.

- If you choose an analog LCD panel, you'll usually save money and be able to use your existing video card, but image quality for both text and graphics may suffer because of the conversion of the computer's digital signal to analog (at the video card) and back to digital again (inside the LCD panel). The conversion can lead to "pixel jitter" or "pixel swim," in which adjacent LCD cells are turned on and off by the display's inability to determine which cells should stay on and stay off. Most panels come with adjustment software to reduce this display-quality problem, but you may not be able to eliminate it entirely.

- High-quality LCD display panels of either digital or analog type are great for displaying sharp text and graphics, but they often can't display as wide a range of very light and very dark colors as CRTs.

- LCD displays don't react as quickly as CRTs, which can cause full-motion video, full-screen 3D games, and animation to look smeared onscreen.

With prices dropping, sizes increasing, and computer companies such as Compaq already including built-in video connectors especially designed for LCD panels, now is a great time to consider buying an LCD panel for your desktop. Make sure that you use the following criteria when you consider purchasing an LCD monitor:

- Evaluate the panel both at its native resolution and at any other resolutions you plan to use.

- If you're considering an analog LCD panel, try it with the video card(s) you plan to use and be sure to check the panel maker's list of suggested video cards for each model.

- If you're considering a digital LCD panel, determine whether the bundled video card (if any) supports the features you need: for example, OpenGL and high-speed 3D support are important for game players; VGA-to-TV support is important for video producers. If the bundled card lacks the features you need, can you get the features in another card? Because several rival standards exist, make sure any alternative digital display cards support the particular panel you want to buy; PanelLink and its successor, Digital Visual Interface (DVI), are the most popular.

- Make sure your system has a suitable expansion slot for the recommended or bundled video-card type. Many low-cost systems today feature onboard AGP video, which can't be upgraded. As the move to LCD panels continues, more of these systems should feature built-in support for LCD displays, but this could be a problem for some time to come.

- Evaluate the panel and card combo's performance on video clips and animation if you work with full-motion video or animated presentation programs.

- Because most video cards aren't optimized for the pivoting feature found in many LCD panels, the portrait mode's performance is often as much as 10–45 percent slower than the default landscape mode.

- Although active-matrix (analog) and digital LCD monitors have much wider viewing areas than do passive-matrix and dual-scan LCD panels used in low-cost notebook computers, their viewing angles are still usually much less than CRTs. This is an important consideration if you're planning to use your LCD monitor for group presentations. In a test of 29 different 15-inch LCD panels in *PC Magazine*'s April 20, 1999 issue, horizontal viewing angles without noticeable color shift ranged from as little as 50 degrees to as much as 115 degrees (higher is better). Most panels tested had viewing angles between 50–75 degrees, a very narrow viewing angle compared to CRTs. A typical CRT monitor allows viewing up to 120 degrees without noticeable color shift.

- A high-contrast ratio (luminance difference between white and black) makes for sharper text and vivid colors. A typical CRT has a contrast ratio of about 245:1. LCD panels in the April 20, 1999 *PC Magazine* test had contrast ratios ranging from a low of 129:1 to a high of 431:1, with more than half of the units tested exceeding the 245:1 contrast ratio of typical CRTs.

- Features such as integrated speakers and USB (Universal Serial Bus) hubs are pleasant additions, but your eyes should make the final decision about which panel is best for you.

Monitor Selection Criteria

Stores offer a dizzying variety of monitor choices, from the low-cost units bundled with computers to large-screen tubes that cost more than many systems. Because a monitor may account for a large part of the price of your computer system, you need to know what to look for when you shop for a monitor.

Monochrome Versus Color

During the early years of the IBM PC and the compatibles that followed, owners had only two video choices: color using a CGA display adapter and monochrome using an MDA display adapter. Since then, many adapter and display options have hit the market.

Monochrome monitors (now all but obsolete) produce images of one color. In the early days, the most popular color was amber, followed by white and green. The color of the monitor is determined by the color of the phosphors on the CRT screen. Some monochrome monitors with white phosphors can support many shades of gray. Color monitors used more sophisticated technology than monochrome monitors, which accounted for their higher prices. Whereas a monochrome picture tube contains one electron gun, a color tube contains three guns arranged in a triangular shape called a delta configuration. Instead of amber, white, or green phosphors, the monitor screen contains phosphor triads, which consist of one red phosphor, one green phosphor, and one blue phosphor arranged in the same pattern as the electron guns. These three primary colors can be mixed to produce all other colors.

Monochrome monitors are difficult to find these days, which is a shame because they do still have applications. It has always seemed wasteful to me to devote a color monitor to a system running an OS with a mono-color display, such as on a NetWare server. The days of using non-VGA displays are about over because the industry is moving to build systems based on the Microsoft/Intel PC99 Design specifications. This "rulebook" for upcoming PCs mandates the elimination of ISA slots. Because Monochrome Display Adapter (MDA) cards are strictly ISA-based, future servers based on PC99 standards and beyond will have to use VGA, like it or not. Some vendors made monochrome VGA monitors, but these have never been common.

The Right Size

Monitors come in different sizes ranging from 9-inch to 42-inch diagonal measure. The larger the monitor, the higher the price tag—after you get beyond 17-inch displays, the prices skyrocket. The most common monitor sizes are 14, 15, 17, and 21 inches. These diagonal measurements, unfortunately, often represent not the size of the actual image that the screen displays, but the size of the tube.

As a result, comparing one company's 15-inch monitor to that of another may be unfair unless you actually measure the active screen area. The active screen area refers to the diagonal measure of the lighted area on the screen. In other words, if you are running Windows, the viewing area is the actual diagonal measure of the desktop.

This area can vary widely from monitor to monitor, so one company's 17-inch monitor may display a 15-inch image, and another company's 17-inch monitor may present a 15 1/2-inch image.

Table 15.1 shows the monitor's advertised diagonal screen size, along with the approximate diagonal measure of the actual active viewing area for the most common display sizes.

Table 15.1   Advertised Screen Size Versus Actual Viewing Area

Monitor Size (in Inches)	Viewing Area (in Inches)
12	10 1/2
14	12 1/2
15	13 1/2
16	14 1/2
17	15 1/2
18	16 1/2
19	17 1/2
20	18 1/2
21	19 1/2

The size of the actual viewable area varies from manufacturer to manufacturer but tends to be approximately 1 1/2-inches less than the actual screen size. However, you can adjust some monitors—such as some models made by NEC, for example—to display a high-quality image that completely fills the tube from edge to edge. Other makes can fill the screen also, but some of them do so only by pushing the monitor beyond its comfortable limits. The result is a distorted image that is worse than the monitor's smaller, properly adjusted picture.

This phenomenon is a well-known monitor-purchasing caveat, and as a result, most manufacturers and vendors have begun advertising the size of the active viewing area of their monitors along with the screen size. This makes it easier for consumers to compare what they are paying for.

In most cases, the 17-inch monitor is currently the best bargain in the industry. A 17-inch monitor is recommended for new systems, especially when running Windows, and is not much more expensive than a 15-inch display. I recommend a 17-inch monitor as the minimum you should consider for most normal applications. Low-end applications can still get away with a 15-inch display, but you will be limited in the screen resolutions that you can view comfortably. Displays of 18 to 21 inches or larger are recommended for high-end systems, especially where graphics applications are the major focus.

Larger monitors are particularly handy for applications such as CAD and desktop publishing, in which the smallest details must be clearly visible. With a 17-inch or larger display, you can see nearly an entire 8 1/2×11-inch print page in 100 percent view; in other words, what you see onscreen virtually matches the page that will be printed. This feature is called WYSIWYG—short for "what you see is what you get." If you can see the entire page at its actual size, you can save yourself the trouble of printing several drafts before you get it right.

With the popularity of the Internet, monitor size and resolution become even more of an issue. Many Web pages are being designed for 1,024×768 resolution, which requires a 17-inch CRT display as a minimum to handle without eyestrain and inadequate focus. Because of their much tighter dot pitch, LCD displays in laptop computers can handle that resolution easily on 13.3– or even some 12.1-inch displays. Using 1,024×768 resolution means you will be able to view most Web pages without scrolling sideways, which is a major convenience.

Note

Although many monitors smaller than 17 inches are physically capable of running at 1,024x768 and even higher resolutions, most people have trouble reading print at that size.

If you have Windows 98, a partial solution is to enable the larger icons by opening the Display control panel, clicking the Settings tab, and clicking Advanced. In the Font Size drop-down list, choose Large Fonts. With either Windows 95 or 98, you can use Large Fonts, but many programs have problems with font sizes larger than the default Small Fonts setting.

Monitor Resolution

Resolution is the amount of detail a monitor can render. This quantity is expressed in the number of horizontal and vertical picture elements, or pixels, contained in the screen. The greater the number of pixels, the more detailed the images. The resolution required depends on the application. Character-based applications (such as DOS command-line programs) require little resolution, whereas graphics-intensive applications (such as desktop publishing and Windows software) require a great deal.

It's important to realize that CRTs are designed to handle a range of resolutions natively, but LCD panels (both desktop and notebook) are built to run a single native resolution and must scale to other choices.

As PC video technology developed, the screen resolutions supported by video adapters grew at a steady pace. The following list shows standard resolutions used in PC video adapters and the terms commonly used to describe them:

Resolution	Acronym	Standard Designation
640x480	VGA	Video Graphics Array
800x600	SVGA	Super VGA
1,024x768	XGA	eXtended Graphics Array
1,280x1,024	UVGA	Ultra VGA

Today, the term VGA is still in common usage as a reference to the standard 640x480 16-color display that the Windows operating systems use as their default. The 15-pin connector to which you connect the monitor on most video adapters is also often called a VGA plug.

However, the terms SVGA, XGA, and UVGA have fallen into disuse. The industry now describes screen resolutions simply by citing the number of pixels. Nearly all the video adapters sold today support the 640x480, 800x600, and 1,024x768 pixel resolutions at several color depths, and many support 1,280x1,024 and higher as well.

Because all CRT and most new and upcoming LCD displays can handle different resolutions, you have a choice. As you'll see later in this chapter, the combinations of resolution and color depth (number of colors onscreen) that you can choose can be limited by how much RAM your graphics adapter has onboard. But, if your graphics adapter has at least 4MB or more, you're free to choose from many settings based on your needs.

What resolution do you want for your display? Generally, the higher the resolution, the larger the display you will want.

Note

To understand this issue, you might want to try different resolutions on your system. As you change from 640×480 to 800×600 and 1024×768, you'll notice several changes to the appearance of your screen.

At 640×480, text and onscreen icons are very large. Because the screen elements used for the Windows 9x desktop and software menus are at a fixed pixel width and height, you'll notice that they shrink in size onscreen as you change to the higher resolutions. You'll be able to see more of your document or Web page onscreen at the higher resolutions because each object requires less of the screen.

If you are operating at 640×480 resolution, for example, you should find a 14- or 15-inch monitor to be comfortable. At 1,024×768, you probably will find that the display of a 15-inch monitor is too small; therefore, you will prefer to use a larger one, such as a 17-inch monitor. The following list shows the minimum-size monitors I recommend to properly display the resolutions that users typically select:

Resolution	Minimum Recommended Monitor
640×480	13-inch
800×600	15-inch
1,024×768	17-inch
1,280×1,024	21-inch

These minimum recommended display sizes are the advertised diagonal display dimensions of the monitor. Note that these are not necessarily the limits of the given monitors' capabilities, but they are what I recommend. In other words, most 15-inch monitors are able to display resolutions at least up to 1,024×768, but the characters, icons, and other information are too small for most users and can cause eyestrain if you try to run beyond the recommended 800×600 resolution.

One exception to this rule is with the LCD displays used in portable systems and a few desktop monitors. LCD-type displays are always crisp and perfectly focused by nature. Also, the dimensions advertised for the LCD screens represent the exact size of the viewable image, unlike most conventional CRT-based monitors. So, the 12.1-inch LCD panels found on many notebook systems today actually have a viewable area with a 12.1-inch diagonal measurement. This measurement is comparable to a 14-inch or even a 15-inch CRT display in most cases. In addition, the LCD is so crisp that screens of a given size can easily handle resolutions that are higher than what would otherwise be acceptable on a CRT. For example, many of the high-end notebook systems now use 13.3-inch LCD panels that feature 1,024×768 resolution. Although this resolution would be unacceptable on a 14-inch or 15-inch CRT display, it works well on the 13.3-inch LCD panel due to the crystal-clear image.

Dot Pitch

Another important specification that denotes the quality of a given CRT monitor is its dot pitch. In a monochrome monitor, the picture element is a screen phosphor, but in a color monitor, the picture element is a phosphor triad. Dot pitch, which applies only to color monitors, is the distance (in millimeters) between phosphor triads. Screens with a small dot pitch have a smaller space between the phosphor triads. As a result, the picture elements are closer together, producing a sharper picture on the screen. Conversely, screens with a large dot pitch tend to produce images that are less clear.

Note

Dot pitch is not an issue with LCD portable or desktop display panels because of their design.

The original IBM PC color monitor had a dot pitch of 0.43mm, which is considered to be poor by almost any standard. Smaller pitch values indicate sharper images. Most monitors have a dot pitch between 0.25 and 0.30mm, with state-of-the-art monitors at the lower end of the scale. To avoid grainy images, look for a dot pitch of 0.26mm or smaller. Be wary of monitors with anything larger than a 0.28mm dot pitch; they lack clarity for fine text and graphics. Although you can save money by buying monitors with smaller tubes or a higher dot pitch, the trade-off isn't worth it.

The dot pitch is one of the most important specifications of any monitor, but it is not the only specification. It is entirely possible that you may find the image on a monitor with a slightly higher dot pitch superior to that of a monitor with a lower dot pitch. There is no substitute for actually looking at images and text on the monitors you're considering purchasing.

Image Brightness and Contrast (LCD Panels)

As previously mentioned, dot pitch is not a factor in deciding which LCD panel to purchase. A corresponding consideration that applies both to LCDs and CRTs, but that is more important on LCDs, is the brightness of the display.

Although a dim CRT display is almost certainly a sign either of improper brightness control or a dying monitor, brightness in LCD displays can vary a great deal from one model to another. Brightness for LCD panels is measured in candelas per square meter, which for some reason is referred to as a "nit." Typical ratings for analog and digital display panels range from 150–250 nits. A good combination is a high nit rating and a high contrast rating.

Interlaced Versus Noninterlaced

Monitors and video adapters may support interlaced or noninterlaced resolution. In noninterlaced (conventional) mode, the electron beam sweeps the screen in lines from top to bottom, one line after the other, completing the screen in one pass. In interlaced mode, the electron beam also sweeps the screen from top to bottom, but it does so in two passes—sweeping the odd lines first and the even lines second. Each pass takes half the time of a full pass in noninterlaced mode. Thus, a monitor such as IBM's 8514/A unit, which offered an 87Hz interlaced mode, could redraw the screen twice in the same time as a monitor running at a noninterlaced mode of 43.5Hz (43.5×2 = 87).

Note

Hz (hertz) refers to how many times the monitor can refresh (redraw) the picture per second. For example, a monitor rated at 85Hz would redraw the picture 85 times per second.

This technique redraws the screen faster and provides more stable images, but it also produces what is often a very noticeable flicker. If you switch your video adapter to a higher screen resolution and you find that your solid, satisfactory picture suddenly seems flickery, you have probably switched to a resolution that your hardware only supports in interlaced mode. Different users react to interlaced displays differently. To some people, it is hardly noticeable, whereas to others, looking at the screen is unbearable.

Caution

It's not unheard of for people with neurological disorders such as epilepsy to be profoundly affected by the flicker produced by monitors running in interlaced mode or at low refresh rates. These people should take adequate precautions before adjusting their video display setting and, if possible, be aware of their physical limitations.

Monitors that use interlacing can use lower refresh rates, thus lessening their cost. The drawback is that interlacing depends on the ability of the eye to combine two nearly identical lines, separated by a gap, into one solid line. If you are looking for high-quality video, however, you should avoid interlacing at all costs and get a video adapter and monitor that support high-resolution, noninterlaced displays.

If you must use an interlaced display, try using a high-quality, dark-glass, anti-glare filter on the front of the monitor. This reduces the apparent flicker as well as the glare, and it improves your vision and your comfort.

Energy and Safety

A properly selected monitor can save energy. Many PC manufacturers are trying to meet the Environmental Protection Agency's Energy Star requirements. Any PC-and-monitor combination that consumes less than 60 watts (30 watts apiece) during idle periods can use the Energy Star logo. Some research shows that such "green" PCs can save each user about $70 per year in electricity costs.

Power Management

Monitors, one of the most power-hungry computer components, can contribute to those savings. One of the first energy-saving standards for monitors was VESA's Display Power-Management Signaling (DPMS) spec, which defines the signals that a computer sends to a monitor to indicate idle times. The computer or video card decides when to send these signals.

In Windows 9x, you need to enable this feature if you want to use it because it's turned off by default. To enable it, open the Display properties in the control panel, switch to the Screen Saver tab and make sure the Energy Star low-power settings and Monitor shutdown settings are checked. You can adjust how long the system remains idle before the monitor picture is blanked or the monitor shuts down completely.

Intel and Microsoft have jointly developed the Advanced Power Management (APM) specification, which defines a BIOS-based interface between hardware that is capable of power-management functions and an operating system that implements power-management policies. In short, this means that you can configure an OS such as Windows 9x to switch your monitor into a low-power mode after an interval of nonuse, and even to shut it off entirely. For these actions to occur, however, the monitor, the system BIOS, and the operating system must all support the APM standard.

With Windows 98 (and Windows 2000), Microsoft introduced a more comprehensive power management method called Advanced Configuration and Power Interface, or ACPI for short. ACPI also works with displays, hard drives, and other devices supported by APM, as well as allowing the computer to "automatically turn peripherals on and off, such as CD-ROMs, network cards, hard disk drives, printers, as well as consumer devices connected to the PC such as VCRs, televisions, telephones, and stereos."

Although APM compatibility has been standard in common BIOSes for several years, a number of recent-model computers from major manufacturers required BIOS upgrades to add this feature when Windows 98 was introduced.

Note

ACPI support is installed on Windows 98 computers if an ACPI-compliant BIOS is present when Windows 98 is first installed. If an ACPI-compliant BIOS is installed after the Windows 98 installation, it will be ignored. Fortunately, Windows 98 still supports APM as well. See Microsoft's FAQ for ACPI on the Microsoft Web site.

For displays, power management is implemented when DPMS signals the monitor to enter into the various APM modes. The basis of the DPMS standard is the condition of the synchronization signals being sent to the display. By altering these signals, a DPMS-compatible monitor can be forced into the various APM modes by an operating system that supports the power-management standard. You can configure the monitor to enter the standby and suspend modes at predefined intervals when the computer is not in use, and even shift back to the on mode when certain events occur, such as when a modem phone line rings.

The defined monitor states in DPMS are as follows:

- *On*. Refers to the state of the display when it is in full operation.
- *Stand-By*. Defines an optional operating state of minimal power reduction with the shortest recovery time.
- *Suspend*. Refers to a level of power management in which substantial power reduction is achieved by the display. The display can have a longer recovery time from this state than from the Stand-By state.
- *Off*. Indicates that the display is consuming the lowest level of power and is nonoperational. Recovery from this state may optionally require the user to manually power on the monitor.

Table 15.2 summarizes the DPMS modes.

Table 15.2   Display Power Management Signaling

State	Horizontal	Vertical	Video	Power Savings	Recovery Time
On	Pulses	Pulses	Active	None	n/a
Stand-By	No Pulses	Pulses	Blanked	Minimal	Short
Suspend	Pulses	No Pulses	Blanked	Substantial	Longer
Off	No Pulses	No Pulses	Blanked	Maximum	System Dependent

Emissions

Another trend in green monitor design is to minimize the user's exposure to potentially harmful electromagnetic fields. Several medical studies indicate that these electromagnetic emissions may cause health problems, such as miscarriages, birth defects, and cancer. The risk may be low, but if you spend a third of your day (or more) in front of a computer monitor, that risk is increased.

The concern is that VLF (very low frequency) and ELF (extremely low frequency) emissions might affect the body. These two emissions come in two forms: electric and magnetic. Some research indicates that ELF magnetic emissions are more threatening than VLF emissions because they interact with the natural electric activity of body cells. Monitors are not the only culprits; significant ELF emissions also come from electric blankets and power lines.

Note

ELF and VLF are a form of electromagnetic radiation; they consist of radio frequencies below those used for normal radio broadcasting.

These two frequencies are covered by the Swedish monitor-emission standards created by SWEDAC, the Swedish Board for Accreditation and Conformity Assessment, the Swedish regulatory agency. In many European countries, government agencies and businesses buy only low-emission monitors. The degree to which emissions are reduced varies from monitor to monitor. The Swedish government's MPR I standard, which dates back to 1987, is the least restrictive. MPR II, established in 1990, is significantly stronger (adding maximums for ELF and VLF emissions) and is the level that you will most likely find in low-emission monitors today.

A more stringent 1992 standard called TCO further tightens the MPR II requirements. In addition, it is a more broad-based environmental standard that includes power-saving requirements and emission limits. Most of the major manufacturers currently offer monitors that meet the TCO standard. TCO '92, the original standard, covered monitors only. Later version of the standard, TCO '95 and TCO '99, don't change the requirements for monitors but broaden the certification to other parts of the computer system and its manufacturing process. You can get more information about the various levels of TCO certification from its Web site.

Today, virtually all monitors on the market support at least MPR II, but TCO is primarily supported on mid-range to high-end monitors from most vendors.

If you aren't using a low-emission monitor yet, you can take other steps to protect yourself. The most important is to stay at arm's length (about 28 inches) from the front of your monitor.

When you move a couple of feet away, ELF magnetic emission levels usually drop to those of a typical office with fluorescent lights. Likewise, monitor emissions are weakest at the front of a monitor, so stay at least three feet from the sides and backs of nearby monitors and five feet from any photocopiers, which are also strong sources of ELF.

Electromagnetic emissions should not be your only concern; you also should be concerned about screen glare. In fact, some of the antiglare panels that fit in front of a monitor screen not only reduce eyestrain, they also cut ELF and VLF emissions.

Frequencies

One essential trick is to choose a monitor that works with your selected video adapter. Today, virtually all monitors are multiple-frequency (also called multiscanning and multifrequency) units that accommodate a range of standards, including those that are not yet standardized. However, big differences exist in how well different monitors cope with different video adapters.

Tip

High-quality monitors retain their value longer than most other computer components. Although it's common for a newer, faster processor to come out right after you have purchased your computer, or to find the same model with a bigger hard disk for the same money, a good quality monitor should outlast your computer. If you purchase a unit with the expectation that your own personal requirements will grow over the years, you may be able to save money on your next system by reusing your old monitor.

Two essential features are front-mounted controls, which can memorize screen settings, and built-in diagnostics. Built-in diagnostics can save you unnecessary trips to the repair shop.

With multiple-frequency monitors, you must match the range of horizontal and vertical frequencies the monitor accepts with those generated by your video adapter. The wider the range of signals, the more expensive—and more versatile—the monitor. Your video adapter's vertical and horizontal frequencies must fall within the ranges supported by your monitor. The vertical frequency (or refresh/frame rate) determines how stable your image will be. The higher the vertical frequency, the better. Typical vertical frequencies range from 50Hz to 160Hz, but multiple-frequency monitors support different vertical frequencies at different resolutions. You may find that a bargain monitor has a respectable 100Hz vertical frequency at 640×480, but drops to a less desirable 60Hz at 1,024×768. The horizontal frequency (or line rate) typically ranges from 31.5KHz to 90KHz or more.

Refresh Rates

The refresh rate (also called the vertical scan frequency) is the rate at which the screen display is rewritten. This is measured in hertz (Hz). A refresh rate of 72Hz means that the screen is refreshed 72 times per second. A refresh rate that is too low causes the screen to flicker, contributing to eyestrain. The higher the refresh rate, the better for your eyes and your comfort during long sessions at the computer.

A *flicker-free refresh rate* is a refresh rate high enough to prevent you from seeing any flicker. The flicker-free refresh rate varies with the resolution of your monitor setting (higher resolutions require a higher refresh rate) and must be matched by both your monitor and your display card. Because a refresh rate that is too high can slow down your video display, use the lowest refresh rate that is comfortable for you.

One factor that is important to consider when you purchase a monitor is the refresh rate, especially if you are planning to use the monitor at 1,024×768 or higher resolutions. Low-cost monitors often have refresh rates that are too low to achieve flicker-free performance for most users, and thus can lead to eyestrain.

Table 15.3 compares two typical 17-inch CRT monitors and a typical midrange graphics card.

Note the differences in the refresh rates supported by the ATI All-in-Wonder Pro and two different 17-inch CRT monitors from LG-Goldstar.

The LG 760SC is a typical, under-$300 monitor, and the LG 790SC sells for about $80 more. Note the 790SC offers flicker-free refresh rates at higher resolutions than the less-expensive 760SC.

Although the ATI All-in-Wonder Pro video card supports higher refresh rates than either monitor, rates higher than the monitor can support cannot be used safely because rates in excess of the monitor's maximum refresh rate may damage the monitor!

Table 15.3   Refresh Rates Comparison

Resolution	ATI Video Card Vertical Refresh	LG 760SC (17") Monitor Vertical Refresh (Maximum)	LG 790SC (17") Monitor Vertical Refresh (Maximum)
1,024×768	43–150Hz*	87Hz*	124Hz*
1,280×1024	43–100Hz*	65Hz	93Hz*
1,600×1200	52–85Hz*	Not supported	80Hz*

Rates above 72Hz will be flicker-free for many users; VESA standard for flicker-free refresh is 85Hz or above.

To determine the monitor's refresh rates for the resolutions you're planning to use, check out the monitor manufacturer's Web site to get the details for any monitor you own or are planning to purchase.

During installation, Windows 98 and Windows 95B (OSR 2.x) support Plug-and-Play (PnP) monitor configuration. A PnP monitor sends signals to the operating system that indicate which refresh rates it supports as well as other display information, and this data is reflected by the Display Properties sheet for that monitor.

To keep the frequency low, some video adapters use interlaced signals, alternately displaying half the lines of the total image. As discussed earlier in this chapter, interlacing produces a pronounced flicker in the display on most monitors unless the phosphor is designed with a very long persistence. For this reason, you should, if possible, avoid using interlaced video modes. Some older adapters and displays used interlacing as an inexpensive way to attain a higher resolution than what would otherwise be possible. For example, the original IBM XGA adapters and monitors used an interlaced vertical frame rate of 43.5Hz in 1,024×768 mode instead of the higher frame rate that most other adapters and displays use at that resolution.

Note

Because monitors are redrawing the screen many times per second, the change in a noninterlaced screen display is virtually invisible to the naked eye, but it is very obvious when computer screens are photographed, filmed, or videotaped. Because these cameras aren't synchronized to the monitor's refresh cycle, it's inevitable that the photo, film, or videotape will show the refresh in progress as a line across the picture.

In my experience, a 60Hz vertical scan frequency (frame rate) is the minimum anybody should use, and even at this frequency, a flicker will be noticed by most people. Especially on a larger display, this can cause eyestrain and fatigue. If you can select a frame rate (vertical scan frequency) of 72Hz or higher, most people will not be able to discern any flicker. Most modern displays easily handle vertical frequencies of up to 85Hz or more, which greatly reduces the flicker seen by the user. However, note that increasing the frame rate, although improving the quality of the image, can also slow down the video hardware because it now needs to display each image more times per second. In general, I recommend that you set the lowest frame rate you find comfortable.

To adjust the video card's refresh rate with Windows 9x, use the Display icon in control panel and select the Advanced Properties button.

Click the Adapter tab and click the down arrow next to the Refresh Rate menu. You'll see the refresh rates supported by the video card. Optimal is the default setting, but this really is a "safe" setting for any monitor. Select a refresh rate of at least 72Hz or higher to reduce or eliminate flicker. Click Apply to take the new setting. If you choose a refresh rate other than Optimal, you'll see a warning about possible monitor damage.

Click OK to try the new setting. The screen changes to show the new refresh rate. If the screen display looks scrambled, wait a few moments and the screen will be restored to the previous value; you'll see a dialog box asking if you want to keep the new setting. If the display was acceptable, click Yes; otherwise, click No to restore your display. If the screen is scrambled and you can't see your mouse pointer, just press the Enter key on your keyboard because No is the default answer. With some older video drivers, this refresh rate dialog box will not be available. Get an updated video driver, or check with the video card vendor for a separate utility program that will set the refresh rate for you.

If you have a scrambled display with a high refresh rate, but you think the monitor should be able to handle the refresh rate you chose, you may not have the correct monitor selected. To check your Windows 9x monitor selection, click the Monitor tab. If your monitor is listed as Super VGA, Windows is using a generic driver that will work with a wide variety of monitors. This generic driver doesn't support refresh rates above 75Hz because some monitors could be damaged by excessive refresh rates.

Check with your monitor vendor for a driver specific for your model. After you install it, see if your monitor will safely support a higher refresh rate.

Horizontal Frequency

When you shop for a VGA monitor, make sure the monitor supports a horizontal frequency of at least 31.5KHz—the minimum that a VGA card needs to paint a 640×480 screen. The 800×600 resolution requires at least a 72Hz vertical frequency and a horizontal frequency of at least 48KHz. The sharper 1,024×768 image requires a vertical frequency of 60Hz and a horizontal frequency of 58KHz. If the vertical frequency increases to 72Hz, the horizontal frequency must be 58KHz. For a super-crisp display, look for available vertical frequencies of 75Hz or higher and horizontal frequencies of up to 90KHz or more. My favorite 17-inch NEC monitor supports vertical resolutions of up to 75Hz at 1,600×1,200 pixels, 117Hz at 1,024×768, and 160Hz at 640×480!

Virtually all the analog monitors on the market today are, to one extent or another, multiple frequency. Because literally hundreds of manufacturers produce thousands of monitor models, it is impractical to discuss the technical aspects of each monitor model in detail. Suffice it to say that before investing in a monitor, you should check the technical specifications to make sure that the monitor meets your needs. If you are looking for a place to start, check out some of the different magazines that periodically feature reviews of monitors. If you can't wait for a magazine review, investigate monitors at the Web sites run by any of the following vendors: IBM, Sony, Mitsubishi, Viewsonic, and NEC.

Each of these manufacturers creates monitors that set the standards by which other monitors can be judged. Although you typically pay a bit more for these manufacturers' monitors, they offer a known, high-level of quality and compatibility, as well as service and support.

Controls

Most of the newer monitors now use digital controls instead of analog controls. This has nothing to do with the signals that the monitor receives from the computer, but only the controls (or lack of them) on the front panel that enable you to adjust the display. Monitors with digital controls have a built-in menu system that enables you to set parameters such as brightness, contrast, screen size, vertical and horizontal shifts, and even focus. The menu is brought up on the screen by a button, and you use controls to make menu selections and vary the settings. When you complete your adjustments, the monitor saves the settings in NVRAM (nonvolatile RAM) located inside the monitor. This type of memory provides permanent storage for the settings with no battery or other power source. You can unplug the monitor without losing your settings and you can alter them at any time in the future. Digital controls provide a much higher level of control over the monitor and are highly recommended.

Tip

Get a monitor with positioning and image controls that are easy to reach, preferably on the front of the case. Look for more than just basic contrast and brightness controls; a good monitor should enable you to adjust the width and height of your screen images and the placement of the image on the screen. The monitor should also be equipped with a tilt-swivel stand so you can adjust the monitor to the best angle for your use.

Environment

One factor that you may not consider when shopping for a monitor is the size of the desk on which you intend to put it. Before you think about purchasing a monitor larger than 15 inches, be aware that a 17-inch monitor can be 18–24 inches deep and weigh upward of 40 pounds; 21-inch and larger monitors can be truly huge! Some of the rickety computer stands and mechanical arms used to keep monitors off the desktop may not be able to safely hold or support a large unit. Check the weight rating of the computer stand or support arm you're planning to use before you put a monitor on it. It's tragic to save a few dollars on these accessories, only to watch them crumple under the weight of a large monitor and wipe out your monitor investment.

Another important consideration is the lighting in the room where you will use the monitor. The appearance of a CRT display in the fluorescent lighting of an office will be markedly different from that in your home. The presence or absence of sunlight in the room also makes a big difference. Office lighting and sunlight can produce glare that becomes incredibly annoying when you are forced to stare at it for hours on end. Some monitors are equipped with an antiglare coating that can help in these instances. Many manufacturers and third-party vendors also produce after-market filters designed to reduce glare.

Many inexpensive monitors are curved because it is easier to send an electron beam across them. Flat-screen monitors, which are a bit more expensive, look better to most people. As a general rule, the less curvature a monitor has, the less glare it reflects.

Testing a Display

Unlike most of the other components of your computer, you can't really tell whether a monitor will suit you by examining its technical specifications. Price may not be a reliable indicator either. Testing monitors is a highly subjective process, and it is best to "kick the tires" of a few at a dealer showroom (with a liberal return policy) or in the privacy of your home or office.

Testing should also not be simply a matter of looking at whatever happens to be displayed on the monitor at the time. Many computer stores display movies, scenic photos, or other flashy graphics that are all but useless for a serious evaluation and comparison. If possible, you should look at the same images on each monitor you try and compare the manner in which they perform a specific series of tasks.

Before running the tests listed below, set your display to the highest resolution and refresh rate allowed by your combination of display and graphics card.

One good series of tasks is as follows:

- Draw a perfect circle with a graphics program. If the displayed result is an oval, not a circle, this monitor will not serve you well with graphics or design software.

- Using a word processor, type some words in 8- or 10-point type (1 point equals 1/72 inch). If the words are fuzzy, or if the black characters are fringed with color, select another monitor.

- Turn the brightness up and down while examining the corner of the screen's image. If the image blooms or swells, it is likely to lose focus at high brightness levels.

- Display a screen with as much white space as possible and look for areas of color variance. This may indicate a problem only with that individual unit or its location, but if you see it on more than one monitor of the same make, it may be indicative of a manufacturing problem; or it could indicate problems with the signal coming from the graphics card. Move the monitor to another system equipped with a different graphics card model and retry this test to see for certain whether it's the monitor or the video card.

- Load Microsoft Windows to check for uniform focus. Are the corner icons as sharp as the rest of the screen? Are the lines in the title bar curved or wavy? Monitors usually are sharply focused at the center, but seriously blurred corners indicate a poor design. Bowed lines may be the result of a poor video adapter, so don't dismiss a monitor that shows those lines without using another adapter to double-check the effect.

- A good monitor will be calibrated so that rays of red, green, and blue light hit their targets (individual phosphor dots) precisely. If they don't, you have bad convergence. This is apparent when edges of lines appear to illuminate with a specific color. If you have good convergence, the colors will be crisp, clear, and true, provided there isn't a predominant tint in the phosphor.

- If the monitor has built-in diagnostics (a recommended feature), try them as well to test the display independent of the graphics card and system to which it's attached.

Video Display Adapters

A video adapter provides the interface between your computer and your monitor and transmits the signals that appear as images on the display. Throughout the history of the PC, there have been a succession of standards for video display characteristics that represent a steady increase in screen resolution and color depth. The following list of standards can serve as an abbreviated history of PC video-display technology:

> MDA (Monochrome Display Adapter)
>
> HGC (Hercules Graphics Card)
>
> CGA (Color Graphics Adapter)
>
> EGA (Enhanced Graphics Adapter)
>
> VGA (Video Graphics Array)
>
> SVGA (Super VGA)
>
> XGA (Extended Graphics Array)

Most of these standards were pioneered by IBM but were also adopted by the manufacturers of compatible PCs as well. Today, IBM is no longer the industry leader that it once was, and many of these standards are obsolete. Those that aren't obsolete are seldom referred to by these names anymore. The sole exception to this is VGA, which is a term that is still used to refer to a baseline graphics display capability supported by virtually every video adapter on the market today.

When you shop for a video adapter today, you are more likely to see specific references to the screen resolutions and color depths that the device supports than a list of standards such as VGA, SVGA, and XGA. However, reading about these standards gives you a good idea of how video-display technology developed over the years and prepares you for any close encounters you may have with legacy equipment from the dark ages.

Today's VGA and later video adapters can also display most older color graphics software written for CGA, EGA and most other obsolete graphics standards, enabling you to use older graphics software (such as game and educational programs) on your current system. Although not a concern for most users, some older programs wrote directly to hardware registers that are no longer found on current video cards.

Obsolete Display Adapters

Although many types of display systems were at one time considered to be industry standards, few of these are viable standards for today's hardware and software.

Note

If you are interested in reading more about MDA, HGC, CGA, EGA, or MCGA display adapters, see Chapter 8 of *Upgrading and Repairing PCs, Tenth Anniversary Edition*, included on the CD with this book.

VGA Adapters and Displays

When IBM introduced the PS/2 systems on April 2, 1987, it also introduced the Video Graphics Array (VGA) display. On that day, in fact, IBM also introduced the lower resolution MultiColor Graphics Array (MCGA) and higher resolution 8514 adapters. The MCGA and 8514 adapters did not become popular standards like the VGA became, and both were discontinued.

Digital Versus Analog Signals

Unlike earlier video standards, which are digital, the VGA is an analog system. Why have displays gone from digital to analog when most other electronic systems have gone digital? Compact disc players (digital) have replaced most turntables (analog), and newer VCRs and camcorders have digital picture storage for smooth slow-motion and freeze-frame capability. With a digital television set, you can watch several channels on a single screen by splitting the screen or placing a picture within another picture.

Most personal computer displays introduced before the PS/2 are digital. This type of display generates different colors by firing the RGB electron beams in on-or-off mode, which allows for the display of up to eight colors (2 to the third power). In the IBM displays and adapters, another signal doubles the number of color combinations from 8 to 16 by displaying each color at one of two intensity levels. This digital display is easy to manufacture and offers simplicity with consistent color combinations from system to system. The real drawback of the digital display system is the limited number of possible colors.

In the PS/2 systems, IBM went to an analog display circuit. Analog displays work like the digital displays that use RGB electron beams to construct various colors, but each color in the analog display system can be displayed at varying levels of intensity—64 levels, in the case of the VGA. This versatility provides 262,144 possible colors (64 to the third power), of which 256 could be simultaneously displayed. For realistic computer graphics, color depth is often more important than high resolution because the human eye perceives a picture that has more colors as being more realistic. IBM moved to analog graphics to enhance the color capabilities of its systems.

Video Graphics Array (VGA)

PS/2 systems incorporated the primary display adapter circuitry onto the motherboard. A single custom VLSI chip designed and manufactured by IBM implements the circuits, or VGA. To adapt this new graphics standard to the earlier systems, IBM introduced the PS/2 Display Adapter. Also called a VGA card, this adapter contains the complete VGA circuit on a full-length adapter board with an 8-bit interface designed for ISA-slot computers, such as the IBM AT and IBM PC/XT. IBM has long since discontinued its VGA card, but virtually all third-party units on the market represent advanced versions of VGA with many more video modes and features.

Although VGA was introduced with the IBM Microchannel (MCA) computers, such as the PS/2 Model 50 and above, it's impossible today to find a brand-new replacement for VGA that fits in the obsolete MCA-bus systems; however, surplus and used third-party cards may be available.

The VGA BIOS (basic input/output system) is the control software residing in the system ROM for controlling VGA circuits. With the BIOS, software can initiate commands and functions without having to manipulate the VGA directly. Programs become somewhat hardware-independent and can call a consistent set of commands and functions built into the system's ROM-control software.

◀◀ See "Video Adapter BIOS," p. 487.

Other implementations of the VGA differ in their hardware but respond to the same BIOS calls and functions. New features are added as a superset of the existing functions, and VGA remains compatible with the graphics and text BIOS functions built into the PC systems from the beginning. The VGA can run almost any software that was originally written for the CGA or EGA, unless it was written to directly access the hardware registers of these cards.

In a perfect world, software programmers would write to the BIOS interface rather than directly to the hardware and would promote software interchanges between different types of hardware. More frequently, however, programmers want the software to perform better, so they write the programs to control the hardware directly. As a result, these programmers achieve higher-performance applications that are dependent on the hardware for which they were first written.

When bypassing the BIOS, a programmer must ensure that the hardware is 100 percent compatible with the standard so that software written to a standard piece of hardware runs on the system. Just because a manufacturer claims this register level of compatibility does not mean that the product is 100 percent compatible or that all software runs as it would on a true IBM VGA. Most manufacturers have "cloned" the VGA system at the register level, which means that even applications that write directly to the video registers will function correctly. This compatibility makes the VGA a truly universal standard.

The VGA displays up to 256 colors onscreen, from a palette of 262,144 (256KB) colors. Because the VGA outputs an analog signal, you must have a monitor that accepts an analog input.

VGA displays come not only in color, but also in monochrome VGA models, which use color summing. With color summing, 64 gray shades are displayed instead of colors. The summing routine is initiated if the BIOS detects a monochrome display when the system boots. This routine uses an algorithm that takes the desired color and rewrites the formula to involve all three color guns, producing varying intensities of gray. Users who prefer a monochrome display, therefore, can execute color-based applications.

Table 15.4 lists the VGA display modes.

Table 15.4   VGA Display Modes

Resolution	Colors	Mode Type	BIOS Mode	Character Format	Character Box	Vertical (Hz)	Horizontal (KHz)
360×400	16	Text	00/01h	40×25	9×16	70	31.5
720×400	16	Text	02/03h	80×25	9×16	70	31.5
320×200	4	APA	04/05h	40×25	8×8	70	31.5
640×200	2	APA	06h	80×25	8×8	70	31.5
720×400	16	Text	07h	80×25	9×16	70	31.5
320×200	16	APA	0Dh	40×25	8×8	70	31.5
640×200	16	APA	0Eh	80×25	8×8	70	31.5
640×350	4	APA	0Fh	80×25	8×14	70	31.5
640×350	16	APA	10h	80×25	8×14	70	31.5
640×480	2	APA	11h	80×30	8×16	60	31.5
640×480	16	APA	12h	80×30	8×16	60	31.5
320×200	256	APA	13h	40×25	8×8	70	31.5

APA = All points addressable (graphics)

Virtually no video adapters on the market today are limited to supporting only the VGA standard. Instead, VGA, at its 16-color 640×480 resolution, has come to be the baseline for PC graphical display configurations. VGA is accepted as the least common denominator for all Windows systems and must be supported by the video adapters in all systems running Windows. The installation programs of all Windows versions use these VGA settings as their default video configuration. In addition to VGA, most adapters support a range of higher screen resolutions and color depths, depending on the capabilities of the hardware. If a Windows 9x system must be started in safe mode because of a startup problem, the system defaults to VGA in the 640×480, 16-color mode.

XGA and XGA-2

IBM announced the PS/2 XGA Display Adapter/A on October 30, 1990, and the XGA-2 in September 1992. Both adapters are high-performance, 32-bit, bus-mastering adapters for Micro Channel-based systems. These video subsystems, evolved from the VGA, provide greater resolution, more colors, and much better performance.

Combine fast VGA, more colors, higher resolution, a graphics coprocessor, and bus mastering, and you have XGA. In essence, a bus master is an adapter with its own processor that can execute operations independently of the motherboard.

The XGA-2 improved on the performance of the original XGA in several ways. First, the XGA-2 increased the number of colors supported at 1,024×768 resolution to 65,536 (64KB). In addition, because of the circuitry of the XGA-2, it processed data at twice the speed of the XGA. The XGA-2 also works in noninterlaced mode, so it produces less flicker than the XGA does. Virtually all these features have been adopted by video cards that belong to the loosely defined Super VGA family below.

Note

If you are interested in reading more about the XGA and XGA-2 display adapters, see Chapter 8 of *Upgrading and Repairing PCs, Tenth Anniversary Edition*, included on the CD with this book.

Super VGA (SVGA)

When IBM's XGA and 8514/A video cards were introduced, competing manufacturers chose not to attempt to clone these incremental improvements on their VGA products. Instead, they began producing lower-cost adapters that offered even higher resolutions. These video cards fall into a category loosely known as Super VGA (SVGA).

SVGA provides capabilities that surpass those offered by the VGA adapter. Unlike the display adapters discussed so far, SVGA refers not to an adapter that meets a particular specification, but to a group of adapters that have different capabilities.

For example, one card may offer several resolutions (such as 800×600 and 1,024×768) that are greater than those achieved with a regular VGA, whereas another card may offer the same or even greater resolutions but also provide more color choices at each resolution. These cards have different capabilities; nonetheless, both are classified as SVGA.

The SVGA cards look much like their VGA counterparts. They have the same connectors, including the feature adapter shown. Because the technical specifications from different SVGA vendors vary tremendously, it is impossible to provide a definitive technical overview in this book. The connector is shown in Figure 15.1. The pinouts are shown in Table 15.5.

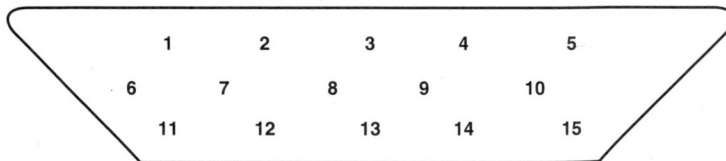

Figure 15.1 SVGA connector.

Table 15.5 Standard 15-pin VGA Connector Pinout

Pin	Function	Direction	Pin	Function	Direction
1	Red Video	Out	9	Key (Plugged Hole)	-_
2	Green Video	Out	10	Sync Ground	-_

Pin	Function	Direction	Pin	Function	Direction
3	Blue Video	Out	11	Monitor ID 0	In
4	Monitor ID 2	In	12	Monitor ID 1	In
5	TTL Ground (monitor self-test)	-	13	Horizontal Sync	Out
6	Red Analog Ground	-	14	Vertical Sync	Out
7	Green Analog Ground	-	15	Monitor ID 3	In
8	Blue Analog Ground	-			

On the VGA cable connector that plugs into your video adapter, pin 9 is often pinless. Pin 5 is used only for testing purposes, and pin 15 is rarely used; these are often pinless as well. To identify the type of monitor connected to the system, some manufacturers use the presence or absence of the monitor ID pins in various combinations.

VESA SVGA Standards

The Video Electronics Standards Association (VESA) includes members from various companies associated with PC and computer video products. In October 1989, VESA, recognizing that programming applications to support the many SVGA cards on the market was virtually impossible, proposed a standard for a uniform programmer's interface for SVGA cards.

The SVGA standard is called the VESA BIOS extension (VBE). If a video card incorporates this standard, a program can easily determine the capabilities of the card and access them. The benefit of the VESA BIOS extension is that a programmer needs to worry about only one routine or driver to support SVGA. Different cards from different manufacturers are accessible through the common VESA interface.

When first proposed, this concept met with limited acceptance. Several major SVGA manufacturers started supplying the VESA BIOS Extension as a separate memory-resident program that you could load when you booted your computer. Over the years, however, other vendors started supplying the VESA BIOS extension as an integral part of their SVGA BIOSes. Today, VBE support is a primary concern for real-mode DOS applications, especially games, and for non-Microsoft operating systems that want to access higher resolutions and color depths. VESA compliance is of virtually no consequence to Windows 9x/NT/2000 users, who use custom video drivers for their graphics cards.

Obviously, if you have a need for VESA compliance, support for VESA in BIOS is a better solution. You do not have to worry about loading a driver or other memory-resident program whenever you want to use a program that expects the VESA extensions to be present.

The current VESA SVGA standard covers just about every video resolution and color-depth combination currently available, up to 1,280×1,024 with 16,777,216 (24-bit) colors. Beyond these resolutions, VESA has adopted a General Timing Format (GTF) that allows a resolution not supported in the BIOS to have standardized timings up to high-definition television resolutions of 1,880×1,440 pixels. Even if an SVGA video adapter claims to be VESA-compatible, however, it still may not work with a particular driver, such as the 800×600, 256-color, SVGA driver that comes with Microsoft Windows. In practice, however, manufacturers continue to provide their own driver software.

Table 15.6 lists the video modes of the Chips and Technologies 65554 SVGA graphics accelerator, a typical chipset used today.

Table 15.6   Chips and Technologies 65554 Graphics Accelerator Chipset Video Modes

BIOS Mode	Mode Type	Resolution	Character	Colors	Scan Freq (Hor./Vert.)
0, 1	VGA Text	40×25 char	9×16	16/256KB	31.5KHz/70Hz
2, 3	VGA Text	80×25 char	9×16	16/256KB	31.5KHz/70Hz
4, 5	VGA Graph	320×200 pels	8×8	4KB/256KB	31.5KHz/70Hz
6	VGA Graph	640×200 pels	8×8	2KB/256KB	31.5KHz/70Hz
7	VGA Text	80×25 char	9×16	Mono	31.5KHz/70Hz
D	VGA Graph	320×200 pels	8×8	16KB/256KB	31.5KHz/70Hz
E	VGA Graph	640×200 pels	8×8	16KB/256KB	31.5KHz/70Hz
F	VGA Graph	640×350 pels	8×14	Mono	31.5KHz/70Hz
10	VGA Graph	640×350 pels	8×14	16KB/256KB	31.5KHz/70Hz
11	VGA Graph	640×480 pels	8×16	2KB/256KB	31.5KHz/60Hz
12	VGA Graph	640×480 pels	8×16	16KB/256KB	31.5KHz/60Hz
13	VGA Graph	320×200 pels	8×8	256KB/256KB	31.5KHz/70Hz
20	SVGA Graph	640×480 pels	8×16	16KB/256KB	31.5KHz/60Hz 37.6KHz/75Hz 43.2KHz/85Hz
22	SVGA Graph	800×600 pels	8×8	16KB/256KB	37.9KHz/60Hz 46.9KHz/75Hz 53.7KHz/85Hz
24	SVGA Graph	1024×768 pels	8×16	16KB/256KB	35.5KHz/87Hz* 48.5KHz/60Hz 60.0KHz/75Hz 68.8KHz/85Hz
28	SVGA Graph	1280×1024 pels	8×16	16KB/256KB	35.5KHz/87Hz* 35.5KHz/60Hz
30	SVGA Graph	640×480 pels	8×16	256KB/256KB	31.5KHz/60Hz 37.6KHz/75Hz 43.2KHz/85Hz
32	SVGA Graph	800×600 pels	8×16	256KB/256KB	37.9KHz/60Hz 46.9KHz/75Hz 53.7KHz/85Hz

BIOS Mode	Mode Type	Resolution	Character	Colors	Scan Freq (Hor./Vert.)
34	SVGA Graph	1024×768 pels	8×16	256KB/256KB	35.5KHz/87Hz*
					48.5KHz/60Hz
					60.0KHz/75Hz
					68.8KHz/85Hz
38	SVGA Graph	1280×1024 pels	8×16	256KB/256KB	35.5KHz/87Hz*
					35.5KHz/60Hz
40	SVGA Graph	640×480 pels	8×16	32KB/32KB	31.5KHz/60Hz
					37.6KHz/75Hz
					43.2KHz/85Hz
41	SVGA Graph	640×480 pels	8×16	64KB/64KB	31.5KHz/60Hz
					37.6KHz/75Hz
					43.2KHz/85Hz
42	SVGA Graph	800×600 pels	8×16	32KB/32KB	37.9KHz/60Hz
					46.9KHz/75Hz
					53.7KHz/85Hz
43	SVGA Graph	800×600 pels	8×16	64KB/64KB	37.9KHz/60Hz
					46.9KHz/75Hz
					53.7KHz/85Hz
44	SVGA Graph	1024×768 pels	8×16	32KB/32KB	48.5KHz/60Hz
45	SVGA Graph	1024×768 pels	8×16	64KB/64KB	48.5KHz/60Hz
50	SVGA Graph	640×480 pels	8×16	16MB/16MB	31.5KHz/60Hz
52	SVGA Graph	800×600 pels	8×16	16MB/16MB	37.9KHz/60Hz

Interlaced

Video Adapter Components

All video display adapters contain certain basic components, such as the following:

- Video BIOS
- Video processor
- Video memory
- Digital-to-analog converter (DAC)
- Bus connector
- Video driver

Many of the popular adapters on the market today include additional modules intended for special purposes, such as 3D acceleration. The following sections examine these components in greater detail.

The Video BIOS

Video adapters include a BIOS (basic input/output system) that is similar in construction but completely separate from the main system BIOS. (Other devices in your system, such as SCSI adapters, may also include their own BIOS.) If you turn your monitor on first and look quickly, you may see an identification banner for your adapter's video BIOS at the very beginning of the system startup process.

Like the system BIOS, the video adapter's BIOS takes the form of a ROM (read-only memory) chip containing basic instructions that provide an interface between the video adapter hardware and the software running on your system. The software that makes calls to the video BIOS can be a standalone application, an operating system, or the main system BIOS. It is the programming in the BIOS chip that enables your system to display information on the monitor during the system POST and boot sequences, before any other software drivers have been loaded from disk.

◀◀ See "BIOS Basics," page 346.

The video BIOS can also be upgraded, just like a system BIOS, in one of two ways. Either the BIOS uses a rewritable chip called an EEPROM (electrically erasable programmable read-only memory) that you can upgrade with a utility that the adapter manufacturer provides, or you may be able to completely replace the chip with a new one—again, if supplied by the manufacturer and if the manufacturer did not hard solder the BIOS to the printed circuit board. A BIOS that you can upgrade using software is referred to as a flash BIOS, and most current-model video cards that offer BIOS upgrades use this method.

Video BIOS upgrades are sometimes necessary to use an existing adapter with a new operating system, or when the manufacturer encounters a significant bug in the original programming. As a general rule, the video BIOS is a component that falls into the "if it ain't broke, don't fix it" category. Try not to let yourself be tempted to upgrade just because you've discovered that a new BIOS revision is available. Check the documentation for the upgrade, and unless you are experiencing a problem that the upgrade addresses, leave it alone.

◀◀ See "Video Adapter BIOS," p. 487.

The Video Processor

The video processor, or chipset, is the heart of any video adapter and essentially defines the card's functions and performance levels. Two video adapters built using the same chipset often have many of the same capabilities and deliver comparable performance. Also, the software drivers that operating systems and applications use to address the video adapter hardware are written primarily with the chipset in mind. You can often use a driver intended for an adapter with a particular chipset on any other adapter using the same chipset. Of course, cards built using the same chipset can differ in the amount and type of memory installed, so performance may vary.

Three main types of processors are used in video adapters:

■ Frame buffer controllers
■ Coprocessors
■ Accelerators

The oldest technology used in creating a video adapter is known as frame-buffer technology. In this scheme, the video adapter is responsible for displaying the individual frames of an image. The video adapter maintains each frame, but it is the main system CPU that performs the calculations necessary to create the frame. This arrangement places a heavy burden on the CPU, which could be busy doing other program-related computing. This method is found today only in very low-cost video cards, normally ISA-based.

At the other end of the spectrum is a chipset technology known as coprocessing. In this scheme, the video adapter includes its own processor, which performs all video-related computations. This arrangement reduces the burden on the system's main CPU, enabling it to perform other tasks. Theoretically, this type of chipset provides the fastest overall system throughput, but performance is, of course, dependent on the hardware being used. This method has been used in specialized video cards, such as those used for CAD and engineering workstations, but it has proven to be far too expensive for normal PC use.

Between these two arrangements is a middle ground—a fixed-function accelerator chip. In this scheme, which is used in most of the graphics accelerator boards on the market today, the circuitry on the video adapter does many of the more time-consuming video tasks (such as drawing lines, circles, and other objects); however, the main CPU still directs the adapter by passing graphics-primitive commands from applications, such as an instruction to draw a rectangle of a given size and color.

When you evaluate video adapters for purchase, you should always know which chipset the devices use. This information gives you a much better basis for comparing that card against others. Product literature and Web sites that provide technical specifications for video adapters should always specify the chipsets used on the devices.

Also, you can often find reviews or opinions concerning specific chipsets that can influence your purchasing decision. You may, for example, read about a great new chipset that has recently been released by a particular manufacturer and, as a result, seek out video adapters using that chipset.

Identifying the chipset on your video adapter also provides you with an additional avenue for drivers and technical support. Most chipset manufacturers maintain Web sites and tech support departments, just as adapter manufacturers do. If you do not receive adequate service from one of the companies, you can always try the other.

The Vendor List on the CD has information on most of the popular video chipset manufacturers, including how to contact them.

The Video RAM

Video adapters rely on their own onboard memory that they use to store video images while processing them. The amount of memory on the adapter determines the maximum screen resolution and color depth that the device can support. You can often select how much memory you want on a particular video adapter; for example, 1MB, 2MB, 4MB, 8MB, 16MB, or 32MB are common choices today. Most cards today come with at least 4MB, and many have 8MB or more. Although adding more memory is not guaranteed to speed up your video adapter, it can increase the speed if it enables a wider bus (from 64 bits wide to 128 bits wide) or provides nondisplay memory as a cache for commonly displayed objects. It also enables the card to generate more colors and higher resolutions.

Many different types of memory are used on video adapters today. These memory types are summarized in Table 15.7 and examined more fully in upcoming sections.

Table 15.7   Memory Types Used in Video Display Adapters

Memory Type/Definition		Relative Speed	Usage
FPM DRAM	Fast Page-Mode RAM	Slow	Low-end ISA cards; obsolete
VRAM*	Video RAM	Very fast	Expensive; rare today
WRAM*	Window RAM	Very fast	Expensive; rare today
EDO DRAM	Extended Data Out DRAM	Moderate	Low-end PCI-bus
SDRAM	Synchronous DRAM	Fast	Midrange PCI/AGP
MDRAM	Multibank DRAM	Fast	Little used; rare
SGRAM	Synchronous Graphics DRAM	Very fast	High-end PCI/AGP

VRAM and WRAM are dual-ported memory types that can read from one port and write data through the other port. This improves performance by reducing wait times for accessing the video RAM.

RAM Calculations

The amount of memory that a video adapter needs to display a particular resolution and color depth is based on a mathematical equation. A location must be present in the adapter's memory array to display every pixel on the screen, and the number of total pixels is determined by the resolution. For example, a screen resolution of 1,024×768 requires a total of 786,432 pixels.

If you were to display that resolution with only two colors, you would need only one bit of memory space to represent each pixel. If the bit has a value of 0, the dot is black, and if its value is 1, the dot is white. If you use 4 bits of memory space to control each pixel, you can display 16 colors because there are 16 possible combinations with a 4-digit binary number (2 to the 4th power equals 16). If you multiply the number of pixels needed for the screen resolution by the number of bits required to represent each pixel, you have the amount of memory that the adapter needs to display that resolution. Here is how the calculation works:

$$1{,}024 \times 768 = 786{,}432 \text{ pixels} \times 4 \text{ bits per pixel}$$
$$= 3{,}145{,}728 \text{ bits}$$
$$= 393{,}216 \text{ bytes}$$
$$= 384\text{KB}$$

As you can see, displaying 16 colors at 1,024×768 resolution requires exactly 384KB of RAM on the video adapter. Because most adapters support memory amounts of only 256KB, 512KB, 1MB, 2MB, or 4MB, you would have to install 512KB to run your system using that resolution and color depth. Increasing the color depth to 8 bits per pixel results in 256 possible colors, and a memory requirement of 786,432 bytes, or 768KB. Again, because no video adapters are equipped with that exact amount, you would have to purchase an adapter with 1MB of memory.

To use the higher resolution modes and greater numbers of colors that are common today, you will need much more memory on your video adapter than the 256KB found on the original IBM VGA. Table 15.8 shows the memory requirements for some of the most commonly used screen resolutions and color depths.

Table 15.8   Video Display Adapter Minimum Memory Requirements

Resolution	Color Depth	No. Colors	Video	Memory Required
640×480	4-bit	16	256KB	153,600 bytes
640×480	8-bit	256	512KB	307,200 bytes
640×480	16-bit	65,536	1MB	614,400 bytes
640×480	24-bit	16,777,216	1MB	921,600 bytes
800×600	4-bit	16	256KB	240,000 bytes
800×600	8-bit	256	512KB	480,000 bytes
800×600	16-bit	65,536	1MB	960,000 bytes
800×600	24-bit	16,777,216	2MB	1,440,000 bytes
1,024×768	4-bit	16	512KB	393,216 bytes
1,024×768	8-bit	256	1MB	786,432 bytes
1,024×768	16-bit	65,536	2MB	1,572,864 bytes
1,024×768	24-bit	16,777,216	4MB	2,359,296 bytes
1,280×1,024	4-bit	16	1MB	655,360 bytes
1,280×1,024	8-bit	256	2MB	1,310,720 bytes
1,280×1,024	16-bit	65,536	4MB	2,621,440 bytes
1,280×1,024	24-bit	16,777,216	4MB	3,932,160 bytes

From this table, you can see that a video adapter with 2MB can display 65,536 colors in 1,024×768 resolution mode, but for a true color (16.8 million colors) display, you would need to upgrade to 4MB.

Although many of the newest video cards on the market today have memory sizes of 8MB, 16MB, or even 32MB, this additional memory isn't required for 24-bit color in high resolutions for 2D graphics.

Note

Although some adapters can operate in a 32-bit mode, this does not necessarily mean that they can produce more than the 16,277,216 colors of a 24-bit true color display. Many video processors and video memory buses are optimized to move data in 32-bit words, and they actually display 24-bit color while operating in a 32-bit mode, instead of the 4,294,967,296 colors that you would expect from a true 32-bit color depth.

If you spend a lot of time working with graphics, you may want to invest in a 24-bit video card with 8MB or more of RAM. Many of the cards today can easily handle 24-bit color, but you will need at least 4MB of RAM to get that capability in the higher resolution modes. With RAM density increasing, prices dropping, and 2D caching and 3D capability improving, 8MB or more of fast SDRAM or SGRAM will make both 2D and 3D programs perform very well.

Note

You can upgrade the RAM on some video adapters by installing a separate module containing the additional memory chips. The module usually takes the form of a daughter card; that is, a small circuit board that plugs into a socket on the video adapter. The design of the daughter board is proprietary, even if the type of memory chips on the board are not. You will have to purchase the module from the manufacturer of the video adapter.

Windows Doesn't Recognize More Than 256 Colors

If you have a video card with 1MB or more of video memory, but the Windows 9x Display Settings properties sheet won't allow you to select a color depth greater than 256 colors, Windows 9x may have misidentified the video card during installation·(this is a common problem with Trident 9680-series video cards, for example).

To see which video card Windows 9x recognizes, click the Advanced Properties button, and then click the Adapter tab if needed. Your adapter type will be listed near the middle of the dialog box. It may be listed either by the video card's brand name and model, or by the video card's chipset maker and chipset model.

If the card model or chipset appears to be incorrect or not specific enough, click Change and see what other drivers your system lists that appear to be compatible. Many video card and chipset makers offer a free utility that you can download from their Web sites that will identify the card model, memory size, and other important information. Use such a utility program to determine which card you have, and then manually install the driver you need.

Video Bus Width

Another issue with respect to the memory on the video adapter is the width of the bus connecting the graphics chipset and the memory on the adapter. The chipset is usually a single large chip on the card that contains virtually all the adapter's functions. It is wired directly to the memory on the adapter through a local bus on the card. Most of the high-end adapters use an internal memory bus that is 64 bits or even 128 bits wide. This jargon can be confusing because video adapters that take the form of separate expansion cards also plug into the main system bus, which has its own speed rating. When you read about a 64-bit or 128-bit video adapter, you must understand that this refers to the local video bus, and that the bus connecting the adapter to the system is actually the 32- or 64-bit PCI or AGP bus on the system's motherboard.

◄◄ See "System Bus Functions and Features," p. 276.

DRAM

Historically, most video adapters have used regular dynamic RAM (DRAM) for this purpose. This type of RAM, although inexpensive, is rather slow. The slowness can be attributed to the need to constantly refresh the information contained within the RAM, and to the fact that DRAM cannot be read at the same time it is being written.

Modern PC graphics adapters need extremely high data transfer rates to and from the video memory. At a resolution of 1,024×768 and a standard refresh rate of 72Hz, the digital-to-analog converter (DAC) on the card needs to read the contents of the video memory frame buffer 72 times per second. In true color (24 bits per pixel) mode, this means that the DAC must be able to read from the video memory at a rate of about 170MB/sec, which is just about the maximum available from a conventional DRAM design. Because of the high bandwidth required for higher refresh rates, resolutions, and color depths, a number of competing memory technologies have emerged over the past several years to meet the performance needs of high-end video memory.

◄◄ See "DRAM," p. 418.

EDO DRAM

One of the more recent memory designs to be incorporated into video adapters is EDO (Extended Data Out) DRAM. EDO provides a wider effective bandwidth by offloading memory precharging to separate circuits, which means that the next access can begin before the last access has fin- · ished. As a result, EDO offers a 10% speed boost over DRAM, at a similar cost. EDO DRAM was introduced by Micron Technologies and was originally designed for use in a PC's main RAM array, but it is now also being used for video adapter memory in low-cost PCI-bus video cards. EDO chips are constructed using the same dies as conventional DRAM chips, and they differ from DRAMs only in how they are wired in final production. This method enables manufacturers to make EDO chips on the same production lines and at the same relative costs as DRAM.

◄◄ See "EDO RAM," p. 427.

High-Speed Video RAM Solutions—Older Types

Over the years, several methods have been used for increasing video RAM speed above the slow DRAM and the only slightly faster EDO RAM. Several, including VRAM, WRAM, and MDRAM were popular for brief periods of time but have been almost completely replaced by SDRAM and SGRAM.

VRAM

VRAM (Video RAM) is designed to be dual-ported, splitting the memory into two sections that can be accessed for reading and writing much faster than single-ported DRAM or EDO memory. This provides much greater performance than standard DRAM or even EDO, but it comes at a higher price.

WRAM

WRAM, or Windows RAM, is a modified VRAM-type, dual-ported memory technology developed by Samsung that is aimed specifically at graphics adapters. WRAM offers marginally better performance than standard VRAM at a lower cost.

MDRAM

MDRAM (Multibank DRAM) is a memory type also explicitly aimed at graphics and video applications. Developed by MoSys Inc., MDRAMs consist of a large number of small (32KB) banks.

MDRAM permits a video card with 2.5MB of RAM to be built, for example; enough to surpass the RAM requirements for 24-bit color at 1,024×768 resolution. Normally, 4MB of video RAM would be required. MDRAM was also designed to be accessed more quickly than even VRAM or WRAM. However, very few video card models ever featured this memory type.

Current High-Speed Video RAM Solutions

SGRAM and SDRAM have all but replaced VRAM, WRAM, and MDRAM as high-speed RAM solutions.

SGRAM

SGRAM, or Synchronous Graphics RAM, is a high-end solution for very fast video adapter designs. Like the SDRAM used in motherboard memory arrays, SGRAM can synchronize itself with the speed of the bus, up to 200MHz. This type of memory can be up to four times as fast as conventional DRAM and can operate at speeds up to 133MHz or faster; it is now being used in many of the highest quality PCI and AGP adapters. SGRAM is one of the most expensive memory technologies now used in video adapters, but it offers superior performance for graphics-intensive applications. The key difference between SGRAM and SDRAM is the inclusion of circuitry to perform block writes that can significantly increase the speed of graphics fill or 3D Z-buffer operations.

SDRAM

SDRAM, or Synchronous DRAM, is the same type of RAM used on Pentium II, Pentium III, and other systems that use DIMM (Dual Inline Memory Modules), although the SDRAMs found on video cards are normally surface-mounted or plugged into a proprietary connector. This memory is designed to work with bus speeds up to 200MHz and provides performance just slightly slower than SGRAM. SDRAM is the memory found in a number of top-line AGP and PCI video cards from some vendors, or in the mid-range and low-end video cards from vendors who use SGRAM for their top-line models.

Emerging High-Speed Video RAM Solutions

The following video RAM types are designed to speed up video RAM access even further, allowing for ever more realistic 3D graphics and full-motion video on your desktop. These emerging technologies should be appearing on high-performance desktops in the near future.

DDR SDRAM

Double-Data-Rate SDRAM is one of the newest video RAM technologies designed to transfer data at speeds twice that of conventional SDRAM. It is fast enough to work with the newest 133MHz-bus motherboards from Intel and other vendors, and is designed to be easily adopted by current users of conventional SDRAM.

Direct RAMBUS DRAM (DRDRAM)

This technology has been developed by Rambus, a company closely linked to Intel, and features a 16-bit data bus (twice that of conventional DRAMS), pipelining, and up to eight simultaneous operations.

Sync Link DRAM (SLDRAM)

This memory technology features very high speeds comparable to DRDRAM with all memory signals on the same line, compared to conventional memory's separate CAS, RAS, address, and data lines.

◀◀ See "SDRAM," p. 428.

The Digital-to-Analog Converter (RAMDAC)

The digital-to-analog converter on a video adapter (commonly called a RAMDAC) does exactly what its name describes. The RAMDAC is responsible for converting the digital images that your computer generates into analog signals that the monitor can display. The speed of the RAMDAC is measured in MHz; the faster the conversion process, the higher the adapter's vertical refresh rate. The speeds of the RAMDACs used in today's high performance video adapters can exceed 200MHz.

On the latest video cards, RAMDAC speeds have increased beyond 200MHz. The benefits of increasing the RAMDAC speed include higher vertical refresh rates, which allows higher resolutions with flicker-free refresh rates (72Hz–85Hz or above).

Table 15.9 shows the effect of faster RAMDAC chips on typical video card chipsets. As RAMDAC increases, higher resolutions with higher vertical-refresh rates are supported.

Table 15.9 Typical Chipset and RAMDAC Pairings and Their Effects on Resolution and Refresh

Chipset	RAMDAC speed	Maximum Resolution	Refresh Rate
Matrox G200	250MHz	1920×1200 (2D) 1920×1080 (3D)	70Hz (2D) 75Hz (3D)
Matrox G400MAX	360MHz	2048×1536 (2D/3D)	85Hz

Note

In some cases, the maximum resolutions and refresh rates listed for any video card may require a RAM upgrade or purchase of a video card with more RAM.

The Bus

You've learned in this chapter that certain video adapters were designed for use with certain system buses. For example, the VGA and XGA both were originally designed for use with IBM's MCA bus. The bus that you use in your computer affects the speed at which your system processes video information. For example, the ISA bus offers a 16-bit data path at speeds of 8.33MHz. The EISA or MCA buses can process 32 bits of data at a time, but they also run at speeds up to 10MHz. These three buses are no longer used for video adapters because IBM has discontinued the MCA bus and the others are too slow.

Note

Don't confuse the system bus speed with the system processor speed, although they are both measured in megahertz (MHz). System processors run at speeds upward of 300MHz, but the system bus is much slower.

The next major improvement in bus speed came with the VESA local bus (VL-Bus) standard, developed in 1992. The VL-Bus connector was typically added to up to three of the ISA slots on an ISA motherboard. Even if it is used in an ISA system, the VL-Bus processes 32 bits of data at a time and at the full-rated external speed of the CPU—up to 50MHz. Thus, you could achieve much greater speeds by using a well-implemented VL-Bus in your system. VL-Bus was a popular feature on many 486-based and early Pentium models, but it has been replaced by PCI. It is an obsolete standard today.

In July 1992, Intel Corporation introduced Peripheral Component Interconnect (PCI) as a blueprint for directly connecting microprocessors and support circuitry; it then extended the design to a full expansion bus with Release 2 in 1993. Popularly termed a mezzanine bus, PCI combines the speed of a local bus with microprocessor independence. PCI video adapters, like VL-Bus adapters, can increase video performance dramatically. PCI video adapters, by their design, are meant to be Plug and Play (PnP), which means that they require little configuration. The PCI standard virtually replaced the older VL-Bus standard overnight and has dominated Pentium-class video until recently. Whereas the PCI bus remains the best general-purpose standard for expansion cards, the new king of high-speed video is AGP.

◄◄ See "Accelerated Graphics Port (AGP)," p. 310.

◄◄ See "The PCI Bus," p. 299.

The most recent system bus innovation is the Accelerated Graphics Port (AGP), a dedicated video bus designed by Intel that delivers a maximum bandwidth four times larger than that of a comparable PCI bus. AGP is essentially an enhancement to the existing PCI bus, intended for use only with video adapters and providing them with high-speed access to the main system memory array. This enables the adapter to process certain 3D video elements, such as texture maps, directly from system memory rather than having to copy the data to the adapter memory before the processing can begin. This saves time and eliminates the need to upgrade the video adapter memory to better support 3D functions.

Although it was designed with the Pentium II in mind, AGP is not processor-dependent. However, it does require support from the motherboard chipset, which means that you cannot upgrade an existing system to use AGP without replacing the motherboard. Currently, Pentium II motherboards with the Intel 440LX, 440EX, 440BX, and 440ZX chipsets support AGP (the 440BX and 400ZX chipsets also support the Pentium III). Intel also makes Celeron-specific chipsets with AGP support, including the 440ZX66, 440LX AGPset, and 440EX AGPset. Although AGP can work with Pentium-class Socket 7 processors, Intel has abandoned new developments in this category, putting all its emphasis on the Pentium II/III/Celeron family. Acer Laboratories Inc. (ALi) offers the Aladdin Pro II chipset that supports AGP X2 for Pentium II Slot 1 motherboards and the Aladdin V Pentium chipset that supports AGP X2 for Pentium Socket 7 motherboards. VIA Technologies' Apollo VP3 and Apollo MVP3 both support AGP for Socket 7 motherboards, and SiS has its SiS 5591, which also supports AGP on a socket 7 motherboard.

◄◄ See "Socket 7 (and Super7)," p. 82.

Even with the proper chipset, however, you cannot take full advantage of AGP's capabilities without the proper operating system support. AGP's DIrect Memory Execute (DIME) feature uses main memory instead of the video adapter's memory for certain tasks, to lessen the traffic to and from the adapter. Windows 98 supports this feature, as will Windows 2000, but Windows 95 does not.

AGP Speeds

AGP support is available in three speeds: AGP 1X, AGP 2X, and AGP 4X. AGP 1X is the original version of AGP, running at 66MHz clock speed and a maximum transfer rate of 266MB/second (twice the speed of 32-bit PCI video cards). It has largely been replaced by AGP 2X, which runs at 133MHz and offers transfer rates up to 533MB/second. The latest version of AGP supports 4X mode, which offers maximum transfer rates in excess of 1GB/second.

Which should you buy? Microsoft states that Windows 98 and Windows 2000 require that a system support AGP 2X or faster to be considered compatible with these operating systems. Because AGP 1X cards are now difficult to find except at the very bottom of the pricing barrel, this isn't a difficult choice to make.

Some vendors are selling AGP 2X cards using chipsets that are really optimized for 2D operation. For best results, buy only AGP cards equipped with true 3D chipsets (see chart below). If you purchase an AGP 2X card with a 2D-optimized chipset, you'll find that AGP 1X cards with a 3D-optimized chipset will be faster in 3D mode because of their superior chipset design.

Should you buy an AGP 4X card? Yes, if you want the very fastest rendering rate for 3D games. These cards achieve their blazing transfer speeds through the use of two data channels that can operate simultaneously. AGP 4X cards are more expensive than their 2X siblings, but they are definitely faster. AGP 4x cards require that the motherboard be AGP version 2.0 compliant.

Should you check motherboard-video card compatibility before you buy? Yes, because early AGP cards (especially those based on Intel's 740 chipset) were designed strictly for the original AGP Pentium II-based motherboards. Many AGP users have Super Socket 7 motherboards instead, and some early AGP cards don't work with these motherboards. Check with both the video card and motherboard vendors before you make your purchase.

◄◄ See "Socket 7 (and Super7)," p. 82.

Many of the high-end video adapters on the market today are already available in both PCI and AGP versions. If your computer has a chipset that supports AGP, you are likely to be well-served by taking advantage of its capabilities.

Note

Many low-cost systems implement AGP video on the motherboard without providing an AGP expansion slot for future upgrades. This will prevent you from changing to a faster or a higher memory AGP video card in the future, although you may be able to use slower PCI video cards. For maximum flexibility, get your AGP video on a card.

VL-Bus, PCI, and AGP have some important differences, as Table 15.10 shows.

Table 15.10   Local Bus Specifications

Feature	VL-Bus	PCI	AGP
Theoretical maximum	132MB/sec	132MB/sec*	533MB/sec throughput (2X) 1.06GB/sec throughput (4X)
Slots**	3 (typical)	4/5 (typical)	1
Plug and Play support	No	Yes	Yes
Cost	Inexpensive	Slightly higher	Slightly higher than PCI
Ideal use	Low-cost 486	High-end 486, Pentium, P6	Pentium II

*At the 66MHz bus speed and 32 bits. Throughput will be higher on the 100MHz system bus.
**More slots are possible through the use of PCI bridge chips.

The Video Driver

The software driver is an essential, and often a problematic, element of a video display subsystem. The driver enables your software to communicate with the video adapter. You can have a video adapter with the fastest processor and the most efficient memory on the market, but still have poor video performance because of a badly written driver.

DOS applications address the video display hardware directly and typically include their own drivers for various types of video adapters. All versions of Windows, however, use a driver that is installed in the operating system. Applications then can use operating system function calls to access the video hardware.

Video drivers are generally designed to support the processor on the video adapter. All video adapters come equipped with drivers supplied by the manufacturer, but often you can use a driver created by the chipset manufacturer as well. Sometimes you may find that one of the two provides better performance than the other or resolves a particular problem you are experiencing.

Most manufacturers of video adapters and chipsets maintain Web sites from which you can obtain the latest drivers. A driver from the chipset manufacturer can be a useful alternative, but you should always try the adapter manufacturer's driver first. Before purchasing a video adapter, it is a good idea to check out the manufacturer's site and see whether you can determine how many driver releases there have been for the adapter you're considering. Frequent driver revisions can be a sign that many users are experiencing problems. Although it may be a good thing to see that the company is responding to complaints, it may also indicate that the hardware is not dependable.

The video driver also provides the interface that you can use to configure the display produced by your adapter. On a Windows 9x system, the Settings page of the Display Control Panel identifies the monitor and video adapter installed on your system and enables you to select the color depth and screen resolution that you prefer. The driver controls the options that are available for these settings, so you can't choose parameters that aren't supported by the hardware. For example, the controls would not allow you to select a 1,024×768 resolution with 24-bit color if the adapter had only 1MB of memory.

When you click the Advanced button on the Settings page, you see the Properties dialog box for your particular video display adapter. The contents of this dialog box can vary, depending on the driver and the capabilities of the hardware. Typically, on the General page of this dialog box, you can select the size of the fonts (large or small) to use with the resolution you've chosen. Windows 98 also adds a control to activate a very convenient feature. The Show Settings Icon on Task Bar check box activates a tray icon that enables you to quickly and easily change resolutions and color depths without having to open the control panel.

The Adapter page displays detailed information about your adapter and the drivers installed on the system, and it enables you to set the Refresh Rate for your display. If your adapter includes a graphics accelerator, the Performance page contains a Hardware Acceleration slider that you can use to control the degree of graphic display assistance provided by your adapter hardware.

Setting the Hardware Acceleration slider to the Full position activates all the adapter's hardware acceleration features.

Moving the slider one notch to the left addresses mouse display problems by disabling the hardware's cursor support in the display driver. This is the equivalent of adding the SWCursor=1 directive to the [Display] section of the System.ini file.

Moving the slider another notch (to the second notch from the right) prevents the adapter from performing certain bit block transfers. With some drivers, this setting also disables memory-mapped I/O. This is the equivalent of adding the Mmio=0 directive to the [Display] section of System.ini and the SafeMode=1 directive to the [Windows] section of Win.ini (and the SWCursor directive mentioned previously).

Moving the slider to the None setting (the far left) adds the SafeMode=2 directive to the [Windows] section of the Win.ini file. This disables all hardware acceleration support and forces the operating system to use only the device-independent bitmap (DIB) engine to display images, rather than bit-block transfers. Use this setting when you experience frequent screen lockups or when you receive invalid page fault error messages.

Note

If you need to disable any of the video hardware features listed earlier, this often indicates a buggy video or mouse driver. Download and install updated video and mouse drivers, and you should be able to revert to full acceleration.

Video Cards for Multimedia

Multimedia has become an important element of the personal computing industry. Technology that was at first relegated to entertainment uses, and therefore dismissed by many computing professionals, has now been assimilated into the corporate world. Live data feeds, video conferencing, and animated presentations are just a few of the technologies that are now commonplace elements of business computing.

As the demand for multimedia content increases, so do the capabilities of the hardware and software used to produce the content. Video is just one, albeit important, element of the multimedia experience, and the graphics adapters on the market today reflect the demand for these increased capabilities. Producing state-of-the-art multimedia content today often requires that the PC be capable of interfacing with other devices, such as cameras, VCRs, and television sets, and many video adapters are now equipped with this capability.

Other multimedia technologies, such as 3D animation, place an enormous burden on a system's processing and data-handling capabilities, and many manufacturers of video adapters are redesigning their products to shoulder this burden more efficiently. The following sections examine some of the video adapter components that make these technologies possible and practical—including VFC, VAFC, VMC, and VESA VIP.

Because none of these specifications for internal video feature connectors have become true industry standards, some manufacturers of auxiliary video products, such as dedicated 3D accelerator boards and MPEG decoders, have taken an alternative route through the standard VGA connector.

The Diamond Monster 3D (and 3D II), for example, works in addition to a system's standard 2D video adapter, not in place of it. However, instead of requiring that the 2D adapter have a particular internal connector, the Monster 3D includes an external pass-through cable. This cable connects the Monster 3D card to your 2D adapter, after which you plug your monitor into the VGA port on the Monster 3D card. Games and any other applications that support the Monster 3D can address that device directly through the PCI bus, and all the signals generated by the 2D adapter pass through the Monster 3D card and are relayed to the monitor.

Video Feature Connectors (VFC)

To extend the capabilities of the VGA standard beyond direct connections to a monitor, several auxiliary connector standards have been devised, first by individual card makers and later by the Video Electronic Standards Association, an industry trade group of monitor and video card makers.

Two early attempts to create a common connector were the Video Feature Connector (VFC) devised by IBM in 1987, and the VESA Advanced Feature Connector (VAFC) and VESA Media Channel (VMC). These connector designs were not widely used.

Note

If you are interested in reading more about VFC, VAFC, and VMC, see Chapter 8 of *Upgrading and Repairing PCs, Tenth Anniversary Edition*, included on the CD with this book.

VESA Video Interface Port (VESA VIP)

The latest attempt at a standard interface between video cards and other video devices today is the VESA Video Interface Port (VESA VIP).

The VESA VIP provides a dedicated connection designed to allow video cards to connect with one or more third-party hardware devices, such as MPEG-2 or HDTV decoders, video digitizers, video encoders, and so on. A dedicated connection prevents competition with other data movement on the PCI bus.

VIP is far more widely supported than previous standards, but it exists in two versions and is implemented in various ways by card vendors. To avoid VESA VIP compatibility problems, check the compatibility list for both the video card and the device you want to connect.

Video Output Devices

When video technology was first introduced, it was based on television. However, a difference exists between the signals used by a television and the signals used by a computer. In the United States, the National Television System Committee (NTSC) established color TV standards in 1953. Some other countries, such as Japan, followed this standard. Many countries in Europe developed more sophisticated standards, including Phase Alternate Line (PAL) and Sequential Couleur Avec Mèmoire (SECAM). Table 15.11 shows the differences among these standards.

Table 15.11   Television Versus Computer Monitors

Standard	Yr. Est.	Country	Lines	Rate
Television				
NTSC	1953 (color) 1941 (b&w)	U.S., Japan	525	60fields/sec
PAL	1941	Europe*	625	50fields/sec
SECAM	1962	France	625	25fields/sec
Computer				
VGA	1987	U.S.	640x480**	72Hz

Field = 1/2 (.5 frame)

*England, Holland, West Germany.

**VGA is based on more lines and uses pixels (480) versus lines; genlocking is used to lock pixels into lines and synchronize computers with TV standards.

A video-output (or VGA-to-NTSC) adapter enables you to display computer screens on a TV set or record them onto videotape for easy distribution. These products fall into two categories: those with genlocking (which enables the board to synchronize signals from multiple video sources or video with PC graphics) and those without. Genlocking provides the signal stability you need to obtain adequate results when recording to tape, but it is not necessary for using a television as a video display.

VGA-to-NTSC converters are available both as internal expansion boards or external boxes that are portable enough to use with a laptop for presentations on the road. Indeed, many laptop and notebook systems these days come equipped with a built-in VGA-to-NTSC converter.

The converter does not replace your existing video adapter but instead connects to the adapter using an external cable. In addition to VGA input and output ports, a video output board has a video output interface for S-Video and composite video.

Most VGA-to-TV converters support the standard NTSC television format and may also support the European PAL format. The resolution that these devices display on a TV set or record on videotape is often limited to straight VGA at 640×480 pixels. The converter may also contain an antiflicker circuit to help stabilize the picture because VGA-to-TV products, as well as TV-to-VGA solutions, often suffer from a case of the jitters.

Still-Image Video Capture Cards

You can install a board into your PC that enables you to capture individual screen images for later editing and playback. There are also external devices that plug into a PC's parallel port. These units capture still images from NTSC video sources such as camcorders or VCRs. Although image quality is limited by the input signal, the results are still good enough for presentations and desktop publishing applications. These devices work with 8-, 16-, and 24-bit VGA cards and usually accept video input from VHS, Super VHS, and Hi-8 devices. As you might expect, however, Super VHS and Hi-8 video sources give better results, as do configurations using more than 256 colors.

Multiple Monitors

Windows 98 includes a video display feature that Macintosh systems have had for years: the capability to use multiple monitors on one system. Windows 98 supports up to nine monitors (and video adapters), each of which can provide a different view of the desktop. When you configure a Windows 98 system to do this, the operating system creates a virtual desktop; that is, a display that exists in video memory that can be larger than the image actually displayed on a single monitor. You use the multiple monitors to display various portions of the virtual desktop, enabling you to place the windows for different applications on separate monitors and move them around at will.

Of course, each monitor that you connect to the system requires its own video adapter, so unless you have nine bus slots free, the prospects of seeing a nine-screen Windows display are slim, for now. However, even two monitors can be a boon to computing productivity.

On a multimonitor Windows 98 system, one display is always considered to be the primary display. The primary display can use any PCI or AGP VGA video adapter that uses a Windows 98 minidriver with a linear frame buffer and a packed (non-planar) format, meaning that most of the brand name adapters sold today are eligible. Additional monitors are called secondaries and are much more limited in their hardware support.

Video cards with the Permedia chipset (not the later Permedia NT and Permedia 2) cannot be used in a multiple-monitor configuration.

The following list of video card chipsets with the specified Microsoft Windows 98 drivers can be used in any combination of primary or secondary adapters. Unlisted chipsets may also work as primary adapters. This list is condensed from Microsoft's Knowledge Base article # Q182/7/08. Check it for updates to this list.

- *ATI.* Mach 64 GX and beyond, including 3D cards, Rage Pro series, Xpert series, and others using the ATIM64.drv or ATIR3.drv
- *S3.* 765 (Trio64V+)S3MM.drv

Note

Only certain updates work. These are 40, 42, 43, 44, 52, 53, and 54. Note that if the card is at one of these updates, Windows 98 recognizes the card as a Trio 64V+, provided the Microsoft driver is used. If the card is not at one of these updates, it is recognized as a Trio 32/64. Some OEM drivers don't care which update is present; be sure to note carefully which Microsoft driver Windows 98 selects when you use this card.

Other S3 chipsets include the Trio64V2, various Diamond, STB, Hercules, Number Nine, and other cards using the Virge or newer chipsets.

- *Cirrus.* 5436, Alpine, 5446, and other cards using the CIRRUSMM.drv
- *Tseng.* Cards with the ET6000 chipset
- *Trident.* 9685/9680/9682/9385/9382/9385 chipsets

It's important that the computer correctly identifies which one of the video adapters is the primary one. This is a function of the system BIOS, and if the BIOS on your computer does not let you select which device should be the primary VGA display, it decides based on the order of the PCI slots in the machine. You should, therefore, install the primary adapter in the highest-priority PCI slot.

◀◀ See "The PCI Bus," p. 299.

After the hardware is in place, you can configure the display for each monitor from the Display control panel's Settings page. The primary display is always fixed in the upper-left corner of the virtual desktop, but you can move the secondary displays to view any area of the desktop you like. You can also set the screen resolution and color depth for each display individually.

Desktop Video (DTV) Boards

You can also capture NTSC (television) signals to your computer system for display or editing. In other words, you can literally watch TV in a window on your computer. When capturing video, you should think in terms of digital versus analog. The biggest convenience of an analog TV signal is efficiency; it is a compact way to transmit video information through a low-bandwidth pipeline. The disadvantage is that although you can control how the video is displayed, you can't edit it.

Actually capturing and recording video from external sources and saving the files onto your PC requires special technology. To do this, you need a device called a video capture board, also called a TV tuner, a video digitizer, or a video grabber.

Note

In this context, the technical nomenclature again becomes confusing because the term video here has its usual connotation; that is, it refers to the display of full-motion photography on the PC monitor. When evaluating video hardware, be sure to distinguish between devices that capture still images from a video source and those that capture full-motion video streams.

One of the uses for analog video is with interactive Computer-Based Training (CBT) programs in which your application sends start, stop, and search commands to a laser disc player that plays discs you have mastered. The software controls the player via an interface that also converts the laser disc's NTSC signal into a VGA-compatible signal for display on your computer's monitor. These types of applications require NTSC-to-VGA conversion hardware.

Whereas a computer can display up to 16 million colors, the NTSC standard allows for approximately only 32,000 colors. Affordable, high-quality video is the Achilles' heel of multimedia. The images are often jerky or less than full-screen. The reason is that full-motion video, such as that which you see on TV, requires 30 images or frames per second (fps), which can be an enormous amount of data.

The typical computer screen was designed to display mainly static images. The storing and retrieving of these images requires managing huge files. Consider this: A single, full-screen color image in an uncompressed format can require as much as 2MB of disk space; a one-second video would therefore require 45MB. Likewise, any video transmission that you want to capture for use on your PC must be converted from an analog NTSC signal to a digital signal that your computer can use. On top of that, the video signal must be moved inside your computer at 10 times the speed of the conventional ISA bus structure. You need not only a superior video card and monitor, but also an excellent expansion bus, such as PCI or AGP.

Considering that full-motion video can consume massive quantities of disk space, it becomes apparent that data compression is all but essential. Compression and decompression (or codec) applies to both video and audio. Not only does a compressed file take up less space, it also performs better; there is simply less data to process. When you are ready to replay the video/audio, the application decompresses the file during playback. In any case, if you are going to work with video, be sure that your hard drive is large enough and fast enough to handle the huge files that can result. There are two types of codecs: hardware-dependent codecs and software (or hardware-independent) codecs. Hardware codecs typically perform better; however, they require additional hardware. Software codes do not require hardware for compression or playback, but they typically do not deliver the same quality or compression ratio. Two of the major codec algorithms are

- *JPEG (Joint Photographic Experts Group).* Originally developed for still images, JPEG can compress and decompress at rates acceptable for nearly full-motion video (30fps). JPEG still uses a series of still images, which makes editing easier. JPEG is typically lossy (meaning that a small amount of the data is lost during the compression process, slightly diminishing the quality of the image), but it can also be lossless. JPEG compression functions by eliminating redundant data for each individual image (intraframe). Compression efficiency is approximately 30:1 (20:1–40:1).

- *MPEG (Motion Pictures Experts Group).* MPEG by itself compresses video at approximately a 30:1 ratio, but with precompression through oversampling, the ratio can climb to 100:1 and higher, while retaining high quality. Thus, MPEG compression results in better, faster videos that require less storage space. MPEG is an interframe compressor. Because MPEG stores only incremental changes, it is not used during editing phases. MPEG decoding can be performed in software on high-performance Pentium systems.

If you will be capturing, compressing, and playing video, you will need Microsoft Video for Windows (VFW), which is included with the Windows 9x and NT operating systems, or QuickTime, which is available as a free download from Apple's Web site. The following codecs are provided along with VFW:

- *Cinepak.* Although Cinepak can take longer to compress, it can produce better quality and higher compression than Indeo. It is also referred to as Compact Video Codec (CVC).

- *Indeo.* Indeo can outperform Cinepak and is capable of real-time compression. An Intel Smart Video board is required for real-time compression.

- *Microsoft Video 1.* Developed by MediaVision (MotiVE) and renamed MS Video 1, this codec is a DCT-based post-processor. A file is compressed after capture.

Many other codecs are freely available from various vendors, providing support for other video formats. Many of the video plug-ins that work with Web browsers supply their codecs and automatically install them on your system. If you look on the Devices page of the Windows 98 Multimedia control panel (or the Advanced page in Windows 95) under Video Compression Codecs, you can view and manage the codecs installed on your computer.

To play or record video on your multimedia PC (MPC), you need some extra hardware and software:

- Video system software, such as Apple's QuickTime for Windows or Microsoft's Video for Windows.

- A compression/digitization video adapter that enables you to digitize and play large video files.

- An NTSC-to-VGA adapter that combines TV signals with computer video signals for output to a VCR. Video can come from a variety of sources: TV, VCR, video camera, or laser disc player. When you record an animation file, you can save it in a variety of different file formats: AVI (Audio Video Interleave), MOV (Apple QuickTime format), or MPG (MPEG format).

When you connect video devices, use the S-Video (S-VHS) connector whenever available. This cable provides the best signal because separate signals are used for color (chroma) and brightness (luma). Otherwise, you will have to use composite video, which mixes luma and chroma. This results in a lower quality signal. The better your signal, the better your video quality will be.

You can also purchase devices that display only NTSC signals on your computer. The way that multimedia technology is advancing, soon you will not be able to tell whether you are using a computer screen or a television. Digital video, in-screen filling, and full-motion color have arrived on desktop platforms with titles, playback boards, and encoding equipment. Soon, MPEG movie clip libraries will be the next form of clip art on CD-ROM. Hardware advances, such as the MMX instructions incorporated into the Pentium architecture, are helping to make motion video more of a useful reality rather than just a novelty.

Table 15.12 provides a breakdown of some common video cards supporting key features. This table is not inclusive and is meant to serve only as a reference example.

Table 15.12   Video Card Support for Key Multimedia Features

Device Type	Example
Built-in TV tuner	ATI All-in-Wonder Pro
TV-tuner attachments	ATI-TV
Parallel-port attachments	ZIPSHOT
USB port	Nogatech USB Live!
Dedicated PCI or ISA card	Video E-Mailer
SCSI card	Iomega BUZ
IEEE-1394 (FireWire) from digital video	Radius MotoDV Studio 2.0

Each of these types of devices has its advantages and potential drawbacks. Table 15.13 provides a summary that will help you decide which solution might be best for you.

Table 15.13   Multimedia Device Comparison

Device Type	Pros	Cons
Graphics card w/built-in TV tuner	Convenience, single-slot solution	Upgrading requires card replacement
TV-tuner attachment	Allows upgrade to existing graphics cards; may be movable to newer models	Can't be used with all graphics cards
Parallel-port attachment	Universal usage on desktop or notebook computer; inexpensive	Frame rate limited by speed of port
USB-port attachment	Easy installation on late-model USB-equipped computers with Windows 98	May not work on Windows 95B OSR 2.x with USB; requires active USB port
Dedicated ISA or PCI interface card	Fast frame rate for realistic video; doesn't require disconnecting parallel printer; works with any graphics card	High resource requirements (IRQ, and so on) on some models; ISA nearly obsolete; requires internal installation
SCSI interface	SCSI card can be used with wide range of other peripherals; fast frame rate for realistic video; external control box for cabling	Requires internal installation
IEEE-1394 (FireWire) connection to digital video	No conversion from analog to digital needed; all-digital image is very high quality without compression artifacts (blocky areas) in video; fast throughput	Requires IEEE-1394 interface card and IEEE-1394 digital video source; new and expensive; card requires internal installation

Troubleshooting Video Capture Devices

Table 15.14 provides some advice for troubleshooting problems with video capture devices.

Table 15.14 Troubleshooting Video Capture Devices

Device Type	Problem	Solutions
Parallel-port attachment	Can't detect device, but printers work okay	Check port settings; device may require IEEE-1284 settings (EPP and ECP); change in BIOS; make sure device is connected directly to port; avoid daisy-chaining devices unless device specifically allows it; check Windows 9x Device Manager for IRQ conflicts.
TV tuners (built-in graphics card or add-on)	No picture	Check cabling; set signal source correctly in software.
All devices	Video capture is jerky	Frame rate is too low; increasing it may require capturing video in a smaller window; use fastest parallel-port setting you can.
All devices	Video playback has pauses, dropped frames	Hard disk may be pausing for thermal recalibration; use AV-tuned SCSI hard drives or new UDMA EIDE drives; install correct bus-mastering EIDE drivers for motherboard chipset to speed things up.
USB devices	Device can't be detected or doesn't work properly	Use Windows 98; late versions of Windows 95 have USB drivers, but they often don't work; if you use a USB hub, make sure it's powered.
Interface cards (all types)	Card can't be detected or doesn't work	Check for IRQ conflicts in Windows 9x Device Manager; consider setting card manually if possible.
All devices	Capture or installation problems	Use the newest drivers available; check manufacturers' Web site for updates, FAQs, and so on.

3D Graphics Accelerators

The latest trend in PC graphic-display technology is the expanded use of 3D images. Three-dimensional imagery has been used for years in the computer gaming world and has even made its way into business computing. Spreadsheet programs such as Microsoft Excel have for years used 3D charts to display spreadsheet data. Of course, the images are not truly three-dimensional because the monitor screen is a 2D medium, but software can produce 3D effects using perspective, textures, and shading.

Abstract shapes such as Excel's 3D bar graphs are not difficult to produce because they consist solely of polygons and other shapes with solid color fills of various shades. You find the truly innovative side of 3D graphics in the so-called virtual-reality environments created in games and in other applications. As with other types of multimedia, however, the techniques that originate in games and other entertainment software will eventually be assimilated into mainstream use.

A 3D image can contain an immense amount of detail, and an animated 3D sequence like those of many games requires a great many images. Obviously, the more images that are needed, the more disk space is required to store them, and the more processing and image-handling speed is needed to display them. To manage all that detail, 3D applications usually store and work with abstractions of the images rather than with the actual images themselves. In essence, the 3D images are generated—or rendered—as needed, rather than simply read from a storage medium.

To construct an animated 3D sequence, a computer can mathematically animate the sequences between keyframes. A keyframe identifies specific points. A bouncing ball, for example, can have three keyframes: up, down, and up. Using these frames as a reference point, the computer can create all the interim images between the top and the bottom. This creates the effect of a smooth-bouncing ball.

After it has created the basic sequence, the system can then refine the appearance of the images by filling them in with color. The most primitive and least effective fill method is called flat shading, in which a shape is simply filled with a solid color. Gouraud shading, a slightly more effective technique, involves the assignment of colors to specific points on a shape. The points are then joined using a smooth gradient between the colors.

The most processor intensive, and by far the most effective type of fill, is called texture mapping. The 3D application includes patterns—or textures—in the form of small bitmaps that it tiles onto the shapes in the image, just as you can tile a small bitmap to form the wallpaper for your Windows desktop. The primary difference is that the 3D application can modify the appearance of each tile by applying perspective and shading to achieve 3D effects.

Until recently, 3D applications had to rely on support from software routines to convert these abstractions into live images. This places a heavy burden on the system processor in the PC, which has a significant impact on the performance not only of the visual display, but also of any other applications that the computer may be running. Now, a new breed of video accelerator chipsets is found on many video adapters that can take on a lot of the tasks involved in rendering 3D images, greatly lessening the load on the system processor and overall system performance.

Prices are dropping rapidly on these 3D accelerators, and more and more software titles are making use of them. Technology that was once available only on high-end graphics workstations is now available on PCs. By rendering images right on the adapter, 3D graphics-accelerator adapters can create smooth, photo-realistic 3D images on a PC at speeds that rival those of low-end graphics workstations.

3D technology has added an entirely new vocabulary to the world of video display adapters. Before purchasing a 3D accelerator adapter, it is a good idea to familiarize yourself with the some of the terms and concepts involved in the 3D image generation process.

The basic function of 3D software is to convert image abstractions into the fully realized images that are then displayed on the monitor. The image abstractions typically consist of the following elements:

- *Vertices*. Locations of objects in three dimensional space, described in terms of their X, Y, and Z coordinates on three axes representing height, width, and depth.

- *Primitives*. The simple geometric objects that the application uses to create more complex constructions, described in terms of the relative locations of their vertices. This serves not only to specify the location of the object in the 2D image, but it also provides perspective because the three axes can define any location in three-dimensional space.

- *Textures*. Two-dimensional bitmap images or surfaces that are designed to be mapped onto primitives. The software enhances the 3D effect by modifying the appearance of the textures, depending on the location and attitude of the primitive; this process is called perspective correction. Some applications use another process called MIP mapping, which utilizes different versions of the same texture that contain varying amounts of detail, depending on how close the object is to the viewer in the three-dimensional space. Another technique, called depth cueing, reduces the color and intensity of an object's fill as the object moves farther away from the viewer.

Using these elements, the abstract image descriptions must then be rendered, meaning that they are converted to visible form. Rendering depends on two standardized functions that convert the abstractions into the completed image that is displayed onscreen. The standard functions performed in rendering are

- *Geometry*. The sizing, orienting, and moving of primitives in space and the calculation of the effects produced by the virtual light sources that illuminate the image.

- *Rasterization*. The converting of primitives into pixels on the video display by filling the shapes with properly illuminated shading, textures, or a combination of the two.

A modern video adapter that includes a chipset capable of 3D video acceleration will have special built-in hardware that can perform the rasterization process much faster than if it is done by software (using the system processor) alone. Most chipsets with 3D acceleration perform the following rasterization functions right on the adapter:

- *Scan conversion*. The determination of which onscreen pixels fall into the space delineated by each primitive.

- *Shading*. The process of filling pixels with smoothly flowing color using the flat or Gouraud shading technique.

- *Texturing*. The process of filling pixels with images derived from a 2D sample picture or surface image.

- *Visible surface determination*. The identification of which pixels in a scene are obscured by other objects closer to the viewer in three-dimensional space.

- *Animation*. The process of switching rapidly and cleanly to successive frames of motion sequences.

Common 3D Techniques

The following techniques are used by virtually all 3D cards. Because they are so common, data sheets for advanced cards frequently don't mention them, although these features are present.

- *Fogging*. Fogging simulates haze or fog in the background of a game screen and helps conceal the sudden appearance of newly rendered objects (buildings, enemies, and so on.)

- *Gouraud Shading*. Interpolates colors to make circles and spheres look more rounded and smooth.

- *Alpha Blending*. One of the first 3D techniques, alpha blending creates translucent objects onscreen, making it a perfect choice for rendering explosions, smoke, water, and glass. Alpha blending can also be used to simulate textures, but it is less realistic than environment-based bump mapping (see "Environment-Based Bump Mapping," later in this chapter).

Advanced 3D Techniques

The following are some of the latest techniques used by leading 3D accelerator cards. Not every card will use every technique.

Stencil Buffering

Stencil buffering is a technique useful for games such as flight simulators, in which a static graphic element—such as a cockpit windshield frame, known as a HUD (Heads Up Display) used by real-life fighter pilots—is placed in front of dynamically changing graphics (such as scenery, other aircraft, sky detail, and so on). In this example, the area of the screen occupied by the cockpit windshield frame is not re-rendered. Only the area seen through the "glass" is re-rendered, saving time and improving frame rates for animation.

Z-Buffering

A closely related technique is Z-buffering, which was originally devised for CAD (Computer Aided Drafting) applications. The Z-buffer portion of video memory holds depth information about the pixels in a scene. As the scene is rendered, the Z-values (depth information) for new pixels are compared to the values stored in the Z-buffer to determine which pixels are in "front" of others and should be rendered. Pixels which are "behind" other pixels are not rendered. This method increases speed and can be used along with stencil buffering to create volumetric shadows and other complex 3D objects.

Environment-Based Bump Mapping

This technique introduces special lighting and texturing effects to simulate the rough texture of rippling water, bricks, and other complex surfaces. It combines three separate texture maps (for colors, for height and depth, and for environment—including lighting, fog, and cloud effects). This creates enhanced realism for scenery in games and could also be used to enhance terrain and planetary mapping, architecture, and landscape-design applications. This represents a significant step beyond alpha blending.

Texture Mapping Filtering Enhancements

To improve the quality of texture maps, several filtering techniques have been developed, including bilinear filtering, trilinear filtering, and anisotropic filtering.

- *Bilinear filtering*. Improves the image quality of small textures placed on large polygons. The stretching of the texture that takes place can create blockiness, but bilinear filtering applies a blur to conceal this visual defect.

- *Trilinear filtering*. Combines bilinear filtering and MIP mapping, calculating the most realistic colors needed for the pixels in each polygon by comparing the values in two MIP maps. This method is superior to either MIP mapping or bilinear filtering alone.

Note

Bilinear and trilinear filtering work well for surfaces viewed straight-on but may not work so well for oblique angles (such as a wall receding into the distance).

■ *Anisotropic filtering.* Some video card makers use another method, called anisotropic filtering, for more realistically rendering oblique-angle surfaces containing text. This technique is used when a texture is mapped to a surface that changes in two of three spatial domains, such as text found on a wall down a roadway (for example, advertising banners at a raceway). The extra calculations used take time, and for that reason, this method is used only by a few video card makers on their fastest video card models.

Single- Versus Multiple-Pass Rendering

Different video card makers handle application of these advanced rendering techniques differently. The current trend is toward applying the filters and the basic rendering in a single pass rather than multiple passes. Video cards with single-pass rendering and filtering normally provide higher frame-rate performance in 3D-animated applications and avoid the problems of visible artifacts caused by errors in multiple floating-point calculations during the rendering process.

Hardware Acceleration Versus Software Acceleration

Compared to software-only rendering, hardware-accelerated rendering provides faster animation than with software alone. Although most software rendering would create more accurate and better-looking images, software rendering is too slow. Using special drivers, these 3D adapters can take over the intensive calculations needed to render a 3D image that were formerly performed by software running on the system processor. This is particularly useful if you are creating your own 3D images and animation, but it is also a great enhancement to the many modern games that rely extensively on 3D effects.

Software Optimization

It's important to realize that the presence of an advanced 3D-rendering feature on any given video card is meaningless unless game and application software designers optimize their software to take advantage of the feature. Although different 3D standards exist (OpenGL, Glide, and Direct 3D), video card makers provide drivers that make their games play with the leading standards. Because some cards do play better with certain games, you'll want to see the reviews in publications such as *Maximum PC* to see how your favorite graphics card performs with the latest games.

Note

If you want to enjoy the features of your newest 3D card right away, make sure you purchase the individual retail-packaged version of the card from a hardware vendor. The lower cost OEM or "white box" versions of video cards are sold without bundled software, come only with driver software, and may differ in other ways from the retail advertised product. Some even use modified drivers or lack special TV-out or other features. Some 3D card makers use different names for their OEM versions to minimize confusion, but others don't. Also, some card makers sell their cards in bulk packs, which are intended for upgrading a large organization with its own support staff. These cards may lack individual documentation and/or driver CDs.

APIs (Application Programming Interface)

An API is an Application Programming Interface. APIs provide hardware and software vendors a means to create drivers and programs that can work fast and reliably across a wide variety of platforms. When APIs exist, drivers can be written to interface with the API rather than directly with the operating system and its underlying hardware.

Leading Game APIs include SGI's OpenGL, 3Dfx's Glide, and Microsoft's Direct 3D. Glide, an enhanced version of OpenGL, is restricted to graphics cards that use 3Dfx chipsets, whereas OpenGL and Direct 3D (part of DirectX) are available for virtually all leading graphics cards. Thus, virtually all recent video cards provide support for OpenGL and Direct 3D.

Whereas OpenGL support is provided by the video card maker, Direct3D support is provided by Microsoft as part of a much larger API called DirectX.

Microsoft DirectX

Microsoft DirectX was developed for Windows 95, Windows 98, and Windows NT 4.0/2000 to provide support for advanced gaming and business graphics, including 3D video, 3D sound, multiplayer support, and other benefits. Although most uses for DirectX thus far have been games, DirectX also supports business applications such as NetMeeting, ActiveMovie, and NetShow, which provide various methods for viewing content and collaborating over the World Wide Web.

Because DirectX features a HAL (Hardware Abstraction layer), software developers can create their software to work on a particular release of DirectX, rather than having to target the increasing numbers of video cards, sound cards, joysticks, and so on, all of which feature different chipsets and would therefore require different direct drivers. DirectX also features a HEL (Hardware Emulation layer), allowing the DirectX software to use software emulation of hardware features as a fallback to support hardware that lacks a specified feature. HEL is obviously slower than HAL, but the thinking is that a software-emulated feature is better than nothing.

DirectX can perform these tasks because DirectX provides drivers for the hardware it supports. Therefore, a simplified way to look at the DirectX relationship between hardware and software is

HARDWARE ⟶ DirectX ⟶ Software

DirectX's design enables hardware to be controlled and accessed by the DirectX software rather than directly by the Windows 9x/NT/2000 operating system. This means that DirectX can be updated independently of the operating system.

DirectX contains a "foundation" layer, which provides direct access to sound, 2D and 3D graphics hardware, input devices, and setup routines. The APIs in the foundation layer with Microsoft DirectX 6.1 are shown in Table 15.15:

Table 15.15   DirectX 6.1 APIs

API Name	Function
DirectDraw	2D graphics
Direct3D	3D graphics
DirectInput	"Force feed" joysticks, steering wheels, and other input devices
DirectSound	Basic sound and mixer effects
DirectSound3D	Creates 3D sound effects with ordinary dual-speaker arrangements
DirectSetup	Automatic setup of software and drivers
DirectMusic	Provides for dynamic, interactive music

Older versions of DirectX will not have all these APIs.

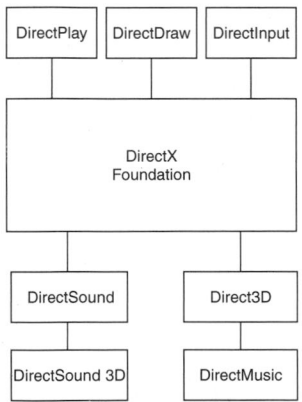

Figure 15.2   The DirectX Foundation layer includes support for the major "building blocks" that make 3D games and applications enjoyable and realistic.

DirectX also contains a Media layer. The APIs in the Media layer with Microsoft DirectX 6.1 are shown in Table 15.16:

Table 15.16   Media Layer APIs

API Name	Function
Direct3D Retained Mode	Manages 3D scene graphs
DirectShow	Formerly known as ActiveMovie—allows playback of streaming media, captures audio and video, and multimedia rendering/streaming
DirectAnimation	Formerly known as ActiveX animation—creates animation, including Dynamic HTML, Java applets, and scripting
DirectX Transform	Allows manipulation of single or multiple images for Web and application use, including morphing, wipes, and more

Older versions of DirectX will not have all these APIs.

The Media layer is shown in Figure 15.3.

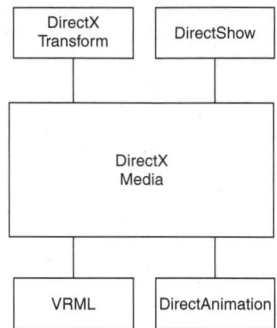

Figure 15.3 The DirectX Media layer allows DirectX services to be used by game, Web, and interactive media designers.

Various releases of DirectX are available from Microsoft as a download, as part of Internet Explorer 4, Internet Explorer 5, Windows 95 OSR 2.x, Windows 2000, Windows 98, and from hardware and software vendors whose products use DirectX.

Most products that require DirectX services check your system to see whether you have the appropriate version of DirectX installed and prompt you to install it from the installation CD or setup program if you don't. It's important to realize the following facts:

DirectX is backward compatible; DirectX 6.1 supports earlier releases of DirectX.

Older DirectX releases will not have all the APIs or the correct APIs found in the latest release. Thus, you cannot use an older version of DirectX if an application or hardware device requires DirectX 6.1, for example.

The latest release of DirectX for Windows NT 4.0 is version 3.0. Version 6.1 or later (with full 3D support and other features) will be supported by Windows 2000.

If you have questions about DirectX support for your hardware, contact your video card, input device, or sound card vendor.

To determine the DirectX version on your computer, check the version number of the DDRAW.DLL file, which is one of the few files that has been part of DirectX since its first release (1.0).

Choose Start, Find, Files or Folders. Type DDRAW.DLL and click Find. After the search is complete, right-click the DDRAW.DLL file and select Properties. Click the Version tab, and scroll down to Product Version (left column). The right column (value) shows the following number, depending on the version. Table 15.17 shows the ActiveX version numbers:

Check the version number of the DDRAW.DLL file, which is one of the few files that has been part of DirectX since its first release (1.0).

To check the version number of the DDRAW.DLL file, use Start, Find Files or Folders; enter DDRAW.DLL, right-click the DDRAW.DLL file, and select Properties. Click the Version tab and scroll down to Product Version (left column). The right column (value) will show the following number, depending upon the version.

Table 15.17   DirectX Version Numbers

DirectX Version	DDRAW.DLL Version Number
1.0	4.02.0095
2.0	4.03.00.1096 (also 2.0a)
3.0	4.04.00.0068* (also 3.0a)
(no version 4.0)	
5.0	4.05.00.0155
6.0	4.06.00.0318
6.1	4.06.02.0436

*Check the version number of the D3DRGBXF.DLL file to determine version 3.0 or 3.0a:
D3DRGBXF.DLL has a version number of 4.04.00.0068 in DirectX 3.0
D3DRGBXF.DLL has a version number of 4.04.00.0070 in DirectX 3.0a

Note

It's normal for some DirectX components to have a different version number than those listed earlier for DDRAW.DLL. This is because Microsoft retained identical files for some DirectX software components from one version to another.

Troubleshooting DirectX

If you have installed DirectX 6.1, a diagnostic program called dxdiag.exe is installed into the \Windows\System folder. DirectX 6.0 has a similar program installed into the C:\Program Files\Directx\Setup. Use this program to check your DirectX setup, including correct files and proper operation.

The most typical cause of problems with DirectX is loading an older version over a newer version. Use the troubleshooting routines supplied with DirectX 6.0 or later to determine whether you have this type of problem, or install the latest version of DirectX available for your operating system. Note that the versions of DirectX supplied on the Windows 95 OSR 2.x and Windows 98 CD-ROMs are not the latest versions. Get the latest version from Microsoft's Web site.

Because DirectX problems can occasionally result in the need to reinstall your operating system, be careful about installing DirectX during a software upgrade or loading process. Some installers don't properly check to see if you have the latest version and want to give you the "correct" version, even if it's out-of-date. If you suspect the software installer is about to slip you an out-of-date version of DirectX, skip that part of the install if you can.

3D Chipsets

As with standard 2D video adapters, there are several manufacturers of popular 3D video chipsets and many more manufacturers of video adapters that use them. Table 15.18 lists the major 3D chipset manufacturers, the various chipsets they make, and the video adapters that use them.

Note

Chipsets marked (3D only) in this table are used on boards that must be connected to and used with an existing 2D or 2D/3D graphics board in your computer. Chipsets marked (2D/3D) are used on boards that provide both features and thus can be used to replace existing boards in your computer.

In each manufacturer's section, the following symbols will be used to provide a ranking within that manufacturer's chipsets only: NEW—RECENT—OLD. Generally, NEW chipsets provide the fastest 3D performance and advanced 3D rendering features. RECENT chipsets, although lacking some of the speed or features of NEW chipsets, are also worthwhile, especially for those on a budget. OLD are generally superseded by RECENT and NEW chipsets and therefore not recommended. Be sure to use this information in conjunction with application-specific and game-specific tests to help you choose the best card/chipset solution for your needs.

Table 15.18   3D Video Chipset Manufacturers

Manufacturer	Chipset	Available Boards
3Dfx Interactive	Voodoo Graphics (3D only OLD)	A-Trend Helios 3D; Canopus Pure 3D; Deltron Flash 3D; Diamond Monster 3D; Guillemot MAXIGamer 3Dfx; Orchid Righteous 3D; Quantum 3D Obsidian series; Skywell Magic 3D
3Dfx Interactive	Voodoo Rush (2D/3D OLD)	California Graphics Emotion 3D; Deltron Flash AT3D Rush; Hercules Stingray 128/3D; Intergraph Intense 3D; Jazz Adrenaline Rush; Viewtop Rush 3D
3Dfx Interactive	Voodoo Banshee (2D/3D RECENT)	Gigabyte GA-630; A-Trend Helios 3d-Banshee Edition Creative Labs 3D Blaster Banshee; Diamond Monster Fusion; ELSA Victory II; Guillemot Maxi Gamer Phoenix; Melco Buffalo WGP-FX; Metabyte Wicked 3D Vengeance; Pace 3D Edge; Quantum 3D Raven; Sky Well Magic Twinpower (Banshee); ASUS AGP-V3200
3Dfx Interactive	Voodoo2 (3D only RECENT)[1]	Aopen PA2000 Voodoo2; A-Trend Helios 3D Voodoo2 Bestdata Arcade Fx Ii 3d; Canopus Pure 3D Ii; Creative 3D Blaster; Diamond Monster 3D II; Gainward Dragon 3000; Guillemot Gamer 3D2 PCI; Metabyte Wicked 3D; Microconversions Game Wizard; Miro Hiscore DLL; Quantum3d Obsidian2 S-Series; Quantum3d Obsidian2 X-Series Single Board SLI; Skywell Magic 3D II; STB Blackmagic 3D; STB Voodoo2 1000; Techworks Power 3D II; Village Tronics 3D Overdrive 2
3Dfx Interactive[2]	Voodoo3 (2D/3D NEW)	3Dfx Voodoo3 2000 AGP; 3Dfx Voodoo3 2000 PCI; 3Dfx Voodoo3 3000 AGP; 3Dfx Voodoo3 3500 AGP
3D labs	Permedia 2(2D/3D RECENT)	Creative Graphics Blaster Exxtreme; Diamond FireGL 1000Pro; Abit V3D; AccelGraphics AccelSTAR II; Alta Technology PMC/Video-3D; Appian Graphics Jeronimo Pro; Biostar Pluto 3D; Boxx Technologies Permedia 2; Britek Electronics AGP Mars-2; Britek Electronics 3D Mars-2; Densan PD200/8A; Elitegroup 3DVision-PAGP; ELSA WINNER 2000/Office; ELSA GLoria Synergy; First International Computer Extremis; Gainward Power 3D II; Giga-Byte GA-600; GVC GA-311; Hercules Dynamite 3D/GL; I-O Data Device GA-PII8/PCI; Iwill 3D Adventure II; Joytech Apollo 3000; Leadtech WinFast 3D L2300; Lung Hwa/EONtronics

Manufacturer	Chipset	Available Boards
		DPB21 PERMEDIA 2; Lung Hwa/EONtronics DAB31 PERMEDIA 2; MaxVision 3DmaxP2; Melco WHP-PS4/PS8; Micro-Labs Ultimate 3D; Micro-Star Int'l MS-4413; Omnicomp Graphics Divine3D; Prolink Microsystems MVGA-3DP2A; Software Integrators Saturn GL; Soyo Computer SY-3DAGPA-Trend
3D labs	Permedia (2D/3D OLD)	Densan 3D MaxiGrafx; Gainward AccuX P200
ATi	RAGE II+ (2D/3D OLD)	3D XPRESSION+; All-in-Wonder; ATi 3D Charger * (may use Rage II/II+ or Rage IIC depending on version)
ATi	Rage IIC (2D/3D OLD)	Gainward CARDEXPERT RAGE II C; Ati 3D Charger (some versions)
ATi	3D RAGE II+DVD (2D/3D OLD)	3D PRO TURBO PC2TV
ATi	Rage Pro (2D/3D RECENT)	ATI All-in-Wonder Pro; ATI XPERT LCD; ATI XPERT@Play 98; ATI XPERT 98; ATI XPERT@Play; ATI XPERT@Work; ATI XPERT XL; ATI 3D Charger
ATi	Rage 128 (2D/3D NEW)	ATI All-in-Wonder 128; ATI RAGE FURY; ATI RAGE MAGNUM; ATI XPERT 128; ATI XPERT 99
ATi	Rage I (2D/3D OLD)	ATI 3D Xpression; ASUS 3DP PCI-V264GT
Intel	740 (2D/3D)	ASUS AGP-V2740; Diamond Stealth II G460; ABIT Intel740; EONTronics Picasso 740; DataExpert DIT5740 (3D Uranus)Real3D StarFighter; Hercules Terminator 2x/I; MaxiGraphics (Guillemot) Gamer 2D/3D AGP
NVIDIA	RIVA 128 (2D/3D RECENT)	ASUS 3D Explorer; Canopus Total 3D 128V; Diamond Viper330; Elsa Erazor Victory; STB Velocity 128
	RIVA 128ZX (RECENT)	STB Lightspeed 128ZX; Yuan AGP-300SZ
	RIVA TNT2 (2D/3D NEW)	Guillemot Maxi Gamer Xentor; Aopen PA3010-A; Aopen PA3010-N; ASUSTeK AGP-V3800 series; Diamond Viper V770; Creative 3D Blaster RIVA TNT2; Yuan AGP-520T; Hercules Dynamite TNT2
	RIVA TNT2 Ultra (2D/3D NEW)	Diamond Viper V770 Ultra; Guillemot Maxi Xentor 32 Ultra; Creative 3D Blaster RIVA TNT2 Ultra; Hercules Dynamite TNT2 Ultra
	RIVA TNT (2D/3D RECENT)	Creative Graphics Blaster RIVA TNT; Diamond Viper 550; Hercules Dynamite TNT
	VANTA NEW)	Yuan AGP-320V
Rendition[3]	(Vérité) v2000 (2D/3D RECENT)	Diamond Stealth S220; DSystems Gladiator; Hercules Thriller 3D; Jazz Outlaw 3D; QDI Vision 1; InnoVISION Warrior 3D; Kasan Blitz2200; Data Expert DVT5200
	v1000 (2D/3D OLD)	Creative 3D Blaster PCI; Intergraph 3D 100; IO Magic Video 3D; Miro miroCRYSTAL VRX; Sierra Screamin' 3D;
	Max 2 Tech 3D	Canopus Total3D

(continues)

Table 15.18 Continued

Manufacturer	Chipset	Available Boards
S3	ViRGE (2D/3D OLD)	Gainward Cardex Genesis SV; Dataexpert Expertcolor; DSV3325P; Diamond Stealth 3D 2000 Pro; Elsa Victory 3D; Expert EVP ViRGE; Genoa Phantom 3D; Hercules Terminator 64/3D; Number Nine 9FX Reality 332; Orchid Fahrenheit Video3D; ASUS 3DP-V375DX; STB Powergraph 64 3D
	Savage3D (2D/3D RECENT)	A-Trend ATG3900; AOPEN NAVIGATOR PA70; Cardexprt ST3D; Colormax Savage 3D; DataExpert Savant 3D DSV5 390; Hercules Terminator BEAST; Galaxie Group Venus Savage 3D; Gainward Cardex GX3; Sigma Savage 3D; Kasan G-Mania Savage 3D
	Savage4 (2D/3D NEW)	Creative Technology 3D Blaster Savage 4; Diamond Stealth III S540; ELSA Winner II
SiS	6326[4]	ASUS AGP-V1326; Aopen PG80/DVD; Aopen PA50D; Aopen PG80; Acorp Intl SiS 6326; DataExpert DSI5326; APAC Multimedia SI600A; Full Yes FYI—SiS 6326; Trumpdale PerformX SiS 6326 AGP; Shuttle HOT-155 AGP; Sertek DCS W821; Koutech Systems KW-750D; Palette Multimedia SiS 6326 AGP; Computer Solutions PA50; Genoa Hornet III DVD; Genoa Hornet III AGP
VideoLogic/NEC	PowerVR PCX2 (3D only RECENT)	Matrox m3D; VideoLogic 3Dx; VideoLogic 5D; VideoLogic 5D Sonic
	PowerVR 250 (2D/3D NEW)	VideoLogic Neon 250

1. *Although the Voodoo2 chipset is a 3D-only product whose cards must be connected to a 2D video card to operate, it remains a popular choice because of SLI (Scan Line Interleaving). By connecting two identical Voodoo2-chipset PCI cards from the same vendor with a special SLI ribbon cable, each card can be used to render alternate lines (card 1 renders lines 1, 3, 5, and so on and card 2 renders lines 2, 4, 6,and so on). This almost doubles fill rates and makes the combination of two Voodoo2 cards a worthy rival for newer 3D chipsets.*

2. *3Dfx acquired video board maker STB in 1999 and began to sell video cards under the 3Dfx name. 3Dfx still supplies Voodoo2 and Voodoo Banshee chipsets to other video card makers.*

3. *Rendition is now owned by PC and memory-maker Micron Technologies, which has renamed the previous Rendition Vérité 2100/2200 chipsets the v2000 (a.k.a v2x00). These chipsets are similar, except for the lack of video-capture features and slower speed in the 2100. A more advanced 2D/3D chipset, known as the V4400, is under development for release in the second half of 1999. PC and memory-maker Micron Technologies now owns Rendition. The previously announced Redline chipset was never released, but the V4400 will be an improved version of this technology.*

4. *The SiS 6326 has relatively weak 3D performance but is a popular choice for built-in video on motherboards using an SiS chipset.*

Upgrading or Replacing Your Video Card

With current developments in rock-bottom video card pricing, improvements in 3D display technology, and massive amounts of high-speed memory available on new video cards (up to 32MB!), it makes little sense today to add most upgrades to an existing video card. The component-level upgrades that can be added include

■ 3D-only cards, such as the cards based on the original 3Dfx Voodoo and Voodoo2 chipsets, which connect to your existing video card with a pass-through cable.

- Memory upgrades to permit higher color depths at a specified screen resolution.
- TV tuners, permitting you to watch cable or broadcast TV on your monitor.
- Video capture devices, allowing you to capture still or moving video to a file.
- 3D-only add-on video cards.

3D-only cards are still available, but their major benefit (adding 3D support to 2D-only cards) has been superseded by improvements in standard video cards. All but the cheapest current-model video cards offer varying levels of 3D support, and most offer better, faster 3D, including advanced rendering features that were not available when 3D-only cards were developed.

3D-only cards must be connected to the system's existing VGA-class graphics card to work. Figure 15.4 shows how a 3D accelerator is linked to a 2D video card.

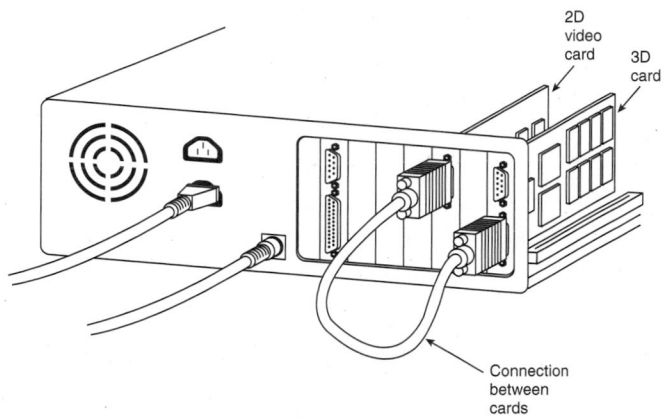

Figure 15.4 Diamond's Monster 3D card (right-side card) has two 15-pin ports. The upper port is used to connect to the monitor. The lower port has a cable connecting it to the original graphics card. 3D-only cards "pass through" standard signals and operate only when requested by a game API, such as OpenGL or Direct 3D/DirectX.

Because of the rise of high-speed, low-cost 2D/3D cards with the same or superior 3D performance, drastic price reductions have been taken by the manufacturers of 3D-only cards. If you're really cost-conscious, this may be tempting, but a better value for most users is replacing your existing 2D-only card with the best 2D/3D card you can afford. One major exception is cards based on the 3Dfx Voodoo2 chipset. By adding a second identical Voodoo2-based card from the same card vendor, you can take advantage of SLI (Scan Line Interleaving) for greatly improved fill rates. SLI draws the first line of the current image with one card, and then uses the other card to draw line 2, and continues to alternate.

Figure 15.5 shows the SLI passthrough connector on a typical Voodoo2-based card, the STB Blackmagic 3D.

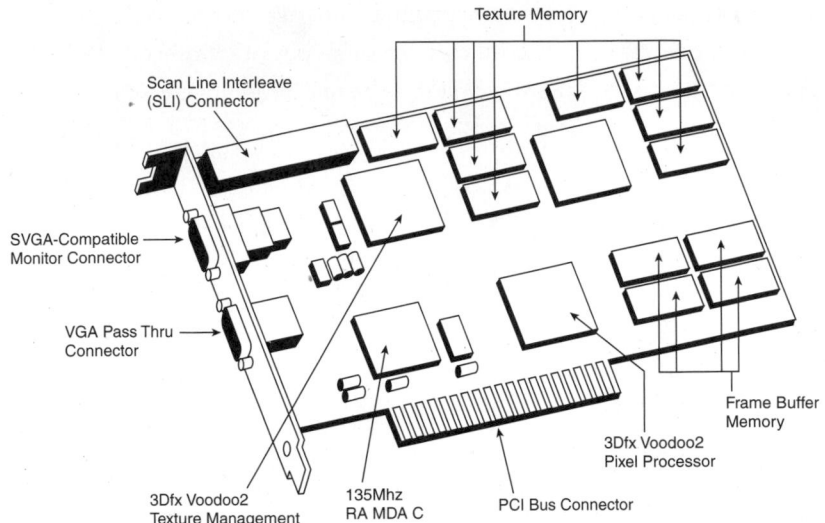

Texture Memory

Scan Line Interleave (SLI) Connector

SVGA-Compatible Monitor Connector

VGA Pass Thru Connector

Frame Buffer Memory

3Dfx Voodoo2 Pixel Processor

3Dfx Voodoo2 Texture Management

135Mhz RA MDA C

PCI Bus Connector

Figure 15.5 The Voodoo2-based STB Blackmagic 3D has a connection for an SLI ribbon cable on the upper-left quadrant of the card (as marked on this figure). To use SLI, the user needs two identical cards designed for SLI and must use the SLI ribbon cable supplied by the card vendor to connect the cards together. STB uses a 3.1-inch cable, so the cards need not be in adjacent slots.

Video Card Memory

Historically, most video cards have had provisions for some sort of memory upgrade, either with individual DIP (Dual Inline Pin) chips or with proprietary modules. Usually, video cards came in two versions: a low-priced variant with built-in memory and a connection for a memory upgrade, and a top-end variant with its memory fully expanded out of the box.

Starting about 1997, video card vendors began to abandon the idea of user-upgradable video card memory, probably for the following reasons:

- Most user-upgradable video cards were never upgraded, but were replaced.

- Recent memory trends have made it difficult to design memory upgrades that would work on more than one or two models.

- Increased use of surface-mount technology, high-capacity memory modules, and similar low-cost, high-reliability production techniques mean that a video card with user-upgradable memory is more expensive to make than a card loaded with 8MB or more of video memory.

- With the massive amounts of video memory available today on video cards (major-brand 32MB AGP-bus video cards retail for under $200), along with the improvements in 2D and 3D technology, it just makes sense to replace your aging 1MB, 2MB, or even 4MB video card with an up-to-date card. When you compare the price of adding 2MB or 4MB of proprietary memory (assuming you can still get it) to your existing video card to the price of a new card with 8–32MB of memory, you'll find the new cards a much better value.

TV Tuner and Video Capture Upgrades

Most video cards don't have TV tuner and video capture uprade features built in, and new cards with these features tend to be in the middle to high range of their manufacturers' price structures.

These features are exciting if you are already into video editing, want to add video to your Web site, or are trying to create CD-R/CD-RW archives of your home video. If you have an up-to-date video card with acceptable 2D and 3D performance and at least 8MB of video RAM, compare the price of the add-ons to the price of a new card with these features. You'll probably find the add-ons to be less expensive. If your card has 4MB of video RAM or less, I'd recommend replacing it with a new card with these features.

Note

If you're planning to upgrade to a new video card in the next year or two, find out if the TV or video add-on you want to buy for your present video card will work with the new model(s). If it's a TV tuner, you might need to consider other cards from the same vendor your current video card came from. If you're unsure of future compatibility, hold off on your purchase or consider buying a card with the desired features included.

Warranty and Support

Because a video card may go through several driver changes during its effective lifetime (about three years or two operating-system revisions), buying a video card from a major manufacturer usually assures you of better support during the card's lifetime. If you buy a card that uses widely available chipsets (such as S3s), you may be able to try a different vendor's version of drivers or use the chipset vendor's "generic" drivers if you don't get satisfactory support from your card vendor.

Keep in mind that using generic drivers (chipset level) or a different brand of drivers may cause problems if your original card's design was "tweaked" from the normal. Look at the vendor's technical support forums or third-party discussions on newsgroups, computer information Web sites such as ZDNET, or magazine Web sites to get a feel for the stability, reliability, and usefulness of a vendor's support and driver services, and for alternatives in case of difficulties.

Video Card Benchmarks

Industry-standard benchmarks such as ZDBOP's Graphics Winmark attempt to measure the performance of different video cards under a controlled testing environment. Unfortunately, especially for gamers, these benchmarks are sometimes "hacked" to allow an artificially high score that doesn't reflect true performance. Also, game performance in particular is partly a function of the APIs the game requires (such as DirectX's Direct3D, Glide, or OpenGL), along with the monitor resolution, color depth, and memory on the card.

Thus, the best way to see how a particular video card will perform for you is to look at the combination of frame rates and rendering quality for popular games. Some of the game standards being used in these comparisons include Quake II (Glide and OpenGL), Forsaken (Direct3D), Hexen II, and Quake (OpenGL). You can use game and video card manufacturers' Web sites and game-review Web sites to see these comparisons. The following game titles offer command-line or menu options that let you generate your own frame-rate reports: Quake/Quake 2, Incoming, Forsaken, Unreal, and Sin.

Microsoft's DirectX is used with virtually all game-oriented video cards, and video card performance can vary according to the version of DirectX in use. If you see drastic differences listed for the same video card and game from different review sources, check to see which version of DirectX was used. The latest version of DirectX is usually faster than previous versions.

Make sure you determine exactly which video card was used to perform the test. Many manufacturers use the same chipset across a line of cards. See the next section to see how this can affect you.

Keep in mind that frame rates are only part of the story. Some vendors support limited color depths to render graphics faster, but because 24-bit color looks more realistic, you might prefer a slightly slower frame rate and have your game look much better onscreen. Use screen shots, live demos (when possible), reviews, as well as frame rates to choose the best 3D card for you.

Comparing Video Cards with the Same Chipset

Many manufacturers create a line of video cards with the same chipset to sell at different pricing points. Why not save some dollars and get the cheapest model? Why not say "price is no object" and get the most expensive one? When you're faced with various cards in the "chipsetX" family, look for differences such as those shown in Table 15.19.

Table 15.19   Comparing Video Cards with the Features

Feature	Effect on You
RAMDAC speed	Less-expensive cards in a family often use a slower RAMDAC. As we saw earlier, this reduces maximum and flicker-free resolutions. If you use a 17-inch or larger monitor, this could be an eye-straining problem. Buy the card with the fastest RAMDAC, especially for use with 17-inch or larger monitors. Faster RAMDACs are often paired with SGRAM or WRAM, which are the fastest types of RAM currently found on video cards.
Amount of RAM	The former standard of 4MB as the practical maximum on a video card has been shattered by the rise of 3D games and applications and low memory prices. Although AGP video cards can use "AGP memory" (a section of main memory borrowed for texturing), it's still faster to perform as much work as possible on the card's own memory. PCI cards must perform all functions within their own memory. Less-expensive cards in a chipset family often have lower amounts of memory onboard, and most current-model cards aren't expandable. Buy a card with enough memory for your games or applications—today and tomorrow.
Memory type	High-end video cards frequently use the new SGRAM (Synchronous Graphics RAM), with SDRAM (Synchronous DRAM) as a popular choice for midrange video cards. The once-popular EDO (Extended Data Out) RAM is fading from view in both main memory and video memory applications. Choose SGRAM, and then SDRAM, in order of preference when possible.

Feature	Effect on You
Memory and core clock speed	Many suppliers adjust the recommended speed of graphics controllers in an effort to provide users with maximum performance. Sometimes the supplier may choose to exceed the rated specification of the graphics chip. Be cautious. Current controller chips are large and they can overheat. An overclocked device in an open system with great airflow may work—or it may fail in a period of months from overstress of the circuitry. If you have questions about the rated speed of a controller, check the chip suppliers' Web site. Many reputable companies do use overclocked parts, but the best vendors supply large heat sinks or even powered fans to avoid overheating.
TV tuner	You can save some money by having it built in, but it's not as important as the other issues listed earlier.

Adapter and Display Troubleshooting

Solving most graphics adapter and monitor problems is fairly simple, although costly, because replacing the adapter or display is the usual procedure. However, before you take this step, make sure that you have exhausted all your other options. One embarrassingly obvious fix to monitor display problems that is often overlooked by many users is to adjust the controls on the monitor, such as the contrast and the brightness. Although most monitors today have a control panel on the front of the unit, other adjustments may be possible as well.

Some NEC monitors, for example, have a focus adjustment screw on the left side of the unit. Because the screw is deep inside the case, the only evidence of its existence is a hole in the plastic grillwork on top of it. To adjust the monitor's focus, you have to stick a long-shanked screwdriver about two inches into the hole and feel around for the screw head. This type of adjustment can save you both an expensive repair bill and the humiliation of being ridiculed by the repair technician. Always examine the monitor case, the documentation, and the manufacturer's Web site or other online services for the locations of adjustment controls.

A defective or dysfunctional adapter or display usually is replaced as a single unit rather than being repaired. Most of today's adapters cost more to service than to replace, and the documentation required to service the hardware properly is not always available. You usually cannot get schematic diagrams, parts lists, wiring diagrams, and other documents for most adapters or monitors. Also, many adapters now are constructed with surface-mount technology that requires a substantial investment in a rework station before you can remove and replace these components by hand. You cannot use a $25 pencil-type soldering iron on these boards!

Servicing monitors is a slightly different proposition. Although a display often is replaced as a whole unit, many displays are too expensive to replace. Your best bet is either to contact the company from which you purchased the display or contact one of the companies that specializes in monitor depot repair.

Depot repair means that you send in your display to repair specialists who either fix your particular unit or return an identical unit they have already repaired. This is normally accomplished for a flat-rate fee; in other words, the price is the same no matter what they have done to repair your actual unit.

Because you will usually get a different (but identical) unit in return, they can ship out your repaired display immediately upon receiving the one you sent in, or even in advance in some cases. This way, you have the least amount of downtime and can receive the repaired display as quickly as possible. In some cases, if your particular monitor is unique or one they don't have in stock, you will have to wait while they repair your specific unit.

Troubleshooting a failed monitor is relatively simple. If your display goes out, for example, a swap with another monitor can confirm that the display is the problem. If the problem disappears when you change the display, the problem is almost certainly in the original display or the cable; if the problem remains, it is likely in the video adapter or PC itself.

Many of the better quality, late-model monitors have built-in self-diagnostic circuitry. Check your monitor's manual for details. Using this feature, if available, can help you determine whether the problem is really in the monitor, or in a cable, or somewhere else in the system. If self diagnostics produce an image onscreen, look to other parts of the video subsystem for your problem.

The monitor cable can sometimes be the source of display problems. A bent pin in the DB-15 connector that plugs into the video adapter can prevent the monitor from displaying images, or it can cause color shifts. Most of the time, you can repair the connector by carefully straightening the bent pin with sharp-nosed pliers.

If the pin breaks off or if the connector is otherwise damaged, you can sometimes replace the monitor cable. Some monitor manufacturers use cables that disconnect from the monitor and the video adapter, whereas others are permanently connected. Depending on the type of connector the device uses at the monitor end, you may have to contact the manufacturer for a replacement.

If you narrow down the problem to the display, consult the documentation that came with the monitor or call the manufacturer for the location of the nearest factory repair depot. Alternative, third-party depot repair service companies are also available that can repair most displays (if they are no longer covered by a warranty); their prices often are much lower than factory service. Check the Vendor List on the CD for several companies that do depot repair of computer monitors and displays.

Caution

You should never attempt to repair a CRT monitor yourself. Touching the wrong component can be fatal. The display circuits can hold extremely high voltages for hours, days, or even weeks after the power is shut off. A qualified service person should discharge the cathode ray tube and power capacitors before proceeding.

For most displays, you are limited to making simple adjustments. For color displays, the adjustments can be quite formidable if you lack experience. Even factory service technicians often lack proper documentation and service information for newer models; they usually exchange your unit for another and repair the defective one later. Never buy a display for which no local factory repair depot is available.

If you have a problem with a display or an adapter, it pays to call the manufacturer, who might know about the problem and make repairs available. Sometimes, when manufacturers encounter numerous problems with a product, they may offer free repair, replacements, or another generous offer that you would never know about if you did not call.

Remember, also, that many of the problems you may encounter with modern video adapters and displays are related to the drivers that control these devices rather than to the hardware. Be sure you have the latest and proper drivers before you attempt to have the hardware repaired; a solution may already be available.

Troubleshooting Monitors

Problem

No Picture

Solution

If the LCD on the front of the monitor is yellow or flashing green, the monitor is in power-saving mode. Move the mouse or press Alt+Tab on the keyboard and wait up to one minute to wake up the system if the system is turned on.

If no lights are on monitor, check the power and the power switch. Check the surge protector or power director to make sure power is going to the monitor. Replace the power cord with a known-working spare if necessary. Retest. Replace the monitor with a known-working spare to make sure the monitor is the problem.

Check data cables at the monitor and video card end.

Check TTL versus analog settings on dual-purpose monitors. TTL is used with EGA cards; analog is used with VGA and SVGA cards.

Problem

Jittery picture quality

LCD monitors. Use display-adjustment software to reduce or eliminate pixel jitter and pixel swim.

All monitors. Check cables for tightness at the video card and the monitor (if removable).

- Remove the extender cable and retest with the monitor plugged directly into the video card. If the extended cable is bad, replace it.
- Check the cables for damage; replace as needed.
- If problems are intermittent, check for interference. (Microwave ovens near monitors can cause severe picture distortion when turned on.)

CRT monitors. Check refresh-rate settings; reduce them until acceptable picture quality is achieved.

- Use onscreen picture adjustments until an acceptable picture quality is achieved.

■ If problems are intermittent and can be "fixed" by waiting or by gently tapping the side of the monitor, the monitor power supply is probably bad or has loose connections internally. Service or replace the monitor.

Troubleshooting Video Cards and Drivers

Problem

Display works in DOS, not in Windows

Solution

If you have an acceptable picture quality in MS-DOS mode (system boot) but no picture in Windows, most likely you have a wrong or corrupted video driver installed in Windows. Boot Windows 9x in safe mode (which uses a VGA driver) or install the VGA driver and restart Windows. If safe mode or VGA works, get the correct driver for the video card and reinstall.

Problem

Can't replace built-in video card with add-on PCI video card

Solution

Check with the video card and system vendor for a list of acceptable replacement video cards. Try another video card with a different chipset. Check the BIOS or motherboard for jumper or configuration settings to disable built-in video. Place the add-on card in a different PCI slot.

DisplayMate

DisplayMate is a unique diagnostic and testing program designed to thoroughly test your video adapter and display. It is somewhat unique in that most conventional PC hardware diagnostics programs do not emphasize video testing the way this program does.

I find it useful not only in testing whether a video adapter is functioning properly, but also in examining video displays. You can easily test the image quality of a display, which allows you to make focus, centering, brightness and contrast, color level, and other adjustments much more accurately than before. If you are purchasing a new monitor, you can use the program to evaluate the sharpness and linearity of the display and to provide a consistent way of checking each monitor that you are considering. If you use projection systems for presentations, as I do in my PC hardware seminars, you will find it invaluable for setting up and adjusting the projector.

DisplayMate can also test a video adapter thoroughly. It will set the video circuits into each possible video mode so you can test all its capabilities. It will also help you to determine the performance level of your card, both with respect to resolution and colors as well as speed. You can then use the program to benchmark the performance of the display, which enables you to compare one type of video adapter system to another.

See the Vendor List on the CD for more information on Sonera Technologies, the manufacturer and distributor of DisplayMate.

Some video-card vendors supply a special version of DisplayMate for use in diagnostics testing.

Serial, Parallel, and Other I/O Interfaces

SOME OF THE MAIN TOPICS IN THIS CHAPTER ARE

Introduction to I/O Ports

This chapter covers the primary peripheral input/output ports on a modern PC system. This includes serial ports, parallel ports, Universal Serial Bus (USB), and IEEE-1394 (i.Link or FireWire). Although SCSI and IDE are also I/O interfaces, they are important enough to warrant their own chapters for more specific and detailed coverage.

The most basic communications ports in any PC system are the serial and parallel ports.

Serial ports (also known as communication or COM ports) were originally used for devices that had to communicate bidirectionally with the system. Such devices include modems, mice, scanners, digitizers, and any other devices that "talk to" and receive information from the PC. Newer parallel port standards now allow the parallel port to perform high-speed bidirectional communications.

Several companies manufacture communications programs that perform high-speed transfers between PC systems using serial or parallel ports. Versions of these file transfer programs have been included with DOS 6.0 and higher (Interlink), and with Windows 95 and newer versions (DCC—Direct Cable Connection). There are currently several products on the market that make non-traditional use of the parallel port. For example, you can purchase network adapters, high-capacity floppy disk drives, CD-ROM drives, or tape backup units that attach to the parallel port.

Serial Ports

The asynchronous serial interface was designed as a system-to-system communications port. Asynchronous means that no synchronization or clocking signal is present, so characters can be sent with any arbitrary time spacing.

Each character that is sent over a serial connection is framed by a standard start-and-stop signal. A single 0 bit, called the start bit, precedes each character to tell the receiving system that the next eight bits constitute a byte of data. One or two stop bits follow the character to signal that the character has been sent. At the receiving end of the communication, characters are recognized by the start-and-stop signals instead of by the timing of their arrival. The asynchronous interface is character-oriented and has about a 20 percent overhead for the extra information that is needed to identify each character.

Serial refers to data that is sent over a single wire, with each bit lining up in a series as the bits are sent. This type of communication is used over the phone system because this system provides one wire for data in each direction. Add-on serial ports for the PC are available from many manufacturers. You can usually find these ports on one of the multifunction boards that is available, or on a board with at least a parallel port. Virtually all modern motherboards include a built-in Super I/O chip that adds one or two serial ports to the motherboard, which means that no additional interface card is required. Older systems normally have the serial ports on a card. Note that card-based modems also incorporate a built-in serial port on the card as part of the modem circuitry. Figure 16.1 shows the standard 9-pin connector that is used with most modern external serial ports. Figure 16.2 shows the original standard 25-pin version.

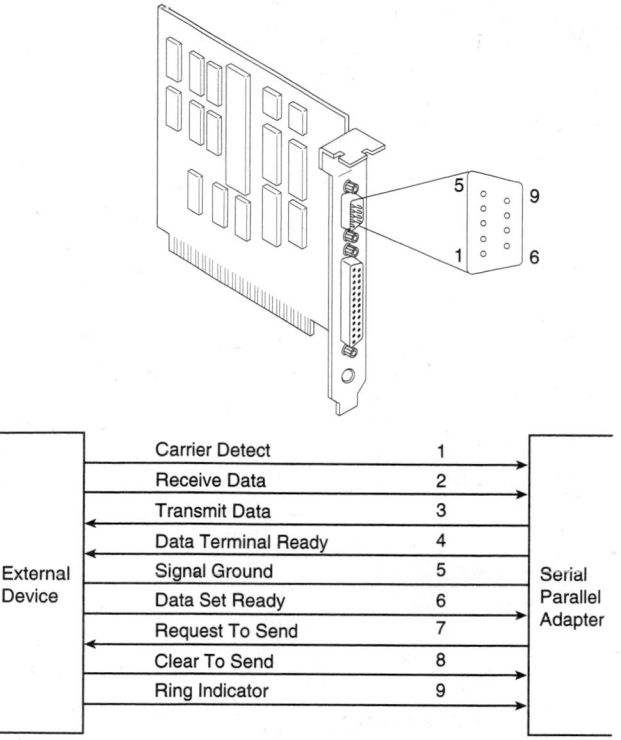

Figure 16.1 AT-style 9-pin serial-port connector specifications.

Serial ports can connect to a variety of devices, such as modems, plotters, printers, other computers, bar code readers, scales, and device control circuits. Basically, anything that needs a two-way connection to the PC uses the industry-standard Reference Standard number 232 revision c (RS-232c) serial port. This device enables data transfer between otherwise incompatible devices.

The official specification recommends a maximum cable length of 50 feet. The limiting factor is the total load capacitance of cable and input circuits of the interface. The maximum capacitance is specified as 2500 pF. There are special low-capacitance cables that can effectively increase the maximum cable length greatly, to as much as 500 feet or more. Also available are line drivers (amplifier/repeaters) that can extend cable length even further.

Tables 16.1, 16.2, and 16.3 show the pinouts of the 9-pin (AT-style), 25-pin, and 9-pin-to-25-pin serial connectors.

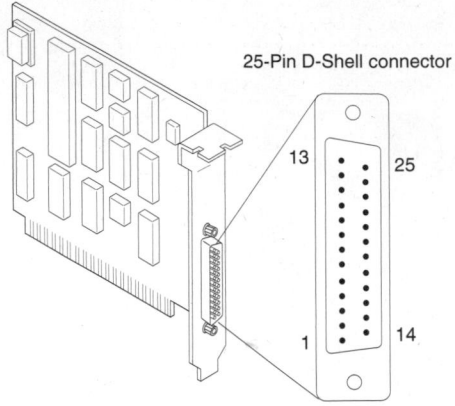

25-Pin D-Shell connector

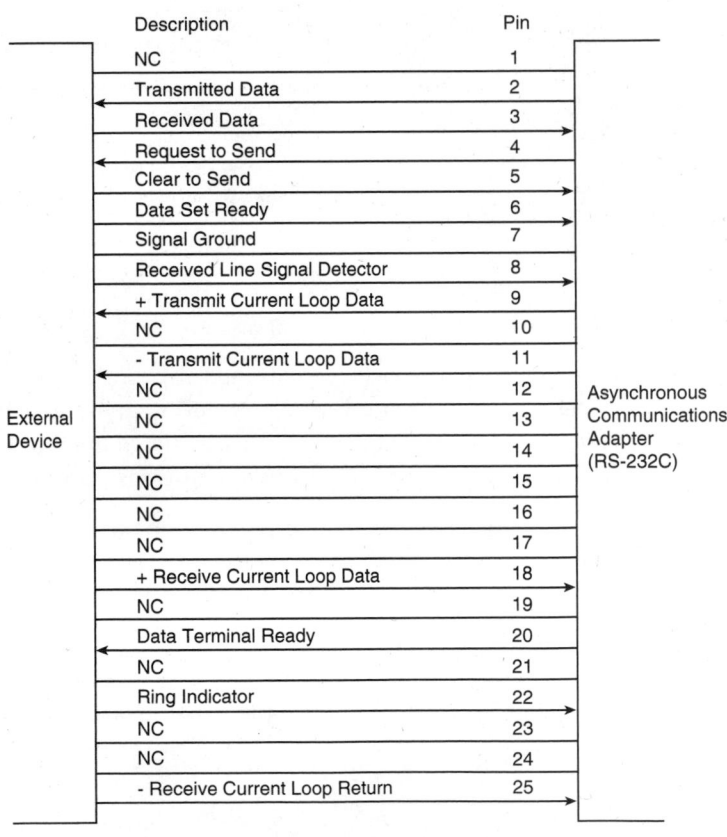

Description	Pin
NC	1
Transmitted Data	2
Received Data	3
Request to Send	4
Clear to Send	5
Data Set Ready	6
Signal Ground	7
Received Line Signal Detector	8
+ Transmit Current Loop Data	9
NC	10
- Transmit Current Loop Data	11
NC	12
NC	13
NC	14
NC	15
NC	16
NC	17
+ Receive Current Loop Data	18
NC	19
Data Terminal Ready	20
NC	21
Ring Indicator	22
NC	23
NC	24
- Receive Current Loop Return	25

External Device

Asynchronous Communications Adapter (RS-232C)

Figure 16.2 Standard 25-pin serial-port connector specifications.

Table 16.1   9-Pin (AT) Serial Port Connector

Pin	Signal	Description	I/O
1	CD	Carrier detect	In
2	RD	Receive data	In
3	TD	Transmit data	Out
4	DTR	Data terminal ready	Out
5	SG	Signal ground	-
6	DSR	Data set ready	In
7	RTS	Request to send	Out
8	CTS	Clear to send	In
9	RI	Ring indicator	In

Table 16.2   25-Pin (PC, XT, and PS/2) Serial Port Connector

Pin	Signal	Description	I/O
1	-	Chassis ground	-
2	TD	Transmit data	Out
3	RD	Receive data	In
4	RTS	Request to send	Out
5	CTS	Clear to send	In
6	DSR	Data set ready	In
7	SG	Signal ground	-
8	CD	Carrier detect	In
9	-	+Transmit current loop return	Out
11	-	-Transmit current loop data	Out
18	-	+Receive current loop data	In
20	DTR	Data terminal ready	Out
22	RI	Ring indicator	In
25	-	-Receive current loop return	In

Table 16.3   9-Pin to 25-Pin Serial Cable Adapter Connections

9-Pin	25-Pin	Signal	Description
1	8	CD	Carrier detect
2	3	RD	Receive data
3	2	TD	Transmit data
4	20	DTR	Data terminal ready
5	7	SG	Signal ground
6	6	DSR	Data set ready
7	4	RTS	Request to send
8	5	CTS	Clear to send
9	22	RI	Ring indicator

Note

Macintosh systems use a similar serial interface, defined as RS-422. Most external modems that are in use today can interface with either RS-232 or RS-422, but it is safest to make sure that the external modem you get for your PC is designed for a PC, not a Macintosh.

UARTs

The heart of any serial port is the Universal Asynchronous Receiver/Transmitter (UART) chip. This chip completely controls the process of breaking the native parallel data within the PC into serial format, and later converting serial data back into the parallel format.

There are several types of UART chips on the market. The original PC and XT used the 8250 UART, which was used for many years in low-priced serial cards. Starting with the first 16-bit systems, the 16450 UART was usually used. The only difference between these chips is their suitability for high-speed communications. The 16450 is better suited for high-speed communications than is the 8250; otherwise, both chips appear identical to most software.

The 16550 UART was the first serial chip used in the IBM PS/2 line, and other 386 and higher systems rapidly adopted it. This chip functioned as the earlier 16450 and 8250 chips, but it also included a 16-byte buffer that aided in faster communications. This is sometimes referred to as a FIFO (First In First Out) buffer. Unfortunately, the early 16550 chips had a few bugs, particularly in the buffer area. These bugs were corrected with the release of the 16550A. The most current version of the chip is the 16550D, which is produced by National Semiconductor.

Tip

The high-speed buffered 16550A (or newer) UART chip is pin-for-pin compatible with the 16450 UART. If your 16450 UART is socketed, a cheap and easy way to improve serial performance is to install a 16550 UART chip in the socket.

Because the 16550 is a faster, more reliable chip than its predecessors, it is best to ensure that your serial ports either have that chip or an equivalent. Most motherboards today that have built-in serial ports use a Super I/O chip that contains the serial port UARTs within it. If you are in doubt about which type of UART you have in your system, you can use the Microsoft MSD program (provided with Windows, MS DOS 6.x, and Windows 95) to determine the type of UART you have.

Note

Another way to tell if you have a 16650 UART in Windows 95 or 98 is to click the Start menu, and then choose Settings, Control Panel. Next, double-click Modems, and then click the Diagnostics tab. The Diagnostics tab shows a list of all COM ports in the system, even if they don't have a modem attached to them. Select the port you want to check in the list and click More Info. Windows 95 or 98 communicates with the port to determine the UART type, and that information is listed in the Port Information portion of the More Info box. If a modem was attached, additional information about the modem is displayed.

The original designer of these UARTs is National Semiconductor (NS). So many other manufacturers are producing clones of these UARTs that you probably don't have an actual NS brand part in your system. Even so, the part you have will be compatible with one of the NS parts, hopefully the 16550. In other words, check to see that whatever UART chip you have does indeed feature the 16-byte FIFO buffer, as found in the NS 16550 part.

Most motherboards now include Super I/O integrated chips that take on the functions of multiple separate chips. Most of these integrated chips function as a 16550 does; however, some that are used on older motherboards might not.

◄◄ See "Super I/O Chips," p. 267.

8250

IBM used this original chip in the PC serial port card. This chip had no transmit/receive buffer, which means that it was very slow. The chip also had several bugs, none of which were serious. The PC and XT ROM BIOSes were written to anticipate at least one of the bugs. The 8250B replaced this chip.

8250A

Do not use the second version of the 8250 in any system. This upgraded chip fixes several bugs in the 8250, including one in the interrupt enable register, but because the PC and XT ROM BIOSes expect the bug, this chip does not work properly with those systems. The 8250A works in an AT system that does not expect the bug, but it does not work adequately at 9600bps.

8250B

The last version of the 8250 fixes bugs from the previous two versions. The interrupt enable bug in the original 8250, which is expected by the PC and XT ROM BIOS software, has been put back into this chip, making the 8250B the most desirable chip for any non-AT serial port application. The 8250B chip might work in an AT under DOS, but it does not run properly at 9600bps because, like all 8250s, it has no transmit/receive buffer.

16450

IBM selected the higher-speed version of the 8250 for the AT. The higher performance mainly comes from a 1-byte transmit/receive buffer that is contained within the chip. Because this chip has fixed the aforementioned interrupt enable bug, the 16450 does not operate properly in many PC or XT systems because they expect this bug to be present. OS/2 requires this chip as a minimum; otherwise, the serial ports do not function properly. It also adds a scratch-pad register as the highest register. The 16450 is used primarily in AT systems because of its increase in throughput over the 8250B.

16550A

This chip is pin-compatible with the 16450, but is much faster due to a built-in 16-character Transmit and Receive FIFO buffer. It also allows multiple DMA channel access. The original version of this chip did not allow the buffer to work, but all 16550A or later revisions had the bug fixed. The last version that was produced by National Semiconductor was called the 16550D. Use a version of this UART in your serial port if you do any communications at 9600bps or higher. If your communications program makes use of the FIFO—and all of them do today—it can greatly increase communications speed and eliminate lost characters and data at the higher speeds. Virtually all Super I/O chips contain the equivalent of dual 16550A or later chips. Most 16550 UARTs have a maximum communications speed of 115Kbps (bits per second).

16650

Several companies have produced versions with larger buffers that they have called 16650 and 16750. These chips are not from National Semiconductor, and the designations only imply that they are compatible with the 16550 but have a larger buffer. The 16650 chips normally have a 32-byte buffer, and the 16750 chips have a 64-byte buffer. These larger buffered versions allow speeds of 230Kbps or 460Kbps and are recommended when you are running a high-speed external communications link such as an ISDN terminal adapter. These are discussed more in the following section.

High-Speed Serial Ports (ESP and Super ESP)

Some modem manufacturers have gone a step further in improving serial data transfer by introducing Enhanced Serial Ports (ESP) or Super High Speed Serial Ports. These ports enable a 28.8Kbps or faster modem to communicate with the computer at data rates up to 921.6Kbps. The extra speed on these ports is generated by increasing the buffer size. These ports are usually based on a 16550, 16650, or 16750 UART, and some even include more buffer memory on the card. Most allow raw port speed settings of 230Kbps or 460Kbps, which is valuable when connecting a PC to a high-speed external component that is connected to a serial port, such as an ISDN terminal adapter. You can't really get the full-speed benefit of an external ISDN modem (terminal adapter) unless your serial port can go at least 230Kbps. Lava Computer Mfg. is one company that offers a complete line of high-speed serial and parallel port cards (see the Vendor List on the accompanying CD).

As the need for additional serial devices continues to increase, users are beginning to need more than the standard two COM ports that are built into most modern motherboards. As a result, multiport serial cards were created. These cards generally have 2–32 ports on them. Often, they also provide higher baud rates than can be achieved on a standard serial port.

Most of the multiport serial cards on the market use standard 16550 UARTs with a processor (typically an 80X86 based processor) and some memory. These cards can improve performance slightly because the processor is dedicated to handling serial information. However, it's not always the best method for high-performance applications.

Some of the better multiport serial cards have broken the model of the 16550 UART in favor of a single integrated circuit. These cards have the advantage of higher sustainable throughput without loss.

Various manufacturers make versions of the 16550; National Semiconductor was the first. The current version is a 40-pin DIP (Dual In-line Pin package) chip called the NS16550D. You can contact Fry's Electronics or Jameco Electronics to obtain the NS16550D, for example.

Note that modern systems don't use these individual UART chips; instead, there will be a component on the motherboard called a *super I/O* chip. This normally has two serial port UARTs as well as a multimode parallel port, floppy controller, keyboard controller, and sometimes the CMOS memory, all built in to a single tiny chip. Still, this chip acts as if all these separate devices were installed: That is, from a software point of view, both the operating system and applications still act as if separate UART chips were installed on serial port adapter cards. Super I/O chips are discussed throughout this chapter and in Chapter 4, "Motherboards and Buses."

Serial Port Configuration

Each time a character is received by a serial port, it has to get the attention of the computer by raising an Interrupt Request Line (IRQ). Eight-bit ISA bus systems have eight of these lines, and systems with a 16-bit ISA bus have 16 lines. The 8259 interrupt controller chip usually handles these requests for attention. In a standard configuration, COM 1 uses IRQ4, and COM 2 uses IRQ3.

When a serial port is installed in a system, it must be configured to use specific I/O addresses (called ports), and interrupts (called IRQs for Interrupt Request). The best plan is to follow the existing standards for how these devices are to be set up. For configuring serial ports, use the addresses and interrupts indicated in Table 16.4.

Table 16.4   Standard Serial I/O Port Addresses and Interrupts

COM x	I/O Ports	IRQ
COM 1	3F8-3FFh	IRQ4
COM 2	2F8-2FFh	IRQ3
COM 3	3E8-3EFh	IRQ4*
COM 4	2E8-2EFh	IRQ3*

Note that although many serial ports can be set up to share IRQ 3 and 4 with COM 1 and COM 2, it is not recommended. The best recommendation is setting COM 3 to IRQ 10 and COM4 to IRQ 11 (if available). If ports above COM 3 are required, it is recommended that you purchase a special multiport serial board.

Make sure that if you are adding more than the standard COM 1 and COM 2 serial ports, they use unique and non-conflicting interrupts. If you purchase a serial port adapter card and intend to use it to supply ports beyond the standard COM1 and COM2, be sure that it can use interrupts other than IRQ3 and IRQ4.

Note that BIOS manufacturers never built support for COM 3 and COM 4 into the BIOS. Therefore, DOS cannot work with serial ports above COM 2 because DOS gets its I/O information from the BIOS. The BIOS finds out what is installed in your system, and where it is installed, during the POST (power on self test). The POST checks only for the first two installed ports. This is not a problem at all under Windows because both Windows 95/98 and NT have built-in support for up to 128 ports.

With support for up to 128 serial ports in Windows, it is much easier to use multiport boards in the system. Multiport boards give your system the capability to collect or share data with multiple devices while using only one slot and one interrupt.

Caution

Sharing interrupts between COM ports—or any devices—can function properly sometimes and not others. It is recommended that you never share interrupts between multiple serial ports. Trying to track down drivers, patches, and updates to allow this to work successfully—if it's even possible at all in your system—can cause you hours of frustration.

◄◄ See "Resolving Resource Conflicts," p. 326.

Testing Serial Ports

You can perform several tests on serial and parallel ports. The two most common types of tests are those that involve software only, and those that involve both hardware and software. The software-only tests are done with diagnostic programs such as Microsoft's MSD, whereas the hardware and software tests involve using a wrap plug to perform loopback testing.

▶▶ See "Testing Parallel Ports," p. 890.

▶▶ See "Advanced Diagnostics Using Loopback Testing," p. 882.

Microsoft Diagnostics (MSD)

MSD is a diagnostic program that is supplied with MS-DOS 6.x, Microsoft Windows, and Windows 9x. Early versions of the program were also shipped with some Microsoft applications, such as Microsoft Word for DOS. Note that with Windows 95 this program can be found on the CD-ROM in the \other\msd directory. In Windows 98, you can find it on the CD-ROM in the \tools\oldmsdos directory. MSD is not automatically installed when you install the operating system. To use it, you must run it from the CD-ROM directly or copy the program from the CD-ROM to your hard disk.

For the most accurate results, many diagnostics programs, such as MSD, are best run in a DOS-only environment. Because of this, you need to restart the machine in DOS mode before using them. Then, to use MSD, switch to the directory in which it is located. This is not necessary, of course, if the directory that contains the program is in your search path, which is often the case with the DOS 6.x or Windows-provided versions of MSD. Then simply type MSD at the DOS prompt and press Enter. Soon you see the MSD screen.

Choose the Serial Ports option. Notice that you are given information about which type of serial chip you have in your system, as well as information about which ports are available. If any of the ports are in use (with a mouse, for example), that information is provided as well.

MSD is helpful in at least determining whether your serial ports are responding. If MSD cannot determine the existence of a port, it does not provide the report that indicates that the port exists. This sort of "look-and-see" test is the first action I usually take to determine why a port is not responding.

Troubleshooting I/O Ports in Windows

Windows 95/98 can tell you whether your ports are functioning. First, you need to verify that the required communications files are present to support the serial ports in your system:

1. Verify the file sizes and dates of both COMM.DRV (16-bit serial driver) and SERIAL.VXD (32-bit serial driver) in the SYSTEM directory, compared to the original versions of these files from the Windows 9x CD-ROM.

2. Confirm that the following lines are present in SYSTEM.INI:

```
[boot]
comm.drv=comm.drv
[386enh]
device=*vcd
```

The SERIAL.VXD driver is not loaded in SYSTEM.INI; instead, it is loaded through the Registry. If both drivers are present and accounted for, you can determine if a particular serial port's I/O address and IRQ settings are properly defined by following these steps:

1. Right-click the System icon and select Properties. Click on the Device Manager tab, Ports, and then select a specific port (such as COM 1).

2. Click the Properties button, and then click the Resources tab to display the current resource settings (IRQ, I/O) for that port.

3. Check the Conflicting Devices List to see if the port is using resources that conflict with other devices. If the port is in conflict with other devices, click the Change Setting button, and then select a configuration that does not cause resource conflicts. You might need to experiment with these settings until you find the right one.

4. If the resource settings cannot be changed, most likely they must be changed via the BIOS Setup. Shut down and restart the system, enter the BIOS setup, and change the port configurations there.

◀◀ See "Resolving Resource Conflicts," p. 326.

A common problem occurs when people try to use a modem on COM 3 with a serial mouse or other device on COM 1. Normally, COM 1 and COM 3 ports use the same IRQ, meaning that they cannot be used simultaneously. The COM 2 and COM 4 ports have the same problem sharing IRQs. If possible, change the COM 3 or COM 4 port to an IRQ setting that is not in conflict with COM1 or COM 2. Note also that some video adapters have an automatic address conflict with COM 4.

Advanced Diagnostics Using Loopback Testing

One of the most useful types of diagnostic test is the loopback test, which can be used to ensure the correct function of the serial port and any attached cables. Loopback tests are basically internal (digital) or external (analog). You can run internal tests by simply unplugging any cables from the port and executing the test via a diagnostics program.

The external loopback test is more effective. This test requires that a special loopback connector or wrap plug be attached to the port in question. When the test is run, the port is used to send data out to the loopback plug, which simply routes the data back into the port's receive pins so that the port is transmitting and receiving at the same time. A loopback or wrap plug is nothing more than a cable that is doubled back on itself. Most diagnostics programs that run this type of test include the loopback plug, and if not, these types of plugs can be purchased easily or even built.

Following is a list of the wiring needed to construct your own loopback or wrap plugs:

- Standard IBM type 25-Pin Serial (Female DB25S) Loopback Connector (Wrap Plug). Connect the following pins:

    1 to 7

    2 to 3

    4 to 5 to 8

    6 to 11 to 20 to 22

    15 to 17 to 23

    18 to 25

- Norton Utilities (Symantec) 25-Pin Serial (Female DB25S) Loopback Connector (Wrap Plug). Connect the following pins:

    2 to 3

    4 to 5

    6 to 8 to 20 to 22

- Standard IBM type 9-Pin Serial (Female DB9S) Loopback Connector (Wrap Plug). Connect the following pins:

    1 to 7 to 8

    2 to 3

    4 to 6 to 9

- Norton Utilities (Symantec) 9-Pin Serial (Female DB9S) Loopback Connector (Wrap Plug). Connect the following pins:

    2 to 3

    7 to 8

    1 to 4 to 6 to 9

◄◄ See "Serial Ports," p. 872.

To make these loopback plugs, you need a connector shell with the required pins installed. Then wire wrap or solder wires, interconnecting the appropriate pins inside the connector shell as specified in the preceding list. In most cases, it is less expensive to purchase a set of loopback connectors that are premade than it is to make them yourself. Most companies that sell diagnostics software, such as Symantec (Norton Utilities), can also sell you a set of loopback plugs.

One advantage of using loopback connectors is that you can plug them into the ends of a cable that is included in the test. This can verify that both the cable and the port are working properly.

If you need to test serial ports further, refer to Chapter 25, "PC Diagnostics, Testing, and Maintenance," which describes third-party testing software.

Parallel Ports

Parallel ports are normally used for connecting printers to a PC. Even though that was their sole original intention, parallel ports have become much more useful over the years as a more general-purpose, relatively high-speed interface between devices. Originally the ports were one way only; modern parallel ports can send and receive data.

Parallel ports are so named because they have eight lines for sending all the bits that comprise one byte of data simultaneously across eight wires. This interface is fast and has traditionally been used for printers. However, programs that transfer data between systems have always used the parallel port as an option for transmitting data because it can do so four bits at a time rather than one bit at a time as with a serial interface.

The following section looks at how these programs transfer data between parallel ports. The only problem with parallel ports is that their cables cannot be extended for any great length without amplifying the signal, or errors occur in the data. Table 16.5 shows the pinout for a standard PC parallel port.

Table 16.5   25-Pin PC-Compatible Parallel Port Connector

Pin	Description	I/O	Pin	Description	I/O
1	-Strobe	Out	14	-Auto Feed	Out
2	+Data Bit 0	Out	15	-Error	In
3	+Data Bit 1	Out	16	-Initialize Printer	Out
4	+Data Bit 2	Out	17	-Select Input	Out
5	+Data Bit 3	Out	18	-Data Bit 0 Return (GND)	In
6	+Data Bit 4	Out	19	-Data Bit 1 Return (GND)	In
7	+Data Bit 5	Out	20	-Data Bit 2 Return (GND)	In
8	+Data Bit 6	Out	21	-Data Bit 3 Return (GND)	In
9	+Data Bit 7	Out	22	-Data Bit 4 Return (GND)	In
10	-Acknowledge	In	23	-Data Bit 5 Return (GND)	In
11	+Busy	In	24	-Data Bit 6 Return (GND)	In
12	+Paper End	In	25	-Data Bit 7 Return (GND)	In
13	+Select	In			

IEEE 1284 Parallel Port Standard

The IEEE 1284 standard, called "Standard Signaling Method for a Bidirectional Parallel Peripheral Interface for Personal Computers," was approved for final release in March 1994. This standard defines the physical characteristics of the parallel port, including data transfer modes and physical and electrical specifications.

IEEE 1284 defines the electrical signaling behavior external to the PC for a multimodal parallel port that can support 4-bit modes of operation. Not all modes are required by the 1284 specification, and the standard makes some provision for additional modes.

The IEEE 1284 specification is targeted at standardizing the behavior between a PC and an attached device, specifically attached printers. However, the specification is of interest to vendors of parallel port peripherals (disks, LAN adapters, and so on).

IEEE 1284 is a hardware and line control-only standard and does not define how software is to talk to the port. An offshoot of the original 1284 standard has been created to define the software interface. The IEEE 1284.3 committee was formed to develop a standard for software that is used with IEEE 1284-compliant hardware. This standard, designed to address the disparity among providers of parallel port chips, contains a specification for supporting EPP mode via the PC's system BIOS.

IEEE 1284 allows for much higher throughput in a connection between a computer and a printer or two computers. The result is that the printer cable is no longer the standard printer cable. The IEEE 1284 printer cable uses twisted-pair technology, which results in a much more reliable and error-free connection.

The IEEE-1284 standard also defines the parallel port connectors, including the two pre-existing types (called Type A and Type B), as well as an additional high-density Type C connector. Type A refers to the standard DB25 connector that is used on most PC systems for parallel port connections, whereas Type B refers to the standard 36-pin Centronics style connector found on most printers. Type C is a new high-density 36-pin connector that can be found on some of the newer printers on the market, such as those from HP. The three connectors are shown in Figure 16.3.

The IEEE 1284 parallel port standard defines five different port operating modes, emphasizing the higher speed EPP and ECP modes. Some of the modes are input only, whereas others are output only. These five modes combine to create four different types of ports, as shown in the following table:

Parallel Port Type	Input Mode	Output Mode	Comments
SPP (Standard Parallel Port)	Nibble	Compatible	4-bit input, 8-bit output
Bidirectional	Byte	Compatible	8-bit I/O
EPP (Enhanced Parallel Port)	EPP	EPP	8-bit I/O
ECP (Enhanced Capabilities Port)	ECP	ECP	8-bit I/O, uses DMA

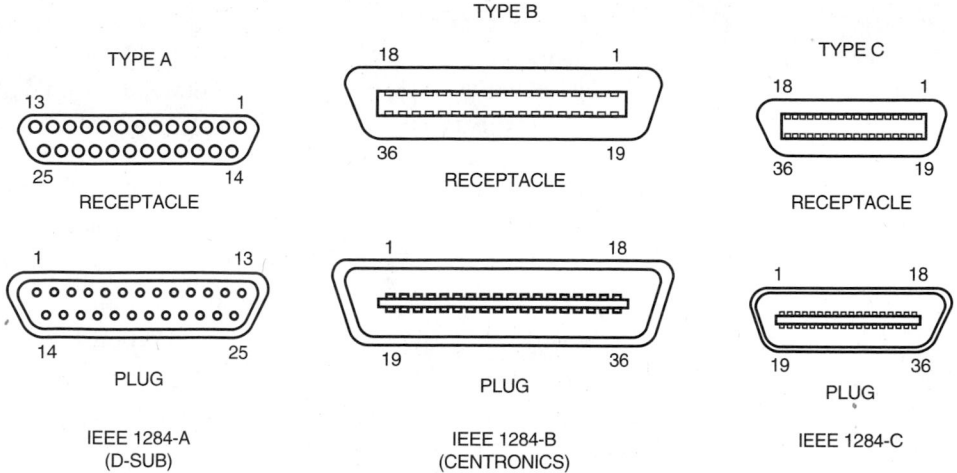

Figure 16.3 The three different types of IEEE 1284 parallel port connectors.

The 1284 defined Parallel Port Modes are shown in the following table, which also shows the approximate transfer speeds:

Parallel Port Mode	Direction	Transfer Rate
Nibble (4-bit)	Input only	50KB/sec
Byte (8-bit)	Input only	150KB/sec
Compatible	Output only	150KB/sec
EPP (Enhanced Parallel Port)	Input/Output	500KB–2MB/sec
ECP (Enhanced Capabilities Port)	Input/Output	500KB–2MB/sec

Each of the port types and modes are discussed in the following sections.

Standard Parallel Ports (SPP)

Older PCs did not have different types of parallel ports available. The only available port was the parallel port that was used to send information from the computer to a device such as a printer. The unidirectional nature of the original PC parallel port is consistent with its primary use—that is, sending data to a printer. There were times, however, when it was desirable to have a bidirectional port—for example, when it was necessary to receive feedback from a printer, which is common with PostScript printers. This could not be done easily with the original unidirectional ports.

Although it was never intended to be used for input, a clever scheme was devised in which four of the signal lines can be used as a 4-bit input connection. Thus, these ports can do 8-bit (byte) output (called Compatible mode) and 4-bit input (called nibble mode). This is still very common on low-end desktop systems. Systems built after 1993 are likely to have more capable parallel ports, such as bidirectional, EPP, or ECP.

Standard parallel ports are capable of effective transfer rates of about 150KBytes/sec output, and about 50KBytes/sec input.

Bidirectional (8-bit) Parallel Ports

With the introduction of the PS/2 series of machines in 1987, IBM introduced the bidirectional parallel port. These are commonly found in PC-compatible systems today and can be designated "bidirectional," "PS/2 type," or "extended" parallel ports. This port design opened the way for true communication between the computer and the peripheral across the parallel port. This was done by defining a few of the previously unused pins in the parallel connector, and by defining a status bit to indicate in which direction information was traveling across the channel. This allows for a true 8-bit (called byte mode) input.

These ports can do both 8-bit input and output using the standard eight data lines, and are considerably faster than the 4-bit ports when used with external devices. Bidirectional ports are capable of approximately 150KB/sec transfer rates on both output and input.

Enhanced Parallel Port (EPP)

EPP is a newer specification, sometimes referred to as the Fast Mode parallel port. The EPP was developed by Intel, Xircom, and Zenith Data Systems, and was announced in October 1991. The first products to offer EPP were Zenith Data Systems laptops, Xircom Pocket LAN Adapters, and the Intel 82360 SL I/O chip. Currently, almost all systems include a multimode parallel port, usually built into the super I/O chip on the motherboard, that supports EPP mode.

EPP operates at almost ISA bus speed and offers a tenfold increase in the raw throughput capability over a conventional parallel port. EPP is especially designed for parallel port peripherals such as LAN adapters, disk drives, and tape backups. EPP has been included in the new IEEE 1284 Parallel Port standard. Transfer rates of up to 2MB/sec are possible with EPP.

Since the original Intel 82360 SL I/O chip in 1992, other major chip vendors (such as National Semiconductor, SMC, Western Digital, and VLSI) have also produced I/O chipsets that offer some form of EPP capability. One problem is that the procedure for enabling EPP across the various chips differs widely from vendor to vendor, and many vendors offer more than one I/O chip.

EPP version 1.7 (March 1992) identifies the first popular version of the hardware specification. With minor changes, this has since been abandoned and folded into the IEEE 1284 standard. Some technical reference materials have erroneously made reference to "EPP specification version 1.9," causing confusion about the EPP standard. Note that "EPP version 1.9" technically does not exist, and any EPP specification after the original version 1.7 is more accurately referred to as a part of the IEEE 1284 specification.

Unfortunately, this has resulted in two somewhat incompatible standards for EPP parallel ports: the original EPP Standards Committee version 1.7 standard, and the IEEE 1284 Committee standard, normally called EPP version 1.9. The two standards are similar enough that new peripherals can be designed to support both standards, but older EPP 1.7 peripherals might not operate with EPP 1284 (EPP 1.9) ports. For this reason, many multimode ports allow configuration in either EPP 1.7 or 1.9 modes, normally selected via the BIOS Setup.

EPP ports are now supported in virtually all Super I/O chips that are used on modern motherboards. Because the EPP port is defined in the IEEE 1284 standard, it has also gained software and driver support, including support in Windows NT.

Enhanced Capabilities Port (ECP)

Another type of high-speed parallel port, the ECP (Enhanced Capabilities Port), was jointly developed by Microsoft and Hewlett-Packard and was formally announced in 1992. Like EPP, ECP offers improved performance for the parallel port and requires special hardware logic.

Since the original announcement, ECP is included in IEEE 1284—just like EPP. Unlike EPP, however, ECP is not tailored to support portable PCs' parallel port peripherals; its purpose is to support an inexpensive attachment to a very high-performance printer or scanner. Furthermore, ECP mode requires the use of a DMA channel, which EPP did not define and which can cause troublesome conflicts with other devices that use DMA. Most PCs with newer super I/O chips can support either EPP or ECP mode.

Most new systems are being delivered with ECP ports that support high throughput communications. In most cases, the ECP ports can be turned into EPP or standard parallel ports via BIOS. However, it's recommended that the port be placed in ECP mode for the best throughput.

Upgrading to EPP/ECP Parallel Ports

If you are purchasing a system today, I recommend one that has a so-called Super I/O chip that supports both EPP and ECP operation. If you want to test the parallel ports in a system, especially to determine what type they are, I highly recommend a utility called Parallel. This is a handy parallel port information utility that examines your system's parallel ports and reports the Port Type, I/O address, IRQ level, BIOS name, and an assortment of informative notes and warnings in a compact and easy-to-read display. The output can be redirected to a file for tech support purposes. Parallel uses very sophisticated techniques for port and IRQ detection, and it is aware of a broad range of quirky port features. You can get it from Parallel Technologies (see the Vendor's List on the CD-ROM).

If you have an older system that does not include an EPP/ECP port and you want to upgrade, there are several companies that now offer boards with the correct Super I/O chips to implement these features. I recommend that you check with Farpoint Communications, Byterunner Technologies, or Lava Computer Mfg.; they are listed in the Vendor List on the CD accompanying this book.

High speed parallel ports such as EPP and ECP type are often used for supporting external peripherals such as Zip drives, CD-ROM drives, tape drives, and even hard disks. Most of these devices attach to the parallel port using a pass-through connection. This means that your local printer can still work through the port, along with the device. The device will have its own drivers that mediate both the communications with the device and the printer pass-through. Using EPP or ECP modes, communications speeds that are as high as 2MB/sec can be achieved. This can allow a relatively high speed device to function almost as if it were connected to the system bus internally.

Parallel Port Configuration

The configuration of parallel ports is not as complicated as it is for serial ports. Even the original IBM PC had BIOS support for three LPT ports. Table 16.6 shows the standard I/O address and interrupt settings for parallel port use.

Table 16.6   Parallel Interface I/O Port Addresses and Interrupts

Standard LPTx	Alternate LPTx	I/O Ports	IRQ
LPT1	-	3BC-3BFh	IRQ7
LPT1	LPT2	378-37Ah	IRQ5
LPT2	LPT3	278h-27Ah	IRQ5

Because the BIOS and DOS have always provided three definitions for parallel ports, problems with older systems are infrequent. Problems can arise, however, from the lack of available interrupt-driven ports for ISA/PCI bus systems. Normally, an interrupt-driven port is not absolutely required for printing operations; in fact, many programs do not use the interrupt-driven capability. Many programs do use the interrupt, however, such as network print programs and other types of background or spooler-type printer programs.

Also, high-speed laser-printer utility programs often use the interrupt capabilities to allow for printing. If you use these types of applications on a port that is not interrupt driven, you see the printing slow to a crawl—if it works at all. The only solution is to use an interrupt-driven port. MS-DOS and Windows 95/98 now support up to 128 parallel ports.

To configure parallel ports in ISA/PCI bus systems, you normally use the BIOS setup program for ports that are built into the motherboard, or maybe set jumpers and switches for adapter card based ports. Because each board on the market is different, you always want to consult the OEM manual for that particular card if you need to know how the card needs to be configured.

◄◄ See "BIOS Hardware/Software," p. 347.

Linking Systems with Parallel Ports

The original IBM PC designers envisioned that the parallel port would be used only for communicating with a printer. Over the years, the number of devices that can be used with a parallel port has increased tremendously. You now can find everything from tape backup units to LAN adapters to CD-ROMs that connect through your parallel port. Some modem manufacturers now have modems that connect to the parallel port instead of the serial port for faster data transfer.

Perhaps one of the most common uses of bidirectional parallel ports is to transfer data between your system and another, such as a laptop computer. If both systems use an EPP/ECP port, you can actually communicate at rates of up to 2MB/sec, which rivals the speed of some hard disk drives. This capability has led to an increase in software to serve this niche of the market. If you are interested in such software (and the parallel ports necessary to facilitate the software), refer to the reviews that periodically appear in sources such as *PC Magazine*.

Connecting two computers with standard unidirectional parallel ports requires a special cable known as a null modem cable. Most programs sell or provide these cables with their software. However, if you need to make one for yourself, Table 16.7 provides the wiring diagram you need.

Table 16.7   Null Modem/Lap Link Cable Wiring

25-pin	Signal Descriptions		Signal Descriptions	25-pin
pin 2	Data Bit 0	÷	-Error	pin 15
pin 3	Data Bit 1	÷	Select	pin 13
pin 4	Data Bit 2	÷	Paper End	pin 12
pin 5	Data Bit 3	÷	-Acknowledge	pin 10
pin 6	Data Bit 4	÷	Busy	pin 11
pin 15	-Error	÷	Data Bit 0	pin 2
pin 13	Select	÷	Data Bit 1	pin 3
pin 12	Paper End	÷	Data Bit 2	pin 4
pin 10	-Acknowledge	÷	Data Bit 3	pin 5
pin 11	Busy	÷	Data Bit 4	pin 6
pin 25	Ground	÷	Ground	pin 25

Tip

Even though cables are usually provided for data transfer programs, notebook users might want to look for an adapter that makes the appropriate changes to a standard parallel cable. This can make traveling lighter by preventing the need for additional cables. Most of the time, these adapters attach to the Centronics end of the cable and provide a standard DB25 connection on the other end. They're sold under a variety of names; however, null modem cable, Laplink adapter, or Laplink converter are the most common names.

Although the wiring configuration and premade interlink cables listed in Table 16.7 work for connecting two machines with ECP/EPP ports, they can't take advantage of the advanced transfer rates of these ports. Special cables are needed to communicate between ECP/EPP ports. Parallel Technologies is a company that sells ECP/EPP cables for connecting to other ECP/EPP computers, as well as a universal cable for connecting any two parallel ports in order to use the highest speed. Connect Air is on the Vendor's List on the CD.

Windows 95 and newer versions include a special program called DCC (Direct Cable Connection), which allows two systems to be networked together via a null modem/LapLink cable. Consult the Windows documentation for information on how to establish a DCC connection. A company called Parallel Technologies (see the Vendor's List on the CD-ROM) has been contracted by Microsoft to supply the special DCC cables used to connect the systems. They have one special type of cable that uses active electronics to ensure a reliable high-speed interconnection.

Parallel to SCSI Converters

Parallel ports can also be used to connect peripherals such as SCSI drives, scanners, or other devices to a PC. This is done by attaching a parallel to SCSI converter to the parallel port, and then you can attach any SCSI device to the SCSI port on the converter. Adaptec is the major supplier of such converters, but they are available from other companies as well.

With a parallel to SCSI converter, you can connect any type of SCSI device such as hard disks, CD-ROM drives, tape drives, Zip drives, or scanners to your PC, all via the parallel port. In order to connect to a SCSI device and also continue to be able to print, most parallel to SCSI converters include a pass-through connection for a printer.

This means that at one end of the converter you have a connection to your parallel port, and at the other end you have both SCSI and parallel port connections. Thus, you can plug an SCSI device (or even multiple devices via a SCSI daisy chain), and still connect your printer as well. The drivers for the parallel to SCSI converter automatically pass through any information to the printer, so the printer works normally.

Testing Parallel Ports

Testing parallel ports is, in most cases, simpler than testing serial ports. The procedures are effectively the same as those used for serial ports, except that when you use the diagnostics software, you choose the obvious choices for parallel ports rather than serial ports.

Not only are the software tests similar, but the hardware tests require the proper plugs for the loopback tests on the parallel port. Several different loopback plugs are required, depending on what software you are using. Most use the IBM style loopback, but some use the style that originated in the Norton Utilities diagnostics.

The following wiring is needed to construct your own loopback or wrap plugs to test a parallel port:

- IBM 25-Pin Parallel (Male DB25P) Loopback Connector (Wrap Plug). Connect the following pins:

  1 to 13

  2 to 15

  10 to 16

  11 to 17

- Norton Utilities 25-Pin Parallel (Male DB25P) Loopback Connector (Wrap Plug). Connect the following pins:

  2 to 15

  3 to 13

  4 to 12

  5 to 10

  6 to 11

USB and 1394 (i.Link) FireWire—Serial and Parallel Port Replacements

Two new high-speed serial-bus architectures for desktop and portable are becoming available: the Universal Serial Bus (USB) and IEEE 1394, which is also called i.Link or FireWire. These are high-speed communications ports that far outstrip the capabilities of the standard serial and parallel ports most systems contain today. They can be used as an alternative to SCSI for high-speed peripheral connections. In addition to performance, these new ports will offer I/O device consolidation, which means that all types of external peripherals will connect to these ports.

The recent trend in high-performance peripheral bus design is to use a serial architecture, where one bit at a time is sent down a wire. Parallel architecture uses 8, 16, or more wires to send bits simultaneously. At the ne clock speed, the parallel bus is faster; however, it is much easier to increase the clock speed of a serial connection than that of a parallel connection.

Parallel connections suffer from several problems, the biggest being signal skew and jitter. Skew and jitter are the reasons that high-speed parallel buses such as SCSI are limited to short distances of three meters or less. The problem is that although the eight or 16 bits of data are fired from the transmitter at the same time, by the time they reach the receiver, propagation delays have conspired to allow some bits to arrive before the others. The longer the cable, the longer the time between the arrival of the first and last bits at the other end! This signal skew, as it is called, prevents you from running a high-speed transfer rate or a longer cable—or both. Jitter is the tendency for the signal to reach its target voltage and float above and below for a short period of time.

With a serial bus, the data is sent one bit at a time. Because there is no worry about when each bit will arrive, the clocking rate can be increased dramatically.

With a high clock rate, parallel signals tend to interfere with each other. Serial again has an advantage because with only one or two signal wires, crosstalk and interference between the wires in the cable are negligible.

Parallel cables are very expensive. In addition to the many additional wires needed to carry the multiple bits in parallel, the cable also needs to be specially constructed to prevent crosstalk and interference between adjacent data lines. This is one reason external SCSI cables are so expensive. Serial cables, on the other hand, are very inexpensive. For one thing, they have very few wires. Furthermore, the shielding requirements are far simpler, even at very high speeds. Because of this, it is also easier to transmit serial data reliably over longer distances, which is why parallel interfaces have shorter recommended cable lengths than do serial interfaces. If you go by specifications, serial cables are to be no longer than 10 feet, whereas parallel cables are to be no longer than 50 feet.

It is for these reasons—in addition to the need for new Plug-and-Play external peripheral interfaces and the elimination of the physical port crowding on portable computers—that these new high-performance serial buses have been developed. Both USB and 1394 are available on desktop and portable PCs today.

USB (Universal Serial Bus)

USB is the peripheral bus standard—developed by PC and telecom industry leaders including Compaq, DEC, IBM, Intel, Microsoft, NEC, and Northern Telecom—that will bring Plug and Play of computer peripherals outside the PC. USB will eliminate the need to install cards into dedicated computer slots and reconfigure the system, saving on important system resources such as interrupts (IRQs). Personal computers that are equipped with USB will allow computer peripherals to be automatically configured as soon as they are physically attached, without the need to reboot or run setup. USB will also allow up to 127 devices to run simultaneously on a computer, with peripherals such as monitors and keyboards acting as additional plug-in sites, or hubs. USB cables, connectors, and peripherals can be identified by a graphic icon, as shown in Figure 16.4.

Figure 16.4   This icon is used to identify USB cables, connectors, and peripherals.

Intel has been the primary proponent of USB, and all their PC chipsets starting with the PIIX3 South Bridge component (used with the 430HX Triton II) have included USB support as standard. Six other companies have worked with Intel in co-developing the USB, including Compaq, Digital, IBM, Microsoft, NEC, and Northern Telecom. Together, these companies have established the USB Implementers Forum to develop, support, and promote the USB architecture.

◄◄ See "Chipsets," p. 235.

The USB is a 12Mbit/sec (1.5MByte/sec) interface over a simple four-wire connection. The bus supports up to 127 devices and uses a tiered star topology, built on expansion hubs that can reside in the PC, any USB peripheral, or even standalone hub boxes. Note that although the standard allows for up to 127 devices to be attached, they would all have to share the 1.5MB/sec bandwidth, meaning that for every device you add, the bus slows down some. In practical reality, few people will have more than eight devices attached at any one time.

For low-performance peripherals such as pointing devices and keyboards, the USB also has a slower 1.5Mbit/sec subchannel. The subchannel connection is used for slower interface devices such as keyboards and mice.

USB devices are either *hubs* or *functions*, or they are both. Hubs provide additional attachment points to the USB, allowing the attachment of additional hubs or functions. Functions are the individual devices that attach to the USB, for example a keyboard, mouse, camera, printer, telephone, and so on. The initial ports in the PC system unit are called the root hub, and they are the starting point for the USB. Most motherboards have two USB ports, either of which can be connected to functions or additional hubs.

Hubs are essentially wiring concentrators, and through a star-type connection they allow the attachment of multiple devices. Each attachment point is referred to as a port. Most hubs have either four or eight ports, but more are possible. For more expandability, you can connect additional hubs to the ports on an existing hub. The hub controls both the connection and distribution of power to each of the connected functions. A typical hub is shown in Figure 16.5.

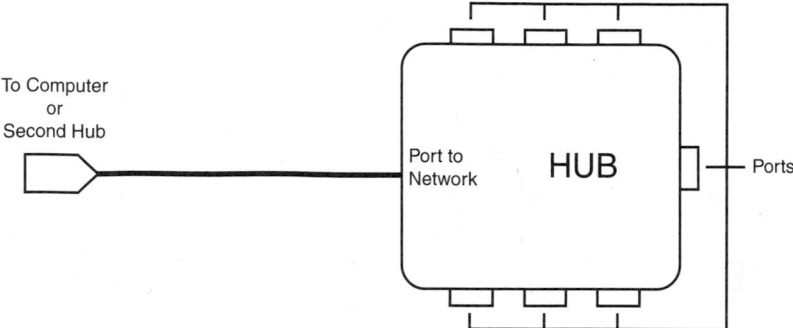

Figure 16.5 A typical USB hub with eight ports.

Maximum cable length between two full-speed (12Mbit/sec) devices or a device and a hub (see Figure 16.6) is five meters using twisted pair shielded cable with 20 gauge wire. Maximum cable length for low speed (1.5Mbit/sec) devices using non-twisted pair wire is three meters. These distance limits are shorter if smaller-gauge wire is used (see Table 16.8).

Table 16.8   Maximum Cable Lengths Versus Wire Gauge

Gauge	Resistance (in Ohms/meter Ω/m)	Length (Max.)
28	0.232 Ω/m	0.81m
26	0.145 Ω/m	1.31m
24	0.091 Ω/m	2.08m
22	0.057 Ω/m	3.33m
20	0.036 Ω/m	5.00m

Although USB is not as fast at data transfer as FireWire or SCSI, it is still more than adequate for the types of peripherals for which it is designed.

There are two different connectors that are specified for USB, called Series A and Series B. The Series A connector is designed for devices where the cable remains permanently attached, such as hubs, keyboards, and mice. The USB ports on most motherboards are also normally a Series A connector. Series B connectors are designed for devices that require detachable cables, such as printers, scanners, modems, telephones, and speakers. The physical USB plugs are small and, unlike a typical serial or parallel cable, the plug is not attached by screws or thumbscrews. The USB plugs (shown in Figure 16.7) snap into place on the USB connector. Table 16.9 shows the pinout for the USB 4-wire connector and cable.

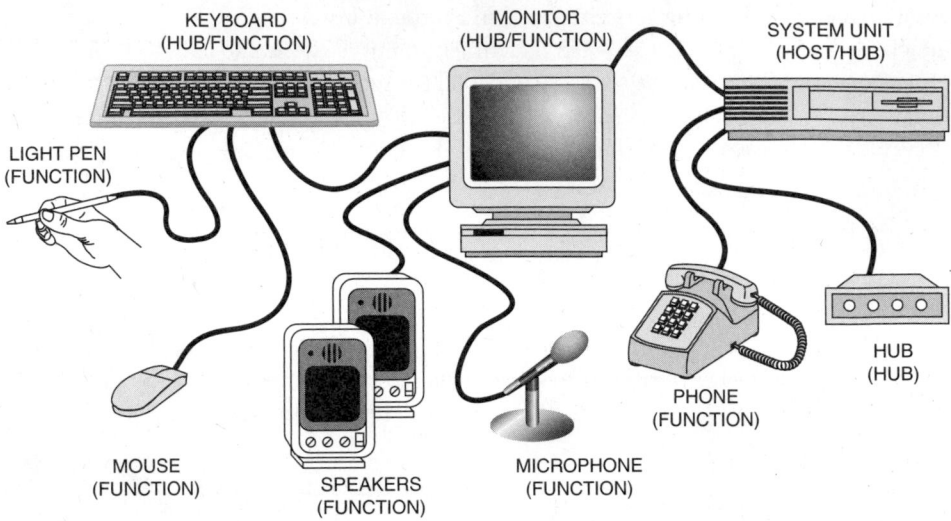

Figure 16.6 A typical PC with USB devices can use multiple USB hubs to support a variety of different peripherals, connected to whichever hub is most convenient.

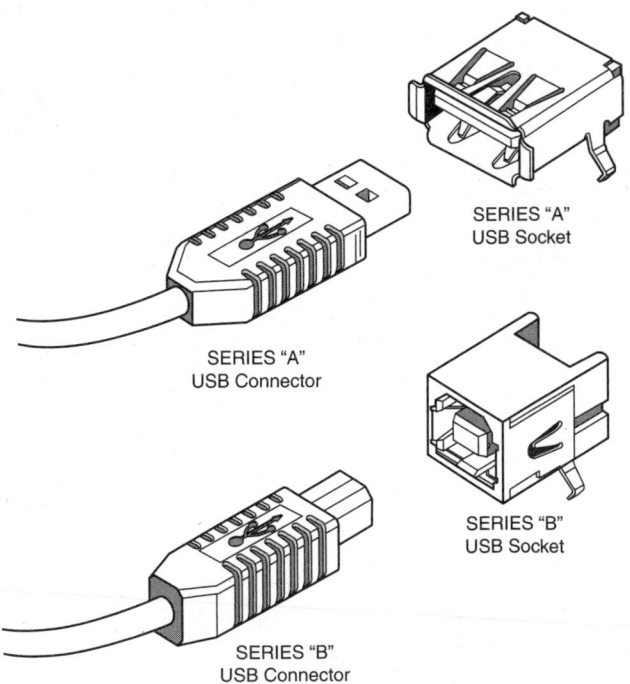

Figure 16.7 USB Series A and Series B plugs and receptacles.

Table 16.9   USB Connector Pinout

Pin	Signal Name	Comment
1	VCC	Cable power
2	- Data	
3	+ Data	
4	Ground	Cable ground

USB conforms to Intel's Plug-and-Play (PnP) specification, including hot plugging, which means that devices can be plugged in dynamically without powering down or rebooting the system. Simply plug in the device, and the USB controller in the PC detects the device and automatically determines and allocates the required resources and drivers. Microsoft has developed USB drivers and included them automatically in Windows 95C, 98, and Windows 2000.

Note that the Windows 95B release or later is required for USB support; the necessary drivers are not present in the original Windows 95 or 95A. Windows 98 includes full USB support, as does Windows 2000. With Windows 95B, the USB drivers are not automatically included; they are provided separately, although a late release of Windows 95—Windows 95C—includes USB support. USB support will also be required in the BIOS, which will be included in newer systems with USB ports built in. Aftermarket boards are also available for adding USB to systems that don't include it as standard on the motherboard. USB peripherals will include modems, telephones, joysticks, keyboards, and pointing devices such as mice and trackballs.

One interesting feature of USB is that all attached devices will be powered by the USB bus. The PnP aspects of USB allow the system to query the attached peripherals as to their power requirements and issue a warning if available power levels are being exceeded. This will be important for USB when it is used in portable systems because the battery power that is allocated to run the external peripherals might be limited.

Another of the benefits of the USB specification is the self-identifying peripheral, a feature that should greatly ease installations because you don't have to set unique IDs or identifiers for each peripheral—the USB handles that automatically. Also, USB devices can be "hot" plugged or unplugged, meaning that you will not have to turn off your computer or reboot every time you want to connect or disconnect a peripheral.

Virtually all motherboards built in the last few years have support for USB built in. One thing to keep in mind before purchasing USB peripherals is that your operating system must offer USB support. Whereas the original Windows 95 upgrade and Windows NT 4.0 do not support USB, the later OSR-2 (OEM Service Release 2) release of Windows 95 (also called 95B) does. Windows 95B will require that you add or install the USB drivers, while Windows 95C has them included on the Windows CD-ROM. Windows 98 and Windows NT 5.0 have full support for USB. Because the USB standard shows promise, it should become an important bus technology in the years to come.

One of the biggest advantages of an interface such as USB is that it only requires a single interrupt from the PC. This means that you can connect up to 127 devices and they will not use separate interrupts as they might if each were connected over a separate interface. With modern PCs suffering from an interrupt shortage, this is a major benefit, and should spur the adoption of this interface for lower-speed peripherals.

There are some unique USB devices available, including USB to Serial and USB to Ethernet converters. USB to Serial Converters allow an easy way to connect legacy RS232 interface peripherals such as modems and serial printers to a USB port. USB to Ethernet Adapters provide a LAN connection through a USB port. Drivers that are supplied with these devices allow them to fully emulate a standard serial port or Ethernet adapter.

IEEE-1394 (Also Called i.Link or FireWire)

IEEE-1394 (or just 1394 for short) is a relatively new bus technology; it is the result of the large data-moving demands of today's audio and video multimedia devices. It is extremely fast, with data transfer rates up to an incredible 400Mbits/sec, and even faster speeds are being developed. The IEEE-1394 (as it is officially known) specification was published by the IEEE Standards Board in late 1995. IEEE is shorthand for *The Institute of Electrical and Electronic Engineers*, the group that wrote the standard. The number comes from the fact that this happened to be the 1394th standard that they published.

1394 also goes under two other common names: i.Link and FireWire. i.Link is a recently unveiled IEEE-1394 designation initiated by Sony in an effort to put a more user-friendly name on IEEE-1394 technology. Most companies that produce 1394 products for PCs have endorsed this new name initiative. The term FireWire is an Apple-specific trademark. Companies that want to include the FireWire name in a 1394 product must first sign a licensing agreement with Apple, something not all companies that are producing PC products have done.

The IEEE-1394 standard currently exists with three different signaling rates—100-, 200-, and 400Mbits/sec (12.5-, 25-, 50MBytes/sec)—and there are gigabit-per-second versions in the works! Most PC adapter cards support the 200Mbits/sec rate, even though current devices generally only operate at 100Mbits/sec. A maximum of 63 devices can be connected to a single IEEE-1394 adapter card by way of daisy chaining. Cables for IEEE-1394 devices use Nintendo GameBoy-derived connectors and consist of six conductors: Four wires are used for data transmission and two conduct power. Connection with the motherboard is made either by a dedicated IEEE-1394 interface or by a PCI adapter card. Figure 16.8 shows the 1394 cable, socket, and connector.

The 1394 bus derived from the FireWire bus that was originally developed by Apple and Texas Instruments, and it is also a part of the new Serial SCSI standard that is discussed later in this chapter.

1394 uses a simple six-wire cable with two differential pairs of clock and data lines, plus two power lines. Just as with USB, 1394 is fully PnP, including the capability for hot plugging (insertion and removal of components without powering down). Unlike the much more complicated parallel SCSI bus, 1394 does not require complicated termination, and devices that are connected to the bus can draw up to 1.5 amps of electrical power. 1394 offers equal or greater performance compared to ultra-wide SCSI, with a much less expensive and less complicated connection.

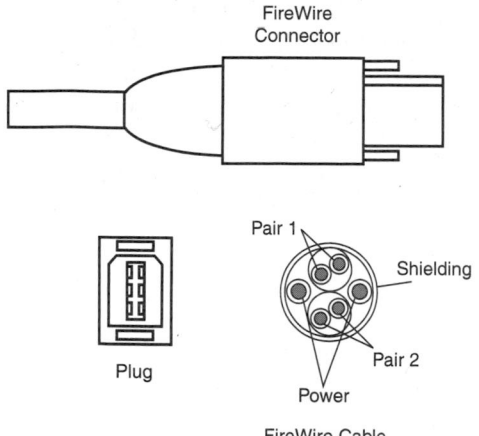

Figure 16.8   IEEE-1394 cable, socket, and connector plug.

1394 is built on a daisy-chained and branched topology, and it allows up to 63 nodes, with a chain of up to 16 devices on each node. If this is not enough, the standard also calls for up to 1,023 bridged buses, which can interconnect more than 64,000 nodes! Additionally, as with SCSI, 1394 can support devices with different data rates on the same bus. Most 1394 adapters have three nodes, each of which can support 16 devices in a daisy-chain arrangement.

The types of devices that will be connected to the PC via 1394 include practically anything that might use SCSI today. This includes all forms of disk drives, including hard disk, optical, floppy, CD-ROM, and the new DVD (Digital Video Disc) drives. Also, digital cameras, tape drives, and many other high-speed peripherals that feature 1394 have interfaces built in. Expect the 1394 bus to be implemented in both desktop and portable computers as a replacement for other external high-speed buses such as SCSI.

Chipsets and PCI adapters for the 1394 bus are already available. Microsoft has developed drivers to support 1394 in Windows 95/98 and Windows NT. As of this writing, devices that conform to the IEEE-1394 standard are limited primarily to camcorders and VCRs with digital video (DV) capability. Sony was among the first to release such devices, although its products have a unique four-wire connector that requires an adapter cord to be used with IEEE-1394 PC cards. DV products are also available from Panasonic and Matsushita, and future IEEE-1394 applications should include DV conferencing devices, satellite audio and video data streams, audio synthesizers, DVD, and other high-speed disc drives.

Because of the current DV emphasis for IEEE-1394 peripherals, most PC cards that are currently offered by Adaptec, FAST Multimedia, Matrox, and others involve DV capturing and editing. If you're willing to spend $1,000 or more on DV camera or recording equipment, these items will probably provide substantial video editing and dubbing capabilities on your PC. Of course, you need IEEE-1394 I/O connectivity, which is still a rarity on current motherboards. Fortunately, Adaptec and Texas Instruments both offer PCI adapter cards that support IEEE-1394.

Because of the similarity in both the form and function of USB and 1394, there has been some confusion about the two. The following table summarizes the differences between the two technologies:

	IEEE-1394 (i.Link) (FireWire)	USB
PC-Host Required	No	Yes
Maximum Number of Devices	63	127
Hot-Swappable	Yes	Yes
Maximum Cable Length Between Devices	4.5 meters	5 meters
Current Transfer Rate	200Mbps (25MB/sec)	12Mbps (1.5MB/sec)
Future Transfer Rates	400Mbps (50MB/sec) 800Mbps (100MB/sec) 1Gbps+ (125MB/sec+)	None
Typical Devices	-DV Camcorders -High-Res. Digital Cameras -HDTV -Set-Top Boxes -High-Speed Drives -High-Res. Scanners	-Keyboards -Mice -Joysticks -Low-Resolution Digital Cameras -Low-Speed Drives -Modems -Printers -Low-Res. Scanners

The main difference is speed. Currently, 1394 offers a data transfer rate that is more than 16 times faster than that of USB. This speed differential will become even greater in the future as higher speed versions of 1394 debut. In the future, PCs will likely include both USB and 1394 interfaces. Together, these two buses can replace most of the standard connections found on the back of a typical PC. Due to the performance differences, USB is clearly designed for low-speed peripherals such as keyboards, mice, modems, and printers, whereas 1394 will be used to connect high-performance computer and digital video electronics products.

Another important benefit of 1394 is that a PC host connection is not required. As such, 1394 can be used to directly connect a Digital Video (DV) camcorder and a DV-VCR for dubbing tapes or editing.

IEEE-1394 stands to offer unprecedented multimedia capabilities to current and future PC users. Current peripherals—particularly DV devices—are fairly expensive, but as with any emerging technology, prices should come down in the future, opening the door wide for new PC uses in both the home and office. A great number of people would gain the capability to do advanced audio and video editing. If you anticipate having multimedia needs on your PC in the future, IEEE-1394 connectivity is a must.

Input Devices

SOME OF THE MAIN TOPICS IN THIS CHAPTER ARE

Keyboards

Keyboard Technology

Keyboard Troubleshooting and Repair

Disassembly Procedures and Cautions

Pointing Devices

Keyboards

One of the most basic system components is the keyboard, which is the primary input device. It is used for entering commands and data into the system. This section looks at the keyboards available for PC-compatible systems, examining the different types of keyboards, how the keyboard functions, the keyboard-to-system interface, and keyboard troubleshooting and repair.

In the years since the introduction of the original IBM PC, IBM has created three different keyboard designs for PC systems; Microsoft has augmented one of them. These designs have become de facto standards in the industry and are shared by virtually all PC manufacturers. With the introduction of Windows 95, a modified version of the standard 101-key design (created by Microsoft) appeared, called the 104-key Windows keyboard.

The primary keyboard types are as follows:

- 101-key Enhanced keyboard
- 104-key Windows keyboard
- 83-key PC and XT keyboard (obsolete)
- 84-key AT keyboard (obsolete)

This section discusses the 101-key Enhanced keyboard and the 104-key Windows keyboard, showing the layout and physical appearance of both. Although you can still find old systems that use the 83-key and 84-key designs, these are rare today. Because all new systems today use the 101- and 104-key keyboard designs, these versions are covered here.

Note

If you need to learn more about the 83-key PC and XT keyboard or the 84-key AT keyboard, see Chapter 7 of *Upgrading and Repairing PCs, Tenth Anniversary Edition*, on the CD included with this book.

Enhanced 101-Key (or 102-Key) Keyboard

In 1986, IBM introduced the "corporate" Enhanced 101-key keyboard for the newer XT and AT models (see Figure 17.1). I use the word corporate because this unit first appeared in IBM's RT PC, which was a RISC (Reduced Instruction Set Computer) system designed for scientific and engineering applications. Keyboards with this design were soon supplied with virtually every type of system and terminal that IBM sold. Other companies quickly copied this design, which has been the standard on Intel-based PC systems ever since.

The layout of this universal keyboard was improved over that of the 84-key unit, with perhaps the exception of the Enter key, which reverted to a smaller size. The 101-key Enhanced keyboard was designed to conform to international regulations and specifications for keyboards. In fact, other companies, such as Digital Equipment Corporation (DEC) and Texas Instruments (TI), had already been using designs similar to the IBM 101-key unit. The IBM 101-key units originally came in versions with and without the status indicator LEDs, depending on whether the unit was sold with an XT or AT system. Now there are many other variations to choose from, including some with integrated pointing devices.

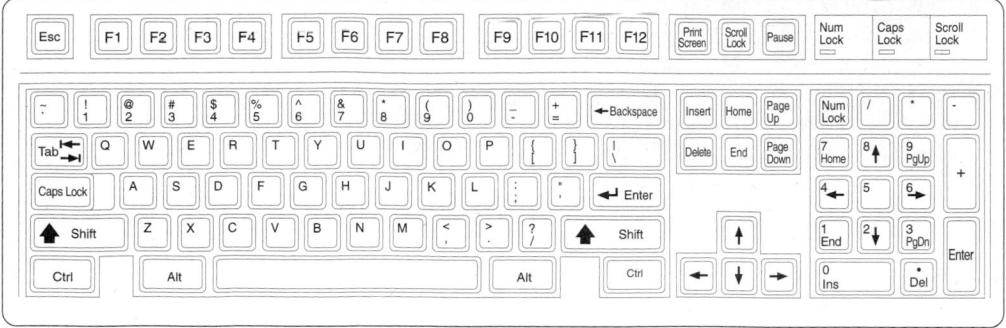

Figure 17.1   101-key Enhanced keyboard layout.

The Enhanced keyboard is available in several different variations, but all are basically the same electrically and all can be interchanged. IBM and its Lexmark keyboard and printer subsidiary have produced a number of keyboards, including versions with built-in pointing devices and new ergonomic layouts. Some of the Enhanced keyboards still attach to the system via the five-pin DIN (an acronym from the German Deutsche Industrie Norm) connector, but most today come with cables for the six-pin mini-DIN connector introduced on the IBM PS/2s. Although the connectors might be physically different, the keyboards are not, and you can either interchange the cables or use a cable adapter to plug one type into the other.

The 101-key keyboard layout can be divided into the following four sections:

- Typing area
- Numeric keypad
- Cursor and screen controls
- Function keys

The 101-key arrangement is similar to the Selectric keyboard layout, with the exception of the Enter key. The Tab, Caps Lock, Shift, and Backspace keys have a larger striking area and are located in the familiar Selectric locations. Ctrl and Alt keys are on each side of the spacebar. The typing area and numeric keypad have home-row identifiers for touch typing.

The cursor- and screen-control keys have been separated from the numeric keypad, which is reserved for numeric input. (As with other PC keyboards, you can use the numeric keypad for cursor and screen control when the keyboard is not in Num Lock mode.) A division-sign key and an additional Enter key have been added to the numeric keypad.

The cursor-control keys are arranged in the inverted T format that is now expected on all computer keyboards. The Insert, Delete, Home, End, Page Up, and Page Down keys, located above the dedicated cursor-control keys, are separate from the numeric keypad. The function keys, spaced in groups of four, are located across the top of the keyboard. The keyboard also has two additional function keys: F11 and F12. The Esc key is isolated in the upper-left corner of the keyboard. Dedicated Print Screen/Sys Req, Scroll Lock, and Pause/Break keys are provided for commonly used functions.

Foreign language versions of the Enhanced keyboard include 102 keys and a slightly different layout from the 101-key U.S. versions.

One of the many useful features of the enhanced keyboard is removable keycaps. This permits the replacement of broken keys and provides access for easier cleaning. Also, with clear keycaps and paper inserts, you can customize the keyboard. Keyboard templates are also available to provide specific operator instructions.

The 101-key Enhanced keyboard or one of its variations will probably continue to be furnished with all desktop PC systems for some time to come. It is by far the most popular design and does not show any signs of being replaced in the future. Because most PCs use this same type of keyboard, it is easy to move from one system to another without relearning the layout. Also, as a relatively inexpensive component, you can easily replace a broken or uncomfortable keyboard.

104-Key (Windows 95/98 Keyboard)

If you are a touch typist as I am, you probably really hate to take your hands off the keyboard to use a mouse. Windows 95 and 98 make this even more of a problem because they use both mouse buttons (the right button is used to open shortcut menus). Many new keyboards, especially those in portable computers, include a variation of the IBM TrackPoint or the Alps Glidepoint pointing devices (discussed later in this chapter), which allow touch typists to keep their hands on the keyboard even while moving the pointer. However, there is still another alternative that can help. Microsoft has come up with a specification that calls for three new Windows-specific keys to be added to the keyboard. These new keys help with functions that would otherwise require multiple keystrokes or mouse clicks.

The Microsoft Windows keyboard specification outlines a set of new keys and key combinations. The familiar 101-key layout has now grown to 104 keys, with the addition of left and right Windows keys and an Application key. These keys are used for operating-system and application-level keyboard combinations, similar to today's Ctrl and Alt combinations. You don't need the new keys to use Windows 95/98 or NT or Windows 2000, but software vendors are starting to add specific functions to their Windows products that make use of the new Application key (which provides the same functionality as clicking the right mouse button). Figure 17.2 shows the standard Windows keyboard layout, including the three new keys.

The recommended Windows keyboard layout calls for the Left and Right Windows keys (called WIN keys) to flank the Alt keys on each side of the spacebar, as well as an Application key on the right of the Right Windows key. Note that the exact placement of these keys is up to the keyboard designer, so you will see variations from keyboard to keyboard.

The WIN keys open the Windows 95 Start menu, which you can then navigate with the cursor keys. The Application key simulates the right mouse button; in most applications, it brings up a context-sensitive pop-up menu. Several WIN key combinations offer preset macro commands as well. For example, you press WIN+E to launch the Windows Explorer application. The following table shows a list of all the Windows 95 and Windows 98 key combinations.

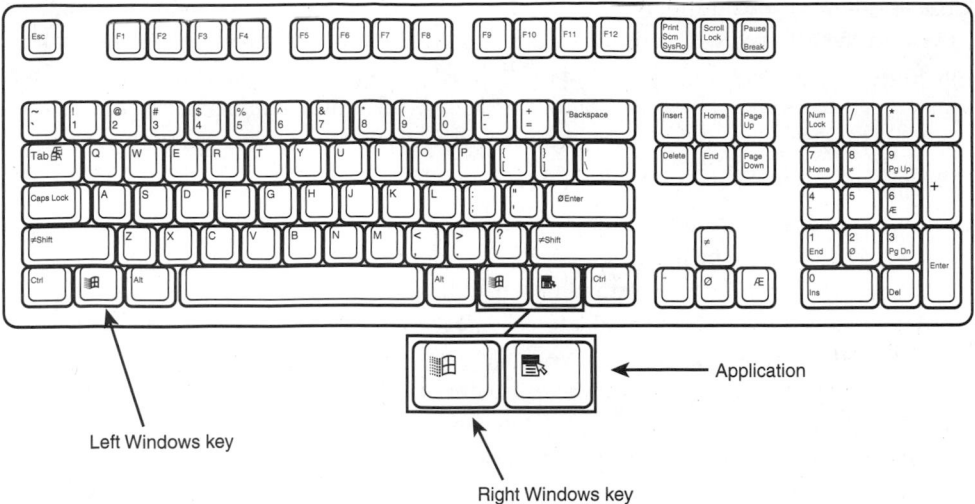

Left Windows key

Right Windows key

Application

Figure 17.2 104-key Windows keyboard layout.

Key Combination	Resulting Action
WIN+R	Run dialog box
WIN+M	Minimize All
Shift+WIN+M	Undo Minimize All
WIN+F1	Help
WIN+E	Windows Explorer
WIN+F	Find Files or Folders
Ctrl+WIN+F	Find Computer
WIN+Tab	Cycle through taskbar buttons
WIN+Break	System Properties dialog box
Application key	Displays a context menu for the selected item

When a 104-key Windows keyboard is used with Microsoft IntelliType Software installed, the following additional key combinations can be used:

Key Combination	Resulting Action
WIN+L	Log off Windows
WIN+P	Opens Print Manager
WIN+C	Opens the control panel
WIN+V	Opens Clipboard
WIN+K	Opens Keyboard Properties dialog box
WIN+I	Opens Mouse Properties dialog box
WIN+A	Opens Accessibility options (if installed)
WIN+spacebar	Displays the list of IntelliType hotkeys
WIN+S	Toggles the Caps Lock key on and off

The Windows keyboard specification requires that keyboard makers increase the number of trilograms in their keyboard designs. A *trilogram* is a combination of three rapidly pressed keys that perform a special function, such as Ctrl+Alt+Delete. Designing a keyboard so that the switch matrix will correctly register trilograms is expensive, and this feature, plus the additional Windows keys, will cause the price of these keyboards to rise. Volume sales, however, as well as the natural market competition, should keep the price reasonable.

Many keyboard manufacturers are now producing keyboards with these Windows-specific keys. Some are also combining these new keys with other features. For example, besides the new Windows keys, the Microsoft Natural Keyboard includes ergonomic features, such as split keypads that are rotated out from the middle to encourage a straight wrist position. For users accustomed to the standard key arrangement, these designs can take some getting used to. Unfortunately, this keyboard (made by Keytronics for Microsoft) does not have nearly as comfortable a feel as the mechanical switch designs such as Alps, Lite-On, or NMB. Nor does it have the extremely high-quality feel of the Lexmark and Unicomp keyboards. In addition to the Windows keys, other companies, such as Lexmark, NMB, and Alps, have licensed a new spacebar design from Keyboard Enhancements, Inc. called Erase-Ease. This new design splits the spacebar into two parts, using the shorter left (or optionally the right) half as an additional Backspace key. If you see a keyboard advertising 105 keys, it probably has both the three additional Windows keys and the extra Backspace key next to the spacebar.

Although they can make it easier for both experienced touch typists and novice users to access some of the functions of Windows and their applications, note that the new Windows keys are not mandatory when running Windows. In fact there are pre-existing standard key combinations that perform the same functions as these new keys. I have also noticed that few people who have these extra keys on their keyboards actually use them. Because of these factors and the fact that adding these keys increases the cost of the keyboard, the new keys have not been universally accepted by all PC manufacturers. Some manufacturers have added browser control or other keys that, although are not standard, can make them easier to use for viewing Web pages.

Portable Keyboards

One of the biggest influences on keyboard design in recent years has been the proliferation of laptop and notebook systems. Because of size limitations, it is obviously not possible to utilize the standard keyboard layout for a portable computer. Manufacturers have come up with many different solutions. Unfortunately, none of these solutions has become an industry standard, as is the 101-key layout. Because of the variations in design, and because a portable system keyboard is not as easily replaceable as that of a desktop system, the keyboard arrangement should be an important part of your purchasing decision.

Early laptop systems often used smaller than normal keys to minimize the size of the keyboard, which resulted in many complaints from users. Today, the keytops on portable systems are usually comparable in size to that of a desktop keyboard, although some systems include half-sized keytops for the function keys and other lesser-used keyboard elements. In addition, consumer demand has caused most manufacturers to retain the inverted-T design for the cursor keys after a few abortive attempts at changing their arrangement.

Of course, the most obvious difference in a portable system keyboard is the sacrifice of the numeric keypad. Most systems now embed the keypad into the standard alphabetical part of the keyboard, as shown in Figure 17.3. To switch the keys from their standard values to their keypad values, you typically must press a key combination involving a proprietary function key, often labeled Fn.

Figure 17.3 Most portable systems today embed the numeric keypad into an oddly shaped block of keys on the alphabetical part of the keyboard.

This is an extremely inconvenient solution, and many users abandon their use of the keypad entirely on portable systems. Unfortunately, some activities, such as the entry of ASCII codes using the Alt key, require the use of the keypad numbers, which can be quite frustrating on systems using this arrangement.

In addition to keypad control, the Fn key is often used to trigger other proprietary features in portable systems, such as toggling between an internal and external display and controlling screen brightness and sound volume.

Some portable system manufacturers have gone to great lengths to provide users with adequate keyboards. For a short time, IBM marketed systems with a keyboard that used a "butterfly" design. The keyboard was split into two halves that rested on top of one another when the system was closed. When you opened the lid, the two halves separated to rest side by side, forming a keyboard that was actually larger than the computer case.

Ironically, the trend toward larger-sized displays in portable systems has made this sort of arrangement unnecessary. Many manufacturers have increased the footprint of their notebook computers to accommodate 12- and even 14-inch display panels, leaving more than adequate room for a full-sized keyboard.

▶▶ See "Keyboards," p. 1241.

Compatibility

The Enhanced keyboards from IBM are universal. They are also auto-switchable, which means they work in virtually any system—from the XT to the PS/2 or any PC-compatible—after you plug them in. Some might also require that a switch be moved on the keyboard to make it compatible with PC/XT systems that do not have the 8042-type keyboard controller on the motherboard. In some cases, you might also need to switch to a cable with the proper system end connector or use an adapter.

Although the Enhanced keyboard is electrically compatible with any AT-type motherboard and even most PC/XT-type motherboards, many older systems will have software problems using these keyboards. IBM changed the ROM on the systems to support the new keyboard properly, and the compatible vendors followed suit. Very old (1986 or earlier) machines may require a ROM upgrade to properly use some of the features on the 101-key Enhanced keyboards, such as the F11 and F12 keys. If the individual system ROM BIOS is not capable of operating the 101-key keyboard correctly, the 101-key keyboard might not work at all (as with all three ROM versions of the IBM PC). The additional keys (F11 and F12 function keys) may not work, or you may have problems with keyboard operation in general. In some cases, these compatibility problems cause improper characters to appear when keys are typed (causing the system to beep), and general keyboard operation is a problem. These problems can often be solved by a ROM upgrade to a newer version that has proper support for the Enhanced keyboard.

In an informal test, I plugged the new keyboard in to an earlier XT. The keyboard seemed to work well. None of the keys that did not exist previously, such as F11 and F12, were operable, but the new arrow keys and numeric keypad worked. The Enhanced keyboard seems to work on XT or AT systems, but it does not function on the original PC systems because of BIOS and electrical interface problems. Many compatible versions of the 101-key Enhanced keyboards have a manual XT/AT switch on the bottom that might enable the keyboard to work in an original PC system.

Tip

If you have an older IBM system, you can tell whether your system has complete ROM BIOS support for the 101-key unit. When you plug in the keyboard and turn on the system unit, the Num Lock light automatically comes on and the numeric keypad portion of the keyboard is enabled. This method of detection is not 100 percent accurate, but if the light goes on, your BIOS generally supports the keyboard. A notable exception is the IBM AT BIOS, dated 06/10/85. It turns on the Num Lock light, but still does not properly support the Enhanced keyboard. All IBM BIOS versions dated since 11/15/85 have proper support for the Enhanced keyboards.

Num Lock

On IBM systems that support the Enhanced keyboard, when the system detects the keyboard on power-up, it enables the Num Lock feature and the light goes on. If the system detects an older 84-key AT-type keyboard, it does not enable the Num Lock function because these keyboards do not have cursor keys separate from the numeric keypad. When the Enhanced keyboards first appeared in 1986, many users (including me) were irritated to find that the numeric keypad was automatically enabled every time the system booted. Most system manufacturers subsequently began integrating a function into the BIOS setup that enabled you to specify the Num Lock status imposed during the boot process.

Some users thought that the automatic enabling of Num Lock was a function of the Enhanced keyboard because none of the earlier keyboards seemed to operate in this way. Remember that this function is not really a keyboard function but instead a function of the motherboard ROM BIOS, which identifies an Enhanced 101-key unit and turns on the Num Lock as a "favor." In systems with a BIOS that cannot control the status of the numeric keypad, you can use the DOS 6.0 or higher version NUMLOCK= parameter in CONFIG.SYS to turn Num Lock on or off, as desired. If you are running a version of DOS earlier than 6.0, you can use one of the many public domain programs available for controlling the Num Lock function. Running the program from the AUTOEXEC.BAT file can set the numeric keypad status whenever the system reboots.

Keyboard Technology

The technology that makes up a typical PC keyboard is very interesting. This section focuses on all the aspects of keyboard technology and design, including the keyswitches, the interface between the keyboard and the system, the scan codes, and the keyboard connectors.

Keyswitch Design

Today's keyboards use any one of several switch types to create the action for each key. Most keyboards use a variation of the mechanical keyswitch. A mechanical keyswitch relies on a mechanical momentary contact type switch to make the electrical contact that forms a circuit. Some high-end keyboards use a totally different nonmechanical design that relies on capacitive switches. This section discusses these switches and the highlights of each design.

The most common type of keyswitch is the mechanical type, available in the following variations:

- Pure mechanical
- Foam element
- Rubber dome
- Membrane

Pure Mechanical Switches

The pure mechanical type is just that—a simple mechanical switch that features metal contacts in a momentary contact arrangement. The switch often includes a tactile feedback mechanism, consisting of a clip and spring arrangement designed to give a "clicky" feel to the keyboard and offer some resistance to the keypress. Several companies, including Alps Electric, Lite-On, and NMB Technologies, manufacture this type of keyboard using switches obtained primarily from Alps Electric. Mechanical switches are very durable, usually have self-cleaning contacts, and are normally rated for 20 million keystrokes, which is second only to the capacitive switch in longevity. They also offer excellent tactile feedback.

Foam Element Switches

Foam element mechanical switches were a very popular design in some older keyboards. Most of the older PC keyboards, including those made by Keytronics and many others, use this technology. These switches are characterized by a foam element with an electrical contact on the bottom. This foam element is mounted on the bottom of a plunger that is attached to the key (see Figure 17.4).

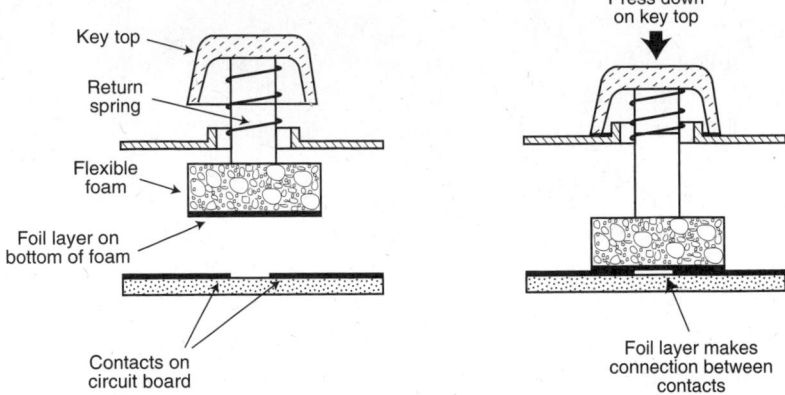

Figure 17.4   Typical foam element mechanical keyswitch.

When the switch is pressed, a foil conductor on the bottom of the foam element closes a circuit on the printed circuit board below. A return spring pushes the key back up when the pressure is released. The foam dampens the contact, helping to prevent bounce, but unfortunately gives these keyboards a "mushy" feel. The big problem with this type of keyswitch design is that there is often little tactile feedback. These types of keyboards send a clicking sound to the system speaker to signify that contact has been made. Compaq has used keyboards of this type (made by Keytronics) in many of their systems. Preferences in keyboard feel are somewhat subjective; I personally do not favor the foam element switch design.

Another problem with this type of design is that it is more subject to corrosion on the foil conductor and the circuit board traces below. When this happens, the key strikes may become intermittent, which can be frustrating. Fortunately, these keyboards are among the easiest to clean. By disassembling the keyboard completely, you can usually remove the circuit board portion—without removing each foam pad separately—and expose the bottoms of all the pads. Then you can easily wipe the corrosion and dirt off the bottom of the foam pads and the circuit board, thus restoring the keyboard to a "like-new" condition. Unfortunately, over time, the corrosion problem will occur again. I recommend using some Stabilant 22a from D.W. Electrochemicals to improve the switch contact action and prevent future corrosion. Because of such problems, the foam element design is not used much anymore and has been superseded in popularity by the rubber dome design.

Rubber Dome Switches

Rubber dome switches are mechanical switches that are similar to the foam element type but are improved in many ways. Instead of a spring, these switches use a rubber dome that has a carbon button contact on the underside. As you press a key, the key plunger presses on the rubber dome, causing it to resist and then collapse all at once, much like the top of an oil can. As the rubber dome collapses, the user feels the tactile feedback, and the carbon button makes contact between the circuit board traces below. When the key is released, the rubber dome re-forms and pushes the key back up.

The rubber eliminates the need for a spring and provides a reasonable amount of tactile feedback without any special clips or other parts. Rubber dome switches use a carbon button because it is resistant to corrosion and because it has a self-cleaning action on the metal contacts below. The rubber domes themselves are formed into a sheet that completely protects the contacts below from dirt, dust, and even minor spills. This type of switch design is the simplest, and it uses the fewest parts. This makes the rubber dome keyswitch very reliable and helps make the keyboards that use it the most popular in service today.

If the rubber dome keyboard has any drawback, it is that the tactile feedback is not as good as many users would like. Although many people find its touch acceptable, some users prefer more tactile feedback than rubber dome keyboards normally provide.

Membrane Switches

The membrane keyboard is a variation on the rubber dome type. The keys themselves are no longer separate, but instead are formed together in a sheet that sits on the rubber dome sheet. This arrangement severely limits key travel. For this reason, membrane keyboards are not considered usable for normal touch typing. However, they are ideal for use in extremely harsh environments. Because the sheets can be bonded together and sealed from the elements, membrane keyboards can be used in situations in which no other type could survive. Many industrial applications use membrane keyboards for terminals that do not require extensive data entry but are used instead to operate equipment, such as cash registers.

Capacitive switches are the only nonmechanical types of keyswitch in use today (see Figure 17.5). The capacitive switch is the Cadillac of keyswitches. It is much more expensive than the more common mechanical rubber dome, but is more resistant to dirt and corrosion and offers the highest-quality tactile feedback of any type of switch.

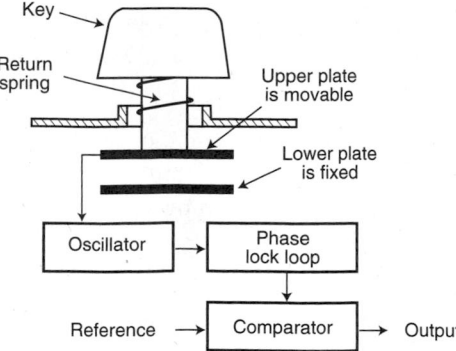

Figure 17.5   A capacitive keyswitch.

A capacitive switch does not work by making contact between conductors. Instead, two plates usually made of plastic are connected in a switch matrix designed to detect changes in the capacitance of the circuit.

When the key is pressed, the plunger moves the top plate in relation to the fixed bottom plate. Usually a mechanism provides for a distinct over-center tactile feedback with a resounding "click." As the top plate moves, the capacitance between the two plates changes. The comparator circuitry in the keyboard detects this change.

Because this type of switch does not rely on metal contacts, it is nearly immune to corrosion and dirt. These switches are very resistant to the key bounce problems that result in multiple characters appearing from a single strike. They are also the most durable in the industry—rated for 25 million or more keystrokes, as opposed to 10 to 20 million for other designs. The tactile feedback is unsurpassed because the switch provides a relatively loud click and a strong over-center feel. The only drawback to the design is the cost. Capacitive switch keyboards are among the most expensive designs. The quality of the feel and their durability make them worth the price, however.

Traditionally, the only vendors of capacitive keyswitch keyboards have been IBM and the inheritors of its keyboard technology, Lexmark and Unicomp.

The Keyboard Interface

A keyboard consists of a set of switches mounted in a grid or array called the *key matrix*. When a switch is pressed, a processor in the keyboard identifies which key is pressed by determining which grid location in the matrix shows continuity. The keyboard processor, which also interprets how long the key is pressed, can even handle multiple keypresses at the same time. A 16-byte hardware buffer in the keyboard can handle rapid or multiple keypresses, passing each one to the system in succession.

When you press a key, the contact bounces slightly in most cases, meaning that there are several rapid on/off cycles just as the switch makes contact. This is called *bounce*. The processor in the keyboard is designed to filter this, or debounce the keystroke. The keyboard processor must distinguish bounce from a double keystrike that the keyboard operator intends to make. This is fairly easy because the bouncing is much more rapid than a person could simulate by striking a key quickly several times.

The keyboard in a PC is actually a computer itself. It communicates with the main system through a special serial data link. This link transmits and receives data in 11-bit packets of information, consisting of eight data bits, plus framing and control bits. Although it is indeed a serial link (in that the data flows on one wire), the keyboard interface is not compatible with the standard RS-232 serial port commonly used to connect modems.

The processor in the original PC keyboard was an Intel 8048 microcontroller chip. Newer keyboards often use an 8049 version that has built-in ROM or other microcontroller chips compatible with the 8048 or 8049. For example, in its Enhanced keyboards, IBM has always used a custom version of the Motorola 6805 processor, which is compatible with the Intel chips. The keyboard's built-in processor reads the key matrix, debounces the keypress signals, converts the keypress to the appropriate scan code, and transmits the code to the motherboard. The processors built into the keyboard contain their own RAM, possibly some ROM, and a built-in serial interface.

In the original PC/XT design, the keyboard serial interface is connected to an 8255 Programmable Peripheral Interface (PPI) chip on the motherboard of the PC/XT. This chip is connected to the interrupt controller IRQ1 line, which is used to signal to the system that keyboard data is available. The data is sent from the 8255 to the processor via I/O port address 60h. The IRQ1 signal causes the main system processor to run a subroutine (INT 9h) that interprets the keyboard scan code data and decides what to do.

In an AT-type keyboard design, the keyboard serial interface is connected to a special keyboard controller on the motherboard. This controller is an Intel 8042 Universal Peripheral Interface (UPI) slave microcontroller chip in the original AT design. This microcontroller is essentially another processor that has its own 2KB of ROM and 128 bytes of RAM. An 8742 version that uses EPROM (Erasable Programmable Read Only Memory) can be erased and reprogrammed. In the past, when you purchased a motherboard ROM upgrade from a motherboard manufacturer for an older system, the upgrade included a new keyboard controller chip as well because it had somewhat dependent and updated ROM code in it. Some systems may use the 8041 or 8741 chips, which differ only in the amount of built-in ROM or RAM, whereas other systems now have the keyboard controller built into the main system chipset.

In an AT system, the (8048-type) microcontroller in the keyboard sends data to the (8042-type) keyboard controller on the motherboard. The motherboard-based controller can also send data back to the keyboard. When the keyboard controller on the motherboard receives data from the keyboard, it signals the motherboard with an IRQ1 and sends the data to the main motherboard processor via I/O port address 60h, just as in the PC/XT. Acting as an agent between the keyboard and the main system processor, the 8042-type keyboard controller can translate scan codes and perform several other functions as well. The system can also send data to the 8042 keyboard controller via port 60h, which then passes it on to the keyboard. Additionally, when the system needs to send commands to or read the status of the keyboard controller on the motherboard, it reads or writes through I/O port 64h. These commands are usually followed by data sent back and forth via port 60h.

In older systems, the 8042 keyboard controller is also used by the system to control the A20 memory address line, which provides access to system memory greater than 1MB. More modern motherboards usually incorporate this functionality directly into the motherboard chipset.

Typematic Functions

If a key on the keyboard is held down, it becomes *typematic*, which means the keyboard repeatedly sends the keypress code to the motherboard. In the AT-style keyboards, the typematic rate is adjusted by sending the appropriate commands to the keyboard processor. This is not possible for the earlier PC/XT keyboard types because the keyboard interface for these types is not bidirectional.

AT-style keyboards have programmable typematic repeat rate and delay parameters. Most operating systems include functions that enable you to adjust these parameters to your own specifications. In Windows 9x and Windows NT, you use the Keyboard control panel. In DOS, you use the MODE command.

Adjusting Keyboard Parameters in Windows

To modify the default values for the typematic repeat rate and delay parameters in any version of Windows, you open the Keyboard control panel. In Windows 95, 98, and NT, the controls are located on the Speed page, as shown in Figure 17.6. The Repeat Delay slider controls the amount of times a key must be pressed before the character begins to repeat, and the Repeat Rate slider controls how fast the character repeats after the delay has elapsed.

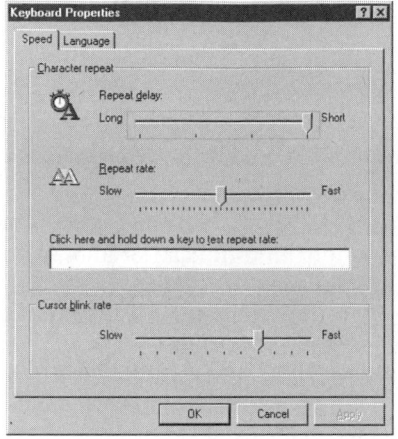

Figure 17.6   Windows 9x and NT provide graphical controls for the keyboard typematic parameters.

Note

The increments on the Repeat Delay and Repeat Rate sliders in the Keyboard control panel correspond to the timings given for the **MODE** command's **RATE** and **DELAY** values, as listed in Tables 17.1 and 17.2 later in this chapter. In those tables you can see that each mark in the Repeat Delay slider adds about 0.25 seconds to the delay, and the marks in the Repeat Rate slider are worth about one character per second each.

The dialog box also contains a text box you can use to test the settings you have chosen before committing them to your system. When you click in the box and press a key, the keyboard reacts using the settings currently specified by the sliders, even if you have not yet applied the changes to the Windows environment.

Note

In Windows 3.1, the settings in the Keyboard control panel override any typematic settings you may have applied in DOS using the **MODE** command.

Adjusting Keyboard Parameters in DOS

In DOS versions 4.0 and later, the MODE command enables you to set the keyboard typematic (repeat) rate, as well as the delay, before typematic action begins. The default value for the RATE parameter (r) is 20 for most PC systems and 21 for IBM PS/2 systems. The default value for the

DELAY parameter (d) is 2. Therefore, for most systems, the standard keyboard typematic speed is 10cps (characters per second), and the delay before typematic action occurs is 0.5 seconds.

To use the DOS MODE command to reset the keyboard typematic rate and delay, use the following command:

```
MODE CON[:] [RATE=r DELAY=d]
```

The acceptable values for the rate r and the resulting typematic rate in cps are shown in Table 17.1.

Table 17.1   DOS 4.0+ *MODE* Command Keyboard Typematic Rate Parameters

Rate No.	Rate ± 20%	Rate No.	Rate ± 20%	Rate No.	Rate ± 20%
32	30.0cps	21	10.9cps	10	4.3cps
31	26.7cps	20	10.0cps	9	4.0cps
30	24.0cps	19	9.2cps	8	3.7cps
29	21.8cps	18	8.6cps	7	3.3cps
28	20.0cps	17	8.0cps	6	3.0cps
27	18.5cps	16	7.5cps	5	2.7cps
26	17.1cps	15	6./cps	4	2.5cps
25	16.0cps	14	6.0cps	3	2.3cps
24	15.0cps	13	5.5cps	2	2.1cps
23	13.3cps	12	5.0cps	1	2.0cps
22	12.0cps	11	4.6cps		

Table 17.2 shows the values for DELAY and the resulting delay time in seconds.

Table 17.2   DOS *MODE* Command Keyboard Typematic Delay Parameters

DELAY No.	Delay Time
1	0.25sec
2	0.50sec
3	0.75sec
4	1.00sec

For example, when running DOS, I always place the following command in my AUTOEXEC.BAT file:

```
MODE CON: RATE=32 DELAY=1
```

This command sets the typematic rate to the maximum speed possible, or 30cps. It also trims the delay to the minimum of 0.25 seconds before repeating begins. This command "turbocharges" the keyboard and makes operations requiring repeated keystrokes work much faster, such as moving within a file by using arrow keys. The quick typematic action and short delay can be disconcerting to some keyboard operators. Slower typists might want to leave their keyboard speed at the default until they become more proficient.

Note

Note that if you are working on a very old system or keyboard, you might get the following message:

`Function not supported on this computer`

This indicates that your system, keyboard, or both do not support the bidirectional interface or the commands required to change the typematic rate and delay. Upgrading the BIOS or the keyboard might enable this function, but it is probably not cost effective to do it on an older system.

Note

Some BIOS versions feature keyboard speed selection capability; however, not all of them allow for full control over the speed and delay.

Keyboard Key Numbers and Scan Codes

When you press a key on the keyboard, the processor built into the keyboard (8048- or 6805-type) reads the keyswitch location in the keyboard matrix. The processor then sends to the motherboard a serial packet of data containing the scan code for the key that was pressed.

This is called the *Make code*. When the key is released, a corresponding *Break code* is sent, indicating to the motherboard that the key has been released. The Break code is equivalent to the Make scan code plus 80h. For example, if the Make scan code for the "A" key is 1Eh, the Break code would be 9Eh. By using both Make and Break scan codes, the system can determine if a particular key has been held down and determine whether multiple keys are being pressed.

In AT-type motherboards that use an 8042-type keyboard controller, the 8042 chip translates the actual keyboard scan codes into one of up to three different sets of system scan codes, which are sent to the main processor. It can be useful in some cases to know what these scan codes are, especially when troubleshooting keyboard problems or when reading the keyboard or system scan codes directly in software.

When a keyswitch on the keyboard sticks or otherwise fails, the Make scan code of the failed keyswitch is usually reported by diagnostics software, including the POST (power on self test), as well as conventional disk-based diagnostics. That means you have to identify the malfunctioning key by its scan code. Tables 17.3 through 17.5 list all the scan codes for every key on the 101-key, 102-key foreign language, and 104-key Windows keyboards. By looking up the reported scan code on these charts, you can determine which keyswitch is defective or needs to be cleaned.

Note

The 101-key Enhanced keyboards are capable of three different scan code sets. Set 1 is the default. Some systems, including some of the IBM PS/2 machines, use one of the other scan code sets during the POST. For example, my IBM P75 uses Scan Code Set 2 during the POST, but switches to Set 1 during normal operation. This is rare, and it really threw me off in diagnosing a stuck key problem one time. It is useful to know if you are having difficulty interpreting the scan code number, however.

IBM also assigns each key a unique key number to distinguish it from the others. This is important when you are trying to identify keys on foreign keyboards, which might use different symbols or characters than the U.S. models do. In the Enhanced keyboard, most foreign models are missing one of the keys (key 29) found on the U.S. version and have two additional keys (keys 42 and 45). This accounts for the 102-key total instead of the 101 keys found on the U.S. version.

Note

The following figures and tables show the keyboard numbering and character locations for modern keyboards. If you need this information for the original 83-key PC keyboard or the 84-key AT keyboard, see Chapter 7 of *Upgrading and Repairing PCs, Tenth Anniversary Edition*, included on the CD with this book.

Figure 17.7 shows the keyboard numbering and character locations for the 101-key Enhanced keyboard. Table 17.3 shows each of the three scan code sets for each key in relation to the key number and character. Scan Code Set 1 is the default; the other two are rarely used. Figure 17.8 shows the layout of a typical foreign language 102-key version of the Enhanced keyboard—in this case, a U.K. version.

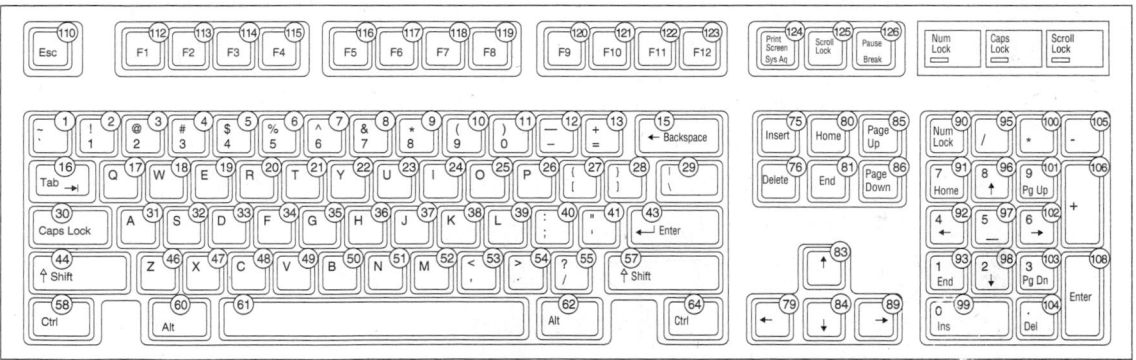

Figure 17.7 101-key Enhanced keyboard key number and character locations (U.S. version).

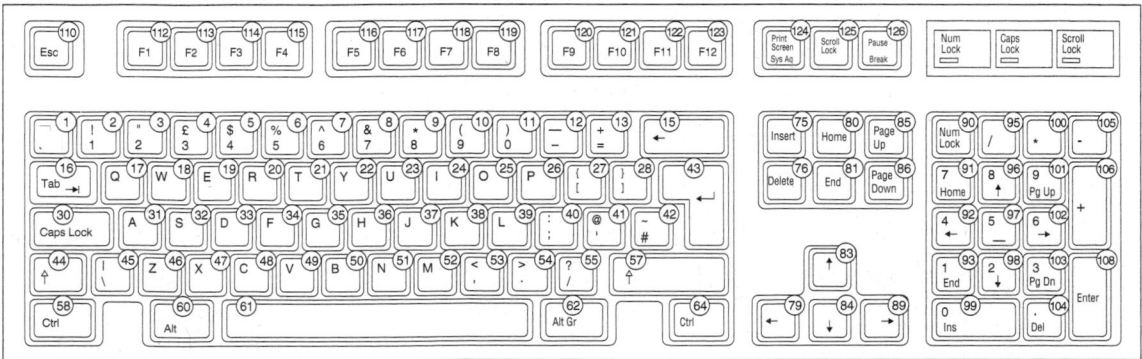

Figure 17.8 102-key Enhanced keyboard key number and character locations (U.K. English version).

Table 17.3   101/102-Key (Enhanced) Keyboard Key Numbers and Scan Codes

Key Number	Key/Character	Scan Code Set 1	Scan Code Set 2	Scan Code Set 3
1	`	29	0E	0E
2	1	2	16	16
3	2	3	1E	1E
4	3	4	26	26
5	4	5	25	25
6	5	6	2E	2E
7	6	7	36	36
8	7	8	3D	3D
9	8	9	3E	3E
10	9	0A	46	46
11	0	0B	45	45
12	-	0C	4E	4E
13	=	0D	55	55
15	Backspace	0E	66	66
16	Tab	0F	0D	0D
17	Q	10	15	15
18	W	11	1D	1D
19	E	12	24	24
20	R	13	2D	2D
21	T	14	2C	2C
22	Y	15	35	35
23	U	16	3C	3C
24	I	17	43	43
25	O	18	44	44
26	P	19	4D	4D
27	[	1A	54	54
28	]	1B	5B	5B
29	\ (101-key only)	2B	5D	5C
30	Caps Lock	3A	58	14
31	A	1E	1C	1C
32	S	1F	1B	1B
33	D	20	23	23
34	F	21	2B	2B
35	G	22	34	34
36	H	23	33	33
37	J	24	3B	3B
38	K	25	42	42
39	L	26	4B	4B
40	;	27	4C	4C

Key Number	Key/Character	Scan Code Set 1	Scan Code Set 2	Scan Code Set 3
41	'	28	52	52
42	# (102-key only)	2B	5D	53
43	Enter	1C	5A	5A
44	Left Shift	2A	12	12
45	\ (102-key only)	56	61	13
46	Z	2C	1A	1A
47	X	2D	22	22
48	C	2E	21	21
49	V	2F	2A	2A
50	B	30	32	32
51	N	31	31	31
52	M	32	3A	3A
53	,	33	41	41
54	.	34	49	49
55	/	35	4A	4A
57	Right Shift	36	59	59
58	Left Ctrl	1D	14	11
60	Left Alt	38	11	19
61	Spacebar	39	29	29
62	Right Alt	E0,38	E0,11	39
64	Right Ctrl	E0,1D	E0,14	58
75	Insert	E0,52	E0,70	67
76	Delete	E0,53	E0,71	64
79	Left arrow	E0,4B	E0,6B	61
80	Home	E0,47	E0,6C	6E
81	End	E0,4F	E0,69	65
83	Up arrow	E0,48	E0,75	63
84	Down arrow	E0,50	E0,72	60
85	Page Up	E0,49	E0,7D	6F
86	Page Down	E0,51	E0,7A	6D
89	Right arrow	E0,4D	E0,74	6A
90	Num Lock	45	77	76
91	Keypad 7 (Home)	47	6C	6C
92	Keypad 4 (Left arrow)	4B	6B	6B
93	Keypad 1 (End)	4F	69	69
95	Keypad /	E0,35	E0,4A	77
96	Keypad 8 (Up arrow)	48	75	75
97	Keypad 5	4C	73	73
98	Keypad 2 (Down arrow)	50	72	72

(continues)

Table 17.3   Continued

Key Number	Key/Character	Scan Code Set 1	Scan Code Set 2	Scan Code Set 3
99	Keypad 0 (Ins)	52	70	70
100	Keypad *	37	7C	7E
101	Keypad 9 (PgUp)	49	7D	7D
102	Keypad 6 (Left arrow)	4D	74	74
103	Keypad 3 (PgDn)	51	7A	7A
104	Keypad . (Del)	53	71	71
105	Keypad -	4A	7B	84
106	Keypad +	4E	E0,5A	7C
108	Keypad Enter	E0,1C	E0,5A	79
110	Escape	1	76	8
112	F1	3B	5	7
113	F2	3C	6	0F
114	F3	3D	4	17
115	F4	3E	0C	1F
116	F5	3F	3	27
117	F6	40	0B	2F
118	F7	41	83	37
119	F8	42	0A	3F
120	F9	43	1	47
121	F10	44	9	4F
122	F11	57	78	56
123	F12	58	7	5E
124	Print Screen	E0,2A,E0,37	E0,12,E0,7C	57
125	Scroll Lock	46	7E	5F
126	Pause	E1,1D,45, E1,9D,C5	E1,14,77, E1,F0,14, F0,77	62

The new keys on a 104-key Windows keyboard have their own unique scan codes. Table 17.4 shows the scan codes for the new keys.

Table 17.4   104-Key Windows Keyboard New Key Scan Codes

New Key	Scan Code Set 1	Scan Code Set 2	Scan Code Set 3
Left Windows	E0,5B	E0,1F	8B
Right Windows	E0,5C	E0,27	8C
Application	E0,5D	E0,2F	8D

Knowing these key number figures and scan codes are useful when you are troubleshooting stuck or failed keys on a keyboard. Diagnostics can report the defective keyswitch by the scan code, which varies from keyboard to keyboard on the character it represents and its location.

International Keyboard Layouts

After the keyboard controller in the system receives the scan codes generated by the keyboard and passes them to the main processor, the operating system converts the codes into the appropriate alphanumeric characters. In the United States, these characters are the letters, numbers, and symbols found on the standard American keyboard.

However, no matter what characters you see on the keytops, it is a relatively simple matter to adjust the scan code conversion process to map different characters to the keys. Windows 9x and Windows NT take advantage of this capability by enabling you to install multiple keyboard layouts to support different languages.

When you open the Keyboard control panel and select the Language page, you see a screen like Figure 17.9. The Language box should display the keyboard layout you selected when you installed the operating system. By clicking the Add button, you can select any one of several additional keyboard layouts supporting other languages.

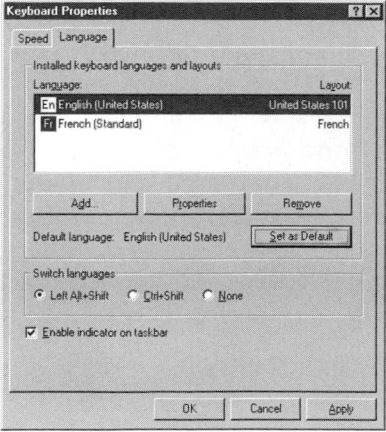

Figure 17.9   The Language page of the Keyboard control panel provides support for multiple character sets.

These keyboard layouts map different characters to certain keys on the standard keyboard. The standard French layout provides easy access to the accented characters commonly used in that language. For example, pressing the 2 key produces the é character. To type the numeral 2, you press the Shift+2 key combination. Other French-speaking countries have different keyboard conventions for the same characters, so Windows includes support for several keyboard layout variations for some languages, based on nationality.

Note

It is important to understand that this feature is not the same as installing the operating system in a different language. These keyboard layouts do not modify the text already displayed on the screen; they only alter the characters generated when you press certain keys.

The alternative keyboard layouts also do not provide support for non-Roman alphabets, such as Russian and Chinese. The accented characters and other symbols used in languages such as French and German are part of the standard ASCII character set. They are always accessible to English-language users through the Windows Character Map utility or through the use of Alt+keypad combinations. An alternative keyboard layout simply gives you an easier way to access the characters used in certain languages.

If you work on documents using more than one language, you can install as many keyboard layouts as necessary and switch between them at will. When you click the Enable Indicator on Taskbar check box on the Language page of the Keyboard control panel, a selector appears in the taskbar's tray area that enables you to switch languages easily. On the same page, you can enable a key combination that switches between the installed keyboard layouts.

Keyboard/Mouse Interface Connectors

Keyboards have a cable with one of two primary types of connectors at the system end. On most aftermarket keyboards, the cable is connected inside the keyboard case on the keyboard end, requiring you to open up the keyboard case to disconnect or test it. Enhanced keyboards manufactured by IBM use a unique cable assembly that plugs into both the keyboard and the system unit. This makes cable interchange or replacement an easy plug-in affair. A special connector called an *SDL* (*Shielded Data Link*) is used at the keyboard end, and the appropriate DIN connector is used at the PC end. Any IBM keyboard or cable can be ordered separately as a spare part. The newer Enhanced keyboards come with an externally detachable keyboard cable that plugs into the keyboard port with a special connector, much like a telephone connector. The other end of the cable is one of the following two types:

- *5-pin DIN connector.* Used on most PC systems with Baby-AT form factor motherboards.
- *6-pin mini-DIN connector.* Used on PS/2 systems and most PCs with LPX, ATX, and NLX motherboards.

Figure 17.10 and Table 17.5 show the physical layout and pinouts of all the respective keyboard connector plugs and sockets.

Table 17.5   Keyboard Connector Signals

Signal Name	5-Pin DIN	6-Pin Mini-DIN	6-Pin SDL
Keyboard Data	2	1	B
Ground	4	3	C
+5v	5	4	E
Keyboard Clock	1	5	D

Signal Name	5-Pin DIN	6-Pin Mini-DIN	6-Pin SDL
Not Connected	—	2	A
Not Connected	—	6	F
Not Connected	3	—	—

DIN = German Industrial Norm (Deutsche Industrie Norm), a committee that sets German dimensional standards.

SDL = Shielded Data Link, a type of shielded connector created by AMP and used by IBM and others for keyboard cables.

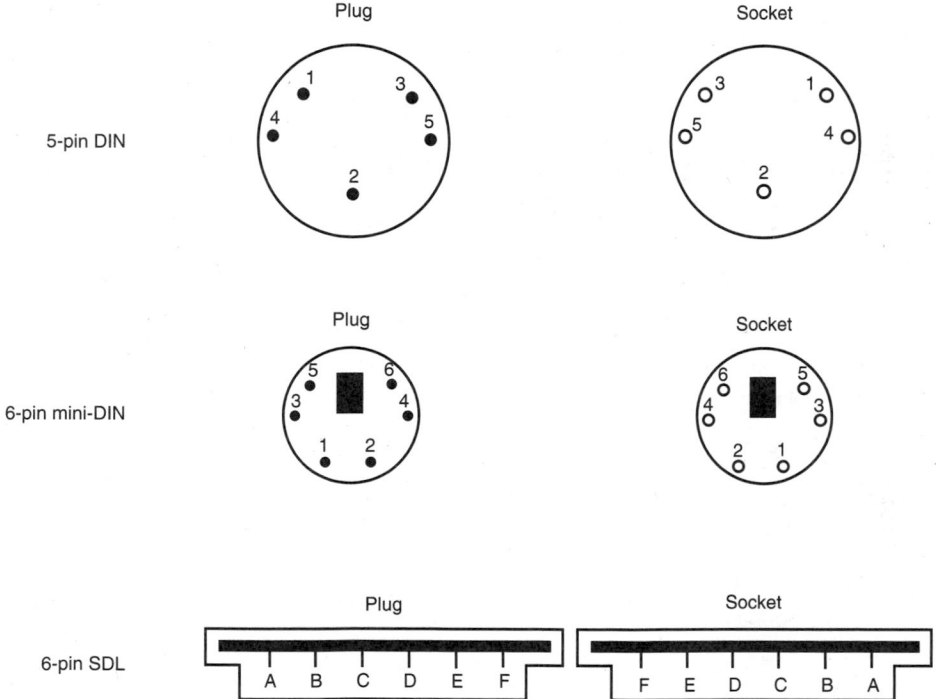

Figure 17.10   Keyboard and mouse connectors.

Motherboard mouse connectors also use the 6-pin mini-DIN connector and have the same pinout and signal descriptions as the keyboard connector; however, the data packets are incompatible. That means you can easily plug a motherboard mouse (PS/2 style) into a mini-DIN keyboard connector or plug the mini-DIN keyboard connector into a motherboard mouse port; however, neither one will work properly in this situation.

Caution

I have also seen PCs with external power supplies that used the same standard DIN connectors to attach the keyboard and the power supply. Although cross-connecting the mini-DIN connectors of a mouse and a keyboard is a harmless annoyance, connecting a power supply to a keyboard socket can be disastrous.

USB Keyboards and Mice

The latest innovation in keyboard (and pointing device) interfacing is connecting them to the PC via a USB (Universal Serial Bus) connection instead of the standard keyboard and mouse ports. Because USB is a universal bus, a single USB port in a system can replace the standard serial and parallel ports as well as the keyboard and mouse ports. Current systems still include both USB and the standard ports, but future systems might forego the others in lieu of a single USB port.

Several keyboard manufacturers have been marketing USB keyboards and pointing devices, including Microsoft with the Natural Keyboard Elite. This is a newer version of its Natural keyboard, which can work in the standard keyboard port as well as via the USB port in newer systems. The Natural Keyboard Elite looks like a standard Natural keyboard as it has a standard 6-pin mini-DIN connector that plugs into the keyboard port on all modern motherboards, but it also includes a special USB adapter that allows it to plug in directly via a USB port.

Note

Note that the internal electronics of this keyboard are different, and the USB adapter included with the Natural Keyboard Elite will not work on other standard keyboards, such as the original Microsoft Natural keyboard version 1.0.

Not all systems accept USB keyboards, even those with USB ports, because the standard PC BIOS has a keyboard driver that expects a standard keyboard port interface keyboard to be present. When a USB keyboard is installed, the system can't use it because there is no driver in the BIOS to make it work. In fact, some systems see the lack of a standard keyboard as an error and halt the boot process until one is installed.

To use a keyboard connected via the USB port, you must meet three requirements:

- Have a USB port in the system
- Run either Microsoft Windows 98 or Microsoft Windows NT 5.0 (which include USB keyboard drivers)
- Have what is referred to as USB Legacy support in your BIOS

USB Legacy support means your motherboard ROM BIOS includes drivers to recognize a USB keyboard. Without this BIOS, you can't use a USB keyboard when in MS-DOS or when installing Windows on the system for the first time. Also, should the Windows installation fail and require manipulation outside of Windows, the USB keyboard will not function unless it is supported in the BIOS. Virtually all 1998 and newer systems with USB ports include a BIOS with USB Legacy (meaning USB Keyboard) support.

For more information on USB, see Chapter 16, "Serial, Parallel, and Other I/O Interfaces."

Keyboards with Special Features

A number of keyboards on the market have special features not found in standard designs. These additional features range from simple things, such as built-in calculators and clocks, to more complicated features, such as integrated pointing devices, special character layouts, shapes, and even programmable keys.

The Dvorak Keyboard

Over the years, many people have attempted to change the design of the standard keyboard to improve typing speed and ergonomics. The standard QWERTY layout (so named for the first six letters below the number keys) we're all familiar with today was designed primarily to facilitate the mechanical needs of early manual typewriters (see Figure 17.11). The arrangement of the letters helped prevent the keys from jamming together as they flew up to strike the paper. Around 1936, August Dvorak and William Dealy developed a modified character layout called the Simplified Keyboard, shown in Figure 17.12, that was intended to replace the QWERTY layout. It was designed with the typist's needs in mind.

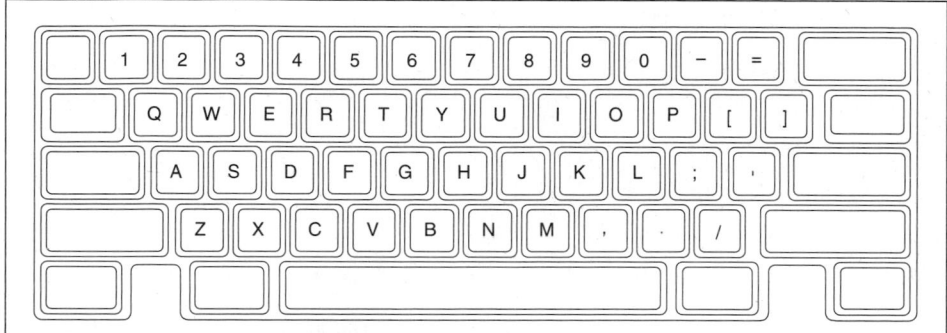

Figure 17.11 QWERTY keyboard layout.

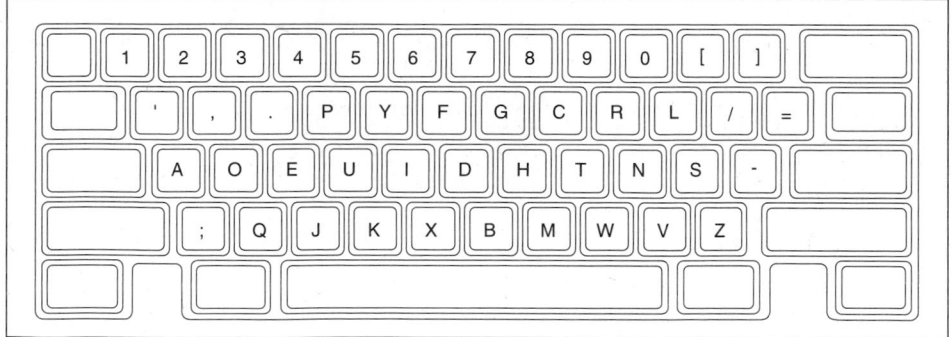

Figure 17.12 Dvorak keyboard layout.

The Dvorak-Dealy Simplified keyboard design is normally called the Dvorak keyboard probably because after they published the initial design, Dvorak alone spent many years perfecting and fine-tuning the layout. The Dvorak keyboard was finally accepted as an ANSI standard in 1982. The different character positions on the keys are designed to promote the alternation of hands during typing. The characters are arranged so that the vowels are in the home row under the left hand, and the consonants used most frequently are placed in the home row under the right hand. This rearrangement results in about 70 percent of all letters typed being on the home row, compared with about 31 percent for QWERTY. Additionally, the letters are arranged so that a drumming pattern, similar to the way people drum their fingers on a table, is encouraged. Some say (although it has not been proved) that the Dvorak layout might also help reduce problems with carpal tunnel syndrome and other repetitive motion injuries.

Although you can purchase Dvorak keyboards from several different keyboard companies, it is possible to convert to the Dvorak layout without spending a penny. By changing the operating system drivers, your existing QWERTY keyboard can function as though it were a Dvorak Keyboard. After changing drivers, you can buy or make stickers to go on the keys to show their new positions, or you can pull the keycaps off and physically rearrange them in the Dvorak layout.

To convert to the Dvorak layout in Windows 95/98, perform the following steps:

1. Open the control panel.
2. Double-click on the Keyboard icon.
3. Select the Language tab.
4. Click Properties, and change the layout to United States-Dvorak.

Instead of changing the properties (layout) of the existing English language keyboard, you can also add a language, complete with its own layout. After adding an additional language, make sure the Enable Indicator on Taskbar box below is checked. This option causes a language indicator to appear on the taskbar. You can then click the taskbar indicator on the desktop to display a menu that lists all installed languages (and layouts), allowing you to quickly switch between them.

To activate the Dvorak layout in Windows 3.1, follow these steps:

1. Open the control panel.
2. Select International.
3. Select Country = U.S.
4. Select Language = English (American).
5. Select Keyboard = U.S. Dvorak.

To change the layout under DOS 5.0 through 6.22, you need the MS-DOS supplemental disk. It contains several utility files, including the Dvorak keyboard layouts. If you don't have this disk, you can download it from the Microsoft Web site.

The Dvorak keyboard design still has its devotees, but it has not achieved widespread popularity, largely because of the difficulty of switching from the familiar QWERTY layout, which is still by far the most commonly used design. Although there are advantages to the Dvorak layout, it has proved difficult to show conclusively that it can actually improve typing speed.

For more information on the Dvorak layout, you can check with Dvorak International (see the Vendor List on the CD), a nonprofit organization dedicated to the Dvorak keyboard layout.

Ergonomic Keyboards

A more recent trend is to change the shape of the keyboard instead of altering the character layout. This trend has resulted in a number of different so-called ergonomic designs. The goal is to shape the keyboard to better fit the human hand. The most common of these designs splits the keyboard in the center, bending the sides outward. Some of these designs allow the angle between the sides to be adjusted, such as the Lexmark Select-Ease design. Others, such as the Microsoft Natural keyboard, are fixed. These split or bent designs more easily conform to the hands' natural angle while typing than the standard keyboard. They can improve productivity and typing speed and help prevent repetitive strain injuries, such as carpal tunnel syndrome (tendon inflammation).

Virtually every keyboard company now has some form of similar ergonomic keyboard, and the same criteria for quality and feel apply as with standard keyboard designs. One of the most popular ergonomic keyboards, the Microsoft Natural Keyboard, is manufactured for Microsoft by Keytronics. It uses the inexpensive soft-touch foam pad or rubber dome keyswitches Keytronics is known for. For those who prefer a more rugged keyboard with higher-quality switches, I recommend the Lexmark Select-Ease, Alps, NMB Technologies, or Lite-On keyboards. These keyboards are available with very high-quality mechanical switches that have a positive tactile feel to them. The Lexmark design, in particular, allows you to adjust the angle between the two sides of the keyboard from fully closed, like a standard keyboard, to split at practically any angle. You can even separate the two halves completely. It also features built-in palm rests, an oversized spacebar, and cursor keys on both sides of the keyboard.

Because of their novelty and their trendy appeal, some ergonomic keyboards can be considerably more expensive than traditional designs, but for users with medical problems caused or exacerbated by improper positioning of the wrists at the keyboard, they can be an important remedy to a serious problem. General users, however, are highly resistant to change, and these designs have yet to significantly displace the standard keyboard layout.

Programmable Keyboards

Several companies, including Maxi-Switch, have introduced keyboards that feature programmable keys. You can assign different keystrokes or macros to keys, or even reprogram the entire keyboard layout. This type of keyboard has been supplied in the past by some of the major PC vendors, such as Gateway 2000.

At one time I used a number of these keyboards in the seminars I teach. Unfortunately, I found the programming functions difficult to remember. Accidentally pressing the programming control keys often put the keyboard into an altered state, requiring it to be reset. In a business environment, this phenomenon resulted in an annoying number of technical support calls from mystified users wondering why their keyboards were locked up.

One other problem was that the extra keys added width to the keyboard, making it wider than most other standard designs. I quickly decided that the programming functions were so rarely used that they were simply not worth the hassle, so I specified standard keyboards for future purchases.

Keyboard Troubleshooting and Repair

Keyboard errors are usually caused by two simple problems. Other more difficult, intermittent problems can arise, but they are much less common. The most frequent problems are as follows:

- Defective cables
- Stuck keys

Defective cables are easy to spot if the failure is not intermittent. If the keyboard stops working altogether or every keystroke results in an error or incorrect character, the cable is likely the culprit. Troubleshooting is simple, especially if you have a spare cable on hand. Simply replace the suspected cable with one from a known, working keyboard to verify whether the problem still exists. If it does, the problem must be elsewhere. You can also test the cable for continuity when it is removed from the keyboard by using a Digital Multi-Meter (DMM). DMMs that have an audible continuity tester built in make this procedure much easier to perform. Wiggle the ends of the cable as you check each wire to make sure there are no intermittent connections. If you discover a problem with the continuity in one of the wires, replace the cable or the entire keyboard, whichever is cheaper. Because replacement keyboards are so inexpensive, sometimes it can be cheaper to replace the entire unit than to get a new cable.

Many times you first discover a problem with a keyboard because the system has an error during the POST. Most systems use error codes in a 3xx numeric format to distinguish the keyboard. If you have any such errors during the POST, write them down. Some BIOS versions do not use cryptic numeric error codes; they simply state something like the following:

```
Keyboard stuck key failure
```

This message is normally displayed by a system with a Phoenix BIOS if a key is stuck. Unfortunately, the message does not identify which key it is!

If your system displays a 3xx (keyboard) error preceded by a two-digit hexadecimal number, the number is the scan code of a failing or stuck keyswitch. Look up the scan code in the tables provided in this section to determine which keyswitch is the culprit. By removing the keycap of the offending key and cleaning the switch, you can often solve the problem.

For a simple test of the motherboard keyboard connector, you can check voltages on some of the pins. Using Figure 17.14 as a guide, measure the voltages on various pins of the keyboard connector. To prevent possible damage to the system or keyboard, turn off the power before disconnecting the keyboard. Then unplug the keyboard and turn the power back on. Make measurements between the ground pin and the other pins according to Table 17.6. If the voltages are within these specifications, the motherboard keyboard circuitry is probably okay.

Table 17.6   Keyboard Connector Specifications

DIN Connector Pin	Mini-DIN Connector Pin	Signal	Voltage
1	5	Keyboard Clock	+2.0v to +5.5v
2	1	Keyboard Data	+4.8v to +5.5v
3	-	Reserved	—
4	3	Ground	—
5	4	+5v Power	+2.0v to +5.5v

If your measurements do not match these voltages, the motherboard might be defective. Otherwise, the keyboard cable or keyboard might be defective. If you suspect that the cable is the problem, the easiest thing to do is replace the keyboard cable with a known good one. If the system still does not work normally, you might have to replace the entire keyboard or the motherboard.

In many newer systems, the motherboard's keyboard and mouse connectors are protected by a fuse that can be replaced. Look for any type of fuse on the motherboard in the vicinity of the keyboard or mouse connectors. Other systems may have a socketed keyboard controller chip (8042-type). In that case, it might be possible to repair the motherboard keyboard circuit by replacing this chip. Because these chips have ROM code in them, it is best to get the replacement from the motherboard or BIOS manufacturer.

Following is a list of standard POST and diagnostics keyboard error codes:

Error Code	Description
3xx	Keyboard errors
301	Keyboard reset or stuck-key failure (XX 301; XX = scan code in hex)
302	System unit keylock switch is locked
302	User-indicated keyboard test error
303	Keyboard or system-board error; keyboard controller failure
304	Keyboard or system-board error; keyboard clock high
305	Keyboard +5v error; PS/2 keyboard fuse (on motherboard) blown
341	Keyboard error
342	Keyboard cable error
343	Keyboard LED card or cable failure
365	Keyboard LED card or cable failure
366	Keyboard interface cable failure
367	Keyboard LED card or cable failure

Disassembly Procedures and Cautions

Repairing and cleaning a keyboard often requires you to take it apart. When performing this task, you must know when to stop! Some keyboards come apart into literally hundreds of little pieces that are almost impossible to reassemble. An IBM keyboard generally has these four major parts:

- Cable
- Case
- Keypad assembly
- Keycaps

You can easily break down a keyboard into these major components and replace any of them, but don't disassemble the keypad assembly, or you will be showered with hundreds of tiny springs, clips, and keycaps. Finding all these parts—several hundred of them—and piecing the unit back together is not a fun way to spend your time, and you might not be able to reassemble the keyboard properly. Figure 17.13 shows a typical keyboard with the case opened.

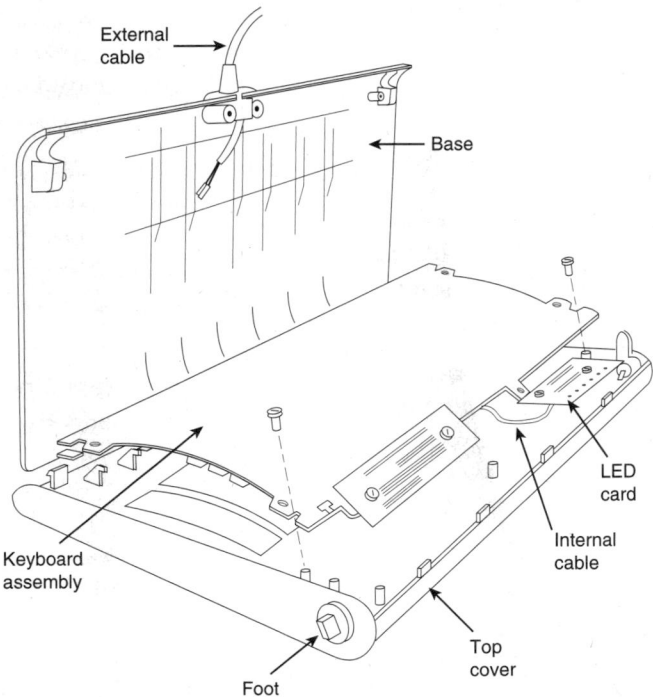

Figure 17.13   Typical keyboard components.

Another problem is that you cannot purchase the smaller parts separately, such as contact clips and springs. The only way to get these parts is from another keyboard. If you ever have a keyboard that is beyond repair, keep it around for these parts. They might come in handy someday.

Most repair operations are limited to changing the cable or cleaning some component of the keyboard, from the cable contact ends to the key contact points. The keyboard cable takes quite a lot of abuse and, therefore, can fail easily. The ends are stretched, tugged, pulled, and generally handled roughly. The cable uses strain reliefs, but you still might have problems with the connectors making proper contact at each end or even with wires that have broken inside the cable. You might want to carry a spare cable for every type of keyboard you have.

All keyboard cables plug into the keyboard and PC with connectors, and you can change the cables easily without having to splice wires or solder connections. With the earlier 83-key PC and 84-key AT keyboards, you must open the case to access the connector to which the cable attaches. On the newer 101-key Enhanced keyboards from IBM, Lexmark, and Unicomp, the cable plugs into the keyboard from the outside of the case, using a modular jack and plug similar to a telephone jack. This design also makes the IBM/Lexmark/Unicomp keyboards universally usable on nearly any system (except the original PC) by simply switching the cable.

The only difference, for example, between the Enhanced keyboards for an IBM AT and an IBM PS/2 system is the attached cable. PS/2 systems use a tan cable with a smaller plug on the computer side. The AT cable is black and has the larger DIN-type plug on the computer side. You can interchange the Enhanced keyboards as long as you use the correct cable for the system.

The only feasible way to repair a keyboard is to replace the cable and to clean the individual keyswitch assemblies, the entire keypad, or the cable contact ends. Other than cleaning a keyboard, the only thing you can do is replace the entire keypad assembly (virtually the entire keyboard) or the cable.

Cleaning a Keyboard

One of the best ways to keep a keyboard in top condition is periodic cleaning. As preventive maintenance, you should vacuum the keyboard weekly, or at least monthly. When vacuuming, it is best to use a soft brush attachment; this will help dislodge the dust. Also note that many keyboards have key caps that can come off easily, be careful or you'll have to dig them out of the vacuum cleaner.

You can also use canned compressed air to blow the dust and dirt out instead of using a vacuum. Before you dust a keyboard with the compressed air, turn the keyboard upside down so that the particles of dirt and dust collected inside can fall out.

On all keyboards, each keycap is removable, which can be handy if a key sticks or acts erratically. For example, a common problem is a key that does not work every time you press it. This problem usually results from dirt collecting under the key. An excellent tool for removing keycaps on almost any keyboard is the U-shaped chip-puller included in many computer tool kits. Simply slip the hooked ends of the tool under the keycap, squeeze the ends together to grip the underside of the keycap, and lift up. IBM sells a tool designed specifically for removing keycaps from its keyboards, but the chip puller works even better. After removing the cap, spray some compressed air into the space under the cap to dislodge the dirt. Then replace the cap and check the action of the key.

Caution

When you remove the keycaps, be careful not to remove the spacebar on the original 83-key PC and the 84-key AT-type keyboards. This bar is difficult to reinstall. The newer 101-key units use a different wire support that can be removed and replaced much more easily.

Spills can be a problem, too. If you tip a soft drink or cup of coffee into a keyboard, you do not necessarily have a disaster. However, you should immediately (or as soon as possible) flush out the keyboard with distilled water. Partially disassemble the keyboard and use the water to wash the components. (See the previous section, "Dissasembly Procedures and Cautions," for disassembly instructions.) If the spilled liquid has dried, soak the keyboard in some of the water for a while. When you are sure the keyboard is clean, pour another gallon or so of distilled water over it and through the keyswitches to wash away any residual dirt. After the unit dries completely, it should be perfectly functional. You might be surprised to know that drenching your keyboard with water does not harm the components. Just make sure you use distilled water, which is free from residue or mineral content. Also make sure the keyboard is fully dry before you try to use it, or some of the components might short out.

Replacement Keyboards

In most cases, it is cheaper or more cost effective to replace a keyboard rather than repair it. This is especially true if the keyboard has an internal malfunction or if one of the keyswitches is defective. Replacement parts for keyboards are almost impossible to procure, and installing any repair part is usually difficult. In addition, many of the keyboards supplied with lower-cost PCs leave much to be desired. They often have a mushy feel, with little or no tactile feedback. A poor keyboard can make using a system a frustrating experience, especially if you are a touch typist. For all these reasons, it is often a good idea to replace an existing keyboard with something better.

Perhaps the highest quality keyboards in the entire computer industry are those made by IBM, or, more accurately, Unicomp. Several years ago, IBM spun off its keyboard and printer divisions as a separate company called Lexmark. Lexmark used to manufacture most IBM-brand keyboards and printers and sold them not only to IBM, but also to other PC vendors and end users. In 1996, Lexmark sold its keyboard technology to a company called Unicomp, which now maintains an extensive selection of over 1,400 keyboards.

Table 17.7 shows the part numbers of all IBM-labeled keyboards and cables. These numbers can serve as a reference when you are seeking a replacement IBM keyboard from IBM directly or from third-party companies. Many third-party companies sell IBM label keyboards for much less than IBM, in both new and refurbished form. Remember that you can also purchase these same keyboards through Unicomp, although they do not come with an IBM label.

Table 17.7   IBM Keyboard and Cable Part Numbers

Description	Part Number
83-key U.S. PC keyboard assembly with cable	8529297
Cable assembly for 83-key PC keyboard	8529168

Description	Part Number
84-key U.S. AT keyboard assembly with cable	8286165
Cable assembly for 84-key keyboard	8286146
101-key U.S. keyboard without LED panel	1390290
101-key U.S. keyboard with LED panel	6447033
101-key U.S. keyboard with LED panel (PS/2 logo)	1392090
6-foot cable for Enhanced keyboard (DIN plug)	6447051
6-foot cable for Enhanced keyboard (mini-DIN plug)	61X8898
6-foot cable for Enhanced keyboard (shielded mini-DIN plug)	27F4984
10-foot cable for Enhanced keyboard (mini-DIN plug)	72X8537

Notice that the original 83/84-key IBM keyboards are sold with a cable that has the larger, five-pin DIN connector already attached. IBM Enhanced keyboards are always sold (at least by IBM) without a cable. You must order the proper cable as a separate item. Cables are available to connect the keyboards to either the older system units that use the larger DIN connector or to PS/2 systems (and many compatibles) that use the smaller mini-DIN connector.

Recently, IBM has started selling complete keyboard assemblies under a program called IBM Options. This program is designed to sell these components in the retail channel to end users of both IBM and compatible systems from other vendors. Items under the IBM Options program are sold through normal retail channels, such as CompUSA and Computer Discount Warehouse (CDW). These items are also priced much cheaper than items purchased as spare parts. They include a full warranty and are sold as complete packages, including cables. Table 17.8 lists some of the IBM Options keyboards and part numbers.

Table 17.8   IBM Options Keyboards (Sold Retail)

Description	Part Number
IBM Enhanced keyboard (cable w/ DIN plug)	92G7454
IBM Enhanced keyboard (cable w/ mini-DIN plug)	92G7453
IBM Enhanced keyboard, built-in Trackball (cable w/ DIN plug)	92G7456
IBM Enhanced keyboard, built-in Trackball (cable w/ mini-DIN plug)	92G7455
IBM Enhanced keyboard, integrated TrackPoint II (cables w/ mini-DIN plugs)	92G7461

The extremely positive tactile feedback of the IBM/Lexmark/Unicomp design is also a benchmark for the rest of the industry. Although keyboard feel is an issue of personal preference, I have never used a keyboard that feels better than the IBM/Lexmark/Unicomp designs. I now equip every system I use with a Unicomp keyboard, including the many non-IBM systems I use. You can purchase these keyboards directly from Unicomp at very reasonable prices. Also, you can sometimes find IBM-labeled models selling for under $100 available from advertisers in computer magazines.

Unicomp sells other keyboards for reasonable prices, too. Many different models are available, including some with a built-in trackball or even the revolutionary TrackPoint pointing device.

(TrackPoint refers to a small stick mounted between the G, H, and B keys.) This device was first featured on the IBM ThinkPad laptop systems, although the keyboards are now sold for use on other manufacturers' PCs. The technology is being licensed to many other manufacturers, including Toshiba. Other manufacturers of high-quality keyboards that are similar in feel to the IBM/Lexmark/Unicomp units are Alps, Lite-On, and NMB Technologies. These keyboards have excellent tactile feedback, with a positive click sound. They are my second choice, after a Unicomp unit. Maxi-Switch also makes a high-quality aftermarket keyboard, which is used by a number of PC manufacturers, including Gateway 2000. They have a good feel, too, and are recommended. Many of these companies can make their keyboards with your own company logo on them (such as the Maxi-Switch models used by Gateway 2000), which is ideal for clone manufacturers looking for name-brand recognition.

Pointing Devices

The mouse was invented in 1964 by Douglas Englebart, who at the time was working at the Stanford Research Institute (SRI), a think tank sponsored by Stanford University. The mouse was officially called an X-Y Position Indicator for a Display System. Xerox later applied the mouse to its revolutionary Alto computer system in 1973. At the time, unfortunately, these systems were experimental and used purely for research.

In 1979, several people from Apple, including Steve Jobs, were invited to see the Alto and the software that ran the system. Steve Jobs was blown away by what he saw as the future of computing, which included the use of the mouse as a pointing device and the GUI (graphical user interface) it operated. Apple promptly incorporated these features into what was to become the Lisa computer and lured away 15 to 20 Xerox scientists to work on the Apple system.

Although Xerox released the Star 8010 computer that used this technology in 1981, it was expensive, poorly marketed, and perhaps way ahead of its time. Apple released the Lisa computer, its first system that used the mouse, in 1983. It was not a runaway success, largely because of its $10,000 list price, but by then Jobs already had Apple working on the low-cost successor to the Lisa, the Macintosh. The Apple Macintosh was introduced in 1984. Although it was not an immediate hit, the Macintosh has grown in popularity since that time.

Many credit the Macintosh with inventing the mouse and GUI, but as you can see, this technology was actually borrowed from others, including SRI and Xerox. Certainly the Macintosh, and now Microsoft Windows and OS/2, have gone on to popularize this interface and bring it to the legion of Intel-based PC systems.

Although the mouse did not catch on quickly in the PC marketplace, today the GUIs for PC systems such as Windows and OS/2 practically demand the use of a mouse. Therefore, it is common for a mouse to be sold with nearly every new system on the market.

Mice come in many shapes and sizes from many different manufacturers. Some have taken the standard mouse design and turned it upside down, creating the trackball. In the trackball devices, you move the ball with your hand directly rather than the unit itself. IBM even produced a very cool mouse/trackball convertible device called the TrackPoint (p/n 1397040). The TrackPoint could be used as either a mouse (ball side down) or as a trackball (ball side up). In most cases, the dedicated trackballs have a much larger ball than would be found on a standard mouse. Other than the orientation and perhaps the size of the ball, a trackball is identical to a mouse in design, basic function, and electrical interface.

The largest manufacturers of mice are Microsoft and Logitech. Even though mice may come in different varieties, their actual use and care differ very little. The standard mouse consists of several components:

- A housing that you hold in your hand and move around on your desktop
- A roller ball that signals movement to the system
- Buttons (usually two) for making selections
- A cable for connecting the mouse to the system
- An interface connector to attach the mouse to the system

The housing, which is made of plastic, consists of very few moving parts. On top of the housing, where your fingers normally lie, are buttons. There may be any number of buttons, but in the PC world, there are typically only two. If additional buttons are on your mouse, specialized software is required for them to operate. On the bottom of the housing is a small rubber ball that rolls as you move the mouse across the tabletop. The movements of this rubber ball are translated into electrical signals transmitted to the computer across the cable. Some mice use a special optical sensor that detects movement over a grid. These optical mice have fallen into disfavor because they work only if you use a special grid pad underneath them.

The cable can be any length, but it is typically between four and six feet long.

Tip

If you have a choice on the length of cable to buy, go for a longer one. This allows easier placement of the mouse in relation to your computer.

After the mouse is connected to your computer, it communicates with your system through the use of a device driver, which can be loaded explicitly or built into the operating system software. For example, no separate drivers are needed to use a mouse with Windows or OS/2, but using the mouse with most DOS-based programs requires a separate driver to be loaded from the CONFIG.SYS or AUTOEXEC.BAT file. Regardless of whether it is built in or not, the driver translates the electrical signals sent from the mouse into positional information and indicates the status of the buttons.

Internally, a mouse is very simple, too. The ball usually rests against two rollers, one for translating the X-axis movement and the other for translating the Y-axis movement. These rollers are usually connected to small disks with shutters that alternately block and allow the passage of light. Small optical sensors detect movement of the wheels by watching an internal infrared light blink on and off as the shutter wheel rotates and "chops" the light. These blinks are translated into movement along the axes. This type of setup, called an *opto-mechanical mechanism*, is by far the most popular in use today (see Figure 17.14).

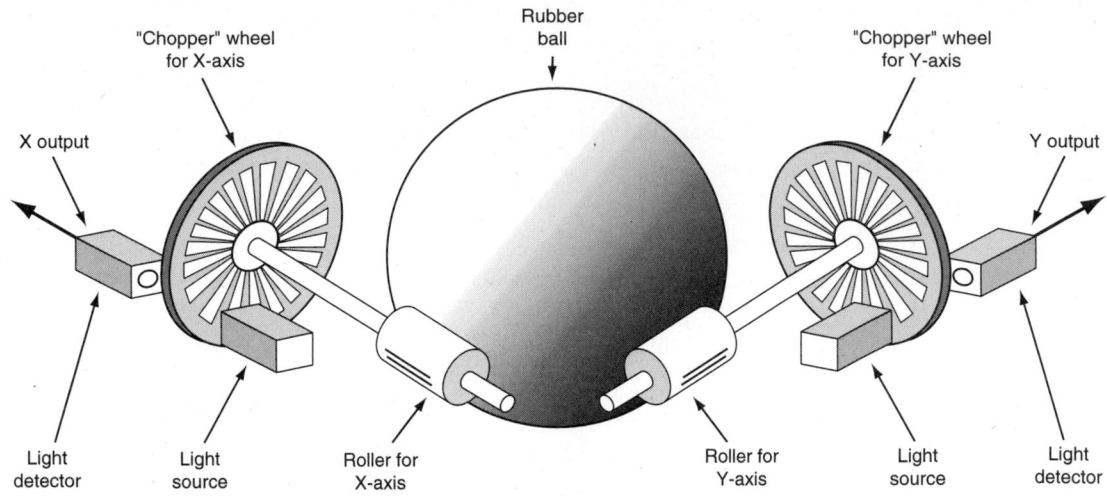

Figure 17.14 Typical opto-mechanical mouse mechanism. Note that for clarity, this figure only shows two optical detectors. Mice use at least two—and sometimes three—sensors per wheel.

Pointing Device Interface Types

The connector used to attach your mouse to the system depends on the type of interface you are using. Three basic interfaces are used for mouse connections, with a fourth combination device possible as well. Mice are most commonly connected to your computer through the following three interfaces:

- Serial interface
- Dedicated motherboard mouse port
- Bus-card interface

Serial

A popular method of connecting a mouse to older PCs is through the standard serial interface. As with other serial devices, the connector on the end of the mouse cable is either a 9-pin or 25-pin male connector. Only a couple of pins in the DB-9 or DB-25 connectors are used for communications between the mouse and the device driver, but the mouse connector typically has all 9 or 25 pins present.

Because most PCs come with two serial ports, a serial mouse can be plugged into either COM 1: or COM 2:. The device driver, when initializing, searches the ports to determine which one the mouse is connected to.

Because a serial mouse does not connect to the system directly, it does not use system resources by itself. Instead, the resources used are those used by the serial port to which it is connected. For example, if you have a mouse connected to COM2, it most likely uses IRQ3 and I/O port addresses 2F8h-2FFh.

◀◀ See "Serial Ports," p. 872.

Motherboard Mouse Port (PS/2)

Most newer computers now come with a dedicated mouse port built into the motherboard. This practice was introduced by IBM with the PS/2 systems in 1987, so this interface is often referred to as a *PS/2 mouse interface*. This term does not imply that such a mouse can work only with a PS/2; instead, it means the mouse can connect to any system that has a dedicated mouse port on the motherboard. Refer to Figure 17.14.

From a hardware perspective, a motherboard mouse connector is usually exactly the same as the mini-DIN connector used for newer keyboards. In fact, the motherboard mouse port is connected to the 8042-type keyboard controller found on the motherboard. All the PS/2 computers include mini-DIN keyboard and mouse port connectors on the back. Most compatible Slimline computers also have these same connectors for space reasons. Other motherboards have a pin-header type connector for the mouse port because most standard cases do not have a provision for the mini-DIN mouse connector. If that is the case, an adapter cable is usually supplied with the system. This cable adapts the pin-header connector on the motherboard to the standard mini-DIN type connector used for the motherboard mouse.

Caution

As mentioned in the "Keyboard/Mouse Interface Connectors" section earlier in this chapter, the mini-DIN sockets used for both keyboard and mouse connections on many systems are physically and electrically interchangeable, but the data packets they carry are not. Be sure to plug each device into the correct socket or neither will function correctly.

Connecting a mouse to the built-in mouse port is the best method of connection because you do not sacrifice any of the system's interface slots or any serial ports, and the performance is not limited by the serial port circuitry. The standard resource usage for a motherboard (or PS/2) mouse port is IRQ12, as well as I/O port addresses 60h and 64h. Because the motherboard mouse port uses the 8042-type keyboard controller chip, the port addresses are those of this chip. IRQ12 is an interrupt that is usually free on most systems and it, of course, must remain free on any ISA bus systems that have a motherboard mouse port because interrupt sharing is not allowed with the ISA bus.

Serial and Motherboard Mouse Port (PS/2)

A hybrid type of mouse can plug into a serial port or a motherboard mouse port connection. This combination serial-PS/2 mouse is more flexible than the single design types. Circuitry in this mouse automatically detects the type of port to which it is connected and configures the mouse automatically. These mice usually come with a mini-DIN connector on the end of their cable and an adapter that converts the mini-DIN to a 9- or 25-pin serial port connector.

Sometimes people use adapters to try to connect a serial mouse to a motherboard mouse port or a motherboard mouse to a serial port. That this does not work is not the fault of the adapter. If the mouse does not explicitly state that it is both a serial and a PS/2-type mouse, it works only on the single interface for which it was designed. Most of the time, you find the designation for what type of mouse you have printed on its underside.

Bus

A bus mouse is typically used in systems that do not have a motherboard mouse port or any available serial ports. The name *bus mouse* is derived from the fact that the mouse requires a special bus interface board, which occupies a slot in your computer and communicates with the device driver across the main motherboard bus. Although the user can't detect whether it's a bus mouse (there is no operational difference between a bus mouse and other types of mice), many people view a bus mouse as less desirable than other types because it occupies a slot that could be used for other peripherals.

Another drawback to the bus mouse is that it is electrically incompatible with the other types of mice. Because they are not very popular, bus mice can be hard to find in a pinch. Likewise, the bus adapters are typically available only for ISA slots; because they are always 8-bit cards, you are limited in the choice of nonconflicting hardware interrupts. A bus mouse can also be dangerous because it uses a mini-DIN connector—similar to the motherboard (PS/2)-type mouse—except with nine pins instead of only five. The Figure 17.15 shows a typical bus mouse connector.

Figure 17.15   Bus mouse nine-pin mini-DIN connector.

Bus mouse adapter cards usually have a selectable interrupt and I/O port address setting, but the IRQ selection is limited to 8-bit interrupts. This usually means you must choose IRQ5 in most systems that already have two serial ports because all the other 8-bit interrupts are in use. If you are already using another 8-bit-only card that needs an interrupt, like some sound cards, you can't run both devices in the same system without conflicts. All in all, I think bus mice should be avoided.

Note

Microsoft sometimes calls a bus mouse an *inport mouse*, which is its proprietary name for a bus mouse connection.

USB

The newest interface for PC keyboards, and virtually every other type of peripheral you can name, is the Universal Serial Bus (USB). USB keyboards connect to a PC through the universal four-wire connector used by all USB devices. Because you can plug up to 127 devices into a single USB port on your PC, these keyboards frequently include additional USB sockets built into the housing, enabling them to function as hubs for other USB devices.

Alternatively, the USB plug that connects to your PC may have a *pass-through* connector. This is a standard USB plug with an integrated USB socket, so you can connect another device using the same port on the computer. Some USB keyboards also include a standard PS/2 mouse port, so you can connect your existing mouse directly to the keyboard instead of to the computer. If your system has a conventional mouse port, I recommend you use it over a USB mouse, as there is no advantage to a USB mouse, and they generally cost more.

Mouse Troubleshooting

If you are experiencing problems with your mouse, you need to look in only two general places—hardware or software. Because mice are basically simple devices, looking at the hardware takes very little time. Detecting and correcting software problems can take a bit longer, however.

Cleaning Your Mouse

If you notice that the mouse pointer moves across the screen in a jerky fashion, it may be time to clean your mouse. This jerkiness is caused when dirt and dust get trapped around the mouse's ball-and-roller assembly, thereby restricting its free movement.

From a hardware perspective, the mouse is a simple device, so cleaning it is easy. The first step is to turn the mouse housing over so that you can see the ball on the bottom. Notice that surrounding the ball is an access panel that you can open. Sometimes instructions indicate how the panel is to be opened. (Some off-brand mice might require you to remove some screws to get at the roller ball.) Remove the panel to see more of the roller ball and the socket in which it rests.

If you turn the mouse back over, the rubber roller ball should fall into your hand. Take a look at the ball. It may be gray or black, but it should have no visible dirt or other contamination. If it does, wash it in soapy water or a mild solvent, such as contact lens cleaner solution or alcohol, and dry it off.

Now take a look at the socket in which the roller ball normally rests. You will see two or three small wheels or bars against which the ball normally rolls. If you see dust or dirt on or around these wheels or bars, you need to clean them. The best way is to use a compressed air duster, which can blow out any dust or dirt. You also can use some electrical contact cleaner to clean the rollers. Remember: Any remaining dirt or dust impedes the movement of the roller ball and results in the mouse not working as it should.

Put the mouse back together by inserting the roller ball into the socket and then securely attaching the cover panel. The mouse should look just as it did before you removed the panel, except that it will be noticeably cleaner.

Interrupt Conflicts

Interrupts are internal signals used by your computer to indicate when something needs to happen. With a mouse, an interrupt is used whenever the mouse has information to send to the mouse driver. If a conflict occurs and the same interrupt used by the mouse is used by a different device, the mouse will not work properly—if at all.

Interrupt conflicts do not normally occur if your system uses a mouse port, but they can occur with the other types of mouse interfaces. Mouse ports built into modern motherboards are almost always set to IRQ12. If your system has a motherboard mouse port, be sure you don't set any other adapter cards to IRQ12, or a conflict will result.

When you are using a serial mouse, interrupt conflicts typically occur if you add a third and fourth serial port, using either an expansion card or an internal serial device, such as a modem. This happens because in ISA bus systems, the odd-numbered serial ports (1 and 3) are usually configured to use the same interrupts, as are the even-numbered ports (2 and 4). Therefore, if your mouse is connected to COM 2: and an internal modem uses COM 4:, they both might use the same interrupt, and you cannot use them at the same time.

Because the mouse generates interrupts only when it is moved, you may find that the modem functions properly until you touch the mouse, at which point the modem is disconnected. You might be able to use the mouse and modem at the same time by moving one of them to a different serial port. For instance, if your mouse uses COM 1: and the modem still uses COM 4:, you can use them both at once because odd and even ports use different interrupts.

The best way around these interrupt conflicts is to make sure no two devices use the same interrupt. Serial port adapters are available for adding COM 3: and COM 4: serial ports that do not share the interrupts used by COM 1: and COM 2:. These boards enable the new COM ports to use other normally available interrupts, such as IRQs 10, 11, 12, 15, or 5. I never recommend configuring a system with shared interrupts; it is a sure way to run into problems later.

If you suspect an interrupt problem with a bus-type mouse, you can use the Device Manager built into Windows 9x (which is accessible from the System control panel) or even a program such as Microsoft Diagnostics (MSD) to help you identify what interrupt is being used by the mouse. You get MSD free with Windows 3.0 or later, as well as with MS-DOS 6.0 or later.

▶▶ See "Operating System Diagnostics," p. 1298.

Be aware that programs, such as MSD, that attempt to identify IRQ usage are not always 100 percent accurate—in fact, they are inaccurate in many cases—and they usually require that the device driver for the particular device be loaded to work.

The Device Manager in Windows 9x is part of the Plug-and-Play (PnP) software for the system, and it is usually 100 percent accurate on PnP hardware. Although some of these interrupt-reporting programs can have problems, most can easily identify the mouse IRQ if the mouse driver has been loaded. After the IRQ is identified, you might need to change the IRQ setting of the bus mouse adapter or one or more other devices in your system so that everything works together properly.

If your driver refuses to recognize the mouse at all, regardless of its type, try using a different mouse that you know works. Replacing a defective mouse with a known good one might be the only way to know whether the problem is indeed caused by a bad mouse.

I have had problems in which a bad mouse caused the system to lock right as the driver loaded or even when diagnostics such as MSD tried to access the mouse. You can easily ferret out this type of problem by loading MSD with the /I option, which causes MSD to bypass its initial hardware detection. Then run each of the tests separately, including the mouse test, to see whether the system locks. If the system locks during the mouse test, you have found a problem with the mouse or the mouse port. Try replacing the mouse to see whether that helps. If it does not, you might need to replace the serial port or bus mouse adapter. If a motherboard-based mouse port goes bad, you can replace the entire motherboard—which is usually expensive—or you can just disable the motherboard mouse port via jumpers or the system BIOS setup program and install a serial or bus mouse instead. This method enables you to continue using the system without having to replace the motherboard.

Driver Software

To function properly, the mouse requires the installation of a device driver. In DOS, you have to load the driver manually through your CONFIG.SYS or AUTOEXEC.BAT file, but the driver is automatically loaded in all versions of Windows. I normally recommend using the default drivers built into the Windows or OS/2 operating systems. In those environments, no additional external driver is necessary. The only reason for loading an external driver (via CONFIG.SYS) is if you want the mouse to work with DOS applications in Windows 3.1. Windows 9x drivers support the use of the mouse in DOS applications by default.

If you need the mouse to work in standard DOS—in other words, outside Windows or OS/2—you must load a device driver through your CONFIG.SYS file or your AUTOEXEC.BAT file. This driver, if loaded in the CONFIG.SYS file, is typically called MOUSE.SYS. The version that loads in the AUTOEXEC.BAT file is called MOUSE.COM. (It is possible that your mouse drivers have different names, depending on who manufactured your mouse.) Again, remember that if you use a mouse only in Windows or OS/2, no external drivers are required because the mouse driver is built in.

The first step to installing a DOS mouse driver is to make sure the proper command to load the driver is in your CONFIG.SYS or AUTOEXEC.BAT file. If it isn't, add the proper line, according to the information supplied with your mouse. For instance, the proper command to load the mouse driver through the CONFIG.SYS file for a Microsoft mouse is as follows:

```
DEVICEHIGH=\DOS\MOUSE.SYS
```

The actual syntax of the command could vary, depending on whether you are loading the device into upper memory and where the device driver is located on your disk.

One of the biggest problems with the separate mouse driver is getting it loaded into an Upper Memory Block (UMB). The older Microsoft mouse drivers—versions 9.0 and earlier—require a large block of 40–56KB UMB to load; upon loading, they shrink down to less than 20KB. Even though they take only 20KB or less after loading, you still need a very large area to get them "in the door."

The best tip I can give you for these separate drivers is to use the newest drivers available from Microsoft. These drivers are included with the newer Microsoft mice and are sold separately as an upgrade. The Microsoft driver works with any type of Microsoft-compatible mouse, which basically means just about any mouse at all. Microsoft requires that you pay about $50 for an upgrade to the newer versions of the mouse driver. You can also get the new driver with a new mouse for $35 or less, which makes the driver-only purchase not very cost effective. Microsoft still includes only the older driver with MS-DOS 6.22 or earlier. IBM included the new driver with PC DOS 6.3 but switched back to the 8.2 driver in PC DOS 17.0.

If you use version 9.01 or later, the driver requires less memory than previous versions and automatically loads into high memory. One of the best features is that the driver first loads into low memory, shrinks down to about 24KB, and then moves into upper memory automatically. In addition, the driver seeks out the smallest UMB that can hold it instead of trying only the largest, as would happen if you used the DEVICEHIGH, LOADHIGH, or LH commands to load the driver. Previous versions of the driver could not fit into an upper memory block unless that block was at least 40–56KB or larger, and they would certainly not move into upper memory automatically. The enhanced self-loading capability of the Microsoft DOS mouse driver 9.01 and higher can save much memory space. It is well worth having.

◀◀ See "Upper Memory Area (UMA)," p. 481.

After placing the proper driver load command in your CONFIG.SYS or AUTOEXEC.BAT file, reboot the system with the mouse connected and make sure the driver loads properly. If the proper command is in place and the driver is not loading, watch your video screen as your system boots. At some point, you should see a message from the mouse driver indicating that it is loaded. If you see a message indicating that the driver failed to load, you must determine why. For example, the driver might not be able to load because not enough memory is available. After you determine why the driver is not loading, you need to rectify the situation and make sure the driver loads.

DOS Application Software

If your mouse does not work with a specific piece of DOS application software, check the setup information or configuration section of the program. Make sure you indicated to the program (if necessary) that you are using a mouse. If it still does not work and the mouse works with other software you are using, contact the technical support department of the application software company.

Microsoft IntelliMouse/IBM Scrollpoint

Late in 1996, Microsoft introduced a new variation of its popular mouse, called the IntelliMouse. This device looks exactly like the standard Microsoft mouse except for a miniature gray wheel rising up between the two buttons. This wheel represents the only major change in external mouse design in many years.

The wheel has two main functions. The primary function is to act as a scrolling device, enabling you to scroll through documents or Web pages by manipulating the wheel with your index finger. The wheel also functions as a third mouse button when you press it.

Although three-button mice have been available for years, the scrolling function is a real breakthrough. No longer do you have to move the mouse pointer to click the scrollbar on the right side of your screen or take your hand off the mouse to use the arrow keys on the keyboard. You just push or pull on the wheel. This is a major convenience, especially when browsing Web pages or working with word processing documents or spreadsheets. Also, unlike three-button mice from other vendors, the IntelliMouse's wheel-button doesn't seem to get in the way and you are less likely to click it by mistake.

The major drawback to the IntelliMouse is that the wheel functions only in software that is written to support it. At the time the IntelliMouse debuted, Microsoft Internet Explorer had already been modified to use the new wheel, and all the applications in Office 97 support it as well. For example, most Office 97 applications allow you to hold down the Ctrl key while turning the wheel to zoom in and out. Manipulating the wheel while holding down the Shift key expands and collapses outlines. As new and updated versions of other software come out, you can expect that they will also support the new wheel functions.

The IntelliMouse 2.0 driver combines features from earlier versions of Microsoft's mouse driver with some interesting new functions. A feature called ClickLock allows you to drag items without holding down the primary mouse button. You can customize this feature by specifying how long you have to hold the button down to activate ClickLock. You can also configure the wheel to scroll a specified number of lines or scroll a screen with each click of the wheel.

You can also set the driver software so that the wheel-button ignores all application-specific functions and instead performs one of four preset functions in all Windows applications. The four choices are as follows:

- Double left-click
- Open an application's Help file
- Switch to Windows Explorer
- Bring up the Windows Start menu

Other driver features retained from earlier versions include a Snap To feature, which moves the pointer to the default button of a dialog box, and functions that add trails when the pointer moves and make the pointer disappear when you start typing.

IBM has released an improved version of the IntelliMouse called the Scrollpoint mouse, which uses a button strain gauge (similar to the TrackPoint pointing device covered in the next section) instead of the wheel. The scrollpointer in the center of the mouse allows you to smoothly scroll through documents without having to lift your finger to roll the wheel, as you do on the Microsoft version, which makes it much easier and more convenient to use. Because there are no moving parts, the Scrollpoint is also more reliable than the IntelliMouse.

TrackPoint II/III

On October 20, 1992, IBM introduced a revolutionary new pointing device called TrackPoint II as an integrated feature of its new ThinkPad 700 and 700C computers. Often referred to as a *pointing stick device*, it consists primarily of a small rubber cap that appears on the keyboard right above the B key, between the G and H keys. This was the first significant new pointing device since the mouse had been invented nearly 30 years earlier!

This device occupies no space on a desk, does not have to be adjusted for left-handed or right-handed use, has no moving parts to fail or become dirty, and—most importantly—does not require you to move your hands from the home row to use it. This is an absolute boon for touch typists.

I was fortunate enough to meet the actual creator and designer of this device in early 1992 at the spring Comdex/Windows World in Chicago. He was in a small corner of the IBM booth showing off his custom-made keyboards with a small silicone rubber nub in the middle. In fact, the devices he had were hand-built prototypes installed in standard desktop keyboards, and he was there trying to get public reaction and feedback on his invention.

I was invited to play with one of the keyboards, which was connected to a demonstration system. By pressing on the stick with my index finger, I could move the mouse pointer on the screen. The stick itself did not move, so it was not a joystick. Instead, it had a silicone rubber cap that was connected to pressure transducers that measured the amount of force my finger was applying and the direction of the force and moved the mouse pointer accordingly. The harder I pressed, the faster the pointer moved. I could move the pointer in any direction smoothly by slightly changing the direction of push or pull. The silicone rubber gripped my finger even though I had been sweating from dashing about the show. After playing around with it for just a few minutes, the movements became automatic—almost as though I could just "think" about where I wanted the pointer to go.

After reflecting on this for a minute, it really hit me: This had to be the most revolutionary pointing device since the mouse itself! Not only would it be a natural replacement for a mouse, but it would also be a boon for touch typists like me who don't like to take their hands off the keyboard.

The gentleman at the booth turned out to be Ted Selker, the primary inventor of the device. He and Joseph Rutledge created this integrated pointing device at the IBM T.J. Watson Research Center. When I asked him when such keyboards would become available, he could not answer. At the time, there were apparently no plans for production, and he was only trying to test user reaction to the device.

Just over six months later, IBM announced the ThinkPad 700, which included this revolutionary device, then called the TrackPoint II Integrated Pointing Device. Since the original version came out, an enhanced version with greater control and sensitivity called the TrackPoint III has become available.

Note

The reason the device was called TrackPoint II is that IBM had previously been selling a convertible mouse/trackball device called the TrackPoint. No relationship exists between the original TrackPoint mouse/trackball, which has since been discontinued, and the TrackPoint II integrated device. Since the original TrackPoint II came out, an improved version called TrackPoint III is now available. It is basically an improved version of the same design. In the interest of simplicity, I will refer to all the TrackPoint II, III, and successive devices as just *TrackPoint*.

In its final production form, the TrackPoint consists of a small red silicone rubber knob nestled between the G, H, and B keys on the keyboard. The primary and secondary mouse buttons are placed below the spacebar where you can easily reach them with your thumbs without taking your hands off the keyboard.

IBM studies conducted by Selker found that the act of removing your hand from the keyboard to reach for a mouse and replacing the hand on the keyboard takes approximately 1.75 seconds. If you type 60wpm, that can equal nearly two lost words per minute, not including the time lost while you regain your train of thought. Almost all this time can be saved each time you use TrackPoint to move the pointer or make a selection (click or double-click). The combination of the buttons and the positioning knob also enable you to perform drag-and-drop functions easily.

IBM's research also found that people can get up to 20 percent more work accomplished using the TrackPoint instead of a mouse, especially when the application involves a mix of typing and pointing activities, such as with word processing, spreadsheets, and other typical office applications. In usability tests with the TrackPoint III, IBM gave a group of desktop computer users a TrackPoint and a traditional mouse. After two weeks, 80 percent of the users had unplugged their mice and switched solely to the TrackPoint device. Selker is convinced (as am I) that the TrackPoint is the best pointing solution for both laptop and desktop systems.

Another feature of the TrackPoint is that a standard mouse can be connected to the system at the same time to allow for dual-pointer use. In this case, a single mouse pointer would still be on the screen, but both the TrackPoint and the connected mouse could move the pointer. This setup not only enables a single person to use both devices, but also enables two people to use the TrackPoint and the mouse simultaneously to move the pointer on the screen. The first pointing device that moves (thus issuing a system interrupt) takes precedence and retains control over the mouse pointer on the screen until it completes its movement action. The second pointing device is automatically locked out until the primary device is stationary. This enables the use of both devices and prevents each one from interfering with the other.

Recognizing the significance of the TrackPoint, especially for portable systems, several other manufacturers of laptop and notebook portable computers, such as Toshiba and Texas Instruments, have licensed the TrackPoint pointing device from IBM. They often give the device a different name, but the technology and operation are the same. For example, Toshiba calls its pointing stick the Accupoint.

I have compared the TrackPoint device to other pointing devices for notebooks, such as the trackballs and even the capacitive touch pads, but nothing compares in terms of accuracy and control—and, of course, you don't have to take your hands off the keyboard!

Unfortunately, many of the lower-end portable system manufacturers have chosen not to license the IBM TrackPoint technology, but instead have attempted to copy it using inferior transducers and control software. The major drawback to these nonlicensed TrackPoint type devices is that they simply do not perform as well as the official versions licensed from IBM. They are usually slow to respond, sluggish in operation, and lack the sensitivity and accuracy found in the IBM-designed versions.

One way of telling whether the TrackPoint device is licensed from IBM and uses the IBM technology is if it accepts IBM TrackPoint II or III rubber caps. They have a square hole in them and will properly lock on to any of the licensed versions, such as those found in Toshiba systems.

IBM has upgraded its pointing stick and now calls it TrackPoint III. There are two main differences in the III system, but the most obvious one is in the rubber cap. IBM always uses red caps in its TrackPoint device, but other companies use different colors (Toshiba uses green or gray, for example). However, the main difference in the new TrackPoint III caps is in the rubber composition, not the color.

The IBM TrackPoint II and Toshiba Accupoint caps are made from silicone rubber, which is grippy and works well in most situations. However, if the user has greasy fingers, the textured surface of the rubber can absorb some of the grease and become slippery. Cleaning the cap (and the user's hands) solves the problem, but it can be annoying at times. The new TrackPoint III caps are made from a different type of rubber, which Selker calls "plastic sandpaper." This type of cap is much more grippy and does not require cleaning except for cosmetic purposes. I have used both types of caps and can say for certain that the TrackPoint III cap is superior!

Note

Because the Accupoint device used in the Toshiba notebooks is licensed from IBM, it uses the same hardware (a pressure transducer called a *strain gauge*) and takes the same physical caps. I ordered a set of the new TrackPoint III caps and installed them on my Toshiba portable systems, which dramatically improved the grip. You can get these caps by ordering them from IBM Parts directly or from others who sell IBM parts, such as DakTech, under IBM part number 84G6536. The cost is approximately $9 for a set of two "plastic sandpaper" red caps.

Replacing the cap is easy—grab the existing cap with your fingers and pull straight up; it pops right off. Then push on the new red IBM TrackPoint III cap in its place. You will thank me when you feel how you can grip the new IBM cap much more easily than you can grip the designs used by others.

The other difference between the TrackPoint II and III from IBM is in the control software. IBM added routines that implement a subtle technique Selker calls "negative inertia," which is marketed under the label *QuickStop response*. This software not only takes into account how far you push the pointer in any direction, but also how quickly you push or release it. Selker found that this improved software (and the sandpaper cap) allows people to make selections up to 8 percent faster.

The TrackPoint is obviously an ideal pointing device for a portable system in which lugging around an external mouse or trackball can be inconvenient. The trackballs and mini-trackballs built into some laptop keyboards are difficult to use and usually require removing your hands from the home row. Mouse and trackball devices are notorious for becoming sticky because the ball picks up dirt that affects the internal roller motion. This problem is especially noticeable with the smaller mini-trackball devices.

Many newer notebook systems include a touch pad, and although this seemed like a good idea at first, it pales in comparison with the TrackPoint. The touch pads are based on a capacitive effect, and pointer operation can become erratic if your skin is too dry or too moist. Their biggest drawback is that they are positioned on the keyboard below the spacebar, which means you have to remove your hand from the home row to place your index finger on the pad, or try to use the pad with your thumb, which has too wide a contact area for precise movement and control.

The bottom line is that anyone who touch types should strongly consider only portable systems that include an IBM-licensed TrackPoint device (such as Toshiba). TrackPoints are far superior to other pointing devices, such as the touch pads, because the TrackPoint is faster to use (you don't have to take your hands off the keyboard's home row), easier to adapt to (especially for speedy touch typists), and far more precise.

The benefits of the TrackPoint are not limited to portable systems, however. Because I use a notebook so often and have found the TrackPoint so fast and easy to use, I wanted to use it on my desktop systems, too. For desktop systems, I use a Lexmark keyboard with the IBM-licensed TrackPoint device built in. This makes for a more consistent interface between desktop and notebook use because I can use the same pointing device in both environments. One drawback for some older systems is that the TrackPoint device in these keyboards works only with systems that used a PS/2- or motherboard-type mouse connector—no serial version is available. I list the part number for the IBM Enhanced keyboard with the TrackPoint in the section "Replacement Keyboards," earlier in this chapter. You can also buy these keyboards directly from Unicomp, which has purchased Lexmark's keyboard technology.

Glidepoint/Track Pads

In response to the TrackPoint, other companies have adopted new pointing device technologies. For example, Alps Electric has introduced a touch pad (also called a *track pad*) pointing device called the Glidepoint. The Glidepoint uses a flat, square pad that senses finger position through body capacitance. This is similar to the capacitance-sensitive elevator button controls you sometimes encounter in office buildings or hotels. Instead of sitting between the keys, the Glidepoint is mounted below the spacebar, and it detects pressure applied by your thumbs or fingers. Transducers under the pad convert finger movement into pointer movement. Several laptop and notebook manufacturers have licensed this technology from Alps and are incorporating it into their portable systems. Apple was one of the first to adopt it in its portable systems.

Although it seems to have gained wide acceptance, this technology has a number of drawbacks. Operation of the device can be erratic, depending on skin resistance and moisture content. The biggest drawback is that to operate the touch pad, users have to remove their hands from the home row on the keyboard, which dramatically slows their progress. In addition, the operation of the touch pad can be imprecise, depending on how pointy your finger or thumb is!

On the other hand, if you're not a touch typist, removing your hands from the keyboard to operate the touch pad might be easier than using a TrackPoint. Even with their drawbacks, touch pad pointing devices are still vastly preferable to using a trackball or a cumbersome external mouse with portable systems.

Running Windows Without a Mouse

Many people do not know that it is possible to dramatically enhance the use of Windows by using the keyboard as an adjunct to the mouse for system control. There are many keyboard shortcuts and other key commands that can greatly increase the speed and efficiency with which you operate Windows, especially if you are creating a document, spreadsheet, email message, and so forth, and even more so if you are an accomplished touch typist. Because I use my PC mainly for writing, I find that taking my hand off the keyboard to use a mouse noticeably slows me down. By augmenting Windows operations with the keyboard, you can control them more efficiently and accurately than with a mouse alone.

In some cases, it is not only desirable, but necessary, to use the keyboard instead of a mouse, such as when your mouse is not functioning properly or is missing altogether. Because technicians often find themselves operating or testing equipment that is not fully functional, it is even more important for them to know how to operate Windows with the keyboard.

The following are the general keyboard-only commands for Windows 95/98:

Key Combination	Resulting Action
F1	Starts Windows Help.
F10	Activates menu bar options.
Shift+F10	Opens a context menu (shortcut menu) for the selected item.
Ctrl+Esc	Opens the Start menu. Use the arrow keys to select an item.
Ctrl+Esc, Esc	Selects the Start button. Press Tab to select the taskbar, or press Shift+F10 for a context menu.
Alt+Tab	Switch to another running application. Hold down the Alt key and then press the Tab key to view the task-switching window.
Shift	Press down and hold the Shift key while you insert a CD-ROM to bypass the AutoPlay feature.
Alt+spacebar	Displays the main window's System menu. From the System menu, you can restore, move, resize, minimize, maximize, or close the window.
Alt+- (hyphen)	Displays the Multiple Document Interface (MDI) child window's System menu. From the MDI child window's System menu, you can restore, move, resize, minimize, maximize, or close the child window.
Ctrl+Tab	Switches to the next child window of a MDI application.
Alt+<underlined letter in menu>	Opens the corresponding menu.
Alt+F4	Closes the current window.
Ctrl+F4	Closes the current MDI window.
Alt+F6	Switches between multiple windows in the same program. For example, when Notepad's Find dialog box is displayed, Alt+F6 switches between the Find dialog box and the main Notepad window.

Here are the Windows dialog box keyboard commands:

Key Combination	Resulting Action
Tab	Move to the next control in the dialog box.
Shift+Tab	Move to the previous control in the dialog box.

Key Combination	Resulting Action
Spacebar	If the current control is a button, this keyboard command clicks the button. If the current control is a check box, it toggles the check box. If the current control is an option button, it selects the option button.
Enter	Equivalent to clicking the selected button (the button with the outline).
Esc	Equivalent to clicking the Cancel button.
Alt+<underlined letter in dialog box item>	Move to the corresponding item.
Ctrl+Tab/Ctrl+Shift+Tab	Move through the property tabs.

These are the keyboard combinations for Windows Explorer tree controls:

Key Combination	Resulting Action
Numeric Keypad *	Expands everything under the current selection.
Numeric Keypad +	Expands the current selection.
Numeric Keypad -	Collapses the current selection.
Right arrow	Expands the current selection if it is not expanded; otherwise, goes to the first child.
Left arrow	Collapses the current selection if it is expanded; otherwise, goes to the parent.

Here are the general Windows folder/shortcut controls:

Key Combination	Resulting Action
F4	Selects the Go To a Different Folder box and moves down the entries in the box (if the toolbar is active in Windows Explorer).
F5	Refreshes the current window.
F6	Moves among panes in Windows Explorer.
Ctrl+G	Opens the Go To Folder tool (in Windows 95 Windows Explorer only).
Ctrl+Z	Undoes the last command.
Ctrl+A	Selects all the items in the current window.
Backspace	Switches to the parent folder.
Shift+click	Selects the close button. (For folders, closes the current folder plus all parent folders.)

These are general folder and Windows Explorer shortcuts for a selected object:

Key Combination	Resulting Action
F2	Renames object.
F3	Finds all files.
Ctrl+X	Cuts.
Ctrl+C	Copies.
Ctrl+V	Pastes.
Shift+Del	Deletes selection immediately, without moving the item to the Recycle Bin.
Alt+Enter	Opens the property sheet for the selected object.
To copy a file	Press down and hold the Ctrl key while you drag the file to another folder.
To create a shortcut	Press down and hold Ctrl+Shift while you drag a file to the desktop or a folder.

Future Pointing Devices

Pointer technology is progressing in ways that were undreamed of when the first mice were developed. Hardware developers are beginning to take advantage of the bidirectional interfaces on PCs to develop input devices that react to a user's actions. A company called Immersion Corp. has developed a mouse called FEELit, which is mounted to a specially designed pad that houses a processor for generating real-time simulations.

An electromagnetic drive inside the pad generates sensations, enabling you to feel three-dimensional icons, window edges, scroll buttons, and other Windows artifacts. You can click and drag objects with variable pressure and feel the elasticity of shapes as you stretch them. Developers can write applications using special function calls that allow them to incorporate the feelings generated by textures, surfaces, liquids, and vibrations into their programs.

Other companies are developing pointing devices that track the user's retina, allowing you to point and click with merely a look. Combined with a virtual screen mounted in front of the user's eye, it will allow people to operate a computer mostly hands-free and without a bulky display. This type of technology has great promise for making computers truly interactive and for enhancing the reality of games and other simulated environments.

Internet Connectivity

SOME OF THE MAIN TOPICS IN THIS CHAPTER ARE

Relating Internet and LAN Connectivity

Asynchronous Modems

Modem Standards

Integrated Services Digital Network (ISDN)

Leased Lines

CATV Networks

DirecPC—Internet Connectivity via Satellite

DSL (Digital Subscriber Line)

Comparing High-Speed Internet Access

Sharing Your High-Speed Internet Access over a LAN—Safely

Modem Troubleshooting

Relating Internet and LAN Connectivity

Communications between computers is a major part of the PC computing industry. Thanks to the World Wide Web (WWW), no computer user is an island. Whether by using a modem or a faster technology, virtually all PCs can be connected to other computers, enabling them to share files, send and receive email, and access the Internet. This chapter explores the various technologies you can use to expand the reach of your PC around the block and around the world.

It may surprise you to see discussions of protocols and networking setup in both this chapter and the LAN chapter of this book, but a modem connection is really just another form of networking. In fact, the Windows 9x and Windows NT operating systems have all but blended the two services into a single entity.

The reason for this combination is that the typical target for a modem connection has changed over the years. For a long time, PC users dialed in to *bulletin board systems* (or BBSes)—proprietary services that provided terminal access to other computers. Online services such as America Online and CompuServe have also been around for many years, but they traditionally used proprietary clients and protocols, quite different from those found on local area networks (LANs).

With the explosive growth of the Internet, modem and network technologies were joined, because both could use the same client software and protocols. Today, the most popular suite of networking protocols—TCP/IP—is used on both LANs and the Internet. When you dial in to an Internet service provider (ISP), you are actually connecting to a network using a modem instead of a network interface card.

Asynchronous Modems

For PCs that are not connected to a network by some other means, a modem has become virtually a standard piece of equipment. For many home users, connecting to the Internet is their primary reason for owning a computer. Whether for business, entertainment, or just keeping in touch with friends and family, a modem connection takes an isolated system and makes it a part of a worldwide network.

The word *modem* (from MOdulator/DEModulator) basically describes a device that converts the digital data used by computers into analog signals suitable for transmission over a telephone line, and converts the analog signals back to digital data at the destination. The typical PC modem is an asynchronous device, meaning that it transmits data in an intermittent stream of small packets. The receiving system takes the data in the packets and reassembles it into a form the computer can use.

Asynchronous modems transmit each byte of data individually as a separate packet. One byte equals 8 bits, which, using the standard ASCII codes, is enough data to transmit a single alphanumeric character. For a modem to transmit asynchronously, it must identify the beginning and end of each byte to the receiving modem. It does this by adding a start bit before and after every byte of data, thus using 10 bits to transmit each byte (see Figure 18.1). For this reason, asynchronous communications have sometimes been referred to as start-stop communications. This is in contrast to synchronous communications, in which a continuous stream of data is transmitted at a steady rate.

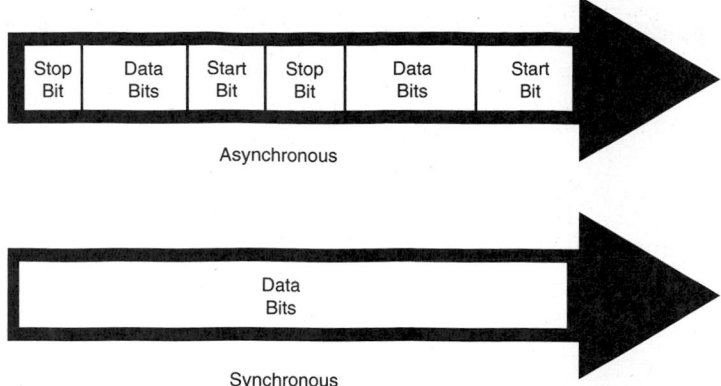

| Stop Bit | Data Bits | Start Bit | Stop Bit | Data Bits | Start Bit |

Asynchronous

Data Bits

Synchronous

Figure 18.1 Asynchronous modems frame each byte of data with a start bit and a stop bit, while synchronous communications use an uninterrupted stream of data.

Synchronous modems are generally used in leased-line environments and in conjunction with multiplexers to communicate between terminals to UNIX-based servers and mainframe computers. Thus, this type of modem is outside the scope of this book.

Whenever modems are referred to in this book, I will be discussing the asynchronous variety. (Synchronous modems are not found in typical computer stores, and aren't included in normal computer configurations, so you may not ever see one unless you go into the data center of a corporation that uses them).

Note

During high-speed modem communications, the start and stop bits are usually not transmitted over the telephone line. Instead, they are eliminated by the data compression algorithm implemented by the modem. However, these bits are part of the data packets generated by the communications software in the computer, and they exist until they reach the modem hardware.

The use of a single start bit is required in all forms of asynchronous communication, but some protocols use more than one stop bit. To accommodate systems with different protocols, communications software products usually enable you to modify the format of the frame used to transmit each byte. The standard format used to describe an asynchronous communications format is parity-data bits–stop bits. Almost all asynchronous connections today are therefore abbreviated as N-8-1 (No parity/8 data bits/1 stop bit). The meanings for each of these parameters and their possible variations are as follows:

- *Parity.* Before error-correction protocols became standard modem features, a simple parity mechanism was used to provide basic error checking at the software level. Today, this is almost never used, and the value for this parameter is nearly always set to none. Other possible parity values that you might see in a communications software package are odd, even, mark, and space.

- *Data Bits.* This parameter indicates how many bits are actually carried in the data portion of the packet (exclusive of the start and stop bits). PCs typically use 8 data bits, but some types of computers use a 7-bit byte, and others may call for other data lengths. Communications programs provide this option to prevent a system from confusing a stop bit with a data bit.

■ *Stop Bits.* This parameter specifies how many stop bits are appended to each byte. PCs typically use one stop bit, but other types of protocols may call for the use of 1.5 or 2 stop bits.

In most situations, you will never have to modify these parameters manually, but the controls are almost always provided. In Windows 9x, for example, if you open the Modems control panel and look at the Connection page of your modem's Properties dialog box, you will see Data Bits, Parity, and Stop Bits selectors, as shown in Figure 18.2.

Unless you use the Windows 9x HyperTerminal program to establish a direct connection to another computer via phone lines, you might never need to modify these parameters. However, if you need to call a mainframe computer to perform *terminal emulation* for e-banking, checking a library's catalog, or working from home, you may need to adjust these parameters. (Terminal emulation means using software to make your PC keyboard and screen act like a terminal such as a DEC VT-100, etc.) Many mainframe computers use even parity and a 7-bit word length. If your PC is set wrong, you'll see garbage text on your monitor instead of the other system's log-in or welcome screen.

Note

Because it has become such a familiar term, even to inexperienced computers users, the word modem is frequently used to describe devices that are, strictly speaking, not modems at all. Later in this chapter, you will learn about ISDN, and the latest Internet-access standards, such as cable modems, DirecPC, and xDSL, none of which convert digital information to analog signals. However, because these devices look something like a standard modem and are used to connect PCs to the Internet or to other networks, they are called modems.

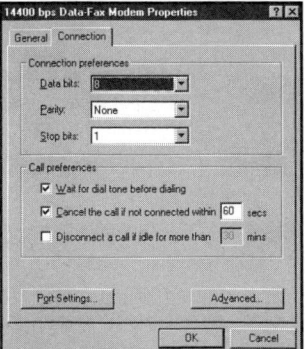

Figure 18.2 The Windows 9x control panel enables you to adjust the connection preferences for your modem.

Modem Standards

For two modems to communicate, they must share the same *protocol*. A protocol is a specification that determines how two entities will communicate. Just as humans must share a common language and vocabulary to speak with each other, two computers or two modems must share a common protocol. In the case of modems, the protocol determines the nature of the analog signal that the device creates from the computer's digital data.

Through the years, there have been many standards for modem communications, most of them developed by bipartisan committees and accepted by nearly all modem manufacturers. As the hardware technology has improved, modem communications have become faster and more efficient, and new standards are constantly being developed to take advantage of the hardware's capabilities.

Note

The term *protocol* is also used to describe software standards that must be established between different computers to allow them to communicate, such as TCP/IP.

Bell Labs and the CCITT are two of the bodies that have set standards for modem protocols. CCITT is an acronym for Comité Consultatif International Téléphonique et Télégraphique, a French term that translates into English as the Consultative Committee on International Telephone and Telegraph. The organization was renamed the International Telecommunication Union (ITU) in the early 1990s, but the protocols developed under the old name are often referred to as such. Newly developed protocols are referred to as ITU-T standards, which refers to the Telecommunication Standardization Sector of the ITU. Bell Labs no longer sets new standards for modems, although several of its older standards are still used. Most modems built in recent years conform to the standards developed by the CCITT.

The ITU, headquartered in Geneva, Switzerland, is an international body of technical experts responsible for developing data communications standards for the world. The group falls under the organizational umbrella of the United Nations, and its members include representatives from major modem manufacturers, common carriers (such as AT&T), and governmental bodies. The ITU establishes communications standards and protocols in many areas, so one modem often adheres to many different standards, depending on its various features and capabilities. Modem standards can be grouped into the following three areas:

■ **Modulation**	ITU V.32bis
Bell 103	ITU V.34
Bell 212A	ITU V.90
CCITT V.21	■ **Error Correction**
ITU V.22bis	ITU V.42
ITU V.29	■ **Data Compression**
ITU V.32	ITU V.42bis

▶▶ See "Modulation Standards," p. 956.

Other standards have been developed by different companies (not Bell Labs or the ITU). These are sometimes called proprietary standards, even though most of these companies publish the full specifications of their protocols so that other manufacturers can develop modems to work with them. The following list shows some of the proprietary standards that have been popular over the years:

- **Modulation**
  HST
  K56flex
  X2

- **Error Correction**
  MNP 1-4
  Hayes V-series

- **Data Compression**
  MNP 5 CSP

Note

K56flex and X2 were competing, proprietary methods for reaching a maximum download speed of up to 56Kbps. K56flex was developed by modem chipset makers Rockwell and Lucent, while X2 was developed by U.S. Robotics (now part of 3Com). These two quasi-standards have now been replaced by the ITU V.90 standard for 56Kbps downloads, but are still supported by many ISPs.

In the interests of backward compatibility, modem manufacturers typically add support for new standards as they are developed, leaving the support for the old standards in place. As a result, when you evaluate modems, you are likely to see long lists of the standards they support, like those just shown. In most cases, you will want to know whether a modem supports the most recent standards, so support for an archaic and seldom-used protocol should not govern your purchasing decision.

Modem manufacturers used to claim to be Hayes-compatible, a phrase that became as meaningless as IBM-compatible when referring to PCs. Today modem manufacturers instead say that they support standard AT command sets, which is what being Hayes-compatible meant. AT commands are text strings sent to the modem by software to activate the modem's features. For example, the ATDT command, followed by a telephone number, causes the modem to dial that number using tone dialing mode. Applications that use modems typically generate AT commands for you, but you can control a modem directly using a communications program with a terminal mode, or even the DOS ECHO command. For this reason, not to mention the recent closure of Hayes, the term Hayes-compatible is seldom used anymore.

Assuming that you have a modem connected to your PC's COM2 port, you can demonstrate this capability by issuing the following command from the DOS command line:

```
ECHO ATH1 > COM2
```

This command sends the ATH1 command string out through your computer's COM2 port to the modem, causing it to go "off hook." If your modem has a speaker, you should hear a dial tone. To hang up, issue the following command:

```
ECHO ATH0 > COM2
```

Because almost every modem uses the Hayes command set, this compatibility is a given and should not really affect your purchasing decisions about modems. The basic modem commands may vary slightly from manufacturer to manufacturer, depending on a modem's special features, but the basic AT command set is all but universal. Some modems, most notably U.S. Robotics (now part of 3Com), allow you to query the command set by sending the string AT$ to the modem. To query the modem's command set, launch a terminal program, such as Windows 9x HyperTerminal, set up a new connection, and type **AT$** in the terminal window. The results of querying a U.S. Robotics (3COM) x2 56K PnP internal modem are shown in Figure 18.3.

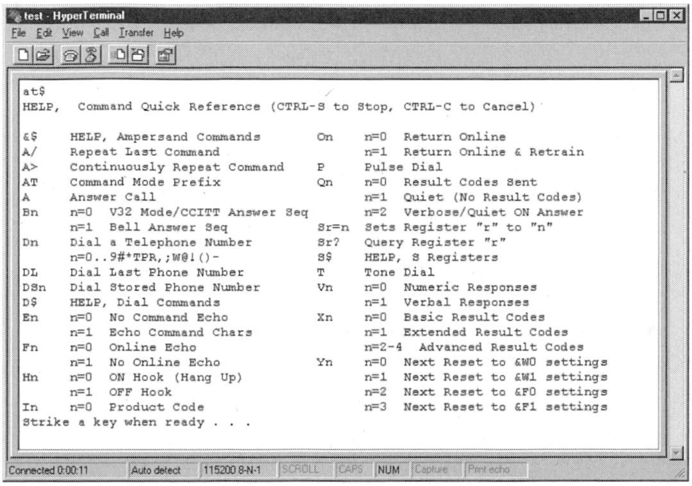

Figure 18.3   The commands and command options that will work with a U.S Robotics/3COM 56k x2 modem are shown here.

Note

A list of the basic **AT** commands can be found in the "Technical Reference" section on the CD. However, the best source for the commands used by your modem is the manual that came with the device.

It's very important you keep manual that came with your modem so you have this information. Although most Windows 9x/NT communications programs use the standard .INF file setup for the modem, some MS-DOS–based programs and some specialized Windows programs might require you to enter or edit an *initialization string*, which is a series of commands sent to the modem before dialing. If these commands are not correct, the modem will not work with these programs!

Baud Versus Bits per Second (bps)

When discussing modem transmission speeds, the terms *baud rate* and *bit rate* are often confused. Baud rate (named after a Frenchman named Emile Baudot, the inventor of the asynchronous telegraph printer) is the rate at which a signal between two devices changes in one second. If a signal between two modems can change frequency or phase at a rate of 300 times per second, for example, that device is said to communicate at 300 baud.

Thus, baud is a signaling rate, not a data-transmission rate. The number of bits transmitted by each baud is used to determine the actual data-transmission rate (properly expressed as bps or Kbps).

(continues)

Sometimes a single modulation change is used to carry a single bit. In that case, 300 baud also equals 300 bps.

If the modem could signal two bit values for each signal change, the bps rate would be twice the baud rate, or 600bps at 300 baud. Most modems transmit several bits per baud, so that the actual baud rate is much slower than the bps rate. In fact, people often use the term baud incorrectly. We normally are not interested in the raw baud rate, but in the bps rate, which is the true gauge of communications speed. As the chart below shows, more recent modems can signal multiple bit values with each signal change:

Baud rate	# of bits/baud	Actual modem bps
600	4	2,400
2400	4	9,600
2400	6	14,400
3200	9	28,800

As before, the baud rate is multiplied by the number of bits/baud to determine the actual bps speed of the modem.

It can be difficult to reach rates above 2,400 baud on normal telephone lines, which explains why a 28.8Kbps (28,800bps) modem may not work above 19,200bps when telephone line quality is poor. As we'll see later, the so-called 56Kbps modems don't use baud as above, but work in a completely different manner.

Modulation Standards

Modems start with modulation, which is the electronic signaling method used by the modem (from modulator to demodulator). Modulation is a variance in some aspect of the transmitted signal. By modulating the signal using a predetermined pattern, the modem encodes the computer data and sends it to another modem that demodulates (or decodes) the signal. Modems must use the same modulation method to understand each other. Each data rate uses a different modulation method, and sometimes more than one method exists for a particular rate.

Regardless of the modulation method, all modems must perform the same task: change the digital data used inside the computer (ON-OFF, 1-0) into the analog (variable tone and volume) data used by the telephone company's circuits, which were built over a period of years and never intended for computer use. That's the "Mo(dulate)" in modem. When the analog signal is received by the other computer, the signal is changed back from the analog waveform into digital data (see Figure 18.4). That's the "Dem(odulate)" in modem.

The three most popular modulation methods are

- *Frequency-shift keying (FSK).* A form of frequency modulation, otherwise known as FM. By causing and monitoring frequency changes in a signal sent over the phone line, two modems can send information.

- *Phase-shift keying (PSK).* A form of phase modulation in which the timing of the carrier signal wave is altered and the frequency stays the same.

- *Quadrature amplitude modulation (QAM).* A modulation technique that combines phase changes with signal-amplitude variations, resulting in a signal that can carry more information than the other methods.

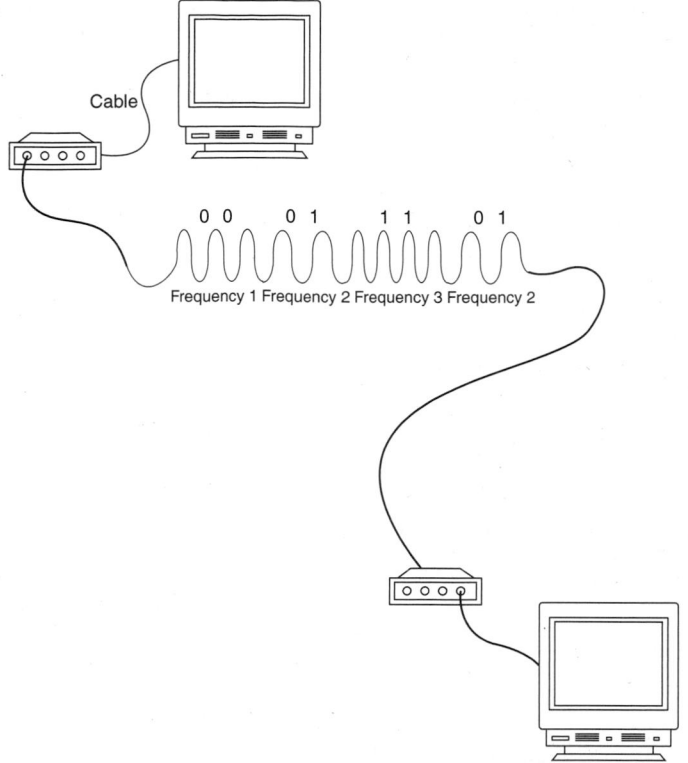

Figure 18.4 The modem at each computer changes digital (computer) signals to analog (telephone) signals when transmitting data, or analog back to digital when receiving data.

Table 18.1 lists the protocols that define the modulation standards used by asynchronous modems, along with their maximum transmission rates and duplex modes. A full duplex protocol is one in which communications can travel in both directions at the same time and at the same speed. A telephone call, for example, is full duplex, because both parties can speak at the same time. In half duplex mode, communications can travel in both directions, but only one side can transmit at a time. A radio call in which only one party can speak at a time is an example of half duplex communications.

These protocols are automatically negotiated between your modem and the modem at the other end of the connection. Basically, the modems start with the fastest protocol common to both and work their way down to a speed/protocol combination that will work under the line conditions existing at the time of the call. The ITUV.90, V.34, and V.32 family are the industry-standard protocols most commonly used today.

Table 18.1   Modem Modulation Standards and Transmission Rates

Protocol	Maximum Transmission Rate (bits per second)	Duplex Mode
Bell 103	300bps	Full
CCITT V.21	300bps	Full
Bell 212A	1200bps	Full
ITU V.22	1200bps	Half
ITU V.22bis	2400bps	Full
ITU V.23	1200/75bps	Pseudo-Full
ITU V.29	9600bps	Half
ITU V.32	9600bps	Full
ITU V.32bis	14400bps (14.4Kbps)	Full
ITU V.32fast	28800bps (28.8Kbps)	Full
ITU V.34	28800bps (28.8Kbps)	Full
ITU V.90	56000bps (56Kbps)*	Full

While the ITU V.90 (successor to the proprietary 56Kflex and X2 standards) allows for this speed of transmission, the U.S. FCC (Federal Communications Commission) allows only 53000 bps (53Kbps) at this time.

Each of these protocols is discussed in the following sections.

Bell 103

Bell 103 is the U.S. and Canadian 300bps modulation standard. It uses FSK modulation at 300 baud to transmit 1 bit per baud. Most higher speed modems are still capable of communicating using this protocol, even though it is obsolete.

V.21

V.21 is an international data-transmission standard for 300bps communications, similar to Bell 103. Because of some differences in the frequencies they use, Bell 103 modems are not compatible with V.21 modems. This standard was used primarily outside the United States.

Bell 212A

Bell 212A is the U.S. and Canadian 1,200bps modulation standard. It uses differential phase-shift keying (DPSK) at 600 baud to transmit 2 bits per baud.

V.22

V.22 is an international 1,200bps data-transmission standard. This standard is similar to the Bell 212A standard but is incompatible in some areas, especially when answering a call. This standard was used primarily outside the United States.

V.22bis

V.22bis is a data-transmission standard for 2,400bps communications. Bis is derived from the Latin meaning *second*, indicating that this data transmission is an improvement to, or follows,

V.22. This international standard is used inside and outside the United States. V.22bis uses QAM at 600 baud and transmits 4 bits per baud to achieve 2,400bps.

V.23

V.23 is a split data-transmission standard, operating at 1,200bps in one direction and 75bps in the reverse direction. Therefore, the modem is only pseudo full-duplex, meaning that it can transmit data in both directions simultaneously, but not at the maximum data rate. This standard was developed to lower the cost of 1,200bps modem technology, which was expensive in the early 1980s. This standard was used primarily in Europe.

V.29

V.29 is a data-transmission standard for 9600bps communications, which defines a half-duplex (one-way) modulation technique. This standard generally is used in Group III facsimile (fax) transmissions, and only rarely in modems. Because V.29 is a half-duplex method, it is substantially easier to implement this high-speed standard than a high-speed full-duplex standard. As a modem standard, V.29 has not been fully defined, so V.29 modems of different brands seldom can communicate with each other. This does not affect fax machines, however, which have a fully defined standard.

V.32

V.32 is a full-duplex (two-way) data transmission standard that runs at 9,600bps. It is a full modem standard and also includes forward error-correcting and negotiation standards. V.32 uses TCQAM (trellis coded quadrature amplitude modulation) at 2,400 baud to transmit 4 bits per baud, resulting in the 9,600bps transmission speed.

The trellis coding is a special forward error-correction technique that creates an additional bit for each packet of four. This extra check bit is used to allow on-the-fly error correction to take place at the receiving end of the transmission. It also greatly increases the resistance of V.32 to noise on the telephone line.

In the past, V.32 has been expensive to implement because the technology it requires is complex. Because a one-way, 9,600bps stream uses almost the entire bandwidth of the phone line, V.32 modems implement echo cancellation, meaning that they cancel out the overlapping signal that their own modems transmit and listen to the other modem's signal. This procedure is complicated and was at one time costly. Advances in lower cost chipsets made these modems inexpensive, and they were the de facto 9,600bps standard for some time.

V.32bis

V.32bis is a 14,400bps extension to V.32. This protocol uses TCQAM modulation at 2,400 baud to transmit 6 bits per baud, for an effective rate of 14,400bps. The trellis coding makes the connection more reliable. This protocol is also a full-duplex modulation protocol, with a fallback to V.32 if the phone line is impaired.

V.32fast

V.32fast, or V.FC (Fast Class) as it is also called, is a standard that was developed by Rockwell and introduced before V.34. V.32fast is an extension to V.32 and V.32bis, but offers a transmission speed of 28,800bps. It has since been superseded by V.34. If you buy a used 28,800bps modem, make sure it is not one of the devices that supports V.32fast instead of V.34. Modems like this are incompatible with many of the V.34 devices now in general use.

V.34

V.34 has superseded all the other 28.8Kbps standards and is the current state-of-the-art in purely analog modem communications. It has been proven as the most reliable standard of communication at 28.8Kbps. A recent annex to the V.34 standard also defines optional higher speeds of 31.2 and 33.6Kbps. Most of the V.34 modems now being produced are capable of transmitting at these higher speeds, and existing V.34 modems that are designed using sophisticated Digital Signal Processors (DSPs) can easily be upgraded to 33.6Kbps. In most cases, you do this by downloading a Modem ROM upgrade from the manufacturer, and then running a program to "flash" the modem's ROM with the new code.

V.34 is the fastest communication now possible over an analog serial connection. Because of limitations inherent in the telephone system, it is also very likely to be the fastest that *purely* analog communications are going to get.

Note

The 56k standards that represent the highest current increment in modem communication speed require a digital connection at one end, and are therefore not purely analog. Other high-speed communication technologies such as ISDN and cable network connections eschew analog communications entirely, so they should not be called modems, strictly speaking.

V.90

V.90 is the ITU-T designation for a 56Kbps communication standard that reconciles the conflict between the U.S. Robotics (3Com) X2 and Rockwell K56Flex modem specifications.

▶▶ See "56K Modems," p. 965.

Error-Correction Protocols

Error correction refers to the capability of some modems to identify errors during a transmission, and to automatically resend data that appears to have been damaged in transit. Although it is also possible to implement error correction using software, this places an additional burden on the computer's expansion bus and processor. By performing error correction using dedicated hardware in the modem, errors are detected and corrected before any data is passed to the computer's CPU.

As with modulation, both modems must adhere to the same standard for error correction to work. Fortunately, most modem manufacturers use the same error correction protocols.

MNP 1-4

This is a proprietary standard that was developed by Microcom to provide basic error correction. The Microcom Networking Protocol (MNP) is examined in greater detail in the "Proprietary Standards" section, later in this chapter.

V.42

V.42 is an error-correction protocol, with fallback to MNP 4; version 4 is an error-correction protocol as well. Because the V.42 standard includes MNP compatibility through Class 4, all MNP 4-compatible modems can establish error-controlled connections with V.42 modems.

This standard uses a protocol called LAPM (Link Access Procedure for Modems). LAPM, like MNP, copes with phone line impairments by automatically retransmitting data corrupted during transmission, assuring that only error-free data passes between the modems. V.42 is considered to be better than MNP 4 because it offers approximately a 20 percent higher transfer rate due to its more intelligent algorithms.

Data-Compression Standards

Data compression refers to a built-in capability in some modems to compress the data they're sending, thus saving time and money for modem users. Depending on the type of files the modem is sending, data can be compressed to nearly one-fourth its original size, effectively quadrupling the speed of the modem. For example, a 14,400bps modem with compression can yield transmission rates of up to 57,600bps, a 28,800bps can yield up to 115,200bps, and a 56,000bps modem up to 224,000bps (download only)—at least in theory. This assumes that the modem has V.42bis data compression built-in (true since about 1990) *and* that the data hasn't already been compressed by software. Thus, in reality, the higher throughput caused by data compression applies only to HTML and plain-text files on the Web. Graphics and ZIP or EXE archives have already been compressed, as have most PDF (Adobe Acrobat Reader) files.

Can Non-56Kbps Modems Achieve Throughput Speeds Above 115,200bps?

Yes. To achieve speeds above 115,200bps, a better UART chip than the standard 16550-series chip found in modern PC serial ports and internal modems is required. 16650 UARTs have a 32-byte buffer, as opposed to the 16-byte buffer found in the standard 16650 UART. The 16650 is seldom used in PCs' built-in serial ports or as part of an internal modem.

Thus, to achieve the highest possible speeds, you need the following: an external modem capable of running at 230.4Kbps throughput, a 16650 UART chip in the serial (COM) port connected to the modem, and appropriate software drivers for the modem. Note that a 56K-compatible modem isn't required! 230.4Kbps connections are available with anything from V.34bis to ISDN modems *if* the device is designed for that speed and you have the correct UART chip and drivers. But, as with the lower speed throughput rates mentioned earlier, these speeds apply only to data that has not been compressed already.

As with error correction, data compression can also be performed with software. Data can only be compressed once, so if you are transmitting files that are already in a compressed form, such as

ZIP archives or GIF images, there will be no palpable increase in speed from the modem's hardware compression. The transmission of plain text files (such as HTML pages) and uncompressed bitmaps, however, is accelerated greatly by modem compression.

MNP 5

Microcom continued the development of its MNP protocols to include a compression protocol called MNP 5. This protocol is examined more fully in the section "Proprietary Standards," later in this chapter.

V.42bis

V.42bis is a CCITT data-compression standard similar to MNP Class 5, but provides about 35 percent better compression. V.42bis is not actually compatible with MNP Class 5, but nearly all V.42bis modems include the MNP 5 data-compression capability as well.

This protocol can sometimes quadruple throughput, depending on the compression technique. This fact has led to some deceptive advertising; for example, a 2,400bps V.42bis modem might advertise "9,600bps throughput" by including V.42bis as well, but this would be possible in only extremely optimistic cases, such as when sending text files that are very loosely packed. In the same manner, many 9,600bps V.42bis makers now advertise "up to 38.4Kbps throughput" by virtue of the compression. Just make sure that you see the truth behind such claims.

V.42bis is superior to MNP 5 because it analyzes the data first, and then determines whether compression would be useful. V.42bis only compresses data that needs compression. MNP 5 always attempts to compress the data, which slows down throughput on previously compressed files.

To negotiate a standard connection using V.42bis, V.42 also must be present. Therefore, a modem with V.42bis data compression is assumed to include V.42 error correction. When combined, these two protocols result in an error-free connection that has the maximum data compression possible.

Proprietary Standards

In addition to the industry-standard protocols for modulation, error correction, and data compression that are generally defined and approved by the ITU-T, several protocols in these areas were invented by various companies and included in their products without any official endorsement by any standards body. Some of these protocols have been quite popular at times and became pseudo-standards of their own.

The most successful proprietary protocols are the MNP (Microcom Networking Protocol) standards developed by Microcom. These error-correction and data-compression protocols are supported widely by other modem manufacturers as well.

Another company that has been successful in establishing proprietary protocols as limited standards is U.S. Robotics (now part of 3Com), with its HST (high-speed technology) modulation protocols. Because of an aggressive marketing campaign with BBS operators, HST modems captured a large portion of the market in the 1980s.

Note that many proprietary protocols are limited to the modems made by one particular manufacturer. In those cases, both the sender and receiver would need to have modems of the same brand equipped with the same proprietary protocol to make use of that protocol's features. The use of proprietary protocols is declining because the modems that feature them can't work at their maximum performance when communicating with modems that lack those protocols.

The following sections examine these and other proprietary modem protocols.

HST

HST is a 14,400bps and 9,600bps modified half-duplex proprietary modulation protocol developed by U.S. Robotics. Although commonly used by BBSes in the 1980s, the HST was made all but extinct by the introduction of V.32 modems at very competitive prices. HST modems run at 9,600bps or 14,400bps in one direction and 300bps or 450bps in the other direction. This is an ideal protocol for interactive sessions. Because echo-cancellation circuitry is not required, costs are lower.

U.S. Robotics also marketed modems that used the ITU-T standard protocols and the U.S. Robotics proprietary standard. These dual-standard modems incorporated both V.32bis and HST protocols, giving you the best of the standard and proprietary worlds and enabling you to connect to virtually any other system at the maximum communications rate. They were at one time among the best modems available; I used and recommended them for many years.

DIS

DIS is a 9,600bps proprietary modulation protocol by CompuCom, which uses Dynamic Impedance Stabilization (DIS), with claimed superiority in noise rejection over V.32. Implementation was very inexpensive, but like HST, only one company made modems that supported the DIS standard. Because of the lower costs of V.32 and V.32bis, this proprietary standard quickly disappeared.

MNP

MNP offers end-to-end error correction, meaning that the modems are capable of detecting transmission errors and requesting retransmission of corrupted data. Some levels of MNP also provide data compression.

As MNP evolved, different classes of the standard were defined, describing the extent to which a given MNP implementation supports the protocol. Most current implementations support Classes 1–5. Higher classes usually are unique to modems manufactured by Microcom, Inc. because they are proprietary.

MNP generally is used for its error-correction capabilities, but MNP Classes 4 and 5 also provide performance increases, with Class 5 offering real-time data compression. The lower classes of MNP are not important to today's modem user, but they are included in the following list for the sake of completeness:

- *MNP Class 1 (block mode).* Uses asynchronous, byte-oriented, half-duplex (one-way) transmission. This method provides about 70 percent efficiency and error correction only, so it's rarely used today.

- *MNP Class 2 (stream mode).* Uses asynchronous, byte-oriented, full-duplex (two-way) transmission. This class also provides error correction only. Because of *protocol overhead* (the time it takes to establish the protocol and operate it), throughput at Class 2 is only about 84 percent of that for a connection without MNP, delivering about 202cps (characters per second) at 2,400bps (240cps is the theoretical maximum). Class 2 is used rarely today.

- *MNP Class 3.* Incorporates Class 2 and is more efficient. It uses asynchronous, bit-oriented, full-duplex method. The improved procedure yields throughput about 108 percent of that of a modem without MNP, delivering about 254cps at 2,400bps.

- *MNP Class 4.* A performance-enhancement class that uses Adaptive Packet Assembly and Optimized Data Phase techniques. Class 4 improves throughput and performance by about 5 percent, although actual increases depend on the type of call and connection, and can be as high as 25–50 percent.

- *MNP Class 5.* A data-compression protocol that uses a real-time adaptive algorithm. It can increase throughput up to 50 percent, but the actual performance of Class 5 depends on the type of data being sent. Raw text files allow the highest increase, although program files cannot be compressed as much and the increase in throughput is smaller. On precompressed data (files already compressed with PKZIP, for example), MNP 5 decreases performance, and therefore was often disabled on BBS systems and online services that dealt primarily with precompressed files.

V-Series

The Hayes V-series is a proprietary error-correction protocol from Hayes that was used in some of its modems. However, the advent of lower cost V.32 and V.32bis modems (even from Hayes) made the V-series all but extinct. These modems used a modified V.29 protocol, which is sometimes called a ping-pong protocol, because it has one high-speed channel and one low-speed channel that alternate back and forth.

CSP

The CSP (CompuCom Speed Protocol) is an error-correction and data-compression protocol available on CompuCom DIS modems.

Fax Modem Standards

Facsimile technology is a science unto itself, although it has many similarities to data communications. These similarities have led to the combination of data and fax capabilities into the same modem. Virtually all the modems on the market today support fax and data communications.

Over the years, the ITU has set international standards for fax transmission. This has led to the grouping of faxes into one of four groups. Each group (I through IV) uses different technology and standards for transmitting and receiving faxes. Groups I and II are relatively slow and provide results that are unacceptable by today's standards, and are therefore not discussed in detail here. Group III is the universal standard in use today by virtually all fax machines, including those combined with modems.

The Group III Fax Protocol

The Group III protocol specifies a maximum fax transmission rate of 9,600 baud and two levels of image resolution: standard (203×98 pixels) and fine (303×196 pixels). The protocol also calls for the use of a data-compression protocol defined by the CCITT (called T.4) and V.29 modulation.

There are two general subdivisions within the Group III fax standard: Class 1 and Class 2. The difference between the two is that in Class 1 faxing, the fax software generates the images and handles the session protocol and timing with the receiving system. In Class 2, the software generates an image for each page and passes it to the fax modem, which handles the session protocol and timing. Thus, with Class 1, compatibility with other fax devices is more the responsibility of the software, while with Class 2, compatibility is more the responsibility of the modem. While both classes call for additional fax-related AT commands to be recognized and acted on by the modem, the Class 2 command set is much larger, consisting of over 40 new instructions.

The Class 1 specification was readily accepted and ratified by the CCITT in 1988, but the Class 2 document was rejected repeatedly. However, some manufacturers have designed Class 2 modems using the draft (that is, unratified) version of the standard. Today, nearly all fax modems support the Group III, Class 1 standard, and this should be the minimum acceptable requirement for any fax modem you intend to purchase. Class 2 support is an additional benefit, but by itself does not provide the almost universal compatibility of Class 1.

The Group IV Fax Protocol

Whereas Groups I through III are analog in nature (such as modems) and are designed to use standard analog telephone lines, the Group IV specification calls for the digital transmission of fax images and requires an ISDN or other digital connection to the destination system. Group IV supports fax resolutions of up to 400dpi and uses a newer CCITT data compression protocol called T.6.

For a digital solution such as Group IV faxing to function, the connection between the source and the destination system must be fully digital. This means that even though your office might use a PBX-based telephone system that is digital, and your telephone carrier might use digital connections, it is very likely that there is at least some analog communication involved in the circuit, such as between the PBX and the local telephone service. Until the telephone system has been converted to a fully digital network (a monumental task), Group IV fax systems will not be capable of replacing Group III systems.

56K Modems

In the ever-continuing quest for speed, modem manufacturers have overcome what was considered to be an unbreakable ceiling for asynchronous data transfer rates over standard telephone lines, and have released modems that support speeds of up to 56,000bps (or 56Kbps). To understand how this additional speed was achieved, you must consider the basic principle of modem technology, that is, the digital-to-analog conversion.

As you've learned, a traditional modem converts data from digital to analog form so it can travel over the Public Switched Telephone Network (PSTN). At the destination system, another modem converts the analog data back to its digital form. This conversion from digital to analog and back causes some speed loss. Even though the phone line is physically capable of carrying data at 56Kbps or more, the effective maximum speed because of the conversions is about 33.6Kbps. A man by the name of Shannon came up with a law (Shannon's Law) stating that the maximum possible error-free data communications rate over the PSTN is approximately 35Kbps, depending on the noise present.

However, Shannon's Law assumes a fully analog connection between the two modems. That is not the case in most of the United States today. In urban areas, most circuits are digital until they reach the telephone company's central office (CO) to which your phone line is connected. The CO converts the digital signal into an analog signal before sending it to your home.

Considering the fact that the phone system is largely digital, you can—in some cases—omit the initial digital-to-analog conversion and send a purely digital signal over the PSTN to the recipient's CO. Thus, there is only one digital-to-analog conversion needed, instead of two or more. The result is that you can theoretically increase the speed of the data transmission, in one direction only, beyond the 35Kbps specified by Shannon's Law, to nearly the 56Kbps speed supported by the telephone network. The transmission in the other direction is still limited to the V.34 maximum of 33.6Kbps.

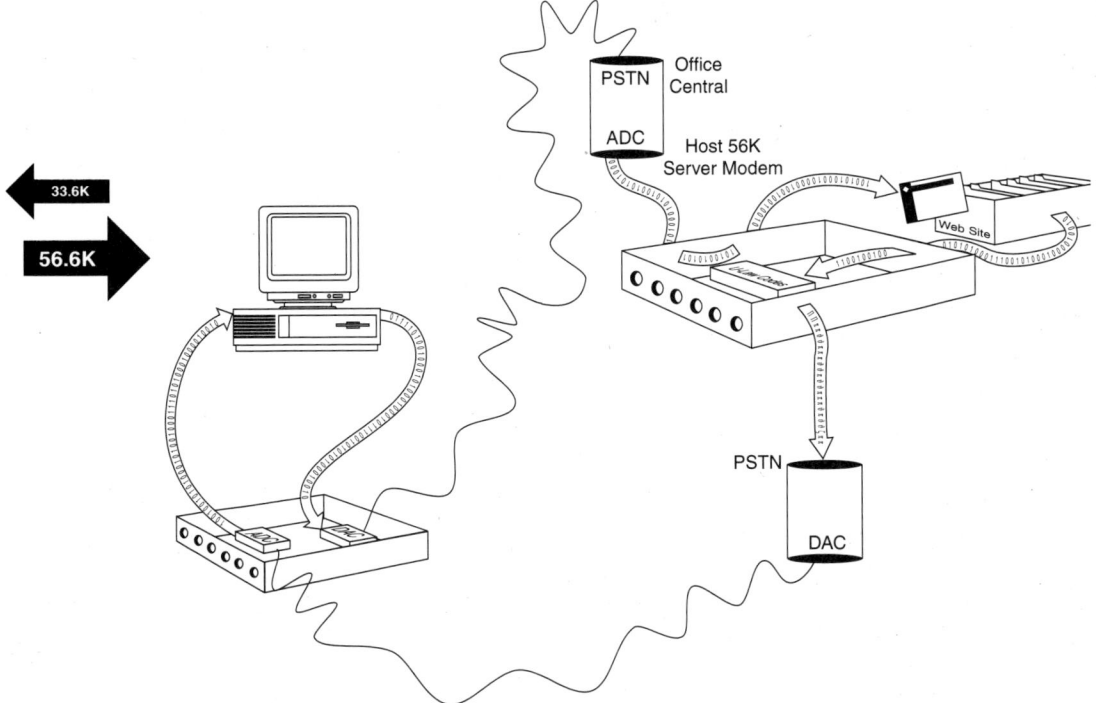

Figure 18.5 56K connections allow you to send data at standard analog modem rates (36,000bps maximum), but allow you to receive data nearly twice as fast.

56K Limitations

Thus, 56K modems can increase data transfer speeds beyond the limits of V.34 modems, but they are subject to certain limitations. Unlike standard modem technologies, you cannot buy two 56K modems, install them on two computers, and achieve 56Kbps speeds. One side of the connection must use a special digital modem that connects directly to the PSTN without a digital-to-analog conversion.

56K modems, therefore, can be used only to connect to ISPs or other hosting services that have invested in the necessary infrastructure to support the connection. Because the ISP has the digital connection to the PSTN, its downstream transmissions to your computer are accelerated, while your communications back to the ISP are not. On a practical level, this means you can surf the Web and download files more quickly, but if you host a Web server on your PC, your users will realize no speed gain, because the upstream traffic is not accelerated.

Also, there can only be one digital-to-analog conversion in the downstream connection from the ISP to your computer. This is dictated by the nature of the physical connection to your local telephone carrier. If additional conversions are involved in your connection, 56K technology will not work for you; 33.6Kbps will be your maximum possible speed. The leading Web site for line testing is the one created by 3Com's U.S. Robotics division, located at:

www.3com.com/56k/need4_56k/linetest.html

This site provides a toll-free number and a simple procedure for you to use in testing your line with your existing modem. Although 33.6Kbps and slower modems have virtually disappeared from the market, it's still useful to know if buying a 56Kbps modem will give you faster speed at your current location.

Since the line test is specific to your location, test the line you'll actually be using for the modem. With the way that the telephone system has had to grow to accommodate new exchanges and devices, even neighbors down the street from each other might have different results.

Caution

56K modem communications are also highly susceptible to slowdowns caused by line noise. Your telephone line may be perfectly adequate for voice communications, and even lower speed modem communications, but inaudible noise can easily degrade a 56K connection to the point at which there is only a marginal increase over a 33.6Kbps modem, or even no increase at all. If you do have a problem with line noise, it would help if you got a surge suppressor with noise filtration.

If you plan to use a PCMCIA/PC Card modem in a notebook computer, be aware that your hotel room will soon host the world's slowest 56K modem—yours! The connection quality of the separate analog phone jacks or the "data port" in the side of the typical hotel guest telephone is usually poor, and you'll be lucky to see even a 24Kbps transmission rate. The analog-digital conversions that happen between your room's telephone and the hotel's digital PBX system eliminate the possibility of using any of the 56K standards the modem supports, because they depend on a direct digital connection to the central switch (CS).

56K Standards

To achieve a high-speed connection, both modems and your ISP (or other hosting service to which you connect), must support the same 56KB technology. Here rises the biggest issue surrounding 56K compatibility. As is often the case, modem manufacturers were anxious to bring the latest technology to market, so two companies released products using competing 56K standards. U.S. Robotics (now part of 3Com) introduced a line of 56K modems using Texas Instruments chipsets that they called X2, while Rockwell, a manufacturer of modem chipsets, released another 56K standard that it called K56flex. Naturally, these two standards were not compatible, and the rest of the modem industry rapidly polarized, supporting one standard or the other. The result was a latter-day version of the Beta-VHS conflict of the 1970s.

Note

To complicate matters further, it was discovered only days before U.S. Robotics shipped its first X2 modems that an old FCC regulation known as Part 68 specifies the maximum amount of power that you can run through a PSTN phone line. Because faster communications require more power, this regulation effectively limits modem communications to a maximum speed of approximately 53Kbps. The regulation was created because increasing the power transmitted over a line beyond a certain point causes increased interference, called *crosstalk*, on neighboring lines. The FCC implemented this regulation long ago, not intending it to apply specifically to modems, and is currently reevaluating its position. This reevaluation process began in the fall of 1998, and is still ongoing.

As a result of having two standards, users were forced to wait and see which technology their ISPs would adopt or commit to one of the two standards, and then find an ISP that supported it. Because the investment in 56K technology was so much more substantial for an ISP, many of them waited to see which of the two standards would win out by becoming either a de facto or a de jure standard.

During this time, it was not uncommon for people to wind up with the "wrong" modem, since many ISPs initially supported only one of the rival standards. As the sales and popularity of both X2 and K56flex increased, many ISPs were forced to create separate dial-up phone numbers for each standard, increasing their costs, but making their users happier.

V.90

Fortunately, this problem has been resolved. On February 5, 1998, the ITU-T approved a "determination" for a 56K modem standard called V.90. The standard was ratified on September 15, 1998. Now that an official standard exists, all modem manufacturers have upgraded their current products to support V.90, and interoperability between devices supporting the two earlier standards should be possible

Because the X2 and K56flex implementations are fundamentally similar in the hardware requirements described earlier, it should be possible to modify existing modems of either type to support V.90 by upgrading their firmware using a flash update or a simple chip replacement. However, this is for the individual modem manufacturers to decide.

If you purchased your modem before the V.90 standard became official, see your modem vendor's Web site for information about upgrading to V.90.

Depending on your modem model, one of three outcomes is likely:

- Some users will be able to download software to "flash" their BIOS firmware to the new V.90 standard.

- Others will need to do a physical modem swap.

- A few, especially those whose modems came from now-defunct companies such as Hayes, Practical Peripherals, and Cardinal Technologies, will be out of luck, and need to continue with their non-V.90 standard or replace their modems.

Note

Don't update your modem to V.90 standard until your ISP has updated its service. Check your ISP's Web site to determine their V.90 status and see which dial-up phone numbers support what standards.

Since the adoption of V.90, users with X2 modems who have updated their firmware to V.90 standards have generally had good luck in connecting, often obtaining higher speeds. However, there have been a number of reports of K56flex users having problems in a V.90 world, even after updating their modems to the V.90 standard. According to one ISP (Florida's Suncoast Networking), some of the K56flex modems affected included Zoltrix, Zoom, and WinLT. If you have problems connecting reliably or speedily after doing a V.90 update from K56flex, try these tips:

Troubleshooting the V.90 (ex-K56flex) Modems

1. Make sure you have the latest firmware release. Even if you have just purchased your modem, your vendor might have put a firmware update on its Web site. To get there for the update, if you're having problems making the connection, dial in with your modem on a 33.6Kbps line, or "pretend" that your modem is an older model by installing it as a 33.6Kbps model from the same vendor.

2. See if you can continue to use the modem as a K56flex. Some modems' firmware ROM (read-only memory) chips have enough room for both K56flex and V.90 code, while others have space for just one or the other (Zoom Telephonics, for example, calls their modems with provision for both standards "Dualmode"). Typically, modems with a 1MB ROM chip can only handle one type of firmware, while modems with a 2MB ROM chip have room for both. If you can't have both code types in your modem at the same time, download both K56flex and V.90 firmware to your system, try each one, and see which works better for you. As long as your ISP has a K56flex-specific modem pool, you don't really need to change to V.90. A good vendor-specific example of these issues can be found at: www.zoomtel.com/techsprt/readme/Zoom-Uploader.html.

3. If your vendor has several versions of firmware available for download, try some of the earlier versions, as well as the latest version. An earlier version might actually work better for you.

4. If you are using your modem in a country other than the United States or Canada, you might need an "international" update. Zoom Telephonic's Web site, for example, lists separate K56flex-to-V.90 updates for Australia, Belgium, Denmark, Finland, France, Germany, Holland (the Netherlands), Italy, Portugal, Sweden, Switzerland, and the United Kingdom (Great Britain and Northern Ireland).

5. Don't forget that your operating system drivers for your modem might also need to be updated.

Note

The problems with moving from K56flex to V.90 do not apply to users who have updated their V.34 modems directly to the V.90 standard, whether by a downloadable firmware update or by a physical modem or chip swap. Even if your V.34 modem was made by a company that later made K56flex modems, you don't need to worry about this unless you updated to K56flex. Then, the troubleshooting advice given earlier applies to you as well.

Modem Recommendations

A modem for a PC can take the form either of an external device with its own power supply that plugs into a PC's serial port, or an internal expansion card that you insert into a bus slot inside the computer. Most manufacturers of modems have both internal and external versions of the same models.

External versions are slightly more expensive because they include a separate case and power supply. Both are equally functional, however, and the decision as to which type you use should typically depend on whether you have a free bus slot or serial port, how much room you have on your desk, the capabilities of your system's internal power supply, and how comfortable you are with opening up your computer.

I have often preferred external modems because of the visual feedback they provide through indicator lights. These lights make it easy to see if the modem is still connected and transmitting or receiving data. However, some communication programs today include onscreen simulations of the lights, providing the same information.

There are other situations, too, where an internal modem is preferable. In case your computer's serial ports do not have buffered UART chips such as the 16550, many internal modems include an onboard 16550 UART. This onboard UART with the modem saves you the trouble of upgrading the UART serial port. Also, external 56K modems can be hampered from achieving their full speed by the limitations of the computer's serial port. An internal model may be preferable instead. Use Table 18.2 to see how internal and external units compare.

Table 18.2—External Versus Internal Modems

Features	External	Internal
Built-in 16550 UART or higher	No (uses computer's serial port UART or may use USB)	Yes (if 14.4Kbps or faster)
Price comparison	Higher	Lower
Extras to buy	RS-232 Modem Interface cable or USB cable	Nothing
Ease of moving to another computer	Easy—unplug the cables and go! (USB modems require a functioning USB port on the other computer)	Difficult—must open case and remove card, open other PC's case and insert card

Features	External	Internal
Power supply	Plugs into wall ("brick" type)	None—powered by host PC
Reset if modem hangs	Turn modem off, and then on again	Restart computer
Monitoring operation	Easy—External signal lights	Difficult—unless your communication software simulates the signal lights
Interface type	Almost always via the RS-232 port, although USB modems are now on the market. Parallel-port modems were made a few years ago, but never proved popular	Traditionally ISA, but many models now available in PCI, which should work better in new machines, allow mapping of COM 3 and 4 away from COM 1 and 2 to avoid IRQ sharing, and be usable in machines of the future which will lack ISA slots

◀◀ See "UARTs," p. 876.

Not all modems that function at the same speed have the same functionality. Many modem manufacturers produce modems running at the same speed, but with different feature sets at different price points. The more expensive modems usually support advanced features such as distinctive ring support, caller ID, voice and data, and even video teleconferencing. When purchasing a modem, be sure that it supports all the features you need. It's also a good idea to make sure the software you plan to use, including the operating system, has been certified for use with the modem you select.

If you live in a rural area, or in an older city neighborhood, your telephone line quality may influence your decision. Look at comparison test results carefully and pay particular attention to how well different modems perform with noisy lines. If your phone line sounds "crackly" during a rainstorm, that poor-quality line makes reliable modem communications difficult too.

Most of the brand-name modems on the market today support a wide range of modulation, error-correction, and data-connection standards. This is because most modems are *auto-negotiating*; that is, when they connect to another modem they implement the most efficient set of protocols they have in common. Even if the two modems do not agree on the most advanced protocol of a particular type, they are likely to have at least one protocol in common.

Another feature to consider is the modem's resistance to electrical damage. Some brands feature built-in power protection to shield against damage from digital telephone lines (higher powered and not compatible with modems) or power surges. However, every modem should be used with a surge protector that allows you to route the RJ-11 telephone cable through the unit for protection against high-voltage surges.

Virtually all modems on the market today support V.90, and even if your particular location can't support those speeds, your modem may still offer advanced features such as voicemail or simultaneous voice and data. Keep in mind that V.90 connections seem to work better for many users if their modem also supports X2. If you prefer a modem made by a vendor which also supports K56flex, try to buy a modem that contains both types of standards in its firmware.

Note

Each type of Internet connection will use a particular combination of TCP/IP settings. TCP/IP is the protocol (software rules) used by all computers on the Internet. We'll learn more about TCP/IP in Chapter 19, "Networking," but for now keep in mind that different TCP/IP settings are required for modem access and access through a NIC or USB port device (cable modem, xDSL, and DirecPC). Modems usually have an IP address provided dynamically by the ISP when the modem connects with the ISP. The other types of Internet access devices normally have a static IP address that doesn't change. IP addresses are just one of the network settings that, if changed, will prevent you from getting on the Internet. See the discussion in Chapter 19 for details.

Integrated Services Digital Network (ISDN)

To get past the speed limitations of asynchronous modems, you have to go completely digital, and ISDN is the next step in telecommunications. ISDN makes the break from the old technology of analog data transfer to the newer digital data transfer. With ISDN, you can connect to the Internet at speeds of up to 128Kbps.

ISDN has been available for over 10 years but has only recently become a practical solution for private users. This was mostly due to the difficulties involved in arranging for the installation of the service with the telephone company. Three years ago, it was difficult to find someone at most regional phone companies who had even heard of ISDN, but there are now quite a few businesses that provide turnkey solutions, including ISP services, ISDN hardware, and negotiations with the phone company.

While it can be used for voice communications, ISDN is not like a normal telephone connection, even though it uses your existing telephone wiring. To achieve high speeds, both ends of the connection must be digital, so you would typically set up an ISDN line specifically for connecting to an ISP that also uses ISDN. Businesses also use higher bandwidth ISDN connections for Internet access or to connect LANs in remote offices.

ISDN is also not like a leased telephone line, however, which permanently connects two specific locations. Your software still dials the number of your intended destination (although it is a special ISDN number), and breaks the connection (that is, hangs up) when the session is finished. Thus, you can change to a different ISP that supports ISDN, if necessary, without dealing with the phone company again.

What Does ISDN Really Mean for Computer Users?

Since ISDN carries two signals, it allows "integrated services" that can include combinations such as voice+data, data+data, voice+fax, fax+data, etc.

The "Digital" in ISDN represents the end of the need for your venerable telecom pal, the modem. ISDN connections are digital from the origination straight to your PC—no digital-analog conversions needed. Thus, the so-called ISDN modem used to hook your PC to an ISDN line is more properly called a *terminal adapter*.

The "Network" in ISDN refers to its capability to interconnect with other ISDN devices around the world. Unlike the earlier high-speed access method for business, the leased line, ISDN isn't limited to making fast connections to a single computer. In fact, if your ISDN equipment includes support for analog services, your ISDN connection can "reach out and touch" regular telephones, fax machines, and other Plain Old Telephone Service (POTS) devices (see Figure 18.6).

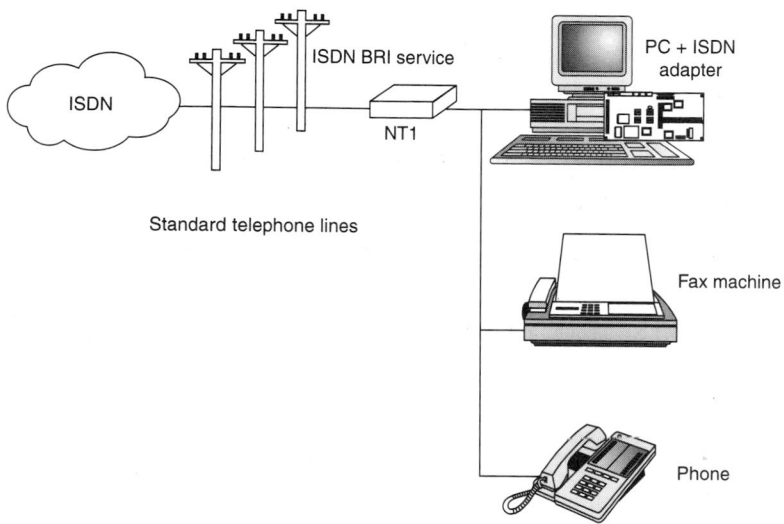

Figure 18.6 This typical ISDN configuration shows how ISDN can link your advanced telecommunications devices with both the ISDN and analog worlds.

An excellent Web resource for ISDN is www.isdnzone.com.

How ISDN Works

On an ISDN connection, bandwidth is divided into bearer channels (B channels) that run at 64Kbps and a delta channel (D channel) that runs at 16Kbps or 64Kbps, depending on the type of service. The B channels carry voice transmissions or user data, and the D channel carries control traffic. In other words, you talk, surf, or fax through the B-channel lines. The typical BRI service would allow you to use one B channel to talk at 64Kbps and one B channel to run your computer for Web surfing at 64Kbps. Hang up the phone, and both B channels become available. If your ISDN service is configured appropriately, your Web browsing becomes supercharged, because you're now running at 128Kbps.

There are two types of ISDN service: Basic Rate Interface (BRI) and Primary Rate Interface (PRI). The BRI service is intended for private and home users and consists of two B channels and one 16Kbps D channel, for a total of 144Kbps. The PRI service is oriented more toward business use, such as for PBX connections to the telephone company's CO. In North America and Japan, the PRI service consists of 23 B channels and one 64Kbps D channel for a total of 1536Kbps, running over a standard T1 interface. In Europe, the PRI service is 30 B channels and one 64Kbps D channel, totaling 1,984Kbps, corresponding to the E1 telecommunications standard. For businesses that require more bandwidth than one PRI connection provides, it's possible to use one D channel to support multiple PRI channels using Non-Facility Associated Signaling (NFAS).

Always on with Dynamic ISDN

Earlier, I compared ISDN with leased-line services, and pointed out that for many users ISDN would be a superior solution. However, conventional ISDN isn't the answer when you want to keep a continuous connection available at minimal cost.

A *nailed-up* connection is continuously kept up for uninterrupted remote access to a LAN. This uses up the resources of at least one B channel, even though the full capacity of the channel is seldom in use at one time. Because traffic will vary greatly over an "always on" connection, Dynamic ISDN was developed to use the power of ISDN more flexibly.

Dynamic ISDN combines the circuit-switching of a traditional phone system connection with the packet-switching of LANs and the WWW.

The D channel is used to make each connection using the X.31 protocol that runs over the normal telco packet-switched network. Normally used for signaling, the D channel has sufficient bandwidth to carry such low-demand traffic as email notification (or even email itself), channel subscription, and PointCast+ "push" information to users.

The high-speed B channels are activated only when needed for high-bandwidth uses such as file transfer. The D channel can automatically switch this type of traffic to either one or both B channels (one provides 64Kbps transfer rates; both would provide 128Kbps transfer rates). The B channels are automatically released when the heavy traffic uses are finished and are free to handle voice or fax traffic until high-volume computer traffic requires their use.

Thus, Dynamic ISDN makes the potential of ISDN a reality by allowing intelligent allocation of resources.

This is the best type of ISDN to get if you want to use ISDN for more than just high-speed Internet access. Check with your ISDN vendor for price and availability in your area.

ISDN Hardware

To connect a PC to an ISDN connection, you must have a hardware component called a *terminal adapter* (TA). The terminal adapter takes the form of an expansion board or an external device connected to a serial port, much like a modem. In fact, terminal adapters are often mistakenly referred to as ISDN modems. Actually, they are not modems at all, because they do not perform analog/digital conversions.

There are two different interfaces to the ISDN service. The U-interface consists of a single pair of wires leading to the telephone company's CO. The Subscriber/Termination (S/T) interface consists of two pairs of wires that typically run from a wall jack to your terminal adapter. The device that converts the U-interface signal to the S/T interface is called a *network termination device*, or NT-1.

Some terminal adapters include an NT-1 integrated into the hardware, enabling you to connect the U-interface directly to the computer. This is an excellent solution as long as the computer is the only device that you plan to connect to the ISDN line. If you want to connect multiple devices, or if your terminal adapter does not include an NT-1, you must purchase an NT-1 separately. Another alternative is to get a network-ready terminal adapter that you can connect to your current NIC. This is an especially good alternative if you have several PCs, as you can share one TA among them.

Caution

When purchasing an ISDN terminal adapter, you will almost always want to invest in an internal version. A terminal adapter with compression can easily exceed a serial port's capability to reliably send and receive data. Consider that even a moderate 2:1 compression ratio exceeds the maximum rated speed of 232Kbps, which most high-speed COM ports support.

Leased Lines

For users with high bandwidth requirements (and deep pockets), dedicated leased lines provide digital service between two locations at speeds that can far exceed ISDN. A *leased line* is a permanent 24-hour connection to a particular location that can only be changed by the telephone company. Businesses use leased lines to connect LANs in remote locations or to connect to the Internet through a service provider. Leased lines are available at various speeds, as described in the following sections.

T-1 and T-3 Connections

To connect networks in distant locations, networks that must support a large number of Internet users, or especially organizations that will be hosting their own Internet services, a T-1 connection might be the wise investment. A *T-1* is a digital connection running at 1.55Mbps. This is more than 10 times faster than an ISDN link. A T-1 may be split (or fractioned), depending on how it is to be used. It can be split into 24 individual 64Kbps lines or left as a single high-capacity pipeline. Some ISPs allow you to lease any portion of a T-1 connection that you want (in 64Kbps increments).

An individual user of the Internet interacts with a T-1 line only indirectly. If you're accessing the Internet via a dial-up (modem) or ISDN connection, your ISP will normally have a connection to one or more T-1 or T-3 lines, which represent the "backbone" of the Internet. This connection to the backbone is sometimes referred to as a *point of presence*. When you make your dial-up connection to the Internet, your ISP shares a small chunk of that T-1 pipe with you. Depending on how many other users are accessing the Internet at your ISP or elsewhere, you might experience very fast to slow throughput, even if your modem connection speed remains constant. It's a bit like splitting up a pizza into smaller and smaller slices to accommodate more people at a party: the more users of a high-speed connection, the slower each individual part of it will be. To keep user connections fast while growing, ISPs will add full or fractional T-1 lines to their point of presence. Or, they might switch from a T-1 connection to the even faster T-3 if available.

Note

Equivalent in throughput to approximately 30 T-1 lines, a T-3 connection runs at 45Mbps, and is suitable for use by very large networks and university campuses. Pricing information falls into the "if you have to ask, you can't afford it" category.

If your Internet connection is on a corporate LAN or your office is located in a downtown building, your relationship to a T-1 line may be much closer. If your building or office is connected directly to a T-1, you're sharing the capacity of that line with just a relative few other users rather than with the hundreds or thousands of dial-up users that a normal ISP is hosting at one time. T-1 links in the United States usually cost several thousand dollars per month, plus a substantial installation fee. But, for a large organization that requires a lot of bandwidth, it can be more economical to install a higher-capacity service and grow into it, rather than constantly upgrade the link.

CATV Networks

Although ISDN represents a significant increase in speed over standard modem technologies, the installation difficulties and the expense (especially when there are connect-time charges) may not be justified. The next step up in speed is a cable TV (CATV) network connection. This service, when available, is usually less expensive than ISDN.

Connecting to the Internet with a "Cable Modem"

As with ISDN, the device used to connect a PC to a CATV network is somewhat inaccurately called a modem. In fact, the so-called cable modem (a name I will continue to use, for the sake of convenience) is actually a great deal more. The device does indeed modulate and demodulate, but it also functions as a tuner, a network bridge, an encryptor, an SNMP agent, and a hub.

To connect your PC to a CATV network, you do not use a serial port as with standard modem technologies. Instead, the most typical connection used today requires that you install a standard Ethernet network interface adapter into a bus slot. The Ethernet adapter connects to the cable modem with the same type of twisted-pair cable used on LANs. In fact, your PC and the cable modem actually form a two-node LAN, with the modem functioning as a hub. There are PCI-based internal and USB-based external cable modems now under development.

The cable modem also connects to the CATV network using the same coaxial cable connection as your cable TV service (see Figure 18.9). Thus, the cable modem functions as a bridge between the tiny twisted-pair network in your home and the hybrid fiber/coax (HFC) network that connects all the cable customers in your neighborhood.

A few cable modem CATV systems have been built using the older one-way (download-only) coax cable, but this type of cable is much slower for cable modem use and is obsolete for both CATV and data communications. The industry has largely replaced coax with HFC.

Up to the present, the cable modems have not been for sale, but have been leased by the CATV companies offering Internet access. This is because each cable modem on a particular CATV network had to match the proprietary technology used by the network. In late 1998, DOCSIS-compliant cable modems began to be used by some CATV companies. DOCSIS refers to devices that meet the Data Over Cable Service Interface Specification standards. These are already for sale in limited markets, and will be available in most markets in 2000.

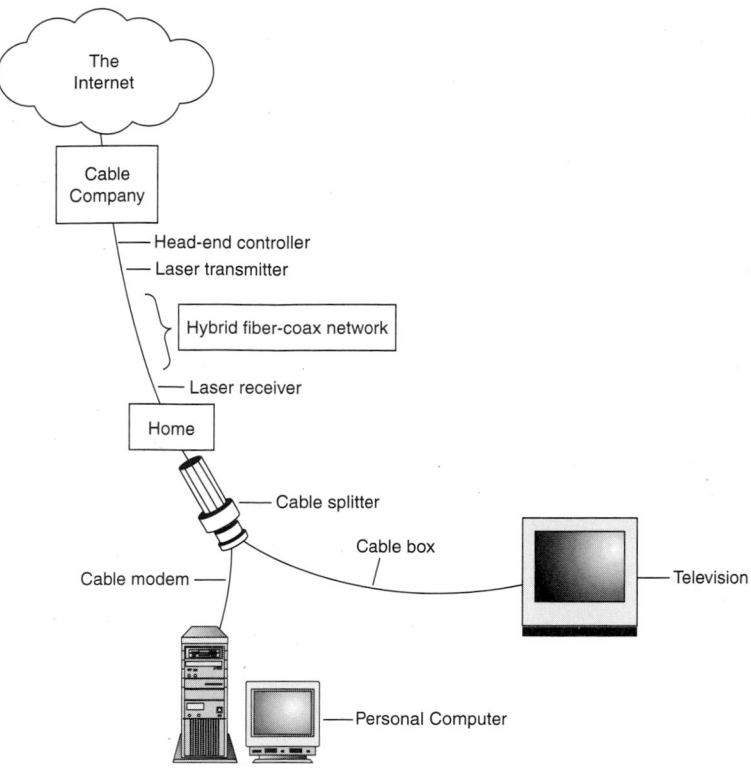

Figure 18.9   A basic cable modem connection to the Internet.

CATV Bandwidth

Cable TV uses what is known as a *broadband network*, meaning that the bandwidth of the connection is split to carry many signals at the same time. These various signals correspond to the various channels you see on your TV. A typical HFC network provides approximately 750MHz of bandwidth, and each channel requires 6MHz. Therefore, because the television channels start at about 50MHz, you would find channel 2 in the 50MHz–56MHz range, channel 3 at 57MHz–63MHz, and continuing on up the frequency spectrum. At this rate, an HFC network can support about 110 channels.

For data networking purposes, cable systems typically allocate one channel's worth of bandwidth in the 50MHz–750MHz range for downstream traffic (that is, traffic coming into the cable modem from the CATV network). In this way, the cable modem functions as a tuner, just like your cable TV box, ensuring that your PC receives signals from the correct frequency.

Upstream traffic (data sent from your PC to the network) uses a different channel. Cable TV systems commonly reserve the bandwidth from 5MHz–42MHz for upstream signals of various types (such as those generated by cable TV boxes that enable you to order pay-per-view programming). Depending on the bandwidth available, you might find that your CATV provider does not furnish the same high speed upstream as it does downstream. This is called an *asymmetrical network*.

Typical upstream traffic modulation techniques include

- *QPSK (Quadrature Phase Shift Keying).* A digital frequency modulation method that's easy to implement and resists noise well. This is the most common method for sending upstream traffic.

- *DQPSK (Differential Quadrature Phase Shift Keying).* Provides narrower bands and thus a wider choice of noise-free channels; it's often used with cellular communications.

- *S-CDMA (Synchronous Code Division Multiple Access).* A method that scatters data across a wide frequency band and allows multiple subscribers to send and receive data concurrently. It provides a high level of security and noise resistance.

- *VSB (Vestigial Side Band).* A digital frequency modulation technique that is faster than QPSK, but more vulnerable to noise.

The method used depends on the CATV provider.

Note

Because the upstream speed often does not match the downstream speed (and to minimize noise, which tends to accumulate because of the tree-and-branch nature of the network), cable TV connections are usually not practical for hosting WWW servers and other Internet services. This is largely deliberate, as most CATV providers are currently targeting their traditional home user market. As the technology matures, however, this type of Internet connection is likely to spread to the business world as well. There are now specialized domain name services that can be used to "point" Web surfers to your cable modem or xDSL connection.

The amount of data throughput that the single 6MHz downstream channel can support is dependent on the type of modulation used at the head end (that is, the system to which your PC connects over the network). Using a technology called 64 QAM (quadrature amplitude modulation), the channel might be capable of carrying up to 27Mbps of downstream data. A variant called 256 QAM can boost this to 36Mbps.

You must realize, however, that you will not achieve anything even approaching this throughput on your PC. First of all, the Ethernet adapter used to connect to the cable modem is limited to 10Mbps, but even this is well beyond the real-life results you will achieve. As with any LAN, you are sharing the available bandwidth with other users. All your neighbors who also subscribe to the service make use of the same 6MHz channel. As more users are added, more systems are contending for the same bandwidth, and throughput goes down.

CATV Security

Because your PC is sharing a network with other users in your neighborhood, and because the traffic is bidirectional, the security of your PC and the network becomes an issue. In most cases, some form of encryption is involved to prevent unauthorized access to the network. As with your cable TV box, the cable modem may contain encryption circuitry that is needed to access the network. Your CATV provider may also supply encryption software that uses a special protocol to log you on to the network. This protects the CATV provider from non-paying users, but it doesn't protect you. The security features vary according to which cable modem is used by your CATV provider.

If you use an operating system such as Windows 9x that has built-in peer networking capabilities, you might be able to see your neighbors' computers on the network. The operating system has settings that enable you to specify whether other network users can access your drives. If these settings are configured improperly, your neighbors may be able to view, access, and even delete the files on your hard drives. Be sure that the technician from the cable company installing the service addresses this problem. If you want to use a cable modem along with sharing access on your computer (for printing, file storage, etc.), I'd recommend that you use passwords for any shared drives. A free utility called Shareclean enables you to have one-button access to turning off drive sharing. This utility was developed by the Privacy Software Corporation and can be downloaded from the Web. You can also use firewall and proxy-server software available from many vendors.

CATV Performance

The fact that you are sharing the CATV network with other users doesn't mean that the performance of a cable modem isn't usually spectacular. Typically, the realized throughput hovers around 512Kbps, almost 10 times that of the fastest modem connection and four times that of ISDN. You will find the WWW to be an entirely new experience at this speed. Those huge audio and video clips you avoided in the past now download in seconds, and you will soon fill your hard drives with all the free software available.

Add to this the fact that the service is typically quite reasonably priced. Remember that the CATV provider is replacing both the telephone company and your ISP in your Internet access solution. The price may be about $40 per month, twice that of a normal dial-up ISP account, but it is far less than ISDN, does not require a telephone line, and provides you with 24-hour access to the Internet. The only drawback is that the service may not yet be available in your area. In my opinion, this technology exceeds all the other Internet access solutions available today in speed, economy, and convenience.

DirecPC—Internet Connectivity via Satellite

If you're in an area where cable TV doesn't exist, or you already have a DirecTV satellite dish, take a look at the southern sky from your home, condo, or apartment building. If you have a good, clear 45-degree window view to the southern sky and you want fast downloads of big files, DirecPC might be the high-speed choice for you.

How DirecPC Works

DirecPC is a *hybrid* system, meaning that incoming and outgoing data streams and other operations are actually routed two ways. DirecPC's much-vaunted 400Kbps satellite connection is for downloads, and downloads only. You'll not only upload by using a conventional modem, but you'll also request pages (Web surfing) with that creaky modem as well. This makes DirecPC a great choice for download junkies, but not the best choice for researchers or others with an impatient mouse-clicker finger. While ISDN offers up to 128Kbps in both directions, DirecPC downloads are typically as much as three times faster. DirecPC works as shown in Figure 18.10.

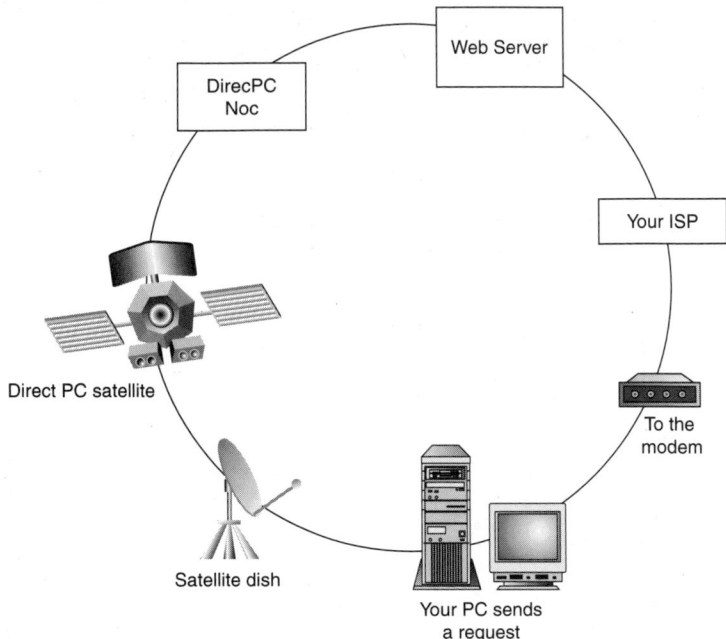

Figure 18.10   DirecPC routes your request for Web pages, graphics, and files using a modem. The speed advantage comes when you receive your data, with a download speed of 400Kbps, thanks to a satellite link.

DirecPC Requirements

DirecPC requires a small satellite dish, similar but not compatible to those used for DirecTV and USSB satellite services (DirecDuo combines DirecPC and DirecTV into a single service, using the same type of dish as DirecPC). The dish is connected to a 32-bit PCI-based Ethernet card for data receiving. You use a conventional modem for sending out page requests or for uploading data. While all services beyond 33.6Kbps are *asymmetrical*—faster for downloading than uploading— except ISDN, the only other fast-download Internet service with a similarly poky speed for uploads is the 56K V.90 modem and its proprietary predecessors (X2 and K56flex).

Installing DirecPC

A DirecPC installation combines the dangers of satellite-TV installation with the usual issues involved in connecting a network-style device to your computer. You'll need an unobstructed 45-degree clear line of sight to the south and room for the 21" satellite dish. Until recently, the PC connection to the DirecPC dish required installing a PCI-based Ethernet card or reconfiguring your existing Ethernet card. Now, Windows 98 users with USB ports can choose a USB-based solution. If you're running Windows 95 or NT, you'll still need your screwdriver and a free PCI slot for the NIC.

Since the DirecPC satellite link uses a single satellite in the southern sky, dish positioning and aiming is much more important than with USSB-type TV dishes.

The DirecPC "Getting Started" guide strongly suggests that DirecPC installers have experience with normal satellite dishes or TV antennas, because issues such as running coaxial cable, proper electrical grounding to code, and other challenges await. Detailed installation instructions for the antenna and other DirecPC components are found on the CD-ROM that comes with the self-installation kit for DirecPC, but are not available on the Web site. Consider professional installation for a carefree, reliable, and safe setup at a reasonable price.

When you install DirecPC on a system that already has a PCI-based Ethernet card, you can choose to have both DirecPC and your existing network use the card, or use the card just with DirecPC. This choice affects the TCP/IP bindings configuration.

Make sure you have your IP addresses handy; you'll need them to complete the installation.

DirecPC's minimum configurations have specified Pentium-class processors, but if you're considering putting that old P-100 to work as a Web-surfer, think again. The latest DirecDuo (DirecPC + DirecTV) data-sheet is now requiring a Pentium 200-class processor.

Purchasing DirecPC

After the complex price structure based on transfer rate of the original version of DirecPC (1.0), DirecPC 2.0 and above now use a simplified pricing structure that ranges from about $30 a month for 25 hours to more than $100 a month for 200 hours.

DirecPC pricing includes ISP service and a single email account (or four if you buy the 200 hours/month service).

The typical retail cost of DirecPC is about $300, which includes hardware and software, but not installation.

DirecPC's FAP—Brakes on High-Speed Downloading?

A big concern for those wanting to exploit the high-speed download feature is DirecPC's Fair Access Policy (FAP), which was introduced long after the service was started. FAP uses unpublished guidelines to determine who is "abusing" the service with large downloads. Abusers have their download bandwidth reduced by about 50 percent until their behavior changes. A class-action lawsuit was filed in July 1998, by DirecPC users who objected to this policy. Users said that Hughes Network Systems, Inc., the developer of DirecPC, was simultaneously selling the system on the basis of very fast download times, and then punishing those who wanted to use it in the way DirecPC had sold to the public.

Excellent discussions of the problems that FAP is causing for many DirecPC users along with some suggestions for dealing with FAP can be found at: http://charon.punk.net/fap/fap.html and http://208.240.252.169/direcpc/.

Technical Problems and Solutions

Because DirecPC uses both land and satellite routing for information, the DirecPC setup program must be properly configured to provide correct (modem-only) routing for DNS lookups and some email applications.

Some Windows 98 users of DirecPC need to uninstall and reinstall the DirecPC software to solve a DLL error. Get more information at the DirecPC Web site.

Users of the popular Matrox Millenium II video cards and chipset need to get the latest Matrox driver, or reduce video acceleration to solve a problem with the video card's use of Automatic PCI Bus Retries, which can cause intermittent signal loss from the DirecPC unit. The new Matrox driver has a setting that will turn off this feature. Other video card drivers that lack this feature should adjust video acceleration down one notch. A new driver for DirecPC can also be downloaded to help with this problem.

Note

While shared high-speed Internet access has been a ticklish issue for some types of products, DirecPC offers detailed information on their Web site about sharing software and its configuration.

Real-World Performance

Benchmark addicts will find that DirecPC will perform poorly on ping tests, because the complex pathway your data must travel (ground to space and back again) means that pings will take at least 400 to 600 ms. Interactive benchmarks are also disappointing. However, real-world speeds in excess of 225Kbps can be reached when downloading big files. To see how DirecPC compares to other methods of online connectivity, see Figure 18.11.

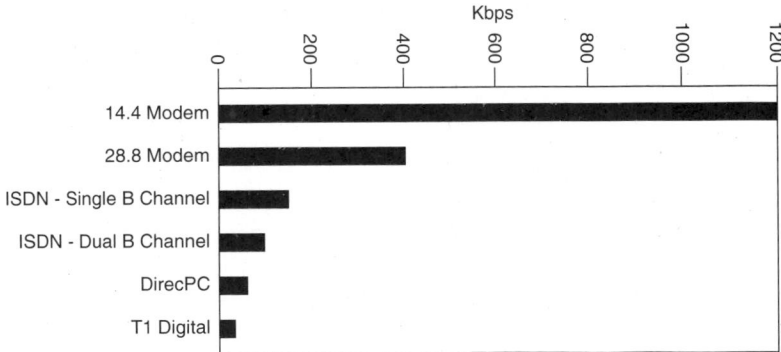

Figure 18.11 DirecPC offers maximum download speeds of up to 400Kbps, but downloads at these speeds will occur only when downloading a large file because of the delays caused by the hybrid nature of DirecPC's connection to the Web. Thus, the Kbps speeds listed in this chart reflect a "best-case" situation.

DirecPC has been a controversial choice for fast Internet access because of the confusing pricing of the original version, concerns about FAP, and its unusual hybrid architecture. However, it performs well for downloads up to 50–70MB at a time. (Many users report that FAP limitations often drastically cut speeds on downloads larger than this.) If you can't get cable-modem or xDSL Internet access, consider DirecPC or the TV/PC combo called DirecDuo. If you want to get more user-oriented information about DirecPC, join the DirecPC newsgroup: `alt.satellite.direcpc`.

DSL (Digital Subscriber Line)

The newest solution to the high-speed Internet-access problem is Digital Subscriber Line, also called xDSL. The *x* stands for the various versions of DSL that are being proposed, and in a small but growing number of cases, actually being offered by a few local telephone companies.

DSL appeals to the telephone companies, who can use the existing Plain Old Telephone Service (POTS) analog wiring to provide high-speed Internet access. Not every type of DSL is suitable for existing wiring, however, all but the fastest, most expensive types can be used with the existing POTS plant. DSL is also appealing to businesses which don't have access to cable modems, but are looking for an alternative to the expensive ISDN services that top out at 128Kbps.

One advantage of DSL compared to its most popular rival, cable modems, is that cable modems are sharing common bandwidth, which means that a lot of simultaneous use by your neighbors can slow your connection down. DSL users don't have this concern; whatever bandwidth speed you paid for is yours—period.

Who Can Use DSL—and Who Can't

DSL services are slowly rolling out across the country, first to major cities, and then to smaller cities and towns. As with 56Kbps modems, rural and small-town users are probably out of luck, and should consider satellite-based DirecPC or cable modems if available for a faster-than-56Kbps experience.

Just as we saw that distance to a telephone company's central switch (CS) was an important consideration for people purchasing an ISDN connection, distance also impacts who can use DSL in the markets offering it. Micron Internet Services' DSL FAQ states that you must be within about 18,000 feet (about three miles) *wire distance* (not a straight line!) to a telco offering DSL. Repeaters or a local loop that's been extended by the telco with fiber-optic line may provide longer distances. The speed of your DSL connection will vary with distance: The closer you are to the telco, the faster your DSL access will be. Many telcos that offer some type of DSL service provide Web sites that will help you determine if, and what type of, DSL is available to you.

Note

If you want to connect a DSL to your SOHO or office LAN, check first to see what the provider's attitude is. Some users report good cooperation, while others indicate they were told "we can't help you" or were told that DSL "couldn't be connected to a LAN." Again, check around for the best policies. You can find more information about connecting DSL to a LAN from these newsgroups: `comp.dcom.xdsl` and `pbinet.adsl`. For "field-tested" ADSL information, check out `users.deltanet.com/~ochen/adsl/index.html`.

Major Types of DSL

- *ADSL (Asymmetrical DSL)*. The type of DSL used most often. The name refers to the downstream speeds being much faster than upstream speeds. For most users, this is no problem as we've already seen, because downloads of Web pages, graphics, and files are the major uses of Internet connections. Maximum downstream speeds are up to 1.6Mbps, with up to 640Kbps upstream. Most vendors who offer ADSL will provide varying levels of service at lower speeds and prices as well. Voice calls are routed over the same wire using a small amount of bandwidth, making it possible to have a single-line service that does voice and data. ADSL is more expensive to set up than some other forms of DSL because a splitter must be installed at the customer site, meaning that you must pay for a service call as part of the initial setup charge.

- *CDSL (Consumer DSL).* A slower (1Mbps upstream) form of DSL that was developed by modem chipset maker Rockwell. It doesn't require a service call because there's no splitter required at the customer site.

- *G.Lite (Universal DSL, and also called DSL Lite or splitterless DSL).* Another version that splits the line at the telco end rather than at the consumer end. Downstream speeds range from 1.544–6.0 Mbps, and upstream speeds can be from 128–384Kbps upstream. This may become the most popular form of DSL.

Table 18.3 summarizes the various types of DSL.

Table 18.3   DSL Type Comparison

DSL Type	Description	Data Rate Downstream; Upstream	Distance Limit	Application
IDSL	ISDN Digital Subscriber Line	128Kbps	18,000 feet on 24 gauge wire	Similar to the ISDN BRI service but data only (no voice on the same line)
CDSL	Consumer DSL from Rockwell	1Mbps downstream; less upstream	18,000 feet on 24 gauge wire	Splitterless home and small business service; similar to DSL Lite
DSL Lite (same as G.Lite)	Splitterless DSL without the "truck roll"	From 1.544 Mbps to 6Mbps downstream, depending on the subscribed service	18,000 feet on 24 gauge wire	The standard ADSL; sacrifices speed for not having to install a splitter at the user's home or business
G.Lite (same as DSL Lite)	Splitterless DSL without the "truck roll"	From 1.544 Mbps to 6Mbps, depending on the subscribed service	18,000 feet on 24 gauge wire	The standard ADSL; sacrifices speed for not having to install a splitter at the user's home or business
HDSL	High bit-rate Digital Subscriber Line	1.544Mbps duplex on two twisted-pair lines; 2.048Mbps duplex on three twisted-pair lines	12,000 feet on 24 gauge wire	T-1/E1 service between server and phone company or within a company; WAN, LAN, server access
SDSL	Single-line DSL	1.544Mbps duplex (U.S. and Canada); 2.048Mbps (Europe) on a single duplex line downstream and upstream	12,000 feet on 24 gauge wire	Same as for HDSL but requiring only one line of twisted pair

DSL Type	Description	Data Rate Downstream; Upstream	Distance Limit	Application
ADSL	Asymmetric Digital Subscriber Line	1.544 to 6.1Mbps downstream; 16 to 640Kbps upstream	1.544Mbps at 18,000 feet; 2.048Mbps at 16,000 feet; 6.312Mpbs at 12,000 feet; 8.448Mbps at 9,000 feet	Used for Internet and Web access, motion video, video on demand, remote LAN access
RADSL	Rate-Adaptive DSL from Westell	Adapted to the line, 640Kbps to 2.2Mbps downstream; 272Kbps to 1.088Mbps upstream	Not provided	Similar to ADSL
UDSL	Uni-directional DSL proposed by a company in Europe	Not known	Not known	Similar to HDSL
VDSL	Very high Digital Subscriber Line	12.9 to 52.8Mbps downstream; 1.5 to 2.3 Mbps upstream; 1.6Mbps to 2.3Mbps downstream	4,500 feet at 12.96Mbps; 3,000 feet at 25.82Mbps; 1,000 feet at 51.84Mbps	ATM networks; Fiber to the Neighborhood

Table copyrighted by and used with permission of whatis.com Inc.

DSL Pricing

DSL pricing is "all over the map," with different telephone companies offering widely different speeds of DSL and different rates. One thing that's true about the most commonly used flavors of DSL is that it is usually another asymmetrical service—with download speeds faster than upload speeds.

For unlimited use, typical DSL pricing ranges anywhere from $25–$500 a month depending on the download speed, ranging from 256Kbps–1.5Mbps.

The wide variance is partly due to the upload speeds permitted. The lower-cost plans typically use a lower upload speed (some variation on ADSL or G.Lite), but not always. Check carefully with your vendor, because your traditional telephone company may not be the only xDSL game in town. Some major cities might have as many as a half-dozen vendors selling various flavors of xDSL.

Time Versus Access

So-called *Personal DSL* plans give you an interesting puzzle: time online versus data transfers.

Before the advent of unlimited Internet access, the time you spent online and the speed of your modem were the two variables used to calculate the cost per-hour of services such as the original CompuServe. I remember looking for files on CIS at 2400bps because surfing the site was cheaper that way, noting the files needed, and then hanging up and downloading them at the "blazing" speed of 9,600bps (a speed that cost you extra to use some years ago).

Some Personal DSL plans have gone back to a consumption-based pricing scheme. But with Personal DSL plans, the speed of your connection or the time you spend are unimportant: It's the amount of data transfer you do.

For many people, this won't be a major issue. Micron Internet Service's Personal DSL plan allows up to 500MB of data transfer per month before a surcharge ($10.00 per additional 500MB) is incurred, for example.

Unless you're routinely downloading massive software service packs or working beyond the fringes of legality by downloading entire CDs, this limitation is more apparent than real. Even though every Web page and graphic you view on the Web counts as a file transfer, the sizes of GIF, JPG, and HTML pages are usually miniscule. Still, find out what the file-transfer limitations are before you sign up for any type of metered DSL.

Comparing High-Speed Internet Access

One way of making sense out of the confusing morass of plans available from cable modem, xDSL, and DirecPC vendors is to calculate the average cost per Mbps of data downloaded.

According to *PC Magazine* (April 20, 1999), the cost per Mbps for DirecPC was $229 per Mbps, based on an average FTP download speed of 223.2Kbps. xDSLs provided a wide variance in cost, from as little as $115 per Mbps to as high as $1,091 per Mbps. Cable modems provided the best cost factors, coming in at a range of $67–$184 per Mbps. How did a V.90 modem fare? A whopping $977 per Mbps, based on an average throughput of only 20.9Kbps!

As the study shows, cable modems offer the best performance of the Internet connections tested. Some DSL services were comparable to the medium-priced cable modems, but some were outlandishly expensive for their performance level, providing a higher cost per-Mbps than the V.90 modem.

DirecPC is a good choice for those who lack a reasonably priced cable modem or DSL provider in their area.

Sharing Your High-Speed Internet Access over a LAN—Safely

Because most faster-than-modem Internet access services use a NIC to connect your system to the Internet, it may seem like a good idea to simply run your cable to your Ethernet hub. This creates a built-in security problem (see Figure 18.12).

For safety, add a proxy server or firewall program to your network; or for the best protection, add a router with firewall features (see Figure 18.13). There are many vendors you can choose from.

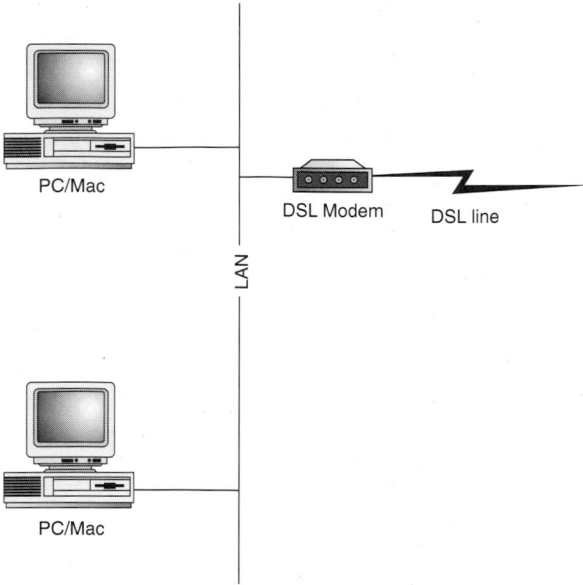

Figure 18.12   With the xDSL or cable modem connection running directly into your network, you can access the Internet, or people on the Internet can access your computer!

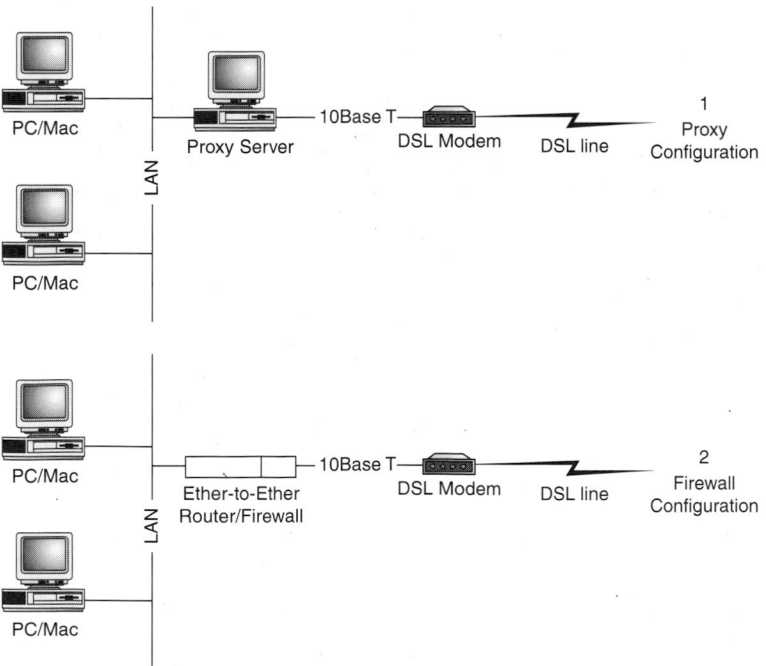

Figure 18.13   Proxy server or firewall software, or a router with firewall support allow your network to access the Internet without risking outside hacking. Combine these with password-protected shared resources for best protection.

Note

Proxy servers and firewalls are an enormous topic which go far beyond the scope of this book. If you want to learn more, I suggest you pick up a copy of *Upgrading and Repairing Networks*, *Second Edition*, also published by Que.

Modem Troubleshooting

Modem Fails to Dial

1. Check line and phone jacks on modem. Use the line jack to attach the modem to the telephone line. The phone jack takes the same RJ-11 silver cord cable, but it's designed to let you daisy-chain a telephone to your modem, so you need only a single line for modem and telephone use. If you've reversed these cables, you'll get no dial tone.

2. If the cables are attached properly, check the cable for cuts or breaks. The shielding used on RJ-11 telephone cables is minimal. If the cable looks bad, replace it.

3. If the modem is external, make sure the RS-232 modem cable is running from the modem to a working serial port on your computer and that it is switched on. Signal lights on the front of the modem can be used to determine if the modem is on and if it is responding to dialing commands.

4. If the modem is a PCMCIA/PC Card, make sure it is fully plugged into the PCMCIA/PC slot. With Windows 9x, you should see a small PCMCIA/PC Card icon on the Toolbar. Double-click on it to view the cards that are currently connected (see Figure 18.14). If your modem is properly attached, it should be visible. Otherwise, remove it, reinsert it into the PCM-CIA/PC Card slot, and see if the computer detects it.

Figure 18.14 This notebook computer has a network card properly installed in its PCMCIA slots, but not a modem. If the modem isn't pushed into the slot firmly, it will appear to be missing.

Connecting a PCMCIA Modem Card via a Dongle

Most PCMCIA modem cards don't use a standard RJ-11 cable because the card is too thin. Instead, they use a connection called a *dongle*, which runs from the PCMCIA Card to the telephone. If this proprietary cable is damaged, your modem is useless. It's a good idea to purchase a spare from the modem vendor and carry it with you. And, if you find the dongle is too short to reach the data jacks in a hotel room, buy a coupler from your local Radio Shack or telephone-parts department and attach a standard RJ-11 cable to your dongle via the coupler.

5. Make sure your modem has been properly configured by your OS. With Windows 9x, use the Modems control panel to view and test your modem configuration. Select your modem and click the Diagnostics tab. This displays the COM (serial) ports in your computer. Select the COM port used by the modem, and click on the More Info tab. This sends test signals to your modem. A properly working modem responds with information about the port and the modem (see Figure 18.15).

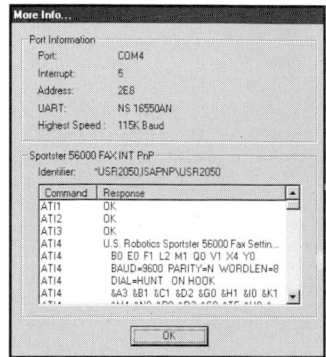

Figure 18.15   The U.S. Robotics 56000 PnP modem was configured to a non-standard IRQ of 5 when it was installed. It contains an up-to-date 16550 UART chip.

6. If you get a `Couldn't Open Port` error message, your modem isn't connected properly. It may be in use already, or there might be an IRQ or I/O port address conflict with another card in your computer. Whether you have a modem installed or not, every COM port that's working will display its IRQ, I/O port address, and UART (Universal Asynchronous Receive-Transmit) chip type when you run Diagnostic. The UART type should be 16550 or above for use with any modern modem.

Note

You can also test your modem response by setting up a HyperTerminal session (discussed earlier) to send the modem commands. If the modem fails to respond, this is another indication of a problem with the modem-PC connection.

Computer Locks Up After Installing Internal Modem

Most likely, you've stumbled across the curse of the shared IRQ. COM 3 shares IRQ 4 with COM 1, and COM 4 shares IRQ 3 with COM 2 by default. The problem is that IRQ sharing for ISA devices (like your COM ports) works when only one device at a time is using the IRQ. The most likely cause for your problem is that your mouse is connected to COM 1, your internal modem is using COM 3, and both COM ports are using the default IRQ of 4. There's no problem as long as the mouse has IRQ 4 all to itself, but the moment you try to use the modem, the computer can't handle two devices trying to use IRQ 4 and locks up. The only solution is to get the internal modem and mouse working on a *separate*, non-conflicting IRQs. You have two options: Move the mouse to another port or disable COM 2 in your computer to make room for an internal modem on COM 2.

Move the Mouse to Another Port

Any mouse that can work on COM 1 can also work on COM 2, usually without any software changes. If both COM 1 and COM 2 are the typical AT-style 9-pin ports, turn off the computer, unplug the mouse from COM 1, plug it back into COM 2, and restart the computer. You should be able to use your mouse and modem at the same time.

If your modem is using COM 4 and your mouse is using COM 2, move the mouse to COM 1 instead. With Windows 9x, use the System Properties Device Manager tab to determine which devices are using what IRQs.

On a few computers, the COM 2 port might be a 25-pin connector. If your mouse didn't ship with an adapter, any computer store will have one. (The 9-pin and 25-pin COM ports are both RS-232, and the adapter will make a device wired for one type of port work with the other.)

If your computer has a PS/2 (6-pin round) mouse port, use it for your mouse instead of tying up a serial port. The PS/2 port uses IRQ 12. If your Pentium-class PC doesn't have a visible PS/2 port, check your system/motherboard instruction manual to see if the motherboard has provision for a PS/2 mouse port header cable. Most Pentium-class baby-AT motherboards have the connector, but some companies don't provide the header cable unless you think to request it (and pay extra!). Check with your system vendor.

Disable COM 2

COM 2, the second serial port, is found on the motherboard of most Pentium-class PCs. To disable it, go into your computer's BIOS setup program, look for the screen that controls built-in ports (such as Onboard Peripherals), and disable the port. Save the changes, exit the setup program, and the system reboots. To see if COM 2 is disabled, use the Windows 9x System Properties sheet Device Manager. Then, set your modem for COM 2, IRQ 3, and install it.

Computer Can't Detect External Modem

1. Make sure the modem has been connected to the computer with the correct type of cable.

   For most external modems, you need an RS-232 modem cable, which will have a 9-pin connector on one end and a 25-pin connector on the other end. Since RS-232 is a very flexible standard encompassing many different pinouts, make sure the cable is constructed according to the following diagram:

PC (with 9-pin COM port - male)		Modem (25-pin port - female)
3	TX data	2
2	RX data	3
7	RTS	4
8	CTS	5
6	DSR	6
5	SIG GND	7
1	CXR	8
4	DTR	20
9	RI	22

If you purchase an RS-232 modem cable prebuilt at a store, you'll have a cable that works with your PC and your modem. However, you can use the preceding chart to build your own cable or, by using a cable tester, determine whether an existing RS-232 cable in your office is actually made for modems or some other device.

2. Make sure the COM (serial) port the modem is connected to is working.

The Windows 9x diagnostics test listed earlier can be useful in this regard, but third-party testing programs such as Touchstone Software's CheckIt, AMIDIAG, and many others have more thorough methods for testing the system's COM ports. These programs can use loop-back plugs to test the serial ports. The loopback plug loops signals that would be sent to the modem or other serial device back to the serial port. These programs normally work best when run from the MS-DOS prompt.

Touchstone Software's CheckIt PRO software uses a loopback plug to test serial ports. You can build the loopback plug yourself, or buy it from the vendor. Loopback plugs will vary in design depending on the vendor.

3. Check the power cord and power switch.

4. Check the USB connector or hub (for USB-based models).

Local Area Networking

SOME OF THE MAIN TOPICS IN THIS CHAPTER ARE

Local Area Networks

Packet Switching Versus Circuit Switching

The Networking Stack

The OSI Reference Model

LAN Hardware Components

Data Link Layer Protocols

High-Speed Networking Technologies

Building a Peer-to-Peer Network

Network Client Software

TCP/IP

Direct Cable Connections

Troubleshooting Network Software Setup

Troubleshooting Networks in Use

Troubleshooting TCP/IP

Troubleshooting Direct Cable Connections

Local Area Networks

A local area network (LAN) enables you to do the following: share files, applications, printers, disk space, modems, faxes, tape backup drives, and CD-ROM drives among different systems; use client/server software products; send electronic mail; and otherwise make a collection of computers work as a team.

In today's world, there are many ways to construct a LAN. As you have seen, a LAN can be as simple as two computers connected via either their serial or parallel ports. Although the term "network" is not often used for this sort of arrangement, it does satisfy the definition.

In most cases, however, computers are connected to a network using a network interface adapter that either takes the form of an expansion card (called a network interface card, or NIC) or is integrated into the computer's motherboard. The adapter in each computer then connects to a cable installation in such a way as to permit any computer on the network to communicate with any other.

Note

Although the vast majority of networked computers are connected by cables, it is also possible to use various wireless technologies such as infrared, lasers, or microwaves as the network medium.

Nearly all LANs are baseband networks, meaning that when a computer transmits its data, the signal occupies the entire bandwidth of the network medium. This is in contrast to a broadband network, on which multiple signals can travel as one. A cable TV network is an example of a broadband network because the signals carrying many different TV channels are all transmitted simultaneously.

Some corporate networks are broadband, such as in cases when PCs are used with terminal-emulation software to communicate with mainframe computers. From the standpoint of the PC user, the change from one band to another is transparent. The user simply switches from a Web browser, for example, to the terminal-emulation program.

Unless the computers that are connected together know they are connected together and agree on a common means of communication and what resources are to be shared, they cannot work together. Networking software is just as important as networking hardware because it establishes the logical connections that make the physical connections work.

At a minimum, each network requires the following:

- Physical (cable) or wireless (IRDA or radio-frequency) connections between computers.
- A common set of communications rules, known as a network protocol.
- Software that enables resources to be shared with other PCs, known as a network operating system.
- Resources that can be shared, such as printers, disk drives, and CD-ROMs.

■ Software that enables computers to access the computer(s) with shared resources, provides some level of access control, and provides some means of distinguishing which computers are active on the network—a network client allows a workstation to access the shared resources on the network.

These rules apply to the simplest, the most powerful, and all networks in between, regardless of their nature.

Client/Server Versus Peer-to-Peer

Although every computer on a LAN is connected to every other, they do not necessarily all communicate with each other. There are two basic types of LANs, based on the communication patterns between the machines, called client/server networks and peer-to-peer networks.

On a client/server network, every computer has a distinct role, either that of a client or a server. A server is designed to share its resources among the client computers on the network. Typically, servers are located in secured areas, such as locked closets and data centers, because they hold the organization's most valuable data and do not have to be accessed by operators on a continuous basis. The rest of the computers on the network function as clients (see Figure 19.1).

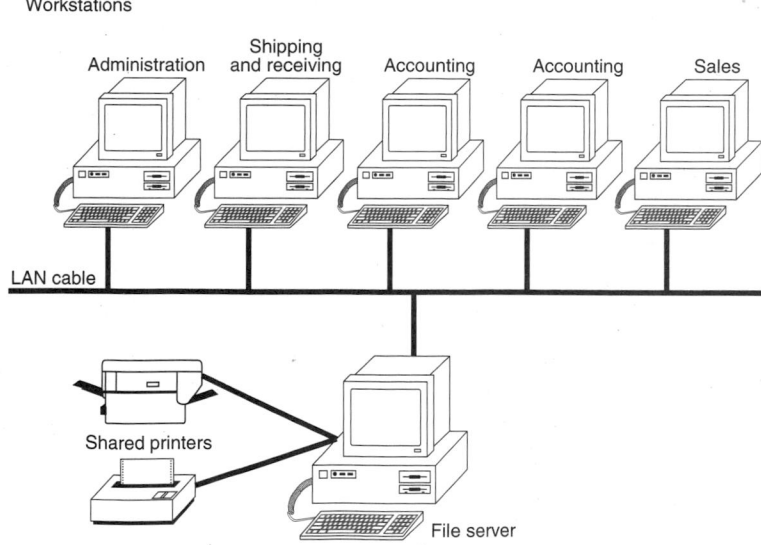

Figure 19.1 The components of a client/server LAN.

A dedicated server computer typically has a faster processor, more memory, and more storage space than a client, as it might have to service dozens or even hundreds of users at the same time. The server runs a special network operating system, such as NetWare, that is designed solely to facilitate the sharing of its resources. These resources can reside on a single server or on a group of servers. When more than one server is used, each server can "specialize" in a particular task (file server, print server, fax server, email server, and so on) or provide redundancy (duplicate servers) in case of server failure. For very demanding computing tasks, several servers can act as a single unit by parallel processing.

A client computer communicates only with servers, not with other clients. A client system is a standard PC that is running an operating system such as DOS or Windows. The only difference is the addition of a client software package that enables the computer to access the resources shared by servers.

By contrast, on a peer-to-peer network, every computer is equal and can communicate with any other computer on the network to which it has been granted access rights (see Figure 19.2). Essentially, every computer on a peer-to-peer network functions as both a server and a client. This is why you might hear about client and server activities, even when the discussion is about a peer-to-peer network. Peer-to-peer networks can be as small as two computers or as large as hundreds of units.

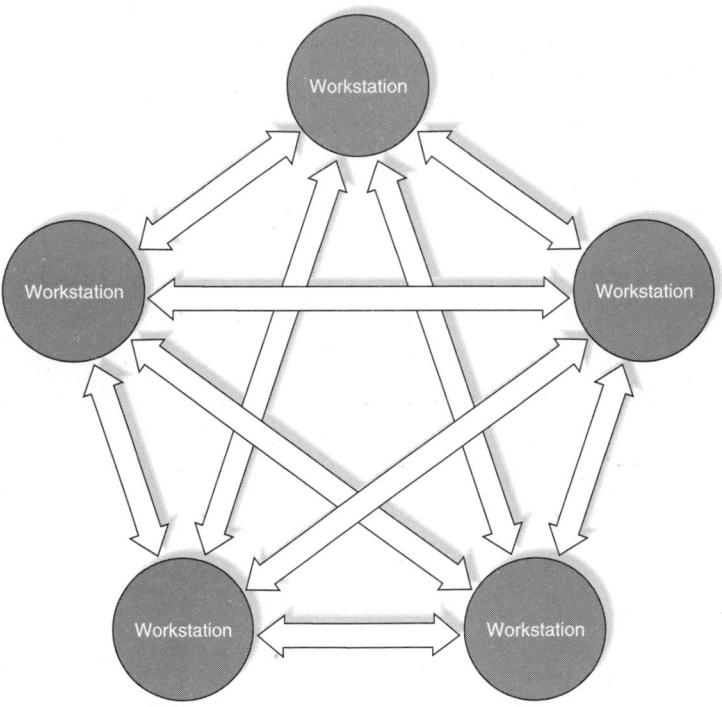

Figure 19.2 The logical architecture of a typical peer-to-peer network.

Peer-to-peer networks are more common in small offices or within a single department of a larger organization. The advantage of a peer-to-peer network is that you don't have to dedicate a computer to function as a file server. Instead, every computer can share its resources with any other. The potential disadvantages to a peer-to-peer network are that there is typically less security and less control because users normally administer their own systems, while client/server networks have the advantage of centralized administration.

Client/server LANs offer enhanced security for shared resources, greater performance, increased backup efficiency for network-based data, and the potential for use of redundant power supplies and RAID drive arrays. Client/server LANs also have a much greater cost to purchase and maintain. Table 19.1 compares client/server and peer-to-peer server networking.

Table 19.1—Comparing Client/Server and Peer-to-Peer Networking

Item	Client/Server	Peer-to-Peer
Access control	Via user/group lists of permissions; single password provides user access to only the resources on his list; users can be given several different levels of access	Via password lists by resource; each resource requires a separate password; all-or-nothing access; no centralized user list
Security	High because access is controlled by user or by group identity	Low because knowing the password gives anybody access to a shared resource
Performance	High because server doesn't waste time or resources handling workstation tasks	Low because servers often act as workstations.
Hardware Cost	High, due to specialized design of server, high-performance nature of hardware, redundancy features	Low because any workstation can become a server by sharing resources
Software Cost	License fees per workstation user are part of the cost of the Network Operating System server software (Windows NT and Windows 2000 Server, Novell NetWare)	Free; all client software is included with any release of Windows 9x and Windows NT Workstation and Windows 2000 Professional
Backup	Centralized when data is stored on server; enables use of high-speed, high-capacity tape backups with advanced cataloging	Left to user decision; usually mixture of backup devices and practices at each workstation
Redundancy	Duplicate power supplies, hot-swappable drive arrays, and even redundant servers are common; network OS normally capable of using redundant devices automatically	No true redundancy among either peer "servers" or clients; failures require manual intervention to correct with high possibility of data loss

Windows 9x and Windows NT have peer-to-peer networking capabilities built into them. Because of Plug-and-Play technology, it is a relatively easy matter to install network interface cards in a collection of Windows 9x systems, connect them with the right kind of cable, and build your own peer-to-peer network.

Packet Switching Versus Circuit Switching

The computers on a LAN must share the same baseband medium, so their communications have to be designed to provide each system with the opportunity to transmit its data. To make this possible, computers break down the data to be transmitted into individual units, called *packets*. The system transmits the packets one at a time, and they travel over the network to the destination, intermingled with packets generated by other machines. At the destination system, the packets are reassembled into their original form. This type of network is called a packet switching network. This method of data handling is used not just in local area network data handling, but also by WANs (wide area networks), the World Wide Web, and other parts of the Internet.

By contrast, a circuit-switching network establishes a connection between the two communicating systems that fully occupies a designated bandwidth all during the session. The two systems transmit their signals over this connection in an unbroken stream because they do not have to share the medium with other systems. The telephone system is an example of a circuit-switching network. One of the challenges of using computers to communicate over telephone lines has been the fundamentally different nature of computer data versus telephone transmissions.

The Networking Stack

Because network client software operates at many levels within each computer, it is often referred to as a stack, that is, a series of modules and services layered atop one another. Earlier in this chapter, you learned about the different types of protocols that modems use to communicate with one another. Networked computers use protocols, too, for the same reason. For two systems to communicate, they must be speaking the same language.

A LAN connection is more complicated than a modem connection, however, and there are many more protocols involved at every layer of the networking stack. For this reason, the networking software is sometimes called the protocol stack. When designing a LAN, there are different protocols available at the various layers of the stack that a network administrator can select to suit a particular environment.

The OSI Reference Model

One of the most commonly used teaching and reference tools in local area networking is called the OSI (Open Systems Interconnection) Reference Model. Developed by the International Organization for Standardization (abbreviated as the ISO) in the 1980s, the OSI model splits a computer's networking stack into seven discrete layers (see Figure 19.3). Each layer provides specific services to the layers above and below it.

At the bottom of the model is the physical side of the network, including cables, NICs, and other hardware. At the top of the model is the application interface that enables you to use your word processor to open a file on a network drive as easily as you can open one on your local drive. In between are layers describing additional services; all combine to make network communications possible. Descriptions of the seven layers follow:

- *Physical*. This part of the OSI model specifies the physical and electrical characteristics of the connections that make up the network (twisted-pair cables, fiber-optic cables, coaxial cables, connectors, repeaters, and other hardware). You can think of this layer as the hardware layer. Although the rest of the layers might be implemented as firmware (that is, chip-level functions on the network adapter) rather than actual software, the other layers are software in relation to this first layer.

- *Data Link*. This layer controls how the electrical impulses enter or leave the network cable. The network's electrical representation of your data (bit patterns, encoding methods, and tokens) is known to this layer and only to this layer. It is here that most errors are detected and corrected (by requesting retransmissions of corrupted packets). In some networking systems, the data link layer is subdivided into a Media Access Control (MAC) layer and a Logical Link Control (LLC) layer. The MAC layer deals with network access (token-passing or collision-sensing) and network control. The LLC layer, operating just above the MAC layer, is concerned with sending and receiving the user data messages. Ethernet and Token Ring are data link layer protocols.

■ *Network*. This layer switches and routes the packets as necessary to get them to their destinations and is responsible for addressing and delivering message packets. Whereas the data link layer is conscious only of the immediately adjacent computers on the network, the network layer is responsible for the entire route of a packet, from source to destination. IP and IPX are examples of network-layer protocols.

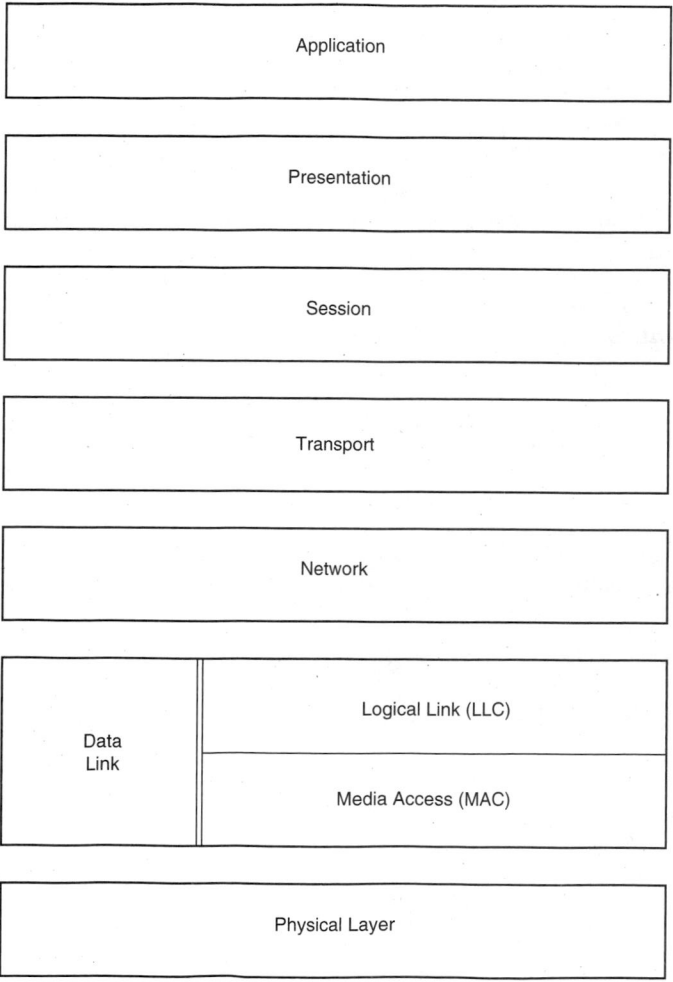

Figure 19.3   The OSI reference model.

Note

The physical, data link, and network layers are all hardware-based, whereas the transport, session, presentation, and application layers are software-based.

■ *Transport*. When more than one packet is in process at any time, such as when a large file must be split into multiple packets for transmission, the transport layer controls the sequencing of the message components and regulates inbound traffic flow. If a duplicate packet arrives, this layer recognizes it as a duplicate and discards it. TCP and SPX are transport-layer protocols.

■ *Session*. The functions in this layer enable applications running at two workstations to coordinate their communications into a single session (which you can think of in terms of a highly structured dialogue). The session layer supports the creation of the session, the management of the packets sent back and forth during the session, and the termination of the session.

■ *Presentation*. When IBM, Apple, DEC, NeXT, and Linux-based computers want to talk to one another, obviously a certain amount of translation and byte reordering needs to be done. The presentation layer converts data into an interim format for transmission over the network and back into the machine's native format afterward.

■ *Application*. This layer defines the interface to the applications running on a networked computer. Application-layer protocols can be programs in themselves (such as FTP), or they can be used by other programs (as SMTP, the Simple Mail Transfer Protocol, is used by most email applications) to redirect data to the network.

It is important to understand that although the OSI model was designed to be a model for the development of actual networking software, the products used on today's LANs do not exactly correspond to these layers. Although you might find that certain protocols fall neatly within the boundaries between the layers, others might overlap or provide services that span several layers. As mentioned earlier, the model is primarily used as a tool for teaching networking and as a reference tool for networking professionals.

As Figure 19.4 shows, when multiple computers are involved in carrying data between the source and destination computers (as on the WWW), only the first three layers of the OSI model are used by the intermediate computers. The sending and receiving computers must perform the tasks listed in all seven layers of the OSI model.

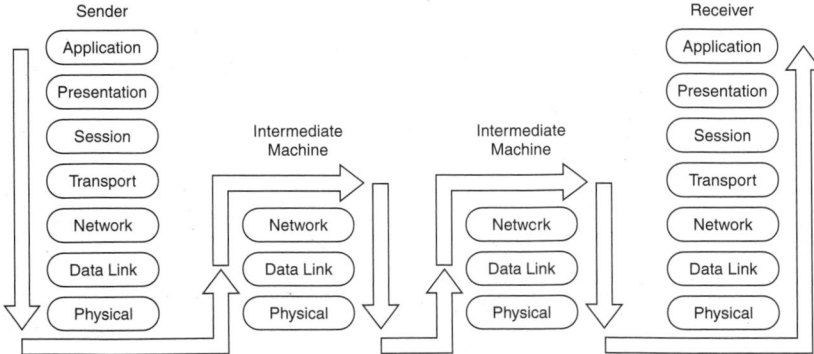

Figure 19.4 Only the first three layers of the OSI model are used by intermediate computers.

Different networks have different names for the software and hardware components they use to correspond to the OSI seven-layer model. In some cases, networks use a single protocol to perform the tasks in two adjacent OSI layers.

Data Encapsulation

The data packets transmitted over a LAN originate at the top of a computer's protocol stack, at the application layer of the OSI model. This is the application data in its simplest form, such as a request for a file stored on another machine or a print job destined for a network printer. As the data travels down through the layers of the protocol stack, it is packaged for its trip across the network. This packaging consists of information provided by each protocol in the stack and intended for the equivalent protocol in the destination computer. Each protocol adds its own information to the data it receives from the layer above in the form of a frame. A frame consists of a header and sometimes a footer added to the beginning (and possibly the end) of a packet. The header and footer are simply additional bytes of data containing specialized control information used to get the packet to its destination.

Thus, when a file request is passed down from the application layer, the next protocol it encounters is usually at the transport layer (because there are no specific presentation layer and session layer protocols). The transport layer takes the data from the application layer, adds its own header, and passes it down to the network layer. The network takes the transport-layer data (including the transport header) and adds its own header before passing it down to the data link layer. The data link layer protocol is unique in that it adds a footer in addition to a header.

This process is called *data encapsulation*. By the time the packet is introduced to the network cable, it has been encapsulated three times or more and consists of a frame within a frame within a frame (see Figure 19.5).

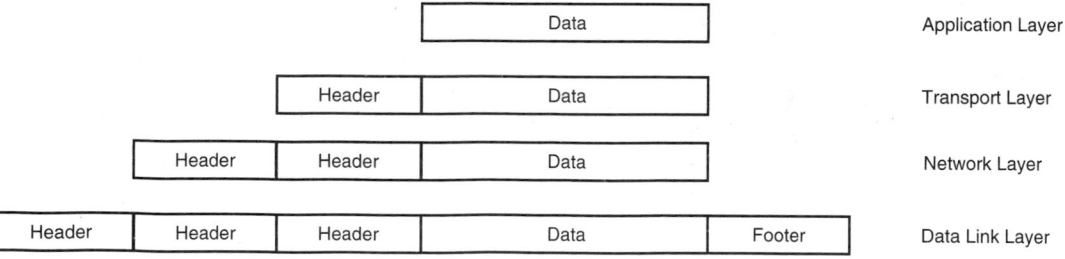

Figure 19.5   Each protocol in a computer's networking stack encapsulates the data it receives from the layer above by adding its own header.

When the packet arrives at its destination, it travels up through the protocol stack, and each frame is removed in the reverse order from which it was applied. In this way, the protocols at each layer in the stack communicate indirectly with their equivalent protocols in the other computer (see Figure 19.6).

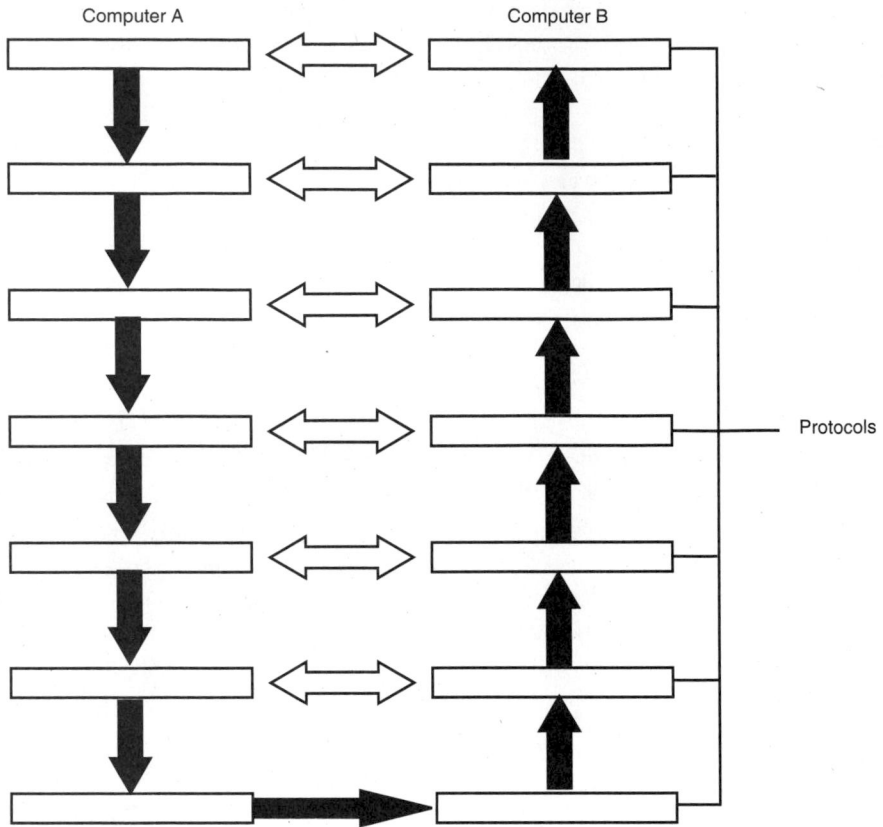

Figure 19.6 Protocols in the networking stack communicate indirectly with their equivalent protocols in other computers.

LAN Hardware Components

Although you can connect virtually any PC to a network, you should use a different set of hardware evaluation criteria when building or purchasing a computer specifically for network use. The following sections examine the types of computers typically found on networks and the other hardware involved, such as network interface adapters and cable types.

Although all the PCs on a network use the same basic components as a standalone system, tradition and experience have resulted in two major hardware profiles: client workstations (which I will refer to simply as "client PCs" to avoid confusion with CAD and graphics workstations) and servers. Client PCs are usually operated by users on their individual desktops, whereas servers are usually located in a secured area. On a client/server network, the client PC is used only by the person sitting in front of it, whereas a server enables many people to share its resources. As a general rule, servers are more powerful machines than client PCs because they must service many different users at once.

On a peer-to-peer network, however, the distinction begins to blur. Because client PCs might also function as servers, it can be necessary to equip them with more powerful components. Technically, there is no reason why you cannot buy a PC marketed as a client PC or a standalone system and use it as a server, as long as it has sufficient resources to run the server software. However, most PC manufacturers sell computers that are specifically designed to function as servers. These machines might have specialized components designed for heavy use and fault tolerance, and you pay more as a result.

Client PCs

The configuration of a client PC is largely dependent on the operating system that you intend to use. DOS and Windows 3.1, for example, can get by on 8MB of RAM, whereas Windows 9x needs at least 16–32MB, and Windows NT should have a minimum of 32MB, with 64MB of RAM desirable, especially for machines that will be upgraded to Windows 2000. In the same way, a Windows NT or Windows 2000 machine should have a faster processor and more hard drive space. Today, the minimum system you can buy typically features a 333MHz or higher Pentium-class processor, but client PCs tend to use the lower-speed versions that have been on the market for a while and are therefore lower in price. The big difference between a client PC and a stand-alone system, however, is that you should consider what resources will be available on the network. If you plan to have users storing their data on network drives, for example, you can equip workstations with smaller hard drives. In the same way, you might want to question whether your client PCs need CD-ROMs if you can provide access to networked units.

You also should consider the environment in which the workstations will be used. It might not be a good idea to equip PCs with audio adapters and speakers if you are going to have a lot of computers in a single room. Of course, if sound support is needed, headphones could be used in place of speakers. Also, computers that use a Slimline case might be appreciated by users with limited workspace.

Servers

A network server is far more likely to be a top-of-the-line PC with the fastest processor available, a lot of RAM, and a large amount of hard disk space. Servers must be high-quality, heavy-duty machines because in serving the whole network, they do many times the work of an ordinary workstation computer. You might type on the server's keyboard only a couple of times a day, and you might glance at its monitor only infrequently. The server's CPU and hard disk drives, however, take the brunt of responding to the file-service requests of all the workstations on the LAN.

Server Processors

The processor in a server should be the most advanced and the fastest that you can afford. Right now, a Pentium II Xeon or Pentium III Xeon is preferable, but new models are being released at shorter and shorter intervals. Servers do more multitasking than any workstation, and the faster the processor is, the more efficient the server will be. However, reliability should also be a major concern. A server is not the place to test out new technology. A client/server network such as Microsoft Windows 2000 Server, Windows NT Server, Novell NetWare, or IBM OS/2 will support multiple processors for support of large numbers of workstations. If you want your server to be able to support two or more processors, make sure that it has provision for multiple processors. Depending on your needs and system configuration, multiple-processor systems can provide these benefits:

■ Scalability for growing networks to keep server performance at a high level as more workstations are growing.

■ Redundancy, enabling another processor to take over if the primary unit fails.

◀◀ See "P6 (686) Sixth-Generation Processors," p. 151.

Server Memory

Servers often require large amounts of memory, much more than workstations. The minimum is usually 64MB these days, but you might need more, depending on the software you intend to run and how much disk space you have installed in the server. Both Windows NT and NetWare run better when they have more than the recommended amount of memory.

It's also a good idea when shopping for a server to be aware of the number of memory slots on the motherboard and the maximum amount of RAM that it supports. Check also how the memory that comes with the computer is configured. A machine with a single 64MB DIMM is easier to upgrade than one with 16MB modules filling all four slots.

For added reliability, consider using memory that supports ECC (Error Correcting) functions if your server supports this feature. ECC memory, when used with a motherboard chip set for ECC support, can actually correct single-bit memory errors and detect multibit memory errors.

◀◀ See "Physical RAM Memory," p. 435.

Server Storage

Hard disk drives are often the most important components in a server. File sharing is one of the primary reasons for networking computers, and the server's hard drives need to be durable, reliable, and geared to the task of serving multiple users simultaneously. For this reason, SCSI hard drives are preferred over IDE drives in today's servers. Although very fast IDE drives are now available, SCSI is still the preferred solution because of its intelligence (causing lower CPU utilization), faster spin rates (equaling higher transfer rates), very high drive-to-unit data-transfer rates with Ultra2Wide SCSI, and time-tested support for drive redundancy with RAID (see the following).

For peer-to-peer networking, IDE drives are quite sufficient, but client/server networking needs the extra performance and reliability features of SCSI, despite the higher cost of the drives and interface cards.

◀◀ See "Small Computer System Interface (SCSI)," p. 530.

The hard disk drives should be large and fast, although in some cases the highest capacity drive available is not necessarily the best choice. When you consider that the server will be processing the file requests of many users simultaneously, it can be more efficient to have, for example, nine 1GB SCSI hard drives rather than one 9GB drive. That way, the requests can be spread across several different units, rather than queued up waiting for one device.

Aside from standard hard disk drives, there are also more elaborate mass storage products on the market that are specifically designed for use with servers. Hard drive arrays can house large numbers of drives and use disk mirroring or RAID (Redundant Array of Inexpensive Disks) to provide fault tolerance. These are technologies that automatically store multiple copies of the server data on various hard drives, so in the event of a drive failure, all the data remains available to users. On some of these arrays, the drives might even be hot-swappable, meaning that you can replace a malfunctioning drive while the machine is still running.

The best version of RAID for use on servers is RAID 5, supported by all current versions of client/server network operating systems. RAID 5 "stripes" the data across multiple SCSI drives, enabling the contents of a single crashed drive to be rebuilt from information on the other drives in the array. When combined with a server that enables "hot-swapping" of drives and power supplies, RAID 5 helps you move closer to continuous 24×7 uptime for your server.

Table 19.2 summarizes the major levels of RAID available.

Table 19.2   RAID Levels Summary

RAID Level	Features	Notes
0	Data transferred in parallel across several drives; no redundancy	Creates a single logical drive from several drives without any failure recovery capabilities; useful for high-bandwidth data handling such as video and image editing
1	Disk mirroring; data written to one drive is duplicated on another	Has been implemented on EIDE as well as SCSI-based drive pairs; requires only two identical drives and special interface card; can be implemented on client PCs as well as servers; hardware implementation more reliable and faster than software implementations
2	Bit interleaving across 32 drives with parity information created on 7 drives	Very expensive in hardware costs, but offers fast performance; suitable for enterprise-level servers
3	Data striping across multiple drives; parity information stored on a dedicated drive; implemented at byte level	Popular choice for data integrity at a relatively low hardware cost; three drive minimum
4	Data striping across multiple drives; parity information stored on a dedicated drive; implemented at block level	Not widely supported on PC servers; difficult to rebuild lost data in case of drive replacement; poor performance
5	Error-correction data striped across all drives in the array; concurrent read/write	Most powerful form of RAID; allows easy "hot swapping" of any failed drive with appropriate server hardware; three drive minimum

Although a server will usually have a CD-ROM drive in it to install software, if nothing else, you might want to have additional CD-ROM drives to share with network users. There are many

CD-ROM changer and drive-array products on the market that enable you to provide users with continuous access to large amounts of CD-ROM–based information.

A CD-ROM changer is a device that holds multiple disks and swaps them in and out of one or more drives. A CD-ROM drive array is a collection of drives in a single housing that share one power supply. A drive array is more expensive than a changer, but all the disks are immediately available.

Server Backups

If you value the data stored on your server at all, making regular backups of your server drives is a necessity. For this purpose, you will probably want to install a SCSI tape drive on your server. Not every server needs its own tape drive, however, because network backup software products can use a single drive to protect data from multiple servers and workstations.

Server Power Supplies

In a server, the power supply is an important but often overlooked item. As with any PC, be sure that the power supply delivers enough current to run all the devices in the computer. On a server, this might require a 400-watt supply or more, as servers typically contain more drives than client PCs do. Client PCs typically have 200-watt power supplies if they are built on a midtower chassis; Slimline clients, such as those based on the NLX chassis, typically have even smaller power supplies, such as the 145-watt units used on the Toshiba Equium series.

Power supply failures and malfunctions can also cause problems elsewhere in the computer that are difficult to diagnose. Your file server might display a message indicating that a RAM chip has failed and then stop; the cause of the problem might indeed be a failed RAM chip, or the problem might be in the power supply.

▶▶ See "Power Supply Troubleshooting," p. 1124.

Power supply fans sometimes stop working or become obstructed with dust and dirt. As a result, the computer overheats and fails completely or acts strangely. Cleaning the fan(s)—after unplugging the computer from the wall outlet, of course—should be a part of the regular maintenance of your file server.

Some servers include redundant fans and power supplies that enable the computer to keep running even when a power supply fails. In other models, the redundant power supplies are hot-swappable, providing even more fault tolerance.

You should also take steps to protect your server from variances in the voltage of its AC power supply (sags and spikes). To make your server as reliable as possible, you should install an uninterruptible power supply (UPS) between the electric power source and the server. The UPS not only provides electricity in case of a power failure, but it also conditions the line to protect the server from voltage fluctuations.

Many UPSs also include a cable that connects to the server's serial port and software that automatically shuts down the operating system when the AC power fails for a given period of time. This ensures that server data is not corrupted by an improper system shutdown.

Server Keyboards, Monitors, and Mice

One area where you can safely skimp when purchasing a server is the user interface components, such as the keyboard, monitor, and mouse (if any). Because these items receive far less use than their workstation counterparts, you can use lower quality, less-expensive components here. A typical file server runs unattended and might go for hours or days without interaction from you. You can turn off the monitor for these long periods.

Network Interface Adapters

The network interface adapter is the PC's link to all the other computers on the network. All file requests and other network communications enter and leave the computer through the network adapter. Figure 19.7 shows a typical network interface adapter card that you might install in a server or workstation. Although servers for small networks might well use the same network interface card (NIC) as the client PCs do, there are increasingly popular NICs designed for server use. It serves no purpose to install a high-speed adapter in a server if the network clients do not also support that same speed. The only difference that you might find is that a server might have more than one adapter to connect to multiple networks.

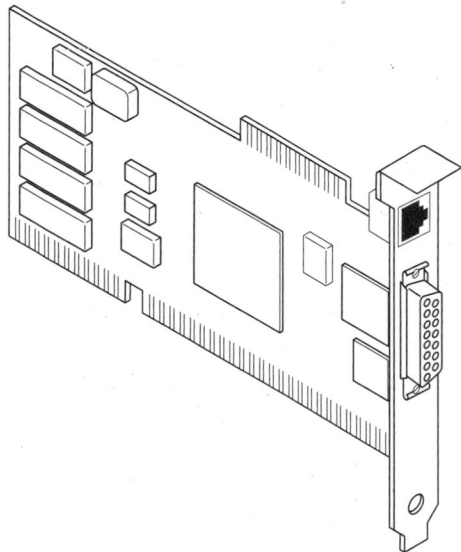

Figure 19.7   The network interface adapter sends and receives messages to and from all the computers on the LAN.

All the network interface adapters on a LAN are designed to use Ethernet, Token Ring, or some other data link layer protocol. Before you purchase adapter cards (or network cables, for that matter), you must decide which data link protocol you want to use. You can find network interface adapters for each of these protocols, however, that perform better than others. A particular network adapter might be faster at processing messages because it has a large amount of onboard memory (RAM), because it contains its own microprocessor, or perhaps because the adapter uses a PCI bus rather than ISA and thus can transfer more data to and from the CPU at one time.

Table 19.3 summarizes the major types of network protocols.

Table 19.3   Network Protocol Summary

Network Type	Speed	Maximum Number of Stations	Cable Types	Notes
ARCnet	2.5Mbps	255 stations	RG-62 coax UTP/Type 1 STP	Obsolete for new instalations; was used to replace IBM 3270 terminals (which used the same coax cable)
Ethernet	10Mbps	Per segment: 10BaseT- 2 10Base2- 30 10Base5-100 10BaseFL-2	UTP Cat 3 (10BaseT), Thicknet (coax; 10Base5), Thinnet (RG-58 coax; 10Base2), Fiber optic (10BaseF)	Being replaced by Fast Ethernet; can be interconnected with Fast Ethernet by use of dual-speed hubs and switches; use switches and routers to overcome "5-4-3" rule in building very large networks
Fast Ethernet	100Mbps	Per segment: 2	Cat 5 UTP	Fast Ethernet can be interconnected with standard Ethernet through use of dual-speed hubs, switches, and routers
Token Ring	4Mbps or 16Mbps	72 on UTP 250-260 on type 1 STP	UTP, Type 1 STP, and Fiber Optic	High price for NICs and MAUs to interconnect clients; primarily used with IBM mid-size and mainframe systems

On most computers, the network interface adapter takes the form of a network interface card, or NIC, that fits into a slot in each computer. Some systems incorporate the network interface adapter onto the motherboard, but this practice is more commonly found in workstations and rarely in servers because most network administrators prefer to select their own.

Ethernet and Token-Ring adapters have unique hardware addresses coded into their firmware. The data link layer protocol uses these addresses to identify the other systems on the network. A packet gets to the right destination because its data link layer protocol header contains the hardware addresses of both the sending and receiving systems.

Network adapters range in price from well under $100 to as much as $300. What do you get for your money?

- First, you get speed. The faster adapters can push data faster onto the cable, which means that a server can receive a request more quickly and send back a response more quickly. The speed of a network adapter is based in large part on its bus type (see the following) and the network type it supports.

- Second, you get special server features to improve reliability. Although a file server's NIC can be the same as a workstation's, there are special features available that should be considered in choosing a NIC for server use.

Bus Type

The EISA bus, a 32-bit version of the venerable 16-bit ISA bus, was never popular for workstation use, but has found itself in frequent use in older servers. If your server gives you a choice between ISA and EISA NICs, choose EISA because of its wider data bus. Even though EISA was designed to enable the use of ISA cards, using them can slow down the entire bus.

Most modern servers now feature PCI expansion slots, which offer both a 32-bit data bus and slot speeds up to four times faster than ISA. Servers also frequently feature a newer version of PCI that uses three bus connectors, rather than two on each card. This is a 64-bit version of PCI, providing twice the data bus of normal 32-bit PCI and eight times the data bus width of ISA. Use a 64-bit PCI NIC if you have this type of slot.

For servers, it's important to purchase NICs that have the desired server-optimized features (see the preceding text) and the fastest bus speed. Table 19.4 summarizes the bus choices you have for server NICs.

Table 19.4   Bus Choices for Server NICs

Slot Type	Speed	Bus Width	Preference
PCI 64-bit	33MHz[1]	64-bit	Best
PCI 32-bit	33MHz[1]	32-bit	Second choice
EISA	8.33MHz[2]	32-bit	Third choice

1 PCI speed of 33MHz assumes a motherboard (frontside bus) speed of 66MHz or 100MHz; other motherboard speeds would cause this to vary.

2 ISA speed of 8.33MHz assumes default of PCI clock speed/4; variations in motherboard speed or PCI clock divisor could cause this to vary.

Data Transfer Speeds on a LAN

Electrical engineers and networking professionals measure the speed of a network in megabits per second (Mbps). Because a byte of information consists of 8 bits, you can divide the megabits per second rating by 8 to find out how many millions of characters (bytes) per second the network can theoretically handle. In practice, however, a LAN is slower than its rated speed. In fact, a LAN is no faster than its slowest component. A slow hard disk drive can make it seem as though the LAN is performing poorly, when the problem is actually inside one of the computers. This multitude of possible causes can make diagnosing networking problems difficult.

Network Adapter Connectors

Ethernet adapters typically have a connector that looks like a large telephone jack called an RJ45 (for 10BaseT cables), a single BNC connector (for Thinnet), or a D-shaped 15-pin connector called a DB15 (for Thicknet). Some adapters have a combination of two or all three of these connector types. Token Ring adapters can have a 9-pin connector called a DB9 or sometimes an RJ45 jack. Figure 19.8 shows a high-performance Token-Ring adapter with both kinds of connectors.

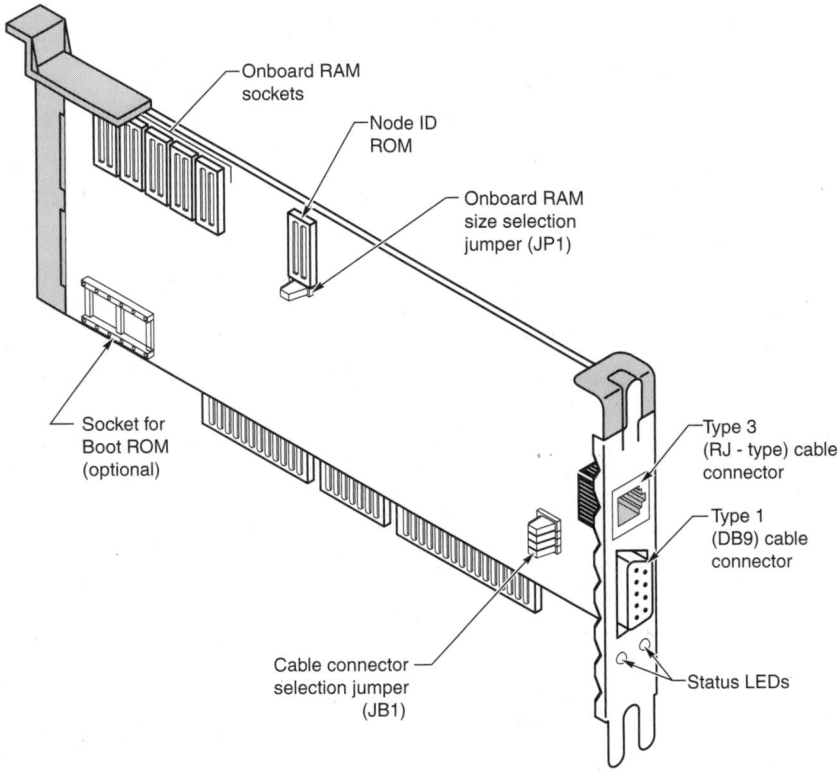

Figure 19.8 The Thomas-Conrad 16/4 Token-Ring adapter (with DB9 and RJ45 connectors).

Cards with two or more connectors enable you to choose from a wider variety of LAN cables. An Ethernet card with two connectors, for example, can enable you to use either unshielded twisted-pair (UTP) or thin Ethernet (Thinnet) cable. You cannot use both connectors at the same time, however, except on special adapters designed specifically for this purpose.

Network Adapter Functions

The LAN adapter card in your PC receives all the traffic going by on the network cable, accepts only the packets destined for your computer, and discards the rest. The adapter then hands these packets over to the system CPU for further processing. The packets then begin their journey up the rest of the networking stack to the application that is their final destination.

When your computer wants to transmit data, the network adapter waits for the appropriate time (determined by which data link layer protocol it uses) and inserts the packets into the data stream. The receiving system notifies your computer as to whether the message arrived intact; if it was garbled, your machine resends.

The network adapter, along with the adapter driver installed on the computer, also participates in the preparation of the data for transmission. A network adapter performs seven major functions during the process of sending or receiving every packet. When sending data out to the network, the adapter performs the steps in the order presented in the following list. When it receives data, the steps are reversed. The seven steps are as follows:

1. *Data transfer.* Data is transferred from PC memory (RAM) to the network interface adapter or from the adapter to PC memory via DMA, shared memory, or programmed I/O.

2. *Buffering.* While being processed by the network adapter, data is stored in a buffer. The buffer enables the adapter to access an entire frame simultaneously so that it can manage the difference between the data rate of the network and the rate at which the PC can process data.

3. *Frame formation.* The network adapter breaks up the data into manageable chunks (or on reception, reassembles it). On an Ethernet network, these chunks are about 1,500 bytes. Token-Ring networks generally use a frame size of about 4KB. The adapter encapsulates the data packet with a header and footer, forming the data link layer frame. At this point, the packet is complete and ready for transmission. (For inbound packets, the adapter reads and removes the header and footer at this stage.)

4. *Media access.* The network adapter uses the appropriate media access control mechanism for the data link layer protocol to regulate its transmissions. On an Ethernet network, the network adapter ensures that the line is quiet before sending its data (or retransmits its data if a collision occurs). On a Token-Ring network, the adapter waits until it receives a token that it can claim. When it has a token, the adapter can transmit its data. (These steps are not applicable to incoming traffic, of course.)

5. *Parallel/serial conversion.* The network adapter receives (or sends) data over the system bus in parallel fashion, either 16 or 32 bits at a time, and stores it in the buffer. The data in the buffer must be sent or received through the network cables in serial fashion with one bit following the next. The adapter card converts between these two formats in the split second before transmission (or after reception).

6. *Encoding/decoding.* The network adapter encodes the data it receives over the system bus into the electrical signals that are carried by the network cable and decodes the signals arriving from the network. Ethernet adapters use a technique called Manchester encoding, whereas Token-Ring adapters use a slightly different scheme called Differential Manchester. These techniques have the advantage of incorporating timing information into the data through the use of bit periods. Instead of representing a 0 as the absence of electricity and a 1 as its presence, the 0s and 1s are represented by changes in polarity as they occur in relation to very small time periods.

7. *Sending/receiving impulses.* The adapter takes the electrically encoded impulses that comprise the data (frame), amplifies them, and sends them through the wire. (On reception, the adapter passes the incoming impulses to the decoding step.)

Of course, the execution of all these steps takes only a fraction of a second. While you were reading about these steps, thousands of frames could have been sent across the LAN.

Network adapter cards and the support software recognize and handle errors that occur when electrical interference, packet collisions (in Ethernet networks), or malfunctioning equipment cause some portion of a frame to be corrupted. Adapters generally detect errors through the use of a cyclic redundancy check (CRC) value computed by the sending system and included in the outgoing frame's footer. The same CRC calculation is performed by the receiving system. If its own calculated CRC doesn't match the value of the CRC in the frame, the receiver tells the sender about the error and requests retransmission of the bad frame.

Cables and Connectors

Generally speaking, the cabling systems described in the next few sections use one of three distinct cable types. These are twisted-pair (in shielded and unshielded varieties known as STP and UTP, 10BaseT, or 100BaseT), coaxial in thin and thick varieties (known as 10Base2 and 10Base5, respectively), and fiber optic. The kind of cable you use depends mostly on the data link layer protocol that you elect to use, the conditions at the network site, and of course, your budget. All the major data link layer protocols used on LANs (such as Ethernet and Token Ring) include highly specific guidelines for the installation of the network cable as part of their specifications. Technically, these guidelines are part of the physical layer, but this is one example of how protocols in the real world do not conform exactly to the OSI model.

Twisted-Pair Cable

Twisted-pair cable is just what its name implies: insulated wires within a protective casing with a specified number of twists per foot. Twisting the wires reduces the effect of electromagnetic interference (that can be generated by nearby cables, electric motors, and fluorescent lighting) on the signals being transmitted. Shielded twisted pair (STP) refers to the amount of insulation around the cluster of wires and therefore its immunity to noise. You are probably familiar with unshielded twisted-pair (UTP) cable; it is often used for telephone wiring. Figure 19.9 shows unshielded twisted-pair cable; Figure 19.10 illustrates shielded twisted-pair cable.

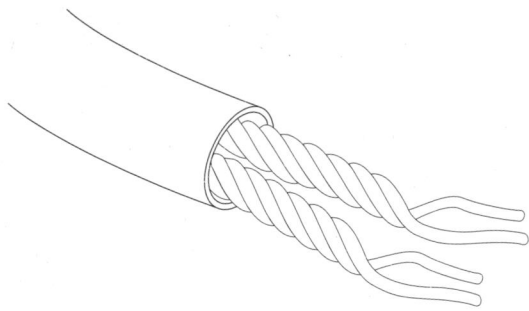

Figure 19.9   An unshielded twisted-pair cable.

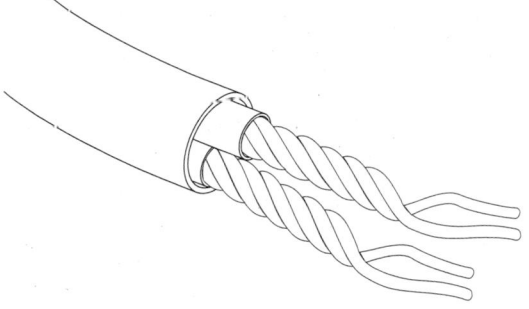

Figure 19.10   A shielded twisted-pair cable.

Shielded Versus Unshielded Twisted Pair

When cabling was being developed for use with computers, it was first thought that shielding the cable from external interference was the best way to reduce interference and provide for greater transmission speeds. However, it was discovered that twisting the pairs of wires is a more effective way to prevent interference from disrupting transmissions. As a result, earlier cabling scenarios relied on shielded cables rather than the unshielded cables more commonly in use today.

Shielded cables also have some special grounding concerns because one, and only one, end of a shielded cable should be connected to an earth ground; issues arose where people inadvertently caused grounding loops to occur by connecting both ends or caused the shield to act as an antenna because it wasn't grounded.

Grounding loops are situations where two different grounds are tied together. This is a bad situation because each ground can have a slightly different potential, resulting in a circuit that has very low voltage but infinite amperage. This causes undue stress on electrical components and can be a fire hazard.

Coaxial Cable

Coaxial cable is fairly prevalent in your everyday life, as it is the standard medium used both by cable TV networks and for antenna connections. Thin and thick, of course, refer to the diameter of the coaxial cable itself. Standard Ethernet cable (Thick Ethernet), rarely used for networking today, is as thick as your thumb. Thin Ethernet cable (sometimes called Thinnet or CheaperNet; RG-58) is slightly narrower than your little finger. The thick cable has a greater degree of noise immunity, is more difficult to damage, and requires a vampire tap (a connector with teeth that pierce the tough outer insulation) and a drop cable to connect to a workstation. Although thin coaxial cable carries the signal over shorter distances than the thick cable, it is lower in cost (hence the name CheaperNet) and uses a simple, bayonet-locking connector called a BNC (Bayonet-Neill-Concelman) connector to attach to workstations. Thin Ethernet was at one time the standard for Ethernet networking, but it has since been replaced by 10BaseT (unshielded twisted pair). Thinnet is wired directly to the back of each computer on the network and generally installs much more easily than Thicknet, but it is more prone to signal interference and physical connection problems.

Figure 19.11 shows an Ethernet BNC coaxial T-connector, and Figure 19.12 illustrates the design of coaxial cable.

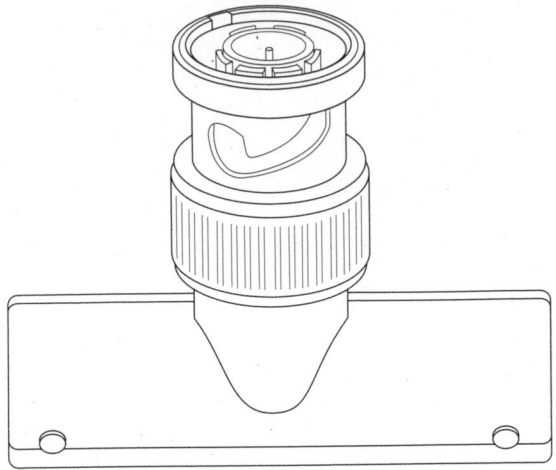

Figure 19.11   An Ethernet coaxial cable T-connector.

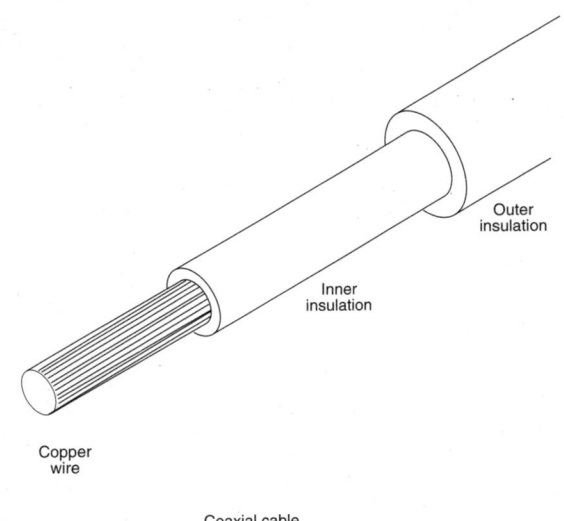

Figure 19.12   Coaxial cable.

Fiber-Optic Cable

Fiber-optic cable uses pulses of light rather than electrical signals to carry information. It is therefore completely resistant to the electromagnetic interference that limits the length of copper cables. Attenuation (the weakening of a signal as it traverses the cable) is also less of a problem, enabling fiber to send data over huge distances at high speeds. It is, however, very expensive and difficult to install and maintain. Splicing the cable, installing connectors, and using the few available diagnostic tools for finding cable faults are skills that very few people have.

Tip

Fiber-optic cable is often used to connect buildings together in a campus network environment for two very important reasons. One is that fiber can travel approximately 2.2km, whereas copper-based technologies are significantly more restricted. The other reason is that because fiber does not use electrical signals, it eliminates the problems with differing ground sources.

Fiber-optic cable is simply designed but unforgiving of bad connections. It usually consists of a core of glass thread with a diameter measured in microns (millionths of a meter), surrounded by a solid glass cladding. This, in turn, is covered by a protective sheath. The first fiber-optic cables were made of glass, but plastic fibers also have been developed. The light source for fiber-optic cable is a light-emitting diode (LED); information usually is encoded by varying the intensity of the light. A detector at the other end of the cable converts the incoming signal back into electrical impulses. Two types of fiber-optic cable exist: single mode and multimode. Single mode has a smaller diameter, is more expensive, and can carry signals over a greater distance.

Figure 19.13 illustrates fiber-optic cables and their connectors. Multimode has a diameter five to ten times greater than single mode, making it easier to connect. This ease of use makes it the most commonly used fiber. However, multimode suffers from higher distortion and lower bandwidth.

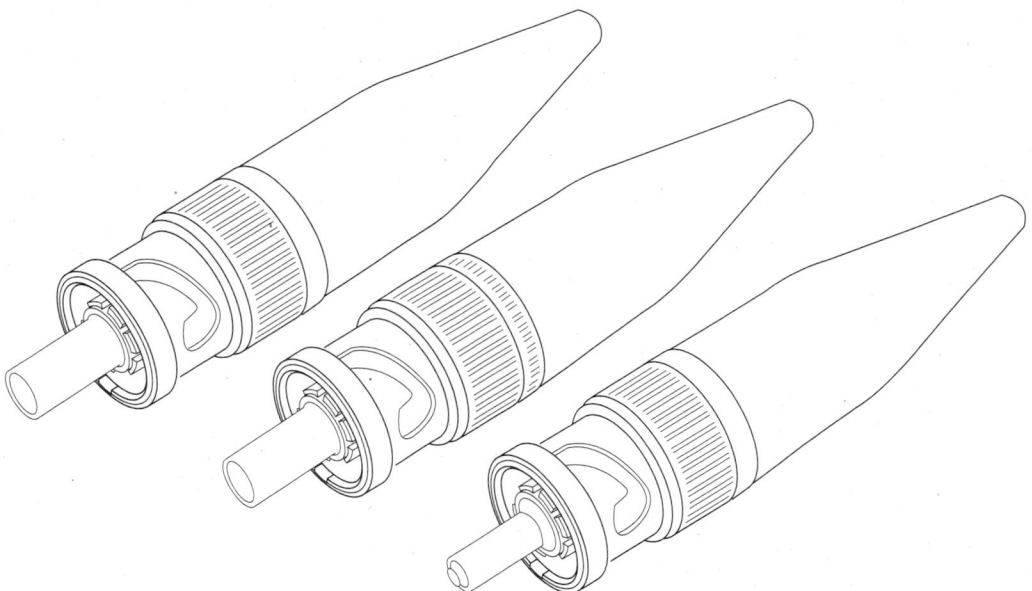

Figure 19.13   Fiber-optic cables use light to carry LAN messages. The ST connector is commonly used with fiber-optic cables. ·

Network Topologies

Each computer on the network is connected to the other computers with cable (or some other medium). Sometimes a single piece of cable winds from station to station, visiting all the network's computers along the way. This cabling arrangement is called a *bus topology*, as shown in Figure 19.14. (A topology is a description of the way the workstations and servers are physically connected.) The potential disadvantage to this type of wiring is that if one computer or cable connection malfunctions, it can cause all the stations beyond it on the bus to lose their network connections. Thin and thick Ethernet coaxial cables are typically installed using a bus topology.

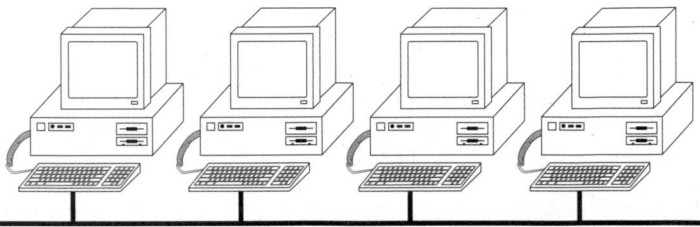

Figure 19.14 The linear bus topology, attaching all network devices to a common cable.

Another type of topology uses separate cables to connect each computer to a central wiring nexus, often called a hub or a concentrator. Figure 19.15 shows this arrangement, which is called a *star topology*. Because each computer uses a separate cable, the failure of a network connection affects only the single machine involved. The other computers can continue to function normally. Bus cabling schemes use less cable than the star but are harder to diagnose or bypass when problems occur. At this time, Ethernet using 10BaseT cable in a star topology is the most commonly implemented type of LAN.

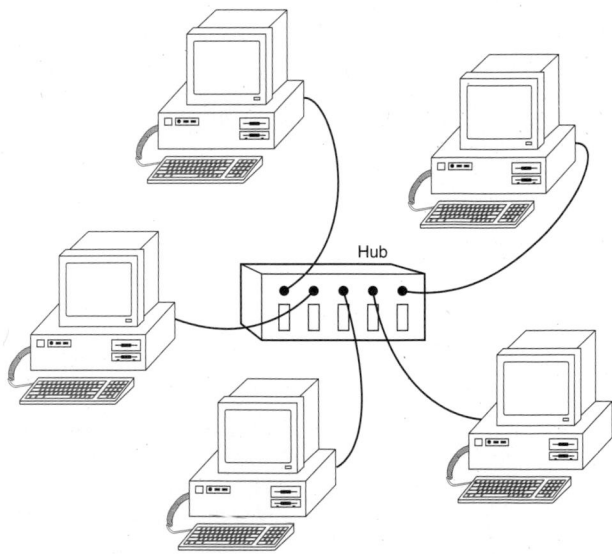

Figure 19.15 The star topology, linking the LAN's computers and devices to one or more central hubs, or access units.

The other topology often listed in discussions of this type is a *ring*, in which each workstation is connected to the next, and the last workstation is connected to the first again (essentially a bus topology with the two ends connected). Data travels around a Token-Ring network in this fashion, for example. However, the ring is not physically evident in the cabling layout for the network. In fact, the ring exists only within the hub (called a multistation access unit or MSAU on a Token-Ring network). See Figure 19.16.

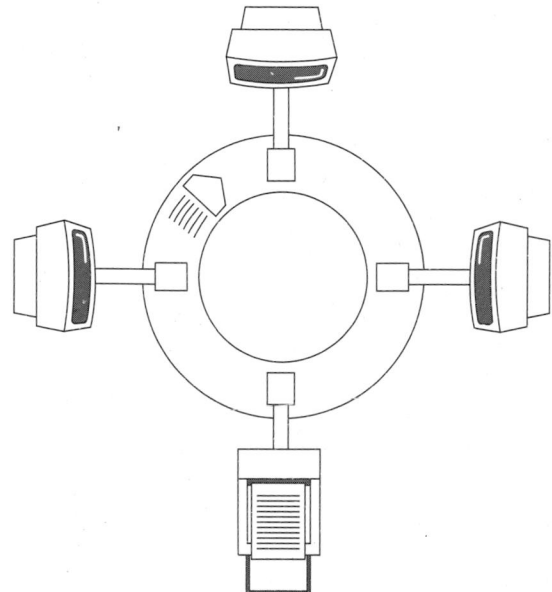

Figure 19.16   All computers and printers are connected to the same circuit, creating a loop.

Signals generated from one computer travel to the hub, are sent out to the next computer, and then go back to the hub again. The data is then passed to each system in turn until it arrives back at the computer that originated it, where it is removed from the network. Therefore, although the physical wiring topology is a star, the data path is theoretically a ring. This is called a *logical ring*.

The logical ring is preferable to a physical ring topology because it affords a greater degree of fault tolerance. As on a bus network, a cable break anywhere in a physical ring would affect the entire network. On a Token-Ring network, the MSAU can effectively remove a malfunctioning computer from the logical ring, enabling the rest of the network to function normally.

These different topologies are often mixed, forming what is called a hybrid network. For example, you can link the hubs of several star networks together with a bus, forming a star-bus network. Rings can be connected in the same way.

Network Cable Installations

If you have to run cables (of any type) through existing walls and ceilings, the cable installation can be the most expensive part of setting up a LAN. At every branching point, special fittings connect the intersecting wires. Sometimes, you also need various additional components along the way, such as hubs, repeaters, or MSAUs.

Note

A few companies, such as Motorola, market LAN technologies that do not require cables at all. Wireless LAN uses infrared, lasers, or radio waves to carry network signals from computer to computer. These technologies are uniquely suited to certain specialized environments but have not yet achieved the speed, reliability, and distance needed for general use.

With the development of easy-to-build (or prebuilt) category 5 twisted-pair cabling, high-speed and low-cost NICs and hubs, and built-in basic networking in current versions of Windows, it's far easier to install and set up a network today than ever before. For small cubicle-office networking in which no wire must be routed through walls and in which Windows 9x peer networking software will be used, you should be able to set up the network yourself if you're comfortable with the technical information in this book.

If your wiring must go through walls, be run through dropped ceilings, be piggy-backed on air ducts, or be run between floors, you might want to have the cable installed professionally by network-cable specialists. A good company will know the following:

- When UTP (unshielded twisted pair) cabling is adequate
- Where STP (shielded twisted pair) cabling might be necessary to avoid excessive cable runs to avoid interference
- How to route cable between rooms, floors, and non-adjacent offices
- How to use wall panels to make cable attachments look better and more professional
- When you must use fireproof Plenum cable
- How to deal with sources of electrical interference such as elevator motors, transmitters, alarm systems, and even florescent office lighting by using fiber-optic or shielded cable

If you want to create TP cables yourself, make sure your cable pairs match the color-coding of any existing cable or the color-coding of any prebuilt cabling you want to add to your new network. Because there are eight wires in TP cables, many incorrect combinations are possible. There are several standards for TP cabling; be consistent.

The most common standard is the Electronic Industry Association/Telecommunications Industry Association's Standard 568B. Table 19.5 lists the wire pairing and placement within the standard RJ-45 connector.

Table 19.5   RJ-45 Connector Wire Pairing and Placement

Wire Pairing	Wire Connected to Pin #	Pair Used For
White/blue and blue	White/blue - #5 Blue - #4	Data
white/orange and orange	White/orange - #1 Orange - #2	Data
white/green and green	white/green - #3 Green - #6	Not used
white/brown - brown	White/brown - #7 Brown - #8	Not used

Thus, a completed cable that follows the 568B standard should look like this when viewed from the flat side of the RJ-45 connector (from left to right):

> orange/white, orange, green/white, blue, blue/white, green, brown/white, brown

If your 10BaseT network will have multiple hubs and run many hundreds or thousands of feet, use hubs that offer the BNC (bayonet) connector and can use Thinnet (RG-58) cable. Although this cable is obsolete for normal network use between workstations, its durability, resistance to interference, and longer maximum distance make it a good choice as a backbone between hubs. Note that some low-cost Ethernet hubs don't offer BNC connectors, and you will need the appropriate T-connectors and terminators.

With any flavor of Ethernet, be sure not to exceed the limits of the network cables you're using.

Tip

By stacking hubs, you create a "virtual hub" that enables you to create a larger network with longer physical distances between the hubs because the hub-to-hub distance is effectively zero.

Planning the cable layout, cutting the cable, attaching connectors, and installing the cables and fittings are jobs usually best left to experienced workers.

Selecting the Proper Cable

As the demands of network users continue for ever-increasing amounts of bandwidth and as manufacturers develop new networking systems to accommodate them, it soon becomes necessary to examine the capabilities of the most fundamental part of the network infrastructure: the cable itself. 100BaseT (Fast Ethernet) networks are now the network of choice because dual-speed hubs enable them to be interconnected with existing 10BaseT networks, and 10BaseT networks that use Category 5 (CAT 5) cable can be upgraded to Fast Ethernet without replacing the cable.

The original type of UTP cable used for Ethernet networks was also the same as that used for business telephone wiring. This is known as Category 3, or voice grade UTP cable, measured according to a scale that quantifies the cable's data-transmission capabilities. The cable itself is 24 AWG

(American Wire Gauge, a standard for measuring the diameter of a wire), copper tinned with solid conductors, 100–105 ohm characteristic impedance, and a minimum of two twists per foot. Category 3 cable is adequate for networks running at up to 16Mbps. This cable usually looks like "silver" telephone cable, but with the larger RJ-45 connector.

Newer, faster network types require greater performance levels, however. Fast Ethernet technologies that run at 100Mbps using the same number of wires as standard Ethernet need a greater resistance to signal crosstalk and attenuation. Therefore, the use of Category 5 UTP cabling is essential (it can be mixed with the Category 3 cabling you already have if you are running at only 10Mbps speeds). If, when you are building a LAN, you can use Category 3 wiring that is already in place, you can do so if you are satisfied with 10BaseT's 10Mbps peak speeds. If, however, you are pulling new cable for your network, the use of Category 5 cable or even better grades is recommended.

Caution

A chain is only as strong as its weakest link, and the same rule holds true for a network cable installation. If you choose to install Category 5 UTP cable, make sure that all the connectors, wall plates, and other hardware components involved are also Category 5.

If you are trying to connect prebuilt Category 5 cabling together on a Fast Ethernet network, use Category-5–grade connectors, or you'll create a substandard section that might fail in your network.

The people who design computer systems love to find ways to circumvent limitations. Manufacturers of Ethernet products have made it possible to build networks in star, branch, and tree designs that overcome the basic limitations already mentioned. You can have thousands of computers on a complex Ethernet network.

LANs are local because the network adapters and other hardware components typically cannot send LAN messages more than a few hundred feet. Table 19.6 lists the distance limitations of different kinds of LAN cable. In addition to the limitations shown in the table, keep in mind that you cannot connect more than 30 computers on a single Thinnet Ethernet segment, more than 100 computers on a Thicknet Ethernet segment, more than 72 computers on a UTP Token-Ring cable, or more than 260 computers on an STP Token-Ring cable.

Table 19.6   Network Distance Limitations

Network Adapter	Cable Type	Maximum	Minimum
Ethernet	Thin*	607 ft.	20 in.
	Thick (drop cable)*	164 ft.	8 ft.
	Thick (backbone)*	1,640 ft.	8 ft.
	UTP	328 ft.	8 ft.
Token Ring	STP	328 ft.	8 ft.
	UTP	148 ft.	8 ft.
ARCnet* (passive hub)		393 ft.	Depends on cable
ARCnet* (active hub)	*	1,988 ft.	Depends on cable

* indicates obsolete for new installations; may be found in existing installations

Data Link Layer Protocols

The protocol that you choose to run at the data link layer is the single most important decision you make when designing a local area network. This protocol defines the speed of the network, the medium access control mechanism it uses, the types of cables you can use, the network interface adapters that you must buy, and the adapter drivers that you install in the network client software.

The Institute of Electrical and Electronic Engineers (IEEE) has defined and documented a set of standards for the physical characteristics of both collision-sensing and token-passing networks. These standards are known as IEEE 802.3 (Ethernet) and IEEE 802.5 (Token Ring). Be aware, however, that the colloquial names Ethernet and Token Ring actually refer to earlier versions of these protocols, upon which the IEEE standards were based. There are minor differences between the frame definitions for true Ethernet and true IEEE 802.3. In terms of the standards, IBM's 16Mbps Token-Ring products are an extension of the IEEE 802.5 standard. There is also an older data link protocol called ARCnet that is now rarely used.

The following sections examine these data link layer protocols.

ARCnet

ARCnet is one of the oldest types of LAN. It originally was a proprietary scheme of the Datapoint Corporation, but other companies also began to manufacture ARCnet-compatible hardware. By modern standards, ARCnet is very slow, but it is forgiving of minor errors in installation. It is known for solid reliability, and ARCnet cable/adapter problems are easy to diagnose. ARCnet generally costs less than Ethernet, but hardware prices for Ethernet adapters have plummeted so much in recent years that the difference in price between the two is no longer that great an issue. ARCnet operates something like Token Ring, but at the slower rate of 2.5Mbps.

Ethernet

With over 20 million installed computers, Ethernet is the most widely used data link layer protocol in the world. Ethernet-based LANs enable you to interconnect a wide variety of equipment, including UNIX workstations, Apple computers, printers, and PCs. You can buy Ethernet adapters from dozens of competing manufacturers, supporting all three of the cable types defined in the standard: Thinnet, Thicknet, and UTP. Traditional Ethernet operates at a speed of 10Mbps, but the more recent Fast Ethernet standards push this speed to 100Mbps.

Fast Ethernet requires adapters, hubs, and cables designed to support the higher speed, but you can buy combination devices that run at both 10Mbps and 100Mbps, enabling you to gradually upgrade your network by installing new NICs and hubs over an extended period of time.

The Ethernet specification consists of three elements:

- *Physical Layer Specifications*. A set of cabling guidelines for the installation of UTP, Thinnet, or Thicknet cable.
- *The Ethernet Frame*. A frame format that defines what information goes into the header and footer applied to every packet of network-layer data by the Ethernet protocol. The frame

includes the hardware addresses of the systems sending and receiving the packet and the CRC value used for error detection and correction.

- *Media Access Control.* A mechanism used to regulate access to the shared network medium by multiple computers.

Because computers on a LAN share a common network medium (usually a cable), there must be a scheme to arbitrate each system's access to the network. If two computers transmit a packet at the same time, a collision can result, garbling both packets and causing data loss. This arbitration scheme is called a *media access control (MAC)* mechanism, and Ethernet networks use a MAC mechanism called *carrier sense multiple access with collision detection (CSMA/CD)*.

When a computer on an Ethernet network wants to transmit, it first listens to the network to see if the network is currently in use. If another computer is transmitting, the system waits for a while and then listens again. If the network is clear, the system transmits its data. This is not a foolproof method, however, as it is possible for two computers to detect a clear network and transmit at the same time, causing a collision.

Collisions are a regular and accepted occurrence on an Ethernet LAN, and a good deal of the technology is devoted to detecting them. When a computer realizes that its transmission has collided with another packet, it waits for a random period of time (called a backoff interval) and transmits the same packet again. Because the two computers involved in the collision use a backoff calculation method called pseudo-random backoff multiplier, the chances of a second collision are reduced because most of the time, different backoff intervals will be calculated for the computers involved. A certain number of collisions are normal and expected on an Ethernet network; however, with higher amounts of traffic, the frequency of collisions rises, and response times increase. A saturated Ethernet network actually can spend more time recovering from collisions than it does sending data. For this reason, it is important not to overburden a single Ethernet segment with too many computers.

On an Ethernet network, the number of computer connections and their intervening distances are the network's limiting factors. Each cable type is subject to its own distance limitations, beyond which an electrical device called a repeater is needed to amplify the signal. Without repeaters, standing waves (additive signal reflections) would distort the signal and cause errors.

Because the Ethernet collision-detection mechanism is highly dependent on timing, you can have only five 200-meter segments and four repeaters wired in series, with a maximum of three segments connected to computers, before the signal propagation delay becomes longer than the maximum allowed period for the detection of a collision. Otherwise, the computers farthest from the sender would be unable to determine whether a collision had occurred. This is known as the Ethernet 5-4-3 rule. See the preceding table for cabling distances. To extend the network beyond the rated cabling distances, you can use repeaters, bridges, or routers.

Token Ring

Token-Ring networks differ substantially from Ethernet. Originally designed by IBM to run at 4Mbps over STP or UTP cable in a logical ring topology, the standard was revised to include a

16Mbps version, which is what most installations use today. Token-Ring adapters and hubs (MSAUs) are considerably more expensive than their Ethernet counterparts, but this cost can often be justified by the protocol's greater speed and its excellent performance even at high traffic levels.

It takes several seconds to open the adapter connection on a Token-Ring LAN. During this time, the MSAU and the Token-Ring adapter perform a small diagnostic check, after which the MSAU establishes the computer as a new neighbor on the ring. After being established as an active workstation, your computer is linked on both sides to your upstream and downstream neighbors (as defined by your position on the MSAU). In its turn, your Token-Ring adapter card accepts the token or frame, regenerates its electrical signals, and sends the token or frame through the MSAU in the direction of your downstream neighbor.

Token-Ring networks use a different type of MAC mechanism than Ethernet LANs, called token passing. On a Token-Ring network, computers continuously pass a special packet called a token among themselves. The token is just a short message indicating that the computer possessing it is allowed to transmit. If a computer has no data to send, it passes the token on to the next downstream computer as soon as it receives it. Only the computer holding the token can transmit data onto the LAN. Every packet transmitted on the network circulates through all the computers on the ring, including its intended destination, and eventually ends up back at the computer that sent it. The sender is then responsible for removing the packet from the network and generating a new token, thus releasing control of the network to the next system.

Because it is not possible for two computers to transmit at the same time on a properly functioning Token-Ring network, there are no collisions, and because every computer has an equal opportunity to transmit, network performance does not degrade at high traffic levels. In special situations, it is also possible to assign priorities to certain computers so they get more frequent access to the LAN. Sometimes a station fumbles and "drops" the token, however. When this happens, the computers on the LAN monitor each other and use a procedure called beaconing to detect the location of the problem and regenerate a lost token.

Although the lack of collisions greatly reduces the need to retransmit "lost" data, Token-Ring networks have been and continue to be a relatively small part of the networking marketplace. The cost of NICs and MSAUs is extremely high; it's possible to pay two to eight times as much for a 16Mbps Token-Ring card as for a 100Mbps Fast Ethernet card, for example.

The performance of Token Ring in high-volume networks, the ease of failure detection and removal of broken nodes, and Token Ring's easy connectivity to IBM mid-sized and mainframe computers make Token Ring a good choice for large networks with IBM mainframe connectivity as a concern.

Early Token Release

On a momentarily idle Token-Ring LAN, workstations circulate a token. The LAN becomes busy (carries information) when a computer takes possession of the token and transmits a data frame targeted at another computer on the network. After receipt by the target node, the data frame continues circulating around the LAN until it returns to its

(continues)

(continued)

source node. The source node removes the data frame and generates a new token that circulates until a downstream node needs it. So far, so good—these are just standard Token-Ring concepts.

When a client sends a file request to a server, it consists of only a few bytes, far fewer than the transmission that returns the actual file to the client. If the request packet has to pass through many other systems to circulate the ring and if the data frame is small, latency occurs. Latency is the unproductive delay that occurs while the source node waits for its upstream neighbor to return the data frame.

During the latency period, the source node appends idle characters onto the LAN following the data frame until the frame circulates the entire LAN and arrives back at the source node. The typical latency period of a 16Mbps ring will result in the transmission of 400 or more bytes' worth of idle characters.

Early Token Release, available only on 16Mbps networks, is a feature that enables the originating workstation to transmit a new token immediately after sending its data frame, thus avoiding the latency period. Downstream nodes pass along the data frame and then receive the token, giving them the opportunity to transmit data themselves. If you were to perform a protocol analysis of a network using Early Token Release, you would see tokens and other data frames immediately following the file request, instead of a long trail of idle characters.

High-Speed Networking Technologies

If you have fast computers on your network, you might want a fast network as well. Even the 16Mbps of a Token-Ring network might be too slow if your applications are data-intensive. The explosive growth of multimedia, groupware, and other technologies that require enormous amounts of data has forced network administrators to consider the need for high-speed network connections to individual desktop systems.

Networking technologies that run at speeds above 16Mbps have been around for several years, and greatly reduced prices on hardware are now making it possible for every network from a small two-station peer-to-peer network to a large departmental network to use 100Mbps networking speed. Real-time data feeds from financial services, videoconferencing, video editing, and high-color graphics processing are just some of the tasks now being performed on PCs that benefit from today's faster network transmission speeds.

Fiber Distributed Data Interface

FDDI has been available for several years, but it is still a much newer protocol than Ethernet or Token Ring. Designed by the X3T9.5 Task Group of ANSI (the American National Standards Institute), FDDI passes tokens and data frames around a double ring of optical fiber cable at a rate of 100Mbps. Two separate rings (called the primary and the secondary rings) with traffic traveling in opposite directions provide fault tolerance in case of a cable break or other malfunction. FDDI classifies the computers on the network as either Class A (connected to both rings) or Class B (connected to the primary ring only).

FDDI was designed to be as much like the IEEE 802.5 Token Ring standard as possible, above the physical layer. Differences occur only where necessary to support the faster speeds and longer transmission distances of FDDI.

If FDDI were to use the same bit-encoding scheme used by Token Ring, every bit would require two optical signals: a pulse of light and then a pause of darkness. This means that FDDI would need to send 200 million signals per second to have a 100Mbps transmission rate. Instead, the scheme used by FDDI—called NRZI 4B/5B—encodes four bits of data into five bits for transmission so that fewer signals are needed to send a byte of information. The five-bit codes (symbols) were chosen carefully to ensure that they meet network timing requirements. The NRZI 4B/5B scheme, at a 100Mbps transmission rate, sends 125 million signals per second (this is 125 megabaud). Also, because each carefully selected light pattern symbol represents four bits (a half byte, or nibble), FDDI hardware can operate at the nibble and byte level rather than at the bit level, making it easier to achieve the high data rate.

There are two major differences in the way that FDDI and IEEE 802.5 Token Rings manage their respective tokens. In traditional Token Ring, a new token is circulated only after a sending system gets back the frame that it sent. In FDDI, a new token is circulated immediately by the sending system after it finishes transmitting a frame, a technique that has since been adapted for use in Token-Ring networks and called Early Token Release. FDDI classifies the computers on the network as either asynchronous (systems that are not rigid about the time periods that occur between network accesses) or synchronous (systems having very stringent requirements regarding the timing between transmissions). FDDI uses a complex algorithm to allocate network access to the two classes of devices.

Although it provides superior performance, FDDI's acceptance as a desktop networking solution has been hampered by its higher installation and maintenance costs. An alternative using a more conventional copper cable, called CDDI (Copper Distributed Data Interface), is easier to install and maintain but does not provide the resistance to interference that enables fiber-optic cable to span such long distances.

100Mbps Ethernet

One of the largest barriers to the implementation of high-speed networking has been the need for a complete replacement of the networking infrastructure. Most companies cannot afford the downtime needed to rewire the entire network, replace all the hubs and NICs, and then configure everything to operate properly. As a result of this, some of the new 100Mbps technologies are designed to make the upgrade process easier in several ways. First, they can often use the network cable that is already in place, and second, they are compatible enough with the existing installation to enable a gradual changeover to the new technology, system by system. Obviously, these factors also minimize the expense associated with such an upgrade.

The two systems that take this approach are 100BaseT (also known as Fast Ethernet), first developed by the Grand Junction Corp., and 100VG AnyLAN, advocated by Hewlett-Packard and AT&T. Both of these systems run at 100Mbps over standard UTP cable, but that is where the similarities end. In fact, of the two, only 100BaseT can truly be called an Ethernet network. 100BaseT uses the same CSMA/CD media access control mechanism and the same frame layout defined in the IEEE 802.3 standard. In fact, 100BaseT has been ratified as an extension to that standard, called 802.3u.

To accommodate existing cable installations, the 802.3u document defines three different cabling standards, as shown in Table 19.7.

Table 19.7   100BaseT Cabling Standards

Standard	Cable Type	Segment Length
100BaseTX	Category 5 (2 pairs)	100 meters
100BaseT4	Category 3, 4, or 5 (4 pairs)	100 meters
100BaseFX	62.6 micrometer Multimode fiber	400 meters (2 strands)

Sites with Category 3 cable already installed can use the system without the need for rewiring, as long as the full four pairs in a typical run are available. However, because Category 3 cable was often used to enable telephony, voice, and computer data to travel over the same wires (using two pairs for each task), you might well need to rewire with Category 5 cabling.

Note

Despite the apparent wastefulness, it is not recommended that data and voice traffic be mixed within the same cable, even if sufficient wire pairs are available. Digital phone traffic could possibly coexist, but normal analog voice lines will definitely inhibit the performance of the data network.

100BaseT also requires the installation of new hubs and new NICs, but because the frame type used by the new system is identical to that of the old, this replacement can be performed gradually to spread the labor and expense over a protracted period of time. You could replace one hub with a 100BaseT model and then switch computers over to it, one at a time, as time permits. Most PCI-based and PC card-based NICs available today can operate at both 10Mbps and 100Mbps speeds to make the changeover even easier.

100VG-(voice grade) AnyLAN also runs at 100Mbps and is specifically designed to use existing Category 3 UTP cabling. Like 100BaseT4, it requires four pairs of cable strands for its communications. There is also a separate Category 5 cable option in the standard. Beyond the cabling, 100VG-AnyLAN is quite different from 100BaseT and indeed from Ethernet.

Whereas 10BaseT and 100BaseT networks both reserve one pair of wires for collision detection, 100VG-AnyLAN is able to transmit over all four pairs simultaneously. This technique is called quartet signaling. 100VG-AnyLAN also uses a different signal-encoding scheme called 5B/6B NRZ, which sends 2.5 times more bits per cycle than an Ethernet network's Manchester encoding scheme. Multiplied by the four pairs of wires (as compared to 10BaseT's one), you have a tenfold increase in transmission speed.

The fourth pair of wires is available for transmitting data because there is no need for collision detection on a 100VG-AnyLAN network. Instead of the CSMA/CD media access system that defines an Ethernet network, 100VG-AnyLAN uses a brand-new technique called demand priority. Individual network computers have to request and be granted permission to transmit by the hub before they can send their data.

100VG-AnyLAN can use the same frame formats as IEEE 802.3 Ethernet and IEEE 802.5 Token Ring so that its traffic can coexist on a LAN with that of existing Ethernet or Token Ring systems. Like 100BaseT, combination 10/100Mbps NICs are available, and the network can be gradually migrated to the new technology.

Support for 100VG-AnyLAN has almost completely disappeared from the market due to the cost of the adapters and the popularity of 10/100Mbps Fast Ethernet adapters. Fast Ethernet is the popularly priced, high-speed network of choice.

Asynchronous Transfer Mode

Asynchronous Transfer mode, or ATM, is one of the newest of the high-speed technologies. It has been in an "emerging" state for some time now without having developed into its full potential. ATM defines a physical-layer protocol in which a standard sized 53-byte packet (called a cell) is used to simultaneously transmit voice, data, and real-time video over the same cable. The cells contain identification information that enables high-speed ATM switches (wiring hubs) to separate the data types and ensure that the cells are reassembled in the right order.

The basic ATM standard runs at 155Mbps, but some implementations can go as high as 660Mbps. There is also an ATM desktop standard that runs at 25Mbps, but this doesn't seem to be enough of a gain over Token-Ring's 16Mbps to be worth the adoption of an entirely new networking technology.

ATM is a radically different concept, and there are no convenient upgrade paths as there are with the 100Mbps standards described earlier. All the networking hardware must be replaced, and the prices of ATM products are significantly higher than those of Fast Ethernet and other high-speed technologies. For this reason, ATM is being used primarily for WAN links at this time. When the delivery of real-time video over the network becomes more of a practical reality than it is now, ATM might find its rightful place. For now, it remains a niche technology.

Upper-Layer Protocols

When you add network client software to a PC, the first step is to install a driver for the network interface adapter in the machine. This driver not only identifies the adapter hardware, but it implements the data link layer protocol. The next step is to install support for the protocols running above the data link layer. There are usually several different protocols operating at the upper layers, but for the purposes of a client installation, they are treated as a single entity.

For example, after installing a driver for the Ethernet adapter in your PC, you can select a protocol suite such as TCP/IP or IPX to work at the upper layers. Both TCP/IP and IPX actually consist of several different protocols, but you install them as one module that operating systems such as Windows 9x and Windows NT somewhat confusingly refer to by the term *protocol*.

In nearly all cases, you can also install multiple protocol suites to support different networking clients on the same computer. For example, a single Ethernet adapter can use IPX to access NetWare servers and TCP/IP to share Windows NT resources at the same time.

Building a Peer-to-Peer Network

For many PC users, their first exposure to networking is a peer-to-peer network, in which each station on the network can both share resources and use those shared resources. In practice, most peer-to-peer networks are set up to enable the sharing of a few particular resources, such as high-performance laser and inkjet printers, large hard drives, and CD-ROM drives. The computers that are directly connected to these resources are called peer servers because they can still be used for individual computer tasks as well as serve up resources to other computers. The computers that use the shared resources are called client workstations, just as in client/server networking.

At one time, investing in a peer-to-peer network was risky. The peer-to-peer networks of the late 1980s used proprietary network hardware and network operating system software. If you outgrew your network, you had to replace your network cards, your network software, and even your network cable.

Today, peer-to-peer networking for small-office/home-office and departmental use in larger organizations makes a great deal of sense. Because the network operating system software for both server and workstation tasks is built into Windows 9x and Windows NT, it costs nothing to try it. The network interface cards (NICs) and cables used by peer-to-peer networks are the very same ones that can be used for client/server networking with Microsoft Windows NT, Windows 2000, and Novell NetWare. Setup is relatively simple, and if you find that you need the extra speed and security of a client/server network later, your network hardware is ready to take you into the new network.

Peer-to-Peer Networking Hardware

At a minimum, a two-station peer-to-peer network for printer or drive sharing requires the following hardware:

- Two NICs (network interface cards), one per station
- Sufficient cable to bridge the systems
- Connectors and cabling hardware (specific connectors depend upon the cable)

A network for more than two stations needs some way to extend the network to additional users. With the preferred types of solutions, this is easy.

Preferred Solutions for Peer-to-Peer Networking

A minimally acceptable networking solution should include the following:

- PCI-based Ethernet cards with RJ-45 connectors for twisted-pair cabling (for desktop/tower computers).
- PC card or CardBus Ethernet cards with RJ-45 connectors (for notebook computers).
- Stackable hub with at least two unused connectors. A stackable hub can be connected to another hub with standard cabling to enable your network to expand. The unused connectors enable this stacking, either through the use of the "uplink" port on hubs designed to be stacked or though a crossover cable.

Previously, I would have recommended standard 10BaseT Ethernet cards and hubs, or dual-speed 10/100 Ethernet cards and a standard 10BaseT hub. However, prices on Fast Ethernet hubs have now dropped to prices comparable to standard Ethernet. With the ten-times-faster data transmission rate of Fast Ethernet and the near-universal use of Fast Ethernet-compliant Category 5 twisted pair cabling, choosing Fast Ethernet is easy. If you are adding to an existing 10BaseT network, use a dual-speed hub so you can interconnect your new high-speed network with your existing 10BaseT network.

Solutions to Avoid in a Peer-to-Peer Network

Many stores sell so-called instant networks. One company, LinkSys, calls theirs a "Network in a Box." These prepackaged network kits can save you money but might lead to compromises you'll regret later, depending on the components. Avoid pre-packaged network kits (or separately purchased network components) that feature the following:

■ *ISA Network Interface Cards (NICs)*. The ISA bus, as discussed in Chapter 16, "Serial, Parallel, and Other I/O Interfaces," is both extremely slow and extremely out of date. Although current Pentium-class motherboards still have 1-3 ISA slots, this 16-bit, 8.33MHz 1984-vintage slot design is being eliminated from PCs that follow the PC99 guidelines published by Microsoft and Intel. Any ISA-based network card you buy today will not be able to be moved to newer systems tomorrow and will give you slow performance and high CPU utilization (which slows down the rest of your system) in the meantime.

◄◄ See "PC 9x Specifications," p. 25.

■ *Thin Ethernet cabling*. Thin coaxial cable, also known as 10Base2, Thinnet, or Cheapernet, was the second type of cabling to be used with Ethernet networking. Easier to work with than Thicknet (10Base5) cabling, it was the most popular way to build a small network into the early '90s. Today, its flaws when compared to unshielded twisted-pair cabling are very obvious. Thinnet cabling must be strung from unit to unit, with one termination point at the server and the other termination point at the last workstation. The cable bayonets onto T-shaped connectors that in turn bayonet onto a BNC connector coming out of the back of the NIC. A failure of the cable, the T-adapter, or the terminator cripples the entire network. This type of topology is called a bus topology. This is one bus you should not catch.

Peer-to-Peer Solutions via Dial-Up Networking

You can also network two Windows 9x, Windows NT, or Windows 2000 PCs using modems and the operating system's Dial-Up Networking feature. Dial-Up Networking uses the same network client software as standard Windows 9x networking but substitutes a modem connection for the network interface adapter. You can use this technology to connect to your office PC from your home computer and even to access other resources on your office network.

Windows 2000 offers these enhancements to your dial-up networking capability:

■ Offline access to network resources, enabling you to work seamlessly on- or offline

■ Improved Plug-and-Play capabilities

■ Network Connection Wizard, which handles dial-up networking, LAN networking, or Internet connections, and Virtual Private Networking services (VPN)

■ Improved Add Printer Wizard, which works with local, network, and Web-based printers

It is important to know that client/server and peer-to-peer networks are not mutually exclusive. You can have dedicated servers on your network and still share your local resources with other users, for example. In fact, this type of mixed network is very popular today, as many organizations are running both NetWare (a client/server operating system) and Windows NT (which can function as either a peer-to-peer operating system or a client/server operating system).

Network Client Software

To access network resources with a PC, whether it is connected to a client/server or a peer-to-peer network, you must install network client software on the computer. The network client can be part of the operating system or a separate product, but it is this software that enables the system to use the network interface adapter to communicate with other machines.

On a properly configured network workstation, accessing network resources is no different from accessing local ones (except that they might be slightly slower). You can open a file on a network drive just as you would open the same file on your local hard disk. This is because the network client software is completely integrated into every level of the computer's operating system.

In most cases, the network client software is part of the operating system. Windows 9x, for example, includes all the software you need to participate in a peer-to-peer Windows network or to connect to Windows NT, Windows 2000, and Novell NetWare servers. To connect to a network using DOS or Windows 3.1, however, you must install a separate client software package.

Configuring Your Network Software

You might have few problems installing your NICs. They might pass their diagnostics flawlessly. But until each station on your network can speak the same language, has correct client or server software setups, and uses the same protocols, your network will not function properly.

Table 19.8 shows the minimum network software configuration you must install for a Windows 9x, Windows NT, and Windows 2000 peer-to-peer networking:

Table 19.8   Minimum Network Software for Peer-to-Peer Networking

Item	Workstation	Server
Windows Network client	Yes	No
NetBEUI protocol	Yes	Yes
File and Print Sharing for Microsoft Networks	No	Yes
NIC installed and bound to protocols and services above	Yes	Yes
Workgroup identification (same for all PCs in workgroup)	Yes	Yes
Computer Name (each PC needs a unique name)	Yes	Yes

Use the Network control panel to choose your network settings. You'll need the following software to set up the network—operating system CDs, diskettes, or hard-disk image files; and NIC drivers. You'll be prompted to insert a CD or disk or browse to the appropriate files during the installation procedure, if they're not available on the Windows 9x CD-ROM.

After you complete the installation of the preceding list of items, click OK in the Networks protocol. You'll need to reboot your PC to complete the process. After this is completed, you'll be ready to share resources.

Setting Up Users, Groups, or Resources

Depending on the network operating system software you choose, you can control access in a variety of different ways.

Peer-to-peer Windows 9x-style networking (also applies to Windows for Workgroups, Windows NT, and Windows 2000 Professional) provides access control on a resource-by-resource basis.

Client/server-based networks such as Windows NT, Windows 2000 Server, and Novell NetWare control resources on a user-permission or group-permission basis. The following example demonstrates the differences in these approaches:

- Users 1, 2, 3, and 4 need to access a CD-ROM drive, two network hard drives, a laser printer, and an inkjet printer.
- Users 1 and 4 need read/write/create access to the \Msoffice folder on hard disk #1 and access to the laser printer. User 4 also needs read-only access to the \Photoshop folder on hard disk #2 and access to the inkjet printer.
- User 3 needs read-only access to the \Msoffice folder on hard disk #1, read/write/create access to the \Photoshop folder on hard disk #2, and access to the inkjet printer.
- User 2 needs access to the laser printer only.

With a peer-to-peer network, the security settings that would be required to secure the resources are shown in Table 19.9

Table 19.9   Peer-to-Peer Security Settings

Resource	Passwords	Reason for Second Password
CD-ROM	one	
\Msoffice	two	1 password for full access
		1 password for read-only access
\Photoshop	two	1 password for full access
		1 password for read-only access
Laser printer	one	
Inkjet printer	one	

This means that there are a total of seven passwords on the system. The number of passwords needed by each user would be as follows:

- User 1—two passwords needed
- User 2—one password needed
- User 3—three passwords needed
- User 4—four passwords needed

This simple example demonstrates the not-so-simple problem of trying to control network resources. The Windows 9x-type peer-to-peer network has no way to create user lists or group permissions and therefore must assign a password to every resource. Even if all the users can remember their passwords (or store them in a password list), the challenge isn't over. Suppose the passwords are revealed to others who shouldn't have access. The authorized users will need to memorize up to four additional (new) passwords after the passwords are changed, assuming that the unauthorized users don't take over the system first.

In addition to the limitations of what Microsoft calls share-level access control, another flaw in the peer-to-peer network scheme is that nobody is really in charge of the network. There is no administrator or "superuser" who can set up and change passwords for all resources. Instead, the user of the computer with the shared resource can add, change, or delete shared resource settings unless user profiles are set up on each machine that eliminate access to the Windows Explorer and Printers folder for the normal user(s) of that computer.

With a client/server network, a single password is assigned to each user by a network administrator, and users can be divided into groups based on similar access needs. Using the previous example, this scenario would create security settings that look like the ones in Tables 19.10 and 19.11.

Table 19.10   Client/Server Network Sample Groups

User	Groups Belonged To
User 1	OfficeCreate, Laserprinter
User 2	Laserprinter
User 3	OfficeRead, PhotoCreate, Inkjet
User 4	OfficeCreate, Laserprinter, PhotoRead, Inkjet

Table 19.11   Client/Server Network Sample Security

Group	Rights	Members
Laserprinter	Use	User 2, User 1, User 4
Inkjet	Use	User 4, User 3
OfficeCreate	Read, write, create	User 1, User 4
OfficeRead	Read	User 3
PhotoCreate	Read, write, create	User 3
PhotoRead	Read	User 4
Administrator	Full network control	

Although the client/server network looks more complex at first glance, it's actually an easier and more secure network. It's easier because each user has a single password, regardless of the number of resources he or she will access. It's easier to administer because rights can be changed for an entire group or for any member(s) of a group. It's more secure because a full-time Network Administrator is able to set up and control all user and group rights to access all network devices. It's more secure because access rights can be controlled more precisely than with a peer-to-peer network's full access, read-only access, or no access options. Because users can have read/write/create but not delete access to a specified resource, a program can be used without the possibility of its being deleted by the user.

This discussion is not designed to minimize the benefits of peer-to-peer networking. Fast, easy to set up, and flexible, peer-to-peer networking should be used in situations in which low cost is an important factor and security is a relatively unimportant concern. If security and performance are important, use a client/server network instead.

Note

To learn more about client/server networking, see *Upgrading and Repairing Networks, Second Edition*, published by Que.

TCP/IP

TCP/IP stands for Transmission Control Protocol/Internet Protocol. TCP and IP are separate transport- and network-layer protocols, respectively, but TCP/IP is the colloquial name given to the entire suite of networking protocols developed for use by the Internet, of which TCP and IP are only two. Later, the TCP/IP protocols were adopted by the UNIX operating systems, and they have now become the most commonly used protocol suite on PC LANs. Virtually every operating system with networking capabilities supports TCP/IP, and it is well on its way to displacing all the other competing protocols. Novell NetWare 5 and Windows 2000 both use TCP/IP as their native protocol for most services.

TCP/IP is an extensive collection of protocols operating at the application, transport, network, and data link layers. The protocols were originally developed by the U.S. Department of Defense in the 1970s as a platform- and hardware-independent medium for communication over what was to become known as the Internet. A good example of this independence is the capability of DOS, Windows 3.1, Windows 9x, and Windows NT systems to access information and transfer files on the Internet, which is a mixed-platform environment. The primary advantages of TCP/IP are the following:

- *Platform Independence.* TCP/IP is not designed for use in any single hardware or software environment. It can be used and is being used on computers and networks of all types.
- *Absolute Addressing.* TCP/IP provides a means of uniquely identifying every machine on the Internet.
- *Open Standards.* The TCP/IP specifications are publicly available to users and developers alike. Suggestions for changes to the standard can be submitted by anyone.
- *Application Protocols.* TCP/IP enables dissimilar environments to communicate. High-level protocols such as FTP and Telnet have become ubiquitous in TCP/IP environments on all platforms.

Although they have been the protocols of choice on UNIX networks for many years, the explosive growth of the Internet has brought the TCP/IP protocols onto all kinds of LANs as well. Many network administrators are finding that they can configure all their network operating systems to use TCP/IP and thus lessen the network traffic problems that can be caused by running several different sets of protocols on the same network.

Some of the most important protocols of the TCP/IP suite are as follows:

- *Internet Protocol (IP).* Operating at the network layer, IP is the main protocol of the TCP/IP suite. It supplies network data with addressing and routing information and splits packets into smaller fragments as needed during the trip to their destination. The data generated by nearly all the other TCP/IP protocols is carried within IP packets, called datagrams. This corresponds to the OSI layer 3, the Network layer.

- *Transmission Control Protocol (TCP).* TCP is a reliable, connection-oriented protocol operating at the transport layer. A reliable protocol is one in which the destination system returns acknowledgment messages to the sender, verifying that the packets were received without errors. A connection-oriented protocol is one in which the two computers exchange messages before transmitting any user data. These messages establish a connection that remains open until the data transmission is completed. TCP is used to transmit relatively large amounts of data, such as FTP file transfers and HTTP Web page transactions.

- *User Datagram Protocol (a.k.a.* Unacknowledged Datagram Protocol*).* Also operating at the transport layer, UDP is a connectionless, unreliable protocol and the counterpart to TCP. A connectionless protocol transmits its data without knowing if the destination system is ready to receive it or even if the destination system exists. An unreliable protocol is one in which the destination system does not transmit explicit acknowledgment messages. Actually, UDP is far from unreliable in the literal sense because it is mostly used for short query/response transactions in which the response functions as an acknowledgment. The Internet's Domain Name System (DNS) uses UDP for much of its communications. TCP and UDP correspond to the OSI layer 4—Transport.

The remaining layers below correspond to the OSI layers 5 and 6, Session and Presentation:

- *Internet Control Message Protocol (ICMP).* ICMP does not carry user data but is instead a control and diagnostic protocol that is used to inform other systems of conditions and errors on the network. The TCP/IP PING utility uses ICMP to determine if another system on a TCP/IP network is functioning.

- *Address Resolution Protocol (ARP).* ARP is a protocol that IP uses to convert its own network layer addresses into data link layer hardware addresses.

- *Point-to-Point Protocol (PPP).* PPP is a data link layer protocol but is not for use on LANs. PPP is used to establish a direct connection between two computers, usually using a modem connection. If you use Windows 9x or Windows NT's Dial-Up Networking feature to connect to the Internet, you are probably using PPP.

Note

Some ISPs that began life as proprietary dial-up networks, such as CompuServe, use a nonstandard version of PPP (CISPPP in the case of CompuServe). If you can't make connections with your modem, make sure you're using the correct version of PPP.

- *File Transfer Protocol (FTP).* FTP is an application layer protocol used to transfer files between TCP/IP systems. Unlike most protocols, FTP actually defines the user interface for an application. Virtually every TCP/IP implementation includes a text-based FTP program, and many of the commands are the same no matter what operating system you are using.

- *Hypertext Transfer Protocol (HTTP).* Operating at the application layer, HTTP is the fundamental protocol of the World Wide Web. When you type a URL in your Web browser, the program transmits an HTTP request to the server you've specified. The server then responds with an HTTP reply containing the file you requested.

■ *Simple Mail Transfer Protocol (SMTP)*. SMTP is the application-layer protocol used by most email applications to send mail over the Internet.

How TCP/IP Differs on LANs Versus Dial-Up Networking

TCP/IP, unlike the other network protocols listed here, is also a protocol used by people who have never seen a NIC. People who access the Internet via modems (with what Windows 9x calls "Dial-Up Networking") use TCP/IP just as those whose Web access is done with their existing LAN. Although the same protocol is used in both cases, the settings vary a great deal.

Table 19.12 summarizes the differences you're likely to encounter. If you access the Internet with both modems and a LAN, you will need to make sure that the TCP/IP properties for modems and LANs are set correctly. You might also need to adjust your browser settings to indicate which connection type you are using. Table 19.12 provides general guidelines; your ISP or network administrator will give you the specific details.

Table 19.12   TCP/IP Properties by Connection Type—Overview

TCP/IP Property Tab	Setting	Modem Access (Dial-Up Adapter)	LAN Access (XYZ Network Card)
IP Address	IP Address	Automatically assigned by ISP	Specified (get value from network administrator)
WINS Configuration	Enable/Disable WINS Resolution	Disabled	Indicate server or enable DHCP to allow NetBIOS over TCP/IP
Gateway	Add Gateway/ List of Gateways	None (PPP is used to connect modem to Internet)	IP Address of Gateway used to connect LAN to internet
DNS Configuration	Enable/ Disable Host Domain	Usually disabled, unless Proxy server used by ISP	Enabled, with Host and Domain specified (get value from network administrator)

As you can see from the preceding table, correct settings for LAN access to the Internet and Dial-up Networking (modem) settings are almost always completely different. In general, the best way to get your Dial-up Networking connection working correctly is to use your ISP's automatic setup software. This is usually supplied as part of your ISP's signup software kit. After the setup is working, view the properties.

Note

In Windows 98, Microsoft suggests that TCP/IP properties be viewed through the Dial-Up Networking icon for the connection, rather than through the Networks icon in the control panel.

IPX

The IPX protocol suite is the collective term for the proprietary protocols created by Novell for their NetWare operating system. Although based loosely on some of the TCP/IP protocols, the

IPX protocol standards are privately held by Novell. However, this has not prevented Microsoft from creating its own IPX-compatible protocol for the Windows operating systems.

IPX (Internetwork Packet Exchange) itself is a connectionless, unreliable, network layer protocol that is equivalent in function to IP. The suite's equivalent to TCP is the Sequenced Packet Exchange (SPX) protocol, which provides connection-oriented, reliable service at the transport layer.

The IPX protocols are typically used today only on networks with NetWare servers and are often installed along with another protocol suite such as TCP/IP. Even NetWare, however, is phasing out its use of IPX and making the move over to TCP/IP, along with the rest of the networking industry. NetWare 5 uses IPX/SPX only for specialized operations. Most of the product uses TCP/IP.

NetBEUI

NetBEUI (NetBIOS Extended User Interface) is a protocol used primarily on small Windows NT networks. It was the default protocol in Windows NT 3.1, the first version of that operating system. Later versions, however, use the TCP/IP protocols as their default.

NetBEUI is a simple protocol that lacks many of the features which enable protocol suites such as TCP/IP to support networks of almost any size. NetBEUI is not routable, so it cannot be used on large internetworks. It is suitable for small peer-to-peer networks, but any serious Windows NT network installation should use TCP/IP.

NetBEUI is still useful for creating "instant networks" with the Direct Cable Connection (see the following section), and it is the minimum protocol required for use in a Windows 9x peer-to-peer network.

Direct Cable Connections

When you have a large amount of data that you want to transfer from one computer to another in the same room, you have several possible solutions. You can copy the data to floppy disks, but for any more than a few megabytes, this is not convenient. Zip drives and other removable disk technologies hold more data, but you must either have the same type of drive on both systems or move the drive from one system to another and install the appropriate software drivers. A network connection would be the fastest solution but is not worth setting up for occasional or one-time use. Finally, you could use modems to dial up one computer from the other and transfer files. This method also works, but it requires two modems and two telephone lines. As an alternative, you can establish a "modem" connection between the two computers without using modems! Using a special type of cable called a null modem (or laplink) cable, you can connect the serial or parallel ports on two computers, forming a simple two-node network, and transfer files between them. This is particularly useful when you have both a desktop and a laptop system on which you want to use the same data.

Null Modem Cables

A null modem cable is a special cable that has its circuits crossed so the transmit data (TD) pin on each serial port connector leads to the receive data (RD) pin on the other. A cable that connects the systems' parallel ports in this way is called a parallel data-transfer cable. Cables like these are usually available at any computer store that sells cables. They are sometimes called Laplink cables, after one of the first software products to introduce the concept of the direct cable connection. FastLynx and other parallel-connection cables supplied for MS-DOS and Windows 3.x will also work. A good rule of thumb is this: If the cable works for LapLink or the MS-DOS INTERLNK file transfer utility, you can use it for Direct Cable Connection as well.

You can also build your own null modem or parallel data-transfer cable using the wiring tables that follow. Table 19.13 shows the pins that you must connect for a serial cable, using either DB-9 (9-pin) or DB-25 (25-pin) connectors. Table 19.14 shows the connections for a parallel port cable. The parallel cable is slightly harder to build, but it is recommended because of its much higher transfer speed and because it will not interfere with existing modems and mouse drivers on the computers.

Table 19.13   3-Wire Serial Null Modem Cable Pinouts

PC#1	DB-9	DB-25	DB-25	DB-9	PC#2
TD	3	2 <———> 3		2	RD
RD	2	3 <———> 2		3	TD
SG	5	7 <———> 7		5	SG

Table 19.14   11-Wire Parallel Data-Transfer Cable Pinouts

PC #1	PC #2
2 <———> 15	
15 <———> 2	
3 <———> 13	
13 <———> 3	
4 <———> 12	
12 <———> 4	
5 <———> 10	
10 <———> 5	
6 <———> 11	
11 <———> 6	
25 <———> 25	

Direct Connect Software

After you have the hardware in place, you need the proper software for the two systems to communicate. At one time, you had to purchase a third-party product (such as LapLink) to do this, but the capability is now part of most operating systems, including DOS 6, Windows 9x, and Windows NT.

In DOS, the software consists of two executable files, called INTERSVR.EXE and INTERLNK.EXE. On Windows 9x and Windows NT, the feature is called Direct Cable Connection. The software functions in basically the same way in either case. One computer is designated the host, and the other is the guest. The software enables a user, working at the guest machine, to transfer files to and from the host.

In the DOS version, you run the INTERSVR program on the host computer. This system can be running a different version of DOS; you simply have to copy the INTERSVR.EXE program to it from a DOS 6 machine (using a floppy disk). On Windows 9x, you click the Start menu and then select Programs, Accessories, Direct Cable Connection (on some systems it might be stored in a Communications folder beneath the Accessories folder). Then choose the Host option button. In both cases, you are prompted to select the COM or LPT port to which you have connected the cable.

On the other computer, you run the INTERLNK.EXE program in DOS or select the same Direct Cable Connection menu item in Windows 9x and choose the Guest option button. Again, you are prompted to choose the correct port, after which the software establishes a connection between the two machines. After this is done, the guest computer mounts the drives from the host in its own file system, assigning them the next available drive letters with Interlink. With the Windows 9x Direct Cable Connection, you can either access the shared drive as a folder or map a drive letter to it with Windows Explorer.

At this point, you can use the drive letters or folders representing the host system just as though they were local resources. You can copy files back and forth using any standard file-management tool, such as the DOS COPY command or Windows Explorer. The only difference is that file transfers will, of course, be slower than local hard drive operations.

Wireless Direct Cable Connection

With Windows 98, you can skip the cable if you're content with the slow-as-molasses serial port speeds *and* if both host and guest computers have an Infrared connector. Just select the device during the setup routine (Microsoft's default Infrared Monitor utility maps the infrared port to a COM or LPT port). Check your Windows Explorer or Toolbar for the Infrared port to see if it's enabled and what ports it's mapped to. When it's enabled you can use it for slow (but cableless) file transfers.

Direct Cable Connection (and Interlink) Tricks

Because both DCC- and Interlink-shared folders can be mapped to drive letters (the mapping is automatic with Interlink; DCC requires that you use Windows Explorer), you can use either utility to perform these useful tricks:

- Use DCC/Interlink to perform backups of your host's drive to a backup device (tape, Zip, Jaz, and so on) attached to your guest computer.
- Use DCC/Interlink to set up a shared CD-ROM drive on the host to install software to a guest computer.

Faster Direct Cable Connections

If you're planning to use Direct Cable Connections more than occasionally and would like to spend less time in file transfers, check with the creators of DCC for a faster and smarter cable. Parallel Technologies created Direct Cable Connection for Microsoft, and their DirectParallel cables ($69.95) provide much faster transmission rates (up to 10× faster!) and also much greater flexibility. The DirectParallel cable comes with several useful utilities for determining parallel port type and monitoring transfers. Because the cable has a "guest" and a "host" end, the DirectParallel cable can be used to provide a guest computer a gateway into a larger network that the host is already connected to. See Parallel Technologies' Web site for further information.

Troubleshooting Network Software Setup

Problem

Duplicate computer IDs

Solution

Make sure that every computer on the network has a unique ID (use control panel, Network, Identification to view this information). Otherwise, you'll get an error message when you reboot the workstations with networking cables attached.

Problem

Different workgroup names

Solution

Make sure that every computer that's supposed to be working together has the same workgroup name. The Windows 9x/NT Network Neighborhood displays computers by workgroup name. Different workgroup names actually create different workgroups, and you'd need to access them by browsing via Entire Network. This wastes time.

Problem

Shared resources not available

Solution

Make sure that shared resources have been set for any servers on your network (including "peer servers" on Windows 9x). If you can't share a resource through Windows Explorer on the peer server, make sure that File and Printer Sharing has been installed.

Problem

Network doesn't work after making changes

Solution

Did you reboot? Any change in the Network icon in Windows 9x control panel requires a system reboot!

Did you log in? No network resources can be accessed unless you log in when prompted. You can use the Start, Shutdown, and Close All Programs and Logon as a New User to recover quickly from a failure to log on.

Troubleshooting Networks in Use

Problem

A user can't access any shared resources (but others can)

Solution

First, have user use Start, Close All Programs and Logon as "new" User. Pressing Cancel or Esc instead of logging in would keep a user off the network.

Next, check cable connections at the server and workstation. Loose terminators or BNC T-connectors will cause trouble for all workstations on a Thinnet cable segment.

Problem

Wrong access level

Solution

If you save your passwords in a password cache, entering the read-only password instead of the full-access password will limit your access with peer servers. Try unsharing the resource and try to reshare it, or have the user of that peer server set up new full-access and read-only passwords. Alternatively, don't use password caching by unchecking the Save Password box when you log on to a shared resource. With a client/server network with user lists and rights, check with your network administrator because she will need to change the rights for you.

Troubleshooting TCP/IP

Problem

Incorrect settings in Network Properties

Solution

Get the correct TCP/IP settings from the administrator and enter them; restart the PC

Problem

Can't keep connection running in Dial-Up Networking

Solution

You might have the wrong version of PPP running (classic CompuServe uses CISPPP instead of normal PPP); change the server type in Properties under Dial-Up Networking, not Networks.

Problem

Message about duplicate IP addresses—can't connect to anything

Solution

Duplicate IP addresses will disable both TCP/IP and NetBEUI networking. If you're trying to share your Internet connection, use software such as Artisoft's Ishare, or check with your networking hardware vendor for their recommendations. If your LAN uses a proxy server for connection, some sharing products might not work. A proxy server serves as a middle ground between your Internet client and the Internet. Any requests for data on the Internet are routed to the proxy server, which then fetches the data from the Internet. When your station receives the data, it's actually coming from the proxy server. Proxy servers are used by corporate networks along with security software to prevent outside access to the corporate network, as well as by filtered Internet services such as Integrity Online.

Troubleshooting Direct Cable Connections

Microsoft's Direct Cable Connection troubleshooter (Windows 95) and DCC Setup Wizard (Windows 95/98) both make a critical mistake in their coverage of setting up DCC: the lack of coverage of networking protocols (protocols aren't required for LapLink or for the MS-DOS Interlink programs). If the same networking protocol isn't set up for both the host and guest PCs, DCC can't work.

To solve problems with DCC, use this checklist:

- Make sure the same networking protocols are installed on both the host and guest machines. The simplest protocol to install is NetBEUI, and that's what Parallel Technologies (creator of DCC) recommends for a basic DCC "mininetwork".

- Use the parallel (LPT) ports for DCC; although serial (COM) port transfers will work, they are unbearably slow.

- Make sure that both host and guest LPT ports are working correctly with no shared IRQ problems. Use the Windows 9x Device Manager to check for IRQ conflicts with the parallel port you're using.

- Make sure the person using the guest computer knows the network "name" of the host computer (set through the Networks icon in control panel, Identification). With a simple protocol such as NetBEUI, it might be necessary to enter the name to log on to the host machine.

- Install the client for Microsoft networks on the guest computer.

- Don't print to the printers on the port using DCC; it won't work! Also, allow any print jobs to finish (or delete them) on any port you want to use for DCC before you set up your cables.

- Make sure that the host computer is sharing a drive so that the guest computer can copy files from it or move files to it. The sharing is done in the same way that peer-to-peer network sharing is done.

- Make sure the Infrared ports on both computers are enabled for use in Windows 98 if you want to use this slow but cable-free method of DCC.

Audio Hardware

SOME OF THE MAIN TOPICS IN THIS CHAPTER ARE

Audio Adapter Applications

Audio Adapter Concepts and Terms

Audio Adapter Features

Choosing an Audio Adapter

Audio Adapter Installation (Overview)

Troubleshooting Sound Card Problems

Speakers

Microphones

When the PC was first created, it did not include audio capabilities other than rudimentary beeping or tone generation. Part of the reason for this was that the PC standard originated in '81, and most of the other computers of that time had similar rudimentary capabilities. Another reason was that there really were no important applications for anything other than the most basic sounds. Computers used beeps for little other than to signal problems such as a full keyboard buffer or errors during the POST (power on self test) sequence.

Systems that were designed later, such as the Macintosh that debuted in 1984, did include high-quality audio capabilities as an integral part of the system hardware and software. Although there still is no universal audio hardware and software standard for PC-compatible systems, the inherent expandability of the PC platform enables users to easily add audio capability to existing systems, and at least one de facto audio standard has emerged.

Today's PC audio hardware usually takes the form of an audio adapter on an expansion card that you install into a bus slot in the computer. As with video adapters, some systems today include the audio hardware directly on the motherboard. The adapter provides jacks for speakers, a microphone, and sometimes other devices such as joysticks and MIDI hardware. On the software side, the audio adapter requires the support of a driver that you install either directly from an application or in your computer's operating system. This chapter focuses on the audio products found in today's PCs, their uses, and how you install and operate them.

Audio Adapter Applications

At first, consumer audio adapters were used only for games. Several companies, including AdLiB, Roland, and Creative Labs, released products by the late 1980s. In 1989, Creative Labs introduced the Game Blaster, which provided stereo sound to a handful of computer games. The question for many buyers was "Why spend $100 for a card that adds sound to a $50 game?" More importantly, because no sound standards existed at the time, the sound card you selected might turn out to be useless with other games.

Note

About the same time as the release of the Game Blaster, hardware supporting the Musical Instrument Digital Interface (MIDI) became available for the PC. At this time, however, such hardware was used only in very specialized recording applications. As MIDI support became a more common feature in musical instruments, it also became a more affordable PC add-on.

A few months after releasing the Game Blaster, Creative Labs announced the Sound Blaster audio adapter. The Sound Blaster was compatible with the AdLiB sound card and Creative Labs' own Game Blaster card. It included a built-in microphone jack and a MIDI port for connecting the PC to a synthesizer or other electronic musical instrument. Finally, the audio adapter had the potential for uses other than games.

Unfortunately, as of 1989, there was still no official standard for PC audio adapters. In many areas of the computer industry, standards often evolve informally due to the widespread acceptance of the market leader's products in a particular segment of the marketplace. These are called de facto standards, as contrasted with de jure standards, which are officially ratified by the manufacturers involved in the development process. For example, Hewlett-Packard printers use a page description language called PCL that has become a de facto standard because a great many of their printers have been sold and most software supports them. Other printer manufacturers then strive to create products that emulate the Hewlett-Packard printers so that they don't require unique commands and can use the same drivers as a Hewlett-Packard printer. This is how a de facto standard is born. The process is essentially based on popularity and economic factors. Although other standards for page description languages exist, Hewlett-Packard's standard is supported by most PC-compatible printers because failure to support it would all but guarantee a marketing disaster.

Over the past few years, some manufacturers of audio adapters have fought for dominance over the market, and there are several popular brands. Historically, the leader in the field has been Creative Labs, whose Sound Blaster audio adapters continue to dominate the marketplace and have established the de facto "Sound Blaster Pro" standard for the industry.

Compatibility with Sound Blaster continues to be important for DOS-based games, but as Windows-based sound APIs such as Microsoft DirectX, Aureal's A3d, and Creative Labs' own Sound Blaster Live! are surpassing DOS support in popularity, support for these newer standards is just as important. The original Sound Blaster and Sound Blaster Pro became a widely supported standard because of broad software support. As the industry accelerates its move to Windows, choosing a sound card still means choosing the card that works best with the applications you want to run. As you'll see later, the change from the resource-gobbling ISA bus to the faster PCI bus has also changed how sound cards work and what must be done for those occasions when "classic" Sound Blaster compatibility is required.

Today, audio adapters have many uses, including the following:

- Adding stereo sound to multimedia entertainment (game) software
- Increasing the effectiveness of educational software, particularly for young children
- Adding sound effects to business presentations and training software
- Creating music by using MIDI hardware and software
- Adding voice notes to files
- Audioconferencing and network telephony
- Adding sound effects to operating system events
- Enabling a PC to read
- Enabling PC use by handicapped individuals
- Playing audio CDs
- Playing MP3 audio files
- Playing audio-video clips
- Playing DVD films with audio
- Providing support for voice-control computer software
- Providing support for voice-dictation and playback software (speech-to-text/text-to-speech)

Games

As with other multimedia technologies, audio adapters were originally designed to play games. In fact, many adapters include a game adapter interface, which is a connector for adding a game control device (usually an analog joystick, control paddles, or a steering wheel). Some adapters also use this interface to connect a plug providing a MIDI connector. The game port is a potential area of conflict because other cards, such as the multi-I/O type cards that many PCs use to provide serial and parallel ports, also have a game interface. This can result in an I/O port address conflict because most game interfaces use the same I/O port addresses. In these cases, it is usually best to use the game adapter interface on the audio adapter and disable any others in your system, especially if you plan to use MIDI devices.

Note

If you have invested in a high-performance game port designed for fast PCs and sophisticated controllers such as driving wheels, force-feedback joysticks, and so on, you should disable the sound card's game port and use the separate one you installed.

By adding an audio adapter, game playing takes on a new dimension. Sound adds a level of realism that would otherwise be impossible even with the best graphics. For example, some games use digitized human voices or real recorded dialogue. Many TV and film actors such as *Star Wars'* Mark Hamill have enjoyed a second career providing voice-overs or even "live" performances in interactive games such as *Wing Commander*. In addition to realistic sounds and effects, games can also have musical scores, which adds to the excitement and entertainment.

Most recent sound cards also offer 3D sound, which uses multiple speakers to provide highly realistic game play and environmental sounds. When coupled with special controllers and powerful new speakers, these sound cards make games extra realistic.

Multimedia

A sound card is a prerequisite if you want to turn your PC into a Multimedia PC (MPC). What is multimedia? The term embraces a number of PC technologies, but it primarily deals with video, sound, and storage. Basically, PC multimedia means the capability to merge images, data, and sound on a computer into a unified perceptual experience. In a practical sense, multimedia usually means adding an audio adapter and a CD-ROM drive to your system.

An organization called the Multimedia PC (MPC) Marketing Council was originally formed by Microsoft to generate standards for MPCs. They have created several MPC standards and license their logo and trademark to manufacturers whose hardware and software conform to these standards.

More recently, the MPC Marketing Council formally transferred responsibility for their standards to the Software Publishers Association's Multimedia PC Working Group. This group includes many of the same members as the original MPC and is now the body governing the MPC specifications. The first thing this group did was create a new MPC standard.

The MPC Marketing Council originally developed two primary standards for multimedia. They are called the MPC Level 1 and MPC Level 2 standards. Under the direction of the Software Publishers Association (SPA), these first two standards have been augmented by a third standard called MPC Level 3, which was introduced in June of 1995. These standards define the minimum capabilities for an MPC. Table 20.1 shows these standards.

Table 20.1   Multimedia Standards

	MPC Level 1	**MPC Level 2**	**MPC Level 3**
Processor	16MHz 386SX	25MHz 486SX	75mhz Pentium
RAM	2MB	4MB	8MB
Hard disk	30MB	160MB	540MB
Floppy disk	1.44MB 3 1/2-inch	1.44MB 3 1/2-inch	1.44MB 3 1/2-inch
CD-ROM drive	Single-speed	Double-speed	Quad-speed
Audio	8-bit	16-bit	16-bit
VGA video	640×480	640×480	640×480
Resolution	16KB colors	64KB colors	64KB colors
Other I/O	Serial, Parallel, MIDI, Game	Serial, Parallel, MIDI, Game	Serial, Parallel, MIDI, Game
Minimum Software	Microsoft Windows 3.1	Microsoft Windows 3.1	Microsoft Windows 3.1
Date introduced	1990	May 1993	June 1995

The MPC-3 specifications should be considered the absolute bare minimums for any multimedia system. In fact, all new and recent-model computers exceed the Level 3 specification by a substantial margin in every area. With Windows 95 or 98 as the standard operating system, I would normally recommend a system that includes at least 32MB of RAM, a 200MHz Pentium processor, and 2GB of hard drive space. A faster CD-ROM drive and a higher video resolution also enhance the multimedia experience. Note that although speakers or headphones are technically not a part of the MPC specification, they are certainly required for sound reproduction.

In addition to hardware specifications, the MPC specifications also define the minimum audio capabilities of a multimedia system. These capabilities must include digital audio recording and playback (linear PCM sampling), music synthesis, and audio mixing. The Software Publishers Association has a special section of its Web site devoted to MPC issues at www.spa.org/mpc, although the organization doesn't plan to provide any new MPC standards. All recent and current PCs with CD-ROM and sound exceed the MPC-3 standards by a comfortable margin.

Because the MPC specifications increasingly reflect multimedia's past, users who want to know what comes next need somewhere else to turn for guidance. Microsoft and Intel jointly manage the PC Design Guide Web site at www.pcdesguide.com, where the PC97, PC98, and PC99 specifications and addenda can be read and reviewed. These standards are widely followed by the industry and point the way to the end of ISA-bus audio and many other enhancements for audio hardware and software in the Windows environment.

Sound Files

You can use two basic types of files to store audio on your PC. One type is generically called a sound file and uses formats such as WAV, VOC, AU, and AIFF. Sound files contain waveform data, which means they are analog audio recordings that have been digitized for storage on a computer. Just as you can store graphic images at different resolutions, you can have sound files that use various resolutions, trading off sound quality for file size. The three default sound resolution levels used in Windows 9x are shown in Table 20.2.

Table 20.2   Windows 9x Sound File Resolutions

Resolution	Frequency	Bandwidth	File Size
Telephone quality	11,025Hz	8-bit mono	11KB/sec
Radio quality	22,050Hz	8-bit mono	22KB/sec
CD quality	44,100Hz	16-bit stereo	172KB/sec

Many new sound cards also support a 48KHz standard designed to match the requirements of DVD audio playback and Dolby AC-3 audio compression technologies. As you can see, the difference in file sizes between the highest and lowest audio resolution levels is substantial. CD quality sound files can occupy enormous amounts of disk space. At this rate, just 60 seconds of audio would require over 10MB of storage. For applications that don't require or benefit from such high resolution, such as voice annotation, telephone quality audio is sufficient and generates much smaller files.

In addition to these standard quality designations, you can create your own combinations of frequency and bandwidth with virtually any audio recording program, including the Sound Recorder applet supplied with Windows 9x.

Audio Compression

By using audio-editing software such as RealPlayer's RealProducer G2, you can compress high-quality sound for use on Web sites with a minimal loss of quality, but a large reduction in file size.

The latest example of a sound format being popularized by the Web is the popular MP3 file type, a digital sound-only flavor of MPEG that has become an overwhelmingly popular downloadable sound format on the World Wide Web. MP3 files have near-CD quality but are far smaller than normal CD-quality WAV files.

MP3 enables both downloading of these compact, quality music files and transformation of the CDs you now own into individual MP3 tracks. Although MP3-creation programs (also called rippers) can work at different sampling rates, the standard is 120Kb/second encoding. A five-minute song that rips to a CD-quality 50MB WAV file would convert to an MP3 file that is less than 4MB.

Thanks to MP3, many PCs around the country are doubling as stereo systems without the need to flip CDs and with the capability to construct custom music playlists. MP3 provides music lovers with the capability to store just the songs they want and to create customized CDs for personal use. MP3 files are being distributed legally by musicians wanting to build an audience or gain publicity for a new CD album or upcoming tour. Unfortunately, many MP3 Web sites are stuffed full of unauthorized MP3 tracks. Despite the problems of "pirate" MP3 files on the Web, MP3 promises to be the leading edge of a consumer-friendly music revolution: helping you get just the songs you want in the media you want, whether it's portable player (such as Diamond Multimedia's RIO), computer storage, or music CD.

Caution

Although MP3 is an exciting method used legally by many artists to attract new audiences, be careful about what you download. Distributing MP3 sound files from copyrighted artists without permission is both unethical and illegal. If you find MP3 files on the Web and are unsure about their legitimacy, don't download them.

MIDI Files

The second type of audio file is a MIDI file, which is as different from a WAV as a vector graphic is from a bitmap. MIDI files, which use MID or RMI extensions, are wholly digital files that do not contain recordings of sound; instead, they contain the instructions that the audio hardware uses to create the sound. Just as 3D video adapters use instructions and textures to create images for the computer to display, MIDI-capable audio adapters use MIDI files as instructions to guide the synthesis of music.

MIDI is a powerful programming language developed in the 1980s to permit electronic musical instruments to communicate. MIDI was the breakthrough standard in the electronic music industry, an industry that to this day shuns nearly all attempts at hardware standardization in favor of proprietary systems. With MIDI you can create, store, edit, and play back music files on your computer either in tandem with a MIDI-compatible electronic musical instrument (typically a keyboard synthesizer) or with just the computer.

Unlike the other types of sound files, MIDI messages require relatively little storage space. An hour of stereo music stored in MIDI format requires less than 500KB. Many games use MIDI sounds instead of recorded ones to supply large amounts of music while conserving disk space. Because they are not recordings, the use of various resolutions does not apply to MIDI files.

A MIDI file is actually a digital representation of a musical score. It is composed of a collection of separate channels, each of which represents a different musical instrument or type of sound. Each channel specifies the frequencies and duration of the notes to be "played" by that instrument, just as a piece of sheet music does. Thus, a MIDI file of a string quartet contains four channels representing two violins, a viola, and a cello.

Note

MIDI files are not intended to be a replacement for sound files such as WAVs; they should be considered a complementary technology. The biggest drawback of MIDI is that the playback technology is limited to sounds that are readily synthesizable. The most obvious shortcoming is that MIDI files are incapable of producing voices (except for synthesized choir effects). Therefore, when you download a MIDI file of your favorite song from the Internet, you'll have to do the singing.

(continues)

(continued)

A more significant limitation of MIDI also stems from its synthetic nature; the quality of your sound card directly influences what MIDI sounds like when you play it back. Because MIDI files can be played back with FM synthesis or wavetable synthesis, older low-cost sound cards without wavetable features will produce MIDI music that sounds like an orchestra of kazoos. Unfortunately, even with a high-quality wavetable sound card, some MIDI files still sound bad because they were produced for playback on FM-synthesis sound cards. Even though most sound cards sold today feature some form of wavetable synthesis, the number of instruments and the quality of the patch sets (the digital samples) can vary widely from card to card. Inexpensive wavetable cards might support only 32 voices, whereas better cards can support 256 or more.

All three MPC specifications as well as the PC9x specifications call for all audio adapters to support MIDI. The general MIDI standard used by most of the audio adapters on the market provide for up to 16 channels in a single MIDI file, but this does not necessarily limit you to 16 instruments. A single channel can represent the sound of a group of instruments, such as a violin section, enabling you to synthesize an entire orchestra.

Because MIDI files consist of digital instructions, you can edit them much more easily than you can a sound file such as a WAV file. With the appropriate software, you can select any channel of a MIDI file and change the notes, the instrument used to play them, and many other attributes that affect the sound the PC produces.

Some software packages can even produce a manuscript of the music in a MIDI file by using standard musical notation. A composer can write a piece of music directly on the computer, edit it as needed, and then print out sheet music for live musicians to read. This is an enormous benefit for professional musicians, who historically have had to either employ music copyists or publishers or spend long hours copying music by hand.

Playing MIDI Files

When you play a MIDI file on your PC, you are not playing back a recording. Your system is actually creating music from scratch. To do this, the computer requires a synthesizer, and every MIDI-capable audio adapter has one. As the system reads the MIDI file, the synthesizer generates the appropriate sound for each channel, using the instructions in the file to create the proper pitches and note lengths and using a predefined patch to simulate the sound of a specific musical instrument. A patch is a set of instructions that the synthesizer uses to create sound similar to a particular instrument. You can control the speed at which the music plays and its volume in real time with the MIDI player software.

The synthesizer on an audio adapter is similar electronically to those found in actual electronic keyboard instruments, but it is usually not as capable. The MPC specifications call for audio adapters to contain FM synthesizer chips that are capable of playing at least six melodic notes and two percussive notes simultaneously.

FM Synthesis

Until the mid-1990s, most low-cost sound boards generated sounds by using FM (frequency modulation) synthesis, a technology first pioneered in 1976. By using one sine wave operator to modify another, FM synthesis creates an artificial sound that mimics an instrument. The MIDI standard supported by the adapter specifies an array of preprogrammed sounds containing most of the instruments used by pop bands and orchestras.

Over the years, the technology has progressed (some FM synthesizers now use four operators) to a point where FM synthesis can sound moderately good, but it is still noticeably artificial. The trumpet sound, for example, is vaguely similar to that of a trumpet, but it would never be confused with the real thing. Today, virtually all new sound cards use more realistic wavetable sound (see the following section), although many still offer FM synthesis as an option.

Wavetable Synthesis

Today, few sound cards use FM synthesis because even at its best, the sound it produces is not a realistic simulation of a musical instrument. More realistic, inexpensive sound was pioneered by Ensoniq Corp., the makers of professional keyboards, in 1984.

Using a technology that was theorized at about the same time as FM synthesis, Ensoniq developed a method of sampling any instrument—including pianos, violins, guitars, flutes, trumpets, and drums—and storing the digitized sound in a wavetable. Stored either in ROM chips or on disk, the wavetable supplies an actual digitized sound of an instrument that the audio adapter can manipulate as needed. Soon after Ensoniq's discovery, other keyboard makers replaced their FM synthesizers with wavetable synthesis.

Today, Ensoniq is owned by Creative Labs, makers of the de facto industry-standard Sound Blaster line of sound cards. Ensoniq continues to create professional keyboards while also supplying OEM sound hardware to many computer vendors. Ensoniq technology has also been added to the Sound Blaster sound-card product line.

A number of low-cost, high-quality PCI-based sound cards using Ensoniq chipsets are also available from various vendors.

A wavetable synthesizer can take a sample of an instrument playing a single note and modify its frequency to play any note on the scale. Some adapters produce better sound by using several samples of the same instrument. The highest note on a piano differs from the lowest note in more than just pitch, and the closer the pitch of the sample is to the note being synthesized, the more realistic the sound is.

Thus, the size of the wavetable has a powerful effect on the quality and variety of sounds that the synthesizer can produce. The best quality wavetable adapters on the market usually have several megabytes of memory on the card for storing samples. Some support optional daughtercards for the installation of additional memory and enable you to customize the samples in the wavetable to your own specifications.

To save money without compromising quality, many current PCI-based wavetable sound cards use so-called "soft wavetable" techniques, which borrow 1–8MB from main computer memory for storage of wavetable samples.

MIDI Connectivity

The advantages of MIDI go beyond the internal functions of your computer. You can also use your audio adapter's MIDI interface to connect an electronic keyboard, sound generator, drum machine, or other MIDI device to your computer. You can then play MIDI files by using the synthesizer in the keyboard instead of the one on your adapter or create your own MIDI files by playing notes on the keyboard. With the right software, you can compose an entire symphony by playing the notes of each instrument separately into its own channel and then playing back all the channels together. Many professional musicians and composers use MIDI to create music directly on computers, bypassing traditional instruments altogether.

Some manufacturers even offer high-end MIDI cards that can operate in full-duplex mode, meaning that you can play back prerecorded audio tracks as you record a new track into the same MIDI file. This is technology that only a few years ago required the services of a professional recording studio with equipment costing hundreds of thousands of dollars.

To connect a MIDI device to your PC, you need an audio adapter that has the MIDI ports defined by the MIDI specification. MIDI uses two round 5-pin DIN ports (see Figure 20.1) for separate input (MIDI-IN) and output (MIDI-OUT). Many devices also have a MIDI-THRU port that passes the input from a device directly to output, but audio adapters generally do not have this. Interestingly, MIDI sends data through only pins 1 and 3 of the connector. Pin 2 is shielded and pins 4 and 5 are unused.

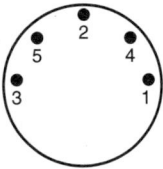

Figure 20.1   The MIDI specification calls for the use of two or three 5-pin DIN connectors.

The primary function of the audio adapter's MIDI interface is to convert the parallel data bytes used on a computer's system bus into the serial MIDI data format. MIDI uses asynchronous serial ports that run at 31.25Kbaud. MIDI communications use 8 data bits, with one start bit and one stop bit, for a speed of 320 microseconds per serial byte.

Note

You can obtain the most recent specifications for the MIDI standard for a modest fee from the MIDI Manufacturers Association's sales-fulfillment address: MMA, PO Box 3173, La Habra, CA 90632-3173 USA.

The MIDI Manufacturers Association also has a Web site at **www.midi.org**.

MIDI runs over special unshielded twisted-pair cables that can have a maximum length of up to 50 feet (although most of the cables sold are 10 or 20 feet long). You can also daisy chain multiple MIDI devices together to combine their capabilities. The total length of the MIDI chain is not limited as long as each individual cable is less than 50 feet.

Many audio adapters do not have MIDI ports directly on the adapter card. Instead, they use a separate connector that plugs into the adapter's game port and provides the MIDI ports. Unfortunately, this connector is rarely included in the box with the adapter. You have to purchase it separately from the audio-card manufacturer.

MIDI Software

Windows 9x includes basic software that enables you to play MIDI files in the form of its Media Player application, and it also includes a selection of MIDI music files. For full MIDI capabilities, however, you'll need sequencing software to either manipulate the tempo of MIDI files and the sounds used to play them or to cut and paste together various prerecorded music sequences.

Many audio adapters come with a selection of software products that provide some MIDI capabilities, and there are shareware and freeware tools available on the Internet, but the truly powerful software that enables you to create, edit, and manipulate MIDI files must be purchased separately.

Presentations

Businesses are rapidly discovering that integrating graphics, animation, and sound into their presentations is more impressive than a simple slide show and is more likely to keep their audiences awake. An audio adapter adds impact to any presentation or classroom.

A variety of business-presentation software and high-end training and authoring packages that can take advantage of a PC's audio capabilities already exists, and you don't have to be a programmer to get your own show on the road. Popular software packages such as Microsoft PowerPoint now include sound and animation features for their presentation files.

Presentation software packages support WAV, AVI, and MIDI files. With these products, you can synchronize sounds with objects. When a presentation displays a picture of your new product, for example, you can add a roaring round of applause. You can even pull in sound from an audio CD in your CD-ROM drive. Many presentation software packages also include clip-media libraries with audio files that you can use license-free.

You can even take your show on the road. Many laptop and notebook computers include sound capability and even have built-in CD-ROM drives and speakers. There are also external audio adapters and even CD-ROM drives available to provide multimedia on the go.

An audio adapter can make many computing tasks (such as learning how to use software) easier. PC software manufacturers have taken an early lead in this area. Many publishers are taking advantage of the space on the CD-ROMs they now use to distribute their products by including animated tutorials and online help, replete with music.

Sound has also found its place on the World Wide Web. Because of their relatively small size, MIDI files are an excellent choice for providing background music when users arrive at your Web site. A catchy tune can help people remember your site out of the many others they see each day, but setting your tune to repeat incessantly can drive Web-surfers crazy. If you want to MIDIfy your Web sites, I suggest that you choose subtle MIDI tracks and give users a control for turning the music off and on, especially if you are considering repeating the MIDI track.

If you want to add digitized voice or music to your site, the leading plug-in with very wide support is RealPlayer; use the RealProducer G2 series to process your sound files for Web use, preserving essential qualities while causing amazing reductions in file size.

Recording

Virtually all audio adapters have an audio input jack. With a microphone, you can record your voice. Using the Sound Recorder application included with all versions of Microsoft Windows, you can play, edit, or record a sound file in the WAV format. From the Windows Sounds Control Panel, you can assign specific WAV files to certain Windows events. I always get a laugh when I exit Windows and hear the sound of a flushing toilet!

This capability is not just an entertaining novelty, however. You can also use specific sounds to notify you of important events, such as when your system experiences an error ("Call extension 999 for help") or when you receive new email ("You've got mail!"). The Windows operating system ships with a collection of basic WAV files that you can assign as needed. Windows 9x also includes collections of WAV files called sound schemes that provide a unified environment for your system based on a given subject. The Musica sound scheme, for example, automatically assigns sound files of various musical instruments to many of the standard system events. Many applications add their own events to the operating system, enabling you to configure sounds for activities specific to that product.

By recording the sound of your own voice (or anything else), you can create your own WAV files and assign them to certain events, instead of using the default Windows WAVs. On most multimedia systems, you can record directly from an audio CD in your CD-ROM drive to the WAV format. You can also attach your stereo system or VCR to the audio input jack and record any sound to a WAV file.

With this simple connection, users have amassed libraries consisting of thousands of WAV files celebrating popular songs, movies, and TV shows.

Tip

By using a CD-R/CD-RW drive and recording software such as Adaptec Easy CD Creator with its music-oriented "Spin Doctor" feature, older analog sound sources such as scratchy LPs and deteriorated cassette and 8-track tapes can be improved during the conversion to digital CD storage. Spin Doctor and similar utilities can remove or minimize the click and hiss common to old recordings. Spin Doctor can also be used to produce a customized CD of your favorite selections from recordings you already own.

Voice Annotation

By using WAV files, you can record voice messages and embed them in your Windows documents. For example, a business executive could pick up a microphone and, by embedding a message in a contract or spreadsheet, give her secretary explicit instructions. This message is called a voice annotation. I like to think of it as a verbal Post-It Note.

With voice annotation, you can embed voice messages, suggestions, or questions in a document and send it to a colleague. To leave such messages, your Windows application must support Windows' object linking and embedding (OLE). OLE is a technology that enables you to take objects created by one application and embed them in a document created in another application. Activating the embedded object in the target application by double-clicking it automatically launches the object's source application. Sound files can also be distributed through the Distributed Common Object Model (DCOM), a refinement of OLE that extends the concept to ActiveX controls. For example, if you embed a portion of a Microsoft Excel spreadsheet into a Word document, you will see the grid of the spreadsheet on the page in Word. However, when you double-click the spreadsheet, Excel launches and temporarily replaces the Word menu and button bars with those of Excel. Clicking another part of the Word document returns you to the normal Word environment.

Embedding a sound in a document works the same way. Imagine that you're editing an Excel spreadsheet and you want to insert a voice note next to a total that looks questionable. Place the cursor in the cell next to the total and then select Edit, Insert, Object, Sound to call up Windows' Sound Recorder. Click the Record button and begin speaking. After you finish recording, the sound appears as an icon in the selected cell. Because the sound file is actually an embedded part of the spreadsheet file, you can copy it to a disk or email it to another user. That user can then double-click the icon and hear your voice.

Although Windows 9x ships with the Sound Recorder applet, this utility limits original recordings to very short time periods, varying with the quality of the recording (higher quality = shorter duration). To record clips of more than about 10 or 15 seconds, use a third-party application.

Tip

Voice annotation is typically an area where sound quality is not a major issue. Be sure to configure your system to use telephone-quality (that is, the lowest quality) audio for this purpose, or you could end up with files that are enormously inflated in size by the addition of embedded audio.

Voice Recognition

Some audio adapters are equipped with software that is capable of voice recognition. You can also get voice recognition for your current adapter in the form of add-on software. Voice recognition, as the name implies, is when your computer is "taught" to recognize spoken word forms and react to them. Voice recognition products generally take two forms: those that are designed to provide a simple voice interface to basic computer functions, and those that can accept vocal dictation and insert the spoken text into an application such as a word processor. The minimum standard for most voice-recognition software is a Sound Blaster 16 or equivalent sound card.

Voice Command Software

The voice interface application is clearly the simpler of the two, as the software only has to recognize a limited vocabulary of words. With this type of software, you can sit in front of your computer and say the words "file open" to access the menu in your active Windows application.

For the average user, this type of application is of dubious value. For a time, Compaq was shipping computers to corporate clients with a microphone and an application of this type at little or no additional cost. The phenomenon of dozens of users in an office talking to their computers was interesting, to say the least. The experiment resulted in virtually no increased productivity, a lot of wasted time as users experimented with the software, and a noisier office.

However, for users with physical handicaps that limit their ability to use a keyboard, this type of software can represent a whole new avenue of communication. For this reason alone, continued development of voice recognition technology is essential.

Note

Voice recognition applications, by necessity, have to be somewhat limited in their scope. For example, it quickly becomes a standard office joke for someone to stick their head into another person's cubicle and call out "Format C!," as though this command would erase the user's hard drive. Obviously, the software must not be able to damage a user's system because of a misinterpreted voice command.

Voice Dictation Software

The other type of voice recognition software is far more complex. Converting standard speech into text is an extraordinarily difficult task, given the wide variation in human speech patterns. For this reason, nearly all software of this type (and some of the basic voice command applications, as well) must be "trained" to understand a particular user's voice. You do this training by reading prepared text samples supplied with the software to the computer. Because the software knows what you're supposed to be saying beforehand, it can associate certain words with the manner in which you speak them.

Users' results with this sort of application vary widely, probably due in no small part to their individual speech patterns. I've heard people rave about being able to dictate pages of text without touching the keyboard, whereas others claim that correcting the many typographical errors is more trouble than typing the text manually.

There are many variables that can account for such wide variances in the quality of voice dictation. Early versions of these products required users to separate words and speak "robotically - like - this" to get the computer to recognize the text. These "discrete speech" products are now obsolete and should be replaced by newer "continuous speech" products.

A second factor is the "trainability" of the software. My experience with trainable and "no-training-needed" programs suggest that training a voice-dictation program to recognize your speech patterns and accent is still a good idea for best results.

A third factor is the program's active and total vocabulary. Given identical voice-recognition engines, the program with the larger active vocabulary will react more quickly to dictation, and the program with the larger total vocabulary will be able to store more user-specific words.

If you're involved in medicine or law or other professions with specialized vocabularies, you might find it saves time (and ultimately money) to purchase industry-specific versions of your favorite voice-recognition program. These programs offer enlarged vocabularies tailored to your line of work.

Other features to look for include voice commands for computer operations, text-to-speech translation to let your computer "read" to you, and Web-browser compliance (which might require a separate program at this point).

Whatever the program you choose, some prerequisites for success include the following:

- A quiet room with little change in background sound.
- A microphone specially designed for voice-recognition (a low-cost one normally comes with the software, but better models are available). *Using a poor-quality microphone or an inadequate sound card will cause problems for even the finest voice-dictation program.*
- Completing sound setup and user training, if offered, to set software for your voice and vocabulary.
- Retraining difficult-to-distinguish words.
- Using the most advanced version of the software you can afford.

Note

The voice-dictation software versions bundled with office suites such as IBM's Lotus SmartSuite and Corel WordPerfect Suite are usually not the top-of-the-line version, but they will usually qualify you for upgrade pricing to move to the best version available.

Voice recognition technology is still a young technology and is sensitive to changes in a person's voice. Illness and stress can often change a person's voice enough to throw off most of the "consumer" voice recognition products. You will also need a fast computer, at least a Pentium, to achieve response times that are quick enough to keep up with your speech. Because voice-recognition technology (especially voice-dictation) can also help users avoid the debilitating effects of repetitive stress injuries on wrists, fingers, and arms from typing too long without a break, it should become increasingly popular as system speeds increase and the software improves.

Note

As with any resource-hungry product, your system should exceed the "minimum requirements" for RAM, CPU speed, and free disk space by a factor of two or three if you want to be really happy with your software.

However, advances in this technology are rapidly developing to a point where more and more of us are able to use continuous speech to write with computers, rather than typing.

Conferencing

One of the newest applications in the world of multimedia is video and audio conferencing over the Internet. These applications range from point-to-point products, such as VocalTec's Internet Phone, to multiuser-conferencing packages, such as Microsoft's NetMeeting. Other applications, such as RealNetworks' Real Player and Microsoft's Media Player, can play back audio (with or without video) as it is received over the Internet, a process called streaming.

For all these applications, the audio adapter is an integral part of the technology. Depending on the speed of your Internet connection, the data compression technology that the software uses, and whether you elect to stream video along with audio, the quality of the sound delivered by conferencing software can range from poor to rather good.

As with voice recognition, this is a technology that is still very young. Over a 33.6Kbps modem connection (which frequently does not reach a full 33.6), one-way audio and video streaming generally works tolerably well, but full-duplex communications, even when audio-only, tend to drop words. However, as faster Internet connections and better data compression techniques become available, audioconferencing and videoconferencing are likely to become as reliable as the telephone network.

Proofreading

You can also use an audio adapter as an inexpensive proofreading tool. Many adapters include a text-to-speech utility that you can use to read a list of numbers or text back to you. This type of software can read back highlighted words or even an entire file.

Having text read back to you enables you to more easily spot forgotten words or awkward phrases. Accountants can double-check numbers, and busy executives can listen to their email while they are doing paperwork.

As I mentioned previously, this is a popular feature of many of the leading voice-dictation programs on the market.

Audio CDs

One convenient and entertaining use of a CD-ROM drive is to play audio CDs while you are working on something else. Virtually all CD-ROM drives support audio CDs, and the music can be piped not only through a pair of speakers (and even a subwoofer) connected to the audio adapter, but also through headphones plugged into the jack provided on most CD-ROM drives. Most sound cards include a CD-player utility, as does Windows 9x, and free versions are available for download on the Internet. These programs usually present a visual display similar to the control panel of an audio CD player. You operate the controls with a mouse or the keyboard and can listen to audio CDs as you work on other things.

If you want to hear CDs through your system's speakers, make sure that your CD audio cable is attached to both the CD-ROM drive and your sound card. Some new systems feature digital speakers attached to the USB (Universal Serial Bus) connection. These can provide excellent sound, but if used with older or cheaper CD-ROM drives, they might produce no sound at all.

USB-based speakers *must* be used with CD-ROM drives that support a feature called "digital audio extraction" if you want CD-based music to play through them. Check your CD-ROM drive's spec sheet for information about this feature.

Note

If you have a CD-R/CD-RW drive as well as an IDE-based CD-ROM, don't forget to check the recordable drive. Many of these do feature digital audio extraction, enabling you to play your music in that drive and use your (normally faster) CD-ROM for program loading and data access.

If your system is equipped with DVD drives, make sure your audio CD player software is DVD-compatible. You might need an update or a different program to work with your DVD drive.

Note

See Chapter 13, "Optical Storage," to learn more about CD audio.

Sound Mixer

On a multimedia PC, it is often possible for two or more sound sources to require the services of the audio adapter at the same time. Any time you have multiple sound sources that you want to play through a single set of speakers, a mixer is necessary.

Most audio adapters include a mixer that enables all the different audio sources, MIDI, WAV, line in, and the CD to use the single line-out jack. Although a separate recording mixer was often used with Windows 3.1x systems, Windows 9x/NT use a single mixer for both recording and playback features. Normally, the adapter ships with software that displays visual sliders like you would see on an actual audio mixer in a recording studio. With these controls, you can set the relative volume of each of the sound sources.

Is an Audio Adapter Necessary?

In the preceding sections, you read about the various ways that high-quality audio can improve the computing experience. Certainly, for recreational computer users, audio greatly enhances the entertainment value of games and other multimedia software. The question still remains, however, of whether audio is suited to the business world.

There are definitely applications, such as voice annotation and audioconferencing, that can be useful to business computer users. In training and other educational environments, audio can be a necessity in some cases. However, three other factors that can make the assimilation of PC audio into the business office problematic are the following:

- Expense
- Productivity
- Noise

The price of adding basic audio capabilities to a PC, like that of virtually all computer hardware, has plummeted during the past few years. Business applications do not require high-end audio features such as wavetable synthesis, so a simple adapter that conforms to the MPC specification is sufficient. You can usually buy a serviceable audio adapter and speakers for about $50, or less when you are buying in volume.

However, this is not an insignificant expenditure when you are talking about hundreds or thousands of PCs. Added to that is the cost of the manpower needed to install and configure all this new hardware.

The easiest solution to this problem is to purchase PCs with integrated audio adapters on the motherboard. Because these systems usually arrive preconfigured or are automatically configured by the operating system, integrated audio eliminates the time and expense of installation and provides basic audio capabilities at the lowest possible cost. If you want to make audio upgrades easier in the future, make sure that your systems come with removable audio cards or that you can easily disable the onboard audio. In either case, most business PCs offer either feature as a standard, making audio a virtual "standard" option on today's computers.

Employee productivity is another important concern. Many network administrators and company executives are only now coming to grips with the effect that Internet access has had on the workforce. Audio definitely has its uses in the business world, as does the World Wide Web, but the question remains as to whether it will be seen by many supervisors as just another time-wasting toy.

The answer to this problem is not so simple. Administrators can take steps to limit users' access to the operating system's sound configuration controls using Windows 9x system policies, but they cannot easily prevent users from downloading or recording sound files and playing them back without limiting the audio hardware's usefulness. As with the Web, however, it is likely that when the novelty of the new capabilities wears off, users will waste less time playing with audio and more time using it productively.

The final problem is the obvious one of the noise produced by the individual speakers attached to a large fleet of PCs. The degree of difficulty is, of course, dependent on the architectural layout of the workplace. For users working in small or private offices, the noise level should be minimal. For workers in cubicles, the situation should be tolerable, as long as the users exercise some restraint in the volume. In an open office with many computers, however, the noise could be a severe problem. Using headphones that plug into the speaker jack on the rear of the sound card or system is a solution that enables the use of sound while eliminating the "over-the-cubicle" noise-irritation factor that can be a problem in many offices.

Network administrators should consider these factors when deciding which users should be furnished with audio hardware.

Audio Adapter Concepts and Terms

To fully understand audio adapters and their functions, you need to understand various concepts and terms. Terms such as 16-bit, CD quality, and MIDI port are just a few. Concepts such as sampling and digital-to-audio conversion (DAC) are often sprinkled throughout stories about new sound products. You've already learned about some of these terms and concepts; the following sections describe many others.

The Nature of Sound

To understand an audio adapter, you have to understand the nature of sound. Every sound is produced by vibrations that compress air or other substances. These sound waves travel in all directions, expanding in balloon-like fashion from the source of the sound. When these waves reach your ear, they cause vibrations that you perceive as sound.

Two of the basic properties of any sound are its pitch and its intensity.

Pitch is the rate at which vibrations are produced. It is measured in the number of hertz (Hz), or cycles per second. One cycle is a complete vibration back and forth. The number of Hz is the frequency of the tone; the higher the frequency, the higher the pitch.

Humans cannot hear all possible frequencies. Very few people can hear sounds with frequencies less than 16Hz or greater than about 20KHz (kilohertz; 1KHz equals 1,000Hz). In fact, the lowest note on a piano has a frequency of 27Hz, and the highest note a little more than 4KHz. Frequency-modulation (FM) radio stations can broadcast notes with frequencies as high as 15KHz.

The intensity of a sound is called its *amplitude*. This intensity determines the sound's volume and depends on the strength of the vibrations producing the sound. A piano string, for example, vibrates gently when the key is struck softly. The string swings back and forth in a narrow arc, and the tone it sends out is soft. If the key is struck more forcefully, however, the string swings back and forth in a wider arc, producing a greater amplitude and a greater volume. The loudness of sounds is measured in decibels (db). The rustle of leaves is rated at 20db, average street noise at 70db, and nearby thunder at 120db.

Game Standards

Most audio adapters emulate some version of the Sound Blaster, by Creative Labs, which is the current entertainment audio standard for DOS-based game and educational programs. AdLiB was a company whose audio adapters at one time rivaled those of Creative Labs in the PC game industry. They were involved in the development of the MSC Level 1 and 2 standards, and for some time AdLiB and Creative Labs were running neck and neck as the de facto standard, until AdLiB declined and went out of business for a time. Now, the company is back in business as AdLiB Multimedia, but they no longer hold a position comparable to that of Creative Labs.

To hear sounds in most DOS games, you must configure the game by selecting one of the audio adapter drivers included with the program. If you plan to play the game through in DOS mode, you might be able to run the game directly from its icon, or you might need to run a DOS-compatibility driver first. Because it's difficult for most of today's Windows-oriented PCI-based sound cards to emulate Sound Blaster at the hardware level demanded by many older games, don't discard that ancient SB Pro or SB 16. You might want to keep it around as long as you have DOS-based games. Older Windows-based games will work with virtually any Windows-supported sound card. For most modern Windows-based games, for best sound quality and features, check to see whether the card is supported by Microsoft's DirectSound3D API (part of DirectX), Aureal's A3D 2.0 Positional Audio API, or Creative Labs' SB Live! standards, depending on what the game uses for its sound APIs.

The ideal combination for a versatile sound card will be one that supports Sound Blaster Pro or 16 without TSR drivers and is supported by DirectX and at least one of the third-party game APIs.

Tip

If you want to save money while still getting near-perfect Sound Blaster compatibility, choose either the Ensoniq-labeled PCI sound card sold by Creative Labs or the many OEM versions. Since Ensoniq is part of the Creative Labs/Sound Blaster family, its cards perform well for both DOS gaming and basic Windows applications.

Many games are now being written for the Windows 9x operating system, which eliminates the problem of audio adapter compatibility. In Windows 9x, you install the driver in the operating system, and any application can take advantage of it. As long as you have a Windows 9x driver for your adapter, you can run any game designed for the OS, although some games will provide enhanced sound if the card also supports the audio APIs listed previously.

Note

Using Windows 9x software also means that the hardware settings used by your sound card (see the following section) need no longer match the traditional Sound Blaster defaults when running a game in a DOS box and under Windows. Legacy applications that run in real-mode DOS will still need to use the legacy defaults. Overall, Windows makes configuring today's crowded systems much easier than it was in the past.

The latest games support 3D standards such as Sound Blaster Live! and Aureal's A3D technology.

Frequency Response

The quality of an audio adapter is often measured by two criteria: frequency response (or range) and total harmonic distortion.

The frequency response of an audio adapter is the range in which an audio system can record or play at a constant and audible amplitude level. Many cards support 30Hz to 20KHz. The wider the spread, the better the adapter.

The total harmonic distortion measures an audio adapter's linearity, the straightness of a frequency response curve. In layman's terms, the harmonic distortion is a measure of accurate sound reproduction. Any nonlinear elements cause distortion in the form of harmonics. The smaller the percentage of distortion, the better. This harmonic distortion factor might make the difference between cards that use the same audio chipset. Cards with cheaper components might have greater distortion, making them produce poorer quality sound.

Sampling

With an audio adapter, a PC can record waveform audio. Waveform audio (also known as sampled or digitized sound) uses the PC as a recording device (such as a tape recorder). Small computer chips built into the adapter, called analog-to-digital converters (ADCs), convert analog sound waves into digital bits that the computer can understand. Likewise, digital-to-analog converters (DACs) convert the recorded sounds to an audible analog format.

Sampling is the process of turning the original analog sound waves (see Figure 20.2) into digital (binary) signals that the computer can save and later replay. The system samples the sound by taking snapshots of its frequency and amplitude at regular intervals. For example, at time X the sound might be measured with an amplitude of Y. The higher (or more frequent) the sample rate, the more accurate the digital sound replicates its real-life source is and the larger the amount of disk space needed to store it is.

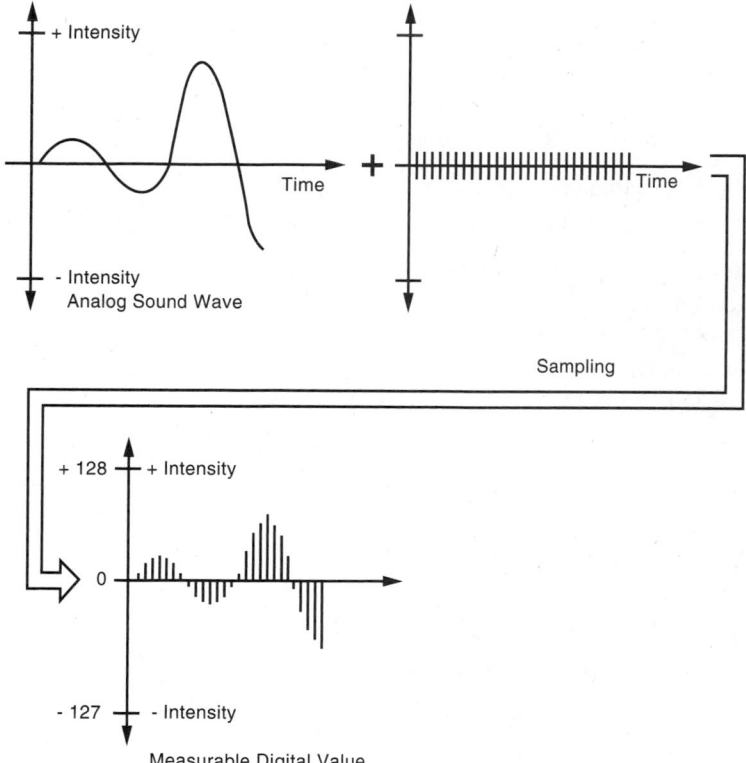

Figure 20.2   Sampling turns a changing sound wave into measurable digital values.

8-Bit Versus 16-Bit

The original MPC specifications required audio adapters to provide 8-bit sound. This doesn't mean the audio adapter must fit into an 8-bit instead of a 16-bit expansion slot. Rather, 8-bit audio means that the adapter uses eight bits to digitize each sound sample. This translates into 256 (2^8) possible digital values to which the sample can be pegged (less quality than the 65,536 values possible with a 16-bit sound card). Generally, 8-bit audio is adequate for recorded speech, whereas 16-bit sound is best for the demands of music. Figure 20.3 shows the difference between 8- and 16-bit sound.

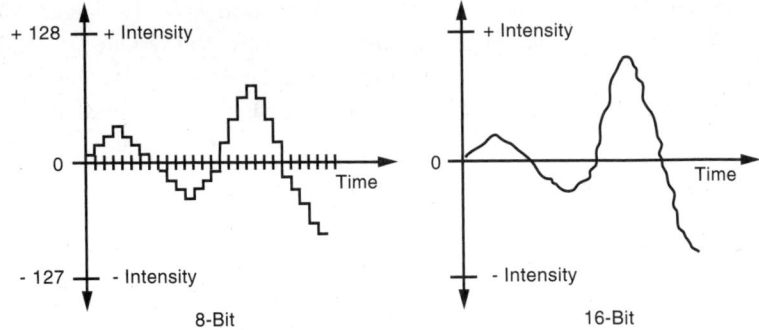

Figure 20.3   16-bit resolution provides more accurate sound reproduction than 8-bit resolution.

Many of the older audio adapters did only 8-bit sound reproduction. Today, all sound cards offer 16-bit reproduction, which offers very high resolution.

Besides resolution, the sampling rate or frequency determines how often the audio adapter measures the level of the sound being recorded or played back. Basically, you have to sample at about two times the highest frequency you want to produce, plus an extra 10 percent to keep out unwanted signals. Humans can hear up to 20,000 cycles per second, or 20KHz. If you double this number and add 10 percent, you get a 44.1KHz sampling rate, the same sampling rate used by high-fidelity audio CDs.

Sound recorded at the telephone-quality rate of 11KHz (capturing 11,000 samples per second) is fuzzier than sound sampled at the radio quality rate of 22KHz. A sound sampled in 16-bit stereo (two channel) at 44KHz (CD-audio quality) requires as much as 10.5MB per minute of disk space. The same sound sample in 8-bit mono (single channel) at 11KHz takes 1/16th the space.

Remember that for best use of your disk space (and to improve Web download times for online sounds), you should match the sound quality to the type of sound you're recording.

You can experiment with the effects of different sampling rates by recording sound with the Windows Sound Recorder or a third-party application set to CD-quality sound. Save the sound and play it back at that highest quality setting. Then convert the file to a lower-quality setting. Save the sound file again with a different name. Play back the different versions, and determine the lowest-quality (and smallest file size) that you can use without serious degradation to sound quality.

Audio Adapter Features

To make an intelligent purchasing decision, you should be aware of some audio adapter basic components and the features they provide. The following sections discuss the features you should consider while evaluating audio adapters for your PC.

Connectors

Most audio adapters have the same connectors. These 1/8-inch minijack connectors provide the means of passing sound signals from the adapter to speakers, headphones, and stereo systems, and of receiving sound from a microphone, CD player, tape player, or stereo. The four types of connectors your audio adapter should have are shown in Figure 20.4.

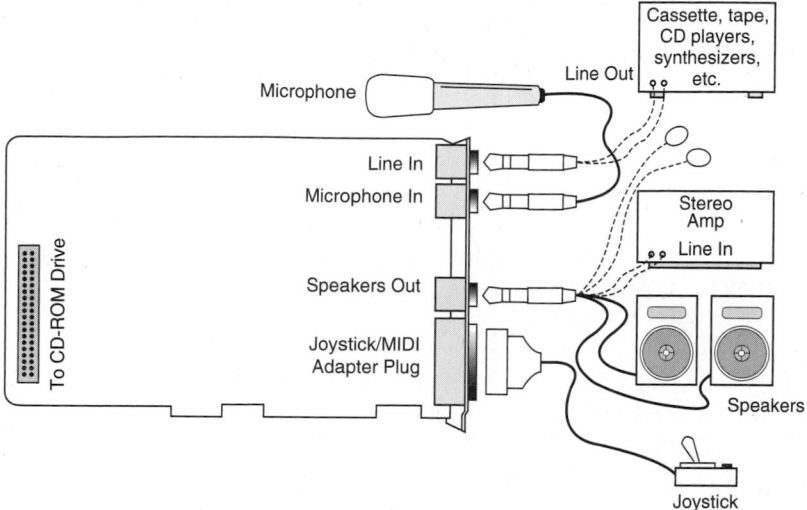

Figure 20.4 The basic input and output connectors that most audio adapters have in common.

- *Stereo line, or audio, out connector.* The line-out connector is used to send sound signals from the audio adapter to a device outside the computer. You can hook up the cables from the line-out connector to stereo speakers, a headphone set, or your stereo system. If you hook up the PC to your stereo system, you can have amplified sound. Some adapters, such as the Microsoft Windows Sound System, provide two jacks for line out. One is for the left channel of the stereo signal; the other is for the right channel.

- *Stereo line, or audio, in connector.* With the line-in connector, you can record or mix sound signals from an external source, such as a stereo system or VCR, to the computer's hard disk.

- *Speaker/headphone connector.* The speaker/headphone connector is provided on most audio adapters, but not necessarily all of them. Instead, the line out (described earlier) doubles as a way to send stereo signals from the adapter to your stereo system or speakers. When the adapter provides both a speaker/headphone and a line-out connector, the speaker/headphone connector provides an amplified signal that can power your headphones or small bookshelf speakers. Most adapters can provide up to four watts of power to drive your speakers. The signals that the adapter sends through the line-out connector are not amplified. The line-out connector generally provides better sound reproduction because it relies on the external amplifier built into your stereo system or speakers, which is typically more powerful than the small amplifier on the audio adapter.

- *Microphone, or mono, in connector.* The mono in connector is used to connect a microphone for recording your voice or other sounds to disk. This microphone jack records in mono, not in stereo, and is therefore not suitable for high quality music recordings. Many audio adapters cards use Automatic Gain Control (AGC) to improve recordings. This feature adjusts the recording levels on-the-fly. A 600–10,000ohm dynamic or condenser microphone works best with this jack. Some inexpensive audio adapters use the line-in connector instead of a separate microphone jack.

- *Joystick connector.* The joystick connector is a 15-pin, D-shaped connector that can connect to any standard joystick or game controller. Sometimes the joystick port can accommodate two joysticks if you purchase an optional Y-adapter. Many computers already contain a joystick port as part of a multifunction I/O circuit on the motherboard or an expansion card. If this is the case, you must take note of which port your operating system or application is configured to use when connecting the game controller.

- *MIDI connector.* Audio adapters typically use the same joystick port as their MIDI connector. Two of the pins in the connector are designed to carry signals to and from a MIDI device, such as an electronic keyboard. In most cases, you must purchase a separate MIDI connector from the audio adapter manufacturer that plugs in to the joystick port and contains the two round, 5-pin DIN connectors used by MIDI devices, plus a connector for a joystick. Because their signals use separate pins, you can connect the joystick and a MIDI device at the same time. You need only this connector if you plan to connect your PC to external MIDI devices. You can still play the MIDI files found on many Web sites by using the audio adapter's internal synthesizer.

- *Internal pin-type connector.* Most audio adapters have an internal pin-type connector that you can use to plug an internal CD-ROM drive directly into the adapter, using a ribbon cable. This connection enables you to channel audio signals from the CD-ROM directly to the audio adapter, so you can play the sound through the computer's speakers. Note that this connector is different from the CD-ROM controller connector found on some audio adapters. This connector does not carry data from the CD-ROM to the system bus; it only provides the CD-ROM drive with direct audio access to the speakers. If your adapter lacks this connector, you can still play CD audio through the computer speakers by connecting the CD-ROM drive's headphone jack to the audio adapter's line-in jack with an external cable.

Tip

The line-in, line-out, and speaker connectors on an audio adapter all use the same 1/8-inch minijack socket. The three jacks are usually labeled, but when setting up a computer on or under a desk, these labels on the back of the PC can be difficult to read. One of the most common reasons why a PC fails to produce any sound is that the speakers are plugged into the wrong socket.

Volume Control

Some audio adapters include a thumbwheel volume control next to the input/output jacks, although sophisticated sound cards have no room for it. This control is usually redundant, as the operating system or the software included with the adapter typically provides a combination of keys or a visual slider control that you can use to adjust the volume. In fact, the volume wheel can be troublesome; if you aren't aware of its existence and it is turned all the way down, you might be puzzled by the adapter's failure to produce sufficient sound.

Synthesis

At one time, when evaluating audio adapters, you had to decide whether to buy a monophonic or stereophonic card. Today, virtually all audio adapters are stereophonic.

Stereophonic cards produce many voices concurrently and from two different sources. A voice is a single sound produced by the adapter. A string quartet uses four voices, one for each instrument, whereas a polyphonic instrument such as a piano requires one voice for each note of a chord. Thus, to fully reproduce the capabilities of a pianist requires ten voices, one for each finger. The more voices an audio adapter is capable of producing, the better the sound fidelity. The best audio adapters on the market today can produce up to 340 simultaneous voices.

Most of the audio adapters that use FM synthesis to imitate musical instruments use synthesizer chips developed by Yamaha. Older and less-expensive adapters use the 11-voice YM3812 or OPL2 chip. Better models use the stereophonic 20-voice YMF262 or OPL3 chip.

Imitated musical instruments are not as impressive as the real thing. Wavetable audio adapters use digital recordings of real instruments and sound effects. Often, several megabytes of these sound clips are embedded in ROM chips on the card. For example, some sound cards use the Ensoniq chip set (a type of circuit design) that does wavetable synthesis of musical instruments. Instead of synthesizing the sound of a trombone playing a D flat, the Ensoniq chip set accesses a digitized sample of an actual trombone playing that note.

If your primary interest in an audio adapter is for entertainment or for use in educational or business settings, FM synthesis quality might be good enough. If you are a music enthusiast or plan to work extensively with MIDI, a wavetable adapter is preferable.

Note

To enhance the MIDI capabilities of Sound Blaster adapters that use FM synthesis, Creative Labs created the Wave Blaster. The Wave Blaster is a daughtercard that plugs into the Sound Blaster card. When the system plays MIDI music, the adapter looks to the Wave Blaster for any of 213 CD-quality, digitally recorded, musical instrument sounds. Without the Wave Blaster, the Sound Blaster would imitate these sounds through FM synthesis. With the Wave Blaster, the music sounds as though it's being played by real instruments—because it is. Although the Wave Blaster is no longer part of Creative Labs' current product line, some vendors might still have inventory.

A hardware-based alternative that is currently available is Yamaha's DB50XG. The DB50XG is designed to attach to Wave Blaster-compatible sound cards from Creative Labs and others. The card supports both General MIDI and Yamaha's advanced XG feature, which supports over 500 voices, compared to General MIDI's limit of 128. This daughtercard sells for about $80, which is more expensive than many PCI-based audio cards available today.

If your sound card is one of the low-priced PCI models that offers only 32 voices, check with your vendor for a software upgrade to a higher number for better MIDI reproduction. All Ensoniq-based 32-voice sound cards from any OEM vendor can be upgraded to 64 voices through software available at Ensoniq's Web site: www.ensoniq.com/multimedia/mm_html/html/drivers.htm.

Data Compression

Most sound cards today can easily produce CD-quality audio, which is sampled at 44.1KHz. At this rate, recorded files (even of your own voice) can consume over 10MB for every minute of recording. To counter this demand for disk space, many audio adapters include their own data-compression capability. For example, the Sound Blaster ASP 16 includes on-the-fly compression of sound files in ratios of 2:1, 3:1, or 4:1.

Some manufacturers of audio adapters use an algorithm called Adaptive Differential Pulse Code Modulation (ADPCM) compression to reduce file size by more than 50 percent. However, a simple fact of audio technology is that when you use such compression, you lose sound quality.

Because it degrades sound quality, there is no standard for the use of ADPCM. Creative Labs uses a proprietary hardware approach, whereas Microsoft is promoting the Business Audio ADPCM design, developed with Compaq.

The most popular compression standard is the Motion Pictures Experts Group (MPEG) standard, which works with both audio and video compression and is gaining support in the non-PC world from products such as the new crop of DVD players now hitting the market. MPEG by itself provides a potential compression ratio of 30:1, and largely because of this, full-motion-video MPEG DVD and CD-ROM titles are now available. The popular MP3 sound compression scheme is an MPEG format, and it can be played back on the latest versions of Microsoft's Windows 9x Media Player, as well as by MP3-only player programs.

Multipurpose Digital Signal Processors

Many audio adapters use digital signal processors (DSPs) to add intelligence to the adapter, freeing the system processor from work-intensive tasks, such as filtering noise from recordings or compressing audio on-the-fly.

The Sound Blaster AWE32's programmable DSP, for example, features compression algorithms for processing text-to-speech data and enables the card's QSound surround-sound 3D audio, along with reverb and chorus effects. DSPs enable an audio adapter to be a multipurpose device. IBM uses its DSP to add a fax modem and digital answering machine to its WindSurfer Communications Adapter.

CD-ROM Connectors

A few older audio adapters double as a CD-ROM controller, or interface, card. Before the EIDE interface made the CD-ROM a ubiquitous PC component, connecting the drive to the audio adapter was an inexpensive means of adding multimedia capabilities to a system. Although some adapters provide a SCSI port that you can theoretically use to connect any SCSI device, others used a proprietary connection that accommodates only a select few CD-ROM drives that support the same interface. The proprietary connectors once used by Creative Labs' early Sound Blaster multimedia upgrade kits have long been obsolete, and cannot be used with today's standard IDE and SCSI-interface CD-ROM drives.

If you're seeking to add both an audio adapter and a CD-ROM drive to an existing system, check for an unused 40-pin IDE connector on an IDE interface cable. If your system has an unused connector, any standard IDE (ATAPI) CD-ROM can be connected there. You can then buy a sound card and IDE CD-ROM drive as a kit or separately. If your sound card has an IDE port built in, disable it to keep it from interfering with the IDE ports on your system board. This might require rejumpering the board, running setup software, or a special command added to the CONFIG.SYS statement for the board during system startup.

Note

In my experience, you'll usually have better, faster choices if you purchase these items separately, rather than as a kit. The only reason to purchase a multimedia kit today is to have a single source for multimedia technical support because the sound cards and CD-ROM drive typically found in kits are often low-end devices with limited features.

Although an integrated audio/CD-ROM controller can be a quick and easy multimedia solution for older systems, I generally recommend that users connect the CD-ROM through a standard EIDE or SCSI interface and avoid the CD-ROM connector on the audio adapter. Virtually all new systems sold today include an EIDE interface, and a SCSI adapter enables you to attach other devices to the same interface, such as hard disks, tape drives, and scanners. The software driver support and performance of a dedicated driver interface will be much better than those provided by audio/CD-ROM combination cards.

◀◀ For more information on adding a CD-ROM drive to your system, see Chapter 13, p. 705.

Sound Drivers

As with many PC components, a software driver provides a vital link between an audio adapter and the application or operating system that uses it. Operating systems such as Windows 9x and Windows NT include a large library of drivers for most of the audio adapters on the market. In most cases, these drivers are written by the manufacturer of the audio adapter and only distributed by Microsoft. You might find that the drivers that ship with the adapter are more recent than those included with the operating system. As always, the best place to find the most recent drivers for a piece of hardware is the manufacturer's own Web site or other online service.

DOS applications do not usually include as wide a range of driver support as an operating system, but you should find that most games and other programs support the Sound Blaster adapters. If you are careful to buy an adapter that is Sound Blaster-compatible, you should have no trouble finding driver support for all your applications. It's preferable to have this support through hardware rather than software. If your game program locks up when you try to detect the sound card during configuration, set the card type and settings manually. This is often a symptom of inadequate emulation for Sound Blaster by a third-party card.

Choosing an Audio Adapter

What are some key features to consider in a sound card? Although some aspects are subjective, the following sections describe some key buying points.

Consumer or Producer?

Different users require varying degrees of performance and different features from an audio adapter. One simple way of classifying audio users is to divide them into business consumers, game consumers, and producers of sound.

Many users need only basic audio capabilities. They want to listen to audio CDs as they work and hear sound effects and music when they play a few games or view Web sites. These are business consumers of sound. They obtain audio from outside sources such as CD-ROMs and the Internet and play them over their speakers. For this type of user, a modest audio adapter is all that is needed. The adapter should provide 16-bit audio, but an FM synthesizer might be sufficient for sound production. Users who want more realistic MIDI music should consider the vast array of low-cost wavetable cards on the market, but they don't need to purchase the top-of-the-line models.

A game consumer who lives in a "dangerous" 3D world of pixelated enemies, desktop flights around the world, or console Grand Prix racing is a far more demanding customer. The increasing realism of all types of games has changed both video and audio standards. Mere stereo playback isn't good enough for hardcore gamers who want to be able to hear monsters behind them or feel the impact of a car crash. These users should choose sound cards with support for four or more speakers and some form of "directional sound," such as Creative Labs' EAX technology used in the Sound Blaster Live! or Aureal's A3D technology used by other brands. As with 3D video cards (see Chapter 15, "Video Hardware"), the 3D audio standard(s) supported by these users' favorite games will help them determine which cards to choose from.

The underlying issue common to all 3D sound cards is that of HRTF (Head Related Transfer Function), which refers to how the shape of the ear and the angle of the listener's head changes the perception of sound. Because HRTF factors mean that a "realistic" sound at one listener's head angle might sound artificial when the listener turns to one side or the other, the addition of multiple speakers that "surround" the user, as well as sophisticated sound algorithms that add controlled reverberation to the mix, are making computer-based sound more and more "real."

Producers are people who intend to create their own sound files. These can range from casual business users recording low-fidelity voice annotations to professional musicians and MIDI maniacs. These users need an adapter that can perform as much of the audio processing as possible itself, so as not to place an additional burden on the system processor. Adapters that use DSPs to perform compression and other tasks are highly recommended in this case. Musicians will certainly want an adapter with as many voices as possible and a wavetable synthesizer. Adapters with expandable memory arrays and the capability to create and modify custom wavetables are also preferable. Many of the best "hardcore gamer"-type soundcards will also be suitable for sound producers by adding the appropriate sound-editing programs such as Sound Forge.

Compatibility

Although there are no official audio adapter standards, Creative Labs' popular Sound Blaster line has become a de facto standard. The Sound Blaster—the first widely distributed audio adapter—is supported by the greatest number of software programs, especially DOS-based programs. An audio adapter advertised as Sound Blaster-compatible should be able to run with virtually any application that supports sound. Most adapters also support the MPC Level 2 or Level 3 specifications, enabling you to play sound files in Windows and more.

Caution

Beware of audio adapters that require special drivers to be Sound Blaster-compatible. These drivers can cause problems and will take up additional memory that otherwise would be available to your applications.

Some wavetable sound cards require you to retain your Sound Blaster card for DOS game compatibility. This wastes a slot and might also create shortages of other hardware resources. I recommend that you look for PCI-based sound cards that feature good Sound Blaster game compatibility and wavetable features in a single slot instead.

Bundled Software

A software bundle can sometimes make the difference between a good buy on an audio adapter and a great one. Audio adapters usually include several sound utilities so you can begin using your adapter right away. Some of the types of software you might receive are as follows:

■ Text-to-speech conversion programs

■ Applications for playing, editing, and recording audio files

■ Audio CD-player programs

■ Stereo sound-mixer programs

■ Sequencer software, which helps you create, edit, and play back MIDI music files

■ Various sound clips

Audio Adapter Installation (Overview)

Installing an audio adapter is no more intimidating than installing an internal modem or a video adapter, especially if you are using Windows 9x and the adapter conforms to the Plug-and-Play specification, as most do. Typically, you follow these steps:

1. Open your computer.

2. Configure your sound card (if it isn't Plug and Play).

3. Insert the audio adapter into a bus slot and attach the CD-ROM drive to the CD Audio In connector, if present.

4. Close your computer.

5. Boot the system, causing Windows 9x to locate and install the driver for the adapter (or install the sound card software for non–Plug–and–Play devices).

6. Attach your speakers and other sound accessories.

Tip

When Windows 9x detects new hardware, it might ask you to reboot after finding a single new item. Because most sound cards today contain multiple features (Sound Blaster compatibility, MPU-401 MIDI compatibility, FM synthesis, digital signal processor, and so on), don't reboot when directed to after the drivers for the first item are loaded. Click No, and you'll often see the system find additional hardware items. Why? A single add-on card might contain multiple hardware components. Reboot only after the Windows 9x desktop has been displayed.

Installing the Sound Card (Detailed Procedure)

After your computer is open, you can install the audio adapter. A few low-cost adapters today use a 16-bit ISA slot, although most mid-range to high-end adapters now use the PCI bus. The migration from ISA to PCI in the audio-adapter industry has been slower than that for other components, such as video-display adapters. The first PCI audio cards were much more expensive than standard commercial models and were intended for professional applications, but most manufacturers, including Creative Labs, Diamond Multimedia Voyetra/Turtle Beach, VideoLogic, and many others, are now marketing PCI adapters for the home PC market.

If you have several empty bus slots from which to choose, install the audio adapter in the slot that is as far away as possible from the other cards in the computer. This reduces any possible electromagnetic interference; that is, it reduces stray radio signals from one card that might affect the sound card. The analog components on audio adapters are highly susceptible to interference, and even though they are shielded, they should be protected as well as possible. Next, you must remove the screw that holds the metal cover over the empty expansion slot you've chosen. Remove your audio adapter from its protective packaging. When you open the bag, carefully grab the card by its metal bracket and edges. Do not touch any of the components on the card. Any static electricity you might transmit can damage the card. Also, do not touch the gold-edge connectors. You might want to invest in a grounding wrist strap, which continually drains you of static build-up as you work on your computer.

If your adapter is not Plug and Play, you might have to set jumpers or DIP switches to configure the adapter to use the appropriate hardware resources in your computer. For example, you might have to adjust an IRQ or DMA setting or turn off the adapter's joystick port because your joystick is already connected to your PC elsewhere. See the instructions that came with your audio adapter. Use the Windows 9x Device Manager to see existing hardware settings, and compare them to the sound card's default settings. Use the default settings if possible. If you're installing a Plug-and-Play sound card into an older system that doesn't have a Plug-and-Play BIOS, you'll also install a program called an "enumerator" that runs early in the startup process to set the card.

◀◀ See "Plug-and-Play BIOS," p. 400.

If your system has an internal CD-ROM drive with an audio cable, connect the audio cable to the adapter's CD Audio In connector. This connector is keyed so that you can't insert it improperly. Note that there is no true standard for this audio cable, so be sure that you get the right one that matches your drive and adapter. If you need to purchase one, you can find cables with multiple connectors designed for different brands of CD-ROM drives.

Next, insert the adapter's edge connector in the bus slot, but first touch a metal object, such as the inside of the computer's cover, to drain yourself of static electricity. When the card is firmly in place, attach the screw to hold the expansion card and then reassemble your computer.

After the adapter card is installed, you can connect small speakers to the speaker jack. Typically, sound cards provide four watts of power per channel to drive bookshelf speakers. If you are using speakers rated for less than four watts, do not turn up the volume on your sound card to the maximum; your speakers might burn out from the overload. You'll get better results if you plug your sound card into powered speakers—that is, speakers with built-in amplifiers.

> ### Tip
>
> If you have powered speakers but don't have batteries in them or have them connected to an AC adapter, don't turn on the speakers! Turning on the speakers without power will prevent you from hearing anything at all. Use the volume control built into your sound card's mixer software instead. Powered speakers sound better, but most small models can run without power in an emergency.

When the sound card installation is finished, you should have a speaker icon in the Windows 9x System Tray. If the speaker icon (indicating the Volume Control) isn't visible, you can install it through the Control Panel's Add/Remove Programs icon. Choose the Windows Setup tab and open the Multimedia section. Put a check mark next to Volume Control and insert the Windows 9x CD-ROM or diskette if requested to complete the installation.

Use the Volume Control to make sure your speakers are receiving a sound signal. The mixer sometimes defaults to Mute. You can usually adjust volume separately for wave files, MIDI, microphone, and other components.

Using Your Stereo Instead of Speakers

Another alternative is to patch your sound card into your stereo system for greatly amplified sound. Check the plugs and jacks at both ends of the connection. Most stereos use pin plugs—also called RCA or phono plugs—for input. Although pin plugs are standard on some sound cards, most use miniature 1/8-inch plugs, which require an adapter when connecting to your stereo system. From Radio Shack, for example, you can purchase an audio cable that provides a stereo 1/8-inch miniplug on one end and phono plugs on the other (Cat. No. 42-2481A).

Make sure that you get stereo, not mono, plugs, unless your sound card supports only mono. To ensure that you have enough cable to reach from the back of your PC to your stereo system, get a six-foot long cable.

Hooking up your stereo to an audio adapter is a matter of sliding the plugs into the proper jacks. If your audio adapter gives you a choice of outputs—speaker/headphone and stereo line out—choose the stereo line-out jack for the connection. This will give you the best sound quality because the signals from the stereo line-out jack are not amplified. The amplification is best left to your stereo system.

Connect this cable output from your audio adapter to the auxiliary input of your stereo receiver, preamp, or integrated amplifier. If your stereo doesn't have an auxiliary input, other input options include—in order of preference—tuner, CD, or Tape 2. (Do not use phono inputs, however, because the level of the signals will be uneven.) You can connect the cable's single stereo miniplug to the sound card's Stereo Line-out jack, for example, and then connect the two RCA phono plugs to the stereo's Tape/VCR 2 Playback jacks.

The first time you use your audio adapter with a stereo system, turn down the volume on your receiver to prevent blown speakers. Barely turn up the volume control and then select the proper input (such as Tape/VCR 2) on your stereo receiver. Finally, start your PC. Never increase the volume to more than three-fourths of the way up. Any higher and the sound might become distorted.

Note

If your stereo speakers are not magnetically shielded, you might hear a lot of crackling if they are placed close to your computer. Try moving them away from the computer, or use magnetically-shielded speakers.

Tricks for Using the Tape Monitor Circuit of Your Stereo

Your receiver might be equipped with something called a tape monitor. This outputs the sound coming from the tuner, tape, or CD to the tape-out port on the back, and it then expects the sound to come back in on the tape in port. These ports, in conjunction with the line-in and line-out ports on your audio adapter, enable you to play computer sound and the radio through the same set of speakers.

Here's how you do it:

1. Turn off the tape monitor circuit on your receiver.

2. Turn down all the controls on the sound card's mixer application.

3. Connect the receiver's tape-out ports to the audio adapter's line-in port.

4. Connect the audio adapter's line-out port to the receiver's tape-in ports.

5. Turn on the receiver, select some music, and set the volume to a medium level.

6. Turn on the tape monitor circuit.

7. Slowly adjust the line-in and main out sliders in the audio adapter's mixer application until the sound level is about the same as before.

8. Disengage and re-engage the tape monitor circuit while adjusting the output of the audio adapter so that the sound level is the same regardless of whether the tape monitor circuit is engaged.

9. Start playing a WAV file.

10. Slowly adjust up the volume slider for the WAV file in the audio adapter's mixer application until it plays at a level (slightly above or below the receiver) that is comfortable.

Now you can get sounds from your computer and the radio through the receiver's speakers.

Different connectors might be needed if you have digital surround speakers and newer PCI-based sound cards. Check your speakers and sound card before you start this project.

Troubleshooting Sound Card Problems

To operate, an audio adapter needs hardware resources, such as IRQ numbers, a base I/O address, and DMA channels that don't conflict with other devices. Most adapters come preconfigured to use the standard Sound Blaster resources that have come to be associated with audio adapters. However, problems occasionally arise even with Plug-and-Play adapters. Troubleshooting might mean that you have to change board jumpers or switches or even reconfigure the other devices in your computer. No one said life was fair.

Hardware (Resource) Conflicts

The most common problem for audio adapters is that they conflict with other devices installed in your PC. You might notice that your audio adapter simply doesn't work (no sound effects or music), repeats the same sounds over and over, or causes your PC to freeze. This situation is called a device, or hardware, conflict. What are they fighting over? Mainly the same bus signal lines or channels (called resources) used for talking to your PC. The sources of conflict in audio adapter installations are generally threefold:

- *Interrupt Requests (IRQs).* Hardware devices use IRQs to "interrupt" your PC and get its attention.
- *Direct Memory Access (DMA) channels.* DMA channels move information directly to your PC's memory, bypassing the system processor. DMA channels enable sound to play while your PC is doing other work.
- *Input/output (I/O) port addresses.* Your PC uses I/O port addresses to channel information between the hardware devices on your audio adapter and your PC. The addresses usually mentioned in a sound card manual are the starting or base addresses. An audio adapter has several devices on it, and each one uses a range of addresses starting with a particular base address.

Most audio adapters include installation software that analyzes your PC and attempts to notify you should any of the standard settings be in use by other devices. The Windows 9x Device Manager (accessed from the System Control Panel) can also help you to resolve conflicts. Although these detection routines can be fairly reliable, unless a device is operating during the analysis, it might not always be detectable.

Some of the newer PCI-based sound cards and Intel-chipset motherboards might not properly support ISA-type I/O addresses used by Sound Blaster-compatible software to communicate with the card. If you have problems getting older games to work with your system, check with your sound card and system board/computer supplier for help, and check with the game developer for possible patches and workarounds.

Table 20.3 shows the default resources used by the components on a typical Sound Blaster 16 card.

Table 20.3   Default Sound Blaster Resource Assignments

Device	Interrupt	I/O Ports	16-Bit DMA	8-Bit DMA
Audio	IRQ 5	220h-233h	DMA 5	DMA 1
MIDI Port	—	330h-331h	—	—
FM Synthesizer	—	388h-38Bh	—	—
Game Port	—	200h-207h	—	—

All these resources are used by a single sound card in your system. No wonder many people have conflicts and problems with audio adapter installations! In reality, working out these conflicts is not all that hard, as you shall see. You can change most of the resources that audio adapters use to alternate settings, should there be conflicts with other devices; even better, you can change the settings of the other device to eliminate the conflict. Note that some devices on the audio adapter, such as the MIDI Port, FM Synthesizer, and Game Port, do not use resources such as IRQs or DMA channels.

It is always best to install an audio adapter by using the default settings whenever possible. This is mainly because of poorly written software that cannot work properly with alternative settings, even if they do not cause conflicts. In other words, if you are having a conflict with another type of adapter, modify the settings of the other device, rather than those of the audio adapter. Take this from experience; otherwise, you will have to explain to your five-year old why the new Dinosaur program you just installed does not make any sounds! This problem is primarily associated with DOS-based game programs, but some older Windows-based programs have also been unable to work with alternative hardware settings.

Resolving Resource Conflicts

The audio portion of a sound card has a default IRQ setting, but it also supports any of several alternative interrupts. As stated earlier, you should endeavor to leave the audio IRQ at the default setting (usually IRQ 5) and change those of other adapters where possible.

If your audio adapter is set to the same IRQ as another device in your system, you might see symptoms such as skipping, jerky sound, or system lockups.

A typical ISA-based audio adapter requires the use of two simultaneous DMA channels. These are usually split into a requirement for an 8-bit DMA and a 16-bit DMA channel. Most adapters use DMA 1 for 8-bit sound (Creative Labs calls this Low DMA), and DMA 5 for 16-bit sound (High DMA). The primary symptom of a DMA conflict in your system is that you hear no sound at all.

Note

PCI-based sound cards don't require DMA settings unless you are using them in "legacy" mode to emulate a Sound Blaster for game support.

If your sound card is part of a multifunction card such as IBM's Mwave series, you'll not only need to have available hardware resources for the sound card, but you'll also need IRQs and I/O port addresses for the card's digital signal processor (DSP) and modem serial port. These cards can be difficult to install in today's resource-starved systems.

Solving Hardware Conflicts

If you use Windows 9x, the Device Manager application can tell you which devices are using a particular resource. If not, you might have to manually resolve any resource conflicts you find.

The best way to manually locate a hardware conflict is to gather all the documentation for your PC and its various devices, such as the SCSI interface adapters, CD-ROM drives, and so on. This topic is discussed more completely in Chapter 16, "Serial, Parallel, and Other I/O Interfaces."

The most common causes of system resource conflicts are the following:

- SCSI host adapters
- Network interface cards
- Bus mouse adapter cards
- Serial port adapter cards for COM3: or COM4:
- Parallel port adapter cards for LPT2:

- Internal modems
- Scanner interface cards

One way to find which device is conflicting with your audio adapter is to temporarily remove all the expansion cards from your system except for the audio adapter and essential devices (such as the video adapter). Then replace each of the cards you removed, one at a time, until your audio adapter no longer works. The last card you added is the troublemaker.

Having found the card that's causing the conflict, you can either switch the settings for the device that is conflicting with your audio adapter or change the settings of the audio adapter. In either case, you will have to change the IRQ, DMA, or I/O address. To do this, you might have to either set jumpers or DIP switches on the adapter or use a configuration program supplied with the adapter to change its settings.

Note

If you are using an LPT2 port card for a slow-speed device such as a dot-matrix or low-end inkjet printer, you can often free up its default IRQ 5 by disabling EPP/ECP/IEEE-1284 modes. These modes require use of an IRQ (ECP also uses a DMA channel). Reverting to standard printing will cause most LPT ports to use only I/O port addresses. This will permit you to use the port for printing and its IRQ 5 for a sound card.

Other Sound Card Problems

Like the common cold, audio adapter problems have common symptoms. Use the following sections to diagnose your problem.

No Sound

If you don't hear anything from your audio adapter, consider these solutions:

- Make sure that the audio adapter is set to use all default resources and that all other devices using these resources have been either reconfigured or removed.
- Are the speakers connected? Check that the speakers are plugged into the sound card's Stereo Line Out or speaker jack (not the Line In or microphone jack).
- Are the mixer settings high enough? Many audio adapters include a sound mixer application. The mixer controls the volume settings for various sound devices, such as the microphone or the CD player. There might be separate controls for both recording and playback. Increase the master volume or speaker volume when you are in the play mode.

  If the Mute option is selected in your sound mixer software, you won't hear anything.

- Use your audio adapter's setup or diagnostic software to test and adjust the volume of the adapter. Such software usually includes sample sounds used to test the adapter.
- Turn off your computer for one minute and then turn it back on. A hard reset (as opposed to pressing the Reset button or pressing Ctrl+Alt+Delete) might clear the problem.
- If your computer game lacks sound, check that it is designed to work with your audio adapter. For example, some games might require the exact settings of IRQ 7 (or IRQ 5), DMA 1, and I/O address 220 to be Sound Blaster-compatible.

One-Sided Sound

If you hear sound coming from only one speaker, check out these possible causes:

- Are you using a mono plug in the stereo jack? A common mistake is to use a mono plug into the sound card's speaker or stereo out jacks. Seen from the side, a stereo connector has two darker stripes. A mono connector has only one stripe.

- If you're using amplified speakers, are they powered on? Check the strength of the batteries or the AC adapter's connection to the electrical outlet.

- Are the speakers wired correctly? When possible, use keyed and color-coded connectors to avoid mistakes, such as those found on the Altec Lansing ACS-340 and others.

- Is the audio adapter driver loaded? Some sound cards provide only left-channel sound if the driver is not loaded correctly. Re-run your adapter's setup software or reinstall it in the operating system.

- Are both speakers set to the same volume? Some speakers use separate volume controls on each speaker. Balance them for best results. Separate speaker volume controls can be an advantage if one speaker must be further away from the user than the other.

Volume Is Low

If you can barely hear your sound card, try these solutions:

- Are the speakers plugged into the proper jack? Speakers require a higher level of drive signal than headphones. Again, adjust the volume level in your mixer application.

- Are the mixer settings too low? Again, adjust the volume level in your mixer application.

- Is the initial volume too low? If your audio adapter has a thumbwheel volume control, check to make sure that it is not turned down too low.

- Are the speakers too weak? Some speakers might need more power than your audio adapter can produce. Try other speakers or put a stereo amplifier between your sound card and speakers.

Scratchy Sound

Scratchy or staticky sound can be caused by several different problems. Improving the sound might be as simple as rearranging your hardware components. The following list suggests possible solutions to the problem of scratchy sound:

- Is your audio adapter near other expansion cards? The adapter might be picking up electrical interference from other expansion cards inside the PC. Move the audio card to an expansion slot as far away as possible from other cards.

- If your audio adapter is ISA-based, it requires a lot of CPU attention. Frequent hard disk access can cause dropouts due to the CPU's switching between managing the sound card and the hard drive.

- Are your speakers too close to your monitor? The speakers might pick up electrical noise from your monitor. Move them farther away. Subwoofers should *never* be placed near the monitor because their powerful magnets might interfere with the picture. They should be on the floor to maximize low-frequency transmission.

■ Are you using a cheaper audio adapter with an FM synthesizer? Some of the adapters that use FM synthesis instead of wavetable sound generation have very poor quality output. Many people have been fooled into thinking they had a defective sound card, when in reality it was just a poor-quality FM synthesis card that simply does not sound good. You can test this by comparing the sound of a MIDI file (which uses the FM synthesizer) with that of a sound file such as a WAV (which doesn't). If the problem is the synthesizer, I recommend upgrading to an adapter that does wavetable synthesis so you can get the full benefit of high quality sound.

Your Computer Won't Start

If your computer won't start at all, you might not have inserted the audio adapter completely into its slot. Turn off the PC and then press firmly on the card until it is seated correctly.

If you install an Ensoniq-based PCI sound card and get an "IOS error" after restarting Windows 95, the installation software should include an IOS fix-up program. You can start Windows 95 in command-prompt mode to get access to the CD-ROM to install this if needed, or it might be on one of the installation diskettes. Check the sound card's Readme file for more information.

Parity Errors or Other Lockups

Your computer might display a memory parity error message or simply crash. This is normally caused by resource conflicts in one of the following areas:

■ IRQ (Interrupt ReQuest)

■ DMA (Direct Memory Access)

■ I/O (Input/Output) ports

If other devices in your system are using the same resources as your audio adapter, crashes, lockups, or parity errors can result. You must ensure that multiple devices in your system do not share these resources. Follow the procedures outlined earlier in this chapter to resolve the resource conflicts.

Joystick Troubleshooting

If your joystick won't work, consider the following list of cures:

■ Are you using two game ports? If you already have a game port installed in your PC, the game or joystick port provided on your audio adapter might conflict with it. Usually it is best to disable any other game ports and use the one on the audio adapter. Many of the Multi-I/O or Super-I/O adapters that come in PC-compatible systems feature game ports that you should disable when you install an audio adapter.

■ Is your computer too fast? Some fast computers get confused by the inexpensive game ports. During the heat of virtual combat, for example, you might find yourself flying upside down or spiraling out of control. This is one sign that your game port is inadequate. Most of the game adapters built into audio adapters work better than the ones on the Multi-I/O adapters. There are also dedicated game cards available that can work with faster computers. These game cards include software to calibrate your joystick and dual ports so that you can enjoy a game with a friend. Another solution is to run your computer at a slower speed, which on some systems is as easy as pressing some type of "de-turbo" button on the case.

Other Problems

Sometimes sound problems can be difficult to solve. Due to quirks and problems with the way DMA is implemented in some motherboard chipsets, there can be problems interacting with certain cards or drivers. Sometimes altering the Chipset Setup options in your CMOS settings can resolve problems. These kinds of problems can take a lot of trial and error to solve.

The PC "standard" is based loosely on the cooperation among a handful of companies. Something as simple as one vendor's BIOS or motherboard design can make the standard nonstandard.

Speakers

Successful business presentations, multimedia applications, and MIDI work demand external high-fidelity stereo speakers. Although you can use standard stereo speakers, they are often too big to fit on or near your desk. Smaller bookshelf speakers are better.

Sound cards offer little or none of the amplification needed to drive external speakers. Although some sound cards have small four-watt amplifiers, they are not powerful enough to drive quality speakers. Also, conventional speakers sitting near your display might create magnetic interference, which can distort colors and objects onscreen or jumble the data recorded on nearby floppy disks or other magnetic media.

To solve these problems, computer speakers need to be small, efficient, and self-powered. Also, they should be provided with magnetic shielding, either in the form of added layers of insulation in the speaker cabinet or electronic cancellation of the magnetic distortion.

Caution

Although most computer speakers are magnetically shielded, do not leave recorded tapes, watches, credit cards, or floppy disks in front of the speakers for long periods of time.

Quality sound depends on quality speakers. A 16-bit audio adapter might provide better sound to computer speakers, but even an 8-bit adapter sounds good from a good speaker. Conversely, an inexpensive speaker makes both 8-bit and 16-bit adapters cards sound tinny.

There are now dozens of models of PC speakers on the market ranging from inexpensive minispeakers from Sony, Koss, and LabTech to larger self-powered models from prestigious audio companies such as Bose and Altec Lansing. Many of the higher-end speaker systems even include subwoofers to provide additional bass response. To evaluate speakers, it helps to know the jargon. Speakers are measured by three criteria:

- *Frequency response.* A measurement of the range of high and low sounds a speaker can reproduce. The ideal range is from 20Hz to 20KHz, the range of human hearing. No speaker system reproduces this range perfectly. In fact, few people hear sounds above 18KHz. An exceptional speaker might cover a range of 30Hz to 23,000KHz. Lesser models might cover only 100Hz to 20,000Hz. Frequency response is the most deceptive specification because identically rated speakers can sound completely different.

- *Total Harmonic Distortion (THD).* An expression of the amount of distortion or noise created by amplifying the signal. Simply put, distortion is the difference between the sound sent to the speaker and the sound you hear. The amount of distortion is measured in percentages.

An acceptable level of distortion is less than .1 percent (one-tenth of one percent). For some CD-quality recording equipment, a common standard is .05 percent. Some speakers have a distortion of 10 percent or more. Headphones often have a distortion of about 2 percent or less.

■ *Watts.* Usually stated as watts per channel, the amount of amplification available to drive the speakers. Check that the company means "per channel" (or RMS) and not total power. Many audio adapters have built-in amplifiers, providing up to eight watts per channel (most provide four watts). This wattage is not enough to provide rich sound, however, which is why many speakers have built-in amplifiers. With the flick of a switch or the press of a button, these speakers amplify the signals they receive from the audio adapter. If you do not want to amplify the sound, you typically leave the speaker switch set to "direct." In most cases, you'll want to amplify the signal.

PC speakers often use batteries to power the amplifiers. Because these speakers require so much power, you might want to invest in an AC adapter or purchase speakers that use AC power. With an AC adapter, you won't have to buy new batteries every few weeks. If your speakers didn't come with an AC adapter, you can pick one up from your local Radio Shack or hardware store. Be sure that the adapter you purchase matches your speakers in voltage and polarity.

You can control the volume and other sound attributes of your speakers in various ways, depending on their complexity and cost. Typically, each speaker has a volume knob, although some share a single volume control. If one speaker is farther away than the other, you might want to adjust the volume accordingly. Many computer speakers include a dynamic bass boost (DBB) switch. This button provides a more powerful bass and clearer treble, regardless of the volume setting. Other speakers have separate bass and treble boost switches or a three-band equalizer to control low, middle, and high frequencies. When you rely on your audio adapter's power rather than your speakers' built-in amplifier, the volume and dynamic bass boost controls have no effect. Your speakers are at the mercy of the adapter's power.

For best audio quality, adjust the master volume on the sound card near the high end, and use the volume control on powered speakers to adjust the volume. Otherwise, your speakers will try to amplify any distortions coming from the low-power input from the PC's audio adapter.

An 1/8-inch stereo minijack connects from the audio adapter's output jack to one of the speakers. The speaker then splits the signal and feeds through a separate cable from the first speaker to the second one (often referred to as the "satellite speaker").

Before purchasing a set of speakers, check that the cables between the speakers are long enough for your computer setup. For example, a tower case sitting alongside one's desk might require longer speaker wires than a desktop computer.

Beware of speakers that have a tardy built-in "sleep" feature. Such speakers, which save electricity by turning themselves off when they are not in use, might have the annoying habit of clipping the first part of a sound after a period of inactivity.

Speakers that are USB-based will not be able to play CD music unless the CD-ROM drive can perform digital audio extraction. Check your drive's specifications for information.

Headphones are an option when you can't afford a premium set of speakers. Headphones also provide privacy and enable you to play your PC audio as loud as you like.

For best results with newer sound cards that support four speakers or more, check the properties sheet for the audio adapter and set whether you're using headphones, stereo speakers, or a larger number of speakers.

Microphones

Some audio adapters come complete with a microphone, but most do not. You'll need one to record your voice to a WAV file. Selecting a microphone is quite simple. You need one that has an 1/8-inch minijack to plug into your audio adapter's microphone, or audio in, jack. Most microphones have an on/off switch.

Like speakers, microphones are measured by their frequency range. This is not an important buying factor, however, because the human voice has a limited range. If you are recording only voices, consider an inexpensive microphone that covers a limited range of frequencies. An expensive microphone's recording capabilities extend to frequencies outside the voice's range. Why pay for something you won't be needing?

If you are recording music, invest in an expensive microphone, but make sure that your audio adapter can do justice to the signal produced by the microphone. A high-quality microphone can produce mediocre results when paired with a cheap 8-bit audio adapter.

Your biggest decision is to select a microphone that suits your recording style. If you work in a noisy office, you might want an unidirectional microphone that will prevent extraneous noises from being recorded. An omnidirectional microphone is best for recording a group conversation.

Most higher priced audio adapters include a microphone of some type. This can be a small lapel microphone, a hand-held microphone, or one with a desktop stand. If you want to keep your hands free, you might want to shun the traditional hand-held microphone for a lapel or desktop model. If your audio adapter does not come with a microphone, see your local stereo or electronics parts store. Be sure that any microphone you purchase has the correct impedance to match the audio adapter's input.

If you're using software such as L&H's Voice Express series, Dragon Naturally Speaking, IBM Via Voice, Philips FreeSpeech, or other voice-recognition software, use the microphone supplied with the software or choose from alternative models the software vendor recommends. Run the microphone setup program again if your software has trouble recognizing your voice.

If you're talking but your voice-recognition or recording software isn't responding, check the following:

- Incorrect jack; it's easy to plug the microphone into the wrong jack. Try using a magic marker to color-code the microphone wire and jack to make matching up easier.
- Check the recording volume in the mixer control. This usually defaults to Mute to avoid spurious noise.
- Make sure the microphone is On in the voice-recognition or recording software. You must click the Record button in recording software, and many voice-recognition programs let you "pick up" the microphone for use or "put it down" when you need to answer the phone. Look for an onscreen microphone icon in the Windows 9x System Tray for fast toggling between modes.

Power Supply and Chassis/Case

SOME OF THE MAIN TOPICS IN THIS CHAPTER ARE

Considering the Importance of the Power Supply

The power supply is not only one of the most important parts in a PC, but it is unfortunately also the most overlooked. In the immortal words of a famous comedian, the power supply gets no respect! People will spend hours discussing their processor speeds, memory capacity, disk storage capacity and speed, video adapter performance, monitor size, and so forth, but rarely even mention or consider their power supply. When a system is put together to meet the lowest possible price point, what component do you think the manufacturer will skimp on? Yes, the power supply. To most people, the power supply is a rather non-descript metal box that sits inside their system, something to which they pay virtually no attention at all. The few who do pay any mind seem only concerned with how many watts of power it is rated to put out (even though there is no practical way to verify those ratings), without regard as to whether the power that is being produced is stable, direct current, and not a wildly variable signal full of noise, hash, spikes, and surges.

On the other hand, I have always placed great emphasis on selecting a power supply for my systems. I consider the power supply the core of the system and am willing to spend more to get a higher quality unit. The power supply function is critical because it supplies electrical power to every other component in the system. In my experience, the power supply is also one of the most failure-prone components in any computer system, especially due to the fact that so many system assemblers use the cheapest ones they can find. A malfunctioning power supply can not only cause other components in the system to malfunction, but it can also damage the other components in your computer by delivering an improper or erratic voltage. Because of its importance to proper and reliable system operation, you should understand both the function and limitations of a power supply, as well as its potential problems and their solutions.

This chapter covers the power supply in detail. I will not only focus on the electrical functions of the supply, but also the mechanical form factors and physical designs that have been used in PC systems in the past as well as today. Because the physical shape (form factor) of the power supply relates to the case, some of this information also relates to the type of chassis or case you have.

Power Supply Function and Operation

The basic function of the power supply is to convert the type of electrical power available at the wall socket to the type the computer circuitry can use. The power supply in a conventional desktop system is designed to convert the American 120-volt, 60Hz, AC (alternating current) power into +3.3v, +5v, and +12v DC (direct current) power. Usually, the digital electronic components and circuits in the system (motherboard, adapter cards, and disk drive logic boards) use the +3.3v or +5v power, and the motors (disk drive motors and any fans) use the +12v power. The power supply must deliver a good, steady supply of DC power so that the system can operate properly.

Signal Functions

If you look at a specification sheet for a typical PC power supply, you can see that the supply generates not only +3.3v, +5v, and +12v, but also -5v and -12v. The positive voltages seemingly power everything in the system (logic and motors), so what are the negative voltages used for? The answer is, not much! Some communications circuits have used the -12v power as a bias current, but rarely is the -5v used at all today. Some of the newest power supply designs such as the SFX (Small form factor) design no longer include the -5v signal for that reason. The only reason it has been around at all is that it is a required signal on the ISA (Industry Standard Architecture) bus for full backward compatibility.

Note

When Intel began releasing processors that required a +3.3v power source, power supplies that supplied the additional output voltage were not yet available. As a result, motherboard manufacturers began adding voltage regulators to their boards, which convert +5v current to +3.3v. Voltage regulators, however, also generate a lot of heat in the conversion process, which should be avoided as much as possible in a PC. Newer DIMM (Dual In-line Memory Module) memory also runs on +3.3v, so to minimize the onboard voltage regulator functions, these boards are usually designed to require a +3.3v signal.

◄◄ See "CPU Operating Voltages," p. 91.

Although -5v and -12v are supplied to the motherboard via the power supply connectors, the motherboard uses only the +5v. The -5v signal is simply routed to the ISA bus on pin B5. The motherboard does not use it. Originally, the analog data separator circuits found in older floppy controllers used -5v, so it was supplied to the bus. Because modern controllers do not need the -5v, most systems no longer use it. It is still required, however, because it is part of the ISA bus standard.

Note

Power supplies in systems with a Micro Channel Architecture (MCA bus) as well as the newer SFX (Small form factor) power supplies used in micro-ATX systems do not supply -5v. If necessary for backward compatibility, the motherboard should use an onboard regulator to supply the -5v signal to the ISA bus. PCI-only systems can be produced that do not need -5v current.

The motherboard logic doesn't use the +12v and -12v signals either. They are routed to pins B9 and B7 of the ISA bus (respectively). Any adapter card on the bus can make use of these voltages if needed, but typically they are used by serial port driver/receiver circuits. If the motherboard has integrated serial ports, it can use the +12v and -12v signals for those ports.

Note

The load placed on the +12v and -12v signals by a serial port is very small. For example, the PS/2 Dual Async adapter uses only 35mA of +12v and 35mA of -12v (0.035 amps each) to operate two ports.

Most newer serial port circuits no longer use 12v driver/receiver circuits. Instead, they now use circuits that run on only +3.3 or +5v. If you have serial ports such as these in your system, the -12v signal from your power supply will probably not be used.

The main function of the +12v power is to run disk drive motors. Usually, a large amount of current is available, especially in systems with a large number of drive bays (such as in a tower configuration). Besides disk drive motors, the +12v supply is used by any cooling fans in the system—which, of course, should always be running. A single cooling fan can draw between 100mA and 250mA (0.1–0.25 amps); however, most newer fans use the lower 100mA figure. Note that although most fans in desktop systems run on +12v, portable systems can use fans that run on +5v, or even +3.3v.

In addition to supplying power to run the system, the power supply also ensures that the system does not run unless the power supplied is sufficient to operate the system properly. In other words, the power supply actually prevents the computer from starting up or operating until all the correct power levels are present.

Each power supply completes internal checks and tests before allowing the system to start. If the tests are successful, the power supply sends a special signal to the motherboard called Power_Good. If this signal is not present continuously, the computer does not run. Therefore, when the AC voltage dips and the power supply becomes overstressed or overheated, the Power_Good signal goes down and forces a system reset or complete shutdown. If you have ever worked on a system that seems dead when the power switch is on and the fan and hard disks are running, you know the effects of losing the Power_Good signal.

▶▶ See "The Power_Good Signal," page 1109.

IBM originally implemented this conservative design so that the computer would not operate if the power became low or the supply, overheated or overstressed, caused output power to falter.

Note

You even can use the Power_Good feature as a method of designing and implementing a reset switch for the PC. The Power_Good line is wired to the clock generator circuit, which controls the clock and reset lines to the microprocessor. When you ground the Power_Good line with a switch, the chip and related circuitry stop the processor. They do so by killing the clock signal and then resetting the processor when the Power_Good signal appears after you release the switch. The result is a full hardware reset of the system. Later in this chapter, you can find instructions for installing such a reset switch in a system not already equipped with one.

Most systems with newer motherboard form factors, such as the ATX, micro-ATX, or NLX, include another special signal. This feature, called PS_ON, can be used to turn the power supply (and thus the system) on or off via software. It is sometimes known as the soft-power feature. PS_ON is most evident when you use it with an operating system that supports the Advanced Power Management (APM) or Advanced Configuration and Power Interface (ACPI) specifications such as Windows 9x. When you select the Shut Down the Computer option from the Start menu, Windows automatically turns the computer off after it completes the OS shutdown sequence. A system without this feature only displays a message that it's safe to shut down the computer.

Power Supply Form Factors

The shape and general physical layout of a component is called the form factor. Items that share a form factor are generally interchangeable, at least as far as their size and fit are concerned. When designing a PC, the engineers can choose to use one of the popular standard PSU (power supply unit) form factors, or they can elect to build their own. Choosing the former means that a virtually inexhaustible supply of inexpensive replacement parts will be available in a variety of quality and power output levels. Going the custom route means additional time and expense for development. In addition, the PSU will be unique to the system and available only from the original manufacturer.

If you can't tell already, I am a fan of the industry-standard form factors! In the early days of PCs, the computer industry was dominated by companies—such as IBM—that manufactured most of their own proprietary components. When other manufacturers began to clone PCs on a large scale, this philosophy became increasingly impractical. The drive toward the standardization of PC components, which began at that time, continues today.

Until the introduction of Intel's ATX architecture in 1995, the form factors of the power supplies used in PC systems differed primarily in their size and their orientation in the computer case. ATX and related standards introduced some new features (such as the PS_ON signal), but virtually all the power supplies used in PCs now conform to the same basic electronic design.

Technically, the PSU in your PC is described as a constant voltage half-bridge forward converting switching power supply:

- Constant voltage means that the PSU puts out the same voltage to the computer's internal components, no matter what the voltage of AC current running it or the capacity (wattage) of the power supply.
- Half-bridge forward converting refers to the PSU's switching design and its power regulation technique. This type of power supply is sometimes known as a switching supply. Compared to other types of power supplies, this design provides an efficient power source and generates a minimum amount of heat. It also maintains a small size and a low price.

Note

Although two power supplies can share the same basic design and form factor, they can differ greatly in quality and efficiency. Later in this chapter, you'll learn about some of the features and specifications to look for when evaluating PC power supplies.

There have been seven main power supply form factors that can be called industry standard. Of these, only three are used in most modern systems; the others are pretty much obsolete. These different form factors are as follows:

Obsolete:	Modern:
PC/XT style	LPX style
AT/Desk style	ATX style
AT/Tower style	SFX style
Baby-AT style	

Each of these power supply styles are available in numerous different configurations and power output levels. The LPX style power supply had been the standard used on most systems up until about four years ago, when the ATX form factor came on the scene. Since then, ATX has become by far the dominant form factor for power supplies, with the new SFX style being added recently to replace ATX for use in very compact systems. The earlier form factors have been largely obsolete for some time now.

Power supply form factors relate to motherboard form factors in often non-obvious ways. For example, most systems with Baby-AT motherboards use LPX style power supplies, and systems with NLX motherboards use ATX power supplies. Here is a cross reference showing the most common type of power supply used with different motherboards:

Motherboard Form Factor:	Most Common PS Form Factor used:	Other PS Form Factors used:
Baby-AT	LPX style	Baby-AT, AT/Tower, or AT/Desk
LPX	LPX style	None
ATX	ATX style	None
Micro-ATX	ATX style	SFX style
NLX	ATX style	None

◀◀ See "Motherboard Form Factors," p. 204.

As you can see, most systems today use the ATX form factor power supply, and some might use the SFX or LPX styles as well.

Note that although the names of these styles of supplies seem to be the same as those of motherboard form factors, the power supply form factor is more related to the system case than the motherboard. All Baby-AT, LPX, and AT/Tower type power supplies use the same two six-pin connectors to plug into the motherboard, and will therefore work with the same boards. For them to physically work in the system, they must fit the case. This can be very misleading because most all cases today that aren't a variation of ATX or NLX will use the LPX style power supply, even tower cases. The bottom line is that it is up to you to make sure the power supply you are purchasing will fit the case you will be installing it into.

PC/XT Style

IBM's XT used the same basic power supply shape as the original PC, except that the new XT supply had more than double the power output capability. Because they were identical in external appearance and the type of connectors they used, you could easily install the higher output XT supply as an upgrade for a PC system. The tremendous popularity of the original PC and XT design led a number of manufacturers to begin building systems that mimicked their shape and layout. These clones, as they have been called, could interchange virtually all components with the IBM systems, including the power supply. Numerous manufacturers then began producing these components. Most of these components follow the form factor of one or more IBM systems. The PC/XT power supply and connectors are shown in Figure 21.1. This form factor is rarely, if at all, used in modern systems today.

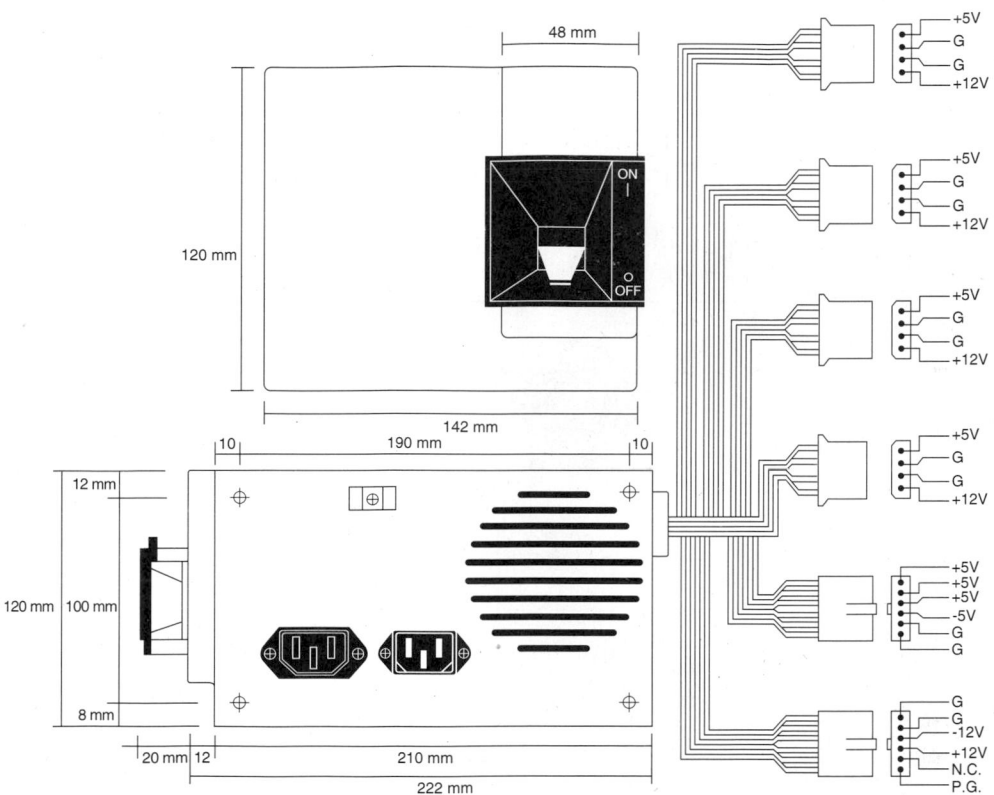

Figure 21.1   PC/XT form factor power supply.

AT/Desk Style

The AT desktop system, introduced by IBM after the XT, had a larger power supply and a different form factor than the original PC/XT. This system, which was rapidly cloned, represented the basis for many IBM-compatible designs. The power supply used in these systems was called the AT/Desktop-style power supply (see Figure 21.2). Hundreds of manufacturers began making motherboards, power supplies, cases, and other components that were physically interchangeable with the original IBM AT. This form factor is rarely, if at all, used today.

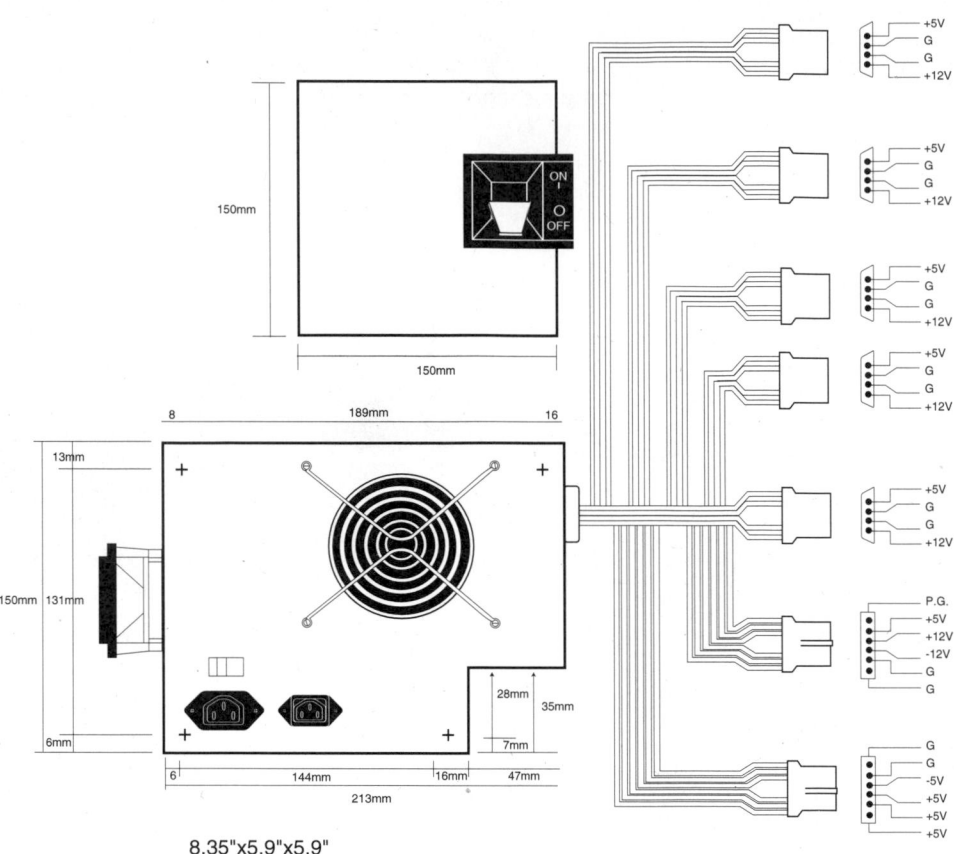

Figure 21.2 AT/Desktop form factor power supply.

AT/Tower Style

The early PC-compatible market came up with some other variations on the AT theme that became quite popular. The AT/Tower configuration was basically a full-sized AT-style desktop system running on its side. The power supply and motherboard form factors were largely the same in the tower system as they were in the desktop. The tower configuration is not new; in fact, even IBM's original AT had a specially mounted logo that could be rotated when you ran the system on its side in the tower configuration.

The type of power supply used in a tower system is identical to that used in a desktop system, except for the location of the power switch. On most AT/Desktop systems, the power switch is located on the power supply (usually in the form of a large toggle switch). Most AT/Tower systems use an external switch attached to the power supply through a short four-wire cable. A full-sized AT power supply with a remote switch is called an AT/Tower form factor power supply (see Figure 21.3). This form factor is rarely, if at all, used today.

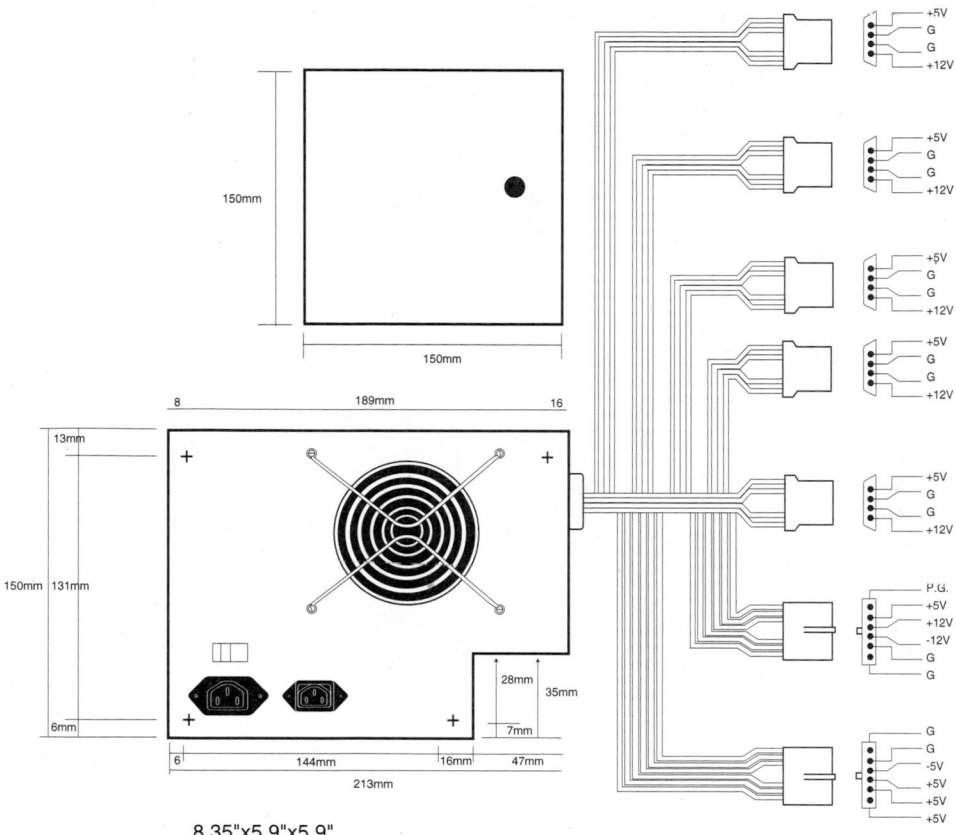

8.35"x5.9"x5.9"

Figure 21.3   AT/Tower form factor power supply.

Baby-AT Style

Another type of AT-based form factor is the so-called Baby-AT, which is a shortened version of the full-sized AT system. The power supply in these systems is shortened in one dimension but matches the AT design in all other respects. Baby-AT–style power supplies can fit into both a Baby-AT chassis and the larger AT-style chassis; however, the full-sized AT/Tower power supply does not fit in the Baby-AT chassis (see Figure 21.4). Because the Baby-AT PSU performed all the same functions as the AT-style power supply, but was in a smaller package, it became the preferred form factor until overtaken by later designs. This form factor is rarely used today.

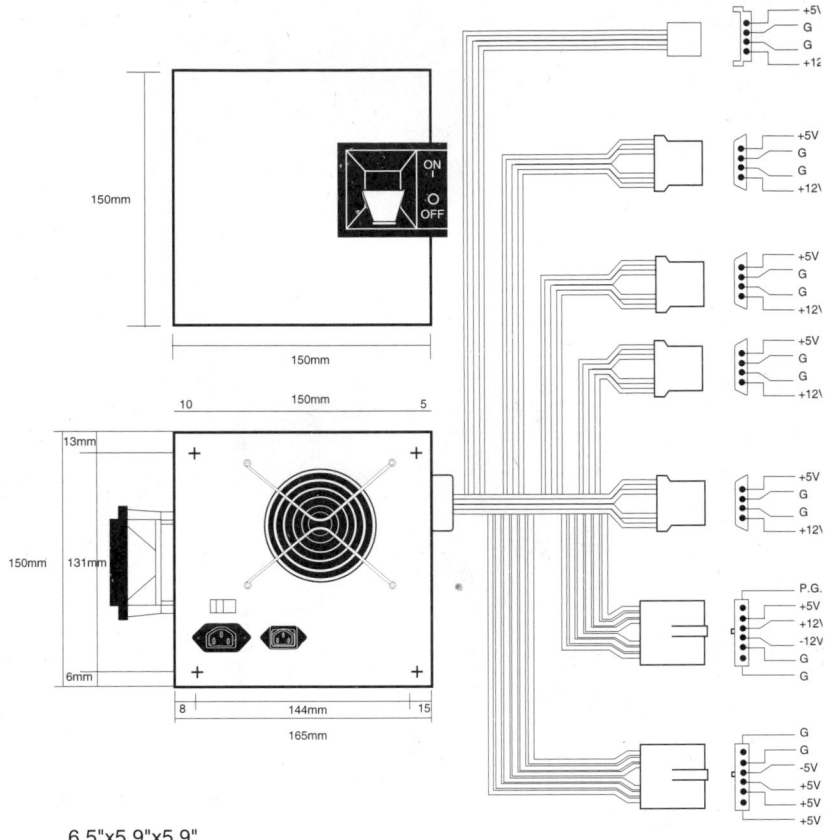

6.5"x5.9"x5.9"

Figure 21.4 Baby-AT form factor power supply.

LPX Style

The next PSU form factor to gain popularity was the LPX style, also called the PS/2 type, Slimline or slim style (see Figure 21.5). The LPX-style power supply has the exact same motherboard and disk drive connectors as the previous standard power supply form factors; it differs mainly in the shape. LPX systems were designed to have a smaller footprint and a lower height than AT-sized systems. These computers used a different motherboard configuration that mounts the expansion bus slots on a "riser" card that plugs into the motherboard. The expansion cards plug into this riser and are mounted sideways in the system, parallel to the motherboard. Because of its smaller case, an LPX system needed a smaller power supply. The PSU designed for LPX systems is smaller than the Baby-AT style in every dimension and takes up less than half the space of its predecessor.

Note

IBM used this type of power supply in some of its PS/2 systems in the late 1980s; hence it is sometimes called a PS/2-type supply.

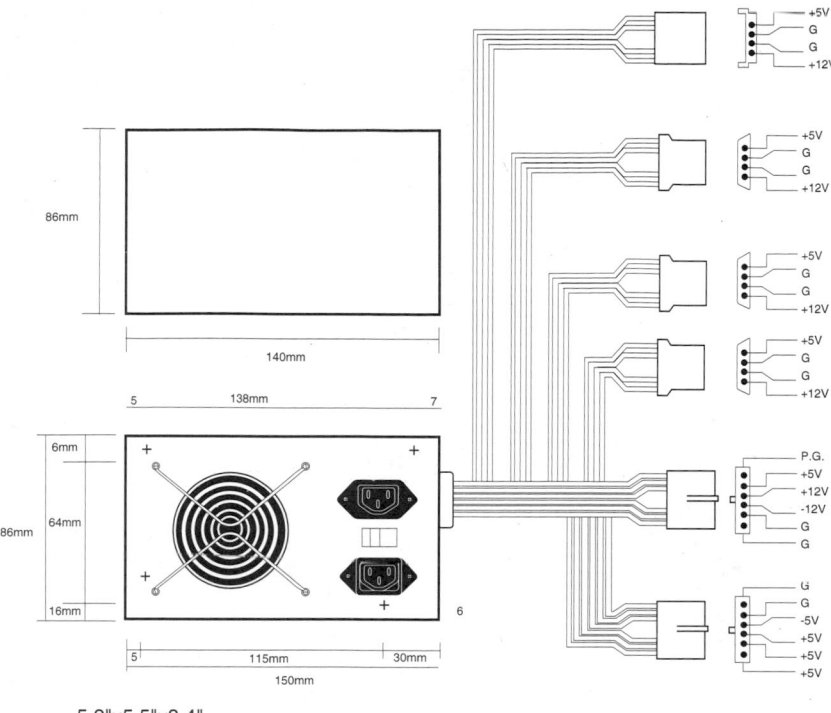

Figure 21.5 LPX form factor power supply.

As with the Baby-AT design in its time, the LPX power supply does the same job as its predecessor, but comes in a smaller package. The LPX power supply quickly found its way into many manufacturers' systems, soon becoming a de facto standard. This style of power supply became the staple of the industry for many years, coming in everything from low profile systems using actual LPX motherboards to full sized towers using Baby-AT or even full-sized AT motherboards. It is still used in some of the PCs produced today, however in the last four years the popularity of LPX has been overshadowed by the increasing popularity of the ATX design.

ATX Style

One of the newer standards in the industry today is the ATX form factor (see Figure 21.6). The ATX specification, now in version 2.01, defines a new motherboard shape, as well as a new case and power supply form factor. The shape of the ATX power supply is based on the LPX design, but there are some important differences worth noting.

One difference is that the ATX specification originally called for the fan to be mounted along the inner side of the supply, where it could blow air across the motherboard and draw it in from outside the case at the rear. This kind of airflow runs in the opposite direction as most standard supplies, which blow air out the back of the supply through a hole in the case where the fan protrudes. The reverse-flow cooling provided by some ATX-style power supplies forces air over the hottest components of the board, such as the processor, memory modules, and expansion slots, which are located in such a way as to take maximum advantage of the airflow. This often eliminates the need for multiple fans in the system—including the CPU fans common in many systems today—the amount of noise produced by the system, and the amount of power needed to run the system.

Another benefit of the reverse-flow cooling is that the system remains cleaner, free from dust and dirt. The case is essentially pressurized, so air is continuously forced out of the cracks in the case—the opposite of what happens with earlier designs. For this reason, the reverse-flow cooling design is often referred to as a positive-pressure-ventilation design. For example, if you held a lit cigarette in front of your floppy drive on a normal system, the smoke would be sucked in through the front of the drive and could contaminate the heads. On an ATX system with reverse-flow cooling, the smoke would be blown out away from the drive because the only air intake would be the single fan vent on the power supply at the rear. For systems that operate in extremely harsh environments, you can add a filter to the fan intake vent to further ensure that all the air entering the system is clean and free of dust.

Although this is theoretically an excellent way to ventilate a system, a properly designed positive-pressure system needs to use a more powerful fan to pull the required amount of air through a filter and to pressurize the case. Also, the filter has to be serviced on a periodic basis—depending upon operating conditions, it can need changing or cleaning as often as every week. In addition, the heat load from the power supply on a fully loaded system exhausts heated air over the CPU, reducing its cooling capability. As newer CPUs create more and more heat, the cooling capability of the airflow becomes absolutely critical. In common practice, using a standard negative-pressure system with an exhaust fan on the power supply and an additional high-quality cooling fan blowing right on the CPU is the best solution. For this reason, the ATX power supply specification has been amended to allow for the older method of negative-pressure ventilation.

Despite the advantages a positive-pressure cooling system can provide, a standard negative pressure system—where air is exhausted out the rear of the power supply and ingested through various vents in the system—offers the most cooling capacity for a given fan airspeed and flow. This is why most of the newer ATX-style power supplies use the negative-pressure cooling system.

The ATX specification was first released by Intel in 1995. In 1996, it became increasingly popular in Pentium and Pentium Pro-based PCs, capturing 18 percent of the motherboard market. With the introduction of the Pentium II in 1997, and now the Pentium III in 1999, ATX has become the dominant motherboard form factor, displacing the previously popular Baby-AT. ATX and its derivatives are likely to remain the most popular form factor for several years to come.

The ATX form factor (see Figure 21.7) addresses several problems with the Baby-AT and mini-AT form factors. Two main problems with the power supply persist. One is that the traditional PC power supply has two connectors that plug into the motherboard. If you insert these connectors backward or out of their normal sequence, you will fry the motherboard. Most responsible system manufacturers "key" the motherboard and power supply connectors so that you cannot install them backward or out of sequence. However, some vendors of cheaper systems do not feature this keying on the boards or supplies they use.

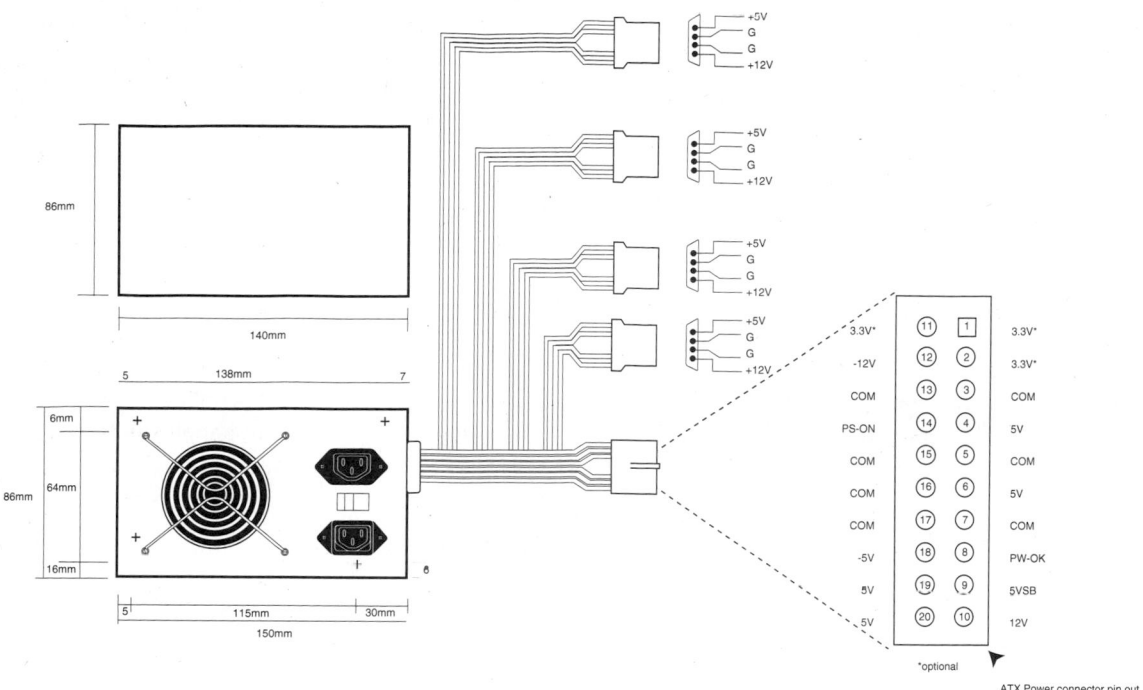

5.9"x5.5"x3.4"

Figure 21.6 ATX form factor power supply, used with both ATX and NLX systems.

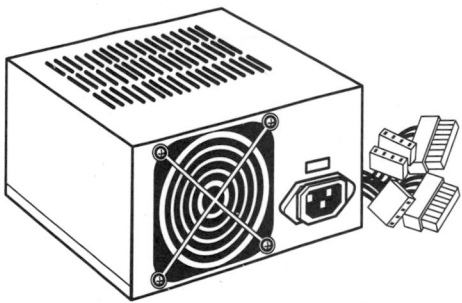

Figure 21.7 ATX/NLX form factor power supply.

The ATX form factor includes a new power plug for the motherboard to prevent users from plugging in their power supplies incorrectly. This new connector has 20 pins and is keyed, which makes it virtually impossible to plug it in backward. Because there is one connector instead of two almost identical ones, it eliminates the problem of plugging in the connectors out of sequence. The new ATX connector also supplies +3.3v, reducing the need for voltage regulators on the motherboard to power the CPU and other +3.3v circuits.

Besides the new +3.3v signals, another set of signals is furnished by the ATX PSU that is not normally seen on standard power supplies. The set consists of the Power_On (PS_On) and 5v_Standby (5VSB) signals, known collectively as Soft Power. Power_On is a motherboard signal that operating systems such as Windows 9x use to power the system on or off via software. This allows features to be implemented such as Wake on Wing or Wake on LAN, in which a signal from a modem or network adapter can actually cause a PC to wake up and power on. Many such systems also have the option of setting a wake up time, upon which the PC can automatically turn on to perform scheduled tasks. These signals can also allow for the optional use of the keyboard to power the system on—exactly like Apple Macintosh systems. The 5v Standby signal is always active, giving the motherboard a limited source of power even when off and enabling these features. Check your BIOS Setup for control over these features.

The other problem solved by an ATX form factor power supply with reverse-cooling airflow is that of keeping today's system processors cool. But it only works in industrial applications, in which an industrial-duty power supply has been designed properly for the heat-load of the intended system and in which constant maintenance is provided. Most of the high-end Pentium and Pentium Pro systems on the market use active heat sinks on the processor, which means there is a small fan on the CPU designed to cool it. Intel and other manufacturers now package cooling fans with the CPU—some are actually permanently mounted on the CPU. For best results, use CPU fans only from reputable manufacturers because a CPU fan can be one of the most critical components for reliable operation.

Note

The cooling method described here was originally recommended by the ATX specification, but it is not required and might not even be preferred. Manufacturers can use alternative methodologies, such as the traditional outblowing (negative pressure) fan arrangement, as well as active or passive heat sinks, on a system with an ATX motherboard. In fact, this might be a better solution for nonindustrial applications for which periodic maintenance of the power-supply filter is not assured.

NLX Style

The NLX specification, also developed by Intel, defines a low-profile case and motherboard with many of the same attributes as the ATX. In fact for interchangeability, NLX systems were designed to use ATX power supplies, even though the case and motherboard dimensions may be different.

As in previous Slimline systems, the NLX motherboard uses a riser board for the expansion bus slots. The NLX motherboard is also designed for easy maintenance access; releasing a simple catch enables you to slide the entire motherboard out of the chassis in about 30 seconds! This is made possible by having nothing connect to the motherboard internally except the riser. The power supply connects to the riser, as do the disk drives, front panel, and multimedia connectors. No boards or cables have to be removed to take out the motherboard, you simply slide it out on rails and slide the replacement in place, all in less than a minute on average.

Just as the standardized ATX architecture functionally replaced the Baby-AT form factor in full-sized desktop and tower systems, NLX is intended to replace the cumbersome and semi-proprietary LPX form factor for smaller desktop systems. For interchangeability with ATX, the NLX specification does not define a new power supply form factor, but uses the ATX type power supply directly instead. NLX is targeted more at the corporate computer market, which has servicibility and maintenance requirements quite different from those of home users. Adoption of the NLX standard is dragging slightly behind that of ATX, but quite a few computer manufacturers have announced systems that take advantage of the lower prices, smaller footprints, and easier maintenance that the new form factor can provide.

SFX Style (Micro-ATX Motherboards)

Intel has recently released a third new motherboard specification, called micro-ATX, that is intended for low-end systems, which are designed with an even smaller footprint than NLX and with potentially smaller power supply requirements. The new smaller micro-ATX motherboards and cases can be designed to use the ATX power supply by default, as well as a new very small power supply called SFX for Small form factor (see Figure 21.8).

The SFX power supply is specifically designed for use in small systems containing a limited amount of hardware. The PSU can provide 90 watts of continuous power (135 watts at its peak) in four voltages (+5, +12, -12, and +3.3v). This amount of power has proved to be sufficient for a small system with a Pentium II processor, an AGP interface, up to four expansion slots, and three peripheral devices—such as hard drives and CD-ROMs.

Note

The SFX power supply does not provide the -5v current required for full compliance with the ISA bus standard. Micro-ATX systems are supposed to use the PCI bus or the AGP interface for all the expansion cards installed in the computer, omitting the ISA bus entirely.

Although Intel designed the SFX power supply specification with the micro-ATX motherboard form factor in mind, SFX is a wholly separate standard that is compliant with other motherboards as well. SFX power supplies use the same 20-pin connector defined in the ATX standard and include both the Power_On and 5v_Standby signals. Whether you will use an ATX or SFX power supply with a micro-ATX system is dependent on the case or chassis, not the motherboard. Each has the same electrical connectors; the difference is which one the case is physically designed to accept.

On a standard model SFX power supply, a 60mm diameter cooling fan is located on the surface of the housing, facing the inside of the computer's case. The fan draws the air into the power supply housing from the system cavity and expels it through a port at the rear of the system. Internalizing the fan in this way reduces system noise and results in a standard negative pressure design. In many cases, additional fans may be needed in the system to cool the processor (see Figure 21.8).

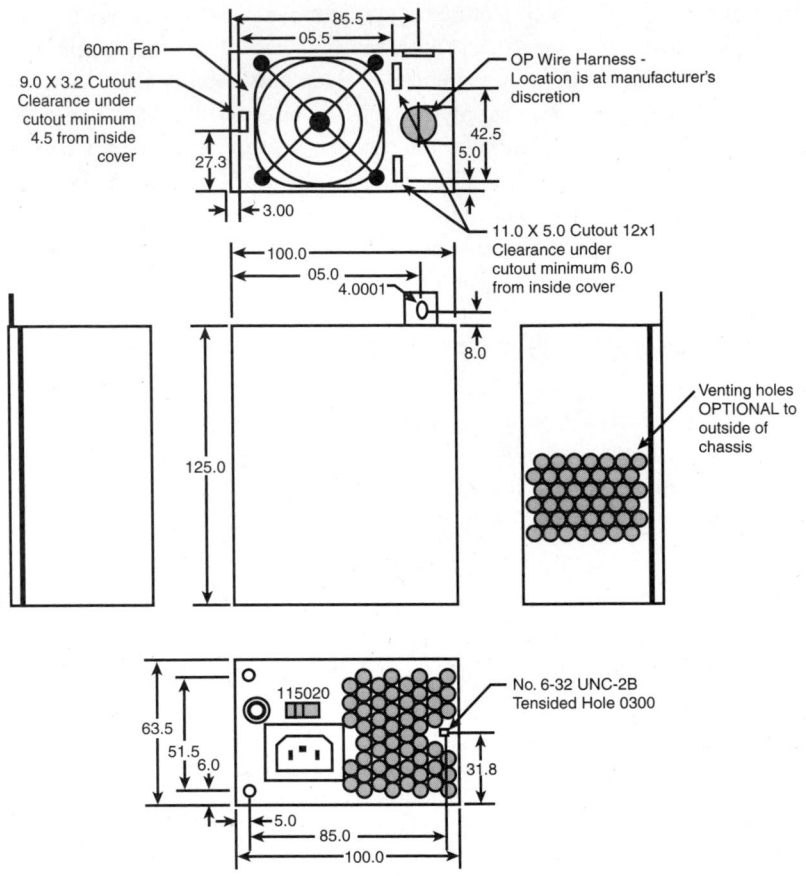

Figure 21.8   SFX form factor power-supply dimensions with standard internal 60mm fan.

For systems that require more cooling capability, there is also a version that allows for a larger 90mm top-mounted cooling fan. The larger fan provides more cooling capability and airflow for systems that need it (see Figure 21.9).

Figure 21.10 shows a picture of an SFX style power supply with the 90mm top-mounted cooling fan.

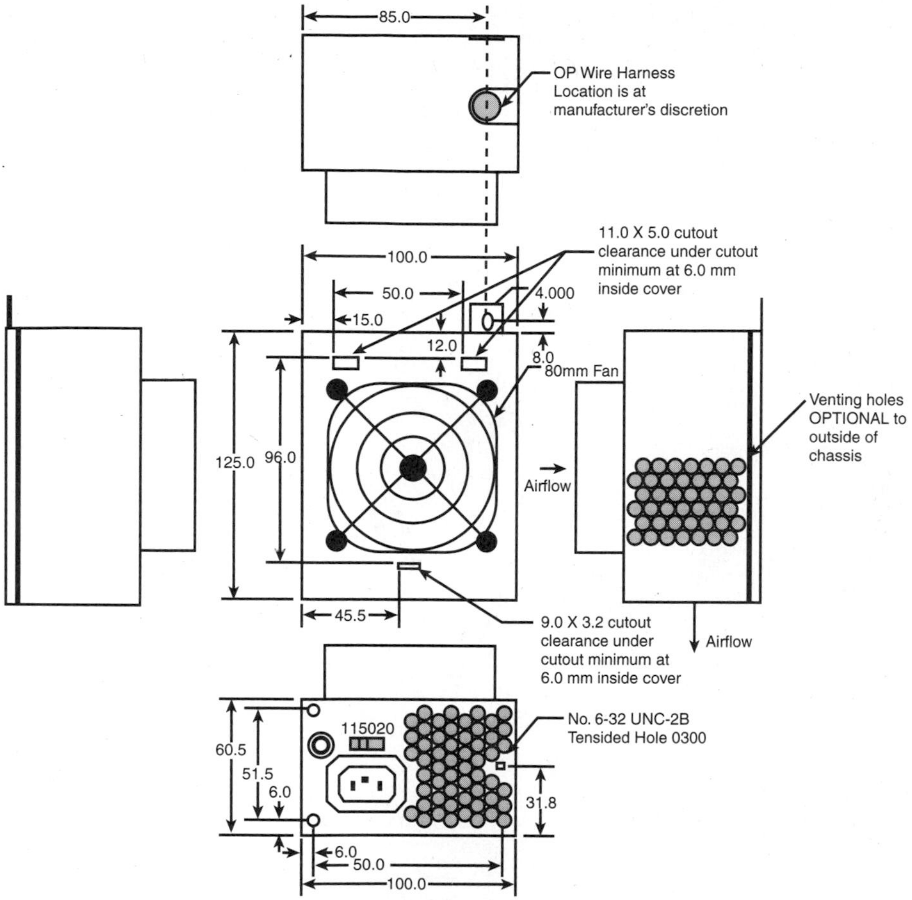

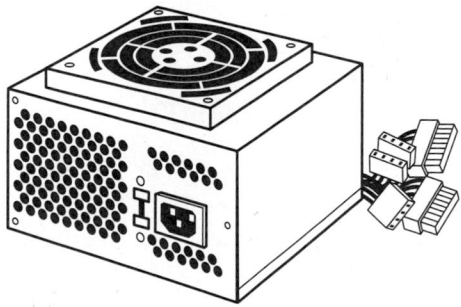

85.0

OP Wire Harness
Location is at
manufacturer's discretion

11.0 X 5.0 cutout
clearance under cutout
minimum at 6.0 mm
inside cover

100.0

50.0

4.000

15.0

12.0

8.0

80mm Fan

Venting holes
OPTIONAL to
outside of
chassis

125.0   96.0

Airflow

45.5

9.0 X 3.2 cutout
clearance under
cutout minimum at
6.0 mm inside cover

Airflow

No. 6-32 UNC-2B
Tensided Hole 0300

60.5

115020

51.5

6.0

31.8

6.0

50.0

100.0

Figure 21.9   SFX form factor power-supply dimensions with internal 90mm top-mounted fan.

Figure 21.10   SFX style supply with 90mm top-mounted cooling fan.

Power Supply Connectors

Table 21.1 shows the pinouts for most LPX-, Baby-AT-, standard AT-, and PC/XT-compatible systems. The two six-pin connectors (P8 and P9) attach the power supply to the motherboard, whereas P10 through P13 are identical four-pin connectors that you use to supply power to internal peripherals, such as floppy and hard disk drives. Figure 21.11 shows the P8 and P9 connectors (sometimes also called P1/P2).

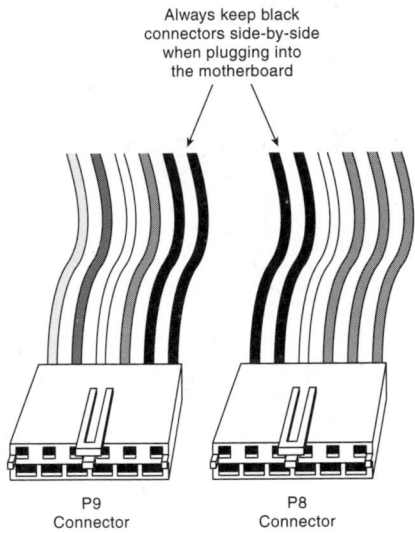

Figure 21.11   Motherboard P8/P9 (sometimes also called P1/P2) power connectors.

All standard PC power supplies that use the P8 and P9 connectors have them installed end-to-end so that the two black-colored wires (ground connections) on both power cables are next to each other. Note the designations P8 and P9 are not fully standardized, although most use those designations because that is what IBM used on the originals. Some power supplies have them labeled as P1/P2 or possibly something else. Because these connectors usually have a clasp that prevents them from being inserted backward on the pins on the motherboards, the major concern is getting them in the correct order and not missing a pin on either side. Following the black-on-black rule keeps you safe. You must take care, however, to make sure no unconnected motherboard pins are between or on either side of the two connectors when you install them. A properly installed connector connects to and covers every motherboard power pin—if any power pins are showing on either side of the connectors, the entire connector assembly is installed incorrectly, which can result in catastrophic failure for the motherboard and everything plugged into it at the time of power-up.

Some systems may have more or fewer drive connectors. For example, IBM's AT system power supplies have only three disk drive power connectors, although most AT/Tower-type power supplies have four drive connectors. Depending on their power ratings, some ATX supplies have as many as eight drive connectors.

If you are adding drives and need additional disk drive power connectors, Y splitter cables (see Figure 21.12) are available from many electronics supply houses (including Radio Shack). These cables can adapt a single power connector to service two drives. As a precaution, make sure that your total power supply output is capable of supplying the additional power.

Table 21.1 shows typical PC/XT and AT power supply connections.

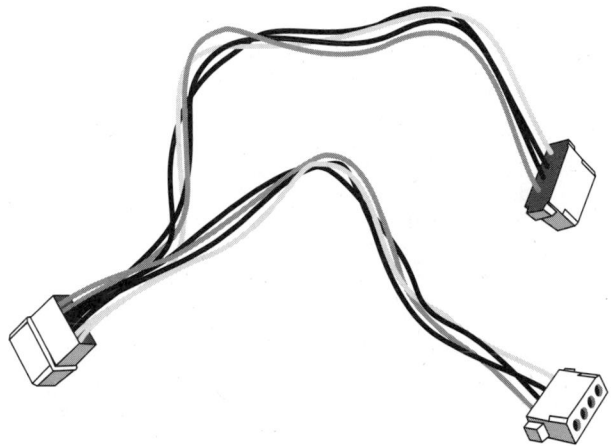

Figure 21.12   A common Y-adapter power cable.

Table 21.1   Typical PC/XT and AT Power Supply Connections

Connector	AT Type	PC/XT Type
P8-1	Power_Good (+5V)	Power_Good (+5v)
P8-2	+5v	Key (No connect)
P8-3	+12v	+12v
P8-4	-12v	-12v
P8-5	Ground (0)	Ground (0)
P8-6	Ground (0)	Ground (0)
P9-1	Ground (0)	Ground (0)
P9-2	Ground (0)	Ground (0)
P9-3	-5v	-5v
P9-4	+5v	+5v
P9-5	+5v	+5v
P9-6	+5v	+5v
P10-1	+12v	+12v
P10-2	Ground (0)	Ground (0)
P10-3	Ground (0)	Ground (0)
P10-4	+5v	+5v

(continues)

Table 21.1   Continued

Connector	AT Type	PC/XT Type
P11-1	+12v	+12v
P11-2	Ground (0)	Ground (0)
P11-3	Ground (0)	Ground (0)
P11-4	+5v	+5v
P12-1	+12v	-
P12-2	Ground (0)	-
P12-3	Ground (0)	-
P12-4	+5v	-
P13-1	+12v	-
P13-2	Ground (0)	-
P13-3	Ground (0)	-
P13-4	+5v	-

Notice that all the power supplies from the AT/Desk through the Baby-AT and LPX power supplies use the same pin configuration. The only other industry standard PSU-to-motherboard connector is the Molex 39-29-9202 (or equivalent) 20-pin ATX style connector (see Figure 21.13). First used in the ATX form factor power supply, it is also used in the SFX form factor. This is a 20-pin keyed connector with pins configured, as shown in Table 21.2. The colors for the wires are those recommended by the ATX standard; however, they are not required for compliance to the specification (in other words, the colors could vary from manufacturer to manufacturer).

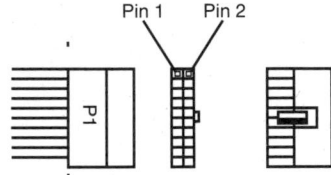

Figure 21.13   ATX style 20-pin motherboard power connector.

Tip

Although the PC/XT power supplies do not have any signal on pin P8-2, you can still use them on AT-type motherboards, or vice versa. The presence or absence of the +5v signal on that pin has little or no effect on system operation.

Table 21.2   ATX Power Supply Connections

Color	Signal	Pin	Pin	Signal	Color
Orange*	+3.3v	11	1	+3.3v	Orange
Blue	-12v	12	2	+3.3v	Orange
Black	GND	13	3	GND	Black
Green	PS_On	14	4	+5v	Red
Black	GND	15	5	GND	Black
Black	GND	16	6	+5v	Red
Black	GND	17	7	GND	Black
White	-5v	18	8	Power_Good	Gray
Red	+5v	19	9	+5VSB (Standby)	Purple
Red	+5v	20	10	+12v	Yellow

* = *May also be Brown, indicating +3.3v Sense feedback.*

Note

The ATX supply features several signals not seen before, such as the +3.3v, Power_On, and +5v_Standby signals. Therefore, it is difficult to adapt a standard LPX form factor supply to make it work properly in an ATX system, even though the shapes of the power supplies themselves are virtually identical.

ATX Optional Power Connector

In addition to the main 20-pin power connector (see Figure 21.14), the ATX specification defines an optional six-pin connector (two rows of three pins each) to provide the signals shown in Table 21.3. The computer can use these signals to monitor and control the cooling fan, monitor the voltage of the +3.3v signal to the motherboard, and provide power and grounding to devices compliant with the IEEE 1394 (FireWire) standard.

Table 21.3   ATX Optional Power Supply Connections

Color	Signal	Pin	Pin	Signal	Color
	Reserved	4	1	FanM	White
Gray	1394	5	2	FanC	Blue
	Reserved	6	3	+3.3v sense	Brown

The FanM signal enables the operating system to monitor the status of the power supply's cooling fan so that it can take appropriate actions, such as shutting down the system if the fan fails.

An operating system can use the FanC signal with variable voltages to control the operation of the power supply's fan, shifting it into a low power state or shutting it off completely when the system is in sleep or standby mode. The ATX standard specifies that a voltage of +1v or less indicates that the fan is to shut down, whereas +10.5v or more instructs the fan to operate at full speed. The system designer can define intermediate voltages to operate variable-speed fans at various levels. If the power supply does not include a variable-speed fan circuit, any voltage level higher than +1v on the FanC signal is interpreted as a command to run the fan at its full (and only) speed.

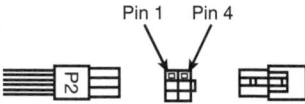

Figure 21.14   ATX optional power supply connections.

Note

The SFX specification also defines the use of a six-pin control connector, but uses it only to provide a fan control signal on one pin. The other five pins are all reserved for future use.

Power Switch Connectors

Most of the power supplies used today employ a remote power switch that is accessible from the front of the computer case. In contrast, earlier form factors, such as the AT desktop and Baby-AT, used a switch that was integrated into the power supply housing. Because the power supply was mounted in a rear corner of the case, the switch was inconveniently located on the back of the computer case.

Pre-ATX power supplies use a remote switch that is connected to the power supply through a standard four-wire cable. The ends of the cable are fitted with spade connector lugs, which plug onto the spade connectors on the power switch. The switch is usually a part of the case, so the power supply comes with the cable and no switch.

The cable from the power supply to the switch in the case contains four color-coded wires. There may also be a fifth wire supplying a ground connection to the case.

Caution

The remote power switch leads carry 110v AC current at all times. You could be electrocuted if you touch the ends of these wires with the power supply plugged in! Always make sure the power supply is unplugged before connecting or disconnecting the remote power switch.

The four or five wires are color coded as follows:

- The brown and blue wires are the live and neutral feed wires from the 110v power cord to the power supply. These wires are always hot when the power supply is plugged in.

- The black and white wires carry the AC feed from the switch back to the power supply. These leads should be hot only when the power supply is plugged in and the switch is turned on.

- A green wire or a green wire with a yellow stripe is the ground lead. It should be connected to the PC case and should help ground the power supply to the case.

On the switch, the tabs for the leads are usually color coded; if not, you can still connect them easily. If no color coding is on the switch, plug the blue and brown wires onto the tabs that are parallel to each other and the black and white wires to the tabs that are angled away from each other. See Figure 21.15 as a guide.

Caution

Although these wire color codings are used on most power supplies, they are not necessarily 100 percent universal. I have encountered power supplies that did not use the same coloring scheme described here. Unless you can verify the color codes with the power supply manufacturer, always disconnect the power supply from the wall socket before handling any of these wires.

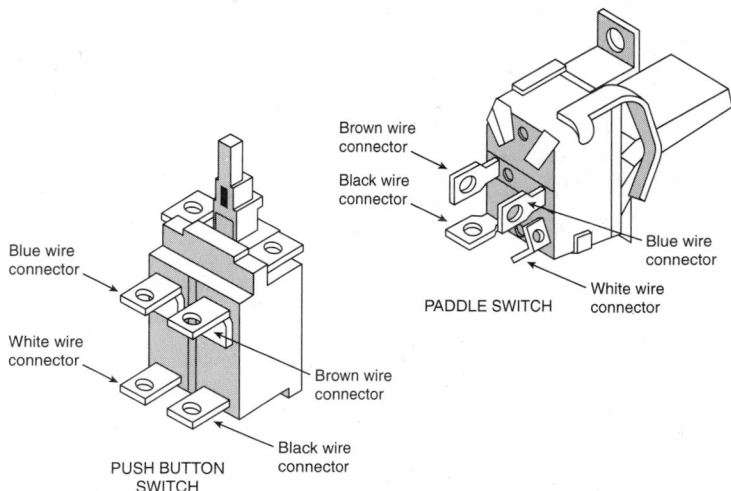

Figure 21.15   Power supply remote switch connections for two styles of switches.

As long as the blue and brown wires are on the one set of tabs and the black and white leads are on the other, the switch and supply will work properly. If you incorrectly mix the leads, you will likely blow the circuit breaker for the wall socket, because mixing them can create a direct short circuit.

All ATX and subsequent power supplies that employ the 20-pin motherboard connector use the PS_ON signal to power up the system. As a result, the remote switch does not physically control the power supply's access to the 110v AC power, as in the older style PSUs. Instead, the power supply's on or off status is toggled by a PS_ON signal received on pin 14 of the ATX connector.

The PS_ON signal can be generated physically by the computer's power switch or electronically by the operating system. PS_ON is an active low signal, meaning that all the DC power signals generated by the PSU are deactivated when PS_ON is held high, with the exception of the +5VSB (standby) signal on pin 9, which is active whenever the power supply is connected to an AC power source. The +5VSB signal provides the power for the remote switch on the case to operate while the computer is off. Thus, the remote switch in an ATX-style system (which should include most NLX and SFX systems) carries only +5v of DC power, rather than the full 110v AC current that is in the older form factors.

Caution

The continuous presence of the +5VSB signal on pin 9 of the ATX connector means that the motherboard is always receiving power from the PSU when connected to an AC source, even when the computer is turned off. As a result, it is even more crucial to unplug an ATX system from the power source before working inside the case than it is on an earlier model system.

Disk Drive Power Connectors

The disk drive connectors on power supplies are fairly universal with regard to pin configuration and even wire color. Table 21.4 shows the standard disk drive power connector pinout and wire colors.

Table 21.4   Disk Drive Power Connector Pinout

Pin	Wire Color	Signal
1	Yellow	+12v
2	Black	Gnd
3	Black	Gnd
4	Red	+5v

This information applies whether the drive connector is the larger Molex version or the smaller mini-version used on most 3 1/2-inch floppy drives. In each case, the pinouts and wire colors are the same. To determine the location of pin 1, look at the connector carefully. It is usually embossed in the plastic connector body; however, it is often tiny and difficult to read. Fortunately, these connectors are keyed and therefore difficult to insert incorrectly. Figure 21.16 shows the keying with respect to pin numbers on the larger drive power connector.

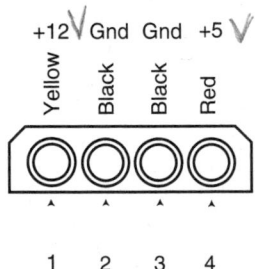

Figure 21.16   A disk drive female power supply cable connector.

Note

Some drive connectors may supply only two wires—usually the +5v and a single ground (pins 3 and 4)—because the floppy drives in most newer systems run on only +5v and do not use the +12v at all.

Physical Connector Part Numbers

The physical connectors used in industry-standard PC power supplies were originally specified by IBM for the supplies used in the original PC/XT/AT systems. They used a specific type of connector between the power supply and the motherboard (the P8 and P9 connectors) and specific connectors for the disk drives. The motherboard connectors used in all the industry-standard power supplies were unchanged from 1981 (when the IBM PC appeared) until 1995 (when Intel released the ATX standard). The original PC's four-pin disk drive connector was augmented by a smaller (also four-pin) power connector when 3 1/2-inch floppy drives appeared in 1986. Table 21.5 lists the standard connectors used for motherboard and disk drive power.

Table 21.5   Physical Power Connectors

Connector Description	Female (on Power Cable)	Male (on Component)
ATX/NLX/SFX (20-pin)	Molex 39-29-9202	Molex 39-01-2200
ATX Optional (6-pin)	Molex 39-01-2960	Molex 39-30-1060
PC/AT/LPX Motherboard P8/P9	Burndy GTC6P-1	Burndy GTC 6RI
Disk Drive (large style)	AMP 1-480424-0	AMP 1-480426-0
Floppy Drive (small style)	AMP 171822-4	AMP 171826-4

You can get these raw connectors through the electronics supply houses (Allied, Newark, and Digi-Key, for example) found in the Vendor List, on the CD. You also can get complete cable assemblies, including drive adapters that convert the large connectors into small connectors; disk drive Y splitter cables; and motherboard power extension cables from a number of the cable and miscellaneous supply houses, such as Ci Design and Key Power.

Caution

Before you install additional connectors to your power supply using Y splitters or any other type of connector, be sure your power supply is capable of delivering sufficient power for all your internal peripherals. Overloading the power supply can cause damage to electrical components and stored data.

▶▶ See "Power Supply Ratings," p. 1112.

The Power_Good Signal

The Power_Good signal (sometimes called Power_OK or POK) is a +5v signal (with variation from +3.0 through +6.0v generally being considered acceptable) generated in the power supply when it has passed its internal self tests and the outputs have stabilized. This normally takes place anywhere from 0.1 to 0.5 seconds after you turn on the power supply switch. This power supply sends the signal to the motherboard, where it is received by the processor timer chip, which controls the reset line to the processor.

In the absence of Power_Good, the timer chip continually resets the processor, which prevents the system from running under bad or unstable power conditions. When the timer chip receives the Power_Good signal, it stops resetting the processor, and the processor begins executing whatever code is at address FFFF:0000 (usually the ROM BIOS).

If the power supply cannot maintain proper outputs (such as when a brownout occurs), the Power_Good signal is withdrawn, and the processor is automatically reset. When the power output returns to its proper levels, the PSU regenerates the Power_Good signal and the system again begins operation (as if you had just powered on). By withdrawing Power_Good, the system never sees the bad power because it is stopped quickly (reset) rather than being allowed to operate using unstable or improper power levels, which can cause memory parity errors and other problems.

◀◀ See "Parity Checking," p. 459.

On pre-ATX systems, the Power_Good connection is made via connector P8-1 (P8 Pin 1) from the power supply to the motherboard. ATX and later systems use pin 8 of the 20-pin connector.

A well-designed power supply delays the arrival of the Power_Good signal until all the PSU's voltages stabilize after you turn the system on. Badly designed power supplies, which are found in many low-cost systems, often do not delay the Power_Good signal properly and enable the processor to start too soon. (The normal Power_Good delay is from 0.1 to 0.5 seconds.) Improper Power_Good timing also causes CMOS memory corruption in some systems.

Note

If you find that a system consistently fails to boot up properly the first time you turn on the switch but that it subsequently boots up if you press the reset or Ctrl+Alt+Delete warm boot command, you likely have a problem with the Power_Good timing. You must install a new, high-quality power supply and see if that solves the problem.

Some cheaper power supplies do not have proper Power_Good circuitry and may just tie any +5v line to that signal. Some motherboards are more sensitive to an improperly designed or improperly functioning Power_Good signal than others. Intermittent startup problems are often the result of improper Power_Good signal timing. A common example is when you replace a motherboard in a system and then find that the system intermittently fails to start properly when you turn the power on. This can be very difficult to diagnose, especially for the inexperienced technician, because the problem appears to be caused by the new motherboard. Although it seems as though the new motherboard is defective, it usually turns out that the power supply is poorly designed. It either cannot produce stable enough power to properly operate the new board, or it has an improperly wired or timed Power_Good signal (which is more likely). In these situations, replacing the supply with a high-quality unit, in addition to the new motherboard, is the proper solution.

Power Supply Loading

PC power supplies are of a *switching* rather than a *linear* design. The switching type of design uses a high-speed oscillator circuit to convert the higher wall-socket AC voltage to the much lower DC voltage used to power the PC and PC components. Switching type power supplies are noted for being very efficient in size, weight, and energy in comparison to the linear design, which uses a large internal transformer to generate different outputs. This type of transformer-based design is inefficient in at least three ways. First, the output voltage of the transformer linearly follows the input voltage (hence the name, linear), so any fluctuations in the AC power going into the system can cause problems with the output. Second, the high current level (power) requirements of a PC system require the use of heavy wiring in the transformer. Third, the 60Hz (hertz) frequency of the AC power supplied from your building is difficult to filter out inside the power supply, requiring large and expensive filter capacitors and rectifiers.

The switching supply, on the other hand, uses a switching circuit that chops up the incoming power at a relatively high frequency. This allows for the use of high-frequency transformers that are much smaller and lighter. Also, the higher frequency is much easier and cheaper to filter out at the output, and the input voltage can vary widely. Input ranging from 90–135 volts still produces the proper output levels, and many switching supplies can automatically adjust to 220v input.

One characteristic of all switching-type power supplies is that they do not run without a *load*. This means that you must have the supply plugged into something drawing power for the supply to work. If you simply have the power supply on a bench with nothing plugged into it, the supply either burns up or its protection circuitry shuts it down. Most power supplies are protected from no-load operation and shut down automatically. Some of the cheap clone supplies, however, lack the protection circuit and relay. They are destroyed after a few seconds of no-load operation. A few power supplies have their own built-in load resistors, so they can run even though no normal load is plugged in.

According to IBM specifications for the standard 192-watt power supply used in the original AT, a minimum load of 7.0 amps was required at +5v and a minimum of 2.5 amps was required at +12v for the supply to work properly.

Because floppy drives present no +12v load unless they are spinning, systems without a hard disk drive often do not operate properly. Some power supplies have a minimum load requirement for both the +5v and +12v sides. If you fail to meet this minimum load, the supply shuts down.

Because of this characteristic, when IBM used to ship the original AT systems without a hard disk, they plugged the hard disk drive power cable into a large 5-ohm 50-watt sandbar resistor, which was mounted in a little metal cage assembly where the drive would have been. The AT case had screw holes on top of where the hard disk would go, specifically designed to mount this resistor cage.

Note

Several computer stores I knew of in the mid-80s would order the diskless AT and install their own 20MB or 30MB drives, which they could get more cheaply from other sources than from IBM. They were throwing away the load resistors by the hundreds! I managed to grab a couple at the time, which is how I know the type of resistor they used.

This resistor would be connected between pin 1 (+12v) and pin 2 (Ground) on the hard disk power connector. This would place a 2.4-amp load on the supply's +12v output, drawing 28.8 watts of power (it would get hot!) and thus enabling the supply to operate normally. Note that the cooling fan in most power supplies draws approximately 0.1 to 0.25 amps, bringing the total load to 2.5 amps or more. If the load resistor were missing, the system would intermittently fail to start up or operate properly. The motherboard would draw +5v at all times, but +12v would normally be used only by motors, and the floppy drive motors would be off most of the time.

Most of the power supplies in use today do not require as much of a load as the original IBM AT power supply. In most cases, a minimum load of 0 to 0.3 amps at +3.3v; 2.0 to 4.0 amps at +5v; and 0.5 to 1.0 amps at +12v is considered acceptable. Most motherboards easily draw the minimum +5v current by themselves. The standard power supply cooling fan draws only 0.1 to 0.25 amps, so the +12v minimum load may still be a problem for a diskless workstation. Generally, the higher the rating on the supply, the more minimum load required; however, there are exceptions, so this is a specification you want to check when evaluating power supplies.

Some high-quality switching power supplies have built-in load resistors and can run under a no-load situation because the supply loads. Other high-quality power supplies, such as those from PC Power and Cooling, have no internal load resistors. They only require a small load on the +5v line to operate properly. Many of the cheaper clone supplies, which often do not have built-in load resistors, may require +3.3v, +5v, and +12v loads to work.

If you want to bench test a power supply, make sure you place loads on all the PSU's positive voltage outputs. This is one reason why it is best to test the supply while it is installed in the system instead of testing it separately on the bench. For impromptu bench testing, you can use a spare motherboard and hard disk drive to load the outputs.

Power-Supply Ratings

A system manufacturer should be able to provide you with the technical specifications of the power supplies it uses in its systems. This type of information can be found in the system's technical-reference manual, as well as on stickers attached directly to the power supply. Power-supply manufacturers can also supply this data, which is preferable if you can identify the manufacturer and contact them directly or via the Web.

Tables 21.6 and 21.7 list power-supply specifications for several of IBM's units, from which the power supplies of many other systems are derived. The input specifications are listed as voltages, and the output specifications are listed as amps at several voltage levels. IBM reports output wattage level as "specified output wattage." If your manufacturer does not list the total wattage, you can convert amperage to wattage by using the following simple formula:

$$\text{Watts} = \text{Volts} \times \text{Amps}$$

For example, if a motherboard is listed as drawing 6 amps of +5v current, that would be 30 watts of power, according to the formula.

By multiplying the voltage by the amperage available at each output and then adding the results, you can calculate the total capable output wattage of the supply.

Table 21.6   Power-Supply Output Ratings for IBM Classic Systems

	PC	Port-PC	XT	XT-286	AT
Minimum Input Voltage	104	90	90	90	90
Maximum Input Voltage	127	137	137	137	137
110/220v Switching	No	Yes	No	Auto	Yes
Output Current (amps):					
+5v	7.0	11.2	15.0	20.0	19.8
-5v	0.3	0.3	0.3	0.3	0.3
+12v	2.0	4.4	4.2	4.2	7.3
-12v	0.25	0.25	0.25	0.25	0.3
Calculated output wattage	63.5	113.3	129.9	154.9	191.7
Specified output wattage	63.5	114.0	130.0	157.0	192.0

Table 21.6 shows the standard power supply output levels available in industry-standard form factors. Most manufacturers offer supplies with ratings from 100 watts to 450 watts or more. Table 21.7 shows the rated outputs at each of the voltage levels for supplies with different manufacturer-specified output ratings. To compile the table, I referred to the specification sheets for supplies from Astec Standard Power and PC Power and Cooling. Although most of the ratings are accurate, they are somewhat misleading for the higher wattage units.

Table 21.7   Typical Compatible Power-Supply Output Ratings

Specified Output Wattage	100W	150W	200W	250W	300W	375W	450W
Output Current (amps):							
+5v	10.0	15.0	20.0	25.0	32.0	35.0	45.0
-5v	0.3	0.3	0.3	0.5	1.0	0.5	0.5
+12v	3.5	5.5	8.0	10.0	10.0	13.0	15.0
-12v	0.3	0.3	0.3	0.5	1.0	0.5	1.0
Calculated output wattage	97.1	146.1	201.1	253.5	297.0	339.5	419.5

Adding a +3.3v signal to the power supply modifies the equation significantly. Table 21.8 contains data for various ATX power supplies that include a +3.3v signal.

Table 21.8   ATX Power-Supply Output Ratings

Specified Output Wattage	235W	275W	300W	400W
Output Current (amps):				
+3.3v	14.0	14.0	14.0	28.0
+5v	22.0	30.0	30.0	30.0
Max +3.3/+5v	125	150	150	215
-5v	0.5	0.5	0.5	1.0
+12v	8.0	10.0	12.0	14.0
-12v	1.0	1.0	1.0	1.0

If you compute the total output using the formula described earlier, these PSUs seem to produce an output that is much higher than their ratings. The 300W model, for example, comes out at 354.7 watts. However, notice that the supply also has a maximum combined output for the +3.3v and +5v signals of 150 watts. This brings the total output to a more logical 308.5 watts.

Most PC power supplies have ratings between 150 and 300 watts. Although lesser ratings are not usually desirable, it is possible to purchase heavy-duty power supplies for most systems that have outputs as high as 500 watts.

The 300-watt and larger units are excellent for enthusiasts who are building fully optioned desktops or tower systems. These supplies run any combination of motherboard and expansion card, as well as a large number of disk drives and other peripherals. In most cases, you cannot exceed the ratings on these power supplies—the system will be out of room for additional items first!

Most power supplies are considered to be universal, or worldwide. That is, they can also run on the 220v, 50-cycle current used in Europe and many other parts of the world. Many power supplies that can switch from 110v to 220v input do so automatically, but a few require you to set a switch on the back of the power supply to indicate which type of power you will access.

Caution

If your supply does not switch input voltages automatically, make sure the voltage setting is correct. If you plug the power supply into a 110v outlet while set in the 220v setting, no damage will result, but the supply will certainly not operate properly until you correct the setting. On the other hand, if you are in a foreign country with a 220v outlet and have the switch set for 110v, you may cause damage.

Power-Supply Specifications

In addition to power output, many other specifications and features go into making a high-quality power supply. I have had many systems over the years. My experience has been that if a brownout occurs in a room with several systems running, the systems with higher-quality power supplies and higher output ratings are far more likely to make it through the power disturbances unscathed, whereas others choke.

High-quality power supplies also help protect your systems. A power supply from a vendor such as Astec or PC Power and Cooling will not be damaged if any of the following conditions occur:

- A 100 percent power outage of any duration
- A brownout of any kind
- A spike of up to 2,500v applied directly to the AC input (for example, a lightning strike or a lightning simulation test)

Decent power supplies have an extremely low current leakage to ground of less than 500 microamps. This safety feature is important if your outlet has a missing or improperly wired ground line.

As you can see, these specifications are fairly tough and are certainly representative of a high-quality power supply. Make sure that your supply can meet these specifications.

You can also use many other criteria to evaluate a PSU. The power supply is a component many users ignore when shopping for a PC, and it is therefore one that some system vendors may choose to skimp on. After all, a dealer is far more likely to be able to increase the price of a computer by spending money on additional memory or a larger hard drive than by installing a better power supply.

When buying a computer (or a replacement PSU), it is always a good idea to learn as much as possible about the power supply. However, many consumers are intimidated by the vocabulary and the statistics found in a typical PSU specification. Here are some of the most common parameters found on power supply specification sheets, along with their meanings:

■ *Mean Time Between Failures (MTBF) or Mean Time To Failure (MTTF)*. The (calculated) average interval, in hours, that the power supply is expected to operate before failing. Power supplies typically have MTBF ratings (such as 100,000 hours or more) that are clearly not the result of real-time empirical testing. In fact, manufacturers use published standards to calculate the results, based on the failure rates of the power supply's individual components. MTBF figures for power supplies often include the load to which the PSU was subjected (in the form of a percentage) and the temperature of the environment in which the tests were performed.

■ *Input Range (or Operating Range)*. The range of voltages that the power supply is prepared to accept from the AC power source. For 110v AC current, an input range of 90 to 135V is common; for 220v current, a 180–270v range is typical.

■ *Peak Inrush Current*. The greatest amount of current drawn by the power supply at a given moment immediately after it is turned on, expressed in terms of amps at a particular voltage. The lower the current, the less thermal shock the system experiences.

■ *Holdup Time*. The amount of time (in milliseconds) that a power supply's output remains within the specified voltage ranges after its input ceases. Values of 15–25 milliseconds are common for today's PSUs.

■ *Transient Response*. The amount of time (in microseconds) a power supply takes to bring its output back the specified voltage ranges after a steep change of the output current. In other words, the amount of time it takes for the output power levels to stabilize after a device in the system starts or stops drawing power. Power supplies sample the current being used by the computer at regular intervals. When a device stops drawing power during one of these intervals (such as when a floppy drive stops spinning), the PSU may supply too high a voltage to the output for a brief time. This excess voltage is called overshoot, and the transient response is the time that it takes for the voltage to return to the specified level. Once a major problem that came with switching power supplies, overshoot has been greatly reduced in recent years. Transient response values are sometimes expressed in time intervals, and at other times are expressed in terms of a particular output change, such as "power output levels stay within regulation during output changes of up to 20 percent."

■ *Overvoltage Protection*. The trip points for each output at which the power supply shuts down or squelches the signal for that output. Values can be expressed as a percentage (for example, 120 percent for +3.3 and +5v) or as raw voltages (for example, +4.6v for the +3.3v output and 7.0v for the +5v output).

- *Maximum Load Current.* The largest amount of current (in amps) that can be safely delivered through a particular output. Values are expressed as individual amperages for each output voltage. With these figures, you can calculate not only the total amount of power the PSU can supply, but also how many devices using those various voltages it can support.

- *Minimum Load Current.* The smallest amount of current (in amps) that must be drawn from a particular output for that output to function. If the current drawn from an output falls below the minimum, the power supply could be damaged or could automatically shut down.

- *Load Regulation (or Voltage Load Regulation).* When the current drawn from a particular output increases or decreases, the voltage changes slightly as well, usually increasing as the current rises. Load regulation is the change in the voltage for a particular output as it transitions from its minimum load to its maximum load (or vice versa). Values, expressed in terms of a +/- percentage, typically range from +/-1 percent to +/-5 percent for the +3.3, +5, and +12v outputs.

- *Line Regulation.* The change in output voltage as the AC input voltage transitions from the lowest to the highest value of the input range. A power supply should be capable of handling any AC voltage in its input range with a change in its output of 1 percent or less.

- *Efficiency.* The ratio of a PSU's power input to its power output, expressed in terms of a percentage. Values of 65–85 percent are common for power supplies today. The remaining 15–35 percent of the power input is converted to heat during the AC/DC conversion process. Although greater efficiency means less heat inside the computer (always a good thing) and lower electric bills, it should not be emphasized at the expense of precision, as evidenced in the PSU's load regulation and other parameters.

- *Ripple (or Ripple and Noise, or AC Ripple, or PARD [Periodic and Random Deviation]).* The average voltage of all AC components' effects on the power supply's outputs, usually measured in millivolts peak-to-peak or RMS. The effects can be caused by internal switching transients, feed through of the rectified line frequency, and other random noise.

Power-Supply Certifications

Many agencies around the world certify electric and electronic components for safety and quality. The most commonly known agency in the United States is Underwriters Laboratories, Inc. (UL). UL standard #1950—the *Standard for Safety of Information Technology Equipment, Including Electrical Business Equipment, Third Edition*—covers power supplies and other PC components. It is always a good idea to purchase power supplies and other devices that are UL-certified. It has often been said that, although not every good product is UL-certified, no bad products are.

In Canada, electric and electronic products are certified by the Canadian Standards Agency (CSA). The German equivalents are TÜV Rheinland and VDE. NEMKO operates in Norway. These three agencies are responsible for certification of products throughout Europe. Power supply manufacturers that sell to an international market should have products that are certified at least by UL, the CSA, and TÜV—if not by all the agencies listed, and more.

Apart from UL-type certifications, many power-supply manufacturers, even the most reputable ones, claim that their products have a Class B certification from the Federal Communications Commission, meaning that they meet FCC standards for electromagnetic and radio frequency interference (EMI/RFI). This is a contentious point, however, because the FCC does not certify power supplies as individual components. Title 47 of the Code of Federal Regulations, Part 15, Section 15.101(c) states as follows:

> "The FCC does NOT currently authorize motherboards, cases, and internal power supplies. Vendor claims that they are selling 'FCC-certified cases,' 'FCC-certified motherboards,' or 'FCC-certified internal power supplies' are false."

In fact, an FCC certification can be issued collectively only to a base unit consisting of a computer case, motherboard, and a power supply. Thus, a power supply purported to be FCC-certified was actually certified along with a particular case and motherboard—not necessarily the same case and motherboard you are using in your system. This does not mean, however, that the manufacturer is being deceitful, or that the power supply is inferior. If anything, this means that when evaluating power supplies, you should place less weight on the FCC certification than on other factors, such as UL certification.

Power-Use Calculations

When expanding or upgrading your PC, it is important to be sure your power supply is capable of providing sufficient current to power all the system's internal devices. One way to see whether your system is capable of expansion is to calculate the levels of power drain in the different system components and deduct the total from the maximum power supplied by the PSU. This calculation can help you decide whether you must upgrade the power supply to a more capable unit. Unfortunately, these calculations can be difficult to make because many manufacturers do not publish power consumption data for their products.

It can be difficult to get power-consumption data for many +5v devices, including motherboards and adapter cards. Motherboards can consume different power levels, depending on numerous factors. Most motherboards consume about 5 amps or so, but try to get information on the one you are using. For adapter cards, if you can find the actual specifications for the card, use those figures. To be on the conservative side, however, I usually go by the maximum available power levels set forth in the respective bus standards.

For example, consider the power-consumption figures for components in a modern PC, such as a desktop or Slimline system with a 200-watt power supply rated for 20 amps at +5V and 8 amps at +12v. The ISA specification calls for a maximum of 2.0 amps of +5v and 0.175 amps of +12v power for each slot in the system. Most systems have eight slots, and you can assume that four are filled for the purposes of calculating power draw. The following calculation shows what happens when you subtract the amount of power necessary to run the different system components:

5v Power:	20.0 Amps
Less:	Motherboard -5.0 amps
	4 slots filled at 2.0 each -8.0 amps
	3 1/2- and 5 1/4-inch floppy drives -1.5 amps
	3 1/2-inch hard disk drive -0.5 amp
	CD-ROM drive -1.0 amp
=Remaining power:	4.0 amps

12v Power:	8.0 Amps
Less:	4 slots filled at 0.175 each -0.7 amp 3 1/2-inch hard disk drive -1.0 amp 3 1/2- and 5 1/4-inch floppy drives -1.0 amp Cooling fan -0.1 amp CD-ROM drive -1.0 amp
=Remaining power:	4.2 amps

In the preceding example, everything seems all right for the present. With half the slots filled, two floppy drives, and one hard disk, the system still has room for more. Problems with the power supply could come up, however, if this system were expanded to the extreme. With every slot filled and two or more hard disks, there definitely would be problems with the +5v current. However, the +12v does seem to have room to spare. You could add a CD-ROM drive or a second hard disk without worrying too much about the +12v power, but the +5v power would be strained.

If you anticipate loading up a system to the extreme—as in a high-end multimedia system, for example—you may want to invest in the insurance of a higher output power supply. For example, a 250-watt supply usually has 25 amps of +5v and 10 amps of +12v current, whereas a 300-watt unit has 32 amps of +5v power. These supplies enable you to fully load the system and are likely to be found in full-sized desktop or tower case configurations in which this type of expansion is expected.

Motherboards can draw anywhere from four to fifteen amps or more of +5v power to run. In fact, a single Pentium 66MHz CPU draws up to 3.2 amps of +5v power all by itself. A 200MHz Pentium Pro CPU or 400MHz Pentium II consumes up to 15 amps. Considering that systems with two or more processors are now becoming common, you could have 30 amps or more drawn by the processors alone. A motherboard such as this—with two CPUs and 128MB or more of RAM for each CPU—might draw more than 40 amps all by itself. Very few "no-name" power supplies can supply this kind of current. For these applications, you should consider only high-quality, high-capacity power supplies from a reputable manufacturer, such as PC Power and Cooling.

In these calculations, bus slots are allotted maximum power in amps, as shown in Table 21.9.

Table 21.9   Maximum Power Consumption in Amps per Bus Slot

Bus Type	+5v Power	+12v Power	+3.3v Power
ISA	2.0	0.175	n/a
EISA	4.5	1.5	n/a
VL-bus	2.0	n/a	n/a
16-bit MCA	1.6	0.175	n/a
32-bit MCA	2.0	0.175	n/a
PCI	5	0.5	7.6

As you can see from the table, ISA slots are allotted 2.0 amps of +5v and 0.175 amp of +12v power. Note that these are maximum figures; not all cards draw this much power. If the slot has a VL-bus extension connector, an additional 2.0 amps of +5v power are allowed for the VL-bus.

Floppy drives can vary in power consumption, but most of the newer 3 1/2-inch drives have motors that run on +5v current in addition to the logic circuits. These drives usually draw 1.0 amps of +5v power and use no +12v at all. 5 1/4-inch drives use standard +12v motors that draw about 1.0 amps. These drives also require about 0.5 amps of +5v for the logic circuits. Most cooling fans draw about 0.1 amps of +12v power, which is negligible.

Typical 3 1/2-inch hard disks today draw about 1 amp of +12v power to run the motors and only about 0.5 amps of +5v power for the logic. 5 1/4-inch hard disks, especially those that are full-height, draw much more power. A typical full-height hard drive draws 2.0 amps of +12v power and 1.0 amps of +5v power.

Another problem with hard disks is that they require much more power during the spinup phase of operation than during normal operation. In most cases, the drive draws double the +12v power during spinup, which can be 4.0 amps or more for the full-height drives. This tapers off to normal after the drive is spinning.

The figures that most manufacturers report for maximum power supply output are full duty-cycle figures. The PSU can supply these levels of power continuously. You usually can expect a unit that continuously supplies a given level of power to be capable of exceeding this level for some noncontinuous amount of time. A supply usually can offer 50 percent greater output than the continuous figure indicates for as long as one minute. Systems often use this cushion to supply the necessary power to spin up a hard disk drive. After the drive has spun to full speed, the power draw drops to a value within the system's continuous supply capabilities. Drawing anything over the rated continuous figure for any extended length of time causes the power supply to run hot and fail early and can also create nasty symptoms in the system.

Tip

If you are using internal SCSI hard drives, you can ease the startup load on your power supply. The key is to enable the SCSI drive's Remote Start option, which causes the drive to start spinning only when it receives a startup command over the SCSI bus. The effect is that the drive remains stationary (drawing very little power) until the very end of the POST and spins up right when the SCSI portion of the POST is begun.

If you have multiple SCSI drives, they all spin up sequentially based on their SCSI ID setting. This is designed so that only one drive is spinning up at any one time and so that no drives start spinning until the rest of the system has had time to start. This greatly eases the load on the power supply when you first power the system on.

In most cases, you enable Remote Start through your SCSI host adapter's setup program. This program may be supplied with the adapter on separate media, or it may be integrated into the adapter's BIOS and activated with a specific key combination at boot time.

The biggest cause of power-supply overload problems has historically been filling up the expansion slots and adding more drives. Multiple hard drives, CD-ROM drives, and floppy drives can create quite a drain on the system power supply. Make sure that you have enough +12v power to run all the drives you plan to install. Tower systems can be especially problematic because they have so many drive bays. Just because the case has room for the devices doesn't mean the power supply can support them. Make sure you have enough +5v power to run all your expansion cards, especially PCI cards. It pays to be conservative, but remember that most cards draw less than the maximum allowed. Today's newest processors can have very high current requirements for the +5- or +3.3-volt supplies. When selecting a power supply for your system, be sure to take into account any future processor upgrades.

Many people wait until an existing component fails before they replace it with an upgraded version. If you are on a tight budget, this "if it ain't broke, don't fix it" attitude may be necessary. Power supplies, however, often do not fail completely all at once; they can fail in an intermittent fashion or allow fluctuating power levels to reach the system, which results in unstable operation. You might be blaming system lockups on software bugs when the culprit is an overloaded power supply. If you have been running your original power supply for a long time and have upgraded your system in other ways, you should expect some problems.

Although there is certainly an appropriate place for the exacting power-consumption calculations you've read about in this section, a great many experienced PC users prefer the "don't worry about it" power calculation method. This technique consists of buying a system with a good quality 300- or 350-watt power supply (or installing such a supply yourself) and then upgrading the system freely, without concern for power consumption. Unless you plan to build a system with six SCSI drives and a dozen other peripherals, you will probably not exceed the capabilities of the PSU, and this method certainly requires far less effort.

Power Off When Not in Use

Should you turn off a system when it is not in use? To answer this frequent question, you should understand some facts about electrical components and what makes them fail. Combine this knowledge with information on power consumption, cost, and safety to come to your own conclusion. Because circumstances can vary, the best answer for your own situation might be different than for others, depending on your particular needs and applications.

Frequently, powering a system on and off does cause deterioration and damage to the components. This seems logical, but the simple reason is not obvious to most people. Many believe that flipping system power on and off frequently is harmful because it electrically "shocks" the system. The real problem, however, is temperature or thermal shock. As the system warms up, the components expand; and as it cools off, the components contract. In addition, various materials in the system have different thermal expansion coefficients, which means that they expand and contract at different rates. Over time, thermal shock causes deterioration in many areas of a system.

From a pure system-reliability viewpoint, it is desirable to insulate the system from thermal shock as much as possible. When a system is turned on, the components go from ambient (room) temperature to as high as 185° F (85° C) within 30 minutes or less. When you turn the system off, the same thing happens in reverse, and the components cool back to ambient temperature in a short period of time.

Thermal expansion and contraction remain the single largest cause of component failure. Chip cases can split, allowing moisture to enter and contaminate them. Delicate internal wires and contacts can break, and circuit boards can develop stress cracks. Surface-mounted components expand and contract at different rates than the circuit board they are mounted on, which causes enormous stress at the solder joints. Solder joints can fail due to the metal hardening from the repeated stress, resulting in cracks in the joint. Components that use heat sinks, such as processors, transistors, or voltage regulators, can overheat and fail because the thermal cycling causes heat sink adhesives to deteriorate, breaking the thermally conductive bond between the device and the heat sink. Thermal cycling also causes socketed devices and connections to loosen or "creep," which can cause a variety of intermittent contact failures.

◄◄ See "SIMMs and DIMMs," p. 437.

Thermal expansion and contraction affect not only chips and circuit boards, but also things such as hard disk drives. Most hard drives today have sophisticated thermal compensation routines that make adjustments in head position relative to the expanding and contracting platters. Most drives perform this thermal compensation routine once every five minutes for the first 30 minutes the drive is running, and then every 30 minutes thereafter. In many drives, this procedure can be heard as a rapid "tick-tick-tick-tick" sound. In essence, anything you can do to keep the system at a constant temperature prolongs the life of the system, and the best way to accomplish this is to leave the system either permanently on or off. Of course, if the system is never turned on in the first place, it should last a long time indeed!

Now, I am not saying that you should leave all systems on 24 hours a day. A system powered on and left unattended can be a fire hazard (I have had monitors spontaneously catch fire—luckily, I was there at the time), is a data security risk (from cleaning crews and other nocturnal visitors), can be easily damaged if moved while running, and wastes electrical energy.

I currently pay 11 cents for a kilowatt-hour of electricity. A typical desktop-style PC with display consumes at least 300 watts (0.3 kilowatt) of electricity (and that is a conservative estimate). This means that it would cost 3.3 cents to run my typical PC for an hour. Multiplying by 168 hours in a week means that it would cost $5.54 per week to run this PC continuously. If the PC were turned on at 9 a.m. and off at 5 p.m., it would be on only 40 hours per week and would cost only $1.32—a savings of $4.22 per week! Multiply this savings by 100 systems, and you are saving $422 per week. Multiply this by 1,000 systems, and you are saving $4,220 per week! Using systems certified under the new EPA Energy Star program (that is, green PCs) would account for an additional savings of around $1 per system per week—or $1,000 per week for 1,000 systems. The great thing about Energy Star systems is that the savings are even greater if the systems are left on for long periods of time because the power management routines are automatic.

Based on these facts, my recommendations are that you power the systems on at the beginning of the workday and off at the end of the workday. Do not power the systems off for lunch, breaks, or any other short durations of time. If you are a home user, leave it on if you are going to be using it later in the day or if instant access is important. I'd normally recommend home users turn the system off when leaving the house or when sleeping. Servers, of course, should be left on continuously. This seems to be the best compromise of system longevity with pure economics. No matter what, these are just guidelines; if it works better for you to leave your system on 24 hours a day, seven days a week, then make it so.

Power Management

As the standard PC configuration has grown to include capabilities formerly considered options, the power requirements of the system have increased steadily. Larger displays, CD-ROM drives, and audio adapters all need more power to run, and the cost of operating a PC rises steadily. To address these concerns, several programs and standards are now being developed that are intended to reduce the power needed to run a PC as much as possible.

For standard desktop systems, power management is a matter of economy and convenience. By turning off specific components of the PC when they are not in use, you can reduce the electric bill and avoid having to power the computer up and down manually.

For portable systems, power management is far more important. Adding CD-ROMs, speakers, and other components to a laptop or notebook computer reduces what is in many cases a short battery life even further. By adding new power management technology, a portable system can supply power only to the components it actually needs to run, thus extending the life of the battery charge.

Energy Star Systems

The EPA has started a certification program for energy-efficient PCs and peripherals. To be a member of this program, the PC or display must drop to a power draw at the outlet of 30 watts or less during periods of inactivity. Systems that conform to this specification get to wear the Energy Star logo. This is a voluntary program; however, many PC manufacturers are finding that it helps them sell their systems if they can advertise these systems as energy efficient.

One problem with this type of system is that the motherboard and disk drives literally can go to sleep, which means they can enter a standby or sleep mode, in which they draw very little power. This causes havoc with some of the older power supplies because the low power draw does not provide enough of a load for them to function properly. Most of the newer supplies on the market, which are designed to work with these systems, have a very low minimum load specification. I suggest that you ensure that the minimum load will be provided by the equipment in your system if you buy a power supply upgrade. Otherwise, when the PC goes to sleep, it may take a power switch cycle to wake it up again. This problem would be most noticeable if you invested in a very high output supply and used it in a system that draws very little power to begin with.

Advanced Power Management

Advanced Power Management (APM) is a specification jointly developed by Intel and Microsoft that defines a series of interfaces between power management-capable hardware and a computer's operating system. When it is fully implemented, APM can automatically switch a computer between five states, depending on the system's current activity. Each state represents a further reduction in power use, accomplished by placing unused components into a low-power mode.

The five system states are as follows:

- *Full On.* The system is completely operational, with no power management occurring.

- *APM Enabled.* The system is operational, with some devices being power managed. Unused devices may be powered down and the CPU clock slowed or stopped.

- *APM Standby.* The system is not operational, with most devices in a low-power state. The CPU clock may be slowed or stopped, but operational parameters are retained in memory. When triggered by a specific user or system activities, the system can return to the APM Enabled state almost instantaneously.

- *APM Suspend.* The system is not operational, with most devices unpowered. The CPU clock is stopped and operational parameters are saved to disk for later restoration. When triggered by a wakeup event, the system returns to the APM Enabled state relatively slowly.

- *Off.* The system is not operational. The power supply is off.

APM requires support from both hardware and software to function. In this chapter, you've already seen how ATX-style power supplies can be controlled by software commands using the Power_On signal and the six-pin optional power connector. Manufacturers are also integrating the same sort of control features into other system components, such as motherboards, monitors, and disk drives.

Operating systems that support APM, such as Windows 9x, trigger power management events by monitoring the activities performed by the computer user and the applications running on the system. However, the OS does not address the power management capabilities of the hardware directly.

A system can have many different hardware devices and many different software functions participating in APM functions, which makes communication difficult. To address this problem, both the operating system and the hardware have an abstraction layer that facilitates communication between the various elements of the APM architecture.

The operating system runs an APM driver that communicates with the various applications and software functions that trigger power management activities, while the system's APM-capable hardware devices all communicate with the system BIOS. The APM driver and the BIOS communicate directly, completing the link between the OS and the hardware.

Thus, for APM to function, there must be support for the standard built into the system's individual hardware devices, the system BIOS, and the operating system (which includes the APM driver). Without all of these components, APM activities cannot occur.

Advanced Configuration and Power Interface (ACPI)

ACPI is a newer power management standard supported by newer system BIOS software running Windows 98 and later operating systems. If your BIOS and operating system supports ACPI, full power management control is now done by the operating system, rather than by the BIOS. ACPI is intended to offer a single place for power management control; in the past, with APM you would often be able to make power management settings in the BIOS setup as well as the operating system that often overlapped or could have conflicting settings. ACPI is supported in newer systems in lieu of APM.

Tip

If, for any reason, you find that power management activities cause problems on your system, such as operating system freeze-ups or hardware malfunctions, the easiest way to disable APM is through the system BIOS. Most BIOSes that support APM include an option to disable it. This breaks the chain of communication between the operating system and the hardware, causing all power management activities to cease. Although it is also possible to achieve the same end by removing the APM driver from the operating system, Windows 9x's Plug-and-Play (PnP) feature detects the system's APM capabilities whenever you restart the computer and attempts to reinstall the APM driver.

If you have a newer system with ACPI, you can disable the power management settings via the Power Management icon in the Windows control panel.

Power Supply Troubleshooting

Troubleshooting the power supply basically means isolating the supply as the cause of problems within a system and, if necessary, replacing it.

Caution

It is rarely recommended that an inexperienced user open a power supply to make repairs because of the dangerous high voltages present. Even when unplugged, power supplies can retain dangerous voltage and must be discharged (like a monitor) before service. Such internal repairs are beyond the scope of this book and are specifically not recommended unless the technician knows what he or she is doing.

Many symptoms lead me to suspect that the power supply in a system is failing. This can sometimes be difficult for an inexperienced technician to see because at times there appears to be little connection between the symptom and the cause—the power supply.

For example, in many cases a parity check error message can indicate a problem with the power supply. This may seem strange because the parity check message specifically refers to memory that has failed. The connection is that the power supply powers the memory, and memory with inadequate power fails.

It takes some experience to know when this type of failure is power related, not caused by the memory. One clue is the repeatability of the problem. If the parity check message (or other problem) appears frequently and identifies the same memory location each time, I would suspect defective memory is the problem. However, if the problem seems random, or if the memory location the error message cites as having failed seems random, I would suspect improper power as the culprit. The following is a list of PC problems that often are power supply-related:

- Any power-on or system startup failures or lockups.
- Spontaneous rebooting or intermittent lockups during normal operation.
- Intermittent parity check or other memory-type errors.
- Hard disk and fan simultaneously failing to spin (no +12v).
- Overheating due to fan failure.

- Small brownouts cause the system to reset.
- Electric shocks felt on the system case or connectors.
- Slight static discharges disrupt system operation.

In fact, just about any intermittent system problem can be caused by the power supply. I always suspect the supply when flaky system operation is a symptom. Of course, the following fairly obvious symptoms point right to the power supply as a possible cause:

- System is completely dead (no fan, no cursor)
- Smoke
- Blown circuit breakers

If you suspect a power supply problem, some of the simple measurements and the more sophisticated tests outlined in this section can help you determine whether the power supply is at fault. Because these measurements may not detect some intermittent failures, you might have to use a spare power supply for a long-term evaluation. If the symptoms and problems disappear when a "known good" spare unit is installed, you have found the source of your problem.

Following is a simple flowchart to help you zero in on common power supply related problems:

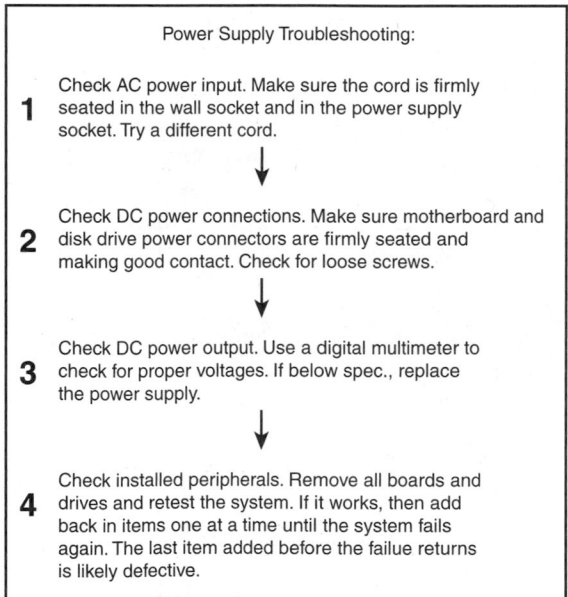

Power Supply Troubleshooting:

1. Check AC power input. Make sure the cord is firmly seated in the wall socket and in the power supply socket. Try a different cord.

2. Check DC power connections. Make sure motherboard and disk drive power connectors are firmly seated and making good contact. Check for loose screws.

3. Check DC power output. Use a digital multimeter to check for proper voltages. If below spec., replace the power supply.

4. Check installed peripherals. Remove all boards and drives and retest the system. If it works, then add back in items one at a time until the system fails again. The last item added before the failue returns is likely defective.

There are many different types of symptoms that can indicate problems with the power supply. Because the power supply literally powers everything else in the system, everything from disk drive problems to memory problems to motherboard problems can often be traced back to the power supply as the root cause.

Overloaded Power Supplies

A weak or inadequate power supply can put a damper on your ideas for system expansion. Some systems are designed with beefy power supplies, as if to anticipate a great deal of system add-ons and expansion components. Most desktop or tower systems are built in this manner. Some systems have inadequate power supplies from the start, however, and cannot adequately service the power-hungry options you might want to add.

The wattage rating can sometimes be very misleading. Not all 300-watt supplies are created the same. People familiar with high-end audio systems know that some watts are better than others. This goes for power supplies, too. Cheap power supplies may in fact put out the rated power, but what about noise and distortion? Some of the supplies are under-engineered to just barely meet their specifications, whereas others may greatly exceed their specifications. Many of the cheaper supplies provide noisy or unstable power, which can cause numerous problems with the system. Another problem with under-engineered power supplies is that they can run hot and force the system to do so as well. The repeated heating and cooling of solid-state components eventually causes a computer system to fail, and engineering principles dictate that the hotter a PC's temperature, the shorter its life. Many people recommend replacing the original supply in a system with a heavier duty model, which solves the problem. Because power supplies come in common form factors, finding a heavy-duty replacement for most systems is easy, as is the installation process.

Inadequate Cooling

Some of the available replacement power supplies have higher capacity cooling fans than the originals, which can greatly prolong system life and minimize overheating problems, especially for the newer, hotter-running processors. If system noise is a problem, models with special fans can run more quietly than the standard models. These PSUs often use larger-diameter fans that spin more slowly, so they run more quietly and move the same amount of air as the smaller fans. PC Power and Cooling specializes in heavy-duty and quiet supplies; Astec has several heavy-duty models as well.

Ventilation in a system is also important. You must ensure adequate airflow to cool the hotter items in the system. Many processors today use passive heat sinks that require a steady stream of air to cool the chip. If the processor heat sink has its own fan, this is not much of a concern. If you have free expansion slots, it's a good idea to space out the boards in your system to permit airflow between them. Place the hottest running boards nearest the fan or the ventilation holes in the system. Make sure that there is adequate airflow around the hard disk drive, especially for those that spin at high rates of speed. Some hard disks can generate quite a bit of heat during operation. If the hard disks overheat, data can be lost.

Always make sure you run your computer with the case cover on, especially if you have a loaded system. Removing the cover can actually cause a system to overheat. With the cover off, the power supply fan no longer draws air through the system. Instead, the fan ends up cooling the supply only, and the rest of the system must be cooled by simple convection. Although most systems do not immediately overheat for this reason, several of my own systems, especially those that are fully expanded, have overheated within 15–30 minutes when run with the case cover off.

In addition, be sure that any empty slot positions have the filler brackets installed. If you leave these brackets off after removing a card, the resultant hole in the case disrupts the internal air-flow and may cause higher internal temperatures.

If you experience intermittent problems that you suspect are related to overheating, a higher-capacity replacement power supply is usually the best cure. Specially designed supplies with additional cooling fan capacity also can help. At least one company sells a device called a fan card, but I am not convinced these are a good idea. Unless the fan is positioned to draw air to or from outside the case, all it does is blow hot air around inside the system and provide a spot cooling effect for anything it is blowing on. In fact, adding fans in this manner contributes to the overall heat inside the system because the fan consumes power and generates heat.

CPU-mounted fans are an exception because they are designed only for spot cooling of the CPU. Many of the newer processors run so much hotter than the other components in the system that a conventional finned aluminum heat sink cannot do the job. In this case, a small fan placed directly over the processor provides a spot cooling effect that keeps the processor temperatures down. One drawback to these active processor cooling fans is that the processor overheats instantly and can be damaged if they fail. Whenever possible, try to use the biggest passive (finned aluminum) heat sink you can find and purchase a CPU fan from a reputable vendor.

Using Digital Multi-Meters

One simple test you can perform on a power supply is to check the output voltages. This shows whether a power supply is operating correctly and whether the output voltages are within the correct tolerance range. Note that you must measure all voltages with the power supply connected to a proper load, which usually means testing while the power supply is still installed in the system.

Selecting a Meter

You need a simple Digital Multi-Meter (DMM) or Digital Volt-Ohm Meter (DVOM) to perform voltage and resistance checks on electronic circuits (see Figure 21.17). You should use only a DMM instead of the older needle-type multi-meters because the older meters work by injecting a 9v signal into the circuit when measuring resistance, which damages most computer circuits.

A DMM uses a much smaller voltage (usually 1.5v) when making resistance measurements, which is safe for electronic equipment. You can get a good DMM with many different features from several sources. I prefer the small pocket-sized meters for computer work because they are easy to carry around.

Some features to look for in a good DMM are as follows:

- *Pocket size*. This is self-explanatory, but small meters are available that have many, if not all, of the features of larger ones. The elaborate features found on some of the larger meters are not really needed for computer work.

- *Overload protection*. This means that if you plug the meter into a voltage or current beyond the meter's capability to measure, the meter protects itself from damage. Cheaper meters lack this protection and can be easily damaged by reading current or voltage values that are too high.

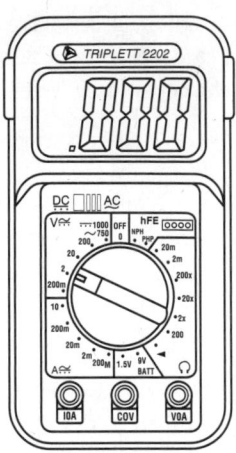

Figure 21.17 A typical DMM.

- *Autoranging.* This means that the meter automatically selects the proper voltage or resistance range when making measurements. This is preferable to the manual range selection; however, really good meters offer both autoranging capability and a manual range override.

- *Detachable probe leads.* The leads can be easily damaged, and sometimes a variety of differently shaped probes are required for different tests. Cheaper meters have the leads permanently attached, which means that you cannot easily replace them. Look for a meter with detachable leads that plug into the meter.

- *Audible continuity test.* Although you can use the ohm scale for testing continuity (0 ohms indicates continuity), a continuity test function causes the meter to produce a beep noise when continuity exists between the meter test leads. By using the sound, you can quickly test cable assemblies and other items for continuity. After you use this feature, you will never want to use the ohms display for this purpose again.

- *Automatic power off.* These meters run on batteries, and the batteries can easily be worn down if the meter is accidentally left on. Good meters have an automatic shutoff that turns off the unit when it senses no readings for a predetermined period of time.

- *Automatic display hold.* This feature enables you to hold the last stable reading on the display even after the reading is taken. This is especially useful if you are trying to work in a difficult-to-reach area single-handedly.

- *Minimum and maximum trap.* This feature enables the meter to trap the lowest and highest readings in memory and hold them for later display, which is especially useful if you have readings that are fluctuating too quickly to see on the display.

Although you can get a basic pocket DMM for as little as $20, one with all of these features is priced in the $100–$200 range. Radio Shack carries some nice inexpensive units, and you can purchase the high-end models from electronics supply houses, such as Newark or Digi-Key.

Measuring Voltage

To measure voltages on a system that is operating, you must use a technique called *back probing* on the connectors (see Figure 21.18). You cannot disconnect any of the connectors while the system is running, so you must measure with everything connected. Nearly all the connectors you need to probe have openings in the back where the wires enter the connector. The meter probes are narrow enough to fit into the connector alongside the wire and make contact with the metal terminal inside. The technique is called back probing because you are probing the connector from the back. You must use this back probing technique to perform virtually all of the following measurements.

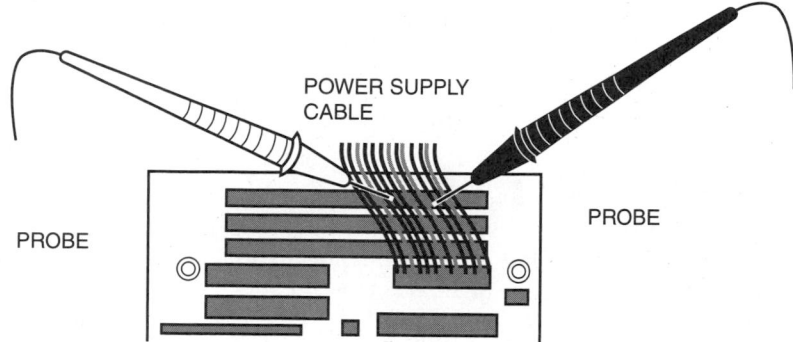

Figure 21.18 Back probing the power-supply connectors.

To test a power supply for proper output, check the voltage at the Power_Good pin (P8-1 on AT, Baby-AT, and LPX supplies; pin 8 on the ATX-type connector) for +3v to +6v of power. If the measurement is not within this range, the system never sees the Power_Good signal and therefore does not start or run properly. In most cases, the power supply is bad and must be replaced.

Continue by measuring the voltage ranges of the pins on the motherboard and drive power connectors. If you are measuring voltages for testing purposes, any reading within 10 percent of the specified voltage is considered acceptable, although most manufacturers of high-quality power supplies specify a tighter 5 percent tolerance. For ATX power supplies, the specification requires that voltages must be within 5 percent of the rating, except for the 3.3v current, which must be within 4 percent. The following table shows the voltage ranges within these tolerances.

Desired Voltage	Loose Tolerance Min. (-10%)	Max. (+8%)	Tight Tolerance Min. (−5%)	Max. (+5%)
+3.3v	2.97v	3.63v	3.135	3.465
+/-5.0v	4.5v	5.4v	4.75	5.25
+/-12.0v	10.8v	12.9v	11.4	12.6

The Power_Good signal has tolerances that are different from the other signals, although it is nominally a +5v signal in most systems. The trigger point for Power_Good is about +2.5v, but most systems require the signal voltage to be within the tolerances listed:

Signal	Minimum	Maximum
Power_Good (+5v)	3.0v	6.0v

Replace the power supply if the voltages you measure are out of these ranges. Again, it is worth noting that any and all power-supply tests and measurements must be made with the power supply properly loaded, which usually means that it must be installed in a system and the system must be running.

Specialized Test Equipment

You can use several types of specialized test gear to test power supplies more effectively. Because the power supply is one of the most failure-prone items in PCs today, it is wise to have these specialized items if you service many PC systems.

Load Resistors for Bench Testing a Power Supply

Bench testing a power supply requires some special setup because all PC power supplies require a load to operate.

Variable Voltage Transformer

When testing power supplies, it is sometimes desirable to simulate different AC voltage conditions at the wall socket to observe how the supply reacts. A variable voltage transformer is a useful test device for checking power supplies because it enables you to exercise control over the AC line voltage used as input for the power supply (see Figure 21.19). This device consists of a large transformer mounted in a housing with a dial indicator that controls the output voltage. You plug the line cord from the transformer into the wall socket and plug the PC power cord into the socket provided on the transformer. The knob on the transformer can be used to adjust the AC line voltage received by the PC.

Most variable transformers can adjust their AC output from 0v to 140v, no matter what the AC input (wall socket) voltage is. Some can cover a range from 0v to 280v as well. You can use the transformer to simulate brownout conditions, enabling you to observe the PC's response. Thus, you can check a power supply for proper Power_Good signal operation, among other things.

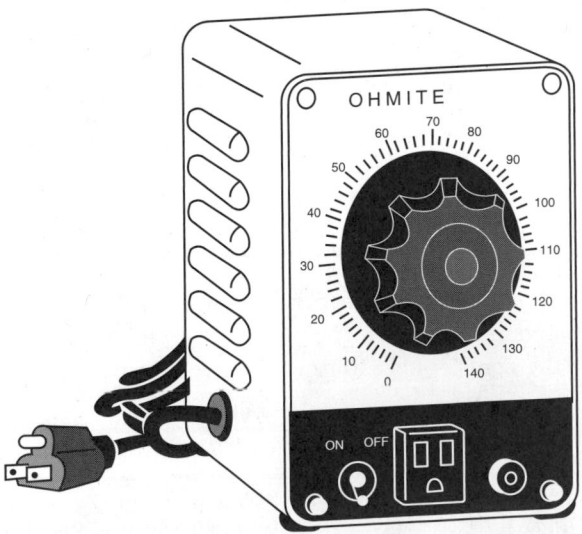

Figure 21.19 A variable voltage transformer.

By running the PC and dropping the voltage until the PC shuts down, you can see how much reserve is in the power supply for handling a brownout or other voltage fluctuations. If your transformer can output voltages in the 200v range, you can test the capability of the power supply to run on foreign voltage levels. A properly functioning supply should operate between 90v to 135v but should shut down cleanly if the voltage is outside that range.

One indication of a problem is seeing parity check-type error messages when you drop the voltage to 80v. This indicates that the Power_Good signal is not being withdrawn before the power supply output to the PC fails. The PC should simply stop operating as the Power_Good signal is withdrawn, causing the system to enter a continuous reset loop.

Variable voltage transformers are sold by a number of electronic parts supply houses, such as Newark and Digi-Key. You should expect to pay anywhere from $100–$300 for this device.

Repairing the Power Supply

Hardly anyone actually repairs power supplies anymore, primarily because it is usually cheaper simply to replace the supply with a new one. Even high-quality power supplies are not that expensive when compared to the labor required to repair them.

A defective power supply is usually discarded unless it happens to be one of the higher quality or more expensive units. In that case, it is usually wise to send the supply out to a company that specializes in repairing power supplies and other components. These companies usually provide what is called depot repair, which means you send the supply to them, and they repair it and return it to you. If time is of the essence, most of the depot repair companies immediately send you a functional equivalent to your defective supply and take yours in as a core charge. Depot repair is the recommended way to service many PC components, such as power supplies, monitors, and printers. If you take your PC in to a conventional service outlet, they often determine which component has the problem and send it out to be depot repaired. You can do that yourself and save the markup that the repair shop normally charges in such cases.

For those with experience around high voltages, it might be possible to repair a failing supply with two relatively simple operations; however, these require opening the supply. I do not recommend doing so but I mention it only as an alternative to replacement in some cases.

Most manufacturers try to prevent you from entering the supply by sealing it with special tamper-proof Torx screws. These screws use the familiar Torx star driver, but also have a tamper-prevention pin in the center that prevents a standard driver from working. Most tool companies such as Jensen or Specialized sell sets of TT (tamperproof Torx) bits, which remove the tamper-resistant screws. Other manufacturers rivet the power supply case shut, which means you must drill out the rivets to gain access.

Caution

The manufacturers place these obstacles there for a reason—to prevent entry by those who are inexperienced with high voltage. Consider yourself warned!

Most power supplies have an internal fuse that is part of the overload protection. If this fuse is blown, the supply does not operate. It is possible to replace this fuse if you open the supply. Be aware, however, that in most cases an underlying power supply problem caused the fuse to blow, and replacing it only causes it to blow again until you address the root cause of the problem. In this case, you are better off sending the unit to a professional depot repair company. The Vendor List, on the CD, lists several companies that do depot repair on power supplies and other components.

PC power supplies have an internal voltage adjustment control that the manufacturer calibrates and sets at the factory. Over time, the condition of some of the components in the supply can change, thus altering the output voltages. If this is the case, you may be able to access the adjustment control and tweak it to bring the voltages back to where they should be.

Several adjustable controls are in the supply—usually small variable resistors that you can turn with a screwdriver.

Caution

You should use a nonconductive tool, such as a fiberglass or plastic screwdriver designed for this purpose. If you dropped a metal tool into an operating supply, dangerous sparks and possibly fire could result—not to mention the danger of electrocution and damage to the supply.

You also have to figure out which of the adjustments are for voltage and which are for each voltage signal. This requires some trial-and-error testing. You can mark the current positions of all the resistors, begin measuring a single voltage signal, and try moving each adjuster slightly until you see the voltage change. If you move an adjuster and nothing changes, put it back to the original position you marked. Through this process, you can locate and adjust each of the voltages to the standard 3.3v, 5v, and 12v levels.

Obtaining Replacement Units

Most of the time, it is simply easier, safer, or less expensive (considering the time and materials involved) to replace the power supply rather than to repair it. As mentioned earlier, replacement power supplies are available from many manufacturers. Before you can shop for a supplier, however, you should consider other purchasing factors.

Deciding on a Power Supply

When you are shopping for a new power supply, you should take several factors into account. First, consider the power supply's shape, or form factor. For example, the power supply used in an AT-style system differs in size from the one used in a Slimline computer. The larger AT form factor power supplies simply will not fit into a Slimline case.

Apart from electrical considerations, power supply form factors can differ physically in their size, shape, screw-hole positions, connector type, number of connectors, fan location, and switch position. However, systems that use the same form factor can easily interchange power supplies. When ordering a replacement supply, you need to know which form factor your system requires.

Some systems use proprietary power supply designs, which makes replacement more difficult. If a system uses one of the common form factor power supplies, replacement units are available from hundreds of vendors. An unfortunate user of a system with a nonstandard form factor supply does not have this kind of choice and must get a replacement from the original manufacturer of the system—and usually pay through the nose for the unit. Although you can find standard form factor supplies for under $100, the proprietary units from some manufacturers run as high as $400 or more. PC buyers often overlook this and discover too late the consequences of having nonstandard components in a system.

◀◀ See "Power Supply Form Factors," p. 1088.

Companies such as Hewlett-Packard and Compaq are notorious for using proprietary form factor power supplies. Be sure you consider this if you intend on owning these types of systems out of warranty. Personally, I always insist on systems that use industry standard power supplies like the ATX form factor supply found in many systems today.

Sources for Replacement Power Supplies

Because one of the most failure-prone items in PC systems is the power supply, I am often asked to recommend a replacement. Literally hundreds of companies manufacture PC power supplies, and I certainly have not tested them all. I can, however, recommend some companies whose products I have come to know and trust.

Although other high-quality manufacturers are out there, at this time I recommend power supplies from either Astec Standard Power or PC Power and Cooling.

Astec makes the power supplies used in most of the high-end systems by IBM, Hewlett-Packard, Apple, and many other name-brand systems. They have power supplies available in a number of standard form factors (AT/Tower, Baby-AT, LPX, and ATX) and a variety of output levels. They have power supplies with ratings of up to 450 watts and power supplies especially designed for Green PCs, which meet the EPA Energy Star requirements for low-power consumption. Their Green power supplies are specifically designed to achieve high efficiency at low-load conditions. Be aware that high-output supplies from other manufacturers may have problems with very low loads. Astec also makes a number of power supplies for laptop and notebook PC systems and has numerous non-PC type supplies.

PC Power and Cooling has a complete line of power supplies for PC systems. They make supplies in all the standard PC form factors used today. Versions are available in a variety of different quality and output levels, from inexpensive replacements to very high-quality high-output models with ratings of up to 450 watts. They even have versions with built-in battery backup, redundant power systems, and a series of special models with high-volume, low-speed (quiet) fan assemblies. Their quiet models are especially welcome to people who work in quiet homes or offices and are annoyed by the fan noise that some power supplies emanate.

PC Power and Cooling also has units available that fit some of Compaq's proprietary designs. This can be a real boon if you have to service or repair Compaq systems because the PC Power and Cooling units are available in higher output ratings than Compaq's. These units cost much less than Compaq's and bolt in as direct replacements.

The support offered by PC Power and Cooling is excellent also, and they have been in business a long time, which is rare in this industry. Besides power supplies, they also have an excellent line of cases.

A high-quality power supply from either of these vendors can be one of the best cures for intermittent system problems and can go a long way toward ensuring trouble-free operation in the future.

Using Power-Protection Systems

Power-protection systems do just what the name implies: They protect your equipment from the effects of power surges and power failures. In particular, power surges and spikes can damage computer equipment, and a loss of power can result in lost data. In this section, you learn about the four primary types of power-protection devices available and when you should use them.

Before considering any further levels of power protection, you should know that a good quality power supply already affords you a substantial amount of protection. High-end power supplies from the vendors I recommend are designed to provide protection from higher-than-normal voltages and currents, and they provide a limited amount of power-line noise filtering. Some of the inexpensive aftermarket power supplies probably do not have this sort of protection. If you have an inexpensive computer, further protecting your system might be wise.

Caution

All the power protection features in this chapter and the protection features in the power supply inside your computer require that the computer's AC power cable be connected to a ground.

Many older homes do not have three-prong (grounded) outlets to accommodate grounded devices.

Do not use a three-pronged adapter (that bypasses the three-prong requirement and enables you to connect to a two-prong socket) to plug in a surge suppressor, computer, or UPS into a two-pronged outlet. They often don't provide a good ground and can inhibit the capabilities of your power-protection devices.

It is also a good idea to test your power sockets to make sure they are grounded. Sometimes outlets, despite having three-prong sockets, are not connected to a ground wire; an inexpensive socket tester (available at most hardware stores) can detect this condition.

Of course, the easiest form of protection is to turn off and unplug your computer equipment (including your modem) when a thunderstorm is imminent. When this is not possible, however, there are other alternatives.

Power supplies should stay within operating specifications and continue to run a system if any of these power line disturbances occur:

- Voltage drop to 80v for up to 2 seconds
- Voltage drop to 70v for up to .5 seconds
- Voltage surge of up to 143v for up to 1 second

IBM also states that neither their power supplies nor systems will be damaged by the following occurrences:

- Full power outage
- Any voltage drop (brownout)
- A spike of up to 2,500v

Because of their internal protection, many computer manufacturers that use high-quality PSUs state in their documentation that external surge suppressors are not needed with their systems.

To verify the levels of protection built into the existing power supply in a computer system, an independent laboratory subjected several unprotected PC systems to various spikes and surges of up to 6,000v—considered the maximum level of surge that can be transmitted to a system through an electrical outlet. Any higher voltage would cause the power to arc to the ground within the outlet. None of the systems sustained permanent damage in these tests. The worst thing that happened was that some of the systems rebooted or shut down if the surge was more than 2,000v. Each system restarted when the power switch was toggled after a shutdown.

I do not use any real form of power protection on my systems, and they have survived near-direct lightning strikes and powerful surges. The most recent incident, only 50 feet from my office, was a direct lightning strike to a brick chimney that blew the top of the chimney apart. None of my systems (which were running at the time) were damaged in any way from this incident; they just shut themselves down. I was able to restart each system by toggling the power switches. An alarm system located in the same office, however, was destroyed by this strike. I am not saying that lightning strikes or even much milder spikes and surges cannot damage computer systems—another nearby lightning strike did destroy a modem and serial adapter installed in one of my systems. I was just lucky that the destruction did not include the motherboard.

This discussion points out an important oversight in some power-protection strategies: Do not forget to provide protection from spikes and surges on the phone line.

The automatic shutdown of a computer during power disturbances is a built-in function of most high-quality power supplies. You can reset the power supply by flipping the power switch from on to off and back on again. Some power supplies even have an auto-restart function. This type of power supply acts the same as others in a massive surge or spike situation: It shuts down the system. The difference is that after normal power resumes, the power supply waits for a specified delay of three to six seconds and then resets itself and powers the system back up. Because no manual switch resetting is required, this feature may be desirable in systems functioning as network servers or in those found in other unattended locations.

The first time I witnessed a large surge cause an immediate shutdown of all my systems, I was extremely surprised. All the systems were silent, but the monitor and modem lights were still on. My first thought was that everything was blown, but a simple toggle of each system-unit power switch caused the power supplies to reset, and the units powered up with no problem. Since that first time, this type of shutdown has happened to me several times, always without further problems.

The following types of power-protection devices are explained in the sections that follow:

- Surge suppressors
- Line conditioners
- Standby power supplies (SPS)
- Uninterruptible power supplies (UPS)

Surge Suppressors (Protectors)

The simplest form of power protection is any one of the commercially available surge protectors—that is, devices inserted between the system and the power line. These devices, which cost between $20 and $200, can absorb the high-voltage transients produced by nearby lightning strikes and power equipment. Some surge protectors can be effective for certain types of power problems, but they offer only very limited protection.

Surge protectors use several devices, usually metal-oxide varistors (MOVs), that can clamp and shunt away all voltages above a certain level. MOVs are designed to accept voltages as high as 6,000v and divert any power above 200v to ground. MOVs can handle normal surges, but powerful surges such as a direct lightning strike can blow right through them. MOVs are not designed to handle a very high level of power and self-destruct while shunting a large surge. These devices therefore cease to function after either a single large surge or a series of smaller ones. The real problem is that you cannot easily tell when they no longer are functional. The only way to test them is to subject the MOVs to a surge, which destroys them. Therefore, you never really know if your so-called surge protector is protecting your system.

Some surge protectors have status lights that let you know when a surge large enough to blow the MOVs has occurred. A surge suppressor without this status indicator light is useless because you never know when it has stopped protecting.

Underwriters Laboratories has produced an excellent standard that governs surge suppressors, called UL 1449. Any surge suppressor that meets this standard is a very good one and definitely offers a line of protection beyond what the power supply in your PC already offers. The only types of surge suppressors worth buying, therefore, should have two features:

- Conformance to the UL 1449 standard
- A status light indicating when the MOVs are blown

Units that meet the UL 1449 specification say so on the packaging or directly on the unit. If this standard is not mentioned, it does not conform. Therefore, you should avoid it.

Another good feature to have in a surge suppressor is a built-in circuit breaker that can be manually reset rather than a fuse. The breaker protects your system if it or a peripheral develops a short. These better surge suppressors usually cost about $40.

Phone Line Surge Protectors

In addition to protecting the power lines, it is critical to provide protection to your systems from any connected phone lines. If you are using a modem or fax board that is plugged into the phone system, any surges or spikes that travel through the phone line can damage your system. In many areas, the phone lines are especially susceptible to lightning strikes, which are the largest cause of fried modems and damage to the computer equipment attached to them.

Several companies manufacture or sell simple surge protectors that plug in between your modem and the phone line. These inexpensive devices can be purchased from most electronics supply houses. Most of the cable and communication products vendors listed in Appendix A sell these phone line surge protectors. Some of the standard power line surge protectors include connectors for phone line protection as well.

Line Conditioners

In addition to high-voltage and current conditions, other problems can occur with incoming power. The voltage might dip below the level needed to run the system, resulting in a brownout. Forms of electrical noise other than simple voltage surges or spikes might travel through the power line, such as radio-frequency interference or electrical noise caused by motors or other inductive loads.

Remember two things when you wire together digital devices (such as computers and their peripherals):

- Any wire can act as an antenna and have voltage induced in it by nearby electromagnetic fields, which can come from other wires, telephones, CRTs, motors, fluorescent fixtures, static discharge, and, of course, radio transmitters.
- Digital circuitry responds with surprising efficiency to noise of even a volt or two, making those induced voltages particularly troublesome. The electrical wiring in your building can act as an antenna, picking up all kinds of noise and disturbances.

A line conditioner can handle many of these types of problems. A line conditioner is designed to remedy a variety of problems. It filters the power, bridges brownouts, suppresses high-voltage and current conditions, and generally acts as a buffer between the power line and the system. A line conditioner does the job of a surge suppressor, and much more. It is more of an active device, functioning continuously, rather than a passive device that activates only when a surge is present. A line conditioner provides true power conditioning and can handle myriad problems. It contains transformers, capacitors, and other circuitry that can temporarily bridge a brownout or low-voltage situation. These units usually cost from $100–$300, depending on the power-handling capacity of the unit.

Backup Power

The next level of power protection includes backup power-protection devices. These units can provide power in case of a complete blackout, which provides the time needed for an orderly system shutdown. Two types are available: the standby power supply (SPS) and the uninterruptible power supply (UPS). The UPS is a special device because it does much more than just provide backup power: It is also the best kind of line conditioner you can buy.

Standby Power Supplies (SPS)

A standby power supply is known as an offline device: It functions only when normal power is disrupted. An SPS system uses a special circuit that can sense the AC line current. If the sensor detects a loss of power on the line, the system quickly switches over to a standby battery and power inverter. The power inverter converts the battery power to 110v AC power, which is then supplied to the system.

SPS systems do work, but sometimes a problem occurs during the switch to battery power. If the switch is not fast enough, the computer system shuts down or reboots anyway, which defeats the purpose of having the backup power supply. A truly outstanding SPS adds to the circuit a ferroresonant transformer, a large transformer with the capability to store a small amount of power and deliver it during the switch time. This device functions as a buffer on the power line, giving the SPS almost uninterruptible capability.

SPS units also may or may not have internal line conditioning of their own. Under normal circumstances, most cheaper units place your system directly on the regular power line and offer no conditioning. The addition of a ferroresonant transformer to an SPS gives it additional regulation and protection capabilities because of the buffer effect of the transformer. SPS devices without the ferroresonant transformer still require the use of a line conditioner for full protection. SPS systems usually cost from a couple hundred to several thousands of dollars, depending on the quality and power-output capacity.

Uninterruptible Power Supplies (UPS)

Perhaps the best overall solution to any power problem is to provide a power source that is conditioned and that cannot be interrupted—which is the definition of an uninterruptible power supply. UPSs are known as online systems because they continuously function and supply power to your computer systems. Because some companies advertise ferroresonant SPS devices as though they were UPS devices, many now use the term true UPS to describe a truly online system. A true UPS system is constructed in much the same way as an SPS system; however, because the computer is always operating from the battery, there is no switching circuit.

In a true UPS, your system always operates from the battery. A voltage inverter converts from 12v DC to 110v AC. You essentially have your own private power system that generates power independently of the AC line. A battery charger connected to the line or wall current keeps the battery charged at a rate equal to or greater than the rate at which power is consumed.

When the AC current supplying the battery charger fails, a true UPS continues functioning undisturbed because the battery-charging function is all that is lost. Because the computer was already running off the battery, no switch takes place, and no power disruption is possible. The battery begins discharging at a rate dictated by the amount of load your system places on the unit, which (based on the size of the battery) gives you plenty of time to execute an orderly system shutdown. Based on an appropriately scaled storage battery, the UPS functions continuously, generating power and preventing unpleasant surprises. When the line power returns, the battery charger begins recharging the battery, again with no interruption.

Note

Occasionally, a UPS can accumulate too much storage and not enough discharge. When this occurs, the UPS emits a loud alarm, alerting you that it's full. Simply unplugging the unit from the AC power source for a while can discharge the excess storage (as it powers your computer) and drain the UPS of the excess.

Many SPS systems are advertised as though they are true UPS systems. The giveaway is the unit's switch time. If a specification for switch time exists, the unit cannot be a true UPS because UPS units never switch. However, a good SPS with a ferroresonant transformer can virtually equal the performance of a true UPS at a lower cost.

Note

Many UPSs today come equipped with a cable and software that enables the protected computer to shut down in an orderly manner on receipt of a signal from the UPS. This way, the system can shut down properly even if the computer is unattended. Some operating systems, such as Windows NT, contain their own UPS software components.

UPS cost is a direct function of both the length of time it can continue to provide power after a line current failure and how much power it can provide. You should therefore purchase a UPS that provides you with enough power to run your system and peripherals and enough time to close files and provide an orderly shutdown. Remember, however, to manually perform a system shutdown procedure during a power outage. You will probably need your monitor plugged into the UPS and the computer. Be sure the UPS you purchase can provide sufficient power for all the devices you must connect to it.

Because of a true UPS's almost total isolation from the line current, it is unmatched as a line conditioner and surge suppressor. The best UPS systems add a ferroresonant transformer for even greater power conditioning and protection capability. This type of UPS is the best form of power protection available. The price, however, can be high. To find out just how much power your computer system requires, look at the UL sticker on the back of the unit. This sticker lists the maximum power draw in watts, or sometimes in just volts and amperes. If only voltage and amperage are listed, multiply the two figures to calculate the wattage.

As an example, if the documentation for a system indicates that the computer can require as much as 110v at a maximum current draw of 5 amps, the maximum power the system can draw is about 550 watts. This wattage is for a system with every slot full, two hard disks, and one floppy—in other words, a system at the maximum possible level of expansion. The system should never draw any more power than that; if it does, a five-ampere fuse in the power supply will blow. This type of system normally draws an average of 300 watts; to be safe when you make calculations for UPS capacity, however, be conservative. Use the 550-watt figure. Adding a monitor that draws 100 watts brings the total to 650 watts or more. Therefore, to run two fully loaded systems, you'll need a 1,100-watt UPS. Don't forget two monitors, each drawing 100 watts. Therefore, the total is 1,300 watts. A UPS of that capacity or greater will cost approximately $500–$700. Unfortunately, that is what the best level of protection costs. Most companies can justify this type of expense only for critical-use PCs, such as network servers.

Note

The highest-capacity UPS sold for use with a conventional 15-amp outlet is about 1,400 watts. If it's any higher, you risk tripping a 15-amp circuit when the battery is charging heavily and the inverter is drawing maximum current.

In addition to the total available output power (wattage), several other factors can differentiate one UPS from another. The addition of a ferroresonant transformer improves a unit's power conditioning and buffering capabilities. Good units also have an inverter that produces a true sine wave output; the cheaper ones may generate a square wave. A square wave is an approximation of a sine wave with abrupt up-and-down voltage transitions. The abrupt transitions of a square wave signal are not compatible with some computer equipment power supplies. Be sure that the UPS you purchase produces a signal compatible with your computer equipment. Every unit has a specification for how long it can sustain output at the rated level. If your systems draw less than the rated level, you have some additional time.

Caution

Be careful! Most UPS systems are not designed for you to sit and compute for hours through an electrical blackout. They are designed to provide power only to essential components and to remain operating long enough to allow for an orderly shutdown. You pay a large amount for units that provide power for more than 15 minutes or so. At some point, it becomes more cost effective to buy a generator than to keep investing in extended life for a UPS.

Some of the many sources of power protection equipment include American Power Conversion (APC), Tripp Lite, and Best Power. These companies sell a variety of UPS, SPS, line, and surge protector products.

Caution

Don't connect a laser printer to a backed-up socket in any SPS or UPS unit. They are both electrically noisy and have widely varying current draws. This can be hard on the inverter in an SPS or UPS, frequently causing the inverter to fail or detect an overload and shut down. Either case means that your system will lose power, too.

Printers are normally noncritical because whatever is being printed can be reprinted. Don't connect them to a UPS unless there's a good business need to do so.

Some UPSs and SPSs have sockets that are conditioned, but not backed up—that is, they do not draw power from the battery. In cases such as this, you can safely plug printers and other peripherals into these sockets.

RTC/NVRAM Batteries (CMOS Chips)

All 16-bit and higher systems have a special type of chip in them that combines a real-time clock (RTC) with at least 64 bytes (including the clock data) of Non-Volatile RAM (NVRAM) memory. This chip is officially called the RTC/NVRAM chip, but is often referred to as the CMOS chip or CMOS RAM because the type of chip used is produced using a CMOS (Complementary Metal Oxide Semiconductor) process. CMOS design chips are known for very low power consumption. This special RTC/NVRAM chip is designed to run off of a battery for several years.

The original chip of this type used in the IBM AT was the Motorola 146818 chip. Although the chips used today have different manufacturers and part numbers, they are all designed to be compatible with this original Motorola part.

These chips include a real-time clock. Its function should be obvious. The clock enables software to read the date and time and preserves the date and time data even when the system is powered off or unplugged.

The NVRAM portion of the chip has another function. It is designed to store basic system configuration, including the amount of memory installed, types of floppy and hard disk drives, and other information. Some of the more modern motherboards use extended NVRAM chips with as much as 2KB or more of space to hold this configuration information. This is especially true for Plug-and-Play systems, which store not only the motherboard configuration, but also the configuration of adapter cards. This system can then read this information every time you power on the system.

These chips are normally powered by some type of battery while the system is off. This battery preserves the information in the NVRAM and powers the clock. Most systems use a lithium-type battery because they have a very long life, especially at the low power draw from the typical RTC/NVRAM chip.

Most of the higher-quality modern systems sold today have a new type of chip that has the battery embedded within it. These are made by several companies—including Dallas Semiconductor and Benchmarq. These chips are notable for their long life. Under normal conditions, the battery will last for 10 years—which is, of course, longer than the useful life of the system. If your system uses one of the Dallas or Benchmarq modules, the battery and chip must be replaced as a unit because they are integrated. Most of the time, these chip/battery combinations are installed in a socket on the motherboard just in case a problem requires an early replacement. You can get new modules direct from the manufacturers for $18 or less, which is often less than the cost of the older separate battery alone.

Some systems do not use a battery at all. Hewlett-Packard, for example, includes a special capacitor in many of their systems that is automatically recharged anytime the system is plugged in. Note that the system does not have to be running for the capacitor to charge; it only has to be plugged in. If the system is unplugged, the capacitor will power the RTC/NVRAM chip for up to a week or more. If the system remains unplugged for a duration longer than that, the NVRAM information is lost. In that case, these systems can reload the NVRAM from a backup kept in a special flash ROM chip contained on the motherboard. The only pieces of information that will actually be missing when you repower the system will be the date and time, which will have to be re-entered. By using the capacitor combined with a NVRAM backup in flash ROM, these systems have a very reliable solution that will last indefinitely.

Many systems use only a conventional battery, which may be either directly soldered into the motherboard or plugged in via a battery connector. For those systems with the battery soldered in, there is normally a spare battery connector on the motherboard where you can insert a conventional plug-in battery, should the original ever fail. In most cases, you would never have to replace the motherboard battery, even if it were completely dead.

Conventional batteries come in many forms. The best are of a lithium design because they will last from two to five years or more. I have seen systems with conventional alkaline batteries mounted in a holder; these are much less desirable because they fail more frequently and do not last as long. Also, they can be prone to leak, and if a battery leaks on the motherboard, the motherboard may be severely damaged.

Besides the different battery types, the chip can require any one of several different voltages. The batteries in PCs are normally 3.6v, 4.5v, or 6v. If you are replacing the battery, make sure that your replacement is the same voltage as the one you removed from the system. Some motherboards can use batteries of several different voltages. Use a jumper or switch to select the different settings. If you suspect your motherboard has this capability, consult the documentation for instructions on changing the settings. Of course, the easiest thing to do is to replace the existing battery with another of the same type.

Symptoms that indicate that the battery is about to fail include having to reset the clock on your PC every time you shut down the system (especially after moving it) and problems during the system's POST, such as drive-detection difficulties. If you experience problems such as these, it is a good idea to make note of your system's CMOS settings and replace the battery as soon as possible.

Caution

When you replace a PC battery, be sure that you get the polarity correct or you will damage the RTC/NVRAM (CMOS) chip. Because the chip is soldered onto most motherboards, this can be an expensive mistake! The battery connector on the motherboard and the battery are normally keyed to prevent a backward connection. The pinout of this connector is on the CD, but should also be listed in your system documentation.

When you replace a battery, in most cases the existing data stored in the NVRAM is lost. Sometimes, however, the data will remain intact for several minutes (I have observed NVRAM retain information with no power for an hour or more), so if you make the battery swap quickly, the information in the NVRAM might be retained. Just to be sure, it is recommended that you record all the system configuration settings stored in the NVRAM by your system Setup program. In most cases, you would want to run the BIOS Setup program and copy or print out all the screens showing the different settings. Some Setup programs offer the capability to save the NVRAM data to a file for later restoration if necessary.

Tip

If your system BIOS is password protected and you forget the password, one possible way to bypass the block is to remove the battery for a few minutes and then replace it. This will reset the BIOS to its default settings, removing the password protection.

After replacing a battery, power up the system and use the Setup program to check the date and time setting and any other data that was stored in the NVRAM.

Printers and Scanners

SOME OF THE MAIN TOPICS IN THIS CHAPTER ARE

The Evolution of Printing and Scanning Technology

The capability to produce a printed version (often called a hard copy) of a document is a primary function of a PC, and along with modems, printers have become a required accessory. This is not to say, however, that every PC requires its own printer. One of the main reasons for the rise in local area networking in the business world has been the capability to share printers among multiple users.

Scanners, once a specialized device found only in the art department of major companies, are finding their way onto corporate and SOHO desks alike. Because their use, their features, and even their most common interface (parallel), complement printers, they will also be discussed in this chapter.

Due in part to this network market, there are a wide variety of printers on the market supporting a multitude of both features and speeds. This chapter examines the underlying concepts of all printer technology, the basic types of printers available today and how they function, and how to install and troubleshoot a printer on your PC.

Printer Technology

There are three basic types of printer technologies used with PCs, which are defined by the method in which the image is produced on the paper. These three technologies are as follows:

- *Laser*. Laser printers function by creating an electrostatic image of an entire page on a photosensitive drum with a laser beam. When an ultrafine colored powder called a toner is applied to the drum, it adheres only to the sensitized areas corresponding to the letters or images on the page. The drum spins and is pressed against a sheet of paper, transferring the toner to the page and creating the image. This is the same basic technology used by copiers.

- *Inkjet*. Inkjet printers, as their name implies, have tiny nozzles that spray ionized ink onto a page. Magnetized plates direct the ink onto the page in the proper pattern to form letters and images.

- *Dot matrix*. Dot-matrix printers use an array of round-headed pins to press an inked ribbon against a page. The pins are arranged in a rectangular grid (called a matrix); different combinations of pins form the various characters and images.

Note

A fourth option, Daisywheel, which created fully-formed characters similar to typewriting, was popular in law offices during the early days of PCs, but has been replaced by laser printers.

In general, laser printers provide the best quality output, followed closely by inkjet, with dot-matrix printers coming in a distant third. As with most computer equipment, the prices of printers have dropped tremendously in recent years, making the laser printers that used to be a high-ticket item accessible to users at almost every level. Dot-matrix printers have become largely relegated to commercial applications requiring continuous feed and multipart forms. Inkjet printers have become important parts of SOHO (small office-home office) printing because of their high print quality (rivaling less-expensive lasers for text), color capabilities, versatility, and inclusion in many popular "all-in-one" printer-scanner-fax units.

Except for these specialized uses, laser printers are superior to inkjet and dot-matrix printers in almost every way. Most printers use the same basic terminology to describe their features and capabilities. The following sections examine some of this technology, how (or if) it applies to the various printer types, and what you should look for when shopping for a printer.

Print Resolution

The term resolution is used to describe the sharpness and clarity of the printed output. All these printer technologies create images by laying down a series of dots on the page. The size and number of these dots determine the printer's resolution and the quality of the output. If you look at a page of text produced by a low-resolution dot-matrix printer, for example, the pattern of dots that forms the individual characters is immediately obvious to the naked eye. This is because the dots are relatively large and of a uniform size. On high-resolution laser printer output, however, the characters look solid because the dots are much smaller and often can be of different sizes.

Printer resolution is usually measured in dots per inch (dpi). This refers to the number of separate dots that the printer can produce in a straight line one inch long. Most printers function at the same resolution both horizontally and vertically, so a specification such as 300dpi implies a 300×300 dot one-inch square. A 300dpi printer can therefore print 90,000 dots in a square inch of space. There are some printers, however, that specify different resolutions in each direction, such as 600×1,200dpi, which means that the printer can produce 720,000 dots in one square inch.

It's important to realize that the resolution of a printed page is far higher than that of a typical PC monitor. The word *resolution* is used to quantify PC video displays also, usually in terms of the number of pixels, such as 640×480 or 800×600. By print standards, however, the typical PC video display has a resolution of only 50–80dpi. By measuring the actual height and width of an image on your screen and comparing it to the image's dimensions in pixels, you can determine the dpi for your display.

As a result, the claims of WYSIWYG (what you see is what you get) output by software and hardware manufacturers are valid only in the roughest sense. All but the lowest resolution printers should produce output that is far superior to that of your screen display.

90,000 dots per square inch might sound like an extraordinary amount of detail, but at 300dpi, printed characters can have noticeably jagged diagonal lines. There are two ways to improve the quality of the printed output and eliminate the "jaggies." One way is to increase the resolution. Today's laser printers usually operate at a minimum of 600dpi, with some high-end models reaching as high as 1,200dpi. Commercial offset printing (as used in the printing of this book, for example), by contrast, usually runs from 1,200 to 2,400dpi. By itself, 600dpi resolution is sufficient to eliminate the obvious jaggedness in the print output.

A second benefit of improved print resolution is the effect higher resolutions have on photographic reproduction. Higher resolutions enable laser and inkjet printers in particular to create more detailed and finer-grained photo printouts. The newest photo-realistic inkjet printers combine high resolutions (600dpi and above) with smaller ink droplets and special color printing techniques to create prints that rival snapshot quality when viewed from a short distance.

600dpi and above laser printers also achieve better photographic reproduction, but through different means. The higher resolution enables them to use smaller dots to simulate half-toning, thus producing better quality photo printing.

Resolution Enhancement

It is also possible to increase the quality of the print output without increasing the resolution by varying the size of the dots. This is a technique that was originated by Hewlett Packard that they call Resolution Enhancement Technology (RET). RET uses smaller dots to fill in the jagged edges created by larger dots.

Because the dots are so small, the cumulative effect to the naked eye is a straight diagonal line. Other manufacturers have developed their own versions of this concept by using other names, such as "edge enhancement." This type of enhancement is only possible for laser and inkjet printers. Because dot-matrix printers produce images by having pins physically strike the page (through an inked ribbon), it is not possible to use variable-sized dots.

Interpolation

There are also many printers that produce higher resolution output by means of a process called *interpolation*. Printer resolution is not just a physical matter of how small the dots created by a laser or inkjet can be; a higher resolution image also means that the printer must process more data. A 600dpi printer has to work with up to 360,000 dots per square inch, whereas a 300dpi printer uses only 90,000 dots.

The higher resolution image, therefore, requires four times more memory than its lower resolution counterpart (at minimum) and a great deal more processing time. Some printers are built with the capability to physically print at a higher resolution but without the required memory and processing power. Thus, the printer can process an image at 600dpi and then interpolate (or scale) the results up to 1,200dpi. Although an interpolated 1,200dpi image is better than a 600dpi image without interpolation, a printer that operates at a true 1,200dpi resolution should produce noticeably better output than an interpolated 1,200dpi, and it will probably cost significantly more as well. It is important when you evaluate printers that you check to see whether the resolution specified by the manufacturer is interpolated.

Paper Quality

Whereas laser printers produce their images by fusing toner to the paper, inkjet printers place the ink on top of the paper. While many "general purpose" papers supposedly suitable for laser, copier, and inkjet printers are sold, using anything less than true inkjet paper will degrade the actual print resolution. This is because inkjet paper should be smoother than laser/copier paper, and promote rapid drying of ink. Paper that lacks these features will have loose fibers causing the ink to "wick," causing a fuzzy appearance to inkjet printing. Photorealistic printing at resolutions above 720dpi requires the use of photo-quality paper that is heavy, very smooth, and very fast drying. Many users' disappointments with inkjet print quality stem from improper paper choices.

Dot-Matrix Print Quality

Dot-matrix printers are different from inkjet and laser printers in several fundamental ways. Most importantly, dot-matrix printers do not process an entire page's worth of data at a time like lasers, but rather work with streams of characters. The print resolution of a dot-matrix printer is based not on its memory or its processing power, but rather on its mechanical capabilities. The grid of dots that a dot-matrix printer uses to create characters is not a data set in a memory array or a pattern on a photosensitive drum; rather, the grid is formed by a set of metal pins that physically strike the page in various combinations. The resolution of the printer is therefore determined by the quantity of its pins, which is usually either 9 or 24. Because it uses more pins to create characters of the same size, a 24-pin printer has pins that are necessarily smaller than those of a 9-pin printer, and the dots they create are smaller as well. As with the other printer types, smaller dots result in fewer jagged edges to the printed characters and a better appearance to the document overall. However, techniques such as resolution enhancement and interpolation do not apply to dot-matrix technology, making the resolution of the printer a far less important statistic. Beyond checking to see whether the printer has 9 or 24 pins, you will not see differences in print quality that are the result of print resolution technology.

Note

Twenty-four–pin dot-matrix printers are often described by manufacturers as producing "near letter quality" output. In a literal sense I suppose this is true because the output that these printers produce is near (but not quite) what you would want to send to a correspondent. Dot-matrix printers still have their place in the professional world, such as for printing multipart forms and carbon copies, but when it comes to printing letters and other general office documents, they lack the resolution needed to produce a professional-looking product.

While any dot-matrix printer is vulnerable to printhead damage (the "pins" are actually fine wires), 24-pin dot-matrix printers are particularly sensitive to incorrectly set head gaps or worn ribbons. These problems can cause the extra-fine wires to be broken, causing gaps in the printing. When evaluating dot-matrix printers for heavy-duty printing, find out what the replacement or repair costs of a printhead will be.

Page Description Languages (PDL)

Both laser and inkjet printers are known as page printers because they assemble an entire page in memory before committing it to paper. This is in contrast to dot-matrix printers, which are character-based. When your PC communicates with a page printer, it does so using a specialized language called a *page description language*, or *PDL*. A PDL is simply a means of coding every aspect of a printed document into a data stream that can be transmitted to the printer. After the PDL code arrives at the printer, internal firmware converts the code to the pattern of dots that are printed on the page. There are currently two PDLs in use today that have become de facto standards in the computer industry: PCL and PostScript. These languages are discussed in the following sections.

Printers that do not support a PDL use escape code sequences to control the printer's features in combination with standard ASCII text for the body of the document (see the section, "Escape Codes," later in this chapter). It is the printer driver loaded on your PC that is responsible for producing print output that is understood by your printer, whether it uses escape codes or a PDL. No matter what the source of the document you are printing and no matter what format is used to store the original document, the data must be converted into a PDL data stream or an ASCII text stream with escape codes to be printed.

PCL (Printer Control Language)

PCL is a page description language that was developed by Hewlett Packard for use in its printers in the early 1980s. As a result of HP's dominance in the printer market, PCL has become a standard that is emulated by many other printer manufacturers. Apart from the actual text being printed, PCL consists largely of commands that are designed to trigger various features and capabilities of the printer. These commands fall into four categories:

- *Control codes*. Standard ASCII codes that represent a function rather than a character, such as Carriage Return (CR), Form Feed (FF), and Line Feed (LF).

- *PCL commands*. Basically the same type of escape code sequences used by dot-matrix printers. These commands comprise the majority of a PCL file's control code and include printer-specific equivalents to document parameters, such as page formatting and font selection.

- *HP-GL/2 (Hewlett-Packard Graphics Language) commands*. Commands that are specific to the printing of vector graphics as part of a compound document. An HP-GL/2 command consists of a two-letter mnemonic that might be followed by one or more parameters that specify how the printer should process the command.

- *PJL (Printer Job Language) commands*. Enable the printer to communicate with the PC bidirectionally, exchange job status and printer identification information, and control the PDL that the printer should use for a specific job and other printer control panel functions. PJL commands are limited to job-level printer control and are not involved in the printing of individual documents.

PCL has evolved over the years as printer capabilities have improved. PCL versions 1 and 2 were used by Hewlett-Packard inkjet and daisywheel impact printers in the early 1980s and could not be considered to be full-fledged page description languages. The first LaserJet printer released in 1984 used PCL 3, and the latest models contain PCL 6. Table 22.1 lists the various versions of PCL, the major capabilities added to each new version, and the HP laser printer models that use them.

Table 22.1   Hewlett-Packard Printer Control Language (PCL) Versions

Version	Date	Models	Benefits
PCL 3	May 1984	LaserJet LaserJet Plus	Full page formatting; vector graphics
PCL 4	Nov 1985	LaserJet Series II	Added typefaces; downloadable macros; support for larger bitmapped fonts and graphics
PCL 4e	Sep 1989	LaserJet IIP, raster IIP Plus	Compressed bitmap fonts; images

Version	Date	Models	Benefits
PCL 5	Mar 1990	LaserJet III, IIID, IIIP, IIIsi, HP-GL/2	Scalable typefaces; outline fonts; (vector) graphics
PCL 5e	Oct 1992	LaserJet 4, 4M, 4L, 4ML, 4P, 4MP, 4 Plus, 4M Plus, 5P, 5MP, 5L, 5L-FS, 5Lxtra, 6L, 6Lxi, 6Lse, 6P, 6MP, 6Psi, 6Pse	600dpi support; bidirectional communication between printer and PC; additional fonts for Microsoft Windows
PCL 5c	Oct 1994	Color LaserJet, Color LaserJet 5, 5M	Color extensions
PCL 6	Apr 1996	LaserJet 5, 5se, LaserJet 6, 6Pse, 6Psi, 6MP	Faster graphics printing and return to application
PCL XL	1996	LaserJet 6P, 6MP	Enhanced graphics commands, multipage printing on one sheet, watermark, smaller file sizes

Although PCL is wholly owned and developed by Hewlett-Packard, this company's long-term dominance in the printer market has made it a de facto standard. Many other companies manufacture printers that use PCL and often advertise these printers as being compatible with a specific Hewlett Packard model.

Note

Most HP inkjet printers use stripped-down versions of PCL; see the particular printer's documentation for information on which PCL features it supports.

PostScript

PostScript is a page description language that was developed by Adobe and first introduced in the Apple LaserWriter printer in 1985. PostScript possessed capabilities at its inception, such as scalable type and vector graphics support, that were only added to PCL years later. For this reason, PostScript quickly became and still remains the industry standard for desktop publishing and graphics work. Adobe licenses the PostScript language to many different printer manufacturers, including those that make the high-resolution image setters used by service bureaus to produce camera-ready output for the offset printing processes used by newspaper, magazine, and book printers.

PostScript does not use escape code sequences such as PCL; it is more like a standard programming language. PostScript is called an object-oriented language because the printer sends images to the printer as geometrical objects rather than bitmaps. This means that to produce type using a particular font, the printer driver specifies a font outline and a specific size. The font outline is a template for the creation of the font's characters at any size. The printer actually generates the images of the characters from the outline, rather than calling on a stored bitmap of each character at each size. This type of image that is generated specifically for use on a particular page is called a vector graphic, as opposed to a bitmap graphic, which arrives at the printer as a fully formed dot pattern. PCL did not have the capability to print scalable type until version 5 was introduced in 1990.

When it comes to printing fonts, outlines simplify the process by enabling printers to be equipped with more internal fonts that can be printed at any size. Bitmapped fonts, on the other hand, usually must be downloaded to the printer from the PC. When graphic images are involved, the difference between a vector-based object and a bitmap can often be seen in the printed output. Because a vector image is actually generated inside the printer, its quality is based on the printer's capabilities. Printing a vector image on a 600dpi printer produces a much better quality product than printing the same image on a 300dpi printer. A bitmap image, on the other hand, will generate the same output on either printer.

At first, modifications to the PostScript language were based on the evolving capabilities of the Apple laser printers that were its primary outlet. These minor modifications eventually became numerous enough for Adobe to release a new baseline version of the language called PostScript Level 2 in 1992. The evolution continued, and PostScript 3 was introduced in 1997. These updates improved the speed and performance of PostScript printers and accommodated their physical changes, such as increased amounts of memory and added paper trays, but they did not introduce revolutionary new features the way that the PCL updates did. PostScript had its most powerful features from the very beginning, and the succeeding revisions of the language remain backward compatible. For more information about PostScript's standard and optional features and uses, see Adobe's Web site.

Note

For users who want to retrofit the graphics power of PostScript to an existing printer but cannot get a hardware upgrade, there are many RIP (Raster Image Processing) programs available that provide for PostScript imaging on common SOHO and office laser and inkjet printers. These programs serve two purposes: They improve printed output, and they enable a user with a low-cost color or monochrome inkjet or laser printer to be able to use that printer as an accurate preview device for preparing PostScript files for output by a high-end typesetter. One of the leading low-cost RIPs that supports most inkjet and laser printers is Zenographics' SuperPrint, now in version 5. Get more information from Zenographics' Web site.

PDL Support

When you are evaluating printers, the decision as to what PDL you want to use should be based primarily on your interaction with other parties, their documents, and their printers. Today, PCL and PostScript are comparable in their capabilities (although this was not always the case), and for your own personal use, either one can produce excellent printed output. However, if you plan to produce documents that are to be passed on to other parties, such as service bureaus for pre-press work, PostScript support is strongly recommended because it is still the dominant standard in the world of professional graphics, printing, and publishing.

You might also come across documents on the Internet and in other places that are provided in the PostScript format. For a long time, a PostScript output file (usually with a PS extension) was the most convenient, platform-independent format for distributing a document containing graphical content.

For example, the specifications for the TCP/IP networking protocols are freely distributed on the Internet in ASCII text form. A few of the documents, however, have diagrams and other graphics that can't be represented in ASCII, so they are published in PostScript format. Any user with a PostScript printer, regardless of the computing platform, can simply copy the file to the printer and produce a hard copy of the document, including all the graphics and fonts found in the original. Although the practice of releasing raw PostScript files is less frequent now that platform-independent formats such as Adobe Acrobat are available, this can still be a valid reason for having a PostScript printer available.

Both PCL and PostScript are available in a wide variety of printers. The Macintosh printing platform is designed around PostScript, which is standard equipment in all Apple's laser printers. Obviously because Hewlett-Packard developed the PCL standard, all their printers use that PDL by default. However, most of the HP laser printers are available in a version with PostScript as well. In addition, most HP laser printers can accept a special add-on module that provides the printer with PostScript support. Very few inkjet printer models contain a PostScript interpreter, and those few are normally B-size (11"×17" paper) or larger units designed for graphics-arts prepress work.

Note

Different HP printers use different levels of PCL. You should also know that printers that nominally use the same level of PCL might vary in their implementations of PCL commands. Search HP's Web site for details about an HP printer model's use of PCL.

Many other manufacturers also use PCL or PostScript (or both), which they have either licensed from HP or Adobe or emulated themselves for their printers. The question of whether a printer has genuine, licensed versions of its PDLs can be very important. There have been numerous instances throughout the history of these PDLs in which unauthorized or poorly emulated versions of PCL and PostScript have been foisted on the public as the real thing. In the mid-1980s, the term "LaserJet Plus Emulation" came to have as little meaning as "Hayes compatible" did for modems. Nowadays, most of the PCL (usually version 5) emulations used in other manufacturers' printers are quite good, but PostScript is a far more complex language and is more difficult to emulate. It is still possible to find discrepancies between an emulated version of a PDL and the real thing that result in visible differences in the printed output.

Here again, the PDL emulation issue is largely dependent on your interactions with other users. If you have a printer with an emulated version of PostScript and a printer driver that accurately addresses that emulated printer firmware, it matters little if the language does not conform precisely to the Adobe specifications. If you are sending your PostScript output to a service bureau for printing on an image setter, however, the discrepancies between an emulated PostScript and the real thing can make a vast difference.

Whenever possible, it is recommended that you purchase a printer that uses the genuine PDL licensed from its creator. A minimum of PCL 5 or PostScript Level 2 is preferable.

Many laser printers support both PCL and PostScript, and you should check to see how a printer handles mixed jobs using different PDLs. The best printers detect the PDL of each job as it arrives in the printer and automatically switch to the appropriate language. If a printer does not have this feature, you might have to send a command with each print job triggering the mode change. For a single user on a standalone system, this is not much of a problem. For a printer connected to a network, it is often hard to be certain of the order in which jobs are printed unless someone constantly monitors the print queue, and manual mode changes can be difficult to organize.

Escape Codes

Virtually all laser printers and most inkjet printers support at least one page description language, but some printers (especially dot-matrix) do not, and in this case the printer driver usually communicates with the printer using escape code sequences. Similar to the PCL commands described earlier, escape codes are control sequences used to activate the features of a particular printer. Escape codes are so named because the ASCII value for the Esc key is used as the first character of the code to signal to the printer that what follows is an instruction code and not a textual element of the document being printed.

On a dot-matrix printer, it might be possible to select different resolutions, fonts, and speeds, depending on the printer's capabilities. The printer driver that you install on your PC is designed to generate the appropriate escape codes based on the options you specify in your application and your printer driver configuration. If your printer driver cannot generate the codes you desire, you can normally set a particular font, size, and enhancement for an entire document through the printer's control panel or control software.

Escape codes are not as standardized as PDLs; you might see different printers use different codes for the same function. Epson, for example, has long been a market leader in the dot-matrix printer industry, and their escape codes have come to be accepted by some other manufacturers, but the acceptance of the codes has not been general enough for them to be called an industry standard.

Epson's escape code standards are ESC/P for their older dot-matrix printers and ESC/P2 for newer dot-matrix printers and most inkjet printer models. ESC/P was the original Epson version and didn't support built-in scalable fonts. ESC/P2 does support built-in scalable fonts found in Epson's newer dot-matrix and inkjet printers and works well with Windows 3.x and 9x.

Host-Based/GDI

Some inkjet and dot-matrix printers don't use either "classic" PDL (PostScript or HP-PCL) but instead use the computer to render the page for printing. These printers are called *host-based* printers. Some variations on host-based printing include printers that use the Windows GDI (graphics device interface) engine to image the page (GDI printers) and Hewlett-Packard's line of Printing Performance Architecture (PPA) printers. In theory, these printers have some advantages:

- *Low cost.* Because the computer has already rendered the page, the printer doesn't need to include a PDL, reducing the printer price.
- *Faster computer means faster printing.* Because most of the printing work is being done by the host computer, speeding up the computer by adding RAM, increasing processor speed, or

using IEEE-1284 bidirectional printer connections (EPP/ECP ports and cables) can improve printing speed. In 1996 tests by *PC Magazine*, the improvements ranged from a modest 5 percent to 87 percent, with complex images showing a bigger improvement than simple text-only print jobs.

■ *Flexible architecture with PPA*. Hewlett-Packard's PPA, depending upon the printer, might have virtually all printer functions performed in the computer (for economy) or might move some features into the printer (for performance).

Although host-based printing has its advantages, there are several key disadvantages:

■ *No direct connection equals no printing*. Host-based printers *must* be tied directly to the host for printing because all they do is produce the finished image. This "gotcha" becomes apparent when your new SOHO or departmental network can't print because the printers no longer have a true host to work with. This affects both GDI-based printers and HP's PPA product line. The need for a host prevents these printers from working with network print servers such as HP's JetDirect series. This can also be an issue with sharing a printer via peer networking.

■ *Problems with printing from non-Windows applications*. Depending upon how the host-based printer is designed, it might not be able to print from any operating system other than Windows. Some printers can print from a "DOS box"—an MS-DOS session that runs within Windows. The issue of support for operating systems such as Linux could also be a big problem for some users.

The more flexible your printing needs, the less likely it is that a host-based printer can meet them. If you plan to use nothing but Windows or Macintosh as an environment, a host-based printer might suffice. Choose carefully.

Printer Memory

Printers have memory chips in them just as PCs do, and laser and inkjet printers usually have a processor as well, making the printer a computer unto itself, albeit a highly specialized one. Printers can use their internal memory for several purposes: as a buffer to hold print job data while it is being fed to the actual print engine; as a workspace to hold data during the processing of images, fonts, and commands; and as permanent and semipermanent storage for outline fonts and other data.

For laser printers, the amount of memory in a page printer is an extremely important gauge of its capabilities. The printer must be able to assemble a bitmap image of an entire page to print it, and the graphic images and fonts that are used on that page all take up memory. Even vector graphics and outline fonts must be processed into bitmaps before they can be printed. The larger the graphics on the page and the more fonts used, the more memory is required. This is in addition to the memory needed to store the PDL interpreter and the printer's permanent fonts.

You might find that your printer has sufficient memory to print an average page of mixed text and graphics, but not enough to print a full-page graphic or a page with many different fonts. The result of this might be a graphic split in half over two pages (a problem sometimes referred to as *guillotining*), missing fonts, or even no output at all. Fortunately, most printers can accept additional memory to extend their capabilities.

Expansion memory for printers can come in many different forms. Some printers use standard memory modules such as SIMMs or DIMMs, whereas others use proprietary designs that you must purchase from the manufacturer (at an inflated price, of course). As with a PC, extra memory installed in a printer is almost never wasted. In addition to the capability of processing larger graphics and more fonts, printers might be able to use extra memory to process the data for one page while printing another and to buffer larger amounts of data received from the PC.

Tip

Because many laser printers use data-compression techniques to print graphics with a small amount of memory, some laser printers print graphics-rich pages much faster after a memory upgrade. This is because the printer needs to spend less time calculating whether the page will fit into memory and little or no time compressing the data to fit.

A printer with additional memory can accept more data from the PC at one time. Depending on your PC's operating system and its printer driver configuration, this can result in a noticeable difference to your system's performance. When you print a document in a DOS application, you cannot proceed with your work (in most cases) until the entire print job has been transmitted to the printer. Multitasking operating systems such as Windows 9x can usually print in the background, enabling work to proceed as the PC processes the print job, but performance might still suffer until the print job is completed. The larger the printer's memory buffer, the faster the print job data leaves the PC, returning the PC to its normal operation.

Simply learning how much memory is installed in the printer you plan to buy is not sufficient to make an intelligent purchasing decision. You must also be aware of how much memory is utilized by the PDLs and resident fonts and how much is left free for print job data. Different PDLs, page sizes, and resolutions require different amounts of memory. As an example, for a 300dpi letter size (8 1/2"×11") printer using PCL, 12MB is a great deal of memory. For a 600dpi tabloid size (11"×17") PostScript printer, it is barely enough. Check with the printer manufacturer and the application software developer for memory guidelines, but keep in mind that one of the best upgrades for a laser printer, as well as for a computer, is more RAM.

The SIMM module sockets on some printers, notably some HP LaserJet models, can be used for more than memory expansion. HP offers PostScript upgrades for certain models that are packaged as a SIMM.

Note

The issue of memory expansion is applicable only to page printers such as lasers. Most dot-matrix and inkjet printers receive data from the PC as a stream of ASCII characters, and because they do not have to assemble an entire page at a time, they can maintain a much smaller buffer, usually only a few kilobytes. Even graphic images are processed by the PC and transmitted to the printer as a bit stream, so it is rarely possible to augment a dot-matrix printer's memory.

Some large-format inkjet printers such as HP's DesignJet series offer memory expansion, but this is not common on normal SOHO and office inkjet printers using letter-sized paper.

Fonts

Fonts are one of the most commonly used and most entertaining printer features. Having quality fonts and using them correctly can make the difference between a professional-looking document and an amateurish one. The term *font* refers to a particular typeface in a particular typestyle at a particular size. A typeface is a design for a set of alphanumeric characters in which the letters, numbers, and symbols all work well together to form an attractive and readable presentation. There are thousands of typefaces available, with many new designs being produced all the time. Some of the basic typefaces included with the Windows operating systems are called Times New Roman, Arial, and Courier. A *typestyle* is a variation on a typeface, such as bold or italic. A typeface can have only one style, or it can have a dozen or more.

Typefaces are often classified by characteristics they have in common. For example, Times New Roman is known as a serif typeface because all its characters have little decorative strokes known as serifs. A typeface such as Arial, which lacks these strokes, is called a sans serif typeface. Courier is called a monospaced typeface because all its letters occupy the same width on the page as on a typewriter. In contrast, Arial and Times New Roman are both proportional typefaces because the characters are designed to fit together based on their widths. The letter "i" in a proportional typeface occupies less horizontal space on the page than the letter "w."

Technically, the term font refers to a typeface at a particular size, usually measured in points (72 points equals one inch). 10-point Courier and 12-point Courier would be considered two separate fonts. This is because in traditional printing and in the first PC printers, each size of a particular typeface was a separate entity. On an old-time printing press, each character on a page was printed by a separate wood or metal slug that would be pressed against the paper to make an impression. Slugs of different sizes were needed to produce different sized characters. In the same way, printers originally used bitmaps to create type. In this printing technique, every character of a typeface exists as a separate pattern of dots ready to be sent to the printer. In essence, each character existed as an individual, tiny graphic. To print the same typeface at various sizes requires individual graphics for each different size. These are called *bitmap fonts*.

Today, printers nearly always use *scalable* fonts. This is a technology in which a typeface requires only a single outline for each character to produce type of any size. The printer retains the outline in memory and generates bitmaps of the text characters at the size required for each job. The bitmaps are stored in a temporary font cache, but only for the duration of the job. The printer can also rotate a scalable font to any angle, whereas bitmaps can be rotated only in 90 degree increments. Outline fonts take up less memory space in the printer and provide a wider range of variations for each typeface. Also because they utilize what amounts to a vector graphic technology, scalable fonts can take advantage of the printer's full resolution, whereas bitmap fonts look the same at any resolution. The drawback to scalable fonts is that they require more processing power from the print engine, but when compared to the advantages they offer, this is a small sacrifice.

Note

Although bitmap fonts are seldom used any longer for normal business documents, some professionals prefer them for certain high resolution printing tasks because they can be customized to suit a particular need. Bitmap fonts are also sometimes used by graphical operating systems such as Windows 3.1 for screen displays because scalable fonts do not look good at the low resolution of the typical monitor. However, a technology called antialiasing, which uses pixels of varying shades of gray (instead of just black and white) to smooth out jagged lines, has largely replaced the use of bitmap fonts on screen displays. Popularized by Adobe Type Manager (with Type 1 fonts), antialiasing has become more widespread for Windows users thanks to the font smoothing features in the Microsoft Plus! add-on for Windows 95 and the built-in font smoothing in Windows 98.

Because antialiasing can occasionally cause problems because of incompatibilities with a few display drivers, it can be turned off.

As a result of this evolution in technology, the terms font and typeface have come to be confused. In the old days, when you purchased a typeface, you would receive the same character set in a variety of sizes, with each size being called a font. Today, when you purchase a typeface, you receive only a single outline font that your printer can scale to any size.

In the days when bitmap fonts were common, there were several different ways to get the bitmaps to the printer. Because bitmap fonts take up more memory space than outlines, it is not practical to store a large number of fonts in the printer permanently. You could buy bitmap fonts as software (called soft fonts) and use a special utility to download them to the printer when needed, or you could purchase fonts on cartridges that you could insert into the printer and remove at will.

Few (if any) of the printers manufactured today have cartridge slots any more, and the process of manually downloading soft fonts, although still technologically possible, is too much trouble to be worthwhile. Today, scalable type is all but universal, and although printers are usually equipped with a selection of font outlines permanently stored in memory, this is more for reasons of speed and convenience than necessity. The printer driver on your PC can automatically download font outlines to the printer as needed or generate scalable type just as your printer can. Technologies such as the TrueType fonts found on both Windows and Macintosh systems can provide you with access to hundreds of typefaces in many styles and at almost any size.

▶▶ See "Driver Problems," p. 1191.

Although all outline fonts function in basically the same way, there are different types of scalable fonts available. PostScript was the original scalable font technology, and Adobe has built up a library of typefaces over the years that is without peer in the digital type industry. Most PostScript printers are equipped with a collection of 39 basic fonts stored internally, but you can choose from thousands of others by browsing Adobe's online services or their Type On Call CD-ROM. In either case, after you purchase these PostScript Type 1 font outlines, you install them on your computer along with a utility called Adobe Type Manager, which is responsible for downloading the appropriate font outlines to your printer as needed.

The other major scalable font technology in use today is TrueType. Developed about six years after PostScript, TrueType is the result of a joint project between Apple and Microsoft. Both companies wanted to integrate a PostScript-style scalable font engine into their respective operating systems, but neither of them wanted to delegate the control over an important element of their OS to a third-party company such as Adobe. Microsoft Windows 9x makes it easy to view your existing TrueType fonts and to compare fonts to each other by using the Windows Explorer's special menus in the Fonts folder.

Although there are substantial technical differences in the way that their font outlines are created, PostScript and TrueType function in much the same way. The primary advantage of TrueType is that it is already integrated into the Windows and Macintosh operating systems and does not require external software such as Adobe Type Manager. Most type foundries now produce their fonts in both PostScript Type 1 and TrueType versions, and any difference between the two in the final product is usually quite difficult to spot.

As with PostScript, many printers include an internal collection of TrueType fonts that the operating system makes available to your applications. You should consider the number of fonts supplied with your printer primarily as a bonus when you evaluate various products. Any typeface provided as an internal TrueType font in your printer can just as easily be produced using a software version, although you might have to purchase it separately.

Note

There are thousands of TrueType and PostScript Type 1 fonts available today at a wide range of prices. Many fonts are available free for the downloading from the Internet or on bargain CD-ROMs, whereas others (such as those offered by Adobe) are quite expensive by comparison. Be aware that there can be profound differences in the quality of these fonts, and although it is not always true that more expensive is better, there are a great many more cheap bad fonts than there are expensive bad fonts.

Printer Drivers

As with many peripherals, printers are highly reliant on a driver installed on the PC. The printer driver provides the software interface between the printer and your application or operating system. The primary function of the driver is to inform the PC about the capabilities of the printer, such as the PDLs it uses, the types of paper it handles, and the fonts installed. When you print a document in an application, the print options you select are supplied by the printer driver, although they appear to be part of the application.

In DOS, printer drivers are integrated into individual applications. A few major software packages provide drivers for a full range of printers, but most include only a few generic drivers. At times like these, the best thing to do is to select a driver that supports the same PDL revision as your printer. For example, a LaserJet III driver uses PCL 5, which will support all the LaserJet III and 4 models, even if it does not use all the printer's features. It is quite possible that a DOS application that doesn't have a driver for your exact printer model might not be able to take advantage of all your printer's capabilities.

In all versions of Windows, you install the printer driver as part of the operating system, not in the individual applications. The Windows product includes drivers for a wide range of printers, and individual drivers are almost always available from the printer manufacturer's online services. Note that the drivers included with Windows are usually developed by the manufacturer of the printer, not by Microsoft, and are included in the Windows package for the sake of convenience.

Although the printer manufacturer develops the drivers for any printer model used with Windows 9x, there might be significant differences between the printer drivers included with Windows 9x and those shipped with the printer or available online. Drivers included with Windows normally provide access to a printer's basic features, whereas the enhanced drivers provided by the manufacturer on CD-ROMs included with the printer or via download might include deluxe color-matching, enhanced spooling, improved dialogs, or other benefits. Be sure to try both types of drivers to see which one works best for you.

PostScript Printer Descriptions (PPDs)

Whereas printers that use PCL or escape sequences all have completely separate Windows drivers, PostScript printers use a single generic driver to support the PDL. For all versions of Windows, this driver is called PSCRIPT.DRV. To support the various capabilities of individual printers, the driver uses plug-in modules called PPDs (PostScript Printer Descriptions). The PPD provides information on the specific mechanical capabilities of the printer, such as paper trays and sizes, whereas the language support is provided by the PostScript driver. To support multiple PostScript printers in Windows, you install additional PPDs to the existing driver architecture.

In addition to the module included with Windows, there is also a PostScript driver called AdobePS that is freely available from Adobe, the owners of the PostScript language. If you have a printer that uses true Adobe PostScript, this driver is recommended because it provides more complete support for the language and all its capabilities. Although the PostScript driver is provided by Microsoft or Adobe, you typically obtain new PPDs from the manufacturer of your printer.

How Printers Operate

Each of the three main printer types uses a different method to create images on a page, as well as a different substance: powdered toner, liquid ink, or a fabric ribbon. The following sections examine how each type of printer creates images on the page.

Laser Printers

The process of printing a document on a laser printer consists of the following stages:

- Communications
- Processing
- Formatting
- Rasterizing
- Laser scanning
- Toner application
- Toner fusing

Different printers perform these procedures in various ways, but the steps are fundamentally the same. Less expensive printers, for example, might rely on the PC to perform more of the processing tasks, whereas others have the internal hardware to do the processing themselves.

Communications

The first step in the printing process is to get the print job data from the PC to the printer. PCs traditionally use the parallel port to communicate with a printer, although many printers can use a serial port. Some devices can even use both types of ports at the same time to connect to two different computers. Network printers often bypass these ports entirely and use an internal adapter to connect directly to the network cable. The newest SOHO and office printers offer USB connections, either as their only port or along with a parallel port.

◄◄ See "Parallel Ports," p. 883.

◄◄ See "USB and 1394 (i.Link)—Serial and Parallel Port Replacements", page 891.

Communications between the printer and the PC obviously consist largely of print job data sent from the computer to the printer. However, communications flow in the other direction, as well. The printer also sends signals back to the PC for the purpose of flow control, that is, to inform the computer when to stop sending data and when to resume. The printer typically has an internal memory buffer that is smaller than the average print job and can only handle a certain amount of data at a time. As pages are actually printed, the printer purges data from its buffer and signals the PC to continue transmitting. This is commonly called *handshaking*. The handshaking protocols used for this communication are dependent on the port used to connect the printer to the PC.

The amount of data that a printer can hold varies widely, and you read earlier in this chapter how you can often enlarge the buffer by installing additional memory. Some printers even contain internal hard disk drives and can store large amounts of print data and collections of fonts. The process of temporarily storing multiple print jobs as they await processing is known as print *spooling*.

Many printers today support even more advanced communications with a PC, enabling a user to interrogate the printer for its current status using a software application and even to configure parameters that previously were accessible only from the control panel on the printer. This type of communication requires that the PC have a bidirectional, ECP, or EPP port.

Processing

After the printer receives the data from the PC, it begins the process of interpreting the code. Most laser printers are really computers in themselves, containing a microprocessor and a memory array that functions much like the equivalent components in your PC. This part of the printer is often called the controller or the interpreter and includes the firmware supporting the page description language(s) that the printer uses.

The first step of the interpretation process is the examination of the incoming data to distinguish the control commands from the actual content of the document. The printer's processor reads the code and evaluates the commands that it finds, organizing those that are to be part of the formatting process and executing others that require physical adjustments to the printer configuration, such as paper tray selection and simplex (single sided) or duplex (double sided) printing. Some printers also convert the document formatting commands into a specialized code that streamlines the formatting process to come, whereas others leave these commands in their raw form.

Note

A common error after changing printers is failing to set the new printer as the default printer. This often leads to sending the wrong printer commands to the new printer, resulting in many sheets of paper covered with gibberish because the printer doesn't understand the (incorrect) commands being sent to it. This is also a concern when using a two-printer-to-one-PC switchbox.

Formatting

The formatting phase of the data interpretation process involves the interpretation of the commands that dictate how the content is to be placed on the page. Again, this is a process that can differ depending on the processing capabilities of the printer. With low-end printers, the PC does much of the formatting, sending highly specific instructions to the printer that describe the exact placement of every character on the page. More capable printers perform these formatting tasks themselves, and you might be surprised to find just how much work your printer does in this respect.

Your application might display your document in a WYSIWYG format that looks very much like the printed output, but this is not necessarily how the printer driver sends the document data to the printer. In most cases, the printer actually lays out the document all over again by interpreting a series of commands that dictate parameters such as the paper size, the location of the margins, and the line spacing. The controller then places the text and graphics on the page within these guidelines, often performing complex procedures such as text justification within the printer.

The formatting process also includes the processing of outline fonts and vector graphics to convert them into bitmaps. In response to a command specifying the use of a particular font at a particular size, for example, the controller accesses the font outline and generates a set of character bitmaps at the correct size. These bitmaps are stored in a temporary font cache where the controller can access them as needed while laying out the text on the page.

Rasterizing

The result of the formatting process is a detailed set of commands defining the exact placement of every character and graphic on each page of the document. In the final stage of the data interpretation process, the controller processes the formatting commands to produce the pattern of tiny dots that will be applied to the page. This process is called *rasterization*. The array of dots is typically stored in a page buffer while it awaits the actual printing process.

The efficiency of this buffering process depends on the amount of memory in the printer and the resolution of the print job. On a monochrome printer, each dot requires one bit of memory, so a letter-sized page at 300dpi requires 1,051,875 bytes of memory ([{8 1/2×11}×300²]/8), or just over 1MB. At 600dpi, the memory requirement jumps to 4,207,500 bytes—over 4MB. Some printers have sufficient memory to buffer an entire page while the formatting of the next page proceeds. Others might lack enough memory to store even one full page and use what are called *band buffers* instead.

Printers that use band buffers divide a page into several horizontal strips, or bands. The controller rasterizes one band's worth of data at a time and sends it to the print engine, clearing the buffer for the next band. This way, the printer can process a page gradually, with the entire array only coming together on the photosensitive drum in the print engine. The band buffer method is cheaper than a full page buffer because it uses less memory, but it is also slower and more prone to errors. In recent years, the price of memory has dropped so much that band buffers are rarely used in laser printers.

Band buffers are used primarily by inkjet printers, which convert each line of text or graphics into a band.

Tip

Some printer drivers enable you to control whether graphics are sent to the printer in vector or raster form. In general, vector graphics provide better speed, but if you experience problems with the placement of the graphics on the page, you can switch to the raster option. Most printer drivers that offer this feature place the control on the Graphics page of the printer's Properties dialog box. However, some drivers might place the control elsewhere or not provide it at all.

A common reason for switching to raster graphics is when a multilayer graphic doesn't print properly. This can be a problem with PCL5 laser printers and some presentation programs such as Microsoft PowerPoint or Lotus Freelance Graphics.

Laser Scanning

After the rasterized image of a page is created by the controller and stored in memory, the processing of that page passes to the print engine, the physical part of the printing process. *Print engine* is a collective term that is used to refer to the actual imaging technology in the printer, including the laser scanning assembly, the photoreceptor, the toner container, the developer unit, the corotrons, the discharge lamp, the fuser, and the paper transport mechanisms. These components are often treated as a collective unit because the print engine is essentially the same hardware that is used in copy machines. Most printer manufacturers build their products around a print engine that they obtain from another manufacturer, such as Canon. A PC printer differs from a copy machine primarily in its data-acquisition and processing procedures. A copier has a built-in scanner, whereas a printer receives and processes digital data from the PC. After the raster image reaches the print engine, however, the procedure that produces the actual document is fundamentally identical.

Figure 22.1 illustrates the laser writing process.

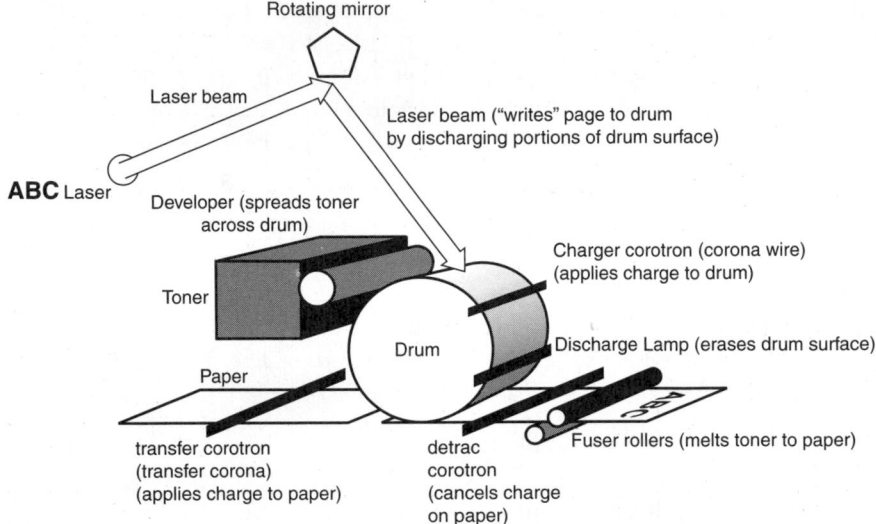

Figure 22.1   The stages of laser imaging with a typical laser printer are shown here.

The laser assembly in a laser printer, sometimes called a raster output scanner (ROS), is used to create an electrostatic pattern of dots on a photosensitive drum (called the photoreceptor) that corresponds to the image stored in the page buffer. The laser assembly consists of the laser, a rotating mirror, and a lens. The laser always remains stationary. To create the pattern of dots across the horizontal width of the drum, the mirror rotates laterally, and the lens adjusts to focus the beam so that the dots on the outer edges of the drum are not distorted by having been farther from the light source. The vertical motion is provided by the slow and steady turning of the drum.

Caution

Because the drum is sensitive to any form of light, it should not be exposed to room light or daylight for extended periods of time. Some printers have a protective mechanism that shields the drum from exposure to light whenever you open up the printer's service compartment. Even when this is the case, however, you should leave the compartment open long enough only to service the printer or change the toner cartridge.

The photoreceptor drum, which in some printers might actually be a belt, is coated with a smooth material that holds an electrostatic charge that can be discharged on specific areas of its surface by exposure to light. The initial charge over the entire surface of the drum is applied by a device called the *charger corotron*. A corotron is a wire carrying a very high voltage that causes the air immediately around it to ionize. This ionization charges the drum's surface and also produces ozone, the source of the smell that is characteristic of laser printers. Some smaller printers use charged rollers instead of corotrons specifically to avoid the production of ozone.

Note

Some laser printer manufacturers such as HP refer to "coronas" instead of "corotrons." They perform the same functions.

Caution

Ozone is a noxious and corrosive gas that should be avoided in closed, unventilated spaces. Although ozone is used to deodorize air and purify water, working in close proximity to laser printers for extended periods of time without a sufficient fresh air supply can cause health problems.

Many laser printers have replaceable ozone filters that should be changed after several thousand pages have been printed. Check your printer documentation to determine when the ozone filter should be changed. Use the self-test feature on the printer to print a page showing the number of pages the printer has produced to help you determine how many more pages you can print before you change the filter (or if you're overdue).

The drum is sensitive to any type of light, but a laser can produce fine enough dots to support the high resolutions required for professional-looking documents. Every spot that the laser light touches on the drum is electrically discharged, leaving the pattern of the page's characters and images on its surface. The laser in a printer discharges the areas of the drum corresponding to the black parts of the page, that is, the characters and images that comprise the document's content. This is known as write-black printing. By contrast, copiers discharge the background areas of the page, a process called write-white printing.

Toner Application

As the photoreceptor drum rotates, the portion of its surface that the laser has discharged next passes by the developer unit (see Figure 22.2). The developer is a roller coated with fine magnetic particles that function as a "brush" for the toner. Toner is an extremely fine black plastic powder that will actually form the image on the printed page. As the developer roller rotates, it passes by the toner container and picks up an even coating of the particles on its magnetic surface. This same developer roller is also located right next to the photoreceptor drum. When its surface passes by the roller, the toner particles are attracted to the areas that have been discharged by the laser, thus forming the image of the page on the drum using the toner particles as a color medium.

As the drum continues its slow rotation, it next passes close to the surface of the paper. The printer has an entirely separate mechanism for extracting one sheet of paper at a time from the supply tray and passing it through the print engine so that its flat surface passes underneath the drum (without actually touching it) at the same speed that the drum is rotating. Beneath the sheet of paper, there is another corotron (called the *transfer corotron*) that charges the paper, causing it to attract the toner particles from the drum in the exact pattern of the document image. After the toner is transferred to the page, the continued rotation of the drum causes it to pass by a discharge lamp (usually a row of LEDs) that "erases" the image of the page by completely discharging the surface of the drum. By this time, the drum has completed a full revolution, and the entire charging and discharging process can begin again for the next page of the document.

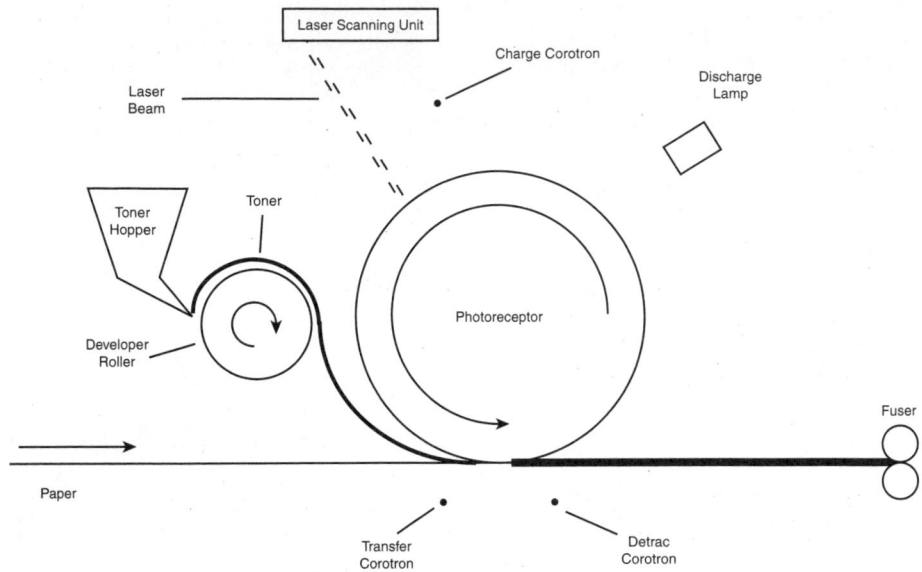

Figure 22.2 A laser printer's print engine largely revolves around a photoreceptor drum that receives the document image from the laser and applies it to the page as it slowly rotates.

As you might imagine, these processes leave little margin for error when it comes to the proximity of the components involved. The drum must pass very close to the corotrons, the developer roller, and the paper surface for the toner to be applied properly. For this reason, many print engines (including Canon and HP) combine these components into a single integrated cartridge that you replace every time you replenish the printer's toner supply. This increases the price of the toner cartridge, but it also enables you to easily replace the most sensitive parts of the printer on a regular basis, thus keeping the printer in good repair.

Toner Fusing

After the toner is transferred from the photoreceptor drum to the page, the page continues its journey through the printer by passing over yet another corotron, called the *detrac corotron*. This corotron essentially cancels the charge that was originally applied by the transfer corotron just before the application of the toner. This is necessary because an electrostatically charged piece of paper tends to stick to anything it contacts, such as the printer's paper handling rollers or other pieces of paper.

At this point in the printing process, you have a sheet of paper with toner sitting on it in the pattern of the printed page (see Figure 22.3). The toner is still in its powdered form, and because the page is no longer statically charged, there is nothing holding it in place except gravity. A slight breeze or tremor can ruin the image at this point. To permanently fuse the toner to the page, it passes through a pair of rollers heated to 400° Fahrenheit or more. This heat causes the plastic toner particles to melt and adhere to the fibers of the paper. At this point, the printing process is complete, and the page exits the printer. It is the nature of the toner and the fusing process that causes the characters of a laser-printed document to have a raised feel and appearance to them that is very attractive, whereas an inked page feels perfectly flat.

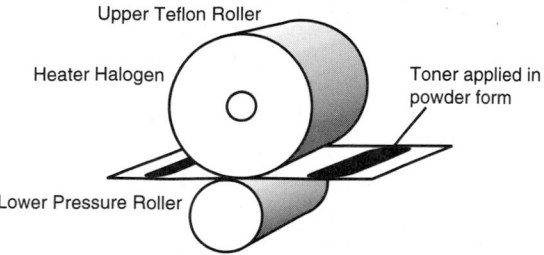

Figure 22.3   Laser printing produces an attractive "embossed" appearance because the toner is fused to the surface of the paper. Extremely rough paper can cause imaging problems, although laser printers can handle many more types of paper than inkjet printers can.

LED Page Printers

LED page printers, pioneered by Okidata, represent an excellent alternative to a "true" laser printer. Both technologies use a rotating drum and copier-like fusing mechanism to create high-quality printing. The difference is that LED page printers use an LED (light-emitting diode) array, rather than a laser beam, to place the image data upon the imaging drum (see Figure 22.4). This difference in imaging enables a straight-through paper path and a longer warranty on the print-head compared to laser printers.

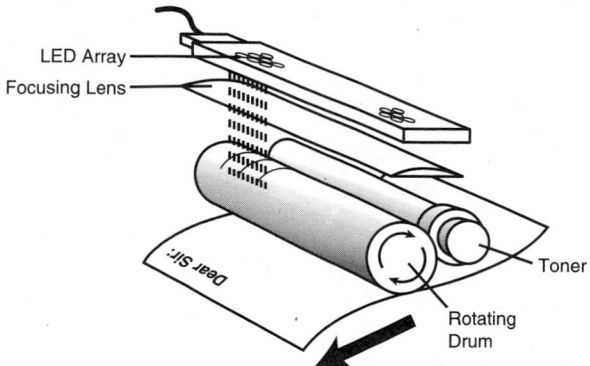

Figure 22.4   LED printers use a light-emitting diode to place the image on the imaging drum.

From the standpoint of print quality and speed, LED page printers produce quality comparable to similar laser printers. In essence, LED page printers are "laserless laser printers."

Inkjet Printers

The data interpretation stages of the inkjet printing process are fundamentally similar to those of a laser printer. The main difference is that because many inkjets tend to occupy the low end of the printer market, they are less likely to have the powerful processors and large amounts of memory found in lasers. You are therefore likely to find more inkjet printers on the market with relatively small memory buffers that rely on the PC for the majority of their processing activities. These printers can print graphics using band buffers instead of full page buffers. Higher-end inkjets, however, can have virtually the same processing capabilities and memory capacities as laser printers.

The primary difference between an inkjet printer and a laser printer, however, is the way that the image is applied to the page. Inkjet printing technology is far simpler than laser printing, requires fewer and less expensive parts, and takes up much less space. Instead of an elaborate process by which toner is applied to a drum and then transferred from the drum to the page, inkjet printers use tiny nozzles to spray liquid ink directly onto the paper in the same dot patterns used by laser printers. For these reasons, inkjet technology is more easily adapted for use in portable printers.

There are two basic types of inkjet printing in use today: thermal and piezo (discussed in the following sections). These terms describe the technology used to force the ink out of the cartridge through the nozzles. The inkjet cartridge typically consists of a reservoir for the liquid ink and the tiny (as small as one micron) nozzles through which the ink is expelled onto the page. The number of nozzles is dependent on the printer's resolution; configurations using anywhere from 21 to 128 nozzles per color are common. Color inkjet printers use four reservoirs with different color inks (cyan, magenta, yellow, and black). By mixing the four inks, the printer can produce virtually any color. (Most inkjets use one replaceable cartridge to hold the reservoirs for the three colors: cyan, magenta, and yellow.)

Thermal Inkjet Printing

Thermal inkjet printers function by superheating the ink in the cartridge to approximately 400 degrees. This causes vapor bubbles to form inside the cartridge that rise to the top of the reservoir. The pressure from the vapor forces ink out of the cartridge through the nozzles in tiny droplets that form the dots on the page. The vacuum caused by the expelled ink draws more ink down into the nozzles, making a constant stream of droplets as needed.

The thermal type of inkjet printing was the first to be developed and is still the most popular. Because of the vapor bubbles that form in the cartridge, Canon began calling its inkjet printers "BubbleJets," a name that has become almost synonymous with this technology.

Piezo Inkjet Printing

Piezo inkjet printing is a newer technology than thermal printing, and it presents distinct advantages. Instead of heat, these printers apply an electric charge to piezoelectric crystals inside the cartridge nozzles. These crystals change their shape as a result of the electric current, forcing the ink out through the nozzles.

Removing the high temperatures from the inkjet printing process presents two important advantages. First, the selection of inks that can withstand 400 degree heat is very limited; piezo technology enables printers to use ink formulations that are better suited to the printing process and less prone to smearing, which is a traditional problem with inkjet printing. Second, spray nozzles that are not exposed to extreme heat can last far longer than those traditional thermal cartridges. Epson pioneered the use of piezo inkjet printing.

Inkjet Limitations

Because it is more difficult to create fine dots with liquid ink than with toner, inkjet printers tend to have lower resolutions than lasers. Inkjet printing is also quite a bit slower than laser printing. Although it is possible to build high-end laser printers that can produce 16 pages per minute (ppm) or more, inkjets are limited in how fast they can actually dispense liquid ink and rarely go above a maximum of eight pages per minute, if that.

The biggest problem with most inkjet printers, however, is that the ink they use has a tendency to smear on standard paper stock. There are special inkjet papers that prevent this problem, but they are more expensive and offer far less variety than the laser printer papers on the market.

Inkjet printers must also use special transparency stock with a roughened (sandpaper-like) surface to promote proper ink drying. The extra cost of special paper and other print media, along with the relatively high cost and limited print life of inkjet cartridges, makes them a high cost-per-page type of printing.

Portable Printers

Portable printers typically use two different imaging technologies: Models made by Citizen use a nonimpact thermal transfer technique that uses special ribbons and a 60-cell printhead to fuse the image to the paper. This "thermal fusion" process provides for a very quiet (under 50db) printer and a nonsmear image, but a limited ribbon life (30 pages maximum for black, five pages maximum for color) and relatively low print resolution (360dpi maximum). Portable printers made by Canon and Brother represent a miniaturization of the normal desktop inkjet printers and provide for resolutions up to 720dpi with an ink cartridge life of hundreds of pages.

Although portable printers offer high print quality similar to their desktop siblings of a similar technology, they must make compromises in other areas to reach the desired goals of light weight (under five lbs) and compact size. They normally feature limited paper-handling with small-capacity paper trays or sometimes manual feed only. They often use only a single ink cartridge, requiring a swap to print in color. A rechargeable battery might be included, or the printer might use a PC card (PCMCIA) interface for both power and data transfer. Other typical features include infrared printing and optional scanning heads (which replace the normal print head). Although portable printers can't compete in features or speed with desktop printers, they enable travelers to deliver a high-quality printout anywhere.

Dot-Matrix Printers

Dot-matrix printers were, at one time, the most popular type of printer on the market because they were small, inexpensive to buy and to run, and fairly reliable. As the price of laser printers steadily dropped, however, and inkjet printers came to market that offered far superior output quality at virtually the same price, the market for dot-matrix printers reduced dramatically. Although they continue to perform certain tasks quite well, dot-matrix printers generally are too noisy, offer mediocre print quality, and have poor paper handling.

Unlike lasers and most inkjets, dot-matrix printers do not process documents a page at a time. Instead, they work primarily with a stream of ASCII characters up to a line at a time, and therefore require very small memory buffers. As a result, their speed is measured in characters per second (cps) instead of pages per minute. There is also very little processing performed in the printer when compared to a laser printer. Dot-matrix printers do not use complex page description languages such as PCL and PostScript. The data stream from the computer contains escape sequences used to set basic printer parameters such as page size and print quality, but any complex processing required is performed by the PC.

Dot-matrix printers work by advancing paper vertically around a rubberized roller, called a *platen*, one line at a time. At the same time, a print head travels back and forth horizontally on a metal bar. The print head contains a matrix of metal pins (usually either 9 or 24) that it extends in various combinations to make a physical impression on the paper. Between the pins and the paper is an inked ribbon, much like that used in a typewriter. The pins pressing through the ribbon onto the page make a series of small dots, forming typographic characters on the page. Dot-matrix printers also usually have rudimentary graphical capabilities, enabling them to produce low-resolution bitmaps using their limited memory as a band buffer.

Dot-matrix printers are usually associated with continuous sheet paper, driven by pinholes on the edges. Most models can also handle single sheets, although rarely with the accuracy found in most laser or inkjet printers. Because they are impact printers, meaning that there is actual physical contact between the print head and the paper, dot-matrix printers can do one thing that lasers and inkjets can't: print multipart forms and carbon copies. Many printers enable you to adjust the pressure of the impact to support various numbers of copies. Dot-matrix printers are rarely used for correspondence and general office printing anymore. Instead, they have found their place in commercial applications, such as for banks and hotels.

Note

Visit the Epson Web site for an interactive product finder for its impact printers. Okidata offers a similar service, which also includes its LED printers and fax machines. Both of these services will ask you detailed questions about your printer requirements and match your answers to the models that fit your requirements most closely.

Color Printing

At one time limited to graphics professionals and other high-end users, color printers have now become a commonplace PC accessory. The simplicity of inkjet printer technology has made it possible for manufacturers to build very low-cost printers that produce color output that, although not up to professional standards, is sufficient for basic personal and business needs.

There are several different types of color printers; most of them are adaptations of existing monochrome technologies. In most cases, color printers function by using the same printing medium in several colors (usually four). Thus, a color inkjet printer uses four colored inks, and a color laser uses toner in four colors. As in process color offset printing, it is possible to create virtually any color by combining cyan, magenta, yellow, and black in various proportions. This is called the *CMYK color model* and is referred to as four-color printing. Some inexpensive inkjet printers use only three colors, eliminating the black. These printers create a simulated black by combining the maximum proportions of the other three colors, but the result is far less effective than a true black medium as well as costly.

Depending on the color medium, there are different processes for combining the four colors. For most color printers, it is not possible to actually mix the four colors to achieve the desired result as you would mix paint. Instead, the printer applies the four colors very close to one another in the correct proportion to achieve the desired result. For example, an inkjet printer works by creating an interlaced pattern of dots, with each dot using one of the four inks. This is known as *bi-level printing*. The proportion of dots of each color and the pattern in which they're interlaced dictates the final color. This process of mixing different colored dots to form another color is called *dithering*. The process is similar to the display on your color monitor that creates the color for each pixel by placing red, green, and blue dots of varying intensities very close to one another.

In most cases, dithering is only a moderately successful color process. The resolution of many color printers is not high enough to prevent you from seeing the individually colored dots if you look carefully. The cumulative effect is of a solid color when seen from a distance, but close up, the dithering pattern is discernible to the naked eye. Some methods of overcoming these limitations include HP's use of color layering, Canon's use of variable-sized ink droplets (similar to laser printer "font smoothing" technologies), many vendors' use of more ink colors, and increasing printer resolution used along with high-gloss papers.

Printing in color necessarily complicates the language that the printer uses to communicate with the PC. Only the PostScript page description language has supported color from its inception. A version of PCL 5 with extensions to accommodate color, called PCL 5c, was introduced by Hewlett Packard in 1994. Many printer manufacturers, however, have their own proprietary color printing technologies, usually employing the printer driver to perform the additional processing required within the PC.

There are obviously many different applications for color printing, but the true test of any color printer is photographic reproduction. Dithered color that is acceptable for use in a bar chart, for example, might be totally inappropriate for printing photographs. Some relatively low-cost printers use special techniques, such as six inks instead of four, to produce better photographic reproductions, but the general rule is that to achieve photographic color prints that are comparable with those you see every day in magazines, you need equipment that is far beyond that which is typically used with PCs.

Graphics professionals, in most cases, use PC-based color printers as a proofing medium. In the past, it would often be necessary for an artist or designer to send a file to a service bureau for color printing to see a proof of the results of their work in hard copy. Now, rather than endure the delay and expense of that process, a relatively low-cost color printer can streamline the entire creative process. PostScript RIP software makes proofing more realistic if the printer doesn't have PostScript built in.

Note

In the world of color printing, "low-cost" is a highly relative term. To a professional graphic artist or designer, a $5,000 color laser printer is a low-cost alternative to the enormously expensive printing systems used by service bureaus. To the average PC user with far more modest color requirements, low-cost color inkjet printers are available in the $200–300 range.

Color printing suffers in comparison to monochrome printing in two significant areas: speed and cost. In most cases, color printers are designed to sacrifice speed to achieve the best possible printing quality. For this reason, it is a good idea to separate your color from your monochrome printing tasks in any sort of production environment. If you use inkjet printers in a business office, for example, it is usually better to have a separate printer dedicated to color output than to force users to wait for a color job to complete to print a simple letter. Although the best inkjet printers today produce black printing that's as good as color printing, the speed of color printing still lags behind black printing. Also, Canon has pioneered the use of an extra-large black cartridge with a wider print head for extra-fast black printing. Printers from Canon and other vendors that use this feature replace the normal black-and-colors ink cartridges with the single high-speed black cartridge.

The cost of a color printer can range from under a hundred to many thousands of dollars, but one aspect of printing in color that many users do not anticipate is the cost of consumables. People accustomed with monochrome printing rarely contemplate the cost of the ink or toner the printer uses and the paper they print on. A single toner cartridge for a laser printer typically produces thousands of pages, and there is a wide range of paper types and qualities available at varying prices.

Color printers, however, are usually far more expensive to run than monochrome. Depending on the color technology it uses, the printer might require special paper that is more expensive than standard printer paper. In addition, the color medium, whether ink, toner, or ribbon, is usually far more expensive than the monochrome alternative and yields fewer prints. The price of consumables per printed page is dependent on the coverage; a full page photograph obviously uses far more color than a page of text with a small color chart embedded in it, but color printing costs of fifty cents or more per page are common, as compared to a few pennies for monochrome printing.

The following sections examine the various color printer technologies intended for the PC market.

Color Inkjet Printers

Inkjet printers are the easiest to adapt to color use and are the most inexpensive. In fact, most of the inkjet printers on the market are capable of printing in color; there are few that are mono-chrome-only. The most typical arrangement is for the printer to use two cartridges: one contain-ing black ink only and one containing the other three colors. The advantage of this arrangement is that you have fewer individual ink containers to replace, but the disadvantage is that when any one of the color reservoirs is empty, you have to replace the entire three-color cartridge, thus dri-ving up the cost. Some printers (such as a few of the HP DeskJet models) also accept a second three-color cartridge in place of the black one, providing a six-color printing solution that achieves better results in photographic printing. Some mid-range and high-end color inkjet print-ers use a separate tank for each color, which provides for more economy in color use, especially for people who use a single color frequently.

Inkjet printers vary widely in their capabilities and their prices. Low-end models typically operate at 150–300dpi, support only letter-sized paper, and print at 2 or 3ppm. As you move up the price scale, resolutions and speeds increase, and printers might be able to use larger page sizes. One specialized breed of printer that often uses inkjet technology is designed to print poster-sized images on paper up to 36-inch wide.

One variation on the inkjet concept, called solid inkjet, wax jet, or phase change printing, uses solid, dyed wax as the color medium rather than liquid ink. As the printer works, it melts the wax and sprays it onto the page. Solid inkjet printers are generally slower and more expensive than traditional inkjets, but they tend to produce more vivid colors and are more resistant to smearing, enabling you to use virtually any type of paper.

Color Laser Printers

Color laser printers are a relatively new development when compared to the other technologies discussed here. The technology is the same as that of a monochrome laser printer except that there are four toners in different colors. Unlike the other types of color printers, which apply all the colors at the same time, many color lasers actually print each color on the page individually. Because the printer has only a single photoreceptor drum, the entire print engine cycle repeats four times for each page, applying the colored toners on top of each other.

This method greatly complicates the printer's paper handling. In a monochrome printer, the page passes beneath the photoreceptor drum at a speed equal to the drum's rotation so that the toner can be applied evenly onto the page. In a color printer, the page must reverse so that it can pass under the drum four times. In addition, the page must be in precisely the same position for each pass (registration) so that the individual dots of different colors fall directly on top of one another.

To overcome the speed and registration problems of conventional color laser printers, the LED page printer mechanism (using light-emitting diodes instead of a laser) pioneered in desktop printers by Okidata is now being used by both Okidata and Lexmark in some color page printer models. Printers using LEDs can print color pages at the same speed as monochrome pages because they can place all four colors in a single pass. There are some lasers that mix the toner on the drum by applying each toner in turn, after which all four colors are laid onto the paper at once. This eases the paper handling difficulties but presents other problems when applying the toner to the drum. In either case, the result is four toner colors mixed on the page and passing through the fuser assembly at once. This technique provides results that are vastly superior to dithered inks and other media. However, color laser printers are still very expensive with PostScript-compatible models starting at $2,000–$3,000. Also, because the drum must rotate four times for each page, these printers are significantly slower than monochrome lasers. Although new developments in host-based color laser printers designed for Windows 9x and NT have dropped the price of some models below $1,300, host-based printers are generally not suitable for elaborate graphics printing.

In addition to the relatively high initial costs of color laser printers, the type and costs of consumables and accessories should also be considered before acquiring a color laser printer. Some models use solid ink "crayons" that are melted and then applied to the paper, but most models use a separate drum and toner cartridge for each primary color. Therefore, the cost-per-page will be much higher for color printing than for black.

Dye Sublimation Printers

Dye sublimation, also called thermal dye transfer, is a printing technique that uses ribbons containing four colored dyes that the printer heats directly into a gas. This way, the four colors are mixed before the printer applies them to the paper. These printers can produce 256 hues for each of the four colors, which combine into a palette totaling 16.7 million different colors. This results in continuous tone (that is, undithered) images that come very close to photographic quality.

Dye sublimation printers produce excellent output, but they suffer in almost every other way. They are slow and costly, both to buy and to run. They require a special paper type that is quite expensive, as are the ribbon cartridges they use. However, dye sublimation technology is quite compatible with thermal wax transfer printing; the two differ primarily in the color medium they use. Several manufacturers make dual mode printers that can use both thermal wax transfer, which is less expensive, and dye sublimation. This enables you to use the cheaper thermal wax mode for proofing and everyday printing, saving the dye sublimation mode for the final product and other special uses.

One of the pioneers of this technology, Fargo Electronics, has turned its attention to card printers, but many other vendors, including Alps, Kodak Digital Science, Mitsubishi, Olympus Seiko Instruments, and others, have introduced dye-sublimation printers for uses ranging from inexpensive snapshot printing to high-end graphic arts.

Thermal Wax Transfer Printers

Thermal wax transfer printers use wax-based inks, somewhat like those used in solid inkjets, that the printer melts before applying them to the page. The process is faster than dye sublimation and does not require a special type of paper, but the printer applies the inks as dots, meaning that the colors must be dithered. The print quality suffers as a result when compared to continuous tone output, but it is generally better than the output from inkjets and other dithered color technologies.

In printers that offer both dye-sublimation and thermal wax transfer options, the thermal wax transfer is used for proofing, and the dye-sublimation mode is used for final results. To see the differences in print quality represented by these technologies, see the Seiko Instruments Web site.

Thermal Fusion Printers

Some portable printers from Citizen and IBM/Lexmark use a variation of the thermal wax transfer technology, using a thermal-transfer dot-matrix printhead and a choice of a multistrike ribbon for draft work and a one-time use film ribbon for final copies. These "thermal fusion" printers are very tiny, approximating a foot-long French bread loaf, making them a good choice for travel. The latest models can also print in color.

Their extremely compact size and low travel weight is balanced by extremely slow printing speeds, relatively low resolution (360dpi tops), limited availability of ribbons, short ribbon life, and the requirement for single-sheet hand-feeding. Citizen is the main maker of these printers today, but the technology is also used by many bar-code printers from a number of vendors.

Choosing a Printer Type

There are hundreds of printers on the market, and you might have a tough time deciding which technology is best suited to your needs. Obviously, price is a major factor, but there are many other criteria that you should consider before making your decision, such as those presented in the following sections.

How Many Printers?

If you are buying a single printer for your personal use, you should consider all your needs and try to find a product that satisfies them. For casual use and particularly for families with kids, an inkjet printer with color capabilities can satisfy most serious needs and provide a lot of fun at the same time.

Note

For best quality and lowest operating cost, make sure that the inkjet printer can accommodate both color and black ink cartridges at the same time (a dual-cartridge printer). Many ultra–low-cost inkjet printers make you switch cartridges depending on whether you want the color or black one in. These single cartridge printers are typically the ones that retail stores bundle in with inexpensive computer/monitor/printer package deals.

If, however, you need top quality output for business correspondence or other professional documents, it might be a good idea to sacrifice the color capabilities and buy a laser printer. There are now small, personal models that are quite affordable for home use.

For businesses, you should consider whether it is a better idea to satisfy all your needs with one printer or consider buying two units with complementary features, such as an inkjet for colored

or ink refill kits. The ink refill kits are the most cost-effective way to save money, but you need to check availability for your brand and model of printer, compare the quality, and do your refills with regard for the mess that squeezing bottles of liquid ink can cause. Check printer warranties also before you try these.

Use of electricity can also be a major concern. Laser printers in particular use a large amount of power, and many businesses leave them running continuously. Printers that have power-saver features that automatically place the unit into a low-power standby mode after a period of inactivity can provide significant savings and, again, help the environment. Because of the high power demands of laser printers, they should never be hooked up to a battery backup unit.

Installing Printer Support

As soon as you connect a typical printer to your PC's parallel or serial port, it is capable of receiving and processing ASCII text input. Even before you install a driver, you can issue a simple DOS command like the following:

```
dir > LPT1
```

The greater than sign in this command redirects the directory listing to the PC's parallel port. A printer connected to that port will receive and print the listing using the printer's default page format. If the printer connected to your PC processes data a page at a time, you will have to manually eject the current page to see the printed results. This is because the echo command does not include the form feed escape sequence that causes the printer to eject the page.

You can also redirect a text file to the printer port using a command such as the following:

```
copy readme.txt > LPT1
```

These commands prove that the PC's parallel or serial port provides a fully functional interface to the printer, but to exercise any further control over the print job, you must install a printer driver. However, if you are troubleshooting a system problem that prevents you from loading the Windows printer drivers, this capability can be useful for printing documentation files or other documents.

Note

These simple tests will not work with most host-based printers. A few can perform these DOS-based tests from within a DOS session running under Windows (a "DOS box"), but most require that printer drivers be installed first.

PostScript-only printers must receive PostScript commands to print. A simple printer test that does work with PostScript printers is part of the venerable Microsoft MSD utility shipped with MS-DOS and Windows 3.1 and found on the Windows 95 CD-ROM. A dual-mode printer with both PostScript and PCL modes will use the PCL mode for this print test if PCL is the default mode.

DOS Drivers

Many DOS programs use no printer drivers, relying instead on the capabilities of the printer and the ASCII characters that represent control codes (such as carriage return and line feed). Larger applications, however, such as word processors and spreadsheets, typically do include drivers for specific printers. Normally, the driver selection is part of the program's installation process.

There are only a few DOS applications that provide driver support for a large selection of printers. WordPerfect, for example, traditionally took pride in its comprehensive printer support, but most applications tend to include a few generic drivers that enable you to specify your printer only in the most general sense. These days, the decline of DOS has resulted in the virtual cessation of DOS application development, meaning that you will probably have a difficult time finding support for a new model printer even in a product such as WordPerfect.

If you have a laser printer that is not specified in the applications list of drivers, you should be able to use a driver supporting the same version of the page description language that your printer uses. A LaserJet III driver, for example, will function with any of the LaserJet III variants, such as the IIId and the IIIsi, because they all use PCL 5. The same driver should also work with the LaserJet 4 and 5 lines if needed because the versions of PCL these printers use are backward compatible with PCL 5.

These more generic drivers might not support all your printer's paper trays and the other features that distinguish the various models. For example, you will not be able to print at 600dpi on your LaserJet 5 printer with a PCL 5 (not PCL 5e) driver. However, you should be able to expect reasonably good results with this type of driver support.

Caution

DOS printing support, once a given except for PostScript-only printers, is slowly becoming a missing feature, especially with low-cost laser and inkjet printers. Some models offer printing from within a "DOS box" under Windows, but this is of no help if you need to print BIOS setup screens or if you need to print from a DOS program without Windows in the background. The lack of DOS support in new printers is a good reason to keep older inkjet or dot-matrix printers around for utility jobs.

Windows Drivers

Printer drivers in Windows differ from those in DOS in that they are part of the operating system instead of the application and in that you should always be able to find a driver for your exact model printer. Windows 3.1, Windows 9x, and Windows NT might use different drivers to support the same printer, and the interface you use to add printer support might be different in each operating system, but the process of installing a driver is fundamentally the same. The process consists mainly of the selection of a printer manufacturer, a model, and an interface port.

All the Windows operating systems have a Printers Control Panel that is the central location for all printer driver configuration activities. You can install drivers for as many printers as you need, including multiple drivers for the same printer, drivers for network printers, and even drivers for printers that do not exist. This last feature enables you to create an "imaginary" printer (see the following text).

If you have a printer that offers a choice of PDLs, you can install a driver for each of the supported languages (typically PostScript and PCL) and select either one when you print a document. Experience will teach you that each language has its strengths and when to use a particular language. Normally, PCL is better for text-heavy documents, whereas PostScript is better for elaborate graphics, especially those created with programs such as Adobe Illustrator and CorelDRAW.

If you have a network client installed on your system, you can install drivers for the printers that you regularly access on the network. The Printers Control Panel enables you to browse the network by using your client and to select the objects representing your network printers.

You might also encounter situations in which it is convenient to "print" a document to an imaginary printer. If, for example, you have to submit a desktop publishing document for pre-press work, you can install the appropriate driver for their image setter on your PC and save the print job data to a file instead of sending it out through a parallel or serial port.

The PDL code created by a printer driver is simply ASCII text, and as such, you can store it as a normal file on your PC. All Windows and most DOS printer drivers enable you to select an output destination of FILE as an alternative to a parallel or serial port. When you actually print a document, the system prompts you for the name and location of the output file to be created.

You can then transport the print file to a system with the appropriate printer by using a disk, a modem, or any other standard medium. After the file is there, you can simply direct it out the appropriate printer port by using the COPY command shown earlier. Because the printer driver has already processed the job, you do not need to have the application that created the document or the printer driver installed on the system. All the commands are in the output file, and you simply have to get it to the printer.

Windows 9x Driver Installation

Windows 9x and Windows NT include a wizard for installing printer drivers that walks you through the entire process. The procedure in Windows 3.1 is fundamentally the same, although the screens are somewhat different in appearance. When you click the Add Printer icon in the Printers Control Panel, the wizard first asks whether you are installing a driver for a printer connected to the local machine or to the network. Then, you are presented with a dialog box as in Figure 22.5 in which you can select the manufacturer of your printer and the specific model.

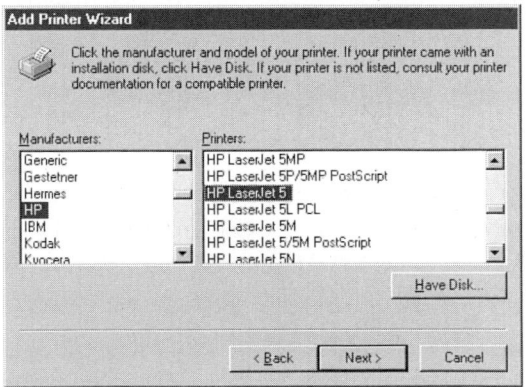

Figure 22.5   The Printer Selector screen from the Windows 98 Add Printer Wizard.

The operating systems include a comprehensive selection of printer drivers and a Have Disk button that enables you to install drivers that you have obtained from the manufacturer of your printer or from other sources.

After selecting the printer type, you specify the port to which the printer is attached. The Available Ports option (see Figure 22.6) lists all the COM and LPT ports installed on your system and the FILE entry for saving print jobs to disk files.

The wizard also asks whether you intend to use the printer with DOS applications. If you answer yes, the wizard configures your system to redirect all output sent to the LPT1 printer port to the printer driver. This is needed when you are configuring a network printer because DOS applications usually do not have support for network printing.

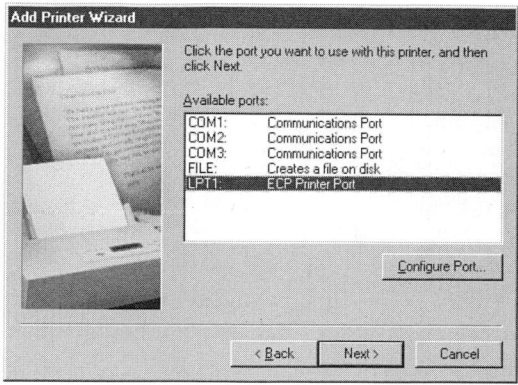

Figure 22.6   The Add Printer Wizard's Available Ports dialog box.

After you specify whether you want to make the new printer your default Windows printer, the wizard creates a new icon in the Printers control panel. This makes the printer available to all your Windows applications and provides access to the printer's Properties dialog box, which you can use to configure the driver and manipulate your print jobs.

Windows 9x Driver Configuration

The Properties dialog box for a particular printer typically contains numerous settings apart from those for selecting the port that the printer is to use. The features and the appearance of this dialog box are dependent on the printer driver you have installed; however, in most cases it enables you to select items such as the size and orientation of the paper that the printer will use, the tray that the paper is loaded in, and the number of copies of each page to print.

Many printer drivers provide settings that enable you to adjust the way that the driver handles print elements such as fonts and graphics. A typical Graphics page such as that for the HP LaserJet 5P driver might contain the following parameters:

- *Resolution.* Enables you to select from the print resolutions supported by the printer. A lower resolution provides faster printing and uses less printer memory. This setting doesn't affect text quality on most recent laser printers; the text will still print at the printer's maximum resolution (600dpi on this model).

■ *Dithering*. Enables you to select various types of dithering for the shades of gray or colors produced by your printer. The various dithering types provide different results depending on the nature of the image and the resolution at which you are running the printer.

Note

You might find that choosing "coarse dithering" for graphics that will be photocopied later actually produces a better quality copy than "fine dithering." This is because normal (nondigital) copiers tend to smear the dots making up the photographic image. If you're planning to photocopy your original for distribution, always make a test copy and evaluate it before you make your high-volume copy run. You might need to adjust your printer options and reprint the original to get acceptable results by varying dither, darkness, contrast, and other options.

■ *Intensity*. Enables you to control how dark the graphic images in your documents should be printed.

■ *Graphics mode*. Enables you to select whether the driver should send graphic images to the printer as vectors to be rasterized by the printer or the driver should rasterize the images in the computer and send the resulting bitmaps to the printer. If you're printing complex slides from a program such as Lotus Freelance Graphics to an HP LaserJet printer, you might find that the layers become "transparent" if you use the default vector graphics setting but print as intended with the bitmap setting.

Caution

If you're planning to use the printer to produce multiple copies of pages with vector graphics from presentation or draw-type software such as Freelance Graphics, Microsoft PowerPoint, CorelDRAW, or Adobe Illustrator, do a single-copy test print first to see if you have problems before running your high-volume print job.

Many printer drivers include a Fonts page that lets you control how the driver treats the TrueType fonts in the documents you print. The usual options are as follows:

■ *Download TrueType fonts as outline soft fonts*. Causes the driver to send the fonts to the printer as vector outlines so that the printer can rasterize them into bitmaps of the proper size. This option generally provides the fastest performance.

■ *Download TrueType fonts as bitmap soft fonts*. Causes the driver to rasterize the fonts in the computer and send the resulting bitmaps to the printer. This option is slightly slower than sending the font outlines but uses less printer memory.

■ *Print TrueType as graphics*. Causes the driver to rasterize the fonts into bitmaps and send them to the printer as graphic images. This is the slowest of the three options, but it enables you to overlap text and graphics without blending them.

The Device Options provided by many printer drivers enables you to specify values for the following options:

■ *Print quality*. Enables you to select the level of text quality for your documents. Lower qualities print faster but have a coarser appearance.

■ *Printer memory*. Enables you to specify how much memory is installed in the printer. The setting displays the amount of memory that ships with the printer, but if you install additional memory, be sure to modify this setting. This setting is used by the Printer Memory Tracking feature (see the following option) to calculate compression and the likelihood of the print job's being completed successfully.

■ *Printer memory tracking.* Enables you to control how aggressively the printer driver will use the amount of memory configured in the printer memory parameter. When it processes a print job, the driver computes the amount of printer memory needed and compares it to the amount installed in the printer. If the job requires a great deal more memory than the printer has, it will abort the job and generate an error message. When the amount of memory required is close to the amount installed, this setting determines whether the driver will attempt to send the job to the printer, at the risk of incurring an out-of-memory error, or behave conservatively by aborting the job.

Printer Sharing via a Network

Windows 9x and Windows NT enable you to share local printers with other users on a Windows network. To do this, you must explicitly create a share representing the printer from the Sharing page of its Properties dialog box (see Figure 22.7). On this page, you specify a NetBIOS name that will become the share name for the printer and a password if you want to limit access to certain users.

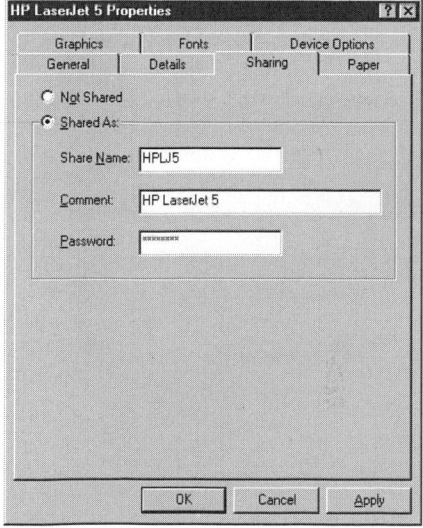

Figure 22.7 Windows 9x and Windows NT can share printers with other network users.

After you have created the share, the printer appears to other users on the network just like a shared drive. To access the printer, a network user must install the appropriate driver for the printer and specify the name of the share instead of a local printer port. To avoid having to type out the path, you can drag an icon representing a network printer from the Network Neighborhood and drop it onto the Add New Printer icon in the Printers Control Panel. After this, you need only select the appropriate driver and answer the default printer and printer test page questions to complete the printer installation.

Caution

Before you try to network your printer, make sure it's network compatible. Many low-cost printers today are host-based and cannot be shared over a network. Check with the printer vendor for details.

Remote Drivers

Windows NT 4.0 differs from Windows 9x in that it can store and distribute the printer drivers for multiple operating systems. When you share a printer in Windows NT, the dialog box contains an Alternate Drivers selector (see Figure 22.8) that enables you to choose the operating systems used by the other computers on your network.

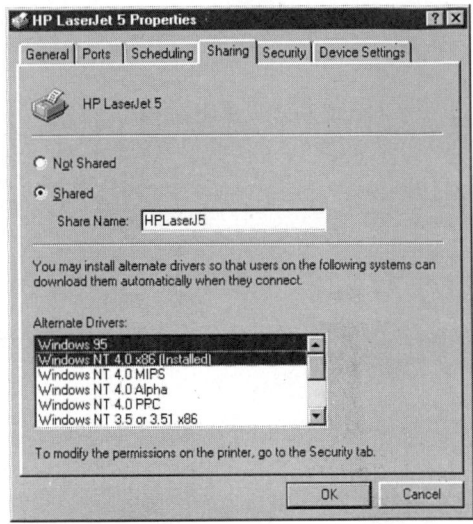

Figure 22.8 Windows NT can automatically supply printer drivers to network client systems.

After the wizard installs the driver for the Windows NT system, it prompts you for the appropriate media containing the drivers for the other operating systems you've selected. This way, when a client selects that Windows NT printer share, it automatically downloads the proper driver from the Windows NT system and installs it, preventing the user from having to identify the printer manufacturer and model.

Print Sharing via Switchboxes

As an alternative to networking, there are a variety of printer-sharing devices available at low cost. The easiest, cheapest way to share a single printer with two to four computers nearby is with an auto-sensing switchbox, available from cable makers such as Belkin and many others.

Printer switchboxes have an output plug where the cable to the printer is connected and two or more input plugs where the cables from the computers are connected. Computers are normally connected to the box by 25-pin straight-through cables, and the connection from the box to the printer uses a standard DB-25 to Centronics printer cable.

Manual Switchboxes

Simple switchboxes use a rotary switch to determine which computer has control of the printer. Although these units are still on the market, they're not recommended for use with laser or inkjet printers or non-printer parallel devices because these devices can be damaged by the switching process and the boxes normally lack IEEE-1284 bidirectional features.

Auto-sensing Switchboxes

Auto-sensing switchboxes are powered by either an external powerpack or the data cables; they continuously switch from one port to the next until a print job is sensed. At that point, the box "locks on" to the print job until the printer has been sent the last page. For use with MS-DOS printing (which often cannot wait for the switchbox to scan the port), many of these boxes also provide the capability for the desired port to be set manually. Most recent models support bidirectional IEEE-1284 modes such as EPP and ECP. Auto-sensing switchboxes that support IEEE-1284 modes will work with most modern laser and inkjet printers, and they will also enable sharing of peripherals such as scanners, tape backups, and other parallel-port devices. IEEE-1284–compliant autosensing switchboxes are available from Hewlett-Packard, Belkin, and many other vendors. Many of these devices are reversable, enabling a single computer to access multiple printers from a single parallel port.

Other Options for Sharing Printers

For sharing a printer among more than four users or for long-distance printing (over 25 feet between printer and computer), there are a variety of solutions available that use a special type of telephone-style cable. Here are a few of the products available, all of which will print more slowly than the previously mentioned switchboxes because they convert short-distance parallel ports into long-distance serial communications:

Products that plug into the MIO port found on many HP LaserJet models include Excellink's JetCard for up to ten users and BayTech's LaserShare for up to eight users. Products that create a "mini-LAN" that can daisy-chain many computers together to any parallel printer (except host-based) include the following: DataDocs's Max-A-Laser, which provides for up to thirty users at distances up to 2,000 feet away. Another option is Linksys's MultiShare for up to eight printers and up to 24 computers at distances up to 1,200 feet.

Support for Other Operating Systems

If your office contains a mixture of Macintoshes and PCs, make sure that the printer offers Macintosh support. Many "personal" printers are basically host-based, requiring Windows 9x or NT to function. Users of the increasingly popular Linux operating system must also shop carefully, as Linux support is still primarily provided by the Linux software vendors, not by the printer makers themselves. For example, Red Hat's popular version of Linux supports PostScript printers natively but uses a PostScript-type interpreter called "ghostscript" to support certain non-Postscript models. Look for the hardware compatibility list at Red Hat's Web site. Also, see *Upgrading and Repairing PCs, Linux Edition*, published by Que.

Preventative Maintenance

Printers are traditionally one of the most annoying devices to troubleshoot for computer professionals because they are prone to many mechanical problems that PCs and other networking devices are not. Variability in the quality of consumables and improper handling by users can exacerbate these problems, resulting in printers that require more attention and maintenance than other devices.

As with PCs, preventative maintenance for printers is largely based on common sense. If you keep the unit clean and treat it properly, it will last longer and produce better quality output than if you don't.

Keep the exterior of your printer clean and free of smudges by wiping it with a soft cloth dampened with water.

Laser and Inkjet Printers

For laser printers, the best preventative maintenance regimen results from purchasing a printer that uses toner cartridges with photoreceptor and developer assemblies. These are the components that regularly come in contact with the toner, so replacing them on a regular basis ensures that these vital parts are clean and undamaged. If your printer does not use this type of cartridge, you should take extra care to clean the inside of the printer whenever you replenish the toner, following the manufacturer's recommendations. Some printers include a special brush or other tool for this purpose.

Caution

It is particularly important to follow the manufacturer's recommendations regarding safety whenever you are working inside a laser printer. Apart from the obvious danger caused by live electrical connections, be aware that some components are very delicate and can be damaged either by rough handling (such as the developer unit and the corotrons or corona wires) or by excessive exposure to light (such as the photoreceptor). In addition, the printer's fusing mechanism is designed to heat up to 400 degrees Farenheit or more and might remain very hot for some time after you unplug the unit. Always allow the printer to cool down for at least 15 minutes before performing any internal maintenance that brings you near the fusing rollers.

Most inkjet cartridges contain new nozzles and a new ink supply, which prevents problems caused by nozzles that have become clogged with dried ink. Like lasers, thermal inkjet printers also rely on a powerful heat source, so you should take precautions before touching the internal components.

Low-cost inkjet cleaning kits can be purchased to help keep your inkjet printer free of ink build-up. Some work with a specially textured cleaning sheet that you spray with the cleaning fluid provided with the kit and then run through the printer by printing a few words; these work with all brands. Others let you clean the printhead after you remove it from the printer; these work with Canon and HP models.

To avoid inkjet problems, make sure that you turn off the printer with its own power switch, not the surge protector or power director! The printer's own power switch initiates a controlled shutdown of the printer, including capping the printheads to keep them from drying out. If you turn off the power externally (with a surge protector, for example), the printheads might dry out because they're exposed to the air, which eventually clogs them beyond user adjustment.

Minor clogging of inkjet cartridges can sometimes be cured by using the printer's diagnostics routines, accessible either through pushbuttons on the printer or through the printer's property sheets in Windows 9x.

Dot-Matrix Printers

Dot-matrix printers are more prone to collecting dirt and dust than any other type of printer. This is due both to the physical contact between the inked ribbon and the print head and to the use of continuous feed paper. As the printer runs, a fabric ribbon turns within its cartridge to keep a freshly inked surface in front of the print head. This lateral movement of the ribbon, combined with the continuous high-speed back-and-forth motion of the pins within the print head, tends to produce an ink-saturated lint that can clog the print heads and smudge the printed characters. Film ribbons can help reduce these problems and provide better print quality, but at the cost of a shorter ribbon life.

Continuous feed paper presents another problem. This paper has perforated borders on both edges with holes that the printer uses to pull the paper through the printer. Depending on the quality of the paper you purchase, some of the dots punched out to produce the holes might be left in the pad of paper. As the paper passes through the printer, these dots can be left behind and can eventually interfere with the paper handling mechanism. Keep dot-matrix printers clean by removing the dots and dust with canned air or a vacuum cleaner and swabbing the print heads regularly with alcohol.

Choosing the Best Paper

Both laser and inkjet printers use cut-sheet paper exclusively, and are therefore prone to paper handling problems such as paper jams and clumping (multiple sheets feeding simultaneously). You can minimize these problems by making sure that you use paper that is intended for your printer type. This is especially true when you are printing on unusual media such as heavy card stock, adhesive labels, or transparencies.

Printer manufacturers usually specify a range of paper weights that the printer is designed to support, and exceeding these can affect the quality of your results. Even more dangerous, using labels or transparencies in a laser printer that are not designed for laser use can be catastrophic. These media are usually not capable of withstanding the heat generated by the fusing process, and might actually melt inside the printer, causing severe or irreparable damage.

It is also important to take precautions when storing your printer paper supply. Damp paper is one of the chief causes of paper jams, clumping, and bad toner coverage. Always store your paper in a cool, dry place, with the reams lying flat, and do not open a package until you are ready to use the paper. When you load paper into your printer, it's always a good idea to riffle through the pad first. This helps the individual pages to separate when the printer extracts them from the paper tray.

Common Printing Problems

You can avoid many printing problems with regular preventative maintenance procedures, but there are still likely to be occasions when you find that the output from your printer is not up to its usual standards or that the printer is not functioning at all. When you are faced with a printing problem, it can sometimes be difficult to determine whether the problem originates in your application, in the computer's printer driver, or in the printer hardware.

In many cases, you can apply standard troubleshooting methodology to printing problems. For example, if you experience the same printing problem when you generate a test page from the printer's control panel as when you print a document from your PC, you can rule out the computer, the driver, and the printer connection as the source of the problem and begin examining the printer. If you experience the same printing problem with different drivers, then you can probably rule out the driver as the cause (unless the manufacturer produced several versions of the driver with the same bug).

Consistency is also an important factor when troubleshooting printer problems. If one page in ten exhibits the problem, you can generally rule out software as the cause and begin looking at the hardware, such as the connecting cable and the printer.

The following sections examine some of the most commonly seen printer problems, categorizing them according to the source of the problem. However, these categories must be taken loosely because some of the problems can have several different causes.

It's important to understand that none of the procedures described in the following sections should take the place of the maintenance and troubleshooting instructions provided with your printer. Your printer might use components and designs that differ substantially from those described in this chapter, and the manufacturer should always be the ultimate authority for hardware maintenance and problem-solving procedures.

Printer Hardware Problems

Problems with the printer usually result from the consumables, such as toner and paper. If the toner cartridge is nearly empty or if the printer's internal components become encrusted with loose toner, the quality of the print output can degrade in various ways. In the same way, paper that is damp, bent, wrinkled, or inserted into the tray improperly can cause myriad problems. You should always check these elements before assuming that printer's internal hardware is at fault:

■ *Fuzzy print.* On a laser printer, characters that are suddenly fuzzy or unclear are probably the result of using paper that is slightly damp. On an inkjet printer, fuzzy or smeary characters can result when you use various types of paper not specifically intended for inkjet printing. This can also occur if there is a problem with the connection between the print cartridge and the cradle. Try reinstalling the print cartridge.

■ *Variable print density.* If you find that some areas of the page are darker than others when using a laser printer, the problem is probably due to the distribution of the toner on the photoreceptor. The most common cause for this is uneven dispensation of the toner as its container empties. Removing the toner cartridge and shaking it from side to side redistributes the toner and should cause it to flow evenly. You can also use this technique to get a few more pages out of a toner cartridge after the printer has registered a "toner low" error. If your printer consistently produces pages with the same varied print density, the problem could be the printer's location. If the unit is not resting on a level surface, the toner can shift to one side of the cartridge, affecting the distribution of the toner on the page. It is also possible that your printer might have a light leak that is causing one area of the photoreceptor to be exposed to more ambient light than others. Moving the printer away from a bright light source can sometimes remedy this problem.

■ *Dirty or damaged corotrons*. A laser printer's corotrons (corona wires) apply electrostatic charges to the photoreceptor and the paper. If the transfer corotron (which charges the paper) has clumps of toner or paper fragments on it, it can apply an uneven charge to the paper, and you might see faint or fuzzy white lines running vertically down your printed pages. All black or all white pages can be caused by a broken charger or transfer corotron (respectively). A toner cartridge that contains the photoreceptor drum typically includes the charger corotron as well, so replacing the cartridge can remedy some of these problems. You can also (gently!) clean a dirty corotron with a cotton swab or other material recommended by the manufacturer. The transfer corotron is usually built into the printer (and not the cartridge) and will require professional servicing if it is broken. These components are made of fragile wires, so be very careful when you clean them.

■ *Sharp vertical white lines*. A sharp white line extending vertically down the entire length of your laser-printed pages that does not go away when you shake the toner cartridge is probably caused by dirt or debris in the developer unit that is preventing the unit from evenly distributing the toner onto the photoreceptor. Again, if the toner cartridge includes the developer unit, replacing it is the simplest fix. If not, your printer might have a mechanism that enables you to remove the developer roller for cleaning or even a tool designed to remove dirt from the roller while it is in place. It might also be possible to clean the roller by slipping the corner of a sheet of paper down the slots between the roller and the metal blades on either side of it.

■ *Regularly spaced spots*. If your laser-printed pages have a spot or spots that are consistently left unprinted, the cause might be a scratch or other flaw in the photoreceptor drum or a buildup of toner on the fusing roller. You can often tell the difference between these two problems by the distance between the spots on the page. If the spots occur less than three inches apart (vertically), the problem is probably caused by the fusing roller. Because the photoreceptor drum has a larger diameter than the fusing roller, the spots it produces would be farther apart or perhaps only one on a page. Replacing a toner cartridge that contains the photoreceptor drum and the fuser cleaning pad (an oil-impregnated pad that presses against the fuser roller to remove excess toner) should solve either of these problems. Otherwise, you will probably have to replace the drum assembly or the fuser cleaning pad separately. Some printers require professional servicing to replace the photoreceptor drum.

■ *Gray print or gray background*. As the photoreceptor drum in a laser printer wears, it begins to hold less of a charge, and less toner adheres to the drum, resulting in printing that is gray rather than black. On printers that include the drum as part of the toner cartridge, this is not usually a problem because the drum is changed frequently. Printers that use the drum for longer periods of time often have a print density control that enables you to gradually increase the amount of toner dispensed by the developer unit as the drum wears. Eventually, however, you will have to replace the drum; at that point, you must lower the print density back to its original setting, or you might find that your prints have a gray background because the developer is applying too much toner to the photoreceptor drum.

- *Loose toner.* If the pages emerging from your laser printer have toner on them that you can rub or brush off, they have not been properly fused. Usually, this means that the fuser is not reaching the temperature needed to completely melt the toner and fuse it to the page. A problem of this type nearly always requires professional service.

- *Solid vertical black line.* A vertical black line running down the entire length of several consecutive pages is a sign that your laser printer's toner cartridge might be nearly empty. Shaking the cartridge can usually eliminate the problem, but eventually you will have to replace it.

- *Frequent paper jams.* Paper handling can be a delicate part of the printer mechanism that is affected by several elements. Printer jams can result when paper is loaded incorrectly into the feed tray, when the paper is damp or wrinkled, or when you use the wrong kind of paper. Occasional jams are normal, but frequent jamming can indicate that you are using paper stock that is too heavy or textured in such a way as to be improper for laser printing. Jams can also result when the printer is not resting on a level surface.

  Envelope handling is often the weak spot in paper handling, especially with older laser printers or low-cost inkjet printers. Because of their uneven thickness, they tend to produce a high percentage of jams. Even if your printer is designed to handle multiple envelopes, consider feeding them one at a time if you have problems, or use alternative addressing means such as clear labels.

- *Blank pages appear between printed pages.* Paper that is damp, wrinkled, or too tightly compressed can cause two or more sheets to run through the printer at one time. To prevent this, store your paper in a cool, dry place, don't stack the reams too high, and riffle through the stack of paper before you insert it in the feed tray. This can also be caused by different paper types or sizes loaded in the IN tray at the same time.

Note

Before you look for a paper problem, be sure to check the printer setup. Some printers, especially on networks, are set to use a blank page to separate print jobs.

- *Memory overflow/printer overrun errors.* These errors indicate that the job you sent to the printer was too complex or consisted of more data than its buffers could handle. This can be caused by the use of too many fonts, text that is too dense, or graphics that are too complex. You can resolve this problem by simplifying your document or installing more memory in the printer. You can also try adjusting the page-protection setting in your printer driver (see the previous option).

Connection Problems

- *Gibberish.* If your page printer produces page after page of seemingly random "garbage" characters, the problem is probably that the printer has failed to recognize the PDL used by the print job. For example, a PostScript print job must begin with the two characters %!. If the printer fails to receive these characters, all the remaining data in the job prints as ASCII. This kind of problem is usually the result of some sort of communications failure between the PC and the printer. Check that the cable connections are secure and the cable is not damaged. If the problem occurs consistently, it might be the result of an improperly configured port in the PC, particularly if you are using a serial port. Check the port's parameters in the operating system. A serial port should be configured to use 8 data bits, 1 stop bit, and no parity (N-8-1).

Using the wrong printer driver will also cause gibberish printing. If you had an inkjet printer as your default and switched to a laser printer but failed to set the laser printer as the default, your print jobs will produce garbage printing unless you specifically send jobs to the laser printer. Similarly, failing to flip a switchbox to use the intended printer will also cause this type of printing error. Thus, many of these printing problems are due to operator error. Whenever you change to a new printer, make sure you set it as the default. Also, to avoid printer-switch errors, consider adding a second parallel port for the other printer or use the new USB-compatible printers if your system is compatible with them.

■ *Printer not available error.* When Windows 9x does not receive a response from a printer over the designated port, it switches the driver to offline mode, which enables you to print jobs and store them in the print spooler until the printer is available. The printer might be unavailable because the parallel or serial port is incorrectly configured, the printer cable is faulty, or the printer is turned off, offline, or malfunctioning. A malfunctioning port can be caused by an IRQ conflict (LPT1 uses IRQ 7, and COM 1 and COM 2 use IRQs 4 and 3, by default) or in the case of a serial port, incorrect start/stop/parity bit settings could be the culprit. A switchbox that is supposed to automatically scan for print jobs but has been set to manual mode or has been turned off can also cause this error.

■ *Printer does not notify Windows when it is out of paper, jammed, or other problem.* This is usually indicative of a communications problem between the printer and the PC. Check the printer cable and its connections at both ends. Some manufacturers recommend that you use a cable that is compliant with the IEEE 1284 standard.

Note

IEEE-1284 cables don't work in their advanced EPP/ECP modes unless your printer port is also set for an IEEE-1284 mode. Check your system documentation for details.

■ *Intermittent or failed communications or a partial print job followed by gibberish.* Interruptions in the communication between the computer and the printer can cause data to be lost in transit, resulting in partial print jobs or no print output at all. Aside from a faulty cable, these problems can result from the use of additional hardware between the printer port and the printer. Switchboxes used to share a printer among several computers and peripherals that share the parallel port with the printer (such as CD-ROM drives) are particularly prone to causing problems such as this.

■ *Port is busy error or printer goes offline.* These errors can occur when an ECP sends data to a printer at a rate faster than it can handle. You can remedy the problem by using the Windows 9x System Control Panel to load the standard printer port driver instead of the ECP driver.

Driver Problems

The best way to determine whether a printer driver is causing a particular problem is to stop using it. If a problem printing from a Windows application disappears when you print a directory listing by issuing the DIR > LPT1 command from the DOS prompt, you can safely say that you need to install a new printer driver. Other driver problems include the following:

■ *Form feed light comes on but nothing prints.* This indicates that the printer has less than a full page of data in its buffer and that the computer has failed to send a form feed command to eject the page. This is a common occurrence when you print from a DOS prompt or application without the benefit of a printer driver or use the Print-Screen key from DOS or within your BIOS setup screens, but it can also be the result of a malfunctioning driver. Some drivers (particularly PostScript drivers) provide an option to send an extra form feed at the end of every print job. Otherwise, you must eject the page manually from the printer's control panel.

■ *Incorrect fonts printing.* Virtually all laser printers have a selection of fonts built into the printer, and by default, most drivers use these fonts in place of similar TrueType or PostScript Type 1 fonts installed on the computer. Sometimes, there can be noticeable differences between the two fonts, however, and the printed text might not look exactly like that on the screen. Slight size discrepancies between the fonts can also cause the page breaks in the printed output to differ from those on the screen.

Note

Because different printers will use TrueType or Type 1 fonts differently, you should select the printer your document will be printed with before you save the document. After you select the printer, scroll through the document and check for problems due to page breaks being shifted, margins changing, or other problems.

You should also perform this procedure before you fax your document using a fax modem. Because fax resolution is a maximum of 200dpi in most cases, this lower resolution can cause major layout changes, even with scalable fonts such as TrueType or PostScript Type 1.

Application Problems

■ *Margins out of range error.* Most laser printers have a border around all four sides of the page of approximately one third of an inch where the toner cannot reach. If you configure an application to use margins smaller than this border, some drivers can generate this error message, whereas others simply truncate the output to fit the maximum printable page size. If your application or driver does not generate an error message and does not give you an opportunity to enter a correct margin setting, be sure to check your printer manual to find the possible margin settings before printing.

Note

Some applications offer a "print-to-fit" option that automatically adjusts the document to fit on the page in case you've made a margin-setting mistake. These options work by changing the font size or by readjusting line and page breaks. This option can be useful, but preview it before you use it blindly.

Scanners

Scanners provide you with a way to convert documents and photographs of many different types into computer-readable form. Similar to the scanning element on a copier, a scanner works by transferring digital signals representing the document to the computer for processing.

Regardless of the final use for the scanned document, all scans are received by the computer as a digital image.

Scanners differ in how the signals are created, how the scanner is interfaced with the computer, and what types of documents can be scanned. After the document is scanned, a scanning utility program provided with the scanner sends the scan to application software. This software determines whether the scan will be saved as an image or converted into computer-readable text.

The Hand Scanner

The oldest type of scanner is the now obsolete hand scanner, developed in the late 1980s by input-device companies such as Logitech and Genius. Hand scanners work by reflecting a narrow beam of light from an LED onto the document to be scanned. The user moves the scanner slowly down the document to be scanned, transmitting data to a lens and CCD (charge-coupled device), which converts the data into digital form. The document is converted into lines of data by the scanner, and the software in the computer reassembles it into a digital image. Depending on the scanner, the data might be captured as black or white, shades of gray, or if one of a few late-model scanners, color up to 24-bit level (16.8 million colors).

Sliding controls on the scanner were used to determine the resolution (dpi) used for scanning, along with the brightness of the scan. On black-and-white scanners, there was also a switch used for line art or dithered scans (dithered was used for photos).

Interfacing a Hand Scanner to Your Computer

Early-model hand scanners used proprietary interface cards that often required an IRQ, a DMA channel, and an I/O port address to work. As PCs became more crowded with resource-hungry devices, and more and more users wanted these low-cost devices but didn't want to wrestle with the complexities of installation, this type of interfacing was replaced by the parallel port (LPT port) connection.

Benefits of a Hand Scanner

- *Low cost.* Hand scanners, because the user provides the "motor" that moves the scanner, have very few moving parts and thus cost little to make or purchase. They have been many users' first scanner.

- *Portable.* When the parallel-port connection replaced the dedicated proprietary interface card, the hand scanner became a truly "universal" device that was able to work on desktop or notebook computers with parallel ports.

- *Scan a book without breaking it.* Hand scanners can be used to scan books whose bindings won't permit them to be scanned with ordinary flatbed scanners. Because only the page scanned needs to be flat, this minimizes strain on old and rare books and makes the scanning of pages from bulky volumes possible.

Drawbacks of the Hand Scanner

- *The user as motor.* The number one problem that virtually all users of hand scanners had was getting a straight scan. Early models made it virtually impossible to keep the scanner going in a straight line because they required users to keep a button on the side of the scanner pressed to keep the unit on. Although later models made the button a toggle, the amount of wavy scans that were discarded was colossal. Some vendors even introduced scan trays with guides to help scans be straight. This helped but worked directly against the portability and low-cost nature of the scanner.

  Even when improvements in scanner design made getting a straight scan less than impossible, the movement away from a dithered black-and-white image (mixing small dots to produce the illusion of gray tones) toward true grayscale and then color meant that scanning speed became more critical. Countless users had to rescan color photos again and again because their attempt to get 300dpi scans meant their hand was quicker than the mechanical "eye" it was pushing.

■ *The picture is bigger than the scanner.* The second major drawback of hand scanners was their built-in size limitation: A photo of about four inches wide was all they were designed to scan. Although later models of hand scanners came with "stitching" software that was designed to enable two or more overlapping scans to become a single final image, this method sounded better than it actually worked.

Sheetfed Scanners—"Faxing" Without the Fax

Hand scanners have been replaced by more powerful, less fussy scanner technologies that are now often similarly low in price.

A sheetfed scanner uses motor-driven rollers to pull the document or photograph to be scanned past a fixed imaging sensor. The design is virtually identical to the scanner built into fax machines. This fact made it easy for even the first multifunction office machines (see preceding sections) to incorporate limited scanning capabilities.

Sheetfed scanners such as Visioneer's PaperPort work well for letter-sized documents, and later models proved competent at handling photographs.

Advantages of the Sheetfed Scanner

■ *Easy interfacing.* Almost all sheetfed scanners take advantage of the "hidden" bidirectional features of the parallel (LPT) port and provide a second port to enable printers to "daisy-chain" to the scanner.

■ *Low cost.* Because the sheetfed scanner uses a simple, rigid imaging device and a straightforward motorized-roller mechanism, its production and selling costs are low.

■ *Size.* The sheetfed scanner is very compact and portable. It can easily fit into a briefcase.

Drawbacks of the Sheetfed Scanner

■ *Scanning limited by resolution, origins of mechanism.* As an outgrowth of fax imaging, sheetfed scanners were originally intended for line art or text scanning only. Although later models could also support grayscale and finally color scanning, the mechanism's limitations mean that resolutions are limited to 400dpi. This is adequate for same-sized scanning but precludes serious enlargements of small originals.

■ *Limited media handling.* Because the sheetfed scanner is essentially a computer-controlled fax scanner, it's subject to the same limitations as a fax machine. It can't handle books or even anything thicker than a piece of paper. It might jam or pull the document through unevenly, producing some unintentionally "creative" effects. It can't work with any type of transparent media such as negatives or slides and will even have problems with smaller than letter-sized documents or snapshot-sized photos.

Although some late-model sheetfed scanners were supplied with a transparent sleeve to hold odd-sized originals, the inability to work with anything beyond individual sheets is a serious limitation.

For these reasons, sheetfed scanners are becoming harder to find as standalone devices but are continuing to be an important part of the jack-of-all-trades multifunction office machine.

Flatbed Scanners

Take the toner, drum, and paper feed off a copier and add a computer interface, and you have the basic understanding of a flatbed scanner, the current favorite among after-the-fact imaging technologies.

As with other types of scanners, reflected light is used to start the imaging process, but flatbed scanners require a more precise design than hand or sheetfed scanners because the light that reflects off the document has a long way to go afterward (and even before because scanning colored images requires the light to go through red, green, and blue filters first). See Figure 22.9.

The light that bounces off the document is reflected through a series of mirrors to light-sensing diodes that convert the light into electricity. The electricity is sent to an analog to digital converter (ADC) that converts the electricity into digital pixels that can represent black-and-white or gray tones or color (if the original was scanned in color). The digital information is sent to the computer, where your application determines its future as text, graphics, or a bad scan that must be redone.

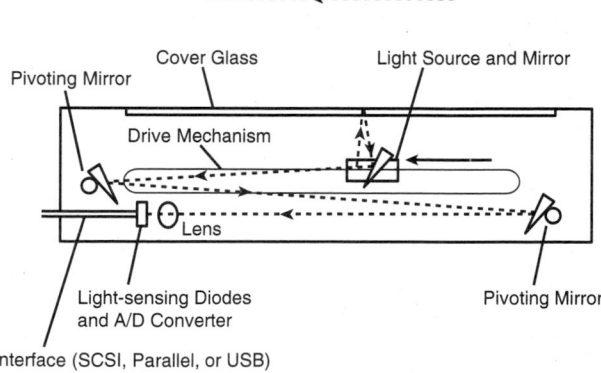

Figure 22.9 The path from the light source to the A/D converter is shown here.

Advantages of Flatbed Scanners

■ *Flexible media handling.* Even the simplest flatbed scanners, like flatbed copiers, can handle documents of varying sizes from small scraps of paper and wallet-sized photos to letter-sized documents as well as books. More-sophisticated scanners with automatic document feeders can even handle legal-sized 8.5"×14" documents. Add a transparency adapter, which shines light through the item to be scanned, and your scanner can also handle negatives, slides, and filmstrips of varying sizes.

There are several different ways of handling transparency media. The least expensive way is an adapter that will reflect light from the normal scanner mechanism behind and through the media. This unit, which can handle single 35mm slides only, is intended for casual use. More serious users will opt for a true transparency adapter, which is a device that replaces the normal scanner cover and contains its own light source and mirror mechanism. The scanner driver is used to select this adapter as the scanning source, and the normal light source inside the main scanner body is turned off. The most sophisticated variation found in very high-priced scanners is a media drawer that slides open and enables transparencies to be slid into the body of the scanner. Of these three, only the media drawer technology provides for true high-resolution scanning of small 35mm slides and negatives.

■ *High resolution made even higher through interpolation.* Unlike simpler types of scanners, flatbed scanners actually have two resolutions: optical and interpolated. Optical resolution refers to the actual resolution of the scanning optics—the hardware. To achieve higher resolution, flatbed scanners also offer a second resolution in which the scanner's software driver fills in fine details lost when detailed line art or text is scanned. This second method is called *interpolation* and usually increases the maximum resolution of the scanner by a factor of at least 4×. Thus, a scanner with a 600dpi optical resolution has an interpolated resolution of at least 2,400dpi. Because the interpolated resolution is software, not hardware-based, poorly-written scanner drivers can cause you to have poor results when using these higher resolutions. However, most scanners feature excellent interpolated modes that can produce much better results when scanning line art or text for OCR use. Although these modes can also be used for photographs, this is seldom needed because of the resolution limitations inherent in photographs (see the following). Interpolated resolutions should not be used to scan 35mm transparencies, either.

Drawbacks of Flatbed Scanners

■ *Size and bulk.* Because flatbed scanners are designed to handle letter-sized documents, they take up a fairly large amount of desk space, although some newer models are hardly larger than the 8.5"×11" letter size paper they handle as a maximum size.

■ *Reflective media limitations.* The least expensive flatbed scanners have no provision for transparency adapters, but most mid-range to high-end models have optional adapters for 35mm and larger negatives and slides. The scanning quality is very high when scanning 4"×5" and larger negatives (I've scanned hundreds of 1920-vintage glass negatives for a university archiving project). However, because of the limits of optical resolution, they're not the best choice for small negatives and slides.

Interfacing the Flatbed Scanner

There are three interface methods used on recent and current-model flatbed scanners: parallel-port, SCSI, and USB.

Parallel (LPT) Port Interfacing

Parallel-port scanners are primarily limited to low-end and mid-range models. This interface type often takes advantage of the higher data-transfer rates of the IEEE-1284 compatible port settings, such as EPP and ECP, and always takes advantage of bidirectional or PS/2-style printer ports. Because virtually all computers have a parallel port, parallel-port scanners are universal scanners capable of working virtually everywhere.

Parallel-port scanners have some significant disadvantages, though. First, it can be difficult to juggle any combination of devices beyond a scanner and a printer. With Zip, LS-120, CD-R/CD-RW, tape backup, and other types of removable-media drives often fighting for the parallel port, the order in which devices are connected to the computer can be critical. Should the Zip drive or the scanner be connected first? The printer must be the last item in the daisy-chain because printers lack the pass-through ports used by the other devices. You'll need to experiment or add a second LPT port to separate your scanner and printer from other devices.

A second disadvantage is scanning speed. Even if your scanner can use the fastest ECP or ECP/EPP port modes, the parallel port can't lay a glove on the faster SCSI or USB ports. Use parallel-port scanners for light-duty operation or when other types of expansion aren't feasible.

SCSI Interfacing

As you saw in Chapter 8, "The SCSI Interface," SCSI interfacing is extremely flexible, providing for daisy-chains of up to seven SCSI devices of varying types and even more with advanced SCSI interface cards. The SCSI Interface is covered in more detail in Chapter 8, "The SCSI Interface."

In tests, a typical scanner equipped with both SCSI and USB ports scanned an 8"×10" color image in about half the time using the SCSI port as compared to when the USB port was used. SCSI is the best choice for users who need speed and flexibility and who already have a SCSI interface or don't mind the extra cost of the card (some scanners come with an appropriate interface card).

USB Interfacing

The Universal Serial Bus is the latest widely available port and will replace serial and parallel ports sometime in the next few years. For users needing to mix the "no-brainer" installation typical of parallel-port devices with the flexibility of SCSI device handling, USB is the way to go for hobbyist use on the latest machines with Windows 98, which is the first version of Windows sold at retail to include USB drivers. USB is covered in more detail in Chapter 16, "Serial, Parallel, and Other I/O Interfaces."

Slide Scanners

Slide scanners use a motorized film holder that pulls a 35mm slide or filmstrip holder past a scanning mechanism. Even though the moving parts in the scanner are limited to the film holder, the high optical resolution of these scanners (1,900–2,700dpi are typical), the resulting precision of the motors, and the relatively small market for transparency film all make slide scanners relatively expensive.

Slide scanners use SCSI interfacing almost exclusively and are usually limited to 35mm film, although some models can be fitted with adapters for the new Advanced Picture System (APS) film holders or microscope slides. A few slide scanners can handle media up to 4"×5".

Although the high cost and tricky operation of slide scanners means that they're not for casual users, they represent the best way to maximize the quality of the small 24mm×36mm (approximately 1"×1.5") 35mm negative or slide at a reasonable cost. They often feature advanced software for automatically correcting color based on the characteristics of the slide or print films being scanned and even automatic digital dust removal.

Photo Scanners

This newest type of scanner is designed for users who want to scan both snapshots and 35mm transparencies and who don't want to pay a bundle to do it. This young product category has only a couple of participants at this time: HP and Artec.

HP's PhotoSmart provides a 300dpi snapshot resolution for prints up to 5"×7" and a 2,400dpi high-resolution scan for 35mm negatives and slides.

Note

Although the differences in scanning resolution between prints and slides/negatives seems startling, there's a good reason for it. Most prints don't provide better quality if scanned at more than 300dpi because of the loss of fine details in prints. Also, prints are at or near the size they'll be when reprinted after scanning. However, slides and negatives are only 24mm×36mm (about 1"×1.5") and must be enlarged a great deal for typical printing or even Internet Web page use. Scanning them at a higher resolution makes sense.

Although the original version required users to wrestle with SCSI interfacing, a newer version, the PhotoSmart S20, uses a USB port instead. Both units provide very high image quality, especially with slides and negatives, but the included software has been the source of many complaints. Lenik Terenin has developed a free replacement for the standard HP scanner software for the PhotoSmart units. You can download his Pscan32 free from the Web. Another replacement PhotoSmart scanner program is Ed Hamrick's shareware VueScan.

Artec's ScanROM 4E is an updated version of their original ScanROM Photo. The ScanROM name comes from the CD-ROM–style loading tray each unit features for media handling. The 4E offers resolutions of up to 4,800dpi, whereas the ScanROM Photo's resolution is 300dpi with Windows 3.1 and up to 1,200dpi with Windows 9x. These units use the EPP-type parallel port for interfacing, making them slower in operation than the HP models but easier to use with a wide range of computers. For more information, see the Artec Web site.

Drum Scanners

Despite the quality improvements in flatbed scanners and the development of slide and transparency scanners, the ultimate image scanners remain drum scanners. Whereas high-resolution flatbed scanners can achieve optical resolutions of 3,000dpi, drum scanners can reach as high as 8,000dpi, making them the perfect choice for creating color separations for professional glossy magazine and catalog reproduction.

Drum scanners attach the media to be scanned to a rotating drum that spins at thousands of rpms (revolutions per minute). Light passes through the drum and image and is converted to digital format by PMTs (Photo Multiplier Tubes).

Drum scanners' superior optical resolution is matched by their capability to pick up fine details (resolving power) and handling of a very wide range of light to dark tones (dynamic range). High-quality drum scanners can handle the entire dynamic range from 0 (pure white) to 4.0 (dead black) optical density (OD). This exceeds the needs of typical prints (0.05–2.2 OD) and even transparencies (0.25–3.2 OD). Some models even perform color separations within the scanner itself.

Although drum scanners are far too expensive for all but high-end graphics studios to purchase (typical models sell for $10–30 thousand and above), many companies offer drum scanning on a per-item basis for graphics that need to be of ultimate quality, such as for high-quality color image setting.

TWAIN

Regardless of which interface you choose for the scanner, a scanner can't work without driver software. One of the hidden factors driving the popularity of scanners is a standard called *TWAIN*.

TWAIN, the "acronym that isn't" (see the following Note), is the collective name for a very popular type of software driver that enables virtually any application to drive virtually any scanner or digital camera.

Note

TWAIN, according to the official TWAIN online site, is short for nothing ("TWAIN is TWAIN"). However, one unofficial name that's made the rounds for years is "Technology Without an Interesting Name."

Before TWAIN, each scanner maker had to provide device drivers and an image-scanning program that was "hard-wired" to the scanner. These programs were usually limited, and most users preferred to perform most image-editing with other programs such as Adobe Photoshop. To get a scanned image into Photoshop, for example, you had to close Photoshop, start the image-scanning program, scan the image, save it, and load it into Photoshop. When combined with the limited multitasking capabilities of early versions of Windows, this clunky process made scanning very difficult for most users. OCR software vendors such as Caere, creators of OmniPage, were among the first to need to have direct access to the scanner, and before TWAIN this meant they had to write direct-support drivers for every scanner they wanted to support.

The result was that new scanners would often not work with existing OCR and graphics programs and that you had to make sure that your scanner and software combination would work together.

TWAIN was created in 1992 by a group of industry vendors in the scanning hardware and OCR/imaging software fields. Over 175 vendors form the TWAIN Coalition, which reviews standards developed by the TWAIN Working Group.

TWAIN provides a hardware-specific driver that can be integrated into OCR, imaging, word processing, and other types of applications. Any TWAIN-compliant application can use any TWAIN device installed on the system. A common use for TWAIN is to enable programs such as Adobe Photoshop to access scanners within the program.

TWAIN devices (scanners and now digital cameras) come with a driver that enables all TWAIN-compliant applications access to the device. Although a user with two scanners (like this writer's Epson and Polaroid scanners) will have a TWAIN driver for each device, either device can be used with any software that supports TWAIN. Instead of each application needing a separate driver routine for every scanner, each application only needs to have TWAIN compatibility to use *any* TWAIN device on the system.

This integration enables a Photoshop user, for example, to choose a TWAIN device as an image source, start the device (a scanner, for example), scan the image, and have the resulting image appear in the Photoshop window for editing—all without the need to close down or reopen Photoshop. TWAIN also opens the door to direct scanner support in word-processing and page-layout programs, as well as in the traditional graphics-editing, photo-editing, and OCR programs.

Because TWAIN provides a standardized interface at the application level, creators of photo editors, OCR programs, and other typical scanner-driven programs no longer need to write customized drivers for the increasing numbers of scanners on the market.

TWAIN also minimizes the chances of scanners becoming outdated due to a lack of software support. Because all the scanner manufacturer has to do is write a single TWAIN driver for each operating system/scanner combination, older scanners can be supported for several years.

ISIS (Image and Scanner Interface Specification)

Image and Scanner Interface Specification (ISIS), created and controlled by Pixel Translations, is another popular imaging-software interface standard. Unlike TWAIN, ISIS is designed to provide support for not only image acquisition, but also image processing and image handling with languages such as Java and Visual Basic OCXs and applications created with these languages.

Pixel Translations provides free toolkits enabling vendors to create ISIS-compliant drivers and also supplies customized drivers to many major scanner vendors. If your scanner provides both ISIS and TWAIN support, try each of them to see which provides you with better performance and features. Because TWAIN, despite its more limited role, is more popular than ISIS, Pixel Translations will be releasing drivers that that will enable any ISIS application to use TWAIN drivers.

If your software lists a File option such as Acquire or Import, your application probably supports TWAIN or ISIS scanner control. If you have multiple TWAIN or ISIS devices, you'll normally have a menu option to Select Source, enabling you to choose which scanner or other digital source to use for image acquisition.

Getting the Most from Your Scanner's Hardware Configuration

1. *Use the fastest interface your scanner offers.*

   If your scanner offers either SCSI and USB or SCSI and parallel, it's worth the extra time and expense (both minimal with Windows 9x) to buy and install a SCSI interface card (some scanners come with the appropriate SCSI card). SCSI is the fastest of the three major interfaces, and speed is a critical factor in scanning, especially with large originals and high scanning resolutions. If you're already using a SCSI card for any other device, you should be able to attach your scanner to it if it's an Adaptec ASPI-compliant SCSI card and scanner.

2. *Set your LPT port for best performance.*

   Generally, bidirectional, EPP, or ECP/EPP modes are recommended for scanners that use parallel ports. (Check your documentation for details.) As you saw with other parallel-port devices, using the fastest possible settings that are compatible with all LPT devices you use is the best route to follow.

3. *Get SCSI right.*

   Although SCSI interfacing is the fastest interface for scanners and many other peripherals, it offers several challenges.

   If your scanner will be added to a daisy-chain of existing SCSI devices, you might need to purchase a different cable from the one that came with your scanner.

   If you'll be using a scanner bundled with a SCSI card and cable, the cable you receive will work fine, but you must make sure that your scanner's terminator is turned on or connected to end the SCSI bus at the scanner. If in the future you add another SCSI device to your system by connecting it to the scanner, turn off the scanner's terminator and turn on or install the new device's terminator.

Scanner Troubleshooting

Scanner Fails to Scan

If the scanner's on a parallel port, make sure you've loaded the correct DOS-based parallel-port driver as well as the scanner driver for Windows. Epson scanners use EPSN.SYS in the computer's CONFIG.SYS file, for example. These device drivers normally require configuration options to indicate the correct LPT port address.

Also, make sure the parallel port is set correctly. At a minimum, parallel-port scanners require the bidirectional or PS/2-style port setting. Some might work with the later IEEE-1284 EPP or ECP modes, but others don't.

If the scanner's SCSI-based, make sure the scanner's device ID isn't in use by other SCSI devices. If your SCSI interface card is made by Adaptec, for example, you can use the included SCSI Interrogator to make sure your scanner and other SCSI-based devices are available.

Make sure that terminators are set correctly for SCSI devices; the last device in the "daisy chain" needs to be terminated.

If you've just updated a Windows 95 system to Windows 98, an important TWAIN driver file might have been replaced. Use the Microsoft Windows 98 Version Conflict Manager (VCM) to check for a changed file called TWAIN.DLL, and replace the one installed during the Windows 98 upgrade with the one you were using (that worked!).

Can't Detect Scanner (SCSI or Parallel)

Scanners must already be turned on when the system starts to be detected. In some cases with a SCSI-based device, you can open the Device Manager (Control Panel, System, Properties Sheet) for Windows 9x and hit the Refresh button after resetting or turning on the scanner. If this fails or if the scanner's a parallel-port model, you must turn on the scanner and restart the computer to get the scanner to be recognized.

Can't Use "Acquire" from Software to Start Scanning

To see if the scanner or the application is at fault, use the scanner's own driver to scan directly (it's normally added to the Windows 9x/NT/2000 menu). If it scans correctly, you might have a problem with TWAIN registration in your application's File, Import/Acquire option. Check your application's documentation for help; the fix might require reinstalling your scanner drivers.

Distorted Graphic Appearance During Scan

Most scanners are designed to handle a wide range of originals, from black-and-white pencil drawings to full-color photographs. You need to correctly identify the image type to get good results. Check your document or image type against the checklist given. You have probably selected the wrong scan type for the document.

Use Table 22.2 as a quick-reference to help determine the best scanning mode for your documents.

Table 22.2   Recommended Scanning Modes for Document Types

Document Type/ Scanning Mode	Color photo	Drawing	Text	Black-and-white photo
Line Art	No	Yes	Yes	No
OCR	No	No	Yes	No
Grayscale	No	Yes[1]	No	Yes
Color Photograph	Yes	No	No	Yes[2]
Color Halftone	Yes[3]	No	No	No
Color Drawing	No	Yes	No	No
256-color	No	Yes	No	No
Copy/Fax	Yes[4]	Yes[4]	Yes[4]	Yes[4]

[1] *Recommended only for drawings containing pencil shading and ink wash effects*

[2] *Use to convert color to b&w if photo-editing software conversion is unavailable or produces inferior results*

[3] *Adjust halftone options to match output device's requirements*

[4] *Use to prepare scanned image for sending as fax or when image will be photocopied; converts all tones to digital halftones*

Graphic Looks Clear on Screen, but Prints Poorly

■ *Colors don't match.* You must use a color-management tool (that might be included with your scanner or must be purchased separately), and you must color-calibrate your scanner and your monitor. See the documentation for your photo-editing program and/or scanner for compatible color-management tools.

■ *Print is fuzzy, lacks definition.* You might have scanned the photograph at 72dpi instead of 200dpi or higher (depending on the printer). Because inkjet and laser printers have many more dots per inch than displays do, a display-optimized scan will become very small and still lack sharpness when printed on a printer with a higher resolution.

OCR Text Is Garbled

- *Check the quality of your document.* Photocopies of documents scanned after handwritten notes and highlighters were used on the original will be very difficult for even the most accurate page-recognition program to decipher.

- *Scan at a minimum of 300dpi or higher if your scanner permits it.* Compare the results at 300dpi to those at 600dpi or even higher; standardize on the resolution that provides the best results. The higher resolutions might take a bit more time, but quality is king! You can't recognize data that doesn't exist.

- *Check the straightness of your document.* Deskew the scan, or reinsert the original and rescan it.

- *The fonts in the document might be excessively stylized—such as script, black letter Gothic, and others.* If you have a hard time telling an "A" from a "D," for example, it's equally difficult for a page-recognition program to decipher it. If you plan to scan documents using the same hard-to-recognize fonts frequently, consider taking the time to "train" your page-recognition program to understand the "new' alphabet, numbers, and symbols.

- *Try manually zoning the document (drawing boxes around what you want scanned).* Check the expected data type in each zone. The program might be mistaking a graphics box for a text area or a table for ordinary text.

Portable PCs

23

SOME OF THE MAIN TOPICS IN THIS CHAPTER ARE

Evolution of the Portable Computer

Portable System Designs

Form Factors

Upgrading and Repairing Portables

Portable System Hardware

Peripherals

The Traveler's Survival Kit

Evolution of the Portable Computer

Portable computers, like their desktop counterparts, have evolved a great deal since the days when the word portable could refer to a desktop-sized case with a handle on it. Today, portable systems can rival the performance of their desktop counterparts in nearly every way. It is to the point that many systems are now being marketed as "desktop replacements," which companies are providing to traveling employees as their primary systems. This chapter examines the types of portable computers available and the technologies designed specifically for use in mobile systems.

Portables started out as suitcase-sized systems that differed from desktops mainly in that all the components, including the monitor, were installed into a single case. Compaq was among the first to market portable computers like these in the 1980s, and although their size, weight, and appearance were almost laughable when compared to today's portables, they were cutting-edge technology for the time. The components themselves were not very different from those in standard computers. Most portable systems are now approximately the size of the notebook they are often named for, and are built using the clamshell design that has become an industry standard, with nearly every component developed specifically for use in mobile systems.

All my professional life I have been on the road teaching PC hardware and software. Since I am almost never home or at a single desk, I have had to rely on portable systems, usually as my primary if not only system. In fact I have used portable systems even before there were PCs. I had some experience with the original Osborne portable, as well as several different Kaypro systems. These were sewing machine sized portables that ran CP/M, the most popular operating system before DOS existed.

My first DOS portable was the original Compaq sewing machine sized portable, and from there I graduated to an IBM Portable PC (also sewing machine sized), and then to a succession of brief-case sized portables. I had to use these larger AC powered systems in lieu of laptop or notebook systems because I needed a system with desktop power, performance, and storage. In 1995, laptop and notebook systems reached parity with desktop systems in power and storage, and I was able to graduate to laptop/notebook systems, which I have been using ever since.

Every version of this book, starting with my first self-published manuscripts in 1985, has been written on a portable system of one kind or another. With the processing power of modern notebook systems moving even closer to desktop systems, I look forward to carrying even smaller and lighter systems in the future.

Portable computers have settled into a number of distinct roles that now determine the size and capabilities of the systems available. Traveling users have specific requirements of portable computers, and the added weight and expense incurred by additional features makes it less likely for a user to carry a system more powerful than is needed.

Portable System Designs

Obviously, portable systems are designed to be smaller and lighter than desktops, and much of the development work that has been done on desktop components has certainly contributed to this end. The 2 1/2-inch hard drives typically used in portables today are a direct extension of the size reductions that have occurred in all hard drives over the past few years. However, two other issues have created a need for the development of new technologies specifically for portable systems; those issues are power and heat.

Environmental concerns are leading to the development of more efficient power management technologies, but, obviously, operating a computer from a battery imposes system limitations that designers of desktop systems never had to consider before the advent of portable systems. What's more, the demand for additional features such as CD-ROM drives, larger displays, and ever faster processors has increased the power drain on the typical system enormously. The problem of conserving power and increasing the system's battery life is typically addressed in three ways:

- *Low power components*. Nearly all the components in today's portable systems are specifically designed to use less power than their desktop counterparts.

- *Increased battery efficiency*. Newer battery technologies such as lithium ion or lithium polymer are making batteries and power supplies more consistent and reliable, and allowing for longer battery life on a single charge.

- *Power management*. Operating systems and utilities that turn off specific system components, such as disk drives when they are not in use, can greatly increase battery life.

Perhaps a more serious problem than battery life in portable systems is heat. The moving parts in a computer, such as disk drives, generate heat through friction, which must somehow be dissipated. In desktop systems, this is accomplished by using fans to continuously ventilate the empty spaces inside the system. Portable systems must be designed to run fan-free most of the time, using innovative systems for moving and dissipating heat.

The worst culprit, as far as heat is concerned, is the system processor. When they were first released, the amount of heat generated by Intel's 486 and Pentium processors was a problem even in desktop systems. Heat sinks and tiny fans mounted on top of the CPU became standard components in most systems. More modern Pentium II/III and Celeron systems benefit from newer processor technology featuring lower voltages, smaller die, integrated cache, and in general lower power consumption than their predecessors.

Because many portable systems are now being designed as replacements for desktops, users are not willing to compromise on processing power. Even the newest and fastest processors designed for desktop systems, like the Pentium III, are quickly adapted for use in mobile systems. However, for reasons of power consumption, noise, and space, fans in portable computers must be much smaller or omitted entirely, and there is very little empty space within the case for ventilation.

To address this problem, Intel has created special methods for packaging its mobile processors that are designed to keep heat output to a minimum. Intel's mobile processors also reduce heat through use of extra-low voltage designs and reduced amounts of Level 2 cache, now often integrated directly on the processor die. Other components are also designed to withstand the heat within a portable computer, which is usually greater than that of a desktop, in any case.

Form Factors

There are three basic form factors that describe most of the portable computers on the market today: laptops, notebooks, and subnotebooks. The definitions of the three types are fluid, however, with the options available on some systems causing particular models to ride the cusp of two categories. The categories are based primarily on size and weight, but these factors have a natural relationship to the capabilities of the system, because a larger case obviously can fit more into it. The three form factors are described in the following sections. Note that these designations are somewhat vague, and the marketing departments in most companies like to come up with their own terms for what they think a particular system might conform to. So don't be surprised if you see a system I might refer to as a laptop be called a notebook, or vice versa, by the manufacturer.

Laptops

As the original name coined for the clamshell-type portable computer, the laptop is the largest of the three basic form factors. Typically, a laptop system weighs seven pounds or more, and is approximately 9×12×2 inches in size, although the larger screens now arriving on the market are causing all portable system sizes to increase. Originally the smallest possible size for a computer, laptops today have become the high-end machines, offering features and performance that are comparable to a desktop system.

Indeed, many laptops are being positioned in the market either as desktop replacements or as multimedia systems suitable for delivering presentations on the road. Because of their greater weight, laptops are typically used by salespeople and other travelers who require the features they provide. However, many high-performance laptops are now being issued to users as their sole computer, even if they only travel from the office to the home. Large active-matrix displays, 32MB to 256MB of RAM, and hard drives of up to 20GB or more in size are all but ubiquitous, with virtually all systems now carrying fast CD-ROM or DVD drives, onboard speakers, and connectivity options that enable the use of external display, storage, and sound systems.

To use them as a desktop replacement, you can equip many laptops with a docking station (or a less-expensive port replicator) that functions as the user's "home base," enabling connection to a network and the use of a full-size monitor and keyboard. For someone who travels frequently, this arrangement often works better than separate desktop and portable systems, on which data must continually be kept in sync. Naturally, you pay a premium for all this functionality. Cutting-edge laptop systems can now cost as much as $2,500–$4,500 or more, at least twice the price of a comparable desktop.

Notebooks

A notebook system is designed to be somewhat smaller than a laptop in nearly every way: size, weight, features, and price. Note that the dividing line between what we might call a notebook or laptop system is somewhat fuzzy. You'll find that these categorizations are somewhat flexible. Weighing five to seven pounds, notebooks typically have smaller and less capable displays and lack the high-end multimedia functions of laptops, but they need not be stripped-down machines. Many notebooks have hard drive and memory configurations comparable to laptops, and virtually all are equipped with CD-ROM drives and sound capabilities.

Designed to function as an adjunct to a desktop system rather than a replacement, a notebook can actually be used as a primary desktop replacement for all but the most power hungry users. Notebooks typically have a wide array of options, as they are targeted at a wider audience, from the power user who can't quite afford (or who doesn't want the size and weight of) the top-of-the-line laptop to the bargain hunter who requires only basic services. Prices can range from under $1,200 to more than $2,500.

Subnotebooks

Subnotebooks are substantially smaller than both notebooks and laptops, and are intended for users who must enter and work with data on the road, as well as connect to the office network. Weighing four to five pounds, and often less than an inch thick, the subnotebook is intended for the traveler who feels overburdened by the larger machines and doesn't need their high-end capabilities.

Usually, the first component omitted in a subnotebook design is the internal floppy drive, although some include external units. You also will not find CD-ROM drives and other bulky hardware components built-in; although, some machines, such as IBM's ThinkPad 570 use a detachable module (or "slice") that fits under the main system to carry CD-ROM or DVD drives and floppy drives. However, many subnotebooks do include large, high-quality displays, plenty of hard drive space, and a full-size keyboard (by portable standards).

As is common in the electronics world, devices become more inexpensive as they get smaller, but only up to a certain point at which small size becomes a commodity and prices begin to go up. Some subnotebooks are intended (and priced) for the high-end market, such as for the executive who uses the system for little else but email and scheduling, but wants a lightweight, elegant, and impressive-looking system. Subnotebooks range in price from under $2,000 to around $4,000, depending on features.

Palmtop (Handheld Mini-Notebooks)

There is also a category of systems that are so incredibly small, they fit in the palm of your hand. I am not referring to the PDAs (Personal Digital Assistants) or the non-PC type systems that run Windows CE, but to systems that although tiny, are fully functional PCs that run the same operating systems and applications as your normal desktop systems. Portable PC systems are no longer constrained by the standard keyboard design and spacing. They normally offer a standard layout of keys, but with the keys spaced much more closely together than with a standard keyboard. As such, this class of system is very difficult to use for extensive typing, but for simple field work, email or internet access, or anything that doesn't require a lot of data entry, they are incredibly useful.

Palmtop computers are typified by the Libretto series from Toshiba, which weigh about 2lbs, have screens of 8-inch or less in size, and a tiny keyboard with integral Trackpoint device. These systems don't offer the faster or more power-hungry processors, but are fully functional PCs that run normal Windows and normal applications. This type of system is ideal as a secondary system for somebody who travels and demands the smallest and lightest, yet fully functional PC.

Upgrading and Repairing Portables

The portable systems manufactured today are less upgradable or repairable in general than desktop systems, mainly due to the lack of standard form factors for cases, motherboards, keyboards, displays, and even batteries. Even so, in some ways a portable can be easier to upgrade than a desktop because portable systems typically use modular components with snap-in connectors that eliminate the need for ribbon cables, mounting rails, and separate electrical connections. Thus, common upgrades like adding memory and swapping out a hard drive (on models with modular drive bays) can usually be accomplished in seconds.

The problem with replacing components in portables is that the hardware tends to be much less generic than it is in desktops. The exceptions are for PC cards, which are interchangeable by definition, memory, and in some cases hard drives. Purchasing a component that is not specifically intended for use in your exact system model can be risky.

In some cases, these compatibility problems are a matter of simple logistics. Portable system manufacturers jam a great deal of machinery into a very small case, and sometimes a new device just will not fit in the space left by the old one. This is particularly true of devices that must be accessible from the outside of the case, such as CD-ROM and floppy drives. Keyboards and monitors, the most easily replaceable of desktop components, are so completely integrated into the case of a portable system that they may not be practically removed at all.

In other cases, your upgrade path may be deliberately limited by the options available in the system BIOS. For example, manufacturers might limit the hard drive types supported by the system to force you to buy a replacement drive from them (at an inflated price), and not a third party. This is something you should check when shopping for a portable system by asking whether the BIOS is upgradable and finding out how much the vendor charges for replacement components.

◄◄ See "Upgrading the BIOS," p. 363.

Most of the time, components for portable systems are sold by referencing the system model number, even when third parties are involved. If you look through a catalog for desktop memory, for example, you see parts listed generically by attributes such as chip speed, form factor, and parity or non-parity. The memory listings for portable systems, on the other hand, will very likely consist of a series of systems manufacturers' names and model numbers, plus the amount of memory in the module.

There are always exceptions to the rule, of course. However, purchasing compatible components that fit together properly is certainly more of a challenge than it is for a desktop system. Table 23.1 explains which portable PC components can be upgraded.

Note

Generally speaking, purchasing a preassembled portable system from a reputable manufacturer is strongly recommended, as is purchasing only replacement components that are advertised as being specifically designed for your system.

Table 23.1   Upgradable Portable System Components

Component	Upgradable	Sources	Notes
CPU	No[1]	n/a	Adoption of newer Intel CPU/chipset packaging allows designers to more easily incorporate new CPUs into existing system designs, but this is not intended for upgrades
Memory	Yes	OEM vendor and third parties	Modules are not interchangeable among many models; only one upgrade socket in most systems
Hard Disk	Varies	OEM vendor and third parties	For systems that lack a modular bay, upgrade requires partial disassembly of system; PC card-based data transfer kit recommended to move data to new hard drive
Video Adapter/ Chipset	No	n/a	Get fastest video circuitry with 4MB or more memory if true-color display needed; some systems offer MPEG2 decoder upgrades for DVD video
Video Display	No	n/a	Get active-matrix if available
Removable-media drives	Varies	n/a	For systems that lack modular bays, use PC card or CardBus-interface LS-120, Zip, Jaz, CD-ROM, and so on

[1] *Note that there are a few companies that will upgrade the processor in your portable. When you send the system to them, they will desolder or remove the original processor and solder or plug in a replacement. Most of the time these upgrades are limited in nature, costly to perform, and the result might include overheating or battery life problems in the future. For the costs involved and the limited benefits, I don't consider processor upgrades to be a viable option for portable systems, except in rare or unique circumstances.*

Most portable systems, especially the smaller laptop or notebook designs, are difficult to disassemble. They have many more screws, which are often hidden under stickers or covers, and usually feature thin plastic parts that interlock. Unlike desktops, once you've taken one portable apart, they are not all alike.

Normally there are no special tools required, but the best advice I can give you is to get the manufacturer specific service manual for your system. One of the reasons I like the IBM Thinkpad series so much is that IBM makes the service/repair and technical reference manuals available free on their Web site. These documents include complete disassembly and reassembly instructions, and a complete parts list including detailed exploded diagrams and part numbers.

Toshiba also has detailed service and technical reference manuals, although you have to purchase them through a dealer. With systems from other manufacturers, you'll have to check to see if such documentation is available. I personally avoid any systems where I can't get this type of information from the manufacturer. I make it a point to get the service and technical reference manuals for any portable system I own. Obtaining these manuals makes future repairs and upgrades much easier.

Portable System Hardware

From a technical standpoint, some of the components used in portable systems are similar to those in desktop computers, while others are completely different. The following sections examine the various subsystems found in portable computers and how they differ from their desktop counterparts.

Displays

Perhaps the most obvious difference between a portable system and a desktop is the display screen. Gone is the box with an emitter bombarding a concave glass tube with electrons. In its place is a flat screen, which is less than half an inch thick. This is called an LCD, or liquid crystal display. Virtually all the screens in portable systems today are color, although monochromes were at one point the industry standard, just as in standard monitors.

An LCD consists of two sheets of a flexible, polarizing material with a layer of liquid crystal solution between them. If you press gently on an LCD screen while it is lit, you can see how it gives slightly, displacing the liquid inside. When an electric current is passed through the liquid, the crystals align and become semi-permeable to light.

◀◀ See "LCD Displays," p. 806.

The display is usually the single most expensive component in a portable system, often costing the manufacturer $1,000 or more. In fact, it is sometimes more economical to replace the entire computer rather than have a broken display replaced. In the first laptops with color screens, the display was a poor replacement for a standard VGA monitor. Today's portable screens are much improved, with some high-end displays even rivaling the performance of a good monitor and providing excellent performance, suitable even for graphic-intensive applications such as bitmap editing and videoconferencing. In fact, there are even LCD displays now being manufactured for use with non-portable systems.

The LCD display in a portable system is designed to operate at a specific resolution. This is because the size of the pixels on an LCD panel cannot be changed. On a desktop system, the signal output from the video adapter can change the resolution on the monitor, thus changing the number of pixels created on the screen. Obviously, as you switch from a resolution of 640×480 to 800×600, the pixels must be smaller to fit into the same space. Systems are currently available with the following resolutions:

- VGA   640×480
- SVGA   800×600
- XGA   1,024×768
- SXGA   1,280×1,024

Be careful when selecting notebooks or laptops with the XGA or SXGA displays, the higher resolution will often result in smaller text and icons than the typical desktop user is accustomed to. Even so, the typical LCD screens are much sharper and clearer than an analog desktop monitor, so even though they are smaller, they are often more readable with less eye strain.

An LCD panel, on the other hand, should be thought of as a grid ruled off to a specified resolution, with transistors controlling the color displayed by each individual pixel. The arrangement of the transistors defines the two major types of LCD displays used in portable systems today: dual scan and active matrix. While dual-scan displays ruled the notebook/laptop market for a long time, recent price drops in active-matrix displays have made them the display of choice for all except the most price-conscious shopper. Many manufacturers are now making solely active-matrix systems, because the costs have come down and the technology is superior.

Even though the prices for these displays have come down, they are still one of the most expensive parts of a portable system. They are also fragile. If you drop your laptop or notebook, you will likely fracture the display, which means it must be replaced. Often the replacements are close to the same cost as purchasing a new system, and accidents such as dropping are not covered under the standard warranty. Another common way people damage their screens is to close the system with a pen, pencil or other item on or above the keyboard. Make sure this area is clear before closing the system.

Dual-Scan (Passive-Matrix) Displays

The dual-scan display, sometimes called a passive-matrix display, has an array of transistors running down the X and Y axes of two sides of the screen. The number of transistors determines the screen's resolution. For example, a dual-scan display with 640 transistors along the X axis and 480 along the Y creates a grid like that shown in Figure 23.1. Each pixel on the screen is controlled by the two transistors representing its coordinates on the X and Y axes.

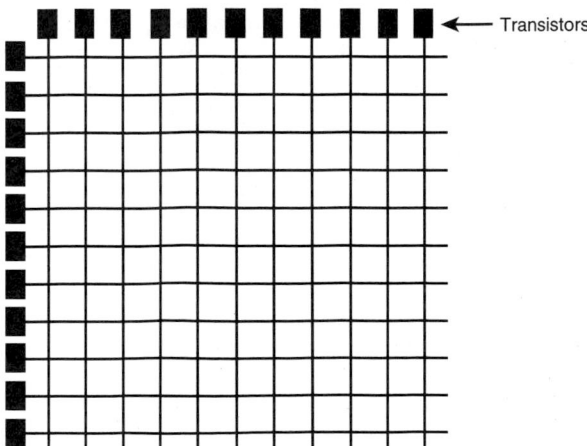

Figure 23.1 Dual scan LCD displays use a combination of two transistors on intersecting axes to control the color of each pixel.

If a transistor in a dual-scan display should fail, a whole line of pixels is disabled, causing a black line across the screen (either horizontally or vertically). There is no solution for this problem other than to replace the display or just live with it. The term dual scan comes from the fact that the processor redraws half of the screen at a time, which speeds up the refresh process somewhat.

Dual-scan displays are generally inferior to active-matrix screens. Dual-scan displays tend to be dimmer, because the pixels work by modifying the properties of reflected light (either room light or, more likely, a white light source behind the screen), rather than generating their own. Dual-scan panels are also prone to ghost images and are difficult to view from an angle, making it hard for two or more people to view the same screen.

However, newer passive-matrix technologies such as color super-twist nematic (CSTN), double-layer super-twist nematic (DSTN), and especially high-performance addressing (HPA) screens have come a long way in making passive-matrix displays a viable, lower-cost alternative to active-matrix technology. These newer displays offer better response rates and contrast—problems that plagued many of the earlier display types—but they are still not as sharp or as fast as an active matrix screen.

◄◄ See "LCD Displays," p. 806.

Of course, passive-matrix displays are also far less expensive than active matrix screens. The drawbacks of a passive matrix display are most noticeable during video-intensive applications, such as presentations, full-color graphics, video, fast-moving games, or under bright lighting conditions, such as in a window seat on an airplane, outdoors, or in offices with a lot of window lighting. For computing tasks that consist largely of reading words on the screen, like word processing and email, the passive matrix display is quite serviceable, even for long periods of time.

The standard size for a dual-scan display has been 10 1/2 inches (measured diagonally), running at 640×480, but most newer systems have 12.1-inch displays that run at 800×600 resolution. If you are familiar with the dual-scan display of an older portable, you will find that today's models are greatly improved.

One major advantage that dual-scan displays still possess is the cost of replacement in case of breakage (a major concern for notebook-equipped travelers). Breakage insurance tends to be far less expensive for dual-scan displays than for active-matrix. The cost of breakage insurance for both types of displays should be considered along with other price factors when choosing a system.

Active-Matrix Displays

An active-matrix display differs from a dual scan in that it contains at least one transistor for every pixel onscreen, rather than just at the edges. The transistors are arranged on a grid of conductive material, with each connected to a horizontal and a vertical member (see Figure 23.2). Selected voltages are applied by electrodes at the perimeter of the grid to address each pixel individually.

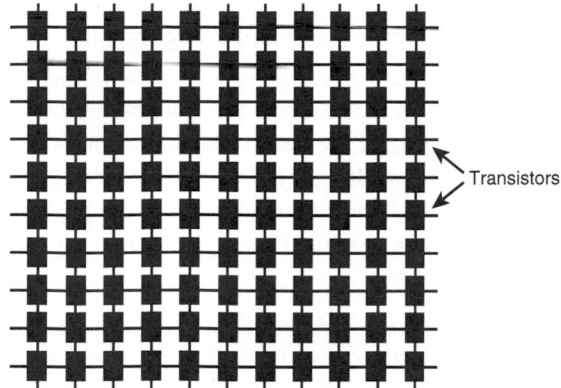

Transistors

Figure 23.2 Active-matrix LCD displays contain a transistor for each pixel on the screen. The pixels generate their own light for a brighter display.

Most active-matrix displays use a thin film transistor (TFT) array. TFT is a method for packaging one to four transistors per pixel within a flexible material that is the same size and shape as the display, so the transistors for each pixel lie directly behind the liquid crystal cells they control.

Two different TFT manufacturing processes account for most of the active-matrix displays on the market today: hydrogenated amorphous silicon (a-Si) and low temperature polysilicon (p-Si). These processes differ primarily in their cost. At first, most TFT displays were manufactured using the a-Si process because it required lower temperatures (less than 400° Celsius) than the p-Si process of the time. Now, lower temperature p-Si manufacturing processes are making this method an economically viable alternative to p-Si.

Although a TFT display has a great many transistors—from 480,000 to 1,920,000 for an 800×600 display—each pixel does not have its own signal connection. Instead, voltages are applied through connections for each row and column, much like the transistors in a passive matrix display.

Because every pixel is individually powered, each one generates its own light of the appropriate color, creating a display that is much brighter and more vivid than a dual-scan panel. The viewing angle is also greater, allowing multiple viewers to gather around the screen, and refreshes are faster and crisper, without the fuzziness of the dual scans, even in the case of games or full-motion video.

On the downside, it should be no surprise that, with 480,000 or more transistors rather than 1,400 (on an 800×600 screen), an active-matrix display requires a lot more power than a dual scan. It drains batteries faster and costs a great deal more, as well.

With all these transistors, it is not uncommon for failures to occur, resulting in displays with one or more "dead pixels," due to malfunctioning transistors. Unlike a dual-scan display, in which the failure of a single transistor causes an immediate and obvious flaw, a single black pixel is far less noticeable. However, many buyers feel (and rightly so) that a computer costing thousands of dollars should be perfect, and have attempted to return systems to the manufacturer solely for this reason.

Intel's advanced 0.25 micron process technology now used for the Pentium II/III/Celeron, as well. Since then, Intel added 300MHz, 266MHz, and 166MHz mobile Pentium/MMX processors also made on the 0.25 micron process. Mobile processors in general provide notebook manufacturers with a unique opportunity to offer users better battery life along with features and functionality that are on par with desktop systems.

The 0.25 micron manufacturing process and Intel's voltage reduction technology decrease the core voltage from 2.45 volts to 1.8 volts (2.0 volts for the 266MHz version) and the I/O interface from 3.3 volts to 2.5 volts, relative to previous generation processors. Intel's new 0.25 micron manufacturing process increases chip speed up to 60 percent, while reducing power consumption (up to 53 percent) when compared to 166MHz mobile Pentium processors with MMX technology on the 0.35 micron process. This reduction in voltages allows for higher speeds with less battery power use and less heat production. Typical power consumption can be reduced from 7.7 watts for 166MHz mobile Pentium processors with MMX technology on the 0.35 process to 3.9 watts for the 233MHz processor. These improvements represent nearly a 50 percent decrease in power consumption.

While Intel has largely replaced their mobile Pentium processors with mobile Pentium II/III and mobile Celeron processors, the power and heat savings pioneered in the mobile Pentium line live on in improved form in these newer processors for portable systems.

◄◄ See "Pentium Processors," p. 129.

◄◄ See "Pentium-MMX Processors," p. 137.

◄◄ See "Pentium II Processors," p. 162.

◄◄ See "Celeron," p. 174.

Intel also manufactured regular (non-MMX) Pentium chips at speeds of 75-, 100-, 120-, 133-, and 150MHz for use in low-end portable systems. These chips also use voltage reduction technology (VRT), which means that they draw the standard 3.3v from the motherboard, but internally they operate on only 2.9v (3.1v for the 150MHz model). Although not as dramatic a reduction as that evidenced in the 0.25 micron process chips, VRT still reduces the overall power consumption and heat production of these processors. These processors are no longer being manufactured, but will appear in older notebook computers you may have or encounter.

Mobile Pentium II

On April 2, 1998 Intel announced the first mobile Pentium II processors. Running at 233MHz and 266MHz, these processors are also manufactured using the 0.25 micron process. With a core voltage of 1.7v and an I/O buffer voltage of 1.8v, they run at even lower voltage levels than their Pentium/MMX counterparts. Although at 8.6 watts, a 266MHz Pentium II consumes more power overall than a Pentium/MMX running at the same speed, you must take into account that the Pentium II includes an integrated L2 cache, while the Pentium/MMX, at 4.5 watts, does not.

To reduce power consumption and heat buildup while preserving speed, Intel redesigned the mobile Pentium II in late 1998 to use a different method for accessing L2 cache. While the original mobile Pentium IIs used a 512KB L2 cache running at half CPU speed, just like the desktop Pentium II processor, the revised design changed to an integrated on-die L2 cache of just 256KB, but running at the same speed as the CPU. By manufacturing this cache directly on the processor die, it runs at the same speed as the processor core, and uses less power than slower external cache.

◀◀ See "Pentium II Processors," p. 162.

Table 23.2 lists the speed, manufacturing process, and voltage specifications for the mobile Pentium, Pentium/MMX, and Pentium II processors currently manufactured by Intel.

Table 23.2   Intel Mobile Processor Specifications

Processor Voltage	Speed	Mfg. Process	Core Voltage	I/O Buffer
Pentium	75MHz	0.35 micron	2.9v	3.3v
Pentium	100MHz	0.35 micron	2.9v	3.3v
Pentium	120MHz	0.35 micron	2.9v	3.3v
Pentium	133MHz	0.35 micron	2.9v	3.3v
Pentium	150MHz	0.35 micron	3.1v	3.3v
Pentium/MMX	120MHz	0.35 micron	2.45v	3.3v
Pentium/MMX	133MHz	0.35 micron	2.45v	3.3v
Pentium/MMX	150MHz	0.35 micron	2.45v	3.3v
Pentium/MMX	166MHz	0.35 micron	2.45v	3.3v
Pentium/MMX	166MHz	0.25 micron	1.8v	2.5v
Pentium/MMX	200MHz	0.25 micron	1.8v	2.5v
Pentium/MMX	233MHz	0.25 micron	1.8v	2.5v
Pentium/MMX	266MHz	0.25 micron	2.0v	2.5v
Pentium/MMX	300MHz	0.25 micron	2.0v	2.5v
Pentium II	233MHz	0.25 micron	1.7v	1.8v
Pentium II	266MHz	0.25 micron	1.7v	1.8v
Pentium II	300MHz	0.25 micron	1.6v 1.5v*	
Pentium II	333MHz	0.25 micron	1.6v	1.5v*
Pentium II	366MHz	0.25 micron	1.6v 1.5v*	
Pentium II	400MHz	0.25 micron	1.6v 1.5v*	

1.6v for mini-cartridge packaging, 1.5v for BGA (ball grid array) packaging

Intel Mobile Pentium Processor Steppings

As with Intel's desktop processor, the chips of the mobile processor line undergo continual development, and are modified in the form of steppings that incorporate corrections and refinements into the hardware manufacturing process. Tables 23.3 and 23.4 list the steppings for the mobile Pentium and Pentium/MMX processor lines, respectively.

Table 23.3   Mobile Pentium Processor Versions and Steppings

Type	Family	Model	Stepping	Mfg. Stepping	Speed	Spec. Number	Comments
0	5	2	1	B1	75-50	Q0601	TCP
0	5	2	2	B3	75-50	Q0606	TCP
0	5	2	2	B3	75-50	SX951	TCP
0/2	5	2	4	B5	75-50	Q0704	TCP
0	5	2	4	B5	75-50	SX975	TCP
0	5	2	5	C2	75-50	Q0725	TCP
0	5	2	5	C2	75-50	SK079	TCP
0	5	2	5	mA1	75-50	Q0686	VRT,TCP
0	5	2	5	mA1	75-50	Q0689	VRT
0	5	2	5	mA1	90-60	Q0694	VRT,TCP
0	5	2	5	mA1	90-60	Q0695	VRT
0	5	2	5	mA1	75-50	SK089	VRT,TCP
0	5	2	5	mA1	75-50	SK091	VRT
0	5	2	5	mA1	90-60	SK090	VRT,TCP
0	5	2	5	mA1	90-60	SK092	VRT
0	5	2	B	mcB1	100-66	Q0884	VRT,TCP
0	5	2	B	mcB1	120-60	Q0779	VRT,TCP
0	5	2	B	mcB1	120-60	Q0808	
0	5	2	B	mcB1	100-66	SY029	VRT,TCP
0	5	2	B	mcB1	120-60	SK113	VRT,TCP
0	5	2	B	mcB1	120-60	SK118	VRT,TCP
0	5	2	B	mcB1	120-60	SX999	
0	5	7	0	mA4	75-50	Q0848	VRT,TCP
0	5	7	0	mA4	75-50	Q0851	VRT
0	5	7	0	mA4	90-60	Q0849	VRT,TCP
0	5	7	0	mA4	90-60	Q0852	VRT
0	5	7	0	mA4	100-66	Q0850	VRT,TCP
0	5	7	0	mA4	100-66	Q0853	VRT
0	5	7	0	mA4	75-50	SK119	VRT,TCP
0	5	7	0	mA4	75-50	SK122	VRT
0	5	7	0	mA4	90-60	SK120	VRT,TCP

Type	Family	Model	Stepping	Mfg. Stepping	Speed	Spec. Number	Comments
0	5	7	0	mA4	90-60	SK123	VRT
0	5	7	0	mA4	100-66	SK121	VRT,TCP
0	5	7	0	mA4	100-66	SK124	VRT
0	5	2	C	mcC0	100-66	Q0887	VRT,TCP
0	5	2	C	mcC0	120-60	Q0879	VRT,TCP
0	5	2	C	mcC0	120-60	Q0880	3.1v
0	5	2	C	mcC0	133-66	Q0881	VRT,TCP
0	5	2	C	mcC0	133-66	Q0882	3.1v
0	5	2	C	mcC0	150-60	Q024	VRT,TCP
0	5	2	C	mcC0	150-60	Q0906	TCP,3.1v
0	5	2	C	mcC0	150-60	Q040	VRT
0	5	2	C	mcC0	75-50	SY056	VRT/TCP
0	5	2	C	mcC0	100-66	SY020	VRT/TCP
0	5	2	C	mcC0	100-66	SY046	3.1v
0	5	2	C	mcC0	120-60	SY021	VRT,TCP
0	5	2	C	mcC0	120-60	SY027	3.1v
0	5	2	C	mcC0	120-60	SY030	
0	5	2	C	mcC0	133-66	SY019	VRT,TCP
0	5	2	C	mcC0	133-66	SY028	3.1v
0	5	2	C	mcC0	150-60	SY061	VRT,TCP
0	5	2	C	mcC0	150-60	SY043	TCP,3.1v
0	5	2	C	mcC0	150-60	SY058	VRT
0	5	2	6	E0	75-50	Q0846	TCP
0	5	2	6	E0	75-50	SY009	TCP

Table 23.4   Mobile Pentium MMX Processor Versions and Steppings

Type	Family	Model	Stepping	Mfg. Stepping	Speed	Spec. Number	Comments
0	5	4	4	mxA3	150-60	Q016	ES,TCP,2.285V
0	5	4	4	mxA3	150-60	Q061	ES,PPGA,2.285V
0	5	4	4	mxA3	166-66	Q017	ES,TCP,2.285V
0	5	4	4	mxA3	166-66	Q062	ES,PPGA,2.285V
0	5	4	4	mxA3	150-60	SL22G	TCP,2.285V
0	5	4	4	mxA3	150-60	SL246	PPGA,2.285V
0	5	4	4	mxA3	166-66	SL22F	TCP,2.285V
0	5	4	4	mxA3	166-66	SL23Z	PPGA,2.285V

(continues)

Table 23.4   Continued

Type	Family	Model	Stepping	Mfg. Stepping	Speed	Spec. Number	Comments
0	5	4	3	mxB1	120-60	Q230	ES,TCP,2.2v
0	5	4	3	mxB1	133-66	Q130	ES,TCP,2.285V
0	5	4	3	mxB1	133-66	Q129	ES,PPGA,2.285V
0	5	4	3	mxB1	150-60	Q116	ES,TCP,2.285V
0	5	4	3	mxB1	150-60	Q128	ES,PPGA,2.285V
0	5	4	3	mxB1	166-66	Q115	ES,TCP,2.285V
0	5	4	3	mxB1	166-66	Q127	ES,PPGA,2.285V
0	5	4	3	mxB1	133-66	SL27D	TCP, 2.285V
0	5	4	3	mxB1	133-66	SL27C	PPGA,2.285V
0	5	4	3	mxB1	150-60	SL26U	TCP,2.285V
0	5	4	3	mxB1	150-60	SL27B	PPGA,2.285V
0	5	4	3	mxB1	166-66	SL26T	TCP,2.285V
0	5	4	3	mxB1	166-66	SL27A	PPGA,2.285V
0	5	8	1	myA0	166-66	Q255	TCP,1.8v
0	5	8	1	myA0	200-66	Q146	TCP,1.8v
0	5	8	1	myA0	233-66	Q147	TCP,1.8v
0	5	8	1	myA0	200-66	SL28P	TCP,1.8v
0	5	8	1	myA0	233-66	SL28Q	TCP,1.8v
0	5	8	1	myA0	266-66	Q250	TCP,2.0v

ES = Engineering Sample. These chips were not sold through normal channels, but were designed for development and testing purposes.

STP = The cB1 stepping is logically equivalent to the C2 step, but on a different manufacturing process. The mcB1 step is logically equivalent to the cB1 step (except it does not support DP, APIC, or FRC). The mcB1, mA1, mA4, and mcC0 steps also use Intel's VRT (voltage reduction technology), and are available in the TCP or SPGA package, primarily to support mobile applications. The mxA3 is logically equivalent to the xA3 stepping (except it does not support DP or APIC).

TCP = Tape Carrier Package

PPGA = Plastic PGA

VRT = Voltage Reduction Technology

2.285v = This is a mobile Pentium processor with MMX technology with a core operating voltage of 2.285v–2.665v.

1.8v = This is a mobile Pentium processor with MMX technology with a core operating voltage of 1.665v–1.935v and an I/O operating voltage of 2.375v–2.625v.

2.2v = This is a mobile Pentium processor with MMX technology with a core operating voltage of 2.10v–2.34v.

2.0v = This is a mobile Pentium processor with MMX technology with a core operating voltage of 1.850v–2.150v and an I/O operating voltage of 2.375v–2.625v.

Table 23.5 lists the steppings for mobile Pentium II processors in the mobile module, mobile mini-cartridge, and other forms.

Table 23.5   Mobile Pentium II Processor Steppings

Family	Model	Core Stepping	L2 Cache Size (KB)	L2 Cache Speed	S-Spec	Core/Bus	Notes
6	5	mdA0	512	1/2 core	SL2KH	233/66	MC, 1.7v
6	5	mdA0	512	1/2 core	SL2KJ	266/66	MC, 1.7v
6	5	mmdA0	512	1/2 core	PMD233	233/66	MMO, 1.7v
6	5	mmdA0	512	1/2 core	PMD266	266/66	MMO, 1.7v
6	5	mdB0	512	1/2 core	SL2RS	300/66	MC, 1.6v1
6	5	mdB0	512	1/2 core	SL2RR	266/66	MC, 1.6v1
6	5	mdB0	512	1/2 core	SL2RQ	233/66	MC, 1.6v1
6	5	mdxA0	256	core	SL32M	266/66	MC, 1.6v1
6	5	mdxA0	256	core	SL32N	300/66	MC, 1.6v1
6	5	mdxA0	256	core	SL32P	333/66	MC, 1.6v1
6	5	mdxA0	256	core	SL36Z	366/66	MC1.6v1
6	5	mdbA0	256	core	SL32Q	266/66	BG, 1.6v2
6	5	mdbA0	256	core	SL32R	300/66	BG, 1.6v2
6	5	mdbA0	256	core	SL32S	333/66	BG, 1.6v2
6	5	mdbA0	256	core	SL3AG	366/66	BG, 1.6v2
6	5	mdbA0	256	core	SL3DR	266/66	BG, 1.5v
6	5	mdbA0	256	core	SL3HH	266/66	PG, 1.6v2
6	5	mdbA0	256	core	SL3HJ	300/66	PG, 1.6v2
6	5	mdbA0	256	core	SL3HK	333/66	PG, 1.6v2
6	5	mdbA0	256	core	SL3HL	366/66	PG, 1.6v2

1.7v = Core processor voltage is 1.7v for these mobile Pentium processors
1.6v1 = Core processor voltage is 1.6v +/- 120mV for these processors
1.6v2 = Core processor voltage is 1.6v +/- 135mV for these processors
1.5v = Core processor voltage is 1.6v +/- 135mV for this processor
MC = Mobile Pentium II processor mounted in a mini-cartridge
MMO = Mobile Pentium II processor mounted in a mobile module including the 440BX North Bridge
BG = Mobile Pentium II processor in BGA packaging for low-profile surface mounting
PG = Mobile Pentium II processor in a (upsilon symbol) PGA1 package

◄◄ See "Pentium Processor Models and Steppings," p. 141.

Instead of metal pins inserted into a socket on the motherboard, a TCP processor is essentially a raw die encased in an oversized piece of polyamide film. The film is similar to photographic film. The die is attached to the film using a process called tape automated bonding (TAB), the same process used to connect electrical connections to LCD panels. The film, called the tape, is laminated with copper foil that is etched to form the leads that will connect the processor to the motherboard (see Figure 23.4). This is similar to the way electrical connections are photographically etched onto a printed circuit board.

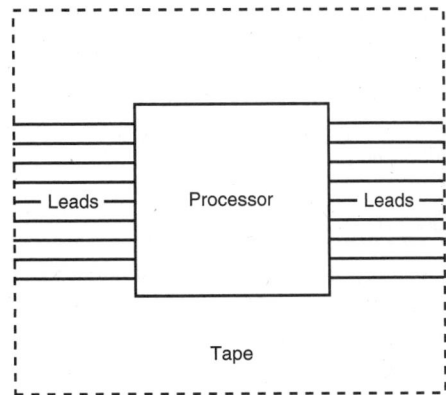

Figure 23.4   A processor that is mounted using the tape carrier package is attached to a piece of copper-laminated film that replaces the pins used in standard desktop processors.

After the leads are formed, they are plated with gold to allow bonding to a gold bump on the silicon die and to guard against corrosion. Next, they are bonded to the processor chip itself, and then the whole package is coated with a protective polyamide siloxane resin and mounted on a filmstrip reel for machine assembly. To get a feel for the small size of this processor, look at Figure 23.5, where it is shown next to a standard-size push-pin for comparison.

After testing, the processor ships to the motherboard manufacturer in this form. The reels of TCP chips are loaded into special machines that stamp-solder them directly to the portable system's motherboard. As such, the installation is permanent; a TCP processor can never be removed from the board for repair or upgrade. Because there is no heat sink or physical container directly attached to the processor, the motherboard becomes the conduit to a heat sink mounted underneath it, thus using the portable system's chassis to pull heat away. Some faster portable systems include thermostatically controlled fans to further aid in heat removal.

Mounting the TCP to the system circuit board requires specific tooling available from all major board assembly equipment vendors. A special tool cuts the tape containing the processor to the proper size and folds the ends containing the leads into a modified gull-wing shape that contacts the circuit board, leaving the processor suspended just above the board (see Figure 23.6). Another tool dispenses a thermally conductive paste to the circuit board prior to placement of the tape containing the processor. This is done so that the heat can be dissipated through a sink on the underside of the motherboard while it is kept away from the soldered connections.

Figure 23.5 Pentium MMX processor in TCP Mobile Package. Photograph used by permission of Intel Corporation.

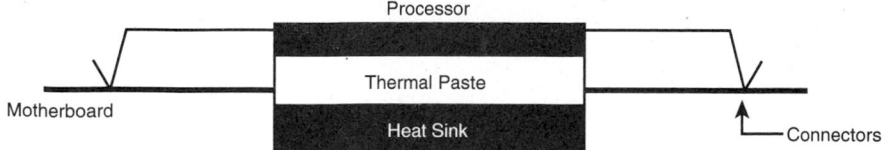

Figure 23.6 The tape keeps the processor's connections to the motherboard away from the chip and allows the underside of the processor to be thermally bonded to the motherboard.

Finally, a hot bar soldering tool connects the leads on the tape to the circuit board. The pinouts for the mobile Pentium TCP are shown in Figure 23.7. The completed TCP assembly forms an efficient thermal contact directly from the die to the motherboard, allowing the processor to run within its temperature limits even in such a raw state. By eliminating the package and essentially bonding the die directly to the motherboard, a significant amount of size and weight are saved.

Note

It should be noted that there are manufacturers of portable systems who use standard desktop PGA processors, sometimes accompanied by fans. Apart from a greatly diminished battery life, systems like these can sometimes be too hot to touch comfortably. For this reason, it is a good idea to determine the exact model processor used in a system that you intend to purchase, and not just the speed.

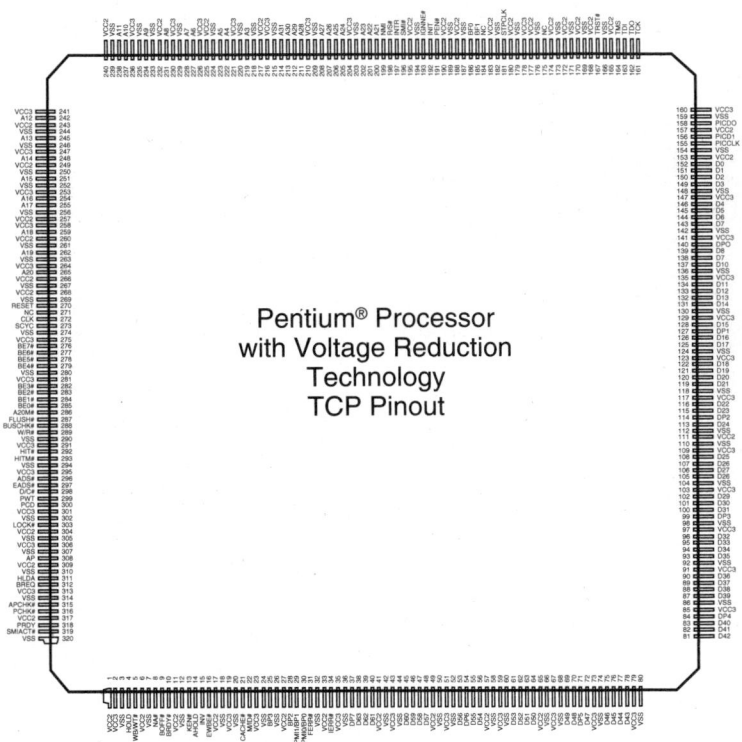

Figure 23.7   Intel mobile Pentium tape carrier package pinout.

Mobile Module

Portable system manufacturers can purchase Pentium processors in raw TCP form and mount the processors to their motherboards themselves. Intel has also introduced another form of processor packaging called the mobile module, or MMO (see Figure 23.8).

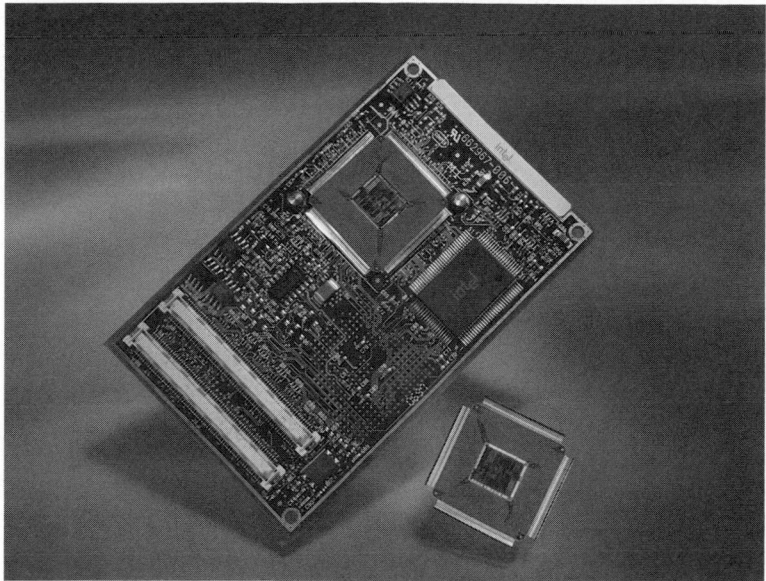

Figure 23.8 Mobile Pentium processors in mobile module or raw tape carrier package form. Photograph used by permission of Intel Corporation.

The mobile module consists of a Pentium or Pentium II processor in its TCP form, mounted on a small daughterboard along with the power supply for the processor's unique voltage require-ments, the system's Level 2 cache memory, and the North Bridge part of the motherboard chipset. This is the core logic that connects the processor to standard system buses containing the South Bridge part of the chipset, as shown in the block diagram in Figure 23.9. North Bridge and South Bridge describe what has come to be an accepted method for dividing the functionality of the chipset into halves that are mounted on separate modules. In a typical portable system design, the manufacturer purchases the mobile module (complete with the North Bridge) from Intel, and uses a motherboard designed by another company that contains the South Bridge.

In many ways, the MMO is similar to the Pentium II Single Edge Cartridge (SEC) design, and in the future will allow the cache memory to run at higher speeds on a separate bus from the rest of the system.

◄◄ See "Intel Chipsets," p. 237.

◄◄ See "Single Edge Contact (SEC) and Single Edge Processor (SEP) Packaging," p. 71.

Pentium® Processor with MMX™ Technology

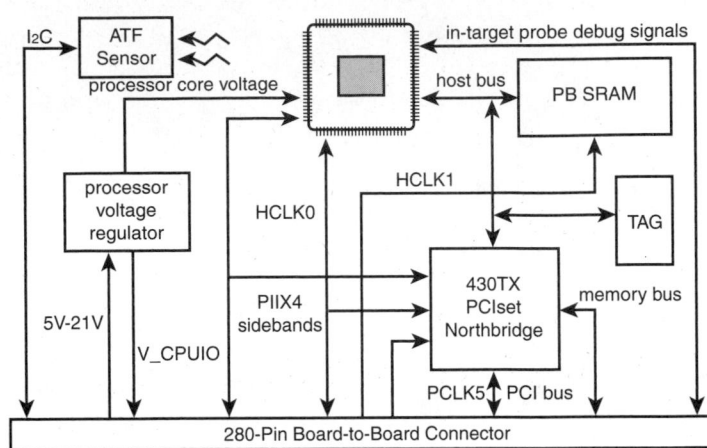

Figure 23.9 Intel Pentium mobile module block diagram.

The module interfaces electrically to its host system via a 3.3v PCI bus, a 3.3v memory bus, and Intel chipset control signals bridging the half of the chipset on the module to the other half of the chipset on the system motherboard. The Intel mobile module also incorporates a single thermal connection that carries all the module's thermal output to the mobile PC's main cooling mechanisms.

The MMO is mounted with screws and alignment guides to secure the module against the typical shock and vibration associated with mobile PC usage. The MMO (shown in Figure 23.10) is 4 inches (101.6mm) long by 2.5 inches (63.5mm) wide by 0.315 inch (8mm) high (0.39 inch or 10mm high at connector).

Figure 23.10 Intel Pentium MMX mobile module, including the processor, chipset, and L2 cache. Photograph used by permission of Intel Corporation.

The mobile module greatly simplifies the process of installing a Pentium or Pentium II processor into a portable system, permits manufacturers to build more standardization into their portable computer designs, and eliminates the need for manufacturers to invest in the special tools needed to mount TCP processors on circuit boards themselves. The module also provides a viable processor upgrade path that was unavailable with a TCP processor permanently soldered to the motherboard.

IBM has adopted the MMO in the latest ThinkPad systems, which should allow them to come out with new designs more quickly because the MMO part of the system will remain an industry standard. The size of the MMO precludes its use in some very thin notebooks, so IBM and others still use the raw TCP processor version for many portable designs as well.

Mini-Cartridge

The mobile versions of the Pentium II processor are available in the mobile module package, with the North Bridge portion of the Intel 440BX AGP chipset. However, Intel has also introduced another new package for the Pentium II called the mini-cartridge. The mini-cartridge is designed especially for use in ultralight portable computers in which the height or bulk of the mobile module would interfere with the system design. It contains only the processor core and 512KB of L2 cache memory in a stainless steel case that exposes the connector and the processor die.

◀◀ See "Intel 440BX," p. 258.

The mini-cartridge is approximately 51mm×47mm in size and 4.5mm in height. Overall, the package is about one-fourth the weight, one-sixth the size, and consumes two-thirds of the power of a desktop Pentium II processor using the Single Edge Connector (SEC). To connect to the socket on the motherboard, the mini-cartridge has a 240-pin connector at one end of the bottom side, with the pins arranged in an 8×30 ball grid array (BGA), as shown in Figure 23.11.

BGA packaging uses solder balls on the bottom of the device, which means that after it is soldered in, there are no visible pins. The unique features of BGA packaging makes it one of the smallest physical packages, and the soldered-in design is thermally more stable than most others; it also allows better heat transfer from the device to the board.

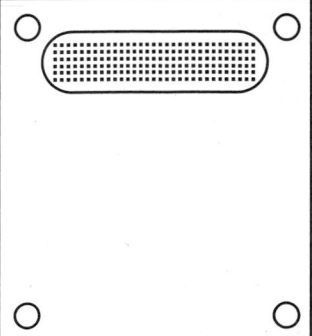

Figure 23.11　Bottom side of the Pentium II mini-cartridge package.

◀◀ To learn more about BGA packaging, see "Pentium II Processors" p. 162.

The BGA packaging is also used in some versions of AMD's mobile K6 family.

Chipsets

As in the desktop market, Intel has come to dominate the mobile chipset industry by creating products that support the advanced features of each new processor they release. The recent mobile Pentium II processor releases were accompanied by the introduction of the mobile 440BX AGPset, which provides support for the accelerated graphics port, 100MHz memory and system buses, and processor power-management capabilities designed to extend battery life.

A similar chipset, but optimized for the mobile Celeron processors and their 66MHz system bus, is the 440ZX-66M AGPset.

Intel's other current chipsets intended for mobile systems are the 430TX PCIset for the Pentium/MMX and the 430MX PCIset for the Pentium.

◀◀ See "Fifth-Generation (P5 Pentium Class) Chipsets," p. 129.

◀◀ See "Sixth-Generation (P6 Pentium Pro/Pentium II Class) Chipsets," p. 151.

Intel's most recent chipset innovation, however, is intended to accommodate the mobile module package for the Pentium/MMX and Pentium II processors. In this design, the chipset's two halves, called the North Bridge and South Bridge, are located on the mobile module and the system motherboard, respectively.

In the 440BX AGPset, for example, the host bridge system controller consists of two VLSI devices. The first of these, the 443BX host bridge (the North Bridge) is part of the mobile module. The other device is the PIIX4 PCI/ISA bridge, which the system manufacturer must incorporate into the motherboard design for the portable computer. This forms the South Bridge. The mobile module connects to the motherboard through a 3.3v PCI bus, a 3.3v memory bus, and some 443BX host bridge control signals. It is these signals that combine the North Bridge and the South Bridge into a single functional chipset.

The new 440MX chipset, designed for mobile Celeron systems, brings chipset integration to a new level, because it combines both North Bridge and South Bridge functions into a single chip. In addition to reducing the chip count at the chipset level, the 440MX provides audio and modem support at a performance level comparable to PCI-based hardware modems and sound cards, with just slightly higher CPU utilization rates.

Clearly, innovations like the mobile module accentuate the association between a computer's processor and its motherboard chipset. Now that the development cycles for new processors tend to be measured in months, not years, it is rapidly becoming a foregone conclusion that to get the most out of the latest Intel processor, you have to use an Intel chipset as well. As when shopping for a desktop system, you should be aware of what chipset is used in the portable computer you plan to buy, and whether it fully supports the capabilities of the processor and the system's other components.

Memory

Adding memory is one of the most common upgrades performed on computers, and portables are no exception. However, most portable systems are exceptional in the design of their memory chips. Unlike desktop systems, in which there are only a few basic types of slots for additional RAM, there are literally dozens of different memory chip configurations that have been designed to shoehorn RAM upgrades into the tightly packed cases of portable systems.

Most portables use a type of DIMM called a Small Outline DIMM (SO-DIMM), which is physically smaller but similar electrically to the standard DIMMs used in desktop systems. SO-DIMMs are normally available in EDO (Extended Data Out) or SDRAM (Synchronous DRAM) form, with various speeds and voltages available. The latest portables are starting to use SO-RIMMs (Small Outline Rambus Inline Memory Modules) similar to the RIMMs used in desktop systems, but again physically smaller. Some systems in the past used proprietary memory cartridges that look like PC cards, but which plug into a dedicated IC (integrated circuit) memory socket, but this isn't common anymore. In any case, appearance is not a reliable measure of compatibility, make sure the memory you are purchasing will work with your system or that you can get a refund or replacement if it doesn't. It is strongly recommended that you install only memory modules that have been designed for your system, in the configurations specified by the manufacturer.

◀◀ See "SIMMs and DIMMs," p. 437.

This recommendation does not necessarily limit you to purchasing memory upgrades only from the manufacturer. There are now many companies that manufacture memory upgrade modules for dozens of different portable systems, by reverse-engineering the original vendor's products. This adds a measure of competition to the market, usually making third-party modules much cheaper than those of a manufacturer that is far more interested in selling new computers for several thousand dollars rather than memory chips for a few hundred.

Note

Some companies have developed memory modules that exceed the original specifications of the system manufacturer, allowing you to install more memory than you could with the maker's own modules. Some manufacturers, such as IBM, have certification programs to signify their approval of these products. Otherwise, there is an element of risk involved in extending the system's capabilities in this way.

Inside the memory modules, the components are not very different from those of desktop systems. Portables use the same types of DRAM and SRAM as desktops, including memory technologies such as EDO (Enhanced Data Out), SDRAM (Synchronous DRAM), or RDRAM (Rambus DRAM). At one time, portable systems tended not to have memory caches because the SRAM chips typically used for this purpose generate a lot of heat. Advances in thermal management have now made this less of an issue, however, and you should expect a high-end system to include SRAM cache memory.

The best philosophy to take when adding RAM to a notebook or laptop computer is "fill 'er up!". Because of the proprietary (non-reusable) nature of portable memory modules, and because adding memory will speed up operations and extend battery life (due to less use of the hard drive for virtual memory swapping), it's wise to bring a notebook up to 64MB or RAM or higher, depending on the chipset and processor. I don't recommend installing more than 64MB in Pentium systems, because the chipsets do not support caching for any memory over 64MB. Pentium II/III or Celeron systems can cache 512MB or 4GB, so in those systems you can install as much memory as you can afford. Keep in mind that more memory means more power consumption and shorter battery life, so exceeding your needs by a wide margin won't help performance but will drain the battery faster. Since most notebook/laptop computers only have a single RAM connector, you need to keep that in mind when you upgrade, because any future upgrades will not add to what you already have, but replace it instead.

Hard Disk Drives

Hard disk drive technology is also largely unchanged in portable systems, except for the size of the disks and their packaging. Enhanced IDE drives are all but universal in portable computers. Internal hard drives typically use 2 1/2-inch platters and are 12.5mm or 19mm tall, depending on the size of the system.

As with memory modules, systems manufacturers have different ways of mounting hard drives in the system, which can cause upgrade compatibility problems. Some systems use a caddy to hold the drive and make the electrical and data connections to the system. This makes the physical part of an upgrade as easy as inserting a new drive into the caddy, and then mounting it in the system. In other cases, you might have to purchase a drive that has been specifically designed for your system, with the proper connectors built into it.

In many portables, replacing a hard drive is much simpler than in a desktop system. Quite a few manufacturers now design their portable systems with external bays that let you easily swap out hard drives without opening the case. Multiple users can share a single machine by snapping in their own hard drives, or you can use the same technique to load different operating systems on the same computer.

The most important aspect of hard drive upgrades that you must be aware of is the drive support provided by the system's BIOS. The BIOS in some systems, and particularly older ones, may offer limited hard drive size options. This is particularly true if your system was manufactured before 1995, when EIDE hard drives came into standard use. BIOSes made before this time support a maximum drive size of 528MB. In some cases, flash BIOS upgrades, which provide support for additional drives, might be available for your system.

◀◀ See "Motherboard BIOS," p. 349.

Many manufacturers have adapted the compact 2 1/2-inch hard drives on the market for after-market use in older notebooks, many of which have drives under 2GB in size. The kits usually start at about 3GB and can be as large as 20GB in size. Normally, you'll pay about two to three times per MB what you would for a desktop hard drive.

To make your upgrade of these systems as easy as possible, make sure you buy a data-transfer kit with the drive. These kits should come with a high-speed PC card (PCMCIA) connector for the new drive and data-transfer/drive preparation software to automate the switchover. Some of these kits can then be used to make the old hard drive a portable model that you can use through a connection via the PC card slot.

Another option for extending hard drive space is PC card hard drives. These are devices that fit into a type III PC card slot and can provide as much as 520MB of disk space in a remarkably tiny package (usually with a remarkably high price). You can also connect external drives to a portable PC, using a PC card SCSI host adapter or specialized parallel port drive interface. This frees you from the size limitations imposed by the system's case, and you can use any size SCSI drive you want, without concern for BIOS limitations.

Removable Media

Apart from hard disk drives, portable systems are now being equipped with other types of storage media that can provide access to larger amounts of data. CD-ROM drives are now available in many laptop and notebook systems, while a few include removable cartridge drives, such as Iomega's Zip drive. This has been made possible by the enhanced IDE specifications that let other types of devices share the same interface as the hard drive.

Another important issue is that of the floppy drive. Smaller systems (those under five pounds) often omit the floppy drive to save space, sometimes including an external unit. Some other systems enable you to substitute a second hard drive or battery for the floppy drive. For certain types of users, the lack of a floppy drive may or may not be an acceptable inconvenience. Many users of portables, especially those that frequently connect to networks, have little use for a floppy drive. This is now true even for the installation of applications, as virtually all software now ships on CD-ROMs.

One of the features that is becoming increasingly common in notebook systems is swappable drive bays that you can use to hold any one of several types of components. This arrangement lets you customize the configuration of your system to suit your immediate needs. For example, when traveling you might remove the floppy drive and replace it with an extra battery, or install a second hard drive when your storage needs increase. Notebook vendors and magazine reviews may refer to the number of spindles when discussing the number of drives a notebook can have installed simultaneously. For example, a computer that can use a floppy drive, CD-ROM, and hard drive simultaneously is a three-spindle system. If a system has two spindles, the most common configuration is a hard drive along with a bay that you can swap a floppy drive, CD-ROM drive, battery, or second hard drive in and out of. When evaluating your notebook needs and hardware, be sure to determine which devices included with a model can be used simultaneously and which require removing another device. If lightweight travel is a concern, determine which parts you don't need for travel that can be swapped out. Swappable bays should come with a cover or faceplate for the open bay to prevent dirt and foreign objects from entering when the bay is empty.

If you aren't satisfied with the removable media drives your current notebook offers, the PC card slot is once again your gateway to virtually unlimited choices. All the popular desktop choices, such as Zip, Jaz, LS-120 SuperDrive, CD-R, and CD-RW can be attached via either a dedicated PC card version of the drive or by using a SCSI PC card with a SCSI version of the drive.

While parallel port drives are also popular, you'll normally suffer a big speed drop for large file transfers, especially if you don't use the high-speed EPP/ECP IEEE-1284 LPT port modes. Also, consider using your USB ports, if your notebook/laptop computer is so equipped.

PC Cards (PCMCIA)

In an effort to give notebook computers the kind of expandability that users have grown used to in desktop systems, the Personal Computer Memory Card International Association (PCMCIA) has established several standards for credit card size expansion boards that fit into a small slot on laptops and notebooks. The development of the PC card interface is one of the few successful feats of hardware standardization in a market full of proprietary designs.

The PC card standards, which were developed by a consortium of more than 300 manufacturers (including IBM, Toshiba, and Apple), have been touted as being a revolutionary advancement in mobile computing. PC card laptop and notebook slots enable you to add memory expansion cards, fax/modems, SCSI adapters, network interface adapters, and many other types of devices to your system. If your computer has PC card slots that conform to the standard developed by the PCMCIA, you can insert any type of PC card (built to the same standard) into your machine and expect it to be recognized and usable.

The promise of PC card technology is enormous. There are not only PC card memory expansion cards, tiny hard drives, and wireless modems available, but also ISDN adapters, MPEG decoders, network interface adapters, sound cards, CD-ROM controllers, and even GPS systems, which use global positioning satellites to help you find your way by locating your exact position on Earth. Besides having use in nautical and aircraft environments, many newer automobiles include in-dash GPS systems that not only pinpoint your exact location, but give you directions to anywhere you'd like to go. If your car is not equipped with a factory-installed GPS system, you can use a notebook or laptop with a GPS receiver and mapping software to provide the same function.

Originally designed as a standard interface for memory cards, the PCMCIA document defines both the PC card hardware and the software support architecture used to run it. The PC cards defined in version 1 of the standard, called Type I, are credit card size (3.4×2.1 inches) and 3.3mm thick. The standard has since been revised to support cards with many other functions. The third version, called PC Card Specification - February 1995, defines three types of cards, with the only physical difference being their thickness. This was done to support the hardware for different card functions.

Most of the PC cards on the market today, such as modems and network interface adapters, are 5mm-thick Type II devices. Type III cards are 10.5mm thick, and are typically used for PC card hard drives. All the card types are backward compatible; you can insert a Type I card into a Type

II or III slot. The standard PC card slot configuration for portable computers is two Type II slots, with one on top of the other. This way, you can also insert a single Type III card, taking up both slots but using only one of the connectors.

Note

There was also a Type IV PC card, thicker still than the Type III, which was designed for higher capacity hard drives. This card type is not recognized by the PCMCIA, however, and is not included in the standard document. There is, therefore, no guarantee of compatibility between Type IV slots and devices, and they should generally be avoided.

The latest version of the standard, published in March 1997, includes many features designed to increase the speed and efficiency of the interface, such as

- DMA (direct memory access) support.
- 3.3v operation.
- Support for APM (Advanced Power Management).
- Plug-and-Play support.
- The PC card ATA standard, which lets manufacturers use the AT Attachment protocols to implement PC card hard disk drives.
- Support for multiple functions on a single card (such as a modem and a network adapter).
- The Zoomed Video (ZV) interface, a direct video bus connection between the PC card adapter and the system's VGA controller, allowing high-speed video displays for videoconferencing applications and MPEG decoders.
- A thermal ratings system that can be used to warn users of excessive heat conditions.
- CardBus, a 32-bit interface that runs at 33MHz and provides 32-bit data paths to the computer's I/O and memory systems, as well as a new shielded connector that prevents CardBus devices from being inserted into slots that do not support the latest version of the standard. This is a vast improvement over the 8- or 16-bit bus width and 8MHz speed of the original PC Card-16 interface. If you connect your portable computer to a 100Mbps network, CardBus can provide the high-speed interface that, in a desktop system, would be provided by PCI.

◄◄ See "DMA Channels," p. 320.

◄◄ See "Plug and Play BIOS," p. 400.

◄◄ See "ATA IDE," p. 512.

The PC card usually has a sturdy metal case, and is sealed except for the interface to the PCMCIA adapter in the computer at one end, which consists of 68 tiny pinholes. The other end of the card may contain a connector for a cable leading to a telephone line, a network, or some other external device.

The pinouts for the PC Card interface are shown in Table 23.8.

Table 23.8   Pinouts for a PCMCIA Card

Pin	Signal Name	Pin	Signal Name
1	Ground	35	Ground
2	Data 3	36	-Card Detect 1
3	Data 4	37	Data 11
4	Data 5	38	Data 12
5	Data 6	39	Data 13
6	Data 7	40	Data 14
7	-Card Enable 1	41	Data 15
8	Address 10	42	-Card Enable 2
9	-Output Enable	43	Refresh
10	Address 11	44	RFU (-IOR)
11	Address 9	45	RFU (–IOW)
12	Address 8	46	Address 17
13	Address 13	47	Address 18
14	Address 14	48	Address 19
15	-Write Enable/-Program	49	Address 20
16	Ready/-Busy (IREQ)	50	Address 21
17	+5V	51	+5V
18	Vpp1	52	Vpp2
19	Address 16	53	Address 22
20	Address 15	54	Address 23
21	Address 12	55	Address 24
22	Address 7	56	Address 25
23	Address 6	57	RFU
24	Address 5	58	RESET
25	Address 4	59	-WAIT
26	Address 3	60	RFU (-INPACK)
27	Address 2	61	-Register Select
28	Address 1	62	Battery Voltage Detect 2 (-SPKR)
29	Address 0	63	Battery Voltage Detect 1 (-STSCHG)
30	Data 0	64	Data 8
31	Data 1	65	Data 9
32	Data 2	66	Data 10
33	Write Protect (-IOIS16)	67	-Card Detect 2
34	Ground	68	Ground

PC Card Software Support

PC cards are by definition *hot-swappable*, meaning that with the proper software support you can remove a card from a slot and replace it with a different one without having to reboot the system. If your PC card devices and your operating system conform to the Plug-and-Play standard, inserting a new card into the slot causes the appropriate drivers for the device to be loaded and configured automatically.

To make this possible, two separate software layers are needed on the computer that provide the interface between the PCMCIA adapter (that controls the card slots) and the applications that use the services of the PC card devices (see Figure 23.12). These two layers are called Socket Services and Card Services. A third module, called an enabler, actually configures the settings of the PC cards.

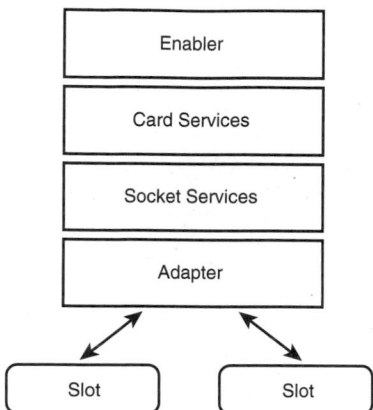

Figure 23.12 The Card and Socket Services enable an operating system to recognize the PC card inserted into a slot and configure the appropriate system hardware resources for the device.

Socket Services

The PCMCIA adapter that provides the interface between the card slots and the rest of the computer is one of the only parts of the PCMCIA architecture that is not standardized. There are many different adapters available to portable systems manufacturers and, as a result, an application or operating system cannot address the slot hardware directly, as it can a parallel or serial port.

Instead, there is a software layer called Socket Services that is designed to address a specific make of PCMCIA adapter hardware. The Socket Services software layer isolates the proprietary aspects of the adapter from all the software operating above it. The communications between the driver and the adapter may be unique, but the other interface, between the Socket Services driver and the Card Services software, is defined by the PCMCIA standard.

Socket Services can take the form of a device driver, a TSR program run from the DOS prompt (or the AUTOEXEC.BAT file), or a service running on an operating system such as Windows 9x or Windows NT. It is possible for a computer to have PC card slots with different adapters, as in the case of a docking station that provides extra slots in addition to those in the portable computer itself. In this case, the computer can run multiple Socket Services drivers, which all communicate with the same Card Services program.

Card Services

The Card Services software communicates with Socket Services and is responsible for assigning the appropriate hardware resources to PC cards. PC cards are no different from other types of bus expansion cards, in that they require access to specific hardware resources to communicate with the computer's processor and memory subsystems. If you have ever inserted an ISA network interface card into a desktop system, you know that you must specify a hardware interrupt, and maybe an I/O port or memory address for the card to operate.

A PC card network adapter requires the same hardware resources, but you don't manually configure the device using jumpers or a software utility as you would an ISA card. The problem is also complicated by the fact that the PCMCIA standard requires that the computer be capable of assigning hardware resources to different devices as they are inserted into a slot. Card Services addresses this problem by maintaining a collection of various hardware resources that it allots to devices as needed, and reclaims as the devices are removed.

If, for example, you have a system with two PC card slots, the Card Services software might be configured to use two hardware interrupts, two I/O ports, and two memory addresses, regardless of whether any cards are in the slots at boot time. No other devices in the computer can use those interrupts. When cards are inserted, Card Services assigns configuration values for the settings requested by the devices, ensuring that the settings allotted to each card are unique.

Card Services is not the equivalent of Plug and Play, although the two may seem similar. In fact, in Windows 9x, Card Services obtains the hardware resources it assigns to PC cards using Plug and Play. For other operating systems, the resources may be allotted to the Card Services program using a text file or command-line switches. In a non–Plug-and-Play system, you must configure the hardware resources assigned to Card Services with the same care that you would configure an ISA board. Although Card Services won't allow two PC cards to be assigned the same interrupt, there is nothing in the PCMCIA architecture to prevent conflicts between the resources assigned to Card Services and those of other devices in the system.

You can have multiple Socket Services drivers loaded on one system, but there can be only one Card Services program. Socket Services must always be loaded before Card Services.

Enablers

One of the oldest rules of PC configuration is that the software configuration must match that of the hardware. For example, if you configure a network interface card to use interrupt 10, you must also configure the network driver to use the same interrupt, so it can address the device. Today, this can be confusing because most hardware is configured not by physically manipulating jumpers or DIP switches, but by running a hardware configuration utility.

In spite of their other capabilities, neither Socket Services nor Card Services is capable of actually configuring the hardware settings of PC cards. This job is left to a software module called an enabler. The enabler receives the configuration settings assigned by Card Services and actually communicates with the PC card hardware itself to set the appropriate values.

Like Socket Services, the enabler must be designed to address the specific PC card that is present in the slot. In most cases, a PCMCIA software implementation includes a generic enabler, that is, one that can address many different types of PC cards. This, in most cases, lets you insert a completely new card into a slot and have it be recognized and configured by the software.

The problem with a generic enabler, and with the PCMCIA software architecture in general, is it requires a significant amount of memory to run. Because it must support many different cards, a generic enabler can require 50KB of RAM or more, plus another 50KB for the Card and Socket Services. For systems running DOS (with or without Windows 3.1), this is a great deal of conventional memory just to activate one or two devices. Once installed and configured, the PC card devices may also require additional memory for network, SCSI, or other device drivers.

Note

Windows 9x or Windows 2000 are the preferred operating systems for running PC card devices. The combination of their advanced memory management, Plug-and-Play capabilities, and the integration of the Card and Socket Services into the operating system makes the process of installing a PC card (usually) as easy as inserting it into the slot.

With Windows NT 4.0, for example, you have to shut down the system and reboot to change the PC card in a slot. What's more, it can be difficult to find Windows NT drivers for many of the PC cards on the market.

When memory is scarce, there can be an alternative to the generic enabler. A specific enabler is designed to address only a single specific PC card, and uses much less memory for that reason. Some PC cards ship with specific enablers that you can use in place of a generic enabler. However, it is also possible to use a specific enabler when you have a PC card that is not recognized by your generic enabler. You can load the specific enabler to address the unrecognized card, along with the generic enabler to address any other cards that you may use. This practice, of course, increases the memory requirements of the software.

Finally, you can avoid the overhead of generic enablers and the Card and Socket Services entirely by using what is known as a point enabler. A *point enabler* is a software module that is included with some PC cards that addresses the hardware directly, eliminating the need for Card and Socket Services. As a result, the point enabler removes the capability to hot swap PC cards and have the system automatically recognize and configure them. If, however, you intend to use the same PC cards all the time and have no need for hot swapping, point enablers can save you a tremendous amount of memory.

Keyboards

Unlike desktop systems, portables have keyboards that are integrated into the one-piece unit. This makes them difficult to repair or replace. The keyboard should also be an important element of your system purchasing decision, because manufacturers are forced to modify the standard 101-key desktop keyboard layout to fit in a smaller case.

The numeric keypad is always the first to go in a portable system's keyboard. Usually, its functionality is embedded into the alphanumeric keyboard and activated by a Function key combination. The Function (or Fn) key is an additional control key used on many systems to activate special features such as the use of an alternate display or keyboard.

Most portable systems today have keyboards that approach the size and usability of desktop models. This is a vast improvement over some older designs in which the keys were reduced to a point at which you could not comfortably touch-type with both hands. Standard conventions like the "inverted T" cursor keys also were modified, causing extreme user displeasure.

Some systems still have half-sized function keys, but one of the by-products of the larger screens found in many of today's portable systems is more room for the keyboard. Thus, many manufacturers are taking advantage of the extra space.

If you plan to perform a lot of numeric data entry with your portable computer, look for numeric keypads that plug into your system and override the embedded keypad on the right side of your keyboard, or use a standard 101-key keyboard if you're at your desk.

Standard keyboards are covered in depth in Chapter 17.

Pointing Devices

As with the layout and feel of the keyboard, pointing devices are a matter of personal taste. Most portable systems have pointing devices that conform to one of the three following types:

- *Trackball.* A small ball (usually about 1/2-inch) partially embedded in the keyboard below the spacebar, which is rolled by the user. While serviceable and accurate, trackballs have become unpopular, primarily due to their tendency to gather dust and dirt in the well that holds the ball, causing degraded performance.

- *Trackpoint.* Developed by IBM and adopted by many other manufacturers, the trackpoint is a small (about 1/4-inch) rubberized button located between the G, H, and B keys of the keyboard. It looks like a pencil eraser and can be nudged in any direction to move the cursor around the screen. The trackpoint is convenient because you can manipulate it without taking your hands off the keyboard. On some earlier models, the rubber cover tended to wear off after heavy use. Newer versions are made of sturdier materials with a grippy surface similar to a cat's tongue.

  The Trackpoint is generally considered the best pointing device for portable systems— certainly for those who touch type. It is the most efficient, easiest to use (for most people), and the most reliable.

- *Trackpad.* The trackpad or touchpad is an electromagnetically sensitive pad, usually about 1×2 inches, that responds to the movement of a finger across its surface. Mouse clicks can be simulated by tapping the pad. Trackpads have great potential, but tend to be overly sensitive to accidental touches, causing undesired cursor movements and especially unwanted mouse clicks. Trackpads are also sensitive to humidity and moist fingers, resulting in unpredictable performance.

Some systems allow users a choice by providing both a trackpoint and a trackpad. Unfortunately, on most of the systems that do this, the two devices use the same interrupt, forcing you to select one device or the other in the system BIOS, rather than letting you use both at the same time.

Note

If you have a trackpad-equipped computer and want to use a mouse with it, don't assume that the trackpad is disabled automatically by the presence of the mouse. Regardless of whether you use a PS/2 mouse or a serial mouse, it may be necessary on some systems to go into the portable's BIOS Setup program and disable the trackpad to avoid accidental cursor movement.

Another important part of the pointer arrangement is the location of the primary and secondary buttons. Some systems locate the buttons in peculiar configurations that require unnatural contortions to perform a click-and-drag operation. Pointing devices are definitely a feature of a portable system that you should test drive before you make a purchase. As an alternative, remember that nearly all portables have a serial port or PS/2 port that you can use to attach an external mouse to the system, when your workspace permits.

Batteries

Battery life is one of the biggest complaints users have about portable systems. Although a great deal has been done to improve the power management capabilities of today's portable computers, the hardware configuration of a fully equipped portable system dissipates 90 percent more power than it did three years ago, and that trend is still continuing. The efficiency of a computer's power use may also have doubled in the last two years, but battery technology has not improved at anything approaching the same rate, leaving the battery life of a typical portable system approximately the same as it was before.

The goal sought by many mobile users has been the same for many years: a full-featured portable system that can run on a single battery for the entire duration of a transcontinental U.S. airplane flight. Unfortunately, the industry seems to be no closer to approaching this goal than it was several years ago. Users typically have to carry two or more battery packs for a six-hour flight, and while mobile power technologies are improving, so are the demands of today's systems. However, while typical battery life has remained in the two- to three-hour range for most reputable manufacturers, the new notebooks have the advantage of having larger hard drives, bigger and brighter screens, more RAM, faster processors, integrated speakers, and CD-ROM drives. Based on the increasing popularity of these notebook systems, the buying consumer has clearly voiced that a more powerful notebook with continuing average battery life is more important and useful than a system that would run for 6–10 hours but sacrifice features they have grown used to using.

For users who simply must have a system that can run for 6–10 hours, check for airlines that are adding at-seat power connections designed for notebook computers. Or, consider using a Windows CE computer equipped with a reasonable facsimile of your favorite word-processor or spreadsheet program.

Battery Types

The battery technology also plays a major role in the portable power issue, of course. Most portable systems today use one of four battery types:

- *Nickel Cadmium (NiCad)*. As the oldest of the four technologies, nickel cadmium batteries are rarely used in portable systems today, because of their shorter life and sensitivity to improper charging and discharging. The life of the battery's charge can be shortened by as much as 40 percent if the battery is not fully discharged before recharging, or if it is overcharged. Permanent damage to the cell can be prevented by periodically discharging it to 1 volt or less. Despite this "memory" effect, however, NiCad batteries hold a charge well when not in use, losing 10 percent of their capacity in the first 24 hours and approximately 10 percent per month after that, and can be recharged 1,500 times or more.

- *Nickel Metal-Hydride (NiMH).* More expensive than NiCads, NiMH batteries have approximately a 30 percent longer life than NiCads, are less sensitive to the memory effect caused by improper charging and discharging, and do not use the environmentally dangerous substances found in NiCads. They have a recommended discharge current that is lower than that of a NiCad battery (one-fifth to one-half of the rated capacity), a self-discharge rate that is 1 1/2 to 2 times greater than that of a NiCad, and can be recharged as many as 500 times. NiMH batteries also require nearly twice as long to recharge as NiCads. While they are still used in many portable systems, NiMH batteries are now found mostly in computers at the lower end of the price range.

- *Lithium-Ion (Li-ion).* As the current industry standard, Li-ion batteries are longer-lived than either NiCad or NiMH technologies, cannot be overcharged, and hold a charge well when not in use. Batteries that use lithium—one of the lightest of all metals, with the greatest electrochemical potential, and providing the largest energy content—have been manufactured since the 1970s. However, lithium is also an unstable substance, and some battery explosions resulted in a large number of battery recalls in the early 1990s. Subsequent models were manufactured using lithium ions from chemicals such as lithium-cobalt dioxide (LiCoO2). Despite a slightly lower energy density, Li-ion batteries are much safer than the lithium designs. Various types of Li-ion batteries use different active materials for their negative electrodes; there are coke and two graphite versions that have slightly different voltage characteristics. Li-ion batteries can also support the heavy-duty power requirements of today's high-end systems, and modern versions can be recharged up to 1,000 times or more. Unlike NiCad and NiMH batteries, which can be used in the same system without modification to the circuitry, Li-ion batteries can only be used in systems specifically designed for them. Inserting a Li-ion battery into a system designed for a NiCad or NiMH can result in a fire. Although the most expensive of the four technologies, Li-ion batteries have come to be used in all but the very low end of the portable system market.

- *Lithium-Ion Polymer.* This is a fourth battery type that has been in development for several years, but which is only now appearing on the market. Lithium-ion polymer batteries are manufactured using a lithium ion and cobalt oxide cell with a proprietary polymer electrolyte, and can be formed into flat sheets as small as 1mm thick and of almost any size. Thus, a thin battery panel can be fitted into a portable computer behind the LCD panel. Lithium-ion polymer batteries provide an energy density that is four times better than a NiCad and a charge life that is 40 percent longer than a Li-ion battery, at one-fifth the weight. This battery technology provides up to 500 charges and is immune to the memory effect that can prevent NiCad and NiMH batteries from recharging fully. Once they are manufactured in sufficient quantities, lithium-ion polymer batteries could replace the bulky battery packs used today in portable systems.

Note

All the battery types in use today function best when they are completely discharged before being recharged. In fact, batteries that have gone unused for several months should be conditioned by putting them through three full discharge/recharge cycles. Lithium-ion batteries are affected the least by incomplete discharging and have a higher discharge cut-off point (2.5–3v versus 1v for NiCads), but the effect on the life of future charges is still noticeable. When storing charged batteries, refrigerating them helps them to retain their charges for longer periods, although you should always allow the battery to return fully to room temperature and be sure that it is dry before putting it in the computer to prevent condensation from forming in the computer.

Unfortunately, buying a portable computer with a more efficient battery does not necessarily mean that you will realize a longer charge life. Power consumption depends on the components installed in the system, the power management capabilities provided by the system software, and the size of the battery itself. Some manufacturers, for example, when moving from NiMH to Li-ion batteries, see this as an opportunity to save some space inside the computer. They decide that because they are using a more efficient power storage technology, they can make the battery smaller and still deliver the same performance.

Battery technology trails behind nearly all the other subsystems found in a portable computer, as far as the development of new innovations is concerned. Because of the continuing trend of adding more features and components to mobile computers, their power consumption has risen enormously in recent years, and power systems have barely been capable of keeping up. On a high-end laptop system, a battery life of three hours is very good, even with all the system's power-management features activated.

One other way that manufacturers are addressing the battery life problem is by designing systems that are capable of carrying two batteries. The inclusion of multipurpose bays within the system's case enables users to replace the floppy or CD-ROM drive with a second battery pack, effectively doubling the computer's charge life.

Power Management

There are various components in a computer that do not need to run continuously while the system is turned on. Mobile systems often conserve battery power by shutting down these components based on the activities of the user. If, for example, you open a text file in an editor and the entire file is read into memory, there is no need for the hard drive to spin while you are working on the file.

After a certain period of inactivity, a power management system can park the hard drive heads and stop the platters from spinning until you save the file to disk or issue any other command that requires drive access. Other components, such as floppy and CD-ROM drives and PC cards, can also be powered down when not in use, resulting in a significant reduction of the power needed to run the system.

Most portables also have systemic power saver modes that suspend the operation of the entire system when it is not in use. The names assigned to these modes can differ, but there are usually two system states that differ in that one continues to power the system's RAM while the other does not. Typically, a "suspend" mode shuts down virtually the entire system after a preset period of inactivity except for the memory. This requires only a small amount of power and allows the system to be reawakened almost instantaneously.

Portable systems usually have a "hibernate" mode, as well, which writes the current contents of the system's memory to a special file on the hard disk, and then shuts down the system, erasing memory as well. When the computer is reactivated, it reads the contents of the file back into memory and work can continue. The reactivation process takes a bit longer in this case, but the system conserves more power by shutting down the memory array.

Note

The memory swap file used for hibernate mode may, in some machines, be located in a special partition on the hard drive dedicated to this purpose. If you inadvertently destroy this partition, you may need a special utility from the system manufacturer to re-create the file.

In most cases, these functions are defined by the APM (Advanced Power Management) standard, a document developed jointly by Intel and Microsoft that defines an interface between an operating system power-management policy driver and the hardware-specific software that addresses devices with power-management capabilities. This interface is usually implemented in the system BIOS.

◄◄ See "Advanced Power Management," p. 1122.

However, as power management techniques continue to develop, it becomes increasingly difficult for the BIOS to maintain the complex information states needed to implement more advanced functions. There is, therefore, another standard that has been developed by Intel, Microsoft, and Toshiba called ACPI (the Advanced Configuration and Power Interface), which is designed to implement power-management functions in the operating system. Microsoft Windows 98 automatically uses ACP if ACPI functions are found in the system BIOS when Windows 98 is first installed. The need to update system BIOSes for ACPI support is one reason many computer vendors have recommended performing a BIOS update before installing Windows 98.

◄◄ See "Power Management Menu," p. 391.

Placing power management under the control of the OS allows for a greater interaction with applications. For example, a program can indicate to the operating system which of its activities are crucial, forcing an immediate activation of the hard drive, and which can be delayed until the next time that the drive is activated for some other reason.

Peripherals

There are a great many add-on devices available for use with portable systems that provide functions that cannot practically or economically be included inside the system itself. Many of the most common uses for portable systems may require additional hardware, either because of the computer's location or the requirements of the function. The following sections discuss some of the most common peripherals used with portable systems.

External Displays

High-end laptop systems are often used to host presentations to audiences that can range in size from the boardroom to the auditorium. For all but the smallest groups of viewers, some means of enlarging the computer display is needed. Most portable systems are equipped with a standard VGA jack that allows the connection of an external monitor.

Systems typically allow the user to choose whether the display should be sent to the internal, the external, or both displays, as controlled by a keystroke combination or the system BIOS. Depending on the capabilities of the video display adapter in the computer, you may be able to use a greater display resolution on an external monitor than you would on the LCD panel.

For environments where the display of a standard monitor is not large enough, there are several alternatives, as discussed in the following sections.

◄◄ See "LCD Displays," p. 806.

Overhead LCD Display Panels

An LCD display panel is something like the LCD screen in your computer except that there is no back on it, making the display transparent. The display technologies and screen resolution options are the same as those for the LCD displays in portable systems, although most of the products on the market use active-matrix displays.

You use an LCD panel by placing it on an ordinary overhead projector, causing the image on the panel to be projected onto a screen (or wall). Because they are not intended solely for use with portable systems, these devices typically include a pass-through cable arrangement, allowing a connection to a standard external monitor, as well as the panel.

While they are serviceable for training and internal use, overhead display panels do not usually deliver the depth and vibrancy of color that can add to the excitement of a sales presentation. The quality of the image is also dependent on the brightness of the lamp used to display it. While the panel itself is fairly small and lightweight, overhead projectors frequently are not. Overhead projectors with sufficient power to produce a bright display through an LCD panel are very expensive and sometimes difficult to rent. If a projector is already available at the presentation site, the LCD panel is a convenient way of enlarging your display. If, however, you are in a position where you must travel to a remote location and supply the overhead projector yourself, you are probably better off with a self-contained LCD projector.

Overhead display panels are not cheap. You will probably have to pay more for one than you paid for your computer. However, on a few models of the IBM ThinkPad, you can remove the top cover that serves as the back of the display and use the computer's own LCD screen as an overhead panel.

LCD Projectors

An LCD projector is essentially a self-contained unit that is a combination of a transparent display panel and a projector. The unit connects to a VGA jack, such as a regular monitor, and frequently includes speakers that connect with a separate cable. Not all LCD projectors are portable; some are intended for permanent installations. The portable models vary in weight, display technologies, and the brightness of the lamp, which is measured in lumens.

A 16-pound unit delivering 500 ANSI lumens is usually satisfactory for a conference room environment; a larger room may require a projector delivering 750 ANSI lumens or more and weighing up to 25 pounds. LCD projectors tend to deliver images that are far superior to those of overhead panels, and they offer a one-piece solution to the image-enlargement problem. However, you have to pay dearly for the convenience. Prices of LCD projectors can range from $3,000 to well over $10,000, but if your business relies on your presentations, the cost may be justified.

For best results, match the resolution of your projector to the native resolution of your notebook computer. If your notebook computer has a 1024×768 resolution screen, make sure your projector offers this same resolution without tricks like scaling or compression. Having the projector and your built-in screen match will permit most systems to use simultaneous display, a great benefit for presenters.

TV-Out

One of the simplest display solutions is a feature that is being incorporated into many of the high-end laptop systems on the market today. It allows you to connect the computer to a standard television set. Called TV-out, various systems provide support for either the North American NTSC television standard, the European PAL standard, or both. Once connected, a software program lets you calibrate the picture on the TV screen.

TV-out is becoming a popular feature on high-end video adapters for desktop systems as well as portables. There are also some manufacturers that are producing external boxes that plug into any computer's VGA port and a television set to provide an external TV display solution. The products convert the digital VGA signal to an analog output that typically can be set to use the NTSC or PAL standard.

Obviously, TV-out is an extremely convenient solution, as it provides an image size that is limited only by the type of television available, costs virtually nothing, and adds no extra weight to the presenter's load (unless you have to bring the TV yourself). You can also connect your computer to a VCR and record your presentation on standard videotape. However, the display resolution of a television set does not approach that of a computer monitor, and the picture quality suffers as a result. This is particularly noticeable when displaying images that contain a lot of text, such as presentation slides and Web pages. It is recommended that you test the output carefully with various size television screens before using TV-out in a presentation environment.

Use simple sans-serif fonts like Arial or Helvetica in presentations and limit the amount of text on any given screen to achieve best results with TV-out devices.

Docking Stations

Now that many portable systems are being sold as replacements for standard desktop computers, docking stations are becoming increasingly popular. A *docking station* is a desktop unit to which you attach (or dock) your portable system when you are at your home or office. At the very least, a docking station provides an AC power connection, a full-size keyboard, a standard desktop mouse, a complete set of input and output ports, and a VGA jack for a standard external monitor.

Once docked, the keyboard and display in the portable system are deactivated, but the other components—particularly the processor, memory, and hard drive—remain active. You are essentially running the same computer but using a standard full-size desktop interface. Docking stations can also contain a wide array of other features, such as a network interface adapter, external speakers, additional hard disk or CD-ROM drives, additional PC card slots, and a spare battery charger.

An operating system such as Windows 9x or Windows 2000 can maintain multiple hardware profiles for a single machine. A *hardware profile* is a collection of configuration settings for the devices accessible to the system. To use a docking station, you create one profile for the portable system in its undocked state, and another that adds support for the additional hardware available while docked.

The use of a docking station eliminates much of the tedium involved in maintaining separate desktop and portable systems. With two machines, you must install your applications twice and continually keep the data between the two systems synchronized. This is traditionally done using a network connection or the venerable null modem cable (a crossover cable used to transfer files between systems by connecting their parallel or serial ports). With a docking station and a suitably equipped portable, you can achieve the best of both worlds.

Docking stations are highly proprietary items that are designed for use with specific computer models. Prices vary widely depending on the additional hardware provided, but because a docking station lacks a CPU, memory, and a display, the cost is usually not excessive.

For systems that lack the docking station option or for those which seem too expensive, consider the less expensive port replicator. While it lacks drive bays and may not feature a network interface card, even the simplest ones offer connectors for video, printer, serial, and keyboard/mouse, which enables you to use more comfortable devices. Because a port replicator is simpler, you may not even need to use the multiple hardware profiles of Windows 9x.

One economic concern for both docking stations and port replicators is that any given model will work with just a few computer models at most. If you plan to change computers frequently and are also looking to increase the number of printer and serial ports you have, consider the Universal Port Replicators available from Mobility Electronics. These units feature serial, parallel, PS/2 mouse and PS/2 keyboard connectors, as well as a PC card slot. Mobility also offers model-specific port replicators for most popular notebook computer models.

Connectivity

One of the primary uses for portable computers is to keep in touch with the home office while traveling by using a modem. Because of this, many hotels and airports are starting to provide telephone jacks for use with modems, but there are still many places where finding a place to plug into a phone line can be difficult. There are products on the market, however, which can help you overcome these problems, even if you are traveling overseas.

Line Testers

Many hotels use digital PBXs for their telephone systems, which typically carry more current than standard analog lines. This power is needed to operate additional features on the telephone, such as message lights and LCD displays. This additional current can permanently damage your modem without warning, and unfortunately, the jacks used by these systems are the same standard RJ-11 connectors used by traditional telephones.

To avoid this problem, you can purchase a line-testing device for about $50 that plugs into a wall jack and measures the amount of current on the circuit. It then informs you whether it is safe to plug in your modem.

Acoustic Couplers

On those occasions when you cannot plug your modem into the phone jack, or when there is no jack available (such as at a pay phone), the last resort is an acoustic coupler. The acoustic coupler is an ancient telecommunications device that predates the system of modular jacks used to connect telephones today. To connect to a telephone line, the coupler plugs into your modem's RJ-11 jack at one end and clamps to a telephone handset at the other end. A speaker at the mouthpiece and a microphone at the earpiece allow the audible signals generated by the modem and the phone system to interact.

The acoustic coupler may be an annoying bit of extra baggage to have to carry with you, but it is the one foolproof method for connecting to any telephone line without having to worry about international standards, line current, or wiring.

The Traveler's Survival Kit

For successful computing on the road, have these with you at all times:

- Your operating system installation files (on CD-ROM or on your hard drive)
- A 56Kbps modem and 10BaseT or dual-speed Ethernet card (can be combo)
- Replacement "dongle" connectors for the modem and network card(s)
- Portable surge protector with RJ11 phone-line protection
- Line couplers that allow you to extend your modem and network card "dongles" with standard RJ11 and RJ45 cables
- Lightweight "Christmas-tree style" extension cord for powering your notebook computer (if it uses ungrounded polarized line cord)
- List of local dial-up numbers for your national ISP (America Online, CompuServe, CompuServe 2000, and so on)
- Spare media for your diskette, ZIP, LS-120 drive
- Tech-support Web sites and phone numbers

Building or Upgrading Systems

SOME OF THE MAIN TOPICS IN THIS CHAPTER ARE

System Components
Case and Power Supply
Motherboard
Floppy Disk and Removable Drives
Hard Disk Drive
CD/DVD-ROM Drive
Keyboard and Pointing Device (Mouse)
Video Card and Display
Sound Card and Speakers
USB Peripherals
Accessories
Hardware and Software Resources
System Assembly and Disassembly
Assembly Preparation
Motherboard Installation
Troubleshooting New Installations
Installing the Operating System
Disassembly/Upgrading Preparation

System Components

In these days of commodity parts and component pricing, building your own system from scratch is no longer the daunting process it once was. Every component necessary to build a PC system is available off the shelf at competitive pricing. In many cases, the system you build can use the same or even better components than the top name-brand systems.

There are, however, some cautions to heed. The main thing to note is that you rarely save money when building your own system; purchasing a complete system from a mail-order vendor or mass merchandiser is almost always less expensive. The reason for this is simple: Most system vendors who build systems to order use many, if not all the same components you can use when building your own system. The difference is that they buy these components in quantity and receive a much larger discount than you can by purchasing only one of a particular item.

In addition, there is only one shipping and handling charge when you purchase a complete system instead of the multiple shipping charges when you purchase separate components. In fact, the shipping, handling, and phone charges from ordering all the separate parts needed to build a PC often add up to $100 or more. This cost rises if you encounter problems with any of the components and have to make additional calls or send improper or malfunctioning parts back for replacement.

It is clear that the reasons for building a system from scratch often have less to do with saving money and more to do with the experience you gain and the results you achieve. In the end, you have a custom system that contains the exact components and features you have selected. Most of the time when you buy a preconfigured system, you have to compromise in some way. For example, you may get the video adapter you want, but you would prefer a different make or model of motherboard. By building your own system, you can select the exact components you want and build the ultimate system for your needs. The experience is also very rewarding. You know exactly how your system is constructed and configured because you have done it yourself. This makes future support and installation of additional accessories much easier.

Another benefit of building your own system is that you are guaranteed a non-proprietary system that will be easily upgradable in the future. Of course if you have been reading the book up to this point, you already know everything you need to ensure any preassembled systems you purchase would be non-proprietary and, therefore, upgradable and repairable in the future.

It may be possible to save some money using components from your current system when building your new system. You might have recently upgraded your hard drive and memory in an attempt to extend the life of your current computer. In most cases, you can take those components with you to the new system if you plan appropriately. For example, if you used 72-pin SIMMs in your old system, you can buy a new motherboard that supports both 72-pin SIMMs and 168-pin DIMMs. Unfortunately, most of these boards won't allow mixing SIMMs and DIMMs, meaning you can either use your old memory or get new DIMM memory, but not use both in the same board. Boards that use the newer RIMM modules won't accept any of your existing memory.

So if you are interested in a rewarding experience, want a customized and fully upgradable system that is not exactly the same as that offered by any vendor, are able to take on all system repair and troubleshooting tasks, want to save some money by reusing some of the components from your current system, and are not in a hurry, building your own PC might be the way to go. On the other hand, if you are interested in getting a PC with the most value for the best price, you want one-stop support for in-warranty repairs and technical problems, and you need an operational system quickly, building your own system should definitely be avoided.

This chapter details the components needed to assemble your own system, explains the assembly procedures, and lists some recommendations for components and their sources.

The components used in building a typical PC are

- Case and power supply
- Motherboard
- Processor with heat sink
- Memory
- Floppy drive
- Hard disk drive
- CD-ROM/DVD drive
- Keyboard
- Pointing device (mouse)
- Video card and display
- Sound card and speakers
- Cooling fans
- Cables
- Hardware (nuts, bolts, screws, and brackets)
- Operating system software

Each of these components is discussed in the following sections.

Case and Power Supply

The case and power supply are usually sold as a unit, although some vendors do sell them separately. There are several designs to choose from, usually dependent on the motherboard form factory you want to use, the number of drive bays available, and whether the system is desktop or floor mounted. For most custom-built systems, an ATX mid-tower case and power supply is the recommended choice. Cases designed for the older Baby-AT motherboard form factor are still available, but the ATX architecture offers considerable improvements. The size and shape of the case, power supply, and even the motherboard are called the *form factor*. Themost popular case form factors are

- Full Tower
- Mini-Tower

Since the chipset really *is* the motherboard, the chipset used in a given motherboard has a profound effect on the performance of the board. It dictates all the performance parameters and limitations of the board, such as memory size and speed, processor types and speeds, supported buses and their speeds, and more. If you plan to incorporate newer technologies such as the Accelerated Graphics Port (AGP) or the Universal Serial Bus (USB) into your system, you must be sure that your motherboard has a chipset that supports these features.

Because chipsets are constantly being introduced and improved over time, I cannot list all of them and their functions, however you will find a detailed description of many of them in Chapter 4. There are several popular high-performance chipsets on the market today. The best of these offer support for SDRAM (Synchronous DRAM) or RDRAM (Rambus DRAM) memory, PCI and AGP busses, Advanced Configuration and Power Interface (ACPI), and Ultra-DMA ATA (IDE) support.

Intel is by far the most popular manufacturer of chipsets in the world, which is not surprising as the development of new chipsets parallels the introduction of new processors. There are other chipset manufacturers, but as Intel releases new processor models at an ever increasing rate, it becomes more difficult for other developers to keep up. In many cases you can use the Intel-compatible processors manufactured by other companies, such as AMD and Cyrix, with motherboards containing Intel chipsets.

◀◀ See "Chipsets," p. 235.

◀◀ See "Knowing What to Look For," p. 338.

Clearly, the selection of a chipset must be based largely on the processor you choose and the additional components you intend to install in the computer.

However, no matter what chipset you look for, I recommend checking for the following supported features:

- SDRAM or RDRAM (main memory)
- ECC (Error Correcting Code) memory support
- ACPI (Advanced Configuration and Power Interface) energy-saving functions
- AGP 2x or 4x
- Dual Ultra-ATA33 or Ultra-ATA66 ATA interfaces

Most of the better chipsets on the market today should have these features. If you are intent on building the ultimate PC (at least by this week's standards), you will also want to consider the fastest processors available. Chipsets designed for these processors should include support for the latest technologies, such as the 133MHz system bus and the accelerated graphics port (AGP). Be sure not to waste your investment on the most capable processor by using a chipset that doesn't fully exploit its capabilities.

Most motherboards manufactured today use both the ISA and PCI expansion buses, although the ISA bus is being eliminated from many newer motherboards. When you are designing your system, carefully consider the number and type of expansion cards that you intend to install. Then, make sure that the motherboard you select has the correct number of slots and that they are of the correct bus type for your peripherals (ISA, PCI, and AGP). Because many newer boards don't have ISA slots, it might be time to get rid of any ISA boards you have and replace them with more capable PCI versions.

When you buy a motherboard, I highly recommend you contact the chipset manufacturer and obtain the documentation (usually called the data book) for your particular chipset. This will explain how the memory and cache controllers, as well as many other devices in the system, operate. This documentation should also describe the Advanced Chipset Setup functions in your system's Setup program. With this information, you may be able to fine-tune the motherboard configuration by altering the chipset features. Because chipsets are frequently discontinued and replaced with newer models, don't wait too long to get the chipset documentation, as most manufacturers make it available only for chips currently in production.

Note

One interesting fact about chipsets is that in the volume that the motherboard manufacturers purchase them, the chipsets usually cost about $40 each. If you have an older motherboard that needs repair, you normally cannot purchase the chipset because they are usually not stocked by the manufacturer after they are discontinued. Not to mention that most chipsets feature surface mounting with ball grid array (BGA) packages that are extremely difficult to remove manually and replace. The low-cost chipset is one of the reasons why motherboards have become disposable items that are rarely, if ever, repaired.

BIOS

Another important feature on the motherboard is the BIOS (basic input/output system). This is also called the ROM BIOS because the code is stored in a read-only memory (ROM) chip. There are several things to look for here. One is that the BIOS is supplied by one of the major BIOS manufacturers such as AMI (American Megatrends International), Phoenix, Award, or Microid Research. Also, make sure that the BIOS is contained in a special type of reprogrammable chip called a Flash ROM or EEPROM (Electrically Erasable Programmable Read Only Memory). This will allow you to download BIOS updates from the manufacturer and, using a program they supply, easily update the code in your BIOS. If you do not have the Flash ROM or EEPROM type, you will have to physically replace the chip if an update is required.

◄◄ See "Upgrading the BIOS," p. 363.

Make sure that the motherboard and BIOS support the Plug-and-Play (PnP) specification. This will make installing new cards, especially PnP cards, much easier. PnP automates the installation and uses special software built into the BIOS and the operating system (such as Windows 95/98 and Windows 2000) to automatically configure adapter cards and resolve adapter resource conflicts.

◄◄ See "See Plug-and-Play BIOS," p. 400.

Memory

Older systems had L2 cache memory on the motherboard, but for almost all newer systems this cache is now a part of the processor. Socket 7 or Super7 motherboards do still include cache on-board, and it is normally soldered in and non-removable or upgradable.

◀◀ See "Cache Memory: SRAM," p. 419.

Most Super7 motherboards support at least 1–2MB of cache memory.

For Pentium Pro/II/III and Celeron systems, no additional L2 memory is needed because the processors have the cache memory integrated into the processor package.

Main memory is normally installed in the form of SIMMs (Single Inline Memory Modules), DIMMs (Dual Inline Memory Modules), or RIMMs (Rambus Inline Memory Modules). There are three different physical types of main memory modules used in PC systems today, with several variations of each. The three main types are as follows:

- 72-pin SIMMs
- 168-pin DIMMs
- 184-pin RIMMs

The 168-pin DIMMs are by far the most common type of memory module used today; however, just a few years ago, most systems came with 72-pin SIMMs. Most systems use the DIMMs because they are 64 bits wide and can be used as a single bank on a Pentium or higher class processors that have a 64-bit external data bus. The newest and fastest systems use the RIMMs, which offer the greatest performance of the available memory types.

◀◀ See "Physical RAM Memory," p. 435.

A 64-bit Pentium class system requires two 72-pin SIMMs (32 bits wide each) or a single 168-pin DIMM (64 bits wide) to make a single bank.

Memory modules can include an extra bit for each eight for parity checking or ECC use. Make sure your chipset (and motherboard) supports ECC before purchasing the more expensive ECC modules.

◀◀ See "Parity and ECC," p. 457.

Another thing to watch out for is the type of metal on the memory module contacts. They are available with either tin- or gold-plated contacts. Although it might seem that gold-plated contacts are better (they are), you should not use them in all systems. You should instead always match the type of plating on the module contacts to what is also used on the socket contacts. In other words, if the motherboard SIMM, DIMM, or RIMM sockets have tin-plated contacts, you must use modules with tin-plated contacts. Most motherboards with SIMM sockets used tin-plated ones requiring tin-plated SIMMs, while most DIMM and RIMM sockets are gold-plated, requiring gold-plated DIMMs and RIMMs.

If you mix dissimilar metals (tin with gold), corrosion on the tin side is rapidly accelerated, and tiny electrical currents are generated. The combination of the corrosion and tiny currents causes havoc, and all types of memory problems and errors may occur. In some systems, I have observed that everything seems fine for about a year, during which the corrosion develops. After that, random memory errors result. Removing and cleaning the memory module and socket contacts postpones the problem for another year, and then the problems return again. How would you like this problem if you had 100 or more systems to support? Of course, you can avoid these problems if you insist on using SIMMs with contacts whose metal matches the metal found in the sockets in which they will be installed.

◀◀ See "Gold Versus Tin," p. 453.

For more information on PC memory of all types, see Chapter 6, "Memory."

I/O Ports

Most motherboards today have built-in I/O ports. If these ports are not built in, they will have to be supplied via a plug-in expansion board that, unfortunately, wastes an expansion slot. The following ports should be included in any new system you assemble:

- Keyboard connector (mini-DIN type)
- Mouse port (mini-DIN type)
- One or two serial ports (16550A buffered UART type)
- Parallel port (EPP/ECP type)
- Dual USB ports
- Optional display connector (integrated video)
- Optional audio/game connectors (MIDI/joystick, speaker, and microphone)
- Two local bus enhanced IDE ports (primary and secondary)
- Floppy controller

Many motherboards feature the optional integrated video and sound interfaces.

All the integrated ports are supported either directly by the motherboard chipset or by an additional super I/O chip and additional interface components. Adding the optional video and sound interfaces directly to the motherboard saves both money and the use of an expansion slot, especially important in the less expensive systems sold today.

If these devices are not present on the motherboard, various super or multi-I/O boards that implement all these ports are available. Again, most of the newer versions of these boards use a single-chip implementation because it is cheaper and more reliable.

◀◀ See "Super I/O Chips," p. 267.

It has become an increasingly popular practice in recent years (especially in Slimline-style systems) to integrate other standard computer functions into the motherboard design, such as video, sound, and even network adapters. The advantages of this practice include freeing up expansion slots that would normally be occupied by separate adapter cards and saving money. The price difference between a motherboard with integrated video and sound and one without would be far less than the cost of good-quality sound and video cards.

The drawback, of course, is that you have little or no choice about the features or quality of the integrated adapters. Integrated components like these are nearly always of serviceable quality, but they certainly do not push the performance envelope of higher end expansion cards. Most people who decide to build a system themselves do so because they want optimum performance from every component, which you do not get from integrated video and sound.

Buying a motherboard with integrated adapters, however, does not preclude you from adding expansion devices of the same type. You can usually install a video or sound card into a system with an integrated sound adapter without major problems, except that the additional cost of the integrated component is wasted. You may also encounter difficulties with the automated hardware detection routines in operating systems, such as Windows 9x detecting the wrong adapter in your system, but you can remedy this by manually identifying the expansion card to the OS.

Note that if your motherboard has integrated devices such as video and sound, you must normally go into the BIOS Setup to disable these devices if you want to add a card-based replacement device. Check your BIOS Setup menus for an Enable/Disable setting for any integrated devices.

Floppy Disk and Removable Drives

Since the advent of the CD-ROM, the floppy disk drive has largely been relegated to a minor role as an alternative system boot device. Usually, today's systems are equipped with a 1.44MB 3 1/2-inch drive, but 2.88MB drives and 120MB SuperDisk drives are also available. All boards today have full support for the LS-120 (SuperDisk) drives, which is a floppy drive that can read and write not only the standard 720KB and 1.44MB formats, but a high-capacity 120MB format as well. Because, unlike Zip drives, they are fully BIOS supportable and therefore bootable. They are a true non-proprietary industry standard, and they are much more reliable than Zip drives. I recommend the SuperDisk drives over Zip unless you must exchange data with other systems that already have Zip drives.

There is another advantage of the SuperDisk drive over Zip. Since the SuperDisk drive functions as a standard floppy as well as a 120MB floppy, you don't need a standard floppy along with a SuperDisk drive. If you use a Zip drive, you will need to install a conventional floppy for backward compatibility, system configuration, and system maintenance issues. Note that many newer motherboards only support a single floppy drive, not two like in most previous boards.

For additional removable storage, I recommend a CD-R (CD-Recordable) or CD-RW (CD-Rewritable) drive. These are now relatively inexpensive and the CD-R media is incredibly cheap. This allows an easy way to back up or archive up to 650MB of data.

Hard Disk Drive

Your system also needs at least one hard disk drive. In most cases, a drive with a minimum capacity of 10GB is recommended, although in some cases you can get away with less for a low-end configuration. High-end systems should have drives of 20GB or higher. One of the cardinal rules of computer shopping is that you can never have too much storage. Buy as much as you can afford, and you'll almost certainly end up filling it anyway.

Tip

If you are an Internet user, one informal method of estimating how much disk space you will need is to go by the speed of your Internet connection. If you have a high-speed link such as that provided by an ISDN connection, a cable modem, or a LAN, you will find that the ease of downloading large amounts of data fills disk drives amazingly quickly. I would recommend at least a 20GB hard drive in these cases, and a removable storage system with a large capacity, such as a Jaz or CD-R drive, is also a good idea.

The most popular hard drive interface for desktop systems is ATA (IDE), though SCSI is preferable for use with multitasking OSes. ATA generally offers greater performance for single-drive installations, but SCSI is better for use with two or more drives or with multitasking operating systems such as Windows 95/98 and NT/2000. This is because of the greater intelligence in the SCSI interface, which removes some of the I/O processing burden from the system's CPU. This is especially important if you are using Windows NT or Windows 2000 in a server role, where it is supporting multiple users and much heavier file access.

Note

In most cases, a system's ATA adapter is integrated into the motherboard. With SCSI, this is much less common. Although it is sometimes possible to purchase a motherboard with an integrated SCSI adapter, you are more likely to have to purchase a separate SCSI host adapter and install it into one of your system's expansion slots. It is recommended that you select an SCSI adapter that uses the fastest expansion bus that your system supports, which in most cases today is PCI. Good quality SCSI host adapters are considerably more complex than an EIDE adapter, and are therefore more expensive. Be sure to consider this additional expense and the need for an additional slot when deciding on a hard drive interface for your system.

SCSI adapters and hard disk drives cost considerably more than their ATA counterparts, but they offer greater expandability (up to 7 or even 15 devices, depending on the SCSI type) and better performance when several different processes are accessing the same devices. If you are building a relatively simple standalone system containing one or two hard disk drives and a CD-ROM, ATA is probably more than sufficient for your needs. However, if you plan on adding other peripherals such as tape drives, cartridge drives, and scanners, or if you plan to share your drives with other users over a network, SCSI might be a worthwhile investment.

Tip

For removable storage devices that require a consistent stream of data to function properly, such as CD-R and tape drives, SCSI is strongly recommended. EIDE devices do not handle multiple tasks nearly as well as SCSI, and can result in buffer underruns, slower data transfer rates, and less efficient storage capacity when used with these types of devices.

◄◄ See "How to Reliably Make CD-Rs," p. 742.

◄◄ See "SCSI Versus IDE," p. 557.

There are several brands of high-quality hard disk drives to choose from, and most of them offer similar performance within their price and capacity categories. In fact, you may notice that the capacities and specifications of the various ATA and SCSI drives offered by certain manufacturers are remarkably similar. This is because a single drive assembly is manufactured for use with both interfaces. The same ATA drive, for example, with the addition of a SCSI interface chip on the logic board, becomes a SCSI drive, often at a substantially higher price.

CD/DVD-ROM Drive

A CD/DVD-ROM drive should be considered a mandatory item in any PC you construct these days. This is because virtually all software is now being distributed on CD-ROM, and many newer titles are on DVD. DVD drives can read CD-ROMs as well as DVD-ROMs, so they are more flexible. Systems can now even boot from CD-ROM drives as long as the system BIOS provides the proper support.

DVD-ROM is a high-density data storage format that uses a CD-sized disc to store a great deal more data than a CD-ROM—from 4.7–17GB, depending on the format. These drives can read standard CD-ROMs and audio CDs, as well as the higher capacity DVD data and video discs.

◄◄ See "DVD (Digital Versatile Disc)," p. 751.

There are several types of CD-ROM or DVD drives to consider these days, but I generally recommend a minimum of a 24x CD-ROM or a 2x DVD-ROM drive connected using the integrated ATA interface found on all modern motherboards. This results in the best possible performance with the minimum amount of hassle. If you plan on using SCSI for your hard drives, however, you might want to select an SCSI CD- or DVD-ROM drive; you'll improve your multitasking performance.

You might also consider purchasing a writable CD-ROM drive, generally known as a CD-R drive. If you do, I recommend you get this in addition to your existing CD-ROM or DVD-ROM drive, that way you can easily copy existing CDs. This is also a good idea because the recordable drives are usually much slower than the ROM-only versions.

CD-R

Burning your own CDs can be a convenient and relatively inexpensive data storage method. Most of the writable CD-ROM drives are WORM (write once/read many) devices that also provide read-only support for standard CD-ROMs. There are now rewritable CD-ROM drives on the market, called CD-RWs, but unlike a CD-R, a CD-RW can be read only by "multiread" drives because the reflection rate of the disc is only 25–35 percent that of a standard CD.

Keyboard and Pointing Device (Mouse)

Obviously, your system needs a keyboard and some type of pointing device, such as a mouse. Different people prefer different types of keyboards, and the "feel" of one type can vary considerably from other types. If possible, I suggest you try a variety of keyboards until you find the type that suits you best. I prefer a stiff action with tactile feedback myself, but others prefer a lighter, quieter touch.

Because two types of keyboard connectors are found in systems today, make sure that the keyboard you purchase matches the connector on your motherboard. Most Baby-AT boards use the larger five-pin DIN connector, and most ATX boards use the six-pin, mini-DIN connector; however, the trend now seems to be changing to the mini-DIN connector for all boards. On some motherboards, you have an option of choosing either connector when you purchase the board. If you end up with a keyboard and motherboard that do not match, there are several companies that sell adapters to mate either type of keyboard to either type of motherboard connector. You can also purchase extension cables for both keyboards and mice that enable you to comfortably place a tower system under a desk or table while the keyboard and mouse remain on the work surface.

◄◄ See "Keyboards," p. 900.

◄◄ See "Keyboard Technology," p. 907.

The same selection concept also applies to mice or other pointing devices; there are a number of different choices that suit different individuals. Try several before deciding on the type you want. If your motherboard includes a built-in mouse port, make sure you get a mouse designed for that interface. This mouse is often called a PS/2 type mouse because the IBM PS/2 systems introduced this type of mouse port. Many systems use a serial mouse connected to a serial port, but a motherboard-integrated mouse port is preferable because it leaves both serial ports free for other devices.

Note that it is possible to purchase keyboards and mice that plug into the USB connector, but I don't recommend these unless your system lacks the standard mini-DIN keyboard and mouse ports.

Tip

You might be tempted to skimp on your keyboard and mouse in order to save a few dollars. Don't! You do all your interacting with your new PC through these devices, and cheap ones make their presence known every time you use your system. I insist on high-quality mechanical switch type keyboards on all my systems.

◄◄ See "Pointing Devices," p. 932.

Video Card and Display

You need a video adapter and a monitor or display to complete your system. There are numerous choices in this area, but the most important piece of advice I have to give is to choose a good monitor. The display is your main interface to the system and can be the cause of many hours of either pain or pleasure, depending on what monitor you choose.

I usually recommend a minimum of a 17-inch display these days. Anything smaller cannot acceptably display a 1,024×768 pixel resolution. If you opt for a 15-inch or smaller display, you might find that the maximum tolerable resolution is 800×600. This may be confusing because many 15-inch monitors are capable of displaying 1,024×768 resolution or even higher, but the characters and features are so small onscreen at that resolution that excessive eyestrain and headaches are often the result. If you spend a lot of time in front of your system and want to work in the higher screen resolutions, a 17-inch display should be considered mandatory. If you can afford it, I recommend a 19-inch display; they work even better at the higher resolutions and have come down in price somewhat from previous years.

Your video card and monitor should be compatible in terms of refresh rate. The minimum refresh rate for a solid, nonflickering display is 70–72Hz—the higher the better. If your new video card can display 16 million colors at a resolution of 1,024×768 and a refresh rate of 76Hz, but your monitor's maximum refresh rate at 1,024×768 is 56Hz, you can't use the video card to its maximum potential. Configuring a video adapter to deliver signals that the monitor cannot support is one of the few software configuration processes that can physically damage the system hardware. Pushing a monitor beyond its capabilities can cause it irreparable harm.

Video adapters in recent years have become standardized on the accelerated graphics port (AGP) interface, although many older systems used PCI-based video cards. You may need to use a PCI video card if you are adding a secondary video adapter to your system to run a second monitor. Windows 98 and Windows 2000 supports this feature and it can be very useful for some applications.

If you are into gaming, you will want one of the newer high-performance 3D video cards on the market. Modern games are very video-intensive, so be sure to check with the game software companies as to what cards they would recommend. It is possible to use separate cards for 2D and 3D graphics (by linking the cards), but I recommend getting a single 2D/3D combination card; they are much easier to set up and generally work better.

◄◄ See "Accelerated Graphics Port (AGP)," p. 310.

◄◄ See "3D Graphics Accelerators," p. 851.

Sound Card and Speakers

You need a sound card and a set of external speakers for any system that you want to be multimedia capable. Although the sound card should be compatible with the Creative Labs Sound Blaster cards, which set the early standards for DOS audio, it is increasingly important to purchase a sound card that is compatible with Windows-based sound APIs, such as DirectX and A3D.

Getting a sound card with an upgradable memory (the same SIMMs you use for your main memory) enables you to download additional sound samples. For best performance, I recommend you get a PCI-based sound card instead of an older ISA bus design. There can be some problems with support for older DOS-based games with some of the new cards, but most of these issues have been addressed by special drivers for the newer cards.

Speakers designed for use with PCs range from tiny, underpowered devices to large audiophile systems. Many of the top manufacturers of stereo speakers are now producing speaker systems for PCs. Let your budget be your guide.

USB Peripherals

The Universal Serial Bus (USB) promises to render the standard I/O ports on the PC obsolete. Essentially, USB brings PnP support to external peripherals by enabling you to plug up to 127 devices into a single port supporting data transfer rates up to 12Mbps. Typically, you plug in a USB hub to a port integrated into the motherboard, and then plug other devices into that. Virtually all current motherboards support USB, and there are numerous external USB devices to connect.

◄◄ See "USB and 1394 (i.Link) FireWire—Serial and Parallel Port Replacements," p. 891.

There are virtually no limits to the types of devices available for USB. Modems, keyboards, mice, CD-ROM drives, speakers, joysticks, tape and floppy drives, scanners, cameras, and printers are just some of the devices available. However, before you start buying all USB peripherals for your new system, be aware that there can be performance problems with a lot of devices on a single bus, and sometimes compatibility problems as well.

Accessories

Apart from the major components, you need a number of other accessories to complete your system. These are the small parts that can make the assembly process a pleasure or a chore. If you are purchasing your system components from mail-order sources, you should make a complete list of all the parts you need, right down to the last cable and screw, and be sure you have everything before you begin the assembly process. It is excruciating to have to wait several days with a half-assembled system for the delivery of a forgotten part.

Heat Sinks/Cooling Fans

Most of today's faster processors produce a lot of heat, and this heat has to be dissipated or your system will operate intermittently or even fail completely. Heat sinks are available in two main types: passive and active.

Passive heat sinks are simply finned chunks of metal (usually aluminum) that are clipped or glued to the top of the processor. They act as a radiator, and in effect give the processor more surface area to dissipate the heat. I normally recommend this passive-design type of heat sink because there are no mechanical parts to fail; however, an active heat sink does cool better for a given size. Often you will have no control over which heat sink you use because it comes already attached to the processor. If you have to attach it yourself, you should use a thermal transfer grease or sticky tape to fill any air gaps between the heat sink and the processor. This allows for maximum heat transfer and the best efficiency.

An active heat sink includes a fan. These can offer greater cooling capacity than the passive types, and some processors are sold with the fan already attached. If you rely on a CPU fan to cool your processor, be sure to buy a high quality one that runs from the computer's internal power. I've seen some battery-operated fans, and even some lower quality system-powered ones, fail without warning; this can result in damage to the processor from excessive heat.

Note

The newer ATX form factor motherboards and chassis are designed to improve system cooling. These systems move the processor and memory near the power supply for better cooling. They often feature secondary case-mounted cooling fans for extra insurance. Note that many processors today come with the heat sink integrated as a part of the unit, often an active type with a high-quality ball bearing cooling fan built-in.

Cables

PC systems need a number of different cables to hook up everything. These can include power cables or adapters, disk drive cables, internal or external CD-ROM cables, and many others. Most of the time, the motherboard will include the cables for any of the internal ports such as floppy or hard drives; other external devices you purchase will come with included cables, but in some cases, they aren't supplied. The Vendor List, on the CD, contains contact information for several cable and small parts suppliers that can get you the cables or other parts you need to complete your system.

Another advantage of the ATX motherboard form factor is that these boards feature externally accessible I/O connectors directly mounted to the rear of the board. This eliminates the "rat's nest" of cables found in the common Baby-AT form factor systems and also makes the ATX system a little cheaper and more reliable.

If you build your system using all OEM (white box) components, be aware that these sometimes don't include the accessories such as cables and additional documentation that you would get with a normal boxed-retail version of the same component.

Hardware

You will need screws, standoffs, mounting rails, and other miscellaneous hardware to assemble your system. Most of these parts are included with the case or your other system components. This is especially true of any card or disk drive brackets or screws. When you purchase a component such as a hard disk drive, some vendors offer you the option of purchasing the bare drive or a kit containing the required cables and mounting hardware for the device. Most of the time bare drives don't include any additional hardware, but you might not need it anyway if the mounting hardware comes with your case. Even so, spending the few additional dollars for the complete drive kit is rarely a waste of money. Even if you're left with some extra bits and pieces after assembling your system, they will probably come in handy someday.

In situations where you need other hardware not included with your system components, you can consult the Vendor List for suppliers of small parts and hardware needed to get your system operational.

Hardware and Software Resources

When you are planning to build a system, it is important to consider how all your selected components will work together and how the software you run must support them. It is not enough to be sure that you have sufficient slots on the motherboard for all your expansion cards and enough bays in the case for all your drives. You must also consider the resources required for all the components.

For example, not only should you be certain that you have enough hardware interrupts (IRQs) to support all your components, you should also know which IRQs are supported by each device. Otherwise, you might find yourself stuck with hardware that you can't install, even though you have interrupts free. Essentially, you should completely configure the system before you begin ordering any parts. Planning a system to this level of detail can be a lot of work, which is one reason why the vast majority of PCs are pre-built.

Another consideration is the operating system and other software you will need. Pre-built systems nearly always arrive with the operating system installed, but when you build your own, you must be prepared with a copy of your selected operating system, including a system disk so that you can boot the system the first time. Since nearly any operating system in use today is distributed on CD-ROM, you'll have to get your computer to recognize the CD-ROM drive before you can install an operating system. To make this process simpler, you might want to create a bootable CD.

◀◀ See "Making a Bootable CD-ROM for Emergencies," p. 763.

The operating system that you select for your new computer is another important decision. You must be certain that the OS supports all the hardware you've selected, which can occasionally be a difficult task. If, for example, you intend to use USB devices, you must run, at the very least, Windows 95 OSR 2.1, which consists of the operating system plus an additional USB support module. To obtain the Windows 95 OSR 2 release, you must purchase it with a new system or, alternatively, a new motherboard or hard drive. Fortunately, USB support is fully integrated into the Windows 98 retail product.

Drivers for specific hardware components might also be a problem. It is a good idea to gather all the latest driver revisions for your hardware, as well as BIOS flashes, firmware updates, and other software components and have them available when you begin the assembly process. Floppy disks are preferable for this, because your CD-ROM drive and connectivity hardware may not yet be operative.

System Assembly and Disassembly

Actually assembling the system is easy after you have lined up all the components! In fact, you will find the parts procurement phase the most lengthy and trying of the entire experience.

Completing the system is basically a matter of screwing everything together, plugging in all the cables and connectors, and configuring everything to operate properly together.

In short order, you will find out whether your system operates as you had planned or whether there are some incompatibilities between some of the components. Be careful and pay attention to how you install all your components. It is rare that a newly assembled system operates perfectly the first time, even for people who are somewhat experienced. It is very easy to forget a jumper, switch, or cable connection that later causes problems in system operation. Most people's first reaction when there are problems is to blame defective hardware, but that is usually not the source. Usually, the problem can be traced to some missed step or error made in the assembly process.

Above all, the most crucial rule of assembling your own system is to save every piece of documentation and software that comes with every component in your system. This material can be indispensable in troubleshooting problems you encounter during the assembly process or later on. You should also retain all the packing materials used to ship mail order components to you until you are certain that they will not have to be returned.

The process of physically assembling a PC requires only a few basic tools: a 1/4-inch nut driver or Phillips-head screwdriver for the external screws that hold the cover in place and a 3/16-inch nut driver or Phillips-head screwdriver for all the other screws. Needle-nose pliers can also help in removing motherboard standoffs, jumpers, and stubborn cable connectors. It is because of marketplace standardization that only a couple of different types and sizes of screws (with a few exceptions) are used to hold a system together. Also, the physical arrangement of the major components is similar even among different manufacturers.

The following sections cover the assembly and disassembly procedure in the following sections:

- Case or cover assembly
- Power supply
- Adapter boards
- Motherboard
- Disk drives

Later, you will learn how to install and remove these components for several different types of systems. With regard to assembly and disassembly, it is best to consider each system by the type of case that it uses. All systems that have AT-type cases, for example, are assembled and disassembled in much the same manner. Tower cases are basically AT-type cases turned sideways, so the same basic instructions apply. Most Slimline and XT-style cases are similar; these systems are assembled and disassembled in much the same way.

The following section lists assembly and disassembly instructions for several case types.

Assembly Preparation

Before you begin assembling any system, one of the issues you must be aware of is ESD (electrostatic discharge) protection. The other is recording the configuration of the system, with regard to the physical aspects of the system (such as jumper or switch settings and cable orientations) and to the logical configuration of the system (especially in terms of elements such as CMOS settings).

ESD Protection

When you are working on the internal components of a computer, you need to take the necessary precautions to prevent accidental static discharges to the components. At any time, your body can hold a large static voltage charge that can easily damage components of your system. Before I ever put my hands into an open system, I first touch a grounded portion of the chassis, such as the power supply case. This action serves to equalize the electrical charges that the device and your body may be carrying. Be sure the power supply is unplugged during all phases of the assembly process. Some will claim that you should leave the system plugged into provide an earth ground through the power cord and outlet, but that is unnecessary.

By touching the chassis or using a wrist strap connecting you and the chassis, all electrical charges will be equalized. It is not important to be earth grounded, the only thing that is important is that you and the components you are working on carry the same relative charge. If you leave the system plugged in, you open yourself up to other problems such as accidentally turning it on or leaving it on when installing a board or device, which can damage the motherboard or other devices.

Caution

Also note that ATX power supplies used in many systems today deliver a +5v current to the motherboard continuously, that is whenever they are plugged in. Bottom line: Make sure any system you are working on is completely unplugged from the wall outlet.

High-end workbenches at repair facilities have the entire bench grounded, so it's not as big of a problem; however, you need something to be a good ground source to prevent a current from building up in you.

A more sophisticated way to equalize the charges between you and any of the system components is to use an ESD protection kit. These kits consist of a wrist strap and mat, with ground wires for attachment to the system chassis. When you are going to work on a system, you place the mat next to or partially below the system unit. Next, you clip the ground wire to both the mat and the system's chassis, tying the grounds together. You then put on the wrist strap and attach that wire to a ground. Because the mat and system chassis are already wired together, you can attach the wrist-strap wire to the system chassis or to the mat. If you are using a wrist strap without a mat, clip the wrist-strap wire to the system chassis. When clipping these wires to the chassis, be sure to use an area that is free of paint so a good ground contact can be achieved. This setup ensures that any electrical charges are carried equally by you and any of the components in the system, preventing the sudden flow of static electricity that can damage the circuits.

As you install or remove disk drives, adapter cards, and especially delicate items such as the entire motherboard, SIMMs, or processors, you should place these components on the static mat. Sometimes people put the system unit on top of the mat, but the unit should be alongside the mat so you have room to lay out all the components as you work with them. If you are going to remove the motherboard from a system, be sure that you leave enough room for it on the mat.

If you do not have such a mat, place the removed circuits and devices on a clean desk or table. Always pick up a loose adapter card by the metal bracket used to secure the card to the system. This bracket is tied into the ground circuitry of the card, so by touching the bracket first, you prevent a discharge from damaging the components of the card. If the circuit board has no metal bracket (a motherboard, for example), handle the board carefully by the edges, and try not to touch any of the connectors or components. If you don't have proper ESD equipment such as a wrist strap or mat, be sure to periodically touch the chassis while working inside the system to equalize any charge you might have built up.

Caution

Some people have recommended placing loose circuit boards and chips on sheets of aluminum foil. This procedure is absolutely *not* recommended and can actually result in an explosion! Many motherboards, adapter cards, and other circuit boards today have built-in lithium or ni-cad batteries. These batteries react violently when they are shorted out, which is exactly what you would be doing by placing such a board on a piece of aluminum foil. The batteries will quickly overheat and possibly explode like a large firecracker (with dangerous shrapnel). Because you will not always be able to tell whether a board has a battery built into it somewhere, the safest practice is to never place any board on any conductive metal surface.

Recording Physical Configuration

While you are assembling a system, it is a good idea to record all the physical settings and configurations of each component, including jumper and switch settings, cable orientations and placement, ground-wire locations, and even adapter board placement. Keep a notebook handy for recording these items, and write down all the settings.

It is especially important to record all the jumper and switch settings on every card that you install in the system, as well as those on the motherboard. If you accidentally disturb these jumpers or switches, you will know how they were originally set. This knowledge is very important if you do not have all the documentation for the system handy. Even if you do, undocumented jumpers and switches often do not appear in the manuals but must be set a certain way for the item to function. Also, record all cable orientations. Most name-brand systems use cables and connectors that are keyed so that they cannot be plugged in backward, but some generic PCs do not have this added feature. In addition, it is possible to mix up hard disk and floppy cables. You should mark or record what each cable was plugged into and its proper orientation. Ribbon cables usually have an odd-colored (red, green, blue, or black) wire at one end that indicates pin 1. There may also be a mark on the connector such as a triangle or even the number 1. The devices into which the cables are plugged are also marked in some way to indicate the orientation of pin 1. Often, there will be a dot next to the pin 1 side of the connector, or there might be a 1 or other mark.

Although cable orientation and placement seem to be very simple, we rarely get through the entire course of my PC troubleshooting seminars without at least one group of people having cable-connection problems. Fortunately, in most cases (except power cables), plugging any of the ribbon cables inside the system backward rarely causes any permanent damage.

Power and battery connections are exceptions; plugging them in backward in most cases will cause damage. In fact, plugging the motherboard power connectors in backward or in the wrong plug location will put 12v where only 5v should be—a situation that can cause components of the board to violently explode. I know of several people who have facial scars caused by shrapnel from exploding components caused by improper power supply connections! As a precaution, I always turn my face away from the system when I power it on for the first time. If you are using an ATX board and power supply, there is little chance of this happening because of the superior type of power connector used.

Plugging in the CMOS battery backward can damage the CMOS chip, which usually is soldered into the motherboard; in such a case, the motherboard must be replaced.

Finally, it is a good idea to record miscellaneous items such as the placement of any ground wires, adapter cards, and anything else that you might have difficulty remembering later. Some configurations and setups may be particular about the slots in which the adapter cards are located; it usually is a good idea to put everything back exactly the way it was originally.

Motherboard Installation

When you are installing your system's motherboard, unpack the motherboard and check to make sure you have everything that should be included. If you purchase a new board, normally you get at least the motherboard, some I/O cables, and a manual. If you ordered the motherboard with a processor or memory, it will normally be installed on the board for you but may also be included separately. Some board kits will include an anti-static wrist strap to help prevent damage due to static electricity when installing the board.

Prepare the New Motherboard

Before your new motherboard is installed, you should install the processor and memory. This will normally be much easier to do before the board is installed in the chassis. Some motherboards have jumpers that control both the CPU speed and the voltage supplied to it. If these are set incorrectly, the system may not operate at all, may operate erratically, or possibly even damage the CPU. If you have any questions about the proper settings, contact the vendor who sold you the board before making any jumper changes.

◄◄ See "CPU Operating Voltages," p. 91.

Most processors today run hot enough to require some form of heat sink to dissipate heat from the processor. To install the processor and heat sink, use the following procedures:

1. Take the new motherboard out of the anti-static bag it was supplied in, and set it on the bag or the anti-static mat, if you have one.

2. Install the processor. There are two procedures, one for socketed processors, the other for slot based processors. Follow the appropriate instructions for the type you are installing.

- *For socketed processors, the procedure is as follows:* Find pin 1 on the processor; it is usually denoted by a corner of the chip that is marked by a dot or a bevel. Next, find the corresponding pin 1 of the ZIF socket for the CPU on the motherboard; it is also usually marked on the board, or there may be a bevel in one corner of the socket. Insert the CPU into the ZIF socket by lifting the release lever until it is vertical. Then align the pins on the processor with the holes in the socket and drop it down into place. If the processor does not go all the way into the socket, check for possible interference or pin alignment problems, but make sure it is fully seated and there is no gap between the bottom of the processor and the socket. If the processor does not seem to want to drop in all the way, remove it to check for proper alignment and any possibly bent pins. If necessary, use a small needle nose pliers or a hemostat to carefully straighten any pins. Don't bend them too much or they will break off. When the processor is fully seated in the socket, push the locking lever on the socket down until it latches to secure the processor.

- *For slot based processors, the procedure is different.* You will need the processor, the universal retention mechanism brackets with included fasteners, and the heat sink supports. Most slot based processors already come with either an active or passive heat sink already installed. Start by positioning the two universal retention mechanism brackets on either side of the processor slot so that the holes in the brackets line up with the holes in the motherboard (see Figure 24.1). Push the included fasteners through the mounting holes in the retention bracket and the motherboard until you feel them snap into place. Insert the fastener retainer pins through the holes in the fastener to lock them into place. Then slide the processor/heat sink down between the brackets until it is firmly seated in the slot. The latches on the top sides of the processor will lock into place when the processor is fully seated. Install the heat sink supports into the holes provided in the motherboard and processor.

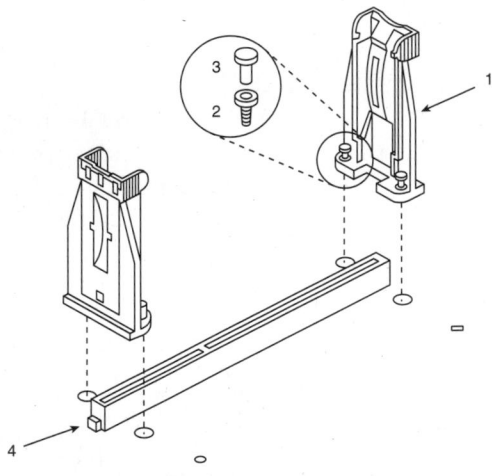

| 1 | Retention bracket | 3 | Fastener retainer pins |
| 2 | Press-fit fasteners | 4 | 242-contact connector (Slot-1) |

Figure 24.1   Universal Retention Mechanism for slot-based processors. Illustration used by permission of Intel Corporation.

3. If the CPU does not already have a heat sink attached to it, attach it now. Most heat sinks will either clip directly to the CPU or to the socket with one or more retainer clips (see Figure 24.2). Be careful when attaching the clip to the socket; you don't want it to scrape against the motherboard, which might damage circuit traces or components. In most cases, it is a good idea to put a dab of heat sink thermal transfer compound (normally a white-colored grease) on the CPU before installing the heat sink. This prevents any air gaps and allows the heat sink to work more efficiently.

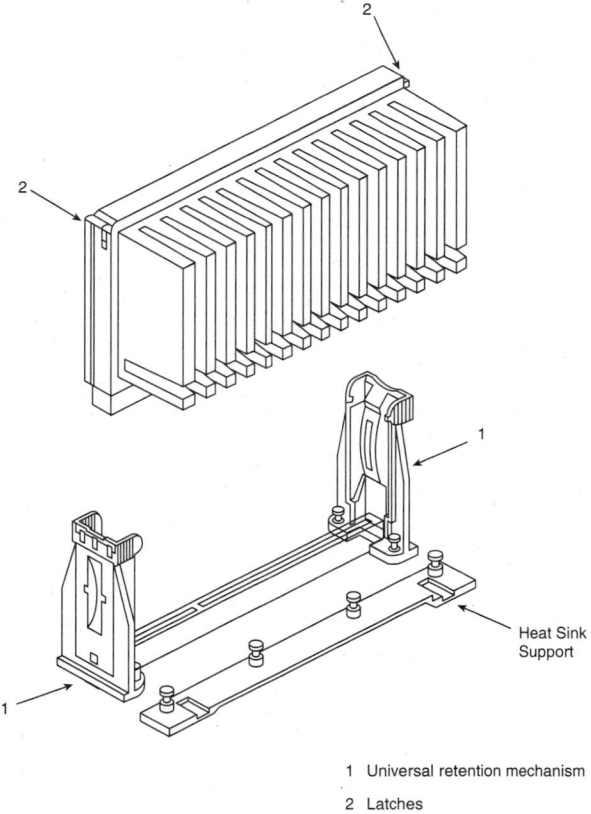

1 Universal retention mechanism

2 Latches

Figure 24.2 Installing a slot-based processor. Illustration used by permission of Intel Corporation.

4. Refer to the motherboard manufacturer's manual to set the jumpers, if any, to match the CPU you are going to install. Look for the diagram of the motherboard to find the jumper location, and look for the tables for the right settings for your CPU. If the CPU was supplied already installed on the motherboard, the jumpers should already be correctly set for you, but it is still a good idea to check them.

Install Memory Modules

In order to function, the motherboard must have memory installed on it. Modern motherboards use either DIMMs or RIMMs. Depending on the module type, it will have a specific method of sliding into and clipping to the sockets. Normally, you install modules in the lowest numbered sockets or banks first. Note that some boards will require modules to be installed in pairs or even four at a time. Consult the motherboard documentation for more information on which sockets to use first and in what order, and how to install the specific modules the board uses.

◄◄ See "Memory Banks," p. 451.

Memory modules are normally keyed to the sockets by a notch on the side or on the bottom, so they can go in only one way.

Caution

Be careful not to damage the connector. If you damage the motherboard memory connector, you could be facing an expensive repair. Never force the module; it should come out easily. If it doesn't, you are doing something wrong.

Mount the New Motherboard in the Case

The motherboard attaches to the case with one or more screws and often several plastic standoffs. If you are using a new case, you might have to attach one or more metal spacers or plastic standoffs in the proper holes before you can install the motherboard. Use the following procedure to install the new motherboard in the case:

1. Find the holes in the new motherboard for the metal spacers and plastic standoffs. You should use metal spacers wherever there is a ring of solder around the hole. Use plastic standoffs where there is no ring of solder (see Figure 24.3). Screw any metal spacers into the new case in the proper positions to align with the screw holes in the motherboard.

2. Insert any plastic standoffs directly into the new motherboard from underneath until they snap into place (see Figure 24.3). Install the I/O shield (if provided loose) over the connectors on the back of the board.

3. Install the new motherboard into the case by setting it down so any standoffs engage the case. Make sure you align the I/O shield with the case or the ports on the back of the board with the I/O shield already in the case. Often you will have to set the board into the case and slide it sideways to engage the standoffs into the slots in the case. When the board is in the proper position, the screw holes in the board should be aligned with all the metal spacers or screw holes in the case.

   Some cases and boards, particularly ATX types, don't use any plastic spacers. Instead they use up to seven screws into metal standoffs that are installed in the case (see Figure 24.4). These are somewhat easier to install because the board drops into place and doesn't require that it be slid to the side to engage any standoffs.

4. Take the screws and any plastic washers that were supplied with the new motherboard and screw the board into the case.

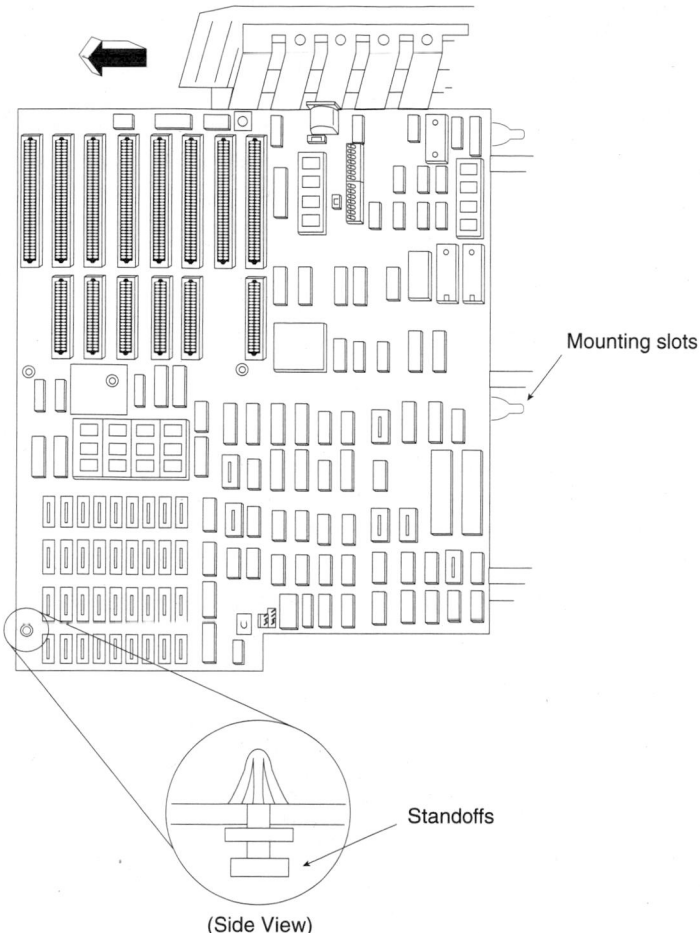

Figure 24.3   Insert standoffs into their mounting slots.

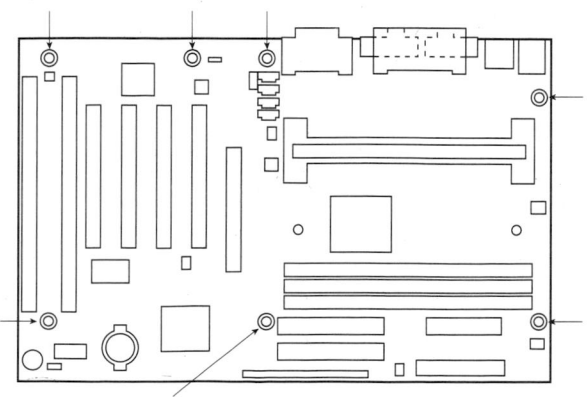

Figure 24.4   Mounting screw holes in a typical ATX motherboard. The arrows mark the screw holes for mounting the motherboard to the case.

the ports and push them out, removing the metal piece covering the hole. Unscrew the hex nuts on each side of the port connector and position the connector in the hole. Install the hex nuts back in through the case to hold the port connector in place.

5. Most newer motherboards also include a built-in mouse port. If the connector for this port is not built into the back of the motherboard (usually next to the keyboard connector), you will probably have a card bracket type connector to install. In that case, plug the cable into the motherboard mouse connector and then attach the external mouse connector bracket to the case.

6. Attach the front panel switch, LED, and internal speaker wires from the case front panel to the motherboard. If they are not marked on the board, check where each one is on the diagram in the motherboard manual.

Install Bus Expansion Cards

Most systems use expansion cards for video, network interface, sound, and SCSI adapters. These cards are plugged into the bus slots present on the motherboard (see Figure 24.7). To install these cards, follow these steps:

1. Insert each card by holding it carefully by the edges, making sure not to touch the chips and circuitry. Put the bottom edge finger connector into a slot that fits. Firmly press down on the top of the card, exerting even pressure, until it snaps into place.

2. Secure each card bracket with a screw.

3. Attach any internal cables you may have removed earlier from the cards.

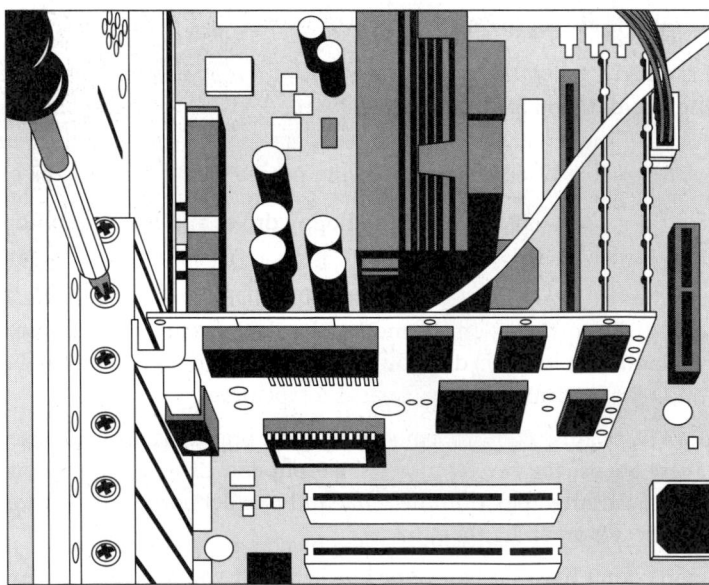

Figure 24.7 Insert the adapter into a slot and screw it in place.

Replace the Cover and Connect External Cables

Now the system should be nearly assembled. All that remains is installing the cover assembly and connecting any external devices that are cabled to the system. I usually don't like to install the case cover screws until I have tested the system and I am sure everything is working properly (see Figure 24.8). Often, I will find that a cable has been connected improperly, or some jumper setting is not correct, requiring that I remove the cover to repair the problem. Use the following procedure to complete the assembly:

1. Slide the cover onto the case.

2. Before powering up the system, connect any external cables. Most of the connectors are D-shaped and go in only one way.

3. Plug the 15-pin monitor cable into the video card female connector.

4. Attach the phone cord to the modem, if any.

5. Plug the round keyboard cable into the keyboard connector, and plug the mouse into the mouse port or serial port (if you are using a serial mouse).

6. If you have any other external cabling, such as joystick or audio jacks to a sound card, attach them now.

Figure 24.8   Insert the screws that hold the cover in place.

Run the Motherboard BIOS Setup Program (CMOS Setup)

Now that everything is connected, you can power up the system and run the system configuration or Setup program. This will enable you to configure the motherboard to access the installed devices and set the system date and time. The system will also test itself to determine whether there are any problems:

1. Power on the monitor first, and then the system unit. Observe the operation via the screen and listen for any beeps from the system speaker.

2. The system should automatically go through a power-on self test (POST) consisting of video BIOS checking, RAM test, and usually an installed component report. If there is a fatal error during the POST, you may not see anything onscreen and the system might beep several times, indicating a specific problem. Check the motherboard or BIOS documentation to determine what the beep codes mean.

3. If there are no fatal errors, you should see the POST display onscreen. Depending on the type of motherboard BIOS such as Phoenix, AMI, Award, or others, you need to press a key or series of keys to interrupt the normal boot sequence and get to the Setup program screens that allow you to enter important system information. Normally, the system will indicate via the onscreen display which key to press to activate the BIOS setup program during the POST, but if not, check the motherboard manual for the key(s) to press to enter the BIOS setup.

4. After the Setup program is running, use the Setup program menus to enter the current date and time, your hard drive settings, floppy drive types, video cards, keyboard settings, and so on. Most newer motherboard BIOSes can autodetect the hard drive, so you should not have to manually enter any parameters for it.

5. Most systems feature an autodetect or auto type setting for the drive; I recommend you choose that if available. This will cause the BIOS to read the parameters directly from the drive, which eliminates a chance for errors, especially if the builder is less experienced. Most systems will also let you set a *user-definable type*, which means that the cylinder, head, and sector counts for this type were entered manually and are not constant. If you set a user-definable type, it is especially important to write down the exact settings you use because this information might be very difficult to figure out if it is ever lost.

   Modern enhanced IDE drives will also have additional configuration items that you should record. These include the translation mode and transfer mode. With drives larger than 528MB, it is important to record the translation mode, which will be expressed differently in different BIOS versions. Look for settings such as CHS (Cylinder Head Sector), ECHS (Extended CHS), Large (which equals ECHS), or LBA (Logical Block Addressing). Normally you would set LBA or Large for any drive over 528MB.

6. Once you have checked over all the settings in the BIOS Setup, follow the instructions on the screen or in the motherboard manual to save the settings and exit the Setup menu.

◄◄ See "Running or Accessing the CMOS Setup Program," p. 375.

Troubleshooting New Installations

At this point, the system should reset and attempt to boot normally from either a floppy disk or hard disk. With the operating system startup disk in drive A:, the system should boot and either reach an installation menu or an A: prompt. If there are any problems, here are some basic items to check:

- If the system won't power up at all, check the power cord. If the cord is plugged into a power strip, make sure the strip is switched on. There is usually a power switch on the front of the case, but some power supplies have a switch on the back as well.

- Check to see if the power switch is connected properly inside the case. There is a connection from the switch to the motherboard, check both ends to see that they are connected properly.

- Check the main power connector from the supply to the board. Make sure the connector(s) are seated fully and if the board is a Baby-AT type, make sure they are plugged in with the correct orientation and sequence.

- If the system appears to be running but you don't see anything on the display, check the monitor to ensure that it is plugged in, turned on, and properly connected to the video card. Make sure the monitor cord is securely plugged into the card.

- Check the video card to be sure it is fully seated in the motherboard slot. Remove and reseat the video card, and possibly try a different slot if it is a PCI card.

- If the system beeps more than once, the BIOS is reporting a fatal error of some kind. See the BIOS Error code listings in Chapter 5, "BIOS," for more information on what these codes mean, as they are dependent on the type and version of BIOS you have. Also consult your motherboard documentation—look in the BIOS section for a table of beep codes.

- If the LED on your floppy drive, hard drive, or CD/DVD-ROM drive stays on continuously, the data cable is probably installed backward or is off by some pins. Check to see that the stripe on the cable is properly oriented toward pin 1 on both the drive and board connector ends. Also check the drive jumpers for proper master/slave relationships.

When you are sure the system is up and running successfully, power it off and screw the chassis cover securely to the case. Now your new system should be ready for the operating system installation.

Installing the Operating System

If you are starting with a new drive, you will need to install the operating system. If you are using a non-Windows operating system, follow the documentation for the installation procedures. Here I will cover installing Windows 9x on an IDE hard drive.

Partitioning the Drive

From the A:> prompt, with the startup disk inserted in the floppy drive, type the following command:

```
FDISK
```

This command is used to partition your drive. Follow the menus to create either a single partition for the entire drive or to create multiple partitions. Normally the first partition must also be made active, which means it will be bootable. I recommend you answer Yes to the prompt "Do you wish to enable large disk support (Y/N)?" This will allow Windows 95B or later (including Windows 98) to install using the FAT32 file system. Then you can continue accepting default entries for all the prompts to partition the drive as a single bootable partition that covers the entire drive.

Next, exit FDISK, this will cause the system to restart.

Note

If you'd rather not use FDISK to partition your drive, you can use Partition Magic to easily create drive partitions. Que's Edition of Partition Magic is included on the CD.

Note

Using FDISK is covered extensively in Chapter 27, "File Systems and Data Recovery."

Format the Drive

After rebooting on the startup floppy, you then need to format each partition you created. The first partition has to be formatted with the operating system startup files using the FORMAT command as follows:

```
FORMAT C: /S
```

All other partitions would be formatted without the /S (system) parameter. After the FORMAT command completes on all the drives, you should reboot again from the startup floppy. Now you are ready to install Windows.

Note

Drive formatting is covered extensively in Chapter 27. See Chapter 14, "Physical Drive Installation and Configuration," for more details on installing and setting up a hard drive.

Loading the CD-ROM Driver

Before you can install Windows, you will have to make sure your startup disk is properly configured to support the CD/DVD drive in your system. This requires that real mode (DOS-based) drivers be installed on the disk that is compatible with your drive. The easiest solution is to use a Windows 98 startup disk, because it is already prepared with the proper drivers for 99 percent of all systems on the market. Even if you are installing Windows 95, you can still use the Windows 98 startup disk to start the process.

If you are using a Windows 95 startup disk and you don't have the CD-ROM drivers on it, you should look for a CD-ROM driver disk that normally comes with your drive. It should have a driver installation batch file on it, which if run, will copy the drivers to your startup disk and create the appropriate CONFIG.SYS and AUTOEXEC.BAT files to enable CD-ROM support.

After you have successfully created a startup disk with the CD-ROM drivers, install the Windows CD-ROM in your CD/DVD drive. After booting from the startup floppy, change to the CD/DVD drive letter, and at that prompt run the SETUP command. This will start the Windows installation program. From here you can follow the prompts to install Windows as you see fit. This procedure can be somewhat lengthy, so be prepared to spend some time. You will not only be installing Windows, but also the drivers for any hardware detected during the installation process.

Note

If you'd like to create a bootable CD containing your Windows installation files, see Chapter 13. For more information about installing CD/DVD drives, see Chapter 14.

After Windows is installed, you can install any additional drivers or application programs you like. At this point your system should be fully operational.

Disassembly/Upgrading Preparation

After you've built your system, you probably will have to open it up again sometime to perform a repair or upgrade. Before you power off the system for the last time and begin to open the case, you should learn and record several things about your computer. Often, when working on a system, you intentionally or accidentally wipe out the CMOS setup information. Most systems use a special battery-powered $I~building;systems;upgrading>CMOS clock and data chip that is used to store the system's configuration information. If the battery is disconnected, or if certain pins are accidentally shorted, you can discharge the CMOS memory and lose the setup. The CMOS memory in most systems is used to store simple things such as how many and what type of floppy drives are connected, how much memory is in the system, and the date and time.

A critical piece of information is the hard disk type settings. Although you or the system can easily determine the other settings the next time you power on the system, the hard disk type information may be another story. Most modern BIOS software can read the type information directly from most IDE and all SCSI drives. With older BIOS software, however, you have to explicitly tell the system the parameters of the attached hard disk. This means that you need to know the current settings for cylinders, heads, and sectors per track.

If you reconfigure a system and do not set the same drive translation as was used originally with that drive, all the data may be inaccessible. Most modern BIOS have an Autodetect feature that automatically reads the drive's capabilities and sets the CMOS settings appropriately. Even so, there have been some problems with the BIOS not reading the drive settings properly or where someone had overridden the settings in the previous installation. With translation, you have to match the setting to what the drive was formatted under previously if you want to read the data properly.

The speed setting is a little more straightforward. Older IDE drives can run up a speed of 8.3MB/sec, which is PIO (Programmed I/O) mode 2. Newer EIDE drives can run PIO Mode 3 (11.1MB/sec), PIO Mode 4 (16.6MB/sec), or several DMA modes including Ultra DMA33 or Ultra DMA66. Most BIOSes today allow you to set the mode specifically, or you can use the Autodetect feature to automatically set the speed. For more information on the settings for hard disk drives, refer to Chapter 7, "The IDE Interface" and Chapter 10, "Hard Disk Storage."

If you do not enter the correct hard disk type information in the CMOS Setup program, you will not be able to access the data on the hard disk. I know of several people who lost some or all their data because they did not enter the correct type information when they reconfigured their systems. If this information is incorrect, the usual results are a missing operating system error message when the systems starts and the inability to access the C: drive.

Some people think that it's possible to figure out the parameters by looking up the particular hard disk in a table. (I have included a table of popular hard disk drive parameters in the Technical Reference on the CD-ROM. This table has proved to be useful to me time and time again.) Unfortunately, this method works only if the person who set up the system originally entered the correct parameters. I have encountered a large number of systems in which the hard disk parameters were not entered correctly; the only way to regain access to the data is to determine, and then use, the same incorrect parameters that were used originally. As you can see, no matter what, you should record the hard disk information from your setup program.

Most systems have the setup program built right into the ROM BIOS software. These built-in Setup programs are activated by a hotkey sequence such as Ctrl+Alt+Esc or Ctrl+Alt+S. Other ROMs prompt you for the setup program every time the system boots, such as with the popular AMI BIOS. With the AMI, you simply press the Delete key when the prompt appears onscreen during a reboot.

The major vendors have standardized on these following keystrokes to enter the BIOS Setup:

- *AMI BIOS.* Press Del during POST.
- *Phoenix BIOS.* Press F2 during POST.
- *Award BIOS.* Press Del or Ctrl+Alt+Esc during POST.
- *Microid Research BIOS.* Press Esc during POST.

If your system will not respond to one of these common keystroke settings, you might have to contact the manufacturer or read the system documentation to find the correct keystrokes to enter setup.

Some unique ones I have encountered are as follows:

- *IBM Aptiva/Valuepoint.* F1 during POST.
- *Older Phoenix BIOS.* Boot to a safe mode DOS command prompt, and then press Ctrl+Alt+Esc, or Ctrl+Alt+S.
- *Compaq.* F10 during POST.

◀◀ See "Running or Accessing the CMOS Setup Program,"" p. 375.

Once you're in the BIOS Setup main screen, you'll usually find a main menu allowing access to other menus and submenus offering different sections or screens. When you get the setup program running, record all the settings. The easiest way to do this is to print it. If a printer is connected, press Shift+Print Screen; a copy of the screen display will be sent to the printer. Some setup programs have several pages of information, so you should record the information on each page.

Many setup programs allow for specialized control of the particular chipset used in the motherboard. These complicated settings can take up to several screens of information—all should be recorded. Most systems will return these settings to a BIOS default if the CMOS battery is removed, and you will lose any customized settings you might have changed. See Chapter 5 for more information on the BIOS settings.

PC Diagnostics, Testing, and Maintenance

SOME OF THE MAIN TOPICS IN THIS CHAPTER ARE

PC Diagnostics

Diagnostics Software

PC Maintenance Tools

Preventive Maintenance

Basic Troubleshooting Guidelines

PC Diagnostics

No matter how well-built your PC is, and how well-written its software, something is eventually going to go wrong, and there might not always be a support system available to resolve the problem for you. Diagnostic software, the kind that comes with your computer, as well as that available from third parties, can be vitally important to you any time your computer malfunctions or you begin the process of upgrading a system component or adding a new device. This chapter examines the types of software that are available, and particularly those that you might already own because they are included with common operating system and hardware products.

You might also find that your system problems are caused by a hardware malfunction and that you have to open up the computer case to perform repairs. This chapter also examines the tools and testers used to upgrade and repair PCs—both the basic items that every user should own and some of the more advanced devices.

Of course, the best way to deal with a problem is to prevent it from happening in the first place. The preventive maintenance sections of this chapter describe the procedures that you should perform on a regular basis to keep your system in good working order.

This chapter describes three levels of diagnostic software (POST, system, and advanced) included with your computer or available from your computer manufacturer. The chapter describes how you can get the most from this software. It also details IBM's audio codes and error codes, which are similar to the error codes used by most computer manufacturers, and examines aftermarket diagnostics and public-domain diagnostic software.

Diagnostics Software

Several types of diagnostic software are available for PCs. Some diagnostic functions are integrated into the PC hardware or into peripheral devices such as expansion cards, whereas others take the form of operating system utilities or separate software products. This software, some of which is included with the system when purchased, assists users in identifying many problems that can occur with a computer's components. In many cases, these programs can do most of the work in determining which PC component is defective or malfunctioning. The types of diagnostic software are as follows:

- *POST*. The power on self test operates whenever any PC is powered up (switched on).

- *Manufacturer supplied diagnostics software*. Many of the larger manufacturers—especially high-end, name-brand manufacturers such as IBM, Compaq, Hewlett-Packard, Dell, and others—make special diagnostics software that is expressly designed for their systems. This manufacturer-specific software normally consists of a suite of tests that thoroughly examines the system. In some cases, you can download these diagnostics from the manufacturer's online services, or you might have to purchase them. Many vendors such as Gateway include a limited version of one of the aftermarket packages that has been customized for use with their systems. In some older IBM and Compaq systems, the diagnostic software is installed on a special partition on the hard drive and can be accessed during startup. This was a convenient way for those system manufacturers to make sure that you always had diagnostics available.

■ *Peripheral diagnostics software.* Many hardware devices ship with specialized diagnostics software designed to test their particular functions. Adaptec SCSI host adapters, for example, include diagnostic functions in the card's BIOS that you can access with a keystroke (Ctrl+A) at boot time. Sound cards normally include a diagnostic program on a disk along with the driver that tests and verifies all the card's functions. Network adapters usually include a diagnostic specific to that adapter, on a disk normally with the drivers. Other devices or adapters might also provide a diagnostic program or disk, usually included with the drivers for the device.

■ *Operating system diagnostics software.* Operating systems such as Windows 9x and Windows NT/2000 include a wide variety of diagnostic software designed to identify and monitor the performance of various components in the computer.

■ *Aftermarket diagnostics software.* A number of manufacturers make general purpose diagnostics software for PCs. This type of software is often bundled with other system maintenance and repair utilities to form a general PC software toolkit.

The Power On Self Test (POST)

When IBM first began shipping the original PC in 1981, it included safety features that had never been seen in a personal computer. These features were the POST and parity-checked memory. Although parity-checked memory is being phased out on many systems, every PC still executes a POST when you turn it on. The following sections provide more detail on the POST, a series of program routines buried in the motherboard ROM-BIOS chip that tests all the main system components at power-on time. This series of routines is partially responsible for the delay when you turn on your PC; the computer executes the POST before loading the operating system.

◀◀ See "Parity and ECC," p. 457.

What Is Tested?

Whenever you start up your computer, it automatically performs a series of tests that checks the primary components in your system, such as the CPU, ROM, motherboard support circuitry, memory, and major peripherals such as the expansion chassis. These tests are brief and are designed to catch hard (not intermittent) errors. The POST procedures are not very thorough compared with available disk-based diagnostics. The POST process provides error or warning messages whenever it encounters a faulty component.

Although the diagnostics performed by the system POST are not very thorough, they are the first line of defense, especially when it comes to detecting severe motherboard problems. If the POST encounters a problem severe enough to keep the system from operating properly, it halts the system boot process and generates an error message that often identifies the cause of the problem. These POST-detected problems are sometimes called fatal errors because they prevent the system from booting. The POST tests normally provide three types of output messages: audio codes, onscreen text messages, and hexadecimal numeric codes that are sent to an I/O port address.

POST Audio Error Codes

POST audio error codes take the form of a series of beeps that identify the faulty component. When your computer is functioning normally, you should usually hear one short beep when the system starts up at the completion of the POST, although some systems (such as Compaq's) do not do this. If a problem is detected, a different number of beeps sound, sometimes in a combination of short and long tones. These BIOS-dependent codes can vary among different BIOS manufacturers, and even among different BIOS from the same manufacturer. It is best if you consult your motherboard manufacturer for the codes specific to your board and BIOS. If that fails, the BIOS manufacturer might have this information.

Note

Tables showing the most current and common BIOS error codes are included in the Technical Reference section on the CD. Consider printing out the codes for your BIOS and keeping them in a safe location.

POST Visual Error Codes

On most PCs, the POST also displays the results of its system memory test on the monitor. The last number displayed is the amount of memory that tested successfully. For example, a system might display the following message:

```
32768 KB OK
```

The number displayed by the memory test should agree with the total amount of memory installed on the system motherboard. Some older systems display a slightly lower total because they deduct part or all of the 384KB of UMA (Upper Memory Area) from the count. On old systems that use expanded memory cards, the memory on the card is not tested by the POST and does not count in the numbers reported. Also, this memory test is performed before any system software loads, so many memory managers or device drivers you might have installed do not affect the results of the test. If the POST memory test stops short of the expected total, the number displayed can indicate how far into the system memory array a memory error lies. This number can help you to identify the exact module that is at fault and can be a valuable troubleshooting aid in itself.

If an error is detected during the POST procedures, an error message might be displayed onscreen. These messages usually are in the form of a numeric code several digits long—for example, 1790-Disk 0 Error. You should check the documentation for your motherboard or system BIOS for information about these errors. The major BIOS manufacturers also maintain Web sites where this information should be available.

Note

I've also included BIOS error messages for AMI Award, Phoenix, Microid Research (MR BIOS), and IBM on the CD, in the Technical Reference section. You should print the codes for your BIOS and keep them in a safe place in case you need them.

I/O Port POST Codes

A lesser-known feature of the POST is that at the beginning of each POST, the BIOS sends test codes to a special I/O port address. These POST codes can be read only by a special adapter card plugged in to one of the system slots. These cards originally were designed to be used by system manufacturers for burn-in testing of the motherboard, to prevent the need for a video display adapter and display. Several companies now make these cards available to technicians. Micro 2000, JDR Microdevices, Data Depot, Ultra-X, and Trinitech are just a few manufacturers that market these POST cards.

When you plug one of these POST cards into a slot, during the POST you see two-digit hexadecimal numbers flash on the card's display. If the system stops unexpectedly or hangs, you can identify the test in progress during the hang from the two-digit code. This step usually identifies the malfunctioning component.

Most of the system BIOSes on the market output the POST codes to I/O port address 80h.

Most POST cards plug in to the 8-bit connector that is a part of the ISA or EISA bus. Because most systems, even those with PCI slots, still have ISA connectors, those cards are adequate. In the future, however, there will be PCs with no ISA slots at all, and an ISA POST card won't work. Micro2000 has a card called the Post-Probe, which has both ISA and PCI connectors on the same board. The Post-Probe also includes a MicroChannel (MCA) bus adapter, making it one of the most flexible POST cards available. Data Depot also offers slot adapters that enable their existing ISA bus cards to work in MCA bus systems. I recommend looking for POST cards that are designed to work in PCI slots. These will certainly become more prevalent as more PCI-only systems (no ISA slots) come on the market. Another ISA/PCI card is the POSTPlus from ForeFront Direct.

Note

A listing of POST I/O port error codes for various BIOSes (including AMI Award, Phoenix, Microid Research, and IBM) can be found in the Technical Reference section of the CD. Also, see Chapter 5 "BIOS" to learn more about working with your BIOS. Remember to consult your motherboard documentation for codes specific to your BIOS version. Also the documentation included with the various POST cards covers most older as well as newer BIOS versions.

Hardware Diagnostics

Many types of diagnostic software are used with specific hardware products. This software can be integrated into the hardware, included with the hardware purchase, or sold as a separate product. The following sections examine several different types of hardware-specific diagnostics.

Note

IBM included specialized diagnostic software for their older PS/2 systems. For more information on this software, see the sixth edition of *Upgrading and Repairing PCs* on the CD-ROM included with this book.

SCSI Diagnostics

Unlike the IDE drive support that is built into the system BIOS of virtually every PC, SCSI is an add-on technology, and most SCSI host adapters contain their own BIOS that enables you to boot the system from a SCSI hard drive. In some cases, the SCSI BIOS also contains configuration software for the adapter's various features, and diagnostics software as well.

The most popular manufacturer of SCSI host adapters is Adaptec, and most of their host adapters contain these features. An Adaptec SCSI adapter normally includes a BIOS that can be enabled or disabled. When the BIOS is activated, you see a message on the monitor as the system boots, identifying the model of the adapter and the revision number of the BIOS. The message also instructs you to press Ctrl+A to access what Adaptec calls its SCSISelect utility.

The SCSISelect utility identifies the Adapter host adapters installed in the system and, if there is more than one, enables you to choose the adapter you want to work with by selecting its port address. After you do this, you are presented with a menu of the functions built into the adapter's BIOS. Every adapter BIOS contains a configuration program and a SCSI Disk Utilities feature that scans the SCSI bus, identifying the devices connected to it. For each hard disk drive connected to the bus, you can perform a low-level disk format or scan the disk for defects, remapping any bad blocks that are found.

For SCSI adapters that use DMA (Direct Memory Access), there is also a Host Adapter Diagnostics feature that tests the communication between the adapter and the main system memory array by performing a series of DMA transfers. If this test should fail, you are instructed how to configure the adapter to use a lower DMA transfer rate.

Network Interface Diagnostics

As with SCSI adapters, many network interface adapters are equipped with their own diagnostics, designed to test their own specialized functions. The EZSTART program included with all SMC network interface cards, for example, contains two adapter test modes. The Basic mode performs the following internal tests on the SMC8000 adapter:

- Bus Interface Controller test
- LAN Address ROM test
- Network Interface Controller test
- RAM test
- ROM test
- Interrupt Generation
- Loopback test

The Two Node test sequence requires that you have another node installed on the same network with an SMC adapter. By running the EZSTART software on both computers, you can configure one adapter as the Responder and the other as the Initiator. The Initiator transmits test messages to the Responder that echoes the same messages back again. If the adapters and the network are functioning properly, the messages should return to the Initiator system in exactly the same form as they were transmitted.

Other network adapters have similar testing capabilities, although the names of the tests might not be exactly the same. The software for the 3Com 3C509B adapter, for example, performs the following tests:

- Register Access test
- EEPROM Vital Data test
- EEPROM Configurable Data test
- FIFO Loopback test
- Interrupt test
- Ethernet Core Loopback test
- Encoder/Decoder Loopback test
- Echo Exchange test (requires two adapters on the same network)

Both the SMC and 3Com diagnostics programs are integrated into the software you use to configure the hardware resources used by the adapters and their other features. The software is not integrated into the hardware; it takes the form of a separate program that ships with the devices and that you can also download free of charge from the manufacturers' respective Web sites.

General-Purpose Diagnostics Programs

A large number of third-party diagnostics programs are available for PC systems. Specific programs are available also to test memory, floppy drives, hard disks, video adapters, and most other areas of the system. Although some of these utility packages should be considered essential in any toolkit, many fall short of the level needed by professional-level troubleshooters. Many products, geared more toward end users, lack the accuracy, features, and capabilities needed by technically proficient people who are serious about troubleshooting. Most of the better diagnostics on the market offer several advantages over end-user products. They are usually better at determining where a problem lies within a system, and often include the serial- and parallel-port loopback connectors that are required to properly diagnose and test serial and parallel ports.

Many of these programs can run in a batch mode, which enables you to run a series of tests without operator intervention. You then can set up automated test suites, which can be especially useful when burning in a system or executing the same tests on many systems.

These programs test all types of memory, including conventional (base) memory, extended memory, and expanded memory. Failures can usually be identified down to the individual memory chip or module (SIMM or DIMM).

Tip

Before trying a commercial diagnostic program to solve your problem, look in your operating system. Most operating systems today provide at least some of the diagnostic functions that diagnostic programs do. You might be able to save some time and money. Operating system-based diagnostics are covered in Chapter 26, "Operating Systems Software and Troubleshooting."

Unfortunately, there is no clear leader in the area of diagnostic software. Each program presented here has unique advantages. As a result, no program is universally better than another. When deciding which diagnostic programs, if any, to include in your arsenal, look for the features that you need.

AMIDiag

AMI (American Megatrends, Inc.) is one of the largest manufacturers of PC ROM BIOS software today. The AMI BIOS can be found on many PCs, and if you've seen the AMI BIOS, you know that most versions have a built-in diagnostic program. Few people know, however, that AMI also markets an enhanced disk-based version of the same diagnostic software that is built into the AMI ROM.

AMIDiag, as the program is called, has numerous features and enhancements not found in the simpler ROM version. AMIDiag is a comprehensive, general-purpose diagnostic that is designed for use on any PC, not just those with an AMI ROM BIOS. Regularly updated over the years, AMIDiag's extensive reporting and diagnostics functions support virtually all the latest hardware found in PCs today, including the latest MMX processors, systems with multiple (up to 16) processors, memory arrays up to 4GB in size, the Intel Universal Serial Bus controller, SCSI devices, PCI, Advanced Power Management, and Plug and Play.

AMIDiag also provides an extensive suite of multimedia diagnostics that can isolate problems with CD-ROM drives, audio adapters, and video displays, as well as modem and network tests.

CheckIt Pro

TouchStone Software Corporation's CheckIt products offer an excellent suite of testing capabilities, including tests of the system CPU; conventional, extended, and expanded memory; hard and floppy drives; and video adapter and monitor (including VESA-Standard cards and monitors, mouse, and keyboard). Several versions of the CheckIt product are available; CheckIt Professional Edition is the company's most complete hardware diagnostic program. The package includes CheckIt versions for both Windows 9x and DOS, TouchStone's PC-cillin antivirus program, and loopback plugs for testing parallel and serial ports.

CheckIt Professional Edition provides benchmarking capabilities and diagnostic tests for most system components and gives detailed information about your system hardware such as total installed memory, hard drive type and size, current memory allocation (including upper memory usage), IRQ availability and usage, modem/fax modem speed, and a variety of other items important to someone troubleshooting a PC.

The product also includes a variety of features that enable you to track the state of your operating system, such as a utility that reports on changes made to important system files and a backup and restore application for the Windows 9x Registry. Although the package centers around the Windows 9x version of the program, the inclusion of the DOS version is a thoughtful addition, in case a system problem prevents you from loading the Windows interface.

Micro-Scope

Micro-Scope by Micro 2000 is a full-featured, general purpose diagnostic program for PC systems. It has many features and capabilities that can be very helpful in troubleshooting or diagnosing hardware problems.

Micro-Scope has a hardware interrupt and I/O port address check feature that is more accurate than the same feature in most other diagnostic software products. It enables you to accurately identify the interrupt or I/O port address that a certain adapter or hardware device in your system is using—a valuable capability in solving conflicts between adapters. Some user-level diagnostics programs have this feature, but the information they report can be grossly inaccurate, and they often miss items installed in the system.

Micro-Scope is particularly useful because the program has its own proprietary operating system, bypassing DOS, and its tests can bypass the ROM BIOS when necessary. This eliminates the masking that occurs when these elements operate in between the system hardware and a diagnostics program. For this reason, the program is also useful for PCs that run other operating systems, such as UNIX or Novell NetWare. For convenience, you can also install Micro-Scope on a hard disk and run it under regular DOS.

Like other diagnostics packages, Micro-Scope is updated regularly to accommodate new hardware as it is released. The current version detects and tests the latest processors by Intel, AMD, and Cyrix and the latest motherboard and video BIOS releases. It also provides support for hardware peripherals such as CD-ROM and DVD-ROM drives and audio adapters. Micro-Scope includes disk repair tools, such as a sector editor that can edit and repair the master and volume boot sectors on a hard disk drive.

Micro-Scope comes complete with the serial and parallel port loopback plugs that you need to completely and accurately test these devices. A loopback plug is a wireless module that attaches to the port and diverts all the signals transmitted through the port's outputs right back to its inputs. With testing software like that included in Micro-Scope, you can verify that every element of a parallel or serial port is operating properly.

Finally, Micro 2000 offers excellent telephone technical support. Its operators do much more than explain how to operate the software—they help you with real troubleshooting problems. This information is augmented by good documentation and online help built in to the software so that, in many cases, you don't have to refer to the manual.

Norton Utilities Diagnostics

When you consider that Norton Diagnostics (NDIAGS) comes with the Norton Utilities, and that Norton Utilities is already an essential collection of system data safeguarding, troubleshooting, testing, and repairing utilities, NDIAGS probably is one of the best values in diagnostic programs.

The current versions of Norton Utilities are 8.0 for the DOS/Windows version and 3.0 for the Windows 95 version. If you don't already have Norton Utilities, you'll want to strongly consider this package, not only for NDIAGS, but also for the other utilities such as Speedisk, Disk Doctor, and Calibrate. These three hard drive utilities basically represent the state of the art in hard drive diagnostics and software-level repair. SYSINFO still handles benchmarking for the Norton Utilities, and it does as good a job as any other diagnostic package on the market.

NDIAGS adds diagnostic capabilities that previously were not provided by the Norton Utilities, including comprehensive information about the overall hardware configuration of your system: the CPU, system BIOS, math coprocessor, video adapter, keyboard and mouse type, hard and floppy drive types, amount of installed memory, bus type, and the number of serial and parallel ports. Unlike some other programs, loopback plugs do not come in the box for NDIAGS, but a coupon is included that entitles you to free plugs by mail. Note that this program uses loopback plugs that are wired slightly differently from those used by most other programs. The different wiring enables you to run some additional tests. Fortunately, the documentation includes a diagram for these plugs, which you can use to make your own if you desire.

NDIAGS thoroughly tests the major system components and enables you to check minor details such as the NumLock, CapsLock, and ScrollLock LEDs on your keyboard. NDIAGS also provides an onscreen grid you can use to center the image on your monitor and test for various kinds of distortion that might indicate a faulty monitor.

PC Technician

PC Technician by Windsor Technologies was one of the first PC diagnostics products on the market in 1984, and since then, it has been highly refined and continuously updated to reflect the changing PC market.

PC Technician is a full-featured comprehensive hardware diagnostic and troubleshooting tool and tests all major areas of a system. Like several of the other more capable programs, PC Technician has its own operating system that isolates it from problems caused by software conflicts. The program is written in assembly language and has direct access to the hardware in the system for testing. This program also includes all the loopback plugs needed for testing serial and parallel ports.

PC Technician has long been a favorite with field service companies who equip their technicians with the product for troubleshooting. This program was designed for the professional service technician; however, it is easy for the amateur to use. As a bonus, PC Technician costs much less than many of the other programs in its class.

PC Technician is deliberately designed to concentrate on the basic PC hardware, and includes a large battery of diagnostic tests for processors, memory, disk drives, I/O ports, and video adapters.

You will not find tests for multimedia devices and other peripherals in PC Technician, but you will find core system testing capabilities that meet or exceed in most areas the other products described in this section.

Although PC Technician is designed for the PC hardware professional, Windsor also has a product called PC-Diagnosys that is geared more toward the end user. PC-Diagnosys includes many of the same tests and features as PC Technician, but lacks the loopback testing and some of the more advanced features of the larger product. Windsor also has a low-end diagnostic product called #1-TuffTEST in both end-user and professional versions that you can download from the company's Web site for a low fee.

QAPlus/FE

QAPlus/FE by Diagsoft is an advanced diagnostic program for Intel-based computers. Its testing is thorough, and its menu-based interface makes it easy to use, even for someone who is not particularly experienced with diagnosing problems with personal computers. QAPlus/FE also includes some of the most accurate system benchmarks you can get, which can be used to find out whether that new system you are thinking of buying is really that much faster than the one you already have. More importantly, QAPlus/FE comes on bootable 3 1/2- and 5 1/4-inch disks that (regardless of your operating system) can start the computer system when problems are so severe that your system hardware cannot even find the hard drive.

Many people already have a less-comprehensive version of this program called QAPlus, which is oriented toward end users. The basic QAPlus version is often included with systems sold by a number of different PC system vendors. Although the simple QAPlus program is okay, the full-blown QAPlus/FE (Field Engineer) version is much better for serious troubleshooting.

QAPlus/FE can test your motherboard, system RAM, video adapter, hard drive, floppy drives, CD-ROM drive, mouse, keyboard, printer, and parallel and serial ports (the QAPlus/FE package includes loopback plugs for full testing of these ports). QAPlus/FE also provides exhaustive information on your system configuration, including the hardware installed on your system, its CPU, and the total amount of RAM installed on your system. It provides full interrupt mapping—crucial when installing new adapter boards and other hardware devices—and gives you a full picture of the device drivers and other programs loaded in memory, as well as other information about DOS and system memory use.

QAPlus/FE also includes various other utilities that are more likely to appeal to the serious PC troubleshooter than to the average PC user. These special capabilities include a CMOS editor that can be used to change system date and time, the hard drive type, installed memory size, and other CMOS information; a COM port debugger; a hard drive test and low-level formatting utility; a floppy drive test utility; and a configuration file editor. The product also includes a remote system communication host program that enables service people with the full remote package to operate your computer via modem.

Unlike some diagnostics programs, QAPlus/FE has a system burn-in capability, meaning it can run your system non-stop under a full load of computations and hardware activity for the purpose of determining whether any system component is likely to fail in real life use. Many people use a burn-in utility when they receive a new system, and then again just before the warranty runs out. A true system burn-in usually lasts 48–72 hours, or even longer. You can configure the amount of time that QAPlus/FE will burn in a system by setting the number of times that the selected tests are to run.

Operating System Diagnostics

In many cases, it might not be necessary to purchase third-party diagnostic software because your operating system has all the diagnostic tools you need. Windows 95, 98, and NT include a large selection of programs that enable you to view, monitor, and troubleshoot the hardware in your system. The following sections examine some of these tools and their functions.

Microsoft Diagnostics (MSD)

MS-DOS 6.x, Windows 3.1, and Windows for Workgroups all include a basic tool called Microsoft Diagnostics (MSD). MSD is a simple, DOS-based program that displays information about your system hardware. Designed in 1993 for use with these older operating systems, however, MSD does not recognize much of the new hardware in use today, such as Pentium processors.

Although MSD has garnered a reputation for incorrectly identifying certain hardware, such as the UART chips in PC serial ports and the interrupt usage listing, it is one of the best tools for identifying memory usage in the Upper Memory Area, which is a common source of conflicts between add-on adapter cards. It is also quite useful for documenting the version numbers of the system BIOS, Video BIOS, and other drivers.

MSD also ships on the Windows 9x CD-ROM, although it is somewhat hidden and is not automatically installed during the Windows setup procedure. You can copy MSD from the CD-ROM directly to your hard drive and run it from any DOS prompt. It does provide better information, however, if you first shut down Windows and choose Restart the Computer in MS-DOS Mode.

Windows 9x Device Manager

Windows 9x's Device Manager is a far more useful hardware inventory tool than MSD. When you select the Device Manager page from the System control panel, you see an expandable list of the types of devices found in the system (see Figure 25.1). Expanding each type displays the actual hardware installed in the computer. Each entry has a Properties dialog box that enables you to configure the device, view the hardware resources that it is using, and update its driver.

By clicking the View Devices By Connection option button, the display is sorted by the computer's various ports and interfaces.

Another lesser-known feature of the Device Manager is that when you double-click the Computer entry at the top of the list, you see the Computer Properties dialog box, shown in Figure 25.2. From this dialog box, you can examine all the IRQs, I/O ports, DMA channels, and memory addresses in your system, and the devices that are using them.

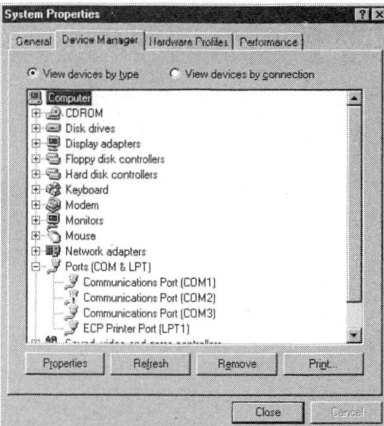

Figure 25.1 The Windows 9x Device Manager.

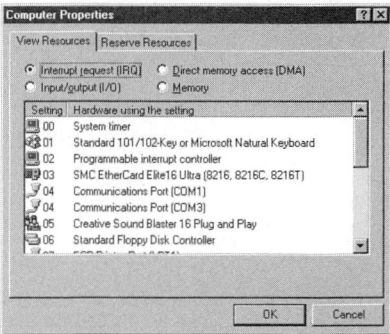

Figure 25.2 The Computer Properties dialog box.

In cases where Windows 9x's Plug-and-Play feature cannot assign system resources for you, the Device Manager is an excellent tool for resolving device conflicts. The Properties dialog box for each device displays the resources supported by that particular device and indicates whether other devices are already using those resources, and which resources the device hardware is configured to use.

Windows 9x Resource Meter

The Windows 9x Resource Meter launches as an icon in the tray area of the toolbar. This application continually monitors the Windows 9x system, user, and GDI (graphics device interface) resources. As you load more programs and open more windows, the icon in the tray indicates the diminishing available resources in the system by growing smaller. When you double-click the Tray icon, you see a more detailed presentation, as shown in Figure 25.3.

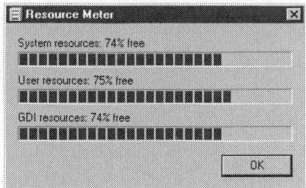

Figure 25.3 The Windows 9x resource meter.

System Monitor/Performance Monitor

The Windows 9x System Monitor and the Windows NT Performance Monitor perform roughly the same function. Both programs track specific elements of a system's performance and display them in a graphical format, as shown in Figure 25.4. By default, you can choose to display various statistics pertaining to the computer's kernel, memory manager, file system, and other core functions.

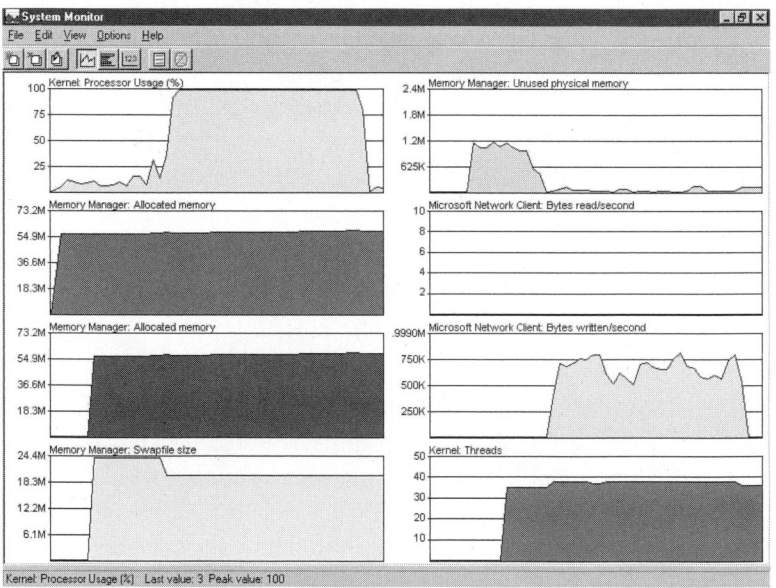

Figure 25.4 The Windows 9x system monitor.

Both of these programs, however, are extensible. Installing additional applications and services on the computer can add new categories of statistics. For example, installing a NetWare client on the system adds a collection of statistics regarding incoming and outgoing traffic generated by that client.

System Information and Diagnostics

Windows 98's System Information program is an excellent addition to the operating system that provides an extensive profile of the computer's hardware and software, rivaling some of the best third-party products on the market (see Figure 25.5). And, although it uses a different display format, Windows NT Diagnostics provides much of the same information.

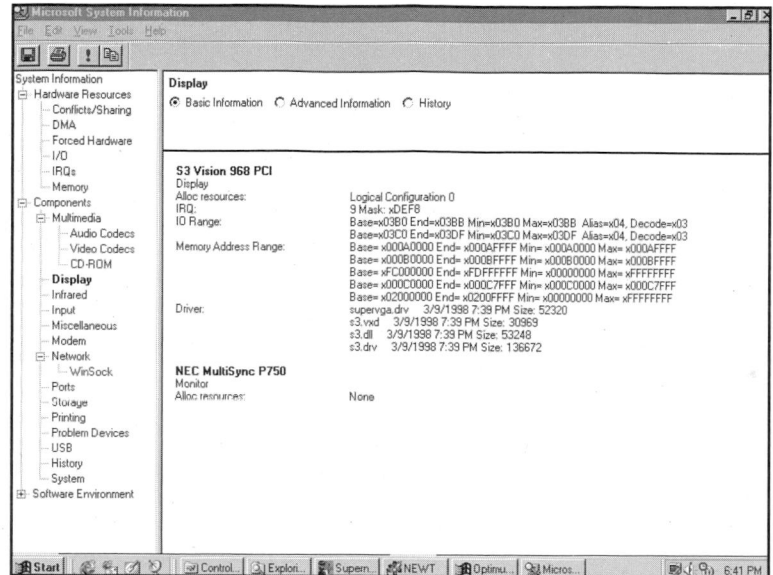

Figure 25.5 Windows 98 system information.

These programs enable you to save, export, or print the information they discover, making it a simple matter to document the entire configuration of a Windows 98 or Windows NT system in great detail. If you should ever have to reinstall the operating system due to a disk failure or other malfunction, having this information handy can simplify the process considerably.

Windows NT Event Viewer

The Event Viewer is Windows NT's primary system message and logging tool. Whenever a significant event occurs in one of three areas—system operation, security, or application execution—it is entered into one of three separate logs.

PC Maintenance Tools

To troubleshoot and repair PC systems properly, you need a few basic tools. If you intend to troubleshoot and repair PCs professionally, there are many more specialized tools you will want to purchase. These advanced tools enable you to more accurately diagnose problems and make jobs easier and faster. The basic tools that should be in every troubleshooter's toolbox are

- Simple hand tools for basic disassembly and reassembly procedures, including a flat blade and Phillips screwdrivers (both medium and small sizes), tweezers, an IC extraction tool, and a parts grabber or hemostat. Most of these items are included in $10–$20 starter toolkits found at most computer stores.

- Diagnostics software and hardware for testing components in a system.

- A multimeter that provides accurate measurements of voltage and resistance, as well as a continuity checker for testing cables and switches.

- Chemicals, such as contact cleaners, component freeze sprays, and compressed air for cleaning the system.

- Foam swabs, or lint-free cotton swabs if foam isn't available.

- Small nylon wire ties for "dressing" or organizing wires.

Some environments might also have the resources to purchase the following devices, although they're not required for most work:

- Memory testing machines, used to evaluate the operation of SIMMs (single inline memory modules), DIMMs (dual inline memory modules), DIP (dual inline pin) chips, and other memory modules

- Serial and parallel loopback (or wrap) plugs to test serial and parallel ports

- A network cable scanner (if you work with networked PCs)

- A serial breakout box (if you use systems that operate over serial cables, such as UNIX dumb terminals)

In addition, an experienced troubleshooter will probably want to have soldering and desoldering tools to fix bad serial cables. These tools are discussed in more detail in the following sections.

Hand Tools

When you work with PC systems, the tools required for nearly all service operations are simple and inexpensive. You can carry most of the required tools in a small pouch. Even a top-of-the-line "master mechanics" set fits inside a briefcase-sized container. The cost of these tool kits ranges from about $20 for a small service kit to $500 for one of the briefcase-sized deluxe kits. Compare these costs with what might be necessary for an automotive technician. An automotive service technician would have to spend $5,000 to $10,000 or more for a complete set of tools. Not only are PC tools much less expensive, but I can tell you from experience that you don't get nearly as dirty working on computers as you do working on cars.

In this section, you learn about the tools required to assemble a kit that is capable of performing basic, board-level service on PC systems. One of the best ways to start such a set of tools is to purchase a small kit sold especially for servicing PCs.

The following list shows the basic tools that you can find in one of the small PC tool kits that sell for about $20:

- 3/16-inch nut driver
- 1/4-inch nut driver
- Small Phillips screwdriver
- Small flat-blade screwdriver
- Medium Phillips screwdriver
- Medium flat-blade screwdriver
- Chip extractor
- Chip inserter
- Tweezers
- Claw-type parts grabber
- T10 and T15 Torx drivers

Note

Some tools aren't recommended because they are of limited use. However, they normally come with these types of kits.

You use nut drivers to remove the hexagonal-headed screws that secure the system-unit covers, adapter boards, disk drives, and power supplies in most systems. The nut drivers work much better than conventional screwdrivers.

Because some manufacturers have substituted slotted or Phillips-head screws for the more standard hexagonal-head screws, standard screwdrivers can be used for those systems.

Caution

When working in a cramped environment such as the inside of a computer case, screwdrivers with magnetic tips can be a real convenience, especially for retrieving that screw you dropped into the case. However, although I have used these types of screwdrivers many times with no problems, you must be aware of the damage that a magnetic field can cause to memory chips and magnetic storage devices such as hard drives and floppy disks. Laying the screwdriver down on or near a floppy or working too close to a hard drive can damage the data on the disk.

Chip-extraction and insertion tools are rarely needed these days because memory chips are mounted on SIMMs or DIMMs and processors use ZIF (zero insertion force) sockets or other user-friendly connectors. The ZIF socket has a lever that, when raised, releases the grip on the pins of the chip, allowing you to easily lift it out with your fingers.

However, if you work with older systems, you must use a chip extractor (see Figure 25.6) to install or remove memory chips (or other smaller chips) without bending any pins on the chip. Usually, you pry out larger chips, such as microprocessors or ROMs, with the small screwdriver. Larger processors require a chip extractor if they are mounted in the older LIF (low insertion force) socket. These chips have so many pins on them that a large amount of force is required to remove them, despite the fact that they call the socket "low insertion force." If you use a screwdriver on a large physical size chip such as a 486, you risk cracking the case of the chip and permanently damaging it. The chip extractor tool for removing these chips has a very wide end with tines that fit between the pins on the chip to distribute the force evenly along the chip's underside. This will minimize the likelihood of breakage. Most of these types of extraction tools must be purchased specially for the chip you're trying to remove.

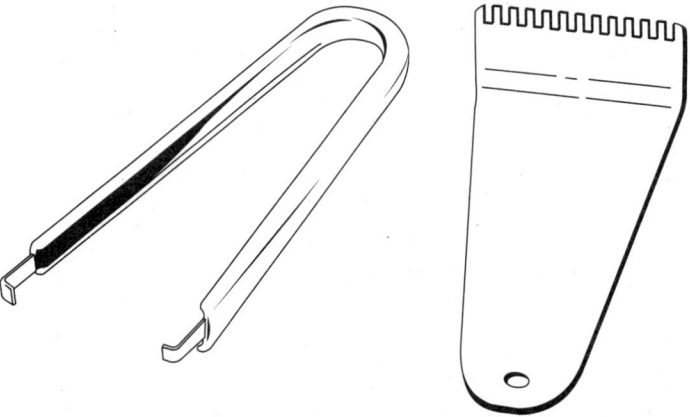

Figure 25.6   The chip extractor (left) would be used to remove an individual RAM or ROM chip from a socket but it would not be useful for a larger processor. Use an extractor such as the one on the right for extracting socketed processors—if the processor does not use a ZIF socket.

The tweezers and parts grabber can be used to hold any small screws or jumper blocks that are difficult to hold in your hand. The parts grabber (see Figure 25.7) is especially useful when you drop a small part into the interior of a system; usually, you can remove the part without completely disassembling the system.

Finally, the Torx driver is a special, star-shaped driver that matches the special screws found in most Compaq systems and in many other systems as well (see Figure 25.8). You can also purchase tamperproof Torx drivers that can remove Torx screws with the tamper-resistant pin in the center of the screw. A tamperproof Torx driver has a hole drilled in it to allow clearance for the pin.

Although this basic set is useful, you should supplement it with some other small hand tools, such as

- Needlenose pliers
- Vise or clamp
- Hemostat
- File

- Wire cutter or wire stripper
- Small flashlight

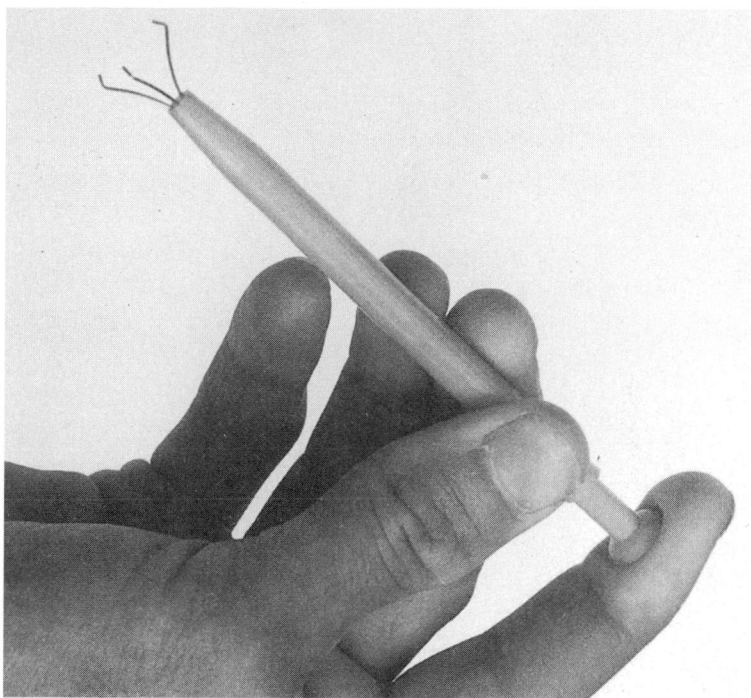

Figure 25.7   The parts grabber has three small metal prongs that can be extended to grab a part.

Pliers are useful for straightening pins on chips, applying or removing jumpers, crimping cables, or grabbing small parts.

Hemostats are especially useful for grabbing small components, such as jumpers.

The wire cutter or stripper, obviously, is useful for making or repairing cables or wiring.

You can use a vise to install connectors on cables, to crimp cables to the shape you want, and to hold parts during delicate operations. In addition to the vise, Radio Shack sells a nifty "extra hands" device that has two movable arms with alligator clips on the end. This type of device is very useful for making cables or for other delicate operations where an extra set of hands to hold something might be useful.

You can use the file to smooth rough metal edges on cases and chassis and to trim the faceplates on disk drives for a perfect fit.

You might often need a flashlight to illuminate system interiors, especially when the system is cramped and the room lighting is not good, or when you are working on a system underneath a user's desk. I consider this tool to be essential.

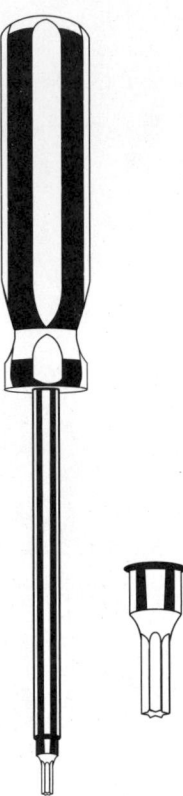

Figure 25.8   A Torx driver and bit.

Another consideration for your tool kit is an ESD (electrostatic discharge) protection kit. This kit consists of a wrist strap with a ground wire and a specially conductive mat with its own ground wire. Using a kit like this when working on a system will help ensure that you never accidentally damage any of the components with a static discharge. You can also get just the wrist strap or the anti-static mat separately.

Note

You can work without an ESD protection kit, if you're disciplined and careful about working on systems. If you don't have an ESD kit available, you should discharge yourself by touching some metallic part of the case while the computer is still plugged in to the AC power source, and then unplug the computer. Many systems today continue to feed power to the motherboard through the soft off connection whenever the computer is plugged in, even when the power switch is turned off. It can be very dangerous to work inside a PC that is still connected to a power source.

The ESD kits, as well as all the other tools and much more, are available from a variety of tool vendors. Specialized Products Company and Jensen Tools are two of the most popular vendors of computer and electronic tools and of service equipment. Their catalogs show an extensive selection of very high-quality tools. (These companies and several others are listed in the Vendor List, on the CD) With a simple set of hand tools, you will be equipped for nearly every PC repair or installation situation. The total cost of these tools should be less than $150, which is not much considering the capabilities they give you.

A Word About Hardware

This section discusses some problems that you might encounter with the hardware (screws, nuts, bolts, and so on) used in assembling a system.

Types of Hardware

One of the biggest aggravations that you encounter in dealing with various systems is the different hardware types and designs that hold the units together.

For example, most systems use screws that fit 1/4-inch or 3/16-inch hexagonal nut drivers. IBM used these screws in all its original PC, XT, and AT systems, and most other system manufacturers use this standard hardware as well. Some manufacturers use different hardware, however. Compaq, for example, uses Torx screws extensively in many of its systems. A Torx screw has a star-shape hole driven by the correct-size Torx driver. These drivers carry size designations such as T-8, T-9, T-10, T-15, T-20, T-25, T-30, and T-40.

A variation on the Torx screw is the tamperproof Torx screw found in power supplies and other assemblies. These screws are identical to the regular Torx screws, except that a pin sticks up from the middle of the star-shape hole in the screw. This pin prevents the standard Torx driver from entering the hole to grip the screw; a special tamperproof driver with a corresponding hole for the pin is required. An alternative is to use a small chisel to knock out the pin in the screw. Usually, a device that is sealed with these types of screws is considered to be a replaceable unit that rarely, if ever, needs to be opened.

Many manufacturers also use the more standard slotted-head and Phillips-head screws. Using tools on these screws is relatively easy, but tools do not grip these fasteners as well as hexagonal head or Torx screws do, and the heads can be stripped more easily than the other types. Extremely cheap versions tend to lose bits of metal as they're turned with a driver, and the metal bits can fall onto the motherboard. Stay away from cheap fasteners whenever possible; the headaches of dealing with stripped screws aren't worth it.

Some system manufacturers now use cases that snap together or use thumb screws. These are usually advertised as "no-tool" cases because you literally do not need any tools to take off the cover and access the major assemblies.

A company called Curtis sells special nylon plastic thumb screws that fit most normal cases and can be used to replace the existing screws to make opening the case a no-tool proposition. However, you should still always use metal screws to install internal components such as adapter cards, disk drives, power supplies, and the motherboard because the metal screws provide a ground point for these devices.

English Versus Metric

Another area of aggravation with hardware is the fact that there are two types of thread systems: English and metric. IBM used mostly English-threaded fasteners in its original line of systems, but many other manufacturers used metric-threaded fasteners.

The difference between the two becomes especially apparent with disk drives. American-manufactured drives typically use English fasteners, whereas drives made in Japan or Taiwan usually use metric. Whenever you replace a floppy drive in an older PC, you encounter this problem. Try to buy the correct screws and any other hardware, such as brackets, with the drive because they might be difficult to find as separate items. Many drive manufacturers offer retail drive kits that include all the required mounting components. The OEM's drive manual lists the correct data about a specific drive's hole locations and thread size.

Hard disks can use either English or metric fasteners; check your particular drive to see which type it uses. Most drives today use metric hardware.

Caution

Some screws in a system can be length-critical, especially screws that are used to retain hard disk drives. You can destroy some hard disks by using a mounting screw that's too long; the screw can puncture or dent the sealed disk chamber when you install the drive and fully tighten the screw. When you install a new drive in a system, always make a trial fit of the hardware to see how far the screws can be inserted into the drive before they interfere with its internal components. When you're in doubt, the drive manufacturer's OEM documentation will tell you precisely what screws are required and how long they should be.

Soldering and Desoldering Tools

In certain situations—such as repairing a broken wire, making cables, reattaching a component to a circuit board, removing and installing chips that are not in a socket, or adding jumper wires or pins to a board—you must use a soldering iron to make the repair.

Although virtually all repairs these days are done by simply replacing the entire failed board and many PC technicians never touch a soldering iron, you might find one useful in some situations. The most common case would be where there is physical damage to a system, such as when someone rips the keyboard connector off of a motherboard by pulling on the cable improperly. Simple soldering skills can save the motherboard in this case.

Most motherboards these days include I/O components such as serial and parallel ports. Many of these ports are fuse-protected on the board; however, the fuse is usually a small soldered-in component. These fuses are designed to protect the motherboard circuits from being damaged by an external source. If a short circuit or static charge from an external device blows these fuses, the motherboard can be saved if you can replace them.

To perform minor repairs such as these, you need a low-wattage soldering iron—usually about 25 watts. More than 30 watts generates too much heat and can damage the components on the board. Even with a low-wattage unit, you must limit the amount of heat to which you subject the board and its components. You can do this with quick and efficient use of the soldering iron and with the use of heat-sinking devices clipped to the leads of the device being soldered. A heat sink is a small metal clip-on device designed to absorb excessive heat before it reaches the component that the heat sink is protecting. In some cases, you can use a pair of hemostats as an effective heat sink when you solder a component.

To remove components that are soldered into place on a printed circuit board, you can use a soldering iron with a solder sucker. This device normally takes the form of a small tube with an air chamber and a plunger-and-spring arrangement. (I do not recommend the squeeze-bulb type of solder sucker.) The unit is "cocked" when you press the spring-loaded plunger into the air chamber. When you want to remove a device from a board, you use the soldering iron from the underside of the board, and heat the point at which one of the component leads joins the circuit board until the solder melts. As soon as melting occurs, move the solder-sucker nozzle into position, and press the actuator. When the plunger retracts, it creates a momentary suction that draws the liquid solder away from the connection and leaves the component lead dry in the hole.

Always do the heating and suctioning from the underside of a board, not from the component side. Repeat this action for every component lead joined to the circuit board. When you master this technique, you can remove a small component in a minute or two with only a small likelihood of damage to the board or other components. Larger chips that have many pins can be more difficult to remove and resolder without damaging other components or the circuit board.

Tip

These procedures are intended for Through-Hole devices only. These are components whose pins extend all the way through holes in the board to the underside. Surface mount devices are removed with a completely different procedure, using much more expensive tools. Working on surface-mounted components is beyond the capabilities of all but the most well-equipped shops.

If you intend to add soldering and desoldering skills to your arsenal of abilities, you should practice. Take a useless circuit board and practice removing various components from the board; then, reinstall the components. Try to remove the components from the board by using the least amount of heat possible. Also, perform the solder-melting operations as quickly as possible, limiting the time that the iron is applied to the joint. Before you install any components, clean out the holes through which the leads must project and mount the component in place. Then, apply the solder from the underside of the board, using as little heat and solder as possible.

Attempt to produce joints as clean as the joints that the board manufacturer produced by machine. Soldered joints that do not look clean can keep the component from making a good connection with the rest of the circuit. This "cold-solder joint" is normally created because you have not used enough heat. Remember that you should not practice your new soldering skills on the motherboard of a system that you are attempting to repair! Don't attempt to work on real boards until you are sure of your skills. I always keep a few junk boards around for soldering practice and experimentation.

Tip

When first learning to solder, you might be tempted to set the iron on the solder and leave it there until the solder melts. If the solder doesn't melt immediately when you apply the iron to it, you're not transferring the heat from the iron to the solder efficiently. This means that either the iron is dirty or there is debris between it and the solder. To clean the iron, take a wet sponge and drag it across the tip of the iron.

If after cleaning the iron there's still some resistance, try to scratch the solder with the iron when it's hot. Generally, this removes any barriers to heat flow and instantly melts the solder.

No matter how good you get at soldering and desoldering, some jobs are best left to professionals. Components that are surface-mounted to a circuit board, for example, require special tools for soldering and desoldering, as do other components that have high pin densities.

Test Equipment

In some cases, you must use specialized devices to test a system board or component. This test equipment is not expensive or difficult to use, but it can add much to your troubleshooting abilities.

Electrical Testing Equipment

I consider a voltmeter to be required gear for proper system testing (refer to Figure 21.10 in Chapter 21). A multimeter can serve many purposes, including checking for voltage signals at different points in a system, testing the output of the power supply, and checking for continuity in a circuit or cable. An outlet tester is an invaluable accessory that can check the electrical outlet for proper wiring. This capability is useful if you believe that the problem lies outside the computer system.

Loopback Connectors (Wrap Plugs)

For diagnosing serial- and parallel-port problems, you need loopback connectors (also called wrap plugs), which are used to circulate, or wrap, signals (see Figure 25.9). The plugs enable the serial or parallel port to send data to itself for diagnostic purposes.

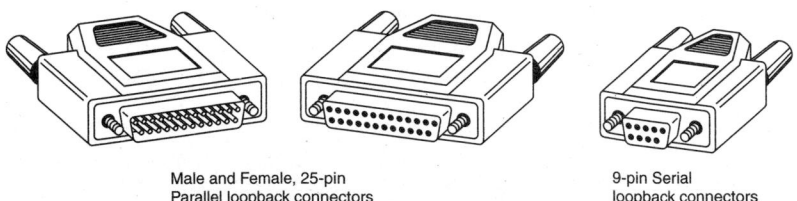

Male and Female, 25-pin
Parallel loopback connectors

9-pin Serial
loopback connectors

Figure 25.9 Typical wrap plugs including 25-pin and 9-pin serial and 25-pin parallel versions

Different types of loopback connectors are available. To accommodate all the ports you might encounter, you need one for the 25-pin serial port, one for the 9-pin serial port, and one for the 25-pin parallel port. Many companies, including IBM, sell the plugs separately, but be aware that you also need diagnostic software that can use them. Some diagnostic software products, such as Micro 2000's Micro-Scope, include loopback connectors with the product.

IBM sells a special combination plug that includes all three connector types in one compact unit. The device costs approximately $30 from IBM. If you're handy, you can even make your own wrap plugs for testing. I include wiring diagrams for the three types of wrap plugs in Chapter 16, "Serial, Parallel, and Other I/O Interfaces." In that chapter, you also will find a detailed discussion of serial and parallel ports.

Besides simple loopback connectors, you might also want to have a breakout box for your toolkit. A breakout box is a DB25 connector device that enables you to make custom temporary cables or even to monitor signals on a cable. For most PC troubleshooting uses, a "mini" breakout box works well and is inexpensive.

Meters

Some troubleshooting procedures require that you measure voltage and resistance. You take these measurements by using a handheld Digital Multi-Meter (DMM). The meter can be an analog device (using an actual meter) or a digital-readout device. The DMM has a pair of wires called test leads or probes. The test leads make the connections so that you can take readings. Depending on the meter's setting, the probes measure electrical resistance, direct-current (DC) voltage, or alternating-current (AC) voltage.

Usually, each system-unit measurement setting has several ranges of operation. DC voltage, for example, usually can be read in several scales, to a maximum of 200 millivolts (mv), 2v, 20v, 200v, and 1,000v. Because computers use both +5v and +12v for various operations, you should use the 20v maximum scale for making your measurements. Making these measurements on the 200mv or 2v scale could "peg the meter" and possibly damage it because the voltage would be much higher than expected. Using the 200v or 1,000v scale works, but the readings at 5v and 12v are so small in proportion to the maximum that accuracy is low.

If you are taking a measurement and are unsure of the actual voltage, start at the highest scale and work your way down. Most of the better meters have autoranging capability—the meter automatically selects the best range for any measurement. This type of meter is much easier to operate. You simply set the meter to the type of reading you want, such as DC volts, and attach the probes to the signal source. The meter selects the correct voltage range and displays the value. Because of their design, these types of meters always have a digital display rather than a meter needle.

Caution

Whenever using a multimeter to test any voltage that could potentially be 110v or above, always use one hand to do the testing, not two. Either clip one lead to one of the sources and probe with the other or hold both leads in one hand.

If you hold a lead in each hand and accidentally slip, you can very easily become a circuit, allowing power to conduct or flow through you. When power flows from arm to arm, the path of the current is directly across the heart. Hearts tend to quit working when subjected to high voltages. They're funny that way.

I prefer the small digital meters; you can buy them for only slightly more than the analog style, and they're extremely accurate and much safer for digital circuits. Some of these meters are not much bigger than a cassette tape; they fit in a shirt pocket. Radio Shack sells a good unit (made for Radio Shack by Beckman) in the $25 price range; the meter is a half-inch thick, weighs 3 1/2 ounces, and is digital and autoranging, as well. This type of meter works well for most, if not all, PC troubleshooting and test uses.

Caution

You should be aware that many analog meters can be dangerous to digital circuits. These meters use a 9v battery to power the meter for resistance measurements. If you use this type of meter to measure resistance on some digital circuits, you can damage the electronics because you essentially are injecting 9v into the circuit. The digital meters universally run on 3-5v or less.

Logic Probes and Logic Pulsers

A logic probe (see Figure 25.10) can be useful for diagnosing problems in digital circuits. In a digital circuit, a signal is represented as either high (+5v) or low (0v). Because these signals are present for only a short time (measured in millionths of a second) or oscillate (switch on and off) rapidly, a simple voltmeter is useless. A logic probe is designed to display these signal conditions easily.

Logic probes are especially useful for troubleshooting a dead system. By using the probe, you can determine whether the basic clock circuitry is operating and whether other signals necessary for system operation are present. In some cases, a probe can help you cross-check the signals at each pin on an integrated circuit chip. You can compare the signals present at each pin with the signals that a known-good chip of the same type would show—a comparison that is helpful in isolating a failed component. Logic probes can also be useful for troubleshooting some disk drive problems by enabling you to test the signals present on the interface cable or drive-logic board.

A companion tool to the probe is the logic pulser. A pulser is designed to test circuit reaction by delivering a logical high (+5v) pulse into a circuit, usually lasting 1 1/2–10 millionths of a second. Compare the reaction with that of a known-functional circuit. This type of device normally is used much less frequently than a logic probe, but in some cases, it can be helpful for testing a circuit.

Outlet Testers

Outlet testers are very useful test tools. These simple, inexpensive devices, sold in hardware stores, test electrical outlets. You simply plug in the device, and three LEDs light in various combinations, indicating whether the outlet is wired correctly.

Although you might think that badly wired outlets would be a rare problem, I have seen a large number of installations in which the outlets were wired incorrectly. Most of the time, the problem is in the ground wire. An improperly wired outlet can result in unstable system operation, such as random parity checks and lockups. With an improper ground circuit, currents can begin flowing on the electrical ground circuits in the system. Because the system uses the voltage on the ground circuits as a comparative signal to determine whether bits are 0 or 1, a floating ground can cause data errors in the system.

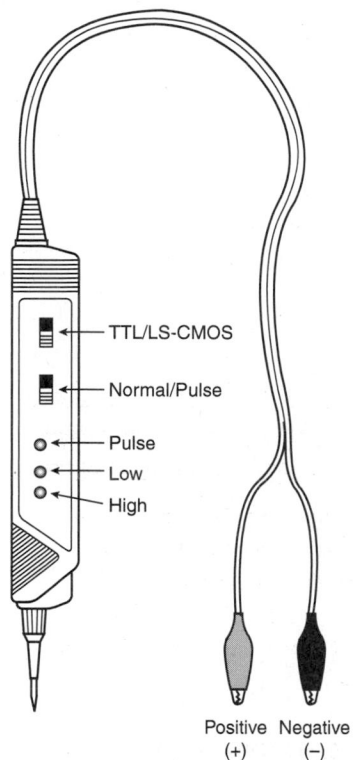

Figure 25.10   A typical logic probe

Once, while running one of my PC troubleshooting seminars, I used a system that I literally could not approach without locking it up. Whenever I walked past the system, the electrostatic field generated by my body interfered with the system, and the PC locked up, displaying a parity-check error message. The problem was that the hotel at which I was giving the seminar was very old and had no grounded outlets in the room. The only way I could prevent the system from locking up was to run the class in my stocking feet because my leather-soled shoes were generating the static charge.

Other symptoms of bad ground wiring in electrical outlets are continual electrical shocks when you touch the case or chassis of the system. These shocks indicate that voltages are flowing where they should not be. This problem can also be caused by bad or improper grounds within the system. By using the simple outlet tester, you can quickly determine whether the outlet is at fault.

If you just walk up to a system and receive an initial shock, it's probably only static electricity. Touch the chassis again without moving your feet. If you receive another shock, there is something very wrong. In this case, the ground wire actually has voltage applied to it. You should have a professional electrician check the outlet immediately.

If you don't like being a human rat in an electrical experiment, you can test the outlets with your multimeter. First, remember to hold both leads in one hand. Test from one blade hole to another. This should read between 110v and 125v depending on the electrical service in the area. Then check from each blade to the ground (the round hole). One blade hole, the smaller one, should show a voltage almost identical to the one that you got from the blade hole to blade hole test. The larger blade hole when measured to ground should show less than 0.5v.

Because ground and neutral are supposed to be tied together at the electrical panel, a large difference in these readings indicates that they are not tied together. However, small differences can be accounted for by current from other outlets down the line flowing on the neutral, when there isn't any on the ground.

If you don't get the results you expect, call an electrician to test the outlets for you. More weird computer problems are caused by improper grounding and other power problems than people like to believe.

Memory Testers

I now consider a memory test machine an all-but-mandatory piece of equipment for anyone serious about performing PC troubleshooting and repair as a profession. The tester is a small device designed to evaluate SIMMs, DIMMs, and other types of memory modules, including individual chips such as those used as cache memory. These testers can be somewhat expensive, costing upwards of $1,000 to $2,500, but these machines are the only truly accurate way to test memory.

Without one of these testers, you are reduced to testing memory by running a diagnostic program on the PC and testing the memory as it is installed. This can be very problematic, as the memory diagnostic program can only do two things to the memory: write and read. A SIMM tester can do many things that a memory diagnostic running in a PC cannot do, such as

- Identify the type of memory
- Identify the memory speed
- Identify whether the memory has parity or is using bogus parity emulation
- Vary the refresh timing and access speed timing
- Locate single bit failures
- Detect power- and noise-related failures
- Detect solder opens and shorts
- Isolate timing-related failures
- Detect data retention errors

No conventional memory diagnostic software can do these things because it has to rely on the fixed access parameters set up by the memory controller hardware in the motherboard chipset. This prevents the software from being able to alter the timing and methods used to access the memory. You might have memory that fails in one system and works in another when the chips are actually bad. This type of intermittent problem is almost impossible to detect with diagnostic software.

The bottom line is that there is no way that you can test memory with true accuracy while it is installed in a PC; a memory tester is required for comprehensive and accurate testing. Although the price of a typical 32MB memory module can be less than $50, the price of a memory tester can be justified very easily in a shop environment where a lot of PCs are tested, because many software and hardware upgrades today require the addition of new memory. With the large increases in the amount of memory in today's systems and stricter timing requirements of newer motherboard designs, it has become even more important to be able to identify or rule out memory as a cause of system failure. One of the memory testers I recommend is the SIGMA LC by Darkhorse Systems. See the Vendor List on the CD for more information. Also see Chapter 6, "Memory," for more information on memory in general.

Preventive Maintenance

Preventive maintenance is the key to obtaining years of trouble-free service from your computer system. A properly administered preventive maintenance program pays for itself by reducing problem behavior, data loss, and component failure and by ensuring a long life for your system. In several cases, I have "repaired" an ailing system with nothing more than a preventive maintenance session. Preventive maintenance can also increase your system's resale value because it will look and run better.

Developing a preventive maintenance program is important to everyone who uses or manages personal computer systems. There are two types of preventive maintenance procedures: active and passive.

An active preventive maintenance program includes procedures that promote a longer, trouble-free life for your PC. This type of preventive maintenance primarily involves the periodic cleaning of the system and its components. The following sections describe several active preventive maintenance procedures, including cleaning and lubricating all major components, reseating chips and connectors, and reformatting hard disks.

Passive preventive maintenance includes steps you can take to protect a system from the environment, such as using power-protection devices; ensuring a clean, temperature-controlled environment; and preventing excessive vibration. In other words, passive preventive maintenance means treating your system well.

Active Preventive Maintenance Procedures

How often you should perform active preventive maintenance procedures depends on the system's environment and the quality of the system's components. If your system is in a dirty environment, such as a machine shop floor or a gas station service area, you might need to clean your system every three months or less. For normal office environments, cleaning a system every one to two years is usually fine. However, if you open your system after one year and find dust bunnies inside, you should probably shorten the cleaning interval.

Other hard disk preventive maintenance procedures include making periodic backups of your data and critical areas such as boot sectors, file allocation tables (FATs), and directory structures on the disk. Also, defragment hard disks periodically to maintain disk efficiency and speed.

System Backups

One of the most important preventive maintenance procedures is the performance of regular system backups. A sad reality in the computer repair and servicing world is that hardware can always be repaired or replaced, but data cannot. Many hard disk troubleshooting and service procedures, for example, require that you repartition or reformat the disk, which overwrites all existing data.

The hard disk drive capacity in a typical PC has grown far beyond the point at which floppy disks are a viable backup solution. Backup solutions that employ floppy disk drives, such as the DOS backup software, are insufficient and too costly for hard disk backups in today's systems. It would take 2,867 1.44MB floppy disks, for example, to back up the 4GB hard disk in my portable system! That would cost more than $1,000 in disks, not to mention the time involved.

The traditional alternative to floppies is magnetic tape. A DAT (digital audio tape) or Travan tape system can store 4GB to 8GB or more on a single tape costing less than $30. The increasing popularity of removable cartridge (such as Iomega Zip and Jaz drives) and writable CD-ROM drives presents even more alternatives.

Although a tape drive can cost up to $500 or more, the media costs are really far more significant than the cost of the drive. If you do responsible backups, you should have at least three sets of media for each system you are backing up. You should use each media set on a rotating basis, and store one of them offsite at all times, in case of fire or theft. You should also introduce new media to the rotation after approximately a year to prevent excessive wear. If you are backing up multiple systems, these media costs can add up quickly.

You should also factor in the cost of your time. If a backup requires manual intervention to change the media during the job, I don't recommend it. A backup system should be capable of fitting a complete backup on a single tape so that you can schedule the job to run unattended. If someone has to hang around to switch tapes every so often, backups become a real chore and are more likely to be overlooked. Also, every time a media change occurs, there is a substantial increase in the likelihood of errors and problems that you might not see until you attempt to perform a restore operation. Backups are far more important than most people realize, and spending a little more on a quality piece of hardware such as a Travan or DAT drive will pay off in the long run with greater reliability, lower media costs, higher performance, and unattended backups that contain the entire system file structure.

With the increasing popularity of removable bulk storage media such as cartridge drives, including Iomega's Zip and Jaz drives, and rewritable CD-ROMs (CD-RWs), many people are using these devices to perform system backups. In most cases, however, although these drives are excellent for storing backup copies of selected data, they are impractical solutions for regular system backups. This can be due both to the capacity of the media in relation to today's hard disk drives and to the cost of the media.

Although the media for a CD-RW drive are quite inexpensive, it would take several discs to back up a multi-gigabyte hard drive, adding a measure of inconvenience to the backup process that makes it far less likely to be performed on a regular basis. Even the Iomega Jaz drive that can store up to 2GB on a single cartridge can require several media changes to complete a single system backup. Add this to the fact that the Jaz cartridges can cost $150 or more each, and you have a backup solution that is both inconvenient and expensive.

Tip

No matter what backup solution you use, the entire exercise is pointless if you cannot restore your data from the storage medium. You should test your backup system by performing random file restores at regular intervals to ensure the viability of your data.

Cleaning a System

One of the most important operations in a good preventive maintenance program is regular and thorough cleaning of the system. Dust buildup on the internal components can lead to several problems. One is that the dust acts as a thermal insulator, which prevents proper system cooling. Excessive heat shortens the life of system components and adds to the thermal stress problem caused by greater temperature changes between the system's power-on and power-off states. Additionally, the dust can contain conductive elements that can cause partial short circuits in a system. Other elements in dust and dirt can accelerate corrosion of electrical contacts, resulting in improper connections. In all, the regular removal of any layer of dust and debris from within a computer system benefits that system in the long run.

Most non-ATX and some ATX PCs use a forced-air cooling system that provides even cooling inside the case. A fan is mounted in, on, or near the power supply and pushes air outside. This depressurizes the interior of the system relative to the outside environment. The lower pressure inside the system causes outside air to be drawn in through openings in the system chassis and cover. This draw-through, or depressurization, is the most efficient cooling system that can be designed without an air filter. Air filters typically are not used with depressurization systems because there is no easy way to limit the air intake to a single port that can be covered by a filter.

Some industrial computers and ATX (as well as NLX) systems use a forced-air system that uses the fan to pressurize, rather than to depressurize, the case. This system forces air to exhaust from any holes in the chassis and case or cover. The key to the pressurization system is that all air intake for the system is at a single location—the fan. You can therefore filter the air flowing into the system by integrating a filter assembly into the fan housing. The filter must be cleaned or changed periodically, however, to prevent it from becoming clogged with dust.

Because the interior of the case is pressurized relative to the outside air, airborne contaminants are not drawn into the system even though it might not be completely sealed. Any air entering the system must pass through the fan and filter housing, which removes the contaminants. Pressurization cooling systems were originally designed for use in industrial computer models intended for extremely harsh environments. However, with the growing popularity of the ATX and NLX architectures, pressurization systems are more common.

A recent trend in ATX case and power supply design, however, has reverted to the negative-pressurization design. Some claim that using the fan in the power supply to cool the CPU directly is not effective because the air is preheated by the power supply, especially if it is heavily loaded. Another important reason is that the single biggest advantage of the positive-pressure system, the capability to filter the incoming air, is either not included in the system design or not maintained properly.

Most of the PCs now in use are depressurization systems. Mounting any sort of air filter on these types of systems is impossible because air enters the system from too many sources. With any cooling system in which incoming air is not filtered, dust and other chemical matter in the environment is drawn in and builds up inside the computer. This buildup can cause severe problems if left unchecked.

Tip

Cigarette smoke contains chemicals that can conduct electricity and cause corrosion of computer parts. The smoke residue can infiltrate the entire system, causing corrosion and contamination of electrical contacts and sensitive components such as floppy drive read/write heads and optical drive lens assemblies. You should avoid smoking near computer equipment and encourage your company to develop and enforce a similar policy.

Floppy disk drives are particularly vulnerable to the effects of dirt and dust. A floppy drive is essentially a large "hole" in the system case through which air continuously flows. Therefore, these drives accumulate a large amount of dust and chemical buildup within a short time. Hard disk drives do not present quite the same problem. Because the head disk assembly (HDA) in a hard disk is a sealed unit with a single barometric vent, no dust or dirt can enter without passing through the barometric vent filter. This filter ensures that contaminating dust or particles cannot enter the interior of the HDA. Thus, cleaning a hard disk requires blowing off the dust and dirt from outside the drive. No internal cleaning is required.

Disassembly and Cleaning Tools

To properly clean the system and all the boards inside requires certain supplies and tools. In addition to the tools required to disassemble the unit, you should have these items:

- Contact cleaning solution
- Canned air
- A small brush
- Lint-free foam cleaning swabs
- Anti-static wrist-grounding strap

You also might want to acquire these optional items:

- Foam tape
- Low-volatile room-temperature vulcanizing (RTV) sealer
- Silicone-type lubricant
- Computer vacuum cleaner

These simple cleaning tools and chemical solutions enable you to perform most common preventive maintenance tasks.

Chemicals

Chemicals can be used to help clean, troubleshoot, and even repair a system. You can use several different types of cleaning solutions with computers and electronic assemblies. Most fall into the following categories:

- Standard cleaners
- Contact cleaner/lubricants
- Dusters

Tip

The makeup of many of the chemicals used for cleaning electronic components has been changing because many of the chemicals originally used are now considered environmentally unsafe. They have been attributed to damaging the earth's ozone layer. Chlorine atoms from chlorofluorocarbons (CFCs) and chlorinated solvents attach themselves to ozone molecules and destroy them. Many of these chemicals are now strictly regulated by federal and international agencies in an effort to preserve the ozone layer. Most of the companies that produce chemicals used for system cleaning and maintenance have had to introduce environmentally safe replacements. The only drawback is that many of these safer chemicals cost more and usually do not work as well as those they replace.

Standard Cleaners

For the most basic function—cleaning components, electrical connectors, and contacts—one of the most useful chemicals is 1,1,1 trichloroethane. This substance is a very effective cleaner that was at one time used to clean electrical contacts and components because it does not damage most plastics and board materials. In fact, trichloroethane could be very useful for cleaning stains on the system case and keyboard as well. Unfortunately, trichloroethane is now being regulated as a chlorinated solvent, along with CFCs (chlorofluorocarbons) such as Freon, but electronic chemical-supply companies are offering several replacements.

Alternative cleaning solutions are available in a variety of types and configurations. You can use pure isopropyl alcohol, acetone, Freon, trichloroethane, or a variety of other chemicals. Most board manufacturers and service shops are now leaning toward alcohol, acetone, or other chemicals that do not cause ozone depletion and comply with government regulations and environmental safety.

Recently, new biodegradable cleaners described as "citrus-based cleaners" have become popular in the industry, and in many cases are more effective and more economical for circuit board and contact cleaning. These cleaners are commonly known as d-limonene or citrus terpenes and are derived from orange peels, which gives them a strong (but pleasant) citric odor. Another type of terpene is called a-pinene, and is derived from pine trees. You must exercise care when using these cleaners, however, because they can cause swelling of some plastics, especially silicone rubber and PVC.

You should be sure that your cleaning solution is designed to clean computers or electronic assemblies. In most cases, this means that the solution should be chemically pure and free from contaminants or other unwanted substances. You should not, for example, use drugstore rubbing alcohol for cleaning electronic parts or contacts because it is not pure and could contain water or perfumes. The material must be moisture-free and residue-free. The solutions should be in liquid form, not a spray. Sprays can be wasteful, and you almost never spray the solution directly on components. Instead, wet a foam or chamois swab used for wiping the component. These electronic-component cleaning solutions are available at any good electronics parts store.

Contact Cleaner/Lubricants

These chemicals are similar to the standard cleaners but include a lubricating component. The lubricant eases the force required when plugging and unplugging cables and connectors, reducing strain on the devices. The lubricant coating also acts as a conductive protectant that insulates the contacts from corrosion. These chemicals can greatly prolong the life of a system by preventing intermittent contacts in the future.

A unique type of contact enhancer and lubricant called Stabilant 22 is currently on the market. This chemical, which you apply to electrical contacts, greatly enhances the connection and lubricates the contact point; it is much more effective than conventional contact cleaners or lubricants.

Stabilant 22 is a liquid-polymer semiconductor; it behaves like liquid metal and conducts electricity in the presence of an electric current. The substance also fills the air gaps between the mating surfaces of two items that are in contact, making the surface area of the contact larger and also keeping out oxygen and other contaminants that can corrode the contact point.

This chemical is available in several forms. Stabilant 22 is the concentrated version, whereas Stabilant 22a is a version diluted with isopropanol in a 4:1 ratio. An even more diluted 8:1-ratio version is sold in many high-end stereo and audio shops under the name Tweek. Just 15ml of Stabilant 22a sells for about $40; a liter of the concentrate costs about $4,000!

As you can plainly see, Stabilant 22 is fairly expensive, but little is required in an application, and nothing else has been found to be as effective in preserving electrical contacts. (NASA uses the chemical on spacecraft electronics.) An application of Stabilant can provide protection for up to 16 years, according to its manufacturer, D.W. Electrochemicals. You will find the company's address and phone number in the Vendor List on the CD.

Stabilant is especially effective on I/O slot connectors, adapter-card edge and pin connectors, disk drive connectors, power-supply connectors, and virtually any connector in the PC. In addition to enhancing the contact and preventing corrosion, an application of Stabilant lubricates the contacts, making insertion and removal of the connector easier.

Dusters

Compressed gas often is used as an aid in system cleaning. You use the compressed gas as a blower to remove dust and debris from a system or component. Originally, these dusters used CFCs (chlorofluorocarbons) such as Freon, whereas modern dusters now use either HFCs (hydrofluorocarbons such as difluoroethane) or carbon dioxide, neither of which is known to damage the ozone layer. Be careful when you use these devices because some of them can generate a static charge when the compressed gas leaves the nozzle of the can. Be sure that you are using the kind approved for cleaning or dusting off computer equipment, and consider wearing a static grounding strap as a precaution. The type of compressed-air cans used for cleaning camera equipment can sometimes differ from the type used for cleaning static-sensitive computer components.

When using these compressed air products, make sure you hold the can upright so that only gas is ejected from the nozzle. If you tip the can, the raw propellant will come out as a cold liquid, which not only is wasteful but can damage or discolor plastics. You should only use compressed gas on equipment that is powered off, to minimize any chance of damage through short circuits.

Closely related to compressed-air products are chemical-freeze sprays. These sprays are used to quickly cool down a suspected failing component, which often temporarily restores it to normal operation. These substances are not used to repair a device, but to confirm that you have found a failed device. Often, a component's failure is heat-related and cooling it temporarily restores it to normal operation. If the circuit begins operating normally, the device you are cooling is the suspect device.

Vacuum Cleaners

Some people prefer to use a vacuum cleaner instead of canned gas dusters for cleaning a system. Canned gas is usually better for cleaning in small areas. A vacuum cleaner is more useful when you are cleaning a system loaded with dust and dirt. You can use the vacuum cleaner to suck out the dust and debris instead of simply blowing it around on the other components, which sometimes happens with canned air. For on-site servicing (when you are going to the location of the equipment instead of the equipment coming to you), canned air is easier to carry in a tool kit than a small vacuum cleaner. There are also tiny vacuum cleaners available for system cleaning. These small units are easy to carry and can serve as an alternative to compressed air cans.

There are special vacuum cleaners specifically designed for use on and around electronic components. They are designed to minimize electrostatic discharge (ESD) while in use. If you are using a regular vacuum cleaner and not one specifically designed with ESD protection, you should take precautions such as wearing a grounding wrist strap. Also, if the cleaner has a metal nozzle, be careful not to touch it to the circuit boards or components you are cleaning.

Brushes and Swabs

You can use a small makeup, photographic, or paint brush to carefully loosen the accumulated dirt and dust inside a PC before spraying it with canned air or using the vacuum cleaner. Be careful about generating static electricity, however. In most cases, you should not use a brush directly on circuit boards, but only on the case interior and other parts such as fan blades, air vents, and keyboards. Wear a grounded wrist strap if you are brushing on or near any circuit boards, and brush slowly and lightly to prevent static discharges from occurring.

Use cleaning swabs to wipe off electrical contacts and connectors, disk drive heads, and other sensitive areas. The swabs should be made of foam or synthetic chamois material that does not leave lint or dust residue. Unfortunately, proper foam or chamois cleaning swabs are more expensive than typical cotton swabs. Do not use cotton swabs because they leave cotton fibers on everything they touch. Cotton fibers are conductive in some situations and can remain on drive heads, which can scratch disks. Foam or chamois swabs can be purchased at most electronics supply stores.

One item to avoid is an eraser for cleaning contacts. Many people (including me) have recommended using a soft pencil-type eraser for cleaning circuit-board contacts. Testing has proven this to be bad advice for several reasons. One reason is that any such abrasive wiping on electrical contacts generates friction and an ESD. This ESD can be damaging to boards and components, especially the newer low-voltage devices. These devices are especially static-sensitive, and cleaning the contacts without a proper liquid solution is not recommended. Also, the eraser will wear off the gold coating on many contacts, exposing the tin contact underneath, which will rapidly corrode when exposed to air. Some companies sell premoistened contact cleaning pads that are soaked in a proper contact cleaner and lubricant. These pads are safe to wipe on conductor and contacts with no likelihood of ESD damage or abrasion of the gold plating.

Silicone Lubricants

You can use a silicone lubricant such as WD-40 to lubricate the door mechanisms on floppy disk drives and any other part of the system that might require clean, non-oily lubrication. Other items that you can lubricate are the disk drive head slider rails and even printer-head slider rails, to provide smoother operation.

Using silicone instead of conventional oils is important because silicone does not gum up and collect dust and other debris. Always use the silicone sparingly. Do not spray it anywhere near the equipment because it tends to migrate and will end up where it doesn't belong (such as on drive heads). Instead, apply a small amount to a toothpick or foam swab and dab the silicone lubricant on the components where needed. You can use a lint-free cleaning stick soaked in silicone to lubricate the metal print-head rails in a printer.

Obtaining Required Tools and Accessories

You can obtain most of the cleaning chemicals and tools discussed in this chapter from an electronics supply house, or even your local Radio Shack. A company called Chemtronics specializes in chemicals for the computer and electronics industry. These and other companies that supply tools, chemicals, and other computer and electronic cleaning supplies are listed in the Vendor List on the CD. With all these items on hand, you should be equipped for most preventive maintenance operations.

Disassembling and Cleaning Procedures

To properly clean your system, you must at least partially disassemble it. Some people go as far as to remove the motherboard. Removing the motherboard results in the best possible access to other areas of the system; but in the interest of saving time, you probably need to disassemble the system only to the point at which the motherboard is completely visible.

To do this, remove all the system's plug-in adapter cards and the disk drives. Complete system disassembly and reassembly procedures are listed in Chapter 24 "Building or Upgrading Systems." Although you can clean the heads of a floppy drive with a cleaning disk without opening the system unit's cover, you probably will want to do more thorough cleaning. In addition to the drive heads, you also should clean and lubricate the door mechanism and clean any logic boards and connectors on the drive. This procedure usually requires removing the drive.

Next, do the same thing with the hard disk drives: Clean the logic boards and connectors, and lubricate the grounding strap. To do this, you must remove the hard disk assembly. As a precaution, be sure your data is backed up first.

Reseating Socketed Chips

Another primary preventive maintenance function is to undo the effects of chip creep. As your system heats and cools, it expands and contracts, and the physical expansion and contraction can cause components that are plugged in to sockets to gradually work their way out of those sockets. This process is called chip creep. To correct its effects, you must find all socketed components in the system and make sure that they are properly reseated.

In most of today's systems, the memory chips are installed in socketed SIMMs or DIMMs. SIMM/DIMM devices are retained securely in their sockets by a positive latching mechanism and cannot creep out. The Memory SIPP (single inline pin package) devices (SIMMs with pins rather than contacts) used in older systems are not retained by a latching mechanism, however, and therefore can creep out of their sockets. Standard socketed memory chips are prime candidates for chip creep. Most other logic components are soldered in. On an older system, you might also find the ROM chips, a math coprocessor, and even the main system processor in sockets. Newer systems place the CPU in a ZIF socket, which has a lever that releases the grip of the socket on the chip. In most cases, there is very little creep with a ZIF socket. In most current systems, the memory (in SIMMs or DIMMs) and the processor are the only components that you will find in sockets; all others are soldered in.

Exceptions, however, might exist. A socketed component in one system might not be socketed in another—even if both are from the same manufacturer. Sometimes this difference results from a parts-availability problem when the boards are manufactured. Rather than halt the assembly line when a part is not available, the manufacturer adds a socket instead of the component. When the component becomes available, it is plugged in and the board is finished.

To make sure that all components are fully seated in their sockets, place your hand on the underside of the board and then apply downward pressure with the thumb of your other hand (from the top) on the chip to be seated. For larger chips, seat the chip carefully in the socket, and press separately on each end of the chip with your thumb to be sure that the chip is fully seated. (The processor and math coprocessor chips can usually be seated in this manner.) In most cases, you should hear a crunching sound as the chip makes its way back into the socket. Because of the great force that is sometimes required to reseat the chips, this operation is difficult if you do not remove the board.

For motherboards, forcibly seating chips can be dangerous if you do not directly support the board from the underside with your hand. Too much pressure on the board can cause it to bow or bend in the chassis, and the pressure can crack it before the chip is fully seated. The plastic standoffs that hold the board up off the metal chassis are spaced too far apart to properly support the board under this kind of stress. Try this operation only if you can remove and support the board adequately from underneath.

You might be surprised to know that, even if you fully seat a chip, it might need reseating again within a year. The creep usually is noticeable within a year or less.

Cleaning Boards

After reseating any socketed devices that might have crept out of their sockets, the next step is to clean the boards and all connectors in the system. For this step, use the cleaning solutions and the lint-free swabs mentioned earlier.

First, clean the dust and debris off the board and then clean any connectors on the board. To clean the boards, it is usually best to use a vacuum cleaner designed for electronic assemblies and circuit boards or a duster can of compressed gas. The dusters are especially effective at blasting any dust and dirt off the boards.

Also, blow any dust out of the power supply, especially around the fan intake and exhaust areas. You do not need to disassemble the power supply to do this; simply use a duster can and blast the compressed air into the supply through the fan exhaust port. This will blow the dust out of the supply and clean off the fan blades and grill, which will help with system airflow.

Caution

Be careful with ESD, which can cause damage when you are cleaning electronic components. Take extra precautions in the dead of winter or in extremely dry, high-static environments. You can apply anti-static sprays and treatments to the work area to reduce the likelihood of ESD damage.

An anti-static wrist-grounding strap is recommended. This should be connected to a ground on the card or board you are wiping. This strap ensures that no electrical discharge occurs between you and the board. An alternative method is to keep a finger or thumb on the ground of the motherboard or card as you wipe it off.

Cleaning Connectors and Contacts

Cleaning the connectors and contacts in a system promotes reliable connections between devices. On a motherboard, you will want to clean the slot connectors, power supply connectors, keyboard and mouse connectors, and speaker connector. For most plug-in cards, you will want to clean the edge connectors that plug in to slots on the motherboard and any other connectors, such as external ones mounted on the card bracket.

Submerge the lint-free swabs in the liquid cleaning solution. If you are using the spray, hold the swab away from the system and spray a small amount on the foam end until the solution starts to drip. Then, use the soaked foam swab to wipe the connectors on the boards. Presoaked wipes are the easiest to use. Simply wipe them along the contacts to remove any accumulated dirt and leave a protective coating behind.

On the motherboard, pay special attention to the slot connectors. Be liberal with the liquid; resoak the foam swab repeatedly, and vigorously clean the connectors. Don't worry whether some of the liquid drips on the surface of the motherboard. These solutions are entirely safe for the whole board and will not damage the components.

Use the solution to wash the dirt off the gold contacts in the slot connectors, and then clean any other connectors on the board. Clean the keyboard and mouse connectors, the grounding positions where screws ground the board to the system chassis, power-supply connectors, speaker connectors, and the battery connectors.

If you are cleaning a plug-in board, pay special attention to the edge connector that mates with the slot connector on the motherboard. When people handle plug-in cards, they often touch the gold contacts on these connectors. Touching the gold contacts coats them with oils and debris, which prevents proper contact with the slot connector when the board is installed. Make sure these gold contacts are free of all finger oils and residue. It is a good idea to use one of the contact cleaners that has a conductive lubricant, which makes it easier to push the adapter into the slot and also protects the contacts from corrosion.

You will also want to use the swab and solution to clean the ends of ribbon cables or other types of cables or connectors in a system. Clean the floppy drive cables and connectors, the hard disk cables and connectors, and any others you find. Don't forget to clean the edge connectors that are on the disk drive logic boards, as well as the power connectors to the drives.

Cleaning the Keyboard and Mouse

Keyboards and mice are notorious for picking up dirt and garbage. If you have ever opened up an older keyboard, you often will be amazed at the junk you will find in there.

To prevent problems, it is a good idea to periodically clean the keyboard with a vacuum cleaner. An alternative method is to turn the keyboard upside down and shoot it with a can of compressed air. This will blow out the dirt and debris that has accumulated inside the keyboard and possibly prevent future problems with sticking keys or dirty keyswitches.

If a particular key is stuck or making intermittent contact, you can soak or spray that switch with contact cleaner. The best way to do this is to first remove the keycap and then spray the cleaner into the switch. This usually does not require complete disassembly of the keyboard. Periodic vacuuming or compressed gas cleaning will prevent more serious problems with sticking keys and keyswitches.

Most mice are easy to clean. In most cases, there is a twist-off locking retainer that keeps the mouse ball retained in the body of the mouse. By removing the retainer, the ball will drop out. After removing the ball, you should clean it with one of the electronic cleaners. I would recommend a pure cleaner instead of a contact cleaner with lubricant because you do not want any lubricant on the mouse ball. Then you should wipe off the rollers in the body of the mouse with the cleaner and some swabs.

Periodic cleaning of a mouse in this manner will eliminate or prevent skipping or erratic movement. I also recommend a mouse pad for most ball-type mice because the pad will prevent the mouse ball from picking up debris from your desk.

Other pointing devices requiring little or no maintenance are the IBM-designed Track-point and similar systems introduced by other manufacturers, such as the Glidepoint by Alps. These devices are totally sealed, and use pressure transducers to control pointer movement. Because they are sealed, cleaning need only be performed externally, and is as simple as wiping the device off with a mild cleaning solution to remove oils and other deposits that have accumulated from handling them.

Hard Disk Maintenance

Certain preventive maintenance procedures protect your data and ensure that your hard disk works efficiently. Some of these procedures actually minimize wear and tear on your drive, which will prolong its life. Additionally, a high level of data protection can be implemented by performing some simple commands periodically. These commands provide methods for backing up (and possibly later restoring) critical areas of the hard disk that, if damaged, would disable access to all your files.

Defragmenting Files

Over time, as you delete and save files to a hard disk, the files become fragmented. This means that they are split into many noncontiguous areas on the disk. One of the best ways to protect both your hard disk and the data on it is to periodically defragment the files on the disk. This serves two purposes. One is that by ensuring that all the files are stored in contiguous sectors on the disk, head movement and drive wear and tear will be minimized. This has the added benefit of improving the speed at which the drive retrieves files by reducing the head thrashing that occurs every time it accesses a fragmented file.

The second major benefit, and in my estimation the more important of the two, is that in the case of a disaster where the FATs and root directory are severely damaged, the data on the drive can usually be recovered easily if the files are contiguous. On the other hand, if the files are split up in many pieces across the drive, it is virtually impossible to figure out which pieces belong to which files without an intact FAT and directory system. For the purposes of data integrity and protection, I recommend defragmenting your hard disk drives on a monthly basis.

There are three main functions in most defragmentation programs:

- File defragmentation
- File packing (free space consolidation)
- File sorting

Defragmentation is the basic function, but most other programs also add file packing. Packing the files is optional on some programs because it usually takes additional time to perform. This function packs the files at the beginning of the disk so that all free space is consolidated at the end of the disk. This feature minimizes future file fragmentation by eliminating any empty holes on the disk. Because all free space is consolidated into one large area, any new files written to the disk will be able to be written in a contiguous manner with no fragmentation.

The last function, file sorting (sometimes called disk optimizing), is not usually necessary and is performed as an option by many defragmenting programs. This function adds a tremendous amount of time to the operation, and has little or no effect on the speed at which information is accessed. It can be somewhat beneficial for disaster recovery purposes because you will have an idea of which files came before or after other files if a disaster occurs. Not all defragmenting programs offer file sorting, and the extra time it takes is probably not worth any benefits you will receive. Other programs can sort the order that files are listed in directories, which is a quick and easy operation compared to sorting the file ordering the disk.

Windows 9x includes a disk defragmentation program with the operating system that you can use on both the FAT16 and FAT32 file systems that the OS supports. For DOS and Windows systems, you must purchase a third-party defragmentation program. Norton Utilities includes a disk defragmenter, as do many other utility packages. If you elect to use a third-party product on a Windows 9x system, be certain that it supports the file system you use on your drives. Running a FAT16 defragmentation program on a FAT32 drive can cause severe problems.

Before you defragment your disks, it is a good idea to run a disk repair program such as Windows 9x's ScanDisk or Norton Disk Doctor, even if you are not experiencing any problems. This ensures that your drives are in good working order before you begin the defragmentation process.

Windows 98 Maintenance Wizard

Windows 98 includes a Task Scheduler program that enables you to schedule programs for automatic execution at specified times. The Windows 98 Maintenance Wizard walks you through the steps of scheduling regular disk defragmentations, disk error scans, and deletions of unnecessary files. You can schedule these processes to execute during nonworking hours, so regular system activities are not disturbed.

Virus Checking

Viruses are a danger to any system, and it's a good idea to make scans with an antivirus program a regular part of your preventive maintenance program. Although both Microsoft and IBM provide antivirus software in MS- and PC-DOS, respectively, if you run Windows 9x or Windows NT, you must obtain a third-party program to scan your system. There are many aftermarket utility packages available that scan for and remove viruses. No matter which of these programs you use, you should perform a scan for virus programs periodically, especially before making hard disk backups. This helps ensure that you catch any potential virus problem before it spreads and becomes a major catastrophe. In addition, it is important to select an antivirus product from a vendor that provides regular updates to the program's virus signatures. The signatures determine which viruses the software can detect and cure, and because there are new viruses constantly being introduced, these updates are essential.

Passive Preventive Maintenance Procedures

Passive preventive maintenance involves taking care of the system by providing the best possible environment—both physical and electrical—for the system. Physical concerns are conditions such as ambient temperature, thermal stress from power cycling, dust and smoke contamination, and disturbances such as shock and vibration. Electrical concerns are items such as ESD, power-line noise, and radio-frequency interference. Each of these environmental concerns is discussed in the following sections.

Examining the Operating Environment

Oddly enough, one of the most overlooked aspects of microcomputer preventive maintenance is protecting the hardware—and the sizable financial investment it represents—from environmental abuse. Computers are relatively forgiving, and they are generally safe in an environment that is comfortable for people. Computers, however, are often treated with no more respect than desktop calculators. The result of this type of abuse is many system failures.

Before you set up a new PC, prepare a proper location for it that is free of airborne contaminants such as smoke or other pollution. Do not place your system in front of a window; the computer should not be exposed to direct sunlight or temperature variations. The environmental temperature should be as constant as possible. Power should be provided through properly grounded outlets and should be stable and free from electrical noise and interference. Keep your system away from radio transmitters or other sources of radio frequency energy.

Heating and Cooling

Thermal expansion and contraction from ambient temperature changes places stress on a computer system. Therefore, keeping the temperature in your office or room relatively constant is important to the successful operation of your computer system.

Temperature variations can lead to serious problems. You might encounter excessive chip creep, for example. If extreme variations occur over a short period, signal traces on circuit boards can crack and separate, solder joints can break, and contacts in the system can undergo accelerated corrosion. Solid-state components such as chips can be damaged also, and a host of other problems can develop.

Temperature variations can play havoc with hard disk drives. Writing to a disk at different ambient temperatures can, on some drives, cause data to be written at different locations relative to the track centers. This can cause read and write problems at a later time.

To ensure that your system operates in the correct ambient temperature, you must first determine your system's specified functional range. Most manufacturers provide data about the correct operating temperature range for their systems. Two temperature specifications might be available, one indicating allowable temperatures during operation and another indicating allowable temperatures under non-operating conditions. IBM, for example, indicates the following temperature ranges as acceptable for most of its systems:

> System on: 60–90° Fahrenheit
>
> System off: 50–110° Fahrenheit

For the safety of the disk and the data it contains, avoid rapid changes in ambient temperatures. If rapid temperature changes occur—for example, when a new drive is shipped to a location during the winter and then brought indoors—let the drive acclimate to room temperature before turning it on. In extreme cases, condensation can form on the platters inside the drive HDA, which is disastrous for the drive if you turn it on before the condensation has a chance to evaporate. Most drive manufacturers specify a timetable to use as a guide in acclimating a drive to room temperature before operating it. You usually must wait several hours to a day before a drive is ready to use after it has been shipped or stored in a cold environment. Manufacturers normally advise that you leave the drive in its packing until it is acclimated. Removing the drive from a shipping carton when extremely cold increases the likelihood of condensation forming as the drive warms up.

Most office environments provide a stable temperature in which to operate a computer system, but some do not. Be sure to give some consideration to the placement of your equipment.

Power Cycling (On/Off)

As you have just learned, the temperature variations that a system encounters greatly stress the system's physical components. The largest temperature variations a system encounters, however, are those that occur during the warmup period right after you turn on the computer. Powering on a cold system subjects it to the greatest possible internal temperature variations. If you want a system to have the longest and most trouble-free life possible, you should limit the temperature variations in its environment. You can limit the extreme temperature cycling in two simple ways during a cold startup: Leave the system off all the time or leave it on all the time. Of these two possibilities, of course, you will probably want to choose the latter option. Leaving the power on is the best way I know to promote system reliability. If your only concern is system longevity, the simple recommendation would be to keep the system unit powered on (or off!) continuously. In the real world, however, there are more variables to consider, such as the cost of electricity, the potential fire hazard of unattended running equipment, and other concerns, as well.

If you think about the way light bulbs typically fail, you can begin to understand how thermal cycling can be dangerous. Light bulbs burn out most often when you first turn them on because the filament must endure incredible thermal stress as it changes temperature, in less than one second, from ambient to several thousands of degrees. A bulb that remains on continuously lasts longer than one that is turned on and off repeatedly.

The place where problems are most likely to occur immediately at power-on is in the power supply. The start-up current draw for the system during the first few seconds of operation is very high compared to the normal operating-current draw. Because the current must come from the power supply, the supply has an extremely demanding load to carry for the first few seconds of operation, especially if several disk drives must be started. Motors have an extremely high power-on current draw. This demand often overloads a marginal circuit or component in the supply and causes it to burn or break with a "snap." I have seen several power supplies die the instant a system was powered up. To enable your equipment to have the longest possible life, try to keep the temperature of solid-state components relatively constant, and limit the number of startups on the power supply. The only way I know to do this is to leave the system on.

Although it sounds like I am telling you to leave all your computer equipment on 24 hours a day, seven days a week, I no longer recommend this type of operation. A couple of concerns have tempered my urge to leave everything running continuously. One is that an unattended system that is powered on represents a fire hazard. I have seen monitors catch fire after internally shorting, and systems whose cooling fans have frozen, causing the power supply and the entire system to overheat. I do not leave any system running in an unattended building. Another problem is wasted electrical power. Many companies have adopted austerity programs that involve turning off lights and other items when not in use. The power consumption of some of today's high-powered systems and accessories is not trivial. Also, an unattended operating system is more of a security risk than one that is powered off and locked.

Realities—such as the fire hazard of unattended systems running during night or weekend hours, security problems, and power-consumption issues—might prevent you from leaving your system on all the time. Therefore, you must compromise. Power on the system only one time daily. Don't power the system on and off several times every day. This good advice is often ignored, especially when several users share systems. Each user powers on the system to perform work on the PC and then powers off the system. These systems tend to have many more problems with component failures.

If you are in a building with a programmable thermostat, you have another reason to be concerned about temperatures and disk drives. Some buildings have thermostats programmed to turn off the heat overnight or over the weekend. These thermostats are programmed also to quickly raise the temperature just before business hours every day. In Chicago, for example, outside temperatures in the winter can dip to -20° (excluding the windchill factor). An office building's interior temperature can drop as low as 50° during the weekend. When you arrive Monday morning, the heat has been on for only an hour or so, but the hard disk platters might not yet have reached even 60° when you turn on the system. During the first 20 minutes of operation, the disk platters rapidly rise in temperature to 120° or more. If you have an inexpensive stepper motor hard disk and begin writing to the disk at these low temperatures, you are setting yourself up for trouble.

Tip

If you do not leave a system on continuously; at least give it 15 minutes or more to warm up after a cold start before writing to the hard disk. This practice does wonders for the reliability of the data on your disk.

If you do leave your system on for long periods of time, make sure that the screen is blank or displays a random image if the system is not in use. The phosphor on the picture tube can burn if a stationary image is left onscreen continuously. Higher-persistence phosphor monochrome screens are most susceptible, and the color displays with low-persistence phosphors are the least susceptible. Most of the monitors used with today's PCs will not show the effect of a screen burn. If you ever have seen a monochrome display with the image of some program permanently burned in—even with the display off—you know what I mean. Look at the monitors that display flight information at the airport; they usually show some of the effects of phosphor burn.

Most modern displays that have power-saving features can automatically enter a standby mode on command by the system. If your system has these power-saving functions, enable them, as they will help to reduce energy costs and preserve the monitor.

Static Electricity

Static electricity can cause numerous problems within a system. The problems usually appear during the winter months when humidity is low or in extremely dry climates where the humidity is low year-round. In these cases, you might need to take special precautions to ensure that your PC is not damaged.

Static discharges outside a system-unit chassis are rarely a source of permanent problems within the system. Usually, the worst possible effect of a static discharge to the case, keyboard, or even a location near the computer is a parity check (memory) error or a system lockup. In some cases, I have been able to cause parity checks or system lockups by simply walking past a PC. Most static-sensitivity problems are caused by improper grounding of the system power. Be sure that you always use a three-prong, grounded power cord plugged in to a properly grounded outlet. If you are unsure about the outlet, you can buy an outlet tester such as those described earlier in this chapter at most electronics supply or hardware stores for only a few dollars.

Whenever you open a system unit or handle circuits removed from the system, you must be much more careful with static. You can permanently damage a component with a static discharge if the charge is not routed to a ground. I usually recommend handling boards and adapters first by a grounding point such as the bracket to minimize the potential for static damage.

An easy way to prevent static problems is with good power-line grounding, which is extremely important for computer equipment. A poorly designed power-line grounding system is one of the primary causes of poor computer design. The best way to prevent static damage is to prevent the static charge from getting into the computer in the first place. The chassis ground in a properly designed system serves as a static guard for the computer that redirects the static charge safely to the ground. For this ground to be complete, therefore, the system must be plugged in to a properly grounded three-wire outlet.

If the static problem is extreme, you can resort to other measures. One is to use a grounded static mat underneath the computer. Touch the mat first before you touch the computer to ensure that any static charges are routed to ground and away from the system unit's internal parts. If problems still persist, you might want to check out the building's electrical ground. I have seen installations that had three-wire outlets that were rendered useless by the building's ungrounded electrical service.

Power-Line Noise

To run properly, a computer system requires a steady supply of clean noise-free power. In some installations, however, the power line serving the computer serves heavy equipment also, and the voltage variations resulting from the on/off cycling of this equipment can cause problems for the computer. Certain types of equipment on the same power line also can cause voltage spikes—short transient signals of sometimes 1,000v or more—that can physically damage a computer. Although these spikes are rare, they can be crippling. Even a dedicated electrical circuit used only by a single computer can experience spikes and transients, depending on the quality of the power supplied to the building or circuit.

During the site-preparation phase of a system installation, you should be aware of these factors to ensure a steady supply of clean power:

- If possible, the computer system should be on its own circuit with its own circuit breaker. This setup does not guarantee freedom from interference, but it helps.
- The circuit should be checked for a good, low-resistance ground, proper line voltage, freedom from interference, and freedom from brownouts (voltage dips).
- A three-wire circuit is a must, but some people substitute grounding-plug adapters to adapt a grounded plug to a two-wire socket. This setup is not recommended; the ground is there for a reason.
- Power-line noise problems increase with the resistance of the circuit, which is a function of wire size and length. To decrease resistance, therefore, avoid extension cords unless absolutely necessary, and then use only heavy-duty extension cords.
- Inevitably, you will want to plug in other equipment later. Plan ahead to avoid the temptation to connect too many items to a single outlet. If possible, provide a separate power circuit for non-computer-related devices.

Air conditioners, coffee makers, copy machines, laser printers, space heaters, vacuum cleaners, and power tools are some of the worst corrupters of a PC system's power. Any of these items can draw an excessive amount of current and play havoc with a PC system on the same electrical circuit. I've seen offices in which all the computers begin to crash at about 9:05 a.m. daily, which is when all the coffee makers are turned on!

Also, try to ensure that copy machines and laser printers do not share a circuit with other computer equipment. These devices draw a large amount of power.

Another major problem in some companies is partitioned offices. Many of these partitions are prewired with their own electrical outlets and are plugged in to one another in a sort of power-line daisy chain, similar to chaining power strips together. I pity the person in the cubicle at the end of the electrical daisy chain, who is likely to have very erratic power!

As a real-world example of too many devices sharing a single circuit, I can describe several instances in which a personal computer had a repeating parity check problem. All efforts to repair the system had been unsuccessful. The reported error locations from the parity check message were inconsistent, which normally indicates a problem with power. The problem could have been the power supply in the system unit or the external power supplied from the wall outlet. This problem was solved one day as I stood watching the system. The parity check message was displayed at the same instant someone two cubicles away turned on a copy machine. Placing the computers on a separate line solved the problem.

By following the guidelines in this section, you can create the proper power environment for your systems and help to ensure trouble-free operation.

Radio-Frequency Interference

Radio-frequency interference (RFI) is easily overlooked as a problem factor. The interference is caused by any source of radio transmissions near a computer system. Living next door to a 50,000-watt commercial radio station is one sure way to get RFI problems, but less-powerful transmitters can cause problems, too. I know of many instances in which cordless telephones have caused sporadic random keystrokes to appear, as though an invisible entity were typing on the keyboard. I also have seen RFI cause a system to lock up. Solutions to RFI problems are more difficult to state because every case must be handled differently. Sometimes, simply moving the system eliminates the problem because radio signals can be directional in nature. At other times, you must invest in specially shielded cables for external devices such as the keyboard and the monitor.

One type of solution to an RFI noise problem with cables is to pass the cable through a toroidal iron core, a doughnut-shaped piece of iron placed around a cable to suppress both the reception and transmission of electromagnetic interference (EMI). Many monitors include a toroid on the cable that connects to the computer. If you can isolate an RFI noise problem in a particular cable, you often can solve the problem by passing the cable through a toroidal core. Because the cable must pass through the center hole of the core, it often is difficult, if not impossible, to add a toroid to a cable that already has end connectors installed.

Radio Shack sells a special snap-together toroid designed specifically to be added to cables already in use. This toroid looks like a thick-walled tube that has been sliced in half. You simply lay the cable in the center of one of the halves, and snap the other half over the first. This type of construction makes it easy to add the noise-suppression features of a toroid to virtually any existing cable.

The best, if not the easiest, way to eliminate an RFI problem is to correct it at the source. It is not likely that you'll be able to convince the commercial radio station near your office to shut down, but if you are dealing with a small radio transmitter that is generating RFI, sometimes you can add a filter to the transmitter that suppresses spurious emissions. Unfortunately, problems sometimes persist until the transmitter is either switched off or moved some distance away from the affected computer.

Dust and Pollutants

Dirt, smoke, dust, and other pollutants are bad for your system. The power-supply fan carries airborne particles through your system, and they collect inside. If your system is used in an extremely harsh environment, you might want to investigate some of the industrial systems on the market designed for harsh conditions.

Many companies make special hardened versions of their systems for harsh environments. Industrial systems usually use a different cooling system from the one used in a regular PC. A large cooling fan is used to pressurize the case rather than depressurize it. The air pumped into the case passes through a filter unit that must be cleaned and changed periodically. The system is pressurized so that no contaminated air can flow into it; air flows only outward. The only way air can enter is through the fan and filter system.

These systems also might have special keyboards impervious to liquids and dirt. Some flat-membrane keyboards are difficult to type on, but are extremely rugged; others resemble the standard types of keyboards but have a thin, plastic membrane that covers all the keys. You can add this membrane to normal types of keyboards to seal them from the environment.

A new breed of humidifier can cause problems with computer equipment. This type of humidifier uses ultrasonics to generate a mist of water sprayed into the air. The extra humidity helps cure problems with static electricity resulting from a dry climate, but the airborne water contaminants can cause many problems. If you use one of these systems, you might notice a white ash-like deposit forming on components. The deposit is the result of abrasive and corrosive minerals suspended in the vaporized water. If these deposits collect on the system components, they can cause all kinds of problems. The only safe way to run one of these ultrasonic humidifiers is to use distilled water. If you use a humidifier, be sure it does not generate these deposits.

If you do your best to keep the environment for your computer equipment clean, your system will run better and last longer. Also, you will not have to open your unit as often for complete preventive maintenance cleaning.

Basic Troubleshooting Guidelines

This section lists basic and general system troubleshooting procedures and guidelines. For specific procedures for troubleshooting a component in the system, see the chapter or section dedicated to that part of the PC.

Before starting any system troubleshooting, there are a few basic steps that should be performed to ensure a consistent starting point and to allow isolating the failed component.

1. Turn off the system and any peripheral devices. Disconnect all external peripherals from the system, except for the keyboard and the video display.

2. Make sure the system is plugged in to a properly grounded power outlet.

3. Make sure the keyboard and video displays are connected to the system. Turn on the video display, and turn up the brightness and contrast controls to at least two-thirds of the maximum. Some displays have onscreen controls that may not be intuitive. Consult the display documentation for more information on how to adjust these settings.

4. To allow the system to boot from a hard disk, make sure there is no floppy disk in the floppy drive. Or put a known good bootable floppy with DOS or diagnostics on it in the floppy drive for testing.

5. Turn on the system. Observe the power supply and chassis fans (if any), and the lights on either the system front panel or power supply. If the fans don't spin and the lights don't light, the power supply or motherboard might be defective.

6. Observe the power on self test (POST). If no errors are detected, the system beeps once and boots up. Errors that display on the screen (*non-fatal* errors) and which do not lock up the system display a text message that varies according to BIOS type and version. Record any errors that occur and refer to Chapter 5 in the section titled "BIOS Error Codes" for more information on any specific codes you see. Errors that lock up the system (*fatal* errors), are indicated by a series of audible beeps. Refer to Chapter 5 for any beep error codes.

7. Confirm that the operating system loads successfully.

Problems During the POST

Problems that occur during the POST are usually caused by incorrect hardware configuration or installation. Actual hardware failure is a far less frequent cause. If you have a POST error, check the following:

1. Are all cables correctly connected and secured?

2. Are the configuration settings correct in Setup?

3. Are all drivers properly installed?

4. Are switches and jumpers on the baseboard correct, if changed from the default settings?

5. Are all resource settings on add-in boards and peripheral devices set so that there are no conflicts, for example, two add-in boards sharing the same interrupt?

6. Is the power supply set to the proper input voltage (110/220v)?

7. Are adapter boards and disk drives installed correctly?

8. Is there a keyboard attached?

9. Is a bootable hard disk (properly partitioned and formatted) installed?

10. Does the BIOS support the drive you have installed, and if so are the parameters entered correctly?

11. Is a bootable floppy disk installed in drive A:?

12. Are all memory SIMMs or DIMMs installed correctly? Try reseating them.

13. Is the operating system properly installed?

Hardware Problems After Booting

If problems occur after the system has been running, and without having made any hardware or software changes, it is possible a hardware fault has occurred. Here is a list of items to check in that case:

1. Try reinstalling the software that has crashed or refuses to run.

2. Try clearing CMOS RAM and running Setup.

3. Check for loose cables, a marginal power supply, or other random component failures.

4. A transient voltage spike, power outage, or brownout might have occurred. Symptoms of voltage spikes include a flickering video display, unexpected system reboots, and the system not responding to user commands. Reload the software and try again.

5. Try reseating the memory modules (SIMMs, DIMMs or RIMMs).

Problems Running Software

Problems running application software (especially new software) are usually caused by or related to the software itself, or that the software is incompatible with the system.

1. Does the system meet the minimum hardware requirements for the software? Check the software documentation to be sure.

2. Check to see that the software is correctly installed. Reinstall if necessary.

3. Check to see that the latest drivers are installed.

4. Scan the system for viruses using the latest antivirus software.

Problems with Adapter Cards

Problems related to add-in boards are usually related to improper board installation or resource (interrupt, DMA or I/O address) conflicts. Also check drivers for the latest versions and be sure the card is compatible with your system and the operating system version you are using.

Operating System Software and Troubleshooting

SOME OF THE MAIN TOPICS IN THIS CHAPTER ARE

Operating Systems from DOS to Windows 2000

DOS and DOS Components

Windows 3.1

Windows 9x

Windows NT and Windows 2000

Linux

Operating Systems from DOS to Windows 2000

This chapter focuses on the operating systems most commonly used on PCs today and their relationships to the PC hardware. Information about operating systems may seem out of place in a book about hardware upgrade and repair, but if you ignore the operating system and other software when you troubleshoot a system, you can miss a number of problems. The best system troubleshooters and diagnosticians know the entire system—hardware and software.

Most of the PCs in use today run a version of Windows, with Windows 9x being the most popular, followed by NT/2000 or older DOS/Windows 3.x versions. Windows NT/2000 is a more advanced alternative that is constantly growing in popularity, mostly in networked or corporate environments. Other non-Microsoft operating systems are available, such as Linux, which offer a great deal of power and flexibility. In particular Linux has gone from an underground operating system to one that is now being supported by major companies such as IBM. This chapter examines the basic structure of the popular operating systems, their components, the system boot process, and how to distinguish a software problem from a hardware problem.

DOS is the original and most basic of PC operating systems. By itself, it is considered to be underpowered and incapable of supporting the full capabilities of much of today's hardware. However, the underlying concepts of DOS form the basis for the more advanced operating systems used today, such as Windows 95 and Windows 98. With the exceptions of Windows NT/2000 and Linux, all the operating systems discussed in this chapter rely on DOS structures for their basic functions.

Operating System Basics

The operating system is just one component in a total system architecture. A PC system has a distinct hierarchy of software that controls the system at all times. Even when you are working in an application such as a word processor or spreadsheet, there are several other programming layers always executing underneath the application. Ultimately, these software layers provide access to the hardware, such as storage media, memory, and the system processor. Usually the layers can be defined distinctly, but sometimes the boundaries are vague. Figure 26.1 shows these layers and how they may differ between two typical PCs.

In most cases, communications occur only between adjoining layers in the system architecture, but this rule is not absolute. Some programs ignore the services provided by the layer directly beneath them and eliminate the middleman by skipping one or more layers. An example of this is when a program ignores the OS and BIOS video routines and communicates directly with the video display hardware in the interest of the highest possible screen performance. Although the high performance goal is admirable, protected mode operating systems (such as Windows 9x and Windows NT/2000) no longer permit direct access to the hardware. This generally results in a more stable operating environment with fewer crashes and system conflicts. Programs that do not play by the rules must be rewritten to run in these new environments.

The hardware is at the lowest level of the system hierarchy. By placing various bytes of information at certain ports or locations within a system's memory structure, you can control virtually any device connected to the CPU. Maintaining control at the hardware level is difficult; doing so requires a complete and accurate knowledge of the system architecture. The attention to detail required to write software operating at this level is most intense. To issue commands to the system at this level, you must use machine language, which consists of binary groups of information applied directly to the microprocessor. Machine language instructions are limited in their function; a great many of them are required to perform even the smallest amount of useful work. However, the large number of instructions required is not a great burden on the system because these instructions are executed extremely rapidly, wasting few system resources.

Programmers can write code consisting of machine language instructions, but generally they use a tool—an assembler—to ease the process. They write programs using an editor, and then use the assembler to convert the editor's output to pure machine language. Assembler commands are still very low-level, and using them effectively requires that the programmer be extremely knowledge-able. No one (in their right mind) writes directly in machine code anymore; assembly language is the lowest level programming environment typically used today. Even assembly language, however, is losing favor among programmers because of the amount of knowledge and work required to complete even simple tasks, and because of the difficulty in translating (or porting) the code to work with another system.

When you start a PC system, a series of machine code programs, the ROM BIOS, assumes control. This set of programs, always present in a system, communicates directly (using machine code) with the hardware. The BIOS accepts or interprets commands generated by programs above it in the system hierarchy. It then translates them to machine code commands that are passed on to the microprocessor. Commands at this level typically are called interrupts or services. A programmer can use nearly any language to supply these instructions to the BIOS.

◀◀ See "BIOS Basics," p. 346.

An operating system (OS) is made up of several components. It attaches to the BIOS so that part of the OS actually becomes an extension of the BIOS, providing more interrupts and services for other programs to use. The OS provides a communication buffer between the BIOS and software running at higher layers in the system hierarchy (such as applications). Because an OS provides the application programmer with interrupts and services they can use in addition to those provided by the BIOS, a lot of "reinventing the wheel" in programming routines is eliminated. For example, Windows provides a rich set of functions that can open, close, find, delete, create, and rename files, as well as perform other file-handling tasks. When programmers want to include these functions in their programs, they can rely on Windows to do most of the work, rather than have to develop routines that perform these functions themselves.

Note

This integration of hardware functions into the operating system has been one of the basic tenets of operating system development over the years. Successive versions of Windows have built on the original DOS model by adding more functions to the OS, thus preventing applications from having to address the hardware directly.

This standard set of functions that applications use to read data from and write it to disks makes data recovery operations possible. Imagine how tough writing programs and using computers would be if every application program had to implement its own custom disk interface, with a proprietary directory and file retrieval system. Every application would require its own special disks. Fortunately, each OS provides a standard set of documented file storage and retrieval routines that all software applications can use.

Another primary function of an OS is to load and run other programs. As it performs that function, the OS provides the shell, or user interface, within which the other program is executed. The OS strives to provide a consistent user interface that all programs can work in. Note that while a graphical interface is now the operational standard in Windows, you can still execute commands at a command prompt.

The System BIOS

Think of the BIOS in a system as a form of compatibility glue that sits between the PC hardware and the operating system. Why is it that DOS can run on the original IBM PC and on the latest Pentium III systems—two very different hardware platforms? How can Windows 9x run on systems from the 386 to the Pentium III? If the OS were written to communicate directly with the hardware on all systems, it would be a very hardware-specific program and require extensive modifications for different hardware configurations. Instead, IBM developed an original set of standard services and functions that each system should be capable of performing, and coded them as programs in the ROM BIOS. Over the years, this BIOS has been extended, but always in a backward compatible way. Each system gets a completely customized ROM BIOS, along with custom device drivers designed specifically for that hardware, which can talk directly to the hardware in the system and know exactly how to perform each specific function on that hardware only.

This convention enables the operating system to be written to what is essentially a standard interface that can support many different types of hardware. Any applications written to the operating system can use that standard interface to access the system hardware. Figure 26.1 shows that two very different hardware platforms can each have a custom BIOS, made up of a ROM BIOS combined with additional device drivers, which can talk directly to the hardware and still provide a standard interface to an operating system.

The two different hardware platforms described in Figure 26.1 can run not only the exact same operating system, but also the same application programs, because of the standard interfaces provided by the BIOS and the OS. Keep in mind, however, that the actual BIOS code differs among the specific machines, and that it is usually not possible to run a BIOS designed for one system in a different system. BIOS upgrades must come from a source that has an intimate understanding of the specific motherboard on which the chip will be installed, because the ROM must be custom written for that particular hardware.

◀◀ See "Upgrading the BIOS," p. 345.

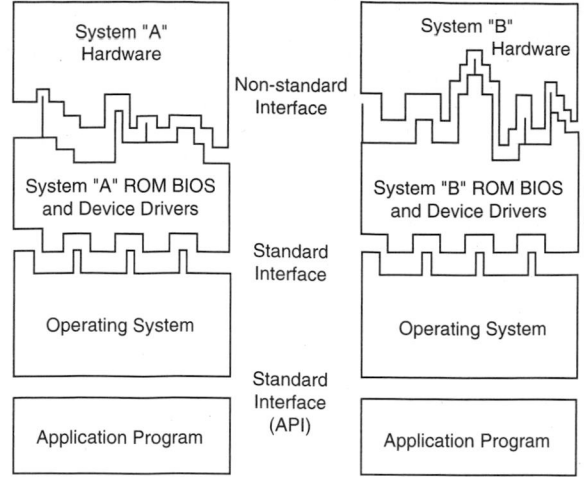

Figure 26.1 A representation of the software layers in a PC system.

Figure 26.1 represents a simplified view of the system; some subtle but important differences exist. Ideally, application programs are insulated from the hardware by the BIOS and OS, but some programs are written to communicate directly with the hardware, circumventing both the OS and the BIOS. Although this was common under DOS, protected-mode operating systems such as Windows 9x, NT/2000, Linux, OS/2, etc. will not allow this to happen. If they do, you'll see a `protection violation` error, because any program that attempts to break the rules will be stopped dead in its tracks. Since system setup, configuration, and diagnostics programs often require direct access to the hardware, they must be run outside of these protected-mode operating systems, either via their own OS or under DOS. This is one reason I still find myself using DOS a great deal on systems—most of the better hardware diagnostics programs require it.

Some utility programs absolutely must communicate directly with the system hardware to perform their function. Another type of system-specific utility, called a memory manager, enables extended memory in a DOS system to function as expanded memory. These drivers work by accessing the system processor directly and using specific features of the chip. Memory managers are no longer used with Windows 9x or NT/2000, as all memory management is now done directly within the operating system itself.

DOS and DOS Components

DOS consists of two primary components: the input/output (I/O) system and the shell. The I/O system consists of the underlying programs that reside in memory while the system is running; these programs load when DOS first boots. The I/O system is stored in the IO.SYS and MSDOS.SYS (or IBMBIO.COM and IBMDOS.COM) files that are flagged with the hidden attribute on a bootable DOS disk. No matter what the exact names are, the function of these two files is basically the same for all versions of DOS.

The user interface program, or shell, is stored in the COMMAND.COM file, which also loads during a normal DOS boot sequence. The shell is the portion of DOS that the user employs to communicate with the system, providing the DOS prompt and internal commands such as COPY and DIR.

The following sections examine the DOS I/O system and shell in more detail to help you properly identify and solve problems that are related to DOS rather than hardware. Also included is a discussion on how DOS allocates disk file space.

IO.SYS (or IBMBIO.COM)

IO.SYS is one of the hidden files found on any DOS system (bootable) disk. This file contains the low-level programs that interact directly with devices on the system and the ROM BIOS. During startup, the DOS volume boot sector loads the file into low memory and gives it control of the system. The entire file, except for the system initializer portion, remains in memory during normal system operation.

For a disk to be bootable, IO.SYS or its equivalent must be listed as the first file in the directory of the disk, and it must occupy at least the first cluster on the disk (cluster number 2). The remainder of the file might be placed in clusters anywhere across the rest of the disk. The file normally is marked with hidden, system, and read-only attributes, and placed on a disk by the FORMAT utility (with the /S switch) or by the SYS utility.

Creating a Boot Disk

Writing the DOS system boot files to a hard or floppy disk is a process that involves more than simply copying the files. To create a bootable disk, you must use either the DOS FORMAT.COM program or the SYS.COM program. When you run FORMAT with the /S switch, as in **FORMAT A: /S**, the program proceeds to format the disk in the usual manner. It then copies the IO.SYS, MSDOS.SYS, and COMMAND.COM files from the drive used to boot the computer, setting the appropriate attributes.

The SYS.COM program copies the same files and sets the same attributes, but without formatting the disk first. You must have sufficient space on the disk for SYS.COM to store the boot files.

Windows 9x includes the FORMAT.COM and SYS.COM utilities as well, but also provides a GUI alternative for creating boot disks. When you select a drive in Windows 9x Explorer and choose Format from the context menu, you are given the option to copy the system files to the disk as part of the formatting process. You can also create a boot disk by launching the Add/Remove Programs control panel and following the instructions on the Startup Disk page.

Creating a Bootable CD-ROM

Newer operating systems such as Windows 98 and 2000 come on bootable CDs. Most systems with a BIOS that supports the Phoenix El Torito bootable CD-ROM extensions can boot from these CDs. Using the capabilities of these newer systems, you can create your own bootable CDs for system recovery.

A bootable CD-ROM is different than most people expect. You just can't boot directly into the CD volume; instead the CD contains two volumes. The first is an image of a boot floppy, which becomes A: when you boot from the CD (your standard floppy becomes B:). The second volume is the actual CD itself, which will be seen as your standard CD-ROM drive letter, such as D: if your hard disk has a single C: partition, or E: if your hard disk has two partitions (C: and D:).

For example, to install Windows 98 on my new system, I didn't need a boot floppy at all. I booted directly from the floppy volume on the Windows 98 CD, used the **FDISK** and **FORMAT** commands on that volume (appearing as A: on my system) to prepare my hard disk, and then changed to E: (my hard disk has two partitions, C: and D:) to run the Windows Setup program. All this was accomplished without using any floppy disks.

A bootable CD can be used as a system backup copy of your bootable hard disk partition C: up to about 675MB in capacity. For example, you can create a bootable CD with your installed version of Windows and your major applications on it, from which you could restore at anytime if there are problems.

If you want to create your own bootable CD, see "Making a Bootable CD-ROM for Emergencies" in Chapter 13.

One important note: If your system does not boot from the CD and boots from the hard disk instead, run your BIOS Setup and ensure that you have the boot sequence set to check the CD-ROM drive *before* the hard disk in the sequence. If your BIOS doesn't offer a boot sequence control, or the CD-ROM drive isn't listed as a choice, your system might not support the Phoenix El Torito bootable CD-ROM specification. Check with your motherboard manufacturer; they might have a newer BIOS available that provides this support.

MSDOS.SYS (or IBMDOS.COM)

MSDOS.SYS, the core of DOS, contains the DOS disk and device handling programs. MSDOS.SYS is loaded into low memory at system startup by the DOS volume boot sector and remains resident in memory during normal system operation.

MSDOS.SYS or its equivalent originally had to be listed as the second entry in the root directory of any bootable disk. Most file management utilities list the files in a given directory in alphabetical order, but this is not necessarily the order in which they are stored on the drive. At one time, the only way for the IO.SYS and MSDOS.SYS files to be read sequentially was for them to be the first two physical files on the disk. The MSDOS.SYS file is flagged with the hidden, system, and read-only attributes, and like IO.SYS, is placed on a disk by the FORMAT /S command or the SYS command. There are now no special requirements for the physical positioning of this file on a disk.

The Shell or Command Processor (COMMAND.COM)

The DOS command processor COMMAND.COM is the portion of DOS with which users normally interact. This file is also written to a system disk by the FORMAT /S and SYS commands, but the file is left visible, unlike IO.SYS and MSDOS.SYS. DOS loads COMMAND.COM into memory after the two system files, providing the command prompt and access to DOS system commands. These commands can be categorized into two types according to how they are made available: resident or transient.

Resident commands are built into COMMAND.COM and are available whenever the DOS prompt is present. They are generally the simpler, frequently used commands such as COPY, CLS, and DIR. Resident commands execute rapidly because the instructions for them are already loaded into memory; they are memory resident.

When you look up a command in a DOS manual, you generally find some indication of whether the command is resident or transient. You can then determine what is required to execute that command. A simple rule is that, at a DOS prompt, all resident commands are instantly available for execution, with no loading of additional files required. Resident commands are also sometimes called internal commands. Commands that run from a separate program on disk are termed external, or transient commands, and are also often called utilities.

Transient commands are not resident in the computer's memory; the instructions to execute these commands must be located on a disk. Because the instructions are loaded into memory only for the execution of the command, and then are overwritten in memory after they are used, they are called transient commands. Most DOS commands are transient; otherwise, the memory requirements for DOS would be much larger than they are. Transient commands are used less frequently than resident commands and take longer to execute, because their disk files must be found and loaded before they can run. DOS's transient commands take the form of individual executable files, such as FORMAT.COM and XCOPY.COM, that are located in the DOS home directory (typically C:\DOS, or C:\WINDOWS\COMMAND in Windows 9x).

Most executable files operate like transient DOS commands. The instructions to execute the command must be located on a disk. The instructions are loaded into memory only for execution and are overwritten in memory after the program is no longer being used.

Note that COMMAND.COM is the same program that Windows runs to produce a DOS command window. By creating a shortcut to the COMMAND.COM file included with Windows, you can call up MS-DOS prompt sessions at will. Placing such a shortcut on your desktop gives you quick access to an MS-DOS prompt window for entering commands. I still find myself using commands and batch files all the time; they are often much more efficient than the point-and-click method.

DOS Command File Search Procedure

One of the most common DOS errors is the Bad command or filename message that appears when you attempt to issue a command that DOS cannot process. This can happen for a number of reasons, and your troubleshooting efforts should begin at the highest level—the software—before you begin to suspect that a hardware problem may be at fault.

Whenever you issue a transient command or run a software application's executable file, DOS attempts to find the instructions needed to execute that command by looking in several places, in a specific order. The instructions that represent the command or program are located in files on one or more disk drives. Files that contain execution instructions have an extension of COM (command files), EXE (executable files), or BAT (batch files). COM and EXE files are machine code programs; BAT files contain ASCII text specifying a series of commands and instructions using the DOS batch facilities. DOS attempts to locate these executable files by searching the current directory and the directories specified in the PATH command.

In other words, if you type several characters, such as WIN, at the DOS prompt, and then press Enter, DOS attempts to find and run a program named WIN by performing a two- or three-level search for the program instructions (the file). The first step in looking for command instructions is to see whether the command is resident in COMMAND.COM and, if so, to run it from the program code already loaded in memory. If the command is not resident, DOS looks in the current directory for a file called WIN with a COM, EXE, or BAT extension (in that order), and loads and executes the first file it finds with the specified name. Therefore, if two files in that directory are called WIN.COM and WIN.BAT, the WIN.COM file will always be executed in response to the WIN command.

If the command is not resident and no file by that name is found in the current directory, DOS looks in each of the directories specified in the DOS PATH environment variable in turn, searching for the file using the same extension order just indicated. (You specify the directories for the PATH environment variable using the PATH command, usually from the AUTOEXEC.BAT file.) Finally, if DOS still fails to locate the required instructions, it displays the error message Bad command or filename. As you can see, this error message can be misleading. You may puzzle at the incapability of DOS to run a command file that clearly is on the disk. This might lead you to suspect a hardware problem concerning the disk drive itself, when the problem actually stems from the fact that the command instructions are missing from the search areas.

A common practice is to place all simple command files or utility programs (transient commands) in one directory and set the PATH to point to that directory. Each of those programs (or commands) is then instantly available by typing its name from any DOS prompt, just as though it were resident in memory.

This practice works well only for single-load programs such as DOS transient commands and other utilities. Major applications often consist of many individual files and might have problems if they are called up from a remote directory or drive using the DOS PATH. This is because the PATH variable has no effect when the application looks for its overlay and accessory files.

On a hard disk system, users typically install all transient commands and utilities in subdirectories and ensure that the PATH points to those directories. The PATH literally is a list of directories and subdirectories specified in the AUTOEXEC.BAT file that tells DOS where to search for files when the command cannot be found in the current directory. A PATH on such a hard drive may look like this:

```
PATH=C:\DOS;C:\BAT;C:\UTILS;
```

In the previous example, all the ancillary programs included with the DOS operating system will be immediately locatable because of the inclusion of C:\DOS in the PATH command.

The PATH normally cannot exceed 128 characters in length (including spaces, colons, semicolons, and backslashes). As a result of this limitation, you cannot have a PATH that contains all your directories if the directory names exceed 128 characters.

Note

On Windows 9x systems, directories can have names up to 255 characters in length and can contain spaces and other characters that DOS directories cannot. However, because the file system always maintains a truncated directory name using the standard DOS 8.3 naming convention, you can use these short names in the **PATH** command. To include directory names containing spaces in the **PATH** command, you must enclose the name in quotes, as in `"C:\Program Files"`.

You can also completely circumvent the DOS command search procedure by entering the complete PATH to the file at the command prompt. For example, rather than include `C:\DOS` in the PATH and enter this command:

    CHKDSK

You can enter the full name of the program:

    C:\DOS\CHKDSK.COM

The latter command immediately locates and loads the CHKDSK program with no search through the current directory or PATH setting. This method of calling up a program speeds the location and execution of the program and works especially well to increase the speed of DOS batch file execution. It also enables you to immediately eliminate path problems as the source of the `Bad command or filename` message.

DOS Versions

In more than a decade and a half of development, a great many DOS versions have been released. IBM released version 1.0 of the operating system in 1981, but by version 3.x, Microsoft also began releasing its own DOS, using the same version numbers as IBM in most cases. Early versions of DOS were frequently designed for the hardware configurations of specific machines. At one time, IBM, Compaq, and other original equipment manufacturers would have their own versions of DOS (created by IBM or Microsoft), designed to support only their hardware. You could not, in many cases, boot an IBM computer using a Compaq DOS boot disk and still gain full functionality.

Over the years, DOS has added a number of commands to the repertoire. In dealing with different versions, it has always been difficult to remember if a particular version included a certain command. Table 26.1 is a list of external MS-DOS command programs, MS-DOS versions they were included with, and the file extension used.

Table 26.1   External MS-DOS Commands by DOS version:

Command	Version 2.0	2.1	3.0	3.1/3.2	3.3	4.0	5.0	6.0	6.2	6.2x
APPEND	—	—	—	—	EXE	EXE	EXE	EXE	EXE	EXE
ASSIGN	COM	COM	COM	COM	COM	COM	COM	—	—	—
ATTRIB	—	—	EXE	EXE	EXE	EXE	EXE	EXE	EXE	EXE
BACKUP	COM	COM	COM	COM	COM	COM	EXE	—	—	—
BASIC	COM	COM	COM	COM	—	—	—	—	—	—

Command	Version 2.0	2.1	3.0	3.1/3.2	3.3	4.0	5.0	6.0	6.2	6.2x
BASICA	COM	COM	COM	COM	—	—	—	—	—	—
CHKDSK	COM	COM	COM	COM	COM	COM	EXE	EXE	EXE	EXE
CHOICE	—	—	—	—	—	—	—	COM	COM	COM
COMMAND	COM	COM	COM	COM	COM	COM	COM	COM	COM	COM
COMP	COM	COM	COM	COM	COM	COM	EXE	—	—	—
DBLSPACE	—	—	—	—	—	—	—	EXE	EXE	—
DEBUG	COM	COM	COM	COM	COM	COM	EXE	EXE	EXE	EXE
DEFRAG	—	—	—	—	—	—	—	EXE	EXE	EXE
DELTREE	—	—	—	—	—	—	—	EXE	EXE	EXE
DISKCOMP	COM	COM	COM	COM	COM	COM	COM	COM	COM	COM
DISKCOPY	COM	COM	COM	COM	COM	COM	COM	COM	COM	COM
DOSKEY	—	—	—	—	—	—	COM	COM	COM	COM
DOSSHELL	—	—	—	—	—	COM	COM	EXE	—	—
DOSSWAP	—	—	—	—	—	—	EXE	EXE	—	—
DRVSPACE	—	—	—	—	—	—	—	—	—	EXE
EDIT	—	—	—	—	—	—	COM	COM	COM	COM
EDLIN	COM	COM	COM	COM	COM	COM	EXE	—	—	—
EMM386	—	—	—	—	—	—	EXE	EXE	EXE	EXE
EXE2BIN	—	EXE	EXE	EXE	EXE	EXE	EXE	—	—	—
EXPAND	—	—	—	—	—	—	EXE	EXE	EXE	EXE
FASTHELP	—	—	—	—	—	—	—	EXE	EXE	EXE
FASTOPEN	—	—	—	—	EXE	EXE	EXE	EXE	EXE	EXE
FC	—	—	—	—	EXE	EXE	EXE	EXE	EXE	EXE
FDISK	COM	COM	COM	COM	COM	EXE	EXE	EXE	EXE	EXE
FILESYS	—	—	—	—	—	EXE	—	—	—	—
FIND	EXE	EXE	EXE	EXE	EXE	EXE	EXE	EXE	EXE	EXE
FORMAT	COM	COM	COM	COM	COM	COM	COM	COM	COM	COM
GRAFTABL	—	—	COM	COM	COM	COM	COM	—	—	—
GRAPHICS	COM	COM	COM	COM	COM	COM	COM	COM	COM	COM
GWBASIC	—	—	—	—	EXE	EXE	—	—	—	—
HELP	—	—	—	—	—	—	EXE	COM	COM	COM
IFSFUNC	—	—	—	—	—	EXE	—	—	—	—
INTERLNK	—	—	—	—	—	—	—	EXE	EXE	EXE
INTERSVR	—	—	—	—	—	—	—	EXE	EXE	EXE
JOIN	—	—	—	EXE	EXE	EXE	EXE	—	—	—
KEYB	—	—	—	—	COM	COM	COM	COM	COM	COM
KEYBFR	—	—	COM	COM	—	—	—	—	—	—

(continues)

Table 26.1 Continued

Command	Version 2.0	2.1	3.0	3.1/3.2	3.3	4.0	5.0	6.0	6.2	6.2x
KEYBGR	—	—	COM	COM	—	—	—	—	—	—
KEYBIT	—	—	COM	COM	—	—	—	—	—	—
KEYBSP	—	—	COM	COM	—	—	—	—	—	—
KEYBUK	—	—	COM	COM	—	—	—	—	—	—
LABEL	—	—	COM	COM	COM	COM	EXE	EXE	EXE	EXE
LINK	EXE	EXE	EXE	EXE	EXE	EXE	—	—	—	—
LOADFIX	—	—	—	—	—	—	COM	COM	COM	COM
MEM	—	—	—	—	—	EXE	EXE	EXE	EXE	EXE
MEMMAKER	—	—	—	—	—	—	—	EXE	EXE	EXE
MIRROR	—	—	—	—	—	—	COM	—	—	—
MODE	COM	COM	COM	COM	COM	COM	COM	COM	COM	COM
MORE	COM	COM	COM	COM	COM	COM	COM	COM	COM	COM
MOVE	—	—	—	—	—	—	—	EXE	EXE	EXE
MSBACKUP	—	—	—	—	—	—	—	EXE	EXE	EXE
MSCDEX	—	—	—	—	—	—	—	EXE	EXE	EXE
MSD	—	—	—	—	—	—	—	EXE	EXE	EXE
MWAV	—	—	—	—	—	—	—	EXE	EXE	EXE
MWAVTSR	—	—	—	—	—	—	—	EXE	EXE	EXE
MWBACKUP	—	—	—	—	—	—	—	EXE	EXE	EXE
MWUNDEL	—	—	—	—	—	—	—	EXE	EXE	EXE
NLSFUNC	—	—	—	—	EXE	EXE	EXE	EXE	EXE	EXE
POWER	—	—	—	—	—	—	—	EXE	EXE	EXE
PRINT	COM	COM	COM	COM	COM	COM	EXE	EXE	EXE	EXE
QBASIC	—	.	—	—	—	—	EXE	EXE	EXE	EXE
RECOVER	COM	COM	COM	COM	COM	COM	EXE	—	—	—
REPLACE	—	—	EXE	—	EXE	EXE	EXE	EXE	EXE	EXE
RESTORE	COM	COM	COM	COM	COM	COM	EXE	EXE	EXE	EXE
SCANDISK	—	—	—	—	—	—	—	—	EXE	EXE
SELECT	—	—	COM	COM	COM	COM	—	—	—	—
SETVER	—	—	—	—	—	—	EXE	EXE	EXE	EXE
SHARE	—	—	EXE	EXE	EXE	EXE	EXE	EXE	EXE	EXE
SIZER	—	—	—	—	—	—	—	EXE	EXE	EXE
SMARTDRV	—	—	—	—	—	—	—	EXE	EXE	EXE
SMARTMON	—	—	—	—	—	—	—	EXE	EXE	—
SORT	EXE	EXE	EXE	EXE	EXE	EXE	EXE	EXE	EXE	EXE
SUBST	—	—	—	EXE	EXE	EXE	EXE	EXE	EXE	EXE
SYS	COM	COM	COM	COM	COM	COM	COM	COM	COM	COM

Command	Version 2.0	2.1	3.0	3.1/3.2	3.3	4.0	5.0	6.0	6.2	6.2x
TREE	COM	COM	COM	COM	COM	COM	COM	COM	COM	COM
UNDELETE	—	—	—	—	—	—	EXE	EXE	EXE	EXE
UNFORMAT	—	—	—	—	—	—	COM	COM	COM	COM
VSAFE	—	—	—	—	—	—	—	COM	COM	COM
XCOPY	—	—	—	—	EXE	EXE	EXE	EXE	EXE	EXE

— = not included with that version

DOS 5.x

By the time that DOS 5.0 was released by Microsoft, however, this situation was all but eliminated. DOS 5.0 was the first version of the operating system to be marketed on a retail level, and users turned out in droves to upgrade their systems. Both the IBM and Microsoft versions of DOS 5.0 and later can be used on almost any system, although later versions may be required to use some of the latest hardware available.

DOS 5.0 offered vastly improved memory management and incorporated many of the features into the operating system that users had grown used to finding in third-party utilities. At this time, there are some people who still swear by DOS 5.0 and resist upgrading to DOS 6 (or higher), which, truth to tell, is more of an enhancement than a major overhaul. However, there is no reason any DOS version below 5.0 should still be in use on any computer (except for museum pieces that can handle nothing but their native versions).

IBM and MS-DOS 6.xx

After DOS 5.0, there were several different versions of DOS 6.xx from both Microsoft and IBM. The original release of MS-DOS 6.0 came from Microsoft. One of the new features included in 6.0 was DoubleSpace disk compression, an automatic compression engine that could effectively double the computer's disk space, in most cases. Unfortunately, DoubleSpace had some problems with certain system configurations and hardware types. In the meantime, IBM took DOS 6.0 from Microsoft, updated it to fix several small problems, removed the disk compression feature, and sold it as IBM DOS 6.1. Microsoft had many problems with the DoubleSpace disk compression used in 6.0 and released 6.2 as a free bug-fix upgrade.

Microsoft then ran into legal problems in the form of a lawsuit brought by Stacker Corporation that accused Microsoft of having infringed on its rights to the compression algorithm used by its Stacker software product. As a result of the suit, Microsoft removed the DoubleSpace compression feature from DOS 6.2, which was re-released as 6.21. Microsoft then quickly developed a non-infringing disk compression utility called DriveSpace, which they released in version 6.22, along with several minor bug fixes. IBM skipped over the 6.2 version number and released DOS 6.3 (now called PC DOS), which also included a different type of compression program than that used by Microsoft. By avoiding the DoubleSpace software, IBM also avoided the bugs and legal problems that Microsoft had encountered. Also included in the updated IBM releases were enhanced PCMCIA and power management commands.

DOS 7.xx

The development of DOS as a standalone product effectively ceased with MS-DOS 6.22 and PC-DOS 7. However, the Windows 95 and 98 operating systems are based on the DOS model. If you run a utility such as MS-DOS 6.x's MSD (Microsoft Diagnostics) on a Windows 95 or Windows 98 machine, you will see that the operating system identifies itself as MS-DOS version 7.0 or 7.10, the next step in the evolution of the operating system.

Potential DOS Upgrade Problems

You already know that the DOS system files have special placement requirements on a hard disk. Sometimes these special requirements cause problems when you are upgrading from one version of DOS to another.

If you have attempted to upgrade a PC system from one version of DOS to another, you know that you can use the DOS SYS command to replace the old system files with new ones. The SYS command copies the existing system files (stored on a bootable disk with hidden, system, and read-only attributes) to the disk, in the correct position and with the correct names and attributes. The COPY command does not copy hidden or system files (nor would it place the system files in the required positions on the destination disk if you modify the file attributes to use COPY). In addition to transferring the two hidden system files from one disk to another, SYS also copies the COMMAND.COM file and updates the DOS volume boot sector on the destination disk so it is correct for the new version of DOS.

When you execute the SYS command, you are usually greeted by one of two messages:

```
System transferred
```

or

```
No room for system on destination disk
```

In DOS versions 3.3 and earlier, if a disk has data on it before you try to write the system files to it, the SYS command will probably fail, because it is not capable of moving other files out of the way. The SYS command in DOS 4.0 and higher versions rarely fails, because it can move files out of the way to put the system files in the correct places.

Some users think that the cause of the No room message on a system with an older version of DOS is that the system files in the newer DOS version are larger than those of the previous version, and that the new files cannot fit into the space allocated for the older versions. They believe that the command fails because this space cannot be provided at the beginning of the disk without moving other data away. This is incorrect. The SYS command fails in these cases because you are trying to install a version of DOS that has different filenames than those already on the disk. There is no normal reason for the SYS command to fail when you update the system files on a disk that already has them.

The system files can be located virtually anywhere on the disk, except that the first cluster (or allocation unit) of the disk must contain the first cluster of the IO.SYS file (or its equivalent). As long as that requirement is met, the IO.SYS and MSDOS.SYS files can be fragmented and scattered about on the disk like any other files, and the SYS command implements them with no problems whatsoever. The only other requirement is that the names IO.SYS and MSDOS.SYS (or their equivalents) must use the first and second directory entries.

DOS 4.0 and Later Versions

Because the system files must use the first two entries in the root directory of the disk and the first cluster (cluster 2) of the disk, the versions of the SYS command in DOS 4.0 and later automatically move any files occupying the first two entries (other than the two system files) to other available entries in the root directory. The SYS command also moves the portion of any foreign file occupying the first cluster to other clusters on the disk.

The SYS command in DOS versions 5.0 and 6.x go one step further: They replace old system files with the new ones. Even if the old system files had other names, DOS 5.0 and higher ensure that they are overwritten by the new system files. With the enhanced SYS command in DOS 4.0 and later versions, it is difficult to make a DOS upgrade fail.

Windows 95

When you install Windows 95 on a system running DOS, the Setup program renames the existing system files with a DOS extension and replaces them with the Windows 95 versions of IO.SYS and MSDOS.SYS. After the operating system is installed, you can invoke a boot menu by pressing the F8 key as the computer starts, which enables you to boot the system to the old DOS version, if needed. To do this, the OS simply renames the Windows 95 system files with the extension W95 and renames the DOS files back to SYS. Windows 98 and 2000 do not incorporate this exact function; you can still boot to a DOS prompt, just not your older version of DOS.

The Boot Process

The term boot comes from the word bootstrap and describes the method by which the PC becomes operational. Just as you pull on a large boot by the small strap attached to the back, a PC loads a large operating system by first loading a small program that can then pull the operating system into memory. The chain of events begins with the application of power, and finally results in a fully functional computer system with software loaded and running. Each event is triggered by the event before it and initiates the event after it.

Tracing the system boot process might help you find the location of a problem if you examine the error messages that the system displays when the problem occurs. If you see an error message that is displayed only by a particular program, you can be sure the program in question was at least loaded and partially running. Combine this information with the knowledge of the boot sequence, and you can at least tell how far along the system's startup procedure has progressed before the problem occurred. You usually want to look at whatever files or disk areas were being accessed during the failure in the boot process. Error messages displayed during the boot process and those displayed during normal system operation can be hard to decipher. However, the first step in decoding an error message is to know where the message came from—what program actually generated or displayed it. The following programs are capable of displaying error messages during the boot process:

- Motherboard ROM BIOS
- Adapter card ROM BIOS extensions
- Master partition boot sector
- DOS volume boot sector
- System files (IO.SYS./IBMBIO.COM and MSDOS.SYS/IBMDOS.COM)
- Device drivers (loaded through CONFIG.SYS or the Win 9x Registry SYSTEM.DAT)
- Shell program (COMMAND.COM in DOS)
- Programs run by AUTOEXEC.BAT, the Windows 9x Startup group, and the Registry
- Windows (WIN.COM)

The following section examines the system startup sequence and provides a detailed account of many of the error messages that might occur during this process.

How DOS Loads and Starts

If you have a problem with your system during startup and you can determine where in this sequence of events your system has stalled, you know what events have occurred and you probably can eliminate each of them as a cause of the problem. The following steps occur in a typical system startup:

1. You switch on electrical power to the system.

2. The power supply performs a self-test (known as the POST—power on self test). When all voltages and current levels are acceptable, the supply indicates that the power is stable and sends the Power_Good signal to the motherboard. The time from switch-on to Power_Good is normally between .1 and .5 seconds.

3. The microprocessor timer chip receives the Power_Good signal, which causes it to stop generating a reset signal to the microprocessor.

◄◄ See "The Power_Good Signal," p. 1109.

4. The microprocessor begins executing the ROM BIOS code, starting at memory address FFFF:0000. Because this location is only 16 bytes from the very end of the available ROM space, it contains a JMP (jump) instruction to the actual ROM BIOS starting address.

◄◄ See "Motherboard BIOS," p. 349.

5. The ROM BIOS performs a test of the central hardware to verify basic system functionality. Any errors that occur are indicated by audio "beep" codes because the video system has not yet been initialized.

6. The BIOS performs a video ROM scan of memory locations C000:0000 through C780:0000, looking for video adapter ROM BIOS programs contained on a video adapter found either on a card plugged into a slot or integrated into the motherboard. If the scan locates a video ROM BIOS, it is tested by a checksum procedure. If the video BIOS passes the checksum test, the ROM is executed; the video ROM code initializes the video adapter and a cursor appears onscreen. If the checksum test fails, the following message appears:

```
C000 ROM Error
```

7. If the BIOS finds no video adapter ROM, it uses the motherboard ROM video drivers to initialize the video display hardware, and a cursor appears onscreen.

8. The motherboard ROM BIOS scans memory locations C800:0000 through DF80:0000 in 2KB increments for any other ROMs located on any other adapter cards (such as SCSI adapters). If any ROMs are found, they are checksum-tested and executed. These adapter ROMs can alter existing BIOS routines and establish new ones.

9. Failure of a checksum test for any of these ROM modules causes this message to appear:

    XXXX ROM Error

where the address XXXX indicates the segment address of the failed ROM module.

10. The ROM BIOS checks the word value at memory location 0000:0472 to see whether this start is a cold start or a warm start. A word value of 1234h in this location is a flag that indicates a warm start, which causes the BIOS to skip the memory test portion of the POST (Power On Self Test). Any other word value in this location indicates a cold start and the BIOS performs the full POST procedure. Some system BIOSes let you control various aspects of the POST procedure, making it possible to skip the memory test, for example, which can be lengthy on a system with a lot of RAM.

◄◄ See "POST Audio Error Codes," p. 1290.

11. If this is a cold start, the POST executes. Any errors found during the POST are reported by a combination of audio and displayed error messages. Successful completion of the POST is indicated by a single beep.

12. The ROM BIOS searches for a partition or volume boot record at cylinder 0, head 0, sector 1 (the very first sector) on the default boot drive. At one time, the default boot drive was always the first floppy disk, or A: drive. However, the BIOSes on today's systems often enable you to select the default boot device and the order that the BIOS will look for other devices to boot from if needed, using a floppy disk, hard disk, or even a CD-ROM drive in any order you choose. This sector is loaded into memory at 0000:7C00 and tested. If a disk is in the drive but the sector cannot be read, or if no disk is present, the BIOS continues with the next step.

Tip

If you do want to boot from a CD-ROM, make sure the CD-ROM drive is specified first in the boot devices menu in your BIOS setup. To ensure that you can boot from an emergency disk, set your floppy drive as the second device in the boot order. A hard disk containing your operating system should be the third drive in the boot order. This allows you to always be ready for an emergency. So long as you do not boot with a CD or floppy loaded, the BIOS will bypass both the CD and floppy disk drives and boot from the hard drive.

13. If the first byte of the partition boot record loaded from the disk in the default boot drive is less than 06h, or if the first byte is greater than or equal to 06h and the first nine words contain the same data pattern, this error message appears and the system stops:

    602-Diskette Boot Record Error

14. If the disk was prepared with FORMAT or SYS using DOS 3.3 or an earlier version and the specified system files are not the first two files in the directory, or if a problem was encountered loading them, the following message appears:

```
Non-System disk or disk error
Replace and strike any key when ready
```

15. If the disk was prepared with FORMAT or SYS using DOS 3.3 or an earlier version and the boot sector is corrupt, you might see this message:

```
Disk Boot failure
```

16. If the disk was prepared with FORMAT or SYS using DOS 4.0 and later versions, and the specified system files are not the first two files in the directory, or if a problem was encountered loading them, or the boot sector is corrupt, this message appears:

```
Non-System disk or disk error
Replace and press any key when ready
```

17. If no partition boot record can be read from drive A:, the BIOS looks for a master boot record (MBR) at cylinder 0, head 0, sector 1 (the very first sector) of the first fixed disk. If this sector is found, it is loaded into memory address 0000:7C00 and tested for a signature.

18. If the last two (signature) bytes of the MBR are not equal to 55AAh, software interrupt 18h (Int 18h) is invoked on most systems.

   This causes the BIOS to display an error message that can vary for different BIOS manufacturers, but which is often something like one of the following messages, depending on which BIOS you have:

   IBM BIOS

```
The IBM Personal Computer Basic_
Version C1.10 Copyright IBM Corp 1981
62940 Bytes free_
Ok_
```

   Or, some newer IBM computers display a graphic depicting the front of a floppy drive, a 3 1/2-inch diskette, and arrows prompting you to put a disk in the drive and press the F1 key to proceed.

   AMI BIOS

```
NO ROM BASIC - SYSTEM HALTED
```

   Compaq BIOS

```
Non-System disk or disk error
replace and strike any key when ready
```

Award BIOS

```
DISK BOOT FAILURE, INSERT SYSTEM DISK AND PRESS ENTER
```

Phoenix BIOS

```
No boot device available -
strike F1 to retry boot, F2 for setup utility
```

or

```
No boot sector on fixed disk -
strike F1 to retry boot, F2 for setup utility
```

Although the messages vary from BIOS to BIOS, the cause for each relates to specific bytes in the MBR, which is the first sector of a hard disk at the physical location cylinder 0, head 0, sector 1.

The problem involves a disk that has either never been partitioned or has had the Master Boot Sector corrupted. During the boot process, the BIOS checks the last two bytes in the MBR (first sector of the drive) for a signature value of 55AAh. If the last two bytes are not 55AAh, an Interrupt 18h is invoked, which calls the subroutine that displays one of the error messages just shown, which basically instruct the user to insert a bootable floppy to proceed.

The MBR (including the signature bytes) is written to the hard disk by the DOS FDISK program. Immediately after a hard disk is low-level formatted, all the sectors are initialized with a pattern of bytes, and the first sector does not contain the 55AAh signature. In other words, these ROM error messages are exactly what you see if you attempt to boot from a hard disk that has been low-level formatted, but has not yet been partitioned.

19. The MBR program searches its partition table for an entry with a system indicator byte designating an extended partition. If the program finds such an entry, it loads the extended partition boot sector at the location indicated. The extended partition boot sector also has a table that is searched for another extended partition. If another extended partition entry is found, that extended partition boot sector is loaded from the location indicated. The search continues until either no more extended partitions are indicated or the maximum number of 24 total partitions has been reached.

20. The MBR searches its partition table for a boot indicator byte marking an active partition.

21. If none of the partitions is marked active (bootable), the BIOS displays a disk error message.

22. If any boot indicator in the MBR table is invalid or if more than one indicates an active partition, the following message is displayed, and the system stops:

```
Invalid partition table
```

23. If an active partition is found in the MBR, the partition boot record from the active partition is loaded and tested.

24. If the partition boot record cannot be read successfully from the active partition within five retries because of read errors, this message appears and the system stops:

```
Error loading operating system
```

25. The hard disk's partition boot record is tested for a signature. If it does not contain a valid signature of 55AAh as the last two bytes in the sector, this message appears and the system stops:

```
Missing operating system
```

26. The partition boot record is executed as a program. This program checks the root directory to ensure that the first two files are IO.SYS (or IBMBIO.COM) and MSDOS.SYS (or IBM-DOS.COM). If these files are present, they are loaded.

27. If the disk was prepared with FORMAT or SYS using DOS 3.3 or an earlier version and the specified system files are not the first two files in the directory, or if a problem is encountered loading them, the following message appears:

```
Non-System disk or disk error
Replace and strike any key when ready
```

28. If the disk was prepared with FORMAT or SYS using DOS 3.3 or an earlier version and the boot sector is corrupt, you might see this message:

```
Disk Boot failure
```

29. If the disk was prepared with FORMAT or SYS using DOS 4.0 or a later version and the specified system files are not the first two files in the directory, if a problem is encountered loading them, or if the boot sector is corrupt, the following message appears:

```
Non-System disk or disk error
Replace and press any key when ready
```

30. If no problems occur, the DOS volume boot sector executes IO.SYS/IBMBIO.COM. On a Windows 9x system, if you activate the boot menu by pressing the F8 key at this time, you can select the operating system files that you want to load.

31. The initialization code in IO.SYS/IBMBIO.COM copies itself into the highest region of contiguous DOS memory and transfers control to the copy. The initialization code copy then relocates MSDOS.SYS over the portion of IO.SYS in low memory that contains the initialization code, because the initialization code no longer needs to be in that location. Windows 9x's IO.SYS combines the functions of DOS's IO.SYS and MSDOS.SYS.

32. The initialization code executes MSDOS.SYS (or IBMDOS.COM), which initializes the base device drivers, determines equipment status, resets the disk system, resets and initializes attached devices, and sets the system default parameters.

33. The full DOS file system is active, and control is returned to the IO.SYS initialization code.

34. The IO.SYS initialization code reads the CONFIG.SYS file multiple times. In Windows 9x, IO.SYS also looks for the SYSTEM.DAT Registry file.

35. When loading CONFIG.SYS, the DEVICE statements are first processed in the order in which they appear. Any device driver files named in those DEVICE statements are loaded and executed. Then any INSTALL statements are processed in the order in which they appear; the programs named are loaded and executed. The SHELL statement is processed and loads the specified command processor with the specified parameters. If the CONFIG.SYS file contains no SHELL statement, the default \COMMAND.COM processor is loaded with default parameters. Loading the command processor overwrites the initialization code in memory (because the job of the initialization code is finished).

In Windows 9x, the system looks in the Registry's Hkey_Local_Machine\System\ CurrentControlSet key to load the device drivers and other parameters specified there before executing the CONFIG.SYS file. The COMMAND.COM program is loaded at this time only if an AUTOEXEC.BAT file exists, so it can process the commands contained within it. The Windows 9x boot menu also provides a safe mode option. This option bypasses the loading of the drivers for the specific hardware in the system and instead loads a set of generic drivers designed to get the system up and running with only minimal functionality. This enables the computer to boot the Windows GUI in situations where a malfunctioning driver or device would otherwise prevent access to the system.

During the final reads of CONFIG.SYS, all the remaining statements are read and processed in a predetermined order. Thus, the order of appearance for statements other than DEVICE, INSTALL, and SHELL in CONFIG.SYS is of no significance.

36. If AUTOEXEC.BAT is present, COMMAND.COM loads and runs AUTOEXEC.BAT. After the commands in AUTOEXEC.BAT have been executed, the DOS prompt appears (unless the AUTOEXEC.BAT calls an application program or shell of some kind, in which case the user might operate the system without ever seeing a DOS prompt).

37. If no AUTOEXEC.BAT file is present, COMMAND.COM executes the internal DATE and TIME commands, displays a copyright message, and displays the DOS prompt.

In Windows 9x, IO.SYS automatically loads HIMEM.SYS, IFSHLP.SYS, and SETVER.EXE. Finally, it loads WIN.COM and Windows 9x is officially started. For more information on how Windows 9x loads, see the section, "The Windows 9x Boot Process," later in this chapter.

Some minor variations from this scenario are possible, such as those introduced by other ROM programs in the various adapters that might be plugged into an expansion slot. Also, depending on the exact ROM BIOS programs involved, some of the error messages and sequences might vary. Generally, however, a computer follows this chain of events while "coming to life."

You can modify the system startup procedures by altering the CONFIG.SYS and AUTOEXEC.BAT files or the Windows 9x Registry or Startup folder. These files control the configuration of DOS or Windows 9x and allow special startup programs to be executed every time the system starts.

File Management

DOS uses several elements and structures to store and retrieve information on a disk. These elements and structures enable DOS to communicate properly with both the ROM BIOS and with application programs to process file storage and retrieval requests. Understanding these structures and how they interact helps you troubleshoot and even repair these structures.

On demand, DOS allocates disk space for a file (space is not preallocated). The space is allocated one cluster (or allocation unit) at a time. A cluster always consists of one or more sectors.

The clusters are arranged on a disk to minimize head movement for multisided media. DOS allocates all the space on a disk cylinder before moving to the next cylinder. It does this by using the sectors under the first head and then all the sectors under each successive head, until all sectors of all heads of the cylinder are used. The next sector DOS uses is sector 1 of head 0 on the next cylinder.

The algorithm that DOS 3.0 and later versions use for file allocation is called the Next Available Cluster algorithm. In this algorithm, the search for available clusters in which to write a file starts not at the beginning of the disk, as in previous DOS versions, but rather from where the last write occurred. Therefore, the disk space freed by erasing a file is not necessarily reused immediately. Rather, DOS maintains a Last Written Cluster pointer and begins its search from that point. This pointer is maintained in system RAM and is lost when the system is reset or rebooted, or when a disk is changed in a floppy drive.

The Next Available Cluster algorithm is faster than the First Available Cluster algorithm of earlier DOS versions and helps to minimize fragmentation. Sometimes this type of algorithm is called elevator seeking because write operations occur at higher and higher clusters until the heads reach the end of the disk area. At that time, the pointer is reset, and write operations work their way from the beginning of the disk again.

Files still end up becoming fragmented using the Next Available Cluster algorithm, because the pointer is reset after a reboot, a disk change operation, or when the end of the disk is reached. Nevertheless, a great benefit of the method is that it makes unerasing files more likely to succeed even if the disk has been written to since the erasure, because the file just erased is not likely to be the target of the next write operation. In fact, it might be some time before the clusters occupied by the erased file are reused.

Even when DOS overwrites a file, it does not reuse the clusters occupied by the original file during the overwrite. For example, if you accidentally save a file using the same name as an important file that already exists, DOS marks the existing file clusters as available, and writes the new file (with the same name) to the disk in other clusters. It is often possible, therefore, to recover the original copy of the file.

This is often how undelete utilities such as the UNDELETE command in DOS and other third-party products are capable of recovering deleted files. Safety utilities such as the Windows 9x Recycle

Bin, however, do not work in the same way. The Recycle Bin is actually just a directory to which the system moves deleted files. The file system continues to register the space occupied by the "deleted" files as in use. The Recycle Bin directory is configured with a maximum possible size that, when reached, causes the system to delete the oldest files stored there.

Interfacing to Disk Drives

DOS uses a combination of disk management components to make files accessible. These components differ slightly between floppies and hard disks and between disks of different sizes. They determine how a disk appears to DOS and applications. Each component used to describe the disk system fits as a layer into the complete system. Each layer communicates with the layer above and below it. When all the components work together, an application can access the disk to find and store data.

There are four primary interface layers between an application program running on a system and the disk drives attached to the system. They consist of software routines that can perform various functions, usually to communicate with the adjacent layers. These layers are as follows:

- DOS Interrupt 21h (Int 21h) routines
- DOS Interrupt 25/26h (Int 25/26h) routines
- ROM BIOS disk Interrupt 13h (Int 13h) routines
- Disk controller I/O port commands

Each layer accepts various commands, performs different functions, and generates results. These interfaces are available for both floppy disk drives and hard disks, although the floppy disk and hard disk Int 13h routines differ widely. The floppy disk controllers and hard disk controllers are very different as well, but all the layers perform the same functions for both floppy disks and hard disks.

Interrupt 21h

The DOS Int 21h routines exist at the highest level and provide the most functionality with the least amount of work. For example, if an application program needs to create a subdirectory on a disk, it can call Int 21h, Function 39h. This function performs all the operations necessary to create the subdirectory, including updating the appropriate directory and FAT sectors. The only information this function needs is the name of the subdirectory to create. DOS Int 21h would do much more work by using one of the lower-level access methods to create a subdirectory. Most applications access the disk through this level of interface.

Interrupt 25h and 26h

The DOS Int 25h and Int 26h routines provide much lower level access to the disk than the Int 21h routines. Int 25h reads only specified sectors from a disk, and Int 26h only writes specified sectors to a disk. If you were to write a program that used these functions to create a subdirectory on a disk, the amount of work would be much greater than that required by the Int 21h method. For example, your program would have to perform all these tasks:

- Calculate exactly which directory and FAT sectors need to be updated
- Use Int 25h to read these sectors
- Modify the sectors appropriately to add the new subdirectory information
- Use Int 26h to write the sectors back to the disk

The number of steps is even greater when you factor in the difficulty in determining exactly what sectors have to be modified. According to Int 25/26h, the entire DOS-addressable area of the disk consists of sectors numbered sequentially from 0. A program designed to access the disk using Int 25h and Int 26h must know the correct disk locations by sector number. A program designed this way might have to be modified to handle disks with different numbers of sectors or different directory and FAT sizes and locations. Because of all the overhead required to get the job done, most programmers do not choose to access the disk in this manner and instead use the higher level Int 21h, which does all the work automatically.

Typically, only disk- and sector-editing programs access disk drives at the Int 25h and Int 26h level. Programs that work at this level of access can edit only areas of a disk that have been defined to DOS as a logical volume (drive letter). For example, the DOS DEBUG program can read sectors from and write sectors to disks with this level of access.

Interrupt 13h

The next lower level of communications with drives, the ROM BIOS Int 13h routines, usually are found in ROM chips on the motherboard or on an adapter card in an expansion slot. However, an Int 13h handler also can be implemented by using a device driver loaded at boot time. Because DOS requires Int 13h access to boot from a drive (and a device driver cannot be loaded until after boot-up), only drives with ROM BIOS-based Int 13h support can be bootable. Int 13h routines communicate directly with the controller using the I/O ports on the controller.

Table 26.2 lists the different functions available at the Interrupt 13h BIOS interface. Some functions are available to floppy drives or hard drives only, whereas others are available to both types of drives.

Table 26.2   Int 13h BIOS Disk Functions

Function	Floppy Disk	Hard Disk	Description
00h	×	×	Reset disk system
01h	×	×	Get status of last operation
02h	×	×	Read sectors
03h	×	×	Write sectors
04h	×	×	Verify sectors
05h	×	×	Format track
06h		×	Format bad track
07h		×	Format drive
08h	×	×	Read drive parameters

Function	Floppy Disk	Hard Disk	Description
09h		×	Initialize drive characteristics
0Ah		×	Read long
0Bh		×	Write long
0Ch		×	Seek
0Dh		×	Alternate hard disk reset
0Eh		×	Read sector buffer
0Fh		×	Write sector buffer
10h		×	Test for drive ready
11h		×	Recalibrate drive
12h		×	Controller RAM diagnostic
13h		×	Controller drive diagnostic
14h		×	Controller internal diagnostic
15h	×	×	Get disk type
16h	×		Get floppy disk change status
17h	×		Set floppy disk type for format
18h	×		Set media type for format
19h		×	Park hard disk heads
1Ah		×	ESDI—Low-level format
1Bh		×	ESDI—Get manufacturing header
1Ch		×	ESDI—Get configuration

Table 26.3 shows the error codes that might be returned by the BIOS INT 13h routines. In some cases, you may see these codes when running a low-level format program, disk editor, or other program that can directly access a disk drive through the BIOS.

Table 26.3   BIOS INT 13h Error Codes

Code	Description
00h	No error
01h	Bad command
02h	Address mark not found
03h	Write protect
04h	Request sector not found
05h	Reset failed
06h	Media change error
07h	Initialization failed
09h	Cross 64KB DMA boundary
0Ah	Bad sector flag detected
0Bh	Bad track flag detected

(continues)

Table 26.3   Continued

Code	Description
10h	Bad ECC on disk read
11h	ECC corrected data error
20h	Controller has failed
40h	Seek operation failed
80h	Drive failed to respond
AAh	Drive not ready
BBh	Undefined error
CCh	Write fault
OEh	Register error
FFh	Sense operation failed

Few high-powered disk utility programs, other than some basic disk formatting applications, can talk to the disk at the Int 13h level. The DOS FDISK program communicates at the Int 13h level, as does the Norton Utilities' DISKEDIT program when it is in its absolute sector mode; these are some of the few disk-repair utilities that can do so. These programs are important because you can use them for the worst data recovery situations in which the partition tables have been corrupted. Because the partition tables, and any non-DOS partitions, exist outside the area of a disk that is defined by DOS, only programs that work at the Int 13h level can access them. Most utility programs for data recovery work only at the DOS Int 25/26h level, which makes them useless for accessing areas of a disk outside of DOS's domain.

Disk Controller I/O Port Commands

At the lowest interface level, programs communicate directly with the disk controller in the controller's own specific native language. To do this, a program must send controller commands through the I/O ports to which the controller responds.

◄◄ See "IDE Origins," p. 510.

Figure 26.2 shows that most application programs work through the Int 21h interface. This interface passes commands to the ROM BIOS as Int 13h commands; the ROM BIOS then converts these commands into direct controller commands. The controller executes the commands and returns the results through the layers until the desired information reaches the application. This process enables developers to write applications without worrying about such low-level system details, leaving them instead up to DOS and the ROM BIOS. This also enables applications to run on widely different types of hardware, as long as the correct ROM BIOS and DOS support is in place.

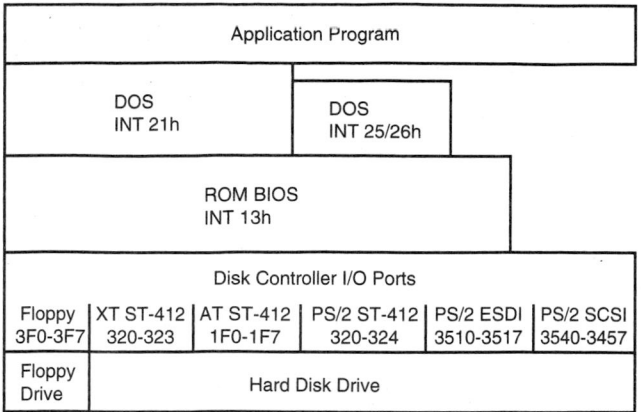

Figure 26.2 Relationships between various interface levels.

Any software can bypass any level of interface and communicate with the level below it, but doing so requires much more work. The lowest level of interface available is direct communication with the controller using I/O port commands. As Figure 26.2 shows, each type of controller has different I/O port locations. With different controllers there are also differences among the commands presented at the ports. Only the controller can talk directly to the disk drive.

If not for the ROM BIOS Int 13h interface, a unique DOS would have to be written for each available type of hard and floppy disk drive. Instead, DOS communicates with the ROM BIOS using standard Int 13h function calls translated by the Int 13h interface into commands for the specific hardware. Because of the standard ROM BIOS interface, DOS is relatively independent from the disk hardware and can support many different types of drives and controllers.

Windows 3.1

The 16-bit Windows platforms—Windows 3.1, Windows 3.11, and Windows for Workgroups—cannot strictly be called operating systems. They are instead graphical environments that operate on top of DOS, using much of the same disk access technology described earlier in this chapter. Windows, however, takes advantage of microprocessor capabilities first introduced in the Intel 80386 chip in ways that DOS cannot.

◀◀ See "Processor Modes," p. 58.

Windows also expands on some of the basic concepts introduced in DOS to make the application programmer's job easier. You read earlier how DOS, in combination with the system ROM BIOS, provides an interface to the PC disk storage devices. This interface enables programmers to use general function calls for disk access that can be applied to any type of hardware by the operating system. However, when you install a DOS application, you often have to select drivers for components such as your video display adapter, audio adapter, and printer, because DOS does not provide anything but the most rudimentary access to these devices.

Windows, on the other hand, does support the unique capabilities of your system hardware. When you install Windows, you select drivers for your specific video, audio, and printer hardware that support all the capabilities of these devices. As a result, Windows applications do not need their own drivers for these devices, because the environment provides a standard set of function calls that offer a universal interface to whatever hardware you have installed in the system.

16-bit Windows Versions

The environment that is commonly referred to as 16-bit Windows or Windows 3.1 can actually be any one of three products. The differences between the versions are rather slight, and the three are largely indistinguishable in terms of the user interface. In general, when this chapter refers to Windows 3.1, any one of the three products can be inferred.

Windows 3.1 was released in 1992 and is the standard graphical 16-bit platform for Intel-based systems. Windows 3.11 was released in 1994, and consisted of updates to the following key Windows files:

- COMMDLG.DLL
- GDI.EXE
- KRNL386.EXE
- PSCRIPT.DRV
- SHELL.DLL
- UNIDRV.DLL
- USER.EXE

The Windows 3.11 upgrade did not result in significant improvements in system performance, and was therefore ignored by many users and administrators responsible for the maintenance of Windows systems.

Both Windows 3.1 and 3.11 contain no networking support whatsoever. At the time they were released, NetWare was the dominant networking platform in the business world and supplied the client software needed to connect a DOS or Windows system to NetWare servers. At the same time, however, Microsoft began to promote their own networking environment, originally released as Windows for Workgroups in 1992 and finally culminating in the initial release of Windows NT in 1993.

Windows for Workgroups is an environment almost identical to Windows 3.1, except that it includes a Windows network client that enables the system to connect either to Windows NT servers or to other Windows for Workgroup systems on a peer-to-peer basis. Windows for Workgroups also supports external clients like those for NetWare, making it possible to run a heterogeneous network containing both Microsoft and Novell network resources.

At the time of its initial release, Windows for Workgroups and other Microsoft networking products relied on the NetBEUI protocol for network communications. As time passed, however, TCP/IP grew to be the industry standard protocol suite, and Microsoft released a TCP/IP client add-in for Windows for Workgroups called TCP/IP-32. There are still a great many PCs today that use this combination of products for business networking.

Loading Windows 3.1

As mentioned earlier, Windows 3.1 is not an operating system in itself. You must always boot the PC to a standard DOS prompt before loading the Windows environment. The system boot process, therefore, is identical to that outlined earlier in this chapter. However, as Windows loads, it changes the operating mode of the system processor and provides an additional interface layer between the system hardware and your applications.

When you load Windows 3.1 by typing WIN at the DOS prompt, the system executes the WIN.COM program that examines the capabilities of the hardware in the system and loads Windows in the appropriate mode to support that hardware. At the time Windows 3.1 was first released, the PC world was on the cusp between the eras of the 286 processor and the 386. If you had a 286-based system, Windows loaded in standard mode; 386-based and higher systems loaded in 386 enhanced mode. Today, of course, anything less than a Pentium is all but extinct and nearly all systems run Windows in 386 enhanced mode, now normally called protected mode on all Intel processors since the 386.

Both Windows modes require access to XMS (extended memory specification) memory, as provided by an extended Memory Manager such as HIMEM.SYS, that is loaded by the CONFIG.SYS file during the system boot sequence. To access XMS, WIN.COM shifts the processor from real mode to protected mode, something that DOS cannot do. In protected mode, a program can be allotted a specific area of memory that is protected from interference by other programs.

Note

Note that real mode and protected mode are attributes of the system processor and should be distinguished from the terms standard mode and 386 enhanced mode, which are Windows software states.

When WIN.COM detects a 286 processor or less, it loads Windows in standard mode by executing a file called DOSX.EXE (the MS-DOS Extended for Windows). In standard mode, a Windows system is capable of accessing extended memory for the purpose of task swapping. Task swapping is when the system is running two or more applications, but only the active window actually has access to the system processor. The system executes two files, WSWAP.EXE and DSWAP.EXE, to support the task swapping of Windows applications and DOS applications, respectively.

When Windows loads in 386 enhanced mode, WIN.COM executes a file called WIN386.EXE that in turn loads the drivers specified in the [386enh] section of the SYSTEM.INI file. 386 enhanced mode makes it possible for Windows to use virtual memory, that is, disk space on a local hard drive that emulates RAM to provide a greater memory address space in which to run applications. With the aid of this virtual memory, a Windows system in 386 enhanced mode can multitask, in other words, run multiple programs at the same time with each program receiving regular access to the processor.

Note

Although true multitasking requires a separate processor for each task, the term has come to be used to refer to the sharing of a single processor's clock cycles, as in a typical Windows PC.

Disk access times are obviously far slower than memory access times (the two being measured in milliseconds, thousandths of a second, versus nanoseconds, billionths of a second), so virtual memory is nowhere near as efficient as actual RAM. However, the capability to swap data from active memory to virtual memory at will gives the system the capability to run more code than it would with RAM alone.

Core Windows Files

After loading the files to support the appropriate mode, Windows loads the core components that provide the basic functions of the environment. These components are as follows:

- KRNL286.EXE or KRNL386.EXE. The kernel file (appropriate to the processor in the system) is responsible for managing system resources such as memory and processor cycles, as well as loading applications and scheduling system events.

- USER.EXE. User is responsible for the manipulation of the windows, icons, and other elements that make up the Windows user interface. When you use the mouse or the keyboard to open, close, move, or resize a window, USER.EXE passes the input to the application associated with the window.

- GDI.EXE. GDI. The graphical device interface, responsible for the generation of screen images and other graphics operations.

After the core files execute, Windows loads an array of device drivers to support the hardware installed in the system. These drivers provide the interface that Windows applications use to access the system hardware. Unlike DOS, few Windows applications access the system hardware directly. The exceptions, again like DOS, tend to be disk utilities that require lower level access than the Windows disk drivers provide.

32-bit Disk Access

Under normal conditions, the hardware interface provided by the Windows device drivers operates in addition to the other interfaces provided by DOS and the system BIOS. When a Windows application needs access to the video display, for example, it makes a function call to the Windows video driver. However, for access to a hard disk drive, the same application would typically use a standard Int 21h request, just like a DOS application. DOS then generates an Int 13h request to the system BIOS, which then communicates with the hard drive controller.

The problem with this arrangement is that although Windows and its applications run the system processor in protected mode, DOS and the BIOS require that the processor run in real mode (called virtual 8086 mode in Windows). Thus, during the disk access procedure, the processor that is operating in protected mode to run the application must switch to virtual mode to process the Int 21h request, and then revert back to protected mode. When DOS finishes processing the Int 21h request, it generates the Int 13h request for the BIOS, and again the processor must switch to virtual mode and back again to trap that interrupt. After the request reaches the disk controller, the hard drive reads the desired information from the disk, and the whole process begins again in reverse to return the requested disk data to the application.

All this mode switching by the processor slows down the disk access routine, as does the relatively slow speed of most system BIOS implementations. Windows 3.1 includes a feature called 32-bit disk access (or fastdisk) that speeds up the process by eliminating the calls to the system BIOS and some of the processor mode shifts.

Fastdisk is essentially a protected mode device driver that communicates directly with the hard disk drive controller, replacing the system BIOS. Applications operate as they normally do, by generating DOS Int 21h requests, forcing the processor to switch to virtual mode. However, when the processor switches back to protected mode to trap the Int 13h request generated by DOS, it does not pass this request to the system BIOS. Instead, the fastdisk driver processes the Int 13h request and communicates directly with the disk controller, all the time in protected mode.

Because the fastdisk driver communicates directly with the disk controller, it only supports hardware that conforms to the Western Digital 1003 controller model, which is used by all manufacturers of IDE drives. You cannot use fastdisk with SCSI drives.

◄◄ See "ATA Commands," p. 519.

Many systems show a distinct improvement in their Windows disk access times as a result of using fastdisk. Fastdisk also makes it possible to run more non-Windows programs in the same amount of memory. Because DOS is not occupied by communications with the BIOS, it is more readily available for use by the virtual machines.

Hardware Problems Versus Software Problems

One of the most aggravating situations in computer repair is opening a system and troubleshooting all the hardware, just to find that the cause of the problem is a software program, not the hardware. Many people have spent large sums of money on replacement hardware, all on the assumption that the hardware was causing problems, when software was actually the culprit. To eliminate these aggravating, sometimes embarrassing, and often expensive situations, you should be able to distinguish a hardware problem from a software problem.

Fortunately, making this distinction can be relatively simple. Software problems often are caused by the device drivers and memory-resident programs loaded from the CONFIG.SYS and AUTOEXEC.BAT files on many systems. One of the first things to do when you begin having problems with your system is boot the system from a DOS disk that has no CONFIG.SYS or AUTOEXEC.BAT configuration files on it. Then test for the problem. If it has disappeared, the cause was probably something in one or both of those files.

To find the problem, begin restoring device drivers and memory-resident programs to CONFIG.SYS and AUTOEXEC.BAT one at a time (starting with CONFIG.SYS). For example, add one program back to CONFIG.SYS, reboot your system, and then determine if the problem has reappeared. When you discover the device driver or memory-resident program causing the problem, you might be able to solve the problem by editing CONFIG.SYS and AUTOEXEC.BAT to change the order in which device drivers and memory-resident programs are loaded. Or, you might have to upgrade or even eliminate the problem device driver or memory-resident program.

Windows 9x

Windows 9x is the next step in the evolution of the operating systems that began with DOS. Although it is a fully 32-bit operating system and improves on Windows 3.1 in many ways, Windows 9x is not the radical innovation that it was purported to be before its release. In fact, Windows 95 is actually a combination of a new version of MS-DOS (called DOS 7.00, according to the VER command) and a new Windows interface (called the Explorer).

As such, Windows 9x can indeed be called an operating system, as it marries DOS and the Windows environment into a more cohesive environment than the DOS/Windows 3.1 combination. Booting a Windows 9x system automatically loads the GUI, but changing one character of the MSDOS.SYS text file causes the computer to boot to a DOS prompt, after which you must type WIN to load the Windows interface. Sound familiar?

Windows 9x and DOS Compared

Much of Windows 9x is based on the same concepts as DOS and Windows 3.1, but developed to the next logical stage. The same two system files, IO.SYS and MSDOS.SYS, still exist in Windows 9x, except that all the system file code is now located in IO.SYS. The MSDOS.SYS file is now an ASCII text file that contains configuration settings for the system's boot behavior.

During the system startup process, the initial procedures are very similar to those of a DOS system, as outlined earlier in this chapter. In Windows 9x, however, IO.SYS automatically loads the equivalents of HIMEM.SYS, IFSHLP.SYS, and SETVER.EXE into memory. You can still use CONFIG.SYS and AUTOEXEC.BAT files to load real-mode device drivers and memory-resident programs, but the 32-bit device drivers designed specifically for use with Windows 9x, as well as most of its configuration settings, are loaded from entries in the Windows 9x Registry. Finally, the WIN.COM file is executed and Windows 9x is officially started.

The Registry is a database of reference information, configuration settings, and application parameters that is continuously available to all Windows 9x modules. It replaces not only the functionality of the CONFIG.SYS and AUTOEXEC.BAT files, but the Windows 3.1 INI files as well.

Note

Be aware that when upgrading a Windows 3.1 computer to Windows 9x, many of the application and operating system settings located in configuration files, such as SYSTEM.INI and WIN.INI, are copied to the Windows 9x Registry. Once this has occurred, changing those settings in these INI files has no effect on the system, because the actual operative setting is located in the Registry.

The Registry takes the form of two disk files called SYSTEM.DAT and USER.DAT. SYSTEM.DAT contains machine-specific settings; USER.DAT contains the settings specific to the user who logs in to the system. By maintaining multiple USER.DAT files, different people can share the same computer, with each user maintaining his or her own system configuration and desktop preferences. Registry files can be imported, exported, modified, backed up, and restored to maintain, modify, and protect the settings for a particular user or machine.

As far as disk storage is concerned, Windows 9x by default still uses the same FAT file system that DOS does, maintaining familiar structures such as the Master Boot Record (MBR), DOS Boot Record (DBR), FATs, and directories. The primary enhancement to the file system is the capability to use file and directory names that are up to 255 characters in length, while retaining backward compatibility with existing FAT file systems and utilities.

▶▶ See "File Allocation Tables (FATs)," p. 1391.

Windows 9x does this by maintaining two names for every file and directory—a long name and a truncated name that fits the standard DOS 8.3 format. This way, you can open a Windows 9x file with any DOS or Windows 3.1 application, although saving the file again will strip away the long filename. If, for example, you ran an older version of a disk repair utility such as Norton Disk Doctor on a Windows 9x FAT volume, you could lose the long names of all the files and directories on your system.

Windows 9x Versions

Since the initial release of Windows 95, quite a few patches and feature updates have been released by Microsoft, as well as two major releases. The Windows 95 OEM Service Release 2 (OSR2) and OSR 2.5 were available only with the purchase of a new computer or hard drive from an authorized Microsoft OEM (original equipment manufacturer). OSR 2.5 adds integrated USB support to OSR2. USB support could be added to OSR2, and the result was often called OSR 2.1. Besides optional or integral USB support, the most important feature in these upgrades was a new file system called FAT32 that is designed to support with greater efficiency the larger hard disk drives now being found in PCs.

The OSR2 and 2.5 versions of Windows 95 were released in this way not to thwart and irritate millions of users (which it has), but to prevent a backlash of incompatibilities that might occur when the operating system is installed on older hardware. Most of the other patches and improvements to the operating system that are included in the OSR2.x release can be applied to Windows 95 installations and are freely available from Microsoft's Web site.

The Windows 98 release adds FAT32 as part of a retail product for the first time, and makes it possible to convert existing FAT16 partitions to FAT32. There are also numerous other new features and accessories in Windows 98, but very little else about the operating system's relationship to the PC hardware is changed from the OSR2 product.

Windows 9x Architecture

Much of the Windows 9x system architecture is similar to that of Windows 3.1, but rewritten in 32-bit code. The core elements of the operating system are still the kernel, the user, and the GDI, but all three now exist in both 32-bit and 16-bit versions. The 32-bit versions generally provide better performance and support for 32-bit applications, while the 16-bit versions are retained for backward compatibility.

Virtual Machine Manager

Windows 9x runs applications in separate, isolated environments called virtual machines. Created by the Virtual Machine Manager (which replaces the Windows 3.1 WIN386.EXE module), each virtual machine contains all the services needed for an application to run. By isolating each application in its own environment, Windows 9x is capable of preventing the rest of the system from being affected by a single malfunctioning application.

Plug and Play (PnP)

Perhaps the largest improvement in Windows 9x from a hardware standpoint is the introduction of support for Plug and Play (PnP). Plug and Play is a standard that enables the operating system to automatically negotiate for the system resources needed by a particular device and configure the hardware to use them. Most of the PC peripherals manufactured today support PnP, making the installation of new hardware as simple as inserting an expansion card into a slot or plugging it into a port.

To implement this functionality, Windows 9x uses a module called the Configuration Manager. The Configuration Manager consists of multiple bus enumerators that are responsible for scanning the system's various expansion buses for the devices connected to them. The enumerators then build a hardware tree containing all the buses and devices in the system.

When this inventory of the system hardware is completed, the Configuration Manager loads a driver for each device in the hardware tree. The Windows 9x drivers are all 32-bit, protected mode modules, permitting them to be loaded into system memory much more easily than their real mode counterparts from Windows 3.1, which require conventional memory (memory below 640KB) to load.

With the drivers loaded, the Configuration Manager then uses resource arbitrators to negotiate the hardware resources that are to be allocated to each device. These arbitrators reconcile any resource conflicts that might exist between devices and determine the best combination of operational settings for the hardware.

FAT32

The primary advantage of the FAT32 file system is its capability to support larger hard drives. The original FAT system used 16-bit numbers to track the clusters or allocation units on a disk. This means that if you consider each cluster a "room," the room numbers were 16 digits long (and in binary). The length of a number dictates the maximum value that can be assigned, for example, a hotel using two-digit (base 10) numbers would be limited to only 100 rooms (00–99). Similarly a 16-bit long number is limited to managing 65,536 clusters. This may seem like a lot, but with the ever increasing capacity of hard disks, it has proven to be quite a severe limitation.

Before FAT32, all you could do was split the drive into multiple partitions or increase the size of the clusters in a given partition. With only just over 65,000 rooms available in a partition, the rooms had to be large, wasting a significant amount of disk space if you were storing smaller files. With FAT32, you have a 32-bit number for tracking clusters, meaning you can have over 4.2 billion clusters total! Because you can split a drive into more separately manageable pieces, the pieces can be smaller, and there is less wasted space.

Surely no one involved in the development of the original FAT file system could ever have dreamed that a modest home computer would come with a 10GB hard drive, but that is now the minimum found in many if not most systems sold today. The largest disk partition size supported by the FAT file system is only 2GB, meaning such a drive would need to be split into at least 5 volumes or partitions, each assigned a different drive letter. The other problem with FAT is that the larger cluster sizes used with high-capacity hard drives are extremely wasteful in terms of the disk space lost to the slack caused by unused bits in allocated clusters.

FAT32 addresses both of these problems by supporting drives and individual partitions up to 2TB (2 terabytes, or about 2,000 GB) in size, and with much smaller clusters. A 2GB FAT16 partition uses 32KB clusters, while the clusters on the same size FAT32 partition are only 4KB. This results in a file system that is more efficient by a factor of 10–15 percent when it comes to storing the maximum possible amount of data on a hard drive.

Note

Although 2TB may seem to be an outrageously large amount of data, consider that a typical PC hard drive has gone from 10MB to 10GB in about 15 years—an increase of 100,000 percent! At this rate of growth, your home computer in the year 2010 should be equipped with a 1000TB hard drive (probably running the FAT256 file system).

FAT32 also overcomes some of the other obvious limitations of the FAT system. For example, FAT32 still has two file allocation tables, but it can now make use of either one, switching to the backup if the first table is corrupted. Also, the root directory of a drive is no longer restricted to a specific size. It is composed of cluster chains like any other directory, and can be located any-where on the disk. FAT32 volumes are implemented by the FDISK program included with the OSR2x Windows 95 and Windows 98 releases. When you attempt to create a partition larger than 512MB, the program asks if you want to enable large disk support. Choosing Yes causes all partitions larger than 512MB to use the FAT32 file system.

FAT32, like Windows 9x, is designed to provide the greatest possible backward compatibility, along with its advanced features. It will continue to support real mode DOS programs and today's protected mode applications. This means that you will be able to boot from any DOS disk and still access FAT32 drives. However, applications designed for use on FAT16 drives that address the hardware directly, such as disk repair programs, will not function on (and may damage) FAT32 volumes.

▶▶ See "FAT32," p. 1399.

The Windows 9x Boot Process

Knowing exactly how Windows 9x loads and starts can be helpful when troubleshooting startup problems. The Windows 9x boot process can be broken into five phases:

- The ROM BIOS bootstrap.
- The Master Boot Record (MBR) and partition boot sector.

- The IO.SYS file is loaded and run.
- Real mode configuration takes place.
- The WIN.COM file is loaded and run.

Phase 1—The ROM BIOS Bootstrap

1. The power on self test (POST) occurs. If your computer has a Plug and Play BIOS, the steps 2–8 steps are performed.

2. The Plug-and-Play BIOS checks non-volatile random access memory (RAM) for input/ output (I/O) port addresses, interrupt request lines (IRQs), direct memory access (DMA) channels, and other settings needed to configure PnP devices on the computer.

3. All Plug-and-Play devices found by the Plug-and-Play BIOS are disabled.

4. A map of used and unused resources is created.

5. The Plug-and-Play devices are configured and re-enabled, one at a time. If your computer does not have a Plug-and-Play BIOS, PnP devices are initialized using their default settings. These devices may be reconfigured dynamically when Windows 9x starts. At that point, the Windows 9x Configuration Manager queries the Plug-and-Play BIOS for device information, and then queries each Plug and Play device for its configuration.

6. The A: drive is checked for the existence of a boot disk.

7. If a boot disk is not found in the A: drive, the ROM BIOS bootstrap loader program checks for a hard disk. If a hard disk is found, the ROM transfers control to the operating system loader.

8. The master boot record and partition table are read.

Phase 2—The Master Boot Record (MBR) and Partition Boot Sector

1. The MBR determines the location of the boot partition by reading the partition table located at the end of the master boot record.

2. The MBR passes control to the partition boot sector in the bootable (active) partition. The partition boot sector contains the disk boot program and a table of disk characteristics.

3. The partition boot sector checks the BIOS Parameter Block (BPB) to find the location of the root directory, and then copies the IO.SYS file from the root directory into memory.

Phase 3—Loading and Running the IO.SYS File

1. A minimal FAT file system is loaded.

2. The MSDOS.SYS file is read.

3. The Starting Windows message is displayed for <n> seconds, or until you press a Windows function key. The amount of time the message is displayed is determined by the BootDelay=<n> line in the MSDOS.SYS file; the default is 2 seconds.

4. If you have multiple hardware profiles, you receive the following message and must choose a hardware configuration to use:

   ```
   Windows cannot determine what configuration your computer is in.
   ```

5. The LOGO.SYS file is loaded and displays a startup image on the screen.

6. If the DRVSPACE.INI or DBLSPACE.INI files exist, they are loaded into memory.

7. The IO.SYS file checks the system Registry files (SYSTEM.DAT and USER.DAT) for valid data.

8. IO.SYS opens the SYSTEM.DAT file. If the SYSTEM.DAT file is not found, the SYSTEM.DA0 file is used for start up. If Windows 9x starts successfully, the SYSTEM.DA0 file is copied to the SYSTEM.DAT file.

9. The DBLBUFF.SYS file is loaded if the `DoubleBuffer=1` is in the MSDOS.SYS file, or if double buffering is enabled under the following Registry key:

   ```
   HKLM\System\CurrentControlSet\Control\WinBoot\DoubleBuffer
   ```

Note

Windows 9x Setup automatically enables double buffering if it detects that it is required.

10. If you have multiple hardware profiles, the hardware profile you chose is loaded from the Registry.

11. The IO.SYS file processes the CONFIG.SYS file.

Phase 4—Real Mode Configuration

Some older hardware devices and programs require that drivers or files be loaded in real mode (16-bit mode) in order for them to work properly. To ensure backward compatibility, Windows 9x processes the CONFIG.SYS and AUTOEXEC.BAT files if they exist.

1. The CONFIG.SYS file is read if it exists, and the statements within are processed, including the loading of drivers into memory. If the CONFIG.SYS file does not exist, the IO.SYS file loads the following required drivers:

   IFSHLP.SYS

   HIMEM.SYS

   SETVER.EXE

   IO.SYS obtains the location of these files from the `WinBootDir=` line of the MSDOS.SYS file, and must be on the hard disk.

2. Windows reserves all global upper memory blocks (UMBs) for the Windows 9x operating system use or for expanded memory support (EMS).

3. The AUTOEXEC.BAT file is processed if present, and any terminate-and-stay resident (TSR) programs listed within are loaded into memory.

Phase 5—Loading and Running the WIN.COM File

1. WIN.COM is loaded and run.

2. WIN.COM file accesses the VMM32.VXD file. If there is enough available RAM, the VMM32.VXD file loads into memory, otherwise, it is accessed from the hard disk (resulting in a slower startup time).

3. The real-mode virtual device driver loader checks for duplicate virtual device drivers (VxDs) in the WINDOWS\SYSTEM\VMM32 folder and the VMM32.VXD file. If a VxD exists in both the WINDOWS\SYSTEM\VMM32 folder and the VMM32.VXD file, the duplicate VxD is "marked" in the VMM32.VXD file so that it is not loaded.

4. VxDs that are not already loaded by the VMM32.VXD file are loaded from the [386 Enh] section of the WINDOWS\SYSTEM.INI file.

Required VxDs

Some VxDs are required for Windows to run properly. These required VxDs are loaded automatically and do not require a Registry entry. The following VxDs are required by Windows 9x:

*BIOSXLAT	*CONFIGMG	*DYNAPAGE
*DOSMGR	*EBIOS	*IFSMGR
*INT13	*IOS	*PAGESWAP
*SHELL	*V86MMGR	*VCD
*VCACHE	*VCOMM	*VCOND
*VDD	*VDMAD	*VFAT
*VKD	*VMCPD	*VPICD
*VTD	*VTDAPI	*VWIN32
*VXDLDR		

5. The real-mode virtual device driver loader checks that all required VxDs loaded successfully. If not, it attempts to load the drivers again.

6. Once the real-mode virtual device driver loading is logged, driver initialization occurs. If there are any VxDs that require real-mode initialization, they begin their process in real mode.

7. VMM32 switches the computer's processor from real mode to protected mode.

8. A three-phase VxD initialization process occurs in which the drivers are loaded according to their InitDevice instead of the order in which they are loaded into memory.

9. After all the VxDs are loaded, the KRNL32.DLL, GDI.EXE, USER.EXE, and EXPLORER.EXE (the default Windows 9x GUI shell) files are loaded.

10. If a network is specified, load the network environment and multiuser profiles. The user is prompted to log on to the network that is installed. Windows 9x allows multiple users to save their custom desktop settings. When a user logs on to Windows, his or her desktop settings are loaded from the Registry. If the user does not log on, the desktop configuration uses a default desktop.

11. Programs in the StartUp group and the RunOnce Registry key are run during the last phase of the startup process. After each program in the RunOnce Registry key is started, the program is removed from the key.

Windows NT and Windows 2000

Whereas DOS, Windows 3.x, and Windows 9x can be seen as successive steps in the continuing evolution of an operating system, Windows NT and Windows 2000 are wholly new concepts from the ground up (when compared to Windows 3.x or Windows 9x). Windows NT and Windows 2000 are true 32-bit operating systems that were designed from the ground up to point toward the future of both network and desktop computing. The primary problem that consistently holds back the advancement of computing technology is backward compatibility. It is difficult to sell a product that forces users to junk the investment that they have already made in software or hardware.

Windows 9x has some DOS/Windows 3.x remnants or 16-bit code within it for this very reason. Corporations hesitate to convert to a new operating system on a large scale if it forces them to waste millions of dollars spent on older 16-bit software and user training. Windows NT was just such a product, and its acceptance in the marketplace since its original release in 1993 has been gradual but steady. Windows NT 4.0 had become a viable competitor to Windows 9x in the desktop marketplace, and Windows 2000 (which was originally going to be called NT 5.0) has continued that trend. The growing trend toward Windows 2000 can be largely attributed to the Windows 9x marketing program that led to a massive 32-bit software development effort. Most 32-bit Windows applications can run on Windows 9x, Windows NT, or Windows 2000, and the backward compatibility issue is fading steadily as 16-bit applications are phased out.

Windows NT and Windows 2000 are completely different operating systems from DOS. Although you can open a DOS session window from within the GUI, it is not a shell in the traditional sense. It is rather a DOS emulation that is designed to provide a familiar command-line interface to users who want it. Many DOS programs will not run in a Windows NT DOS session, nor is it possible to boot the Windows NT operating system to a character-based state that precedes the loading of the graphical interface, as with Windows 9x.

Like Windows 9x, Windows NT and Windows 2000 use a Registry to load device drivers and store their configuration settings. There are no CONFIG.SYS, AUTOEXEC.BAT, or INI files. Windows NT can use the FAT16 file system, which enables you to boot the computer using a DOS disk and still access its drives. Some of Windows 2000's most advanced features, however, are provided by the NT File System (NTFS). NTFS (like FAT32) allows you to create partitionsup to 2TB in size, but it also provides the file compression, security, and auditing features that are important to Windows NT computers in network environments. Beginning in Windows 2000, support will be provided for the FAT32 file system as well.

During the Windows NT installation process, the initial setup is performed on a FAT drive, which can be converted to NTFS at the end of the installation process, if you so desire. You can also convert the drives later, using a CONVERT.EXE utility provided with the operating system. From the time a partition is converted to NTFS, however, it is not accessible by any other operating system. If you use a DOS disk to boot a system with NTFS partitions, you will have access to the floppy drive only, just as if there were no hard drives installed in the computer. To switch the machine back to Windows 9x, Windows 3.1, or DOS, you must delete the NTFS partitions (and their data) and create new FAT partitions from scratch.

Windows 2000 allows you to install to either a FAT32 or NTFS drive.

Versions

The first version of Windows NT was called 3.1, because it was released in 1993 when Windows 3.1 was the current 16-bit Windows product. The graphical interface was identical to that of Windows 3.1, even if the underlying infrastructure was completely different.

Subsequent versions (3.5 and 3.51) drew greater distinctions between the Server and Workstation versions of the operating system by adding the capability to create groupings of Windows NT machines called domains. These versions also provided bug fixes, implemented some architectural changes, such as making TCP/IP the default networking protocol, and added new services like DHCP and WINS.

Windows NT 4.0 was the first release to make substantial changes to the appearance of the operating system, by adding the same Explorer interface used by Windows 9x. Windows 2000 continues that trend, finally adding the Plug-and-Play capabilities of Windows 9x, and further enhancing the desktop and user interface.

Windows NT and Windows 2000 Startup

When you start a Windows NT or Windows 2000 system, the boot process is identical to that of a DOS or Windows 9.x system, up until the time when the system reads the partition boot record from the active partition. Instead of the IO.SYS and MSDOS.SYS files, Windows NT/2000 use an OS loader program called NTLDR that begins the hardware detection process and enables you to select the operating system to load. If, for example, you have installed Windows NT or Windows 2000 on a system already running another OS, you have the option of booting either operating system. The boot options are stored in a file called BOOT.INI.

Once you elect to load Windows NT or Windows 2000, a file called NTDETECT.COM loads and detects the hardware in the computer. Then, the Windows NT Kernel (NTOSKRNL.EXE) and the hardware abstraction layer (HAL.DLL) are loaded into memory. The kernel is responsible for initializing most of the operating system, including the device drivers, the Windows NT subsystems and services, and the memory paging file. It isn't until you press the Ctrl+Alt+Delete key combination and log on to the system that the startup process is considered to be complete.

Windows NT and Windows 2000 Components

The Windows NT and Windows 2000 kernel is responsible for scheduling tasks and managing threads. The thread is the smallest unit of processor activity Windows NT can handle. Because Windows NT is a multithreaded operating system, the kernel is responsible for ensuring that the threads of the various processes running on the system at any one time receive the appropriate access to the processor, based on their priorities.

Windows NT was designed to be a modular operating system and to be portable to different hardware (that is, processor) platforms. To make this possible, a module called the hardware abstraction layer (HAL) creates a virtual interface to the system hardware. The operating system kernel and the device drivers then use this interface to communicate with the hardware, rather than accessing it directly. Because the interface is machine-independent, it is a relatively simple matter to port the kernel, drivers, and other components to other platforms, such as Digital's Alpha processor.

Windows NT and Windows 2000 have two operational modes: kernel and user. Kernel mode provides access to all system resources and processor instructions. The OS kernel and the HAL both run in kernel mode, as does the Windows NT Executive. The Executive consists of the following operating system components:

- *Object Manager*. All Windows NT resources, including files and directories, threads and processes, and memory segments and sections, are represented by abstract formations known as objects. The Object Manager provides a hierarchical naming system for these objects, which makes it possible to track their creation and use.

- *I/O Manager*. The I/O Manager is responsible for all Windows NT's input and output functions and maintains communications with the various device drivers for the system hardware to make this possible.

- *Security Reference Monitor*. The Security Reference Monitor (SRM) works together with the user mode security subsystem to control access to Windows NT objects. All requests for access to an object pass through the SRM, which checks its access control list for the appropriate rights.

- *Process Manager*. The Process Manager controls the creation and deletion of process objects and the threads that make up the processes.

- *Virtual Memory Manager*. The Virtual Memory Manager is responsible for allocating a protected memory address space to each process running on the system. As with Windows 9x, Windows NT can use disk space as virtual memory, and allocate a total amount of memory that is larger than the RAM installed in the system.

- *Local Procedure Call*. The Local Procedure Call facility provides communications between client and server processes on the same system, just as Remote Procedure Calls are used for client/server communications between different systems.

User mode is a less privileged mode that keeps the processes running in it isolated from parts of the OS that could be crashed. User mode interacts with the user and the user applications. This split in modes allows applications designed for Windows as well as some native OS/2 and POSIX applications to run without giving these other applications direct access to the kernel.

Linux

Linux is a freely distributed version of UNIX written by Linus Torvalds along with assistance from people all across the Internet. Linux has all the features you would expect of a modern UNIX implementation, including true multitasking, virtual memory, shared libraries, demand loading, shared executables, proper memory management, and integrated TCP/IP networking.

Linux runs on 386 and higher PCs (mainly Pentium and higher), using the 32-bit mode and facilities of the Intel processor family. Although written originally for Intel processors, ports to other architectures are becoming available.

One of the most interesting aspects of Linux is its open nature. The Linux kernel copyright belongs to Linus Torvalds, however, he has placed it under the GNU General Public License. This means that you may freely copy, change, and distribute it, but you may not impose any restrictions on further distribution, and you must make the source code available. This has encouraged others to add to the operating system, as well as write applications for it, at a very rapid pace. The main operating system and utilities can be downloaded from several Internet sites, as well as ordered on CD-ROM from companies such as Caldera or Red Hat for a reasonable distribution fee.

There are numerous applications available for Linux, most of which can also be downloaded over the Net or purchased very reasonably on disc. Linux doesn't run Windows software, but windows type applications (including popular applications, such as WordPerfect, and games, such as Quake) have been ported over. Linux does include a DOS emulator, so most DOS programs can be run. Of course, it also includes a full suite of UNIX type commands and programs as well.

For more information on Linux, especially as it relates to upgrading and repairing PCs, we now have a version of this book titled Upgrading and Repairing PCs for Linux. It is available from any bookstore or from the publisher direct under ISBN 0-7897-2075-2.

File Systems and Data Recovery

SOME OF THE MAIN TOPICS IN THIS CHAPTER ARE

FAT Disk Structures

VFAT and Long Filenames

FAT32

FAT File System Errors

FAT File System Utilities

NTFS

Common Drive Error Messages and Solutions

General File System Troubleshooting

FAT Disk Structures

Physically it is the hard disks and other media that provide the basic technology for storing data. Logically however, it is the file system that provides the hierarchical structure of volumes and directories in which you store individual files and the organizational model that makes it possible for the system to locate data anywhere on a given disk or drive. File systems are normally an integrated part of an operating system (OS), and many of the newer OSes provide support for several file systems from which you can choose.

The most commonly used file systems today are based on a file allocation table (FAT), which keeps track of the data stored in each cluster on a disk. There are several varieties of the FAT system called FAT12, FAT16, and FAT32, all of which are differentiated by the number of digits used in the allocation table numbers. In other words, FAT32 uses 32-bit numbers to keep track of data clusters; FAT16 uses 16-bit numbers, and so on. The different FAT systems are normally used as follows:

- *FAT12.* Used on all volumes smaller than 16MB (for example, floppies)
- *FAT16.* Used on volumes from 16MB through 2GB
- *FAT32.* Optionally used on volumes from 512MB through 2TB

FAT12 and FAT16 are the file systems originally used by DOS and Windows, and are supported by virtually every other PC operating system in use today. Most PC drives or volumes today are formatted under one of the FAT file systems.

Fat32 is supported by Windows 95B and later versions, including 95C and 98, as well as Windows 2000 (which also supports NTFS). Although all PC operating systems I am aware of support at least FAT12 and FAT16, some have support for non-FAT file systems as well. Windows NT introduced the NT File System (NTFS), which is unique to NT and Windows 2000 and not supported by Windows 9x. OS/2 1.2 introduced the High Performance File System (HPFS), which is unique to OS/2, although NT versions 3.x also supported it.

This chapter examines these file systems in more detail. Because of the popularity of the FAT file systems, they are emphasized, although the additional capabilities provided by HPFS or NTFS are also discussed.

To manage files on a disk and enable all application programs to see a consistent interface to the file system no matter what type of storage hardware is being used, the operating system (OS) creates several structures on the disk. These structures are the same for any OS that supports the FAT file system, including Windows 9x, NT, and Windows 2000. The following list shows all the structures and areas that FAT uses to manage a disk, in roughly the same order that they appear on the media:

- Master and extended partition boot records (sectors)
- Volume boot record
- Root directory
- File allocation tables (FATs)

- Clusters (allocation units in the data area)
- Diagnostic read-and-write cylinder

All these structures are detailed later in this section. A hard disk has all these disk-management structures, and a floppy disk has all but the master and extended partition boot records and diagnostic cylinder. The volume boot record through data area structures are repeated for each partition or volume on a drive. These structures are created on hard disk drives or other high-capacity media by the FDISK program included with all operating systems. You cannot use FDISK on a floppy disk because floppy disks cannot be partitioned. Figure 27.1 is a simple diagram showing the relative locations of these FAT disk-management structures on a 2,111MB Western Digital hard disk.

Note

Some removable cartridge drives, such as the SuperDisk (LS-120) and Iomega Zip drive, function like high-capacity floppy disk drives. They lack a master boot record (MBR) and diagnostic cylinder and cannot be partitioned like hard disk drives. Other higher capacity removable drives, such as the Iomega Jaz, can be partitioned like a hard disk drive.

Figure 27.1 shows the placement and arrangement of the file management structures on a typical drive. This particular example uses a Western Digital Caviar AC12100, but all PC hard drives using the FAT file system would be similar except for the number of cylinders.

Each disk area has a purpose and function. If one of these special areas is damaged, serious consequences can result. Damage to one of these sensitive structures usually causes a domino effect, limiting access to other areas of the disk or causing further problems in using the disk. For example, the OS cannot normally access a drive at all if the MBR is corrupted. Therefore, you should understand these data structures well enough to be able to repair them when necessary. Rebuilding these special tables and areas of the disk is essential to the art of data recovery.

Master Partition Boot Record

The first PC OS to support hard disks, DOS 2.0 released in 1983, was also the first to introduce the 16-bit FAT and the capability to partition a drive. *Partitioning* is basically dividing the drive into multiple volumes. One concept easily misunderstood is that all drives that *can* be partitioned *must* be partitioned; that is, you have to partition the drive even if you are only going to set it up with only one partition. Another name for a partition is a *logical volume*, because the partition shows up as an additional drive letter or volume to the OS.

Although the primary use for partitioning today is to divide a single drive into multiple volumes for use by the same OS, originally it was intended to allow multiple different OSes, each with different file systems, to co-exist on a single drive. This multi-OS capability still exists today, although often additional aftermarket utilities are required to manage and boot from multiple OSes on a single machine.

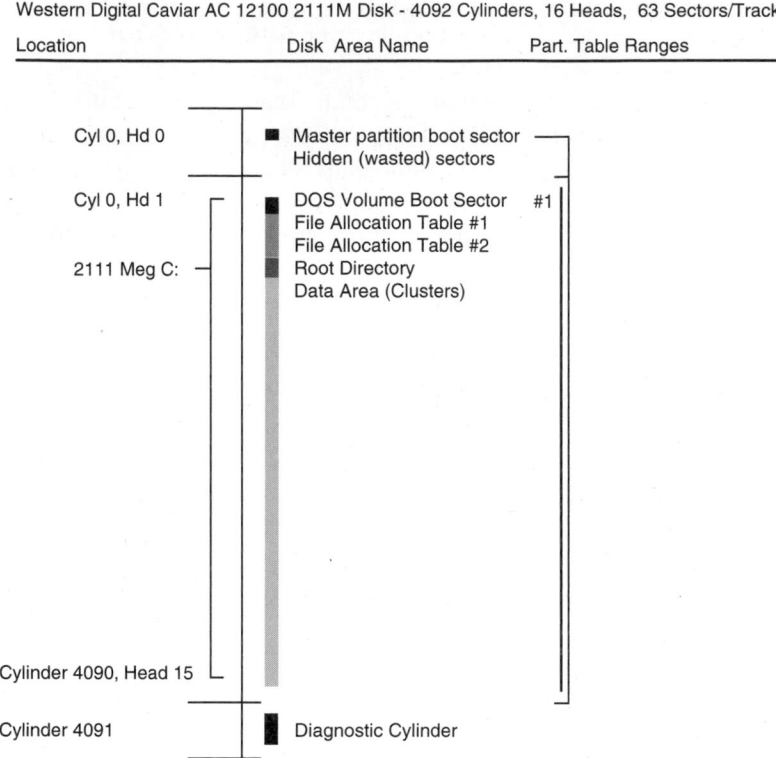

Figure 27.1 FAT file management structures on a typical drive.

To use a hard disk with different operating systems, you can logically divide the disk by creating partitions. You can, for example, use FDISK to create one or more FAT partitions for use with DOS or Windows 9x, and leave the rest of the disk storage area for use by another OS's file system. Each of the FAT partitions will appear to the OS as a separate drive letter.

Note

For more information about creating and formatting partitions, see Chapter 14, "Physical Drive Installation and Configuration."

Information about each of the partitions on the disk is stored in a partition (or volume) boot record at the beginning of each partition. There is also a main table listing the partitions embedded in the master partition boot record.

The master partition boot record (or master boot sector) is always located in the first sector of the entire disk (cylinder 0, head 0, sector 1) and consists of the following structures:

■ *Master partition table*. Contains a list of the partitions on the disk and the locations of their volume boot records. This table is very small and can contain only four entries at the most. Therefore, to accommodate more partitions, operating systems such as DOS can divide a single extended partition into multiple logical volumes.

■ *Master boot code.* A small program that is executed by the system BIOS, the main function of which is to pass control of the system to the partition that has been designated as active (or bootable).

Primary and Extended FAT Partitions

Most OSes are designed to support up to 24 partitions on a single hard disk drive (represented by the drive letters C: through Z:), but the partition table in the master partition boot record can have a maximum of only four entries. To resolve this discrepancy, the FDISK program enables you to create two types of FAT partitions: a primary partition and an extended partition. The first FAT partition that you create on a disk should be the primary, which is listed in the master partition table and appears to the operating system as a single drive letter.

An extended partition is listed in the master partition table like the primary, but it differs in that you can use its disk space to create multiple logical partitions, or volumes. You can create only one extended partition on a single drive, meaning that there will never normally be more than two entries in the master partition table devoted to FAT volumes.

The logical volumes that you create in the extended partition appear as separate drive letters to the operating system, but they are not listed in the master partition table. Logical volumes cannot be active partitions, and are therefore not bootable. You can create up to 23 volumes out of a single extended partition (assuming that you have already created a primary FAT partition, which brings the total to 24).

Each of the logical partitions (or volumes) in an extended partition includes an extended partition table that contains information about that volume. The master partition table's entry for the extended partition contains a reference to the first volume's extended partition table. This table in turn contains a reference detailing the location of the second volume's table. This chain of references continues, linking all the volumes in the extended partition to the master partition table.

Of course, few people have any reason to create 24 FAT partitions on a single disk drive, but the extended partition makes it possible to exceed the four-entry limitation of the master partition table.

Because the master boot record contains the first program that the system executes when you boot a PC, it is frequently a target for creators of computer viruses. A virus that infects or destroys the master boot record can make it impossible for the BIOS to find the active partition, thus preventing the operating system from loading. Because the master boot record contains the first program executed by the system, a virus stored there loads before any antivirus code can detect it. To remove a master boot record virus, you must first boot the system from a clean, uninfected floppy disk and then run an antivirus program.

Each partition on a disk contains a volume boot record as its first sector, which is listed in the master partition table. With the FDISK utility, you can designate a single partition as active (or bootable). The master partition boot record causes the active partition's volume boot record to receive control whenever the system is started or reset. You can also create additional disk partitions for Novell NetWare, Windows NT's NTFS, OS/2's HPFS, AIX (UNIX), XENIX, or other file systems, using disk utilities provided with the operating systems that support them. These partitions are listed in the master partition table, even though they may use different structures within the partition.

However, you cannot access the data stored on these foreign operating system partitions with DOS. In some cases, you cannot access FAT partitions using other operating systems either, although OS/2 and Windows NT do support FAT in addition to their own file systems: HPFS and NTFS. You must create at least one partition on a hard disk for it to be accessible by an operating system. Creating a partition adds an entry to the master partition table.

Table 27.1 shows the format of the Master Boot Record (MBR) and its partition tables. The table lists the fields in each of the master partition table's four entries, the location on the disk where each field begins (the offset), and its length. Some of the fields are stored as *Dwords*—four bytes read in reverse order—because of the internal structure of the Intel processors.

Table 27.1   Master Boot Record (Partition Tables)

Master Partition Table Entry #1

Offset	Length	Description
1BEh 446	1 byte	Boot indicator byte (80h = active, else 00h)
1BFh 447	1 byte	Starting head (or side) of partition
1C0h 448	16 bits	Starting cylinder (10 bits) and sector (6 bits)
1C2h 450	1 byte	System indicator byte (see Table 27.2)
1C3h 451	1 byte	Ending head (or side) of partition
C4h 452	16 bits	Ending cylinder (10 bits) and sector (6 bits)
1C6h 454	1 dword	Relative sector offset of partition
1CAh 458	1 dword	Total number of sectors in partition

Partition Table Entry #2

Offset	Length	Description
1CEh 462	1 byte	Boot indicator byte (80h = active, else 00h)
1CFh 463	1 byte	Starting head (or side) of partition
1D0h 464	16 bits	Starting cylinder (10 bits) and sector (6 bits)
D2h 466	1 byte	System indicator byte (see Table 27.2)
1D3h 467	1 byte	Ending head (or side) of partition
1D4h 468	16 bits	Ending (10 bits) and sector (6 bits)
1D6h 470	1 dword	Relative sector offset of partition
1DAh 474	1 dword	Total number of sectors in partition

Partition Table Entry #3

Offset	Length	Description
1DEh 478	1 byte	Boot indicator byte (80h = active, else 00h)
1DFh 479	1 byte	Starting head (or side) of partition
1E0h 480	16 bits	Starting cylinder (10 bits) and sector (6 bits)

Offset		Length	Description
1E2h	482	1 byte	System indicator byte (see Table 27.2)
1E3h	483	1 byte	Ending head (or side) of partition
1E4h	484	16 bits	Ending cylinder (10 bits) and sector (6 bits)
1E6h	486	1 dword	Relative sector offset of partition
1EAh	490	1 dword	Total number of sectors in partition

Partition Table Entry #4

Offset		Length	Description
1EEh	494	1 byte	Boot indicator byte (80h = active, else 00h)
1EFh	495	1 byte	Starting head (or side) of partition
1F0h	496	16 bits	Starting cylinder (10 bits) and sector (6 bits)
1F2h	498	1 byte	System indicator byte (see Table 27.2)
F3h	499	1 byte	Ending head (or side) of partition
1F4h	500	16 bits	Ending cylinder (10 bits) and sector (6 bits)
1F6h	502	1 dword	Relative sector offset of partition
1FAh	506	1 dword	Total number of sectors in partition

Signature Bytes

Offset		Length	Description
1FEh	510	2 bytes	Boot sector signature (55AAh)

A word equals 2 bytes read in reverse order, and a dword equals two words read in reverse order.

The data in the partition table entries tells the system where each partition starts and ends on the drive, how big it is, whether it is bootable, and what type of file system is contained in the partition. Each entry in the Master Partition Table contains a system indicator byte that identifies the file system type used in the partition referenced by that entry. Table 27.2 shows the standard values and meanings of the system indicator bytes.

Table 27.2   Standard System Indicator Byte Values

Value	Partition Type	Translation Mode	Partition Size
00h	None	—	—
01h	Primary FAT12	CHS	0–15MB
04h	Primary FAT16	CHS	16MB–32MB
05h	Extended	CHS	16MB–32MB
06h	Primary FAT16	CHS	32MB–2GB
0Eh	Primary FAT16	LBA	32MB–2GB
0Fh	Extended	LBA	32MB–2GB
0Bh	Primary FAT32	LBA	512MB–2TB
0Ch	Extended	LBA	512MB–2TB

Table 27.3   Non-Standard System Indicator Byte Values

Value	Partition Type
02h	MS-XENIX Root Partition
03h	MS-XENIX usr Partition
07h	OS/2 HPFS Partition
08h	AIX File System Partition
09h	AIX boot Partition
50h	Ontrack Disk Manager READ-ONLY Partition
51h	Ontrack Disk Manager READ/WRITE Partition
56h	Golden Bow Vfeature Partition
61h	Storage Dimensions Speedstor Partition
63h	IBM 386/ix or UNIX System V/386 Partition
64h	Novell NetWare Partition
75h	IBM PCIX Partition
DBh	DR Concurrent DOS/CPM-86 Partition
F2h	Some OEM DOS 3.2+ second Partition
FFh	UNIX Bad Block Table Partition

These values can be useful for somebody trying to manually repair a partition table using a disk editor such as the Diskedit program included with the Norton Utilties.

Undocumented FDISK

FDISK is a very powerful program. In DOS 5 and later versions, including Windows 9x, Windows NT, and Windows 2000, it gained some additional capabilities. Unfortunately, these capabilities were never documented in any of the Microsoft documentation for Windows or DOS. The most important undocumented parameter in FDISK is the **/MBR** (Master Boot Record) parameter, which causes FDISK to rewrite the Master Boot Record code area, leaving the partition table area intact.

The **/MBR** parameter is tailor-made for eliminating boot-sector virus programs that infect the Master Partition Boot Record (cylinder 0, head 0, sector 1) of a hard disk. To use this feature, enter the following:

```
FDISK /MBR
```

FDISK then rewrites the boot record code, leaving the partition tables intact. This should not cause any problems on a normally functioning system, but just in case, I recommend backing up the partition table information to floppy disk before trying it. You can do this by using a third-party product such as Norton Utilities.

Be aware that using FDISK with the **/MBR** switch will overwrite the partition tables if the two signature bytes at the end of the sector (55AAh) are damaged. This situation is highly unlikely, however. In fact, if these signature bytes were damaged, you would know; the system would not boot and would act as though there were no partitions at all.

Volume Boot Records

The volume boot record is the first sector on any area of a drive addressed as a partition or volume (or logical DOS disk). On a floppy disk or removable cartridge (such as a Zip disk), for example, this sector is the first one on the disk because DOS recognizes the disk as a volume without the need for partitioning. On a hard disk, the volume boot record or sectors are located as the first sector within any disk area allocated as a nonextended partition, or any area recognizable as a DOS volume. Refer to Figure 27.1 for an idea of the physical relationship between this volume boot record and the other data structures on a disk. The volume boot record resembles the master partition boot record in that it contains two elements, which are as follows:

- *Disk parameter block.* Sometimes called the media parameter block, the disk parameter block contains specific information about the volume, such as its size, the number of disk sectors it uses, the size of its clusters, and the volume label name.

- *Volume boot code.* The program that begins the process of loading the operating system. For DOS and Windows 9x systems, this is the IO.SYS file.

◀◀ See "IO.SYS (or IBMBIO.COM)," p. 1342

The volume boot record of the active partition on a disk is loaded by the system ROM BIOS for floppy disks or by the master partition boot record on a hard disk. The program code in the volume boot record is given control of the system; it performs some tests and then attempts to load the first system file (in DOS/Windows, this is IO.SYS). The volume boot record, such as the master boot record, is transparent to the running system; it is outside the data area of the disk on which files are stored.

Note

Many of the systems today are capable of booting from drives other than standard floppy disk and hard disk drives. In these cases, the boot drive must be specifically supported by system BIOS. For example, some BIOS products enable you to select an ATAPI CD-ROM as a boot device, in addition to the floppy and hard disk drives.

Other types of removable media, such as Zip cartridges and LS-120 disks, can also be made bootable. When properly supported by the BIOS, an LS-120 drive can replace the existing floppy disk drive as drive A:.

On a FAT partition, you create a volume boot record with the FORMAT command (high-level format) included with DOS and Windows 9x. Hard disks on FAT systems have a volume boot record at the beginning of every DOS logical drive area allocated on the disk, in both the primary and extended partitions. Although all the logical drives contain the program area as well as a data table area, only the program code from the volume boot record in the active partition on a hard disk is executed. The others are read by the operating system files during boot-up to obtain their data tables and determine the volume parameters.

The volume boot record contains program code and data. The single data table in this sector is called the media parameter block or disk parameter block. The operating system needs the information this table contains to verify the capacity of the disk volume as well as the location of important structures such as the FAT. The format of this data is very specific.

Table 27.3 shows the format and layout of the DOS boot record (DBR), including the location of each field within the record (the offset) in both hexadecimal and decimal notation and the length of each field.

Table 27.3 DOS Boot Record (DBR) Format Offset

Hex	Dec	Field Length	Description
00h	0	3 bytes	Jump instruction to boot program code
03h	3	8 bytes	OEM name and DOS version (IBM 5.0)
0Bh	11	1 word	Bytes/sector (usually 512)
0Dh	13	1 byte	Sectors/cluster (must be a power of 2)
0Eh	14	1 word	Reserved sectors (boot sectors, usually 1)
10h	16	1 byte	FAT copies (usually 2)
11h	17	1 word	Maximum root directory entries (usually 512)
13h	19	1 word	Total sectors (if partition <= 32MB, else 0)
15h	21	1 byte	Media descriptor byte (F8h for hard disks)
16h	22	1 word	Sectors/FAT
18h	24	1 word	Sectors/track
1Ah	26	1 word	Number of heads
1Ch	28	1 dword	Hidden sectors (If partition <= 32MB, 1 word only)

For DOS 4.0 or Higher Only, Else 00h

Hex	Dec	Field Length	Description
20h	32	1 dword	Total Sectors (if partition > 32MB, else 0)
24h	36	1 byte	Physical drive no. (00h=floppy, 80h=hard disk)
25h	37	1 byte	Reserved (00h)
26h	38	1 byte	Extended boot record signature (29h)
27h	39	1 dword	Volume serial number (32-bit random number)
2Bh	43	11 bytes	Volume label (NO NAME stored if no label)
36h	54	8 bytes	File system ID (FAT12 or FAT16)

For All Versions of DOS

Hex	Dec	Field Length	Description
3Eh	62	448 bytes	Boot Program Code
1FEh	510	2 bytes	Signature Bytes (55AAh)

A word is 2 bytes read in reverse order, and a dword is two words read in reverse order.

Root Directory

A *directory* is a simple database containing information about the files stored on a FAT partition. Each record in this database is 32 bytes long, with no delimiters or separating characters between the fields or records. A directory stores almost all the information that the operating system knows about a file, including the following:

■ *Filename and extension.* The 8-character name and 3-character extension of the file. The dot between the name and the extension is implied, but not included in the entry.

Note

To see how Windows 9x extends filenames to allow 255 characters within the 8.3 directory structure, see "VFAT and Long Filenames," later in this chapter.

- *File attribute byte.* The byte containing the flags representing the standard DOS file attributes, using the format shown in Table 27.5.
- *Date/Time of last change.* The date and time that the file was created or last modified.
- *File size.* The size of the file, in bytes.
- *Link to start cluster.* The number of the cluster in the partition where the beginning of the file is stored. To learn more about clusters, see "Clusters (Allocation Units)" later in this chapter.

There is information that a directory does not contain about a file. This includes where the rest of its clusters in the partition are located and whether the file is contiguous or fragmented. This information is contained in the FAT.

There are two basic types of directories: the root directory and subdirectories. Any given volume can have only one root directory. The root directory is always stored on a disk in a fixed location immediately following the two copies of the FAT. Root directories vary in size because of the different types and capacities of disks, but the root directory of a given disk is fixed. After a root directory is created by the FORMAT command, it has a fixed length and cannot be extended to hold more entries. The root directory entry limits are shown in Table 27.4. Subdirectories are stored as files in the data area of the disk and can grow in size dynamically, therefore they have no fixed length limits.

Table 27.4   Root Directory Entry Limits

Drive Type	Maximum Root Directory Entries
Hard disk	512
1.44MB floppy disk	224
2.88MB floppy disk	448
Jaz and Zip	512
LS-120	512
Sparq	512

Note

One of the advantages of the FAT32 file system is that the root directory can be located anywhere on the disk, and it can have an unlimited number of entries. FAT32 is discussed in more detail later in this chapter.

Every directory, whether it is the root directory or a subdirectory, is organized in the same way. Entries in the directory database store important information about individual files and how files are named on the disk. The directory information is linked to the FAT by the starting cluster entry. In fact, if no file on a disk were longer than one single cluster, the FAT would be unnecessary. The directory stores all the information needed by DOS to manage the file, with the exception of the list of clusters that the file occupies other than the first one. The FAT stores the remaining information about the other clusters that the file occupies.

To trace a file on a disk, use a disk editor such as the DISKEDIT program that comes with the Norton Utilities. Start by looking up the directory entry to get the information about the starting cluster of the file and its size. Then, using the appropriate editor commands, go to the FAT where you can follow the chain of clusters that the file occupies until you reach the end of the file. By using the directory and FAT in this manner, you can visit all the clusters on the disk that are occupied by the file. This type of technique can be useful when these entries are corrupted and when you are trying to find missing parts of a file.

FAT directory entries are 32 bytes long and are in the format shown in Table 27.5, which shows the location (or offset) of each field within the entry (in both hexadecimal and decimal form) and the length of each field.

Table 27.5   FAT Directory Format

Offset (Hex)	Offset (Dec)	Field Length	Description
00h	0	8 bytes	Filename
08h	8	3 bytes	File extension
0Bh	11	1 byte	File attributes
0Ch	12	10 bytes	Reserved (00h)
16h	22	1 word	Time of creation
18h	24	1 word	Date of creation
1Ah	26	1 word	Starting cluster
1Ch	28	1 dword	Size in bytes

Filenames and extensions are left-justified and padded with spaces, (which are represented as ASCII 32h bytes). In other words, if your filename is "AL", it is really stored as "AL------", where the dashes are spaces. The first byte of the filename indicates the file status for that directory entry, shown in Table 27.6:

Table 27.6   Directory Entry Status Byte (first byte)

Hex	File Status
00h	Entry never used; entries past this point not searched.
05h	Indicates that the first character of the filename is actually E5h.
E5h	s (lowercase sigma). Indicates that the file has been erased.
2Eh	. (period). Indicates that this entry is a directory. If the second byte is also 2Eh, the cluster field contains the cluster number of the parent directory (0000h, if the parent is the root).

A word is 2 bytes read in reverse order, and a dword is two words read in reverse order.

Table 27.7 describes the FAT directory file attribute byte. Attributes are one-bit flags that control specific properties of a file, such as whether it is hidden or designated as read-only. Each flag is individually activated (1) or deactivated (0) by changing the bit value. The combination of the eight bit values can be expressed as a single hexadecimal byte value; for example 07h translates to 00000111, and the 1 bits in positions 3, 2, and 1 indicate the file is System, Hidden, and Read-Only.

Table 27.7 FAT Directory File Attribute Byte

Bit Positions 7 6 5 4 3 2 1 0	Hex Value	Description
0 0 0 0 0 0 0 1	01h	Read-only file
0 0 0 0 0 0 1 0	02h	Hidden file
0 0 0 0 0 1 0 0	04h	System file
0 0 0 0 1 0 0 0	08h	Volume label
0 0 0 1 0 0 0 0	10h	Subdirectory
0 0 1 0 0 0 0 0	20h	Archive (updated since backup)
0 1 0 0 0 0 0 0	40h	Reserved
1 0 0 0 0 0 0 0	80h	Reserved

Examples

0 0 0 0 0 1 1 1	07h	System, hidden, read-only
0 0 1 0 0 0 0 1	21h	Read-only, archive
0 0 1 1 0 0 1 0	32h	Hidden, subdirectory, archive
0 0 1 0 0 1 1 1	27h	Read-only, hidden, system, archive

File Allocation Tables (FATs)

The file allocation table (FAT) is a list of numerical entries describing how each cluster in the partition is allocated. The data area of the partition has a single entry in the table for each of its clusters. Sectors in the nondata area of the partition are outside the range of the disk controlled by the FAT. Thus, the sectors that comprise the boot records, FATs, and the root directory are outside the range of sectors controlled by the FAT.

▶▶ See "The Data Area," p. 1396.

The FAT does not manage every data sector specifically, but rather allocates space in groups of sectors called clusters or allocation units. A cluster is a unit of storage consisting of one or more sectors. The size of a cluster is determined by the FDISK program during the creation of the partition, based on the partition's size. The smallest space that a file can occupy in a partition is one cluster; all files use space in integer (whole) cluster units. If a file is one byte larger than one cluster, two whole clusters are used.

You can think of the FAT as a type of spreadsheet that tracks the allocation of the disk's clusters. Each cell in the spreadsheet corresponds to a single cluster on the disk. The number stored in that cell is a code indicating whether the cluster is used by a file and, if so, where the next cluster of the file is located. Thus, to determine which clusters a particular file is using, you would start by looking at the first FAT reference in the file's directory entry. When you look up the referenced cluster in the FAT, the table contains a reference to the file's next cluster. Each FAT reference therefore points to the next cluster in what is called a FAT chain, until you reach the cluster containing the end of the file. Numbers stored in the FAT are hexadecimal numbers that are either 12 or 16 bits long. The 16-bit FAT numbers are easy to follow in a disk sector editor because they take an even two bytes of space. The 12-bit numbers are 1 1/2 bytes long, which presents a problem because most disk sector editors show data in byte units. To edit a 12-bit FAT, you must do some hex/binary math to convert the displayed byte units to FAT numbers. Fortunately (unless you are using the DOS DEBUG program), most of the available tools and utility programs have a FAT-editing mode that automatically converts the numbers for you. Most of them also show the FAT numbers in decimal form, which most people find easier to handle. Table 27.8 shows the relationship between the directory and FAT for a given file (assuming that the file is not fragmented).

Table 27.8 Directory and FAT Relationship (file not fragmented)

Directory

Name	Starting Cluster	Size
USCONST.TXT	1000	4

FAT16 File Allocation Table

FAT Cluster #	Value	Meaning
00002	0	First Cluster available
...	...	...
00999	0	Cluster available
01000	1001	In use, points to next cluster
01001	1002	In use, points to next cluster
01002	1003	In use, points to next cluster
01003	FFFFh	End Of File
01004	0	Cluster available
01005	0	Cluster available
...	...	...
65526	0	Last Cluster available

In this example, the directory entry states that the file starts in cluster number 1000. In the FAT, that cluster has a non-zero value, which indicates that it is in use; the specific value indicates where the file that is using it would continue. In this case the entry for cluster 1000 is 1001, which means the file continues in cluster 1001. The entry in 1001 points to 1002, and from 1002 the entry points to 1003. The entry for 1003 is FFFFh, which is an indication that the cluster is in use, but that the file ends here and uses no additional clusters.

The use of the FAT becomes more clear when you see that files can be fragmented. Let's say that before the USCONST.TXT file was written, another file already occupied clusters 1002 and 1003. If USCONST.TXT was written starting at 1000, it would not have been capable of being completely written before running into the other file. As such, the operating system would skip over the used clusters and continue the file in the next available cluster. The end result is shown in Table 27.9.

Table 27.9   Directory and FAT Relationship (fragmented file)

Directory

Name	Starting Cluster	Size
PLEDGE.TXT	1002	2
USCONST.TXT	1000	4

FAT16 File Allocation Table

FAT Cluster #	Value	Meaning
00002	0	First Cluster available
…	…	…
00999	0	Cluster available
01000	1001	In use, points to next cluster
01001	1004	In use, points to next cluster
01002	1003	In use, points to next cluster
01003	FFFFh	End Of File
01004	1005	In use, points to next cluster
01005	FFFFh	End Of File
…	…	…
65526	0	Last Cluster available

In this example, the USCONST.TXT was interrupted by the PLEDGE.TXT file that was previously written, so those clusters are skipped over, and the pointers in the FAT reflect that. Note that the defrag programs included with DOS and Windows will take an example like this and move the files so they are contiguous, one after the other.

The first two entries in the FAT are reserved and contain information about the table itself. All remaining entries correspond to specific clusters on the disk. Most FAT entries consist of a reference to another cluster containing the next part of a particular file. However, some FAT entries contain hexadecimal values with special meanings, as follows:

- *0000h*. Indicates that the cluster is not in use by a file.
- *FFF7h*. Indicates that at least one sector in the cluster is damaged and that it should not be used to store data.
- *FFFF8h–FFFFh*. Indicates that the cluster contains the end of a file and that no reference to another cluster is needed.

The FDISK program determines whether a 12-bit or 16-bit FAT is placed on a disk, even though the FAT isn't written until you perform a high-level format (using the FORMAT utility). On today's systems, usually only floppy disks use 12-bit FATs, but FDISK also creates a 12-bit FAT if you create a hard disk volume that is smaller than 16MB (32,756 sectors). On hard disk volumes of more than 16MB, FDISK creates a 16-bit FAT. On drives larger than 512MB, the FDISK program included in Windows 95 OSR2 and Windows 98 enables you to create 32-bit FATs.

FDISK creates two copies of the FAT. Each one occupies contiguous sectors on the disk, and the second FAT copy immediately follows the first. Unfortunately, the operating system uses the second FAT copy only if sectors in the first FAT copy become unreadable. If the first FAT copy is corrupted, which is a much more common problem, the operating system does not use the second FAT copy. Even the CHKDSK command does not check or verify the second FAT copy. Moreover, whenever the OS updates the first FAT, it automatically copies large portions of the first FAT to the second FAT. If the first copy was corrupted and subsequently updated by the OS, a large portion of the first FAT would be copied over to the second FAT copy, damaging it in the process. After the update, the second copy is usually a mirror image of the first one, complete with any corruption. Two FATs rarely stay out of sync for very long. When they are out of sync and the OS writes to the disk, it updates the first FAT and also overwrites the second FAT with the first. This is why disk repair and recovery utilities warn you to stop working as soon as you detect a FAT problem. Programs such as Norton Disk Doctor use the second copy of the FAT as a reference to repair the first one, but if the OS has already updated the second FAT, repair may be impossible.

Clusters (Allocation Units)

The term cluster was changed to allocation unit in DOS 4.0 (although many people continue to use the old term). Allocation unit is appropriate because a single cluster is the smallest unit of the disk that the operating system can handle when it writes or reads a file. A cluster is equal to one or more 512-byte sectors, in a power of two. Although a cluster can be a single disk sector, it is usually more than one. Having more than one sector per cluster reduces the size and processing overhead of the FAT and enables the operating system to run faster because it has fewer individual units to manage. The trade-off is in wasted disk space. Because operating systems manage space only in full-cluster units, every file consumes space on the disk in increments of one cluster.

Table 27.10 shows the default cluster (or allocation unit) sizes for the various floppy disk formats used over the years.

Table 27.10   Default Floppy Disk Cluster (Allocation Unit) Sizes

Drive Type	Cluster (Allocation Unit) Size	Density
5 1/4-inch 360KB	2 sectors (1,024 bytes)	Low
5 1/4-inch 1.2MB	1 sector (512 bytes)	High
3 1/2-inch 720KB	2 sectors (1,024 bytes)	Low
3 1/2-inch 1.44MB	1 sector (512 bytes)	High
3 1/2-inch 2.88MB	2 sectors (1,024 bytes)	Extra

It seems strange that the high-density disks, which have many more individual sectors than low-density disks, sometimes have smaller cluster sizes. The larger the FAT, the more entries the operating system must manage, and the slower it seems to function. This sluggishness is due to the excessive overhead required to manage all the individual clusters; the more clusters to be managed, the slower things become. The trade-off is in the minimum cluster size. High-density floppy disk drives are faster than their low-density counterparts, so perhaps IBM and Microsoft determined that the decrease in cluster size balances the drive's faster operation and offsets the use of a larger FAT.

Because the operating system can allocate only whole clusters, there is inevitably a certain amount of wasted storage space. File sizes rarely fall on cluster boundaries, so the last cluster allocated to a particular file is rarely filled completely. The extra space left over between the actual end of the file and the end of the cluster is called *slack*. A partition with large clusters has more slack space, whereas smaller clusters generate less slack.

For hard disks, the cluster size varies greatly among different partition sizes. The field in the disk parameter block that specifies the cluster size is two bytes long, meaning that its maximum possible value is 65,535. Thus, the largest possible cluster is 32KB, because a 64KB cluster would require a value of 65,536 in this field. Table 27.11 shows the cluster sizes that FDISK selects for a particular volume size.

Table 27.11   Default Hard Disk Cluster (Allocation Unit) Sizes

Hard Disk Volume Size	Cluster (Allocation Unit) Size	FAT Type
0MB to less than 16MB	8 sectors or 4,096 bytes	12-bit
16MB through 128MB	4 sectors or 2,048 bytes	16-bit
More than 128–256MB	8 sectors or 4,096 bytes	16-bit
More than 256B–512MB	16 sectors or 8,192 bytes	16-bit
More than 512B–1,024MB	32 sectors or 16,384 bytes	16-bit
More than 1,024B–2,048MB	64 sectors or 32,768 bytes	16-bit

The effect of larger cluster sizes on disk utilization can be substantial. A 2GB partition containing about 5,000 files, with average slack of one-half of the last 32KB cluster used for each file, wastes over 78MB [5000×(.5×32)KB] of file space.

The cluster size, in combination with the structure of the FAT, also dictates the maximum possible FAT partition size. Because the FAT uses 16-byte entries to reference the clusters in the partition, there can be a maximum of only 65,536 (216) clusters. At 32KB per cluster, this means that the largest possible FAT partition is 2,096,832KB or 2,047.6875MB in size.

Even if the 2-byte cluster size field could contain the value indicating 64KB clusters, the maximum partition size would still be constrained. The maximum partition size would be limited by the field in the disk parameter block that specifies the number of sectors per cluster. This field is only one byte long and its value must be a power of two. This makes its highest possible value 128 sectors, which equates to a maximum cluster size of 64KB. 65,536 clusters at 64K each equals a maximum partition size of 4GB.

Note

Windows NT does support the use of 64KB clusters on FAT16 partitions, enabling you to create partitions up to 4GB in size. However, the huge amount of slack that generally results from clusters this large makes this practice undesirable.

The Data Area

The data area of a partition is the place where the actual files are stored. It is located following the boot record, file allocation tables, and root directory. This is the area of the disk that is divided into clusters and managed by the FAT and root directory.

Diagnostic Read-and-Write Cylinder

The FDISK partitioning program always reserves the last cylinder of a hard disk for use as a special diagnostic read-and-write test cylinder. Because this cylinder is reserved is one reason FDISK always reports fewer total cylinders than the drive manufacturer states are available. Operating systems do not use this cylinder for any normal purpose because it lies outside the partitioned area of the disk.

◄◄ See "Disk Formatting," p. 594.

On systems with IDE or SCSI disk interfaces, the drive and controller might also allocate an additional area past the logical end of the drive for a bad-track table and spare sectors. This situation might account for additional discrepancies between the FDISK and the drive manufacturer's reported sizes.

The diagnostics area enables software such as a manufacturer-supplied diagnostics disk to perform read-and-write tests on a hard disk without corrupting any user data.

VFAT and Long Filenames

The original Windows 95 release uses what is essentially the same FAT file system as DOS, except for a few important enhancements. Like much of the rest of Windows 95, the operating system support for the FAT file system was rewritten using 32-bit code and called *VFAT* (virtual file allocation table). VFAT works in combination with the 32-bit protected mode VCACHE (that replaces the 16-bit real mode SMARTDrive cache used in DOS and Windows 3.1) to provide better file system performance. However, the most obvious improvement in VFAT is its support for long filenames. DOS and Windows 3.1 had been encumbered by the standard 8.3 file naming convention for many years, and adding long filename support was a high priority in Windows 95, particularly in light of the fact that Macintosh and OS/2 users had long enjoyed this capability.

The problem for the Windows 95 designers, as is often the case in the PC industry, was backward compatibility. It is no great feat to make long filenames possible when you are designing a new file system from scratch, as Microsoft did years before with Windows NT's NTFS. However, the Windows 95 developers wanted to add long filenames to the existing FAT file system, and still make it possible to store those names on existing DOS volumes and for previous versions of DOS and Windows to access the files.

VFAT provides the capability to assign file and directory names that are up to 255 characters in length (including the length of the path). The three-character extension is maintained because, like previous Windows versions, Windows 95 relies on the extensions to associate file types with specific applications. VFAT's long filenames can also include spaces, as well as the following characters, which standard DOS 8.3 names cannot: +,;=[].

The first problem when implementing the long filenames was how to make them usable to previous versions of DOS and 16-bit Windows applications that support only 8.3 names. The resolution to this problem is to give each file two names: a long filename and an alias that uses the traditional 8.3 naming convention. When you create a file with a long filename in Windows 9x, VFAT uses the following process to create an equivalent 8.3 alias name:

1. The first three characters after the last dot in the long filename become the extension of the alias.

2. The first six characters of the long filename (excluding spaces, which are ignored) are converted into uppercase, and become the first six characters of the alias filename. If any of these six characters are illegal under the standard 8.3 naming rules (that is, +,;=[or]), VFAT converts those characters into underscores.

3. VFAT adds the two characters ~1 as the seventh and eighth characters of the alias filename, unless this will result in a name conflict, in which case it uses ~2, ~3, and so on, as needed.

Aliasing in Windows NT

Note that Windows NT creates aliases differently than Windows 9x (as shown later):

NT begins by taking the first six legal characters in the LFN and follows them with a tilde and number. If the first six characters are unique, and then a number 1 follows the tilde.

If the first six characters aren't unique, a number 2 is added. NT uses the first three legal characters following the last period in the LFN for a file extension.

At the fifth iteration of this process, NT takes only the first two legal characters, performs a hash on the filename to produce four hexidecimal characters, places the four hex characters after the first 2 legal characters and appends a ~5. The ~5 remains for all subsequent aliases; only the hex numbers change.

Tip

You can modify the behavior of the VFAT filename truncation mechanism to make it use the first eight characters of the long filename instead of the first six characters plus ~1. To do this, you must add a new binary value to the HKEY_LOCAL_MACHINE\System\CurrentControlSet\control\FileSystem Registry key called NameNumericTail, with a value of 0. Changing the value to 1 returns the truncation process to its original state.

VFAT stores this alias filename in the standard name field of the file's directory entry. Any version of DOS or 16-bit Windows can therefore access the file using the alias name. The big problem that still remains, however, is where to store the long filenames. Clearly, it is not possible to store a 255-character filename in a 32-byte directory entry (because each character requires one byte). However, modifying the structure of the directory entry would make the files unusable by previous DOS versions.

The developers of VFAT resolved this problem by using additional directory entries to store the long filenames. Each of the directory entries is still 32 bytes long, so up to eight may be required for each long name, depending on its length. To ensure that these additional directory entries are not misinterpreted by earlier DOS versions, VFAT flags them with a combination of attributes that is not possible for a normal file: read-only, hidden, system, and volume label. These attributes cause DOS to ignore the long filename entries, while preventing them from being mistakenly overwritten.

Caution

When using long filenames on a standard FAT partition, it is a good idea to avoid storing them in the root directory. Files with long names that take up multiple directory entries can more easily use up the limited number of entries allotted to the root directory than files with 8.3 names. On FAT32 drives, this is not a problem, because the root directory has an unlimited number of entries.

This solution for implementing backward compatible long filenames in Windows 9x is ingenious, but it is not without its problems. Most of these problems stem from the use of applications that can access only the 8.3 alias names assigned to files. In some cases, if you open a file with a long name using one of these programs and save it again, the connection to the additional directory entries containing the long name is severed and the long name is lost.

This is especially true for older versions of disk utilities, such as Norton Disk Doctor, that are not designed to support VFAT. Most older applications ignore the additional directory entries because of the combination of attributes assigned to them, but disk repair utilities are usually designed to detect and "correct" discrepancies of this type. The result is that running an old version of Norton Disk Doctor on a partition with long filenames will result in the loss of all the long names. In the same way, backup utilities not designed for use with VFAT can strip off the long filenames from a partition.

Note

When using VFAT's long filename capabilities, it is definitely preferable that you use disk and backup utilities that are intended to support VFAT. Windows 9x includes VFAT-compatible disk repair, defragmentation, and backup programs. If, however, you are for some reason inclined to use an older program that does not support VFAT, Windows 9x includes a clumsy, but effective, solution.

There is a program included on the Windows 9x CD-ROM called LFNBK.EXE. It doesn't install with the operating system, but you can use it to strip the long filenames from a VFAT volume and store them in a text file called LFNBK.DAT. You can then work with the files on the volume as though they were standard 8.3 FAT files. Afterward, you can use LFNBK.EXE to restore the long filenames to their original places (assuming the file and directory structure has not changed). This is not a convenient solution, nor is it recommended for use in anything but extraordinary circumstances, but the capability is there if needed.

Another problem with VFAT's long filenames involves the process by which the file system creates the 8.3 alias names. VFAT creates a new alias every time you create or copy a file into a new directory, meaning that it is possible for the alias to change. For example, you might have a file called Expenses-January98.doc stored in a directory with the alias EXPENS~1.DOC. If you use

Windows 9x Explorer to copy this file to directory that already contains a file called Expenses-December97.doc, you are likely to find that this existing file is already using the alias EXPENS~1.DOC. In this case, VFAT will assign EXPENS~2.DOC as the alias of the newly copied file, with no warning to the user. This is not a problem for applications that support VFAT because the long filenames are unchanged, but a user running an older application may open the EXPENS~1.DOC file expecting to find the list of January 1998 expenses, and see the December 1997 expenses list instead.

FAT32

When the FAT file system was being developed, 2GB hard disk drives were a fantasy, and no one expected the partition size limitation imposed by the combination of 16-bit FAT entries and 32KB cluster sizes to be a problem. Today, however, even low-end PCs come equipped with hard drives holding at least 2GB, and 6 or 8GB drives are common. When you use the standard FAT file system with these larger drives, you have to create several partitions, each no larger than approximately 2GB. To many users, having multiple drive letters representing a single disk is confusing, making it difficult to organize and locate files.

To address this problem, Microsoft has released an enhanced version of the FAT file system, called FAT32. FAT32 works just like the standard FAT, the only difference is that it uses numbers with more digits, meaning it can manage more clusters on a disk. Unlike VFAT, which is a Windows 9x innovation that makes use of existing file system structures, FAT32 is an enhancement of the FAT file system itself. In other words, while VFAT is implemented as part of the Windows 9x Virtual Machine Manager (Vmm.vxd), FAT32 is implemented by the FDISK program before the Windows GUI is even loaded. FAT32 was first included in the Windows 95 OEM Service Release 2 (OSR2), and is also part of Windows 98. Windows NT 5.0 will also provide support for FAT32.

Note

Because the FAT32 file system is implemented by the FDISK utility when you partition the drive, you cannot use FAT32 on a floppy disk or any removable cartridge that does not utilize a partition table. However, any medium that you can partition with FDISK, such as an Iomega Jaz cartridge, can use FAT32.

The most obvious improvement in FAT32 is that by using 32-bit values for FAT entries instead of 16-bit ones, the maximum number of clusters allowed in a single partition jumps from 65,536 (2^{16}) to 268,435,456. This value is equivalent to 2^{28}, not 2^{32}, because four bits out of the 32 are reserved for other uses. FAT32 also uses 32-bit values for the low-level operating system calls used to retrieve a specific disk sector.

These expanded values blow the top off of the 2GB limit on partition sizes; FAT32 partitions can theoretically be up to 2TB in size (1 terabyte = 1,024 gigabytes). This figure is derived from a new maximum of 4,294,967,296 (2^{32}) possible 512-byte sectors. Individual files can be up to 4GB in size; they are limited by the size field in the directory entry, which is 4 bytes long. Because the clusters are numbered using 32-bit values instead of 16-bit ones, the format of the directory entries on a FAT32 partition must be changed slightly. The 2-byte Link to Start Cluster field is increased to 4 bytes, using two of the ten bytes (bytes 12 to 21) in the directory entry that were reserved for future use.

Another important difference in FAT32 partitions is the nature of the root directory. In a FAT32 partition, the root directory does not occupy a fixed position on the disk as in a FAT16 partition. Instead, it can be located anywhere in the partition and expand to any size. This eliminates the preset limit on root directory entries and provides the infrastructure needed to make FAT32 partitions dynamically resizable. Microsoft has not yet implemented this feature in Windows 9x, but there are third-party products such as PowerQuest's PartitionMagic that take advantage of this capability.

The primary drawback of FAT32 is that it is not compatible with previous versions of DOS and Windows 95. You cannot boot to a previous version of DOS or (pre-OSR2) Windows 95 from a FAT32 drive, nor will a system started with an old DOS or Windows 95 boot disk be capable of seeing FAT32 partitions. Apart from Windows 95 OSR2, Windows 98, and Windows 2000, the only operating system that natively supports FAT32 is Linux.

FAT32 Cluster Sizes

Because FAT32 partitions can have so many more clusters than FAT16 partitions, the clusters themselves can be smaller. Using smaller clusters reduces the wasted disk space caused by slack. For example, the same 2GB partition with 5,000 files on it mentioned earlier would use 4KB clusters with FAT32 instead of 32KB clusters with FAT16. Assuming the same amount of slack for each file, the smaller cluster size reduces the average amount of wasted space on that partition from over 78MB to under 10MB.

To compare FAT16 and FAT32, you can look at how a file would be stored on each. For FAT16, I'll use the same example as before. With FAT16 the cluster numbers are stored as 16-bit entries, from 0000h–FFFFh. The largest value possible is FFFFh, which corresponds to 65,535 in decimal, but several numbers at the beginning and end are reserved for special use. The actual cluster numbers allowed in a FAT16 system range from 0002h–FFF6h, which is 2–65,526 in decimal. All files have to be stored in cluster numbers within that range. That leaves only 65,524 valid clusters to use for storing files (cluster numbers below 2 and above 65,526 are reserved), meaning a partition has to be broken up into that many clusters or less. A typical file entry under FAT16 might look like Table 27.12:

Table 27.12   FAT16 File Entries

Directory

Name	Starting Cluster	Size
USCONST.TXT	1000	4

FAT16 File Allocation Table

FAT Cluster #	Value	Meaning
00002	0	First Cluster available
…	…	…
00999	0	Cluster available
01000	1001	In use, points to next cluster
01001	1002	In use, points to next cluster

FAT16 File Allocation Table

FAT Cluster #	Value	Meaning
01002	1003	In use, points to next cluster
01003	FFFFh	End Of File
01004	0	Cluster available
...	...	...
65526	0	Last Cluster available

With FAT32, the cluster numbers range from 00000000h to FFFFFFFFh, which is from 0 to 4,294,967,295 in decimal. Again some values at the low and high end are reserved, and only values from between 00000002h and FFFFFFF6h are valid, which is to say from 2 through 4,294,967,286 are valid. This leaves 4,294,967,284 valid entries, which means the drive must be split into that many clusters or less. Since a drive can be split into so many more clusters, they can be smaller, which conserves on disk space. The same file as shown above might be stored on a FAT32 system as shown in Table 27.13:

Table 27.13   FAT32 File Entries

Directory

Name	Starting Cluster	Size
USCONST.TXT	1000	8

FAT32 File Allocation Table

FAT Cluster #	Value	Meaning
0000000002	0	First Cluster available
...	...	...
0000000999	0	Cluster available
0000001000	1001	In use, points to next cluster
0000001001	1002	In use, points to next cluster
0000001002	1003	In use, points to next cluster
0000001003	1004	In use, points to next cluster
0000001004	1005	In use, points to next cluster
0000001005	1006	In use, points to next cluster
0000001006	1007	In use, points to next cluster
0000001007	FFFFFFFFh	End Of File
0000001008	0	Cluster available
...	...	...
4,294,967,286	0	Last Cluster available

Because the FAT32 system allows for many more clusters to be allocated, the cluster size is usually smaller. So, while files overall use more individual clusters, there is less wasted space because the last cluster is, on average, only half filled.

Note

PC Magazine has released a free DOS utility called CHKDRV that calculates the slack on a FAT16 or FAT32 partition. You can download this program from `ftp://ftp.zdnet.com/pcmag/1995/0627/chkdrv.zip`.

Table 27.14 lists the cluster sizes for various FAT32 partition sizes.

Table 27.14   FAT32 Cluster Sizes

Partition Size	Cluster Size
0MB to less than 260MB	512 bytes
260MB–8GB	4,096 bytes
6–16GB	8,192 bytes
16–32GB	16,384 bytes
32GB–2TB	32,768 bytes

Of course, using smaller clusters means there must be many more of them, and more entries in the FAT as well. A 2GB partition using FAT32 requires 524,288 FAT entries, while the same drive needs only 65,536 entries using FAT16. Thus, the size of one copy of the FAT16 table is 128KB (65,536 entries × 16 bits = 1,048,576 bits/8 = 131,072 bytes/1,024 = 128KB), while the FAT32 table is 2MB in size.

The size of the FAT has a definite impact on the performance of the file system. Windows 9x uses its VCACHE to try to keep the FAT in memory at all times to improve file system performance. The use of 4KB clusters for drives up to 8GB in size is, therefore, a reasonable compromise for the average PC's memory capacity. If the file system were to use clusters that are equal to one disk sector (1 sector = 512KB) in an attempt to minimize slack as much as possible, the FAT table for a 2GB drive would contain 4,194,304 entries and be 16MB in size.

This would monopolize a substantial portion of the memory in the average system, probably resulting in noticeably degraded performance. Although at first it may seem as though even a 2MB FAT is quite large when compared to 128KB, keep in mind that hard disk drives are a great deal faster now than they were when the FAT file system was originally designed. In practice, implementing FAT32 on a Windows 9x system typically results in a minor (less than 5 percent) improvement in file system performance. However, systems that perform a great many sequential disk writes may see an equally minor degradation in performance.

FAT Mirroring

FAT32 also takes greater advantage of the two copies of the FAT stored on a disk partition. On a FAT16 partition, the first copy of the FAT is always the primary copy and replicates its data to the secondary FAT, sometimes corrupting it in the process. On a FAT32 partition, when the system detects a problem with the primary copy of the FAT, it can switch to the other copy, which then becomes the primary. The system can also disable the FAT mirroring process to prevent the viable FAT from being corrupted by the other copy. This provides a greater degree of fault tolerance to FAT32 partitions, often making it possible to repair a damaged FAT without an immediate system interruption or a loss of table data.

Creating FAT32 Partitions

Despite the substantial changes provided by FAT32, the new file system does have a large effect on the procedures you use to create and manage partitions. You create new FAT32 partitions in Windows 9x using the FDISK utility from the command prompt, just like you would create FAT16 partitions. When you launch FDISK, the program examines your hard disk drives and, if they have a capacity greater than 512MB, presents the following message:

```
Your computer has a disk larger than 512 MB. This version of Windows
includes improved support for large disks, resulting in more efficient
use of disk space on large drives, and allowing disks over 2 GB to be
formatted as a single drive.

IMPORTANT: If you enable large disk support and create any new drives on this
disk, you will not be able to access the new drive(s) using other operating
systems, including some versions of Windows 95 and Windows NT, as well as
earlier versions of Windows and MS-DOS. In addition, disk utilities that
were not designed explicitly for the FAT32 file system will not be able
to work with this disk. If you need to access this disk with other operating
systems or older disk utilities, do not enable large drive support.

Do you wish to enable large disk support (Y/N)...........? [N]
```

If you answer Yes to this question, any partitions you create that are larger than 512MB will be FAT32 partitions. If you want to create partitions larger than 2GB, you must use FAT32. Otherwise, you can choose which file system you prefer. All the screens following this one are the same as those in previous versions of FDISK.

Normally, the FDISK utility determines the cluster size that will be used when you format the partition, based on the partition's size and the file system used. However, you can override FDISK using an undocumented switch for the FORMAT utility. If you use the command

```
FORMAT /Z:n
```

where n multiplied by 512 equals the desired cluster size in bytes, you can create a partition that uses cluster sizes that are larger or smaller than the defaults for the file system.

Caution

The /Z switch does not override the 65,536 cluster limit on FAT16 partitions, so it is recommended that you use it only with FAT32. In addition, you should not use this switch on a production system without extensive testing first. Modifying the cluster size might increase or reduce the amount of slack on the partition, but it also might have a pronounced effect on the performance of the drive.

Converting FAT16 to FAT32

The Windows 95 OSR2 release can create FAT32 partitions only out of empty disk space. If you want to convert an existing FAT16 partition to FAT32, you have to back up the data, destroy the

FAT16 partition, create a new FAT32 partition, and then restore the data. Windows 98, on the other hand, includes a FAT32 Conversion Wizard that enables you to migrate existing partitions in place.

The wizard gathers the information needed to perform the conversion, informs you of the consequences of implementing FAT32, and attempts to prevent data loss and other problems. After you have selected the drive that you want to convert (see Figure 27.2), the wizard performs a scan for applications (such as disk utilities) that might not function properly on the converted partition. The wizard gives you the opportunity to remove these and warns you to back up the data on the partition before proceeding with the conversion. Even if you don't use the Microsoft Backup utility that the wizard offers, backing up your data is a strongly recommended precaution.

After you answer all the wizard's prompts and confirm that you want to continue with the conversion, the system reboots to a DOS prompt. The actual conversion is a DOS process, making it possible to convert even the partition on which Windows 98 is installed. Because the conversion must deal with the existing partition data in addition to creating new volume boot record information, FATs, and clusters, the process can take far longer than partitioning and formatting an empty drive. Depending on the amount of data involved and the new cluster size, the conversion might take several hours to complete.

After you convert a FAT16 partition to FAT32, you cannot convert it back with Windows 98's tools, except by destroying the partition and using FDISK to create a new one. Therefore, be sure to carefully consider your actions before proceeding. It is also a good idea to take other precautions before beginning the conversion process, such as connecting the system to a UPS. A power failure during the conversion could result in a loss of data.

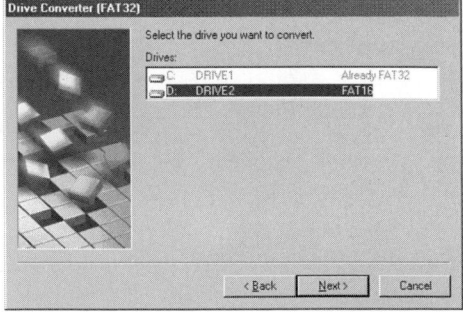

Figure 27.2 The FAT32 Conversion Wizard enables Windows 98 users to convert existing FAT16 partitions to FAT32.

FAT32 and PartitionMagic

Windows 95 OSR2 and Windows 98 include only basic tools for creating FAT32 partitions, but there is a product called PartitionMagic, from PowerQuest, which provides many other partition manipulation features. PartitionMagic can convert FAT16 partitions to FAT32 in place, as the Windows 98 FAT32 Conversion Wizard can, but unlike Windows 98, it can also convert FAT32 partitions back to FAT16.

Among many other things, this product can also resize FAT16 and FAT32 partitions without destroying the data they contain, shrink and expand FAT clusters, and tell you how much disk space you will save as the result of changing the cluster size. PartitionMagic takes advantage of the inherent capabilities of the FAT16 and FAT32 file systems to provide features that will probably be added to Windows 9x at some future time.

FAT File System Errors

File system errors can, of course, occur because of hardware problems, but you are more likely to see them result from software crashes and improper system handling. Turning off a system without shutting down Windows properly, for example, can result in errors that cause clusters to be incorrectly listed as in use when they are not. Some of the most common file system errors that occur on FAT partitions are described in the following sections.

Lost Clusters

Probably the most common file system error, lost clusters are clusters that the FAT designates as being in use when they actually are not. Most often caused by an interruption of a file system process due to an application crash or a system shutdown, for example, the FAT entry of a lost cluster may contain a reference to a subsequent cluster. However, the FAT chain stemming from the directory entry has been broken somewhere along the line.

Lost clusters would appear in the file structure as shown in Table 27.15:

Table 27.15   Lost Clusters in a File Structure

Directory

Name	Starting Cluster	Size
(no entry)	0	0

FAT16 File Allocation Table

FAT Cluster #	Value	Meaning
00002	0	First Cluster available
...	...	...
00999	0	Cluster available
01000	1001	In use, points to next cluster
01001	1002	In use, points to next cluster
01002	1003	In use, points to next cluster
01003	FFFFh	End Of File
01004	0	Cluster available
...	...	...
65526	0	Last Cluster available

The operating system sees a valid chain of clusters in the FAT, but no corresponding directory entry to back it up. This is most often caused by programs that are terminated before they can close their open files. The operating system normally modifies the FAT chain as the file is written, and the final step when closing is to create a matching directory entry. If the system is interrupted before the file is closed, lost clusters are the result.

Disk repair programs check for lost clusters by tracing the FAT chain for each file and subdirectory in the partition and building a facsimile of the FAT in memory. After compiling a list of all the FAT entries that indicate properly allocated clusters, the program compares this facsimile with the actual FAT. Any entries denoting allocated clusters in the real FAT that do not appear in the facsimile are lost clusters because they are not part of a valid FAT chain.

The utility typically gives you the opportunity to save the data in the lost clusters as a file before it changes the FAT entries to show them as unallocated clusters. If your system crashed or lost power while you were working with a word processor data file, for example, you might be able to retrieve text from the lost clusters in this way. When left unrepaired, lost clusters are unavailable for use by the system, reducing the storage capacity of your drive.

The typical choices you have for correcting lost clusters are to assign them a made up name or zero out the FAT entries. If you assign them a name, you can at least look at the entries as a valid file, and then delete the file if you find it useless. The CHKDSK program is designed to fix lost clusters by assigning them names starting with FILE0001.CHK. If there is more than one lost chain, sequential numbers following the first one will be used. The lost clusters shown earlier could be corrected by CHKDSK, as shown in Table 27.16:

Table 27.16   Finding Lost Clusters

Directory

Name	Starting Cluster	Size
FILE0001.CHK	1000	4

FAT16 File Allocation Table

FAT Cluster #	Value	Meaning
00002	0	First Cluster available
...	...	...
00999	0	Cluster available
01000	1001	In use, points to next cluster
01001	1002	In use, points to next cluster
01002	1003	In use, points to next cluster
01003	FFFFh	End Of File
01004	0	Cluster available
...	...	...
65526	0	Last Cluster available

As you can see, a new entry was created to match the FAT entries. The name is made up because there is no way for the repair utility to know what the original name of the file might have been.

Cross-Linked Files

Cross-linked files occur when two directory entries improperly reference the same cluster in their Link to Start Cluster fields. The result is that each file utilizes the same FAT chain. Because the clusters can store data from only one file, working with one of the two files can inadvertently overwrite the other file's data.

Cross-linked files would appear in the file structure as shown in Table 27.17:

Table 27.17   Cross-Linked Files

Directory

Name	Starting Cluster	Size
USCONST.TXT	1000	4
PLEDGE.TXT	1002	2

FAT16 File Allocation Table

FAT Cluster #	Value	Meaning
00002	0	First Cluster available
...	...	...
00999	0	Cluster available
01000	1001	In use, points to next cluster
01001	1002	In use, points to next cluster
01002	1003	In use, points to next cluster
01003	FFFFh	End Of File
01004	0	Cluster available
...	...	...
65526	0	Last Cluster available

In this case there are two files that claim ownership of clusters 1002 and 1003. These files are said to be cross-linked on 1002. When a situation like this arises, normally one of the files is valid and the other is corrupt, being that only one actual given set of data can occupy a given cluster. The normal repair is to copy both files involved to new names, which will duplicate their data separately in another area of the disk, and then delete *all* the files that are cross-linked. It is important to delete them all because by deleting one of them, the FAT chain will be zeroed, which will further damage the other entries. Then you can examine the files you copied to determine which one is good and which is corrupt.

Detecting cross-linked files is a relatively easy task for a disk repair utility because it has to examine only the partition's directory entries, and not the file clusters themselves. However, by the time that the utility detects the error, the data from one of the two files is probably already lost, although you may be able to recover parts of it from lost clusters.

Invalid Files or Directories

Sometimes the information in a directory entry for a file or subdirectory can be corrupted to the point at which the entry is not just erroneous (as in cross-linked files) but invalid. The entry may have a cluster or date reference that is invalid or may violate the rules for the entry format in some other way. In most cases, disk repair software can correct these problems, permitting access to the file.

FAT Errors

As discussed earlier, corruption of the FAT can sometimes be repaired by accessing its duplicate copy. Disk repair utilities typically rely on this technique to restore a damaged FAT to its original state, as long as the copy has not been corrupted by the mirroring process. FAT32 tables are more likely to be repairable, because their more advanced mirroring capabilities make it less likely for the copy to be corrupted.

An example of a damaged FAT might appear to the operating system shown in Table 27.18.

Table 27.18 Damaged FAT

Directory

Name	Starting Cluster	Size
USCONST.TXT	1000	4

FAT16 File Allocation Table

FAT Cluster #	Value	Meaning
00002	0	First Cluster available
...	...	...
00999	0	Cluster available
01000	1001	In use, points to next cluster
01001	0	Cluster Available
01002	1003	In use, points to next cluster
01003	FFFFh	End Of File
01004	0	Cluster available
...	...	...
65526	0	Last Cluster available

This single error would cause multiple problems to appear. The file USCONST.TXT would now come up as having an *allocation error*—where the size in the directory no longer matches the number of clusters in the FAT chain. The file would end after cluster 1001 in this example, and the rest of the data would be missing if one loaded this file for viewing. Also there would be two lost clusters; that is, 1002 and 1003 appear to have no directory entry that owns them. When multiple problems like this appear, it is often due to a single incident of damage. The repair in this case could involve copying the data from the backup FAT back to the primary FAT, but in most cases the backup will be similarly damaged. Normal utilities would truncate the file and create an entry for a second file out of the lost clusters. You would have to figure out yourself that they really belong together. This is where having knowledge in data recovery can help over using automated utilities that cannot think for themselves.

FAT File System Utilities

The CHKDSK, RECOVER, and SCANDISK commands are the DOS damaged disk recovery team. These commands are crude, and their actions sometimes are drastic, but at times they are all that is available or needed. RECOVER is best known for its function as a data recovery program. CHKDSK usually is used for inspection of the file structure. Many users are unaware that CHKDSK can implement repairs to a damaged file structure. DEBUG, a crude, manually controlled program, can help in the case of a disk disaster, if you know exactly what you are doing.

SCANDISK is a safer, more automated, more powerful replacement for CHKDSK and RECOVER. It should be used in their place if you are running DOS 6 or higher or Windows 9x.

The *CHKDSK* Command

The useful and powerful DOS CHKDSK command is frequently misunderstood. To casual users, the primary function of CHKDSK seems to be providing a disk space allocation report for a given volume as well as a memory allocation report. CHKDSK does those things, but its primary value is in discovering, defining, and repairing problems with the DOS directory and FAT system on a disk volume. In handling data recovery problems, CHKDSK is a valuable tool, although it is crude and simplistic compared to some of the aftermarket utilities that perform similar functions.

The output of the CHKDSK command when it runs on a typical hard disk is as follows:

```
Volume 4GB_SCSI    created 01-31-1998 5:05p
Volume Serial Number is 1882-18CF

2,146,631,680 bytes total disk space
      163,840 bytes in 3 hidden files
   16,220,160 bytes in 495 directories
  861,634,560 bytes in 10,355 user files
1,268,613,120 bytes available on disk

       32,768 bytes in each allocation unit
       65,510 total allocation units on disk
       38,715 available allocation units on disk

      655,360 total bytes memory
      632,736 bytes free
```

A little-known CHKDSK function is its capability to report on a specified file's (or group of files') level of fragmentation. CHKDSK can also produce a list of all files (including hidden and system files) on a particular volume, such as a super DIR command. By far, the most important CHKDSK capabilities are its detection and correction of problems in the FAT file system.

The name of the CHKDSK program is misleading: It seems to be a contraction of CHECK DISK. The program does not actually check a disk, or even the files on a disk, for integrity. CHKDSK cannot even truly show how many bad sectors are on a disk, much less locate and mark them. The real function of CHKDSK is to inspect the directories and FATs to see whether they correspond with each other or contain discrepancies. CHKDSK does not detect (and does not report on) damage in a file; it checks only the FAT and directory areas of a disk.

CHKDSK also can test files for contiguity. Files loaded into contiguous tracks and sectors of a disk or floppy disk naturally are more efficient. Files spread over wide areas of the disk make access operations take longer. DOS always knows the location of all a file's fragments by using the cluster references in the FAT. Sometimes, for various reasons, these references might be lost or corrupted and leave DOS incapable of locating some portion of a file. Using CHKDSK can alert you to this condition and even enable you to reclaim the unused file space.

CHKDSK Command Syntax

The syntax of the CHKDSK command is as follows:

```
CHKDSK [d:\path\] [filename] [/F] [/V]
```

The d: switch specifies the disk volume to analyze. The \path and filename options specify files to check for fragmentation in addition to the volume analysis. Wildcards are permitted in the filename specification, to specify multiple files in a specified directory for fragmentation analysis. One limitation of the fragmentation analysis is that it does not check for fragmentation across directory boundaries, only within a specified directory.

The /F (Fix) switch enables CHKDSK to perform repairs if it finds problems with the directories and FATs. If /F is not specified, the program cannot write to the disk and no repairs are performed.

The /V (Verbose) switch causes the program to list all the entries in all the directories on a disk and give detailed information in cases where it encounters errors.

The drive, path, and file specifiers are optional. If you add no parameters for the command, CHKDSK processes the default volume or drive and does not check files for contiguity. If you specify [path] and [filename] parameters, CHKDSK checks all specified files to see whether they are stored contiguously on the disk. The program displays one of two messages as a result:

```
All specified file(s) are contiguous
```

or

```
[filename] Contains xxx non-contiguous blocks
```

CHKDSK displays the second message for each file on the disk that it finds to be fragmented and displays the number of fragments that compose the file. A fragmented file is one that is scattered around the disk in pieces rather than existing in one contiguous area of the disk. Fragmented files are slower to load than contiguous files, which reduces disk performance. Fragmented files are also much more difficult to recover if a problem with the FAT or directory on the disk occurs.

If you have only DOS, there are several ways to accomplish a full defragmentation. To defragment files on a floppy disk, you can format a new floppy disk and use COPY or XCOPY to copy all the files from the fragmented disk to the replacement. For a hard disk, you must completely back up, format, and then restore the disk. This procedure is time-consuming and dangerous, which is why there are so many third-party defragmenting utilities available.

CHKDSK Operation

CHKDSK reports problems found in a disk volume's FAT or directory system with one of several descriptive messages that vary to fit the specific error. Sometimes the messages are cryptic or misleading. CHKDSK does not specify how an error should be handled. It does not tell you whether CHKDSK can repair the problem, whether you must use some other utility, or what the consequences of the error and the repair will be. Neither does CHKDSK tell you what caused the problem nor how to avoid repeating the problem.

The primary function of CHKDSK is to compare the directory and FAT to determine whether they agree with each other—that is, whether all the data in the directory entries for the files (such as the starting cluster and size information) corresponds to what is in the FAT (such as chains of clusters with end-of-chain indicators). CHKDSK also checks subdirectory file entries, as well as the special "dot" (.) and "double dot" (..) entries that tie the subdirectory system together.

The second function of CHKDSK is to implement repairs to the disk structure. CHKDSK patches the disk so that the directory and FAT are in alignment and agreement. From a repair standpoint, understanding CHKDSK is relatively easy. CHKDSK almost always modifies the directories on a disk to correspond to what it finds in the FAT. There are only a few special cases in which CHKDSK modifies the FAT. When it does, the FAT modifications are always the same type of simple change.

Think of CHKDSK's repair capability as a directory patcher. Because CHKDSK cannot repair most types of FAT damage effectively, it simply modifies the disk directories to match whatever problems it finds in the FAT.

CHKDSK is not a very smart repair program and often can do more damage repairing the disk than if it had left the disk alone. In many cases, the information in the directories is correct and can be used (by some other utility) to help repair the FAT tables. If you have run CHKDSK with the /F parameter, however, the original directory information no longer exists, and a good FAT repair is impossible.

Caution

You should never run CHKDSK with the /F parameter without first running it in read-only mode (without the /F parameter) to determine whether and to what extent damage exists.

Only after carefully examining the disk damage and determining how CHKDSK would fix the problems should you run CHKDSK with the /F parameter. If you do not specify the /F parameter when you run CHKDSK, the program does not make corrections to the disk. Rather, it performs repairs in a mock fashion. This limitation is a safety feature because you do not want CHKDSK to take action until you have examined the problem. After deciding whether CHKDSK will make the correct assumptions about the damage, you might want to run it with the /F parameter.

Caution

Sometimes people place a **CHKDSK** /**F** command in their AUTOEXEC.BAT file; this is a very dangerous practice. If a system's disk directories and FAT system become damaged, attempting to load a program whose directory and FAT entries are damaged might lock the system. If, after you reboot, CHKDSK is fixing the problem because it is in the AUTOEXEC.BAT, it can irreparably damage the file structure of the disk. In many cases, CHKDSK ends up causing more damage than originally existed, and no easy way exists to undo the CHKDSK repair. Because CHKDSK is a simple utility that often makes faulty assumptions in repairing a disk, you must run it with great care when you specify the /**F** parameter.

Problems reported by CHKDSK are usually problems with the software and not the hardware. You rarely see a case in which lost clusters, allocation errors, or cross-linked files reported by CHKDSK were caused directly by a hardware fault, although it is certainly possible. The cause is usually a defective program or a program that was stopped before it could close files or purge buffers. A hardware fault certainly can stop a program before it can close files, but many people think that these error messages signify fault with the disk hardware, which is almost never the case.

The *RECOVER* Command

The DOS RECOVER command is designed to mark clusters as bad in the FAT when the clusters cannot be read properly. When the system cannot read a file because of a problem with a sector on the disk going bad, the RECOVER command can mark the FAT so that those clusters are not used by another file. When used improperly, this program is highly dangerous. The RECOVER utility has not been included in DOS since version 5 and is not supplied in Windows 9x, as its functionality has been replaced by SCANDISK.

Caution

Be very careful when you use RECOVER. Used improperly, it can do severe damage to your files and the FAT. If you enter the **RECOVER** command without a filename for it to work on, the program assumes that you want every file on the disk recovered, and operates on every file and subdirectory on the disk. It converts all subdirectories to files, places all filenames in the root directory, and gives them new names (FILE0000.REC, FILE0001.REC, and so on). This process essentially wipes out the file system on the entire disk. Do not use RECOVER without providing a filename for it to work on. This program should be considered as dangerous as the **FORMAT** command.

SCANDISK

It's a good idea to check your FAT partitions regularly for the problems discussed in this chapter and any other difficulties that may arise. By far an easier and more effective solution for disk diagnosis and repair than CHKDSK and RECOVER is the SCANDISK utility, included with DOS 6 and higher versions as well as with Windows 9x. This program is more thorough and comprehensive than CHKDSK or RECOVER, and can perform the functions of both of them—and a great deal more. Windows 95 OSR2 and Windows 98 include SCANDISK versions that support FAT32 partitions.

SCANDISK is like a scaled-down version of third-party disk repair programs such as Norton Disk Doctor, and it can verify both file structure and disk sector integrity. If SCANDISK finds problems, it can repair directories and FATs. If the program finds bad sectors in the middle of a file, it marks the clusters (allocation units) containing the bad sectors as bad in the FAT, and attempts to read the file data by rerouting around the defect.

Windows 9x includes both DOS and Windows versions of SCANDISK, which are named SCAN-DISK.EXE and SCANDSKW.EXE, respectively. Windows 9x scans your drives at the beginning of the operating system installation process and automatically loads the DOS version of SCANDISK whenever you restart your system after turning it off without completing the proper shutdown procedure. You can also launch SCANDISK.EXE from a DOS prompt or from a batch file using the following syntax.

```
Scandisk x: [/a] [/n] [/p] [dblspace.nnn/drvspace.nnn]
x: - designator of the drive that you want to scan
/a - scans all local fixed hard disks
/n - noninteractive mode; requires no user input
/p - scans only, without correcting errors
/custom - runs Scandisk with the options configured in the
➥[CUSTOM] section of the Scandisk.ini file
dblspace.nnn or drvspace.nnn - scans a compressed volume file,
➥where nnn is replaced by the file extension (such as 001)
```

The SCANDISK.INI file, located in the C:\WINDOWS\COMMAND directory on a Windows 9x system by default, contains extensive and well-documented parameters that you can use to control the behavior of SCANDISK.EXE. Note that the options in the SCANDISK.INI file are applied only to the DOS version of the utility and have no effect on the Windows GUI version.

You can also run the GUI version of the utility by opening the Start menu and choosing Programs, Accessories, System Tools. Both versions scan and repair the FAT and the directory and file structures, repair problems with long filenames, and scan volumes that have been compressed with DriveSpace or DoubleSpace.

SCANDISK provides two basic testing options: Standard and Thorough. The difference between the two is that the Thorough option causes the program to scan the entire surface of the disk for errors in addition to the items just mentioned. You can also select whether to run the program interactively or let it automatically repair any errors that it finds.

The DOS and Windows 9x versions of SCANDISK also test the FAT in different ways. The DOS version scans and, if necessary, repairs the primary copy of the file allocation table. After this it copies the repaired version of the primary to the backup copy. The Windows version, however, scans both copies of the FAT. If the program finds discrepancies between the two copies, it uses the data from the copy that it judges to be correct and reassembles the primary FAT using the best data from both copies.

SCANDISK also has an Advanced Options dialog box that enables you to set the following parameters:

- Whether the program should display a summary of its findings
- Whether the program should log its findings
- How the program should repair cross-linked files (two directory entries pointing to the same cluster)
- How the program should repair lost file fragments
- Whether to check files for invalid names, dates, and times

Although SCANDISK is good, and is certainly a vast improvement over CHKDSK, I would recommend using one of the commercial packages, such as the Norton Utilities, for any major disk problems. These utilities go far beyond what is included in DOS or Windows 9x.

Disk Defragmentation

The entire premise of the FAT file systems is based on the storage of data in clusters that can be located anywhere on the disk. This enables the computer to store a file of nearly any size at any time. The process of following a FAT chain to locate all the clusters holding the data for a particular file can force the hard disk drive to access many different locations on the disk. Because of the physical work involved in moving the disk drive heads, reading a file that is heavily fragmented in this way is slower than reading one that is stored on consecutive clusters.

As you regularly add, move, and delete files on a disk over a period of time, the files become increasingly fragmented, which can slow down disk performance. You can relieve this problem by periodically running a disk defragmentation utility on your drives, such as the one included with Windows 9x. When you run Disk Defragmenter, the program reads each of the files in the disk, using the FAT table to access its clusters, wherever they might be located.

The program then writes the file to a series of contiguous clusters and deletes the original. By progressively reading, erasing, and writing files, the program eventually leaves the disk in a state where all its files exist on contiguous clusters. As a result, the drive is capable of reading any file on the disk with a minimum of head movement, thus providing what is often a noticeable performance increase.

The Windows 95 Disk Defragmentation utility provides this basic defragmenting function. It also enables you to select whether you want to arrange the files on the disk to consolidate the empty clusters into one contiguous free space (which takes longer). The Windows 98 version adds a feature that examines the files on the disk and arranges them with the most often used program files grouped together at the front of the disk, which can make programs load faster.

To show how defragmenting works, see the example of a fragmented file shown in Table 27.19:

Table 27.19   Fragmented File

Directory

Name	Starting Cluster	Size
PLEDGE.TXT	1002	2
USCONST.TXT	1000	4

FAT16 File Allocation Table

FAT Cluster #	Value	Meaning
00002	0	First cluster available
...	...	...
00999	0	Cluster available
01000	1001	In use, points to next cluster
01001	1004	In use, points to next cluster
01002	1003	In use, points to next cluster
01003	FFFFh	End of file
01004	1005	In use, points to next cluster
01005	FFFFh	End of file
...	...	...
65526	0	Last cluster available

In the preceding example, the file USCONST.TXT is fragmented in two pieces. If we ran a defragmenting program, the files would be read off the disk and rewritten in a contiguous fashion. One possible outcome is shown in Table 27.20:

Table 27.20   Defragmented File

Directory

Name	Starting Cluster	Size
PLEDGE.TXT	1004	2
USCONST.TXT	1000	4

FAT16 File Allocation Table

FAT Cluster #	Value	Meaning
00002	0	First cluster available
...	...	...
00999	0	Cluster available
01000	1001	In use, points to next cluster
01001	1002	In use, points to next cluster
01002	1003	In use, points to next cluster
01003	FFFFh	End of file

(continues)

Table 27.20   Continued

FAT16 File Allocation Table

FAT Cluster #	Value	Meaning
01004	1005	In use, points to next cluster
01005	FFFFh	End of file
...	...	...
65526	0	Last cluster available

Although it doesn't look like much was changed, you can see that now both files are in one piece, stored one right after the other. Because defragmenting involves reading and rewriting a possibly large number of files on your drive, it can take a long time, especially if you have a lot of fragmented files and not very much free working space on the drive.

Third-party defragmentation utilities, such as the Speed Disk program included in the Norton Utilities, provide additional features, such as the capability to select specific files that should be moved to the front of the disk. Speed Disk can also defragment the Windows 9x swap file and files that are flagged with the system and hidden attributes, which Disk Defragmenter will not touch.

Caution

Although the Disk Defragmentation utilities included with Windows 9x and third-party products are usually quite safe, you should always be aware that defragmenting a disk is an inherently dangerous procedure. The program reads, erases, and rewrites every file on the disk and has the potential to cause damage to your data when interrupted improperly. Although I have never seen a problem result from the process, an unforeseen event such as a power failure during a defragmentation procedure can conceivably be disastrous. I strongly recommend that you always run a disk repair utility such as SCANDISK on your drives before defragmenting them, and have a current backup ready.

Third-Party Programs

When you get a Sector not found error reading drive C:, the best course of action is to use one of the third-party disk repair utilities on the market, rather than DOS's RECOVER or even SCAN-DISK. The Norton Utilities by Symantec stands as perhaps the premier data recovery package on the market today. This package is comprehensive and automatically repairs most types of disk problems.

Programs such as the Norton Disk Doctor can perform much more detailed repairs with a greater amount of safety. If the error is on a floppy disk, use Norton's DiskTool before you use Disk Doctor. DiskTool is specially designed to help you recover data from floppy disks. Disk Doctor and DiskTool preserve as much of the data in the file as possible, and can mark the FAT so the bad sectors or clusters of the disk are not used again. These programs also save Undo information, making it possible for you to reverse any data recovery operation.

Disk Doctor and DiskTool are part of Symantec's Norton Utilities package, which includes a great many other useful tools. For example, Norton Utilities has an excellent sector editor that enables you to view and edit any part of a disk, including the master and volume boot records, FATs, and other areas that fall outside of the disk's normal data area. Currently, there is no other program as comprehensive or as capable of editing disks at the sector level. The disk editor included with the Norton Utilities can give the professional PC troubleshooter or repairperson the ability to work directly with any sector on the disk, but this does require extensive knowledge of sector formats and disk structures. The documentation with the package is excellent and can be very helpful if you are learning data recovery on your own.

Note

Data recovery is a lucrative service that the more advanced technician can provide. People are willing to pay much more to get their data back than to replace a hard drive.

For more automatic recovery that anybody can perform, Norton Utilities has several other useful modules. Disk Doctor and Calibrate are two of the modules included with the Norton Utilities (both version 8.0 for DOS/Windows and version 3.0 for Windows 95). Together, these two utilities provide exhaustive testing of the data structures and sectors of a hard drive. Disk Doctor works with both hard disks and floppy disks. It tests the capability of the drive to work with the system in which it is installed, including the drive's boot record, FATs, file structure, and data areas. Calibrate, which is used for the most intensive testing of the data area of a drive, also tests the hard drive controller electronics.

You can also use Calibrate to perform deep-pattern testing of IDE and SCSI drives. This process writes millions of bytes of data to every sector of the drive to see whether it can properly retain data. It moves data if the sector where the data is stored is flawed. Bad sectors are then marked as bad in the FAT.

Because of the excellent disk editor, anybody serious about data recovery needs a copy of Norton Utilities. The many other modules that are included are excellent as well. The latest versions now include NDIAGS, which is a comprehensive PC hardware diagnostic.

The most important consideration when you purchase third-party disk utilities is to choose products that support your file system. Norton Utilities, for example, is available in a DOS version and a Windows 9x version, and only the latter supports FAT32 partitions.

NTFS

NTFS is Windows NT's native file system. Although NT supports FAT partitions, NTFS provides many advantages over FAT, including long filenames, support for larger files and partitions, extended attributes, and increased security. NTFS, like all of Windows NT, was newly designed from the ground up. Backward compatibility with previous Microsoft operating systems was not a concern, because the developers were intent on creating an entirely new 32-bit platform. As a result, no operating systems other than Windows NT can read NTFS partitions.

This is an important consideration. All the other Windows operating systems are fundamentally based on DOS and leave you the alternative of booting to a DOS prompt in special situations. Whether you have to run a special DOS utility to configure a piece of hardware or perform an emergency disk repair, the DOS option is always there.

Windows NT is not DOS-based. You can open a window that provides a DOS-like command prompt in Windows NT, but this is actually a DOS emulation, not a true shell. You cannot boot the system to a command prompt, avoiding the GUI, as you can with Windows 9x. You can, of course, bypass NT entirely by starting the system with a DOS boot disk, but if you have NTFS partitions on your drives, you will not be able to access them from the DOS prompt.

NTFS supports filenames of up to 255 characters, using spaces, multiple periods, and any other standard characters except the following: *?/\;<>|. Because NTFS file offsets are 64 bits long, files and partitions can be truly enormous: up to 16EB (exabytes) in size (16 exabytes = 2^{64} bytes = 17,179,869,184 gigabytes)! To give you an idea of just how much data this is, it is estimated that all the words ever spoken by human beings throughout history would occupy 5EB of storage.

NTFS Architecture

Although NTFS partitions are very different from FAT partitions internally, they do comply with the extra-partitional disk structures described earlier in this chapter. NTFS partitions are listed in the master partition table of a disk drive's master boot record, just like FAT partitions, and they have a volume boot record as well, although it is formatted somewhat differently.

An NTFS partition is based on a structure called the Master File Table, or MFT. The MFT concept expands on that of the FAT. Instead of using a table of cluster references, the MFT contains much more detailed information about the files and directories in the partition. In some cases, it even contains the files and directories themselves.

The first record in the MFT is called the descriptor, which contains information about the MFT itself. The volume boot record for an NTFS partition contains a reference that points to the location of this descriptor record. The second record in the MFT is a mirror copy of the descriptor, which provides fault tolerance, should the first copy be damaged.

The third record is the log file record. All NTFS transactions are logged to a file that can be used to restore data in the event of a disk problem. The bulk of the MFT consists of records for the files and directories that are stored on the partition. NTFS files take the form of objects that have both user- and system-defined attributes. Attributes on NTFS partitions are more comprehensive than the few simple flags used on FAT partitions. All the information on an NTFS file is stored as attributes of that file. In fact, even the file data itself is an attribute. Unlike FAT files, the attributes of NTFS files are part of the file itself; they are not listed separately in a directory entry. Directories exist as MFT records as well, but they consist mainly of indexes listing the files in the directory; they do not contain the size, date, time, and other information about the individual files.

Thus, an NTFS drive's MFT is much more than a cluster list, like a FAT; it is actually the primary data storage structure on the partition. If a file or directory is relatively small (less than approximately 1,500 bytes), the entire thing may even be stored in the MFT. For larger amounts of storage, the MFT record for a file or directory contains pointers to external clusters in the partition. These external clusters are called extents. All the records in the MFT, including the descriptors and the log file, are capable of using extents for storage of additional attributes. The attributes of a file that are part of the MFT record are called resident attributes. Those stored in extents are called nonresident attributes.

NTFS Compatibility

Although NTFS partitions are not directly accessible by DOS and other operating systems, Windows NT is designed for network use, and NTFS files are expected to be accessed by other operating systems. For this reason, NTFS continues to support the standard DOS file attributes and the 8.3 FAT naming convention.

One of the main reasons for using NTFS is the security that it provides for its files and directories. NTFS security attributes are called *permissions*, and are designed to enable system administrators to control access to files and directories by granting specific rights to users and groups. This is a much more granular approach than the FAT file system attributes, which apply to all users.

However, you can still set the FAT-style attributes on NTFS files using the standard Windows NT file management tools, including Windows NT Explorer and even the DOS ATTRIB command. When you copy FAT files to an NTFS drive over the network, the FAT-style attributes remain in place until you explicitly remove them. This can be an important consideration, because the FAT-style attributes take precedence over the NTFS permissions. A file on an NTFS drive that is flagged with the FAT read-only attribute, for example, cannot be deleted by a Windows NT user, even if that user has NTFS permissions that grant them full access.

To enable DOS and 16-bit Windows systems to access files on NTFS partitions over a network, the file system maintains an 8.3 alias name for every file and directory on the partition. The algorithm for deriving the alias from the long filename is the same as that used by Windows 95's VFAT. Windows NT also provides its FAT partitions with the same type of long filename support used by VFAT, allocating additional directory entries to store the long filenames as needed.

Creating NTFS Drives

NTFS is for use on hard disk drives. You cannot create an NTFS floppy disk (although you can format removable media such as Iomega Zip and Jaz cartridges to use NTFS). Three basic ways to create an NTFS disk partition are as follows:

- Create a new NTFS volume out of unpartitioned disk space during the Windows NT installation process or after the installation with the Disk Administrator utility.
- Format an existing partition to NTFS (destroying its data in the process) using the Windows NT Format dialog box (accessible from Windows NT Explorer or Disk Administrator), or the FORMAT command (with the /fs:ntfs switch) from the command prompt.
- Convert an existing FAT partition to NTFS (preserving its data) during the Windows NT installation process or after the installation with the command-line CONVERT utility.

NTFS Tools

Because it uses a fundamentally different architecture, virtually none of the troubleshooting techniques outlined earlier in this chapter are applicable when dealing with NTFS partitions, nor can the disk utilities intended for use on FAT partitions address them. Windows NT has a rudimentary capability to check a disk for file system errors and bad sectors, but apart from that, the operating system contains no other disk repair or defragmentation utilities.

The NTFS file system, however, does have its own automatic disk repair capabilities. In addition to Windows NT's fault-tolerance features, such as disk mirroring (maintaining the same data on two separate drives) and disk striping with parity (splitting data across several drives with parity information for data reconstruction), the OS also uses a disk error recover technique called *cluster remapping*.

With cluster remapping, when Windows NT detects a bad sector on an NTFS partition, it automatically remaps the data in that cluster to another cluster. If the drive is part of a fault-tolerant drive array, any lost data is reconstructed from the duplicate data on the other drive(s).

Despite these features, however, there is still a real need for disk repair and defragmentation utilities for Windows NT. They have been a long time in coming, but there are now finally third-party utilities that can repair and defragment NTFS drives. One I recommend is the Norton Utilities for NT, by Symantec.

Common Drive Error Messages and Solutions

There are several common error messages that are associated with problems in the file system or drives. This section covers the common ones, listing their cause and possible solutions.

Some of the most common file system errors are shown in the following list:

- Missing Operating System
- NO ROM BASIC - SYSTEM HALTED
- Boot error Press F1 to retry
- Invalid drive specification
- Invalid Media Type
- Hard Disk Controller Failure

These normally occur when booting the system or when trying to log in to or access a drive. The following section describes each of these errors and offers possible solutions.

Missing Operating System

This error indicates problems in the master boot record (MBR) or partition table entries. The partition table entries might be pointing to a sector that is not the actual beginning of a partition. This can also be caused by invalid BIOS settings, caused in some cases by a dead or dying battery. In fact in my experience, corrupt or improper BIOS settings are the number one cause of this problem. Another cause can be virus damage to the MBR. This error can also occur if there is no active partition defined in the partition table.

The normal solution is to correct the invalid BIOS settings. The BIOS settings for drive parameters must be set to the same values as when the drive was partitioned and formatted to read the drive correctly. If the MBR is damaged or virus infected, you can try FDISK/MBR to repair. Other types of damage will require more sophisticated use of a disk editor utility or repartitioning and reformatting the drive to start over.

NO ROM BASIC - SYSTEM HALTED

This error is generated by the AMI BIOS when the boot sector or master boot record of the boot drive is damaged or missing. This error can also occur if the boot device has been improperly configured, or is not configured at all in the BIOS. In this case, data in the partition might be valid and undamaged, but there is no bootable partition.

IBM systems in this situation used to drop into a built-in BIOS version of BASIC, but most non-IBM BIOS manufacturers did not license this code from Microsoft. So instead of dropping into BASIC, they would display this cryptic message. Because the most common cause of this type of error is a failure to set at least one partition as active (bootable), the normal solution is to run FDISK and set the primary partition as active. If this is not the problem, the solution would be to repair the damaged MBR or to correct the improper BIOS settings.

Boot Error Press F1 to Retry

This error is generated by the Phoenix BIOS when the hard disk is missing a master boot record or boot sector, or when there is a problem accessing the boot drive. This has the same meaning as NO ROM BASIC. The most common cause of this message is having no partitions defined as active (bootable).

Invalid Drive Specification

This error occurs when you attempt to log in to a drive that has not been partitioned, or for which the partition table entry has been damaged or is incorrect. Use FDISK to partition the drive or to check out the existing partitions. If they are damaged, you will normally want to use a data recovery utility such as the Norton Utilities to correct the problem. Another solution is to repartition the drive from scratch, but this will cause any existing data on the drive to be overwritten.

Invalid Media Type

This indicates the partition table is valid, but the volume boot sector, directory, or file allocation tables are corrupt, damaged, or not yet initialized. For example, this is the standard error you would receive if you tried to access a drive that had been partitioned but not yet formatted. The FORMAT command is what creates the volume boot record (VBR), file allocation tables (FATs), and directories on the disk.

The repair usually involves using a data recovery utility, such as the Norton Utilities, or reformatting the drive.

Hard Disk Controller Failure

This message indicates the hard disk controller has failed, the hard disk controller is not set up properly in the BIOS, or the controller cannot communicate with the attached drive(s), such as with cable problems.

The solution is to check out the drive installation and make sure the cables to the drive are properly installed, the drive is receiving power, it is spinning, and the BIOS Setup definitions are correct. If all these are correct, the drive, cable, or controller might be physically damaged. Replace them with known good spares one at a time until the problem is solved.

General File System Troubleshooting

Here are some general procedures to follow for troubleshooting drive access, file system, or boot problems:

1. Start the system using a Windows startup disk, or any bootable MS-DOS disk that contains FDISK.EXE, FORMAT.COM, SYS.COM, and SCANDISK.EXE (Windows 95B or later versions preferred).

2. If your system cannot boot from the floppy, you might have more serious problems with your hardware. Check the floppy drive and the motherboard for proper installation and configuration.

3. Run FDISK from the Windows startup disk. Select option 4 (Display partition information).

4. If the partitions are listed, make sure that the bootable partition (normally the primary partition) is defined as active (look for an uppercase A in the Status column.)

5. If there are no partitions listed and you do not want to recover any of the data existing on the drive now, use FDISK to create new partitions, and then use FORMAT to format the partitions. This will overwrite any previously existing data on the drive.

6. If you want to recover the data on the drive and no partitions are being shown, you will need to use a data recovery program, such as the Norton Utilities by Symantec or Lost and Found by PowerQuest, to recover the data.

7. If all the partitions appear in FDISK.EXE, and one is defined as active, run the SYS command as follows to restore the system files to the hard disk:

        SYS C:

8. For this to work properly, it is important that the disk you boot from be a startup disk from the same operating system (or version of Windows) you have on your hard disk.

9. You should receive the message System Transferred if the command works properly. Remove the disk from drive A: and restart the system. If you still have the same error as before after you restart your computer, your drive might be improperly configured or damaged.

10. Run SCANDISK from the Windows startup disk or an aftermarket data recovery utility such as the Norton Utilities to check for problems with the hard disk.

11. Using SCANDISK, perform a surface scan. If ScanDisk reports any physically damaged sectors on the hard disk, the drive may need to be replaced.

A Final Word

28

SOME OF THE MAIN TOPICS IN THIS CHAPTER ARE

Manuals (Documentation)

Magazines

Online Resources

Seminars

Machines

CompTIA A+ Core Examination Objective Map

In Conclusion

The contents of this book cover the components of a PC-compatible system. In this book, you have discovered how all the components operate and interact, and how they should be set up and installed. You have seen the ways that components fail and learned the symptoms of these failures. You reviewed steps in diagnosing and troubleshooting the major components in a system so you can locate and replace a failing component. You also learned about upgrades for components, including what upgrades are available, the benefits of an upgrade, and how to obtain and perform the actual upgrade. Because failing components so often are technically obsolete, it is often desirable to combine repair and upgrade procedures to replace a failing part with an upgraded or higher performance part.

The information I have presented in this book represents many years of research, along with years of hands-on, practical experience with PC-compatible systems. A great deal of research and investigation have gone into each section. This information and knowledge have saved many companies and even individuals many thousands of dollars. By reading this book, you can also take advantage of this wealth of information; the information presented may save you and your company time, energy, and, most importantly, money!

Bringing PC service and support in-house is one of the best ways to save money. Eliminating service contracts for most systems and reducing downtime are just two of the benefits of applying the information presented in this book. As I have indicated many times, you can also save a lot of money on component purchases by eliminating the middleman and purchasing the components directly from distributors or manufacturers.

The Vendor List on the CD provides the best of these sources for you to contact. If you intend to build your own systems, the vendor list will be extremely useful, as I have listed sources for all the components needed to assemble a complete system—from the screws and brackets all the way to the cases, power supplies, and motherboards. I have found that this list is one of the most frequently used parts of this book; I use it myself all the time. In the past, people have been unable to make direct purchases because doing so required a new level of understanding of the components involved. Also, many of the manufacturers and direct distributors of products are unable to provide support for beginning users; this is why they often rely on the middlemen to sell and support their products. Of course, armed with this knowledge, you can now purchase products from more direct sources, eliminating the middleman and paying less for the products in the process. This book can give you the deeper level of knowledge and understanding you need so you can purchase the components you want directly from the vendors who manufacture and distribute them, saving a great deal of money in the long run.

Not only can you use this book to save money, but the information contained within will allow you to have the knowledge and confidence to select exactly the components you need to build a custom and yet nonproprietary system to your own specifications. Such a system would be fully upgradable and maintainable using inexpensive industry-standard components.

I used many sources to gather the information in this book, starting with my own real-world experiences. I have also taught this information to thousands of people in the hundreds of seminars presented over the last 18 years by my company, Mueller Technical Research. In fact, my PC Hardware seminars are the longest-running seminars on the subject. During these seminars, I am often asked where more technical information can be obtained and whether I have any "secrets" for acquiring this knowledge. Well, I won't keep any secrets! I can freely share the following five key sources of information that can help you become a verifiable expert in PC upgrading and repairing:

- Manuals
- Magazines (documentation)
- Modems (online resources such as the Internet)
- Meetings (seminars)
- Machines (hands-on work with actual systems)

The last thing I'll show you in this chapter is how this book can be a great resource to prepare for the CompTIA A+ certification exam. Thousands of A+-certified PC technicians have used this book as part of their training (and continue to use it in their jobs).

Note

To learn more about A+ Certification, I recommend that you pick up a copy of *Upgrading and Repairing PCs: A+ Certification Study Guide*, published by Que.

Manuals (Documentation)

Manuals and documentation are the single most important sources of computer information. Unfortunately, these also are the most frequently overlooked sources of information. Much of my knowledge has come from poring over technical-reference manuals and other original equipment manufacturers' (OEM) manuals.

One of the biggest problems in troubleshooting, servicing, or upgrading a system is having proper documentation. I believe that good documentation is critical for system support and future upgrade capability. Because it can be a problem getting documentation on older systems or components, the best time to acquire documentation is when the system or components are new.

Oftentimes, these manuals must be obtained from the OEM (original equipment manufacturer) of the equipment you purchase, meaning the vendor or reseller will not supply them. Wherever possible, you should make an effort to discover who the real OEM of each component in your system is, so you can obtain documentation on the product or component.

A simple analogy explains the importance of manuals and other issues concerning repair and maintenance of a system. Compare your business use of computers to a taxicab company. The company has to purchase automobiles to use as cabs. The owners purchase not one car but an entire fleet of cars. Do you think that they would purchase a fleet of automobiles based solely on reliability, performance, or even gas-mileage statistics? Would they neglect to consider ongoing maintenance and service of these automobiles? Would they purchase a fleet of cars that could be serviced only by the original manufacturer and for which parts could not be obtained easily or inexpensively? Do you think that they would buy a car that did not have available a detailed service and repair manual? Would they buy an automobile for which parts were scarce and that was supported by a sparse dealer network with few service and parts outlets, making long waits for parts and service inevitable? The answer (of course) to all these questions is no, no, no!

You can see why most taxicab companies and police departments use "standard" automobiles such as the Chevrolet Caprice or Ford Crown Victoria. If ever there were "generic" cars, these models would qualify! Dealers, parts, and documentation for these particular models are everywhere. These cars share parts with many other automobiles as well, which makes them easy to service and maintain.

Your business (especially if it is large) also amounts to a "fleet" of computers. Think of this fleet as being similar to the cars of a cab company, which would go out of business quickly if these cars could not be kept running smoothly and inexpensively. Now you know why the old Checker Marathon automobile used to be so popular with cab companies: Its design barely changed from the time it was introduced in 1956, until it was discontinued in July 1982. This meant that parts interchanged and service procedures remained largely the same over the entire 26-year life of the product.

In many ways, the industry-standard PC-compatible systems are like the venerable Checker Marathon. You can get technical information by the shelfful for these systems. You can get parts and upgrade material from so many sources that anything you need is always immediately available and at a discounted price. These are the benefits of purchasing industry-standard systems using standard motherboard and chassis form factors. This results in systems that are easily supported, repaired, and upgraded. An additional benefit is that when these standards are followed, the systems in a company can be easily maintained using largely interchangeable parts.

Several types of documentation are available to cover a given system:

- *System-level documentation.* The system-specific manual(s) put together by the system manufacturer or assembler. Some companies break this down further into Operations, Technical Reference, and Service manuals.

- *Component or board-level documentation.* The specific OEM manuals for each major component, such as the motherboard, video card, hard disk, floppy disk drive, CD-ROM drive, modem, network card, SCSI adapter, and so on.

- *Chip- and chipset-level documentation.* The most specific and technical manuals that cover items such as the processor, motherboard chipset, Super I/O chip, BIOS, memory modules, video chipset, and various disk controller, SCSI bus interface, network interface, and other chips used throughout the system.

The system- and component-level documentation is essential for even the most basic troubleshooting and upgrading tasks. More technical literature, such as the chip- and chipset-level documentation, is probably necessary only for software and hardware developers who have more special requirements. However, if you are like me and really want to know as much about a system as possible, you will find that having the chip- and chipset-level documentation can give you insights and information about a system you simply can't get otherwise. This section will examine all this documentation and, most importantly, explain how to get it!

Basic System Documentation

When you purchase a complete system, it should include a basic set of documentation. What you actually get will vary widely, depending on what type of system you get and who put it together.

Name-brand manufacturers such as IBM, Compaq, Hewlett-Packard, Toshiba, Packard Bell, and others will almost certainly include custom user-level manuals they have developed specifically for each system they sell. These manuals are often very basic and contain only enough information for basic system setup, installation, and minor troubleshooting. Most of the bigger name manufacturers who design and manufacture their own motherboards have much more technical documentation available. For example, IBM, HP, Toshiba, and Compaq have technical reference and service manuals available for their systems that contain much more information than the books that come free with their systems.

These technical reference manuals contain detailed information about the components used in the system—information that would be useful to technicians or sophisticated users wanting to know more details. Service manuals contain detailed instructions on system disassembly and reassembly, troubleshooting flowcharts, problem-solving guides, and a complete parts listing. Service manuals are particularly useful for laptop and notebook computers, where the disassembly and reassembly is often not intuitive and where virtually all the parts are custom. You should contact the manufacturer or a manufacturer-authorized service center to find out about any service or technical reference documentation that might be available.

Companies who assemble or build systems out of industry-standard components such as most of the well-known mail-order brands may either produce their own documentation or include the documentation that is supplied with the components they install in their systems. Most of the larger system assemblers, such as Dell, Gateway, Micron, Midwest Micro, Quantex, and others, will also have their own custom-produced documentation for the main system unit, and might even have custom manuals for many of the individual system components.

This type of documentation is useful for people setting up a system for the first time or for performing simple upgrades. However, it often lacks the detailed technical reference information needed by someone who might be troubleshooting the system or upgrading it beyond what the manufacturer or assembler had originally intended. In that case, you are better off with any of the OEM component manuals that are available directly from the component or peripheral manufacturers themselves.

Most of the smaller system assemblers will forego any custom-produced system documentation and simply include the component-level manuals for the components they are including in the assembled system. For example, if an Asus motherboard and STB video card were included in a particular system, the manuals from Asus and STB that originally came with those products would be included with the assembled system.

Getting Documentation from an Assembler

Some system assemblers like to keep the component documentation and not include it with the systems they build. This forces the purchaser of the systems to go back to the assembler for any support or technical information. It also tends to make the purchaser believe that the assembler actually manufactured the system rather than assembling it using off-the-shelf components. In other cases, system assemblers use special OEM versions of products that come in plain white boxes with little or no documentation. In that case, the system assembler is expected to provide the documentation in their custom manual. If you get the generic OEM product versions with your system, I recommend contacting the actual OEM component manufacturer for more detailed and specific documentation.

The standard manuals included with most system components and peripherals contain basic instructions for system setup, operation, testing, relocation, and option installation. Some sort of basic diagnostics disk (sometimes called a Diagnostics and Setup or Reference Disk) normally is included with a system as well. Often the diagnostics are simply a custom-labeled version of a commonly available commercial diagnostic program.

Tip

Most system vendors and equipment manufacturers have jumper settings and manuals available on their Web sites in downloadable form. Appendix A, "Web Site List," contains a list of vendors and their Web sites.

Component and Peripheral Documentation

It is a well-known fact that many systems sold today are not really manufactured as a custom unit by a single company but instead are assembled out of standard off-the-shelf components that are available on the open market. In fact, I normally recommend that people purchase exactly that type of system, because all the components conform to known standards and can easily be replaced or upgraded later.

Even proprietary manufactured systems such as IBM, Compaq, Hewlett-Packard, Packard Bell, and others use at least some off-the-shelf standard components (disk drives, for example). To fully document a system, I recommend you take an inventory of the standard components used, and then collect all the OEM documentation or product manuals for them.

This process is simple; when I am supporting a given system, first I disassemble it and write down all the information on each of the components inside. Sometimes, you will need to do a little more investigating or even ask the company that assembled the system exactly what components they included. Most components, such as hard disks, CD-ROM drives, video cards, sound cards, network cards, and more, are pretty easy to identify. Somewhere on the device or card there should be a label indicating at least the manufacturer and usually also the model number. From this, you can look up the manufacturer in the Vendor List on the CD. Using that information, you can contact the company via telephone, fax, or Internet Web site to obtain the complete documentation on their products.

If you are running a fully Plug-and-Play-compatible operating system such as Windows 95/98 or Windows 2000, you can find out the manufacturers and model numbers of many of the devices in your system by using the Device Manager program.

Motherboards can be tricky to identify because not all manufacturers mark them clearly. In fact, the largest manufacturer of motherboards, Intel, does not mark its boards with either the name or the model number! This is because the major system assemblers who use the boards (Dell, Gateway, Micron, and many others) don't really want people to know where the board originally came from. In some cases, the system assembler will even stamp their own name on the board, even though they did not manufacture it.

If there are no motherboard manufacturer markings, you should contact the company that sold you the computer to ask them exactly what motherboard you have. I would not even consider purchasing a new system unless I knew exactly whose motherboard was being included and exactly what model it was. Don't be afraid to ask the system assembler company exactly what motherboard or other components they are installing in the systems they sell. If they can't or won't answer, you may be better off purchasing from a different company in the future. If the company who sold the system is no longer available or cannot help, check the paperwork that came with the system. Sometimes there are clues in the original paperwork that might indicate what motherboard your system includes. Most of the popular motherboard manufacturers are listed.

Note

Every electronic component in your computer is required to have an FCC (Federal Communications Commission) ID number. If you are having trouble determining the original manufacturer of a component, use the FCC ID number to look up the name and other information on the company who produced the device. The FCC maintains a searchable database of these ID numbers on their official site at `http://www.fcc.gov/oet/fccid/`. I find this site invaluable when trying to determine the origin of some unmarked products.

As an example, one system I recently worked on is a Dell Dimension XPS R450 (Pentium II) 450MHz system that included the following industry-standard components:

Motherboard:	Intel SE440BX "Seattle"
Processor:	Intel Pentium II 450
Video Card:	ATI Xpert 98D
Hard Disk:	Maxtor DiamondMax 91296
Floppy Disk Drive:	Teac FD-235HG
DVD-ROM Drive:	Toshiba SD-M1202

Most of the larger system assemblers such as Dell, Gateway, Micron, and others have been using Intel motherboards. Most motherboards today use Intel processors and chipsets, but some people might not be aware that Intel makes complete PC motherboards, as well. Even so, Dell did not include the actual Intel motherboard or other component manuals but instead included their own custom manuals for the motherboard, video card, hard disk, and CD-ROM drive. By contacting the individual companies directly over the Internet and via the telephone, I was able to obtain more detailed documentation on all these products. Many times, the OEM documentation or product manuals can be downloaded directly from the respective companies' Web sites, often in the form of Adobe Acrobat .PDF files, which you can read with the Acrobat reader available for free downloading from Adobe.

Chip and Chipset Documentation

If you really want the ultimate in documentation for your system, I highly recommend getting the documentation for the various chips and chipsets in your system. This would include specific manuals for each of the major chip-level components in the system—such as the processor, motherboard chipset, BIOS, Super I/O chipset, and so on. Before you can get this documentation, you must first identify all the relevant chips and chipsets in your system.

The process is relatively simple. Look at the documentation for each major component, especially the motherboard. The OEM motherboard documentation should tell you which chipset is used on the board, which processors are supported, and which Super I/O chip is used. From the OEM documentation you have on your system components, you should be able to find out what the following major chip and chipsets are:

> Processor
>
> Motherboard Chipset
>
> ROM BIOS
>
> Super I/O Chip
>
> Video Chipset

If your motherboard has an integrated video card, the video chipset type will be listed there also. If you have a separate video card, look in the video card manual, which should clearly identify the video chipset used.

The most important chips you will want to identify are on the motherboard. The first thing you would want to identify is the processor. This should be relatively easy; most PC systems use Intel processors. A small percentage of systems use AMD or Cyrix processors, or versions of these processors sold under other names. The documentation that comes with the system will normally identify which brand of processor you have and which model and speed it is. Often times the processor will be hidden under a heat sink, which means you might have to remove the processor from its socket to see the markings on the bottom. Intel Pentium II and III processors, which come in the SEC (Single Edge Contact) cartridge, are usually easier to identify because their markings are along the top edge and not covered by the heat sink.

If you aren't sure what processor is in the system, software programs such as the MSD (Microsoft Diagnostics) program can tell you. It's included with Windows 3.1, the System control panel in Windows 9x, or a system diagnostic you purchase, such as the Norton Utilities. Commercial utilities like Norton Utilities can give you more detailed information about your processor, often including the speed it is running at and other pertinent information, such as whether it supports MMX instructions.

Normally, the processor is the largest chip on the motherboard, and can often be identified by reading the information stamped on it. In some cases, the processor will have a heat sink or fan attached to the top. In this case, you may have to remove either the heat sink or fan to read the information stamped on top of the chip, or remove the entire processor and heat sink or fan assembly to read the information stamped on the bottom of the chip.

Note

You should check to see that the processor in your system is really rated to run at the speed your system is set for. Many of the smaller system assemblers have been installing overclocked CPUs in their systems. For example, they might have sold you a 266MHz system but only have a 233MHz processor installed. The only way to verify the actual chip rating is to check the chip manufacturer markings stamped or printed on the chip. Some vendors have even resorted to wiping off the original markings and remarking the chips at a higher speed, carefully placing an official-looking sticker over the original marks, or even installing new forged casings over the processor. Unfortunately, these remarked chips can be difficult to spot for the less experienced. These types of scams are one reason for recommending the bigger name-brand system assemblers. Intel has more recently been building over-clock protection circuitry into their chips that is designed to help prevent this; unfortunately, the remarkers have found ways to bypass this circuitry.

The motherboard chipset type can be difficult for software to determine, so you will normally have to find out which chipset you have from the motherboard documentation or by firsthand inspection. The motherboard chipset usually consists of two or more large chips on the board; however, there are chipsets that use anywhere from one to six chips. Generally, each chip in the set will have a part number stamped on it, but the chipset will be named after the main chip. The Pentium Pro board I mentioned had two chips labeled 82441FX and 82442FX; these two chips are called the North Bridge or primary components of the chipset. There was also an 82371SB South Bridge chip that is also called the PIIX3 (PCI/IDE/ISA eXcelerator). All three chips are a part of what Intel calls the 440FX chipset. Most of their newer chipsets, such as the 440LX and 440BX, consist of only two chips—one for the North Bridge and one for the South Bridge.

◄◄ See "Chipsets," p. 235.

Finding out the manufacturer of the motherboard BIOS is easy; it is normally found in the motherboard manual. It is also normally displayed, along with the exact version number you have, every time you power the system on. Most systems today use an AMI, Award, or Phoenix BIOS, but there are several other manufacturers as well.

Virtually all motherboards built in the 1990s (and later) include a special interface chip called a Super I/O chip. This is a single-chip device that normally includes the following components:

- Primary and secondary IDE host adapters
- Floppy disk drive controller
- Two serial ports
- One parallel port

Many of the more recent Super I/O chips do not include the IDE host adapters, such as the National Semiconductor 87308 or 87309 or SMsC FCD37M707 chips used in the Intel Pentium Pro and Pentium II/III motherboards. That is because the IDE ports are already built into the various Intel 82371 South Bridge chips. The National Semiconductor Super I/O chips also include an 8042-style keyboard and mouse controller. Some Super I/O chips include an MC146818-style real-time clock with nonvolatile CMOS RAM, although that is also normally a part of the Intel chipset South Bridge. Other Super I/O chips may include a game (joystick) interface as well. Obtaining the documentation for your particular Super I/O chip will, of course, tell you exactly what its capabilities are.

Another important chipset in a system is the video chipset. This is normally found on the video card or on the motherboard, if the motherboard has built-in video. The OEM video card or motherboard documentation should tell you exactly which video chipset you have. If not, you can use free software such as MSD or commercial programs such as Norton Utilities to identify which chipset you have without even opening the case. A last resort would be to open the system and read the part number right off of the video chipset, which is usually the largest chip on the video card.

Using a Pentium III 500MHz system as an example, I found it contained the following main chip and chipset components:

Processor:	Intel Pentium III
Motherboard Chipset:	Intel 440BX
ROM BIOS:	Phoenix/Intel
Super I/O Chip:	SMsC FDC37M707
Video Chipset:	ATI Rage Pro Turbo

Note that this particular motherboard did not have the video integrated, so the video chipset was on the video card.

From the documentation on these chips, I was able to get more information on the various serial, parallel, and disk controllers contained in the Super I/O chip. And, I learned more about the advanced CMOS settings in the BIOS Setup routines as they pertain to the 440BX motherboard chipset.

For example, I often get questions about the Advanced CMOS settings. Most people assume that these settings are described in their ROM BIOS documentation because the ROM-based CMOS Setup program in their system controls these settings. If you contact the BIOS manufacturer or read the BIOS documentation, you will quickly find that the ROM BIOS manufacturer knows little or nothing about these settings. In fact, these settings actually have little or nothing to do with the particular ROM BIOS used and everything to do with the particular motherboard chipset used. You can find descriptions of all these settings in the documentation for your motherboard chipset, which can be obtained from the chipset manufacturer.

Manufacturer System-Specific Documentation

If your system is from a name-brand manufacturer—such as IBM, Compaq, Hewlett-Packard, Toshiba, and others—there may be a wealth of information available in manufacturer-specific manuals and documentation. Because of the specific nature of the information in these types of manuals, you most likely will have to obtain it from the manufacturer of the system.

Large manufacturers such as Intel, IBM, Compaq, Hewlett-Packard, and others both manufacture their own components and purchase components from other sources. Many of these manufacturers also make available complete libraries of technical documentation for their systems. IBM, HP, and Compaq also make their technical libraries available in CD-ROM versions, which are not only very comprehensive but also very convenient and easy to search. These CD-ROMs contain detailed information about PC systems and peripherals from these companies. If you have an IBM, Compaq, or HP system, contact the manufacturer to see about ordering their CD-ROM reference library. Normally, these are offered as subscriptions for $250 or so annually.

The process of obtaining other manufacturers' manuals may (or may not) be easy. Most large companies run responsible service and support operations that provide technical documentation. Other companies either do not have or are unwilling to part with such documentation, in an effort to protect their service departments (and their dealers' service departments) from competition. Contact the manufacturer directly; they can direct you to the correct department so that you can inquire about this information. Information on how to contact most PC manufacturers can be found in the Vendor List on the CD.

Magazines

The next source of information—magazines—is one of the best sources for up-to-date reviews and technical data. Featured are "bug fixes," problem alerts, and general industry news. Keeping a printed book up to date with the latest events in the computer industry is extremely difficult or even impossible. Things move so fast that the magazines themselves barely keep pace. I subscribe to most of the major computer magazines and am hard-pressed to pick one as the best. They all are important to me, and each one provides different information or the same information with a different angle or twist. Although the reviews usually leave me wanting, the magazines still are a valuable way to at least hear about products, most of which I never would have known about without the magazines' reports and advertisements. Most computer magazines are also available on CD-ROM, which can ease the frantic search for a specific piece of information you remember reading about. If CD-ROM versions are too much for your needs, be aware that you can access and search most major magazines on the Internet. This capability is valuable when you want to research everything you can about a specific subject.

One of the best kept secrets in the computer industry is the excellent trade magazines that offer free subscriptions. Although many of these magazines are directed toward the wholesale or technical end of the industry, I like to subscribe to them. Some of my favorite magazines in this category include the following:

- *Computer Design*
- *Computer Hotline*
- *Electronic News*
- *Computer Reseller News*
- *Electronic Products*
- *Electronic Design News*
- *Processor*
- *Electronic Buyer's News*
- *Service News*
- *Electronic Engineering Times*
- *Test and Measurement World*

Most of these magazines offer free subscriptions to anyone who qualifies. Aimed at people in the computer and electronics industries, these magazines offer a much greater depth and breadth of technical and industry information than the more "public" magazines that most people are familiar with. You'll find these and other recommended magazines on the CD.

Online Resources

With a modem, you can tie into everything from the Internet (World Wide Web) to local electronic bulletin board systems (BBSes) to major information networks such as CompuServe and AOL. Many hardware and software companies offer technical support and even software upgrades over the Internet. Through the Internet and other online resources, you can reach computer enthusiasts, technical-support people from various organizations, and experts in virtually all areas of computer hardware and software. You can also collect useful utility and help programs that can make your job much easier. The world of public-domain and user-supported software awaits, as does more technical information and related experiences than you can imagine.

The Vendor List not only includes the names, addresses, and voice phone numbers for companies, but also the Internet addresses (Web sites) or BBS numbers, where available. If you need more information on a vendor's products, or need technical support, try using the vendor's online connection. Many companies today provide online services to facilitate obtaining updated software or driver files that you can download quickly and easily. When a vendor provides an online connection, I consider that service a major advantage in comparison to other vendors who do not provide such a service. Using vendor-provided online connections either through the Internet or via a private BBS or even CompuServe has saved me money and countless hours of time.

In fact, the Internet is probably the most efficient method of reaching me. My email address is scottmueller@compuserve.com. If you have questions, a comment, or useful information you think I might be interested in, send me a message. Because of the extra steps in processing, my standard mail can get backed up, and it can take me quite a while to answer a regular postal letter. Electronic mail, however, involves fewer steps for me to send, and always seems to have a higher priority. If you do send a regular letter, be sure to include a SASE (self-addressed, stamped envelope) so I will be able to reply.

Seminars

Public and private seminars are a very valuable resource. This is, in fact, how I got my start writing; I teach PC hardware seminars, and I had to write a course book to go along with the seminars! Seminars are an excellent way to have information explained in person, often filling in gaps and adding visual information that isn't nearly as easy to present in a printed book alone.

Seminars come in two main types, public and on-site. A public course is just that, offered to the general public so anybody can sign up and attend. These are most often conducted in hotels or at specific training facilities around the country. On-site seminars are conducted at a particular company's location and only for employees of that company. These seminars are often customized to company's individual needs.

Machines

The term *machines* refers to the systems themselves—that is, hands-on experience. Actual experience on live systems is one of my best sources of information. For example, suppose that I need to answer the question "Will the XYZ SCSI host adapter work with the ABC tape drive?" The answer is as simple as plugging everything in and flipping the switch. (Simple to talk about, that is; actual testing can take quite a bit of time!)

Seriously, experimenting with and observing running systems are some of the best learning tools at your disposal. I recommend that you try everything; rarely will anything you try harm the equipment. Harming valuable data is definitely possible, if not likely, however, so make regular backups as insurance. You should not use a system you depend on for day-to-day operations as an experimental system; if possible, use a secondary machine. People sometimes are reluctant to experiment with systems that cost a lot of money, but much can be learned through direct tests and studies of the system. I often find that vendor claims about a product are somewhat misleading when I actually install it and run some tests. If you are unsure that something will really work, make sure that the company has a return policy that allows you to return the item for a refund if it does not meet your expectations.

Support people in larger companies have access to quantities of hardware and software I can only dream about. Some larger companies have toy stores where they regularly purchase equipment solely for evaluation and testing. Dealers and manufacturers also have access to an enormous variety of equipment. If you are in this position, take advantage of this access to equipment and learn from this resource. When new systems are purchased, take notes on their construction and components.

Every time I encounter a system I have not previously worked with, I immediately open it and start taking notes. I want to know the make and model of all the internal components, such as disk drives, power supplies, and motherboards. As far as motherboards are concerned, I like to record the numbers of the primary IC chips on the board, such as the processor (of course), integrated chipsets, floppy drive controller chips, keyboard controller chips, video chipsets, and any other major chips on the board. By knowing which chipset your system uses, you can often infer other capabilities of the system, such as enhanced setup or configuration capabilities.

I like to know which BIOS version is in the system, and I even make a copy of the BIOS on disk for backup and further study purposes. I want to know the hard drive tables from the BIOS, and any other particulars involved in setting up and installing a system. Write down the type of battery a system uses so that you can obtain spares. Note any unique brackets or construction techniques such as specialized hardware (Torx screws, for example) so that you can be prepared for servicing the system later. Some programs have been designed to help you maintain an inventory of systems and components, but I find that these fall far short of the detail I am talking about here.

This discussion brings up a pet peeve of mine. Nothing burns me up as much as reading a review of computer systems in a major magazine, in which reviewers test systems and produce benchmark and performance results for, let's say, the hard disks or video displays in a system. Then, they do not open up the machines and tell me (and the world) exactly which components the manufacturer of the system is using! I want to know exactly which disk controller, hard drive, BIOS, motherboard, video adapter, and so on are found in each system. Without this information, their review and benchmark tests are useless to me.

Then, these reviewers run a test of disk performance between two systems with the same disk controller and drives, and say (with a straight face) that the one that came out a few milliseconds ahead of the other wins the test. With the statistical variation that normally occurs in any manufactured components, these results are meaningless. The point is perhaps to be very careful of whom you trust in a normal magazine review. If it tells me exactly which components were tested, I can draw my own conclusions and even make comparisons to other systems not included in that review.

You can always search the Net for unbiased reviews written by individuals about a given product. Some products with poor support or reliability problems often have anti-product Web sites put up by disgruntled individuals. Although one person's experience with a product may not be indicative of the normal performance, when you see hundreds of messages or sites complaining about something, you usually get the idea. Similarly, you might also find great praise for a product, or messages indicating how people have found uses that are out of the ordinary.

CompTIA A+ Core Examination Objective Map

CompTIA is the organization that sets the objectives for the A+ certification. As with many computing fields, earning your certification can increase your job security or increase your value to prospective employers.

The A+ exam consists of two parts. The part that is most closely related to the topics in this book is the Core exam, which mostly covers hardware.

To become A+ certified, you must also pass the DOS/Windows Module exam. Although this book does cover many of the topics tested by the DOS/Windows module in the course of discussing hardware, this book does not pretend to be a thorough reference to DOS or Windows, so those objectives are not listed here. I highly recommend the *Upgrading and Repairing PCs: A+ Certification Study Guide* (ISBN: 0-7897-2095-7).

Tip

The CD-ROM that comes with this book includes test preparation software with 150 questions to help you prepare for the A+ Core exam. These 150 questions are part of a larger test prep program from Marcraft. Their complete program covers both components of the A+ exam and contains over 900 sample questions. For more information about this program and a special discount offer for purchasers of this book, see the page describing it near the end of the book.

The CompTIA organization has established the following objectives for the Core portion of the A+ Certification exam.

1.0 Installation, Configuration, and Upgrading

This section challenges the test taker to identify, install, configure, and upgrade microcomputer modules and peripherals. Established procedures for system assembly and disassembly must be followed. Test elements include the ability to identify and configure IRQs, DMAs, and I/O addresses, and to properly set configuration switches and jumpers.

1.1 Identify basic terms, concepts, and functions of system modules, including how each module should work during normal operation. Examples of concepts and modules include the following:

- System board
- Power supply
- CPU/microprocessor
- Memory
- Storage devices
- Monitor
- Modem
- Firmware
- Boot process
- BIOS
- CMOS

1.2 Identify basic procedures for adding and removing field-replaceable modules. Examples of modules include

- System board
- Power supply
- CPU/microprocessor
- Memory
- Storage devices
- Input devices

1.3 Identify available IRQs, DMAs, and I/O addresses with procedures for configuring them for device installation. Examples include

- Standard IRQ settings
- Modems
- Floppy disk drives
- Hard drives

1.4 Identify common peripheral ports, associated cables, and their connectors. Examples include

- Cable types
- Cable orientation
- Serial versus parallel
- Pin connections

Examples of connector types include

- DB-9
- DB-25
- RJ-11
- BNC
- RJ-45
- PS2/Mini-DIN

1.5 Identify proper procedures for installing and configuring IDE/EIDE devices. Examples include

- Master/slave
- Devices per channel

1.6 Identify proper procedures for installing and configuring SCSI devices. Topics include

- Address/termination conflicts
- Cabling
- Types (standard, wide, fast, ultra wide)
- Internal versus external
- Switch and jumper settings

1.7 Identify proper procedures for installing and configuring peripheral devices. Topics include

- Monitor/video card
- Modem
- Storage devices

1.8 Identify procedures for upgrading BIOS. Topics include

- Methods for upgrading
- When to upgrade

1.9 Identify hardware methods of system optimization and when to use them. Examples include

- Memory
- Hard drives
- CPU/microprocessors
- Cache memory

2.0 Diagnosing and Troubleshooting

This item requires the test taker to apply knowledge relating to diagnosing and troubleshooting common module problems and system malfunctions. This includes knowledge of the symptoms relating to common problems.

2.1 Identify common symptoms and problems associated with each module and how to troubleshoot and isolate the problems. Contents may include

- Processor/memory symptoms
- Keyboards/mouse/trackball/pen/microphones/touch pad
- Floppy drive failures
- Parallel ports/scanners/tape drives
- Hard drives
- Sounds card/audio
- Monitor/video
- Motherboards
- Modems
- BIOS
- CMOS
- Power supply
- Slot covers
- POST audible/visual error codes
- Troubleshooting tools; for example, multimeter

2.2 Identify basic troubleshooting procedures and good practices for eliciting problem symptoms from customers. Topics include

- Troubleshooting/isolation/problem determination
- Determine whether hardware or software problem

Gather information from the user regarding

- Customer environment
- Symptoms/error codes
- Situation when the problem occurred

3.0 Safety and Preventive Maintenance

This section requires the test taker to show knowledge of safety and preventive maintenance. With regard to safety, it includes the potential hazards to personnel and equipment when working with lasers, high-voltage equipment, ESD (Electrostatic Discharge), and items that require special disposal procedures that comply with environmental guidelines. With regard to preventive maintenance, this includes knowledge of preventive maintenance products, procedures, environmental hazards, and precautions when working on microcomputer systems.

3.1 Identify the purpose of various types of preventive maintenance products and procedures, and when to use or perform them. Examples include

- Liquid cleaning compounds
- Types of materials to clean contacts and connections
- Vacuum-out systems, power supplies, fans

3.2 Identify procedures and devices for protecting against environmental hazards. Examples include

- UPS (uninterruptible power supply)/suppressors/noise filters/plug strips
- Determining the signs of power issues
- Proper methods of component storage for future use

3.3 Identify the potential hazards and proper safety procedures relating to lasers and high-voltage equipment. Examples include

- Lasers can cause blindness.
- High-voltage equipment can cause electrocution; for example, power supply/CRT.

3.4 Identify items that require special disposal procedures that comply with environmental guidelines. Examples include

- Batteries
- Toner kits/cartridges
- Chemical solvents and cans
- CRTs
- MSDS (Material Safety Data Sheet)

3.5 Identify ESD (Electrostatic Discharge) precautions and procedures, including the use of ESD protection devices. Examples include

- What ESD can do, and how it may be apparent or hidden
- Common ESD protection devices
- Situations that could present a danger or hazard

4.0 Motherboard/Processors/Memory

This section requires the test taker to demonstrate knowledge of specific terminology, and facts, ways, and means of dealing with classifications, categories, and principles of motherboards, processors, and memory in microcomputer systems.

4.1 Distinguish between the popular CPU chips in terms of their basic characteristics. Popular CPU chips include

- Popular CPU chips

Characteristics include

- Physical size
- Voltage
- Speeds
- Onboard cache or not
- Sockets
- Number of pins

4.2 Identify the categories of RAM (Random Access Memory) terminology, their locations, and physical characteristics. Terminology includes

- EDO RAM (Extended Data Output RAM)
- DRAM (Dynamic Random Access Memory)
- SRAM (Static RAM)
- VRAM (Video RAM)
- WRAM (Windows Accelerator Card RAM)

Locations and physical characteristics include

- Memory bank
- Memory chips (8-bit, 16-bit, and 32-bit)
- SIMMS (Single Inline Memory Module)
- DIMMS (Dual Inline Memory Module)
- Parity chips versus non-parity chips

4.3 Identify the most popular type of motherboards, their components, and their architecture (for example, bus structures and power supplies).

Types of motherboards include

- AT (Full and Baby)
- ATX

Motherboard components include

- Communication ports
- SIMM and DIMM
- Processor sockets
- External cache memory (Level 2)

Bus architecture includes

- ISA
- EISA
- PCI
- USB (Universal Serial Bus)
- VESA local bus (VL-BUS)
- PC Card (PCMCIA)

Basic compatibility guidelines

4.4 Identify the purpose of CMOS (Complementary Metal-Oxide Semiconductor), what it contains, and how to change its basic parameters. Examples include

- Printer parallel port: Unidirectional/bidirectional, disable/enable, ECP/EPP
- COM/serial port: memory address, interrupt request, disable
- Hard drive: size and drive type
- Floppy drive: enable/disable drive or boot, speed, density
- Boot sequence
- Memory: parity, non-parity
- Date/time
- Passwords

5.0 Printers

This domain requires knowledge of basic types of printers, basic concepts, printer components, how they work, how they print onto a page, paper path, care and service techniques, and common problems.

5.1 Identify basic concepts, printer operations, printer components, and field-replaceable units in primary printer types.

Types of printers include

- Laser
- Inkjet
- Dot matrix

Paper feeder mechanisms

5.2 Identify care and service techniques and common problems with primary printer types. Examples include

- Feed and output
- Errors
- Paper jam
- Print quality
- Safety precautions
- Preventive maintenance

5.3 Identify the types of printer connections and configurations. Topics include

- Parallel
- Serial
- Network

6.0 Portable Systems

This section requires the test taker to demonstrate knowledge of portable computers and their unique components and problems.

6.1 Identify the unique components of portable systems and their unique problems. Examples include

- Battery
- LCD
- AC adapter
- Docking stations
- Hard drive
- Types I, II, III cards
- Network cards
- Memory

7.0 Basic Networking

This section requires the test taker to demonstrate knowledge of basic network concepts and terminology, ability to determine whether a computer is networked, knowledge of procedures for swapping and configuring network interface cards, and knowledge of the ramifications of repairs when a computer is networked.

7.1 Identify basic networking concepts, including how a network works. Examples include the following:

- Network access
- Protocol
- Network interface cards
- Full duplexing
- Cabling/twisted-pair, coaxial, fiber optic
- Ways to network a PC

7.2 Identify procedures for swapping and configuring network interface cards.

7.3 Identify ramifications of repairs on the network. Examples include

- Reduced bandwidth
- Loss of data
- Network slowdown

8.0 Customer Satisfaction

No one can underestimate the value and importance of customer satisfaction, especially personal computer repair technicians who must deal with customers who are often under stress because their computer has crashed. The CompTIA A+ Core exam has several objectives dealing with customer service. As important as this topic is, it is not covered in this book, which is really about the nuts and bolts of PC repair.

In Conclusion

Last year this book achieved a milestone in computer book publishing—that is, it had been published for over 10 years! This year marks the 11th anniversary of this book. This was the first book of its kind on the market, and it has since spawned an entire series of clone books from other competitors, many with surprisingly similar names. Despite the similar (in name only) competitor books, this is still the longest-running, best-selling, most popular book of its kind. Some may find it interesting to know that this book was previously published as my own seminar manual for several years prior to this incarnation, so it has been around in one form or another even longer than the edition number indicates.

No other book currently on the market contains such a complete and informative technical reference, which is one reason why so many large companies and educational institutions have standardized on this book for their technicians and students. This book is currently being used as an official textbook for many corporate and college-level computer training courses, as well as for my own PC training seminars, for which the book was originally designed.

I'd like to personally thank all the people who have supported the book over the years, especially those who have written with comments and suggestions.

I hope that *Upgrading and Repairing PCs, Eleventh Edition*, is beneficial to you; and I hope that you have enjoyed reading it as much as I have enjoyed writing it over the last 11 years. If you have questions about this book, or if you have ideas for future versions, I can be reached at the following address:

> Scott Mueller
>
> Mueller Technical Research
>
> 21 Spring Lane
>
> Barrington Hills, IL 60010-9009
>
> Phone: (847) 854-6794
>
> Fax: (847) 854-6795
>
> Email: scottmueller@compuserve.com
>
> Web Address: http://www.m-tr.com

Time constraints normally prevent me from responding to regular mail. If you do need a response through the mail, please include a self-addressed, stamped envelope so that I can reply to you. If you are interested in one of my many intensive PC training seminars or videotapes, please call my office.

Thank you again for reading this book. And a special thanks to those people who have been loyal readers since the first edition came out in December, 1988.

Sincerely,

Scott Mueller

Address	Description
elaine.teleport.com/%7Ecurt/modems.html	High speed modem FAQ
hardware.pairnet.com	Links to hardware news and reviews
infopad.eecs.berkeley.edu/CIC	CPU information
pclt.cis.yale.edu/pclt/PCHW/PLATYPUS.HTM	General overview of PC hardware technologies
tx.scitexdv.com/SCSI2/SCSI2.html	SCSI 2 specification
Web.idirect.com/~frank/index.html	Hard drive and CD-ROM specifications
www.56k.com	News and information on KFlex, X2, and v.90 standard modems
www.agpforum.org	AGP specifications and information
www.anandtech.com	Reviews of motherboards, processors, and more
www.atipa.com/InfoSheets/irqs.shtml	Troubleshooting COM and IRQ conflicts
www.cd-info.com	Compact disc development and production technology
www.chipanalyst.com/q/	Microprocessor design resources
www.chipset.com	Links to chipset vendor Web sites
www.cis.ohio-state.edu/hypertext/faq/usenet	SCSI FAQs from USENET/scsi-faq/top.html
www.cis.ohio-state.edu/hypertext/faq/usenet-faqs/bygroup/comp/sys/ibm/pc/hardware/top.html	Links to several hardware-related Usenet group FAQs
www.cpu-central.com	CPU specifications, information, and reviews
www.drivershq.com	Links to hardware drivers
www.driverupdate.com	Windows 95 and 3.1 hardware drivers
www.erols.com/chare/main.htm	Links to processors specifications and FAQs
www.firewire.org	FireWire specification and information
www.hardwarecentral.com	Reviews, FAQs, and more about most PC hardware components
www.heartlab.rri.uwo.ca/vidfaq/chipset.html	Video chipset FAQ
www.irda.org	Infrared technology standards
www.isdn.ocn.com	ISDN information and FAQs
www.itu.ch	International Telecommunication Union (standards body for modems and other telecommunications)
www.k56.org	Specifications on the KFlex version of 56K modems
www.lemig.umontreal.ca/bios/bios_sg.htm	The BIOS survival guide
www.motherboards.org	Motherboard reviews, tips, and performance comparisons
www.mrdriver.com	Links to hardware drivers for many operating systems
www.pc-card.com	PC Card and PCMCIA standards
www.pcengines.com/simm.htm	Memory buyer's guide
www.pcguide.com	General PC hardware information
www.pcisig.com	PCI specifications and developments
www.pcWebopedia.com	PC technology encyclopedia and search engine
www.ping.be/bios/numbers.shtml	Identifies BIOS by ID numbers
www.scsita.org	SCSI Trade Association's SCSI information
www.sig.net/~slogan/hardware.htm	Hardware advice, reviews, and links
www.sldram.com	Information on new SLDRAM memory technology
www.spa.org	MPC specifications
www.storagereview.com	Reviews and benchmarks of SCSI and ATA IDE hard drives
www.symbios.com/x3t10	I/O information, mainly about SCSI
www.sysopt.com	System optimization and performance with special emphasis on motherboards
www.teleport.com/~nlx/	NLX motherboard specifications
www.the-view.com	Hardware reviews and news

Address	Description
www.tomshardware.com	Reviews and analysis of motherboards, processors, video cards, and more
www.tweakit.oom	Reviews and performance comparisons of new hardware
www.twinight.org/chipdir/	Directory of chips, manufacturers, pinouts, and so on
www.usb.org	USB specifications and information
www.vesa.org	VESA standards
www.west.net/~jay/modem	Modem initialization strings
www.windrivers.com	Hardware drivers for all Windows versions
www.winfiles.com/drivers	Windows 95 hardware drivers
www.x86.org	"Secrets" about Intel processors and technologies
wwwcsif.cs.ucdavis.edu/~wen/intel.html	Guide to Intel chipsets

Glossary

This glossary contains computer and electronics terms that are applicable to the subject matter in this book. The glossary is meant to be as comprehensive as possible on the subject of upgrading or repairing PCs. Many terms correspond to the latest technology in disk interfaces, modems, video and display equipment, and standards that govern the PC industry. Although a glossary is a resource not designed to be read from beginning to end, you should find that scanning through this one is interesting, if not enlightening, with respect to some of the newer PC technology.

The computer industry is filled with acronyms used as shorthand for a number of terms. This glossary defines many acronyms, as well as the term on which the acronym is based. The definition of an acronym usually is included under the acronym. For example, Video Graphics Array is defined under the acronym VGA rather than under Video Graphics Array. This organization makes it easier to look up a term—IDE, for example—even if you do not know in advance what it stands for (Integrated Drive Electronics).

For additional reference, *Que's Computer Dictionary* (ISBN: 0-7897-1670-4) is a comprehensive dictionary of computer terminology.

These Web sites can also help you with terms that are not included in this glossary:

```
http://zeppo.cnet.com/Resources/Info/Glossary/
http://www-edlab.ucdavis.edu/ed180/hardwarepracticum.html
http://www.webopedia.com
```

.INF file   A Windows driver and device information file used to install new drivers or services.

100BaseT   A 100Mbps CSMA/CD Ethernet local area network (LAN) that works on Category 5 twisted-pair wiring. 100BaseT Ethernet LANs work on a "star" configuration in which the wire from each workstation routes directly to a central 100BaseT hub. This is the new standard for 100Mbps Ethernet.

100BaseVG   The joint Hewlett-Packard-AT&T proposal for Fast Ethernet running at 100Mbps. It uses four pairs of Category 5 cable using the 10BaseT twisted-pair wiring scheme to transmit or receive. 100BaseVG splits the signal across the four wire pairs at 25MHz each. This standard has not found favor with corporations and has been almost totally replaced by 100BaseT.

10Base2   IEEE standard for baseband Ethernet at 10Mbps over RG-58 coaxial cable to a maximum distance of 185 meters. Also known as Thin Ethernet (Thinnet) or IEEE 802.3.

10Base5   IEEE standard for baseband Ethernet at 10Mbps over thick coaxial cable to a maximum distance of 500 meters. Also known as Thick Ethernet or Thicknet.

10BaseT   A 10Mbps CSMA/CD Ethernet LAN that works on Category 3 or better twisted-pair wiring that is very similar to standard telephone cabling. 10BaseT Ethernet LANs work on a "star" configuration in which the wire from each workstation routes directly to a 10BaseT hub. Hubs may be joined together.

286   See *80286*.

386   See *80386*.

486   See *80486*.

56K   The generic term for modems that can receive data at 56Kbps. *See also* V.90, X2, Kflex.

586   A generic term used to refer to fifth-generation processors similar to the Intel Pentium.

640KB barrier   The limit imposed by the PC-compatible memory model using DOS mode. DOS programs can address only 1MB total memory, and PC-compatibility generally requires the top 384KB to be reserved for the system, leaving only the lower 640KB for DOS or other real-mode applications.

80286   An Intel microprocessor with 16-bit registers, a 16-bit data bus, and a 24-bit address bus. It can operate in both real and protected virtual modes.

80287   An Intel math coprocessor designed to perform floating-point math with much greater speed and precision than the main CPU. The 80287 can be installed in most 286- and some 386DX-based systems, and adds more than 50 new instructions to what is available in the primary CPU alone.

80386   See *80386DX*.

80386DX   An Intel microprocessor with 32-bit registers, a 32-bit data bus, and a 32-bit address bus. This processor can operate in real, protected virtual, and virtual real modes.

80386SX   An Intel microprocessor with 32-bit registers, a 16-bit data bus, and a 24-bit address bus. This processor, designed as a low-cost version of the 386DX, can operate in real, protected virtual, and virtual real modes.

80387   An Intel math coprocessor designed to perform floating-point math with much greater speed and precision than the main CPU. The 80387 can be installed in most 386DX-based systems, and adds more than 50 new instructions to those available in the primary CPU alone.

80486   See *80486DX*.

80486DX   An Intel microprocessor with 32-bit registers, a 32-bit data bus, and a 32-bit address bus. The 486DX has a built-in cache controller with 8KB of cache memory as well as a built-in math coprocessor equivalent to a 387DX. The 486DX can operate in real, protected virtual, and virtual real modes.

80486DX2   A version of the 486DX with an internal clock doubling circuit that causes the chip to run at twice the motherboard clock speed. If the motherboard clock is 33MHz, the DX2 chip will run at 66MHz. The DX2 designation applies to chips sold through the OEM market, while a retail version of the DX2 is sold as an overdrive processor.

80486DX4   A version of the 486DX with an internal clock tripling circuit that causes the chip to run at three times the motherboard clock speed. If the motherboard clock is 33.33MHz, the DX4 chip will run at 100MHz.

80486SX   An Intel microprocessor with 32-bit registers, a 32-bit data bus, and a 32-bit address bus. The 486SX is the same as the 486DX except that it lacks the built-in math coprocessor function, and was designed as a low-cost version of the 486DX. The 486SX can operate in real, protected virtual, and virtual real modes.

8086   An Intel microprocessor with 16-bit registers, a 16-bit data bus, and a 20-bit address bus. This processor can operate only in real mode.

8087   An Intel math coprocessor designed to perform floating-point math with much greater speed and precision than the main CPU. The 8087 can be installed in most 8086- and 8088-based systems, and adds more than 50 new instructions to those available in the primary CPU alone.

8088   An Intel microprocessor with 16-bit registers, an 8-bit data bus, and a 20-bit address bus. This processor can operate only in real mode, and was designed as a low-cost version of the 8086.

8514/A   An analog video display adapter from IBM for the PS/2 line of personal computers. Compared to previous display adapters such as EGA and VGA, it provides a high resolution of 1,024×768 pixels with as many as 256 colors or 64 shades of gray. It provides a video coprocessor that performs two-dimensional graphics functions internally, thus relieving the CPU of graphics tasks. It uses an interlaced monitor; it scans every other line every time the screen is refreshed.

abend   Short for abnormal end. A condition occurring when the execution of a program or task is terminated unexpectedly because of a bug or crash.

absolute address   An explicit identification of a memory location, device, or location within a device.

AC (Alternating current)   The frequency is measured in cycles per seconds (cps), or hertz (Hz). The standard value running through the wall outlet is 120 volts at 60Hz, through a fuse or circuit breaker that usually can handle about 15 or 20 amps.

accelerator board   An add-in board replacing the computer's CPU with circuitry that enables the system to run faster. See graphics accelerator.

access light   The LED on the front of a drive or other device (or on the front panel of the system) that indicates the computer is reading or writing data on the device.

access mechanism   See *actuator*.

access time   The time that elapses from the instant information is requested to the point that delivery is completed. Usually described in nanoseconds (ns) for memory chips, and in milliseconds (ms) for disk drives. Most manufacturers rate average access time on a hard disk as the time required for a seek across one third of the total number of cylinders plus one half of the time for a single revolution of the disk platters (latency).

accumulator   A register (temporary storage) in which the result of an operation is formed.

acoustic coupler   A device used to connect a computer modem to a phone line by connecting to the handset of a standard AT&T-style phone. The audible sounds to and from the modem are transmitted to the handset through the coupler while the handset is resting in the coupler. Although often thought of as obsolete, an acoustic coupler can be used to ensure the availability of a modem connection when traveling and access to an RJ-11 jack is unavailable.

ACPI (Advanced Configuration and Power Interface)   A standard developed by Intel, Microsoft, and Toshiba that is designed to implement power management functions in the operating system. ACPI is a replacement for APM. See also *APM*.

active high   Designates a digital signal that has to go to a high value to be true. Synonymous with positive.

active low   Designates a digital signal that has to go to a low value to be true. Synonymous with negative.

active matrix   A type of LCD screen that contains at least one transistor for every pixel on the screen. Color active-matrix screens use three transistors for each pixel, one each for the red, green, and blue dots. The transistors are arranged on a grid of conductive material, with each connected to a horizontal and a vertical member. See also *TFT*.

actuator   The device that moves a disk drive's read/write heads across the platter surfaces. Also known as an access mechanism.

adapter description files (ADF)   Refers to the setup and configuration files and drivers necessary to install an adapter card such as a network adapter card. Primarily used with Micro Channel Architecture bus cards.

adapter   The device that serves as an interface between the system unit and the devices attached to it. Often synonymous with circuit board, circuit card, or card, but may also refer to a connector or cable adapter, which changes one type of connector to another.

add-in board   See *expansion card.*

address   Refers to where a particular piece of data or other information is found in the computer. Also can refer to the location of a set of instructions.

address bus   One or more electrical conductors used to carry the binary-coded address from the microprocessor throughout the rest of the system.

ADSL (Asymmetric Digital Subscriber Line)   A high-speed transmission technology originally developed by Bellcore and now standardized by ANSI as T1.413. ADSL uses existing UTP copper wires to communicate digitally at high speed between the telephone company central office (CO) and the subscriber. ADSL sends information asymmetrically, meaning it is faster one way than the other. The original ADSL speed was T-1 (1.536Mbps) downstream from the carrier to the subscriber's premises and 16Kbps upstream. However, ADSL is available in a variety of configurations and speeds. See *DSL.*

AGP (Accelerated Graphics Port)   Developed by Intel, a fast dedicated interface between the video adapter or chipset and the motherboard chipset North Bridge. AGP is 32 bits wide, runs at 66MHz, and can transfer 1 or 2 bits per cycle (1x or 2x modes).

aliasing   Undesirable visual effects (sometimes called artifacts) in computer-generated images, caused by inadequate sampling techniques. The most common effect is jagged edges along diagonal or curved object boundaries. *See also* anti-aliasing.

allocation unit   See *cluster.*

alphanumeric characters   A character set that contains only letters (A–Z) and digits (0–9). Other characters, such as punctuation marks, may also be allowed.

ampere   The basic unit for measuring electrical current. Also called amp.

analog loopback   A modem self-test in which data from the keyboard is sent to the modem's transmitter, modulated into analog form, looped back to the receiver, demodulated into digital form, and returned to the screen for verification.

analog signals   Continuously variable signals. Analog circuits are more subject to distortion and noise than are digital circuits but are capable of handling complex signals with relatively simple circuitry. See also *digital signals.*

analog   The representation of numerical values by physical variables such as voltage, current, and so on; continuously variable quantities whose values correspond to the quantitative magnitude of the variables. See also *digital.*

analog-to-digital converter   An electronic device that converts analog signals to digital form.

AND   A logic operator having the property that if P is a statement, Q is a statement, R is a statement..., and then the AND of P, Q, R... is true if all statements are true and is false if any statement is false.

AND gate   A logic gate in which the output is 1 only if all inputs are 1.

animation   The process of displaying a sequential series of still images to achieve a motion effect.

ANSI (American National Standards Institute)   A nongovernmental organization founded in 1918 to propose, modify, approve, and publish data processing standards for voluntary use in the United States. Also the U.S. representative to the International Standards Organization (ISO) in Paris and the International Electrotechnical Commission (IEC). For more information, see the Vendor List on the CD. Contact ANSI, 1430 Broadway, New York, NY 10018.

answer mode   A state in which the modem transmits at the predefined high frequency of the communications channel and receives at the low frequency. The transmit/receive frequencies are the reverse of the calling modem, which is in originate mode. See also originate mode.

anti-aliasing   Software adjustment to make diagonal or curved lines appear smooth and continuous in computer-generated images. See also aliasing.

anti-static mat   A pad placed next to a computer upon which components are placed while servicing the system to prevent static damage. Also can refer to a larger sized mat below an entire computer desk and chair to discharge static from a user before he touches the computer.

antivirus   Software that prevents files containing viruses from running on a computer or software that detects, repairs, cleans, or removes virus-infected files.

APA   All points addressable. A mode in which all points of a displayable image can be controlled by the user or a program.

aperture grille   A type of shadow mask used in CRTs. The most common is used in Sony's Trinitron monitors, which use vertical phosphor stripes and vertical slots in the mask, compared to the traditional shadow mask that uses phosphor dots and round holes in the mask. See also shadow mask.

API (Application Program Interface)   A system call (routine) that gives programmers access to the services provided by the operating system. In IBM-compatible systems, the ROM BIOS and DOS together present an API that a programmer can use to control the system hardware.

APM (Advanced Power Management)   A specification sponsored by Intel and Microsoft originally proposed to extend the life of batteries in battery-powered computers. It is now used in desktop computers, as well. APM allows application programs, the system BIOS, and the hardware to work together to reduce power consumption. An APM-compliant BIOS provides built-in power management services to the operating system. The application software communicates power-saving data via predefined APM interfaces. Replaced in newer systems by ACPI. See also *ACPI*.

application   End-user oriented software such as a word processor, spreadsheet, database, graphics editor, game, or Web browser.

arbitration   A method by which multiple devices attached to a single bus can bid or arbitrate to get control of that bus.

archive bit   The bit in a file's attribute byte that sets the archive attribute. Tells whether the file has been changed since it last was backed up.

archive medium   A storage medium (floppy disk, tape cartridge, or removable cartridge) to hold files that need not be accessible instantly.

ARCnet (Attached Resource Computer Network)   A baseband, token-passing LAN technology offering a flexible bus/star topology for connecting personal computers. Operating at 2.5Mbit/sec, it is one of the oldest LAN systems and was popular in low-cost networks. Originally developed by John Murphy of Datapoint Corporation, although ARCnet interface cards are available from a variety of vendors.

areal density   A calculation of the bit density (bits per inch, or BPI) multiplied by the track density (tracks per inch, or TPI), which results in a figure indicating how many bits per square inch are present on the disk surface.

ARQ (Automatic repeat request)   A general term for error-control protocols that feature error detection and automatic retransmission of defective blocks of data.

ASCII (American Standard Code for Information Interchange)   A standard 7-bit code created in 1965 by Robert W. Bemer to achieve compatibility among various types of data processing equipment. The standard ASCII character set consists of 128 decimal numbers ranging from 0 through 127, which are assigned to letters, numbers, punctuation marks, and the most common special characters. In 1981, IBM introduced the extended ASCII character set with the IBM PC, extending the code to 8 bits and adding characters from 128 through 255 to represent additional special mathematical, graphics, and foreign characters.

ASCII character   A 1-byte character from the ASCII character set, including alphabetic and numeric characters, punctuation symbols, and various graphics characters.

ASME (American Society of Mechanical Engineers) (http://www.asme.org/)   ASME International has nearly 600 codes and standards in print, and its many committees involve more than 3,000 individuals, mostly engineers but not necessarily members of the society. The standards are used in more than 90 countries throughout the world.

aspect ratio   The measurement of a film or television viewing area in terms of relative height and width. The aspect ratio of most modern motion pictures varies between 3:5 to as large as 3:7, which creates a problem when a wide-format motion picture is transferred to the more square-shaped television screen, with its aspect ratio of 3:4.

assemble   The act of translating a program expressed in an assembler language into a computer machine language.

assembler language   A computer-oriented language whose instructions are usually in one-to-one correspondence with machine language instructions.

asymmetrical modulation   A duplex transmission technique that splits the communications channel into one high-speed channel and one slower channel. During a call under asymmetrical modulation, the modem with the greater amount of data to transmit is allocated the high-speed channel. The modem with less data is allocated the slow, or back, channel. The modems dynamically reverse the channels during a call if the volume of data transfer changes.

asynchronous communication   Data transmission in which the length of time between transmitted characters may vary. Timing is dependent on the actual time for the transfer to take place, as opposed to synchronous communication, which is timed rigidly by an external clock signal. Because the receiving modem must be signaled about when the data bits of a character begin and end, start and stop bits are added to each character. See also *synchronous communication*.

asynchronous memory   Memory that runs using a different timing or clock rate (usually slower) than the motherboard speed.

AT clock   Refers to the Motorola 146818 real-time clock (RTC) and CMOS RAM chip which first debuted in the IBM AT and whose function has been present in all PC-compatible systems since. Keeps track of the time of day and makes this data available to the operating system or other software.

ATA (AT Attachment interface)   An IDE disk interface standard introduced in March 1989 that defines a compatible register set and a 40-pin connector and its associated signals. See also *IDE*.

ATA-2   The second generation AT Attachment interface specification. This version defines faster transfer modes and logical block addressing schemes to allow high-performance large-capacity drives. Also called Fast ATA, Fast ATA-2, and enhanced IDE (EIDE).

ATAPI   AT Attachment Packet Interface   A specification that defines device-side characteristics for an IDE-connected peripheral, such as CD-ROM or tape drives. ATAPI is essentially an adaptation of the SCSI command set to the IDE interface.

ATM (Asynchronous Transfer Mode)   A high-bandwidth, low-delay, packet-like switching and multiplexing technique. Usable capacity is segmented into fixed-size cells consisting of header and information fields, allocated to services on demand.

attribute byte   A byte of information, held in the directory entry of any file, that describes various attributes of the file, such as whether it is read-only or has been backed up since it last was changed. Attributes can be set by the DOS ATTRIB command.

ATX   A motherboard and power supply form factor standard designed by Intel and introduced in 1995 that is characterized by a double row of rear external I/O connectors on the motherboard; a single keyed power supply connector; memory and processor locations that are designed not to interfere with the installation of adapter cards; and an improved cooling flow.

audio   A signal that can be heard, such as through the speaker of the PC. Many PC diagnostics tests use both visual (onscreen) codes and audio signals.

audio frequencies Frequencies that can be heard by the human ear (approximately 20–20,000Hz).

auto answer A setting in modems enabling them to answer incoming calls over the phone lines automatically.

auto dial A feature in modems enabling them to dial phone numbers without human intervention.

auto-disconnect A modem feature that allows a modem to hang up the telephone line when the modem at the other end hangs up.

AUTOEXEC.BAT A special batch file that DOS executes at startup. Contains any number of DOS commands that are executed automatically, including the capability to start programs at startup. See also batch file.

automatic head parking Disk drive head parking performed whenever the drive is powered off. Found in all modern hard disk drives with a voice-coil actuator.

auto-redial A modem or software feature that automatically redials the last number dialed if the number is busy or does not answer.

available memory Memory currently not in use by the operating system, drivers, or applications that may be used to load additional software.

average access time The average time it takes a disk drive to begin reading any data placed anywhere on the drive. This includes the average seek time, which is when the heads are moved, as well as the latency, which is the average amount of time required for any given data sector to pass underneath the heads. Together, these factors make up the average access time. See also *average seek time* and *latency*.

average latency The average time required for any byte of data stored on a disk to rotate under the disk drive's read/write head. Equal to one half the time required for a single rotation of a platter.

average seek time The average amount of time it takes to move the heads from one random cylinder location to another, usually including any head settling time. In many cases, the average seek time is defined as the seek time across one third of the total number of cylinders.

AVI (Audio Video Interleave) A storage technique developed by Microsoft for its Video for Windows product that combines audio and video into a single frame or track, saving valuable disk space and keeping audio in synchronization with the corresponding video.

backbone The portion of the Internet or wide area network (WAN) transmission wiring that connects the main Internet/WAN servers and routers and is responsible for carrying the bulk of the Internet/WAN data.

backplane A rarely used motherboard design in which the components normally found on a motherboard are located instead on an expansion adapter card plugged into a slot. In these systems, the board with the slots is the backplane.

backup disk   Contains information copied from another disk. Used to make sure that original information is not destroyed or altered.

backup   The process of duplicating a file or library onto a separate piece of media. Good insurance against the loss of an original.

backward compatibility   The design of software and hardware to work with previous versions of the same software or hardware.

bad sector   A disk sector that cannot hold data reliably because of a media flaw or damaged format markings.

bad track table   A label affixed to the casing of a hard disk drive that tells which tracks are flawed and cannot hold data. The listing is entered into the low-level formatting program.

balanced signal   Refers to signals consisting of equal currents moving in opposite directions. When balanced or nearly balanced signals pass through twisted-pair lines, the electromagnetic interference effects such as crosstalk caused by the two opposite currents largely cancel each other out. Differential signaling is a method that uses balanced signals.

balun   Short for balanced/unbalanced. A type of transformer that enables balanced cables to be joined with unbalanced cables. Twisted-pair (balanced) cables, for example, can be joined with coaxial (unbalanced) cables if the proper balun transformer is used.

bandwidth   1) Generally, the measure of the range of frequencies within a radiation band required to transmit a particular signal. The difference between the lowest and highest signal frequencies. The bandwidth of a computer monitor is a measure of the rate that a monitor can handle information from the display adapter. The wider the bandwidth, the more information the monitor can carry, and the greater the resolution. 2) Used to describe the data-carrying capacity of a given communications circuit or pathway. The bandwidth of a circuit is a measure of the rate at which information can be passed.

bank   The collection of memory chips or modules that make up a block of memory readable or writable by the processor in a single cycle. This block, therefore, must be as large as the data bus of the particular microprocessor. In PC systems, the processor data bus (and therefore the bank size) is usually 8, 16, 32, or 64 bits wide. Optionally, some systems also incorporate an additional parity or ECC bit for each 8 data bits, resulting in a total of 9, 18, 36, or 72 bits (respectively) for each bank. Memory in a PC must always be added or removed in full-bank increments.

bar code   The code used on consumer products and inventory parts for identification purposes. Consists of bars of varying thickness that represent characters and numerals that are read with an optical reader. The most common version is called the Universal Product Code (UPC).

base address   Starting location for consecutive string of memory or I/O addresses/ports.

base memory   The amount of memory available to the operating system or application programs within the first megabyte, accessible in the processor's real mode.

base-2 Refers to the computer numbering system that consists of two numerals: 0 and 1. Also called binary.

baseband transmission The transmission of digital signals over a limited distance. ARCnet and Ethernet local area networks use baseband signaling. Contrasts with broadband transmission, which refers to the transmission of analog signals over a greater distance.

BASIC (Beginner's All-purpose Symbolic Instruction Code) A popular computer programming language. Originally developed by John Kemeny and Thomas Kurtz in the mid-1960s at Dartmouth College. Normally, an interpretive language, meaning that each statement is translated and executed as it is encountered, but can be a compiled language, in which all the program statements are compiled before execution.

batch file A set of commands stored in a disk file for execution by the operating system. A special batch file called AUTOEXEC.BAT is executed by DOS each time the system is started. All DOS batch files have a BAT file extension.

baud A unit of signaling speed denoting the number of discrete signal elements that can be transmitted per second. The word baud is derived from the name of J.M.E. Baudot (1845–1903), a French pioneer in the field of printing telegraphy and the inventor of Baudot code. Although technically inaccurate, baud rate commonly is used to mean bit rate. Because each signal element or baud may translate into many individual bits, bits per second (bps) normally differs from baud rate. A rate of 2,400 baud means that 2,400 frequency or signal changes per second are being sent, but each frequency change may signal several bits of information. For example, 33.6Kbps modems actually transmit at only 2,400 baud.

Baudot code A 5-bit code used in many types of data communications, including teletype (TTY), radio teletype (RTTY), and telecommunications devices for the deaf (TDD). Baudot code has been revised and extended several times. See also *baud*.

bay An opening in a computer case or chassis that holds disk drives.

BBS (bulletin board system) A computer that operates with a program and a modem to enable other computers with modems to communicate with it, often on a round-the-clock basis. Thousands of PC IBM- and Apple-related BBSes offer a wealth of information and public-domain software that can be downloaded.

B-channel The two bearer channels in ISDN that run at 64Kbps each and that carry the data.

bezel A cosmetic panel that covers the face of a drive or some other device.

Bézier curve A mathematical method for describing a curve, often used in illustration and CAD programs to draw complex shapes.

bidirectional 1) Refers to lines over which data can move in two directions, such as a data bus or a telephone line. 2) Refers to the capability of a printer to print from right to left and from left to right alternately.

binary   Refers to the computer numbering system that consists of two numerals: 0 and 1. Also called base-2.

BIOS (basic input/output system)   The part of an operating system that handles the communications between the computer and its peripherals. Often burned into read-only memory (ROM) chips or rewritable flash (EEPROM) memory chips.

bipolar   A category of semiconductor circuit design, which was used to create the first transistor and the first integrated circuit. Bipolar and CMOS are the two major transistor technologies. Most all personal computers use CMOS technology chips. CMOS uses far less energy than bipolar.

bisynchronous (binary synchronous control)   An earlier protocol developed by IBM for software applications and communicating devices operating in synchronous environments. The protocol defines operations at the link level of communications—for example, the format of data frames exchanged between modems over a phone line.

bit Binary digit   Represented logically by 0 or 1 and electrically by 0 volts and (typically) 5 volts. Other methods are used to represent binary digits physically (tones, different voltages, lights, and so on), but the logic is always the same.

bit density   Expressed as bits per inch (BPI). Defines how many bits can be written onto one linear inch of a track. Sometimes also called linear density.

bit depth   The number of bits used to describe the color of each pixel on a computer display. For example, a bit depth of two means that the monitor can display only black and white pixels; a bit depth of four means the monitor can display 16 different colors; a bit depth of eight allows for 256 colors; and so on.

bit map   A method of storing graphics information in memory in which a bit devoted to each pixel (picture element) onscreen indicates whether that pixel is on or off. A bit map contains a bit for each point or dot on a video display screen and allows for fine resolution because any point or pixel onscreen can be addressed. A greater number of bits can be used to describe each pixel's color, intensity, and other display characteristics.

blank or blanking interval   A period in which no video signal is received by a monitor, while the videodisc or digital video player searches for the next video segment or frame to display.

block   A string of records, words, or characters formed for technical or logic reasons and to be treated as an entity.

block diagram   The logical structure or layout of a system in graphics form. Does not necessarily match the physical layout and does not specify all the components and their interconnections.

BMP   A Windows graphics format that may be device dependent or independent. Device-independent BMP files (DIB) are coded for translation to a wide variety of displays and printers.

BNC (Bayonet-Neill-Concelman)   Also known as British-Naval-Connector, Baby-N-Connector, or Bayonet-Nut-Coupler; nobody seems to be quite sure what the actual name is. This bayonet- locking connector is noted for its excellent shielding and impedance-matching characteristics, resulting in low noise and minimal signal loss at any frequency up to 4GHz. It is used in Ethernet 10Base2 networks (also known as IEEE 802.3, or Thinnet) to terminate coaxial cables. It is also used for some high-end video monitors.

bonding   In ISDN, joining two 64Kbps B-channels to achieve 128Kbps speed.

Boolean operation   Any operation in which each of the operands and the result take one of two values.

boot record   The first sector on a disk or partition that contains disk parameter information for the BIOS and operating system as well as bootstrap loader code that instructs the system how to load the operating system files into memory, thus beginning the initial boot sequence to boot the machine.

boot sector   See *boot record*.

boot sector virus   A virus designed to occupy the boot sector of a disk. Any attempt to start or boot a system from this disk will transfer the virus to the hard disk, after which it will subsequently be loaded every time the system is started. Most PC viruses are boot sector viruses.

boot   To load a program into the computer. The term comes from the phrase "pulling a boot on by the bootstrap."

bootstrap   A technique or device designed to bring itself into a desired state by means of its own action. The term is used to describe the process by which a device such as a PC goes from its initial power-on condition to a running condition without human intervention. See also *boot*.

boule   Purified, cylindrical silicon crystals from which semiconducting electronic chips including microprocessors, memory, and other chips in a PC are manufactured.

bps (bits per second)   The number of binary digits, or bits, transmitted per second. Sometimes confused with baud.

branch prediction   A feature of fifth-generation (Pentium and higher) processors that attempts to predict whether a program branch will be taken or not and then fetches the appropriate following instructions.

bridge   In local area networks, an interconnection between two similar networks. Also the hardware equipment used to establish such an interconnection.

broadband transmission   A term used to describe analog transmission. Requires modems for connecting terminals and computers to the network. Using frequency division multiplexing, many different signals or sets of data can be transmitted simultaneously. The alternate transmission scheme is baseband, or digital, transmission.

brownout   An AC supply voltage drop in which the power does not shut off entirely but continues to be supplied at lower than normal levels.

bubble memory A special type of nonvolatile read/write memory introduced by Intel in which magnetic regions are suspended in crystal film and data is maintained when the power is off. A typical bubble memory chip contains about 512KB, or more than four million bubbles. Bubble memory failed to catch on because of slow access times measured in several milliseconds. It has, however, found a niche use as solid-state "disk" emulators in environments where conventional drives are unacceptable, such as in military or factory use.

buffer A block of memory used as a holding tank to store data temporarily. Often positioned between a slower peripheral device and the faster computer. All data moving between the peripheral and the computer passes through the buffer. A buffer enables the data to be read from or written to the peripheral in larger chunks, which improves performance. A buffer that is x bytes in size usually holds the last x bytes of data that moved between the peripheral and CPU. This method contrasts with that of a cache, which adds intelligence to the buffer so that the most often accessed data rather than the last accessed data remains in the buffer (cache). A cache can improve performance greatly over a plain buffer.

bug An error or defect in a program.

burn-in The operation of a circuit or equipment to establish that its components are stable and to screen out defective ports or assemblies.

burst mode A memory cycling technology that takes advantage of the fact that most memory accesses are consecutive in nature. After setting up the row and column addresses for a given access, using burst mode can then access the next three adjacent addresses with no additional latency.

Burst Static RAMs (BSRAMs) Short for Pipeline Burst SRAM, BSRAMs are a common type of static RAM chip used for memory caches where access to subsequent memory locations after the first byte is accessed takes fewer machine cycles.

bus A linear electrical signal pathway over which power, data, and other signals travel. It is capable of connecting to three or more attachments. A bus is generally considered to be distinct from radial or point-to-point signal connections. The term comes from the Latin "omnibus" meaning "for all." When used to describe a topology, bus always implies a linear structure.

bus mouse An obsolete type of mouse used in the 1980s that plugs into a special mouse expansion board instead of a serial port or motherboard mouse port. The bus mouse connector looks like a motherboard mouse (sometimes called PS/2 mouse) connector, but the pin configurations are different and not compatible.

busmaster An intelligent device that when attached to the Micro Channel, EISA, VLB, or PCI bus can bid for and gain control of the bus to perform its specific task without processor intervention.

byte A collection of bits that makes up a character or other designation. Generally, a byte is 8 data bits. When referring to system RAM, an additional parity (error-checking) bit is also stored (see parity), making the total 9 bits.

C   A high-level computer programming language. A frequently used programming language on mainframes, minis, and PC computer systems. C++ is a popular variant.

cache   An intelligent buffer. By using an intelligent algorithm, a cache contains the data that is accessed most often between a slower peripheral device and the faster CPU. See also *L2 cache*, *L1 cache*, and *disk cache*.

CAM (Common Access Method)   A committee formed in 1988 that consists of a number of computer peripheral suppliers and is dedicated to developing standards for a common software interface between SCSI peripherals and host adapters.

capacitor   A device consisting of two plates separated by insulating material and designed to store an electrical charge.

card   A printed circuit board containing electronic components that form an entire circuit, usually designed to plug into a connector or slot. Sometimes also called an adapter.

card edge connector   See *edge connector*.

CardBus   A PC card specification for a 32-bit interface that runs at 33MHz and provides 32-bit data paths to the computer's I/O and memory systems, as well as a new shielded connector that prevents CardBus devices from being inserted into slots that do not support the latest version of the PC card standard.

carpal tunnel syndrome   A painful hand injury that gets its name from the narrow tunnel in the wrist that connects ligament and bone. When undue pressure is put on the tendons, they can swell and compress the median nerve, which carries impulses from the brain to the hand, causing numbness, weakness, tingling, and burning in the fingers and hands. Computer users get carpal tunnel syndrome primarily from improper keyboard ergonomics that result in undue strain on the wrist and hand.

carrier   A continuous frequency signal capable of being either modulated or impressed with another information-carrying signal. The reference signal used for the transmission or reception of data. The most common use of this signal with computers involves modem communications over phone lines. The carrier is used as a signal on which the information is superimposed.

carrier detect signal   A modem interface signal that indicates to the attached data terminal equipment (DTE) that it is receiving a signal from the distant modem. Defined in the RS-232 specification. Same as the received line-signal detector.

cathode ray tube (CRT)   A device that contains electrodes surrounded by a glass sphere or cylinder and displays information by creating a beam of electrons that strike a phosphor coating inside the display unit. This device is most commonly used in computer monitors and terminals.

CAV (Constant Angular Velocity)   An optical disk recording format where the data is recorded on the disk in concentric circles. CAV disks are rotated at a constant speed. This is similar to the recording technique used on floppy disk drives. CAV limits the total recorded capacity compared to CLV (Constant Linear Velocity), which is also used in optical recording.

CCITT An acronym for the Comit[ac]e Consultatif International de Télégraphique et Téléphonique (in English, the International Telegraph and Telephone Consultative Committee or the Consultative Committee for International Telegraph and Telephone). Renamed ITU (International Telecommunications Union). See *ITU*.

CCS (Common Command Set) A set of SCSI commands specified in the ANSI SCSI-1 Standard X3.131-1986 Addendum 4.B. All SCSI devices must be capable of using the CCS to be fully compatible with the ANSI SCSI-1 standard.

CD (compact disc or compact audio disc) A 4.75-inch (12cm) optical disc that contains information encoded digitally in the constant linear velocity (CLV) format. This popular format for high-fidelity music offers 90 decibels signal/noise ratio, 74 minutes of digital sound, and no degradation of quality from playback. The standards for this format (developed by NV Philips and Sony Corporation) are known as the Red Book. The official (and rarely used) designation for the audio-only format is CD-DA (compact disc-digital audio). The simple audio format is also known as CD-A (compact disc-audio). A smaller (3-inch) version of the CD is known as CD-3.

CD Video A CD format introduced in 1987 that combined 20 minutes of digital audio and 6 minutes of analog video on a standard 4.75-inch CD. Upon introduction, many firms renamed 8-inch and 12-inch videodiscs as CDV, in an attempt to capitalize on the consumer popularity of the audio CD. The term fell out of use in 1990 and was replaced in some part by laserdisc and more recently, DVD.

CD+G Compact Disc-Graphics A CD format that includes extended graphics capabilities as written into the original CD-ROM specifications. Includes limited video graphics encoded into the CD subcode area. Developed and marketed by Warner New Media.

CD+MIDI (Compact Disc-Musical Instrument Digital Interface) A CD format that adds to the CD+G format digital audio, graphics information, and musical instrument digital interface (MIDI) specifications and capabilities. Developed and marketed by Warner New Media.

CD-DA (Compact Disc Digital Audio) Also known as Red Book Audio and is the digital sound format used by audio CDs. CD-DA uses a sampling rate of 44.1KHz and stores 16 bits of information for each sample. CD audio is not played through the computer, but through a special chip in the CD-ROM drive. Fifteen minutes of CD-DA sound can require about 80MB. The highest quality sound that can be used by multimedia PC is the CD-DA format at 44.1KHz sample rate. See *CD*.

CD-I (Compact Disc-Interactive) A compact disc format released in October 1991 that provides audio, digital data, still graphics, and motion video. The standards for this format (developed by NV Philips and Sony Corporation) are known as the Green Book. CD-I did not catch on with consumers and is now considered obsolete.

CD-R (Compact Disc-Recordable, sometimes also called CD-Writable) CD-R disks are compact discs that can be recorded and read as many times as desired. CD-R is part of the Orange Book Standard defined by ISO. CD-R technology is used for mass production of multimedia applications. CD-R discs can be compatible with CD-ROM, CD-ROM XA, and CD audio. Orange Book specifies multi-session capabilities, which allow data recording on the disc at different times in several recording sessions. Kodak's Photo CD is an example of CD-R technology and fits up to 100 digital photographs on a single CD. Multi-session capability allows several rolls of 35mm film to be added to a single disc on different occasions.

CD-ROM (Compact Disc-Read Only Memory)   A 4.75-inch laser-encoded optical memory storage medium with the same constant linear velocity (CLV) spiral format as audio CDs and some videodiscs, CD-ROMs can hold about 650MB of data. CD-ROMs require more error-correction information than the standard prerecorded compact audio disc. The standards for this format (developed by NV Philips and Sony Corporation) are known as the Yellow Book. See also *CD-ROM XA*.

CD-ROM drive   A device that retrieves data from a CD-ROM disc; differs from a standard audio CD player by the incorporation of additional error-correction circuitry. CD-ROM drives usually can also play music from audio CDs.

CD-ROM XA (Compact Disc-Read Only Memory eXtended Architecture)   The XA standard was developed jointly by Sony, Philips, and Microsoft in 1988 and is now part of the Yellow Book standard. XA is a built-in feature of newer CD-ROM drives, and supports simultaneous sound playback with data transfer. Non-XA drives support either sound playback or data transfer, but not both simultaneously. XA also provides for data compression right on the disk, which can also increase data transfer rates.

CD-RW (Compact Disc-ReWritable)   A type of rewritable CD-ROM technology defined in Part III of the Orange Book standard that uses a different type of disc that the drive can rewrite at least one thousand times. CD-RW drives can also be used to write CD-R discs, and they can read CD-ROMs. CD-RWs have a lower reflectivity than standard CD-ROMs, and CD-ROM drives must be of the newer multiread variety to read them. CD-RW was initially known as CD-E (for CD-Erasable).

CD-WO (Compact Disc-Write Once)   A variant on CD-ROM that can be written to once and read many times; developed by NV Philips and Sony Corporation. Also known as CD-WORM (CD-write once/read many), CD-Recordable, or CD-Writable. Standards for this format are known as the Orange Book.

CD-WORM   See *CD-WO*.

Centronics connector   Refers to one of two types of cable connectors used with either parallel or SCSI devices.

ceramic substrate   A thin, flat, fired ceramic part used to hold an IC chip (usually made of beryllium oxide or aluminum oxide).

CERN Conseil Européen pour la Recherche Nucléaire (The European Laboratory for Particle Physics)   The site in Geneva where the World Wide Web was created in 1989.

CGA (Color Graphics Adapter)   A type of PC video display adapter introduced by IBM on August 12, 1981, that supports text and graphics. Text is supported at a maximum resolution of

80×25 characters in 16 colors with a character box of 8×8 pixels. Graphics is supported at a maximum resolution of 320×200 pixels in 16 colors or 640×200 pixels in two colors. The CGA outputs a TTL (digital) signal with a horizontal scanning frequency of 15.75KHz, and supports TTL color or NTSC composite displays.

channel   1) Any path along which signals can be sent. 2) In ISDN, data bandwidth is divided into two B-channels that bear data and one D-channel that carries information about the call.

character   A representation, coded in binary digits, of a letter, number, or other symbol.

character set   All the letters, numbers, and characters that a computer can use to represent data. The ASCII standard has 256 characters, each represented by a binary number from 1 to 256. The ASCII set includes all the letters in the alphabet, numbers, most punctuation marks, some mathematical symbols, and other characters.

charge coupled device   A light sensing and storage device used in scanners and digital cameras to capture the pixels.

check bit   See *parity*.

checksum   Short for summation check, a technique for determining whether a package of data is valid. The package, a string of binary digits, is added up and compared with the expected number.

chip   Another name for an IC, or integrated circuit. Housed in a plastic or ceramic carrier device with pins for making electrical connections.

chip carrier   A ceramic or plastic package that carries an integrated circuit.

chipset   A single chip or pair of chips that integrates into it the clock generator, bus controller, system timer, interrupt controller, DMA controller, CMOS RAM/clock, and keyboard controller. See also *North Bridge* and *South Bridge*.

CHS (Cylinder Head Sector)   The term used to describe the nontranslating scheme used by the BIOS to access IDE drives that are less than or equal to 528MB in capacity. See *LBA*.

CIF (Common Image Format)   The standard sample structure that represents the picture information of a single frame in digital HDTV, independent of frame rate and sync/blank structure. The uncompressed bit rate for transmitting CIF at 29.97 frames/sec is 36.45Mbps.

circuit   A complete electronic path.

circuit board   The collection of circuits gathered on a sheet of plastic, usually with all contacts made through a strip of pins. The circuit board usually is made by chemically etching metal-coated plastic.

CISC (Complex Instruction Set Computer)   Refers to traditional computers that operate with large sets of processor instructions. Most modern computers, including the Intel 80xxx processors, are in this category. CISC processors have expanded instruction sets that are complex in nature and require several to many execution cycles to complete. This structure contrasts with

RISC (reduced instruction set computer) processors, which have far fewer instructions that execute quickly.

clean room   1) A dust-free room in which certain electronic components (such as chips or hard disk drives) must be manufactured and serviced to prevent contamination. Rooms are rated by Class numbers. A Class 100 clean room must have fewer than 100 particles larger than 0.5 microns per cubic foot of space. 2) A legal approach to copying software or hardware where one team analyzes the product and writes a detailed description, followed by a second team who reads the description written by the first and who then develops a compatible version of the product. When done correctly, such a design methodology will survive a legal attack.

client/server   A type of network in which every computer is either a server with a defined role of sharing resources with clients or a client that can access the resources on the server.

clock multiplier   A processor feature where the internal core runs at a higher speed than the motherboard or processor bus. See also *overclocking*.

clock speed   A measurement of the rate at which the clock signal for a device oscillates, usually expressed in millions of cycles per second (MHz).

clock   The source of a computer's timing signals. Synchronizes every operation of the CPU.

clone   Originally referred to an IBM-compatible computer system that physically as well as electrically emulates the design of one of IBM's personal computer systems. More currently, it refers to any PC system running an Intel or compatible processor in the 80x86 family.

cluster   Also called allocation unit. A group of one or more sectors on a disk that forms a fundamental unit of storage to the operating system. Cluster or allocation unit size is determined by the operating system when the disk is formatted. Larger clusters generally offer faster system performance but waste disk space.

CLV (Constant Linear Velocity)   An optical recording format where the spacing of data is consistent throughout the disk, and the rotational speed of the disk varies depending on what track is being read. Additionally, more sectors of data are placed on the outer tracks compared to the inner tracks of the disk, which is similar to zone recording on hard drives. CLV drives will adjust the rotational speed to maintain a constant track velocity as the diameter of the track changes. CLV drives rotate faster near the center of the disk and slower toward the edge. Rotational adjustment maximizes the amount of data that can be stored on a disk. CD audio and CD-ROM use CLV recording.

CMOS (complementary metal-oxide semiconductor)   A type of chip design that requires little power to operate. In PCs, a battery-powered CMOS memory and clock chip is used to store and maintain the clock setting and system configuration information.

CMYK (Cyan Magenta Yellow Black)   The standard four-color model used for printing.

coated media   Hard disk platters coated with a reddish iron-oxide medium on which data is recorded.

coaxial cable   Also called coax cable. A data-transmission medium noted for its wide bandwidth, immunity to interference, and high cost compared to other types of cable. Signals are transmitted inside a fully shielded environment, in which an inner conductor is surrounded by a solid insulating material and then an outer conductor or shield. Used in many local area network systems such as Ethernet and ARCnet.

COBOL (Common Business-Oriented Language)   A high-level computer programming language primarily used by some larger companies. It has never achieved popularity on personal and small business computers.

code page   A table used in DOS 3.3 and later that sets up the keyboard and display characters for various foreign languages.

code page switching   A DOS feature in versions 3.3 and later that changes the characters displayed onscreen or printed on an output device. Primarily used to support foreign-language characters. Requires an EGA or better video system and an IBM-compatible graphics printer.

CODEC (CODer-DECoder)   A device that converts voice signals from their analog form to digital signals acceptable to more modern digital PBXs and digital transmission systems. It then converts those digital signals back to analog so that you may hear and understand what the other party is saying.

coercivity   A measurement in units of oersteds of the amount of magnetic energy to switch or "coerce" the flux change in the magnetic recording media. High-coercivity disk media requires a stronger write current.

cold boot   Starting or restarting a computer by resetting or turning on the power supply. See also *warm boot*.

collision detection/avoidance   A process used on a LAN to prevent data packets from interfering with each other and to determine whether data packets have encountered a collision and initiate a resend of the affected packets.

collision   In a LAN, if two computers transmit a packet of data at the same time on the network, the data may become garbled, which is known as a collision.

Color Graphics Adapter   See *CGA*.

color palette   The colors available to a graphics adapter for display.

COM port   A serial port on a PC that conforms to the RS-232 standard. See also *RS-232*.

COMDEX   The largest international computer trade show and conference in the world. COMDEX/Fall is held in Las Vegas during October, and COMDEX/Spring usually is held in Chicago or Atlanta during April.

command   An instruction that tells the computer to start, stop, or continue an operation.

command interpreter   The operating system program that controls a computer's shell or user interface. The command interpreter for MS-DOS is COMMAND.COM. The command interpreter for Windows is WIN.COM.

COMMAND.COM   An operating system file that is loaded last when the computer is booted. The command interpreter or user interface and program-loader portion of DOS.

common mode noise   Noise or electrical disturbances that can be measured between a current- or signal-carrying line and its associated ground. Common mode noise is frequently introduced to signals between separate computer equipment components through the power distribution circuits. It can be a problem when single-ended signals are used to connect different equipment or components that are powered by different circuits.

common   The ground or return path for an electrical signal. If a wire, it usually is colored black.

CompactFlash   An ATA flash memory card physical format that is approximately one third the size of a standard PC card. Often abbreviated CF, CompactFlash cards are identical in function to standard ATA Flash PC cards, but use 50 pin connectors instead of 68. ATA flash cards contain built-in disk controller circuitry to enable the card to function as a solid-state disk drive. CF cards can plug into a CompactFlash socket or with an adapter into a standard Type I or II PC-card slot.

compatible   1) In the early days of the PC industry when IBM dominated the market, a term used to refer to computers from other manufacturers that had the same features as a given IBM model. 2) In general, software or hardware that conforms to industry standards or other de facto standards so that it can be used in conjunction with or in lieu of other versions of software or hardware from other vendors in a like manner.

compiler   A program that translates a program written in a high-level language into its equivalent machine language. The output from a compiler is called an object program.

complete backup   A backup of all information on a hard disk, including the directory tree structure.

composite video   Television picture information and sync pulses combined. The complete wave form of the color video signal composed of chrominance and luminance picture information; blanking pedestal; field, line, and color sync pulses; and field equalizing pulses. Some video cards have an RCA jack that outputs a composite video signal. See also *RGB*.

compressed file   A file that has been reduced in size via one or more compression techniques.

computer   Device capable of accepting data, applying prescribed processes to this data, and displaying the results or information produced.

computer-based training (CBT)   The use of a computer to deliver instruction or training; also known as Computer-Aided (or Assisted) Instruction (CAI), Computer-Aided Learning (CAL), Computer-Based Instruction (CBI), and Computer-Based Learning (CBL).

CONFIG.SYS   A file that can be created to tell DOS how to configure itself when the machine starts up. Can load device drivers, set the number of DOS buffers, and so on.

configuration file   A file kept by application software to record various aspects of the software's configuration, such as the printer it uses.

console   The unit, such as a terminal or a keyboard, in your system with which you communicate with the computer.

contiguous   Touching or joined at the edge or boundary, in one piece.

continuity   In electronics, an unbroken pathway. Testing for continuity normally means testing to determine whether a wire or other conductor is complete and unbroken (by measuring 0 ohms). A broken wire shows infinite resistance (or infinite ohms).

control cable   The wider of the two cables that connect an ST-506/412 or ESDI hard disk drive to a controller card. A 34-pin cable that carries commands and acknowledgments between the drive and controller.

controller card   An adapter holding the control electronics for one or more devices such as hard disks. Ordinarily occupies one of the computer's slots.

controller   The electronics that control a device such as a hard disk drive and intermediate the passage of data between the device and the computer.

conventional memory   The first megabyte or first 640KB of system memory accessible by an Intel processor in real mode. Sometimes called base memory.

convergence   Describes the capability of a color monitor to focus the three colored electron beams on a single point. Poor convergence causes the characters onscreen to appear fuzzy and can cause headaches and eyestrain.

coprocessor   An additional computer processing unit designed to handle specific tasks in conjunction with the main or central processing unit.

copy protection   A hardware or software scheme to prohibit making illegal copies of a program.

core   An "old-fashioned" term for computer memory.

core speed   The internal speed of a processor. With all modern processors, this speed is faster than the system bus speed and that speed relationship is regulated by the clock multiplier in the processor.

CP/M (Control Program for Microcomputers, originally Control Program/Monitor)   An operating system created by Gary Kildall, the founder of Digital Research. Created for the old 8-bit microcomputers that used the 8080, 8085, and Z-80 microprocessors. Was the dominant operating system in the late 1970s and early 1980s for small computers used in a business environment.

cps (Characters per second)   A data transfer rate generally estimated from the bit rate and the character length. At 2,400bps, for example, 8-bit characters with start and stop bits (for a total of 10 bits per character) are transmitted at a rate of approximately 240cps. Some protocols, such as V.42 and MNP, employ advanced techniques such as longer transmission frames and data compression to increase characters per second.

CPU (Central Processing Unit)   The computer's microprocessor chip; the brains of the outfit. Typically, an IC using VLSI (very-large-scale integration) technology to pack several different functions into a tiny area. The most common electronic device in the CPU is the transistor, of which several thousand to several million or more are found.

crash   A malfunction that brings work to a halt. A system crash usually is caused by a software malfunction, and ordinarily you can restart the system by rebooting the machine. A head crash, however, entails physical damage to a disk and probable data loss.

CRC (Cyclic Redundancy Checking)   An error-detection technique consisting of a cyclic algorithm performed on each block or frame of data by both sending and receiving modems. The sending modem inserts the results of its computation in each data block in the form of a CRC code. The receiving modem compares its results with the received CRC code and responds with either a positive or negative acknowledgment. In the ARQ protocol implemented in high-speed modems, the receiving modem accepts no more data until a defective block is received correctly.

crosstalk   The electromagnetic coupling of a signal on one line with another nearby signal line. Crosstalk is caused by electromagnetic induction, where a signal traveling through a wire creates a magnetic field that induces a current in other nearby wires.

CRT (cathode-ray tube)   A term used to describe a television or monitor screen tube.

current   The flow of electrons, measured in amperes, or amps.

cursor   The small flashing hyphen that appears onscreen to indicate the point at which any input from the keyboard will be placed.

cycle   Time for a signal to transition from leading edge to the next leading edge.

cyclic redundancy checking   See *CRC*.

cylinder   The set of tracks on a disk that are on each side of all the disk platters in a stack and are the same distance from the center of the disk. The total number of tracks that can be read without moving the heads. A floppy drive with two heads usually has 160 tracks, which are accessible as 80 cylinders. A typical 4GB hard disk has 10 platters with 20 heads (19 for data and one servo head) and 4,000 cylinders, in which each cylinder is composed of 19 tracks.

D/A Converter (DAC)   A device that converts digital signals to analog form.

daisy chain   Stringing up components in such a manner that the signals move serially from one to the other. Most microcomputer multiple disk drive systems are daisy-chained. The SCSI bus system is a daisy-chain arrangement, in which the signals move from computer to disk drives to tape units, and so on.

daisywheel printer   An impact printer that prints fully formed characters one at a time by rotating a circular print element composed of a series of individual spokes, each containing two characters that radiate from a center hub. Produces letter-quality output.

DAT (Digital Audio Tape)   A small cassette containing 4mm-wide tape used for storing large amounts of digital information. DAT technology emerged in Europe and Japan in 1986 as a way to produce high-quality, digital audio recordings and was modified in 1988 to conform to the

DDS (digital data storage) standard for storing computer data. Raw capacities for a single tape are 2GB for DDS, 4GB for DDS-2, and 12GB for DDS-3, with double that for compressed data.

data 1) Groups of facts processed into information. A graphic or textural representation of facts, concepts, numbers, letters, symbols, or instructions used for communication or processing. 2) An android from the 24th century with a processing speed of 60 trillion operations per second and a storage capacity of 800 quadrillion bits, and who serves on the USS Enterprise NCC-1701-D with the rank of lieutenant commander.

data bus The connection that transmits data between the processor and the rest of the system. The width of the data bus defines the number of data bits that can be moved into or out of the processor in one cycle.

data cable Generically, a cable that carries data. Specific to HD connections, the narrower (20 pin) of two cables that connects an ST-506/412 or ESDI hard disk drive to a controller card.

data communications A type of communication in which computers and terminals can exchange data over an electronic medium.

data compression A technique where mathematical algorithms are applied to the data in a file to eliminate redundancies and therefore reduce the size of the file. See *lossy compression* and *lossless compression.*

data link layer In networking, the layer of the OSI reference model that controls how the electrical impulses enter or leave the network cable. Ethernet and Token Ring are the two most common examples of data link layer protocols.

data separator A device that separates data and clock signals from a single encoded signal pattern. Usually, the same device does both data separation and combination and is sometimes called an endec, or encoder/decoder.

data transfer rate The maximum rate at which data can be transferred from one device to another.

daughterboard Add-on board to increase functionality and/or memory. Attaches to existing board.

DB-25 25-pin D-shell connector, primarily used for PC parallel ports.

DB-9 9-pin D-shell connector, primarily used for PC serial ports.

DC Direct current, such as that provided by a power supply or batteries.

DC-600 (Data Cartridge 600) a data-storage medium invented by 3MB in 1971 that uses a quarter-inch-wide tape 600 feet in length.

DCE (Data Communications Equipment) The hardware that performs the communication—usually a dial-up modem that establishes and controls the data link through the telephone network. See also *DTE.*

D-channel   In ISDN, a 16Kbps channel that is used to transmit control data about a connection.

DDE (Dynamic Data Exchange)   A form of interprocess communications used by Microsoft Windows to support the exchange of commands and data between two applications running simultaneously. This capability has been enhanced further with object linking and embedding (OLE).

de facto standard   A software or hardware technology that is not officially made a standard by any recognized standards organization but that is used as a reference for consumers and vendors due to its dominance in the marketplace.

DEBUG   The name of a utility program included with DOS used for specialized purposes such as altering memory locations, tracing program execution, patching programs and disk sectors, and performing other low-level tasks.

decibel (dB)   A logarithmic measure of the ratio between two powers, voltages, currents, sound intensities, and so on. Signal-to-noise ratios are expressed in decibels.

dedicated line   A user-installed telephone line that connects a specified number of computers or terminals within a limited area, such as a single building. The line is a cable rather than a public-access telephone line. The communications channel also may be referred to as nonswitched because calls do not go through telephone company switching equipment.

dedicated servo surface   In voice-coil-actuated hard disk drives, one side of one platter given over to servo data that is used to guide and position the read/write heads.

default   Any setting assumed at startup or reset by the computer's software and attached devices and operational until changed by the user. An assumption the computer makes when no other parameters are specified. When you type DIR without specifying the drive to search, for example, the computer assumes that you want it to search the default drive. The term is used in software to describe any action the computer or program takes on its own with embedded values.

defect map   A list of unusable sectors and tracks coded onto a drive during the low-level format process.

defragmentation   The process of rearranging disk sectors so files are stored on consecutive sectors in adjacent tracks.

degauss   1) To remove magnetic charges, or to erase magnetic images. Normal applications include monitors and disks or tapes. Most monitors incorporate a degaussing coil, which surrounds the CRT, and automatically energize this coil for a few seconds when powered up to remove color or image distorting magnetic fields from the metal mask inside the tube. Some monitors include a button or control that can be used for additional applications of this coil to remove more stubborn magnetic traces. 2) Also the act of erasing or demagnetizing a magnetic disk or tape using a special tool called a degaussing coil.

density   The amount of data that can be packed into a certain area on a specific storage media.

desktop   A personal computer that sits on a desk.

device driver   A memory-resident program loaded by CONFIG.SYS that controls an unusual device, such as an expanded memory board.

Dhrystone   A benchmark program used as a standard figure of merit indicating aspects of a computer system's performance in areas other than floating-point math performance. Because the program does not use any floating-point operations, performs no I/O, and makes no operating system calls, it is most useful for measuring the processor performance of a system. The original Dhrystone program was developed in 1984 and was written in Ada, although the C and Pascal versions became more popular by 1989.

diagnostics   Programs used to check the operation of a computer system. These programs enable the operator to check the entire system for any problems and to indicate in what area the problems lie.

dial-up adapter   In Windows 9x, a software program that uses a modem to emulate a network interface card for networking. Most commonly used to connect to an Internet service provider or a dial-up server for remote access to a LAN.

die   An individual chip (processor, RAM, or other integrated circuit) cut from a finished silicon chip wafer and built into the physical package that will connect it to the rest of the PC or a circuit board.

differential   An electrical signaling method where a pair of lines are used for each signal in "push-pull" fashion. In most cases, differential signals are balanced so that the same current flows on each line in opposite directions. This is unlike single-ended signals, which use only one line per signal referenced to a single ground. Differential signals have a large tolerance for common-mode noise and little crosstalk when used with twisted-pair wires even in long cables. Differential signaling is expensive because two pins are required for each signal.

digital loopback   A test that checks the modem's RS-232 interface and the cable that connects the terminal or computer and the modem. The modem receives data (in the form of digital signals) from the computer or terminal and immediately returns the data to the screen for verification.

digital signals   Discrete, uniform signals. In this book, the term refers to the binary digits 0 and 1.

digitize   To transform an analog wave to a digital signal that a computer can store. Conversion to digital data and back is performed by a Digital to Analog Converter (DAC), often a single-chip device. How closely a digitized sample represents an analog wave depends on the number of times the amplitude of a wave is measured and recorded (the rate of digitization) as well as the number of different levels that can be specified at each instance. The number of possible signal levels is dictated by the resolution in bits.

DIMM (Dual Inline Memory Module)   A 64-bit wide, 168-pin memory module used in Pentium and newer PCs. They are available in several versions, including 5v or 3v, buffered or unbuffered, with FPM/EDO or SDRAM memory, and in 64-bit (non-ECC/parity) or 72-bit (ECC/parity) form.

Most Pentium and newer PCs require 3.3v unbuffered SDRAM DIMMs in either non-ECC or ECC versions (ECC recommended).

DIP (Dual Inline Package)   A family of rectangular, integrated-circuit flat packages that have leads on the two longer sides. Package material is plastic or ceramic.

DIP switch   A tiny switch (or group of switches) on a circuit board. Named for the form factor of the carrier device in which the switch is housed.

direct memory access (DMA)   A process by which data moves between a disk drive (or other device) and system memory without direct control of the central processing unit, thus freeing it up for other tasks.

Direct Rambus DRAM   See *RDRAM*.

directory   An area of a disk that stores the titles given to the files saved on the disk and serves as a table of contents for those files. Contains data that identifies the name of a file, the size, the attributes (system, hidden, read-only, and so on), the date and time of creation, and a pointer to the location of the file. Each entry in a directory is 32 bytes long.

disc   Flat, circular, rotating medium that can store various types of information, both analog and digital. "Disc" is often used in reference to optical storage media, while "disk" refers to magnetic storage media. Disc is often used as a short form for videodisc or compact audio disc (CD).

disk access time   See *access time*.

disk   Alternative spelling for "disc" that generally refers to magnetic storage medium on which information can be accessed at random. Floppy disks and hard disks are examples.

disk cache   A portion of memory on the PC motherboard or on a drive interface card or controller used to store frequently accessed information from the drive (such as the file allocation table (FAT) or directory structure) to speed up disk access. With a larger disk cache, additional data from the data portion of a drive can be cached as well. See also cache, L1 cache, and L2 cache.

disk partition   See *partition*.

display adapter   The interface between the computer and the monitor that transmits the signals that appear as images on the display. This can take the form of an expansion card or a chip built into the motherboard.

dithering   The process of creating more colors and shades from a given color palette. In monochrome displays or printers, dithering will vary the black and white dot patterns to simulate shades of gray. Grayscale dithering is used to produce different shades of gray when the device can only produce limited levels of black or white outputs. Color screens or printers use dithering to create additional colors by mixing and varying the dot sizing and spacing. For example, when converting from 24-bit color to 8-bit color (an 8-bit palette has only 256 colors compared to the 24-bit palette's millions), dithering adds pixels of different colors to simulate the original color. Dithering is also known as error diffusion.

DLL (Dynamic Link Library)   An executable driver program module for Microsoft Windows that can be loaded on demand and linked in at runtime and subsequently unloaded when the driver is no longer needed.

DMA   See *direct memory access*.

DMI (Desktop Management Interface)   DMI is an operating system- and protocol-independent standard developed by the Desktop Management Task Force (DMTF) for managing desktop systems and servers. DMI provides a bidirectional path to interrogate all the hardware and software components within a PC, allowing hardware and software configurations to be monitored from a central station in a network.

docking station   Equipment that allows a laptop or notebook computer to use peripherals and accessories normally associated with desktop systems.

doping   Adding chemical impurities to silicon (which is naturally a nonconductor), creating a material with semiconductor properties that is then used in the manufacturing of electronic chips.

DOS (Disk Operating System)   A collection of programs stored on the DOS disk that contain routines enabling the system and user to manage information and the hardware resources of the computer. DOS must be loaded into the computer before other programs can be started.

dot pitch   A measurement of the width of the dots that make up a pixel. The smaller the dot pitch, the sharper the image.

dot-matrix printer   An impact printer that prints characters composed of dots. Characters are printed one at a time by pressing the ends of selected wires against an inked ribbon and paper.

double density (DD)   An indication of the storage capacity of a floppy drive or disk in which eight or nine sectors per track are recorded using MFM encoding. See MFM.

downtime   Operating time lost because of a computer malfunction.

DPMI (DOS Protected Mode Interface)   An industry standard interface that allows DOS applications to execute program code in the protected mode of the 286 or later Intel processor. The DPMI specification is available from Intel.

DPMS (Display Power Management Signaling)   A VESA standard for signaling a monitor or display to switch into energy conservation modes. DPMS provides for two low energy modes: standby and suspend.

DRAM (Dynamic Random Access Memory)   The most common type of computer memory, DRAM can be made very inexpensively compared to other types of memory. DRAM chips are small and inexpensive because they normally require only one transistor and a capacitor to represent each bit. The capacitors must be energized every 15ms or so (hundreds of times per second) to maintain their charges. DRAM is volatile, meaning it will lose data with no power or without regular refresh cycles.

drive   A mechanical device that manipulates data storage media.

driver   A program designed to interface a particular piece of hardware to an operating system or other standard software.

drum   The cylindrical photoreceptor in a laser printer that receives the document image from the laser and applies it to the page as it slowly rotates.

DSL (Digital Subscriber Line)   A high-speed digital modem technology. DSL is either symmetric or asymmetric. Asymmetric provides faster downstream speeds, which is suited for Internet usage and video on demand. Symmetric provides the same rate coming and going. See *ADSL*.

DSM (Digital Storage Media)   A digital storage or transmission device or system.

DSP (Digital Signal Processor)   Dedicated, limited function processor often found in modems, sound cards, cellular phones, and so on.

DTE (Data Terminal [or Terminating] Equipment)   The device, usually a computer or terminal, that generates or is the final destination of data. See also DCE.

dual cavity pin grid array   Chip packaging designed by Intel for use with the Pentium Pro processor that houses the processor die in one cavity of the package and the L2 cache memory in a second cavity within the same package.

Dual Independent Bus (DIB) Architecture   A processor technology with the existence of two independent buses on the processor—the L2 cache bus and the processor-to-main-memory system bus. The processor can use both buses simultaneously, thus getting as much as two times more data into and out of the processor than a single bus architecture processor. The Intel Pentium Pro, Pentium II, and newer processors have DIB architecture.

dual scan display   A lower quality but economical type of LCD color display that has an array of transistors running down the x and y axes of two sides of the screen. The number of transistors determines the screen's resolution.

duplex   Indicates a communications channel capable of carrying signals in both directions.

DVD (Digital Versatile Disc)   originally called Digital Video Disc. A new type of high-capacity CD-ROM disc and drive format with up to 28 times the capacity of standard CD-ROM. The disc is the same diameter as a CD-ROM but can be recorded on both sides and on two layers for each side. Each side holds 4.7GB on a single layer disc, while dual-layer versions hold 8.5GB per side, for a maximum of 17GB total if both sides and both layers are used, which is the equivalent of 28 CD-ROMs. DVD drives can read standard audio CDs and CD-ROMs.

DVI (Digital Video Interactive)   A standard that was originally developed at RCA Laboratories and sold to Intel in 1988. DVI integrates digital motion, still video, sound, graphics, and special effects in a compressed format. DVI is a highly sophisticated hardware compression technique used in interactive multimedia applications.

Dvorak keyboard   A keyboard design by August Dvorak that was patented in 1936 and approved by ANSI in 1982. Provides increased speed and comfort and reduces the rate of errors by placing the most frequently used letters in the center for use by the strongest fingers. Finger motions and awkward strokes are reduced by more than 90 percent in comparison with the familiar QWERTY keyboard. The Dvorak keyboard has the five vowel keys, AOEUI, together under the left hand in the center row and the five most frequently used consonants, DHTNS, under the fingers of the right hand.

dynamic execution   A processing technique that allows the processor to dynamically predict the order of instructions and execute them out of order internally if necessary for an improvement in speed. Makes use of the three techniques Multiple Branch Prediction, Data Flow Analysis, and Speculative Execution.

EBCDIC (Extended Binary Coded Decimal Interchange Code)   An IBM-developed 8-bit code for the representation of characters. It allows 256 possible character combinations within a single byte. EBCDIC is the standard code on IBM mini-computers and mainframes, but not on the IBM microcomputers, where ASCII is used instead.

ECC (Error Correcting Code)   A type of system memory or cache that is capable of detecting and correcting some types of memory errors without interrupting processing.

ECP (Enhanced Capabilities Port)   A type of high-speed parallel port jointly developed by Microsoft and Hewlett-Packard that offers improved performance for the parallel port and requires special hardware logic.

edge connector   The part of a circuit board containing a series of printed contacts that is inserted into an expansion slot or connector.

EDO (Extended Data Out) RAM   A type of RAM chips that allow for a timing overlap between successive accesses, thus improving memory cycle time.

EEPROM (Electrically Erasable Programmable Read Only Memory)   A type of nonvolatile memory chip used to store semipermanent information in a computer such as the BIOS. An EEPROM can be erased and reprogrammed directly in the host system without special equipment. This is used so manufacturers can upgrade the ROM code in a system by supplying a special program that erases and reprograms the EEPROM chip with the new code. Also called a flash ROM.

EGA (Enhanced Graphics Adapter)   A type of PC video display adapter first introduced by IBM on September 10, 1984, that supports text and graphics. Text is supported at a maximum resolution of 80×25 characters in 16 colors with a character box of 8×14 pixels. Graphics is supported at a maximum resolution of 640×350 pixels in 16 (from a palette of 64) colors. The EGA outputs a TTL (digital) signal with a horizontal scanning frequency of 15.75, 18.432, or 21.85KHz, and supports TTL color or TTL monochrome displays.

EIA (Electronic Industries Association)   An organization that defines electronic standards in the United States.

EIDE (Enhanced Integrated Drive Electronics)   A specific Western Digital implementation of the ATA-2 specification. See *ATA-2*.

EISA (Extended Industry Standard Architecture)   An extension of the Industry Standard Architecture (ISA) bus developed by IBM for the AT. The EISA design was led by Compaq Corporation. Later, eight other manufacturers (AST, Epson, Hewlett-Packard, NEC, Olivetti, Tandy, Wyse, and Zenith) joined Compaq in a consortium founded September 13, 1988. This group became known as the "gang of nine." The EISA design was patterned largely after IBM's Micro Channel Architecture (MCA) in the PS/2 systems, but unlike MCA, EISA allows for backward compatibility with older plug-in adapters.

electronic mail (email)   A method of transferring messages from one computer to another.

electrostatic discharge (ESD)   The grounding of static electricity. A sudden flow of electricity between two objects at different electrical potentials. ESD is a primary cause of integrated circuit damage or failure.

embedded controller   In disk drives, a controller built into the same physical unit that houses the drive rather than on a separate adapter card. IDE and SCSI drives both use embedded controllers.

embedded servo data   Magnetic markings embedded between or inside tracks on disk drives that use voice-coil actuators. These markings enable the actuator to fine-tune the position of the read/write heads.

EMM (Expanded Memory Manager)   A driver that provides a software interface to expanded memory. EMMs were originally created for expanded memory boards, but can also use the memory management capabilities of the 386 or later processors to emulate an expanded memory board. EMM386.EXE is an example of an EMM that comes with DOS.

EMS (Expanded Memory Specification)   Sometimes also called the LIM spec because it was developed by Lotus, Intel, and Microsoft. Provides a way for microcomputers running under DOS to access additional memory. EMS memory management provides access to a maximum of 32MB of expanded memory through a small (usually 64KB) window in conventional memory. EMS is a cumbersome access scheme designed primarily for pre-286 systems that could not access extended memory.

emulator   A piece of test apparatus that emulates or imitates the function of a particular chip.

encoding   The protocol by which data is carried or stored by a medium.

encryption   The translation of data into unreadable codes to maintain security.

endec (encoder/decoder)   A device that takes data and clock signals and combines or encodes them using a particular encoding scheme into a single signal for transmission or storage. The same device also later separates or decodes the data and clock signals during a receive or read operation. Sometimes called a data separator.

Energy Star   A certification program started by the Environmental Protection Agency. Energy Star certified computers and peripherals are designed to draw less than 30 watts of electrical energy from a standard 110-volt AC outlet during periods of inactivity. Also called Green PCs.

Enhanced Graphics Adapter   See *EGA*.

Enhanced Small Device Interface   See *ESDI*.

EPP (Enhanced Parallel Port)   A type of parallel port developed by Intel, Xircom, and Zenith Data Systems that operates almost at ISA bus speed and offers a tenfold increase in the raw throughput capability over a conventional parallel port. EPP is especially designed for parallel port peripherals such as LAN adapters, disk drives, and tape backups.

EPROM (Erasable Programmable Read-Only Memory)   A type of read-only memory (ROM) in which the data pattern can be erased to allow a new pattern. EPROM usually is erased by ultraviolet light and recorded by a higher-than-normal voltage programming signal.

equalization   A compensation circuit designed into modems to counteract certain distortions introduced by the telephone channel. Two types are used: fixed (compromise) equalizers and those that adapt to channel conditions (adaptive). Good-quality modems use adaptive equalization.

error control   Various techniques that check the reliability of characters (parity) or blocks of data. V.42, MNP, and HST error-control protocols use error detection (CRC) and retransmission of error frames (ARQ).

error message   A word or combination of words to indicate to the user that an error has occurred somewhere in the program.

ESCD (Extended System Configuration Data)   Area in CMOS or Flash/NVRAM where Plug-and-Play information is stored.

ESDI (Enhanced Small Device Interface)   A hardware standard developed by Maxtor and standardized by a consortium of 22 disk drive manufacturers on January 26, 1983. A group of 27 manufacturers formed the ESDI steering committee on September 15, 1986, to enhance and improve the specification. A high-performance interface used primarily with hard disks, ESDI provides for a maximum data transfer rate to and from a hard disk of between 10 and 24Mbit/sec.

Ethernet   A type of network protocol developed in the late 1970s by Bob Metcalf at Xerox Corporation and endorsed by the IEEE. One of the oldest LAN communications protocols in the personal computing industry, Ethernet networks use a collision-detection protocol to manage contention.

expanded memory   Otherwise known as EMS memory, memory that conforms to the EMS specification. Requires a special device driver and conforms to a standard developed by Lotus, Intel, and Microsoft.

expansion card   An integrated circuit card that plugs into an expansion slot on a motherboard to provide access to additional peripherals or features not built into the motherboard. Also referred to as an add-in board.

expansion slot   A slot on the motherboard that physically and electrically connects an expansion card to the motherboard and the system buses.

eXtended Graphics Array   See *XGA*.

extended memory   Direct processor-addressable memory that is addressed by an Intel (or compatible) 286, 386, or 486 processor in the region beyond the first megabyte. Addressable only in the processor's protected mode of operation.

extended partition   A nonbootable DOS partition containing DOS volumes. Starting with DOS v3.3, the DOS FDISK program can create two partitions that serve DOS: an ordinary, bootable partition (called the primary partition) and an extended partition, which may contain as many as 23 volumes from D:–Z:.

external device   A peripheral that is installed outside of the system case.

extra-high density (ED)   An indication of the storage capacity of a floppy drive or disk in which 36 sectors per track are recorded using a vertical recording technique with MFM encoding.

fast-ATA (fast AT attachment interface)   Also called fast ATA-2, these are specific Seagate and Quantum implementations of the ATA-2 interface. See ATA-2.

Fast Page Mode RAM   A type of RAM that improves on standard DRAM speed by allowing for faster access to all the data within a given row of memory by keeping the row address the same and changing only the column.

FAT (file allocation table)   A table held near the outer edge of a disk that tells which sectors are allocated to each file and in what order.

FAT32   A disk file allocation system from Microsoft that uses 32-bit values for FAT entries instead of 16-bit values used by the original FAT system, enabling partition sizes up to 2TB (terabytes). FAT32 first appeared in Windows 95B and is also found in Windows 98 and Windows NT 5.0.

fax/modem   A peripheral that integrates the capabilities of a fax machine and a modem in one expansion card or external unit.

FDISK   The name of the disk-partitioning program under several operating systems to create the master boot record and allocate partitions for the operating system's use.

feature connector   On a video adapter, a connector that allows an additional video feature card such as a separate 3D accelerator, video capture card, or MPEG decoder to be connected to the main video adapter and display.

FIFO (first-in, first-out) A method of storing and retrieving items from a list, table, or stack so that the first element stored is the first one retrieved.

file A collection of information kept somewhere other than in random-access memory.

file attribute Information held in the attribute byte of a file's directory entry.

file compression See *compressed file.*

filename The name given to the disk file. For DOS, it must be one to eight characters long and may be followed by a filename extension, which can be one to three characters long. Windows 95 eases these constraints by allowing filenames of up to 255 characters.

FireWire Also called IEEE 1394. A serial I/O interface standard that is extremely fast, with data transfer rates up to 400MB/sec, 800MB/sec, or 3.2GB/sec, depending on the version of standard used.

firmware Software contained in a read-only memory (ROM) device. A cross between hardware and software.

fixed disk Also called a hard disk, a disk that cannot be removed from its controlling hardware or housing. Made of rigid material with a magnetic coating and used for the mass storage and retrieval of data.

flash ROM A type of EEPROM developed by Intel that can be erased and reprogrammed in the host system. See *EEPROM.*

flicker A monitor condition caused by refresh rates that are too low in which the display flashes visibly. This can cause eyestrain or more severe physical problems.

floating-point unit (FPU) Sometimes called the math coprocessor; handles the more complex calculations of the processing cycle.

floppy disk A removable disk using flexible magnetic media enclosed in a semirigid or rigid plastic case.

floppy disk controller The logic and interface that connects a floppy disk drive to the system.

floppy tape A tape standard that uses drives connecting to an ordinary floppy disk controller.

floptical drive A special type of high-capacity removable disk drive that uses an optical mechanism to properly position the drive read/write heads over the data tracks on the disk, allowing for more precise control of the read/write positioning and therefore narrower track spacing and more data packed into a smaller area than traditional floppy disks.

flow control A mechanism that compensates for differences in the flow of data input to and output from a modem or other device.

FM encoding Frequency modulation encoding. An outdated method of encoding data on the disk surface that uses up half the disk space with timing signals.

FM synthesis   An audio technology that uses one sine wave operator to modify another and create an artificial sound that mimics an instrument.

folder   In a graphical user interface, a simulated file folder that holds documents (text, data, or graphics), applications, and other folders. A folder is like a DOS subdirectory.

form factor   The physical dimensions of a device. Two devices with the same form factor are physically interchangeable. The IBM PC, XT, and XT Model 286, for example, all use power supplies that are internally different but have exactly the same form factor.

FORMAT   The DOS format program that performs both low- and high-level formatting on floppy disks but only high-level formatting on hard disks.

formatted capacity   The total number of bytes of data that can fit on a formatted disk. The unformatted capacity is higher because space is lost defining the boundaries between sectors.

formatting   Preparing a disk so that the computer can read or write to it. Checks the disk for defects and constructs an organizational system to manage information on the disk.

FORTRAN (Formula translator)   A high-level programming language developed in 1954 by John Backus at IBM, primarily for programs dealing with mathematical formulas and expressions similar to algebra and used primarily in scientific and technical applications.

fragmentation   The state of having a file scattered around a disk in pieces rather than existing in one contiguous area of the disk. Fragmented files are slower to read than files stored in contiguous areas and can be more difficult to recover if the FAT or a directory becomes damaged.

frame   1) A data communications term for a block of data with header and trailer information attached. The added information usually includes a frame number, block size data, error-check codes, and start/end indicators. 2) Also a single, complete picture in a video or film recording. A video frame consists of two interlaced fields of either 525 lines (NTSC) or 625 lines (PAL/SECAM), running at 30 frames per second (NTSC) or 25 frames per second (PAL/SECAM).

frame buffer   A memory device that stores, pixel by pixel, the contents of an image. Frame buffers are used to refresh a raster image. Sometimes they incorporate local processing capability. The "depth" of the frame buffer is the number of bits per pixel, which determines the number of colors or intensities that can be displayed.

frame rate   The speed at which video frames are scanned or displayed, 30 frames per second for NTSC, 25 frames a second for PAL/SECAM.

FTP (File Transfer Protocol)   A method of transferring files over the Internet. FTP can be used to transfer files between two machines on which the user has accounts. Anonymous FTP can be used by a user to retrieve a file from a server without having an account on that server.

full duplex   Signal flow in both directions at the same time. In microcomputer communications, also may refer to the suppression of the online local echo.

full-height drive   A drive unit that is 3 1/4 inches high, 5 3/4 inches wide, and 8 inches deep.

full-motion video   A video sequence displayed at full television standard resolutions and frame rates. In the U.S., this would equate to NTSC video at 30 frames per second.

function keys   Special-purpose keys that can be programmed to perform various operations. Serve many different functions depending on the program being used.

gas-plasma display   Commonly used in portable systems, a type of display that operates by exciting a gas, usually neon or an argon-neon mixture, through the application of a voltage. When sufficient voltage is applied at the intersection of two electrodes, the gas glows an orange-red. Because gas-plasma displays generate light, they require no backlighting.

gateway   Officially, an application-to-application conversion program or system. For example, an email gateway would convert between SMTP (Internet) email format to MHS (Novell) email format. The term gateway is also used as a slang term for router. See also *router*.

gender   When describing connectors for PCs, connectors are described as male if they have pins or female if they have receptacles designed to accept the pins of a male connector.

genlocking   The process of aligning the data rate of a video image with that of a digital device to digitize the image and enter it into computer memory. The machine that performs this function is known as a genlock.

GIF (Graphics Interchange Format)   A popular raster graphics file format developed by CompuServe that handles 8-bit color (256 colors) and uses the LZW method to achieve compression ratios of approximately 1.5:1 to 2:1.

giga   A multiplier indicating 1 billion (1,000,000,000) of some unit. Abbreviated as g or G. When used to indicate a number of bytes of memory storage, the multiplier definition changes to 1,073,741,824. One gigabit, for example, equals 1,000,000,000 bits, and one gigabyte equals 1,073,741,824 bytes.

gigabyte (GB)   A unit of information storage equal to 1,073,741,824 bytes.

graphics accelerator   A video processor or chipset specially designed to speed display and rendering of graphical objects onscreen.

graphics adapter   See *video adapter*.

Green Book   The standard for Compact Disc-Interactive (CD-I). Philips developed CD-I technology for the consumer market, to be connected to a television instead of a computer monitor. CD-I is not a computer system but a consumer device that made a small splash in the market and disappeared. CD-I disks require special code and are not compatible with standard CD-ROMs. A CD-ROM cannot be played on the CD-I machine, but Red Book audio can be played on CD-I devices.

GUI (Graphical User Interface)   A type of program interface that allows users to choose commands and functions by pointing to a graphical icon using either a keyboard or pointing device such as a mouse. Windows and OS/2 are the most popular GUIs available for PC systems.

half duplex   Signal flow in both directions but only one way at a time. In microcomputer communications, half duplex may refer to activation of the online local echo, which causes the modem to send a copy of the transmitted data to the screen of the sending computer.

half-height drive   A drive unit that is 1.625 inches high, and either 5.75 or 4 inches wide and 4 or 8 inches deep.

halftoning   A process that uses dithering to simulate a continuous tone image such as a photograph or shaded drawing using various sizes of dots. Newspapers, magazines, and many books use halftoning. The human eye will merge the dots to give the impression of gray shades.

hard disk   A high-capacity disk storage unit characterized by a normally nonremovable rigid substrate medium. The platters in a hard disk normally are constructed of aluminum or glass/ceramic. Also sometimes called a fixed disk.

hard error   An error in reading or writing data that is caused by damaged hardware.

hardware   Physical components that make up a microcomputer, monitor, printer, and so on.

HDLC (High-Level Data Link Control)   A standard protocol developed by the ISO for software applications and communicating devices operating in synchronous environments. Defines operations at the link level of communications—for example, the format of data frames exchanged between modems over a phone line.

head   A small electromagnetic device inside a drive that reads, records, and erases data on the media.

head actuator   The device that moves read/write heads across a disk drive's platters. Most drives use a stepper-motor or a voice-coil actuator.

head crash   A (usually) rare occurrence in which a read/write head strikes a platter surface with sufficient force to damage the magnetic medium.

head parking   A procedure in which a disk drive's read/write heads are moved to an unused track so that they will not damage data in the event of a head crash or other failure.

head seek   The movement of a drive's read/write heads to a particular track.

heat sink   A mass of metal attached to a chip carrier or socket for the purpose of dissipating heat.

helical scan   A type of recording technology that has vastly increased the capacity of tape drives. Invented for use in broadcast systems and now used in VCRs. Conventional longitudinal recording records a track of data straight across the width of a single-track tape. Helical scan recording packs more data on the tape by positioning the tape at an angle to the recording heads. The heads spin to record diagonal stripes of information on the tape.

hexadecimal number   A number encoded in base-16, such that digits include the letters A through F as well as the numerals 0–9 (for example, 8BF3, which equals 35,827 in base-10).

hidden file   A file that is not displayed in DOS directory listings because the file's attribute byte holds a special setting.

high density (HD)   An indication of the storage capacity of a floppy drive or disk in which 15 or 18 sectors per track are recorded using MFM encoding.

high sierra format   A standard format for placing files and directories on CD-ROMs, proposed by an ad hoc committee of computer vendors, software developers, and CD-ROM system integrators. (Work on the format proposal began at the High Sierra Hotel at Lake Tahoe, Nevada.) A revised version of the format was adopted by the ISO as ISO 9660.

high-definition television (HDTV)   Video formats offering greater visual accuracy (or resolution) than current NTSC, PAL, or SECAM broadcast standards. HDTV formats generally range in resolution from 655 to 2,125 scanning lines, having an aspect ration of 5:3 (or 1.67:1) and a video bandwidth of 30–MHz (5+ times greater than NTSC standard). Digital HDTV has a bandwidth of 300MHz. HDTV is subjectively comparable to 35mm film.

high-level formatting   Formatting performed by the DOS FORMAT program. Among other things, it creates the root directory and FATs.

history file   A file created by utility software to keep track of earlier use of the software. Many backup programs, for example, keep history files describing earlier backup sessions.

hit ratio   In describing the efficiency of a disk or memory cache, the ratio of the number of times the data is found in the cache to the total number of data requests is the hit ratio. 1:1 would be a perfect hit ratio, meaning that every data request was found in the cache. The closer to 1:1 the ratio is, the more efficient the cache.

HMA (High Memory Area)   The first 64KB of extended memory, which is controlled typically by the HIMEM.SYS device driver. Real-mode programs can be loaded into the HMA to conserve conventional memory. Normally, DOS 5.0 and later use the HMA exclusively to reduce the DOS conventional memory footprint.

horizontal scan rate   In monitors, the speed at which the electron beam moves laterally across the screen. Normally expressed as a frequency; typical monitors range from 31.5KHz to 90KHz, with the higher frequencies being more desirable.

HPT (High-Pressure Tin)   A PLCC socket that promotes high forces between socket contacts and PLCC contacts for a good connection.

HST (High-Speed Technology)   The USRobotics proprietary high-speed modem-signaling scheme, developed as an interim protocol until the V.32 protocol could be implemented in a cost-effective manner.

HTML (Hypertext Markup Language)   A language used to describe and format plain-text files on the Web. HTML is based on pairs of tags that allow you to mix graphics with text, change the appearance of text, and create hypertext documents with links to other documents.

HTTP (Hypertext Transfer Protocol)   The protocol that describes the rules that a browser and server use to communicate over the World Wide Web. HTTP allows a Web browser to request HTML documents from a Web server. See also *hypertext*.

Huffman coding   A technique that minimizes the average number of bytes required to represent the characters in a text. Huffman coding works for a given character distribution by assigning short codes to frequently occurring characters and longer codes to infrequently occurring characters.

hypertext   A technology that allows for quick and easy navigation between and within large documents. Hypertext links are pointers to other sections within the same document, other documents, or other resources such as FTP sites, images, or sounds.

Hz   An abbreviation for hertz, a frequency measurement unit used internationally to indicate one cycle per second.

I/O (input/output)   A circuit path that enables independent communications between the processor and external devices.

I/O port (input/output port)   Used to communicate to and from devices, such as a printer or disk.

IBMBIO.COM   One of the DOS system files required to boot the machine. The first file loaded from disk during the boot. Contains extensions to the ROM BIOS.

IBMDOS.COM   One of the DOS system files required to boot the machine. Contains the primary DOS routines. Loaded by IBMBIO.COM, it in turn loads COMMAND.COM.

IC (integrated circuit)   A complete electronic circuit contained on a single chip. May consist of only a few or thousands of transistors, capacitors, diodes, or resistors, and generally is classified according to the complexity of the circuitry and the approximate number of circuits on the chip. SSI (small-scale integration) equals 2 to 10 circuits. MSI (medium-scale integration) equals 10 to 100 circuits. LSI (large-scale integration) equals 100 to 1,000 circuits. VLSI (very-large-scale integration) equals 1,000 to 10,000 circuits. ULSI (ultra-large-scale integration) equals more than 10,000 circuits.

IDE (Integrated Drive Electronics)   Describes a hard disk with the disk controller circuitry integrated within it. The first IDE drives commonly were called hard cards. Also refers to the ATA interface standard, the standard for attaching hard disk drives to ISA bus IBM-compatible computers. IDE drives typically operate as though they were standard ST-506/412 drives. See also *ATA*.

IEEE 1394   See *FireWire*.

IEEE 802.3   See *10Base2*.

incremental backup   A backup of all files that have changed since the last backup.

inductive   A property where energy can be transferred from one device to another via the magnetic field generated by the device even though no direct electrical connection is established between the two.

initiator   A device attached to the SCSI bus that sends a command to another device (the target) on the SCSI bus. The SCSI host adapter plugged into the system bus is an example of a SCSI initiator.

inkjet printer   A type of printer that sprays one or more colors of ink on the paper. Can produce output with quality approaching that of a laser printer at a lower cost.

input   Data sent to the computer from the keyboard, telephone, video camera, another computer, paddles, joysticks, and so on.

instruction   Program step that tells the computer what to do for a single operation.

integrated circuit   See *IC*.

interface   A communications device or protocol that enables one device to communicate with another. Matches the output of one device to the input of the other device.

interlacing   A method of scanning alternate lines of pixels on a display screen. The odd lines are scanned first from top to bottom and left to right. The electron gun goes back to the top and makes a second pass, scanning the even lines. Interlacing requires two scan passes to construct a single image. Because of this additional scanning, interlaced screens often seem to flicker unless a long persistence phosphor is used in the display.

interleave ratio   The number of sectors that pass beneath the read/write heads before the "next" numbered sector arrives. When the interleave ratio is 3:1, for example, a sector is read, two pass by, and then the next is read. A proper interleave ratio, laid down during low-level formatting, enables the disk to transfer information without excessive revolutions due to missed sectors.

interleaved memory   The process of alternating access between two banks of memory to overlap accesses, thus speeding up data retrieval.

internal command   In DOS, a command contained in COMMAND.COM so that no other file must be loaded to perform the command. DIR and COPY are two examples of internal commands.

internal device   A peripheral device that is installed inside the main system case either in an expansion slot or in a drive bay.

internal drive   A disk or tape drive mounted inside one of a computer's disk drive bays (or a hard disk card, which is installed in one of the computer's slots).

Internet   A computer network that joins many government, university, and private computers together over phone lines. The Internet traces its origins to a network set up in 1969 by the Department of Defense. You can connect to the Internet through many online services such as CompuServe and America Online, or you can connect through local Internet service providers

(ISPs). Internet computers use the TCP/IP communications protocol. There are several million hosts on the Internet. A host is a mainframe, mini, or workstation that directly supports the Internet protocol (the IP in TCP/IP).

interpreter   A program for a high-level language that translates and executes the program at the same time. The program statements that are interpreted remain in their original source language, the way the programmer wrote them—that is, the program does not need to be compiled before execution. Interpreted programs run slower than compiled programs and always must be run with the interpreter loaded in memory.

interrupt   A suspension of a process, such as the execution of a computer program, caused by an event external to that process and performed in such a way that the process can be resumed. An interrupt can be caused by internal or external conditions such as a signal indicating that a device or program has completed a transfer of data.

interrupt vector   A pointer in a table that gives the location of a set of instructions that the computer should execute when a particular interrupt occurs.

IO.SYS   One of the DOS system files required to boot the machine. The first file loaded from disk during the boot. Contains extensions to the ROM BIOS.

IPX (Internet Packet eXchange)   Novell NetWare's native LAN communications protocol used to move data between server and/or workstation programs running on different network nodes. IPX packets are encapsulated and carried by the packets used in Ethernet and the similar frames used in Token-Ring networks.

IRQ (interrupt request)   Physical connections between external hardware devices and the interrupt controllers. When a device such as a floppy controller or a printer needs the attention of the CPU, an IRQ line is used to get the attention of the system to perform a task. On PC and XT IBM-compatible systems, eight IRQ lines are included, numbered IRQ0 through IRQ7. On the AT and PS/2 systems, 16 IRQ lines are numbered IRQ0 through IRQ15. IRQ lines must be used only by a single adapter in the ISA bus systems, but Micro Channel Architecture (MCA) adapters can share interrupts.

ISA bus clock   Clock that operates the ISA bus at normally 8.33MHz.

ISA (Industry Standard Architecture)   The bus architecture that was introduced as an 8-bit bus with the original IBM PC in 1981 and later expanded to 16 bits with the IBM PC/AT in 1984. ISA slots are still found in PC systems today.

ISDN (Integrated Services Digital Network)   An international telecommunications standard that enables a communications channel to carry digital data simultaneously with voice and video information.

ISO 9660   An international standard that defines file systems for CD-ROM discs, independent of the operating system. ISO (International Standards Organization) 9660 has two levels. Level one provides for DOS file system compatibility, while Level two allows file names of up to 32 characters. See also *high sierra format*.

ISO (International Standards Organization)   The ISO, based in Paris, develops standards for international and national data communications. The U.S. representative to the ISO is the American National Standards Institute (ANSI). See also *high sierra format*.

ITU (International Telecommunications Union)   Formerly called CCITT. An international committee organized by the United Nations to set international communications recommendations, which frequently are adopted as standards, and to develop interface, modem, and data network recommendations. The Bell 212A standard for 1,200bps communication in North America, for example, is observed internationally as CCITT V.22. For 2,400bps communication, most U.S. manufacturers observe V.22bis, while V.32, V.32bis, V34 and V34+ are standards for 9,600, 14,400, 28,800, and 33,600bps, respectively. The V.90 standard recently was defined for 56Kbps modems.

Java   An object-oriented programming language and environment similar to C or C++. Java was developed by Sun Microsystems and is used to create network-based applications.

Jaz drive   A proprietary type of removable media drive with a magnetic hard disk platter in a rigid plastic case. Developed by Iomega and currently available in 1GB and 2GB sizes.

JEDEC (Joint Electronic Devices Engineering Council)   A group that establishes standards for the electronics industry.

J-lead   J-shaped leads on chip carriers, which can be surface-mounted on a PC board or plugged into a socket that then is mounted on a PC board, usually on .050-inch centers.

joystick   An input device generally used for game software usually consisting of a central upright stick that controls horizontal and vertical motion and one or more buttons to control discrete events such as firing guns. More complex models may resemble flight yokes and steering wheels or may incorporate tactile feedback.

JPEG (Joint Photographic Experts Group)   The international consortium of hardware, software, and publishing interests who, under the auspices of the ISO, has defined a universal standard for digital compression and decompression of still images for use in computer systems. JPEG compresses at about a 20:1 ratio before visible image degradation occurs. A lossy data compression standard that was originally designed for still images but can also compress real-time video (30 frames per second) and animation. Lossy compression permanently discards unnecessary data, resulting in some loss of precision.

jukebox   A type of CD-ROM drive that allows several CD-ROM disks to be in the drive at the same time. The drive itself determines which disk is needed by the system and loads the disks into the reading mechanism as needed.

jumper   A small, plastic-covered metal clip that slips over two pins protruding from a circuit board. Sometimes also called a shunt. When in place, the jumper connects the pins electrically and closes the circuit. By doing so, it connects the two terminals of a switch, turning it "on."

Kermit   A protocol designed for transferring files between microcomputers and mainframes. Developed by Frank DaCruz and Bill Catchings at Columbia University (and named after the talking frog on *The Muppet Show*), Kermit is widely accepted in the academic world.

kernel   Operating system core component.

key disk   In software copy protection, a distribution floppy disk that must be present in a floppy disk drive for an application program to run.

keyboard macro   A series of keystrokes automatically input when a single key is pressed.

keyboard   The primary input device for most computers consisting of keys with letters of the alphabet, digits, punctuation, and function control keys.

keylock   Physical locking mechanism to preventing internal access to the system unit or peripherals.

KFlex   A proprietary standard for 56Kbps modem transmissions developed by Rockwell and implemented in modems from a variety of vendors. Superseded by the official V.90 standard for 56Kbps modems. See also *X2* and *V.90*.

kilo   A multiplier indicating one thousand (1,000) of some unit. Abbreviated as k or K. When used to indicate a number of bytes of memory storage, the multiplier definition changes to 1,024. One kilobit, for example, equals 1,000 bits, and one kilobyte equals 1,024 bytes.

kilobyte (KB)   A unit of information storage equal to 1,024 bytes.

L1 cache (level one)   A memory cache that is built into the CPU core of 486 and later generation processors. See *cache* and *disk cache*.

L2 cache (level two)   A second-level memory cache that is external to the processor core, usually larger and slower than L1. Normally found on the motherboard of 386, 486, and Pentium systems and inside the processor package or module in Pentium Pro and Pentium II systems. Moving the L2 cache onto the processor in the Pentium Pro and Pentium II allows it to run at speeds up to full processor speed rather than motherboard speed. See *SEC (single edge contact) cartridge*, *cache*, and *disk cache*.

landing zone   An unused track on a disk surface on which the read/write heads can land when power is shut off. The place that a parking program or a drive with an autopark mechanism parks the heads.

LAPM (link-access procedure for modems)   An error-control protocol incorporated in CCITT Recommendation V.42. Like the MNP and HST protocols, uses cyclic redundancy checking (CRC) and retransmission of corrupted data (ARQ) to ensure data reliability.

laptop computer   A computer system smaller than a briefcase but larger than a notebook that usually has a clamshell design in which the keyboard and display are on separate halves of the system, which are hinged together. These systems normally run on battery power.

large mode   Another name for the LBA translation scheme used by IDE drives to translate the cylinder, head, and sector specifications of the drive to those usable by an enhanced BIOS.

large scale integration   See *IC*.

laser printer   A type of printer that is a combination of an electrostatic copying machine and a computer printer. The output data from the computer is converted by an interface into a raster feed, similar to the impulses that a TV picture tube receives. The impulses cause the laser beam to scan a small drum that carries a positive electrical charge. Where the laser hits, the drum is discharged. A toner, which also carries a positive charge, is then applied to the drum. This toner, a fine black powder, sticks only to the areas of the drum that have been discharged electrically. As it rotates, the drum deposits the toner on a negatively charged sheet of paper. Another roller then heats and bonds the toner to the page.

latency   1) The amount of time required for a disk drive to rotate half of a revolution. Represents the average amount of time to locate a specific sector after the heads have arrived at a specific track. Latency is part of the average access time for a drive. 2) The initial setup time required for a memory transfer in DRAM to select the row and column addresses for the memory to be read/written.

LBA (Logical Block Addressing)   A method used with SCSI and IDE drives to translate the cylinder, head, and sector specifications of the drive to those usable by an enhanced BIOS. LBA is used with drives that are larger than 528MB and causes the BIOS to translate the drive's logical parameters to those usable by the system BIOS.

LCC (Leadless Chip Carrier)   A type of integrated circuit package that has input and output pads rather than leads on its perimeter.

LCD (Liquid Crystal Display)   A display that uses liquid crystal sealed between two pieces of polarized glass. The polarity of the liquid crystal is changed by an electric current to vary the amount of light that can pass through. Because LCD displays do not generate light, they depend on either the reflection of ambient light or backlighting the screen. The best type of LCD, the active-matrix or thin-film transistor (TFT) LCD, offers fast screen updates and true color capability.

LED (Light-Emitting Diode)   A semiconductor diode that emits light when a current is passed through it.

LIF (Low Insertion Force)   A type of socket that requires only a minimum of force to insert a chip carrier.

light pen   A handheld input device with a light-sensitive probe or stylus connected to the computer's graphics adapter board by a cable. Used for writing or sketching onscreen or as a pointing device for making selections. Unlike mice, not widely supported by software applications.

line voltage   The AC voltage available at a standard wall outlet, nominally 110-120v.

Lithium Ion   A portable system battery type that is longer-lived than either NiCad or NiMH technologies, cannot be overcharged, and holds a charge well when not in use. Lithium Ion batteries are also lighter weight than the either NiCad or NiMH technologies. Because of these superior features, Li-ion batteries have come to be used in all but the very low end of the portable system market.

local area network (LAN)   The connection of two or more computers, usually via a network adapter card or NIC.

local bus   A generic term used to describe a bus that is directly attached to a processor and which operates at the processor's speed and data transfer width.

local echo   A modem feature that enables the modem to send copies of keyboard commands and transmitted data to the screen. When the modem is in command mode (not online to another system), the local echo normally is invoked through an ATE1 command, which causes the modem to display your typed commands. When the modem is online to another system, the local echo is invoked by an ATF0 command, which causes the modem to display the data it transmits to the remote system.

logical drive   A drive as named by a DOS drive specifier, such as C: or D:. Under DOS 3.3 or later, a single physical drive can act as several logical drives, each with its own specifier.

logical unit number   See *LUN*.

lossless compression   A compression technique that preserves all the original information in an image or other data structures. ▪

lossy compression   A compression technique that achieves optimal data reduction by discarding redundant and unnecessary information in an image.

lost clusters   Clusters that have been marked accidentally as "unavailable" in the FAT even though they don't belong to any file listed in a directory. See also clusters and allocation units.

low-level formatting   Formatting that divides tracks into sectors on the platter surfaces. Places sector-identifying information before and after each sector and fills each sector with null data (usually hex F6). Specifies the sector interleave and marks defective tracks by placing invalid checksum figures in each sector on a defective track.

LPT port   Line Printer port, a common system abbreviation for a parallel printer port.

LPX   A semi-proprietary motherboard design used in many Low Profile or Slimline case systems. Because there is no formal standard, these are typically not interchangeable between vendors and are often difficult to find replacement parts for repair or upgrade.

luminance   Measure of brightness usually used in specifying monitor brightness.

LUN (Logical Unit Number)   A number given to a device (a logical unit) attached to a SCSI physical unit and not directly to the SCSI bus. Although as many as eight logical units can be attached to a single physical unit, normally a single logical unit is a built-in part of a single physical unit. A SCSI hard disk, for example, has a built-in SCSI bus adapter that is assigned a physical unit number or SCSI ID, and the controller and drive portions of the hard disk are assigned a LUN (usually 0). Also see *PUN*.

LZH (Lempel Zev Welch) A compression scheme used in the GIF graphic format.

machine address A hexadecimal (hex) location in memory.

machine language Hexadecimal program code that a computer can understand and execute. It can be output from assembler or compiler.

magnetic domain A tiny segment of a track just large enough to hold one of the magnetic flux reversals that encode data on a disk surface.

magneto-optical recording An erasable optical disk recording technique that uses a laser beam to heat pits on the disk surface to the point at which a magnet can make flux changes.

magneto-resistive A technology originally developed by IBM and commonly used for the read element of a read/write head on a high-density magnetic disk. Based on the principle that the resistance to electricity changes in a material when brought in contact with a magnetic field, in this case, the read element material and the magnetic bit. Such drives use a magnetoresistive read sensor for reading and a standard inductive element for writing. A magnetoresistive read head is more sensitive to magnetic fields than inductive read heads.

mask A photographic map of the circuits for a particular layer of a semiconductor chip used in manufacturing the chip.

master partition boot sector On hard disks, a one-sector record that gives essential information about the disk and tells the starting locations of the various partitions. Always the first physical sector of the disk.

math coprocessor A processing chip designed to quickly handle complex arithmetic computations involving floating-point arithmetic, offloading these from the main processor. Originally contained in a separate coprocessor chip, starting with the 486 family of processors, Intel has incorporated the math coprocessor into the main processors in what is called the floating-point unit.

MCA (Micro Channel Architecture) Developed by IBM for the PS/2 line of computers and introduced on April 2, 1987. Features include a 16- or 32-bit bus width and multiple master control. By allowing several processors to arbitrate for resources on a single bus, the MCA is optimized for multitasking, multiprocessor systems. Offers switchless configuration of adapters, which eliminates one of the biggest headaches of installing older adapters.

MCGA (MultiColor Graphics Array) A type of PC video display circuit introduced by IBM on April 2, 1987, that supports text and graphics. Text is supported at a maximum resolution of 80×25 characters in 16 colors with a character box of 8×16 pixels. Graphics is supported at a maximum resolution of 320×200 pixels in 256 (from a palette of 262,144) colors or 640×480 pixels in two colors. The MCGA outputs an analog signal with a horizontal scanning frequency of 31.5KHz, and supports analog color or analog monochrome displays.

MCI (Media Control Interface) A device-independent specification for controlling multimedia devices and files. MCI is a part of the multimedia extensions and offers a standard interface set of device control commands. MCI commands are used for audio recording and playback and animation playback. Device types include CD audio, digital audio tape players, scanners, MIDI sequencers, videotape players or recorders, and audio devices that play digitized waveform files.

MDA Monochrome Display Adapter (also, MGA—Mono Graphics Adapter)   A type of PC video display adapter introduced by IBM on August 12, 1981, that supports text only. Text is supported at a maximum resolution of 80×25 characters in four colors with a character box of 9×14 pixels. Colors, in this case, indicate black, white, bright white, and underlined. Graphics modes are not supported. The MDA outputs a digital signal with a horizontal scanning frequency of 18.432KHz, and supports TTL monochrome displays. The IBM MDA also included a parallel printer port.

mean time between failure   See *MTBF*.

mean time to repair   See *MTTR*.

medium   The magnetic coating or plating that covers a disk or tape.

mega   A multiplier indicating 1 million (1,000,000) of some unit. Abbreviated as m or M. When used to indicate a number of bytes of memory storage, the multiplier definition changes to 1,048,576. One megabit, for example, equals 1,000,000 bits, and one megabyte equals 1,048,576 bytes.

megabyte (MB)   A unit of information storage equal to 1,048,576 bytes.

memory   Any component in a computer system that stores information for future use.

memory caching   A service provided by extremely fast memory chips that keeps copies of the most recent memory accesses. When the CPU makes a subsequent access, the value is supplied by the fast memory rather than by relatively slow system memory.

memory-resident program   A program that remains in memory after it has been loaded, consuming memory that otherwise might be used by application software.

menu software   Utility software that makes a computer easier to use by replacing DOS commands with a series of menu selections.

MFM encoding (Modified Frequency Modulation encoding)   A method of encoding data on the surface of a disk. The coding of a bit of data varies by the coding of the preceding bit to preserve clocking information.

MHz   An abbreviation for megahertz, a unit of measurement indicating the frequency of one million cycles per second. One hertz (Hz) is equal to one cycle per second. Named after Heinrich R. Hertz, a German physicist who first detected electromagnetic waves in 1883.

MI/MIC (Mode Indicate/Mode Indicate Common)   Also called forced or manual originate. Provided for installations in which equipment other than the modem does the dialing. In such installations, the modem operates in dumb mode (no auto-dial capability), yet must go off-hook in originate mode to connect with answering modems.

micro (µ)   A prefix indicating one millionth (1/1,000,000 or .000001) of some unit.

Micron   A unit of measurement equaling one millionth of a meter. Often used in measuring the size of circuits in chip manufacturing processes. Current state-of-the-art chip fabrication builds chips with 0.25 micron circuits.

microprocessor   A solid-state central processing unit much like a computer on a chip. An integrated circuit that accepts coded instructions for execution.

microsecond (μs)   A unit of time equal to one millionth (1/1,000,000 or .000001) of a second.

MIDI (Musical Instrument Digital Interface)   An interface and file format standard for connecting a musical instrument to a microcomputer and storing musical instrument data. Multiple musical instruments can be daisy-chained and played simultaneously with the help of the computer and related software. The various operations of the instruments can be captured, saved, edited, and played back. A MIDI file contains note information, timing (how long a note is held), volume, and instrument type for as many as 16 channels. Sequencer programs are used to control MIDI functions such as recording, playback, and editing. MIDI files store only note instructions and not actual sound data.

milli (m)   A prefix indicating one thousandth (1/1,000 or .001) of some unit.

millisecond (ms)   A unit of time equal to one thousandth (1/1,000 or .001) of a second.

mini-tower   A type of PC system case that is shorter than a full or mid-sized tower.

MIPS (million instructions per second)   Refers to the average number of machine-language instructions a computer can perform or execute in one second. Because different processors can perform different functions in a single instruction, MIPS should be used only as a general measure of performance among different types of computers.

MMX   An Intel processor enhancement that adds 57 new instructions designed to improve multimedia performance. MMX also implies a doubling of the internal L1 processor cache.

mnemonic   An abbreviated name for something that is used in a manner similar to an acronym. Computer processor instructions are often abbreviated with a mnemonic such as JMP (Jump), CLR (Clear), STO (Store), INIT (Initialize). A mnemonic name for an instruction or an operation makes it easy to remember and convenient to use.

MNP (Microcom Networking Protocol)   Asynchronous error-control and data-compression protocols developed by Microcom, Inc., and now in the public domain. Ensures error-free transmission through error detection (CRC) and retransmission of erred frames. MNP Levels 1–4 cover error control and have been incorporated into CCITT Recommendation V.42. MNP Level 5 includes data compression but is eclipsed in superiority by V.42bis, an international standard that is more efficient. Most high-speed modems will connect with MNP Level 5 if V.42bis is unavailable.

MO (Magneto-Optical)   MO drives use both magnetic and optical storage properties. MO technology is erasable and recordable, as opposed to CD-ROM (Read-Only) and WORM (Write-Once) drives. MO uses laser and magnetic field technology to record and erase data.

Mobile module (MMO)   A type of processor packing from Intel for mobile computers consisting of a Pentium or Pentium II processor in its TCP form, mounted on a small daughterboard along with the power supply for the processor's unique voltage requirements, the system's L2 cache memory, and the "North Bridge" part of the motherboard chipset.

modem (modulator/demodulator)   A device that converts electrical signals from a computer into an audio form transmittable over telephone lines, or vice versa. Modulates, or transforms, digital signals from a computer into the analog form that can be carried successfully on a phone line; also demodulates signals received from the phone line back to digital signals before passing them to the receiving computer.

module   An assembly that contains a complete circuit or subcircuit.

Monochrome Display Adapter   See *MDA*.

MOS (metal-oxide semiconductor)   Refers to the three layers used in forming the gate structure of a field-effect transistor (FET). MOS circuits offer low-power dissipation and enable transistors to be jammed close together before a critical heat problem arises. PMOS, the oldest type of MOS circuit, is a silicon-gate P-channel MOS process that uses currents made up of positive charges. NMOS is a silicon-gate N-channel MOS process that uses currents made up of negative charges and is at least twice as fast as PMOS. CMOS, Complementary MOS, is nearly immune to noise, runs off almost any power supply, and is an extremely low-power circuit technique.

motherboard   The main circuit board in the computer. Also called planar, system board, or backplane.

mouse   An input device invented by Douglas Engelbart of Stanford Research Center in 1963 and popularized by Xerox in the 1970s. A mouse consists of a roller ball and a tracking mechanism on the underside that relays the mouse's horizontal and vertical position to the computer, allowing precise control of the pointer location on the screen. The top side features two or three buttons and possibly a small wheel used to select or click items on screen.

MPC   A trademarked abbreviation for Multimedia Personal Computer. The original MPC specification was developed by Tandy Corporation and Microsoft as the minimum platform capable of running multimedia software. In the summer of 1995, the MPC Marketing Council introduced an upgraded MPC 3 standard. The MPC 1 Specification defines the following minimum standard requirements: a 386SX or 486 CPU; 2MB RAM; 30MB hard disk; VGA video display; 8-bit digital audio subsystem; CD-ROM drive; and systems software compatible with the applications programming interfaces (APIs) of Microsoft Windows version 3.1 or later. The MPC 2 specification defines the following minimum standard requirements: 25MHz 486SX with 4MB RAM; 160MB hard disk; 16-bit sound card; 65,536 color video display; double-speed CD-ROM drive; and systems software compatible with the applications programming interfaces (APIs) of Microsoft Windows version 3.1 or later. The MPC 3 Specification defines the following minimum standard requirements: 75MHz Pentium with 8MB RAM; 540MB hard disk; 16-bit sound card; 65,536 color video display; quad speed CD-ROM drive; OM-1-compliant MPEG-1 video, and systems software compatible with the applications programming interfaces (APIs) of Microsoft Windows version 3.1 and DOS 6.0 or later.

MPEG (Motion Picture Experts Group)   A working ISO committee that has defined standards for lossy digital compression and decompression of motion video/audio for use in computer systems. Also see lossy. The MPEG-1 standard delivers decompression data at 1.2 to 1.5MB/sec, allowing CD players to play full-motion color movies at 30 frames per second. MPEG-1 compresses at about a 50:1 ratio before image degradation occurs, but compression ratios as high as 200:1 are attainable. MPEG-2 extends to the higher data rates (2–15Mbps) needed for signals delivered from remote sources (such as broadcast, cable, or satellite). MPEG-2 is designed to support a range of picture aspect ratios, including 4:3 and 16:9. MPEG compression produces about a 50 percent volume reduction in file size.

MPR   The Swedish government standard for maximum video terminal radiation. The current version is called MPR II.

MSDOS.SYS   One of the DOS system files required to boot the machine. Contains the primary DOS routines. Loaded by IO.SYS, it in turn loads COMMAND.COM.

MTBF (Mean Time Between Failure)   A statistically derived measure of the probable time a device will continue to operate before a hardware failure occurs, usually given in hours. Because no standard technique exists for measuring MTBF, a device from one manufacturer can be significantly more or significantly less reliable than a device with the same MTBF rating from another manufacturer.

MTTR (Mean Time To Repair)   A measure of the probable time it will take a technician to service or repair a specific device, usually given in hours.

Multicolor Graphics Array   See *MCGA*.

multimedia   The integration of sound, graphic images, animation, motion video, and text in one environment on a computer. It is a set of hardware and software technologies that are rapidly changing and enhancing the computing environment.

multisession   A term used in CD-ROM recording to describe a recording event. Multi-session capabilities allow data recording on the disk at different times in several recording sessions. Kodak's Photo CD is an example of CD-R technology. See also *session* (single or multisession).

multitask   To run several programs simultaneously.

multithread   To concurrently process more than one message by an application program. OS/2, Windows 95, and Windows NT are examples of multithreaded operating systems. Each program can start two or more threads, which carry out various interrelated tasks with less overhead than two separate programs would require.

multiuser system   A system in which several computer terminals share the same central processing unit (CPU).

nano (n)   A prefix indicating one billionth (1/1,000,000,000 or .000000001) of some unit.

nanosecond (ns)   A unit of time equal to one billionth (1/1,000,000,000 or .000000001) of a second.

NetBEUI (NetBIOS Extended User Interface)   A network protocol used primarily by Windows NT and most suitable for small peer-to-peer networks.

NetBIOS (Network Basic Input/Output System)   A commonly used network protocol originally developed by IBM and Sytek for PC local area networks. NetBIOS provides session and transport services (Layers 4 and 5 of the OSI model).

network   A system in which a number of independent computers are linked to share data and peripherals, such as hard disks and printers.

Network Interface Card (NIC)   An adapter that connects a PC to a network.

network layer   In the OSI reference model, the layer that switches and routes the packets as necessary to get them to their destinations. This layer is responsible for addressing and delivering message packets.

NiCad   The oldest of the three battery technologies used in portable systems, nickel cadmium batteries are rarely used in portable systems today because of their shorter life and their sensitivity to improper charging and discharging. See also NiMH and Lithium Ion.

NiMH   A battery technology used in portable systems. Nickel Metal-Hydride batteries have approximately a 30 percent longer life than NiCads, are less sensitive to the memory effect caused by improper charging and discharging, and do not use the environmentally dangerous substances found in NiCads. Newer Lithium Ion (Li-ion) batteries are far superior.

NLX   A new low-profile motherboard form factor standard that is basically an improved version of the semiproprietary LPX design. Designed to accommodate larger processor and memory form factors and incorporate newer bus technologies such as AGP and USB. Besides design improvements, it is fully standardized, which means you should be able to replace one NLX board with another from a different manufacturer, something that was not normally possible with LPX.

noninterlaced monitor   A desirable monitor design where the electron beam sweeps the screen in lines from top to bottom, one line after the other, completing the entire screen in one pass.

nonvolatile memory (NVRAM)   Random-access memory whose data is retained when power is turned off. Sometimes NVRAM is retained without any power whatsoever, as in EEPROM or flash memory devices. In other cases, the memory is maintained by a small battery. NVRAM that is battery maintained is sometimes also called CMOS memory. CMOS NVRAM is used in IBM-compatible systems to store configuration information. True NVRAM often is used in intelligent modems to store a user-defined default configuration loaded into normal modem RAM at power-up.

nonvolatile RAM disk   A RAM disk powered by a battery supply so that it continues to hold its data during a power outage.

North Bridge   The Intel term for the main portion of the motherboard chipset that incorporates the interface between the processor and the rest of the motherboard. The North Bridge contains the cache, main memory, and AGP controllers as well as the interface between the high-speed (normally 66MHz or 100MHz) processor bus and the 33MHz PCI (Peripheral Component Interconnect) or 66MHz AGP (Accelerated Graphics Port) buses. See also *chipset* and *South Bridge*.

notebook computer   A very small personal computer approximately the size of a notebook.

NTSC   The National Television Standards Committee, which governs the standard for television and video playback and recording in the United States. The NTSC was originally organized in 1941 when TV broadcasting first began on a wide scale in black and white, and the format was revised in 1953 for color. The NTSC format has 525 scan lines, a field frequency of 60Hz, a broadcast bandwidth of 4MHz, line frequency of 15.75KHz, frame frequency of 1/30 of a second, and a color subcarrier frequency of 3.58MHz. It is an interlaced signal, which means that it scans every other line each time the screen is refreshed. The signal is generated as a composite of red, green, and blue signals for color and includes an FM frequency for audio and a signal for stereo. See also PAL and SECAM, which are incompatible systems used in Europe. NTSC is also called composite video.

null modem   A serial cable wired so that two data terminal equipment (DTE) devices, such as personal computers, or two data communication equipment (DCE) devices, such as modems or mice, can be connected. Also sometimes called a modem-eliminator or a LapLink cable. To make a null-modem cable with DB-25 connectors, you wire these pins together: 1-1, 2-3, 3-2, 4-5, 5-4, 6-8-20, 20-8-6, and 7-7.

numeric coprocessor   See *math coprocessor*.

NVRAM (Nonvolatile Random Access Memory)   Memory that retains data without power. Flash memory and battery-backed CMOS RAM are examples of NVRAM.

object hierarchy   Occurs in a graphical program when two or more objects are linked and one object's movement is dependent on the other object. This is known as a parent-child hierarchy. In an example using a human figure, the fingers would be child objects to the hand, which is a child object to the arm, which is a child to the shoulder, and so on. Object hierarchy provides much control for an animator in moving complex figures.

OCR (Optical Character Recognition)   An information-processing technology that converts human-readable text into computer data. Usually a scanner is used to read the text on a page, and OCR software converts the images to characters.

ODI (Open Data-link Interface)   A device driver standard from Novell that allows you to run multiple protocols on the same network adapter card. ODI adds functionality to Novell's NetWare and network computing environments by supporting multiple protocols and drivers.

OEM (original equipment manufacturer)   Any manufacturer that sells its product to a reseller. Usually refers to the original manufacturer of a particular device or component. Most Compaq hard disks, for example, are made by Conner Peripherals, who is considered the OEM.

OLE (object linking and embedding)   An enhancement to the original Dynamic Data Exchange (DDE) protocol that allows you to embed or link data created in one application in a document created in another application and subsequently edit that data directly from the final document.

online fallback   A feature that enables high-speed error-control modems to monitor line quality and fall back to the next lower speed if line quality degrades. Some modems fall forward as line quality improves.

open architecture   A system design in which the specifications are made public to encourage third-party vendors to develop add-on products. The PC is a true open architecture system, but the Macintosh is proprietary.

operating system (OS)   A collection of programs for operating the computer. Operating systems perform housekeeping tasks such as input and output between the computer and peripherals and accepting and interpreting information from the keyboard. DOS and OS/2 are examples of popular OSes.

optical disk   A disk that encodes data as a series of reflective pits that are read (and sometimes written) by a laser beam.

Orange Book   The standard for recordable compact discs (like CD-ROM, but recordable instead of read-only). Recordable compact discs are called CD-R and are becoming popular with the widespread use of multimedia. Part of the Orange Book standard defines rewritable Magneto-Optical disks and another section defines optical write-once, read-many (WORM) disks.

originate mode   A state in which the modem transmits at the predefined low frequency of the communications channel and receives at the high frequency. The transmit/receive frequencies are the reverse of the called modem, which is in answer mode. See also answer mode.

OS/2   An operating system originally developed through a joint effort by IBM and Microsoft Corporation and later by IBM alone. Originally released in 1987, OS/2 is a 32-bit operating system designed to run on computers using the Intel 386 or later microprocessors. The OS/2 Workplace Shell, an integral part of the system, is a graphical interface similar to Microsoft Windows and the Apple Macintosh system.

OSI (Open Systems Interconnection)   Reference Model Developed by the International Organization for Standardization (abbreviated as the ISO) in the 1980s, the OSI model splits a computer's networking stack into seven discrete layers. Each layer provides specific services to the layers above and below it.

output   Information processed by the computer, or the act of sending that information to a mass storage device such as a video display, a printer, or a modem.

over-clocking   The process of running a processor at a speed faster than the officially marked speed by using a higher clock multiplier or faster bus speed. Not recommended or endorsed by processor manufacturers. See also *clock multiplier*.

OverDrive   An Intel trademark name for its line of upgrade processors.

overlay   Part of a program that is loaded into memory only when it is required.

overrun   A situation in which data moves from one device faster than a second device can accept it.

overscanning A technique used in consumer display products that extends the deflection of a CRT's electron beam beyond the physical boundaries of the screen to ensure that images will always fill the display area. See also *underscanning*.

overwrite To write data on top of existing data, thus erasing the existing data.

package A device that includes a chip mounted on a carrier and sealed.

pairing Combining processor instructions for optimal execution on superscalar processors.

PAL 1) Phase Alternating Line system. Invented in 1961, a system of TV broadcasting used in England and other European countries (except France). PAL's image format is 4:3, 625 lines, 50Hz, and 4MHz video bandwidth with a total 8MHz of video channel width. With its 625-line picture delivered at 25 frames per second, PAL provides a better image and an improved color transmission over the NTSC system used in North America. 2) PAL also stands for Programmable Array Logic, a type of chip that has logic gates specified by a device programmer.

palmtop computer A computer system smaller than a notebook that is designed so that it can be held in one hand while being operated by the other. Many are now called PDAs or personal digital assistants.

parallel A method of transferring data characters in which the bits travel down parallel electrical paths simultaneously—for example, eight paths for 8-bit characters. Data is stored in computers in parallel form but may be converted to serial form for certain operations.

parity A method of error checking in which an extra bit is sent to the receiving device to indicate whether an even or odd number of binary 1 bits were transmitted. The receiving unit compares the received information with this bit and can obtain a reasonable judgment about the validity of the character. The same type of parity (even or odd) must be used by two communicating computers, or both may omit parity. When parity is used, a parity bit is added to each transmitted character. The bit's value is 0 or 1, to make the total number of 1s in the character even or odd, depending on which type of parity is used.

park program A program that executes a seek to the highest cylinder or just past the highest cylinder of a drive so that the potential of data loss is minimized if the drive is moved.

partition A section of a hard disk devoted to a particular operating system. Most hard disks have only one partition, devoted to DOS. A hard disk can have as many as four partitions, each occupied by a different operating system. DOS v3.3 or later can occupy two of these four partitions.

Pascal A high-level programming language named for the French mathematician Blaise Pascal (1623–1662). Developed in the early 1970s by Niklaus Wirth for teaching programming and designed to support the concepts of structured programming.

passive matrix Another name for dual scan display type LCDs.

PC card (PCMCIA) Personal Computer Memory Card International Association A credit card-sized expansion adapter for notebook and laptop PCs. PC card is the official PCMCIA trademark;

however, both PC card and PCMCIA card are used to refer to these standards. PCMCIA cards are removable modules that can hold numerous types of devices including memory, modems, fax/modems, radio transceivers, network adapters, solid state disks, and hard disks.

PCI (Peripheral Component Interconnect)   A standard bus specification initially developed by Intel that bypasses the standard ISA I/O bus and uses the system bus to increase the bus clock speed and take full advantage of the CPU's data path.

PCL (Printer Control Language)   Developed by Hewlett-Packard in 1984 as a language for the HP LaserJet printer. PCL is now the de facto industry standard for PC printing. PCL defines a standard set of commands, enabling applications to communicate with HP or HP-compatible printers, and is supported by virtually all printer manufacturers.

peer-to-peer   A type of network in which any computer can act as both a server (by providing access to its resources to other computers) and a client (by accessing shared resources from other computers).

PEL   See pixel.

Pentium   An Intel microprocessor with 32-bit registers, a 64-bit data bus, and a 32-bit address bus. The Pentium has a built-in L1 cache that is segmented into a separate 8KB cache for code and another 8KB cache for data. The Pentium includes an FPU or math coprocessor. The Pentium is backward compatible with the 486 and can operate in real, protected virtual, and virtual real modes.

Pentium II   An Intel sixth-generation processor similar to the Pentium Pro, but with MMX capabilities and SEC cartridge packaging technology.

Pentium Pro   An Intel sixth-generation processor with 32-bit registers, a 64-bit data bus, and a 36-bit address bus. The Pentium Pro has the same segmented Level 1 cache as the Pentium but also includes a 256KB, 512KB, or 1MB of L2 cache on separate die inside the processor package. The Pentium Pro includes a FPU or math coprocessor. The Pentium Pro is backward compatible with the Pentium and can operate in real, protected, and virtual real modes.

peripheral   Any piece of equipment used in computer systems that is an attachment to the computer. Disk drives, terminals, and printers are all examples of peripherals.

persistence   In a monitor, the quality of the phosphor chemical that indicates how long the glow caused by the electrons striking the phosphor will remain onscreen.

PGA   1) Pin Grid Array. A chip package that has a large number of pins on the bottom designed for socket mounting. 2) Also a Professional Graphics Adapter, a limited-production, high-resolution graphics card for XT and AT systems from IBM.

Photo CD   A technology developed by Eastman Kodak and Philips that stores photographic images on a CD-R recordable compact disc. Images stored on the Photo CD may have resolutions as high as 2,048×3,072 pixels. Up to 100 true-color images (24-bit color) can be stored on one disk. Photo CD images are created by scanning film and digitally recording the images on compact discs (CDs). The digitized images are indexed (given a 4-digit code), and thumbnails of each image on the disc are shown on the front of the case along with its index number. Multisession capability allows several rolls of film to be added to a single disk on different occasions.

photolithography   The photographic process used in electronic chip manufacturing that creates transistors and circuit and signal pathways in semiconductors by depositing different layers of various materials on the chip.

photoresist   A chemical used to coat a silicon wafer in the semiconductor manufacturing process that makes the silicon sensitive to light for photolithography.

physical drive   A single disk drive. DOS defines logical drives, which are given a specifier, such as C: or D:. A single physical drive may be divided into multiple logical drives. Conversely, special software can span a single logical drive across two physical drives.

physical unit number   See *PUN*.

PIF (Program Information File)   A file that contains information about a non-Windows application specifying optimum settings for running the program under Windows 3.x. These are called property sheets in Windows 95.

pin   1) The lead on a connector, chip, module or device. 2) Personal Identification Number. A personal password used for identification purposes.

pin compatible   Chips having the same pinout functions.

pinout   A listing of which pins have what functions on a chip, socket, slot, or other connector.

PIO mode (programmed input/output mode)   The standard data transfer modes used by IDE drives that use the processor's registers for data transfer. This is in contrast with DMA modes, which transfer data directly between main memory and the device. The slowest PIO mode is 0 and the fastest current mode is mode 4.

pipeline   A path for instructions or data to follow.

pixel   A mnemonic term meaning picture element. Any of the tiny elements that form a picture on a video display screen. Also called a pel.

planar board   A term equivalent to motherboard, used by IBM in some of its literature.

plated media   Hard disk platters plated with a form of thin metal film medium on which data is recorded.

platter   A disk contained in a hard disk drive. Most drives have two or more platters, each with data recorded on both sides.

PLCC (Plastic Leaded-Chip Carrier)   A popular chip-carrier package with J-leads around the perimeter of the package.

Plug and Play (PnP)   A hardware and software specification developed by Intel that allows a PnP system and PnP adapter cards to automatically configure themselves. PnP cards are free from switches and jumpers and are configured via the PnP BIOS in the host system, or via supplied programs for non-PnP systems.

polling   A communications technique that determines when a device is ready to send data. The system continually interrogates polled devices in a round-robin sequence. If a device has data to send, it sends back an acknowledgment and the transmission begins. Contrasts with interrupt-driven communications, in which the device generates a signal to interrupt the system when it has data to send.

port address   One of a system of addresses used by the computer to access devices such as disk drives or printer ports. You may need to specify an unused port address when installing any adapter boards in a system unit.

port   Plug or socket that enables an external device such as a printer to be attached to the adapter card in the computer. Also a logical address used by a microprocessor for communications between it and various devices.

port replicator   For mobile computers, a device that plugs into the laptop and provides all of the ports for connecting external devices. The advantage of using a port replicator is that the external devices can be left connected to the replicator and the mobile computer connected to them all at once by connecting to the replicator, rather than connecting to each individual device. A port replicator differs from a docking station in that the latter can provide additional drive bays and expansion slots not found in port replicators.

portable computer   A computer system smaller than a transportable system but larger than a laptop system. Most portable systems conform to the lunchbox style popularized by Compaq or the briefcase style popularized by IBM, each with a fold-down (removable) keyboard and built-in display. These systems characteristically run on AC power and not on batteries, include several expansion slots, and can be as powerful as full desktop systems.

POS (Programmable Option Select)   The Micro Channel Architecture's POS eliminates switches and jumpers from the system board and adapters by replacing them with programmable registers. Automatic configuration routines store the POS data in a battery-powered CMOS memory for system configuration and operations. The configuration utilities rely on adapter description files (ADF) that contain the setup data for each card.

POST (power on self test)   A series of tests run by the computer at power-on. Most computers scan and test many of their circuits and sound a beep from the internal speaker if this initial test indicates proper system performance.

PostScript   A page-description language developed primarily by John Warnock of Adobe Systems for converting and moving data to the laser-printed page. Instead of using the standard method of transmitting graphics or character information to a printer, telling it where to place dots one-by-one on a page, PostScript provides a way for the laser printer to interpret mathematically a full page of shapes and curves.

POTS (Plain Old Telephone Service)   Standard analog telephone service.

power management   Systems used initially in mobile computers (and now also used in desktop systems) to decrease power consumption by turning off or slowing down devices during periods of inactivity. See *APM*.

power supply   An electrical/electronic circuit that supplies all operating voltage and current to the computer system.

PPGA (Plastic Pin Grid Array)   A chip-packaging form factor used by Intel as an alternative to traditional ceramic packaging.

PPP (Point-to-Point Protocol)   A protocol that allows a computer to use the Internet with a standard telephone line and a high-speed modem. PPP is a new standard that replaces SLIP. PPP is less common than SLIP; however, it is increasing in popularity.

precompensation   A data write modification required by some older drives on the inner cylinders to compensate for the higher density of data on the (smaller) inner cylinders.

primary partition   An ordinary, single-volume bootable partition. See also extended partition.

processor   See *microprocessor.*

processor speed   The clock rate at which a microprocessor processes data. A typical Pentium PC, for example, operates at 200MHz (200 million cycles per second).

program   A set of instructions or steps telling the computer how to handle a problem or task.

PROM (Programmable Read-Only Memory)   A type of memory chip that can be programmed to store information permanently—information that cannot be erased.

proprietary   Anything invented by one company and that uses components only available from that one company. Especially applies to cases in which the inventing company goes to lengths to hide the specifications of the new invention or to prevent other manufacturers from making similar or compatible items. The opposite of standard or open architecture. Computers with nonstandard components that are available only from the original manufacturer, such as Apple Macintosh systems, are known as proprietary.

protected mode   A mode available in all Intel and compatible processors except the first-generation 8086 and 8088. In this mode, memory addressing is extended beyond the 1MB limits of the 8088 and real mode, and restricted protection levels can be set to trap software crashes and control the system.

protocol   A system of rules and procedures governing communications between two or more devices. Protocols vary, but communicating devices must follow the same protocol to exchange data. The data format, readiness to receive or send, error detection, and error correction are some of the operations that may be defined in protocols.

PS/2 mouse   A mouse designed to plug into a dedicated mouse port (a round, 6-pin DIN connector) on the motherboard, rather than plug into a serial port. The name comes from the fact that this port was first introduced on the IBM PS/2 systems.

PUN (Physical Unit Number)   A term used to describe a device attached directly to the SCSI bus. Also known as a SCSI ID. As many as eight SCSI devices can be attached to a single SCSI bus, and each must have a unique PUN or ID assigned from 7 to 0. Normally, the SCSI host adapter is assigned the highest-priority ID, which is 7. A bootable hard disk is assigned an ID of 0, and other nonbootable drives are assigned higher priorities.

QAM (Quadrature Amplitude Modulation)   A modulation technique used by high-speed modems that combines both phase and amplitude modulation. This technique enables multiple bits to be encoded in a single time interval.

QIC (Quarter-Inch Committee)   An industry association that sets hardware and software standards for tape-backup units that use quarter-inch-wide tapes.

QWERTY keyboard   The standard typewriter or computer keyboard, with the characters Q, W, E, R, T, and Y on the top row of alpha keys. Because of the haphazard placement of characters, this keyboard can hinder fast typing.

rails   Plastic strips attached to the sides of disk drives mounted in IBM ATs and compatibles so that the drives can slide into place. These rails fit into channels in the side of each disk drive bay position.

RAM disk   A "phantom disk drive" in which a section of system memory (RAM) is set aside to hold data, just as though it were a number of disk sectors. To DOS, a RAM disk looks like and functions like any other drive.

RAM (random-access memory)   All memory accessible at any instant (randomly) by a microprocessor.

RAMBUS Dynamic RAM   See *RDRAM*.

random-access file   A file in which all data elements (or records) are of equal length and written in the file end to end, without delimiting characters between. Any element (or record) in the file can be found directly by calculating the record's offset in the file.

random-access memory   See *RAM*.

raster   A pattern of horizontal scanning lines normally on a computer monitor. An electromagnetic field causes the beam of the monitor's tube to illuminate the correct dots to produce the required characters.

raster graphics   A technique for representing a picture image as a matrix of dots. It is the digital counterpart of the analog method used in TV. There are several raster graphics standards.

RCA jack   Also called a phono connector. A plug and socket for a two-wire coaxial cable used to connect audio and video components. The plug is a 1/8-inch thick prong that sticks out 5/16-inch from the middle of a cylinder.

RDRAM (Rambus DRAM)   A high-speed dynamic RAM technology developed by Rambus, Inc., which will be supported by Intel's 1999 and later motherboard chipsets. RDRAM transfers data at 1G/sec or faster, which is significantly faster than SDRAM and other technologies and which will be capable of keeping up with future-generation high-speed processors. Memory modules with RDRAM chips are called RIMMs (Rambus Inline Memory Modules). Rambus licenses its technology to other semiconductor companies, who manufacture the chips and RIMMs.

read/write head   A tiny magnet that reads and writes data on a disk track.

read-only file   A file whose attribute setting in the file's directory entry tells DOS not to allow software to write into or over the file.

read-only memory   See *ROM*.

real mode   A mode available in all Intel 8086-compatible processors that enables compatibility with the original 8086. In this mode, memory addressing is limited to 1MB.

real-time   The actual time in which a program or event takes place. In computing, real-time refers to an operating mode under which data is received and processed and the results returned so quickly that the process appears instantaneous to the user. The term is also used to describe the process of simultaneous digitization and compression of audio and video information.

reboot   The process of restarting a computer and reloading the operating system.

Red Book   More commonly known as Compact Disc-Digital Audio (CD-DA), and is one of four compact disc standards. Red Book got its name from the color of the manual used to describe the CD Audio specifications. The Red Book audio standard requires that digital audio be sampled at a 44.1KHz sample rate using 16 bits for each sample. This is the standard used by audio CDs and many CD-ROMs. See also *CD-A* and *CD-DA*.

refresh cycle   A cycle in which the computer accesses all memory locations stored by DRAM chips so that the information remains intact. DRAM chips must be accessed several times a second, or else the information fades.

refresh rate   Another term for the vertical scan frequency of monitors.

register   Storage area in memory having a specified storage capacity, such as a bit, a byte, or a computer word, and intended for a special purpose.

Registry   The system configuration files used by Windows 9x and Windows NT to store settings about installed hardware and drivers, user preferences, installed software, and other settings required to keep Windows running correctly. Replaces the WIN.INI and SYSTEM.INI files from Windows 3.x.

remote digital loopback   A test that checks the phone link and a remote modem's transmitter and receiver. Data entered from the keyboard is transmitted from the initiating modem, received by the remote modem's receiver, looped through its transmitter, and returned to the local screen for verification.

remote echo   A copy of the data received by the remote system, returned to the sending system, and displayed onscreen. A function of the remote system.

resolution   1) A reference to the size of the pixels used in graphics. In medium-resolution graphics, pixels are large. In high-resolution graphics, pixels are small. 2) A measure of the number of horizontal and vertical pixels that can be displayed by a video adapter and monitor.

RFI (Radio Frequency Interference)   A high frequency signal radiated by improperly shielded conductors, particularly when signal path lengths are comparable to or longer than the signal wavelengths. The FCC now regulates RFI in computer equipment sold in the U.S. under FCC Regulations Part 15, Subpart J.

RGB (Red-Green-Blue)   A type of computer color display output signal comprised of separately controllable red, green, and blue signals; as opposed to composite video, in which signals are combined prior to output. RGB monitors typically offer higher resolution than composite monitors.

ribbon cable   Flat cable with wires running in parallel, such as those used for internal IDE or SCSI.

RIMM (Rambus Inline Memory Module)   A type of memory module made using RDRAM chips. See *RDRAM*.

RISC (Reduced Instruction Set Computer)   Differentiated from CISC, Complex Instruction Set Computer. RISC processors have simple instruction sets requiring only one or a few execution cycles. These simple instructions can be used more effectively than CISC systems with appropriately designed software, resulting in faster operations. See also *CISC*.

RJ-11   The standard 2-wire connector type used for single-line telephone connections.

RJ-14   The standard 4-wire connector type used for two-line telephone connections.

RJ-45   A standard connector type used in networking with twisted-pair cabling. Resembles an RJ-11/14 telephone jack, but RJ-45 is larger with more wires.

RLL (Run-Length Limited)   A type of encoding that derives its name from the fact that the techniques used limit the distance (run length) between magnetic flux reversals on the disk platter. Several types of RLL encoding techniques exist, although only two are commonly used. (1,7) RLL encoding increases storage capacity by about 30 percent over MFM encoding and is most popular in the very highest capacity drives due to a better window margin, while (2,7) RLL encoding increases storage capacity by 50 percent over MFM encoding and is used in the majority of RLL implementations. Most IDE, ESDI, and SCSI hard disks use one of these forms of RLL encoding.

RMA number (Return-Merchandise Authorization Number)   A number given to you by a vendor when you arrange to return an item for repairs. Used to track the item and the repair.

ROM BIOS (read-only memory basic input/output system)   A BIOS encoded in a form of read-only memory for protection. Often applied to important startup programs that must be present in a system for it to operate.

ROM (read-only memory)   A type of memory that has values permanently or semi-permanently burned in. These locations are used to hold important programs or data that must be available to the computer when the power initially is turned on.

root directory   The main directory of any hard or floppy disk. Has a fixed size and location for a particular disk volume and cannot be resized dynamically the way subdirectories can.

router Hardware that routes messages from one local area network to another. It is used to internetwork similar and dissimilar networks and can select the most expedient route based on traffic load, line speeds, costs, and network failures.

routine Set of frequently used instructions. May be considered as a subdivision of a program with two or more instructions that are related functionally.

RS-232 An interface introduced in August 1969 by the Electronic Industries Association. The RS-232 interface standard provides an electrical description for connecting peripheral devices to computers.

scan codes The hexadecimal codes actually sent by the keyboard to the motherboard when a key is pressed.

scan lines The parallel lines across a video screen, along which the scanning spot travels in painting the video information that makes up a monitor picture. NTSC systems use 525 scan lines to a screen; PAL systems use 625.

scanning frequency A monitor measurement that specifies how often the image is refreshed. See also vertical scan frequency.

scratch disk A disk that contains no useful information and can be used as a test disk. IBM has a routine on the Advanced Diagnostics disks that creates a specially formatted scratch disk to be used for testing floppy drives.

SCSI (Small Computer System Interface) A standard originally developed by Shugart Associates (then called SASI for Shugart Associates System Interface) and later approved by ANSI in 1986. SCSI-2 was approved in 1994, and SCSI-3 is currently in the development process. Normally uses a 50-pin connector and permits multiple devices (up to eight including the host) to be connected in daisy-chain fashion.

SDLC (Synchronous Data Link Control) A protocol developed by IBM for software applications and communicating devices operation in IBM's Systems Network Architecture (SNA). Defines operations at the link level of communications—for example, the format of data frames exchanged between modems over a phone line.

SDRAM (Synchronous DRAM) RAM that runs at the same speed as the main system bus.

SEC (Single Edge Contact) cartridge An Intel processor packaging design in which the processor along with several L2 cache chips are mounted on a small circuit board (much like an oversized memory SIMM), which is then sealed in a metal and plastic cartridge. The cartridge is then plugged into the motherboard through an edge connector called Slot 1 or Slot 2, which looks very much like an adapter card slot.

SECAM Sequential Couleur A M[ac]emoire (sequential color with memory), the French color TV system also adopted in Russia. The basis of operation is the sequential recording of primary colors in alternate lines. The image format is 4:3, 625 lines, 50Hz, and 6MHz video bandwidth with a total 8MHz of video channel width.

sector   A section of one track defined with identification markings and an identification number. Most sectors hold 512 bytes of data.

security software   Utility software that uses a system of passwords and other devices to restrict an individual's access to subdirectories and files.

seek time   The amount of time required for a disk drive to move the heads across one third of the total number of cylinders. Represents the average time it takes to move the heads from one cylinder to another randomly selected cylinder. Seek time is a part of the average access time for a drive.

semiconductor   A substance, such as germanium or silicon, whose conductivity is poor at low temperatures but is improved by minute additions of certain substances or by the application of heat, light, or voltage. Depending on the temperature and pressure, a semiconductor can control a flow of electricity. Semiconductors are the basis of modern electronic-circuit technology.

sequencer   A software program that controls MIDI file messages and keeps track of music timing. Because MIDI files store note instructions instead of actual sounds, a sequencer is needed to play, record, and edit MIDI sounds. Sequencer programs allow for recording and playback of MIDI files by storing the instrument, note pitch (frequency), duration (in real time) that each note is held, and loudness (amplitude) of each musical or sound-effect note.

sequential file   A file in which varying-length data elements are recorded end to end, with delimiting characters placed between each element. To find a particular element, you must read the whole file up to that element.

serial mouse   A mouse designed to connect to a computer's serial port.

serial port   An I/O connector used to connect to serial devices.

serial   The transfer of data characters one bit at a time, sequentially, using a single electrical path.

servo   The mechanism in a drive that enables the head positioner to adjust continuously so that it is precisely placed above a given cylinder in the drive.

servo data   Magnetic markings written on disk platters to guide the read/write heads in drives that use voice-coil actuators.

session (single or multisession)   A term used in CD-ROM recording to describe a recording event. In a single session, data is recorded on a CD-ROM and an index is created. If additional space is left on the disc, another session can be used to record additional files along with another index. Some older CD-ROM drives do not expect additional recording sessions and therefore will be unable to read the additional session data on the disk. The advent of Kodak's Photo CD propelled the desire for multisession CD-ROM XA (extended architecture) drives.

settling time   The time required for read/write heads to stop vibrating after they have been moved to a new track.

shadow mask   A thin screen full of holes that adheres to the inside of a color CRT. The electron beam is aimed through the holes in the mask onto the phosphor dots. See also aperture grille.

shadow ROM   A copy of a system's slower access ROM BIOS placed in faster access RAM, usually during the startup or boot procedure. This setup enables the system to access BIOS code without the penalty of additional wait states required by the slower ROM chips. Also called shadow RAM.

shell   The generic name of any user interface software. COMMAND.COM is the standard shell for DOS. OS/2 comes with three shells: a DOS command shell, an OS/2 command shell, and the OS/2 Presentation Manager, a graphical shell.

shielded twisted-pair (STP)   Unshielded twisted-pair (UTP) network cabling with a metal sheath or braid around it to reduce interference, usually used in Token-Ring networks.

shock rating   A rating (usually expressed in G force units) of how much shock a disk drive can sustain without damage. Usually two different specifications exist for a drive powered on or off.

signal-to-noise (S/N) ratio   The strength of a video or audio signal in relation to interference (noise). The higher the S/N ratio, the better the quality of the signal.

SIMM (Single Inline Memory Module)   An array of memory chips on a small PC board with a single row of I/O contacts.

single-ended   An electrical signaling method where a single line is referenced by a ground path common to other signals. In a single-ended bus intended for moderately long distances, there is commonly one ground line between groups of signal lines to provide some resistance to signal crosstalk. Single-ended signals require only one driver or receiver pin per signal, plus one ground pin per group of signals. Single-ended signals are vulnerable to common mode noise and crosstalk but are much less expensive than differential signaling methods.

SIP (Single Inline Package)   A DIP-like package with only one row of leads.

skinny dip   Twenty-four- and twenty-eight-position DIP devices with .300-inch row-to-row centerlines.

sleep   See *suspend*.

SLIP (Serial Line Internet Protocol)   An Internet protocol that is used to run the Internet Protocol (IP) over serial lines such as telephone circuits. IP allows a packet to traverse multiple networks on the way to its final destination.

slot   A physical connector on a motherboard to hold an expansion card, SIMMs and DIMMs, or a processor card in place and make contact with the electrical connections.

Slot 1   The motherboard connector designed by Intel to accept its SEC cartridge processor design used by the Pentium II.

Slot 2   A motherboard connector for Pentium II Xeon processors intended mainly for fileserver applications. Slot 2 systems support up to four-way symmetric multiprocessing.

SMBIOS   A BIOS that incorporates system management functions and reporting compatible with the Desktop Management Interface (DMI).

SMPTE time code   An 80-bit standardized edit time code adopted by SMPTE, the Society of Motion Picture and Television Engineers. The SMPTE time code is a standard used to identify individual video frames in the video-editing process. SMPTE time code controls such functions as play, record, rewind, and forward of video tapes. SMPTE time code displays video in terms of hours, minutes, seconds, and frames for accurate video editing.

snow   A flurry of bright dots that can appear anywhere onscreen on a monitor.

socket   A receptacle, usually on a motherboard although sometimes also found on expansion cards, that processors or chips can be plugged into.

Socket 1–8   The Intel specifications for eight different sockets to accept various Intel processors in the 486, Pentium, and Pentium Pro families.

soft error   An error in reading or writing data that occurs sporadically, usually because of a transient problem such as a power fluctuation.

software   A series of instructions loaded in the computer's memory that instructs the computer in how to accomplish a problem or task.

SO-J (Small Outline J-lead)   A small DIP package with J-shaped leads for surface mounting or socketing.

South Bridge   The Intel term for the lower-speed component in the chipset that has always been a single individual chip. Also called the PIIX (PCI, ISA, IDE eXcelerator), the South Bridge connects to the 33MHz PCI bus and contains the IDE interface ports and the interface to the 8MHz ISA bus. It also normally contains the USB interface and even the CMOS RAM and real-time clock functions. The South Bridge contains all of the components that make up the ISA bus, including the interrupt and DMA controllers. See also *chipset* and *North Bridge*.

spindle   The central post on which a disk drive's platters are mounted.

spindle count   In notebook and laptop computers with interchangeable drives, spindle count refers to how many drives can be installed and used at the same time.

SRAM (Static Random Access Memory)   A form of high-speed memory. SRAM chips do not require a refresh cycle like DRAM chips and can be made to operate at very high-access speeds. SRAM chips are very expensive because they normally require six transistors per bit. This also makes the chip larger than conventional DRAM chips. SRAM is volatile, meaning it will lose data with no power.

ST-506/412   A hard disk interface invented by Seagate Technology and introduced in 1980 with the ST-506 5MB hard drive.

stair-stepping   Jagged raster representation of diagonals or curves; corrected by anti-aliasing.

standby   Defines an optional operating state of minimal power reduction with the shortest recovery time.

standby power supply   A backup power supply that quickly switches into operation during a power outage.

Standoff   In a motherboard and case design, small nonconductive spacers (usually plastic or nylon) used to keep the underside of the motherboard from contacting the metallic case, therefore preventing short circuits of the motherboard.

start/stop bits   The signaling bits attached to a character before and after the character is transmitted during asynchronous transmission.

starting cluster   The number of the first cluster occupied by a file. Listed in the directory entry of every file.

stepper motor actuator   An assembly that moves disk drive read/write heads across platters by a sequence of small partial turns of a stepper motor.

stepping   The code used to identify the revision of a processor. New masks are introduced to build each successive stepping, incorporating any changes needed to fix known bugs in prior steppings.

storage   Device or medium on or in which data can be entered or held and retrieved at a later time. Synonymous with memory.

streaming   In tape backup, a condition in which data is transferred from the hard disk as quickly as the tape drive can record the data so that the drive does not start and stop or waste tape.

string   A sequence of characters.

subdirectory   A directory listed in another directory. Subdirectories themselves exist as files.

subroutine   A segment of a program that can be executed by a single call. Also called program module.

superscalar execution   The capability of a processor to execute more than one instruction at a time.

surface mount   Chip carriers and sockets designed to mount to the surface of a PC board.

surge protector   A device in the power line that feeds the computer and provides protection against voltage spikes and other transients.

suspend   Refers to a level of power management in which substantial power reduction is achieved by the display or other components. The components can have a longer recovery time from this state than from the standby state.

SVGA (Super VGA) Originally, this referred to a video adapter or monitor capable of 800×600 resolution. However, this term is now often misused and used to refer to any video adapter or monitor that can display any resolution greater than 640×480.

S-Video (Y/C) Type of video signal used in the Hi8 and S-VHS videotape formats in which the luminance and chrominance (Y/C) components are kept separate, providing greater control and quality of each image. S-video transmits luminance and color portions separately, thus avoiding the NTSC encoding process and its inevitable loss of picture quality.

SWEDAC (Swedish Board for Technical Accreditation) Regulatory agency establishing standards such as MPR1 and MPR2, which specify maximum values for both alternating electric fields and magnetic fields and provide monitor manufacturers with guidelines in creating low-emission monitors.

synchronous communication A form of communication in which blocks of data are sent at strictly timed intervals. Because the timing is uniform, no start or stop bits are required. Compare with asynchronous communication. Some mainframes support only synchronous communications unless a synchronous adapter and appropriate software have been installed. See also asynchronous communication.

system crash A situation in which the computer freezes up and refuses to proceed without rebooting. Usually caused by faulty software. Unlike a hard disk crash, no permanent physical damage occurs.

system files Files with the system attribute. Normally, the hidden files that are used to boot the operating system. The MS-DOS and Windows 9x system files include IO.SYS and MSDOS.SYS; the IBM DOS system files are IBMBIO.COM and IBMDOS.COM.

System Management Mode (SMM) Circuitry integrated into Intel processors that operates independently to control the processor's power use based on its activity level. It allows the user to specify time intervals after which the CPU will be powered down partially or fully and also supports the suspend/resume feature that allows for instant power on and power off.

target A device attached to a SCSI bus that receives and processes commands sent from another device (the initiator) on the SCSI bus. A SCSI hard disk is an example of a target.

TCM (Trellis-coded modulation) An error-detection and correction technique employed by high-speed modems to enable higher-speed transmissions that are more resistant to line impairments.

TCO 1) Refers to the Swedish Confederation of Professional Employees, which has set stringent standards for devices that emit radiation. See MPR II. 2) Total Cost of Ownership. The cost of using a computer. It includes the cost of the hardware, software, and upgrades as well as the cost of the in-house staff and consultants that provide training and technical support.

TCP (Tape Carrier Package)   A method of packaging processors for use in portable systems that reduces the size, the power consumed, and the heat generated by the chip. A processor in the TCP form factor is essentially a raw die encased in an oversized piece of polyamide film. The film is laminated with copper foil that is etched to form the leads that will connect the processor to the motherboard.

TCP/IP (Transmission Control Protocol/Internet Protocol)   A set of protocols developed by the U.S. Department of Defense (DoD) to link dissimilar computers across many kinds of networks. This is the primary protocol used by the Internet.

temporary backup   A second copy of a work file, usually having the extension BAK. Created by application software so that you easily can return to a previous version of your work.

temporary file   A file temporarily (and usually invisibly) created by a program for its own use.

tera   A multiplier indicating 1 trillion (1,000,000,000,000) of some unit. Abbreviated as t or T. When used to indicate a number of bytes of memory storage, the multiplier definition changes to 1,099,511,627,776. One terabit, for example, equals 1,000,000,000,000 bits, and one terabyte equals 1,099,511,627,776 bytes.

terabyte (TB)   A unit of information storage equal to 1,099,511,627,776 bytes.

terminal   A device whose keyboard and display are used for sending and receiving data over a communications link. Differs from a microcomputer in that it has no internal processing capabilities. Used to enter data into or retrieve processed data from a system or network.

terminal mode   An operational mode required for microcomputers to transmit data. In terminal mode, the computer acts as though it were a standard terminal such as a teletypewriter rather than a data processor. Keyboard entries go directly to the modem, whether the entry is a modem command or data to be transmitted over the phone lines. Received data is output directly to the screen. The more popular communications software products control terminal mode and enable more complex operations, including file transmission and saving received files.

terminator   Hardware or circuits that must be attached to or enabled at both ends of an electrical bus. Functions to prevent the reflection or echoing of signals that reach the ends of the bus and to ensure that the correct impedance load is placed on the driver circuits on the bus. Most commonly used with the SCSI bus.

TFT (Thin Film Transistor)   The highest quality and brightest LCD color display type. A method for packaging one to four transistors per pixel within a flexible material that is the same size and shape as the LCD display, so that the transistors for each pixel lie directly behind the liquid crystal cells that they control.

thin Ethernet   See *10base2* or *IEEE 802.3*.

thin-film media   Hard disk platters that have a thin film (usually three-millionths of an inch) of medium deposited on the aluminum substrate through a sputtering or plating process.

Thinnet   See *10base2* or *IEEE 802.3*.

through-hole   Chip carriers and sockets equipped with leads that extend through holes in a PC board.

throughput   The amount of user data transmitted per second without the overhead of protocol information such as start and stop bits or frame headers and trailers.

TIFF (Tagged Image File Format)   A way of storing and exchanging digital image data. Developed by Aldus Corporation, Microsoft Corporation, and major scanner vendors to help link scanned images with the popular desktop publishing applications. Supports three main types of image data: black-and-white data, halftones or dithered data, and grayscale data.

time code   A frame-by-frame address code time reference recorded on the spare track of a videotape or inserted in the vertical blanking interval. The time code is an eight-digit number encoding time in hours, minutes, seconds, and video frames.

Token Ring   A type of local area network in which the workstations relay a packet of data called a token in a logical ring configuration. When a station wants to transmit, it takes possession of the token, attaches its data, and then frees the token after the data has made a complete circuit of the electrical ring. Transmits at speeds of 16Mbps. Because of the token-passing scheme, access to the network is controlled, unlike the slower 10BaseX Ethernet system in which collisions of data can occur, which wastes time. The Token-Ring network uses shielded twisted-pair wiring, which is cheaper than the coaxial cable used by 10Base2 and 10Base5 Ethernet and ARCnet.

toner   The ultrafine colored plastic powder used in laser printers and photocopiers to produce the image on paper.

tower   A personal computer that normally sits on the floor and that is mounted vertically rather than horizontally.

TPI (tracks per inch)   Used as a measurement of magnetic track density. Standard 5 1/4-inch 360KB floppy disks have a density of 48 TPI, and the 1.2MB disks have a 96 TPI density. All 3 1/2-inch disks have a 135.4667 TPI density, and hard disks can have densities greater than 3,000 TPI.

track   One of the many concentric circles that holds data on a disk surface. Consists of a single line of magnetic flux changes and is divided into some number of 512-byte sectors.

track density   Expressed as tracks per inch (TPI); defines how many tracks are recorded in one inch of space measured radially from the center of the disk. Sometimes also called radial density.

track-to-track seek time   The time required for read/write heads to move between adjacent tracks.

transport layer   In the OSI reference model, when more than one packet is in process at any time, such as when a large file must be split into multiple packets for transmission, this is the layer that controls the sequencing of the message components and regulates inbound traffic flow.

transportable computer   A computer system larger than a portable system and similar in size and shape to a portable sewing machine. Most transportables conform to a design similar to the original Compaq portable, with a built-in CRT display. These systems are characteristically very heavy and run only on AC power. Because of advances primarily in LCD and plasma-display technology, these systems are largely obsolete and have been replaced by portable systems.

troubleshooting   The task of determining the cause of a problem.

true-color images   Also called 24-bit color images because each pixel is represented by 24 bits of data, allowing for 16.7 million colors. The number of colors possible is based on the number of bits used to represent the color. If 8 bits are used, there are 256 possible color values (2 to the 8th power). To obtain 16.7 million colors, each of the primary colors (red, green, and blue) is represented by 8 bits per pixel, which allows for 256 possible shades for each of the primary red, green, and blue colors or 256×256×256 = 16.7 million total colors.

TSR (Terminate-and-Stay-Resident)   A program that remains in memory after being loaded. Because they remain in memory, TSR programs can be reactivated by a predefined keystroke sequence or other operation while another program is active. Usually called resident programs.

TTL (Transistor-to-Transistor Logic)   Digital signals often are called TTL signals. A TTL display is a monitor that accepts digital input at standardized signal voltage levels.

twisted pair   A type of wire in which two small, insulated copper wires are wrapped or twisted around each other to minimize interference from other wires in the cable. Two types of twisted-pair cables are available: unshielded and shielded. Unshielded twisted-pair (UTP) wiring commonly is used in telephone cables and provides little protection against interference. Shielded twisted-pair (STP) wiring is used in some networks or any application in which immunity from electrical interference is more important. Twisted-pair wire is much easier to work with than coaxial cable and is cheaper as well.

typematic   The keyboard repeatedly sending the keypress code to the motherboard for a key that is held down. The delay before the code begins to repeat and the speed at which it repeats are user adjustable.

UART (Universal Asynchronous Receiver Transmitter)   A chip device that controls the RS-232 serial port in a PC-compatible system. Originally developed by National Semiconductor, several UART versions are in PC-compatible systems: The 8250B is used in PC- or XT-class systems, and the 16450 and 16550A are used in AT-class systems.

unformatted capacity   The total number of bytes of data that can fit on a disk. The formatted capacity is lower because space is lost defining the boundaries between sectors.

uninterruptible power supply (UPS)   A device that supplies power to the computer from batteries so that power will not stop, even momentarily, during a power outage. The batteries are recharged constantly from a wall socket.

Universal Asynchronous Receiver Transmitter   See *UART*.

UPC (Universal Product Code)   A 10-digit computer-readable bar code used in labeling retail products. The code in the form of vertical bars includes a five-digit manufacturer identification number and a five-digit product code number.

update To modify information already contained in a file or program with current information.

Upper Memory Area (UMA) The 384KB of memory between 640KB and 1MB.

URL (Uniform Resource Locator) The primary naming scheme used to identify a particular site or file on the World Wide Web. URLs combine information about the protocol being used, the address of the site where the resource is located, the subdirectory location at the site, and the name of the particular file (or page) in question.

USB (Universal Serial Bus) A 12Mbit/sec (1.5MB/sec) interface over a simple four-wire connection. The bus supports up to 127 devices and uses a tiered star topology built on expansion hubs that can reside in the PC, any USB peripheral, or even standalone hub boxes.

utility Programs that carry out routine procedures to make computer use easier.

UTP (Unshielded Twisted Pair) A type of wire often used indoors to connect telephones or computer devices. Comes with two or four wires twisted inside a flexible plastic sheath or conduit and uses modular plugs and phone jacks.

V.21 An ITU standard for modem communications at 300bps. Modems made in the U.S. or Canada follow the Bell 103 standard but can be set to answer V.21 calls from overseas. The actual transmission rate is 300 baud and employs FSK (frequency shift keying) modulation, which encodes a single bit per baud.

V.22 An ITU standard for modem communications at 1,200bps, with an optional fallback to 600bps. V.22 is partially compatible with the Bell 212A standard observed in the U.S. and Canada. The actual transmission rate is 600 baud, using DPSK (differential-phase shift keying) to encode as much as two bits per baud.

V.22bis An ITU standard for modem communications at 2,400bps. Includes an automatic link-negotiation fallback to 1,200bps and compatibility with Bell 212A/V.22 modems. The actual transmission rate is 600 baud, using QAM (quadrature amplitude modulation) to encode as much as four bits per baud.

V.23 An ITU standard for modem communications at 1,200 or 600bps with a 75bps back channel. Used in the United Kingdom for some videotext systems.

V.25 An ITU standard for modem communications that specifies an answer tone different from the Bell answer tone used in the U.S. and Canada. Most intelligent modems can be set with an ATB0 command so that they use the V.25 2,100Hz tone when answering overseas calls.

V.32 An ITU standard for modem communications at 9,600bps and 4,800bps. V.32 modems fall back to 4,800bps when line quality is impaired and fall forward again to 9,600bps when line quality improves. The actual transmission rate is 2,400 baud using QAM (quadrature amplitude modulation) and optional TCM (trellis-coded modulation) to encode as much as four data bits per baud.

V.32bis An ITU standard that extends the standard V.32 connection range and supports 4,800; 7,200; 9,600; 12,000; and 14,400bps transmission rates. V.32bis modems fall back to the next lower speed when line quality is impaired, fall back further as necessary, and fall forward to the next higher speed when line quality improves. The actual transmission rate is 2,400 baud using QAM (quadrature amplitude modulation) and TCM (trellis-coded modulation) to encode as much as six data bits per baud.

V.32terbo   A proprietary standard proposed by several modem manufacturers that will be cheaper to implement than the standard V.32 fast protocol but that will only support transmission speeds of up to 18,800bps. Because it is not an industry standard, it is not likely to have widespread industry support.

V.34   An ITU standard that extends the standard V.32bis connection range, supporting 28,800bps transmission rates as well as all the functions and rates of V.32bis. This was called V.32fast or V.fast while under development.

V.34+   An ITU standard that extends the standard V.34 connection range, supporting 33,600bps transmission rates as well as all the functions and rates of V.34.

V.42   An ITU standard for modem communications that defines a two-stage process of detection and negotiation for LAPM error control. Also supports MNP error-control protocol, Levels 1–4.

V.42bis   An extension of CCITT V.42 that defines a specific data-compression scheme for use with V.42 and MNP error control.

V.90   ITU-T designation for a defining the standard for 56Kbps communication. Supercedes the proprietary X2 schemes from U.S. Robotics (3Com) and K56Flex from Rockwell.

vaccine   A type of program used to locate and eradicate virus code from infected programs or systems.

VCPI (Virtual Control Program Interface)   A 386 and later processor memory management standard created by Phar Lap software in conjunction with other software developers. VCPI provides an interface between applications using DOS extenders and 386 memory managers.

Vertical Blanking Interval (VBI)   The top and bottom lines in the video field, in which frame numbers, picture stops, chapter stops, white flags, closed captions, and more may be encoded. These lines do not appear on the display screen but maintain image stability and enhance image access.

vertical scan frequency   The rate at which the electron gun in a monitor scans or refreshes the entire screen each second.

Very Large Scale Integration   See *IC*.

VESA (Video Electronics Standards Association)   Founded in the late 1980s by NEC Home Electronics and eight other leading video board manufacturers, with the main goal to standardize the electrical, timing, and programming issues surrounding 800×600 resolution video displays, commonly known as Super VGA. VESA has also developed the Video Local Bus (VL-Bus) standard for connecting high-speed adapters directly to the local processor bus.

VFAT (virtual file allocation table)   A file system used in Windows for Workgroups and Windows 95/98. VFAT provides 32-bit protected mode access for file manipulation and supports long filenames (LFNs)—up to 255 characters in Windows 95 and later. VFAT compatible with the standard DOS 16-bit FAT. VFAT was called 32-bit file access in Windows for Workgroups. VFAT is not the same as FAT32.

VGA (Video Graphics Array)   A type of PC video display circuit (and adapter) first introduced by IBM on April 2, 1987, that supports text and graphics. Text is supported at a maximum resolution of 80×25 characters in 16 colors with a character box of 9×16 pixels. Graphics is supported at a maximum resolution of 320×200 pixels in 256 (from a palette of 262,144) colors or 640×480 pixels in 16 colors. The VGA outputs an analog signal with a horizontal scanning frequency of 31.5KHz and supports analog color or analog monochrome displays.

VHS (Video Home System)   A popular consumer videotape format developed by Matsushita and JVC.

video   A system of recording and transmitting primarily visual information by translating moving or still images into electrical signals. The term video properly refers only to the picture, but as a generic term, video usually embraces audio and other signals that are part of a complete program. Video now includes not only broadcast television but many nonbroadcast applications such as corporate communications, marketing, home entertainment, games, teletext, security, and even the visual display units of computer-based technology.

Video 8 or **8mm Video**   Video format based on the 8mm videotapes popularized by Sony for camcorders.

video adapter   An expansion card or chipset built into a motherboard that provides the capability to display text and graphics onscreen. If the adapter is part of an expansion card, it also includes the physical connector for the monitor cable. If the chipset is on the motherboard, the video connector will be on the motherboard as well.

video graphics array   See *VGA*.

video-on-CD or **video CD**   A full-motion digital video format using MPEG video compression and incorporating a variety of VCR-like control capabilities. See also *White Book*.

virtual disk   A RAM disk or "phantom disk drive" in which a section of system memory (usually RAM) is set aside to hold data, just as though it were a number of disk sectors. To DOS, a virtual disk looks like and functions like any other "real" drive.

virtual memory   A technique by which operating systems (including OS/2) load more programs and data into memory than they can hold. Parts of the programs and data are kept on disk and constantly swapped back and forth into system memory. The applications' software programs are unaware of this setup and act as though a large amount of memory is available.

virtual real mode   A mode available in all Intel 80386-compatible processors. In this mode, memory addressing is limited to 4,096MB, restricted protection levels can be set to trap software crashes and control the system, and individual real-mode compatible sessions can be set up and maintained separately from one another.

virus   A type of resident program designed to replicate itself. Usually at some later time when the virus is running, it causes an undesirable action to take place.

VL-Bus (VESA Local Bus)   A standard 32-bit expansion slot bus specification used in 486 PCs. Now replaced by PCI bus.

VMM (Virtual Memory Manager)   A facility in Windows enhanced mode that manages the task of swapping data in and out of 386 and later processor virtual real-mode memory space for multiple non-Windows applications running in virtual real mode.

voice-coil actuator   A device that moves read/write heads across hard disk platters by magnetic interaction between coils of wire and a magnet. Functions somewhat like an audio speaker, from which the name originated.

voltage reduction technology   An Intel processor technology that allows a processor to draw the standard voltage from the motherboard but run the internal processor core at a lower voltage.

voltage regulator   A device that smoothes out voltage irregularities in the power fed to the computer.

volume   A portion of a disk signified by a single drive specifier. Under DOS v3.3 and later, a single hard disk can be partitioned into several volumes, each with its own logical drive specifier (C:, D:, E:, and so on).

volume label   An identifier or name of up to 11 characters that names a disk.

VPN (virtual private network)   A private network that is operated within a public network. In order to maintain privacy, VPNs use access control and encryption.

VRAM (video random-access memory)   VRAM chips are modified DRAMs on video boards that enable simultaneous access by the host system's processor and the processor on the video board. A large amount of information thus can be transferred quickly between the video board and the system processor. Sometimes also called dual-ported RAM.

VxD (virtual device driver)   A special type of Windows driver. VxDs run at the most privileged CPU mode (ring 0) and allow low-level interaction with the hardware and internal Windows functions.

wafer   A thin circular piece of silicon from which processors, memory, and other semiconductor electronics are manufactured.

wait states   Pause cycles during system operation that require the processor to wait one or more clock cycles until memory can respond to the processor's request. Enables the microprocessor to synchronize with lower-cost, slower memory. A system that runs with "zero wait states" requires none of these cycles because of the use of faster memory or a memory cache system.

warm boot   Rebooting a system by means of a software command rather than turning the power off and back on. See also *cold boot.*

wave table synthesis   A method of creating synthetic sound on a sound card that uses actual musical instrument sounds sampled and stored on ROM (or RAM) on the sound card. The sound card then modifies this sample to create any note needed for that instrument. Produces much better sound quality than FM synthesis.

Whetstone   A benchmark program developed in 1976 and designed to simulate arithmetic-intensive programs used in scientific computing. Remains completely CPU-bound and performs no I/O or system calls. Originally written in ALGOL, although the C and Pascal versions became more popular by the late 1980s. The speed at which a system performs floating-point operations often is measured in units of Whetstones.

White Book   A standard specification developed by Philips and JVC in 1993 for storing MPEG standard video on CDs. An extension of the Red Book standard for digital audio, Yellow Book standard for CD-ROM, Green Book standard for CD-I, and Orange Book standard for CD write-once.

Whitney technology   A term referring to a magnetic disk design that usually has oxide or thin film media, thin film read/write heads, low floating-height sliders, and low-mass actuator arms that together allow higher-bit densities than the older Winchester technology. Whitney technology was first introduced with the IBM 3370 disk drive, circa 1979.

wide area network (WAN)   A LAN that extends beyond the boundaries of a single building.

Winchester drive   Any ordinary, nonremovable (or fixed) hard disk drive. The name originates from a particular IBM drive in the 1960s that had 30MB of fixed and 30 of removable storage. This 30-30 drive matched the caliber figure for a popular series of rifles made by Winchester, so the slang term Winchester was applied to any fixed-platter hard disk.

Winchester technology   The term Winchester is loosely applied to mean any disk with a fixed or nonremovable recording medium. More precisely, the term applies to a ferrite read/write head and slider design with oxide media that was first employed in the IBM 3340 disk drive, circa 1973. Most drives today actually use Whitney technology.

Wintel   The common name given to computers running Microsoft Windows using Intel processors. A slang term for the PC standard.

wire frames   The most common technique used to construct a three-dimensional object for animation. A wire frame is given coordinates of length, height, and width. Wire frames are then filled with textures, colors, and movement. Transforming a wire frame into a textured object is called rendering.

word length   The number of bits in a data character without parity, start, or stop bits.

World Wide Web (WWW)   Also called the Web. A graphical information system based on hypertext that enables a user to easily access documents located on the Internet.

WORM (write-once, read-many or multiple)   An optical mass-storage device capable of storing many megabytes of information but that can be written to only once on any given area of the disk. A WORM disk typically holds more than 200MB of data. Because a WORM drive cannot write over an old version of a file, new copies of files are made and stored on other parts of the disk whenever a file is revised. WORM disks are used to store information when a history of older versions must be maintained. Recording on a WORM disk is performed by a laser writer that burns pits in a thin metallic film (usually tellurium) embedded in the disk. This burning process is called ablation. WORM drives are frequently used for archiving data.

write precompensation   A modification applied to write data by a controller to alleviate partially the problem of bit shift, which causes adjacent 1s written on magnetic media to read as though they were farther apart. When adjacent 1s are sensed by the controller, precompensation is used to write them closer together on the disk, thus enabling them to be read in the proper bit cell window. Drives with built-in controllers normally handle precompensation automatically. Precompensation normally is required for the inner cylinders of oxide media drives.

write protect   Preventing a removable disk from being overwritten by means of covering a notch or repositioning a sliding switch, depending on the type of media.

X2   A proprietary modem standard developed by U.S. Robotics (since acquired by 3Com) that allows modems to receive data at up to 56Kbps. This has been superseded by the V.90 standard. See also V.90.

x86   A generic term referring to Intel and Intel-compatible PC microprocessors. Although the Pentium, Pentium Pro, and Pentium II do not have a numeric designation due to trademark law, they are later generations of this family.

XGA (eXtended Graphics Array)   A type of PC video display circuit (and adapter) first introduced by IBM on October 30, 1990, that supports text and graphics. Text is supported at a maximum resolution of 132×60 characters in 16 colors with a character box of 8×6 pixels. Graphics is supported at a maximum resolution of 1024×768 pixels in 256 (from a palette of 262,144) colors or 640×480 pixels in 65,536 colors. The XGA outputs an analog signal with a horizontal scanning frequency of 31.5 or 35.52KHz and supports analog color or analog monochrome displays.

XMM (eXtended Memory Manager)   A driver that controls access to extended memory on 286 and later processor systems. HIMEM.SYS is an example of an XMM that comes with DOS.

Xmodem   A file-transfer protocol—with error checking—developed by Ward Christensen in the mid-1970s and placed in the public domain. Designed to transfer files between machines running the CP/M operating system and using 300 or 1,200 bps modems. Until the late 1980s, because of its simplicity and public-domain status, Xmodem remained the most widely used microcomputer file-transfer protocol. In standard Xmodem, the transmitted blocks are 128 bytes. 1KB-Xmodem is an extension to Xmodem that increases the block size to 1,024 bytes. Many newer file-transfer protocols that are much faster and more accurate than Xmodem have been developed, such as Ymodem and Zmodem.

XMS (eXtended Memory Specification)   A Microsoft-developed standard that provides a way for real-mode applications to access extended memory in a controlled fashion. The XMS standard is available from Microsoft.

XON/XOFF   Standard ASCII control characters used to tell an intelligent device to stop or resume transmitting data. In most systems, typing Ctrl+S sends the XOFF character. Most devices understand Ctrl+Q as XON; others interpret the pressing of any key after Ctrl+S as XON.

Y-connector   A Y-shaped splitter cable that divides a source input into two output signals.

Yellow Book   The standard used by Compact Disc-Read Only Memory (CD-ROM). Multimedia applications most commonly use the Yellow Book standard, which specifies how digital information is to be stored on the CD-ROM and read by a computer. Extended Architecture (XA) is currently an extension of the Yellow Book that allows for the combination of different data types (audio and video, for example) onto one track in a CD-ROM. Without XA, a CD-ROM can access only one data type at a time. Many CD-ROM drives are now XA capable.

Yellow Book standards   See *CD-ROM*.

Ymodem   A file-transfer protocol first released as part of Chuck Forsberg's YAM (yet another modem) program. An extension to Xmodem designed to overcome some of the limitations of the original. Enables information about the transmitted file, such as the file name and length, to be sent along with the file data and increases the size of a block from 128 to 1,024 bytes. Ymodem-batch adds the capability to transmit "batches" or groups of files without operator interruption. YmodemG is a variation that sends the entire file before waiting for an acknowledgment. If the receiving side detects an error in midstream, the transfer is aborted. YmodemG is designed for use with modems that have built-in error-correcting capabilities.

ZIF (Zero Insertion Force)   Sockets that require no force for the insertion of a chip carrier. Usually accomplished through movable contacts and uses primarily 486, Pentium, and Pentium Pro processor systems.

zip drive   An external drive manufactured by Iomega that supports 100MB magnetic media on a 3 1/2-inch removable drive.

ZIP (Zigzag Inline Package)   A DIP package that has all leads on one edge in a zigzag pattern and mounts in a vertical plane.

Zmodem   A file-transfer protocol commissioned by Telenet and placed in the public domain. Like Ymodem, it was designed by Chuck Forsberg and developed as an extension to Xmodem to overcome the inherent latency when using Send/ Ack-based protocols such as XModem and YModem. It is a streaming, sliding- window protocol.

zoned recording   In hard drives, a way to increase the capacity of a hard drive is to format more sectors on the outer cylinders than on the inner ones. Zoned recording splits the cylinders into groups called zones, with each successive zone having more and more sectors per track as you move out from the inner radius of the disk. All the cylinders in a particular zone have the same number of sectors per track.

zoomed video   A direct video bus connection between the PC card adapter and a mobile system's VGA controller, allowing high-speed video displays for videoconferencing applications and MPEG decoders.

Making the Most Of PartitionMagic and Drive Image

SOME OF THE MAIN TOPICS IN THIS CHAPTER ARE

Putting PartitionMagic to Work

Putting Drive Image to Work

The Que versions of PowerQuest's popular and powerful utilities PartitionMagic 4.0 and Drive Image 3.0 are an incredible pair of tools for the professional PC repair technician or the occasional PC upgrader. Wherever you fall in this spectrum, you are sure to find many uses for these programs.

The online documentation and readme files with the programs cover all the functionality in both very well. For that reason, and because this book is already very big (I'm short on space), this appendix looks at some practical uses and applications for PartitionMagic and Drive Image rather than going through a dry explanation of all the features.

Putting PartitionMagic to Work

Before using PartitionMagic the first time, be aware that along with its power comes some element of risk. It is possible to misuse this program and accidentally destroy the entire contents of your hard drive. As you select options (particularly the option to delete or reformat a specific partition) take extra care to be sure you have chosen the correct partition that you want to work on. I know several people who thought they were deleting and writing over an unneeded partition, carelessly chose the wrong partition, and deleted what they intended to save. With that said, here are some of the basic tasks you can perform with PartitionMagic to fine-tune your PC hard drive organization and structure:

- Divide a single large hard drive into several smaller partitions
- Convert a partition from one file format to another
- Resize existing partitions without erasing or destroying any of the data on them
- Change cluster sizes to optimize drive space usage, again without reformatting the drive or destroying data

Let's look at some of the practical applications of these features.

The Benefits of Several Partitions

When hard drives were less than 500MB, a single partition for a whole drive made sense if your operating system could handle it. With drive sizes in dozens of gigabytes today (I saw an announcement and advertisement for a 50GB drive from IBM this week), a single large partition has many drawbacks. You should divide a larger drive into smaller partitions for any of the following reasons:

- *With one partition you can run one operating system.* If you want to run Windows 95 or 98 and have it dual boot with Windows NT or Linux (or triple boot with all three, or quadruple boot with an old version of DOS) you need to have a partitioned drive. If you have a large enough drive, divide it into enough different partitions to allow for one partition for each operating system. If you already have an operating system loaded and the drive is one single large partition, run PartitionMagic to divide the drive into smaller partitions. When you install Windows NT or Linux, they each include their own boot manager that allow you to choose the right operating system at boot time. Or you can install a more flexible boot manager such as Mattsoft Boot Manager, which is also included on the CD with this book.

■ *Put your data on different partitions than your operating systems.* If an operating system has a bad crash and you have to delete everything and reinstall it from scratch, you are much less likely to lose your data files if you have them on a separate partition. If you use several different operating systems, especially different versions of Windows, and want to conveniently and safely access data files from any operating system, you shouldn't keep your data files on the same drive as an operating system. And, if you make good backups of your data files, it will be easier and faster to make and maintain your data file backups if they aren't mixed in with your operating system and program files.

■ *Make it easier to find data on a large drive.* Dividing a drive into partitions gives you another level of organization. If you have thousands of files on a 20GB drive in one partition, you had better be the world's best organizer if you plan to find anything.

■ *Make a separate partition to store image files from Drive Image.* If you plan to use Drive Image to keep backup images (and why shouldn't you use it since it's included with the book?), the fastest and easiest way to make and restore these images is onto another partition. Of course, these image files are relatively large and eventually you'll need to move some to a removable medium such as CD-R or Jaz. But, for speed and performance, you can write and restore 500–1,000MB of data from one partition on a drive to a Drive Image file on another partition in less than 10 minutes on a typical system. Read more about Drive Image later in this appendix.

■ *Do you have a CD-R or CD-RW?* If you make data or music CDs with it, make one or two extra 650MB partitions on your drive to store your data to. This allows you to put all the files that you want to burn onto a CD into the exact organization that you want them without having to dig through different directories or drives while you are in the CD recording process. By making these 650MB, you are ensured that you always have enough space to burn your CD from.

There are many more reasons for separate partitions that I'm sure you will discover.

Changing Partition File Formats

Windows 95 OSR2 and Windows 98 both added the FAT32 file system and the capability to convert a FAT16 drive to FAT32. But they both left out the capability to convert back from FAT32 to FAT16. This is an important capability you need that PartitionMagic provides. Many low-level system utilities that boot from a DOS floppy disk and DOS itself (both MS-DOS and third-party versions) are incapable of reading FAT32 drives. PartitionMagic can convert from FAT16 to FAT32 and back without losing any data. If you do decide to convert from FAT16 to FAT32, PartitionMagic is much faster for doing this than the built-in Windows utility.

Likewise with the secure NTFS file system in Windows NT 4, you might want to convert a partition to NTFS. Windows NT gives you this option when you install it. If you run PartitionMagic from Windows NT, you can also convert to NTFS using PartitionMagic if you didn't when you installed NT. PartitionMagic disables the options to convert to or from NTFS if you are not running in NT.

Making More Room on a Partition

With the ever increasing size of software programs and the data files they create, everyone comes to a time when their drive or a partition within a drive won't hold it all. If the drive itself is too small, you need to upgrade, and Drive Image will come in handy, as discussed later in the chapter. If you outgrow one partition, especially your primary partition containing Windows, you're in for a hassle without PartitionMagic. Without it you'll need to back up all your data to another drive or removable media, use FDISK to delete the partition that is too small, and then delete another partition to take some space from (you need to have it backed up if you need anything on it). Then, recreate a new partition at the right size and reload your backup. This whole process can easily take hours.

When you need more space on a partition, run PartitionMagic; find a partition with some extra unused space and adjust it to make it a little smaller while making the other partition larger. The graphical interface for PartitionMagic even lets you drag the partition to the size you want. It does all this without destroying any existing data and, therefore, there's no need to reload a backup when it finishes. The whole process is much faster and less error prone than backing up, deleting, recreating, and restoring partitions with FDISK.

Increase Drive Performance

As discussed in Chapter 27, "File Systems and Data Recovery," seek and read times on large drives can be affected by cluster size. Additionally, wasted space from partially filled clusters can take up a significant portion of a drive with many files. PartitionMagic helps improve performance and limit wasted space by resizing clusters. You can use PartitionMagic to find out how much space is wasted by the current cluster size and then to change to a cluster size that reduces the waste. As with other PartitionMagic operations, this can be done without affecting any of the data already on a drive.

A similar operation allows you to change the size of the root directory on a FAT16 system. (FAT32 root directories can grow as needed so this feature isn't needed with them.) While it is generally not a good idea to have too many files in the root, there might be special circumstances when you need more files in the root than the directory will allow. This is especially likely of you use a lot of long filenames in the root, which take up more directory space. PartitionMagic does allow you to change this directory size to increase the allowable number of files. (PowerQuest points out that there is a small chance that this operation will move the first few files on the partition and if this is a partition containing an operating system, this can prevent the system from booting. The files are not gone; there is a way to move them back. Contact PowerQuest technical support if you run into this and need to know how to do it.)

Putting Drive Image to Work

Drive Image by itself is a powerful backup and upgrading tool. Used together with PartitionMagic, the two are a great combination. The primary uses of this single user license of Drive Image are

- To make an identical copy of a drive's contents onto another drive or partition
- To make or restore a backup image of a partition's entire contents

With either of these operations, Drive Image works with common file system formats including FAT16, FAT32, and NTFS. Drive Image includes system files and hidden files, and correctly keeps all long filenames. The next few sections explore a few uses for these operations.

Upgrading to a New Hard Drive with Drive Image

One of the most unnecessarily complicated upgrade procedures is getting the files from your old hard drive to your new one. If you are installing your new drive as secondary drive, that's not a problem; you don't need to copy files, and you'll boot to your old drive. But if you just bought a new 20GB drive to replace your old 500MB or 2GB model, you probably want to use the bigger, faster drive as the primary one. You can't just copy the files over from DOS without trashing the long filenames. Many new drives come with simple utilities for transferring files, but they can be slower than Drive Image and don't have some of the options. And, if you bought a new drive that doesn't include these features or are upgrading to a used drive, you need Drive Image.

In this situation, you'll want to install Drive Image on your existing drive before making the upgrade. When you install, you get an option to make a bootable floppy disk and a Drive Image program disk that will run after booting from this floppy. This is the best way to perform the upgrade. Install and configure the new drive as described in Chapter 14, "Physical Drive Installation and Configuration." After you have the BIOS configured to recognize both drives, boot from the floppy. Then use Drive Image to copy the entire old drive to the new drive. Even for several gigabytes of data, this will take just a few minutes. Once it is copied, connect and configure the new drive as the primary drive, and you will be ready to boot from it. (In fact, you can even connect it as the primary drive prior to copying. Because you will be booting from a floppy, the new drive doesn't need to be bootable to make the copy.)

After that, you can refigure the old drive as a secondary drive or remove it from the system.

Upgrading to a New Drive from a Drive Image Image File

Typically, the scenario described in the previous section is the fastest way to upgrade to a new drive with Drive Image. But,e from a previous image file created from Drive Image. Those situations could include

- A failed (crashed) drive
- Not enough physical space or available interface connections for both drives
- You want to load the new drive with something other than the current contents of the old drive

In any of these situations, Drive Image will restore an image file to the new CD with all the contents of the old drive. If your old drive has crashed, hopefully you kept your image files on another drive or removable media. Once you get your BIOS to recognize the new drive, boot from the Drive Image floppies and restore the image file. If you need to restore from a removable media device, be sure to include the drivers for your removable device on the boot floppy. Drive Image will not create images directly to a CD-R (the last section of this appendix discusses how to use it with a CD-R). Drive Image will create images directly to a Jaz drive (or a Zip drive if your image files are small) or other removable media which has DOS drivers that allow Drive Image to write to the drive through a DOS drive letter. Drive Image can also restore images from a CD as long as the DOS drivers for the CD-ROM are loaded and the CD-ROM as a DOS drive letter.

After you have restored the image file to the new drive, you can set the BIOS to boot from the new drive; it should boot immediately. There is no need to transfer any system files, reload any settings, or make any other changes. Everything that was on the partition when you imaged it will be on the new drive.

Creating Backup Image Files

Whenever you are making images with Drive Image, the best option is Low Compression. This will make the image file about 40 percent smaller than the amount of data on the partition you are imaging. (For example, if you have a 2GB partition with 1GB used, the image will be about 600MB.) Higher compression will save only about 10 percent more space in most cases and is much slower. On most drives, low compression is very fast and you won't notice much slowdown compared to the No Compression setting.

You cannot create an image file of a partition on the same partition. This makes using PartitionMagic along with Drive Image a great combination. Keep a spare partition with some space on it for your images so that creating the image files goes quickly. Then you can restore directly from these images or copy and move these images to removable media to save space. As long as you have a way to access the removable media when you boot to DOS, you can restore directly from the removable media. Or, you can copy the image you need to restore from to another partition.

Many Que editors and writers use Drive Image and PartitionMagic extensively when working with beta versions of software. This gives them an easy way to keep a working copy of their system that can easily be restored. Every time there is a new beta, it's easy to restore the working copy of the system from prior to the beta software and the load the new copy of the beta. This allows you to keep a "clean" baseline copy of your system that you can restore and load new software onto whenever you need to test something. When you are done testing it, simply restore the system and it's gone. This eliminates the problem of programs (beta or otherwise) that can't be completely uninstalled through their uninstaller, and is much more effective than third-party uninstaller programs if you need to keep a clean system. Of course, any other software that you install or settings you change after installing the software to test will also be gone when you restore the previous clean image. In addition to software testing, this is useful if you need to test many different hardware and driver variations and need a clean baseline system to test them on.

Restoring Image File Backups

Restoring an image file from Drive Image is quick and easy. All you need to do is select the drive containing the image, select the image file itself, and select where to restore it. If you are restoring to a partition that is not empty, Drive Image will warn you that you are about to overwrite an existing partition. When you restore from Drive Image, it does not restore individual files; it replaces the entire contents of the partition with the contents of the image. If there is anything on the partition you are restoring onto that you need to keep, stop the process, exit Drive Image, and move the files that you need before restoring the image.

As Drive Image restores the image, it will progress through several stages and verify what it restores as it goes. If the partition you are restoring to does not have enough space to restore the image, Drive Image will prompt you to resize the partition. If you are restoring the image to a larger drive with more space, you can also set Drive Image to create a larger partition than the original image came from, which will have the effect of restoring the image into a partition with more free space. If Drive Image can't resize the partition to fit, this is a good place to stop Drive Image and start PartitionMagic.

You will need to reboot if you have restored the image to your primary bootable partition.

Making Bootable Backup Image File CDs

As mentioned earlier, Drive Image currently does not support writing images directly to a CD-R. However, once you have an image file created, it is very easy to use your CD recording software to burn a CD with a copy of your image. You can either use this as a backup or delete the image file from the drive to save space. If you are going to be making CD-Rs with your image files, be sure to keep the images small enough to fit on a CD, less than 650MB. In fact, to make sure the CD-R does the best possible job writing the CD, keep the images under 600MB. Drive Image has an option to slip image files into multiple files, so if you have an image that will be bigger than 600MB, you can copy it to more than one CD.

Making CDs with image files is easy, and you can copy these images directly or restore from them if your CD's DOS drivers are loaded. To take this one step further, you can make the CD bootable using the techniques for creating bootable CDs discussed in Chapter 13, "Optical Storage." When you do this, be sure that the autoexec.bat and config.sys files that will be in the bootable CD have the right DOS CD-ROM drivers specified and that those drivers are included on the CD. In addition to the boot files, you'll want to include the Drive Image files from the program floppy and the image(s) that you want to be able to restore.

With this bootable CD-ROM you can then put a clean drive with no other bootable drive in the system and boot from your CD-ROM. After the system has booted, start Drive Image from the CD and select and restore an image from the CD. Even if you have a fast CD-ROM drive, restoring from a CD with Drive Image running from the CD will be slower. But, this gives you a permanent and almost indestructible copy of your image to boot from and saves you from having to keep bootable floppy disks and a Drive Image program disk separate from your image CD.

Exploring the Professional Uses of Drive Image

One of the most valuable uses of Drive Image for PC technicians and IT support staffs is to be able to create a single image that can be used to configure several identical machines with the exact same software and settings. It is important to note that Que's version of Drive Image (as well as the standard version of Drive Image sold in retail outlets) is not licensed for this purpose. This is a single-user/single-machine license. PowerQuest sells a Professional version for use by corporations and others who need this multiple system rollout license. However, all the features that you have seen will work for rolling out the same image to many machines.

If you do purchase the Professional license for Drive Image, keep in mind that the systems you are configuring from each image need to be identical. They need to have the same video cards, CD-ROM drives, and other components and peripherals. If they don't, the Windows drivers and settings from the image won't work when you restore the image to another system.

Multiple system rollout is a great use for creating your images on removable media or making bootable CD-Rs with your images.

List of Acronyms

Symbols

305 RAMAC (Random Access Method of Accounting), IBM
82C836 SCAT (Single Chip AT) chipset

A

AAD (Analog Alignment Diskette)
ACPI (Advanced Configuration and Power Interface)
ADCs (analog-to-digital converters)
ADPCM (Adaptive Differential Pulse Code Modulation)
ADSL (Asymmetrical DSL)
AGC (Automatic Gain Control)
AGP (Accelerated Graphics Port)
AMD (Advanced Micro Devices)
ANSI (American National Standards Institute)
API (Application Program Interface)
APIC (Advanced Programmable Interrupt Controller)
APM (Advanced Power Management)
ARLL (Advanced Run Length Limited)
ARP (Address Resolution Protocol)
ASPI (Advanced SCSI Programming Interface)
ATAPI (AT Attachment Packet Interface)
ATM (Asynchronous Transfer Mode)

B

BASIC (Beginners All-Purpose Symbolic Instruction Code)
BBSs (bulletin board systems)
BEDO (Burst Extended-Data-Out) DRAM
BF (bus frequency) pins
BGA (Ball Grid Array)
BiCMOS (bipolar complementary metal oxide semi-conductor)

BIOS (basic input/output system)
BNC (Bayonet-Neill-Concelman) connectors
BPB (BIOS Parameter Block)
BPI (bits per inch)
BPS (bits per second)
BRI (Basic Rate Interface)
BSRAMs (Burst Static RAMs)
BTB (Branch Target Buffer)

C

CACP (Central Arbitration Control Point)
CAD (Computer Aided Drafting)
CAM (Common Access Method)
CAM ATA (Common Access Method AT Attachment)
CAV (Constant Angular Velocity)
CBT (Computer-Based Training)
CCITT (Consultative Committee on International Telephone and Telegraph)
CD-R (CD-Recordable)
CD-ROM (Compact Disc-Read Only Memory)
CD-RW (CD-Rewritable)
CDSL (Consumer DSL)
CFCs (chlorofluorocarbons)
CHS (Cylinder Head Sector)
CISC (Complex Instruction Set Computer)
CLKMUL (Clock Multiplier)
CLV (Constant Linear Velocity)
CMOS (Complementary Metal-Oxide Semiconductor)
CP/M (Control Program for Microprocessors)
CPUs (Central Processing Units)
CRC (cyclical redundancy checking)
CRTs (cathode ray tubes)
CSA (Canadian Standards Agency)
CSEL (Cable Select) signals
CSMA/CD (carrier sense multiple access with collision detection)

CSN (Card Select Number)
CSP (CompuCom Speed Protocol)
CSTN (color super-twist nematic)
CVC (Compact Video Codec)

D

DAC (Digital to Analog Converter)
DASP (Drive Active/Slave Present) signals
DAT (digital audio tape)
db (decibels)
DBB (dynamic bass boost)
DBR (DOS Boot Record)
DDD (Digital Diagnostic Diskette)
DDR (Double Data Rate)
DDR SDRAM (Double-Data-Rate SDRAM)
DDWG (Digital Display Work Group) standard
DIB (device-independent bitmap)
DIB (Dual Independent Bus)
DIME (Direct Memory Execute)
DIMMs (Dual Inline Memory Modules)
DIN (Deutsche Industrie Norm)
DIP (Dual Inline Package) chips
DIS (dynamic impedance stabilization)
DLT (Digital Linear Tape)
DMA (Direct Memory Access)
DMI (Desktop Management Interface)
DMM (Digital Multi-Meter)
DOS (Disk Operating System)
DPMI (DOS protected mode interface)
DPMS (Display Power-Management Signaling)
DQPSK (Differential Quadrature Phase Shift Keying)
DRAM (Dynamic RAM)
DRDRAM (Direct RAMBUS DRAM)
DSL (Digital Subscriber Line)
DSPs (digital signal processors)
DSTN (double-layer super-twist nematic)
DTV (Desktop Video) boards
DV (digital video)
DVD (Digital Versatile Disc)
DVOM (Digital Volt-Ohm Meters)

E

ECC (Error Correcting Code)
ECHS (Extended Cylinder Head Sector)
ECM (Electronic Control Module)
ECP (Enhanced Capabilities Port)
EDC (Error Detection Code)
EDO (Extended Data Out) memory/RAM
EEPROM (Electrically Erasable Programmable Read-Only Memory)
EIDE (Enhanced IDE)
EISA (Extended Industry Standard Architecture)
ELF (extremely low frequency)
EMI (electromagnetic interference)
EMS (expanded memory support)
EPIC (Explicitly Parallel Instruction Computing)
EPP (Enhanced Parallel Port)

EPROM (Erasable Programmable Read-Only Memory)
ESD (electrostatic discharge)
ESDI (Enhanced Small Device Interface)
ESP (Enhanced Serial Ports)

F-G

FAP (Fair Access Policy)
FAT (file allocation table)
FCC (Federal Communications Commission)
FDDI (fiber distributed data interface)
FDIV (Floating Point Divide)
FIFO (First In First Out)
FIT (Failures in Time)
FM (Frequency Modulation)
FPM (Fast Page Mode) memory
FPUs (floating point units)
FSK (frequency-shift keying)
FTP (File Transfer Protocol)
FWH (Firmware Hub)

GMCH (Graphics Memory Controller Hub)
GUIs (graphical user interfaces)

H

HAL (Hardware Abstraction Layer)
HDAs (Head Disk Assemblies)
HELs (Hardware Emulation Layers)
HERS (hard error rates)
HFC (hybrid fiber/coax)
HFCs (hydrofluorocarbons)
HLF (High-Level Formatting)
HMA (High Memory Area)
HP-GL/2 (Hewlett Packard Graphics Language)
HPA (high performance addressing)
HPFS (High Performance File System)
HRD (High-Resolution Diagnostic Diskette)
HST (high-speed protocol)
HTTP (Hypertext Transfer Protocol)
HUD (Heads Up Display)
HVD (High Voltage Differential) signaling
Hz (Hertz)

I-K

ICH (Integrated Controller Hub)
ICMP (Internet Control Message Protocol)
iCOMP (Intel Comparative Microprocessor Performance) index
ICs (integrated circuits)
IDE (Integrated Drive Electronics)
IDE/ATAPI (Integrated Drive Electronics/AT Attachment Packet Interface)
IDT (Integrated Device Technology)
IEEE (Institute of Electrical and Electronic Engineers)
IML (Initial Microcode Load)
IP (Internet Protocol)
IPL (Initial Program Load) ROM

IPX (Internetwork Packet Exchange)
IrDA (Infrared Data) connectors
IRQs (Interrupt Requests)
ISA (Industry Standard Architecture)
ISDN (Integrated Services Digital Network)
ISIS (Image and Scanner Interface Specification)
ISO (International Organization for Standardization)
ITU (International Telecommunications Union)

JEDEC (Joint Electronic Devices Engineering Council)
JPEG (Joint Photographic Experts Group)

L

LANs (local area networks)
LAPM (Link Access Procedure for Modems)
LBA (Logical Block Addressing)
LCDs (liquid crystal displays)
Li-ion (lithium-ion) batteries
LIF (Low Insertion Force)
LIM (Lotus Intel Microsoft)
LLC (Logical Link Control)
LLF (Low-Level Formatting)
LVD (Low Voltage Differential) signaling

M

MAC (Media Access Control)
Mbps (megabits per second)
MBR (master boot record)
MCA (Micro Channel Architecture)
MCM (Multi-Chip Module)
MDRAM (Multibank DRAM)
MFM (Modified Frequency Modulation)
MFT (Master File Table)
MIC (Memory Interface Controller)
MIDI (Musical Instrument Digital Interface)
MIG (Metal-In-Gap)
MMO (mobile module)
MMU (memory management unit)
MMX (Multi-Media eXtensions)
MNP (Microcom Networking Protocol)
MOVs (metal-oxide varistors)
MPC (Multimedia PC)
MPEG (Motion Pictures Experts Group)
MPS (Multi-Processor Specification)
MR (Magneto-Resistive) heads
MSCDEX (Microsoft CD-ROM Extensions)
MSD (Microsoft Diagnostics)
MTBF (Mean Time Between Failures)
MTTF (Mean Time To Failure)

N

NCITS (National Committee on Information Technology Standards)
NCs (Network Computers)
NDP (numeric data processor)

NEAT (New Enhanced AT) CS8221 chipset
NetBEUI (NetBIOS Extended User Interface)
NFAS (Non-Facility Associated Signaling)
NiCad (nickel cadmium) batteries
NICs (Network Interface Cards)
NiMH (nickel metal-hydride) batteries
NMI (non-maskable interrupt)
NTFS (NT File System)
NTSC (National Television System Committee)
NVRAM (Non-Volatile RAM)

O

OEM (original equipment manufacturer)
OLE (object linking and embedding)
OLGA (Organic Land Grid Array)
OSI (Open Systems Interconnection)
OSR2 (OEM Service Release 2)
OSR2.5 (OEM Service Release 2.5)
OTP (one time programmable) chips

P

PAC (Pin Array Cartridge)
PARD (Periodic and Random Deviation)
PCI (Peripheral Component Interconnect)
PCI ISA IDE Xcelerator (PIIX) chips
PCL (Printer Control Language)
PCMCIA (Personal Computer Memory Card International Association)
PDL (Page Description Language)
PFA (Predictive Failure Analysis)
PGA (Pin Grid Array)
PIIX (PCI ISA IDE Xcelerator) chips
PIO (Programmed I/O)
PJL (Printer Job Language)
PLGA (Plastic Land Grid Array)
PMTs (Photo Multiplier Tubes)
PnP (Plug and Play)
POST (power on self test)
PPA (Printing Performance Architecture)
PPDs (PostScript Printer Descriptions)
PPGA (Plastic Pin Grid Array) package
PPI (Programmable Peripheral Interface)
PPP (Point-to-Point Protocol)
PQFP (Plastic Quad Flat Pack) packaging
PRI (Primary Rate Interface)
PRML (Partial Response, Maximum-Likelihood) electronics
PSK (phase-shift keying)
PSTN (Public Switched Telephone Network)
PSU (power supply unit)

Q

QAM (quadrature-amplitude modulation)
QFP (Quad Flat Pack)
QIC (Quarter-Inch Committee)
QPSK (Quadrature Phase Shift Keying)

R

RAID (Redundant Array of Inexpensive Disks)
RAM (Random Access Memory)
RAMDACs (Digital-to-Analog Converters)
RDRAM (Rambus Dynamic RAM)
RET (Resolution Enhancement Technology)
RFI (radio-frequency interference)
RIMMs (Rambus Inline Memory Modules)
RIP (Raster Image Processing) applications
RISC (Reduced Instruction Set Computer) chips
RLL (Run Length Limited)
RNG (Random Number Generator)
ROM (Read Only Memory)
ROS (raster output scanner)
RTC (Real Time Clock)
RTC/NVRAM (Real-Time Clock/Non-Volatile Memory) chip

S

S-CDMA (Synchronous Code Division Multiple Access)
S.M.A.R.T. (Self-Monitoring, Analysis, and Reporting Technology)
S/T (Subscriber/Termination) Interface
SAM (SCSI Architectural Model)
SASI (Shugart Associates System Interface)
SBIC (SCSI Bus Adapter Chip)
SCAT (82C836 Single Chip AT) chipset
SCSI (Small Computer System Inteface)
SDL (Shielded Data Link)
SDRAM (Synchronous Dynamic RAM)
SEC (Single Edge Cartridge)
SEC (Single Edge Contact)
SEC-DED (Single-Bit Error Correction-Double-Bit Error Detection)
SECC2 (Single Edge Contact Cartridge 2)
SEP (Single Edge Processor)
SERS (soft error rates)
SEUs (single event upsets)
SGRAM (Synchronous Graphics RAM)
SIMD (Single Instruction, Multiple Data)
SIMMs (Single Inline Memory Modules)
SIPPs (single inline pinned packages)
SIR (Serial Infra Red)
SMI (System Management Interrupt)
SMM (System Management Mode)
SMTP (Simple Mail Transfer Protocol)
SPD (Serial Presence Detect) device
SPGA (Staggered Pin Grid Array)
SPP (Standard Parallel Port)
SPS (Standby Power Supplies)
SPSYNC (Spindle Synchronization) signals
SRAM (Static RAM)
SRM (Security Reference Monitor)
SSE (Streaming SIMD Extensions)
STP (shielded twisted pair)
SVGA (Super VGA)

T

TAB (tape automated bonding)
TCP (tape carrier package)
TCP (Transmission Control Protocol)
TCQAM (trellis coded quadrature amplitude modulation)
TF (thin-film) heads
TFT (thin-film transistors)
THD (Total Harmonic Distortion)
TIP (Trouble in Paradise) diagnosis program
TLB (Translation Lookaside Buffer)
TPI (tracks per inch)
TSOP (Thin Small Outline Package)

U

UART (Universal Asynchronous Receiver/Transmitter)
UDP (User Datagram Protocol)
UL (Underwriters Laboratories, Inc.)
Ultra VGA (UVGA)
UMA (upper memory area)
UMA (Unified Memory Architecture)
UMB (Upper Memory Block)
UPI (Universal Peripheral Interface)
UPS (Uninterruptible Power Supplies)
USB (Universal Serial Bus)
UTP (unshielded twisted-pair) cables
UVGA (Ultra VGA)

V

VESA (Video Electronics Standards Association)
VESA VIP (VESA Video Interface Port)
VFAT (virtual file allocation table)
VFW (Microsoft Video for Windows)
VGA (Video Graphics Array)
VID (Voltage Identification)
VL (VESA Local) bus
VLF (very low frequency)
VLSI (very large scale integration)
VRAM (Video RAM)
VRM (Voltage Regulator Module)
VRT (Voltage Reduction Technology)
VSB (Vestigal Side Band)
VTOC (Volume Table of Contents)
VxDs (virtual device drivers)

W

WORM (write-once, read many)
WRAM (Window RAM)
WYSIWYG (what you see is what you get)

X-Z

XGA (eXtended Graphics Array)
XMS (extended memory specification)
ZIF (Zero Insertion Force)
ZV (Zoomed Video)

INDEX

A

cylinders 586, 588

W

Other Related Titles

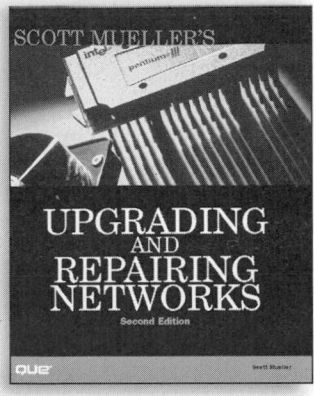

Upgrading and Repairing Networks Second Edition
by Terry Olgetree
ISBN: 0-7897-2034-5
$49.99 USA/
$74.95 CAN

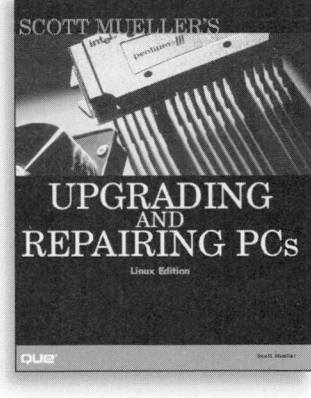

Upgrading and Repairing PCs Linux Edition
by Joe DeVita
ISBN: 0-7897-2075-2
$49.99 USA/
$74.95 CAN

Upgrading and Repairing PCs Portable Technical Reference
by Scott Mueller
ISBN: 0-7897-2096-5
$19.99 USA/$29.95 CAN

Practical Cisco Routers
by Joe Habraken
ISBN: 0-7897-2103-1
$29.99 USA/$44.95 CAN

Special Edition Using Windows 98 Second Edition
by Ed Bott
ISBN: 0-7897-2203-8
$39.99 US

Special Edition Using Windows 2000 Pro
by Bob Coward
ISBN: 0-7897-2125-2
$39.99 US

Special Edition Using Windows 2000 Server
by Robert Reinstein
ISBN: 0-7897-2141-4
$29.99 US

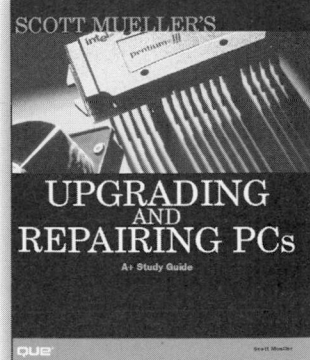

Upgrading and Repairing PCs: A+ Study Guide
by Scott Mueller
ISBN: 0-7897-2095-7
$19.99 USA/
$29.95 CAN

www.quecorp.com

All prices are subject to change.

License Agreement

By opening this package, you are agreeing to be bound by the following agreement:

You may not copy or redistribute the entire CD-ROM as a whole; copying and redistribution of individual software programs on the CD-ROM is governed by terms set by individual copyright holders.

The installer and code from the author(s) are copyrighted by the publisher and the author(s). Individual programs and other items on the CD-ROM are copyrighted or are under GNU license by their various authors or other copyright holders.

This software is sold *as is* without warranty of any kind, either expressed or implied, including but not limited to the implied warranties of merchantability and fitness for a particular purpose. Neither the publisher nor its dealers or distributors assumes any liability for any alleged or actual damages arising from the use of this program. (Some states do not allow for the exclusion of implied warranties, so the exclusion might not apply to you.)

Upgrading and Repairing PCs, Eleventh Edition

by Scott Mueller

Thank you for making *Upgrading and Repairing PCs* by Scott Mueller the best-selling PC hardware repair book ever. Please help us tailor the content of the next edition to best fit your needs. Take a few minutes to answer these questions and return this self-addressed form, or you can answer the questions on our Web site: www.quecorp.com/surveys.

---

1. **Does your job involve upgrading, repairing, building, or troubleshooting PCs on a regular basis?**
   - ❑ Yes   ❑ No

2. **Why did you buy this book?**
   - ❑ Professional use   ❑ Personal use

3. **Where did you buy this book?**
   - ❑ Bookstore   ❑ Internet site   ❑ Consumer electronics store
   - ❑ Office club   ❑ Computer store   ❑ Other _____

4. **Which of the following certifications have you earned or do you plan to earn in the next six months?**

A+:	❑ Have	❑ Plan to have
MCSE:	❑ Have	❑ Plan to have
Network+:	❑ Have	❑ Plan to have
Other _____	❑ Have	❑ Plan to have

5. **What types of processors are in the computers that you currently use, upgrade, repair, build, or troubleshoot?**
   - ❑ Pentium III   ❑ Mobile Pentium   ❑ AMD-K6
   - ❑ Pentium II/Celeron/Zeon   ❑ 486   ❑ AMD-K5
   - ❑ Mobile Pentium II   ❑ 386   ❑ Cyrix Media GX
   - ❑ Pentium Pro   ❑ AMD-K7   ❑ Cyrix 6x86/6x86MX
   - ❑ Pentium/Pentium MMX   ❑ AMD-K6 II   ❑ Other _____

6. **Which of the following processor architectures do you prefer or recommend in your systems:**
   - ❑ Slot 1/Slot 2   ❑ Socket 370   ❑ Super Socket 7   ❑ No Preference

7. **What type of bus slots are in use in the systems that you currently use, upgrade, repair, build, or troubleshoot?**
   - ❑ AGP   ❑ EISA   ❑ 16-bit ISA   ❑ VL-Bus
   - ❑ PCI   ❑ MCA   ❑ 8-bit ISA

8. **What types of removable magnetic media drives are currently in use in the systems that you use, upgrade, repair, build, or troubleshoot?**
   - ❑ 360KB 5 1/4" floppy   ❑ 2.88MB floppy   ❑ Jaz
   - ❑ 1.2MB 5 1/4" floppy   ❑ 21MB floptical   ❑ SyQuest or other optical
   - ❑ 720KB 3 1/2" floppy   ❑ LS-120 (120MB)   ❑ Sparq
   - ❑ 1.44MB 3 1/2" floppy   ❑ Zip   ❑ Other

9. **What type of hard drive interfaces are currently in use in the systems that you use, upgrade, repair, build, or troubleshoot?**
   - ❑ ST-506/412   ❑ IDE   ❑ SCSI   ❑ ESDI

10. **What operating systems are currently in use in the systems that you use, upgrade, repair, build, or troubleshoot?**
    - ❑ MS DOS 5 or earlier DOS versions   ❑ Windows 98   ❑ Windows 2000
    - ❑ MS DOS 6.x   ❑ Windows NT 3.5x   ❑ Linux
    - ❑ Windows 95   ❑ Windows NT 4   ❑ Other _____

11. **What troubleshooting, diagnostic, or configuration software do you use to upgrade, repair, build, or troubleshoot PCs?**
   - ❑ PartitionMagic
   - ❑ DriveImage
   - ❑ Disk Manager
   - ❑ Windows 98 System Information
   - ❑ Norton Utilities
   - ❑ Checkit
   - ❑ Tools provided with operating system (MSD, Control Panel, System Information)
   - ❑ MicroScope
   - ❑ Other _____

12. **What hardware or tools do you use to upgrade, repair, build, or troubleshoot PCs?**
   - ❑ POST card
   - ❑ Memory tester
   - ❑ Loopback connectors (wrap plugs)
   - ❑ Logic probe
   - ❑ Digital multi-meter
   - ❑ Other (please specify) _____

13. **Please list the chapter numbers of the three chapters in this book that you find *most* useful:**
   Most useful _____   2nd most useful _____   3rd most useful _____

14. **Please list the chapter numbers of the three chapters in this book that you find *least* useful:**
   Least useful _____   2nd least useful _____   3rd least useful _____

15. **Please list any other upgrading, repairing, troubleshooting, or hardware configuration topics that are not covered in this book that you would like to see covered or that are covered that you would like to see covered in more detail:**

16. **What other books in the Scott Mueller Library do you plan on purchasing in the next six months?**
   - ❑ *Upgrading and Repairing PCs Linux Edition*
   - ❑ *Upgrading and Repairing Networks Second Edition*
   - ❑ *Upgrading and Repairing PCs: Technician's Portable Reference*
   - ❑ *Upgrading and Repairing PCs: A+ Certification Study Guide*

If you would agree to be contacted for follow-up surveys or questions regarding this book or other Que books, please list the following information. Otherwise you can leave this blank:

Name _____

Address _____

City _____   State _____   ZIP Code _____

Phone Number _____   email address _____